FILM ACTORS GUIDE

Second Edition

COMPILED AND EDITED STEVEN A. LUKANIC

LONE EAGLE PUBLISHING CO.
Los Angeles, California

FILM
ACTORS
GUIDE

FILM ACTORS GUIDE   2nd Edition
Copyright © 1995 by Steven A. LuKanic

LONE EAGLE PUBLISHING CO.
2337 Roscomare Road, Suite Nine
Los Angeles, CA 90077-1851
310/471-8066

Printed in the United States of America

Cover design by Heidi Frieder
Logo Art by Liz and Frank Ridenour

This book was entirely typeset using an Apple Quadra 950, New Gen Turbo Printer, Microsoft Word and Aldus Pagemaker.

Printed by McNaughton & Gunn, Saline, Michigan 48176
Printed entirely on recycled paper.

ISBN: 0-943728-63-0
ISSN 1055-0836

NOTE: We have made every reasonable effort to ensure that the information contained herein is as accurate as possible. However, errors and omissions are sure to occur and are unintentional. We would appreciate your notifying us of any which you may find.

Lone Eagle Publishing is a division of Lone Eagle Productions, Inc.

LONE EAGLE PUBLISHING STAFF
Publishers .... Joan V. Singleton
Ralph S. Singleton
VP - Editorial .... Bethann Wetzel
Customer Service .... Douglas Deacon
Art Director .... Heidi Frieder
Computer Consultant .... Clive McKay

ii

LETTER FROM THE PUBLISHERS

The **Second Edition** of the **Film Actors Guide** represents a quantum leap in credits heretofore unavailable to the reader unless you were willing to spend hours—or days—of research time trying to get this information from agents or the Screen Actors Guild. Now in one, albeit huge, volume, you can find the credits for over 5,400 working actors and actresses.

Due to the overwhelming response of our readers, we have made the following improvements and enhancements. You can now look up credits in the index. There are over 42,000 separate index entries. As Steve LuKanic so aptly notes, this index does not list every film made, nor does it list every actor or actress in every film. If an actor has died, then chances are, his or her credits are not contained in the index. We just don't have enough room. It is, however, an index to every film and actor listed in this book. Now if you can't remember the name of the other actors who were in "An Officer and A Gentleman," you don't have to despair. . . you can find it in the Index.

Steve has taken great pains to include all actors who have speaking parts in films—not just big films or big actors. So, don't be surprised when you find credits for Rockets Redglare in addition to those for Robert Redford.

Another enhancement is a listing showing actors and their agents. Producers, directors and studio executives have told us they would like a quick cross-reference of actors and their agents, and so here it is. It will make brainstorming for casting ideas a lot more fruitful. The one draw-back, if Steve couldn't find your agent, or your agent wasn't willing to give us information about whom they represent, then an actor's name won't appear here. This should be a warning to all actors. Please keep us advised of your agent so we can update this information. Remember, you can't get hired if no one can find you!

The Academy Award information is a godsend for movie buffs as well as for those professionals in the industry. How terrific to not only be able to look up information by year, but also by person. And Katharine Hepburn's record is still unbroken.

The Third Edition of Film Actors Guide will most likely be available on-line as well as in print. We will be adding photos. For those of you who are interested, please drop us a note and we will send information to you about having your photo included.

As always, we welcome all comments, pro and con.

Joan V. Singleton and Ralph S. Singleton
Publishers

TABLE OF CONTENTS

LETTER FROM THE PUBLISHERS iii

INTRODUCTION vii

KEY TO ABBREVIATIONS viii

HOW TO USE THIS BOOK ix

FILM ACTORS
    Alphabetical Listing 3

INDEX BY FILM TITLE 391

INDICES
    Academy Award Nominees and Winners by Year 589
    Academy Award Nominees and Winners by Actor 603
    Index by Actor—Male 621
    Index by Actor—Female 643
    Index of Actor and Agent 657
    Guilds 672
    Agents and Managers 673
    Advertisers 679

ABOUT THE EDITOR 680

INTRODUCTION

Digging out from under the piles of *Hollywood Reporter, Daily Varity*, L.A. Times *Calendar* sections and *Premiere* magazines used in researching the second edition of the FILM ACTORS GUIDE, I'm aware of two things. One, newspapers and magazines attract bugs, and two, I could never be an actor myself. Not that I wouldn't mind the $7 million paycheck or resting between takes in my own Star Waggon. But the road to making a living as an actor can be a bumpy one at best, and I tip my hat to anyone brave enough to make the journey.

Movies have always fascinated me, and I guess in part, so have movie actors. We see their faces on the screen, their names on the marquees—in some cases, their hand and footprints in cement—and before the eyes of the world, these once "ordinary" people become bigger than life. But, as is often the case, fame and success can be fleeting, particularly in a profession where fading looks, personal crises and opening weekend box office receipts can determine whether or not an actor "will ever work in this town again." And that's not even considering the thousands of souls who spend years taking lessons, workshops, stapling resumés to 8x10s, auditioning, auditioning, and auditioning some more . . . and *never* seeing their faces on the screen or their names on a marquee.

But they keep going. And in true Hollywood fashion, the old pros know there's always such a thing as a comeback, and the newcomers hold high the hope of being discovered . . . or at least getting their SAG card.

Like them, we too keep plugging along in our efforts to make this the definitive book on film actors, be they famous, not so famous, infamous, or virtual "nobodies" on their way to becoming famous. As with any reference book, this is still a work-in-progress, and it seems a bit overwhelming keeping up with the careers of every working actor in Hollywood. Nevertheless, we do our best, and with future editions, we will only continue to add more information to make this a better book.

My thanks to all the people who helped contribute to this project in one way or another, including: Mark Katchur, Kathie Foley, Matt Grigsby, Brett Born, and Barbara Rosing Hoke. Special thanks this year to Samantha Crisp at the William Morris Agency and to my friends Tom Meyer, Molly Shaw, Mike Green, Susan Avallone and Kim Krivanek for their invaluable information and assistance. Also, my deepest appreciation to Alice and John Novak for continually checking up on me; to Lori Tan for her neverending support and encouragement; to Brigette Lester for stepping over all the newspapers, and to Jana Howington for her patience and understanding. I couldn't do this without them.

Finally, to everyone in the "Eagle's Nest"—Ralph and Joan Singleton, Doug Deacon, and particularly Bethann Wetzel, who works harder than anyone I know and takes as much pride in this book as I do—thank you. Your continued enthusiasm and optimism make all the long hours of research worth the effort.

Steven A. LuKanic
Los Angeles, California

KEY TO ABBREVIATIONS

(TF) = TELEFEATURE
Motion pictures made for television with an on-air running time of 1-1/2 hours to 4-1/2 hours on commercial television; or 1 hour to 4 hours on non-commercial television.

(CTF) = CABLE TELEFEATURE
Motion pictures made for cable television with an on-air running time of 1 hour to 4 hours.

(MS) = MINISERIES
Motion pictures made for television with an on-air running time of 4-1/2 hours or more on commercial television; or 4 hours or more on non-commercial television.

(CMS) = CABLE MINISERIES
Motion pictures made for cable television with an on-air running time of 4 hours or more.

(FD) = FEATURE DOCUMENTARY
Documentary films made for theatrical distribution or feature length (1 or more hours.)

(AF) = ANIMATED FEATURE

(AS) = ANIMATED SHORT

KEY TO SYMBOLS

★★ = Academy Award Win for Best Performance by an Actor or Actress in a Leading Role

★ = Academy Award Nomination for Best Performance by an Actor or Actress in a Leading Role

✪✪ = Academy Award Win for Best Performance by an Actor or Actress in a Supporting Role

✪ = Academy Award Nomination for Best Performance by an Actor or Actress in a Supporting Role

† = after an actor's name denotes deceased

HOW TO USE THIS BOOK

The main purpose of this book is to provide an easy, practical and comprehensive reference to film actors and their work. The actors are listed alphabetically by name with a rundown of their credits by year. We do not editorialize their listings—their credits speak for themselves.

We also believe in the old saying that there are no small parts, just small actors, so this book lists credits for box office superstars as well as actors who may have only uttered one or two lines in a film. The only requirement is that the actor's name must be listed in the credits of a particular feature film, television or cable movie or miniseries in order to have that credit listed in the book (with exception to uncredited cameo appearances which are noted accordingly). We've primarily listed actors who are currently active in the industry or have worked in features or television during the past ten years. There are a few exceptions (e.g. Doris Day, Ronald Reagan), but the book's primary focus is on working actors in the feature film world of today. Thus, credits for deceased actors are not listed (although we have included their names under many of the films listed in the new INDEX BY FILM TITLE. These credits are noted with a "†" next to their names). As the book went to press, sadly the film world lost the wonderful talents of Jessica Tandy, Burt Lancaster, Raul Julia, Martha Raye and Patrick O'Neal. We've left their credits in as a tribute to their illustrious and celebrated careers.

Please note, the book does *not* include credits for stage productions, episodic television and cable series, commercials, infomercials, music videos, exercise videos, porn flicks, industrial films, courtroom appearances or murder trials. We *do*, however, list credits for a few noteworthy short films (e.g. Michael Jackson and Anjelica Huston in *CAPTAIN EO*).

Keeping this criteria in mind, be assured that we will never intentionally omit an actor or credit; likewise, we try to verify all names and credits listed and are constantly revising, updating, and cross-checking for accuracy against many different, reliable sources. Should you find errors or omissions, please bring them to our attention so that we can continue to improve the book.

A few other explanations as you use the book:

NAMES: If an actor was born with a different name or has been credited in a film under a different name, that name (or names) is listed in italics directly beneath the name listed, e.g.,

R O S E A N N E
(Roseanne Arnold/Roseanne Barr)

Actors with un-hyphenated last names and alter egos continue to pose a challenge as to where we place them in the alphabet (e.g., Helena Bonham Carter; Paul Reubens/Pee Wee Herman). To help alleviate some of the confusion, if you look up a particular actor in the "wrong" section, you'll usually find a note indicating where in the book they are actually listed.

BIRTHDATE & BIRTHPLACE INFORMATION: We have included this information when available.

CONTACT INFORMATION: Undoubtedly, this is the most difficult information to obtain and maintain, not only because it changes daily, but because so many agencies refuse to provide us the names of the clients they represent. Our apologies to the actors listed in the book who don't have contact information listed; we encourage them to inform their agents to work with us in future editions and allow us that information, or keep us updated on your whereabouts. If you'd like to get in touch with someone in the book and no contact information is listed, or it has changed since publication call the Screen Actors Guild.

FILM TITLES: From the script to the screen, films often change titles (e.g., *COP TIPS WAITRESS $2 MILLION TIP* became *IT COULD HAPPEN TO YOU.*) International distribution only adds to the confusion as films take on new foreign titles, and to complicate things further, many films change titles *again* when they're released on video or broadcast on television. We've tried to simplify all this by using the following guidelines:

Most American films are listed by their original U.S.-theatrical release titles. In some cases, alternate or foreign titles for these releases are listed in italics, e.g.,

WHO'LL STOP THE RAIN *DOG SOLDIERS* United Artists, 1978

In most cases, we have not included any alternate video or television titles for American theatrical releases; however, we *have* listed made-for-television or cable movies and miniseries by their original broadcast titles. Also, while there are numerous films which bypass theatrical distribution and are released solely on video, or are intentionally made for the video market, most are not included in this book.

In the case of foreign films from English-speaking countries, we have listed and italicized their original titles if different from their American release titles, e.g.,

GOSPEL ACCORDING TO VIC *HEAVENLY PURSUITS* Skouras Pictures, 1985, British

As for foreign films from non English-speaking countries, we have listed and italicized their original titles if different in meaning from their American release titles, e.g.,

THE WONDERFUL CROOK *PAS SI MÉCHANT QUE ÇA* New Yorker, 1974, Swiss-French

Foreign films which were either not released in the U.S. or released here without changing titles are listed by their original foreign titles, e.g.,

GERMINAL   Sony Pictures Classics, 1993, French

DISTRIBUTORS AND PRODUCTION COMPANIES: Original American distributors are listed after feature film titles. Foreign films released in the U.S. will usually have their U.S. distributors or production companies listed; in the case of foreign films not released in the U.S., original distributors or production companies are listed wherever possible. Television movies and miniseries are identified not by the network on which they aired but rather by the name of their production companies (with a few exceptions where the names of the production companies were not available at press time). Feature films without distributors are also listed with the names of their production companies.

YEAR OF RELEASE: For American films, we have generally listed the year in which the film was first shown theatrically in the U.S., regardless of whether it was released nationwide. If a movie opened in New York or Los Angeles on the last day of 1991, we have indicated that year as the release date. If a film was completed in one year and then shelved for release until several years later, we have indicated the year of release, and in some cases, the year in which it was filmed. For films not yet released, the dates listed are projections.

In the case of foreign films, we have listed the year of release in the country of origin, which often differs from the U.S. release date anywhere from one to five years.

COUNTRY OF ORIGIN: So many factors are involved when determining this—where the film is made, who's making it, who's paying for it, etc. Therefore, we have taken the information at hand and made decisions based on that.

ACADEMY AWARDS: Best Actor, Actress, Supporting Actor and Supporting Actress nominees and winners are noted, both under individual actors' listings as well as in the two Academy Award sections in the back of the book. If you can't remember all the Best Actor or Actress nominees in 1992, for example, just look in the INDEX BY YEAR section. If you can't remember all the films which have earned Robert De Niro Oscar nods, look under "De Niro" in the INDEX BY NAME section.

ADDITIONAL INFORMATION: Voiceover work in animated films, narration and other non-visual acting skills often contribute so much to a particular film, so we've included those credits and list them as follows:

PCAHONTAS (AF)   Buena Vista, 1995 (voice)

We've also indicated where actors have directed or co-directed the film(s) in which they appear, an accomplishment which seems well worth noting.

★ ★ ★

FILM ACTORS

A

ANGELA AAMES
SCARFACE   Universal, 1983
THE LOST EMPIRE   JGM Enterprises, 1984
BASIC TRAINING   The Movie Store, 1985

WILLIE AAMES
(William Upton)
b. July 15, 1960 - California

FRANKENSTEIN (TF)   Dan Curtis Productions, 1973
SCAVENGER HUNT   20th Century Fox, 1979
PARADISE   Avco Embassy, 1982, Canadian
ZAPPED!   Embassy, 1982
CUT AND RUN   1985, Italian
KILLING MACHINE   Golden Sun Productions, 1986, Spanish
EIGHT IS ENOUGH: A FAMILY REUNION (TF)   Lorimar TV, 1987
AN EIGHT IS ENOUGH WEDDING (TF)   Lorimar TV, 1989

CAROLINE AARON
Agent: William Morris Agency - Beverly Hills, 310/274-7451

CRIMES AND MISDEMEANORS   Orion, 1989
EDWARD SCISSORHANDS   20th Century Fox, 1990
ALICE   Orion, 1990

ALLAN AARONS
ADVENTURES IN BABYSITTING   Buena Vista, 1987

BRUCE ABBOTT
OUT OF TIME (TF)   Columbia TV, 1988
TRAPPED (CTF)   MCA/Cine Enterprises, 1989
JOHNNY RYAN (TF)   Dan Curtis TV Productions/MGM-UA TV/
   NBC Productions, 1990

DIAHNNE ABBOTT
b. 1945 - New York, New York

NEW YORK, NEW YORK   United Artists, 1977
JO JO DANCER, YOUR LIFE IS CALLING   Columbia, 1986

KAREEM ABDUL-JABBAR
GAME OF DEATH   Columbia, 1979, U.S.-Hong Kong
AIRPLANE!   Paramount, 1980

IAN ABERCROMBIE
KICKS (TF)   ABC Circle Films, 1985
ZANDALEE   Electric Pictures/ITC Entertainment Group, 1991

F. MURRAY ABRAHAM
b. October 24, 1939 - Pittsburgh, Pennsylvania
Agent: William Morris Agency - Beverly Hills, 310/274-7451

THEY MIGHT BE GIANTS   Universal, 1971
SERPICO   Paramount, 1973
THE SUNSHINE BOYS   MGM/United Artists, 1975
ALL THE PRESIDENT'S MEN   Warner Bros., 1976
THE RITZ   Warner Bros., 1976
MADMAN   1978, Israeli
THE BIG FIX   Universal, 1978
SCARFACE   Universal, 1983
AMADEUS ★★   Orion, 1984
DREAM WEST (MS)   Sunn Classic Pictures, 1986
THE NAME OF THE ROSE   20th Century Fox, 1986,
   West German-Italian-French

AN INNOCENT MAN   Buena Vista, 1989
THE BONFIRE OF THE VANITIES   Warner Bros., 1990 (uncredited)
MOBSTERS   Universal, 1991
BY THE SWORD   The Movie Group, 1992
LAST ACTION HERO   Columbia, 1993
SURVIVING THE GAME   New Line Cinema, 1994
NOSTRADAMUS   Orion Classics, 1994, British

JIM ABRAHAMS
b. May 10, 1944 - Milwaukee, Wisconsin
Agent: UTA - Beverly Hills, 310/273-6700

KENTUCKY FRIED MOVIE   United Film Distribution, 1977
AIRPLANE!   Paramount, 1980 (also co-directed)

VICTORIA ABRIL
THE LOVERS   Aries Film Releasing, 1990, Spanish
TIE ME UP! TIE ME DOWN!   *ATAME*   Miramax Films,
   1990, Spanish
HIGH HEELS   Miramax Films, 1991, Spanish-French
INTRUSO   1992
KIKA   1993
JIMMY HOLLYWOOD   Paramount, 1994

SHARON ACKER
Agent: The Characters Talent Agency, Ltd. - Toronto, Canada,
   416/964-8522

LUCKY JIM   Kingsley International, 1957, British
WAITING FOR CAROLINE   1967, Canadian
POINT BLANK   MGM, 1967
THE FIRST TIME   United Artists, 1969
ACT OF THE HEART   Universal, 1970, Canadian
A CLEAR AND PRESENT DANGER (TF)   Universal TV, 1970
HEC RAMSEY (TF)   Universal TV/Mark VII Ltd., 1972
THE STRANGER (TF)   Bing Crosby Productions, 1973
THE HANGED MAN (TF)   Fenady Associates/Bing Crosby
   Productions, 1974
OUR MAN FLINT: DEAD ON TARGET (TF)   20th Century
   Fox TV, 1976
THE HOSTAGE HEART (TF)   Andrew J. Fenady Associates/
   MGM TV, 1977
THE MURDER THAT WOULDN'T DIE (TF)   Universal TV, 1980
HAPPY BIRTHDAY TO ME   Columbia, 1981, Canadian

JOSS ACKLAND
b. February 29, 1928 - London, England
Agent: Susan Smith & Associates - Beverly Hills, 213/852-4777

THE GHOST SHIP   RKO Radio, 1943
SEVEN DAYS TO NOON   Mayer-Kinglsey, 1950, British
RASPUTIN—THE MAD MONK   *I KILLED RASPUTIN*
   20th Century Fox, 1966, British-French-Italian
MR. FORBUSH AND THE PENGUINS   1971
THE HOUSE THAT DRIPPED BLOOD   Cinerama Releasing
   Corporation, 1971, British
VILLAIN   MGM, 1971, British
CRESCENDO   Warner Bros., 1972, British
THE HAPPINESS CAGE   *THE MIND SNATCHERS*   Cinerama
   Releasing Corporation, 1972
ENGLAND MADE ME   Cine Globe, 1973, British
HITLER: THE LAST TEN DAYS   1973, U.S.-Italian
PENNY GOLD   Scotia-Barber, 1973, British
THE THREE MUSKETEERS   20th Century Fox, 1974, British
THE BLACK WINDMILL   Universal, 1974, British
S*P*Y*S   20th Century Fox, 1974, British-U.S.
THE LITTLE PRINCE   Paramount, 1974, British
GREAT EXPECTATIONS (TF)   Transcontinental Film Productions,
   1974, British
OPERATION DAYBREAK   *PRICE OF FREEDOM*   Warner Bros.,
   1975, British
ONE OF OUR DINOSAURS IS MISSING   Buena Vista,
   1975, U.S.-British
ROYAL FLASH   20th Century Fox, 1976, British
WATERSHIP DOWN (AF)   Avco Embassy, 1978, British (voice)
SILVER BEARS   Columbia, 1978

WHO IS KILLING THE GREAT CHEFS OF EUROPE?
 Warner Bros., 1978
SAINT JACK   New World, 1979
THE APPLE   Cannon, 1980, U.S.-West German
ROUGH CUT   Paramount, 1980
DANGEROUS DAVIES - THE LAST DETECTIVE   ITC/Inner Circle/
 Maidenhead Films, 1980, British
A ZED AND TWO NOUGHTS   Skouras Pictures, 1985,
 British-Dutch
LADY JANE   Paramount, 1985, British
THE SICILIAN   20th Century Fox, 1987
WHITE MISCHIEF   Columbia, 1987, British
LETHAL WEAPON 2   Warner Bros., 1989
JEKYLL & HYDE (TF)   King-Phoenix Entertainment/London
 Weekend TV, 1990, U.S.-British
THE SECRET LIFE OF IAN FLEMING (CTF)   Saban-Scherick
 Productions, 1990, U.S.-British
THE OBJECT OF BEAUTY   Avenue Pictures, 1991
BILL & TED'S BOGUS JOURNEY   Orion, 1991
THE MIGHTY DUCKS   Buena Vista, 1992
MOTHER'S BOYS   Dimension/Miramax Films, 1994
THE PRINCESS AND THE GOBLIN (AF)   Hemdale, 1994 (voice)
MIRACLE ON 34TH STREET   20th Century Fox, 1994

DEBORAH ADAIR
RICH MEN, SINGLE WOMEN (TF)   Aaron Spelling
 Productions, 1990

BRANDON ADAMS
D2: THE MIGHTY DUCKS   Buena Vista, 1994

BROOKE ADAMS
b. 1949 - New York, New York
Agent: Susan Smith & Associates - Beverly Hills, 213/852-4777

MURDER ON FLIGHT 502 (TF)   Spelling-Goldberg
 Productions, 1975
SHOCK WAVES   Joseph Brenner Associates, 1977
INVASION OF THE BODY SNATCHERS   United Artists, 1978
DAYS OF HEAVEN   Paramount, 1978
THE GREAT TRAIN ROBBERY   *THE FIRST GREAT TRAIN
 ROBBERY*   United Artists, 1979, British
A MAN, A WOMAN AND A BANK   Avco Embassy,
 1979, Canadian
CUBA   United Artists, 1979
TELL ME A RIDDLE   Filmways, 1980
UTILITIES   1981, Canadian
THE DEAD ZONE   Paramount, 1983, Canadian
ALMOST YOU   TLC Films/20th Century Fox, 1984
LACE (MS)   Lorimar Productions, 1984
SPECIAL PEOPLE: BASED ON A TRUE STORY (TF)   Joe Cates
 Productions/CTV Broadcasting Corporation, 1984,
 U.S.-Canadian
KEY EXCHANGE   TLC Films/20th Century Fox, 1985
LACE II (MS)   Lorimar Productions, 1985
THE STUFF   New World, 1985
THE LION OF AFRICA (CTF)   HBO Pictures/Lois Luger
 Productions, 1987
BRIDESMAIDS (TF)   Motown Productions/Qintex Entertainment/
 Deaune Productions, 1989
THE UNBORN   Califilm, 1991

CATLIN ADAMS
THE JERK   Universal, 1979
THE JAZZ SINGER   AFD, 1980

DON ADAMS
b. April 13, 1926 - New York, NY

THE NUDE BOMB   Universal, 1980
GET SMART, AGAIN! (TF)   Phoenix Entertainment Group/
 IndieProd Co., 1989

EDIE ADAMS
(Elizabeth Edith Enke)
b. April 16, 1927 - Kingston, Pennsylvania

THE APARTMENT   United Artists, 1960
LOVER COME BACK   Universal, 1962
CALL ME BWANA   United Artists, 1963
IT'S A MAD MAD MAD MAD WORLD   United Artists, 1963
UNDER THE YUM YUM TREE   Columbia, 1963
LOVE WITH THE PROPER STRANGER   Paramount, 1964
THE BEST MAN   United Artists, 1964
MADE IN PARIS   MGM, 1966
THE OSCAR   Embassy, 1966
THE HONEY POT   United Artists, 1967, British-U.S.-Italian
EVIL ROY SLADE (TF)   Universal TV, 1971
THE RETURN OF JOE FORRESTER   *COP ON THE BEAT* (TF)
 Columbia, 1975
UP IN SMOKE   Paramount, 1978

JANE ADAMS
MRS. PARKER AND THE VICIOUS CIRCLE   Fine Line Features/
 New Line Cinema, 1994

JOEY LAUREN ADAMS
SLEEP WITH ME   MGM/UA, 1994

MASON ADAMS
b. February 26, 1919 - New York, New York

ADAM (TF)   Alan Landsburg Productions, 1983
PASSIONS (TF)   Carson Production Group/Wizan TV
 Enterprises, 1984
THE NIGHT THEY SAVED CHRISTMAS (TF)
 Robert Halmi, Inc., 1984
UNDER SIEGE (TF)   Ohlmeyer Communications Company/
 Telepictures Productions, 1986
F/X   Orion, 1986
RAGE OF ANGELS: THE STORY CONTINUES (MS)
 NBC Productions, 1986
HOUSEGUEST   Buena Vista, 1995

MAUD ADAMS
(Maud Wikstrom)
b. February 12, 1945 - Lulea, Sweden

THE BOYS IN THE BAND   National General, 1970
THE CHRISTIAN LICORICE STORE   National General, 1971
THE GIRL IN BLUE   *U-TURN*   Cinerama Releasing Corporation,
 1973, Canadian
THE MAN WITH THE GOLDEN GUN   United Artists, 1974, British
ROLLERBALL   United Artists, 1975
KILLER FORCE   American International, 1975, British-Swiss
L'UOMO SENZA PIETA   1977, Italian
PLAYING FOR TIME (TF)   Syzygy Productions, 1980
THE HOSTAGE TOWER (TF)   Jerry Leider Productions, 1980
TATTOO   20th Century Fox, 1981
OCTOPUSSY   MGM/UA, 1983, British
NAIROBI AFFAIR (TF)   Robert Halmi, Inc., 1984
TARGET EAGLE   1984, Spanish-Mexican
BLACKE'S MAGIC (TF)   Universal TV, 1986
THE WOMEN'S CLUB   Weintraub-Cloverleaf/Scorsese
 Productions, 1987
JANE AND THE LOST CITY   Marcel-Robertson Productions/Glen
 Films Productions, 1987, British
MAN OF PASSION   Golden Sun Productions, 1988, Spanish

WESLEY ADDY
b. August 4, 1913 - Omaha, Nebraska

THE FIRST LEGION   United Artists, 1951
MY SIX CONVICTS   Universal, 1952
KISS ME DEADLY   United Artists, 1955
THE BIG KNIFE   United Artists, 1955
TIMETABLE   1956
THE GARMENT JUNGLE   1957
TEN SECONDS TO HELL   United Artists, 1959, British

WHAT EVER HAPPENED TO BABY JANE?   Warner Bros., 1962
FOUR FOR TEXAS   1963
HUSH...HUSH, SWEET CHARLOTTE   20th Century-Fox, 1964
SECONDS   Paramount, 1966
MISTER BUDDWING   MGM, 1966
TORA! TORA! TORA!   20th Century Fox, 1970, U.S.-Japanese
THE GRISSOM GANG   Cinerama Releasing Corporation, 1971
NETWORK   MGM/United Artists, 1976
THE EUROPEANS   Levitt-Pickman, 1979, British
THE VERDICT   20th Century Fox, 1982
THE BOSTONIANS   Almi Pictures, 1984

JEAN CLAUDE ADELIN
CHOCOLAT   Orion Classics, 1988, French

ISABELLE ADJANI
b. June 27, 1955 - Paris, France

LE PETIT BOUGNAT   1969, French
FAUSTINE AND THE BEAUTIFUL SUMMER   1971, French
THE SLAP   1974, French
THE STORY OF ADELE H ★   New World, 1975, French
THE TENANT   Paramount, 1976, French-U.S.
BAROCCO   1976
VIOLETTE ET FRANCOIS   1977, French
THE DRIVER   20th Century Fox, 1978
NOSFERATU *THE VAMPYRE*   20th Century Fox, 1979,
   West German-French-U.S.
THE BRONTE SISTERS   1979, French-British
CLARA ET LES CHICS TYPES   1980
POSSESSION   1981, French-West German
QUARTET   New World, 1981, British-French
ONE DEADLY SUMMER   1983, French
SUBWAY   Island Pictures, 1985, French
ISHTAR   Columbia, 1987
CAMILLE CLAUDEL ★   Orion Classics, 1988, French

SUZANNE ADKINSON
RACING WITH THE MOON   Paramount, 1984

MATT ADLER
FLIGHT OF THE NAVIGATOR   Buena Vista, 1986
NORTH SHORE   Universal, 1987
WHITE WATER SUMMER   Columbia, 1987
DREAM A LITTLE DREAM   Vestron, 1989
DIVING IN   Skouras Pictures, 1990

FRANK ADONIS
EYES OF LAURA MARS   Columbia, 1978
RAGING BULL   United Artists, 1980

SADE ADU
ABSOLUTE BEGINNERS   Orion, 1986, British

ALAR AEDMA
SADIE AND SON (TF)   Norton Wright Productions/Kenny Rogers
   Organization/ITC Productions, 1987

BEN AFFLECK
Agent: Paradigm - Los Angeles, 310/277-4400

SCHOOL TIES   Paramount, 1992

CASEY AFFLECK
UNTITLED VAN SANT/ZISKIN   Columbia, 1995

BEHROOZ AFRAKHAN
Agent: The Tyler Kjar Agency - Toluca Lake, 818/760-0321

DYING YOUNG   20th Century Fox, 1991

ROBERT AGINS
THE COLOR OF MONEY   Buena Vista, 1986

HAILEY ELLEN AGNEW
b. November 4, 1986 - Palo Alto, California

FOR KEEPS   TriStar, 1988

JENNY AGUTTER
b. December 20, 1952 - Taunton, Devonshire, England
Agent: Gersh Agency - Beverly Hills, 310/274-6611

EAST OF SUDAN   Columbia, 1964, British
GATES TO PARADISE   1967, British
STAR! *THOSE WERE THE HAPPY TIMES*
   20th Century Fox, 1968
I START COUNTING   United Artists, 1969, British
THE RAILWAY CHILDREN   Universal, 1971, British
WALKABOUT   20th Century Fox, 1971, British-Australian
THE SNOW GOOSE (TF)   NBC, 1971
A WAR OF CHILDREN (TF)   Tomorrow Entertainment, 1972
LOGAN'S RUN   MGM/United Artists, 1976
THE EAGLE HAS LANDED   Columbia, 1977, British
EQUUS   United Artists, 1977, British
THE MAN IN THE IRON MASK (TF)   Norman Rosemont
   Productions/ITC, 1977, U.S.-British
DOMINIQUE   Sword and Sworcery Productions, 1979, British
CHINA 9, LIBERTY 37   Titanus, 1978, Italian
THE RIDDLE OF THE SANDS   1979, British
SWEET WILLIAM   Kendon Films, 1980, British
THE SURVIVOR   Hemdale, 1981, Australian
AMY   Buena Vista, 1981
AN AMERICAN WEREWOLF IN LONDON   Universal, 1981
SECRET PLACES   TLC Films/20th Century Fox, 1984, British
SILAS MARNER (TF)   BBC, 1985, British
CHILD'S PLAY 2   Universal, 1990
DARKMAN   Universal, 1990 (uncredited)

MICHAEL AHERNE
THE COMMITMENTS   20th Century Fox, 1991

DANNY AIELLO
b. June 20, 1935 - New York, New York
Agent: UTA - Beverly Hills, 310/273-6700

BANG THE DRUM SLOWLY   Paramount, 1973
THE GODFATHER, PART II   Paramount, 1974
THE FRONT   Columbia, 1976
FINGERS   Brut Productions, 1978
BLOODBROTHERS   Warner Bros., 1978
LOVEY: A CIRCLE OF CHILDREN, PART II (TF)   Time-Life
   Productions, 1978
DEFIANCE   American International, 1980
HIDE IN PLAIN SIGHT   MGM/United Artists, 1980
CHU CHU AND THE PHILLY FLASH   20th Century-Fox, 1981
FORT APACHE, THE BRONX   20th Century Fox, 1981
AMITYVILLE II: THE POSSESSION   Orion, 1982
A QUESTION OF HONOR (TF)   Roger Gimbel Productions/EMI TV/
   Sonny Grosso Productions, 1982
BLOOD FEUD (TF)   20th Century Fox TV/Glickman-Selznick
   Productions, 1983
DEATHMASK   1984
OLD ENOUGH   Orion Classics, 1984
ONCE UPON A TIME IN AMERICA   The Ladd Company/
   Warner Bros., 1984, U.S.-Italian-Canadian
KEY EXCHANGE   TLC Films/20th Century Fox, 1985
LADY BLUE (TF)   David Gerber Productions/MGM-UA TV, 1985
THE PROTECTOR   Warner Bros., 1985, U.S.-Hong Kong
THE PURPLE ROSE OF CAIRO   Orion, 1985
THE STUFF   New World, 1985
DADDY (TF)   Robert Greenwald Productions, 1987
MAN ON FIRE   TriStar, 1987, Italian-French
MOONSTRUCK   MGM/UA, 1987
THE PICK-UP ARTIST   20th Century Fox, 1987
RADIO DAYS   Orion, 1987
ALONE IN THE NEON JUNGLE (TF)   Robert Halmi, Inc., 1988
THE JANUARY MAN   MGM/UA, 1989
THE THIRD SOLUTION *RUSSICUM* (TF)   1989, Italian
THE PREPPIE MURDER (TF)   Jack Grossbart Productions/
   Spectator Films, 1989
DO THE RIGHT THING ○   Universal, 1989

HARLEM NIGHTS   Paramount, 1989
THE CLOSER   Ion Pictures, 1990
JACOB'S LADDER   TriStar, 1990
ONCE AROUND   Universal, 1991
HUDSON HAWK   TriStar, 1991
29TH STREET   20th Century Fox, 1991
RUBY   Triumph Releasing Corporation, 1992
MISTRESS   Tribeca Films, 1992
THE CEMETERY CLUB   Buena Vista, 1993
THE PICKLE   Columbia, 1993
ME AND THE KID   Orion, 1993
THE PROFESSIONAL   Columbia, 1994
PRET-A-PORTER   Miramax Films, 1994
CITY HALL   Columbia, 1995

RICK AIELLO

Agent: The Artists Agency - Los Angeles, 310/277-7779

STREETS OF GOLD   20th Century Fox, 1986
LAST EXIT TO BROOKLYN   Cinecom, 1989, West German-U.S.
DO THE RIGHT THING   Universal, 1989
HARLEM NIGHTS   Paramount, 1989
THE CLOSER   Ion Pictures, 1990
29TH STREET   20th Century Fox, 1991

ANOUK AIMÉE
(Françoise Sorya Dreyfus)
b. April 27, 1932 - Paris, France

LA MAISON SOUS LA MER   1947, French
THE LOVERS OF VERONA   1949, French
THE GOLDEN SALAMANDER   Eagle Lion, 1950, British
LE RIDEAU CRAMOISI   1951, French
THE MAN WHO WATCHED TRAINS GO BY   *THE PARIS EXPRESS*
   1952, British
LES MAUVAISES RENCONTRES   1955, French
CONTRABAND SPAIN   1955, British
POT BOUILLE   *THE HOUSE OF LOVERS*   Continental,
   1957, French
MONTPARNASSE 19   1958, French
LA TETE CONTRE LES MURS   1959, French
THE CHASERS   1959, French
THE JOURNEY   MGM, 1959
LA DOLCE VITA   Astor, 1960, Italian
THE JOKER   Lopert, 1961, French
LOLA   Films Around the World, 1961, French
IL GIUDIZIO UNIVERSALE   1961, Italian
SODOM AND GOMORRAH   20th Century Fox, 1961,
   Italian-French-U.S.
8 1/2   Embassy, 1963, Italian
OF FLESH AND BLOOD   *LES GRANDS CHEMINS*   Times,
   1963, French-Italian
IL SUCCESSO   1963, Italian-French
WHITE VOICES   Rizzoli, 1964, Italian-French
LA FUGA   1965, Italian
A MAN AND A WOMAN ★   Allied Artists, 1966, French
JUSTINE   20th Century Fox, 1969
THE MODEL SHOP   Columbia, 1969
THE APPOINTMENT   MGM, 1969
SECOND CHANCE   *SI C'ÉTAIT A REFAIRE*   United Artists
   Classics, 1976, French
FIRST LOVE   *MON PREMIER AMOUR*   1978, French
TRAGEDY OF A RIDICULOUS MAN   The Ladd Company/
   Warner Bros., 1981, Italian
GENERAL OF THE DEAD ARMY   1983
SUCCESS IS THE BEST REVENGE   Triumph/Columbia,
   1984, British
LONG LIVE LIFE   1984
A MAN AND A WOMAN: 20 YEARS LATER   Warner Bros.,
   1986, French
PRET-A-PORTER   Miramax Films, 1994

FRANKLYN AJAYE
CAR WASH   Universal, 1976
CONVOY   United Artists, 1978
THE JAZZ SINGER   AFD, 1980
GET CRAZY   Embassy, 1983
THE WRONG GUYS   New World, 1988

ANDRA AKERS
DESERT HEARTS   Samuel Goldwyn Company, 1985

KAREN AKERS
b. October 13, 1945 - New York, New York

THE PURPLE ROSE OF CAIRO   Orion, 1985

PHIL AKIN
SADIE AND SON (TF)   Norton Wright Productions/Kenny Rogers
   Organization/ITC Productions, 1987

JOE ALASKEY
CASPER   Universal, 1995

LOU ALBANO
WISE GUYS   MGM/UA, 1986

EDDIE ALBERT
(Edward Albert Heimberger)
b. April 22, 1908 - Rock Island, Illinois

BROTHER RAT   Warner Bros., 1938
ON YOUR TOES   Warner Bros., 1939
FOUR WIVES   Warner Bros., 1939
BROTHER RAT AND A BABY   Warner Bros., 1940
AN ANGEL FROM TEXAS   Warner Bros., 1940
MY LOVE CAME BACK   Warner Bros., 1940
A DISPATCH FROM REUTERS   Warner Bros., 1940
FOUR MOTHERS   Warner Bros., 1941
THE WAGONS ROLL AT NIGHT   Warner Bros., 1941
OUT OF THE FOG   Warner Bros., 1941
THIEVES FALL OUT   Warner Bros., 1941
THE GREAT MR. NOBODY   1941
TREAT 'EM ROUGH   Universal, 1942
EAGLE SQUADRON   Universal, 1942
LADIES' DAY   1943
LADY BODYGUARD   Paramount, 1943
BOMBARDIER   1943
STRANGE VOYAGE   1945
RENDEZVOUS WITH ANNIE   Republic, 1946
THE PERFECT MARRIAGE   Paramount, 1946
SMASH-UP   *SMASH-UP—THE STORY OF A WOMAN*
   Universal, 1947
TIME OUT OF MIND   Universal, 1947
HIT PARADE OF 1947   1947
THE DUDE GOES WEST   Allied Artists, 1948
YOU GOTTA STAY HAPPY   Universal, 1948
THE FULLER BRUSH GIRL   Columbia, 1950
MEET ME AFTER THE SHOW   1951
YOU'RE IN THE NAVY NOW   *U.S.S. TEAKETTLE*
   20th Century Fox, 1951
ACTORS AND SIN   United Artists, 1952
CARRIE   Paramount, 1952
ROMAN HOLIDAY ✪   Paramount, 1953
THE GIRL RUSH   Paramount, 1955
OKLAHOMA!   Magna, 1955
I'LL CRY TOMORROW   MGM, 1955
ATTACK!   United Artists, 1956
TEAHOUSE OF THE AUGUST MOON   MGM, 1956
THE SUN ALSO RISES   20th Century Fox, 1957
THE JOKER IS WILD   *ALL THE WAY*   Paramount, 1957
THE GUN RUNNERS   United Artists, 1958
THE ROOTS OF HEAVEN   20th Century Fox, 1958
ORDERS TO KILL   United Motion Picture Organization,
   1958, British
BELOVED INFIDEL   20th Century Fox, 1959
THE YOUNG DOCTORS   United Artists, 1961
THE TWO LITTLE BEARS   1961
MADISON AVENUE   20th Century Fox, 1962
THE LONGEST DAY   20th Century Fox, 1962
WHO'S GOT THE ACTION?   Paramount, 1962
MIRACLE OF THE WHITE STALLIONS   Buena Vista, 1963
CAPTAIN NEWMAN, M.D.   Universal, 1963
7 WOMEN   MGM, 1965
THE PARTY'S OVER   Allied Artists, 1966, British

SEE THE MAN RUN (TF)   Universal TV, 1971
THE HEARTBREAK KID ✪   20th Century Fox, 1972
FIREBALL FORWARD (TF)   20th Century Fox TV, 1972
McQ   Warner Bros., 1972
THE TAKE   1974
THE LONGEST YARD   Paramount, 1974
ESCAPE TO WITCH MOUNTAIN   Buena Vista, 1975
THE DEVIL'S RAIN   Bryanston, 1975, U.S.-Mexican
PROMISE HIM ANYTHING (TF)   ABC Circle Films, 1975
HUSTLE   Paramount, 1975
WHIFFS   20th Century Fox, 1975
BIRCH INTERVAL   Gamma III, 1976
MOVING VIOLATION   20th Century Fox, 1976
THE WORD (MS)   Charles Fries Productions/Stonehenge
     Productions, 1978
FOOLIN' AROUND   Columbia, 1979
EVENING IN BYZANTIUM (TF)   Universal TV, 1979
THE CONCORDE—AIRPORT '79   Universal, 1979
YESTERDAY   1980, Canadian
HOW TO BEAT THE HIGH COST OF LIVING   American
     International, 1980
GOLIATH AWAITS (TF)   Larry White Productions/Hugh Benson
     Productions/Columbia TV, 1981
TAKE THIS JOB AND SHOVE IT   Avco Embassy, 1981
YES, GIORGIO   MGM/UA, 1982
THE ACT   Artists Releasing Corporation/Film Ventures
     International, 1984
DREAMSCAPE   20th Century Fox, 1984
BURNING RAGE (TF)   Gilbert Cates Productions, 1984
STITCHES   International Film Marketing, 1985
IN LIKE FLYNN (TF)   Glen A. Larson Productions/20th Century Fox
     TV/Astral Film Productions, 1985, U.S.-Canadian
DRESS GRAY (MS)   von Zerneck Productions/Warner
     Bros. TV, 1986
HEAD OFFICE   TriStar, 1986
MERCY OR MURDER? (TF)   John J. McMahon Productions/
     MGM-UA TV, 1987
RETURN TO GREEN ACRES (TF)   JaYgee Productions/
     Orion TV, 1990

EDWARD ALBERT
b. February 20, 1951 - Los Angeles, California

THE FOOL KILLER   Allied Artists, 1965
BUTTERFLIES ARE FREE   Columbia, 1972
40 CARATS   Columbia, 1973
MIDWAY   Universal, 1976
THE SQUEEZE   *THE RIP-OFF*   Maverick International,
     1976, Italian-U.S.
THE DOMINO PRINCIPLE   Avco Embassy, 1977
THE PURPLE TAXI   *UN TAXI MAUVE*   1977, French-Italian-Irish
THE GREEK TYCOON   Universal, 1978
THE WORD (MS)   Charles Fries Productions/Stonehenge
     Productions, 1978
SILENT VICTORY: THE KITTY O'NEIL STORY (TF)
     Channing-Debin-Locke Company, 1979
THE LAST CONVERTIBLE (MS)   Universal TV, 1979
WHEN TIME RAN OUT   Warner Bros., 1980
GALAXY OF TERROR   *MINDWARP: AN INFINITY OF HORRORS/
     PLANET OF HORRORS*   New World, 1981
BUTTERFLY   Analysis, 1981, U.S.-Canadian
THE HOUSE WHERE EVIL DWELLS   MGM/UA, 1982,
     U.S.-Japanese
BLOOD FEUD (TF)   20th Century Fox TV/Glickman-Selznick
     Productions, 1983
A TIME TO DIE   *SEVEN GRAVES FOR ROGAN*   Almi Films, 1983
ELLIE   Shapiro Entertainment, 1984
GETTING EVEN   American Distribution Group, 1986
DISTORTIONS   Cori Films, 1987
THE RESCUE   Buena Vista, 1988

ALAN ALDA
b. January 28, 1936 - New York, New York
Agent: UTA - Beverly Hills, 310/273-6700

GONE ARE THE DAYS!   *PURLIE VICTORIOUS*   Trans-Lux, 1963
PAPER LION   United Artists, 1968
THE EXTRAORDINARY SEAMAN   MGM, 1969

CATCH-22   Paramount, 1970
THE MOONSHINE WAR   MGM, 1970
JENNY   Cinerama Releasing Corporation, 1970
THE MEPHISTO WALTZ   20th Century Fox, 1971
TO KILL A CLOWN   20th Century Fox, 1972
THE GLASS HOUSE   *TRUMAN CAPOTE'S THE GLASS
     HOUSE* (TF)   Tomorrow Entertainment, 1972
PLAYMATES (TF)   ABC Circle Films, 1972
ISN'T IT SHOCKING? (TF)   ABC Circle Films, 1973
KILL ME IF YOU CAN (TF)   Columbia TV, 1977
CALIFORNIA SUITE   Columbia, 1978
SAME TIME, NEXT YEAR   Universal, 1978
THE SEDUCTION OF JOE TYNAN   Universal, 1979
THE FOUR SEASONS   Universal, 1981 (also directed)
SWEET LIBERTY   Universal, 1986 (also directed)
A NEW LIFE   Paramount, 1988 (also directed)
CRIMES AND MISDEMEANORS   Orion, 1989
BETSY'S WEDDING   Buena Vista, 1990 (also directed)
WHISPERS IN THE DARK   Paramount, 1992
MANHATTAN MURDER MYSTERY   TriStar, 1993
AND THE BAND PLAYED ON (CTF)   HBO Pictures/Spelling
     Entertainment, 1993
WHITE MILE (CTF)   HBO Pictures, 1994
CANADIAN BACON   MGM/UA, 1994

BEATRICE ALDA
THE FOUR SEASONS   Universal, 1981
A NEW LIFE   Paramount, 1988

ELIZABETH ALDA
THE FOUR SEASONS   Universal, 1981

RUTANYA ALDA
CAN ELLEN BE SAVED? (TF)   ABC Circle Films, 1974
THE DEER HUNTER   Universal, 1978
MOMMIE DEAREST   Paramount, 1981
AMITYVILLE II: THE POSSESSION   Orion, 1982
RACING WITH THE MOON   Paramount, 1984
APPRENTICE TO MURDER   New World, 1987, Canadian
PRANCER   Orion, 1989
THE DARK HALF   Orion, 1993

NORMAN ALDEN
OPERATION BOTTLENECK   1961
MAN'S FAVORITE SPORT?   Universal, 1964
THE DEVIL'S BRIGADE   United Artists, 1968
TORA! TORA! TORA!   20th Century Fox, 1970, U.S.-Japanese
KANSAS CITY BOMBER   MGM, 1972
SEMI-TOUGH   United Artists, 1977

TOM ALDRICH
WHAT ABOUT BOB?   Buena Vista, 1991

NORMA ALEANDRO
THE OFFICIAL STORY   Historias Cinematograficas,
     1985, Argentine
GABY - A TRUE STORY ✪   TriStar, 1987, U.S.-Mexican
COUSINS   Paramount, 1989
DARK HOLIDAY (TF)   Peter Nelson-Lou Antonio Productions/The
     Finnegan-Pinchuk Company/Orion TV, 1989
VITAL SIGNS   20th Century Fox, 1990

AKI ALEONG
BRADDOCK: MISSING IN ACTION III   Cannon, 1988
FAREWELL TO THE KING   Orion, 1989

JACE ALEXANDER
Agent: Writers & Artists Agency - Los Angeles, 310/820-2240

MATEWAN   Cinecom, 1987
"CROCODILE" DUNDEE II   Paramount, 1988, U.S.-Australian
EIGHT MEN OUT   Orion, 1988
WHEN WE WERE YOUNG (TF)   Richard & Esther Shapiro
     Entertainment, 1989
MENENDEZ: A KILLING IN BEVERLY HILLS (MS)   Zev Braun
     Pictures/TriStar Television, 1994

JANE ALEXANDER
(Jane Quigley)
b. October 28, 1939 - Boston, Massachusetts
Agent: William Morris Agency - Beverly Hills, 310/274-7451

THE GREAT WHITE HOPE ★ 20th Century Fox, 1970
A GUNFIGHT Paramount, 1971
WELCOME HOME, JOHNNY BRISTOL (TF) Cinema Center, 1971
THE NEW CENTURIONS Columbia, 1972
MIRACLE ON 34TH STREET (TF) 20th Century Fox TV, 1973
THIS IS THE WEST THAT WAS (TF) Universal TV, 1974
DEATH BE NOT PROUD (TF) Good Housekeeping Productions/
    Westfall Productions, 1975
ALL THE PRESIDENT'S MEN ✪ Warner Bros., 1976
ELEANOR AND FRANKLIN (TF) Talent Associates, 1976
ELEANOR AND FRANKLIN: THE WHITE HOUSE YEARS (TF)
    Talent Associates, 1977
THE BETSY Allied Artists, 1978
KRAMER VS. KRAMER ✪ Columbia, 1979
BRUBAKER 20th Century Fox, 1980
PLAYING FOR TIME (TF) Syzygy Productions, 1980
NIGHT CROSSING Buena Vista, 1982
TESTAMENT ★ Paramount, 1983
CALAMITY JANE (TF) CBS Entertainment, 1983
CITY HEAT Warner Bros., 1984
MALICE IN WONDERLAND *THE RUMOR MILL* (TF)
    ITC Productions, 1985
SWEET COUNTRY Cinema Group, 1986, Greek
BLOOD AND ORCHIDS (MS) Lorimar Productions, 1986
IN LOVE AND WAR (TF) Carol Schreder Productions/Tisch-Avnet
    Productions, 1987
SQUARE DANCE Island Pictures, 1987
OPEN ADMISSIONS (TF) The Mount Company/Viacom
    Productions, 1988
GLORY TriStar, 1989 (uncredited)
DAUGHTER OF THE STREETS (TF) Adam Productions/20th
    Century Fox TV, 1990

JASON ALEXANDER
b. September 23, 1959 - Newark, New Jersey
Agent: William Morris Agency - Beverly Hills, 310/274-7451

ROCKABYE (TF) Roger Gimbel Productions/Peregrine
    Entertainment/Bertinelli Productions, 1986
PRETTY WOMAN Buena Vista, 1990
JACOB'S LADDER TriStar, 1990
CONEHEADS Paramount, 1993
THE PAPER Universal, 1994
THE RETURN OF JAFAR (AV) Buena Vista, 1994 (voice)
NORTH Columbia, 1994
BLANKMAN Columbia, 1994
STRANGER THINGS Columbia, 1995 (also directed)

CONSTANTIN ALEXANDROV
GORILLAS IN THE MIST Warner Bros./Universal, 1988

DENNIS ALEXIO
KICKBOXER Cannon, 1989

MUHAMMAD ALI
(Cassius Clay)
b. January 17, 1938

REQUIEM FOR A HEAVYWEIGHT Columbia, 1962
THE GREATEST Columbia, 1977
FREEDOM ROAD (TF) Zev Braun Productions/Freedom Road
    Films, 1979

ANA ALICIA
COWARD OF THE COUNTY (TF) Kraco Productions, 1981
ROMERO Four Seasons Entertainment, 1989

LISA ALIFF
DRAGNET Universal, 1987

MICHAEL ALLDREDGE
ABOUT LAST NIGHT... TriStar, 1986
ROBOTJOX Triumph Releasing Corporation, 1990

BILL ALLEN
RAD TriStar, 1986

CHAD ALLEN
TERRORVISION Empire Pictures, 1986

COREY ALLEN
b. June 29, 1934 - Cleveland, Ohio

THE BRIDGES AT TOKO-RI Paramount, 1954
THE MAD MAGICIAN Columbia, 1954
THE NIGHT OF THE HUNTER United Artists, 1955
REBEL WITHOUT A CAUSE Warner Bros., 1955
SHADOW ON THE WINDOW Columbia, 1957
PARTY GIRL MGM, 1958
PRIVATE PROPERTY Citation, 1960
SWEET BIRD OF YOUTH MGM, 1962
THE CHAPMAN REPORT Warner Bros., 1962

DEBBIE ALLEN
b. January 16, 1950 - Houston, Texas

JO JO DANCER, YOUR LIFE IS CALLING Columbia, 1986
BLANK CHECK Buena Vista, 1994

JO HARVEY ALLEN
TRUE STORIES Warner Bros., 1986
THE CLIENT Warner Bros., 1994

JOAN ALLEN
b. August 20, 1956 - Rochelle, Illinois

COMPROMISING POSITIONS Paramount, 1985
ALL MY SONS (TF) 1986
PEGGY SUE GOT MARRIED TriStar, 1986
MANHUNTER DEG, 1986
TUCKER - THE MAN AND HIS DREAM Paramount, 1988
IN COUNTRY Warner Bros., 1989
THE JAMES BRADY STORY (CTF) HBO Pictures/Enigma TV, 1991
SEARCHING FOR BOBBY FISCHER Paramount, 1993
JOSH AND S.A.M. Columbia, 1993
MAD LOVE Buena Vista, 1995

KAREN ALLEN
b. October 5, 1951 - Carrollton, Illinois

NATIONAL LAMPOON'S ANIMAL HOUSE Universal, 1978
MANHATTAN United Artists, 1979
THE WANDERERS Orion/Warner Bros., 1979
A SMALL CIRCLE OF FRIENDS United Artists, 1980
CRUISING United Artists, 1980
RAIDERS OF THE LOST ARK Paramount, 1981
SHOOT THE MOON MGM/United Artists, 1982
SPLIT IMAGE Orion, 1982
STARMAN Columbia, 1984
UNTIL SEPTEMBER MGM/UA, 1984
BACKFIRE New Century/Vista, 1987, U.S.-Canadian
THE GLASS MENAGERIE Cineplex Odeon, 1987
SCROOGED Paramount, 1988
ANIMAL BEHAVIOR Millimeter Films, 1989
CHALLENGER (TF) The IndieProd Company/King Phoenix
    Entertainment/George Englund, Jr. Productions, 1990
SECRET WEAPON (CTF) Griffin-Elysian Productions/TVS/
    ABC-Australia, 1990, U.S.-British-Australian
SWEET TALKER New Line Cinema, 1991
KING OF THE HILL Gramercy Pictures, 1993
GHOST IN THE MACHINE 20th Century Fox, 1993

KEITH ALLEN
THE SUPERGRASS Hemdale, 1985, British
CHICAGO JOE AND THE SHOWGIRL New Line Cinema, 1990
SECOND BEST Warner Bros., 1994

MIKKI ALLEN
REGARDING HENRY Paramount, 1991

NANCY ALLEN
b. June 24, 1950 - New York, New York

THE LAST DETAIL Columbia, 1973
CARRIE United Artists, 1976
I WANNA HOLD YOUR HAND Universal, 1978
1941 Universal/Columbia, 1979
HOME MOVIES United Artists Classics, 1979
DRESSED TO KILL Filmways, 1980
BLOW OUT Filmways, 1981
STRANGE INVADERS Orion, 1983, Canadian
THE BUDDY SYSTEM 20th Century Fox, 1984
NOT FOR PUBLICATION Samuel Goldwyn Company,
   1984, U.S.-British
THE PHILADELPHIA EXPERIMENT New World, 1984
TERROR IN THE AISLES (FD) Universal, 1984
ROBOCOP Orion, 1987
SWEET REVENGE Concorde, 1987
POLTERGEIST III MGM/UA, 1988
LIMIT UP MCEG, 1989
ROBOCOP 2 Orion, 1990
MEMORIES OF MURDER (CTF) Houston Lady Productions/
   Viacom, 1990
ROBOCOP 3 Orion, 1993

PATRICK ALLEN
ROMAN HOLIDAY (TF) Jerry Ludwig Enterprises, Inc./
   Paramount TV, 1987

STEVE ALLEN
b. December 26, 1921 - New York, New York

DOWN MEMORY LANE Eagle Lion, 1949
I'LL GET BY 1950
THE BENNY GOODMAN STORY 1956
THE BIG CIRCUS 1959
COLLEGE CONFIDENTIAL Universal, 1960
DON'T WORRY, WE'LL THINK OF A TITLE 1966
A MAN CALLED DAGGER MGM, 1967
WARNING SHOT Paramount, 1967
NOW YOU SEE IT, NOW YOU DON'T (TF) Universal TV, 1968
WHERE WERE YOU WHEN THE LIGHTS WENT OUT?
   MGM, 1968
THE COMIC Columbia, 1969
THE SUNSHINE BOYS MGM/United Artists, 1975
HEART BEAT Orion/Warner Bros., 1980
THE RATINGS GAME (CTF) Imagination-New Street
   Productions, 1984
AMAZON WOMEN ON THE MOON Universal, 1987
GREAT BALLS OF FIRE Orion, 1989
THE PLAYER Fine Line Features/New Line Cinema, 1992

TIM ALLEN
THE SANTA CLAUSE Buena Vista, 1994

TODD ALLEN
WYATT EARP Warner Bros., 1994

WOODY ALLEN
(Allen Stewart Konigsberg)
b. December 1, 1935 - Brooklyn, New York
Agent: ICM - New York, 212/556-5600

WHAT'S NEW PUSSYCAT? United Artists, 1965, British
WHAT'S UP, TIGER LILY? American International,
   1966 (also directed)
CASINO ROYALE Columbia, 1967, British

TAKE THE MONEY AND RUN Cinerama Releasing Corporation,
   1969 (also directed)
BANANAS United Artists, 1971 (also directed)
PLAY IT AGAIN, SAM Paramount, 1972
EVERYTHING YOU ALWAYS WANTED TO KNOW ABOUT SEX*
   (*BUT WERE AFRAID TO ASK) United Artists,
   1972 (also directed)
SLEEPER United Artists, 1973 (also directed)
LOVE AND DEATH United Artists, 1975 (also directed)
THE FRONT Columbia, 1976
ANNIE HALL ★ United Artists, 1977 (also directed)
MANHATTAN United Artists, 1979 (also directed)
STARDUST MEMORIES United Artists, 1980 (also directed)
A MIDSUMMER NIGHT'S SEX COMEDY Orion/Warner Bros.,
   1982 (also directed)
ZELIG Orion/Warner Bros., 1983 (also directed)
BROADWAY DANNY ROSE Orion, 1984 (also directed)
HANNAH AND HER SISTERS Orion, 1986 (also directed)
RADIO DAYS Orion, 1987 (voice) (also directed)
KING LEAR Cannon, 1987, U.S.-Swiss
NEW YORK STORIES Buena Vista, 1989
   (also directed his segment)
CRIMES AND MISDEMEANORS Orion, 1989 (also directed)
SCENES FROM A MALL Buena Vista, 1991
SHADOWS AND FOG Orion, 1992 (also directed)
HUSBANDS AND WIVES TriStar, 1992 (also directed)
MANHATTAN MURDER MYSTERY TriStar, 1993 (also directed)
DON'T DRINK THE WATER (TF) ABC, 1994 (also directed)

KIRSTIE ALLEY
b. January 12, 1955 - Wichita, Kansas
Agent: Metropolitan Talent Agency - Los Angeles, 213/857-4500

STAR TREK II: THE WRATH OF KHAN Paramount, 1982
CHAMPIONS Embassy, 1983, British
BLIND DATE New Line Cinema, 1984, British-Greek
RUNAWAY TriStar, 1984
NORTH AND SOUTH (MS) Wolper Productions/Warner
   Bros. TV, 1985
A BUNNY'S TALE (TF) Stan Margulies Company/ABC Circle
   Films, 1985
NORTH AND SOUTH, BOOK II (MS) Wolper Productions/
   Robert A. Papazian Productions/Warner Bros. TV, 1986
PRINCE OF BEL AIR (TF) Leonard Hill Films, 1986
INFIDELITY (TF) Mark-Jett Productions/ABC Circle Films, 1987
SUMMER SCHOOL Paramount, 1987
SHOOT TO KILL Buena Vista, 1988
LOVERBOY TriStar, 1989
LOOK WHO'S TALKING TriStar, 1989
MADHOUSE Orion, 1990
SIBLING RIVALRY Columbia, 1990
LOOK WHO'S TALKING TOO TriStar, 1990
LOOK WHO'S TALKING NOW TriStar, 1993
DAVID'S MOTHER (TF) Hearst Entertainment, 1994
VILLAGE OF THE DAMNED Universal, 1995

GREGG ALLMAN
b. December 8, 1947 - Nashville, Tennessee

RUSH MGM-Pathe, 1991

CHRISTOPHER ALLPORT
Agent: Susan Smith & Associates - Beverly Hills, 213/852-4777

CHINA BEACH (TF) Sacret, Inc. Productions/Warner
   Bros. TV, 1988
DAVID (TF) Tough Boys, Inc./Donald March Productions/ITC
   Entertainment Group, 1988

JUNE ALLYSON
(Ella Geisman)
b. October 7, 1917 - Bronx, New York
Agent: Shapiro-Lichtman - Los Angeles, 310/859-8877

BEST FOOT FORWARD MGM, 1943
GIRL CRAZY MGM, 1943
THOUSANDS CHEER MGM, 1943

TWO GIRLS AND A SAILOR   MGM, 1944
MEET THE PEOPLE   MGM, 1944
MUSIC FOR MILLIONS   MGM, 1944
HER HIGHNESS AND THE BELLBOY   MGM, 1945
THE SAILOR TAKES A WIFE   MGM, 1945
TWO SISTERS FROM BOSTON   MGM, 1946
TILL THE CLOUDS ROLL BY   MGM, 1946
THE SECRET HEART   MGM, 1946
HIGH BARBAREE   MGM, 1947
GOOD NEWS   MGM, 1947
THE BRIDE GOES WILD   MGM, 1948
THE THREE MUSKETEERS   MGM, 1948
WORDS AND MUSIC   MGM, 1948
LITTLE WOMEN   MGM, 1949
THE STRATTON STORY   MGM, 1949
THE REFORMER AND THE REDHEAD   MGM, 1950
RIGHT CROSS   MGM, 1950
TOO YOUNG TO KISS   MGM, 1951
THE GIRL IN WHITE   MGM, 1952
BATTLE CIRCUS   MGM, 1953
REMAINS TO BE SEEN   MGM, 1953
THE GLENN MILLER STORY   Universal, 1954
EXECUTIVE SUITE   MGM, 1954
WOMAN'S WORLD   20th Century-Fox, 1954
STRATEGIC AIR COMMAND   Paramount, 1955
THE McCONNELL STORY   Warner Bros., 1955
THE SHRIKE   Universal, 1955
THE OPPOSITE SEX   MGM, 1956
YOU CAN'T RUN AWAY FROM IT   Columbia, 1956
INTERLUDE   Universal, 1957
MY MAN GODFREY   Universal, 1957
STRANGER IN MY ARMS   1959
THEY ONLY KILL THEIR MASTERS   1972
CURSE OF THE BLACK WIDOW (TF)   Dan Curtis Productions/
   ABC Circle Films, 1977
BLACKOUT   1978, Canadian-French
THE KID WITH THE BROKEN HALO (TF)   Satellite
   Productions, 1982
THAT'S ENTERTAINMENT! III (FD)   MGM/UA, 1994

MARIA CONCHITA ALONSO
b. June 29, 1957 - Cuba

MOSCOW ON THE HUDSON   Columbia, 1984
A FINE MESS   Columbia, 1986
TOUCH AND GO   TriStar, 1986
EXTREME PREJUDICE   TriStar, 1987
THE RUNNING MAN   TriStar, 1987
COLORS   Orion, 1988
VAMPIRE'S KISS   Hemdale, 1989
PREDATOR 2   20th Century Fox, 1990
McBAIN   Shapiro-Glickenhaus, 1991
THE HOUSE OF THE SPIRITS   Miramax Films, 1993, U.S.-German

CAROL ALT
b. December 1, 1960

PORTFOLIO   1983
BYE BYE BABY   Prism Entertainment, 1989

HECTOR ALTERIO
THE NEST   1981, Spanish
CAMILA   European Classics, 1985, Argentine-Spanish
THE OFFICIAL STORY   Historias Cinematograficas,
   1985, Argentine

BRUCE ALTMAN
THE PAPER   Universal, 1994

JEFF ALTMAN
Agent: David Shapira & Associates - Sherman Oaks, 818/906-0322

AMERICAN HOT WAX   Paramount, 1978
DOIN' TIME   The Ladd Company/Warner Bros., 1984
SOUL MAN   New World, 1986

TRINI ALVARADO
b. 1967 - New York, New York
Agent: J. Michael Bloom & Associates - Los Angeles, 310/275-6800

RICH KIDS   United Artists, 1979
TIMES SQUARE   AFD, 1980
MRS. SOFFEL   MGM/UA, 1984
SWEET LORRAINE   Angelika Films, 1987
FRANK NITTI: THE ENFORCER (TF)   Len Hill Films, 1988
SATISFACTION   20th Century Fox, 1988
STELLA   Buena Vista, 1990
THE BABE   Universal, 1992
LITTLE WOMEN   Columbia, 1994

LEON AMES
(Leon Wycoff)
b. January 20, 1903 - Portland, Indiana

MURDERS IN THE RUE MORGUE   Universal, 1932
THIRTEEN WOMEN   1932
PARACHUTE JUMPER   Warner Bros., 1933
THE COUNT OF MONTE CRISTO   Universal, 1934
RECKLESS   MGM, 1935
STOWAWAY   20th Century Fox, 1936
CHARLIE CHAN ON BROADWAY   1937
MYSTERIOUS MR. MOTO   20th Century Fox, 1938
SUEZ   20th Century Fox, 1938
CODE OF THE STREETS   1939
ELLERY QUEEN AND THE MURDER RING   1941
NO GREATER SIN   1941
CRIME DOCTOR   Columbia, 1943
MEET ME IN ST. LOUIS   MGM, 1944
THE THIN MAN GOES HOME   MGM, 1944
THIRTY SECONDS OVER TOKYO   MGM, 1944
SON OF LASSIE   MGM, 1945
WEEK-END AT THE WALDORF   MGM, 1945
YOLANDA AND THE THIEF   MGM, 1945
THE POSTMAN ALWAYS RINGS TWICE   MGM, 1946
SONG OF THE THIN MAN   MGM, 1947
A DATE WITH JUDY   MGM, 1948
THE VELVET TOUCH   MGM, 1948
LITTLE WOMEN   MGM, 1949
BATTLEGROUND   MGM, 1949
AMBUSH   MGM, 1949
CRISIS   MGM, 1950
ON MOONLIGHT BAY   Warner Bros., 1951
IT'S A BIG COUNTRY   MGM, 1951
LET'S DO IT AGAIN   Columbia, 1953
PEYTON PLACE   20th Century Fox, 1957
FROM THE TERRACE   20th Century Fox, 1960
THE ABSENT-MINDED PROFESSOR   Buena Vista, 1961
THE MISADVENTURES OF MERLIN JONES   Buena Vista, 1964
THE MONKEY'S UNCLE   Buena Vista, 1965
ON A CLEAR DAY YOU CAN SEE FOREVER   Paramount, 1970
TORA! TORA! TORA!   20th Century Fox, 1970, U.S.-Japanese
HAMMERSMITH IS OUT   Cinerama Releasing Corporation, 1972
TIMBER TRAMP   Alaska Pictures, 1973
THE MEAL   *DEADLY ENCOUNTER*   1975
JUST YOU AND ME, KID   Columbia, 1979
TESTAMENT   Paramount, 1983
JAKE SPEED   New World, 1986
PEGGY SUE GOT MARRIED   TriStar, 1986

MADCHEN AMICK
I'M DANGEROUS TONIGHT (CTF)   BBK Productions, 1990
STEPHEN KING'S SLEEPWALKERS   Columbia, 1992
TWIN PEAKS: FIRE WALK WITH ME   New Line Cinema,
   1992, U.S.-French
LOVE, CHEAT AND STEAL (CTF)   Showtime, 1993
DREAM LOVER   Gramercy Pictures, 1994
TRAPPED IN PARADISE   20th Century Fox, 1994

SUZY AMIS
b. January 5, 1958 - Oklahoma City, Oklahoma
Agent: ICM - Beverly Hills, 310/550-4000

FANDANGO   Warner Bros., 1985
THE BIG TOWN   Columbia, 1987

PLAIN CLOTHES   Paramount, 1988
ROCKET GIBRALTAR   Columbia, 1988
WHERE THE HEART IS   Buena Vista, 1990
RICH IN LOVE   MGM/UA, 1993
THE BALLAD OF LITTLE JO   Fine Line Features/New
    Line Cinema, 1993
TWO SMALL BODIES   Castle Hill Pictures, 1994
BLOWN AWAY   MGM/UA, 1994

JOHN AMOS
b. December 27, 1940 - Newark, New Jersey
Agent: The Artists Agency - Los Angeles, 310/277-7779

SWEET SWEETBACK'S BAADASSSSS SONG   Cinemation, 1971
THE WORLD'S GREATEST ATHLETE   Buena Vista, 1973
LET'S DO IT AGAIN   Warner Bros., 1975
TOUCHED BY LOVE   *TO ELVIS, WITH LOVE*   Columbia, 1980
THE BEASTMASTER   MGM/UA, 1982
JUNGLE HEAT   1984
AMERICAN FLYERS   Warner Bros., 1985
COMING TO AMERICA   Paramount, 1988
LOCK UP   TriStar, 1989
DIE HARD 2   20th Century Fox, 1990

MOREY AMSTERDAM
SIDE BY SIDE (TF)   Avnet-Kerner Productions, 1988

LUANA ANDERS
Agent: Media Artists Group - Beverly Hills, 213/658-5050

LIFE BEGINS AT 17   Columbia, 1958
THE PIT AND THE PENDULUM   American International, 1961
THE YOUNG RACERS   American International, 1963
DEMENTIA 13   American International, 1963
THE TRIP   American International, 1967
EASY RIDER   Columbia, 1969
THAT COLD DAY IN THE PARK   Commonwealth United,
    1969, U.S.-Canadian
THE MANIPULATOR   1971
WHEN THE LEGENDS DIE   20th Century Fox, 1972
SHAMPOO   Columbia, 1975
THE MISSOURI BREAKS   United Artists, 1976
GOIN' SOUTH   Paramount, 1978
ONE FROM THE HEART   Columbia, 1982
PERSONAL BEST   The Geffen Company/Warner Bros., 1982
MOVERS & SHAKERS   MGM/UA, 1985

DANA ANDERSEN
UNDER THE INFLUENCE (TF)   CBS Entertainment, 1986
GINGERALE AFTERNOON   Skouras Pictures, 1989

BRIDGETTE ANDERSON
A SUMMER TO REMEMBER (TF)   Interplanetary Productions, 1985

DARYL ANDERSON
THE PEOPLE ACROSS THE LAKE (TF)   Bill McCutchen
    Productions/Columbia TV, 1988

DAVE ANDERSON
GOSPEL ACCORDING TO VIC   *HEAVENLY PURSUITS*
    Skouras Pictures, 1986, British

DION ANDERSON
DYING YOUNG   20th Century Fox, 1991

ERICH ANDERSON
(E. Erich Anderson)
Agent: Paradigm - Los Angeles, 310/277-4400

FRIDAY THE 13TH - THE FINAL CHAPTER   Paramount, 1984
WELCOME TO 18   American Distribution Group, 1986
BAT 21   TriStar, 1988

ERIKA ANDERSON
ZANDALEE   Electric Pictures/ITC Entertainment Group, 1991

HARRY ANDERSON
b. October 14, 1952 - Newport, Rhode Island
Agent: CAA - Beverly Hills, 310/288-4545

SPIES, LIES AND NAKED THIGHS (TF)   Qintex
    Entertainment, 1988
IT (TF)   Konigsberg-Sanitsky Productions/Green-Epstein
    Productions/Lorimar TV, 1990

HASKELL V. ANDERSON
KICKBOXER   Cannon, 1989

ISA ANDERSON
NIGHT ANGEL   Fries Distribution Company, 1990

JO ANDERSON
DEAD AGAIN   Paramount, 1991
MENENDEZ: A KILLING IN BEVERLY HILLS (MS)   Zev Braun
    Pictures/TriStar Television, 1994

JOHN ANDERSON
b. 1922 - Clayton, Illinois
Agent: Paul Kohner, Inc. - Los Angeles, 310/550-1060

AGAINST ALL FLAGS   Universal, 1952
TARGET ZERO   1955
THE TRUE STORY OF LYNN STUART   1958
PSYCHO   Paramount, 1960
WALK ON THE WILD SIDE   Columbia, 1962
RIDE THE HIGH COUNTRY   MGM, 1962
THE SATAN BUG   United Artists, 1965
THE HALLELUJAH TRAIL   United Artists, 1965
NAMU, THE KILLER WHALE   United Artists, 1966
WELCOME TO HARD TIMES   MGM, 1967
DAY OF THE EVIL GUN   MGM, 1968
HEAVEN WITH A GUN   MGM, 1969
YOUNG BILLY YOUNG   United Artists, 1969
COTTON COMES TO HARLEM   United Artists, 1970
SOLDIER BLUE   Avco Embassy, 1970
FIREHOUSE   Metromedia Productions/Stonehenge
    Productions, 1972
MAN AND BOY   Levitt-Pickman, 1972
THE STEPMOTHER   Crown International, 1973
EXECUTIVE ACTION   National General, 1973
THE DOVE   Paramount, 1974
THE SPECIALIST   Crown International, 1975
PETER LUNDY AND THE MEDICINE HAT STALLION (TF)
    Ed Friendly Productions, 1977
THE LINCOLN CONSPIRACY   Sunn Classic, 1977
THE DEERSLAYER (TF)   Sunn Classic Productions, 1978
DONNER PASS: THE ROAD TO SURVIVAL (TF)   Sunn Classic
    Productions, 1978
BACKSTAIRS AT THE WHITE HOUSE (MS)   Ed Friendly
    Productions, 1979
SMOKEY AND THE BANDIT II   Universal, 1980
STARMAN   Columbia, 1984
DREAM WEST (MS)   Sunn Classic Pictures, 1986
SCORPION   Crown International, 1986
AMERICAN HARVEST (TF)   Roth-Stratton Productions/The
    Finnegan Company, 1987
EIGHT MEN OUT   Orion, 1988

KEVIN ANDERSON
Agent: CAA - Beverly Hills, 310/288-4545

ORPHANS   Lorimar, 1987
MILES FROM HOME   Cinecom, 1988
IN COUNTRY   Warner Bros., 1989
SLEEPING WITH THE ENEMY   20th Century Fox, 1991
LIEBESTRAUM   MGM-Pathe, 1991
THE NIGHT WE NEVER MET   Miramax Films, 1993
RISING SUN   20th Century Fox, 1993
BALTO (AF)   Universal, 1995 (voice)

F
I
L
M

A
C
T
O
R
S

LINDSAY ANDERSON
CHARIOTS OF FIRE   The Ladd Company/Warner Bros.,
  1981, British

LONI ANDERSON
b. August 5, 1945 - St. Paul, Minnesota
Agent: CAA - Beverly Hills, 310/288-4545

THE MAGNIFICENT MAGNET OF SANTA MESA (TF)
  Columbia TV, 1977
THREE ON A DATE (TF)   ABC Circle Films, 1978
THE JAYNE MANSFIELD STORY (TF)   Alan Landsburg
  Productions, 1980
STROKER ACE   Universal, 1983
A LETTER TO THREE WIVES (TF)   Michael Filerman Productions/
  20th Century Fox TV, 1985
STRANDED (TF)   Tim Flack Productions/Columbia TV, 1986
NECESSITY (TF)   Barry-Enright Productions/Alexander
  Productions, 1988
A WHISPER KILLS (TF)   Sandy Hook Productions/Steve Tisch
  Company/Phoenix Entertainment Group, 1988
TOO GOOD TO BE TRUE (TF)   Newland-Raynor Productions, 1988
SORRY, WRONG NUMBER (CTF)   Jack Grossbart Productions/
  Wilshire Court Productions, 1989
ALL DOGS GO TO HEAVEN (AF)   MGM/UA, 1989 (voice)

LOUIE ANDERSON
CLOAK & DAGGER   Universal, 1984
RATBOY   Warner Bros., 1986
QUICKSILVER   Columbia, 1986
COMING TO AMERICA   Paramount, 1988

MELISSA ANDERSON
(Melissa Sue Anderson)
b. September 26, 1969 - Berkeley, California

LITTLE HOUSE ON THE PRAIRIE (TF)   NBC Productions, 1974
THE LONELIEST RUNNER (TF)   NBC Productions, 1976
JAMES AT 15 (TF)   20th Century Fox TV, 1977
HAPPY BIRTHDAY TO ME   Columbia, 1981, Canadian
FIRST AFFAIR (TF)   CBS Entertainment, 1983
CHATTANOOGA CHOO CHOO   April Fools, 1984

MELODY ANDERSON
b. 1955 - Canada

BEVERLY HILLS MADAM (TF)   NLS Productions/Orion TV, 1986
THE BOY IN BLUE   20th Century Fox, 1986, Canadian
DEEP DARK SECRETS (TF)   Gross-Weston Productions/
  Fries Entertainment, 1987
FINAL NOTICE (CTF)   Wilshire Court Productions/Sharm Hill
  Productions, 1989

MITCHELL ANDERSON
Agent: Gersh Agency - Beverly Hills, 310/274-6611

THE KAREN CARPENTER STORY (TF)   Weintraub Entertainment
  Group, 1989
THE COMEBACK (TF)   CBS Entertainment, 1989

RICHARD ANDERSON
b. August 8, 1926 - Long Branch, New Jersey

TWELVE O'CLOCK HIGH   20th Century Fox, 1949
THE MAGNIFICENT YANKEE   MGM, 1950
PAYMENT ON DEMAND   RKO Radio, 1951
ACROSS THE WIDE MISSOURI   MGM, 1951
THE PEOPLE AGAINST O'HARA   MGM, 1951
JUST THIS ONCE   MGM, 1952
SCARAMOUCHE   MGM, 1952
THE STORY OF THREE LOVES   MGM, 1953
ESCAPE FROM FORT BRAVO   MGM, 1953
THE STUDENT PRINCE   MGM, 1954
HIT THE DECK   MGM, 1955
FORBIDDEN PLANET   MGM, 1956
THE SEARCH FOR BRIDEY MURPHY   Paramount, 1956

THE BUSTER KEATON STORY   Paramount, 1957
PATHS OF GLORY   United Artists, 1957
THE LONG HOT SUMMER   MGM, 1958
THE CURSE OF THE FACELESS MAN   1958
COMPULSION   20th Century Fox, 1959
THE WACKIEST SHIP IN THE ARMY   1960
A GATHERING OF EAGLES   Universal, 1963
JOHNNY COOL   United Artists, 1963
SEVEN DAYS IN MAY   Paramount, 1964
SECONDS   Paramount, 1966
THE RIDE TO HANGMAN'S TREE   Universal, 1967
TORA! TORA! TORA!   20th Century Fox, 1970, U.S.-Japanese
MACHO CALLAHAN   Avco Embassy, 1970
DOCTORS' WIVES   Columbia, 1971
THE HONKERS   1972
PLAY IT AS IT LAYS   Universal, 1972
THE SIX MILLION DOLLAR MAN (TF)   Universal TV, 1973
BLACK EYE   Warner Bros., 1974
COVER UP (TF)   Glen A. Larson Productions/20th
  Century Fox TV, 1984
PERRY MASON RETURNS (TF)   Intermedia Productions/Strathmore
  Productions/Viacom Productions, 1985
THE STEPFORD CHILDREN (TF)   Edgar J. Scherick Productions/
  Taft Entertainment TV, 1987
RETURN OF THE SIX MILLION DOLLAR MAN AND THE BIONIC
  WOMAN (TF)   Michael Sloan Productions/Universal TV, 1987
BIONIC SHOWDOWN: THE SIX MILLION DOLLAR MAN AND
  THE BIONIC WOMAN (TF)   Universal TV, 1989

SONJA G. ANDERSON
Contact: 213/276-3211

TANGO & CASH   Warner Bros., 1989
DIE HARD 2   20th Century Fox, 1990
BODIES   Allison Entertainment/JAD Films, Intl., 1990

STANLEY ANDERSON
DECEIVED   Buena Vista, 1991
ROBOCOP 3   Orion, 1993

BIBI ANDERSSON
(Birgitta Andersson)
b. November 11, 1935 - Stockholm, Sweden

SIR ARNE'S TREASURE   1954, Swedish
SMILES OF A SUMMER NIGHT   Janus, 1955, Swedish
THE SEVENTH SEAL   Janus, 1956, Swedish
WILD STRAWBERRIES   Janus, 1957, Swedish
THE MAGICIAN   Janus, 1958, Swedish
BRINK OF LIFE   Janus, 1958, Swedish
THE DEVIL'S EYE   Janus, 1960, Swedish
THE PLEASURE GARDEN   1961, Swedish
SHORT IS THE SUMMER   1962, Swedish
THE SWEDISH MISTRESS   1962, Swedish
ALL THESE WOMEN   Janus, 1964, Swedish
THE ISLAND   1966, Swedish
MY SISTER MY LOVE   SYSKONBADD 1782   Sigma III,
  1966, Swedish
PERSONA   United Artists, 1966, Swedish
DUEL AT DIABLO   United Artists, 1966
THE RAPE   1967, French-Swedish
THE PASSION OF ANNA   United Artists, 1969, Swedish
THE KREMLIN LETTER   20th Century Fox, 1970
THE TOUCH   Cinerama Releasing Corporation,
  1971, U.S.-Swedish
CRIES AND WHISPERS   New World, 1972, Swedish
SCENES FROM A MARRIAGE   Cinema 5, 1973, Swedish
IT IS RAINING ON SANTIAGO   1975, French-Bulgarian
BLONDY   1976, French
I NEVER PROMISED YOU A ROSE GARDEN   New World, 1977
AN ENEMY OF THE PEOPLE   Warner Bros., 1978
L'AMOUR EN QUESTION   1978, French
QUINTET   20th Century Fox, 1979
THE CONCORDE—AIRPORT '79   Universal, 1979
EXPOSED   MGM/UA, 1983

STARR ANDREEFF
Agent: Badgley/Connor - Los Angeles, 310/278-9313

THE TERROR WITHIN   Concorde, 1989

FREDERIC ANDREI
DIVA   United Artists Classics, 1982, French

URSULA ANDRESS
b. March 19, 1936 - Bern, Switzerland

SINS OF CASANOVA   *LE AVVENTURE DI GIACOMO CASANOVA*
   1954, Italian-French
AN AMERICAN IN ROME   *UN AMERICANO A ROMA*   1954, Italian
LA CATENA DELL'ODIO   1955, Italian
DR. NO   United Artists, 1962, British
FUN IN ACAPULCO   Paramount, 1963
4 FOR TEXAS   Warner Bros., 1964
NIGHTMARE IN THE SUN   1965
SHE   MGM, 1965, British
WHAT'S NEW PUSSYCAT?   United Artists, 1965, British
THE 10TH VICTIM   *LA DECIMA VITTIMA*   Embassy,
   1965, Italian-French
UP TO HIS EARS   *LES TRIBULATIONS D'UN CHINOIS EN CHINE*
   Lopert, 1965, French-Italian
THE BLUE MAX   20th Century Fox, 1966, British-U.S.
ONCE BEFORE I DIE   7 Arts, 1967, U.S.-Filipino
CASINO ROYALE   Columbia, 1967, British
ANYONE CAN PLAY   *LE DOLCI SIGNORE*   1968, Italian-French
THE SOUTHERN STAR   *L'ETOILE DU SUD*   Columbia,
   1969, French-British
PERFECT FRIDAY   Chevron, 1970, British
RED SUN   *SOLEIL ROUGE*   National General, 1972,
   French-Italian-Spanish
L'ULTIMA *CHANCE*   1973, Italian
LOADED GUNS   1974
AFRICA EXPRESS   1975, Italian
L'INFERMIERA   1976, Italian
40 GRADA SOTTO LE LENZULOA   1976, Italian
THE LOVES AND TIMES OF SCARAMOUCHE   *SCARAMOUCHE*
   1976, Italian-Yugoslavian
CASANOVA E COMPAGNI   1978, Italian
UNA STRANA COPPIO DI GANGSTERS   1979, Italian
LETTI SELVAGGI   1979, Italian
THE FIFTH MUSKETEER   Columbia, 1979, Austrian
CLASH OF THE TITANS   MGM/United Artists, 1981, British
MAN AGAINST THE MOB: THE CHINATOWN MURDERS (TF)
   von Zerneck-Sertner Productions, 1989

ANTHONY ANDREWS
b. 1948 - London, England
Agent: Gersh Agency - Beverly Hills, 310/274-6611

A WAR OF CHILDREN (TF)   Tomorrow Entertainment, 1972
QB VII (MS)   Screen Gems/Columbia TV/The Douglas Cramer
   Company, 1974
IT'S NOT THE SIZE THAT COUNTS   *PERCY'S PROGRESS*
   Joseph Brenner Associates, 1974, British
OPERATION DAYBREAK   *PRICE OF FREEDOM*   Warner Bros.,
   1976, British
THE SCARLET PIMPERNEL (TF)   London Films Ltd., 1982, British
IVANHOE (TF)   1982
BRIDESHEAD REVISITED (MS)   Granada TV/WNET-13/NDR
   Hamburg, 1982, British-U.S.-West German
AGATHA CHRISTIE'S 'SPARKLING CYANIDE' (TF)
   Stan Margulies Productions/Warner Bros. TV, 1983
UNDER THE VOLCANO   Universal, 1984
THE HOLCROFT COVENANT   Universal, 1985, British
SUSPICION (TF)   Hemisphere, 1986, British
THE SECOND VICTORY   Filmworld Distributors, 1987,
   Australian-British
THE LIGHTHORSEMEN   Cinecom, 1987, Australian
BLUEGRASS (MS)   The Landsburg Company, 1988
THE WOMAN HE LOVED (TF)   The Larry Thompson Organization/
   HTV/New World TV, 1988, U.S.-British
HANNA'S WAR   Cannon, 1988
HANDS OF A MURDERER (TF)   Storke-Fuisz Productions/
   Yorkshire TV, 1990, British-U.S.
LOST IN SIBERIA   1991

DAVID ANDREWS
Agent: Paradigm - Los Angeles, 310/277-4400

WILD HORSES (TF)   Wild Horses Productions/Telepictures
   Productions, 1985
CHERRY 2000   Orion, 1988
A SON'S PROMISE (TF)   Marian Rees Associates, 1990
STEPHEN KING'S GRAVEYARD SHIFT   Paramount, 1990
WYATT EARP   Warner Bros., 1994

JULIE ANDREWS
(Julia Elizabeth Welles)
b. October 1, 1935 - Walton-on-Thames, England
Agent: William Morris Agency - Beverly Hills, 310/274-7451

MARY POPPINS ★★   Buena Vista, 1964
THE AMERICANIZATION OF EMILY   MGM, 1964
THE SOUND OF MUSIC ★   20th Century Fox, 1965
TORN CURTAIN   Universal, 1966
HAWAII   United Artists, 1966
THOROUGHLY MODERN MILLIE   Universal, 1967
STAR!   *THOSE WERE THE HAPPY TIMES*
   20th Century Fox, 1968
DARLING LILI   Paramount, 1970
THE TAMARIND SEED   Avco Embassy, 1974
THE PINK PANTHER STRIKES AGAIN   United Artists,
   1976, British (uncredited)
10   Orion/Warner Bros., 1979
LITTLE MISS MARKER   Universal, 1980
S.O.B.   Paramount, 1981
VICTOR/VICTORIA ★   MGM/United Artists, 1982
THE MAN WHO LOVED WOMEN   Columbia, 1983
THAT'S LIFE!   Columbia, 1986
DUET FOR ONE   Cannon, 1986
OUR SONS (TF)   Robert Greenwald Productions, 1991
A FINE ROMANCE   *TCHIN-TCHIN*   Castle Hill Productions,
   1992, U.S.-Italian

JACK ANGEL
BALTO (AF)   Universal, 1995 (voice)

VANESSA ANGEL
Agent: APA - Los Angeles, 310/273-0744

SLEEP WITH ME   MGM/UA, 1994

ANGELYNE
EARTH GIRLS ARE EASY   Vestron, 1989

JEAN-HUGUES ANGLADE
Agent: William Morris Agency - Beverly Hills, 310/274-7451

BETTY BLUE   Alive Films, 1986, French
ESPECIALLY ON SUNDAY   Miramax Films, 1993

PHILIP ANGLIM
Agent: Writers & Artists Agency - Los Angeles, 310/820-2240

TESTAMENT   Paramount, 1983

FRANCESCA ANNIS
b. 1944 - London, England

THE CAT GANG   1958
BEWARE OF CHILDREN   *NO KIDDING*   American International,
   1960, British
CLEOPATRA   20th Century Fox, 1963, U.S.-British
THE EYES OF ANNIE JONES   1964, U.S.-British
THE PLEASURE GIRLS   Times, 1965
THE WALKING STICK   MGM, 1970, British
MACBETH   Columbia, 1971, British
COMING OUT OF THE ICE (TF)   The Konigsberg Company, 1982
KRULL   Columbia, 1983, U.S.-British
DUNE   Universal, 1984
UNDER THE CHERRY MOON   Warner Bros., 1986
I'LL TAKE MANHATTAN (MS)   Steve Krantz Productions, 1987

ANN-MARGRET
(Ann-Margaret Olsson)
b. April 28, 1941 - Valsjobyn, Sweden
Agent: William Morris Agency - Beverly Hills, 310/274-7451

POCKETFUL OF MIRACLES   United Artists, 1961
STATE FAIR   20th Century Fox, 1962
BYE BYE BIRDIE   Columbia, 1963
VIVA LAS VEGAS   MGM, 1964
KITTEN WITH A WHIP   Universal, 1964
THE PLEASURE SEEKERS   20th Century Fox, 1964
BUS RILEY'S BACK IN TOWN   Universal, 1965
ONCE A THIEF   MGM, 1965
THE CINCINNATI KID   MGM, 1965
MADE IN PARIS   MGM, 1966
STAGECOACH   20th Century Fox, 1966
THE SWINGER   Paramount, 1966
MURDERERS' ROW   Columbia, 1966
THE TIGER AND THE PUSSYCAT   *IL TIGRE*   Embassy,
   1967, Italian-U.S.
CRIMINAL AFFAIR   1967
THE PROPHET   Joseph Green Pictures, 1967, Italian
R.P.M.   Columbia, 1970
C.C. AND COMPANY   Avco Embassy, 1970
CARNAL KNOWLEDGE ✪   Avco Embassy, 1971
THE TRAIN ROBBERS   Warner Bros., 1973
THE OUTSIDE MAN   *UN HOMME EST MORT*   United Artists,
   1973, French-Italian
TOMMY ★   Columbia, 1975, British
THE TWIST   *FOLIES BOURGEOISES*   FFCM, 1976,
   French-Italian-West German
JOSEPH ANDREWS   Paramount, 1977, British
THE LAST REMAKE OF BEAU GESTE   Universal, 1977
THE CHEAP DETECTIVE   Columbia, 1978
MAGIC   20th Century Fox, 1978
THE VILLAIN   Columbia, 1979
MIDDLE AGE CRAZY   20th Century Fox, 1980, Canadian-U.S.
THE RETURN OF THE SOLDIER   European Classics, 1981, British
I OUGHT TO BE IN PICTURES   20th Century Fox, 1982
LOOKIN' TO GET OUT   Paramount, 1982
WHO WILL LOVE MY CHILDREN? (TF)   ABC Circle Films, 1983
A STREETCAR NAMED DESIRE (TF)   Keith Barish
   Productions, 1984
TWICE IN A LIFETIME   The Yorkin Company, 1985
52 PICK-UP   Cannon, 1986
THE TWO MRS. GRENVILLES (MS)   Lorimar-Telepictures, 1987
A TIGER'S TALE   Atlantic Releasing Corporation, 1987
A NEW LIFE   Paramount, 1988
OUR SONS (TF)   Robert Greenwald Productions, 1991
NEWSIES   Buena Vista, 1992
GRUMPY OLD MEN   Warner Bros., 1993
NOBODY'S CHILDREN (CTF)   1994
SCARLETT (MS)   1994

SUSAN ANSPACH
b. November 23, 1939 - New York, New York
Agent: Harris & Goldberg - Los Angeles, 310/553-5200

THE LANDLORD   United Artists, 1970
FIVE EASY PIECES   Columbia, 1970
PLAY IT AGAIN, SAM   Paramount, 1972
BLUME IN LOVE   Warner Bros., 1973
NASHVILLE   Paramount, 1975
MAD BULL   Steckler Productions/Filmways, 1977
THE BIG FIX   Universal, 1978
RUNNING   Columbia, 1979, Canadian-U.S.
THE DEVIL AND MAX DEVLIN   Buena Vista, 1981
GAS   Paramount, 1981, Canadian
MONTENEGRO   *MONTENEGRO, OR PIGS AND PEARLS*
   Atlantic Releasing Corporation, 1981, Swedish-British
DEADLY ENCOUNTER (TF)   Roger Gimbel Productions/
   EMI TV, 1982
GONE ARE THE DAYS (CTF)   Walt Disney Productions, 1984
SPACE (MS)   Stonehenge Productions/Paramount TV, 1985
BLUE MONKEY   Spectrafilm, 1987, Canadian

ADAM ANT
Agent: Harris & Goldberg - Los Angeles, 310/553-5200

NOMADS   Atlantic Releasing Corporation, 1986
COLD STEEL   CineTel, 1987
SLAMDANCE   Island Pictures, 1987
OUT OF TIME (TF)   Columbia TV, 1988
WORLD GONE WILD   Lorimar, 1988

LYSETTE ANTHONY
Agent: William Morris Agency - Beverly Hills, 310/274-7451

KRULL   Columbia, 1983, U.S.-British
WITHOUT A CLUE   Orion, 1988
HUSBANDS AND WIVES   TriStar, 1992
LOOK WHO'S TALKING NOW   TriStar, 1993
THE ADVOCATE   Miramax Films, 1994
THE HARD TRUTH (CTF)   HBO Pictures, 1994
TARGET OF SUSPICION (CTF)   HBO Pictures, 1994
DR. JEKYLL AND MS. HYDE   Savoy Pictures, 1995

STEVE ANTIN
THE LAST AMERICAN VIRGIN   Cannon, 1982
THE ACCUSED   Paramount, 1988
SURVIVAL QUEST   MGM/UA, 1990
WITHOUT YOU I'M NOTHING   MCEG, 1990

SUSAN ANTON
b. October 12, 1950 - Yucaipa, California
Agent: The Irv Schechter Company - Beverly Hills, 310/278-8070

GOLDENGIRL   Avco Embassy, 1979
SPRING FEVER   Comworld, 1983, Canadian
CANNONBALL RUN II   Warner Bros., 1984
LENA'S HOLIDAY   Crown International, 1991

JIM ANTONIO
REARVIEW MIRROR (TF)   Simon-Asher Entertainment/Sunn Classic
   Pictures, 1984
MAYFLOWER MADAM (TF)   Robert Halmi, Inc., 1987

GABRIELLE ANWAR
Agent: UTA - Beverly Hills, 310/273-6700

MANIFESTO   Cannon, 1988, U.S.-Yugoslavian
THE MYSTERIES OF THE DARK JUNGLE (MS)   RCS-TV/RAI/
   Beta Film/ZDF/ORF/TF1/TVE, 1990,
   Italian-West German-French
IF LOOKS COULD KILL   Warner Bros., 1991
WILD HEARTS CAN'T BE BROKEN   Buena Vista, 1991
SCENT OF A WOMAN   Universal, 1992
FOR LOVE OR MONEY   Universal, 1993
THE THREE MUSKETEERS   Buena Vista, 1993
BODY SNATCHERS   Warner Bros., 1994
THINGS TO DO IN DENVER WHEN YOU'RE DEAD
   Miramax Films, 1995

MARIA ANZ
AMERICAN ANTHEM   Columbia, 1986

JOHN APICELLA
DAD   Universal, 1989

APOLLONIA
(Patricia Apollonia Kotero)
Agent: Shapiro-Lichtman - Los Angeles, 310/859-8877

PURPLE RAIN   Warner Bros., 1984
MINISTRY OF VENGEANCE   MPCA, 1989

PETER APPEL
MAN 2 MAN   Buena Vista, 1995

CHRISTINA APPLEGATE
b. November 25, 1971 - Los Angeles, California

DON'T TELL MOM THE BABYSITTER'S DEAD   Warner Bros., 1991
ACROSS THE MOON   Hemdale, 1994
WILD BILL   MGM/UA, 1995

JOHN APREA
Agent: The Artists Group, Ltd. - Los Angeles, 310/552-1100

GETTING PHYSICAL (TF)   CBS Entertainment, 1984
AMERICAN ANTHEM   Columbia, 1986
CYBER-TRACKER   PM Entertainment, 1994

MICHAEL APTED
b. February 10, 1941 - Aylesbury, England
Agent: CAA - Beverly Hills, 310/288-4545

SPIES LIKE US   Warner Bros., 1985

AMY AQUINO
Agent: William Morris Agency - Beverly Hills, 310/274-7451

BOYS ON THE SIDE   Warner Bros., 1995

ANGELICA ARAGON
A WALK IN THE CLOUDS   20th Century Fox, 1995

FRANK ARAGON
Agent: Sutter/Walls Associates, Inc. - Los Angeles, 213/658-8200

ANGEL TOWN   Taurus Entertainment, 1990

ALFONSO ARAU
THREE AMIGOS   Orion, 1986
STONES FOR IBARRA (TF)   Titus Productions, 1988

GABRIEL ARCAND
THE DECLINE OF THE AMERICAN EMPIRE   Cineplex Odeon,
    1986, Canadian

ANNE ARCHER
b. August 25, 1947 - Los Angeles, California
Agent: ICM - Beverly Hills, 310/550-4000

THE HONKERS   1972
CANCEL MY RESERVATION   Warner Bros., 1972
THE ALL-AMERICAN BOY   Warner Bros., 1973
THE MARK OF ZORRO (TF)   20th Century Fox, 1974
LIFEGUARD   Paramount, 1976
TRACKDOWN   United Artists, 1976
HAROLD ROBBINS' THE PIRATE   *THE PIRATE* (TF)
    Howard W. Koch Productions/Warner Bros. TV, 1978
PARADISE ALLEY   Universal, 1978
GOOD GUYS WEAR BLACK   American Cinema, 1979
HERO AT LARGE   MGM/United Artists, 1980
RAISE THE TITANIC   AFD, 1980, British-U.S.
GREEN ICE   Universal/AFD, 1981, British
WALTZ ACROSS TEXAS   Atlantic Releasing Corporation, 1983
THE SKY'S THE LIMIT (TF)   Palance-Levy Productions, 1984
TOO SCARED TO SCREAM   The Movie Store, 1984
THE NAKED FACE   Cannon, 1985
THE CHECK IS IN THE MAIL   Ascot Entertainment Group, 1986
A DIFFERENT AFFAIR (TF)   Rogers-Samuels Productions, 1987
FATAL ATTRACTION ✪   Paramount, 1987
LEAP OF FAITH (TF)   Hart, Thomas & Berlin Productions, 1988
LOVE AT LARGE   Orion, 1990
NARROW MARGIN   TriStar, 1990
EMINENT DOMAIN   Triumph Releasing Corporation, 1990,
    Canadian-French-Israeli
NAILS (CTF)   Viacom Pictures, 1992
PATRIOT GAMES   Paramount, 1992
FAMILY PRAYERS   Arrow Entertainment, 1993 (filmed in 1991)
BODY OF EVIDENCE   MGM/UA, 1993
SHORT CUTS   Fine Line Features/New Line Cinema, 1993
CLEAR AND PRESENT DANGER   Paramount, 1994

FANNY ARDANT
AFRAID OF THE DARK   New Line Cinema, 1991

NIELS ARESTRUP
SINCERELY CHARLOTTE   New Line Cinema, 1986, French
MEETING VENUS   Warner Bros., 1991

CARMEN ARGENZIANO
MOMENT OF TRUTH: CRADLE OF CONSPIRACY (TF)
    O'Hara/Horowitz Productions, 1994

VICTOR ARGO
OFF BEAT   Buena Vista, 1986
HER ALIBI   Warner Bros., 1989
KING OF NEW YORK   New Line Cinema, 1990
McBAIN   Shapiro-Glickenhaus Entertainment, 1991

ADAM ARKIN
UNDER THE RAINBOW   Orion/Warner Bros., 1981
HEATWAVE (CTF)   The Avnet-Kerner Company/
    Propaganda Films, 1990
THE DOCTOR   Buena Vista, 1991

ALAN ARKIN
b. March 26, 1934 - New York, New York
Agent: William Morris Agency - Beverly Hills, 310/274-7451

THE RUSSIANS ARE COMING, THE RUSSIANS ARE COMING ★
    United Artists, 1966
WOMAN TIMES SEVEN   Avco Embassy, 1967, French-Italian-U.S.
WAIT UNTIL DARK   Warner Bros., 1967
INSPECTOR CLOUSEAU   United Artists, 1968, British
THE HEART IS A LONELY HUNTER ★   Warner Bros., 1968
THE MONITORS   Commonwealth United, 1969
POPI   United Artists, 1969
CATCH-22   Paramount, 1970
LITTLE MURDERS   20th Century Fox, 1971 (also directed)
DEADHEAD MILES   Paramount, 1971
LAST OF THE RED HOT LOVERS   Paramount, 1972
FREEBIE AND THE BEAN   Warner Bros., 1974
RAFFERTY AND THE GOLD DUST TWINS   Warner Bros., 1975
HEARTS OF THE WEST   MGM/United Artists, 1975
THE SEVEN PERCENT SOLUTION   Universal, 1976, British
THE OTHER SIDE OF HELL (TF)   Aubrey-Lyon Productions, 1978
FIRE SALE   20th Century Fox, 1977 (also directed)
THE MAGICIAN OF LUBLIN   Cannon, 1979,
    Israeli-West German-U.S.
THE IN-LAWS   Columbia, 1979
SIMON   Orion/Warner Bros., 1980
IMPROPER CHANNELS   Crown International, 1981, Canadian
CHU CHU AND THE PHILLY FLASH   20th Century Fox, 1981
FULL MOON HIGH   Filmways, 1981
THE RETURN OF CAPTAIN INVINCIBLE   *LEGEND IN LEOTARDS*
    New World, 1983, Australian
JOSHUA THEN AND NOW   20th Century Fox, 1985, Canadian
BAD MEDICINE   20th Century Fox, 1985
A DEADLY BUSINESS (TF)   Thebaut-Frey Productions/Taft
    Entertainment TV, 1986
BIG TROUBLE   Columbia, 1986
ESCAPE FROM SOBRIBOR (TF)   Rule-Starger Productions/Zenith
    Productions, 1987, U.S.-British
COUPE DE VILLE   Universal, 1990
EDWARD SCISSORHANDS   20th Century Fox, 1990
HAVANA   Universal, 1990
THE ROCKETEER   Buena Vista, 1991
GLENGARRY GLEN ROSS   New Line Cinema, 1992
INDIAN SUMMER   Buena Vista, 1993
SO I MARRIED AN AXE MURDERER   TriStar, 1993
NORTH   Columbia, 1994
BULLETS OVER BROADWAY   Miramax Films, 1994
THE JERKY BOYS   Buena Vista, 1994

ROBERT ARKINS
THE COMMITMENTS   20th Century Fox, 1991

ELIZABETH ARLEN
THE FIRST POWER   Orion, 1990

DIMITRA ARLYS
(Dimitra Arliss)
THE SKI BUM   Avco Embassy, 1971
THE STING   Universal, 1973
DEATH SCREAM   *THE WOMAN WHO CRIED MURDER* (TF)
   RSO Films, 1975
THE OTHER SIDE OF MIDNIGHT   20th Century Fox, 1977
HAROLD ROBBINS' THE PIRATE   *THE PIRATE* (TF)
   Howard W. Koch Productions/Warner Bros. TV, 1978
A PERFECT COUPLE   20th Century Fox, 1979
GUYANA TRAGEDY: THE STORY OF JIM JONES (TF)
   The Konigsberg Company, 1980
XANADU   Universal, 1980
MURDER IN TEXAS (TF)   Dick Clark Productions/
   Billy Hale Films, 1981
THE FALL OF THE HOUSE OF USHER (TF)   Sunn Classic
   Productions, 1982
FIREFOX   Warner Bros., 1982
ELENI   Warner Bros., 1985
THE RICHEST MAN IN THE WORLD: THE ARISTOTLE ONASSIS
   STORY (TF)   The Konigsberg-Sanitsky Company, 1988

PEDRO ARMENDARIZ, JR.
THE MAGNIFICENT SEVEN RIDE   United Artists, 1972
THE DEADLY TRACKERS   Warner Bros., 1973
EARTHQUAKE   Universal, 1974
EVITA PERON (TF)   Hartwest Productions/Zephyr
   Productions, 1981
WALKER   Universal, 1987, U.S.-Nicaraguan
LICENCE TO KILL   MGM/UA, 1989, British
OLD GRINGO   Columbia, 1989

VIJAY ARMITRAJ
OCTOPUSSY   MGM/UA, 1983, British

ALUN ARMSTRONG
b. Annfield Plain, England

GET CARTER   MGM, 1971, British
A BRIDGE TOO FAR   United Artists, 1977, British
THE DUELLISTS   Paramount, 1978, British
THE FRENCH LIEUTENANT'S WOMAN   United Artists,
   1981, British
KRULL   Columbia, 1983, U.S.-British
WHITE HUNTER, BLACK HEART   Warner Bros., 1990
AMERICAN FRIENDS   Prominent Features, 1991, British
LONDON KILLS ME   Fine Line Features/New Line Cinema,
   1992, British
PATRIOT GAMES   Paramount, 1992
BLUE ICE   M&M Productions/HBO Pictures, 1992, British-U.S.
BLACK BEAUTY   Warner Bros., 1994, British-U.S.
AN AWFULLY BIG ADVENTURE   Fine Line Features/New Line
   Cinema, 1995, British

BESS ARMSTRONG
Agent: William Morris Agency - Beverly Hills, 310/274-7451

GETTING MARRIED (TF)   Paramount TV, 1978
HOW TO PICK UP GIRLS!   King-Hitzig Productions, 1978
THE FOUR SEASONS   Universal, 1981
JEKYLL AND HYDE...TOGETHER AGAIN   Paramount, 1982
HIGH ROAD TO CHINA   Warner Bros., 1983, U.S.-Yugoslavian
JAWS 3-D   Universal, 1983
LACE (MS)   Lorimar Productions, 1984
NOTHING IN COMMON   TriStar, 1986
SECOND SIGHT   Warner Bros., 1989
DREAM LOVER   Gramercy Pictures, 1994

CURTIS ARMSTRONG
Agent: Paradigm - Los Angeles, 310/277-4400

RISKY BUSINESS   The Geffen Company/Warner Bros., 1983
REVENGE OF THE NERDS   20th Century Fox, 1984

BAD MEDICINE   20th Century Fox, 1985
THE CLAN OF THE CAVE BEAR   Warner Bros., 1986
ONE CRAZY SUMMER   Warner Bros., 1986
REVENGE OF THE NERDS II: NERDS IN PARADISE
   20th Century Fox, 1987

GEORGINA ARMSTRONG
BLACK BEAUTY   Warner Bros., 1994, British-U.S.

HUGH ARMSTRONG
HOW TO GET AHEAD IN ADVERTISING   Warner Bros.,
   1989, British

KERRY ARMSTRONG
DADAH IS DEATH (MS)   Steve Krantz Productions/Roadshow,
   Coote & Carroll Productions/Samuel Goldwyn TV,
   1988, U.S.-Australian

R.G. ARMSTRONG
GARDEN OF EDEN   1957
FROM HELL TO TEXAS   20th Century Fox, 1958
THE FUGITIVE KIND   United Artists, 1960
RIDE THE HIGH COUNTRY   MGM, 1962
HE RIDES TALL   Universal, 1964
MAJOR DUNDEE   Columbia, 1965
EL DORADO   Paramount, 1967
80 STEPS TO JONAH   Warner Bros., 1969
THE BALLAD OF CABLE HOGUE   Warner Bros., 1970
THE GREAT WHITE HOPE   20th Century Fox, 1970
J.W. COOP   Columbia, 1972
THE GREAT NORTHFIELD, MINNESOTA RAID   Universal, 1972
PAT GARRETT AND BILLY THE KID   MGM, 1973
WHITE LIGHTNING   United Artists, 1973
MY NAME IS NOBODY   1974, Italian-French-West German
WHO FEARS THE DEVIL   *LEGEND OF HILL BILLY JOHN*
   Jack H. Harris Enterprises, 1974
RACE WITH THE DEVIL   20th Century Fox, 1975
WHITE LINE FEVER   Columbia, 1975
STAY HUNGRY   United Artists, 1976
MR. BILLION   20th Century Fox, 1977
THE CAR   Universal, 1977
THE PACK   *THE LONG, DARK NIGHT*   Warner Bros., 1977
HEAVEN CAN WAIT   Paramount, 1978
TEXAS DETOUR   Cinema Shares International, 1978
WHERE THE BUFFALO ROAM   Universal, 1980
REDS   Paramount, 1981
HAMMETT   Orion/Warner Bros., 1982
EVILSPEAK   The Frank Moreno Company, 1982
THE BEST OF TIMES   Universal, 1986
LBJ: THE EARLY YEARS (TF)   Louis Rudolph Films/Fries
   Entertainment, 1987
DICK TRACY   Buena Vista, 1990

DESI ARNAZ, JR.
b. January 19, 1953 - Los Angeles, California

RED SKY AT MORNING   Universal, 1970
MARCO   Cinerama Releasing Corporation, 1973
SHE LIVES! (TF)   ABC Circle Films, 1973
BILLY TWO HATS   *THE LADY AND THE OUTLAW*   United Artists,
   1974, British
JOYRIDE   American International, 1977
HOW TO PICK UP GIRLS! (TF)   King-Hitzig Productions, 1978
A WEDDING   20th Century Fox, 1978
THE NIGHT THE BRIDGE FELL DOWN (TF)   Irwin Allen
   Productions/Warner Bros. TV, 1983
THE MAMBO KINGS   Warner Bros., 1992

LUCIE ARNAZ
b. July 17, 1951 - Hollywood, California
Agent: William Morris Agency - Beverly Hills, 310/274-7451

WHO IS THE BLACK DAHLIA? (TF)   Douglas S. Cramer
   Productions, 1975
DEATH SCREAM   *THE WOMAN WHO CRIED MURDER* (TF)
   RSO Films, 1975

BILLY JACK GOES TO WASHINGTON   Taylor-Laughlin, 1977
THE MATING SEASON (TF)   Highgate Pictures, 1980
THE JAZZ SINGER   AFD, 1980
SECOND THOUGHTS   Universal, 1983
WHO GETS THE FRIENDS? (TF)   CBS Entertainment, 1988

DENIS ARNDT
BASIC INSTINCT   TriStar, 1992

JAMES ARNESS
(James Aurness)
b. May 26, 1923 - Minneapolis, Minnesota

THE FARMER'S DAUGHTER   RKO Radio, 1947
BATTLEGROUND   MGM, 1949
WAGON MASTER   RKO Radio, 1950
THE THING   1951
THE PEOPLE AGAINST O'HARA   MGM, 1951
CARBINE WILLIAMS   MGM, 1952
BIG JIM McLAIN   1952
HORIZONS WEST   Universal, 1952
LONE HAND   Universal, 1953
HONDO   Warner Bros., 1953
THEM!   Warner Bros., 1954
HER TWELVE MEN   MGM, 1954
MANY RIVERS TO CROSS   MGM, 1954
THE SEA CHASE   Warner Bros., 1955
FLAME OF THE ISLANDS   1955
THE FIRST TRAVELLING SALESLADY   RKO Radio, 1956
McCLAIN'S LAW (TF)   Eric Bercovici Productions/
   Epipsychidion, Inc., 1982
THE ALAMO: 13 DAYS TO GLORY (TF)   Briggle, Hennessy,
   Carrothers Productions/The Finnegan Company/
   Fries Entertainment, 1987
GUNSMOKE: RETURN TO DODGE (TF)   CBS Entertainment, 1987
RED RIVER (TF)   Catalina Production Group/MGM-UA TV, 1988
GUNSMOKE: THE LAST APACHE (TF)   CBS Entertainment/
   Galatea Productions, 1990

ROSEANNE ARNOLD
(See ROSEANNE)

TOM ARNOLD
Agent: William Morris Agency - Beverly Hills, 310/274-7451

FREDDY'S DEAD: THE FINAL NIGHTMARE
   New Line Cinema, 1991
BACKFIELD IN MOTION (TF)   Think Entertainment/
   The Avnet-Kerner Company, 1991
UNDERCOVER BLUES   MGM/UA, 1993
TRUE LIES   20th Century Fox, 1994
NINE MONTHS   20th Century Fox, 1995

DAVID ARNOTT
CRISSCROSS   MGM-Pathe Communications, 1992

JUDIE ARONSON
AMERICAN NINJA   Cannon, 1985

ALEXIS ARQUETTE
TERMINAL BLISS   Cannon, 1992

DAVID ARQUETTE
WILD BILL   MGM/UA, 1995

LEWIS ARQUETTE
NOBODY'S FOOL   Island Pictures, 1986
SLEEP WITH ME   MGM/UA, 1994

PATRICIA ARQUETTE
Agent: UTA - Beverly Hills, 310/273-6700

DADDY (TF)   Robert Greenwald Productions, 1987
FAR NORTH   Alive Films, 1988

THE INDIAN RUNNER   MGM-Pathe, 1991
TRUE ROMANCE   Warner Bros., 1993
HOLY MATRIMONY   Buena Vista, 1994
ED WOOD   Buena Vista, 1994
HEAVEN'S PRISONERS   Savoy Pictures, 1994
INFINITY   1995

ROSANNA ARQUETTE
b. August 10, 1959 - New York, New York
Agent: ICM - Beverly Hills, 310/550-4000

ZUMA BEACH (TF)   Edgar J. Scherick Associates/Warner
   Bros. TV, 1978
THE ORDEAL OF PATTY HEARST (TF)   Finnegan Associates/David
   Paradine TV, 1979
MORE AMERICAN GRAFFITI   Universal, 1979
GORP   American International, 1980
S.O.B.   Paramount, 1981
JOHNNY BELINDA (TF)   Dick Berg-Stonehenge Productions/Lorimar
   Productions, 1982
THE EXECUTIONER'S SONG (TF)
   Film Communications Inc., 1982
THE WALL (TF)   Cinetex International/Time-Life Productions,
   1982, U.S.-Polish
BABY IT'S YOU   Paramount, 1983
OFF THE WALL   Jensen Farley Pictures, 1983
THE AVIATOR   MGM/UA, 1985
DESPERATELY SEEKING SUSAN   Orion, 1985
SILVERADO   Columbia, 1985
AFTER HOURS   The Geffen Company/Warner Bros., 1985
8 MILLION WAYS TO DIE   TriStar, 1986
NOBODY'S FOOL   Island Pictures, 1986
AMAZON WOMEN ON THE MOON   Universal, 1987
PROMISED A MIRACLE (TF)   Dick Clark Productions/Republic
   Pictures/Roni Weisberg Productions, 1988
THE BIG BLUE   Columbia, 1988
NEW YORK STORIES   Buena Vista, 1989
SWEET REVENGE (CTF)   The Movie Group, 1990, French-U.S.
FLIGHT OF THE INTRUDER   Paramount, 1991
BLACK RAINBOW   Miramax Films, 1991, British
NOWHERE TO RUN   Columbia, 1993
PULP FICTION   Miramax Films, 1994
SEARCH AND DESTROY   October Films, 1995

MARIO ARRAMBIDE
THE MILAGRO BEANFIELD WAR   Universal, 1988

JERI ARREDONDO
SILENT TONGUE   Trimark Pictures, 1994, U.S.-French

LISA C. ARRINDELL
LIVIN' LARGE!   Samuel Goldwyn Company, 1991

BEATRICE ARTHUR
(Beatrice Frankel)
b. May 13, 1924 - New York, New York

THAT KIND OF WOMAN   Paramount, 1959
LOVERS AND OTHER STRANGERS   Cinerama Releasing
   Corporation, 1970
MAME   Warner Bros., 1974
MY FIRST LOVE (TF)   The Avnet-Kerner Company, 1988
STRANGER THINGS   Columbia, 1995

MONTY ASH
TOUGH GUYS   Buena Vista, 1986

ROCHELLE ASHANA
KICKBOXER   Cannon, 1989

LORRAINE ASHBOURNE
DISTANT VOICES, STILL LIVES   Alive Films, 1988, British

DANA ASHBROOK
Agent: William Morris Agency - Beverly Hills, 310/274-7451

RETURN OF THE LIVING DEAD PART II   Lorimar, 1988
WAXWORK   Vestron, 1988
TWIN PEAKS: FIRE WALK WITH ME   New Line Cinema, 1992,
   U.S.-French

DAPHNE ASHBROOK
THAT SECRET SUNDAY (TF)   CBS Entertainment, 1986
CARLY'S WEB (TF)   MTM Enterprises, 1987
LONGARM (TF)   Universal TV, 1988
ROCK HUDSON (TF)   The Konigsberg-Sanitsky Company, 1990
AUTOMATIC   Active Entertainment, 1994

LINDEN ASHBY
Agent: APA - Los Angeles, 310/273-0744

NIGHT ANGEL   Fries Distribution Company, 1990
WYATT EARP   Warner Bros., 1994
MORTAL KOMBAT   New Line Cinema, 1995

RENEE ASHERSON
ROMANCE ON THE ORIENT EXPRESS (TF)   von Zerneck
   Productions/Yorkshire TV, 1985, U.S.-British

ELIZABETH ASHLEY
(Elizabeth Ann Cole)
b. August 30, 1939 - Ocala, Florida
Agent: Gersh Agency - Beverly Hills, 310/274-6611

THE CARPETBAGGERS   Paramount, 1963
SHIP OF FOOLS   Columbia, 1965
THE THIRD DAY   Warner Bros., 1965
HARPY (TF)   Cinema Center 100, 1970
MARRIAGE OF A YOUNG STOCKBROKER
   20th Century Fox, 1971
WHEN MICHAEL CALLS (TF)   Palomar International, 1971
THE FACE OF FEAR (TF)   QM Productions, 1971
SECOND CHANCE (TF)   Metromedia Productions, 1971
YOUR MONEY OR YOUR WIFE (TF)   Brentwood Productions, 1972
THE HEIST (TF)   Paramount TV, 1972
THE MAGICIAN (TF)   Paramount TV, 1973
PAPERBACK HERO   1973, Canadian
GOLDEN NEEDLES   *THE CHASE FOR THE GOLDEN NEEDLES*
   American International, 1974
RANCHO DeLUXE   United Artists, 1975
92 IN THE SHADE   United Artists, 1975
ONE OF MY WIVES IS MISSING   Spelling-Goldberg
   Productions, 1976
THE GREAT SCOUT AND CATHOUSE THURSDAY
   American International, 1976
THE WAR BETWEEN THE TATES (TF)   Talent Associates, 1977
A FIRE IN THE SKY (TF)   Bill Driskill Productions, 1978
COMA   MGM/United Artists, 1978
WINDOWS   United Artists, 1980
PATERNITY   Paramount, 1981
SPLIT IMAGE   Orion, 1982
SVENGALI (TF)   Robert Halmi Productions, 1983
HE'S FIRED, SHE'S HIRED (TF)   CBS Entertainment, 1984
STAGECOACH (TF)   Raymond Katz Productions/Heritage
   Entertainment, 1986
WARM HEARTS, COLD FEET (TF)   Lorimar-Telepictures, 1987
THE TWO MRS. GRENVILLES (MS)   Lorimar-Telepictures, 1987
DRAGNET   Universal, 1987
MAN OF PASSION   Golden Sun Productions, 1988, Spanish
VAMPIRE'S KISS   Hemdale, 1989

FRANK ASHMORE
AIRPLANE!   Paramount, 1980

JOHN ASHTON
Agent: Harris & Goldberg - Los Angeles, 310/553-5200

BEVERLY HILLS COP   Paramount, 1984
A DEATH IN CALIFORNIA (MS)   Mace Neufeld Productions/Lorimar
   Productions, 1985

KING KONG LIVES   DEG, 1986
SOME KIND OF WONDERFUL   Paramount, 1987
BEVERLY HILLS COP II   Paramount, 1987
MIDNIGHT RUN   Universal, 1988
I KNOW MY FIRST NAME IS STEVEN (MS)   Andrew Adelson
   Company/Lorimar TV, 1989
LITTLE BIG LEAGUE   Columbia, 1994
TRAPPED IN PARADISE   20th Century Fox, 1994

ED ASNER
(Edward Asner)
b. November 15, 1929 - Kansas City, Kansas
Agent: Paradigm - Los Angeles, 310/277-4400

THE SATAN BUG   United Artists, 1965
THE SLENDER THREAD   Paramount, 1965
VENETIAN AFFAIR   MGM, 1967
EL DORADO   Paramount, 1967
GUNN   Warner Bros., 1967
CHANGE OF HABIT   Universal, 1969
THEY CALL ME MISTER TIBBS!   United Artists, 1970
THE TODD KILLINGS   *A DANGEROUS FRIEND*
   National General, 1971
SKIN GAME   Warner Bros., 1971
DEATH SCREAM   *THE WOMAN WHO CRIED MURDER* (TF)
   RSO Films, 1975
HEY, I'M ALIVE! (TF)   Charles Fries Productions/Worldvision, 1975
GUS   Buena Vista, 1976
RICH MAN, POOR MAN (MS)   Universal TV, 1976
THE LIFE AND ASSASSINATION OF THE KINGFISH (TF)
   Tomorrow Entertainment, 1977
ROOTS (MS)   Wolper Productions, 1977
THE GATHERING (TF)   Hanna-Barbera Productions, 1977
FORT APACHE, THE BRONX   20th Century Fox, 1981
O'HARA'S WIFE   Davis-Panzer Productions, 1982
DANIEL   Paramount, 1983
ANATOMY OF AN ILLNESS (TF)   Hamner Productions/CBS
   Entertainment, 1984
VITAL SIGNS (TF)   CBS Entertainment, 1986
KATE'S SECRET (TF)   Andrea Baynes Productions/
   Columbia TV, 1986
THE CHRISTMAS STAR (TF)   Lake Walloon Productions/Catalina
   Production Group/Walt Disney TV, 1986
CRACKED UP (TF)   Aaron Spelling Productions, 1987
MOON OVER PARADOR   Universal, 1988, U.S.-Brazilian
NOT A PENNY MORE, NOT A PENNY LESS (CMS)   BBC/
   Paramount TV/Revcom, 1990
SWITCHED AT BIRTH (MS)   Morrow-Heus Productions/
   O'Hara-Horowitz Productions/Columbia TV, 1991
JFK   Warner Bros., 1991
HAPPILY EVER AFTER (AF)   First National Film Corporation,
   1993 (voice)
GYPSY (TF)   RHI Entertainment, 1993
CATS DON'T DANCE (AF)   Turner Pictures, 1996 (voice)

ARMAND ASSANTE
b. October 4, 1949 - New York, New York
Agent: CAA - Beverly Hills, 310/288-4545

HAROLD ROBBINS' THE PIRATE   *THE PIRATE* (TF)
   Howard W. Koch Productions/Warner Bros. TV, 1978
PARADISE ALLEY   Universal, 1978
LADY OF THE HOUSE (TF)   Metromedia Productions, 1978
PROPHECY   Paramount, 1979
LITTLE DARLINGS   Paramount, 1980
PRIVATE BENJAMIN   Warner Bros., 1980
LOVE AND MONEY   Paramount, 1982
I, THE JURY   20th Century Fox, 1982
UNFAITHFULLY YOURS   20th Century Fox, 1984
EVERGREEN (MS)   Edgar J. Scherick Associates/Metromedia
   Producers Corporation, 1985
A DEADLY BUSINESS (TF)   Thebaut-Frey Productions/Taft
   Entertainment TV, 1986
BELIZAIRE THE CAJUN   Skouras Pictures, 1986
RAGE OF ANGELS: THE STORY CONTINUES (MS)
   NBC Productions, 1986
HANDS OF A STRANGER (MS)   Edgar J. Scherick Productions/Taft
   Entertainment TV, 1987

STRANGER IN MY BED (TF)   Edgar J. Scherick Productions/Taft
   Entertainment TV, 1987
NAPOLEON AND JOSEPHINE: A LOVE STORY (MS)
   David L. Wolper Productions/Warner Bros. TV, 1987
JACK THE RIPPER (MS)   Euston Films/Thames TV/Hill-O'Connor
   Entertainment/Lorimar TV, 1988, British-U.S.
PASSION AND PARADISE (MS)   Picturebase International/
   Primedia Productions/Leonard Hill Films, 1989,
   U.S.-Canadian
ANIMAL BEHAVIOR   Millimeter Films, 1989
Q&A   TriStar, 1990
ETERNITY   Academy Entertainment, 1990
FEVER (CTF)   HBO Pictures/Saban-Scherick Productions, 1991
THE MARRYING MAN   Buena Vista, 1991
THE MAMBO KINGS   Warner Bros., 1992
1492: CONQUEST OF PARADISE   Paramount,
   1992, British-Spanish
HOFFA   20th Century Fox, 1992
FATAL INSTINCT   MGM/UA, 1993
TRIAL BY JURY   Warner Bros., 1994
CANAAN'S WAY (CTF)   HBO Pictures, 1994
JUDGE DREDD   Buena Vista, 1995

JOHN ASTIN
b. March 30, 1930 - Baltimore, Maryland

WEST SIDE STORY   United Artists, 1961
THAT TOUCH OF MINK   Universal, 1962
THE WHEELER DEALERS   MGM, 1963
THE SPIRIT IS WILLING   Paramount, 1967
CANDY   1968, U.S.-Italian-French
VIVA MAX!   Commonwealth United, 1969
BUNNY O'HARE   American International, 1971
EVIL ROY SLADE (TF)   Universal TV, 1971
EVERY LITTLE CROOK AND NANNY   MGM, 1972
GET TO KNOW YOUR RABBIT   Warner Bros., 1972
THE BROTHERS O'TOOLE   1973
FREAKY FRIDAY   Buena Vista, 1977
BODY SLAM   DEG, 1987

MACKENZIE ASTIN
b. 1973 - Los Angeles, California
Agent: William Morris Agency - Beverly Hills, 310/274-7451

THE FACTS OF LIFE DOWN UNDER (TF)   Embassy TV/
   Crawford Productions, 1987, U.S.-Australian
IRON WILL   Buena Vista, 1994

PATTY DUKE ASTIN
(See Patty DUKE)

SEAN ASTIN
b. 1971 - Los Angeles, California
Agent: William Morris Agency - Beverly Hills, 310/274-7451

THE GOONIES   Warner Bros., 1985
STAYING TOGETHER   Hemdale, 1989
THE WAR OF THE ROSES   20th Century Fox, 1989
MEMPHIS BELLE   Warner Bros., 1990
TOY SOLDIERS   TriStar, 1991
ENCINO MAN   Buena Vista, 1992
WHERE THE DAY TAKES YOU   New Line Cinema, 1992
RUDY   TriStar, 1993
SAFE PASSAGE   New Line Cinema, 1994

WILLIAM ATHERTON
b. July 30, 1947 - Orange, Connecticut
Agent: Gersh Agency - Beverly Hills, 310/274-6611

THE NEW CENTURIONS   Columbia, 1972
CLASS OF '44   Warner Bros., 1973
THE SUGARLAND EXPRESS   Universal, 1974
THE GREAT GATSBY   Paramount, 1974
THE DAY OF THE LOCUST   Paramount, 1975
THE HINDENBURG   Universal, 1975
LOOKING FOR MR. GOODBAR   Paramount, 1977

MALIBU (TF)   Hamner Productions/Columbia TV, 1983
GHOSTBUSTERS   Columbia, 1984
REAL GENIUS   TriStar, 1985
NO MERCY   TriStar, 1986
DIE HARD   20th Century Fox, 1988
INTRIGUE (TF)   Crew Neck Productions/Linnea Productions/
   Columbia TV, 1988
BURIED ALIVE (CTF)   Niki Marvin Productions/
   MCA Entertainment, 1990
DIE HARD 2   20th Century Fox, 1990
OSCAR   Buena Vista, 1991
THE PELICAN BRIEF   Warner Bros., 1993

FEODOR ATKINE
SORCERESS   European Classics, 1988, French

CHRISTOPHER ATKINS
b. February 21, 1961 - Rye, New York

THE BLUE LAGOON   Columbia, 1980
CHILD BRIDE OF SHORT CREEK (TF)   Lawrence Schiller-Paul
   Monash Productions, 1981
A NIGHT IN HEAVEN   20th Century Fox, 1983

EILEEN ATKINS
INADMISSIBLE EVIDENCE   Paramount, 1968, British
THE DEVIL WITHIN HER   *I DON'T WANT TO BE BORN*
   20th Century Fox, 1975, British
EQUUS   United Artists, 1977, British
OLIVER TWIST (TF)   Claridge Group Ltd./Grafton Films,
   1982, British
THE DRESSER   Columbia, 1983, British
LET HIM HAVE IT   Fine Line Features/New Line Cinema, 1991,
   British-French-Dutch

ROBERT ATKINS
THE COMMITMENTS   20th Century Fox, 1991

TOM ATKINS
Agent: Paradigm - Los Angeles, 310/277-4400

SPECIAL DELIVERY   American International, 1976
LETHAL WEAPON   Warner Bros., 1987

JAYNE ATKINSON
Agent: Susan Smith & Associates - Beverly Hills, 213/852-4777

FREE WILLY   Warner Bros., 1993
BLANK CHECK   Buena Vista, 1994
WILLY II: THE ADVENTURE HOME   Warner Bros., 1995

ROWAN ATKINSON
Agent: William Morris Agency - Beverly Hills, 310/274-7451

THE TALL GUY   Miramax Films, 1990
FOUR WEDDINGS AND A FUNERAL   Gramercy Pictures,
   1994, British
THE LION KING (AF)   Buena Vista, 1994 (voice)

LARRY ATLAS
BRASS (TF)   Carnan Productions/Jaygee Productions/
   Orion TV, 1985

RICHARD ATTENBOROUGH
(Sir Richard Attenborough)
b. August 29, 1923 - Cambridge, England
Agent: CAA - Beverly Hills, 310/288-4545

JURASSIC PARK   Universal, 1993
MIRACLE ON 34TH STREET   20th Century Fox, 1994

ANTONELLA ATTILI
CINEMA PARADISO   *NUOVO CINEMA PARADISO*   Miramax Films,
   1989, Italian-French

RENÉ AUBERJONOIS
b. June 1, 1940 - New York, New York

LILITH Columbia, 1964
PETULIA Warner Bros., 1968, U.S.-British
M*A*S*H* 20th Century Fox, 1970
BREWSTER McCLOUD MGM, 1970
McCABE AND MRS. MILLER Warner Bros., 1971
IMAGES Columbia, 1972, Irish
PETE N' TILLIE Universal, 1972
THE HINDENBURG Universal, 1975
PANACHE (TF) Warner Bros. TV, 1976
THE BIG BUS Paramount, 1976
KING KONG Paramount, 1976
EYES OF LAURA MARS Columbia, 1978
WHERE THE BUFFALO ROAM Universal, 1980
THE CHRISTMAS STAR (TF) Lake Walloon Productions/Catalina
    Production Group/Walt Disney TV, 1986
LONGARM (TF) Universal TV, 1988
THE LITTLE MERMAID (AF) Buena Vista, 1989 (voice)
A CONNECTICUT YANKEE IN KING ARTHUR'S COURT (TF)
    Schaefer-Karpf Productions/Consolidated Productions, 1989

STÉPHANE AUDRAN
b. 1933 - Versailles, France

THE DISCREET CHARM OF THE BOURGEOISIE 20th Century
    Fox, 1972, French
SILVER BEARS Columbia, 1978
THE PRISONER OF ZENDA Universal, 1979
EAGLE'S WING International Picture Show, 1980, British
LA CAGE AUX FOLLES 3: THE WEDDING 1985, Italian-French
BETTY MK2, 1993, French

CLAUDINE AUGER
b. April 26, 1942 - Paris, France

TESTAMENT OF ORPHEUS *LE TESTAMENT D'ORPHÉE*
    1960, French
IN THE FRENCH STYLE *A LA FRANÇAISE* Columbia,
    1963, French-U.S.
GAMES OF DESIRE *DIE LADY* 1964, French-West German
YOYO 1965, French
THE HEAD OF THE FAMILY *IL PADRE DI FAMIGLIA*
    Ultra/CFC/Marianne Productions, 1965, Italian-French
THUNDERBALL United Artists, 1965, British
TRIPLE CROSS Warner Bros., 1966, French-British
THAT MAN GEORGE! *L'HOMME DE MARRAKECH* Allied Artists,
    1966, French-Italian-Spanish
TREASURE OF SAN GENNARO *OPERAZIONE SAN GENNARO*
    Paramount, 1966, Italian-French-West German
THE DEVIL IN LOVE *L'ARCIDIAVOLO* Warner Bros., 1966, Italian
THE KILLING GAME *JEU DE MASSACRE* 1967, French
ANYONE CAN PLAY *LE DOLCI SIGNORE* 1967, Italian
THE BASTARD 1968
ANTEFATTO 1971, Italian
THE BLACK BELLY OF THE TARANTULA 1972, Italian
FLIC STORY Adel Productions/Lira Films/Mondial, 1975, French
EMMENEZ-MOI AU RITZ 1977, French
SOTTO CHOCK 1978, Italian
UN PAPILLON SUR L'EPAULE Action Films, 1978, French
LOVERS AND LIARS *TRAVELS WITH ANITA* Levitt-Pickman,
    1979, Italian-French
FANTASTICA Les Productions du Verseau/El Productions, 1980,
    Canadian-French
SECRET PLACES TLC Films/20th Century Fox, 1984, British

JEAN-PIERRE AUMONT
(Jean-Pierre Salomons)
b. January 5, 1909 - Paris, France

DAY FOR NIGHT *LA NUIT AMERICAINE* Warner Bros.,
    1973, French-Italian
CAT AND MOUSE *LE CHAT ET LA SOURIS* Quartet,
    1975, French
CATHERINE & CO. 1975, French-Italian
THE HAPPY HOOKER Cannon, 1975

MAHOGANY Paramount, 1975
BLACKOUT 1978, Canadian-French
THE BLOOD OF OTHERS *LE SANG DES AUTRES* (CMS) HBO
    Premiere Films/ICC/Filmax Productions, 1984, Canadian-French
SIDNEY SHELDON'S WINDMILLS OF THE GODS *WINDMILLS OF
    THE GODS* (MS) Dove Productions/ITC Productions, 1988

MARCUS AURELIUS
APEX Republic Pictures, 1994

ALANA AUSTIN
NORTH Columbia, 1994

KAREN AUSTIN
ASSASSIN (TF) Sankan Productions, 1986
LAURA LANSING SLEPT HERE (TF) Schaefer-Karpf Productions/
    Gaylord Production Company, 1988

PATTI AUSTIN
b. August 10, 1948 - New York, New York

TUCKER - THE MAN AND HIS DREAM Paramount, 1988

TERI AUSTIN
DANGEROUS LOVE Concorde, 1988
JOHNNY RYAN (TF) Dan Curtis TV Productions/MGM-UA TV/
    NBC Productions, 1990

DANIEL AUTEUIL
JEAN DE FLORETTE Orion Classics, 1986, French
MANON OF THE SPRING Orion Classics, 1986, French
A FEW DAYS WITH ME Galaxy International, 1988, French
MAMA, THERE'S A MAN IN YOUR BED *ROMUALD ET JULIETTE*
    Miramax Films, 1988, French

ALAN AUTRY
b. July 31, 1952 - Shreveport, Louisiana

AT CLOSE RANGE Orion, 1986
DESTINATION: AMERICA (TF) Stephen J. Cannell
    Productions, 1987
PROUD MEN (TF) von Zerneck-Samuels Productions, 1987

FRANKIE AVALON
(Francis Thomas Avallone)
b. September 18, 1939 - Philadelphia, Pennsylvania
Agent: ICM - Beverly Hills, 310/550-4000

JAMBOREE 1957
GUNS OF THE TIMBERLAND 1960
THE ALAMO United Artists, 1960
VOYAGE TO THE BOTTOM OF THE SEA 20th Century Fox, 1961
PANIC IN YEAR ZERO! American International, 1962
BEACH PARTY American International, 1963
THE CASTILIAN 1963, Spanish
DRUMS OF AFRICA MGM, 1963
OPERATION BIKINI 1963
BIKINI BEACH American International, 1964
MUSCLE BEACH PARTY American International, 1964
PAJAMA PARTY American International, 1964
BEACH BLANKET BINGO American International, 1965
I'LL TAKE SWEDEN 1965
SERGEANT DEADHEAD American International, 1965
HOW TO STUFF A WILD BIKINI American International, 1965
DR. GOLDFOOT AND THE BIKINI MACHINE
    American International, 1966
FIREBALL 500 American International, 1966
THE MILLION EYES OF SU-MURU 1967
SKIDOO Paramount, 1968
HORROR HOUSE *THE HAUNTED HOUSE OF HORROR*
    American International, 1970, British-U.S.
THE TAKE 1974
GREASE Paramount, 1978
BACK TO THE BEACH Paramount, 1987

GREG AVELLONE
WYATT EARP   Warner Bros., 1994

JAMES AVERY
TIMESTALKERS (TF)   Fries Entertainment/Newland-Raynor
  Productions, 1987
FULL EXPOSURE: THE SEX TAPES SCANDAL (TF)
  von Zerneck-Sertner Films, 1989

MARGARET AVERY
THE COLOR PURPLE ○   Warner Bros., 1985
HEATWAVE (CTF)   The Avnet-Kerner Company/
  Propaganda Films, 1990

VAL AVERY
THE HARDER THEY FALL   Columbia, 1956
EDGE OF THE CITY   MGM, 1957
KING CREOLE   Paramount, 1958
THE LONG HOT SUMMER   MGM, 1958
TOO LATE BLUES   Paramount, 1962
REQUIEM FOR A HEAVYWEIGHT   Columbia, 1962
HUD   Paramount, 1963
THE HALLELUJAH TRAIL   United Artists, 1965
HOMBRE   20th Century Fox, 1967
THE PINK JUNGLE   Universal, 1968
FACES   Continental, 1968
THE BROTHERHOOD   Paramount, 1968
A DREAM OF KINGS   National General, 1969
THE TRAVELING EXECUTIONER   MGM, 1970
THE ANDERSON TAPES   Columbia, 1971
MINNIE AND MOSCOWITZ   Universal, 1971
BLACK CAESAR   American International, 1973
THE LAUGHING POLICEMAN   20th Century Fox, 1973
LET'S DO IT AGAIN   Warner Bros., 1975
RUSSIAN ROULETTE   Avco Embassy, 1975, U.S.-Canadian
LUCKY LADY   20th Century Fox, 1975
HARRY AND WALTER GO TO NEW YORK   Columbia, 1976
HEROES   Universal, 1977
THE WANDERERS   Orion/Warner Bros., 1979
LOVE AND BULLETS   AFD, 1979, British
COBRA   Warner Bros., 1986

JONATHAN AVILDSEN
THE KARATE KID PART III   Columbia, 1989

RICK AVILES
Agent: Writers & Artists Agency - Los Angeles, 310/820-2240

GHOST   Paramount, 1990
THE SAINT OF FORT WASHINGTON   Warner Bros., 1993

MILI AVITAL
STARGATE   MGM/UA, 1994

HOYT AXTON
b. March 25, 1938 - Duncan, Oklahoma
Agent: Charles H. Stern Agency, Inc. - Los Angeles, 310/479-1788

SMOKY   20th Century Fox, 1966
THE BLACK STALLION   United Artists, 1979
CLOUD DANCER   Blossom, 1980
ENDANGERED SPECIES   MGM/UA, 1982
LIAR'S MOON   Crown International, 1982
HEART LIKE A WHEEL   20th Century Fox, 1983
GREMLINS   Warner Bros., 1984
DALLAS: THE EARLY YEARS (TF)   Roundelay Productions/
  Lorimar Telepictures, 1986
CHRISTMAS COMES TO WILLOW CREEK (TF)   Blue Andre
  Productions/ITC Productions, 1987
RETRIBUTION   Taurus Entertainment, 1988
DISORGANIZED CRIME   Buena Vista, 1989
WE'RE NO ANGELS   Paramount, 1989
BURIED ALIVE (CTF)   Niki Marvin Productions/MCA
  Entertainment, 1990

DAN AYKROYD
b. July 1, 1952 - Ottawa, Canada
Agent: CAA - Beverly Hills, 310/288-4545

LOVE AT FIRST SIGHT   Movietown, 1977, Canadian
MR. MIKE'S MONDO VIDEO   New Line Cinema, 1979
1941   Universal/Columbia, 1979
THE BLUES BROTHERS   Universal, 1980
NEIGHBORS   Columbia, 1981
IT CAME FROM HOLLYWOOD (FD)   Paramount, 1982
DOCTOR DETROIT   Universal, 1983
TRADING PLACES   Paramount, 1983
TWILIGHT ZONE—THE MOVIE   Warner Bros., 1983
INDIANA JONES AND THE TEMPLE OF DOOM   Paramount, 1984
GHOSTBUSTERS   Columbia, 1984
NOTHING LASTS FOREVER   MGM/UA Classics, 1984
INTO THE NIGHT   Universal, 1985
SPIES LIKE US   Warner Bros., 1985
DRAGNET   Universal, 1987
THE COUCH TRIP   Orion, 1988
THE GREAT OUTDOORS   Universal, 1988
CADDYSHACK II   Warner Bros., 1988
MY STEPMOTHER IS AN ALIEN   WEG, 1988
GHOSTBUSTERS II   Columbia, 1989
DRIVING MISS DAISY ○   Warner Bros., 1989
LOOSE CANNONS   TriStar, 1990
NOTHING BUT TROUBLE   Warner Bros., 1991 (also directed)
MY GIRL   Columbia, 1991
THIS IS MY LIFE   20th Century Fox, 1992
SNEAKERS   Universal, 1992
CHAPLIN   TriStar, 1992, U.S.-British
CONEHEADS   Paramount, 1993
MY GIRL 2   Columbia, 1994
NORTH   Columbia, 1994
EXIT TO EDEN   Savoy Pictures, 1994
GETTING AWAY WITH MURDER   Savoy Pictures, 1995

DAVID AYKROYD
PICKING UP THE PIECES (TF)   CBS Entertainment, 1985
NUTCRACKER: MONEY, MADNESS AND MURDER (MS)
  Green Arrow Productions/Warner Bros. TV, 1987
POOR LITTLE RICH GIRL: THE BARBARA HUTTON STORY (MS)
  Lester Persky Productions/ITC Productions, 1987
SIDNEY SHELDON'S WINDMILLS OF THE GODS   *WINDMILLS OF*
  THE GODS (MS)   Dove Productions/ITC Productions, 1988

HANK AZARIA
QUIZ SHOW   Buena Vista, 1994

ANNETTE AZCUY
BILL & TED'S BOGUS JOURNEY   Orion, 1991

TONY AZITO
THE PIRATES OF PENZANCE   Universal, 1983

SHABANA AZMI
MADAME SOUSATZKA   Cineplex Odeon, 1988, British
CITY OF JOY   TriStar, 1992

B

OBBA BABATUNDÉ

Agent: Stone Manners Talent Agency - Los Angeles, 213/654-7575

DEAD AGAIN   Paramount, 1991

BARBARA BABCOCK

Agent: Paradigm - Los Angeles, 310/277-4400

HEAVEN WITH A GUN   MGM, 1969
THE LAST CHILD (TF)   Aaron Spelling Productions, 1971
BANG THE DRUM SLOWLY   Paramount, 1973
CHOSEN SURVIVORS   Columbia, 1974
SALEM'S LOT (TF)   Warner Bros. TV, 1979
THE LORDS OF DISCIPLINE   Paramount, 1983
NEWS AT ELEVEN (TF)   Turman-Foster Productions/Finnegan
   Associates, 1986
HEART OF DIXIE   Orion, 1989
HAPPY TOGETHER   Borde Releasing Corporation, 1990
A FAMILY FOR JOE (TF)   Grosso-Jacobson Productions/NBC
   Productions, 1990
FAR AND AWAY   Universal, 1992

LAUREN BACALL

(Betty Joan Perske)
b. September 16, 1924 - New York, New York
Agent: William Morris Agency - Beverly Hills, 310/274-7451

TO HAVE AND HAVE NOT   Warner Bros., 1944
CONFIDENTIAL AGENT   Warner Bros., 1945
TWO GUYS FROM MILWAUKEE   Warner Bros., 1946 (uncredited)
THE BIG SLEEP   Warner Bros., 1946
DARK PASSAGE   Warner Bros., 1947
KEY LARGO   Warner Bros., 1948
YOUNG MAN WITH A HORN   Warner Bros., 1950
BRIGHT LEAF   Warner Bros., 1950
HOW TO MARRY A MILLIONAIRE   20th Centuy Fox, 1953
WOMAN'S WORLD   20th Century Fox, 1954
THE COBWEB   MGM, 1955
BLOOD ALLEY   Warner Bros., 1955
WRITTEN ON THE WIND   Universal, 1956
DESIGNING WOMAN   MGM, 1957
THE GIFT OF LOVE   20th Century Fox, 1958
FLAME OVER INDIA   *NORTH WEST FRONTIER*
   20th Century Fox, 1959, British
SHOCK TREATMENT   1964
SEX AND THE SINGLE GIRL   Warner Bros., 1964
HARPER   Warner Bros., 1966
MURDER ON THE ORIENT EXPRESS   Paramount, 1974, British
THE SHOOTIST   Paramount, 1976
PERFECT GENTLEMEN (TF)   Paramount TV, 1978
HEALTH   20th Century Fox, 1980
THE FAN   Paramount, 1981
APPOINTMENT WITH DEATH   Cannon, 1988, U.S.-British
MR. NORTH   Samuel Goldwyn Company, 1988
INNOCENT VICTIM   *TREE OF HANDS*   Greenpoint/Granada/
   British Screen, 1989, British
DINNER AT EIGHT (CTF)   Think Entertainment/Turner
   Network TV, 1989
MISERY   Columbia, 1990
ALL I WANT FOR CHRISTMAS   Paramount, 1991
A STAR FOR TWO   InterStar Releasing, 1992, French-Canadian
THE PORTRAIT (CTF)   Robert Greenwald Productions/Atticus
   Corporation/Turner Network TV, 1993
PRET-A-PORTER   Miramax Films, 1994

MICHAEL BACALL

ALL SHOOK UP   Universal, 1991

BARBARA BACH

b. August 27, 1946

THE SPY WHO LOVED ME   United Artists, 1977, British-U.S.
FORCE 10 FROM NAVARONE   American International,
   1978, British
MAD MAGAZINE PRESENTS UP THE ACADEMY   *UP THE
   ACADEMY*   Warner Bros., 1980
CAVEMAN   United Artists, 1981
THE UNSEEN   1981
GIVE MY REGARDS TO BROADSTREET   20th Century Fox,
   1984, British

CATHERINE BACH

HUSTLE   Paramount, 1975
CANNONBALL RUN II   Warner Bros., 1984

BRIAN BACKER

b. December 5, 1956 - New York, New York
Agent: Abrams Artists & Associates - Los Angeles, 310/859-0625

FAST TIMES AT RIDGEMONT HIGH   Universal, 1982
POLICE ACADEMY 4: CITIZENS ON PATROL   Warner Bros., 1987

KEVIN BACON

b. July 8, 1958 - Philadelphia, Pennsylvania
Agent: CAA - Beverly Hills, 310/288-4545

NATIONAL LAMPOON'S ANIMAL HOUSE   Universal, 1978
STARTING OVER   Paramount, 1979
THE GIFT (TF)   The Jozak Company/Cypress Point Productions/
   Paramount TV, 1979
FRIDAY THE 13TH   Paramount, 1980
HERO AT LARGE   MGM/United Artists, 1980
ONLY WHEN I LAUGH   Columbia, 1981
DINER   MGM/United Artists, 1982
FORTY-DEUCE   Island Alive, 1982
FOOTLOOSE   Paramount, 1984
ENORMOUS CHANGES AT THE LAST MINUTE   TC Films
   International, 1985
QUICKSILVER   Columbia, 1986
WHITE WATER SUMMER   *RITES OF SUMMER*   Columbia, 1987
PLANES, TRAINS AND AUTOMOBILES   Paramount, 1987
END OF THE LINE   Orion Classics, 1988
LEMON SKY   American Playhouse Theatrical Films, 1988
SHE'S HAVING A BABY   Paramount, 1988
CRIMINAL LAW   Hemdale, 1989
THE BIG PICTURE   Columbia, 1989
TREMORS   Universal, 1990
FLATLINERS   Columbia, 1990
HE SAID, SHE SAID   Paramount, 1991
QUEENS LOGIC   New Line Cinema, 1991
PYRATES   Seven Arts/New Line Cinema, 1991
JFK   Warner Bros., 1991
A FEW GOOD MEN   Columbia, 1992
THE AIR UP THERE   Buena Vista, 1994
THE RIVER WILD   Universal, 1994
MURDER IN THE FIRST   Warner Bros., 1994
APOLLO 13   Universal, 1995

DIEDRICH BADER

THE BEVERLY HILLBILLIES   20th Century Fox, 1993

MINA BADIE

MRS. PARKER AND THE VICIOUS CIRCLE   Fine Line Features/
   New Line Cinema, 1994

KRISTIN BAER

THE COWBOY WAY   Universal, 1994

ROSS BAGLEY

THE LITTLE RASCALS   Universal, 1994

VERNEL BAGNERIS
PENNIES FROM HEAVEN   MGM/United Artists, 1981
DOWN BY LAW   Island Pictures, 1986

BILL BAILEY
ON THE EDGE   Skouras Pictures, 1986
A CASUALTY OF WAR (CTF)   F.F.S. Productions/Taurus Film/
    Blair Communications, 1990, British
GUILTY BY SUSPICION   Warner Bros., 1991

G.W. BAILEY
Agent: Writers & Artists Agency - Los Angeles, 310/820-2240

POLICE ACADEMY   The Ladd Company/Warner Bros., 1984
RUNAWAY   TriStar, 1984
RUSTLER'S RHAPSODY   Paramount, 1985
A WINNER NEVER QUITS (TF)   Blatt-Singer Productions/
    Columbia TV, 1986
SHORT CIRCUIT   TriStar, 1986
BURGLAR   Warner Bros., 1987
POLICE ACADEMY 4: CITIZENS ON PATROL   Warner Bros., 1987
POLICE ACADEMY 5: ASSIGNMENT MIAMI BEACH
    Warner Bros., 1988
THE GIFTED ONE (TF)   Richard Rothstein Productions/NBC
    Productions, 1989
POLICE ACADEMY 6: CITY UNDER SIEGE   Warner Bros., 1989
DOUBLE CROSS: THE BARRY SEAL STORY (CTF)
    HBO Pictures/Green-Epstein Productions/Lorimar TV, 1991
POLICE ACADEMY: MISSION TO MOSCOW   Warner Bros., 1994

CHUB BAILLY
THE NEW ADVENTURES OF PIPPI LONGSTOCKING
    Columbia, 1988

BARBARA BAIN
b. September 13, 1934 - Chicago, Illinois

MURDER ONCE REMOVED (TF)   Metromedia Productions, 1971
GOODNIGHT MY LOVE   ABC Circle Films, 1972
A SUMMER WITHOUT BOYS (TF)   Playboy Productions, 1973
SKINHEADS   Amazing Movies, 1989

CONRAD BAIN
b. February 4, 1923
Agent: Harris & Goldberg - Los Angeles, 310/553-5200

BANANAS   United Artists, 1971
POSTCARDS FROM THE EDGE   Columbia, 1990

SCOTT BAIO
b. September 22, 1961 - Brooklyn, New York
Agent: Shapiro-Lichtman - Los Angeles, 310/859-8877

BUGSY MALONE   Paramount, 1976, British
SOMETHING FOR JOEY (TF)   MTM Productions, 1977
FOXES   United Artists, 1980
THE BOY WHO DRANK TOO MUCH (TF)   MTM Enterprises, 1980
ZAPPED!   Embassy, 1982
ALICE IN WONDERLAND (MS)   Irwin Allen Productions/
    Procter & Gamble Productions/Columbia TV, 1985

SCOTT BAIRSTOW
WHITE FANG 2: MYTH OF THE WHITE WOLF   Buena Vista, 1994

BLANCHE BAKER
b. December 20, 1956 - New York, New York
Agent: Abrams Artists & Associates - Los Angeles, 310/859-0625

HOLOCAUST (MS)   Titus Productions, 1978
RAW DEAL   DEG, 1986
SHAKEDOWN   Universal, 1988
LIVIN' LARGE!   Samuel Goldwyn Company, 1991

CARROLL BAKER
b. May 28, 1931 - Johnstown, Pennsylvania
Agent: Abrams Artists & Associates - Los Angeles, 310/859-0625

EASY TO LOVE   MGM, 1953
GIANT   Warner Bros., 1956
BABY DOLL ★   Warner Bros., 1956
THE BIG COUNTRY   United Artists, 1958
BUT NOT FOR ME   20th Century Fox, 1959
THE MIRACLE   Warner Bros., 1959
BRIDGE TO THE SUN   MGM, 1961, U.S.-French
SOMETHING WILD   United Artists, 1961
HOW THE WEST WAS WON   MGM/Cinerama, 1962
STATION SIX—SAHARA   Allied Artists, 1963, British-West German
THE CARPETBAGGERS   Paramount, 1964
CHEYENNE AUTUMN   Warner Bros., 1964
SYLVIA   Paramount, 1965
THE GREATEST STORY EVER TOLD   United Artists, 1965
MISTER MOSES   United Artists, 1965, British
HARLOW   Paramount, 1965
JACK OF DIAMONDS   MGM, 1967, U.S.-West German
L'HAREM   1968, Italian-French-West German
PARANOIA   ORGASMO   1968, Italian
THE SWEET BODY OF DEBORAH   1969, Italian-French
A QUIET PLACE TO KILL   PARANOIA   1969, Italian-Spanish
COSI DOLCE...COSI PERVERSA   1970, Italian-French
IN FONDO ALLA PISCINA   1971, Italian-Spanish
CAPTAIN APACHE   Scotia International, 1971, British-Spanish
BLOODY MARY   1972
THE DEVIL HAS SEVEN FACES   1972, Italian
IL COLTELLO DI GHIACCIO   1972, Italian-Spanish
THE MADNESS OF LOVE   1973, Italian-Spanish
BABA YAGA   1973, Spanish
BABA YAGA DEVIL WITCH   1974
THE SKY IS FALLING   1976, Canadian
THE FLOWER WITH THE DEADLY STING   1976, Italian
DOMANI SAREMO RICCHI   1976, Italian-West German
LA MOGLIE VERGINE   1976, Italian
L'APPAT   1976, Austrian-West German-French
CONFESSIONS OF A FRUSTRATED HOUSEWIFE   1976
ANDY WARHOL'S BAD   New World, 1977
THE DEVIL HAS SEVEN FACES   1977
CYCLONE   1977, Mexican
THE WORLD IS FULL OF MARRIED MEN   New Realm,
    1979, British
THE WATCHER IN THE WOODS   Buena Vista, 1980
STAR 80   The Ladd Company/Warner Bros., 1983
THE SECRET DIARY OF SIGMUND FREUD   TLC Films/
    20th Century Fox, 1984
NATIVE SON   Cinecom, 1986
ON FIRE (TF)   Robert Greenwald Productions, 1987
IRONWEED   TriStar, 1987
KINDERGARTEN COP   Universal, 1990

DIANE BAKER
b. February 25, 1938 - Hollywood, California

THE DIARY OF ANNE FRANK   20th Century Fox, 1959
JOURNEY TO THE CENTER OF THE EARTH
    20th Century Fox, 1959
THE BEST OF EVERYTHING   20th Century Fox, 1959
THE WIZARD OF BAGHDAD   20th Century Fox, 1960
TESS OF THE STORM COUNTRY   20th Century Fox, 1960
HEMINGWAY'S ADVENTURES OF A YOUNG MAN
    20th Century Fox, 1962
THE 300 SPARTANS   20th Century Fox, 1962
NINE HOURS TO RAMA   20th Century Fox, 1963, British-U.S.
THE STOLEN HOURS   United Artists, 1963
THE PRIZE   MGM, 1963
STRAIT-JACKET   Columbia, 1964
DELLA (TF)   Four Star, 1964
MARNIE   Universal, 1964
MIRAGE   Universal, 1965
SANDS OF BEERSHEBA   Landau-Unger, 1966, Israeli-U.S.
THE DANGEROUS DAYS OF KIOWA JONES   MGM, 1966
THE HORSE IN THE GRAY FLANNEL SUIT   1968
KRAKATOA EAST OF JAVA   Cinerama Releasing
    Corporation, 1969

THE D.A.: MURDER ONE *MURDER ONE* (TF)   Mark Vii, Ltd./
   Universal TV/Jack Webb Productions, 1969
THE BADGE OR THE CROSS (TF)   1970
WHEELER AND MURDOCH (TF)   1970
THE OLD MAN WHO CRIED WOLF (TF)   Aaron Spelling
   Productions, 1970
DO YOU TAKE THIS STRANGER? (TF)   Universal TV, 1971
A LITTLE GAME (TF)   Universal TV, 1971
KILLER BY NIGHT (TF)   Cinema Center, 1971
CONGRATULATIONS, IT'S A BOY (TF)   Aaron Spelling
   Productions, 1971
A TREE GROWS IN BROOKLYN (TF)   20th Century-Fox TV, 1974
THE DREAM MAKERS (TF)   MGM-TV, 1975
THE LAST SURVIVORS (TF)   Bob Banner Associates, 1975
BAKER'S HAWK   Doty-Dayton, 1976
A WOMAN OF SUBSTANCE (MS)   Artemis Portman Productions,
   1984, British
THE SILENCE OF THE LAMBS   Orion, 1991

DYLAN BAKER
Agent: ICM - Beverly Hills, 310/550-4000

THE WIZARD OF LONELINESS   Skouras Pictures, 1988
THE LONG WALK HOME   Miramax Films, 1990
DELIRIOUS   MGM-Pathe, 1991
LOVE POTION #9   20th Century Fox, 1992

HENRY JUDD BAKER
CLEAN AND SOBER   Warner Bros., 1988

JAY BAKER
Agent: Paradigm - Los Angeles, 310/277-4400

APRIL FOOL'S DAY   Paramount, 1986

JOE DON BAKER
b. February 12, 1936 - Groebeck, Texas
Agent: The Artists Agency - Los Angeles, 310/277-7779

COOL HAND LUKE   Warner Bros., 1967
GUNS OF THE MAGNIFICENT SEVEN   United Artists, 1969
ADAM AT SIX A.M.   National General, 1970
WILD ROVERS   MGM, 1971
MONGO'S BACK IN TOWN (TF)   Bob Banner Associates, 1971
WELCOME HOME SOLDIER BOYS   20th Century-Fox, 1972
JUNIOR BONNER   Cinerama Releasing Corporation, 1972
CHARLEY VARRICK   Universal, 1973
WALKING TALL   Cinerama Releasing Corporation, 1973
THE OUTFIT   MGM, 1974
GOLDEN NEEDLES   American International, 1974
MITCHELL   Allied Artists, 1975
FRAMED   Paramount, 1975
CRASH!   Group 1, 1977
THE PACK   Warner Bros., 1977
TO KILL A COP (TF)   David Gerber Company/Columbia TV, 1978
SPEEDTRAP   First Artists, 1978
POWER (TF)   David Gerber Company/Columbia TV, 1980
JOYSTICKS   Jensen Farley Pictures, 1983
THE NATURAL   TriStar, 1984
FLETCH   Universal, 1985
GETTING EVEN   American Distribution Group, 1986
THE ABDUCTION OF KARI SWENSON (TF)
   NBC Productions, 1987
THE LIVING DAYLIGHTS   MGM/UA, 1987, British
CRIMINAL LAW   Hemdale, 1989
CAPE FEAR   Universal, 1991
REALITY BITES   Universal, 1994
PANTHER   Gramercy Pictures, 1995
OUTBREAK   Warner Bros., 1995

KATHY BAKER
Agent: ICM - Beverly Hills, 310/550-4000

THE RIGHT STUFF   The Ladd Company/Warner Bros., 1983
NOBODY'S CHILD (TF)   Joseph Feury Productions/Gaylord
   Production Company, 1986
STREET SMART   Cannon, 1987

A KILLING AFFAIR   Hemdale, 1988
PERMANENT RECORD   Paramount, 1988
CLEAN AND SOBER   Warner Bros., 1988
JACKNIFE   Cineplex Odeon, 1989
DAD   Universal, 1989
THE IMAGE (CTF)   HBO Pictures/Citadel Entertainment, 1990
EDWARD SCISSORHANDS   20th Century Fox, 1990
ARTICLE 99   Orion, 1992
JENNIFER EIGHT   Paramount, 1992
MAD DOG AND GLORY   Universal, 1993

KENNY BAKER
b. August 24, 1934 - Birmingham, England

CIRCUS OF HORRORS   American International, 1960, British
STAR WARS   20th Century Fox, 1977
THE EMPIRE STRIKES BACK   20th Century Fox, 1980
RETURN OF THE JEDI   20th Century Fox, 1983

RAY BAKER
NOBODY'S CHILD (TF)   Joseph Feury Productions/Gaylord
   Production Company, 1986
SPEECHLESS   MGM/UA, 1994

RAYMOND BAKER
THE SECRETARY   Republic Pictures, 1995

GARY BAKEWELL
BACKBEAT   Gramercy Pictures, 1994, British

BRENDA BAKKE
Agent: APA - Los Angeles, 310/273-0744

DANGEROUS LOVE   Motion Picture Corporation of America, 1988
TWOGETHER   Borde Releasing, 1994
DEMON KNIGHT   Universal, 1995

BRIGITTE BAKO
A MAN IN UNIFORM   I.R.S. Releasing, 1994
STRANGE DAYS   20th Century Fox, 1995

SCOTT BAKULA
b. October 9 - St. Louis, Missouri
Agent: UTA - Beverly Hills, 310/273-6700

QUANTUM LEAP (TF)   Belisarius Productions/Universal TV, 1989
SIBLING RIVALRY   Columbia, 1990
L.A. STORY   TriStar, 1991
NECESSARY ROUGHNESS   Paramount, 1991
COLOR OF NIGHT   Buena Vista, 1994
CATS DON'T DANCE (AF)   Turner Pictures, 1996 (voice)

BOB BALABAN
b. August 16, 1945 - Chicago, Illinois

MIDNIGHT COWBOY   United Artists, 1969
ME, NATALIE   1969
CLOSE ENCOUNTERS OF THE THIRD KIND   Columbia, 1977
ALTERED STATES   Warner Bros., 1980
PRINCE OF THE CITY   Orion/Warner Bros., 1981
WHOSE LIFE IS IT ANYWAY?   MGM/United Artists, 1981
END OF THE LINE   Orion Classics, 1988
DEAD-BANG   Warner Bros., 1989
ALICE   Orion, 1990
LITTLE MAN TATE   Orion, 1991
FOR LOVE OR MONEY   Universal, 1993
GREEDY   Universal, 1994
CITY SLICKERS II: THE LEGEND OF CURLY'S GOLD   Columbia,
   1994 (uncredited)

ADAM BALDWIN
b. 1962 - Chicago, Illinois

RECKLESS   MGM/UA, 1984
POISON IVY (TF)   NBC Productions, 1985
FULL METAL JACKET   Warner Bros., 1987, British

COHEN & TATE   Nelson Entertainment, 1989
NEXT OF KIN   Warner Bros., 1989
GUILTY BY SUSPICION   Warner Bros., 1991
RADIO FLYER   Columbia, 1992
WHERE THE DAY TAKES YOU   New Line Cinema, 1992
WYATT EARP   Warner Bros., 1994

ALEC BALDWIN
b. April 3, 1958 - Massapequa, New York
Agent: CAA - Beverly Hills, 310/288-4545

SWEET REVENGE   *CODE OF HONOR/BITTERSWEET
   REVENGE* (TF)   David Greene Productions/Robert Papazian
   Productions, 1984
LOVE ON THE RUN (TF)   NBC Productions, 1985
DRESS GRAY (MS)   von Zerneck Productions/Warner
   Bros. TV, 1986
THE ALAMO: 13 DAYS TO GLORY (TF)   Briggle, Hennessy,
   Carrothers Productions/The Finnegan Company/Fries
   Entertainment, 1987
FOREVER, LULU   TriStar, 1987
SHE'S HAVING A BABY   Paramount, 1988
BEETLEJUICE   The Geffen Company/Warner Bros., 1988
MARRIED TO THE MOB   Orion, 1988
TALK RADIO   Universal, 1988
WORKING GIRL   20th Century Fox, 1988
GREAT BALLS OF FIRE   Orion, 1989
THE HUNT FOR RED OCTOBER   Paramount, 1990
MIAMI BLUES   Orion, 1990
ALICE   Orion, 1990
THE MARRYING MAN   Buena Vista, 1991
PRELUDE TO A KISS   20th Century Fox, 1992
GLENGARRY GLEN ROSS   New Line Cinema, 1992
MALICE   Columbia, 1993
THE GETAWAY   Universal, 1994
THE SHADOW   Universal, 1994
HEAVEN'S PRISONERS   Savoy Pictures, 1994

DANIEL BALDWIN
Agent: William Morris Agency - Beverly Hills, 310/274-7451

HARLEY DAVIDSON & THE MARLBORO MAN   MGM-Pathe, 1991
ATTACK OF THE 50-FOOT WOMAN (CTF)   HBO Pictures/Lorimar
   Productions, 1993
CAR 54, WHERE ARE YOU?   Orion, 1994

STEPHEN BALDWIN
Agent: UTA - Beverly Hills, 310/273-6700

THE PRODIGIOUS HICKEY (TF)   Ronald J. Kahn Productions/
   American Playhouse, 1987
THE BEAST   Columbia, 1988
BORN ON THE FOURTH OF JULY   Universal, 1989
CROSSING THE BRIDGE   Buena Vista, 1992
8 SECONDS   New Line Cinema, 1994
THREESOME   TriStar, 1994
A SIMPLE TWIST OF FATE   Buena Vista, 1994
MRS. PARKER AND THE VICIOUS CIRCLE   Fine Line Features/
   New Line Cinema, 1994
USUAL SUSPECTS   1995

WILLIAM BALDWIN
b. 1963 - Massapequa, New York
Agent: CAA - Beverly Hills, 310/288-4545

THE PREPPIE MURDER (TF)   Jack Grossbart Productions/
   Spectator Films, 1989
INTERNAL AFFAIRS   Paramount, 1990
FLATLINERS   Columbia, 1990
BACKDRAFT   Universal, 1991
THREE OF HEARTS   New Line Cinema, 1993
SLIVER   Paramount, 1993
A PYROMANIAC'S LOVE STORY   Buena Vista, 1995
FAIR GAME   Warner Bros., 1995

CHRISTIAN BALE
b. 1974 - Bournemouth, England
Agent: William Morris Agency - Beverly Hills, 310/274-7451

EMPIRE OF THE SUN   Warner Bros., 1987
HENRY V   Samuel Goldwyn Company, 1989, British
NEWSIES   Buena Vista, 1992
SWING KIDS   Buena Vista, 1993
LITTLE WOMEN   Columbia, 1994
POCAHONTAS (AF)   Buena Vista, 1995 (voice)

RICHARD BALIN
SCHIZOID   Cannon, 1980
FIRST MONDAY IN OCTOBER   Paramount, 1981
GRADUATION DAY   IFI-Scope III, 1981
TORCHLIGHT   International Film Marketing, 1984, U.S.-Mexican
THAT'S ADEQUATE   South Gate Entertainment, 1989
BEASTMASTER II   MGM-Pathe, 1991
THE RAPE OF DR. WILLIS (TF)   Interprod Productions, 1991

FAIRUZA BALK
Agent: William Morris Agency - Beverly Hills, 310/274-7451

RETURN TO OZ   Buena Vista, 1985
VALMONT   Orion, 1989, French
GAS, FOOD LODGING   I.R.S. Releasing, 1992
SHAME (CTF)   Dalrymple Productions/Steinhardt Baer Pictures/
   Viacom, 1992
MURDER IN THE HEARTLAND (TF)   O'Hara-Horowitz
   Productions, 1993
IMAGINARY CRIMES   Warner Bros., 1994

ANGELINE BALL
THE COMMITMENTS   20th Century Fox, 1991
MY GIRL 2   Columbia, 1994

KAYE BALLARD
(Catherine Gloria Balotta)
b. November 20, 1926 - Cleveland, Ohio

THE GIRL MOST LIKELY   Universal, 1957
A HOUSE IS NOT A HOME   Embassy, 1964
WHICH WAY TO THE FRONT?   Warner Bros., 1970
THE RITZ   Warner Bros., 1976
FREAKY FRIDAY   Buena Vista, 1977
FALLING IN LOVE AGAIN   *IN LOVE*   International Picture Show
   Company, 1980
MODERN LOVE   Triumph Releasing Corporation, 1990
ETERNITY   Preferred Films, 1990

MARK BALLOU
Agent: Paul Kohner, Inc. - Los Angeles, 310/550-1060

BIG   20th Century Fox, 1988

MARTIN BALSAM
b. November 4, 1919 - New York, New York

ON THE WATERFRONT   Columbia, 1954
TWELVE ANGRY MEN   United Artists, 1957
TIME LIMIT   1957
MARJORIE MORNINGSTAR   Warner Bros., 1958
AL CAPONE   Allied Artists, 1959
MIDDLE OF THE NIGHT   Columbia, 1959
PSYCHO   Paramount, 1960
EVERYBODY GO HOME!   *TUTTI A CASA*   Royal Films
   International, 1960, Italian-French
ADA   MGM, 1961
BREAKFAST AT TIFFANY'S   Paramount, 1961
CAPE FEAR   Universal, 1962
CONQUERED CITY   *LA CITTA PRIGIONIERA*   American
   International, 1962, Italian
WHO'S BEEN SLEEPING IN MY BED?   Paramount, 1963
THE CARPETBAGGERS   Paramount, 1964
YOUNGBLOOD HAWKE   Warner Bros., 1964
SEVEN DAYS IN MAY   Paramount, 1964

HARLOW   Paramount, 1965
THE BEDFORD INCIDENT   Columbia, 1965
A THOUSAND CLOWNS ⊙⊙   United Artists, 1965
AFTER THE FOX   United Artists, 1966, Italian-U.S.-British
HOMBRE   20th Century Fox, 1967
ME, NATALIE   1969
TRILOGY (TF)   Allied Artists, 1969
THE GOOD GUYS AND THE BAD GUYS   Warner Bros., 1969
CATCH-22   Paramount, 1970
TORA! TORA! TORA!   20th Century Fox, 1970, U.S.-Japanese
LITTLE BIG MAN   National General, 1970
THE OLD MAN WHO CRIED WOLF (TF)   Aaron Spelling
   Productions, 1970
HUNTERS ARE FOR KILLING (TF)   Cinema Center, 1970
THE ANDERSON TAPES   Columbia, 1971
CONFESSIONS OF A POLICE CAPTAIN   CONFESSIONE DI UN
   COMMISSARIO   1971, Italian
THE MAN (TF)   Paramount, 1972
NIGHT OF TERROR (TF)   Paramount TV, 1972
THE STONE KILLER   Columbia, 1973
SUMMER WISHES, WINTER DREAMS   Columbia, 1973
THE SIX MILLION DOLLAR MAN (TF)   Universal TV, 1973
I CONSIGLIORI   1973, Italian
MONEY TO BURN (TF)   Universal TV, 1974
TRAPPED BENEATH THE SEA (TF)   ABC Circle Films, 1974
THE TAKING OF PELHAM 1-2-3   United Artists, 1974
MURDER ON THE ORIENT EXPRESS   Paramount, 1974, British
COUNSELOR AT CRIME   CORRUZIONE AL PALAZZO DI
   GIUSTIZIA   1974, Italian
MILES TO GO BEFORE I SLEEP (TF)   Tomorrow
   Entertainment, 1975
IL TEMPO DEGLI ASSASSINI   1975, Italian
MITCHELL   Allied Artists, 1975
DEATH AMONG FRIENDS (TF)   Douglas S. Cramer Productions/
   Warner Bros. TV, 1975
ALL THE PRESIDENT'S MEN   Warner Bros., 1976
TWO-MINUTE WARNING   Universal, 1976
THE LINDBERGH KIDNAPPING CASE (TF)   Columbia TV, 1976
RAID ON ENTEBBE (TF)   Edgar J. Scherick Associates/
   20th Century Fox, 1977
THE SENTINEL   Universal, 1977
SILVER BEARS   Columbia, 1978
RAINBOW (TF)   Ten-Four Productions, 1978
THE SEEDING OF SARAH BURNS (TF)   Michael Klein
   Productions, 1979
THE HOUSE ON GARIBALDI STREET (TF)   1979
AUNT MARY (TF)   Henry-Jaffe Enterprises, 1979
CUBA   United Artists, 1979
THE LOVE TAPES (TF)   Christiana Productions/MGM TV, 1980
THERE GOES THE BRIDE   Vanguard, 1980, British
THE SALAMANDER   ITC, 1981, British-Italian-U.S.
LITTLE GLORIA...HAPPY AT LAST (TF)   Edgar J. Scherick
   Associates/Metromedia Producers Corporation, 1982,
   U.S.-Canadian-British
THE GOODBYE PEOPLE   Embassy, 1984
SPACE (MS)   Stonehenge Productions/Paramount TV, 1985
ST. ELMO'S FIRE   Columbia, 1985
DEATH WISH 3   Cannon, 1985
THE DELTA FORCE   Cannon, 1986
SECOND SERVE (TF)   Linda Yellen Productions/Lorimar-
   Telepictures, 1986
PRIVATE INVESTIGATIONS (TF)   MGM/UA, 1987
QUEENIE (TF)   von Zerneck-Samuels Productions/Highgate
   Pictures, 1987
THE CHILD SAVER (TF)   Michael Filerman Productions/NBC
   Productions, 1988
CAPE FEAR   Universal, 1991

TALIA BALSAM
Agent: Writers & Artists Agency - Los Angeles, 213/820-2240

CRAWLSPACE   Empire Pictures, 1986

MICHAEL BALZARY
THE CHASE   20th Century Fox, 1994

DAVID BAMBER
HIGH HOPES   Skouras Pictures, 1988, British

ANNE BANCROFT
(Anna Maria Louise Italiano)
b. September 17, 1931 - Bronx, New York
Agent: ICM - Beverly Hills, 310/550-4000

DON'T BOTHER TO KNOCK   20th Century Fox, 1952
TONIGHT WE SING   20th Century Fox, 1953
THE ROBE   20th Century-Fox, 1953
TREASURE OF THE GOLDEN CONDOR   20th Century Fox, 1953
THE KID FROM LEFT FIELD   1953
DEMETRIUS AND THE GLADIATORS   20th Century Fox, 1954
THE RAID   20th Century Fox, 1954
GORILLA AT LARGE   1954
A LIFE IN THE BALANCE   1955
NEW YORK CONFIDENTIAL   Warner Bros., 1955
THE NAKED STREET   1955
THE LAST FRONTIER   Columbia, 1956
WALK THE PROUD LAND   1956
NIGHTFALL   Columbia, 1956
THE RESTLESS BREED   20th Century Fox, 1957
THE GIRL IN BLACK STOCKINGS   United Artists, 1957
THE MIRACLE WORKER ★★   United Artists, 1962
THE PUMPKIN EATER ★   Royal International, 1964, British
THE SLENDER THREAD   Paramount, 1965
7 WOMEN   MGM, 1966
THE GRADUATE ★   Avco Embassy, 1967
YOUNG WINSTON   Columbia, 1972, British
THE PRISONER OF SECOND AVENUE   Warner Bros., 1975
THE HINDENBURG   Universal, 1975
SILENT MOVIE   20th Century Fox, 1976 (uncredited)
LIPSTICK   Paramount, 1976
THE TURNING POINT ★   20th Century Fox, 1977
JESUS OF NAZARETH (MS)   Sir Lew Grade Productions/ITC,
   1978, British-Italian
FATSO   20th Century Fox, 1980 (also directed)
THE ELEPHANT MAN   Paramount, 1980, British-U.S.
MARCO POLO (MS)   RAI/Franco Cristaldi Productions/Vincenzo
   Labella Productions, 1982, Italian
TO BE OR NOT TO BE   20th Century Fox, 1983
GARBO TALKS   MGM/UA, 1984
AGNES OF GOD ★   Columbia, 1985
'NIGHT, MOTHER   Universal, 1986
84 CHARING CROSS ROAD   Columbia, 1987, British
TORCH SONG TRILOGY   New Line Cinema, 1988
BERT RIGBY, YOU'RE A FOOL   Warner Bros., 1989
NEIL SIMON'S BROADWAY BOUND   BROADWAY BOUND (TF)
   ABC Productions, 1992
HONEYMOON IN VEGAS   Columbia, 1992
LOVE POTION #9   20th Century Fox, 1992
POINT OF NO RETURN   Warner Bros., 1993
MALICE   Columbia, 1993
MR. JONES   TriStar, 1993
HOW TO MAKE AN AMERICAN QUILT   Universal, 1995

BRADFORD BANCROFT
DANGEROUSLY CLOSE   Cannon, 1986

ANTONIO BANDERAS
MATADOR   Cinevista, 1986, Spanish
LAW OF DESIRE   Cinevista/Promovision International,
   1987, Spanish
WOMEN ON THE VERGE OF A NERVOUS BREAKDOWN
   Orion Classics, 1988, Spanish
TIE ME UP! TIE ME DOWN!   ATAME   Miramax Films,
   1990, Spanish
THE MAMBO KINGS   Warner Bros., 1992
PHILADELPHIA   TriStar, 1993
THE HOUSE OF THE SPIRITS   Miramax Films, 1993, U.S.-German
INTERVIEW WITH THE VAMPIRE   Warner Bros., 1994
DESPERADO   Columbia, 1995

VICTOR BANERJEE

A PASSAGE TO INDIA   Columbia, 1984, British
FOREIGN BODY   Orion, 1986, British
DADAH IS DEATH (MS)   Steve Krantz Productions/Roadshow,
   Coote & Carroll Productions/Samuel Goldwyn TV,
   1988, U.S.-Australian

JONATHAN BANKS

b. January 31, 1947 - Washington D.C.
Agent: Paradigm - Los Angeles, 310/277-4400

AIRPLANE!   Paramount, 1980
GREMLINS   Warner Bros., 1984
ARMED AND DANGEROUS   Columbia, 1986
WHO IS JULIA? (TF)   CBS Entertainment, 1986
DOWNPAYMENT ON MURDER (TF)   Adam Productions/
   20th Century Fox TV, 1987
FREEJACK   Warner Bros., 1992

TYRA BANKS

HIGHER LEARNING   Columbia, 1994

IAN BANNEN

b. June 29, 1928 - Airdrie, Scotland
Agent: Harris & Goldberg - Los Angeles, 310/553-5200

PRIVATE'S PROGRESS   DCA, 1956, British
THE THIRD KEY   *THE LONG ARM*   1956, British
THE BIRTHDAY PRESENT   1957
A TALE OF TWO CITIES   Rank, 1958, British
MAN IN A COCKED HAT   *CARLTON BROWNE OF THE F.O.*
   Show Corporation, 1959, British
A FRENCH MISTRESS   Films Around the World, 1960, British
MACBETH   British Lion, 1960, British
THE RISK   *SUSPECT*   Kingsley International, 1961
ON FRIDAY AT ELEVEN   British Lion, 1961, West German-British
STATION SIX—SAHARA   Allied Artists, 1963, British-West German
PSYCHE 59   Royal Films International, 1964, British
MISTER MOSES   United Artists, 1965, British
ROTTEN TO THE CORE   Cinema 5, 1965, British
THE HILL   MGM, 1965, British
THE FLIGHT OF THE PHOENIX ✪   20th Century Fox, 1965
PENELOPE   MGM, 1966
THE SAILOR FROM GIBRALTAR   Lopert, 1967, British
LOCK UP YOUR DAUGHTERS   1969, British
TOO LATE THE HERO   Cinerama Releasing Corporation, 1970
THE DESERTER   *LA SPINA DORSALE DEL DIAVOLO*
   Paramount, 1971, Italian-Yugoslavian
JANE EYRE (TF)   Omnibus Productions/Sagittarius Productions,
   1971, British-U.S.
FRIGHT   1971
DOOMWATCH   Avco Embassy, 1972, British
THE OFFENCE   United Artists, 1973, British
THE MACKINTOSH MAN   Warner Bros., 1973, U.S.-British
THE DRIVER'S SEAT   1973, Italian
THE VOYAGE   United Artists, 1974, Italian
BITE THE BULLET   Columbia, 1975
FROM BEYOND THE GRAVE   Howard Mahler Films, 1975, British
SWEENEY   EMI, 1977
BASTARDS WITHOUT GLORY   1978, Italian
THE WATCHER IN THE WOODS   Buena Vista, 1980
EYE OF THE NEEDLE   United Artists, 1981, U.S.-British
GANDHI   Columbia, 1982, British-Indian
NIGHT CROSSING   Buena Vista, 1982
GORKY PARK   Orion, 1983
DEFENSE OF THE REALM   Hemdale, 1985, British
LAMB   Limehouse/Flickers/Channel Four, 1985, British
HOPE AND GLORY   Columbia, 1987, British
PERRY MASON: THE CASE OF THE DESPERATE
   DECEPTION (TF)   The Fred Silverman Company/Dean
   Hargrove Productions/Viacom, 1990
GHOST DAD   Universal, 1990
THE BIG MAN   Miramax Films, 1990, British
DAMAGE   New Line Cinema, 1992, French-British

REGGIE BANNISTER

PHANTASM II   Universal, 1988

CHRISTINE BARANSKI

b. May 2, 1952 - Buffalo, New York

CRACKERS   Universal, 1984
9 1/2 WEEKS   MGM/UA, 1986
REVERSAL OF FORTUNE   Warner Bros., 1990
TO DANCE WITH THE WHITE DOG (TF)   Signboard Hill
   Productions, 1993
THE REF   Buena Vista, 1994

OLIVIA BARASH

PATTY HEARST   Atlantic Releasing Corporation, 1988

ADRIENNE BARBEAU

b. June 11, 1945 - Sacramento, California

RED ALERT (TF)   The Jozak Company/Paramount TV, 1977
SOMEONE'S WATCHING ME! (TF)   Warner Bros. TV, 1978
THE FOG   Avco Embassy, 1981
ESCAPE FROM NEW YORK   Avco Embassy, 1981
SWAMP THING   Avco Embassy, 1982
CREEP SHOW   Warner Bros., 1982
BRIDGE ACROSS TIME (TF)   Fries Entertainment, 1985
BACK TO SCHOOL   Orion, 1986

ANDREA BARBER

THE SKATEBOARD KID II   Concorde, 1995

FRANCES BARBER

SAMMY AND ROSIE GET LAID   Cinecom, 1987, British

GLYNIS BARBER

THE WICKED LADY   MGM/UA/Cannon, 1983, British

URBANO BARBERINI

OTELLO   Cannon, 1986, Italian

GENE BARGE

ABOVE THE LAW   Warner Bros., 1988

PATRICIA BARKER

NUTCRACKER: THE MOTION PICTURE   Atlantic Releasing
   Corporation, 1986

ELLEN BARKIN

b. April 16, 1954 - Bronx, New York
Agent: ICM - Beverly Hills, 310/550-4000

DINER   MGM/United Artists, 1982
DANIEL   Paramount, 1983
EDDIE AND THE CRUISERS   Embassy, 1983
THE ADVENTURES OF BUCKAROO BANZAI: ACROSS THE 8TH
   DIMENSION   20th Century Fox, 1984
HARRY AND SON   Orion, 1984
DESERT BLOOM   Columbia, 1986
DOWN BY LAW   Island Pictures, 1986
MADE IN HEAVEN   Lorimar, 1987
THE BIG EASY   Columbia, 1987
SIESTA   Lorimar, 1987, British
SEA OF LOVE   Universal, 1989
JOHNNY HANDSOME   TriStar, 1989
SWITCH   Warner Bros., 1991
MAN TROUBLE   20th Century Fox, 1992
THIS BOY'S LIFE   Warner Bros., 1993
INTO THE WEST   Miramax Films, 1993, British-Irish-Japanese
THE TOOL SHED   Buena Vista, 1994
WILD BILL   MGM/UA, 1995

PAT BARLOW

APRIL FOOL'S DAY   Paramount, 1986

CHRISTOPHER DANIEL BARNES

THE LITTLE MERMAID (AF)   Buena Vista, 1989 (voice)
THE BRADY BUNCH MOVIE   Paramount, 1995

F
I
L
M

A
C
T
O
R
S

PRISCILLA BARNES
THE LAST MARRIED COUPLE IN AMERICA   Universal, 1980
THE WILD WOMEN OF CHASTITY GULCH (TF)   Aaron Spelling
   Productions, 1982
PERFECT PEOPLE (TF)   Robert Greenwald Productions, 1988
LICENCE TO KILL   MGM/UA, 1989, British
EROTIQUE   Group 1, 1993, U.S.-German-Hong Kong-Brazilian
THE CROSSING GUARD   Miramax Films, 1994

CHARLIE BARNETT
NOBODY'S FOOL   Island Pictures, 1986

SANDY BARON
BROADWAY DANNY ROSE   Orion, 1984
VAMP   New World, 1986

JEAN-MARC BARR
THE BIG BLUE   Columbia, 1988

STEVEN BARR
MEMOIRS OF AN INVISIBLE MAN   Warner Bros., 1992

MARIE-CHRISTINE BARRAULT
b. March 21, 1944 - Paris, France

COUSIN, COUSINE ★   Northal Films, 1976, French
THE MEDUSA TOUCH   Warner Bros., 1978, British
STARDUST MEMORIES   United Artists, 1980

MAJEL BARRETT
(Majel Hudec)
b. February 23, 1939 - Columbus, Ohio

STAR TREK - THE MOTION PICTURE   Paramount, 1979
STAR TREK IV: THE VOYAGE HOME   Paramount, 1986

NANCY BARRETT
BELIZAIRE THE CAJUN   Skouras Pictures, 1986

AMBER BARRETTO
LITTLE MONSTERS   MGM/UA, 1989

BARBARA BARRIE
b. May 23, 1931 - Chicago, Illinois
Agent: Gersh Agency - Beverly Hills, 310/274-6611

ONE POTATO, TWO POTATO   Cinema 5, 1964
SUMMER OF MY GERMAN SOLDIER (TF)   Highgate
   Productions, 1978
THE BELL JAR   Avco Embassy, 1979
BREAKING AWAY ✪   20th Century Fox, 1979
PRIVATE BENJAMIN   Warner Bros., 1980
THE EXECUTION (TF)   Newland-Raynor Productions/Comworld
   Productions, 1985
VITAL SIGNS (TF)   CBS Entertainment, 1986
WINNIE (TF)   All Girl Productions/NBC Productions, 1988
MY FIRST LOVE (TF)   The Avnet-Kerner Company, 1988
END OF THE LINE   Orion Classics, 1988
MY BREAST (TF)   CBS, 1994

ROBERT V. BARRON
BILL & TED'S EXCELLENT ADVENTURE   Orion, 1989

RONNIE BARRON
ABOVE THE LAW   Warner Bros., 1988

MATTHEW BARRY
LUNA   20th Century Fox, 1979, Italian-U.S.
NO WAY OUT   Orion, 1987

NEILL BARRY
b. November 29, 1965 - New York, New York

OLD ENOUGH   Orion Classics, 1984

PATRICIA BARRY
Agent: Paul Kohner Agency - Los Angeles, 310/550-1060

SEA OF LOVE   Universal, 1989
EVERGREEN (MS)   Edgar J. Scherick Associates/Metromedia
   Producers Corporation, 1985

RAYMOND J. BARRY
OUT OF BOUNDS   Columbia, 1986
BORN ON THE FOURTH OF JULY   Universal, 1989
THE REF   Buena Vista, 1994

DREW BARRYMORE
b. February 22, 1975 - Los Angeles, California
Agent: UTA - Beverly Hills, 310/273-6700

ALTERED STATES   Warner Bros., 1980
E.T. THE EXTRA-TERRESTRIAL   Universal, 1982
FIRESTARTER   Universal, 1984
IRRECONCILABLE DIFFERENCES   Warner Bros., 1984
STEPHEN KING'S CAT'S EYE   *CAT'S EYE*   MGM/UA, 1985
BABES IN TOYLAND (TF)   Orion TV/Finnegan-Pinchuk
   Company, 1986
CONSPIRACY OF LOVE (TF)   New World TV, 1987
FAR FROM HOME   Vestron, 1989
SEE YOU IN THE MORNING   Warner Bros., 1989
POISON IVY   New Line Cinema, 1992
MOTORAMA   Two Moon Releasing, 1992
GUNCRAZY   Academy Entertainment, 1992
SKETCH ARTIST (CTF)   Motion Picture Corporation of
   America, 1992
DOPPELGANGER: THE EVIL WITHIN (CTF)
   Planet Productions, 1993
THE AMY FISHER STORY (TF)   Andrew Adelson Productions/
   ABC Productions, 1993
BAD GIRLS   20th Century Fox, 1994
BOYS ON THE SIDE   Warner Bros., 1995
MAD LOVE   Buena Vista, 1995

PAUL BARTEL
b. August 6, 1938 - Brooklyn, New York
Agent: ICM - Beverly Hills, 310/550-4000

EAT MY DUST!   New World, 1976
CANNONBALL   New World, 1976 (also directed)
GRAND THEFT AUTO   New World, 1977
EATING RAOUL   20th Century Fox International Classics,
   1982 (also directed)
HEART LIKE A WHEEL   20th Century Fox, 1983
NOT FOR PUBLICATION   Samuel Goldwyn Company, 1984,
   U.S.-British (also directed)
CADDYSHACK II   Warner Bros., 1988
SCENES FROM THE CLASS STRUGGLE IN BEVERLY HILLS
   Cinecom, 1989 (also directed)
FAR OUT MAN   New Line Cinema, 1990
THE POPE MUST DIET   Miramax Films, 1991
THE JERKY BOYS   Buena Vista, 1994

BONNIE BARTLETT
DEADLY DECEPTION (TF)   CBS Entertainment, 1987
RIGHT TO DIE (TF)   Ohlmeyer Communications, 1987
TWINS   Universal, 1988

ROBIN BARTLETT
Agent: Gersh Agency - Beverly Hills, 310/274-6611

HEAVEN'S GATE   United Artists, 1980
PLAYING FOR TIME (TF)   Syzygy Productions, 1980
SKOKIE (TF)   Titus Productions, 1981
COURAGE (TF)   Highgate Pictures/New World TV, 1986
BABY BOOM   MGM/UA, 1987
MOONSTRUCK   MGM/UA, 1987
SEE YOU IN THE MORNING   Warner Bros., 1989
LEAN ON ME   Warner Bros., 1989
CRIMES AND MISDEMEANORS   Orion, 1989
POSTCARDS FROM THE EDGE   Columbia, 1990

ALICE   Orion, 1990
IF LOOKS COULD KILL   Warner Bros., 1991
DECEIVED   Buena Vista, 1991

ROBERT BARTON
E.T. THE EXTRA-TERRESTRIAL   Universal, 1982

BILLY BARTY
b. October 25, 1924 - Millsboro, Pennsylvania

THE DAY OF THE LOCUST   Paramount, 1975
W.C. FIELDS AND ME   Universal, 1976
THE AMAZING DOBERMANS   Golden, 1976
THE HAPPY HOOKER GOES TO WASHINGTON   Cannon, 1977
FOUL PLAY   Paramount, 1978
THE LORD OF THE RINGS (AF)   United Artists, 1978 (voice)
FIREPOWER   AFD, 1979, British
SKATETOWN, U.S.A.   Columbia, 1979
BEING DIFFERENT (TD)   Astral Films, 1981, Canadian
HARDLY WORKING   20th Century-Fox, 1981
UNDER THE RAINBOW   Orion/Warner Bros., 1981
NIGHT PATROL   New World, 1985
LEGEND   Universal, 1986, British
TOUGH GUYS   Buena Vista, 1986
BODY SLAM   DEG, 1987
RUMPELSTILTSKIN   Cannon, 1987, U.S.-Israeli
WILLOW   MGM/UA, 1988
THE PRINCESS AND THE PEA   21st Century Film
   Corporation, 1995

MIKHAIL BARYSHNIKOV
b. January 27, 1948 - Riga, Latvia
Agent: CAA - Beverly Hills, 310/288-4545

THE TURNING POINT ✪   20th Century Fox, 1977
WHITE NIGHTS   Columbia, 1985
DANCERS   Cannon, 1987
COMPANY BUSINESS   MGM-Pathe, 1991

GARY BASARABA
Agent: Paradigm - Los Angeles, 310/277-4400

NO MERCY   TriStar, 1986
FRIED GREEN TOMATOES   Universal, 1991
MRS. PARKER AND THE VICIOUS CIRCLE   Fine Line Features/
   New Line Cinema, 1994

HARRY BASIL
PEGGY SUE GOT MARRIED   TriStar, 1986
THE SEVENTH SIGN   TriStar, 1988

JOHN BASINGER
CHILDREN OF A LESSER GOD   Paramount, 1986

KIM BASINGER
b. December 8, 1953 - Athens, Georgia
Agent: CAA - Beverly Hills, 310/288-4545

DOG AND CAT (TF)   1977
KATIE: PORTRAIT OF A CENTERFOLD (TF)   Moonlight
   Productions/Warner Bros. TV, 1978
KILLJOY   WHO MURDERED JOY MORGAN? (TF)   Lorimar
   Productions, 1981
HARD COUNTRY   Universal/AFD, 1981
MOTHER LODE   SEARCH FOR THE MOTHER LODE: THE LAST
   GREAT TREASURE   Agamemnon Films, 1982, Canadian
THE MAN WHO LOVED WOMEN   Columbia, 1983
NEVER SAY NEVER AGAIN   Warner Bros., 1983
THE NATURAL   TriStar, 1984
FOOL FOR LOVE   Cannon, 1985
9 1/2 WEEKS   MGM/UA, 1986
NO MERCY   TriStar, 1987
BLIND DATE   TriStar, 1987
NADINE   TriStar, 1987
MY STEPMOTHER IS AN ALIEN   WEG, 1988

BATMAN   Warner Bros., 1989
THE MARRYING MAN   Buena Vista, 1991
FINAL ANALYSIS   Warner Bros., 1992
COOL WORLD   Paramount, 1992
THE REAL McCOY   Universal, 1993
WAYNE'S WORLD 2   Paramount, 1993
THE GETAWAY   Universal, 1994
PRET-A-PORTER   Miramax Films, 1994

ELYA BASKIN
MOSCOW ON THE HUDSON   Columbia, 1984
STREETS OF GOLD   20th Century Fox, 1986
THE NAME OF THE ROSE   20th Century Fox, 1986,
   West German-Italian-French
DEEPSTAR SIX   TriStar, 1989
ENEMIES, A LOVE STORY   20th Century Fox, 1989

ANGELA BASSETT
BOYZ 'N THE HOOD   Columbia, 1991
PASSION FISH   Miramax Films, 1992
MALCOLM X   Warner Bros., 1992
THE JACKSONS: AN AMERICAN DREAM (TF)   Stan Margulies
   Company/de Passe Entertainment/Motown Record Company/
   Polygram Filmed Entertainment, 1992
WHAT'S LOVE GOT TO DO WITH IT ★   Buena Vista, 1993
STRANGE DAYS   20th Century Fox, 1995

LINDA BASSETT
WAITING FOR THE MOON   Skouras Pictures, 1987,
   U.S.-French-British-West German

BILL BASTIANI
MOBSTERS   Universal, 1991

ANTHONY BATE
EMINENT DOMAIN   Triumph Releasing Corporation, 1990,
   Canadian-French-Israeli

JASON BATEMAN
b. January 14, 1968 - Los Angeles, California

CAN YOU FEEL ME DANCING? (TF)   Robert Greenwald
   Productions, 1986
BATES MOTEL (TF)   Universal TV, 1987
TEEN WOLF TOO   Atlantic Releasing Corporation, 1987
CROSSING THE MOB (TF)   Bateman Company Productions/
   Interscope Communications, 1988
MOVING TARGET (TF)   Lewis B. Chesler Productions/Bateman
   Company Productions/Finnegan-Pinchuk Company/
   MGM-UA TV, 1988
NECESSARY ROUGHNESS   Paramount, 1991
BREAKING THE RULES   Miramax Films, 1992
THIS CAN'T BE LOVE (TF)   Davis Entertainment/Pacific Motion
   Pictures/World International Network, 1994

JUSTINE BATEMAN
b. February 19, 1966 - Rye, New York

FAMILY TIES VACATION (TF)   Paramount TV/Ubu Productions/
   NBC Entertainment, 1985
RIGHT TO KILL? (TF)   Wrye-Konigsberg Productions/Taper Media
   Enterprises/Telepictures Productions, 1985
CAN YOU FEEL ME DANCING? (TF)   Robert Greenwald
   Productions, 1986
SATISFACTION   20th Century Fox, 1988
THE CLOSER   Ion Pictures, 1990
THE NIGHT WE NEVER MET   Miramax Films, 1993

ALAN BATES
b. February 17, 1934 - Allestree, Derbyshire, England

THE ENTERTAINER   Continental, 1960, British
WHISTLE DOWN THE WIND   Pathe-America, 1961, British
A KIND OF LOVING   Continental, 1962, British
THE RUNNING MAN   Columbia, 1963, British

THE GUEST *THE CARETAKER* Janus, 1964, British
NOTHING BUT THE BEST Royal Films International, 1964, British
ZORBA THE GREEK 20th Century Fox/International Classics, 1964, Greek
GEORGY GIRL Columbia, 1966, British
KING OF HEARTS *LE ROI DE COEUR* Lopert, 1966, French-British
FAR FROM THE MADDING CROWD MGM, 1967, British
THE FIXER ★ MGM, 1968, British
WOMEN IN LOVE United Artists, 1969, British
THREE SISTERS American Film Theatre, 1970, British
THE GO-BETWEEN Columbia, 1971, British
A DAY IN THE DEATH OF JOE EGG Columbia, 1972, British
STORY OF A LOVE STORY *IMPOSSIBLE OBJECT* Valoria, 1973, British-French
BUTLEY American Film Theatre, 1974, British
THE STORY OF JACOB AND JOSEPH (TF) Screen Gems/Columbia TV, 1974 (voice)
IN CELEBRATION American Film Theatre, 1975, British-Canadian
ROYAL FLASH 20th Century Fox, 1975, British
THE COLLECTION (TF) Granada TV, 1976, British
AN UNMARRIED WOMAN 20th Century Fox, 1978
THE SHOUT Films Inc., 1978, British
THE ROSE 20th Century Fox, 1979
NIJINSKY Paramount, 1980
QUARTET New World, 1981, British-French
VERY LIKE A WHALE (TF) Black Lion, 1981, British
THE RETURN OF THE SOLDIER European Classics, 1981, British
BRITANNIA HOSPITAL United Artists Classics, 1982, British
THE WICKED LADY MGM/UA/Cannon, 1983, British
AN ENGLISHMAN ABROAD (TF) BBC, 1983, British
A VOYAGE ROUND MY FATHER (TF) Thames TV/D.L. Taffner, Ltd., 1983, British
DR. FISCHER OF GENEVA (TF) Consolidated Productions/BBC, 1983, British
DUET FOR ONE Cannon, 1986
A PRAYER FOR THE DYING Samuel Goldwyn Company, 1987, British
PACK OF LIES (TF) Robert Halmi, Inc., 1987
WE THINK THE WORLD OF YOU Cinecom, 1988, British
CLUB EXTINCTION *DR. M* NEF Filmproduktion/Ellepi Film/Clea Productions/Deutsches Fersehen/La Sept/Telefilm GmbH., 1990, West German-Italian-French
MISTER FROST Triumph Releasing Corporation, 1990, French-British
HAMLET Warner Bros., 1990, British
SECRET FRIENDS Whistling Gypsy Productions/Film Four International/Briarpatch Film Corporation, 1992, U.S.-British
SILENT TONGUE Trimark Pictures, 1994, U.S.-French

KATHY BATES
b. June 28, 1948 - Memphis, Tennessee
Agent: Susan Smith & Associates - Beverly Hills, 213/852-4777

TAKING OFF Universal, 1971
STRAIGHT TIME Warner Bros., 1978
COME BACK TO THE 5 & DIME JIMMY DEAN, JIMMY DEAN Cinecom, 1982
JOHNNY BULL (TF) Titus Productions/Eugene O'Neill Memorial Theatre Center, 1986
SUMMER HEAT Atlantic Releasing Corporation, 1987
ARTHUR 2 ON THE ROCKS Warner Bros., 1988
ROE VS. WADE (TF) The Manheim Company/NBC Productions, 1989
SIGNS OF LIFE Avenue Pictures, 1989
MEN DON'T LEAVE Warner Bros., 1990
DICK TRACY Buena Vista, 1990
WHITE PALACE Universal, 1990
MISERY ★★ Columbia, 1990
AT PLAY IN THE FIELDS OF THE LORD Universal, 1991
FRIED GREEN TOMATOES Universal, 1991
SHADOWS AND FOG Orion, 1992
PRELUDE TO A KISS 20th Century Fox, 1992
USED PEOPLE 20th Century Fox, 1992
A HOME OF OUR OWN Gramercy Pictures, 1993
NORTH Columbia, 1994
CURSE OF THE STARVING CLASS Trimark Pictures, 1994
DOLORES CLAIBORNE Columbia, 1994

PAUL BATES
Agent: Gersh Agency - Beverly Hills, 310/274-6611

HOT PURSUIT Paramount, 1987
COMING TO AMERICA Paramount, 1988
CRAZY PEOPLE Paramount, 1990

RANDALL BATINKOFF
Agent: Paradigm - Los Angeles, 310/277-4400

THE STEPFORD CHILDREN (TF) Edgar J. Scherick Productions/Taft Entertainment TV, 1987
FOR KEEPS TriStar, 1988
SCHOOL TIES Paramount, 1992

BRYAN BATT
JEFFREY 1995

PATRICK BAUCHAU
THE RAPTURE New Line Cinema, 1991
THE NEW AGE Warner Bros., 1994

BELINDA BAUER
Agent: David Shapira & Associates - Sherman Oaks, 818/906-0322

FLASHDANCE Paramount, 1983
THE SINS OF DORIAN GRAY (TF) Rankin-Bass Productions, 1983
STARCROSSED (TF) Fries Entertainment, 1985
TONIGHT'S THE NIGHT (TF) Indieprod Productions/Phoenix Entertainment Group, 1987
ROBOCOP 2 Orion, 1990

STEVEN BAUER
(Steven Rocky Echevarria)
b. December 2, 1956 - Havana, Cuba

SCARFACE Universal, 1983
THIEF OF HEARTS Paramount, 1984
RUNNING SCARED MGM/UA, 1986
THE BEAST Columbia, 1988
GLEAMING THE CUBE 20th Century Fox, 1989
DRUG WARS: THE CAMARENA STORY (MS) ZZY, Inc. Productions/World International Network, 1990
RAISING CAIN Universal, 1992

MEREDITH BAXTER
(Meredith Baxter-Birney)
b. June 21, 1947 - Los Angeles, California
Agent: William Morris Agency - Beverly Hills, 310/274-7451

STAND UP AND BE COUNTED Columbia, 1971
BEN Cinerama Releasing Corporation, 1972
THE CAT CREATURE (TF) Screen Gems/Columbia TV, 1973
THE STRANGER WHO LOOKS LIKE ME (TF) Filmways, 1974
THE NIGHT THAT PANICKED AMERICA (TF) Paramount TV, 1975
TARGET RISK (TF) Universal TV, 1975
ALL THE PRESIDENT'S MEN Warner Bros., 1976
THE NOVEMBER PLAN 1976
BITTERSWEET LOVE Avco Embassy, 1976
BEULAH LAND (MS) David Gerber Company/Columbia TV, 1980
THE RAPE OF RICHARD BᴇCK (TF) Robert Papazian Productions/Henerson-Hirsch Productions, 1985
FAMILY TIES VACATION (TF) Paramount TV/Ubu Productions/NBC Entertainment, 1985
KATE'S SECRET (TF) Andrea Baynes Productions/Columbia TV, 1986
THE LONG JOURNEY HOME (TF) Andrea Baynes Productions/Grail Productions/Lorimar-Telepictures, 1987
WINNIE (TF) All Girl Productions/NBC Productions, 1988
SHE KNOWS TOO MUCH (TF) The Fred Silverman Company/Dinnegan-Pinchuk Productions/MGM-UA TV, 1989
THE KISSING PLACE (CTF) Cynthia Cherbak Productions/Wilshire Court Productions, 1990
BURNING BRIDGES (TF) Andrea Baynes Productions/Lorimar TV, 1990

A WOMAN SCORNED (TF) Patchett Kaufman Entertainment, 1992
HER FINAL FURY: BETTY BRODERICK, THE LAST CHAPTER (TF)
   Patchett Kaufman Entertainment/Lowry-Rawls Productions, 1992
ONE MORE MOUNTAIN (TF) Marian Rees Associates, 1994
MY BREAST (TF) CBS, 1994

TURHAN BAY
THE SKATEBOARD KID II Concorde, 1995

NATHALIE BAYE
b. July 6, 1948 - Mainneville, France

DAY FOR NIGHT LA NUIT AMERICAINE Warner Bros.,
   1973, French-Italian
THE GREEN ROOM New World, 1978, French
THE GIRL FROM LORRAINE LA PROVINCIALE New Yorker,
   1980, French-Swiss
LA BALANCE Spectrafilm, 1982, French
THE RETURN OF MARTIN GUERRE European International,
   1982, French
EVERY OTHER WEEKEND MK2, 1991

GARY BAYER
NOT MY KID (TF) Beth Polson Productions/Finnegan
   Associates, 1985
GO TOWARD THE LIGHT (TF) Corapeak Productions/The Polson
   Company, 1988

GEOFFREY BAYLDON
THE STRANGER LEFT NO CARD 1953, British
HORROR OF DRACULA DRACULA Universal, 1958, British
LIBEL MGM, 1959, British
THE WEBSTER BOY RFI, 1963, British
A JOLLY BAD FELLOW THEY ALL DIED LAUGHING
   Continental, 1963, British
KING RAT Columbia, 1965, British
GYPSY GIRL SKY WEST AND CROOKED 1966, British
TO SIR WITH LOVE Columbia, 1966, British
CASINO ROYALE Columbia, 1967, British
OTLEY Columbia, 1969, British
LONG AGO TOMORROW THE RAGING MOON Cinema 5,
   1970, British
SCROOGE National General, 1970, British
ASYLUM Cinerama Releasing Corporation, 1972, British
BULLSHOT! Island Alive, 1983, British
MADAME SOUSATZKA Cineplex Odeon, 1988, British

STACY BAYNE
PERFECT Columbia, 1985

TRACY BAYNE
PERFECT Columbia, 1985

MICHAEL BEACH
Agent: Paradigm - Los Angeles, 310/277-4400

OPEN ADMISSIONS (TF) The Mount Company/Viacom
   Productions, 1988
LEAN ON ME Warner Bros., 1989
INTERNAL AFFAIRS Paramount, 1990
CADENCE New Line Cinema, 1991
THE TOOL SHED Buena Vista, 1994

JENNIFER BEALS
Agent: UTA - Beverly Hills, 310/273-6700

FLASHDANCE Paramount, 1983
THE BRIDE Columbia, 1985, British
VAMPIRE'S KISS Hemdale, 1989
RIDER IN THE DARK Cannon, 1989
BLOOD AND CONCRETE I.R.S. Releasing, 1991
MRS. PARKER AND THE VICIOUS CIRCLE Fine Line Features/
   New Line Cinema, 1994
DEVIL IN A BLUE DRESS TriStar, 1994
LET IT BE ME Savoy Pictures, 1995

REATHEL BEAN
THE GUN IN BETTY LOU'S HANDBAG Buena Vista, 1992

SEAN BEAN
b. Sheffield, England
Agent: ICM - Beverly Hills, 310/550-4000

CARAVAGGIO British Film Institute, 1986, British
STORMY MONDAY Atlantic Releasing Corporation, 1988, British
THE FIELD Avenue Pictures, 1990, Irish-British
PATRIOT GAMES Paramount, 1992
LADY CHATTERLEY Global Arts/London Films/BBC, 1993, British
BLACK BEAUTY Warner Bros., 1994, British-U.S.

ALLYCE BEASLY
b. July 6, 1951 - New York, New York

MOONLIGHTING (TF) Picturemaker Productions/
   ABC Circle Films, 1985

NORMAN BEATON
THE MIGHTY QUINN MGM/UA, 1989

NED BEATTY
b. July 6, 1937 - Louisville, Kentucky

DELIVERANCE Warner Bros., 1972
THE LIFE AND TIMES OF JUDGE ROY BEAN
   National General, 1972
FOOTSTEPS NICE GUYS FINISH LAST (TF) Metromedia
   Productions, 1972
THE THIEF WHO CAME TO DINNER Warner Bros., 1973
WHITE LIGHTNING United Artists, 1973
THE MARCUS-NELSON MURDERS KOJAK AND THE MARCUS-
   NELSON MURDERS (TF) Universal TV, 1973
DYING ROOM ONLY (TF) Lorimar Productions, 1973
THE LAST AMERICAN HERO 20th Century Fox, 1973
THE EXECUTION OF PRIVATE SLOVIK (TF) Universal TV, 1974
ATTACK ON TERROR: THE FBI VS. THE KU KLUX KLAN (TF)
   QM Productions, 1975
THE DEADLY TOWER (TF) MGM TV, 1975
W.W. AND THE DIXIE DANCEKINGS 20th Century-Fox, 1975
NASHVILLE Paramount, 1975
ALL THE PRESIDENT'S MEN Warner Bros., 1976
THE BIG BUS Paramount, 1976
NETWORK ✪ MGM/United Artists, 1976
SILVER STREAK 20th Century Fox, 1976
MIKEY AND NICKY Paramount, 1976
ALAMBRISTA! Bobwin/Films Haus, 1977
TAIL GUNNER JOE (TF) Universal TV, 1977
LUCAN (TF) MGM TV, 1977
EXORCIST II: THE HERETIC Warner Bros., 1977
THE GREAT BANK HOAX SHENANIGANS/THE GREAT GEORGIA
   BANK HOAX Warner Bros., 1977
GRAY LADY DOWN Universal, 1978
SUPERMAN Warner Bros., 1978
A QUESTION OF LOVE (TF) Viacom, 1978
PROMISES IN THE DARK Orion/Warner Bros., 1979
WISE BLOOD New Line Cinema, 1979
FRIENDLY FIRE (TF) Marble Arch Productions, 1979
1941 Universal, 1979
THE AMERICAN SUCCESS COMPANY AMERICAN SUCCESS/
   SUCCESS Columbia, 1979, West German-U.S.
GUYANA TRAGEDY: THE STORY OF JIM JONES (TF)
   The Konigsberg Company, 1980
HOPSCOTCH Avco Embassy, 1980
THE INCREDIBLE SHRINKING WOMAN Universal, 1981
SUPERMAN II Warner Bros., 1981, U.S.-British
THE TOY Columbia, 1982
A WOMAN CALLED GOLDA (TF) Harve Bennett Productions/
   Paramount TV, 1982
STROKER ACE Universal, 1983
TOUCHED Lorimar Productions/Wildwoods Partners, 1983
MURDER, SHE WROTE (TF) Universal TV, 1984
ROBERT KENNEDY AND HIS TIMES (MS) Chris-Rose Productions/
   Columbia TV, 1985
ALFRED HITCHCOCK PRESENTS (TF) Universal TV, 1985
RESTLESS NATIVES Orion Classics, 1985, British

HOSTAGE FLIGHT (TF)   Frank von Zerneck Films, 1985
BACK TO SCHOOL   Orion, 1986
THE FOURTH PROTOCOL   Lorimar, 1987, British
THE BIG EASY   Columbia, 1987
SMOKE   Columbia, 1988
PHYSICAL EVIDENCE   Columbia, 1989
MINISTRY OF VENGEANCE   MPCA, 1989
CHATTAHOOCHEE   Hemdale, 1990
TENNESSEE WALTZ   Condor Productions, 1990
REPOSSESSED   New Line Cinema, 1990
A CRY IN THE WILD   Concorde, 1990
HEAR MY SONG   Miramax Films, 1991, British-Irish
PRELUDE TO A KISS   20th Century Fox, 1992
ED AND HIS DEAD MOTHER   I.R.S. Releasing, 1993
RUDY   TriStar, 1993
RADIOLAND MURDERS   Universal, 1994

WARREN BEATTY
(Henry Warren Beaty)
b. March 30, 1937 - Richmond, Virginia
Agent: CAA - Beverly Hills, 310/288-4545

SPLENDOR IN THE GRASS   Warner Bros., 1961
THE ROMAN SPRING OF MRS. STONE   Warner Bros., 1961
ALL FALL DOWN   MGM, 1962
LILITH   Columbia, 1964
MICKEY ONE   Columbia, 1965
PROMISE HER ANYTHING   Paramount, 1966
KALEIDOSCOPE   Warner Bros., 1966, British
BONNIE AND CLYDE ★   Warner Bros., 1967
THE ONLY GAME IN TOWN   20th Century Fox, 1970
McCABE AND MRS. MILLER   Warner Bros., 1971
$ *DOLLARS*   Columbia, 1971
THE PARALLAX VIEW   Paramount, 1974
SHAMPOO   Columbia, 1975
THE FORTUNE   Columbia, 1975
HEAVEN CAN WAIT ★   Paramount, 1978 (also co-directed)
REDS ★   Paramount, 1981 (also directed)
ISHTAR   Columbia, 1987
DICK TRACY   Buena Vista, 1990 (also directed)
TRUTH OR DARE (FD)   Miramax Films, 1991 (uncredited)
BUGSY ★   TriStar, 1991
LOVE AFFAIR   Warner Bros., 1994

JIM BEAVER
Agent: The Artists Agency - Los Angeles, 310/277-7779

IN COUNTRY   Warner Bros., 1989

TERRY BEAVER
TO DANCE WITH THE WHITE DOG (TF)   Signboard Hill
   Productions, 1993

BILLY BECK
ANOTHER YOU   TriStar, 1991

JENNY BECK
TROLL   Empire Pictures, 1986

JOHN BECK
b. January 28, 1943 - Chicago, Illinois
Agent: Camden ITG - Los Angeles, 310/289-2700

THE SILENT GUN (TF)   Paramount TV, 1969
LAWMAN   United Artists, 1971
PAT GARRETT AND BILLY THE KID   MGM, 1973
SLEEPER   United Artists, 1973
SIDEKICKS (TF)   Warner Bros. TV, 1974
THE LAW (TF)   Universal TV, 1974
THE CALL OF THE WILD (TF)   Charles Fries Productions, 1976
THE BIG BUS   Paramount, 1976
SKY RIDERS   20th Century Fox, 1976
THE OTHER SIDE OF MIDNIGHT   20th Century-Fox, 1977
AUDREY ROSE   United Artists, 1977
ARTHUR HAILEY'S WHEELS   *WHEELS* (MS)   Universal TV, 1978
THE TIME MACHINE (TF)   Sunn Classic Productions, 1978

PERRY MASON: THE CASE OF THE LADY IN THE LAKE (TF)
   The Fred Silverman Company/Strathmore Productions/
   Viacom, 1988
FIRE AND RAIN (CTF)   Wilshire Court Productions, 1989

KIMBERLY BECK
ZUMA BEACH (TF)   Edgar J. Scherick Associates/
   Warner Bros. TV, 1978
FRIDAY THE 13TH - THE FINAL CHAPTER   Paramount, 1984

MICHAEL BECK
Agent: David Shapira & Associates - Sherman Oaks, 818/906-0322

HOLOCAUST (MS)   Titus Productions, 1978
MAYFLOWER: THE PILGRIMS' ADVENTURE (TF)   Syzygy
   Productions, 1979
WARRIORS   Paramount, 1979
XANADU   Universal, 1980
ALCATRAZ: THE WHOLE SHOCKING STORY (TF)   Pierre Cossette
   Productions, 1980
TRIUMPHS OF A MAN CALLED HORSE   Jensen Farley Pictures,
   1983, U.S.-Mexican
REARVIEW MIRROR (TF)   Simon-Asher Entertainment/Sunn Classic
   Pictures, 1984
BLACKOUT (CTF)   HBO Premiere Films/Roger Gimbel Productions/
   Peregrine Entertainment, Ltd./Lee Buck Industries/Alexander
   Smith & Parks, 1985, U.S.-Canadian
HOUSTON: THE LEGEND OF TEXAS (TF)   Taft Entertainment TV/
   J.D. Feigelson Productions, 1986

GRAHAM BECKEL
FAMILY OF SPIES (MS)   King Phoenix Entertainment, 1990
JENNIFER EIGHT   Paramount, 1992

HARTMUT BECKER
ESCAPE FROM SOBRIBOR (TF)   Rule-Starger Productions/Zenith
   Productions, 1987, U.S.-British

IRENE BEDARD
POCAHONTAS (AF)   Buena Vista, 1995 (voice)

ANDREW BEDNARSKI
FAMILY SINS (TF)   London Films, 1987

BONNIE BEDELIA
b. March 25, 1948 - New York, New York

THE GYPSY MOTHS   MGM, 1969
THEY SHOOT HORSES, DON'T THEY?   Cinerama Releasing
   Corporation, 1969
LOVERS AND OTHER STRANGERS   Cinerama Releasing
   Corporation, 1970
THE STRANGE VENGEANCE OF ROSALIE   20th Century
   Fox, 1972
HAWKINS ON MURDER   *DEATH AND THE MAIDEN* (TF)
   Arena-Leda Productions/MGM TV, 1973
A QUESTION OF LOVE (TF)   Viacom, 1978
THE BIG FIX   Universal, 1978
HEART LIKE A WHEEL   20th Century Fox, 1983
THE LADY FROM YESTERDAY (TF)   Barry Weitz Films/Comworld
   Productions, 1985
VIOLETS ARE BLUE   Columbia, 1986
ALEX: THE LIFE OF A CHILD (TF)   Mandy Productions, 1986
THE BOY WHO COULD FLY   20th Century Fox, 1986
WHEN THE TIME COMES (TF)   Jaffe-Lansing Productions/Republic
   Pictures, 1987
DIE HARD   20th Century Fox, 1988
THE PRINCE OF PENNSYLVANIA   New Line Cinema, 1988
FAT MAN AND LITTLE BOY   Paramount, 1989
DIE HARD 2   20th Century Fox, 1990
PRESUMED INNOCENT   Warner Bros., 1990
SOMEBODY HAS TO SHOOT THE PICTURE (CTF)   Alan Barnette
   Productions/Frank Pierson Films/MCA-TV Entertainment/Scholastic
   Productions, 1990
SWITCHED AT BIRTH (MS)   Morrow-Heus Productions/
   O'Hara-Horowitz Productions/Columbia TV, 1991
NEEDFUL THINGS   Columbia, 1993
SPEECHLESS   MGM/UA, 1994

KABIR BEDI
SWASHBUCKLER   Universal, 1976
THE THIEF OF BAGHDAD (TF)   Palm Films, Ltd.,
   1978, British-French
ASHANTI   Columbia, 1979, Swiss-U.S.
OCTOPUSSY   MGM/UA, 1983, British

DANIEL BEER
Agent: Bauman, Hiller & Associates - Los Angeles, 213/857-6666

DYING YOUNG   20th Century Fox, 1991

LESLIE BEGA
ANGELS IN RED   Concorde, 1991
MOBSTERS   Universal, 1991

JASON BEGHE
MONKEY SHINES   Orion, 1988
THE OPERATION (TF)   Moress, Nanas, Golden Entertainment/
   Viacom, 1990
THELMA & LOUISE   MGM-Pathe, 1991
JIMMY HOLLYWOOD   Paramount, 1994

ED BEGLEY, JR.
b. September 16, 1949 - Los Angeles, California
Agent: APA - Los Angeles, 310/273-0744

NOW YOU SEE HIM, NOW YOU DON'T   Buena Vista, 1972
COCKFIGHTER   *BORN TO KILL*   New World, 1974
STAY HUNGRY   United Artists, 1976
BLUE COLLAR   Universal, 1978
THE CONCORDE—AIRPORT 79   Universal, 1979
THE IN-LAWS   Columbia, 1979
YOUNG DOCTORS IN LOVE   20th Century Fox, 1982
EATING RAOUL   20th Century Fox International Classics, 1982
PROTOCOL   Warner Bros., 1984
THIS IS SPINAL TAP   Embassy, 1984
STREETS OF FIRE   Universal, 1984
TRANSYLVANIA 6-5000   New World, 1985
CELEBRATION FAMILY (TF)   Frank von Zerneck Films, 1987
ROMAN HOLIDAY (TF)   Jerry Ludwig Enterprises, Inc./
   Paramount TV, 1987
SPIES, LIES AND NAKED THIGHS (TF)
   Qintex Entertainment, 1988
THE ACCIDENTAL TOURIST   Warner Bros., 1988
SCENES FROM THE CLASS STRUGGLE IN BEVERLY HILLS
   Cinecom, 1989
SHE-DEVIL   Orion, 1989
NOT A PENNY MORE, NOT A PENNY LESS (CMS)
   BBC/Paramount TV/Revcom, 1990
IN THE BEST INTEREST OF THE CHILD (TF)   Papazian-Hirsch
   Entertainment, 1990
MEET THE APPLEGATES   Triton Pictures, 1991
GREEDY   Universal, 1994
EVEN COWGIRLS GET THE BLUES   Fine Line Features/New Line
   Cinema, 1994
RENAISSANCE MAN   Buena Vista, 1994
WORLD WAR II: THEN THERE WERE GIANTS (TF)
   World International Network, 1994
THE PAGEMASTER   20th Century Fox, 1994
HOW MUCH ARE THOSE CHILDREN IN THE WINDOW?
   Concorde, 1995

DORIS BELACK
TOOTSIE   Columbia, 1982
THE HEARST AND DAVIES AFFAIR (TF)   ABC Circle Films, 1985
ALMOST PARTNERS (TF)   South Carolina Educational
   TV Network, 1987

SHARI BELAFONTE-HARPER
THE MIDNIGHT HOUR (TF)   ABC Circle Films, 1985
KATE'S SECRET (TF)   Andrea Baynes Productions/
   Columbia TV, 1986

MARTY BELAFSKY
NEWSIES   Buena Vista, 1992

JOE BELCHER
LINK   Thorn EMI/Cannon, 1986, U.S.-British

JOHN BELL
ROCKET GIBRALTAR   Columbia, 1988
MR. AND MRS. BRIDGE   Miramax Films, 1990

MARSHALL BELL
Agent: UTA - Beverly Hills, 310/273-6700

A NIGHTMARE ON ELM STREET 2: FREDDY'S REVENGE
   New Line Cinema, 1985
TUCKER - THE MAN AND HIS DREAM   Paramount, 1988
TOTAL RECALL   TriStar, 1990
AIR AMERICA   TriStar, 1990
THE VAGRANT   MGM-Pathe, 1991
AIRHEADS   20th Century Fox, 1994
THE PUPPET MASTERS   Buena Vista, 1994

TOBIN BELL
FALSE IDENTITY   RKO Pictures, 1990
THE QUICK AND THE DEAD   TriStar, 1995

VANESSA BELL
THE INKWELL   Buena Vista, 1994

NED BELLAMY
CARNOSAUR   New Horizons Pictures, 1993

KATHLEEN BELLER
Agent: Paradigm - Los Angeles, 310/277-4400

THE GODFATHER, PART II   Paramount, 1974
MARY WHITE (TF)   Radnitz/Mattel Productions, 1977
SOMETHING FOR JOEY (TF)   MTM Productions, 1977
ARE YOU IN THE HOUSE ALONE? (TF)   Charles Fries
   Productions, 1978
THE BETSY   Allied Artists, 1978
PROMISES IN THE DARK   Orion/Warner Bros., 1979
FORT APACHE, THE BRONX   20th Century Fox, 1981
DEADLY MESSAGES (TF)   Columbia TV, 1985

GIL BELLOWS
Agent: William Morris Agency - Beverly Hills, 310/274-7451

THE SHAWSHANK REDEMPTION   Columbia, 1994

PAMELA BELLWOOD-WHEELER
(Pamela Bellwood)
Agent: Paul Kohner Agency - Los Angeles, 310/550-1060

THE WILD WOMEN OF CHASTITY GULCH (TF)   Aaron Spelling
   Productions, 1982
DEEP DARK SECRETS (TF)   Gross-Weston Productions/Fries
   Entertainment, 1987
CELLAR DWELLAR   Empire Pictures, 1988
DOUBLE STANDARD (TF)   Louis Rudolph Productions/Fenton
   Entertainment Group/Fries Entertainment, 1988

ROBERT BELTRAN
Agent: Harris & Goldberg - Los Angeles, 310/553-5200

EATING RAOUL   20th Century Fox International Classics, 1982
NIGHT OF THE COMET   Atlantic Releasing Corporation, 1984
THE MYSTIC WARRIOR (MS)   David L. Wolper-Stan Margulies
   Productions/Warner Bros. TV, 1984
LATINO   Cinecom, 1985
GABY - A TRUE STORY   TriStar, 1987, U.S.-Mexican
SCENES FROM THE CLASS STRUGGLE IN BEVERLY HILLS
   Cinecom, 1989
CRACKDOWN   Concorde, 1991

MARK BELTZMAN
BILLY MADISON   Universal, 1995

JAMES BELUSHI
b. June 15, 1954 - Chicago, Illinois

THIEF   United Artists, 1981
TRADING PLACES   Paramount, 1983
THE MAN WITH ONE RED SHOE   20th Century Fox, 1985
SALVADOR   Hemdale, 1986
ABOUT LAST NIGHT...   TriStar, 1986
JUMPIN' JACK FLASH   20th Century Fox, 1986
LITTLE SHOP OF HORRORS   The Geffen Co./Warner Bros., 1986
REAL MEN   MGM/UA, 1987
THE PRINCIPAL   TriStar, 1987
RED HEAT   TriStar, 1988
WHO'S HARRY CRUMB?   TriStar, 1989
K-9   Universal, 1989
HOMER & EDDIE   Skouras Pictures, 1990
TAKING CARE OF BUSINESS   Buena Vista, 1990
MR. DESTINY   Buena Vista, 1990
ONLY THE LONELY   20th Century Fox, 1991
CURLY SUE   Warner Bros., 1991
ONCE UPON A CRIME   MGM-Pathe, 1992, U.S.-Italian
TRACES OF RED   Samuel Goldwyn Company, 1992
WILD PALMS (MS)   Ixtlan Corporation/Greengrass Prods., Inc., 1993
LAST ACTION HERO   Columbia, 1993
ROYCE (CTF)   Gerber/ITC Productions, 1994
PARALLEL LIVES (CTF)   Showtime Entertainment, 1994
SEPARATE LIVES   Trimark Pictures, 1995
DESTINY TURNS ON THE RADIO   Savoy Pictures, 1995
THE PEBBLE AND THE PENGUIN (AF)   MGM/UA, 1995 (voice)

RICHARD BELZER
FREEWAY   New World, 1988
FLETCH LIVES   Universal, 1989
MISSING PIECES   Orion, 1991
NORTH   Columbia, 1994
THE PUPPET MASTERS   Buena Vista, 1994

CLIFF BEMIS
Agent: Century Artists, Ltd. - Beverly Hills, 310/273-4366

MODERN LOVE   Triumph Releasing Corporation, 1990

BRIAN BENBEN
Agent: UTA - Beverly Hills, 310/273-6700

CLEAN AND SOBER   Warner Bros., 1988
GOD'S PAYROLL   *PHONE CALLS*   1988
RADIOLAND MURDERS   Universal, 1994

DIRK BENEDICT
b. March 1, 1945 - Helen, Montana
Agent: Stone Manners Talent Agency - Los Angeles, 213/654-7575

JOURNEY FROM DARKNESS (TF)   Bob Banner Associates, 1975
CRUISE INTO TERROR (TF)   Aaron Spelling Productions, 1978
SCAVENGER HUNT   20th Century Fox, 1979
BATTLESTAR: GALACTICA   Universal, 1979
UNDERGROUND ACES   Filmways, 1981
THE A-TEAM (TF)   Stephen J. Cannell Productions, 1983
BODY SLAM   DEG, 1987
TRENCHCOAT IN PARADISE (TF)   Ogiens-Kane Company
   Productions/The Finnegan-Pinchuk Company, 1990

PAUL BENEDICT
THEY MIGHT BE GIANTS   Universal, 1971
ARTHUR 2 ON THE ROCKS   Warner Bros., 1988
BABYCAKES (TF)   Konigsberg-Sanitsky Productions, 1989
THE FRESHMAN   TriStar, 1990
THE ADDAMS FAMILY   Paramount, 1991

YVES BENEYTON
EMINENT DOMAIN   Triumph Releasing Corporation, 1990,
   Canadian-French-Israeli

JOHN BENFIELD
HIDDEN AGENDA   Hemdale, 1990

ROBERTO BENIGNI
DOWN BY LAW   Island Pictures, 1986

ANNETTE BENING
b. 1958 - Topeka, Kansas
Agent: Gersh Agency - Beverly Hills, 310/274-6611

HOSTAGE (TF)   CBS Entertainment, 1988
THE GREAT OUTDOORS   Universal, 1988
VALMONT   Orion, 1989, French
POSTCARDS FROM THE EDGE   Columbia, 1990
THE GRIFTERS ✪   Miramax Films, 1990
GUILTY BY SUSPICION   Warner Bros., 1991
REGARDING HENRY   Paramount, 1991
BUGSY   TriStar, 1991
LOVE AFFAIR   Warner Bros., 1994
THE AMERICAN PRESIDENT   Columbia, 1995

PAUL BENJAMIN
A STRANGER WAITS (TF)   Bruce Lansbury Productions/Edgar
   Lansbury Productions/Lewisfilm, Ltd./New Century TV Prods., 1987
DO THE RIGHT THING   Universal, 1989

RICHARD BENJAMIN
b. May 22, 1938 - New York, New York
Agent: Gersh Agency - Beverly Hills, 310/274-6611

THUNDER OVER THE PLAINS   Warner Bros., 1953
CRIME WAVE   1954
GOODBYE, COLUMBUS   Paramount, 1969
DIARY OF A MAD HOUSEWIFE   Universal, 1970
CATCH-22   Paramount, 1970
THE MARRIAGE OF A YOUNG STOCKBROKER
   20th Century Fox, 1971
THE STEAGLE   Avco Embassy, 1971
PORTNOY'S COMPLAINT   Warner Bros., 1972
THE LAST OF SHEILA   Warner Bros., 1973
WESTWORLD   MGM, 1973
THE SUNSHINE BOYS   MGM/United Artists, 1975
HOUSE CALLS   Universal, 1978
LOVE AT FIRST BITE   American International, 1979
SCAVENGER HUNT   20th Century Fox, 1979
THE LAST MARRIED COUPLE IN AMERICA   Universal, 1980
WITCHES' BREW   1980
FIRST FAMILY   Warner Bros., 1980
HOW TO BEAT THE HIGH COST OF LIVING
   American International, 1980
SATURDAY THE 14TH   New World, 1981

DAVID BENNENT
THE TIN DRUM   New World, 1979, West German
LEGEND   Universal, 1986, British

JEFF BENNETT
LAND BEFORE TIME (AF)   Universal, 1995 (voice)

JILL BENNETT
LADY JANE   Paramount, 1985, British
THE SHELTERING SKY   Warner Bros., 1990, British

MARCIA BENNETT
ADVENTURES IN BABYSITTING   Buena Vista, 1987

TONY BENNETT
b. August 3, 1926 - New York, New York

THE SCOUT   20th Century Fox, 1994

AMBER BENSON
BYE BYE LOVE   20th Century Fox, 1995

JODI BENSON
THE LITTLE MERMAID (AF)   Buena Vista, 1989 (voice)
HANS CHRISTIAN ANDERSEN'S THUMBELINA (AF)
   Warner Bros., 1994 (voice)

LYRIC BENSON
MODERN LOVE   Triumph Releasing Corporation, 1990

PERRY BENSON
SID & NANCY   Samuel Goldwyn Company, 1986, British

ROBBY BENSON
(Robby Segal)
b. January 21, 1956 - Dallas, Texas
Agent: Gordon/Rosson Talent Agency - Studio City, 818/509-1900

JORY   1972
JEREMY   United Artists, 1973
DEATH BE NOT PROUD (TF)   Good Housekeeping Productions/
   Westfall Productions, 1975
LUCKY LADY   20th Century Fox, 1975
THE DEATH OF RICHIE (TF)   Henry Jaffe Enterprises, 1977
ODE TO BILLY JOE   Warner Bros., 1976
ONE ON ONE   Warner Bros., 1977
THE END   United Artists, 1978
ICE CASTLES   Columbia, 1979
WALK PROUD   Universal, 1979
DIE LAUGHING   Orion/Warner Bros., 1980
TRIBUTE   20th Century Fox, 1980
NATIONAL LAMPOON'S MOVIE MADNESS *NATIONAL LAMPOON
   GOES TO THE MOVIES*   United Artists, 1981
THE CHOSEN   20th Century Fox International Classics, 1982
HARRY AND SON   Orion, 1984
CALIFORNIA GIRLS (TF)   ABC Circle Films, 1985
CITY LIMITS   Atlantic Releasing Corporation, 1985
RENT-A-COP   Kings Road Productions, 1988
MODERN LOVE   Triumph Releasing Corporation,
   1990 (also directed)
BEAUTY AND THE BEAST (AF)   Buena Vista, 1991 (voice)

FABRIZIO BENTIVOGLIO
APARTMENT ZERO   Skouras Pictures, 1989

JEROME BENTON
UNDER THE CHERRY MOON   Warner Bros., 1986
GRAFFITI BRIDGE   Warner Bros., 1990

PAUL BEN-VICTOR
HOUSEGUEST   Buena Vista, 1995

DANIEL BENZALI
PACK OF LIES (TF)   Robert Halmi, Inc., 1987
MESSENGER OF DEATH   Cannon, 1988

LUCA BERCOVICI
AMERICAN FLYERS   Warner Bros., 1985
CLEAN AND SOBER   Warner Bros., 1988

BLAZE BERDAHL
PET SEMATARY   *STEPHEN KING'S PET SEMATARY*
   Paramount, 1989

TOM BERENGER
(Thomas Michael Moore)
b. May 31, 1949 - Chicago, Illinois
Agent: CAA - Beverly Hills, 310/288-4545

LOOKING FOR MR. GOODBAR   Paramount, 1977
JOHNNY, WE HARDLY KNEW YE (TF)   Talent Associates/Jamel
   Productions, 1977
IN PRAISE OF OLDER WOMEN   Avco Embassy, 1978, Canadian
FLESH AND BLOOD (TF)   The Jozak Company/Cpyress Point
   Productions/Paramount TV, 1979
BUTCH AND SUNDANCE: THE EARLY DAYS
   20th Century Fox, 1979
THE DOGS OF WAR   United Artists, 1981, U.S.-British
BEYOND THE DOOR   Gaumont, 1982, Italian
THE BIG CHILL   Columbia, 1983
EDDIE AND THE CRUISERS   Embassy, 1983

FEAR CITY   Chevy Chase Distribution, 1984
RUSTLER'S RHAPSODY   Paramount, 1985
PLATOON ✪   Orion, 1986
IF TOMORROW COMES (MS)   CBS Entertainment, 1986
SOMEONE TO WATCH OVER ME   Columbia, 1987
SHOOT TO KILL   Buena Vista, 1988
BETRAYED   MGM/UA, 1988
LAST RITES   MGM/UA, 1988
MAJOR LEAGUE   Paramount, 1989
BORN ON THE FOURTH OF JULY   Universal, 1989
LOVE AT LARGE   Orion, 1990
THE FIELD   Avenue Pictures, 1990, Irish-British
SHATTERED   MGM-Pathe, 1991
AT PLAY IN THE FIELDS OF THE LORD   Universal, 1991
SNIPER   TriStar, 1993
SLIVER   Paramount, 1993
GETTYSBURG   New Line Cinema, 1993
MAJOR LEAGUE II   Warner Bros., 1994
CHASERS   Warner Bros., 1994
LAST OF THE DOGMEN   Savoy Pictures, 1995
AVENGING ANGEL (CTF)   Turner Network TV, 1995

CRAIG BERENSON
AIRPLANE!   Paramount, 1980

MARISA BERENSON
DEATH IN VENICE   Warner Bros., 1971, Italian-French
CABARET   Allied Artists, 1972
BARRY LYNDON   Warner Bros., 1975, British
KILLER FISH   *DEADLY TREASURE OF THE PIRANHA*
   Associated Film Distribution, 1978, British-Brazilian-French
S.O.B.   Paramount, 1981
WHITE HUNTER, BLACK HEART   Warner Bros., 1990
JEFFERSON IN PARIS   Buena Vista, 1995

PETER BERG
Agent: ICM - Beverly Hills, 310/550-4000

RACE FOR GLORY   New Century/Vista, 1989
SHOCKER   Universal, 1989
GENUINE RISK   I.R.S., 1990
CROOKED HEARTS   MGM-Pathe, 1991
LATE FOR DINNER   Columbia, 1991
A MIDNIGHT CLEAR   Interstar Releasing, 1992
FIRE IN THE SKY   Paramount, 1993

CANDICE BERGEN
b. May 8, 1946 - Beverly Hills, California
Agent: William Morris Agency - Beverly Hills, 310/274-7451

THE GROUP   United Artists, 1966
THE SAND PEBBLES   20th Century Fox, 1966
LIVE FOR LIFE   *VIVRE POUR VIVRE*   United Artists, 1967,
   French-Italian
THE DAY THE FISH CAME OUT   20th Century Fox,
   1967, British-Greek
THE MAGUS   20th Century Fox, 1968, British
THE ADVENTURERS   Paramount, 1970
GETTING STRAIGHT   Columbia, 1970
SOLDIER BLUE   Avco Embassy, 1970
CARNAL KNOWLEDGE   Avco Embassy, 1971
THE HUNTING PARTY   United Artists, 1971
T.R. BASKIN   Paramount, 1971
11 HARROWHOUSE   *ANYTHING FOR LOVE*   20th Century Fox,
   1974, British
THE WIND AND THE LION   MGM/United Artists, 1975
BITE THE BULLET   Columbia, 1975
THE DOMINO PRINCIPLE   Avco Embassy, 1977
A NIGHT FULL OF RAIN   *THE END OF THE WORLD IN OUR
   USUAL BED IN A NIGHT FULL OF RAIN*   Warner Bros.,
   1978, Italian-U.S.
OLIVER'S STORY   Paramount, 1979
STARTING OVER ✪   Paramount, 1979
RICH AND FAMOUS   MGM/United Artists, 1981
MERLIN & THE SWORD   1982
GANDHI   Columbia, 1982, British-Indian
STICK   Universal, 1985

HOLLYWOOD WIVES (MS)   Aaron Spelling Productions, 1985
ARTHUR THE KING (TF)   Martin Poll Productions/Comworld
    Productions/Jadran Film, 1985, U.S.-Yugoslavian
MURDER: BY REASON OF INSANITY (TF)
    LS Entertainment, 1985
MAYFLOWER MADAM (TF)   Robert Halmi, Inc., 1987

FRANCES BERGEN
Agent: The Craig Agency - Los Angeles, 213/655-0236

AMERICAN GIGOLO   Paramount, 1980

LEWIS BERGEN
HARD EVIDENCE   1995

POLLY BERGEN
b. July 14, 1930 - Knoxville, Tennessee
Agent: William Morris Agency - Beverly Hills, 310/274-7451

KISSES FOR MY PRESIDENT   Warner Bros., 1964
MAKING MR. RIGHT   Orion, 1987
ADDICTED TO HIS LOVE (TF)   Green-Epstein Productions/
    Columbia TV, 1988
SHE WAS MARKED FOR MURDER (TF)   Jack Grossbart
    Productions, 1988
WAR AND REMEMBRANCE (MS)   Dan Curtis Productions/ABC
    Circle Films, 1988-89
MY BROTHER'S WIFE (TF)   Robert Greenwald Productions/
    Adam Productions, 1989
CRY-BABY   Universal, 1990
DR. JEKYLL AND MS. HYDE   Savoy Pictures, 1995

GREGG BERGER
POLICE ACADEMY: MISSION TO MOSCOW   Warner Bros., 1994

HELMUT BERGER
THE DAMNED   *LA CADUTA DEGLI DEI/GOTTERDAMERUNG*
    Warner Bros., 1969, Italian-West German
THE GODFATHER, PART III   Paramount, 1990

WILLIAM BERGER
THE BERLIN AFFAIR   Cannon, 1985, Italian-West German

PATRICK BERGIN
Agent: William Morris Agency - Beverly Hills, 310/274-7451

MOUNTAINS OF THE MOON   TriStar, 1990
SLEEPING WITH THE ENEMY   20th Century Fox, 1991
HIGHWAY TO HELL   Hemdale, 1991
LOVE CRIMES   Millimeter Films, 1992
PATRIOT GAMES   Paramount, 1992
MAP OF THE HUMAN HEART   Miramax Films, 1993,
    British-French-New Zealand

MARY KAY BERGMAN
BEAUTY AND THE BEAST (AF)   Buena Vista, 1991 (voice)

ED BERKE
'NIGHT, MOTHER   Universal, 1986

XANDER BERKELEY
THE GUN IN BETTY LOU'S HANDBAG   Buena Vista, 1992

STEVEN BERKOFF
Agent: The Gage Group - Los Angeles, 213/859-8777

OCTOPUSSY   MGM/UA, 1983, British
BEVERLY HILLS COP   Paramount, 1984
ABSOLUTE BEGINNERS   Orion, 1986, British
UNDER THE CHERRY MOON   Warner Bros., 1986

MILTON BERLE
(Milton Berlinger)
b. July 12, 1908 - New York, New York
Agent: Lenhoff/Robinson Agency - Los Angeles, 310/558-4700

THE PERILS OF PAULINE   1914
TILLIE'S PUNCTURED ROMANCE   Keystone, 1914
EASY STREET   Mutual, 1916
LITTLE BROTHER   1917
HUMORESQUE   Paramount, 1920
THE MARK OF ZORRO   United Artists, 1920
LENA RIVERS   1925
SPARROWS   United Artists, 1926
NEW FACES OF 1937   1937
RADIO CITY REVELS   1938
TALL, DARK AND HANDSOME   20th Century Fox, 1941
SUN VALLEY SERENADE   20th Century Fox, 1941
RISE AND SHINE   20th Century Fox, 1941
A GENTLEMAN AT HEART   1942
WHISPERING GHOSTS   1942
OVER MY DEAD BODY   1943
MARGIN FOR ERROR   20th Century Fox, 1943
ALWAYS LEAVE THEM LAUGHING   Warner Bros., 1949
THE BELLBOY   Paramount, 1960
LET'S MAKE LOVE   20th Century Fox, 1960
IT'S A MAD MAD MAD MAD WORLD   United Artists, 1963
THE LOVED ONE   MGM, 1965
THE OSCAR   Embassy, 1966
DON'T WORRY, WE'LL THINK OF A TITLE   1966
THE HAPPENING   Columbia, 1967
WHO'S MINDING THE MINT?   Columbia, 1967
WHERE ANGELS GO...TROUBLE FOLLOWS!   Columbia, 1968
FOR SINGLES ONLY   Columbia, 1968
CAN HIERONYMOUS MERKIN EVER FORGET MERCY HUMPPE
    AND FIND TRUE HAPPINESS?   Regional, 1969, British
SEVEN IN DARKNESS (TF)   Paramount TV, 1969
EVIL ROY SLADE (TF)   Universal TV, 1971
JOURNEY BACK TO OZ (AF)   1974 (voice)
LEPKE   Warner Bros., 1975
THE LEGEND OF VALENTINO (TF)   Spelling-Goldberg
    Productions, 1975
WON TON TON, THE DOG WHO SAVED HOLLYWOOD
    Paramount, 1976
THE MUPPET MOVIE   AFD, 1979, British
BROADWAY DANNY ROSE   Orion, 1984
SIDE BY SIDE (TF)   Avnet-Kerner Productions, 1988

JEANNIE BERLIN
b. November 1, 1949 - Los Angeles, California

ON A CLEAR DAY YOU CAN SEE FOREVER   Paramount, 1970
GETTING STRAIGHT   Columbia, 1970
MOVE   20th Century Fox, 1970
THE STRAWBERRY STATEMENT   MGM, 1970
THE BABY MAKER   National General, 1970
WHY   *DETENUOT IN ATTESA DI GIUDIZIO*   Documento Film,
    1971, Italian
PORTNOY'S COMPLAINT   Warner Bros., 1972
BONE   Jack H. Harris Enterprises, 1972
THE HEARTBREAK KID ✪   20th Century Fox, 1972
SHEILA LEVINE IS DEAD AND LIVING IN NEW YORK
    Paramount, 1975
IN THE SPIRIT   Castle Hill Productions, 1990

CRYSTAL BERNARD
b. September 30 - Houston, Texas
Agent: William Morris Agency - Beverly Hills, 310/274-7451

SIRINGO   Rysher Entertainment, 1994

JASON BERNARD
Agent: Paul Kohner, Inc. - Los Angeles, 310/550-1060

ALL OF ME   Universal, 1984

THELONIOUS BERNARD
A LITTLE ROMANCE   Orion/Warner Bros., 1979, U.S.-French

SANDRA BERNHARD
b. 1955 - Flint, Michigan

THE KING OF COMEDY   20th Century Fox, 1983
TRACK 29   Island Pictures, 1988
WITHOUT YOU I'M NOTHING   New Line Cinema, 1990
HUDSON HAWK   TriStar, 1991

CORBIN BERNSEN
b. September 7, 1953 - North Hollywood, California
Agent: ICM - Beverly Hills, 310/550-4000

EAT MY DUST!   New World, 1976
KING KONG   Paramount, 1976
S.O.B.   Paramount, 1981
L.A. LAW (TF)   20th Century Fox TV, 1986
BERT RIGBY, YOU'RE A FOOL   Warner Bros., 1989
MAJOR LEAGUE   Paramount, 1989
BREAKING POINT (CTF)   Avnet-Kerner Company, 1989
DISORGANIZED CRIME   Buena Vista, 1989
SHATTERED   MGM-Pathe, 1991
MAJOR LEAGUE II   Warner Bros., 1994
RADIOLAND MURDERS   Universal, 1994
TALES FROM THE HOOD   Savoy Pictures, 1995

ELIZABETH BERRIDGE
THE FUNHOUSE   Universal, 1981
AMADEUS   Orion, 1984
SMOOTH TALK   Spectrafilm, 1985
FIVE CORNERS   Cineplex Odeon, 1988

DANIEL BERRIGAN
THE MISSION   Warner Bros., 1986, British

HALLE BERRY
Agent: William Morris Agency - Beverly Hills, 310/274-7451

JUNGLE FEVER   Universal, 1991
STRICTLY BUSINESS   Universal, 1991
THE LAST BOY SCOUT   The Geffen Company/Warner Bros., 1991
BOOMERANG   Paramount, 1992
QUEEN (MS)   The Wolper Organization/Bernard Sofronski
   Productions, 1993
FATHER HOOD   Buena Vista, 1993
THE PROGRAM   Buena Vista, 1993
THE FLINTSTONES   Universal, 1994
LOSING ISAIAH   Paramount, 1995

JOHN BERRY
'ROUND MIDNIGHT   Warner Bros., 1986, U.S.-French

LLOYD BERRY
APRIL FOOL'S DAY   Paramount, 1986

RICHARD BERRY
LA BALANCE   Spectrafilm, 1982, French
A MAN AND A WOMAN: 20 YEARS LATER   Warner Bros.,
   1986, French

DOROTHÉE BERRYMAN
THE DECLINE OF THE AMERICAN EMPIRE   Cineplex Odeon,
   1986, Canadian

NUMA BERTELL
JFK   Warner Bros., 1991

DEHL BERTI
BULLIES   Universal, 1986, Canadian

ROLAND BERTIN
DIVA   United Artists Classics, 1982, French

VALERIE BERTINELLI
b. April 23, 1960 - Wilmington, Delaware
Agent: William Morris Agency - Beverly Hills, 310/274-7451

YOUNG LOVE, FIRST LOVE (TF)   Lorimar Productions, 1979
SHATTERED VOWS (TF)   Bertinelli-Pequod Productions, 1984
SILENT WITNESS (TF)   Robert Greenwald Productions, 1985
ROCKABYE (TF)   Roger Gimbel Productions/Peregrine
   Entertainment/Bertinelli Productions, 1986
I'LL TAKE MANHATTAN (MS)   Steve Krantz Productions, 1987
PANCHO BARNES (MS)   Blue Andre Productions/Orion TV, 1988
TAKEN AWAY (TF)   Hart, Thomas & Berlin Productions, 1989

ANGELO BERTOLINI
LADY IN WHITE   New Century/Vista, 1988

BIBI BESCH
Agent: Barrett, Benson, McCartt & Weston - Beverly Hills,
   310/247-5500

DISTANCE   1975
STAR TREK II: THE WRATH OF KHAN   Paramount, 1982
THE DAY AFTER (TF)   ABC Circle Films, 1983
BETSY'S WEDDING   Buena Vista, 1990

ARIEL BESSE
BEAU PERE   New Line Cinema, 1981, French

MARTINE BESWICKE
WIDE SARGASSO SEA   Fine Line Features/New Line Cinema,
   1993, British

LAURA BETTI
COURAGE MOUNTAIN   Triumph Releasing Corporation,
   1989, U.S.-French

TROY BEYER
ROOFTOPS   New Visions, 1989

DIDIER BEZACE
THE LITTLE THIEF   Miramax Films, 1989, French

KULDEEP BHAKOO
CHEETAH   Buena Vista, 1989

MICHAEL BIEHN
Agent: ICM - Beverly Hills, 310/550-4000

ZUMA BEACH (TF)   Edgar J. Scherick Associates/
   Warner Bros. TV, 1978
COACH   Crown International, 1978
THE FAN   Paramount, 1981
THE TERMINATOR   Orion, 1984
DEADLY INTENTIONS (MS)   Green-Epstein Productions, 1985
ALIENS   20th Century Fox, 1986
THE SEVENTH SIGN   TriStar, 1988
THE ABYSS   20th Century Fox, 1989
NAVY SEALS   Orion, 1990
NAMELESS   MGM-Pathe, 1991
DEADFALL   Trimark Pictures, 1993
TOMBSTONE   Buena Vista, 1993

CLAUDIO BIGAGLI
FIORILE   Fine Line Features/New Line Cinema, 1993, Italian

HUGH BIGNEY
NUTCRACKER: THE MOTION PICTURE   Atlantic Releasing
   Corporation, 1986

ROXANN BIGGS
Agent: Bauman, Hiller & Associates - Los Angeles, 213/857-6666

GUILTY BY SUSPICION   Warner Bros., 1991

F
I
L
M

A
C
T
O
R
S

THEODORE BIKEL
b. May 2, 1924 - Veinna, Austria
Agent: The Artists Group, Ltd. - Los Angeles, 310/552-1100

THE AFRICAN QUEEN   United Artists, 1951
MELBA   United Artists, 1953, British
DESPERATE MOMENT   Universal, 1953, British
THE LOVE LOTTERY   Continental, 1953, British
THE DIVIDED HEART   Republic, 1954, British
THE LITTLE KIDNAPPERS   *THE KIDNAPPERS*   United Artists,
   1954, British
THE COLDITZ STORY   Republic, 1955, British
THE VINTAGE   1957
THE PRIDE AND THE PASSION   United Artists, 1957
THE ENEMY BELOW   20th Century Fox, 1957
FRAULEIN   20th Century Fox, 1958
THE DEFIANT ONES ✪   United Artists, 1958
I WANT TO LIVE!   United Artists, 1958
THE ANGRY HILLS   MGM, 1959
THE BLUE ANGEL   20th Century Fox, 1959
A DOG OF FLANDERS   20th Century Fox, 1960
MY FAIR LADY   Warner Bros., 1964
SANDS OF THE KALAHARI   Paramount, 1965, British
THE RUSSIANS ARE COMING, THE RUSSIANS ARE COMING
   United Artists, 1966
SWEET NOVEMBER   Warner Bros., 1968
MY SIDE OF THE MOUNTAIN   Paramount, 1969
DARKER THAN AMBER   National General, 1970
200 MOTELS   United Artists, 1971, British
THE LITTLE ARK   National General, 1972
VICTORY AT ENTEBBE (TF)   1976
SEE YOU IN THE MORNING   Warner Bros., 1989

TONY BILL
b. August 23, 1940 - San Diego, California

COME BLOW YOUR HORN   Paramount, 1963
SOLDIER IN THE RAIN   Allied Artists, 1963
NONE BUT THE BRAVE   Warner Bros., 1964, U.S.-Japanese
MARRIAGE ON THE ROCKS   Warner Bros., 1965
YOU'RE A BIG BOY NOW   7 Arts, 1966
ICE STATION ZEBRA   MGM, 1968
CASTLE KEEP   Columbia, 1969
FLAP   1970
SHAMPOO   Columbia, 1975

RAOUL BILLEREY
SORCERESS   European Classics, 1988, French

BARBARA BILLINGSLEY
AIRPLANE!   Paramount, 1980
BAY COVEN (TF)   Guber-Peters Company/Phoenix Entertainment
   Group, 1987
GOING TO THE CHAPEL (TF)   The Furia Organization/
   Finnegan-Pinchuk Productions, 1988

PETER BILLINGSLEY
RUSSKIES   New Century/Vista, 1987
BEVERLY HILLS BRATS   Taurus Entertainment, 1989

BARBARA BINGHAM
FRIDAY THE 13TH PART VII - JASON TAKES MANHATTAN
   Paramount, 1989

JULIETTE BINOCHE
Agent: UTA - Beverly Hills, 310/273-6700

THE UNBEARABLE LIGHTNESS OF BEING   Orion, 1988
WOMEN & MEN: IN LOVE THERE ARE NO RULES (CTF)
   David Brown Productions/HBO Showcase, 1991
DAMAGE   New Line Cinema, 1992, French-British
BLUE   *BLEU-BLANC-ROUGE*   Miramax Films, 1993,
   Swiss-French-Polish

THORA BIRCH
PARADISE   Buena Vista, 1991
ALL I WANT FOR CHRISTMAS   Paramount, 1991
PATRIOT GAMES   Paramount, 1992
HOCUS POCUS   Buena Vista, 1993
MONKEY TROUBLE   New Line Cinema, 1994
CLEAR AND PRESENT DANGER   Paramount, 1994
GASLIGHT ADDITION   New Line Cinema, 1995

BILLIE BIRD
SIXTEEN CANDLES   Universal, 1984
ONE CRAZY SUMMER   Warner Bros., 1986
POLICE ACADEMY 4: CITIZENS ON PATROL   Warner Bros., 1987
HOME ALONE   20th Century Fox, 1990

LARRY BIRD
BLUE CHIPS   Paramount, 1994

JESSE BIRDSALL
GETTING IT RIGHT   MCEG, 1989, U.S.-British

DAVID BIRNEY
b. April 23, 1939 - Washington D.C.

GLITTER (TF)   Aaron Spelling Productions, 1984
THE LONG JOURNEY HOME (TF)   Andrea Baynes Productions/
   Grail Productions/Lorimar-Telepictures, 1987
LOVE AND BETRAYAL (TF)   Gross-Weston Productions/ITC
   Entertainment Group, 1989
ALWAYS REMEMBER I LOVE YOU (TF)   Stephen J. Cannell/
   Gross-Weston Productions, Inc., 1990

DEBBY BISHOP
SID & NANCY   Samuel Goldwyn Company, 1986, British

JOEY BISHOP
b. February 3, 1918 - Bronx, New York

OCEAN'S ELEVEN   Warner Bros., 1960
THE DELTA FORCE   Cannon, 1986
BETSY'S WEDDING   Buena Vista, 1990

KELLY BISHOP
Agent: Abrams Artists & Associates - Los Angeles, 310/859-0625

AN UNMARRIED WOMAN   20th Century Fox, 1978
DIRTY DANCING   Vestron, 1987
ME AND HIM   Columbia, 1988

RUMMY BISHOP
ADVENTURES IN BABYSITTING   Buena Vista, 1987

TROY BISHOP
TERMS OF ENDEARMENT   Paramount, 1983

JACQUELINE BISSET
b. September 13, 1944 - Weybridge, Surrey, England
Agent: William Morris Agency - Beverly Hills, 310/274-7451

THE KNACK...AND HOW TO GET IT   Lopert, 1965, British
ARRIVADERCI, BABY!   *DROP DEAD, DARLING*   Paramount,
   1966, British
CUL-DE-SAC   Sigma III, 1966, British
TWO FOR THE ROAD   20th Century Fox, 1967, British-U.S.
CASINO ROYALE   Columbia, 1967, British
CAPETOWN AFFAIR   1967
THE DETECTIVE   20th Century Fox, 1968
THE SWEET RIDE   20th Century Fox, 1968
BULLITT   Warner Bros., 1968
THE FIRST TIME   United Artists, 1969, U.S.-Canadian
L'ECHELLE BLANCHE   1969, French
SECRET WORLD   *LA PROMESSE*   1969, French
THE GRASSHOPPER   National General, 1969
AIRPORT   Universal, 1970

THE MEPHISTO WALTZ   20th Century Fox, 1971
BELIEVE IN ME   MGM, 1971
SECRETS   Lonestar, 1971, British
STAND UP AND BE COUNTED   Columbia, 1972
THE LIFE AND TIMES OF JUDGE ROY BEAN
   National General, 1972
THE THIEF WHO CAME TO DINNER   Warner Bros., 1973
DAY FOR NIGHT   *LA NUIT AMERICAINE*   Warner Bros.,
   1973, French-Italian
LE MAGNIFIQUE   Cine III, 1973, French
MURDER ON THE ORIENT EXPRESS   Paramount, 1974, British
THE SPIRAL STAIRCASE   1975, British
END OF THE GAME   20th Century Fox, 1975, German-Italian
THE SUNDAY WOMAN   20th Century Fox, 1976, Italian-French
ST. IVES   Warner Bros., 1976
THE DEEP   Columbia, 1977
SECRETS   Lonestar, 1978, British (filmed in 1971)
WHO IS KILLING THE GREAT CHEFS OF EUROPE?
   Warner Bros., 1978
THE GREEK TYCOON   Universal, 1978
AMO NON AMO   1979, Italian
TOGETHER?   *I LOVE YOU, I LOVE YOU NOT*   1979, Italian
WHEN TIME RAN OUT   Warner Bros., 1980
INCHON!   MGM/UA, 1982, South Korean
RICH AND FAMOUS   MGM/United Artists, 1981
CLASS   Orion, 1983
UNDER THE VOLCANO   Universal, 1984
ANNA KARENINA (TF)   Rastar Productions/Colgems
   Productions, 1985
FORBIDDEN (CTF)   HBO Premiere Films/Mark Forstater
   Productions/Clasart/Anthea Productions, 1985,
   U.S.-British-West German
CHOICES (TF)   Robert Halmi, Inc., 1986
NAPOLEON AND JOSEPHINE: A LOVE STORY (MS)
   David L. Wolper Productions/Warner Bros. TV, 1987
HIGH SEASON   Hemdale, 1987, British
SCENES FROM THE CLASS STRUGGLE IN BEVERLY HILLS
   Cinecom, 1989
WILD ORCHID   Triumph Releasing Corporation, 1990

JOSIE BISSETT

Agent: Paul Kohner Agency - Los Angeles, 310/550-1060

BOOK OF LOVE   New Line Cinema, 1991

CLINT BLACK

b. 1962 - Katy, Louisiana
Agent: CAA - Beverly Hills, 310/288-4545

MAVERICK   Warner Bros., 1994

KAREN BLACK

(Karen Ziegler)
b. July 1, 1942 - Park Ridge, Illinois

YOU'RE A BIG BOY NOW   7 Arts, 1966
HARD CONTRACT   20th Century Fox, 1969
EASY RIDER   Columbia, 1969
FIVE EASY PIECES ✪   Columbia, 1970
DRIVE, HE SAID   Columbia, 1971
A GUNFIGHT   Paramount, 1971
BORN TO WIN   United Artists, 1971
CISCO PIKE   Columbia, 1971
PORTNOY'S COMPLAINT   Warner Bros., 1972
THE PYX   Cinerama Releasing Corporation, 1973, Canadian
LITTLE LAURA & BIG JOHN   1973
THE OUTFIT   MGM, 1974
RHINOCEROS   American Film Theatre, 1974
THE GREAT GATSBY   Paramount, 1974
AIRPORT 1975   Universal, 1974
LAW AND DISORDER   Columbia, 1974
TRILOGY OF TERROR (TF)   ABC Circle Films, 1975
AN ACE UP MY SLEEVE   1975, British
THE DAY OF THE LOCUST   Paramount, 1975
NASHVILLE   Paramount, 1975
CRIME AND PASSION   American International, 1976,
   U.S.-West German

FAMILY PLOT   Universal, 1976
BURNT OFFERINGS   United Artists, 1976
THE SQUEEZE   *THE RIP-OFF*   Maverick International,
   1976, Italian-U.S.
THE STRANGE POSSESSION OF MRS. OLIVER (TF)
   The Shpetner Company, 1977
KILLER FISH   *DEADLY TREASURE OF THE PIRANHA*
   Associated Film Distribution, 1978, British-Brazilian-French
CAPRICORN ONE   20th Century Fox, 1978
IN PRAISE OF OLDER WOMEN   Avco Embassy, 1978, Canadian
MR. HORN (TF)   Lorimar Productions, 1979
THE LAST WORD   Samuel Goldwyn Company, 1979
SEPARATE WAYS   1981
CHANEL SOLITAIRE   United Film Distribution, 1981, French-British
COME BACK TO THE 5 & DIME JIMMY DEAN, JIMMY DEAN
   Cinecom, 1982
KILLING HEAT   *THE GRASS IS SINGING*   Satori, 1983,
   British-Swedish-Zambian
CAN SHE BAKE A CHERRY PIE?   Castle Hill Productions/
   Quartet Films, 1983
BAD MANNERS   *GROWING PAINS*   New World, 1984
MARTIN'S DAY   MGM/UA, 1984, British
CUT AND RUN   1985
SAVAGE DAWN   MAG Enterprises/Gregory Earls Productions, 1985
INVADERS FROM MARS   Cannon, 1986
HOSTAGE   1987, South African
IT'S ALIVE III: ISLAND OF THE ALIVE   Warner Bros., 1987
HOMER & EDDIE   Skouras Pictures, 1990
NIGHT ANGEL   Fries Distribution Company, 1990
HAUNTING FEAR   Troma, 1991
SISTER ISLAND   1995

LEWIS BLACK

HANNAH AND HER SISTERS   Orion, 1986

BLACK-EYED SUSAN

IRONWEED   TriStar, 1987
BLOODHOUNDS OF BROADWAY   Columbia, 1989

DAVID BLACKER

ADVENTURES IN BABYSITTING   Buena Vista, 1987

HONOR BLACKMAN

GOLDFINGER   United Artists, 1964
LACE (MS)   Lorimar Productions, 1984

TAUREAN BLACQUE

Agent: Paradigm - Los Angeles, 310/277-4400

DEEPSTAR SIX   TriStar, 1989

RUBÉN BLADES

b. July 16, 1948 - Panama City, Panama
Agent: UTA - Beverly Hills, 310/273-6700

CRITICAL CONDITION   Paramount, 1987
THE MILAGRO BEANFIELD WAR   Universal, 1988
WAITING FOR SALAZAR   Buena Vista, 1988
DEAD MAN OUT (CTF)   HBO Showcase/Citadel Entertainment
   Productions/Granada TV, 1989, U.S.-Canadian-British
DISORGANIZED CRIME   Buena Vista, 1989
THE TWO JAKES   Paramount, 1990
THE LEMON SISTERS   Miramax Films, 1990
PREDATOR 2   20th Century Fox, 1990
THE JOSEPHINE BAKER STORY (CTF)   HBO Pictures/RHI
   Entertainment, Inc./Anglia TV/John Kemeny Productions, 1991
CRAZY FROM THE HEART (CMS)   Papazian-Hirsch Entertainment/
   DeMann Entertainment, 1991
THE SUPER   20th Century Fox, 1991
COLOR OF NIGHT   Buena Vista, 1994

BETSY BLAIR

MARTY ✪   United Artists, 1955
A DELICATE BALANCE   American Film Theatre, 1973
BETRAYED   MGM/UA, 1988

LINDA BLAIR

Agent: Schiowitz, Clay & Rose - Los Angeles, 213/650-7300

THE EXORCIST ✪   Warner Bros., 1973
BORN INNOCENT (TF)   Tomorrow Entertainment, 1974
AIRPORT 1975   Universal, 1974
SARAH T - PORTRAIT OF A TEENAGE ALCOHOLIC (TF)
   Universal TV, 1975
SWEET HOSTAGE (TF)   Brut Productions, 1975
VICTORY AT ENTEBBE (TF)   1976
EXORCIST II: THE HERETIC   Warner Bros., 1977
ROLLER BOOGIE   United Artists, 1979
WILD HORSE HANK   1979, Canadian
HELL NIGHT   Compass International, 1981
RUCKUS   International Vision Productions, 1982
CHAINED HEAT   Jensen Farley Productions, 1983,
   American-German
RED HEAT   TAT Filmproductions/Aida United GM BH/International
   Screen, 1984, West German-U.S.
SAVAGE STREETS   Entermark Corporation, 1984
NIGHT PATROL   New World, 1985
SAVAGE ISLAND   1985, U.S.-Italian-Spanish
NIGHTFORCE   Vestron, 1987
W.B. BLUE AND THE BEAN   The Movie Group, 1988
SILENT ASSASSINS   1988, U.S.-South Korean
BAD BLOOD   Platinum Pictures, 1989
DISTANT   Horizon, 1989
UP YOUR ALLEY   Seymour Borde & Associates, 1989
WITCHERY   1989, Italian
REPOSSESSED   New Line Cinema, 1990
DEAD SLEEP   Warner Village Roadshow, 1990, Australian
FATAL BOND   1991, Australian

LIONEL BLAIR

ABSOLUTE BEGINNERS   Orion, 1986, British

LISA BLAIR

b. October 22, 1986 - Ontario, Canada

THREE MEN AND A BABY   Buena Vista, 1987

MICHELLE BLAIR

b. October 22, 1986 - Ontario, Canada

THREE MEN AND A BABY   Buena Vista, 1987

NICKY BLAIR

THAT'S LIFE   Columbia, 1986
BEACHES   Buena Vista, 1988

GEOFFREY BLAKE

Agent: Harris & Goldberg - Los Angeles, 310/553-5200

ONE TERRIFIC GUY (TF)   CBS Entertainment, 1986
THE ABDUCTION OF KARI SWENSON (TF)
   NBC Productions, 1987
YOUNG GUNS   20th Century Fox, 1988
PHILADELPHIA EXPERIMENT 2   Trimark Pictures, 1993

LISA BLAKE RICHARDS

(See Lisa Blake RICHARDS)

MICHAEL BLAKE

NATIONAL LAMPOON'S SENIOR TRIP   New Line Cinema, 1995

ROBERT BLAKE

(Michael Gubitosi/Bobby Blake)
b. September 18, 1933 - Nutley, New Jersey

MOKEY   MGM, 1942
ANDY HARDY'S DOUBLE LIFE   MGM, 1943
THE BIG NOISE   1944
WOMAN IN THE WINDOW   1944
DAKOTA   1945
PILLOW TO POST   Warner Bros., 1945

THE HORN BLOWS AT MIDNIGHT   Warner Bros., 1945
IN OLD SACRAMENTO   1946
HUMORESQUE   Warner Bros., 1947
THE LAST ROUNDUP   1947
THE RETURN OF RIN TIN TIN   1947
THE TREASURE OF THE SIERRA MADRE   Warner Bros., 1948
THE BLACK ROSE   20th Century Fox, 1950
APACHE WAR SMOKE   1952
TREASURE OF THE GOLDEN CONDOR   20th Century Fox, 1953
RUMBLE ON THE DOCKS   1956
THE TIJUANA STORY   1957
THE BEAST OF BUDAPEST   1958
REVOLT IN THE BIG HOUSE   Allied Artists, 1958
BATTLE FLAME   Allied Artists, 1959
THE PURPLE GANG   1960
TOWN WITHOUT PITY   1961
THE CONNECTION   Films Around the World, 1962
PT-109   Warner Bros., 1963
THE GREATEST STORY EVER TOLD   United Artists, 1965
THIS PROPERTY IS CONDEMNED   Paramount, 1966
IN COLD BLOOD   Columbia, 1967
TELL THEM WILLIE BOY IS HERE   Universal, 1969
RIPPED OFF   *THE BOXER*   1971, Italian
CORKY   *LOOKING GOOD*   1972
ELECTRA GLIDE IN BLUE   United Artists, 1973
BUSTING   United Artists, 1974
COAST TO COAST   Paramount, 1980
SECOND HAND HEARTS   *THE HAMSTER OF HAPPINESS*
   Paramount, 1981
OF MICE AND MEN (TF)   Of Mice and Men Productions, 1981
BLOOD FEUD (TF)   20th Century Fox TV/Glickman-Selznick
   Productions, 1983
FATHER OF HELL TOWN (TF)   Breezy Productions, 1985
HEART OF A CHAMPION: THE RAY MANCINI STORY (TF)
   Rare Titles Productions/Robert Papazian Productions, 1985

SUSAN BLAKELY

b. 1950 - Frankfurt, Germany

SAVAGES   1972
THE WAY WE WERE   Columbia, 1973
THE LORDS OF FLATBUSH   Columbia, 1974
THE TOWERING INFERNO   20th Century Fox/Warner Bros., 1974
REPORT TO THE COMMISSIONER   United Artists, 1975
SHAMPOO   Columbia, 1975
CAPONE   20th Century Fox, 1975
RICH MAN, POOR MAN (MS)   Universal TV, 1976
SECRETS (TF)   The Jozak Company, 1977
DREAMER   20th Century Fox, 1979
THE CONCORDE—AIRPORT '79   Universal, 1979
MAKE ME AN OFFER (TF)   ABC Circle Films, 1980
A CRY FOR LOVE (TF)   Charles Fries Productions/Alan Sacks
   Productions, 1980
THE OKLAHOMA CITY DOLLS (TF)   IKE Productions/
   Columbia TV, 1981
THE BUNKER (TF)   Time-Life Productions/SFP France/Antenne-2,
   1981, U.S.-French
WILL THERE REALLY BE A MORNING? (TF)   Jaffe-Blakely Films/
   Sama Productions/Orion TV, 1983
BLOOD AND ORCHIDS (MS)   Lorimar Productions, 1986
THE ANNIHILATOR (TF)   Universal TV, 1986
THE TED KENNEDY, JR. STORY (TF)   Entertainment
   Partners, 1986
OVER THE TOP   Cannon, 1987
FATAL CONFESSION: A FATHER DOWLING MYSTERY (TF)
   The Fred Silverman Company/Strathmore
   Productions/Viacom, 1987
BROKEN ANGEL (TF)   The Stan Margulies Company/
   MGM-UA TV, 1988
APRIL MORNING (TF)   Robert Halmi, Inc./Samuel
   Goldwyn TV, 1988
LADYKILLERS (TF)   Barry Weitz Films/ABC Cicle Films, 1988
DREAM A LITTLE DREAM   Vestron, 1989
DEAD RECKONING (CTF)   Houston Lady Productions, 1990
THE INCIDENT (TF)   Qintex Entertainment, 1990
MY MOM'S A WEREWOLF   Crown International Pictures, 1990
AGAINST HER WILL: AN INCIDENT IN BALTIMORE (TF)
   RHI Entertainment, 1992

RONEE BLAKLEY
b. 1946 - Stanley, Idaho

NASHVILLE ✪ Paramount, 1975
RENALDO AND CLARA   Circuit, 1978
THE DRIVER   20th Century Fox, 1978
SHE CAME TO THE VALLEY   RGV Pictures, 1979
THE BALTIMORE BULLET   Avco Embassy, 1980

JENNIFER BLANC
BALTO (AF)   Universal, 1995 (voice)

MICHEL BLANC
MENAGE *TENUE DE SOIREE* Cinecom, 1986, French
URANUS   Prestige Films, 1991, French
THE FAVOR, THE WATCH, AND THE VERY BIG FISH
   Trimark Pictures, 1991, French-British
PRET-A-PORTER   Miramax Films, 1994

TIM BLANEY
SHORT CIRCUIT   TriStar, 1986 (voice)
SHORT CIRCUIT 2   TriStar, 1988 (voice)

MARK BLANKFIELD
Agent: Gordon/Rosson Talent Agency - Studio City, 818/509-1900

ANGEL III   New World, 1988

MARTIN MARIA BLAU
GINGER AND FRED   MGM/UA, 1986, Italian-French-West German

BRIAN BLESSED
BROTHERLY LOVE *COUNTRY DANCE* MGM, 1970, British
THE TROJAN WOMEN   Cinerama Releasing Corporation,
   1971, U.S.-Greek
MAN OF LA MANCHA   United Artists, 1972, Italian-U.S.-British
HENRY VIII AND HIS SIX WIVES   Levitt-Pickman, 1973
I CLAUDIUS (MS)   1976
FLASH GORDON   Universal, 1980
HIGH ROAD TO CHINA   Warner Bros., 1983, U.S.-Yugoslavian
WAR AND REMEMBRANCE (MS)   Dan Curtis Productions/
   ABC Circle Films, 1988-89
HENRY V   Samuel Goldwyn Company, 1989, British
PRISONERS OF HONOR (CTF)   HBO Pictures/Dreyfuss-James
   Productions, 1991
ROBIN HOOD: PRINCE OF THIEVES   Warner Bros., 1991

BRENDA BLETHYN
A RIVER RUNS THROUGH IT   Columbia, 1992

CAROLINE BLISS
LICENCE TO KILL   MGM/UA, 1989, British

OLIVER BLOCK
BIG   20th Century Fox, 1988

CLAIRE BLOOM
b. February 15, 1931 - London, England
Agent: Marion Rosenberg Office - Los Angeles, 213/653-7383

THE BLIND GODDESS   1948
LIMELIGHT   United Artists, 1952
INNOCENTS IN PARIS   1953
THE MAN BETWEEN   United Artists, 1953, British
RICHARD III   Lopert, 1956, British
ALEXANDER THE GREAT   United Artists, 1956
THE BROTHERS KARAMAZOV   MGM, 1958
LOOK BACK IN ANGER   Warner Bros., 1958, British
THE BUCCANEER   Paramount, 1958
BRAINWASHED *THE ROYAL GAME* Allied Artists, 1960, German
THE WONDERFUL WORLD OF THE BROTHERS GRIMM
   MGM/Cinerama, 1962
THE CHAPMAN REPORT   Warner Bros., 1962
IL MAESTRO DI VIGEVANO   1963, Italian

THE HAUNTING   MGM, 1963, British-U.S.
80,000 SUSPECTS   Rank, 1963, British
HIGH INFIDELITY   Magna, 1964, Italian-French
THE OUTRAGE   MGM, 1964
THE SPY WHO CAME IN FROM THE COLD   Paramount,
   1965, British
CHARLY   Cinerama Releasing Corporation, 1968
THREE INTO TWO WON'T GO   1969
THE ILLUSTRATED MAN   Warner Bros., 1969
A SEVERED HEAD   Columbia, 1970, British
RED SKY AT MORNING   Universal, 1970
THE GOING UP OF DAVID LEV (TF)   1971
A DOLL'S HOUSE   Paramount, 1973, Canadian-U.S.
ISLANDS IN THE STREAM   Paramount, 1977
BACKSTAIRS AT THE WHITE HOUSE (MS)   Ed Friendly
   Productions, 1979
CLASH OF THE TITANS   MGM/UA, 1981, British
BRIDESHEAD REVISITED (MS)   Granada TV/WNET-13/NDR
   Hamburg, 1981
ELLIS ISLAND (MS)   Pantheon Pictures/Telepictures Productions,
   1984, U.S.-British
FLORENCE NIGHTINGALE (TF)   Cypress Point Productions, 1985
HOLD THE DREAM (TF)   Robert Bradford Productions/Taft
   Entertainment TV, 1986, U.S.-British
LIBERTY (TF)   Robert Greenwald Productions, 1986
ANASTASIA: THE MYSTERY OF ANNA (MS)   Telecom
   Entertainment/Consolidated Productions/Reteitalia,
   1986, U.S.-Italian
QUEENIE (MS)   von Zerneck-Samuels Productions/Highgate
   Pictures, 1987
SAMMY AND ROSIE GET LAID   Cinecom, 1987, British
BERYL MARKHAM: A SHADOW ON THE SUN (TF)
   Tamara Asseyev Productions/New World TV, 1988
THE LADY AND THE HIGHWAYMAN (TF)   The Grade Company/
   Gainsborough Pictures, 1989, British
CRIMES AND MISDEMEANORS   Orion, 1989
THE PRINCESS AND THE GOBLIN (AF)   Hemdale, 1994 (voice)

VERNA BLOOM
MEDIUM COOL   Paramount, 1969
NATIONAL LAMPOON'S ANIMAL HOUSE   Universal, 1978
AFTER HOURS   The Geffen Company/Warner Bros., 1985

CATHIANNE BLORE
AN AMERICAN TAIL (AF)   Universal, 1986 (voice)

ROBERTS BLOSSOM
Agent: Gersh Agency - Beverly Hills, 310/274-6611

FLASHPOINT   TriStar, 1984
ALWAYS   Universal, 1989
HOME ALONE   20th Century Fox, 1990
DOC HOLLYWOOD   Warner Bros., 1991
THE QUICK AND THE DEAD   TriStar, 1995

LISA BLOUNT
Agent: William Morris Agency - Beverly Hills, 310/274-7451

9/30/55 *SEPTEMBER 30, 1955* Universal, 1977
DEAD AND BURIED   Avco Embassy, 1981
AN OFFICER AND A GENTLEMAN   Paramount, 1982
STORMIN' HOME (TF)   CBS Entertainment, 1985
CEASE FIRE   Cineworld, 1985
CUT AND RUN   1985, Italian
THE ANNIHILATOR (TF)   Universal TV, 1986
RADIOACTIVE DREAMS   DEG, 1986
PRINCE OF DARKNESS   Universal, 1987
NIGHTFLYERS   New Century/Vista, 1987
SOUTH OF RENO   Open Road Productions/Pendulum
   Productions, 1987
UNHOLY MATRIMONY (TF)   Edgar J. Scherick Associates/Taft
   Entertainment TV, 1988
GREAT BALLS OF FIRE   Orion, 1989
OUT COLD   TriStar, 1989
BLIND FURY   TriStar, 1990

JACK BLUM
HAPPY BIRTHDAY TO ME   Columbia, 1981, Canadian

MARK BLUM
Agent: APA - Los Angeles, 310/273-0744

DESPERATELY SEEKING SUSAN   Orion, 1985
"CROCODILE" DUNDEE   Paramount, 1986, Australian
CAPITAL NEWS (TF)   MTM Enterprises, 1990

ROBERT BLYTHE
THE ENGLISHMAN WHO WENT UP A HILL, BUT CAME DOWN
   A MOUNTAIN   Miramax Films, 1995

ANNE BOBBY
NIGHTBREED   20th Century Fox, 1990

HART BOCHNER
Business Manager: Perry & Neidorf, 9720 Wilshire Blvd., 3rd Floor,
   Beverly Hills, CA, 310/553-0171

ISLANDS IN THE STREAM   Paramount, 1977
BREAKING AWAY   20th Century Fox, 1979
RICH AND FAMOUS   MGM/United Artists, 1981
THE SUN ALSO RISES (TF)   Furia-Oringer Productions/
   20th Century Fox TV, 1984
SUPERGIRL   Warner Bros., 1984, British
THE WILD LIFE   Universal, 1984
MAKING MR. RIGHT   Orion, 1987
DIE HARD   20th Century Fox, 1988
WAR AND REMEMBRANCE (MS)   Dan Curtis Productions/
   ABC Circle Films, 1988-89
APARTMENT ZERO   Skouras Pictures, 1989
MR. DESTINY   Buena Vista, 1990
BATMAN: MASK OF THE PHANTASM (AF)   Warner Bros.,
   1993 (voice)

LLOYD BOCHNER
MORNING GLORY   Academy Entertainment, 1993

ERIC BOGOSIAN
b. April 24, 1953 - Boston, Massachusetts
Agent: William Morris Agency - Beverly Hills, 310/274-7451

THE CAINE MUTINY COURT-MARTIAL (TF)
   CBS Entertainment, 1988
TALK RADIO   Universal, 1988
LAST FLIGHT OUT (TF)   The Manheim Company/Co-Star
   Entertainment/NBC Productions, 1990
SEX, DRUGS, ROCK & ROLL   Avenue Pictures, 1991
DOLORES CLAIBORNE   Columbia, 1994

GAIL BOGGS
GHOST   Paramount, 1990

IAN BOHEN
WYATT EARP   Warner Bros., 1994

RICHARD BOHRINGER
DIVA   United Artists Classics, 1982, French

CHRISTINE BOISSON
SORCERESS   European Classics, 1988, French

BILL BOLENDER
FATAL DECEPTION: MRS. LEE HARVEY OSWALD (TF)
   David L. Wolper Productions/Bernard Sofronski/Warner Bros.
   Television, 1993

JOSEPH BOLOGNA
Agent: The Blake Agency - Beverly Hills, 310/246-0241

MIXED COMPANY   United Artists, 1974
THE BIG BUS   Paramount, 1976

CHAPTER TWO   Columbia, 1979
MY FAVORITE YEAR   MGM/UA, 1982
BLAME IT ON RIO   20th Century Fox, 1984
A TIME TO TRIUMPH (TF)   Billos-Kauffman Productions/Phoenix
   Entertainment Group, 1986
RAGS TO RICHES (TF)   Leonard Hill Films/New World TV, 1987
PRIME TARGET (TF)   RLC Productions/The Finnegan-Pinchuk
   Company/MGM-UA TV, 1989
IT HAD TO BE YOU   Limelite Studios, 1989
COUPE DE VILLE   Universal, 1990

PAOLO BONACELLI
CAMORRA   *UN COMPLICATO INTRIGO DI DONNE, VICOLI E
   DELITTI*   Cannon, 1986, Italian

CYNTHIA BOND
DEF BY TEMPTATION   Troma, 1990

JAMES BOND III
DEF BY TEMPTATION   Troma, 1990 (also directed)

RALEIGH BOND
ALL NIGHT LONG   Universal, 1981

STEVE BOND
PICASSO TRIGGER   Malibu Bay Films, 1989
TO DIE FOR   Arrowhead Entertainment, 1989

SUDIE BOND
THEY MIGHT BE GIANTS   Universal, 1971
COME BACK TO THE 5 & DIME JIMMY DEAN, JIMMY DEAN
   Cinecom, 1982
SILKWOOD   20th Century-Fox, 1983
JOHNNY DANGEROUSLY   20th Century Fox, 1984

PETER BONERZ
Agent: CAA - Beverly Hills, 310/288-4545

CIRCLE OF VIOLENCE: A FAMILY DRAMA (TF)   Sheldon Pinchuk
   Productions/Rafshoon Communications/Finnegan Associates/
   Telepictures Productions, 1986

LISA BONET
b. November 16, 1967 - San Francisco, California

ANGEL HEART   TriStar, 1987
BANK ROBBER   I.R.S. Releasing, 1993

HELENA BONHAM CARTER
b. May 26, 1966 - London, England
Agent: UTA - Beverly Hills, 310/273-6700

LADY JANE   Paramount, 1985, British
A ROOM WITH A VIEW   Cinecom, 1986, British
MAURICE   Cinecom, 1987, British
A HAZARD OF HEARTS (TF)   The Grade Company/Gainsborough
   Pictures, 1987, British
GETTING IT RIGHT   MCEG, 1989, U.S.-British
HAMLET   Warner Bros., 1990, British
HOWARDS END   Sony Pictures Classics, 1992, British
FATAL DECEPTION: MRS. LEE HARVEY OSWALD (TF)
   David L. Wolper Productions/Bernard Sofronski/Warner Bros.
   Television, 1993
MARY SHELLEY'S FRANKENSTEIN   TriStar, 1994
THE PRINCESS AND THE PEA   21st Century Film
   Corporation, 1995

EVAN BONIFANT
3 NINJAS KICK BACK   TriStar, 1994

SANDRINE BONNAIRE
VAGABOND   *SANS TOIT NI LOI*   Grange Communications/IFEX
   Film, 1985, French
A FEW DAYS WITH ME   Galaxy International, 1988, French

FRANK BONNER
Agent: Paradigm - Los Angeles, 310/277-4400

YOU CAN'T HURRY LOVE   MCEG, 1988

TONY BONNER
THE LAST FRONTIER (TF)   McElroy & McElroy Productions, 1986, Australian
QUIGLEY DOWN UNDER   MGM/UA, 1990

BONO
U2: RATTLE AND HUM (FD)   Paramount, 1988

SONNY BONO
b. February 16, 1935 - Detroit, Michigan

WILD ON THE BEACH   20th Century-Fox, 1965
GOOD TIMES   Columbia, 1967
MURDER ON FLIGHT 502 (TF)   Spelling-Goldberg Productions, 1975
AIRPLANE II: THE SEQUEL   Paramount, 1982
TROLL   Empire Pictures, 1986
HAIRSPRAY   New Line Cinema, 1988

BRIAN BONSALL
BLANK CHECK   Buena Vista, 1994

SORRELL BOOKE
b. January 4, 1930 - Buffalo, New York

GONE ARE THE DAYS!   *PURLIE VICTORIOUS*   Trans-Lux, 1963
BYE BYE BRAVERMAN   Warner Bros., 1968
WHAT'S UP, DOC?   Warner Bros., 1972
SPECIAL DELIVERY   American International, 1976

LESLEY BOONE
STUART SMALLEY   Paramount, 1995

PAT BOONE
(Charles Eugene Boone)
b. June 1, 1934 - Jacksonville, Florida

BERNARDINE   20th Century Fox, 1957
APRIL LOVE   20th Century Fox, 1957
MARDI GRAS   20th Century Fox, 1958
JOURNEY TO THE CENTER OF THE EARTH   20th Century Fox, 1959
ALL HANDS ON DECK   20th Century Fox, 1961
STATE FAIR   20th Century Fox, 1962
THE MAIN ATTRACTION   MGM, 1962, British
THE YELLOW CANARY   20th Century Fox, 1963
NEVER PUT IT IN WRITING   Allied Artists, 1964, British
THE HORROR OF IT ALL   20th Century Fox, 1964, British
GOODBYE, CHARLIE   20th Century Fox, 1964
THE GREATEST STORY EVER TOLD   United Artists, 1965
THE PERILS OF PAULINE   Universal, 1967
THE PIGEON (TF)   Thomas-Spelling Productions, 1969
THE CROSS AND THE SWITCHBLADE   Dick Ross, 1970

CHARLEY BOORMAN
DELIVERANCE   Warner Bros., 1972
THE EMERALD FOREST   Embassy, 1985, British

KATRINE BOORMAN
CAMILLE CLAUDEL   Orion Classics, 1988, French

JAMES BOOTH
Agent: Hillard Elkins - Los Angeles, 213/285-0700

ZULU   Embassy, 1964, British
ZORRO, THE GAY BLADE   20th Century Fox, 1981
AVENGING FORCE   Cannon, 1986
AMERICAN NINJA 4: THE ANNIHILATION   Cannon, 1991

POWERS BOOTHE
A CRY FOR LOVE (TF)   Charles Fries Productions/Alan Sacks Productions, 1980
CRUSING   United Artists, 1980
GUYANA TRAGEDY: THE STORY OF JIM JONES (TF)   The Konigsberg Company, 1980
SOUTHERN COMFORT   20th Century Fox, 1981
PHILIP MARLOWE, PRIVATE EYE   *CHANDLERTOWN* (CMS)   HBO/David Wickes Television Ltd./London Weekend Television, 1983, British
RED DAWN   MGM/UA, 1984
A BREED APART   Orion, 1984
THE EMERALD FOREST   Embassy, 1985, British
EXTREME PREJUDICE   TriStar, 1987
FAMILY OF SPIES (MS)   King Phoenix Entertainment, 1990
BY DAWN'S EARLY LIGHT (CTF)   HBO Pictures/Paravision International U.S.A., 1990
TOMBSTONE   Buena Vista, 1993
BLUE SKY   Orion, 1994

PETER BORETSKI
THE NUTCRACKER PRINCE (AF)   Warner Bros., 1990 (voice)

RIKKE BORGE
TATTOO   20th Century Fox, 1981

ERNEST BORGNINE
(Ermes Effron Borgnine)
b. January 24, 1917 - Hamden, Connecticut
Agent: Selected Artists Agency - Studio City, 818/905-5744

CHINA CORSAIR   1951
THE WHISTLE AT EATON FALLS   Columbia, 1951
THE MOB   Columbia, 1951
THE STRANGER WORE A GUN   Columbia, 1953
FROM HERE TO ETERNITY   Columbia, 1953
JOHNNY GUITAR   Republic, 1954
DEMETRIUS AND THE GLADIATORS   20th Century Fox, 1954
THE BOUNTY HUNTER   Warner Bros., 1954
VERA CRUZ   United Artists, 1954
BAD DAY AT BLACK ROCK   MGM, 1955
MARTY ★★   United Artists, 1955
RUN FOR COVER   Paramount, 1955
VIOLENT SATURDAY   20th Century Fox, 1955
THE LAST COMMAND   Republic, 1955
THE SQUARE JUNGLE   Universal, 1955
JUBAL   Columbia, 1956
THE CATERED AFFAIR   MGM, 1956
THE BEST THINGS IN LIFE ARE FREE   20th Century-Fox, 1956
THREE BRAVE MEN   1957
THE VIKINGS   United Artists, 1958
THE BADLANDERS   MGM, 1958
TORPEDO RUN   MGM, 1958
THE RABBIT TRAP   United Artists, 1959
MAN ON A STRING   Columbia, 1960
PAY OR DIE   Allied Artists, 1960
SEASON OF PASSION   *SUMMER OF THE SEVENTEENTH DOLL*   1961, Australian-British
LES GUERRILLEROS   1961, Spanish
GO NAKED IN THE WORLD   MGM, 1961
IL RE DI POGGIOREALE   1961, Italian
IL GIUDIZIO ITALIANI   1962, Italian
SEDUCTION OF THE SOUTH   1962, Italian
BARABBAS   Columbia, 1962, Italian
McHALE'S NAVY   1964
THE FLIGHT OF THE PHOENIX   20th Century Fox, 1966
THE OSCAR   Embassy, 1966
THE DIRTY DOZEN   MGM, 1967
CHUKA   Paramount, 1967
THE LEGEND OF LYLAH CLARE   MGM, 1968
THE SPLIT   MGM, 1968
ICE STATION ZEBRA   MGM, 1968
THE WILD BUNCH   Warner Bros., 1969
VENGEANCE IS MINE   1969, Italian
A BULLET FOR SANDOVAL   *LOS DESPERADOS*   1970, Spanish-Italian
THE ADVENTURERS   Paramount, 1970

SUPPOSE THEY GAVE A WAR AND NOBODY CAME?
   Cinerama Releasing Corporation, 1970
THE TRACKERS (TF)   Aaron Spelling Productions, 1971
WILLARD   Cinerama Releasing Corporation, 1971
BUNNY O'HARE   American International, 1971
RAIN FOR A DUSTY SUMMER   Do'Bar, 1971, Spanish-U.S.
HANNIE CAULDER   Paramount, 1971, British
RIPPED OFF   *THE BOXER*   1971, Italian
TOUGH GUY   1972
THE REVENGERS   National General, 1972, U.S.-Mexican
WHAT HAPPENED TO THE MYSTERIOUS
   MR. FOSTER? (TF)   1972
THE POSEIDON ADVENTURE   20th Century Fox, 1972
THE NEPTUNE FACTOR   20th Century Fox, 1973, Canadian
EMPEROR OF THE NORTH   *EMPEROR OF THE NORTH POLE*
   20th Century Fox, 1973
SUNDAY IN THE COUNTRY   American International, 1973, British
LAW AND DISORDER   Columbia, 1974
TWICE IN A LIFETIME (TF)   Martin Rackin Productions, 1974
THE DEVIL'S RAIN   Bryanston, 1975, U.S.-Mexican
HUSTLE   Paramount, 1975
CLEAVER AND HAVEN (TF)   1976
FUTURE COP (TF)   Paramount TV, 1976
NATALE IN CASA DI APPUNTAMENTO   1976, Italian
WON TON TON, THE DOG THAT SAVED HOLLYWOOD
   Paramount, 1976
SHOOT   Avco Embassy, 1976, Canadian
FIRE!   Irwin Allen Productions/20th Century Fox TV, 1977
THE GREATEST   Columbia, 1977
CROSSED SWORDS   *THE PRINCE AND THE PAUPER*
   Warner Bros., 1978, British
JESUS OF NAZARETH (TF)   Sir Lew Grade Productions/ITC,
   1978, British-Italian
CONVOY   United Artists, 1978
ALL QUIET ON THE WESTERN FRONT (TF)   Norman Rosemont
   Productions/Marble Arch Productions, 1979
THE DOUBLE McGUFFIN   Mulberry Square, 1979
THE BLACK HOLE   Buena Vista, 1979
WHEN TIME RAN OUT   Warner Bros., 1980
ESCAPE FROM NEW YORK   Avco Embassy, 1981
HIGH RISK   American Cinema, 1981
DEADLY BLESSING   United Artists, 1981
SUPERFUZZ   Avco Embassy, 1981, Italian
BLOOD FEUD (TF)   20th Century Fox TV/Glickman-Selznick
   Productions, 1983
YOUNG WARRIORS   Cannon, 1983
MASQUERADE (TF)   Renee Valente Productions/Glen A. Larson
   Productions/20th Century Fox TV, 1983
AIRWOLF (TF)   Belisarius Productions/Universal TV, 1984
THE LAST DAYS OF POMPEII (TF)   David Gerber Company/
   Columbia TV/Centerpoint Films/RAI, 1984,
   U.S.-British-Italian
LOVE LEADS THE WAY (TF)   Hawkins-Permut Productions, 1984
CODENAME: WILDGEESE   New World, 1984,
   Italian-West German
THE DIRTY DOZEN: THE NEXT MISSION (TF)   MGM-UA TV/
   Jadran Film, 1987, U.S.-Yugoslavian
THE DIRTY DOZEN: THE FATAL MISSION (TF)
   MGM-UA TV, 1988
JAKE SPANNER, PRIVATE EYE (CTF)   Andrew J. Fenady
   Productions/Scotti-Vinnedge TV/USA Network, 1989
APPEARANCES (TF)   Walt Disney Television, 1990
MISTRESS   Tribeca Films, 1992

KATHERINE BOROWITZ

Agent: Gersh Agency - Beverly Hills, 310/274-6611

MEN OF RESPECT   Columbia, 1991

AMARYLLIS BORREGO

SLEEP WITH ME   MGM/UA, 1994

JESSE BORREGO

I LIKE IT LIKE THAT   Columbia, 1994

BRIAN BOSAK

BETRAYED   MGM/UA, 1988

GIULIA BOSCHI

CHOCOLAT   Orion Classics, 1988, French

PHILIP BOSCO

b. September 26, 1930 - Jersey City
Agent: Judy Schoen & Associates - Los Angeles, 213/962-1950

A LOVELY WAY TO DIE   Universal, 1968
TRADING PLACES   Paramount, 1983
THE POPE OF GREENWICH VILLAGE   MGM/UA, 1984
HEAVEN HELP US   TriStar, 1985
FLANAGAN   United Film Distribution, 1985
THE MONEY PIT   Universal, 1986
CHILDREN OF A LESSER GOD   Paramount, 1986
SUSPECT   TriStar, 1987
THREE MEN AND A BABY   Buena Vista, 1987
ANOTHER WOMAN   Orion, 1988
WORKING GIRL   20th Century Fox, 1988
THE DREAM TEAM   Universal, 1989
THE LUCKIEST MAN IN THE WORLD   Co-Star Entertainment, 1989
BLUE STEEL   MGM/UA, 1990
MURDER IN BLACK AND WHITE (TF)   Titus Productions, 1990
QUICK CHANGE   Warner Bros., 1990
F/X 2 - THE DEADLY ART OF ILLUSION   Orion, 1991
TRUE COLORS   Paramount, 1991
STRAIGHT TALK   Buena Vista, 1992
ANGIE   Buena Vista, 1994

TODD BOSLEY

LITTLE GIANTS   Warner Bros., 1994

TOM BOSLEY

b. October 1, 1927 - Chicago, Illinois
Agent: Shapiro-Lichtman - Los Angeles, 310/859-8877

LOVE WITH THE PROPER STRANGER   Paramount, 1963
THE WORLD OF HENRY ORIENT   United Artists, 1964
DIVORCE AMERICAN STYLE   Columbia, 1967
THE SECRET WAR OF HARRY FRIGG   Universal, 1968
YOURS, MINE AND OURS   United Artists, 1968
TO FIND A MAN   *TO FIND A MAN/SEX AND THE TEENAGER*
   Columbia, 1972
MIRACLE ON 34TH STREET (TF)   20th Century-Fox TV, 1973
MIXED COMPANY   United Artists, 1974
WHO IS THE BLACK DAHLIA? (TF)   Douglas S. Cramer
   Productions, 1975
THE NIGHT THAT PANICKED AMERICA (TF)   Paramount TV, 1975
GUS   Buena Vista, 1976
FOR THE LOVE OF IT (TF)   Charles Fries Productions/Neila
   Productions, 1980
O'HARA'S WIFE   Davis-Panzer Productions, 1982
THE JESSE OWENS STORY (TF)   Harve Bennett Productions/
   Paramount TV, 1984
PRIVATE SESSIONS (TF)   The Belle Company/Seltzer-Gimbel
   Productions/Raven's Claw Productions/Comworld
   Productions, 1985
PERRY MASON: THE CASE OF THE NOTORIOUS NUN (TF)
   Intermedia Productions/Strathmore Productions/Viacom
   Productions, 1986
FATAL CONFESSION: A FATHER DOWLING MYSTERY (TF)
   The Fred Silverman Company/Strathmore
   Productions/Viacom, 1987
MILLION DOLLAR MYSTERY   DEG, 1987
WICKED STEPMOTHER   MGM, 1988
FATHER DOWLING MYSTERIES: THE MISSING BODY
   MYSTERY (TF)   The Fred Silverman Company/Dean Hargrove
   Productions, 1989

BARBARA BOSSON

b. November 1, 1939 - Charleroi, Pennsylvania

HOSTAGE FLIGHT (TF)   Frank von Zerneck Films, 1985
JURY DUTY: THE COMEDY (TF)   Steve White Productions/
   Spectator Films, 1990

BARRY BOSTWICK
b. February 24, 1944 - San Mateo, California

JENNIFER ON MY MIND   United Artists, 1971
THE CHADWICK FAMILY (TF)   Universal TV, 1974
THE ROCKY HORROR PICTURE SHOW   20th Century Fox, 1976, British
THE QUINNS (TF)   Daniel Wilson Productions, 1977
MOVIE MOVIE   Warner Bros., 1978
MURDER BY NATURAL CAUSES (TF)   Richard Levinson-William Link Productions, 1979
ONCE UPON A FAMILY (TF)   Universal TV, 1980
MOVIOLA   *THE SILENT LOVERS* (MS)   David L. Wolper-Stan Margulies Productions/Warner Bros. TV, 1980
SCRUPLES (TF)   Lou-Step Productions/Warner Bros. TV, 1980
RED FLAG: THE ULTIMATE GAME (TF)   Marble Arch Productions, 1981
MEGAFORCE   20th Century Fox, 1982
GEORGE WASHINGTON (MS)   David Gerber Company/MGM-UA TV, 1984
A WOMAN OF SUBSTANCE (TF)   Artemis Portman Productions, 1984, British
DECEPTIONS (TF)   Louis Rudolph Productions/Consolidated Productions/Columbia TV, 1985, U.S.-British
BETRAYED BY INNOCENCE (TF)   Inter Planetary Pictures/CBS Entertainment, 1986
PLEASURES (TF)   Catalina Production Group/Columbia TV, 1986
GEORGE WASHINGTON II: THE FORGING OF A NATION (TF)   David Gerber Company/MGM TV, 1986
I'LL TAKE MANHATTAN (MS)   Steve Krantz Productions, 1987
BODY OF EVIDENCE (TF)   CBS Entertainment, 1988
ADDICTED TO HIS LOVE (TF)   Green-Epstein Productions/Columbia TV, 1988
WAR AND REMEMBRANCE (MS)   Dan Curtis Productions/ABC Circle Films, 1988-89
PARENT TRAP III (TF)   Walt Disney TV, 1989
PARENT TRAP: HAWAIIAN HONEYMOON (TF)   Walt Disney TV, 1989
JUDITH KRANTZ'S TILL WE MEET AGAIN   *TILL WE MEET AGAIN* (MS)   Steve Krantz Productions/Yorkshire TV, 1989, U.S.-British
CHALLENGER (TF)   The IndieProd Company/King Phoenix Entertainment/George Englund, Jr. Productions, 1990
WEEKEND AT BERNIE'S II   TriStar, 1993
DANIELLE STEEL'S ONCE IN A LIFETIME   *ONCE IN A LIFETIME* (TF)   The Cramer Company/NBC Productions, 1994
THE SECRETARY   Republic Pictures, 1995

BRIAN BOSWORTH
Agent: The Artists Agency - Los Angeles, 310/277-7779

STONE COLD   Columbia, 1991

SARA BOTSFORD
STILL OF THE NIGHT   MGM/UA, 1982
JUMPIN' JACK FLASH   20th Century Fox, 1986
MY BREAST (TF)   CBS, 1994

JOSEPH BOTTOMS
THE DOVE   Paramount, 1974
CRIME AND PASSION   American International, 1976, U.S.-West German
HOLOCAUST (MS)   Titus Productions, 1978
THE BLACK HOLE   Buena Vista, 1979
CLOUD DANCER   Blossom, 1980
KING OF THE MOUNTAIN   Universal, 1981
THE INTRUDER WITHIN (TF)   1981
SURFACING   Arista, 1981, Canadian
THE SINS OF DORIAN GRAY (TF)   Rankin-Bass Productions, 1983
ISLAND SONS (TF)   Universal TV, 1987

SAM BOTTOMS
Agent: The Agency - Los Angeles, 310/551-3000

THE LAST PICTURE SHOW   Columbia, 1971
CLASS OF '44   Warner Bros., 1973

ZANDY'S BRIDE   *FOR BETTER, FOR WORSE*   Warner Bros., 1974
SAVAGES (TF)   Spelling-Goldberg Productions, 1974
CAGE WITHOUT A KEY (TF)   Columbia TV, 1975
THE OUTLAW JOSEY WALES   Warner Bros., 1976
APOCALYPSE NOW   United Artists, 1979
BRONCO BILLY   Warner Bros., 1980
ISLAND SONS (TF)   Universal TV, 1987
GARDENS OF STONE   TriStar, 1987
HUNTER'S BLOOD   Concorde, 1987

TIMOTHY BOTTOMS
b. August 30, 1950 - Santa Barbara, California
Agent: Bresler, Kelly & Kipperman - Encino, 818/905-1155

JOHNNY GOT HIS GUN   1971
THE LAST PICTURE SHOW   Columbia, 1971
LOVE AND PAIN AND THE WHOLE DAMNED THING   Columbia, 1973, British-U.S.
THE PAPER CHASE   20th Century Fox, 1973
THE WHITE DAWN   Paramount, 1974
THE CRAZY WORLD OF JULIUS VROODER   20th Century Fox, 1974
SEVEN MEN AT DAYBREAK   *PRICE OF FREEDOM*   Warner Bros., 1975, British
ARTHUR HAILEY'S THE MONEYCHANGERS   *THE MONEYCHANGERS* (MS)   Ross Hunter Productions/Paramount TV, 1976
A SMALL TOWN IN TEXAS   American International, 1976
ROLLERCOASTER   Universal, 1977
THE OTHER SIDE OF THE MOUNTIAN PART 2   Universal, 1978
HURRICANE   Paramount, 1979
A SHINING SEASON (TF)   Green-Epstein Productions/T-M Productions/Columbia TV, 1979
JOHN STEINBECK'S EAST OF EDEN   *EAST OF EDEN* (MS)   Mace Neufeld Productions, 1981
THE HIGH COUNTRY   Crown International, 1981, Canadian
HAMBONE AND HILLIE   New World, 1984
LOVE LEADS THE WAY (TF)   Hawkins-Permut Productions, 1984
IN THE SHADOW OF KILLMANJARO   Scotti Brothers, 1986, U.S.-British-Kenya
PERRY MASON: THE CASE OF THE NOTORIOUS NUN (TF)   Intermedia Productions/Strathmore Productions/Viacom Productions, 1986
INVADERS FROM MARS   Cannon, 1986
ISLAND SONS (TF)   Universal TV, 1987
TEXASVILLE   Columbia, 1990
ICE RUNNER   Trident Releasing Corporation, 1991

JACQUES BOUDET
WAITING FOR THE MOON   Skouras Pictures, 1987, U.S.-French-British-West German

EVELYNE BOUIX
A MAN AND A WOMAN: 20 YEARS LATER   Warner Bros., 1986, French

CAROLE BOUQUET
FOR YOUR EYES ONLY   United Artists, 1981, British
NEW YORK STORIES   Buena Vista, 1989

RANDY BOURNE
PEGGY SUE GOT MARRIED   TriStar, 1986

JOY BOUSHEL
THE FLY   20th Century Fox, 1986, U.S.-Canadian

DENNIS BOUTSIKARIS
THE DREAM TEAM   Universal, 1989
THUNDERBOAT ROW (TF)   Stephen J. Cannell Productions, 1989
BOYS ON THE SIDE   Warner Bros., 1995

DAVID BOWE
UHF   Orion, 1989
AIR AMERICA   TriStar, 1990

Bo

**F
I
L
M**

**A
C
T
O
R
S**

MICHAEL BOWEN
Agent: Harris & Goldberg - Los Angeles, 310/553-5200

ECHO PARK   Atlantic Releasing Corporation, 1986, U.S.-Austrian
IRON EAGLE   TriStar, 1986
THE RYAN WHITE STORY (TF)   The Landsburg Company, 1989

MALICK BOWENS
OUT OF AFRICA   Universal, 1985
THE BELIEVERS   Orion, 1987

DAVID BOWER
FOUR WEDDINGS AND A FUNERAL   Gramercy Pictures,
   1994, British

TOM BOWER
THE LIGHTSHIP   Castle Hill Productions, 1985, U.S.-West German

DAVID BOWIE
(David Jones)
b. January 8, 1947 - Brixton, London, England
Agent: ICM - Beverly Hills, 310/550-4000

THE VIRGIN SOLDIERS   Columbia, 1969, British
THE MAN WHO FELL TO EARTH   Cinema 5, 1976, British
JUST A GIGOLO   United Artists Classics, 1978, West German
THE HUNGER   MGM/UA, 1983, British
ZIGGY STARDUST AND THE SPIDERS FROM MARS
   20th Century Fox International Classics/Miramax Films,
   1983, filmed in 1973
MERRY CHRISTMAS MR. LAWRENCE   Universal, 1983,
   British-Japanese
INTO THE NIGHT   Universal, 1985
LABYRINTH   TriStar, 1986, British
ABSOLUTE BEGINNERS   Orion, 1986, British
THE LAST TEMPTATION OF CHRIST   Universal, 1988
TWIN PEAKS: FIRE WALK WITH ME   New Line Cinema, 1992,
   U.S.-French

PETER BOWLES
FOR THE LOVE OF BENJI   Mulberry Square, 1977
BERYL MARKHAM: A SHADOW ON THE SUN (TF)   Tamara
   Asseyev Productions/New World TV, 1988

BRUCE BOXLEITNER
b. May 12, 1950 - Elgin, Illinois
Agent: William Morris Agency - Beverly Hills, 310/274-7451

SIX-PACK ANNIE   1975
KISS ME, KILL ME (TF)   Columbia TV, 1976
HOW THE WEST WAS WON (MS)   MGM TV, 1977
THE BALTIMORE BULLET   Avco Embassy, 1980
WILD TIMES (TF)   Metromedia Producers Corporation/Rattlesnake
   Productions, 1980
KENNY ROGERS AS THE GAMBLER (TF)   Kragen & Co., 1980
JOHN STEINBECK'S EAST OF EDEN   *EAST OF EDEN* (MS)
   Mace Neufeld Productions, 1981
TRON   Buena Vista, 1982
KENNY ROGERS AS THE GAMBLER—THE ADVENTURE
   CONTINUES (TF)   Lion Share Productions, 1983
KENNY ROGERS AS THE GAMBLER III: THE LEGEND
   CONTINUES (TF)   Lion Share Productions, 1987
ANGEL IN GREEN (TF)   Aligre Productions/Taft Hardy Group,
   1987, U.S.-New Zealand
RED RIVER (TF)   Catalina Production Group/MGM-UA TV, 1988
THE TOWN BULLY (TF)   Dick Clark Productions, 1988
FROM THE DEAD OF NIGHT (TF)   Shadowplay Films/Phoenix
   Entertainment Group, 1989
THE ROAD RAIDERS (TF)   New East Entertainment/
   Universal TV, 1989
JUDITH KRANTZ'S TILL WE MEET AGAIN   *TILL WE
   MEET AGAIN* (MS)   Steve Krantz Productions/Yorkshire TV,
   1989, U.S.-British
KUFFS   Universal, 1992
THE BABE   Universal, 1992

SULLY BOYAR
THE JAZZ SINGER   AFD, 1980
THE MANHATTAN PROJECT   20th Century Fox, 1986

ALAN BOYCE
SEVEN MINUTES IN HEAVEN   Warner Bros., 1986

BRITTANY BOYD
LASSIE   Paramount, 1994

GUY BOYD
Agent: Gersh Agency - Beverly Hills, 310/274-6611

STREAMERS   United Artists Classics, 1983
BODY DOUBLE   Columbia, 1984
TANK   Universal, 1984
THE EWOK ADVENTURE (TF)   Lucasfilm, Ltd./Korty Films
   Productions, 1984
JAGGED EDGE   Columbia, 1985
LUCAS   20th Century Fox, 1986
FIREFIGHTER (TF)   Forest Hill Productions/Embassy TV, 1986
WAR PARTY   Hemdale, 1989
THE LAST OF THE FINEST   Orion, 1990
KISS ME A KILLER   Concorde, 1991
SISTER ISLAND   1995

JAN GAN BOYD
ASSASSINATION   Cannon, 1987
HARRY'S HONG KONG (TF)   Aaron Spelling Productions, 1987

SARAH BOYD
OLD ENOUGH   Orion Classics, 1984

TANYA BOYD
JO JO DANCER, YOUR LIFE IS CALLING   Columbia, 1986

PETER BOYDEN
BLOW OUT   Filmways, 1981

BRAD BOYLE
HOOSIERS   Orion, 1986

LARA FLYNN BOYLE
Agent: Judy Schoen & Associates - Los Angeles, 213/962-1950

AMERIKA (MS)   ABC Circle Films, 1987
POLTERGEIST III   MGM/UA, 1988
TERROR ON HIGHWAY 91 (TF)   Katy Film Productions, 1989
HOW I GOT INTO COLLEGE   20th Century Fox, 1989
THE PREPPIE MURDER (TF)   Jack Grossbart Productions/
   Spectator Films, 1989
THE ROOKIE   Warner Bros., 1990
MOBSTERS   Universal, 1991
WAYNE'S WORLD   Paramount, 1992
WHERE THE DAY TAKES YOU   New Line Cinema, 1992
THE TEMP   Paramount, 1993
THREE OF HEARTS   New Line Cinema, 1993
RED ROCK WEST   1993
THREESOME   TriStar, 1994
BABY'S DAY OUT   20th Century Fox, 1994
THE ROAD TO WELLVILLE   Columbia, 1994

PETER BOYLE
b. October 18, 1933 - Philadelphia, Pennsylvania

THE VIRGIN PRESIDENT   1968
MEDIUM COOL   Paramount, 1969
JOE   Cannon, 1970
DIARY OF A MAD HOUSEWIFE   Universal, 1970
T.R. BASKIN   Paramount, 1971
THE CANDIDATE   Warner Bros., 1972
STEELYARD BLUES   Warner Bros., 1973
SLITHER   MGM, 1973
KID BLUE   20th Century Fox, 1973
THE FRIENDS OF EDDIE COYLE   Paramount, 1973

THE MAN WHO COULD TALK TO KIDS (TF)   Tomorrow
   Entertainment, 1973
CRAZY JOE   Columbia, 1974, Italian-U.S.
YOUNG FRANKENSTEIN   20th Century Fox, 1974
TAXI DRIVER   Columbia, 1976
SWASHBUCKLER   Universal, 1976
TAIL GUNNER JOE (TF)   Universal TV, 1977
F.I.S.T.   United Artists, 1978
THE BRINKS JOB   Universal, 1978
BEYOND THE POSEIDON ADVENTURE   Warner Bros., 1979
FROM HERE TO ETERNITY (MS)   Bennett-Katleman Productions/
   Columbia TV, 1979
HARDCORE   Columbia, 1979
IN GOD WE TRU$T   Universal, 1980
WHERE THE BUFFALO ROAM   Universal, 1980
OUTLAND   The Ladd Company/Warner Bros., 1981
HAMMETT   Orion/Warner Bros., 1982
YELLOWBEARD   Orion, 1983, British
JOHNNY DANGEROUSLY   20th Century Fox, 1984
TURK 182   20th Century Fox, 1985
SURRENDER   Warner Bros., 1987
JOSEPH WAMBAUGH'S ECHOES IN THE DARKNESS
   ECHOES IN THE DARKNESS (MS)   Litke-Grossbart
   Productions/New World TV, 1987
RED HEAT   TriStar, 1988
GUTS AND GLORY: THE RISE AND FALL OF OLLIE NORTH (MS)
   Mike Robe Productions/Papazian-Hirsch Entertainment, 1989
THE DREAM TEAM   Universal, 1989
CHALLENGER (TF)   The IndieProd Company/King Phoenix
   Entertainment/George Englund, Jr. Productions, 1990
MEN OF RESPECT   Columbia, 1991
HONEYMOON IN VEGAS   Columbia, 1992
ROYCE (CTF)   Gerber/ITC Productions, 1994
THE SHADOW   Universal, 1994
THE SANTA CLAUSE   Buena Vista, 1994
KATIE   Warner Bros., 1995
WHILE YOU WERE SLEEPING   Buena Vista, 1995

LORRAINE BRACCO
b. 1955 - New York, New York
Agent: CAA - Beverly Hills, 310/288-4545

SOMEONE TO WATCH OVER ME   Columbia, 1987
SING   TriStar, 1989
THE DREAM TEAM   Universal, 1989
GOODFELLAS ✪   Warner Bros., 1990
SWITCH   Warner Bros., 1991
MEDICINE MAN   Buena Vista, 1992
RADIO FLYER   Columbia, 1992
TALENT FOR THE GAME   Paramount, 1992
TRACES OF RED   Samuel Goldwyn Company, 1992
BEING HUMAN   Warner Bros., 1994
EVEN COWGIRLS GET THE BLUES   Fine Line Features/
   New Line Cinema, 1994
THE BASKETBALL DIARIES   1995

ALEJANDRO BRACHO
Agent: Writers & Artists Agency - Los Angeles, 213/820-2240

ROMERO   Four Seasons Entertainment, 1989

EDDIE BRACKEN
b. February 7, 1920 - New York, New York
Agent: William Morris Agency - Beverly Hills, 310/274-7451

OSCAR   Buena Vista, 1991
HOME ALONE 2: LOST IN NEW YORK   20th Century Fox, 1992
ROOKIE OF THE YEAR   20th Century Fox, 1993

GREG BRADFORD
ZAPPED!   Embassy, 1982

JESSE BRADFORD
Agent: William Morris Agency - Beverly Hills, 310/274-7451

KING OF THE HILL   Gramercy Pictures, 1993
YELLOW DOG   20th Century Fox, 1994

RICHARD BRADFORD
Agent: Susan Smith & Associates - Beverly Hills, 213/852-4777

THE TRIP TO BOUNTIFUL   Island Pictures/FilmDallas, 1985
LITTLE NIKITA   Columbia, 1988
THE MILAGRO BEANFIELD WAR   Universal, 1988
HEART OF DIXIE   Orion, 1989
NIGHT GAME   Trans World Entertainment, 1989
INTERNAL AFFAIRS   Paramount, 1990
AMBITION   Miramax Films, 1991
COLD HEAVEN   Hemdale, 1992

DAVID BRADLEY
Agent: Fred Amsel & Associates - Los Angeles, 213/939-1188

AMERICAN NINJA 3: BLOOD HUNT   Cannon, 1989
AMERICAN NINJA 4: THE ANNIHILATION   Cannon, 1991

CATHRYN BRADSHAW
BERT RIGBY, YOU'RE A FOOL   Warner Bros., 1989

TERRY BRADSHAW
THE CANNONBALL RUN   20th Century Fox, 1981

RANDALL BRADY
Agent: Michel Keeler - 213/962-6426

TOP GUN   Paramount, 1986

SONIA BRAGA
Agent: ICM - Beverly Hills, 310/550-4000

DONA FLOR AND HER TWO HUSBANDS   New Yorker,
   1978, Brazilian
GABRIELA   MGM/UA Classics, 1983, Brazilian-Italian
KISS OF THE SPIDER WOMAN   Island Alive/FilmDallas,
   1985, Brazilian-U.S.
THE MILAGRO BEANFIELD WAR   Universal, 1988
MOON OVER PARADOR   Universal, 1988, U.S.-Brazilian
THE ROOKIE   Warner Bros., 1990

KENNETH BRANAGH
b. December 10, 1960 - Belfast, Northern Ireland
Agent: Paradigm - Los Angeles, 310/277-4400

HIGH SEASON   Hemdale, 1987, British
A MONTH IN THE COUNTRY   Orion Classics, 1987, British
HENRY V ★   Samuel Goldwyn Company, 1989,
   British (also directed)
DEAD AGAIN   Paramount, 1991 (also directed)
PETER'S FRIENDS   Samuel Goldwyn Company, 1992,
   British (also directed)
SWING KIDS   Buena Vista, 1993 (uncredited)
MUCH ADO ABOUT NOTHING   Samuel Goldwyn Company, 1993,
   British-U.S. (also directed)
MARY SHELLEY'S FRANKENSTEIN   TriStar, 1994 (also directed)

LILLO BRANCATO
Agent: William Morris Agency - Beverly Hills, 310/274-7451

A BRONX TALE   Savoy Pictures, 1993
RENAISSANCE MAN   Buena Vista, 1994
CRIMSON TIDE   Buena Vista, 1995

DERRICK BRANCHE
MY BEAUTIFUL LAUNDRETTE   Orion Classics, 1985, British

WALKER BRAND
CITY SLICKERS   Columbia, 1991

KLAUS MARIA BRANDAUER
Agent: ICM - Beverly Hills, 310/550-4000

THE SALZBURG CONNECTION   20th Century Fox, 1972
MEPHISTO   Analysis, 1980, Hungarian-West German
NEVER SAY NEVER AGAIN   Warner Bros., 1983
KINDERGARTEN   IFEX Film, 1984, Soviet
THE LIGHTSHIP   Castle Hill Productions, 1985, U.S.-West German
COLONEL REDL   Orion Classics, 1985,
   West German-Austrian-Hungarian
OUT OF AFRICA ✪   Universal, 1985
STREETS OF GOLD   20th Century Fox, 1986
HANUSSEN   Studio Objektiv/CCC Filmkunst/Hungarofilm/MOKEP,
   1988, Hungarian-West German
BURNING SECRET   Vestron, 1988, U.S.-British-West German
THE RUSSIA HOUSE   MGM-Pathe, 1990
WHITE FANG   Buena Vista, 1991
BECOMING COLETTE   Scotti Bros., 1991

JONATHAN BRANDIS
THE NEVERENDING STORY II: THE NEXT CHAPTER
   Warner Bros., 1991
LADYBUGS   Paramount, 1992

LUISINA BRANDO
MISS MARY   New World, 1986, Argentinian

MARLON BRANDO
(Marlon Brando, Jr.)
b. April 3, 1924 - Omaha, Nebraska
Agent: ICM - Beverly Hills, 310/550-4000

THE MEN   *BATTLE STRIPE*   Columbia, 1950
A STREETCAR NAMED DESIRE ★   Warner Bros., 1951
VIVA ZAPATA! ★   20th Century Fox, 1952
JULIUS CAESAR ★   MGM, 1953
THE WILD ONE   Columbia, 1954
ON THE WATERFRONT ★★   Columbia, 1954
DÉSIRÉE   20th Century Fox, 1954
GUYS AND DOLLS   MGM, 1955
TEAHOUSE OF THE AUGUST MOON   MGM, 1956
SAYONARA ★   Warner Bros., 1957
THE YOUNG LIONS   20th Century Fox, 1958
THE FUGITIVE KIND   United Artists, 1960
ONE-EYED JACKS   Paramount, 1961 (also directed)
MUTINY ON THE BOUNTY   MGM, 1962
THE UGLY AMERICAN   Universal, 1963
BEDTIME STORY   Universal, 1964
MORITURI   *THE SABOTEUR, CODE NAME MORITURI*
   20th Century Fox, 1965
THE CHASE   Columbia, 1966
THE APPALOOSA   Universal, 1966
A COUNTESS FROM HONG KONG   Universal, 1967, British
REFLECTIONS IN A GOLDEN EYE   Warner Bros., 1967
CANDY   1968, U.S.-Italian-French
THE NIGHT OF THE FOLLOWING DAY   Universal, 1969
BURN!   *QUEIMADA!*   United Artists, 1969, Italian-French
THE NIGHTCOMERS   Avco Embassy, 1972, British
THE GODFATHER ★★   Paramount, 1972
LAST TANGO IN PARIS ★   United Artists, 1973, Italian-French
THE MISSOURI BREAKS   United Artists, 1976
SUPERMAN   Warner Bros., 1978
ROOTS: THE NEXT GENERATIONS (MS)
   Wolper Productions, 1979
APOCALYPSE NOW   United Artists, 1979
THE FORMULA   MGM/United Artists, 1980
A DRY WHITE SEASON ✪   MGM/UA, 1989
THE FRESHMAN   TriStar, 1990
CHRISTOPHER COLUMBUS: THE DISCOVERY   Warner Bros.,
   1992, British-Spanish
DON JUAN DE MARCO AND THE CENTERFOLD
   New Line Cinema, 1995

MICHAEL BRANDON
Agent: The Artists Agency - Los Angeles, 310/277-7779

LOVERS AND OTHER STRANGERS   Cinerama Releasing
   Corporation, 1970
FM   Universal, 1978
DEADLY MESSAGES (TF)   Columbia TV, 1985

SHARON H. BRANDON
IRON EAGLE II   TriStar, 1988, Canadian-Israeli

NICOLETTA BRASCHI
DOWN BY LAW   Island Pictures, 1986

BENJAMIN BRATT
NASTY BOYS (TF)   NBC Productions/Universal TV, 1989
ONE GOOD COP   Buena Vista, 1991
DEMOLITION MAN   Warner Bros., 1993

ANDRE BRAUGHER
GLORY   TriStar, 1989
SOMEBODY HAS TO SHOOT THE PICTURE (CTF)   Alan Barnette
   Productions/Frank Pierson Films/MCA-TV Entertainment/Scholastic
   Productions, 1990

BART BRAVERMAN
PRINCE OF BEL AIR (TF)   Leonard Hill Films, 1986

THOMAS BRAY
Agent: CAA - Beverly Hills, 310/288-4545

LADY MOBSTER (TF)   Danjul Films/von Zerneck-Samuels
   Productions, 1988
DEEPSTAR SIX   TriStar, 1989

PATRICK BREEN
Agent: Gersh Agency - Beverly Hills, 310/274-6611

NOBODY'S PERFECT   Moviestore Entertainment, 1990

TRACY BREGMAN
HAPPY BIRTHDAY TO ME   Columbia, 1981, Canadian

BEAU BREMANN
BOOK OF LOVE   New Line Cinema, 1991

EILEEN BRENNAN
b. September 3, 1935 - Los Angeles, California
Agent: David Shapira & Associates - Sherman Oaks, 818/906-0322

DIVORCE AMERICAN STYLE   Columbia, 1967
THE LAST PICTURE SHOW   Columbia, 1971
PLAYMATES (TF)   ABC Circle Films, 1972
THE BLUE KNIGHT (TF)   Lorimar Productions, 1973
SCARECROW   Warner Bros., 1973
THE STING   Universal, 1973
DAISY MILLER   Paramount, 1974
MY FATHER'S HOUSE (TF)   1975
THE NIGHT THAT PANICKED AMERICA (TF)   Paramount TV, 1975
AT LONG LAST LOVE   20th Century Fox, 1975
HUSTLE   Paramount, 1975
MURDER BY DEATH   Columbia, 1976
THE DEATH OF RICHIE (TF)   Henry Jaffe Enterprises, 1977
THE GREAT SMOKEY ROADBLOCK   *THE LAST OF THE
   COWBOYS*   Dimension, 1978
FM   Universal, 1978
THE CHEAP DETECTIVE   Columbia, 1978
BLACK BEAUTY (MS)   Universal TV, 1978
MY OLD MAN (TF)   Zeitman-McNichol-Halmi Productions, 1979
PRIVATE BENJAMIN ✪   Warner Bros., 1980
WHEN THE CIRCUS CAME TO TOWN   Entheos Unlimited
   Productions/Meteor Films, 1981
THE FUNNY FARM   New World, 1983, Canadian
PANDEMONIUM   MGM/UA, 1982
CLUE   Paramount, 1985

BLOOD VOWS: THE STORY OF A MAFIA WIFE (TF)
    Louis Rudolph Films/Fries Entertainment, 1987
RENTED LIPS   New Century/Vista, 1988
THE NEW ADVENTURES OF PIPPI LONGSTOCKING
    Columbia, 1988
STICKY FINGERS   Spectrafilm, 1988
GOING TO THE CHAPEL (TF)   The Furia Organization/
    Finnegan-Pinchuk Productions, 1988
IT HAD TO BE YOU   Limelite Studios, 1989
STELLA   Buena Vista, 1990
TEXASVILLE   Columbia, 1990
WHITE PALACE   Universal, 1990

AMY BRENNEMAN

BYE BYE LOVE   20th Century Fox, 1995
CASPER   Universal, 1995
NO FEAR   Universal, 1995

EVE BRENNER

THE GREAT MOUSE DETECTIVE (AF)   Buena Vista, 1986 (voice)

MARTIN BREST

b. August 8, 1951 - New York, New York
Agent: CAA - Beverly Hills, 310/288-4545

FAST TIMES AT RIDGEMONT HIGH   Universal, 1982
SPIES LIKE US   Warner Bros., 1985

MAIA BREWTON

ADVENTURES IN BABYSITTING   Buena Vista, 1987
A FAMILY FOR JOE (TF)   Grosso-Jacobson Productions/NBC
    Productions, 1990

BEAU BRIDGES

(Lloyd Vernet Bridges III)
b. December 9, 1941 - Los Angeles, California
Agent: CAA - Beverly Hills, 310/288-4545

FORCE OF EVIL   MGM, 1948
NO MINOR VICES   MGM, 1948
THE RED PONY   Republic, 1949
ZAMBA   1949
THE EXPLOSIVE GENERATION   United Artists, 1961
VILLAGE OF THE GIANTS   Embassy, 1965
THE INCIDENT   20th Century Fox, 1967
FOR LOVE OF IVY   Cinerama Releasing Corporation, 1968
GAILY GAILY   United Artists, 1969
ADAM'S WOMAN   Warner Bros., 1970, Australian
THE LANDLORD   United Artists, 1970
THE CHRISTIAN LICORICE STORE   National General, 1971
HAMMERSMITH IS OUT   Cinerama Releasing Corporation, 1972
CHILD'S PLAY   Paramount, 1972
YOUR THREE MINUTES ARE UP   1973
LOVIN' MOLLY   Columbia, 1974
THE STRANGER WHO LOOKS LIKE ME (TF)   Filmways, 1974
THE OTHER SIDE OF THE MOUNTAIN   Universal, 1975
MEDICAL STORY (TF)   David Gerber Company/Columbia TV, 1975
ONE SUMMER LOVE *DRAGONFLY*   American International, 1976
SWASHBUCKLER   Universal, 1976
TWO MINUTE WARNING   Universal, 1976
GREASED LIGHTNING   Warner Bros., 1977
THE FOUR FEATHERS (TF)   Norman Rosemont Productions/
    Trident Films Ltd., 1978, U.S.-British
THE PRESIDENT'S MISTRESS (TF)   Stephen Friedman/Kings
    Productions, 1978
THE CHILD STEALER (TF)   The Production Company/
    Columbia TV, 1979
THE FIFTH MUSKETEER   Columbia, 1979, Austrian
THE RUNNER STUMBLES   20th Century Fox, 1979
NORMA RAE   20th Century Fox, 1979
SILVER DREAM RACER   Almi Cinema 5, 1980, British
HONKY TONK FREEWAY   Universal/AFD, 1981
LOVE CHILD   The Ladd Company/Warner Bros., 1982
NIGHT CROSSING   Buena Vista, 1982
DANGEROUS COMPANY (TF)   The Dangerous Company/
    Finnegan Associates, 1982
THE KID FROM NOWHERE (TF)   Cates-Bridges Company,
    1982 (also directed)

WITNESS FOR THE PROSECUTION (TF)   Norman Rosemont
    Productions/United Artists Productions, 1982, U.S.-British
HEART LIKE A WHEEL   20th Century Fox, 1983
THE HOTEL NEW HAMPSHIRE   Orion, 1984
THE RED-LIGHT STING (TF)   J.E. Productions/Universal TV, 1984
SPACE (MS)   Stonehenge Productions/Paramount TV, 1985
OUTRAGE! (TF)   Irwin Allen Productions/Columbia TV, 1986
THE THANKSGIVING PROMISE (TF)   Mark H. Ovitz Productions/
    Walt Disney TV, 1986 (also directed)
THE KILLING TIME   New World, 1987
THE WILD PAIR   Trans World Entertainment, 1987 (also directed)
SEVEN HOURS TO JUDGMENT   Trans World Entertainment,
    1988 (also directed)
THE IRON TRIANGLE   Scotti Bros., 1989
JUST ANOTHER SECRET (CTF)   F.F.S. Productions/Taurusfilm/
    Blair Communications/USA Network, 1989, U.S.-British
EVERYBODY'S BABY: THE RESCUE OF JESSICA McCLURE (TF)
    Dick Berg-Stonehenge Productions/The Campbell Soup Company/
    Interscope Productions, 1989
THE FABULOUS BAKER BOYS   20th Century Fox, 1989
THE WIZARD   Universal, 1989
DADDY'S DYIN'...WHO'S GOT THE WILL?   MGM/UA, 1990
WITHOUT WARNING: THE JAMES BRADY STORY (CTF)   HBO
    Pictures/Enigma TV, 1991
MARRIED TO IT   Orion, 1993
THE POSITIVELY TRUE ADVENTURES OF THE ALLEGED TEXAS
    CHEERLEADER-MURDERING MOM (CTF)   Frederick S. Pierce
    Company/Sudden Entertainment Productions, 1993

JEFF BRIDGES

b. December 4, 1949 - Los Angeles, California
Agent: CAA - Beverly Hills, 310/288-4545

THE COMPANY SHE KEEPS   RKO Radio, 1951
HALLS OF ANGER   United Artists, 1970
IN SEARCH OF AMERICA (TF)   Four Star Productions, 1970
THE YIN AND YANG OF MR. GO   1970
THE LAST PICTURE SHOW ❂   Columbia, 1971
FAT CITY   Columbia, 1972
BAD COMPANY   Paramount, 1972
THE LAST AMERICAN HERO   *HARD DRIVER*
    20th Century Fox, 1973
THE ICEMAN COMETH   American Film Theatre, 1973
LOLLY MADONNA XXX   *THE LOLLY-MADONNA WAR*
    MGM, 1973
THUNDERBOLT AND LIGHTFOOT ❂   United Artists, 1974
RANCHO DeLUXE   United Artists, 1975
HEARTS OF THE WEST   MGM/United Artists, 1975
STAY HUNGRY   United Artists, 1976
KING KONG   Paramount, 1976
SOMEBODY KILLED HER HUSBAND   Columbia, 1978
WINTER KILLS   Avco Embassy, 1979
THE AMERICAN SUCCESS CO.   *SUCCESS*   Columbia, 1979,
    West German-U.S.
HEAVEN'S GATE   United Artists, 1980
CUTTER'S WAY   *CUTTER AND BONE*   United Artists
    Classics, 1981
KISS ME GOODBYE   20th Century Fox, 1982
THE LAST UNICORN (AF)   Jensen Farley Pictures, 1982 (voice)
TRON   Buena Vista, 1982
AGAINST ALL ODDS   Columbia, 1984
STARMAN ★   Columbia, 1984
JAGGED EDGE   Columbia, 1985
8 MILLION WAYS TO DIE   TriStar, 1986
THE MORNING AFTER   20th Century Fox, 1986
THE THANKSGIVING PROMISE (TF)   Mark H. Ovitz Productions/
    Walt Disney TV, 1986 (uncredited)
NADINE   TriStar, 1987
TUCKER - THE MAN AND HIS DREAM   Paramount, 1988
SEE YOU IN THE MORNING   Warner Bros., 1989
COLD FEET   Avenue Pictures, 1989 (uncredited)
THE FABULOUS BAKER BOYS   20th Century Fox, 1989
TEXASVILLE   Columbia, 1990
THE FISHER KING   TriStar, 1991
THE VANISHING   20th Century Fox, 1993
AMERICAN HEART   Triton Pictures, 1993
FEARLESS   Warner Bros., 1993
BLOWN AWAY   MGM/UA, 1994
WILD BILL   MGM/UA, 1995

LLOYD BRIDGES
b. January 15, 1913 - San Leandro, California
Agent: William Morris Agency - Beverly Hills, 310/274-7451

THE LONE WOLF TAKES A CHANCE   1941
HERE COMES MR. JORDAN   Columbia, 1941
TWO LATINS FROM MANHATTAN   1941
ATLANTIC CONVOY   Columbia, 1942
ALIAS BOSTON BLACKIE   Columbia, 1942
SHUT MY BIG MOUTH   1942
THE TALK OF THE TOWN   Columbia, 1942
THE HEAT'S ON   Columbia, 1943
SAHARA   Columbia, 1943
PASSPORT TO SUEZ   Columbia, 1943
LOUISIANA HAYRIDE   1944
THE MASTER RACE   RKO Radio, 1944
THE IMPOSTOR   STRANGE CONFESSION   Universal, 1944
A WALK IN THE SUN   20th Century Fox, 1945
MISS SUSIE SLAGLE'S   Paramount, 1945
ABILENE TOWN   United Artists, 1946
CANYON PASSAGE   Universal, 1946
RAMROD   United Artists, 1947
16 FATHOMS DEEP   1948
MOONRISE   Republic, 1948
HOME OF THE BRAVE   United Artists, 1949
TRAPPED   Eagle Lion, 1949
RED CANYON   Universal, 1949
CALAMITY JANE AND SAM BASS   Universal, 1949
COLT .45   Warner Bros., 1950
ROCKETSHIP X-M   Lippert, 1950
THE WHITE TOWER   1950
THE SOUND OF FURY   TRY AND GET ME   United Artists, 1950
LITTLE BIG HORN   Lippert, 1951
THREE STEPS NORTH   1951
THE WHISTLE AT EATON FALLS   Columbia, 1951
HIGH NOON   United Artists, 1952
PLYMOUTH ADVENTURE   MGM, 1952
CITY OF BAD MEN   1953
THE TALL TEXAN   1953
THE KID FROM LEFT FIELD   1953
THE LIMPING MAN   1953, British
PRIDE OF THE BLUE GRASS   Allied Artists, 1954
APACHE WOMAN   American International, 1955
WICHITA   Allied Artists, 1955
WETBACKS   1956
THE RAINMAKER   Paramount, 1956
RIDE OUT FOR REVENGE   United Artists, 1957
THE GODDESS   Columbia, 1958
AROUND THE WORLD UNDER THE SEA   MGM, 1966
ATTACK ON THE IRON COAST   United Artists, 1968, U.S.-British
DARING GAME   Paramount, 1968
THE HAPPY ENDING   United Artists, 1969
THE LOVE WAR (TF)   Thomas-Spelling Productions, 1970
THE SILENT GUN (TF)   Paramount TV, 1969
SILENT NIGHT, LONELY NIGHT (TF)   Universal TV, 1969
LOST FLIGHT (TF)   1971
TO FIND A MAN   THE BOY NEXT DOOR/SEX AND THE
   TEENAGER   Columbia, 1972
HAUNTS OF THE VERY RICH (TF)   ABC Circle Films, 1972
TROUBLE COMES TO TOWN (TF)   ABC Circle Films, 1973
RUNNING WILD   1973
CRIME CLUB (TF)   CBS, Inc., 1973
DEATH RACE (TF)   Universal TV, 1973
STOWAWAY TO THE MOON (TF)   20th Century Fox TV, 1975
COP ON THE BEAT   THE RETURN OF JOE FORRESTER (TF)
   Columbia TV, 1975
ROOTS (MS)   Wolper Productions, 1977
TELETHON (TF)   ABC Circle Films, 1977
THE GREAT WALLENDAS (TF)   Daniel Wilson Productions, 1978
THE CRITICAL LIST (TF)   MTM Productions, 1978
THE FIFTH MUSKETEER   Columbia, 1979, Austrian
BEAR ISLAND   Taft International, 1980, Canadian-British
AIRPLANE!   Paramount, 1980
JOHN STEINBECK'S EAST OF EDEN   EAST OF EDEN (MS)
   Mace Neufeld Productions, 1981
THE BLUE AND THE GRAY (MS)   Larry White-Lou Reda
   Productions/Columbia TV, 1982
GRACE KELLY (TF)   The Kota Company/Embassy TV, 1983
AIRPLANE II: THE SEQUEL   Paramount, 1982
PAPER DOLLS (TF)   Mandy Productions/MGM-UA TV, 1984

WEEKEND WARRIORS   The Movie Store, 1986
DRESS GRAY (MS)   von Zerneck Productions/
   Warner Bros. TV, 1986
THE THANKSGIVING PROMISE (TF)   Mark H. Ovitz Productions/
   Walt Disney TV, 1986
THE WILD PAIR   Trans World Entertainment, 1987
TUCKER - THE MAN AND HIS DREAM   Paramount,
   1988 (uncredited)
SHE WAS MARKED FOR MURDER (TF)   Jack Grossbart
   Productions, 1988
COUSINS   Paramount, 1989
WINTER PEOPLE   Columbia, 1989
CROSS OF FIRE (TF)   Leonard Hill Films, 1989
CAPITAL NEWS (TF)   MTM Enterprises, 1990
JOE VERSUS THE VOLCANO   Warner Bros., 1990
LEONA HELMSLEY: THE QUEEN OF MEAN (TF)
   Fries Entertainment/Goiman-Taylor Entertainment, 1990
HOT SHOTS!   20th Century Fox, 1991
HONEY, I BLEW UP THE KID   Buena Vista, 1992
HOT SHOTS! PART DEUX   20th Century Fox, 1993
BLOWN AWAY   MGM/UA, 1994

DANIEL BRIERE
THE DECLINE OF THE AMERICAN EMPIRE   Cineplex Odeon,
   1986, Canadian

RICHARD BRIERS
HENRY V   Samuel Goldwyn Company, 1989, British
MARY SHELLEY'S FRANKENSTEIN   TriStar, 1994

RICHARD BRIGHT
PANIC IN NEEDLE PARK   20th Century Fox, 1971
THE GODFATHER   Paramount, 1972
THE GETAWAY   National General, 1972
THE GODFATHER, PART II   Paramount, 1974
MARATHON MAN   Paramount, 1976
RED HEAT   TriStar, 1988
THE REF   Buena Vista, 1994

FRAN BRILL
OLD ENOUGH   Orion Classics, 1984

STEVEN BRILL
Agent: Writers & Artists Agency - Los Angeles, 213/820-2240

sex, lies, and videotape   Miramax Films, 1989

VICTORIA BRILL
JIMMY HOLLYWOOD   Paramount, 1994

NICK BRIMBLE
ROBIN HOOD: PRINCE OF THIEVES   Warner Bros., 1991

WILFORD BRIMLEY
(A. Wilford Brimley)
b. September 27, 1934 - Salt Lake City, Utah

THE ELECTRIC HORSEMAN   Columbia, 1979
THE CHINA SYNDROME   Columbia, 1979
RODEO GIRL (TF)   Steckler Productions/Marble Arch
   Productions, 1980
BRUBAKER   20th Century Fox, 1980
BORDERLINE   AFD, 1980
ABSENCE OF MALICE   Columbia, 1981
DEATH VALLEY   Universal, 1982
THE THING   Universal, 1982
HIGH ROAD TO CHINA   Warner Bros., 1983, U.S.-Yugoslavian
TENDER MERCIES   Universal/AFD, 1983
10 TO MIDNIGHT   Cannon, 1983
TOUGH ENOUGH   20th Century Fox, 1983
HARRY AND SON   Orion, 1984
THE STONE BOY   TLC Films/20th Century Fox, 1984
THE HOTEL NEW HAMPSHIRE   Orion, 1984
THE NATURAL   TriStar, 1984
COUNTRY   Buena Vista, 1984
COCOON   20th Century Fox, 1985

EWOKS: THE BATTLE FOR ENDOR (TF)   Lucasfilm, Ltd., 1985
REMO WILLIAMS: THE ADVENTURE BEGINS   Orion, 1985
AMERICAN JUSTICE   *JACKALS*   The Movie Store, 1986
ACT OF VENGEANCE (CTF)   HBO Premiere Films/Telepix
   Canada Corporation, 1986, U.S.-Canadian
THOMPSON'S LAST RUN (TF)   Cypress Point Productions, 1986
END OF THE LINE   Orion Classics, 1988
COCOON: THE RETURN   20th Century Fox, 1988
ETERNITY   Academy Entertainment, 1990
THE FIRM   Paramount, 1993
HARD TARGET   Universal, 1993

CHRISTIE BRINKLEY
b. February 2, 1954

NATIONAL LAMPOON'S VACATION   Warner Bros., 1983

MORGAN BRITTANY
GYPSY   Warner Bros., 1962
THE BIRDS   Universal, 1963
MARNIE   Universal, 1964
YOURS, MINE AND OURS   United Artists, 1968
THE DAY OF THE LOCUST   Paramount, 1975
GABLE AND LOMBARD   Universal, 1976
SAMURAI (TF)   Danny Thomas Productions/Universal TV, 1979
DEATH CAR ON THE FREEWAY (TF)   Shpetner Productions, 1979
STUNT SEVEN (TF)   Martin Poll Productions, 1979
GLITTER (TF)   Aaron Spelling Productions, 1984
LBJ: THE EARLY YEARS (TF)   Brice Productions/Louis Rudolph
   Films/Fries Entertainment, 1987
PERRY MASON: THE CASE OF THE SCANDALOUS
   SCOUNDREL (TF)   The Fred Silverman Company/Strathmore
   Productions/Viacom, 1987

JIM BROADBENT
Agent: William Morris Agency - Beverly Hills, 310/274-7451

WIDOWS' PEAK   Fine Line Features/New Line Cinema, 1994
PRINCESS CARABOO   TriStar, 1994
ROUGH MAGIC   Savoy Pictures, 1995

JEFFREY BROADHURST
GYPSY (TF)   RHI Entertainment, 1993

KENT BROADHURST
Agent: Silver, Kass & Massetti Agency - Los Angeles, 310/289-0909

THE DARK HALF   Orion, 1993

ANNE BROCHET
Agent: Susan Smith & Associates - Beverly Hills, 213/852-4777

TOUS LES MATINS DU MONDE   October Films, 1992, French

PHIL BROCK
P.O.W. THE ESCAPE   Cannon, 1986

STANLEY BROCK
TIN MEN   Buena Vista, 1987
UHF   Orion, 1989

ROY BROCKSMITH
BIG BUSINESS   Buena Vista, 1988
THE WAR OF THE ROSES   20th Century Fox, 1989
TOTAL RECALL   TriStar, 1990
THE ROAD TO WELLVILLE   Columbia, 1994

MATTHEW BRODERICK
b. March 21, 1962 - New York, New York
Agent: CAA - Beverly Hills, 310/288-4545

MAX DUGAN RETURNS   20th Century Fox, 1983
WARGAMES   MGM/UA, 1983
LADYHAWKE   Warner Bros., 1985

ON VALENTINE'S DAY   Angelika Films, 1986
FERRIS BUELLER'S DAY OFF   Paramount, 1986
ON VALENTINE'S DAY   *STORY OF A MARRIAGE*
   Angelika Films, 1986
PROJECT X   20th Century Fox, 1987
BILOXI BLUES   Universal, 1988
TORCH SONG TRILOGY   New Line Cinema, 1988
FAMILY BUSINESS   TriStar, 1989
GLORY   TriStar, 1989
THE FRESHMAN   TriStar, 1990
OUT ON A LIMB   Universal, 1992
THE NIGHT WE NEVER MET   Miramax Films, 1993
THE LION KING (AF)   Buena Vista, 1994 (voice)
THE ROAD TO WELLVILLE   Columbia, 1994
MRS. PARKER AND THE VICIOUS CIRCLE   Fine Line Features/
   New Line Cinema, 1994
INFINITY   1995

JAMES BROLIN
b. July 18, 1940 - Los Angeles, California

TAKE HER, SHE'S MINE   20th Century Fox, 1963
GOODBYE, CHARLIE   20th Century Fox, 1964
VON RYAN'S EXPRESS   20th Century Fox, 1965
MORITURI   *THE SABOTEUR, CODE NAME MORITURI*
   20th Century Fox, 1965
FANTASTIC VOYAGE   20th Century Fox, 1966
OUR MAN FLINT   20th Century Fox, 1966
THE BOSTON STRANGLER   20th Century Fox, 1968
MARCUS WELBY, M.D.   *A MATTER OF HUMANITIES* (TF)
   Universal TV, 1968
SHORT WALK TO DAYLIGHT (TF)   Universal TV, 1972
SKYJACKED   MGM, 1972
WESTWORLD   MGM, 1973
TRAPPED (TF)   Universal TV, 1973
CLASS OF '63 (TF)   Metromedia Productions/Stonehenge
   Productions, 1973
GABLE AND LOMBARD   Universal, 1976
THE CAR   Universal, 1977
STEEL COWBOY (TF)   Roger Gimbel Productions/EMI TV, 1978
CAPRICORN ONE   20th Century Fox, 1978
THE AMITYVILLE HORROR   American International, 1979
NIGHT OF THE JUGGLER   Columbia, 1980
HIGH RISK   American Cinema, 1981
ARTHUR HAILEY'S HOTEL   *HOTEL* (TF)   Aaron Spelling
   Productions, 1983
PEE-WEE'S BIG ADVENTURE   Warner Bros., 1985
BEVERLY HILLS COWGIRL BLUES (TF)   The Leonard Goldberg
   Company, 1985
INTIMATE ENCOUNTERS (TF)   Larry Thompson Productions/Donna
   Mills Productions/Columbia TV, 1986
DEEP DARK SECRETS (TF)   Gross-Weston Productions/Fries
   Entertainment, 1987
PARALLEL LIVES (CTF)   Showtime Entertainment, 1994

JOSH BROLIN
Agent: ICM - Beverly Hills, 310/550-4000

THE GOONIES   Warner Bros., 1985
THRASHIN'   Fries Entertainment, 1986
PRISON FOR CHILDREN (TF)   Knopf-Simons Productions/Viacom
   Productions, 1987

VALRI BROMFIELD
WHO'S HARRY CRUMB?   TriStar, 1989
NOTHING BUT TROUBLE   Warner Bros., 1991
NEEDFUL THINGS   Columbia, 1993

ELEANOR BRON
b. Edgware, England

HELP!   United Artists, 1965, British
ALFIE   Paramount, 1966, British
BEDAZZLED   20th Century-Fox, 1967, British
TWO FOR THE ROAD   20th Century Fox, 1967, British-U.S.
WOMEN IN LOVE   United Artists, 1970, British
TURTLE DIARY   Samuel Goldwyn Company, 1985, British

LITTLE DORRIT, PART I: NOBODY'S FAULT   Cannon,
   1988, British
LITTLE DORRIT, PART II: LITTLE DORRIT'S STORY   Cannon,
   1988, British
INTRIGUE (TF)   Crew Neck Productions/Linnea Productions/
   Columbia TV, 1988
THE FOOL   Sands Films, Ltd./Film Four International/British
   Screen/John Tyler, 1990, British
BLACK BEAUTY   Warner Bros., 1994, British-U.S.
A LITTLE PRINCESS   Warner Bros., 1994

CHARLES BRONSON
(Charles Bunchinsky/Buchinsky/Buchinski)
b. November 3, 1921 - Ehrenfield, Pennsylvania
Agent: William Morris Agency - Beverly Hills, 310/274-7451

YOU'RE IN THE NAVY NOW   *USS TEAKETTLE*
   20th Century Fox, 1951
THE PEOPLE AGAINST O'HARA   MGM, 1951
THE MOB   Columbia, 1951
RED SKIES OF MONTANA   1952
MY SIX CONVICTS   Universal, 1952
THE MARRYING KIND   Columbia, 1952
PAT AND MIKE   MGM, 1952
DIPLOMATIC COURIER   20th Century Fox, 1952
BLOODHOUNDS OF BROADWAY   1952
HOUSE OF WAX   Warner Bros., 1953
MISS SADIE THOMPSON   Columbia, 1954
CRIME WAVE   1954
TENNESSEE CHAMP   1954
RIDING SHOTGUN   Warner Bros., 1954
APACHE   United Artists, 1954
VERA CRUZ   United Artists, 1954
DRUM BEAT   Warner Bros., 1954
BIG HOUSE, U.S.A.   United Artists, 1955
TARGET ZERO   1955
JUBAL   Columbia, 1956
RUN OF THE ARROW   20th Century Fox, 1957
GANG WAR   1958
SHOWDOWN AT BOOT HILL   1958
MACHINE GUN KELLY   American International, 1958
WHEN HELL BROKE LOOSE   1958
NEVER SO FEW   MGM, 1959
THE MAGNIFICENT SEVEN   United Artists, 1960
MASTER OF THE WORLD   American International, 1961
A THUNDER OF DRUMS   MGM, 1961
X-15   United Artists, 1961
LONELY ARE THE BRAVE   Universal, 1962
KID GALAHAD   United Artists, 1962
THE GREAT ESCAPE   United Artists, 1963
4 FOR TEXAS   Warner Bros., 1963
THE SANDPIPER   MGM, 1965
BATTLE OF THE BULGE   Warner Bros., 1965
THIS PROPERTY IS CONDEMNED   Paramount, 1966
THE DIRTY DOZEN   MGM, 1967
GUNS FOR SAN SEBASTIAN   *LA BATAILLE DE SAN SEBASTIAN*
   MGM, 1968, French-Italian-Mexican
VILLA RIDES!   Paramount, 1968
ADIEU L'AMI   1968, French
ONCE UPON A TIME IN THE WEST   Paramount, 1969, Italian-U.S.
LOLA   *TWINKY*   American International, 1969, British-Italian
RIDER ON THE RAIN   Avco Embassy, 1970, French-Italian
YOU CAN'T WIN 'EM ALL   *THE DUBIOUS PATRIOTS*
   1970, British
THE FAMILY   *VIOLENT CITY*   1970, Italian-French
COLD SWEAT   *DE LA PART DES COPAINS*   Emerson, 1970,
   French-Italian
SOMEONE BEHIND THE DOOR   GSF, 1971, French
SOLEIL ROUGE   1971, French-Italian-Spanish
THE VALACHI PAPERS   *JOE VALACHI: I SEGRETI DI COSA
   NOSTRA*   Columbia, 1972, Italian-French
CHATO'S LAND   United Artists, 1972, Spanish-British
THE MECHANIC   United Artists, 1972
THE VALDEZ HORSES   *CHINO*   Intercontinental, 1973,
   Italian-Spanish-French
THE STONE KILLER   Columbia, 1973, U.S.-British
MR. MAJESTYK   United Artists, 1974
DEATH WISH   Paramount, 1974

BREAKOUT   Columbia, 1975
HARD TIMES   Columbia, 1975
BREAKHEART PASS   United Artists, 1976
ST. IVES   Warner Bros., 1976
FROM NOON TILL THREE   United Artists, 1976
RAID ON ENTEBBE (TF)   Edgar J. Scherick Associates/20th Century
   Fox TV, 1977
THE WHITE BUFFALO   United Artists, 1977
TELEFON   MGM/United Artists, 1977
LOVE AND BULLETS   AFD, 1979, British
CABOBLANCO   Avco Embassy, 1981
DEATH HUNT   20th Century Fox, 1981
DEATH WISH II   Filmways, 1982
10 TO MIDNIGHT   Cannon, 1983
THE EVIL THAT MEN DO   TriStar, 1984
DEATH WISH 3   Cannon, 1985
MURPHY'S LAW   Cannon, 1986
ASSASSINATION   Cannon, 1987
DEATH WISH 4: THE CRACKDOWN   Cannon, 1987
MESSENGER OF DEATH   Cannon, 1988
KINJITE (FORBIDDEN SUBJECTS)   Cannon, 1989
THE INDIAN RUNNER   MGM-Pathe, 1991
DEATH WISH V: THE FACE OF DEATH   Trimark Pictures, 1994

NICKY BRONSON
ROCKET GIBRALTAR   Columbia, 1988

IRINA BROOK
THE GIRL IN THE PICTURE   Samuel Goldwyn Company,
   1986, British

JAYNE BROOK
CLEAN SLATE   MGM/UA, 1994

JACQUELINE BROOKES
Agent: William Morris Agency - Beverly Hills, 310/274-7451

THE GOOD SON   20th Century Fox, 1993

ALBERT BROOKS
b. July 22, 1947 - Los Angeles, California

TAXI DRIVER   Columbia, 1976
REAL LIFE   Paramount, 1979 (also directed)
PRIVATE BENJAMIN   Warner Bros., 1980
MODERN ROMANCE   Columbia, 1981 (also directed)
TERMS OF ENDEARMENT   Paramount, 1983 (voice)
TWILIGHT ZONE—THE MOVIE   Warner Bros., 1983
UNFAITHFULLY YOURS   20th Century Fox, 1984
LOST IN AMERICA   The Geffen Company/Warner Bros.,
   1985 (also directed)
BROADCAST NEWS ✪   20th Century Fox, 1987
DEFENDING YOUR LIFE   The Geffen Company/Warner Bros.,
   1991 (also directed)
I'LL DO ANYTHING   Columbia, 1994
THE SCOUT   20th Century Fox, 1994

JOEL BROOKS
STRANDED (TF)   Tim Flack Productions/Columbia TV, 1986
SKIN DEEP   20th Century Fox, 1989
INDECENT PROPOSAL   Paramount, 1993

MEL BROOKS
(Melvin Kaminsky)
b. June 28, 1926 - New York, New York

PUTNEY SWOPE   Cinema 5, 1969
THE TWELVE CHAIRS   UMC, 1970 (also directed)
BLAZING SADDLES   Warner Bros., 1974 (also directed)
SILENT MOVIE   20th Century Fox, 1976 (also directed)
HIGH ANXIETY   20th Century Fox, 1977
THE MUPPET MOVIE   AFD, 1979, British
HISTORY OF THE WORLD—PART 1   20th Century Fox,
   1981 (also directed)
TO BE OR NOT TO BE   20th Century Fox, 1983

SPACEBALLS   MGM/UA, 1987 (also directed)
LIFE STINKS   MGM-Pathe, 1991 (also directed)
ROBIN HOOD: MEN IN TIGHTS   20th Century Fox,
   1993 (also directed)
THE LITTLE RASCALS   Universal, 1994

RANDI BROOKS
TERRORVISION   Empire Pictures, 1986

RANDY BROOKS
Agent: Paul Kohner, Inc. - Los Angeles, 310/550-1060

8 MILLION WAYS TO DIE   TriStar, 1986

RICHARD BROOKS
THE HIDDEN   New Line Cinema, 1987
84 CHARLIE MOPIC   New Century/Vista, 1989

ANTHONY BROPHY
THE RUN OF THE COUNTRY   Columbia, 1995

PIERCE BROSNAN
b. May 16, 1952 - County Meath, Ireland
Agent: CAA - Beverly Hills, 310/288-4545

THE LONG GOOD FRIDAY   Embassy, 1980, British
THE MANIONS OF AMERICA (MS)   Roger Gimbel Productions/
   EMI TV/Argonaut Films, Ltd., 1981
NANCY ASTOR (TF)   1981
NOMADS   Atlantic Releasing Corporation, 1986
THE FOURTH PROTOCOL   Lorimar, 1987, British
REMINGTON STEELE: THE STEELE THAT WOULDN'T DIE (TF)
   MTM Productions, 1987
JAMES CLAVELL'S NOBLE HOUSE   *NOBLE HOUSE* (MS)
   Noble House Productions, Ltd./De Laurentiis Entertainment
   Group, 1988
TAFFIN   MGM/UA, 1988, U.S.-Irish
THE DECEIVERS   Cinecom, 1988
AROUND THE WORLD IN 80 DAYS (MS)   Harmony/Gold/
   ReteEuropa/Valente-Baerwald Productions, 1989
HEIST (CTF)   HBO Pictures/Chris-Rose Productions/
   Paramount TV, 1989
MISTER JOHNSON   Avenue Pictures, 1991
STEPHEN KING'S THE LAWNMOWER MAN
   New Line Cinema, 1992
MRS. DOUBTFIRE   20th Century Fox, 1993
LOVE AFFAIR   Warner Bros., 1994
ROBINSON CRUSOE   Miramax Films, 1995
GOLDENEYE   MGM/UA, 1995

BROTHER THEODORE
THE 'BURBS   Universal, 1989

BLAIR BROWN
b. 1948 - Washington D.C.
Agent: ICM - Beverly Hills, 310/550-4000

THE CHOIRBOYS   Universal, 1977
THE QUINNS (TF)   Daniel Wilson Productions, 1977
ELEANOR AND FRANKLIN: THE WHITE HOUSE YEARS (TF)
   Talent Associates, 1977
ARTHUR HAILEY'S WHEELS   *WHEELS* (MS)
   Universal TV, 1978
AND I ALONE SURVIVED (TF)   Jerry Leider-OJL
   Productions, 1978
THE CHILD STEALER (TF)   The Production Company/
   Columbia TV, 1979
ONE-TRICK PONY   Warner Bros., 1980
ALTERED STATES   Warner Bros., 1980
CONTINENTAL DIVIDE   Universal, 1981
KENNEDY (MS)   Central Independent Television Productions/
   Alan Landsburg Productions, 1983, British-U.S.
A FLASH OF GREEN   Spectrafilm, 1984
THE BAD SEED (TF)   Hajeno Productions/Warner Bros. TV, 1985
SPACE (MS)   Stonehenge Productions/Paramount TV, 1985

HANDS OF A STRANGER (MS)   Edgar J. Scherick Productions/
   Taft Entertainment TV, 1987
STEALING HOME   Warner Bros., 1988
STRAPLESS   Miramax Films, 1990
PASSED AWAY   Buena Vista, 1992

BRUCE BROWN
THE ENDLESS SUMMER II (FD)   New Line Cinema, 1994
   (narration; also directed)

BRYAN BROWN
b. 1947 - Sydney, Australia
Agent: CAA - Beverly Hills, 310/288-4545

NEWSFRONT   New Yorker, 1978, Australian
BREAKER MORANT   New World/Quartet, 1979, Australian
THE CHANT OF JIMMIE BLACKSMITH   1980
WINTER OF OUR DREAMS   Satori, 1981, Australian
A TOWN LIKE ALICE (MS)   Seven Network/Victorian Film
   Corporation, 1981, Australian
FAR EAST   Filmco Australia, 1983, Australian
THE THORN BIRDS (MS)   David L. Wolper-Stan Margulies
   Productions/Edward Lewis Productions/Warner Bros. TV, 1983
KIM (TF)   London Films, 1984, British
GIVE MY REGARDS TO BROAD STREET   20th Century Fox,
   1984, British
PARKER   Virgin Films, 1985, British
REBEL   Vestron, 1985, Australian
TAI-PAN   DEG, 1986
F/X   Orion, 1986
THE GOOD WIFE   *THE UMBRELLA WOMAN*   Atlantic Releasing
   Corporation, 1986, Australian
THE SHIRALEE (MS)   SAFC Productions, 1988, Australian
COCKTAIL   Buena Vista, 1988
GORILLAS IN THE MIST   Warner Bros./Universal, 1988
F/X 2 - THE DEADLY ART OF ILLUSION   Orion, 1991
SWEET TALKER   New Line Cinema, 1991
PRISONERS OF THE SUN   Skouras Pictures, 1991
BLAME IT ON THE BELLBOY   Buena Vista, 1992, British

CAITLIN BROWN
DON JUAN DE MARCO AND THE CENTERFOLD   New Line
   Cinema, 1995

CLANCY BROWN
Agent: Paradigm - Los Angeles, 310/277-4400

THE BRIDE   Columbia, 1985, British
HIGHLANDER   20th Century Fox, 1986, British-U.S.
THUNDER ALLEY   Cannon, 1986
EXTREME PREJUDICE   TriStar, 1987
SHOOT TO KILL   Buena Vista, 1988
JOHNNY RYAN (TF)   Dan Curtis TV Productions/MGM-UA TV/
   NBC Productions, 1990
BLUE STEEL   MGM/UA, 1990
WAITING FOR THE LIGHT   Triumph Releasing Corporation, 1990
AMBITION   Miramax Films, 1991
LOVECRAFT (CTF)   HBO Pictures/Pacific Western
   Productions, 1991
PAST MIDNIGHT   New Line Cinema, 1992
PET SEMATARY II   Paramount, 1992
LAST LIGHT (CTF)   Showtime Networks, Inc./Stillwater
   Productions, 1993
THE SHAWSHANK REDEMPTION   Columbia, 1994

DWIER BROWN
FIELD OF DREAMS   Universal, 1989
THE GUARDIAN   Universal, 1990

ERNIE BROWN
WISDOM   20th Century Fox, 1986

GARRETT M. BROWN
Agent: Gersh Agency - Beverly Hills, 310/274-6611

ZELIG   Orion/Warner Bros., 1983

GEORG STANFORD BROWN

THE COMEDIANS   MGM, 1967, British
DAYTON'S DEVILS   Commonwealth United, 1968
BULLITT   Warner Bros., 1968
COLOSSUS: THE FORBIN PROJECT   *THE FORBIN PROJECT*
  Universal, 1970
THE MAN   Paramount, 1972
WILD IN THE SKY   *BLACK JACK*   1972
ROOTS (MS)   Wolper Productions, 1977
ROOTS: THE NEXT GENERATIONS (MS)   Wolper Productions,
  1979 (also co-directed)
THE NIGHT THE CITY SCREAMED (TF)   David Gerber
  Company, 1980
STIR CRAZY   Columbia, 1980
IN DEFENSE OF KIDS (TF)   MTM Enterprises, 1983
THE JESSE OWENS STORY (TF)   Harve Bennett Productions/
  Paramount TV, 1984
NORTH AND SOUTH (MS)   Wolper Productions/Warner
  Bros. TV, 1985
ALONE IN THE NEON JUNGLE (TF)   Robert Halmi, Inc.,
  1988 (also directed)

JIM BROWN
(James Nathaniel Brown)
b. February 17, 1935 - St. Simon Island

RIO CONCHOS   20th Century Fox, 1964
THE DIRTY DOZEN   MGM, 1967
DARK OF THE SUN   *THE MERCENARIES*   MGM, 1968, British
THE SPLIT   MGM, 1968
ICE STATION ZEBRA   MGM, 1968
RIOT   Paramount, 1969
100 RIFLES   20th Century Fox, 1969
TICK TICK TICK   MGM, 1970
EL CONDOR   National General, 1970
THE GRASSHOPPER   National General, 1970
KENNER   MGM, 1971
SLAUGHTER   American International, 1972
BLACK GUNN   1972
SLAUGHTER'S BIG RIP-OFF   American International, 1973
I ESCAPED FROM DEVIL'S ISLAND   United Artists, 1973
THE SLAMS   MGM, 1973
THREE THE HARD WAY   1974
TAKE A HARD RIDE   20th Century Fox, 1975
KID VENGEANCE   Irwin Yablans, 1977, U.S.-Israeli
FINGERS   Brut Productions, 1978
ONE DOWN, TWO TO GO   Almi Films, 1982
LADY BLUE (TF)   David Gerber Productions/MGM-UA TV, 1985
CRACK HOUSE   Cannon, 1989
I'M GONNA GIT YOU SUCKA   MGM/UA, 1989

JULIE BROWN
Agent: William Morris Agency - Beverly Hills, 310/274-7451

EARTH GIRLS ARE EASY   Vestron, 1989
SHAKES THE CLOWN   I.R.S. Releasing, 1992

RALPH BROWN
Agent: Susan Smith & Associates - Beverly Hills, 213/852-4777

IMPROMPTU   Hemdale, 1990, U.S.-French
ALIEN 3   20th Century Fox, 1992, U.S.-British
WAYNE'S WORLD 2   Paramount, 1993

REB BROWN
Agent: Fred Amsel & Associates - Los Angeles, 213/939-1188

DEATH OF A SOLDIER   Scotti Brothers, 1986, Australian
CAGE   New Century/Vista, 1989

ROBERT BROWN
LICENCE TO KILL   MGM/UA, 1989, British

ROGER AARON BROWN
TALL TALE   Buena Vista, 1994

RUTH BROWN
HAIR SPRAY   New Line Cinema, 1988
TRUE IDENTITY   Buena Vista, 1991

SALLY BROWN
CRAWLSPACE   Empire Pictures, 1986

SHARON BROWN
FOR KEEPS   TriStar, 1988

THOMAS BROWN
Agent: Century Artists, Ltd. - Beverly Hills, 310/273-4366

HONEY, I SHRUNK THE KIDS   Buena Vista, 1989

WENDELL BROWN
MAD MAGAZINE PRESENTS UP THE ACADEMY   *UP THE*
  ACADEMY   Warner Bros., 1980

W.H. BROWN
THE ACCIDENTAL TOURIST   Warner Bros., 1988

WOODY BROWN
Agent: Gordon/Rosson Talent Agency - Studio City, 818/509-1900

THE ACCUSED   Paramount, 1988

LESLIE BROWNE
THE TURNING POINT ✪   20th Century Fox, 1977
NIJINSKY   Paramount, 1980

ROBERT ALAN BROWNE
PSYCHO III   Universal, 1986

ROSCOE LEE BROWNE
b. May 2, 1925 - Woodbury, New Jersey
Agent: Susan Smith & Associates - Beverly Hills, 213/852-4777

THE CONNECTION   Films Around the World, 1962
BLACK LIKE ME   1964
TERROR IN THE CITY   1966
THE COMEDIANS   MGM, 1967, British
UP TIGHT   Paramount, 1968
TOPAZ   Universal, 1969
THE LIBERATION OF L.B. JONES   Columbia, 1970
CISCO PIKE   Columbia, 1972
THE COWBOYS   Warner Bros., 1972
THE WORLD'S GREATEST ATHLETE   Buena Vista, 1973
SUPERFLY T.N.T.   Paramount, 1973
UPTOWN SATURDAY NIGHT   Warner Bros., 1974
LOGAN'S RUN   MGM/United Artists, 1976
TWILIGHT'S LAST GLEAMING   Allied Artists, 1977,
  U.S.-West German
NOTHING PERSONAL   American International, 1980, Canadian
LEGAL EAGLES   Universal, 1986
JUMPIN' JACK FLASH   20th Century Fox, 1986
STUCK WITH EACH OTHER (TF)   Nexus Productions, 1989
LADY IN A CORNER (TF)   Sagaponack Films/Pantheon Pictures/
  Allan Leicht Productions, 1989

BO BRUNDIN
LATE FOR DINNER   Columbia, 1991

PHILIP BRUNS
BETRAYED BY INNOCENCE (TF)   InterPlanetary Pictures/
  CBS Entertainment, 1986
RETURN OF THE LIVING DEAD PART II   Lorimar, 1988

ERIC BRUSKOTTER
MAJOR LEAGUE II   Warner Bros., 1994

KARIS BRYANT
THE SUBSTITUTE WIFE (TF)   Frederick S. Pierce Company, 1994

LEE BRYANT
AIRPLANE! Paramount, 1980
DEATHMASK 1984

MICHAEL BRYANT
b. April 5, 1928 - London, England

WALK IN THE SHADOW *LIFE FOR RUTH* Continental,
   1962, British
THE MIND BENDERS American International, 1963, British
THE DEADLY AFFAIR Columbia, 1967, British
TORTURE GARDEN Columbia, 1968, British
GOODBYE MR. CHIPS MGM, 1969, British
MUMSY, NANNY ,SONNY AND GIRLY *GIRLY* Cinerama
   Releasing Corporation, 1970, British
NICHOLAS AND ALEXANDRA Columbia, 1971, British
THE RULING CLASS Avco Embassy, 1972, British
CARAVAN TO VACCARES Bryanston, 1976, British-French
GHANDI Columbia, 1982, British-Indian
SAKHAROV (CTF) HBO Premiere Films/Titus Productions,
   1984, U.S.-British

TODD BRYANT
Agent: Ambrosio-Mortimer - Beverly Hills, 310/274-4274

STAR TREK V: THE FINAL FRONTIER Paramount, 1989
THE PUPPET MASTERS Buena Vista, 1994

YVONNE BRYCELAND
JOHNNY HANDSOME TriStar, 1989

LARRY BRYGGMAN
DIE HARD 3 20th Century Fox, 1995

ANDREW BRYNIARSKI
HUDSON HAWK TriStar, 1991

ERIN BUCHANAN
SISTER ISLAND 1995

MILES BUCHANAN
BLISS New World, 1985, Australian

SIMONE BUCHANAN
SHAME Skouras Pictures, 1988, Australian

BETTY BUCKLEY
b. July 3, 1947 - Ft. Worth, Texas

CARRIE United Artists, 1976
THE ORDEAL OF BILL CARNEY (TF) Belle Company/Comworld
   Productions, 1981
TENDER MERCIES Universal/AFD, 1983
THE THREE WISHES OF BILLY GRIER (TF)
   I & C Productions, 1984
EVERGREEN (MS) Edgar J. Scherick Associates/Metromedia
   Producers Corporation, 1985
ROSES ARE FOR THE RICH (TF) Phoenix Entertainment
   Group, 1987
FRANTIC Warner Bros., 1988
ANOTHER WOMAN Orion, 1988
BABYCAKES (TF) Konigsberg-Sanitsky Productions, 1989
WYATT EARP Warner Bros., 1994

KEITH BUCKLEY
HALF MOON STREET 20th Century Fox, 1986, British

SUSAN BUCKNER
GREASE Paramount, 1978
DEADLY BLESSING United Artists, 1981

SUSAN BUGG
VIBES Columbia, 1988

GENEVIEVE BUJOLD
b. July 1, 1942 - Montreal, Quebec, Canada
Agent: The Blake Agency - Beverly Hills, 310/246-0241

FRENCH CAN CAN *ONLY THE FRENCH CAN* United Motion
   Picture Organization, 1954, French
THE ADOLESCENTS 1964, Canadian-French-Italian-Japanese
LA GUERRE EST FINIE Brandon, 1966, French-Swedish
KING OF HEARTS *LE ROI DE COEUR* Lopert, 1967,
   French-Italian
THE THIEF OF PARIS *LE VOLEUR* Lopert, 1967, French-Italian
ISABEL Paramount, 1968, Canadian
ANNE OF THE THOUSAND DAYS ★ Universal, 1969, British
ACT OF THE HEART *ACTE DU COEUR* Universal,
   1970, Canadian
THE TROJAN WOMEN Cinerama Releasing Corporation, 1971,
   British-Greek
JOURNEY EPOH, 1972, Canadian
KAMOURASKA New Line Cinema, 1974, Canadian
EARTHQUAKE Universal, 1974
SWASHBUCKLER Universal, 1976
OBSESSION Columbia, 1976
ALEX & THE GYPSY 20th Century Fox, 1976
ANOTHER MAN, ANOTHER CHANCE United Artists,
   1977, U.S.-French
COMA MGM/United Artists, 1978
MURDER BY DECREE Avco Embassy, 1979, Canadian-British
FINAL ASSIGNMENT Almi Cinema 5, 1980, Canadian
THE LAST FLIGHT OF NOAH'S ARK Buena Vista, 1980
MONSIGNOR 20th Century Fox, 1982
TIGHTROPE Warner Bros., 1984
CHOOSE ME Island Alive/New Cinema, 1984
TROUBLE IN MIND Alive Films, 1985
THE MODERNS Alive Films, 1988
DEAD RINGERS 20th Century Fox, 1988
RED EARTH, WHITE EARTH (TF) Chris-Rose Productions, 1989
FALSE IDENTITY RKO Pictures, 1990
A PAPER WEDDING Capitol Entertainment, 1991

JOYCE BULIFANT
AIRPLANE! Paramount, 1980

FRANCESCA BULLER
Agent: Susan Smith & Associates - Beverly Hills, 213/852-4777

DECEIVED Buena Vista, 1991

SANDRA BULLOCK
Agent: UTA - Beverly Hills, 310/273-6700

BIONIC SHOWDOWN: THE SIX-MILLION DOLLAR MAN AND
   THE BIONIC WOMAN (TF) Universal TV, 1989
FIRE ON THE AMAZON Concorde, 1991
LOVE POTION #9 20th Century Fox, 1992
THE VANISHING 20th Century Fox, 1993
DEMOLITION MAN Warner Bros., 1993
THE THING CALLED LOVE Paramount, 1993
WRESTLING ERNEST HEMINGWAY Warner Bros., 1993
SPEED 20th Century Fox, 1994
WHILE YOU WERE SLEEPING Buena Vista, 1995

ANDY BUMATAI
THE WHOOPEE BOYS Paramount, 1986
ALOHA SUMMER *HANAUMA BAY* Spectrafilm, 1988

GARLAND BUNTING
BLAZE Buena Vista, 1989

CARA BUONO
GLADIATOR Columbia, 1992

CHRISTOPHER BURGARD
84 CHARLIE MOPIC New Century/Vista, 1989

GREGG BURGE
A CHORUS LINE Columbia, 1985

JOHN BURGESS
MISS FIRECRACKER   Corsair Pictures, 1989

DELTA BURKE
b. July 30, 1956 - Orlando, Florida

A BUNNY'S TALE (TF)   Stan Margulies Company/
   ABC Circle Films, 1985
WHERE THE HELL'S THAT GOLD?!!? (TF)   Willie Nelson
   Productions/Brigade Productions/Konigsberg-Sanitsky
   Company, 1988

MICHELLE BURKE
CONEHEADS   Paramount, 1993
MAJOR LEAGUE II   Warner Bros., 1994

ROBERT BURKE
ROBOCOP 3   Orion, 1993

DENNIS BURKLEY
Agent: The Artists Agency - Los Angeles, 310/277-7779

WANTED DEAD OR ALIVE   New World, 1986
PASS THE AMMO   New Century/Vista, 1988
LAMBADA   Warner Bros., 1990

TOM BURLINSON
Agent: Harris & Goldberg Talent & Literary Agency - Los Angeles,
   310/553-5200

THE MAN FROM SNOWY RIVER   20th Century-Fox,
   1982, Australian
PHAR LAP   20th Century Fox, 1983, Australian
FLESH + BLOOD   Orion, 1985, U.S.-Dutch
RETURN TO SNOWY RIVER   Buena Vista, 1988, Australian

LEO BURMESTER
THE ABYSS   20th Century Fox, 1989
A PERFECT WORLD   Warner Bros., 1993

CAROL BURNETT
b. April 26, 1933 - San Antonio, Texas
Agent: ICM - Beverly Hills, 310/550-4000

WHO'S BEEN SLEEPING IN MY BED?   Paramount, 1963
PETE N' TILLIE   Universal, 1972
THE FRONT PAGE   Universal, 1974
A WEDDING   20th Century Fox, 1978
THE GRASS IS ALWAYS GREENER OVER THE SEPTIC TANK (TF)
   Joe Hamilton Productions, 1978
FRIENDLY FIRE (TF)   Marble Arch Productions, 1979
HEALTH   20th Century Fox, 1980
THE FOUR SEASONS   Universal, 1981
CHU CHU AND THE PHILLY FLASH   20th Century Fox, 1981
ANNIE   Columbia, 1982
BETWEEN FRIENDS (CTF)   HBO Premiere Films/Marian Rees
   Associates/Robert Cooper Films III/List-Estrin Productions,
   1983, U.S.-Canadian
FRESNO (MS)   MTM Productions, 1986
PLAZA SUITE (TF)   Kalola Productions, 1987
HOSTAGE (TF)   CBS Entertainment, 1988
NOISES OFF   Buena Vista, 1992

RUSSELL BURNETT
NUTCRACKER: THE MOTION PICTURE   Atlantic Releasing
   Corporation, 1986

GEORGE BURNS
(Nathan Birnbaum)
b. January 20, 1896 - New York, New York

THE BIG BROADCAST   Paramount, 1932
COLLEGE HUMOR   Paramount, 1933
INTERNATIONAL HOUSE   Paramount, 1933
SIX OF A KIND   Paramount, 1934
WE'RE NOT DRESSING   Paramount, 1934

MANY HAPPY RETURNS   Paramount, 1934
LOVE IN BLOOM   Paramount, 1935
THE BIG BROADCAST OF 1936   Paramount, 1935
HERE COMES COOKIE   Paramount, 1935
COLLEGE HOLIDAY   Paramount, 1936
A DAMSEL IN DISTRESS   RKO Radio, 1937
COLLEGE SWING   Paramount, 1938
HONOLULU   MGM, 1939
THE SUNSHINE BOYS ○○   MGM/United Artists, 1975
OH, GOD!   Warner Bros., 1977
SGT. PEPPER'S LONELY HEARTS CLUB BAND   Universal, 1978
MOVIE MOVIE   Warner Bros., 1978
JUST YOU AND ME, KID   Columbia, 1979
GOING IN STYLE   Warner Bros., 1979
OH, GOD! BOOK II   Warner Bros., 1980
TWO OF A KIND (TF)   Lorimar Productions, 1982
OH GOD! YOU DEVIL   Warner Bros., 1984
18 AGAIN   New World, 1988

JERE BURNS
Agent: Harris & Goldberg Talent & Literary Agency - Los Angeles,
   310/553-5200

LET'S GET HARRY   TriStar, 1986
TOUCH AND GO   TriStar, 1986
HIT LIST   New Line Cinema, 1989
WIRED   Taurus Entertainment, 1989
TURN BACK THE CLOCK (TF)   Michael Filerman Productions/
   NBC Productions, 1989
GREEDY   Universal, 1994

JOE BURNS
ONE PLUE TWO EQUALS FOUR   Sierra Sky Entertainment, 1994

WILLIAM S. BURROUGHS
DRUGSTORE COWBOY   Avenue Pictures, 1989
BLOODHOUNDS OF BROADWAY   Columbia, 1989

SAFFRON BURROWS
CIRCLE OF FRIENDS   Savoy Pictures, 1995

ELLEN BURSTYN
(Edna Rae Gillooly/Ellen McRae)
b. December 7, 1932 - Detroit, Michigan
Agent: CAA - Beverly Hills, 310/288-4545

FOR THOSE WHO THINK YOUNG   United Artists, 1964
GOODBYE, CHARLIE   20th Century Fox, 1964
PIT STOP   Distributors International, 1969
TROPIC OF CANCER   Paramount, 1970
ALEX IN WONDERLAND   MGM, 1970
THE LAST PICTURE SHOW ○   Columbia, 1971
THE KING OF MARVIN GARDENS   Columbia, 1972
THE EXORCIST ★   Warner Bros., 1973
THURSDAY'S GAME (TF)   ABC Circle Films, 1974
HARRY AND TONTO   20th Century Fox, 1974
ALICE DOESN'T LIVE HERE ANYMORE ★★   Warner Bros., 1974
PROVIDENCE   Cinema 5, 1977, French-Swiss
A DREAM OF PASSION   Avco Embassy, 1978, Greek-U.S.
SAME TIME, NEXT YEAR ★   Universal, 1978
RESURRECTION ★   Universal, 1980
SILENCE OF THE NORTH   Universal, 1981, Canadian
THE PEOPLE VS. JEAN HARRIS (TF)   1981
THE AMBASSADOR   MGM/UA/Cannon, 1984
SURVIVING (TF)   Telepictures Productions, 1985
TWICE IN A LIFETIME   The Yorkin Company, 1985
ACT OF VENGEANCE (CTF)   HBO Premiere Films/Telepix Canada
   Corporation, 1986, U.S.-Canadian
INTO THIN AIR (TF)   Fries Entertainment, 1986
SOMETHING IN COMMON (TF)   New World TV/Freyda Rothstein
   Productions/Littke-Grossbart Productions, 1986
PACK OF LIES (TF)   Robert Halmi, Inc., 1987
HANNA'S WAR   Cannon, 1988
DYING YOUNG   20th Century Fox, 1991
THE CEMETERY CLUB   Buena Vista, 1993
WHEN A MAN LOVES A WOMAN   Buena Vista, 1994
ROOMMATES   Buena Vista, 1994
HOW TO MAKE AN AMERICAN QUILT   Universal, 1995

CLARISSA BURT
THE NEVERENDING STORY II: THE NEXT CHAPTER
   Warner Bros., 1991

DONALD BURTON
HUDSON HAWK   TriStar, 1991

KATE BURTON
ELLIS ISLAND (MS)   Pantheon Pictures/Telepictures Productions,
   1984, U.S.-British
BIG TROUBLE IN LITTLE CHINA   20th Century Fox, 1986

LeVAR BURTON
b. February 16, 1957 - West Germany
Agent: The Marion Rosenberg Office - Los Angeles, 213/653-7383

ROOTS (MS)   Wolper Productions, 1977
BILLY: PORTRAIT OF A STREET KID (TF)   Mark Carliner
   Productions, 1977
LOOKING FOR MR. GOODBAR   Paramount, 1977
BATTERED (TF)   Henry Jaffe Enterprises, 1978
ONE IN A MILLION: THE RON LeFLORE STORY (TF)
   Roger Gimbel Productions/EMI TV, 1978
DUMMY (TF)   The Konigsberg Company/Warner Bros. TV, 1979
ROOTS: THE NEXT GENERATIONS (MS)   Wolper Prods., 1979
GUYANA TRAGEDY: THE STORY OF JIM JONES TF)
   The Konigsberg Company, 1980
THE HUNTER   Paramount, 1980
GRAMBLING'S WHITE TIGER (TF)   Jenner-Wallach Productions/
   InterPlanetary Productions, 1981
THE JESSIE OWENS STORY (TF)   Harve Bennett Productions/
   Paramount TV, 1984
THE MIDNIGHT HOUR (TF)   ABC Circle Films, 1985
LIBERTY (TF)   Robert Greenwald Productions, 1986
THE SUPERNATURALS   Republic Entertainment/Sandy Howard
   Productions, 1986
A SPECIAL FRIENDSHIP (TF)   Entertainment Partners, 1987
ROOTS: THE GIFT (TF)   Wolper Prods./Warner Bros. TV, 1988
FIRESTORM: 72 HOURS IN OAKLAND (TF)   Gross-Weston Prods./
   Capital Cities-ABC Video Productions/Cannell Entertainment, 1993
PARALLEL LIVES (CTF)   Showtime Entertainment, 1994
STAR TREK GENERATIONS   Paramount, 1994

STEVE BURTON
CYBER-TRACKER   PM Entertainment, 1994

WENDELL BURTON
Agent: Don Gerler & Associates - Los Angeles, 213/850-7386

THE STERILE CUCKOO   Paramount, 1969
FORTUNE AND MEN'S EYES   MGM, 1971, Canadian
BEING THERE   United Artists, 1979
JOHN STEINBECK'S EAST OF EDEN   EAST OF EDEN (MS)
   Mace Neufeld Productions, 1981

STEVE BUSCEMI
Agent: Ambrosio-Mortimer - Beverly Hills, 310/274-4274

PARTING GLANCES   1986
HEART   New World, 1987
CALL ME   Vestron, 1988
NEW YORK STORIES   Buena Vista, 1989
BLOODHOUNDS OF BROADWAY   Columbia, 1989
KING OF NEW YORK   New Line Cinema, 1990
RESERVOIR DOGS   Miramax Films, 1992
ED AND HIS DEAD MOTHER   I.R.S. Releasing, 1993
AIRHEADS   20th Century Fox, 1994
DESPERADO   Columbia, 1995

GARY BUSEY
b. June 29, 1944 - Goose Creek, Texas
Agent: ICM - Beverly Hills, 310/550-4000

DIRTY LITTLE BILLY   Columbia, 1972
LOLLY MADONNA XXX   THE LOLLY-MADONNA WAR   MGM, 1973
THE LAST AMERICAN HERO   HARD DRIVER   20th Century Fox, 1973

HEX   1973
THE EXECUTION OF PRIVATE SLOVIK (TF)   Universal TV, 1974
THUNDERBOT AND LIGHTFOOT   United Artists, 1974
THE LAW (TF)   Universal TV, 1974
THE GUMBALL RALLY   Warner Bros., 1976
A STAR IS BORN   Warner Bros., 1976
STRAIGHT TIME   Warner Bros., 1978
BIG WEDNESDAY   Warner Bros., 1978
THE BUDDY HOLLY STORY ★   Columbia, 1978
FOOLIN' AROUND   Columbia, 1978
CARNY   United Artists, 1980
BARBAROSA   Universal/AFD, 1982, West German
D.C. CAB   Universal, 1983
THE BEAR   Embassy, 1984
INSIGNIFICANCE   Island Alive, 1985, British
SILVER BULLET   STEPHEN KING'S SILVER BULLET
   Paramount, 1985
EYE OF THE TIGER   Scotti Bros., 1986
LET'S GET HARRY   TriStar, 1986
LETHAL WEAPON   Warner Bros., 1987
BULLETPROOF   CineTel Films, 1987
A DANGEROUS LIFE (CMS)   HBO/McElroy & McElroy/FilmAccord
   Corporation/Australian Broadcasting Corporation/Zenith
   Productions, 1988, U.S.-Australian
PREDATOR 2   20th Century Fox, 1990
MY HEROES HAVE ALWAYS BEEN COWBOYS   Samuel Goldwyn
   Company, 1991
POINT BREAK   20th Century Fox, 1991
UNDER SIEGE   Warner Bros., 1992
THE FIRM   Paramount, 1993
ROOKIE OF THE YEAR   20th Century Fox, 1993
SURVIVING THE GAME   New Line Cinema, 1994
DROP ZONE   Paramount, 1994

TIMOTHY BUSFIELD
b. June 12, 1957 - Lansing, Michigan
Agent: William Morris Agency - Beverly Hills, 310/274-7451

STRIPES   Columbia, 1981
REVENGE OF THE NERDS   20th Century Fox, 1984
REVENGE OF THE NERS II: NERDS IN PARADISE
   20th Century Fox, 1987
FIELD OF DREAMS   Universal, 1989
LITTLE BIG LEAGUE   Columbia, 1994
QUIZ SHOW   Buena Vista, 1994

BILLY GREEN BUSH
THE CULPEPPER CATTLE CO.   20th Century Fox, 1972
40 CARATS   Columbia, 1973
ELECTRA GLIDE IN BLUE   United Artists, 1973
ALICE DOESN'T LIVE HERE ANYMORE   Warner Bros., 1975
MACKINTOSH AND T.J.   Penland, 1975
THE JERICHO MILE (TF)   ABC Circle Films, 1979
TOM HORN   Warner Bros., 1980
CRITTERS   New Line Cinema, 1986

CHUCK BUSH
FANDANGO   Warner Bros., 1985

GRAND L. BUSH
COLORS   Orion, 1988
DIE HARD   20th Century Fox, 1988
CHASERS   Warner Bros., 1994

AKOSUA BUSIA
THE COLOR PURPLE   Warner Bros., 1985
NATIVE SON   Cinecom, 1986
LOW BLOW   Crown International, 1986
THE GEORGE McKENNA STORY (TF)   Alan Landsburg
   Productions, 1986
A SPECIAL FRIENDSHIP (TF)   Entertainment Partners, 1987

DICK BUTKUS
b. December 9, 1942 - Chicago, Illinois

MOTHER, JUGS & SPEED   20th Century Fox, 1976
CRACKING UP   SMORGASBORD   Warner Bros., 1983

JOHNNY DANGEROUSLY   20th Century Fox, 1984
HAMBURGER...THE MOTION PICTURE   FM Entertainment, 1986

DEAN BUTLER
THE KID WITH THE 200 I.Q. (TF)   Guillaume-Margo Productions/
  Zephyr Productions, 1983
LITTLE HOUSE: LOOK BACK TO YESTERDAY (TF)
  NBC Productions/Ed Friendly Productions, 1983
LITTLE HOUSE: BLESS ALL THE DEAR CHILDREN (TF)
  NBC Productions/Ed Friendly Productions, 1984
LITTLE HOUSE: THE LAST FAREWELL (TF)   NBC Productions/
  Ed Friendly Productions, 1984
DESERT HEARTS   Samuel Goldwyn Company, 1985

GENE BUTLER
GINGERALE AFTERNOON   Skouras Pictures, 1989

TOM BUTLER
ERNEST RIDES AGAIN   Emshell Producers Group, 1993

YANCY BUTLER
HARD TARGET   Universal, 1993
DROP ZONE   Paramount, 1994
LET IT BE ME   Savoy Pictures, 1995

RED BUTTONS
(Aaron Chwatt)
b. February 5, 1919 - New York, New York

WINGED VICTORY   20th Century Fox, 1944
13 RUE MADELEINE   20th Century Fox, 1946
SAYONARA ∞   Warner Bros., 1957
IMITATION GENERAL   MGM, 1958
THE BIG CIRCUS   1959
ONE, TWO, THREE   United Artists, 1961
FIVE WEEKS IN A BALLOON   20th Century Fox, 1962
HATARI!   Paramount, 1962
THE LONGEST DAY   20th Century Fox, 1962
GAY PUR-EE (AF)   1963 (voice)
A TICKLISH AFFAIR   MGM, 1963
YOUR CHEATIN' HEART   MGM, 1964
UP FROM THE BEACH   20th Century Fox, 1965
HARLOW   Paramount, 1965
STAGECOACH   20th Century Fox, 1966
THEY SHOOT HORSES, DON'T THEY?   Cinerama Releasing
  Corporation, 1969
BREAKOUT (TF)   Universal TV, 1970
WHO KILLED MARY WHAT'S'ER NAME?   Cannon, 1971
THE POSEIDON ADVENTURE   20th Century Fox, 1972
THE NEW ORIGINAL WONDER WOMAN (TF)   1975
LOUIS ARMSTRONG—CHICAGO STYLE (TF)   Charles Fries
  Productions, 1976
GABLE AND LOMBARD   Universal, 1976
VIVA KNIEVEL!   Warner Bros., 1977
PETE'S DRAGON   Buena Vista, 1977
TELETHON (TF)   ABC Circle Films, 1977
VEGA$ (TF)   Aaron Spelling Productions, 1978
MOVIE MOVIE   Warner Bros., 1978
THE USERS (TF)   Aaron Spelling Productions, 1978
C.H.O.M.P.S.   American International, 1979
WHEN TIME RAN OUT   Warner Bros., 1980
THE DREAM MERCHANTS (TF)   Columbia TV, 1980
LEAVE 'EM LAUGHING (TF)   Julian Fowles Productions/Charles
  Fries Productions, 1981
SIDE SHOW   Krofft Entertainment, 1981
REUNION AT FAIRBOROUGH (CTF)   HBO Premiere Films/Alan
  Wagner Productions/Alan King Productions/Columbia TV, 1985
ALICE IN WONDERLAND (MS)   Irwin Allen Productions/
  Procter & Gamble Productions/Columbia TV, 1985
18 AGAIN   New World, 1988
THE AMBULANCE   Triumph Releasing Corporation, 1991
IT COULD HAPPEN TO YOU   TriStar, 1994

RUTH BUZZI
b. July 24, 1936 - Westerly, Rhode Island
Agent: The Artists Group, Ltd. - Los Angeles, 310/552-1100

FREAKY FRIDAY   Buena Vista, 1977
THE APPLE DUMPLING GANG RIDES AGAIN   Buena Vista, 1979
THE VILLAIN   Columbia, 1979
CHU CHU AND THE PHILLY FLASH   20th Century-Fox, 1981
THE BEING   BVF Films, 1983
BAD GUYS *EASTER SUNDAY*   Interpictures, 1986

JOHN BYNER
WHAT'S UP, DOC?   Warner Bros., 1972
THE GREAT SMOKEY ROADBLOCK   *THE LAST OF THE
  COWBOYS*   Dimension, 1976
THE MAN IN THE SANTA CLAUS SUIT   Dick Clark Productions, 1978
STROKER ACE   Universal, 1983
TRANSYLVANIA 6-5000   New World, 1985

ANNE BYRNE
MANHATTAN   United Artists, 1979

DAVID BYRNE
b. May 14, 1952 - Dumbarton, Scotland

TRUE STORIES   Warner Bros., 1986 (also directed)

DEBBIE BYRNE
REBEL   Vestron, 1985, Australian

GABRIEL BYRNE
Agent: ICM - Beverly Hills, 310/550-4000

THE OUTSIDER   Paramount, 1979, U.S.-Irish
EXCALIBUR   Orion/Warner Bros., 1981, British-Irish
THE KEEP   Paramount, 1983
HANNAH K.   Universal Classics, 1983, French
REFLECTIONS (TF)   Court House Films/Film Four International,
  1984, British
CHRISTOPHER COLUMBUS (MS)   RAI/Clesi Cinematografica/
  Antenne-2/Bavaria Atelier/Lorimar Productions, 1985,
  Italian-West German-U.S.-French
DEFENSE OF THE REALM   Hemdale, 1985, British
MUSSOLINI: THE UNTOLD STORY (MS)   Trian Productions, 1985
GOTHIC   Vestron, 1986, British
LIONHEART   Orion, 1987
HELLO AGAIN   Buena Vista, 1987
JULIA AND JULIA   Cinecom, 1987, Italian
SIESTA   Lorimar, 1987, British
MILLER'S CROSSING   20th Century Fox, 1990
SHIPWRECKED   Buena Vista, 1991
COOL WORLD   Paramount, 1992
POINT OF NO RETURN   Warner Bros., 1993
INTO THE WEST   Miramax Films, 1993, British-Irish-Japanese
A DANGEROUS WOMAN   Gramercy Pictures, 1993
A SIMPLE TWIST OF FATE   Buena Vista, 1994
TRIAL BY JURY   Warner Bros., 1994
LITTLE WOMEN   Columbia, 1994
USUAL SUSPECTS   1995
BUFFALO GIRLS (MS)   Lauren Film Productions, Inc./CBS, 1995

MICHAEL BYRNE
THE LONG GOOD FRIDAY   Embassy, 1982, British
CHAMPIONS   Embassy, 1983, British
THE GOOD FATHER   Skouras Pictures, 1986, British
INDIANA JONES AND THE LAST CRUSADE   Paramount, 1989

NIALL BYRNE
THE MIRACLE   Miramax Films, 1991

JOSEPHINE BYRNES
FRAUDS   Australian Film Finance Corporation, 1993, Australian

SUSAN BYUN
Agent: The Rainford Agency - Los Angeles, 213/655-1404

SGT. KABUKIMAN, NYPD   Troma, 1991

C

JAMES CAAN
b. March 26, 1939 - Bronx, New York
Agent: UTA - Beverly Hills, 310/273-6700

IRMA LA DOUCE   United Artists, 1963
LADY IN A CAGE   United Artists, 1964
THE GLORY GUYS   United Artists, 1965
RED LINE 7000   Paramount, 1965
EL DORADO   Paramount, 1967
GAMES   Universal, 1967
COUNTDOWN   Warner Bros., 1968
JOURNEY TO SHILOH   Universal, 1968
SUBMARINE X-I   United Artists, 1968, British
THE RAIN PEOPLE   Warner Bros., 1969
RABBIT, RUN   Warner Bros., 1970
BRIAN'S SONG (TF)   Screen Gems/Columbia TV, 1971
T.R. BASKIN   Paramount, 1971
THE GODFATHER ✪   Paramount, 1972
SLITHER   MGM, 1973
CINDERELLA LIBERTY   20th Century Fox, 1973
THE GAMBLER   Paramount, 1974
FREEBIE AND THE BEAN   Warner Bros., 1974
THE GODFATHER, PART II   Paramount, 1974
FUNNY LADY   Columbia, 1975
ROLLERBALL   United Artists, 1975
GONE WITH THE WEST   International Cinefilm, 1975
THE KILLER ELITE   United Artists, 1975
HARRY AND WALTER GO TO NEW YORK   Columbia, 1976
SILENT MOVIE   20th Century Fox, 1976 (uncredited)
ANOTHER MAN, ANOTHER CHANCE   United Artists,
   1977, U.S.-French
A BRIDGE TOO FAR   United Artists, 1977, British
COMES A HORSEMAN   United Artists, 1978
THE DRIVER   20th Century Fox, 1978
CHAPTER TWO   Columbia, 1979
HIDE IN PLAIN SIGHT   MGM/United Artists, 1980 (also directed)
THIEF   United Artists, 1981
BOLERO   *LES UNS ET LES AUTRES/WITHIN MEMORY*
   Double 13/Sharp Features, 1981, French
KISS ME GOODBYE   20th Century Fox, 1982
GARDENS OF STONE   TriStar, 1987
ALIEN NATION   20th Century Fox, 1988
DICK TRACY   Buena Vista, 1990
MISERY   Columbia, 1990
FOR THE BOYS   20th Century Fox, 1991
HONEYMOON IN VEGAS   Columbia, 1992
THE PROGRAM   Buena Vista, 1993
FLESH AND BONE   Paramount, 1993
THINGS TO DO IN DENVER WHEN YOU'RE DEAD
   Miramax Films, 1995

SELINA CADRELL
NOT QUITE PARADISE   *NOT QUITE JERUSALEM*   New World,
   1986, British

HARRY CAESAR
THE LONGEST YARD   Paramount, 1974
BIRD ON A WIRE   Universal, 1990

SID CAESAR
b. September 8, 1922 - Yonkers, New York
Agent: The Artists Group, Ltd. - Los Angeles, 310/552-1100

TARS AND SPARS   Columbia, 1946
THE GUILT OF JANET AMES   Columbia, 1947
IT'S A MAD MAD MAD MAD WORLD   United Artists, 1963
A GUIDE FOR THE MARRIED MAN   20th Century Fox, 1967

THE BUSY BODY   Paramount, 1967
THE SPIRIT IS WILLING   Paramount, 1967
TEN FROM YOUR SHOW OF SHOWS   1973
AIRPORT 1975   Universal, 1974
SILENT MOVIE   20th Century Fox, 1976
FIRE SALE   20th Century Fox, 1977
THE CHEAP DETECTIVE   Columbia, 1978
GREASE   Paramount, 1978
THE FIENDISH PLOT OF DR. DU MANCHU   Orion/Warner Bros.,
   1980, British
HISTORY OF THE WORLD—PART 1   20th Century Fox, 1981
GREASE 2   Paramount, 1982
CANNONBALL RUN II   Warner Bros., 1984
OVER THE BROOKLYN BRIDGE   MGM/UA-Cannon, 1984
LOVE IS NEVER SILENT (TF)   Marian Rees Associates, 1985
ALICE IN WONDERLAND (MS)   Irwin Allen Productions/
   Procter & Gamble Productions/Columbia TV, 1985
STOOGEMANIA   Atlantic Releasing Corporation, 1985
THE EMPEROR'S NEW CLOTHES   Cannon, 1987, U.S.-Israeli
SIDE BY SIDE (TF)   Avnet-Kerner Productions, 1988

JOSE MARIA CAFFAREL
MAN OF PASSION   Golden Sun Productions, 1988, Spanish

STEPHEN CAFFREY
LONGTIME COMPANION   Samuel Goldwyn Company, 1990

NICOLAS CAGE
(Nicolas Coppola)
b. January 7, 1964 - Long Beach, California
Agent: ICM - Beverly Hills, 310/550-4000

RUMBLE FISH   Universal, 1983
VALLEY GIRL   Atlantic Releasing Corporation, 1983
RACING WITH THE MOON   Paramount, 1984
THE COTTON CLUB   Orion, 1984
BIRDY   TriStar, 1984
THE BOY IN BLUE   20th Century Fox, 1986, Canadian
PEGGY SUE GOT MARRIED   TriStar, 1986
RAISING ARIZONA   20th Century Fox, 1987
MOONSTRUCK   MGM/UA, 1987
VAMPIRE'S KISS   Hemdale, 1989
FIRE BIRDS   Buena Vista, 1990
WILD AT HEART   Samuel Goldwyn Company, 1990
ZANDALEE   Electric Pictures/ITC Entertainment Group, 1991
HONEYMOON IN VEGAS   Columbia, 1992
RED ROCK WEST   1993
DEADFALL   Trimark Pictures, 1993
GUARDING TESS   TriStar, 1994
IT COULD HAPPEN TO YOU   TriStar, 1994
TRAPPED IN PARADISE   20th Century Fox, 1994
KISS OF DEATH   20th Century Fox, 1995
LEAVING LAS VEGAS   1995

MICHAEL CAINE
(Maurice Joseph Micklewhite, Jr.)
b. March 14, 1933 - London, England

HELL IN KOREA   *A HILL IN KOREA*   1956, British
HOW TO MURDER A RICH UNCLE   1957, British
THE KEY   1958, British
BLIND SPOT   1958, Dutch
THE TWO-HEADED SPY   Columbia, 1959
FOXHOLE IN CAIRO   Paramount, 1960, British
THE BULLDOG BREED   1960
THE DAY THE EARTH CAUGHT FIRE   Universal, 1961, British
SOLO FOR SPARROW   1962
THE WRONG ARM OF THE LAW   Continental, 1963, British
ZULU   Embassy, 1964, British
THE IPCRESS FILE   Universal, 1965, British
ALFIE ★   Paramount, 1966, British
THE WRONG BOX   Columbia, 1966, British
GAMBIT   Universal, 1966
FUNERAL IN BERLIN   Paramount, 1967, British
HURRY SUNDOWN   Paramount, 1967
BILLION DOLLAR BRAIN   United Artists, 1967, British
WOMAN TIMES SEVEN   Avco Embassy, 1967, French-Italian-U.S.

TONIGHT LET'S ALL MAKE LOVE IN LONDON (FD)   1968
DEADFALL   20th Century Fox, 1968, British
THE MAGUS   20th Century Fox, 1968, British
PLAY DIRTY   United Artists, 1969, British
THE ITALIAN JOB   Paramount, 1969
BATTLE OF BRITAIN   United Artists, 1969, British
TOO LATE THE HERO   Cinerama Releasing Corporation, 1970
THE LAST VALLEY   Cinerama Releasing Corporation, 1971, British
GET CARTER   MGM, 1971, British
KIDNAPPED   American International, 1971, British
PULP   United Artists, 1972, British
SLEUTH ★   20th Century Fox, 1972
X, Y & ZEE   *ZEE & CO.*   Columbia, 1972, British
THE DESTRUCTORS   *THE MARSEILLES CONTRACT*
  American International, 1974, British-French
THE BLACK WINDMILL   Universal, 1974, British
THE WILBY CONSPIRACY   United Artists, 1975, British
PEEPER   20th Century Fox, 1975
THE ROMANTIC ENGLISHWOMAN   New World, 1975, British
THE MAN WHO WOULD BE KING   Allied Artists, 1975, British
HARRY AND WALTER GO TO NEW YORK   Columbia, 1976
THE EAGLE HAS LANDED   Columbia, 1976, British
A BRIDGE TOO FAR   United Artists, 1977, British
SILVER BEARS   Columbia, 1978
THE SWARM   Warner Bros., 1978
CALIFORNIA SUITE   Columbia, 1978
ASHANTI   Columbia, 1979, Swiss-U.S.
BEYOND THE POSEIDON ADVENTURE   Warner Bros., 1979
THE ISLAND   Universal, 1980
DRESSED TO KILL   Filmways, 1980
VICTORY   Paramount, 1981
THE HAND   Orion/Warner Bros., 1981
DEATHTRAP   Warner Bros., 1982
BEYOND THE LIMIT   *THE HONORARY CONSUL*   Paramount,
  1983, British
EDUCATING RITA ★   Columbia, 1983, British
WATER   Atlantic Releasing Corporation, 1984, British
BLAME IT ON RIO   20th Century Fox, 1984
THE JIGSAW MAN   United Film Distribution, 1984, British
THE HOLCROFT COVENANT   Universal, 1985
SWEET LIBERTY   Universal, 1986
HANNAH AND HER SISTERS ○○   Orion, 1986
MONA LISA   Island Pictures, 1986, British
THE WHISTLE BLOWER   Hemdale, 1986
HALF MOON STREET   20th Century Fox, 1986, British
JAWS THE REVENGE   Universal, 1987
THE FOURTH PROTOCOL   Lorimar, 1987, British
SURRENDER   Warner Bros., 1987
WITHOUT A CLUE   Orion, 1988
JACK THE RIPPER (TF)   Euston Films/Thames TV/Hill-O'Connor
  Entertainment/Lorimar TV, 1988, British-U.S.
DIRTY ROTTEN SCOUNDRELS   Orion, 1988
JEKYLL & HYDE (TF)   King-Phoenix Entertainment/London
  Weekend TV, 1990, U.S.-British
A SHOCK TO THE SYSTEM   Corsair Pictures, 1990
MR. DESTINY   Buena Vista, 1990
NOISES OFF   Buena Vista, 1992
THE MUPPET CHRISTMAS CAROL   Buena Vista, 1992
ON DEADLY GROUND   Warner Bros., 1994
WORLD WAR II: THEN THERE WERE GIANTS (TF)
  World International Network, 1994
BLUE ICE (CTF)   HBO, 1994

FRASER CAINS
THE ENGLISHMAN WHO WENT UP A HILL, BUT CAME
  DOWN A MOUNTAIN   Miramax Films, 1995

PAUL CALDERON
KING OF NEW YORK   New Line Cinema, 1990

SERGIO CALDERON
OLD GRINGO   Columbia, 1989

GENE CALDWELL
MISS FIRECRACKER   Corsair Pictures, 1989

L. SCOTT CALDWELL
THE FUGITIVE   Warner Bros., 1993

ZOE CALDWELL
b. September 14, 1933 - Melbourne, Australia

THE PURPLE ROSE OF CAIRO   Orion, 1985

DAVID CALE
BEETHOVEN   Universal, 1992

JADE CALEGORY
MAC AND ME   Orion, 1988

DON CALFA
10   Orion/Warner Bros., 1979

RORY CALHOUN
(Francis Timothy Durgin)
b. August 8, 1922 - Los Angeles, California

SOMETHING FOR THE BOYS   20th Century Fox, 1944
THE GREAT JOHN L.   1945
THE RED HOUSE   Warner Bros., 1947
ADVENTURE ISLAND   Paramount, 1947
MIRACULOUS JOURNEY   1948
MASSACRE RIVER   1949
SAND   *WILL JAMES' SAND*   1949
A TICKET TO TOMAHAWK   1950
ROGUE RIVER   1950
I'D CLIMB THE HIGHEST MOUNTAIN   20th Century-Fox, 1951
MEET ME AFTER THE SHOW   1951
WITH A SONG IN MY HEART   20th Century Fox, 1952
WAY OF A GAUCHO   1952
POWDER RIVER   1953
HOW TO MARRY A MILLIONAIRE   20th Century Fox, 1953
RIVER OF NO RETURN   20th Century Fox, 1954
DAWN AT SOCORRO   Universal, 1954
FOUR GUNS TO THE BORDER   1954
A BULLET IS WAITING   Columbia, 1954
AIN'T MISBEHAVIN'   Universal, 1955
THE TREASURE OF PANCHO VILLA   Universal, 1955
THE SPOILERS   Universal, 1956
RAW EDGE   1956
RED SUNDOWN   Universal, 1956
FLIGHT TO HONG KONG   1956
THE BIG CAPER   1957
THE HIRED GUN   MGM, 1957
APACHE TERRITORY   1958
THE COLOSSUS OF RHODES   MGM, 1960,
  Italian-French-Spanish
MARCO POLO   American International, 1961, Italian-French
REQUIEM FOR A HEAVYWEIGHT   Columbia, 1962
A FACE IN THE RAIN   Embassy, 1963
THE GUN HAWK   1963
YOUNG FURY   Paramount, 1965
BLACK SPURS   Paramount, 1965
APACHE UPRISING   Paramount, 1966
DAYTON'S DEVILS   Commonwealth United, 1968
NIGHT OF THE LEPUS   MGM, 1972
LOVE AND THE MIDNIGHT AUTO SUPPLY   *MIDNIGHT AUTO
  SUPPLY*   1978
ANGEL   New World, 1984
AVENGING ANGEL   New World, 1985

BRANDON CALL
BLIND FURY   TriStar, 1990

R.D. CALL
Agent: The Agency - Los Angeles, 310/551-3000

AT CLOSE RANGE   Orion, 1986

K CALLAN
Agent: The Gage Group - Los Angeles, 213/859-8777

JOE   Cannon, 1970
FRANKIE & JOHNNY   Paramount, 1991
THE UNBORN   Califilm, 1991

SIMON CALLOW
AMADEUS   Orion, 1984
A ROOM WITH A VIEW   Cinecom, 1986, British
MAURICE   Cinecom, 1987, British
POSTCARDS FROM THE EDGE   Columbia, 1990
MR. AND MRS. BRIDGE   Miramax Films, 1990
FOUR WEDDINGS AND A FUNERAL   Gramercy Pictures,
    1994, British
JEFFERSON IN PARIS   Buena Vista, 1995

VANESSA BELL CALLOWAY
WHAT'S LOVE GOT TO DO WITH IT   Buena Vista, 1993

BILL CALVERT
Agent: Paradigm - Los Angeles, 310/277-4400

HEART AND SOULS   Universal, 1993

DEAN CAMERON
SUMMER SCHOOL   Paramount, 1987
MEN AT WORK   Triumph Releasing Corporation, 1990
SLEEP WITH ME   MGM/UA, 1994

JANE CAMERON
PAIR OF ACES (TF)   Pedernales Films/Once Upon A Time
    Films, Ltd., 1990
THE UNBORN   Califilm, 1991

KIRK CAMERON
b. October 12, 1970 - Panorama City, California
Agent: UTA - Beverly Hills, 310/273-6700

THE BEST OF TIMES   Universal, 1986
LIKE FATHER, LIKE SON   TriStar, 1987
LISTEN TO ME   Columbia, 1989

TONY CAMILIERI
BILL & TED'S EXCELLENT ADVENTURE   Orion, 1989

ROBERT CAMILLETTI
(Rob Camilletti)
LOVERBOY   TriStar, 1989
BORN ON THE FOURTH OF JULY   Universal, 1989
SOAPDISH   Paramount, 1991

COLLEEN CAMP
SMILE   United Artists, 1975
FUNNY LADY   Columbia, 1975
APOCALPYSE NOW   United Artists, 1979
GAME OF DEATH   Columbia, 1979, U.S.-Hong Kong
THEY ALL LAUGHED   United Artists Classics, 1982
VALLEY GIRLS   Atlantic Releasing Corporation, 1983
SMOKEY AND THE BANDIT 3   Universal, 1983
THE CITY GIRL   Moon Pictures, 1984
DOIN' TIME   The Ladd Company/Warner Bros., 1984
JOY OF SEX   Paramount, 1984
POLICE ACADEMY 2: THEIR FIRST ASSIGNMENT
    Warner Bros., 1985
D.A.R.Y.L.   Paramount, 1985
CLUE   Paramount, 1985
POLICE ACADEMY 3: BACK IN TRAINING   Warner Bros., 1986
WALK LIKE A MAN   MGM/UA, 1987
POLICE ACADEMY 4: CITIZENS ON PATROL   Warner Bros., 1987
TRACK 29   Island Pictures, 1988
ILLEGALLY YOURS   MGM/UA, 1988
ADDICTED TO HIS LOVE (TF)   Green-Epstein Productions/
    Columbia TV, 1988
WICKED STEPMOTHER   MGM/UA, 1989
THE VAGRANT   MGM-Pathe, 1991
WAYNE'S WORLD   Paramount, 1992
SLIVER   Paramount, 1993
GREEDY   Universal, 1994
DIE HARD 3   20th Century Fox, 1995

HAMILTON CAMP
b. October 30, 1934 - London, England

HEAVEN CAN WAIT   Paramount, 1978
ALL NIGHT LONG   Universal, 1981
BRIDESMAIDS (TF)   Motown Productions/Qintex Entertainment/
    Deaun Productions, 1989
THE ARENA   Triumph Releasing Corporation, 1991

FRANK CAMPANELLA
HEAVEN CAN WAIT   Paramount, 1978
DICK TRACY   Buena Vista, 1990

JOSEPH CAMPANELLA
b. November 21, 1927 - New York, New York

MURDER, INC.   20th Century Fox, 1960
THE YOUNG LOVERS   MGM, 1964
THE ST. VALENTINE'S DAY MASSACRE   20th Century Fox, 1967
BEN   Cinerama Releasing Corporation, 1972
BODY CHEMISTRY   Concorde, 1990

AMELIA CAMPBELL
THE PAPER   Universal, 1994
MRS. PARKER AND THE VICIOUS CIRCLE   Fine Line Features/
    New Line Cinema, 1994

BILL CAMPBELL
THE ROCKETEER   Buena Vista, 1991
BRAM STOKER'S DRACULA   *DRACULA*   Columbia, 1992

BRUCE CAMPBELL
Agent: APA - Los Angeles, 310/273-0744

MIND WARP   New Line Cinema, 1991
ARMY OF DARKNESS   Universal, 1993

CHERYL CAMPBELL
McVICAR   Crown International, 1981, British
CHARIOTS OF FIRE   The Ladd Company/Warner Bros.,
    1981, British

GLEN CAMPBELL
b. April 22, 1936 - Billstown, Arkansas

ROCK-A-DOODLE (AF)   Samuel Goldwyn Company, 1992 (voice)

J. KENNETH CAMPBELL
WAXWORK   Vestron, 1988
FLIGHT OF THE INTRUDER   Paramount, 1991
COBB   Warner Bros., 1994

JULIA CAMPBELL
Agent: William Morris Agency - Beverly Hills, 310/274-7451

OPPORTUNITY KNOCKS   Universal, 1990
LIVIN' LARGE!   Samuel Goldwyn Company, 1991

MAE E. CAMPBELL
Agent: Artists First, Inc. - Los Angeles, 213/653-5640

AIRPLANE!   Paramount, 1980

NICHOLAS CAMPBELL
CHILDREN OF THE NIGHT (TF)   Robert Guenette
    Productions, 1985
NAKED LUNCH   20th Century Fox, 1991

SCOTT MICHAEL CAMPBELL
RADIOLAND MURDERS   Universal, 1994

TEVIN CAMPBELL
Agent: CAA - Beverly Hills, 310/288-4545

GRAFFITI BRIDGE   Warner Bros., 1990

TISHA CAMPBELL
HOUSE PARTY 3   New Line Cinema, 1994

CRIS CAMPION
PIRATES   Cannon, 1986, French-Tunisian

RAFAEL CAMPOS
WHERE THE BUFFALO ROAM   Universal, 1980

RON CANADA
Agent: Stone Manners Talent Agency - Los Angeles, 213/654-7575

ADVENTURES IN BABYSITTING   Buena Vista, 1987
ARTHUR 2 ON THE ROCKS   Warner Bros., 1988
DOWNTOWN   20th Century Fox, 1990
THE LAST OF THE FINEST   Orion, 1990
HONEY, I BLEW UP THE KID   Buena Vista, 1992
HOME ALONE 2: LOST IN NEW YORK   20th Century Fox, 1992
GETTING EVEN WITH DAD   MGM/UA, 1994
THE RHINEHART THEORY   Rysher Entertainment, 1994

CANDY CANDIDO
THE GREAT MOUSE DETECTIVE (AF)   Buena Vista, 1986 (voice)

DYAN CANNON
(Samille Diane Friesen/Diane Cannon)
b. January 4, 1939 - Tacoma, Washington
Agent: APA - Los Angeles, 310/273-0744

THE RISE AND FALL OF LEGS DIAMOND   Warner Bros., 1960
THIS REBEL BREED   *THREE SHADES OF LOVE*
   Warner Bros., 1960
BOB & CAROL & TED & ALICE ✪   Columbia, 1969
THE BURGLARS   *LE CASSE*   Columbia, 1972, French
THE ANDERSON TAPES   Columbia, 1971
DOCTORS' WIVES   Columbia, 1971
THE LOVE MACHINE   Columbia, 1971
SUCH GOOD FRIENDS   Paramount, 1971
SHAMUS   Columbia, 1973
THE LAST OF SHEILA   Warner Bros., 1973
CHILD UNDER A LEAF   Cinema National, 1974, Canadian
HEAVEN CAN WAIT ✪   Paramount, 1978
LADY OF THE HOUSE (TF)   Metromedia Productions, 1978
REVENGE OF THE PINK PANTHER   United Artists,
   1978, British
HONEYSUCKLE ROSE   Warner Bros., 1980
COAST TO COAST   Paramount, 1980
AUTHOR! AUTHOR!   20th Century Fox, 1982
DEATHTRAP   Warner Bros., 1982
MASTER OF THE GAME (MS)   Rosemont Productions, 1984
ARTHUR THE KING (TF)   Martin Poll Productions/Comworld
   Productions/Jadran Film, 1985, U.S.-Yugoslavian
JENNY'S WAR (TF)   Louis Rudolph Productions/HTV/
   Columbia TV, 1985, U.S.-British
CADDYSHACK II   Warner Bros., 1988
THE END OF INNOCENCE   Skouras Pictures,
   1990 (also directed)
CHRISTMAS IN CONNECTICUT (CTF)   Guber-Peters
   Entertainment/Turner Network TV, 1992
THE PICKLE   Columbia, 1993

J.D. CANNON
AN AMERICAN DREAM   1966
COOL HAND LUKE   Warner Bros., 1967
COTTON COMES TO HARLEM   United Artists, 1970
LAWMAN   United Artists, 1970
TESTIMONY OF TWO MEN (TF)   Universal TV, 1977
KILLING STONE (TF)   Universal TV, 1978
IKE (MS)   ABC Circle Films, 1979
WALKING THROUGH THE FIRE (TF)   Time-Life Films, 1979
RAISE THE TITANIC   AFD, 1980, British-U.S.

DEATH WISH II   Filmways, 1982
THE RETURN OF SAM McCLOUD (TF)   Michael Sloan Productions/
   Universal TV, 1989

MAX CANTOR
FEAR, ANXIETY AND DEPRESSION   Samuel Goldwyn
   Company, 1990

VIRGINIA CAPERS
JO JO DANCER, YOUR LIFE IS CALLING   Columbia, 1986

JOHN CAPODICE
MENENDEZ: A KILLING IN BEVERLY HILLS (MS)   Zev Braun
   Pictures/TriStar Television, 1994

VINNY CAPONE
BIG   20th Century Fox, 1988

FRANCIS CAPRA
Agent: William Morris Agency - Beverly Hills, 310/274-7451

A BRONX TALE   Savoy Pictures, 1993
WILLY II: THE ADVENTURE HOME   Warner Bros., 1995

KATE CAPSHAW
Agent: ICM - Beverly Hills, 310/550-4000

A LITTLE SEX   Universal, 1982
WINDY CITY   Warner Bros., 1984
DREAMSCAPE   20th Century Fox, 1984
BEST DEFENSE   Paramount, 1984
INDIANA JONES AND THE TEMPLE OF DOOM   Paramount, 1984
POWER   20th Century Fox, 1986
SPACECAMP   20th Century Fox, 1986
HER SECRET LIFE (TF)   Phoenix Entertainment Group, 1987
BLACK RAIN   Paramount, 1989
INTERNAL AFFAIRS (MS)   Titus Productions, 1988
LOVE AT LARGE   Orion, 1990
MY HEROES HAVE ALWAYS BEEN COWBOYS   Samuel Goldwyn
   Company, 1991
LOVE AFFAIR   Warner Bros., 1994
THE COUPLE NEXT DOOR (CTF)   Showtime, 1994
JUST CAUSE   Warner Bros., 1995

IRENE CARA
b. March 18, 1959 - New York, New York

FAME   MGM/United Artists, 1980
GUYANA TRAGEDY: THE STORY OF JIM JONES (TF)
   The Konigsberg Company, 1980
D.C. CAB   Universal, 1983
CITY HEAT   Warner Bros., 1984

PAUL CARAFOTES
Agent: Badgley/Connor - Los Angeles, 310/278-9313

ALL THE RIGHT MOVES   20th Century Fox, 1983

TANTOO CARDINAL
SILENT TONGUE   Trimark Pictures, 1994, U.S.-French

HARRY CAREY, JR.
b. May 16, 1921 - Saugus, California

PURSUED   Warner Bros., 1947
RED RIVER   United Artists, 1948
SO DEAR TO MY HEART   Buena Vista, 1948
THREE GODFATHERS   MGM, 1949
SHE WORE A YELLOW RIBBON   RKO Radio, 1949
WAGONMASTER   RKO Radio, 1950
RIO GRANDE   Republic, 1950
COPPER CANYON   Paramount, 1950
WARPATH   Paramount, 1951
MONKEY BUSINESS   20th Century Fox, 1952
ISLAND IN THE SKY   Warner Bros., 1953

GENTLEMEN PREFER BLONDES   20th Century-Fox, 1953
BENEATH THE TWELVE-MILE REEF   1953
THE SILVER LODE   RKO Radio, 1954
THE LONG GRAY LINE   Columbia, 1955
MISTER ROBERTS   Warner Bros., 1955
THE SEARCHERS   Warner Bros., 1956
THE RIVER'S EDGE   20th Century Fox, 1957
RIO BRAVO   Warner Bros., 1959
THE GREAT IMPOSTOR   Universal, 1960
THE COMANCHEROS   20th Century Fox, 1961
CHEYENNE AUTUMN   Warner Bros., 1964
SHENANDOAH   Universal, 1965
THE RARE BREED   Universal, 1966
ALVAREZ KELLY   Columbia, 1966
THE WAY WEST   United Artists, 1967
THE DEVIL'S BRIGADE   United Artists, 1968
BANDOLERO!   20th Century Fox, 1968
DEATH OF A GUNFIGHTER   Universal, 1969
THE UNDEFEATED   20th Century Fox, 1969
THE MOONSHINE WAR   MGM, 1970
DIRTY DINGUS MAGEE   MGM, 1970
ONE MORE TIME   United Artists, 1970, British
BIG JAKE   National General, 1971
SOMETHING BIG   National General, 1971
E POI LO CHIAMORONO IL MAGNIFICO   1972, Italian-French
CAHILL U.S MARSHAL   Warner Bros., 1973
TAKE A HARD RIDE   20th Century Fox, 1975
NICKELODEON   Columbia, 1976
THE LONG RIDERS   United Artists, 1980
ENDANGERED SPECIES   MGM/UA, 1982
PRINCESS DAISY (MS)   NBC Productions/Steve Krantz
    Productions, 1983
CROSSROADS   Columbia, 1986
THE WHALES OF AUGUST   Alive Films, 1987
BREAKING IN   Samuel Goldwyn Company, 1989
BACK TO THE FUTURE PART III   Universal, 1990

RON CAREY

SILENT MOVIE   20th Century Fox, 1976
HISTORY OF THE WORLD—PART 1   20th Century-Fox, 1981
JOHNNY DANGEROUSLY   20th Century Fox, 1984

TIMOTHY CAREY

HELLGATE   Lippert, 1952
BLOODHOUNDS OF BROADWAY   1952
WHITE WITCH DOCTOR   20th Century Fox, 1953
ALASKA SEAS   Paramount, 1954
CRIME WAVE   1954
EAST OF EDEN   Warner Bros., 1955
FINGER MAN   1955
THE KILLING   United Artists, 1956
THE LAST WAGON   20th Century Fox, 1956
PATHS OF GLORY   United Artists, 1957
REVOLT IN THE BIG HOUSE   Allied Artists, 1958
ONE-EYED JACKS   Paramount, 1961
CONVICTS FOUR   REPRIEVE   1962
BIKINI BEACH   American International, 1964
WATERHOLE #3   Paramount, 1967
A TIME FOR KILLING   1967
HEAD   Columbia, 1968
WHAT'S THE MATTER WITH HELEN?   United Artists, 1971
MINNIE AND MOSKOWITZ   Universal, 1971
THE OUTFIT   MGM, 1974
THE CONVERSATION   Paramount, 1974
PEEPER   20th Century Fox, 1976
THE KILLING OF A CHINESE BOOKIE   Faces International, 1976
SPEEDTRAP   First Artists, 1978
FAST -WALKING   Pickman Films, 1982
D.C. CAB   Universal, 1983
ECHO PARK   Atlantic Releasing Corporation, 1986, U.S.-Austrian

TIMOTHY CARHART

Agent: Bauman, Hiller & Associates - Los Angeles, 213/857-6666

THE RESCUE   Buena Vista, 1988
BEVERLY HILLS COP III   Paramount, 1994
CANDYMAN 2: FAREWELL TO THE FLESH
    Gramercy Pictures, 1995

GIA CARIDES

Agent: William Morris Agency - Beverly Hills, 310/274-7451

BLISS   New World, 1985, Australian
THE TOOL SHED   Buena Vista, 1994

LEN CARIOU

b. September 30, 1939 - Winnipeg, Canada
Agent: Paradigm - Los Angeles, 310/277-4400

A LITTLE NIGHT MUSIC   New World, 1977, Austrian-U.S.
THE FOUR SEASONS   Universal, 1981
SURVIVING (TF)   Telepictures Productions, 1985
KILLER IN THE MIRROR (TF)   Litke-Grossbart Productions/Warner
    Bros. TV, 1986
LADY IN WHITE   New Century/Vista, 1988
WITNESS TO THE EXECUTION (TF)   NBC, 1994

CARITA

SUMMER   LE RAYON VEIT   Orion Classics, 1985, French

CYNTHIA CARLE

ALAMO BAY   TriStar, 1985

CATHERINE CARLEN

CHOPPER CHICKS IN ZOMBIETOWN   Troma, 1991

GEORGE CARLIN

b. May 12, 1937 - New York, New York
Agent: William Morris Agency - Beverly Hills, 310/274-7451

OUTRAGEOUS FORTUNE   Buena Vista, 1987
BILL & TED'S EXCELLENT ADVENTURE   Orion, 1989
BILL & TED'S BOGUS JOURNEY   Orion, 1991
THE PRINCE OF TIDES   Columbia, 1991

GLORIA CARLIN

Agent: Marshak-Wyckoff & Associates - Los Angeles, 310/278-7222

THE HANOI HILTON   Cannon, 1987
SO PROUDLY WE HAIL (TF)   Lionel Chetwynd Productions/CBS
    Entertainment, 1990

STEVE CARLISLE

SONNY BOY   Triumph Releasing Corporation, 1990

JOEL CARLSON

COMMUNION   MCEG, 1989

LES CARLSON

THE FLY   20th Century Fox, 1986, U.S.-Canadian

JULIE CARMEN

Agent: Metropolitan Talent Agency - Los Angeles, 213/857-4500

THE MILAGRO BEANFIELD WAR   Universal, 1988
NEON EMPIRE (CMS)   Richard Maynard Productions/Fries
    Entertainment, 1989
KISS ME A KILLER   Concorde, 1991
COLD HEAVEN   Hemdale, 1992
IN THE MOUTH OF MADNESS   New Line Cinema, 1994

LOENE CARMEN

THE YEAR MY VOICE BROKE   Avenue Pictures, 1988, Australian

JEAN CARMET

SORCERESS   European Classics, 1988, French

ART CARNEY

(Arthur William Matthew Carney)
b. November 4, 1918 - Mount Vernon, New York

POT O' GOLD   United Artists, 1941
THE YELLOW ROLLS-ROYCE   MGM, 1965, British

Ca

ACTORS
GUIDE

F
I
L
M

A
C
T
O
R
S

A GUIDE FOR THE MARRIED MAN   20th Century-Fox, 1967
HARRY AND TONTO ★★   20th Century Fox, 1974
DEATH SCREAM   *THE WOMAN WHO CRIED MURDER* (TF)
   RSO Films, 1975
KATHERINE (TF)   The Jozak Company, 1975
W.W. AND THE DIXIE DANCEKINGS   20th Century-Fox, 1975
WON TON TON, THE DOG WHO SAVED HOLLYWOOD
   Paramount, 1976
LANIGAN'S RABBI (TF)   Universal TV, 1976
THE LATE SHOW   Warner Bros., 1976
SCOTT JOPLIN   Universal, 1977
HOUSE CALLS   Universal, 1978
MOVIE MOVIE   Warner Bros., 1978
SUNBURN   Paramount, 1979, U.S.-British
GOING IN STYLE   Warner Bros., 1979
STEEL   *LOOK DOWN AND DIE/MEN OF STEEL*
   World Northal, 1980
ROADIE   United Artists, 1980
DEFIANCE   American International, 1980
BITTER HARVEST (TF)   Charles Fries Productions, 1981
ST. HELENS   Davis-Panzer Productions, 1981
TAKE THIS JOB AND SHOVE IT   Avco Embassy, 1981
THE EMPEROR'S NEW CLOTHES   1984
FIRESTARTER   Universal, 1984
THE MUPPETS TAKE MANHATTAN   TriStar, 1984
THE NIGHT THEY SAVED CHRISTMAS (TF)
   Robert Halmi, Inc., 1984
THE NAKED FACE   Cannon, 1985
IZZY AND MOE (TF)   Robert Halmi, Inc., 1985
THE BLUE YONDER   *TIME FLYER* (CTF)   Three Blind Mice
   Productions, 1985
THE UNDERGRADS (CTF)   Sharmhill Productions/The Disney
   Channel, 1985, U.S.-Canadian
MIRACLE OF THE HEART: A BOYS TOWN STORY (TF)
   Larry White Productions/Columbia TV, 1986
WHERE PIGEONS GO TO DIE (TF)   Michael Landon Productions/
   World International Network, 1990
LAST ACTION HERO   Columbia, 1993

LESLIE CARON
b. July 1, 1931 - Boulogne-Billancourt, France
Agent: The Blake Agency - Beverly Hills, 310/246-0241

AN AMERICAN IN PARIS   MGM, 1951
THE MAN WITH A CLOAK   MGM, 1951
GLORY ALLEY   MGM, 1952
THE STORY OF THREE LOVES   MGM, 1953
LILI ★   MGM, 1953
THE GLASS SLIPPER   1955
DADDY LONG LEGS   1955
GABY   1956
GIGI   MGM, 1958
THE DOCTOR'S DILEMMA   MGM, 1958, British
THE MAN WHO UNDERSTOOD WOMEN   20th Century Fox, 1959
THE BATTLE OF AUSTERLITZ   *AUSTERLITZ*   20th Century Fox,
   1960, French
THE SUBTERRANEANS   MGM, 1960
FANNY   Warner Bros., 1961
GUNS OF DARKNESS   Warner Bros., 1962, British
THREE FABLES OF LOVE   *LES QUATRE VÉRITÉS*   1962,
   French-Italian-Spanish
THE L-SHAPED ROOM ★   Columbia, 1963, British
FATHER GOOSE   Universal, 1964
A VERY SPECIAL FAVOR   Universal, 1965
PROMISE HER ANYTHING   Paramount, 1966
IS PARIS BURNING?   *PARIS BRULE-T-IL?*   Paramount,
   1966, French-U.S.
THE HEAD OF THE FAMILY   *IL PADRE DI FAMIGLIA*
   Ultra/CFC/Marianne Productions, 1968, Italian-French
MADRON   Four Star-Excelsior, 1970, U.S.-Israeli
CHANDLER   MGM, 1971
QB VII (MS)   Screen Gems/Columbia TV/The Douglas Cramer
   Company, 1974
SERAIL   1976, French
THE MAN WHO LOVED WOMEN   *L'HOMME QUI AIMAIT
   LES FEMMES*   Cinema 5, 1977, French
VALENTINO   United Artists, 1979, British
GOLDENGIRL   Avco Embassy, 1979
THE CONTRACT   New Yorker, 1980, Polish

IMPERATIV (TF)   TeleCulture, 1982, West German
MASTER OF THE GAME (MS)   Rosemont Productions, 1984
DANGEROUS MOVES   Arthur Cohn Productions, 1984, Swiss
COURAGE MOUNTAIN   Triumph Releasing Corporation,
   1989, U.S.-French
DAMAGE   New Line Cinema, 1992, French-British
LET IT BE ME   Savoy Pictures, 1995

DAVID CARPENTER
CRIMES OF THE HEART   DEG, 1986
P.O.W. THE ESCAPE   Cannon, 1986

JOHN CARPENTER
b. January 16, 1948 - Carthage, New York
Agent: ICM - Beverly Hills, 310/550-4000

SOMETHING WILD   Orion, 1986

DAVID CARRADINE
b. December 8, 1936 - Hollywood, California

TAGGART   Universal, 1964
BUS RILEY'S BACK IN TOWN   Universal, 1965
THE VIOLENT ONES   1967
HEAVEN WITH A GUN   MGM, 1969
YOUNG BILLY YOUNG   United Artists, 1969
THE GOOD GUYS AND THE BAD GUYS   Warner Bros., 1969
THE McMASTERS   Chevron, 1970
MACHO CALLAHAN   Avco Embassy, 1970
BOXCAR BERTHA   American International, 1972
MEAN STREETS   Warner Bros., 1973
YOU AND ME   Filmmakers International, 1975 (also directed)
DEATH RACE 2000   New World, 1975
CANNONBALL   New World, 1976
BOUND FOR GLORY   United Artists, 1976
THE SERPENT'S EGG   Paramount, 1977, West German-U.S.
THUNDER AND LIGHTNING   20th Century Fox, 1977
GRAY LADY DOWN   Universal, 1978
CIRCLE OF IRON   *THE SILENT FLUTE*   Avco Embassy, 1979
OLD BOYFRIENDS   Avco Embassy, 1979
MR. HORN (TF)   Lorimar Productions, 1979
CLOUD DANCER   Blossom, 1980
THE LONG RIDERS   United Artists, 1980
AMERICANA   Crown International, 1981
SAFARI 3000   United Artists, 1982
LONE WOLF McQUADE   Orion, 1983
THE BAD SEED (TF)   Hajeno Productions/Warner Bros. TV, 1985
NORTH AND SOUTH (MS)   Wolper Productions/
   Warner Bros. TV, 1985
ARMED RESPONSE   CineTel, 1986
OCEANS OF FIRE (TF)   Catalina Production Group, 1986
THE MISFIT BRIGADE   *WHEELS OF TERROR*   Trans World
   Entertainment, 1987, U.S.-British
SIX AGAINST THE ROCK (TF)   Schaefer-Karpf-Epstein Productions/
   Gaylord Production Company, 1987
I SAW WHAT YOU DID (TF)   Universal TV, 1988
THE COVER GIRL AND THE COP (TF)   Barry & Enright
   Productions, 1989
THINK BIG   MPCA, 1990
BIRD ON A WIRE   Universal, 1990
SONNY BOY   Triumph Releasing Corporation, 1990
ROADSIDE PROPHETS   New Line Cinema, 1992

KEITH CARRADINE
b. August 8, 1951 - San Mateo, California
Agent: ICM - Beverly Hills, 310/550-4000

McCABE & MRS. MILLER   Warner Bros., 1971
A GUNFIGHT   Paramount, 1971
EMPEROR OF THE NORTH   *EMPEROR OF THE NORTH POLE*
   20th Century Fox, 1973
HEX   1973
ANTOINE ET SEBASTIEN   1973, French
THE GODCHILD (TF)   MGM TV, 1974
THIEVES LIKE US   United Artists, 1974
RUN, RUN, JOE!   1974
IDAHO TRANSFER   Cinemation, 1975

YOU AND ME   Filmmakers International, 1975
NASHVILLE   Paramount, 1975
LUMIERE   New World, 1976, French
WELCOME TO L.A.   United Artists/Lions Gate, 1977
THE DUELLISTS   Paramount, 1978, British
PRETTY BABY   Paramount, 1978
SGT. PEPPER'S LONELY HEARTS CLUB BAND   Universal, 1978
OLD BOYFRIENDS   Avco Embassy, 1979
AN ALMOST PERFECT AFFAIR   Paramount, 1979
THE LONG RIDERS   United Artists, 1980
SOUTHERN COMFORT   20th Century Fox, 1981
CHIEFS (MS)   Highgate Pictures, 1983
CHOOSE ME   Island Alive/New Cinema, 1984
MARIA'S LOVERS   Cannon, 1985
SCORNED AND SWINDLED (TF)   Cypress Point Productions, 1985
TROUBLE IN MIND   Alive Films, 1985
A WINNER NEVER QUITS (TF)   Blatt-Singer Productions/
   Columbia TV, 1986
BACKFIRE   New Century/Vista, 1987
L'INCHIESTA   Italian International, 1987, Italian
MURDER ORDAINED (TF)   Zev Braun Productions/Interscope
   Communications, 1987
EYE ON THE SPARROW (TF)   Sarabande Productions/
   Republic Pictures, 1987
STONES FOR IBARRA (TF)   Titus Productions, 1988
MY FATHER, MY SON (TF)   Fred Weintraub Productions/
   John J. McMahon Productions, 1988
THE MODERNS   Alive Films, 1988
THE REVENGE OF AL CAPONE (TF)   Unity Productions/River City
   Productions, 1989
COLD FEET   Avenue Pictures, 1989
DADDY'S DYIN'...WHO'S GOT THE WILL?   MGM/UA, 1990
CRISSCROSS   MGM-Pathe Communications, 1992
ANDRE   Paramount, 1994
MRS. PARKER AND THE VICIOUS CIRCLE   Fine Line Features/
   New Line Cinema, 1994
WILD BILL   MGM/UA, 1995
THE TIE THAT BINDS   Buena Vista, 1995

ROBERT CARRADINE
b. 1954 - Los Angeles, California
Agent: Innovative Artists - Los Angeles, 310/553-5200
Management: More/Medavoy Management - Los Angeles,
   213/969-0700

THE COWBOYS   Warner Bros., 1972
MEAN STREETS   Warner Bros., 1973
ALOHA, BOBBY AND ROSE   Columbia, 1975
THE POM-POM GIRLS   Crown International, 1976
JACKSON COUNTY JAIL   New World, 1976
CANNONBALL   New World, 1976
MASSACRE AT CENTRAL HIGH   Brian Distributing, 1976
ORCA   Paramount, 1977
JOYRIDE   American International, 1977
COMING HOME   United Artists, 1978
BLACKOUT   1978, Canadian-French
SURVIVAL OF DANA (TF)   EMI TV, 1979
THE BIG RED ONE   United Artists, 1980
THE LONG RIDERS   United Artists, 1980
HEARTACHES   MPM, 1981, Canadian
TAG: THE ASSASSINATION GAME   New World, 1982
WAVELENGTH   New World, 1983
JUST THE WAY YOU ARE   MGM/UA, 1984
REVENGE OF THE NERDS   20th Century Fox, 1984
THE SUN ALSO RISES (MS)   Furia-Oringer Productions/
   20th Century Fox TV, 1984
MONTE CARLO (MS)   New World TV/Phoenix Entertainment Group/
   Collins-Holm Productions/Highgate Pictures, 1986
CONSPIRACY: TRIAL OF THE CHICAGO 8 (CTF)   Jeremy Kagan
   Productions/Inter Planetary Productions, 1987
THE LIBERATORS (TF)   Kenneth Johnson Productions/
   Walt Disney TV, 1987
NUMBER ONE WITH A BULLET   Cannon, 1987
REVENGE OF THE NERDS II: NERDS IN PARADISE
   20th Century Fox, 1987
BUY & CELL   Trans World Entertainment, 1989
I SAW WHAT YOU DID (TF)   Universal TV, 1988
RUDE AWAKENING   Orion, 1989

THE INCIDENT (TF)   Qintex Entertainment, 1990
SOMEBODY HAS TO SHOOT THE PICTURE (CTF)   Alan Barnette
   Productions/Frank Pierson Films/MCA-TV Entertainment/
   Scholastic Productions, 1990
CLARENCE (CTF)   Atlantis Films/South Pacific Pictures, Ltd./North
   Star Entertainment Group/The Family Channel/Television New
   Zealand, 1991, Canadian-U.S.-New Zealand
DOUBLE CROSSED CTF)   Green-Epstein Productions/
   Lorimar TV, 1991
ILLUSIONS   Paul Entertainment/Prism Entertainment, 1991
NERDS: THE NEXT GENERATION (TF)
   20th Century Fox TV, 1992

CARLOS CARRASCO
SPEED   20th Century Fox, 1994

BARBARA CARRERA
THE MASTER GUNFIGHTER   Taylor-Laughlin, 1975
EMBRYO   Cine Artists, 1976
THE ISLAND OF DR. MOREAU   American International, 1977
WHEN TIME RAN OUT   Warner Bros., 1980
LONE WOLF McQUADE   Orion, 1983
NEVER SAY NEVER AGAIN   Warner Bros., 1983
WILD GEESE II   Universal, 1985, British
LOVERBOY   TriStar, 1989
WICKED STEPMOTHER   MGM/UA, 1989
THE FAVORITE   Kings Road, 1989

TIA CARRERE
Agent: ICM - Beverly Hills, 310/550-4000

ALOHA SUMMER   *HANAUMA BAY*   Spectrafilm, 1988
WAYNE'S WORLD   Paramount, 1992
RISING SUN   20th Century Fox, 1993
WAYNE'S WORLD 2   Paramount, 1993
TRUE LIES   20th Century Fox, 1994
JURY DUTY   Sony Pictures, 1995

JIM CARREY
(James Carrey)
b. 1962 - Newmarket, Ontario, Canada
Agent: UTA - Beverly Hills, 310/273-6700

ONCE BITTEN   Samuel Goldwyn Company, 1985
PEGGY SUE GOT MARRIED   TriStar, 1986
THE DEAD POOL   Warner Bros., 1988
EARTH GIRLS ARE EASY   Vestron, 1989
PINK CADILLAC   Warner Bros., 1989
DOING TIME ON MAPLE DRIVE (TF)   FNM Films, 1992
ACE VENTURA: PET DETECTIVE   Warner Bros., 1994
THE MASK   New Line Cinema, 1994
DUMB AND DUMBER   New Line Cinema, 1994
BATMAN FOREVER   Warner Bros., 1995

ROBERT CARRICART
THE MILAGRO BEANFIELD WAR   Universal, 1988

ELPIDIA CARRILLO
THE BORDER   Universal, 1982
BEYOND THE LIMIT   *THE HONORARY CONSUL*
   Paramount, 1983, British

DEBBIE LEE CARRINGTON
Agent: Coralie Jr. Agency - Los Angeles, 213/681-8281

HOWARD THE DUCK   Universal, 1986
TOTAL RECALL   TriStar, 1990
THE BONFIRE OF THE VANITIES   Warner Bros., 1990
DICK AND MARGE SAVE THE WORLD   Warner Bros., 1992
BATMAN RETURNS   Warner Bros., 1992

DIAHANN CARROLL
b. July 17, 1935 - Bronx, New York
Agent: APA - Los Angeles, 310/273-0744

CARMEN JONES   20th Century Fox, 1954
PORGY AND BESS   Columbia, 1959
GOODBYE AGAIN   *AIMEZ-VOUS BRAHMS?*   United Artists,
   1961, French-U.S.
PARIS BLUES   United Artists, 1961
HURRY SUNDOWN   Paramount, 1967
THE SPLIT   MGM, 1968
CLAUDINE ★   20th Century Fox, 1974
DEATH SCREAM   *THE WOMAN WHO CRIED MURDER* (TF)
   RSO Films, 1975
FROM THE DEAD OF NIGHT (TF)   Shadowplay Films/Phoenix
   Entertainment Group, 1989
MURDER IN BLACK AND WHITE (TF)   Titus Productions, 1990
THE FIVE HEARTBEATS   20th Century Fox, 1991

HELENA CARROLL
THE DEAD   Vestron, 1987

JANET CARROLL
Agent: Harris & Goldberg - Los Angeles, 310/553-5200

BLUFFING IT (TF)   Ohlmeyer Communications, 1987
SHARING RICHARD (TF)   Houston Motion Picture Entertainment/
   CBS Entertainment, 1988
FAMILY BUSINESS   TriStar, 1989

LISA HART CARROLL
TERMS OF ENDEARMENT   Paramount, 1983

PAT CARROLL
b. May 5, 1927 - Shreveport, Louisiana

THE LITTLE MERMAID (AF)   Buena Vista, 1989 (voice)

ROCKY CARROLL
Agent: Paradigm - Los Angeles, 310/277-4400

THE CHASE   20th Century Fox, 1994
CRIMSON TIDE   Buena Vista, 1995

RONN CARROLL
DEEPSTAR SIX   TriStar, 1989

HUNTER CARSON
INVADERS FROM MARS   Cannon, 1986

TERENCE T.C. CARSON
LIVIN' LARGE   Samuel Goldwyn Company, 1991

ALICE CARTER
Agent: Bauman, Hiller & Associates - Los Angeles, 213/857-6666

GROSS ANATOMY   Buena Vista, 1989

FINN CARTER
HOW I GOT INTO COLLEGE   20th Century Fox, 1989
REVEALING EVIDENCE (TF)   T.W.S. Productions/Universal TV, 1990

HELENA BONHAM CARTER
(See Helena BONHAM Carter)

JIM CARTER
TOP SECRET!   Paramount, 1984
A PRIVATE FUNCTION   Island Alive, 1985, British
HAUNTED HONEYMOON   Orion, 1986
A MONTH IN THE COUNTRY   Orion Classics, 1987, British
ERIK THE VIKING   Orion, 1989, British
THE WITCHES   Warner Bros., 1990, British
BLAME IT ON THE BELLBOY   Buena Vista, 1992, British

THE HOUR OF THE PIG   Miramax Films, 1993, British-French
BLACK BEAUTY   Warner Bros., 1994, British-U.S.
BALTO (AF)   Universal, 1995 (voice)

LYNDA CARTER
b. July 24, 1951 - Phoenix, Arizona
Agent: William Morris Agency - Beverly Hills, 310/274-7451

STILLWATCH (TF)   Zev Braun Pictures/Interscope Communications/
   Potomac Productions, 1987
MICKEY SPILLANE'S MIKE HAMMER: MURDER TAKES ALL (TF)
   Jay Bernstein Productions/Columbia TV, 1990

MICHAEL PATRICK CARTER
CHILD'S PLAY   MGM/United Artists, 1988
ALL I WANT FOR CHRISTMAS   Paramount, 1991
WAYNE'S WORLD   Paramount, 1992
MILK MONEY   Paramount, 1994

NELL CARTER
b. September 13, 1948 - Birmingham, Alabama
Agent: William Morris Agency - Beverly Hills, 310/274-7451

HOW MUCH ARE THOSE CHILDREN IN THE WINDOW?
   Concorde, 1995

VERONICA CARTWRIGHT
Agent: William Morris Agency - Beverly Hills, 310/274-7451

THE CHILDREN'S HOUR   United Artists, 1961
THE BIRDS   Universal, 1963
INSERTS   United Artists, 1976, British
GOIN' SOUTH   Paramount, 1978
INVASION OF THE BODY SNATCHERS   United Artists, 1978
ALIEN   20th Century Fox, 1979, U.S.-British
GUYANA TRAGEDY: THE STORY OF JIM JONES (TF)
   The Konigsberg Company, 1980
PRIME SUSPECT (TF)   Tisch-Avnet Television, 1982
NIGHTMARES   Universal, 1983
NOT MY KID (TF)   Beth Polson Productions/Finnegan Associates, 1985
ROBERT KENNEDY AND HIS TIMES (MS)   Chris-Rose Productions/
   Columbia TV, 1985
FLIGHT OF THE NAVIGATOR   Buena Vista, 1986
WISDOM   20th Century Fox, 1986
INTIMATE ENCOUNTERS (TF)   Larry Thompson Productions/
   Donna Mills Productions/Columbia TV, 1986
THE WITCHES OF EASTWICK   Warner Bros., 1987
VALENTINO RETURNS   Vidmark International, 1987
DESPERATE FOR LOVE (TF)   Vishudda Productions/Andrew
   Adelson Productions/Lorimar Telepictures, 1989
A SON'S PROMISE (TF)   Marian Rees Associates, 1990
FALSE IDENTITY   RKO Pictures, 1990
MAN TROUBLE   20th Century Fox, 1992
CANDYMAN 2: FAREWELL TO THE FLESH   Gramercy Pictures, 1995

DAVID CARUSO
Agent: UTA - Beverly Hills, 310/273-6700

BLUE CITY   Paramount, 1986
CHINA GIRL   Vestron, 1987
KING OF NEW YORK   New Line Cinema, 1990
HUDSON HAWK   TriStar, 1991
MAD DOG AND GLORY   Universal, 1993
KISS OF DEATH   20th Century Fox, 1995
JADE   Paramount, 1995

DANA CARVEY
b. June 6, 1955 - Missoula, Montana

TOUGH GUYS   Buena Vista, 1986
MOVING   Warner Bros., 1988
OPPORTUNITY KNOCKS   Universal, 1990
WAYNE'S WORLD   Paramount, 1992
WAYNE'S WORLD 2   Paramount, 1993
CLEAN SLATE   MGM/UA, 1994
THE ROAD TO WELLVILLE   Columbia, 1994
TRAPPED IN PARADISE   20th Century Fox, 1994

SALVATORE CASCIO
CINEMA PARADISO *NUOVO CINEMA PARADISO*
Miramax Films, 1989, Italian-French

NICHOLAS CASCONE
Agent: Susan Smith & Associates - Beverly Hills, 213/852-4777

84 CHARLIE MOPIC   New Century/Vista, 1989

MAX CASELLA
Agent: William Morris Agency - Beverly Hills, 310/274-7451

NEWSIES   Buena Vista, 1992
ED WOOD   Buena Vista, 1994

CHIARA CASELLI
ESPECIALLY ON SUNDAY   Miramax Films, 1993

BERNIE CASEY
SHARKY'S MACHINE   Orion/Warner Bros., 1981
SPIES LIKE US   Warner Bros., 1985
RENT-A-COP   Kings Road Productions, 1988
BILL & TED'S EXCELLENT ADVENTURE   Orion, 1989
I'M GONNA GIT YOU SUCKA   MGM/UA, 1989
ANOTHER 48 HRS.   Paramount, 1990

JOHNNY CASH
b. February 26, 1932 - Kingsland, Arkansas
Agent: APA - Los Angeles, 310/273-0744

FIVE MINUTES TO LIVE *DOOR-TO-DOOR MANIAC*   1961
A GUNFIGHT   Paramount, 1971
THE PRIDE OF JESSE HALLAM (TF)   The Konigsberg
   Company, 1981
MURDER IN COWETA COUNTY (TF)   Telecom Entertainment/
   The International Picture Show Co., 1983
THE BARON AND THE KID (TF)   Telecom Entertainment, 1984
THE LAST DAYS OF FRANK AND JESSE JAMES (TF)
   Joseph Cates Productions, 1986
STAGECOACH (TF)   Raymond Katz Productions/Heritage
   Entertainment, 1986

ROSALIND CASH
b. December 31, 1938 - Atlantic City, New Jersey
Agent: John Sekura/A Talent Agency - Los Angeles, 213/962-6290

KLUTE   Warner Bros., 1971
THE OMEGA MAN   Warner Bros., 1971
THE ALL-AMERICAN BOY   Warner Bros., 1971
THE NEW CENTURIONS   Columbia, 1972
HICKEY AND BOGGS   United Artists, 1972
UPTOWN SATURDAY NIGHT   Warner Bros., 1974
AMAZING GRACE   United Artists, 1974
CORNBREAD EARL AND ME   American International, 1975
DR. BLACK, MR. HYDE   Dimension, 1976
THE MONKEY HUSTLE   American International, 1976
THE CLASS OF MISS MACMICHAEL   Brut Productions,
   1979, British
GUYANA TRAGEDY: THE STORY OF JIM JONES (TF)
   The Konigsberg Company, 1980
WRONG IS RIGHT   Columbia, 1982

KATRINA CASPARY
Agent: Booh Schut Agency - Studio City, 818/760-6669

MAC AND ME   Orion, 1988

NICK CASSAVETES
MASK   Universal, 1985
THE WRAITH   New Century/Vista, 1986
BLACK MOON RISING   New World, 1986
BACKSTREET DREAMS   Trimark Pictures, 1990
BLIND FURY   TriStar, 1990
THE DOORS   TriStar, 1991
TWOGETHER   Borde Releasing, 1994

THE GODS OF SKID ROW   1994
MRS. PARKER AND THE VICIOUS CIRCLE   Fine Line Features/
   New Line Cinema, 1994

VIRGINIA CASSAVETES
TWOGETHER   Borde Releasing, 1994

JEAN-PIERRE CASSEL
(Jean-Pierre Crochon)
b. October 27, 1932 - Paris, France

THOSE MAGNIFICENT MEN IN THEIR FLYING MACHINES
   20th Century Fox, 1965, British
OH! WHAT A LOVELY WAR   Paramount, 1969, British
THE DISCREET CHARM OF THE BOURGEOISIE
   20th Century Fox, 1972, French
THE THREE MUSKETEERS   20th Century Fox, 1974, British
MURDER ON THE ORIENT EXPRESS   Paramount, 1974, British
THE FOUR MUSKETEERS   20th Century Fox, 1975, British
WHO IS KILLING THE GREAT CHEFS OF EUROPE?
   Warner Bros., 1978

SEYMOUR CASSEL
Agent: William Morris Agency - Beverly Hills, 310/274-7451

TOO LATE BLUES   Paramount, 1962
THE KILLERS   Universal, 1964
THE SWEET RIDE   20th Century Fox, 1968
COOGAN'S BLUFF   Universal, 1968
FACES ✪   Continental, 1968
THE REVOLUTIONARY   United Artists, 1970
MINNIE AND MOSKOWITZ   Universal, 1971
THE LAST TYCOON   Paramount, 1975
THE KILLING OF A CHINESE BOOKIE   Faces International, 1976
SCOTT JOPLIN   Universal, 1977
BLACK OAK CONSPIRACY   1977
DEATH GAME *THE SEDUCERS*   1977
VALENTINO   United Artists, 1977, British
CONVOY   United Artists, 1978
CALIFORNIA DREAMING   American International, 1979
TIN MEN   Buena Vista, 1987
TRACK 29   Island Pictures, 1988
DICK TRACY   Buena Vista, 1990
WHITE FANG   Buena Vista, 1991
HONEYMOON IN VEGAS   Columbia, 1992
IN THE SOUP   Triton Pictures, 1992,
   U.S.-Japanese-German-French-Spanish-Italian
INDECENT PROPOSAL   Paramount, 1993
IT COULD HAPPEN TO YOU   TriStar, 1994
THINGS TO DO IN DENVER WHEN YOU'RE DEAD
   Miramax Films, 1995

GABRIEL CASSEUS
NEW JERSEY DRIVE   Gramercy Pictures, 1994

JOANNA CASSIDY
b. August 2, 1944 - Camden, New Jersey

BULLITT   Warner Bros., 1968
FOOLS   Cinerama Releasing Corporation, 1970
THE LAUGHING POLICEMAN   20th Century Fox, 1974
THE OUTFIT   MGM, 1974
BANK SHOT   1974
NIGHT CHILD   1975
STAY HUNGRY   United Artists, 1976
THE LATE SHOW   Warner Bros., 1977
STUNTS *WHO IS KILLING THE STUNTMEN?*
   New Line Cinema, 1977
BLADE RUNNER   The Ladd Company/Warner Bros., 1982
UNDER FIRE   Orion, 1983
CODENAME: FOXFIRE (TF)   Universal TV, 1985
HOLLYWOOD WIVES (MS)   Aaron Spelling Productions, 1985
THE CHILDREN OF TIMES SQUARE (TF)   Gross-Weston
   Productions/Fries Entertainment, 1986
PLEASURES (TF)   Catalina Production Group/Columbia TV, 1986
CLUB PARADISE   Warner Bros., 1986

THE FOURTH PROTOCOL   Lorimar, 1987, British
A FATHER'S REVENGE (TF)   Shadowplay-Rosco Productions/
    Phoenix Entertainment Group, 1988
WHO FRAMED ROGER RABBIT   Buena Vista, 1988
1969   Atlantic Releasing Corporation, 1988
NIGHTMARE AT BITTER CREEK (TF)   Swanton Films/Guber-Peters
    Entertainment Company/Phoenix Entertainment Group, 1988
THE PACKAGE   Orion, 1989
WHERE THE HEART IS   Buena Vista, 1990
WHEELS OF TERROR (CTF)   Once Upon A Time Productions/
    Wilshire Court Productions, 1990
DON'T TELL MOM THE BABYSITTER'S DEAD   Warner Bros., 1991
LONELY HEARTS   Live Entertainment, 1991

PATRICK CASSIDY

SOMETHING IN COMMON (TF)   New World TV/Freyda Rothstein
    Productions/Littke-Grossbart Productions, 1986
DRESS GRAY (MS)   von Zerneck Prods./Warner Bros. TV, 1986
THREE ON A MATCH (TF)   Belisarius Productions/TriStar TV, 1987
NAPOLEON AND JOSEPHINE: A LOVE STORY (MS)
    David L. Wolper Productions/Warner Bros. TV, 1987
FOLLOW YOUR HEART (TF)   Force Ten Productions/Jabberwocky/
    NBC Productions, 1990
LONGTIME COMPANION   Samuel Goldwyn Company, 1990
I'LL DO ANYTHING   Columbia, 1994

SHAUN CASSIDY

ONCE UPON A TEXAS TRAIN (TF)   Robert Papazian Productions/
    Brigade Productions/Rastar, 1988
ROOTS: THE GIFT (TF)   Wolper Productions/
    Warner Bros. TV, 1988

RALPH CASTELLI

BEATLEMANIA   American Cinema, 1981

DAN CASTELLANETA

THE RETURN OF JAFAR (AV)   Buena Vista, 1994 (voice)

SERGIO CASTELLITTO

THE BIG BLUE   Columbia, 1988

CHRISTOPHER CASTILE

BEETHOVEN   Universal, 1992

JOHN CASTLE

Agent: Paradigm - Los Angeles, 310/277-4400

THE LION IN WINTER   Avco Embassy, 1968, British
ANTONY AND CLEOPATRA   Rank, 1973, British-Spanish-Swiss
MAN OF LA MANCHA   United Artists, 1972, Italian-U.S.
THE INCREDIBLE SARAH   Reader's Digest, 1976, British
EAGLE'S WING   International Picture Show, 1979, British
ROBOCOP 3   Orion, 1993

ANALIA CASTRO

THE OFFICIAL STORY   Historias Cinematograficas,
    1985, Argentine

GEORGINA CATES

AN AWFULLY BIG ADVENTURE   Fine Line Features/New Line
    Cinema, 1995, British

PHOEBE CATES

Agent: UTA - Beverly Hills, 310/273-6700

PARADISE   Avco Embassy, 1982, Canadian
FAST TIMES AT RIDGEMONT HIGH   Universal, 1982
BABY SISTER (TF)   Moonlight Productions II, 1983
PRIVATE SCHOOL   Universal, 1983
LACE (MS)   Lorimar Productions, 1984
GREMLINS   Warner Bros., 1984
LACE II (MS)   Lorimar Productions, 1985
BRIGHT LIGHTS, BIG CITY   MGM/UA, 1988
HEART OF DIXIE   Orion, 1989

I LOVE YOU TO DEATH   TriStar, 1990 (uncredited)
GREMLINS 2 THE NEW BATCH   Warner Bros., 1990
DROP DEAD FRED   New Line Cinema, 1991
BODIES, REST & MOTION   Mainline Films, 1993
PRINCESS CARABOO   TriStar, 1994

REG E. CATHEY

TANK GIRL   MGM/UA, 1995

LLOYD CATLETT

BLOWN AWAY   MGM/UA, 1994

JULIETTE CATON

COURAGE MOUNTAIN   Triumph Releasing Corporation,
    1989, U.S.-French

KIM CATTRALL

Agent: William Morris Agency - Beverly Hills, 310/274-7451

POLICE ACADEMY   The Ladd Company/Warner Bros., 1984
TURK 182   20th Century Fox, 1985
BIG TROUBLE IN LITTLE CHINA   20th Century Fox, 1986
MANNEQUIN   20th Century Fox, 1987
MASQUERADE   MGM/UA, 1988
THE BONFIRE OF THE VANITIES   Warner Bros., 1990
STAR TREK VI: THE UNDISCOVERED COUNTRY
    Paramount, 1991
WILD PALMS (MS)   Ixtlan Corporation/Greengrass
    Productions, Inc., 1993
THE RHINEHART THEORY   Rysher Entertainment, 1994
LIVE NUDE GIRLS   Republic Pictures, 1995

MAXWELL CAULFIELD

Agent: Harris & Goldberg - Los Angeles, 310/553-5200

GREASE 2   Paramount, 1982
THE BOYS NEXT DOOR   New World, 1985
DANCE WITH DEATH   Concorde, 1991
GETTYSBURG   New Line Cinema, 1993

CATHY CAVADINI

AN AMERICAN TAIL: FIEVEL GOES WEST (AF)   Universal,
    1991 (voice)

CHRISTINE CAVANAGH

BALTO (AF)   Universal, 1995 (voice)

MEGAN CAVANAGH

A LEAGUE OF THEIR OWN   Columbia, 1992

DICK CAVETT

b. November 19, 1936 - Gibbon, Nebraska

ANNIE HALL   United Artists, 1977
HEALTH   20th Century Fox, 1980
A NIGHTMARE ON ELM STREET, PART 3: DREAM WARRIORS
    New Line Cinema, 1987
BEETLEJUICE   Warner Bros., 1988

JAMES CAVIEZEL

WYATT EARP   Warner Bros., 1994

CHRISTOPHER CAZENOVE

Agent: Paul Kohner, Inc. - Los Angeles, 310/550-1060

ROYAL FLASH   20th Century Fox, 1975, British
ZULU DAWN   American Cinema, 1979, British
EYE OF THE NEEDLE   United Artists, 1981, British
FROM A FAR COUNTRY   Trans World Film/ITC/RAI/Film Polski,
    1981, British-Italian-Polish
THE LETTER (TF)   Hajero Productions/Warner Bros. TV, 1982
HEAT AND DUST   Universal Classics, 1983, British
MATA HARI   Cannon, 1985

JENNY'S WAR (TF)   Louis Rudolph Productions/HTV/Columbia TV,
    1985, U.S.-British
LACE II (MS)   Lorimar Productions, 1985
THE FANTASIST   ITC, 1986, Irish
SIDNEY SHELDON'S WINDMILLS OF THE GODS   *WINDMILLS OF
    THE GODS* (MS)   Dove Productions/ITC Productions, 1988
THE LADY AND THE HIGHWAYMAN (TF)   The Grade Company/
    Gainsborough Pictures, 1989, British
THREE MEN AND A LITTLE LADY   Buena Vista, 1990
ACES: IRON EAGLE III   New Line Cinema, 1991

DANIEL CECCALDI
TWISTED OBSESSION   Majestic Films International, 1990

JANE CECIL
SEPTEMBER   Orion, 1987

CLEMENTINE CÉLARIE
BETTY BLUE   Alive Films, 1986, French

STEVEN CEPELLO
GRUNT! THE WRESTLING MOVIE   New World, 1986

BRIAN CESAK
FANDANGO   Warner Bros., 1985

JUNE CHADWICK
THIS IS SPINAL TAP   Embassy, 1984

KATHLEEN CHALFANT
MISS FIRECRACKER   Corsair Pictures, 1989

FEODOR CHALIAPIN, ;JR.
THE NAME OF THE ROSE   20th Century Fox, 1986,
    West German-Italian-French
MOONSTRUCK   MGM/UA, 1987
STANLEY & IRIS   MGM/UA, 1990

GARY CHALK
THE FLY II   20th Century Fox, 1989

RICHARD CHAMBERLAIN
(George Richard Chamberlain)
b. March 31, 1935 - Beverly Hills, California
Agent: CAA - Beverly Hills, 310/288-4545

THE SECRET OF THE PURPLE REEF   20th Century-Fox, 1960
A THUNDER OF DRUMS   1961
TWILIGHT OF HONOR   MGM, 1963
JOY IN THE MORNING   MGM, 1965
PETULIA   1968, U.S.-British
THE MADWOMAN OF CHAILLOT   Warner Bros., 1969, British
JULIUS CAESAR   American International, 1971, British
THE MUSIC LOVERS   United Artists, 1971, British
LADY CAROLINE LAMB   United Artists, 1973, British
THE LAST OF THE BELLES (TF)   1974
THE THREE MUSKETEERS   20th Century Fox, 1974, British
THE TOWERING INFERNO   20th Century Fox/Warner Bros., 1974
THE FOUR MUSKETEERS   20th Century Fox, 1975, British
THE SLIPPER AND THE ROSE: THE STORY OF CINDERELLA
    Universal, 1976, British
THE COUNT OF MONTE CRISTO   Norman Rosemont
    Productions/ITC, 1976, U.S.-British
THE MAN IN THE IRON MASK (TF)   Norman Rosemont
    Productions/ITC, 1977
THE SWARM   Warner Bros., 1978
CENTENNIAL (MS)   Universal TV, 1978
THE LAST WAVE   World Northal, 1978, Australian
SHOGUN (MS)   Paramount TV/NBC Entertainment,
    1980, U.S.-Japanese
MURDER BY PHONE   New World, 1983, Canadian
THE THORN BIRDS (MS)   David L. Wolper-Stan Margulies
    Productions/Edward Lewis Productions/Warner Bros. TV, 1983
KING SOLOMON'S MINES   Cannon, 1985

WALLENBERG: A HERO'S STORY (MS)   Dick Berg-Stonehenge
    Productions/Paramount TV, 1985
DREAM WEST (MS)   Sunn Classic Pictures, 1986
CASANOVA (TF)   Konigsberg-Sanitsky Company/Reteitalia,
    1987, U.S.-Italian
ALLAN QUATERMAIN AND THE LOST CITY OF GOLD
    Cannon, 1987
THE BOURNE IDENTITY (MS)   Alan Shayne Productions/
    Warner Bros. TV, 1988
THE RETURN OF THE MUSKETEERS   Universal, 1989

WILT CHAMBERLAIN
CONAN THE DESTROYER   Universal, 1984

MICHAEL "BOOGALOO SHRIMP" CHAMBERS
BREAKIN'   MGM/UA/Cannon, 1984
BREAKIN' 2 ELECTRIC BOOGALOO   TriStar/Cannon, 1985

JO CHAMPA
Agent: Metropolitan Talent Agency - Los Angeles, 213/857-4500

SALOME   Cannon, 1986, Italian-French
THE FAMILY   *LA FAMIGLIA*   Vestron, 1987, Italian
THE DARK SUN   Cecchi Gori/Tiger/Reteitalia, 1990, Italian
OUT FOR JUSTICE   Warner Bros., 1991
DON JUAN DE MARCO AND THE CENTERFOLD
    New Line Cinema, 1995

MICHAEL CHAMPION
TOTAL RECALL   TriStar, 1990

DENNIS CHAN
KICKBOXER   Cannon, 1989

JACKIE CHAN
THE CANNONBALL RUN   20th Century Fox, 1981

MICHELE CHAN
Agent: Twentieth Century Artists - Los Angeles, 213/850-5516

AMERICAN NINJA 3: BLOOD HUNT   Cannon, 1989

MELISSA CHAN
THE GIRL WHO CAME BETWEEN THEM (TF)   Saban-Scherick
    Productions, 1990

ESTEE CHANDLER
TERMINAL BLISS   Cannon, 1992

JARED CHANDLER
FLIGHT OF THE INTRUDER   Paramount, 1991

JOHN CHANDLER
ADVENTURES IN BABYSITTING   Buena Vista, 1987

KYLE CHANDLER
THE COLOR OF EVENING   1991

SARI CHANG
Agent: Abrams Artists & Associates - Los Angeles, 310/859-0625

CHINA GIRL   Vestron, 1987

CAROL CHANNING
b. January 31, 1923 - Seattle, Washington

HAPPILY EVER AFTER (AF)   First National Film Corporation,
    1993 (voice)
HANS CHRISTIAN ANDERSEN'S THUMBELINA (AF)
    Warner Bros., 1994 (voice)

STOCKARD CHANNING
(Susan Stockard)
b. February 13, 1944 - New York, New York
Agent: ICM - Beverly Hills, 310/550-4000

THE HOSPITAL   United Artists, 1971
UP THE SANDBOX   National General, 1972
THE GIRL MOST LIKELY TO... (TF)   ABC Circle Films, 1973
THE FORTUNE   Columbia, 1975
SWEET REVENGE   *DANDY, THE ALL AMERICAN GIRL*
   MGM/United Artists, 1976
THE BIG BUS   Paramount, 1976
LUCAN (TF)   MGM TV, 1977
THE CHEAP DETECTIVE   Columbia, 1978
GREASE   Paramount, 1978
SILENT VICTORY: THE KITTY O'NEIL STORY (TF)
   Channin-Debin-Locke Company, 1979
THE FISH THAT SAVED PITTSBURGH   United Artists, 1979
SAFARI 3000   United Artists, 1982
WITHOUT A TRACE   20th Century Fox, 1983
NOT MY KID (TF)   Beth Polson Productions/Finnegan
   Associates, 1985
THE MEN'S CLUB   Atlantic Releasing Corporation, 1986
HEARTBURN   Paramount, 1986
THE ROOM UPSTAIRS (TF)   Marian Rees Associates/The
   Alexander Group, 1987
JOSEPH WAMBAUGH'S ECHOES IN THE DARKNESS
   ECHOES IN THE DARKNESS (MS)   Litke Grossbart Productions/
   New World TV, 1987
A TIME OF DESTINY   Columbia, 1988
STAYING TOGETHER   Hemdale, 1989
PERFECT WITNESS (CTF)   HBO Pictures/Granger
   Productions, 1989
MEET THE APPLEGATES   Triton Pictures, 1991
MARRIED TO IT   Orion, 1993
SIX DEGREES OF SEPARATION ★   MGM/UA, 1993
SMOKE   Miramax Films, 1995
TO WONG FOO, THANKS FOR EVERYTHING, JULIE NEWMAR
   Universal, 1995

ROSALIND CHAO
THE JOY LUCK CLUB   Buena Vista, 1993

DAMIAN CHAPA
MENENDEZ: A KILLING IN BEVERLY HILLS (MS)   Zev Braun
   Pictures/TriStar Television, 1994
STREET FIGHTER   Universal, 1994

GERALDINE CHAPLIN
b. July 31, 1944 - Santa Monica, California
Agent: William Morris Agency - Beverly Hills, 310/274-7451

LIMELIGHT   United Artists, 1952
DOCTOR ZHIVAGO   MGM, 1965, British
STRANGER IN THE HOUSE   *COP-OUT*   1967, British
THE COUNTESS FROM HONG KONG   Universal, 1967, British
I KILLED RASPUTIN   *J'AI TUÉ RASPOUTINE*   1967,
   French-Italian-West German
HONEYCOMB   *LA MADRIGUERA*   CineGlobe, 1969, Spanish
THE HAWAIIANS   United Artists, 1970
SUR UN ARBRE PERCHÉ   1971, French
LA CASA SIN FRONTERAS   1972, Spanish
Z.P.G.   Paramount, 1972, British
INNOCENT BYSTANDERS   1973, British
VERFLUCHT DIES AMERIKA!   1974, West German
LA BANDA DE JAIDER   1974, Spanish-West German
THE THREE MUSKETEERS   20th Century Fox, 1974, British
THE FOUR MUSKETEERS   20th Century Fox, 1975, British
NASHVILLE   Paramount, 1975
BUFFALO BILL AND THE INDIANS or SITTING BULL'S HISTORY
   LESSON   United Artists, 1976
CRIA!   *CRIA CUERVOS*   Jason Allen, 1976, Spanish
WELCOME TO L.A.   United Artists/Lions Gate, 1977
ELISA, MY LOVE   *ELISA, VIDA MIA*   Elias Querejeta
   Productions, 1977, Spanish
NOROIT   1977, French
IN MEMORIAM   1977, Spanish
UNE PAGE D'AMOUR   1977, Belgian-French

ROSELAND   Cinema Shares International, 1977
LOS OJOS VENDADOS   Elias Querejeta Productions,
   1978, Spanish
A WEDDING   20th Century Fox, 1978
REMEMBER MY NAME   Columbia/Lagoon Associates, 1978
THE MIRROR CRACK'D   AFD, 1980, British
VOYAGE EN DOUCE   1980, French
BOLERO   *LES UNS ET LES AUTRES/WITHIN MEMORY*
   Double 13/Sharp Features, 1982, French
LOVE ON THE GROUND   Spectrafilm, 1984, French
THE CORSICAN BROTHERS (TF)   Rosemont Productions,
   1985, British-U.S.
HEARTBURN   Paramount, 1986
THE MODERNS   Alive Films, 1988
CHAPLIN   TriStar, 1992, U.S.-British

JUDITH CHAPMAN
DEAD SPACE   Concorde, 1991

LONNY CHAPMAN
Agent: Contemporary Artists - Santa Monica, 310/395-1800

YOUNG AT HEART   Warner Bros., 1954
BABY DOLL   Warner Bros., 1956
THE BIRDS   Universal, 1963
THE REIVERS   National General, 1969
THE COWBOYS   Warner Bros., 1972
WHERE THE RED FERN GROWS   1974
MOVING VIOLATION   20th Century Fox, 1976
NORMA RAE   20th Century Fox, 1979
52 PICK-UP   Cannon, 1986

DAVE CHAPPELLE
ROBIN HOOD: MEN IN TIGHTS   20th Century Fox, 1993

PATRICIA CHARBONNEAU
Agent: Harris & Goldberg - Los Angeles, 310/553-5200

DESERT HEARTS   Samuel Goldwyn Company, 1985
CALL ME   Vestron, 1988
SHAKEDOWN   Universal, 1988
DISASTER AT SILO 7 (TF)   Mark Carliner Productions, 1988
DESPERADO: BADLANDS JUSTICE (TF)   Desperado
   Productions, 1989

JON CHARDIET
BEAT STREET   Orion, 1984

TARA CHARENDOFF
NATIONAL LAMPOON'S SENIOR TRIP   New Line Cinema, 1995

CYD CHARISSE
(Tula Ellice Finklea)
b. March 8, 1921 - Amarillo, Texas
Agent: Shapiro-Lichtman - Los Angeles, 310/859-8877

MISSION TO MOSCOW   Warner Bros., 1943
SOMETHING TO SHOUT ABOUT   Columbia, 1943
THE HARVEY GIRLS   MGM, 1946
SIEGFIELD FOLLIES   MGM, 1946
THREE WISE FOOLS   MGM, 1946
TILL THE CLOUDS ROLL BY   MGM, 1946
FIESTA   MGM, 1947
THE UNFINISHED DANCE   MGM, 1947
ON AN ISLAND WITH YOU   MGM, 1948
WORDS AND MUSIC   MGM, 1948
THE KISSING BANDIT   MGM, 1948
EAST SIDE, WEST SIDE   MGM, 1949
TENSION   MGM, 1949
MARK OF THE RENEGADE   Universal, 1951
SINGIN' IN THE RAIN   MGM, 1952
THE WILD NORTH   MGM, 1952
SOMBRERO   MGM, 1953
THE BAND WAGON   MGM, 1953
EASY TO LOVE   MGM, 1953 (uncredited)
BRIGADOON   MGM, 1954

DEEP IN MY HEART   MGM, 1954
IT'S ALWAYS FAIR WEATHER   MGM, 1955
MEET ME IN LAS VEGAS   MGM, 1956
INVITATION TO THE DANCE   MGM, 1956
SILK STOCKINGS   MGM, 1957
TWILIGHT FOR THE GODS   Universal, 1958
PARTY GIRL   MGM, 1958
BLACK TIGHTS   *UN DEUX TROIS QUATRE/
   LES COLLANTS NOIRS*   Magna, 1960, French
FIVE GOLDEN HOURS   *CINQUE ORE IN CONTANTI*
   1961, British
TWO WEEKS IN ANOTHER TOWN   MGM, 1962
ASSASSINATION IN ROME   *ASSASSINIO/MADE IN ITALY*
   1963, Italian
THE SILENCERS   Columbia, 1966
MAROC 7   Paramount, 1967, British
CALL HER MOM (TF)   Screen Gems/Columbia TV, 1972
WARLORDS OF ATLANTIS   Columbia, 1978, British
PORTRAIT OF AN ESCORT (TF)   Moonlight Productions/
   Filmways, 1980
SWIMSUIT (TF)   Musifilm Productions/American First
   Run Studios, 1989
THAT'S ENTERTAINMENT! III (FD)   MGM/UA, 1994

DAVID CHARLES
JULIA HAS TWO LOVERS   South Gate Entertainment, 1991

JOSH CHARLES
HAIRSPRAY   New Line Cinema, 1988
DEAD POETS SOCIETY   Buena Vista, 1989
DON'T TELL MOM THE BABYSITTER'S DEAD   Warner Bros., 1991
CROSSING THE BRIDGE   Buena Vista, 1992
THREESOME   TriStar, 1994
THINGS TO DO IN DENVER WHEN YOU'RE DEAD
   Miramax Films, 1995

RAY CHARLES
b. September 23, 1930 - Albany, Georgia
Agent: William Morris Agency - Beverly Hills, 310/274-7451

THE BLUES BROTHERS   Universal, 1980

CHARO
b. January 15, 1951 - Murcia, Spain

THE CONCORDE—AIRPORT '79   Universal, 1979
MOON OVER PARADOR   Universal, 1988, U.S.-Brazilian
HANS CHRISTIAN ANDERSEN'S THUMBELINA (AF)
   Warner Bros., 1994 (voice)

CHEVY CHASE
b. October 8, 1943 - New York, New York
Agent: CAA - Beverly Hills, 310/288-4545

TUNNELVISION   World Wide, 1976
FOUL PLAY   Paramount, 1978
SEEMS LIKE OLD TIMES   Columbia, 1980
OH, HEAVENLY DOG   20th Century Fox, 1980
CADDYSHACK   Orion/Warner Bros., 1980
MODERN PROBLEMS   20th Century Fox, 1981
UNDER THE RAINBOW   Orion/Warner Bros., 1981
NATIONAL LAMPOON'S VACATION   Warner Bros., 1983
DEAL OF THE CENTURY   Warner Bros., 1983
FLETCH   Universal, 1985
NATIONAL LAMPOON'S EUROPEAN VACATION   Warner Bros., 1985
SPIES LIKE US   Warner Bros., 1985
THREE AMIGOS   Orion, 1986
FUNNY FARM   Warner Bros., 1988
CADDYSHACK II   Warner Bros., 1988
FLETCH LIVES   Universal, 1989
NATIONAL LAMPOON'S CHRISTMAS VACATION   Warner Bros., 1989
L.A. STORY   TriStar, 1991 (uncredited)
NOTHING BUT TROUBLE   Warner Bros., 1991
MEMOIRS OF AN INVISIBLE MAN   Warner Bros., 1992
HERO   Columbia, 1992 (uncredited)
LAST ACTION HERO   Columbia, 1993
COPS & ROBBERSONS   TriStar, 1994
MAN 2 MAN   Buena Vista, 1995

INGRID CHAVEZ
GRAFFITI BRIDGE   Warner Bros., 1990

MAURY CHAYKIN
Agent: Gersh Agency - Beverly Hills, 310/274-6611

IRON EAGLE II   TriStar, 1988, Canadian-Israeli
BREAKING IN   Samuel Goldwyn Company, 1989
DANCES WITH WOLVES   Orion, 1990
UNSTRUNG HEROES   Buena Vista, 1995

DON CHEADLE
DEVIL IN A BLUE DRESS   TriStar, 1994

JOAN CHEN
Agent: William Morris Agency - Beverly Hills, 310/274-7451

LITTLE FLOWER   1980, Chinese
AWAKENING   1980, Chinese
TAI-PAN   DEG, 1986
THE LAST EMPEROR   Columbia, 1987, British-Chinese
THE BLOOD OF HEROES   New Line Cinema, 1990
TWIN PEAKS (TF)   Lynch-Frost Productions/Propaganda Films/
   World Vision Enterprises, 1990
WEDLOCK (CTF)   HBO Pictures/Spectacor Films, 1991
WHERE SLEEPING DOGS LIE   August Entertainment, 1992
HEAVEN AND EARTH   Warner Bros., 1993
GOLDEN GATE   Samuel Goldwyn Company, 1994
ON DEADLY GROUND   Warner Bros., 1994
JUDGE DREDD   Buena Vista, 1995
THE WILDSIDE   August Entertainment, 1995

MOIRA CHEN
(Laura Gemser)
LOVE IS FOREVER (TF)   Michael Landon-Hall Bartlett Films/
   NBC-TV/20th Century Fox TV, 1983

CHER
(Cherilyn Sarkesian)
b. May 20, 1946 - El Centro, California
Agent: CAA - Beverly Hills, 310/288-4545

WILD ON THE BEACH   20th Century-Fox, 1965
GOOD TIMES   Columbia, 1967
CHASTITY   1969
COME BACK TO THE 5 & DIME JIMMY DEAN, JIMMY DEAN
   Cinecom, 1982
SILKWOOD ✪   20th Century Fox, 1983
MASK   Universal, 1985
MOONSTRUCK ★★   MGM/UA, 1987
THE WITCHES OF EASTWICK   Warner Bros., 1987
SUSPECT   TriStar, 1987
MERMAIDS   Orion, 1990
THE PLAYER   Fine Line Features/New Line Cinema, 1992
FAITHFUL   Savoy Pictures, 1995

COLBY CHESTER
SALVADOR   Hemdale, 1986

MORRIS CHESTNUT
THE INKWELL   Buena Vista, 1994
UNDER SIEGE 2   Warner Bros., 1995

KEVIN CHEVALIA
HOMEWARD BOUND: THE INCREDIBLE JOURNEY
   Buena Vista, 1993

SAM CHEW
OSCAR   Buena Vista, 1991

SONNY CHIBA
ACES: IRON EAGLE III   New Line Cinema, 1991

MICHAEL CHIKLIS
WIRED   Taurus Entertainment, 1989

JULIA CHILD
WE'RE BACK! A DINOSAUR'S STORY (AF)   Universal, 1993 (voice)

LOIS CHILES
Agent: APA - Los Angeles, 310/273-0744

THE WAY WE WERE   Columbia, 1973
THE GREAT GATSBY   Paramount, 1974
COMA   MGM/United Artists, 1978
DEATH ON THE NILE   Paramount, 1978, British
MOONRAKER   United Artists, 1979, British-French
COURAGE   *RAW COURAGE*   New World, 1984
SWEET LIBERTY   Universal, 1986
CREEPSHOW 2   New World, 1987
BROADCAST NEWS   20th Century Fox, 1987
SAY ANYTHING   20th Century Fox, 1989 (uncredited)
BURNING BRIDGES (TF)   Andrea Baynes Prods./Lorimar TV, 1990

JOEY CHIN
KING OF NEW YORK   New Line Cinema, 1990

TSAI CHIN
THE JOY LUCK CLUB   Buena Vista, 1993

KIEU CHINH
Agent: The Light Company - Los Angeles, 213/826-2230

OPERATION C.I.A.   1965
GLEAMING THE CUBE   20th Century Fox, 1989
THE JOY LUCK CLUB   Buena Vista, 1993

ANNA CHLUMSKY
Agent: William Morris Agency - Beverly Hills, 310/274-7451

MY GIRL   Columbia, 1991
MY GIRL 2   Columbia, 1994
TRADING MOM   Trimark Pictures, 1994
GOLD DIGGERS   Universal, 1995

RAE DAWN CHONG
b. 1961 - California
Agent: William Morris Agency - Beverly Hills, 310/274-7451

QUEST FOR FIRE   20th Century Fox, 1982, Canadian-French
BEAT STREET   Orion, 1984
CHOOSE ME   Island Alive/New Cinema, 1984
FEAR CITY   Chevy Chase Distribution, 1984
AMERICAN FLYERS   Warner Bros., 1985
COMMANDO   20th Century Fox, 1985
RUNNING OUT OF LUCK   Nitrate Film Ltd./Julien Temple Productino Company, 1985, British
THE COLOR PURPLE   Warner Bros., 1985
SOUL MAN   New World, 1986
THE PRINCIPAL   TriStar, 1987
CURIOSITY KILLS (CTF)   Dutch Productions, 1990
TALES FROM THE DARKSIDE: THE MOVIE   Paramount, 1990
FAR OUT MAN   New Line Cinema, 1990

THOMAS CHONG
(Tommy Chong)
b. May 24, 1938 - Edmonton, Canada

UP IN SMOKE   Paramount, 1978
CHEECH & CHONG'S NEXT MOVIE   Universal, 1980 (also directed)
CHEECH & CHONG'S NICE DREAMS   Columbia, 1981 (also directed)
IT CAME FROM HOLLYWOOD (FD)   Paramount, 1982
CHEECH & CHONG: STILL SMOKIN'   Paramount, 1983 (also directed)
CHEECH & CHONG'S THE CORSICAN BROTHERS   Orion, 1984 (also directed)

AFTER HOURS   The Geffen Company/Warner Bros., 1985
FAR OUT MAN   New Line Cinema, 1990 (also directed)
NATIONAL LAMPOON'S SENIOR TRIP   New Line Cinema, 1995

NAVIN CHOWDHRY
MADAME SOUSATZKA   Cineplex Odeon, 1988, British

JENNY CHRISINGER
AN UNREMARKABLE LIFE   Continental Film Group, 1989

CLAUDIA CHRISTIAN
Agent: Abrams Artists & Associates - Los Angeles, 310/859-0625

HOUSTON: THE LEGEND OF TEXAS (TF)   Taft Entertainment TV/ J.D. Feigelson Productions, 1987
THE HIDDEN   New Line Cinema, 1987
CLEAN AND SOBER   Warner Bros., 1988
UPWORLD   Vestron, 1989
THINK BIG   MPCA, 1990
THE ARENA   Triumph Releasing Corporation, 1991
HEXED   Columbia, 1993
THE CHASE   20th Century Fox, 1994

JULIE CHRISTIE
b. April 14, 1941 - Chukua, Assam, India
Agent: ICM - Beverly Hills, 310/550-4000

CROOKS   1962, British
ANONYMOUS   1962, British
THE FAST LADY   Rank, 1962, British
BILLY LIAR   Continental, 1963, British
YOUNG CASSIDY   MGM, 1965, British
DARLING ★★   Embassy, 1965, British
DOCTOR ZHIVAGO   MGM, 1965, British
FAHRENHEIT 451   Universal, 1967, British
FAR FROM THE MADDING CROWD   MGM, 1967, British
PETULIA   Warner Bros., 1968, U.S.-British
IN SEARCH OF GREGORY   1970, British
THE GO-BETWEEN   Columbia, 1971, British
McCABE & MRS. MILLER ★   Warner Bros., 1971
DON'T LOOK NOW   Paramount, 1973, British-Italian
SHAMPOO   Columbia, 1975
NASHVILLE   Paramount, 1975
DEMON SEED   MGM/United Artists, 1977
HEAVEN CAN WAIT   Paramount, 1978
MEMOIRS OF A SURVIVOR   EMI, 1981, British
THE RETURN OF THE SOLDIER   European Classics, 1981, British
HEAT AND DUST   Universal Classics, 1983, British
THE GOLD DIGGERS   British Film Institute/Channel Four, 1984, British
MISS MARY   New World, 1986, Argentinian
POWER   20th Century Fox, 1986
DADAH IS DEATH (MS)   Steve Krantz Productions/Roadshow, Coote & Carroll Productions/Samuel Goldwyn TV, 1988, U.S.-Australian
FOOLS OF FORTUNE   New Line Cinema, 1990
DRAGONHEART   Universal, 1995

BRIAN CHRISTOPHER
MILK MONEY   Paramount, 1994

DENNIS CHRISTOPHER
A WEDDING   20th Century Fox, 1978
9/30/55   *SEPTEMBER 30, 1955*   Universal, 1977
BREAKING AWAY   20th Century Fox, 1979
CALIFORNIA DREAMING   American International, 1979
FADE TO BLACK   American Cinema, 1980
CHARIOTS OF FIRE   The Ladd Company/Warner Bros., 1981, British
DON'T CRY, IT'S ONLY THUNDER   Sanrio, 1982, U.S.-Japanese
THE FLIGHT OF THE SPRUCE GOOSE   Michael Hausman/ Filmhaus, 1986
JAKE SPEED   New World, 1986
ALIEN PREDATOR   Trans World Entertainment, 1987
IT (TF)   Konigsberg-Sanitsky Productions/Green-Epstein Productions/Lorimar TV, 1990

JORDAN CHRISTOPHER
STAR 80   The Ladd Company/Warner Bros., 1983

DAVID CHUNG
THE BALLAD OF LITTLE JO   Fine Line Features/
   New Line Cinema, 1993

THOMAS CHURCH
DEMON KNIGHT   Universal, 1995

JUDE CICCOLELLA
MAD LOVE   Buena Vista, 1995

CHARLES CIOFFI
Agent: Paradigm - Los Angeles, 310/277-4400

KLUTE   Warner Bros., 1971
PETER GUNN (TF)   The Blake Edwards Company/
   New World TV, 1989
NEWSIES   Buena Vista, 1992

RALPH CLANTON
DEATH BE NOT PROUD (TF)   Good Housekeeping Productions/
   Westfall Productions, 1975

GORDON CLAPP
Agent: Paul Kohner, Inc. - Los Angeles, 310/550-1060

RETURN OF THE SECAUCUS SEVEN   Libra/Specialty Films, 1980
MATEWAN   Cinecom, 1987
EIGHT MEN OUT   Orion, 1988
SMALL SACRIFICES (MS)   Louis Rudolph Films/Motown
   Productions/Allarcom Ltd./Fries Entertainment, 1989,
   U.S.-Canadian

ERIC CLAPTON
b. March 30, 1945 - Surrey, England
Agent: CAA - Beverly Hills, 310/288-4545

TOMMY   Columbia, 1975, British
THE SECRET POLICEMAN'S OTHER BALL (FD)   Miramax,
   1982, British
WATER   Atlantic Releasing Corporation, 1984, British (uncredited)

BETSY CLARK
BOXING HELENA   Orion Classics, 1993

BLAKE CLARK
Agent: APA - Los Angeles, 310/273-0744

JOHNNY HANDSOME   TriStar, 1989

BRET BAXTER CLARK
DEATHSTALKER IV   Concorde, 1991

CANDY CLARK
FAT CITY   Columbia, 1972
AMERICAN GRAFFITI ✪   Universal, 1973
I WILL I WILL...FOR NOW   20th Century Fox, 1976
THE MAN WHO FELL TO EARTH   Cinema 5, 1976, British
CITIZENS BAND   HANDLE WITH CARE   Paramount, 1977
THE BIG SLEEP   United Artists, 1978, British
WHEN YOU COMIN' BACK, RED RYDER?   Columbia, 1979
MORE AMERICAN GRAFFITI   Universal, 1979
BLUE THUNDER   Columbia, 1983
AMITYVILLE 3-D   Orion, 1983
AT CLOSE RANGE   Orion, 1986
POPEYE DOYLE (TF)   20th Century Fox TV, 1986
THE BLOB   TriStar, 1988
ORIGINAL INTENT   Studio Three, 1991

JOSH CLARK
BIG   20th Century Fox, 1988

MATT CLARK
Agent: Paul Kohner, Inc. - Los Angeles, 310/550-1060

WILL PENNY   Paramount, 1968
MONTE WALSH   National General, 1970
EMPEROR OF THE NORTH POLE   EMPEROR OF THE NORTH
   20th Century Fox, 1973
WHITE LIGHTNING   United Artists, 1973
HEARTS OF THE WEST   MGM/United Artists, 1975
KID VENGEANCE   Irwin Yablans, 1977, U.S.-Israeli
BRUBAKER   20th Century Fox, 1980
THE LEGEND OF THE LONE RANGER   Universal/AFD, 1981
HONKEYTONK MAN   Warner Bros., 1982
LOVE LETTERS   MY LOVE LETTERS   New World, 1983
COUNTRY   Buena Vista, 1984
RETURN TO OZ   Buena Vista, 1985
TUFF TURF   New World, 1985
LOVE, MARY (TF)   CBS Entertainment, 1985
OUT OF THE DARKNESS (TF)   Grosso-Jacobson Productions/
   Centerpoint Productions, 1985
KENNY ROGERS AS THE GAMBLER III: THE LEGEND
   CONTINUES (TF)   Lion Share Productions, 1987
TERROR ON HIGHWAY 91 (TF)   Katy Film Productions, 1989
BLIND WITNESS (TF)   King Phoenix Entertainment Group, 1989
BACK TO THE FUTURE PART III   Universal, 1990

RON CLARK
TOP GUN   Paramount, 1986

SUSAN CLARK
b. March 8, 1940 - Sarnid, Ontario, Canada

BANNING   Universal, 1967
MADIGAN   Universal, 1968
COOGAN'S BLUFF   Universal, 1968
SOMETHING FOR A LONELY MAN (TF)   Universal TV, 1968
TELL THEM WILLIE BOY IS HERE   Universal, 1969
THE CHALLENGERS (TF)   Universal TV, 1970
SKULLDUGGERY   Universal, 1970
COLOSSUS: THE FORBIN PROJECT   THE FORBIN PROJECT
   Universal, 1970
THE ASTRONAUT (TF)   Universal TV, 1971
VALDEZ IS COMING   United Artists, 1971
SKIN GAME   Warner Bros., 1971
SHOWDOWN   Universal, 1973
TRAPPED (TF)   Universal TV, 1973
THE MIDNIGHT MAN   Universal, 1974
AIRPORT 1975   Universal, 1974
NIGHT MOVES   Warner Bros., 1975
THE APPLE DUMPLING GANG   Buena Vista, 1975
BABE (TF)   MGM TV, 1975
AMELIA EARHART (TF)   Universal TV, 1976
THE NORTH AVENUE IRREGULARS   Buena Vista, 1979
MURDER BY DECREE   Avco Embassy, 1979, British-Canadian
CITY ON FIRE   Avco Embassy, 1979, Canadian
PROMISES IN THE DARK   Orion/Warner Bros., 1979
DOUBLE NEGATIVE   Best Vilm and Video, 1980, Canadian
NOBODY'S PERFEKT   Columbia, 1981
PORKY'S   20th Century Fox, 1982, U.S.-Canadian
MAID IN AMERICA (TF)   CBS Entertainment, 1982

CAITLIN CLARKE
MAYFLOWER MADAM (TF)   Robert Halmi, Inc., 1987
BLOWN AWAY   MGM/UA, 1994

JOANNA CLARKE
COURAGE MOUNTAIN   Triumph Releasing Corporation,
   1989, U.S.-French

WARREN CLARKE
CRUSOE   Island Pictures, 1988, U.S.-British

PATRICIA CLARKSON
THE UNTOUCHABLES   1987
THE DEAD POOL   Warner Bros., 1988
ROCKET GIBRALTAR   Columbia, 1988
EVERYBODY'S ALL-AMERICAN   Warner Bros., 1988

ANDREW DICE CLAY
(Andrew Clay Silverstein)
WACKO   Jensen Farley Pictures, 1981
MAKING THE GRADE   MGM/UA-Cannon, 1984
PRETTY IN PINK   Paramount, 1986
CASUAL SEX?   Universal, 1988
THE ADVENTURES OF FORD FAIRLANE   20th Century Fox, 1990
DICE RULES (FD)   Seven Arts, 1991

NICHOLAS CLAY
Agent: Susan Smith & Associates - Beverly Hills, 213/852-4777

THE NIGHT DIGGER   MGM, 1971, British
THE DARWIN ADVENTURE   20th Century Fox, 1972, British
TRISTAN AND ISOLDE   *LOVESPELL*   Clar Productions,
   1979, British
ZULU DAWN   American Cinema, 1979, British
EXCALIBUR   Orion/Warner Bros., 1981, British-Irish
LADY CHATTERLY'S LOVER   Cannon, 1981, French-British
EVIL UNDER THE SUN   Universal/AFD, 1982, British
THE CORSICAN BROTHERS (TF)   Rosemont Productions,
   1985, British-U.S.

JILL CLAYBURGH
b. April 30, 1944 - New York, New York
Agent: William Morris Agency - Beverly Hills, 310/274-7451

THE WEDDING PARTY   Powell Productions Plus/Ondine, 1969
THE TELEPHONE BOOK   1971
PORTNOY'S COMPLAINT   Warner Bros., 1972
THE THIEF WHO CAME TO DINNER   Warner Bros., 1973
THE TERMINAL MAN   Warner Bros., 1974
THE ART OF CRIME (TF)   Universal TV, 1975
HUSTLING (TF)   Filmways, 1974
GABLE AND LOMBARD   Universal, 1976
SILVER STREAK   20th Century Fox, 1976
GRIFFIN AND PHOENIX: A LOVE STORY (TF)
   ABC Circle Films, 1976
SEMI-TOUGH   United Artists, 1977
AN UNMARRIED WOMAN ★   20th Century Fox, 1978
LUNA   20th Century Fox, 1979, Italian-U.S.
STARTING OVER ★   Paramount, 1979
IT'S MY TURN   Columbia, 1980
FIRST MONDAY IN OCTOBER   Paramount, 1981
I'M DANCING AS FAST AS I CAN   Paramount, 1982
HANNAH K.   Universal Classics, 1983, French
WHERE ARE THE CHILDREN?   Columbia, 1986
MILES TO GO... (TF)   Keating-Shostak Productions,
   1986, U.S.-Canadian
SHY PEOPLE   Cannon, 1987
WHO GETS THE FRIENDS? (TF)   CBS Entertainment, 1988
FEAR STALK (TF)   Donald March Productions/ITC Entertainment
   Group/CBS Entertainment, 1989
UNSPEAKABLE ACTS (TF)   The Landsburg Company, 1990
WHISPERS IN THE DARK   Paramount, 1992
FIRESTORM: A CATASTROPHE IN OAKLAND (TF)   ABC, 1993
RICH IN LOVE   MGM/UA, 1993
NAKED IN NEW YORK   Fine Line Features/New Line Cinema, 1994
HONOR THY FATHER AND MOTHER: THE TRUE STORY OF THE
   MENENDEZ BROTHERS (TF)   Saban Entertainment, 1994

ADAM CLAYTON
U2: RATTLE AND HUM (FD)   Paramount, 1988

MERRY CLAYTON
MAID TO ORDER   New Century/Vista, 1987

JOHN F. CLEARY
CHILDREN OF A LESSER GOD   Paramount, 1986

JOHN CLEESE
b. October 27, 1939 - Somerset, England

INTERLUDE   Columbia, 1968, British
THE BEST HOUSE IN LONDON   MGM, 1969, British

THE RISE AND RISE OF MICHAEL RIMMER   Warner Bros.,
   1970, British
AND NOW FOR SOMETHING COMPLETELY DIFFERENT
   1972, British
THE LOVE BAN   1973, British
MONTY PYTHON AND THE HOLY GRAIL   Cinema 5, 1974, British
MONTY PYTHON'S LIFE OF BRIAN   Orion/Warner Bros.,
   1979, British
TIME BANDITS   Avco Embassy, 1981, British
THE SECRET POLICEMAN'S OTHER BALL (FD)   Miramax,
   1982, British
MONTY PYTHON LIVE AT THE HOLLYWOOD BOWL   Columbia,
   1982, British
PRIVATES ON PARADE   Orion Classics, 1982, British
MONTY PYTHON'S THE MEANING OF LIFE   Universal,
   1983, British
YELLOWBEARD   Orion, 1983, British
SILVERADO   Columbia, 1985
CLOCKWISE   Universal, 1986, British
A FISH CALLED WANDA   MGM/UA, 1988, British
ERIK THE VIKING   Orion, 1989, British
AN AMERICAN TAIL: FIEVEL GOES WEST (AF)   Universal,
   1991 (voice)
SPLITTING HEIRS   Universal, 1993, British-U.S.
MARY SHELLEY'S FRANKENSTEIN   TriStar, 1994
THE JUNGLE BOOK   Buena Vista, 1994
THE SWAN PRINCESS (AF)   New Line Cinema, 1995 (voice)

CHRISTIAN CLEMENSON
Agent: Susan Smith & Associates - Beverly Hills, 213/852-4777

HANNAH AND HER SISTERS   Orion, 1986
BROADCAST NEWS   20th Century Fox, 1987
BAD INFLUENCE   Triumph Releasing Corporation, 1990
CAPITAL NEWS (TF)   MTM Enterprises, 1990
AND THE BAND PLAYED ON (CTF)   HBO Pictures/Spelling
   Entertainment, 1993

DAVID CLENNON
STAR 80   The Ladd Company/Warner Bros., 1983
FALLING IN LOVE   Paramount, 1984
SWEET DREAMS   TriStar, 1985
LEGAL EAGLES   Universal, 1986
BETRAYED   MGM/UA, 1988
MAN TROUBLE   20th Century Fox, 1992
AND THE BAND PLAYED ON (CTF)   HBO Pictures/Spelling
   Entertainment, 1993

JIMMY CLIFF
THE HARDER THEY COME   1973, Jamaican
CLUB PARADISE   Warner Bros., 1986

GEORGE CLINTON
GRAFFITI BRIDGE   Warner Bros., 1990

DEL CLOSE
FERRIS BUELLER'S DAY OFF   Paramount, 1986

GLENN CLOSE
b. March 19, 1947 - Greenwich, Connecticut
Agent: CAA - Beverly Hills, 310/288-4545

TOO FAR TO GO (TF)   Sea Cliff Productions, 1979
ORPHAN TRAIN (TF)   Roger Gimbel Productions/EMI TV, 1979
THE WORLD ACCORDING TO GARP ✪   Warner Bros., 1982
THE BIG CHILL ✪   Columbia, 1983
THE STONE BOY   TLC Films/20th Century Fox, 1984
THE NATURAL ✪   TriStar, 1984
GREYSTOKE: THE LEGEND OF TARZAN, LORD OF THE APES
   Warner Bros., 1984, British-U.S. (voice; uncredited)
SOMETHING ABOUT AMELIA (TF)   Leonard Goldberg
   Productions, 1984
MAXIE   Orion, 1985
JAGGED EDGE   Columbia, 1985
FATAL ATTRACTION ★   Paramount, 1987
DANGEROUS LIAISONS ★   Warner Bros., 1988

LIGHT YEARS (AF)   1988, French (voice)
STONES FOR IBARRA (TF)   Titus Productions, 1988
IMMEDIATE FAMILY   Columbia, 1989
REVERSAL OF FORTUNE   Warner Bros., 1990
HAMLET   Warner Bros., 1990, British
SARAH, PLAIN AND TALL (TF)   Self Help Productions/Trillium
   Productions, 1991
MEETING VENUS   Warner Bros., 1991
HOOK   TriStar, 1991
SKYLARK (TF)   Self Help Productions/Trillium Productions, 1993
THE HOUSE OF THE SPIRITS   Miramax Films, 1993, U.S.-German
THE PAPER   Universal, 1994
MARY REILLY   TriStar, 1995

JOHN SCOTT CLOUGH
Agent: APA - Los Angeles, 310/273-0744

GROSS ANATOMY   Buena Vista, 1989

FRANÇOIS CLUZET
'ROUND MIDNIGHT   Warner Bros., 1986, U.S.-French
CHOCOLAT   Orion Classics, 1988, French
PARIS MATCH   20th Century Fox, 1995

KIM COATES
THE CLIENT   Warner Bros., 1994

RANDALL (TEX) COBB
Agent: The Blake Agency - Beverly Hills, 310/246-0241

THE GOLDEN CHILD   Paramount, 1986
CRITICAL CONDITION   Paramount, 1987
RAISING ARIZONA   20th Century Fox, 1987
BUY & CELL   Empire Pictures, 1989
FLETCH LIVES   Universal, 1989
BLIND FURY   TriStar, 1990

BILL COBBS
THE COLOR OF MONEY   Buena Vista, 1986
THE BODYGUARD   Warner Bros., 1992
FLUKE   MGM/UA, 1994

JAMES COBURN
b. August 31, 1928 - Laurel, Nebraska

RIDE LONESOME   Columbia, 1959
FACE OF A FUGITIVE   Columbia, 1959
THE MAGNIFICENT SEVEN   United Artists, 1960
HELL IS FOR HEROES   Paramount, 1962
THE GREAT ESCAPE   United Artists, 1963
CHARADE   Universal, 1963
THE MAN FROM GALVESTON   Warner Bros., 1964
THE AMERICANIZATION OF EMILY   MGM, 1964
MAJOR DUNDEE   Columbia, 1965
A HIGH WIND IN JAMAICA   20th Century Fox, 1965, British
THE LOVED ONE   MGM, 1965
OUR MAN FLINT   20th Century Fox, 1966
WHAT DID YOU DO IN THE WAR, DADDY?   United Artists, 1966
DEAD HEAT ON A MERRY-GO-ROUND   Paramount, 1966
IN LIKE FLINT   20th Century Fox, 1967
WATERHOLE # 3   Paramount, 1967
THE PRESIDENT'S ANALYST   Paramount, 1967
DUFFY   Columbia, 1968, U.S.-British
CANDY   1968, U.S.-French-Italian
HARD CONTRACT   20th Century Fox, 1969
THE LAST OF THE MOBILE HOTSHOTS   Warner Bros., 1970
DUCK YOU SUCKER!   A FISTFUL OF DYNAMITE   United Artists,
   1972, Italian-Spanish
THE HONKERS   1972
THE CAREY TREATMENT   MGM, 1972
PAT GARRETT & BILLY THE KID   MGM, 1973
THE LAST OF SHEILA   Warner Bros., 1973
HARRY IN YOUR POCKET   1973
A REASON TO LIVE, A REASON TO DIE   MASSACRE AT FORT
   HOLMAN   1974, Italian

THE INTERNECINE PROJECT   Allied Artists, 1974, British
JACKPOT   1975, Italian
BITE THE BULLET   Columbia, 1975
HARD TIMES   Columbia, 1975
SKY RIDERS   20th Century Fox, 1976, U.S.-West German
THE LAST HARD MEN   20th Century Fox, 1976
MIDWAY   Universal, 1976
WHIT E ROCK (FD)   EMI, 1977, British
CROSS OF IRON   Avco Embassy, 1977, British-West German
THE DAIN CURSE (TF)   Martin Poll Productions, 1978
CALIFORNIA SUITE   Columbia, 1978
FIREPOWER   AFD, 1979, British
THE MUPPET MOVIE   AFD, 1979, British
GOLDENGIRL   Avco Embassy, 1979
LOVING COUPLES   20th Century Fox, 1980
THE BALTIMORE BULLET   Avco Embassy, 1980
MR. PATMAN   Film Consortium, 1980, Canadian
LOOKER   The Ladd Company/Warner Bros., 1981
HIGH RISK   American Cinema, 1981
MALIBU (TF)   Hamner Productions/Columbia TV, 1983
DIGITAL DREAMS   Ripple Productions, Ltd., 1983
DRAW!   HBO Premiere Films/Astral Film Productions/Bryna
   Company, 1984, U.S.-Canadian
MARTIN'S DAY   MGM/UA, 1984, British
SINS OF THE FATHER (TF)   Fries Entertainment, 1985
DEATH OF A SOLDIER   Scotti Brothers, 1986, Australian
HUDSON HAWK   TriStar, 1991
SISTER ACT 2: BACK IN THE HABIT   Buena Vista, 1993
MAVERICK   Warner Bros., 1994

IMOGENE COCA
b. November 18, 1908 - Philadelphia, Pennsylvania

UNDER THE YUM YUM TREE   Columbia, 1963
TEN FROM YOUR SHOW OF SHOWS   1973
RABBIT TEST   Avco Embassy, 1978
RETURN OF THE BEVERLY HILLBILLIES (TF)   CBS, 1981
NATIONAL LAMPOON'S VACATION   Warner Bros., 1983
NOTHING LASTS FOREVER   MGM/UA Classics, 1984
PAPA WAS A PREACHER   1986
BUY & CELL   Empire Pictures, 1989

CAMILLE CODURI
KING RALPH   Universal, 1991

GEORGE COE
Agent: Gersh Agency - Beverly Hills, 310/274-6611

THE DOVE   Paramount, 1974
THE STEPFORD WIVES   Columbia, 1975
KRAMER VS. KRAMER   Columbia, 1979
THE FIRST DEADLY SIN   Filmways, 1980
BLIND DATE   TriStar, 1987
SHOOTDOWN (TF)   Leonard Hill Films, 1988
COUSINS   Paramount, 1989

JOEL COEN
Agent: UTA - Beverly Hills, 310/273-6700

SPIES LIKE US   Warner Bros., 1985

PAUL COEUR
WHITE FANG 2: MYTH OF THE WHITE WOLF   Buena Vista, 1994

SCOTT COFFEY
Agent: Harris & Goldberg - Los Angeles, 310/553-5200

ALL SHOOK UP   Universal, 1991
TANK GIRL   MGM/UA, 1995

JOHN COFFEY
WAR OF THE BUTTONS   Warner Bros., 1994

Co

FILM
ACTORS
GUIDE

**F
I
L
M**

**A
C
T
O
R
S**

FRED COFFIN
Agent: Susan Smith & Associates - Beverly Hills, 213/852-4777

THE DELIBERATE STRANGER (MS)   Stuart Phoenix Productions/
    Lorimar-Telepictures, 1986
THE BEDROOM WINDOW   DEG, 1987
SHOOT TO KILL   Buena Vista, 1988
HARD TO KILL   Warner Bros., 1990
FULLY LOADED   Buena Vista, 1991

JEFF COHEN
(Jeffrey Jay Cohen)
THE GOONIES   Warner Bros., 1985
BACK TO THE FUTURE   Universal, 1985
FIRE WITH FIRE   Paramount, 1986

JESSICA LYNN COHEN
GEORGE BALANCHINE'S THE NUTCRACKER   Warner Bros., 1993

MINDY COHN
Agent: The Light Company - Los Angeles, 213/826-2230

THE BOY WHO COULD FLY   20th Century Fox, 1986
THE FACTS OF LIFE DOWN UNDER (TF)   Embassy TV/Crawford
    Productions, 1987, U.S.-Australian

GARY COLE
b. September 20, 1957 - Park Ridge, Illinois
Agent: ICM - Beverly Hills, 310/550-4000

HEART OF STEEL (TF)   Beowulf Productions, 1983
FATAL VISION (MS)   NBC Productions, 1984
VITAL SIGNS (TF)   CBS Entertainment, 1986
JOSEPH WAMBAUGH'S ECHOES IN THE DARKNESS
    ECHOES IN THE DARKNESS (MS)   Litke-Grossbart
    Productions/New World TV, 1987
THOSE SHE LEFT BEHIND (TF)   NBC Productions, 1989
THE OLD MAN AND THE SEA (TF)   Storke Enterprises/Green
    Pond Productions/Yorkshire TV, 1990
SON OF THE MORNING STAR (MS)   Mount Company/Preston
    Stephen Fisher Company/Republic Pictures, 1991
IN THE LINE OF FIRE   Columbia, 1993
THE BRADY BUNCH MOVIE   Paramount, 1995

GEORGE COLE
MARY REILLY   TriStar, 1995

NATALIE COLE
b. February 6, 1950 - Los Angeles, California
Agent: William Morris Agency - Beverly Hills, 310/274-7451

CATS DON'T DANCE (AF)   Turner Pictures, 1996 (voice)

CHARLOTTE COLEMAN
FOUR WEDDINGS AND A FUNERAL   Gramercy Pictures,
    1994, British

DABNEY COLEMAN
b. January 3, 1932 - Austin, Texas
Agent: ICM - Beverly Hills, 310/550-4000

THE SLENDER THREAD   Paramount, 1965
THIS PROPERTY IS CONDEMNED   Paramount, 1966
THE SCALPHUNTERS   United Artists, 1968
DOWNHILL RACER   Paramount, 1969
I LOVE MY WIFE   Universal, 1970
THE BROTHERHOOD OF THE BELL (TF)   Cinema Center, 1970
DYING ROOM ONLY (TF)   Lorimar Productions, 1973
BAD RONALD (TF)   Lorimar Productions, 1974
CINDERELLA LIBERTY   20th Century Fox, 1974
THE DOVE   Paramount, 1974
THE TOWERING INFERNO   20th Century Fox/Warner Bros., 1974
RETURNING HOME (TF)   Lorimar Productions/Samuel Goldwyn
    Productions, 1975
ATTACK ON TERROR: THE FBI VS. THE KU KLUX KLAN (TF)
    QM Productions, 1975

BITE THE BULLET   Columbia, 1975
THE OTHER SIDE OF THE MOUNTAIN   Universal, 1975
KISS ME, KILL ME (TF)   Columbia TV, 1976
MANEATERS ARE LOOSE! (TF)   Mona Productions/Finnegan
    Associates, 1978
VIVA KNIEVEL!   Warner Bros., 1978
NORTH DALLAS FORTY   Paramount, 1979
NOTHING PERSONAL   American International, 1980, Canadian
HOW TO BEAT THE HIGH COST OF LIVING
    American International, 1980
MELVIN AND HOWARD   Universal, 1980
NINE TO FIVE   20th Century Fox, 1980
ON GOLDEN POND   Universal/AFD, 1981
MODERN PROBLEMS   20th Century Fox, 1981
YOUNG DOCTORS IN LOVE   20th Century Fox, 1982
TOOTSIE   Columbia, 1982
WARGAMES   MGM/UA, 1983
CLOAK AND DAGGER   Universal, 1984
THE MUPPETS TAKE MANHATTAN   TriStar, 1984
THE MAN WITH ONE RED SHOE   20th Century Fox, 1985
MURROW (CTF)   HBO Premiere Films/Titus Productions/TVS Ltd.
    Productions, 1986, U.S.-British
FRESNO (MS)   MTM Productions, 1986
GUILTY OF INNOCENCE: THE LENELL GETER STORY (TF)
    Embassy TV, 1987
SWORN TO SILENCE (TF)   Daniel H. Blatt/Robert Singer
    Productions, 1987
DRAGNET   Universal, 1987
PLAZA SUITE (TF)   Kalola Productions, 1987
BABY M (MS)   ABC Circle Films, 1988
HOT TO TROT   Warner Bros., 1988
MAYBE BABY (TF)   Perry Lafferty Productions/von Zerneck-Samuels
    Productions, 1988
WHERE THE HEART IS   Buena Vista, 1990
SHORT TIME   20th Century Fox, 1990
MEET THE APPLEGATES   Triton Pictures, 1991
THE BEVERLY HILLBILLIES   20th Century Fox, 1993
CLIFFORD   Orion, 1994

GARY COLEMAN
b. February 8, 1968 - Zion, Illinois

ON THE RIGHT TRACK   20th Century Fox, 1981
THE KID WITH THE BROKEN HALO (TF)   Satellite Productions, 1982
JIMMY THE KID   New World, 1983
THE KID WITH THE 200 I.Q. (TF)   Guillaume-Margo Productions/
    Zephyr Productions, 1983
THE FANTASTIC WORLD OF D.C. COLLINS (TF)   Guillaume-Margo
    Productions/Zephyr Productions, 1984
PLAYING WITH FIRE (TF)   Zephyr Productions, 1985

MARGARET COLIN
Agent: ICM - New York, 212/556-5600

SOMETHING WILD   Orion, 1986
PRETTY IN PINK   Paramount, 1986
THE RETURN OF SHERLOCK HOLMES (TF)   CBS Entertainment,
    1987, British
WARM HEARTS, COLD FEET (TF)   Lorimar-Telepictures, 1987
THREE MEN AND A BABY   Buena Vista, 1987
MARTIANS GO HOME   Taurus Entertainment, 1990
THE BUTCHER'S WIFE   Paramount, 1991

CHRISTOPHER COLLET
FIRSTBORN   Paramount, 1984
RIGHT TO KILL? (TF)   Wrye-Konigsberg Productions/Taper Media
    Enterprises/Telepictures Productions, 1985
THE MANHATTAN PROJECT   20th Century Fox, 1986

KEN COLLEY
WALLENBERG: A HERO'S STORY (MS)   Dick Berg-Stonehenge
    Productions/Paramount TV, 1985
A SUMMER STORY   Atlantic Releasing Corporation, 1988

ALBERT COLLINS
ADVENTURES IN BABYSITTING   Buena Vista, 1987

BLAKE COLLINS
THE LITTLE RASCALS   Universal, 1994

JOAN COLLINS
b. May 23, 1933 - London, England

I BELIEVE IN YOU   1952, British
DECAMERON NIGHTS   1953, British
THE SLASHER   *COSH BOY*   Lippert, 1953, British
TURN THE KEY SOFTLY   1953, British
THE GOOD DIE YOUNG   United Artists, 1954, British
THE ADVENTURES OF SADIE   *OUR GIRL FRIDAY*   1955, British
LAND OF THE PHARAOHS   Warner Bros., 1955
THE VIRGIN QUEEN   20th Century Fox, 1955
THE GIRL IN THE RED VELVET SWING   20th Century-Fox, 1955
THE OPPOSITE SEX   MGM, 1956
SEA WIFE   1957, British
STOPOVER TOKYO   1957
THE WAYWARD BUS   1957
ISLAND IN THE SUN   20th Century Fox, 1957
THE BRAVADOS   20th Century Fox, 1958
RALLY ROUND THE FLAG, BOYS!   20th Century-Fox, 1958
SEVEN THIEVES   20th Century Fox, 1960
ESTHER AND THE KING   20th Century Fox, 1960, Italian-U.S.
THE ROAD TO HONG KONG   United States, 1962, British-U.S.
WARNING SHOT   Paramount, 1967
DRIVE HARD, DRIVE FAST (TF)   Universal TV, 1969
SUBTERFUGE   1969, British
CAN HIERONYMOUS MERKIN EVER FORGET MERCY HUMPPE
   AND FIND TRUE HAPPINESS?   Regional, 1969, British
UP IN THE CELLAR   American International, 1970
THE EXECUTIONER   Columbia, 1970, British
QUEST FOR LOVE   Rank, 1971, British
INN OF THE FRIGHTENED PEOPLE   *TERROR FROM UNDER
   THE HOUSE/REVENGE*   Hemisphere, 1971
TALES FROM THE CRYPT   Cinerama Releasing Corporation, 1972
FEAR IN THE NIGHT   International Co-Productions, 1972, British
TALES THAT WITNESS MADNESS   Paramount, 1973
DARK PLACES   Cinerama Releasing Corporation, 1974, British
ALFIE DARLING   *OH! ALFIE*   1975, British
THE DEVIL WITHIN HER   *I DON'T WANT TO BE BORN*
   20th Century Fox, 1975, British
THE BAWDY ADVENTURES OF TOM JONES   Universal, 1976
ARTHUR HAILEY'S THE MONEYCHANGERS
   THE MONEYCHANGERS (MS)   Ross Hunter Productions/
   Paramount TV, 1976
EMPIRE OF THE ANTS   American International, 1977
THE STUD   Trans-American, 1978, British
THE BIG SLEEP   United Artists, 1978, British
ZERO TO SIXTY   First Artists, 1978, Canadian
THE BITCH   Brent Walker Productions, 1979, British
GAME FOR VULTURES   New Line Cinema, 1979, British
SUNBURN   Paramount, 1979, U.S.-British
PAPER DOLLS (TF)   Leonard Goldberg Productions, 1982
THE WILD WOMEN OF CHASTITY GULCH (TF)   Aaron Spelling
   Productions, 1982
NUTCRACKER   Rank, 1983, British
THE MAKING OF A MALE MODEL (TF)   Aaron Spelling
   Productions, 1983
HER LIFE AS A MAN (TF)   LS Entertainment, 1984
THE CARTIER AFFAIR (TF)   Hill-Mandelker Productions, 1984
SINS (MS)   New World TV/The Greif-Dore Company/Collins-Holm
   Productions, 1986
MONTE CARLO (MS)   New World TV/Phoenix Entertainment Group/
   Collins-Holm Productions/Highgate Pictures, 1986

PAULINE COLLINS
b. September 30, 1940 - Exmouth, England
Agent: Susan Smith & Associates - Beverly Hills, 213/852-4777

SHIRLEY VALENTINE ★   Paramount, 1989, British
CITY OF JOY   TriStar, 1992

PHIL COLLINS
b. January 30, 1951
Agent: Camden ITG - Los Angeles, 310/289-2700

BUSTER   Hemdale, 1988, British
HOOK   TriStar, 1991

AND THE BAND PLAYED ON (CTF)   HBO Pictures/Spelling
   Entertainment, 1993
FRAUDS   Australian Film Finance Corporation, 1993, Australian
BALTO (AF)   Universal, 1995 (voice)

STEPHEN COLLINS
Agent: William Morris Agency - Beverly Hills, 310/274-7451

ALL THE PRESIDENT'S MEN   Warner Bros., 1976
BETWEEN THE LINES   Midwest Film Productions, 1977
THE PROMISE   Universal, 1979
STAR TREK - THE MOTION PICTURE   Paramount, 1979
LOVING COUPLES   20th Century Fox, 1980
THREESOME (TF)   CBS Entertainment, 1984
BREWSTER'S MILLIONS   Universal, 1985
CHOKE CANYON   United Film Distribution, 1986
JUMPIN' JACK FLASH   20th Century Fox, 1986
THE TWO MRS. GRENVILLES (MS)   Lorimar-Telepictures, 1987
WEEKEND WAR (TF)   Pompian-Atamvan Productions/
   Columbia TV, 1988
STELLA   Buena Vista, 1990
SCARLETT (MS)   1994

TYLER COLLINS
A RAGE IN HARLEM   Miramax Films, 1991, U.S.-British

FRANK COLLISON
MOBSTERS   Universal, 1991

ALEX COLON
THE MIGHTY QUINN   MGM/UA, 1989

KAREN COLSTON
SWEETIE   Avenue Pictures, 1990, Australian

ROBBIE COLTRANE
Agent: William Morris Agency - Beverly Hills, 310/274-7451

DEFENSE OF THE REALM   Hemdale, 1985, British
MONA LISA   Island Pictures, 1986, British
CARAVAGGIO   British Film Institute, 1986, British
BERT RIGBY, YOU'RE A FOOL   Warner Bros., 1989
HENRY V   Samuel Goldwyn Company, 1989, British
NUNS ON THE RUN   20th Century Fox, 1990
THE POPE MUST DIET   Miramax Films, 1991
PERFECTLY NORMAL   Four Seasons Entertainment, 1991
THE ADVENTURES OF HUCK FINN   Buena Vista, 1993

MICHAEL COLYAR
HOLLYWOOD SHUFFLE   Samuel Goldwyn Company, 1987
HOT SHOTS! PART DEUX   20th Century Fox, 1993
HOUSE PARTY 3   New Line Cinema, 1994

JEFFREY COMBS
Agent: Borinstein/Oreck/Bogart Agency - Los Angeles, 213/658-8600

H.P. LOVECRAFT'S RE-ANIMATOR   *RE-ANIMATOR*
   Empire Pictures, 1985
FROM BEYOND   Empire Pictures, 1986
CELLAR DWELLAR   Empire Pictures, 1988

RAY COMBS
OVERBOARD   MGM/UA, 1987

JEFF CONAWAY
JENNIFER ON MY MIND   United Artists, 1971
THE EAGLE HAS LANDED   Columbia, 1977, British
GREASE   Paramount, 1978
BREAKING UP IS HARD TO DO (TF)   Green-Epstein Productions/
   Columbia TV, 1979
COVERGIRL   New World, 1984, Canadian
THE PATRIOT   Crown International, 1986
ELVIRA, MISTRESS OF THE DARK   New World, 1988

GINO CONFROTI
HANS CHRISTIAN ANDERSEN'S THUMBELINA (AF)
Warner Bros., 1994 (voice)

COLTON CONKLIN
THE SUBSTITUTE WIFE (TF)   Frederick S. Pierce Company, 1994

DIDI CONN
Agent: The Agency - Los Angeles, 310/551-3000

YOU LIGHT UP MY LIFE   Columbia, 1977
GREASE   Paramount, 1978
GREASE 2   Paramount, 1982

JEAN-PAUL CONNART
LA BALANCE   Spectrafilm, 1982, French

BILLY CONNELLY
WATER   Atlantic Releasing Corporation, 1984, British
THE BIG MAN   Miramax Films, 1990, British

JENNIFER CONNELLY
Agent: ICM - Beverly Hills, 310/550-4000

ONCE UPON A TIME IN AMERICA   The Ladd Company/Warner
Bros., 1984, U.S.-Italian-Canadian
LABYRINTH   TriStar, 1986, British
SEVEN MINUTES IN HEAVEN   Warner Bros., 1986
SOME GIRLS   MGM/UA, 1989
THE HOT SPOT   Orion, 1990
CAREER OPPORTUNITIES   Universal, 1991
THE ROCKETEER   Buena Vista, 1991
HIGHER LEARNING   Columbia, 1994

JASON CONNERY
Agent: Paradigm - Los Angeles, 310/277-4400

BYE BYE BABY   Prism Entertainment, 1989
THE SECRET LIFE OF IAN FLEMING (CTF)   Saban-Scherick
Productions, 1990, U.S.-British

SEAN CONNERY
(Thomas Connery)
b. August 25, 1930 - Edinburgh, Scotland
Agent: CAA - Beverly Hills, 310/288-4545

NO ROAD BACK   1956, British
HELL DRIVERS   Rank, 1957, British
TIME LOCK   DCA, 1957, British
ACTION OF THE TIGER   MGM, 1957, British
ANOTHER TIME, ANOTHER PLACE   Paramount, 1958
A NIGHT TO REMEMBER   Paramount, 1958
DARBY O'GILL AND THE LITTLE PEOPLE   Buena Vista, 1959
TARZAN'S GREATEST ADVENTURE   Paramount,
1959, British-U.S.
ON THE FIDDLE   *OPERATION SNAFU/OPERATION WARHEAD*
1961, British
THE FRIGHTENED CITY   1962
THE LONGEST DAY   20th Century Fox, 1962
DR. NO   United Artists, 1962, British
FROM RUSSIA WITH LOVE   United Artists, 1963, British
MARNIE   Universal, 1964
WOMAN OF STRAW   United Artists, 1964, British
GOLDFINGER   United Artists, 1964, British
THE HILL   MGM, 1965, British
THUNDERBALL   United Artists, 1965, British
A FINE MADNESS   Warner Bros., 1966
YOU ONLY LIVE TWICE   United Artists, 1967, British
SHALAKO!   Cinerama Releasing Corporation, 1968, British
THE RED TENT   Paramount, 1969, Italian-Soviet
THE MOLLY MAGUIRES   Paramount, 1970
THE ANDERSON TAPES   Columbia, 1971
DIAMONDS ARE FOREVER   United Artists, 1971, British
THE OFFENCE   United Artists, 1973, British
ZARDOZ   20th Century Fox, 1974, British
MURDER ON THE ORIENT EXPRESS   Paramount, 1974, British

THE TERRORISTS   *RANSOM*   20th Century Fox, 1975, British
THE WIND AND THE LION   MGM/United Artists, 1975
THE MAN WHO WOULD BE KING   Allied Artists, 1975, British
THE NEXT MAN   Allied Artists, 1976
ROBIN AND MARIAN   Columbia, 1976, British
A BRIDGE TOO FAR   United Artists, 1977, British
METEOR   American International, 1979
THE GREAT TRAIN ROBBERY   United Artists, 1979, British
CUBA   United Artists, 1979
TIME BANDITS   Avco Embassy, 1981, British
OUTLAND   The Ladd Company/Warner Bros., 1981
WRONG IS RIGHT   Columbia, 1982
FIVE DAYS ONE SUMMER   The Ladd Company/Warner Bros.,
1982, British
SWORD OF THE VALIANT   1982
NEVER SAY NEVER AGAIN   Warner Bros., 1983
HIGHLANDER   20th Century Fox, 1986, British-U.S.
THE NAME OF THE ROSE   20th Century Fox, 1986,
West German-Italian-French
THE UNTOUCHABLES ⊙⊙   Paramount, 1987
THE PRESIDIO   Paramount, 1988
MEMORIES OF ME   MGM/UA, 1988
INDIANA JONES AND THE LAST CRUSADE   Paramount, 1989
ERIK THE VIKING   Orion, 1989, British (uncredited)
FAMILY BUSINESS   TriStar, 1989
THE HUNT FOR RED OCTOBER   Paramount, 1990
THE RUSSIA HOUSE   MGM-Pathe, 1990
HIGHLANDER II - THE QUICKENING   Entertainment Film
Distributors, 1991, British-U.S.
ROBIN HOOD: PRINCE OF THIEVES   Warner Bros., 1991 (uncredited)
MEDICINE MAN   Buena Vista, 1992
RISING SUN   20th Century Fox, 1993
A GOOD MAN IN AFRICA   Gramercy Pictures, 1994
JUST CAUSE   Warner Bros., 1995
FIRST KNIGHT   Columbia, 1995
DRAGONHEART   Universal, 1995

HARRY CONNICK, JR.
b. 1967 - New Orleans, Louisiana

MEMPHIS BELLE   Warner Bros., 1990
LITTLE MAN TATE   Orion, 1991
COPYCAT   Warner Bros., 1995

BILLY CONNOLLY
INDECENT PROPOSAL   Paramount, 1993

BART CONNOR
RAD   TriStar, 1986

TOM CONNOR
THE MILAGRO BEANFIELD WAR   Universal, 1988

CHRISTIAN CONRAD
CHARLEY HANNAH (TF)   A. Shane Company, 1986
HIGH MOUNTAIN RANGERS (TF)   A. Shane Company,
1987 (also directed)
JESSE HAWKES (TF)   A. Shane Company, 1989 (also directed)

ROBERT CONRAD
(Conrad Robert Falk)
b. March 1, 1935 - Chicago, Illinois
Agent: David Shapira & Associates - Sherman Oaks, 818/906-0322

THUNDERING JETS   1958
PALM SPRINGS WEEKEND   Warner Bros., 1963
YOUNG DILLINGER   1965
THE D.A.: MURDER ONE (TF)   Mark VII, Ltd./Universal TV/
Jack Webb Productions, 1969
WEEKEND OF TERROR (TF)   Paramount TV, 1970
THE D.A.: CONSPIRACY TO KILL (TF)   Universal TV/
Mark VII, Ltd., 1971
FIVE DESPERATE WOMEN (TF)   Aaron Spelling Productions, 1971
THE ADVENTURES OF NICK CARTER (TF)   Universal TV, 1972
THE LAST DAY (TF)   Paramount TV, 1975
LOVE A LITTLE, STEAL A LOT   1975

SMASH-UP ON INTERSTATE 5 (TF)   Filmways, 1976
SUDDEN DEATH   Topar, 1977, U.S.-Filipino
CENTENNIAL (MS)   Universal TV, 1978
THE WILD, WILD WEST REVISITED (TF)
   CBS Entertainment, 1979
BREAKING UP IS HARD TO DO (TF)   Green-Epstein Productions/
   Columbia TV, 1979
WRONG IS RIGHT   Columbia, 1982
WILL: G. GORDON LIDDY (TF)   A. Shane Company, 1982
CONFESSIONS OF A MARRIED MAN (TF)   Gloria Monty
   Productions/Comworld Productions, 1983
HARD KNOX (TF)   A. Shane Company, 1984
TWO FATHERS' JUSTICE (TF)   A. Shane Company, 1985
THE FIFTH MISSILE (TF)   Bercovici-St. Johns Productions/
   MGM-UA TV, 1986
ASSASSIN (TF)   Sankan Productions, 1986
CHARLEY HANNAH (TF)   A. Shane Company, 1986
ONE POLICE PLAZA (TF)   CBS Entertainment, 1986
HIGH MOUNTAIN RANGERS (TF)   A. Shane Company,
   1987 (also directed)
GLORY DAYS (TF)   A. Shane Company/Sibling Rivalries,
   1988 (also directed)
JESSE HAWKES (TF)   A. Shane Company, 1989 (also directed)
ANYTHING TO SURVIVE (TF)   Saban-Scherick Productions/ATL
   Productions/B.C. Films, 1990
SWORN TO VENGEANCE (TF)   CBS, 1993

FRANCES CONROY
AMAZING GRACE AND CHUCK   TriStar, 1987
TERRORIST ON TRIAL: THE UNITED STATES VS.
   SALIM AJAMI (TF)   George Englund Productions/Robert
   Papazian Productions, 1988
ROCKET GIBRALTAR   Columbia, 1988
DIRTY ROTTEN SCOUNDRELS   Orion, 1988

KEVIN CONROY
Agent: Paradigm - Los Angeles, 310/277-4400

BATMAN: MASK OF THE PHANTASM (AF)   Warner Bros.,
   1993 (voice)

RUAIDHRI CONROY
INTO THE WEST   Miramax Films, 1993, British-Irish-Japanese

MICHAEL CONSTANTINE
THE LAST MILE   United Artists, 1959
THE HUSTLER   20th Century Fox, 1961
ISLAND OF LOVE   Warner Bros., 1963
BEAU GESTE   Universal, 1966
HAWAII   United Artists, 1966
SKIDOO   Paramount, 1968
IF IT'S TUESDAY, THIS MUST BE BELGIUM   United Artists, 1969
THE REIVERS   National General, 1969
PEEPER   FAT CHANCE   20th Century Fox, 1975
VOYAGE OF THE DAMNED   Avco Embassy, 1976, British
RAID ON ENTEBBE (TF)   Edgar J. Scherick Associates/
   20th Century Fox TV, 1977
THE NORTH AVENUE IRREGULARS   Buena Vista, 1979
SUMMER OF MY GERMAN SOLDIER (TF)
   Highgate Productions, 1978
EVITA PERON (TF)   Hartwest Productions/Zephyr
   Productions, 1981
LEAP OF FAITH (TF)   Hart, Thomas & Berlin Productions, 1988
PRANCER   Orion, 1989
MY LIFE   Columbia, 1993

TOM CONTI
FLAME   Goodtime Enterprises, 1975, British
GALILEO   American Film Theatre, 1975, British-Canadian
THE HAUNTING OF JULIA   FULL CIRCLE   Discovery Films,
   1976, British-Canadian
THE DUELLISTS   Paramount, 1978, British
BLADE ON THE FEATHER (TF)   London Weekend TV,
   1980, British
THE WALL (TF)   Cinetex International/Time-Life Productions,
   1982, U.S.-Polish

REUBEN, REUBEN ★   20th Century Fox International
   Classics, 1983
MERRY CHRISTMAS, MR. LAWRENCE   Universal, 1983,
   British-Japanese
AMERICAN DREAMER   Warner Bros., 1984
GOSPEL ACCORDING TO VIC   HEAVENLY PURSUITS
   Skouras Pictures, 1986, British
SAVING GRACE   Columbia, 1986
MIRACLES   Orion, 1986
NAZI HUNTER: THE BEATE KLARSFELD STORY (TF)
   William Kayden Productions/Orion TV/Silver Chalice/Revcom/
   George Walker TV/TF1/SFP, 1986, U.S.-British-French
BEYOND THERAPY   New World, 1987
ROMAN HOLIDAY (TF)   Jerry Ludwig Enterprises, Inc./
   Paramount TV, 1987
SHIRLEY VALENTINE   Paramount, 1989, British

PATRICIO CONTRERAS
THE OFFICIAL STORY   Historias Cinematograficas,
   1985, Argentine
OLD GRINGO   Columbia, 1989

PEGGY CONVERSE
THE ACCIDENTAL TOURIST   Warner Bros., 1988

WILLIAM CONVERSE-ROBERTS
STONE PILLOW (TF)   Schaefer-Karpf Productions/Gaylord
   Productions, 1985
ON VALENTINE'S DAY   STORY OF A MARRIAGE
   Angelika Films, 1986

KEVIN CONWAY
b. May 29, 1942 - New York, New York
Agent: Badgley/Connor - Los Angeles, 310/278-9313

FLASHPOINT   TriStar, 1984
ONE GOOD COP   Buena Vista, 1991
RAMBLING ROSE   New Line Cinema, 1991
JENNIFER EIGHT   Paramount, 1992
GETTYSBURG   New Line Cinema, 1993
THE QUICK AND THE DEAD   TriStar, 1995

TIM CONWAY
b. December 15, 1933 - Willoughby, Ohio

McHALE'S NAVY   1964
McHALE'S NAVY JOINS THE AIR FORCE   1965
THE WORLD'S GREATEST ATHLETE   Buena Vista, 1973
THE APPLE DUMPLING GANG   Buena Vista, 1975
GUS   Buena Vista, 1976
THE SHAGGY D.A.   Buena Vista, 1976
THE BILLION DOLLAR HOBO   1978
THE APPLE DUMPLING GANG RIDES AGAIN   Buena Vista, 1979
THE PRIZE FIGHTER   New World, 1979
THE PRIVATE EYES   New World, 1980
THE LONGSHOT   Orion, 1986

KEITH COOGAN
ADVENTURES IN BABYSITTING   Buena Vista, 1987
HIDING OUT   DEG, 1987
UNDER THE BOARDWALK   New World, 1989
CHEETAH   Buena Vista, 1989
COUSINS   Paramount, 1989
BOOK OF LOVE   New Line Cinema, 1991
TOY SOLDIERS   TriStar, 1991
DON'T TELL MOM THE BABYSITTER'S DEAD   Warner Bros., 1991

BARBARA COOK
HANS CHRISTIAN ANDERSEN'S THUMBELINA (AF)   Warner Bros.,
   1994 (voice)

BART ROBINSON COOK
GEORGE BALANCHINE'S THE NUTCRACKER
   Warner Bros., 1993

PETER COOK
b. November 17, 1937 - Torquay, England

THE WRONG BOX   Columbia, 1966, British
BEDAZZLED   20th Century Fox, 1967, British
A DANDY IN ASPIC   Columbia, 1968, British
THOSE DARING YOUNG MEN IN THEIR JAUNTY JALOPIES
   MONTE CARLO OR BUST   Paramount, 1969,
   British-Italian-French
THE BED-SITTING ROOM   United Artists, 1969, British
THE RISE AND RISE OF MICHAEL RIMMER   Warner Bros.,
   1970, British
THE ADVENTURES OF BARRY MCKENZIE   Double Head
   Productions, 1972, Australian
THE HOUND OF THE BASKERVILLES   Atlantic Releasing
   Corporation, 1978, British
DEREK AND CLIVE GET THE HORN (PF)   Peter Cook Productions,
   1981, British
THE SECRET POLICEMAN'S OTHER BALL (FD)   Miramax,
   1982, British
YELLOWBEARD   Orion, 1983, British
SUPERGIRL   Warner Bros., 1984, British
THE PRINCESS BRIDE   20th Century Fox, 1987
GETTING IT RIGHT   MCEG, 1989, U.S.-British
GREAT BALLS OF FIRE   Orion, 1989
BLACK BEAUTY   Warner Bros., 1994, British-U.S.

JENNIFER COOKE
FRIDAY THE 13TH, PART VI: JASON LIVES   Paramount, 1986

DANNY COOKSEY
MAC AND ME   Orion, 1988

KEVIN COONEY
Agent: The Gage Group - Los Angeles, 213/859-8777

THE TRIP TO BOUNTIFUL   Island Pictures/FilmDallas, 1985
FULL MOON IN BLUE WATER   Trans World Entertainment, 1988

ALICE COOPER
SGT. PEPPER'S LONELY HEARTS CLUB BAND   Universal, 1978
FREDDY'S DEAD: THE FINAL NIGHTMARE
   New Line Cinema, 1991
WAYNE'S WORLD   Paramount, 1992

CAMI COOPER
SHOCKER   Universal, 1989

CHARLES COOPER
STAR TREK V: THE FINAL FRONTIER   Paramount, 1989
BLIND FURY   TriStar, 1990

CHRIS COOPER
Agent: APA - Los Angeles, 310/273-0744

MATEWAN   Cinecom, 1987
GUILTY BY SUSPICION   Warner Bros., 1991

GARRY COOPER
CARAVAGGIO   British Film Institute, 1986, British

INDIA COOPER
ABOVE THE LAW   Warner Bros., 1988

JACKIE COOPER
(John Cooper, Jr.)
b. September 15, 1922 - Los Angeles, California
Agent: Contemporary Artists - Santa Monica, 310/395-1800

FOX MOVIETONE FOLLIES   Fox, 1929
SUNNY SIDE UP   Fox, 1929
SKIPPY ★   Paramount, 1931
DONOVAN'S KID   1931
THE CHAMP   MGM, 1931

SOOKY   Paramount, 1931
WHEN A FELLER NEEDS A FRIEND   MGM, 1932
DIVORCE IN THE FAMILY   MGM, 1932
BROADWAY TO HOLLYWOOD   MGM, 1933
THE BOWERY   United Artists, 1933
LONE COWBOY   MGM, 1934
TREASURE ISLAND   MGM, 1934
PECK'S BAD BOY   Fox, 1934
DINKY   1935
O'SHAUGHNESSY'S BOY   MGM, 1935
TOUGH GUY   MGM, 1936
THE DEVIL IS A SISSY   MGM, 1936
BOY OF THE STREETS   1937
WHITE BANNERS   Warner Bros., 1938
GANGSTER'S BOY   1938
THAT CERTAIN AGE   1938
NEWSBOYS' HOME   1938
SCOUTS TO THE RESCUE   1939
SPIRIT OF CULVER   1939
STREETS OF NEW YORK   1939
TWO BRIGHT BOYS   1939
WHAT A LIFE   Paramount, 1939
THE BIG GUY   Universal, 1939
SEVENTEEN   Paramount, 1940
THE RETURN OF FRANK JAMES   20th Century-Fox, 1940
GALLANT SONS   MGM, 1940
LIFE WITH HENRY   Paramount, 1941
ZIEGFELD GIRL   MGM, 1941
HER FIRST BEAU   1941
GLAMOUR BOY   Paramount, 1941
SYNCOPATION   RKO Radio, 1942
MEN OF TEXAS   Universal, 1942
THE NAVY COMES THROUGH   RKO Radio, 1942
WHERE ARE YOUR CHILDREN?   1944
STORK BITES MAN   United Artists, 1947, British
KILROY WAS HERE   Monogram, 1947
FRENCH LEAVE   1948
EVERYTHING'S DUCKY   Columbia, 1961
SHADOW ON THE LAND (TF)   Screen Gems/Columbia TV, 1968
THE ASTRONAUT (TF)   Universal TV, 1971
THE LOVE MACHINE   Columbia, 1971
MAYBE I'LL COME HOME IN THE SPRING (TF)   Metromedia
   Productions, 1971
CHOSEN SURVIVORS   Columbia, 1974
THE DAY THE EARTH MOVED (TF)   ABC Circle Films, 1974
THE INVISIBLE MAN (TF)   Universal TV, 1975
MOBILE TWO (TF)   Universal TV/Mark Vii, Ltd., 1975
OPERATION PETTICOAT (TF)   Universal TV, 1977
SUPERMAN   Warner Bros., 1978
SUPERMAN II   Warner Bros., 1981, U.S.-British
SUPERMAN III   Warner Bros., 1983, U.S.-British
SUPERMAN IV: THE QUEST FOR PEACE   Warner Bros., 1987

JEREMY COOPER
THE REFLECTING SKIN   Miramax Films, 1991

LUKE COOPER
BYE BYE BLUES   Circle Releasing, 1989, Canadian

ROY COOPER
Agent: APA - Los Angeles, 310/273-0744

DOLORES CLAIBORNE   Columbia, 1994

JOAN COPELAND
A LITTLE SEX   Universal, 1982
HER ALIBI   Warner Bros., 1989
MURDER IN BLACK AND WHITE (TF)   Titus Productions, 1990

SOFIA COPPOLA
PEGGY SUE GOT MARRIED   TriStar, 1986
THE GODFATHER, PART III   Paramount, 1990

JEFF CORBETT
TALENT FOR THE GAME   Paramount, 1992

JOHN CORBETT
Agent: CAA - Beverly Hills, 310/288-4545

TOMBSTONE   Buena Vista, 1993

BARRY CORBIN
Agent: Writers & Artists Agency - Los Angeles, 213/820-2240

STIR CRAZY   Columbia, 1980
THE BEST LITTLE WHOREHOUSE IN TEXAS   Universal, 1982
THE MAN WHO LOVED WOMEN   Columbia, 1983
WARGAMES   MGM/UA, 1983
THE BALLAD OF GREGORIO CORTEZ   Embassy, 1983
NOTHING IN COMMON   TriStar, 1986
WARM HEARTS, COLD FEET (TF)   Lorimar-Telepictures, 1987
THE PEOPLE ACROSS THE LAKE (TF)   Bill McCutchen
    Productions/Columbia TV, 1988
WHO'S HARRY CRUMB?   TriStar, 1989
SHORT TIME   20th Century Fox, 1990

JEFF COREY
b. August 10, 1914 - New York, New York

THE DEVIL AND DANIEL WEBSTER ALL THAT MONEY CAN
    BUYDANIEL AND THE DEVIL   RKO Radio, 1941
THE MAN WHO WOULDN'T DIE   1942
MY FRIEND FLICKA   1943
THE KILLERS   Universal, 1946
BRUTE FORCE   Warner Bros., 1947
JOAN OF ARC   RKO Radio, 1948
HOME OF THE BRAVE   United Artists, 1949
BRIGHT LEAF   Warner Bros., 1950
RAWHIDE DESPERATE SIEGE   20th Century Fox, 1951
FOURTEEN HOURS   20th Century Fox, 1951
ONLY THE VALIANT   Warner Bros., 1951
RED MOUNTAIN   Paramount, 1951
THE BALCONY   Continental, 1963
LADY IN A CAGE   United Artists, 1964
MICKEY ONE   Columbia, 1965
THE CINCINATTI KID   MGM, 1965
SECONDS   Paramount, 1967
IN COLD BLOOD   Columbia, 1967
THE BOSTON STRANGLER   20th Century Fox, 1968
TRUE GRIT   Paramount, 1969
BUTCH CASSIDY AND THE SUNDANCE KID
    20th Century Fox, 1969
BENEATH THE PLANET OF THE APES   20th Century-Fox, 1970
GETTING STRAIGHT   Columbia, 1970
THEY CALL ME MISTER TIBBS!   United Artists, 1970
LITTLE BIG MAN   National General, 1970
IMPASSE   1970
SHOOT-OUT   Universal, 1971
CATLOW   MGM, 1971, U.S.-Spanish
PAPER TIGER   Joseph E. Levine Presents, 1975, British
THE PREMONITION   Avco Embassy, 1976
THE LAST TYCOON   Paramount, 1976
MOONSHINE COUNTY EXPRESS   New World, 1977
OH, GOD!   Warner Bros., 1977
THE WILD GEESE   Allied Artists, 1978, British
JENNIFER   1978
BUTCH AND SUNDANCE: THE EARLY DAYS
    20th Century Fox, 1979
BATTLE BEYOND THE STARS   New World, 1979
THE SWORD AND THE SORCERER   Group 1, 1982
CONAN THE DESTROYER   Universal, 1984
FINAL JEOPARDY (TF)   Frank von Zerneck Productions, 1985
BIRD ON A WIRE   Universal, 1990
SURVIVING THE GAME   New Line Cinema, 1994

DAN CORKILL
ROCKET GIBRALTAR   Columbia, 1988

ANNIE CORLEY
THE BRIDGES OF MADISON COUNTY   Warner Bros., 1995

SHARON CORLEY
NEW JERSEY DRIVE   Gramercy Pictures, 1994

MADDIE CORMAN
Agent: The Agency - Los Angeles, 310/551-3000

SEVEN MINUTES IN HEAVEN   Warner Bros., 1986
THE ADVENTURES OF FORD FAIRLANE   20th Century Fox, 1990

ELLIE CORNELL
Agent: The Gage Group, Inc. - Los Angeles, 213/859-8777

HALLOWEEN IV - THE RETURN OF MICHAEL MYERS
    Galaxy, 1988
HALLOWEEN 5 - THE REVENGE OF MICHAEL MYERS
    Galaxy, 1989

GEORGE CORRAFACE
Agent: William Morris Agency - Beverly Hills, 310/274-7451

IMPROMPTU   Hemdale, 1990, U.S.-French
CHRISTOPHER COLUMBUS: THE DISCOVERY   Warner Bros.,
    1992, British-Spanish

NICK CORRI
Agent: The Marion Rosenberg Office - Los Angeles, 213/653-7383

A NIGHTMARE ON ELM STREET   New Line Cinema, 1984
THE COTTON CLUB   Orion, 1984
WILDCATS   Warner Bros., 1986
SLAVES OF NEW YORK   TriStar, 1989

BUD CORT
(Walter Edward Cox)
Agent: Judy Schoen & Associates - Los Angeles, 213/962-1950

M*A*S*H   20th Century Fox, 1970
THE TRAVELING EXECUTIONER   MGM, 1970
BREWSTER McCLOUD   MGM, 1970
HAROLD AND MAUDE   Paramount, 1971
WHY SHOOT THE TEACHER?   Quartet, 1977, Canadian
HITLER'S SON   1978, British
DIE LAUGHING   Orion/Warner Bros., 1980
SHE DANCES ALONE   Continental, 1982, Australian
LOVE LETTERS   New World, 1983
ELECTRIC DREAMS   MGM/UA, 1984, British (voice)
MARIA'S LOVERS   Cannon, 1984
INVADERS FROM MARS   Cannon, 1986
BATES MOTEL (TF)   Universal TV, 1987
TED & VENUS   Double Helix Films, 1991

ELAINE CORTADELLAS
VAGABOND SANS TOIT NI LOI   Grange Communications/
    IFEX Film, 1985, French

DAN CORTESE
Agent: William Morris Agency - Beverly Hills, 310/274-7451

TWO GUYS TALKING ABOUT GIRLS   Trimark Pictures, 1995

JESSE CORTI
BEAUTY AND THE BEAST (AF)   Buena Vista, 1991 (voice)

BILL COSBY
(William H. Cosby, Jr.)
b. July 12, 1937 - Philadelphia, Pennsylvania
Agent: William Morris Agency - Beverly Hills, 310/274-7451

TO ALL MY FRIENDS ON SHORE (TF)   Jemmin & Jamel
    Productions, 1972
MAN AND BOY   Levitt-Pickman, 1972
HICKEY AND BOGGS   United Artists, 1972
UPTOWN SATURDAY NIGHT   Warner Bros., 1974
LET'S DO IT AGAIN   Warner Bros., 1975
MOTHER, JUGS & SPEED   20th Century Fox, 1976
A PIECE OF THE ACTION   Warner Bros., 1977
TOP SECRET (TF)   Jemmin, Inc./Sheldon Leonard
    Productions, 1978

THE DEVIL AND MAX DEVLIN   Buena Vista, 1981
CALIFORNIA SUITE   Columbia, 1978
LEONARD PART 6   Columbia, 1987
GHOST DAD   Universal, 1990
THE METEOR MAN   MGM/UA, 1993
I SPY RETURNS (TF)   CBS, 1994

ROBERT COSTANZO
THE LIGHTSHIP   Castle Hill Productions, 1985, U.S.-West German
DELUSION   I.R.S. Releasing, 1991
MAN'S BEST FRIEND   New Line Cinema, 1993
BATMAN: MASK OF THE PHANTASM (AF)   Warner Bros.,
    1993 (voice)
NORTH   Columbia, 1994
STRANGER THINGS   Columbia, 1995

BOB COSTAS
THE SCOUT   20th Century Fox, 1994

NICOLAS COSTER
Agent: The Artists Group, Ltd. - Los Angeles, 310/552-1100

BETSY'S WEDDING   Buena Vista, 1990

KEVIN COSTNER
b. January 18, 1955 - Los Angeles, California
Business: Tig Productions, 4000 Warner Blvd., Burbank, CA 91523,
    818/954-4500
Agent: CAA - Beverly Hills, 310/288-4545

SHADOWS RUN BLACK   1981
NIGHT SHIFT   The Ladd Company/Warner Bros., 1982
CHASING DREAMS   1982
FRANCES   Universal/AFD, 1982
STACY'S KNIGHTS   1983
TABLE FOR FIVE   Warner Bros., 1983
TESTAMENT   Paramount, 1983
THE BIG CHILL   Columbia, 1983
THE GUNRUNNER   1984, Canadian
AMERICAN FLYERS   Warner Bros., 1985
FANDANGO   Warner Bros., 1985
SILVERADO   Columbia, 1985
SIZZLE BEACH, U.S.A.   1986 (filmed in 1974)
THE UNTOUCHABLES   Paramount, 1987
NO WAY OUT   Orion, 1987
BULL DURHAM   Orion, 1988
FIELD OF DREAMS   Universal, 1989
REVENGE   Columbia, 1990
DANCES WITH WOLVES ★   Orion, 1990 (also directed)
TRUTH OR DARE (FD)   Miramax Films, 1991 (uncredited)
ROBIN HOOD: PRINCE OF THIEVES   Warner Bros., 1991
JFK   Warner Bros., 1991
THE BODYGUARD   Warner Bros., 1992
A PERFECT WORLD   Warner Bros., 1993
WYATT EARP   Warner Bros., 1994
THE WAR   Universal, 1994
WATERWORLD   Universal, 1995

JOHN COTHRAN, JR.
JIMMY HOLLYWOOD   Paramount, 1994

BERNIE COULSON
BULLIES   Universal, 1986, Canadian
THE ACCUSED   Paramount, 1988
LOVERBOY   TriStar, 1989
EDDIE AND THE CRUISERS II: EDDIE LIVES   Scotti Bros., 1989

CLOTILDE COURAU
Agent: William Morris Agency - Beverly Hills, 310/274-7451

THE PICKLE   Columbia, 1993

MARGARET COURTENAY
DUET FOR ONE   Cannon, 1986

TOM COURTENAY
b. February 25, 1937 - Hull, England

THE LONELINESS OF THE LONG DISTANCE RUNNER
    Continental, 1962, British
PRIVATE POTTER   MGM, 1964, British
BILLY LIAR   Continental, 1963, British
KING AND COUNTRY   Allied Artists, 1964, British
OPERATION CROSSBOW   *THE GREAT SPY MISSION*   MGM,
    1965, British-Italian
KING RAT   Columbia, 1965, British
DOCTOR ZHIVAGO ✪   MGM, 1965, British
NIGHT OF THE GENERALS   Columbia, 1967, British-French
THE DAY THE FISH CAME OUT   20th Century Fox, 1967,
    British-Greek
A DANDY IN ASPIC   Columbia, 1968, British
OTLEY   Columbia, 1969, British
ONE DAY IN THE LIFE OF IVAN DENISOVITCH   Cinerama
    Releasing Corporation, 1971, British-Norwegian
TO CATCH A SPY   *CATCH ME A SPY*   Rank, 1971, British-French
THE DRESSER ★   Columbia, 1983, British
HAPPY NEW YEAR   Columbia, 1987
LEONARD PART 6   Columbia, 1987
THE LAST BUTTERFLY   Arrow Releasing, 1993

BRIAN COUSINS
LONGTIME COMPANION   Samuel Goldwyn Company, 1990

CHRISTIAN COUSINS
KINDERGARTEN COP   Universal, 1990

JOSEPH COUSINS
KINDERGARTEN COP   Universal, 1990

FRANKLIN COVER
WALL STREET   20th Century Fox, 1987

TOM COVIELLO
BIG   20th Century Fox, 1988

NICHOLAS COWAN
SURF NINJAS   New Line Cinema, 1993

MATTHEW COWLES
WHITE FANG 2: MYTH OF THE WHITE WOLF   Buena Vista, 1994

BRIAN COX
Agent: The Marion Rosenberg Office - Los Angeles, 213/653-7383

MANHUNTER   DEG, 1986
MURDER BY MOONLIGHT (TF)   Tamara Asseyev Productions/
    London Weekend TV/Viacom, 1989, U.S.-British
HIDDEN AGENDA   Hemdale, 1990
IRON WILL   Buena Vista, 1994
ROB ROY   MGM/UA, 1995

COURTENEY COX
b. Birmingham, Alabama
Agent: CAA - Beverly Hills, 310/288-4545

DOWN TWISTED   Cannon, 1987
MASTERS OF THE UNIVERSE   Cannon, 1987
IF IT'S TUESDAY, IT STILL MUST BE BELGIUM (TF)
    Eisenstock & Mintz Productions, 1987
COCOON: THE RETURN   20th Century Fox, 1988
I'LL BE HOME FOR CHRISTMAS (TF)   NBC Productions, 1988
JUDITH KRANTZ'S TILL WE MEET AGAIN   *TILL WE
    MEET AGAIN* (MS)   Steve Krantz Productions/Yorkshire TV,
    1989, U.S.-British
CURIOSITY KILLS (CTF)   Dutch Productions, 1990
MR. DESTINY   Buena Vista, 1990
BLUE DESERT   Neo Films/First Look Films, 1991
SHAKING THE TREE   Castle Hill Productions, 1992
THE OPPOSITE SEX (AND HOW TO LIVE WITH THEM)
    Miramax Films, 1993
ACE VENTURA: PET DETECTIVE   Warner Bros., 1994

E'LON COX
JO JO DANCER, YOUR LIFE IS CALLING   Columbia, 1986

JENNIFER COX
THE BRADY BUNCH MOVIE   Paramount, 1995

MITCHELL COX
Personal Manager: Marc Rindner - Los Angeles, 213/461-6334

PROTOTYPE X29A   Vidmark, 1991
RULE #3   Arrow Releasing, 1993
APEX   Republic Pictures, 1994

RONNY COX
b. August 23, 1938 - Clouderoft, New Mexico

DELIVERANCE   Warner Bros., 1972
THE HAPPINESS CAGE   THE MIND SNATCHERS
   Cinerama Releasing Corporation, 1972
BOUND FOR GLORY   United Artists, 1976
THE CAR   Universal, 1977
THE ONION FIELD   Avco Embassy, 1979
TAPS   20th Century Fox, 1981
THE BEAST WITHIN   United Artists, 1982
FALLEN ANGEL (TF)   Green-Epstein Productions/
   Columbia TV, 1981
BEVERLY HILLS COP   Paramount, 1984
ROBOCOP   Orion, 1987
BEVERLY HILLS COP II   Paramount, 1987
THE COMEBACK (TF)   CBS Entertainment, 1989
LOOSE CANNONS   TriStar, 1990
TOTAL RECALL   TriStar, 1990
PAST MIDNIGHT   New Line Cinema, 1992
HARD EVIDENCE   1995

VEANNE COX
MISS FIRECRACKER   Corsair Pictures, 1989

PETER COYOTE
SOUTHERN COMFORT   20th Century Fox, 1981
STRANGER'S KISS   Orion, 1984
HEARTBREAKERS   Orion, 1984
E.T. THE EXTRA-TERRESTRIAL   Universal, 1982
JAGGED EDGE   Columbia, 1985
OUTRAGEOUS FORTUNE   Buena Vista, 1987
SWORN TO SILENCE (TF)   Daniel H. Blatt/Robert Singer
   Productions, 1987
JOSEPH WAMBAUGH'S ECHOES IN THE DARKNESS
   ECHOES IN THE DARKNESS (MS)   Litke-Grossbart Productions/
   New World TV, 1987
HEART OF MIDNIGHT   Virgin Vision, 1989
CROOKED HEARTS   MGM-Pathe Communications, 1991
BITTER MOON   Fine Line Features/New Line Cinema, 1993,
   French-British

CHARMAINE CRAIG
WHITE FANG 2: MYTH OF THE WHITE WOLF   Buena Vista, 1994

ROGER CRAIG
NAKED OBSESSION   Concorde, 1991

INGRID CRAIGIE
THE DEAD   Vestron, 1987

JOEY CRAMER
RUNAWAY   TriStar, 1984
FLIGHT OF THE NAVIGATOR   Buena Vista, 1986

BARBARA CRAMPTON
Agent: The Artists Agency - Los Angeles, 310/277-7779

FROM BEYOND   Empire Pictures, 1986

KENNETH CRANHAM
PRIME SUSPECT   Columbia, 1991

MATT CRAVEN
Agent: ICM - Beverly Hills, 310/550-4000

HAPPY BIRTHDAY TO ME   Columbia, 1981, Canadian
JACOB'S LADDER   TriStar, 1990
INDIAN SUMMER   Buena Vista, 1993
CRIMSON TIDE   Buena Vista, 1995

MIMI CRAVEN
THE SECRETARY   Republic Pictures, 1995

WES CRAVEN
b. August 2, 1949 - Cleveland, Ohio

WES CRAVEN'S NEW NIGHTMARE   New Line Cinema,
   1994 (also directed)

ELLEN CRAWFORD
SISTER ISLAND   1995

MICHAEL CRAWFORD
(Michael Dumble-Smith)
b. January 19, 1942 - Salisbury, England

SOAP BOX DERBY   1958, British
TWO LIVING, ONE DEAD   Emerson Films, 1961, British-Swedish
THE WAR LOVER   Columbia, 1962, British
TWO LEFT FEET   1963, British
THE KNACK...AND HOW TO GET IT   Lopert, 1965, British
A FUNNY THING HAPPENED ON THE WAY TO THE FORUM
   United Artists, 1966, British
THE JOKERS   Universal, 1967, British
HOW I WON THE WAR   United Artists, 1967, British
HELLO, DOLLY!   20th Century Fox, 1969
THE GAMES   20th Century Fox, 1970, British
HELLO—GOODBYE   20th Century Fox, 1970
ALICE'S ADVENTURES IN WONDERLAND   1972

WAYNE CRAWFORD
JAKE SPEED   New World, 1986
McNELLY'S RANGERS   Warner Bros., 1995

DENNIS CREAGHAN
THE TED KENNEDY, JR. STORY (TF)   Entertainment
   Partners, 1986

BRUNO CREMER
MENAGE   TENUE DE SOIREE   Cinecom, 1986, French

RICHARD CRENNA
b. November 30, 1926 - Los Angeles, California
Agent: CAA - Beverly Hills, 310/288-4545

RED SKIES OF MONTANA   1952
THE PRIDE OF ST. LOUIS   1952
IT GROWS ON TREES   Universal, 1952
OUR MISS BROOKS   1956
OVER-EXPOSED   1956
JOHN GOLDFARB, PLEASE COME HOME   20th Century-Fox, 1965
MADE IN PARIS   MGM, 1966
THE SAND PEBBLES   20th Century Fox, 1966
WAIT UNTIL DARK   Warner Bros., 1967
STAR!   THOSE WERE THE HAPPY TIMES
   20th Century-Fox, 1968
MIDAS RUN   Cinerama Releasing Corporation, 1969
MAROONED   Columbia, 1969
THE DESERTER   Paramount, 1971, Italian-Yugoslavian
THIEF (TF)   Metromedia Productions/Stonehenge Productions, 1971
CATLOW   MGM, 1971, U.S.-Spanish
RED SKY AT MORNING   Universal, 1971
DOCTORS' WIVES   Columbia, 1971
UN FLIC   DIRTY MONEY   1972, French
THE MAN CALLED NOON   1973
DOUBLE INDEMNITY (TF)   Universal TV, 1973
NIGHTMARE (TF)   CBS, Inc., 1974
BREAKHEART PASS   United Artists, 1976

THE WAR BETWEEN THE TATES (TF)   Talent Associates, 1977
THE EVIL   New World, 1978
HARD RIDE TO RANTAN   1979, Canadian
STONE COLD DEAD   Dimension, 1979, Canadian
BODY HEAT   The Ladd Company/Warner Bros., 1981
FIRST BLOOD   Orion, 1982, Canadian
TABLE FOR FIVE   Warner Bros., 1983
THE FLAMINGO KID   20th Century Fox, 1984
PASSIONS (TF)   Carson Production Group/Wizan
   TV Enterprises, 1984
THE RAPE OF RICHARD BECK (TF)   Robert Papazian Productions/
   Henerson-Hirsch Productions, 1985
RAMBO: FIRST BLOOD PART II   TriStar, 1985
DOUBLETAKE (MS)   Titus Productions, 1985
POLICE STORY: THE FREEWAY KILLINGS (TF)   David Gerber
   Productions/MGM-UA TV/Columbia TV, 1987
KIDS LIKE THESE (TF)   Taft Entertainment/Nexus
   Productions, 1987
PLAZA SUITE (TF)   Kalola Productions, 1987
RAMBO III   TriStar, 1988
STUCK WITH EACH OTHER (TF)   Nexus Productions, 1989
THE CASE OF THE HILLSIDE STRANGLERS (TF)   ABC, 1989
MURDER IN BLACK AND WHITE (TF)   Titus Productions, 1990
MONTANA (CTF)   HBO Productions/Zoetrope Studios/
   Roger Gimbel Productions, 1990
THE FORGET-ME-NOT MURDERS (TF)   CBS, 1994

MARSHALL CRENSHAW
LA BAMBA   Columbia, 1987

WENDY CREWSON
THE GOOD SON   20th Century Fox, 1993
CORRINA, CORRINA   New Line Cinema, 1994
THE SANTA CLAUSE   Buena Vista, 1994

MISSY CRIDER
EYES OF TERROR (TF)   Bar-Gene Productions/Freyda Rothstein
   Productions/Hearst Entertainment, 1994

QUENTIN CRISP
ORLANDO   Sony Pictures Classics, 1992,
   British-Russian-Italian-French-Dutch

ANTHONY CRIVELLO
SPELLBINDER   MGM/UA, 1988

CARLENE CROCKETT
SISTER ISLAND   1995

BILL CROFT
BULLIES   Universal, 1986, Canadian

JONATHAN CROMBIE
BULLIES   Universal, 1986, Canadian

JAMES CROMWELL
Agent: Century Artists, Ltd. - Los Angeles, 310/273-4366

THE RESCUE   Buena Vista, 1988
THE BABE   Universal, 1992

GAIL CRONAUER
THE SUBSTITUTE WIFE (TF)   Frederick S. Pierce Company, 1994

DAVID CRONENBERG
b. March 15, 1943 - Toronto, Ontario, Canada
Agent: CAA - Beverly Hills, 310/288-4545

THE FLY   20th Century Fox, 1986, U.S.-Canadian (also directed)
NIGHTBREED   20th Century Fox, 1990

LAUREL CRONIN
BEETHOVEN   Universal, 1992

WALTER CRONKITE
WE'RE BACK! A DINOSAUR'S STORY (AF)   Universal,
   1993 (voice)

HUME CRONYN
b. July 18, 1911 - London, Ontario, Canada
Agent: ICM - Beverly Hills, 310/550-4000

SHADOW OF A DOUBT   Universal, 1943
PHANTOM OF THE OPERA   Universal, 1943
THE CROSS OF LORRAINE   MGM, 1943
LIFEBOAT   20th Century Fox, 1944
THE SEVENTH CROSS ✪   MGM, 1944
MAIN STREET AFTER DARK   MGM, 1944
A LETTER FOR EVIE   MGM, 1945
THE SAILOR TAKES A WIFE   MGM, 1945
ZIEGFELD FOLLIES   MGM, 1945
THE GREEN YEARS   MGM, 1946
THE POSTMAN ALWAYS RINGS TWICE   MGM, 1946
THE BEGINNING OR THE END   MGM, 1946
BRUTE FORCE   Warner Bros., 1947
THE BRIDE GOES WILD   MGM, 1948
TOP O' THE MORNING   Paramount, 1949
PEOPLE WILL TALK   20th Century Fox, 1951
CROWDED PARADISE   1956
SUNRISE AT CAMPOBELLO   1960
CLEOPATRA   20th Century Fox, 1963
HAMLET   1964
THE ARRANGEMENT   Warner Bros., 1969
GAILY GAILY   United Artists, 1969
THERE WAS A CROOKED MAN...   Warner Bros., 1970
CONRACK   20th Century Fox, 1974
THE PARALLAX VIEW   Paramount, 1974
ROLLOVER   Orion/Warner Bros., 1981
HONKY TONK FREEWAY   Universal/AFD, 1981
THE WORLD ACCORDING TO GARP   Warner Bros., 1982
IMPULSE   20th Century Fox, 1984
BREWSTER'S MILLIONS   Universal, 1985
COCOON   20th Century Fox, 1985
BATTERIES NOT INCLUDED   Universal, 1987
FOXFIRE (TF)   Marian Rees Associates, 1987
COCOON: THE RETURN   20th Century Fox, 1988
DAY ONE (TF)   Aaron Spelling Productions/Paragon Motion Pictures/
   David W. Rintels Productions, 1989
TO DANCE WITH THE WHITE DOG (TF)   Signboard Hill
   Productions, 1993
THE PELICAN BRIEF   Warner Bros., 1993

TANDY CRONYN
THE JANUARY MAN   MGM/UA, 1989

ANNETTE CROSBIE
ORDEAL BY INNOCENCE   Cannon, 1984, British

DENISE CROSBY
Agent: Gersh Agency - Beverly Hills, 310/274-6611

48 HRS.   Paramount, 1982
ELIMINATORS   Empire Pictures, 1986
PET SEMATARY   STEPHEN KING'S PET SEMATARY
   Paramount, 1989
SKIN DEEP   20th Century Fox, 1989
TENNESSEE WALTZ   Condor Productions, 1989

LUCINDA CROSBY
THE NAKED CAGE   Cannon, 1986

MARY CROSBY
CONFESSIONS OF A MARRIED MAN (TF)   Gloria Monty
   Productions/Comworld Productions, 1983
THE ICE PIRATES   MGM/UA, 1983
STAGECOACH (TF)   Raymond Katz Productions/Heritage
   Entertainment, 1986
QUICKER THAN THE EYE   Condor Productions, 1988,
   French-Swiss
BODY CHEMISTRY   Concorde, 1990
THE DAY THE WALL CAME DOWN   Concorde, 1991

BEN CROSS
b. December 16, 1947 - London, England
Agent: APA - Los Angeles, 310/273-0744

CHARIOTS OF FIRE   The Ladd Company/Warner Bros.,
   1981, British
THE FAR PAVILIONS (CMS)   Geoff Reeve & Associates/
   Goldcrest, 1984, British
THE ASSISI UNDERGROUND   Cannon, 1985, Italian-British
NIGHTLIFE (CTF)   Cine Enterprises Mexico/MTE,
   1989, U.S.-Mexican
DEEP TROUBLE (CTF)   USA Cable, 1993
FIRST KNIGHT   Columbia, 1995

HARLEY CROSS
Agent: William Morris Agency - Beverly Hills, 310/274-7451

THE BELIEVERS   Orion, 1987
COHEN & TATE   Nelson Entertainment, 1989
THE FLY II   20th Century Fox, 1989
STANLEY & IRIS   MGM/UA, 1990
TO DANCE WITH THE WHITE DOG (TF)   Signboard Hill
   Productions, 1993

LINDSAY CROUSE
(Lindsay Ann Crouse)
b. May 12, 1948 - New York, New York
Agent: Susan Smith & Associates - Beverly Hills, 213/852-4777

ALL THE PRESIDENT'S MEN   Warner Bros., 1976
ELEANOR AND FRANKLIN (TF)   Talent Associates, 1976
SLAP SHOT   Universal, 1977
BETWEEN THE LINES   Midwest Film Productions, 1977
THE VERDICT   20th Century Fox, 1982
DANIEL   Paramount, 1983
ICEMAN   Universal, 1984
PLACES IN THE HEART ✪   TriStar, 1984
HOUSE OF GAMES   Orion, 1987
LEMON SKY   American Playhouse Theatrical Films, 1988
COMMUNION   MCEG, 1989
BEING HUMAN   Warner Bros., 1994
PARALLEL LIVES (CTF)   Showtime Entertainment, 1994
BYE BYE LOVE   20th Century Fox, 1995

ASHLEY CROW
Agent: William Morris Agency - Beverly Hills, 310/274-7451

THE GOOD SON   20th Century Fox, 1993
LITTLE BIG LEAGUE   Columbia, 1994

CORY CROW
THE NEW ADVENTURES OF PIPPI LONGSTOCKING
   Columbia, 1988

RUSSELL CROWE
Agent: ICM - Beverly Hills, 310/550-4000

THE CROSSING (MFV)   Republic Pictures, 1993
PROOF   New Line Cinema, 1995
THE QUICK AND THE DEAD   TriStar, 1995
ROMPER STOMPER   New Line Cinema, 1995
ROUGH MAGIC   Savoy Pictures, 1995

KEVIN CROWLEY
THE PACKAGE   Orion, 1989

TOM CRUISE
(Thomas Cruise Mapother IV)
b. July 3, 1962 - Syracuse, New York
Agent: CAA - Beverly Hills, 310/288-4545

ENDLESS LOVE   Universal, 1981
TAPS   20th Century Fox, 1981
ALL THE RIGHT MOVES   20th Century Fox, 1983
RISKY BUSINESS   The Geffen Company/Warner Bros., 1983
LOSIN' IT   Embassy, 1983, Canadian-U.S.

THE OUTSIDERS   Warner Bros., 1983
LEGEND   Universal, 1985, British
TOP GUN   Paramount, 1986
THE COLOR OF MONEY   Buena Vista, 1986
COCKTAIL   Buena Vista, 1988
RAIN MAN   MGM/UA, 1988
BORN ON THE FOURTH OF JULY ★   Universal, 1989
DAYS OF THUNDER   Paramount, 1990
FAR AND AWAY   Universal, 1992
A FEW GOOD MEN   Columbia, 1992
THE FIRM   Paramount, 1993
INTERVIEW WITH THE VAMPIRE   Warner Bros., 1994
MISSION: IMPOSSIBLE   Paramount, 1995

CELIA CRUZ
THE MAMBO KINGS   Warner Bros., 1992
THE PEREZ FAMILY   Samuel Goldwyn Company, 1994

RAYMOND CRUZ
CLEAR AND PRESENT DANGER   Paramount, 1994

JON CRYER
PRETTY IN PINK   Paramount, 1986
HIDING OUT   DEG, 1987
DUDES   New Century/Vista, 1987
HOT SHOTS!   20th Century Fox, 1991

BILLY CRYSTAL
b. March 14, 1948 - Long Beach, New York
Agent: ICM - Beverly Hills, 310/550-4000

HUMAN FEELINGS (TF)   Crestview Productions/Worldvision, 1978
RABBIT TEST   Avco Embassy, 1978
ANIMALYMPICS (AF)   Lisberger Studios, 1979 (voice)
BREAKING UP IS HARD TO DO (TF)   Green-Epstein Productions/
   Columbia TV, 1979
ENOLA GAY (TF)   The Production Company/Viacom, 1980
THIS IS SPINAL TAP   Embassy, 1984
RUNNING SCARED   MGM/UA, 1986
THE PRINCESS BRIDE   20th Century Fox, 1987
THROW MOMMA FROM THE TRAIN   Orion, 1987
MEMORIES OF ME   MGM/UA, 1988
WHEN HARRY MET SALLY...   Columbia, 1989
CITY SLICKERS   Columbia, 1991
MR. SATURDAY NIGHT   Columbia, 1992 (also directed)
CITY SLICKERS II: THE LEGEND OF CURLY'S GOLD
   Columbia, 1994
FORGET PARIS   Columbia, 1995 (also directed)

LINDSAY CRYSTAL
CITY SLICKERS II: THE LEGEND OF CURLY'S GOLD
   Columbia, 1994

MELINDA CULEA
A LITTLE SEX   Universal, 1982

KIERAN CULKIN
HOME ALONE   20th Century Fox, 1990
FATHER OF THE BRIDE   Buena Vista, 1991
HOME ALONE 2: LOST IN NEW YORK   20th Century Fox, 1992
NOWHERE TO RUN   Columbia, 1993
IT RUNS IN THE FAMILY   MGM/UA, 1994

MACAULAY CULKIN
b. August 26, 1980 - New York, New York
Agent: ICM - Beverly Hills, 310/550-4000

ROCKET GIBRALTAR   Columbia, 1988
SEE YOU IN THE MORNING   Warner Bros., 1989
UNCLE BUCK   Universal, 1989
JACOB'S LADDER   TriStar, 1990 (uncredited)
HOME ALONE   20th Century Fox, 1990
ONLY THE LONELY   20th Century Fox, 1991
MY GIRL   Columbia, 1991
HOME ALONE 2: LOST IN NEW YORK   20th Century Fox, 1992
THE GOOD SON   20th Century Fox, 1993

GEORGE BALANCHINE'S THE NUTCRACKER   Warner Bros., 1993
GETTING EVEN WITH DAD   MGM/UA, 1994
THE PAGEMASTER   20th Century Fox, 1994
RICHIE RICH   Warner Bros., 1994

QUINN CULKIN
THE GOOD SON   20th Century Fox, 1993

JOHN CULLUM
(John David Cullum)
b. March 2, 1930 - Knoxville, Tennessee
Agent: ICM - Beverly Hills, 310/550-4000

HAWAII   United Artists, 1966
1776   Columbia, 1972
THE DAY AFTER (TF)   ABC Circle Films, 1983
GLORY   TriStar, 1989

JOSEPH CULP
DREAM LOVER   MGM/UA, 1986

ROBERT CULP
b. August 16, 1930 - Berkeley, California

PT-109   Warner Bros., 1963
THE RAIDERS   Universal, 1963
SUNDAY IN NEW YORK   MGM, 1963
RHINO!   MGM, 1964
BOB & CAROL & TED & ALICE   Columbia, 1969
SEE THE MAN RUN (TF)   Universal TV, 1971
HANNIE CAULDER   Paramount, 1972, British
HICKEY AND BOGGS   United Artists, 1972 (also directed)
THE CASTAWAY COWBOY   Buena Vista, 1974
A CRY FOR HELP (TF)   Universal TV, 1975
INSIDE OUT   *HITLER'S GOLD/THE GOLDEN HEIST*
   Warner Bros., 1975, British
SKY RIDERS   20th Century Fox, 1976, U.S.-West German
BREAKING POINT   20th Century Fox, 1976, Canadian
THE GREAT SCOUT AND CATHOUSE THURSDAY
   American International, 1976
GOLDENGIRL   Avco Embassy, 1979
THE GREATEST AMERICAN HERO (TF)   Stephen J. Cannell
   Productions, 1981
TURK 182   20th Century Fox, 1985
WHAT PRICE VICTORY? (TF)   Wolper Productions/
   Warner Bros. TV, 1988
NAMELESS   MGM-Pathe, 1991
THE PELICAN BRIEF   Warner Bros., 1993
I SPY RETURNS (TF)   CBS, 1994

STEVEN CULP
JASON GOES TO HELL—THE FINAL FRIDAY
   New Line Cinema, 1993

JIM CUMMINGS
THE LION KING (AF)   Buena Vista, 1994 (voice)
BALTO (AF)   Universal, 1995 (voice)

QUINN CUMMINGS
Agent: Susan Smith & Associates - Beverly Hills, 213/852-4777

THE GOODBYE GIRL ✪   MGM/Warner Bros., 1977
INTIMATE STRANGERS (TF)   Charles Fries Productions, 1977
THE BABYSITTER (TF)   Moonlight Productions/Filmways, 1980

BRIAN CUMMINS
BEAUTY AND THE BEAST (AF)   Buena Vista, 1991 (voice)

KENDALL CUNNINGHAM
HANS CHRISTIAN ANDERSEN'S THUMBELINA (AF)
   Warner Bros., 1994 (voice)

LIAM CUNNINGHAM
WAR OF THE BUTTONS   Warner Bros., 1994
A LITTLE PRINCESS   Warner Bros., 1994

JAMES CURLEY
IN THE LINE OF FIRE   Columbia, 1993

RICHARD CURNOCK
PARADISE   Avco Embassy, 1982, Canadian

LYNETTE CURRAN
BLISS   New World, 1985, Australian

SONDRA CURRIE
THE SECRETARY   Republic Pictures, 1995

TIM CURRY
Agent: UTA - Beverly Hills, 310/273-6700

THE ROCKY HORROR PICTURE SHOW   20th Century- Fox,
   1976, British
THE SHOUT   Films, Inc., 1979, British
TIMES SQUARE   AFD, 1980
OLIVER TWIST (TF)   Claridge Group Ltd./Grafton Films,
   1982, British
ANNIE   Columbia, 1982
THE PLOUGHMAN'S LUNCH   Samuel Goldwyn Company,
   1983, British
CLUE   Paramount, 1985
LEGEND   Universal, 1986, British
THE HUNT FOR RED OCTOBER   Paramount, 1990
IT (TF)   Konigsberg-Sanitsky Productions/Green-Epstein
   Productions/Lorimar TV, 1990
OSCAR   Buena Vista, 1991
PASSED AWAY   Buena Vista, 1992
HOME ALONE 2: LOST IN NEW YORK   20th Century Fox, 1992
NATIONAL LAMPOON'S LOADED WEAPON 1
   New Line Cinema, 1993
THE THREE MUSKETEERS   Buena Vista, 1993
THE SHADOW   Universal, 1994
CONGO   Paramount, 1995
THE PEBBLE AND THE PENGUIN (AF)   MGM/UA, 1995 (voice)

JANE CURTIN
b. September 6, 1947 - Cambridge, Massachusetts

HOW TO BEAT THE HIGH COST OF LIVING   American
   International, 1980
MAYBE BABY (TF)   Perry Lafferty Productions/von Zerneck-Samuels
   Productions, 1988
COMMON GROUND (MS)   Daniel H. Blatt Productions/
   Lorimar TV, 1990
CONEHEADS   Paramount, 1993

VALERIE CURTIN
Agent: CAA - Beverly Hills, 310/288-4545

MAXIE   Orion, 1985
DOWN AND OUT IN BEVERLY HILLS   Buena Vista, 1986

JAMIE LEE CURTIS
b. November 22, 1958 - Los Angeles, California
Agent: CAA - Beverly Hills, 310/288-4545

OPERATION PETTICOAT (TF)   Universal TV, 1977
HALLOWEEN   Compass International, 1978
THE FOG   Avco Embassy, 1980
PROM NIGHT   Avco Embassy, 1980, Canadian
TERROR TRAIN   20th Century Fox, 1980, Canadian
SHE'S IN THE ARMY NOW (TF)   ABC Circle Films, 1981
ROAD GAMES   Avco Embassy, 1981, Australian
HALLOWEEN II   Universal, 1981
DEATH OF A CENTERFOLD: THE DOROTHY STRATTEN
   STORY (TF)   Wilcox Productions/MGM TV, 1981
MONEY ON THE SIDE (TF)   Green-Epstein Productions/Hal Landers
   Productions/Columbia TV, 1982
LOVE LETTERS   New World, 1983
TRADING PLACES   Paramount, 1983
GRANDVIEW, U.S.A.   Warner Bros., 1984

THE ADVENTURES OF BUCKAROO BANZAI: ACROSS THE
8TH DIMENSION   20th Century Fox, 1984
PERFECT   Columbia, 1985
AS SUMMERS DIE (TF)   HBO Premiere Films/Chris-Rose
Productions/Baldwin/Aldrich Productions/Lorimar-Telepictures
Productions, 1986
AMAZING GRACE AND CHUCK   TriStar, 1987
A MAN IN LOVE   Cinecom, 1987, French
DOMINICK AND EUGENE   Orion, 1988
A FISH CALLED WANDA   MGM/UA, 1988, British
BLUE STEEL   MGM/UA, 1990
QUEENS LOGIC   New Line Cinema, 1991
MY GIRL   Columbia, 1991
FOREVER YOUNG   Warner Bros., 1992
MY GIRL 2   Columbia, 1994
MOTHER'S BOYS   Dimension/Miramax Films, 1994
TRUE LIES   20th Century Fox, 1994

KEENE CURTIS

b. February 15, 1923 - Salt Lake City, Utah

SLIVER   Paramount, 1993

LIANE CURTIS

HARD CHOICES   Lorimar, 1986

ROBIN CURTIS

STAR TREK III: THE SEARCH FOR SPOCK   Paramount, 1984
STAR TREK IV: THE VOYAGE HOME   Paramount, 1986

SONIA CURTIS

TERMINAL BLISS   Cannon, 1992

TONY CURTIS

(Bernard Schwartz/Anthony Curtis)
b. June 3, 1925 - Bronx, New York
Agent: The Blake Agency - Beverly Hills, 310/246-0241

CRISS CROSS   Universal, 1949
CITY ACROSS THE RIVER   Universal, 1949
THE LADY GAMBLES   Universal, 1949
JOHNNY STOOL PIGEON   Universal, 1949
FRANCIS   Universal, 1950
I WAS A SHOPLIFTER   Universal, 1950
WINCHESTER '73   Universal, 1950
SIERRA   Universal, 1950
KANSAS RAIDERS   Universal, 1950
THE PRINCE WHO WAS A THIEF   Universal, 1951
FLESH AND FURY   Universal, 1952
NO ROOM FOR THE GROOM   Universal, 1952
SON OF ALI BABA   Universal, 1952
HOUDINI   Paramount, 1953
THE ALL-AMERICAN   1953
FORBIDDEN   Universal, 1953
BEACHHEAD   United Artists, 1954
JOHNNY DARK   Universal, 1954
THE BLACK SHIELD OF FALWORTH   Universal, 1954
SIX BRIDGES TO CROSS   Universal, 1955
SO THIS IS PARIS   Universal, 1955
THE PURPLE MASK   Universal, 1955
THE SQUARE JUNGLE   Universal, 1955
TRAPEZE   United Artists, 1956
THE RAWHIDE YEARS   Universal, 1956
MISTER CORY   MGM, 1957
SWEET SMELL OF SUCCESS   United Artists, 1957
THE MIDNIGHT STORY   Universal, 1957
THE VIKINGS   United Artists, 1958
KINGS GO FORTH   United Artists, 1958
THE DEFIANT ONES ★   United Artists, 1958
THE PERFECT FURLOUGH   Universal, 1959
SOME LIKE IT HOT   United Artists, 1959
OPERATION PETTICOAT   Universal, 1959
PEPE   Columbia, 1960
WHO WAS THAT LADY?   Columbia, 1960
THE RAT RACE   Paramount, 1960
SPARTACUS   Universal, 1960

THE GREAT IMPOSTER   Universal, 1961
THE OUTSIDER   Universal, 1961
TARAS BULBA   United Artists, 1962
FORTY POUNDS OF TROUBLE   Universal, 1963
THE LIST OF ADRIAN MESSENGER   Universal, 1963
CAPTAIN NEWMAN, M.D.   Universal, 1963
WILD AND WONDERFUL   Universal, 1964
GOODBYE, CHARLIE   20th Century Fox, 1964
PARIS WHEN IT SIZZLES   Paramount, 1964
SEX AND THE SINGLE GIRL   Warner Bros., 1965
THE GREAT RACE   Warner Bros., 1965
BOEING BOEING   Paramount, 1965
NOT WITH MY WIFE YOU DON'T!   Warner Bros., 1966
CHAMBER OF HORRORS   Warner Bros., 1966
ARRIVEDERCI, BABY!   *DROP DEAD, DARLING*   Paramount,
1966, British
DON'T MAKE WAVES   MGM, 1967
THE BOSTON STRANGLER   20th Century Fox, 1968
ON MY WAY TO THE CRUSADES I MET A GIRL WHO...
THE CHASTITY BELT   Warner Bros., 1969, Italian-U.S.
THOSE DARING YOUNG MEN IN THEIR JAUNTY JALOPIES
MONTE CARLO OR BUST   Paramount, 1969,
British-Italian-French
YOU CAN'T WIN 'EM ALL   *THE DUBIOUS PATRIOTS*
1970, British
SUPPOSE THEY GAVE A WAR AND NOBODY CAME?
Cinerama Releasing Corporation, 1970
THE PERSUADERS   1971, British
THE THIRD GIRL FROM THE LEFT (TF)
Playboy Productions, 1973
CAPONE   20th Century Fox, 1975
LEPKE   Warner Bros., 1975
THE COUNT OF MONTE CRISTO (TF)   Norman Rosemont
Productions/ITC, 1975, U.S.-British
THE LAST TYCOON   Paramount, 1976
CASANOVA & CO.   *SEX ON THE RUN*   1976,
Austrian-Italian-French-West German
THE MANITOU   1978
SEXTETTE   Crown International, 1978
THE BAD NEWS BEARS GO TO JAPAN   Paramount, 1978
IT RAINED ALL NIGHT THE DAY I LEFT   Caneuram/Israfilm/COFCI,
1978, Canadian-Israeli-French
VEGA$ (TF)   Aaron Spelling Productions, 1978
THE USERS (TF)   Aaron Spelling Productions, 1978
TITLE SHOT   Arista, 1978, Canadian
LITTLE MISS MARKER   Universal, 1980
THE MIRROR CRACK'D   AFD, 1980, British
MOVIOLA   *THE SCARLETT O'HARA WARS* (MS)   David L. Wolper-
Stan Margulies Productions/Warner Bros. TV, 1980
INMATES: A LOVE STORY (TF)   Henerson-Hirsch Productions/
Finnegan Associates, 1981
PORTRAIT OF A SHOWGIRL (TF)   Hamner Productions, 1982
BRAINWAVES   MPM, 1983
INSIGNIFICANCE   Island Alive, 1985, British
KING OF THE CITY   *CLUB LIFE*   Troma, 1986
MAFIA PRINCESS (TF)   Jack Farren Productions/Group W
Productions, 1986
AGATHA CHRISTIE'S "MURDER IN THREE ACTS" (TF)
Warner Bros. TV, 1986
TARZAN IN MANHATTAN (TF)   American First Run Studios, 1989
CENTER OF THE WEB   AIP, 1992
NAKED IN NEW YORK   Fine Line Features/New Line Cinema, 1994

PIERRE CURZI

THE DECLINE OF THE AMERICAN EMPIRE   Cineplex Odeon,
1986, Canadian

ANN CUSACK

A LEAGUE OF THEIR OWN   Columbia, 1992

DICK CUSACK

MY BODYGUARD   20th Century Fox, 1980
THE LOST HONOR OF KATHRYN BECK (TF)   Open Road
Productions, 1984
EIGHT MEN OUT   Orion, 1988
THINGS CHANGE   Columbia, 1988
THE PACKAGE   Orion, 1989
CRAZY PEOPLE   Paramount, 1990

JOAN CUSACK
b. October 11, 1962 - Evanston, Illinois
Agent: ICM - Beverly Hills, 310/550-4000

MY BODYGUARD   20th Century Fox, 1980
SIXTEEN CANDLES   Universal, 1984
THE ALLNIGHTER   Universal, 1987
BROADCAST NEWS   20th Century Fox, 1987
MARRIED TO THE MOB   Orion, 1988
WORKING GIRL ✪   20th Century Fox, 1988
SAY ANYTHING   20th Century Fox, 1989 (uncredited)
MEN DON'T LEAVE   Warner Bros., 1990
MY BLUE HEAVEN   Warner Bros., 1990
HERO   Columbia, 1992
TOYS   20th Century Fox, 1992
ADDAMS FAMILY VALUES   Paramount, 1993
CORRINA, CORRINA   New Line Cinema, 1994
NINE MONTHS   20th Century Fox, 1995

JOHN CUSACK
b. June 28, 1966 - Evanston, Illinois
Agent: William Morris Agency - Beverly Hills, 310/274-7451

CLASS   Orion, 1983
GRANDVIEW, U.S.A.   Warner Bros., 1984
SIXTEEN CANDLES   Universal, 1984
BETTER OFF DEAD   Warner Bros., 1985
THE JOURNEY OF NATTY GANN   Buena Vista, 1985
THE SURE THING   Embassy, 1985
ONE CRAZY SUMMER   Warner Bros., 1986
STAND BY ME   Columbia, 1986
HOT PURSUIT   Paramount, 1987
BROADCAST NEWS   20th Century Fox, 1987
EIGHT MEN OUT   Orion, 1988
TAPEHEADS   Avenue Pictures, 1988
FAT MAN AND LITTLE BOY   Paramount, 1989
SAY ANYTHING   20th Century Fox, 1989
THE GRIFTERS   Miramax Films, 1990
TRUE COLORS   Paramount, 1991
SHADOWS AND FOG   Orion, 1992
THE PLAYER   Fine Line Features/New Line Cinema, 1992
ROADSIDE PROPHETS   New Line Cinema, 1992
BOB ROBERTS   Paramount/Miramax Films, 1992
MAP OF THE HUMAN HEART   Miramax Films, 1993,
   British-French-New Zealand
MONEY FOR NOTHING   Buena Vista, 1993
BULLETS OVER BROADWAY   Miramax Films, 1994
THE ROAD TO WELLVILLE   Columbia, 1994
CITY HALL   Columbia, 1995
GROSSE POINT BLANK   MGM/UA, 1995

SINEAD CUSACK
ROCKET GIBRALTAR   Columbia, 1988
BAD BEHAVIOUR   October Films, 1993, British

IAIN CUTHBERTSON
GORILLAS IN THE MIST   Warner Bros./Universal, 1988

LISE CUTTER
DESPERADO (TF)   Walter Mirisch Productions/Charles E. Sellier
   Productions/Universal TV, 1987
BUY & CELL   Empire Pictures, 1989
EQUAL JUSTICE (TF)   The Thomas Carter Company/Orion TV, 1990

JULIE CYPHER
WAITING FOR SALAZAR   Buena Vista, 1988

CHARLES CYPHERS
HALLOWEEN   Compass International, 1978
HALLOWEEN II   Universal, 1981
GLEAMING THE CUBE   20th Century Fox, 1989
MAJOR LEAGUE   Paramount, 1989

HENRY CZERNY
Agent: William Morris Agency - Beverly Hills, 310/274-7451

ULTIMATE BETRAYAL (TF)   Hearst Entertainment, 1994
CLEAR AND PRESENT DANGER   Paramount, 1994

AUGUSTA DABNEY
VIOLETS ARE BLUE   Columbia, 1986
THE PAPER   Universal, 1994

MARYAM D'ABO
BEHIND ENEMY LINES (TF)   TVS Productions/MTM Enterprises,
   1985, British-U.S.
SOMETHING IS OUT THERE (MS)   Columbia TV, 1988
NIGHTLIFE (CTF)   Cine Enterprises Mexico/MTE, 1989,
   U.S.-Mexican
NOT A PENNY MORE, NOT A PENNY LESS (CMS)   BBC/
   Paramount TV/Revcom, 1990
THE LIVING DAYLIGHTS   MGM/UA, 1987, British

OLIVIA D'ABO
Agent: ICM - Beverly Hills, 310/550-4000

CONAN THE DESTROYER   Universal, 1984
BOLERO   Cannon, 1984
REALLY WEIRD TALES (CTF)   HBO/Atlantis Films, 1987,
   U.S.-Canadian
BULLIES   Universal, 1986, Canadian
BANK ROBBER   I.R.S. Releasing, 1993
GREEDY   Universal, 1994
CLEAN SLATE   MGM/UA, 1994
LIVE NUDE GIRLS   Republic Pictures, 1995

WILLEM DAFOE
(William Dafoe)
b. July 22, 1955 - Appleton, Wisconsin
Agent: CAA - Beverly Hills, 310/288-4545

HEAVEN'S GATE   United Artists, 1980
THE LOVELESS   Atlantic Releasing Corporation, 1981
THE HUNGER   MGM/UA, 1983, British
THE COMMUNISTS ARE COMFORTABLE (AND THREE
   OTHER STORIES)   1984
ROADHOUSE 66   Atlantic Releasing Corporation, 1984
NEW YORK NIGHTS   International Talent Marketing, 1984
STREETS OF FIRE   Universal, 1984
TO LIVE AND DIE IN L.A.   MGM/UA, 1985
PLATOON ✪   Orion, 1986
DEAR AMERICA: LETTERS HOME FROM VIETNAM (FD)
   Taurus Entertainment, 1987 (voice)
OFF LIMITS   20th Century Fox, 1988
THE LAST TEMPTATION OF CHRIST   Universal, 1988
MISSISSIPPI BURNING   Orion, 1988
BORN ON THE FOURTH OF JULY   Universal, 1989
TRIUMPH OF THE SPIRIT   Triumph Releasing Corporation, 1989
CRY-BABY   Universal, 1990
WILD AT HEART   Samuel Goldwyn Company, 1990
FLIGHT OF THE INTRUDER   Paramount, 1991
WHITE SANDS   Warner Bros., 1992
LIGHT SLEEPER   Fine Line Features/New Line Cinema, 1992
BODY OF EVIDENCE   MGM/UA, 1993
CLEAR AND PRESENT DANGER   Paramount, 1994
VICTORY   Miramax Films, 1995

JENSEN DAGGETT
Agent: The Agency - Los Angeles, 310/551-3000

FRIDAY THE 13TH PART VIII - JASON TAKES MANHATTAN
   Paramount, 1989

E.G. DAILY
Agent: Flick East/West Talent, Inc. - Los Angeles, 213/463-6333 or
    New York, 212/307-1850

LOVERBOY   TriStar, 1989

CYNTHIA DALE
THE BOY IN BLUE   20th Century Fox, 1986, Canadian
SADIE AND SON (TF)   Norton Wright Productions/Kenny Rogers
    Organization/ITC Productions, 1987

KATHRYN DALEY
SCORPION   Crown International, 1986

JOE DALLESANDRO
Agent: Flick East/West Talent, Inc. - Los Angeles, 213/463-6333 or
    New York, 212/307-1850

FLESH   Warhol, 1968
TRASH   Warhol, 1970
HEAT   Warhol, 1972
ANDY WARHOL'S FRANKENSTEIN   *FLESH FOR FRANKENSTEIN*
    Bryanston, 1974, Italian-French
ANDY WARHOL'S DRACULA   *BLOOD FOR DRACULA*
    Bryanston, 1974, Italian-French
THE COTTON CLUB   Orion, 1984
CRITICAL CONDITION   Paramount, 1987
SUNSET   TriStar, 1988
DOUBLE REVENGE   Smart Egg Releasing, 1989
CRY-BABY   Universal, 1990

ABBY DALTON
b. August 15, 1932 - Las Vegas, Nevada

CYBER-TRACKER   PM Entertainment, 1994

FRED DALTON THOMPSON
(See Fred Dalton THOMPSON)

SUSANNA DALTON
A LITTLE SEX   Universal, 1982

TIMOTHY DALTON
b. March 21, 1944 - Wales
Agent: ICM - Beverly Hills, 310/550-4000

THE LION IN WINTER   Avco Embassy, 1968, British
CROMWELL   1970, British
WUTHERING HEIGHTS   American International, 1970, British
MARY, QUEEN OF SCOTS   Universal, 1971, British
LADY CAROLINE LAMB   United Artists, 1972, British
PERMISSION TO KILL   1975, British-Australian
EL HOMBRE QUE SUPO AMAR   1976, Spanish
SEXTETTE   Crown International, 1978
AGATHA   Warner Bros., 1979, British
FLASH GORDON   Universal, 1980, British
CHANEL SOLITAIRE   United Film Distribution, 1981, French-British
MISTRAL'S DAUGHTER (MS)   Steve Krantz Productions/R.T.L.
    Productions/Antenne-2, 1984, U.S.-French
FLORENCE NIGHTINGALE (TF)   Cypress Point Productions, 1985
THE DOCTOR AND THE DEVILS   20th Century Fox, 1985, British
SINS (MS)   New World TV/The Greif-Dore Company/Collins-Holm
    Productions, 1986
THE LIVING DAYLIGHTS   MGM/UA, 1987, British
LICENCE TO KILL   MGM/UA, 1989, British
HAWKS   Skouras Pictures, 1989
THE ROCKETEER   Buena Vista, 1991
BRENDA STARR   New World, 1992
NAKED IN NEW YORK   Fine Line Features/New Line Cinema, 1994
SCARLETT (MS)   1994

ROGER DALTREY
b. March 1, 1944 - London, England
Agent: APA - Los Angeles, 310/273-0744

TOMMY   Columbia, 1975, British
LISTZOMANIA   Warner Bros., 1975, British

THE LEGACY   Universal, 1979
McVICAR   Crown International, 1981, British
MACK THE KNIFE   21st Century Distribution, 1989

ANNA DALVA
GUARDIAN ANGEL   PM Entertainment, 1994

TIMOTHY DALY
b. March 1, 1958 - Suffern, New Jersey
Agent: Gersh Agency - Beverly Hills, 310/274-6611

DINER   MGM/United Artists, 1982
I MARRIED A CENTERFOLD (TF)   Moonlight II Productions, 1984
MIRRORS (TF)   Leonard Hill Films, 1985
I'LL TAKE MANHATTAN (MS)   Steve Krantz Productions, 1987
MADE IN HEAVEN   Lorimar, 1987
SPELLBINDER   MGM/UA, 1988
RED EARTH, WHITE EARTH (TF)   Chris-Rose Productions, 1989
LOVE OR MONEY   Hemdale, 1990
YEAR OF THE COMET   Columbia, 1992
WITNESS TO THE EXECUTION (TF)   NBC, 1994
DR. JEKYLL AND MS. HYDE   Savoy Pictures, 1995

TYNE DALY
b. February 21, 1947 - Madison, Wisconsin
Agent: The Blake Agency - Beverly Hills, 310/246-0241

JOHN AND MARY   20th Century Fox, 1969
ANGEL UNCHAINED   American International, 1970
HEAT OF ANGER (TF)   Metromedia Productions, 1971
A HOWLING IN THE WOODS (TF)   Universal TV, 1971
PLAY IT AS IT LAYS   Universal, 1972
THE ADULTRESS   1973
THE ENTERTAINER (TF)   RSO Films, 1975
THE ENFORCER   Warner Bros., 1976
INTIMATE STRANGERS (TF)   Charles Fries Productions, 1977
TELEFON   MGM/United Artists, 1977
SPEEDTRAP   First Artists, 1977
BETTER LATE THAN NEVER (TF)   Ten-Four Productions, 1979
THE WOMEN'S ROOM (TF)   Philip Mandelker Productions/
    Warner Bros. TV, 1980
ZOOT SUIT   Universal, 1981
CAGNEY & LACEY (TF)   Mace Neufeld Productions/Filmways, 1981
THE AVIATOR   MGM/UA, 1985
MOVERS & SHAKERS   MGM/UA, 1985
KIDS LIKE THESE (TF)   Taft Entertainment/Nexus
    Productions, 1987
STUCK WITH EACH OTHER (TF)   Nexus Productions, 1989
THE LAST TO GO (TF)   Freyda Rothstein Productions/Interscope
    Productions, 1991
FACE OF A STRANGER (TF)   Linda Gottlieb Productions/Viacom
    Productions, 1991
SCATTERED DREAMS: THE KATHY MESSENGER
    STORY (TF)   1993
THE FORGET-ME-NOT MURDERS (TF)   CBS, 1994
CHRISTY (TF)   CBS, 1994
CAGNEY & LACEY: THE RETURN (TF)   The Rosenzweig
    Company, 1994
CAGNEY & LACEY: TOGETHER AGAIN (TF)   The Rosenzweig
    Company, 1995

JACQUES D'AMBOISE
OFF BEAT   Buena Vista, 1986

FRANC D'AMBROSIO
Agent: Gersh Agency - Beverly Hills, 310/274-6611

THE GODFATHER PART III   Paramount, 1990

LEO DAMIAN
Agent: CNA & Associates - Los Angeles, 310/556-4343

PRO & CON   Fountainhead Filmworks, 1989
GHOSTS CAN'T DO IT   Triumph Releasing Corporation, 1990

SOLVEIG DAMMARTIN
UNTIL THE END OF THE WORLD   Warner Bros., 1991,
    West German-French

GABRIEL DAMON
STRANGER IN MY BED (TF)   Edgar J. Scherick Productions/Taft
   Entertainment TV, 1987
ROBOCOP 2   Orion, 1990
NEWSIES   Buena Vista, 1992

MATT DAMON
Agent: UTA - Beverly Hills, 310/273-6700

RISING SON (CTF)   Sarabande Productions, 1990
SCHOOL TIES   Paramount, 1992
GERONIMO - AN AMERICAN LEGEND   Columbia, 1993

STUART DAMON
STAR 80   The Ladd Company/Warner Bros., 1983

MIKE DAMUS
LOST IN YONKERS   Columbia, 1993

MALCOLM DANARE
Agent: John Crosby - Los Angeles, 213/655-2255

THE CURSE   Trans World Entertainment, 1987
POPCORN   Studio Three, 1991

CHARLES DANCE
Agent: William Morris Agency - Beverly Hills, 310/274-7451

FOR YOUR EYES ONLY   United Artists, 1981, British
SAIGON - YEAR OF THE CAT (TF)   Thames TV, 1983, British
THE JEWEL IN THE CROWN (TF)   Granada TV, 1984, British
THE McGUFFIN   BBC, 1985, British
PLENTY   20th Century Fox, 1985, British
THE GOLDEN CHILD   Paramount, 1986
GOOD MORNING, BABYLON   Vestron, 1987, Italian-French-U.S.
WHITE MISCHIEF   Columbia, 1987, British
OUT ON A LIMB (MS)   Stan Margulies Company/ABC
   Circle Films, 1987
PASCALI'S ISLAND   Avenue Entertainment, 1988, British-U.S.
THE PHANTOM OF THE OPERA (MS)   Saban-Scherick
   Productions, 1990
ALIEN 3   20th Century Fox, 1992, U.S.-British
LAST ACTION HERO   Columbia, 1993
CHINA MOON   Orion, 1994

LAWRENCE DANE
Agent: The Artists Group, Ltd. - Los Angeles, 310/552-1100

FATAL ATTRACTION   *HEAD ON*   Greentree Productions,
   1980, Canadian
HAPPY BIRTHDAY TO ME   Columbia, 1981, Canadian
FIND THE LADY   Danton, 1975, Canadian-British
NOTHING PERSONAL   American International, 1980, Canadian
SCANNERS   Avco Embassy, 1981, Canadian
OF UNKNOWN ORIGIN   Warner Bros., 1983, Canadian
ROLLING VENGEANCE   Apollo Pictures, 1987, U.S.-Canadian
NATIONAL LAMPOON'S SENIOR TRIP   New Line Cinema, 1995

CLAIRE DANES
LITTLE WOMEN   Columbia, 1994

BEVERLY D'ANGELO
b. 1954 - Columbus, Ohio
Agent: William Morris Agency - Beverly Hills, 310/274-7451

ANNIE HALL   United Artists, 1977
FIRST LOVE   Paramount, 1977
THE SENTINEL   Universal, 1977
EVERY WHICH WAY BUT LOOSE   Warner Bros., 1978
HAIR   United Artists, 1979
COAL MINER'S DAUGHTER   Universal, 1980
PATERNITY   Paramount, 1981
HONKY TONK FREEWAY   Universal/AFD, 1981
NATIONAL LAMPOON'S VACATION   Warner Bros., 1983
FINDERS KEEPERS   Warner Bros., 1984
NATIONAL LAMPOON'S EUROPEAN VACATION   Warner Bros., 1985

DOUBLETAKE (MS)   Titus Productions, 1985
SLOW BURN (CTF)   Joel Schumacher Productions/
   Universal Pay TV, 1986
BIG TROUBLE   Columbia, 1986
IN THE MOOD   *THE WOO WOO KID*   Lorimar, 1987
HANDS OF A STRANGER (MS)   Edgar J. Scherick Productions/Taft
   Entertainment TV, 1987
MAID TO ORDER   New Century/Vista, 1987
NATIONAL LAMPOON'S CHRISTMAS VACATION   Warner Bros., 1989
DADDY'S DYIN'...WHO'S GOT THE WILL?   MGM/UA, 1990
PACIFIC HEIGHTS   20th Century Fox, 1990
THE POPE MUST DIET   Miramax Films, 1991
LONELY HEARTS   Live Entertainment, 1991
THE MIRACLE   Miramax Films, 1991
MAN TROUBLE   20th Century Fox, 1992
LIGHTNING JACK   Savoy Pictures, 1994, Australian-U.S.
MENENDEZ: A KILLING IN BEVERLY HILLS (MS)   Zev Braun
   Pictures/TriStar Television, 1994
PTERODACTYL WOMAN FROM BEVERLY HILLS   Experimental
   Pictures, 1994
HOW MUCH ARE THOSE CHILDREN IN THE WINDOW?
   Concorde, 1995

RODNEY DANGERFIELD
b. November 22, 1922 - Babylon, New York

THE PROJECTIONIST   Maron Films Limited, 1971
CADDYSHACK   Orion/Warner Bros., 1980
EASY MONEY   Orion, 1983
BACK TO SCHOOL   Orion, 1986
ROVER DANGERFIELD (AF)   Warner Bros., 1991 (voice)
LADYBUGS   Paramount, 1992
NATURAL BORN KILLERS   Warner Bros., 1994

ISA DANIELI
CAMORRA   *UN COMPLICATO INTRIGO DI DONNE, VICOLI E
   DELITTI*   Cannon, 1986, Italian

ALEX DANIELS
Agent: Herb Tannen & Associates - Los Angeles, 213/466-6191

CYBORG   Cannon, 1989

ANTHONY DANIELS
STAR WARS   20th Century Fox, 1977
THE EMPIRE STRIKES BACK   20th Century Fox, 1980
RETURN OF THE JEDI   20th Century Fox, 1983

JEFF DANIELS
b. 1955 - Georgia

Agent: ICM - Beverly Hills, 310/550-4000

TERMS OF ENDEARMENT   Paramount, 1983
MARIE   MGM/UA, 1985
THE PURPLE ROSE OF CAIRO   Orion, 1985
SOMETHING WILD   Orion, 1986
HEARTBURN   Paramount, 1986
RADIO DAYS   Orion, 1987
THE HOUSE ON CARROLL STREET   Orion, 1988
THE CAINE MUTINY COURT-MARTIAL (TF)
   CBS Entertainment, 1988
SWEET HEARTS DANCE   TriStar, 1988
CHECKING OUT   Warner Bros., 1989
NO PLACE LIKE HOME (TF)   Feury-Grant Productions/Orion TV, 1989
LOVE HURTS   Vestron, 1990
ARACHNOPHOBIA   Buena Vista, 1990
WELCOME HOME ROXY CARMICHAEL   Paramount, 1990
THE BUTCHER'S WIFE   Paramount, 1991
GETTYSBURG   New Line Cinema, 1993
SPEED   20th Century Fox, 1994
DUMB AND DUMBER   New Line Cinema, 1994

PHIL DANIELS
QUADROPHENIA   World Northal, 1979, British
BREAKING GLASS   Paramount, 1980, British
BAD BEHAVIOUR   October Films, 1993, British

WILLIAM DANIELS
b. March 31, 1927 - Brooklyn, New York
Agent: The Artists Agency - Los Angeles, 310/277-7779

FAMILY HONEYMOON   1949
LADYBUG, LADYBUG   United Artists, 1963
A THOUSAND CLOWNS   United Artists, 1965
THE PRESIDENT'S ANALYST   Paramount, 1967
THE GRADUATE   Avco Embassy, 1967
TWO FOR THE ROAD   20th Century Fox, 1967, British-U.S.
MARLOWE   MGM, 1969
1776   Columbia, 1972
THE PARALLAX VIEW   Paramount, 1974
BLACK SUNDAY   Paramount, 1977
OH, GOD!   Warner Bros., 1977
KILLER ON BOARD (TF)   Lorimar Productions, 1977
THE ONE AND ONLY   Paramount, 1978
SUNBURN   Paramount, 1979, U.S.-British
THE BLUE LAGOON   Columbia, 1980
CITY IN FEAR (TF)   Trans World International, 1980
ALL NIGHT LONG   Universal, 1981
REDS   Paramount, 1981
REHEARSAL FOR MURDER (TF)   Levinson-Link Productions/
   Robert Papazian Productions, 1982
BLIND DATE   TriStar, 1987
THE LITTLE MATCH GIRL (TF)   NBC Productions, 1987
HER ALIBI   Warner Bros., 1989
HOWARD BEACH: MAKING THE CASE FOR MURDER (TF)
   Patchett-Kaufmann Entertainment, 1989

ELI DANKER
Agent: The Actors Group Agency - Los Angeles, 310/657-7113

WANTED DEAD OR ALIVE   New World, 1986
THE TAKING OF FLIGHT 847: THE ULI DERICKSON STORY (TF)
   Columbia TV, 1988

BLYTHE DANNER
b. February 3, 1943 - Philadelphia, Pennsylvania

DR. COOK'S GARDEN (TF)   Paramount TV, 1970
1776   Columbia, 1972
TO KILL A CLOWN   20th Century Fox, 1972
LOVIN' MOLLY   Columbia, 1974
SIDEKICKS (TF)   Warner Bros. TV, 1974
HEARTS OF THE WEST   MGM/United Artists, 1975
FUTUREWORLD   American International, 1976
A LOVE AFFAIR: THE ELEANOR AND LOU GEHRIG STORY (TF)
   Charles Fries Productions/Stonehenge Productions, 1978
ARE YOU IN THE HOUSE ALONE? (TF)   Charles Fries
   Productions, 1978
TOO FAR TO GO (TF)   Sea Cliff Productions, 1979
THE GREAT SANTINI   THE ACE   Orion/Warner Bros., 1980
INSIDE THE THIRD REICH (TF)   ABC Circle Films, 1982
MAN, WOMAN AND CHILD   Paramount, 1983
GUILTY CONSCIENCE (TF)   Levinson-Link Productions/Robert
   Papazian Productions, 1985
BRIGHTON BEACH MEMOIRS   Universal, 1986
ANOTHER WOMAN   Orion, 1988
MONEY, POWER, MURDER (TF)   Skids Productions/CBS
   Entertainment, 1989
MR. AND MRS. BRIDGE   Miramax Films, 1990
ALICE   Orion, 1990
THE PRINCE OF TIDES   Columbia, 1991
HUSBANDS AND WIVES   TriStar, 1992
TO WONG FOO, THANKS FOR EVERYTHING, JULIE NEWMAR
   Universal, 1995

ROYAL DANO
b. November 16, 1922 - New York, New York

UNDERCOVER GIRL   Universal, 1950
UNDER THE GUN   1951
THE RED BADGE OF COURAGE   MGM, 1951
FLAME OF ARABY   1951
BEND OF THE RIVER   Universal, 1952
JOHNNY GUITAR   Republic, 1954

THE FAR COUNTRY   Universal, 1955
THE TROUBLE WITH HARRY   Paramount, 1955
TRIBUTE TO A BAD MAN   MGM, 1956
SANTIAGO   Warner Bros., 1956
MOBY DICK   Warner Bros., 1956, British
TENSION AT TABLE ROCK   1956
CRIME OF PASSION   United Artists, 1957
TROOPER HOOK   1957
ALL MINE TO GIVE   Universal, 1957
MAN IN THE SHADOW   Universal, 1957
SADDLE THE WIND   MGM, 1958
HANDLE WITH CARE   1958
MAN OF THE WEST   United Artists, 1958
NEVER STEAL ANYTHING SMALL   1959
THESE THOUSAND HILLS   20th Century Fox, 1959
HOUND DOG MAN   20th Century Fox, 1959
FACE OF FIRE   Allied Artists, 1959
THE ADVENTURES OF HUCKLEBERRY FINN   MGM, 1960
CIMARRON   MGM, 1960
POSSE FROM HELL   1961
KING OF KINGS   MGM, 1961
SAVAGE SAM   1963
SEVEN FACES OF DR. LAO   MGM, 1964
GUNPOINT   Universal, 1966
THE DANGEROUS DAYS OF KIOWA JONES (TF)   MGM TV, 1966
WELCOME TO HARD TIMES   MGM, 1967
THE LAST CHALLENGE   MGM, 1967
DAY OF THE EVIL GUN   MGM, 1968
IF HE HOLLERS LET HIM GO   1968
THE UNDEFEATED   20th Century Fox, 1969
BACKTRACK (TF)   Universal, 1969
RUN SIMON, RUN (TF)   Aaron Spelling Productions, 1970
MOON OF THE WOLF (TF)   Filmways, 1972
THE GREAT NORTHFIELD, MINNESOTA RAID   Universal, 1972
THE CULPEPPER CATTLE COMPANY   20th Century-Fox, 1972
ACE ELI AND RODGER OF THE SKIES   20th Century-Fox, 1973
CAHILL, U.S. MARSHALL   Warner Bros., 1973
ELECTRA GLIDE IN BLUE   United Artists, 1973
BIG BAD MAMA   New World, 1974
MANHUNTER (TF)   QM Productions, 1974
THE WILD PARTY   American International, 1975
HUCKLEBERRY FINN (TF)   ABC Circle Films, 1975
CAPONE   20th Century Fox, 1975
MESSIAH OF EVIL   International Cinefilm, 1975
DRUM   United Artists, 1976
THE OUTLAW JOSEY WALES   Warner Bros., 1976
THE KILLER INSIDE ME   Warner Bros., 1976
MURDER IN PEYTON PLACE (TF)   20th Century-Fox TV, 1977
DONNER PASS: THE ROAD TO SURVIVAL (TF)   Sunn Classic
   Productions, 1978
STRANGERS: THE STORY OF A MOTHER AND A DAUGHTER (TF)
   Chris-Rose Productions, 1979
TAKE THIS JOB AND SHOVE IT   Avco Embassy, 1981
HAMMETT   Orion/Warner Bros., 1982
SOMETHING WICKED THIS WAY COMES   Buena Vista, 1983
THE RIGHT STUFF   The Ladd Company/Warner Bros., 1983
WILL THERE REALLY BE A MORNING? (TF)   Jaffe-Blakely Films/
   Sama Productions/Orion TV, 1983
TEACHERS   MGM/UA, 1984

GERALDINE DANON
BUSINESS TRIP   MGM-Pathe, 1991

TED DANSON
b. December 29, 1947 - San Diego, California
Agent: CAA - Beverly Hills, 310/288-4545

THE ONION FIELD   Avco Embassy, 1979
OUR FAMILY BUSINESS (TF)   Lorimar Productions, 1981
BODY HEAT   The Ladd Company/Warner Bros., 1981
CREEPSHOW   Warner Bros., 1982
SOMETHING ABOUT AMELIA (TF)   Leonard Goldberg
   Productions, 1984
LITTLE TREASURE   TriStar, 1985
A FINE MESS   Columbia, 1986
JUST BETWEEN FRIENDS   Orion, 1986
WHEN THE BOUGH BREAKS (TF)   Taft Entertainment TV/TDF
   Productions, 1986

WE ARE THE CHILDREN (TF)   Paulist Pictures/Dan Fauci-Ted
   Danson Productions/The Furia Organization, 1987
THREE MEN AND A BABY   Buena Vista, 1987
COUSINS   Paramount, 1989
DAD   Universal, 1989
THREE MEN AND A LITTLE LADY   Buena Vista, 1990
MADE IN AMERICA   Warner Bros., 1993
GETTING EVEN WITH DAD   MGM/UA, 1994
PONTIAC MOON   Paramount, 1994
LOCH NESS   Gramercy Pictures, 1995

MICHAEL DANTE
(Ralph Vitti)
b. 1935 - Stamford, Connecticut

FORT DOBBS   Warner Bros., 1958
WESTBOUND   Warner Bros., 1959
SEVEN THIEVES   20th Century Fox, 1960
KID GALAHAD   United Artists, 1962
OPERATION BIKINI   1963
THE NAKED KISS   Allied Artists, 1964
APACHE RIFLES   20th Century Fox, 1964
HARLOW   1965
ARIZONA RAIDERS   Columbia, 1965
WILLARD   Cinerama Releasing Corporation, 1971
WINTERHAWK   Howco International, 1975
SHINING STAR   *THAT'S THE WAY OF THE WORLD*
   United Artists, 1975
THE FARMER   Columbia, 1977
BEYOND EVIL   IFI-Scope III, 1980
THE BIG SCORE   Almi Distribution, 1983
CAGE   New Century/Vista, 1989

TONY DANZA
b. April 21, 1950 - New York, New York
Agent: ICM - Beverly Hills, 310/550-4000

GOING APE!   Paramount, 1981
SINGLE BARS, SINGLE WOMEN (TF)   Carsey-Werner Productions/
   Sunn Classic Pictures, 1984
DOING LIFE (TF)   Castilian Productions/Phoenix Entertainment
   Group, 1986
FREEDOM FIGHTER (TF)   HTV/Columbia TV/Embassy TV,
   1988, U.S.-British
SHE'S OUT OF CONTROL   Columbia, 1989
RENAISSANCE MAN   Buena Vista, 1994
ANGELS IN THE OUTFIELD   Buena Vista, 1994

INGEBORGA DAPKUNAITE
FATAL DECEPTION: MRS. LEE HARVEY OSWALD (TF)
   David L. Wolper Productions/Bernard Sofronski/Warner Bros.
   Television, 1993

PATTI D'ARBANVILLE
Agent: Harris & Goldberg - Los Angeles, 310/553-5200

FLESH   Warhol, 1968
BILITIS   Topar, 1976, French
BIG WEDNESDAY   Warner Bros., 1978
TIME AFTER TIME   Orion/Warner Bros., 1979
THE FIFTH FLOOR   Film Ventures International, 1980
MODERN PROBLEMS   20th Century Fox, 1981
THE BOYS NEXT DOOR   New World, 1985
CALL ME   Vestron, 1988
FRESH HORSES   WEG, 1988
CROSSING THE MOB (TF)   Bateman Company Productions/
   Interscope Communications, 1988
WIRED   Taurus Entertainment, 1989
SNOW KILL (CTF)   Wilshire Court Productions, 1990

PATRIKA DARBO
Agent: Booh Schut Agency - Studio City, 818/760-6669

DADDY'S DYIN'...WHO'S GOT THE WILL?   MGM/UA, 1990
THE VAGRANT   MGM-Pathe, 1991

KIM DARBY
(Deborah Zerby)
b. July 8, 1948 - Hollywood, California

BYE BYE BIRDIE   Columbia, 1963
BUS RILEY'S BACK IN TOWN   Universal, 1965
TRUE GRIT   Paramount, 1969
GENERATION   Avco Embassy, 1969
THE STRAWBERRY STATEMENT   MGM, 1970
NORWOOD   Paramount, 1970
THE GRISSOM GANG   Cinerama Releasing Corporation, 1971
THE PEOPLE (TF)   Metromedia Productions/American
   Zoetrope, 1971
DON'T BE AFRAID OF THE DARK (TF)   Lorimar Productions, 1973
THE PINK TELEPHONE   SJ International, 1975, French
RICH MAN, POOR MAN (MS)   Universal TV, 1976
THE ONE AND ONLY   Paramount, 1978
FLATBED ANNIE & SWEETIE PIE: LADY TRUCKERS (TF)
   Moonlight Productions/Filmways, 1979
THE LAST CONVERTIBLE (MS)   Roy Huggins Productions/
   Universal TV, 1979
ENOLA GAY: THE MEN, THE MISSION, THE ATOMIC BOMB (TF)
   The Production Company/Viacom, 1980
FIRST STEPS (TF)   CBS Entertainment, 1985
BETTER OFF DEAD   Warner Bros., 1985
TEEN WOLF TOO   Atlantic Releasing Corporation, 1987

SEVERN DARDEN
DEAD HEAT ON A MERRY-GO-ROUND   Paramount, 1966
THE PRESIDENT'S ANALYST   Paramount, 1967
LUV   Columbia, 1967
PUSSYCAT, PUSSYCAT, I LOVE YOU   United Artists, 1970, British
VANISHING POINT   20th Century Fox, 1971
THE HIRED HAND   Universal, 1971
CISCO PIKE   Columbia, 1971
PLAYMATES (TF)   ABC Circle Films, 1972
THE WAR BETWEEN MEN AND WOMEN   National General, 1972
WHO FEARS THE DEVIL   *THE LEGEND OF HILLBILLY JOHN*
   Jack H. Harris, 1974
THE DISAPPEARANCE OF AIMEE (TF)   Tomorrow
   Entertainment, 1976
IN GOD WE TRU$T   Universal, 1980
WHY WOULD I LIE?   MGM/United Artists, 1980
SATURDAY THE 14TH   New World, 1981
BACK TO SCHOOL   Orion, 1986
THE TELEPHONE   New World, 1988

LINDA DARLOW
IMMEDIATE FAMILY   Columbia, 1989

GÉRARD DARMON
DIVA   United Artists Classics, 1982, French
BETTY BLUE   Alive Films, 1986, French

MICHAEL DARRELL
Agent: Erika Wain Agency - Los Angeles, 213/460-4224

E.T. THE EXTRA-TERRESTRIAL   Universal, 1982

DANIELLE DARRIEUX
A FEW DAYS WITH ME   Galaxy International, 1988, French

HENRY DARROW
THE LAST OF THE FINEST   Orion, 1990
MAVERICK   Warner Bros., 1994

STACEY DASH
Agent: The Actors Group Agency - Los Angeles, 310/657-7113

TENNESSEE WALTZ   Condor Productions, 1989
MO' MONEY   Columbia, 1992
RENAISSANCE MAN   Buena Vista, 1994

NIGEL DAVENPORT
b. May 23, 1928 - Shelford Cambridge, England

LOOK BACK IN ANGER   Warner Bros., 1958, British
PEEPING TOM   Astor, 1960, British
IN THE COOL OF THE DAY   1963
THE THIRD SECRET   20th Century Fox, 1964, British
A HIGH WIND IN JAMAICA   20th Century Fox, 1965, British-U.S.
SANDS OF THE KALAHARI   Paramount, 1965, British
LIFE AT THE TOP   Columbia, 1965, British
WHERE THE SPIES ARE   MGM, 1965, British
A MAN FOR ALL SEASONS   Columbia, 1966, British
RED AND BLUE   1967, British
SEBASTIAN   Paramount, 1968, British
THE STRANGE AFFAIR   Paramount, 1968, British
PLAY DIRTY   United Artists, 1968, British
SINFUL DAVEY   United Artists, 1969, British
THE ROYAL HUNT OF THE SUN   National General,
    1969, British-U.S.
THE VIRGIN SOLDIERS   Columbia, 1969, British
THE MIND OF MR. SOAMES   Columbia, 1970, British
NO BLADE OF GRASS   MGM, 1970, British
THE LAST VALLEY   Cinerama Releasing Corporation, 1971, British
VILLAIN   MGM, 1971, British
MARY QUEEN OF SCOTS   Universal, 1971, British-U.S.
LIVING FREE   Columbia, 1972, British
DRACULA (TF)   Universal TV/Dan Curtis Productions, 1973
CHARLEY-ONE-EYE   Paramount, 1973, British
PHASE IV   Paramount, 1974
STAND UP VIRGIN SOLDIERS   1977, British
THE ISLAND OF DR. MOREAU   American International, 1977
AN EYE FOR AN EYE   Avco Embassy, 1981, British
ZULU DAWN   American Cinema, 1979, British
THE LONDON AFFAIR   1979, British-U.S.
CHARIOTS OF FIRE   The Ladd Company/Warner Bros.,
    1981, British
NIGHTHAWKS   Universal, 1981
A CHRISTMAS CAROL (TF)   Entertainment Partners, Ltd.,
    1984, U.S.-British
CARAVAGGIO   British Film Institute, 1986, British

BELINDA DAVEY
DEATH OF A SOLDIER   Scotti Brothers, 1986, Australian

ROBERT DAVI
Agent: APA - Los Angeles, 310/273-0744

THE GOONIES   Warner Bros., 1985
RAW DEAL   DEG, 1986
WILD THING   Atlantic Releasing Corporation, 1987, U.S.-Canadian
TERRORIST ON TRIAL: THE UNITED STATES VS.
    SALIM AJAMI (TF)   George Englund Productions/Robert
    Papazian Productions, 1988
ACTION JACKSON   Lorimar, 1988
DIE HARD   20th Century Fox, 1988
LICENCE TO KILL   MGM/UA, 1989, British
DECEPTIONS (CTF)   Sugar Entertainment/Alpha Entertainment
    Productions, 1990
THE TAKING OF BEVERLY HILLS   Orion, 1991
CENTER OF THE WEB   AIP, 1992
COPS & ROBBERSONS   TriStar, 1994

ELEANOR DAVID
SYLVIA   MGM/UA Classics, 1985, New Zealand
84 CHARING CROSS ROAD   Columbia, 1987, British

KEITH DAVID
PLATOON   Orion, 1986
ALWAYS   Universal, 1989
MEN AT WORK   Triumph Releasing Corporation, 1990
MARKED FOR DEATH   20th Century Fox, 1990
FINAL ANALYSIS   Warner Bros., 1992
ARTICLE 99   Orion, 1992
THE PUPPET MASTERS   Buena Vista, 1994
THE QUICK AND THE DEAD   TriStar, 1995
CLOCKERS   Universal, 1995

LOLITA DAVIDOVICH
(Lolita David)
b. July 15, 1961
Agent: ICM - Beverly Hills, 310/550-4000

THE BIG TOWN   Columbia, 1987
ADVENTURES IN BABYSITTING   Buena Vista, 1987
BLAZE   Buena Vista, 1989
THE OBJECT OF BEAUTY   Avenue Pictures, 1991
THE INNER CIRCLE   Columbia, 1991
KEEP THE CHANGE (CTF)   The Steve Tisch Company/High
    Horse Films, 1992
RAISING CAIN   Universal, 1992
LEAP OF FAITH   Paramount, 1992
BOILING POINT   Warner Bros., 1993
INTERSECTION   Paramount, 1994
COBB   Warner Bros., 1994
STRANGER THINGS   Columbia, 1995

EILEEN DAVIDSON
Agent: Metropolitan Talent Agency - Los Angeles, 213/857-4500

SHARING RICHARD (TF)   Houston Motion Picture Entertainment/
    CBS Entertainment, 1988
EASY WHEELS   Fries Entertainment, 1989
ETERNITY   Academy Entertainment, 1990

JAYE DAVIDSON
THE CRYING GAME ✪   Miramax Films, 1992, Irish-British
STARGATE   MGM/UA, 1994

JOHN DAVIDSON
b. December 13, 1941 - Pittsburgh, Pennsylvania

THE HAPPIEST MILLIONAIRE   1967
THE ONE AND ONLY GENUINE, ORIGINAL FAMILY BAND
    Buena Vista, 1968
COFFEE, TEA OR ME? (TF)   CBS, Inc., 1973
SHELL GAME (TF)   Thoroughbred Productions, 1975
THE CONCORDE—AIRPORT '79   Universal, 1979
EDWARD SCISSORHANDS   20th Century Fox, 1990

TOMMY DAVIDSON
Agent: William Morris Agency - Beverly Hills, 310/274-7451

STRICTLY BUSINESS   Warner Bros., 1991

EMBETH DAVIDTZ
Agent: William Morris Agency - Beverly Hills, 310/274-7451

SCHINDLER'S LIST   Universal, 1993
MURDER IN THE FIRST   Warner Bros., 1994

JOHN RHYS-DAVIES
(See John RHYS-DAVIES)

RAY DAVIES
ABSOLUTE BEGINNERS   Orion, 1986, British

RUDI DAVIES
THE OBJECT OF BEAUTY   Avenue Pictures, 1991

ANN B. DAVIS
b. May 5, 1926 - Schenectady, New York

THE BRADY GIRLS GET MARRIED (TF)   Sherwood Schwartz
    Productions, 1981
A VERY BRADY CHRISTMAS (TF)   Sherwood Schwartz
    Productions/Paramount TV, 1988
THE BRADYS (TF)   Brady Productions/Paramount TV, 1990
NAKED GUN 33 1/3: THE FINAL INSULT   Paramount, 1994
THE BRADY BUNCH MOVIE   Paramount, 1995

CAROLE DAVIS
THE FLAMINGO KID   20th Century Fox, 1984
LET'S GET HARRY   TriStar, 1986

MANNEQUIN   20th Century Fox, 1987
PRINCESS ACADEMY   Empire Pictures, 1987,
   U.S.-French-Yugoslavian
BAJA OKLAHOMA (CTF)   HBO Pictures/Rastar Productions, 1988
SHRIMP ON THE BARBIE   Vestron, 1990, U.S.-New Zealand
IF LOOKS COULD KILL   Warner Bros., 1991

GEENA DAVIS
b. January 21, 1957 - Wareham, Massachusetts
Agent: CAA - Beverly Hills, 310/288-4545

TOOTSIE   Columbia, 1982
SECRET WEAPONS (TF)   Goodman-Rosen Prods./ITC Prods., 1985
FLETCH   Universal, 1985
THE FLY   20th Century Fox, 1986, U.S.-Canadian
BEETLEJUICE   The Geffen Company/Warner Bros., 1988
THE ACCIDENTAL TOURIST ○○   Warner Bros., 1988
EARTH GIRLS ARE EASY   Vestron, 1989
QUICK CHANGE   Warner Bros., 1990
THELMA & LOUISE ★   MGM-Pathe, 1991
A LEAGUE OF THEIR OWN   Columbia, 1992
HERO   Columbia, 1992
ANGIE   Buena Vista, 1994
SPEECHLESS   MGM/UA, 1994
CUTTHROAT ISLAND   MGM/UA, 1995

GUY DAVIS
BEAT STREET   Orion, 1984

JUDY DAVIS
b. 1956 - Perth, Australia

MY BRILLIANT CAREER   Analysis, 1979, Australian
WINTER OF OUR DREAMS   Satori, 1981, Australian
HOODWINK   CB Films, 1982, Australian
HEATWAVE   New Line Cinema, 1982, Australian
THE FINAL OPTION   *WHO DARES WINS*   MGM/UA, 1982
A WOMAN CALLED GOLDA (TF)   Harve Bennett Productions/
   Paramount TV, 1982
A PASSAGE TO INDIA ★   Columbia, 1984, British
KANGAROO   Cineplex Odeon, 1986, Australian
HIGH TIDE   TriStar, 1987, Australian
ALICE   Orion, 1990
IMPROMPTU   Hemdale, 1991
BARTON FINK   20th Century Fox, 1991
NAKED LUNCH   20th Century Fox, 1991, Canadian-British
HUSBANDS AND WIVES ○   TriStar, 1992
THE REF   Buena Vista, 1994
THE NEW AGE   Warner Bros., 1994

KIMBERLEE M. DAVIS
BIG   20th Century Fox, 1988

MAC DAVIS
b. January 21, 1942 - Lubbock, Texas

NORTH DALLAS FORTY   Paramount, 1979
CHEAPER TO KEEP HER   American Cinema, 1980
THE STING II   Universal, 1983
WHAT PRICE VICTORY? (TF)   Wolper Productions/
   Warner Bros. TV, 1988

METTA DAVIS
ABOVE THE LAW   Warner Bros., 1988

MILTON DAVIS, JR.
ANGELS IN THE OUTFIELD   Buena Vista, 1994

NANCY DAVIS
(Anne Frances Robbins/Nancy Reagan)
b. July 6, 1921 - New York, New York

THE DOCTOR AND THE GIRL   MGM, 1949
SHADOW ON THE WALL   MGM, 1949
NIGHT INTO MORNING   MGM, 1951
IT'S A BIG COUNTRY   MGM, 1952

DONOVAN'S BRAIN   United Artists, 1953
HELLCATS OF THE NAVY   Columbia, 1957
CRASH LANDING   Columbia, 1958

OSSIE DAVIS
b. December 18, 1917 - Cogdell, Georgia
Agent: The Artists Agency - Los Angeles, 310/277-7779

NO WAY OUT   20th Century Fox, 1950
THE JOE LOUIS STORY   1953
GONE ARE THE DAYS!   *PURLIE VICTORIOUS*   Trans-Lux, 1963
THE CARDINAL   Columbia, 1963
SHOCK TREATMENT   1964
THE HILL   MGM, 1965, British
A MAN CALLED ADAM   Embassy, 1966
THE SCALPHUNTERS   United Artists, 1968
SAM WHISKEY   United Artists, 1969
SLAVES   Continental, 1969
MALCOLM X (FD)   1972
LET'S DO IT AGAIN   Warner Bros., 1975
COUNTDOWN AT KUSINI   Columbia, 1976,
   U.S.-Nigerian (also directed)
ROOTS (MS)   Wolper Productions, 1977
HOT STUFF   Columbia, 1979
HARRY AND SON   Orion, 1984
AVENGING ANGEL   New World, 1985
DO THE RIGHT THING   Universal, 1989
JOE VERSUS THE VOLCANO   Warner Bros., 1990
JUNGLE FEVER   Universal, 1991
GLADIATOR   Columbia, 1992
QUEEN (MS)   The Wolper Organization/Bernard Sofronski
   Productions, 1993
GRUMPY OLD MEN   Warner Bros., 1993
THE CLIENT   Warner Bros., 1994

PHILIP DAVIS
HIGH HOPES   Skouras Pictures, 1988, British

SAMMI DAVIS
HOPE AND GLORY   Columbia, 1987, British
THE RAINBOW   Vestron, 1989, British
CHERNOBYL: THE FINAL WARNING (CTF)   1991
SHADOW OF CHINA   New Line Cinema, 1991

VIVEKA DAVIS
Agent: The Gordon/Rosson Company - Studio City, 818/509-1900

SHOOT THE MOON   MGM/United Artists, 1982
A DANGEROUS WOMAN   Gramercy Pictures, 1993

WARWICK DAVIS
RETURN OF THE JEDI   20th Century Fox, 1983
THE EWOK ADVENTURE (TF)   Lucasfilm Ltd./Korty Films, 1984
EWOKS: THE BATTLE FOR ENDOR (TF)   Lucasfilm Ltd., 1985
WILLOW   MGM/UA, 1988
LEPRECHAUN   Trimark Pictures, 1993
LEPRECHAUN 2   Trimark Pictures, 1994

BRUCE DAVISON
Agent: William Morris Agency - Beverly Hills, 310/274-7451

LAST SUMMER   Allied Artists, 1969
THE STRAWBERRY STATEMENT   MGM, 1970
WILLARD   Cinerama Releasing Corporation, 1971
THE JERUSALEM FILE   MGM, 1972, U.S.-Israeli
ULZANA'S RAID   Universal, 1972
THE AFFAIR (TF)   Spelling-Goldberg Productions, 1973
MAME   Warner Bros., 1974
MOTHER, JUGS & SPEED   20th Century Fox, 1976
SHORT EYES   *SLAMMER*   The Film League, 1977
BRASS TARGET   MGM/United Artists, 1978
SUMMER OF MY GERMAN SOLDIER (TF)   Highgate Prods., 1978
HIGH RISK   American Cinema, 1981
CRIMES OF PASSION   New World, 1984
SPIES LIKE US   Warner Bros., 1985
THE LADIES CLUB   New Line Cinema, 1986
POOR LITTLE RICH GIRL: THE BARBARA HUTTON STORY (MS)
   Lester Persky Productions/ITC Productions, 1987

LONGTIME COMPANION ✪ Samuel Goldwyn Company, 1990
OSCAR Buena Vista, 1991
SHORT CUTS Fine Line Features/New Line Cinema, 1993
SIX DEGREES OF SEPARATION MGM/UA, 1993
YELLOW DOG 20th Century Fox, 1994
THE SKATEBOARD KID II Concorde, 1995

PETER DAVISON
ALL CREATURES GREAT AND SMALL (TF) Talent Associates/
EMI TV, 1975, British
BLACK BEAUTY Warner Bros., 1994, British-U.S.

PAM DAWBER
b. October 18, 1951 - Farmington Hills, Michigan
Agent: ICM - Beverly Hills, 310/550-4000

THIS WIFE FOR HIRE (TF) The Belle Company/Guillaume-Margo
Productions/Comworld Productions, 1985
AMERICAN GEISHA (TF) Interscope Communications/Stonehenge
Productions, 1986
WILD HORSES (TF) Wild Horses Productions/Telepictures
Productions, 1985
QUIET VICTORY: THE CHARLIE WEDEMEYER STORY (TF)
The Landsburg Company, 1988
DO YOU KNOW THE MUFFIN MAN? (TF) The Avnet-Kerner
Company, 1989

RICHARD DAWSON
b. November 20, 1932 - Hampshire, England

THE RUNNING MAN TriStar, 1987

DORIS DAY
(Doris von Kappelhoff)
b. April 3, 1924 - Cincinnati, Ohio

ROMANCE ON THE HIGH SEAS Warner Bros., 1948
MY DREAM IS YOURS Warner Bros., 1949
IT'S A GREAT FEELING Warner Bros., 1949
YOUNG MAN WITH A HORN Warner Bros., 1950
TEA FOR TWO Warner Bros., 1950
THE WEST POINT STORY Warner Bros., 1950
STORM WARNING Warner Bros., 1951
LULLABY OF BROADWAY Warner Bros., 1951
ON MOONLIGHT BAY Warner Bros., 1951
I'LL SEE YOU IN MY DREAMS Warner Bros., 1951
STARLIFT Warner Bros., 1951
THE WINNING TEAM Warner Bros., 1952
APRIL IN PARIS Warner Bros., 1952
BY THE LIGHT OF THE SILVERY MOON Warner Bros., 1953
CALAMITY JANE Warner Bros., 1953
LUCKY ME Warner Bros., 1954
YOUNG AT HEART Warner Bros., 1954
LOVE ME OR LEAVE ME MGM, 1955
THE MAN WHO KNEW TOO MUCH Paramount, 1956
JULIE MGM, 1956
THE PAJAMA GAME Warner Bros., 1957
TEACHER'S PET Paramount, 1958
THE TUNNEL OF LOVE MGM, 1958
IT HAPPENED TO JANE *TWINKLE AND SHINE* Columbia, 1959
PILLOW TALK ★ Universal, 1959
PLEASE DON'T EAT THE DAISIES MGM, 1960
MIDNIGHT LACE Universal, 1960
LOVER, COME BACK Universal, 1962
THAT TOUCH OF MINK Universal, 1962
JUMBO *BILLY ROSE'S JUMBO* MGM, 1962
THE THRILL OF IT ALL Universal, 1963
MOVE OVER, DARLING 20th Century Fox, 1963
SEND ME NO FLOWERS Universal, 1964
DO NOT DISTURB 20th Century Fox, 1965
THE GLASS BOTTOM BOAT MGM, 1966
CAPRICE 20th Century Fox, 1967
THE BALLAD OF JOSIE Universal, 1968
WHERE WERE YOU WHEN THE LIGHTS WENT OUT?
MGM, 1968
WITH SIX YOU GET EGGROLL National General, 1968

MORRIS DAY
PURPLE RAIN Warner Bros., 1984
THE ADVENTURES OF FORD FAIRLANE 20th Century Fox, 1990
GRAFFITI BRIDGE Warner Bros., 1990

ASSAF DAYAN
THE DELTA FORCE Cannon, 1986

DANIEL DAY-LEWIS
b. April 29, 1957 - London, England
Agent: William Morris Agency - Beverly Hills, 310/274-7451

SUNDAY, BLOODY SUNDAY United Artists, 1971, British
GANDHI Columbia, 1982, British-Indian
THE BOUNTY Orion, 1984, British
MY BEAUTIFUL LAUNDRETTE (TF) Orion Classics, 1985, British
A ROOM WITH A VIEW Cinecom, 1986, British
THE UNBEARABLE LIGHTNESS OF BEING Orion, 1988
STARS AND BARS Columbia, 1988
MY LEFT FOOT ★★ Miramax Films, 1989, Irish-British
EVERSMILE, NEW JERSEY J&M Entertainment, 1989,
Argentine-British
THE LAST OF THE MOHICANS 20th Century Fox, 1992
THE AGE OF INNOCENCE Columbia, 1993
IN THE NAME OF THE FATHER ★ Universal, 1993, Irish-British

KIM DEACON
REBEL Vestron, 1985, Australian

LUCY DEAKINS
THE BOY WHO COULD FLY 20th Century Fox, 1986
LITTLE NIKITA Columbia, 1988
CHEETAH Buena Vista, 1989

JOAQUIM DE ALMEIDA
CLEAR AND PRESENT DANGER Paramount, 1994
ONLY YOU TriStar, 1994

LAURA DEAN
ALMOST YOU TLC Films/20th Century Fox, 1984

LOREN DEAN
PLAIN CLOTHES Paramount, 1988
SAY ANYTHING 20th Century Fox, 1989
BILLY BATHGATE Buena Vista, 1991

RICK DEAN
THE UNBORN Califilm, 1991

RON DEAN
Agent: The Geddes Agency - Los Angeles, 213/651-2401

ABOVE THE LAW Warner Bros., 1988
THE PACKAGE Orion, 1989
THE CLIENT Warner Bros., 1994

GINA DEANGELIS
COUSINS Paramount, 1989

JUSTIN DEAS
Agent: Paradigm - Los Angeles, 310/277-4400

DREAM LOVER MGM/UA, 1986
WACO & RHINEHART (TF) Touchstone Films TV, 1987
A STRANGER WAITS (TF) Bruce Lansbury Productions/Edgar
Lansbury Prods./Lewisfilm Ltd./New Century TV Productions, 1987
MONTANA (CTF) HBO Productions/Zoetrope Studios/Roger Gimbel
Productions, 1990

JEAN DEBAER
Agent: Writers & Artists Agency - Los Angeles, 310/820-2240

84 CHARING CROSS ROAD Columbia, 1987, British

ISAACH DE BANKOLE
CHOCOLAT   Orion Classics, 1988, French

YVONNE DE CARLO
(Peggy Yvonne Middleton)
b. September 1, 1922 - Vancouver, British Columbia, Canada
Agent: Ruth Webb Enterprises, Inc. - Los Angeles, 213/874-1700

HARVARD HERE I COME!   Columbia, 1942
THIS GUN FOR HIRE   Paramount, 1942
ROAD TO MOROCCO   Paramount, 1942
LUCKY JORDAN   Paramount, 1942
YOUTH ON PARADE   1942
RHYTHM PARADE   1943
THE CRYSTAL BALL   United Artists, 1943
SALUTE FOR THREE   Paramount, 1943
FOR WHOM THE BELL TOLLS   Paramount, 1943
SO PROUDLY WE HAIL!   Paramount, 1943
LET'S FACE IT   Paramount, 1943
TRUE TO LIFE   Paramount, 1943
THE DEERSLAYER   Columbia, 1943
STANDING ROOM ONLY   Paramount, 1944
THE STORY OF DR. WASSELL   Paramount, 1944
RAINBOW ISLAND   Paramount, 1944
KISMET   MGM, 1944
PRACTICALLY YOURS   Paramount, 1944
HERE COME THE WAVES   Paramount, 1944
BRING ON THE GIRLS   Paramount, 1945
SALOME—WHERE SHE DANCED   1945
FRONTIER GAL   1945
SONG OF SCHEHEREZADE   1947
BRUTE FORCE   Warner Bros., 1947
SLAVE GIRL   1947
BLACK BART   Universal, 1948
CASBAH   Universal, 1948
RIVER LADY   Universal, 1948
CRISS CROSS   Universal, 1949
CALAMITY JANE AND SAM BASS   Universal, 1949
THE GAL WHO TOOK THE WEST   1949
BUCCANEER'S GIRL   1950
THE DESERT HAWK   1950
TOMAHAWK   Universal, 1951
HOTEL SAHARA   United Artists, 1951, British
SILVER CITY   Paramount, 1951
THE SAN FRANCISCO STORY   Warner Bros., 1952
SCARLET ANGEL   1952
HURRICANE SMITH   Paramount, 1952
SOMBRERO   MGM, 1953
SHE DEVILS   1953
FORT ALGIERS   United Artists, 1953
THE CAPTAIN'S PARADISE   1953, British
LA CASTIGLIONE   1954, French-Italian
BORDER RIVER   Universal, 1954
TONIGHT'S THE NIGHT   1954, British-U.S.
PASSION   RKO Radio, 1954
SHOTGUN   Allied Artists, 1955
FLAME OF THE ISLANDS   1955
MAGIC FIRE   Republic, 1956
RAW EDGE   1956
DEATH OF A SCOUNDREL   1956
THE TEN COMMANDMENTS   Paramount, 1956
BAND OF ANGELS   Warner Bros., 1957
MARY MAGDALENE   1958, Italian
TIMBUKTU   United Artists, 1959
McLINTOCK!   United Artists, 1963
A GLOBAL AFFAIR   MGM, 1964
LAW OF THE LAWLESS   Paramount, 1964
MUNSTER, GO HOME   Universal, 1966
HOSTILE GUNS   Paramount, 1967
THE POWER   MGM, 1968
ARIZONA BUSHWHACKERS   Paramount, 1968
THE DELTA FACTOR   American International, 1970
THE SEVEN MINUTES   20th Century Fox, 1971
THE GIRL ON THE LATE LATE SHOW (TF)   Screen Gems/
     Columbia TV, 1974
THE MARK OF ZORRO (TF)   20th Century Fox TV, 1974
IT SEEMED LIKE A GOOD IDEA AT THE TIME   Selective Cinema,
     1974, British-Canadian

WON TON TON, THE DOG WHO SAVED HOLLYWOOD
     Paramount, 1976
SATAN'S CHEERLEADERS   World Amusement, 1977
NOCTURNA   Compass International, 1979
SILENT SCREAM   American Cinema, 1980
GUYANA: CULT OF THE DAMNED   1980, Mexican
THE MAN WITH BOGART'S FACE   SAM MARLOW, PRIVATE EYE
     20th Century Fox, 1980
THE MUNSTERS' REVENGE (TF)   Universal TV, 1981
LIAR'S MOON   Crown International, 1982
FLESH AND BULLETS   1985
A MASTERPIECE OF MURDER (TF)   20th Century Fox TV, 1986
AMERICAN GOTHIC   Vidmark, 1987, British
CELLAR DWELLAR   Empire Pictures, 1988
OSCAR   Buena Vista, 1991

RUBY DEE
(Ruby Ann Wallace)
b. October 27, 1924 - Cleveland, Ohio
Agent: The Artists Agency - Los Angeles, 310/277-7779

NO WAY OUT   20th Century Fox, 1950
THE JACKIE ROBINSON STORY   Eagle Lion, 1950
THE TALL TARGET   MGM, 1951
GO MAN GO!   1954
EDGE OF THE CITY   MGM, 1957
ST. LOUIS BLUES   Paramount, 1958
TAKE A GIANT STEP   United Artists, 1960
VIRGIN ISLAND   1960
A RAISIN IN THE SUN   Columbia, 1961
GONE ARE THE DAYS!   PURLIE VICTORIOUS   Trans-Lux, 1963
THE BALCONY   Continental, 1963
THE INCIDENT   20th Century Fox, 1967
UPTIGHT   Paramount, 1968
BUCK AND THE PREACHER   Columbia, 1972
BLACK GIRL   Cinerama Releasing Corporation, 1972
COUNTDOWN AT KUSINI   Columbia, 1976, U.S.-Nigerian
CAT PEOPLE   Universal, 1982
DO THE RIGHT THING   Universal, 1989
LOVE AT LARGE   Orion, 1990
SIDNEY SHELDON'S WINDMILLS OF THE GODS   WINDMILLS OF
     THE GODS (MS)   Dove Productions/ITC Productions, 1988
JUNGLE FEVER   Universal, 1991
COP AND A HALF   Universal, 1993

SANDRA DEE
(Alexandra Zuck)
b. April 23, 1942 - Bayonne, New Jersey

UNTIL THEY SAIL   MGM, 1957
THE RELUCTANT DEBUTANTE   MGM, 1958
THE RESTLESS YEARS   1958
IMITATION OF LIFE   Universal, 1959
GIDGET   Columbia, 1959
A SUMMER PLACE   Warner Bros., 1959
PORTRAIT IN BLACK   Universal, 1960
ROMANOFF AND JULIET   Universal, 1961
TAMMY TELL ME TRUE   1961
COME SEPTEMBER   Universal, 1961
IF A MAN ANSWERS   Universal, 1962
TAMMY AND THE DOCTOR   1963
TAKE HER, SHE'S MINE   20th Century Fox, 1963
I'D RATHER BE RICH   Universal, 1964
THAT FUNNY FEELING   Universal, 1965
A MAN COULD GET KILLED   Universal, 1966
DOCTOR, YOU'VE GOT TO BE KIDDING   MGM, 1967
ROSIE!   Universal, 1968
THE DUNWICH HORROR   American International, 1970
AD EST DI MARSA MATRUH   1971, Italian
THE DAUGHTERS OF JOSHUA CABE (TF)   Spelling-Goldberg
     Productions, 1972
HOUSTON, WE'VE GOT A PROBLEM (TF)   1974
THE MANHUNTER (TF)   Universal TV, 1976
FANTASY ISLAND (TF)   Spelling-Goldberg Productions, 1977

RICK DEES
LA BAMBA   Columbia, 1987
THE FLINTSTONES   Universal, 1994

EDDIE DEEZEN

GREASE   Paramount, 1978
THE WHOOPEE BOYS   Paramount, 1986
ROCK-A-DOODLE (AF)   Samuel Goldwyn Company, 1992 (voice)

CALVERT DEFOREST

MY DEMON LOVER   New Line Cinema, 1987

GUY DEGHY

WALLENBERG: A HERO'S STORY (MS)   Dick Berg-Stonehenge
   Productions/Paramount TV, 1985

MICHAEL DeGOOD

EYES OF TERROR (TF)   Bar-Gene Productions/Freyda Rothstein
   Productions/Hearst Entertainment, 1994

CONSUELO DE HAVILLAND

BETTY BLUE   Alive Films, 1986, French

OLIVIA DE HAVILLAND

b. July 1, 1916 - Tokyo, Japan

A MIDSUMMER NIGHT'S DREAM   Warner Bros., 1935
ALIBI IKE   Warner Bros., 1935
THE IRISH IN US   Warner Bros., 1935
CAPTAIN BLOOD   Warner Bros., 1935
ANTHONY ADVERSE   Warner Bros., 1936
THE CHARGE OF THE LIGHT BRIGADE   Warner Bros., 1936
CALL IT A DAY   Warner Bros., 1937
THE GREAT GARRICK   Warner Bros., 1937
IT'S LOVE I'M AFTER   Warner Bros., 1937
GOLD IS WHERE YOU FIND IT   Warner Bros., 1938
THE ADVENTURES OF ROBIN HOOD   Warner Bros., 1938
FOUR'S A CROWD   Warner Bros., 1938
HARD TO GET   Warner Bros., 1938
WINGS OF THE NAVY   Warner Bros., 1939
DODGE CITY   Warner Bros., 1939
THE PRIVATE LIVES OF ELIZABETH AND ESSEX
   ELIZABETH THE QUEEN   Warner Bros., 1939
GONE WITH THE WIND ✪   MGM, 1939
RAFFLES   United Artists, 1940
MY LOVE CAME BACK   Warner Bros., 1940
SANTA FE TRAIL   Warner Bros., 1940
THE STRAWBERRY BLONDE   Warner Bros., 1941
HOLD BACK THE DAWN ★   Paramount, 1941
THEY DIED WITH THEIR BOOTS ON   Warner Bros., 1941
THE MALE ANIMAL   Warner Bros., 1942
IN THIS OUR LIFE   Warner Bros., 1942
THANK YOUR LUCKY STARS   Warner Bros., 1943
PRINCESS O'ROURKE   Warner Bros., 1943
GOVERNMENT GIRL   Warner Bros., 1943
DEVOTION   Warner Bros., 1946
THE WELL-GROOMED BRIDE   Paramount, 1946
TO EACH HIS OWN ★★   Paramount, 1946
THE DARK MIRROR   Universal, 1946
THE SNAKE PIT ★   20th Century Fox, 1948
THE HEIRESS ★★   Paramount, 1949
MY COUSIN RACHEL   20th Century Fox, 1952
THAT LADY   20th Century Fox, 1955, British
NOT AS A STRANGER   United Artists, 1955
THE AMBASSADOR'S DAUGHTER   1956
THE PROUD REBEL   Buena Vista, 1958
LIBEL   MGM, 1959, British
THE LIGHT IN THE PIAZZA   MGM, 1962
LADY IN A CAGE   United Artists, 1964
HUSH...HUSH, SWEET CHARLOTTE   20th Century-Fox, 1964
THE ADVENTURERS   Paramount, 1970
POPE JOAN   *THE DEVIL'S IMPOSTER*   Columbia, 1972, British
THE SCREAMING WOMAN (TF)   Universal TV, 1972
THE FIFTH MUSKETEER   Columbia, 1979, Austrian
AIRPORT '77   Universal, 1977
THE SWARM   Warner Bros., 1978
ROOTS: THE NEXT GENERATIONS (MS)   Wolper Productions, 1979
MURDER IS EASY (TF)   David L. Wolper-Stan Margulies
   Productions/Warner Bros. TV, 1982
THE ROYAL ROMANCE OF CHARLES AND DIANA (TF)
   Chrysalis-Yellen Productions, 1982

ANASTASIA: THE MYSTERY OF ANNA (TF)   Telecom
   Entertainment/Consolidated Productions/Reteitalia, 1986,
   U.S.-Italian
THE WOMAN HE LOVED (TF)   The Larry Thompson Organization/
   HTV/New World TV, 1988, U.S.-British

KIM DELANEY

CRACKED UP (TF)   Aaron Spelling Productions, 1987
CHRISTMAS COMES TO WILLOW CREEK (TF)   Blue Andre
   Productions/ITC Productions, 1987
SOMETHING IS OUT THERE (TF)   Columbia TV, 1988
TAKE MY DAUGHTERS, PLEASE (TF)   NBC Productions, 1988

MICHAEL DELANO

IRON FIST   Century Film Partners, 1994

CATHLEEN DELANY

THE DEAD   Vestron, 1987

DANA DELANY

b. March 13, 1957 - New York, New York
Agent: ICM - Beverly Hills, 310/550-4000

ALMOST YOU   TLC Films/20th Century Fox, 1984
THREESOME (TF)   CBS Entertainment, 1984
WHERE THE RIVER RUNS BLACK   MGM/UA, 1986
PATTY HEARST   Atlantic Releasing Corporation, 1988
CHINA BEACH (TF)   Sacret, Inc. Productions/
   Warner Bros. TV, 1988
HOUSESITTER   Universal, 1992
LIGHT SLEEPER   Fine Line Features/New Line Cinema, 1992
WILD PALMS (MS)   Ixtlan Corporation/Greengrass
   Productions, Inc., 1993
TOMBSTONE   Buena Vista, 1993
BATMAN: MASK OF THE PHANTASM (AF)   Warner Bros.,
   1993 (voice)
EXIT TO EDEN   Savoy Pictures, 1994
LIVE NUDE GIRLS   Republic Pictures, 1995
BLACK AND WHITE   Warner Bros., 1995

SIMON DE LA BROSSE

THE LITTLE THIEF   Miramax Films, 1989, French

DANNY DE LA PAZ

Agent: The Agency - Los Angeles, 310/551-3000

BOULEVARD NIGHTS   Warner Bros., 1979

GEORGE DE LA PEÑA

Agent: The Lantz Office - New York, 212/586-0200

NIJINSKY   Paramount, 1980

DEREK DE LINT

THE UNBEARABLE LIGHTNESS OF BEING   Orion, 1988
BURNING BRIDGES (TF)   Andrea Baynes Productions/
   Lorimar TV, 1990

JOSEPH DeLISI

THE PRINCE OF PENNSYLVANIA   New Line Cinema, 1988

ANTHONY DELON

CHRONICLE OF A DEATH FORETOLD   Island Pictures, 1988

JULIE DELPY

Agent: William Morris Agency - Beverly Hills, 310/274-7451

THE THREE MUSKETEERS   Buena Vista, 1993
BEFORE SUNRISE   Columbia, 1995

BENICIO DEL TORO

LICENCE TO KILL   MGM/UA, 1989, British
CHINA MOON   Orion, 1994

DOM DeLUISE
b. August 1,1933 - Brooklyn, New York

FAIL SAFE   Columbia, 1964
THE GLASS BOTTOM BOAT   MGM, 1966
THE BUSY BODY   Paramount, 1967
WHAT'S SO BAD ABOUT FEELING GOOD?   Universal, 1968
NORWOOD   Paramount, 1970
THE TWELVE CHAIRS   UMC, 1970
EVERY LITTLE CROOK AND NANNY   MGM, 1972
BLAZING SADDLES   Warner Bros., 1974
THE ADVENTURE OF SHERLOCK HOLMES' SMARTER BROTHER
    20th Century Fox, 1975
SILENT MOVIE   20th Century Fox, 1976
THE WORLD'S GREATEST LOVER   20th Century Fox, 1977
SEXTETTE   Crown International, 1978
THE END   United Artists, 1978
THE CHEAP DETECTIVE   Columbia, 1978
HOT STUFF   Columbia, 1979 (also directed)
THE MUPPET MOVIE   AFD, 1979, British
FATSO   20th Century Fox, 1980
SMOKEY AND THE BANDIT II   Universal, 1980
THE LAST MARRIED COUPLE IN AMERICA   Universal, 1980
WHOLLY MOSES   Columbia, 1980
THE CANNONBALL RUN   20th Century Fox, 1981
HISTORY OF THE WORLD—PART 1   20th Century-Fox, 1981
THE BEST LITTLE WHOREHOUSE IN TEXAS   Universal, 1982
HAPPY (TF)   Bacchus Films, Inc., 1983
CANNONBALL RUN II   Warner Bros., 1984
JOHNNY DANGEROUSLY   20th Century Fox, 1984
HAUNTED HONEYMOON   Orion, 1986
AN AMERICAN TAIL (AF)   Universal, 1986 (voice)
ALL DOGS GO TO HEAVEN (AF)   MGM/UA, 1989 (voice)
LOOSE CANNONS   TriStar, 1989
AN AMERICAN TAIL: FIEVEL GOES WEST (AF)   Universal,
    1991 (voice)
HAPPILY EVER AFTER (AF)   First National Film Corporation,
    1993 (voice)
ROBIN HOOD: MEN IN TIGHTS   20th Century Fox, 1993

MICHAEL DeLUISE
CLASS CRUISE (TF)   Portoangelo Productions, 1989
SUNSET BEAT (TF)   Patrick Hasburgh Productions, 1990

PETER DeLUISE
RESCUE ME   Cannon, 1993

MARIA DE MEDEIROS
Agent: William Morris Agency - Beverly Hills, 310/274-7451

HENRY & JUNE   Universal, 1990
PULP FICTION   Miramax Films, 1994

CHRIS DEMETRAL
BLANK CHECK   Buena Vista, 1994

REBECCA DE MORNAY
b. 1962 - Los Angeles, California
Agent: ICM - Beverly Hills, 310/550-4000

ONE FROM THE HEART   Columbia, 1982
RISKY BUSINESS   The Geffen Company/Warner Bros., 1983
TESTAMENT   Paramount, 1983
THE SLUGGER'S WIFE   NEIL SIMON'S THE SLUGGER'S WIFE
    Columbia, 1985
THE TRIP TO BOUNTIFUL   Island Pictures/FilmDallas, 1985
RUNAWAY TRAIN   Cannon, 1985
THE MURDERS IN THE RUE MORGUE (TF)   Robert Halmi, Inc./
    International Film Productions, 1986
AND GOD CREATED WOMAN   Vestron, 1988
FEDS   Warner Bros., 1988
HEART RAGE   Windmill Entertainment, 1989
DEALERS   Skouras Pictures, 1989, British
BY DAWN'S EARLY LIGHT (CTF)   HBO Pictures/Paravision
    International, 1990
BACKDRAFT   Universal, 1991
AN INCONVENIENT WOMAN (TF)   ABC Productions, 1991

THE HAND THAT ROCKS THE CRADLE   Buena Vista, 1992
GUILTY AS SIN   Buena Vista, 1993
THE THREE MUSKETEERS   Buena Vista, 1993

PATRICK DEMPSEY
Agent: CAA - Beverly Hills, 310/288-4545

HEAVEN HELP US   TriStar, 1985
MEATBALLS III   SUMMER JOB   TMS Pictures, 1986, Canadian
IN THE MOOD   THE WOO WOO KID   Lorimar, 1987
CAN'T BUY ME LOVE   Buena Vista, 1987
IN A SHALLOW GRAVE   Skouras Pictures, 1988
LOVERBOY   TriStar, 1989
COUPE DE VILLE   Universal, 1990
HAPPY TOGETHER   Borde Releasing Corporation, 1990
RUN   Buena Vista, 1991
MOBSTERS   Universal, 1991
BANK ROBBER   I.R.S. Releasing, 1993
WITH HONORS   Warner Bros., 1994
OUTBREAK   Warner Bros., 1995

JEFFREY DEMUNN
A TIME TO LIVE (TF)   Blue Andre Productions/ITC
    Productions, 1985
THE HITCHER   TriStar, 1986
THE BLOB   TriStar, 1988
BETRAYED   MGM/UA, 1988
BLAZE   Buena Vista, 1989
SETTLE THE SCORE (TF)   Steve Sohmer Inc. Productions/ITC
    Entertainment Group, 1989

JUDI DENCH
THE THIRD SECRET   20th Century Fox, 1964, British
A STUDY IN TERROR   Columbia, 1965, British
FOUR IN THE MORNING   West One, 1965, British
HE WHO RIDES A TIGER   Sigma III, 1966, British
A MIDSUMMER NIGHT'S DREAM   Eagle, 1968, British
DEAD CERT   United Artists, 1973, British
SAIGON - YEAR OF THE CAT (TF)   Thames TV, 1983, British
LUTHER   American Film Theatre, 1974
WETHERBY   MGM/UA Classics, 1985, British
A ROOM WITH A VIEW   Cinecom, 1986, British
84 CHARING CROSS ROAD   Columbia, 1987, British
A HANDFUL OF DUST   New Line Cinema, 1988
HENRY V   Samuel Goldwyn Company, 1989, British

CATHERINE DENEUVE
(Catherine Dorléac)
b. October 22, 1943 - Paris, France

LES COLLÉGIENNES   1967, French
WILD ROOTS OF LOVE   LES PETITS CHATS   1959, French
LES PORTES CLAQUENT   1960, French
TALES OF PARIS   LES PARISIENNES   1962, French
VICE AND VIRTUE   VICE ET LA VERTU   1963, French
VACANCES PORTUGAISES   1963, French
THE UMBRELLAS OF CHERBOURG   LES PARAPLUIES DE
    CHERBOURG   1964, French
MALE HUNT   LA CHASSE A L'HOMME   1964, French
MALE COMPANION   UN MONSIEUR DE COMPAGNIE
    1964, French
REPULSION   Royal Films International, 1965, British
LE CHANT DU MONDE   1965, French
LA VIE DE CHATEAU   1966, French
LES CRÉATURES   1966, French
THE YOUNG GIRLS OF ROCHEFORT   LES DEMOISELLES DE
    ROCHEFORT   1967, French
BELLE DU JOUR   1967, French
BENJAMIN   1968, French
MANON 70   1968, French
MAYERLING   1968, French-British
LA CHAMADE   1968, French
THE APRIL FOOLS   1969
MISSISSIPPI MERMAID   LA SIRENE DE MISSISSIPPI
    1969, French
TRISTANA   1970
DONKEY SKIN   PEAU D'ANE   1971, French

IT ONLY HAPPENS TO OTHERS   *ÇA N'ARRIVE QU'AUX AUTRES*
   1971, French
LIZA   *LA CAGNA*   Horizon, 1972, Italian-French
DIRTY MONEY   *UN FLIC*   1972, French
A SLIGHTLY PREGNANT MAN   SJ International, 1973, French
THE WOMAN WITH RED BOOTS   1973, French
FATTI DI GENTE PERBENE   *LA GRANDE BOURGEOISE*
   Filmarpa Film/Lira Film, 1974, Italian-French
ACT OF AGGRESSION   *L'AGRESSION*   1975, French
LOVERS LIKE US   *LE SAUVAGE/THE SAVAGE*   1975, French
HUSTLE   Paramount, 1975
SECOND CHANCE   *SI C'ÉTAIT A REFAIRE*   United Artists
   Classics, 1976, French
ANIMA PERSA   Dean Film/Les Productions Fox Europe, 1977,
   Italian-French
MARCH OR DIE   Columbia, 1977, British
L'ARGENT DES AUTRES   1978, French
ECOUTE VOIR...   1978, French
SI JE SUIS COMME ÇA C'EST LA FAUTE A PAPA   1979, French
AN ADVENTURE FOR TWO   *A NOUS DEUX*   AMLF, 1979,
   French-Canadian
ILS SONT GRAND CES PETITS   1979, French
THE LAST MÉTRO   United Artists Classics, 1980, French
ABATTRE   1980, French
THE HUNGER   MGM/UA, 1983, British
THE AFRICAN   1984
FORT SAGANNE   1985
THE SCENE OF THE CRIME   1986
INDOCHINE ★   Sony Pictures Classics, 1992, French

JAKE DENGEL
AT CLOSE RANGE   Orion, 1986

LYDIE DENIER
Agent: The Craig Agency - Los Angeles, 213/655-0236

BLOOD RELATIONS   Miramax Films, 1988
GUARDIAN ANGEL   PM Entertainment, 1994
PERFECT ALIBI   Rysher Entertainment, 1994

ROBERT DE NIRO
b. August 17, 1943 - New York, New York
Agent: CAA - Beverly Hills, 310/288-4545

GREETINGS   Sigma III, 1968
SAM'S SONG   1969
THE WEDDING PARTY   Powell Productions Plus/Ondine, 1969
HI, MOM!   Sigma III, 1970
BLOODY MAMA   American International, 1970
BORN TO WIN   United Artists, 1971
THE GANG THAT COULDN'T SHOOT STRAIGHT   MGM, 1971
JENNIFER ON MY MIND   United Artists, 1971
BANG THE DRUM SLOWLY   Paramount, 1973
MEAN STREETS   Warner Bros., 1973
THE GODFATHER, PART II ⊙⊙   Paramount, 1974
TAXI DRIVER ★   Columbia, 1976
THE LAST TYCOON   Paramount, 1976
1900   Paramount, 1977, Italian
NEW YORK, NEW YORK   United Artists, 1977
THE DEER HUNTER ★   Universal, 1978
RAGING BULL ★★   United Artists, 1980
TRUE CONFESSIONS   United Artists, 1981
THE KING OF COMEDY   20th Century Fox, 1983
FALLING IN LOVE   Paramount, 1984
ONCE UPON A TIME IN AMERICA   The Ladd Company/Warner
   Bros., 1984, U.S.-Italian-Canadian
BRAZIL   Universal, 1985, British
THE MISSION   Warner Bros., 1986, British
ANGEL HEART   TriStar, 1987
THE UNTOUCHABLES   Paramount, 1987
DEAR AMERICA: LETTERS HOME FROM VIETNAM (FD)
   Taurus Entertainment, 1987 (voice)
MIDNIGHT RUN   Universal, 1988
JACKNIFE   Cineplex Odeon, 1989
WE'RE NO ANGELS   Paramount, 1989
STANLEY & IRIS   MGM/UA, 1990
GOODFELLAS   Warner Bros., 1990
AWAKENINGS ★   Columbia, 1990

GUILTY BY SUSPICION   Warner Bros., 1991
BACKDRAFT   Universal, 1991
CAPE FEAR ★   Universal, 1991
MISTRESS   Tribeca Films, 1992
NIGHT AND THE CITY   20th Century Fox, 1992
MAD DOG AND GLORY   Universal, 1993
THIS BOY'S LIFE   Warner Bros., 1993
A BRONX TALE   Savoy Pictures, 1993 (also directed)
MARY SHELLEY'S FRANKENSTEIN   TriStar, 1994
CASINO   Universal, 1995
HEAT   Warner Bros., 1995

JACQUES DENIS
CHOCOLAT   Orion Classics, 1988, French

ANTHONY DENISON
(Anthony John Denison)
Agent: Paradigm - Los Angeles, 310/277-4400

I LOVE YOU PERFECT (TF)   Gross-Weston Productions/Susan Dey
   Productions/Stephen J. Cannell Productions, 1989
THE GIRL WHO CAME BETWEEN THEM (TF)   Saban-Scherick
   Productions, 1990
ANGEL OF DESIRE   Trimark Pictures, 1994
BRILLIANT DISGUISE   Prism Pictures, 1994

MICHAEL DENISON
SHADOWLANDS   Savoy Pictures, 1993, U.S.-British

BRIAN DENNEHY
b. July 9, 1938 - Bridgeport, Connecticut
Agent: Susan Smith & Associates - Beverly Hills, 213/852-4777

JOHNNY, WE HARDLY KNEW YE (TF)   Talent Associates/Jamel
   Productions, 1977
IT HAPPENED AT LAKEWOOD MANOR   *PANIC AT LAKEWOOD
   MANOR/ANTS* (TF)   1977
SEMI-TOUGH   United Artists, 1977
FOUL PLAY   Paramount, 1978
RUBY AND OSWALD   *FOUR DAYS IN DALLAS* (TF)
   Alan Landsburg Productions, 1978
A DEATH IN CANAAN (TF)   Chris-Rose Productions/
   Warner Bros. TV, 1978
A REAL AMERICAN HERO (TF)   Bing Crosby Productions, 1978
PEARL (MS)   Silliphant-Konigsberg Productions/
   Warner Bros. TV, 1978
SILENT VICTORY: THE KITTY O'NEIL STORY (TF)
   Channing-Debin-Locke Company, 1979
BUTCH AND SUNDANCE: THE EARLY DAYS
   20th Century Fox, 1979
10   Orion/Warner Bros., 1979
LITTLE MISS MARKER   Universal, 1980
A RUMOUR OF WAR (MS)   Charles Fries Productions, 1980
SPLIT IMAGE   Orion, 1982
FIRST BLOOD   Orion, 1982, Canadian
GORKY PARK   Orion, 1983
NEVER CRY WOLF   Buena Vista, 1983
THE RIVER RAT   Paramount, 1984
HUNTER (TF)   Stephen J. Cannell Productions, 1984
EVERGREEN (MS)   Edgar J. Scherick Associates/Metromedia
   Producers Corporation, 1985
COCOON   20th Century Fox, 1985
SILVERADO   Columbia, 1985
TWICE IN A LIFETIME   The Yorkin Company, 1985
ACCEPTABLE RISKS (TF)   ABC Circle Films, 1986
F/X   Orion, 1986
LEGAL EAGLES   Universal, 1986
THE BELLY OF AN ARCHITECT   1987, British-Italian
BEST SELLER   Orion, 1987
A FATHER'S REVENGE (TF)   Shadowplay-Rosco Productions/
   Phoenix Entertainment Group, 1988
MILES FROM HOME   Cinecom, 1988
COCOON: THE RETURN   20th Century Fox, 1988
DAY ONE (TF)   Aaron Spelling Productions/Paragon Motion Pictures/
   David W. Rintels Productions, 1989
PERFECT WITNESS (CTF)   HBO Pictures/Granger
   Productions, 1989

PRIDE AND EXTREME PREJUDICE (CTF)   F.F.S. Productions/
   Taurusfilm/Blair Communications, 1990,
   British-West German-U.S.
KILLING IN A SMALL TOWN (TF)   The IndieProd Co./Hearst
   Entertainment Productions, 1990
RISING SON (CTF)   Sarabande Productions, 1990
THE LAST OF THE FINEST   Orion, 1990
PRESUMED INNOCENT   Warner Bros., 1990
IN BROAD DAYLIGHT (TF)   Force Ten Productions/
   New World TV, 1991
F/X 2 - THE DEADLY ART OF ILLUSION   Orion, 1991
GLADIATOR   Columbia, 1992
TO CATCH A KILLER (TF)   Schreckinger-Kinberg Productions/
   Creative Entertainment Group/Tribune Entertainment/Saban
   International, 1992, U.S.-Canadian
THE STARS FELL ON HENRIETTA   Warner Bros., 1995
BILLY THE THIRD   Paramount, 1995

WINSTON DENNIS

THE ADVENTURES OF BARON MUNCHAUSEN   Columbia, 1989

JOHN DENVER
b. December 31, 1943 - Roswell, New Mexico
Agent: William Morris Agency - Beverly Hills, 310/274-7451

OH, GOD!   Warner Bros., 1977
THE CHRISTMAS GIFT (TF)   Rosemont Productions/Sunn Classic
   Pictures, 1986
FOXFIRE (TF)   Marian Rees Associates, 1987
HIGHER GROUND (TF)   Green-Epstein Productions/
   Columbia TV, 1988

GÉRARD DEPARDIEU
b. December 27, 1948 - Chateauroux, Frnace
Agent: CAA - Beverly Hills, 310/288-4545

LE CRI DU CORMORAN LE SOIR AUDESSUS DES JONQUES
   1970, French
UN PEU DE SOLEIL DANS L'EAU FROIDE   SNC, 1971, French
LE TUEUR   1971, French
L'AFFAIRE DOMINICI   1972, French
AU RENDEZ-VOUS DE LA MORT JOYEUSE   United Artists,
   1972, French
LA SCOUMOUNE   1972, French
LE VIAGER   1972, French
DEUX HOMMES DANS LA VILLE   1972, French
NATHALIE GRANGER   Films Moliere, 1973, French
RUDE JOURNÉE POUR LA REINE   1973, French
THE HOLES   LES GASPARDS   1973, French
GOING PLACES   LES VALSEUSES   Cinema 5, 1974, French
STAVISKY   Cinemation, 1974, French
VINCENT, FRANÇOIS, PAUL, AND THE OTHERS   Joseph Green
   Pictures, 1974, French-Italian
THE WONDERFUL CROOK   PAS SI MÉCHANT QUE ÇA
   New Yorker, 1975, Swiss-French
7 MORTS SUR ORDONNANCE   1975, French
MAITRESSE   Tinc, 1976, French
JE T'AIME MOI NON PLUS   1975, French
THE LAST WOMAN   LA DERNIERE FEMME   Columbia,
   1976, Italian-French
BAROCCO   1976, French
BAXTER—VERA BAXTER   Sun Child Productions, 1977, French
1900   Paramount, 1977, Italian
RENÉ LA CANNE   1977, French
LE CAMION   Films Moliere, 1977, French
VIOLANTA   1977, Swiss
LA NUIT TOUS LES CHATS SONT GRIS   1977, French
DITES-LUI QUE JE L'AIME   1977, French
THE LEFT-HANDED WOMAN   1977, French
GET OUT YOUR HANDKERCHIEFS   PRÉPAREZ VOS
   MOUCHOIRS   New Line Cinema, 1978, French
REVE DE SINGE   1977, French
BYE BYE MONKEY   Fida, 1978, Italian-French
LE SUCRE   1978, French
LES CHIENS   1978, French
L'INGORGO   1978, French
LE GRAND EMBOUTEILLAGE   1978, French

BUFFET FROID   Parafrance, 1979, French
LOULOU   Gaumont, 1979, French
MON ONCLE D'AMÉRIQUE   New World, 1980, French
ROSY LA BOURRASQUE   1979, French
THE LAST METRO   United Artists Classics, 1980, French
JE VOUS AIME   Renn Films/FR3/Cinevog, 1980, French
INSPECTEUR LA BAVURE   1980, French
THE WOMAN NEXT DOOR   United Artists Classics, 1981, French
LE CHOIX DES ARMES   1981, French
LE CHEVRE   European International, 1981, French
THE RETURN OF MARTIN GUERRE   European International,
   1981, French
LE GRAND FRERE   National, 1983, French
DANTON   Triumph/Columbia, 1983, French-Polish
THE MOON IN THE GUTTER   Triumph/Columbia,
   1983, French-Italian
LES COMPERES   European International, 1983, French
FORT SAGANNE   1984, French
LE TARTUFFE   1984, French (also directed)
RIVE DROITE, RIVE GAUCHE   1984, French
ONE WOMAN OR TWO   Orion Classics, 1985, French
POLICE   Island Pictures, 1985, French
MÉNAGE   TENUE DE SOIREE   Cinecom, 1986, French
RUE DU DÉPART   1986, French
JEAN DE FLORETTE   Orion Classics, 1987, French
LES FUGITIFS   Gaumont, 1986, French
UNDER THE SUN OF SATAN   Alive Films, 1987, French
CAMILLE CLAUDEL   Orion Classics, 1988, French
DROLE D'ENDROIT POUR UNE RENCONTRE   1988, French
DEUX   1988, French
TOO BEAUTIFUL FOR YOU   Orion Classics, 1989, French
JE VEUX RENTRER A LA MAISON   1989, French
CYRANO DE BERGERAC ★   Orion Classics, 1990, French
GREEN CARD   Buena Vista, 1990
URANUS   Prestige Films, 1991, French
1492: CONQUEST OF PARADISE   Paramount,
   1992, British-Spanish
TOUS LES MATINS DU MONDE   October Films, 1992, French
GERMINAL   Sony Pictures Classics, 1993, French
MY FATHER, THE HERO   Buena Vista, 1994
BOGUS   Warner Bros., 1995

JOHNNY DEPP
b. June 9, 1963 - Owensboro, Kentucky
Agent: ICM - Beverly Hills, 310/550-4000

A NIGHTMARE ON ELM STREET   New Line Cinema, 1984
PRIVATE RESORT   TriStar, 1985
PLATOON   Orion, 1986
CRY-BABY   Universal, 1990
EDWARD SCISSORHANDS   20th Century Fox, 1990
FREDDY'S DEAD: THE FINAL NIGHTMARE
   New Line Cinema, 1991
BENNY & JOON   MGM/UA, 1993
WHAT'S EATING GILBERT GRAPE   Paramount, 1993
ED WOOD   Buena Vista, 1994
ARIZONA DREAMER   Warner Bros., 1995
DON JUAN DE MARCO AND THE CENTERFOLD
   New Line Cinema, 1995

BO DEREK
(Mary Kathleen Collins)
b. November 20, 1955 - Long Beach, California
Agent: ICM - Beverly Hills, 310/550-4000

AND ONCE UPON A TIME   FANTASIES   Joseph Brenner
   Associates, 1973
ORCA   Paramount, 1977
10   Orion/Warner Bros., 1979
A CHANGE OF SEASONS   20th Century Fox, 1980
TARZAN THE APE MAN   MGM/United Artists, 1981
BOLERO   Cannon, 1984
GHOSTS CAN'T DO IT   Triumph Releasing Corporation, 1990
BILLY THE THIRD   Paramount, 1995

EDDIE DERHAM
LITTLE GIANTS   Warner Bros., 1994

BRUCE DERN
b. June 4, 1936 - Chicago, Illinois
Agent: CAA - Beverly Hills, 310/288-4545

WILD RIVER   20th Century Fox, 1960
HUSH...HUSH, SWEET CHARLOTTE   20th Century Fox, 1964
MARNIE   Universal, 1964
THE WILD ANGELS   American International, 1966
THE ST. VALENTINE'S DAY MASSACRE   20th Century Fox, 1967
WATERHOLE #3   Paramount, 1967
THE TRIP   American International, 1967
THE WAR WAGON   Universal, 1967
PSYCH-OUT   American International, 1968
WILL PENNY   Paramount, 1968
HANG 'EM HIGH   United Artists, 1968
SUPPORT YOUR LOCAL SHERIFF   United Artists, 1969
CASTLE KEEP   Columbia, 1969
NUMBER ONE   United Artists, 1969
THEY SHOOT HORSES, DON'T THEY?   Cinerama Releasing
    Corporation, 1969
CYCLE SAVAGES   Trans American, 1970
BLOODY MAMA   American International, 1970
DRIVE, HE SAID   Columbia, 1971
THE INCREDIBLE TWO-HEADED TRANSPLANT   1971
THE COWBOYS   Warner Bros., 1972
SILENT RUNNING   Universal, 1972
THE KING OF MARVIN GARDENS   Columbia, 1972
THE LAUGHING POLICEMAN   20th Century Fox, 1973
THE GREAT GATSBY   Paramount, 1974
SMILE   United Artists, 1975
POSSE   Paramount, 1975
FAMILY PLOT   Universal, 1976
WON TON TON, THE DOG WHO SAVED HOLLYWOOD
    Paramount, 1976
FOLIES BOURGEOISES   1976, French
BLACK SUNDAY   Paramount, 1976
COMING HOME ✪   United Artists, 1978
THE DRIVER   20th Century Fox, 1978
MIDDLE AGE CRAZY   20th Century Fox, 1980, Canadian-U.S.
TATTOO   20th Century Fox, 1981
HARRY TRACY, DESPERADO   Quartet/Films, Inc.,
    1982, Canadian
THAT CHAMPIONSHIP SEASON   Cannon, 1982
SPACE (MS)   Stonehenge Productions/Paramount TV, 1985
TOUGHLOVE (TF)   Fries Entertainment, 1985
ON THE EDGE   Skouras Pictures, 1986
THE BIG TOWN   Columbia, 1987
ROSES ARE FOR THE RICH (MS)   Phoenix Entertainment
    Group, 1987
1969   Atlantic Releasing Corporation, 1988
WORLD GONE WILD   Lorimar, 1988
THE 'BURBS   Universal, 1989
AFTER DARK, MY SWEET   Avenue Pictures, 1990
TRENCHCOAT IN PARADISE (TF)   Ogiens-Kane Company
    Productions/The Finnegan-Pinchuk Company, 1990
DIGGSTOWN   MGM-Pathe Entertainment, 1992
WILD BILL   MGM/UA, 1995

LAURA DERN
b. February 10, 1967 - Los Angeles, California
Agent: UTA - Beverly Hills, 310/273-6700

ALICE DOESN'T LIVE HERE ANYMORE   Warner Bros., 1974
FOXES   United Artists, 1980
LADIES AND GENTLEMEN, THE FABULOUS STAINS
    Paramount, 1982
TEACHERS   MGM/UA, 1984
MASK   Universal, 1985
SMOOTH TALK   Spectrafilm, 1985
BLUE VELVET   DEG, 1986
HAUNTED SUMMER   Cannon, 1988
FAT MAN AND LITTLE BOY   Paramount, 1989
WILD AT HEART   Samuel Goldwyn Company, 1990
RAMBLING ROSE ★   New Line Cinema, 1991
AFTERBURN (CTF)   HBO Pictures, 1992
JURASSIC PARK   Universal, 1993
A PERFECT WORLD   Warner Bros., 1993

PORTIA DE ROSSI
SIRENS   Miramax Films, 1993, Australian-British-German

CLEAVANT DERRICKS
Agent: Susan Smith & Associates - Beverly Hills, 213/852-4777

MOSCOW ON THE HUDSON   Columbia, 1984
OFF BEAT   Buena Vista, 1986

STEFAN DESALLE
RUSSKIES   New Century/Vista, 1987

ANNE DESALVO
Agent: Gersh Agency - Beverly Hills, 310/274-6611

PERFECT   Columbia, 1985
COMPROMISING POSITIONS   Paramount, 1985
BURGLAR   Warner Bros., 1987
TAKING CARE OF BUSINESS   Buena Vista, 1990

STANLEY DeSANTIS
ANNIE HALL   United Artists, 1977
SATURDAY NIGHT FEVER   Paramount, 1977
THE BEST LITTLE WHOREHOUSE IN TEXAS   Universal, 1982
TAKING CARE OF BUSINESS   Buena Vista, 1990
POSTCARDS FROM THE EDGE   Columbia, 1990
ED WOOD   Buena Vista, 1994

MARY JO DESCHANEL
Agent: Bauman Hiller & Associates - Los Angeles, 213/857-6666

THE RIGHT STUFF   The Ladd Company/Warner Bros., 1983

ROBERT DESIDERIO
Agent: Gersh Agency - Beverly Hills, 310/274-6611

ORIGINAL SIN (TF)   Larry A. Thompson Organization/
    New World TV, 1989
GROSS ANATOMY   Buena Vista, 1989

JIM DESMOND
EIGHT MEN OUT   Orion, 1988

ROSANA DE SOTO
THE IN-LAWS   Columbia, 1979
CANNERY ROW   MGM/United Artists, 1982
THE BALLAD OF GREGORIO CORTEZ   Embassy, 1983
LA BAMBA   Columbia, 1987
FAMILY BUSINESS   TriStar, 1989
STAR TREK VI: THE UNDISCOVERED COUNTRY
    Paramount, 1991

MARUSCHKA DETMERS
Agent: William Morris Agency - Beverly Hills, 310/274-7451

HANNA'S WAR   Cannon, 1988
THE MAMBO KINGS   Warner Bros., 1992

CHARLOTTE de TURCKHEIM
JEFFERSON IN PARIS   Buena Vista, 1995

KURT DEUTSCH
MOMENT OF TRUTH: CRADLE OF CONSPIRACY (TF)
    O'Hara/Horowitz Productions, 1994

WILLIAM DEVANE
b. September 5, 1937 - Albany, New York
Agent: APA - Los Angeles, 310/273-0744

THE PURSUIT OF HAPPINESS   Columbia, 1971
THE 300 YEAR WEEKEND   Cinerama Releasing Corporation, 1971
MY OLD MAN'S PLACE   GLORY BOY   Cinerama Releasing
    Corporation, 1972

McCABE AND MRS. MILLER Warner Bros., 1971
LADY LIBERTY *MORTADELLA* United Artists, 1971, Italian
IRISH WHISKEY REBELLION *A CHANGE IN THE WIND*
  Cinerama Releasing Corporation, 1972
CRIME CLUB (TF) CBS, Inc., 1973
REPORT TO THE COMMISSIONER United Artists, 1975
FEAR ON TRIAL (TF) Alan Landsburg Productions, 1975
FAMILY PLOT Universal, 1976
MARATHON MAN Paramount, 1976
RED ALERT (TF) The Jozak Company/Paramount TV, 1977
THE BAD NEWS BEARS IN BREAKING TRAINING
  Paramount, 1977
BLACK BEAUTY (MS) Universal TV, 1978
ROLLING THUNDER American International, 1978
FROM HERE TO ETERNITY (MS) Bennett-Katleman Productions/
  Columbia TV, 1979
YANKS Universal, 1979, British
THE DARK Film Ventures International, 1979
RED FLAG: THE ULTIMATE GAME (TF) Marble Arch
  Productions, 1981
HONKY TONK FREEWAY Universal/AFD, 1981
TESTAMENT Paramount, 1983
JANE DOE (TF) ITC, 1983
TIMESTALKERS (TF) Fries Entertainment/Newland-Raynor
  Productions, 1987
THE PREPPIE MURDER (TF) Jack Grossbart Productions/
  Spectator Films, 1989
CHIPS, THE WAR DOG (CTF) W.G. Productions, 1990
VITAL SIGNS 20th Century Fox, 1990

RICHARD DEVIA
BIG 20th Century Fox, 1988

LORETTA DEVINE
LITTLE NIKITA Columbia, 1988

DANNY DEVITO
b. November 17, 1944 - Asbury Park, New Jersey
Agent: CAA - Beverly Hills, 310/288-4545

LADY LIBERTY *MORTADELLA* United Artists, 1971, Italian
SCALAWAG Paramount, 1973, U.S.-Italian
ONE FLEW OVER THE CUCKOO'S NEST United Artists, 1975
THE VAN 1976
THE WORLD'S GREATEST LOVER 20th Century Fox, 1977
GOIN' SOUTH Paramount, 1979
GOING APE! Paramount, 1981
TERMS OF ENDEARMENT Paramount, 1983
THE RATINGS GAME (CTF) Imagination-New Street Productions,
  1984 (also directed)
JOHNNY DANGEROUSLY 20th Century Fox, 1984
ROMANCING THE STONE 20th Century Fox, 1984
THE JEWEL OF THE NILE 20th Century Fox, 1985
HEAD OFFICE TriStar, 1986
MY LITTLE PONY - THE MOVIE (AF) DEG, 1986 (voice)
WISE GUYS MGM/UA, 1986
RUTHLESS PEOPLE Buena Vista, 1986
TIN MEN Buena Vista, 1987
THROW MOMMA FROM THE TRAIN Orion, 1987 (also directed)
TWINS Universal, 1988
THE WAR OF THE ROSES 20th Century Fox, 1989 (also directed)
OTHER PEOPLE'S MONEY Warner Bros., 1991
BATMAN RETURNS Warner Bros., 1992
HOFFA 20th Century Fox, 1992 (also directed)
JACK THE BEAR 20th Century Fox, 1992
LOOK WHO'S TALKING NOW TriStar, 1993 (voice)
RENAISSANCE MAN Buena Vista, 1994
JUNIOR Universal, 1994

KARLA DEVITO
MODERN LOVE Triumph Releasing Corporation, 1990

SUSAN DEY
b. December 10, 1952 - Pekin, Illinois
Agent: ICM - Beverly Hills, 310/550-4000

SKYJACKED MGM, 1972
TERROR ON THE BEACH (TF) 20th Century Fox TV, 1973
CAGE WITHOUT A KEY (TF) Columbia TV, 1975
MARY JANE HARPER CRIED LAST NIGHT (TF)
  Paramount TV, 1977
FIRST LOVE Paramount, 1977
LOOKER The Ladd Company/Warner Bros., 1981
LOVE LEADS THE WAY (TF) Hawkins-Permut Productions, 1984
ECHO PARK Atlantic Releasing Corporation, 1986, U.S.-Austrian
L.A. LAW (TF) 20th Century Fox TV, 1986
ANGEL IN GREEN (TF) Aligre Productions/Taft Hardy Group, 1987,
  U.S.-New Zealand
THE TROUBLE WITH DICK FilmDallas, 1988
I LOVE YOU PERFECT (TF) Gross-Weston Productions/Susan Dey
  Productions/Stephen J. Cannell Productions, 1989

CLIFF DE YOUNG
SUNSHINE (TF) Universal TV, 1973
HARRY AND TONTO 20th Century Fox, 1974
THE NIGHT THAT PANICKED AMERICA (TF) Paramount TV, 1975
THE LINDBERGH KIDNAPPING CASE (TF) Columbia TV, 1976
BLUE COLLAR Universal, 1978
KING (MS) Abby Mann Productions/Filmways, 1978
SHOCK TREATMENT 20th Century Fox, 1981, British
THE HUNGER MGM/UA, 1983, British
PROTOCOL Warner Bros., 1984
RECKLESS MGM/UA, 1984
ROBERT KENNEDY AND HIS TIMES (MS) Chris-Rose Productions/
  Columbia TV, 1985
FLIGHT OF THE NAVIGATOR Buena Vista, 1986
F/X Orion, 1986
RUDE AWAKENING Orion, 1989
GLORY TriStar, 1989
FLASHBACK Paramount, 1990
DEADLY INTENTIONS (MS) Green-Epstein Productions, 1985
F/X Orion, 1986
FLIGHT OF THE NAVIGATOR Buena Vista, 1986
HER SECRET LIFE (TF) Phoenix Entertainment Group, 1987
WHERE PIGEONS GO TO DIE (TF) Michael Landon Productions/
  World International Network, 1990
CRACKDOWN Concorde, 1991
INFINITY 1995

NEIL DIAMOND
b. January 24, 1941 - Brooklyn, New York

THE JAZZ SINGER AFD, 1980

REED EDWARD DIAMOND
MEMPHIS BELLE Warner Bros., 1990

CAMERON DIAZ
Agent: ICM - Beverly Hills, 310/550-4000

THE MASK New Line Cinema, 1994
THE PHANTOM Paramount, 1995

LEONARDO DICAPRIO
Agent: CAA - Beverly Hills, 310/288-4545

THIS BOY'S LIFE Warner Bros., 1993
WHAT'S EATING GILBERT GRAPE ✪ Paramount, 1993
THE QUICK AND THE DEAD TriStar, 1995
THE BASKETBALL DIARIES 1995

GEORGE DICENZO
BACK TO THE FUTURE Universal, 1985
ABOUT LAST NIGHT... TriStar, 1986
THE NEW ADVENTURES OF PIPPI LONGSTOCKING
  Columbia, 1988
FACE OF THE ENEMY 1988
SING TriStar, 1989

ANDY DICK
REALITY BITES Universal, 1994
IN THE ARMY NOW Buena Vista, 1994

GEORGE DICKERSON
Agent: Badgley/Connor - Los Angeles, 310/278-9313

BLUE VELVET DEG, 1986
AFTER DARK, MY SWEET Avenue Pictures, 1990
DEATH WARRANT MGM/UA, 1990

LUCINDA DICKEY
BREAKIN' MGM/UA/Cannon, 1984
BREAKIN' 2 ELECTRIC BOOGALOO TriStar/Cannon, 1985

ANGIE DICKINSON
(Angeline Brown)
b. September 30, 1931 - Kulm, North Dakota
Agent: The Blake Agency - Beverly Hills, 310/246-0241

LUCKY ME Warner Bros., 1954
MAN WITH THE GUN United Artists, 1955
TENNESSEE'S PARTNER RKO Radio, 1955
THE RETURN OF JACK SLADE Allied Artists, 1955
GUN THE MAN DOWN *ARIZONA MISSION* United Artists, 1956
HIDDEN GUNS Republic, 1956
THE BLACK WHIP 20th Century Fox, 1956
TENSION AT TABLE ROCK Universal, 1956
SHOOTOUT AT MEDICINE BEND Warner Bros., 1957
CALYPSO JOE Allied Artists, 1957
CHINA GATE 20th Century Fox, 1957
I MARRIED A WOMAN Universal, 1958
CRY TERROR MGM, 1958
RIO BRAVO Warner Bros., 1959
THE BRAMBLE BUSH Warner Bros., 1960
OCEAN'S ELEVEN Warner Bros., 1960
THE SINS OF RACHEL CADE Warner Bros., 1961
A FEVER IN THE BLOOD Warner Bros., 1961
ROME ADVENTURE Warner Bros., 1962
JESSICA United Artists, 1962, U.S.-Italian-French
CAPTAIN NEWMAN, M.D. Universal, 1963
THE KILLERS Universal, 1964
THE ART OF LOVE Universal, 1965
THE CHASE Columbia, 1966
CAST A GIANT SHADOW United Artists, 1966
POINT BLANK MGM, 1967
THE LAST CHALLENGE MGM, 1967
SAM WHISKEY United Artists, 1969
YOUNG BILLY YOUNG United Artists, 1969
SOME KIND OF NUT United Artists, 1969
THE LOVE WAR (TF) Thomas-Spelling Productions, 1970
THIEF (TF) Metromedia, 1971
PRETTY MAIDS ALL IN A ROW MGM, 1971
THE RESURRECTION OF ZACHARY WHEELER 1971
SEE THE MAN RUN (TF) Universal TV, 1971
THE NORLISS TAPES (TF) Metromedia Producers
    Corporation, 1973
THE OUTSIDE MAN *UN HOMME EST MORT* United Artists,
    1973, French-Italian
PRAY FOR THE WILDCATS (TF) ABC Circle Films, 1974
BIG BAD MAMA New World, 1974
PEARL (MS) Silliphant-Konigsberg Productions/Warner
    Bros. TV, 1978
KLONDIKE FEVER *JACK LONDON'S KLONDIKE FEVER* 1980
DRESSED TO KILL Filmways, 1980
DEATH HUNT 20th Century Fox, 1981
CHARLIE CHAN AND THE CURSE OF THE DRAGON QUEEN
    American Cinema, 1981
A TOUCH OF SCANDAL (TF) Doris M. Keating Productions/
    Columbia TV, 1984
HOLLYWOOD WIVES (MS) Aaron Spelling Productions, 1985
POLICE STORY: THE FREEWAY KILLINGS (TF) David Gerber
    Productions/MGM-UA TV/Columbia TV, 1987
STILLWATCH (TF) Zev Braun Pictures/Interscope
    Communications/Potomac Productions, 1987
ONCE UPON A TEXAS TRAIN (TF) Robert Papazian Productions/
    Brigade Productions/Rastar, 1988

FIRE AND RAIN (CTF) Wilshire Court Productions, 1989
PRIME TARGET (TF) RLC Productions/The Finnegan-Pinchuk
    Company/MGM-UA TV, 1989
WILD PALMS (MS) Ixtlan Corporation/Greengrass
    Productions, Inc., 1993
EVEN COWGIRLS GET THE BLUES Fine Line Features/New Line
    Cinema, 1994
THE MADDENING Trimark Pictures, 1995

J.D. DICKINSON
THE NEW ADVENTURES OF PIPPI LONGSTOCKING
    Columbia, 1988

SANDRA DICKINSON
BALTO (AF) Universal, 1995 (voice)

BO DIDDLEY
b. December 20, 1928 - McComb, Mississippi

EDDIE AND THE CRUISERS: EDDIE LIVES Scotti Bros., 1989

JOHN DIEHL
ANGEL New World, 1984
GLITZ (TF) Lorimar-Telepictures/Robert Cooper Films, 1988
MADHOUSE Orion, 1990
MO' MONEY Columbia, 1992
THE NEW AGE Warner Bros., 1994

MARSHA DIETLEIN
RETURN OF THE LIVING DEAD PART II Lorimar, 1988

VICTORIA DILLARD
OUT OF SYNC BET Films, 1994

PHYLLIS DILLER
(Phyllis Diller)
b. July 17, 1917 - Lima, Ohio
Contact: Milton B. Suchin - Los Angeles, 213/550-1133

SPLENDOR IN THE GRASS Warner Bros., 1961
BOY, DID I GET A WRONG NUMBER! United Artists, 1966
THE FAT SPY Magna, 1966
EIGHT ON THE LAM United Artists, 1967
MAD MONSTER PARTY? (AF) Embassy, 1967 (voice)
THE PRIVATE NAVY OF SGT. O'FARRELL United Artists, 1968
DID YOU HEAR THE ONE ABOUT THE TRAVELING SALESLADY?
    Universal, 1968
THE ADDING MACHINE 1969, U.S.-British
PINK MOTEL 1983
THE NUTCRACKER PRINCE (AF) Warner Bros., 1990 (voice)
HAPPILY EVER AFTER (AF) First National Film Corporation,
    1993 (voice)

BRADFORD DILLMAN
b. April 14, 1930 - San Francisco, California
Agent: The Artists Group, Ltd. - Los Angeles, 310/552-1100

A CERTAIN SMILE 20th Century Fox, 1958
IN LOVE AND WAR 20th Century Fox, 1958
COMPULSION 20th Century Fox, 1959
CRACK IN THE MIRROR 20th Century Fox, 1960
CIRCLE OF DECEPTION 1961, British
SANCTUARY 20th Century Fox, 1961
FRANCIS OF ASSISI 20th Century Fox, 1961
A RAGE TO LIVE United Artists, 1965
THE PLAINSMAN Universal, 1966
THE HELICOPTER SPIES 1967
SERGEANT RYKER Universal, 1968
JIGSAW Universal, 1968
THE BRIDGE AT REMAGEN United Artists, 1969
SUPPOSE THEY GAVE A WAR AND NOBODY CAME
    Cinerama Releasing Corporation, 1970
BROTHER JOHN Columbia, 1971
THE MEPHISTO WALTZ 20th Century Fox, 1971
ESCAPE FROM THE PLANET OF THE APES
    20th Century Fox, 1971

THE RESURRECTION OF ZACHARY WHEELER   1971
THE ICEMAN COMETH   American Film Theatre, 1973
THE WAY WE WERE   Columbia, 1973
99 AND 44/100% DEAD   20th Century Fox, 1974
CHOSEN SURVIVORS   Columbia, 1974
GOLD   Allied Artists, 1974, British
BUG   Paramount, 1975
THE ENFORCER   Warner Bros., 1976
THE LINCOLN CONSPIRACY   Sunn Classic, 1977
THE AMSTERDAM KILL   Columbia, 1978, U.S.-Hong Kong
MASTERMIND   Goldstone, 1977
THE SWARM   Warner Bros., 1978
PIRANHA   New World, 1978
LOVE AND BULLETS   AFD, 1979, British
GUYANA: CULT OF THE DAMNED   1980, Mexican
SUDDEN IMPACT   Warner Bros., 1983

PAMELA DILLMAN
Management: Braverman, Gekis & Bloom - Los Angeles,
   310/203-8700

BYE BYE LOVE   20th Century Fox, 1995

KEVIN DILLON
Agent: ICM - Beverly Hills, 310/550-4000

HEAVEN HELP US   TriStar, 1985
PLATOON   Orion, 1986
THE RESCUE   Buena Vista, 1988
THE BLOB   TriStar, 1988
WAR PARTY   Hemdale, 1989
IMMEDIATE FAMILY   Columbia, 1989
WHEN HE'S NOT A STRANGER (TF)
   Ohlmeyer Communications, 1989
THE DOORS   TriStar, 1991
A MIDNIGHT CLEAR   Interstar Releasing, 1992
NO ESCAPE   Savoy Pictures, 1994

MATT DILLON
b. February 18, 1964 - New Rochelle, New York
Agent: ICM - Beverly Hills, 310/550-4000

OVER THE EDGE   Orion/Warner Bros., 1979
MY BODYGUARD   20th Century Fox, 1980
LITTLE DARLINGS   Paramount, 1980
LIAR'S MOON   Crown International, 1982
TEX   Buena Vista, 1982
THE OUTSIDERS   Warner Bros., 1983
RUMBLE FISH   Universal, 1983
THE FLAMINGO KID   20th Century Fox, 1984
TARGET   Warner Bros., 1985
REBEL   Vestron, 1985, Australian
NATIVE SON   Cinecom, 1986
THE BIG TOWN   Columbia, 1987
KANSAS   Trans World Entertainment, 1988
DRUGSTORE COWBOY   Avenue Pictures, 1989
BLOODHOUNDS OF BROADWAY   Columbia, 1989
A KISS BEFORE DYING   Universal, 1991
WOMEN & MEN: IN LOVE THERE ARE NO RULES (CTF)
   David Brown Productions/HBO Showcase, 1991
SINGLES   Warner Bros., 1992
MR. WONDERFUL   Warner Bros., 1993
THE SAINT OF FORT WASHINGTON   Warner Bros., 1993
GOLDEN GATE   Samuel Goldwyn Company, 1994
UNTITLED VAN SANT/ZISKIN   Columbia, 1995

MELINDA DILLON
THE APRIL FOOLS   National General, 1969
SLAP SHOT   Universal, 1977
CLOSE ENCOUNTERS OF THE THIRD KIND ✪   Columbia, 1977
BOUND FOR GLORY   United Artists, 1978
THE CRITICAL LIST (TF)   MTM Productions, 1978
F.I.S.T.   United Artists, 1978
ABSENCE OF MALICE ✪   Columbia, 1981
FALLEN ANGEL (TF)   Green-Epstein Productions/
   Columbia TV, 1981
SPACE (MS)   Stonehenge Productions/Paramount TV, 1985

SHATTERED SPIRITS (TF)   Sheen-Greenblatt Productions/Robert
   Greenwald Productions, 1986
HARRY AND THE HENDERSONS   Universal, 1987
SHATTERED INNOCENCE (TF)   Green-Epstein Productions/
   Lorimar TV, 1988
STAYING TOGETHER   Hemdale, 1989
SPONTANEOUS COMBUSTION   Taurus Entertainment, 1990
THE PRINCE OF TIDES   Columbia, 1991
DEMOLITION MAN   Warner Bros., 1993
SIOUX CITY   I.R.S. Releasing, 1994
TO WONG FOO, THANKS FOR EVERYTHING, JULIE NEWMAR
   Universal, 1995

RICHARD DIMITRI
Agent: Paradigm - Los Angeles, 310/277-4400

JOHNNY DANGEROUSLY   20th Century Fox, 1984

YI DING
LITTLE PANDA   Warner Bros., 1995

ERNIE DINGO
"CROCODILE" DUNDEE II   Paramount, 1988, U.S.-Australian

JERRY DINOME
DANGEROUSLY CLOSE   Cannon, 1986

JOHN DISANTI
Agent: Stone Manners Talent Agency - Los Angeles, 310/275-9599

EYES OF A STRANGER   Warner Bros., 1981

BOB DISHY
THE TIGER MAKES OUT   Columbia, 1967
LOVERS AND OTHER STRANGERS   Cinerama Releasing
   Corporation, 1970
THE BIG BUS   Paramount, 1976
FIRST FAMILY   Warner Bros., 1980
THE LAST MARRIED COUPLE IN AMERICA   Universal, 1980
AUTHOR! AUTHOR!   20th Century Fox, 1982
BRIGHTON BEACH MEMOIRS   Universal, 1986
CRITICAL CONDITION   Paramount, 1987
DON JUAN DE MARCO AND THE CENTERFOLD
   New Line Cinema, 1995

HARRY DITSON
TOP SECRET!   Paramount, 1984

ANDREW DIVOFF
ANOTHER 48 HRS.   Paramount, 1990
STEPHEN KING'S GRAVEYARD SHIFT   Paramount, 1990
TOY SOLDIERS   TriStar, 1991
A LOW DOWN DIRTY SHAME   Buena Vista, 1994

DONNA DIXON
DOCTOR DETROIT   Universal, 1983
SPIES LIKE US   Warner Bros., 1985
BEVERLY HILLS MADAM (TF)   NLS Productions/Orion TV, 1986
LUCKY STIFF   *MR. CHRISTMAS DINNER*   New Line Cinema, 1988
IT HAD TO BE YOU   Limelight Studios, 1989
WAYNE'S WORLD   Paramount, 1992

MACINTYRE DIXON
FUNNY FARM   Warner Bros., 1988

WILLIE DIXON
RICH GIRL   Studio Three, 1991

BADJA DJOLA
THE LIGHTSHIP   Castle Hill Productions, 1985, U.S.-West German
AN INNOCENT MAN   Buena Vista, 1989
A RAGE IN HARLEM   Miramax Films, 1991, U.S.-British
HEAVEN'S PRISONERS   Savoy Pictures, 1994

KEVIN DOBSON
b. March 18, 1944 - New York, New York
Agent: Century Artists, Ltd. - Beverly Hills, 310/273-4366

MIDWAY   Universal, 1976
ALL NIGHT LONG   Universal, 1981
SWEET REVENGE (TF)   David Greene Productions/Robert
   Papazian Productions, 1984
MONEY, POWER, MURDER (TF)   Skids Productions/CBS
   Entertainment, 1989

PETER DOBSON
SING   TriStar, 1989
LAST EXIT TO BROOKLYN   Cinecom, 1989, West German-U.S.
THE MARRYING MAN   Buena Vista, 1991
WHERE THE DAY TAKES YOU   New Line Cinema, 1992

JOHN DOE
Agent: William Morris Agency - Beverly Hills, 310/274-7451

SALVADOR   Hemdale, 1986
SLAM DANCE   Island Pictures, 1987
GREAT BALLS OF FIRE   Orion, 1989
ROADSIDE PROPHETS   New Line Cinema, 1992

MATT DOHERTY
D2: THE MIGHTY DUCKS   Buena Vista, 1994

SHANNEN DOHERTY
Agent: William Morris Agency - Beverly Hills, 310/274-7451

HEATHERS   New World, 1989

AMI DOLENZ
Agent: Gersh Agency - Beverly Hills, 310/274-6611

SHE'S OUT OF CONTROL   Columbia, 1989
RESCUE ME   Cannon, 1993

BÉATRICE DOLLE
BETTY BLUE   Alive Films, 1986, French

ARIELLE DOMBASLE
PAULINE AT THE BEACH   Orion Classics, 1983, French
LACE (MS)   Lorimar Productions, 1984
LACE II (MS)   Lorimar Productions, 1985
TWISTED OBSESSION   Majestic Films International, 1990

SOLVEIG DOMMARTIN
UNTIL THE END OF THE WORLD   Warner Bros., 1991,
   West German-French

ELINOR DONAHUE
Agent: Fred Amsel & Associates, Inc. - Los Angeles, 213/939-1188

PRETTY WOMAN   Buena Vista, 1990

TROY DONAHUE
(Merle Johnson, Jr.)
b. January 27, 1936 - New York, New York

MAN AFRAID   Universal, 1957
THIS HAPPY FEELING   Universal, 1958
THE VOICE IN THE MIRROR   Universal, 1958
MONSTER ON THE CAMPUS   Universal, 1958
SUMMER LOVE   Universal, 1958
WILD HERITAGE   Universal, 1958
THE PERFECT FURLOUGH   Universal, 1959
IMITATION OF LIFE   Universal, 1959
A SUMMER PLACE   Warner Bros., 1959
THE CROWDED SKY   Warner Bros., 1960
PARRISH   Warner Bros., 1961
SUSAN SLADE   Warner Bros., 1961
ROME ADVENTURE   Warner Bros., 1962
PALM SPRINGS WEEKEND   Warner Bros., 1963

A DISTANT TRUMPET   Warner Bros., 1964
MY BLOOD RUNS COLD   Warner Bros., 1965
COME SPY WITH ME   1967
THOSE FANTASTIC FLYING FOOLS   *BLAST-OFF/JULES VERNE'S
   ROCKET TO THE MOON*   American International,   1967, British
SWEET SAVIOR   1971
COCKFIGHTER   *BORN TO KILL/WILD DRIFTER/GAMBLIN' MAN*
   New World, 1974
SEIZURE   Cinerama Releasing Corporation, 1974, Canadian
THE GODFATHER, PART II   Paramount, 1974
MALIBU (TF)   Hamner Productions/Columbia TV, 1983
BAD BLOOD   Platinum Pictures, 1989
CRY-BABY   Universal, 1990

JULI DONALD
THE MUPPETS TAKE MANHATTAN   TriStar, 1984
THE PURPLE ROSE OF CAIRO   Orion, 1985
DRAGNET   Universal, 1987

PETER DONAT
Agent: Gersh Agency - Beverly Hills, 310/274-6611

MY OLD MAN'S PLACE   1971
THE GODFATHER, PART II   Paramount, 1974
RUSSIAN ROULETTE   Avco Embassy, 1975, U.S.-Canadian
THE HINDENBURG   Universal, 1975
F.I.S.T.   United Artists, 1978
A DIFFERENT STORY   Avco Embassy, 1978
THE CHINA SYNDROME   Columbia, 1979
TUCKER - THE MAN AND HIS DREAM   Paramount, 1988
SKIN DEEP   20th Century Fox, 1989
THE WAR OF THE ROSES   20th Century Fox, 1989

DONAL DONNELLY
THE DEAD   Vestron, 1987
THE GODFATHER, PART III   Paramount, 1990

PATRICE DONNELLY
PERSONAL BEST   The Geffen Company/Warner Bros., 1982
AMERICAN ANTHEM   Columbia, 1986

ROBERT DONNER
Agent: J. Carter Gibson Agency - Los Angeles, 310/274-8813

THE MAN WHO LOVED CAT DANCING   MGM, 1973
ALLAN QUATERMAIN AND THE LOST CITY OF GOLD
   Cannon, 1987

VINCENT D'ONOFRIO
(Vincent Philip D'Onofrio)
FULL METAL JACKET   Warner Bros., 1987, British
ADVENTURES IN BABYSITTING   Buena Vista, 1987
MYSTIC PIZZA   Samuel Goldwyn Company, 1988
THE BLOOD OF HEROES   New Line Cinema, 1990
CROOKED HEARTS   MGM-Pathe, 1991
DYING YOUNG   20th Century Fox, 1991
CROOKED HEARTS   MGM-Pathe, 1991
THE PLAYER   Fine Line Features/New Line Cinema, 1992
HOUSEHOLD SAINTS   Fine Line Features/New Line Cinema, 1993
BEING HUMAN   Warner Bros., 1994
IMAGINARY CRIMES   Warner Bros., 1994
ED WOOD   Buena Vista, 1994
STUART SMALLEY   Paramount, 1995
STRANGE DAYS   20th Century Fox, 1995

AMANDA DONOHOE
Agent: William Morris Agency - Beverly Hills, 310/274-7451

FOREIGN BODY   Orion, 1986, British
CASTAWAY   Cannon, 1986, British
THE LAIR OF THE WHITE WORM   Vestron, 1988, British
THE RAINBOW   Vestron, 1989, British
DARK OBSESSION   *DIAMOND SKULLS*   Circle Releasing,
   1989, British
PAPER MASK   FFI/British Screen, 1990, British
THE SUBSTITUTE (CTF)   Showtime, 1993
THE MADNESS OF GEORGE III   Samuel Goldwyn Company, 1995

ERIN DONOVAN
Agent: Selected Artists Agency - Studio City, 818/905-5744

MACK THE KNIFE   21st Century Distribution, 1989

TATE DONOVAN
Agent: Gersh Agency - Beverly Hills, 310/274-6611

NORTH BEACH AND RAWHIDE (MS)   CBS Entertainment, 1985
INTO THIN AIR (TF)   Fries Entertainment, 1986
SPACECAMP   20th Century Fox, 1986
NUTCRACKER: MONEY, MADNESS AND MURDER (MS)
   Green Arrow Productions/Warner Bros. TV, 1987
CLEAN AND SOBER   Warner Bros., 1988
DEAD-BANG   Warner Bros., 1989
MEMPHIS BELLE   Warner Bros., 1990
LITTLE NOISES   Monument Pictures, 1991
LOVE POTION #9   20th Century Fox, 1992
HOLY MATRIMONY   Buena Vista, 1994

ALISON DOODY
A VIEW TO A KILL   MGM/UA, 1985, British
A PRAYER FOR THE DYING   Samuel Goldwyn Company,
   1987, British
TAFFIN   MGM/UA, 1988, U.S.-Irish
INDIANA JONES AND THE LAST CRUSADE   Paramount, 1989
MAJOR LEAGUE II   Warner Bros., 1994

JAMES DOOHAN
STAR TREK - THE MOTION PICTURE   Paramount, 1979
STAR TREK II: THE WRATH OF KHAN   Paramount, 1982
STAR TREK III: THE SEARCH FOR SPOCK   Paramount, 1984
STAR TREK IV: THE VOYAGE HOME   Paramount, 1986
STAR TREK V: THE FINAL FRONTIER   Paramount, 1989
STAR TREK VI: THE UNDISCOVERED COUNTRY
   Paramount, 1991
STAR TREK GENERATIONS   Paramount, 1994

PAUL DOOLEY
Agent: ICM - Beverly Hills, 310/550-4000

SLAP SHOT   Universal, 1977
A WEDDING   20th Century Fox, 1978
A PERFECT COUPLE   20th Century Fox, 1979
BREAKING AWAY   20th Century Fox, 1979
RICH KIDS   United Artists, 1979
HEALTH   20th Century Fox, 1980
POPEYE   Paramount, 1980
PATERNITY   Paramount, 1981
ENDANGERED SPECIES   MGM/UA, 1982
KISS ME GOODBYE   20th Century Fox, 1982
GOING BERSERK   Universal, 1983, Canadian
SIXTEEN CANDLES   Universal, 1984
BIG TROUBLE   Columbia, 1985
O.C. AND STIGGS   MGM/UA, 1987
LAST RITES   MGM/UA, 1988
WHEN HE'S NOT A STRANGER (TF)
   Ohlmeyer Communications, 1989
FLASHBACK   Paramount, 1990
A DANGEROUS WOMAN   Gramercy Pictures, 1993

JOHN DOOLITTLE
Agent: Badgley/Connor - Los Angeles, 310/278-9313

THE CLAN OF THE CAVE BEAR   Warner Bros., 1986

ROBERT DOQUI
Agent: The Gage Group - Los Angeles, 213/859-7777

NASHVILLE   Paramount, 1975
ROBOCOP   Orion, 1987
ROBOCOP 3   Orion, 1993

EDNA DORE
HIGH HOPES   Skouras Pictures, 1988, British

STEPHEN DORFF
THE GATE   New Century/Vista, 1987, Canadian
I KNOW MY FIRST NAME IS STEVEN (TF)   Andrew Adelson
   Company/Lorimar TV, 1989
DO YOU KNOW THE MUFFIN MAN? (TF)   The Avnet-Kerner
   Company, 1989
A SON'S PROMISE (TF)   Marian Rees Associates, 1990
ALWAYS REMEMBER I LOVE YOU (TF)   Stephen J. Cannell/
   Gross-Weston Productions, Inc., 1990
THE POWER OF ONE   Warner Bros., 1992
JUDGMENT NIGHT   Universal, 1993
RESCUE ME   Cannon, 1993
BACKBEAT   Gramercy Pictures, 1994, British
S.F.W.   Gramercy Pictures, 1994

MICHAEL DORN
STAR TREK VI: THE UNDISCOVERED COUNTRY
   Paramount, 1991
STAR TREK GENERATIONS   Paramount, 1994

SARAH ROWLAND DOROFF
THREE FUGITIVES   Buena Vista, 1989

JOE DORSEY
BAT 21   TriStar, 1988

JOHN DOSSETT
LONGTIME COMPANION   Samuel Goldwyn Company, 1990
THAT NIGHT   Warner Bros., 1993

ROY DOTRICE
b. May 26, 1923 - Guernsey, England
Agent: The Lantz Office - New York, 212/586-0200

THE HEROES OF TELEMARK   Columbia, 1965, British
A TWIST OF SAND   United Artists, 1968, British
LOCK UP YOUR DAUGHTERS   1969
ONE OF THOSE THINGS   1971
NICHOLAS AND ALEXANDRA   Columbia, 1971, British
FAMILY REUNION (TF)   Creative Projects, Inc./Columbia TV, 1981
AMADEUS   Orion, 1984
ELIMINATORS   Empire Pictures, 1986
YOUNG HARRY HOUDINI (TF)   Walt Disney TV, 1987
THE LADY FORGETS (TF)   Leonard Hill Films, 1989
THE CUTTING EDGE   MGM-Pathe Communications, 1992

DAVID DOTY
Agent: The Gage Group - Los Angeles, 213/859-8777

FULL MOON IN BLUE WATER   Trans World Entertainment, 1988

DOUG E. DOUG
Agent: William Morris Agency - Beverly Hills, 310/274-7451

COOL RUNNINGS   Buena Vista, 1993
OPERATION DUMBO DROP   Buena Vista, 1995

ILEANNA DOUGLAS
GUILTY BY SUSPICION   Warner Bros., 1991
SEARCH AND DESTROY   October Films, 1995
UNTITLED VAN SANT/ZISKIN   Columbia, 1995

KIRK DOUGLAS
(Issur Danielovitch Demsky)
b. December 9, 1916 - Amsterdam, New York
Agent: CAA - Beverly Hills, 310/288-4545

THE STRANGE LOVE OF MARTHA IVERS   Paramount, 1946
MOURNING BECOMES ELECTRA   RKO Radio, 1947
OUT OF THE PAST   RKO Radio, 1947
I WALK ALONE   Paramount, 1947
THE WALLS OF JERICHO   20th Century Fox, 1948
MY DEAR SECRETARY   1948
A LETTER TO THREE WIVES   20th Century Fox, 1949
CHAMPION ★   United Artists, 1949

YOUNG MAN WITH A HORN   Waner Bros., 1950
THE GLASS MENAGERIE   Waner Bros., 1950
ALONG THE GREAT DIVIDE   Waner Bros., 1951
THE BIG CARNIVAL   *ACE IN THE HOLE*   Paramount, 1951
DETECTIVE STORY   Paramount, 1951
THE BIG TREES   1952
THE BIG SKY   RKO Radio, 1952
THE BAD AND THE BEAUTIFUL ★   MGM, 1952
THE STORY OF THREE LOVES   MGM, 1953
THE JUGGLER   Columbia, 1953
ACT OF LOVE   United Artists, 1954, U.S.-French
20,000 LEAGES UNDER THE SEA   Buena Vista, 1954
THE RACERS   20th Century Fox, 1955
ULYSSES   1955, Italian
MAN WITHOUT A STAR   Universal, 1955
THE INDIAN FIGHTER   United Artists, 1955
LUST FOR LIFE ★   MGM, 1956
TOP SECRET AFFAIR   Warner Bros., 1957
GUNFIGHT AT THE O.K. CORRAL   Paramount, 1957
PATHS OF GLORY   United Artists, 1957
THE VIKINGS   United Artists, 1958
LAST TRAIN FROM GUN HILL   Paramount, 1959
THE DEVIL'S DISCIPLE   United Artists, 1959, British
STRANGERS WHEN WE MEET   Columbia, 1960
SPARTACUS   Universal, 1960
THE LAST SUNSET   Universal, 1961
TOWN WITHOUT PITY   United Artists, 1961, U.S.-German-Swiss
LONELY ARE THE BRAVE   Universal, 1962
TWO WEEKS IN ANOTHER TOWN   MGM, 1962
THE HOOK   MGM, 1963
THE LIST OF ADRIAN MESSENGER   Universal, 1963
FOR LOVE OR MONEY   Universal, 1963
SEVEN DAYS IN MAY   Paramount, 1964
IN HARM'S WAY   Paramount, 1965
THE HEROES OF TELEMARK   Columbia, 1965, British
CAST A GIANT SHADOW   United Artists, 1966
IS PARIS BURNING?   *PARIS BRULE-T-IL?*   Paramount,
   1966, U.S.-French
THE WAY WEST   United Artists, 1967
THE WAR WAGON   Universal, 1967
A LOVELY WAY TO DIE   Universal, 1968
THE BROTHERHOOD   Paramount, 1968
THE ARRANGEMENT   Warner Bros., 1969
THERE WAS A CROOKED MAN   Warner Bros., 1970
THE LIGHT AT THE EDGE OF THE WORLD   National General,
   1971, U.S.-Spanish
A GUNFIGHT   Paramount, 1971
CATCH ME A SPY   Rank, 1971, British
HEARTS AND MINDS   1972, Italian
SCALAWAG   Paramount, 1973, U.S.-Italian (also directed)
MOUSEY (TF)   Universal TV/Associated British Films,
   1974, U.S.-British
JACQUELINE SUSANN'S ONCE IS NOT ENOUGH
   ONCE IS NOT ENOUGH   Paramount, 1975
POSSE   Paramount, 1975 (also directed)
ARTHUR HAILEY'S THE MONEYCHANGERS
   THE MONEYCHANGERS (MS)   Ross Hunter Productions/
   Paramount TV, 1976
VICTORY AT ENTEBBE (TF)   1976
THE CHOSEN   *HOLOCAUST 2000*   20th Century Fox International
   Classics, 1978, Italian-British
THE FURY   20th Century Fox, 1978
THE VILLAIN   Columbia, 1979
SATURN 3   AFD, 1980
HOME MOVIES   United Artists Classics, 1979
THE FINAL COUNTDOWN   United Artists, 1980
THE MAN FROM SNOWY RIVER   20th Century Fox,
   1982, Australian
REMEMBRANCE OF LOVE (TF)   Doris Quinlan Productions/
   Comworld Productions, 1982
EDDIE MACON'S RUN   Universal, 1983
AMOS (TF)   The Bryna Company/Vincent Pictures
   Productions, 1985
TOUGH GUYS   Buena Vista, 1986
QUEENIE (TF)   von Zerneck-Samuels Productions/Highgate
   Pictures, 1987
INHERIT THE WIND (TF)   Vincent Pictures Productions/
   David Greene-Robert Papazian Productions, 1988
OSCAR   Buena Vista, 1991
GREEDY   Universal, 1994

MICHAEL DOUGLAS
b. September 25, 1944 - New Brunswick, New Jersey
Agent: CAA - Beverly Hills, 310/288-4545

HAIL, HERO!   National General, 1969
ADAM AT SIX A.M.   National General, 1970
SUMMERTREE   Columbia, 1971
WHEN MICHAEL CALLS (TF)   Palomar International, 1971
NAPOLEON AND SAMANTHA   Buena Vista, 1972
THE STREETS OF SAN FRANCISCO (TF)   QM Productions, 1972
COMA   MGM/United Artists, 1978
THE CHINA SYNDROME   Columbia, 1979
RUNNING   Universal, 1979
IT'S MY TURN   Columbia, 1980
THE STAR CHAMBER   20th Century Fox, 1983
ROMANCING THE STONE   20th Century Fox, 1984
A CHORUS LINE   Columbia, 1985
THE JEWEL OF THE NILE   20th Century Fox, 1985
FATAL ATTRACTION   Paramount, 1987
WALL STREET ★★   20th Century Fox, 1987
BLACK RAIN   Paramount, 1989
THE WAR OF THE ROSES   20th Century Fox, 1989
SHINING THROUGH   20th Century Fox, 1992
BASIC INSTINCT   TriStar, 1992
FALLING DOWN   Warner Bros., 1993
DISCLOSURE   Warner Bros., 1994
THE AMERICAN PRESIDENT   Columbia, 1995

SARAH DOUGLAS
Agent: Stone Manners Talent Agency - Los Angeles, 310/275-9599

SUPERMAN II   Warner Bros., 1981, U.S.-British
CONAN THE DESTROYER   Universal, 1984
SOLARBABIES   MGM/UA, 1986
NIGHTFALL   Concorde, 1988

SUZZANE DOUGLAS
TAP   TriStar, 1989
THE INKWELL   Buena Vista, 1994
JASON'S LYRIC   1994

ROBYN DOUGLASS
BREAKING AWAY   20th Century Fox, 1979
ROMANTIC COMEDY   MGM/UA, 1983
HER LIFE AS A MAN (TF)   LS Entertainment, 1984

BRAD DOURIF
ONE FLEW OVER THE CUCKOO'S NEST ✪   United Artists, 1975
EYES OF LAURA MARS   Columbia, 1978
WISE BLOOD   New Line Cinema, 1979
GUYANA TRAGEDY: THE STORY OF JIM JONES (TF)
   The Konigsberg Company, 1980
HEAVEN'S GATE   United Artists, 1980
RAGTIME   Paramount, 1981
DUNE   Universal, 1984
IMPURE THOUGHTS   ASA Communications, 1986
BLUE VELVET   DEG, 1986
RAGE OF ANGELS: THE STORY CONTINUES (MS)
   NBC Productions, 1986
VENGEANCE: THE STORY OF TONY CIMO (TF)   Nederlander
   TV and Film Productions/Robirdie Pictures, 1986
CHILD'S PLAY   MGM/United Artists, 1988
MISSISSIPPI BURNING   Orion, 1988
SPONTANEOUS COMBUSTION   Taurus Entertainment, 1990
THE EXORCIST III   20th Century Fox, 1990
SONNY BOY   Triumph Releasing Corporation, 1990
STEPHEN KING'S GRAVEYARD SHIFT   Paramount, 1990
CHILD'S PLAY 2   Universal, 1990 (voice)
HIDDEN AGENDA   Hemdale, 1990
CHILD'S PLAY 3   Universal, 1991 (voice)
WILD PALMS (MS)   Ixtlan Corporation/Greengrass
   Productions, Inc., 1993
COLOR OF NIGHT   Buena Vista, 1994

ANN DOWD
IT COULD HAPPEN TO YOU   TriStar, 1994

CHRIS DOWDEN
BIG   20th Century Fox, 1988

FREDA DOWIE
DISTANT VOICES, STILL LIVES   Alive Films, 1988, British

KATHRYN DOWLING
ULTIMATE BETRAYAL (TF)   Hearst Entertainment, 1994

RACHAEL DOWLING
THE DEAD   Vestron, 1987

LESLEY-ANNE DOWN
b. March 17, 1954 - London, England

IN THE DEVIL'S GARDEN   *ASSAULT/TOWER OF TERROR*
   Hemisphere, 1971, British
COUNTESS DRACULA   20th Century Fox, 1972, British
ALL THE RIGHT NOISES   20th Century Fox, 1971, British
POPE JOAN   *THE DEVIL'S IMPOSTER*   Columbia, 1972, British
SCALAWAG   Paramount, 1973, U.S.-Italian
FROM BEYOND THE GRAVE   *CREATURES*   Howard Mahler
   Films, 1973, British
BRANNIGAN   United Artists, 1975, British-U.S.
THE PINK PANTHER STRIKES AGAIN   United Artists,
   1976, British
A LITTLE NIGHT MUSIC   New World, 1977, Austrian-U.S.
THE BETSY   Allied Artists, 1978
THE ONE AND ONLY ORIGINAL PHYLLIS DIXEY (TF)
   Thames TV, 1979, British
THE GREAT TRAIN ROBBERY   *THE FIRST GREAT TRAIN
   ROBBERY*   United Artists, 1979, British
HANOVER STREET   Columbia, 1979
ROUGH CUT   Paramount, 1980
SPHINX   Orion/Warner Bros., 1981
THE HUNCHBACK OF NOTRE DAME (TF)   Norman Rosemont
   Productions/Columbia TV, 1982, U.S.-British
MURDER IS EASY (TF)   David L. Wolper-Stan Margulies
   Productions/Warner Bros. TV, 1982
THE LAST DAYS OF POMPEII (MS)   David Gerber Company/
   Columbia TV/Centerpoint Films/RAI, 1984,U.S.-British-Italian
ARCH OF TRIUMPH (TF)   Newland-Raynor Productions/HTV,
   1985, U.S.-British
NORTH AND SOUTH (MS)   Wolper Productions/
   Warner Bros. TV, 1985
NOMADS   Atlantic Releasing Corporation, 1986
INDISCREET (TF)   Karen Mack Productions/HTV/Republic
   Pictures, 1988, U.S.-British
LADYKILLERS (TF)   Barry Weitz Films/ABC Circle Films, 1988
NIGHT WALK (TF)   CBS Entertainment/Galatea Productions, 1989
DEATH WISH V: THE FACE OF DEATH   Trimark Pictures, 1994

MORTON DOWNEY, JR.
Agent: The Agency - Los Angeles, 310/551-3000

PREDATOR 2   20th Century Fox, 1990

ROBERT DOWNEY, JR.
b. April 4, 1965 - New York, New York
Agent: CAA - Beverly Hills, 310/288-4545

GREASER'S PALACE   Greaser's Palace, 1972
MAD MAGAZINE PRESENTS UP THE ACADEMY
   Warner Bros., 1980
THIS AMERICA THE MOVIE, NOT THE COUNTRY
BABY IT'S YOU   Paramount, 1983
FIRSTBORN   Paramount, 1984
TUFF TURF   New World, 1985
WEIRD SCIENCE   Universal, 1985
BACK TO SCHOOL   Orion, 1986
THE PICK-UP ARTIST   20th Century Fox, 1987
LESS THAN ZERO   20th Century Fox, 1987
JOHNNY BE GOOD   Orion, 1988
RENTED LIPS   Cineworld, 1988
1969   Atlantic Releasing Corporation, 1988
CHANCES ARE   TriStar, 1989
TRUE BELIEVER   Columbia, 1989

AIR AMERICA   TriStar, 1990
TOO MUCH SUN   New Line Cinema, 1991
SOAPDISH   Paramount, 1991
CHAPLIN ★   TriStar, 1992, U.S.-British
HEART AND SOULS   Universal, 1993
SHORT CUTS   Fine Line Features/New Line Cinema, 1993
NATURAL BORN KILLERS   Warner Bros., 1994
ONLY YOU   TriStar, 1994
RESTORATION   Miramax Films, 1994

DAVID DOYLE
b. December 1, 1929 - Lincoln, Nebraska
Agent: The Gage Group - Los Angeles, 213/859-8777

PAPER LION   United Artists, 1968
PARADES   Cinerama Releasing Corporation, 1972
LADY LIBERTY   *MORTADELLA*   1972, Italian
MIRACLE ON 34TH STREET (TF)   20th Century-Fox TV, 1973
CHARLIE'S ANGELS (TF)   Spelling-Goldberg Productions, 1976
THE COMEBACK   *THE DAY THE SCREAMING STOPPED*
   Enterprise, 1978, British
MAYBE BABY (TF)   Perry Lafferty Productions/von Zerneck-Samuels
   Productions, 1988

BRIAN DOYLE-MURRAY
Agent: Abrams Artists & Associates - Los Angeles, 310/859-0625

MODERN PROBLEMS   20th Century Fox, 1981
CLUB PARADISE   Warner Bros., 1986
SCROOGED   Paramount, 1988
THE EXPERTS   Paramount, 1989
HOW I GOT INTO COLLEGE   20th Century Fox, 1989
JFK   Warner Bros., 1991
WAYNE'S WORLD   Paramount, 1992
JURY DUTY   Sony Pictures, 1995

BILLY DRAGO
VAMP   New World, 1986
HERO AND THE TERROR   Cannon, 1988
FREEWAY   New World, 1988
DELTA FORCE 2 - OPERATION STRANGLEHOLD   MGM/UA, 1990
NEVER SAY DIE   Nu World, 1994

FABIA DRAKE
VALMONT   Orion, 1989, French

LARRY DRAKE
b. February 21 - Tulsa, Oklahoma

TOO GOOD TO BE TRUE (TF)   Newland-Raynor Productions, 1988
DARKMAN   Universal, 1990
THE JOURNEY OF AUGUST KING   Miramax Films, 1995

POLLY DRAPER
GOLD DIGGERS   Universal, 1995

FRAN DRESCHER
Agent: Gersh Agency - Beverly Hills, 310/274-6611

SATURDAY NIGHT FEVER   Paramount, 1977
DOCTOR DETROIT   Universal, 1983
THIS IS SPINAL TAP   Embassy, 1984
LOVE AND BETRAYAL (TF)   Gross-Weston Productions/ITC
   Entertainment Group, 1989
UHF   Orion, 1989
THE BIG PICTURE   Columbia, 1989
IT HAD TO BE YOU   Limelite Studios, 1989
CADILLAC MAN   Orion, 1990
CAR 54, WHERE ARE YOU?   Orion, 1994

RICHARD DREYFUSS
b. October 29, 1948 - Brooklyn, New York
Agent: ICM - Beverly Hills, 310/550-4000

VALLEY OF THE DOLLS   20th Century Fox, 1967
THE GRADUATE   Avco Embassy, 1967

THE YOUNG RUNAWAYS MGM, 1968
HELLO DOWN THERE Paramount, 1969
DILLINGER American International, 1973
AMERICAN GRAFFITI Universal, 1973
THE APPRENTICESHIP OF DUDDY KRAVITZ Paramount,
   1974, Canadian
JAWS Universal, 1975
INSERTS United Artists, 1976, British
VICTORY AT ENTEBBE (TF) 1976
CLOSE ENCOUNTERS OF THE THIRD KIND Columbia, 1977
THE GOODBYE GIRL ★★ MGM/Warner Bros., 1977
THE BIX FIX Universal, 1978
THE COMPETITION Columbia, 1980
WHOSE LIFE IS IT ANYWAY? MGM/UA, 1981
THE BUDDY SYSTEM 20th Century Fox, 1984
DOWN AND OUT IN BEVERLY HILLS Buena Vista, 1986
STAND BY ME Columbia, 1986
TIN MEN Buena Vista, 1987
STAKEOUT Buena Vista, 1987
NUTS Warner Bros., 1987
MOON OVER PARADOR Universal, 1988, U.S.-Brazilian
LET IT RIDE Paramount, 1989
ALWAYS Universal, 1989
POSTCARDS FROM THE EDGE Columbia, 1990
ONCE AROUND Universal, 1991
ROSENCRANTZ & GUILDENSTERN ARE DEAD Cinecom, 1991
WHAT ABOUT BOB? Buena Vista, 1991
PRISONERS OF HONOR (CTF) HBO Pictures/Dreyfuss-James
   Productions, 1991
LOST IN YONKERS Columbia, 1993
ANOTHER STAKEOUT Buena Vista, 1993
SILENT FALL Warner Bros., 1994
MR. HOLLAND'S OPUS Buena Vista, 1995

BRIAN DRILLINGER
BRIGHTON BEACH MEMOIRS Universal, 1986

MINNIE DRIVER
CIRCLE OF FRIENDS Savoy Pictures, 1995

SOO DROUET
ROBIN HOOD: PRINCE OF THIEVES Warner Bros., 1991

JOHN DRUMMOND
ABOVE THE LAW Warner Bros., 1988

FRED DRYER
b. July 6, 1946 - Hawthorne, California

HUNTER (TF) Stephen J. Cannell Productions, 1984

JA'NET DUBOIS
Agent: Fred Amsel & Associates - Los Angeles, 213/939-1188

I'M GONNA GIT YOU SUCKA MGM/UA, 1989

CECILE DUCASSE
CHOCOLAT Orion Classics, 1988, French

DAVID DUCHOVNY
JULIA HAS TWO LOVERS South Gate Entertainment, 1991
THE RAPTURE New Line Cinema, 1991
BEETHOVEN Universal, 1992
CHAPLIN TriStar, 1992, U.S.-British
KALIFORNIA Gramercy Pictures, 1993

RICK DUCOMMUN
Agent: William Morris Agency - Beverly Hills, 310/274-7451

A FINE MESS Columbia, 1986
SPACEBALLS MGM/UA, 1987
DIE HARD 20th Century Fox, 1988
THE EXPERTS Paramount, 1989
THE 'BURBS Universal, 1989
LITTLE MONSTERS MGM/UA, 1989
THE HUNT FOR RED OCTOBER Paramount, 1990
BLANK CHECK Buena Vista, 1994

MICHAEL DUDIKOFF
Agent: The Craig Agency - Los Angeles, 213/655-0236

AMERICAN NINJA Cannon, 1985
AVENGING FORCE Cannon, 1986
RADIOACTIVE DREAMS DEG, 1986
RIVER OF DEATH Cannon, 1989, British
AMERICAN NINJA 4: THE ANNIHILATION Cannon, 1991
THE HUMAN SHIELD Cannon, 1992
RESCUE ME Cannon, 1993

KAREN DUFFY
BLANK CHECK Buena Vista, 1994

PATRICK DUFFY
b. March 17, 1949 - Townsend, Montana
Agent: Writers & Artists Agency - Los Angeles, 310/820-2240

UNHOLY MATRIMONY (TF) Edgar J. Scherick Associates/Taft
   Entertainment TV, 1988
TOO GOOD TO BE TRUE (TF) Newland-Raynor Productions, 1988

THOMAS F. DUFFY
WAGONS EAST TriStar, 1994

DENNIS DUGAN
Agent: Gersh Agency - Beverly Hills, 310/274-6611

HARRY AND WALTER GO TO NEW YORK Columbia, 1976
WATER Atlantic Releasing Corporation, 1984, British
THE TOUGHEST MAN IN THE WORLD (TF) Guber-Peters
   Productions/Centerpoint Productions, 1984
SHADOW CHASERS (TF) Johnson-Grazer Productions/
   Warner Bros. TV, 1985
THE NEW ADVENTURES OF PIPPI LONGSTOCKING
   Columbia, 1988
PARENTHOOD Universal, 1989

TOM DUGAN
Agent: Atkins & Associates - Los Angeles, 213/658-1025

PERFECT VICTIMS Vertigo Pictures, 1988

JOHN DUKAKIS
JAWS 2 Universal, 1978

OLYMPIA DUKAKIS
b. 1931 - Lowell, Massachusetts
Agent: William Morris Agency - Beverly Hills, 310/274-7451

DEATH WISH Paramount, 1974
MOONSTRUCK ○○ MGM/UA, 1987
WORKING GIRL 20th Century Fox, 1988
LOOK WHO'S TALKING TriStar, 1989
DAD Universal, 1989
STEEL MAGNOLIAS TriStar, 1989
IN THE SPIRIT Castle Hill Productions, 1990
LOOK WHO'S TALKING TOO TriStar, 1990
THE CEMETERY CLUB Buena Vista, 1993
LOOK WHO'S TALKING NOW TriStar, 1993
I LOVE TROUBLE Buena Vista, 1994
MR. HOLLAND'S OPUS Buena Vista, 1995
JEFFREY 1995

BILL DUKE
AMERICAN GIGOLO Paramount, 1980
ACTION JACKSON Lorimar, 1988
BIRD ON A WIRE Universal, 1990

PATTY DUKE
(Anna Marie Duke/Patty Duke Astin)
b. December 14, 1946 - Elmhurst, New York
Agent: William Morris Agency - Beverly Hills, 310/274-7451

I'LL CRY TOMORROW MGM, 1955
SOMEBODY UP THERE LIKES ME MGM, 1956
COUNTRY MUSIC HOLIDAY 1958

THE GODDESS   Columbia, 1958
HAPPY ANNIVERSARY   United Artists, 1959
.4-D MAN   1959
THE POWER AND THE GLORY   (TF)   1962
THE MIRACLE WORKER ∞   United Artists, 1962
BILLIE   United Artists, 1965
VALLEY OF THE DOLLS   20th Century-Fox, 1967
ME, NATALIE   1969
MY SWEET CHARLIE (TF)   Universal TV, 1970
TWO ON A BENCH (TF)   Universal TV, 1971
IF TOMORROW COMES (TF)   Aaron Spelling Productions, 1971
SHE WAITS (TF)   Metromedia Productions, 1971
YOU'LL LIKE MY MOTHER   Universal, 1972
DEADLY HARVEST (TF)   CBS, Inc., 1972
NIGHTMARE (TF)   CBS, Inc., 1974
CAPTAINS AND THE KINGS (TF)   Universal TV, 1976
KILLER ON BOARD (TF)   Lorimar Productions, 1977
A FAMILY UPSIDE DOWN (TF)   Ross Hunter-Jacques Mapes Film/
   Paramount TV, 1978
THE SWARM   Warner Bros., 1978
HANGING BY A THREAD (TF)   1979
THE MIRACLE WORKER (TF)   Katz-Gallin Productions/Half-Pint
   Productions, 1979
BEFORE AND AFTER (TF)   The Konigsberg Company, 1979
BEST KEPT SECRETS (TF)   ABC Circle Films, 1984
GEORGE WASHINGTON: THE FORGING OF A NATION (MS)
   David Gerber Company/MGM TV, 1986
A TIME TO TRIUMPH (TF)   Billos-Kaufman Productions/Phoenix
   Entertainment Group, 1986
FIGHT FOR LIFE (TF)   Fries Entertainment, 1987
PERRY MASON: THE CASE OF THE AVENGING ACE (TF)
   The Fred Silverman Company/Strathmore Productions/
   Viacom, 1988
FATAL JUDGMENT (TF)   Jack Farren Productions/Group W
   Productions, 1988
EVERYBODY'S BABY: THE RESCUE OF JESSICA McCLURE (TF)
   Dick Berg-Stonehenge Productions/The Campbell Soup Company/
   Interscope Productions, 1989
AMITYVILLE: THE EVIL ESCAPES (TF)   Steve White Productions/
   Spectator Films, 1990
ALWAYS REMEMBER I LOVE YOU (TF)   Stephen J. Cannell/
   Gross-Weston Productions, Inc., 1990
ABSOLUTE STRANGERS (TF)   Cates-Doty Productions/Fries
   Entertainment, 1991
PRELUDE TO A KISS   20th Century Fox, 1992

ROBIN DUKE

CLUB PARADISE   Warner Bros., 1986

DAVID DUKES

b. June 6, 1945 - San Francisco, California
Agent: ICM - Beverly Hills, 310/550-4000

A FIRE IN THE SKY (TF)   Bill Driskill Productions, 1978
A LITTLE ROMANCE   Orion/Warner Bros., 1979, U.S.-French
THE FIRST DEADLY SIN   Filmways, 1980
ONLY WHEN I LAUGH   Columbia, 1981
WITHOUT A TRACE   20th Century Fox, 1983
THE WINDS OF WAR (MS)   Paramount TV/Dan Curtis
   Productions, 1983
SENTIMENTAL JOURNEY (TF)   Lucille Ball Productions/
   Smith-Richmond Productions/20th Century Fox TV, 1984
SPACE (MS)   Stonehenge Productions/Paramount TV, 1985
KANE AND ABEL (MS)   Schrekinger Communications/
   Embassy TV, 1985
THE MEN'S CLUB   Atlantic Releasing Corporation, 1986
WAR AND REMEMBRANCE (MS)   Dan Curtis Productions/
   ABC Circle Films, 1988-89
SEE YOU IN THE MORNING   Warner Bros., 1989
TURN BACK THE CLOCK (TF)   Michael Filerman Productions/
   NBC Productions, 1989
THE JOSEPHINE BAKER STORY (CTF)   HBO Pictures/RHI
   Entertainment/Anglia TV/John Kemeny Productions, 1991
AND THE BAND PLAYED ON (CTF)   HBO Pictures/Spelling
   Entertainment, 1993

KEIR DULLEA

b. May 30, 1936 - Cleveland, Ohio

2001: A SPACE ODYSSEY   MGM, 1968, British
THE HOSTAGE TOWER (TF)   Jerry Leider Productions, 1980

DENISE DUMMONT

Agent: Artists First, Inc. - Los Angeles, 213/653-5640

HEART OF MIDNIGHT   Virgin Vision, 1989

DENNIS DUN

YEAR OF THE DRAGON   MGM/UA, 1985
THE LAST EMPEROR   Columbia, 1987, British-Chinese
BIG TROUBLE IN LITTLE CHINA   20th Century Fox, 1986
PRINCE OF DARKNESS   Universal, 1987

FAYE DUNAWAY

b. January 14, 1941 - Bascam, Florida
Agent: ICM - Beverly Hills, 310/550-4000

THE HAPPENING   Columbia, 1967
HURRY SUNDOWN   Paramount, 1967
BONNIE AND CLYDE ★   Warner Bros., 1967
THE THOMAS CROWN AFFAIR   United Artists, 1968
THE EXTRAORDINARY SEAMAN   MGM, 1969
A PLACE FOR LOVERS   *GLI AMANTI*   MGM, 1969, Italian-French
THE ARRANGEMENT   Warner Bros., 1969
PUZZLE OF A DOWNFALL CHILD   Universal, 1970
LITTLE BIG MAN   National General, 1970
DOC   United Artists, 1971
THE DEADLY TRAP   *LA MAISON SOUS LES ARBRES*
   National General, 1971, French-Italian
OKLAHOMA CRUDE   Columbia, 1973
THE THREE MUSKETEERS   20th Century Fox, 1974, British
CHINATOWN ★   Paramount, 1974
THE TOWERING INFERNO   20th Century Fox/Warner Bros., 1974
THE FOUR MUSKETEERS   20th Century Fox, 1975, British
THREE DAYS OF THE CONDOR   Paramount, 1975
VOYAGE OF THE DAMNED   Avco Embassy, 1976, British
NETWORK ★★   MGM/United Artists, 1976
THE DISAPPEARANCE OF AIMEE (TF)
   Tomorrow Entertaiment, 1976
EYES OF LAURA MARS   Columbia, 1978
THE CHAMP   MGM/United Artists, 1979
THE FIRST DEADLY SIN   Filmways, 1980
MOMMIE DEAREST   Paramount, 1981
EVITA PERON (TF)   Hartwest Productions/Zephyr
   Productions, 1981
THE WICKED LADY   MGM/UA/Cannon, 1983, British
CHRISTOPHER COLUMBUS (MS)   RAI/Ciesi Cinematografica/
   Antenne-2/Bavaria Atelier/Lorimar Productions, 1985,
   Italian-West German-U.S.-French
SUPERGIRL   Warner Bros., 1984, British
ORDEAL BY INNOCENCE   Cannon, 1984, British
AGATHA CHRISTIE'S "THIRTEEN AT DINNER" (TF)
   Warner Bros. TV, 1985
BEVERLY HILLS MADAM (TF)   NLS Productions/Orion TV, 1986
CASANOVA (TF)   Konigsberg-Sanitsky Company/Reteitalia, 1987,
   U.S.-Italian
BARFLY   Cannon, 1987
BURNING SECRET   Vestron, 1988, U.S.-British-West German
COLD SASSY TREE (CTF)   Faye Dunaway Productions/Ohlmeyer
   Communications/Turner Network TV, 1989
THE HANDMAID'S TALE   Cinecom, 1990
THE TEMP   Paramount, 1993
ARIZONA DREAMER   Warner Bros., 1995
DON JUAN DE MARCO AND THE CENTERFOLD
   New Line Cinema, 1995

ADRIAN DUNBAR

Agent: William Morris Agency - Beverly Hills, 310/274-7451

MY LEFT FOOT   Miramax Films, 1989, Irish-British
WIDOWS' PEAK   Fine Line Features/New Line Cinema, 1994

ANDREW DUNCAN

THE GIG   Castle Hill Productions, 1985

SANDY DUNCAN

b. February 20, 1946 - Henderson, Texas

$1,000,000 DUCK   Buena Vista, 1971
STAR SPANGLED GIRL   Paramount, 1971
ROOTS (MS)   Wolper Productions, 1977
THE CAT FROM OUTER SPACE   Buena Vista, 1978
MY BOYFRIEND'S BACK (TF)   Interscope Communications, 1989
ROCK-A-DOODLE (AF)   Samuel Goldwyn Company, 1992 (voice)
THE SWAN PRINCESS (AF)   New Line Cinema, 1995 (voice)

VIC DUNLOP

Agent: CNA & Associates - Los Angeles, 310/556-4343

MARTIANS GO HOME   Taurus Entertainment, 1990

KEVIN DUNN

Agent: Paradigm - Los Angeles, 310/277-4400

TAKEN AWAY (TF)   Hart, Thomas & Berlin Productions, 1989
THE BONFIRE OF THE VANITIES   Warner Bros., 1990
ONLY THE LONELY   20th Century Fox, 1991
HOT SHOTS!   20th Century Fox, 1991
CHAPLIN   TriStar, 1992, U.S.-British
DAVE   Warner Bros., 1993
LITTLE BIG LEAGUE   Columbia, 1994
MAD LOVE   Buena Vista, 1995

NORA DUNN

WORKING GIRL   20th Century Fox, 1988
HOW I GOT INTO COLLEGE   20th Century Fox, 1989
MIAMI BLUES   Orion, 1990
PASSION FISH   Miramax Films, 1992
I LOVE TROUBLE   Buena Vista, 1994

GRIFFIN DUNNE

b. June 8, 1955 - New York, New York
Agent: UTA - Beverly Hills, 310/273-6700

HEAD OVER HEELS   CHILLY SCENES OF WINTER
   United Artists, 1979
THE FAN   Paramount, 1981
AN AMERICAN WEREWOLF IN LONDON   Universal, 1981
THE WALL (TF)   Cinetex International/Time-Life Productions,
   1982, U.S.-Polish
COLD FEET   Cinecom, 1984
ALMOST YOU   TLC Films/20th Century Fox, 1984
JOHNNY DANGEROUSLY   20th Century Fox, 1984
AFTER HOURS   The Geffen Company/Warner Bros., 1985
WHO'S THAT GIRL?   Warner Bros., 1987
THE BIG BLUE   Columbia, 1988
ME AND HIM   Columbia, 1989
SECRET WEAPON (CTF)   Griffin-Elysian Productions/TVS/
   ABC-Australia, 1990, U.S.-British-Australian
ONCE AROUND   Universal, 1991
MY GIRL   Columbia, 1991
STEPKIDS   New Line Cinema, 1991
STRAIGHT TALK   Buena Vista, 1992
I LIKE IT LIKE THAT   Columbia, 1994
SEARCH AND DESTROY   October Films, 1995

KIRSTEN DUNST

INTERVIEW WITH THE VAMPIRE   Warner Bros., 1994
LITTLE WOMEN   Columbia, 1994

PETER DUPRE

EYES OF A STRANGER   Warner Bros., 1981

V.C. DUPREE

Agent: Brooke, Dunn & Oliver - Los Angeles, 310/859-1405

FRIDAY THE 13TH PART VIII - JASON TAKES MANHATTAN
   Paramount, 1989

MARC DURET

THE BIG BLUE   Columbia, 1988

CHARLES DURNING

b. February 28, 1933 - Highland Falls, New York
Agent: Paradigm - Los Angeles, 310/277-4400

HARVEY MIDDLEMAN, FIREMAN   Columbia, 1965
I WALK THE LINE   Columbia, 1970
HI, MOM!   Sigma III, 1970
THE PURSUIT OF HAPPINESS   Columbia, 1971
DEADHEAD MILES   1972
DEALING: OR THE BERKELEY-TO-BOSTON FORTY-BRICK
   LOST-BAG BLUES   Warner Bros., 1972
SISTERS   American International, 1973
THE CONNECTION (TF)   D'Antoni Productions, 1973
THE STING   Universal, 1973
THE FRONT PAGE   Universal, 1974
DOG DAY AFTERNOON   Warner Bros., 1975
THE HINDENBURG   Universal, 1975
THE TRIAL OF CHAPLAIN JENSEN (TF)
   20th Century Fox TV, 1975
QUEEN OF THE STARDUST BALLROOM (TF)
   Tomorrow Entertainment, 1975
SWITCH (TF)   Universal TV, 1975
THE RIVALRY (TF)   NBC-TV, 1975
CAPTAINS AND THE KINGS (MS)   Universal TV, 1976
BREAKHEART PASS   United Artists, 1976
HARRY AND WALTER GO TO NEW YORK   Columbia, 1976
TWILIGHT'S LAST GLEAMING   Allied Artists, 1977,
   U.S.-West German
THE CHOIRBOYS   Universal, 1977
SPECIAL OLYMPICS   A SPECIAL KIND OF LOVE (TF)
   Roger Gimbel Productions/EMI TV, 1978
THE FURY   20th Century Fox, 1978
THE GREEK TYCOON   Universal, 1978
AN ENEMY OF THE PEOPLE   Warner Bros., 1978
STUDS LONIGAN (MS)   Lorimar Productions, 1979
THE MUPPET MOVIE   AFD, 1979, British
NORTH DALLAS FORTY   Paramount, 1979
TILT   Warner Bros., 1979
STARTING OVER   Paramount, 1979
WHEN A STRANGER CALLS   Columbia, 1979
DIE LAUGHING   Orion/Warner Bros., 1980
THE FINAL COUNTDOWN   United Artists, 1980
TRUE CONFESSIONS   United Artists, 1981
SHARKY'S MACHINE   Orion/Warner Bros., 1981
THE BEST LITTLE WHOREHOUSE IN TEXAS ✪   Universal, 1982
TOOTSIE   Columbia, 1982
TWO OF A KIND   20th Century Fox, 1983
TO BE OR NOT TO BE ✪   20th Century Fox, 1983
MASS APPEAL   Universal, 1984
DEATH OF A SALESMAN (TF)   Roxbury and Punch
   Productions, 1985
STICK   Universal, 1985
THE MAN WITH ONE RED SHOE   20th Century Fox, 1985
STAND ALONE   New World, 1985
SOLARBABIES   MGM/UA, 1986
WHERE THE RIVER RUNS BLACK   MGM/UA, 1986
TOUGH GUYS   Buena Vista, 1986
BIG TROUBLE   Columbia, 1986
HAPPY NEW YEAR   Columbia, 1987
A TIGER'S TALE   Atlantic Releasing Corporation, 1987
CASE CLOSED (TF)   Houston Motion Picture Entertainment, Inc./
   CBS Entertainment, 1988
COP   Atlantic Releasing Corporation, 1988
FAR NORTH   Alive Films, 1988
UNHOLY MATRIMONY (TF)   Edgar J. Scherick Associates/Taft
   Entertainment TV, 1988
PRIME TARGET (TF)   RLC Productions/The Finnegan-Pinchuk
   Company/MGM-UA TV, 1989
DINNER AT EIGHT (CTF)   Think Entertainment/Turner
   Network TV, 1989
DICK TRACY   Buena Vista, 1990
THE KENNEDYS OF MASSACHUSETTS (MS)   Edgar J. Scherick
   Associates/Orion TV, 1990
V.I. WARSHAWSKI   Buena Vista, 1991
WHEN A STRANGER CALLS BACK (CTF)   Krost-Chapin
   Productions/The Producers Entertainment Group/MTE, 1993
THE MUSIC OF CHANCE   I.R.S. Releasing, 1993
THE HUDSUCKER PROXY   Warner Bros., 1994
THE GOLDEN GOOSE   21st Century Film Corporation, 1995

MICHAEL DURRELL
MENENDEZ: A KILLING IN BEVERLY HILLS (MS)   Zev Braun
    Pictures/TriStar Television, 1994

MARJ DUSAY
Agent: Fred Amsel & Associates - Los Angeles, 213/939-1188

MADE IN HEAVEN   Lorimar, 1987

ANN DUSENBERRY
Agent: J. Michael Bloom & Associates - New York, 212/529-6500

HE'S NOT YOUR SON (TF)   CBS Entertainment, 1984
BASIC TRAINING   The Movie Store, 1985
THE MEN'S CLUB   Atlantic Releasing Corporation, 1986

ELIZA DUSHKU
THAT NIGHT   Warner Bros., 1993
TRUE LIES   20th Century Fox, 1994
BYE BYE LOVE   20th Century Fox, 1995

CHARLES S. DUTTON
Agent: CAA - Beverly Hills, 310/288-4545

"CROCODILE" DUNDEE II   Paramount, 1988, U.S.-Australian
AN UNREMARKABLE LIFE   Continental Film Group, 1989
JACKNIFE   Cineplex Odeon, 1989
Q&A   TriStar, 1990
ALIEN 3   20th Century Fox, 1992, U.S.-British
RUDY   TriStar, 1993
SURVIVING THE GAME   New Line Cinema, 1994
A LOW DOWN DIRTY SHAME   Buena Vista, 1994

ROBERT DUVALL
b. January 5, 1931 - San Diego, California
Agent: William Morris Agency - Beverly Hills, 310/274-7451

TO KILL A MOCKINGBIRD   Universal, 1962
CAPTAIN NEWMAN, M.D.   Universal, 1963
NIGHTMARE IN THE SUN   1964
THE CHASE   Columbia, 1966
COUNTDOWN   Warner Bros., 1968
THE DETECTIVE   Warner Bros., 1968
BULLITT   Warner Bros., 1968
TRUE GRIT   Paramount, 1969
THE RAIN PEOPLE   Warner Bros., 1969
M*A*S*H   20th Century Fox, 1970
THE REVOLUTIONARY   United Artists, 1970
THX 1138   Warner Bros., 1971
LAWMAN   United Artists, 1971
THE GODFATHER ✪   Paramount, 1972
THE GREAT NORTHFIELD, MINNESOTA RAID   Universal, 1972
JOE KIDD   Universal, 1972
TOMORROW   Filmgroup, 1972
BADGE 373   Paramount, 1973
LADY ICE   National General, 1973
THE CONVERSATION   Paramount, 1974 (uncredited)
THE OUTFIT   MGM, 1974
THE GODFATHER, PART II   Paramount, 1974
BREAKOUT   Columbia, 1975
THE KILLER ELITE   United Artists, 1975
NETWORK   MGM/United Artists, 1976
THE SEVEN-PER-CENT SOLUTION   Universal, 1976, British
THE EAGLE HAS LANDED   Columbia, 1977, British
THE GREATEST   Columbia, 1977
THE BETSY   Allied Artists, 1978
INVASION OF THE BODY SNATCHERS   United Artists, 1978
IKE: THE WAR YEARS (MS)   ABC Circle Films, 1979
APOCALYPSE NOW ✪   United Artists, 1979
THE GREAT SANTINI   THE ACE ★   Orion/Warner Bros., 1980
TRUE CONFESSIONS   United Artists, 1981
THE PURSUIT OF D.B. COOPER   Universal, 1981
TENDER MERCIES ★★   Universal/AFD, 1983
THE STONE BOY   TLC Films/20th Century Fox, 1984
THE NATURAL   TriStar, 1984
THE LIGHTSHIP   Castle Hill Productions, 1985, U.S.-West German

BELIZAIRE THE CAJUN   Skouras Pictures, 1986
HOTEL COLONIAL   Hemdale, 1987, U.S.-Italian
LET'S GET HARRY   TriStar, 1987
COLORS   Orion, 1988
LONESOME DOVE (MS)   Motown Productions/Pangaea/Qintex
    Entertainment, Inc., 1989
THE HANDMAID'S TALE   Cinecom, 1990
A SHOW OF FORCE   Paramount, 1990
DAYS OF THUNDER   Paramount, 1990
RAMBLING ROSE   New Line Cinema, 1991
NEWSIES   Buena Vista, 1992
FALLING DOWN   Warner Bros., 1993
GERONIMO - AN AMERICAN LEGEND   Columbia, 1993
WRESTLING ERNEST HEMINGWAY   Warner Bros., 1993
THE PAPER   Universal, 1994
THE STARS FELL ON HENRIETTA   Warner Bros., 1995
A SCARLET LETTER   Buena Vista, 1995

SHELLEY DUVALL
b. 1950 - Houston, Texas
Agent: Gersh Agency - Beverly Hills, 310/274-6611

BREWSTER McCLOUD   MGM, 1970
McCABE AND MRS. MILLER   Warner Bros., 1971
THIEVES LIKE US   United Artists, 1974
NASHVILLE   Paramount, 1975
BUFFALO BILL AND THE INDIANS or SITTING BULL'S HISTORY
    LESSON   United Artists, 1976
ANNIE HALL   United Artists, 1977
3 WOMEN   20th Century Fox, 1977
POPEYE   Paramount, 1980
THE SHINING   Warner Bros., 1980, British
TIME BANDITS   Avco Embassy, 1981, British
LILY (TF)   Platypus Productions/Viacom Productions, 1986
ROXANNE   Columbia, 1987
MOTHER GOOSE ROCK 'N' RHYME (CTF)
    Think Entertainment, 1990
SUBURBAN COMMANDO   New Line Cinema, 1991

ROBERT DVI
ACTION JACKSON   Lorimar, 1988

SALLY DWORSKY
THE LION KING (AF)   Buena Vista, 1994 (voice)

JOHN DYE
BEST OF THE BEST   Taurus Entertainment/SVS Films, 1989
THE PERFECT WEAPON   Paramount, 1991

BOB DYLAN
(Robert Zimmerman)
b. May 24, 1941 - Hibbing, Minnesota

DON'T LOOK BACK (FD)   Leacock-Pennebaker, 1967
PAT GARRETT & BILLY THE KID   MGM, 1973
RENALDO AND CLARA   Circuit, 1978 (also directed)
HEARTS OF FIRE   Lorimar, 1987, U.S.-British

RICHARD DYSART
b. March 30, 1929 - Augusta, Maine
Agent: Writers & Artists Agency - Los Angeles, 310/820-2240

THE HINDENBURG   Universal, 1975
MALICE IN WONDERLAND (TF)   ITC Productions, 1985
BLOOD AND ORCHIDS (MS)   Lorimar Productions, 1986
L.A. LAW (TF)   20th Century Fox TV, 1986
THE LAST DAYS OF PATTON (TF)   Entertainment Partners, 1986
SIX AGAINST THE ROCK (TF)   Schaefer-Karpf-Epstein Productions/
    Gaylord Production Company, 1987
MOVING TARGET (TF)   Lewis B. Chesler Productions/Bateman
    Company Productions/Finnegan-PinchukCompany/
    MGM-UA TV, 1988
DAY ONE (TF)   Aaron Spelling Productions/Paragon Motion Pictures/
    David W. Rintels Productions, 1989
BACK TO THE FUTURE PART III   Universal, 1990

GEORGE DZUNDZA
b. July 19, 1945 - Rosenheim, Germany

THE DEER HUNTER   Universal, 1978
STREAMERS   United Artists Classics, 1983
BROTHERLY LOVE (TF)   CBS Entertainment, 1985
NO MERCY   TriStar, 1986
ONE POLICE PLAZA (TF)   CBS Entertainment, 1986
THE BEAST   Columbia, 1988
SOMETHING IS OUT THERE (MS)   Columbia TV, 1988
TERROR ON HIGHWAY 91 (TF)   Katy Film Productions, 1989
THE RYAN WHITE STORY (TF)   The Landsburg Company, 1989
IMPULSE   Warner Bros., 1990
WHITE HUNTER, BLACK HEART   Warner Bros., 1990
THE BUTCHER'S WIFE   Paramount, 1991
BASIC INSTINCT   TriStar, 1992
CRIMSON TIDE   Buena Vista, 1995

DAISY EAGAN
LOSING ISAIAH   Paramount, 1995

JEFF EAST
Agent; The Artists Group, Ltd. - Los Angeles, 310/552-1100

DEADLY BLESSING   United Artists, 1981
THE DAY AFTER (TF)   ABC Circle Films, 1983

LESLIE EASTERBROOK
Agent: The Marion Rosenberg Office - Los Angeles, 213/653-7383

POLICE ACADEMY   The Ladd Company/Warner Bros., 1984
POLICE ACADEMY 3: BACK IN TRAINING   Warner Bros., 1986
POLICE ACADEMY 4: CITIZENS ON PATROL
   Warner Bros., 1987
THE TAKING OF FLIGHT 847: THE ULI DERICKSON STORY (TF)
   Columbia TV, 1988
POLICE ACADEMY 5: ASSIGNMENT MIAMI BEACH
   Warner Bros., 1988
POLICE ACADEMY 6: CITY UNDER SIEGE   Warner Bros., 1989
POLICE ACADEMY: MISSION TO MOSCOW   Warner Bros., 1994

RICHARD EASTON
Agent: Bauman, Hiller & Associates - Los Angeles, 213/857-6666

DEAD AGAIN   Paramount, 1991

ROBERT EASTON
Contact: 213/463-4811

WORKING GIRL   20th Century Fox, 1988
THE BEVERLY HILLBILLIES   20th Century Fox, 1993

CLINT EASTWOOD
b. May 31, 1930 - San Francisco, California
Business: Malpaso Productions, 4000 Warner Blvd., Burbank,
   CA 91522, 818/954-3367
Agent: William Morris Agency - Beverly Hills, 310/274-7451

REVENGE OF THE CREATURE   Universal, 1955
FRANCIS IN THE NAVY   Universal, 1955
LADY GODIVA   Universal, 1955
TARANTULA   Universal, 1955
NEVER SAY GOODBYE   Universal, 1956
THE FIRST TRAVELING SALESLADY   RKO Radio, 1956
STAR IN THE DUST   1956

ESCAPADE IN JAPAN   Universal, 1957
AMBUSH AT CIMARRON PASS   1958
LAFAYETTE ESCADRILLE   Warner Bros., 1958
A FISTFUL OF DOLLARS   United Artists, 1964,
   Italian-Spanish-West German
FOR A FEW DOLLARS MORE   United Artists, 1965,
   Italian-Spanish-West German
THE GOOD, THE BAD AND THE UGLY   United Artists, 1967,
   Italian-Spanish
THE WITCHES   Lopert, 1967, Italian-French
HANG 'EM HIGH   United Artists, 1968
COOGAN'S BLUFF   Universal, 1968
WHERE EAGLES DARE   MGM, 1969, British
PAINT YOUR WAGON   Paramount, 1969
TWO MULES FOR SISTER SARA   Universal, 1970, U.S.-Mexican
KELLY'S HEROES   MGM, 1970, U.S.-Yugoslavia
THE BEGUILED   Universal, 1971
PLAY MISTY FOR ME   Universal, 1971 (also directed)
DIRTY HARRY   Warner Bros., 1971
JOE KIDD   Universal, 1972
HIGH PLAINS DRIFTER   Universal, 1973 (also directed)
MAGNUM FORCE   Warner Bros., 1973
THUNDERBOLT AND LIGHTFOOT   United Artists, 1974
THE EIGER SANCTION   Universal, 1975 (also directed)
THE OUTLAW JOSEY WALES   Warner Bros.,
   1976 (also directed)
THE ENFORCER   Warner Bros., 1976
THE GAUNTLET   Warner Bros., 1977 (also directed)
EVERY WHICH WAY BUT LOOSE   Warner Bros., 1978
ESCAPE FROM ALCATRAZ   Paramount, 1979
ANY WHICH WAY YOU CAN   Warner Bros., 1980
BRONCO BILLY   Warner Bros., 1980 (also directed)
FIREFOX   Warner Bros., 1982 (also directed)
HONKYTONK MAN   Warner Bros., 1982 (also directed)
SUDDEN IMPACT   Warner Bros., 1983 (also directed)
TIGHTROPE   Warner Bros., 1984
CITY HEAT   Warner Bros., 1984
PALE RIDER   Warner Bros., 1985 (also directed)
HEARTBREAK RIDGE   Warner Bros., 1986 (also directed)
THE DEAD POOL   Warner Bros., 1988
PINK CADILLAC   Warner Bros., 1989
WHITE HUNTER, BLACK HEART   Warner Bros.,
   1990 (also directed)
THE ROOKIE   Warner Bros., 1990 (also directed)
UNFORGIVEN ★   Warner Bros., 1992 (also directed)
IN THE LINE OF FIRE   Columbia, 1993
A PERFECT WORLD   Warner Bros., 1993 (also directed)
THE BRIDGES OF MADISON COUNTY   Warner Bros.,
   1995 (also directed)

KYLE EASTWOOD
HONKYTONK MAN   Warner Bros., 1982

DAVID EBERTS
BURNING SECRET   Vestron, 1988, U.S.-British-West German

CHRISTINE EBERSOLE
Agent: ICM - Beverly Hills, 310/550-4000

AMADEUS   Orion, 1984
ACCEPTABLE RISKS (TF)   ABC Circle Films, 1986
MAC AND ME   Orion, 1988
DEAD AGAIN   Paramount, 1991
GYPSY (TF)   RHI Entertainment, 1993
MY GIRL 2   Columbia, 1994
RICHIE RICH   Warner Bros., 1994

BUDDY EBSEN
b. April 2, 1908 - Belleville, Illinois

THE BEVERLY HILLBILLIES   20th Century Fox, 1993

JAMES ECKHOUSE
Agent: Writers & Artists Agency - Los Angeles, 213/820-2240

BLUE HEAVEN   Vestron/Shapiro Entertainment, 1984
BIG   20th Century Fox, 1988

HERB EDELMAN
b. November 5, 1933 - Brooklyn, New York

BAREFOOT IN THE PARK   Paramount, 1967
THE ODD COUPLE   Paramount, 1968
THE YAKUZA   *BROTHERHOOD OF THE YAKUZA*
   Warner Bros., 1975
CALIFORNIA SUITE   Columbia, 1978
MARATHON (TF)   Alan Landsburg Productions, 1980
SMORGASBORD   *CRACKING UP*   Warner Bros., 1983

BARBARA EDEN
(Barbara Huffman)
b. August 23, 1934 - Tucson, Arizona
Agent: William Morris Agency - Beverly Hills, 310/274-7451

BACK FROM ETERNITY   RKO Radio, 1956
THE WAYWARD GIRL   Republic, 1957
A PRIVATE'S AFFAIR   20th Century Fox, 1959
TWELVE HOURS TO KILL   1960
FLAMING STAR   20th Century Fox, 1960
FROM THE TERRACE   20th Century Fox, 1960
ALL HANDS ON DECK   20th Century Fox, 1961
VOYAGE TO THE BOTTOM OF THE SEA   20th Century Fox, 1961
THE WONDERFUL WORLD OF THE BROTHERS GRIMM
   MGM/Cinerama, 1962
SWINGIN' ALONG   *DOUBLE TROUBLE*   1962
FIVE WEEKS IN A BALLOON   20th Century Fox, 1962
THE YELLOW CANARY   20th Century Fox, 1963
THE BRASS BOTTLE   1964
THE SEVEN FACES OF DR. LAO   MGM, 1964
THE NEW INTERNS   Columbia, 1964
RIDE THE WILD SURF   Columbia, 1964
THE FEMINIST AND THE FUZZ (TF)   Screen Gems/
   Columbia TV, 1970
QUICK, LET'S GET MARRIED   *SEVEN DIFFERENT WAYS*   1971
THE WOMAN HUNTER (TF)   Bing Crosby Productions, 1972
A HOWLING IN THE WOODS (TF)   Universal TV, 1971
THE STRANGER WITHIN (TF)   Lorimar Productions, 1974
THE AMAZING DOBERMANS   Golden, 1976
HOW TO BREAK UP A HAPPY DIVORCE (TF)   Charles Fries
   Productions, 1976
HARPER VALLEY P.T.A.   April Fools, 1978
CHATTANOOGA CHOO CHOO   April Fools, 1984
I DREAM OF JEANNIE: 15 YEARS LATER (TF)   Can't Sing
   Can't Dance Productions/Columbia TV, 1985
THE STEPFORD CHILDREN (TF)   Edgar J. Scherick Productions/
   Taft Entertainment TV, 1987
THE SECRET LIFE OF KATHY McCORMICK (TF)
   Tamara Asseyev Productions/New World TV, 1988
YOUR MOTHER WEARS COMBAT BOOTS (TF)
   Kushner-Locke Productions, 1989
A BRAND NEW LIFE: THE HONEYMOON (TF)
   NBC Productions, 1989
HER WICKED WAYS (TF)   Lois Luger Productions/Freyda Rothstein
   Productions/Bar-Gene Productions/ITC Entertainment, 1990
I STILL DREAM OF JEANNIE (TF)   Jeannie Entertainment/Carla
   Singer Productions/Bar-Gene Productions, 1991
EYES OF TERROR (TF)   Bar-Gene Productions/Freyda Rothstein
   Productions/Hearst Entertainment, 1994

EDGE
(The Edge)
U2: RATTLE AND HUM (FD)   Paramount, 1988

BEATIE EDNEY
HIGHLANDER   20th Century Fox, 1986, British-U.S.
MISTER JOHNSON   Avenue Pictures, 1991

RICHARD EDSON
STRANGER THAN PARADISE   Samuel Goldwyn Company, 1984
DESPERATELY SEEKING SUSAN   Orion, 1985
FERRIS BUELLER'S DAY OFF   Paramount, 1986
HOWARD THE DUCK   Universal, 1986
PLATOON   Orion, 1986
GOOD MORNING VIETNAM   Buena Vista, 1987
WALKER   Universal, 1987, U.S.-Nicaraguan
EIGHT MEN OUT   Orion, 1988

DO THE RIGHT THING   Universal, 1989
BLOODHOUNDS OF BROADWAY   Columbia, 1989
STRANGE DAYS   20th Century Fox, 1995

ANTHONY EDWARDS
b. January 19, 1962 - Santa Barbara, California

FAST TIMES AT RIDGEMONT HIGH   Universal, 1982
HEART LIKE A WHEEL   20th Century Fox, 1983
REVENGE OF THE NERDS   20th Century Fox, 1984
GOING FOR THE GOLD: THE BILL JOHNSON STORY (TF)
   ITC Productions/Sullivan-Carter Interests/Goodman-Rosen
   Productions, 1985
GOTCHA!   Universal, 1985
THE SURE THING   Embassy, 1985
TOP GUN   Paramount, 1986
REVENGE OF THE NERDS II: NERDS IN PARADISE
   20th Century Fox, 1987
SUMMER HEAT   Atlantic Releasing Corporation, 1987
MR. NORTH   Samuel Goldwyn Company, 1988
HOW I GOT INTO COLLEGE   20th Century Fox, 1989
MIRACLE MILE   Hemdale, 1989
HAWKS   Skouras Pictures, 1989
EL DIABLO (CTF)   HBO Pictures/Wizan-Black Films, 1990
DOWNTOWN   20th Century Fox, 1990
PET SEMATARY II   Paramount, 1992
THE CLIENT   Warner Bros., 1994

CASSANDRA EDWARDS
VASECTOMY, A DELICATE MATTER   Seymour Borde &
   Associates, 1986

ERIC EDWARDS
NATIONAL LAMPOON'S SENIOR TRIP   New Line Cinema, 1995

JENNIFER EDWARDS
Agent: Gersh Agency - Beverly Hills, 310/274-6611

S.O.B.   Paramount, 1981
THE MAN WHO LOVED WOMEN   Columbia, 1983
A FINE MESS   Columbia, 1986
THAT'S LIFE!   Columbia, 1986
SUNSET   TriStar, 1988
PETER GUNN (TF)   The Blake Edwards Company/
   New World TV, 1990

KRISTLE EDWARDS
THE LION KING (AF)   Buena Vista, 1994 (voice)

LUKE EDWARDS
THE WIZARD   Universal, 1989
I KNOW MY FIRST NAME IS STEVEN (MS)   Andrew Adelson
   Company/Lorimar TV, 1989
GUILTY BY SUSPICION   Warner Bros., 1991
NEWSIES   Buena Vista, 1992
MOTHER'S BOYS   Dimension/Miramax Films, 1994
LITTLE BIG LEAGUE   Columbia, 1994

PADDI EDWARDS
THE LITTLE MERMAID (AF)   Buena Vista, 1989 (voice)

RONNIE CLAIRE EDWARDS
8 SECONDS   New Line Cinema, 1994

SEBASTIAN RICE EDWARDS
HOPE AND GLORY   Columbia, 1987, British

VINCE EDWARDS
(Vincent Edward Zoimo)
b. July 9, 1928 - New York, New York

MR. UNIVERSE   1951
SAILOR BEWARE   Paramount, 1952
HIAWATHA   Allied Artists, 1952
ROGUE COP   1954
THE NIGHT HOLDS TERROR   Columbia, 1955

CELL 2455 DEATH ROW   1955
SERENADE   Warner Bros., 1956
THE KILLING   United Artists, 1956
THE THREE FACES OF EVE   20th Century Fox, 1957
THE HIRED GUN   1957
MURDER BY CONTRACT   Columbia, 1958
CITY OF FEAR   Columbia, 1959
TOO LATE BLUES   Paramount, 1962
THE VICTORS   Columbi,a 1964
THE DEVIL'S BRIGADE   United Artists, 1968
HAMMERHEAD   Columbia, 1968, British
THE DESPERADOES   Columbia, 1969
THE MAD BOMBER   Cinemation, 1972
EVENING IN BYZANTIUM (TF)   Universal TV, 1978
THE SEDUCTION   Avco Embassy, 1981
SPACE RAIDERS   New World, 1983
DEAL OF THE CENTURY   Warner Bros., 1983
THE DIRTY DOZEN: THE DEADLY MISSION (TF)
   MGM-UA TV/Jadran Film, 1987, U.S.-Yugoslavian
RETURN TO HORROR HIGH   New World, 1987
CELLAR DWELLAR   Empire Pictures, 1988
THE GUMSHOE KID   Argus Entertainment, 1989

PETER EGAN
THE HIRELING   Columbia, 1973, British
CALLAN   Cinema National, 1974, British
HENNESSY   American International, 1975, British
CHARIOTS OF FIRE   The Ladd Company/Warner Bros.,
   1981, British
A WOMAN OF SUBSTANCE (MS)   Artemis Portman
   Productions, 1984, British

SAMANTHA EGGAR
b. March 5, 1939 - London, England
Agent: The Craig Agency - Los Angeles, 213/655-0236

THE WILD AND THE WILLING   YOUNG AND WILLING
   Universal, 1962, British
DOCTOR CRIPPEN   1963, British
DOCTOR IN DISTRESS   Governor, 1963, British
PSYCHE 59   1964, British
THE COLLECTOR ★   Columbia, 1965, U.S.-British
RETURN FROM THE ASHES   United Artists, 1965, U.S.-British
WALK, DON'T RUN   Columbia, 1966
DOCTOR DOLITTLE   20th Century Fox, 1967
THE MOLLY MAGUIRES   Paramount, 1970
THE WALKING STICK   MGM, 1970, British
THE LADY IN A CAR WITH GLASSES AND A GUN   Columbia,
   1970, French-U.S.
THE LIGHT AT THE EDGE OF THE WORLD   National General,
   1971, U.S.-Italian-Spanish
THE DEAD ARE ALIVE   1972, Italian-Yugoslavian-West German
A NAME FOR EVIL   1972
DOUBLE INDEMNITY (TF)   Universal TV, 1973
ALL THE KIND STRANGERS (TF)   Cinemation, 1974
THE SEVEN PER-CENT SOLUTION   Universal, 1976, British
THE KILLER WHO WOULDN'T DIE (TF)   Paramount TV, 1976
WHY SHOOT THE TEACHER?   Quartet, 1977, Canadian
THE UNCANNY   1977
WELCOME TO BLOOD CITY   EMI, 1977, Canadian-British
ZIEGFELD: THE MAN AND HIS WOMEN (TF)   Frankovich
   Productions/Columbia TV, 1978
THE GREAT BATTLE   BATTLE FORCE   1978,
   West German-Yugoslavian
THE BROOD   New World, 1979, Canadian
THE EXTERMINATOR   Avco Embassy, 1980
CURTAINS   Jensen Farley Pictures, 1983, Canadian
LOVE AMONG THIEVES (TF)   Robert A. Papazian
   Productions, 1987
A GHOST IN MONTE CARLO (CTF)   The Grade Company/
   Gainsborough Pictures, 1990, British

STAN EGI
COME SEE THE PARADISE   20th Century Fox, 1990

JENNIFER EHLE
BACKBEAT   Gramercy Pictures, 1994, British

LISA EICHHORN
b. February 4, 1952 - Reading, Pennsylvania
Agent: Writers & Artists Agency - Los Angeles, 213/820-2240

THE EUROPEANS   Levitt-Pickman, 1979, British
YANKS   Universal, 1979, British
CUTTER'S WAY   CUTTER AND BONE   United Artists Classics, 1981
WILDROSE   Troma, 1984
BLIND JUSTICE (TF)   CBS Entertainment, 1986
OPPOSING FORCE   HELL CAMP   Orion, 1986
PRIDE AND EXTREME PREJUDICE (CTF)   F.F.S. Productions/
   Taurusfilm/Blair Communications, 1990, British-West German-U.S.
KING OF THE HILL   Gramercy Pictures, 1993

JILL EIKENBERRY
b. January 21, 1947 - New Haven, Connecticut
Agent: William Morris Agency - Beverly Hills, 310/274-7451

THE DEADLIEST SEASON (TF)   Titus Productions, 1977
BETWEEN THE LINES   Midwest Film Productions, 1977
A NIGHT FULL OF RAIN   THE END OF THE WORLD IN OUR USUAL
   BED IN A NIGHT FULL OF RAIN   Warner Bros., 1978, Italian-U.S.
AN UNMARRIED WOMAN   20th Century Fox, 1978
BUTCH AND SUNDANCE: THE EARLY DAYS
   20th Century Fox, 1979
RICH KIDS   United Artists, 1979
ORPHAN TRAIN (TF)   Roger Gimbel Productions/EMI TV, 1979
HIDE IN PLAIN SIGHT   MGM/United Artists, 1980
SWAN SONG (TF)   Renee Valente Productions/Topanga
   Services Ltd./20th Century Fox, 1980
ARTHUR   Orion, 1981
SESSIONS (TF)   Roger Gimbel Productions/EMI TV/Sarabande
   Productions, 1983
KANE & ABEL (MS)   Schrekinger Communications/Embassy TV, 1985
GRACE QUIGLEY   THE ULTIMATE SOLUTION OF GRACE
   QUIGLEY   Cannon, 1985
THE MANHATTAN PROJECT   20th Century Fox, 1986
L.A. LAW (TF)   20th Century Fox TV, 1986
ASSAULT AND MATRIMONY (TF)   Michael Filerman Productions/
   NBC Productions, 1987
FAMILY SINS (TF)   London Films, Inc., 1987
A STONING IN FULHAM COUNTY (TF)   The Landsburg
   Company, 1988
MY BOYFRIEND'S BACK (TF)   Interscope Communications, 1989
CAST THE FIRST STONE (TF)   Mench Productions/
   Columbia TV, 1989
PARALLEL LIVES (CTF)   Showtime Entertainment, 1994

LISA EILBACHER
Agent: APA - Los Angeles, 310/273-0744

THE WAR BETWEEN MEN AND WOMEN   National General, 1972
ARTHUR HAILEY'S WHEELS   WHEELS (MS)   Universal TV, 1978
10 TO MIDNIGHT   Cannon, 1983
THE WINDS OF WAR (MS)   Paramount TV/Dan Curtis
   Productions, 1983
BEVERLY HILLS COP   Paramount, 1984
THUNDER ALLEY   Cannon, 1986
MONTE CARLO (MS)   New World TV/Phoenix Entertainment Group/
   Collins-Holm Productions/Highgate Pictures, 1986
DEADLY DECEPTION (TF)   CBS Entertainment, 1987
MANHUNT: SEARCH FOR THE NIGHT STALKER (TF)
   Leonard Hill Films, 1989

JANET EILBER
Agent: The Light Company - Los Angeles, 213/826-2230

WHOSE LIFE IS IT ANYWAY?   MGM/United Artists, 1981
ROMANTIC COMEDY   MGM/UA, 1983
HARD TO HOLD   Universal, 1984

JACK EISEMAN
MAC AND ME   Orion, 1988

NED EISENBERG
HIDING OUT   DEG, 1987
AIR AMERICA   TriStar, 1990

DEBRA EISENSTADT
OLEANNA   Samuel Goldwyn Company, 1995

BRITT EKLAND
(Britt-Marie Eklund)
b. October 6, 1942 - Stockholm, Sweden

SHORT IS THE SUMMER   1962, Swedish-Norwegian
IL COMMANDANTE   1963, Italian
AFTER THE FOX   United Artists, 1966, Italian-U.S.-British
TOO MANY THIEVES (TF)   1966
THE BOBO   Warner Bros., 1967, British
THE DOUBLE MAN   Warner Bros., 1967, British
THE NIGHT THEY RAIDED MINSKY'S   United Artists, 1968
MACHINE GUN McCAIN   *GLI INTOCCABILI*   1968, Italian
THE CANNIBALS   1969, Italian
STILETTO   Avco Embassy, 1969
GET CARTER   MGM, 1971, British
PERCY   MGM, 1971, British
A TIME FOR LOVING   1971
NIGHT HAIR CHILD   Hemdale, 1971, British
ASYLUM   Cinerama Releasing Corporation, 1972, British
BAXTER!   National General, 1972, British
ENDLESS NIGHT   1972
THE ULTIMATE THRILL   General Cinema, 1974
THE MAN WITH THE GOLDEN GUN   United Artists, 1974, British
THE WICKER MAN   Warner Bros., 1975, British
ROYAL FLASH   20th Century Fox, 1975, British
HIGH VELOCITY   1977
CASANOVA & CO.   1977, Austrian-West German-Italian
SLAVERS   1977, West German
KING SOLOMON'S TREASURE   Filmco Ltd., 1977, Canadian
THE GREAT WALLENDAS (TF)   Daniel Wilson Productions, 1977
RING OF PASSION (TF)   20th Century Fox TV, 1979
THE HOSTAGE TOWER (TF)   Jerry Leider Productions, 1980
THE MONSTER CLUB   ITC, 1981, British
MOON IN SCORPIO   Trans World Entertainment, 1988
SCANDAL   Miramax Films, 1989

ERIKA ELENIAK
Agent: Abrams Artists & Associates - Los Angeles, 310/859-0625

E.T. THE EXTRA-TERRESTRIAL   Universal, 1982
UNDER SIEGE   Warner Bros., 1992
THE BEVERLY HILLBILLIES   20th Century Fox, 1993
CHASERS   Warner Bros., 1994
A PYROMANIAC'S LOVE STORY   Buena Vista, 1995

DANNY ELFMAN
TIM BURTON'S THE NIGHTMARE BEFORE CHRISTMAS
   Buena Vista, 1993 (voice)

CHRISTINE ELISE
CHILD'S PLAY 2   Universal, 1990
BODY SNATCHERS   Warner Bros., 1994

EVANGELINA ELIZONDO
A WALK IN THE CLOUDS   20th Century Fox, 1995

HECTOR ELIZONDO
b. December 22, 1944 - New York, New York
Agent: William Morris Agency - Beverly Hills, 310/274-7451

VALDEZ IS COMING   United Artists, 1971
BORN TO WIN   United Artists, 1971
STAND UP AND BE COUNTED   Columbia, 1972
POCKET MONEY   National General, 1972
THE TAKING OF PELHAM 1-2-3   United Artists, 1974
REPORT TO THE COMMISSIONER   United Artists, 1975
THIEVES   Paramount, 1977
THE DAIN CURSE (MS)   Martin Poll Productions, 1978
CUBA   United Artists, 1979
AMERICAN GIGOLO   Paramount, 1980
THE FAN   Paramount, 1981
YOUNG DOCTORS IN LOVE   20th Century Fox, 1982
THE FLAMINGO KID   20th Century Fox, 1984

PRIVATE RESORT   TriStar, 1985
MURDER: BY REASON OF INSANITY (TF)
   LS Entertainment, 1985
OUT OF THE DARKNESS (TF)   Grosso-Jacobson Productions/
   Centerpoint Productions, 1985
NOTHING IN COMMON   TriStar, 1986
COURAGE (TF)   Highgate Pictures/New World TV, 1986
YOUR MOTHER WEARS COMBAT BOOTS (TF)   Kushner-Locke
   Productions, 1989
LEVIATHAN   MGM/UA, 1989, U.S.-Italian
PRETTY WOMAN   Buena Vista, 1990
TAKING CARE OF BUSINESS   Buena Vista, 1990
NECESSARY ROUGHNESS   Paramount, 1991
FRANKIE & JOHNNY   Paramount, 1991
PAY DIRT   Paramount, 1991
BEING HUMAN   Warner Bros., 1994
BEVERLY HILLS COPS III   Paramount, 1994
GETTING EVEN WITH DAD   MGM/UA, 1994
EXIT TO EDEN   Savoy Pictures, 1994

ROBERT ELLENSTEIN
STAR TREK IV: THE VOYAGE HOME   Paramount, 1986

CHRIS ELLIOT
MANHUNTER   DEG, 1986
NEW YORK STORIES   Buena Vista, 1989

BOB ELLIOTT
b. March 26, 1923 - Boston, Massachusetts

AUTHOR! AUTHOR!   20th Century Fox, 1982

CHRIS ELLIOTT
Agent: William Morris Agency - Beverly Hills, 310/274-7451

THE ABYSS   20th Century Fox, 1989
GROUNDHOG DAY   Columbia, 1993
CB4   Universal, 1993
CABIN BOY   Buena Vista, 1994

SAM ELLIOTT
b. August 9, 1944 - Sacramento, California
Agent: William Morris Agency - Beverly Hills, 310/274-7451

THE GAMES   20th Century Fox, 1970, British
FROGS   American International, 1972
MOLLY AND LAWLESS JOHN   Producers Distribution
   Corporation, 1972
THE BLUE KNIGHT (TF)   Lorimar Productions, 1973
I WILL FIGHT NO MORE FOREVER (TF)   Wolper Productions, 1975
LIFEGUARD   Paramount, 1976
ONCE AN EAGLE (TF)   Universal TV, 1976
THE LAST CONVERTIBLE (TF)   Roy Huggins Productions/
   Universal TV, 1979
ASPEN (MS)   Universal TV, 1979
THE SACKETS (TF)   Douglas Netter Enterprises/M.B. Scott
   Productions/Shalako Enterprises, 1979
THE LEGACY   Universal, 1979
WILD TIMES (TF)   Metromedia Producers Corporation/Rattlesnake
   Productions, 1980
MURDER IN TEXAS (TF)   Dick Clark Productions/
   Billy Hale Films, 1981
THE SHADOW RIDERS (TF)   The Pegasus Group, Ltd./
   Columbia TV, 1982
TRAVIS McGEE (TF)   Hajeno Productions/Warner Bros. TV, 1983
MASK   Universal, 1985
A DEATH IN CALIFORNIA (MS)   Mace Neufeld Productions/Lorimar
   Productions, 1985
THE BLUE LIGHTNING (TF)   Alan Sloan Productions/The Seven
   Network/Coote-Carroll Australia/Roadshow, 1986, U.S.-Australian
HOUSTON: THE LEGEND OF TEXAS (TF)   Taft Entertainment TV/
   J.D. Feigelson Productions, 1986
FATAL BEAUTY   MGM/UA, 1987
THE QUICK AND THE DEAD (CTF)   HBO Pictures/Joseph Cates
   Company, 1987
SHAKEDOWN   Universal, 1988
ROAD HOUSE   MGM/UA, 1989

PRANCER   Orion, 1989
SIBLING RIVALRY   Columbia, 1990
RUSH   MGM-Pathe, 1991
GETTYSBURG   New Line Cinema, 1993
TOMBSTONE   Buena Vista, 1993
BUFFALO GIRLS (MS)   Lauren Film Productions, Inc./CBS, 1995

STEPHEN ELLIOTT
Agent: Harris & Goldberg - Los Angeles, 310/553-5200

DEATH WISH   Paramount, 1974
THE GOLDEN HONEYMOON (TF)   Learning in Focus, 1980
ASSASSINATION   20th Century Fox, 1981
ARTHUR   Orion, 1981
ROADHOUSE 66   Atlantic Releasing Corporation, 1984
ARTHUR 2 ON THE ROCKS   Warner Bros., 1988

ROWAN ELMES
A DRY WHITE SEASON   MGM/UA, 1989

ROBERT ELSON
THE ENGLISHMAN WHO WENT UP A HILL, BUT CAME DOWN
   A MOUNTAIN   Miramax Films, 1995

ELVIRA
(See Cassandra PETERSON)

CARY ELWES
Agent: UTA - Beverly Hills, 310/273-6700

OXFORD BLUES   MGM/UA, 1984, British
LADY JANE   Paramount, 1985, British
THE PRINCESS BRIDE   20th Century Fox, 1987
GLORY   TriStar, 1989
DAYS OF THUNDER   Paramount, 1990
HOT SHOTS!   20th Century Fox, 1991
LEATHER JACKETS   Triumph Releasing Corporation, 1992
BRAM STOKER'S DRACULA   *DRACULA*   Columbia, 1992
THE CRUSH   Warner Bros., 1993
ROBIN HOOD: MEN IN TIGHTS   20th Century Fox, 1993
THE JUNGLE BOOK   Buena Vista, 1994
MARTIN EDEN   1995

JONATHAN EMERSON
84 CHARLIE MOPIC   New Century/Vista, 1989

MICHAEL EMIL
TRACKS   Castle Hill Productions, 1977
CAN SHE BAKE A CHERRY PIE?   Castle Hill Productions/
   Quartet Films, 1983
ALWAYS   Samuel Goldwyn Company, 1985
INSIGNIFICANCE   Island Alive, 1985, British
SOMEONE TO LOVE   Rainbow/Castle Hill Productions, 1987

JESSE EMMETT
AIRPLANE!   Paramount, 1980

ALEX ENGLISH
AMAZING GRACE AND CHUCK   TriStar, 1987

ZACH ENGLISH
THE REAL McCOY   Universal, 1993

ROBERT ENGLUND
b. June 6, 1948 - Hollywood, California

HOBSON'S CHOICE (TF)   CBS Entertainment, 1983
A NIGHTMARE ON ELM STREET   New Line Cinema, 1984
A NIGHTMARE ON ELM STREET 2: FREDDY'S REVENGE
   New Line Cinema, 1985
INFIDELITY (TF)   Mark-Jett Productions/ABC Circle Films, 1987
A NIGHTMARE ON ELM STREET 3: DREAM WARRIORS
   New Line Cinema, 1987
A NIGHTMARE ON ELM STREET 4: THE DREAM MASTER
   New Line Cinema, 1988

A NIGHTMARE ON ELM STREET 5: THE DREAM CHILD
   New Line Cinema, 1989
THE PHANTOM OF THE OPERA   Century Film Corporation, 1989
THE ADVENTURES OF FORD FAIRLANE   20th Century Fox, 1990
FREDDY'S DEAD: THE FINAL NIGHTMARE
   New Line Cinema, 1991
WES CRAVEN'S NEW NIGHTMARE   New Line Cinema, 1994

RICHARD EPCAR
MEMOIRS OF AN INVISIBLE MAN   Warner Bros., 1992

OMAR EPPS
Agent: Gersh Agency - Beverly Hills, 310/274-6611

JUICE   Paramount, 1992
THE PROGRAM   Buena Vista, 1993
MAJOR LEAGUE II   Warner Bros., 1994
HIGHER LEARNING   Columbia, 1994

ALVIN EPSTEIN
BEAUTY AND THE BEAST (AF)   Buena Vista, 1991 (voice)

PIERRE EPSTEIN
INDECENT PROPOSAL   Paramount, 1993

KATHRYN ERBE
Agent: William Morris Agency - Beverly Hills, 310/274-7451

WHAT ABOUT BOB?   Buena Vista, 1991
RICH IN LOVE   MGM/UA, 1993
D2: THE MIGHTY DUCKS   Buena Vista, 1994
KISS OF DEATH   20th Century Fox, 1995

TAMI ERIN
THE NEW ADVENTURES OF PIPPI LONGSTOCKING
   Columbia, 1988

LEE ERMEY
(R. Lee Ermey)
Agent: Harris & Goldberg - Los Angeles, 310/553-5200

FULL METAL JACKET   Warner Bros., 1987, British
FLETCH LIVES   Universal, 1989

DUKE ERNSBERGER
ERNEST RIDES AGAIN   Emshell Producers Group, 1993

LAURA ERNST
TOO MUCH SUN   New Line Cinema, 1991

GIANCARLO ESPOSITO
Agent: Badgley/Connor - Los Angeles, 310/278-9313

SWEET LORRAINE   Angelika Films, 1987
SCHOOL DAZE   Columbia, 1988
DO THE RIGHT THING   Universal, 1989
MO' BETTER BLUES   Universal, 1990
KING OF NEW YORK   New Line Cinema, 1990
BOB ROBERTS   Paramount/Miramax Films, 1992
FRESH   Miramax Films, 1994

CHRISTINE ESTABROOK
ALMOST YOU   TLC Films/20th Century Fox, 1984

EMILIO ESTEVEZ
b. May 12, 1963 - Los Angeles, California

TEX   Buena Vista, 1982
NIGHTMARES   Universal, 1983
THE OUTSIDERS   Warner Bros., 1983
REPO MAN   Universal, 1984
THE BREAKFAST CLUB   Universal, 1985
ST. ELMO'S FIRE   Columbia, 1985

**F
I
L
M

A
C
T
O
R
S**

THAT WAS THEN, THIS IS NOW   Paramount, 1985
MAXIMUM OVERDRIVE   DEG, 1986
WISDOM   20th Century Fox, 1986 (also directed)
STAKEOUT   Buena Vista, 1987
YOUNG GUNS   20th Century Fox, 1988
YOUNG GUNS II   20th Century Fox, 1990
MEN AT WORK   Triumph Releasing Corporation,
   1990 (also directed)
FREEJACK   Warner Bros., 1992
THE MIGHTY DUCKS   Buena Vista, 1992
NATIONAL LAMPOON'S LOADED WEAPON 1
   New Line Cinema, 1993
ANOTHER STAKEOUT   Buena Vista, 1993
JUDGMENT NIGHT   Universal, 1993
D2: THE MIGHTY DUCKS   Buena Vista, 1994
THE WAR AT HOME   Buena Vista, 1995 (also directed)

RAMON ESTEVEZ
MAN OF PASSION   Golden Sun Productions, 1988, Spanish
CADENCE   New Line Cinema, 1991

RENEE ESTEVEZ
HEATHERS   New World, 1989

ERIK ESTRADA
b. May 16, 1949 - New York, New York

THE NEW CENTURIONS   Columbia, 1972
TRACKDOWN   United Artists, 1976
FIRE! (TF)   Irwin Allen Productions/20th Century Fox TV, 1977
HOUR OF THE ASSASSIN   Concorde, 1987, U.S.-Peruvian
THE DIRTY DOZEN: THE FATAL MISSION (TF)
   MGM-UA TV, 1988
SHE KNOWS TOO MUCH (TF)   The Fred Silverman Company/
   Dinnegan-Pinchuk Productions/MGM-UA TV, 1989
SPIRITS   American Independent, 1991

ANGELO EVANS
ANGELO, MY LOVE   Cinecom, 1983

ART EVANS
RUTHLESS PEOPLE   Buena Vista, 1986
JO JO DANCER, YOUR LIFE IS CALLING   Columbia, 1986
NATIVE SON   Cinecom, 1986
WHITE OF THE EYE   Palisades Entertainment, 1987, British
THE MIGHTY QUINN   MGM/UA, 1989
FORCED EXPOSURE   Concorde, 1991
THE LOOTERS   Universal, 1992

EVANS EVANS
DEAD-BANG   Warner Bros., 1989

JOSH EVANS
DREAM A LITTLE DREAM   Vestron, 1989
BORN ON THE FOURTH OF JULY   Universal, 1989
RICOCHET   Warner Bros., 1991

LINDA EVANS
b. November 18, 1942 - Hartford, Connecticut
Agent: William Morris Agency - Beverly Hills, 310/274-7451

TWILIGHT OF HONOR   MGM, 1963
THOSE CALLOWAYS   1964
BEACH BLANKET BINGO   American International, 1965
FEMALE ARTILLERY (TF)   Universal TV, 1973
THE KLANSMAN   Paramount, 1974
MITCHELL   Allied Artists, 1975
NOWHERE TO RUN (TF)   MTM Enterprises, 1978
AVALANCHE EXPRESS   20th Century Fox, 1979
TOM HORN   Warner Bros., 1980
DYNASTY (TF)   Aaron Spelling Productions/Fox-Cat
   Productions, 1981
KENNY ROGERS AS THE GAMBLER—THE ADVENTURE
   CONTINUES (TF)   Lion Share Productions, 1983
THE LAST FRONTIER (TF)   McElroy & McElroy Productions,
   1986, Australian

TROY EVANS
ARTICLE 99   Orion, 1992
UNDER SIEGE   Warner Bros., 1992
ACE VENTURA: PET DETECTIVE   Warner Bros., 1994

CHAD EVERETT
(Raymond Cramton)
b. June 11, 1936 - South Bend, Indiana
Agent: Camden ITG - Los Angeles, 310/289-2700

CLAUDELLE INGLISH   Warner Bros., 1961
THE CHAPMAN REPORT   Warner Bros., 1962
ROME ADVENTURE   Warner Bros., 1962
GET YOURSELF A COLLEGE GIRL   MGM, 1964
THE SINGING NUN   MGM, 1966
MADE IN PARIS   MGM, 1966
JOHNNY TIGER   Universal, 1966
FIRST TO FIGHT   1967
THE LAST CHALLENGE   MGM, 1967
THE IMPOSSIBLE YEARS   MGM, 1968
THE FIRECHASERS (TF)   Rank, 1971, British
THE FRENCH ATLANTIC AFFAIR (TF)   Aaron Spelling Productions/
   MGM TV, 1979
THE INTRUDER WITHIN (TF)   1981
AIRPLANE II: THE SEQUEL   Paramount, 1982
THE ROUSTERS (TF)   Stephen J. Cannell Productions, 1983
FEVER PITCH   MGM/UA, 1985
THUNDERBOAT ROW (TF)   Stephen J. Cannell Productions, 1989

RUPERT EVERETT
PRINCESS DAISY (TF)   NBC Productions/Steve Krantz
   Productions, 1983
ANOTHER COUNTRY   Orion Classics, 1984, British
DANCE WITH A STRANGER   Samuel Goldwyn Company,
   1985, British
DUET FOR ONE   Cannon, 1986
THE RIGHT HAND MAN   FilmDallas, 1987, Australian
HEARTS OF FIRE   Lorimar, 1987, U.S.-British
CHRONICLE OF A DEATH FORETOLD   Island Pictures, 1988
THE COMFORT OF STRANGERS   Skouras Pictures, 1990, British
PRET-A-PORTER   Miramax Films, 1994
THE MADNESS OF GEORGE III   Samuel Goldwyn Company, 1995

TOM EVERETT
BEST OF THE BEST   Taurus Entertainment, 1989

NANCY EVERHARD
Agent: The Light Company - Los Angeles, 213/826-2230

DOUBLE REVENGE   Smart Egg Releasing, 1988
DEEPSTAR SIX   TriStar, 1989
THE TRIAL OF THE INCREDIBLE HULK (TF)   Bixby-Brandon
   Productions/New World TV, 1989
THE CHINA LAKE MURDERS (CTF)   Papazian-Hirsch
   Entertainment/MCA TV, 1990
THIS GUN FOR HIRE (CTF)   USA Cable, 1991

REX EVERHART
BEAUTY AND THE BEAST (AF)   Buena Vista, 1991 (voice)

GREG EVIGAN
b. October 14, 1953 - South Amboy, New Jersey
Agent: The Blake Agency - Beverly Hills, 310/246-0241

SCENE OF THE CRIME (TF)   J.E. Productions/Universal TV, 1984
STRIPPED TO KILL   Concorde, 1987
DEEPSTAR SIX   TriStar, 1989
THE LADY FORGETS (TF)   Leonard Hill Films, 1989

BARBARA EWING
WHEN THE WHALES CAME   20th Century Fox, 1989, British

BLAKE EWING
THE LITTLE RASCALS   Universal, 1994

MAYNARD EZIASHI
MISTER JOHNSON   Avenue Pictures, 1991
A GOOD MAN IN AFRICA   Gramercy Pictures, 1994

DANIEL EZRALOW
CAMORRA *UN COMPLICATO INTRIGO DI DONNE,*
   VICOLI E DELITTI   Cannon, 1986, Italian

AVA FABIAN
DRAGNET   Universal, 1987
WELCOME HOME ROXY CARMICHAEL   Paramount, 1990

JAQUES FABBRI
DIVA   United Artists Classics, 1982, French

FRANCO FABRIZI
GINGER AND FRED   MGM/UA, 1986, Italian-French-West German

WARREN FABRO
ALOHA SUMMER   *HANAUMA BAY*   Spectrafilm, 1988

JEFF FAHEY
PSYCHO III   Universal, 1986
CURIOSITY KILLS (CTF)   Dutch Productions, 1990
THE LAST OF THE FINEST   Orion, 1990
IMPULSE   Warner Bros., 1990
PARKER KANE (TF)   Parker Kane Productions/Silver Pictures TV/
   Orion TV, 1990
WHITE HUNTER, BLACK HEART   Warner Bros., 1990
BODY PARTS   Paramount, 1991
IRON MAZE   Castle Hill Productions, 1991, U.S.-Japanese
STEPHEN KING'S THE LAWNMOWER MAN
   New Line Cinema, 1992
WYATT EARP   Warner Bros., 1994

MAX FAIRCHILD
DEATH OF A SOLDIER   Scotti Brothers, 1986, Australian

MORGAN FAIRCHILD
b. February 3, 1950 - Dallas, Texas
Agent: Camden ITG - Los Angeles, 310/289-2700

THE DREAM MERCHANTS (TF)   Columbia TV, 1980
FLAMINGO ROAD (TF)   MF Productions/Lorimar Productions, 1980
THE SEDUCTION   Avco Embassy, 1981
PAPER DOLLS (TF)   Mandy Films Productions/MGM-UA TV, 1984
PEE-WEE'S BIG ADVENTURE   Warner Bros., 1985
CAMPUS MAN   Paramount, 1987
STREET OF DREAMS (TF)   Bill Stratton-Myrtos Productions/
   Phoenix Entertainment Group, 1988
HOW TO MURDER A MILLIONAIRE (TF)   Robert Greenwald
   Productions, 1990

HEATHER FAIRFIELD
A DEADLY SILENCE (TF)   Robert Greenwald Productions, 1989
THE WAR OF THE ROSES   20th Century Fox, 1989

ADAM FAITH
McVICAR   Crown International, 1981, British

LISANNE FALK
Agent: Gersh Agency - Beverly Hills, 310/274-6611

HEATHERS   New World, 1989

PETER FALK
b. September 16, 1927 - New York, New York
Agent: ICM - Beverly Hills, 310/550-4000

WIND ACROSS THE EVERGLADES   Warner Bros., 1958
THE BLOODY BROOD   1959, Canadian
PRETTY BOY FLOYD   1960
MURDER, INC. ✪   20th Century Fox, 1960
THE SECRET OF THE PURPLE REEF   1960
POCKETFUL OF MIRACLES ✪   United Artists, 1961
PRESSURE POINT   United Artists, 1962
THE BALCONY   Continental, 1963
IT'S A MAD MAD MAD MAD WORLD   United Artists, 1963
ROBIN AND THE SEVEN HOODS   Warner Bros., 1964
ITALIANO BRAVA GENTE   1965, Italian-Soviet
THE GREAT RACE   Warner Bros., 1965
TOO MANY THIEVES (TF)   1966
PENELOPE   MGM, 1966
LUV   Columbia, 1967
PRESCRIPTION MURDER (TF)   Universal TV, 1967
ANZIO   *LO SBARCO DI ANZIO*   Columbia, 1968, Italian
MACHINE GUN McCAIN   *GLI INTOCCABILI*   1969,
   Italian-Yugoslavian
CASTLE KEEP   Columbia, 1969
A STEP OUT OF LINE (TF)   Cinema Center, 1970
HUSBANDS   Columbia, 1970
OPERATION SNAFU   *SITUATION NORMAL ALL FOULED UP*
   1970, Italian-Yugoslavian
RANSOM FOR A DEAD MAN (TF)   Universal TV, 1971
A WOMAN UNDER THE INFLUENCE   Faces International, 1974
MURDER BY DEATH   Columbia, 1976
MIKEY AND NICKY   Paramount, 1976
GRIFFIN AND PHOENIX (TF)   ABC Circle Films, 1976
THE CHEAP DETECTIVE   Columbia, 1978
THE BRINK'S JOB   Universal, 1978
THE IN-LAWS   Columbia, 1979
...ALL THE MARBLES   MGM/United Artists, 1981
BIG TROUBLE   Columbia, 1986
HAPPY NEW YEAR   Columbia, 1987
THE PRINCESS BRIDE   20th Century Fox, 1987
WINGS OF DESIRE   *DER HIMMEL UBER BERLIN*   Orion Classics,
   1988, West German-French
VIBES   Columbia, 1988
COOKIE   Warner Bros., 1989
IN THE SPIRIT   Castle Hill Productions, 1990
TUNE IN TOMORROW   Cinecom, 1990
THE PLAYER   Fine Line Features/New Line Cinema, 1992
ROOMMATES   Buena Vista, 1994

SIOBHAN FALLON
THE PAPER   Universal, 1994
GREEDY   Universal, 1994

STEPHANIE FARACY
HEAVEN CAN WAIT   Paramount, 1978
WHEN YOU COMIN' BACK, RED RYDER?   Columbia, 1979
CLASSIFIED LOVE (TF)   CBS Entertainment, 1986
THE GREAT OUTDOORS   Universal, 1988

DANIEL FARALDO
WACO & RINEHART (TF)   Touchstone Films TV, 1987
ABOVE THE LAW   Warner Bros., 1988

DEBRAH FARENTINO
MENENDEZ: A KILLING IN BEVERLY HILLS (MS)   Zev Braun
   Pictures/TriStar Television, 1994
XXX'S & OOO'S (TF)   Moving Target Productions/New World
   Entertainment, 1994

Fa

**F
I
L
M

A
C
T
O
R
S**

JAMES FARENTINO
b. February 24, 1938 - Brooklyn, New York

PSYCHOMANIA *VIOLENT MIDNIGHT* 1963
ENSIGN PULVER Warner Bros., 1964
THE WAR LORD Universal, 1965
THE PAD AND HOW TO USE IT Universal, 1966
BANNING 1967
ROSIE! Universal, 1967
ME, NATALIE 1969
STORY OF A WOMAN 1970
JESUS OF NAZARETH (MS) Sir Lew Grade Productions/ITC,
    1978, British-Italian
SON-RISE: A MIRACLE OF LOVE (TF) 1979
THE FINAL COUNTDOWN United Artists, 1980
DEAD AND BURIED Avco Embassy, 1981
EVITA PERON (TF) Hartwest Productions/Zephyr
    Productions, 1981
A SUMMER TO REMEMBER (TF) Interplanetary Productions, 1985
THAT SECRET SUNDAY (TF) CBS Entertainment, 1986
FAMILY SINS (TF) London Films, Inc., 1987
THE RED SPIDER (TF) CBS Entertainment, 1988
WHO GETS THE FRIENDS? (TF) CBS Entertainment, 1988
NAKED LIE (TF) Shadowplay Films/Phoenix Entertainment
    Group, 1989
HER ALIBI Warner Bros., 1989
COMMON GROUND (MS) Daniel H. Blatt Productions/
    Lorimar TV, 1990
DAZZLED (TF) 1994
HONOR THY FATHER AND MOTHER: THE TRUE STORY OF
    THE MENENDEZ MURDERS (TF) Saban Entertainment, 1994

ANTONIO FARGAS
Agent: Gersh Agency - Beverly Hills, 310/274-6611

PUTNEY SWOPE Cinema 5, 1969
SHAFT MGM,, 1971
CLEOPATRA JONES Warner Bros., 1973
THE GAMBLER Paramount, 1974
CAR WASH Universal, 1976
NEXT STOP, GREENWICH VILLAGE 20th Century-Fox, 1976
PRETTY BABY Paramount, 1978
SHAKEDOWN Universal, 1988
I'M GONNA GIT YOU SUCKA MGM/UA, 1989

DENNIS FARINA
Agent: Getty's Agency - Chicago, 312/348-3333

THIEF United Artists, 1981
JO JO DANCER, YOUR LIFE IS CALLING Columbia, 1986
MANHUNTER DEG, 1986
MIDNIGHT RUN Universal, 1988
OPEN ADMISSIONS (TF) The Mount Company/Viacom
    Productions, 1988
THE CASE OF THE HILLSIDE STRANGLER (TF)
    Kenwood Productions/Fries Entertainment, 1989
BLIND FAITH (MS) NBC Productions, 1990
PEOPLE LIKE US (TF) ITC Productions, 1990
MEN OF RESPECT Columbia, 1991
SERIOUS MONEY New Line Cinema, 1991
ANOTHER STAKEOUT Buena Vista, 1993
STRIKING DISTANCE Columbia, 1993
LITTLE BIG LEAGUE Columbia, 1994

CHRIS FARLEY
Agent: CAA - Beverly Hills, 310/288-4545

THE CONEHEADS Paramount, 1993
AIRHEADS 20th Century Fox, 1994
BILLY THE THIRD Paramount, 1995

GARY FARMER
POWWOW HIGHWAY Warner Bros., 1989, U.S.-British
THE DARK WIND New Line Cinema, 1991

RICHARD FARNSWORTH
Agent: Twentieth Century Artists - Los Angeles, 213/850-5516

THE DUCHESS AND THE DIRTWATER FOX
    20th Century Fox, 1976
COMES A HORSEMAN O United Artists, 1978
TOM HORN Warner Bros., 1980
RESURRECTION Universal, 1908
THE GREY FOX United Artists Classics, 1983, Canadian
WALTZ ACROSS TEXAS Atlantic Releasing Corporation, 1983
THE NATURAL TriStar, 1984
RHINESTONE 20th Century Fox, 1984
SYLVESTER Columbia, 1985
SPACE RAGE Vestron, 1985
RUCKUS International Vision Productions, 1982
RED EARTH, WHITE EARTH (TF) Chris-Rose Productions, 1989
THE TWO JAKES Paramount, 1990
MISERY Columbia, 1990
THE GETAWAY Universal, 1994
LASSIE Paramount, 1994

JAMIE FARR
b. July 1, 1934 - Toledo, Ohio

RIDE BEYOND VENGEANCE Columbia, 1966
WHO'S MINDING THE MINT? Columbia, 1967
WITH SIX YOU GET EGG ROLL National General, 1968
THE BLUE KNIGHT (TF) Lorimar Productions, 1973
AMATEUR NIGHT AT THE DIXIE BAR AND GRILL (TF)
    Motown/Universal TV, 1979
THE CANNONBALL RUN 20th Century Fox, 1981
CANNONBALL RUN II Warner Bros., 1984
FOR LOVE OR MONEY (TF) Robert Papazian Productions/
    Henerson-Hirsch Productions, 1984
COMBAT HIGH (TF) Frank von Zerneck Productions/Lynch-Biller
    Productions, 1986
SCROOGED Paramount, 1988

MIKE FARRELL
b. February 6, 1939 - St. Paul, Minnesota
Agent: Paradigm - Los Angeles, 310/277-4400

THE GRADUATE Avco Embassy, 1967
PRIVATE SESSIONS (TF) The Belle Company/Seltzer-Gimbel
    Prods./Raven's Claw Productions/Comworld Productions, 1985
VANISHING ACT (TF) Robert Cooper Productions, 1986,
    U.S.-Canadian
A DEADLY SILENCE (TF) Robert Greenwald Productions, 1989
INCIDENT AT DARK RIVER (CTF) Farrell-Minoff Productions/Turner
    Network TV, 1989

TERRY FARRELL
Agent: Flick East/West Talent, Inc. - Los Angeles, 213/463-6333 or
    New York, 212/307-1850

BACK TO SCHOOL Orion, 1986

MIA FARROW
b. February 9, 1945 - Los Angeles, California
Agent: UTA - Beverly Hills, 310/273-6700

GUNS AT BATASI 20th Century Fox, 1964, British-U.S.
A DANDY IN ASPIC Columbia, 1968, British
ROSEMARY'S BABY Paramount, 1968
SECRET CEREMONY Universal, 1968, British-U.S.
JOHN AND MARY 20th Century Fox, 1969
SEE NO EVIL *BLIND TERROR* Columbia, 1971, British
FOLLOW ME! Rank Film Distributors, 1971, British
GOODBYE, RAGGEDY ANN (TF) Metromedia Producers
    Corporation, 1971
THE PUBLIC EYE Universal, 1972, British
HIGH HEELS *DOCTEUR POPAUL/SCOUNDREL IN WHITE*
    Les Films La Boetie, 1972, French-Italian
THE GREAT GATSBY Paramount, 1974
THE TEMPEST 1975, West German-French
THE HAUNTING OF JULIA *FULL CIRCLE* Discovery Films,
    1977, British-Canadian

AVALANCHE   New World Pictures, 1978
A WEDDING   20th Century Fox, 1978
DEATH ON THE NILE   Paramount, 1978, British
HURRICANE   Paramount, 1979
A MIDSUMMER NIGHT'S SEX COMEDY   Orion/Warner Bros., 1982
ZELIG   Orion/Warner Bros., 1983
BROADWAY DANNY ROSE   Orion, 1984
SUPERGIRL   Warner Bros., 1984, British
THE PURPLE ROSE OF CAIRO   Orion, 1985
HANNAH AND HER SISTERS   Orion, 1986
RADIO DAYS   Orion, 1987
SEPTEMBER   Orion, 1987
ANOTHER WOMAN   Orion, 1988
NEW YORK STORIES   Buena Vista, 1989
CRIMES AND MISDEMEANORS   Orion, 1989
ALICE   Orion, 1990
SHADOWS AND FOG   Orion, 1992
HUSBANDS AND WIVES   TriStar, 1992
WIDOWS' PEAK   Fine Line Features/New Line Cinema, 1994

STEPHANIE FARROW
ZELIG   Orion/Warner Bros., 1983
THE PURPLE ROSE OF CAIRO   Orion, 1985

LENA FARUGIA
THE GODS MUST BE CRAZY II   Columbia, 1990

BEN FAULKNER
SILENT FALL   Warner Bros., 1994

MICHAEL FAUSTINO
BLANK CHECK   Buena Vista, 1994

FARRAH FAWCETT
(Farrah Fawcett-Majors)
b. February 2, 1946 - Corpus Christi, Texas
Agent: William Morris Agency - Beverly Hills, 310/274-7451

LOVE IS A FUNNY THING   UN HOMME QUI ME PLAIT
   United Artists, 1970, French-Italian
MYRA BRECKINRIDGE   20th Century Fox, 1970
THE FEMINIST AND THE FUZZ (TF)   Screen Gems/
   Columbia TV, 1970
THE GREAT AMERICAN BEAUTY CONTEST (TF)
   ABC Circle Films, 1973
MURDER ON FLIGHT 502 (TF)   Spelling-Goldberg
   Productions, 1975
LOGAN'S RUN   MGM/United Artists, 1976
CHARLIE'S ANGELS (TF)   Spelling-Goldberg Productions, 1976
SOMEBODY KILLED HER HUSBAND   Columbia, 1978
SUNBURN   Paramount, 1979, U.S.-British
AN ALMOST PERFECT AFFAIR   Paramount, 1979
SATURN 3   AFD, 1980
MURDER IN TEXAS (TF)   Dick Clark Productions/
   Billy Hale Films, 1981
THE CANNONBALL RUN   20th Century Fox, 1981
THE RED-LIGHT STING (TF)   J.E. Productions/Universal TV, 1984
THE BURNING BED (TF)   Tisch-Avnet Productions, 1984
BETWEEN TWO WOMEN (TF)   The Jon Avnet Company, 1986
EXTREMITIES   Atlantic Releasing Corporation, 1986
NAZI HUNTER: THE BEATE KLARSFELD STORY (TF)
   William Kayden Productions/Orion TV/Silver Chalice/Revcom/
   George Walker TV/TF1/SFP, 1986, U.S.-British-French
POOR LITTLE RICH GIRL: THE BARBARA HUTTON STORY (MS)
   Lester Persky Productions/ITC Productions, 1987
SEE YOU IN THE MORNING   Warner Bros., 1989
MARGARET BOURKE-WHITE (CTF)   Turner Network TV/
   Project VII/Central TV Enterprises, 1989, U.S.-Canadian
SMALL SACRIFICES (MS)   Louis Rudolph Films/Motown
   Productions/Allarcom Ltd./Fries Entertainment, 1989,
   U.S.-Canadian
THE SUBSTITUTE WIFE (TF)   Frederick S. Pierce Company, 1994
MAN 2 MAN   Buena Vista, 1995

PAUL FEIG
HEAVYWEIGHTS   Buena Vista, 1994

MICHAEL FEINSTEIN
THIS CAN'T BE LOVE (TF)   Davis Entertainment/Pacific Motion
   Pictures/World International Network, 1994

FRITZ FELD
b. October 15, 1900 - Berlin, Germany

BARFLY   Cannon, 1987

COREY FELDMAN
Agent: APA - Los Angeles, 310/273-0744

TIME AFTER TIME   Orion/Warner Bros., 1979
FRIDAY THE 13TH   Paramount, 1980
FRIDAY THE 13TH - THE FINAL CHAPTER   Paramount, 1984
GREMLINS   Warner Bros., 1984
THE GOONIES   Warner Bros., 1985
STAND BY ME   Columbia, 1986
THE LOST BOYS   Warner Bros., 1987
LICENSE TO DRIVE   20th Century Fox, 1988
DREAM A LITTLE DREAM   Vestron, 1989
THE 'BURBS   Universal, 1989

TOVAH FELDSHUH
b. December 27, 1952 - New York, New York
Agent: William Morris Agency - Beverly Hills, 310/274-7451

SCREAM PRETTY PEGGY (TF)   Universal TV, 1973
THE AMAZING HOWARD HUGHES (TF)   Roger Gimbel
   Productions/EMI TV, 1977
TERROR OUT OF THE SKY (TF)   Alan Landsburg Productions, 1978
THE TRIANGLE FACTORY FIRE SCANDAL (TF)   Alan Landsburg
   Productions/Don Kirshner's Productions, 1979
CHEAPER TO KEEP HER   American Cinema, 1980
THE WOMEN'S ROOM (TF)   Philip Mandelken Productions/Warner
   Bros. TV, 1980
THE IDOLMAKER   United Artists, 1980
DANIEL   Paramount, 1983

NORMAN FELL
b. March 24, 1924 - Philadelphia, Pennsylvania

PORK CHOP HILL   United Artists, 1959
OCEAN'S ELEVEN   Warner Bros., 1960
THE GRADUATE   Avco Embassy, 1967
BULLITT   Warner Bros., 1968
IF IT'S TUESDAY, THIS MUST BE BELGIUM   United Artists, 1969
THE STONE KILLER   Columbia, 1973
GUARDIAN OF THE WILDERNESS   1976
THE END   United Artists, 1978
ON THE RIGHT TRACK   20th Century Fox, 1981
PATERNITY   Paramount, 1981
STRIPPED TO KILL   Concorde, 1987
FOR THE BOYS   20th Century Fox, 1991

JULIAN FELLOWES
BABY—SECRET OF THE LOST LEGEND   Buena Vista, 1985

FREDDY FENDER
THE MILAGRO BEANFIELD WAR   Universal, 1988

SHERILYN FENN
Agent: The Agency - Los Angeles, 310/551-3000

TWO MOON JUNCTION   Lorimar, 1988
WILD AT HEART   Samuel Goldwyn Company, 1990
OF MICE AND MEN   MGM-Pathe Communications, 1992
THREE OF HEARTS   New Line Cinema, 1993
BOXING HELENA   Orion Classics, 1993
FATAL INSTINCT   MGM/UA, 1993

LANCE FENTON
HEATHERS   New World, 1989

SARAH JANE FENTON
A GOOD MAN IN AFRICA   Gramercy Pictures, 1994

SIMON FENTON
MATINEE   Universal, 1993

JUAN FERNANDEZ
"CROCODILE" DUNDEE II   Paramount, 1988, U.S.-Australian
KINJITE (FORBIDDEN SUBJECTS)   Cannon, 1989
ACES: IRON EAGLE III   New Line Cinema, 1991

NANCY FERRARA
DANGEROUS GAME   MGM/UA, 1993

CONCHATA FERRELL
b. March 28, 1943 - Charleston, West Virginia

A DEATH IN CANAAN (TF)   Chris-Rose Productions/Warner
   Bros. TV, 1978
HEARTLAND   Levitt-Pickman, 1979
THE GIRL CALLED HATTER FOX (TF)   Roger Gimbel Productions/
   EMI TV, 1980
THE SEDUCTION OF MISS LEONA (TF)   Edgar J. Scherick
   Productions, 1981
RAPE AND MARRIAGE: THE RIDEOUT CASE (TF)   Stonehenge
   Productions/Blue Greene Productions/Lorimar Productions, 1981
NORTH BEACH AND RAWHIDE (MS)   CBS Entertainment, 1985
WHERE THE RIVER RUNS BLACK   MGM/UA, 1986
EYE ON THE SPARROW (TF)   Sarabande Productions/Republic
   Pictures, 1987
FOR KEEPS   TriStar, 1988
YOUR MOTHER WEARS COMBAT BOOTS (TF)   Kushner-Locke
   Productions, 1989
EDWARD SCISSORHANDS   20th Century Fox, 1990

TYRA FERRELL
JUNGLE FEVER   Universal, 1991
BOYZ N THE HOOD   Columbia, 1991
WHITE MEN CAN'T JUMP   20th Century Fox, 1992
POETIC JUSTICE   Columbia, 1993

MEL FERRER
(Melchior Gaston Ferrer)
b. August 25, 1917 - Elberon, New Jersey

LOST BOUNDARIES   1949
BORN TO BE BAD   RKO Radio, 1950
THE BRAVE BULLS   Columbia, 1951
RANCHO NOTORIOUS   RKO Radio, 1952
SCARAMOUCHE   MGM, 1952
LILI   MGM, 1953
KNIGHTS OF THE ROUND TABLE   MGM, 1954, British
SAADIA   MGM, 1954
FORBIDDEN   *PROIBITO*   1954, Italian
OH, ROSALINDA!   Associated British Picture Corporation,
   1955, British
WAR AND PEACE   Paramount, 1956, U.S.-Italian
PARIS DOES STRANGE THINGS   *ELENA ET LES HOMMES*
   Warner Bros., 1956, French-Italian
THE VINTAGE   MGM, 1957
THE SUN ALSO RISES   20th Century Fox, 1957
FRAULEIN   20th Century Fox, 1958
THE WORLD, THE FLESH AND THE DEVIL   MGM, 1959
L'HOMME A FEMMES   1960, French
BLOOD AND ROSES   *ET MOURIR DE PLAISIR*   Paramount,
   1960, French-Italian
THE HANDS OF ORLAC   *LES MAINS D'ORLAC*   1961,
   French-British
LEGGE DI GUERRA   1961, Italian
I LANCIERI NERI   1961, Italian
THE DEVIL AND THE TEN COMMANDMENTS   Union Films,
   1962, French-Italian
THE LONGEST DAY   20th Century Fox, 1962, U.S.-French
THE FALL OF THE ROMAN EMPIRE   Paramount, 1964
PARIS WHEN IT SIZZLES   Paramount, 1964
SEX AND THE SINGLE GIRL   Warner Bros., 1964
EL SEÑOR DE LA SALLE   1964, Spanish
EL GRECO   20th Century Fox, 1966, Italian-French
BRANNIGAN   United Artists, 1975, British-U.S.

GIRL FROM THE RED CABARET   1975, Spanish
DAS NETZ   1976, West German
IL CORSARO NERO   1976, Italian
EATEN ALIVE   *DEATH TRAP*   Virgo International, 1976
LA RAGAZZA IN PIGIAMA GIALLO   1978, Italian
THE NORSEMEN   American International, 1978
THE TEMPTER   *L'ANTI CRISTO*   1978, Italian
GUYANA: CULT OF THE DAMNED   1980, Mexican
THE FIFTH FLOOR   Film Ventures International, 1980
THE TOP OF THE HILL (TF)   Fellows-Keegan Company/
   Paramount TV, 1980
THE MEMORY OF EVA RYKER (TF)   Irwin Allen Productions, 1981
FUGITIVE FAMILY (TF)   Aubrey Hamner Productions, 1981
SEDUCED (TF)   Catalina Production Group/Comworld
   Productions, 1985
OUTRAGE! (TF)   Irwin Allen Productions/Columbia TV, 1986
DREAM WEST (MS)   Sunn Classic Pictures, 1986

MIGUEL FERRER
Agent: William Morris Agency - Beverly Hills, 310/274-7451

FLASHPOINT   TriStar, 1984
ROBOCOP   Orion, 1987
C.A.T. SQUAD: PYTHON WOLF (TF)   NBC Productions, 1988
DEEPSTAR SIX   TriStar, 1989
SHANNON'S DEAL (TF)   Stan Rogow Productions/
   NBC Productions, 1989
BLANK CHECK   Buena Vista, 1994
ROYCE (CTF)   Gerber/ITC Productions, 1994

MARTIN FERRERO
JURASSIC PARK   Universal, 1993

EVE FERRET
ABSOLUTE BEGINNERS   Orion, 1986, British

LOU FERRIGNO
THE INCREDIBLE HULK (TF)   Universal TV, 1977
THE INCREDIBLE HULK RETURNS (TF)   B&B Productions/New
   World TV, 1988
CAGE   New Century/Vista, 1989
THE TRIAL OF THE INCREDIBLE HULK (TF)   Bixby-Brandon
   Productions/New World TV, 1989
THE DEATH OF THE INCREDIBLE HULK (TF)   Bixby-Brandon
   Productions/New World TV, 1990

DEBRA FEUER
NIGHT ANGEL   Fries Distribution Company, 1990

MILES FEULNER
Agent: Susan Smith & Associates - Beverly Hills, 213/852-4777

LITTLE BIG LEAGUE   Columbia, 1994

WILLIAM FICHTNER
STRANGE DAYS   20th Century Fox, 1995

JOHN FIEDLER
b. Platville, Wisconsin - February 3, 1925

TWELVE ANGRY MEN   United Artists, 1957
STAGE STRUCK   RKO Radio, 1958
THAT TOUCH OF MINK   Universal, 1962
THE WORLD OF HENRY ORIENT   United Artists, 1964
KISS ME STUPID   Lopert, 1964
FITZWILLY   United Artists, 1967
THE ODD COUPLE   Paramount, 1968
TRUE GRIT   Paramount, 1969
MAKING IT   20th Century Fox, 1971
THE SHAGGY D.A.   Buena Vista, 1976
THE CANNONBALL RUN   20th Century Fox, 1981
SHARKY'S MACHINE   Orion/Warner Bros., 1981
SAVANNAH SMILES   Embassy, 1982

CHELSEA FIELD
Agent: Gersh Agency - Beverly Hills, 310/274-6611

NIGHTINGALES (TF)   Aaron Spelling Productions, 1988
SKIN DEEP   20th Century Fox, 1989
AN INCONVENIENT WOMAN (TF)   ABC Productions, 1991
HARLEY DAVIDSON & THE MARLBORO MAN   MGM-Pathe, 1991
THE LAST BOY SCOUT   The Geffen Company/Warner Bros., 1991
LOVE POTION #9   20th Century Fox, 1992
THE DARK HALF   Orion, 1993
THE BIRDS II: LAND'S END (CTF)   Showtime Entertainment, 1994
ROYCE (CTF)   Gerber/ITC Productions, 1994
ANDRE   Paramount, 1994

SALLY FIELD
b. November 6, 1946 - Pasadena, California
Agent: CAA - Beverly Hills, 310/288-4545

THE WAY WEST   United Artists, 1967
MAYBE I'LL COME HOME IN THE SPRING (TF)
   Metromedia Productions, 1970
HOME FOR THE HOLIDAYS (TF)   ABC Circle Films, 1972
MARRIAGE: YEAR ONE (TF)   Universal TV, 1971
STAY HUNGRY   United Artists, 1976
SYBIL (TF)   Lorimar Productions, 1976
SMOKEY AND THE BANDIT   Universal, 1977
HEROES   Universal, 1977
HOOPER   Warner Bros., 1978
THE END   United Artists, 1978
BEYOND THE POSEIDON ADVENTURE   Warner Bros., 1979
NORMA RAE ★★   20th Century Fox, 1979
SMOKEY AND THE BANDIT II   Universal, 1980
BACK ROADS   Warner Bros., 1981
ABSENCE OF MALICE   Columbia, 1981
KISS ME GOODBYE   20th Century Fox, 1982
PLACES IN THE HEART ★★   TriStar, 1984
MURPHY'S ROMANCE   Columbia, 1985
SURRENDER   Warner Bros., 1987
PUNCHLINE   Columbia, 1988
STEEL MAGNOLIAS   TriStar, 1989
NOT WITHOUT MY DAUGHTER   MGM-Pathe, 1991
SOAPDISH   Paramount, 1991
HOMEWARD BOUND: THE INCREDIBLE JOURNEY
   Buena Vista, 1993 (voice)
MRS. DOUBTFIRE   20th Century Fox, 1993
FORREST GUMP   Paramount, 1994
A WOMAN OF INDEPENDENT MEANS (MS)   Robert Greenwald
   Productions, 1995

SHIRLEY ANNE FIELD
b. June 27, 1938 - London, England

IT'S NEVER TOO LATE   1956, British
THE GOOD COMPANIONS   Rank, 1957, British
THE SILKEN AFFAIR   1957, British
HORRORS OF THE BLACK MUSEUM   1959, British
UPSTAIRS AND DOWNSTAIRS   20th Century Fox, 1959, British
ONCE MORE, WITH FEELING   Columbia, 1960
PEEPING TOM   Astor, 1960, British
THE ENTERTAINER   Continental, 1960, British
SATURDAY NIGHT AND SUNDAY MORNING   Continental,
   1960, British
WILD FOR KICKS   *BEAT GIRL*   1962, British
THESE ARE THE DAMNED   *THE DAMNED*   Columbia,
   1962, British
THE WAR LOVER   Columbia, 1962, British
LUNCH HOUR   Bryanston, 1962, British
KINGS OF THE SUN   United Artists, 1963
MAN IN THE MIDDLE   20th Century Fox, 1964, British-U.S.
CARNABY M.D.   *DOCTOR IN CLOVER*   Continental, 1966, British
ALFIE   Paramount, 1966, British
HOUSE OF THE LIVING DEAD   1977, British
MY BEAUTIFUL LAUNDRETTE (TF)   Orion Classics, 1985, British
GETTING IT RIGHT   MCEG, 1989, U.S.-British
HEAR MY SONG   Miramax Films, 1991

TODD FIELD
GROSS ANATOMY   Buena Vista, 1989
SLEEP WITH ME   MGM/UA, 1994

MAURIE FIELDS
DEATH OF A SOLDIER   Scotti Brothers, 1986, Australian

TONY FIELDS
TRICK OR TREAT   DEG, 1986

ROBERT FIELDSTEEL
MISS FIRECRACKER   Corsair Pictures, 1989

RALPH FIENNES
SCHINDLER'S LIST ⊙   Universal, 1993
QUIZ SHOW   Buena Vista, 1994
STRANGE DAYS   20th Century Fox, 1995
OLD FRIENDS   TriStar, 1995

HARVEY FIERSTEIN
Agent: Gersh Agency - Beverly Hills, 310/274-6611

TORCH SONG TRILOGY   New Line Cinema, 1988
MRS. DOUBTFIRE   20th Century Fox, 1993
BULLETS OVER BROADWAY   Miramax Films, 1994

TRAVIS FINE
Agent: Susan Smith & Associates - Beverly Hills, 213/852-4777

MENENDEZ: A KILLING IN BEVERLY HILLS (MS)   Zev Braun
   Pictures/TriStar Television, 1994

NATALIE FINLAND
LABYRINTH   TriStar, 1986, British

GEORGE FINN
YOUNGBLOOD   MGM/UA, 1986

JOHN FINN
Agent: Susan Smith & Associates - Beverly Hills, 213/852-4777

GLORY   TriStar, 1989

JOHN FINNEGAN
AN AMERICAN TAIL (AF)   Universal, 1986 (voice)

ALBERT FINNEY
b. May 9, 1936 - Salford, England
Agent: ICM - Beverly Hills, 310/550-4000

THE ENTERTAINER   Continental, 1960, British
SATURDAY NIGHT AND SUNDAY MORNING   Continental,
   1960, British
TOM JONES ★   Lopert, 1963, British
THE VICTORS   Columbia, 1963
NIGHT MUST FALL   Embass, 1964, British
TWO FOR THE ROAD   20th Century Fox, 1967, British-U.S.
CHARLIE BUBBLES   Regional, 1968, British (also directed)
THE PICASSO SUMMER   Warner Bros., 1969
SCROOGE   National General, 1970, British
GUMSHOE   Columbia, 1971, British
ALPHA BETA   Cine III, 1973, British
MURDER ON THE ORIENT EXPRESS ★   Paramount, 1974, British
THE DUELLISTS   Paramount, 1978, British
WOLFEN   Orion/Warner Bros., 1980
LOOPHOLE   MGM/United Artists, 1980, British
LOOKER   The Ladd Company/Warner Bros., 1981
SHOOT THE MOON   MGM/United Artists, 1982
ANNIE   Columbia, 1982
THE DRESSER ★   Columbia, 1983, British
UNDER THE VOLCANO ★   Universal, 1984
ORPHANS   Lorimar, 1987
THE ENDLESS GAME (CTF)   TVS Films/Reteitalia/Pixit, 1990,
   British-Italian
THE IMAGE (CTF)   HBO Pictures/Citadel Entertainment, 1990
MILLER'S CROSSING   20th Century Fox, 1990
THE PLAYBOYS   Samuel Goldwyn Company, 1992, Irish-British
RICH IN LOVE   MGM/UA, 1993
THE BROWNING VERSION   Paramount, 1994, British
THE RUN OF THE COUNTRY   Columbia, 1995

LINDA FIORENTINO
Agent: UTA - Beverly Hills, 310/273-6700

VISION QUEST   Warner Bros., 1985
GOTCHA!   Universal, 1985
AFTER HOURS   The Geffen Company/Warner Bros., 1985
THE MODERNS   Alive Films, 1988
NEON EMPIRE (CMS)   Richard Maynard Productions/Fries
   Entertainment, 1989
QUEENS LOGIC   New Line Cinema, 1991
THE LAST SEDUCTION   1994

RICHARD FIRE
POLTERGEIST III   MGM/UA, 1988

COLIN FIRTH
CAMILLE (TF)   Rosemont Productions, 1984, U.S.-British
ANOTHER COUNTRY   Orion Classics, 1984, British
DUTCH GIRLS (TF)   London Weekend TV, 1984, British
CAMILLE (TF)   Rosemont Productions, 1984, British
LOST EMPIRES (TF)   Granada TV, 1986, British
APARTMENT ZERO   Skouras Pictures, 1989
VALMONT   Orion, 1989, French
THE ADVOCATE   Miramax Films, 1994

PETER FIRTH
b. October 27, 1953 - Yorkshire, England
Agent: Susan Smith & Associates - Beverly Hills, 213/852-4777

BROTHER SUN, SISTER MOON   Paramount, 1973, Italian-British
DIAMONDS ON WHEELS   Buena Vista, 1972, U.S.-British
ACES HIGH   Cinema Shares International, 1977, British
EQUUS ✪   United Artists, 1977
JOSEPH ANDREWS   Paramount, 1977, British
WHEN YOU COMIN' BACK, RED RYDER?   Columbia, 1979
TESS   Columbia, 1980, French-British
THE AERODROME (TF)   BBC, 1983, British
LIFEFORCE   TriStar, 1985, British
LETTER TO BREZHNEV   Circle Releasing, 1985, British
THE INCIDENT (TF)   Qintex Entertainment, 1990
PRISONERS OF HONOR (CTF)   HBO Pictures/Dreyfuss-James
   Productions, 1991
SHADOWLANDS   Savoy Pictures, 1993, U.S.-British
AN AWFULLY BIG ADVENTURE   Fine Line Features/New Line
   Cinema, 1995, British

KATE FISCHER
SIRENS   Miramax Films, 1993, Australian-British-German

LAURENCE FISHBURNE
(Larry Fishburne)
Agent: Paradigm - Los Angeles, 310/277-4400

CORNBREAD, EARL AND ME   American International, 1975
FAST BREAK   Columbia, 1979
APOCALYPSE NOW   United Artists, 1979
WILLIE AND PHIL   20th Century Fox, 1980
DEATH WISH II   Filmways, 1982
RUMBLE FISH   Universal, 1983
THE COTTON CLUB   Orion, 1984
THE COLOR PURPLE   Warner Bros., 1985
QUICKSILVER   Columbia, 1986
GARDENS OF STONE   TriStar, 1987
A NIGHTMARE ON ELM STREET, PART 3: DREAM WARRIORS
   New Line Cinema, 1987
RED HEAT   TriStar, 1988
SCHOOL DAZE   Columbia, 1988
KING OF NEW YORK   New Line Cinema, 1990
CADENCE   New Line Cinema, 1991
BOYZ 'N THE HOOD   Columbia, 1991
WHAT'S LOVE GOT TO DO WITH IT ★   Buena Vista, 1993
SEARCHING FOR BOBBY FISCHER   Paramount, 1993
THE TOOL SHED   Buena Vista, 1994
HIGHER LEARNING   Columbia, 1994
JUST CAUSE   Warner Bros., 1995
WATERWORLD   Universal, 1995

CARRIE FISHER
b. October 21, 1956 - Los Angeles, California
Agent: CAA - Beverly Hills, 310/288-4545

SHAMPOO   Columbia, 1975
STAR WARS   20th Century Fox, 1977
LEAVE YESTERDAY BEHIND (TF)   ABC Circle Films, 1978
MR. MIKE'S MONDO VIDEO   New Line Cinema, 1979
THE EMPIRE STRIKES BACK   20th Century Fox, 1980
THE BLUES BROTHERS   Universal, 1980
UNDER THE RAINBOW   Orion/Warner Bros., 1981
RETURN OF THE JEDI   20th Century Fox, 1983
GARBO TALKS   MGM/UA, 1984
THE MAN WITH ONE RED SHOE   20th Century Fox, 1985
LIBERTY (TF)   Robert Greenwald Productions, 1986
HANNAH AND HER SISTERS   Orion, 1986
HOLLYWOOD VICE SQUAD   Concorde/Cinema Group, 1986
AMAZON WOMEN ON THE MOON   Universal, 1987
THE TIME GUARDIAN   Hemdale, 1987, Australian
APPOINTMENT WITH DEATH   Cannon, 1988, U.S.-British
THE 'BURBS   Universal, 1989
LOVERBOY   TriStar, 1989
WHEN HARRY MET SALLY...   Columbia, 1989
SWEET REVENGE (CTF)   The Movie Group, 1990, French-U.S.
SIBLING RIVALRY   Columbia, 1990
DROP DEAD FRED   New Line Cinema, 1991
SOAPDISH   Paramount, 1991
THIS IS MY LIFE   20th Century Fox, 1992

EDDIE FISHER
(Edwin Jack Fisher)
b. August 10, 1928 - Philadelphia, Pennsylvania

ALL ABOUT EVE   20th Century Fox, 1950
BUNDLE OF JOY   RKO Radio, 1956
BUTTERFIELD 8   MGM, 1960
NOTHING LASTS FOREVER   MGM/UA Classics, 1984

FRANCES FISHER
Agent: UTA - Beverly Hills, 310/273-6700

TOUGH GUYS DON'T DANCE   Cannon, 1987
PATTY HEARST   Atlantic Releasing Corporation, 1988
COLD SASSY TREE (CTF)   Faye Dunaway Productions/Ohlmeyer
   Communications/Turner Network TV, 1989
LUCY & DESI: BEFORE THE LAUGHTER (TF)   Larry Thompson
   Entertainment, 1991
UNFORGIVEN   Warner Bros., 1992
ATTACK OF THE 50-FOOT WOMAN (CTF)   HBO Pictures/Lorimar
   Productions, 1993
BABYFEVER   Rainbow Releasing, 1994
THE STARS FELL ON HENRIETTA   Warner Bros., 1995

GREGOR FISHER
THE GIRL IN THE PICTURE   Samuel Goldwyn Company,
   1986, British

TRICIA LEIGH FISHER
Agent: The Gordon/Rosson Company - Studio City, 818/509-1900

STICK   Universal, 1985
STRANGE VOICES (TF)   Forrest Hills Productions/Dacks-Geller
   Productions/TLC, 1987
BOOK OF LOVE   New Line Cinema, 1991

CIARAN FITZGERALD
INTO THE WEST   Miramax Films, 1993, British-Irish-Japanese

GERALDINE FITZGERALD
b. November 24, 1914 - Dublin, Ireland

BLIND JUSTICE   1934, British
OPEN ALL NIGHT   1934, British
THE LAD   1935, British
ACE OF SPADES   1935, British
THREE WITNESSES   1935, British
DEPARTMENT STORE   1935, British

LT. DARING R.N.   1935, British
TURN OF THE TIDE   1935, British
DEBT OF HONOR   1936, British
CAFE MASCOT   1936, British
THE MILL ON THE FLOSS   1937, British
WUTHERING HEIGHTS ✪   United Artists, 1939
DARK VICTORY   Warner Bros., 1939
A CHILD IS BORN   Warner Bros., 1940
'TILL WE MEET AGAIN   1940
FLIGHT FROM DESTINY   Warner Bros., 1941
SHINING VICTORY   Warner Bros., 1941
THE GAY SISTERS   Warner Bros., 1942
WATCH ON THE RHINE   Warner Bros., 1943
LADIES COURAGEOUS   1944
WILSON   20th Century Fox, 1944
UNCLE HARRY   THE STRANGE AFFAIR OF UNCLE HARRY
   Universal, 1945
THREE STRANGERS   Warner Bros., 1946
O.S.S.   Paramount, 1946
NOBODY LIVES FOREVER   Warner Bros., 1946
SO EVIL MY LOVE   Paramount, 1948, U.S.-British
THE OBSESSED   THE LATE EDWINA BLAKE   1951, British
TEN NORTH FREDERICK   1958
THE FIERCEST HEART   20th Century Fox, 1961
THE PAWNBROKER   Landau/Allied Artists, 1965
RACHEL RACHEL   Warner Bros., 1968
BELIEVE IN ME   MGM, 1971
THE LAST AMERICAN HERO   HARD DRIVER
   20th Century Fox, 1973
HARRY AND TONTO   20th Century Fox, 1974
ECHOES OF A SUMMER   THE LAST CASTLE   Cine Artists,
   1976, U.S.-Canadian
YESTERDAY'S CHILD (TF)   Paramount TV, 1977
THE QUINNS (TF)   Daniel Wilson Productions, 1977
THE MANGO TREE   1977, Australian
BYE BYE MONKEY   Fida, 1978, French-Italian
TRISTAN AND ISOLDE   LOVESPELL   Clar Productions, 1979, British
ARTHUR   Orion, 1981
EASY MONEY   Orion, 1983
KENNEDY (MS)   Central Independent Television Productions/Alan
   Landsburg Productions, 1983, British-U.S.
DO YOU REMEMBER LOVE? (TF)   Dave Bell Productions, 1985
POLTERGEIST II: THE OTHER SIDE   MGM/UA, 1986
CIRCLE OF VIOLENCE: A FAMILY DRAMA (TF)   Sheldon Pinchuk
   Productions/Rafshoon Communications/Finnegan Associates/
   Telepictures Productions, 1986
NIGHT OF COURAGE (TF)   Titus Productions, 1987
ARTHUR 2 ON THE ROCKS   Warner Bros., 1988

GREG FITZGERALD

WAR OF THE BUTTONS   Warner Bros., 1994

TARA FITZGERALD

Agent: William Morris Agency - Beverly Hills, 310/274-7451

HEAR MY SONG   Miramax Films, 1991, British-Irish
SIRENS   Miramax Films, 1993, Australian-British-German

FANNIE FLAGG

Agent: CAA - Beverly Hills, 310/288-4545

FIVE EASY PIECES   Columbia, 1970
STAY HUNGRY   United Artists, 1976
SEX AND THE MARRIED WOMAN (TF)   Universal TV, 1977
RABBIT TEST   Avco Embassy, 1978
GREASE   Paramount, 1978
FRIED GREEN TOMATOES   Universal, 1991 (uncredited)

JOE FLAHERTY

CLUB PARADISE   Warner Bros., 1986
ONE CRAZY SUMMER   Warner Bros., 1986
BACK TO THE FUTURE PART II   Universal, 1989

FIONNULA FLANAGAN

b. December 10, 1941 - Dublin, Ireland

YOUNGBLOOD   MGM/UA, 1986
WHITE MILE (CTF)   HBO Pictures, 1994

ED FLANDERS

b. December 29, 1934 - Minneapolis, Minnesota

GOODBYE, RAGGEDY ANN (TF)   Metromedia Producers
   Corporation, 1971
INDICT AND CONVICT (TF)   Universal TV, 1974
THE LEGEND OF LIZZIE BORDEN (TF)   Paramount TV, 1975
ELEANOR AND FRANKLIN (TF)   Talent Associates, 1976
THE AMAZING HOWARD HUGHES (TF)   Roger Gimbel
   Productions/EMI TV, 1977
MacARTHUR   Universal, 1977
BACKSTAIRS AT THE WHITE HOUSE (MS)   Ed Friendly
   Productions, 1979
SALEM'S LOT (TF)   Warner Bros. TV, 1979
THE NINTH CONFIGURATION   TWINKLE, TWINKLE,
   "KILLER" KANE   Warner Bros., 1980
TRUE CONFESSIONS   United Artists, 1981
THE PURSUIT OF D.B. COOPER   Universal, 1981
FINAL DAYS (TF)   The Samuels Film Company, 1989
THE EXORCIST III   20th Century Fox, 1990
THE PERFECT TRIBUTE (CTF)   Dorothea Petrie Productions/
   Proctor & Gamble Productions/World International Network, 1991

JAMES FLEET

FOUR WEDDINGS AND A FUNERAL   Gramercy Pictures,
   1994, British

SUSAN FLEETWOOD

THE SACRIFICE   Orion Classics, 1986, Swedish-French

CHARLES FLEISCHER

Agent: APA - Los Angeles, 310/273-0744

DEADLY FRIEND   Warner Bros., 1986
WHO FRAMED ROGER RABBIT   Buena Vista, 1988 (voice)
TUMMY TROUBLE (AS)   Buena Vista, 1989 (voice)
BACK TO THE FUTURE PART II   Universal, 1989
ROLLERCOASTER RABBIT (AS)   Buena Vista, 1990 (voice)
DICK TRACY   Buena Vista, 1990
STRAIGHT TALK   Buena Vista, 1992
THE PAGEMASTER   20th Century Fox, 1994 (voice)

NOAH FLEISS

JOSH AND S.A.M.   Columbia, 1993

DEXTER FLETCHER

CARAVAGGIO   British Film Institute, 1986, British
THE RACHEL PAPERS   MGM/UA, 1989, U.S.-British
TWISTED OBSESSION   Majestic Films International, 1990

LOUISE FLETCHER

b. 1934 - Birmingham, Alabama
Agent: Gersh Agency - Beverly Hills, 310/274-6611

CAN ELLEN BE SAVED? (TF)   ABC Circle Films, 1974
THIEVES LIKE US   United Artists, 1974
RUSSIAN ROULETTE   Avco Embassy, 1975, U.S.-Canadian
ONE FLEW OVER THE CUCKOO'S NEST ★★   United Artists, 1975
EXORCIST II: THE HERETIC   Warner Bros., 1977
THE CHEAP DETECTIVE   Columbia, 1978
THOU SHALT NOT COMMIT ADULTERY (TF)   Edgar J. Scherick
   Associates, 1978
THE LADY IN RED   GUNS, SIN AND BATHTUB GIN
   New World, 1979
THE MAGICIAN OF LUBLIN   Cannon, 1979,
   Israeli-West German-U.S.
THE LUCKY STAR   Pickman Films, 1980, Canadian
MAMA DRACULA   1980, French-Belgian
STRANGE BEHAVIOR   DEAD KIDS   World Northal, 1981,
   New Zealand-Australian
STRANGE INVADERS   Orion, 1983, Canadian
BRAINSTORM   MGM/UA, 1983
FIRESTARTER   Universal, 1984
A SUMMER TO REMEMBER (TF)   Interplanetary Productions, 1985
THE BOY WHO COULD FLY   20th Century Fox, 1986 (uncredited)
INVADERS FROM MARS   Cannon, 1986

NOBODY'S FOOL   Island Pictures, 1986
FLOWERS IN THE ATTIC   New World, 1987
TWO MOON JUNCTION   Lorimar, 1988
THE KAREN CARPENTER STORY (TF)   Welntraub Entertainment
   Group, 1989
BEST OF THE BEST   Taurus Entertainment/SVS Films, 1989
FINAL NOTICE (CTF)   Wilshire Court Productions/Sharm Hill
   Productions, 1989
BLUE STEEL   MGM/UA, 1990
THE PLAYER   Fine Line Features/New Line Cinema, 1992

DARLANNE FLEUGEL
Agent: Harris & Goldberg - Los Angeles, 310/553-5200

ONCE UPON A TIME IN AMERICA   The Ladd Company/Warner
   Bros., 1984, U.S.-Italian-Canadian
RUNNING SCARED   MGM/UA, 1986
TOUGH GUYS   Buena Vista, 1986
FREEWAY   New World, 1988
LOCK UP   TriStar, 1989

DANN FLOREK
FLIGHT OF THE INTRUDER   Paramount, 1991

KIM FLOWERS
NOBODY'S PERFECT   Moviestore Entertainment, 1990

CHARLES R. FLOYD
P.O.W. THE ESCAPE   Cannon, 1986

LARA FLYNN BOYLE
(See Lara Flynn BOYLE)

MIRIAM FLYNN
FOR KEEPS   TriStar, 1988

NINA FOCH
(Nina Consuelo Maud Fock)
b. April 20, 1924 - Leyden, Holland
Agent: William Morris Agency - Beverly Hills, 310/274-7451

THE RETURN OF THE VAMPIRE   Columbia, 1943
NINE GIRLS   Columbia, 1943
CRY OF THE WEREWOLF   Columbia, 1944
SHADOWS IN THE NIGHT   Columbia, 1944
A SONG TO REMEMBER   Columbia, 1945
MY NAME IS JULIA ROSS   Columbia, 1945
I LOVE A MYSTERY   Columbia, 1945
ESCAPE IN THE FOG   Columbia, 1945
PRISON SHIP   Columbia, 1945
JOHNNY O'CLOCK   Columbia, 1947
THE GUILT OF JANET AMES   Columbia, 1947
THE DARK PAST   Columbia, 1948
THE UNDERCOVER MAN   Columbia, 1949
JOHNNY ALLEGRO   1949
AN AMERICAN IN PARIS   MGM, 1951
ST. BENNY THE DIP   United Artists, 1951
SCARAMOUCHE   MGM, 1952
YOUNG MAN WITH IDEAS   MGM, 1952
FAST COMPANY   MGM, 1953
SOMBRERO   MGM, 1953
EXECUTIVE SUITE ○   MGM, 1954
FOUR GUNS TO THE BORDER   1954
YOU'RE NEVER TOO YOUNG   Paramount, 1955
ILLEGAL   Warner Bros., 1955
THE TEN COMMANDMENTS   Paramount, 1956
THREE BRAVE MEN   1957
CASH McCALL   Warner Bros., 1959
SPARTACUS   Universal, 1960
PRESCRIPTION: MURDER (TF)   Universal TV, 1968
GIDGET GROWS UP (TF)   Screen Gems/Columbia TV, 1969
SUCH GOOD FRIENDS   Paramount, 1971
FEMALE ARTILLERY (TF)   Universal TV, 1973
SALTY   1975
MAHOGANY   Paramount, 1975

THE GREAT HOUDINIS (TF)   ABC Circle Films, 1976
JENNIFER   1978
SHADOW CHASERS (TF)   Johnson-Grazer Productions/
   Warner Bros. TV, 1985
OUTBACK BOUND (TF)   Andrew Gottlieb Productions/
   CBS Entertainment, 1988
SKIN DEEP   20th Century Fox, 1989
SLIVER   Paramount, 1993
MORNING GLORY   Academy Entertainment, 1993

DAVID FOIL
sex, lies, and videotape   Miramax Films, 1989

DAVID FOLEY
Agent: William Morris Agency - Beverly Hills, 310/274-7451

IT'S PAT   Buena Vista, 1994

ELLEN FOLEY
Agent: Gersh Agency - Beverly Hills, 310/274-6611

HAIR   United Artists, 1979
FATAL ATTRACTION   Paramount, 1987
MARRIED TO THE MOB   Orion, 1988

ALISON FOLLAND
UNTITLED VAN SANT/ZISKIN   Columbia, 1995

MEGAN PORTER FOLLOWS
(Megan Follows)
Agent: Susan Smith & Associates - Beverly Hills, 213/852-4777

SIN OF INNOCENCE (TF)   Renee Valente Productions/Jeremac
   Productions/20th Century Fox TV, 1986
INHERIT THE WIND (TF)   Vincent Pictures Productions/David
   Greene-Robert Papazian Productions, 1988
THE NUTCRACKER PRINCE (AF)   Warner Bros., 1990 (voice)

BRIDGET FONDA
Agent: UTA - Beverly Hills, 310/273-6700

ARIA   Miramax Films, 1988, British
YOU CAN'T HURRY LOVE   MCEG, 1988
SHAG   Hemdale, 1988
OUT OF THE RAIN   Acme Company, 1989
SCANDAL   Miramax Films, 1989
STRAPLESS   Miramax Films, 1990
ROGER CORMAN'S FRANKENSTEIN UNBOUND
   FRANKENSTEIN UNBOUND   20th Century Fox, 1990
THE GODFATHER, PART III   Paramount, 1990
DROP DEAD FRED   New Line Cinema, 1991
DOC HOLLYWOOD   Warner Bros., 1991
IRON MAZE   Castle Hill Productions, 1991, U.S.-Japanese
LEATHER JACKETS   Triumph Releasing Corporation, 1991
SINGLE WHITE FEMALE   Columbia, 1992
SINGLES   Warner Bros., 1992
POINT OF NO RETURN   Warner Bros., 1993
BODIES, REST & MOTION   Fine Line Features/
   New Line Cinema, 1993
LITTLE BUDDHA   Miramax Films, 1994, British-French
IT COULD HAPPEN TO YOU   TriStar, 1994
CAMILLA   Miramax Films, 1994, British-Canadian
THE ROAD TO WELLVILLE   Columbia, 1994
ROUGH MAGIC   Savoy Pictures, 1995
CITY HALL   Columbia, 1995

JANE FONDA
b. December 21, 1937 - New York, New York
Agent: CAA - Beverly Hills, 310/288-4545

TALL STORY   Warner Bros., 1960
WALK ON THE WILD SIDE   Columbia, 1962
THE CHAPMAN REPORT   Warner Bros., 1962
PERIOD OF ADJUSTMENT   MGM, 1962
IN THE COOL OF THE DAY   1963

SUNDAY IN NEW YORK   MGM, 1963
JOY HOUSE   *LES FÉLINS/THE LOVE CAGE*   MGM, 1964, French
CIRCLE OF LOVE   *LA RONDE*   Continental, 1964, French-Italian
CAT BALLOU   Columbia, 1965
THE CHASE   Columbia, 1966
THE GAME IS OVER   *LA CURÉE*   Royal Films International,
   1966, French-Italian
ANY WEDNESDAY   Warner Bros., 1966
HURRY SUNDOWN   Paramount, 1967
BAREFOOT IN THE PARK   Paramount, 1966
SPIRITS OF THE DEAD   *HISTOIRES EXTRAORDINAIRES*
   ("Metzengerstein" episode)   American International, 1968, French
BARBARELLA   Paramount, 1968, Italian-French
THEY SHOOT HORSES, DON'T THEY? ★   Cinerama Releasing
   Corporation, 1969
KLUTE ★★   Warner Bros., 1971
TOUT VA BIEN   New Yorker, 1972, French-Italian
F.T.A.   *FREE THE ARMY*   American International, 1972
STEELYARD BLUES   Warner Bros., 1973
A DOLL'S HOUSE   Paramount, 1973, Canadian-U.S.
INTRODUCTION TO THE ENEMY (FD)   1974
THE BLUE BIRD   20th Century Fox, 1976, U.S.-Soviet
FUN WITH DICK AND JANE   Columbia, 1977
JULIA ★   20th Century Fox, 1977
COMING HOME ★★   United Artists, 1978
COMES A HORSEMAN   United Artists, 1978
CALIFORNIA SUITE   Columbia, 1978
THE CHINA SYNDROME ★   Columbia, 1979
THE ELECTRIC HORSEMAN   Columbia, 1979
NO NUKES (FD)   Warner Bros., 1980
NINE TO FIVE   20th Century Fox, 1980
ON GOLDEN POND ⊙   Universal/AFD, 1981
ROLLOVER   Orion/Warner Bros., 1981
THE DOLLMAKER (TF)   Finnegan Associates/IPC Films, Inc./
   Dollmaker Productions, 1984
AGNES OF GOD   Columbia, 1985
THE MORNING AFTER ★   20th Century Fox, 1986
LEONARD PART 6   Columbia, 1987
OLD GRINGO   Columbia, 1989
STANLEY & IRIS   MGM/UA, 1990

PETER FONDA
b. February 23, 1939 - New York, New York

TAMMY AND THE DOCTOR   1963
THE VICTORS   Columbia, 1963
LILITH   Columbia, 1964
THE YOUNG LOVERS   1964
THE WILD ANGELS   American International, 1966
THE TRIP   American International, 1967
SPIRITS OF THE DEAD   *HISTOIRES EXTRAORDINAIRES*
   ("Metzengerstein" episode)   American International, 1968, French
EASY RIDER   Columbia, 1969
THE HIRED HAND   Universal, 1971 (also directed)
THE LAST MOVIE   Universal, 1971
TWO PEOPLE   Universal, 1973
DIRTY MARY CRAZY LARRY   20th Century Fox, 1974
OPEN SEASON   1974, Spanish
RACE WITH THE DEVIL   20th Century Fox, 1975
92 IN THE SHADE   United Artists, 1975
THE DIAMOND MERCENARIES   *KILLER FORCE*   American
   International, 1975, British-Swiss
FUTUREWORLD   American International, 1976
FIGHTING MAD   20th Century Fox, 1976
OUTLAW BLUES   Warner Bros., 1977
HIGH-BALLIN'   1978
WANDA NEVADA   United Artists, 1979 (also directed)
THE HOSTAGE TOWER (TF)   Jerry Leider Productions, 1980
THE CANNONBALL RUN   20th Century Fox, 1981
SPLIT IMAGE   Orion, 1982
A REASON TO LIVE (TF)   Rastar Productions/Robert Papazian
   Productions, 1985
BODIES, REST & MOTION   Fine Line Features/
   New Line Cinema, 1993

PHIL FONDACARO
TROLL   Empire Pictures, 1986

HALLIE FOOTE
Agent: The Blake Agency - Beverly Hills, 310/246-0241

ON VALENTINE'S DAY   *STORY OF A MARRIAGE*
   Angelika Films, 1986

HORTON FOOTE, JR.
ON VALENTINE'S DAY   *STORY OF A MARRIAGE*
   Angelika Films, 1986

JUNE FORAY
DUCK TALES THE MOVIE: THE SECRET OF THE LOST LAMP (AF)
   Buena Vista, 1990 (voice)
HANS CHRISTIAN ANDERSEN'S THUMBELINA (AF)
   Warner Bros., 1994 (voice)

MICHELLE FORBES
Agent: UTA - Beverly Hills, 310/273-6700

KALIFORNIA   Gramercy Pictures, 1993

FAITH FORD
b. September 14 - Alexandria, Virginia
Agent: UTA - Beverly Hills, 310/273-6700

NORTH   Columbia, 1994

HARRISON FORD
b. July 13, 1942 - Chicago, Illinois
Contact: McQueeney Management - Los Angeles, 310/277-1882

DEAD HEAT ON A MERRY-GO-ROUND   Paramount, 1966
A TIME FOR KILLING   *THE LONG RIDE HOME*   Columbia, 1967
LUV   Columbia, 1967
JOURNEY TO SHILOH   Universal, 1968
THE INTRUDERS (TF)   Universal TV, 1970
ZABRISKIE POINT   MGM, 1970
GETTING STRAIGHT   Columbia, 1970
AMERICAN GRAFFITI   Universal, 1973
THE CONVERSATION   Paramount, 1974
THE POSSESSED (TF)   Warner Bros. TV, 1977
HEROES   Universal, 1977
STAR WARS   20th Century Fox, 1977
FORCE 10 FROM NAVARONE   American International, 1978
HANOVER STREET   Columbia, 1979
THE FRISCO KID   Warner Bros., 1979
APOCALYPSE NOW   United Artists, 1979
THE EMPIRE STRIKES BACK   20th Century-Fox, 1980
RAIDERS OF THE LOST ARK   Paramount, 1981
BLADE RUNNER   The Ladd Company/Warner Bros., 1982
RETURN OF THE JEDI   20th Century Fox, 1983
INDIANA JONES AND THE TEMPLE OF DOOM   Paramount, 1984
WITNESS ★   Paramount, 1985
THE MOSQUITO COAST   Warner Bros., 1986
FRANTIC   Warner Bros., 1988
WORKING GIRL   20th Century Fox, 1988
INDIANA JONES AND THE LAST CRUSADE   Paramount, 1989
PRESUMED INNOCENT   Warner Bros., 1990
REGARDING HENRY   Paramount, 1991
PATRIOT GAMES   Paramount, 1992
THE FUGITIVE   Warner Bros., 1993
JIMMY HOLLYWOOD   Paramount, 1994 (uncredited)
CLEAR AND PRESENT DANGER   Paramount, 1994
SABRINA   Paramount, 1995

MARIA FORD
DANCE WITH DEATH   Concorde, 1991
DEATHSTALKER IV   Concorde, 1991

MICK FORD
HOW TO GET AHEAD IN ADVERTISING   Warner Bros.,
   1989, British

STEVEN FORD
WHEN HARRY MET SALLY...   Columbia, 1989

TOMMY FORD
HARLEM NIGHTS   Paramount, 1989

KEN FOREE
FROM BEYOND   Empire Pictures, 1986

AMANDA FOREMAN
SLIVER   Paramount, 1993

DEBORAH FOREMAN
VALLEY GIRL   Atlantic Releasing Corporation, 1983
MY CHAUFFEUR   Crown International, 1985
APRIL FOOL'S DAY   Paramount, 1986
WAXWORK   Vestron, 1988
THE EXPERTS   Paramount, 1989

CLAIRE FORIANI
POLICE ACADEMY: MISSION TO MOSCOW   Warner Bros., 1994

RICHARD FORONJY
THE MORNING AFTER   20th Century Fox, 1986
MIDNIGHT RUN   Universal, 1988

VERONICA FORQUE
WHAT HAVE I DONE TO DESERVE THIS?   Cinevista,
   1985, Spanish

FREDERIC FORREST
Agent: Camden ITG - Los Angeles, 310/289-2700

WHEN THE LEGENDS DIE   20th Century Fox, 1972
THE DON IS DEAD   Universal, 1973
THE CONVERSATION   Paramount, 1974
THE GRAVY TRAIN   *THE DION BROTHERS*   Columbia, 1974
LARRY (TF)   Tomorrow Entertainment, 1974
HUCKLEBERRY FINN (TF)   ABC Circle Films, 1975
PROMISE HIM ANYTHING (TF)   ABC Circle Films, 1975
PERMISSION TO KILL   1975, British
THE MISSOURI BREAKS   United Artists, 1977
IT LIVES AGAIN   Warner Bros., 1978
RUBY AND OSWALD (TF)   Alan Landsburg Productions, 1978
APOCALYPSE NOW   United Artists, 1979
THE ROSE ✪   20th Century Fox, 1979
ONE FROM THE HEART   Columbia, 1982
HAMMETT   Orion/Warner Bros., 1982
SAIGON—YEAR OF THE CAT (TF)   Thames TV, 1983, British
VALLEY GIRL   Atlantic Releasing Corporation, 1983
WHO WILL LOVE MY CHILDREN? (TF)   ABC Circle Films, 1983
CALAMITY JANE (TF)   CBS Entertainment, 1983
BEST KEPT SECRETS (TF)   ABC Circle Films, 1984
THE STONE BOY   TLC Films/20th Century Fox, 1984
QUO VADIS (TF)   1985, Italian
RETURN   Silver Productions, 1985
RIGHT TO KILL? (TF)   Wrye-Konigsberg Productions/Taper Media
   Enterprises/Telepictures Productions, 1985
WHERE ARE THE CHILDREN? (TF)   Columbia, 1985
THE DELIBERATE STRANGER (MS)   Stuart Phoenix Productions/
   Lorimar-Telepictures, 1986
STACKING   *SEASON OF DREAMS*   Spectrafilm, 1987
LITTLE GIRL LOST (TF)   Marian Rees Associates, 1988
BERYL MARKHAM: A SHADOW ON THE SUN (MS)
   Tamara Asseyev Productions/New World TV, 1988
TUCKER - THE MAN AND HIS DREAM   Paramount, 1988
LONESOME DOVE (MS)   Motown Productions/Pangaea/Qintex
   Entertainment, Inc., 1989
MUSIC BOX   TriStar, 1989
THE TWO JAKES   Paramount, 1990
THE GAME   Shapiro Glickenhaus Entertainment, 1991
FALLING DOWN   Warner Bros., 1993
LASSIE   Paramount, 1994

STEVE FORREST
(William Forrest Andrews)
b. September 29, 1924 - Huntsville, Texas

THE BAD AND THE BEAUTIFUL   MGM, 1952
THE CLOWN   MGM, 1953
BATTLE CIRCUS   MGM, 1953
DREAM WIFE   MGM, 1953
SO BIG   Warner Bros., 1953
TAKE THE HIGH GROUND   MGM, 1953
PHANTOM OF THE RUE MORGUE   Warner Bros., 1954
PRISONER OF WAR   MGM, 1954
ROGUE COP   MGM, 1954
BEDEVILLED   MGM, 1955
THE LIVING IDOL   MGM, 1957
IT HAPPENED TO JANE   Columbia, 1959
FIVE BRANDED WOMEN   Paramount, 1960, Italian-Yugoslavian
HELLER IN PINK TIGHTS   Paramount, 1960
FLAMING STAR   20th Century Fox, 1960
THE SECOND TIME AROUND   20th Century-Fox, 1961
THE LONGEST DAY   20th Century Fox, 1962
THE YELLOW CANARY   20th Century Fox, 1963
RASCAL   1969
THE WILD COUNTRY   Buena Vista, 1971
THE LATE LIZ   1971
WANTED: THE SUNDANCE WOMAN (TF)
   20th Century Fox TV, 1976
NORTH DALLAS FORTY   Paramount, 1979
MOMMIE DEAREST   Paramount, 1981
THE MANIONS OF AMERICA (MS)   Roger Gimbel Productions/EMI
   TV/Argonaut Films, Ltd., 1981
MALIBU (TF)   Hamner Productions/Columbia TV, 1983
HOLLYWOOD WIVES (MS)   Aaron Spelling Productions, 1985
SPIES LIKE US   Warner Bros., 1985
GUNSMOKE: RETURN TO DODGE (TF)   CBS Entertainment, 1987

SUSAN FORRISTAL
Agent: Flick East/West Talent, Inc. - Los Angeles, 213/463-6333 or
   New York, 212/307-1850

L.A. STORY   TriStar, 1991

ROBERT FORSTER
(Robert Foster, Jr.)
b. July 13, 1941 - Rochester, New York
Agent: APA - Los Angeles, 310/273-0744

REFLECTIONS IN A GOLDEN EYE   Warner Bros., 1967
THE STALKING MOON   National General, 1969
JUSTINE   20th Century Fox, 1969
MEDIUM COOL   Paramount, 1969
PIECES OF DREAMS   United Artists, 1970
COVER ME BABE   20th Century Fox, 1970
JOURNEY THROUGH ROSEBUD   GSF, 1972
THE DEATH SQUAD (TF)   Spelling-Goldberg Productions, 1973
THE DON IS DEAD   Universal, 1973
NAKIA (TF)   1974
STUNTS   *WHO IS KILLING THE STUNTMENT?*
   New Line Cinema, 1977
AVALANCHE   New World, 1978
STANDING TALL (TF)   QM Productions, 1978
THE BLACK HOLE   Buena Vista, 1979
ALLIGATOR   Group 1, 1980
GOLIATH AWAITS (MS)   Larry White Productions/Hugh Benson
   Productions/Columbia TV, 1981
VIGILANTE   *STREET GANG*   Artists Releasing Corporation/Film
   Ventures International, 1983
THE DELTA FORCE   Cannon, 1986
29TH STREET   20th Century Fox, 1991
SCANNER COP 2   Republic Pictures, 1994

JOHN FORSYTHE
b. January 29, 1918 - Penns Grove, New Jersey
Agent: Paradigm - Los Angeles, 310/277-4400

DESTINATION TOKYO   Warner Bros., 1943
THE CAPTIVE CITY   United Artists, 1952
THE GLASS WEB   Universal, 1953

IT HAPPENS EVERY THURSDAY   Universal, 1953
ESCAPE FROM FORT BRAVO   MGM, 1953
THE TROUBLE WITH HARRY   Paramount, 1955
THE AMBASSADOR'S DAUGHTER   1956
SEE HOW THEY RUN (TF)   Universal TV, 1964
KITTEN WITH A WHIP   Universal, 1964
MADAME X   Universal, 1966
IN COLD BLOOD   Columbia, 1967
TOPAZ   Universal, 1969
THE HAPPY ENDING   United Artists, 1969
MURDER ONCE REMOVED (TF)   Metromedia Productions, 1971
THE HEALERS (TF)   Warner Bros. TV, 1975
CHARLIE'S ANGELS (TF)   Spelling-Goldberg Productions,
   1976 (voice; uncredited)
TAIL GUNNER JOE (TF)   Universal TV, 1977
GOODBYE AND AMEN   Cineriz, 1978, Italian-French
THE USERS (MS)   Aaron Spelling Productions, 1979
...AND JUSTICE FOR ALL   Columbia, 1979
DYNASTY (TF)   Aaron Spelling Productions/Fox-Cat
   Productions, 1981
ON FIRE (TF)   Robert Greenwald Productions, 1987
SCROOGED   Paramount, 1988

WILLIAM FORSYTHE
(Bill Forsythe)
Agent: UTA - Beverly Hills, 310/273-6700

CLOAK & DAGGER   Universal, 1984
ONCE UPON A TIME IN AMERICA   The Ladd Company/
   Warner Bros., 1984, U.S.-Italian-Canadian
THE LIGHTSHIP   Castle Hill Productions, 1985, U.S.-West German
RAISING ARIZONA   20th Century Fox, 1987
EXTREME PREJUDICE   TriStar, 1987
WEEDS   DEG, 1987
PATTY HEARST   Atlantic Releasing Corporation, 1988
DEAD-BANG   Warner Bros., 1989
TORRENTS OF SPRING   Millimeter Films, 1989, Italian-French
BLIND FAITH (MS)   NBC Productions, 1990
DICK TRACY   Buena Vista, 1990
CAREER OPPORTUNITES   Universal, 1991
OUT FOR JUSTICE   Warner Bros., 1991
STONE COLD   Columbia, 1991
THE WATERDANCE   Samuel Goldwyn Company, 1992
THE GUN IN BETTY LOU'S HANDBAG   Buena Vista, 1992
THINGS TO DO IN DENVER WHEN YOU'RE DEAD
   Miramax Films, 1995

NICK APOLLO FORTE
BROADWAY DANNY ROSE   Orion, 1984

JODIE FOSTER
b. November 19, 1962 - Bronx, New York
Agent: ICM - Beverly Hills, 310/550-4000

NAPOLEON AND SAMANTHA   Buena Vista, 1972
KANSAS CITY BOMBER (TF)   MGM, 1972
TOM SAWYER   United Artists, 1973
ONE LITTLE INDIAN   Buena Vista, 1973
ALICE DOESN'T LIVE HERE ANYMORE   Warner Bros., 1974
ECHOES OF A SUMMER   *THE LAST CASTLE*   Cine Artists,
   1976, U.S.-Canadian
TAXI DRIVER ✪   Columbia, 1976
BUGSY MALONE   Paramount, 1976, British
FREAKY FRIDAY   Buena Vista, 1977
THE LITTLE GIRL WHO LIVES DOWN THE LANE
   American International, 1977, U.S.-Canadian-French
IL COSOTTO   1977, Italian
MOI FLEUR BLEUE   1977, French
CANDLESHOE   Buena Vista, 1977
CARNY   United Artists, 1980
FOXES   United Artists, 1980
O'HARA'S WIFE   Davis-Panzer Productions, 1982
SVENGALI (TF)   Robert Halmi Productions, 1983
THE HOTEL NEW HAMPSHIRE   Orion, 1984
THE BLOOD OF OTHERS   *LE SANG DES AUTRES* (CMS)   HBO
   Premiere Films/ICC/Filmax Productions, 1984, Canadian-French
MESMERIZED   RKO/Challenge Corporation Services, 1986,
   New Zealand-Australian-British

SIESTA   Lorimar, 1987
FIVE CORNERS   Cineplex Odeon, 1988
STEALING HOME   Warner Bros., 1988
THE ACCUSED ★★   Paramount, 1988
BACKTRACK   *CATCHFIRE*   Vestron, 1991
THE SILENCE OF THE LAMBS ★★   Orion, 1991
LITTLE MAN TATE   Orion, 1991 (also directed)
SHADOWS AND FOG   Orion, 1992
SOMMERSBY   Warner Bros., 1993
MAVERICK   Warner Bros., 1994
NELL   20th Century Fox, 1994

KIMBERLY FOSTER
Agent: APA - Los Angeles, 310/273-0744

ONE CRAZY SUMMER   Warner Bros., 1986
DRAGNET   Universal, 1987

MEG FOSTER
THE DEATH OF ME YET (TF)   Aaron Spelling Productions, 1971
SUNSHINE (TF)   Universal TV, 1973
THINGS IN THEIR SEASON (TF)   Tomorrow Entertainment, 1974
JAMES DEAN (TF)   The Jozak Company, 1976
A DIFFERENT STORY   Avco Embassy, 1979
THE LEGEND OF SLEEPY HOLLOW   Sunn Classic Pictures, 1979
CARNY   United Artists, 1980
GUYANA TRAGEDY: THE STORY OF JIM JONES (TF)
   The Konigsberg Company, 1980
TICKET TO HEAVEN   United Artists Classics, 1981, Canadian
THE OSTERMAN WEEKEND   20th Century Fox, 1983
THE EMERALD FOREST   Embassy, 1985, British
THEY LIVE   Universal, 1988
RELENTLESS   New Line Cinema, 1989
BLIND FURY   TriStar, 1990
DEAD ON   New Line Cinema, 1991
FUTUREKICK   Conocrde, 1991

STACIE FOSTER
CYBER-TRACKER   PM Entertainment, 1994

DENYS FOUQUERAY
EMINENT DOMAIN   Triumph Releasing Corporation, 1990,
   Canadian-French-Israeli

EDWARD FOX
A BRIDGE TOO FAR   United Artists, 1977, British
SKULLDUGGERY   Universal, 1970
GANDHI   Columbia, 1982, British-Indian
THE BOUNTY   Orion, 1984, British
ANASTASIA: THE MYSTERY OF ANNA (MS)   Telecom
   Entertainment/Consolidated Productions/Reteitalia, 1986,
   U.S.-Italian
A HAZARD OF HEARTS (TF)   The Grade Company/Gainsborough
   Pictures, 1987, British

JAMES FOX
b. May 19, 1939 - London, England

THOROUGHLY MODERN MILLIE   Universal, 1967
PERFORMANCE   Warner Bros., 1970, British
GREYSTOKE: THE LEGEND OF TARZAN, LORD OF THE APES
   Warner Bros., 1984, British-U.S.
A PASSAGE TO INDIA   Columbia, 1984, British
ABSOLUTE BEGINNERS   Orion, 1986, British
BERYL MARKHAM: A SHADOW ON THE SUN (MS)
   Tamara Asseyev Productions/New World TV, 1988
FAREWELL TO THE KING   Orion, 1989
THE MIGHTY QUINN   MGM/UA, 1989
THE RUSSIA HOUSE   MGM-Pathe, 1990
AFRAID OF THE DARK   New Line Cinema, 1991
PATRIOT GAMES   Paramount, 1992
THE REMAINS OF THE DAY   Columbia, 1993, British

KIRK FOX
WYATT EARP   Warner Bros., 1994

MICHAEL J. FOX
b. June 9, 1961 - Edmonton, Alberta, Canada
Agent: CAA - Beverly Hills, 310/288-4545

MIDNIGHT MADNESS   Buena Vista, 1980
CLASS OF 1984   United Film Distribution, 1982, Canadian
POISON IVY (TF)   NBC Productions, 1985
BACK TO THE FUTURE   Universal, 1985
TEEN WOLF   Atlantic Releasing Corporation, 1985
FAMILY TIES VACATION (TF)   Paramount TV/Ubu Productions/
   NBC Entertainment, 1985
THE SECRET OF MY SUCCESS   Universal, 1987
LIGHT OF DAY   TriStar, 1987
DEAR AMERICA: LETTERS HOME FROM VIETNAM (FD)
   Taurus Entertainment, 1987 (voice)
BRIGHT LIGHTS, BIG CITY   MGM/UA, 1988
CASUALTIES OF WAR   Columbia, 1989
BACK TO THE FUTURE PART II   Universal, 1989
BACK TO THE FUTURE PART III   Universal, 1990
THE HARD WAY   Universal, 1991
DOC HOLLYWOOD   Warner Bros., 1991
HOMEWARD BOUND: THE INCREDIBLE JOURNEY
   Buena Vista, 1993 (voice)
LIFE WITH MIKEY   Buena Vista, 1993
FOR LOVE OR MONEY   Universal, 1993
GREEDY   Universal, 1994
DON'T DRINK THE WATER (TF)   ABC, 1994
THE AMERICAN PRESIDENT   Columbia, 1995

SEAN FOX
3 NINJAS KICK BACK   TriStar, 1994

ROBERT FOXWORTH
b. November 1, 1941 - Houston, Texas
Agent: APA - Los Angeles, 310/273-0744

FRANKENSTEIN (TF)   Dan Curtis Productions, 1973
THE DEVIL'S DAUGHTER (TF)   Paramount TV, 1973
THE QUESTOR TAPES (TF)   Universal TV, 1974
MRS. SUNDANCE (TF)   20th Century Fox TV, 1974
JAMES DEAN (TF)   The Jozak Company, 1976
TREASURE OF MATECUMBE   Buena Vista, 1976
IT HAPPENED AT LAKEWOOD MANOR (TF)   Alan Landsburg
   Productions, 1977
DEATH MOON (TF)   Roger Gimbel Productions/EMI TV, 1978
DAMIEN: OMEN II   20th Century Fox, 1978
PROPHECY   Paramount, 1979
THE BLACK MARBLE   Avco Embassy, 1980
PERSONAL CHOICE   Moviestore Entertainment, 1988
THE RETURN OF DESPERADO (TF)   Walter Mirisch Productions/
   Charles E. Sellier, Jr. Productions/Universal TV, 1988
DOUBLE STANDARD (TF)   Louis Rudolph Productions/Fenton
   Entertainment Group/Fries Entertainment, 1988
FACE TO FACE (TF)   Qintex Productions, 1990

VICTORIA FOYT
BABYFEVER   Rainbow Releasing, 1994

CARLA FRACCI
NIJINSKY   Paramount, 1980

JONATHAN FRAKES
Agent: Paradigm - Los Angeles, 310/277-4400

STAR TREK GENERATIONS   Paramount, 1994

ANTHONY (TONY) FRANCIOSA
(Anthony Papaleo)
b. October 28, 1928 - New York, New York

A FACE IN THE CROWD   Warner Bros., 1957
THIS COULD BE THE NIGHT   MGM, 1957
A HATFUL OF RAIN ★   20th Century Fox, 1957
WILD IS THE WIND   Paramount, 1957
THE LONG HOT SUMMER   MGM, 1958
THE NAKED MAJA   United Artists, 1959, Italian-U.S.

CAREER   Paramount, 1959
THE STORY ON PAGE ONE   1960
SENILITA   Zebra Film/Aera Film, 1961, Italian-French
GO NAKED IN THE WORLD   MGM, 1961
PERIOD OF ADJUSTMENT   MGM, 1962
RIO CONCHOS   20th Century Fox, 1964
THE PLEASURE SEEKERS   20th Century Fox, 1964
A MAN COULD GET KILLED   Universal, 1966
ASSAULT ON A QUEEN   Paramount, 1966
THE SWINGER   Paramount, 1966
FATHOM   20th Century Fox, 1967, British
THE SWEET RIDE   20th Century Fox, 1968
IN ENEMY COUNTRY   1968
A MAN CALLED GANNON   Universal, 1969
ACROSS 110TH STREET   United Artists, 1972
THE DROWNING POOL   Warner Bros., 1975
THE WORLD IS FULL OF MARRIED MEN   New Realm,
   1979, British
FIREPOWER   AFD, 1979, British
DEATH WISH II   Filmways, 1982
UNSANE   *TENEBRAE*   Bedford Entertainment/Film Gallery,
   1982, Italian
STAGECOACH (TF)   Raymond Katz Productions/Heritage
   Entertainment, 1986
BLOOD VOWS: THE STORY OF A MAFIA WIFE (TF)
   Louis Rudolph Films/Fries Entertainment, 1987

DON FRANCKS
JOHNNY MNEMONIC   TriStar, 1994

CHARLES FRANK
A LETTER TO THREE WIVES (TF)   Michael Filerman Productions/
   20th Century Fox TV, 1985

JOANNA FRANK
ALWAYS   Samuel Goldwyn Company, 1985

MARILYN DODDS FRANK
GRUNT! THE WRESTLING MOVIE   New World, 1986

TONY FRANK
RUSH   MGM-Pathe, 1991
THE SUBSTITUTE WIFE (TF)   Frederick S. Pierce Company, 1994

AL FRANKEN
ONE MORE SATURDAY NIGHT   Columbia, 1986
STUART SMALLEY   Paramount, 1995

WILLIAM FRANKFATHER
ALAMO BAY   TriStar, 1985

ARETHA FRANKLIN
b. March 25, 1942 - Memphis, Tennessee
Agent: William Morris Agency - Beverly Hills, 310/274-7451

THE BLUES BROTHERS   Universal, 1980

DIANE FRANKLIN
Agent: Special Artists Agency - Beverly Hills, 310/859-9688

THE LAST AMERICAN VIRGIN   Cannon, 1982
AMITYVILLE II: THE POSSESSION   Orion, 1982
TERRORVISION   Empire Pictures, 1986

JOE FRANKLIN
b. 1925 - New York, New York

BROADWAY DANNY ROSE   Orion, 1984

JOHN FRANKLIN
THE ADDAMS FAMILY   Paramount, 1991
ADDAMS FAMILY VALUES   Paramount, 1993

DENNIS FRANZ
b. October 28, 1944 - Chicago, Illinois
Agent: Paradigm - Los Angeles, 310/277-4400

DRESSED TO KILL   Filmways, 1980
BLOW OUT   Filmways, 1981
BODY DOUBLE   Columbia, 1984
DEADLY MESSAGES (TF)   Columbia TV, 1985
KISS SHOT (TF)   London Productions/Whoop, Inc., 1989
THE PACKAGE   Orion, 1989

BRENDAN FRASER
Agent: William Morris Agency - Beverly Hills, 310/274-7451

ENCINO MAN   Buena Vista, 1992
SCHOOL TIES   Paramount, 1992
GUILTY UNTIL PROVEN INNOCENT (TF)   NBC, 1993
WITH HONORS   Warner Bros., 1994
IN THE ARMY NOW   Buena Vista, 1994
AIRHEADS   20th Century Fox, 1994
THE SCOUT   20th Century Fox, 1994
BALTO (AF)   Universal, 1995 (voice)

RUPERT FRAZER
EMPIRE OF THE SON   Warner Bros., 1987

RON FRAZIER
Agent: Susan Smith & Associates - Beverly Hills, 213/852-4777

HEAD OFFICE   TriStar, 1986
FAT MAN AND LITTLE BOY   Paramount, 1989

LEILA FRECHET
CHANEL SOLITAIRE   United Film Distribution, 1981, French-British

AL FREEMAN, JR.
b. March 21, 1934 - San Antonio, Texas

MALCOLM X   Warner Bros., 1992

J.E. FREEMAN
MILLER'S CROSSING   20th Century Fox, 1990
IT COULD HAPPEN TO YOU   TriStar, 1994

JONATHAN FREEMAN
ALADDIN (AF)   Buena Vista, 1992 (voice)

KATHLEEN FREEMAN
Agent: Henderson/Hogan - Beverly Hills, 310/274-7815

WILD HARVEST   Paramount, 1947
THE NAKED CITY   Universal, 1948
THE SAXON CHARM   1948
MR. BELVEDERE GOES TO COLLEGE   20th Century-Fox, 1949
A PLACE IN THE SUN   Paramount, 1951
SINGIN' IN THE RAIN   MGM, 1952
THE BAD AND THE BEAUTIFUL   MGM, 1952
THE GREATEST SHOW ON EARTH   Paramount, 1952
LONELY HEART BANDITS   1952
BONZO GOES TO COLLEGE   1952
FULL HOUSE   1952
THE AFFAIRS OF DOBIE GILLIS   MGM, 1953
ATHENA   1954
THE FAR COUNTRY   Universal, 1954
THE FLY   20th Century Fox, 1958
NORTH TO ALASKA   20th Century Fox, 1960
THE LADIES MAN   Paramount, 1961
THE ERRAND BOY   Paramount, 1962
THE NUTTY PROFESSOR   Paramount, 1963
THE DISORDERLY ORDERLY   Paramount, 1964
MARRIAGE ON THE ROCKS   Warner Bros., 1965
THE ROUNDERS   MGM, 1965
THREE ON A COUCH   Columbia, 1966
SUPPORT YOUR LOCAL GUNFIGHTER   United Artists, 1971
STAND UP AND BE COUNTED   Columbia, 1972
THE BLUES BROTHERS   Universal, 1980

DRAGNET   Universal, 1987
GREMLINS 2 THE NEW BATCH   Warner Bros., 1990

MORGAN FREEMAN
b. June 1, 1937 - Memphis, Tennessee
Agent: William Morris Agency - Beverly Hills, 310/274-7451

TEACHERS   MGM/UA, 1984
THE ATLANTA CHILD MURDERS (MS)   Mann-Rafshoon
   Productions/Finnegan Associates, 1985
THAT WAS THEN...THIS IS NOW   Paramount, 1985
RESTING PLACE (TF)   Marian Rees Associates, 1986
FIGHT FOR LIFE (TF)   Fries Entertainment, 1987
STREET SMART ✪   Cannon, 1987
CLEAN AND SOBER   Warner Bros., 1988
LEAN ON ME   Warner Bros., 1989
JOHNNY HANDSOME   TriStar, 1989
DRIVING MISS DAISY ★   Warner Bros., 1989
GLORY   TriStar, 1989
THE BONFIRE OF THE VANITIES   Warner Bros., 1990
ROBIN HOOD: PRINCE OF THIEVES   Warner Bros., 1991
THE POWER OF ONE   Warner Bros., 1992
UNFORGIVEN   Warner Bros., 1992
THE SHAWSHANK REDEMPTION   Columbia, 1994
OUTBREAK   Warner Bros., 1995
THE AMERICAN PRESIDENT   Columbia, 1995

PAUL FREEMAN
RAIDERS OF THE LOST ARK   Paramount, 1981
SHANGHAI SURPRISE   MGM/UA, 1986, British-U.S.
WITHOUT A CLUE   Orion, 1988
ACES: IRON EAGLE III   New Line Cinema, 1991

STEPHANE FREISS
VAGABOND   *SANS TOIT NI LOI*   Grange Communications/
   IFEX Film, 1985, French

SUSAN FRENCH
HOUSE   New World, 1986

MATT FREWER
Agent: Paradigm - Los Angeles, 310/277-4400

FAR FROM HOME   Vestron, 1989
HONEY, I SHRUNK THE KIDS   Buena Vista, 1989
SHORT TIME   20th Century Fox, 1990
THE TAKING OF BEVERLY HILLS   Orion, 1991
NATIONAL LAMPOON'S SENIOR TRIP   New Line Cinema, 1995

SAMI FREY
BLACK WIDOW   20th Century Fox, 1987
WAR AND REMEMBRANCE (MS)   Dan Curtis Productions/
   ABC Circle Films, 1988-89

BRENDA FRICKER
Agent: Writers & Artists Agency - Los Angeles, 213/820-2240

MY LEFT FOOT ✪✪   Miramax Films, 1989, Irish-British
THE FIELD   Avenue Pictures, 1990, Irish-British
HOME ALONE 2: LOST IN NEW YORK   20th Century Fox, 1992
SO I MARRIED AN AXE MURDERER   TriStar, 1993
ANGELS IN THE OUTFIELD   Buena Vista, 1994

TOM FRIDLEY
FRIDAY THE 13TH, PART VI: JASON LIVES   Paramount, 1986

LISA FRIEDE
DANGEROUS LOVE   Motion Picture Corporation of America, 1988

PETER FRIEDMAN
Agent: Gersh Agency - New York, 212/997-1818

THE SEVENTH SIGN   TriStar, 1988
SINGLE WHITE FEMALE   Columbia, 1992
BLINK   New Line Cinema, 1994

COLIN FRIELS
MALCOLM Vestron, 1986, Australian
HIGH TIDE TriStar, 1987, Australian
GROUND ZERO Avenue Pictures, 1988
DARKMAN Universal, 1990
A GOOD MAN IN AFRICA Gramercy Pictures, 1994

DAVID FRISHBERG
BREAKING IN Samuel Goldwyn Company, 1989

SADIE FROST
BRAM STOKER'S DRACULA *DRACULA* Columbia, 1992
A PYROMANIAC'S LOVE STORY Buena Vista, 1995

CATHERINE FROT
SORCERESS European Classics, 1988, French

TOBY FROUD
LABYRINTH TriStar, 1986, British

STEPHEN FRY
Agent: William Morris Agency - Beverly Hills, 310/274-7451

PETER'S FRIENDS Samuel Goldwyn Company, 1992, British
I.Q. Paramount, 1994

SEAN FRYE
E.T. THE EXTRA-TERRESTRIAL Universal, 1982

LEO FUCHS
AVALON TriStar, 1990

ALAN FUDGE
MY DEMON LOVER New Line Cinema, 1987
TOO YOUNG TO DIE? (TF) von Zerneck-Sertner Films, 1990

JOHN FUJIOKA
AMERICAN NINJA Cannon, 1985

KURT FULLER
GHOSTBUSTERS II Columbia, 1989
NO HOLDS BARRED New Line Cinema, 1989
CAPITAL NEWS (TF) MTM Enterprises, 1990
WAYNE'S WORLD Paramount, 1992

ROBERT FULLER
MAVERICK Warner Bros., 1994

ANNETTE FUNICELLO
b. October 22, 1942 - Utica, New York

JOHNNY TREMAIN Buena Vista, 1957
THE SHAGGY DOG Buena Vista, 1959
BABES IN TOYLAND Buena Vista, 1961
BEACH PARTY American International, 1963
MUSCLE BEACH PARTY American International, 1963
BIKINI BEACH American International, 1964
THE MISADVENTURES OF MERLIN JONES Buena Vista, 1964
THE MONKEY'S UNCLE Buena Vista, 1965
BEACH BLANKET BINGO American International, 1965
HOW TO STUFF A WILD BIKINI American International, 1965
FIREBALL 500 American International, 1966
BACK TO THE BEACH Paramount, 1987

EDWARD FURLONG
TERMINATOR 2: JUDGMENT DAY TriStar, 1991
PET SEMATARY II Paramount, 1992
AMERICAN HEART Triton Pictures, 1993
A HOME OF OUR OWN Gramercy Pictures, 1993
BRAINSCAN Triumph Releasing Corporation, 1994
LITTLE ODESSA New Line Cinema, 1994
BEFORE AND AFTER Buena Vista, 1995

JOHN FURLONG
WYATT EARP Warner Bros., 1994

DEBORRA-LEE FURNESS
SHAME Skouras Pictures, 1988, Australian
THE LAST OF THE FINEST Orion, 1990

STEPHEN FURST
NATIONAL LAMPOON'S ANIMAL HOUSE Universal, 1978
SWIM TEAM 1979
TAKE DOWN Buena Vista, 1979
MIDNIGHT MADNESS Buena Vista, 1980
THE UNSEEN 1981
SILENT RAGE Columbia, 1982
NATIONAL LAMPOON'S CLASS REUNION 20th Century Fox, 1982
UP THE CREEK Orion, 1984
IF IT'S TUESDAY, IT STILL MUST BE BELGIUM (TF)
   Eisenstock & Mintz Productions, 1987
THE DREAM TEAM Universal, 1989

SASSON GABAI
STEAL THE SKY (CTF) HBO Pictures/Yoram Ben Ami Productions/
   Paramount TV, 1988

EVA GABOR
b. 1921 - Hungary

PACIFIC BLACKOUT 1941
FORCED LANDING 1941
A ROYAL SCANDAL 20th Century Fox, 1945
THE WIFE OF MONTE CRISTO Producers Releasing Corporation, 1946
SONG OF SURRENDER Paramount, 1949
PARIS MODEL Columbia, 1953
THE MAD MAGICIAN Columbia, 1954
THE LAST TIME I SAW PARIS MGM, 1954
ARTISTS AND MODELS Paramount, 1955
MY MAN GODFREY Universal, 1957
DON'T GO NEAR THE WATER MGM, 1957
GIGI MGM, 1958
THE TRUTH ABOUT WOMEN 1958
IT STARTED WITH A KISS MGM, 1959
LOVE ISLAND 1960
A NEW KIND OF LOVE Paramount, 1963
YOUNGBLOOD HAWKE Warner Bros., 1964
THE ARISTOCATS (AF) Buena Vista, 1970 (voice)
THE RESCUERS (AF) Buena Vista, 1977 (voice)
THE PRINCESS ACADEMY Empire Pictures, 1987
RETURN TO GREEN ACRES (TF) JaYgee Prods./Orion TV, 1990
THE RESCUERS DOWN UNDER (AF) Buena Vista, 1990 (voice)

ZSA ZSA GABOR
b. Hungary

LOVELY TO LOOK AT MGM, 1952
MOULIN ROUGE United Artists, 1952, British
THE STORY OF THREE LOVES MGM, 1953
LILI MGM, 1953
THREE RING CIRCUS Paramount, 1954
PUBLIC ENEMY NUMBER ONE 1954, French
DEATH OF A SCOUNDREL 1956
THE GIRL IN THE KREMLIN 1957
THE MAN WHO WOULDN'T TALK British Lion, 1958, British
TOUCH OF EVIL Universal, 1958
QUEEN OF OUTER SPACE Allied Artists, 1958
PEPE Columbia, 1960
BOYS' NIGHT OUT MGM, 1962

PICTURE MOMMY DEAD   Embassy, 1966
ARRIVEDERCI, BABY!   *DROP DEAD DARLING*   Paramount, 1966
JACK OF DIAMONDS   MGM, 1967, U.S.-West German
UP THE FRONT   1972, British
EVERY GIRL SHOULD HAVE ONE   1978
THE NAKED GUN 2 1/2: THE SMELL OF FEAR   Paramount, 1991
HAPPILY EVER AFTER (AF)   First National Film Corporation,
   1993 (voice)
THE BEVERLY HILLBILLIES   20th Century Fox, 1993

PETER GABRIEL
b. February 13, 1950 - London, England

NEW YORK STORIES   Buena Vista, 1989

JENNY GAGO
Agent: Paul Kohner, Inc. - Los Angeles, 310/550-1060

UNDER FIRE   Orion, 1983
IRRECONCILABLE DIFFERENCES   Warner Bros., 1984
NO MAN'S LAND   Orion, 1987
INNERSPACE   Warner Bros., 1987
BEST SELLER   Orion, 1987
CONVICTED: A MOTHER'S STORY (TF)   NBC Productions, 1987
OUT ON A LIMB (MS)   Stan Marhulies Company/
   ABC Circle Films, 1987
OLD GRINGO   Columbia, 1989

BOYD GAINES
HEARTBREAK RIDGE   Warner Bros., 1986

COURTNEY GAINS
THE 'BURBS   Universal, 1989
MEMPHIS BELLE   Warner Bros., 1990

CHARLOTTE GAINSBOURG
Agent: William Morris Agency - Beverly Hills, 310/274-7451

THE LITTLE THIEF   Miramax Films, 1989, French
THE CEMENT GARDEN   October Films, 1993,
   German-British-French

MICHEL GALABRU
LA CAGE AUX FOLLES 3: THE WEDDING   1985, Italian-French

ANNA GALIENA
BEING HUMAN   Warner Bros., 1994

MEGAN GALLACHER
THE BIRDS II: LAND'S END (CTF)   Showtime Entertainment, 1994

PETER GALLAGHER
Agent: ICM - Beverly Hills, 310/550-4000

THE IDOLMAKER   United Artists, 1980
SUMMER LOVERS   Filmways, 1982
THE CAINE MUTINY COURTMARTIAL (TF)
   CBS Entertainment, 1988
THE MURDER OF MARY PHAGAN (MS)   George Stevens, Jr.
   Productions/Century Tower Productions, 1988
I'LL BE HOME FOR CHRISTMAS (TF)   NBC Productions, 1988
sex, lies, and videotape   Miramax Films, 1989
LOVE AND LIES (TF)   Freyda Rothstein Productions/
   ITC Entertainment Group, 1990
TUNE IN TOMORROW   Cinecom, 1990
MORTAL THOUGHTS   Columbia, 1991
LATE FOR DINNER   Columbia, 1991
THE PLAYER   Fine Line Features/New Line Cinema, 1992
BOB ROBERTS   Paramount/Miramax Films, 1992
MALICE   Columbia, 1993
SHORT CUTS   Fine Line Features/New Line Cinema, 1993
MOTHER'S BOYS   Dimension/Miramax Films, 1994
WHITE MILE (CTF)   HBO Pictures, 1994
MRS. PARKER AND THE VICIOUS CIRCLE   Fine Line Features/
   New Line Cinema, 1994
WHILE YOU WERE SLEEPING   Buena Vista, 1995

GINA GALLEGO
Agent: Belson & Klass Associates - Beverly Hills, 310/274-9169

THE MEN'S CLUB   Atlantic Releasing Corporation, 1986
MY DEMON LOVER   New Line Cinema, 1987
PERSONALS (CTF)   Sharmhill Productions/Wilshire Court
   Productions, 1990, Canadian-U.S.

ZACH GALLIGAN
JACOBO TIMERMAN: PRISONER WITHOUT A NAME, CELL
   WITHOUT A NUMBER (TF)   Chrysalis-Yellin Productions, 1983
NOTHING LASTS FOREVER   MGM/UA Classics, 1984
GREMLINS   Warner Bros., 1984
SURVIVING (TF)   Telepictures Productions, 1985
WAXWORK   Vestron, 1988
GREMLINS 2 THE NEW BATCH   Warner Bros., 1990
ZANDALEE   Electric Pictures/ITC Entertainment Group, 1991

VINCENT GALLO
THE HOUSE OF THE SPIRITS   Miramax Films, 1993, U.S.-German

DON GALLOWAY
THE BIG CHILL   Columbia, 1983

RITA GAM
DISTORTIONS   Cori Films, 1987

MASON GAMBLE
DENNIS THE MENACE   Warner Bros., 1993

MICHAEL GAMBON
Agent: Paradigm - Los Angeles, 310/277-4400

TURTLE DIARY   Samuel Goldwyn Company, 1985, British
MOBSTERS   Universal, 1991
TOYS   20th Century Fox, 1992
CLEAN SLATE   MGM/UA, 1994

ROBIN GAMMEL
Agent: The Blake Agency - Beverly Hills, 310/246-0241

NIGHTMARES   Universal, 1983
GUILTY BY SUSPICION   Warner Bros., 1991

JAMES GAMMON
Agent: The Blake Agency - Beverly Hills, 310/246-0241

URBAN COWBOY   Paramount, 1980
THE BALLAD OF GREGORIO CORTEZ   Embassy, 1983
FATHER OF HELL TOWN (TF)   Breezy Productions, 1985
THE MILAGRO BEANFIELD WAR   Universal, 1988
MAJOR LEAGUE   Paramount, 1989
REVENGE   Columbia, 1990
CRISSCROSS   MGM-Pathe Communications, 1992
MAJOR LEAGUE II   Warner Bros., 1994
WILD BILL   MGM/UA, 1995

JAMES GANDOLFINI
ANGIE   Buena Vista, 1994
TERMINAL VELOCITY   Buena Vista, 1994
CRIMSON TIDE   Buena Vista, 1995

BRUNO GANZ
THE MARQUISE OF O...   New Line Cinema, 1976,
   French-West German
LUMIERE   New World, 1976, French
THE AMERICAN FRIEND   New Yorker, 1977, West German-French
THE BOYS FROM BRAZIL   20th Century Fox, 1978
NOSFERATU THE VAMPYRE   20th Century Fox, 1979,
   West German-French-U.S.
CIRCLE OF DECEIT   *FALSE WITNESS*   United Artists Classics,
   1982, West German-French
STRAPLESS   Miramax Films, 1990
ESPECIALLY ON SUNDAY   Miramax Films, 1993

ANDY GARCIA

b. April 12, 1956 - Havana, Cuba
Agent: Paradigm - Los Angeles, 310/277-4400

BLUE SKIES AGAIN   Warner Bros., 1983
A NIGHT IN HEAVEN   20th Century Fox, 1983
THE LONELY GUY   Universal, 1984
THE MEAN SEASON   Orion, 1985
8 MILLION WAYS TO DIE   TriStar, 1986
THE UNTOUCHABLES   Paramount, 1987
STAND AND DELIVER   Warner Bros., 1988
AMERICAN ROULETTE   Film Four International/British Screen/
   Mandemar Group, 1988, British
BLACK RAIN   Paramount, 1989
INTERNAL AFFAIRS   Paramount, 1990
A SHOW OF FORCE   Paramount, 1990
THE GODFATHER, PART III ✪   Paramount, 1990
DEAD AGAIN   Paramount, 1991
HERO   Columbia, 1992
JENNIFER EIGHT   Paramount, 1992
WHEN A MAN LOVES A WOMAN   Buena Vista, 1994
THINGS TO DO IN DENVER WHEN YOU'RE DEAD
   Miramax Films, 1995

MAGALI GARCIA

SALSA   Cannon, 1988

STENIO GARCIA

AT PLAY IN THE FIELDS OF THE LORD   Universal, 1991

ALLEN GARFIELD

(Allen Goorwitz)
b. November 22, 1939 - Newark, New Jersey

ORGY GIRLS '69   1968
GREETINGS   Sigma III, 1968
PUTNEY SWOPE   Cinema 5, 1969
MARCH OF THE SPRING   1969
ROOMMATES   *HARE*   1969
HI, MOM!   Sigma III, 1970
THE OWL AND THE PUSSYCAT   Columbia, 1970
TAKING OFF   Universal, 1971
BANANAS   United Artists, 1971
CRY UNCLE!   Cambist, 1971
BELIEVE IN ME   MGM, 1971
YOU'VE GOT TO WALK IT LIKE YOU TALK IT OR YOU'LL LOSE
   YOUR BEAT   1971
GET TO KNOW YOUR RABBIT   Warner Bros., 1972
THE CANDIDATE   Warner Bros., 1972
THE ORGANIZATION   United Artists, 1972
SLITHER   MGM, 1973
BUSTING   United Artists, 1974
THE CONVERSATION   Paramount, 1974
THE FRONT PAGE   Universal, 1974
NASHVILLE   Paramount, 1975
PACO   Cinema National, 1975
GABLE AND LOMBARD   Universal, 1976
MOTHER, JUGS & SPEED   20th Century Fox, 1976
SKATEBOARD   Universal, 1978
THE BRINKS JOB   Universal, 1978
ONE-TRICK PONY   Warner Bros., 1980
THE STUNT MAN   20th Century Fox, 1980
CONTINENTAL DIVIDE   Universal, 1981
ONE FROM THE HEART   Columbia, 1982
THE BLACK STALLION RETURNS   MGM/UA, 1983
GET CRAZY   Embassy, 1983
THE COTTON CLUB   Orion, 1984
DESERT BLOOM   Columbia, 1986
CRY DEVIL   Premiere Pictures, 1989
DICK TRACY   Buena Vista, 1990

ART GARFUNKEL

b. November 5, 1941 - New York, New York

CATCH-22   Paramount, 1970
CARNAL KNOWLEDGE   Avco Embassy, 1971
BAD TIMING/A SENSUAL OBSESSION   World Northal, 1980, British

GOOD TO GO   Island Pictures, 1986
BOXING HELENA   Orion Classics, 1993

LEE GARLINGTON

Agent: Paul Kohner, Inc. - Los Angeles, 310/550-1060

COBRA   Warner Bros., 1986
PSYCHO III   Universal, 1986
KILLING IN A SMALL TOWN (TF)   The IndieProd Co./Hearst
   Entertainment Productions, 1990

JAMES GARNER

(James Baumgarner)
b. April 7, 1928 - Norman, Oklahoma
Agent: ICM - Beverly Hills, 310/550-4000

TOWARD THE UNKNOWN   Warner Bros., 1956
THE GIRL HE LEFT BEHIND   Warner Bros., 1956
SHOOT-OUT AT MEDICINE BEND   Warner Bros., 1957
SAYONARA   Warner Bros., 1957
DARBY'S RANGERS   Warner Bros., 1958
UP PERISCOPE   Warner Bros., 1959
CASH McCALL   Warner Bros., 1960
THE CHILDREN'S HOUR   United Artists, 1962
BOYS' NIGHT OUT   MGM, 1962
THE GREAT ESCAPE   United Artists, 1963
THE THRILL OF IT ALL   Universal, 1963
THE WHEELER DEALERS   MGM, 1963
MOVE OVER, DARLING   20th Century Fox, 1963
THE AMERICANIZATION OF EMILY   MGM, 1964
36 HOURS   MGM, 1965
THE ART OF LOVE   Universal, 1965
A MAN COULD GET KILLED   Universal, 1966
DUEL AT DIABLO   United Artists, 1966
MISTER BUDDWING   MGM, 1966
GRAND PRIX   MGM, 1966
HOUR OF THE GUN   United Artists, 1967
HOW SWEET IT IS   Buena Vista, 1968
THE PINK JUNGLE   Universal, 1968
MARLOWE   MGM, 1969
SUPPORT YOUR LOCAL SHERIFF   United Artists, 1969
A MAN CALLED SLEDGE   1970, Italian
SUPPORT YOUR LOCAL GUNFIGHTER   United Artists, 1971
SKIN GAME   Warner Bros., 1971
THEY ONLY KILL THEIR MASTERS   1972
ONE LITTLE INDIAN   Buena Vista, 1973
THE CASTAWAY COWBOY   Buena Vista, 1974
THE ROCKFORD FILES (TF)   Universal TV, 1974
THE NEW MAVERICK (TF)   Cherokee Productions/
   Warner Bros. TV, 1978
HEALTH   20th Century Fox, 1980
THE FAN   Paramount, 1981
VICTOR/VICTORIA   MGM/United Artists, 1982
THE LONG SUMMER OF GEORGE ADAMS (TF)
   Warner Bros. TV, 1982
TANK   Universal, 1984
HEARTSOUNDS (TF)   Embassy TV, 1984
MURPHY'S ROMANCE ★   Columbia, 1985
SPACE (MS)   Stonehenge Productions/Paramount TV, 1985
PROMISE (TF)   Garner-Duchow Productions/Warner Bros. TV, 1986
MY NAME IS BILL W. (TF)   Garner-Duchow Productions, 1989
SUNSET   TriStar, 1988
DECORATION DAY (TF)   Hallmark Hall of Fame, 1990
FIRE IN THE SKY   Paramount, 1993
BREATHING LESSONS (TF)   Signboard Hill Productions, 1994
MAVERICK   Warner Bros., 1994

GALE GARNETT

MR. AND MRS. BRIDGE   Miramax Films, 1990

RICHARD GARNETT

LINK   Thorn EMI/Cannon, 1986, U.S.-British

JANEANE GAROFALO

REALITY BITES   Universal, 1994
BYE BYE LOVE   20th Century Fox, 1995
COLDBLOODED   MPCA, 1995

TERI GARR

b. December 11, 1945 - Lakewood, Ohio
Agent: CAA - Beverly Hills, 310/288-4545

THE MOONSHINE WAR   MGM, 1970
YOUNG FRANKENSTEIN   20th Century Fox, 1974
OH, GOD!   Warner Bros., 1977
CLOSE ENCOUNTERS OF THE THIRD KIND   Columbia, 1977
MR. MIKE'S MONDO VIDEO   New Line Cinema, 1979
THE BLACK STALLION   United Artists, 1979
HONKY TONK FREEWAY   Universal/AFD, 1981
ONE FROM THE HEART   Columbia, 1982
TOOTSIE ✪   Columbia, 1982
MR. MOM   20th Century Fox, 1983
THE BLACK STALLION RETURNS   MGM/UA, 1983
THE STING II   Universal, 1983
THE WINTER OF OUR DISCONTENT (TF)
   Lorimar Productions, 1983
FIRSTBORN   Paramount, 1984
AFTER HOURS   The Geffen Company/Warner Bros., 1985
INTIMATE STRANGERS (TF)   Nederlander TV & Film Productions/
   Telepictures Productions, 1986
MIRACLES   Orion, 1986
FRESNO (MS)   MTM Productions, 1986
PACK OF LIES (TF)   Robert Halmi, Inc., 1987
FULL MOON IN BLUE WATER   Trans World Entertainment, 1988
OUT COLD   TriStar, 1989
LET IT RIDE   Paramount, 1989
MOTHER GOOSE ROCK 'N' RHYME (CTF)
   Think Entertainment, 1990
SHORT TIME   20th Century Fox, 1990
WAITING FOR THE LIGHT   Triumph Releasing Corporation, 1990
THE PLAYER   Fine Line Features/New Line Cinema, 1992
DICK AND MARGE SAVE THE WORLD   Warner Bros., 1992
DUMB AND DUMBER   New Line Cinema, 1994
PRET-A-PORTER   Miramax Films, 1994
PERFECT ALIBI   Rysher Entertainment, 1995

BRAD GARRETT

EIGHT MEN OUT   Orion, 1988
CASPER   Universal, 1995

ELIZA GARRETT

LOVE IS A GUN   Trimark Pictures, 1994

HANK GARRETT

THE BOYS NEXT DOOR   New World, 1985

BARBARA GARRICK

THE FIRM   Paramount, 1993

JIM GARRISON

JFK   Warner Bros., 1991

GREER GARSON

b. September 29, 1908 - County Down, Ireland

GOODBYE, MR. CHIPS ★   MGM, 1939, British
REMEMBER?   MGM, 1939
PRIDE AND PREJUDICE   MGM, 1940
BLOSSOMS IN THE DUST ★   MGM, 1941
WHEN LADIES MEET   MGM, 1941
MRS. MINIVER ★★   MGM, 1942
RANDOM HARVEST   MGM, 1942
THE YOUNGEST PROFESSION   MGM, 1943
MADAME CURIE ★   MGM, 1943
MRS. PARKINGTON ★   MGM, 1944
THE VALLEY OF DECISION ★   MGM, 1945
ADVENTURE   MGM, 1946
DESIRE ME   MGM, 1947
JULIA MISBEHAVES   MGM, 1948
THAT FORSYTE WOMAN THE FORSYTE SAGA   MGM, 1949
THE MINIVER STORY   MGM, 1950
THE LAW AND THE LADY   MGM, 1951
JULIUS CAESAR   MGM, 1953
SCANDAL AT SCOURIE   MGM, 1953
HER TWELVE MEN   MGM, 1954
STRANGE LADY IN TOWN   Warner Bros., 1955
SUNRISE AT CAMPOBELLO ★   Warner Bros., 1960
PEPE   Columbia, 1960
THE SINGING NUN   MGM, 1966
THE HAPPIEST MILLIONAIRE   Buena Vista, 1967
LITTLE WOMEN (TF)   Universal TV, 1978

STEVE GARVEY

BLOODFIST VI   New Horizon Pictures, 1994

LINDA GARY

LAND BEFORE TIME (AF)   Universal, 1995 (voice)

LORRAINE GARY

JAWS   Universal, 1975
I NEVER PROMISED YOU A ROSE GARDEN   New World, 1977
JAWS 2   Universal, 1978
1941   Universal, 1979
JUST YOU AND ME KID   Columbia, 1979
JAWS: THE REVENGE   Universal, 1987

VINCENT GAUTHIER

SUMMER LE RAYON VEIT   Orion Classics, 1985, French
NAZI HUNTER: THE BEATE KLARSFELD STORY (TF)   William
   Kayden Productions/Orion TV/Silver Chalice/Revcom/George
   Walker TV/TF1/SFP, 1986, U.S.-British-French

JOHN GAVIN

(John Anthony Golenor)
b. April 8, 1928 - Los Angeles, California

BEHIND THE HIGH WALL   1956
FOUR GIRLS IN TOWN   Universal, 1957
QUANTEZ   1957
A TIME TO LOVE AND A TIME TO DIE   Universal, 1958
IMITATION OF LIFE   Universal, 1959
PSYCHO   Paramount, 1960
SPARTACUS   Universal, 1960
MIDNIGHT LACE   Universal, 1960
A BREATH OF SCANDAL   Paramount, 1960
ROMANOFF AND JULIET   Universal, 1961
TAMMY TELL ME TRUE   1961
BACK STREET   Universal, 1961
THOROUGHLY MODERN MILLIE   Universal, 1967
THE MADWOMAN OF CHAILLOT   Warner Bros., 1969, British
PUSSYCAT PUSSYCAT, I LOVE YOU   United Artists, 1970, British
RICH MAN, POOR MAN (MS)   Universal TV, 1976
JENNIFER   1978
HISTORY OF THE WORLD—PART 1   20th Century Fox, 1981

JACKIE GAYLE

TIN MEN   Buena Vista, 1987
BERT RIGBY, YOU'RE A FOOL   Warner Bros., 1989

MITCH GAYLORD

AMERICAN ANTHEM   Columbia, 1986

GEORGE GAYNES

(George Jongejans)
Agent: William Morris Agency - Beverly Hills, 310/274-7451

THE GROUP   United Artists, 1965
DOCTORS' WIVES   Columbia, 1971
THE WAY WE WERE   Columbia, 1973
NICKELODEON   Columbia, 1976
HARRY AND WALTER GO TO NEW YORK   Columbia, 1976
RICH MAN, POOR MAN (MS)   Universal TV, 1976
WASHINGTON: BEHIND CLOSED DOORS (MS)
   Paramount TV, 1977
DEAD MEN DON'T WEAR PLAID   Universal, 1979
BREAKING UP IS HARD TO DO (TF)   Green-Epstein Productions/
   Columbia TV, 1979
ALTERED STATES   Warner Bros., 1980
SCRUPLES II   Lou-Step Productions/Warner Bros. TV, 1981

TOOTSIE   Columbia, 1982
TO BE OR NOT TO BE   20th Century Fox, 1983
POLICE ACADEMY   The Ladd Company/Warner Bros., 1984
MICKI & MAUDE   Columbia, 1984
POLICE ACADEMY 2: THEIR FIRST ASSIGNMENT
   Warner Bros., 1985
POLICE ACADEMY 3: BACK IN TRAINING   Warner Bros., 1986
POLICE ACADEMY 4: CITIZENS ON PATROL   Warner Bros., 1987
POLICE ACADEMY 5: ASSIGNMENT MIAMI BEACH
   Warner Bros., 1988
POLICE ACADEMY 6: CITY UNDER SIEGE   Warner Bros., 1989
POLICE ACADEMY: MISSION TO MOSCOW   Warner Bros., 1994

WENDY GAZELLE
TRIUMPH OF THE SPIRIT   Triumph Releasing Corporation, 1989

BEN GAZZARA
b. August 28, 1930 - New York, New York

THE STRANGE ONE   *END AS A MAN*   Columbia, 1957
ANATOMY OF A MURDER   Columbia, 1959
THE PASSIONATE THIEF   *RISATE DI GIOIA*   Embassy,
   1960, Italian
THE YOUNG DOCTORS   United Artists, 1961
CONVICTS FOUR   1962
CONQUERED CITY   *LA CITTA PRIGIONIERA*
   American International, 1962, Italian
A RAGE TO LIVE   United Artists, 1965
IF IT'S TUESDAY, THIS MUST BE BELGIUM   United Artists, 1969
THE BRIDGE AT REMAGEN   United Artists, 1969
HUSBANDS   Columbia, 1970
WHEN MICHAEL CALLS (TF)   Palomar International, 1971
PURSUIT (TF)   ABC Circle Films, 1972
FIREBALL FORWARD (TF)   20th Century Fox TV, 1972
THE FAMILY RICO (TF)   CBS, Inc., 1972
INDICT AND CONVICT (TF)   Universal TV, 1973
THE NEPTUNE FACTOR   *AN UNDERWATER ODYSSEY/
   THE NEPTUNE DISASTER*   20th Century Fox, 1973, Canadian
MANEATER (TF)   Universal TV, 1973
QB VII (MS)   Screen Gems/Columbia TV/The Douglas Cramer
   Company, 1974
CAPONE   20th Century Fox, 1975
THE KILLING OF A CHINESE BOOKIE   Faces International, 1976
VOYAGE OF THE DAMNED   Avco Embassy, 1976, British
THE SICILIAN CONNECTION   Joseph Green Pictures, 1977, Italian
HIGH VELOCITY   1977
THE DEATH OF RICHIE (TF)   Henry Jaffe Enterprises, 1977
THE TRIAL OF LEE HARVEY OSWALD (MS)   Charles Fries
   Productions, 1977
OPENING NIGHT   Faces International, 1978
SAINT JACK   New World, 1979
SIDNEY SHELDON'S BLOODLINE   *BLOODLINE*   Paramount, 1979
THEY ALL LAUGHED   United Artists Classics, 1981
INCHON!   MGM/UA, 1982, South Korean
TALES OF ORDINARY MADNESS   Fred Baker Films,
   1983, Italian-French
AN EARLY FROST (TF)   NBC Productions, 1985
A LETTER TO THREE WIVES (TF)   Michael Filerman Productions/
   20th Century Fox TV, 1985
POLICE STORY: THE FREEWAY KILLINGS (TF)   David Gerber
   Productions/MGM-UA TV/Columbia TV, 1987
DOWNPAYMENT ON MURDER (TF)   Adam Productions/
   20th Century Fox TV, 1987
QUICKER THAN THE EYE   Condor Productions, 1988,
   French-Swiss
ROAD HOUSE   MGM/UA, 1989
PEOPLE LIKE US (TF)   ITC Productions, 1990
PARALLEL LIVES (CTF)   Showtime Entertainment, 1994

MICHAEL V. GAZZO
THE GODFATHER, PART II ✪   Paramount, 1974
THE WINTER OF OUR DISCONTENT (TF)
   Lorimar Productions, 1983
FEAR CITY   Chevy Chase Distribution, 1984
COOKIE   Warner Bros., 1989

ANTHONY GEARY
THE IMPOSTER (TF)   Gloria Monty Productions/Comworld
   Productions, 1984
KICKS (TF)   ABC Circle Films, 1985
CRACK HOUSE   Cannon, 1989
YOU CAN'T HURRY LOVE   MCEG, 1989
UHF   Orion, 1989
DANGEROUS LOVE   Motion Picture Corporation of America, 1989

CYNTHIA GEARY
8 SECONDS   New Line Cinema, 1994

JASON GEDRICK
Agent: UTA - Beverly Hills, 310/273-6700

IRON EAGLE   TriStar, 1986
THE ZOO GANG   New World, 1986
PROMISED LAND   Vestron, 1988
ROOFTOPS   New Visions, 1989
BACKDRAFT   Universal, 1991
CROSSING THE BRIDGE   Buena Vista, 1992

MARTHA GEHMAN
Agent: Flick East/West Talent, Inc. - Los Angeles, 213/463-6333 or
   New York, 212/307-1850

F/X   Orion, 1986

GRATIEN GELINAS
AGNES OF GOD   Columbia, 1985

TONY GENARO
THE MILAGRO BEANFIELD WAR   Universal, 1988

BRYAN GENESSE
SKIN DEEP   20th Century Fox, 1989

AVRIL GENTLES
MISS FIRECRACKER   Corsair Pictures, 1989

STEPHEN GEOFFREYS
AT CLOSE RANGE   Orion, 1986

BABS GEORGE
THE SUBSTITUTE WIFE (TF)   Frederick S. Pierce Company, 1994

CHIEF LEONARD GEORGE
MAN 2 MAN   Buena Vista, 1995

JOSEPH GEORGE
SYLVIA   MGM/UA Classics, 1985, New Zealand

SUSAN GEORGE
b. July 26, 1950 - London, England

BILLION DOLLAR BRAIN   United Artists, 1967, British
THE SORCERERS   1967
THE STRANGE AFFAIR   Paramount, 1968
ALL NEAT IN BLACK STOCKINGS   National General, 1969, British
LOLA   *TWINKEY*   American International, 1969, British-Italian
SPRING AND PORT WINE   1970
THE LOOKING GLASS WAR   Columbia, 1970, British
DIE SCREAMING MARIANNE   1971, British
SUDDEN TERROR   *EYEWITNESS*   National General, 1971
STRAW DOGS   Cinerama Releasing Corporation, 1971, British
FRIGHT   1971, British
SONNY AND JED   1973, Italian-Spanish
DIRTY MARY, CRAZY LARRY   20th Century Fox, 1974
MANDINGO   Paramount, 1975
OUT OF SEASON   Athenaeum, 1975, British
A SMALL TOWN IN TEXAS   American International, 1976
TOMORROW NEVER COMES   1977, British-Canadian
ENTER THE NINJA   Cannon, 1981

VENOM   Paramount, 1982
THE JIGSAW MAN   United Film Distribution, 1984, British
LIGHTNING, THE WHITE STALLION   Cannon, 1986
JACK THE RIPPER (TF)   Euston Films/Thames TV/Hill-O'Connor
   Entertainment/Lorimar TV, 1988, British-U.S.

GIL GERARD
AIRPORT '77   Universal, 1977
RANSOM FOR ALICE! (TF)   Universal TV, 1977
KILLING STONE (TF)   Universal TV, 1978
BUCK ROGERS IN THE 25TH CENTURY   Universal, 1979
HEAR NO EVIL (TF)   Paul Pompian Productions/MGM-TV, 1982
FOR LOVE OR MONEY (TF)   Robert Papazian Productions/
   Henerson-Hirsch Productions, 1984
STORMIN' HOME (TF)   CBS Entertainment, 1985
INTERNATIONAL AIRPORT (TF)   Aaron Spelling Productions, 1985
FINAL NOTICE (CTF)   Wilshire Court Productions/Sharm Hill
   Productions, 1989

JOAN GERBER
DUCK TALES THE MOVIE: THE SECRET OF THE LOST LAMP (AF)
   Buena Vista, 1990 (voice)

GEORGE GERDES
IRON WILL   Buena Vista, 1994

RICHARD GERE
b. August 31, 1949 - Philadelphia, Pennsylvania
Agent: ICM - Beverly Hills, 310/550-4000

STRIKE FORCE (TF)   D'Antoni-Weitz Television Productions, 1975
REPORT TO THE COMMISSIONER   United Artists, 1975
BABY BLUE MARINE   Columbia, 1976
LOOKING FOR MR. GOODBAR   Paramount, 1977
BLOODBROTHERS   Warner Bros., 1978
DAYS OF HEAVEN   Paramount, 1978
YANKS   Universal, 1979, British
AMERICAN GIGOLO   Paramount, 1980
AN OFFICER AND A GENTLEMAN   Paramount, 1982
BREATHLESS   Orion, 1983
BEYOND THE LIMIT   THE HONORARY CONSUL   Paramount,
   1983, British
THE COTTON CLUB   Orion, 1984
KING DAVID   Paramount, 1985, U.S.-British
POWER   20th Century Fox, 1986
NO MERCY   TriStar, 1986
MILES FROM HOME   Cinecom, 1988
INTERNAL AFFAIRS   Paramount, 1990
PRETTY WOMAN   Buena Vista, 1990
RHAPSODY IN AUGUST   Orion Classics, 1991, Japanese
FINAL ANALYSIS   Warner Bros., 1992
SOMMERSBY   Warner Bros., 1993
AND THE BAND PLAYED ON (CTF)   HBO Pictures/Spelling
   Entertainment, 1993
MR. JONES   TriStar, 1993
INTERSECTION   Paramount, 1994
FIRST KNIGHT   Columbia, 1995

GREG GERMANN
MISS FIRECRACKER   Corsair Pictures, 1989
ONCE AROUND   Universal, 1991

SAVINA GERSAK
Agent: Century Artists, Ltd. - Beverly Hills, 310/273-4366

SONNY BOY   Triumph Releasing Corporation, 1990

GINA GERSHON
PRETTY IN PINK   Paramount, 1986

ALEXANDRA GERSTEN
FEAR, ANXIETY AND DEPRESSION   Samuel Goldwyn
   Company, 1990

JAMI GERTZ
Agent: ICM - Beverly Hills, 310/550-4000

CROSSROADS   Columbia, 1986
QUICKSILVER   Columbia, 1986
SOLARBABIES   MGM/UA, 1986
THE LOST BOYS   Warner Bros., 1987
LESS THAN ZERO   20th Century Fox, 1987
LISTEN TO ME   Columbia, 1989
RENEGADES   Universal, 1989
DON'T TELL HER IT'S ME   Hemdale, 1990
SIBLING RIVALRY   Columbia, 1990
THIS CAN'T BE LOVE (TF)   Davis Entertainment/Pacific Motion
   Pictures/World International Network, 1994

BALTHAZAR GETTY
Agent: William Morris Agency - Beverly Hills, 310/274-7451

YOUNG GUNS II   20th Century Fox, 1990
MY HEROES HAVE ALWAYS BEEN COWBOYS   Samuel Goldwyn
   Company, 1991
THE POPE MUST DIET   Miramax Films, 1991
WHERE THE DAY TAKES YOU   New Line Cinema, 1992
NATURAL BORN KILLERS   Warner Bros., 1994
JUDGE DREDD   Buena Vista, 1995

ESTELLE GETTY
b. July 25, 1924 - New York, New York
Agent: Jack Rose Agency - Los Angeles, 310/274-4673

TOOTSIE   Columbia, 1982
MASK   Universal, 1985
COPACABANA (TF)   Dick Clark Productions/Stiletto, Ltd., 1985
STOP! OR MY MOM WILL SHOOT   Universal, 1992

JOHN GETZ
Agent: Gersh Agency - Beverly Hills, 310/274-6611

TATTOO   20th Century Fox, 1981
THIEF OF HEARTS   Paramount, 1984
BLOOD SIMPLE   Circle Releasing Corporation, 1984
THE FLY   20th Century Fox, 1986, U.S.-Canadian
THE FLY II   20th Century Fox, 1989
BORN ON THE FOURTH OF JULY   Universal, 1989
MEN AT WORK   Triumph Releasing Corporation, 1990
CURLY SUE   Warner Bros., 1991
DON'T TELL MOM THE BABYSITTER'S DEAD   Warner Bros., 1991

ALICE GHOSTLEY
b. August 14, 1926 - Eve, Missouri
Agent: APA - Los Angeles, 310/273-0744

NEW FACES   1954
TO KILL A MOCKINGBIRD   Universal, 1962
MY SIX LOVES   1963
THE FLIM FLAM MAN   20th Century Fox, 1967
THE GRADUATE   Avco Embassy, 1967
VIVA MAX!   Commonwealth United, 1969
ACE ELI AND RODGER OF THE SKIES   20th Century Fox, 1973
GATOR   United Artists, 1976
GREASE   Paramount, 1978

LOUIS GIAMBALVO
Agent: Gersh Agency - Beverly Hills, 310/274-6611

SEE NO EVIL, HEAR NO EVIL   TriStar, 1989

GIANCARLO GIANNINI
b. August 1, 1942 - Spezia, Italy

SWEPT AWAY BY AN UNUSUAL DESTINY IN THE BLUE SEA
   OF AUGUST   Cinema 5, 1974, Italian
SEVEN BEAUTIES ★   Cinema 5, 1976, Italian
AMERICAN DREAMER   Warner Bros., 1984
NEW YORK STORIES   Buena Vista, 1989
ONCE UPON A CRIME   MGM-Pathe, 1992, U.S.-Italian
A WALK IN THE CLOUDS   20th Century Fox, 1995

IAN GIATTI
THE RESCUE   Buena Vista, 1988

BARRY GIBB
b. September 1, 1946

SGT. PEPPER'S LONELY HEARTS CLUB BAND   Universal, 1978

CYNTHIA GIBB
Agent: William Morris Agency - Beverly Hills, 310/274-7451

SALVADOR   Hemdale, 1986
MODERN GIRLS   Atlantic Releasing Corporation, 1986
YOUNGBLOOD   MGM/UA, 1986
SHORT CIRCUIT 2   TriStar, 1988
THE KAREN CARPENTER STORY (TF)   Weintraub Entertainment
    Group, 1989
WHEN WE WERE YOUNG (TF)   Richard & Esther Shapiro
    Entertainment, 1989
DEATH WARRANT   MGM/UA, 1990
GYPSY (TF)   RHI Entertainment, 1993

MAURICE GIBB
SGT. PEPPER'S LONELY HEARTS CLUB BAND   Universal, 1978

ROBIN GIBB
SGT. PEPPER'S LONELY HEARTS CLUB BAND   Universal, 1978

LEEZA GIBBONS
Agent: William Morris Agency - Beverly Hills, 310/274-7451

SOAPDISH   Paramount, 1991

MARLA GIBBS
b. June 14, 1931 - Chicago, Illinois

THE METEOR MAN   MGM/UA, 1993

HENRY GIBSON
b. September 21, 1935 - Germantown, Pennsylvania

KISS ME STUPID   Lopert, 1964
EVIL ROY SLADE (TF)   Universal TV, 1972
CHARLOTTE'S WEB (AF)   Paramount, 1973 (voice)
NASHVILLE   Paramount, 1975
THE LAST REMAKE OF BEAU GESTE   1977
AMATEUR NIGHT AT THE DIXIE BAR AND GRILL (TF)
    Motown/Universal TV, 1979
A PERFECT COUPLE   20th Century Fox, 1979
HEALTH   20th Century Fox, 1980
THE BLUES BROTHERS   Universal, 1980
THE INCREDIBLE SHRINKING WOMAN   Universal, 1981
SWITCHING CHANNELS   Columbia, 1988
THE 'BURBS   Universal, 1989

MEL GIBSON
b. January 3, 1956 - Peekskill, New York
Agent: ICM - Beverly Hills, 310/550-4000

SUMMER CITY   1977, Australian
MAD MAX   American International, 1979, Australian
TIM   Satori, 1979, Australian
ATTACK FORCE Z   John McCallum Productions/Central Motion
    Picture Corporation, 1980, Australian-Taiwanese
GALLIPOLI   Paramount, 1981, Australian
THE ROAD WARRIOR   MAD MAX 2   Warner Bros.,
    1981, Australian
THE YEAR OF LIVING DANGEROUSLY   MGM/UA,
    1983, Australian
THE BOUNTY   Orion, 1984, British
MRS. SOFFEL   MGM/UA, 1984
THE RIVER   Universal, 1984
MAD MAX BEYOND THUNDERDOME   Warner Bros.,
    1985, Australian
LETHAL WEAPON   Warner Bros., 1987
TEQUILA SUNRISE   Warner Bros., 1988

LETHAL WEAPON 2   Warner Bros., 1989
BIRD ON A WIRE   Universal, 1990
AIR AMERICA   TriStar, 1990
HAMLET   Warner Bros., 1990, British
LETHAL WEAPON 3   Warner Bros., 1992
FOREVER YOUNG   Warner Bros., 1992
THE MAN WITHOUT A FACE   Warner Bros., 1993 (also directed)
MAVERICK   Warner Bros., 1994
BRAVE HEART   Paramount, 1995 (also directed)
POCAHONTAS (AF)   Buena Vista, 1995 (voice)

THOMAS GIBSON
SLEEP WITH ME   MGM/UA, 1994

RAY GIDEON
MADE IN HEAVEN   Lorimar, 1987

JOHN GIELGUD
(Sir John Gielgud)
b. April 14, 1904 - London, England
Agent: ICM - Beverly Hills, 310/550-4000

WHO IS THE MAN?   1924, British
THE CLUE OF THE NEW PIN   1929, British
INSULT   1932, British
THE GOOD COMPANIONS   Gaumont-British, 1933, British
SECRET AGENT   Gaumont-British, 1936, British
THE PRIME MINISTER   1941, British
JULIUS CAESAR   MGM, 1953
ROMEO AND JULIET   1954, British (voice)
RICHARD III   Lopert, 1956, British
AROUND THE WORLD IN 80 DAYS   United Artists, 1956
THE BARRETTS OF WIMPOLE STREET   MGM, 1957, U.S.-British
SAINT JOAN   United Artists, 1957
BECKET ✪   Paramount, 1964, British
THE LOVED ONE   MGM, 1965
CHIMES AT MIDNIGHT   FALSTAFF   Peppercorn-Wromser, 1966,
    Spanish-Swiss
SEBASTIAN   Paramount, 1968, British
THE CHARGE OF THE LIGHT BRIGADE   United Artists,
    1968, British
THE SHOES OF THE FISHERMAN   MGM, 1968
ASSIGNMENT TO KILL   1969
OH! WHAT A LOVELY WAR   Paramount, 1969, British
JULIUS CAESAR   American International, 1970, British
EAGLE IN A CAGE   National General, 1971, British-Yugoslavian
PROBE (TF)   Warner Bros. TV, 1972
LOST HORIZON   Columbia, 1972
FRANKENSTEIN: THE TRUE STORY (TF)   Universal TV, 1973
QB VII (MS)   Screen Gems/Columbia TV/The Douglas Cramer
    Company, 1974
11 HARROWHOUSE   ANYTHING FOR LOVE   20th Century Fox,
    1974, British
LUTHER   American Film Theatre, 1974
GOLD   Allied Artists, 1974, British
MURDER ON THE ORIENT EXPRESS   Paramount, 1974, British
GALILEO   American Film Theatre, 1975, British-Canadian
ACES HIGH   Cinema Shares International, 1977, British
JOSEPH ANDREWS   Paramount, 1977, British
PROVIDENCE   Cinema 5, 1977, French-Swiss
CALIGULA   CALIGOLA   Analysis Film Releasing, 1977, Italian-U.S.
LES MISÉRABLES (TF)   Norman Rosemont Productions/ITV
    Entertainment, 1978
MURDER BY DECREE   Avco Embassy, 1979, Canadian-British
LION OF THE DESERT   United Film Distribution, 1979
A PORTRAIT OF THE ARTIST AS A YOUNG MAN   1981,
    Libyan-British
THE HUMAN FACTOR   United Artists, 1979, British
THE ELEPHANT MAN   Paramount, 1980, British-U.S.
THE FORMULA   MGM/United Artists, 1980
ARTHUR ✪✪   Orion, 1981
SPHINX   Orion/Warner Bros., 1981
CHARIOTS OF FIRE   The Ladd Company/Warner Bros.,
    1981, British
PRIEST OF LOVE   Filmways, 1981, British
BRIDESHEAD REVISITED (MS)   Granada TV/WNET-13/NDR
    Hamburg, 1982, British-U.S.-West German
GANDHI   Columbia, 1982, British-Indian
INSIDE THE THIRD REICH (MS)   ABC Circle Films, 1982

MARCO POLO (MS)   RAI/Franco Cristaldi Productions/Vincenzo
   Labella Productions, 1982, Italian
WAGNER (MS)   London Trust Productions/Richard Wagner
   Productions/Ladbroke Productions/Hungarofilm, 1983,
   British-Hungarian-Austrian
THE SCARLET AND THE BLACK (TF)   Bill McCutchen Productions/
   ITC/RAI, 1983, U.S.-Italian
THE WICKED LADY   MGM/UA/Cannon, 1983, British
INVITIATION TO THE WEDDING   Chancery Lane Films,
   1984, British
THE SHOOTING PARTY   European Classics, 1984, British
SCANDALOUS   Orion, 1984
THE FAR PAVILIONS (CMS)   Geoff Reeve & Associates/Goldcrest,
   1984, British
THE MASTER OF BALLANTRAE (TF)   Larry White-Hugh Benson
   Productions/HTV/Columbia TV, 1984, U.S.-British
CAMILLE (TF)   Rosemont Productions, 1984, U.S.-British
ROMANCE ON THE ORIENT EXPRESS (TF)   von Zerneck
   Productions/Yorkshire TV, 1985, U.S.-British
PLENTY   20th Century Fox, 1985, British
THE WHISTLE BLOWER   Hemdale, 1986, British
APPOINTMENT WITH DEATH   Cannon, 1988, U.S.-British
ARTHUR 2 ON THE ROCKS   Warner Bros., 1988
A MAN FOR ALL SEASONS (CTF)   Agamemnon Films/British Lion,
   1988, U.S.-British
GETTING IT RIGHT   MCEG, 1989, U.S.-British
WAR AND REMEMBRANCE (MS)   Dan Curtis Productions/ABC
   Circle Films, 1988-89
PROSPERO'S BOOKS   Miramax Films, 1991
SHINING THROUGH   20th Century Fox, 1992
THE POWER OF ONE   Warner Bros., .1992

STEFAN GIERASCH
Agent: Paradigm - Los Angeles, 310/277-4400

PERFECT   Columbia, 1985

GLORIA GIFFORD
CALIFORNIA SUITE   Columbia, 1978

ROLAND GIFT
SAMMY AND ROSIE GET LAID   Cinecom, 1987, British
SCANDAL   Miramax Films, 1989

MELISSA GILBERT
(Melissa Gilbert-Brinkman)
b. May 8, 1964 - Los Angeles, California
Agent: William Morris Agency - Beverly Hills, 310/274-7451

LITTLE HOUSE ON THE PRAIRIE (TF)   NBC Productions, 1974
THE MIRACLE WORKER (TF)   Katz-Gallin Productions/Half-Pint
   Productions,1979
LITTLE HOUSE: LOOK BACK TO YESTERDAY (TF)
   NBC Productions/Ed Friendly Productions, 1984
LITTLE HOUSE: BLESS ALL THE DEAR CHILDREN (TF)
   NBC Productions/Ed Friendly Productions, 1984
LITTLE HOUSE: THE LAST FAREWELL (TF)   NBC Productions/
   Ed Friendly Productions, 1984
SYLVESTER   Columbia, 1985
CHOICES (TF)   Robert Halmi, Inc., 1986
BLOOD VOWS: THE STORY OF A MAFIA WIFE (TF)
   Louis Rudolph Films/Fries Entertainment, 1987
KILLER INSTINCT (TF)   Millar-Bromberg Productions/ITC
   Entertaiment, 1988
WITHOUT HER CONSENT (TF)   Raymond Katz Enterprises/Half
   Pint Productions/Carla Singer Productions, 1990
FORBIDDEN NIGHTS (TF)   Tristine Rainer Productions/Warner
   Bros. TV, 1990

SARA GILBERT
Agent: William Morris Agency - Beverly Hills, 310/274-7451

POISON IVY   New Line Cinema, 1992

PAMELA GILDAY
THRASHIN'   Fries Entertainment, 1986

NANCY GILES
Agent: The Agency - Los Angeles, 310/551-3000

BIG   20th Century Fox, 1988

LINDA GILLEN
Agent: Gersh Agency - Beverly Hills, 310/274-6611

BIG   20th Century Fox, 1988

ANITA GILLETTE
b. August 16, 1938 - Baltimore, Maryland

MOONSTRUCK   MGM/UA, 1987
BOYS ON THE SIDE   Warner Bros., 1995

TERRY GILLIAM
b. November 12, 1940 - Minneapolis, Minnesota
Agent: CAA - Beverly Hills, 310/288-4545

AND NOW FOR SOMETHING COMPLETELY DIFFERENT
   1972, British
MONTY PYTHON AND THE HOLY GRAIL   Cinema 5, 1974,
   British (also co-directed)
MONTY PYTHON'S LIFE OF BRIAN   Orion/Warner Bros.,
   1979, British
MONTY PYTHON LIVE AT THE HOLLYWOOD BOWL   Columbia,
   1982, British
MONTY PYTHON'S THE MEANING OF LIFE   Universal,
   1983, British
SPIES LIKE US   Warner Bros., 1985

RICHARD GILLILAND
CHALLENGE OF A LIFETIME (TF)   Moonlight Productions, 1985
KILLING IN A SMALL TOWN (TF)   The IndieProd Co./Hearst
   Entertainment Productions, 1990

HUGH GILLIN
PSYCHO III   Universal, 1986
WANTED DEAD OR ALIVE   New World, 1986
ELVIS AND ME (MS)   Navarone Productions/New World TV, 1988

JACK GILPIN
SOMETHING WILD   Orion, 1986
FUNNY FARM   Warner Bros., 1988

CLARENCE GILYARD, JR.
TOP GUN   Paramount, 1986

ROBERT GINTY
b. November 14, 1948 - New York, New York

HAWAIIAN HEAT (TF)   James D. Parriott Productions/
   Universal TV, 1984
LOVERBOY   TriStar, 1989
MADHOUSE   Orion, 1990
HARLEY DAVIDSON & THE MARLBORO MAN   MGM-Pathe, 1991
LONELY HEARTS   Live Entertainment, 1991

FRANK GIO
MARRIED TO THE MOB   Orion, 1988

REMY GIRARD
THE DECLINE OF THE AMERICAN EMPIRE   Cineplex Odeon,
   1986, Canadian

FRANK GIRARDEAU
ALL I WANT FOR CHRISTMAS   Paramount, 1991

RAY GIRARDIN
LOVERBOY   TriStar, 1989

ANNABETH GISH
Agent: ICM - Beverly Hills, 310/550-4000

DESERT BLOOM   Columbia, 1986
HIDING OUT   DEG, 1987
MYSTIC PIZZA   Samuel Goldwyn Company, 1988
WHEN HE'S NOT A STRANGER (TF)   Ohlmeyer
   Communications, 1989
COUPE DE VILLE   Universal, 1990
WYATT EARP   Warner Bros., 1994

SHEILA GISH
HIGHLANDER   20th Century Fox, 1986, British-U.S.

GUDRUN GISLADOTTIR
THE SACRIFICE   Orion Classics, 1986, Swedish-French

NEIL GIUNTOLI
MEMPHIS BELLE   Warner Bros, 1990

ROBIN GIVENS
b. November 27, 1964 - New York, New York

BEVERLY HILLS MADAM (TF)   NLS Productions/Orion TV, 1986
THE PENTHOUSE (TF)   Greene-White Productions/
   Spectator Films, 1989
THE WOMEN OF BREWSTER PLACE (MS)   Harpo Productions/
   Phoenix Entertainment Group, 1989
A RAGE IN HARLEM   Miramax Films, 1991, U.S.-British
BOOMERANG   Paramount, 1992
FOREIGN STUDENT   Gramercy Pictures, 1994
BLANKMAN   Columbia, 1994
BRILLIANT DISGUISE   Prism Pictures, 1994

RON GLASS
HOUSEGUEST   Buena Vista, 1995

ISABEL GLASSER
PURE COUNTRY   Warner Bros., 1992
FOREVER YOUNG   Warner Bros., 1992

PHILLIP GLASSER
AN AMERICAN TAIL (AF)   Universal, 1986 (voice)
AN AMERICAN TAIL: FIEVEL GOES WEST (AF)   Universal,
   1991 (voice)

ROBERT GLAUDINI
PARASITE   Embassy, 1982
GRUNT! THE WRESTLING MOVIE   New World, 1986

MATTHEW GLAVE
Agent: Susan Smith & Associates - Beverly Hills, 213/852-4777

BABY'S DAY OUT   20th Century Fox, 1994

JOANNA GLEASON
HEARTBURN   Paramount, 1986
HANNAH AND HER SISTERS   Orion, 1986
CRIMES AND MISDEMEANORS   Orion, 1989
THE BOYS (TF)   William Link Productions/Papazian-Hirsch
   Productions, 1991
F/X 2 - THE DEADLY ART OF ILLUSION   Orion, 1991
FOR RICHER, FOR POORER FATHER, SON AND THE
   MISTRESS (CTF)   Citadel Entertainment Productions, 1992

PAUL GLEASON
THE GREAT SANTINI THE ACE   Orion/Warner Bros., 1980
FORT APACHE, THE BRONX   20th Century Fox, 1981
ARTHUR   Orion, 1981
THE PURSUIT OF D.B. COOPER   Universal, 1982
TENDER MERCIES   Universal/AFD, 1983
TRADING PLACES   Paramount, 1983
THE BREAKFAST CLUB   Universal, 1985
FOREVER, LULU   TriStar, 1987
MORGAN STEWART'S COMING HOME   New Century/Vista, 1987

SUPERCARRIER (TF)   Fries Entertainment/Richard Hayward-Real
   Tinsel Productions, 1988
SHE'S HAVING A BABY   Paramount, 1988
JOHNNY BE GOOD   Orion, 1988
DIE HARD   20th Century Fox, 1988
NIGHT GAME   Trans World Entertainment, 1989
RICH GIRL   Studio Three, 1991

IAIN GLEN
MOUNTAINS OF THE MOON   TriStar, 1990
FOOLS OF FORTUNE   New Line Cinema, 1990
ROSENCRANTZ & GUILDENSTERN ARE DEAD   Cinecom, 1991

SCOTT GLENN
b. January 26, 1942 - Pittsburg, Pennsylvania

THE BABY MAKER   National General, 1970
ANGELS HARD AS THEY COME   1971
HEX   1973
NASHVILLE   Paramount, 1975
FIGHTING MAD   20th Century Fox, 1976
APOCALYPSE NOW   United Artists, 1979
URBAN COWBOY   Paramount, 1980
PERSONAL BEST   The Geffen Company/Warner Bros., 1982
THE CHALLENGE   Embassy, 1982
THE RIGHT STUFF   The Ladd Company/Warner Bros., 1983
THE RIVER   Universal, 1984
WILD GEESE II   Universal, 1985, British
SILVERADO   Columbia, 1985
OFF LIMITS   20th Century Fox, 1988
VERNE MILLER   Alive Films, 1988
INTRIGUE (TF)   Crew Neck Productions/Linnea Productions/
   Columbia TV, 1988
THE OUTSIDE WOMAN (TF)   Green-Epstein Productions, 1989
MISS FIRECRACKER   Corsair Pictures, 1989
THE HUNT FOR RED OCTOBER   Paramount, 1990
THE SILENCE OF THE LAMBS   Orion, 1991
MY HEROES HAVE ALWAYS BEEN COWBOYS   Samuel Goldwyn
   Company, 1991
BACKDRAFT   Universal, 1991
WOMEN & MEN: IN LOVE THERE ARE NO RULES (CTF)
   David Brown Productions/HBO Showcase, 1991
THE PLAYER   Fine Line Features/New Line Cinema, 1992
NIGHT OF THE RUNNING MAN   Trimark Pictures, 1994
TALL TALE   Buena Vista, 1994
FLIGHT OF THE DOVE   Concorde, 1995

SHARON GLESS
b. May 31, 1943 - Los Angeles, California
Agent: William Morris Agency - Beverly Hills, 310/274-7451

AIRPORT 1975   Universal, 1974
SWITCH (TF)   Universal TV, 1975
THE IMMIGRANTS (MS)   Universal TV, 1978
THE LAST CONVERTIBLE (TF)   Roy Huggins Productions/
   Universal TV, 1979
CENTENNIAL (MS)   Universal TV, 1980
HARDHAT & LEGS (TF)   Syzygy Productions, 1980
MOVIOLA: THE SCARLETT O'HARA WAR (MS)   David L.
   Wolper-Stan Margulies Productions/Warner Bros. TV, 1980
THE MIRACLE OF KATHY MILLER (TF)   Rothman-Wohl
   Productions/Universal TV, 1981
HOBSON'S CHOICE (TF)   CBS Entertainment, 1983
THE STAR CHAMBER   20th Century Fox, 1983
LETTING GO (TF)   Adam Productions/ITC Productions, 1985
THE OUTSIDE WOMAN (TF)   Green-Epstein Productions, 1989
SEPARATED BY MURDER (TF)   1994
CAGNEY & LACEY: THE RETURN (TF)   The Rosenzweig
   Company, 1994
CAGNEY & LACEY: TOGETHER AGAIN (TF)   The Rosenzweig
   Company, 1995

STACEY GLICK
BRIGHTON BEACH MEMOIRS   Universal, 1986

BRIAN GLOVER
KES   United Artists, 1970, British
MR. QUILP THE OLD CURIOSITY SHOP   Avco Embassy,
   1975, British
JABBERWOCKY   Cinema 5, 1977, British

DIRTY KNIGHT'S WORK *TRIAL BY COMBAT/CHOICE OF WEAPONS* Gamma III, 1976, British
THE GREAT TRAIN ROBBERY *THE FIRST GREAT TRAIN ROBBERY* United Artists, 1979, British
AN AMERICAN WEREWOLF IN LONDON Universal, 1981
BRITANNIA HOSPITAL United Artists Classics, 1982, British
ALIEN 3 20th Century Fox, 1992, U.S.-British

CRISPIN GLOVER
RACING WITH THE MOON Paramount, 1984
RIVER'S EDGE Island Films, 1987
BACK TO THE FUTURE Universal, 1985
AT CLOSE RANGE Orion, 1986
WHERE THE HEART IS Buena Vista, 1990
WILD AT HEART Samuel Goldwyn Company, 1990
THE DOORS TriStar, 1991
LITTLE NOISES Monument Pictures, 1991
EVEN COWGIRLS GET THE BLUES Fine Line Features/New Line Cinema, 1994

DANNY GLOVER
b. July 22, 1947 - San Francisco, California
Agent: William Morris Agency - Beverly Hills, 310/274-7451

ICEMAN Universal, 1984
WITNESS Paramount, 1985
SILVERADO Columbia, 1985
LETHAL WEAPON Warner Bros., 1987
BAT 21 TriStar, 1988
DEAD MAN OUT (CTF) HBO Showcase/Citadel Entertainment Productions/Granada TV, 1989, U.S.-Canadian-British
LONESOME DOVE (MS) Motown Productions/Pangaea/Qintex Entertainment, Inc., 1989
LETHAL WEAPON 2 Warner Bros., 1989
PREDATOR 2 20th Century Fox, 1990
TO SLEEP WITH ANGER Samuel Goldwyn Company, 1990
FLIGHT OF THE INTRUDER Paramount, 1991
A RAGE IN HARLEM Miramax Films, 1991, U.S.-British
PURE LUCK Universal, 1991
GRAND CANYON 20th Century Fox, 1991
LETHAL WEAPON 3 Warner Bros., 1992
BOPHA! Paramount, 1993
THE SAINT OF FORT WASHINGTON Warner Bros., 1993
MAVERICK Warner Bros., 1994 (uncredited)
ANGELS IN THE OUTFIELD Buena Vista, 1994
OPERATION DUMBO DROP Buena Vista, 1995

EILEEN GLOVER
SYLVIA MGM/UA Classics, 1985, New Zealand

JOHN GLOVER
ANNIE HALL United Artists, 1977
JULIA 20th Century Fox, 1977
LAST EMBRACE United Artists, 1979
A LITTLE SEX Universal, 1982
AN EARLY FROST (TF) NBC Productions, 1985
52 PICK-UP Cannon, 1986
NUTCRACKER: MONEY, MADNESS AND MURDER (MS) Green Arrow Productions/Warner Bros. TV, 1987
A KILLING AFFAIR Hemdale, 1988
THE CHOCOLATE WAR MCEG, 1988
MASQUERADE MGM/UA, 1988
ROCKET GIBRALTAR Columbia, 1988
MOVING TARGET (TF) Lewis B. Chesler Productions/Bateman Company Productions/Finnegan-Pinchuk Company/MGM-UA TV, 1988
DAVID (TF) Tough Boys Inc./Donald March Productions/ITC Entertainment Group, 1988
HOT PAINT (TF) Catalina Production Group/MGM-UA TV, 1988
SCROOGED Paramount, 1988
BREAKING POINT (CTF) Avnet-Kerner Company, 1989
TWIST OF FATE (TF) Henry Plitt-Larry White Productions/HTV/Columbia TV, 1989, British-U.S.
GREMLINS 2 THE NEW BATCH Warner Bros., 1990
EL DIABLO (CTF) HBO Pictures/Wizan-Black Films, 1990
ED AND HIS DEAD MOTHER I.R.S. Releasing, 1993
NIGHT OF THE RUNNING MAN Trimark Pictures, 1994
AUTOMATIC Active Entertainment, 1994

JULIAN GLOVER
TOM JONES Lopert, 1963, British
THE GIRL WITH GREEN EYES United Artists, 1964, British
TIME LOST AND TIME REMEMBERED *I WAS HAPPY HERE* Continental, 1966, British
ALFRED THE GREAT MGM, 1969, British
THE ADDING MACHINE 1969, U.S.-British
WUTHERING HEIGHTS American International, 1970, British
NICHOLAS AND ALEXANDRA Columbia, 1971, British
DEAD CERT United Artists, 1973, British
JUGGERNAUT United Artists, 1974, British
THE BRUTE Rank, 1976, British
FOR YOUR EYES ONLY United Artists, 1981, British
HEAT AND DUST Universal Classics, 1983, British
CRY FREEDOM Universal, 1987, British-U.S.
INDIANA JONES AND THE LAST CRUSADE Paramount, 1989
TREASURE ISLAND (CTF) Agamemnon Films/British Lion, 1990, British-U.S.
KING RALPH Universal, 1991

SAVION GLOVER
TAP TriStar, 1989

TAWNY SUNSHINE GLOVER
HANS CHRISTIAN ANDERSEN'S THUMBELINA (AF) Warner Bros., 1994 (voice)

CARLIN GLYNN
Agent: William Morris Agency - Beverly Hills, 310/274-7451

THREE DAYS OF THE CONDOR Paramount, 1975
THE TRIP TO BOUNTIFUL Island Pictures/FilmDallas, 1985
NIGHT GAME Trans World Entertainment, 1989

TAMARA GLYNN
HALLOWEEN 5 - THE REVENGE OF MICHAEL MYERS Galaxy, 1989

HENRY GODINEZ
ABOVE THE LAW Warner Bros., 1988

ALEXANDER GODUNOV
b. November 28, 1949 - Sakhalin Island, Russia

WITNESS Paramount, 1985
THE MONEY PIT Universal, 1986
DIE HARD 20th Century Fox, 1988
NORTH Columbia, 1994

ANGELA GOETHALS
ROCKET GIBRALTAR Columbia, 1988
FULLY LOADED Buena Vista, 1991

SARA GOETHALS
ROCKET GIBRALTAR Columbia, 1988

PETER MICHAEL GOETZ
KING KONG LIVES DEG, 1986
JUMPIN' JACK FLASH 20th Century Fox, 1986
PROMISE (TF) Garner-Duchow Productions/Warner Bros. TV, 1986
RIGHT TO DIE (TF) Ohlmeyer Communications, 1987
THE KAREN CARPENTER STORY (TF) Weintraub Entertainment Group, 1989
DAD Universal, 1989
ANOTHER YOU TriStar, 1991

JOANNA GOING
Agent: William Morris Agency - Beverly Hills, 310/274-7451

WYATT EARP Warner Bros., 1994

BRANDY GOLD
OH, GOD! YOU DEVIL Warner Bros., 1984
WILDCATS Warner Bros., 1986

TRACEY GOLD
SHOOT THE MOON   MGM/United Artists, 1982
A REASON TO LIVE (TF)   Rastar Productions/Robert Papazian
   Productions, 1985

WHOOPI GOLDBERG
(Caryn Johnson)
b. November 13, 1950 - New York, New York
Agent: CAA - Beverly Hills, 310/288-4545

THE COLOR PURPLE ★   Warner Bros., 1985
JUMPIN' JACK FLASH   20th Century Fox, 1986
FATAL BEAUTY   MGM/UA, 1987
BURGLAR   Warner Bros., 1987
THE TELEPHONE   New World, 1988
CLARA'S HEART   Warner Bros., 1988
KISS SHOT (TF)   London Productions/Whoop, Inc., 1989
HOMER & EDDIE   Skouras Pictures, 1990
GHOST ∞   Paramount, 1990
THE LONG WALK HOME   Miramax Films, 1990
SOAPDISH   Paramount, 1991
THE PLAYER   Fine Line Features/New Line Cinema, 1992
SISTER ACT   Buena Vista, 1992
SARAFINA!   Miramax Films/Buena Vista, 1992,
   South African-British-French
MADE IN AMERICA   Warner Bros., 1993
SISTER ACT 2: BACK IN THE HABIT   Buena Vista, 1993
NAKED IN NEW YORK   Fine Line Features/New Line Cinema, 1994
THE LION KING (AF)   Buena Vista, 1994 (voice)
CORRINA, CORRINA   New Line Cinema, 1994
THE PAGEMASTER   20th Century Fox, 1994 (voice)
STAR TREK GENERATIONS   Paramount, 1994
BOYS ON THE SIDE   Warner Bros., 1995
MOONLIGHT AND VALENTINO   Gramercy Pictures, 1995
T. REX   New Line Cinema, 1995
BOGUS   Warner Bros., 1995

JEFF GOLDBLUM
b. October 22, 1952 - Pittsburg, Pennsylvania

DEATH WISH   Paramount, 1974
CALIFORNIA SPLIT   Columbia, 1974
NASHVILLE   Paramount, 1975
NEXT STOP, GREENWICH VILLAGE   20th Century-Fox, 1976
BETWEEN THE LINES   Midwest Film Productions, 1977
ANNIE HALL   United Artists, 1977
INVASION OF THE BODY SNATCHERS   United Artists, 1978
REMEMBER MY NAME   Columbia/Lagoon Associates, 1978
THANK GOD IT'S FRIDAY   Columbia, 1978
TENSPEED AND BROWNSHOE (TF)   Stephen J. Cannell
   Productions, 1980
REHEARSAL FOR MURDER (TF)   Levinson-Link Productions/
   Robert Papazian Productions, 1982
THRESHOLD   20th Century Fox International Classics,
   1983, Canadian
THE BIG CHILL   Columbia, 1983
THE RIGHT STUFF   The Ladd Company/Warner Bros., 1983
THE ADVENTURES OF BUCKAROO BONZAI: ACROSS THE
   8TH DIMENSION   20th Century Fox, 1984
INTO THE NIGHT   Universal, 1985
TRANSYLVANIA 6-5000   New World, 1985
SILVERADO   Columbia, 1985
THE FLY   20th Century Fox, 1986, U.S.-Canadian
BEYOND THERAPY   New World, 1987
VIBES   Columbia, 1988
EARTH GIRLS ARE EASY   Vestron, 1989
TWISTED OBSESSION   Majestic Films International, 1990
THE TALL GUY   Miramax Films, 1990
THE PLAYER   Fine Line Features/New Line Cinema, 1992
DEEP COVER   New Line Cinema, 1992
THE FAVOR, THE WATCH, AND THE VERY BIG FISH   Trimark
   Pictures, 1991, French-British
JURASSIC PARK   Universal, 1993
HIDEAWAY   TriStar, 1995
NINE MONTHS   20th Century Fox, 1995

ANNIE GOLDEN
THE PEBBLE AND THE PENGUIN (AF)   MGM/UA, 1995 (voice)

NORMAN D. GOLDEN II
COP AND A HALF   Universal, 1993

MICHAEL GOLDFINGER
HARLEM NIGHTS   Paramount, 1989

RICKY PAULL GOLDIN
Agent: Metropolitan Talent Agency - Los Angeles, 213/857-4500

LOVE LIVES ON (TF)   ABC Circle Films, 1985
LAMBADA   Warner Bros., 1990

MARCY GOLDMAN
b. Chicago, Illinois
Agent: Rickey Barr Agency - Los Angeles, 213/276-0887

EVERYTHING YOU ALWAYS WANTED TO KNOW ABOUT SEX*
   (*BUT WERE AFRAID TO ASK)   United Artists, 1972
THE KENTUCKY FRIED MOVIE   United Film Distribution, 1977
AIRPLANE!   Paramount, 1980
SUBURBAN COMMANDO   New Line Cinema, 1991
HER FINAL FURY: BETTY BRODERICK, THE LAST CHAPTER (TF)
   Patchett Kaufman Entertainment/Lowry-Rawls Productions, 1992
NAKED GUN 33 1/3: THE FINAL INSULT   Paramount, 1994
MONKEY TROUBLE   New Line Cinema, 1994
NIGHT OF THE RUNNING MAN   Trimark Pictures, 1994

DANNY GOLDRING
ABOVE THE LAW   Warner Bros., 1988

BERT GOLDSTEIN
BIG   20th Century Fox, 1988

JENETTE GOLDSTEIN
Agent: Harris & Goldberg - Los Angeles, 310/553-5200

ALIENS   20th Century Fox, 1986
NEAR DARK   DEG, 1987

BOB GOLDTHWAIT
(Bobcat Goldthwait)
b. 1962 - Syracuse, New York

POLICE ACADEMY 2: THEIR FIRST ASSIGNMENT
   Warner Bros., 1985
POLICE ACADEMY 3: BACK IN TRAINING   Warner Bros., 1986
ONE CRAZY SUMMER   Warner Bros., 1986
BURGLAR   Warner Bros., 1987
POLICE ACADEMY 4: CITIZENS ON PATROL   Warner Bros., 1987
HOT TO TROT   Warner Bros., 1988
SCROOGED   Paramount, 1988
SHAKES THE CLOWN   I.R.S. Releasing, 1992 (also directed)
FREAKED   20th Century Fox, 1993

TONY GOLDWYN
Agent: CAA - Beverly Hills, 310/288-4545

GHOST   Paramount, 1990
KUFFS   Universal, 1992
TRACES OF RED   Samuel Goldwyn Company, 1992
THE PELICAN BRIEF   Warner Bros., 1993

VALERIA GOLINO
Agent: CAA - Beverly Hills, 310/288-4545

A JOKE OF DESTINY LYING IN WAIT AROUND THE CORNER LIKE
   A STREET BANDIT   Samuel Goldwyn Company, 1983, Italian
BIG TOP PEE-WEE   Paramount, 1988
RAIN MAN   MGM/UA, 1988
TORRENTS OF SPRING   Millimeter Films, 1990
HOT SHOTS!   20th Century Fox, 1991
THE INDIAN RUNNER   MGM-Pathe, 1991
YEAR OF THE GUN   Columbia, 1991
HOT SHOTS! PART DEUX   20th Century Fox, 1993
CLEAN SLATE   MGM/UA, 1994
IMMORTAL BELOVED   Columbia, 1994

JAIME GOMEZ
CRIMSON TIDE   Buena Vista, 1995

MATEO GOMEZ
DELTA FORCE 2 - OPERATION STRANGLEHOLD
   MGM/UA, 1990

ALISON GOMPF
CHILDREN OF A LESSER GOD   Paramount, 1986

CAROLINE GOODALL
CLIFFHANGER   TriStar, 1993
SCHINDLER'S LIST   Universal, 1993
DISCLOSURE   Warner Bros., 1994

CAROL GOODHEART
ON VALENTINE'S DAY *STORY OF A MARRIAGE*
   Angelika Films, 1986

CUBA GOODING, JR.
BOYZ 'N THE HOOD   Columbia, 1991
GLADIATOR   Columbia, 1992
DAYBREAK (CTF)   Foundation Entertainment Productions/
   HBO Showcase, 1993
JUDGMENT NIGHT   Universal, 1993
LIGHTNING JACK   Savoy Pictures, 1994, Australian-U.S.
LOSING ISAIAH   Paramount, 1995
OUTBREAK   Warner Bros., 1995

DEAN GOODMAN
TUCKER - THE MAN AND HIS DREAM   Paramount, 1988

JOHN GOODMAN
b. June 20, 1953 - St. Louis, Missouri
Agent: Gersh Agency - Beverly Hills, 310/274-6611

C.H.U.D.   New World, 1984
REVENGE OF THE NERDS   20th Century Fox, 1984
SWEET DREAMS   TriStar, 1985
TRUE STORIES   Warner Bros., 1986
RAISING ARIZONA   20th Century Fox, 1987
BURGLAR   Warner Bros., 1987
THE BIG EASY   Columbia, 1987
PUNCHLINE   Columbia, 1988
EVERYBODY'S ALL-AMERICAN   Warner Bros., 1988
SEA OF LOVE   Universal, 1989
ALWAYS   Universal, 1989
STELLA   Buena Vista, 1990
ARACHNOPHOBIA   Buena Vista, 1990
KING RALPH   Universal, 1991
BARTON FINK   20th Century Fox, 1991
THE BABE   Universal, 1992
MATINEE   Universal, 1993
BORN YESTERDAY   Buena Vista, 1993
WE'RE BACK! A DINOSAUR'S STORY (AF)   Universal,
   1993 (voice)
THE FLINTSTONES   Universal, 1994
HUEY LONG (CTF)   Turner Network TV, 1995

DEBORAH GOODRICH
Agent: CNA & Associates - Los Angeles, 310/556-4343

APRIL FOOL'S DAY   Paramount, 1986
LIBERACE (TF)   The Liberace Foundation/Dick Clark Productions/
   Republic Pictures, 1988

JAMIE GOODWIN
LET IT BE ME   Savoy Pictures, 1995

MICHAEL GOODWIN
BUY & CELL   Empire Pictures, 1989

THATCHER GOODWIN
STEALING HOME   Warner Bros., 1988

MICHAEL GOORJIAN
Agent: APA - Los Angeles, 310/273-0744

NEWSIES   Buena Vista, 1992
DAVID'S MOTHER (TF)   Hearst Entertainment, 1994
SAFE PASSAGE   New Line Cinema, 1994

DON GORDON
Z.P.G.   Paramount, 1972, British
SKIN DEEP   20th Century Fox, 1989

EVE GORDON
AVALON   TriStar, 1990
THE BOYS (TF)   William Link Productions/Papazian-Hirsch
   Productions, 1991
PARADISE   Buena Vista, 1991

HILARY GORDON
THE MOSQUITO COAST   Warner Bros., 1986

KEITH GORDON
DRESSED TO KILL   Filmways, 1980
CHRISTINE   Columbia, 1983
SINGLE BARS, SINGLE WOMEN (TF)   Carsey-Werner Productions/
   Sunn Classic Pictures, 1984
BACK TO SCHOOL   Orion, 1986
COMBAT HIGH (TF)   Frank von Zerneck Productions/Lynch-Biller
   Productions, 1986

JOHN GORDON-SINCLAIR
THE GIRL IN THE PICTURE   Samuel Goldwyn Company,
   1986, British

BREON GORMAN
CHEETAH   Buena Vista, 1989

CLIFF GORMAN
Agent: Paradigm - Los Angeles, 310/277-4400

JUSTINE   20th Century Fox, 1969
THE BOYS IN THE BAND   National General, 1970
COPS AND ROBBERS   United Artists, 1973
STRIKE FORCE (TF)   D'Antoni-Weitz Television Productions, 1975
ROSEBUD   United Artists, 1975
AN UNMARRIED WOMAN   20th Century Fox, 1978
ALL THAT JAZZ   20th Century Fox, 1979
NIGHT OF THE JUGGLER   Columbia, 1980
ANGEL   New World, 1984
DOUBLETAKE (MS)   Titus Productions, 1985
INTERNAL AFFAIRS (MS)   Titus Productions, 1988
MURDER IN BLACK AND WHITE (TF)   Titus Productions, 1990
NIGHT AND THE CITY   20th Century Fox, 1992

ROBERT GORMAN
THE ACCIDENTAL TOURIST   Warner Bros., 1988
MR. NANNY   New Line Cinema, 1993

KAREN LYNN GORNEY
Agent: Lucy Kroll Agency - New York, 212/877-0556

DAVID AND LISA   Continental, 1962
SATURDAY NIGHT FEVER   Paramount, 1977

MARJOE GORTNER
THE MARCUS NELSON MURDERS (TF)   Universal TV, 1973
EARTHQUAKE   Universal, 1974
THE GUN AND THE PULPIT (TF)   Danny Thomas Productions, 1974
FOOD OF THE GODS   American International, 1976
BOBBIE JOE AND THE OUTLAW   American International, 1976
SIDEWINDER ONE   Avco Embassy, 1977
VIVA KNIEVEL!   Warner Bros., 1977
ACAPULCO GOLD   R.C. Riddell, 1978
STARCRASH   New World, 1979, Italian
WHEN YOU COMIN' BACK, RED RYDER?   Columbia, 1979

HELL HOLE   Arkoff International Pictures, 1985
AMERICAN NINJA 3: BLOOD HUNT   Cannon, 1989
WILD BILL   MGM/UA, 1995

LOUIS GOSSETT JR.
b. May 27, 1936 - Brooklyn, New York
Agent: CAA - Beverly Hills, 310/288-4545

A RAISIN IN THE SUN   Columbia, 1961
COMPANIONS IN NIGHTMARE (TF)   1968
THE LANDLORD   United Artists, 1970
TRAVELS WITH MY AUNT   MGM, 1972, British
IT'S GOOD TO BE ALIVE (TF)   Metromedia Productions, 1974
SIDEKICKS (TF)   Warner Bros. TV, 1974
THE WHITE DAWN   Paramount, 1974
DELANCEY STREET (TF)   Paramount TV, 1975
THE RIVER NIGER   Cine Artists, 1976
THE DEEP   Columbia, 1977
ROOTS (MS)   Wolper Productions, 1977
THE CHOIRBOYS   Universal, 1977
LITTLE LADIES OF THE NIGHT (TF)   Spelling-Goldberg
   Productions, 1978
TO KILL A COP (TF)   David Gerber Company/Columbia TV, 1978
THE CRITICAL LIST (TF)   MTM Productions, 1978
BACKSTAIRS AT THE WHITE HOUSE (MS)   Ed Friendly
   Productions, 1979
THE LAZARUS SYNDROME (TF)   Blinn-Thorpe Productions/
   Viacom, 1979
THIS MAN STANDS ALONE (TF)   Roger Gimbel Productions/
   EMI TV/Abby Mann Productions, 1979
DON'T LOOK BACK (TF)   TBA Productions/Satie Productions/
   TRISEME, 1981
BENNY'S PLACE (TF)   Titus Productions, 1982
AN OFFICER AND A GENTLEMAN ⚭⚭   Paramount, 1982
SADAT (TF)   Blatt-Singer Productions/Columbia TV, 1983
JAWS 3-D   Universal, 1983
FINDERS KEEPERS   Warner Bros., 1984
THE GUARDIAN (CTF)   HBO Premiere Films/Robert Cooper
   Productions/Stanley Chase Productions, 1984, U.S.-Canadian
ENEMY MINE   20th Century Fox, 1985
FIREWALKER   Cannon, 1986
IRON EAGLE   TriStar, 1986
A GATHERING OF OLD MEN (TF)   Consolidated Productions/
   Jennie & Company/Zenith Productions, 1987
FIREWALKER   Cannon, 1987
THE PRINCIPAL   TriStar, 1987
THE FATHER CLEMENTS STORY (TF)   Zev Braun Productions/
   Interscope Communications, 1987
IRON EAGLE II   TriStar, 1988, Canadian-Israeli
ROOTS: THE GIFT (TF)   Wolper Productions/Warner
   Bros. TV, 1988
THE PUNISHER   New World, 1989
EL DIABLO (CTF)   HBO Pictures/Wizan-Black Films, 1990
THE JOSEPHINE BAKER STORY (CTF)   HBO Pictures/RHI
   Entertainment/Anglia TV/John Kemeny Productions, 1991
TOY SOLDIERS   TriStar, 1991
ACES: IRON EAGLE III   New Line Cinema, 1992
DIGGSTOWN   MGM-Pathe Entertainment, 1992
A GOOD MAN IN AFRICA   Gramercy Pictures, 1994

ROBERT GOSSETT
MENENDEZ: A KILLING IN BEVERLY HILLS (MS)   Zev Braun
   Pictures/TriStar Television, 1994

WALTER GOTELL
HOT MONEY GIRL   *THE TREASURE OF SAN TERESA*
   United Producers Releasing Corporation, 1959, British
THE GUNS OF NAVARONE   Columbia, 1961, U.S.-British
THE DAMNED   Columbia, 1961, British
OUR MISS FRED   1972
THE SPY WHO LOVED ME   United Artists, 1977,
   British-U.S.
THE BOYS FROM BRAZIL   20th Century Fox, 1978
FOR YOUR EYES ONLY   United Artists, 1980, British
BASIC TRAINING   The Movie Store, 1985

GILBERT GOTTFRIED
Agent: William Morris Agency - Beverly Hills, 310/274-7451

THE ADVENTURES OF FORD FAIRLANE   20th Century Fox, 1990
ALADDIN (AF)   Buena Vista, 1992 (voice)
HOUSE PARTY 3   New Line Cinema, 1994
HANS CHRISTIAN ANDERSEN'S THUMBELINA (AF)   Warner Bros.,
   1994 (voice)
THE RETURN OF JAFAR (AV)   Buena Vista, 1994 (voice)

THOMAS GOTTSCHALK
THINK BIG   MPCA, 1990

MICHAEL GOUGH
b. November 23, 1917 - Malaya
Agent: Gersh Agency - Beverly Hills, 310/274-6611

BLANCHE FURY   1947
ANNA KARENINA   20th Century Fox, 1948, British
SARABAND   *SARABAND FOR DEAD LOVERS*   Eagle Lion,
   1948, British
THE SMALL BACK ROOM   *HOUR OF GLORY*   Snader Productions,
   1949, British
THE MAN IN THE WHITE SUIT   Rank, 1951, British
NO RESTINGPLACE   1951
THE SWORD AND THE ROSE   1953
ROB ROY   1953
RICHARD III   Lopert, 1956
HORROR OF DRACULA   *DRACULA*   Universal, 1958, British
HORRORS OF THE BLACK MUSEUM   1958
THE HORSE'S MOUTH   United Artists, 1959, British
KONGA   1961
CANDIDATE FOR MURDER   1962
THE PHANTOM OF THE OPERA   Universal, 1962, British
BLACK ZOO   1963
DR. TERROR'S HOUSE OF HORRORS   Paramount, 1965, British
THE SKULL   Paramount, 1965, British
THEY CAME FROM BEYOND SPACE   Embassy, 1967, British
BERSERK   Columbia, 1967, British
A WALK WITH LOVE AND DEATH   20th Century Fox, 1969, British
WOMEN IN LOVE   United Artists, 1970, British
JULIUS CAESAR   American International, 1970, British
TROG   Warner Bros., 1970, British
THE GO-BETWEEN   Columbia, 1971, British
SAVAGE MESSIAH   MGM, 1972, British
HENRY VIII AND HIS SIX WIVES   Levitt-Pickman, 1972, British
GALILEO   American Film Theatre, 1975, British-Canadian
THE BOYS FROM BRAZIL   20th Century Fox, 1978
THE DRESSER   Columbia, 1983, British
MEMED MY HAWK   Filmworld Distributors, 1983, British-Yugoslavian
TOP SECRET!   Paramount, 1984
LACE II (MS)   Lorimar Productions, 1985
OUT OF AFRICA   Universal, 1985
CARAVAGGIO   British Film Institute, 1986, British
BATMAN   Warner Bros., 1989
LET HIM HAVE IT   Fine Line Features/New Line Cinema, 1991,
   British-French-Dutch
BATMAN RETURNS   Warner Bros., 1992
NOSTRADAMUS   Orion Classics, 1994, British
BATMAN FOREVER   Warner Bros., 1995

ELLIOTT GOULD
(Elliott Goldstein)
b. August 29, 1938 - Brooklyn, New York
Agent: Shapira & Associates - Sherman Oaks, 818/906-0322

THE NIGHT THEY RAIDED MINSKY'S   United Artists, 1968
BOB & CAROL & TED & ALICE ⚭   Columbia, 1969
M*A*S*H   20th Century Fox, 1970
GETTING STRAIGHT   Columbia, 1970
MOVE   20th Century Fox, 1970
I LOVE MY WIFE   Universal, 1970
THE TOUCH   Cinerama Releasing Corporation, 1971, Swiss-U.S.
LITTLE MURDERS   20th Century Fox, 1971
THE LONG GOODBYE   United Artists, 1973
BUSTING   United Artists, 1974
S*P*Y*S   20th Century Fox, 1974, British-U.S.
CALIFORNIA SPLIT   Columbia, 1974

WHO? Allied Artists, 1975
NASHVILLE Paramount, 1975
WHIFFS 20th Century Fox, 1975
MEAN JOHNNY BARROWS Atlas, 1976
I WILL I WILL...FOR NOW 20th Century Fox, 1976
HARRY AND WALTER GO TO NEW YORK Columbia, 1976
A BRIDGE TOO FAR United Artists, 1977, British
THE SILENT PARTNER EMC Film/Aurora, 1978, Canadian
CAPRICORN ONE 20th Century Fox, 1978
MATILDA American International, 1978
THE LADY VANISHES Rank, 1979, British
ESCAPE TO ATHENA AFD, 1979, British
THE MUPPET MOVIE AFD, 1979, British
FALLING IN LOVE AGAIN *IN LOVE* International Picture Show
     Company, 1980
THE LAST FLIGHT OF NOAH'S ARK Buena Vista, 1980
DIRTY TRICKS Avco Embassy, 1981, Canadian
THE DEVIL AND MAX DEVLIN Buena Vista, 1981
THE MUPPETS TAKE MANHATTAN TriStar, 1984
THE NAKED FACE Cannon, 1985
INSIDE OUT Hemdale, 1986
VANISHING ACT (TF) Robert Cooper Productions,
     1986, U.S.-Canadian
THE TELEPHONE New World, 1988
DANGEROUS LOVE Motion Picture Corporation of America, 1988
CRY DEVIL Premiere Pictures, 1989
STOLEN: ONE HUSBAND (TF) King Phoenix Entertainment, 1990
THE LEMON SISTERS Miramax Films, 1990
DEAD MEN DON'T DIE JGM Enterprises, 1991
BUGSY TriStar, 1991
LET IT BE ME Savoy Pictures, 1995

HAROLD GOULD
b. December 10, 1923 - Schenectady, New York

HE AND SHE 1969
WHERE DOES IT HURT? American International, 1971, British
THE STING Universal, 1973
LOVE AND DEATH United Artists, 1975
THE BIG BUS Paramount, 1976
SILENT MOVIE 20th Century Fox, 1976
WASHINGTON: BEHIND CLOSED DOORS (MS)
     Paramount TV, 1977
SEEMS LIKE OLD TIMES Columbia, 1980
THE MAN IN THE SANTA CLAUS SUIT (TF) Dick Clark
     Productions, 1980
MOVIOLA (MS) David L. Wolper-Stan Margulies Productions/
     Warner Bros. TV, 1980
THE ONE AND ONLY Paramount, 1978
MRS. DELAFIELD WANTS TO MARRY (TF) Schaefer-Karpf
     Productions/Gaylord Production Company, 1986
GET SMART, AGAIN! (TF) Phoenix Entertainment Group/IndieProd
     Company, 1989
ROMERO Four Seasons Entertainment, 1989

JASON GOULD
THE BIG PICTURE Columbia, 1989
THE PRINCE OF TIDES Columbia, 1991

RAY GOULDING
AUTHOR! AUTHOR! 20th Century Fox, 1982

ROBERT GOULET
b. November 26, 1933 - Lawrence, Massachusetts

HONEYMOON HOTEL MGM, 1963
I'D RATHER BE RICH Universal, 1964
ATLANTIC CITY Paramount, 1981, Canadian-French
SCROOGED Paramount, 1988
THE NAKED GUN 2 1/2: THE SMELL OF FEAR Paramount, 1991

CYNTHIA GOUW
STAR TREK V: THE FINAL FRONTIER Paramount, 1989

GREGORY GOUYER
THE ACCIDENTAL TOURIST Warner Bros., 1988

DAVID GOW
MRS. PARKER AND THE VICIOUS CIRCLE Fine Line Features/
     New Line Cinema, 1994

HARRY GOZ
MOMMIE DEAREST Paramount, 1981

JOHN CHRISTIAN GRAAS
PHILADELPHIA EXPERIMENT 2 Trimark Pictures, 1993

NICKOLAS GRACE
DIAMOND'S EDGE Kings Road Entertainment, 1990

DAVID GRAF
b. April 16, 1950 - Lancaster, Ohio

FOUR FRIENDS Filmways, 1981
THE LONG SUMMER OF GEORGE ADAMS (TF)
     Warner Bros. TV, 1982
IRRECONCILABLE DIFFERENCES Warner Bros., 1984
POLICE ACADEMY The Ladd Company/Warner Bros., 1984
POLICE AC ADEMY 2: THEIR FIRST ASSIGNMENT
     Warner Bros., 1985
POLICE ACADEMY 3: BACK IN TRAINING Warner Bros., 1986
POLICE ACADEMY 4: CITIZENS ON PATROL Warner Bros., 1987
THE TOWN BULLY (TF) Dick Clark Productions, 1988
LOVE AT STAKE *BURNIN' LOVE* TriStar, 1988
POLICE ACADEMY 5: ASSIGNMENT MIAMI BEACH
     Warner Bros., 1988
POLICE ACADEMY 6: CITY UNDER SIEGE Warner Bros., 1989
THE BRADY BUNCH MOVIE Paramount, 1995

ILENE GRAFF
LADYBUGS Paramount, 1992

TODD GRAFF
NOT QUITE PARADISE *NOT QUITE JERUSALEM* New World,
     1986, British
SWEET LORRAINE Angelika Films, 1987
DOMINICK AND EUGENE Orion, 1988
FIVE CORNERS Cineplex Odeon, 1988
THE ABYSS 20th Century Fox, 1989
HARD RAIN Buena Vista, 1989
OPPORTUNITY KNOCKS Universal, 1990

BILLY GRAHAM
BUGSY TriStar, 1991

C.J. GRAHAM
FRIDAY THE 13TH, PART VI: JASON LIVES Paramount, 1986

GARY GRAHAM
Agent: Metropolitan Talent Agency - Los Angeles, 213/857-4500

ROBOTJOX Triumph Releasing Corporation, 1990

GERRITT GRAHAM
Agent: Gersh Agency - Beverly Hills, 310/274-6611

PHANTOM OF THE PARADISE 20th Century-Fox, 1974
USED CARS Columbia, 1980
TERRORVISION Empire Pictures, 1986
POLICE ACADEMY 6: CITY UNDER SIEGE Warner Bros., 1989
CHILD'S PLAY 2 Universal, 1990
PHILADELPHIA EXPERIMENT 2 Trimark Pictures, 1993

HEATHER GRAHAM
Agent: CAA - Beverly Hills, 310/288-4545

LICENSE TO DRIVE 20th Century Fox, 1988
DRUGSTORE COWBOY Avenue Pictures, 1989
GUILTY AS CHARGED I.R.S. Media, 1991
ALL SHOOK UP Universal, 1991
DIGGSTOWN MGM-Pathe Entertainment, 1992
MRS. PARKER AND THE VICIOUS CIRCLE Fine Line Features/
     New Line Cinema, 1994

HEPBURN GRAHAM
CRUSOE   Island Pictures, 1988, U.S.-British

GAWN GRAINGER
AUGUST   Granada Films, 1995

SETH GRANGER
THE ACCIDENTAL TOURIST   Warner Bros., 1988

BETH GRANT
SPEED   20th Century Fox, 1994
TO WONG FOO, THANKS FOR EVERYTHING, JULIE NEWMAR
   Universal, 1995

DAVID MARSHALL GRANT
(David Grant)
b. Westport, Connecticut
Agent: ICM - Beverly Hills, 310/550-4000

FRENCH POSTCARDS   Paramount, 1979
HAPPY BIRTHDAY, GEMINI   United Artists, 1980
KENT STATE (TF)   Inter Planetary Productions/Osmond
   Communications, 1981
SESSIONS (TF)   Roger Gimbel Productions/EMI TV/Sarabande
   Productions, 1983
AMERICAN FLYERS   Warner Bros., 1985
DALLAS: THE EARLY YEARS (TF)   Roundelay Productions/
   Lorimar Telepictures, 1986
THE BIG TOWN   Columbia, 1987
BAT 21   TriStar, 1988
AIR AMERICA   TriStar, 1990
STRICTLY BUSINESS   Warner Bros., 1991

FAYE GRANT
THE JANUARY MAN   MGM/UA, 1989
THE GUN IN BETTY LOU'S HANDBAG   Buena Vista, 1992

HUGH GRANT
MAURICE   Cinecom, 1987, British
IMPROMPTU   Hemdale, 1990, U.S.-French
OUR SONS (TF)   Robert Greenwald Productions, 1991
THE REMAINS OF THE DAY   Columbia, 1993, British
SIRENS   Miramax Films, 1993, Australian-British-German
BITTER MOON   Fine Line Features/New Line Cinema, 1993,
   French-British
FOUR WEDDINGS AND A FUNERAL   Gramercy Pictures,
   1994, British
RESTORATION   Miramax Films, 1994
NINE MONTHS   20th Century Fox, 1995
AN AWFULLY BIG ADVENTURE   Fine Line Features/New Line
   Cinema, 1995, British

LEE GRANT
(Lyova Rosenthal)
b. October 31, 1927 - New York, New York
Agent: Camden ITG - Los Angeles, 310/289-2700

DETECTIVE STORY ✪   Paramount, 1951
STORM FEAR   United Artists, 1956
MIDDLE OF THE NIGHT   Columbia, 1959
THE BALCONY   Continental, 1963
AN AFFAIR OF THE SKIN   1963
TERROR IN THE CITY   1966
DIVORCE AMERICAN STYLE   Columbia, 1967
IN THE HEAT OF THE NIGHT   United Artists, 1967
VALLEY OF THE DOLLS   20th Century Fox, 1967
BUONA SERA, MRS. CAMPBELL   United Artists, 1969
THE BIG BOUNCE   Warner Bros., 1969
MAROONED   Columbia, 1969
THE LANDLORD ✪   United Artists, 1970
THERE WAS A CROOKED MAN   Warner Bros., 1970
NIGHT SLAVES (TF)   Bing Crosby Productions, 1970
PLAZA SUITE   Paramount, 1971
THE NEON CEILING (TF)   Universal TV, 1971
LIEUTENANT SCHUSTER'S WIFE (TF)   Universal TV, 1972

PORTNOY'S COMPLAINT   Warner Bros., 1972
PARTNERS IN CRIME (TF)   Universal TV, 1973
WHAT ARE BEST FRIENDS FOR? (TF)   ABC Circle Films, 1973
THE INTERNECINE PROJECT   Allied Artists, 1974, British
SHAMPOO ✪✪   Columbia, 1975
VOYAGE OF THE DAMNED ✪   Avco Embassy, 1976, British
AIRPORT '77   Universal, 1977
THE SPELL (TF)   Charles Fries Productions, 1977
DAMIEN—OMEN II   20th Century Fox, 1978
THE MAFU CAGE   *MY SISTER, MY LOVE/THE DAGE*
   Clouds Productions, 1978
THE SWARM   Warner Bros., 1978
BACKSTAIRS AT THE WHITE HOUSE (MS)   Ed Friendly
   Productions, 1979
WHEN YOU COMIN' BACK, RED RYDER?   Columbia, 1979
YOU CAN'T GO HOME AGAIN (TF)   CBS Entertainment, 1979
LITTLE MISS MARKER   Universal, 1980
FOR LADIES ONLY (TF)   The Catalina Production Group/
   Viacom, 1981
CHARLIE CHAN AND THE CURSE OF THE DRAGON QUEEN
   American Cineman, 1981
VISITING HOURS   20th Century Fox, 1982, Canadian
WILL THERE REALLY BE A MORNING? (TF)   Jaffe-Blakely Films/
   Sarna Productions/Orion TV, 1983
TEACHERS   MGM/UA, 1984
MUSSOLINI: THE UNTOLD STORY (MS)   Trian Productions, 1985
THE BIG TOWN   Columbia, 1987
THE HIJACKING OF THE ACHILLE LAURO (TF)   Tamara Asseyev
   Productions/Spectator Films/New World TV, 1989
DEFENDING YOUR LIFE   The Geffen Company/Warner Bros., 1991

MICAH GRANT
TERMINAL BLISS   Cannon, 1992

RICHARD E. GRANT
HOW TO GET AHEAD IN ADVERTISING   Warner Bros.,
   1989, British
HENRY & JUNE   Universal, 1990
WARLOCK   Trimark Pictures, 1991
L.A. STORY   TriStar, 1991
HUDSON HAWK   TriStar, 1991
THE PLAYER   Fine Line Features/New Line Cinema, 1992
BRAM STOKER'S DRACULA   *DRACULA*   Columbia, 1992
THE AGE OF INNOCENCE   Columbia, 1993
PRET-A-PORTER   Miramax Films, 1994

RODNEY A. GRANT
Agent: The Geddes Agency - Los Angeles, 213/651-2401

SON OF THE MORNING STAR (TF)   Republic Pictures/The Mount
   Company, 1990
DANCES WITH WOLVES   Orion, 1990
WAGONS EAST   TriStar, 1994

KAREN GRASSLE
WYATT EARP   Warner Bros., 1994

JUDY GRAUBART
AUTHOR! AUTHOR!   20th Century Fox, 1982

PETER GRAVES
(Peter Aurness)
b. March 18, 1925 - Minneapolis, Minnesota

ROGUE RIVER   1950
FORT DEFIANCE   1951
RED PLANET MARS   1952
STALAG 17   Paramount, 1953
BENEATH THE TWELVE MILE REEF   1953
THE RAID   20th Century Fox, 1954
BLACK TUESDAY   United Artists, 1954
THE LONG GRAY LINE   Columbia, 1955
THE NIGHT OF THE HUNTER   United Artists, 1955
THE COURT-MARTIAL OF BILLY MITCHELL   Warner Bros., 1955
IT CONQUERED THE WORLD   American International, 1956
THE BEGINNING OF THE END   Republic, 1957

WOLF LARSEN   1958
A RAGE TO LIVE   United Artists, 1965
TEXAS ACROSS THE RIVER   Universal, 1966
VALLEY OF MYSTERY   1967
THE BALLAD OF JOSIE   Universal, 1968
SERGEANT RYKER   Universal, 1968
THE FIVE MAN ARMY   MGM, 1970, Italian
CALL TO DANGER (TF)   Paramount TV, 1973
THE PRESIDENT'S PLANE IS MISSING (TF)
   ABC Circle Films, 1973
SCREAM OF THE WOLF (TF)   Metromedia Producers
   Corporation, 1974
THE UNDERGROUND MAN (TF)   Paramount TV, 1974
WHERE HAVE ALL THE PEOPLE GONE? (TF)
   Metromedia Productions, 1974
DEAD MAN ON THE RUN (TF)   Sweeney-Finnegan
   Productions, 1975
SIDECAR RACERS   Universal, 1975, Australian
THE MYSTERIOUS MONSTERS   *BIGFOOT, THE MYSTERIOUS
   MONSTER*   Sunn Classic, 1976
CRUISE MISSILE   Eichberg Film/Cinelux-Romano Film/Mundial
   Film/Cine-Luce/Noble Productions/FPDC, 1978,
   West German-Spanish-U.S.-Iranian
THE REBELS (TF)   Universal TV, 1979
AIRPLANE!   Paramount, 1980
DEATH CAR ON THE FREEWAY (TF)   Shpetner Productions, 1980
THE MEMORY OF EVA RYKER (TF)   Irwin Allen Productions, 1980
AIRPLANE II: THE SEQUEL   Paramount, 1982
SAVANNAH SMILES   Embassy, 1982
THE WINDS OF WAR (MS)   Paramount TV/Dan Curtis
   Productions, 1983
NUMBER ONE WITH A BULLET   Cannon, 1987
IF IT'S TUESDAY, IT STILL MUST BE BELGIUM (TF)
   Eisenstock & Mintz Productions, 1987
MISSION IMPOSSIBLE - THEGOLDEN SERPENT (TF)
   Paramount TV, 1989

RUPERT GRAVES

Agent: William Morris Agency - Beverly Hills, 310/274-7451

A HANDFUL OF DUST   New Line Cinema, 1988
DAMAGE   New Line Cinema, 1992, French-British
THE MADNESS OF GEORGE III   Samuel Goldwyn Company, 1995

BRUCE GRAY

DRAGNET   Universal, 1987

DAVID BARRY GRAY

GERONIMO - AN AMERICAN LEGEND   Columbia, 1993

ERIN GRAY

b. January 7, 1952 - Honolulu, Hawaii

JASON GOES TO HELL—THE FINAL FRIDAY
   New Line Cinema, 1993

LINDA GRAY

b. September 12, 1940 - Santa Monica, Califronia

KENNY ROGERS AS THE GAMBLER III: THE LEGEND
   CONTINUES (TF)   Lion Share Productions, 1987
OSCAR   Buena Vista, 1991

SAM GRAY

STEAL THE SKY (CTF)   HBO Pictures/Yoram Ben Ami
   Productions/Paramount TV, 1988

SPALDING GRAY

THE FARMER'S DAUGHTER   1973
VARIETY   1983
ALMOST YOU   TLC Films/20th Century Fox, 1984
THE COMMUNISTS ARE COMFORTABLE (AND THREE
   OTHER STORIES)   1984
THE KILLING FIELDS   Warner Bros., 1984, British
HARD CHOICES   Lorimar, 1986
SEVEN MINUTES IN HEAVEN   Warner Bros., 1986

TRUE STORIES   Warner Bros., 1986
SWIMMING TO CAMBODIA (PF)   Cinecom, 1987
CLARA'S HEART   Warner Bros., 1988
BEACHES   Buena Vista, 1988
HEAVY PETTING   1988
STARS AND BARS   1988
SPALDING GRAY'S MONSTER IN A BOX   *MONSTER IN A
   BOX* (PF)   Fine Line Features/New Line Cinema, 1991, British
STRAIGHT TALK   Buena Vista, 1992
KING OF THE HILL   Gramercy Pictures, 1993
THE PAPER   Universal, 1994

JOE GRECO

ABOUT LAST NIGHT...   TriStar, 1986
ABOVE THE LAW   Warner Bros., 1988

BILLY GREEN BUSH

(See Billy Green BUSH)

FRANK ROZELAAR GREEN

THE PRINCESS AND THE GOBLIN (AF)   Hemdale, 1994 (voice)

JANET LAINE GREEN

BULLIES   Universal, 1986, Canadian

KERRI GREEN

LUCAS   20th Century Fox, 1986

SETH GREEN

RADIO DAYS   Orion, 1987
AIRBORNE   Warner Bros., 1993

SHON GREENBLATT

NEWSIES   Buena Vista, 1992

DANIEL GREENE

ARTHUR 2 ON THE ROCKS   Warner Bros., 1988
ELVIRA, MISTRESS OF THE DARK   New World, 1988

ELLEN GREENE

Agent: William Morris Agency - Beverly Hills, 310/274-7451

NEXT STOP, GREENWICH VILLAGE   20th Century-Fox, 1976
LITTLE SHOP OF HORRORS   The Geffen Company/
   Warner Bros., 1986
ME AND HIM   Columbia, 1988
TALK RADIO   Universal, 1988
DINNER AT EIGHT (CTF)   Think Entertainment/Turner
   Network TV, 1989
PUMP UP THE VOLUME   New Line Cinema, 1990
STEPPING OUT   Paramount, 1991
ROCK-A-DOODLE (AF)   Samuel Goldwyn Company, 1992 (voice)
WAGONS EAST   TriStar, 1994

GRAHAM GREENE

Agent: Susan Smith & Associates - Beverly Hills, 213/852-4777

DANCES WITH WOLVES ✪   Orion, 1990
THUNDERHEART   TriStar, 1992
BENEFIT OF THE DOUBT   Miramax Films, 1993
NORTH   Columbia, 1994
DIE HARD 3   20th Century Fox, 1995

H. RICHARD GREENE

MENENDEZ: A KILLING IN BEVERLY HILLS (MS)   Zev Braun
   Pictures/TriStar Television, 1994

JAMES GREENE

PHILADELPHIA EXPERIMENT 2   Trimark Pictures, 1993

MICHAEL GREENE

LORD OF THE FLIES   Columbia, 1990

MICHELLE GREENE

PERRY MASON: THE CASE OF THE NOTORIOUS NUN (TF)
Intermedia Productions/Strathmore Productions/Viacom
Productions, 1986
DOUBLE STANDARD (TF)   Louis Rudolph Productions/Fenton
Entertainment Group/Fries Entertainment, 1988

PETER GREENE

JUDGMENT NIGHT   Universal, 1993

SHECKY GREENE

b. April 8, 1926 - Chicago, Illinois

HISTORY OF THE WORLD—PART 1   20th Century-Fox, 1981

BRAD GREENQUIST

THE BEDROOM WINDOW   DEG, 1987
PET SEMATARY   *STEPHEN KING'S PET SEMATARY*
Paramount, 1989

BRUCE GREENWOOD

Agent: APA - Los Angeles, 310/273-0744

DESTINATION: AMERICA (TF)   Stephen J. Cannell
Productions, 1987
IN THE LINE OF DUTY: THE FBI MURDERS (TF)   Telecom
Entertainment/World International Network, 1988
TWIST OF FATE (MS)   Henry Plitt-Larry White Productions/HTV/
Columbia TV, 1989, British-U.S.
SPY (CTF)   Deadly Productions/Wilshire Cour Productions, 1989
SUMMER DREAMS: THE STORY OF THE BEACH BOYS (TF)
Leonard Hill Films, 1990
THE LITTLE KIDNAPPERS (CTF)   Jones Maple Leaf Productions/
The Disney Channel/CBC/Resnick-Margellos Productions,
1990, Canadian

JANE GREER
(Bettejane Greer)

b. September 9, 1924 - Washington, D.C.

TWO O'CLOCK COURAGE   RKO Radio, 1945
PAN AMERICANA   RKO Radio, 1945
GEORGE WHITE'S SCANDALS   RKO Radio, 1945
DICK TRACY, DETECTIVE   RKO Radio, 1945
THE FALCON'S ALIBI   RKO Radio, 1946
THE BAMBOO BLONDE   RKO Radio, 1946
SUNSET PASS   RKO Radio, 1946
SINBAD THE SAILOR   RKO Radio, 1947
THEY WON'T BELIEVE ME   RKO Radio, 1947
OUT OF THE PAST   RKO Radio, 1947
STATION WEST   RKO Radio, 1948
THE BIG STEAL   RKO Radio, 1949
THE COMPANY SHE KEEPS   RKO Radio, 1951
YOU'RE IN THE NAVY NOW   *U.S.S. TEAKETTLE*
20th Century Fox, 1951
YOU FOR ME   MGM, 1952
THE PRISONER OF ZENDA   MGM, 1952
DESPERATE SEARCH   MGM, 1952
THE CLOWN   MGM, 1953
DOWN AMONG THE SHELTERING PALMS
20th Century Fox, 1953
RUN FOR THE SUN   United Artists, 1956, British
MAN OF A THOUSAND FACES   Universal, 1957
WHERE LOVE HAS GONE   Paramount, 1964
BILLIE   United Artists, 1965
THE OUTFIT   MGM, 1974
THE SHADOW RIDERS (TF)   The Pegasus Group, Ltd./
Columbia TV, 1982
AGAINST ALL ODDS   Columbia, 1984
JUST BETWEEN FRIENDS   Orion, 1986
IMMEDIATE FAMILY   Columbia, 1989

BRADLEY GREGG

Agent: Paradigm - Los Angeles, 310/277-4400

CLASS OF 1999   Vestron, 1989
MADHOUSE   Orion, 1990

VIRGINIA GREGG

EVITA PERON (TF)   Hartwest Productions/Zephyr
Productions, 1981

ANDRE GREGORY

Agent: William Morris Agency - Beverly Hills, 310/274-7451

MY DINNER WITH ANDRE   New Yorker, 1981
ALWAYS   Samuel Goldwyn Company, 1985
THE MOSQUITO COAST   Warner Bros., 1986
STREET SMART   Cannon, 1987
DEMOLITION MAN   Warner Bros., 1993

KIM GREIST

C.H.U.D.   New World, 1984
BRAZIL   Universal, 1985, British
MANHUNTER   DEG, 1986
THROW MOMMA FROM THE TRAIN   Orion, 1987
PUNCHLINE   Columbia, 1988
HOMEWARD BOUND: THE INCREDIBLE JOURNEY
Buena Vista, 1993
HOUSEGUEST   Buena Vista, 1995

GOOGY GRESS

MAXIE   Orion, 1985
AMERICAN ANTHEM   Columbia, 1986
VIBES   Columbia, 1988
BLOODHOUNDS OF BROADWAY   Columbia, 1989

LAURENT GREVILL

CAMILLE CLAUDEL   Orion Classics, 1988, French

JENNIFER GREY

Agent: CAA - Beverly Hills, 310/288-4545

RED DAWN   MGM/UA, 1984
THE COTTON CLUB   Orion, 1984
AMERICAN FLYERS   Warner Bros., 1985
FERRIS BUELLER'S DAY OFF   Paramount, 1986
DIRTY DANCING   Vestron, 1987
BLOODHOUNDS OF BROADWAY   Columbia, 1989
MURDER IN MISSISSIPPI (TF)   Wolper Productions/Bernard
Sofronski Productions/Warner Bros. TV, 1990
CRIMINAL JUSTICE (CTF)   HBO Pictures, 1991
WIND   TriStar, 1992, U.S.-Japanese

JOEL GREY
(Joel Katz)

b. April 11, 1932 - Cleveland, Ohio
Agent: William Morris Agency - Beverly Hills, 310/274-7451

ABOUT FACE   Warner Bros., 1952
CALYPSO HEAT WAVE   1957
COME SEPTEMBER   Universal, 1961
CABARET OO   Allied Artists, 1972
MAN ON A SWING   Paramount, 1974
BUFFALO BILL AND THE INDIANS or SITTING BULL'S HISTORY
LESSON   United Artists, 1976
THE SEVEN-PER-CENT SOLUTION   Universal, 1976, British
REMO WILLIAMS: THE ADVENTURE BEGINS   Orion, 1985
QUEENIE (TF)   von Zerneck-Samuels Productions/Highgate
Pictures, 1987
THE MUSIC OF CHANCE   I.R.S. Releasing, 1993

RICHARD GRIECO

Agent: CAA - Beverly Hills, 310/288-4545

IF LOOKS COULD KILL   Warner Bros., 1991
MOBSTERS   Universal, 1991

DAVID ALAN GRIER
Agent: William Morris Agency - Beverly Hills, 310/274-7451
Manager: Amy Howard Management - Los Angeles, 310/475-6020

BOOMERANG   Paramount, 1992
IN THE ARMY NOW   Buena Vista, 1994
BLANKMAN   Columbia, 1994
TALES FROM THE HOOD   Savoy Pictures, 1995

PAM GRIER
Agent: APA - Los Angeles, 310/273-0744

BEYOND THE VALLEY OF THE DOLLS   20th Century Fox, 1970
THE BIG DOLL HOUSE   New World, 1971
THE BIG BIRD CAGE   New World, 1972
HIT MAN   MGM, 1972
TWILIGHT PEOPLE   Dimension, 1972, U.S.-Filipino
BLACK MAMA, WHITE MAMA   American International, 1973
COFFY   American International, 1973
SCREAM, BLACULA, SCREAM!   1973
THE ARENA   New World, 1974
FOXY BROWN   American International, 1974
SHEBA BABY   1975
BUCKTOWN   American International, 1975
FRIDAY FOSTER   American International, 1975
DRUM   United Artists, 1976
GREASED LIGHTNING   Warner Bros., 1977
FORT APACHE, THE BRONX   20th Century Fox, 1981
SOMETHING WICKED THIS WAY COMES   Buena Vista, 1983
ON THE EDGE   Skouras Pictures, 1986
ABOVE THE LAW   Warner Bros., 1988
THE PACKAGE   Orion, 1989
CLASS OF 1999   Vestron, 1989
BILL & TED'S BOGUS JOURNEY   Orion, 1991

JONATHAN GRIES
Agent: Susan Smith & Associates - Beverly Hills, 213/852-4777

TERRORVISION   Empire Pictures, 1986
RUNNING SCARED   MGM/UA, 1986

JOE GRIFASI
BAD MEDICINE   20th Century Fox, 1985
F/X   Orion, 1986
MATEWAN   Cinecom, 1987
BEACHES   Buena Vista, 1988

SIMONE GRIFFETH
THE PATRIOT   Crown International, 1986

EDDIE GRIFFIN
Agent: William Morris Agency - Beverly Hills, 310/274-7451

THE METEOR MAN   MGM/UA, 1993
JASON'S LYRIC   1994

LORIE GRIFFIN
ALOHA SUMMER   *HANAUMA BAY*   Spectrafilm, 1988

MERV GRIFFIN
b. July 6, 1925 - San Mateo, California

SLAPSTICK OF ANOTHER KIND   *SLAPSTICK*   Entertainment
   Releasing Corporation/International Film Marketing, 1983

MICHAEL GRIFFIN
SONNY BOY   Triumph Releasing Corporation, 1990

ANDY GRIFFITH
(Andrew Samuel Griffith)
b. June 1, 1926 - Mount Airy, North Carolina
Agent: William Morris Agency - Beverly Hills, 310/274-7451

A FACE IN THE CROWD   Warner Bros., 1957
NO TIME FOR SERGEANTS   Warner Bros., 1958
ONIONHEAD   Warner Bros., 1958
THE SECOND TIME AROUND   20th Century Fox, 1961

ANGEL IN MY POCKET   Universal, 1969
WINTER KILL (TF)   Andy Griffith Enterprises/MGM TV, 1974
HEARTS OF THE WEST   MGM/United Artists, 1975
WASHINGTON: BEHIND CLOSED DOORS (MS)   Paramount TV, 1977
THE GIRL IN THE EMPTY GRAVE (TF)   NBC TV, 1977
DEADLY GAME (TF)   MGM TV, 1977
CENTENNIAL (MS)   Universal TV, 1978
FROM HERE TO ETERNITY (TF)   Bennett-Katleman Productions/
   Columbia TV, 1979
ROOTS: NEXT GENERATIONS (MS)   Wolper Productions, 1979
FATAL VISION (MS)   NBC Productions, 1984
CRIM EOF INNOCENCE (TF)   Ohlmeyer Communications, 1985
DIARY OF A PERFECT MURDER (TF)   Viacom Productions, 1986
RETURN TO MAYBERRY (TF)   Strathmore Productions/Viacom
   Productions, 1986
UNDER THE INFLUENCE (TF)   CBS Entertainment, 1986
MATLOCK: THE HUNTING PARTY (TF)   The Fred Silverman
   Company/Dean Hargrove Productions/Viacom, 1989

MELANIE GRIFFITH
b. August 9, 1957 - New York, New York
Agent: ICM - Beverly Hills, 310/550-4000

THE HARRAD EXPERIMENT   Cinerama Releasing Corporation, 1973
SMILE   United Artists, 1975
NIGHT MOVES   Warner Bros., 1975
THE DROWNING POOL   Warner Bros., 1975
JOYRIDE   American International, 1977
ONE ON ONE   Warner Bros., 1977
STEEL COWBOY (TF)   Roger Gimbel Productions/EMI TV, 1978
THE STAR MAKER (TF)   Channing-Debin-Locke Company/Carson
   Productions, 1981
SHE'S IN THE ARMY NOW (TF)   ABC Circle Films, 1981
ROAR   1981
BODY DOUBLE   Columbia, 1984
FEAR CITY   Chevy Chase Distribution, 1984
ALFRED HITCHCOCK PRESENTS (TF)   Universal TV, 1985
SOMETHING WILD   Orion, 1986
CHERRY 2000   Orion, 1988 (filmed in 1986)
THE MILAGRO BEANFIELD WAR   Universal, 1988
STORMY MONDAY   Atlantic Releasing Corporation, 1988, British
WORKING GIRL ★   20th Century Fox, 1988
IN THE SPIRIT   Castle Hill Productions, 1990
PACIFIC HEIGHTS   20th Century Fox, 1990
WOMEN & MEN: STORIES OF SEDUCTION (CTF)
   HBO Showcase/David Brown Productions, 1990
THE BONFIRE OF THE VANITIES   Warner Bros., 1990
PARADISE   Buena Vista, 1991
SHINING THROUGH   20th Century Fox, 1992
A STRANGER AMONG US   Buena Vista, 1992
BORN YESTERDAY   Buena Vista, 1993
MILK MONEY   Paramount, 1994
NOBODY'S FOOL   Paramount, 1994
GASLIGHT ADDITION   New Line Cinema, 1995
BUFFALO GIRLS (MS)   Lauren Film Productions, Inc./CBS, 1995

RICHARD GRIFFITHS
Agent: William Morris Agency - Beverly Hills, 310/274-7451

KING RALPH   Universal, 1991

THOMAS IAN GRIFFITH
Agent: CAA - Beverly Hills, 310/288-4545

THE KARATE KID PART III   Columbia, 1989
ROCK HUDSON (TF)   The Konigsberg-Sanitsky Company, 1990

TRACY GRIFFITH
THE FIRST POWER   Orion, 1990
DESERT SHIELD   21st Century Distribution, 1991

RICHARD GRIFFITHS
GORKY PARK   Orion, 1983
GREYSTOKE: THE LEGEND OF TARZAN, LORD OF THE APES
   Warner Bros., 1984, British-U.S.
A PRIVATE FUNCTION   Island Alive, 1984, British
SHANGHAI SURPRISE   MGM/UA, 1986, British-U.S.
BLAME IT ON THE BELLBOY   Buena Vista, 1992, British

SCOTT GRIMES

Agent: Metropolitan Talent Agency - Los Angeles, 213/857-4500

CRITTERS   New Line Cinema, 1986

TAMMY GRIMES

b. January 30, 1934 - Lynn, Massachusetts

THREE BITES OF THE APPLE   1967
ARTHUR ARTHUR   1969
THE OTHER MAN (TF)   Universal TV, 1970
PLAY IT AS IT LAYS   Universal, 1972
THE BORROWERS (TF)   Walt DeFaria Productions/
   20th Century Fox TV, 1973
HORROR AT 37,000 FEET (TF)   CBS, Inc., 1973
SOMEBODY KILLED HER HUSBAND   Columbia, 1978
YOU CAN'T GO HOME AGAIN (TF)   CBS Entertainment, 1979
THE RUNNER STUMBLES   20th Century Fox, 1979
CAN'T STOP THE MUSIC   AFD, 1980
MR. NORTH   Samuel Goldwyn Company, 1988

TIM GRIMM

CLEAR AND PRESENT DANGER   Paramount, 1994

SKIP GRIPARIS

MAJOR LEAGUE II   Warner Bros., 1994

GEORGE GRIZZARD

b. April 1, 1928 - Roanoke Rapids, North Carolina
Agent: Paradigm - Los Angeles, 310/277-4400

FROM THE TERRACE   20th Century Fox, 1960
ADVISE AND CONSENT   Columbia, 1962
WARNING SHOT   Paramount, 1967
HAPPY BIRTHDAY WANDA JUNE   Columbia, 1971
TRAVIS LOGAN, D.A. (TF)   QM Productions, 1971
INDICT AND CONVICT (TF)   Universal TV, 1974
THE STRANGER WITHIN (TF)   Lorimar Productions, 1974
ATTACK ON TERROR: THE FBI VS. THE KU KLUX KLAN (TF)
   QM Productions, 1975
COMES A HORSEMAN   United Artists, 1978
THE NIGHT RIDER (TF)   Stephen J. Cannell Productions/
   Universal TV, 1979
FIREPOWER   AFD, 1979, British
SEEMS LIKE OLD TIMES   Columbia, 1980
BACHELOR PARTY   20th Century Fox, 1984
THE DELIBERATE STRANGER (MS)   Stuart Phoenix Productions/
   Lorimar-Telepictures, 1986
THAT SECRET SUNDAY (TF)   CBS Entertainment, 1986
DAVID (TF)   Tough Boys, Inc./Donald March Productions/ITC
   Entertainment Group, 1988
FALSE WITNESS (TF)   Valente-Kritzer-EPI Productions/
   New World TV, 1989
CAROLINE? (TF)   Barry & Enright Productions, 1990
GHOSTS CAN'T DO IT   Triumph Releasing Corporation, 1990

CHARLES GRODIN

b. April 21, 1935 - Pittsburgh, Pennsylvania
Agent: UTA - Beverly Hills, 310/273-6700

ROSEMARY'S BABY   Paramount, 1968
SEX AND THE COLLEGE GIRL   1970
CATCH-22   Paramount, 1970
THE HEARTBREAK KID   20th Century Fox, 1972
11 HARROWHOUSE   1974
KING KONG   Paramount, 1976
THIEVES   Paramount, 1977
HEAVEN CAN WAIT   Paramount, 1978
JUST ME AND YOU (TF)   Roger Gimbel Productions/EMI, 1978
THE GRASS IS ALWAYS GREENER OVER THE SEPTIC TANK (TF)
   Joe Hamilton Productions, 1978
SUNBURN   Paramount, 1979, U.S.-British
REAL LIFE   Paramount, 1979
IT'S MY TURN   Columbia, 1980
SEEMS LIKE OLD TIMES   Columbia, 1980
THE GREAT MUPPET CAPER   Universal/AFD, 1981, British

THE INCREDIBLE SHRINKING WOMAN   Universal, 1981
THE WOMAN IN RED   Orion, 1984
THE LONELY GUY   Universal, 1984
MOVERS & SHAKERS   MGM/UA, 1985
LAST RESORT   Concorde/Cinema Group, 1986
FRESNO (MS)   MTM Productions, 1986
ISHTAR   Columbia, 1987
THE COUCH TRIP   Orion, 1988
YOU CAN'T HURRY LOVE   MCEG, 1989
MIDNIGHT RUN   Universal, 1988
TAKING CARE OF BUSINESS   Buena Vista, 1990
BEETHOVEN   Universal, 1992
DAVE   Warner Bros., 1993
SO I MARRIED AN AXE MURDERER   TriStar, 1993
HEART AND SOULS   Universal, 1993
BEETHOVEN'S 2ND   Universal, 1993
CLIFFORD   Orion, 1994
IT RUNS IN THE FAMILY   MGM/UA, 1994

GARY GROOMES

WIRED   Taurus Entertainment, 1989

ARYE GROSS

Agent: William Morris Agency - Beverly Hills, 310/274-7451

SOUL MAN   New World, 1986
THE EXPERTS   Paramount, 1989
COUPE DE VILLE   Universal, 1990
A MIDNIGHT CLEAR   Interstar Releasing, 1992
SHAKING THE TREE   Castle Hill Productions, 1992
THE OPPOSITE SEX (AND HOW TO LIVE WITH THEM)
   Miramax Films, 1993
HEXED   Columbia, 1993

MARY GROSS

CLUB PARADISE   Warner Bros., 1986
BABY BOOM   MGM/UA, 1987
CASUAL SEX?   Universal, 1988
FEDS   Warner Bros., 1988
TROOP BEVERLY HILLS   Columbia, 1989

MICHAEL GROSS

b. June 21, 1947 - Chicago, Illinois

FAMILY TIES VACATION (TF)   Paramount TV/Ubu Productions/
   NBC Entertainment, 1985
A LETTER TO THREE WIVES (TF)   Michael Filerman Productions/
   20th Century Fox TV, 1985
RIGHT TO DIE (TF)   Ohlmeyer Communications, 1987
BIG BUSINESS   Buena Vista, 1988
IN THE LINE OF DUTY: THE FBI MURDERS (TF)   Telecom
   Entertainment/World International Network, 1988
A CONNECTICUT YANKEE IN KING ARTHUR'S COURT (TF)
   Schaefer-Karpf Productions/Consolidated Productions, 1989
TREMORS   Universal, 1990
FIRESTORM: A CATASTROPHE IN OAKLAND (TF)   ABC, 1993

PAUL GROSS

XXX'S & OOO'S (TF)   Moving Target Productions/New World
   Entertainment, 1994

GARY GRUBBS

Agent: Paradigm - Los Angeles, 310/277-4400

GUILTY OF INNOCENCE: THE LENELL GETER STORY (TF)
   Embassy TV, 1986
FOXFIRE (TF)   Marian Rees Associates, 1987
JFK   Warner Bros., 1991

OLIVIER GRUNER

NEMESIS   Imperial Entertainment, 1993

HARRY GUARDINO
b. December 23, 1925 - Brooklyn, New York
Agent: The Artists Group - Los Angeles, 310/552-1100

FLESH AND FURY   Universal, 1952
HOLD BACK TOMORROW   1955
HOUSEBOAT   Paramount, 1958
PORK CHOP HILL   United Artists, 1959
THE FIVE PENNIES   Paramount, 1959
FIVE BRANDED WOMEN   *JOVANKA E LE ALTRE*   Paramount,
    1960, Italian-Yugoslavian
KING OF KINGS   MGM, 1961
HELL IS FOR HEROES   Universal, 1962
THE PIGEON THAT TOOK ROME   Paramount, 1962
RHINO!   MGM, 1964
TREASURE OF SAN GENNARO   *OPERAZIONE SAN GENNARO*
    Paramount, 1966, Italian-French-West German
THE ADVENTURES OF BULLWHIP GRIFFIN   Buena Vista, 1967
VALLEY OF MYSTERY   1967
MADIGAN   Universal, 1968
JIGSAW   Universal, 1968
THE HELL WITH HEROES   Universal, 1968
LOVERS AND OTHER STRANGERS   Cinerama Releasing
    Corporation, 1970
RED SKY AT MORNING   Universal, 1970
DIRTY HARRY   Warner Bros., 1971
THEY ONLY KILL THEIR MASTERS   MGM, 1972
CAPONE   20th Century Fox, 1975
ST. IVES   Warner Bros., 1976
THE ENFORCER   Warner Bros., 1976
STREET KILLING (TF)   ABC Circle Films, 1976
ROLLERCOASTER   Universal, 1977
MATILDA   American International, 1978
EVENING IN BYZANTIUM (TF)   Universal TV, 1978
GOLDENGIRL   Avco Embassy, 1979
ANY WHICH WAY YOU CAN   Warner Bros., 1980

CASTULO GUERRA
Agent: Paradigm - Los Angeles, 310/277-4400

WHERE THE RIVER RUNS BLACK   MGM/UA, 1986

CHRISTOPHER GUEST
Agent: CAA - Beverly Hills, 310/288-4545

DEATH WISH   Paramount, 1974
THIS IS SPINAL TAP   Embassy, 1984
LITTLE SHOP OF HORRORS   The Geffen Company/
    Warner Bros., 1986
THE PRINCESS BRIDE   20th Century Fox, 1987
STICKY FINGERS   Spectrafilm, 1988
A FEW GOOD MEN   Columbia, 1992

LANCE GUEST
HALLOWEEN II   Universal, 1981
THE WIZARD OF LONELINESS   Skouras Pictures, 1988
FAVORITE SON (MS)   NBC Productions, 1988

FRANÇOIS GUETARY
LACE II (MS)   Lorimar Productions, 1985

NACHA GUEVARA
MISS MARY   New World, 1986, Argentina

CARLA GUGINO
Agent: William Morris Agency - Beverly Hills, 310/274-7451

SON-IN-LAW   Buena Vista, 1993

PAUL GUILFOYLE
BILLY GALVIN   Vestron, 1986
HOWARD THE DUCK   Universal, 1986
FINAL ANALYSIS   Warner Bros., 1992

ROBERT GUILLAUME
b. November 30, 1937 - St. Louis, Missouri
Agent: The Blake Agency - Beverly Hills, 310/246-0241

SEEMS LIKE OLD TIMES   Columbia, 1980
WANTED DEAD OR ALIVE   New World, 1986
PERRY MASON: THE CASE OF THE SCANDALOUS SCOUNDREL (TF)
    The Fred Silverman Company/Strathmore Productions/Viacom, 1987
THE PENTHOUSE (TF)   Greene-White Productions/
    Spectator Films, 1989
LEAN ON ME   Warner Bros., 1989
DEATH WARRANT   MGM/UA, 1990
THE METEOR MAN   MGM/UA, 1993
THE LION KING (AF)   Buena Vista, 1994 (voice)

TIM GUINEE
Agent: William Morris Agency - Beverly Hills, 310/274-7451

TAI-PAN   DEG, 1986
ONCE AROUND   Universal, 1991

ALEC GUINNESS
(Sir Alec Guinness)
b. April 2, 1914 - London, England

EVENSONG   Gaumont-British, 1934, British
GREAT EXPECTATIONS   Universal, 1946, British
OLIVER TWIST   United Artists, 1948, British
KIND HEARTS AND CORONETS   General Film Distributors,
    1949, British
A RUN FOR YOUR MONEY   1949, British
LAST HOLIDAY   1950, British
THE MUDLARK   20th Century Fox, 1950, British
THE LAVENDER HILL MOB ★   Universal, 1951, British
THE MAN IN THE WHITE SUIT   Rank, 1951, British
THE PROMOTER   *THE CARD*   Universal, 1952, British
THE CAPTAIN'S PARADISE   1953, British
THE MALTA STORY   Universal, 1953, British
FATHER BROWN   *THE DETECTIVE*   Columbia, 1954, British
TO PARIS WITH LOVE   General Film Distributors, 1955, British
THE PRISONER   Columbia, 1955, British
THE LADYKILLERS   Continental, 1955, British
THE SWAN   MGM, 1956
ALL AT SEA   *BARNACLE BILL*   1958, British
THE BRIDGE ON THE RIVER KWAI ★★   Columbia, 1957, British
THE HORSE'S MOUTH   United Artists, 1958, British
THE SCAPEGOAT   1959, British
OUR MAN IN HAVANA   1959, British
TUNES OF GLORY   Lopert, 1960, British
A MAJORITY OF ONE   Warner Bros., 1962
DAMN THE DEFIANT!   *H.M.S. DEFIANT*   Columbia, 1962, British
LAWRENCE OF ARABIA   Columbia, 1962, British
THE FALL OF THE ROMAN EMPIRE   Paramount, 1964
SITUATION HOPELESS—BUT NOT SERIOUS   Paramount, 1965
DOCTOR ZHIVAGO   MGM, 1965, British
HOTEL PARADISO   MGM, 1966, British
THE QUILLER MEMORANDUM   Paramount, 1966, British
THE COMEDIANS   MGM, 1967, British
CROMWELL   Columbia, 1970, British
SCROOGE   National General, 1970, British
BROTHER SUN SISTER MOON   Paramount, 1973, Italian-British
HITLER: THE LAST TEN DAYS   1973, Italian-British
MURDER BY DEATH   Columbia, 1976
STAR WARS ✪   20th Century Fox, 1977
TINKER, TAILOR, SOLDIER, SPY (TF)   BBC/Paramount TV,
    1979, British
THE EMPIRE STRIKES BACK   20th Century Fox, 1980
RAISE THE TITANIC   AFD, 1980, British-U.S.
LITTLE LORD FAUNTLEROY (TF)   Norman Rosemont Productions,
    1980, U.S.-British
SMILEY'S PEOPLE (MS)   BBC/Paramount TV, 1982, British
RETURN OF THE JEDI   20th Century Fox, 1983
LOVESICK   The Ladd Company/Warner Bros., 1983
A PASSAGE TO INDIA   Columbia, 1984, British
MONSIGNOR QUIXOTE (TF)   Thames TV, 1985, British
LITTLE DORRIT ✪   Cannon, 1987, British
A HANDFUL OF DUST   New Line Cinema, 1988
ERIK THE VIKING   Orion, 1989, British

JEWELL N. GUION
MISS FIRECRACKER   Corsair Pictures, 1989

TOM GUIRY
THE SANDLOT   20th Century Fox, 1993
LASSIE   Paramount, 1994

CLU GULAGER
THE KILLERS   Universal, 1964
WINNING   Universal, 1969
SAN FRANCISCO INTERNATIONAL AIRPORT (TF)
   Universal TV, 1970
THE LAST PICTURE SHOW   Columbia, 1971
THE GLASS HOUSE   *TRUMAN CAPOTE'S THE
   GLASS HOUSE* (TF)   Tomorrow Entertainment, 1972
FOOTSTEPS (TF)   Metromedia Productions, 1972
A CALL TO DANGER (TF)   Paramount TV, 1973
McQ   Warner Bros., 1974
THE KILLER WHO WOULDN'T DIE (TF)   Paramount TV, 1976
THE OTHER SIDE OF MIDNIGHT   20th Century-Fox, 1977
A FORCE OF ONE   American Cinema, 1979
TOUCHED BY LOVE   Columbia, 1980
THE RETURN OF THE LIVING DEAD   Orion, 1985
A NIGHTMARE ON ELM STREET 2: FREDDY'S REVENGE
   New Line Cinema, 1986
HUNTER'S BLOOD   Concorde, 1986
I'M GONNA GIT YOU SUCKA   MGM/UA, 1989

DAVID GULPILIL
"CROCODILE" DUNDEE   Paramount, 1986, Australian

MOSES GUNN
b. October 2, 1929 - St. Louis, Missouri

NOTHING BUT A MAN   Cinema 5, 1964
WHAT'S SO BAD ABOUT FEELING GOOD?   Universal, 1968
THE GREAT WHITE HOPE   20th Century Fox, 1970
CARTER'S ARMY (TF)   Thomas-Spelling Productions, 1970
WUSA   Paramount, 1970
WILD ROVERS   MGM, 1971
SHAFT   MGM, 1971
EAGLE IN A CAGE   National General, 1971, British-Yugoslavian
THE HOT ROCK   20th Century Fox, 1972
SHAFT'S BIG SCORE   MGM, 1972
HAUNTS OF THE VERY RICH (TF)   ABC Circle Films, 1972
THE ICEMAN COMETH   American Film Theatre, 1973
AMAZING GRACE   United Artists, 1974
CORNBREAD EARL AND ME   American International, 1975
ROLLERBALL   United Artists, 1975
AARON LOVES ANGELA   1975
REMEMBER MY NAME   Columbia/Lagoon Associates, 1978
THE NINTH CONFIGURATION   *TWINKLE, TWINKLE,
   "KILLER" KANE*   Warner Bros., 1980
RAGTIME   Paramount, 1981
AMITYVILLE II: THE POSSESSION   Orion, 1982
FIRESTARTER   Universal, 1984
HEARTBREAK RIDGE   Warner Bros., 1986
BATES MOTEL   Universal TV, 1987
THE WOMEN OF BREWSTER PLACE (MS)   Harpo Productions/
   Phoenix Entertainment Group, 1989

MORTY GUNTY
BROADWAY DANNY ROSE   Orion, 1984

BOB GUNTON
MATEWAN   Cinecom, 1987
COOKIE   Warner Bros., 1989
GLORY   TriStar, 1989
WILD PALMS (MS)   Ixtlan Corporation/Greengrass
   Productions, Inc., 1993
DEMOLITION MAN   Warner Bros., 1993
THE SHAWSHANK REDEMPTION   Columbia, 1994
DOLORES CLAIBORNE   Columbia, 1994

ERIC GURRY
AUTHOR! AUTHOR!   20th Century Fox, 1982
THE ZOO GANG   New World, 1986

SEREZHA GUSAK
KINDERGARTEN   IFEX Film, 1984, Soviet

LOUIS GUSS
MOONSTRUCK   MGM/UA, 1987

ARLO GUTHRIE
ROADSIDE PROPHETS   New Line Cinema, 1992

CAROLINE GUTHRIE
b. July 10, 1947 - New York, New York

THE GIRL IN THE PICTURE   Samuel Goldwyn Company,
   1986, British

STEVE GUTTENBERG
b. August 24, 1958 - Brooklyn, New York
Agent: William Morris Agency - Beverly Hills, 310/274-7451

SOMETHING FOR JOEY (TF)   MTM Productions, 1977
THE CHICKEN CHRONICLES   Avco Embassy, 1977
THE BOYS FROM BRAZIL   20th Century Fox, 1978
PLAYERS   Paramount, 1979
TO RACE THE WIND (TF)   Walter Grauman Productions, 1980
CAN'T STOP THE MUSIC   AFD, 1980
MIRACLE ON ICE (TF)   Moonlight Productions/Filmways, 1981
DINER   MGM/United Artists, 1982
THE MAN WHO WASN'T THERE   Paramount, 1983
THE DAY AFTER (TF)   ABC Circle Films, 1983
POLICE ACADEMY   The Ladd Company/Warner Bros., 1984
BAD MEDICINE   20th Century Fox, 1985
COCOON   20th Century Fox, 1985
POLICE ACADEMY 2: THEIR FIRST ASSIGNMENT
   Warner Bros., 1985
SHORT CIRCUIT   TriStar, 1986
POLICE ACADEMY 3: BACK IN TRAINING   Warner Bros., 1986
THE BEDROOM WINDOW   DEG, 1987
POLICE ACADEMY 4: CITIZENS ON PATROL   Warner Bros., 1987
SURRENDER   Warner Bros., 1987
THREE MEN AND A BABY   Buena Vista, 1987
COCOON: THE RETURN   20th Century Fox, 1988
HIGH SPIRITS   TriStar, 1988, British
DON'T TELL HER IT'S ME   Hemdale, 1990
THREE MEN AND A LITTLE LADY   Buena Vista, 1990

LUCY GUTTERIDGE
TOP SECRET!   Paramount, 1984
A CHRISTMAS CAROL (TF)   Entertainment Partners Ltd.,
   1984, U.S.-British
HITLER'S S.S.: PORTRAIT IN EVIL (TF)   Colason Limited
   Productions/Edgar J. Scherick Associates, 1985, British-U.S.
THE WOMAN HE LOVED (TF)   The Larry Thompson Organization/
   HTV/New World TV, 1988, U.S.-British

RONALD GUTTMAN
HER ALIBI   Warner Bros., 1989
JOSH AND S.A.M.   Columbia, 1993

JASMINE GUY
b. March 10, 1964 - Boston, Massachusetts

HARLEM NIGHTS   Paramount, 1989

MICHAEL C. GWYNNE
Agent: Susan Smith & Associates - Beverly Hills, 213/852-4777

SPECIAL DELIVERY   American International, 1976
BUTCH AND SUNDANCE: THE EARLY DAYS
   20th Century-Fox, 1979
SEDUCED (TF)   Catalina Production Group/Comworld
   Productions, 1985

H

LUKAS HAAS
Agent: CAA - Beverly Hills, 310/288-4545

TESTAMENT   Paramount, 1983
WITNESS   Paramount, 1985
SHATTERED SPIRITS (TF)   Sheen-Greenblatt Productions/
   Robert Greenwald Productions, 1986
SOLARBABIES   MGM/UA, 1986
LADY IN WHITE   New Century/Vista, 1988
THE WIZARD OF LONELINESS   Skouras Pictures, 1988
THE RYAN WHITE STORY (TF)   The Landsburg Company, 1989
SEE YOU IN THE MORNING   Warner Bros., 1989
MUSIC BOX   TriStar, 1989
THE PERFECT TRIBUTE (CTF)   Dorothea Petrie Productions/
   Proctor & Gamble Productions/World International
   Network, 1991
RAMBLING ROSE   New Line Cinema, 1991
LEAP OF FAITH   Paramount, 1992
ALAN AND NAOMI   Triton Pictures, 1993
BOYS   Buena Vista, 1995

OLIVIA HACK
THE BRADY BUNCH MOVIE   Paramount, 1995

SHELLEY HACK
ANNIE HALL   United Artists, 1977
IF EVER I SEE YOU AGAIN   Columbia, 1978
TIME AFTER TIME   Orion/Warner Bros., 1979
SINGLE BARS, SINGLE WOMEN (TF)   Carsey-Werner
   Productions/Sunn Classic Pictures, 1984
KICKS (TF)   ABC Circle Films, 1985
TROLL   Empire Pictures, 1986
THE STEPFATHER   New Century/Vista, 1987
BRIDESMAIDS (TF)   Motown Productions/Qintex Entertainment/
   Deaune Productions, 1989
A CASUALTY OF WAR (CTF)   F.F.S. Productions/Taurus Film/
   Blair Communications, 1990, British

BUDDY HACKETT
(Leonard Hacker)
b. August 31, 1924 - Brooklyn, New York

WALKING MY BABY BACK HOME   Universal, 1953
GOD'S LITTLE ACRE   United Artists, 1958
ALL HANDS ON DECK   20th Century-Fox, 1961
EVERYTHING'S DUCKY   Columbia, 1961
THE WONDERFUL WORLD OF THE BROTHERS GRIMM
   MGM/Cinerama, 1962
THE MUSIC MAN   Warner Bros., 1962
IT'S A MAD MAD MAD MAD WORLD   United Artists, 1963
MUSCLE BEACH PARTY   American International, 1964
THE GOLDEN HEAD   Cinerama, 1965, Hungarian-U.S.
THE LOVE BUG   Buena Vista, 1969
THE GOOD GUYS AND THE BAD GUYS   Warner Bros.,
   1969 (uncredited)
BUD AND LOU (TF)   Bob Banner Associates, 1978
LOOSE SHOES   *COMING ATTRACTIONS*   Atlantic Releasing
   Corporation, 1980
SCROOGED   Paramount, 1988
THE LITTLE MERMAID (AF)   Buena Vista, 1989 (voice)

GENE HACKMAN
(Eugene Alder)
b. January 30, 1931 - San Bernardino, California
Agent: CAA - Beverly Hills, 310/288-4545

MAD DOG COLL   Columbia, 1961
LILITH   Columbia, 1964
HAWAII   United Artists, 1966
A COVENANT WITH DEATH   Warner Bros., 1967
BANNING   Universal, 1967
BONNIE AND CLYDE ✪   Warner Bros., 1967
FIRST TO FIGHT   Warner Bros., 1967
THE SPLIT   MGM, 1968
SHADOW ON THE LAND (TF)   Screen Gems/Columbia TV, 1968
DOWNHILL RACER   Paramount, 1969
THE GYPSY MOTHS   MGM, 1969
MAROONED   Columbia, 1969
RIOT   Paramount, 1969
I NEVER SANG FOR MY FATHER ✪   Columbia, 1970
THE HUNTING PARTY   United Artists, 1970
CISCO PIKE   Columbia, 1971
DOCTORS' WIVES   Columbia, 1971
THE FRENCH CONNECTION ★★   20th Century Fox, 1971
THE POSEIDON ADVENTURE   20th Century-Fox, 1972
PRIME CUT   National General, 1972
SCARECROW   Warner Bros., 1973
THE CONVERSATION   Paramount, 1974
YOUNG FRANKENSTEIN   20th Century-Fox, 1974
ZANDY'S BRIDE   *FOR BETTER, FOR WORSE*
   Warner Bros., 1974
BITE THE BULLET   Columbia, 1975
FRENCH CONNECTION II   20th Century-Fox, 1975
LUCKY LADY   20th Century-Fox, 1975
NIGHT MOVES   Warner Bros., 1975
A BRIDGE TOO FAR   United Artists, 1977, British
THE DOMINO PRINCIPLE   Avco Embassy, 1977
MARCH OR DIE   Columbia, 1977, British
SUPERMAN   Warner Bros., 1978, U.S.-British
SUPERMAN II   Warner Bros., 1981, U.S.-British
ALL NIGHT LONG   Universal, 1981
REDS   Paramount, 1981
UNCOMMON VALOR   Paramount, 1983
UNDER FIRE   Orion, 1983
TWO OF A KIND   20th Century-Fox, 1983 (voice)
EUREKA   MGM/UA Classics, 1984, British (filmed in 1981)
MISUNDERSTOOD   MGM/UA, 1984
TWICE IN A LIFETIME   The Yorkin Company, 1985
TARGET   Warner Bros., 1985
HOOSIERS   Orion, 1986
POWER   20th Century Fox, 1986
NO WAY OUT   Orion, 1987
SUPERMAN IV: THE QUEST FOR PEACE   Warner Bros., 1987
FULL MOON IN BLUE WATER   Trans World Entertainment, 1988
SPLIT DECISIONS   New Century/Vista, 1988
BAT 21   TriStar, 1988
ANOTHER WOMAN   Orion, 1988
MISSISSIPPI BURNING ★   Orion, 1988
THE PACKAGE   Orion, 1989
LOOSE CANNONS   TriStar, 1990
POSTCARDS FROM THE EDGE   Columbia, 1990
NARROW MARGIN   TriStar, 1990
CLASS ACTION   20th Century Fox, 1991
COMPANY BUSINESS   MGM-Pathe, 1991
UNFORGIVEN ✪✪   Warner Bros., 1992
THE FIRM   Paramount, 1993
GERONIMO - AN AMERICAN LEGEND   Columbia, 1993
WYATT EARP   Warner Bros., 1994
THE QUICK AND THE DEAD   TriStar, 1995
CRIMSON TIDE   Buena Vista, 1995

DAYLE HADDON
THE CHEATERS   1976, Italian
SEX WITH A SMILE   1976, Italian
NORTH DALLAS FORTY   Paramount, 1979
BEDROOM EYES   Film Gallery/Aquarius, 1984, Canadian
CYBORG   Cannon, 1989

RON HADDRICK
QUIGLEY DOWN UNDER MGM/UA, 1990

ROSS HAGEN
NIGHT CREATURE *OUT OF THE DARKNESS* Dimension, 1978
AVENGING ANGEL New World, 1985
ARMED RESPONSE CineTel, 1986
COMMANDO SQUAD Trans World Entertainment, 1987

MOLLY HAGAN
DALLAS: THE EARLY YEARS (TF) Roundelay Productions/
  Lorimar Telepictures, 1986
SOME KIND OF WONDERFUL Paramount, 1987
SHOOTDOWN (TF) Leonard Hill Films, 1988

JULIE HAGERTY
AIRPLANE! Paramount, 1980
A MIDSUMMER NIGHT'S SEX COMEDY Orion/Warner Bros., 1982
AIRPLANE II: THE SEQUEL Paramount, 1982
GOODBYE, NEW YORK Castle Hill Productions, 1985, U.S.-Israeli
LOST IN AMERICA The Geffen Company/Warner Bros., 1985
BAD MEDICINE 20th Century Fox, 1985
BEYOND THERAPY New World, 1987
RUDE AWAKENING Orion, 1989
BLOODHOUNDS OF BROADWAY Columbia, 1989
WHAT ABOUT BOB? Buena Vista, 1991
NOISES OFF Buena Vista, 1992

LARRY HAGMAN
(Larry Hageman)
b. September 21, 1931 - Fort Worth, Texas

ENSIGN PULVER Warner Bros., 1964
FAIL SAFE Columbia, 1964
IN HARM'S WAY Paramount, 1965
THE GROUP United Artists, 1966
UP IN THE CELLAR *THREE IN THE CELLAR* American
  International, 1970
VANISHED (TF) Universal TV, 1971
A HOWLING IN THE WOODS (TF) Universal TV, 1971
BEWARE! THE BLOB *SON OF BLOB* Jack H. Harris Enterprises,
  1972 (also directed)
THE ALPHA CAPER (TF) Universal TV, 1973
HARRY AND TONTO 20th Century-Fox, 1974
STARDUST Columbia, 1975, British
MOTHER, JUGS & SPEED 20th Century-Fox, 1976
THE BIG BUS Paramount, 1976
INTIMATE STRANGERS (TF) Charles Fries Productions, 1977
THE EAGLE HAS LANDED Columbia, 1977, British
S.O.B. Paramount, 1981
DEADLY ENCOUNTER (TF) Roger Gimbel Productions/
  EMI TV, 1982
DALLAS: THE EARLY YEARS (TF) Roundelay Productions/
  Lorimar Telepictures, 1986

CHARLES HAID
b. June 2, 1944 - San Francisco, California
Agent: William Morris Agency - Beverly Hills, 310/274-7451

ALTERED STATES Warner Bros., 1980
CHILDREN IN THE CROSSFIRE (TF) Schaefer-Karpf Productions/
  Prendergast-Brittcadia Productions/Gaylord Production
  Company, 1984
SIX AGAINST THE ROCK (TF) Schaefer-Karpf-Epstein
  Productions/Gaylord Production Company, 1987
WEEKEND WAR (TF) Pompian-Atamian Productions/
  Columbia TV, 1988
COP Atlantic Releasing Corporation, 1988
THE RESCUE Buena Vista, 1988
THE GREAT ESCAPE II: THE UNTOLD STORY (MS)
  Michael Jaffe Films/Spectacor Films, 1988
THE REVENGE OF AL CAPONE (TF) Unity Productions/River City
  Productions, 1989
A DEADLY SILENCE (TF) Robert Greenwald Productions, 1989
FIRE AND RAIN (CTF) Wilshire Court Productions, 1989
MAN AGAINST THE MOB: THE CHINATOWN MURDERS (TF)
  von Zerneck-Sertner Productions, 1989
NIGHTBREED 20th Century Fox, 1990

DAVID HAID
A WINNER NEVER QUITS (TF) Blatt-Singer Productions/
  Columbia TV, 1986

SID HAIG
C.C. AND COMPANY Avco Embassy, 1970
BEYOND ATLANTIS Dimension, 1973, U.S.-Filipino
COMMANDO SQUAD Trans World Entertainment, 1987
THE FORBIDDEN DANCE Columbia, 1990

KENNETH HAIGH
BAD GIRL *TEENAGE BAD GIRL/MY TEENAGE DAUGHTER*
  British Lion, 1956, British
HIGH FLIGHT 1958, British
SAINT JOAN United Artists, 1957
CLEOPATRA 20th Century-Fox, 1963
A HARD DAY'S NIGHT United Artists, 1964, British
THE DEADLY AFFAIR Columbia, 1967, British
A LOVELY WAY TO DIE Universal, 1968
EAGLE IN A CAGE National General, 1972, British-Yugoslavian
MAN AT THE TOP 1975, British
ROBIN AND MARIAN Columbia, 1976, British
THE BITCH Brent Walker Productions, 1979, British

COREY HAIM
b. 1971 - Toronto, Canada
Agent: APA - Los Angeles, 310/273-0744

FIRSTBORN Paramount, 1984
SECRET ADMIRER Orion, 1985
SILVER BULLET *STEPHEN KING'S SILVER BULLET*
  Paramount, 1985
MURPHY'S ROMANCE Columbia, 1985
A TIME TO LIVE (TF) Blue Andre Productions/
  ITC Productions, 1985
LUCAS 20th Century Fox, 1986
THE LOST BOYS Warner Bros., 1987
LICENSE TO DRIVE 20th Century Fox, 1988
WATCHERS Universal, 1988
DREAM A LITTLE DREAM Vestron, 1989

BARBARA HALE
b. April 18, 1921 - DeKalb, Illinois
Agent: David Shapira & Associates - Sherman Oaks, 818/906-0322

GILDERSLEEVE'S BAD DAY RKO Radio, 1943
THE SEVENTH VICTIM RKO Radio, 1943
THE IRON MAJOR RKO Radio, 1943
HIGHER AND HIGHER RKO Radio, 1944
THE FALCON OUT WEST RKO Radio, 1944
THE FALCON IN HOLLYWOOD RKO Radio, 1944
WEST OF THE PECOS RKO Radio, 1945
FIRST YANK INTO TOKYO RKO Radio, 1945
LADY LUCK RKO Radio, 1946
A LIKELY STORY RKO Radio, 1947
THE BOY WITH GREEN HAIR RKO Radio, 1948
THE CLAY PIGEON RKO Radio, 1949
THE WINDOW RKO Radio, 1949
JOLSON SINGS AGAIN Columbia, 1949
AND BABY MAKES THREE Columbia, 1949
EMERGENCY WEDDING Columbia, 1950
THE JACKPOT 20th Century-Fox, 1950
LORNA DOONE Columbia, 1951
THE FIRST TIME Columbia, 1952
SEMINOLE Universal, 1953
LONE HAND Universal, 1953
A LION IS IN THE STREETS Warner Bros., 1953
UNCHAINED Warner Bros., 1955
THE FAR HORIZONS Paramount, 1955
THE HOUSTON STORY Columbia, 1956
SEVENTH CAVALRY Columbia, 1956
THE OKLAHOMAN Allied Artists, 1957
DESERT HELL 20th Century-Fox, 1958
BUCKSKIN Paramount, 1968
AIRPORT Universal, 1970
THE GIANT SPIDER INVASION Group 1, 1976
BIG WEDNESDAY Warner Bros., 1978

PERRY MASON RETURNS (TF)   Intermedia Productions/
   Strathmore Productions/Viacom Productions, 1985
PERRY MASON: THE CASE OF THE NOTORIOUS NUN (TF)
   Intermedia Productions/Strathmore Productions/Viacom
   Productions, 1986
PERRY MASON: THE CASE OF THE SHOOTING STAR (TF)
   Intermedia Productions/Strathmore Productions/Viacom
   Productions, 1986
PERRY MASON: THE CASE OF THE SCANDALOUS
   SCOUNDREL (TF)   The Fred Silverman Company/Strathmore
   Productions/Viacom, 1987
PERRY MASON: THE CASE OF THE LOST LOVE (TF)   The Fred
   Silverman Company/Strathmore Productions/Viacom, 1987
PERRY MASON: THE CASE OF THE MURDERED MADAM (TF)
   The Fred Silverman Company/Strathmore Productions/
   Viacom, 1987
PERRY MASON: THE CASE OF THE SINISTER SPIRIT (TF)
   The Fred Silverman Company/Strathmore Productions/Viacom
   Productions, 1987
PERRY MASON: THE CASE OF THE AVENGING ACE (TF)
   The Fred Silverman Company/Strathmore Productions/
   Viacom, 1988
PERRY MASON: THE CASE OF THE LADY IN THE LAKE (TF)
   The Fred Silverman Company/Strathmore Productions/
   Viacom, 1988
PERRY MASON: THE CASE OF THE LETHAL LESSON (TF)
   The Fred Silverman Company/Dean Hargrove Productions/
   Viacom, 1989
PERRY MASON: THE CASE OF THE MUSICAL MURDER (TF)
   The Fred Silverman Company/Dean Hargrove Productions/
   Viacom, 1989
PERRY MASON: THE CASE OF THE ALL-STAR ASSASSIN (TF)
   The Fred Silverman Company/Dean Hargrove Productions/
   Viacom, 1989
PERRY MASON: THE CASE OF THE PARISIAN PARADOX (TF)
   The Fred Silverman Company/Dean Hargrove Productions/
   Viacom, 1990
PERRY MASON: THE CASE OF THE POISONED PEN (TF)
   The Fred Silverman Company/Dean Hargrove Productions/
   Viacom, 1990
PERRY MASON: THE CASE OF THE DESPERATE DECEPTION (TF)
   The Fred Silverman Company/Dean Hargrove Productions/
   Viacom, 1990

BRIAN HALEY
BABY'S DAY OUT   20th Century Fox, 1994

JACKIE EARLE HALEY
THE DAY OF THE LOCUST   Paramount, 1975
THE BAD NEWS BEARS   Paramount, 1976
DAMNATION ALLEY   20th Century-Fox, 1977
THE BAD NEWS BEARS IN BREAKING TRAINING
   Paramount, 1977
THE BAD NEWS BEARS GO TO JAPAN   Paramount, 1978
BREAKING AWAY   20th Century-Fox, 1979
LOSIN' IT   Embassy, 1983, Canadian-U.S.

ALBERT HALL
BETRAYED   MGM/UA, 1988
MALCOLM X   Warner Bros., 1992

ANTHONY MICHAEL HALL
NATIONAL LAMPOON'S VACATION   Warner Bros., 1983
SIXTEEN CANDLES   Universal, 1984
THE BREAKFAST CLUB   Universal, 1985
WEIRD SCIENCE   Universal, 1985
OUT OF BOUNDS   Columbia, 1986
JOHNNY BE GOOD   Orion, 1988
UPWORLD   Vestron, 1989
EDWARD SCISSORHANDS   20th Century Fox, 1990

ARSENIO HALL
b. February 12, 1955 - Cleveland, Ohio
Agent: CAA - Beverly Hills, 310/288-4545

AMAZON WOMEN ON THE MOON   Universal, 1987
COMING TO AMERICA   Paramount, 1988
HARLEM NIGHTS   Paramount, 1989

BRAD HALL
TROLL   Empire Pictures, 1986
LIMIT UP   MCEG, 1989
THE GUARDIAN   Universal, 1990

BUG HALL
THE LITTLE RASCALS   Universal, 1994

DAISY HALL
I'M DANGEROUS TONIGHT (CTF)   BBK Productions, 1990

DIEDRE HALL
b. October 31, 1948 - Milwaukee, Wisconsin

A REASON TO LIVE (TF)   Papazian Productions, 1985
TAKE MY DAUGHTERS, PLEASE (TF)   NBC Productions, 1988

HANNA R. HALL
b. Denver, Colorado

FORREST GUMP   Paramount, 1994

HARRIET HALL
HIT LIST   New Line Cinema, 1989

JERRY HALL
RUNNING OUT OF LUCK   Nitrate Film Ltd./Julien Temple Productino
   Company, 1985, British
BATMAN   Warner Bros., 1989

PHILIP BAKER HALL
THE SPIRIT (TF)   von Zerneck-Samuels Productions/
   Warner Bros. TV, 1987

RICH HALL
TRUE BLUE (TF)   Grosso-Jacobson Productions/
   NBC Productions, 1989

RODGER HALL
DANCE WITH DEATH   Concorde, 1991

CHARLES HALLAHAN
WILD PALMS (MS)   Ixtlan Corporation/Greengrass Prods., Inc., 1993

JOHN HALLAM
MURPHY'S WAR   Paramount, 1971, British
WHEN THE WHALES CAME   20th Century Fox, 1989, British

DEAN HALLO
Agent: Judy Schoen & Associates - Los Angeles, 213/962-1950

CITY SLICKERS   Columbia, 1991

RODGER HALLSTON
OF UNKNOWN ORIGIN   Concorde, 1994

JOHNNY HALLYDAY
THE IRON TRIANGLE   Scotti Bros., 1989

VERONICA HAMEL
b. November 20, 1943 - Philadelphia, Pennsylvania
Agent: William Morris Agency - Beverly Hills, 310/274-7451

CANNONBALL   New World, 1976
BEYOND THE POSEIDON ADVENTURE   Warner Bros., 1979
WHEN TIME RAN OUT   Warner Bros., 1980
SESSIONS (TF)   Roger Gimbel Productions/EMI TV/Sarabande
   Productions, 1983
KANE AND ABEL (MS)   Schrekinger Communications/Embassy TV, 1985
A NEW LIFE   Paramount, 1988
TWIST OF FATE (MS)   Henry Plitt-Larry White Productions/HTV/
   Columbia TV, 1989, British-U.S.
TAKING CARE OF BUSINESS   Buena Vista, 1990

BRIAN HAMILL
THE PICK-UP ARTIST   20th Century Fox, 1987

MARK HAMILL
b. September 25, 1952 - Oakland, California
Agent: APA - Los Angeles, 310/273-0744

SARAH T - PORTRAIT OF A TEENAGE ALCOHOLIC (TF)
   Universal TV, 1975
ERIC (TF)   Lorimar Productions, 1975
DELANCEY STREET: THE CRISIS WITHIN (TF)
   Paramount TV, 1975
MALLORY: CIRCUMSTANTIAL EVIDENCE (TF)   Universal TV/
   Crescendo Productions/R.B. Productions, 1976
THE CITY (TF)   QM Productions, 1977
STAR WARS   20th Century-Fox, 1977
WIZARDS (AF)   20th Century-Fox, 1977 (voice)
CORVETTE SUMMER   MGM/United Artists, 1978
THE BIG RED ONE   United Artists, 1980
THE EMPIRE STRIKES BACK   20th Century-Fox, 1980
THE NIGHT THE LIGHTS WENT OUT IN GEORGIA
   Avco Embassy, 1981
BRITANNIA HOSPITAL   United Artists Classics, 1982, British
RETURN OF THE JEDI   20th Century-Fox, 1983
SLIPSTREAM   Entertainment Film Productions, 1989, British
STEPHEN KING'S SLEEPWALKERS *SLEEPWALKERS*
   Columbia, 1992 (uncredited)
THE GUYVER   Imperial Entertainment, 1991,
   U.S.-Japanese-Taiwanese-South Korean
TIME RUNNER   1993, Canadian-U.S.
VILLAGE OF THE DAMNED   Universal, 1995

ANTONY HAMILTON
MIRRORS (TF)   Leonard Hill Films, 1985

CARRIE HAMILTON
Agent: The Blake Agency - Beverly Hills, 310/246-0241

HOSTAGE (TF)   CBS Entertainment, 1988
TOKYO POP   Spectrafilm, 1988

ERIN HAMILTON
PLAZA SUITE (TF)   Kalola Productions, 1987

GEORGE HAMILTON
b. August 12, 1939 - Memphis, Tennessee
Agent: APA - Los Angeles, 310/273-0744

CRIME & PUNISHMENT, USA   Allied Artists, 1959
HOME FROM THE HILL   MGM, 1960
ALL THE FINE YOUNG CANNIBALS   MGM, 1960
WHERE THE BOYS ARE   MGM, 1960
ANGEL BABY   Allied Artists, 1961
BY LOVE POSSESSED   United Artists, 1961
A THUNDER OF DRUMS   MGM, 1961
LIGHT IN THE PIAZZA   MGM, 1962
TWO WEEKS IN ANOTHER TOWN   MGM, 1962
THE VICTORS   Columbia, 1963
ACT ONE   Warner Bros., 1963
LOOKING FOR LOVE   MGM, 1964
YOUR CHEATIN' HEART   MGM, 1964
VIVA MARIA!   United Artists, 1965, French-Italian
THAT MAN GEORGE!   *L'HOMME DE MARRAKECH*   Allied Artists,
   1966, French-Italian-Spanish
DOCTOR, YOU'VE GOT TO BE KIDDING   MGM, 1967
JACK OF DIAMONDS   MGM, 1967, U.S.-West German
A TIME FOR KILLING   *THE LONG RIDE HOME*   Columbia, 1967
THE POWER   MGM, 1968
EVEL KNIEVEL   Fanfare, 1972
THE MAN WHO LOVED CAT DANCING   MGM, 1973
JACQUELINE SUSANN'S ONCE IS NOT ENOUGH
   ONCE IS NOT ENOUGH   Paramount, 1975
THE DEAD DON'T DIE (TF)   Douglas S. Cramer Productions, 1975
ROOTS (MS)   Wolper Productions, 1977
THE STRANGE POSSESSION OF MRS. OLIVER (TF)
   The Shpetner Company, 1977
KILLER ON BOARD (TF)   Lorimar Productions, 1977

THE HAPPY HOOKER GOES TO WASHINGTON   Cannon, 1977
THE USERS (TF)   Aaron Spelling Productions, 1978
SEXTETTE   Crown International, 1978
INSTITUTE FOR REVENGE (TF)   Gold-Driskill Productions/
   Columbia TV, 1979
LOVE AT FIRST BITE   American International, 1979
FROM HELL TO VICTORY   1979, French-Italian-Spanish
ZORRO, THE GAY BLADE   20th Century-Fox, 1981
TWO FATHERS' JUSTICE (TF)   A. Shane Company, 1985
MONTE CARLO (MS)   New World TV/Phoenix Entertainment Group/
   Collins-Holm Productions/Highgate Pictures, 1986
POKER ALICE (TF)   New World TV, 1987
THE GODFATHER, PART III   Paramount, 1990
   DOC HOLLYWOOD   Warner Bros., 1991
ONCE UPON A CRIME   MGM-Pathe, 1992, U.S.-Italian

JOSH HAMILTON
Agent: William Morris Agency - Beverly Hills, 310/274-7451

ALIVE   Buena Vista, 1993
WITH HONORS   Warner Bros., 1994

LINDA HAMILTON
b. September 26 - Salisbury, Maryland
Agent: ICM - Beverly Hills, 310/550-4000

CHILDREN OF THE CORN   New World, 1984
THE TERMINATOR   Orion, 1984
SECRET WEAPONS (TF)   Goodman-Rosen Prods./ITC Prods., 1985
CLUB MED (TF)   Lorimar Productions, 1986
BLACK MOON RISING   New World, 1986
KING KONG LIVES   DEG, 1986
GO TOWARD THE LIGHT (TF)   Corapeak Productions/
   The Polson Company, 1988
MR. DESTINY   Buena Vista, 1990
TERMINATOR 2: JUDGMENT DAY   TriStar, 1991
SILENT FALL   Warner Bros., 1994
SEPARATE LIVES   Trimark Pictures, 1995

RICHARD HAMILTON
IN COUNTRY   Warner Bros., 1989

SUZANNA HAMILTON
JOHNNY BULL (TF)   Titus Productions/Eugene O'Neill Memorial
   Theatre Center, 1986

HARRY HAMLIN
b. October 30, 1951 - Pasadena, California

MOVIE MOVIE   Warner Bros., 1978
STUDS LONIGAN (MS)   Lorimar Productions, 1979
KING OF THE MOUNTAIN   Universal, 1981
MAKING LOVE   20th Century-Fox, 1981
CLASH OF THE TITANS   MGM/United Artists, 1981, British
BLUE SKIES AGAIN   Warner Bros., 1983
MAXIE   Orion, 1985
SPACE (MS)   Stonehenge Productions/Paramount TV, 1985
L.A. LAW (TF)   20th Century Fox TV, 1986
LAGUNA HEAT (CTF)   HBO Pictures/Jay Weston Productions, 1987
FAVORITE SON (MS)   NBC Productions, 1988
DINNER AT EIGHT (CTF)   Think Entertainment/Turner Network TV, 1989
DECEPTIONS (CTF)   Sugar Entertainment/Alpha Entertainment
   Productions, 1990

BEN HAMMER
ZABRISKIE POINT   MGM, 1970
THE EXECUTION OF PRIVATE SLOVIK (TF)   Universal TV, 1974
THE COMPETITION   Columbia, 1980
THE WINDS OF WAR (MS)   Paramount TV/Dan Curtis
   Productions, 1983
JAGGED EDGE   Columbia, 1985
SURVIVAL QUEST   MGM/UA, 1990
CRAZY PEOPLE   Paramount, 1990

NICHOLAS HAMMOND
TROUBLE IN PARADISE (TF)   Qintex Entertainment,
   1989, U.S.-Australian

JANE HAMPER
FEAR, ANXIETY AND DEPRESSION   Samuel Goldwyn
   Company, 1990

JAMES HAMPTON
(Jim Hampton)
Agent: The Artists Group, Ltd. - Los Angeles, 310/552-1100

THE LONGEST YARD   Paramount, 1974
W.W. AND THE DIXIE DANCEKINGS   20th CenturyFox, 1975
HAWMPS!   Mulberry Square, 1976
HANGAR 18   Sunn Classic, 1980
CONDORMAN   Buena Vista, 1981
TEEN WOLF   Atlantic Releasing Corporation, 1985
TEEN WOLF TOO   Atlantic Releasing Corporation, 1987

MAGGIE HAN
MURDER IN PARADISE (TF)   Bill McCutchen Productions/
   Columbia TV, 1990

TERRI HANAUER
Agent: Writers & Artists Agency - Los Angeles, 213/820-2240

COMMUNION   MCEG, 1989

HERBIE HANCOCK
b. April 12, 1940 - Chicago, Illinois
Agent: CAA - Beverly Hills, 310/288-4545

INDECENT PROPOSAL   Paramount, 1993

JOHN HANCOCK
STREETS OF JUSTICE (TF)   Universal TV, 1985
THE BONFIRE OF THE VANITIES   Warner Bros., 1990

SHEILA HANCOCK
THREE MEN AND A LITTLE LADY   Buena Vista, 1990

JAMES HANDY
Agent: APA - Los Angeles, 310/273-0744

THE VERDICT   20th Century-Fox, 1982
BRIGHTON BEACH MEMOIRS   Universal, 1986
POPEYE DOYLE (TF)   December 3rd Productions/Robert Singer
   Productions/20th Century Fox TV, 1986
BURGLAR   Warner Bros., 1987
BIRD   Warner Bros., 1988
K-9   Universal, 1989
THE PREPPIE MURDER (TF)   Jack Grossbart Productions/
   Spectator Films, 1989
ARACHNOPHOBIA   Buena Vista, 1990
UNSPEAKABLE ACTS (TF)   The Landsburg Company, 1990
APPEARANCES (TF)   Walt Disney Television, 1990
GOODNIGHT, SWEET WIFE (TF)   1990
THE ROCKETEER   Buena Vista, 1991

ANNE HANEY
BLIND JUSTICE (TF)   CBS Entertainment, 1986

DARYL HANEY
DADDY'S BOYS   Concorde, 1988

HELEN HANFT
THE BUTCHER'S WIFE   Paramount, 1991

LARRY HANKIN
Agent: Gold/Marshak & Associates - Burbank, 818/953-7689

ARMED AND DANGEROUS   Columbia, 1986
HOME ALONE   20th Century Fox, 1990
THE SHADOW   Universal, 1994
IT'S PAT   Buena Vista, 1994
BILLY MADISON   Universal, 1995

TOM HANKS
b. July 9, 1956 - Oakland, California
Agent: CAA - Beverly Hills, 310/288-4545

HE KNOWS YOU'RE ALONE   MGM/United Artists, 1980
MAZES AND MONSTERS (TF)   McDermott Productions/Procter &
   Gamble Productions, 1982
BACHELOR PARTY   20th Century Fox, 1984
SPLASH   Buena Vista, 1984
THE MAN WITH ONE RED SHOE   20th Century Fox, 1985
VOLUNTEERS   TriStar, 1985
EVERY TIME WE SAY GOODBYE   TriStar, 1986, Israeli
THE MONEY PIT   Universal, 1986
NOTHING IN COMMON   TriStar, 1986
DRAGNET   Universal, 1987
BIG ★   20th Century Fox, 1988
PUNCHLINE   Columbia, 1988
THE 'BURBS   Universal, 1989
TURNER & HOOCH   Buena Vista, 1989
JOE VERSUS THE VOLCANO   Warner Bros., 1990
THE BONFIRE OF THE VANITIES   Warner Bros., 1990
RADIO FLYER   Columbia, 1992 (uncredited)
A LEAGUE OF THEIR OWN   Columbia, 1992
SLEEPLESS IN SEATTLE   TriStar, 1993
PHILADELPHIA ★★   TriStar, 1993
FORREST GUMP   Paramount, 1994
APOLLO 13   Universal, 1995

DARYL HANNAH
b. 1961 - Chicago, Illinois
Agent: ICM - Beverly Hills, 310/550-4000

THE FURY   20th Century-Fox, 1978
THE FINAL TERROR   Comworld, 1981
HARD COUNTRY   Universal/AFD, 1981
SUMMER LOVERS   Filmways, 1982
PAPER DOLLS (TF)   Leonard Goldberg Productions, 1982
BLADE RUNNER   The Ladd Company/Warner Bros., 1982
THE FINAL TERROR   Comworld, 1983
SPLASH   Buena Vista, 1984
RECKLESS   MGM/UA, 1984
THE POPE OF GREENWICH VILLAGE   MGM/UA, 1984
THE CLAN OF THE CAVE BEAR   Warner Bros., 1986
LEGAL EAGLES   Universal, 1986
ROXANNE   Columbia, 1987
WALL STREET   20th Century Fox, 1987
HIGH SPIRITS   TriStar, 1988, British
CRIMES AND MISDEMEANORS   Orion, 1989 (uncredited)
STEEL MAGNOLIAS   TriStar, 1989
CRAZY PEOPLE   Paramount, 1990
AT PLAY IN THE FIELDS OF THE LORD   Universal, 1991
MEMOIRS OF AN INVISIBLE MAN   Warner Bros., 1992
ATTACK OF THE 50-FOOT WOMAN (CTF)   HBO Pictures/Lorimar
   Productions, 1993
GRUMPY OLD MEN   Warner Bros., 1993
THE TIE THAT BINDS   Buena Vista, 1995

JOHN HANNAH
FOUR WEDDINGS AND A FUNERAL   Gramercy Pictures,
   1994, British

ADAM HANN-BYRD
LITTLE MAN TATE   Orion, 1991

ALYSON HANNIGAN
MY STEPMOTHER IS AN ALIEN   WEG, 1988

GALE HANSEN
DEAD POETS SOCIETY   Buena Vista, 1989
DESERT SHIELD   21st Century Distribution, 1991

PETER HANSEN
THE WAR OF THE ROSES   20th Century Fox, 1989

MARCIA GAY HARDEN
Agent: William Morris Agency - Beverly Hills, 310/274-7451

MILLER'S CROSSING 20th Century Fox, 1990
LATE FOR DINNER Columbia, 1991
USED PEOPLE 20th Century Fox, 1992

JERRY HARDIN
Agent: Susan Smith & Associates - Beverly Hills, 213/852-4777

WANTED DEAD OR ALIVE New World, 1986
THE MILAGRO BEANFIELD WAR Universal, 1988
BLAZE Buena Vista, 1989
THE FIRM Paramount, 1993

MELORA HARDIN
Agent: Writers & Artists Agency - Los Angeles, 213/820-2240

SOUL MAN New World, 1986
LAMBADA Warner Bros., 1990

KADEEM HARDISON
b. July 24 - New York, New York

DREAM DATE (TF) Golchan-Kosberg Productions/Hoffman-Israel
    Productions, 1989
GUNMEN Dimension/Miramax Films, 1994
RENAISSANCE MAN Buena Vista, 1994
PANTHER Gramercy Pictures, 1995

EDWARD HARDWICKE
SHADOWLANDS Savoy Pictures, 1993, U.S.-British

DORIAN HAREWOOD
b. August 6, 1951 - Dayton, Ohio

SPARKLE Warner Bros., 1976
GRAY LADY DOWN Universal, 1978
LOOKER The Ladd Company/Warner Bros., 1981
AGAINST ALL ODDS Columbia, 1984
THE JESSE OWENS STORY (TF) Harve Bennett Productions/
    Paramount TV, 1984
THE FALCON AND THE SNOWMAN Orion, 1985
AMERIKA (MS) ABC Circle Films, 1987
GUILTY OF INNOCENCE: THE LENELL GETER STORY (TF)
    Embassy TV, 1987
FULL METAL JACKET Warner Bros., 1987, British
GOD BLESS THE CHILD (TF) Indieprod Company/Phoenix
    Entertainment Group, 1988
KISS SHOT (TF) London Productions/Whoop, Inc., 1989

AMY HARGREAVES
BRAINSCAN Triumph Releasing Corporation, 1994

SUSANNAH HARKER
A DRY WHITE SEASON MGM/UA, 1989

WILEY HARKER
GUILTY CONSCIENCE (TF) Levinson-Link Productions/Robert
    Papazian Productions, 1985

JOHN HARKINS
Agent: Susan Smith & Associates - Beverly Hills, 213/852-4777

THIS GUN FOR HIRE (CTF) USA Cable, 1991

DEBORAH HARMON
PRINCE OF BEL AIR (TF) Leonard Hill Films, 1986

MARK HARMON
b. September 2, 1951 - Burbank, California
Agent: UTA - Beverly Hills, 310/273-6700

ELEANOR AND FRANKLIN: THE WHITE HOUSE YEARS (TF)
    Talent Associates, 1977
GETTING MARRIED (TF) Paramount TV, 1978

CENTENNIAL (MS) Universal TV, 1978
COMES A HORSEMAN United Artists, 1978
BEYOND THE POSEIDON ADVENTURE Warner Bros., 1979
THE DREAM MERCHANTS (TF) Columbia TV, 1980
FLAMINGO ROAD (TF) MF Productions/Lorimar Productions, 1980
PRINCE OF BEL AIR (TF) Leonard Hill Films, 1986
LET'S GET HARRY TriStar, 1986
THE DELIBERATE STRANGER (MS) Stuart Phoenix Productions/
    Lorimar-Telepictures, 1986
SUMMER SCHOOL Paramount, 1987
AFTER THE PROMISE (TF) Tamara Asseyev Productions/
    New World TV, 1987
THE PRESIDIO Paramount, 1988
STEALING HOME Warner Bros., 1988
TENNESSEE WILLIAMS' SWEET BIRD OF YOUTH SWEET BIRD
    OF YOUTH (TF) Atlantic/Kushner-Locke Productions, 1989
WORTH WINNING 20th Century Fox, 1989
COLD HEAVEN Hemdale, 1992
WYATT EARP Warner Bros., 1994
NATURAL BORN KILLERS Warner Bros., 1994
GLENORKY Triumph Releasing Corporation, 1995

CHRISTINA HARNOS
THE RESCUE Buena Vista, 1988

JESSICA HARPER
b. 1949 - Chicago, Illinois

PHANTOM OF THE PARADISE 20th Century-Fox, 1974
INSERTS United Artists, 1976, British
SUSPIRIA International Classics, 1977, Italian
THE EVICTORS American International, 1979
STARDUST MEMORIES United Artists, 1980
SHOCK TREATMENT 20th Century-Fox, 1981, British
PENNIES FROM HEAVEN MGM/United Artists, 1981
MY FAVORITE YEAR MGM/UA, 1982
WHEN DREAMS COME TRUE (TF) I & C Productions, 1985
THE IMAGEMAKER Castle Hill Productions, 1986
THE BLUE IGUANA Paramount, 1988

ROBERT HARPER
WANTED DEAD OR ALIVE New World, 1986
MURDER ORDAINED (TF) Zev Braun Productions/Interscope
    Communications, 1987
OUTBACK BOUND (TF) Andrew Gottlieb Productions/CBS
    Entertainment, 1988
FINAL ANALYSIS Warner Bros., 1992

TESS HARPER
b. August 15, 1950 - Mammouth Springs, Arkansas
Agent: William Morris Agency - Beverly Hills, 310/274-7451

CHIEFS (MS) Highgate Pictures, 1983
STARFLIGHT: THE PLANE THAT COULDN'T LAND
    STARFLIGHT ONE (TF) Orgolini-Nelson Productions, 1983
AMITYVILLE 3-D AMITYVILLE: THE DEMON Orion, 1983
TENDER MERCIES Universal/AFD, 1983
FLASHPOINT TriStar, 1984
A SUMMER TO REMEMBER (TF) Interplanetary Productions, 1985
CRIMES OF THE HEART ✪ DEG, 1986
DADDY (TF) Robert Greenwald Productions, 1987
ISHTAR Columbia, 1987
LITTLE GIRL LOST (TF) Marian Rees Associates, 1988
FAR NORTH Alive Films, 1988
HER ALIBI Warner Bros., 1989
CRIMINAL LAW Hemdale, 1989
UNCONQUERED (TF) Alexandra Film Productions/Double Helix
    Films/Dick Lowry Productions, 1989
INCIDENT AT DARK RIVER (CTF) Farrell-Minoff Productions/
    Turner Network TV, 1989
DADDY'S DYIN'...WHO'S GOT THE WILL? MGM/UA, 1990
MY HEROES HAVE ALWAYS BEEN COWBOYS Samuel Goldwyn
    Company, 1991
THE MAN IN THE MOON MGM-Pathe, 1991

VALERIE HARPER
b. August 22, 1940 - Suffern, New York
Agent: William Morris Agency - Beverly Hills, 310/274-7451

FREEBIE AND THE BEAN   Warner Bros., 1974
THURSDAY'S GAME (TF)   ABC Circle Films, 1974
NIGHT TERROR (TF)   Charles Fries Productions, 1977
CHAPTER TWO   Columbia, 1979
THE LAST MARRIED COUPLE IN AMERICA   Universal, 1980
BLAME IT ON RIO   20th Century Fox, 1984
THE EXECUTION (TF)   Newland-Raynor Productions/Comworld
   Productions, 1985
STRANGE VOICES (TF)   Forrest Hills Productions/Dacks-Geller
   Productions/TLC, 1987
DROP-OUT MOTHER (TF)   Fries Entertainment/Comco Prods., 1988
THE PEOPLE ACROSS THE LAKE (TF)   Bill McCutchen
   Productions/Columbia TV, 1988
STOLEN: ONE HUSBAND (TF)   King Phoenix Entertainment, 1990

REBECCA HARRELL
PRANCER   Orion, 1989

WOODY HARRELSON
b. July 23, 1961 - Midland, Texas
Agent: CAA - Beverly Hills, 310/288-4545

HARPER VALLEY PTA   April Fools, 1978
WILDCATS   Warner Bros., 1986
BAY COVEN (TF)   Guber-Peters Company/Phoenix
   Entertainment Group, 1987
KILLER INSTINCT (TF)   Millar-Bromberg Prods./ITC Entertainment, 1988
L.A. STORY   TriStar, 1991
DOC HOLLYWOOD   Warner Bros., 1991
WHITE MEN CAN'T JUMP   20th Century Fox, 1992
INDECENT PROPOSAL   Paramount, 1993
I'LL DO ANYTHING   Columbia, 1994
THE COWBOY WAY   Universal, 1994
NATURAL BORN KILLERS   Warner Bros., 1994
THE MONEY TRAIN   Columbia, 1995

BARBARA HARRIS
b. July 25, 1935 - Evanston, Illinois
Agent: Bresler, Kelly & Kipperman - Encino, 818/905-1155

A THOUSAND CLOWNS   United Artists, 1965
OH DAD, POOR DAD, MAMA'S HUNG YOU IN THE CLOSET
   AND I'M FEELING SO SAD   Paramount, 1967
PLAZA SUITE   Paramount, 1971
WHO IS HARRY KELLERMAN, AND WHY IS HE SAYING THOSE
   TERRIBLE THINGS ABOUT ME? ○   National General, 1971
THE WAR BETWEEN MEN AND WOMEN   National General, 1972
MIXED COMPANY   United Artists, 1974
THE MANCHU EAGLE MURDER CAPER MYSTERY
   United Artists, 1975
NASHVILLE   Paramount, 1975
FAMILY PLOT   Universal, 1976
FREAKY FRIDAY   Buena Vista, 1977
MOVIE MOVIE   Warner Bros., 1978
THE NORTH AVENUE IRREGULARS   Buena Vista, 1979
THE SEDUCTION OF JOE TYNAN   Universal, 1979
SECOND HAND HEARTS   THE HAMSTER OF HAPPINESS
   Paramount, 1981
PEGGY SUE GOT MARRIED   TriStar, 1986
NICE GIRLS DON'T EXPLODE   New World, 1987
DIRTY ROTTEN SCOUNDRELS   Orion, 1988

CYNTHIA HARRIS
IZZY AND MOE (TF)   Robert Halmi, Inc., 1985
A SPECIAL FRIENDSHIP (TF)   Entertainment Partners, 1987
PANCHO BARNES (MS)   Blue Andre Productions/Orion TV, 1988

DANIELLE HARRIS
HALLOWEEN IV - THE RETURN OF MICHAEL MYERS
   Galaxy, 1988
HALLOWEEN 5 - THE REVENGE OF MICHAEL MYERS
   Galaxy, 1989
THE LAST BOY SCOUT   The Geffen Company/Warner Bros., 1991

DAVID HARRIS
BADGE OF THE ASSASSIN (TF)   Blatt-Singer Productions/
   Columbia TV, 1985

ED HARRIS
b. November 28, 1950 - Tenafly, New Jersey
Agent: CAA - Beverly Hills, 310/288-4545

THE AMAZING HOWARD HUGHES (TF)   Roger Gimbel
   Productions/EMI TV, 1977
COMA   MGM/United Artists, 1978
BORDERLINE   AFD, 1980
DREAM ON   1981
KNIGHTRIDERS   United Film Distribution, 1981
CREEPSHOW   Warner Bros., 1982
UNDER FIRE   Orion, 1983
THE RIGHT STUFF   The Ladd Company/Warner Bros., 1983
A FLASH OF GREEN   Spectrafilm, 1984
SWING SHIFT   Warner Bros., 1984
PLACES IN THE HEART   TriStar, 1984
ALAMO BAY   TriStar, 1985
SWEET DREAMS   TriStar, 1985
CODE NAME: EMERALD   MGM/UA, 1985
THE LAST INNOCENT MAN (CTF)   HBO Pictures/Maurice Singer
   Productions, 1987
WALKER   Universal, 1988, U.S.-Nicaraguan
TO KILL A PRIEST   Columbia, 1989
JACKNIFE   Cineplex Odeon, 1989
THE ABYSS   20th Century Fox, 1989
STATE OF GRACE   Orion, 1990
PARIS TROUT (CTF)   Viacom, 1991
GLENGARRY GLEN ROSS   New Line Cinema, 1992
RUNNING MATES (CTF)   HBO Pictures, 1992
THE FIRM   Paramount, 1993
NEEDFUL THINGS   Columbia, 1993
CHINA MOON   Orion, 1994
MILK MONEY   Paramount, 1994
JUST CAUSE   Warner Bros., 1995
APOLLO 13   Universal, 1995

JULIE HARRIS
(Julia Ann Harris)
b. December 2, 1925 - Grosse Pointe, Michigan
Agent: William Morris Agency - Beverly Hills, 310/274-7451

THE MEMBER OF THE WEDDING ★   Columbia, 1952
EAST OF EDEN   Warner Bros., 1955
I AM A CAMERA   1955, British
THE TRUTH ABOUT WOMEN   1958, British
THE POACHER'S DAUGHTER   SALLY'S IRISH ROGUE   1960, Irish
THE HAUNTING   MGM, 1963, British-U.S.
HARPER   Warner Bros., 1966
YOU'RE A BIG BOY NOW   7 Arts, 1966
REFLECTIONS IN A GOLDEN EYE   Warner Bros., 1967
THE SPLIT   MGM, 1968
THE HOUSE ON GREENAPPLE ROAD (TF)   QM Productions, 1970
HOW AWFUL ABOUT ALLAN (TF)   Aaron Spelling Productions, 1970
THE PEOPLE NEXT DOOR   Avco Embassy, 1970
HOME FOR THE HOLIDAYS (TF)   ABC Circle Films, 1972
THE GREATEST GIFT (TF)   Universal TV, 1947
THE HIDING PLACE   World Wide, 1975
VOYAGE OF THE DAMNED   Avco Embassy, 1976, British
BACKSTAIRS AT THE WHITE HOUSE (MS)   Ed Friendly
   Productions, 1979
THE BELL JAR   Avco Embassy, 1979
NUTCRACKER: THE MOTION PICTURE   Atlantic Releasing
   Corporation, 1986 (voice)
THE WOMAN HE LOVED (TF)   The Larry Thompson Organization/
   HTV/New World TV, 1988, U.S.-British
GORILLAS IN THE MIST   Warner Bros./Universal, 1988
TOO GOOD TO BE TRUE (TF)   Newland-Raynor Productions, 1988
SINGLE WOMEN, MARRIED MEN (TF)   CBS Entertainment, 1989
THE DARK HALF   Orion, 1993

JULIUS HARRIS
SLAVES   Continental, 1969
INCIDENT IN SAN FRANCISCO (TF)   QM Productions, 1971
SUPERFLY   1972

SHAFT'S BIG SCORE   MGM, 1972
BLACK CAESAR   American International, 1973
HELL UP IN HARLEM   American International, 1973
A CRY FOR HELP (TF)   Universal TV, 1975
KING KONG   Paramount, 1976
RICH MAN, POOR MAN (MS)   Universal TV, 1976
VICTORY AT ENTEBBE (TF)   1976
ISLANDS IN THE STREAM   Paramount, 1977
LOOKING FOR MR. GOODBAR   Paramount, 1977
RING OF PASSION (TF)   20th Century-Fox TV, 1978
FIRST FAMILY   Warner Bros., 1980
HARLEY DAVIDSON & THE MARLBORO MAN   MGM-Pathe, 1991

LARA HARRIS

THE FOURTH WAR   Cannon, 1990

LEONORE HARRIS

LENA: MY 100 CHILDREN (TF)   Robert Greenwald
   Productions, 1987

M.K. HARRIS

GENUINE RISK   I.R.S., 1990

MEL HARRIS

Agent: Gersh Agency - Beverly Hills, 310/274-6611

WANTED DEAD OR ALIVE   New World, 1986
HARRY'S HONG KONG (TF)   Aaron Spelling Productions, 1987
K-9   Universal, 1989
CROSS OF FIRE (MS)   Leonard Hill Films, 1989
MY BROTHER'S WIFE (TF)   Robert Greenwald Productions/
   Adam Productions, 1989
THE PAGEMASTER   20th Century Fox, 1994
THE SECRETARY   Republic Pictures, 1995

NEIL PATRICK HARRIS

b. June 15, 1973 - Albuquerque, New Mexico
Agent: ICM - Beverly Hills, 310/550-4000

CLARA'S HEART   Warner Bros., 1988
HOME FIRES BURNING (TF)   Marian Rees Associates, 1989
COLD SASSY TREE (CTF)   Faye Dunaway Productions/Ohlmeyer
   Communications/Turner Network TV, 1989

PHIL HARRIS

b. June 24, 1904 - Linton, Indiana

THE JUNGLE BOOK (AF)   Buena Vista, 1967 (voice)
ROCK-A-DOODLE (AF)   Samuel Goldwyn Company, 1992 (voice)

RICHARD HARRIS

b. October 1, 1932 - Limerick, Ireland
Agent: William Morris Agency - Beverly Hills, 310/274-7451

ALIVE AND KICKING   1958, British
SHAKE HANDS WITH THE DEVIL   United Artists, 1959, British
THE WRECK OF THE MARY DEARE   MGM, 1959, British-U.S.
THE NIGHT FIGHTERS   A TERRIBLE BEAUTY   United Artists,
   1960, British
ALL NIGHT LONG   Continental, 1961, British
THE GUNS OF NAVARONE   Columbia, 1961, British-U.S.
THE LONG AND THE SHORT AND THE TALL
   JUNGLE FIGHTERS   1961, British
MUTINY ON THE BOUNTY   MGM, 1962
THIS SPORTING LIFE ★   Continental, 1963, British
RED DESERT   Rizzoli, 1964, Italian-French
I TRE VOLTI   De Laurentis, 1965, Italian
MAJOR DUNDEE   Columbia, 1965
THE HEROES OF TELEMARK   Columbia, 1965, British
THE BIBLE   20th Century-Fox, 1966, Italian-U.S.
HAWAII   United Artists, 1966
CAPRICE   20th Century-Fox, 1967
CAMELOT   Warner Bros., 1967
THE MOLLY MAGUIRES   Paramount, 1970
A MAN CALLED HORSE   National General, 1970
CROMWELL   Columbia, 1970, British

MAN IN THE WILDERNESS   Warner Bros., 1971
THE HERO   BLOOMFIELD   Avco Embassy, 1972,
   Israeli-British (also directed)
THE SNOW GOOSE (TF)   NBC, 1971
THE DEADLY TRACKERS   Warner Bros., 1973
99 AND 44/100% DEAD   20th Century-Fox, 1974
JUGGERNAUT   United Artists, 1974, British
ECHOES OF A SUMMER   THE LAST CASTLE   Cine Artists,
   1976, U.S.-Canadian
ROBIN AND MARIAN   Columbia, 1976, British
THE RETURN OF A MAN CALLED HORSE   United Artists, 1976
THE CASSANDRA CROSSING   Avco Embassy, 1977,
   British-Italian-West German
GULLIVER'S TRAVELS   EMI, 1977, British-Belgian
ORCA   Paramount, 1977
GOLDEN RENDEZVOUS   Rank, 1977, British
THE WILD GEESE   Allied Artists, 1978, British
GAME FOR VULTURES   New Line Cinema, 1979, British
THE LAST WORD   Samuel Goldwyn Company, 1979
HIGHPOINT   1980, Canadian
YOUR TICKET IS NO LONGER VALID   RSL Productions/
   Ambassador, 1981, Canadian
TARZAN THE APE MAN   MGM/United Artists, 1981
TRIUMPH OF A MAN CALLED HORSE   Jensen Farley Pictures,
   1983, U.S.-Mexican
MARTIN'S DAY   MGM/UA, 1984, British
MAIGRET (TF)   Granada TV, 1988, British
MACK THE KNIFE   21st Century Distribution, 1989
THE FIELD ★   Avenue Pictures, 1990, Irish-British
PATRIOT GAMES   Paramount, 1992
UNFORGIVEN   Warner Bros., 1992
WRESTLING ERNEST HEMINGWAY   Warner Bros., 1993
SILENT TONGUE   Trimark Pictures, 1994, U.S.-French
THE ROYAL WAY   Miramax Films, 1995

ROSS HARRIS

TESTAMENT   Paramount, 1983

ROSSIE HARRIS

AIRPLANE!   Paramount, 1980

ZELDA HARRIS

CROOKLYN   Universal, 1994

CATHRYN HARRISON

DUET FOR ONE   Cannon, 1986

GEORGE HARRISON

b. February 25, 1943 - Liverpool, England

WHAT'S HAPPENING: THE BEATLES IN THE USA (FD)   1964
A HARD DAY'S NIGHT   United Artists, 1964, British
HELP!   United Artists, 1965, British
YELLOW SUBMARINE (AF)   1968, British (voice)
LET IT BE (FD)   United Artists, 1970, British
WATER   Atlantic Releasing Corporation, 1984, British (uncredited)
SEDUCED (TF)   Catalina Production Group/Comworld Prods., 1985
SHANGHAI SURPRISE   MGM/UA, 1986, British-U.S. (uncredited)

GREGORY HARRISON

b. May 31, 1950 - Avalon, California
Agent: William Morris Agency - Beverly Hills, 310/274-7451

THE HARRAD EXPERIMENT   Cinerama Releasing
   Corporation, 1973
LOGAN'S RUN (TF)   Goff-Roberts-Steiner Productions/
   MGM TV, 1977
CENTENNIAL (MS)   Universal TV, 1978
FOR LADIES ONLY (TF)   The Catalina Production Group/
   Viacom, 1981
SEDUCED (TF)   Catalina Production Group/Comworld
   Productions, 1985
OCEANS OF FIRE (TF)   Catalina Production Group, 1986
FRESNO (MS)   MTM Productions, 1986
HOT PAINT (TF)   Catalina Production Group/MGM-UA TV, 1988
RED RIVER (TF)   Catalina Production Group/MGM-UA TV, 1988
DANGEROUS PURSUIT (CTF)   Sankan Productions, 1990

LINDA HARRISON

COCOON   20th Century Fox, 1985

KATHRYN HARROLD

Agent: William Morris Agency - Beverly Hills, 310/274-7451

YES, GIORGIO   MGM/UA, 1982
THE SENDER   Paramount, 1982, U.S.-British
INTO THE NIGHT   Universal, 1985
MacGRUDER AND LOUD (TF)   Aaron Spelling Productions, 1985
RAW DEAL   DEG, 1986
MAN AGAINST THE MOB (TF)   Frank von Zerneck Films, 1988

DEBORAH HARRY

(Debbie Harry)
b. July 1, 1945 - Miami, Florida
Agent: William Morris Agency - Beverly Hills, 310/274-7451

VIDEODROME   Universal, 1983, Canadian
HAIRSPRAY   New Line Cinema, 1988
NEW YORK STORIES   Buena Vista, 1989
TALES FROM THE DARKSIDE: THE MOVIE   Paramount, 1990

CHRISTOPHER HART

THE ADDAMS FAMILY   Paramount, 1991
ADDAMS FAMILY VALUES   Paramount, 1993

DAVID HART

IN THE HEAT OF THE NIGHT (TF)   The Fred Silverman Company/
   Jadda Productions/MGM-UA TV, 1988

IAN HART

BACKBEAT   Gramercy Pictures, 1994, British

ROXANNE HART

OLD ENOUGH   Orion Classics, 1984
HIGHLANDER   20th Century Fox, 1986, British-U.S.
SAMARITAN: THE MITCH SNYDER STORY (TF)   Levine-Robbins
   Productions/Fries Entertainment, 1986
VENGEANCE: THE STORY OF TONY CIMO (TF)   Nederlander
   TV and Film Productions/Robirdie Pictures, 1986
ONCE AROUND   Universal, 1991

MARIETTE HARTLEY

b. June 21, 1940 - New York, New York

RIDE THE HIGH COUNTRY   MGM, 1962
DRUMS OF AFRICA   MGM, 1963
MARNIE   Universal, 1964
MAROONED   Columbia, 1969
BARQUERO   United Artists, 1970
EARTH II (TF)   MGM-TV, 1971
SANDCASTLES (TF)   Metromedia Productions, 1972
SKYJACKED   MGM, 1972
GENESIS II (TF)   Warner Bros. TV, 1973
THE KILLER WHO WOULDN'T DIE (TF)   Paramount TV, 1976
THE LAST HURRAH (TF)   O'Connor-Becker Productions/
   Columbia TV, 1977
STONE (TF)   Stephen J. Cannell Productions/Universal TV, 1979
IMPROPER CHANNELS   Crown International, 1981, Canadian
NO PLACE TO HIDE (TF)   1982
M.A.D.D.: MOTHERS AGAINST DRUNK DRIVERS (TF)
   Universal TV, 1983
SILENCE OF THE HEART (TF)   David A. Simons Productions/
   Tisch-Avnet Productions, 1984
ONE TERRIFIC GUY (TF)   CBS Entertainment, 1986
MY TWO LOVES (TF)   Alvin Cooperman Productions/
   Taft Entertainment TV, 1986
1969   Atlantic Releasing Corporation, 1988
PASSION AND PARADISE (MS)   Picturebase International/Primedia
   Productions/Leonard Hill Films, 1989, U.S.-Canadian
ENCINO MAN   Buena Vista, 1992

PHIL HARTMAN

b. September 24, 1948 - Ontario, Canada
Agent: William Morris Agency - Beverly Hills, 310/274-7451

JUMPIN' JACK FLASH   20th Century Fox, 1986
HOW I GOT INTO COLLEGE   20th Century Fox, 1989
FLETCH LIVES   Universal, 1989
CB4   Universal, 1993
GREEDY   Universal, 1994
THE PAGEMASTER   20th Century Fox, 1994 (voice)
HOUSEGUEST   Buena Vista, 1995

LISA HARTMAN-BLACK

(Lisa Hartman)
b. June 1, 1956 - Houston, Texas
Agent: David Shapira & Associates - Sherman Oaks, 818/906-0322

BEVERLY HILLS COWGIRL BLUES (TF)   The Leonard Goldberg
   Company, 1985
ROSES ARE FOR THE RICH (MS)   Phoenix Entertainment
   Group, 1987
FULL EXPOSURE: THE SEX TAPES SCANDAL (TF)
   von Zerneck-Sertner Films, 1989
THE OPERATION (TF)   Moress, Nanas, Golden Entertainment/
   Viacom, 1990
THE TAKE (CTF)   Cine-Nevada, Inc. Productions/MCA-TV, 1990

RAINBOW HARVEST

OLD ENOUGH   Orion Classics, 1984
STREETS OF GOLD   20th Century Fox, 1986

DON HARVEY

Agent: Abrams Artists & Associates - Los Angeles, 310/859-0625

THE UNTOUCHABLES   Paramount, 1987
CREEPSHOW 2   New World, 1987
THE BEAST   Columbia, 1988
EIGHT MEN OUT   Orion, 1988
CASUALTIES OF WAR   Columbia, 1989
HUDSON HAWK   TriStar, 1991
TANK GIRL   MGM/UA, 1995

RODNEY HARVEY

Agent: Flick East/West Talent, Inc. - Los Angeles, 213/463-6333 or
   New York, 212/307-1850

MIXED BLOOD   Sara Films, 1984, U.S.-French
THE RETURN OF BILLY JACK   Billy Jack Productions,
   1986, unfinished
THE INITIATION   International Film Management/Goldfarb
   Distributors, 1987, Australian
FIVE CORNERS   Cineplex Odeon, 1987
SALSA   Cannon, 1988

DAVID HASSELHOFF

b. July 12, 1952 - Baltimore, Maryland

KNIGHT RIDER (TF)   Glen A. Larson Productions/
   Universal TV, 1982
THE CARTIER AFFAIR (TF)   Hill-Mandelker Productions, 1984
BRIDGE ACROSS TIME (TF)   Fries Entertainment, 1985
PERRY MASON: THE CASE OF THE LADY IN THE LAKE (TF)
   The Fred Silverman Company/Strathmore Productions/
   Viacom, 1988
BAYWATCH: PANIC AT MALIBU PIER (TF)
   GTG Entertainment, 1989

MARILYN HASSETT

QUARANTINED (TF)   Paramount TV, 1970
THEY SHOOT HORSES, DON'T THEY?   Cinerama Releasing
   Corporation, 1969
THE OTHER SIDE OF THE MOUNTAIN   Universal, 1975
TWO MINUTE WARNING   Universal, 1976
THE OTHER SIDE OF THE MOUNTAIN PART 2   Universal, 1978
THE BELL JAR   Avco Embassy, 1979
MESSENGER OF DEATH   Cannon, 1988

TERI HATCHER
Agent: William Morris Agency - Beverly Hills, 310/274-7451

THE BIG PICTURE   Columbia, 1989
TANGO & CASH   Warner Bros., 1989
SOAPDISH   Paramount, 1991
STRAIGHT TALK   Buena Vista, 1992
HEAVEN'S PRISONERS   Savoy Pictures, 1994

HURD HATFIELD
b. 1918 - New York, New York

DRAGON SEED   MGM, 1944
THE PICTURE OF DORIAN GRAY   MGM, 1945
THE DIARY OF A CHAMBERMAID   United Artists, 1946
THE BEGINNING OR THE END   MGM, 1947
THE UNSUSPECTED   Warner Bros., 1947
THE CHECKERED COAT   1948
JOAN OF ARC   RKO Radio, 1948
CHINATOWN AT MIDNIGHT   1949
TARZAN AND THE SLAVE GIRL   1950
DESTINATION MURDER   1971
THE LEFT-HANDED GUN   Warner Bros., 1958
EL CID   Allied Artists, 1961
KING OF KINGS   MGM, 1961
MICKEY ONE   Columbia, 1965
HARLOW (TF)   1965
THE BOSTON STRANGLER   20th Century-Fox, 1968
THIEF (TF)   Metromedia Productions/Stonehenge Productions, 1971
VON RICHTHOFEN AND BROWN   United Artists, 1971
THE NORLISS TAPES (TF)   Metromedia Producers
   Corporation, 1973
THE WORD (MS)   Charles Fries Productions/Stonehenge
   Productions, 1978
YOU CAN'T GO HOME AGAIN (TF)   CBS Entertainment, 1979
CRIMES OF THE HEART   DEG, 1986
HER ALIBI   Warner Bros., 1989

AMY HATHAWAY
KINJITE (FORBIDDEN SUBJECTS)   Cannon, 1989
THE CLIENT   Warner Bros., 1994

NOAH HATHAWAY
TROLL   Empire Pictures, 1986

TOM HATTEN
SPIES LIKE US   Warner Bros., 1985

RUTGER HAUER
b. January 23, 1944 - Netherlands
Agent: William Morris Agency - Beverly Hills, 310/274-7451

KEETJE TIPPEL   *CATHY TIPPEL/KATIE'S PASSION*
   Cinema National, 1975, Dutch
MAX HAVELAAR   1976, Dutch-Indonesian
SOLDIER OF ORANGE   Samuel Goldwyn Company, 1979, Dutch
SPETTERS   Samuel Goldwyn Company, 1980, Dutch
NIGHTHAWKS   Universal, 1981
CHANEL SOLITAIRE   United Film Distribution, 1981, French-British
BLADE RUNNER   The Ladd Company/Warner Bros., 1982
INSIDE THE THIRD REICH (TF)   ABC Circle Films, 1982
THE OSTERMAN WEEKEND   20th Century-Fox, 1983
EUREKA   MGM/UA Classics, 1984, British (filmed in 1981)
A BREED APART   Orion, 1984
LADYHAWKE   Warner Bros., 1985
FLESH + BLOOD   Orion, 1985, U.S.-Dutch
THE HITCHER   TriStar, 1986
WANTED DEAD OR ALIVE   New World, 1987
ESCAPE FROM SOBRIBOR (TF)   Rule-Starger Productions/Zenith
   Productions, 1987, U.S.-British
THE LEGEND OF THE HOLY DRINKER   *LA LEGGENDA DEL
   SANTO BEVITORE*   Columbia Italia, 1988, Italian
BLOODHOUNDS OF BROADWAY   Columbia, 1989
THE BLOOD OF HEROES   New Line Cinema, 1990
BLIND FURY   TriStar, 1990
WEDLOCK (CTF)   HBO Pictures/The Frederick S. Pierce Company/
   Spectacor Films, 1991
SPLIT SECOND   InterStar Releasing, 1992, U.S.-British

BUFFY THE VAMPIRE SLAYER   20th Century Fox, 1992
PAST MIDNIGHT (CTF)   CineTel Films, 1992
VOYAGE (CTF)   Davis Entertainment/Quinta Communications/
   USA Network, 1993
SURVIVING THE GAME   New Line Cinema, 1994
AMELIA EARHART - THE FINAL FLIGHT (CTF)
   Turner Network TV, 1994
NOSTRADAMUS   Orion Classics, 1994, British
THE BEANS OF EGYPT, MAINE   I.R.S. Releasing, 1994
FATHERLAND (CTF)   HBO Pictures, 1994

COLE HAUSER
SCHOOL TIES   Paramount, 1992

FAY HAUSER
CANDYMAN 2: FAREWELL TO THE FLESH   Gramercy Pictures, 1995

JERRY HAUSER
THE BRADY GIRLS GET MARRIED (TF)   Sherwood Schwartz
   Productions, 1981
A VERY BRADY CHRISTMAS (TF)   Sherwood Schwartz
   Productions/Paramount TV, 1988
THE BRADYS (TF)   Brady Productions/Paramount TV, 1990

WINGS HAUSER
SWEET REVENGE (TF)   David Greene Productions/Robert
   Papazian Productions, 1984
JO JO DANCER, YOUR LIFE IS CALLING   Columbia, 1986
TOUGH GUYS DON'T DANCE   Cannon, 1987
DEAD MAN WALKING   Metropolis Productions/Hit Films, 1988
TALES FROM THE HOOD   Savoy Pictures, 1995

NIGEL HAVERS
CHARIOTS OF FIRE   The Ladd Company/Warner Bros., 1981, British
A PASSAGE TO INDIA   Columbia, 1984, British
BURKE AND WILLS   Hemdale, 1985, Australian
THE WHISTLE BLOWER   Hemdale, 1987
EMPIRE OF THE SUN   Warner Bros., 1987
FAREWELL TO THE KING   Orion, 1989

ALLAN HAVEY
Agent: William Morris Agency - Beverly Hills, 310/274-7451

CHECKING OUT   Warner Bros., 1989

ETHAN HAWKE
Agent: CAA - Beverly Hills, 310/288-4545

EXPLORERS   Paramount, 1985
DEAD POETS SOCIETY   Buena Vista, 1989
DAD   Universal, 1989
WHITE FANG   Buena Vista, 1991
MYSTERY DATE   Orion, 1991
A MIDNIGHT CLEAR   Interstar Releasing, 1992
ALIVE   Buena Vista, 1993
RICH IN LOVE   MGM/UA, 1993
REALITY BITES   Universal, 1994
SEARCH AND DESTROY   October Films, 1995
BEFORE SUNRISE   Columbia, 1995

CORWIN HAWKINS
A LOW DOWN DIRTY SHAME   Buena Vista, 1994

GOLDIE HAWN
b. November 21, 1945 - Takoma Park, Maryland
Agent: CAA - Beverly Hills, 310/288-4545

THE ONE AND ONLY GENUINE, ORIGINAL FAMILY BAND
   Buena Vista, 1968
CACTUS FLOWER OO   Columbia, 1969
THERE'S A GIRL IN MY SOUP   Columbia, 1970, British
$ *DOLLARS*   Columbia, 1971
BUTTERFLIES ARE FREE   Columbia, 1972
THE SUGARLAND EXPRESS   Universal, 1974
THE GIRL FROM PETROVKA   Universal, 1974
SHAMPOO   Columbia, 1975

THE DUCHESS AND THE DIRTWATER FOX
   20th Century-Fox, 1976
FOUL PLAY   Paramount, 1978
LOVERS AND LIARS *TRAVELS WITH ANITA*   Levitt-Pickman,
   1979, Italian-French
PRIVATE BENJAMIN ★   Warner Bros., 1980
SEEMS LIKE OLD TIMES   Columbia, 1980
BEST FRIENDS   Warner Bros., 1982
SWING SHIFT   Warner Bros., 1984
PROTOCOL   Warner Bros., 1985
WILDCATS   Warner Bros., 1986
OVERBOARD   MGM/UA, 1987
BIRD ON A WIRE   Universal, 1990
DECEIVED   Buena Vista, 1991
CRISSCROSS   MGM-Pathe Communications, 1992
HOUSESITTER   Universal, 1992
DEATH BECOMES HER   Universal, 1992

NIGEL HAWTHORNE
A TALE OF TWO CITIES (TF)   Norman Rosemont Productions/
   Marble Arch Productions, 1980, U.S.-British
THE HUNCHBACK OF NOTRE DAME (TF)   Norman Rosemont
   Productions/Columbia TV, 1982, U.S.-British
FIREFOX   Warner Bros., 1982
GANDHI   Columbia, 1982, British-Indian
DREAMCHILD   Universal, 1985, British
TURTLE DIARY   Samuel Goldwyn Company, 1985, British
JENNY'S WAR (TF)   Louis Rudolph Productions/HTV/
   Columbia TV, 1985, U.S.-British
THE CHAIN   Rank, 1985, British
DEMOLITION MAN   Warner Bros., 1993
THE MADNESS OF GEORGE III   Samuel Goldwyn Company, 1995

KUMIKO HAYAKAWA
KINJITE (FORBIDDEN SUBJECTS)   Cannon, 1989

KARL HAYDEN
DA   FilmDallas Pictures, 1988

JEFF HAYENGA
Agent: The Gage Group - Los Angeles, 213/859-8777

THE PRINCE OF PENNSYLVANIA   New Line Cinema, 1988
THE UNBORN   Califilm, 1991

HELEN HAYES
(Helen Hayes Brown)
b. October 10, 1900 - Washington, D.C.

THE WEAVERS OF LIFE   1917
BABS   1920
THE SIN OF MADELON CLAUDET ★★   MGM, 1931
ARROWSMITH   United Artists, 1931
A FAREWELL TO ARMS   Paramount, 1932
THE SON-DAUGHTER   MGM, 1932
THE WHITE SISTER   MGM, 1933
ANOTHER LANGUAGE   1933
NIGHT FLIGHT   MGM, 1933
CRIME WITHOUT PASSION   Paramount, 1934 (uncredited)
WHAT EVERY WOMAN KNOWS   MGM, 1934
VANESSA, HER LOVE STORY   1935
STAGE DOOR CANTEEN   United Artists, 1943
MY SON JOHN   Paramount, 1952
MAIN STREET TO BROADWAY   MGM, 1953
ANASTASIA   20th Century-Fox, 1956
THIRD MAN ON THE MOUNTAIN   Buena Vista, 1959,
   U.S.-British (uncredited)
AIRPORT ○○   Universal, 1970
DO NOT FOLD, SPINDLE OR MUTILATE (TF)   Lee Rich
   Productions, 1971
THE SNOOP SISTERS *FEMALE INSTINCT* (TF)   Universal TV, 1972
HELEN HAYES: PORTRAIT OF AN AMERICAN ACTRESS (FD)   1974
HERBIE RIDES AGAIN   Buena Vista, 1974
ONE OF OUR DINOSAURS IS MISSING   Buena Vista,
   1975, U.S.-British
VICTORY AT ENTEBBE (TF)   1976
ARTHUR HAILEY'S THE MONEYCHANGERS
   THE MONEYCHANGERS (MS)   Ross Hunter Productions/
   Paramount TV, 1976

CANDLESHOE   Buena Vista, 1977
A FAMILY UPSIDE DOWN (TF)   Ross Hunter-Jacques Mapes Film/
   Paramount TV, 1978
MURDER IS EASY (TF)   David L. Wolper-Stan Margulies
   Productions/Warner Bros. TV, 1982
A CARIBBEAN MYSTERY (TF)   Stan Margulies Productions/
   Warner Bros. TV, 1983
HIGHWAY TO HEAVEN (TF)   Michael Landon Productions, 1984
MURDER WITH MIRRORS (TF)   Hajeno Productions/
   Warner Bros. TV, 1985

ISAAC HAYES
b. August 20, 1942 - Covington, Texas

COUNTERFORCE   Golden Sun Productions, Spanish
I'M GONNA GIT YOU SUCKA   MGM/UA, 1989
GUILTY AS CHARGED   I.R.S. Media, 1991
ROBIN HOOD: MEN IN TIGHTS   20th Century Fox, 1993
OUT OF SYNC   BET Films, 1994

LORI HAYES
MISS FIRECRACKER   Corsair Pictures, 1989

PATRICIA HAYES
CANDLES AT NINE   1944
NICHOLAS NICKLEBY   1947, British
THE LOVE MATCH   1954
THE BATTLE OF THE SEXES   Continental, 1959, British
GOODBYE, MR. CHIPS   MGM, 1969, British
THE CORN IS GREEN (TF)   Warner Bros. TV, 1979
THE NEVER ENDING STORY   Warner Bros., 1984, West German
LITTLE DORRIT   Cannon, 1988, British

JIM HAYNIE
ON THE EDGE   Skouras Pictures, 1986
STAYING TOGETHER   Hemdale, 1989
MEN DON'T LEAVE   Warner Bros., 1990
TOO MUCH SUN   New Line Cinema, 1991

ROBERT HAYS
b. July 24, 1947 - Bethesda, Maryland

YOUNG PIONEERS (TF)   ABC Circle Films, 1976
YOUNG PIONEERS' CHRISTMAS (TF)   ABC Circle Films, 1976
DELTA COUNTY, U.S.A.   Leonard Goldberg Productions/
   Paramount TV, 1977
THE INITIATION OF SARAH (TF)   Charles Fries Productions, 1978
AIRPLANE!   Paramount, 1980
TAKE THIS JOB AND SHOVE IT   Avco Embassy, 1981
THE FALL OF THE HOUSE OF USHER (TF)   Sunn Classic
   Productions, 1982
AIRPLANE II: THE SEQUEL   Paramount, 1982
TOUCHED   Lorimar Productions/Wildwoods Partners, 1983
TRENCHCOAT   Buena Vista, 1983
SCANDALOUS   Orion, 1984
STEPHEN KING'S CAT'S EYE *CAT'S EYE*   MGM/UA, 1985
MURDER BY THE BOOK (TF)   Nelson Productions/Orion TV, 1987
HOMEWARD BOUND: THE INCREDIBLE JOURNEY
   Buena Vista, 1993

DENNIS HAYSBERT
Agent: Paradigm - Los Angeles, 310/277-4400

MR. BASEBALL   Universal, 1992
LOVE FIELD   Orion, 1992
MAJOR LEAGUE II   Warner Bros., 1994

CHRIS HAYWOOD
MALCOLM   Vestron, 1986, Australian
QUIGLEY DOWN UNDER   MGM/UA, 1990

LENA HEADEY
THE JUNGLE BOOK   Buena Vista, 1994

SHARI HEADLEY
Agent: Writers & Artists Agency - Los Angeles, 213/820-2240

COMING TO AMERICA   Paramount, 1988

GLENNE HEADLY
Agent: ICM - Beverly Hills, 310/550-4000

NADINE   TriStar, 1987
MAKING MR. RIGHT   Orion, 1987
DIRTY ROTTEN SCOUNDRELS   Orion, 1988
LONESOME DOVE (MS)   Motown Productions/Pangaea/Qintex
   Entertainment, Inc., 1989
DICK TRACY   Buena Vista, 1990
MORTAL THOUGHTS   Columbia, 1991
AND THE BAND PLAYED ON (CTF)   HBO Pictures/Spelling
   Entertainment, 1993
GETTING EVEN WITH DAD   MGM/UA, 1994
MR. HOLLAND'S OPUS   Buena Vista, 1995

ANTHONY HEALD
SILKWOOD   20th Century-Fox, 1983
TEACHERS   MGM/UA, 1984
OUTRAGEOUS FORTUNE   Buena Vista, 1987
POSTCARDS FROM THE EDGE   Columbia, 1990
THE SILENCE OF THE LAMBS   Orion, 1991
THE CLIENT   Warner Bros., 1994

DAVID HEALY
ELEANOR AND FRANKLIN: THE WHITE HOUSE YEARS (TF)
   Talent Associates, 1977
THE TED KENNEDY, JR. STORY (TF)   Entertainment
   Partners, 1986

KATHERINE HEALY
SIX WEEKS   Universal, 1982

PATRICIA HEALY
ULTRAVIOLET   Concorde, 1992

JOHN HEARD
b. March 7, 1945 - Washington D.C.

FIRST LOVE   Paramount, 1977
BETWEEN THE LINES   Midwest Film Productions, 1977
HEAD OVER HEELS   *CHILLY SCENES OF WINTER*
   United Artists, 1979
ON THE YARD   Midwest Film Productions, 1979
HEART BEAT   Orion/Warner Bros., 1980
CUTTER'S WAY   *CUTTER AND BONE*   United Artists
   Classics, 1981
CAT PEOPLE   Universal, 1982
WILL THERE REALLY BE A MORNING? (TF)   Jaffe-Blakely Films/
   Sama Productions/Orion TV, 1983
HEAVEN HELP US   TriStar, 1985
AFTER HOURS   The Geffen Company/Warner Bros., 1985
THE TRIP TO BOUNTIFUL   Island Pictures/FilmDallas, 1985
OUT ON A LIMB (MS)   Stan Margulies Company/
   ABC Circle Films, 1987
THE TELEPHONE   New World, 1988
THE MILAGRO BEANFIELD WAR   Universal, 1988
NECESSITY (TF)   Barry-Enright Productions/
   Alexander Productions, 1988
BIG   20th Century Fox, 1988
BETRAYED   MGM/UA, 1988
BEACHES   Buena Vista, 1988
THE PACKAGE   Orion, 1989
CROSS OF FIRE (MS)   Leonard Hill Films, 1989
HOME ALONE   20th Century Fox, 1990
THE END OF INNOCENCE   Skouras Pictures, 1990
AWAKENINGS   Columbia, 1990
RAMBLING ROSE   New Line Cinema, 1991
DECEIVED   Buena Vista, 1991
RADIO FLYER   Columbia, 1992
HOME ALONE 2: LOST IN NEW YORK   20th Century Fox, 1992
IN THE LINE OF FIRE   Columbia, 1993
THE PELICAN BRIEF   Warner Bros., 1993

GEORGE HEARN
b. 1935 - Memphis, Tennessee

SEE YOU IN THE MORNING   Warner Bros., 1989
SNEAKERS   Universal, 1992
THE VANISHING   20th Century Fox, 1993

PATRICIA HEARST
CRY-BABY   Universal, 1990
SERIAL MOM   Savoy Pictures, 1994

JOEY HEATHERTON
b. September 14, 1944 - New York, New York

TWILIGHT OF HONOR   MGM, 1963
WHERE LOVE HAS GONE   Paramount, 1964
MY BLOOD RUNS COLD   Warner Bros., 1965
BLUEBEARD   Cinerama Releasing Corporation, 1972,
   Italian-French-West German
THE HAPPY HOOKER GOES TO WASHINGTON   Cannon, 1977
CRY-BABY   Universal, 1990

PATRICIA HEATON
MEMOIRS OF AN INVISIBLE MAN   Warner Bros., 1992
BEETHOVEN   Universal, 1992

TOM HEATON
APRIL FOOL'S DAY   Paramount, 1986

DAVID HEAVENER
EYE OF THE STRANGER   Silver Lake International Pictures, 1993

PAUL HECHT
Agent: Susan Smith & Associates - Beverly Hills, 213/852-4777

TEMPEST   World Northal, 1980, British
ROLLOVER   Orion/Warner Bros., 1981
JOSHUA THEN AND NOW   20th Century Fox, 1985, Canadian
I'LL TAKE MANHATTAN (MS)   Steve Krantz Productions, 1987
A NEW LIFE   Paramount, 1988

EILEEN HECKART
b. March 29, 1919 - Columbus, Ohio
Agent: APA - Los Angeles, 310/273-0744

MIRACLE IN THE RAIN   Warner Bros., 1956
SOMEBODY UP THERE LIKES ME   MGM, 1956
BUS STOP   20th Century-Fox, 1956
THE BAD SEED ✪   Warner Bros., 1956
HOT SPELL   Paramount, 1958
HELLER IN PINK TIGHTS   Paramount, 1960
MY SIX LOVES   1963
UP THE DOWN STAIRCASE   Warner Bros., 1967
NO WAY TO TREAT A LADY   Paramount, 1968
THE TREE   Guenette, 1969
BUTTERFLIES ARE FREE ✪✪   Columbia, 1972
ZANDY'S BRIDE   *FOR BETTER, FOR WORSE*   Warner Bros., 1974
THE HIDING PLACE   World Wide, 1975
BURNT OFFERINGS   United Artists, 1976
SUNSHINE CHRISTMAS (TF)   Universal TV, 1977
SUDDENLY LOVE (TF)   Ross Hunter Productions, 1978
BACKSTAIRS AT THE WHITE HOUSE (MS)   Ed Friendly
   Productions, 1979
WHITE MAMA (TF)   Tomorrow Entertainment, 1980
HEARTBREAK RIDGE   Warner Bros., 1986
STUCK WITH EACH OTHER (TF)   Nexus Productions, 1989

DAN HEDAYA
BLOOD SIMPLE   Circle Releasing Corporation, 1984
RECKLESS   MGM/UA, 1984
COURAGE (TF)   Highgate Pictures/New World TV, 1986
RUNNING SCARED   MGM/UA, 1986
WISEGUYS   MGM/UA, 1986
DOUBLE YOUR PLEASURE (TF)   Steve White Productions, 1989
JOE VERSUS THE VOLCANO   Warner Bros., 1990
THE ADDAMS FAMILY   Paramount, 1991

BOILING POINT   Warner Bros., 1993
BENNY & JOON   MGM/UA, 1993
ROOKIE OF THE YEAR   20th Century Fox, 1993
UNTITLED VAN SANT/ZISKIN   Columbia, 1995

DAVID HEDISON
(Al Hedison)
Agent: Fred Amsel & Associates - Los Angeles, 213/939-1188

THE ENEMY BELOW   20th Century-Fox, 1957
THE FLY   20th Century-Fox, 1958
SON OF ROBIN HOOD   20th Century-Fox, 1959
THE LOST WORLD   20th Century-Fox, 1960
MARINES LET'S GO   20th Century-Fox, 1961
THE GREATEST STORY EVER TOLD   United Artists, 1965
LIVE AND LET DIE   United Artists, 1973, British
THE CAT CREATURE (TF)   Screen Gems/Columbia TV, 1973
ADVENTURES OF THE QUEEN (TF)   20th Century-Fox TV, 1975
THE LIVES OF JENNY DOLAN (TF)   Ross Hunter Productions/
   Paramount TV, 1975
MURDER IN PEYTON PLACE (TF)   20th Century-Fox TV, 1977
THE POWER WITHIN (TF)   Aaron Spelling Productions, 1979
ffolkes   *NORTH SEA HIJACK*   Universal, 1980, British
THE NAKED FACE   Cannon, 1985
SMART ALEC   *THE MOVIE MAKER*   1986
LICENCE TO KILL   MGM/UA, 1989, British

JACK HEDLEY
ROOM AT THE TOP   Continental, 1959, British
MAKE MINE MINK   1960
LAWRENCE OF ARABIA   Columbia, 1962, British
IN THE FRENCH STYLE   Columbia, 1963, French-U.S.
THE CRIMSON BLADE   *THE SCARLET BLADE*   1963
OF HUMAN BONDAGE   MGM, 1964, British
WITCHCRAFT   20th Century-Fox, 1964, British
THE ANNIVERSARY   20th Century-Fox, 1968, British
GOODBYE, MR. CHIPS   MGM, 1969, British
BRIEF ENCOUNTER (TF)   Carlo Ponti Productions/Cecil Clarke
   Productions, 1974, British
SOPHIA LOREN: HER OWN STORY (TF)   Roger Gimbel
   Productions/EMI TV, 1980
FOR YOUR EYES ONLY   United Artists, 1981, British

TIPPI HEDREN
(Nathalie Hedren)
b. 1935 - Lafayette, Minnesota

THE BIRDS   Universal, 1963
MARNIE   Universal, 1964
A COUNTESS FROM HONG KONG   Universal, 1967, British
THE MAN WITH THE ALBATROSS   1969
THE HARRAD EXPERIMENT   Cinerama Releasing Corporation, 1973
ROAR   1981
PACIFIC HEIGHTS   20th Century Fox, 1990

KYLE T. HEFFNER
FLASHDANCE   Paramount, 1983

MARTA HEFLIN
COME BACK TO THE 5 & DIME JIMMY DEAN, JIMMY DEAN
   Cinecom, 1982

KATHERINE HEIGL
MY FATHER, THE HERO   Buena Vista, 1994
UNDER SIEGE 2   Warner Bros., 1995

MARG HELGENBERGER
Agent: Gersh Agency - Beverly Hills, 310/274-6611

CHINA BEACH (TF)   Sacret, Inc. Productions/Warner Bros. TV, 1988
ALWAYS   Universal, 1989
BLIND VENGEANCE (CTF)   Spanish Trail Productions/MCA TV, 1990
CROOKED HEARTS   MGM-Pathe, 1991
SPECIES   MGM/UA, 1995

OCEAN HELLMAN
ANYTHING TO SURVIVE (TF)   Saban-Scherick Productions/
   ATL Productions/B.C. Films, 1990

LEVON HELM
BEST REVENGE   Lorimar Distribution International, 1983, Canadian
THE DOLLMAKER (TF)   Finnegan Associates/IPC Films, Inc./
   Dollmaker Productions, 1984
COAL MINER'S DAUGHTER   Universal, 1980
THE RIGHT STUFF   The Ladd Company/Warner Bros., 1983
SMOOTH TALK   Spectrafilm, 1985
END OF THE LINE   Orion Classics, 1988
STAYING TOGETHER   Hemdale, 1989

KATHERINE HELMOND
b. July 5, 1934 - Galveston, Texas
Agent: William Morris Agency - Beverly Hills, 310/274-7451

DR. MAX (TF)   CBS, Inc., 1974
LOCUSTS (TF)   Paramount TV, 1974
THE LEGEND OF LIZZIE BORDEN (TF)   Paramount TV, 1975
BABY BLUE MARINE   Columbia, 1976
FAMILY PLOT   Universal, 1976
GETTING MARRIED (TF)   Paramount TV, 1978
PEARL (TF)   Silliphant-Konigsberg Prods./Warner Bros. TV, 1978
DIARY OF A TEENAGE HITCHHIKER (TF)
   The Shpetner Company, 1979
TIME BANDITS   Avco Embassy, 1981, British
BRAZIL   Universal, 1985, British
SHADEY   Skouras Pictures, 1985, British
OVERBOARD   MGM/UA, 1987
LADY IN WHITE   New Century/Vista, 1988
THE PERFECT TRIBUTE (CTF)   Dorothea Petrie Productions/
   Proctor & Gamble Productions/World International Network, 1991

DAVID HEMBLEN
A MAN IN UNIFORM   I.R.S. Releasing, 1994

MARGAUX HEMINGWAY
b. February 19, 1955 - Portland, Oregon

LIPSTICK   Paramount, 1976
KILLER FISH   *DEADLY TREASURE OF THE PIRANHA*
   Associated Film Distribution, 1978, British-Brazilian-French
THEY CALL ME BRUCE?   *A FISTFUL OF CHOPSTICKS*
   Artists Releasing Corporation/Film Ventures International, 1982
OVER THE BROOKLYN BRIDGE   MGM/UA, Cannon, 1984
KILLING MACHINE   Golden Sun Productions, 1986, Spanish

MARIEL HEMINGWAY
b. November 21, 1961 - Mill Valley, California
Agent: ICM - Beverly Hills, 310/550-4000

LIPSTICK   Paramount, 1976
I WANT TO KEEP MY BABY (TF)   CBS, Inc., 1976
MANHATTAN ✪   United Artists, 1979
PERSONAL BEST   The Geffen Company/Warner Bros., 1982
STAR 80   The Ladd Company/Warner Bros., 1983
CREATOR   Universal, 1985
THE MEAN SEASON   Orion, 1985
AMERIKA (MS)   ABC Circle Films, 1987
SUPERMAN IV: THE QUEST FOR PEACE   Warner Bros., 1987
SUNSET   TriStar, 1988
DELIRIOUS   MGM-Pathe, 1991
FALLING FROM GRACE   Columbia, 1992

DAVID HEMMINGS
b. November 18, 1941 - Guildford, England

SAINT JOAN   United Artists, 1957
NO TREES IN THE STREET   Associated British Picture Corporation,
   1958, British
THE WIND OF CHANGE   1960, British
MURDER CAN BE DEADLY   *THE PAINTED SMILE*   1962, British
SOME PEOPLE   American International, 1962, British
SING AND SWING   *LIVE IT UP*   1963, British
THE GIRL-GETTERS   *THE SYSTEM*   American International,
   1964, British
DATELINE DIAMONDS   Rank, 1966, British
BLOW-UP   Premier, 1966, British-Italian
EYE OF THE DEVIL   MGM, 1967, British
CAMELOT   Warner Bros., 1967

BARBARELLA   Paramount, 1968, French-Italian
THE CHARGE OF THE LIGHT BRIGADE   United Artists,
   1968, British
THE LONG DAY'S DYING   1968, British
WHEN I LARF   1968
ALFRED THE GREAT   MGM, 1969, British
THE BEST HOUSE IN LONDON   MGM, 1969, British
THE WALKING STICK   MGM, 1970, British
FRAGMENT OF FEAR   Columbia, 1971, British
UNMAN, WITTERING AND ZINGO   Paramount, 1971, British
THE LOVE MACHINE   Columbia, 1971
VOICES   Hemdale, 1973, British
JUGGERNAUT   United Artists, 1974, British
MR. QUILP   *THE OLD CURIOSITY SHOP*   Avco Embassy,
   1975, British
DEEP RED   *PROFONDO ROSSO*   Howard Mahler Films,
   1975, Italian
THE SQUEEZE   Warner Bros., 1977, British
ISLANDS IN THE STREAM   Paramount, 1977
THE DISAPPEARANCE   Levitt-Pickman, 1977, Canadian
CROSSED SWORDS   *THE PRINCE AND THE PAUPER*
   Warner Bros., 1978, British
BLOOD RELATIVES   *LES LIENS DE SANG*   Filmcorp,
   1978, French-Canadian
SQUADRA ANTIRUFFA   1978, Italian
POWER PLAY   Magnum International Pictures/Cowry Film
   Productions, 1978, Canadian-British
JUST A GIGOLO   United Artists Classics, 1978,
   West German (also directed)
MURDER BY DECREE   Avco Embassy, 1979, Canadian-British
CHARLIE MUFFIN (TF)   Euston Films, Ltd., 1979, British
THIRST   1979, Australian
MAN, WOMAN AND CHILD   Paramount, 1983
THE KEY TO REBECCA (MS)   Taft Entertainment TV/Castle
   Combe Productions, 1985, U.S.-British (also directed)
BEVERLY HILLS COWGIRL BLUES (TF)   The Leonard Goldberg
   Company, 1985
HARRY'S HONG KONG (TF)   Aaron Spelling Productions, 1987
THREE ON A MATCH (TF)   Belisarius Productions/TriStar TV, 1987

SHERMAN HEMSLEY
b. February 1, 1938 - Philadelphia, Pennsylvania

COMBAT HIGH (TF)   Frank von Zerneck Productions/
   Lynch-Biller Productions, 1986
ROUGH STUFF   New Line Cinema, 1992
MR. NANNY   New Line Cinema, 1993

GEORGE HENARE
RAPA NUI   Warner Bros., 1994

BILL HENDERSON
GET CRAZY   Embassy, 1983
MURPHY'S LAW   Cannon, 1986
CITY SLICKERS   Columbia, 1991

FLORENCE HENDERSON
b. February 14, 1934 - Dale, Indiana
Agent: APA - Los Angeles, 310/273-0744

SONG OF NORWAY   Cinerama Releasing Corporation, 1970
THE BRADY GIRLS GET MARRIED (TF)   Sherwood Schwartz
   Productions, 1981
A VERY BRADY CHRISTMAS (TF)   Sherwood Schwartz
   Productions/Paramount TV, 1988
THE BRADYS (TF)   Brady Productions/Paramount TV, 1990
THE BRADY BUNCH MOVIE   Paramount, 1995

MAGGIE HENDERSON
INDISCREET (TF)   Karen Mack Productions/HTV/Republic Pictures,
   1988, U.S.-British

SAFFRON HENDERSON
THE FLY II   20th Century Fox, 1989

TONY HENDRA
THIS IS SPINAL TAP   Embassy, 1984

BENJAMIN HENDRICKSON
CONSENTING ADULTS   Buena Vista, 1992

STEVE HENDRICKSON
THE WIZARD OF LONELINESS   Skouras Pictures, 1988

CARRIE HENN
ALIENS   20th Century Fox, 1986

MARILU HENNER
b. April 6, 1952 - Chicago, Illinois
Agent: William Morris Agency - Beverly Hills, 310/274-7451

BETWEEN THE LINES   Midwest Film Productions, 1977
BLOODBROTHERS   Warner Bros., 1978
HAMMETT   Orion/Warner Bros., 1983
THE MAN WHO LOVED WOMEN   Columbia, 1983
CANNONBALL RUN II   Warner Bros., 1984
JOHNNY DANGEROUSLY   20th Century Fox, 1984
STARK (TF)   CBS Entertainment, 1985
RUSTLER'S RHAPSODY   Paramount, 1985
PERFECT   Columbia, 1985
LADYKILLERS (TF)   Barry Weitz Films/ABC Circle Films, 1988
L.A. STORY   TriStar, 1991
NOISES OFF   Buena Vista, 1992

SAM HENNINGS
DROP ZONE   Paramount, 1994

LANCE HENRIKSEN
Agent: APA - Los Angeles, 310/273-0744

PIRANHA II: THE SPAWNING   Saturn International,
   1983, Italian-U.S.
NIGHTMARES   Universal, 1983
STREETS OF JUSTICE (TF)   Universal TV, 1985
ALIENS   20th Century Fox, 1986
CHOKE CANYON   United Film Distribution, 1986
NEAR DARK   DEG, 1987
PUMPKINHEAD   MGM/UA, 1988
HIT LIST   New Line Cinema, 1989
JOHNNY HANDSOME   TriStar, 1989
SURVIVAL QUEST   MGM/UA, 1990
ALIEN 3   20th Century Fox, 1992, U.S.-British
JENNIFER EIGHT   Paramount, 1992
HARD TARGET   Universal, 1993
MAN'S BEST FRIEND   New Line Cinema, 1993
NO ESCAPE   Savoy Pictures, 1994
COLOR OF NIGHT   Buena Vista, 1994
NATURE OF THE BEAST   New Line Cinema, 1994

BUCK HENRY
(Buck Henry Zuckerman)
b. 1930 - New York, New York
Agent: William Morris Agency - Beverly Hills, 310/274-7451

THE TROUBLEMAKER   Janus, 1964
THE GRADUATE   Avco Embassy, 1967
THE SECRET WAR OF HARRY FRIGG   Universal, 1968
CATCH-22   Paramount, 1970
THE OWL AND THE PUSSYCAT   Columbia, 1970
TAKING OFF   Universal, 1971
IS THERE SEX AFTER DEATH?   1971
THE DAY OF THE DOLPHIN   Avco Embassy, 1973 (voice)
THE MAN WHO FELL TO EARTH   Cinema 5, 1976, British
HEAVEN CAN WAIT   Paramount, 1978 (also co-directed)
OLD BOYFRIENDS   Avco Embassy, 1979
FIRST FAMILY   Warner Bros., 1980 (also directed)
GLORIA   Columbia, 1980
ARIA   Miramax Films, 1987, British
RUDE AWAKENING   Orion, 1989
TUNE IN TOMORROW   Cinecom, 1990
DEFENDING YOUR LIFE   Warner Bros., 1991
THE PLAYER   Fine Line Features/New Line Cinema, 1992
SHORT CUTS   Fine Line Features/New Line Cinema, 1993
GRUMPY OLD MEN   Warner Bros., 1993
EVEN COWGIRLS GET THE BLUES   Fine Line Features/
   New Line Cinema, 1994

GREGG HENRY
Agent: Susan Smith & Associates - Beverly Hills, 213/852-4777

BODY DOUBLE   Columbia, 1984
THE PATRIOT   Crown International, 1986
A STONING IN FULHAM COUNTY (TF)   The Landsburg
   Company, 1988

J.M. HENRY
MRS. PARKER AND THE VICIOUS CIRCLE   Fine Line Features/
   New Line Cinema, 1994

JUSTIN HENRY
b. May 25, 1971 - New York, New York
Agent: Susan Smith & Associates - Beverly Hills, 213/852-4777

KRAMER VS. KRAMER ❂   Columbia, 1979
TIGER TOWN (CTF)   Thompson Street Pictures, 1983
SIXTEEN CANDLES   Universal, 1984
MARTIN'S DAY   MGM/UA, 1984, British
SWEET HEARTS DANCE   TriStar, 1988

LENNY HENRY
Agent: William Morris Agency - Beverly Hills, 310/274-7451

TRUE IDENTITY   Buena Vista, 1991

MIKE HENRY
TARZAN AND THE VALLEY OF GOLD   American International,
   1966, U.S.-Swiss
TARZAN AND THE GREAT RIVER   Paramount, 1967
TARZAN AND THE JUNGLE BOY   Paramount, 1968
RIO LOBO   National General, 1970
SKYJACKED   MGM, 1972
THE LONGEST YARD   Paramount, 1974
SMOKEY AND THE BANDIT   Universal, 1977
SMOKEY AND THE BANDIT II   Universal, 1980
SMOKEY AND THE BANDIT 3   Universal, 1983

NATASHA HENSTRIDGE
SPECIES   MGM/UA, 1995

DOREEN HEPBURN
DA   FilmDallas Pictures, 1988

KATHARINE HEPBURN
b. November 8, 1907 - Hartford, Connecticut

A BILL OF DIVORCEMENT   RKO Radio, 1932
CHRISTOPHER STRONG   RKO Radio, 1933
MORNING GLORY ★★   RKO Radio, 1933
LITTLE WOMEN   RKO Radio, 1933
SPITFIRE   RKO Radio, 1934
THE LITTLE MINISTER   RKO Radio, 1934
BREAK OF HEARTS   RKO Radio, 1935
ALICE ADAMS ★   RKO Radio, 1935
SYLVIA SCARLETT   RKO Radio, 1935
MARY OF SCOTLAND   RKO Radio, 1936
A WOMAN REBELS   RKO Radio, 1936
QUALITY STREET   RKO Radio, 1937
STAGE DOOR   RKO Radio, 1937
BRINGING UP BABY   RKO Radio, 1938
HOLIDAY   Columbia, 1938
THE PHILADELPHIA STORY ★   MGM, 1940
WOMAN OF THE YEAR ★   MGM, 1942
KEEPER OF THE FLAME   MGM, 1942
STAGE DOOR CANTEEN   United Artists, 1943
DRAGON SEED   MGM, 1944
WITHOUT LOVE   MGM, 1945
UNDERCURRENT   MGM, 1946
SEA OF GRASS   20th Century-Fox, 1947
SONG OF LOVE   MGM, 1947
STATE OF THE UNION   MGM, 1948
ADAM'S RIB   MGM, 1949
THE AFRICAN QUEEN ★   United Artists, 1951
PAT AND MIKE   MGM, 1952

SUMMERTIME *SUMMER MADNESS* ★   United Artists,
   1955, British
THE RAINMAKER ★   Paramount, 1956
THE IRON PETTICOAT   MGM, 1956, British
DESK SET   20th Century-Fox, 1957
SUDDENLY, LAST SUMMER ★   Columbia, 1959
LONG DAY'S JOURNEY INTO NIGHT ★   Embassy, 1962
GUESS WHO'S COMING TO DINNER ★★   Columbia, 1967
THE LION IN WINTER ★★   Avco Embassy, 1968, British
THE MADWOMAN OF CHAILLOT   Warner Bros., 1969, British
THE TROJAN WOMEN   Cinerama Releasing Corporation,
   1971, U.S.-Greek
THE GLASS MENAGERIE (TF)   Talent Associates, 1973
A DELICATE BALANCE   American Film Theatre, 1973
LOVE AMONG THE RUINS (TF)   ABC Circle Films, 1975
ROOSTER COGBURN   Universal, 1975
OLLY OLLY OXEN FREE *THE GREAT BALLOON
   ADVENTURE* Sanrio, 1978
THE CORN IS GREEN (TF)   Warner Bros. TV, 1979
ON GOLDEN POND ★★   Universal/AFD, 1981
GRACE QUIGLEY *THE ULTIMATE SOLUTION OF
   GRACE QUIGLEY* Cannon, 1985
MRS. DELAFIELD WANTS TO MARRY (TF)   Schaefer-Karpf
   Productions/Gaylord Production Company, 1986
LAURA LANSING SLEPT HERE (TF)   Schaefer-Karpf Productions/
   Gaylord Production Company, 1988
THE MAN UPSTAIRS (TF)   Burt Reynolds Productions, 1992
THIS CAN'T BE LOVE (TF)   Davis Entertainment/Pacific Motion
   Pictures/World International Network, 1994
LOVE AFFAIR   Warner Bros., 1994

BERNARD HEPTON
GET CARTER   MGM, 1971, British
HENRY VIII AND HIS SIX WIVES   Levitt-Pickman, 1973, British
VOYAGE OF THE DAMNED   Avco Embassy, 1976, British
TINKER, TAILOR, SOLDIER, SPY (TF)   BBC/Paramount TV,
   1979, British
GANDHI   Columbia, 1982, British-Indian
SMILEY'S PEOPLE (MS)   BBC/Paramount TV, 1982, British
SHADEY   Skouras Pictures, 1985, British
EMINENT DOMAIN   Triumph Releasing Corporation, 1990,
   Canadian-French-Israeli

RICHARD HERD
Agent: Harris & Goldberg - Los Angeles, 310/553-5200

MARCIANO (TF)   ABC Circle Films, 1979
FUTURE COP *TRANCERS*   Empire Pictures, 1985
MY FIRST LOVE (TF)   The Avnet-Kerner Company, 1988
GLEAMING THE CUBE   20th Century Fox, 1989
FALL FROM GRACE (TF)   NBC Productions, 1990
THE SECRETARY   Republic Pictures, 1995

PEE-WEE HERMAN
(See Paul REUBENS)

PAUL HERMAN
BIG   20th Century-Fox, 1988

LAURA HERRING
THE FORBIDDEN DANCE   Columbia, 1990

EDWARD HERRMANN
b. July 21, 1943 - Washington D.C.
Agent: William Morris Agency - Beverly Hills, 310/274-7451

LADY LIBERTY *MORTADELLA*   United Artists, 1971, Italian
THE PAPER CHASE   20th Century-Fox, 1973
THE DAY OF THE DOLPHIN   Avco Embassy, 1973
THE GREAT GATSBY   Paramount, 1974
THE GREAT WALDO PEPPER   Universal, 1975
ELEANOR AND FRANKLIN (TF)   Talent Associates, 1976
ELEANOR AND FRANKLIN: THE WHITE HOUSE YEARS (TF)
   Talent Associates, 1977
THE BETSY   Allied Artists, 1978
A LOVE AFFAIR: THE ELEANOR AND LOU GEHRIG STORY (TF)
   Charles Fries Productions/Stonehenge Productions, 1978

FREEDOM ROAD (TF)   Zev Braun Productions/Freedom Road
    Films, 1979
THE NORTH AVENUE IRREGULARS   Buena Vista, 1979
PORTRAIT OF A STRIPPER (TF)   Moonlight Productions/
    Filmways, 1979
TAKE DOWN   Buena Vista, 1979
REDS   Paramount, 1981
HARRY'S WAR   Taft International, 1981
ANNIE   Columbia, 1982
A LITTLE SEX   Universal, 1982
MRS. SOFFEL   MGM/UA, 1984
THE PURPLE ROSE OF CAIRO   Orion, 1985
COMPROMISING POSITIONS   Paramount, 1985
THE MAN WITH ONE RED SHOE   20th Century Fox, 1985
MURROW (CTF)   HBO Premiere Films/Titus Productions/TVS Ltd.
    Productions, 1986, U.S.-British
OVERBOARD   MGM/UA, 1987
THE LOST BOYS   Warner Bros., 1987
BIG BUSINESS   Buena Vista, 1988
SO PROUDLY WE HAIL (TF)   Lionel Chetwynd Productions/CBS
    Entertainment, 1990
RICHIE RICH   Warner Bros., 1994

BARBARA HERSHEY
(Barbara Herzstein/Barbara Seagull)
b. February 5, 1948 - Hollywood, California
Agent: CAA - Beverly Hills, 310/288-4545

WITH SIX YOU GET EGGROLL   National General, 1968
HEAVEN WITH A GUN   MGM, 1969
LAST SUMMER   Allied Artists, 1969
THE LIBERATION OF L.B. JONES   Columbia, 1970
THE BABY MAKER   National General, 1970
THE PURSUIT OF HAPPINESS   Columbia, 1971
DEALING: OR THE BERKELEY-TO-BOSTON FORTY-BRICK
    LOST-BAG BLUES   Warner Bros., 1972
BOXCAR BERTHA   American International, 1972
THE CRAZY WORLD OF JULIUS VROODER
    20th Century-Fox, 1974
LOVE COMES QUIETLY   1975
YOU AND ME   Filmmakers International, 1975
DIAMONDS   Avco Embassy, 1975, U.S.-Israeli-Swiss
THE LAST HARD MEN   20th Century-Fox, 1976
DIRTY KNIGHTS' WORK   *CHOICE OF WEAPONS*   Gamma III,
    1976, British
FLOOD! (TF)   Irwin Allen Productions/20th Century-Fox TV, 1976
AMERICANA   Crown International, 1981
THE STUNT MAN   20th Century-Fox, 1980
TAKE THIS JOB AND SHOVE IT   Avco Embassy, 1981
THE ENTITY   20th Century-Fox, 1983
THE RIGHT STUFF   The Ladd Company/Warner Bros., 1983
THE NATURAL   TriStar, 1984
HOOSIERS   Orion, 1986
HANNAH AND HER SISTERS   Orion, 1986
TIN MEN   Buena Vista, 1987
SHY PEOPLE   Cannon, 1987
A WORLD APART   Atlantic Releasing Corporation, 1988, British
THE LAST TEMPTATION OF CHRIST   Universal, 1988
BEACHES   Buena Vista, 1988
KILLING IN A SMALL TOWN (TF)   The IndieProd Co./Hearst
    Entertainment Productions, 1990
TUNE IN TOMORROW   Cinecom, 1990
PARIS TROUT (CTF)   Viacom, 1991
DEFENSELESS   New Line Cinema, 1991
THE PUBLIC EYE   Universal, 1992
FALLING DOWN   Warner Bros., 1993
SWING KIDS   Buena Vista, 1993
SPLITTING HEIRS   Universal, 1993, British-U.S.
A DANGEROUS WOMAN   Gramercy Pictures, 1993
LAST OF THE DOGMEN   Savoy Pictures, 1995

JASON HERVEY
BACK TO THE FUTURE   Universal, 1985
BACK TO SCHOOL   Orion, 1986

JOHN HERZFELD
COBRA   Warner Bros., 1986

GRANT HESLOV
CONGO   Paramount, 1995

SUSAN HESS
DRESS GRAY (MS)   von Zerneck Productions/
    Warner Bros. TV, 1986
WHAT PRICE VICTORY? (TF)   Wolper Productions/
    Warner Bros. TV, 1988

GREGOR HESSE
DEAD AGAIN   Paramount, 1991

HOWARD HESSEMAN
b. February 27, 1940 - Lebanon, Oregon
Agent: APA - Los Angeles, 310/273-0744

THE SUNSHINE BOYS   MGM/United Artists, 1975
THE BIG BUS   Paramount, 1976
TUNNELVISION   World Wide, 1976
LOOSE SHOES   *COMING ATTRACTIONS*   1980
PRIVATE LESSONS   Jensen Farley Pictures, 1981
ONE SHOE MAKES IT MURDER (TF)   The Fellows-Keegan
    Company/Lorimar Productions, 1982
DOCTOR DETROIT   Universal, 1983
SILENCE OF THE HEART (TF)   David A. Simons Productions/
    Tisch-Avnet Productions, 1984
POLICE ACADEMY 2: THEIR FIRST ASSIGNMENT
    Warner Bros., 1985
FLIGHT OF THE NAVIGATOR   Buena Vista, 1986
MY CHAUFFEUR   Crown International, 1986
AMAZON WOMEN ON THE MOON   Universal, 1987
HEAT   New Century/Vista, 1987
SIX AGAINST THE ROCK (TF)   Schaefer-Karpf-Epstein Productions/
    Gaylord Production Company, 1987
THE DIAMOND TRAP (TF)   Jay Bernstein Productions/
    Columbia TV, 1988
OUT OF SYNC   BET Films, 1994

CHARLTON HESTON
(Charles Carter)
b. October 4, 1923 - Evanston, Illinois
Agent: ICM - Beverly Hills, 310/550-4000

DARK CITY   Paramount, 1950
THE GREATEST SHOW ON EARTH   Paramount, 1952
THE SAVAGE   Paramount, 1952
RUBY GENTRY   20th Century-Fox, 1952
THE PRESIDENT'S LADY   20th Century-Fox, 1953
PONY EXPRESS   Paramount, 1953
ARROWHEAD   Paramount, 1953
BAD FOR EACH OTHER   Columbia, 1953
THE NAKED JUNGLE   Paramount, 1954
SECRET OF THE INCAS   Paramount, 1954
THE FAR HORIZONS   Paramount, 1955
THE PRIVATE WAR OF MAJOR BENSON   Universal, 1955
LUCY GALLANT   Paramount, 1955
THE TEN COMMANDMENTS   Paramount, 1956
THREE VIOLENT PEOPLE   Paramount, 1957
TOUCH OF EVIL   Universal, 1958
THE BIG COUNTRY   United Artists, 1958
THE BUCCANEER   Paramount, 1958
THE WRECK OF THE MARY DEARE   MGM, 1959, U.S.-British
BEN-HUR ★★   MGM, 1959
EL CID   Allied Artists, 1961
THE PIGEON THAT TOOK ROME   Paramount, 1962
DIAMOND HEAD   Columbia, 1963
55 DAYS AT PEKING   Allied Artists, 1963
THE GREATEST STORY EVER TOLD   United Artists, 1965
MAJOR DUNDEE   Columbia, 1965
THE AGONY AND THE ECSTASY   20th Century-Fox, 1965
THE WAR LORD   Universal, 1965
KHARTOUM   United Artists, 1966, British
COUNTERPOINT   Universal, 1968
PLANET OF THE APES   20th Century-Fox, 1968
WILL PENNY   Paramount, 1968
NUMBER ONE   United Artists, 1969
JULIUS CAESAR   American International, 1970, British

BENEATH THE PLANET OF THE APES   20th Century-Fox, 1970
THE HAWAIIANS   United Artists, 1970
THE OMEGA MAN   Warner Bros., 1971
CALL OF THE WILD   Constantin, 1972,
    British-West German-French-Italian-Spanish
SKYJACKED   MGM, 1972
ANTONY AND CLEOPATRA   Rank, 1973,
    British-Spanish-Swiss (also directed)
SOYLENT GREEN   MGM, 1973
THE THREE MUSKETEERS   20th Century-Fox, 1974, British
AIRPORT 1975   Universal, 1974
EARTHQUAKE   Universal, 1974
THE FOUR MUSKETEERS   20th Century-Fox, 1975, British
THE LAST HARD MEN   1976
MIDWAY   Universal, 1976
TWO-MINUTE WARNING   Universal, 1976
CROSSED SWORDS   THE PRINCE AND THE PAUPER
    Warner Bros., 1978, British
GRAY LADY DOWN   Universal, 1978
THE MOUNTAIN MEN   Columbia, 1980
THE AWAKENING   Orion/Warner Bros., 1980
MOTHER LODE   SEARCH FOR THE MOTHER LODE:
    THE LAST GREAT TREASURE   Agamemnon Films, 1982,
    Canadian (also directed)
CHIEFS (MS)   Highgate Pictures, 1983
NAIROBI AFFAIR (TF)   Robert Halmi, Inc., 1984
PROUD MEN (TF)   von Zerneck-Samuels Productions, 1987
A MAN FOR ALL SEASONS (CTF)   Agamemnon Filims/British Lion,
    1988, U.S.-British (also directed)
ORIGINAL SIN (TF)   Larry A. Thompson Organization/
    New World TV, 1989
ALMOST AN ANGEL   Paramount, 1990, Australian-U.S.
TREASURE ISLAND (CTF)   Agamemnon Films/British Lion,
    1990, British-U.S.
THE LITTLE KIDNAPPERS (CTF)   Jones Maple Leaf Productions/
    The Disney Channel/CBC/Resnick-Margellos Productions,
    1990, Canadian
WAYNE'S WORLD 2   Paramount, 1993
TOMBSTONE   Buena Vista, 1993
TRUE LIES   20th Century Fox, 1994

MARTIN HEWITT
Agent: ICM - Beverly Hills, 310/550-4000

ENDLESS LOVE   Universal, 1981
OUT OF CONTROL   New World, 1985
ALIEN PREDATOR   Trans World Entertainment, 1987

DAVID HEWLETT
THE PENTHOUSE (TF)   Greene-White Productions/
    Spectator Films, 1989

BARTON HEYMAN
BILLY GALVIN   Vestron, 1986

PAT HEYWOOD
ROMEO AND JULIET   Paramount, 1968, Italian-British
10 RILLINGTON PLACE   Columbia, 1971, British
WHO SLEW AUNTIE ROO?   American International, 1971, British
GETTING IT RIGHT   MCEG, 1989, U.S.-British

JOHN BENJAMIN HICKEY
DOLORES CLAIBORNE   Columbia, 1994

WILLIAM HICKEY
Agent: Harris & Goldberg - Los Angeles, 310/553-5200

PRIZZI'S HONOR ✪   20th Century Fox, 1985
ONE CRAZY SUMMER   Warner Bros., 1986
THE NAME OF THE ROSE   20th Century Fox, 1986,
    West German-Italian-French
A HOBO'S CHRISTMAS (TF)   Joe Byrnne-Falrose Productions/
    Phoenix Entertainment, 1987
DA   FilmDallas Pictures, 1988
IT HAD TO BE YOU   Limelight Studios, 1989
TALES FROM THE DARKSIDE: THE MOVIE   Paramount, 1990
THE JERKY BOYS   Buena Vista, 1994

CATHERINE HICKLAND
Agent: Fred Amsel & Associates - Los Angeles, 213/939-1188

GHOST TOWN   Empire Pictures, 1988
PINK CADILLAC   Warner Bros., 1989

DWAYNE HICKMAN
BRING ME THE HEAD OF DOBIE GILLIS (TF)
    20th Century Fox TV, 1988

CATHERINE HICKS
Agent: Susan Smith & Associates - Beverly Hills, 213/852-4777

GARBO TALKS   MGM/UA, 1984
PEGGY SUE GOT MARRIED   TriStar, 1986
STAR TREK IV: THE VOYAGE HOME   Paramount, 1986
CHILD'S PLAY   MGM/United Artists, 1988
SHE'S OUT OF CONTROL   Columbia, 1989
SPY (CTF)   Deadly Productions/Wilshire Cour Productions, 1989

KEVIN HICKS
BLOOD RELATIONS   Miramax Films, 1988

TARAL HICKS
A BRONX TALE   Savoy Pictures, 1993

ANTHONY HIGGINS
Agent: William Morris Agency - London, 071/434-2191

LACE (MS)   Lorimar Productions, 1984
LACE II (MS)   Lorimar Productions, 1985
FOR LOVE OR MONEY   Universal, 1993
NOSTRADAMUS   Orion Classics, 1994, British

CLARE HIGGINS
BAD BEHAVIOUR   October Films, 1993, British

JOEL HIGGINS
THREESOME (TF)   CBS Entertainment, 1984
LAURA LANSING SLEPT HERE (TF)   Schaefer-Karpf Productions/
    Gaylord Production Company, 1988

MICHAEL HIGGINS
Agent: The Artists Group, Ltd. - Los Angeles, 310/552-1100

ON VALENTINE'S DAY   STORY OF A MARRIAGE
    Angelika Films, 1986
CRUSOE   Island Pictures, 1988, U.S.-British
DEAD-BANG   Warner Bros., 1989

LISE HILBOLDT
SWEET LIBERTY   Universal, 1986

ARTHUR HILL
b. August 1, 1922 - Melfort, Saskatchewan, Canada
Agent: CAA - Beverly Hills, 310/288-4545

I WAS A MALE WAR BRIDE   20th Century-Fox, 1949
MISS PILGRIM'S PROGRESS   Grand National, 1950, British
SALUTE THE TOFF   1952
LIFE WITH THE LYONS   Exclusive, 1954, British
THE DEEP BLUE SEA   20th Century-Fox, 1955, British
THE YOUNG DOCTORS   United Artists, 1961
THE UGLY AMERICAN   Universal, 1963
IN THE COOL OF THE DAY   1963
MOMENT TO MOMENT   Universal, 1966
HARPER   Warner Bros., 1966
PETULIA   Warner Bros., 1968, U.S.-British
THE CHAIRMAN   20th Century-Fox, 1969, U.S.-British
RABBIT, RUN   Warner Bros., 1970
THE PURSUIT OF HAPPINESS   Columbia, 1971
THE ANDROMEDA STRAIN   Universal, 1971
DEATH BE NOT PROUD (TF)   Good Housekeeping Productions/
    Westfall Productions, 1975
THE KILLER ELITE   United Artists, 1975

**F
I
L
M

A
C
T
O
R
S**

FUTUREWORLD   American International, 1976
A BRIDGE TOO FAR   United Artists, 1977, British
BUTCH AND SUNDANCE: THE EARLY DAYS
   20th Century-Fox, 1979
A LITTLE ROMANCE   Orion/Warner Bros., 1979, U.S.-French
THE CHAMP   MGM/United Artists, 1979
DIRTY TRICKS   Avco Embassy, 1981, Canadian
MAKING LOVE   20th Century-Fox, 1982
THE AMATEUR   20th Century-Fox, 1982, Canadian
LOVE LEADS THE WAY (TF)   Hawkins-Permut Productions, 1984
MURDER, SHE WROTE (TF)   Universal TV, 1984
ONE MAGIC CHRISTMAS   Buena Vista, 1985, U.S.-Canadian
PERRY MASON: THE CASE OF THE NOTORIOUS NUN (TF)
   Intermedia Prods./Strathmore Prods./Viacom Productions, 1986
CHRISTMAS EVE (TF)   NBC Productions, 1986

CHARLES C. HILL
WACO & RHINEHART (TF)   Touchstone Films TV, 1987

DANA HILL
Agent: The Artists Group, Ltd. - Los Angeles, 310/552-1100

FALLEN ANGEL (TF)   Green-Epstein Productions/
   Columbia TV, 1981
SHOOT THE MOON   MGM/United Artists, 1982
CROSS CREEK   Universal, 1983
SILENCE OF THE HEART (TF)   David A. Simons Productions/
   Tisch-Avnet Productions, 1984
NATIONAL LAMPOON'S EUROPEAN VACATION
   Warner Bros., 1985
COMBAT HIGH (TF)   Frank von Zerneck Productions/Lynch-Biller
   Productions, 1986

FRANK O. HILL
STROKER ACE   Universal, 1983

GILBERT R. HILL
BEVERLY HILLS COP   Paramount, 1984

LAURYN HILL
SISTER ACT 2: BACK IN THE HABIT   Buena Vista, 1993

MAURICE HILL
AIRPLANE!   Paramount, 1980

RICK HILL
DEATHSTALKER IV   Concorde, 1991

STEVEN HILL
b. February 24, 1922 - Seattle, Washington

A LADY WITHOUT PASSPORT   MGM, 1950
THE GODDESS   Columbia, 1958
A CHILD IS WAITING   United Artists, 1963
THE SLENDER THREAD   Paramount, 1965
IT'S MY TURN   Columbia, 1980
YENTL   MGM/UA, 1983
ON VALENTINE'S DAY   STORY OF A MARRIAGE
   Angelika Films, 1986
LEGAL EAGLES   Universal, 1986
RAW DEAL   DEG, 1986
HEARTBURN   Paramount, 1986
RUNNING ON EMPTY   Warner Bros., 1988
THE FIRM   Paramount, 1993

WENDY HILLER
(Dame Wendy Hiller)
b. August 15, 1912 - Bramshall, Cheshire, England

LANCASHIRE LAD   1937, British
PYGMALION ★   MGM, 1938, British
MAJOR BARBARA   United Artists, 1941, British
I KNOW WHERE I'M GOING   Universal, 1945, British
OUTCAST OF THE ISLANDS   United Artists, 1951, British
SAILOR OF THE KING   SINGLEHANDED   20th Century-Fox, 1953,

SOMETHING OF VALUE   MGM, 1957
HOW TO MURDER A RICH UNCLE   1957, British
SEPARATE TABLES ⊙⊙   United Artists, 1958
SONS AND LOVERS   20th Century-Fox, 1960, British
TOYS IN THE ATTIC   United Artists, 1963
A MAN FOR ALL SEASONS ⊙   Columbia, 1966, British
DAVID COPPERFIELD (TF)   Omnibus Productions/Sagittarius
   Productions, 1970, British-U.S.
MURDER ON THE ORIENT EXPRESS   Paramount, 1974, British
VOYAGE OF THE DAMNED   Avco Embassy, 1976
THE CAT AND THE CANARY   Quartet, 1978, British
THE ELEPHANT MAN   Paramount, 1980, British-U.S.
THE CURSE OF KING TUT'S TOMB (TF)   Stromberg-Kerby
   Productions/Columbia TV/HTV West, 1980
MAKING LOVE   20th Century-Fox, 1982
THE LONELY PASSION OF JUDITH HEARNE   Island Films,
   1987, British

JOHN HILLERMAN
b. December 30, 1932 - Denison, Texas

PAPER MOON   Paramount, 1973
BLAZING SADDLES   Warner Bros., 1974
CHINATOWN   Paramount, 1974
AT LONG LAST LOVE   20th Century-Fox, 1975
LUCKY LADY   20th Century-Fox, 1975
THE DAY OF THE LOCUST   Paramount, 1975
KILL ME IF YOU CAN (TF)   Columbia TV, 1977
SUNBURN   Paramount, 1979, U.S.-British
HISTORY OF THE WORLD—PART 1   20th Century-Fox, 1981
ASSAULT AND MATRIMONY (TF)   Michael Filerman Productions/
   NBC Productions, 1987
STREET OF DREAMS (TF)   Bill Stratton-Myrtos Productions/Phoenix
   Entertainment Group, 1988
AROUND THE WORLD IN 80 DAYS (MS)   Harmony/Gold/
   ReteEuropa/Valente-Baerwald Productions, 1989
HANDS OF A MURDERER (TF)   Storke-Fuisz Productions/
   Yorkshire TV, 1990, British-U.S.

GREGORY HINES
b. February 14, 1946 - New York, New York
Agent: CAA - Beverly Hills, 310/288-4545

HISTORY OF THE WORLD—PART 1   20th Century-Fox, 1981
WOLFEN   Orion/Warner Bros., 1981
THE COTTON CLUB   Orion, 1984
WHITE NIGHTS   Columbia, 1985
RUNNING SCARED   MGM/UA, 1986
OFF LIMITS   20th Century Fox, 1988
TAP   TriStar, 1989
EVE OF DESTRUCTION   Orion, 1991
A RAGE IN HARLEM   Miramax Films, 1991, U.S.-British
RENAISSANCE MAN   Buena Vista, 1994

MAURICE HINES
THE COTTON CLUB   Orion, 1984

PAT HINGLE
b. July 19, 1923 - Denver, Colorado
Agent: The Blake Agency - Beverly Hills, 310/246-0241

ON THE WATERFRONT   Columbia, 1954
THE STRANGE ONE   END AS A MAN   Columbia, 1957
NO DOWN PAYMENT   20th Century-Fox, 1957
SPLENDOR IN THE GRASS   Warner Bros., 1961
THE UGLY AMERICAN   Universal, 1963
ALL THE WAY HOME   1963
INVITATION TO A GUNFIGHTER   United Artists, 1964
NEVADA SMITH   Paramount, 1966
JIGSAW   Universal, 1968
SOL MADRID   MGM, 1968
HANG 'EM HIGH   United Artists, 1968
BLOODY MAMA   American International, 1970
WUSA   Paramount, 1970
NORWOOD   Paramount, 1970
THE CAREY TREATMENT   MGM, 1972
ONE LITTLE INDIAN   Buena Vista, 1973
RUNNING WILD   1973

HAZEL'S PEOPLE *THE GRASS WAS GREEN* 1973
DELIVER US FROM EVIL (TF) Playboy Productions, 1973
THE SUPER COPS MGM, 1974
DEADLY HONEYMOON *NIGHTMARE HONEYMOON* MGM, 1974
THE GAUNTLET Warner Bros., 1977
STONE (TF) Stephen J. Cannell Productions/Universal TV, 1979
WHEN YOU COMIN' BACK, RED RYDER? Columbia, 1979
NORMA RAE 20th Century-Fox, 1979
SUDDEN IMPACT Warner Bros., 1983
BREWSTER'S MILLIONS Universal, 1985
THE FALCON AND THE SNOWMAN Orion, 1985
THE LADY FROM YESTERDAY (TF) Barry Weitz Films/
    Comworld Productions, 1985
THE RAPE OF RICHARD BECK (TF) Robert Papazian
    Productions/Henerson-Hirsch Productions, 1985
MANHUNT FOR CLAUDE DALLAS (TF) London Films, Inc., 1986
MAXIMUM OVERDRIVE DEG, 1986
BABY BOOM MGM/UA, 1987
LBJ: THE EARLY YEARS (TF) Brice Productions/Louis Rudolph
    Films/Fries Entertainment, 1987
KOJAK: THE PRICE OF JUSTICE (TF) MCA/Universal TV, 1987
STRANGER ON MY LAND (TF) Edgar J. Scherick Associates/
    Taft Entertainment TV, 1988
THE TOWN BULLY (TF) Dick Clark Productions, 1988
EVERYBODY'S BABY: THE RESCUE OF JESSICA McCLURE (TF)
    Dick Berg-Stonehenge Productions/The Campbell Soup
    Company/Interscope Productions, 1989
BATMAN Warner Bros., 1989
THE GRIFTERS Miramax Films, 1990
BATMAN RETURNS Warner Bros., 1992
BATMAN FOREVER Warner Bros., 1995

BRENT HINKLEY
ED WOOD Buena Vista, 1994

TOMMY HINKLEY
THE HUMAN SHIELD Cannon, 1992

PAUL HIPP
LIBERACE: BEHIND THE MUSIC (TF) Canadian International
    Studios/Kushner-Locke Productions, 1988, U.S.-Canadian

JUDD HIRSCH
b. March 15, 1935 - New York, New York

THE LAW (TF) Universal TV, 1974
FEAR ON TRIAL (TF) Alan Landsburg Productions, 1975
THE LEGEND OF VALENTINO (TF) Spelling-Goldberg
    Productions, 1975
THE KEEGANS (TF) Universal TV, 1976
KING OF THE GYPSIES Paramount, 1978
SOONER OR LATER (TF) Laughing Willow Company/NBC, 1979
ORDINARY PEOPLE ✪ Paramount, 1980
WITHOUT A TRACE 20th Century-Fox, 1983
THE GOODBYE PEOPLE Embassy, 1984
DETECTIVE IN THE HOUSE (TF) Lorimar-Telepictures, 1985
FIRST STEPS (TF) CBS Entertainment, 1985
BROTHERLY LOVE (TF) CBS Entertainment, 1985
RUNNING ON EMPTY Warner Bros., 1988
THE GREAT ESCAPE II: THE UNTOLD STORY (MS)
    Michael Jaffe Films/Spectacor Films, 1988

CHRISTIANNE HIRT
DOUBLE STANDARD (TF) Louis Rudolph Productions/Fenton
    Entertainment Group/Fries Entertainment, 1988

IGAWA HISASHI
RHAPSODY IN AUGUST Orion Classics, 1991

JUDITH HOAG
Agent: Bauman, Hiller & Associates - Los Angeles, 213/857-6666

TEENAGE MUTANT NINJA TURTLES New Line Cinema, 1990

MICHELLE HOARD
ABOVE THE LAW Warner Bros., 1988

MARA HOBEL
MOMMIE DEAREST Paramount, 1981
DOING LIFE (TF) Castilian Productions/Phoenix Entertainment
    Group, 1986

KANE HODDER
FRIDAY THE 13TH PART VIII - JASON TAKES MANHATTAN
    Paramount, 1989

PATRICIA HODGE
Agent: Susan Smith & Associates - Beverly Hills, 213/852-4777

BETRAYAL 20th Century-Fox International Classics, 1983, British
THE SECRET LIFE OF IAN FLEMING (CTF) Saban-Scherick
    Productions, 1990, U.S.-British
DIAMOND'S EDGE Kings Road Entertainment, 1990

TOM HODGES
HEAVYWEIGHTS Buena Vista, 1994

ISABELLA HOFMANN
Agent: Susan Smith & Associates - Beverly Hills, 213/852-4777

INDEPENDENCE (TF) Sunn Classic Pictures, 1987
THE TOWN BULLY (TF) Dick Clark Productions, 1988

BASIL HOFFMAN
LADY LIBERTY *MORTADELLA* United Artists, 1972, Italian
AT LONG LAST LOVE 20th Century-Fox, 1975
ALL THE PRESIDENT'S MEN Warner Bros., 1976
CLOSE ENCOUNTERS OF THE THIRD KIND Columbia, 1977
THE ELECTRIC HORSEMAN Columbia, 1979
ORDINARY PEOPLE Paramount, 1980
MY FAVORITE YEAR MGM/UA, 1982
COMMUNION New Line Cinema, 1989
LAMBADA Warner Bros., 1990

DOMINIC HOFFMAN
Agent: Silver, Kass & Massetti Agency, Ltd. - Los Angeles,
    310/289-0909

SURVIVAL QUEST MGM/UA, 1990

DUSTIN HOFFMAN
b. August 8, 1937 - Los Angeles, California
Agent: CAA - Beverly Hills, 310/288-4545

THE TIGER MAKES OUT Columbia, 1967
MADIGAN'S MILLIONS American International, 1967, Italian
THE GRADUATE ★ Avco Embassy, 1967
MIDNIGHT COWBOY ★ United Artists, 1969
JOHN AND MARY 20th Century-Fox, 1969
LITTLE BIG MAN National General, 1970
WHO IS HARRY KELLERMAN AND WHY IS HE SAYING THOSE
    TERRIBLE THINGS ABOUT ME? National General, 1971
STRAW DOGS Cinerama Releasing Corporation, 1971, British
ALFREDO ALFREDO Paramount, 1972, Italian
PAPILLON Allied Artists, 1973
LENNY ★ United Artists, 1974
ALL THE PRESIDENT'S MEN Warner Bros., 1976
MARATHON MAN Paramount, 1976
STRAIGHT TIME Warner Bros., 1978
AGATHA Warner Bros., 1979, British
KRAMER VS. KRAMER ★★ Columbia, 1979
TOOTSIE ★ Columbia, 1982
DEATH OF A SALESMAN (TF) Roxbury and Punch
    Productions, 1985
ISHTAR Columbia, 1987
RAIN MAN ★★ MGM/UA, 1988
FAMILY BUSINESS TriStar, 1989
DICK TRACY Buena Vista, 1990
BILLY BATHGATE Buena Vista, 1991
HOOK TriStar, 1991
HERO Columbia, 1992
OUTBREAK Warner Bros., 1995

GABY HOFFMAN
FIELD OF DREAMS   Universal, 1989
UNCLE BUCK   Universal, 1989
THIS IS MY LIFE   20th Century Fox, 1992
SLEEPLESS IN SEATTLE   TriStar, 1993
THE MAN WITHOUT A FACE   Warner Bros., 1993

SUSAN LEE HOFFMAN
OUTBREAK   Warner Bros., 1995

SUSANNA HOFFS
THE ALLNIGHTER   Universal, 1987

MARCO HOFSCHNEIDER
Agent: Gersh Agency - Beverly Hills, 310/274-6611

EUROPA, EUROPA   Orion Classics, 1991, French-German-Polish
FOREIGN STUDENT   Gramercy Pictures, 1994
IMMORTAL BELOVED   Columbia, 1994

HEATHER HOGAN
LAND BEFORE TIME (AF)   Universal, 1995 (voice)

HULK HOGAN
NO HOLDS BARRED   New Line Cinema, 1989
SUBURBAN COMMANDO   New Line Cinema, 1991
ROUGH STUFF   New Line Cinema, 1992
MR. NANNY   New Line Cinema, 1993

PAUL HOGAN
b. October 8, 1939 - New South Wales, Australia
Agent: CAA - Beverly Hills, 310/288-4545

"CROCODILE" DUNDEE   Paramount, 1986, Australian
"CROCODILE" DUNDEE II   Paramount, 1988, U.S.-Australian
ALMOST AN ANGEL   Paramount, 1990, Australian-U.S.
LIGHTNING JACK   Savoy Pictures, 1994, Australian-U.S.

SUSAN HOGAN
WHITE FANG   Buena Vista, 1991

HAL HOLBROOK
(Harold Rowe Holbrook, Jr.)
b. February 17, 1925 - Cleveland, Ohio

THE GROUP   United Artists, 1966
WILD IN THE STREETS   American International, 1968
A CLEAR AND PRESENT DANGER (TF)   Universal TV, 1970
THE PEOPLE NEXT DOOR   Avco Embassy, 1970
THE GREAT WHITE HOPE   20th Century-Fox, 1970
SUDDENLY SINGLE   Chris-Rose Productions, 1971
THAT CERTAIN SUMMER (TF)   Universal TV, 1972
THEY ONLY KILL THEIR MASTERS   1972
JONATHAN LIVINGSTON SEAGULL   Paramount, 1973 (voice)
MAGNUM FORCE   Warner Bros., 1973
THE GIRL FROM PETROVKA   Universal, 1974
ALL THE PRESIDENT'S MEN   Warner Bros., 1976
MIDWAY   Universal, 1976
JULIA   20th Century-Fox, 1977
RITUALS   *THE CREEPER*   1978, Canadian
CAPRICORN ONE   20th Century-Fox, 1978
MURDER BY NATURAL CAUSES (TF)   Richard Levinson-William
   Link Productions, 1979
THE FOG   Avco Embassy, 1980
CREEPSHOW   Warner Bros., 1982
THE STAR CHAMBER   20th Century-Fox, 1983
THE THREE WISHES OF BILLY GRIER (TF)   I & C Productions, 1984
BEHIND ENEMY LINES (TF)   TVS Productions/MTM Enterprises,
   1985, British-U.S.
UNDER SIEGE (TF)   Ohlmeyer Communications Company/
   Telepictures Productions, 1986
DRESS GRAY (MS)   von Zerneck Productions/
   Warner Bros. TV, 1986
WALL STREET   20th Century Fox, 1987
PLAZA SUITE (TF)   Kalola Productions, 1987

MARIO PUZO'S THE FORTUNATE PILGRIM   *THE FORTUNATE
   PILGRIM* (MS)   NBC Productions, 1988
I'LL BE HOME FOR CHRISTMAS (TF)   NBC Productions, 1988
DAY ONE (TF)   Aaron Spelling Productions/Paragon Motion Pictures/
   David W. Rintels Productions, 1989
FLETCH LIVES   Universal, 1989
SORRY, WRONG NUMBER (CTF)   Jack Grossbart Productions/
   Wilshire Court Productions, 1989
THE FIRM   Paramount, 1993
CATS DON'T DANCE (AF)   Turner Pictures, 1996 (voice)

MARJEAN HOLDEN
PHILADELPHIA EXPERIMENT 2   Trimark Pictures, 1993

GEOFFREY HOLDER
b. August 1, 1930 - Trinidad

EVERYTHING YOU ALWAYS WANTED TO KNOW ABOUT SEX*
   (*BUT WERE AFRAID TO ASK)   United Artists, 1972
LIVE AND LET DIE   United Artists, 1973, British
SWASHBUCKLER   Universal, 1976
ANNIE   Columbia, 1982
GHOST OF A CHANCE (TF)   Stuart-Phoenix Productions/Thunder
   Bird Road Productions/Lorimar-Telepictures, 1987

TEDDY HOLIAVKO
BIG   20th Century Fox, 1988

ANTONY HOLLAND
CHRISTMAS COMES TO WILLOW CREEK (TF)   Blue Andre
   Productions/ITC Productions, 1987

DAVID HOLLANDER
AIRPLANE!   Paramount, 1980

STEVE HOLLAR
HOOSIERS   Orion, 1986

POLLY HOLLIDAY
b. July 2, 1937 - Jasper, Alabama
Agent: The Blake Agency - Beverly Hills, 310/246-0241 or
   The Lantz Office - New York, 213/586-0200

THE CATAMOUNT KILLING   Hallmark Releasing, 1975
W.W. AND THE DIXIE DANCEKINGS   20th Century-Fox, 1975
THE FRONT   Columbia, 1976
ALL THE PRESIDENT'S MEN   Warner Bros., 1976
DISTANCE   Cine-Bright, 1977
THE ONE AND ONLY   Paramount, 1978
MISSING CHILDREN: A MOTHER'S STORY (TF)   Kayden-Gleason
   Productions, 1982
THE GIFT OF LOVE: A CHRISTMAS STORY (TF)   Telecom
   Entertainment/Amanda Productions, 1983
GREMLINS   Warner Bros., 1984
MOON OVER PARADOR   Universal, 1988, U.S.-Brazilian

EARL HOLLIMAN
b. September 11, 1928 - Delhi, Louisiana

SCARED STIFF   Paramount, 1953
DESTINATION GOBI   20th Century-Fox, 1953
BROKEN LANCE   20th Century-Fox, 1954
THE BRIDGES OF TOKO-RI   Paramount, 1955
THE BIG COMBO   Allied Artists, 1955
I DIED A THOUSAND TIMES   Warner Bros., 1955
FORBIDDEN PLANET   1956
GIANT   Warner Bros., 1956
THE BURNING HILLS   Warner Bros., 1956
THE RAINMAKER   Paramount, 1956
DON'T GO NEAR THE WATER   MGM, 1957
GUNFIGHT AT THE O.K. CORRAL   Paramount, 1957
TROOPER HOOK   United Artists, 1957
HOT SPELL   Paramount, 1958
THE TRAP   Paramount, 1959
LAST TRAIN FROM GUN HILL   Paramount, 1959
VISIT TO A SMALL PLANET   Paramount, 1960

ARMORED COMMAND   Allied Artists, 1961
SUMMER AND SMOKE   Paramount, 1961
THE SONS OF KATIE ELDER   Paramount, 1965
A COVENANT WITH DEATH   Warner Bros., 1967
ANZIO *THE BATTLE OF ANZIO* Columbia, 1968, Italian
SMOKE   1969
THE POWER   MGM, 1968
THE BISCUIT EATER   Buena Vista, 1972
TRAPPED (TF)   Universal TV, 1973
I LOVE YOU, GOODBYE (TF)   Tomorrow Entertainment, 1974
ALEXANDER: THE OTHER SIDE OF DAWN (TF)   Douglas Cramer
   Productions, 1977
SHARKY'S MACHINE   Orion/Warner Bros., 1981
THE THORN BIRDS (MS)   David L. Wolper-Stan Margulies
   Productions/Edward Lewis Productions/Warner Bros. TV, 1983
AMERICAN HARVEST (TF)   Roth-Stratton Productions/
   The Finnegan Company, 1987
GUNSMOKE: RETURN TO DODGE (TF)   CBS Entertainment, 1987

LAUREN HOLLY
Agent: UTA - Beverly Hills, 310/273-6700

BAND OF THE HAND   TriStar, 1986
SEVEN MINUTES TO HEAVEN   Warner Bros., 1986
ARCHIE: TO RIVERDALE AND BACK AGAIN (TF)   Patchett
   Kaufman Entertainment/DIC Enterprises, 1990
THE ADVENTURES OF FORD FAIRLANE   20th Century Fox, 1990
DRAGON: THE BRUCE LEE STORY   Universal, 1993
DUMB AND DUMBER   New Line Cinema, 1994

CELESTE HOLM
b. April 29, 1919 - New York, New York
Agent: Mishkin Agency - Beverly Hills, 310/274-5261

THREE LITTLE GIRLS IN BLUE   20th Century-Fox, 1946
CARNIVAL IN COSTA RICA   20th Century-Fox, 1947
GENTLEMAN'S AGREEMENT ❍❍   20th Century-Fox, 1947
ROAD HOUSE   20th Century-Fox, 1948
THE SNAKE PIT   20th Century-Fox, 1948
CHICKEN EVERY SUNDAY   20th Century-Fox, 1949
A LETTER TO THREE WIVES   20th Century-Fox, 1949 (voice)
EVERYBODY DOES IT   20th Century-Fox, 1949
COME TO THE STABLE ❍   20th Century-Fox, 1950
CHAMPAGNE FOR CAESAR   Universal, 1950
ALL ABOUT EVE ❍   20th Century-Fox, 1950
THE TENDER TRAP   MGM, 1955
HIGH SOCIETY   MGM, 1956
BACHELOR FLAT   20th Century-Fox, 1961
DOCTOR, YOU'VE GOT TO BE KIDDING!   MGM, 1967
THE DELPHI BUREAU (TF)   Warner Bros. TV, 1972
TOM SAWYER   United Artists, 1973
THE UNDERGROUND MAN (TF)   Paramount TV, 1974
DEATH CRUISE (TF)   Spelling-Goldberg Productions, 1974
CAPTAINS AND THE KINGS (MS)   Universal TV, 1976
BITTERSWEET LOVE   Avco Embassy, 1976
LOVE BOAT II (TF)   Aaron Spelling Productions, 1977
THE PRIVATE FILES OF J. EDGAR HOOVER
   American International, 1978
BACKSTAIRS AT THE WHITE HOUSE (MS)   Ed Friendly
   Productions, 1979
MIDNIGHT LACE (TF)   Four R Productions/Universal TV, 1980
JESSIE (TF)   Lindsay Wagner Productions/MGM-UA TV, 1984
MURDER BY THE BOOK (TF)   Nelson Productions/Orion TV, 1987
THREE MEN AND A BABY   Buena Vista, 1987

IAN HOLM
(Ian Holm Cuthbert)
b. September 12, 1931 - Goodmayes, England
Agent: William Morris Agency - Beverly Hills, 310/274-7451

THE BOFORS GUN   Universal, 1968, British
A MIDSUMMER NIGHT'S DREAM   Eagle, 1968, British
THE FIXER   MGM, 1968, British
OH! WHAT A LOVELY WAR   Paramount, 1969, British
A SEVERED HEAD   Columbia, 1971, British
NICHOLAS AND ALEXANDRA   Columbia, 1971, British
MARY QUEEN OF SCOTS   Universal, 1971, British
YOUNG WINSTON   Columbia, 1972, British

THE HOMECOMING   American Film Theatre, 1973, British
JUGGERNAUT   United Artists, 1974, British
ROBIN AND MARIAN   Columbia, 1976, British
SHOUT AT THE DEVIL   American International, 1976, British
THE MAN IN THE IRON MASK (TF)   Norman Rosemont
   Productions/ITC, 1977, U.S.-British
MARCH OR DIE   Columbia, 1977, British
HOLOCAUST (MS)   Titus Productions, 1978
JESUS OF NAZARETH (MS)   Sir Lew Grade Productions/ITC,
   1978, British-Italian
ALIEN   20th Century-Fox, 1979, U.S.-British
S.O.S. TITANIC (TF)   Roger Gimbel Productions/EMI TV/Argonaut
   Films, Ltd., 1979, U.S.-British
ALL QUIET ON THE WESTERN FRONT (TF)   Norman Rosemont
   Productions/Marble Arch Productions, 1979
TIME BANDITS   Avco Embassy, 1981, British
CHARIOTS OF FIRE ❍   The Ladd Company/Warner Bros.,
   1981, British
RETURN OF THE SOLDIER   European Classics, 1982, British
GREYSTOKE: THE LEGEND OF TARZAN, LORD OF THE APES
   Warner Bros., 1984, British-U.S.
LAUGHTERHOUSE   Film Four International, 1984, British
DANCE WITH A STRANGER   Samuel Goldwyn Company,
   1985, British
WETHERBY   MGM/UA Classics, 1985, British
BRAZIL   Universal, 1985, British
DREAMCHILD   Universal, 1985, British
ANOTHER WOMAN   Orion, 1988
HENRY V   Samuel Goldwyn Company, 1989, British
HAMLET   Warner Bros., 1990, British
MARY SHELLEY'S FRANKENSTEIN   TriStar, 1994
LOCH NESS   Gramercy Pictures, 1995
THE MADNESS OF GEORGE III   Samuel Goldwyn Company, 1995

REX HOLMAN
STAR TREK V: THE FINAL FRONTIER   Paramount, 1989

BRITTANY ASHTON HOLMES
THE LITTLE RASCALS   Universal, 1994

SANDRINE HOLT
RAPA NUI   Warner Bros., 1994

WILL HOLT
ZELIG   Orion/Warner Bros., 1983

MARIA HOLVÖE
WORTH WINNING   20th Century Fox, 1989

EVANDER HOLYFIELD
NECESSARY ROUGHNESS   Paramount, 1991

ARABELLA HOLZBOG
STONE COLD   Columbia, 1991

JAMES HONG
CHINATOWN   Paramount, 1974
AIRPLANE!   Paramount, 1980
MISSING IN ACTION   Cannon, 1984
BIG TROUBLE IN LITTLE CHINA   20th Century Fox, 1986
THE GOLDEN CHILD   Paramount, 1986
THE KAREN CARPENTER STORY (TF)   Weintraub Entertainment
   Group, 1989
THE PERFECT WEAPON   Paramount, 1991
MISSING PIECES   Orion, 1991

HOWARD HONIG
AIRPLANE!   Paramount, 1980

DON HOOD
BLIND VENGEANCE (CTF)   Spanish Trail Productions/
   MCA TV, 1990

JAN HOOKS

b. April 23, 1957 - Decatur, Georgia
Agent: William Morris Agency - Beverly Hills, 310/274-7451

PEE-WEE'S BIG ADVENTURE   Warner Bros., 1986
WILDCATS   Warner Bros., 1986
BATMAN RETURNS   Warner Bros., 1992
A DANGEROUS WOMAN   Gramercy Pictures, 1993

KEVIN HOOKS

b. September 19, 1958 - Philadelphia, Pennsylvania

SOUNDER   20th Century-Fox, 1972
AARON LOVES ANGELA   1975
TAKE DOWN   Buena Vista, 1979
INNERSPACE   Warner Bros., 1987
STRICTLY BUSINESS   Warner Bros., 1991 (also directed)

ROBERT HOOKS

b. April 18, 1937 - Washington, D.C.

SWEET LOVE BITTER   Peppercorn=Wormser, 1967
HURRY SUNDOWN   Paramount, 1967
THE LAST OF THE MOBILE HOTSHOTS   Warner Bros., 1970
CROSSCURRENT   *CABLE CAR MURDER* (TF)
   Warner Bros. TV, 1971
TROUBLE MAN   20th Century-Fox, 1972
TRAPPED (TF)   Universal TV, 1973
THE KILLER WHO WOULDN'T DIE (TF)   Paramount TV, 1976
JUST AN OLD SWEET SONG (TF)   MTM Enterprises, 1976
AIRPORT '77   Universal, 1977
TO KILL A COP (TF)   David Gerber Company/Columbia TV, 1978
A WOMAN CALLED MOSES (TF)   Henry Jaffe Enterprises, 1978
BACKSTAIRS AT THE WHITE HOUSE (MS)   Ed Friendly
   Productions, 1979
HOLLOW IMAGE (TF)   Titus Productions, 1979
FAST-WALKING   Pickman Films, 1982
STAR TREK III: THE SEARCH FOR SPOCK   Paramount, 1984
SUPERCARRIER (TF)   Fries Entertainment/Richard Hayward-Real
   Tinsel Productions, 1988
HEATWAVE (CTF)   The Avnet-Kerner Company/
   Propaganda Films, 1990

WILLIAM HOOTKINS

Agent: Metropolitan Talent Agency - Los Angeles, 213/857-4500

THE RETURN OF SHERLOCK HOLMES (TF)
   CBS Entertainment, 1987
WACO & RHINEHART (TF)   Touchstone Films TV, 1987
THE PRINCESS AND THE GOBLIN (AF)   Hemdale, 1994 (voice)

BOB HOPE

(Leslie Townes Hope)
b. May 29, 1903 - Eltham, England
Agent: ICM - Beverly Hills, 310/550-4000

THE BIG BROADCAST OF 1938   Paramount, 1938
COLLEGE SWING   Paramount, 1938
GIVE ME A SAILOR   Paramount, 1938
THANKS FOR THE MEMORY   Paramount, 1938
NEVER SAY DIE   Paramount, 1939
SOME LIKE IT HOT   *RHYTHM ROMANCE*   Paramount, 1939
THE CAT AND THE CANARY   Paramount, 1939
ROAD TO SINGAPORE   Paramount, 1940
THE GHOST BREAKERS   Paramount, 1940
ROAD TO ZANZIBAR   Paramount, 1941
CAUGHT IN THE DRAFT   Paramount, 1941
NOTHING BUT THE TRUTH   Paramount, 1941
LOUISIANA PURCHASE   Paramount, 1941
MY FAVORITE BLONDE   Paramount, 1942
ROAD TO MOROCCO   Paramount, 1942
STAR SPANGLED RHYTHM   Paramount, 1942
THEY GOT ME COVERED   RKO Radio, 1943
LET'S FACE IT   Paramount, 1943
THE PRINCESS AND THE PIRATE   RKO Radio, 1944
ROAD TO UTOPIA   Paramount, 1945
MONSIEUR BEAUCAIRE   Paramount, 1946

MY FAVORITE BRUNETTE   Paramount, 1947
WHERE THERE'S LIFE   Paramount, 1947
VARIETY GIRL   Paramount, 1947
ROAD TO RIO   Paramount, 1947
THE PALEFACE   Paramount, 1948
SORROWFUL JONES   Paramount, 1949
THE GREAT LOVER   Paramount, 1949
FANCY PANTS   Paramount, 1950
THE LEMON DROP KID   Paramount, 1951
MY FAVORITE SPY   Paramount, 1951
THE GREATEST SHOW ON EARTH   Paramount, 1952
SON OF PALEFACE   Paramount, 1952
ROAD TO BALI   Paramount, 1952
OFF LIMITS   Paramount, 1953
SCARED STIFF   Paramount, 1953
HERE COME THE GIRLS   Paramount, 1953
CASANOVA'S BIG NIGHT   Paramount, 1954
THE SEVEN LITTLE FOYS   Paramount, 1955
THAT CERTAIN FEELING   Paramount, 1956
THE IRON PETTICOAT   MGM, 1956, British
BEAU JAMES   Paramount, 1957
PARIS HOLIDAY   United Artists, 1958
THE FIVE PENNIES   Paramount, 1959
ALIAS JESSE JAMES   United Artists, 1959
THE FACTS OF LIFE   United Artists, 1960
BACHELOR IN PARADISE   MGM, 1961
THE ROAD TO HONG KONG   United Artists, 1962
CRITIC'S CHOICE   Warner Bros., 1963
CALL ME BWANA   United Artists, 1963
A GLOBAL AFFAIR   MGM, 1964
I'LL TAKE SWEDEN   1965
THE OSCAR   Embassy, 1966
NOT WITH MY WIFE YOU DON'T!   Warner Bros., 1966
BOY, DID I GET THE WRONG NUMBER!   United Artists, 1966
EIGHT ON THE LAM   United Artists, 1967
THE PRIVATE NAVY OF SGT. O'FARRELL   United Artists, 1968
HOW TO COMMIT MARRIAGE   Cinerama Releasing
   Corporation, 1969
CANCEL MY RESERVATION   Warner Bros., 1972
THE MUPPET MOVIE   AFD, 1979, British
SPIES LIKE US   Warner Bros., 1985
A MASTERPIECE OF MURDER (TF)   20th Century Fox TV, 1986

LESLIE HOPE

Agent: William Morris Agency - Beverly Hills, 310/274-7451

KANSAS   Trans World Entertainment, 1988
TALK RADIO   Universal, 1988
IT TAKES TWO   1988
MEN AT WORK   Triumph Releasing Corporation, 1990

WILLIAM HOPE

ALIENS   20th Century Fox, 1986

ANTHONY HOPKINS

(Sir Anthony Hopkins)
b. December 31, 1937 - Port Talbot, South Wales
Agent: ICM - Beverly Hills, 310/550-4000

THE LION IN WINTER   Avco Embassy, 1968, British
HAMLET   Columbia, 1969, British
THE LOOKING GLASS WAR   Columbia, 1970, British
WHEN EIGHT BELLS TOLL   Cinerama Releasing Corporation,
   1971, British
YOUNG WINSTON   Columbia, 1972, British
A DOLL'S HOUSE   Paramount, 1973, Canadian-U.S.
ALL CREATURES GREAT AND SMALL (TF)   Talent Associates/
   EMI TV, 1974, U.S.-British
QB VII (MS)   Screen Gems/Columbia TV/The Douglas Cramer
   Company, 1974
THE GIRL FRO MPETROVKA   Universal, 1974
JUGGERNAUT   United Artists, 1974, British
THE LINDBERGH KIDNAPPING CASE (TF)   Columbia TV, 1976
DARK VICTORY (TF)   Universal TV, 1976
VICTORY AT ENTEBBE (TF)   1976
AUDREY ROSE   United Artists, 1977
A BRIDGE TOO FAR   United Artists, 1977, British

INTERNATIONAL VELVET   MGM/United Artists, 1978, British
MAGIC   20th Century-Fox, 1978
MAYFLOWER: THE PILGRIMS' ADVENTURE (TF)
   Syzygy Productions, 1979
THE ELEPHANT MAN   Paramount, 1980, British-U.S.
A CHANGE OF SEASONS   20th Century-Fox, 1980
THE BUNKER (TF)   Time-Life Productions/SFP France/Antenne-2,
   1981, U.S.-French
THE HUNCHBACK OF NOTRE DAME (TF)   Norman Rosemont
   Productions/Columbia TV, 1982, U.S.-British
A MARRIED MAN (TF)   1984, British
THE BOUNTY   Orion, 1984, British
MUSSOLINI: THE DECLINE AND FALL OF IL DUCE (CMS)
   HBO Premiere Films/RAI/Antenne-2/Beta Film/TVE/RTSI, 1985,
   U.S.-Italian-French-West German
HOLLYWOOD WIVES (MS)   Aaron Spelling Productions, 1985
GUILTY CONSCIENCE (TF)   Levinson-Link Productions/Robert
   Papazian Productions, 1985
ARCH OF TRIUMPH (TF)   Newland-Raynor Productions/HTV,
   1985, U.S.-British
BLUNT   1986
84 CHARING CROSS ROAD   Columbia, 1987, British
THE GOOD FATHER   Skouras Pictures, 1987, British
THE DAWNING (TF)   TVS Entertainment/Vista Organization,
   1988, British
THE TENTH MAN (TF)   Rosemont Productions/William Self
   Productions, 1988, U.S.-British
A CHORUS OF DISAPPROVAL   South Gate Entertainment,
   1988, British
GREAT EXPECTATIONS (CMS)   The Disney Channel/
   Primetime TV/HTV/Tesauro TV, 1989, U.S.-British-Spanish
DESPERATE HOURS   MGM/UA, 1990
THE SILENCE OF THE LAMBS ★★   Orion, 1991
FREEJACK   Warner Bros., 1992
HOWARDS END   Sony Pictures Classics, 1992, British
THE EFFICIENCY EXPERT   SPOTSWOOD   Miramax Films,
   1992, Australian
BRAM STOKER'S DRACULA   DRACULA   Columbia, 1992
CHAPLIN   TriStar, 1992, U.S.-British
THE TRIAL   Angelika Films, 1993, British
THE REMAINS OF THE DAY ★   Columbia, 1993, British
SHADOWLANDS   Savoy Pictures, 1993, U.S.-British
THE INNOCENT   Miramax Films, 1994, U.S.-German
THE ROAD TO WELLVILLE   Columbia, 1994
LEGENDS OF THE FALL   Tristar, 1994
IMMORTAL BELOVED   Warner Bros., 1994
AUGUST   Granada Films, 1995 (also directed)
SURVIVING PICASSO   Warner Bros., 1995

BO HOPKINS

b. February 2, 1942 - Greenwood, South Carolina
Agent: The Artists Group, Ltd. - Los Angeles, 310/552-1100

THE WILD BUNCH   Warner Bros., 1969
THE BRIDGE AT REMAGEN   United Artists, 1969
MACHO CALLAHAN   Avco Embassy, 1970
MONTE WALSH   National General, 1970
THE CULPEPPER CATTLE COMPANY   20th Century-Fox, 1972
THE ONLY WAY HOME   Regional, 1972
THE GETAWAY   National General, 1972
THE MAN WHO LOVED CAT DANCING   MGM, 1973
WHITE LIGHTNING   United Artists, 1973
AMERICAN GRAFFITI   Universal, 1973
THE NICKEL RIDE   20th Century-Fox, 1975
THE DAY OF THE LOCUST   Paramount, 1975
POSSE   Paramount, 1975
THE KILLER ELITE   United Artists, 1975
A SMALL TOWN IN TEXAS   American International, 1976
TENTACLES   1977, Italian
ASPEN (MS)   Universal TV, 1977
THADDEUS ROSE AND EDDIE (TF)   CBS, Inc., 1978
MIDNIGHT EXPRESS   Columbia, 1978, British
MORE AMERICAN GRAFFITI   Universal, 1979
THE FIFTH FLOOR   Film Ventures International, 1980
DYNASTY (TF)   Aaron Spelling Productions/Fox-Cat
   Productions, 1981
HOUSTON: THE LEGEND OF TEXAS (TF)   Taft Entertainment TV/
   J.D. Feigelson Productions, 1986
CENTER OF THE WEB   AIP, 1992

DENNIS HOPPER

b. May 17, 1936 - Dodge City, Kansas
Agent: CAA - Beverly Hills, 310/288-4545

I DIED A THOUSAND TIMES   Warner Bros., 1955
REBEL WITHOUT A CAUSE   Warner Bros., 1955
GIANT   Warner Bros., 1956
THE STEEL JUNGLE   Warner Bros., 1956
GUNFIGHT AT THE O.K. CORRAL   Paramount, 1957
THE STORY OF MANKIND   Warner Bros., 1957
FROM HELL TO TEXAS   20th Century-Fox, 1958
THE YOUNG LAND   1959
KEY WITNESS   MGM, 1960
NIGHT TIDE   Universal, 1963
TARZAN AND JANE REGAINED...SORT OF   Film-Makers, 1964
THE SONS OF KATIE ELDER   Paramount, 1965
QUEEN OF BLOOD   American International, 1966
COOL HAND LUKE   Warner Bros., 1967
THE TRIP   American International, 1967
THE GLORY STOMPERS   1967
PANIC IN THE CITY   1968
HANG 'EM HIGH   United Artists, 1968
EASY RIDER   Columbia, 1969 (also directed)
TRUE GRIT   Paramount, 1969
THE AMERICAN DREAMER (FD)   EYR, 1971
THE LAST MOVIE   Universal, 1971 (also directed)
CRUSH PROOF   1972
KID BLUE   20th Century-Fox, 1973
THE SKY IS FALLING   1975, Canadian
MAD DOG MORGAN   MAD DOG   Cinema Shares International,
   1976, Australian
TRACKS   Castle Hill Productions, 1977
LES APPRENTIS SORCIERS   1977, French
THE AMERICAN FRIEND   DER AMERIKANISCHE FREUND
   New Yorker, 1977, West German-French
COULEUR CHAIR   1977, Belgian-French
L'ORDRE ET LA SECURITE DU MONDE   1978 , French
APOCALYPSE NOW   United Artists, 1979
WILD TIMES (TF)   Metromedia Producers Corporation/Rattlesnake
   Productions, 1980
KING OF THE MOUNTAIN   Universal, 1981
WHITE STAR   1981
HUMAN HIGHWAY   1982
REBORN   Diseno y Produccion de Films/Diamant/Laurel, 1982,
   Spanish-Italian-U.S.
OUT OF THE BLUE   Discovery Films, 1982,
   Canadian (also directed)
THE OSTERMAN WEEKEND   20th Centur-Fox, 1983
RUMBLE FISH   Universal, 1983
SLAGSKAMPEN   1984
MY SCIENCE PROJECT   Buena Vista, 1985
STARK (TF)   CBS Entertainment, 1985
RUNNING OUT OF LUCK   Nitrate Film Ltd./Julien Temple Productino
   Company, 1985, British
STARK: MIRROR IMAGE (TF)   CBS Entertainment, 1986
BLUE VELVET   DEG, 1986
HOOSIERS ○   Orion, 1986
THE TEXAS CHAINSAW MASSACRE 2   Cannon, 1986
RIDERS OF THE STORM   THE AMERICAN WAY   Miramax Films,
   1986, British
BLACK WIDOW   20th Century Fox, 1987
O.C. AND STIGGS   MGM/UA, 1987
RIVER'S EDGE   Hemdale, 1987
STRAIGHT TO HELL   Island Films, 1987, British-Spanish
THE PICK-UP ARTIST   20th Century Fox, 1987
BLOOD RED   Hemdale, 1988
MOTION AND EMOTION (TD)   Channel Four, 1989, British
FLASHBACK   Paramount, 1990
HOLLYWOOD MAVERICKS (TD)   American Film Institute/NHK
   Enterprises, 1990, U.S.-Japanese
CHATTAHOOCHEE   Hemdale, 1990
BACKTRACK   CATCHFIRE   Vestron, 1991 (also directed)
PARIS TROUT (CTF)   Viacom, 1991
THE INDIAN RUNNER   MGM-Pathe, 1991
DOUBLE CROSS: THE BARRY SEAL STORY (CTF)   HBO Pictures/
   Green-Epstein Productions/Lorimar TV, 1991
BOILING POINT   Warner Bros., 1993
TRUE ROMANCE   Warner Bros., 1993
RED ROCK WEST   1993

SPEED   20th Century Fox, 1994
SEARCH AND DESTROY   October Films, 1995
WATERWORLD   Universal, 1995

TIM HOPPER
FRANKIE & JOHNNY   Paramount, 1991

LENA HORNE
b. June 30, 1917 - Brooklyn, New York

THE DUKE IS TOPS   1938
PANAMA HATTIE   MGM, 1942
CABIN IN THE SKY   MGM, 1943
STORMY WEATHER   20th Century-Fox, 1943
I DOOD IT   MGM, 1943
THOUSANDS CHEER   MGM, 1943
SWING FEVER   MGM, 1943
BROADWAY RHYTHM   MGM, 1944
TWO GIRLS AND A SAILOR   MGM, 1944
ZIEGFELD FOLLIES   MGM, 1946
TILL THE CLOUDS ROLL BY   MGM, 1946
WORDS AND MUSIC   MGM, 1948
DUCHESS OF IDAHO   MGM, 1950
MEET ME IN LAS VEGAS   *VIVA LAS VEGAS*   MGM, 1956
DEATH OF A GUNFIGHTER   Universal, 1969
THE WIZ   Universal, 1978
THAT'S ENTERTAINMENT! III (FD)   MGM/UA, 1994

WIL HORNEFF
Agent: William Morris Agency - Beverly Hills, 310/274-7451

GHOST IN THE MACHINE   20th Century Fox, 1993
THE YEARLING (TF)   RHI Entertainment, 1994
KATIE   Warner Bros., 1995

ADAM HOROVITZ
Agent: Gersh Agency - Beverly Hills, 310/274-6611

LOST ANGELS   Vestron, 1989
ROADSIDE PROPHETS   New Line Cinema, 1992

JANE HORROCKS
GETTING IT RIGHT   MCEG, 1989, U.S.-British
LIFE IS SWEET   Republic Pictures, 1991
SECOND BEST   Warner Bros., 1994

ANNA MARIA HORSFORD
TAKEN AWAY (TF)   Hart, Thomas & Berlin Productions, 1989

LEE HORSLEY
Agent: Harris & Goldberg - Los Angeles, 310/553-5200

MATT HOUSTON (TF)   Largo Productions/Aaron Spelling
   Productions, 1982
WHEN DREAMS COME TRUE (TF)   I & C Productions, 1985
CROSSINGS (MS)   Aaron Spelling Productions, 1986
INFIDELITY (TF)   Mark-Jett Productions/ABC Circle Films, 1987
SINGLE WOMEN, MARRIED MEN (TF)   CBS Entertainment, 1989

JASON HORST
BROKEN ANGEL (TF)   The Stan Margulies Company/
   MGM-UA TV, 1988

MICHAEL HORTON
Agent: Paul Kohner, Inc. - Los Angeles, 310/550-1060

PRINCE OF BEL AIR (TF)   Leonard Hill Films, 1986
MY FATHER, MY SON (TF)   Fred Weintraub Productions/John J.
   McMahon Productions, 1988

PETER HORTON
Agent: UTA - Beverly Hills, 310/273-6700

CHILDREN OF THE CORN   New World, 1984
WHERE THE RIVER RUNS BLACK   MGM/UA, 1986
SIDE OUT   TriStar, 1990

SHIZUKO HOSHI
THE WASH   Skouras Pictures, 1988
COME SEE THE PARADISE   20th Century Fox, 1990

BOB HOSKINS
b. October 26, 1942 - Bury St. Edmunds, Suffolk, England
Agent: CAA - Beverly Hills, 310/288-4545

THE NATIONAL HEALTH   1973
ROYAL FLASH   20th Century-Fox, 1975, British
INSERTS   United Artists, 1976, British
ZULU DAWN   American Cinema, 1979, British
THE LONG GOOD FRIDAY   Embassy, 1980, British
PINK FLOYD—THE WALL   MGM/UA, 1982, British
BEYOND THE LIMIT   *THE HONORARY CONSUL*   Paramount,
   1983, British
LASSITER   Warner Bros., 1984
THE COTTON CLUB   Orion, 1984
THE DUNERA BOYS (TF)   1985, Australian
MUSSOLINI: THE DECLINE AND FALL OF IL DUCE (CMS)
   HBO Premiere Films/RAI/Antenne-2/Beta Film/TVE/RTSI, 1985,
   U.S.-Italian-French-West German
BRAZIL   Universal, 1985, British
MONA LISA ★   Island Pictures, 1986, British
SWEET LIBERTY   Universal, 1986
A PRAYER FOR THE DYING   Samuel Goldwyn Company,
   1987, British
THE LONELY PASSION OF JUDITH HEARNE   Island Films,
   1987, British
WHO FRAMED ROGER RABBIT   Buena Vista, 1988
THE RAGGEDY RAWNEY   Four Seasons Entertainment, 1988,
   British (also directed)
ERIK THE VIKING   Orion, 1989, British
HEART CONDITION   New Line Cinema, 1990
MERMAIDS   Orion, 1990
SHATTERED   Warner Bros., 1991
THE INNER CIRCLE   Columbia, 1991
HOOK   TriStar, 1991
PASSED AWAY   Buena Vista, 1992
THE FAVOR, THE WATCH, AND THE VERY BIG FISH
   Trimark Pictures, 1991, French-British
SUPER MARIO BROS.   Buena Vista, 1993
WORLD WAR II: THEN THERE WERE GIANTS (TF)
   World International Network, 1994
BALTO (AF)   Universal, 1995 (voice)

AMANDA HOUCK
THE ACCIDENTAL TOURIST   Warner Bros., 1988

CAROLINE HOUCK
THE ACCIDENTAL TOURIST   Warner Bros., 1988

JERRY HOUSER
ANOTHER YOU   TriStar, 1991

WHITNEY HOUSTON
b. August 9, 1963 - East Orange, New Jersey
Agent: William Morris Agency - Beverly Hills, 310/274-7451

THE BODYGUARD   Warner Bros., 1992

ADAM COLEMAN HOWARD
SLAVES OF NEW YORK   TriStar, 1989

ALAN HOWARD
THE COOK, THE THIEF, HIS WIFE & HER LOVER   Miramax Films,
   1989, French-Dutch
JUST ANOTHER SECRET (CTF)   F.F.S. Productions/Taurusfilm/
   Blair Communications/USA Network, 1989, U.S.-British
PRIDE AND EXTREME PREJUDICE (CTF)   F.F.S. Productions/
   Taurusfilm/Blair Communications, 1990, British-West German-U.S.
A CASUALTY OF WAR (CTF)   F.F.S. Productions/Taurus Film/
   Blair Communications, 1990, British

ARLISS HOWARD

SYLVESTER   Columbia, 1985
THE LIGHTSHIP   Castle Hill Productions, 1985, U.S.-West German
HANDS OF A STRANGER (MS)   Edgar J. Scherick Productions/
   Taft Entertainment TV, 1987
I KNOW MY FIRST NAME IS STEVEN (MS)   Andrew Adelson
   Company/Lorimar TV, 1989
MEN DON'T LEAVE   Warner Bros., 1990
SOMEBODY HAS TO SHOOT THE PICTURE (CTF)   Alan Barnette
   Productions/Frank Pierson Films/MCA-TV Entertainment/
   Scholastic Productions, 1990
FOR THE BOYS   20th Century Fox, 1991
CRISSCROSS   MGM-Pathe Communications, 1992
WILDER NAPALM   TriStar, 1993

CLINT HOWARD

COCOON   20th Century Fox, 1985
GUNG HO   Paramount, 1986
END OF THE LINE   Orion Classics, 1988
BACKDRAFT   Universal, 1991
CARNOSAUR   New Horizons Pictures, 1993

JOHN HOWARD

YOUNG EINSTEIN   Warner Bros., 1988, Australian

KEN HOWARD

b. March 28, 1944 - El Centro, California

TELL ME THAT YOU LOVE ME, JUNIE MOON   Paramount, 1970
SUCH GOOD FRIENDS   Paramount, 1971
THE STRANGE VENGEANCE OF ROSALIE
   20th Century-Fox, 1972
1776   Columbia, 1972
SUPERDOME (TF)   ABC Circle Films, 1978
THE CRITICAL LIST (TF)   MTM Productions, 1978
THE VICTIMS (TF)   Hajeno Productions/Warner Bros. TV, 1982
THE THORN BIRDS (MS)   David L. Wolper-Stan Margulies
   Productions/Edward Lewis Productions/Warner Bros. TV, 1983
SECOND THOUGHTS   Universal, 1983
HE'S NOT YOUR SON (TF)   CBS Entertainment, 1984
RAGE OF ANGELS: THE STORY CONTINUES (MS)   NBC
   Productions, 1986
AGATHA CHRISTIE'S 'THE MAN IN THE BROWN SUIT' (TF)
   Alan Shayne Productions/Warner Bros. TV, 1989
OSCAR   Buena Vista, 1991

RON HOWARD

(Ronny Howard)
b. March 1, 1954 - Duncan, Oklahoma
Agent: CAA - Beverly Hills, 310/288-4545

THE JOURNEY   MGM, 1959
FIVE MINUTES TO LIVE   *DOOR-TO-DOOR MANIAC*   1961
THE MUSIC MAN   Warner Bros., 1962
THE COURTSHIP OF EDDIE'S FATHER   MGM, 1963
VILLAGE OF THE GIANTS   Embassy, 1965
THE WILD COUNTRY   Buena Vista, 1971
AMERICAN GRAFFITI   Universal, 1973
HAPPY MOTHER'S DAY...LOVE, GEORGE
   RUN, STRANGER, RUN   Cinema 5, 1973
THE SPIKES GANG   United Artists, 1974
EAT MY DUST!   New World, 1976
THE SHOOTIST   Paramount, 1976
GRAND THEFT AUTO   New World, 1977 (also directed)
MORE AMERICAN GRAFFITI   Universal, 1979
RETURN TO MAYBERRY (TF)   Strathmore Productions/Viacom
   Productions, 1986

MAXINE HOWE

THE PRINCESS AND THE GOBLIN (AF)   Hemdale, 1994 (voice)

C. THOMAS HOWELL

b. December 7, 1966 - Los Angeles, California
Agent: William Morris Agency - Beverly Hills, 310/274-7451

THE OUTSIDERS   Warner Bros., 1983
GRANDVIEW, U.S.A.   Warner Bros., 1984

RED DAWN   MGM/UA, 1984
TANK   Universal, 1984
SECRET ADMIRER   Orion, 1985
SOUL MAN   New World, 1986
THE HITCHER   TriStar, 1986
A TIGER'S TALE   Atlantic Releasing Corporation, 1987
THE RETURN OF THE MUSKETEERS   Universal, 1989
CURIOSITY KILLS (CTF)   Dutch Productions, 1990
SIDE OUT   TriStar, 1990
FAR OUT MAN   New Line Cinema, 1990
THAT NIGHT   Warner Bros., 1993
GETTYSBURG   New Line Cinema, 1993

TOM HOWELL

E.T. THE EXTRA-TERRESTRIAL   Universal, 1982

DAVID HUBAND

POLICE ACADEMY 3: BACK IN TRAINING   Warner Bros., 1986

SEASON HUBLEY

LOLLY MADONNA XXX   *THE LOLLY-MADONNA WAR*
   MGM, 1973
SHE LIVES! (TF)   ABC Circle Films, 1973
CATCH MY SOUL   *SANTA FE SATAN*   Cinerama Releasing
   Corporation, 1974
ELVIS (TF)   Dick Clark Productions, 1979
HARDCORE   Columbia, 1979
ESCAPE FROM NEW YORK   Avco Embassy, 1981
LONDON AND DAVIS IN NEW YORK (TF)   Bloodworth-Thomason
   Mozark Productions/Columbia TV, 1984
THE THREE WISHES OF BILLY GRIER (TF)
   I & C Productions, 1984
UNDER THE INFLUENCE (TF)   CBS Entertainment, 1986
CHRISTMAS EVE (TF)   NBC Productions, 1986
PRETTYKILL   Spectrafilm, 1987, Canadian
SHAKEDOWN ON THE SUNSET STRIP (TF)
   CBS Entertainment, 1988
UNSPEAKABLE ACTS (TF)   The Landsburg Company, 1990
CHILD IN THE NIGHT (TF)   Mike Robe Productions, 1990

WHIP HUBLEY

TOP GUN   Paramount, 1986
RUSSKIES   New Century/Vista, 1987

BOB HUDDLESTON

LOVE IS NEVER SILENT (TF)   Marian Rees Associates, 1985

DAVID HUDDLESTON

ALL THE WAY HOME   Paramount, 1963
A LOVELY WAY TO DIE   Universal, 1968
SLAVES   Continental, 1969
RIO LOBO   National General, 1970
FOOLS' PARADE   Columbia, 1971
BAD COMPANY   Paramount, 1972
BROCK'S LAST CASE (TF)   Talent Associates/Universal TV, 1972
THE GUN AND THE PULPIT (TF)   Danny Thomas
   Productions, 1974
BLAZING SADDLES   Warner Bros., 1974
THE OREGON TRAIL (TF)   Universal TV, 1976
CAPRICORN ONE   20th Century-Fox, 1978
KATE BLISS AND THE TICKERTAPE KID (TF)   Aaron Spelling
   Productions, 1978
SMOKEY AND THE BANDIT II   Universal, 1980
SANTA CLAUS: THE MOVIE   TriStar, 1985, U.S.-British
BLACKE'S MAGIC (TF)   Universal TV, 1986
WHEN THE BOUGH BREAKS (TF)   Taft Entertainment TV/TDF
   Productions, 1986
FRANTIC   Warner Bros., 1988

ERNIE HUDSON

b. Benton Harbor, Michigan
Agent: Gersh Agency - Beverly Hills, 310/274-6611

JOY OF SEX   Paramount, 1984
GHOSTBUSTERS   Columbia, 1984
LOVE ON THE RUN (TF)   NBC Productions, 1985
THE DIRTY DOZEN: THE FATAL MISSION (TF)   MGM-UA TV, 1988

GHOSTBUSTERS II   Columbia, 1989
THE HAND THAT ROCKS THE CRADLE   Buena Vista, 1992
WILD PALMS (MS)   Ixtlan Corporation/Greengrass
   Productions, Inc., 1993
HEART AND SOULS   Universal, 1993
SUGAR HILL   20th Century Fox, 1994
NO ESCAPE   Savoy Pictures, 1994
THE CROW   Dimension/Miramax Films, 1994
THE COWBOY WAY   Universal, 1994
AIRHEADS   20th Century Fox, 1994
SPEECHLESS   MGM/UA, 1994
THE BASKETBALL DIARIES   1995
CONGO   Paramount, 1995

BARNARD HUGHES
b. July 16, 1915 - Bedford, New York

MIDNIGHT COWBOY   United Artists, 1969
WHERE'S POPPA?   United Artists, 1970
THE HOSPITAL   United Artists, 1971
RAGE   Warner Bros., 1972
SISTERS   American International, 1973
OH, GOD!   Warner Bros., 1977
KILL ME IF YOU CAN (TF)   Columbia TV, 1977
BEST FRIENDS   Warner Bros., 1982
TRON   Buena Vista, 1982
MAXIE   Orion, 1985
NIGHT OF COURAGE (TF)   Titus Productions, 1987
THE LOST BOYS   Warner Bros., 1987
A HOBO'S CHRISTMAS (TF)   Joe Byrnne-Falrose Productions/
   Phoenix Entertainment, 1987
DA   FilmDallas Pictures, 1988
HOME FIRES BURNING (TF)   Marian Rees Associates, 1989
DAY ONE (TF)   Aaron Spelling Productions/Paragon Motion
   Pictures/David W. Rintels Productions, 1989
GUTS AND GLORY: THE RISE AND FALL OF OLLIE NORTH (MS)
   Mike Robe Productions/Papazian-Hirsch Entertainment, 1989
THE INCIDENT (TF)   Qintex Entertainment, 1990
DOC HOLLYWOOD   Warner Bros., 1991
SISTER ACT 2: BACK IN THE HABIT   Buena Vista, 1993

BRENDAN HUGHES
TO DIE FOR   Skouras Pictures, 1989

BRUCE HUGHES
DANGER DOWN UNDER (TF)   Weintraub Entertainment Group/
   Hoyts Productions, Ltd., 1988, U.S.-Australian

FINOLA HUGHES
Agent: Gersh Agency - Beverly Hills, 310/274-6611

NUTCRACKER   Rank, 1983, British
STAYING ALIVE   Paramount, 1983
SOAPDISH   Paramount, 1991
ASPEN EXTREME   Buena Vista, 1993

MIKO HUGHES
PET SEMATARY   STEPHEN KING'S PET SEMATARY
   Paramount, 1989
KINDERGARTEN COP   Universal, 1990
JACK THE BEAR   20th Century Fox, 1992
WES CRAVEN'S NEW NIGHTMARE   New Line Cinema, 1994

WENDY HUGHES
HEIST (CTF)   HBO Pictures/Chris-Rose Productions/
   Paramount TV, 1989
PRINCESS CARABOO   TriStar, 1994

TOM HULCE
(Thomas Hulce)
b. December 6, 1953 - Whitewater, Wisconsin
Agent: CAA - Beverly Hills, 310/288-4545

9/30/55   SEPTEMBER 30, 1955   Universal, 1977
NATIONAL LAMPOON'S ANIMAL HOUSE   Universal, 1978
THOSE LIPS, THOSE EYES   United Artists, 1980

AMADEUS ★   Orion, 1984
ECHO PARK   Atlantic Releasing Corporation, 1986, U.S.-Austrian
SLAM DANCE   Island Pictures, 1987
DOMINICK AND EUGENE   Orion, 1988
PARENTHOOD   Universal, 1989
MURDER IN MISSISSIPPI (TF)   Wolper Productions/Bernard
   Sofronski Productions/Warner Bros. TV, 1990
THE INNER CIRCLE   Columbia, 1991
BLACK RAINBOW   Miramax Films, 1991, British
FEARLESS   Warner Bros., 1993
MARY SHELLEY'S FRANKENSTEIN   TriStar, 1994
WINGS OF COURAGE   TriStar, 1995
THE HUNCHBACK OF NOTRE DAME (AF)   Buena Vista,
   1996 (voice)

DIANNE HULL
Agent: Contemporary Artists - Santa Monica, 310/395-1800

ALOHA, BOBBY AND ROSE   Columbia, 1975
THE ONION FIELD   Avco Embassy, 1979
THE FIFTH FLOOR   Film Ventures International, 1980
THE NEW ADVENTURES OF PIPPI LONGSTOCKING
   Columbia, 1988

ERIC HULL
DRUGSTORE COWBOY   Avenue Pictures, 1989

MARY-MARGARET HUMES
HISTORY OF THE WORLD—PART 1   20th Century-Fox, 1981

MARK HUMPHREY
IRON EAGLE II   TriStar, 1988, Canadian-Israeli

MICHAEL CONNER HUMPHREYS
b. Memphis, Tennessee

FORREST GUMP   Paramount, 1994

BONNIE HUNT
BEETHOVEN   Universal, 1992
BEETHOVEN'S 2ND   Universal, 1993
ONLY YOU   TriStar, 1994
GETTING AWAY WITH MURDER   Savoy Pictures, 1995

HELEN HUNT
Agent: CAA - Beverly Hills, 310/288-4545

FUTURE COP   TRANCERS   Empire Pictures, 1985
BILL: ON HIS OWN (TF)   Alan Landsburg Productions, 1983
QUARTERBACK PRINCESS (TF)   CBS Entertainment, 1983
PEGGY SUE GOT MARRIED   TriStar, 1986
PROJECT X   20th Century-Fox, 1987
STEALING HOME   Warner Bros., 1988
NEXT OF KIN   Warner Bros., 1989
INCIDENT AT DARK RIVER (CTF)   Farrell-Minoff Productions/
   Turner Network TV, 1989
THE WATERDANCE   Samuel Goldwyn Company, 1992
BOB ROBERTS   Paramount/Miramax Films, 1992
MR. SATURDAY NIGHT   Columbia, 1992
KISS OF DEATH   20th Century Fox, 1995

LINDA HUNT
b. April 2, 1945 - Conyers, Georgia
Agent: William Morris Agency - Beverly Hills, 310/274-7451

POPEYE   Paramount, 1980
THE YEAR OF LIVING DANGEROUSLY ○○   MGM/UA,
   1983, Australian
DUNE   Universal, 1984
THE BOSTONIANS   Almi Pictures, 1984
ELENI   Warner Bros., 1985
SILVERADO   Columbia, 1985
WAITING FOR THE MOON   Skouras Pictures, 1987,
   U.S.-French-British-West German
THE ROOM UPSTAIRS (TF)   Marian Rees Associates/
   The Alexander Group, 1987

THE ROOM (TF)   Sandcastle 5 Productions/Secret Castle
    Productions, 1987
SHE-DEVIL   Orion, 1989
KINDERGARTEN COP   Universal, 1990
IF LOOKS COULD KILL   Warner Bros., 1991
PRET-A-PORTER   Miramax Films, 1994
POCAHONTAS (AF)   Buena Vista, 1995 (voice)

BILL HUNTER
NEWSFRONT   New Yorker, 1978, Australian
HEATWAVE   New Line Cinema, 1982, Australian
THE HIT   Island Alive, 1984, British
REBEL   Vestron, 1985, Australian
DEATH OF A SOLDIER   Scotti Brothers, 1986, Australian
THE ADVENTURES OF PRISCILLA, QUEEN OF THE DESERT
    Gramercy Pictures, 1994, Australian

HOLLY HUNTER
b. March 20, 1958 - Conyers, Georgia
Agent: ICM - Beverly Hills, 310/550-4000

THE BURNING   Orion, 1981
AN UNCOMMON LOVE (TF)   Beechwood Productions/Lorimar
    Productions, 1983
SVENGALI (TF)   Robert Halmi Productions, 1983
WITH INTENT TO KILL (TF)   London Productions, 1984
SWING SHIFT   Warner Bros., 1984
RAISING ARIZONA   20th Century Fox, 1987
A GATHERING OF OLD MEN (TF)   Consolidated Productions/
    Jennie & Company/Zenith Productions, 1987
BROADCAST NEWS ★   20th Century Fox, 1987
END OF THE LINE   Orion Classics, 1988
MISS FIRECRACKER   Corsair Pictures, 1989
ANIMAL BEHAVIOR   Millimeter Films, 1989
ROE VS. WADE (TF)   The Manheim Company/
    NBC Productions, 1989
ALWAYS   Universal, 1989
ONCE AROUND   Universal, 1991
CRAZY IN LOVE (CTF)   Ohlmeyer Communications/Karen
    Danaher-Dorr Productions, 1992
THE POSITIVELY TRUE ADVENTURES OF THE ALLEGED TEXAS
    CHEERLEADER-MURDERING MOM (CTF)   Frederick S. Pierce
    Company/Sudden Entertainment Productions, 1993
THE FIRM ✪   Paramount, 1993
THE PIANO ★★   Miramax Films, 1993, New Zealand-French
COPYCAT   Warner Bros., 1995
OLD FRIENDS   TriStar, 1995

RONALD HUNTER
THE LAZARUS SYNDROME (TF)   Blinn-Thorpe Productions/
    Viacom, 1979
TEACHERS   MGM/UA, 1984
THREE SOVEREIGNS FOR SARAH (TF)   Night Owl
    Productions, 1985
INTERNAL AFFAIRS (MS)   Titus Productions, 1988

STEPHEN B. HUNTER
BULLIES   New World, 1986, Canadian

TAB HUNTER
(Arthur Gelien)
b. July 1, 1931 - New York, New York

THE LAWLESS   Paramount, 1950
ISLAND OF DESIRE   *SATURDAY ISLAND*   United Artists,
    1952, British
GUN BELT   1953
RETURN TO TREASURE ISLAND   United Artists, 1954
TRACK OF THE CAT   Warner Bros., 1954
BATTLE CRY   Warner Bros., 1955
THE SEA CHASE   Warner Bros., 1955
THE BURNING HILLS   Warner Bros., 1956
THE GIRL HE LEFT BEHIND   Warner Bros., 1956
LAFAYETTE ESCADRILLE   Warner Bros., 1958
GUNMAN'S WALK   Columbia, 1958
DAMN YANKEES   Warner Bros., 1958

THAT KIND OF WOMAN   Paramount, 1959
THEY CAME TO CORDURA   Columbia, 1959
THE PLEASURE OF HIS COMPANY   Paramount, 1961
THE GOLDEN ARROW   *LA FRECCIA D'ORO*   MGM, 1962, Italian
OPERATION BIKINI   1963
RIDE THE WILD SURF   Columbia, 1964
WAR-GODS OF THE DEEP   *CITY UNDER THE SEA*
    American International, 1965
THE LOVED ONE   MGM, 1965
BIRDS DO IT   Columbia, 1966
HOSTILE GUNS   Paramount, 1967
SWEET KILL   *THE AROUSERS*   New World, 1970
THE LIFE AND TIMES OF JUDGE ROY BEAN
    National General, 1972
TIMBER TRAMP   Alaska Pictures, 1973
THE KID FROM LEFT FIELD (TF)   Gary Coleman Productions/
    Deena Silver-Kramer's Movie Company, 1979
GREASE 2   Paramount, 1982
PANDEMONIUM   MGM/UA, 1982
POLYESTER   New Line Cinema, 1981
LUST IN THE DUST   New World, 1985

TROY HUNTER
TOP GUN   Paramount, 1986

ISABELLE HUPPERT
b. March 16, 1955 - Paris, France
Agent: UTA - Beverly Hills, 310/273-6700

FAUSTINE AND THE BEAUTIFUL SUMMER
    FAUSTINE ET LE BEL ETÉ   1971
CESAR AND ROSALIE   *CÉSAR ET ROSALIE*   Cinema 5, 1972,
    French-Italian-West German
L'AMPELOPEDE   1973
GOING PLACES   *LES VALSEUSES*   Cinema 5, 1974
ALOISE   1974
ROSEBUD   United Artists, 1975
LE GRAN DÉLIRE   1975
SÉRIEUX COMME LE PLAISIR   1975
RAPE OF INNOCENCE   *DUPONT LA JOIE*   1975
NO TIME FOR BREAKFAST   *DOCTEUR FRANÇOISE
    GAILLAND*   1975
THE JUDGE AND THE ASSASSIN   *LE JUGE ET L'ASSASSIN*
    Libra, 1976, French
THE LACEMAKER   *LA DENTELLIERE*   New Yorker,
    1977, Swiss-French
LES INDIENS SONT ENCORE LOIN   1977
VIOLETTE   *VIOLETTE NOZIERE*   New Yorker, 1978, French
LA COULEUR DE TEMPS   1978
HEAVEN'S GATE   United Artists, 1980
EVERY MAN FOR HIMSELF   *SAUVE QUI PEUT*   New Yorker/
    Zoetrope, 1980, Swiss-French
CLEAN SLATE   *COUP DE TORCHON*   Biograph/Quartet/
    Films, Inc.,/The Frank Moreno Company, 1982, French
THE TROUT   *LA TRUITE*   1982
ENTRE NOUS   *COUP DE FOUDRE*   United Artists Classics,
    1983, French
MY BEST FRIEND'S GIRL   European International, 1983, French
SINCERELY, CHARLOTTE   New Line Cinema, 1986, French
CACTUS   Spectrafilm, 1986, Australian
THE BEDROOM WINDOW   DEG, 1987

ELLIOTT HURST
POPCORN   Studio Three, 1991

JOHN HURT
b. January 22, 1940 - Chesterfield, England
Agent: William Morris Agency - Beverly Hills, 310/274-7451

THE WILD AND THE WILLING   *YOUNG AND WILLING*   Universal,
    1962, British
THIS IS MY STREET   Anglo-Amalgamated, 1963, British
A MAN FOR ALL SEASONS   Columbia, 1966, British
THE SAILOR FROM GIBRALTAR   Lopert, 1967, British
BEFORE WINTER COMES   Columbia, 1969, British
SINFUL DAVEY   United Artists, 1969, British
IN SEARCH OF GREGORY   1970, British

10 RILLINGTON PLACE   Columbia, 1971, British
CRY OF THE PENGUINS   *MR. FORBUSH AND THE PENGUINS*
   1971, British
THE PIED PIPER   Paramount, 1972, British-West German
THE GHOUL   Rank, 1974, British
LITTLE MALCOLM AND HIS STRUGGLE AGAINST THE EUNUCHS
   Multicetera Investments, 1974, British
THE DISAPPEARANCE   Levitt-Pickman, 1977, British
EAST OF ELEPHANT ROCK   1977, British
SPECTRE (TF)   20th Century-Fox TV, 1977
THE NAKED CIVIL SERVANT (TF)   Thames TV, 1978, British
MIDNIGHT EXPRESS ✪   Columbia, 1978
THE SHOUT   Films, Inc., 1979, British
ALIEN   20th Century-Fox, 1979, U.S.-British
HEAVEN'S GATE   United Artists, 1980
THE ELEPHANT MAN ★   Paramount, 1980
HISTORY OF THE WORLD—PART 1   20th Century-Fox, 1981
NIGHT CROSSING   Buena Vista, 1982
PARTNERS   Paramount, 1982
THE OSTERMAN WEEKEND   20th Century-Fox, 1983
CHAMPIONS   Embassy, 1983, British
1984   Atlantic Releasing Corporation, 1984, British
THE HIT   Island Alive, 1984, British
SUCCESS IS THE BEST REVENGE   Triumph/Columbia,
   1984, British
JAKE SPEED   New World, 1986
FROM THE HIP   DEG, 1987
ARIA   Miramax Films, 1987, British
WHITE MISCHIEF   Columbia, 1988, British
SCANDAL   Miramax Films, 1989
THE INVESTIGATION: INSIDE A TERRORIST BOMBING (CTF)
   Granada Television, 1990
THE FIELD   Avenue Pictures, 1990, Irish-British
KING RALPH   Universal, 1991
HANS CHRISTIAN ANDERSEN'S THUMBELINA (AF)
   Warner Bros., 1994 (voice)
EVEN COWGIRLS GET THE BLUES   Fine Line Features/New Line
   Cinema, 1994
WILD BILL   MGM/UA, 1995
ROB ROY   MGM/UA, 1995

MARY BETH HURT
b. September 26, 1946 - Marshalltown, Iowa

INTERIORS   United Artists, 1978
HEAD OVER HEELS   *CHILLY SCENES OF WINTER*
   United Artists, 1979
THE WORLD ACCORDING TO GARP   1982
D.A.R.Y.L.   Paramount, 1985
COMPROMISING POSITIONS   Paramount, 1985
BABY GIRL SCOTT (TF)   Polson Company Productions/
   The Finnegan-Pinchuk Company, 1987
PARENTS   Vestron, 1989
SLAVES OF NEW YORK   TriStar, 1989
DEFENSELESS   New Line Cinema, 1991
THE AGE OF INNOCENCE   Columbia, 1993
SIX DEGREES OF SEPARATION   MGM/UA, 1993

WILLIAM HURT
b. March 20, 1950 - Washington D.C.

ALTERED STATES   Warner Bros., 1980
EYEWITNESS   20th Century-Fox, 1981
BODY HEAT   The Ladd Company/Warner Bros., 1981
GORKY PARK   Orion, 1983
THE BIG CHILL   Columbia, 1983
KISS OF THE SPIDER WOMAN ★★   Island Alive/FilmDallas,
   1985, Brazilian-U.S.
CHILDREN OF A LESSER GOD ★   Paramount, 1986
BROADCAST NEWS ★   20th Century Fox, 1987
A TIME OF DESTINY   Columbia, 1988
THE ACCIDENTAL TOURIST   Warner Bros., 1988
I LOVE YOU TO DEATH   TriStar, 1990
ALICE   Orion, 1990
THE DOCTOR   Buena Vista, 1991
UNTIL THE END OF THE WORLD   Warner Bros., 1991,
   West German-French
MR. WONDERFUL   Warner Bros., 1993

TRIAL BY JURY   Warner Bros., 1994
SECOND BEST   Warner Bros., 1994
SMOKE   Miramax Films, 1995

ANJELICA HUSTON
b. July 8, 1951 - Santa Monica, California
Agent: ICM - Beverly Hills, 310/550-4000

A WALK WITH LOVE AND DEATH   20th Century-Fox, 1969, British
SINFUL DAVEY   United Artists, 1969, British
HAMLET   Columbia, 1969, British
SWASHBUCKLER   Universal, 1976
THE LAST TYCOON   Paramount, 1976
THE POSTMAN ALWAYS RINGS TWICE   Paramount, 1981
FRANCES   Universal/AFD, 1982
THIS IS SPINAL TAP   Embassy, 1984
THE ICE PIRATES   MGM/UA, 1984
PRIZZI'S HONOR ✪✪   20th Century Fox, 1985
GOOD TO GO   Island Pictures, 1986
GARDENS OF STONE   TriStar, 1987
CAPTAIN EO (Disneyland/Walt Disney World)   1987
THE DEAD   Vestron, 1987
JOHN HUSTON AND THE DUBLINERS   1987
A HANDFUL OF DUST   New Line Cinema, 1988
MR. NORTH   Samuel Goldwyn Company, 1988
JOHN HUSTON: THE MAN, THE MOVIES, THE MAVERICK (CTD)
   Point Blank, 1988
LONESOME DOVE (MS)   Motown Productions/Pangaea/Qintex
   Entertainment, Inc., 1989
CRIMES AND MISDEMEANORS   Orion, 1989
ENEMIES, A LOVE STORY ✪   20th Century Fox, 1989
THE WITCHES   Warner Bros., 1990
THE GRIFTERS ★   Miramax Films, 1990
THE ADDAMS FAMILY   Paramount, 1991
THE PLAYER   Fine Line Features/New Line Cinema, 1992
FAMILY PICTURES (TF)   Alexander, Enright & Associates/Hearst
   Entertainment, 1993
MANHATTAN MURDER MYSTERY   TriStar, 1993
AND THE BAND PLAYED ON (CTF)   HBO Pictures/Spelling
   Entertainment, 1993
ADDAMS FAMILY VALUES   Paramount, 1993
THE CROSSING GUARD   Miramax Films, 1994
THE PEREZ FAMILY   Samuel Goldwyn Company, 1994
BUFFALO GIRLS (MS)   Lauren Film Productions, Inc./CBS, 1995

CAROL HUSTON
SHOOTER (TF)   UBU Productions/Paramount TV, 1988

WILL HUTCHINS
MAVERICK   Warner Bros., 1994

DOUG HUTCHISON
Agent: Gersh Agency - Beverly Hills, 310/274-6611

FRESH HORSES   WEG, 1988

CANDANCE HUTSON
LAND BEFORE TIME (AF)   Universal, 1995 (voice)

LAUREN HUTTON
(Mary Hutton)
b. November 17, 1943 - Charleston, South Carolina
Agent: CAA - Beverly Hills, 310/288-4545

PAPER LION   United Artists, 1968
PIECES OF DREAMS   United Artists, 1970
LITTLE FAUSS AND BIG HALSEY   Paramount, 1970
THE GAMBLER   Paramount, 1974
GATOR   United Artists, 1976
WELCOME TO L.A.   United Artists/Lions Gate, 1977
VIVA KNIEVEL!   Warner Bros., 1977
SOMEONE'S WATCHING ME! (TF)   Warner Bros. TV, 1978
A WEDDING   20th Century-Fox, 1978
INSTITUTE FOR REVENGE (TF)   Gold-Driskill Productions/
   Columbia TV, 1979
AMERICAN GIGOLO   Paramount, 1980

PATERNITY Paramount, 1981
ZORRO, THE GAY BLADE 20th Century-Fox, 1981
STARFLIGHT: THE PLANE THAT COULDN'T LAND
    STARFLIGHT ONE (TF) Orgolini-Nelson Productions, 1983
LASSITER Warner Bros., 1984
SCANDAL SHEET (TF) Fair Dinkum Productions, 1985
ONCE BITTEN Samuel Goldwyn Company, 1985
TIMESTALKERS (TF) Fries Entertainment/Newland-Raynor
    Productions, 1987
MALONE Orion, 1987
PERFECT PEOPLE (TF) Robert Greenwald Productions, 1988
FEAR (CTF) Richard Kobritz-Rockne S. O'Bannon
    Productions, 1990
GUILTY AS CHARGED I.R.S. Media, 1991
MY FATHER, THE HERO Buena Vista, 1994

TIMOTHY HUTTON
b. August 16, 1960 - Malibu, California
Agent: UTA - Beverly Hills, 310/273-6700

ZUMA BEACH (TF) Edgar J. Scherick Associates/Warner
    Bros. TV, 1978
AND BABY MAKES SIX (TF) Alan Landsburg Productions, 1979
YOUNG LOVE, FIRST LOVE (TF) Lorimar Productions, 1979
FRIENDLY FIRE (TF) Marble Arch Productions, 1979
ORDINARY PEOPLE ○○ Paramount, 1980
TAPS 20th Century Fox, 1980
DANIEL Paramount, 1983
ICEMAN Universal, 1984
THE FALCON AND THE SNOWMAN Orion, 1985
TURK 182 20th Century Fox, 1985
MADE IN HEAVEN Lorimar, 1987
A TIME OF DESTINY Columbia, 1988
EVERYBODY'S ALL-AMERICAN Warner Bros., 1988
TORRENTS OF SPRING Millimeter Films, 1990
Q&A TriStar, 1990
THE TEMP Paramount, 1993
THE DARK HALF Orion, 1993
PARIS MATCH 20th Century Fox, 1995

RICHARD HUW
GETTING IT RIGHT MCEG, 1989, U.S.-British

PAM HYATT
THE CARE BEARS MOVIE II: A NEW GENERATION (AF)
    Columbia, 1986, Canadian (voice)

JONATHAN HYDE
Agent: William Morris Agency - Beverly Hills, 310/274-7451

RICHIE RICH Warner Bros., 1994

ALEX HYDE-WHITE
SUPERCARRIER (TF) Fries Entertainment/Richard Hayward-Real
    Tinsel Productions, 1988
KINJITE (FORBIDDEN SUBJECTS) Cannon, 1989
INDIANA JONES AND THE LAST CRUSADE Paramount, 1989
PRETTY WOMAN Buena Vista, 1990
OF UNKNOWN ORIGIN Concorde, 1994

FRANCES HYLAND
HAPPY BIRTHDAY TO ME Columbia, 1981, Canadian

STEPHEN HYTNER
THE MARRYING MAN Buena Vista, 1991

I

PETER IACHANGELO
TATTOO 20th Century-Fox, 1981

MASATO IBU
EMPIRE OF THE SON Warner Bros., 1987

ICE CUBE
Agent: William Morris Agency - Beverly Hills, 310/274-7451

BOYZ 'N THE HOOD Columbia, 1991
THE LOOTERS Universal, 1992
HIGHER LEARNING Columbia, 1994

ICE-T
Agent: UTA - Beverly Hills, 310/273-6700

NEW JACK CITY Warner Bros., 1991
RICOCHET Warner Bros., 1991
THE LOOTERS Universal, 1992
SURVIVING THE GAME New Line Cinema, 1994
JOHNNY MNEMONIC TriStar, 1994
TANK GIRL MGM/UA, 1995

ERIC IDLE
b. March 29, 1943 - England
Agent: William Morris Agency - Beverly Hills, 310/274-7451

AND NOW FOR SOMETHING COMPLETELY DIFFERENT
    1972, British
MONTY PYTHON AND THE HOLY GRAIL Cinema 5, 1974, British
ALL YOU NEED IS CASH *THE RUTLES* (TF) Rutles Corps
    Productions, 1978, British (also co-directed)
MONTY PYTHON'S LIFE OF BRIAN Orion/Warner Bros.,
    1979, British
MONTY PYTHON LIVE AT THE HOLLYWOOD BOWL Columbia,
    1982, British
MONTY PYTHON'S THE MEANING OF LIFE Universal,
    1983, British
YELLOWBEARD Orion, 1983, British
NATIONAL LAMPOON'S EUROPEAN VACATION
    Warner Bros., 1985
THE TRANSFORMERS (AF) DEG, 1986 (voice)
AROUND THE WORLD IN 80 DAYS (MS) Harmony/Gold/
    ReteEuropa/Valente-Baerwald Productions, 1989
THE ADVENTURES OF BARON MUNCHAUSEN Columbia, 1989
NUNS ON THE RUN 20th Century Fox, 1990
TOO MUCH SUN New Line Cinema, 1991
MISSING PIECES Orion, 1991
DICK AND MARGE SAVE THE WORLD Warner Bros., 1992
SPLITTING HEIRS Universal, 1993, British-U.S.
CASPER Universal, 1995

BILLY IDOL
b. November 30, 1955 - London, England

THE DOORS TriStar, 1991

IGGY POP
(See Iggy POP)

IMAN
OUT OF AFRICA Universal, 1985 (uncredited)
STAR TREK VI: THE UNDISCOVERED COUNTRY
    Paramount, 1991
EXIT TO EDEN Savoy Pictures, 1994

GARY IMHOFF
HANS CHRISTIAN ANDERSEN'S THUMBELINA (AF)
Warner Bros., 1994 (voice)

MICHAEL IMPERIOLI
Agent: William Morris Agency - Beverly Hills, 310/274-7451

THE BASKETBALL DIARIES   1995

JOHN INGLE
LAND BEFORE TIME (AF)   Universal, 1995 (voice)

STEVE INWOOD
CONTRACT ON CHERRY STREET (MS)   Columbia TV, 1977
THE REHEARSAL   1979
NIGHT OF THE JUGGLER   Columbia, 1980
FAME   MGM/United Artists, 1980
PRINCE OF THE CITY   Orion/Warner Bros., 1981
JACQUELINE SUSANN'S VALLEY OF THE DOLLS (MS)
   20th Century-Fox TV, 1981
A QUESTION OF HONOR (MS)   Roger Gimbel Productions/
   EMI TV/Sonny Grosso Productions, 1982
FARRELL FOR THE PEOPLE (TF)   InterMedia Entertainment/
   TAL Productions/MGM-UA TV, 1982
THE FIGHTER (TF)   Martin Manulis Productions/The Catalina
   Production Group, 1983
STAYING ALIVE   Paramount, 1983
CRIME OF INNOCENCE (TF)   Ohlmeyer Communications
   Company, 1985
DARK MANSIONS (TF)   Aaron Spelling Productions, 1986
DIARY OF A PERFECT MURDER (TF)   Viacom Productions, 1986
THE HUMAN SHIELD   Cannon, 1992

AHARON IPALE
VIBES   Columbia, 1988

JOHN IRELAND
b. January 30, 1914 - Vancouver, Canada

A WALK IN THE SUN   20th Century-Fox, 1945
BEHIND GREEN LIGHTS   1946
MY DARLING CLEMENTINE   20th Century-Fox, 1946
RAILROADED   Eagle Lion, 1947
THE GANGSTER   1947
OPEN SECRET   1948
RAW DEAL   Eagle Lion, 1948
RED RIVER   United Artists, 1948
JOAN OF ARC   RKO Radio, 1948
A SOUTHERN YANKEE   1948
I SHOT JESSE JAMES   1949
ROUGHSHOD   RKO Radio, 1949
ANNA LUCASTA   1949
THE DOOLINS OF OKLAHOMA   Columbia, 1949
ALL THE KING'S MEN ◉   Columbia, 1949
CARGO TO CAPETOWN   1950
THE RETURN OF JESSE JAMES   1950
VENGEANCE VALLEY   MGM, 1951
THE SCARF   United Artists, 1951
LITTLE BIG HORN   Lippert, 1951
THE BASKETBALL FIX   1951
RED MOUNTAIN   Paramount, 1951
THE BUSHWHACKERS   Realart, 1952
HURRICANE SMITH   Paramount, 1952
THE 49TH MAN   1953
OUTLAW TERRITORY   1953 (also co-directed)
COMBAT SQUAD   1953
SECURITY RISK   1954
THE GOOD DIE YOUNG   United Artists, 1954, British
SOUTHWEST PASSAGE   1954
THE FAST AND THE FURIOUS   American International
   Pictures, 1954
THE STEEL CAGE   United Artists, 1954
QUEEN BEE   Columbia, 1955
HELL'S HORIZON   1955
THE GUNSLINGER   ARC, 1956
GUNFIGHT AT THE O.K. CORRAL   Paramount, 1957

PARTY GIRL   MGM, 1958
NO PLACE TO LAND   1958
FACES IN THE DARK   1960, British
SPARTACUS   Universal, 1960
WILD IN THE COUNTRY   1961
NO TIME TO KILL   1961, British-Swiss-West German
BRUSHFIRE!   1962
55 DAYS AT PEKING   Allied Artists, 1963
THE CEREMONY   1963
THE FALL OF THE ROMAN EMPIRE   Paramount, 1964
DAY OF THE NIGHTMARE   Governor, 1965
I SAW WHAT YOU DID   Universal, 1965
FORT UTAH   Paramount, 1967
CAXAMBU   1967
ARIZONA BUSHWHACKERS   Paramount, 1968
EL CHE GUEVARA   1969, Italian
THE ADVENTURERS   Paramount, 1970
ONE ON TOP OF THE OTHER   1971, Italian-French-Spanish
ESCAPE TO THE SUN   Cinevision, 1972,
   Israeli-West German-French
THE HOUSE OF THE SEVEN CORPSES   1974
WELCOME TO ARROW BEACH   *TENDER FLESH*   1974
THE MAD BUTCHER   1974
FAREWELL, MY LOVELY   Avco Embassy, 1975
IL LETTO IN PIAZZA   1976, Italian
SALON KITTY   American International, 1976,
   Italian-West German-French
SATAN'S CHEERLEADERS   World Amusement, 1977
THE SWISS CONSPIRACY   SJ International, 1977
RANSOM   *ASSAULT ON PARADISE/MANIAC*   New World, 1977
VERANO SANGRIENTO   1977, Spanish-Italian
TOMORROW NEVER COMES   1977, British-Canadian
LOVE AND THE MIDNIGHT AUTO SUPPLY
   MIDNIGHT AUTO SUPPLY   1978
THE SHAPE OF THINGS TO COME   Film Ventures International,
   1979, Canadian
THE COURAGE OF KAVIK THE WOLF DOG   *KAVIK THE
   WOLF DOG*   1980
GUYANA: CULT OF THE DAMNED   1980,
   Mexican-Spanish-Panamanian
THE INCUBUS   Artists Releasing Corporation/Film Ventures
   International, 1982, Canadian
MARTIN'S DAY   MGM/UA, 1984, British
THUNDER RUN   Cannon, 1986
MESSENGER OF DEATH   Cannon, 1988

KATHY IRELAND
NECESSARY ROUGHNESS   Paramount, 1991
THE PLAYER   Fine Line Features/New Line Cinema, 1992
DICK AND MARGE SAVE THE WORLD   Warner Bros., 1992
NATIONAL LAMPOON'S LOADED WEAPON 1
   New Line Cinema, 1993

PABLO IRLANDO
THE SKATEBOARD KID II   Concorde, 1995

JEREMY IRONS
b. September 19, 1948 - Cowes, England
Agent: CAA - Beverly Hills, 310/288-4545

NIJINSKY   Paramount, 1980
THE FRENCH LIEUTENANT'S WOMAN   United Artists,
   1981, British
BRIDESHEAD REVISITED (MS)   Granada TV/WNET-13/NDR
   Hamburg, 1982, British-U.S.-West German
MOONLIGHTING   Universal Classics, 1982, British
BETRAYAL   20th Century-Fox International Classics, 1983, British
THE WILD DUCK   RKR Releasing, 1983, Australian
SWANN IN LOVE   Orion Classics, 1984, French-West German
THE MISSION   Warner Bros., 1986, British
DEAD RINGERS   20th Century Fox, 1988
A CHORUS OF DISAPPROVAL   South Gate Entertainment,
   1988, British
REVERSAL OF FORTUNE ★★   Warner Bros., 1990
KAFKA   Miramax Films, 1991
DAMAGE   New Line Cinema, 1992, French-British

WATERLAND   Fine Line Features/New Line Cinema,
    1992, British-U.S.
M. BUTTERFLY   Warner Bros., 1993
THE HOUSE OF THE SPIRITS   Miramax Films,
    1993, U.S.-German
THE LION KING (AF)   Buena Vista, 1994 (voice)
DIE HARD 3   20th Century Fox, 1995

MICHAEL IRONSIDE
SCANNERS   Avco Embassy, 1981, Canadian
VISITING HOURS   20th Century-Fox, 1982, Canadian
CROSS COUNTRY   New World, 1983, Canadian
THE SINS OF DORIAN GRAY (TF)   Rankin-Bass Productions, 1983
SPACEHUNTER: ADVENTURES IN THE FORBIDDEN ZONE
    Columbia, 1983, Canadian-U.S.
THE SURROGATE   1984, Canadian
JO JO DANCER, YOUR LIFE IS CALLING   Columbia, 1986
TOP GUN   Paramount, 1986
HELLO MARY LOU: PROM NIGHT II   *THE HAUNTING OF
    HAMILTON HIGH*   Samuel Goldwyn Company, 1987, Canadian
EXTREME PREJUDICE   TriStar, 1987
NOWHERE TO HIDE   New Century/Vista, 1987, U.S.-Canadian
WATCHERS   Universal, 1988
TOTAL RECALL   TriStar, 1990
HIGHLANDER II - THE QUICKENING   Entertainment Film
    Distributors, 1991, British-U.S.
McBAIN   Shapiro-Glickenhaus, 1991
THE VAGRANT   MGM-Pathe, 1991
THE NEXT KARATE KID   Columbia, 1994

PAULA IRVINE
PHANTASM II   Universal, 1988

AMY IRVING
b. September 10, 1953 - Palo Alto, California
Agent: William Morris Agency - Beverly Hills, 310/274-7451

CARRIE   United Artists, 1976
PANACHE   Warner Bros. TV, 1976
THE FURY   20th Century-Fox, 1978
VOICES   MGM/United Artists, 1979
HONEYSUCKLE ROSE   Warner Bros., 1980
THE COMPETITION   Columbia, 1980
YENTL ✪   MGM/UA, 1983
THE FAR PAVILIONS (CMS)   Geoff Reeve & Associates/Goldcrest,
    1984, British
MICKI & MAUDE   Columbia, 1984
ANASTASIA: THE MYSTERY OF ANNA (TF)   Telecom
    Entertainment/Consolidated Productions/Reteitalia, 1986,
    U.S.-Italian
RUMPELSTILTSKIN   Cannon, 1987, U.S.-Israeli
WHO FRAMED ROGER RABBIT   Buena Vista,
    1988 (voice; uncredited)
CROSSING DELANCEY   Warner Bros., 1988
A SHOW OF FORCE   Paramount, 1990
AN AMERICAN TAIL: FIEVEL GOES WEST (AF)   Universal,
    1991 (voice)
BENEFIT OF THE DOUBT   Miramax Films, 1993

BILL IRWIN
Agent: ICM - Beverly Hills, 310/550-4000

POPEYE   Paramount, 1980
A NEW LIFE   Paramount, 1988
EIGHT MEN OUT   Orion, 1988
SCENES FROM A MALL   Buena Vista, 1991
HOT SHOTS!   20th Century-Fox, 1991
STEPPING OUT   Paramount, 1991
SILENT TONGUE   Trimark Pictures, 1994, U.S.-French

TOM IRWIN
DECEIVED   Buena Vista, 1991

CHRIS ISAAK
Agent: UTA - Beverly Hills, 310/273-6700

MARRIED TO THE MOB   Orion, 1988
THE SILENCE OF THE LAMBS   Orion, 1991
TWIN PEAKS: FIRE WALK WITH ME   New Line Cinema,
    1992, U.S.-French
LITTLE BUDDHA   Miramax Films, 1994, British-French

TAKAAKI ISHIBASHI
MAJOR LEAGUE II   Warner Bros., 1994

JIM ISHIDA
THE IRON TRIANGLE   Scotti Bros., 1989

ROBERT ITO
AMERICAN GEISHA (TF)   Interscope Communications/Stonehenge
    Productions, 1986

GREGORY ITZIN
AIRPLANE!   Paramount, 1980

ZELJKO IVANEK
OUR SONS (TF)   Robert Greenwald Productions, 1991
INFINITY   1995

BURL IVES
(Burle Icle Ivanhoe)
b. June 14, 1909 - Hunt, Illinois

SMOKY   1946
GREEN GRASS OF WYOMING   1948
STATION WEST   RKO Radio, 1948
SO DEAR TO MY HEART   1948
SIERRA   Universal, 1950
EAST OF EDEN   Warner Bros., 1955
THE POWER AND THE PRIZE   MGM, 1956
DESIRE UNDER THE ELMS   Paramount, 1958
THE BIG COUNTRY ✪✪   United Artists, 1958
WIND ACROSS THE EVERGLADES   Warner Bros., 1958
CAT ON A HOT TIN ROOF   MGM, 1958
DAY OF THE OUTLAW   United Artists, 1959
OUR MAN IN HAVANA   1959, British
LET NO MAN WRITE MY EPITAPH   Columbia, 1960
THE SPIRAL ROAD   Universal, 1962
SUMMER MAGIC   Buena Vista, 1963
THE BRASS BOTTLE   1964
ENSIGN PULVER   Warner Bros., 1964
THE DAYDREAMER   1966 (voice)
JULES VERNE'S ROCKET TO THE MOON   *THOSE FANTASTIC
    FLYING FOOLS/BLAST-OFF*   1967, British
THE OTHER SIDE OF BONNIE AND CLYDE   1968 (voice)
THE McMASTERS   Chevron, 1970
THE MAN WHO WANTED TO LIVE FOREVER   *THE ONLY WAY
    OUT IS DEAD*   1970, Canadian
HUGO THE HIPPO   1976 (voice)
BAKER'S HAWK   Doty-Dayton, 1976
JUST YOU AND ME KID   Columbia, 1979
EARTHBOUND (TF)   Taft International, 1981
UPHILL ALL THE WAY   New World, 1985
POOR LITTLE RICH GIRL: THE BARBARA HUTTON STORY (MS)
    Lester Persky Productions/ITC Productions, 1987
TWO MOON JUNCTION   Lorimar, 1988

DANA IVEY
THE COLOR PURPLE   Warner Bros., 1985
POSTCARDS FROM THE EDGE   Columbia, 1990
THE ADDAMS FAMILY   Paramount, 1991
ADDAMS FAMILY VALUES   Paramount, 1993

LELA IVEY
BIG   20th Century Fox, 1988

JUDITH IVEY
b. September 4, 1951 - El Paso, Texas

THE WOMAN IN RED   Orion, 1984
COMPROMISING POSITIONS   Paramount, 1985
THE LONG HOT SUMMER (TF)   Leonard Hill Productions, 1985
BRIGHTON BEACH MEMOIRS   Universal, 1986
WE ARE THE CHILDREN (TF)   Paulist Pictures/Dan Fauci-Ted
   Danson Productions/The Furia Organization, 1987
HELLO AGAIN   Buena Vista, 1987
SISTER, SISTER   New World, 1987
MILES FROM HOME   Cinecom, 1988
IN COUNTRY   Warner Bros., 1989
LOVE HURTS   Vestron, 1989
EVERYBODY WINS   Orion, 1990
ALICE   Orion, 1990 (uncredited)

J

JACKÉE
b. August 14, 1957 - Winston Salem, North Carolina

LADYBUGS   Paramount, 1992

ANNE JACKSON
b. September 3, 1926 - Allegheny, Pennsylvania

SO YOUNG SO BAD   1950
THE JOURNEY   MGM, 1959
TALL STORY   Warner Bros., 1960
THE TIGER MAKES OUT   Columbia, 1967
HOW TO SAVE A MARRIAGE AND RUIN YOUR LIFE
   Columbia, 1968
THE SECRET LIFE OF AN AMERICAN WIFE   20th Century-Fox, 1968
ZIGZAG   MGM, 1970
THE ANGEL LEVINE   United Artists, 1970
LOVERS AND OTHER STRANGERS   Cinerama Releasing
   Corporation, 1970
DIRTY DINGUS MAGEE   MGM, 1970
NASTY HABITS   Brut Productions, 1977, British
THE BELL JAR   Avco Embassy, 1979
THE SHINING   Warner Bros., 1980, British
A WOMAN CALLED GOLDA (TF)   Harve Bennett Productions/
   Paramount TV, 1982
OUT ON A LIMB (MS)   Stan Margulies Company/
   ABC Circle Films, 1987
BABY M (MS)   ABC Circle Films, 1988

CORDELL JACKSON
THE GUN IN BETTY LOU'S HANDBAG   Buena Vista, 1992

GLENDA JACKSON
b. May 9, 1936 - Birkenhead, England

THIS SPORTING LIFE   Continental, 1963, British
THE PERSECUTION AND ASSASSINATION OF JEAN-PAUL
   MARAT AS PERFORMED BY THE INMATES OF THE ASYLUM
   OF CHARENTON UNDER THE DIRECTION OF THE MARQUIS
   DE SADE   United Artists, 1967, British
TELL ME LIES   Continental, 1968, British
NEGATIVES   Continental, 1968, British
WOMEN IN LOVE ★★   United Artists, 1970, British
THE MUSIC LOVERS   United Artists, 1971, British
SUNDAY, BLOODY SUNDAY ★   United Artists, 1971, British
MARY QUEEN OF SCOTS   Universal, 1971, British
THE BOY FRIEND   MGM, 1971, British (uncredited)
THE TRIPLE ECHO   Altura, 1973, British
THE NELSON AFFAIR   A BEQUEST TO THE NATION
   Universal, 1973, British

A TOUCH OF CLASS ★★   Avco Embassy, 1973
THE MAIDS   American Film Theatre, 1974, British-Canadian
THE TEMPTER   1974
THE ROMANTIC ENGLISHWOMAN   New World, 1975, British
THE DEVIL IS A WOMAN   20th Century-Fox, 1975, British-Italian
HEDDA ★   Brut Productions, 1975, British
THE INCREDIBLE SARAH   Reader's Digest, 1976, British
NASTY HABITS   Brut Productions, 1976, British
HOUSE CALLS   Universal, 1978
STEVIE   First Artists, 1978, Canadian
THE CLASS OF MISS MacMICHAEL   Brut Productions,
   1978, British
LOST AND FOUND   Columbia, 1979
HEALTH   20th Century-Fox, 1979
HOPSCOTCH   Avco Embassy, 1980
THE PATRICIA NEAL STORY (TF)   Lawrence Schiller
   Productions, 1981
RETURN OF THE SOLDIER   European Classics, 1982, British
AND NOTHING BUT THE TRUTH   GIRO CITY   Castle Hill
   Productions, 1983, British
SAKHAROV (CTF)   HBO Premiere Films/Titus Productions,
   1984, U.S.-British
TURTLE DIARY   Samuel Goldwyn Company, 1985, British
BUSINESS AS USUAL   Cannon, 1987, British
BEYOND THERAPY   New World, 1987

JANET JACKSON
b. May 16, 1966 - Gary, Indiana
Agent: CAA - Beverly Hills, 310/288-4545

POETIC JUSTICE   Columbia, 1993

JOHN M. JACKSON
THE HITCHER   TriStar, 1986
GINGERALE AFTERNOON   Skouras Pictures, 1989

JONATHAN JACKSON
CAMP NOWHERE   Buena Vista, 1994

JOSHUA JACKSON
Agent: William Morris Agency - Beverly Hills, 310/274-7451

THE MIGHTY DUCKS   Buena Vista, 1992
D2: THE MIGHTY DUCKS   Buena Vista, 1994
ANDRE   Paramount, 1994

KATE JACKSON
b. October 29, 1948 - Birmingham, Alabama

THE SEVEN MINUTES   20th Century-Fox, 1971
NIGHT OF DARK SHADOWS   MGM, 1971
LIMBO   WOMEN IN LIMBO   Universal, 1972
SATAN'S SCHOOL FOR GIRLS (TF)   Spelling-Goldberg
   Productions, 1973
KILLER BEES (TF)   RSO Films, 1974
DEATH CRUISE (TF)   Spelling-Goldberg Productions, 1974
DEATH SCREAM   THE WOMAN WHO CRIED MURDER (TF)
   RSO Films, 1975
DEATH AT LOVE HOUSE (TF)   Spelling-Goldberg Productions, 1976
CHARLIE'S ANGELS (TF)   Spelling-Goldberg Productions, 1976
THUNDER AND LIGHTNING   20th Century-Fox, 1977
JAMES AT 15 (TF)   20th Century-Fox TV, 1977
TOPPER (TF)   Cosmo Prods./Robert A. Papazian Productions, 1979
INMATES: A LOVE STORY (TF)   Henerson-Hirsch Productions/
   Finnegan Associates, 1981
MAKING LOVE   20th Century-Fox, 1981
DIRTY TRICKS   Avco Embassy, 1981, Canadian
LISTEN TO YOUR HEART (TF)   CBS Entertainment, 1983
LOVERBOY   TriStar, 1989

MICHAEL JACKSON
b. August 29, 1958 - Gary, Indiana
Agent: CAA - Beverly Hills, 310/288-4545

THE WIZ   Universal, 1978
CAPTAIN EO (Disneyland/Walt Disney World)   1987

**F
I
L
M

A
C
T
O
R
S**

PHILIP JACKSON
HIGH HOPES   Skouras Pictures, 1988, British
BAD BEHAVIOUR   October Films, 1993, British

REGGIE JACKSON
THE NAKED GUN: FROM THE FILES OF POLICE SQUAD!
   Paramount, 1988

SAMUEL L. JACKSON
JUNGLE FEVER   Universal, 1991
WHITE SANDS   Warner Bros., 1992
NATIONAL LAMPOON'S LOADED WEAPON 1
   New Line Cinema, 1993
JURASSIC PARK   Universal, 1993
FRESH   Miramax Films, 1994
THE NEW AGE   Warner Bros., 1994
PULP FICTION   Miramax Films, 1994
LOSING ISAIAH   Paramount, 1995
KISS OF DEATH   20th Century Fox, 1995
DIE HARD 3   20th Century Fox, 1995

VICTORIA JACKSON
b. August 2, 1959 - Miami, Florida
Agent: William Morris Agency - Beverly Hills, 310/274-7451

THE PICK-UP ARTIST   20th Century Fox, 1987
BABY BOOM   MGM/UA, 1987
CASUAL SEX?   Universal, 1988
DREAM A LITTLE DREAM   Vestron, 1989
UHF   Orion, 1989
FAMILY BUSINESS   TriStar, 1989

DEREK JACOBI
b. October 22, 1938 - London, England

THE DAY OF THE JACKAL   Universal, 1973, British-French
BLUE BLOOD   Mallard Productions, 1974, British
THE ODESSA FILE   Columbia, 1974, British-West German
THE MEDUSA TOUCH   Warner Bros., 1977, British
THE HUMAN FACTOR   United Artists, 1979, British
THE HUNCHBACK OF NOTRE DAME (TF)   Norman Rosemont
   Productions/Columbia TV, 1982, U.S.-British, 1982
INSIDE THE THIRD REICH (MS)   ABC Circle Films, 1982
ENIGMA   Embassy, 1982, British-French
LITTLE DORRIT   Cannon, 1987, British
THE SECRET GARDEN (TF)   Rosemont Productions,
   1988, U.S.-British
THE TENTH MAN (TF)   Rosemont Productions/William Self
   Productions, 1988, U.S.-British
HENRY V   Samuel Goldwyn Company, 1989, British
DEAD AGAIN   Paramount, 1991

IRENE JACOB
VICTORY   Miramax Films, 1995

LOU JACOBI
b. December 28, 1913 - Toronto, Ontario, Canada

A KID FOR TWO FARTHINGS   Lopert, 1955, British
THE DIARY OF ANNE FRANK   20th Century-Fox, 1959
SONG WITHOUT END   Columbia, 1960
IRMA LA DOUCE   United Artists, 1963
PENELOPE   MGM, 1966
COTTON COMES TO HARLEM   United Artists, 1970
LITTLE MURDERS   20th Century-Fox, 1971
EVERYTHING YOU ALWAYS WANTED TO KNOW ABOUT SEX*
   (BUT WERE AFRAID TO ASK)   United Artists, 1972
NEXT STOP, GREENWICH VILLAGE   20th Century-Fox, 1976
ROSELAND   Cinema Shares International, 1977
ARTHUR   Orion, 1981
THE LUCKY STAR   Pickman Films, 1981, Canadian
THE MAGICIAN   1979, Israeli-West German
MY FAVORITE YEAR   MGM/UA, 1982
AVALON   TriStar, 1990
I.Q.   Paramount, 1994

LAWRENCE-HILTON JACOBS
PARAMEDICS   Vestron, 1988

DEAN JACOBSEN
CHILD'S PLAY 3   Universal, 1991

BOBBY JACOBY
NIGHT OF THE DEMONS 2   Republic Pictures, 1994

SCOTT JACOBY
BAXTER!   National General, 1972
RIVALS   *SINGLE PARENT*   Avco Embassy, 1973
BAD RONALD (TF)   Lorimar Productions, 1974
LOVE AND THE MIDNIGHT AUTO SUPPLY   *MIDNIGHT AUTO
   SUPPLY*   1978
THE LITTLE GIRL WHO LIVES DOWN THE LANE   American
   International, 1977, U.S.-Canadian-French
TO DIE FOR   Arrowhead Entertainment, 1988

YVES JACQUES
THE DECLINE OF THE AMERICAN EMPIRE   Cineplex Odeon,
   1986, Canadian

RICHARD JAECKEL
b. October 10, 1926 - Long Beach, New York
Agent: David Shapira & Associates - Sherman Oaks, 818/906-0322

GUADALCANAL DIARY   20th Century-Fox, 1943
WING AND A PRAYER   20th Century-Fox, 1944
JUNGLE PATROL   1948
CITY ACROSS THE RIVER   1949
BATTLEGROUND   MGM, 1949
SANDS OF IWO JIMA   Republic, 1949
THE GUNFIGHTER   20th Century-Fox, 1950
HOODLUM EMPIRE   1952
COME BACK LITTLE SHEBA   Paramount, 1952
THE BIG LEAGUER   MGM, 1953
THE VIOLENT MEN   Columbia, 1955
ATTACK!   1956
3:10 TO YUMA   Columbia, 1957
COWBOY   Columbia, 1958
THE NAKED AND THE DEAD   Warner Bros., 1958
PLATINUM HIGH SCHOOL   1960
THE GALLANT HOURS   United Artists, 1960
TOWN WITHOUT PITY   1961
THE YOUNG AND THE BRAVE   MGM, 1963
FOUR FOR TEXAS   1963
TOWN TAMER   Paramount, 1965
THE DIRTY DOZEN   MGM, 1967
THE DEVIL'S BRIGADE   United Artists, 1968
THE GREEN SLIME   MGM, 1969
CHISUM   Warner Bros., 1970
SOMETIMES A GREAT NOTION ✪   Universal, 1971
ULZANA'S RAID   Universal, 1972
PAT GARRETT & BILLY THE KID   MGM, 1973
THE OUTFIT   MGM, 1973
CHOSEN SURVIVORS   Columbia, 1974
THE DROWNING POOL   Warner Bros., 1975
TWILIGHT'S LAST GLEAMING   Allied Artists, 1977,
   U.S.-West German
WALKING TALL, PART 2   American International, 1975
GRIZZLY   1976
THE JAWS OF DEATH   *MAKO: THE JAWS OF DEATH*   1976
TWILIGHT'S LAST GLEAMING   Allied Artists, 1977
DAY OF THE ANIMALS   *SOMETHING IS OUT THERE*   1977
DELTA FOX   1977
THE DARK   Film Ventures International, 1978
HERBIE GOES BANANAS   Buena Vista, 1980
...ALL THE MARBLES   MGM/UA, 1981
COLD RIVER   1982
STARMAN   Columbia, 1984
BLACK MOON RISING   New World, 1986
SUPERCARRIER (TF)   Fries Entertainment/Richard Hayward-Real
   Tinsel Productions, 1988
DELTA FORCE 2 - OPERATION STRANGLEHOLD   MGM/UA, 1990

SAEED JAFFREY
MY BEAUTIFUL LAUNDRETTE   Orion Classics, 1985, British
THE DECEIVERS   Cinecom, 1988
DIAMOND'S EDGE   Kings Road Entertainment, 1990

BIANCA JAGGER
THE CANNONBALL RUN   20th Century-Fox, 1981

MICK JAGGER
b. July 26, 1943 - Dartford, England

NED KELLY   United Artists, 1970, British
PERFORMANCE   Warner Bros., 1970, British
GIMME SHELTER (FD)   Cinema 5, 1970
RUNNING OUT OF LUCK   Nitrate Film Ltd./Julien Temple
   Production Company, 1985, British
FREEJACK   Warner Bros., 1992

HENRY JAGLOM
b. January 26, 1941 - London, England
Business: International Rainbow Pictures, The Penthouse,
   9165 Sunset Blvd., Los Angeles, CA 90069, 213/271-0202 or
   888 Seventh Avenue - 34th Floor, New York, NY 10106,
   212/245-8300

SITTING DUCKS   Speciality Films, 1980 (also directed)
ALWAYS   Samuel Goldwyn Company, 1985 (also directed)
SOMEONE TO LOVE   Rainbow/Castle Hill Productions,
   1987 (also directed)
NEW YEAR'S DAY   International Rainbow Pictures,
   1988 (also directed)

LISA JAKUB
MATINEE   Universal, 1993
MRS. DOUBTFIRE   20th Century Fox, 1993

ANTHONY JAMES
UNFORGIVEN   Warner Bros., 1992

BRION JAMES
ARMED AND DANGEROUS   Columbia, 1986
ANOTHER 48 HRS.   Paramount, 1990
THE PLAYER   Fine Line Features/New Line Cinema, 1992
PTERODACTYL WOMAN FROM BEVERLY HILLS
   Experimental Pictures, 1994

CLIFTON JAMES
DAVID AND LISA   Continental, 1962
THE CHASE   Columbia, 1966
COOL HAND LUKE   Warner Bros., 1967
THE REIVERS   National General, 1969
tick...tick...tick   MGM, 1970
THE NEW CENTURIONS   Columbia, 1972
THE ICEMAN COMETH   American Film Theatre, 1973
LIVE AND LET DIE   United Artists, 1973, British
THE LAST DETAIL   Columbia, 1973
JUGGERNAUT   United Artists, 1974, British
THE MAN WITH THE GOLDEN GUN   United Artists, 1974, British
BANK SHOT   1974
SILVER STREAK   20th Century-Fox, 1975
THE BAD NEWS BEARS IN BREAKING TRAINING   Paramount, 1977
SUPERMAN II   Warner Bros., 1981, U.S.-British
THE UNTOUCHABLES   Paramount, 1987
EIGHT MEN OUT   Orion, 1988

DALTON JAMES
MY FATHER, THE HERO   Buena Vista, 1994

GERALDINE JAMES
SWEET WILLIAM   Kendon Films, 1980, British
GANDHI   Columbia, 1982, British-Indian
SHE'S BEEN AWAY   BBC Films, 1989, British
THE WOLVES OF WILLOUGHBY CHASE   Zenith Productions,
   1990, British
THE TALL GUY   Miramax Films, 1990
IF LOOKS COULD KILL   Warner Bros., 1991

HAWTHORNE JAMES
THE FIVE HEARTBEATS   20th Century Fox, 1991
SPEED   20th Century Fox, 1994

JEFF JAMES
THE FORBIDDEN DANCE   Columbia, 1990

JESSICA JAMES
IMMEDIATE FAMILY   Columbia, 1989

MIKE JAMES
ABOVE THE LAW   Warner Bros., 1988

RON K. JAMES
ERNEST RIDES AGAIN   Emshell Producers Group, 1993

STEVE JAMES
AMERICAN NINJA   Cannon, 1985
AVENGING FORCE   Cannon, 1986
P.O.W. THE ESCAPE   Cannon, 1986
HERO AND THE TERROR   Cannon, 1988
AMERICAN NINJA 3: BLOOD HUNT   Cannon, 1989
I'M GONNA GIT YOU SUCKA   MGM/UA, 1989
McBAIN   Shapiro-Glickenhaus Entertainment, 1991

CONRAD JANIS
b. February 11, 1928 - New York, New York

SNAFU   1945
MARGIE   20th Century-Fox, 1946
THE HIGH WINDOW   1946
BEYOND GLORY   Paramount, 1948
KEEP IT COOL   LET'S ROCK   1958
THE DUCHESS AND THE DIRTWATER FOX
   20th Century-Fox, 1976
ROSELAND   Cinema Shares International, 1977
OH, GOD! BOOK II   Warner Bros., 1980
BREWSTER'S MILLIONS   Universal, 1985
NOTHING IN COMMON   TriStar, 1986
SONNY BOY   Triumph Releasing Corporation, 1990

BRUCE JARCHOW
BIG   20th Century Fox, 1988

GABE JARRET
REAL GENIUS   TriStar, 1985

PETER JASON
RIO LOBO   National General, 1970
THE DRIVER   20th Century-Fox, 1978
THE LONG RIDERS   United Artists, 1980
TEXAS LIGHTNING   Film Ventures International, 1981
48 HRS   Paramount, 1982
TRICK OR TREATS   Lone Star, 1983
STREETS OF FIRE   Universal, 1984
BREWSTER'S MILLIONS   Universal, 1985
HEARTBREAK RIDGE   Warner Bros., 1986
PRINCE OF DARKNESS   Universal, 1987
FROM THE DEAD OF NIGHT (TF)   Shadowplay Films/Phoenix
   Entertainment Group, 1989

TONY JAY
BEAUTY AND THE BEAST (AF)   Buena Vista, 1991 (voice)

MARK JOHN JEFFRIES
LOSING ISAIAH   Paramount, 1995

KEN JENKINS
AIR AMERICA   TriStar, 1990

REBECCA JENKINS
BYE BYE BLUES   Circle Releasing Corporation, 1990, Canadian

RICHARD JENKINS
Agent: William Morris Agency - Beverly Hills, 310/274-7451

ON VALENTINE'S DAY *STORY OF A MARRIAGE*
  Angelika Films, 1986
THE MANHATTAN PROJECT 20th Century Fox, 1986
LITTLE NIKITA Columbia, 1988
STEALING HOME Warner Bros., 1988
OUT ON THE EDGE (TF) Rick Dawn Enterprises/The Steve Tisch
  Company/King Phoenix Entertainment, 1989
BLAZE Buena Vista, 1989
WOLF Columbia, 1994
TRAPPED IN PARADISE 20th Century Fox, 1994

BRUCE JENNER
CAN'T STOP THE MUSIC AFD, 1980

LUCINDA JENNEY
PEGGY SUE GOT MARRIED TriStar, 1986
WIRED Taurus Entertainment, 1989
THELMA & LOUISE MGM-Pathe, 1991
AMERICAN HEART Triton Pictures, 1993

JULIA JENNINGS
10 Orion/Warner Bros., 1979
AUNT MARY (TF) Henry Jaffee Enterprises, 1979
XANADU Universal, 1980
MARATHON (TF) Alan Landsburg Productions, 1980
S.O.B. Paramount, 1981
TEACHERS MGM/UA, 1984
BLIND DATE TriStar, 1987
DRAGNET Universal, 1987

WAYLON JENNINGS
b. June 15, 1937 - Littlefield, Texas

STAGECOACH (TF) Raymond Katz Prods/Heritage Entertainment, 1986

SALOME JENS
b. May 8, 1935 - Milwaukee, Wisconsin
Agent: Badgley/Connor - Los Angeles, 310/278-9313

ANGEL BABY Allied Artists, 1961
THE FOOL KILLER Allied Artists, 1965
SECONDS Paramount, 1966
ME, NATALIE 1969
SAVAGES Angelika, 1972
IN THE GLITTER PALACE (TF) The Writers Company/
  Columbia TV, 1977
SHARON: PORTRAIT OF A MISTRESS (TF) Moonlight
  Productions/Paramount TV, 1977
FROM HERE TO ETERNITY (MS) Benett-Katleman Productions/
  Columbia TV, 1979
CLOUD DANCER Blossom, 1980
HARRY'S WAR Taft International, 1981
CLAN OF THE CAVE BEAR Warner Bros., 1985
JUST BETWEEN FRIENDS Orion, 1986

MICHAEL JETER
THE FISHER KING TriStar, 1991
BANK ROBBER I.R.S. Releasing, 1993
GYPSY (TF) RHI Entertainment, 1993
SISTER ACT 2: BACK IN THE HABIT Buena Vista, 1993
DROP ZONE Paramount, 1994

JOAN JETT
b. September 22, 1960 - Philadelphia, Pennsylvania

LIGHT OF DAY TriStar, 1987

PENN JILLETTE
Agent: William Morris Agency - Beverly Hills, 310/274-7451

OFF BEAT Buena Vista, 1986
MY CHAUFFEUR Crown International, 1986
TOUGH GUYS DON'T DANCE Cannon, 1987

ANN JILLIAN
b. January 29, 1950 - Cambridge, Massachusetts
Agent: William Morris Agency - Beverly Hills, 310/274-7451

KILLER IN THE MIRROR (TF) Litke-Grossbart Productions/
  Warner Bros. TV, 1986
CONVICTED: A MOTHER'S STORY (TF) NBC Productions, 1987
PERRY MASON: THE CASE OF THE MURDERED MADAM (TF)
  The Fred Silverman Company/Strathmore Productions/Viacom, 1987
THE ANN JILLIAN STORY (TF) 9J, Inc. Productions/ITC, 1988
ORIGINAL SIN (TF) Larry A. Thompson Organization/
  New World TV, 1989
LITTLE WHITE LIES (TF) Larry Thompson Organization/
  New World TV, 1989
MACSHAYNE: WINNER TAKES ALL (TF) NBC, 1994

YOLANDA JILOT
DIVING IN Skouras Pictures, 1990

BILLY JOEL
b. May 9, 1949 - Bronx, New York

OLIVER & COMPANY (AF) Buena Vista, 1988 (voice)

JAKE JOHANNSEN
MRS. PARKER AND THE VICIOUS CIRCLE Fine Line Features/
  New Line Cinema, 1994

DAVID JOHANSEN
SCROOGED Paramount, 1988
LET IT RIDE Paramount, 1989
TALES FROM THE DARKSIDE: THE MOVIE Paramount, 1990
FREEJACK Warner Bros., 1992
MR. NANNY New Line Cinema, 1993
CAR 54, WHERE ARE YOU? Orion, 1994

PAUL JOHANSSON
THE LAKER GIRLS (TF) Viacom Productions/The Finnegan-Pinchuk
  Company/Valente-Hamilton Productions, 1990
SOAPDISH Paramount, 1991

ALEXANDRA JOHNES
THE NEVERENDING STORY II: THE NEXT CHAPTER
  Warner Bros., 1991

JOHNNY B.
THE JERKY BOYS Buena Vista, 1994

GLYNIS JOHNS
b. October 5, 1923 - Durban, South Africa
Agent: Susan Smith & Associates - Beverly Hills, 213/852-4777

THE REF Buena Vista, 1994
WHILE YOU WERE SLEEPING Buena Vista, 1994

A.J. JOHNSON
SCHOOL DAZE Columbia, 1988
DYING YOUNG 20th Century Fox, 1991

ARNOLD JOHNSON
MY DEMON LOVER New Line Cinema, 1987

ANNE MARIE JOHNSON
(Anne-Marie Johnson)
b. July 18 - Los Angeles, California
Agent: Gordon/Rosson Talent Agency - Studio City, 818/509-1900

HIS MISTRESS (TF) David L. Wolper Productions/
  Warner Bros. TV, 1984
THE ATLANTA CHILD MURDERS (MS) Mann-Rafshoon
  Productions/Finnegan Associates, 1985
HOLLYWOOD SHUFFLE Samuel Goldwyn Company, 1987
IN THE HEAT OF THE NIGHT (TF) The Fred Silverman Company/
  Jadda Productions/MGM-UA TV, 1988

DREAM DATE (TF)   Golchan-Kosberg Productions/Hoffman-Israel
    Productions, 1989
I'M GONNA GIT YOU SUCKA   MGM/UA, 1989
ROBOTJOX   Triumph Releasing Corporation, 1990
THE FIVE HEARTBEATS   20th Century Fox, 1991
JACKIE COLLINS' LUCKY CHANCES (MS)   NBC Productions, 1991
TRUE IDENTITY   Buena Vista, 1991
STRICTLY BUSINESS   Warner Bros., 1991

BEN JOHNSON
b. June 13, 1920 - Pawhuska, Oklahoma

THREE GODFATHERS   MGM, 1948
SHE WORE A YELLOW RIBBON   RKO Radio, 1949
MIGHTY JOE YOUNG   RKO Radio, 1949
THE WAGONMASTER   RKO Radio, 1950
RIO GRANDE   Republic, 1950
FORT DEFIANCE   1951
SHANE   Paramount, 1953
WAR DRUMS   United Artists, 1957
SLIM CARTER   1957
FORT BOWIE   United Artists, 1960
ONE-EYED JACKS   Paramount, 1961
MAJOR DUNDEE   Columbia, 1965
THE RARE BREED   Universal, 1966
WILL PENNY   Paramount, 1968
THE WILD BUNCH   Warner Bros., 1969
THE UNDEFEATED   20th Century-Fox, 1969
CHISUM   Warner Bros., 1970
THE LAST PICTURE SHOW ∞   Columbia, 1971
SOMETHING BIG   National General, 1971
CORKY *LOOKIN' GOOD*   1972
JUNIOR BONNER   Cinerama Releasing Corporation, 1972
THE GETAWAY   National General, 1972
THE TRAIN ROBBERS   Warner Bros., 1973
KID BLUE   20th Century-Fox, 1973
DILLINGER   American International, 1973
THE SUGARLAND EXPRESS   Universal, 1974
BITE THE BULLET   Columbia, 1975
HUSTLE   Paramount, 1975
BREAKHEART PASS   United Artists, 1976
THE TOWN THAT DREADED SUNDOWN
    American International, 1977
THE GREATEST   Columbia, 1977
GRAYEAGLE   American International, 1977
THE SWARM   Warner Bros., 1978
TERROR TRAIN   20th Century-Fox, 1980, Canadian
THE HUNTER   Paramount, 1980
RED DAWN   MGM/UA, 1984
WILD HORSES (TF)   Wild Horses Productions/Telepictures
    Productions, 1985
DREAM WEST (MS)   Sunn Classic Pictures, 1986
LET'S GET HARRY   TriStar, 1986
STRANGER ON MY LAND (TF)   Edgar J. Scherick Associates/
    Taft Entertainment TV, 1988
MY HEROES HAVE ALWAYS BEEN COWBOYS   Samuel Goldwyn
    Company, 1991
McNELLY'S RANGERS   Warner Bros., 1995

BRAD JOHNSON
b. October 24, 1959
Agent: CAA - Beverly Hills, 310/288-4545

NAM ANGELS   Concorde, 1989, U.S.-Filipino
ALWAYS   Universal, 1989
FLIGHT OF THE INTRUDER   Paramount, 1991
AN AMERICAN STORY (TF)   Signboard Hill Productions/RHI
    Entertainment, 1992
NED BLESSING: THE STORY OF MY LIFE AND TIMES (TF)
    Wittliff-Pangaen Productions/Hearst Entertainment/
    CBS Entertainment, 1993
PHILADELPHIA EXPERIMENT 2   Trimark Pictures, 1993
THE BIRDS 2: LAND'S END (CTF)   Showtime, 1994
CRIES UNHEARD: THE DONNA YAKLICH STORY (TF)
    Carla Singer Productions, 1994
SIRINGO   Rysher Entertainment, 1994
XXX'S & OOO'S (TF)   Moving Target Productions/New World
    Entertainment, 1994

DON JOHNSON
b. December 15, 1949 - Flatt Creek, Missouri
Agent: ICM - Beverly Hills, 310/550-4000

ZACHARIAH   Cinerama Releasing Corporation, 1971
THE HARRAD EXPERIMENT   Cinerama Releasing
    Corporation, 1973
RETURN TO MACON COUNTY   American International, 1975
A BOY AND HIS DOG   Pacific Film Enterprises, 1975
LAW OF THE LAND (TF)   QM Productions, 1976
THE CITY (TF)   QM Productions, 1977
SKI LIFT TO DEATH (TF)   1978
AMATEUR NIGHT AT THE DIXIE BAR AND GRILL (TF)
    Motown/Universal TV, 1979
BEULAH LAND (MS)   David Gerber Company/Columbia TV, 1980
MIAMI VICE (TF)   The Michael Mann Company/Universal TV, 1984
THE LONG HOT SUMMER (MS)   Leonard Hill Productions, 1985
SWEET HEARTS DANCE   TriStar, 1988
DEAD-BANG   Warner Bros., 1989
THE HOT SPOT   Orion, 1990
HARLEY DAVIDSON & THE MARLBORO MAN   MGM-Pathe, 1991
PARADISE   Buena Vista, 1991
BORN YESTERDAY   Buena Vista, 1993
GUILTY AS SIN   Buena Vista, 1993

KARL JOHNSON
AVENGING FORCE   Cannon, 1986

LAMONT JOHNSON
b. September 20, 1922 - Stockton, California

ONE ON ONE   Warner Bros., 1977 (also directed)

LYNN-HOLLY JOHNSON
ICE CASTLES   Columbia, 1979
THE WATCHER IN THE WOODS   Buena Vista, 1980
FOR YOUR EYES ONLY   United Artists, 1981, British
WHERE THE BOYS ARE '84   TriStar, 1984
ALIEN PREDATOR   Trans World Entertainment, 1987

MEL JOHNSON, JR.
Agent: Gersh Agency - Beverly Hills, 310/274-6611

TOTAL RECALL   TriStar, 1990

MICHELLE JOHNSON
BLAME IT ON RIO   20th Century Fox, 1984
GUNG HO   Paramount, 1986
WAXWORK   Vestron, 1988
GENUINE RISK   I.R.S., 1990
MENENDEZ: A KILLING IN BEVERLY HILLS (MS)   Zev Braun
    Pictures/TriStar Television, 1994

REGGIE JOHNSON
PLATOON   Orion, 1986

VAN JOHNSON
(Charles Van Johnson)
b. August 25, 1916 - Newport, Rhode Island

TOO MANY GIRLS   RKO Radio, 1940
MURDER IN THE BIG HOUSE   1942
SOMEWHERE I'LL FIND YOU   MGM, 1942
THE WAR AGAINST MRS. HADLEY   MGM, 1942
DR. GILLESPIE'S NEW ASSISTANT   MGM, 1942
THE HUMAN COMEDY   MGM, 1943
PILOT NO. 5   MGM, 1943
MADAME CURIE   MGM, 1943
A GUY NAMED JOE   MGM, 1943
THE WHITE CLIFFS OF DOVER   MGM, 1944
THREE MEN IN WHITE   MGM, 1944
TWO GIRLS AND A SAILOR   MGM, 1944
THIRTY SECONDS OVER TOKYO   MGM, 1944
BETWEEN TWO WOMEN   MGM, 1944
THRILL OF A ROMANCE   MGM, 1945
WEEKEND AT THE WALDORF   MGM, 1945

ZIEGFELD FOLLIES   MGM, 1945
EASY TO WED   MGM, 1946
NO LEAVE, NO LOVE   MGM, 1946
TILL THE CLOUDS ROLL BY   MGM, 1946
HIGH BARBAREE   MGM, 1947
THE ROMANCE OF ROSY RIDGE   MGM, 1947
STATE OF THE UNION   MGM, 1948
THE BRIDE GOES WILD   MGM, 1948
COMMAND DECISION   MGM, 1949
MOTHER IS A FRESHMAN   20th Century-Fox, 1949
SCENE OF THE CRIME   1949
IN THE GOOD OLD SUMMERTIME   MGM, 1949
BATTLEGROUND   MGM, 1949
THE BIG HANGOVER   MGM, 1950
DUCHESS OF IDAHO   MGM, 1950
GROUNDS FOR MARRIAGE   MGM, 1950
THREE GUYS NAMED MIKE   MGM, 1950
GO FOR BROKE   MGM, 1951
TOO YOUNG TO KISS   MGM, 1951
IT'S A BIG COUNTRY   MGM, 1951
INVITATION   MGM, 1951
WHEN IN ROME   MGM, 1952
WASHINGTON STORY   MGM, 1952
PLYMOUTH ADVENTURE   MGM, 1952
CONFIDENTIALLY CONNIE   MGM, 1952
REMAINS TO BE SEEN   MGM, 1953
EASY TO LOVE   MGM, 1953
THE SIEGE AT RED RIVER   20th Century-Fox, 1954
MEN OF THE FIGHTING LADY   MGM, 1954
THE CAINE MUTINY   Columbia, 1954
BRIGADOON   MGM, 1954
THE LAST TIME I SAW PARIS   MGM, 1954
THE END OF THE AFFAIR   Columbia, 1955, British
THE BRASS BOTTLE   1956
MIRACLE IN THE RAIN   Warner Bros., 1956
23 PACES TO BAKER STREET   20th Century-Fox,
   1956, British-U.S.
SLANDER   MGM, 1956
KELLY AND ME   Universal, 1957
ACTION OF THE TIGER   MGM, 1957
THE PIED PIPER OF HAMELIN (TF)   1957
THE LAST BLITZKRIEG   Columbia, 1959
WEB OF EVIDENCE   *BEYOND THIS PLACE*   Allied Artists,
   1959, British
SUBWAY IN THE SKY   1959, British
THE ENEMY GENERAL   Columbia, 1960
WIVES AND LOVERS   Paramount, 1963
DIVORCE AMERICAN STYLE   Columbia, 1967
YOURS MINE AND OURS   United Artists, 1968
WHERE ANGELS GO...TROUBLE FOLLOWS!   Columbia, 1968
BATTLE SQUADRON   *LA BATTAGLIA D'INGHILTERRA*   1969,
   Italian-Spanish-French
IL PREZZO DEL POTERE   1968, Italian
COMPANY OF KILLERS   *THE PROTECTORS*   Universal, 1970
L'OCCHIO DEL RAGNO   1971, Italian
RICH MAN, POOR MAN (MS)   Universal TV, 1976
THE PURPLE ROSE OF CAIRO   Orion, 1985

MIKE JOLLY

Agent: Judy Schoen and Associates - Los Angeles, 213/962-1950

CREATOR   Universal, 1985
BAD GUYS   Interpictures, 1986
FRESNO (MS)   MTM Productions, 1986
THREE O'CLOCK HIGH   Universal, 1987
FATAL BEAUTY   MGM/UA, 1987
WHAT PRICE VICTORY (TF)   Wolper Productions/Warner
   Bros. TV, 1988
BRING ME THE HEAD OF DOBIE GILLIS (TF)
   20th Century Fox TV, 1988
FLIGHT OF THE INTRUDER   Paramount, 1991
EVE OF DESTRUCTION   Orion, 1991
SISTER ACT   Buena Vista, 1992
CLEAN SLATE   MGM/UA, 1994
FORREST GUMP   Paramount, 1994

CHRISTINE JONES

STEALING HOME   Warner Bros., 1988

DEAN JONES
b. January 25, 1935 - Morgan County, Alabama
Agent: The Blake Agency - Beverly Hills, 310/246-0241

TEA AND SYMPATHY   MGM, 1956
TEN THOUSAND BEDROOMS   MGM, 1957
JAILHOUSE ROCK   MGM, 1957
HANDLE WITH CARE   MGM, 1958
IMITATION GENERAL   MGM, 1958
TORPEDO RUN   MGM, 1958
NIGHT OF THE QUARTER MOON   *FLESH AND FLAME*
   MGM, 1958
NEVER SO FEW   MGM, 1959
UNDER THE YUM YUM TREE   Columbia, 1963
THE NEW INTERNS   Columbia, 1964
TWO ON A GUILLOTINE   Warner Bros., 1965
THAT DARN CAT   Buena Vista, 1965
THE UGLY DACHSHUND   Buena Vista, 1966
ANY WEDNESDAY   Warner Bros., 1966
MONKEYS, GO HOME!   Buena Vista, 1967
BLACKBEARD'S GHOST   Buena Vista, 1968
THE HORSE IN THE GRAY FLANNEL SUIT   Buena Vista, 1968
THE LOVE BUG   Buena Vista, 1969
THE $1,000,000 DUCK   Buena Vista, 1971
SNOWBALL EXPRESS   Buena Vista, 1972
MR. SUPERINVISIBLE   Buena Vista, 1973
THE SHAGGY D.A.   Buena Vista, 1976
HERBIE GOES TO MONTE CARLO   Buena Vista, 1977
BORN AGAIN   Avco Embassy, 1978
FIRE AND RAIN (CTF)   Wilshire Court Productions, 1989
OTHER PEOPLE'S MONEY   Warner Bros., 1991
BEETHOVEN   Universal, 1992
CLEAR AND PRESENT DANGER   Paramount, 1994

DEBI JONES
DISTANT VOICES, STILL LIVES   Alive Films, 1989, British

FREDDIE JONES
THE BLISS OF MRS. BLOSSOM   Paramount, 1968, U.S.-British
OTLEY   Columbia, 1969, British
FRANKENSTEIN MUST BE DESTROYED!   Warner Bros.,
   1970, British
GOODBYE GEMINI   Cinerama Releasing Corporation, 1970, British
SITTING TARGET   MGM, 1972, British
ANTONY AND CLEOPATRA   Rank, 1973, British-Spanish-Swiss
COUNT DRACULA AND HIS VAMPIRE BRIDE   *THE SATANIC*
   RITES OF DRACULA   Dynamite Entertainment, 1973, British
THE ELEPHANT MAN   Paramount, 1980, British-U.S.
FIREFOX   Warner Bros., 1982
AND THE SHIP SAILS ON   Triumph/Columbia, 1983, Italian-French
KRULL   Columbia, 1983, U.S.-British
DUNE   Universal, 1984
FIRESTARTER   Universal, 1984
ERIK THE VIKING   Orion, 1989, British

GRACE JONES
b. May 19, 1952 - Spanishtown, Jamaica

CONAN THE DESTROYER   Universal, 1984
A VIEW TO A KILL   MGM/UA, 1985, British
VAMP   New World, 1986

HELEN JONES
BLISS   New World, 1985, Australian

HENRY JONES
b. August 1, 1912 - Philadelphia, Pennsylvania

THE LADY SAYS NO   1951
THE BAD SEED   Warner Bros., 1956
THE GIRL CAN'T HELP IT   20th Century-Fox, 1956
WILL SUCCESS SPOIL ROCK HUNTER?   20th Century-Fox, 1957
3:10 TO YUMA   Columbia, 1957
VERTIGO   Paramount, 1958
CASH McCALL   Warner Bros., 1959
THE BRAMBLE BUSH   Warner Bros., 1960
ANGEL BABY   Allied Artists, 1961

NEVER TOO LATE   Warner Bros., 1965
THE CHAMPAGNE MURDERS   *LE SCANDALE*
   Universal, 1967, French
PROJECT X   Paramount, 1968
STAY AWAY JOE   MGM, 1968
SUPPORT YOUR LOCAL SHERIFF   United Artists, 1969
BUTCH CASSIDY AND THE SUNDANCE KID
   20th Century-Fox, 1969
DIRTY DINGUS MAGEE   MGM, 1970
RABBIT, RUN   Warner Bros., 1970
THE SKIN GAME   Warner Bros., 1971
SUPPORT YOUR LOCAL GUNFIGHTER   United Artists, 1971
PETE 'N' TILLIE   Universal, 1972
TOM SAWYER   United Artists, 1973
THE OUTFIT   MGM, 1974
NINE TO FIVE   20th Century-Fox, 1980
DEATHTRAP   Warner Bros., 1982
CODENAME: FOXFIRE (TF)   Universal TV, 1985
DICK TRACY   Buena Vista, 1990

JAMES EARL JONES
b. January 17, 1931 - Arkabutla, Mississippi
Agent: Bauman, Hiller & Associates - Los Angeles, 213/857-6666

DR. STRANGELOVE: OR HOW I LEARNED TO STOP WORRYING
   AND LOVE THE BOMB   Columbia, 1964, British
THE COMEDIANS   MGM, 1967, British
KING: A FILMED RECORD...MONTGOMERY TO MEMPHIS (FD)
   Maron Films Limited, 1970
END OF THE ROAD   Allied Artists, 1970
THE GREAT WHITE HOPE ★   20th Century-Fox, 1970
MALCOLM X (FD)   1972 (voice)
THE MAN   Paramount, 1972
CLAUDINE   20th Century-Fox, 1974
DEADLY HERO   Avco Embassy, 1976
THE RIVER NIGER   Cine Artists, 1976
THE BINGO LONG TRAVELING ALL-STARS AND MOTOR KINGS
   Universal, 1976
SWASHBUCKLER   Universal, 1976
THE GREATEST   Columbia, 1977
EXORCIST II: THE HERETIC   Warner Bros., 1977
THE LAST REMAKE OF BEAU GESTE   Universal, 1977
STAR WARS   20th Century-Fox, 1977 (voice; uncredited)
A PIECE OF THE ACTION   Warner Bros., 1977
THE GREATEST THING THAT ALMOST HAPPENED (TF)
   Charles Fries Productions, 1977
JESUS OF NAZARETH (MS)   Sir Lew Grade Productions/ITC,
   1978, British-Italian
ROOTS: THE NEXT GENERATIONS (MS)
   Wolper Productions, 1979
THE BUSHIDO BLADE   *THE BLOODY BUSHIDO BLADE*
   Aquarius, 1979, Japanese
THE EMPIRE STRIKES BACK   20th Century-Fox,
   1980 (voice; uncredited)
GUYANA TRAGEDY: THE STORY OF JIM JONES (TF)
   The Konigsberg Company, 1980
CONAN THE BARBARIAN   Universal, 1982
RETURN OF THE JEDI   20th Century-Fox, 1983 (voice; uncredited)
THE LAS VEGAS STRIP WARS (TF)   George Englund
   Productions, 1984
THE ATLANTA CHILD MURDERS (MS)   Mann-Rafshoon
   Productions/Finnegan Associates, 1985
SOUL MAN   New World, 1986
MATEWAN   Cinecom, 1987
ALLAN QUATERMAIN AND THE LOST CITY OF GOLD
   Cannon, 1987
GARDENS OF STONE   TriStar, 1987
COMING TO AMERICA   Paramount, 1988
THREE FUGITIVES   Buena Vista, 1989
FIELD OF DREAMS   Universal, 1989
BEST OF THE BEST   Taurus Entertainment/SVS Films, 1989
THE HUNT FOR RED OCTOBER   Paramount, 1990
LAST FLIGHT OUT (TF)   The Manheim Company/Co-Star
   Entertainment/NBC Productions, 1990
HEATWAVE (CTF)   The Avnet-Kerner Company/
   Propaganda Films, 1990
THE LAST ELEPHANT (CTF)   RHI Entertainment/Qintex
   Entertainment, 1990

THE AMBULANCE   Triumph Releasing Corporation, 1991
SNEAKERS   Universal, 1992
PATRIOT GAMES   Paramount, 1992
SOMMERSBY   Warner Bros., 1993
THE METEOR MAN   MGM/UA, 1993
CLEAN SLATE   MGM/UA, 1994
THE LION KING (AF)   Buena Vista, 1994 (voice)
CLEAR AND PRESENT DANGER   Paramount, 1994

JANET JONES
A CHORUS LINE   Columbia, 1985
AMERICAN ANTHEM   Columbia, 1986
POLICE ACADEMY 5: ASSIGNMENT MIAMI BEACH
   Warner Bros., 1988

JEFFREY JONES
Agent: J. Michael Bloom & Associates - Los Angeles, 310/275-6800

AMADEUS   Orion, 1984
FERRIS BUELLER'S DAY OFF   Paramount, 1986
GEORGE WASHINGTON II: THE FORGING OF A NATION (TF)
   David Gerber Company/MGM TV, 1986
HOWARD THE DUCK   Universal, 1986
THE HANOI HILTON   Cannon, 1987
BEETLEJUICE   The Geffen Company/Warner Bros., 1988
WITHOUT A CLUE   Orion, 1988
WHO'S HARRY CRUMB?   TriStar, 1989
VALMONT   Orion, 1989, French
ENID IS SLEEPING   Vestron, 1990
DICK AND MARGE SAVE THE WORLD   Warner Bros., 1992
OUT ON A LIMB   Universal, 1992
ED WOOD   Buena Vista, 1994
HOUSEGUEST   Buena Vista, 1995

JENNIFER JONES
(Phyllis Isley)
b. March 2, 1919 - Tulsa, Oklahoma

NEW FRONTIER   Republic, 1939
DICK TRACY'S G-MEN   1939
THE SONG OF BERNADETTE ★★   20th Century-Fox, 1943
SINCE YOU WENT AWAY ✪   United Artists, 1944
LOVE LETTERS ★   Paramount, 1945
CLUNY BROWN   20th Century-Fox, 1946
DUEL IN THE SUN ★   Selznick International, 1946, British
PORTRAIT OF JENNIE   Selznick, 1948
WE WERE STRANGERS   Columbia, 1949
MADAME BOVARY   MGM, 1949
THE WILD HEART   *GONE TO EARTH*   RKO Radio, 1950, British
CARRIE   Paramount, 1952
RUBY GENTRY   20th Century-Fox, 1953
INDISCRETION OF AN AMERICAN WIFE   *STAZIONE TERMINI*
   Columbia, 1953, Italian-U.S.
BEAT THE DEVIL   United Artists, 1954, British-U.S.
LOVE IS A MANY-SPLENDORED THING ★
   20th Century-Fox, 1955
GOOD MORNING, MISS DOVE   20th Century-Fox, 1955
THE MAN IN THE GRAY FLANNEL SUIT   20th Century-Fox, 1956
THE BARRETTS OF WIMPOLE STREET   MGM, 1957
A FAREWELL TO ARMS   20th Century-Fox, 1957
TENDER IS THE NIGHT   20th Century-Fox, 1962
THE IDOL   Embassy, 1966, British
CULT OF THE DAMNED   *ANGEL ANGEL DOWN WE GO*   1970
THE TOWERING INFERNO   20th Century-Fox/Warner Bros., 1974

JILL JONES
GRAFFITI BRIDGE   Warner Bros., 1990

L.Q. JONES
THE WILD BUNCH   Warner Bros., 1969
THE BALLAD OF CABLE HOGUE   Warner Bros., 1970
THE HUNTING PARTY   United Artists, 1971
THE BROTHERHOOD OF SATAN   Columbia, 1971
MOTHER, JUGS & SPEED   20th Century-Fox, 1976
RIVER OF DEATH   Cannon, 1989, British
CASINO   Universal, 1995

O-LAN JONES
MARRIED TO THE MOB   Orion, 1988

QUINCY JONES
Agent: William Morris Agency - Beverly Hills, 310/274-7451

LISTEN UP: THE LIVES OF QUINCY JONES   Warner Bros., 1990

RENEE JONES
Agent: Harris & Goldberg - Los Angeles, 310/553-5200

JESSIE (TF)   Lindsay Wagner Productions/MGM-UA TV, 1984
FRIDAY THE 13TH, PART VI: JASON LIVES   Paramount, 1986

SHIRLEY JONES
b. March 31, 1934 - Smithton, Pennsylvania

OKLAHOMA!   Magna, 1955
CAROUSEL   20th Century-Fox, 1956
APRIL LOVE   20th Century-Fox, 1957
NEVER STEAL ANYTHING SMALL   1959
BOBBIKINS   20th Century-Fox, 1960, British
ELMER GANTRY ⊙⊙   United Artists, 1960
PEPE   Columbia, 1960
TWO RODE TOGETHER   Columbia, 1961
THE MUSIC MAN   Warner Bros., 1962
THE COURTSHIP OF EDDIE'S FATHER   MGM, 1963
A TICKLISH AFFAIR   MGM, 1963
DARK PURPOSE   L'INTRIGO   Universal, 1964, Italian-French-U.S.
BEDTIME STORY   Universal, 1964
FLUFFY   Universal, 1965
THE SECRET OF MY SUCCESS   MGM, 1965, British
SILENT NIGHT, LONELY NIGHT (TF)   Universal TV, 1969
THE HAPPY ENDING   United Artists, 1969
BUT I DON'T WANT TO GET MARRIED (TF)   Aaron Spelling
    Productions, 1970
THE CHEYENNE SOCIAL CLUB   National General, 1970
THE GIRLS OF HUNTINGTON HOUSE (TF)
    Lorimar Productions, 1973
THE FAMILY NOBODY WANTED (TF)   Universal TV, 1975
WINNER TAKE ALL (TF)   The Jozak Company, 1975
THE LIVES OF JENNY DOLAND (TF)   Ross Hunter Productions/
    Paramount TV, 1975
YESTERDAY'S CHILD (TF)   Paramount TV, 1977
WHO'LL SAVE OUR CHILDREN? (TF)   Time-Life Productions, 1978
EVENING IN BYZANTIUM (TF)   Universal TV, 1978
A LAST CRY FOR HELP (TF)   Myrt-Hal Productions/Viacom, 1979
BEYOND THE POSEIDON ADVENTURE   Warner Bros., 1979
THE CHILDREN OF AN LAC (TF)   Charles Fries Productions, 1980
INMATES: A LOVE STORY (TF)   Henerson-Hirsch Productions/
    Finnegan Associates, 1981

SIMON JONES
CLUB PARADISE   Warner Bros., 1986
MIRACLE ON 34TH STREET   20th Century Fox, 1994

TERRY JONES
AND NOW FOR SOMETHING COMPLETELY DIFFERENT
    1972, British
MONTY PYTHON AND THE HOLY GRAIL   Cinema 5, 1974,
    British (also co-directed)
MONTY PYTHON'S LIFE OF BRIAN   Orion/Warner Bros., 1979,
    British (also co-directed)
MONTY PYTHON LIVE AT THE HOLLYWOOD BOWL   Columbia,
    1982, British
MONTY PYTHON'S THE MEANING OF LIFE   Universal, 1983,
    British (also co-directed)
ERIK THE VIKING   Orion, 1989, British (also directed)

TOMMY LEE JONES
(Tom Lee Jones)
b. September 15, 1946 - San Saba, Texas
Agent: ICM - Beverly Hills, 310/550-4000

LOVE STORY   Paramount, 1970
JACKSON COUNTY JAIL   New World, 1976
CHARLIE'S ANGELS (TF)   Spelling-Goldberg Productions, 1976
SMASH-UP ON INTERSTATE 5 (TF)   Filmways, 1976
THE AMAZING HOWARD HUGHES (TF)   Roger Gimbel
    Productions/EMI TV, 1977
THE BETSY   Allied Artists, 1978
ROLLING THUNDER   American International, 1978
EYES OF LAURA MARS   Columbia, 1978
COAL MINER'S DAUGHTER   Universal, 1980
BACK ROADS   Warner Bros., 1981
THE EXECUTIONER'S SONG (TF)
    Film Communications Inc., 1982
NATE AND HAYES   SAVAGE ISLANDS   Paramount,
    1983, New Zealand
THE RIVER RAT   Paramount, 1984
BLACK MOON RISING   New World, 1986
YURI NOSENKO, KGB (CTF)   HBO Showcase/BBC/Premiere TV,
    1986, U.S.-British
BROKEN VOWS (TF)   Robert Halmi, Inc., 1987
THE BIG TOWN   Columbia, 1987
STORMY MONDAY   Atlantic Releasing Corporation, 1988, British
STRANGER ON MY LAND (TF)   Edgar J. Scherick Associates/Taft
    Entertainment TV, 1988
APRIL MORNING (TF)   Robert Halmi, Inc./Samuel
    Goldwyn TV, 1988
LONESOME DOVE (MS)   Motown Productions/Pangaea/Qintex
    Entertainment, Inc., 1989
THE PACKAGE   Orion, 1989
FIRE BIRDS   Buena Vista, 1990
JFK ⊙   Warner Bros., 1991
UNDER SIEGE   Warner Bros., 1992
THE FUGITIVE ⊙⊙   Warner Bros., 1993
HOUSE OF CARDS   Miramax Films, 1993
HEAVEN AND EARTH   Warner Bros., 1993
BLOWN AWAY   MGM/UA, 1994
THE CLIENT   Warner Bros., 1994
NATURAL BORN KILLERS   Warner Bros., 1994
BLUE SKY   Orion, 1994
COBB   Warner Bros., 1994
THE GOOD OLD BOYS (CTF)   Turner Network TV,
    1995 (also directed)
BATMAN FOREVER   Warner Bros., 1995

JACKIE JOSEPH
GREMLINS 2 THE NEW BATCH   Warner Bros., 1990

RONALD G. JOSEPH
Agent: Fred Amsel & Associates - Los Angeles, 213/939-1188

THE MILAGRO BEANFIELD WAR   Universal, 1988

ERLAND JOSEPHSON
Agent: Susan Smith & Associates - Beverly Hills, 213/852-4777

SO CLOSE TO LIFE   Janus, 1958, Swedish
HOUR OF THE WOLF   United Artists, 1968, Swedish
A PASSION   1969
CRIES AND WHISPERS   New World, 1972, British
SCENES FROM A MARRIAGE   Cinema 5, 1973, Swedish
FACE TO FACE   Paramount, 1976, Swedish
BEYOND EVIL   IFI-Scope III, 1980
AUTUMN SONATA   New World, 1978, West German
MONTENEGRO   MONTENEGRO, OR PIGS AND PEARLS
    Atlantic Releasing Corporation, 1981, Swedish
AFTER THE REHEARSAL   Triumph/Columbia, 1983,
    Swedish-West German
THE SACRIFICE   Orion Classics, 1986, Swedish-French
THE UNBEARABLE LIGHTNESS OF BEING   Orion, 1988
MEETING VENUS   Warner Bros., 1991
PROSPERO'S BOOKS   Miramax Films, 1991

LARRY JOSHUA
SUGAR HILL   20th Century Fox, 1994

LOUIS JOURDAN
(Louis Gendre)
b. June 19, 1919 - Marseille, France

LE CORSAIRE   1939, French
HER FIRST AFFAIR   *PREMIER RENDEZ-VOUS*   1941, French
L'ARLÉSIENNE   1942, French
FÉLICIE NANTEUIL   1942, French
LA VIE DE BOHEME   1942, French
THE HEART OF A NATION   *UNTEL PERE ET FILS*   1943, French
TWILIGHT   *LA BELLE AVENTURE*   1945, French
THE PARADINE CASE   Selznick Releasing, 1948
LETTER FROM AN UNKNOWN WOMAN   Universal, 1948
NO MINOR VICES   MGM, 1948
MADAME BOVARY   MGM, 1949
BIRD OF PARADISE   20th Century-Fox, 1951
ANNE OF THE INDIES   20th Century-Fox, 1951
THE HAPPY TIME   Columbia, 1952
RUE DE L'ESTRAPADE   1953, French
DECAMERON NIGHTS   RKO Radio, 1953
THREE COINS IN THE FOUNTAIN   20th Century-Fox, 1954
THE SWAN   MGM, 1956
JULIE   MGM, 1956
DANGEROUS EXILE   Rank, 1957, British
THE BRIDE IS MUCH TOO BEAUTIFUL   *LA MARIÉE EST TROP BELLE*   1958, French
GIGI   MGM, 1958
THE BEST OF EVERYTHING   20th Century-Fox, 1959
CAN-CAN   20th Century-Fox, 1960
AMAZONS OF ROME   *LE VEGINI DI ROMA*   1961, Italian-French
THE COUNT OF MONTE CRISTO   *LE COMTE DE MONTE CRISTO*   1961, French-Italian
DISORDER   *IL DISORDINE*   1962, Italian-French
THE V.I.P.s   MGM, 1963, British
MADE IN PARIS   MGM, 1966
TO COMMIT A MURDER   *PEAU D'ESPION*   Cinerama Releasing Corporation, 1967, French-Italian-West German
THE YOUNG REBEL   *CERVANTES*   American International, 1968, Spanish-French-Italian
A FLEA IN HER EAR   1968, U.S.-French
RUN A CROOKED MILE (TF)   Universal TV, 1969
THE COUNT OF MONTE CRISTO (TF)   Norman Rosemont Productions/ITC, 1975, U.S.-British
THE MAN IN THE IRON MASK (TF)   Norman Rosemont Productions/ITC, 1977, U.S.-British
SILVER BEARS   Columbia, 1978
SWAMP THING   Avco Embassy, 1982
OCTOPUSSY   MGM/UA, 1983, British
BEVERLY HILLS MADAM (TF)   NLS Productions/Orion TV, 1986

MILLA JOVOVICH
RETURN TO THE BLUE LAGOON   Columbia, 1991
KUFFS   Universal, 1992
CHAPLIN   TriStar, 1992, U.S.-British

ROBERT JOY
Agent: William Morris Agency - Beverly Hills, 310/274-7451

ATLANTIC CITY   Paramount, 1981
DESPERATELY SEEKING SUSAN   Orion, 1985
THE DARK HALF   Orion, 1993

MARIO JOYNER
HANGIN' WITH THE HOMEBOYS   New Line Cinema, 1991

ASHLEY JUDD
Agent: William Morris Agency - Beverly Hills, 310/274-7451

RUBY IN PARADISE   October Films, 1993
SMOKE   Miramax Films, 1995

ROBERT JUDD
CROSSROADS   Columbia, 1986

RAUL JULIA†
(Raul Rafael Carlos Julia y Arcelay)
b. March 9, 1944 - San Juan, Puerto Rico
d. October 24, 1994

STILETTO   Avco Embassy, 1969
THE PANIC IN NEEDLE PARK   20th Century-Fox, 1971
DEATH SCREAM   *THE WOMAN WHO CRIED MURDER* (TF) RSO Films, 1975
EYES OF LAURA MARS   Columbia, 1978
ONE FROM THE HEART   Columbia, 1982
THE ESCAPE ARTIST   Orion/Warner Bros., 1982
THE TEMPEST   Columbia, 1982
MUSSOLINI: THE UNTOLD STORY (MS)   Trian Productions, 1985
COMPROMISING POSITIONS   Paramount, 1985
KISS OF THE SPIDER WOMAN   Island Alive/FilmDallas, 1985, Brazilian-U.S.
FLORIDA STRAITS (CTF)   HBO Premiere Films/Robert Cooper Productions, 1986
THE MORNING AFTER   20th Century Fox, 1986
LA GRAN FIESTA   Jack R. Crosby/The Frank Moreno Company, 1986, Puerto Rican
THE ALAMO: 13 DAYS TO GLORY (TF)   Briggle, Hennessy, Carrothers Productions/The Finnegan Company/Fries Entertainment, 1987
RICHEST MAN IN THE WORLD: THE ARISTOTLE ONASSIS STORY (MS)   The Konigsberg-Sanitsky Company, 1988
THE PENITENT   Cineworld, 1988
TRADING HEARTS   Cineworld, 1988
MOON OVER PARADOR   Universal, 1988, U.S.-Brazilian
TEQUILA SUNRISE   Warner Bros., 1988
TANGO BAR   Beco Films/Zaga Films, 1988, Puerto Rican-Argentinian
ROMERO   Four Seasons Entertainment, 1989
MACK THE KNIFE   21st Century Distribution, 1989
ROGER CORMAN'S FRANKENSTEIN UNBOUND   *FRANKENSTEIN UNBOUND*   20th Century Fox, 1990
PRESUMED INNOCENT   Warner Bros., 1990
THE ROOKIE   Warner Bros., 1990
HAVANA   Universal, 1990 (uncredited)
THE ADDAMS FAMILY   Paramount, 1991
ADDAMS FAMILY VALUES   Paramount, 1993
STREET FIGHTER   Universal, 1994
DESPERADO   Columbia, 1995

JANET JULIAN
KING OF NEW YORK   New Line Cinema, 1990

GORDON JUMP
b. April 1, 1932 - Dayton, Ohio

CONQUEST OF THE PLANET OF THE APES 20th Century-Fox, 1972
HOUSE CALLS   Universal, 1978
RUBY AND OSWALD   *FOUR DAYS IN DALLAS* (TF) Alan Landsburg Productions, 1978
THE FURY   20th Century-Fox, 1978
ON FIRE (TF)   Robert Greenwald Productions, 1987
PERRY MASON: THE CASE OF THE LOST LOVE (TF)   The Fred Silverman Company/Strathmore Productions/Viacom, 1987

CALVIN JUNG
Agent: Fred Amsel & Associates - Los Angeles, 213/939-1188

AMERICAN NINJA 3: BLOOD HUNT   Cannon, 1989

JOHN JUNKIN
CHICAGO JOE AND THE SHOWGIRL   New Line Cinema, 1990

KATY JURADO
(Maria Cristina Jurado Garcia)
b. 1927 - Guadalajara, Mexico

THE BULLFIGHTER AND THE LADY   Republic, 1951
HIGH NOON   United Artists, 1952
ARROWHEAD   Paramount, 1953
BROKEN LANCE ✪   20th Century-Fox, 1954

THE RACERS   20th Century-Fox, 1955
TRIAL   MGM, 1955
TRAPEZE   United Artists, 1956
MAN FROM DEL RIO   1956
THE BADLANDERS   MGM, 1958
ONE-EYED JACKS   Paramount, 1961
BARABBAS   Columbia, 1962, Italian
SMOKY   20th Century-Fox, 1966
A COVENANT WITH DEATH   Warner Bros., 1967
STAY AWAY JOE   MGM, 1968
PAT GARRETT AND BILLY THE KID   MGM, 1973
EL ELEGIDO   1977, Mexican
LOS ALBANILES   1977, Mexican
EL RECURSO DEL METEDO   Azteca Films, 1978,
   Mexican-French-Cuban
THE CHILDREN OF SANCHEZ   Lone Star, 1978, U.S.-Mexican
EVITA PERON (TF)   Hartwest Productions/Zephyr
   Productions, 1981
UNDER THE VOLCANO   Universal, 1984

LINDA RAE JURGENS
TOP GUN   Paramount, 1986

JANE KACZMAREK
FALLING IN LOVE   Paramount, 1984
THE RIGHT OF THE PEOPLE (TF)   Big Name Films/Fries
   Entertainment, 1986
THE CHRISTMAS GIFT (TF)   Rosemont Productions/Sunn Classic
   Pictures, 1986
I'LL TAKE MANHATTAN (MS)   Steve Krantz Productions, 1987
THE THREE KINGS (TF)   Aaron Spelling Productions, 1987
SPOONER (CTF)   Pipeline Productions, 1989

ELAINE KAGAN
GOODFELLAS   Warner Bros., 1990
ANGIE   Buena Vista, 1994

DAVID KAGEN
Agent: Bauman, Hiller & Associates - Los Angeles, 213/857-6666

FRIDAY THE 13TH, PART VI: JASON LIVES   Paramount, 1986

RODNEY KAGEYAMA
VIBES   Columbia, 1988

STEVE KAHAN
Agent: Paradigm - Los Angeles, 310/277-4400

LETHAL WEAPON 2   Warner Bros., 1989
DEMOLITION MAN   Warner Bros., 1993
WILLY II: THE ADVENTURE HOME   Warner Bros., 1995

WOLF KAHLER
RAIDERS OF THE LOST ARK   Paramount, 1981

MADELINE KAHN
b. September 29, 1942 - Boston, Massachuesetts

WHAT'S UP, DOC?   Warner Bros., 1972
PAPER MOON ✪   Paramount, 1973
BLAZING SADDLES ✪   Warner Bros., 1974
YOUNG FRANKENSTEIN   20th Century-Fox, 1974
AT LONG LAST LOVE   20th Century-Fox, 1975
THE ADVENTURE OF SHERLOCK HOLMES' SMARTER BROTHER
   20th Century-Fox, 1975

WON TON TON, THE DOG WHO SAVED HOLLYWOOD
   Paramount, 1976
HIGH ANXIETY   20th Century-Fox, 1977
THE CHEAP DETECTIVE   Columbia, 1978
THE MUPPET MOVIE   AFD, 1979, British
SIMON   Orion/Warner Bros., 1980
FIRST FAMILY   Warner Bros., 1980
HAPPY BIRTHDAY, GEMINI   United Artists, 1980
WHOLLY MOSES   Columbia, 1980
HISTORY OF THE WORLD—PART 1   20th Century-Fox, 1981
SLAPSTICK OF ANOTHER KIND   SLAPSTICK   Entertainment
   Releasing Corporation/International Film Marketing, 1983
YELLOWBEARD   Orion, 1983, British
CITY HEAT   Warner Bros., 1984
CLUE   Paramount, 1985
MY LITTLE PONY - THE MOVIE (AF)   DEG, 1986 (voice)
AN AMERICAN TAIL (AF)   Universal, 1986 (voice)
BETSY'S WEDDING   Buena Vista, 1990
FOR RICHER, FOR POORER   FATHER, SON AND THE
   MISTRESS (CTF)   Citadel Entertainment Productions, 1992
LIFESAVERS   TriStar, 1994

TONI KALEM
BILLY GALVIN   Vestron, 1986

PATRICIA KALEMBER
Agent: Gersh Agency - Beverly Hills, 310/274-6611

LITTLE GIRL LOST (TF)   Marian Rees Associates, 1988
FLETCH LIVES   Universal, 1989
JACOB'S LADDER   TriStar, 1990

KAMAL
THE JERKY BOYS   Buena Vista, 1994

DANNY KAMEKONA
THE KARATE KID PART II   Columbia, 1986
ROBOTJOX   Triumph Releasing Corporation, 1990

DANA KAMINSKI
BIG   20th Century Fox, 1988

STEVEN KAMPMANN
CLUB PARADISE   Warner Bros., 1986

STEVE KANALY
McNELLY'S RANGERS   Warner Bros., 1995

SEAN KANAN
Agent: Harris & Goldberg - Los Angeles, 310/553-5200

THE KARATE KID PART III   Columbia, 1989
RICH GIRL   Studio Three, 1991

BRAD KANE
ALADDIN (AF)   Buena Vista, 1992 (voice)

CAROL KANE
b. June 18, 1952 - Cleveland, Ohio

IS THIS TRIP REALLY NECESSARY?   1970
CARNAL KNOWLEDGE   Avco Embassy, 1971
DESPERATE CHARACTERS   ITC, 1971
WEDDING IN WHITE   Avco Embassy, 1973, Canadian
THE LAST DETAIL   Columbia, 1973
DOG DAY AFTERNOON   Warner Bros., 1975
HESTER STREET ★   Midwest Films, 1975
HARRY AND WALTER GO TO NEW YORK   Columbia, 1976
ANNIE HALL   United Artists, 1977
THE WORLD'S GREATEST LOVER   20th Century-Fox, 1977
VALENTINO   United Artists, 1977, British
THE MAFU CAGE   MY SISTER, MY LOVE/THE CAGE
   Clouds Productions, 1978
THE MUPPET MOVIE   AFD, 1979, British

WHEN A STRANGER CALLS   Columbia, 1979
STRONG MEDICINE   1979
NORMAN LOVES ROSE   Atlantic Releasing Corporation,
    1981, Australian
BURNING RAGE (TF)   Gilbert Cates Productions, 1984
RACING WITH THE MOON   Paramount, 1984
JUMPIN' JACK FLASH   20th Century Fox, 1986
ISHTAR   Columbia, 1987
THE PRINCESS BRIDE   20th Century Fox, 1987
DROP-OUT MOTHER (TF)   Fries Entertainment/Comco
    Productions, 1988
STICKY FINGERS   Spectrafilm, 1988
LICENSE TO DRIVE   20th Century Fox, 1988
SCROOGED   Paramount, 1988
FLASHBACK   Paramount, 1990
MY BLUE HEAVEN   Warner Bros., 1990
THE LEMON SISTERS   Miramax , 1990
WHEN A STRANGER CALLS BACK (CTF)   Krost-Chapin
    Productions/The Producers Entertainment Group/MTE, 1993
ADDAMS FAMILY VALUES   Paramount, 1993
EVEN COWGIRLS GET THE BLUES   Fine Line Features/
    New Line Cinema, 1994

IVAN KANE

Agent: Judy Schoen & Associates - Los Angeles, 213/962-1950

PLATOON   Orion, 1986

JOHN KANI
SARAFINA!   Miramax Films/Buena Vista, 1992,
    South African-British-French

ALEXIS KANNER
b. May 2, 1952 - Luchon, France

REACH FOR GLORY   Royal Films International, 1963, British
CROSSPLOT   United Artists, 1969, British
GOODBYE GEMINI   Cinerama Releasing Corporation, 1970, British
CONNECTING ROOMS   1971, British
KINGS AND DESPERATE MEN   1983, Canadian (also directed)
NIGHTFALL   Concorde, 1988

WENDY KAPLAN
HALLOWEEN 5 - THE REVENGE OF MICHAEL MYERS
    Galaxy, 1989

SHASHI KAPOOR
THE DECEIVERS   Cinecom, 1988

VALERIE KAPRISKY
BREATHLESS   Orion, 1983

MITZI KAPTURE
Agent: David Shapira & Associates - Sherman Oaks, 818/906-0322

ANGEL III   New World, 1988

RON KARABATSOS
RICH GIRL   Studio Three, 1991

JAMES KAREN
POLTERGEIST   MGM/UA, 1982
INVADERS FROM MARS   Cannon, 1986
WALL STREET   20th Century Fox, 1987
RETURN OF THE LIVING DEAD PART II   Lorimar, 1988
SHATTERED DREAMS (TF)   Roger Gimbel Productions/Carolco
    Television Productions, 1990
THE UNBORN   Califilm, 1991

RITA KARIN
THE BIG FIX   Universal, 1978
ENEMIES, A LOVE STORY   20th Century Fox, 1989

JOHN KARLEN
b. May 28, 1933 - New York, New York
Agent: Gersh Agency - Beverly Hills, 310/274-6611

IMPULSE   20th Century Fox, 1984
RACING WITH THE MOON   Paramount, 1984
WELCOME HOME, BOBBY (TF)   Titus Productions, 1986
NATIVE SON   Cinecom, 1986
DADDY (TF)   Robert Greenwald Productions, 1987
THE COVER GIRL AND THE COP (TF)   Barry & Enright
    Productions, 1989
BABYCAKES (TF)   Konigsberg-Sanitsky Productions, 1989
SURF NINJAS   New Line Cinema, 1993
CAGNEY & LACEY: THE RETURN (TF)   The Rosenzweig
    Company, 1994
CAGNEY & LACEY: TOGETHER AGAIN (TF)   The Rosenzweig
    Company, 1995

SARAH ROSE KARR
BEETHOVEN   Universal, 1992

ALEX KARRAS
b. July 15, 1935 - Gary, Indiana

PAPER LION   United Artists, 1968
HARDCASE (TF)   Hanna-Barbera Productions, 1972
THE 500 POUND JERK (TF)   Wolper Productions, 1973
BLAZING SADDLES   Warner Bros., 1974
BABE (TF)   MGM-TV, 1975
MULLIGAN'S STEW (TF)   Paramount TV, 1977
MAD BULL (TF)   Steckler Productions/Filmways, 1977
CENTENNIAL (MS)   Universal TV, 1978
FM   Universal, 1978
WHEN TIME RAN OUT   Warner Bros., 1980
NOBODY'S PERFEKT   Columbia, 1981
VICTOR/VICTORIA   MGM/United Artists, 1982
AGAINST ALL ODDS   Columbia, 1984

TCHEKY KARYO
SORCERESS   European Classics, 1988, French
THE BEAR   TriStar, 1988, French
NOSTRADAMUS   Orion Classics, 1994, British
BAD BOYS   Columbia, 1995

LINDA KASH
ERNEST RIDES AGAIN   Emshell Producers Group, 1993

DAPHNA KASTNER
JULIA HAS TWO LOVERS   South Gate Entertainment, 1991

ANDREAS KATSULAS
NEXT OF KIN   Warner Bros., 1989
COMMUNION   MCEG, 1989
TRUE IDENTITY   Buena Vista, 1991
BLAME IT ON THE BELLBOY   Buena Vista, 1992, British
THE FUGITIVE   Warner Bros., 1993

NICKY KATT
THE CURE   Universal, 1995

WILLIAM KATT
Agent: APA - Los Angeles, 310/273-0744

CARRIE   United Artists, 1976
FIRST LOVE   Paramount, 1977
BIG WEDNESDAY   Warner Bros., 1978
BUTCH AND SUNDANCE: THE EARLY DAYS
    20th Century-Fox, 1979
THE GREATEST AMERICAN HERO (TF)   Stephen J. Cannell
    Productions, 1981
BABY—SECRET OF THE LOST LEGEND   Buena Vista, 1985
PERRY MASON RETURNS (TF)   Intermedia Productions/Strathmore
    Productions/Viacom Productions, 1985
HOUSE   New World, 1986

PERRY MASON: THE CASE OF THE NOTORIOUS NUN (TF)
Intermedia Productions/Strathmore Productions/Viacom
Productions, 1986
PERRY MASON: THE CASE OF THE SHOOTING STAR (TF)
Intermedia Productions/Strathmore Productions/Viacom
Productions, 1986
PERRY MASON: THE CASE OF THE SCANDALOUS
SCOUNDREL (TF)   The Fred Silverman Company/Strathmore
Productions/Viacom, 1987
PERRY MASON: THE CASE OF THE LOST LOVE (TF)   The Fred
Silverman Company/Strathmore Productions/Viacom, 1987
PERRY MASON: THE CASE OF THE MURDERED MADAM (TF)
The Fred Silverman Company/Strathmore Productions/
Viacom, 1987
PERRY MASON: THE CASE OF THE SINISTER SPIRIT (TF)
The Fred Silverman Company/Strathmore Productions/Viacom
Productions, 1987
PERRY MASON: THE CASE OF THE AVENGING ACE (TF)   The
Fred Silverman Company/Strathmore Productions/Viacom, 1988
PERRY MASON: THE CASE OF THE LADY IN THE LAKE (TF)
The Fred Silverman Company/Strathmore Productions/
Viacom, 1988
SWIMSUIT (TF)   Musifilm Prod.s/American First Run Studios, 1989
NAKED OBSESSION   Concorde, 1991

ERIKA KATZ
BIG   20th Century Fox, 1988

OMRI KATZ
MATINEE   Universal, 1993
HOCUS POCUS   Buena Vista, 1993

JONATHAN KAUFER
b. March 14, 1955 - Los Angeles, California

ALWAYS   Samuel Goldwyn Company, 1985

CHRISTINE KAUFMANN
BAGDAD CAFE   Island Pictures, 1987, West German-U.S.

CAROLINE KAVA
NOBODY'S CHILD (TF)   Joseph Feury Productions/Gaylord
Production Company, 1986
BODY OF EVIDENCE (TF)   CBS Entertainment, 1988
LITTLE NIKITA   Columbia, 1988
BORN ON THE FOURTH OF JULY   Universal, 1989

JULIE KAVNER
BAD MEDICINE   20th Century Fox, 1985
HANNAH AND HER SISTERS   Orion, 1986
RADIO DAYS   Orion, 1987
NEW YORK STORIES   Buena Vista, 1989
AWAKENINGS   Columbia, 1990
ALICE   Orion, 1990
THIS IS MY LIFE   20th Century Fox, 1992
I'LL DO ANYTHING   Columbia, 1994
DON'T DRINK THE WATER (TF)   ABC, 1994
FORGET PARIS   Columbia, 1995

CHARLES KAY
HENRY V   Samuel Goldwyn Company, 1989, British

HADLEY KAY
THE CARE BEARS MOVIE II: A NEW GENERATION (AF)
Columbia, 1986, Canadian (voice)

NORMAN KAYE
CACTUS   Spectrafilm, 1986, Australian

STUBBY KAYE
b. November 11, 1918 - New York, New York

TAXI   20th Century-Fox, 1953
GUYS AND DOLLS   MGM, 1955
LI'L ABNER   Paramount, 1959

40 POUNDS OF TROUBLE   Universal, 1963
SEX AND THE SINGLE GIRL   Warner Bros., 1964
CAT BALLOU   Columbia, 1965
THE WAY WEST   United Artists, 1967
SWEET CHARITY   Universal, 1969
THE COCKEYED COWBOYS OF CALICO COUNTY   MGM, 1970
THE DIRTIEST GIRL I EVER MET   1973
SIX PACK ANNIE   1975
WHO FRAMED ROGER RABBIT   Buena Vista, 1988

LAINIE KAZAN
b. May 15, 1942 - New York, New York

MY FAVORITE YEAR   MGM/UA, 1982
THE DELTA FORCE   Cannon, 1986
BEACHES   Buena Vista, 1988
RUDE AWAKENING   Orion, 1989
ETERNITY   Academy Entertainment, 1990
29TH STREET   20th Century Fox, 1991
HONEYMOON IN VEGAS   Columbia, 1992
THE CEMETERY CLUB   Buena Vista, 1993

TIM KAZURINSKY
MY BODYGUARD   20th Century-Fox, 1980
SOMEWHERE IN TIME   Universal, 1980
CONTINENTAL DIVIDE   Universal, 1981
NEIGHBORS   Columbia, 1982
A BILLION FOR BORIS   Comworld, 1985
POLICE ACADEMY 2: THEIR FIRST ASSIGNMENT
Warner Bros., 1985
POLICE ACADEMY 3: BACK IN TRAINING   Warner Bros., 1986
ABOUT LAST NIGHT...   TriStar, 1986
POLICE ACADEMY 4: CITIZENS ON PATROL   Warner Bros., 1987

JAMES KEACH
b. December 7 - Flushing, New York
Agent: Metropolitan Talent Agency - Los Angeles, 213/857-4500

SUNBURST   Atlantic Releasing Corporation, 1976
DEATH PLAY   New Line, 1976
CANNONBALL   New World, 1976
WELCOME TO L.A.   United Artists/Lions Gate, 1977
KILL ME IF YOU CAN (TF)   Columbia TV, 1977
FM   Universal, 1978
COMES A HORSEMAN   United Artists, 1978
LACY AND THE MISSISSIPPI QUEEN (TF)   Lawrence Gordon
Productions/Paramount TV, 1978
LIKE NORMAL PEOPLE (TF)   Christiana Productions/
20th Century-Fox TV, 1979
HURRICANE   Paramount, 1979
THE LONG RIDERS   United Artists, 1980
THOU SHALT NOT KILL (TF)   Edgar J. Scherick Associates/
Warner Bros. TV, 1982
LOVE LETTERS   New World, 1983
NATIONAL LAMPOON'S VACATION   Warner Bros., 1983
THE RAZOR'S EDGE   Columbia, 1984
MOVING VIOLATIONS   20th Century Fox, 1985
STAND ALONE   New World, 1985
WILDCATS   Warner Bros., 1986
THE EXPERTS   Paramount, 1989

STACY KEACH
(Walter Stacy Keach, Jr.)
b. June 2, 1941 - Savannah, Georgia
Agent: William Morris Agency - Beverly Hills, 310/274-7451

THE HEART IS A LONELY HUNTER   Warner Bros., 1968
END OF THE ROAD   Allied Artists, 1970
THE TRAVELING EXECUTIONER   MGM, 1970
BREWSTER McCLOUD   MGM, 1970
DOC   United Artists, 1971
FAT CITY   Columbia, 1972
THE NEW CENTURIONS   Columbia, 1972
THE LIFE AND TIMES OF JUDGE ROY BEAN   National General, 1972
GOODNIGHT, MIKE   1972
LUTHER   American Film Theatre, 1973, British
THE GRAVY TRAIN   *THE DION BROTHERS*   Columbia, 1974
ALL THE KIND STRANGERS (TF)   Cinemation, 1974

WATCHED! 1974
CONDUCT UNBECOMING Allied Artists, 1975, British
JAMES MICHENER'S DYNASTY (TF) David Paradine TV, 1976
STREET PEOPLE 1976, U.S.-Italian
THE KILLER INSIDE ME Warner Bros., 1976
THE SQUEEZE Warner Bros., 1977, British
JESUS OF NAZARETH (MS) Sir Lew Grade Productions/ITC,
    1978, British-Indian
SLAVE OF THE CANNIBAL GOD 1978
GRAY LADY DOWN Universal, 1978
TWO SOLITUDES New World-Mutual, 1978, Canadian
UP IN SMOKE Paramount, 1978
THE NINTH CONFIGURATION *TWINKLE, TWINKLE,
    "KILLER" KANE* Warner Bros., 1980
THE LONG RIDERS United Artists, 1980
CHEECH & CHONG'S NICE DREAMS Columbia, 1981
ROAD GAMES Avco Embassy, 1981, Australian
BUTTERFLY Analysis, 1982, U.S.-Canadian
THAT CHAMPIONSHIP SEASON Cannon, 1982
PRINCESS DAISY (MS) NBC Productions/Steve Krantz
    Productions, 1983
MISTRAL'S DAUGHTER (MS) Steve Krantz Productions/R.T.L.
    Productions/Antenne-2, 1984, U.S.-French
INTIMATE STRANGERS (TF) Nederlander TV and Film
    Productions/Telepictures Productions, 1986
THE RETURN OF MICKEY SPILLANE'S MIKE HAMMER (TF)
    Jay Bernstein Productions/Columbia TV, 1986
CLASS OF 1999 Vestron, 1989
MICKEY SPILLANE'S MIKE HAMMER: MURDER TAKES ALL (TF)
    Jay Bernstein Productions/Columbia TV, 1989
FALSE IDENTITY RKO Pictures, 1990

MARIE KEAN

THE DEAD Vestron, 1987

STACI KEANAN

LISA MGM/UA, 1990

JAMES KEANE

CANNERY ROW MGM/United Artists, 1982
DICK TRACY Buena Vista, 1990

DIANE KEATON
(Diane Hall)
b. January 5, 1946 - Los Angeles, California
Agent: William Morris Agency - Beverly Hills, 310/274-7451

LOVERS AND OTHER STRANGERS Cinerama Releasing
    Corporation, 1970
THE GODFATHER Paramount, 1972
PLAY IT AGAIN, SAM Paramount, 1972
SLEEPER United Artists, 1973
THE GODFATHER, PART II Paramount, 1974
LOVE AND DEATH United Artists, 1975
I WILL, I WILL..FOR NOW 20th Century-Fox, 1976
HARRY AND WALTER GO TO NEW YORK Columbia, 1976
LOOKING FOR MR. GOODBAR Paramount, 1977
ANNIE HALL ★★ United Artists, 1977
INTERIORS United Artists, 1978
MANHATTAN United Artists, 1979
REDS ★ Paramount, 1981
SHOOT THE MOON MGM/United Artists, 1982
THE LITTLE DRUMMER GIRL Warner Bros., 1984
MRS. SOFFEL MGM/UA, 1984
CRIMES OF THE HEART DEG, 1986
BABY BOOM MGM/UA, 1987
RADIO DAYS Orion, 1987
THE GOOD MOTHER Buena Vista, 1988
THE LEMON SISTERS Miramax Films, 1990
THE GODFATHER, PART III Paramount, 1990
FATHER OF THE BRIDE Buena Vista, 1991
RUNNING MATES (CTF) HBO Pictures/Marvin Worth
    Productions, 1992
MANHATTAN MURDER MYSTERY TriStar, 1993
LOOK WHO'S TALKING NOW TriStar, 1993 (voice)
AMELIA EARHART - THE FINAL FLIGHT (CTF)
    Turner Network TV, 1994
FATHER OF THE BRIDE 2 Buena Vista, 1995

MICHAEL KEATON
(Michael Douglas)
b. September 5, 1951 - Coraopolis, Pennsylvania
Agent: CAA - Beverly Hills, 310/288-4545

NIGHT SHIFT The Ladd Company/Warner Bros., 1982
MR. MOM 20th Century-Fox, 1983
JOHNNY DANGEROUSLY 20th Century Fox, 1984
GUNG HO Paramount, 1986
TOUCH AND GO TriStar, 1987
THE SQUEEZE TriStar, 1987
BEETLEJUICE The Geffen Company/Warner Bros., 1988
CLEAN AND SOBER Warner Bros., 1988
THE DREAM TEAM Universal, 1989
BATMAN Warner Bros., 1989
PACIFIC HEIGHTS 20th Century Fox, 1990
ONE GOOD COP Buena Vista, 1991
BATMAN RETURNS Warner Bros., 1992
MUCH ADO ABOUT NOTHING Samuel Goldwyn Company,
    1993, British-U.S.
MY LIFE Columbia, 1993
THE PAPER Universal, 1994
SPEECHLESS MGM/UA, 1994

ELE KEATS

NEWSIES Buena Vista, 1992

RICHARD KEATS

APEX Republic Pictures, 1994

LILA KEDROVA
b. 1918 - Leningrad, U.S.S.R.

NO WAY BACK *WEG OHNE UMKEHR* 1953, West German
LE DEFROQUÉ 1954, French
RAZZIA *RAZZIA SUR LA CHNOUFF* 1955, French
DES GENS SANS IMPORTANCE 1956, French
THE LOVEMAKER *CALLE MAYOR* 1956, Spanish
MODIGLIANI OF MONTPARNASSE *MONTPARNASSE 19*
    1958, French
THE FEMALE *LA FEMME ET LA PANTIN* 1959, French-Italian
ZORBA THE GREEK ◊◊ 20th Century-Fox/International Classics,
    1964, Greek
A HIGH WIND IN JAMAICA 20th Century-Fox, 1965, U.S.-British
TORN CURTAIN Universal, 1966
PENELOPE MGM, 1966
THE GIRL WHO COULDN'T SAY NO *TENDERLY* Italnoleggio,
    1968, Italian
THE KREMLIN LETTER 20th Century-Fox, 1970
ESCAPE TO THE SUN Cinevision, 1972,
    Israeli-West German-French
UNDERCOVERS HERO *SOFT BEDS AND HARD BATTLES*
    United Artists, 1975, British
PERCHE?! 1975, Italian
ELIZA'S HOROSCOPE 1975, Canadian
THE TENANT Paramount, 1976, French-U.S.
MARCH OR DIE Columbia, 1977, British
MOI FLEUR BLEUE 1977, French
WIDOWS' NEST 1977, U.S.-Spanish
LE CAVALEUR CCFC, 1979, French
TELL ME A RIDDLE Filmways, 1980
SWORD OF THE VALIANT Cannon, 1982, British

ANDREW KEEGAN

THE SKATEBOARD KID II Concorde, 1995

KARI KEEGAN

JASON GOES TO HELL—THE FINAL FRIDAY
    New Line Cinema, 1993

HOWARD KEEL
(Harry Clifford Leek)
b. April 13, 1917 - Gillespie, Illinois
Agent: Abrams Artists & Associates - Los Angeles, 310/859-0625

HIDEOUT *THE SMALL VOICE* Republic, 1949
ANNIE GET YOUR GUN MGM, 1950
PAGAN LOVE SONG MGM, 1950
THREE GUYS NAMED MIKE MGM, 1950
SHOW BOAT MGM, 1951
TEXAS CARNIVAL MGM, 1951
CALLAWAY WENT THATAWAY MGM, 1952
LOVELY TO LOOK AT MGM, 1952
DESPERATE SEARCH MGM, 1952
RIDE VAQUERO! MGM, 1953
FAST COMPANY MGM, 1953
I LOVE MELVIN MGM, 1953
CALAMITY JANE Warner Bros., 1953
KISS ME KATE MGM, 1953
ROSE MARIE MGM, 1954
SEVEN BRIDES FOR SEVEN BROTHERS MGM, 1954
DEEP IN MY HEART MGM, 1954
JUPITER'S DARLING MGM, 1955
KISMET MGM, 1955
FLOODS OF FEAR Universal, 1959, British
THE BIG FISHERMAN Buena Vista, 1959
ARMORED COMMAND Allied Artists, 1961
DAY OF THE TRIFFIDS Allied Artists, 1963, British
THE MAN FROM BUTTON WILLOW (AF) Animation Filmmakers
   Distribution, 1965 (voice)
WACO Paramount, 1966
RED TOMAHAWK Paramount, 1967
THE WAR WAGON Universal, 1967
ARIZONA BUSHWHACKERS Paramount, 1968
THAT'S ENTERTAINMENT! III (FD) MGM/UA, 1994

GEOFFREY KEEN
HIS EXCELLENCY General Film Distributors, 1950
GENEVIEVE 1953
THE LONG ARM 1956
NO LOVE FOR JOHNNIE Embassy, 1961, British
THE SPIRAL ROAD Universal, 1962
LIVE NOW, PAY LATER 1962, British
THE HEROES OF TELEMARK Columbia, 1965, British
DR. ZHIVAGO MGM, 1965, British
BORN FREE Columbia, 1966, British
TASTE THE BLOOD OF DRACULA Warner Bros., 1970, British
LIVING FREE Columbia, 1971, British
DOOMWATCH Avco Embassy, 1972, British
THE SPY WHO LOVED ME United Artists, 1977, British-U.S.
MOONRAKER United Artists, 1979, British-French
FOR YOUR EYES ONLY MGM/UA, 1981, British
A VIEW TO A KILL MGM/UA, 1948, British
THE LIVING DAYLIGHTS MGM/UA, 1987, British

CATHERINE KEENER
SURVIVAL QUEST MGM/UA, 1990

MATT KEESLAR
THE RUN OF THE COUNTRY Columbia, 1995

HARVEY KEITEL
b. May 13, 1939 - Brooklyn, New York
Agent: William Morris Agency - Beverly Hills, 310/274-7451

WHO'S THAT KNOCKING AT MY DOOR? Joseph Brenner
   Associates, 1968
MEAN STREETS Warner Bros., 1973
ALICE DOESN'T LIVE HERE ANYMORE Warner Bros., 1975
SHINING STAR *THAT'S THE WAY OF THE WORLD*
   United Artists, 1975
TAXI DRIVER Columbia, 1976
MOTHER, JUGS & SPEED 20th Century-Fox, 1976
BUFFALO BILL AND THE INDIANS or SITTING BULL'S
   HISTORY LESSON United Artists, 1976
WELCOME TO L.A. United Artists/Lions Gate, 1977

THE DUELLISTS Paramount, 1977, British
FINGERS Brut Productions, 1978
BLUE COLLAR Universal, 1978
EAGLE'S WING International Picture Show, 1979, British
DEATHWATCH Quartet, 1980, French-West German
SATURN 3 AFD, 1980
BAD TIMING/A SENSUAL OBSESSION World Northal,
   1980, British
THE BORDER Universal, 1982
LA NUIT DE VARENNES Triumph/Columbia, 1982, French-Italian
EXPOSED MGM/UA, 1983
CORRUPT *ORDER OF DEATH* New Line Cinema, 1983, Italian
DREAM ONE Columbia, 1984, British-French
FALLING IN LOVE Paramount, 1984
CAMORRA *UN COMPLICATO INTRIGO DI DONNE,*
   VICOLI E DELITTI Cannon, 1986, Italian
OFF BEAT Buena Vista, 1986
THE MEN'S CLUB Atlantic Releasing Corporation, 1986
WISE GUYS MGM/UA, 1986
THE PICK-UP ARTIST 20th Century Fox, 1987
DEAR AMERICA: LETTERS HOME FROM VIETNAM (FD)
   Taurus Entertainment, 1987 (voice)
THE LAST TEMPTATION OF CHRIST Universal, 1988
THE JANUARY MAN MGM/UA, 1989
THE TWO JAKES Paramount, 1990
MORTAL THOUGHTS Columbia, 1991
THELMA & LOUISE MGM-Pathe Communications, 1991
BUGSY ✪ TriStar, 1991
SISTER ACT Buena Vista, 1992
RESERVOIR DOGS Miramax Films, 1992
THE BAD LIEUTENANT Live Entertainment, 1992
POINT OF NO RETURN Warner Bros., 1993
RISING SUN 20th Century Fox, 1993
THE PIANO Miramax Films, 1993, New Zealand-French
DANGEROUS GAME MGM/UA, 1993
MONKEY TROUBLE New Line Cinema, 1994
PULP FICTION Miramax Films, 1994
IMAGINARY CRIMES Warner Bros., 1994
SMOKE Miramax Films, 1995

BRIAN KEITH
b. November 14, 1921 - Bayonne, New Jersey
Agent: The Blake Agency - Beverly Hills, 310/246-0241

PIED PIPER MALONE Paramount, 1924
ARROWHEAD Paramount, 1953
ALASKA SEAS Paramount, 1954
THE VIOLENT MEN Columbia, 1955
TIGHT SPOT Columbia, 1955
FIVE AGAINST THE HOUSE Columbia, 1955
STORM CENTER Columbia, 1956
NIGHTFALL Columbia, 1957
RUN OF THE ARROW 20th Century-Fox, 1957
CHICAGO CONFIDENTIAL 1957
FORT DOBBS Warner Bros., 1958
SIERRA BARON 20th Century-Fox, 1958
THE YOUNG PHILADELPHIANS Warner Bros., 1959
TEN WHO DARED Buena Vista, 1960
THE PARENT TRAP Buena Vista, 1961
TRIGGER HAPPY *THE DEADLY COMPANIONS* 1961
MOON PILOT 1962
SAVAGE SAM 1963
THE RAIDERS Universal, 1964
A TIGER WALKS 1964
THE PLEASURE SEEKERS 20th Century-Fox, 1965
THE HALLELUJAH TRAIL United Artists, 1965
THOSE CALLOWAYS 1965
THE RUSSIANS ARE COMING, THE RUSSIANS ARE COMING
   United Artists, 1966
THE RARE BREED Universal, 1966
NEVADA SMITH Paramount, 1966
REFLECTIONS IN A GOLDEN EYE Warner Bros., 1967
WITH SIX YOU GET EGGROLL National General, 1968
KRAKATOA, EAST OF JAVA *VOLCANO* Cinerama Releasing
   Corporation, 1969
GAILY, GAILY United Artists, 1969
SUPPOSE THEY GAVE A WAR AND NOBODY CAME?
   Cinerama Releasing Corporation, 1970

THE McKENZIE BREAK   United Artists, 1970
SOMETHING BIG   National General, 1971
SCANDALOUS JOHN   Buena Vista, 1971
THE YAKUZA   Warner Bros., 1975
THE WIND AND THE LION   MGM/UA, 1975
THE QUEST (TF)   David Gerber Company/Columbia TV, 1976
JOE PANTHER   Artists Creation & Associates, 1976
NICKELODEON   Columbia, 1976
HOOPER   Warner Bros., 1978
METEOR   American International, 1979
EAGLE'S WING   International Picture Show, 1979, British
THE MOUNTAIN MEN   Columbia, 1980
CHARLIE CHAN AND THE CURSE OF THE DRAGON QUEEN
   American Cinema, 1981
SHARKY'S MACHINE   Orion/Warner Bros., 1981
HARDCASTLE AND McCORMICK (TF)   Stephen J. Cannell
   Productions, 1983
MURDER, SHE WROTE (TF)   Universal TV, 1984
THE ALAMO: 13 DAYS TO GLORY (TF)   Briggle, Hennessy,
   Carrothers Productions/The Finnegan Company/Fries
   Entertainment, 1987
DEATH BEFORE DISHONOR   New World, 1987
YOUNG GUNS   20th Century Fox, 1988
WELCOME HOME   Columbia, 1989
LADY IN A CORNER (TF)   Sagaponack Films/Pantheon Pictures/
   Allen Leicht Productions/Fries Entertainment, 1989

DAVID KEITH
b. May 8, 1954 - Knoxville, Tennessee
Agent: William Morris Agency - Beverly Hills, 310/274-7451

THE ROSE   20th Century-Fox, 1979
BACK ROADS   Warner Bros., 1981
AN OFFICER AND A GENTLEMAN   Paramount, 1982
RED DAWN   MGM/UA, 1984
IF TOMORROW COMES (MS)   CBS Entertainment, 1986
WHITE OF THE EYE   Palisades Entertainment, 1987, British
HEARTBREAK HOTEL   Buena Vista, 1988
GUTS AND GLORY: THE RISE AND FALL OF OLLIE NORTH (MS)
   Mike Robe Productions/Papazian-Hirsch Entertainment, 1989
THE TWO JAKES   Paramount, 1990
OFF AND RUNNING   Orion, 1991
MAJOR LEAGUE II   Warner Bros., 1994
XXX'S & OOO'S (TF)   Moving Target Productions/New World
   Entertainment, 1994

TINA KELLEGHER
THE SNAPPER   Miramax Films, 1993, British

MARTHE KELLER
FUNERAL IN BERLIN   Paramount, 1966, British
THE DEVIL BY THE TAIL   *LE DIABLE PAR LA QUEUE*
   Lopert, 1969, French
GIVE HER THE MOON   *LES CAPRICES DE MARIE*
   United Artists, 1970, French
LA VIEILLE FILLE   1971, French
ELLE COURT ELLE COURT LA BANLIEU   1973, French
LA RAISON DU PLUS FOU   Gaumont, 1973, French
AND NOW MY LOVE   *TOUTE UNE VIE*   Avco Embassy,
   1974, French-Italian
DOWN THE ANCIENT STAIRS   *PER LE ANTICHE SCALE*
   20th Century-Fox, 1975, Italian-French
LE GUEPIER   1976, French
MARATHON MAN   Paramount, 1976
BLACK SUNDAY   Paramount, 1976
BOBBY DEERFIELD   Columbia, 1977
FEDORA   1978, West German-French
THE FORMULA   MGM/United Artists, 1980
THE AMATEUR   20th Century-Fox, 1981, Canadian
THE NIGHTMARE YEARS (CMS)   Consolidated Productions, 1989

SALLY KELLERMAN
b. June 2, 1938 - Long Beach, California
Agent: Gersh Agency - Beverly Hills, 310/274-6611

REFORM SCHOOL GIRL   American International, 1959
THE THIRD DAY   Warner Bros., 1965
THE BOSTON STRANGLER   20th Century-Fox, 1968

THE APRIL FOOLS   National General, 1969
M*A*S*H ✪   20th Century-Fox, 1970
BREWSTER McCLOUD   MGM, 1970
LAST OF THE RED HOT LOVERS   Paramount, 1972
A REFLECTION OF FEAR   Columbia, 1973, British
LOST HORIZON   Columbia, 1973
SLITHER   MGM, 1973
RAFFERTY AND THE GOLD DUST TWINS   Warner Bros., 1975
THE BIG BUS   Paramount, 1976
WELCOME TO L.A.   United Artists/Lions Gate, 1977
MAGEE AND THE LADY   *SHE'LL BE SWEET* (TF)
   Australian Broadcasting Commission/Trans-Atlantic Enterprises,
   1979, Australian
A LITTLE ROMANCE   Orion/Warner Bros., 1979, U.S.-French
FATAL ATTRACTION   *HEAD ON*   Greentree Productions,
   1980, Canadian
FOXES   United Artists, 1980
LOVING COUPLES   20th Century-Fox, 1980
SERIAL   Paramount, 1980
MOVING VIOLATIONS   20th Century Fox, 1985
SECRET WEAPONS (TF)   Goodman-Rosen Productions/
   ITC Productions, 1985
BACK TO SCHOOL   Orion, 1986
THAT'S LIFE!   Columbia, 1986
MEATBALLS III   *SUMMER JOB*   TMS Pictures, 1986, Canadian
YOU CAN'T HURRY LOVE   MCEG, 1989
BORIS AND NATASHA   New Line Cinema, 1990
PRET-A-PORTER   Miramax Films, 1994

DEFOREST KELLEY
b. January 20, 1920 - Atlanta, Georgia
Agent: The Blake Agency - Beverly Hills, 310/246-0241

FEAR IN THE NIGHT   International Co-Productions, 1947, British
HOUSE OF BAMBOO   20th Century-Fox, 1955
WARLOCK   20th Century-Fox, 1959
JOHNNY RENO   Paramount, 1966
STAR TREK - THE MOTION PICTURE   Paramount, 1979
STAR TREK II: THE WRATH OF KHAN   Paramount, 1982
STAR TREK III: THE SEARCH FOR SPOCK   Paramount, 1984
STAR TREK IV: THE VOYAGE HOME   Paramount, 1986
STAR TREK V: THE FINAL FRONTIER   Paramount, 1989
STAR TREK VI: THE UNDISCOVERED COUNTRY
   Paramount, 1991

SHEILA KELLEY
Agent: UTA - Beverly Hills, 310/273-6700

THE FULFILLMENT OF MARY GRAY (TF)   Lee Caplin Productions/
   Indian Neck Entertainment, 1989
STAYING TOGETHER   Hemdale, 1989
BREAKING IN   Samuel Goldwyn Company, 1989
PURE LUCK   Universal, 1991
SINGLES   Warner Bros., 1992
THE SECRETARY   Republic Pictures, 1995

JOHN KELLOGG
VIOLETS ARE BLUE   Columbia, 1986

DANIEL HUGH KELLY
HARDCASTLE AND McCORMICK (TF)   Stephen J. Cannell
   Productions, 1983
NIGHT OF COURAGE (TF)   Titus Productions, 1987
THE GOOD SON   20th Century Fox, 1993

DAVID PATRICK KELLY
THE CROW   Dimension/Miramax Films, 1994

GENE KELLY
(Eugene Curran Kelly)
b. August 23, 1912 - Pittsburgh, Pennsylvania

FOR ME AND MY GAL   MGM, 1942
PILOT NO. 5   MGM, 1943
DU BARRY WAS A LADY   MGM, 1943
THOUSANDS CHEER   MGM, 1943
THE CROSS OF LORRAINE   MGM, 1943

COVER GIRL   Columbia, 1944
CHRISTMAS HOLIDAY   Universal, 1944
ANCHORS AWEIGH ★   MGM, 1945
ZIEGFELD FOLLIES   MGM, 1946
LIVING IN A BIG WAY   MGM, 1947
THE PIRATE   MGM, 1948
THE THREE MUSKETEERS   MGM, 1948
WORDS AND MUSIC   MGM, 1948
TAKE ME OUT TO THE BALL GAME   MGM, 1949
ON THE TOWN   MGM, 1949 (also co-directed)
BLACK HAND   MGM, 1950
SUMMER STOCK   MGM, 1950
AN AMERICAN IN PARIS   MGM, 1951
IT'S A BIG COUNTRY   MGM, 1952
SINGIN' IN THE RAIN   MGM, 1952 (also co-directed)
THE DEVIL MAKES THREE   MGM, 1952
BRIGADOON   MGM, 1954
CREST OF THE WAVE   *SEAGULLS OVER SORRENTO*   MGM, 1954, British
DEEP IN MY HEART   MGM, 1954
IT'S ALWAYS FAIR WEATHER   MGM, 1955 (also co-directed)
INVITIATION TO THE DANCE   MGM, 1956 (also directed)
THE HAPPY ROAD   MGM, 1957 (also co-directed)
LES GIRLS   MGM, 1957
MARJORIE MORNINGSTAR   Warner Bros., 1958
LET'S MAKE LOVE   20th Century-Fox, 1960
INHERIT THE WIND   United Artists, 1960
WHAT A WAY TO GO!   20th Century-Fox, 1964
THE YOUNG GIRLS OF ROCHEFORT   *LES DEMOISELLES DE ROCHEFORT*   Warner Bros., 1968, French
40 CARATS   Columbia, 1973
THAT'S ENTERTAINMENT! (FD)   MGM/United Artists, 1974
THAT'S ENTERTAINMENT, PART 2 (FD)   MGM/United Artists, 1976 (also co-directed)
VIVA KNIEVEL!   Warner Bros., 1977
XANADU   Universal, 1980
THAT'S ENTERTAINMENT! III (FD)   MGM/UA, 1994

JEAN LOUISA KELLY

UNCLE BUCK   Orion, 1989

MOIRA KELLY

THE CUTTING EDGE   MGM-Pathe Communications, 1992
TWIN PEAKS: FIRE WALK WITH ME   New Line Cinema, 1992, U.S.-French
CHAPLIN   TriStar, 1992, U.S.-British
DAYBREAK (CTF)   Foundation Entertainment Productions/HBO Showcase, 1993
WITH HONORS   Warner Bros., 1994
THE TIE THAT BINDS   Buena Vista, 1995

LINDA KELSEY

Agent: Harris & Goldberg - Los Angeles, 310/553-5200

ELEANOR AND FRANKLIN (TF)   Talent Associates, 1976
ELEANOR AND FRANKLIN: THE WHITE HOUSE YEARS (TF)   Talent Associates, 1977
ATTACK ON FEAR (TF)   Tomorrow Entertainment, 1984
NUTCRACKER: MONEY, MADNESS AND MURDER (MS)   Green Arrow Productions/Warner Bros. TV, 1987
BABY GIRL SCOTT (TF)   Polson Company Productions/The Finnegan-Pinchuk Company, 1987

GARY KEMP

THE KRAYS   Miramax Films, 1990
THE BODYGUARD   Warner Bros., 1992

JEREMY KEMP

(Jeremy Walker)
b. February 3, 1935 - Chesterfield, England

CLEOPATRA   20th Century-Fox, 1963
FACE OF A STRANGER   Warner-Pathe, 1964, British
DR. TERROR'S HOUSE OF HORRORS   Paramount, 1965, British
OPERATION CROSSBOW   *THE GREAT SPY MISSION*   MGM, 1965, British-Italian

CAST A GIANT SHADOW   United Artists, 1966
THE BLUE MAX   20th Century-Fox, 1966, British-U.S.
ASSIGNMENT K   Columbia, 1968, British
THE STRANGE AFFAIR   Paramount, 1968, British
A TWIST OF SAND   United Artists, 1968, British
THE GAMES   20th Century-Fox, 1970, British
DARLING LILI   Paramount, 1970
SUDDEN TERROR   *EYEWITNESS*   National General, 1970, British
POPE JOAN   *THE DEVIL'S IMPOSTER*   Columbia, 1972, British
THE BELSTONE FOX   *FREE SPIRIT*   Cine III, 1973, British
THE SEVEN-PER-CENT SOLUTION   Universal, 1976, British
A BRIDGE TOO FAR   United Artists, 1977, British
THE RHINEMANN EXCHANGE (MS)   Universal TV, 1977
EAST OF ELEPHANT ROCK   1978
LEOPARD IN THE SNOW   New World, 1978, Canadian-British
CARAVANS   Universal, 1978, U.S.-Iranian
THE PRISONER OF ZENDA   Universal, 1979
EVITA PERON (TF)   Hartwest Productions/Zephyr Productions, 1981
THE RETURN OF THE SOLDIER   European Classics, 1981, British
THE WINDS OF WAR (MS)   Paramount TV/Dan Curtis Productions, 1983
SADAT (MS)   Blatt-Singer Productions/Columbia TV, 1983
GEORGE WASHINGTON (MS)   David Gerber Company/MGM-UA TV, 1984
TOP SECRET!   Paramount, 1984
PETER THE GREAT (TF)   PTG Productions/NBC Productions, 1986
WHEN THE WHALES CAME   20th Century Fox, 1989, British
PRISONERS OF HONOR (CTF)   HBO Pictures/Dreyfuss-James Productions, 1991
ANGELS AND INSECTS   Samuel Goldwyn Company, 1995

GEORGE KENNEDY

b. February 18, 1925 - New York, New York
Agent: Paradigm - Los Angeles, 310/277-4400

THE LITTLE SHEPHERD OF KINGDOM COME   20th Century-Fox, 1961
LONELY ARE THE BRAVE   Universal, 1962
THE SILENT WITNESS   1962
THE MAN FROM THE DINER'S CLUB   Columbia, 1963
CHARADE   Universal, 1963
ISLAND OF THE BLUE DOLPHINS   20th Century-Fox, 1964
STRAIT-JACKET   Columbia, 1964
McHALE'S NAVY   Universal, 1964
HUSH...HUSH, SWEET CHARLOTTE   20th Century-Fox, 1965
IN HARM'S WAY   Paramount, 1965
MIRAGE   Universal, 1965
SHENANDOAH   Universal, 1965
THE SONS OF KATIE ELDER   Paramount, 1965
THE FLIGHT OF THE PHOENIX   20th Century-Fox, 1966
HURRY SUNDOWN   Paramount, 1967
THE DIRTY DOZEN   MGM, 1967
COOL HAND LUKE ○○   Warner Bros., 1967
THE BALLAD OF JOSIE   Universal, 1967
THE LEGEND OF LYLAH CLARE   MGM, 1968
BANDOLERO!   20th Century-Fox, 1968
THE PINK JUNGLE   Universal, 1968
THE BOSTON STRANGLER   20th Century-Fox, 1968
GUNS OF THE MAGNIFICENT SEVEN   United Artists, 1969
THE GOOD GUYS AND THE BAD GUYS   Warner Bros., 1969
GAILY, GAILY   United Artists, 1969
tick...tick...tick   MGM, 1970
AIRPORT   Universal, 1970
ZIGZAG   MGM, 1970
DIRTY DINGUS MAGEE   MGM, 1970
FOOLS' PARADE   Columbia, 1971
A GREAT AMERICAN TRAGEDY (TF)   Metromedia Productions, 1972
THE FAMILY   *VIOLENT CITY*   1972, Italian-French
LOST HORIZON   Columbia, 1973
CAHILL—U.S. MARSHALL   United Artists, 1973
THUNDERBOLT AND LIGHTFOOT   United Artists, 1974
AIRPORT 1975   Universal, 1974
EARTHQUAKE   Universal, 1974
THE EIGER SANCTION   Universal, 1975
THE HUMAN FACTOR   Bryanston, 1975, British-U.S.
THE BLUE KNIGHT (TF)   Lorimar Productions, 1975

AIRPORT '77   Universal, 1977
PROOF OF THE MAN   1977, Japanese
MEAN DOG BLUES   American International, 1978
DEATH ON THE NILE   Paramount, 1978, British
BRASS TARGET   MGM/United Artists, 1978
BACKSTAIRS AT THE WHITE HOUSE (MS)   Ed Friendly
   Productions, 1979
STEEL   *LOOK DOWN AND DIE/MEN OF STEEL*
   World Northal, 1980
THE DOUBLE McGUFFIN   Mulberry Square, 1979
THE CONCORDE—AIRPORT '79   Universal, 1979
MODERN ROMANCE   Columbia, 1981
BOLERO   Cannon, 1984
A RARE BREED   New World, 1984
CHATTANOOGA CHOO CHOO   April Fools, 1984
SAVAGE DAWN   MAG Enterprises/Gregory Earls Productions, 1985
THE DELTA FORCE   Cannon, 1986
LIBERTY (TF)   Robert Greenwald Productions, 1986
RADIOACTIVE DREAMS   DEG, 1986
CREEPSHOW 2   New World, 1987
KENNY ROGERS AS THE GAMBLER III: THE LEGEND
   CONTINUES (TF)   Lion Share Productions, 1987
WHAT PRICE VICTORY? (TF)   Wolper Productions/
   Warner Bros. TV, 1988
THE NAKED GUN: FROM THE FILES OF POLICE SQUAD!
   Paramount, 1988
THE TERROR WITHIN   Concorde, 1989
MINISTRY OF VENGEANCE   MPCA, 1989
THE NAKED GUN 2 1/2: THE SMELL OF FEAR   Paramount, 1991
NAKED GUN 33 1/3: THE FINAL INSULT   Paramount, 1994

JIHMI KENNEDY
GUNG HO   Paramount, 1986
GLORY   TriStar, 1989

JOHN F. KENNEDY, JR.
A MATTER OF DEGREES   Backbeat Productions/New Font Films/
   Linus Associates/George Gund/Fujisankei Communications, 1990

KRISTINA MARIE KENNEDY
b. September 11, 1985 - West Islip, New York

BABY BOOM   MGM/UA, 1987

MICHELLE LYNN KENNEDY
b. September 11, 1985 - West Islip, New York

BABY BOOM   MGM/UA, 1987

MIMI KENNEDY
BABY GIRL SCOTT (TF)   Polson Company Productions/
   The Finnegan-Pinchuk Company, 1987
IMMEDIATE FAMILY   Columbia, 1989

PATSY KENSIT
THE GREAT GATSBY   Paramount, 1974
THE BLUE BIRD   20th Century-Fox, 1976, U.S.-Soviet
ABSOLUTE BEGINNERS   Orion, 1986, British
LETHAL WEAPON 2   Warner Bros., 1989
CHICAGO JOE AND THE SHOWGIRL   New Line Cinema, 1990
NAMELESS   MGM-Pathe
TWENTY-ONE   Triton Pictures, 1991
BLAME IT ON THE BELLBOY   Buena Vista, 1992, British
TIMEBOMB   MGM-Pathe, 1992
ANGELS AND INSECTS   Samuel Goldwyn Company, 1995

SUZANNE KENT
WHITE FANG   Buena Vista, 1991

MICHAEL KENWORTHY
'NIGHT, MOTHER   Universal, 1986
RETURN OF THE LIVING DEAD PART II   Lorimar, 1988

JOANNA KERNS
b. February 12, 1953 - San Francisco, California

HUNTER (TF)   Stephen J. Cannell Productions, 1984
A BUNNY'S TALE (TF)   Stan Margulies Company/
   ABC Circle Films, 1985
STORMIN' HOME (TF)   CBS Entertainment, 1985
THE RAPE OF RICHARD BECK (TF)   Robert Papazian Productions/
   Henerson-Hirsch Productions, 1985
THOSE SHE LEFT BEHIND (TF)   NBC Productions, 1989
THE PREPPIE MURDER (TF)   Jack Grossbart Productions/
   Spectator Films, 1989
BLIND FAITH (MS)   NBC Productions, 1990

DEBORAH KERR
(Deborah J. Kerr-Trimmer)
b. September 30, 1921 - Helensburgh, Scotland

MAJOR BARBARA   United Artists, 1941, British
LOVE ON THE DOLE   1941, British
COURAGEOUS MR. PENN   *PENN OF PENNSYLVANIA*
   1941, British
HATTER'S CASTLE   1941, British
THE AVENGERS   *THE DAY WILL DAWN*   1942, British
THE LIFE AND DEATH OF COLONEL BLIMP   GFO, 1943, British
VACATION FROM MARRIAGE   *PERFECT STRANGERS*
   MGM, 1945, British
THE ADVENTURESS   *I SEE A DARK STRANGER*   1946, British
BLACK NARCISSUS   Universal, 1946, British
THE HUCKSTERS   MGM, 1947
IF WINTER COMES   MGM, 1948
EDWARD MY SON ★   MGM, 1949
PLEASE BELIEVE ME   MGM, 1950
KING SOLOMON'S MINES   MGM, 1950
QUO VADIS?   MGM, 1951
THE PRISONER OF ZENDA   MGM, 1952
THUNDER IN THE EAST   Paramount, 1953
YOUNG BESS   MGM, 1953
JULIUS CAESAR   MGM, 1953
DREAM WIFE   MGM, 1953
FROM HERE TO ETERNITY ★   Columbia, 1953
THE END OF THE AFFAIR   Columbia, 1955, British
THE PROUD AND THE PROFANE   Paramount, 1956
THE KING AND I ★   20th Century-Fox, 1956
TEA AND SYMPATHY   MGM, 1956
HEAVEN KNOWS, MR. ALLISON ★   20th Century-Fox, 1957
AN AFFAIR TO REMEMBER   20th Century-Fox, 1957
BONJOUR TRISTESSE   Columbia, 1958
SEPARATE TABLES ★   United Artists, 1958
THE JOURNEY   MGM, 1959
COUNT YOUR BLESSINGS   MGM, 1959
BELOVED INFIDEL   20th Century-Fox, 1959
THE SUNDOWNERS ★   Warner Bros., 1960
THE GRASS IS GREENER   Universal, 1960
THE NAKED EDGE   United Artists, 1961, British-U.S.
THE INNOCENTS   20th Century-Fox, 1961, British
THE CHALK GARDEN   Universal, 1964, British
THE NIGHT OF THE IGUANA   MGM, 1964
MARRIAGE ON THE ROCKS   Warner Bros., 1965
EYE OF THE DEVIL   MGM, 1967, British
CASINO ROYALE   Columbia, 1967, British
PRUDENCE AND THE PILL   20th Century-Fox, 1968, British
THE GYPSY MOTHS   MGM, 1969
THE ARRANGEMENT   Warner Bros., 1969
WITNESS FOR THE PROSECUTION (TF)   Norman Rosemont
   Productions/United Artists Productions, 1982, U.S.-British
A WOMAN OF SUBSTANCE (MS)   Artemis Portman Productions,
   1984, British
REUNION AT FAIRBOROUGH (CTF)   HBO Premiere Films/Alan
   Wagner Productions/Alan King Productions/Columbia TV, 1985
THE ASSAM GARDEN   The Moving Picture Company, 1985, British

JAY KERR
AMERICAN HARVEST (TF)   Roth-Stratton Productions/
   The Finnegan Company, 1987

BRIAN KERWIN
b. October 25, 1949
Agent: William Morris Agency - Beverly Hills, 310/274-7451

WET GOLD (TF)   Telepictures Productions, 1984
BLUEGRASS (MS)   The Landsburg Company, 1988
TORCH SONG TRILOGY   New Line Cinema, 1988
SWITCHED AT BIRTH (MS)   Morrow-Heus Productions/
   O'Hara-Horowitz Productions/Columbia TV, 1991
HARD PROMISES   Columbia, 1991
AGAINST HER WILL: AN INCIDENT IN BALTIMORE (TF)
   RHI Entertainment, 1992
LOVE FIELD   Orion, 1992
GETTING AWAY WITH MURDER   Savoy Pictures, 1995
GOLD DIGGERS   Universal, 1995

PERSIS KHAMBATTA
STAR TREK - THE MOTION PICTURE   Paramount, 1979
NIGHTHAWKS   Universal, 1981
MEGAFORCE   20th Century-Fox, 1982

LELETI KHUMALO
SARAFINA!   Miramax Films/Buena Vista, 1992,
   South African-British-French

BLAINE KIA
ALOHA SUMMER   *HANAUMA BAY*   Spectrafilm, 1988

KID
(Kid N' Play)
Agent: William Morris Agency - Beverly Hills, 310/274-7451

A CLASS ACT   Warner Bros., 1992

MICHAEL KIDD
SMILE   United Artists, 1975
SKIN DEEP   20th Century Fox, 1988

MARGOT KIDDER
b. October 17, 1948 - Yellow Knife, Canada
Agent: Marion Rosenberg Office - Los Angeles, 213/653-7383

GAILY, GAILY   United Artists, 1969
QUACKSER FORTUNE HAS A COUSIN IN THE BRONX
   UMC, 1970, British
SUDDENLY SINGLE (TF)   Chris-Rose Productions, 1971
THE BOUNTY MAN (TF)   ABC Circle Films, 1972
SISTERS   American International, 1973
THE GRAVY TRAIN   *THE DION BROTHERS*   Columbia, 1974
HONKY TONK (TF)   MGM-TV, 1974
BLACK CHRISTMAS   *SILENT NIGHT, EVIL NIGHT/*
   STRANGER IN THE HOUSE   Warner Bros., 1975
THE GREAT WALDO PEPPER   Universal, 1975
THE REINCARNATION OF PETER PROUD
   American International, 1975
92 IN THE SHADE   United Artists, 1975
SUPERMAN   Warner Bros., 1978
THE AMITYVILLE HORROR   American International, 1979
WILLIE AND PHIL   20th Century-Fox, 1980
SUPERMAN II   Warner Bros., 1981, U.S.-British
SOME KIND OF HERO   Paramount, 1982
HEARTACHES   MPM, 1982, Canadian
SUPERMAN III   Warner Bros., 1983, U.S.-British
TRENCHCOAT   Buena Vista, 1983
PICKING UP THE PIECES (TF)   CBS Entertainment, 1985
GOBOTS: BATTLE OF THE ROCK LORDS (AF)
   Clubhouse/Atlantic Releasing Corporation, 1986 (voice)
VANISHING ACT (TF)   Robert Cooper Productions, 1986,
   U.S.-Canadian
SUPERMAN IV: THE QUEST FOR PEACE   Warner Bros., 1987
BODY OF EVIDENCE (TF)   CBS Entertainment, 1988

NICOLE KIDMAN
Agent: CAA - Beverly Hills, 310/288-4545

DEAD CALM   Warner Bros., 1989, Australian
DAYS OF THUNDER   Paramount, 1990
BILLY BATHGATE   Buena Vista, 1991
FAR AND AWAY   Universal, 1992
MALICE   Columbia, 1993
MY LIFE   Columbia, 1993
UNTITLED VAN SANT/ZISKIN   Columbia, 1994
BATMAN FOREVER   Warner Bros., 1995
PORTRAIT OF A LADY   Gramercy Pictures, 1995

RICHARD KIEL
THE PHANTOM PLANET   1961
THE MAGIC SWORD   1962
HOUSE OF THE DAMNED   20th Century-Fox, 1962
THE HUMAN DUPLICATORS   1965
A MAN CALLED DAGGER   MGM, 1968
THE LONGEST YARD   Paramount, 1974
SILVER STREAK   20th Century-Fox, 1976
THE SPY WHO LOVED ME   United Artists, 1977, British-U.S.
FORCE 10 FROM NAVARONE   American International, 1978
HUMANOID   1978
THEY WENT THAT-A-WAY AND THAT-A-WAY
   International Picture Show Company, 1978
MOONRAKER   United Artists, 1979, British-French
SO FINE   Warner Bros., 1981
HYSTERICAL   Embassy, 1983
PALE RIDER   Warner Bros., 1985
THINK BIG   Motion Picture Corporation of America, 1990
THE GIANT OF THUNDER MOUNTAIN   New Generation, 1991

UDO KIER
FOR LOVE OR MONEY   Universal, 1993
JOHNNY MNEMONIC   TriStar, 1994

RICHARD KILEY
b. March 31, 1922 - Chicago, Illinois

THE MOB   Columbia, 1951
THE SNIPER   Columbia, 1952
EIGHT IRON MEN   Columbia, 1952
PICKUP ON SOUTH STREET   20th Century-Fox, 1953
THE BLACKBOARD JUNGLE   MGM, 1955
THE PHENIX CITY STORY   Allied Artists, 1955
SPANISH AFFAIR   Paramount, 1958, Spanish
PENDULUM   Columbia, 1969
MURDER ONCE REMOVED (TF)   Metromedia Productions, 1971
THE LITTLE PRINCE   Paramount, 1974, British
FRIENDLY PERSUASION (TF)   International TV Productions/
   Allied Artists, 1975
THE MACAHANS (TF)   Albert S. Ruddy Productions/MGM TV, 1976
LOOKING FOR MR. GOODBAR   Paramount, 1977
ANGEL ON MY SHOULDER (TF)   Mace Neufeld Productions/Barney
   Rosenzweig Productions/Beowulf Productions, 1980
ENDLESS LOVE   Universal, 1981
THE BAD SEED (TF)   Hajeno Productions/Warner Bros. TV, 1985
IF TOMORROW COMES (MS)   CBS Entertainment, 1986
DO YOU REMEMBER LOVE? (TF)   Dave Bell Productions, 1985
A YEAR IN THE LIFE (MS)   Universal TV, 1986
MY FIRST LOVE (TF)   The Avnet-Kerner Company, 1988
FINAL DAYS (TF)   Samuels Film Company, 1989
GUNSMOKE: THE LAST APACHE (TF)   CBS Entertainment/
   Galatea Productions, 1990
ABSOLUTE STRANGERS (TF)   Cates-Doty Productions/Fries
   Entertainment, 1991

VAL KILMER
Agent: CAA - Beverly Hills, 310/288-4545

TOP SECRET!   Paramount, 1984
REAL GENIUS   TriStar, 1985
TOP GUN   Paramount, 1986
THE MURDERS IN THE RUE MORGUE (TF)   Robert Halmi, Inc./
   International Film Productions, 1986
WILLOW   MGM/UA, 1988
KILL ME AGAIN   MGM/UA, 1989

F I L M   A C T O R S

THE DOORS   TriStar, 1991
THUNDERHEART   TriStar, 1992
TRUE ROMANCE   Warner Bros., 1993
THE REAL McCOY   Universal, 1993
TOMBSTONE   Buena Vista, 1993
WINGS OF COURAGE   TriStar, 1995
BATMAN FOREVER   Warner Bros., 1995

PATRICK KILPATRICK
DEATH WARRANT   MGM/UA, 1990
SCANNER COP 2   Republic Pictures, 1994

EVAN KIM
THE DEAD POOL   Warner Bros., 1988

CHARLES KIMBROUGH
b. May 23 - St. Paul, Minnesota
Agent: J. Michael Bloom & Associates - Los Angeles, 310/275-6800

WEEKEND WAR (TF)   Pompian-Atamian Prods./Columbia TV, 1988

ALAN KING
(Irwin Alan Kinberg)
b. December 26, 1927 - Brooklyn, New York
Agent: William Morris Agency - Beverly Hills, 310/274-7451

HIT THE DECK   1955
MIRACLE IN THE RAIN   Warner Bros., 1956
THE GIRL HE LEFT BEHIND   Warner Bros., 1956
THE HELEN MORGAN STORY   Warner Bros., 1957
ON THE FIDDLE   1961, British
OPERATION SNAFU   *ON THE FIDDLE/OPERATION WARHEAD*
   1961, British
BYE BYE BRAVERMAN   Warner Bros., 1968
THE ANDERSON TAPES   Columbia, 1971
JUST TELL ME WHAT YOU WANT   Columbia, 1980
AUTHOR! AUTHOR!   20th Century-Fox, 1982
I, THE JURY   20th Century-Fox, 1982
LOVESICK   The Ladd Company/Warner Bros., 1983
STEPHEN KING'S CAT'S EYE   *CAT'S EYE*   MGM/UA, 1985
MEMORIES OF ME   MGM/UA, 1988
ENEMIES, A LOVE STORY   20th Century Fox, 1989
NIGHT AND THE CITY   20th Century Fox, 1992
CASINO   Universal, 1995

ERIK KING
CASUALTIES OF WAR   Columbia, 1989

LARRY KING
b. November 19, 1933 - New York, New York

EDDIE AND THE CRUISERS: EDDIE LIVES   Scotti Bros., 1989

MABEL KING
THE WIZ   Universal, 1978
SCROOGED   Paramount, 1988

MORGANA KING
THE GODFATHER   Paramount, 1972
THE GODFATHER, PART II   Paramount, 1974
DEADLY INTENTIONS (MS)   Green-Epstein Productions, 1985

PERRY KING
b. April 30, 1948 - Alliance, Ohio
Agent: CAA - Beverly Hills, 310/288-4545

SLAUGHTERHOUSE FIVE   Universal, 1972
THE POSSESSION OF JOEL DELANEY   Paramount, 1972
THE LORDS OF FLATBUSH   Columbia, 1974
MANDINGO   Paramount, 1975
THE WILD PARTY   American International, 1975
CAPTAINS AND THE KINGS (MS)   Universal TV, 1976
LIPSTICK   Paramount, 1976
ANDY WARHOL'S BAD   New World, 1977
THE CHOIRBOYS   Universal, 1977

ASPEN (MS)   Universal TV, 1977
A DIFFERENT STORY   Avco Embassy, 1978
THE CRACKER FACTORY (TF)   Roger Gimbel Productions/
   EMI TV, 1979
THE LAST CONVERTIBLE (MS)   Roy Huggins Productions/
   Universal TV, 1979
LOVE'S SAVAGE FURY (TF)   Aaron Spelling Productions, 1979
SEARCH AND DESTROY   *STRIKING BACK*   Film Ventures
   International, 1981
CLASS OF 1984   United Film Distribution, 1982, Canadian
RIPTIDE (TF)   Stephen J. Cannell Productions, 1984
STRANDED (TF)   Tim Flack Productions/Columbia TV, 1986
I'LL TAKE MANHATTAN (MS)   Steve Krantz Productions, 1987
PERFECT PEOPLE (TF)   Robert Greenwald Productions, 1988
SHAKEDOWN ON THE SUNSET STRIP (TF)
   CBS Entertainment, 1988
DISASTER AT SILO 7 (TF)   Mark Carliner Productions, 1988
ROXANNE: THE PRIZE PULITZER (TF)   Qintex Entertainment, 1989
SWITCH   Warner Bros., 1991
LET IT BE ME   Savoy Pictures, 1995

REGINA KING
POETIC JUSTICE   Columbia, 1993
HIGHER LEARNING   Columbia, 1994

ROWENA KING
Agent: William Morris Agency - Beverly Hills, 310/274-7451

WIDE SARGASSO SEA   Fine Line Features/New Line Cinema,
   1993, British

STEPHEN KING
Agent: CAA - Beverly Hills, 310/288-4545

PET SEMATARY   *STEPHEN KING'S PET SEMATARY*
   Paramount, 1989

BEN KINGSLEY
b. December 31, 1943 - Yorkshire, England
Agent: ICM - Beverly Hills, 310/550-4000

GANDHI ★★   Columbia, 1982, British-Indian
BETRAYAL   20th Century-Fox International Classics, 1983, British
CAMILLE (TF)   Rosemont Productions, 1984, U.S.-British
HAREM   Sara Films, 1985, French
TURTLE DIARY   Samuel Goldwyn Company, 1985, British
TESTIMONY (TF)   European Classics, 1987, British
PASCALI'S ISLAND   Avenue Entertainment, 1988, British-U.S.
WITHOUT A CLUE   Orion, 1988
BUGSY ✪   TriStar, 1991
SNEAKERS   Universal, 1992
DAVE   Warner Bros., 1993
SEARCHING FOR BOBBY FISCHER   Paramount, 1993
SCHINDLER'S LIST   Universal, 1993
DEATH AND THE MAIDEN   Fine Line Features/New Line Cinema, 1994
JOSEPH (CTF)   Turner Network TV, 1994
SPECIES   MGM/UA, 1995

SUSAN KINGSLEY
OLD ENOUGH   Orion Classics, 1984

AMELIA KINKADE
NIGHT OF THE DEMONS 2   Republic Pictures, 1994

ROY KINNEAR
THE PRINCESS AND THE GOBLIN (AF)   Hemdale, 1994 (voice)

TERRY KINNEY
Agent: William Morris Agency - Beverly Hills, 310/274-7451

NO MERCY   TriStar, 1986
MURDER ORDAINED (TF)   Zev Braun Productions/Interscope
   Communications, 1987
TALENT FOR THE GAME   Paramount, 1992
THE FIRM   Paramount, 1993
BODY SNATCHERS   Warner Bros., 1994

LANCE KINSEY
THINGS ARE TOUGH ALL OVER   Columbia, 1982
DR. DETROIT   Universal, 1983
CLASS   Orion, 1983
POLICE ACADEMY 2: THEIR FIRST ASSIGNMENT
    Warner Bros., 1985
POLICE ACADEMY 3: BACK IN TRAINING   Warner Bros., 1986
POLICE ACADEMY 4: CITIZENS ON PATROL   Warner Bros., 1987
POLICE ACADEMY 5: ASSIGNMENT MIAMI BEACH
    Warner Bros., 1988
POLICE ACADEMY 6: CITY UNDER SIEGE   Warner Bros., 1989

NASTASSJA KINSKI
(Nastassia Kinski)
b. January 24, 1961 - Berlin, Germany
Agent: ICM - Beverly Hills, 310/550-4000

TO THE DEVIL A DAUGHTER   EMI, 1976, British-West German
STAY AS YOU ARE   1978, French
TESS   Columbia, 1980, French-British
CAT PEOPLE   Universal, 1982
ONE FROM THE HEART   Columbia, 1982
EXPOSED   MGM/UA, 1983
THE MOON IN THE GUTTER   Triumph/Columbia, 1983,
    French-Italian
THE HOTEL NEW HAMPSHIRE   Orion, 1984
MARIA'S LOVERS   Cannon, 1984
PARIS, TEXAS   TLC Films/20th Century Fox, 1984,
    West German-French
UNFAITHFULLY YOURS   20th Century Fox, 1984
HAREM   Sara Films, 1985, French
REVOLUTION   Warner Bros., 1985, British-Norwegian
TORRENTS OF SPRING   Millimeter Films, 1990
TERMINAL VELOCITY   Buena Vista, 1994

BRUNO KIRBY
b. 1949 - New York, New York
Agent: William Morris Agency - New York, 212/586-5100

THE HARRAD EXPERIMENT   Cinerama Releasing
    Corporation, 1973
BETWEEN THE LINES   Midwest Film Productions, 1977
WHERE THE BUFFALO ROAM   Universal, 1980
THIS IS SPINAL TAP   Embassy, 1984
TIN MEN   Buena Vista, 1987
BERT RIGBY, YOU'RE A FOOL   Warner Bros., 1989
WHEN HARRY MET SALLY...   Columbia, 1989
WE'RE NO ANGELS   Paramount, 1989
THE FRESHMAN   TriStar, 1990
CITY SLICKERS   Columbia, 1991
GOLDEN GATE   Samuel Goldwyn Company, 1994
THE BASKETBALL DIARIES   1995

SALLY KIRKLAND
b. October 31, 1944 - New York, New York

13 MOST BEAUTIFUL WOMEN   Film Makers, 1964
BLUE   Paramount, 1968, British
COMING APART   Kaleidoscope, 1969
FUTZ!   Commonwealth United, 1969
BRAND X   1970
GOING HOME   MGM, 1971
THE YOUNG NURSES   1973
THE WAY WE WERE   Columbia, 1973
THE STING   Universal, 1973
CINDERELLA LIBERTY   20th Century-Fox, 1974
CANDY STRIPE NURSES   New World, 1974
BIG BAD MAMA   New World, 1974
BITE THE BULLET   Columbia, 1975
CRAZY MAMA   New World, 1975
DEATH SCREAM   *THE WOMAN WHO CRIED MURDER* (TF)
    RSO Films, 1975
BREAKHEART PASS   United Artists, 1976
A STAR IS BORN   Warner Bros., 1976
PIPE DREAMS   Avco Embassy, 1976
HOMETOWN, U.S.A.   Film Ventures International, 1979
PRIVATE BENJAMIN   Warner Bros., 1980
THE INCREDIBLE SHRINKING WOMAN   Universal, 1981

FATAL GAMES   1982
HUMAN HIGHWAY   1982
LOVE LETTERS   New World, 1983
TALKING WALLS   Drummond Productions, 1987
ANNA ★   Vestron, 1987
WHITE HOT   *CRACK IN THE MIRROR*   Triax Entertainment
    Group, 1988
COLD FEET   Avenue Pictures, 1989
BEST OF THE BEST   Taurus Entertainment/SVS Films, 1989
REVENGE   Columbia, 1990
HEATWAVE (CTF)   The Avnet-Kerner Company/Propaganda
    Films, 1990
JFK   Warner Bros., 1991
EYE OF THE STRANGER   Silver Lake International Pictures, 1993
GUNMEN   Dimension/Miramax Films, 1994

GENE KIRKWOOD
GUILTY BY SUSPICION   Warner Bros., 1991

MIA KIRSHNER
MR. HOLLAND'S OPUS   Buena Vista, 1995

TERRY KISER
Agent: Bauman, Hiller & Associates - Los Angeles, 213/857-6666

ALL NIGHT LONG   Universal, 1981
WEEKEND AT BERNIE'S   20th Century Fox, 1989
MANNEQUIN TWO ON THE MOVE   20th Century Fox, 1991
WEEKEND AT BERNIE'S II   TriStar, 1993

DARCI KISTLER
GEORGE BALANCHINE'S THE NUTCRACKER   Warner Bros., 1993

TAWNY KITAEN
BACHELOR PARTY   20th Century Fox, 1984
CALIFORNIA GIRLS (TF)   ABC Circle Films, 1985

MICHAEL KITCHEN
OUT OF AFRICA   Universal, 1985
CROSSING TO FREEDOM (TF)   Procter & Gamble Productions/
    Stan Margulies Productions/Granada TV, 1990, U.S.-British
ENCHANTED APRIL   Miramax Films, 1991, British
DANDELION DEAD (TF)   Masterpiece Theatre/PBS, 1994, British

EARTHA KITT
b. January 26, 1928 - North, South Carolina

NEW FACES   1954
THE MARK OF THE HAWK   1957
ST. LOUIS BLUES   Paramount, 1958
ANNA LUCASTA   United Artists, 1958
THE SAINT OF DEVIL'S ISLAND   1961
UNCLE TOM'S CABIN   *ONKEL TOMS HÜTTE*   1965,
    West German-French-Italian-Yugoslavian
SYNANON   Columbia, 1965
LT. SCHUSTER'S WIFE (TF)   1972
FRIDAY FOSTER   American International, 1975
TO KILL A COP (TF)   David Gerber Company/Columbia TV, 1978
ALL BY MYSELF (FD)   Christian Blackwood Productions, 1982
THE PINK CHIQUITAS   1986
THE SERPENT WARRIORS   1986
ERIK THE VIKING   Orion, 1989, British

GARY KLAR
BIG   20th Century Fox, 1988
MARRIED TO THE MOB   Orion, 1988

ROBERT KLEIN
b. February 8, 1942 - New York, New York
Agent: APA - Los Angeles, 310/273-0744

HOOPER   Warner Bros., 1978
THE BELL JAR   Avco Embassy, 1979
POISON IVY (TF)   NBC Productions, 1985
THIS WIFE FOR HIRE (TF)   The Belle Company/Guillaume-Margo
    Productions/Comworld Productions, 1985
LIFESAVERS   TriStar, 1994

ANNA KLEMP
BLUE SKY   Orion, 1994

KEVIN KLINE
b. October 24, 1947 - St. Louis, Missouri
Agent: CAA - Beverly Hills, 310/288-4545

SOPHIE'S CHOICE   Universal/AFD, 1982
THE PIRATES OF PENZANCE   Universal, 1983
THE BIG CHILL   Columbia, 1983
SILVERADO   Columbia, 1985
VIOLETS ARE BLUE   Columbia, 1986
CRY FREEDOM   Universal, 1987, British-U.S.
A FISH CALLED WANDA OO   MGM/UA, 1988, British
THE JANUARY MAN   MGM/UA, 1989
I LOVE YOU TO DEATH   TriStar, 1990
SOAPDISH   Paramount, 1991
GRAND CANYON   20th Century Fox, 1991
CONSENTING ADULTS   Buena Vista, 1992
CHAPLIN   TriStar, 1992, U.S.-British
DAVE   Warner Bros., 1993
GEORGE BALANCHINE'S THE NUTCRACKER   Warner Bros.,
   1993 (voice)
PRINCESS CARABOO   TriStar, 1994
PARIS MATCH   20th Century Fox, 1995
THE HUNCHBACK OF NOTRE DAME (AF)   Buena Vista,
   1996 (voice)

HEIDI KLING
OUT ON A LIMB   Universal, 1992

JACK KLUGMAN
b. April 27, 1922 - Philadelphia, Pennsylvania

TIMETABLE   1956
TWELVE ANGRY MEN   United Artists, 1957
CRY TERROR   MGM, 1958
DAYS OF WINE AND ROSES   Warner Bros., 1962
I COULD GO ON SINGING   United Artists, 1963, British
THE YELLOW CANARY   20th Century-Fox, 1963
ACT ONE   Warner Bros., 1963
HAIL MAFIA!   *JE VOUS SALUE MAFFIA!*   1965, French-Italian
THE DETECTIVE   20th Century-Fox, 1968
THE SPLIT   MGM, 1968
GOODBYE, COLUMBUS   Paramount, 1969
WHO SAYS I CAN'T RIDE A RAINBOW?   1971
TWO-MINUTE WARNING   Universal, 1976
QUINCY, M.E. (TF)   Glen A. Larson Productions/Universal TV, 1976
PARALLEL LIVES (CTF)   Showtime Entertainment, 1994

VINCENT KLYN
CYBORG   Cannon, 1989

ROB KNEPPER
THAT'S LIFE!   Columbia, 1986
RENEGADES   Universal, 1989

BOBBY KNIGHT
BLUE CHIPS   Paramount, 1994

CHRISTOPHER KNIGHT
THE BRADY GIRLS GET MARRIED (TF)   Sherwood Schwartz
   Productions, 1981
A VERY BRADY CHRISTMAS (TF)   Sherwood Schwartz
   Productions/Paramount TV, 1988
THE BRADYS (TF)   Brady Productions/Paramount TV, 1990
THE BRADY BUNCH MOVIE   Paramount, 1995

LILY KNIGHT
AN UNREMARKABLE LIFE   Continental Film Group, 1989

SHIRLEY KNIGHT
b. July 5, 1937 - Goessel, Kansas
Agent: Gersh Agency - Beverly Hills, 310/274-6611

FIVE GATES TO HELL   20th Century-Fox, 1959
ICE PALACE   Warner Bros., 1960
THE DARK AT THE TOP OF THE STAIRS O   Warner Bros., 1960
THE COUCH   1962
SWEET BIRD OF YOUTH O   MGM, 1962
HOUSE OF WOMEN   Warner Bros., 1962
FLIGHT FROM ASHIYA   United Artists, 1964, U.S.-Japanese
THE GROUP   United Artists, 1966
DUTCHMAN   Continental, 1966, British
PETULIA   Warner Bros., 1968, U.S.-British
THE COUNTERFEIT KILLER   1968
THE RAIN PEOPLE   Warner Bros., 1969
SECRETS   Lone Star, 1971, British
JUGGERNAUT   United Artists, 1974, British
BEYOND THE POSEIDON ADVENTURE   Warner Bros., 1979
ENDLESS LOVE   Universal, 1981
THE SENDER   Paramount, 1982, U.S.-British
WITH INTENT TO KILL (TF)   London Productions, 1984
HARD PROMISES   Columbia, 1991
STUART SMALLEY   Paramount, 1994

TRENTON KNIGHT
THE SKATEBOARD KID II   Concorde, 1995

WAYNE KNIGHT
Agent: Gersh Agency - New York, 212/997-1818

DEAD AGAIN   Paramount, 1991
JURASSIC PARK   Universal, 1993
UNTITLED VAN SANT/ZISKIN   Columbia, 1995

ANDREW KNOTT
b. Salford, Manchester, England

THE SECRET GARDEN   Warner Bros., 1993, U.S.-British
BLACK BEAUTY   Warner Bros., 1994, British-U.S.

ROBERT KNOTT
WILD BILL   MGM/UA, 1995

DON KNOTTS
b. July 21, 1924 - Morgantown, West Virginia

NO TIME FOR SERGEANTS   Warner Bros., 1958
WAKE ME WHEN IT'S OVER   20th Century-Fox, 1960
THE LAST TIME I SAW ARCHIE   United Artists, 1961
IT'S A MAD MAD MAD MAD WORLD   United Artists, 1963
MOVE OVER, DARLING   20th Century-Fox, 1963
THE INCREDIBLE MR. LIMPET   Universal, 1964
THE GHOST AND MR. CHICKEN   Universal, 1966
THE RELUCTANT ASTRONAUT   1967
THE SHAKIEST GUN IN THE WEST   Universal, 1968
THE LOVE GOD?   1969
HOW TO FRAME A FIGG   Universal, 1971
THE APPLE DUMPLING GANG   Buena Vista, 1975
NO DEPOSIT, NO RETURN   Buena Vista, 1976
GUS   Buena Vista, 1976
HERBIE GOES TO MONTE CARLO   Buena Vista, 1977
HOT LEAD AND COLD FEET   Buena Vista, 1978
THE APPLE DUMPLING GANG RIDES AGAIN   Buena Vista, 1979
THE PRIVATE EYES   New World, 1980
RETURN TO MAYBERRY (TF)   Strathmore Productions/Viacom
   Productions, 1986
CATS DON'T DANCE (AF)   Turner Pictures, 1996 (voice)

TERENCE KNOX
HEART LIKE A WHEEL   20th Century-Fox, 1983
CITY KILLER (TF)   Stan Shpetner Productions, 1984
J.O.E. AND THE COLONEL (TF)   Mad Dog Productions/
   Universal TV, 1985
CHASE (TF)   CBS Entertainment, 1985

MURDER ORDAINED (MS)   Zev Braun Productions/Interscope
   Communications, 1987
SNOW KILL (CTF)   Wilshire Court Productions, 1990

JEFF KOBER

Agent: Gersh Agency - Beverly Hills, 310/274-6611

THE FIRST POWER   Orion, 1990
TANK GIRL   MGM/UA, 1995

EDWARD I. KOCH

NEW YORK STORIES   Buena Vista, 1989

PETER KOCH

LOVERBOY   TriStar, 1989

WALTER KOENIG

STAR TREK - THE MOTION PICTURE   Paramount, 1979
STAR TREK II: THE WRATH OF KHAN   Paramount, 1982
STAR TREK III: THE SEARCH FOR SPOCK   Paramount, 1984
STAR TREK IV: THE VOYAGE HOME   Paramount, 1986
STAR TREK V: THE FINAL FRONTIER   Paramount, 1989
STAR TREK VI: THE UNDISCOVERED COUNTRY
   Paramount, 1991
STAR TREK GENERATIONS   Paramount, 1994

JAY KOGEN

COLDBLOODED   MPCA, 1995

MARY KOHNERT

Agent: J. Michael Bloom & Associates - Los Angeles, 310/275-6800

L.A. STORY   TriStar, 1991

GUICH KOOCK

AMERICAN NINJA   Cannon, 1985
SQUARE DANCE   Island Pictures, 1987

HARVEY KORMAN

b. February 15, 1927 - Chicago, Illinois

LIVING VENUS   Creative Services, 1960
GYPSY   Warner Bros., 1962
LORD LOVE A DUCK   United Artists, 1966
THREE BITES OF THE APPLE   MGM, 1966
DON'T JUST STAND THERE!   1968
THE APRIL FOOLS   National General, 1969
BLAZING SADDLES   Warner Bros., 1974
HUCKLEBERRY FINN   United Artists, 1974
HIGH ANXIETY   20th Century-Fox, 1977
AMERICATHON   United Artists, 1979
FIRST FAMILY   Warner Bros., 1980
HERBIE GOES BANANAS   Buena Vista, 1980
HISTORY OF THE WORLD—PART 1   20th Century-Fox, 1981
TRAIL OF THE PINK PANTHER   MGM/UA, 1982
CURSE OF THE PINK PANTHER   MGM/UA, 1983
THE LONGSHOT   Orion, 1986
CRASH COURSE (TF)   Fries Entertainment, 1988

CHARLIE KORSMO

MEN DON'T LEAVE   Warner Bros., 1990
DICK TRACY   Buena Vista, 1990
WHAT ABOUT BOB?   Buena Vista, 1991
HOOK   TriStar, 1991

JOSEPH KOSALA

ABOVE THE LAW   Warner Bros., 1988

PAUL KOSLO

Agent: The Artists Agency - Los Angeles, 310/277-7779

ROBOTJOX   Triumph Releasing Corporation, 1990

SHO KOSUGI

ALOHA SUMMER   *HANAUMA BAY*   Spectrafilm, 1988

ELIAS KOTEAS

ONE MAGIC CHRISTMAS   Buena Vista, 1985, U.S.-Canadian
GARDENS OF STONE   TriStar, 1987
SOME KIND OF WONDERFUL   Paramount, 1987
FULL MOON IN BLUE WATER   Trans World Entertainment, 1988
TUCKER - THE MAN AND HIS DREAM   Paramount, 1988
FULL MOON IN BLUE WATER   Trans World Entertainment, 1988
BLOOD RED   Hemdale, 1990
TEENAGE MUTANT NINJA TURTLES   New Line Cinema, 1990
LOOK WHO'S TALKING TOO   TriStar, 1990
ALMOST AN ANGEL   Paramount, 1990, Australian-U.S.

YAPHET KOTTO

b. November 15, 1937 - New York, New York
Agent: The Artists Group, Ltd. - Los Angeles, 310/552-1100

NOTHING BUT A MAN   Cinema 5, 1964
THE THOMAS CROWN AFFAIR   United Artists, 1968
FIVE CARD STUD   Paramount, 1968
THE LIBERATION OF L.B. JONES   Columbia, 1970
MAN AND BOY   Levitt-Pickman, 1972
BONE   Jack H. Harris Enterprises, 1972
THE LIMIT   *TIME LIMIT/SPEED LIMIT 65*   Cannon,
   1972 (also directed)
ACROSS 110TH STREET   United Artists, 1972
LIVE AND LET DIE   United Artists, 1973, British
TRUCK TURNER   American International, 1974
REPORT TO THE COMMISSIONER   United Artists, 1975
SHARKS' TREASURE   United Artists, 1975
FRIDAY FOSTER   American International, 1975
THE MONKEY HUSTLE   American International, 1976
DRUM   United Artists, 1976
BLUE COLLAR   Universal, 1978
ALIEN   20th Century-Fox, 1979, U.S.-British
BRUBAKER   20th Century-Fox, 1980
THE STAR CHAMBER   20th Century-Fox, 1983
PLAYING WITH FIRE (TF)   Zephyr Productions, 1985
WARNING SIGN   20th Century Fox, 1985
HAREM (MS)   Highgate Pictures, 1986
IN SELF DEFENSE (TF)   Leonard Hill Films, 1987
PRETTYKILL   Spectrafilm, 1987, Canadian
THE RUNNING MAN   TriStar, 1987
MIDNIGHT RUN   Universal, 1988
MINISTRY OF VENGEANCE   MPCA, 1989
FREDDY'S DEAD: THE FINAL NIGHTMARE
   New Line Cinema, 1991
OUT OF SYNC   BET Films, 1994

MARIE BUTLER KOUF

DISORGANIZED CRIME   Buena Vista, 1989

MARTIN KOVE

Agent: Stone Manners Agency - Los Angeles, 213/654-7575

THE KARATE KID   Columbia, 1984
THE KARATE KID PART II   Columbia, 1986
STEELE JUSTICE   Atlantic Releasing Corporation, 1987
HIGHER GROUND (TF)   Green-Epstein Productions/
   Columbia TV, 1988
THE KARATE KID PART III   Columbia, 1989

PETE KOWANKO

STARCROSSED (TF)   Fries Entertainment, 1985
SYLVESTER   Columbia, 1985
THE GIFTED ONE (TF)   Richard Rothstein Productions/NBC
   Productions, 1989

SHIGERU KOYAMA

BLACK RAIN   Paramount, 1989

HARLEY JANE KOZAK
(Harley Kozak)
Agent: UTA - Beverly Hills, 310/273-6700

PARENTHOOD   Universal, 1989
SIDE OUT   TriStar, 1990
ARACHNOPHOBIA   Buena Vista, 1990
THE TAKING OF BEVERLY HILLS   Nelson Entertainment, 1991
NECESSARY ROUGHNESS   Paramount, 1991
ALL I WANT FOR CHRISTMAS   Paramount, 1991
THE FAVOR   Orion, 1994

JOHN KOZAK
A NEW LIFE   Paramount, 1988

LINDA KOZLOWSKI
Agent: William Morris Agency - Beverly Hills, 310/274-7451

"CROCODILE" DUNDEE   Paramount, 1986, Australian
"CROCODILE" DUNDEE II   Paramount, 1988, U.S.-Australian
FAVORITE SON (MS)   NBC Productions, 1988
ALMOST AN ANGEL   Paramount, 1990, Australian-U.S.
VILLAGE OF THE DAMNED   Universal, 1995

JEROEN KRABBÉ
Agent: The Marion Rosenberg Office - Los Angeles, 213/653-7383

NO MERCY   TriStar, 1986
JUMPIN' JACK FLASH   20th Century Fox, 1986
THE LIVING DAYLIGHTS   MGM/UA, 1987, British
CROSSING DELANCEY   Warner Bros., 1988
THE PUNISHER   New World, 1989
SECRET WEAPON (CTF)   Griffin-Elysian Productions/TVS/
   ABC-Australia, 1990, U.S.-British-Australian
THE PRINCE OF TIDES   Columbia, 1991
THE FUGITIVE   Warner Bros., 1993
KING OF THE HILL   Gramercy Pictures, 1993
IMMORTAL BELOVED   Columbia, 1994

JANE KRAKOWSKI
STEPPING OUT   Paramount, 1991

SAVELY KRAMAROV
MOSCOW ON THE HUDSON   Columbia, 1984

STEPFANIE KRAMER
HUNTER (TF)   Stephen J. Cannell Productions, 1984
BRIDGE ACROSS TIME (TF)   Fries Entertainment, 1985
TAKE MY DAUGHTERS, PLEASE (TF)   NBC Productions, 1988

J. DAVID KRASSNER
CLEAN AND SOBER   Warner Bros., 1988

BRIAN KRAUSE
Agent: William Morris Agency - Beverly Hills, 310/274-7451

RETURN TO THE BLUE LAGOON   Columbia, 1991
STEPHEN KING'S SLEEPWALKERS   Columbia, 1992

DAVID KRIEGEL
SPEED   20th Century Fox, 1994
SLEEP WITH ME   MGM/UA, 1994

ALICE KRIGE
A TALE OF TWO CITIES (TF)   Norman Rosemont Productions/
   Marble Arch Productions, 1980, U.S.-British
CHARIOTS OF FIRE   The Ladd Company/Warner Bros.,
   1981, British
GHOST STORY   Universal, 1981
ELLIS ISLAND (MS)   Pantheon Pictures/Telepictures Productions,
   1984, U.S.-British
KING DAVID   Paramount, 1985, U.S.-British
WALLENBERG: A HERO'S STORY (MS)   Dick Berg-Stonehenge
   Productions/Paramount TV, 1985

DREAM WEST (MS)   Sunn Classic Pictures, 1986
SECOND SERVE (TF)   Linda Yellen Productions/
   Lorimar-Telepictures, 1986
BARFLY   Cannon, 1987
SEE YOU IN THE MORNING   Warner Bros., 1989
MAX AND HELEN (CTF)   Citadel Entertainment, 1990
STEPHEN KING'S SLEEPWALKERS   Columbia, 1992

SYLVIA KRISTEL
b. September 28, 1952 - Utrecht, Holland

BECAUSE OF THE CATS   1972, Dutch
LIVING APART TOGETHER   1973, Dutch
EMMANUELLE   Columbia, 1974, French
UN LINCEUL N'A PAS DE POCHES   1974, French
LE JEU AVE LE FEU   Arcadic Productions, 1974, French
JULIA: INNOCENCE ONCE REMOVED   *JULIA*   1974,
   French-West German
EMMANUELLE—JOYS OF A WOMAN   *EMMANUELLE II*
   1975, French
LA MARGE   1976, French
ALICE OR THE LAST ESCAPADE   *ALICE OU LA DERNIERE
   FUGUE*   Filmel-PHPG, 1976, French
UNE FEMME FIDELE   FFCM, 1976, French
RENÉ LA CANNE   1977, French
GOODBYE EMMANUELLE   1978, French
MYSTERIES   1979, Dutch
THE CONCORDE—AIRPORT '79   Universal, 1979
THE FIFTH MUSKETEER   Columbia, 1979, Austrian
THE NUDE BOMB   Universal, 1980
PRIVATE LESSONS   Jensen Farley Pictures, 1981
LADY'S CHATTERLEY'S LOVER   Cannon, 1982, French-British
CASANOVA (TF)   Konigsberg-Sanitsky Company/Reteitalia,
   1987, U.S.-Italian

KRIS KRISTOFFERSON
b. June 22, 1936 - Brownsville, Texas
Agent: ICM - Beverly Hills, 310/550-4000

THE LAST MOVIE   Universal, 1971
CISCO PIKE   Columbia, 1972
PAT GARRETT & BILLY THE KID   MGM, 1973
THE GOSPEL ROAD   20th Century-Fox, 1973
BLUME IN LOVE   Warner Bros., 1973
BRING ME THE HEAD OF ALFREDO GARCIA   United Artists, 1974
ALICE DOESN'T LIVE HERE ANYMORE   Warner Bros., 1974
THE SAILOR WHO FELL FROM GRACE WITH THE SEA
   Avco Embassy, 1976, British
VIGILANTE FORCE   United Artists, 1976
A STAR IS BORN   Warner Bros., 1976
SEMI-TOUGH   United Artists, 1977
CONVOY   United Artists, 1978
FREEDOM ROAD (TF)   Zev Braun Productions/Freedom Road
   Films, 1979
HEAVEN'S GATE   United Artists, 1980
ROLLOVER   Orion/Warner Bros., 1981
FLASHPOINT   TriStar, 1984
SONGWRITER   TriStar, 1984
TROUBLE IN MIND   Alive Films, 1985
THE LAST DAYS OF FRANK AND JESSE JAMES (TF)
   Joseph Cates Productions, 1986
BLOOD AND ORCHIDS (MS)   Lorimar Productions, 1986
STAGECOACH (TF)   Raymond Katz Productions/Heritage
   Entertainment, 1986
AMERIKA (MS)   ABC Circle Films, 1987
BIG TOP PEE-WEE   Paramount, 1988
MILLENNIUM   20th Century Fox, 1989
WELCOME HOME   Columbia, 1989
PAIR OF ACES (TF)   Pedernales Films/Once Upon A Time
   Films, Ltd., 1990
ORIGINAL INTENT   Studio Three, 1991
CHRISTMAS IN CONNECTICUT (CTF)   Guber-Peters
   Entertainment/Turner Network TV, 1992

GARY KRUG
THE ADVENTURES OF MARK TWAIN (AF)   Atlantic Releasing
   Corporation, 1985 (voice)

DAVID KRUMHOLTZ
Agent: Carson/Adler Agency - New York, 212/307-1882

ADDAMS FAMILY VALUES   Paramount, 1993
THE SANTA CLAUSE   Buena Vista, 1994

OLEK KRUPPA
THE LAST ELEPHANT (CTF)   RHI Entertainment/Qintex
   Entertainment, 1990

JACK KRUSCHEN
RED, HOT AND BLUE   Paramount, 1949
CONFIDENCE GIRL   United Artists, 1952
A BLUEPRINT FOR MURDER   20th Century-Fox, 1953
THE WAR OF THE WORLDS   Paramount, 1953
MONEY FROM HOME   Paramount, 1954
JULIE   MGM, 1956
CRY TERROR   MGM, 1958
THE DECKS RAN RED   MGM, 1958
THE LAST VOYAGE   MGM, 1960
THE ANGRY RED PLANET   American International, 1960
THE APARTMENT ✪   United Artists, 1960
STUDS LONIGAN   United Artists, 1960
LOVER COME BACK   Universal, 1962
CAPE FEAR   Universal, 1962
REPRIEVE   *CONVICTS FOUR*   1962
McLINTOCK!   United Artists, 1963
THE UNSINKABLE MOLLY BROWN   MGM, 1964
DEAR BRIGITTE   20th Century-Fox, 1965
HARLOW   Paramount, 1965
THE HAPPENING   Columbia, 1967
CAPRICE   20th Century-Fox, 1967
THE $1,000,000 DUCK   Buena Vista, 1971
FREEBIE AND THE BEAN   Warner Bros., 1974
GUARDIAN OF THE WILDERNESS   1977
SATAN'S CHEERLEADERS   World Amusement, 1977
SUNBURN   Paramount, 1979, U.S.-British
UNDER THE RAINBOW   Orion/Warner Bros., 1981

ARMEN KSAJIKIAN
TRUE LIES   20th Century Fox, 1994

JUDY KUHN
POCAHONTAS (AF)   Buena Vista, 1995 (voice)

THOMAS JOSEPH (T.J.) KUHN
b. June 27, 1985 - Phoenix, Arizona

RAISING ARIZONA   20th Century Fox, 1987

WILLIAM KUNSTLER
MALCOLM X   Warner Bros., 1992

SWOOSIE KURTZ
b. September 6, 1944 - Omaha, Nebraska
Agent: APA - Los Angeles, 310/273-0744

FIRST LOVE   Paramount, 1977
WALKING THROUGH THE FIRE (TF)   Time-Life Films, 1979
MARRIAGE IS ALIVE AND WELL (TF)   Lorimar Productions, 1980
THE MATING SEASON (TF)   Highgate Pictures, 1980
THE WORLD ACCORDING TO GARP   Warner Bros., 1982
AGATHA CHRISTIE'S 'A CARIBBEAN MYSTERY' (TF)
   Stan Margulies Productions/Warner Bros. TV, 1983
AGAINST ALL ODDS   Columbia, 1984
GUILTY CONSCIENCE (TF)   Levinson-Link Productions/Robert
   Papazian Productions, 1985
A TIME TO LIVE (TF)   Blue Andre Productions/ITC Productions, 1985
TRUE STORIES   Warner Bros., 1986
WILDCATS   Warner Bros., 1986
BRIGHT LIGHTS, BIG CITY   MGM/UA, 1988
VICE VERSA   Columbia, 1988
DANGEROUS LIAISONS   Warner Bros., 1988
THE IMAGE (CTF)   HBO Pictures/Citadel Entertainment, 1990
STANLEY & IRIS   MGM/UA, 1990
A SHOCK TO THE SYSTEM   Corsair Pictures, 1990

THE POSITIVELY TRUE ADVENTURES OF THE ALLEGED TEXAS
   CHEERLEADER-MURDERING MOM (CTF)   Frederick S. Pierce
   Company/Sudden Entertainment Productions, 1993
AND THE BAND PLAYED ON (CTF)   HBO Pictures/Spelling
   Entertainment, 1993
REALITY BITES   Universal, 1994

NICHOLAS KUSENKO
ABOVE THE LAW   Warner Bros., 1988

DYLAN KUSSMAN
DEAD POETS SOCIETY   Buena Vista, 1989
WILD HEARTS CAN'T BE BROKEN   Buena Vista, 1991

NORA KUZMA
(See Traci LORDS)

NANCY KWAN
DRAGON: THE BRUCE LEE STORY   Universal, 1993

PETER KWONG
ANGEL TOWN   Taurus Entertainment, 1990

BURT KWOUK
GOLDFINGER   United Artists, 1964, British
YOU ONLY LIVE TWICE   United Artists, 1967, British
DEEP END   Paramount, 1970, British-West German
THE RETURN OF THE PINK PANTHER   United Artists,
   1975, British
THE PINK PANTHER STRIKES AGAIN   United Artists, 1976, British
THE LAST REMAKE OF BEAU GESTE   1977
THE FIENDISH PLOT OF DR. FU MANCHU   Orion/Warner Bros.,
   1980, British
TRAIL OF THE PINK PANTHER   MGM/UA, 1982
CURSE OF THE PINK PANTHER   MGM/UA, 1983
PLENTY   20th Century Fox, 1985, British
EMPIRE OF THE SON   Warner Bros., 1987
AIR AMERICA   TriStar, 1990

L

PATTI LABELLE
(Patricia Louise Holt)
b. October 4, 1944 - Philadelphia, Pennsylvania

A SOLDIER'S STORY   Columbia, 1984
UNNATURAL CAUSES (TF)   Blue Andre Productions/
   ITC Productions, 1986
SING   TriStar, 1989

MATTHEW LABORTEAUX
SHATTERED SPIRITS (TF)   Sheen-Greenblatt Productions/Robert
   Greenwald Productions, 1986
DEADLY FRIEND   Warner Bros., 1986

PATRICK LABORTEAUX
PRINCE OF BEL AIR (TF)   Leonard Hill Films, 1986
SUMMER SCHOOL   Paramount, 1987

RONALD LACEY
Agent: The Marion Rosenberg Office - Los Angeles, 213/653-7383

THE LIKELY LADS   EMI, 1976, British
ZULU DAWN   American Cinema, 1979, British
CHARLESTON (TF)   Robert Stigwood Productions/RSO, Inc., 1979
RAIDERS OF THE LOST ARK   Paramount, 1981

FIREFOX   Warner Bros., 1982
INVITATION TO THE WEDDING   Chancery Lane Films, 1984, British
SWORD OF THE VALIANT   Cannon, 1982, British
RED SONJA   MGM/UA, 1985
SKY BANDITS   Galaxy International, 1986, British

STEPHEN LACK
FATAL ATTRACTION   *HEAD ON*   Greentree Productions,
   1980, Canadian

ANDRE LACOMBE
THE BEAR   TriStar, 1988, French

CHERYL LADD
(Cheryl Jean Stoppelmoor)
b. July 12, 1951 - Huron, South Dakota

SATAN'S SCHOOL FOR GIRLS (TF)   Spelling-Goldberg
   Productions, 1973
THE TREASURE OF JAMAICA REEF   *EVIL IN THE DEEP*   1974
GRACE KELLY (TF)   The Kota Company/Embassy TV, 1983
NOW AND FOREVER   1983, Australian
PURPLE HEARTS   The Ladd Company/Warner Bros., 1984
ROMANCE ON THE ORIENT EXPRESS (TF)   von Zerneck
   Productions/Yorkshire TV, 1985, U.S.-British
A DEATH IN CALIFORNIA (MS)   Mace Neufeld Productions/
   Lorimar Productions, 1985
CROSSINGS (MS)   Aaron Spelling Productions, 1986
DEADLY CARE (TF)   Universal TV, 1987
BLUEGRASS (MS)   The Landsburg Company, 1988
THE FULFILLMENT OF MARY GRAY (TF)   Lee Caplin Productions/
   Indian Neck Entertainment, 1989
MILLENNIUM   20th Century Fox, 1989
JEKYLL & HYDE (TF)   King-Phoenix Entertainment/London
   Weekend TV, 1990, U.S.-British
THE GIRL WHO CAME BETWEEN THEM (TF)   Saban-Scherick
   Productions, 1990
LISA   MGM/UA, 1990
DANIELLE STEEL'S 'CHANGES'   *CHANGES* (TF)   The Cramer
   Company/NBC Productions, 1991
POISON IVY   New Line Cinema, 1992

DIANE LADD
(Rose Diane Ladner)
b. November 29, 1932 - Meridian, Mississippi
Agent: The Marion Rosenberg Office - Los Angeles, 213/653-7383

SOMETHING WILD   United Artists, 1961
THE WILD ANGELS   American International, 1966
REBEL ROUSERS   1967
THE REIVERS   National General, 1969
MACHO CALLAHAN   Avco Embassy, 1970
WUSA   Paramount, 1970
WHITE LIGHTNING   United Artists, 1973
CHINATOWN   Paramount, 1974
ALICE DOESN'T LIVE HERE ANYMORE ✪   Warner Bros., 1974
EMBRYO   Cine Artist, 1976
THADDEUS ROSE AND EDDIE (TF)   CBS, Inc., 1978
WILLA   GJL Productions/Dove, Inc., 1979
GUYANA TRAGEDY: THE STORY OF JIM JONES (TF)
   The Konigsberg Company, 1980
ALL NIGHT LONG   Universal, 1981
GRACE KELLY (TF)   The Kota Company/Embassy TV, 1983
SOMETHING WICKED THIS WAY COMES   Buena Vista, 1983
I MARRIED A CENTERFOLD (TF)   Moonlight II Productions, 1984
CRIM EOF INNOCENCE (TF)   Ohlmeyer Communications, 1985
CELEBRATION FAMILY (TF)   Frank von Zerneck Films, 1987
BLUEGRASS (MS)   The Landsburg Company, 1988
WILD AT HEART ✪   Samuel Goldwyn Company, 1990
A KISS BEFORE DYING   Universal, 1991
RAMBLING ROSE ✪   New Line Cinema, 1991
THE CEMETERY CLUB   Buena Vista, 1993
CARNOSAUR   New Horizons Pictures, 1993

PAT LAFFAN
THE SNAPPER   Miramax Films, 1993, British

ART LA FLEUR
COBRA   Warner Bros., 1986
AIR AMERICA   TriStar, 1990
OSCAR   Buena Vista, 1991
JACK THE BEAR   20th Century Fox, 1992
IN THE ARMY NOW   Buena Vista, 1994
MAN 2 MAN   Buena Vista, 1995

BERNADETTE LAFONT
WAITING FOR THE MOON   Skouras Pictures, 1987,
   U.S.-French-British-West German

FELICITY LA FORTUNE
ALL I WANT FOR CHRISTMAS   Paramount, 1991

SAMANTHA LAGPACAN
HEAVEN'S PRISONERS   Savoy Pictures, 1994

CHRISTINE LAHTI
b. April 14, 1950 - Birmingham, Michigan

DR. SCORPION (TF)   Universal TV, 1978
THE LAST TENANT (TF)   Titus Productions, 1978
...AND JUSTICE FOR ALL   Columbia, 1979
WHOSE LIFE IS IT ANYWAY?   MGM/United Artists, 1981
LADIES AND GENTLEMEN, THE FABULOUS STAINS
   Paramount, 1982
THE EXECUTIONER'S SONG (TF)   Film Communications, Inc., 1982
SWING SHIFT ✪   Warner Bros., 1984
SINGLE BARS, SINGLE WOMEN (TF)   Carsey-Werner Productions/
   Sunn Classic Pictures, 1984
LOVE LIVES ON (TF)   ABC Circle Films, 1985
JUST BETWEEN FRIENDS   Orion, 1986
AMERIKA (MS)   ABC Circle Films, 1987
STACKING   *SEASON OF DREAMS*   Spectrafilm, 1987
HOUSEKEEPING   Columbia, 1987
RUNNING ON EMPTY   Warner Bros., 1988
MISS FIRECRACKER   Corsair Pictures, 1989
GROSS ANATOMY   Buena Vista, 1989
NO PLACE LIKE HOME (TF)   Feury-Grant Productions/
   Orion TV, 1989
FUNNY ABOUT LOVE   Paramount, 1990
CRAZY FROM THE HEART (CTF)   Papazian-Hirsch Entertainment/
   DeMann Entertainment, 1991
THE DOCTOR   Buena Vista, 1991
LEAVING NORMAL   Universal, 1992
THE GOOD FIGHT (CTF)   Freyda Rothstein Productions/Hearst
   Entertainment Productions, 1992
HIDEAWAY   TriStar, 1995

LEAH LAIL
HEAVYWEIGHTS   Buena Vista, 1994

RICKI LAKE
Agent: William Morris Agency - Beverly Hills, 310/274-7451

HAIRSPRAY   New Line Cinema, 1988
WORKING GIRL   20th Century Fox, 1988
BABYCAKES (TF)   Konigsberg-Sanitsky Productions, 1989
COOKIE   Warner Bros., 1989
LAST EXIT TO BROOKLYN   Cinecom, 1989, West German-U.S.
CRY-BABY   Universal, 1990
WHERE THE DAY TAKES YOU   New Line Cinema, 1992
SERIAL MOM   Savoy Pictures, 1994

LALA
WATCHERS   Universal, 1988
TEQUILLA SUNRISE   Warner Bros., 1988
DREAM A LITTLE DREAM   Vestron, 1989

LORENZO LAMAS
b. January 20, 1958 - Santa Monica, California
Agent: David Shapira & Associates - Sherman Oaks, 818/906-0322

GREASE   Paramount, 1978
THE KILLING STREETS   21st Century, 1991

CHRISTOPHER LAMBERT
Agent: UTA - Beverly Hills, 310/273-6700

GREYSTOKE: THE LEGEND OF TARZAN, LORD OF THE APES
    Warner Bros., 1984, British-U.S.
SUBWAY   Island Pictures, 1985, French
HIGHLANDER   20th Century Fox, 1986, British-U.S.
THE SICILIAN   20th Century Fox, 1987
TO KILL A PRIEST   Columbia, 1988
HIGHLANDER II - THE QUICKENING   Entertainment Film
    Distributors, 1991, British-U.S.
KNIGHT MOVES   InterStar Releasing, 1993
FORTRESS   Dimension/Miramax Films, 1993, Australian-U.S.
GUNMEN   Dimension/Miramax Films, 1994
ROADFLOWER   Miramax Films, 1994
MORTAL KOMBAT   New Line Cinema, 1995

VASSILI LAMBRINOS
LAST RITES   MGM/UA, 1988

MARK LAMOS
LONGTIME COMPANION   Samuel Goldwyn Company, 1990

JOHN LA MOTTA
AMERICAN NINJA   Cannon, 1985

DOROTHY LAMOUR
(Mary Leta Dorothy Kaumeyer)
b. December 10, 1914 - New Orleans, Louisiana
Agent: Fred Amsel & Associates - Los Angeles, 213/939-1188

THE JUNGLE PRINCESS   Paramount, 1936
SWING HIGH, SWING LOW   Paramount, 1937
COLLEGE HOLIDAY   Paramount, 1937
THE LAST TRAIN FROM MADRID   Paramount, 1937
HIGH WIDE AND HANDSOME   Paramount, 1973
THE HURRICANE   Paramount, 1937
THRILL OF A LIFETIME   Paramount, 1937
THE BIG BROADCAST OF 1938   Paramount, 1938
HER JUNGLE LOVE   Paramount, 1938
SPAWN OF THE NORTH   Paramount, 1938
TROPIC HOLIDAY   Paramount, 1938
ST. LOUIS BLUES   Paramount, 1939
MAN ABOUT TOWN   Paramount, 1939
DISPUTED PASSAGE   Paramount, 1939
JOHNNY APOLLO   20th Century-Fox, 1940
TYPHOON   Paramount, 1940
ROAD TO SINGAPORE   Paramount, 1940
MOON OVER BURMA   Paramount, 1940
CHAD HANNA   20th Century-Fox, 1940
ROAD TO ZANZIBAR   Paramount, 1941
CAUGHT IN THE DRAFT   Paramount, 1941
ALOMA OF THE SOUTH SEAS   Paramount, 1941
THE FLEET'S IN   Paramount, 1942
BEYOND THE BLUE HORIZON   Paramount, 1942
ROAD TO MOROCCO   Paramount, 1942
STAR SPANGLED RHYTHM   Paramount, 1942
THEY GOT ME COVERED   RKO Radio, 1943
DIXIE   Paramount, 1943
RIDING HIGH   Paramount, 1943
AND THE ANGELS SING   Paramount, 1944
RAINBOW ISLAND   Paramount, 1944
A MEDAL FOR BENNY   Paramount, 1945
DUFFY'S TAVERN   Paramount, 1945
MASQUERADE IN MEXICO   Paramount, 1945
ROAD TO UTOPIA   Paramount, 1945
MY FAVORITE BRUNETTE   Paramount, 1947
ROAD TO RIO   Paramount, 1947
WILD HARVEST   Paramount, 1947
VARIETY GIRL   Paramount, 1947
A MIRACLE CAN HAPPEN   *ON OUR MERRY WAY*
    United Artists, 1948
LULU BELLE   1948
THE GIRL FROM MANHATTAN   United Artists, 1948
SLIGHTLY FRENCH   Columbia, 1949
MANHANDLED   Paramount, 1949
THE LUCKY STIFF   1949

HERE COMES THE GROOM   Paramount, 1951
THE GREATEST SHOW ON EARTH   Paramount, 1952
ROAD TO BALI   Paramount, 1952
THE ROAD TO HONG KONG   United Artists, 1962
DONOVAN'S REEF   Paramount, 1963
PAJAMA PARTY   Warner Bros., 1964
THE PHYNX   Warner Bros., 1970
WON TON TON, THE DOG WHO SAVED HOLLYWOOD
    Paramount, 1975
DEATH OF LOVE HOUSE (TF)   Spelling-Goldberg Productions, 1976
CREEPSHOW 2   New World, 1987

ZOHRA LAMPERT
SPENDOR IN THE GRASS   Warner Bros., 1961
PAY OR DIE   Allied Artists, 1960
BYE BYE BRAVERMAN   Warner Bros., 1968
A FINE MADNESS   Warner Bros., 1966
OPENING NIGHT   Faces International, 1978
ALPHABET CITY   Atlantic Releasing Corporation, 1984
TEACHERS   MGM/UA, 1984

CHUS LAMPREAVE
WHAT HAVE I DONE TO DESERVE THIS?   Cinevista,
    1985, Spanish

BURT LANCASTER†
(Burton Stephen Lancaster)
b. November 2, 1913 - New York, New York
d. October 20, 1994

THE KILLERS   Universal, 1946
VARIETY GIRL   Paramount, 1947
BRUTE FORCE   Warner Bros., 1947
DESERT FURY   Paramount, 1947
I WALK ALONE   Paramount, 1948
ALL MY SONS   Universal, 1948
SORRY, WRONG NUMBER   Paramount, 1948
KISS THE BLOOD OFF MY HANDS   Universal, 1948
CRISS CROSS   Universal, 1949
ROPE OF SAND   Paramount, 1949
THE FLAME AND THE ARROW   Warner Bros., 1950
MISTER 880   20th Century-Fox, 1950
VENGEANCE VALLEY   MGM, 1951
JIM THORPE—ALL AMERICAN   Warner Bros., 1951
TEN TALL MEN   1951
THE CRIMSON PIRATE   Warner Bros., 1952, U.S.-British
COME BACK LITTLE SHEBA   Paramount, 1952
SOUTH SEA WOMAN   Warner Bros., 1953
FROM HERE TO ETERNITY ★   Columbia, 1953
HIS MAJESTY O'KEEFE   Warner Bros., 1954
APACHE   United Artists, 1954
VERA CRUZ   United Artists, 1954
THE KENTUCKIAN   United Artists, 1955 (also directed)
THE ROSE TATTOO   Paramount, 1955
TRAPEZE   United Artists, 1956
THE RAINMAKER   Paramount, 1956
GUNFIGHT AT THE O.K. CORRAL   Paramount, 1957
SWEET SMELL OF SUCCESS   United Artists, 1957
RUN SILENT, RUN DEEP   United Artists, 1958
SEPARATE TABLES   United Artists, 1958
THE DEVIL'S DISCIPLE   United Artists, 1959, British-U.S.
THE UNFORGIVEN   United Artists, 1960
ELMER GANTRY ★★   United Artists, 1960
THE YOUNG SAVAGES   United Artists, 1961
JUDGMENT AT NUREMBERG   United Artists, 1961
BIRDMAN OF ALCATRAZ ★   United Artists, 1962
A CHILD IS WAITING   United Artists, 1963
THE LIST OF ADRIAN MESSENGER   Universal, 1963
THE LEOPARD   *IL GATTOPARDO*   20th Century-Fox,
    1963, Italian-French
SEVEN DAYS IN MAY   Paramount, 1964
THE TRAIN   United Artists, 1964, U.S.-French-Italian
THE HALLELUJAH TRAIL   United Artists, 1965
THE PROFESSIONALS   Columbia, 1966
THE SCALPHUNTERS   United Artists, 1968
THE SWIMMER   Columbia, 1968
CASTLE KEEP   Columbia, 1969
THE GYPSY MOTHS   MGM, 1969

KING: A FILMED RECORD...MONTGOMERY TO MEMPHIS (FD)
  Maron Films Limited, 1970
AIRPORT   Universal, 1970
LAWMAN   United Artists, 1971
VALDEZ IS COMING   United Artists, 1971
ULZANA'S RAID   Universal, 1972
SCORPIO   United Artists, 1973
EXECUTIVE ACTION   National General, 1973
THE MIDNIGHT MAN   Universal, 1974 (also co-directed)
CONVERSATION PIECE   *GRUPPO DI FAMIGLIA IN UNO INTERO*
  New Line Cinema, 1975, Italian-French
MOSES (TF)   Avco Embassy, 1976, U.S.-Italian
1900   Paramount, 1976, Italian
BUFFALO BILL AND THE INDIANS or SITTING BULL'S HISTORY
  LESSON   United Artists, 1976
VICTORY AT ENTEBBE (TF)   1976
THE CASSANDRA CROSSING   Avco Embassy, 1977,
  British-Italian-West German
TWILIGHT'S LAST GLEAMING   Allied Artists, 1977,
  U.S.-West German
THE ISLAND OF DR. MOREAU   American International, 1977
GO TELL THE SPARTANS   Avco Embassy, 1978
ZULU DAWN   American Cinema, 1979, British
CATTLE ANNIE AND LITTLE BRITCHES   Universal, 1980
ATLANTIC CITY ★   Paramount, 1981
MARCO POLO (MS)   RAI/Franco Cristaldi Productions/Vincenzo
  Labella Productions, 1982, Italian
LOCAL HERO   Warner Bros., 1983, British-Scottish
THE OSTERMAN WEEKEND   20th Century-Fox, 1983
SCANDAL SHEET (TF)   Fair Dinkum Productions, 1985
LITTLE TREASURE   TriStar, 1985
ON WINGS OF EAGLES (MS)   Edgar J. Scherick Productions/
  Taft Entertainment TV, 1986
TOUGH GUYS   Buena Vista, 1986
BARNUM (TF)   Robert Halmi, Inc./Filmline International, 1986,
  U.S.-Canadian
ROCKET GIBRALTAR   Columbia, 1988
FIELD OF DREAMS   Universal, 1989
THE PHANTOM OF THE OPERA (MS)   Saban-Scherick
  Productions, 1990

JAMES LANCASTER

GETTYSBURG   New Line Cinema, 1993

JONATHAN ISAAC LANDAU

BIG   20th Century Fox, 1988

JULIET LANDAU

ED WOOD   Buena Vista, 1994

MARTIN LANDAU

b. June 20, 1931 - Brooklyn, New York
Agent: William Morris Agency - Beverly Hills, 310/274-7451

PORK CHOP HILL   United Artists, 1959
NORTH BY NORTHWEST   MGM, 1959
THE GAZEBO   MGM, 1960
STAGECOACH TO DANCERS' ROCK   Universal, 1962
CLEOPATRA   20th Century-Fox, 1963
THE GREATEST STORY EVER TOLD   United Artists, 1965
THE HALLELUJAH TRAIL   United Artists, 1965
NEVADA SMITH   Paramount, 1966
THEY CALL ME MISTER TIBBS!   United Artists, 1970
A TOWN CALLED HELL   *A TOWN CALLED BASTARD*
  Scotia International, 1971, British-Spanish
WELCOME HOME, JOHNNY BRISTOL (TF)   Cinema Center, 1971
SAVAGE (TF)   Universal TV, 1973
BLACK GUNN   1972
SAVAGE (TF)   Universal TV, 1973
TOUGH TONY   *TONY SAITTA*   1976, Italian
BLAZING MAGNUMS   *STRANGE SHADOWS IN AN
  EMPTY ROOM*   1977
METEOR   American International, 1979
THE RETURN   *THE ALIEN'S RETURN*   1980
WITHOUT WARNING   *IT CAME WITHOUT WARNING*
  Filmways, 1980
ALONE IN THE DARK   New Line Cinema, 1982
TREASURE ISLAND   Cannon, 1986, French

SWEET REVENGE   Concorde, 1987
EMPIRE STATE   Virgin/Miracle, 1987, British
TUCKER - THE MAN AND HIS DREAM ✪   Paramount, 1988
CRIMES AND MISDEMEANORS ✪   Orion, 1989
NEON EMPIRE (CMS)   Richard Maynard Productions/Fries
  Entertainment, 1989
MAX AND HELEN (CTF)   Citadel Entertainment, 1990
BY DAWN'S EARLY LIGHT (CTF)   HBO Pictures/Paravision
  International, 1990
MISTRESS   Tribeca Films, 1992
SLIVER   Paramount, 1993
EYE OF THE STRANGER   Silver Lake International Pictures, 1993
INTERSECTION   Paramount, 1994
ED WOOD   Buena Vista, 1994
JOSEPH (CTF)   Turner Network TV, 1994
CITY HALL   Columbia, 1995

AUDREY LANDERS

A CHORUS LINE   Columbia, 1985
POPEYE DOYLE (TF)   December 3rd Productions/Robert Singer
  Productions/20th Century Fox TV, 1986

STEVE LANDESBERG

HOW MUCH ARE THOSE CHILDREN IN THE WINDOW?
  Concorde, 1995

TIMOTHY LANDFIELD

CHEETAH   Buena Vista, 1989

GUDRUN LANDGREBE

THE BERLIN AFFAIR   Cannon, 1985, Italian-West German

SONNY LANDHAM

ACTION JACKSON   Lorimar, 1988
LOCK UP   TriStar, 1989

HAL LANDON, JR.

BILL & TED'S BOGUS JOURNEY   Orion, 1991

PAVEL LANDOVSKY

THE UNBEARABLE LIGHTNESS OF BEING   Orion, 1988

VALERIE LANDSBURG

THE RYAN WHITE STORY (TF)   The Landsburg Company, 1989

DIANE LANE

b. January 22, 1963 - New York, New York
Agent: William Morris Agency - Beverly Hills, 310/274-7451

A LITTLE ROMANCE   Orion/Warner Bros., 1979, U.S.-French
LADIES AND GENTLEMEN, THE FABULOUS STAINS
  Paramount, 1982
RUMBLE FISH   Universal, 1983
STREETS OF FIRE   Universal, 1984
THE COTTON CLUB   Orion, 1984
LADY BEWARE   Scotti Brothers, 1987
THE BIG TOWN   Columbia, 1987
LONESOME DOVE (MS)   Motown Productions/Pangaea/Qintex
  Entertainment, Inc., 1989
VITAL SIGNS   20th Century Fox, 1990
FRANKIE & JOHNNY   Paramount, 1991
CHAPLIN   TriStar, 1992, U.S.-British
KNIGHT MOVES   InterStar Releasing, 1993
INDIAN SUMMER   Buena Vista, 1993
THE WORLD'S OLDEST LIVING CONFEDERATE WIDOW
  TELLS ALL (MS)   CBS, 1994
WILD BILL   MGM/UA, 1995
JUDGE DREDD   Buena Vista, 1995

NATHAN LANE

Agent: William Morris Agency - Beverly Hills, 310/274-7451

FRANKIE & JOHNNY   Paramount, 1991
LIFE WITH MIKEY   Buena Vista, 1993
THE LION KING (AF)   Buena Vista, 1994 (voice)

PERRY LANG

ZUMA BEACH (TF)   Edgar J. Scherick Associates/
   Warner Bros. TV, 1978
BIG WEDNESDAY   Warner Bros., 1978
1941   Universal/Columbia, 1979
THE BIG RED ONE   United Artists, 1980
ALLIGATOR   Group 1, 1980
SPRING BREAK   Columbia, 1983
MORTUARY ACADEMY   Landmark Releasing, 1987
EIGHT MEN OUT   Orion, 1988
REVEALING EVIDENCE (TF)   T.W.S. Productions/
   Universal TV, 1990

STEPHEN LANG

b. July 11, 1952 - New York, New York
Agent: William Morris Agency - Beverly Hills, 310/274-7451

DEATH OF A SALESMAN (TF)   Roxbury and Punch
   Productions, 1985
STONE PILLOW (TF)   Schaefer-Karpf Productions/Gaylord
   Productions, 1985
BAND OF THE HAND   TriStar, 1986
MANHUNTER   DEG, 1986
LAST EXIT TO BROOKLYN   Cinecom, 1989, West German-U.S.
THE HARD WAY   Universal, 1991
ANOTHER YOU   TriStar, 1991
GETTYSBURG   New Line Cinema, 1993
BEYOND INNOCENCE   Buena Vista, 1994
LITTLE PANDA   Warner Bros., 1995

SUE ANE LANGDON

THE OUTSIDER   Universal, 1961
THE ROUNDERS   MGM, 1965
A FINE MADNESS   Warner Bros., 1966
A GUIDE FOR THE MARRIED MAN   20th Century-Fox, 1967
THE CHEYENNE SOCIAL CLUB   National General, 1970
WITHOUT WARNING   Filmways, 1980
ZAPPED!   Embassy, 1982

HOPE LANGE

b. November 28, 1931 - Redding Ridge, Connecticut
Agent: Century Artists, Ltd. - Beverly Hills, 310/273-4366

BUS STOP   20th Century-Fox, 1956
THE TRUE STORY OF JESSE JAMES   20th Century-Fox, 1957
PEYTON PLACE ✪   20th Century-Fox, 1957
THE YOUNG LIONS   20th Century-Fox, 1958
IN LOVE AND WAR   1958
THE BEST OF EVERYTHING   20th Century-Fox, 1959
WILD IN THE COUNTRY   1961
POCKETFUL OF MIRACLES   United Artists, 1961
LOVE IS A BALL   United Artists, 1963
JIGSAW   Universal, 1968
CROWHAVEN FARM (TF)   Aaron Spelling Productions, 1970
THAT CERTAIN SUMMER (TF)   Universal TV, 1972
THE 500 POUND JERK (TF)   Wolper Productions, 1972
DEATH WISH   Paramount, 1974
I LOVE YOU, GOODBYE (TF)   Tomorrow Entertainment, 1974
FER DE LANCE (TF)   Leslie Stevens Productions, 1974
THE SECRET NIGHT CALLER (TF)   Charles Fries Productions/
   Penthouse Productions, 1975
LIKE NORMAL PEOPLE (TF)   Christiana Productions/
   20th Century-Fox TV, 1979
THE DAY CHRIST DIED (TF)   Martin Manulis Productions/
   20th Century-Fox TV, 1980
I AM THE CHEESE   Libra Cinema 5, 1983
THE PRODIGAL   World Wide, 1984
A NIGHTMARE ON ELM STREET 2: FREDDY'S REVENGE
   New Line Cinema, 1985
BLUE VELVET   DEG, 1986
CLEAR AND PRESENT DANGER   Paramount, 1994

JESSICA LANGE

b. April 20, 1950 - Cloquet, Minnesota
Agent: CAA - Beverly Hills, 310/288-4545

KING KONG   Paramount, 1976
ALL THAT JAZZ   20th Century-Fox, 1979
HOW TO BEAT THE HIGH COST OF LIVING
   American International, 1980
THE POSTMAN ALWAYS RINGS TWICE   Paramount, 1981
TOOTSIE ✪✪   Columbia, 1982
FRANCES ★   Universal/AFD, 1982
COUNTRY ★   Buena Vista, 1984
SWEET DREAMS ★   TriStar, 1985
CRIMES OF THE HEART   DEG, 1986
EVERYBODY'S ALL-AMERICAN   Warner Bros., 1988
FAR NORTH   Alive Films, 1988
MUSIC BOX ★   TriStar, 1989
MEN DON'T LEAVE   Warner Bros., 1990
CAPE FEAR   Universal, 1991
O PIONEERS! (TF)   Craig Anderson Productions/Lorimar TV/
   Prairie Films, 1992
NIGHT AND THE CITY   20th Century Fox, 1992
BLUE SKY   Orion, 1994
LOSING ISAIAH   Paramount, 1995
ROB ROY   MGM/UA, 1995

FRANK LANGELLA

b. January 1, 1940 - Bayonne, New Jersey
Agent: Harris & Goldberg - Los Angeles, 310/553-5200

THE TWELVE CHAIRS   UMC, 1970
DIARY OF A MAD HOUSEWIFE   Universal, 1970
THE DEADLY TRAP   LA MAISON SOUS LES ARBRES
   National General, 1971, French-Italian
THE WRATH OF GOD   MGM, 1972
THE MARK OF ZORRO (TF)   20th Century-Fox, 1974
DRACULA   Universal, 1979
THOSE LIPS, THOSE EYES   United Artists, 1980
SPHINX   Orion/Warner Bros., 1981
LIBERTY (TF)   Robert Greenwald Productions, 1986
THE MEN'S CLUB   Atlantic Releasing Corporation, 1986
MASTERS OF THE UNIVERSE   Cannon, 1987
AND GOD CREATED WOMAN   Vestron, 1988
TRUE IDENTITY   Buena Vista, 1991
DAVE   Warner Bros., 1993
DOOMSDAY GUN (CTF)   HBO Pictures, 1994
BRAINSCAN   Triumph Releasing Corporation, 1994
JUNIOR   Universal, 1994

HEATHER LANGENKAMP

A NIGHTMARE ON ELM STREET   New Line Cinema, 1984
A NIGHTMARE ON ELM STREET 3: DREAM WARRIORS
   New Line Cinema, 1987
WES CRAVEN'S NEW NIGHTMARE   New Line Cinema, 1994

LISA LANGLOIS

Agent: Bauman, Hiller & Associates - Los Angeles, 213/857-6666

HAPPY BIRTHDAY TO ME   Columbia, 1981, Canadian
THE MAN WHO WASN'T THERE   Paramount, 1983
JOY OF SEX   Paramount, 1984
THE NEST   Concorde, 1988

ANGELA LANSBURY

b. October 16, 1925 - London, England
Agent: William Morris Agency - Beverly Hills, 310/274-7451

GASLIGHT ✪   MGM, 1944
NATIONAL VELVET   MGM, 1944
THE PICTURE OF DORIAN GRAY ✪   MGM, 1945
THE HARVEY GIRLS   MGM, 1946
THE HOODLUM SAINT   MGM, 1946
TILL THE CLOUDS ROLL BY   MGM, 1946
THE PRIVATE AFFAIRS OF BEL AMI   United Artists, 1947
TENTH AVENUE ANGEL   MGM, 1947
IF WINTER COMES   MGM, 1947
STATE OF THE UNION   MGM, 1948

THE THREE MUSKETEERS   MGM, 1948
THE RED DANUBE   MGM, 1949
SAMSON AND DELILAH   Paramount, 1949
KIND LADY   MGM, 1951
MUTINY   Universal, 1952
REMAINS TO BE SEEN   MGM, 1953
A LAWLESS STREET   Columbia, 1955
THE PURPLE MASK   Universal, 1955
PLEASE MURDER ME   1956
THE COURT JESTER   Paramount, 1956
KEY MAN   *A LIFE AT STAKE*   1957, British
THE LONG HOT SUMMER   MGM, 1958
THE RELUCTANT DEBUTANTE   MGM, 1958
SEASON OF PASSION   *SUMMER OF THE 17TH DOLL*
   1959, Australian-British
THE DARK AT THE TOP OF THE STAIRS   Warner Bros., 1960
A BREATH OF SCANDAL   Paramount, 1960
BLUE HAWAII   Paramount, 1961
ALL FALL DOWN   MGM, 1962
THE MANCHURIAN CANDIDATE ✪   United Artists, 1962
IN THE COOL OF THE DAY   MGM, 1963, British
THE WORLD OF HENRY ORIENT   United Artists, 1964
DEAR HEART   Warner Bros., 1964
THE GREATEST STORY EVER TOLD   United Artists, 1965
THE AMOROUS ADVENTURES OF MOLL FLANDERS
   Paramount, 1965, British
HARLOW   Paramount, 1965
MISTER BUDDWING   MGM, 1966
SOMETHING FOR EVERYONE   National General, 1970, British
BEDKNOBS AND BROOMSTICKS   Buena Vista, 1971
DEATH ON THE NILE   Paramount, 1978, British
THE LADY VANISHES   Rank, 1979, British
THE MIRROR CRACK'D   AFD, 1980, British
LITTLE GLORIA...HAPPY AT LAST (MS)   Edgar J. Scherick
   Associates/Metromedia Producers Corporation, 1982,
   U.S.-Canadian-British
THE PIRATES OF PENZANCE   Universal, 1983
THE GIFT OF LOVE: A CHRISTMAS STORY (TF)   Telecom
   Entertainment/Amanda Productions, 1983
LACE (MS)   Lorimar Productions, 1984
THE COMPANY OF WOLVES   Cannon, 1984, British
MURDER, SHE WROTE (TF)   Universal TV, 1984
RAGE OF ANGELS: THE STORY CONTINUES (MS)
   NBC Productions, 1986
SHOOTDOWN (TF)   Leonard Hill Films, 1988
THE SHELL SEEKERS (TF)   Marian Rees Associates/Central
   Films Ltd., 1990, U.S.-British
BEAUTY AND THE BEAST (AF)   Buena Vista, 1991 (voice)

DAVID LANSBURY
PARALLEL LIVES (CTF)   Showtime Entertainment, 1994

WILLIAM LANTEAU
ON GOLDEN POND   Universal/AFD, 1981

CHARLES LANYER
THE STEPFATHER   New Century/Vista, 1987

ANTHONY LaPAGLIA
FRANK NITTI: THE ENFORCER (TF)   Len Hill Films, 1988
GOD'S PAYROLL   *PHONE CALLS*   1988
SLAVES OF NEW YORK   TriStar, 1989
BETSY'S WEDDING   Buena Vista, 1990
CRIMINAL JUSTICE (CTF)   Elysian Films/HBO Showcase, 1990
HE SAID, SHE SAID   Paramount, 1991
ONE GOOD COP   Buena Vista, 1991
29TH STREET   20th Century Fox, 1991
KEEPER OF THE CITY (CTF)   Viacom Pictures, 1992
WHISPERS IN THE DARK   Paramount, 1992
INNOCENT BLOOD   Warner Bros., 1992
SO I MARRIED AN AXE MURDERER   TriStar, 1993
THE CLIENT   Warner Bros., 1994
BULLETPROOF HEART   1994
LIFESAVERS   TriStar, 1994
EMPIRE   Warner Bros., 1995

ALISON LA PLACA
Agent: APA - Los Angeles, 310/273-0744

MADHOUSE   Orion, 1990

BRYAN LARKIN
BORN ON THE FOURTH OF JULY   Universal, 1989
SHE-DEVIL   Orion, 1989

LINDA LARKIN
ALADDIN (AF)   Buena Vista, 1992 (voice)
THE RETURN OF JAFAR (AV)   Buena Vista, 1994 (voice)

SAMANTHA LARKIN
BIG   20th Century Fox, 1988

SHEENA LARKIN
DR. JEKYLL AND MS. HYDE   Savoy Pictures, 1995

JOHN LARROQUETTE
b. November 25, 1947 - New Orleans, Louisiana
Agent: CAA - Beverly Hills, 310/288-4545

HEART BEAT   Orion/Warner Bros., 1980
GREEN ICE   Universal/AFD, 1981, British
STRIPES   Columbia, 1981
STAR TREK III: THE SEARCH FOR SPOCK   Paramount, 1984
CONVICTED (TF)   Larry Thompson Productions, 1986
BLIND DATE   TriStar, 1987
HOT PAINT (TF)   Catalina Production Group/MGM-UA TV, 1988
SECOND SIGHT   Warner Bros., 1989
MADHOUSE   Orion, 1990
RICHIE RICH   Warner Bros., 1994

DARRELL LARSON
MEN AT WORK   Triumph Releasing Corporation, 1990

GARY LARSON
MADE IN HEAVEN   Lorimar, 1987

ERIQ LA SALLE
COMING TO AMERICA   Paramount, 1988

MARTINO LASALLE
ALAMO BAY   TriStar, 1985

ROBERT LaSARDO
DROP ZONE   Paramount, 1994

HARRIS LASKAWAY
NECESSITY (TF)   Barry-Enright Productions/Alexander
   Productions, 1988

LOUISE LASSER
b. April 11, 1941 - New York, New York

WHAT'S NEW, PUSSYCAT?   United Artists, 1965, British
WHAT'S UP, TIGER LILY?   American International, 1966 (voice)
TAKE THE MONEY AND RUN   Cinerama Releasing
   Corporation, 1969
BANANAS   United Artists, 1971
SUCH GOOD FRIENDS   Paramount, 1971
EVERYTHING YOU ALWAYS WANTED TO KNOW ABOUT SEX*
   (*BUT WERE AFRAID TO ASK)   United Artists, 1972
COFFEE, TEA OR ME? (TF)   CBS, Inc., 1973
ISN'T IT SHOCKING? (TF)   ABC Circle Films, 1973
SLITHER   MGM, 1973
JUST ME AND YOU (TF)   Roger Gimbel Productions/EMI, 1978
IN GOD WE TRU$T   Universal, 1980
STARDUST MEMORIES   United Artists, 1980 (uncredited)
SING   TriStar, 1989
RUDE AWAKENING   Orion, 1989
MODERN LOVE   Triumph Releasing Corporation, 1990

SYDNEY LASSICK
SONNY BOY   Triumph Releasing Corporation, 1990

LOUISE LATHAM
Agent: Badgley/Connor - Los Angeles, 310/278-9313

MARNIE   Universal, 1964
FIRECREEK   Warner Bros., 1968
MAKING IT   20th Century-Fox, 1971
WHITE LIGHTNING   United Artists, 1973
THE SUGARLAND EXPRESS   Universal, 1974
THE AWAKENING LAND (MS)   Bensen-Kuhn-Sagal Productions/
   Warner Bros. TV, 1978
LOVE LIVES ON (TF)   ABC Circle Films, 1985
FRESNO (MS)   MTM Productions, 1986
PARADISE   Buena Vista, 1991

MATT LATTANZI
THAT'S LIFE!   Columbia, 1986
DIVING IN   Skouras Pictures, 1990

ELLEN HAMILTON LATZEN
FATAL ATTRACTION   Paramount, 1987

JOE D. LAUCK
ABOVE THE LAW   Warner Bros., 1988

JACK LAUFER
LOST IN YONKERS   Columbia, 1993

TED LAUFER
TEN TO MIDNIGHT   Cannon, 1983

CYNDI LAUPER
b. June 20, 1953 - New York, New York
Agent: William Morris Agency - Beverly Hills, 310/274-7451

VIBES   Columbia, 1988
MOTHER GOOSE ROCK 'N' RHYME (CTF)
   Think Entertainment, 1990
OFF AND RUNNING   Orion, 1991
LIFE WITH MIKEY   Buena Vista, 1993

MATTHEW LAURANCE
EDDIE AND THE CRUISERS   Embassy, 1983
EDDIE AND THE CRUISERS II: EDDIE LIVES   Scotti Bros., 1989

MITCHELL LAURANCE
THE PORTRAIT (CTF)   Robert Greenwald Productions/Atticus
   Corporation/Turner Network TV, 1993

TAMMY LAUREN
THE STEPFORD CHILDREN (TF)   Edgar J. Scherick Productions/
   Taft Entertainment TV, 1987
I SAW WHAT YOU DID (TF)   Universal TV, 1988
THE PEOPLE ACROSS THE LAKE (TF)   Bill McCutchen
   Productions/Columbia TV, 1988
DESPERATE FOR LOVE (TF)   Vishudda Productions/Andrew
   Adelson Productions/Lorimar Telepictures, 1989

VERONICA LAUREN
HOMEWARD BOUND: THE INCREDIBLE JOURNEY
   Buena Vista, 1993

MICHAEL LAURENCE
AIRPLANE!   Paramount, 1980

DAN LAURIA
STAKEOUT   Buena Vista, 1987
DAVID (TF)   Tough Boys, Inc./Donald March Productions/ITC
   Entertainment Group, 1988
HOWARD BEACH: MAKING THE CASE FOR MURDER (TF)
   Patchett-Kaufmann Entertainment, 1989

HUGH LAURIE
Agent: William Morris Agency - Beverly Hills, 310/274-7451

PETER'S FRIENDS   Samuel Goldwyn Company, 1992, British

PIPER LAURIE
(Rosetta Jacobs)
b. January 22, 1932 - Detroit, Michigan
Agent: William Morris Agency - Beverly Hills, 310/274-7451

LOUISA   Universal, 1950
THE MILKMAN   Universal, 1950
THE PRINCE WHO WAS A THIEF   Universal, 1951
FRANCIS GOES TO THE RACES   Universal, 1951
NO ROOM FOR THE GROOM   Universal, 1952
HAS ANYBODY SEEN MY GAL?   Universal, 1952
SON OF ALI BABA   Universal, 1952
THE MISSISSIPPI GAMBLER   Universal, 1953
THE GOLDEN BLADE   Universal, 1953
DANGEROUS MISSION   Universal, 1954
JOHNNY DARK   Universal, 1954
DAWN AT SOCORRO   Universal, 1954
SMOKE SIGNAL   Universal, 1955
AIN'T MISBEHAVIN'   Universal, 1955
KELLY AND ME   Universal, 1957
UNTIL THEY SAIL   MGM, 1957
THE HUSTLER ★   20th Century-Fox, 1961
CARRIE ⊙   United Artists, 1976
RUBY   Dimension, 1977
TIM   Satori, 1979, Australian
SKAG (TF)   NBC, 1980
THE BUNKER (TF)   Time-Life Productions/SFP France/Antenne-2,
   1981, U.S.-French
MAE WEST (TF)   Hill-Mandelker Films, 1982
THE THORN BIRDS (MS)   David L. Wolper-Stan Margulies
   Productions/Edward Lewis Productions/Warner Bros. TV, 1983
TOUGHLOVE (TF)   Fries Entertainment, 1985
RETURN TO OZ   Buena Vista, 1985
TENDER IS THE NIGHT (CMS)   Showtime/BBC/Seven Network,
   1985, U.S.-British-Australian
LOVE, MARY (TF)   CBS Entertainment, 1985
CHILDREN OF A LESSER GOD ⊙   Paramount, 1986
PROMISE (TF)   Garner-Duchow Productions/Warner Bros. TV, 1986
DISTORTIONS   Cori Films, 1987
APPOINTMENT WITH DEATH   Cannon, 1988, U.S.-British
GO TOWARD THE LIGHT (TF)   Corapeak Productions/The Polson
   Company, 1988
DREAM A LITTLE DREAM   Vestron, 1989
TWIN PEAKS (TF)   Lynch-Frost Productions/Propaganda Films/
   World Vision Enterprises, 1990
RISING SON (CTF)   Sarabande Productions, 1990
OTHER PEOPLE'S MONEY   Warner Bros., 1991
RICH IN LOVE   MGM/UA, 1993
WRESTLING ERNEST HEMINGWAY   Warner Bros., 1993

ED LAUTER
b. October 30, 1940 - Long Beach, New York
Agent: Gersh Agency - Beverly Hills, 310/274-6611

THE NEW CENTURIONS   Columbia, 1972
THE LAST AMERICAN HERO   20th Century-Fox, 1973
EXECUTIVE ACTION   National General, 1973
LOLLY MADONNA XXX   *THE LOLLY-MADONNA WAR*
   MGM, 1973
THE LONGEST YARD   Paramount, 1974
LAST HOURS BEFORE MORNING (TF)   Charles Fries
   Productions/MGM TV, 1975
KING KONG   Paramount, 1976
THE CHICKEN CHRONICLES   Avco Embassy, 1977
THE BIG SCORE   Almi Distribution, 1983
CUJO   Warner Bros., 1983
EUREKA   MGM/UA Classics, 1984, British (filmed in 1981)
LASSITER   Warner Bros., 1984
FINDERS KEEPERS   Warner Bros., 1984
THE CARTIER AFFAIR (TF)   Hill-Mandelker Productions, 1984
DEATH WISH 3   Cannon, 1985
YOUNGBLOOD   MGM/UA, 1986

RAW DEAL   DEG, 1986
THE LAST DAYS OF PATTON (TF)   Entertainment
   Partners, 1986
TENNESSEE WALTZ   Condor Productions, 1988
GLEAMING THE CUBE   20th Century Fox, 1989
WAGONS EAST   TriStar, 1994
TRIAL BY JURY   Warner Bros., 1994

DOMINIQUE LAVANANT
A FEW DAYS WITH ME   Galaxy International, 1988, French

LINDA LAVIN
b. October 15, 1937 - Portland, Maine

A PLACE TO CALL HOME (TF)   Big Deal Productions/Crawford
   Productions/Embassy TV, 1987, U.S.-Australian
LENA: MY 100 CHILDREN (TF)   Robert Greenwald
   Productions, 1987
SEE YOU IN THE MORNING   Warner Bros., 1989

ADAM LaVORGNA
29TH STREET   20th Century Fox, 1991
MILK MONEY   Paramount, 1994

JOHN PHILLIP LAW
b. September 7, 1937 - Hollywood, California

HIGH INFIDELITY   *ALTA INFEDELTA*   1964, Italian
THREE NIGHTS OF LOVE   *TRE NOTTI D'AMORE*   1964, Italian
THE RUSSIANS ARE COMING, THE RUSSIANS ARE COMING
   United Artists, 1966
HURRY SUNDOWN   Paramount, 1967
DEATH RIDES A HORSE   *DA UOMO A UOMO*   1969, Italian
DANGER DIABOLIK   *DIABOLIK*   1968, French-Italian
BARBARELLA   Paramount, 1968, French-Italian
SKIDOO   Paramount, 1969
THE SERGEANT   Warner Bros., 1968
THE HAWAIIANS   United Artists, 1970
VON RICHTHOFEN AND BROWN   United Artists, 1971
THE LOVE MACHINE   Columbia, 1971
THE LAST MOVIE   Universal, 1971
THE GOLDEN VOYAGE OF SINBAD   Columbia, 1974, British
OPEN SEASON   1974
DR. JUSTICE   1975, French
TIGERS DON'T CRY   1976, South African
SUSSURI NEL BUIO   1976, Italian
YOUR HEAVEN, MY HELL   1976
COLPO SECCO   1977, Italian
CASSANDRA CROSSING   Avco Embassy, 1977,
   British-Italian-West German
THE CRYSTAL MAN   1979, Italian
TARZAN, THE APE MAN   MGM/United Artists, 1981

BRUNO LAWRENCE
THE EFFICIENCY EXPERT   *SPOTSWOOD*   Miramax Films,
   1992, Australian

MARTIN LAWRENCE
TALKIN' DIRTY AFTER DARK   New Line Cinema, 1991
YOU SO CRAZY   Samuel Goldwyn Company, 1994
BAD BOYS   Columbia, 1995

MATTHEW LAWRENCE
DAVID (TF)   Tough Boys, Inc./Donald March Productions/ITC
   Entertainment Group, 1988
MRS. DOUBTFIRE   20th Century Fox, 1993

ADAM LAWSON
APEX   Republic Pictures, 1994

DENIS LAWSON
LOCAL HERO   Warner Bros., 1983, British-Scottish

LEIGH LAWSON
MADHOUSE MANSION   *GHOST STORY*   1974
IT'S NOT THE SIZE THAT COUNTS   *PERCY'S PROGRESS*
   Joseph Brenner Associates, 1974, British
LOVE AMONG THE RUINS (TF)   ABC Circle Films, 1975
GOLDEN RENDEZVOUS   Rank, 1977, British
THE DEVIL'S ADVOCATE   Filmworld Distributors, 1978,
   West German
TESS   Columbia, 1980, French-British
MURDER IS EASY (TF)   David L. Wolper-Stan Margulies
   Productions/Warner Bros. TV, 1982
SWORD OF THE VALIANT   1982, British
LACE (MS)   Lorimar Productions, 1984
QUEENIE (MS)   von Zerneck-Samuels Productions/Highgate
   Pictures, 1987
MADAME SOUSATZKA   Cineplex Odeon, 1988, British

RICHARD LAWSON
Agent: ICM - Beverly Hills, 310/550-4000

STICK   Universal, 1985
DOUBLE YOUR PLEASURE (TF)   Steve White Productions, 1989

PAUL LAZAR
TRAPPED IN PARADISE   20th Century Fox, 1994

VERONICA LAZAR
LUNA   20th Century-Fox, 1979, Italian-U.S.

GEORGE LAZENBY
ON HER MAJESTY'S SECRET SERVICE   United Artists,
   1969, British
UNIVERSAL SOLDIER   Hemdale, 1971, British
THE MAN FROM HONG KONG   The Movie Company/Golden
   Harvest, 1975, Australian-Hong Kong
COVER GIRLS (TF)   Columbia TV, 1977
EVENING IN BYZANTIUM (TF)   Universal TV, 1978
SAINT JACK   New World, 1979

HIEP THI LE
HEAVEN AND EARTH   Warner Bros., 1993

THUY THU LE
CASUALTIES OF WAR   Columbia, 1989

ROSEMARY LEACH
BRIEF ENCOUNTER (TF)   Carlo Ponti Productions/Cecil Clarke
   Productions, 1974
THAT'LL BE THE DAY   EMI, 1974, British
S.O.S. TITANIC (TF)   Roger Gimbel Productions/EMI TV/Argonaut
   Films, Ltd., 1979, U.S.-British
THE JEWEL IN THE CROWN (MS)   Granada TV, 1984, British
TURTLE DIARY   Samuel Goldwyn Company, 1985, British
A ROOM WITH A VIEW   Cinecom, 1985, British

CLORIS LEACHMAN
b. April 30, 1926 - Des Moines, Iowa
Agent: Metropolitan Talent Agency - Los Angeles, 213/857-4500

KISS ME DEADLY   United Artists, 1955
THE RACK   MGM, 1956
THE CHAPMAN REPORT   Warner Bros., 1962
BUTCH CASSIDY AND THE SUNDANCE KID
   20th Century-Fox, 1969
LOVERS AND OTHER STRANGERS   Cinerama Releasing
   Corporation, 1970
THE PEOPLE NEXT DOOR   Avco Embassy, 1970
WUSA   Paramount, 1970
THE STEAGLE   Avco Embassy, 1971
THE LAST PICTURE SHOW OO   Columbia, 1971
HAUNTS OF THE VERY RICH (TF)   ABC Circle Films, 1972
CHARLEY AND THE ANGEL   Buena Vista, 1973
DILLINGER   American International, 1973
HAPPY MOTHER'S DAY...LOVE, GEORGE
   RUN, STRANGER, RUN   Cinema 5, 1973

DEATH SENTENCE (TF)   Spelling-Goldberg Productions, 1974
HITCHHIKE! (TF)   Universal TV, 1974
DAISY MILLER   Paramount, 1974
YOUNG FRANKENSTEIN   20th Century-Fox, 1974
CRAZY MAMA   New World, 1975
A GIRL NAMED SOONER (TF)   Frederick Brogger Associates/
   20th Century-Fox TV, 1975
DEATH SCREAM *THE WOMAN WHO CRIED MURDER* (TF)
   RSO Films, 1975
HIGH ANXIETY   20th Century-Fox, 1977
THE MOUSE AND HIS CHILD (AF)   Sanrio, 1977 (voice)
THE NORTH AVENUE IRREGULARS   Buena Vista, 1979
BACKSTAIRS AT THE WHITE HOUSE (MS)   Ed Friendly
   Productions, 1979
THE MUPPET MOVIE   AFD, 1979, British
SCAVENGER HUNT   20th Century-Fox, 1979
S.O.S. TITANIC (TF)   Roger Gimbel Productions/EMI TV/Argonaut
   Films, Ltd., 1979, U.S.-British
FOOLIN' AROUND   Columbia, 1980
YESTERDAY   1980, Canadian
HERBIE GOES BANANAS   Buena Vista, 1980
HISTORY OF THE WORLD—PART 1   20th Century-Fox, 1981
DEADLY INTENTIONS (MS)   Green-Epstein Productions, 1985
LOVE IS NEVER SILENT (TF)   Marian Rees Associates, 1985
SHADOW PLAY   New World, 1986
MY LITTLE PONY - THE MOVIE (AF)   DEG, 1986 (voice)
WALK LIKE A MAN   MGM/UA, 1987
THE FACTS OF LIFE DOWN UNDER (TF)   Embassy TV/Crawford
   Productions, 1987, U.S.-Australian
HANSEL AND GRETEL   Cannon, 1987, U.S.-Israeli
GOING TO THE CHAPEL (TF)   The Furia Organization/
   Finnegan-Pinchuk Productions, 1988
LOVE HURTS   Vestron, 1989
PRANCER   Orion, 1989
TEXASVILLE   Columbia, 1990
THE BEVERLY HILLBILLIES   20th Century Fox, 1993

BILL LEADBETTER

TAI-PAN   DEG, 1986

MICHAEL LEARNED
b. April 9, 1939 - Washington D.C.

HURRICANE (TF)   Metromedia Productions, 1974
IT COULDN'T HAPPEN TO A NICER GUY (TF)
   The Jozak Company, 1974
WIDOW (TF)   Lorimar Productions, 1976
LITTLE MO (TF)   Mark VII, Ltd./Worldvision, 1978
TOUCHED BY LOVE   Columbia, 1980

DENIS LEARY
Agent: William Morris Agency - Beverly Hills, 310/274-7451

DEMOLITION MAN   Warner Bros., 1993
JUDGMENT NIGHT   Universal, 1993
GUNMEN   Dimension/Miramax Films, 1994
THE REF   Buena Vista, 1994
THE NEON BIBLE   Miramax Films, 1995
OPERATION DUMBO DROP   Buena Vista, 1995

TIMOTHY LEARY
ROADSIDE PROPHETS   New Line Cinema, 1992

KELLY LeBROCK
THE WOMAN IN RED   Orion, 1984
WEIRD SCIENCE   Universal, 1985
HARD TO KILL   Warner Bros., 1990

ODILE LE CLEZIO
YOUNG EINSTEIN   Warner Bros., 1988, Australian

FREDERICK LEDEBUR
GINGER AND FRED   MGM/UA, 1986, Italian-French-West German

ANN MARIE LEE
THE FLY II   20th Century Fox, 1989

CHRISTOPHER LEE
POLICE ACADEMY: MISSION TO MOSCOW   Warner Bros., 1994

JASON SCOTT LEE
BORN IN EAST L.A.   Universal, 1987
BACK TO THE FUTURE PART II   Universal, 1989
VESTIGE OF HONOR (TF)   Desperado Pictures/Dan Wigutow
   Productions/Envoy Productions/Spanish Trail Productions, 1990
MAP OF THE HUMAN HEART   Miramax Films, 1993,
   British-French-New Zealand
DRAGON: THE BRUCE LEE STORY   Universal, 1993
RAPA NUI   Warner Bros., 1994
THE JUNGLE BOOK   Buena Vista, 1994

JESSE LEE
THE BRADY BUNCH MOVIE   Paramount, 1995

JOIE LEE
SHE'S GOTTA HAVE IT   Island Pictures, 1986
SCHOOL DAZE   Columbia, 1988
DO THE RIGHT THING   Universal, 1989
MO' BETTER BLUES   Universal, 1990
CROOKLYN   Universal, 1994
LOSING ISAIAH   Paramount, 1995

MICHELE LEE
(Michele Dusiak)
b. June 24, 1942 - Los Angeles, California

HOW TO SUCCEED IN BUSINESS WITHOUT REALLY TRYING
   United Artists, 1967
THE LOVE BUG   Buena Vista, 1969
THE COMIC   Columbia, 1969
DARK VICTORY (TF)   Universal TV, 1976
BUD AND LOU (TF)   Bob Banner Associates, 1978
A LETTER TO THREE WIVES (TF)   Michael Filerman Productions/
   20th Century Fox TV, 1985
SINGLE WOMEN, MARRIED MEN (TF)   CBS Entertainment, 1989

PAUL J. Q. LEE
BIG   20th Century Fox, 1988

RUTA LEE
PTERODACTYL WOMAN FROM BEVERLY HILLS
   Experimental Pictures, 1994

SHERYL LEE
Agent: William Morris Agency - Beverly Hills, 310/274-7451

TWIN PEAKS: FIRE WALK WITH ME   New Line Cinema,
   1992, U.S.-French
BACKBEAT   Gramercy Pictures, 1994, British

SPIKE LEE
(Shelton Jackson Lee)
b. March 20, 1957 - Atlanta, Georgia

SHE'S GOTTA HAVE IT   Island Pictures, 1986 (also directed)
SCHOOL DAZE   Columbia, 1988 (also directed)
DO THE RIGHT THING   Universal, 1989 (also directed)
MO' BETTER BLUES   Universal, 1990 (also directed)
JUNGLE FEVER   Universal, 1991 (also directed)
MALCOLM X   Warner Bros., 1992 (also directed)
CROOKLYN   Universal, 1994 (also directed)

PHIL LEEDS
ENEMIES, A LOVE STORY   20th Century Fox, 1989
GHOST   Paramount, 1990
FRANKIE AND JOHNNY   Paramount, 1992

JAMES LE GROS
Agent: William Morris Agency - Beverly Hills, 310/274-7451

SOLARBABIES   MGM/UA, 1986
PHANTASM II   Universal, 1988
DRUGSTORE COWBOY   Avenue Pictures, 1989
BLOOD AND CONCRETE   I.R.S. Releasing, 1991
LEATHER JACKETS   Triumph Releasing Corporation, 1991
WHERE THE DAY TAKES YOU   New Line Cinema, 1992
MRS. PARKER AND THE VICIOUS CIRCLE   Fine Line Features/
   New Line Cinema, 1994
INFINITY   1995
DESTINY TURNS ON THE RADIO   Savoy Pictures, 1995

JOHN LEGUIZAMO
Agent: William Morris Agency - Beverly Hills, 310/274-7451

CASUALTIES OF WAR   Columbia, 1989
WHISPERS IN THE DARK   Paramount, 1992
SUPER MARIO BROS.   Buena Vista, 1993
CARLITO'S WAY   Universal, 1993
A PYROMANIAC'S LOVE STORY   Buena Vista, 1995
TO WONG FOO, THANKS FOR EVERYTHING, JULIE NEWMAR
   Universal, 1995

FREDERIC LEHNE
BILLIONAIRE BOYS CLUB (MS)   Donald March/Gross-Weston
   Productions/ITC Productions, 1987
THIS GUN FOR HIRE (CTF)   USA Cable, 1991
MAN'S BEST FRIEND   New Line Cinema, 1993
DREAM LOVER   Gramercy Pictures, 1994

RON LEIBMAN
b. October 11, 1937 - New York, New York
Agent: Gersh Agency - Beverly Hills, 310/274-6611

WHERE'S POPPA?   United Artists, 1970
THE HOT ROCK   20th Century-Fox, 1972
SLAUGHTERHOUSE FIVE   Universal, 1972
YOUR THREE MINUTES ARE UP   Cinerama Releasing
   Corporation, 1973
THE SUPER COPS   MGM, 1974
THE ART OF CRIME (TF)   Universal TV, 1975
WON TON TON, THE DOG WHO SAVED HOLLYWOOD
   Paramount, 1976
A QUESTION OF GUILT (TF)   Lorimar Productions, 1978
NORMA RAE   20th Century-Fox, 1979
MAD MAGAZINE PRESENTS UP THE ACADEMY
   UP THE ACADEMY   Warner Bros., 1980
RIVKIN: BOUNTY HUNTER (TF)   Chiarascurio Productions/
   Ten-Four Productions, 1981
ZORRO, THE GAY BLADE   20th Century-Fox, 1981
ROMANTIC COMEDY   MGM/UA, 1983
RHINESTONE   20th Century Fox, 1984
CHRISTMAS EVE (TF)   NBC Productions, 1986
TERRORIST ON TRIAL: THE UNITED STATES VS.
   SALIM AJAMI (TF)   George Englund Productions/Robert
   Papazian Productions, 1988

JANET LEIGH
(Jeanette Helen Morrison)
b. July 6, 1927 - Merced, California
Agent: Fred Amsel & Associates - Los Angeles, 213/939-1188

THE ROMANCE OF ROSY RIDGE   MGM, 1947
IF WINTER COMES   MGM, 1948
HILLS OF HOME   MGM, 1948
WORDS AND MUSIC   MGM, 1948
ACT OF VIOLENCE   MGM, 1949
LITTLE WOMEN   MGM, 1949
THE DOCTOR AND THE GIRL   MGM, 1949
THAT FORSYTE WOMAN   *THE FORSYTE SAGA*   MGM, 1949
THE RED DANUBE   MGM, 1949
HOLIDAY AFFAIR   RKO Radio, 1949
STRICTLY DISHONORABLE   MGM, 1951
ANGELS IN THE OUTFIELD   MGM, 1951
TWO TICKETS TO BROADWAY   RKO Radio, 1951

IT'S A BIG COUNTRY   MGM, 1952
JUST THIS ONCE   MGM, 1952
SCARAMOUCHE   MGM, 1952
FEARLESS FAGAN   MGM, 1952
THE NAKED SPUR   MGM, 1953
CONFIDENTIALLY CONNIE   MGM, 1953
HOUDINI   Paramount, 1953
WALKING MY BABY BACK HOME   Universal, 1953
PRINCE VALIANT   20th Century-Fox, 1954
LIVING IT UP   Paramount, 1954
THE BLACK SHIELD OF FALWORTH   Universal, 1954
ROGUE COP   MGM, 1954
PETE KELLY'S BLUES   Warner Bros., 1955
MY SISTER EILEEN   Columbia, 1955
SAFARI   Columbia, 1956, British
JET PILOT   Universal, 1957
TOUCH OF EVIL   Universal, 1958
THE VIKINGS   United Artists, 1958
THE PERFECT FURLOUGH   Universal, 1959
WHO WAS THAT LADY?   Columbia, 1960
PSYCHO ●   Paramount, 1960
PEPE   Columbia, 1960
THE MANCHURIAN CANDIDATE   United Artists, 1962
BYE BYE BIRDIE   Columbia, 1963
WIVES AND LOVERS   Paramount, 1963
KID RODELO   Paramount, 1966
HARPER   Warner Bros., 1966
THREE ON A COUCH   Columbia, 1966
AN AMERICAN DREAM   Warner Bros., 1966
THE SPY IN THE GREEN HAT   MGM, 1967
GRAND SLAM   Paramount, 1968, Italian-Spanish-West German
HELLO DOWN THERE   Paramount, 1969
HONEYMOON WITH A STRANGER (TF)
   20th Century-Fox TV, 1969
THE MONK (TF)   Thomas-Spelling Productions, 1969
THE HOUSE ON GREENAPPLE ROAD (TF)   QM Productions, 1970
DEADLY DREAM (TF)   Universal TV, 1971
ONE IS A LONELY NUMBER   MGM, 1972
NIGHT OF THE LEPUS   MGM, 1972
MURDOCK'S GANG (TF)   Don Fedderson Productions, 1973
MURDER AT THE WORLD SERIES (TF)   ABC Circle Films, 1977
TELETHON (TF)   ABC Circle Films, 1977
BOARDWALK   Atlantic Releasing Corporation, 1979
THE FOG   Avco Embassy, 1980

JENNIFER JASON LEIGH
b. 1958 - Los Angeles, California
Agent: ICM - Beverly Hills, 310/550-4000

EYES OF A STRANGER   Warner Bros., 1981
FAST TIMES AT RIDGEMONT HIGH   Universal, 1982
EASY MONEY   Orion, 1983
FLESH + BLOOD   Orion, 1985, U.S.-Dutch
THE MEN'S CLUB   Atlantic Releasing Corporation, 1986
THE HITCHER   TriStar, 1986
SISTER, SISTER   New World, 1987
HEART OF MIDNIGHT   Virgin Vision, 1989
THE BIG PICTURE   Columbia, 1989
LAST EXIT TO BROOKLYN   Cinecom, 1989, West German-U.S.
BURIED ALIVE (CTF)   Niki Marvin Productions/
   MCA Entertainment, 1990
MIAMI BLUES   Orion, 1990
BACKDRAFT   Universal, 1991
CROOKED HEARTS   MGM-Pathe, 1991
RUSH   MGM-Pathe, 1991
SINGLE WHITE FEMALE   Columbia, 1992
SHORT CUTS   Fine Line Features/New Line Cinema, 1993
THE HUDSUCKER PROXY   Warner Bros., 1994
MRS. PARKER AND THE VICIOUS CIRCLE   Fine Line Features/
   New Line Cinema, 1994
DOLORES CLAIBORNE   Columbia, 1994

SPENCER LEIGH
CARAVAGGIO   British Film Institute, 1986, British

STEVEN LEIGH
IN LOVE AND WAR (TF)   Carol Schreder Productions/Tisch-Avnet
   Productions, 1987

DAVID LEISURE
b. November 16 - San Diego, California
Agent: Harris & Goldberg - Los Angeles, 310/553-5200

AIRPLANE! Paramount, 1980
IF IT'S TUESDAY, IT STILL MUST BE BELGIUM (TF)
 Eisenstock & Mintz Productions, 1987
PERFECT PEOPLE (TF) Robert Greenwald Productions, 1988
GODDESS OF LOVE (TF) Phil Margo Enterprises/New World TV/
 Phoenix Entertainment Group, 1988
YOU CAN'T HURRY LOVE MCEG, 1989

DONOVAN LEITCH
Agent: William Morris Agency - Beverly Hills, 310/274-7451

AND GOD CREATED WOMAN Vestron, 1988
THE BLOB TriStar, 1988
THE IN CROWD Orion, 1988
GLORY TriStar, 1989

PAUL LeMAT
FIREHOUSE (TF) Metromedia Productions/Stonehenge
 Productions, 1972
AMERICAN GRAFFITI Universal, 1973
ALOHA BOBBY AND ROSE Columbia, 1975
CITIZENS BAND *HANDLE WITH CARE* Paramount, 1977
MORE AMERICAN GRAFFITI Universal, 1979
MELVIN AND HOWARD Universal, 1980
DEATH VALLEY Universal, 1982
JIMMY THE KID New World, 1983
STRANGE INVADERS Orion, 1983, Canadian
THE BURNING BED (TF) Tisch-Avnet Productions, 1984
THE HANOI HILTON Cannon, 1987
PRIVATE INVESTIGATIONS MGM/UA, 1987
EASY WHEELS Fries Entertainment, 1989
BLIND WITNESS (TF) King Phoenix Entertainment Group, 1989

JOHN D. LeMAY
JASON GOES TO HELL—THE FINAL FRIDAY
 New Line Cinema, 1993

CHRIS LEMMON
Agent: Gordon/Rosson Talent Agency - Studio City, 818/509-1900

AIRPORT '77 Universal, 1977
THAT'S LIFE! Columbia, 1986
DAD Universal, 1989
LENA'S HOLIDAY Crown International, 1991

JACK LEMMON
(John Uhler Lemmon III)
b. February 8, 1925 - Boston, Massachusetts
Agent: CAA - Beverly Hills, 310/288-4545

IT SHOULD HAPPEN TO YOU Columbia, 1954
PHFFFT! Columbia, 1954
THREE FOR THE SHOW Columbia, 1955
MISTER ROBERTS ○○ Warner Bros., 1955
MY SISTER EILEEN Universal, 1955
YOU CAN'T RUN AWAY FROM IT Columbia, 1956
FIRE DOWN BELOW Columbia, 1957
OPERATION MAD BALL Columbia, 1957
COWBOY Columbia, 1958
BELL, BOOK AND CANDLE Columbia, 1958
SOME LIKE IT HOT ★ United Artists, 1959
IT HAPPENED TO JANE Columbia, 1959
THE APARTMENT ★ United Artists, 1960
PEPE Columbia, 1960
THE WACKIEST SHIP IN THE ARMY 1960
THE NOTORIOUS LANDLADY Columbia, 1962
DAYS OF WINE AND ROSES ★ Warner Bros., 1962
IRMA LA DOUCE United Artists, 1963
UNDER THE YUM YUM TREE Columbia, 1963
GOOD NEIGHBOR SAM Columbia, 1964
HOW TO MURDER YOUR WIFE United Artists, 1965
THE GREAT RACE Warner Bros., 1965

THE FORTUNE COOKIE United Artists, 1966
LUV Columbia, 1967
THE ODD COUPLE Paramount, 1968
THE APRIL FOOLS National General, 1969
THE OUT-OF-TOWNERS Paramount, 1970
THE WAR BETWEEN MEN AND WOMEN National General, 1972
AVANTI! United Artists, 1972, U.S.-Italian
SAVE THE TIGER ★★ Paramount, 1973
THE FRONT PAGE Universal, 1974
THE PRISONER OF SECOND AVENUE Warner Bros., 1975
THE ENTERTAINER (TF) RSO Films, 1975
ALEX & THE GYPSY 20th Century-Fox, 1976
AIRPORT '77 Universal, 1977
THE CHINA SYNDROME ★ Columbia, 1979
TRIBUTE ★ 20th Century-Fox, 1980
BUDDY BUDDY MGM/United Artists, 1981
MISSING ★ Universal, 1982
MASS APPEAL Universal, 1984
MACARONI Paramount, 1985, Italian
THAT'S LIFE! Columbia, 1986
LONG DAY'S JOURNEY INTO NIGHT (TF) 1987
THE MURDER OF MARY PHAGAN (MS) George Stevens, Jr.
 Productions/Century Tower Productions, 1988
DAD Universal, 1989
JFK Warner Bros., 1991
FOR RICHER, FOR POORER *FATHER, SON AND THE
 MISTRESS* (CTF) Citadel Entertainment Productions, 1992
THE PLAYER Fine Line Features/New Line Cinema, 1992
GLENGARRY GLEN ROSS New Line Cinema, 1992
SHORT CUTS Fine Line Features/New Line Cinema, 1993
GRUMPY OLD MEN Warner Bros., 1993
GETTING AWAY WITH MURDER Savoy Pictures, 1995
THE GRASS HARP New Line Cinema, 1995

KASI LEMMONS
SCHOOL DAZE Columbia, 1988
VAMPIRE'S KISS Hemdale, 1988z
THE SILENCE OF THE LAMBS Orion, 1991

GENEVIEVE LEMON
SWEETIE Avenue Pictures, 1990, Australian
THE PIANO Miramax Films, 1993, New Zealand-French

UTE LEMPER
PRET-A-PORTER Miramax Films, 1994

MARK LENARD
STAR TREK - THE MOTION PICTURE Paramount, 1979
STAR TREK III: THE SEARCH FOR SPOCK Paramount, 1984
STAR TREK IV: THE VOYAGE HOME Paramount, 1986
STAR TREK VI: THE UNDISCOVERED COUNTRY
 Paramount, 1991

DINAH LENNEY
BABYFEVER Rainbow Releasing, 1994

HARRY J. LENNIX
Agent: William Morris Agency - Beverly Hills, 310/274-7451

THE FIVE HEARTBEATS 20th Century Fox, 1991
MO' MONEY Columbia, 1992

TEA LEONI
BAD BOYS Columbia, 1995

JAY LENO
b. April 28, 1950 - New Rochelle, New York

SILVER BEARS Columbia, 1978
AMERICAN HOT WAX Paramount, 1978
AMERICATHON United Artists, 1979
DAVE Warner Bros., 1993
WE'RE BACK! A DINOSAUR'S STORY (AF) Universal,
 1993 (voice)
THE FLINTSTONES Universal, 1994

KAY LENZ
Agent: The Gage Group - Los Angeles, 213/859-8777

BREEZY   Universal, 1973
LISA, BRIGHT AND DARK (TF)   Bob Banner Associates, 1973
WHITE LINE FEVER   Columbia, 1975
THE GREAT SCOUT AND CATHOUSE THURSDAY
   American International, 1976
RICH MAN, POOR MAN (MS)   Universal TV, 1976
THE PASSAGE   United Artists, 1979, British
HOUSE   New World, 1986
STRIPPED TO KILL   Concorde, 1987
SMOKE   Columbia, 1988
PHYSICAL EVIDENCE   Columbia, 1989
FALLING FROM GRACE   Columbia, 1992

MELISSA LEO
ALWAYS   Samuel Goldwyn Company, 1985
A TIME OF DESTINY   Columbia, 1988

LEON
Agent: UTA - Beverly Hills, 310/273-6700

THE FIVE HEARTBEATS   20th Century Fox, 1991
CLIFFHANGER   TriStar, 1993
COOL RUNNINGS   Buena Vista, 1993
ABOVE THE RIM   New Line Cinema, 1994

DAVID LEON
BEATLEMANIA   American Cinema, 1981

JOE LEON
ALMOST YOU   TLC Films/20th Century Fox, 1984

ROBERT SEAN LEONARD
Agent: William Morris Agency - Beverly Hills, 310/274-7451

DEAD POETS SOCIETY   Buena Vista, 1989
MR. AND MRS. BRIDGE   Miramax Films, 1990
SWING KIDS   Buena Vista, 1993
MARRIED TO IT   Orion, 1993
MUCH ADO ABOUT NOTHING   Samuel Goldwyn Company,
   1993, British-U.S.
THE AGE OF INNOCENCE   Columbia, 1993
SAFE PASSAGE   New Line Cinema, 1994

AL LEONG
BILL & TED'S EXCELLENT ADVENTURE   Orion, 1989
CAGE   New Century/Vista, 1989

TEA LEONI
BAD BOYS   Columbia, 1995

CHAUNCEY LEOPARDI
HOUSEGUEST   Buena Vista, 1994

PHILIPPE LEOTARD
LA BALANCE   Spectrafilm, 1982, French

KEN LERNER
Agent: Fred Amsel & Associates - Los Angeles, 213/939-1188

HIT LIST   New Line Cinema, 1989
FAST GETAWAY   New Line Cinema, 1991

MICHAEL LERNER
Agent: Gersh Agency - Beverly Hills, 310/274-6611

ALEX IN WONDERLAND   MGM, 1970
THE CANDIDATE   Warner Bros., 1972
BUSTING   United Artists, 1974
ST. IVES   Warner Bros., 1976
OUTLAW BLUES   Warner Bros., 1977
RUBY AND OSWALD   FOUR DAYS IN DALLAS (TF)
   Alan Landsburg Productions, 1978

BORDERLINE   AFD, 1980
COAST TO COAST   Paramount, 1980
THE BALTIMORE BULLET   Avco Embassy, 1980
THE POSTMAN ALWAYS RINGS TWICE   Paramount, 1981
NATIONAL LAMPOON'S CLASS REUNION
   20th Century-Fox, 1982
STRANGE INVADERS   Orion, 1983, Canadian
RITA HAYWORTH: THE LOVE GODDESS (TF)
   The Susskind Co., 1983
BLOOD FEUD (TF)   20th Century-Fox TV/Glickman-Selznick
   Productions, 1983
MOVERS & SHAKERS   MGM/UA, 1985
THE EXECUTION (TF)   Newland-Raynor Productions/Comworld
   Productions, 1985
HANDS OF A STRANGER (MS)   Edgar J. Scherick Productions/
   Taft Entertainment TV, 1987
VIBES   Columbia, 1988
EIGHT MEN OUT   Orion, 1988
HARLEM NIGHTS   Paramount, 1989
THE CLOSER   Ion Pictures, 1990
BARTON FINK ○   20th Century Fox, 1991
NEWSIES   Buena Vista, 1992
BLANK CHECK   Buena Vista, 1994
NO ESCAPE   Savoy Pictures, 1994
RADIOLAND MURDERS   Universal, 1994
A PYROMANIAC'S LOVE STORY   Buena Vista, 1995

PHILIPPE LEROY
THE BERLIN AFFAIR   Cannon, 1985, Italian-West German

PHILIPPINE LEROY-BEAULIEU
JEFFERSON IN PARIS   Buena Vista, 1995

MARK LESTER
b. July 11, 1958 - Oxford, England

THE COUNTERFEIT CONSTABLE   *ALLEZ FRANCE!*   1964
SPACEFLIGHT IC-1   1965, British
FAHRENHEIT 451   Universal, 1967, British
OUR MOTHER'S HOUSE   MGM, 1967, British
OLIVER!   Columbia, 1968, British
RUN WILD, RUN FREE   Columbia, 1969, British
SUDDEN TERROR   *EYEWITNESS*   National General, 1971, British
MELODY   *S.W.A.L.K.*   Levitt-Pickman, 1971, British
BLACK BEAUTY   Paramount, 1971, British-West German-Spanish
WHO SLEW AUNTIE ROO?   American International, 1971, British
NIGHT HAIR CHILD   1971
SCALAWAG   Paramount, 1973, Italian-U.S.
LITTLE ADVENTURER   1975
CROSSED SWORDS   *THE PRINCE AND THE PAUPER*
   Warner Bros., 1978, British

LORI LETHIN
THE DAY AFTER (TF)   ABC Circle Films, 1983

DAVID LETTERMAN
b. April 12, 1947 - Indianapolis, Indiana
Agent: CAA - Beverly Hills, 310/288-4545

CABIN BOY   Buena Vista, 1994

CALVIN LEVELS
ADVENTURES IN BABYSITTING   Buena Vista, 1987

RACHEL LEVIN
THE MEN'S CLUB   Atlantic Releasing Corporation, 1986
DUET FOR ONE   Cannon, 1986
GABY - A TRUE STORY   TriStar, 1987, U.S.-Mexican

ANNA LEVINE
Agent: APA - Los Angeles, 310/273-0744

DESPERATELY SEEKING SUSAN   Orion, 1985
SOMETHING WILD   Orion, 1986
WALL STREET   20th Century Fox, 1987
TALK RADIO   Universal, 1988

JERRY LEVINE
IRON EAGLE   TriStar, 1986
BORN ON THE FOURTH OF JULY   Universal, 1989

TED LEVINE
IRONWEED   TriStar, 1987
BETRAYED   MGM/UA, 1988
LOVE AT LARGE   Orion, 1990
THE SILENCE OF THE LAMBS   Orion, 1991

BARRY LEVINSON
b. June 2, 1932 - Baltimore, Maryland
Agent: CAA - Beverly Hills, 310/288-4545

RAIN MAN   MGM/UA, 1988 (also directed)
QUIZ SHOW   Buena Vista, 1994

STEVE LEVITT
Agent: Badgley/Connor - Los Angeles, 310/278-9313

HUNK   Crown International, 1987

EUGENE LEVY
Agent: William Morris Agency - Beverly Hills, 310/274-7451

ARMED AND DANGEROUS   Columbia, 1986
CLUB PARADISE   Warner Bros., 1986

AL LEWIS
MUNSTER, GO HOME   Universal, 1966
THEY MIGHT BE GIANTS   Universal, 1971
MARRIED TO THE MOB   Orion, 1988
CAR 54, WHERE ARE YOU?   Orion, 1994

CHARLOTTE LEWIS
PIRATES   Cannon, 1986, French-Tunisian
THE GOLDEN CHILD   Paramount, 1986

DAWNN LEWIS
b. August 13, 1960 - New York, New York
Agent: Badgley/Connor - Los Angeles, 310/278-9313

I'M GONNA GIT YOU SUCKA   MGM/UA, 1989

ELBERT LEWIS
SQUARE DANCE   Island Pictures, 1987

FIONA LEWIS
b. September 28, 1946 - Westcliff, England

THE FEARLESS VAMPIRE KILLERS OR: PARDON ME, BUT
   YOUR TEETH ARE IN MY NECK   *DANCE OF THE VAMPIRES*
   MGM, 1967, British
JOANNA   20th Century-Fox, 1968, British
OTLEY   Columbia, 1969, British
WHERE'S JACK?   Paramount, 1969, British
VILLAIN   MGM, 1971, British
DR. PHIBES RISES AGAIN   American International, 1972, British
DRACULA (TF)   Universal TV/Dan Curtis Productions, 1973
LISZTOMANIA   Warner Bros., 1975, British
DRUM   United Artists, 1976
STUNTS   New Line Cinema, 1977
THE FURY   20th Century-Fox, 1978
WANDA NEVADA   United Artists, 1979
STRANGE INVADERS   Orion, 1983, Canadian

GEOFFREY LEWIS
Agent: William Morris Agency - Beverly Hills, 310/274-7451

SMILE   United Artists, 1975
LUCKY LADY   20th Century-Fox, 1975
EVERY WHICH WAY BUT LOOSE   Warner Bros., 1978
ANY WHICH WAY YOU CAN   Warner Bros., 1980
FLETCH LIVES   Universal, 1989
PINK CADILLAC   Warner Bros., 1989

GUNSMOKE: THE LAST APACHE (TF)   CBS Entertainment/
   Galatea Productions, 1990
DOUBLE IMPACT   Columbia, 1991
STEPHEN KING'S THE LAWNMOWER MAN   New Line Cinema, 1992
THE MAN WITHOUT A FACE   Warner Bros., 1993
WHITE FANG 2: MYTH OF THE WHITE WOLF   Buena Vista, 1994

GWEN LEWIS
EYES OF A STRANGER   Warner Bros., 1981

HUEY LEWIS
b. July 5, 1951 - New York, New York

BACK TO THE FUTURE   Universal, 1985
SHORT CUTS   Fine Line Features/New Line Cinema, 1993

JENIFER LEWIS
WHAT'S LOVE GOT TO DO WITH IT   Buena Vista, 1993
CORRINA, CORRINA   New Line Cinema, 1994
RENAISSANCE MAN   Buena Vista, 1994

JENNY LEWIS
THE WIZARD   Universal, 1989

JERRY LEWIS
(Joseph Levitch)
b. March 16, 1926 - Newark, New Jersey
Agent: William Morris Agency - Beverly Hills, 310/274-7451

MY FRIEND IRMA   Paramount, 1949
MY FRIEND IRMA GOES WEST   Paramount, 1950
AT WAR WITH THE ARMY   Paramount, 1950
THAT'S MY BOY   Paramount, 1951
SAILOR BEWARE   Paramount, 1951
JUMPING JACKS   Paramount, 1952
THE STOOGE   Paramount, 1952
SCARED STIFF   Paramount, 1953
THE CADDY   Paramount, 1953
MONEY FROM HOME   Paramount, 1953
LIVING IT UP   Paramount, 1954
THREE-RING CIRCUS   Paramount, 1954
YOU'RE NEVER TOO YOUNG   Paramount, 1955
ARTISTS AND MODELS   Paramount, 1955
PARDNERS   Paramount, 1956
HOLLYWOOD OR BUST   Paramount, 1956
THE DELICATE DELINQUENT   Paramount, 1957
THE SAD SACK   Paramount, 1957
ROCK-A-BYE BABY   Paramount, 1958
THE GEISHA BOY   Paramount, 1958
DON'T GIVE UP THE SHIP   Paramount, 1959
VISIT TO A SMALL PLANET   Paramount, 1960
THE BELLBOY   Paramount, 1960 (also directed)
CINDERFELLA   Paramount, 1960
THE LADIES' MAN   Paramount, 1961 (also directed)
THE ERRAND BOY   Paramount, 1961 (also directed)
IT'S ONLY MONEY   Paramount, 1962
IT'S A MAD MAD MAD MAD WORLD   United Artists, 1963
THE NUTTY PROFESSOR   Paramount, 1963 (also directed)
WHO'S MINDING THE STORE?   Paramount, 1963
THE PATSY   Paramount, 1964 (also directed)
THE DISORDERLY ORDERLY   Paramount, 1964
THE FAMILY JEWELS   Paramount, 1965 (also directed)
BOEING BOEING   Paramount, 1965
THREE ON A COUCH   Columbia, 1966 (also directed)
WAY...WAY OUT   20th Century-Fox, 1966
THE BIG MOUTH   Columbia, 1967 (also directed)
DON'T RAISE THE BRIDGE—LOWER THE RIVER   Columbia,
   1968, British
HOOK, LINE AND SINKER   Columbia, 1969
WHICH WAY TO THE FRONT?   Warner Bros., 1970 (also directed)
HARDLY WORKING   20th Century-Fox, 1981 (also directed)
SLAPSTICK OF ANOTHER KIND   *SLAPSTICK*   Entertainment
   Releasing Corporation/International Film Marketing, 1983
SMORGASBORD   *CRACKING UP*   Warner Bros., 1983 (also directed)
THE KING OF COMEDY   20th Century-Fox, 1983
COOKIE   Warner Bros., 1989
MR. SATURDAY NIGHT   Columbia, 1992
ARIZONA DREAMER   Warner Bros., 1995

JERRY LEE LEWIS
b. September 29, 1935 - Ferriday, Louisiana

AMERICAN HOT WAX   Paramount, 1978
GREAT BALLS OF FIRE   Orion, 1989 (voice)

JULIETTE LEWIS
Agent: William Morris Agency - Beverly Hills, 310/274-7451

CROOKED HEARTS   MGM-Pathe, 1991
CAPE FEAR ✪   Universal, 1991
HUSBANDS AND WIVES   TriStar, 1992
THAT NIGHT   Warner Bros., 1993
KALIFORNIA   Gramercy Pictures, 1993
WHAT'S EATING GILBERT GRAPE   Paramount, 1993
ROMEO IS BLEEDING   Gramercy Pictures, 1994, U.S.-British
NATURAL BORN KILLERS   Warner Bros., 1994
LIFESAVERS   TriStar, 1994
STRANGE DAYS   20th Century Fox, 1995

PHILL LEWIS
Agent: The Artists Agency - Los Angeles, 310/277-7779

HEATHERS   New World, 1989
CITY SLICKERS   Columbia, 1991
ACES: IRON EAGLE III   New Line Cinema, 1991

RAWLE D. LEWIS
COOL RUNNINGS   Buena Vista, 1993

RICHARD LEWIS
b. June 29, 1947 - New York, New York
Agent: ICM - Beverly Hills, 310/550-4000

ONCE UPON A CRIME   MGM-Pathe, 1992, U.S.-Italian
ROBIN HOOD: MEN IN TIGHTS   20th Century Fox, 1993
WAGONS EAST   TriStar, 1994

ZACHARY LEWIS
AIRPLANE!   Paramount, 1980

GONG LI
FAREWELL MY CONCUBINE   Miramax Films, 1992,
   Hong Kong-Chinese

RICHARD LIBERTINI
SHARKY'S MACHINE   Orion/Warner Bros., 1981
BEST FRIENDS   Warner Bros., 1982
ALL OF ME   Universal, 1984
UNFAITHFULLY YOURS   20th Century Fox, 1984
FLETCH   Universal, 1985
BETRAYED   MGM/UA, 1988
ANIMAL BEHAVIOR   Millimeter Films, 1989
FLETCH LIVES   Universal, 1989
DUCK TALES THE MOVIE: THE SECRET OF THE LOST LAMP (AF)
   Buena Vista, 1990 (voice)

NANCY LIEBERMAN
PERFECT PROFILE   Arista Films, 1988

JUDITH LIGHT
b. February 9, 1950 - Trenton, New Jersey

THE RYAN WHITE STORY (TF)   The Landsburg Company, 1989

HEATHER LILLY
SEE YOU IN THE MORNING   Warner Bros., 1989

TRACI LIN
CLASS OF 1999   Vestron, 1989
SURVIVAL QUEST   MGM/UA, 1990

LAR PARK LINCOLN
CHILDREN OF THE NIGHT (TF)   Robert Guenette Productions, 1985
HOUSE II : THE SECOND STORY   New World, 1987

PRINCESS ACADEMY   Empire Pictures, 1987, Yugoslavian-French
FRIDAY THE 13TH PART VII - THE NEW BLOOD   Paramount, 1989

HAL LINDEN
b. March 20, 1931 - New York, New York
Agent: William Morris Agency - Beverly Hills, 310/274-7451

WHEN YOU COMIN' BACK, RED RYDER?   Columbia, 1979
FATHER FIGURE (TF)   Finnegan Associates/Time-Life Prods., 1980
THE OTHER WOMAN (TF)   CBS Entertainment, 1983
MY WICKED, WICKED WAYS: THE LEGEND OF ERROL
   FLYNN (TF)   CBS Entertainment, 1985
A NEW LIFE   Paramount, 1988

VIVECA LINDFORS
b. December 29, 1920 - Uppsala, Sweden
Agent: Paul Kohner, Inc. - Los Angeles, 310/550-1060

PUZZLE OF A DOWNFALL CHILD   Universal, 1970
WELCOME TO L.A.   United Artists/Lions Gate, 1977
THE HAND   Orion/Warner Bros., 1981
SECRET WEAPONS (TF)   Goodman-Rosen Productions/ITC
   Productions, 1985
THE SURE THING   Embassy, 1985
THE ANN JILLIAN STORY (TF)   9J, Inc. Productions/ITC, 1988
ZANDALEE   Electric Pictures/ITC Entertainment Group, 1991

AUDRA LINDLEY
Agent: Badgley/Connor - Los Angeles, 310/278-9313

THE HEARTBREAK KID   20th Century-Fox, 1972
PEARL (MS)   Silliphant-Konigsberg Prods./Warner Bros. TV, 1979
WHEN YOU COMIN' BACK, RED RYDER?   Columbia, 1979
MOVIOLA (MS)   David L. Wolper-Stan Margulies Productions/
   Warner Bros. TV, 1980
CANNERY ROW   MGM/United Artists, 1982
BEST FRIENDS   Warner Bros., 1982
DESERT HEARTS   Samuel Goldwyn Company, 1985
ABSOLUTE STRANGERS (TF)   Cates-Doty Productions/Fries
   Entertainment, 1991

DELROY LINDO
Agent: William Morris Agency - Beverly Hills, 310/274-7451

MALCOLM X   Warner Bros., 1992
MR. JONES   TriStar, 1993
CROOKLYN   Universal, 1994
CLOCKERS   Universal, 1995

VINCENT LINDON
BETTY BLUE   Alive Films, 1986, French

ROBERT LINDSAY
Agent: William Morris Agency - Beverly Hills, 310/274-7451

BERT RIGBY, YOU'RE A FOOL   Warner Bros., 1989
STRIKE IT RICH   Millimeter Films, 1990

RICHARD LINEBACK
SPEED   20th Century Fox, 1994

BAI LING
THE CROW   Dimension/Miramax Films, 1994

REX LINN
CLIFFHANGER   TriStar, 1993
DROP ZONE   Paramount, 1994

MARK LINN-BAKER
b. June 19, 1953 - St. Louis, Missouri

MANHATTAN   United Artists, 1979
MY FAVORITE YEAR   MGM/UA, 1982
NOISES OFF   Buena Vista, 1992

LAURA LINNEY
A SIMPLE TWIST OF FATE   Buena Vista, 1994
CONGO   Paramount, 1995

LARRY LINVILLE
Agent: Stone Manners Talent Agency - Los Angeles, 310/275-9599

EARTH GIRLS ARE EASY   Vestron, 1989

RAY LIOTTA
b. December 18 - Newark, New Jersey
Agent: CAA - Beverly Hills, 310/288-4545

HARDHAT AND LEGS (TF)   Syzygy Productions, 1980
THE LONELY LADY   Universal, 1983
SOMETHING WILD   Orion, 1986
DOMINICK AND EUGENE   Orion, 1988
FIELD OF DREAMS   Universal, 1989
GOODFELLAS   Warner Bros., 1990
WOMEN & MEN: IN LOVE THERE ARE NO RULES (CTF)
   David Brown Productions/HBO Showcase, 1991
ARTICLE 99   Orion, 1992
UNLAWFUL ENTRY   20th Century Fox, 1992
NO ESCAPE   Savoy Pictures, 1994
CORRINA, CORRINA   New Line Cinema, 1994
OPERATION DUMBO DROP   Buena Vista, 1995

MAUREEN LIPMAN
WATER   Atlantic Releasing Corporation, 1984, British

DENNIS LIPSCOMB
Agent: Harris & Goldberg - Los Angeles, 310/553-5200

RETRIBUTION   Taurus Entertainment, 1988

PEGGY LIPTON
KINJITE (FORBIDDEN SUBJECTS)   Cannon, 1989
TWIN PEAKS: FIRE WALK WITH ME   New Line Cinema,
   1992, U.S.-French

TINY LISTER
NO HOLDS BARRED   New Line Cinema, 1989

JOHN LITHGOW
b. October 19, 1945 - Rochester, New York
Agent: CAA - Beverly Hills, 310/288-4545

DEALING: OR THE BERKELEY-TO-BOSTON FORTY-BRICK
   LOST-BAG BLUES   Warner Bros., 1972
OBSESSION   Columbia, 1986
THE BIG FIX   Universal, 1978
ALL THAT JAZZ   20th Century-Fox, 1979
RICH KIDS   United Artists, 1979
BLOW OUT   Filmways, 1981
I'M DANCING AS FAST AS I CAN   Paramount, 1982
THE WORLD ACCORDING TO GARP ✪   Warner Bros., 1982
THE DAY AFTER (TF)   ABC Circle Films, 1983
TERMS OF ENDEARMENT ✪   Paramount, 1983
TWILIGHT ZONE—THE MOVIE   Warner Bros., 1983
THE ADVENTURES OF BUCKAROO BANZAI: ACROSS THE
   8TH DIMENSION   20th Century Fox, 1984
MESMERIZED   RKO/Challenge Corporation Services, 1984,
   New Zealand-Australian-British
FOOTLOOSE   Paramount, 1984
2010   MGM/UA, 1984
SANTA CLAUS: THE MOVIE   TriStar, 1985, U.S.-British
RESTING PLACE (TF)   Marian Rees Associates, 1986
THE MANHATTAN PROJECT   20th Century Fox, 1986
BABY GIRL SCOTT (TF)   Polson Company Productions/
   The Finnegan-Pinchuk Company, 1987
HARRY AND THE HENDERSONS   Universal, 1987
DISTANT THUNDER   Paramount, 1988
OUT COLD   TriStar, 1989
TRAVELING MAN (CTF)   HBO Pictures, 1989
THE LAST ELEPHANT (CTF)   RHI Entertainment/Qintex
   Entertainment, 1990

MEMPHIS BELLE   Warner Bros., 1990
THE BOYS (TF)   William Link Prods./Papazian-Hirsch Productions, 1991
RICOCHET   Warner Bros., 1991
AT PLAY IN THE FIELDS OF THE LORD   Universal, 1991
RAISING CAIN   Universal, 1992
CLIFFHANGER   TriStar, 1993
LOVE, CHEAT AND STEAL (CTF)   Showtime, 1993
THE PELICAN BRIEF   Warner Bros., 1993
WORLD WAR II: THEN THERE WERE GIANTS (TF)
   World International Network, 1994
A GOOD MAN IN AFRICA   Gramercy Pictures, 1994
PRINCESS CARABOO   TriStar, 1994
SILENT FALL   Warner Bros., 1994

MICHELLE LITTLE
Agent: The Agency - Los Angeles, 310/551-3000

RADIOACTIVE DREAMS   DEG, 1986
MY DEMON LOVER   New Line Cinema, 1987

LITTLE RICHARD
b. December 5, 1932 - Macon, Georgia
Agent: William Morris Agency - Beverly Hills, 310/274-7451

DOWN AND OUT IN BEVERLY HILLS   Buena Vista, 1986
GODDESS OF LOVE (TF)   Phil Margo Enterprises/New World TV/
   Phoenix Entertainment Group, 1988
MOTHER GOOSE ROCK 'N' RHYME (CTF)   Think Entertainment, 1990

ROBYN LIVELY
Agent: Abrams Artists & Associates - Los Angeles, 310/859-0625

BRAINSTORM   MGM/UA, 1983
WILDCATS   Warner Bros., 1986
THE BEST OF TIMES   Universal, 1986
THE KARATE KID PART III   Columbia, 1989

LL COOL J
Agent: ICM - Beverly Hills, 310/550-4000

TOYS   20th Century Fox, 1992

DESMOND LLEWELYN
ON HER MAJESTY'S SECRET SERVICE   United Artists, 1969, British
THE MAN WITH THE GOLDEN GUN   United Artists, 1974, British
OCTOPUSSY   MGM/UA, 1983, British
LICENCE TO KILL   MGM/UA, 1989, British

CHRISTOPHER LLOYD
b. October 22, 1938 - Stamford, Connecticut
Agent: Gersh Agency - Beverly Hills, 310/274-6611

ONE FLEW OVER THE CUCKOO'S NEST   United Artists, 1975
GOIN' SOUTH   Paramount, 1979
THE ONION FIELD   Avco Embassy, 1979
MR. MOM   20th Century-Fox, 1983
TO BE OR NOT TO BE   20th Century-Fox, 1983
THE ADVENTURES OF BUCKAROO BANZAI: ACROSS THE
   8TH DIMENSION   20th Century Fox, 1984
JOY OF SEX   Paramount, 1984
STAR TREK III: THE SEARCH FOR SPOCK   Paramount, 1984
BACK TO THE FUTURE   Universal, 1985
CLUE   Paramount, 1985
MIRACLES   Orion, 1986
WHO FRAMED ROGER RABBIT   Buena Vista, 1988
EIGHT MEN OUT   Orion, 1988
TRACK 29   Island Pictures, 1988
THE DREAM TEAM   Universal, 1989
BACK TO THE FUTURE PART II   Universal, 1989
BACK TO THE FUTURE PART III   Universal, 1990
DUCK TALES THE MOVIE: THE SECRET OF THE LOST LAMP (AF)
   Buena Vista, 1990 (voice)
THE ADDAMS FAMILY   Paramount, 1991
DENNIS THE MENACE   Warner Bros., 1993
ADDAMS FAMILY VALUES   Paramount, 1993
ANGELS IN THE OUTFIELD   Buena Vista, 1994
CAMP NOWHERE   Buena Vista, 1994

**F
I
L
M**

**A
C
T
O
R
S**

RADIOLAND MURDERS   Universal, 1994
THE PAGEMASTER   20th Century Fox, 1994
THINGS TO DO IN DENVER WHEN YOU'RE DEAD
   Miramax Films, 1995

CORY LLOYD

THE SUBSTITUTE WIFE (TF)   Frederick S. Pierce Company, 1994

EMILY LLOYD

b. September 29, 1970 - England
Agent: William Morris Agency - Beverly Hills, 310/274-7451

WISH YOU WERE HERE   Atlantic Releasing Corporation,
   1987, British
COOKIE   Warner Bros., 1989
IN COUNTRY   Warner Bros., 1989
CHICAGO JOE AND THE SHOWGIRL   New Line Cinema, 1990
A RIVER RUNS THROUGH IT   Columbia, 1992

ERIC LLOYD

HEART AND SOULS   Universal, 1993
THE SANTA CLAUSE   Buena Vista, 1994

JOHN BEDFORD LLOYD

TOUGH GUYS DON'T DANCE   Cannon, 1987
THE ABYSS   20th Century Fox, 1989
WAITING FOR THE LIGHT   Triumph Releasing Corporation, 1990

NORMAN LLOYD

b. November 8, 1914 - Jersey City, New Jersey

SABOTEUR   Universal, 1942
THE UNSEEN   Paramount, 1945
THE SOUTHERNER   United Artists, 1945
SPELLBOUND   United Artists, 1945
A WALK IN THE SUN   20th Century-Fox, 1946
THE GREEN YEARS   MGM, 1946
THE BEGINNING OR THE END   MGM, 1947
NO MINOR VICES   MGM, 1948
CALAMITY JANE AND SAM BASS   Universal, 1949
SCENE OF THE CRIME   1949
REIGN OF TERROR *THE BLACK BOOK*   Eagle Lion, 1949
THE FLAME AND THE ARROW   Warner Bros., 1950
M   Columbia, 1951
HE RAN ALL THE WAY   United Artists, 1951
LIMELIGHT   United Artists, 1952
AUDREY ROSE   United Artists, 1977
FM   Universal, 1978
THE NUDE BOMB   Universal, 1980
DEAD POETS SOCIETY   Buena Vista, 1989

TONY LoBIANCO

Agent: David Shapira & Associates - Sherman Oaks, 818/906-0322

THE HONEYMOON KILLERS   1970
THE FRENCH CONNECTION   20th Century-Fox, 1971
THE SEVEN UPS   20th Century-Fox, 1973
DEMON *GOD TOLD ME TO*   New World, 1977
JESUS OF NAZARETH (MS)   Sir Lew Grade Productions/ITC,
   1978, British-Italian
BLOODBROTHERS   Warner Bros., 1978
F.I.S.T.   United Artists, 1978
MAGEE AND THE LADY *SHE'LL BE SWEET* (TF)   Australian
   Broadcasting Commission/Trans-Atlantic Enterprises, 1979, Australian
MARCIANO (TF)   ABC Circle Films, 1979
SEPARATE WAYS   Crown International, 1981
CITY HEAT   Warner Bros., 1984
JESSIE (TF)   Lindsay Wagner Productions/MGM-UA TV, 1984
THE ANN JILLIAN STORY (TF)   9J, Inc. Productions/ITC, 1988
BODY OF EVIDENCE (TF)   CBS Entertainment, 1988
CITY OF HOPE   Samuel Goldwyn Company, 1991
BOILING POINT   Warner Bros., 1993, U.S.-French

TONE LOC

THE ADVENTURES OF FORD FAIRLANE   20th Century Fox, 1990
TALKIN' DIRTY AFTER DARK   New Line Cinema, 1991
POSSE   Gramercy Pictures, 1993, U.S.-British

POETIC JUSTICE   Columbia, 1993
SURF NINJAS   New Line Cinema, 1993
ACE VENTURA: PET DETECTIVE   Warner Bros., 1994
BLANK CHECK   Buena Vista, 1994

AMY LOCANE

LOST ANGELS   Vestron, 1989
CRY-BABY   Universal, 1990
SCHOOL TIES   Paramount, 1992
BLUE SKY   Orion, 1994

CAROL LOCATELL

BEST FRIENDS   Warner Bros., 1982

BRUCE LOCKE

ROBOCOP 3   Orion, 1993

SONDRA LOCKE

b. May 28, 1947 - Shelbyville, Tennessee
Agent: Bauer Benedek Agency - Los Angeles, 213/275-2421

THE HEART IS A LONELY HUNTER ✪   Warner Bros., 1968
WILLARD   Cinerama Releasing Corporation, 1971
A REFLECTION OF FEAR   Columbia, 1973, British
THE OUTLAW JOSEY WALES   Warner Bros., 1976
DEATH GAME *THE SEDUCERS*   1976
THE GAUNTLET   Warner Bros., 1977
WISHBONE CUTTER   1978
EVERY WHICH WAY BUT LOOSE   Warner Bros., 1978
ANY WHICH WAY YOU CAN   Warner Bros., 1980
BRONCO BILLY   Warner Bros., 1980
SUDDEN IMPACT   Warner Bros., 1983
RATBOY   Warner Bros., 1987 (also directed)

ANNE LOCKHART

JOYRIDE   American International, 1977
TROLL   Empire Pictures, 1986

JUNE LOCKHART

b. June 25, 1925 - New York, New York
Agent: APA - Los Angeles, 310/273-0744

A CHRISTMAS CAROL   MGM, 1938
ALL THIS AND HEAVEN TOO   Warner Bros., 1940
ADAM HAD FOUR SONS   Columbia, 1941
SERGEANT YORK   Warner Bros., 1941
MISS ANNIE ROONEY   United Artists, 1942
THE WHITE CLIFFS OF DOVER   MGM, 1944
MEET ME IN ST. LOUIS   MGM, 1944
KEEP YOUR POWDER DRY   MGM, 1945
SON OF LASSIE   1945
THE SHE-WOLF OF LONDON   1946
THE YEARLING   MGM, 1947
T-MEN   Eagle Lion, 1947
BURY ME DEAD   1947
TIME LIMIT   1957
LASSIE'S GREATEST ADVENTURE   20th Century-Fox, 1963
THE NIGHT THEY SAVED CHRISTMAS (TF)   Robert Halmi, Inc., 1984
TROLL   Empire Pictures, 1986
A WHISPER KILLS (TF)   Sandy Hook Productions/Steve Tisch
   Company/Phoenix Entertainment Group, 1988
SLEEP WITH ME   MGM/UA, 1994

HEATHER LOCKLEAR

b. September 25, 1961 - Los Angeles, California
Agent: William Morris Agency - Beverly Hills, 310/274-7451

RICH MEN, SINGLE WOMEN (TF)   Aaron Spelling Productions, 1990
WAYNE'S WORLD 2   Paramount, 1993

ROBERT LOGGIA

b. January 3, 1930 - New York, New York
Agent: CAA - Beverly Hills, 310/288-4545

SOMEBODY UP THERE LIKES ME   MGM, 1957
COP HATER   1958

THE NINE LIVES OF ELFEGO BACA (TF)   1959
CATTLE KING   MGM, 1963
THE GREATEST STORY EVER TOLD   United Artists, 1965
CHE!   20th Century Fox, 1969
ARTHUR HAILEY'S THE MONEYCHANGERS
   THE MONEYCHANGERS (MS)   Ross Hunter Productions/
   Paramount TV, 1976
FIRST LOVE   Paramount, 1977
REVENGE OF THE PINK PANTHER   United Artists, 1978, British
THE NINTH CONFIGURATION *TWINKLE, TWINKLE,*
   "KILLER" KANE   Warner Bros., 1980
S.O.B.   Paramount, 1981
AN OFFICER AND A GENTLEMAN   Paramount, 1982
TRAIL OF THE PINK PANTHER   MGM/UA, 1982
A WOMAN CALLED GOLDA (TF)   Harve Bennett Productions/
   Paramount TV, 1982
PSYCHO II   Universal, 1983
CURSE OF THE PINK PANTHER   MGM/UA, 1983
SCARFACE   Universal, 1983
A TOUCH OF SCANDAL (TF)   Doris M. Keating Productions/
   Columbia TV, 1984
PRIZZI'S HONOR   20th Century Fox, 1985
JAGGED EDGE ✪   Columbia, 1985
STREETS OF JUSTICE (TF)   Universal TV, 1985
THAT'S LIFE!   Columbia, 1986
ARMED AND DANGEROUS   Columbia, 1986
GABY - A TRUE STORY   TriStar, 1987, U.S.-Mexican
OVER THE TOP   Cannon, 1987
THE BELIEVERS   Orion, 1987
HOT PURSUIT   Paramount, 1987
JOSEPH WAMBAUGH'S ECHOES IN THE DARKNESS
   ECHOES IN THE DARKNESS (MS)   Litke-Grossbart
   Productions/New World TV, 1987
BIG   20th Century Fox, 1988
INTRIGUE (TF)   Crew Neck Productions/Linnea Productions/
   Columbia TV, 1988
FAVORITE SON (MS)   NBC Productions, 1988
DREAM BREAKERS (TF)   CBS Entertainment, 1989
RELENTLESS   New Line Cinema, 1989
TRIUMPH OF THE SPIRIT   Triumph Releasing Corporation, 1989
OPPORTUNITY KNOCKS   Universal, 1990
THE MARRYING MAN   Buena Vista, 1991
NECESSARY ROUGHNESS   Paramount, 1991
GLADIATOR   Columbia, 1992
INNOCENT BLOOD   Warner Bros., 1992
WILD PALMS (MS)   Ixtlan Corporation/Greengrass
   Productions, Inc., 1993
BAD GIRLS   20th Century Fox, 1994
WHITE MILE (CTF)   HBO Pictures, 1994
I LOVE TROUBLE   Buena Vista, 1994

AARON LOHR
NEWSIES   Buena Vista, 1992

KARINA LOMBARD
Agent: William Morris Agency - Beverly Hills, 310/274-7451

WIDE SARGASSO SEA   Fine Line Features/New Line Cinema,
   1993, British
THE FIRM   Paramount, 1993
LEGENDS OF THE FALL   TriStar, 1994

MICHAEL LOMBARD
"CROCODILE" DUNDEE   Paramount, 1986, Australian
PET SEMATARY *STEPHEN KING'S PET SEMATARY*
   Paramount, 1989

SOL LOMITA
ZELIG   Orion/Warner Bros., 1983

JASON LONDON
Agent: William Morris Agency - Beverly Hills, 310/274-7451

TO WONG FOO, THANKS FOR EVERYTHING, JULIE NEWMAR
   Universal, 1995

JOHN LONE
Agent: UTA - Beverly Hills, 310/273-6700

ICEMAN   Universal, 1984
YEAR OF THE DRAGON   MGM/UA, 1985
THE LAST EMPEROR   Columbia, 1987, British-Chinese
THE MODERNS   Alive Films, 1988
SHADOW OF CHINA   New Line Cinema, 1991
M. BUTTERFLY   Warner Bros., 1993
THE SHADOW   Universal, 1994
THE HUNTED   Universal, 1995

BRAD LONG
HOOSIERS   Orion, 1986

JODI LONG
Agent: Flick East/West Talent, Inc. - Los Angeles, 213/463-6333 or
   New York, 212/307-1850

PATTY HEARST   Atlantic Releasing Corporation, 1988

SHELLEY LONG
b. August 23, 1949 - Fort Wayne, Indiana
Agent: CAA - Beverly Hills, 310/288-4545

NIGHT SHIFT   The Ladd Company/Warner Bros., 1982
IRRECONCILABLE DIFFERENCES   Warner Bros., 1984
THE MONEY PIT   Universal, 1986
OUTRAGEOUS FORTUNE   Buena Vista, 1987
HELLO AGAIN   Buena Vista, 1987
TROOP BEVERLY HILLS   Columbia, 1989
VOICES WITHIN: THE LIVES OF TRUDDI CASE (TF)   Itzbinzo
   Long Productions/P.A. Productions/New World TV, 1990
DON'T TELL HER IT'S ME   Hemdale, 1990
THE BRADY BUNCH MOVIE   Paramount, 1995

TONY LONGO
Agent: Stone Manners Talent Agency - Los Angeles, 310/275-9599

BLOODHOUNDS OF BROADWAY   Columbia, 1989
HOUSEGUEST   Buena Vista, 1995

EMILY LONGSTRETH
THE BIG PICTURE   Columbia, 1989
RISING SON (CTF)   Sarabande Productions, 1990

MICHAEL LONSDALE
MOONRAKER   United Artists, 1979, British-French
THE NAME OF THE ROSE   20th Century Fox, 1986,
   West German-Italian-French
THE REMAINS OF THE DAY   Columbia, 1993, British
JEFFERSON IN PARIS   Buena Vista, 1995

MIKE LOOKINLAND
THE TOWERING INFERNO   20th Century-Fox/Warner Bros., 1974
THE BRADY GIRLS GET MARRIED (TF)   Sherwood Schwartz
   Productions, 1981
A VERY BRADY CHRISTMAS (TF)   Sherwood Schwartz
   Productions/Paramount TV, 1988
THE BRADYS (TF)   Brady Productions/Paramount TV, 1990
THE BRADY BUNCH MOVIE   Paramount, 1995

NANCY LOOMIS
HALLOWEEN   Compass International, 1978

ROD LOOMIS
BILL & TED'S EXCELLENT ADVENTURE   Orion, 1989

BLAISE LOONG
CYBORG   Cannon, 1989

TANYA LOPERT
NAVAJO JOE *UN DOLLARO A TESTA*   United Artists, 1966,
   Italian-Spanish
A FEW DAYS WITH ME   Galaxy International, 1988, French

GERRY LOPEZ
FAREWELL TO THE KING   Orion, 1989

PERRY LOPEZ
CHINATOWN   Paramount, 1974
KINJITE (FORBIDDEN SUBJECTS)   Cannon, 1989
ACTION JACKSON   Lorimar, 1988

TRACI LORDS
(Nora Kuzma)
NOT OF THIS EARTH   Concorde, 1988
FAST FOOD   Fries Distribution, 1989
CRY-BABY   Universal, 1990

SOPHIA LOREN
(Sofia Scicolone)
b. September 20, 1934 - Rome, Italy

CUORI SUL MARE   1950, Italian
IL SOGNO DI ZORRO   1952, Italian
LA FAVORITA   1952, Italian
LA TRATTA DELLA BIANCHE   Excelsa/Ponti/Dino De Laurentiis
    Cinematografica, 1952, Italian
AFRICA SOTTO I MARI   1953, Italian
AIDA   1953, Italian
THE SIGN OF VENUS   1953
THE ANATOMY OF LOVE   *TEMPI NOSTRI*   1953, Italian
NEAPOLITAN CAROUSEL   *CAROSELLO NAPOLITANO*
    1954, Italian
TWO NIGHTS WITH CLEOPATRA   *DUE NOTTI CON CLEOPATRA*
    1954, Italian
ATILLA   1958, Italian-French
THE GOLD OF NAPLES   *L'ORO DI NAPOLI*   DCA, 1954, Italian
A DAY IN COURT   *UN GIORNO IN PRETURA*   1954, Italian
WOMAN OF THE RIVER   *LA DONNA DEL FIUME*   1955, Italian
TOO BAD SHE'S BAD   *PECCATO CHE SIA UNA CANAGLIA*
    1955, Italian
IL SEGNO DI VENERE   Titanus, 1955, Italian
THE MILLER'S BEAUTIFUL WIFE   *LA BELLA MUGNAIA*
    1955, Italian
SCANDAL IN SORRENTO   *PANE AMORE E...*   DCA, 1957, Italian
BOY ON A DOLPHIN   20th Century-Fox, 1957
THE PRIDE AND THE PASSION   United Artists, 1957
LEGEND OF THE LOST   United Artists, 1957
LUCKY TO BE A WOMAN   *LA FORTUNA DI ESSERE DONNA*
    1958, Italian
DESIRE UNDER THE ELMS   Paramount, 1958
THE KEY   Columbia, 1958, British
HOUSE BOAT   Paramount, 1958
THE BLACK ORCHID   Paramount, 1959
THAT KIND OF WOMAN   Paramount, 1959
HELLER IN PINK TIGHTS   Paramount, 1960
IT STARTED IN NAPLES   Paramount, 1960
A BREATH OF SCANDAL   Paramount, 1960
THE MILLIONAIRESS   20th Century-Fox, 1960, British
TWO WOMEN ★★   Embassy, 1960, Italian-French
EL CID   Allied Artists, 1961
MADAME   1962, French
BOCCACCIO '70   Embassy, 1962, Italian-French
FIVE MILES TO MIDNIGHT   *LE COUTEAU DANS LA PLAIE*
    United Artists, 1963, U.S.-French-Italian
THE CONDEMNED OF ALTONA   *I SEQUESTRATI DI ALTONA*
    20th Century-Fox, 1963, Italian-French
YESTERDAY, TODAY AND TOMORROW   *IERI OGGI E DOMANI*
    Embassy, 1964, Italian
THE FALL OF THE ROMAN EMPIRE   Paramount, 1964
MARRIAGE ITALIAN STYLE ★   Embassy, 1964, Italian-French
OPERATION CROSSBOW   *THE GREAT SPY MISSION*   MGM,
    1965, British-Italian
LADY L   MGM, 1966, U.S.-Italian-French
JUDITH   Paramount, 1966, U.S.-British-Israeli
ARABESQUE   Universal, 1966, British-U.S.
A COUNTESS FROM HONG KONG   Universal, 1967, British
MORE THAN A MIRACLE   *C'ERA UNA VOLTA*   MGM,
    1967, Italian-French
GHOSTS ITALIAN STYLE   *QUESTI FANTASMI*   1969, Italian
SUNFLOWER   *I GIRASOLI*   Avco Embassy, 1969, Italian-French
THE PRIEST'S WIFE   Warner Bros., 1971, Italian-French
LADY LIBERTY   *MORTADELLA*   United Artists, 1971, Italian

MAN OF LA MANCHA   United Artists, 1972, Italian-U.S.
WHITE SISTER   *BIANCO ROSSO E...*   Columbia, 1973,
    Italian-French-Spanish
THE VOYAGE   *IL VIAGGIO*   United Artists, 1973, Italian
BRIEF ENCOUNTER (TF)   Carlo Ponti Productions/Cecil Clarke
    Productions, 1974, British
JURY OF ONE   *THE VERDICT*   1974, French-Italian
THE CASSANDRA CROSSING   Avco Embassy, 1977,
    British-Italian-West German
A SPECIAL DAY   *UNA GIORNATA SPECIALE*   Cinema 5,
    1977, Italian-Canadian
ANGELA   1977, Canadian
BRASS TARGET   MGM/United Artists, 1978
SHIMMY LUGANO E TARANTELLE E VINO   1978, Italian
BLOOD FEUD   *REVENGE*   AFD, 1979, Italian
FIREPOWER   AFD, 1979, British
SOPHIA LOREN: HER OWN STORY (TF)   Roger Gimbel
    Productions/EMI TV, 1980
AURORA (TF)   Roger Gimbel Productions/Peregrine Productions/
    Sacis S.P.A. Roma, 1984
COURAGE (TF)   Highgate Pictures/New World TV, 1986
MARIO PUZO'S THE FORTUNATE PILGRIM   *THE FORTUNATE
    PILGRIM* (MS)   NBC Productions, 1988
PRET-A-PORTER   Miramax Films, 1994

JAMES LORINZ
THE JERKY BOYS   Buena Vista, 1994

EB LOTTIMER
DESERT SHIELD   21st Century Distribution, 1991

LORI LOUGHLIN
Agent: William Morris Agency - Beverly Hills, 310/274-7451

RAD   TriStar, 1986
BACK TO THE BEACH   Paramount, 1987

JULIA LOUIS-DREYFUSS
b. January 13, 1961 - New York, New York
Agent: UTA - Beverly Hills, 310/273-6700

SOUL MAN   New World, 1986
TROLL   Empire Pictures, 1986
HANNAH AND HER SISTERS   Orion, 1986
JACK THE BEAR   20th Century Fox, 1993
NORTH   Columbia, 1994

TINA LOUISE
(Tina Blacker)
b. February 11, 1934 - New York, New York

GOD'S LITTLE ACRE   United Artists, 1958
DAY OF THE OUTLAW   United Artists, 1959
THE HANGMAN   Paramount, 1959
THE TRAP   Paramount, 1959
THE SIEGE OF SYRACUSE   *L'ASSEDIO DI SIRACUSA*
    1960, Italian-French
THE WARRIOR EMPRESS   *SAFFO—VENERE DI LESBO*
    1960, Italian-French
ARMORED COMMAND   Allied Artists, 1961
FOR THOSE WHO THINK YOUNG   United Artists, 1964
THE WRECKING CREW   Columbia, 1968
HOW TO COMMIT MARRIAGE   Cinerama Releasing
    Corporation, 1969
THE GOOD GUYS AND THE BAD GUYS   Warner Bros., 1969
THE HAPPY ENDING   United Artists, 1969
DEATH SCREAM   *THE WOMAN WHO CRIED MURDER* (TF)
    RSO Films, 1975
THE STEPFORD WIVES   Columbia, 1975
MEAN DOG BLUES   American International, 1978

CHAD LOVE
SIRINGO   Rysher Entertainment, 1994

DARLENE LOVE
LETHAL WEAPON   Warner Bros., 1987
LETHAL WEAPON 2   Warner Bros., 1989
LETHAL WEAPON 3   Warner Bros., 1992

VICTOR LOVE
Agent: Gersh Agency - Beverly Hills, 310/274-6611

NATIVE SON   Cinecom, 1986

JODY LOVETT
MISS FIRECRACKER   Corsair Pictures, 1989

LYLE LOVETT
THE PLAYER   Fine Line Features/New Line Cinema, 1992
SHORT CUTS   Fine Line Features/New Line Cinema, 1993
PRET-A-PORTER   Miramax Films, 1994

JON LOVITZ
b. July 21, 1957 - Tarzana, California
Agent: CAA - Beverly Hills, 310/288-4545

THE LAST RESORT   Concorde/Cinema Group, 1986
RATBOY   Warner Bros., 1986
BRAVE LITTLE TOASTER (AF)   Hyperion-Kushner-Locke
    Productions, 1987 (voice)
JUMPIN' JACK FLASH   20th Century Fox, 1986
THREE AMIGOS   Orion, 1986
BIG   20th Century Fox, 1988
MY STEPMOTHER IS AN ALIEN   WEG, 1988
MR. DESTINY   Buena Vista, 1990
AN AMERICAN TAIL: FIEVEL GOES WEST (AF)   Universal,
    1991 (voice)
A LEAGUE OF THEIR OWN   Columbia, 1992
DICK AND MARGE SAVE THE WORLD   Warner Bros., 1992
NATIONAL LAMPOON'S LOADED WEAPON 1
    New Line Cinema, 1993
CITY SLICKERS II: THE LEGEND OF CURLY'S GOLD
    Columbia, 1994
NORTH   Columbia, 1994
TRAPPED IN PARADISE   20th Century Fox, 1994

ARVIE LOWE, JR.
NEWSIES   Buena Vista, 1992

CHAD LOWE
Agent: William Morris Agency - Beverly Hills, 310/274-7451

SILENCE OF THE HEART (TF)   David A. Simons Productions/
    Tisch-Avnet Productions, 1984
APRIL MORNING (TF)   Robert Halmi, Inc./Samuel
    Goldwyn TV, 1988
NOBODY'S PERFECT   Moviestore Entertainment, 1990
HIGHWAY TO HELL   Hemdale, 1991

ROB LOWE
b. March 17, 1964 - Charlotteville, Virginia

CLASS   Orion, 1983
THE HOTEL NEW HAMPSHIRE   Orion, 1984
OXFORD BLUES   MGM/UA, 1984, British
ST. ELMO'S FIRE   Columbia, 1985
YOUNGBLOOD   MGM/UA, 1986
ABOUT LAST NIGHT...   TriStar, 1986
SQUARE DANCE   Island Pictures, 1987
MASQUERADE   MGM/UA, 1988
ILLEGALLY YOURS   MGM/UA, 1988
BAD INFLUENCE   Triumph Releasing Corporation, 1990
DESERT SHIELD   21st Century Distribution, 1991
WAYNE'S WORLD   Paramount, 1992
THE STAND (MS)   ABC, 1994
FRANK AND JESSE   Trimark Pictures, 1994
BILLY THE THIRD   Paramount, 1995

CAREY LOWELL
CLUB PARADISE   Warner Bros., 1986
DANGEROUSLY CLOSE   Cannon, 1986
DOWN TWISTED   Cannon, 1987
ME AND HIM   Columbia, 1989
LICENCE TO KILL   MGM/UA, 1989, British
THE GUARDIAN   Universal, 1990
SLEEPLESS IN SEATTLE   TriStar, 1993

RANDY LOWELL
MRS. PARKER AND THE VICIOUS CIRCLE   Fine Line Features/
    New Line Cinema, 1994

MARK LOWENTHAL
BASIC TRAINING   The Movie Store, 1985
CHECKING OUT   Warner Bros., 1989, U.S.-British
SCENES FROM THE CLASS STRUGGLE IN BEVERLY HILLS
    Cinecom, 1989
DEFENSELESS   New Century/Vista, 1989
HEART CONDITION   New Line Cinema, 1990
I COME IN PEACE   Triumph Releasing Corporation, 1990
POSTCARDS FROM THE EDGE   Columbia, 1990
IRON MAZE   Castle Hill Productions, 1991, U.S.-Japanese
ARTICLE 99   Orion, 1992
NEWSIES   Buena Vista, 1992

ANDREW LOWERY
SCHOOL TIES   Paramount, 1992

T.J. LOWTHER
Agent: William Morris Agency - Beverly Hills, 310/274-7451

A PERFECT WORLD   Warner Bros., 1993
MAD LOVE   Buena Vista, 1995

LISA LU
THE JOY LUCK CLUB   Buena Vista, 1993

LISA LUCAS
Agent: Susan Smith & Associates - Beverly Hills, 213/852-4777

HEART AND SOULS   Universal, 1993

LAURENCE LUCKINBILL
b. November 21, 1934 - Fort Smith, Arkansas

THE BOYS IN THE BAND   National General, 1970
SUCH GOOD FRIENDS   Paramount, 1971
THE DELPHI BUREAU (TF)   Warner Bros. TV, 1972
DEATH SENTENCE (TF)   Spelling-Goldberg Productions, 1974
PANIC ON THE 5.22 (TF)   QM Productions, 1974
WINNER TAKE ALL (TF)   The Jozak Company, 1975
THE LINDBERGH KIDNAPPING CASE (TF)   Columbia TV, 1976
IKE (MS)   ABC Circle Films, 1979
THE PROMISE   Universal, 1979
MESSENGER OF DEATH   Cannon, 1988
STAR TREK V: THE FINAL FRONTIER   Paramount, 1989

WILLIAM LUCKING
RESCUE ME   Cannon, 1993

PAMELA LUDWIG
RACE FOR GLORY   New Century/Vista, 1989

CARL LUMBLY
Agent: Writers & Artists Agency - Los Angeles, 310/824-6300

THE BEDROOM WINDOW   DEG, 1987
EVERYBODY'S ALL-AMERICAN   Warner Bros., 1988
PACIFIC HEIGHTS   20th Century Fox, 1990
TO SLEEP WITH ANGER   Samuel Goldwyn Company, 1990

JENNY LUMET
Q & A   TriStar, 1990

JOANNA LUMLEY
SOME GIRLS DO   United Artists, 1968, British
ON HER MAJESTY'S SECRET SERVICE   United Artists,
    1969, British
TAM LIN   *THE DEVIL'S WIDOW*   American International, 1971
THE BREAKING OF BUMBO   1970
GAMES THAT LOVERS PLAY   1970
COUNT DRACULA AND HIS VAMPIRE BRIDE   *SATANIC RITES
    OF DRACULA*   Dynamite Entertainment, 1973, British

DON'T JUST LIE THERE, SAY SOMETHING   1973
TRAIL OF THE PINK PANTHER   MGM/UA, 1982
CURSE OF THE PINK PANTHER   MGM/UA, 1983
MISTRAL'S DAUGHTER (MS)   Steve Krantz Productions/R.T.L.
    Productions/Antenne-2, 1984, U.S.-French

DOLPH LUNDGREN
Agent: William Morris Agency - Beverly Hills, 310/274-7451

ROCKY IV   MGM/UA, 1985
MASTERS OF THE UNIVERSE   1987
THE PUNISHER   New World, 1989
RED SCORPION   Shapiro-Glickenhaus Entertainment, 1989
SHOWDOWN IN LITTLE TOKYO   Warner Bros., 1991
UNIVERSAL SOLDIER   TriStar, 1992
JOHNNY MNEMONIC   TriStar, 1994
MELTDOWN   Trimark Pictures, 1995

STEVE LUNDQUIST
KILLER TOMATOES GO TO FRANCE   20th Century Fox, 1991

JESSICA LUNDY
Agent: William Morris Agency - Beverly Hills, 310/274-7451

MADHOUSE   Orion, 1990

MIN LUONG
GLEAMING THE CUBE   20th Century Fox, 1989

PATTI LUPONE
b. April 21, 1949 - Northport, New York
Agent: Gersh Agency - Beverly Hills, 310/274-6611

WITNESS   Paramount, 1985
WISE GUYS   MGM/UA, 1986
DRIVING MISS DAISY   Warner Bros., 1989

PETER LUPUS
THINK BIG   MPCA, 1990

JOHN LURIE
STRANGER THAN PARADISE   Samuel Goldwyn Company, 1984
DOWN BY LAW   Island Pictures, 1986

THUY AN LUU
DIVA   United Artists Classics, 1982, French

FRANC LUZ
Agent: Judy Schoen & Associates - Los Angeles, 213/962-1950

GHOST TOWN   Empire Pictures, 1988

DAVID LYNCH
b. January 20, 1946 - Missoula, Montana
Agent: CAA - Beverly Hills, 310/288-4545

ZELLY AND ME   Columbia, 1988
TWIN PEAKS: FIRE WALK WITH ME   New Line Cinema, 1992,
    U.S.-French (also directed)

KATE LYNCH
EASY PREY (TF)   New World TV/Rene Malo Productions, 1986
THE ANN JILLIAN STORY (TF)   9J, Inc. Productions/ITC, 1988

KELLY LYNCH
Agent: William Morris Agency - Beverly Hills, 310/274-7451

ROAD HOUSE   MGM/UA, 1989
DRUGSTORE COWBOY   Avenue Pictures, 1989
DESPERATE HOURS   MGM/UA, 1990
CURLY SUE   Warner Bros., 1991
THREE OF HEARTS   New Line Cinema, 1993
IMAGINARY CRIMES   Warner Bros., 1994

THE BEANS OF EGYPT, MAINE   I.R.S. Releasing, 1994
HEAVEN'S PRISONERS   Savoy Pictures, 1994

RICHARD LYNCH
SCARECROW   Warner Bros., 1973
STEEL   LOOK DOWN AND DIE/MEN OF STEEL
    World Northal, 1980
VAMPIRE (TF)   MTM Enterprises, 1979
THE FORMULA   MGM/United Artists, 1980
ALCATRAZ: THE WHOLE SHOCKING STORY (TF)
    Pierre Cossette Productions, 1981
THE SWORD AND THE SORCERER   Group 1, 1982
THE BARBARIANS   Cannon, 1987, Italian
LITTLE NIKITA   Columbia, 1988
THE FORBIDDEN DANCE   Columbia, 1990
McNELLY'S RANGERS   Warner Bros., 1995

VERNON LYNCH, JR.
VAMPIRE IN BROOKLYN   Paramount, 1995

CAROL LYNLEY
(Carolyn Lee)
b. February 13, 1942 - New York, New York

THE LIGHT IN THE FOREST   Buena Vista, 1958
HOLIDAY FOR LOVERS   20th Century-Fox, 1959
BLUE DENIM   20th Century-Fox, 1959
HOUND-DOG MAN   20th Century-Fox, 1959
RETURN TO PEYTON PLACE   20th Century-Fox, 1961
THE LAST SUNSET   Universal, 1961
THE STRIPPER   20th Century-Fox, 1963
UNDER THE YUM YUM TREE   Columbia, 1963
THE CARDINAL   Columbia, 1963
SHOCK TREATMENT   20th Century-Fox, 1964
THE PLEASURE SEEKERS   20th Century-Fox, 1964
BUNNY LAKE IS MISSING   Columbia, 1965, British
HARLOW   Paramount, 1965
THE SHUTTERED ROOM   Warner Bros., 1966, British
DANGER ROUTE   United Artists, 1968, British
THE SMUGGLERS (TF)   1968
THE MALTESE BIPPY   MGM, 1969
ONCE YOU KISS A STRANGER   Warner Bros., 1969
NORWOOD   Paramount, 1970
WEEKEND OF TERROR (TF)   Paramount TV, 1970
CROSSCURRENT   CABLE CAR MURDER (TF)
    Warner Bros. TV, 1971
THE NIGHT STALKER (TF)   ABC, Inc., 1972
BEWARE THE BLOB!   SON OF BLOB   Jack H. Enterprises, 1972
THE POSEIDON ADVENTURE   20th Century-Fox, 1972
COTTER   1973
THE ELEVATOR (TF)   Universal TV, 1974
DEATH STALK (TF)   Wolper Productions, 1975
THE FOUR DEUCES   Avco Embassy, 1975
FLOOD! (TF)   Irwin Allen Productions/20th Century-Fox TV, 1976
BAD GEORGIA ROAD   Dimension, 1976
FANTASY ISLAND (TF)   Spelling-Goldberg Productions, 1977
HAVING BABIES II (TF)   The Jozak Company, 1977
THE COPS AND ROBIN (TF)   Paramount TV, 1978
THE BEASTS ARE ON THE STREETS (TF)   Hanna-Barbera
    Productions, 1978
THE CAT AND THE CANARY   Quartet, 1978, British
THE SHAPE OF THINGS TO COME (TF)   Film Ventures
    International, 1979, Canadian
VIGILANTE   STREET GANG   Artists Releasing Corporation/Film
    Ventures International, 1982
SPIRITS   American Independent, 1991

ROBERT F. LYONS
AVENGING ANGEL   New World, 1985
MURPHY'S LAW   Cannon, 1986

ROBIN LYONS
THE PRINCESS AND THE GOBLIN (AF)   Hemdale, 1994 (voice)

STEVE LYONS
THE PRINCESS AND THE GOBLIN (AF)   Hemdale, 1994 (voice)

M

KATE MABERLY

Agent: William Morris Agency - Beverly Hills, 310/274-7451

THE SECRET GARDEN   Warner Bros., 1993, U.S.-British

ZACHARY MABRY

THE LITTLE RASCALS   Universal, 1994

BERNIE MAC

Agent: UTA - Beverly Hills, 310/273-6700

ABOVE THE RIM   New Line Cinema, 1994

RALPH MACCHIO

b. November 4, 1962 - Huntington, New York
Agent: ICM - Beverly Hills, 310/550-4000

MAD MAGAZINE PRESENTS UP THE ACADEMY
  UP THE ACADEMY   Warner Bros., 1980
DANGEROUS COMPANY (TF)   The Dangerous Company/
  Finnegan Associates, 1982
THE OUTSIDERS   Warner Bros., 1983
THE KARATE KID   Columbia, 1984
THE THREE WISHES OF BILLY GRIER (TF)
  I & C Productions, 1984
THE KARATE KID PART II   Columbia, 1986
CROSSROADS   Columbia, 1986
DISTANT THUNDER   Paramount, 1988
THE KARATE KID PART III   Columbia, 1989
TOO MUCH SUN   New Line Cinema, 1991
MY COUSIN VINNY   20th Century Fox, 1992
NAKED IN NEW YORK   Fine Line Features/New Line Cinema, 1994

SIMON MacCORKINDALE

JESUS OF NAZARETH (MS)   Sir Lew Grade Productions/ITC,
  1978, British-Italian
DEATH ON THE NILE   Paramount, 1978, British
THE RIDDLE OF THE SANDS   Satori, 1979, British
CABO BLANCO   Avco Embassy, 1980
THE MANIONS OF AMERICA (MS)   Roger Gimbel Productions/
  EMI TV/Argonaut Films, Ltd., 1981
THE SWORD AND THE SORCERER   Group 1, 1982
JAWS 3-D   Universal, 1983
OBSESSIVE LOVE (TF)   Onza, Inc./Moonlight Productions, 1984

MIKE MacDONALD

Agent: Spotlite Enterprises - Beverly Hills, 310/657-8004

THE NUTCRACKER PRINCE (AF)   Warner Bros., 1990 (voice)

ANDIE MacDOWELL

b. April 21, 1958 - Gaffney, South Carolina
Agent: ICM - Beverly Hills, 310/550-4000

GREYSTOKE: THE LEGEND OF TARZAN, LORD OF THE APES
  Warner Bros., 1984, British-U.S.
ST. ELMO'S FIRE   Columbia, 1985
sex, lies, and videotape   Miramax Films, 1989
GREEN CARD   Buena Vista, 1990
THE OBJECT OF BEAUTY   Avenue Pictures, 1991
HUDSON HAWK   TriStar, 1991
WOMEN & MEN: IN LOVE THERE ARE NO RULES (CTF)
  David Brown Productions/HBO Showcase, 1991
THE PLAYER   Fine Line Features/New Line Cinema, 1992
GROUNDHOG DAY   Columbia, 1993
SHORT CUTS   Fine Line Features/New Line Cinema, 1993

FOUR WEDDINGS AND A FUNERAL   Gramercy Pictures,
  1994, British
BAD GIRLS   20th Century Fox, 1994
UNSTRUNG HEROES   Buena Vista, 1995

ALI MacGRAW
(Alice Macgraw)
b. April 1, 1938 - Pound Ridge, New York

A LOVELY WAY TO DIE   Universal, 1968
GOODBYE, COLUMBUS   Paramount, 1969
LOVE STORY ★   Paramount, 1970
THE GETAWAY   National General, 1972
CONVOY   United Artists, 1978
PLAYERS   Paramount, 1979
JUST TELL ME WHAT YOU WANT   Columbia, 1980
THE WINDS OF WAR (MS)   Paramount TV/Dan Curtis
  Productions, 1983
CHINA ROSE (TF)   Robert Halmi, Inc., 1983

STEPHEN MACHT

THE TENTH LEVEL (TF)   CBS, Inc., 1976
AMELIA EARHART (TF)   Universal TV, 1976
RAID ON ENTEBBE (TF)   Edgar J. Scherick Associates/
  20th Century-Fox TV, 1977
THE CHOIRBOYS   Universal, 1977
LOOSE CHANGE (TF)   1978
RING OF PASSION (TF)   20th Century-Fox TV, 1978
HUNTERS OF THE REEF (TF)   Writers Company Productions/
  Paramount TV, 1978
THE IMMIGRANTS (MS)   Universal TV, 1978
NIGHTWING   Columbia, 1979
THE MOUNTAIN MEN   Columbia, 1980
GALAXINA   Crown International, 1980
ENOLA GAY: THE MEN, THE MISSION, THE ATOMIC BOMB (TF)
  The Production Company/Viacom, 1980
KILLJOY (TF)   Lorimar Productions, 1981
THE AMERICAN DREAM (TF)   Mace Neufeld Productions/
  Viacom, 1981
AGATHA CHRISTIE'S 'A CARIBBEAN MYSTERY' (TF)
  Stan Margulies Productions/Warner Bros. TV, 1983
THE LAST WINTER   Triumph/Columbia, 1983, Israeli
FLIGHT 90: DISASTER ON THE POTOMAC (TF)   Sheldon Pinchuk
  Productions/Finnegan Associates, 1984
SAMSON AND DELILAH (TF)   Catalina Production Group/Comworld
  Productions, 1984
GEORGE WASHINGTON: THE FORGING OF A NATION (MS)
  David Gerber Company/MGM TV, 1986
THE RETURN OF MICKEY SPILLANE'S MIKE HAMMER (TF)
  Jay Bernstein Productions/Columbia TV, 1986
THE MONSTER SQUAD   TriStar, 1987
STRANGE VOICES (TF)   Forrest Hills Productions/Dacks-Geller
  Productions/TLC, 1987
BLIND WITNESS (TF)   King Phoenix Entertainment Group, 1989
MY BOYFRIEND'S BACK (TF)   Interscope Communications, 1989
FEAR STALK (TF)   Donald March Productions/ITC Entertainment
  Group/CBS Entertainment, 1989
STEPHEN KING'S GRAVEYARD SHIFT   Paramount, 1990
AMITYVILLE 1992: IT'S ABOUT TIME (MFV)   Republic Pictures, 1992
SIRINGO   Rysher Entertainment, 1994

KYLE MacLACHLAN

b. 1960 - Yakima, Washington
Agent: UTA - Beverly Hills, 310/273-6700

DUNE   Universal, 1984
BLUE VELVET   DEG, 1986
THE HIDDEN   New Line Cinema, 1987
DREAM BREAKERS (TF)   CBS Entertainment, 1989
TWIN PEAKS (TF)   Lynch-Frost Productions/Propaganda Films/
  World Vision Enterprises, 1990
DON'T TELL HER IT'S ME   Hemdale, 1990
THE DOORS   TriStar, 1991
TWIN PEAKS: FIRE WALK WITH ME   New Line Cinema,
  1992, U.S.-French
RICH IN LOVE   MGM/UA, 1993
THE TRIAL   Angelika Films, 1993
THE FLINTSTONES   Universal, 1994

SHIRLEY MacLAINE
(Shirley MacLean Beaty)
b. April 24, 1934 - Richmond, Virginia
Agent: ICM - Beverly Hills, 310/550-4000

THE TROUBLE WITH HARRY   Paramount, 1955
ARTISTS AND MODELS   Paramount, 1955
AROUND THE WORLD IN 80 DAYS   United Artists, 1956
THE SHEEPMAN   MGM, 1958
THE MATCHMAKER   Paramount, 1958
HOT SPELL   Paramount, 1958
SOME CAME RUNNING ★   MGM, 1958
ASK ANY GIRL   MGM, 1959
CAREER   Paramount, 1959
OCEAN'S 11   Warner Bros., 1960
CAN-CAN   20th Century-Fox, 1960
THE APARTMENT ★   United Artists, 1960
ALL IN A NIGHT'S WORK   Paramount, 1961
TWO LOVES   MGM, 1961
THE CHILDREN'S HOUR   United Artists, 1962
MY GEISHA   Paramount, 1962
TWO FOR THE SEESAW   United Artists, 1962
IRMA LA DOUCE ★   United Artists, 1963
WHAT A WAY TO GO!   20th Century-Fox, 1964
JOHN GOLDFARB, PLEASE COME HOME   20th Century-Fox, 1964
THE YELLOW ROLLS-ROYCE   MGM, 1965, British
GAMBIT   Universal, 1966
WOMAN TIMES SEVEN   Avco Embassy, 1967, French-Italian-U.S.
THE BLISS OF MRS. BLOSSOM   Paramount, 1968, British
SWEET CHARITY   Universal, 1969
TWO MULES FOR SISTER SARA   Universal, 1970, U.S.-Mexican
DESPERATE CHARACTERS   ITC, 1971
THE POSSESSION OF JOEL DELANEY   Paramount, 1972
THE TURNING POINT ★   20th Century-Fox, 1977
BEING THERE   United Artists, 1979
A CHANGE OF SEASONS   20th Century-Fox, 1980
LOVING COUPLES   20th Century-Fox, 1980
TERMS OF ENDEARMENT ★★   Paramount, 1983
CANNONBALL RUN II   Warner Bros., 1984
OUT ON A LIMB (MS)   Stan Margulies Company/ABC Circle Films, 1987
MADAME SOUSATZKA   Cineplex Odeon, 1988, British
STEEL MAGNOLIAS   TriStar, 1989
POSTCARDS FROM THE EDGE   Columbia, 1990
WAITING FOR THE LIGHT   Triumph Releasing Corporation, 1990
DEFENDING YOUR LIFE   Warner Bros., 1991
USED PEOPLE   20th Century Fox, 1992
WRESTLING ERNEST HEMINGWAY   Warner Bros., 1993
GUARDING TESS   TriStar, 1994
EVENING STAR   Paramount, 1995

ROBERT MacNAUGHTON
E.T. THE EXTRATERRESTRIAL   Universal, 1982
A PLACE TO CALL HOME (TF)   Big Deal Productions/Crawford
   Productions/Embassy TV, 1987, U.S.-Australian

PATRICK MacNEE
b. February 6, 1922 - London, England
Agent: The Irv Schechter Company - Beverly Hills, 310/278-8070

COLONEL BLIMP   *THE LIFE AND DEATH OF COLONEL BLIMP*
   GFO, 1943, British
HAMLET   Universal, 1948, British
FLESH & BLOOD   1951, British
THREE CASES OF MURDER   1954, British
PURSUIT OF THE GRAF SPEE   *THE BATTLE OF THE
   RIVER PLATE*   Rank, 1957, British
LES GIRLS   MGM, 1957
MISTER JERICHO (TF)   ITC, 1969, British
KING SOLOMON'S TREASURE   Filmco Limited, 1977,
   Canadian-British
THE BILLION DOLLAR THREAT (TF)   David Gerber Productions/
   Columbia TV, 1979
THE HOWLING   Avco Embassy, 1981
THE SEA WOLVES   Paramount, 1982, British
YOUNG DOCTORS IN LOVE   20th Century-Fox, 1982
THE RETURN OF THE MAN FROM U.N.C.L.E. (TF)   Michael Sloan
   Productions/Viacom Productions, 1983
A VIEW TO A KILL   MGM/UA, 1985, British
SHADEY   Skouras Pictures, 1985, British

CLUB MED (TF)   Lorimar Productions, 1986
WAXWORK   Vestron, 1988
SORRY, WRONG NUMBER (CTF)   Jack Grossbart Productions/
   Wilshire Court Productions, 1989

TRESS MacNELLIE
LAND BEFORE TIME (AF)   Universal, 1995 (voice)

PETER MacNICOL
SOPHIE'S CHOICE   Universal/AFD, 1982
JOHNNY BULL (TF)   Titus Productions/Eugene O'Neill Memorial
   Theatre Center, 1986
GHOSTBUSTERS II   Columbia, 1989

ELLE MACPHERSON
Agent: ICM - Beverly Hills, 310/550-4000

SIRENS   Miramax Films, 1993, Australian-British-German

BILL MACY
b. May 18, 1922 - Revere, Massachusetts
Agent: Writers & Artists Agency - Los Angeles, 310/820-2240

ALL TOGETHER NOW (TF)   RSO Films, 1975
DEATH AT LOVE HOUSE (TF)   Spelling-Goldberg Productions, 1976
THE LATE SHOW   Warner Bros., 1977
STUNT SEVEN (TF)   Martin Poll Productions, 1979
BAD MEDICINE   20th Century Fox, 1985
MOVERS & SHAKERS   MGM/UA, 1985

WILLIAM H. MACY
THE CLIENT   Warner Bros., 1994
MR. HOLLAND'S OPUS   Buena Vista, 1995
OLEANNA   Samuel Goldwyn Company, 1995

JOHN MADDEN
LITTLE GIANTS   Warner Bros., 1994

JAMES MADDIO
THE BASKETBALL DIARIES   1995

AMY MADIGAN
b. 1957 - Chicago, Illinois
Agent: William Morris Agency - Beverly Hills, 310/274-7451

LOVE CHILD   The Ladd Company/Warner Bros., 1982
THE DAY AFTER (TF)   ABC Circle Films, 1983
LOVE LETTERS   New World, 1983
STREETS OF FIRE   Universal, 1984
PLACES IN THE HEART   TriStar, 1984
ALAMO BAY   TriStar, 1985
TWICE IN A LIFETIME ✪   The Yorkin Company, 1985
NOWHERE TO HIDE   New Century/Vista, 1987, U.S.-Canadian
THE PRINCE OF PENNSYLVANIA   New Line Cinema, 1988
ROE VS. WADE (TF)   The Manheim Company/NBC Productions, 1989
FIELD OF DREAMS   Universal, 1989
UNCLE BUCK   Universal, 1989
THE DARK HALF   Orion, 1993

MADONNA
(Madonna Louise Ciccone)
b. August 16, 1958 - Bay City, Michigan
Agent: CAA - Beverly Hills, 310/288-4545

A CERTAIN SACRIFICE   1979
DESPERATELY SEEKING SUSAN   Orion, 1985
VISION QUEST   Warner Bros., 1985
SHANGHAI SURPRISE   MGM/UA, 1986, British-U.S.
WHO'S THAT GIRL?   Warner Bros., 1987
BLOODHOUNDS OF BROADWAY   Columbia, 1989
DICK TRACY   Buena Vista, 1990
TRUTH OR DARE (FD)   Miramax Films, 1991
SHADOWS AND FOG   Orion, 1992
A LEAGUE OF THEIR OWN   Columbia, 1992
BODY OF EVIDENCE   MGM/UA, 1993
DANGEROUS GAME   MGM/UA, 1993

BRYAN MADORSKY
PARENTS   Vestron, 1989

MICHAEL MADSEN
b. 1958 - Chicago, Illinois
Agent: CAA - Beverly Hills, 310/288-4545

WARGAMES   MGM/UA, 1983
THE NATURAL   TriStar, 1984
OUR FAMILY HONOR (TF)   Lawrence & Charles Gordon
   Productions/Lorimar Productions, 1985
KILL ME AGAIN   MGM/UA, 1989
THE DOORS   TriStar, 1991
THELMA & LOUISE   MGM-Pathe, 1991
STRAIGHT TALK   Buena Vista, 1992
RESERVOIR DOGS   Miramax Films, 1992
FREE WILLY   Warner Bros., 1993
MONEY FOR NOTHING   Buena Vista, 1993
THE GETAWAY   Universal, 1994
WYATT EARP   Warner Bros., 1994
WILLY II: THE ADVENTURE HOME   Warner Bros., 1995
SPECIES   MGM/UA, 1995

VIRGINIA MADSEN
DUNE   Universal, 1984
ELECTRIC DREAMS   MGM/UA, 1984, British
THE HEARST AND DAVIES AFFAIR (TF)
   ABC Circle Films, 1985
MUSSOLINI: THE UNTOLD STORY (MS)
   Trian Productions, 1985
FIRE WITH FIRE   Paramount, 1986
MODERN GIRLS   Atlantic Releasing Corporation, 1986
SLAM DANCE   Island Pictures, 1987
MR. NORTH   Samuel Goldwyn Company, 1988
HOT TO TROT   Warner Bros., 1988
HEART OF DIXIE   Orion, 1989
THE HOT SPOT   Orion, 1990
HIGHLANDER II - THE QUICKENING   Entertainment Film
   Distributors, 1991, British-U.S.

ROMA MAFFIA
THE PAPER   Universal, 1994
DISCLOSURE   Warner Bros., 1994

BRANDON MAGGART
DRESSED TO KILL   Filmways, 1980

PUPELLA MAGGIO
CINEMA PARADISO   *NUOVO CINEMA PARADISO*
   Miramax Films, 1989, Italian-French

JACK MAGNER
AMITYVILLE II: THE POSSESSION   Orion, 1982

ANN MAGNUSON
MAKING MR. RIGHT   Orion, 1987
A NIGHT IN THE LIFE OF JIMMY REARDON
   20th Century Fox, 1988
TEQUILA SUNRISE   Warner Bros., 1988
CHECKING OUT   Warner Bros., 1989
LOVE AT LARGE   Orion, 1990

VALERIE MAHAFFEY
NATIONAL LAMPOON'S SENIOR TRIP   New Line Cinema, 1995

JOSEPH MAHER
Agent: Writers & Artists Agency - Los Angeles, 310/820-2240

HEAVEN CAN WAIT   Paramount, 1978
FUNNY FARM   Warner Bros., 1988
I.Q.   Paramount, 1994

BRUCE MAHLER
FRIDAY THE 13TH PART 3   Paramount, 1982
POLICE ACADEMY   The Ladd Company/Warner Bros., 1985
POLICE ACADEMY 2: THEIR FIRST ASSIGNMENT
   Warner Bros., 1985
POLICE ACADEMY 3: BACK IN TRAINING   Warner Bros., 1986
POLICE ACADEMY 6: CITY UNDER SIEGE   Warner Bros., 1989

JOHN MAHONEY
THE CHICAGO STORY (TF)   Eric Bercovici Productions/
   MGM TV, 1981
LISTEN TO YOUR HEART (TF)   CBS Entertainment, 1983
THE KILLING FLOOR (TF)   Public Forum Productions/
   KERA-Dallas-Ft. Worth, 1984
VOYEUR   Crystal Productions, 1984
CODE OF SILENCE   Orion, 1985
THE MANHATTAN PROJECT   20th Century Fox, 1986
STREETS OF GOLD   20th Century Fox, 1986
TRAPPED IN SILENCE (TF)   Reader's Digest Productions, 1986
TIN MEN   Buena Vista, 1987
SUSPECT   TriStar, 1987
MOONSTRUCK   MGM/UA, 1987
FRANTIC   Warner Bros., 1988
BETRAYED   MGM/UA, 1988
EIGHT MEN OUT   Orion, 1988
FAVORITE SON (MS)   NBC Productions, 1988
SAY ANYTHING   20th Century Fox, 1989
THE IMAGE (CTF)   HBO Pictures/Citadel Entertainment, 1990
LOVE HURTS   Vestron, 1990
THE RUSSIA HOUSE   MGM-Pathe, 1990
BARTON FINK   20th Century Fox, 1991
ARTICLE 99   Orion, 1992
IN THE LINE OF FIRE   Columbia, 1993
STRIKING DISTANCE   Columbia, 1993
REALITY BITES   Universal, 1994

TOM MAHONEY
CANNERY ROW   MGM/United Artists, 1982

SHARON MAIDEN
CLOCKWISE   Universal, 1986, British

STEPHEN MAILER
CRY-BABY   Universal, 1990

TINA MAJORINO
WHEN A MAN LOVES A WOMAN   Buena Vista, 1994
ANDRE   Paramount, 1994
CORRINA, CORRINA   New Line Cinema, 1994
WATERWORLD   Universal, 1995

LEE MAJORS
b. April 23, 1942 - Wyandotte, Michigan
Agent: David Shapira & Associates - Sherman Oaks, 818/906-0322

WILL PENNY   Paramount, 1968
THE BALLAD OF ANDY CROCKER (TF)   Thomas-Spelling
   Productions, 1969
THE LIBERATION OF L.B. JONES   Columbia, 1970
WEEKEND OF TERROR (TF)   Paramount TV, 1970
THE SIX MILLION DOLLAR MAN (TF)   Universal TV, 1973
FRANCIS GARY POWERS: THE TRUE STORY OF THE U-2 SPY
   INCIDENT (TF)   Charles Fries Productions, 1976
JUST A LITTLE INCONVENIENCE (TF)   Universal TV, 1977
THE NORSEMAN   American International, 1978
KILLER FISH   *DEADLY TREASURE OF THE PIRANHA*   Associated
   Film Distribution, 1978, British-Brazilian-French
STEEL   *LOOK DOWN AND DIE/MEN OF STEEL*
   World Northal, 1980
THE NAKED SUN   1979
SHARKS   1979
AGENCY   Taft International, 1980, Canadian
THE FALL GUY (TF)   Glen A. Larson Productions/
   20th Centuy-Fox TV, 1981
STARFLIGHT: THE PLANE THAT COULDN'T LAND
   STARFLIGHT ONE (TF)   Orgolini-Nelson Productions, 1983

THE COWBOY AND THE BALLERINA (TF)
Cowboy Productions, 1984
RETURN OF THE SIX MILLION DOLLAR MAN AND THE BIONIC
WOMAN (TF)   Michael Sloan Productions/Universal TV, 1987
DANGER DOWN UNDER (TF)   Weintraub Entertainment Group/
Hoyts Productions, Ltd., 1988, U.S.-Australian
SCROOGED   Paramount, 1988
BIONIC SHOWDOWN: THE SIX MILLION DOLLAR MAN AND THE
BIONIC WOMAN (TF)   Universal TV, 1989
FIRE! TRAPPED ON THE 37TH FLOOR (TF)   Papazian-Hirsch
Productions/Republic Pictures, 1991

LEE MAJORS II
RETURN OF THE SIX MILLION DOLLAR MAN AND THE BIONIC
WOMAN (TF)   Michael Sloan Productions/Universal TV, 1987

MIRIAM MAKEBA
SARAFINA!   Miramax Films/Buena Vista, 1992,
South African-British-French

CHRIS MAKEPEACE
MEATBALLS   Paramount, 1979, Canadian
MY BODYGUARD   20th Century-Fox, 1980
VAMP   New World, 1986
ALOHA SUMMER   *HANAUMA BAY*   Spectrafilm, 1988

WENDY MAKKENA
SISTER ACT   Buena Vista, 1992
SISTER ACT 2: BACK IN THE HABIT   Buena Vista, 1993
CAMP NOWHERE   Buena Vista, 1994

MAKO
(Jimmy Sakuyama)
THE SAND PEBBLES ✪   20th Century-Fox, 1966
THE HAWAIIANS   United Artists, 1970
THE ISLAND AT THE TOP OF THE WORLD   Buena Vista, 1974
THE KILLER ELITE   United Artists, 1975
THE BIG BRAWL   Warner Bros., 1980
UNDER THE RAINBOW   Orion/Warner Bros., 1981
THE BUSHIDO BLADE   Aquarius, 1982, U.S.-Japanese
CONAN THE BARBARIAN   Universal, 1982
TESTAMENT   Paramount, 1983
CONAN THE DESTROYER   Universal, 1984
HAWAIIAN HEAT (TF)   James D. Parriott Productions/
Universal TV, 1984
ARMED RESPONSE   CineTel, 1986
TUCKER - THE MAN AND HIS DREAM   Paramount, 1988
THE WASH   Skouras Pictures, 1988
AN UNREMARKABLE LIFE   Continental Film Group, 1989
MURDER IN PARADISE (TF)   Bill McCutchen Productions/
Columbia TV, 1990
TAKING CARE OF BUSINESS   Buena Vista, 1990
HIROSHIMA: OUT OF THE ASHES (TF)   Robert Greenwald
Productions, 1990
PACIFIC HEIGHTS   20th Century Fox, 1990
THE PERFECT WEAPON   Paramount, 1991
RISING SUN   20th Century Fox, 1993

BLU MAKUMA
SHOOT TO KILL   Buena Vista, 1988
DISTANT THUNDER   Paramount, 1988
WATCHERS   Universal, 1988

CHRISTOPHE MALAVOY
LA BALANCE   Spectrafilm, 1982, French

CHRISTOPHER MALCOLM
LABYRINTH   TriStar, 1986, British

PAULA MALCOMSON
Agent: Circle Talent Associates - Beverly Hills, 310/285-1585

TOMBSTONE   Buena Vista, 1993

KARL MALDEN
(Malden Sekulovich)
b. March 22, 1914 - Gary, Indiana
Agent: CAA - Beverly Hills, 310/288-4545

THEY KNEW WHAT THEY WANTED   Columbia, 1940
WINGED VICTORY   20th Century-Fox, 1944
13 RUE MADELEINE   20th Century-Fox, 1947
BOOMERANG   20th Century-Fox, 1947
KISS OF DEATH   20th Century-Fox, 1947
THE GUNFIGHTER   20th Century-Fox, 1950
WHERE THE SIDEWALK ENDS   20th Century-Fox, 1950
HALLS OF MONTEZUMA   20th Century-Fox, 1950
A STREETCAR NAMED DESIRE ✪✪   Warner Bros., 1951
THE SELLOUT   1952
DECISION BEFORE DAWN   20th Century-Fox, 1952
OPERATION SECRET   Warner Bros., 1952
DIPLOMATIC COURIER   20th Century-Fox, 1952
RUBY GENTRY   20th Century-Fox, 1953
I CONFESS   Warner Bros., 1953
TAKE THE HIGH GROUND   MGM, 1953
PHANTOM OF THE RUE MORGUE   Warner Bros., 1954
ON THE WATERFRONT ✪   Columbia, 1954
BABY DOLL   Warner Bros., 1956
FEAR STRIKES OUT   Paramount, 1957
BOMBERS B-52   Warner Bros., 1957
THE HANGING TREE   Warner Bros., 1959
POLLYANNA   Buena Vista, 1960
THE GREAT IMPOSTOR   Universal, 1961
PARRISH   Warner Bros., 1961
ONE-EYED JACKS   Paramount, 1961
ALL FALL DOWN   MGM, 1962
BIRDMAN OF ALCATRAZ   United Artists, 1962
GYPSY   Warner Bros., 1962
HOW THE WEST WAS WON   MGM/Cinerama, 1962
COME FLY WITH ME   MGM, 1963
DEAD RINGER   1964
CHEYENNE AUTUMN   Warner Bros., 1964
THE CINCINNATI KID   MGM, 1965
NEVADA SMITH   Paramount, 1966
THE SILENCERS   Columbia, 1966
MURDERERS' ROW   Columbia, 1966
HOTEL   Warner Bros., 1967
THE ADVENTURES OF BULLWHIP GRIFFIN   Buena Vista, 1967
BILLION DOLLAR BRAIN   United Artists, 1967, British
BLUE   Paramount, 1968, British
HOT MILLIONS   MGM, 1968, British
PATTON   20th Century-Fox, 1970
THE CAT O' NINE TAILS   National General, 1971,
Italian-West German-French
WILD ROVERS   MGM, 1971
THE STREETS OF SAN FRANCISCO (TF)   QM Productions, 1972
SUMMERTIME KILLER   French-Italian-Spanish, 1973
CAPTAINS COURAGEOUS (TF)   Norman Rosemont
Productions, 1977
METEOR   American International, 1979
BEYOND THE POSEIDON ADVENTURE   Warner Bros., 1979
WORD OF HONOR (TF)   Georgia Bay Productions, 1981
THE STING II   Universal, 1982
TWILIGHT TIME   MGM/UA, 1983, U.S.-Yugoslavian
WITH INTENT TO KILL (TF)   London Productions, 1984
FATAL VISION (MS)   NBC Productions, 1984
BILLY GALVIN   Vestron, 1986
NUTS   Universal, 1987
MY FATHER, MY SON (TF)   Fred Weintraub Productions/John J.
McMahon Productions, 1988
THE HIJACKING OF THE ACHILLE LAURO (TF)   Tamara Asseyev
Productions/Spectator Films/New World TV, 1989
ABSOLUTE STRANGERS (TF)   Cates-Doty Productions/Fries
Entertainment, 1991

WENDIE MALICK
Agent: Camden ITG - Los Angeles, 310/289-2700

A LITTLE SEX   Universal, 1982

ART MALIK
THE LIVING DAYLIGHTS MGM/UA, 1987, British
CITY OF JOY TriStar, 1992
TRUE LIES 20th Century Fox, 1994

JOSHUA MALINA
MENENDEZ: A KILLING IN BEVERLY HILLS (MS) Zev Braun
  Pictures/TriStar Television, 1994

JUDITH MALINA
ENEMIES, A LOVE STORY 20th Century Fox, 1989
THE ADDAMS FAMILY Paramount, 1991
HOUSEHOLD SAINTS Fine Line Features/New Line Cinema, 1993

ROSS MALINGER
SLEEPLESS IN SEATTLE TriStar, 1993

CLAIRE MALIS
'NIGHT, MOTHER Universal, 1986

JOHN MALKOVICH
b. December 9, 1953 - Christopher, Illinois

PLACES IN THE HEART ✪ TriStar, 1984
THE KILLING FIELDS Warner Bros., 1984, British
DEATH OF A SALESMAN (TF) Roxbury and Punch
  Productions, 1985
ELENI Warner Bros., 1985
MAKING MR. RIGHT Orion, 1987
THE GLASS MENAGERIE Cineplex Odeon, 1987
EMPIRE OF THE SUN Warner Bros., 1987
MILES FROM HOME Cinecom, 1988
DANGEROUS LIAISONS Warner Bros., 1988
THE SHELTERING SKY Warner Bros., 1990, British
QUEENS LOGIC New Line Cinema, 1991
THE OBJECT OF BEAUTY Avenue Pictures, 1991
SHADOWS AND FOG Orion, 1992
OF MICE AND MEN MGM-Pathe Communications, 1992
JENNIFER EIGHT Paramount, 1992
ALIVE Buena Vista, 1993 (uncredited)
IN THE LINE OF FIRE ✪ Columbia, 1993
MARY REILLY TriStar, 1995

BRIAN MALLON
GETTYSBURG New Line Cinema, 1993

BARBARA MALLORY
AIRPLANE! Paramount, 1980

JOHN MALLOY
CANNERY ROW MGM/United Artists, 1982

MATT MALLOY
MRS. PARKER AND THE VICIOUS CIRCLE Fine Line Features/
  New Line Cinema, 1994

MICHAEL MALONEY
HENRY V Samuel Goldwyn Company, 1989, British

STACY MALONEY
AMERICAN ANTHEM Columbia, 1986

MELISSA MANCHESTER
b. February 15, 1951 - Bronx, New York

FOR THE BOYS 20th Century Fox, 1991

RIC MANCINI
ALOHA SUMMER HANAUMA BAY Spectrafilm, 1988

NICK MANCUSO
Agent: Gersh Agency - Beverly Hills, 310/274-6611

DR. SCORPION (TF) Universal TV, 1978
THE HOUSE ON GARIBALDI STREET (TF) 1979
TORN BETWEEN TWO LOVERS (TF) Alan Landsburg
  Productions, 1979
NIGHTWING Columbia, 1979
THE KIDNAPPING OF THE PRESIDENT Crown International,
  1980, Canadian
SCRUPLES (MS) Lou-Step Productions/Warner Bros. TV, 1981
TICKET TO HEAVEN United Artists Classics, 1981, Canadian
MOTHER LODE SEARCH FOR THE MOTHER LODE: THE LAST
  GREAT TREASURE Agamemnon Films, 1982, Canadian
THE LEGEND OF WALKS FAR WOMAN (TF) Roger Gimbel Prods./
  EMI TV/Raquel Welch/Lee Levinson Productions, 1982
HEARTBREAKERS Orion, 1984
STINGRAY (TF) Stephen J. Cannell Productions, 1985
HALF A LIFETIME (CTF) HBO Showcase/Astral Film Enterprises/
  Martin Bergman Productions, 1986, U.S.-Canadian
THE KING OF LOVE (TF) Sarabande Productions/MGM-UA TV, 1987
BURNING BRIDGES (TF) Andrea Baynes Prods./Lorimar TV, 1990
UNDER SIEGE Warner Bros., 1992
WILD PALMS (MS) Ixtlan Corporation/Greengrass
  Productions, Inc., 1993

ROBERT MANDAN
THE BEST LITTLE WHOREHOUSE IN TEXAS Universal, 1982
ZAPPED! Embassy, 1982
PERRY MASON: THE CASE OF THE LOST LOVE (TF) The Fred
  Silverman Company/Strathmore Productions/Viacom, 1987

HOWIE MANDELL
b. November 29, 1955 - Toronto, Ontario
Agent: ICM - Beverly Hills, 310/550-4000

A FINE MESS Columbia, 1986
WALK LIKE A MAN MGM/UA, 1987
LITTLE MONSTERS MGM/UA, 1989

BARBARA MANDRELL
b. December 25, 1948 - Houston, Texas

BURNING RAGE (TF) Gilbert Cates Productions, 1984

COSTAS MANDYLOR
Agent: William Morris Agency - Beverly Hills, 310/274-7451

MOBSTERS Universal, 1991

BARRY MANILOW
b. June 17, 1946 - New York, New York

COPACABANA (TF) Dick Clark Productions/Stiletto, Ltd., 1985

BYRON MANN
STREET FIGHTER Universal, 1994

GLORIA MANN
POINT BREAK 20th Century Fox, 1991
29TH STREET 20th Century Fox, 1991

TERRENCE MANN
CRITTERS New Line Cinema, 1986

DINAH MANOFF
b. January 25, 1958 - New York, New York
Agent: Gersh Agency - Beverly Hills, 310/274-6611

GREASE Paramount, 1978
ORDINARY PEOPLE Paramount, 1980
I OUGHT TO BE IN PICTURES 20th Century-Fox, 1982
CLASSIFIED LOVE (TF) CBS Entertainment, 1986
CHILD'S PLAY MGM/UA, 1988
THE COVER GIRL AND THE COP (TF) Barry & Enright
  Productions, 1989

STAYING TOGETHER   Hemdale, 1989
BLOODHOUNDS OF BROADWAY   Columbia, 1989
WELCOME HOME ROXY CARMICHAEL   Paramount, 1990

GEORGE J. MANOS
HEAVEN CAN WAIT   Paramount, 1978
BIG   20th Century Fox, 1988

PAUL MANTEE
Agent: Flick - Los Angeles, 310/247-1777

ROBINSON CRUSOE ON MARS   Paramount, 1964
AN AMERICAN DREAM   1966
THEY SHOOT HORSES, DON'T THEY?   Cinerama Releasing
   Corporation, 1969
W.C. FIELDS AND ME   Universal, 1976
DAY OF THE ANIMALS   *SOMETHING IS OUT THERE*   1977
THE GREAT SANTINI   *THE ACE*   Orion/Warner Bros., 1980

JOE MANTEGNA
b. November 13, 1947 - Chicago, Illinois
Agent: Peter Strain & Associates - New York, 212/391-0380

COMPROMISING POSITIONS   Paramount, 1985
CRITICAL CONDITION   Paramount, 1987
HOUSE OF GAMES   Orion, 1987
SUSPECT   TriStar, 1987
THINGS CHANGE   Columbia, 1988
ALICE   Orion, 1990
THE GODFATHER, PART III   Paramount, 1990
QUEENS LOGIC   New Line Cinema, 1991
HOMICIDE   Triumph Releasing Corporation, 1991
BUGSY   TriStar, 1991
BODY OF EVIDENCE   MGM/UA, 1993
SEARCHING FOR BOBBY FISCHER   Paramount, 1993
BABY'S DAY OUT   20th Century Fox, 1994
AIRHEADS   20th Century Fox, 1994
THE RHINEHART THEORY   Rysher Entertainment, 1995
STRANGER THINGS   Columbia, 1995
FORGET PARIS   Columbia, 1995

HENRIETTE MANTEL
THE BRADY BUNCH MOVIE   Paramount, 1995

MICHAEL MANTELL
THE BROTHER FROM ANOTHER PLANET   Cinecom, 1984
MATEWAN   Cinecom, 1987
FIVE CORNERS   Cineplex Odeon, 1987
EIGHT MEN OUT   Orion, 1988

KITI MANVER
WHAT HAVE I DONE TO DESERVE THIS?   Cinevista,
   1985, Spanish

LESLEY MANVILLE
HIGH HOPES   Skouras Pictures, 1988, British

MARY MARA
LOVE POTION #9   20th Century Fox, 1992

PETER MARC
Agent: Paul Kohner, Inc. - Los Angeles, 310/550-1060

DANGEROUS LOVE   Motion Picture Corporation of America, 1988

SOPHIE MARCEAU
BRAVE HEART   Paramount, 1995

JANE MARCH
THE LOVER   MGM/UA, 1992, French
COLOR OF NIGHT   Buena Vista, 1994

NANCY MARCHAND
b. June 19, 1928 - Buffalo, New York
Agent: APA - New York, 212/582-1500

THE BACHELOR PARTY   United Artists, 1957
LADYBUG, LADYBUG   United Artists, 1963
TELL ME THAT YOU LOVE ME, JUNIE MOON   Paramount, 1970
THE HOSPITAL   United Artists, 1971
THE BOSTONIANS   Almi Pictures, 1984
FROM THE HIP   DEG, 1987
THE NAKED GUN: FROM THE FILES OF POLICE SQUAD!
   Paramount, 1988

DAVID MARCIANO
Agent: Bauman, Hiller & Associates - Los Angeles, 213/857-6666

HARLEM NIGHTS   Paramount, 1989

TED MARCOUX
GHOST IN THE MACHINE   20th Century Fox, 1993

ANDREA MARCOVICCI
THE FRONT   Columbia, 1976
THE CONCORDE—AIRPORT '79   Universal, 1979
JACK THE BEAR   20th Century Fox, 1992

RICHARD MARCUS
DEADLY FRIEND   Warner Bros., 1986
JESSE (TF)   Turman-Foster Company/Jordan Productions/Republic
   Pictures, 1988

TOM MARDIROSIAN
THE DARK HALF   Orion, 1993

JANET MARGOLIN
b. July 25, 1943 - New York, New York

DAVID AND LISA   Continental, 1962
THE EAVESDROPPER   1964, Argentine
BUS RILEY'S BACK IN TOWN   Universal, 1965
THE GREATEST STORY EVER TOLD   United Artists, 1965
MORITURI   *THE SABOTEUR: CODE NAME MORITURI*
   20th Century-Fox, 1965
NEVADA SMITH   Paramount, 1966
ENTER LAUGHING   Columbia, 1967
BUONA SERA, MRS. CAMPBELL   United Artists, 1968
TAKE THE MONEY AND RUN   Cinerama Releasing Corporation, 1969
THE LAST CHILD (TF)   Aaron Spelling Productions, 1971
FAMILY FLIGHT (TF)   Universal TV, 1972
YOUR THREE MINUTES ARE UP   1973
PRAY FOR THE WILDCATS (TF)   ABC Circle Films, 1974
PLANET EARTH (TF)   Warner Bros. TV, 1974
LANIGAN'S RABBI (TF)   Universal TV, 1976
ANNIE HALL   United Artists, 1977
MURDER IN PEYTON PLACE (TF)   20th Century-Fox TV, 1977
THE TRIANGLE FACTORY FIRE SCANDAL (TF)   Alan Landsburg
   Productions/Don Kirshner Productions, 1979
LAST EMBRACE   United Artists, 1979
GHOSTBUSTERS II   Columbia, 1989

STUART MARGOLIN
b. January 31 - Davenport, Iowa
Agent: ICM - Beverly Hills, 310/550-4000

LIMBO   *WOMEN IN LIMBO*   Universal, 1972
THE STONE KILLER   Columbia, 1973
DEATH WISH   Paramount, 1974
LANIGAN'S RABBI (TF)   Universal TV, 1976
THE BIG BUS   Paramount, 1976
FUTUREWORLD   American International, 1976
DAYS OF HEAVEN   Paramount, 1978
S.O.B.   Paramount, 1981
CLASS   Orion, 1983
A FINE MESS   Columbia, 1986
IRON EAGLE II   TriStar, 1988, Canadian-Israeli
BYE BYE BLUES   Circle Releasing Corporation, 1990, Canadian
GUILTY BY SUSPICION   Warner Bros., 1991

MIRIAM MARGOLYES
Agent: Susan Smith & Associates - Beverly Hills, 213/852-4777

LITTLE DORRIT Cannon, 1987, British
THE BUTCHER'S WIFE Paramount, 1991
DEAD AGAIN Paramount, 1991
THE AGE OF INNOCENCE Columbia, 1993
JAMES AND THE GIANT PEACH Buena Vista, 1995 (voice)

ANN-MARGRET
(See ANN-Margret)

DAVID MARGULIES
DRESSED TO KILL Filmways, 1980
GHOSTBUSTERS II Columbia, 1989

MICHELE MARIANA
THE ADVENTURES OF MARK TWAIN (AF) Atlantic Releasing
    Corporation, 1985 (voice)

AUGUSTO MARIANI
BIG 20th Century Fox, 1988

LISA MARIE
ED WOOD Buena Vista, 1994

JEAN-PIERRE MARIELLE
A FEW DAYS WITH ME Galaxy International, 1988, French

BANDUK MARIKA
CACTUS Spectrafilm, 1986, Australian

CHEECH MARIN
(Richard Marin)
b. July 13, 1946 - Los Angeles, California
Agent: CAA - Beverly Hills, 310/288-4545

UP IN SMOKE Paramount, 1978
CHEECH & CHONG"S NEXT MOVIE Universal, 1980
CHEECH & CHONG'S NICE DREAMS Columbia, 1981
IT CAME FROM HOLLYWOOD (FD) Paramount, 1982
CHEECH & CHONG: STILL SMOKIN' Paramount, 1983
CHEECH & CHONG'S THE CORSICAN BROTHERS Orion, 1984
AFTER HOURS The Geffen Company/Warner Bros., 1985
ECHO PARK Atlantic Releasing Corporation, 1986, U.S.-Austrian
BORN IN EAST L.A. Universal, 1987 (also directed)
OLIVER & COMPANY (AF) Buena Vista, 1988 (voice)
RUDE AWAKENING Orion, 1989
SHRIMP ON THE BARBIE Vestron, 1990, U.S.-New Zealand
THE LION KING (AF) Buena Vista, 1994 (voice)
DESPERADO Columbia, 1995

JASON MARIN
BACK TO THE FUTURE Universal, 1985
THE LITTLE MERMAID (AF) Buena Vista, 1989 (voice)

ED MARINARO
TONIGHT'S THE NIGHT (TF) Indieprod Productions/Phoenix
    Entertainment Group, 1987
SHARING RICHARD (TF) Houston Motion Picture Entertainment/
    CBS Entertainment, 1988
THE DIAMOND TRAP (TF) Jay Bernstein Productions/
    Columbia TV, 1988

DAN MARINO
ACE VENTURA: PET DETECTIVE Warner Bros., 1994

MARKY MARK
(See Mark WAHLBERG)

AVIVA MARKS
PARADISE Avco Embassy, 1982, Canadian

RALPH MARRERO
THE BABE Universal, 1992

KENNETH MARS
THE PRODUCERS Avco Embassy, 1968
BUTCH CASSIDY AND THE SUNDANCE KID 20th Century-Fox, 1969
DESPERATE CHARACTERS ITC, 1971
WHAT'S UP, DOC? Warner Bros., 1972
PAPER MOON Paramount, 1973
THE PARALLAX VIEW Paramount, 1974
YOUNG FRANKENSTEIN 20th Century-Fox, 1974
NIGHT MOVES Warner Bros., 1975
THE APPLE DUMPLING GANG RIDES AGAIN Buena Vista, 1979
RADIO DAYS Orion, 1987
FOR KEEPS TriStar, 1988
GET SMART, AGAIN! (TF) Phoenix Entertainment Group/
    IndieProd Co., 1989
POLICE ACADEMY 6: CITY UNDER SIEGE Warner Bros., 1989
THE LITTLE MERMAID (AF) Buena Vista, 1989 (voice)
SHADOWS AND FOG Orion, 1992
HANS CHRISTIAN ANDERSEN'S THUMBELINA (AF)
    Warner Bros., 1994 (voice)
LAND BEFORE TIME (AF) Universal, 1995 (voice)

BRANFORD MARSALIS
b. August 26, 1960 - New Orleans, Louisiana

THROW MOMMA FROM THE TRAIN Orion, 1987
SCHOOL DAZE Columbia, 1988

JEAN MARSH
b. July 1, 1934 - London, England

THE EAGLE HAS LANDED Columbia, 1977, British
MASTER OF THE GAME (MS) Rosemont Productions, 1984
THE CORSICAN BROTHERS (TF) Norman Rosemont Productions,
    1985, British-U.S.
RETURN TO OZ Buena Vista, 1985
WILLOW MGM/UA, 1988
A CONNECTICUT YANKEE IN KING ARTHUR'S COURT (TF)
    Schaefer-Karpf Productions/Consolidated Productions, 1989

SALLY ANN MARSH
THE PRINCESS AND THE GOBLIN (AF) Hemdale, 1994 (voice)

BRYAN MARSHALL
RETURN TO SNOWY RIVER Buena Vista, 1988, Australian

DAVID ANTHONY MARSHALL
Agent: Geddes Agency - Los Angeles, 213/651-2401

ANOTHER 48 HRS. Paramount, 1990

E. G. MARSHALL
(Everett G. Marshall)
b. June 18, 1910 - Owatonna, Minnesota

THE HOUSE ON 92ND STREET 20th Century-Fox, 1945
13 RUE MADELEINE 20th Century-Fox, 1946
UNTAMED FURY Producers Releasing Corporation, 1948
CALL NORTHSIDE 777 20th Century-Fox, 1948
THE CAINE MUTINY Columbia, 1954
PUSHOVER Columbia, 1954
THE BAMBOO PRISON Columbia, 1954
BROKEN LANCE 20th Century-Fox, 1954
THE SILVER CHALICE Warner Bros., 1954
THE LEFT HAND OF GOD 20th Century-Fox, 1955
THE SCARLET HOUR Paramount, 1956
THE MOUNTAIN Paramount, 1956
TWELVE ANGRY MEN United Artists, 1957
THE BACHELOR PARTY United Artists, 1957
MAN ON FIRE MGM, 1957
THE BUCCANEER Paramount, 1958
THE JOURNEY MGM, 1959
COMPULSION 20th Century-Fox, 1959
CRASH McCALL Warner Bros., 1960

TOWN WITHOUT PITY   United Artists, 1961
THE CHASE   Columbia, 1966
IS PARIS BURNING?   Paramount, 1966, Fench-U.S.
THE POPPY IS ALSO A FLOWER   Comet, 1966, European
THE BRIDGE AT REMAGEN   United Artists, 1969
A CLEAR AND PRESENT DANGER (TF)   Universal TV, 1970
TORA! TORA! TORA!   20th Century-Fox, 1970, U.S.-Japanese
THE PURSUIT OF HAPPINESS   Columbia, 1971
VANISHED (TF)   Universal TV, 1971
THE CITY (TF)   Universal TV, 1971
PURSUIT (TF)   ABC Circle Films, 1972
MONEY TO BURN (TF)   Universal TV, 1973
THE ABDUCTION OF ST. ANNE (TF)   QM Productions, 1975
INTERIORS   United Artists, 1978
THE PRIVATE FILES OF J. EDGAR HOOVER
   American International, 1978
THE LAZARUS SYNDROME (TF)   Blinn-Thorpe Productions/
   Viacom, 1979
SUPERMAN II   Warner Bros., 1981, U.S.-British
CREEPSHOW   Warner Bros., 1982
KENNEDY (MS)   Central Independent Television Productions/Alan
   Landsburg Productions, 1983, British-U.S.
SAIGON - YEAR OF THE CAT (TF)   Thames TV, 1983, British
THE WINTER OF OUR DISCONTENT (TF)
   Lorimar Productions, 1983
POWER   20th Century Fox, 1986
AT MOTHER'S REQUEST (TF)   Vista Organization, Ltd., 1987
THE HIJACKING OF THE ACHILLE LAURO (TF)   Tamara Asseyev
   Productions/Spectator Films/New World TV, 1989
CONSENTING ADULTS   Buena Vista, 1992

GARRY MARSHALL
b. November 13, 1934 - New York, New York
Agent: ICM - Beverly Hills, 310/550-4000

LOST IN AMERICA   The Geffen Company/Warner Bros., 1985
SOAPDISH   Paramount, 1991
A LEAGUE OF THEIR OWN   Columbia, 1992
HOCUS POCUS   Buena Vista, 1993

JAMES MARSHALL
GLADIATOR   Columbia, 1992
TWIN PEAKS: FIRE WALK WITH ME   New Line Cinema,
   1992, U.S.-French
A FEW GOOD MEN   Columbia, 1992

KEN MARSHALL
FEDS   Warner Bros., 1988

PENNY MARSHALL
b. October 15, 1942 - New York, New York
Agent: CAA - Beverly Hills, 310/288-4545

THE SAVAGE SEVEN   American International, 1968
HOW SWEET IT IS!   Buena Vista, 1968
THE FEMINIST AND THE FUZZ (TF)   Screen Gems/
   Columbia TV, 1970
HOW COME NOBODY'S ON OUR SIDE?   American
   Films Ltd., 1975
1941   Universal, 1979
CHALLENGE OF A LIFETIME (TF)   Moonlight Productions, 1985
MOVERS & SHAKERS   MGM/UA, 1985
THE HARD WAY   Universal, 1991
HOCUS POCUS   Buena Vista, 1993

WILLIAM MARSHALL
b. August 19, 1924 - Gary, Indiana

LYDIA BAILEY   20th Century-Fox, 1952
DEMETRIUS AND THE GLADIATORS   20th Century-Fox, 1954
SOMETHING OF VALUE   MGM, 1957
TO TRAP A SPY   MGM, 1966
THE BOSTON STRANGLER   20th Century-Fox, 1968
ZIGZAG   MGM, 1970
SKULLDUGGERY   Universal, 1970
BLACULA   American International, 1972
SCREAM, BLACULA, SCREAM!   American International, 1973

ABBY   1974
TWILIGHT'S LAST GLEAMING   Allied Artists, 1977,
   U.S.-West German
VASECTOMY, A DELICATE MATTER   Seymour Borde &
   Associates, 1986

CRISTINA MARSILLACH
EVERY TIME WE SAY GOODBYE   TriStar, 1986, Israeli

K.C. MARTEL
E.T. THE EXTRA-TERRESTRIAL   Universal, 1982

ANDREA MARTIN
Agent: William Morris Agency - Beverly Hills, 310/274-7451

CLUB PARADISE   Warner Bros., 1986
RUDE AWAKENING   Orion, 1989
TOO MUCH SUN   New Line Cinema, 1991
STEPPING OUT   Paramount, 1991
ALL I WANT FOR CHRISTMAS   Paramount, 1991

DEAN MARTIN
(Dino Paul Crocetti)
b. June 7, 1917 - Steubenville, Ohio

MY FRIEND IRMA   Paramount, 1949
MY FRIEND IRMA GOES WEST   Paramount, 1950
AT WAR WITH THE ARMY   Paramount, 1950
THAT'S MY BOY   Paramount, 1951
SAILOR BEWARE   Paramount, 1951
JUMPING JACKS   Paramount, 1952
THE STOOGE   Paramount, 1952
SCARED STIFF   Paramount, 1953
THE CADDY   Paramount, 1953
MONEY FROM HOME   Paramount, 1953
LIVING IT UP   Paramount, 1954
THREE-RING CIRCUS   Paramount, 1954
YOU'RE NEVER TOO YOUNG   Paramount, 1955
ARTISTS AND MODELS   Paramount, 1955
PARDNERS   Paramount, 1956
HOLLYWOOD OR BUST   Paramount, 1956
TEN THOUSAND BEDROOMS   MGM, 1957
THE YOUNG LIONS   20th Century-Fox, 1958
SOME CAME RUNNING   MGM, 1959
RIO BRAVO   Warner Bros., 1959
CAREER   Paramount, 1959
WHO WAS THAT LADY?   Columbia, 1960
BELLS ARE RINGING   MGM, 1960
OCEAN'S ELEVEN   Warner Bros., 1960
ALL IN A NIGHT'S WORK   Paramount, 1961
ADA   MGM, 1961
SERGEANTS 3   United Artists, 1962
WHO'S GOT THE ACTION?   Paramount, 1962
TOYS IN THE ATTIC   United Artists, 1963
FOUR FOR TEXAS   Warner Bros., 1963
WHO'S BEEN SLEEPING IN MY BED?   Paramount, 1963
WHAT A WAY TO GO!   20th Century-Fox, 1964
ROBIN AND THE SEVEN HOODS   Warner Bros., 1964
KISS ME, STUPID   Lopert, 1964
THE SONS OF KATIE ELDER   Paramount, 1965
MARRIAGE ON THE ROCKS   Warner Bros., 1965
THE SILENCERS   Columbia, 1966
TEXAS ACROSS THE RIVER   Universal, 1966
MURDERERS' ROW   Columbia, 1966
ROUGH NIGHT IN JERICHO   Universal, 1967
THE AMBUSHERS   Columbia, 1967
HOW TO SAVE A MARRIAGE (AND RUIN YOUR LIFE)
   Columbia, 1968
BANDOLERO!   20th Century-Fox, 1968
FIVE CARD STUD   Paramount, 1968
THE WRECKING CREW   Columbia, 1969
AIRPORT   Universal, 1970
SOMETHING BIG   National General, 1971
SHOWDOWN   Universal, 1973
MR. RICCO   MGM, 1975
THE CANNONBALL RUN   20th Century-Fox, 1981
CANNONBALL RUN II   Warner Bros., 1984

D U A N E   M A R T I N
ABOVE THE RIM   New Line Cinema, 1994

G E O R G E   M A R T I N
Agent: ICM - Beverly Hills, 310/550-4000

FALLING IN LOVE   Paramount, 1984
CROSSING DELANCEY   Warner Bros., 1988
DYING YOUNG   20th Century Fox, 1991

G R E G O R Y   P A U L   M A R T I N
MEMOIRS OF AN INVISIBLE MAN   Warner Bros., 1992

H E L E N   M A R T I N
NIGHT ANGEL   Fries Distribution Company, 1990

K E L L I E   M A R T I N
MATINEE   Universal, 1993

M A R Y   C A T H E R I N E   M A R T I N
CLEAN AND SOBER   Warner Bros., 1988

N A N   M A R T I N
PROUD MEN (TF)   von Zerneck-Samuels Productions, 1987

P A M E L A   S U E   M A R T I N
b. January 5, 1953

TO FIND A MAN   *TO FIND A MAN/SEX AND THE TEENAGER*
   Columbia, 1972
THE POSEIDON ADVENTURE   20th Century-Fox, 1972
THE GIRLS OF HUNTINGTON HOUSE (TF)   Lorimar
   Productions, 1973
BUSTER AND BILLIE   Columbia, 1974
THE GUN AND THE PULPIT (TF)   Danny Thomas
   Productions, 1974
THE LADY IN RED   *GUNS, SIN AND BATHTUB GIN*
   New World, 1979
DYNASTY (TF)   Aaron Spelling Productions/Fox-Cat
   Productions, 1981
TORCHLIGHT   International Film Marketing, 1984, U.S.-Mexican
BAY COVEN (TF)   Guber-Peters Company/Phoenix Entertainment
   Group, 1987
A CRY IN THE WILD   Concorde, 1990

S H A R L E N E   M A R T I N
FRIDAY THE 13TH PART VIII - JASON TAKES MANHATTAN
   Paramount, 1989

S H A R O N   M A R T I N
Agent: Metropolitan Talent Agency - Los Angeles, 213/857-4500

PTERODACTYL WOMAN FROM BEVERLY HILLS   Experimental
   Pictures, 1994

S T E V E   M A R T I N
b. April 14, 1945 - Waco, Texas
Agent: ICM - Beverly Hills, 310/550-4000

SGT. PEPPER'S LONELY HEARTS CLUB BAND   Universal, 1978
THE KIDS ARE ALRIGHT (FD)   New World, 1979, British
THE MUPPET MOVIE   AFD, 1979, British
THE JERK   Universal, 1979
PENNIES FROM HEAVEN   MGM/United Artists, 1981
DEAD MEN DON'T WEAR PLAID   Universal, 1982
THE MAN WITH TWO BRAINS   Warner Bros., 1983
THE LONELY GUY   Universal, 1984
ALL OF ME   Universal, 1984
MOVERS & SHAKERS   MGM/UA, 1985
THREE AMIGOS   Orion, 1986
LITTLE SHOP OF HORRORS   The Geffen Company/
   Warner Bros., 1986
ROXANNE   Columbia, 1987
PLANES, TRAINS AND AUTOMOBILES   Paramount, 1987

DIRTY ROTTEN SCOUNDRELS   Orion, 1988
PARENTHOOD   Universal, 1989
MY BLUE HEAVEN   Warner Bros., 1990
L.A. STORY   TriStar, 1991
FATHER OF THE BRIDE   Buena Vista, 1991
GRAND CANYON   20th Century Fox, 1991
HOUSESITTER   Universal, 1992
LEAP OF FAITH   Paramount, 1992
AND THE BAND PLAYED ON (CTF)   HBO Pictures/Spelling
   Entertainment, 1993
A SIMPLE TWIST OF FATE   Buena Vista, 1994
LIFESAVERS   TriStar, 1994
FATHER OF THE BRIDE 2   Buena Vista, 1995
SGT. BILKO   Universal, 1995

A   M A R T I N E Z
Agent: William Morris Agency - Beverly Hills, 310/274-7451

POWWOW HIGHWAY   Warner Bros., 1989, U.S.-British
MANHUNT: SEARCH FOR THE NIGHT STALKER (TF)
   Leonard Hill Films, 1989
SHE-DEVIL   Orion, 1989

S T E V E N   M A R T I N I
MAJOR PAYNE   Universal, 1995

H I L A R Y   M A S O N
ROBOTJOX   Triumph Releasing Corporation, 1990

J A C K I E   M A S O N
b. June 9, 1931 - Sheboygan, Wisconsin

CADDYSHACK II   Warner Bros., 1988

M A D I S O N   M A S O N
Agent: Craig Agency - Los Angeles, 213/655-0236

DANGEROUSLY CLOSE   Cannon, 1986
FLIGHT OF THE INTRUDER   Paramount, 1991

M A R S H A   M A S O N
b. April 3, 1942 - St. Louis, Missouri
Agent: ICM - Beverly Hills, 310/550-4000

HOT ROD HULLABALLO   Allied Artists, 1966
BLUME IN LOVE   Warner Bros., 1973
CINDERELLA LIBERTY ★   20th Century-Fox, 1973
AUDREY ROSE   United Artists, 1977
THE GOODBYE GIRL ★   MGM/Warner Bros., 1977
THE CHEAP DETECTIVE   Columbia, 1978
PROMISES IN THE DARK   Orion/Warner Bros., 1979
CHAPTER TWO ★   Columbia, 1979
ONLY WHEN I LAUGH ★   Columbia, 1981
MAX DUGAN RETURNS   20th Century-Fox, 1983
SURVIVING (TF)   Telepictures Productions, 1985
HEARTBREAK RIDGE   Warner Bros., 1986
TRAPPED IN SILENCE (TF)   Reader's Digest Productions, 1986
DINNER AT EIGHT (CTF)   Think Entertainment/Turner
   Network TV, 1989
STELLA   Buena Vista, 1990
DROP DEAD FRED   New Line Cinema, 1991
I LOVE TROUBLE   Buena Vista, 1994

B E N   M A S T E R S
Agent: J. Michael Bloom & Associates - Los Angeles, 310/275-6800

DREAM LOVER   MGM/UA, 1986
THE DELIBERATE STRANGER (MS)   Stuart Phoenix Productions/
   Lorimar-Telepictures, 1986
KATE'S SECRET (TF)   Andrea Baynes Productions/
   Columbia TV, 1986
RIVIERA (TF)   MTM Productions, 1987
JAMES CLAVELL'S NOBLE HOUSE   *NOBLE HOUSE* (MS)   Noble
   House Productions, Ltd./De Laurentiis Entertainment Group, 1988
STREET OF DREAMS (TF)   Bill Stratton-Myrtos Productions/Phoenix
   Entertainment Group, 1988

FAY MASTERSON
Agent: Susan Smith & Associates - Beverly Hills, 213/852-4777

THE MAN WITHOUT A FACE   Warner Bros., 1993

MARY STUART MASTERSON
b. 1957 - New York, New York
Agent: William Morris Agency - Beverly Hills, 310/274-7451

THE STEPFORD WIVES   Columbia, 1975
HEAVEN HELP US   TriStar, 1985
LOVE LIVES ON (TF)   ABC Circle Films, 1985
MUSSOLINI: THE UNTOLD STORY (MS)   Trian Productions, 1985
MY LITTLE GIRL   Hemdale, 1986
AT CLOSE RANGE   Orion, 1986
SOME KIND OF WONDERFUL   Paramount, 1987
GARDENS OF STONE   TriStar, 1987
MR. NORTH   Samuel Goldwyn Company, 1988
CHANCES ARE   TriStar, 1989
IMMEDIATE FAMILY   Columbia, 1989
FUNNY ABOUT LOVE   Paramount, 1990
FRIED GREEN TOMATOES   Universal, 1991
MARRIED TO IT   Orion, 1993
BENNY & JOON   MGM/UA, 1993
BAD GIRLS   20th Century Fox, 1994
RADIOLAND MURDERS   Universal, 1994
HEAVEN'S PRISONERS   Savoy Pictures, 1994

MARY ELIZABETH MASTRANTONIO
b. November 17, 1958 - Lombard, Illinois
Agent: CAA - Beverly Hills, 310/288-4545

SCARFACE   Universal, 1983
MUSSOLINI: THE UNTOLD STORY (MS)   Trian Productions, 1985
THE COLOR OF MONEY ✪   Buena Vista, 1986
THE JANUARY MAN   MGM/UA, 1989
THE ABYSS   20th Century Fox, 1989
FOOLS OF FORTUNE   New Line Cinema, 1990
CLASS ACTION   20th Century Fox, 1991
ROBIN HOOD: PRINCE OF THIEVES   Warner Bros., 1991
WHITE SANDS   Warner Bros., 1992
CONSENTING ADULTS   Buena Vista, 1992
THREE WISHES   Savoy Pictures, 1995

MARCELLO MASTROIANNI
b. September 28, 1923 - Fontana Liri, Italy

I MISERABILI   1947, Italian
VITA DE CANE   ATA, 1950, Italian
UNA DOMENICA D'AGOSTO   1950, Italian
PARIGI E SEMPRE PARIGI   1951, Italian
SENSUALITA   1952, Italian
THREE GIRLS FROM ROME   LE RAGAZZE DI PIAZZA DI SPAGNA   1952, Italian
THE ANATOMY OF LOVE   TEMPI NOSTRI   1954, Italian
CRONACHE DI POVERI AMANTI   Cooperative Spettori Produtti Cinematografici, 1954, Italian
GIORNI D'AMORE   1954, Italian
HOUSE OF RICORDI   CASA RICORDI   1954, Italian
TOO BAD SHE'S BAD   PECCATO CHE SIA UNA CANAGLIA   1955, Italian
THE MILLER'S BEAUTIFUL WIFE   LA BELLA MUGNAIA   1955, Italian
THE BIGAMIST   IL BIGAMO   1956, Italian
LUCKY TO BE A WOMAN   LA FORTUNA DI ESSERE DONNA   1956, Italian
A TAILOR'S MAID   PADRI E FIGLI   Trans-Lux, 1957, Italian
THE MOST WONDERFUL MOMENT   IL MOMENTO PIU BELLO   1957, Italian
WHITE NIGHTS   LE NOTTI BIANCHE   United Motion Picture Organization, 1957, Italian
THE BIG DEAL ON MADONNA STREET   I SOLITI IGNOTI   United Motion Picture Organization, 1958, Italian
LOVE ON THE RIVIERA   RACCONTI D'ESTATE   1958, Italian
WHERE THE HOT WIND BLOWS   LA LOI/IL LEGGE   MGM, 1958, Italian-French
LA DOLCE VITA   Astor, 1960, Italian
IL BELL'ANTONIO   1960, Italian

LOVE A LA CARTE   ADUA E LE COMPAGNE   1960, Italian
THE NIGHT   LA NOTTE   Lopert, 1961, Italian-French
GHOSTS OF ROME   FANTASMI A ROMA   1961, Italian
THE ASSASSIN   THE LADY KILLER OF ROME   Manson, 1961, Italian
DIVORCE ITALIAN STYLE ★   Embassy, 1961, Italian
A VERY PRIVATE AFFAIR   LA VIE PRIVÉE   MGM, 1962, Italian-French
FAMILY DIARY   CRONACA FAMILIARE   1962, Italian
8 1/2   OTTO E MEZZO   Embassy, 1963, Italian
THE ORGANIZER   I COMPAGNI   Continental, 1963, Italian-French-Yugoslavian
YESTERDAY, TODAY AND TOMORROW   IERI OGGI DOMANI   Embasy, 1963, Italian-French
MARRIAGE ITALIAN STYLE   MATRIMONIO ALL'ITALIANA   1964, Italian
CASANOVA '70   1965, Italian
THE TENTH VICTIM   LA DECIMA VITTIMA   1965, Italian
GHOSTS ITALIAN STYLE   QUESTI FANTASMI   1967, Italian
THE STRANGER   LO STRANIERO   1967, Italian
A PLACE FOR LOVERS   AMANTI   MGM, 1969, Italian-French
SUNFLOWER   I GIRASOLI   1969, Italian
LEO THE LAST   1970, British
THE PIZZA TRIANGLE   DRAMA DELLA GELOSIA   1970, Italian
WHAT?   Avco Embassy, 1973, Italian-French-West German
A SPECIAL DAY ★   Cinema 5, 1977, Italian
GABRIELA   MGM/UA Classics, 1983, Brazilian-Italian
GINGER AND FRED   MGM/UA, 1986, Italian-French-West German
DARK EYES ★   Island Pictures, 1987, Italian-French
EVERYBODY'S FINE   Miramax Films, 1990, Italian
USED PEOPLE   20th Century Fox, 1992
PRET-A-PORTER   Miramax Films, 1994

RICHARD MASUR
Agent: Susan Smith & Associates - Beverly Hills, 213/852-4777

WHIFFS   20th Century-Fox, 1975
SEMI-TOUGH   United Artists, 1977
WHO'LL STOP THE RAIN   DOG SOLDIERS   United Artists, 1978
HANOVER STREET   Columbia, 1979
SCAVENGER HUNT   20th Century-Fox, 1979
WALKING THROUGH THE FIRE (TF)   Time-Life Films, 1979
HEAVEN'S GATE   United Artists, 1980
JOHN STEINBECK'S EAST OF EDEN   EAST OF EDEN (MS)   Mace Neufeld Productions, 1981
FALLEN ANGEL (TF)   Green-Epstein Productions/Columbia TV, 1981
I'M DANCING AS FAST AS I CAN   Paramount, 1982
THE THING   Universal, 1982
UNDER FIRE   Orion, 1983
RISKY BUSINESS   The Geffen Company/Warner Bros., 1983
NIGHTMARES   Universal, 1983
ADAM (TF)   Alan Landsburg Productions, 1983
THE BURNING BED (TF)   Tisch-Avnet Productions, 1984
OBSESSED WITH A MARRIED WOMAN (TF)   Sidaris-Camhe Productions/The Feldman-Meeker Company, 1985
THE MEAN SEASON   Orion, 1985
MY SCIENCE PROJECT   Buena Vista, 1985
WILD HORSES (TF)   Wild Horses Productions/Telepictures Productions, 1985
ADAM: HIS SONG CONTINUES (TF)   Alan Landsburg Productions, 1986
WHEN THE BOUGH BREAKS (TF)   Taft Entertainment TV/TDF Productions, 1986
THE GEORGE McKENNA STORY (TF)   Alan Landsburg Productions, 1986
HEARTBURN   Paramount, 1986
THE BELIEVERS   Orion, 1986
ROSES ARE FOR THE RICH (MS)   Phoenix Entertainment Group, 1987
RENT-A-COP   Kings Road Productions, 1988
SHOOT TO KILL   Buena Vista, 1988
LICENSE TO DRIVE   20th Century Fox, 1988
FAR FROM HOME   Vestron, 1989
SETTLE THE SCORE (TF)   Steve Sohmer Inc. Productions/ITC Entertainment Group, 1989
FLASHBACK   Paramount, 1990
IT (TF)   Konigsberg-Sanitsky Productions/Green-Epstein Productions/Lorimar TV, 1990
ALWAYS REMEMBER I LOVE YOU (TF)   Stephen J. Cannell/Gross-Weston Productions, Inc., 1990

MY GIRL   Columbia, 1991
ENCINO MAN   Buena Vista, 1992
THE MAN WITHOUT A FACE   Warner Bros., 1993
AND THE BAND PLAYED ON (CTF)   HBO Pictures/Spelling
   Entertainment, 1993
SIX DEGREES OF SEPARATION   MGM/UA, 1993
MY GIRL 2   Columbia, 1994
FORGET PARIS   Columbia, 1995

TIM MATHESON
b. December 31, 1947 - Glendale, California
Agent: CAA - Beverly Hills, 310/288-4545

DIVORCE AMERICAN STYLE   Columbia, 1967
YOURS, MINE AND OURS   United Artists, 1968
MAGNUM FORCE   Warner Bros., 1973
NATIONAL LAMPOON'S ANIMAL HOUSE   Universal, 1978
THE APPLE DUMPLING GANG RIDES AGAIN   Buena Vista, 1979
DREAMER   20th Century-Fox, 1979
A LITTLE SEX   Universal, 1982
TO BE OR NOT TO BE   20th Century-Fox, 1983
IMPULSE   20th Century Fox, 1984
OBSESSED WITH A MARRIED WOMAN (TF)   Sidaris-Camhe
   Productions/The Feldman-Meeker Company, 1985
FLETCH   Universal, 1985
BLIND JUSTICE (TF)   CBS Entertainment, 1986
WARM HEARTS, COLD FEET (TF)   Lorimar-Telepictures, 1987
BAY COVEN (TF)   Guber-Peters Company/Phoenix
   Entertainment Group, 1987
BURIED ALIVE (CTF)   Niki Marvin Prods./MCA Entertainment, 1990
DROP DEAD FRED   New Line Cinema, 1991

DAKIN MATHEWS
MENENDEZ: A KILLING IN BEVERLY HILLS (MS)   Zev Braun
   Pictures/TriStar Television, 1994

THOM MATHEWS
Agent: Metropolitan Talent Agency - Los Angeles, 213/857-4500

FRIDAY THE 13TH, PART VI: JASON LIVES   Paramount, 1986
DANGEROUSLY CLOSE   Cannon, 1986
RETURN OF THE LIVING DEAD PART II   Lorimar, 1988

SAMANTHA MATHIS
PUMP UP THE VOLUME   New Line Cinema, 1990
THIS IS MY LIFE   20th Century Fox, 1992
FERNGULLY...THE LAST RAINFOREST (AF)   20th Century Fox,
   1992 (voice)
THE THING CALLED LOVE   Paramount, 1993
LITTLE WOMEN   Columbia, 1994
HOW TO MAKE AN AMERICAN QUILT   Universal, 1995

JAQUES MATHOU
BETTY BLUE   Alive Films, 1986, French

KYALO MATIVO
BABY—SECRET OF THE LOST LEGEND   Buena Vista, 1985

MARLEE MATLIN
b. August 24, 1964 - Morton Grvce, Illinois
Agent: ICM - Beverly Hills, 310/550-4000

CHILDREN OF A LESSER GOD ★★   Paramount, 1986
BRIDGE TO SILENCE (TF)   Fries Entertainment/Briggle,
   Hennessy, Carrothers & Associates, 1989
THE PLAYER   Fine Line Features/New Line Cinema, 1992

WALTER MATTHAU
(Walter Matuschanskavasky)
b. October 1, 1920 - New York, New York
Agent: William Morris Agency - Beverly Hills, 310/274-7451

THE KENTUCKIAN   1955
THE INDIAN FIGHTER   United Artists, 1955
BIGGER THAN LIFE   20th Century-Fox, 1956

A FACE IN THE CROWD   Warner Bros., 1957
SLAUGHTER ON TENTH AVENUE   Universal, 1957
KING CREOLE   Paramount, 1958
THE VOICE IN THE MIRROR   1958
ONIONHEAD   Warner Bros., 1958
RIDE A CROOKED TRAIL   1958
GANGSTER STORY   RCIP-States Rights, 1960 (also directed)
STRANGERS WHEN WE MEET   Columbia, 1960
LONELY ARE THE BRAVE   Universal, 1962
WHO'S GOT THE ACTION?   Paramount, 1962
ISLAND OF LOVE   Warner Bros., 1963
CHARADE   Universal, 1963
ENSIGN PULVER   Warner Bros., 1964
FAIL-SAFE   Columbia, 1964
GOODBYE CHARLIE   20th Century-Fox, 1964
MIRAGE   Universal, 1965
THE FORTUNE COOKIE ○○   United Artists, 1966
A GUIDE FOR THE MARRIED MAN   20th Century-Fox, 1967
THE ODD COUPLE   Paramount, 1968
THE SECRET LIFE OF AN AMERICAN WIFE
   20th Century-Fox, 1968
CANDY   1968, U.S.-Italian-French
HELLO, DOLLY!   20th Century-Fox, 1969
CACTUS FLOWER   Columbia, 1969
A NEW LEAF   Paramount, 1971
PLAZA SUITE   Paramount, 1971
KOTCH ★   Cinerama, 1971
PETE N' TILLIE   Universal, 1972
CHARLIE VARRICK   Universal, 1973
THE LAUGHING POLICEMAN   20th Century-Fox, 1974
THE TAKING OF PELHAM 1-2-3   United Artists, 1974
THE FRONT PAGE   Universal, 1974
EARTHQUAKE   Universal, 1974
THE SUNSHINE BOYS ★   MGM, 1975
THE BAD NEWS BEARS   Paramount, 1976
CASEY'S SHADOW   Columbia, 1978
CALIFORNIA SUITE   Columbia, 1978
HOUSE CALLS   Universal, 1978
LITTLE MISS MARKER   Universal, 1980
HOPSCOTCH   Avco Embassy, 1980
FIRST MONDAY IN OCTOBER   Paramount, 1981
BUDDY BUDDY   MGM/United Artists, 1981
I OUGHT TO BE IN PICTURES   20th Century-Fox, 1982
THE SURVIVORS   Columbia, 1983
MOVERS & SHAKERS   MGM/UA, 1985
PIRATES   Cannon, 1986, French-Tunisian
THE COUCH TRIP   Orion, 1988
THE INCIDENT (TF)   Qintex Entertainment, 1990
JFK   Warner Bros., 1991
AGAINST HER WILL: AN INCIDENT IN BALTIMORE (TF)
   RHI Entertainment, 1992
DENNIS THE MENACE   Warner Bros., 1993
GRUMPY OLD MEN   Warner Bros., 1993
INCIDENT IN A SMALL TOWN (TF)   RHI Entertainment, 1994
I.Q.   Paramount, 1994
THE GRASS HARP   New Line Cinema, 1995

AL MATTHEWS
ROUGH CUT   Paramount, 1980

DAKIN MATTHEWS
Agent: Henderson/Hogan Agency - Beverly Hills, 310/274-7815

CLEAN AND SOBER   Warner Bros., 1988
MY BROTHER'S WIFE (TF)   Robert Greenwald Productions/Adam
   Productions, 1989

LIESEL MATTHEWS
A LITTLE PRINCESS   Warner Bros., 1994

JERRY MATZ
THE GIG   Castle Hill Productions, 1985

MONICA MAUGHAN
CACTUS   Spectrafilm, 1986, Australian

CARMEN MAURA
Agent: William Morris Agency - Beverly Hills, 310/274-7451

WHAT HAVE I DONE TO DESERVE THIS? Cinevista,
1985, Spanish

LOIS MAXWELL
(Lois Hooker)
b. 1927 - Canada

THAT HAGEN GIRL   1947
CORRIDOR OF MIRRORS   Universal, 1948, British
THE DECISION OF CHRISTOPHER BLAKE   1948
WOMEN OF TWILIGHT   1949
THE DARK PAST   Columbia, 1948
THE CRIME DOCTOR'S DIARY   1949
KAZAN   1949
BRIEF RAPTURE *AMORI E VELENI*   1950, Italian
TOMORROW IS TOO LATE *DOMANI E TROPPO TARDI*
   1950, Italian
THE WOMAN'S ANGLE   1952, British
AIDA   1953, Italian
PASSPORT TO TREASON   1955, British
THE HIGH TERRACE   1956, British
SATELLITE IN THE SKY   1956, British
TIME WITHOUT PITY   Astor, 1956, British
KILL ME TOMORROW   Tudor Pictures, 1957, British
THE UNSTOPPABLE MAN   1960, British
LOLITA   MGM, 1962, British
DR. NO   United Artists, 1962, British
COME FLY WITH ME   MGM, 1963
THE HAUNTING   MGM, 1963, British-U.S.
FROM RUSSIA WITH LOVE   United Artists, 1963, British
GOLDFINGER   United Artists, 1964, British
THUNDERBALL   United Artists, 1965, British
OPERATION KID BROTHER *OK CONNERY*   1967, Italian
YOU ONLY LIVE TWICE   United Artists, 1967, British
ON HER MAJESTY'S SECRET SERVICE   United Artists,
   1969, British
THE ADVENTURERS   Paramount, 1970
DIAMONDS ARE FOREVER   United Artists, 1971, British
LIVE AND LET DIE   United Artists, 1973, British
THE MAN WITH THE GOLDEN GUN   United Artists, 1974, British
THE SPY WHO LOVED ME   United Artists, 1977, British-U.S.
MOONRAKER   United Artists, 1979, British-French
OCTOPUSSY   MGM/UA, 1983, British

ELAINE MAY
(Elaine Berlin)
b. April 21, 1932 - Philadelphia, Pennsylvania
Agent: CAA - Beverly Hills, 310/288-4545

LUV   Columbia, 1967
ENTER LAUGHING   Columbia, 1967
A NEW LEAF   Paramount, 1971
CALIFORNIA SUITE   Columbia, 1978
IN THE SPIRIT   Castle Hill Productions, 1990

JODHI MAY
Agent: William Morris Agency - Beverly Hills, 310/274-7451

A WORLD APART   Atlantic Releasing Corporation, 1988, British
EMINENT DOMAIN   Triumph Releasing Corporation, 1990,
   Canadian-French-Israeli
THE LAST OF THE MOHICANS   20th Century Fox, 1992

RIK MAYALL
DROP DEAD FRED   New Line Cinema, 1991
THE PRINCESS AND THE GOBLIN (AF)   Hemdale, 1994 (voice)

CHRISTOPHER MAYER
GLITTER (TF)   Aaron Spelling Productions, 1984

PETER MAYHEW
SINBAD AND THE EYE OF THE TIGER   Columbia, 1977, British
STAR WARS   20th Century-Fox, 1977
THE EMPIRE STRIKES BACK   20th Century-Fox, 1980
RETURN OF THE JEDI   20th Century-Fox, 1983

MIMI MAYNARD
FALSE IDENTITY   RKO Pictures, 1990

GALE MAYRON
HEART OF MIDNIGHT   Virgin Vision, 1989
THE GUN IN BETTY LOU'S HANDBAG   Buena Vista, 1992

MELANIE MAYRON
HARRY AND TONTO   20th Century-Fox, 1974
GABLE AND LOMBARD   Universal, 1976
CAR WASH   Universal, 1976
GIRLFRIENDS   Warner Bros., 1978
HEARTBEEPS   Universal, 1981
MISSING   Universal, 1982
WALLENBERG: A HERO'S STORY (MS)   Dick Berg-Stonehenge
   Productions/Paramount TV, 1985
STICKY FINGERS   Spectrafilm, 1988
CHECKING OUT   Warner Bros., 1989
MY BLUE HEAVEN   Warner Bros., 1990
DROP ZONE   Paramount, 1994

DEBI MAZAR
MONEY FOR NOTHING   Buena Vista, 1993
BEETHOVEN'S 2ND   Universal, 1993
BULLETS OVER BROADWAY   Miramax Films, 1994

PAUL MAZURSKY
b. April 25, 1930 - Brooklyn, New York
Agent: ICM - Beverly Hills, 310/550-4000

FEAR AND DESIRE   Joseph Burstyn, Inc., 1953
THE BLACKBOARD JUNGLE   MGM, 1955
DEATHWATCH   1966
ALEX IN WONDERLAND   MGM, 1970 (also directed)
BLUME IN LOVE   Warner Bros., 1973 (also directed)
A STAR IS BORN   Warner Bros., 1976
AN UNMARRIED WOMAN   20th Century-Fox, 1978 (also directed)
A MAN, A WOMAN AND A BANK   Avco Embassy, 1979, Canadian
HISTORY OF THE WORLD—PART 1   20th Century Fox, 1981
TEMPEST   Columbia, 1982 (also directed)
MOSCOW ON THE HUDSON   Columbia, 1984 (also directed)
INTO THE NIGHT   Universal, 1985
DOWN AND OUT IN BEVERLY HILLS   Buena Vista,
   1986 (also directed)
MOON OVER PARADOR   Universal, 1988,
   U.S.-Brazilian (also directed)
PUNCHLINE   Columbia, 1988
SCENES FROM THE CLASS STRUGGLE IN BEVERLY HILLS
   Cinecom, 1989
ENEMIES, A LOVE STORY   20th Century Fox, 1989 (also directed)
SCENES FROM A MALL   Buena Vista, 1991 (also directed)
MAN TROUBLE   20th Century Fox, 1992
THE PICKLE   Columbia, 1993 (also directed)
CARLITO'S WAY   Universal, 1993
FAITHFUL   Savoy Pictures, 1995 (also directed)

JOSEPH MAZZELLO
RADIO FLYER   Columbia, 1992
JURASSIC PARK   Universal, 1993
SHADOWLANDS   Savoy Pictures, 1993, U.S.-British
THE RIVER WILD   Universal, 1994
THE CURE   Universal, 1995
THREE WISHES   Savoy Pictures, 1995

SCOTT McAFEE
LAND BEFORE TIME (AF)   Universal, 1995 (voice)

DES McALEER
HIDDEN AGENDA   Hemdale, 1990

ALEX McARTHUR
Agent: ICM - Beverly Hills, 310/550-4000

RACE FOR GLORY   New Century/Vista, 1989

TOM McBEATH
THE ACCUSED   Paramount, 1988

RUTH McCABE
MY LEFT FOOT   Miramax Films, 1989, Irish-British
THE SNAPPER   Miramax Films, 1993, British

FRANCES LEE McCAIN
THE LAUGHING POLICEMAN   20th Century-Fox, 1973
REAL LIFE   Paramount, 1979
HONKY TONK FREEWAY   Universal/AFD, 1981
TEX   Buena Vista, 1982
FOOTLOOSE   Paramount, 1984
GREMLINS   Warner Bros., 1984
FIRST STEPS (TF)   CBS Entertainment, 1985
THE RAPE OF RICHARD BECK (TF)   Robert Papazian Productions/
   Henerson-Hirsch Productions, 1985
BACK TO THE FUTURE   Universal, 1985

DAVID McCALLUM
b. September 19, 1933 - Glasgow, Scotland

THE SECRET PLACE   Rank, 1957, British
HELL DRIVERS   Rank, 1957, British
ROBBERY UNDER ARMS   ITC Productions, 1957, Australian
VIOLENT PLAYGROUND   Lopert, 1957, British
A NIGHT TO REMEMBER   Rank, 1958, British
JUNGLE FIGHTERS   THE LONG AND THE SHORT AND THE TALL
   1961, British
JUNGLE STREET GIRLS   JUNGLE STREET   1961, British
BILLY BUDD   Allied Artists, 1962, British
FREUD   Universal, 1962
THE GREAT ESCAPE   United Artists, 1963
THE GREATEST STORY EVER TOLD   United Artists, 1965
THE SPY WITH MY FACE   MGM, 1966
AROUND THE WORLD UNDER THE SEA   MGM, 1966
THREE BITES OF THE APPLE   1967
SOL MADRID   MGM, 1968
MOSQUITO SQUADRON   United Artists, 1970, British
FRANKENSTEIN: THE TRUE STORY (TF)   Universal TV, 1973
DIAMOND HUNTERS   1975
THE KINGFISH CAPER   1976, South African
DOGS   R.C. Riddell, 1977
KING SOLOMON'S TREASURE   Filmco Limited, 1978, Canadian
THE WATCHER IN THE WOODS   Buena Vista, 1980
THE RETURN OF THE MAN FROM UNCLE (TF)   Michael Sloan
   Productions/Viacom Productions, 1983
FREEDOM FIGHTER (TF)   HTV/Columbia TV/Embassy TV, 1988,
   U.S.-British

MERCEDES McCAMBRIDGE
(Carlotta Mercedes Agnes McCambridge)
b. March 17, 1918 - Joliet, Illinois

ALL THE KING'S MEN ⊙⊙   Columbia, 1949
INSIDE STRAIGHT   1951
LIGHTNING STRIKES TWICE   Warner Bros., 1951
THE SCARF   United Artists, 1951
JOHNNY GUITAR   Republic, 1954
GIANT ⊙   Warner Bros., 1956
A FAREWELL TO ARMS   20th Century-Fox, 1957
TOUCH OF EVIL   Universal, 1958
SUDDENLY LAST SUMMER   Columbia, 1959
CIMARRON   MGM, 1960
ANGEL BABY   Allied Artists, 1961
RUN HOME SLOW   1965
THE COUNTERFEIT KILLER   1968
99 WOMEN   1969
THE HOT DEATH   1969, West German
KILLER BY NIGHT (TF)   Cinema Center, 1972
TWO FOR THE MONEY (TF)   Aaron Spelling Productions, 1972

THE GIRLS OF HUNTINGTON HOUSE (TF)
   Lorimar Productions, 1973
THE PRESIDENT'S PLANE IS MISSING (TF)   1973
THE EXORCIST   Warner Bros., 1973 (voice; uncredited)
LIKE A CROW ON A JUNE BUG   SIXTEEN   1974
WHO IS THE BLACK DAHLIA? (TF)   Douglas S. Cramer
   Productions, 1975
THIEVES   Paramount, 1977
THE SACKETTS (TF)   Douglas Netter Enterprises/M.B. Scott
   Productions/Shalako Enterprises, 1979
THE CONCORDE—AIRPORT '79   Universal, 1979

TOM McCAMUS
A MAN IN UNIFORM   I.R.S. Releasing, 1994

CHUCK McCANN
DUCK TALES THE MOVIE: THE SECRET OF THE LOST LAMP (AF)
   Buena Vista, 1990 (voice)

DONAL McCANN
THE DEAD   Vestron, 1987

ANDREW McCARTHY
b. 1963 - New York, New York
Agent: ICM - Beverly Hills, 310/550-4000

CLASS   Orion, 1983
ST. ELMO'S FIRE   Columbia, 1985
PRETTY IN PINK   Paramount, 1986
WAITING FOR THE MOON   Skouras Pictures, 1987,
   U.S.-French-British-West German
KANSAS   Trans World Entertainment, 1988
FRESH HORSES   WEG, 1988
HOT AND COLD   20th Century Fox, 1989
WEEKEND AT BERNIE'S   20th Century Fox, 1989
YEAR OF THE GUN   Columbia, 1991
WEEKEND AT BERNIE'S II   TriStar, 1993
MRS. PARKER AND THE VICIOUS CIRCLE   Fine Line Features/
   New Line Cinema, 1994

KEVIN McCARTHY
b. February 15, 1914 - Seattle, Washington

DEATH OF A SALESMAN ⊙   Columbia, 1951
DRIVE A CROOKED ROAD   Columbia, 1954
AN ANNAPOLIS STORY   Allied Artists, 1955
STRANGER ON HORSEBACK   United Artists, 1955
NIGHTMARE   1956
INVASION OF THE BODY SNATCHERS   Allied Artists, 1956
THE MISFITS   United Artists, 1961
A GATHERING OF EAGLES   Universal, 1963
AN AFFAIR OF THE SKIN   1963
THE PRIZE   MGM, 1963
THE BEST MAN   United Artists, 1964
MIRAGE   Universal, 1965
A BIG HAND FOR THE LITTLE LADY   Warner Bros., 1966
HOTEL   Warner Bros., 1967
IF HE HOLLERS LET HIM GO   1968
TO HELL WITH HEROES   Universal, 1968
REVENGE IN EL PASO   1969
ACE HIGH   1969
KANSAS CITY BOMBER   MGM, 1972
ALIEN THUNDER   1974, Canadian
ORDER TO KILL   EL CLAN DES LOS IMMORALES   1974, Spanish
BUFFALO BILL AND THE INDIANS or SITTING BULL'S
   HISTORY LESSON   United Artists, 1976
THE THREE SISTERS   1977
PIRHANHA   New World, 1978
INVASION OF THE BODY SNATCHERS   United Artists, 1978
CAPTAIN AVENGER   1979
THOSE LIPS, THOSE EYES   United Artists, 1980
THE HOWLING   Avco Embassy, 1981
MY TUTOR   Crown International, 1983
TWILIGHT ZONE—THE MOVIE   Warner Bros., 1983
THE MIDNIGHT HOUR (TF)   ABC Circle Films, 1985
INNERSPACE   Warner Bros., 1987

F
I
L
M

A
C
T
O
R
S

POOR LITTLE RICH GIRL: THE BARBARA HUTTON STORY (MS)
    Lester Persky Productions/ITC Productions, 1987
IN THE HEAT OF THE NIGHT (TF)   The Fred Silverman Company/
    Jadda Productions/MGM-UA TV, 1988
UHF   Orion, 1989
EVE OF DESTRUCTION   Orion, 1991

NOBU McCARTHY
THE KARATE KID PART II   Columbia, 1986
THE WASH   Skouras Pictures, 1988

SHEILA McCARTHY
PARADISE   Buena Vista, 1991
STEPPING OUT   Paramount, 1991
MENENDEZ: A KILLING IN BEVERLY HILLS (MS)   Zev Braun
    Pictures/TriStar Television, 1994

PAUL McCARTNEY
b. June 18, 1942 - Liverpool, England

WHAT'S HAPPENING: THE BEATLES IN THE USA (FD)   1964
A HARD DAY'S NIGHT   United Artists, 1964, British
HELP!   United Artists, 1965, British
YELLOW SUBMARINE (AF)   1968, British (voice)
LET IT BE (FD)   United Artists, 1970, British

CHARLES McCAUGHIN
WAXWORK   Vestron, 1988
V.I. WARSHAWSKI   Buena Vista, 1991

RUE McCLANAHAN
b. February 21, 1936 - Healdton, Oklahoma
Agent: APA - Los Angeles, 310/273-0744

THEY MIGHT BE GIANTS   Universal, 1971
THE LITTLE MATCH GIRL (TF)   NBC Productions, 1987
LIBERACE (TF)   The Liberace Foundation/Dick Clark Productions/
    Republic Pictures, 1988
TAKE MY DAUGHTERS, PLEASE (TF)   NBC Productions, 1988
AGATHA CHRISTIE'S 'THE MAN IN THE BROWN SUIT' (TF)
    Alan Shayne Productions/Warner Bros. TV, 1989
MODERN LOVE   Triumph Releasing Corporation, 1990

KATHLEEN McCLELLAN
MORTAL KOMBAT   New Line Cinema, 1995

SEAN McCLORY
BEYOND GLORY   Paramount, 1948
DESERT FOX   20th Century-Fox, 1951
LES MISÉRABLES   20th Century-Fox, 1952
RING OF FEAR   1954
MOONFLEET   MGM, 1955
DIANE   MGM, 1957
BANDOLERO   20th Century-Fox, 1968
THE DEAD   Vestron, 1987

LEIGH McCLOSKEY
DOUBLE REVENGE   Smart Egg Releasing, 1989

KELY McCLUNG
STICKFIGHTER   Warner Bros., 1994

DOUG McCLURE
b. May 11, 1935 - Glendale, California

THE ENEMY BELOW   20th Century-Fox, 1957
GIDGET   Columbia, 1959
BECAUSE THEY'RE YOUNG   Columbia, 1960
THE UNFORGIVEN   United Artists, 1960
THE LIVELY SET   Universal, 1964
SHENANDOAH   Universal, 1965
BEAU GESTE   Universal, 1966
THE KING'S PIRATE   Universal, 1967
NOBODY'S PERFECT   Universal, 1968
BACKTRACK   Universal, 1969

THE JUDGE AND JAKE WYLER (TF)   Universal TV, 1972
PLAYMATES (TF)   ABC Circle Films, 1972
THE LAND THAT TIME FORGOT   American International,
    1975, British
WHAT CHANGED CHARLEY FARTHING?   Stirling Gold,
    1975, British
AT THE EARTH'S CORE   American International, 1976, British
THE PEOPLE THAT TIME FORGOT   American International,
    1977, British
WARLORDS OF ATLANTIS   Columbia, 1978, British
REBELS (MS)   Universal TV, 1979
HUMANOIDS FROM THE DEEP   New World, 1980
THE HOUSE WHERE EVIL DWELLS   MGM/UA, 1982, U.S.-Japan
CANNONBALL RUN II   Warner Bros., 1984
COVER UP (TF)   Glen Larson Productions/
    20th Century-Fox TV, 1984
52 PICK-UP   Cannon, 1986
MAVERICK   Warner Bros., 1994

MARC McCLURE
SUPERMAN II   Warner Bros., 1981, U.S.-British
SUPERMAN III   Warner Bros., 1983, U.S.-British
SUPERGIRL   Warner Bros., 1984, British
BACK TO THE FUTURE   Universal, 1985

MOLLY McCLURE
DADDY'S DYIN'...WHO'S GOT THE WILL?   MGM/UA, 1990

EDIE McCLURG
b. July 23, 1957 - Kansas City, Missouri

FERRIS BUELLER'S DAY OFF   Paramount, 1986
PLANES, TRAINS AND AUTOMOBILES   Paramount, 1987
THE LITTLE MERMAID (AF)   Buena Vista, 1989 (voice)
CURLY SUE   Warner Bros., 1991
A RIVER RUNS THROUGH IT   Columbia, 1992
NATURAL BORN KILLERS   Warner Bros., 1994

KEN McCLUSKEY
THE COMMITMENTS   20th Century Fox, 1991

HEATHER McCOMB
NEW YORK STORIES   Buena Vista, 1989

MATTHEW McCONAUGHEY
Agent: William Morris Agency - Beverly Hills, 310/274-7451

BOYS ON THE SIDE   Warner Bros., 1995

KENT McCORD
AIRPLANE II: THE SEQUEL   Paramount, 1982
PREDATOR 2   20th Century Fox, 1990

CATHERINE McCORMACK
BRAVE HEART   Paramount, 1995

CAROLYN McCORMICK
b. September 19, 1959

CRIES UNHEARD: THE DONNA YAKLICH STORY (TF)
    Carla Singer Productions, 1994

MAUREEN McCORMICK
THE BRADY GIRLS GET MARRIED (TF)   Sherwood Schwartz
    Productions, 1981
A VERY BRADY CHRISTMAS (TF)   Sherwood Schwartz
    Productions/Paramount TV, 1988
THE BRADY BUNCH MOVIE   Paramount, 1995

PAT McCORMICK
SMOKEY AND THE BANDIT   Universal, 1977
SMOKEY AND THE BANDIT II   Universal, 1980
SMOKEY AND THE BANDIT 3   Universal, 1983
SCROOGED   Paramount, 1988

ALEC McCOWEN
TIME WITHOUT PITY   Astor, 1956, British
TOWN ON TRIAL   Columbia, 1956, British
THE LONELINESS OF THE LONG DISTANCE RUNNER
    Continental, 1962, British
IN THE COOL OF THE DAY   1963
THE AGONY AND THE ECSTASY   20th Century-Fox, 1965
THE WITCHES   Lopert, 1967, Italian-French
THE HAWAIIANS   United Artists, 1970
FRENZY   Universal, 1972
TRAVELS WITH MY AUNT   MGM, 1972, British
STEVIE   First Artists, 1978, British
HANOVER STREET   Columbia, 1979
NEVER SAY NEVER AGAIN   Warner Bros., 1983
THE ASSAM GARDEN   The Moving Picture Company, 1985, British
PERSONAL SERVICES   Vestron, 1987, British
CRY FREEDOM   Universal, 1987, British-U.S.
HENRY V   Samuel Goldwyn Company, 1989, British
THE AGE OF INNOCENCE   Columbia, 1993

MATT McCOY
Agent: Metropolitan Talent Agency - Los Angeles, 213/857-4500

POLICE ACADEMY 5: ASSIGNMENT MIAMI BEACH
    Warner Bros., 1988
DEEPSTAR SIX   TriStar, 1989
POLICE ACADEMY 6: CITY UNDER SIEGE   Warner Bros., 1989
THE HAND THAT ROCKS THE CRADLE   Buena Vista, 1992

PAUL McCRANE
FAME   MGM/United Artists, 1980
ROBOCOP   Orion, 1987
THE PORTRAIT (CTF)   Robert Greenwald Productions/Atticus
    Corporation/Turner Network TV, 1993

KIMBERLY McCULLOUGH
CONSENTING ADULTS   Buena Vista, 1992

MATTHEW McCURLEY
Agent: William Morris Agency - Beverly Hills, 310/274-7451

NORTH   Columbia, 1994
LITTLE GIANTS   Warner Bros., 1994

BILL McCUTCHEON
FAMILY BUSINESS   TriStar, 1989
STEEL MAGNOLIAS   TriStar, 1989
MR. DESTINY   Buena Vista, 1990

DYLAN McDERMOTT
Agent: CAA - Beverly Hills, 310/288-4545

HAMBURGER HILL   Paramount, 1987
TWISTER   Vestron, 1988
STEEL MAGNOLIAS   TriStar, 1989
IN THE LINE OF FIRE   Columbia, 1993
THE COWBOY WAY   Universal, 1994
MIRACLE ON 34TH STREET   20th Century Fox, 1994
DESTINY TURNS ON THE RADIO   Savoy Pictures, 1995

SHANE McDERMOTT
AIRBORNE   Warner Bros., 1993

CHRISTOPHER McDONALD
Agent: William Morris Agency - Beverly Hills, 310/274-7451

THE HEARSE   Crown International, 1980
GREASE 2   Paramount, 1982
WHERE THE BOYS ARE '84   TriStar, 1984
CHATANOOGA CHOO CHOO   April Fools, 1984
BREAKIN'   Cannon, 1984
THE BOYS NEXT DOOR   New World, 1985
OUTRAGEOUS FORTUNE   Buena Vista, 1987
LITTLE GIRL LOST (TF)   Marian Rees Associates, 1988
PARAMEDICS   Vestron, 1988

CHANCES ARE   TriStar, 1989
THE PLAY ROOM   Republic, 1989, Canadian
THELMA & LOUISE   MGM-Pathe, 1991
DUTCH   20th Century-Fox, 1991
BENEFIT OF THE DOUBT   Miramax Films, 1993
GRUMPY OLD MEN   Warner Bros., 1993
MONKEY TROUBLE   New Line Cinema, 1994
QUIZ SHOW   Buena Vista, 1994
TERMINAL VELOCITY   Buena Vista, 1994

KEVIN McDONALD
NATIONAL LAMPOON'S SENIOR TRIP   New Line Cinema, 1995

MIKE McDONALD
DANCE WITH DEATH   Concorde, 1991

NORM McDONALD
BILLY MADISON   Universal, 1995

MARY McDONNELL
Agent: William Morris Agency - Beverly Hills, 310/274-7451

MATEWAN   Cinecom, 1987
DANCES WITH WOLVES ✪   Orion, 1990
GRAND CANYON   20th Century Fox, 1991
SNEAKERS   Universal, 1992
PASSION FISH ★   Miramax Films, 1992
BLUE CHIPS   Paramount, 1994

FRANCES McDORMAND
Agent: William Morris Agency - Beverly Hills, 310/274-7451

BLOOD SIMPLE   Circle Releasing Corporation, 1984
RAISING ARIZONA   20th Century Fox, 1987
MISSISSIPPI BURNING ✪   Orion, 1988
CHATTAHOOCHEE   Hemdale, 1990
DARKMAN   Universal, 1990
HIDDEN AGENDA   Hemdale, 1990
THE BUTCHER'S WIFE   Paramount, 1991
PASSED AWAY   Buena Vista, 1992
SHORT CUTS   Fine Line Features/New Line Cinema, 1993

RODDY McDOWALL
(Roderick Andrew Anthony Jude McDowall)
b. September 17, 1928 - London, England
Agent: Harris & Goldberg Agency - Los Angeles, 310/553-5200

SCRUFFY   1938, British
MURDER IN THE FAMILY   1938, British
HEY! HEY! USA   1938, British
POISON PEN   1939, British
THE OUTSIDER   1939, British
DEAD MAN'S SHOES   1939, British
JUST WILLIAM   1939, British
SALOON BAR   1940, British
THIS ENGLAND   1941, British
MAN HUNT   20th Century-Fox, 1941
HOW GREEN WAS MY VALLEY   20th Century-Fox, 1941
CONFIRM OR DENY   20th Century-Fox, 1941
SON OF FURY   20th Century-Fox, 1942
THE PIED PIPER   20th Century-Fox, 1942
ON THE SUNNY SIDE   1942
MY FRIEND FLICKA   1943
LASSIE COME HOME   MGM, 1943
THE WHITE CLIFFS OF DOVER   MGM, 1944
THE KEYS OF THE KINGDOM   20th Century-Fox, 1944
THUNDERHEAD—HEAD OF FLICKA   1945
MOLLY AND ME   20th Century-Fox, 1945
HOLIDAY IN MEXICO   MGM, 1946
ROCKY   Monogram, 1948
MACBETH   Republic, 1948
KIDNAPPED   Monogram, 1948
TUNA CLIPPER   Monogram, 1949
BLACK MIDNIGHT   Monogram, 1949
KILLER SHARK   Monogram, 1950
THE STEEL FIST   1952

THE SUBTERRANEANS   1960
MIDNIGHT LACE   Universal, 1961
THE LONGEST DAY   20th Century-Fox, 1962
CLEOPATRA   20th Century-Fox, 1963
SHOCK TREATMENT   1964
THE GREATEST STORY EVER TOLD   United Artists, 1965
THE LOVED ONE   MGM, 1965
THAT DARN CAT   Buena Vista, 1965
INSIDE DAISY CLOVER   Warner Bros., 1965
LORD LOVE A DUCK   United Artists, 1966
THE DEFECTOR   *L'ESPION*   1966, French-West German
THE ADVENTURES OF BULLWHIP GRIFFIN   Buena Vista, 1967
THE COOL ONES   Warner Bros., 1967
IT!   1967, British
PLANET OF THE APES   20th Century-Fox, 1968
FIVE CARD STUD   Paramount, 1968
HELLO DOWN THERE   Paramount, 1969
MIDAS RUN   Cinerama Releasing Corporation, 1969
CULT OF THE DAMNED   *ANGEL ANGEL DOWN WE GO*   1969
PRETTY MAIDS ALL IN A ROW   MGM, 1971
ESCAPE FROM THE PLANET OF THE APES
    20th Century-Fox, 1971
BEDKNOBS AND BROOMSTICKS   Buena Vista, 1971
CONQUEST OF THE PLANET OF THE APES
    20th Century-Fox, 1972
THE POSEIDON ADVENTURE   20th Century-Fox, 1972
THE LIFE AND TIMES OF JUDGE ROY BEAN
    National General, 1972
BATTLE FOR THE PLANET OF THE APES   20th Century-Fox, 1973
THE LEGEND OF HELL HOUSE   20th Century-Fox, 1973, British
ARNOLD   Cinerama Releasing Corporation, 1973
MIRACLE ON 34TH STREET (TF)   20th Century-Fox TV, 1973
THE ELEVATOR (TF)   Universal TV, 1974
DIRTY MARY, CRAZY LARRY   20th Century-Fox, 1974
FUNNY LADY   Columbia, 1975
MEAN JOHNNY BARROWS   Atlas, 1976
EMBRYO   Cine Artists, 1976
SIXTH AND MAIN   National General, 1977
LASERBLAST   Irwin Yablans, 1978
RABBIT TEST   Avco Embassy, 1978
THE CAT FROM OUTER SPACE   Buena Vista, 1978
CIRCLE OF IRON   Avco Embassy, 1979
SCAVENGER HUNT   20th Century-Fox, 1979
EVIL UNDER THE SUN   Universal/AFD, 1982, British
CLASS OF 1984   United Film Distribution, 1982, Canadian
LONDON AND DAVIS IN NEW YORK (TF)   Bloodworth-Thomason
    Mozark Productions/Columbia TV, 1984
FRIGHT NIGHT   Columbia, 1985
GOBOTS: BATTLE OF THE ROCK LORDS (AF)   Clubhouse/
    Atlantic Releasing Corporation, 1986 (voice)
DEAD OF WINTER   MGM/UA, 1987
FRIGHT NIGHT PART 2   New Century/Vista, 1989
OF UNKNOWN ORIGIN   Concorde, 1994

MALCOLM McDOWELL
b. June 15, 1943 - Leeds, England

POOR COW   National General, 1967, British
IF...   Paramount, 1967, British
FIGURES IN A LANDSCAPE   National General, 1970, British
LONG AGO TOMORROW   *THE RAGING MOON*   Cinema 5,
    1971, British
A CLOCKWORK ORANGE   Warner Bros., 1971, British
O LUCKY MAN!   Warner Bros., 1973, British
ROYAL FLASH   20th Century-Fox, 1975, British
VOYAGE OF THE DAMNED   Avco Embassy, 1976, British
ACES HIGH   Cinema Shares International, 1977, British
CALIGULA   Analysis Film Releasing, 1977, Italian-U.S.
THE PASSAGE   United Artists, 1979, British
TIME AFTER TIME   Orion/Warner Bros., 1979
CAT PEOPLE   Universal, 1982
BRITANNIA HOSPITAL   United Artists Classics, 1982, British
BLUE THUNDER   Columbia, 1983
CROSS CREEK   Universal/AFD, 1983
GET CRAZY   Embassy, 1983
ARTHUR THE KING (TF)   Martin Poll Productions/Comworld
    Productions/Jadran Film, 1985, U.S.-Yugoslavian
MONTE CARLO (MS)   New World TV/Phoenix Entertainment Group/
    Collins-Holm Productions/Highgate Pictures, 1986

BUY & CELL   Empire Pictures, 1989
CLASS OF 1999   Vestron, 1989
BOPHA!   Paramount, 1993
MILK MONEY   Paramount, 1994
STAR TREK GENERATIONS   Paramount, 1994
TANK GIRL   MGM/UA, 1995

JAMES McEACHIN
PLAY MISTY FOR ME   Universal, 1971
FUZZ   United Artists, 1972
THE ALPHA CAPER (TF)   Universal TV, 1973
EVERY WHICH WAY BUT LOOSE   Warner Bros., 1978
2010   MGM/UA, 1984

JOHN McENERY
b. Birmingham, England

ROMEO AND JULIET   Paramount, 1968, Italian-British
NICHOLAS AND ALEXANDRA   Columbia, 1971, British
BARTLEBY   1972, British
GALILEO   American Film Theatre, 1973, British-Canadian
THE DUELLISTS   Paramount, 1978, British
JAMAICA INN (TF)   HTV/Metromedia Producers Corporation/United
    Media, Ltd./Jamaica Inn Productions, 1985, British-U.S.
GULAG (CTF)   Lorimar Productions/HBO Premiere Films, 1985
TUSITALA (MS)   Australian Broadcasting Corporation/Portman
    Productions/Channel Four, 1986, Australian-British
CODENAME: KYRIL (TF)   HTV/Incito Productions, 1988, British
LITTLE DORRIT, PART I: NOBODY'S FAULT   Cannon,
    1988, British
LITTLE DORRIT, PART II: LITTLE DORRIT'S STORY   Cannon,
    1988, British
HAMLET   Warner Bros., 1990, British
BLACK BEAUTY   Warner Bros., 1994, British-U.S.

REBA McENTIRE
b. March 28, 1954 - McAlester, Oklahoma
Agent: William Morris Agency - Beverly Hills, 310/274-7451

NORTH   Columbia, 1994

GERALDINE McEWAN
HENRY V   Samuel Goldwyn Company, 1989, British
ROBIN HOOD: PRINCE OF THIEVES   Warner Bros., 1991

GATES McFADDEN
STAR TREK GENERATIONS   Paramount, 1994

STEPHANIE McFADDEN
LOVE FIELD   Orion, 1992

PAUL McGANN
DEALERS   Skouras Pictures, 1989
AFRAID OF THE DARK   New Line Cinema, 1991
ALIEN 3   20th Century Fox, 1992, U.S.-British

DARREN McGAVIN
b. May 7, 1922 - Spokane, Washington

FEAR   1945
QUEEN FOR A DAY   United Artists, 1951
SUMMER MADNESS   *SUMMERTIME*   United Artists, 1955, British
THE MAN WITH THE GOLDEN ARM   United Artists, 1955
THE COURT-MARTIAL OF BILLY MITCHELL   Warner Bros., 1955
BEAU JAMES   Paramount, 1957
THE DELICATE DELINQUENT   Paramount, 1957
THE CASE AGAINST BROOKLYN   Columbia, 1958
BULLET FOR A BADMAN   Universal, 1964
RIDE THE HIGH WIND   1965, South African
THE GREAT SIOUX MASSACRE   1965
MISSION MARS   Allied Artists, 1968
TRIBES (TF)   20th Century-Fox TV, 1970
MRS. POLLIFAX—SPY   United Artists, 1971
THE NIGHT STALKER (TF)   ABC, Inc., 1972

THE PETTY STORY   1974
THE NIGHT STRANGLER (TF)   ABC Circle Films, 1974
NO DEPOSIT, NO RETURN   Buena Vista, 1976
AIRPORT '77   Universal, 1977
HOT LEAD AND COLD FEET   Buena Vista, 1978
ZERO TO SIXTY   First Artists, 1979, Canadian
IKE (MS)   ABC Circle Films, 1979
THE MARTIAN CHRONICLES   Charles Fries Productions/
   Stonehenge Productions, 1980
HANGAR 18   1980
TURK 182   20th Century Fox, 1985
FROM THE HIP   DEG, 1987
THE DIAMOND TRAP (TF)   Jay Bernstein Productions/
   Columbia TV, 1988
CHILD IN THE NIGHT (TF)   Mike Robe Productions, 1990
BLOOD AND CONCRETE   I.R.S. Releasing, 1991

PATRICK McGAW
MALICIOUS   Republic Pictures, 1995

JACK McGEE
Agent: Camden ITG - Los Angeles, 310/289-2700

BACKDRAFT   Universal, 1991
MIRACLE ON 34TH STREET   20th Century Fox, 1994

BRUCE McGILL
CITIZENS BAND   *HANDLE WITH CARE*   Paramount, 1977
NATIONAL LAMPOON'S ANIMAL HOUSE   Universal, 1978
THE BALLAD OF GREGORIO CORTEZ   Embassy, 1983
SILKWOOD   20th Century-Fox, 1983
TOUGH ENOUGH   20th Century-Fox, 1983
INTO THE NIGHT   Universal, 1985
WILDCATS   Warner Bros., 1986
WAITING FOR THE MOON   Skouras Pictures, 1987,
   U.S.-French-British-West German
END OF THE LINE   Orion Classics, 1988
OUT COLD   TriStar, 1989
TIMECOP   Universal, 1994

EVERETT McGILL
DUNE   Universal, 1984
LICENCE TO KILL   MGM/UA, 1989, British

KELLY McGILLIS
b. July 9, 1957 - Newport Beach, California
Agent: ICM - Beverly Hills, 310/550-4000

REUBEN, REUBEN   20th Century-Fox International Classics, 1983
SWEET REVENGE (TF)   David Greene Productions/Robert
   Papazian Productions, 1984
WITNESS   Paramount, 1985
TOP GUN   Paramount, 1986
MADE IN HEAVEN   Lorimar, 1987
THE HOUSE ON CARROLL STREET   Orion, 1988
THE ACCUSED   Paramount, 1988
WINTER PEOPLE   Columbia, 1989
THE BABE   Universal, 1992
NORTH   Columbia, 1994

JOHN C. McGINLEY
Agent: Harris & Goldberg - Los Angeles, 310/553-5200

PLATOON   Orion, 1986
WALL STREET   20th Century Fox, 1987
TALK RADIO   Universal, 1988
FAT MAN AND LITTLE BOY   Paramount, 1989
HIGHLANDER II - THE QUICKENING   Entertainment Film
   Distributors, 1991, British-U.S.
ARTICLE 99   Orion, 1992
A MIDNIGHT CLEAR   Interstar Releasing, 1992
CAR 54, WHERE ARE YOU?   Orion, 1994
ON DEADLY GROUND   Warner Bros., 1994
SURVIVING THE GAME   New Line Cinema, 1994
WAGONS EAST   TriStar, 1994
KATIE   Warner Bros., 1995

PATRICK McGOOHAN
b. March 19, 1928 - New York, New York

BRAVEHEART   Paramount, 1995

BARRY McGOVERN
JOE VERSUS THE VOLCANO   Warner Bros., 1990

ELIZABETH McGOVERN
b. July 18, 1961 - Evanston, Illinois

ORDINARY PEOPLE   Paramount, 1980
HEAVEN'S GATE   United Artists, 1980
RAGTIME ⊙   Paramount, 1981
LOVESICK   The Ladd Company/Warner Bros., 1983
RACING WITH THE MOON   Paramount, 1984
ONCE UPON A TIME IN AMERICA   The Ladd Company/
   Warner Bros., 1984, U.S.-Italian-Canadian
NATIVE SON   Cinecom, 1986
THE BEDROOM WINDOW   DEG, 1987
SHE'S HAVING A BABY   Paramount, 1988
JOHNNY HANDSOME   TriStar, 1989
THE HANDMAID'S TALE   Cinecom, 1990
A SHOCK TO THE SYSTEM   Corsair Pictures, 1990
KING OF THE HILL   Gramercy Pictures, 1993
THE FAVOR   Orion, 1994
WINGS OF COURAGE   TriStar, 1995

MAUREEN McGOVERN
b. July 27, 1949 - Youngstown, Ohio

THE TOWERING INFERNO   20th Century-Fox/Warner Bros., 1974
AIRPLANE!   Paramount, 1980
THE BREAKFAST CLUB   Universal, 1985

TERENCE McGOVERN
DUCK TALES THE MOVIE: THE SECRET OF THE LOST LAMP (AF)
   Buena Vista, 1990 (voice)

TOM McGOWAN
MRS. PARKER AND THE VICIOUS CIRCLE   Fine Line Features/
   New Line Cinema, 1994
HEAVYWEIGHTS   Buena Vista, 1994

DEREK McGRATH
POLICE ACADEMY 4: CITIZENS ON PATROL   Warner Bros., 1987

BRUCE McGUIRE
FROM BEYOND   Empire Pictures, 1986

STEPHEN McHATTIE
THE PEOPLE NEXT DOOR   Avco Embassy, 1970
VON RICHTHOFEN AND BROWN   United Artists, 1971
SEARCH FOR THE GODS (TF)   Warner Bros. TV, 1975
THE ULTIMATE WARRIOR   Warner Bros., 1975
LOOK WHAT'S HAPPENED TO ROSEMARY'S BABY (TF)
   Paramount TV, 1976
JAMES DEAN (TF)   The Jozak Company, 1976
MOVING VIOLATION   20th Century-Fox, 1976
GRAY LADY DOWN   Universal, 1978
CENTENNIAL (MS)   Universal TV, 1978
ROUGHNECKS (MS)   Douglas Netter Productions/Metromedia
   Producers Corporations, 1980
DEATH VALLEY   Universal, 1982
BELIZAIRE THE CAJUN   Skouras Pictures, 1986
BLOODHOUNDS OF BROADWAY   Columbia, 1989

MARVIN J. McINTYRE
FANDANGO   Warner Bros., 1985

DAVID McKAY
THE GIRL IN THE PICTURE   Samuel Goldwyn Company,
   1986, British

Mc

FILM
ACTORS
GUIDE

F
I
L
M

A
C
T
O
R
S

243

MICHAEL McKEAN
YOUNG DOCTORS IN LOVE   20th Century-Fox, 1982
THIS IS SPINAL TAP   Embassy, 1984
LIGHT OF DAY   TriStar, 1987
SHORT CIRCUIT 2   TriStar, 1988
EARTH GIRLS ARE EASY   Vestron, 1989
THE BIG PICTURE   Columbia, 1989
FLASHBACK   Paramount, 1990
BOOK OF LOVE   New Line Cinema, 1991
TRUE IDENTITY   Buena Vista, 1991
MEMOIRS OF AN INVISIBLE MAN   Warner Bros., 1992
MAN TROUBLE   20th Century Fox, 1992
AIRHEADS   20th Century Fox, 1994
RADIOLAND MURDERS   Universal, 1994
THE BRADY BUNCH MOVIE   Paramount, 1995

LONETTE McKEE
b. 1954 - Detroit, Michigan

THE COTTON CLUB   Orion, 1984
BREWSTER'S MILLIONS   Universal, 1985
DANGEROUS PASSION (TF)   Stormy Weathers Productions/
    Davis Entertainment TV, 1990
JUNGLE FEVER   Universal, 1991

DANICA McKELLAR
MOMENT OF TRUTH: CRADLE OF CONSPIRACY (TF)
    O'Hara/Horowitz Productions, 1994

IAN McKELLEN
b. May 25, 1939 - Burnley, England
Agent: APA - Los Angeles, 310/273-0744

THE BALLAD OF LITTLE JO   Fine Line Features/
    New Line Cinema, 1993
AND THE BAND PLAYED ON (CTF)   HBO Pictures/Spelling
    Entertainment, 1993
SIX DEGREES OF SEPARATION   MGM/UA, 1993
RESTORATION   Miramax Films, 1994

DOUG McKEON
ON GOLDEN POND   Universal/AFD, 1981
MISCHIEF   20th Century Fox, 1985
HEART OF A CHAMPION: THE RAY MANCINI STORY (TF)
    Rare Titles Productions/Robert Papazian Productions, 1985
AT MOTHER'S REQUEST (TF)   Vista Organization, Ltd., 1987
NORMAN ROCKWELL'S 'BREAKING HOME TIES'
    BREAKING HOME TIES (TF)   ABC, 1987

NANCY McKEON
Agent: William Morris Agency - Beverly Hills, 310/274-7451

STRANGE VOICES (TF)   Forrest Hills Productions/Dacks-Geller
    Productions/TLC, 1987
WHERE THE DAY TAKES YOU   New Line Cinema, 1992

CHARLES McKEOWN
THE ADVENTURES OF BARON MUNCHAUSEN   Columbia, 1989

BILL McKINNEY
(William McKinney)
Agent: The Barry Freed Company - Los Angeles, 310/277-1260

DELIVERANCE   Warner Bros., 1972
JUNIOR BONNER   Cinerama Releasing Corporation, 1972
KANSAS CITY BOMBER   MGM, 1972
THE LIFE AND TIMES OF JUDGE ROY BEAN
    National General, 1972
CLEOPATRA JONES   Warner Bros., 1973
FOR PETE'S SAKE   Columbia, 1974
THE OUTFIT   MGM, 1974
THE PARALLAX VIEW   Paramount, 1974
THUNDERBOLT AND LIGHTFOOT   United Artists, 1974
BREAKHEART PASS   United Artists, 1976
CANNONBALL   New World, 1976
THE OUTLAW JOSEY WALES   Warner Bros., 1976
THE SHOOTIST   Paramount, 1976

THE GAUNTLET   Warner Bros., 1977
VALENTINO   United Artists, 1977, British
EVERY WHICH WAY BUT LOOSE   Warner Bros., 1978
WHEN YOU COMIN' BACK, RED RYDER?   Columbia, 1979
ANY WHICH WAY YOU CAN   Warner Bros., 1980
BRONCO BILLY   Warner Bros., 1980
CARNEY   United Artists, 1980
ST. HELENS   Davis-Panzer Productions, 1981
TEX   Buena Vista, 1982
FIRST BLOOD   Orion, 1982, Canadian
HEART LIKE A WHEEL   20th Century-Fox, 1983
AGAINST ALL ODDS   Columbia, 1984
KINJITE (FORBIDDEN SUBJECTS)   Cannon, 1989
CITY SLICKERS II: THE LEGEND OF CURLY'S GOLD
    Columbia, 1994

RAY McKINNON
THE GUN IN BETTY LOU'S HANDBAG   Buena Vista, 1992

RACHEL McLISH
ACES: IRON EAGLE III   New Line Cinema, 1991

JOHN McMARTIN
WHAT'S SO BAD ABOUT FEELING GOOD?   Universal, 1968
SWEET CHARITY   Universal, 1969
DREAM LOVER   MGM/UA, 1986
NATIVE SON   Cinecom, 1986

SAM McMURRAY
RAISING ARIZONA   20th Century Fox, 1987
THE WIZARD   Universal, 1989
L.A. STORY   TriStar, 1991
STONE COLD   Columbia, 1991

KEVIN McNALLY
THE BERLIN AFFAIR   Cannon, 1985, Italian-West German

BRIAN McNAMARA
CADDYSHACK II   Warner Bros., 1988
MYSTERY DATE   Orion, 1991

WILLIAM McNAMARA
STEALING HOME   Warner Bros., 1988
DREAM A LITTLE DREAM   Vestron, 1989
TEXASVILLE   Columbia, 1990
SURVIVING THE GAME   New Line Cinema, 1994
COPYCAT   Warner Bros., 1995

IAN McNEICE
NO ESCAPE   Savoy Pictures, 1994

KATE McNEIL
MONKEY SHINES   Orion, 1988

KRISTY McNICHOL
b. September 11, 1962 - Los Angeles, California

BLACK SUNDAY   Paramount, 1977
LIKE MOM, LIKE ME (TF)   CBS Entertainment, 1978
THE END   United Artists, 1978
SUMMER OF MY GERMAN SOLDIER (TF)   Highgate Productions, 1978
LITTLE DARLINGS   Paramount, 1980
THE NIGHT THE LIGHTS WENT OUT IN GEORGIA
    Avco Embassy, 1981
ONLY WHEN I LAUGH   Columbia, 1981
WHITE DOG   Paramount, 1982
THE PIRATE MOVIE   20th Century-Fox, 1982, Australian
JUST THE WAY YOU ARE   MGM/UA, 1984
LOVE, MARY (TF)   CBS Entertainment, 1985
DREAM LOVER   MGM/UA, 1986
WOMEN OF VALOR (TF)   Inter Planetary Productions/Jeni
    Productions, 1986
TWO MOON JUNCTION   Lorimar, 1988
YOU CAN'T HURRY LOVE   MCEG, 1989

ARMELIA McQUEEN
GHOST   Paramount, 1990

FRANK McRAE
CANNERY ROW   MGM/United Artists, 1982
48 HOURS   Paramount, 1982
FAREWELL TO THE KING   Orion, 1989
LICENCE TO KILL   MGM/UA, 1989, British
LOCK UP   TriStar, 1989
THE WIZARD   Universal, 1989
LAST ACTION HERO   Columbia, 1993

GERALD McRANEY
b. August 19, 1948 - Collins, Mississippi
Agent: Karg-Weissenback & Associates - Beverly Hills, 310/205-0435

THE PEOPLE ACROSS THE LAKE (TF)   Bill McCutchen
   Productions/Columbia TV, 1988
WHERE THE HELL'S THAT GOLD?!!? (TF)   Willie Nelson
   Productions/Brigade Productions/Konigsberg-Sanitsky
   Company, 1988
MURDER BY MOONLIGHT (TF)   Tamara Asseyev Productions/
   London Weekend TV/Viacom, 1989, U.S.-British
BLIND VENGEANCE (CTF)   Spanish Trail Productions/
   MCA TV, 1990
SCATTERED DREAMS: THE KATHY MESSENGER
   STORY (TF)   1993

PETER McROBBIE
BIG   20th Century Fox, 1988

MICHAEL McSHANE
RICHIE RICH   Warner Bros., 1994

CAROLINE McWILLIAMS
SWORN TO SILENCE (TF)   Daniel H. Blatt/Robert Singer
   Productions, 1987

COURTLAND MEAD
THE LITTLE RASCALS   Universal, 1994

JAYNE MEADOWS
b. September 27, 1920 - Wu Chang, China

CITY SLICKERS   Columbia, 1991

STEPHEN MEADOWS
V.I. WARSHAWSKI   Buena Vista, 1991

COLM MEANEY
THE COMMITMENTS   20th Century Fox, 1991, U.S.-British-Irish
UNDER SIEGE   Warner Bros., 1992
THE SNAPPER   Miramax Films, 1993, British

KEVIN MEANEY
BIG   20th Century Fox, 1988

RUSSELL MEANS
POCAHONTAS (AF)   Buena Vista, 1995 (voice)

ANNE MEARA
b. September 20, 1929 - New York, New York
Agent: Innovative Artists - New York, 212/315-4455

LOVERS AND OTHER STRANGERS   Cinerama Releasing
   Corporation, 1970
KATE McSHANE (TF)   Paramount TV, 1975
NASTY HABITS   Brut Productions, 1977, British
THE BOYS FROM BRAZIL   20th Century-Fox, 1978
FAME   MGM/United Artists, 1980
THE OTHER WOMAN (TF)   CBS Entertainment, 1983
AWAKENINGS   Columbia, 1991
HEAVYWEIGHTS   Buena Vista, 1994

MEAT LOAF
(Marvin Lee Aday)
Agent: William Morris Agency - Beverly Hills, 310/274-7451

THE ROCKY HORROR PICTURE SHOW   20th Century-Fox,
   1975, British
THE GUN IN BETTY LOU'S HANDBAG   Buena Vista, 1992
LEAP OF FAITH   Paramount, 1992

JULIO MECHOSO
(Julio Oscar Mechoso)
MENENDEZ: A KILLING IN BEVERLY HILLS (MS)   Zev Braun
   Pictures/TriStar Television, 1994
A PYROMANIAC'S LOVE STORY   Buena Vista, 1995

JOHN MEILLON
ON THE BEACH   United Artists, 1959
THE SUNDOWNERS   Warner Bros., 1960
OFFBEAT   1961, British
THE VALIANT   United Artists, 1962, British-Italian
BILLY BUDD   Allied Artists, 1962, British
THE RUNNING MAN   Columbia, 1963, British
THEY'RE A WEIRD MOB   Williamson/Powell, 1966, Australian
THE CARS THAT EAT PEOPLE   *THE CARS THAT ATE PARIS*
   New Line Cinema, 1974, Australian
"CROCODILE" DUNDEE   Paramount, 1986, Australian
"CROCODILE" DUNDEE II   Paramount, 1988, U.S.-Australian

JOHN MELLENCAMP
(John Cougar Mellencamp)
Agent: CAA - Beverly Hills, 310/288-4545

FALLING FROM GRACE   Columbia, 1992 (also directed)

STEPHEN MENDEL
SCANNER COP 2   Republic Pictures, 1994

BEN MENDELSOHN
Agent: Susan Smith & Associates - Beverly Hills, 213/852-4777

THE YEAR MY VOICE BROKE   Avenue Pictures, 1988, Australian

ROBERT MENZIES
CACTUS   Spectrafilm, 1986, Australian

HECTOR MERCADO
DELTA FORCE 2 - OPERATION STRANGLEHOLD   MGM/UA, 1990

MARIAN MERCER
b. November 26, 1935 - Akron, Ohio

OUT ON A LIMB   Universal, 1992

MONIQUE MERCURE
NAKED LUNCH   20th Century Fox, 1991

MICOLE MERCURIO
GLEAMING THE CUBE   20th Century Fox, 1989
THE CLIENT   Warner Bros., 1994
WHILE YOU WERE SLEEPING   Buena Vista, 1995

PAUL MERCURIO
STRICTLY BALLROOM   Miramax Films, 1992, Australian
EXIT TO EDEN   Savoy Pictures, 1994
JOSEPH (CTF)   Turner Network TV, 1994
BACK OF BEYOND   Beyond Films, 1995

BURGESS MEREDITH
b. November 16, 1908 - Cleveland, Ohio

WINTERSET   RKO Radio, 1936
THERE GOES THE GROOM   1937
SPRING MADNESS   Paramount, 1938

IDIOT'S DELIGHT   MGM, 1939
OF MICE AND MEN   United Artists, 1939
CASTLE ON THE HUDSON   Warner Bros., 1940
SECOND CHORUS   Paramount, 1940
SAN FRANCISCO DOCKS   Universal, 1941
THAT UNCERTAIN FEELING   United Artists, 1941
TOM, DICK AND HARRY   RKO Radio, 1941
STREET OF CHANCE   Paramount, 1942
THE STORY OF G.I. JOE   United Artists, 1945
DIARY OF A CHAMBERMAID   United Artists, 1946
MAGNIFICENT DOLL   Universal, 1946
MINE OWN EXECUTIONER   1947, British
ON OUR MERRY WAY   *A MIRACLE CAN HAPPEN*
   United Artists, 1948
THE MAN ON THE EIFFEL TOWER   1949 (also directed)
THE GAY ADVENTURE   1953, British
JOE BUTTERFLY   1957
ADVISE AND CONSENT   Columbia, 1962
THE CARDINAL   Columbia, 1963
THE KIDNAPPERS   *MAN ON THE RUN*   1964
IN HARM'S WAY   Paramount, 1965
MADAME X   Universal, 1966
A BIG HAND FOR THE LITTLE LADY   Warner Bros., 1966
BATMAN   20th Century-Fox, 1966
CRAZY QUILT   Farallon, 1966 (voice)
HURRY SUNDOWN   Paramount, 1967
TORTURE GARDEN   Columbia, 1968, British
STAY AWAY, JOE   MGM, 1968
SKIDOO   Paramount, 1969
MACKENNA'S GOLD   Columbia, 1969
HARD CONTRACT   20th Century-Fox, 1969
THE REIVERS   National General, 1969 (voice)
THERE WAS A CROOKED MAN...   Warner Bros., 1970
SUCH GOOD FRIENDS   Paramount, 1971
CLAY PIGEON   MGM, 1971
BEWARE! THE BLOB   *SON OF BLOB*   Jack H. Harris
   Enterprises, 1972
PROBE (TF)   Warner Bros. TV, 1972
A FAN'S NOTES   Warner Bros., 1972, Canadian
THE MAN   Paramount, 1972
GOLDEN NEEDLES   *THE CHASE FOR THE GOLDEN NEEDLES*
   American International, 1974
THE DAY OF THE LOCUST ✪   Paramount, 1975
92 IN THE SHADE   United Artists, 1975
THE HINDENBURG   Universal, 1975
BURNT OFFERINGS   United Artists, 1976
ROCKY ✪   United Artists, 1976
THE SENTINEL   Universal, 1977
THE GREAT BANK HOAX   *SHENANIGANS/THE GREAT
   GEORGIA BANK HOAX*   Warner Bros., 1977
GOLDEN RENDEZVOUS   Rank, 1977, British
TAIL GUNNER JOE (TF)   Universal TV, 1977
THE MANITOU   1978
FOUL PLAY   Paramount, 1978
MAGIC   20th Century-Fox, 1978
ROCKY II   United Artists, 1979
FINAL ASSIGNMENT   Almi Cinema 5, 1980, Canadian
WHEN TIME RAN OUT   Warner Bros., 1980
TRUE CONFESSIONS   United Artists, 1981
THE LAST CHASE   Crown International, 1981, Canadian
CLASH OF THE TITANS   MGM/United Artists, 1981, British
ROCKY III   MGM/UA, 1982
SANTA CLAUS: THE MOVIE   TriStar, 1985, U.S.-British
BROKEN RAINBOW (FD)   Earthworks Films, 1985 (voice)
KING LEAR   Cannon, 1987, U.S-Swiss
FULL MOON IN BLUE WATER   Trans World Entertainment, 1988
ROCKY V   MGM/UA, 1990
GRUMPY OLD MEN   Warner Bros., 1993

MACHA MERIL
DUET FOR ONE   Cannon, 1986

EDA REISS MERIN
DON'T TELL MOM THE BABYSITTER'S DEAD   Warner Bros., 1991

DINA MERRILL
(Nedenia Hutton)
b. December 9, 1925 - New York, New York

DESK SET   20th Century-Fox, 1957
A NICE LITTLE BANK THAT SHOULD BE ROBBED
   20th Century-Fox, 1958
DON'T GIVE UP THE SHIP   Paramount, 1959
OPERATION PETTICOAT   Universal, 1959
BUTTERFIELD 8   MGM, 1960
THE SUNDOWNERS   Warner Bros., 1960
THE YOUNG SAVAGES   United Artists, 1961
THE COURTSHIP OF EDDIE'S FATHER   MGM, 1963
THE PLEASURE SEEKERS   20th Century-Fox, 1964
I'LL TAKE SWEDEN   1965
RUNNING WILD   1973
DELIVER US FROM EVIL (TF)   Playboy Productions, 1973
THE MEAL   1975
THE GREATEST   Columbia, 1977
A WEDDING   20th Century-Fox, 1978
JUST TELL ME WHAT YOU WANT   Columbia, 1980
CADDYSHACK II   Warner Bros., 1988
THE PLAYER   Fine Line Features/New Line Cinema, 1992

THERESA MERRITT
THEY MIGHT BE GIANTS   Universal, 1971
THE WIZ   Universal, 1978
THE GREAT SANTINI   *THE ACE*   Orion/Warner Bros., 1980
THE BEST LITTLE WHOREHOUSE IN TEXAS   Universal, 1982

DANIEL MESGUICH
JEFFERSON IN PARIS   Buena Vista, 1995

AMNON MESKIN
ALWAYS   Samuel Goldwyn Company, 1985

DOLORES MESSINA
BIG   20th Century Fox, 1988

DEBRA MESSING
A WALK IN THE CLOUDS   20th Century Fox, 1995

LAURIE METCALF
b. June 16, 1955 - Carbonville, Illinois
Agent: ICM - Beverly Hills, 310/550-4000

MAKING MR. RIGHT   Orion, 1987
MILES FROM HOME   Cinecom, 1988
INTERNAL AFFAIRS   Paramount, 1990
PACIFIC HEIGHTS   20th Century Fox, 1990
FRANKIE & JOHNNY   Paramount, 1991
JFK   Warner Bros., 1991
MISTRESS   Tribeca Films, 1992
A DANGEROUS WOMAN   Gramercy Pictures, 1993
BLINK   New Line Cinema, 1994

MARK METCALF
WHERE THE BUFFALO ROAM   Universal, 1980

AARON MICHAEL METCHIK
TRADING MOM   Trimark Pictures, 1994

ASHER METCHIK
TRADING MOM   Trimark Pictures, 1994

ART METRANO
THEY SHOOT HORSES, DON'T THEY?   Cinerama Releasing
   Corporation, 1969
THE ALL-AMERICAN BOY   Warner Bros., 1973
CHEAPER TO KEEP HER   American Cinema, 1980
HOW TO BEAT THE HIGH COST OF LIVING   American
   International, 1980
GOING APE!   Paramount, 1981
BREATHLESS   Orion, 1983

TEACHERS   MGM/UA, 1984
POLICE ACADEMY 2: THEIR FIRST ASSIGNMENT
   Warner Bros., 1985
POLICE ACADEMY 3: BACK IN TRAINING   Warner Bros., 1986

JIM METZLER
TEX   Buena Vista, 1982
HOT TO TROT   Warner Bros., 1988
OLD GRINGO   Columbia, 1989
HURRICANE   I.R.S. Releasing, 1991

IRVING METZMAN
"CROCODILE" DUNDEE   Paramount, 1986, Australian

ANNE-LAURE MEURY
L'AMI DE MON AMIE   *FRIEND OF A FRIEND*   Orion Classics,
   1988, French

BESS MEYER
THE INNER CIRCLE   Columbia, 1991

DINA MEYER
JOHNNY MNEMONIC   TriStar, 1994
DRAGONHEART   Universal, 1995

ARI MEYERS
b. April 6, 1969 - San Juan, Puerto Rico

THINK BIG   MPCA, 1990

MICHELLE MEYRINK
REAL GENIUS   TriStar, 1985

CORA MIAO
EAT A BOWL OF TEA   Columbia, 1989, U.S.-Hong Kong

FRANÇOISE MICHAUD
EMINENT DOMAIN   Triumph Releasing Corporation, 1990,
   Canadian-French-Israeli

DOMINIQUE MICHEL
THE DECLINE OF THE AMERICAN EMPIRE   Cineplex Odeon,
   1986, Canadian

HELENA MICHELL
THE DECEIVERS   Cinecom, 1988

DALE MIDKIFF
Agent: Gersh Agency - Beverly Hills, 310/274-6611

STREETWALKIN'   Concorde, 1985
DALLAS: THE EARLY YEARS (TF)   Roundelay Productions/
   Lorimar Telepictures, 1986
CASUAL SEX?   Universal, 1988
ELVIS AND ME (MS)   Navarone Productions/New World TV, 1988
PET SEMATARY   *STEPHEN KING'S PET SEMATARY*
   Paramount, 1989
LOVE POTION #9   20th Century Fox, 1992

BETTE MIDLER
b. December 1, 1945 - Honolulu, Hawaii
Agent: CAA - Beverly Hills, 310/288-4545

HAWAII   United Artists, 1966
THE ROSE ★   20th Century-Fox, 1979
DIVINE MADNESS (FD)   The Ladd Company/Warner Bros., 1980
JINXED!   MGM/UA, 1982
DOWN AND OUT IN BEVERLY HILLS   Buena Vista, 1986
RUTHLESS PEOPLE   Buena Vista, 1986
OUTRAGEOUS FORTUNE   Buena Vista, 1987
BIG BUSINESS   Buena Vista, 1988
OLIVER & COMPANY (AF)   Buena Vista, 1988 (voice)
BEACHES   Buena Vista, 1988
STELLA   Buena Vista, 1990

SCENES FROM A MALL   Buena Vista, 1991
FOR THE BOYS ★   20th Century Fox, 1991
HOCUS POCUS   Buena Vista, 1993
GYPSY (TF)   RHI Entertainment, 1993

JULIA MIGENES
CARMEN   Triumph/Columbia, 1984, Italian-French
MACK THE KNIFE   21st Century Distribution, 1989

TOTO MIGNONE
GINGER AND FRED   MGM/UA, 1986, Italian-French-West German

ALYSSA MILANO
b. December 19, 1972 - New York, New York
Agent: William Morris Agency - Beverly Hills, 310/274-7451

WHERE THE DAY TAKES YOU   New Line Cinema, 1992
NO FEAR   Universal, 1995

CHRISTOPHER CLEARY MILES
SECOND BEST   Warner Bros., 1994

JOANNA MILES
BUG   Paramount, 1975
RIGHT TO DIE (TF)   Ohlmeyer Communications, 1987
ROSENCRANTZ & GUILDENSTERN ARE DEAD   Cinecom, 1991
JUDGE DREDD   Buena Vista, 1995

SARAH MILES
b. December 31, 1941 - Ingatestone, England
Agent: Harris & Goldberg Agency - Los Angeles, 310/553-5200

TERM OF TRIAL   Warner Bros., 1963
THE SERVANT   Landau, 1963, British
THE CEREMONY   1963
THOSE MAGNIFICENT MEN IN THEIR FLYING MACHINES
   20th Century-Fox, 1965, British
TIME LOST AND TIME REMEMBERED   *I WAS HAPPY HERE*
   Continental, 1966, British
BLOW-UP   Premier, 1966, British-Italian
RYAN'S DAUGHTER ★   MGM, 1970
LADY CAROLINE LAMB   United Artists, 1972, British
THE HIRELING   Columbia, 1973
THE MAN WHO LOVED CAT DANCING   MGM, 1973
GREAT EXPECTATIONS (TF)   Transcontinental Film Productions,
   1974, British
BRIDE TO BE   1975
THE SAILOR WHO FELL FROM GRACE WITH THE SEA
   Avco Embassy, 1976, British
THE BIG SLEEP   United Artists, 1978, British
PRIEST OF LOVE   Filmways, 1981, British
VENOM   Paramount, 1982, British
ORDEAL BY INNOCENCE   Cannon, 1984, British
STEAMING   New World, 1985, British
HAREM (MS)   Highgate Pictures1986
QUEENIE (TF)   von Zerneck-Samuels Prods./Highgate Pictures, 1987
HOPE AND GLORY   Columbia, 1987, British
WHITE MISCHIEF   Columbia, 1987, British

SYLVIA MILES
b. September 9, 1932 - New York, New York

MURDER, INC.   20th Century-Fox, 1960
PARRISH   Warner Bros., 1961
PSYCHOMANIA   *VIOLENT MIDNIGHT*   1963
MIDNIGHT COWBOY ✪   United Artists, 1969
THE LAST MOVIE   Universal, 1971
WHO KILLED MARY WHAT'S'ER NAME?   Cannon, 1971
HEAT   Warhol, 1972
92 IN THE SHADE   United Artists, 1975
FAREWELL, MY LOVELY ✪   Avco Embassy, 1975
THE GREAT SCOUT AND CATHOUSE THURSDAY
   American International, 1976
THE SENTINEL   Universal, 1977
SHALIMAR   *THE DEADLY THIEF*   Judson Productions/Laxmi
   Productions, 1978, U.S.-Indian
ZERO TO SIXTY   First Artists, 1979, Canadian

EVIL UNDER THE SUN   Universal/AFD, 1982, British
CRITICAL CONDITION   Paramount, 1987
WALL STREET   20th Century Fox, 1987
CROSSING DELANCEY   Warner Bros., 1988
SHE-DEVIL   Orion, 1989

VERA MILES
(Vera Ralston)
b. August 23, 1929 - Boise City, Oklahoma

TWO TICKETS TO BROADWAY   1951
FOR MEN ONLY *THE TALL LIE*   1952
THE ROSE BOWL STORY   Monogram, 1952
THE CHARGE AT FEATHER CREEK   Warner Bros., 1953
PRIDE OF THE BLUE GRASS   Allied Artists, 1954
TARZAN'S HIDDEN JUNGLE   MGM, 1955
WICHITA   Allied Artists, 1955
THE SEARCHERS   Warner Bros., 1956
AUTUMN LEAVES   Columbia, 1956
23 PACES TO BAKER STREET   20th Century-Fox, 1956, British-U.S.
THE WRONG MAN   Warner Bros., 1957
BEAU JAMES   Paramount, 1957
THE FBI STORY   Warner Bros., 1959
WEB OF EVIDENCE *BEYOND THIS PLACE*   Allied Artists,
    1959, British
FIVE BRANDED WOMEN   Paramount, 1960, Italian-Yugoslavian
A TOUCH OF LARCENY   Paramount, 1960, British
PSYCHO   Paramount, 1960
BACK STREET   Universal, 1961
THE MAN WHO SHOT LIBERTY VALANCE   Paramount, 1962
THE HANGED MAN (TF)   Universal TV, 1964
A TIGER WALKS   Buena Vista, 1964
THOSE CALLOWAYS   Buena Vista, 1965
FOLLOW ME, BOYS!   Buena Vista, 1966
GENTLE GIANT   Paramount, 1967
THE SPIRIT IS WILLING   Paramount, 1967
SERGEANT RYKER   Universal, 1968
KONA COAST   Warner Bros., 1968
HELLFIGHTERS   Universal, 1969
IT TAKES ALL KINDS   1969, U.S.-Australian
THE WILD COUNTRY   Buena Vista, 1971
MOLLY AND LAWLESS JOHN   Producers Distribution
    Corporation, 1972
ONE LITTLE INDIAN   Buena Vista, 1973
THE CASTAWAY COWBOY   Buena Vista, 1974
TWILIGHT'S LAST GLEAMING   Allied Artists, 1977,
    U.S.-West German
THOROUGHBRED *RUN FOR THE ROSES*   Kodiak Films1978
OUR FAMILY BUSINESS (TF)   Lorimar Productions, 1981
PSYCHO II   Universal, 1983
INTO THE NIGHT   Universal, 1985
THE HIJACKING OF THE ACHILLE LAURO (TF)   Tamara Asseyev
    Productions/Spectator Films/New World TV, 1989

PENELOPE MILFORD
COMING HOME ✪   United Artists, 1978
ENDLESS LOVE   Universal, 1981
HEATHERS   New World, 1989

MICHAEL MILHOAN
CRIMSON TIDE   Buena Vista, 1995

FRANK MILITARY
Agent: William Morris Agency - Beverly Hills, 310/274-7451

DEAD-BANG   Warner Bros., 1989

ANN MILLER
b. April 12, 1919 - Houston, Texas

THAT'S ENTERTAINMENT! III (FD)   MGM/UA, 1994

BARRY MILLER
SATURDAY NIGHT FEVER   Paramount, 1977
FAME   MGM/United Artists, 1980
PEGGY SUE GOT MARRIED   TriStar, 1986
THE PICKLE   Columbia, 1993

DENNIS MILLER
b. November 3, 1953 - Pittsburg, Pennsylvania

MADHOUSE   Orion, 1990
DISCLOSURE   Warner Bros., 1994

DICK MILLER
Agent: Contemporary Artists - Santa Monica, 310/395-1800

APACHE WOMAN   American International, 1955
THE UNDEAD   American International, 1956
NOT OF THIS EARTH   Allied Artists, 1957
THUNDER OVER HAWAII   American International, 1957
A BUCKET OF BLOOD   American International, 1959
THE TERROR   American International, 1963
SKI PARTY   American International, 1965
THE DIRTY DOZEN   MGM, 1967
THE GRISSOM GANG   Cinerama Releasing Corporation, 1971
ULZANA'S RAID   Universal, 1972
BIG BAD MAMA   New World, 1974
HUSTLE   Paramount, 1975
CANNONBALL   New World, 1976
PIRANHA   New World, 1978
USED CARS   Columbia, 1980
HEARTBEEPS   Universal, 1981
HEART LIKE A WHEEL   20th Century-Fox, 1983
GREMLINS   Warner Bros., 1984
AFTER HOURS   The Geffen Company/Warner Bros., 1985
EXPLORERS   Paramount, 1985
THE 'BURBS   Universal, 1989
GREMLINS 2 THE NEW BATCH   Warner Bros., 1990

HARVEY MILLER
BIG   20th Century Fox, 1988

JASON MILLER
b. April 22, 1939 - New York, New York

THE EXORCIST ✪   Warner Bros., 1973
THE NICKEL RIDE   20th Century-Fox, 1975
A HOME OF OUR OWN (TF)   QM Productions, 1975
F. SCOTT FITZGERALD IN HOLLYWOOD (TF)   Titus Productions, 1976
THE DAIN CURSE (TF)   Martin Poll Productions, 1978
THE DEVIL'S ADVOCATE   Filmworld Distributors, 1978, West German
THE NINTH CONFIGURATION *TWINKLE, TWINKLE,
    "KILLER" KANE*   Warner Bros., 1980
A TOUCH OF SCANDAL (TF)   Doris M. Keating Productions/
    Columbia TV, 1984
THE EXORCIST III   20th Century Fox, 1990

LARRY MILLER
PRETTY WOMAN   Buena Vista, 1990
L.A. STORY   TriStar, 1991
UNDERCOVER BLUES   MGM/UA, 1993
THE FAVOR   Orion, 1994
DREAM LOVER   Gramercy Pictures, 1994
CORRINA, CORRINA   New Line Cinema, 1994

LINDA MILLER
ELVIS AND ME (MS)   Navarone Productions/New World TV, 1988

MAXINE MILLER
THE CARE BEARS MOVIE II: A NEW GENERATION (AF)
    Columbia, 1986, Canadian (voice)
THIS CAN'T BE LOVE (TF)   Davis Entertainment/Pacific Motion
    Pictures/World International Network, 1994

PENELOPE ANN MILLER
Agent: CAA - Beverly Hills, 310/288-4545

ADVENTURES IN BABYSITTING   Buena Vista, 1987
MILES FROM HOME   Cinecom, 1988
BILOXI BLUES   Universal, 1988
BIG TOP PEE-WEE   Paramount, 1988
DEAD-BANG   Warner Bros., 1989
THE FRESHMAN   TriStar, 1990

AWAKENINGS   Columbia, 1990
KINDERGARTEN COP   Universal, 1990
OTHER PEOPLE'S MONEY   Warner Bros., 1991
YEAR OF THE COMET   Columbia, 1992
THE GUN IN BETTY LOU'S HANDBAG   Buena Vista, 1992
CHAPLIN   TriStar, 1992, U.S.-British
CARLITO'S WAY   Universal, 1993
THE SHADOW   Universal, 1994

REBECCA MILLER
Agent: William Morris Agency - Beverly Hills, 310/274-7451

WIND   TriStar, 1992, U.S.-Japanese
CONSENTING ADULTS   Buena Vista, 1992
MRS. PARKER AND THE VICIOUS CIRCLE   Fine Line Features/
   New Line Cinema, 1994

SIDNEY MILLER
EVERYTHING YOU ALWAYS WANTED TO KNOW ABOUT SEX*
   (BUT WERE AFRAID TO ASK)   United Artists, 1972
STAR 80   The Ladd Company/Warner Bros., 1983

STEPHEN E. MILLER
THE ACCUSED   Paramount, 1988

ANDRA MILLIAN
NIGHTFALL   Concorde, 1988

DONNA MILLS
b. December 11, 1942 - Chicago, Illinois

THE INCIDENT   20th Century-Fox, 1967
PLAY MISTY FOR ME   Universal, 1971
HAUNTS OF THE VERY RICH (TF)   ABC Circle Films, 1972
NIGHT OF TERROR (TF)   Paramount TV, 1972
THE BAIT (TF)   1973
LIVE AGAIN, DIE AGAIN (TF)   Universal TV, 1974
WHO IS THE BLACK DAHLIA? (TF)   Douglas S. Cramer
   Productions, 1975
SMASH-UP ON INTERSTATE 5 (TF)   Filmways, 1976
CURSE OF THE BLACK WIDOW (TF)   Dan Curtis Productions/
   ABC Circle Films, 1977
THE HUNTED LADY (TF)   QM Productions, 1977
SUPERDOME (TF)   ABC Circle Films, 1978
BARE ESSENCE (MS)   Warner Bros. TV, 1982
HE'S NOT YOUR SON (TF)   CBS Entertainment, 1984
THE LADY FORGETS (TF)   Leonard Hill Films, 1989

HAYLEY MILLS
b. April 18, 1946 - London, England
Agent: Susan Smith & Associates - Beverly Hills, 213/852-4777

TIGER BAY   Continental, 1959, British
POLLYANNA   Buena Vista, 1960
THE PARENT TRAP   Buena Vista, 1961
WHISTLE DOWN THE WIND   Pathe-American, 1962, British
IN SEARCH OF THE CASTAWAYS   Buena Vista,
   1962, U.S.-British
SUMMER MAGIC   Buena Vista, 1963
THE CHALK GARDEN   Universal, 1964
THE MOON-SPINNERS   Buena Vista, 1964, U.S.-British
THE TRUTH ABOUT SPRING   Universal, 1965, U.S.-British
THAT DARN CAT   Buena Vista, 1965
THE GYPSY GIRL   SKY WEST AND CROOKED   1966
THE DAYDREAMER   1966 (voice)
THE TROUBLE WITH ANGELS   Columbia, 1966
THE FAMILY WAY   Warner Bros., 1967, British
AFRICA—TEXAS STYLE!   Paramount, 1967, British-U.S.
A MATTER OF INNOCENCE   PRETTY POLLY   1967
TWISTED NERVE   National General, 1969, British
TAKE A GIRL LIKE YOU   Columbia, 1970, British
CRY OF THE PENGUINS   FORBUSH AND THE PENGUINS
   1971, British
ENDLESS NIGHT   AGATHA CHRISTIES' ENDLESS NIGHT
   1971, British
DEADLY STRANGERS   20th Century-Fox/Rank, 1974, British

WHAT CHANGED CHARLEY FARTHING?   Stirling Gold,
   1975, British
THE KINGFISH CAPER   1975, South African
THE FLAME TREES OF THIKA (TF)   London Films, Ltd./
   Consolidated Productions, Ltd., 1980, British
PARENT TRAP II (CTF)   The Landsburg Company/
   Walt Disney TV, 1986
PARENT TRAP III (TF)   Walt Disney TV, 1989
PARENT TRAP: HAWAIIAN HONEYMOON (TF)   Walt Disney TV, 1989

JOHN MILLS
b. February 22, 1908 - North Elmham, England

THE MIDSHIPMAID   1932, British
BRITANNIA OF BILLINGSGATE   1933, British
THE GHOST CAMERA   1933, British
RIVER WOLVES   1934, British
A POLITICAL PARTY   1934, British
THOSE WERE THE DAYS   1934, British
THE LASH   1934, British
BLIND JUSTICE   1934, British
DOCTOR'S ORDERS   1934, British
ROYAL CAVALCADE   1935, British
BORN FOR GLORY   FOREVER ENGLAND   1935, British
CHARING CROSS ROAD   1935, British
FIRST OFFENSE   1936, British
NINE DAYS A QUEEN   TUDOR ROSE   1936, British
YOU'RE IN THE ARMY NOW   OHMS   1937, British
THE GREEN COCKATOO   1937, British
GOODBYE, MR. CHIPS   1939, British
OLD BILL AND SON   1941, British
COTTAGE TO LET   1941, British
THE BLACK SHEEP OF WHITEHALL   1941, British
THE YOUNG MR. PITT   1942, British
THE BIG BLOCKADE   1942, British
IN WHICH WE SERVE   1942, British
WE DIVE AT DAWN   1943, British
THIS HAPPY BREED   1944, British
WATERLOO ROAD   1944, British
JOHNNY IN THE CLOUDS   THE WAY TO THE STARS
   1945, British
GREAT EXPECTATIONS   1946, British
SO WELL REMEMBERED   1947, British
THE OCTOBER MAN   1947, British
SCOTT OF THE ANTARCTIC   1948, British
THE HISTORY OF MR. POLLY   1949, British
THE ROCKING HORSE WINNER   1949, British
OPERATION DISASTER   MORNING DEPARTURE   1950, British
MR. DENNING DRIVES NORTH   1951, British
THE GENTLE GUNMAN   1952, British
THE LONG MEMORY   1952, British
HOBSON'S CHOICE   1954, British
THE COLDITZ STORY   1955, British
THE END OF THE AFFAIR   1955, British
ABOVE US THE WAVES   1955, British
ESCAPADE   1955, British
WAR AND PEACE   1956, U.S.-Italian
IT'S GREAT TO BE YOUNG   1956, British
THE BABY AND THE BATTLESHIP   1956, British
AROUND THE WORLD IN 80 DAYS   1956, British
TOWN ON TRIAL   1957, British
THE CIRCLE   VICIOUS CIRCLE   1957, British
DUNKIRK   1958, British
ICE COLD IN ALEX   1958, British
I WAS MONTY'S DOUBLE   1958, British
TIGER BAY   1959, British
SUMMER OF THE 17TH DOLL   1960, British
TUNES OF GLORY   1960, British
SWISS FAMILY ROBINSON   Buena Vista, 1960
THE CHALK GARDEN   Universal, 1964, British
RYAN'S DAUGHTER OO   MGM, 1970
OKLAHOMA CRUDE   Columbia, 1973
GANDHI   Columbia, 1982, British-Indian

ZEKE MILLS
THE SUBSTITUTE WIFE (TF)   Frederick S. Pierce Company, 1994

JUNO MILLS-COCKELL
PARENTS   Vestron, 1989

JOHN OMIRAH MILUWI
GORILLAS IN THE MIST   Warner Bros./Universal, 1988

LAU SIU MING
EAT A BOWL OF TEA   Columbia, 1989, U.S.-Hong Kong

LIZA MINNELLI
b. March 12, 1946 - Los Angeles, California

IN THE GOOD OLD SUMMERTIME   MGM, 1949
CHARLIE BUBBLES   Regional, 1968, British
THE STERILE CUCKOO ★   Paramount, 1969
TELL ME THAT YOU LOVE ME JUNIE MOON   Paramount, 1970
CABARET ★★   Allied Artists, 1972
JOURNEY BACK TO OZ (AF)   1974 (voice)
THAT'S ENTERTAINMENT! (FD)   MGM/United Artists, 1974
LUCKY LADY   20th Century-Fox, 1975
A MATTER OF TIME   American International, 1976, U.S.-Italian
SILENT MOVIE   20th Century-Fox, 1976 (uncredited)
NEW YORK, NEW YORK   United Artists, 1977
ARTHUR   Orion, 1981
THE KING OF COMEDY   20th Century-Fox, 1983
THE MUPPETS TAKE MANHATTAN   TriStar, 1984
THAT'S DANCING! (FD)   MGM/UA, 1985
A TIME TO LIVE (TF)   Blue Andre Productions/
   ITC Productions, 1985
RENT-A-COP   Kings Road Productions, 1988
ARTHUR 2 ON THE ROCKS   Warner Bros., 1988
STEPPING OUT   Paramount, 1991
PARALLEL LIVES (CTF)   Showtime Entertainment, 1994

KYLIE MINOGUE
STREET FIGHTER   Universal, 1994

KELLY JO MINTER
(Kelly Minter)
THE PRINCIPAL   TriStar, 1987
POPCORN   Studio Three, 1991

ROBERT G. MIRANDA
(Robert Guy Miranda)
Personal Manager: Marc Rindner - Los Angeles, 213/461-6334

CROSSROADS   Columbia, 1986
THE UNTOUCHABLES   Paramount, 1987
MIDNIGHT RUN   Universal, 1988
MY BLUE HEAVEN   Warner Bros., 1990
THE ROCKETEER   Buena Vista, 1991
SISTER ACT   Buena Vista, 1992
NEIL SIMON'S LOST IN YONKERS   LOST IN YONKERS
   Columbia, 1993
MONKEY TROUBLE   New Line Cinema, 1994

HELEN MIRREN
HEROSTRATUS   1967
A MIDSUMMER NIGHT'S DREAM   Eagle, 1968, British
AGE OF CONSENT   Columbia, 1970, Australian
SAVAGE MESSIAH   MGM, 1972
MISS JULIE   1973
O LUCKY MAN!   Warner Bros., 1973, British
CALIGULA   Analysis Film Releasing, 1980, Italian-U.S.
S.O.S. TITANIC (TF)   Roger Gimbel Productions/EMI TV/Argonaut
   Films, Ltd., 1979, U.S.-British
HUSSY   Watchgrove Ltd., 1980, British
THE FIENDISH PLOT OF DR. FU MANCHU   Orion/Warner Bros.,
   1980, British
THE LONG GOOD FRIDAY   Embassy, 1980, British
EXCALIBUR   Orion/Warner Bros., 1981, British-Irish
CAL   Warner Bros., 1984, Irish
2010   MGM/UA, 1984
WHITE NIGHTS   Columbia, 1985
THE MOSQUITO COAST   Warner Bros., 1986
PASCALI'S ISLAND   Avenue Entertainment, 1988, British-U.S.
THE COOK, THE THIEF, HIS WIFE & HER LOVER   Miramax Films,
   1989, Dutch-French
WHEN THE WHALES CAME   20th Century Fox, 1989, British

RED KING, WHITE KNIGHT (CTF)   HBO Pictures/Zenith
   Productions/John Kemeny Productions/Citadel Entertainment,
   1989, U.S.-British-Canadian
THE COMFORT OF STRANGERS   Skouras Pictures, 1990, British
DR. BETHUNE   1994
THE HAWK   Castle Hill Productions, 1994
THE MADNESS OF GEORGE III   Samuel Goldwyn Company, 1995

MR. T
(Lawrence Tero)
ROCKY III   MGM/UA, 1982
THE A-TEAM (TF)   Stephen J. Cannell Productions, 1983
D.C. CAB   Universal, 1983
THE TOUGHEST MAN IN THE WORLD (TF)   Guber-Peters
   Productions/Centerpoint Productions, 1984
FREAKED   20th Century Fox, 1993

DONNA MITCHELL
THE PORTRAIT (CTF)   Robert Greenwald Productions/Atticus
   Corporation/Turner Network TV, 1993

JOHN CAMERON MITCHELL
Agent: Geddes Agency - Los Angeles, 213/651-2401

BAND OF THE HAND   TriStar, 1986

ROBERT MITCHUM
b. August 6, 1917 - Bridgeport, Connecticut
Agent: ICM - Beverly Hills, 310/550-4000

HOPPY SERVES A WRIT   1943
THE LEATHER BURNERS   1943
BORDER PATROL   United Artists, 1943
FOLLOW THE BAND   1943
COLT COMRADES   United Artists, 1943
THE HUMAN COMEDY   MGM, 1943
WE'VE NEVER BEEN LICKED   1943
BEYOND THE LAST FRONTIER   1943
BAR 20   United Artists, 1943
DOUGHBOYS IN IRELAND   Columbia, 1943
CORVETTE K-225   1943
AERIAL GUNNER   1943
LONE STAR TRAIL   1943
FALSE COLORS   1943
THE DANCING MASTERS   1943
RIDERS OF THE DEADLINE   Republic, 1944
CRY HAVOC   MGM, 1943
GUNG HO!   Universal, 1943
JOHNNY DOESN'T LIVE HERE ANY MORE   AND SO THEY
   WERE MARRIED   1944
WHEN STRANGERS MARRY   Columbia, 1944
THE GIRL RUSH   RKO Radio, 1944
THIRTY SECONDS OVER TOKYO   MGM, 1944
NEVADA   1944
WEST OF THE PECOS   1945
THE STORY OF G.I. JOE ✪   United Artists, 1945
TILL THE END OF TIME   RKO Radio, 1946
UNDERCURRENT   MGM, 1946
THE LOCKET   RKO Radio, 1946
PURSUED   Warner Bros., 1947
CROSSFIRE   RKO Radio, 1947
DESIRE ME   MGM, 1947
OUT OF THE PAST   RKO Radio, 1947
RACHEL AND THE STRANGER   RKO Radio, 1948
BLOOD ON THE MOON   RKO Radio, 1948
THE RED PONY   Republic, 1949
THE BIG STEAL   RKO Radio, 1949
HOLIDAY AFFAIR   1949
WHERE DANGER LIVES   RKO Radio, 1950
MY FORBIDDEN PAST   RKO Radio, 1951
HIS KIND OF WOMAN   RKO Radio, 1951
THE RACKET   RKO Radio, 1951
MACAO   RKO Radio, 1952
ONE MINUTE TO ZERO   RKO Radio, 1952
THE LUSTY MEN   RKO Radio, 1952
SECOND CHANCE   RKO Radio, 1953
ANGEL FACE   RKO Radio, 1953

WHITE WITCH DOCTOR   20th Century-Fox, 1953
SHE COULDN'T SAY NO   RKO Radio, 1954
RIVER OF NO RETURN   20th Century-Fox, 1954
TRACK OF THE CAT   Warner Bros., 1954
NOT AS A STRANGER   United Artists, 1955
THE NIGHT OF THE HUNTER   United Artists, 1955
MAN WITH THE GUN   United Artists, 1955
FOREIGN INTRIGUE   1956
BANDIDO   United Artists, 1956
HEAVEN KNOWS MR. ALLISON   20th Century-Fox, 1957
FIRE DOWN BELOW   Columbia, 1957
THE ENEMY BELOW   20th Century-Fox, 1957
THUNDER ROAD   1958
THE HUNTERS   20th Century-Fox, 1958
THE ANGRY HILLS   MGM, 1959
THE WONDERFUL COUNTRY   United Artists, 1959
HOME FROM THE HILL   MGM, 1960
THE SUNDOWNERS   Warner Bros., 1960
THE NIGHT FIGHTERS   *A TERRIBLE BEAUTY*   United Artists,
   1960, British
THE GRASS IS GREENER   Universal, 1960
THE LAST TIME I SAW ARCHIE   United Artists, 1961
CAPE FEAR   Universal, 1962
THE LONGEST DAY   20th Century-Fox, 1962
TWO FOR THE SEESAW   United Artists, 1962
THE LIST OF ADRIAN MESSENGER   Universal, 1963
RAMPAGE   Warner Bros., 1963
MAN IN THE MIDDLE   20th Century-Fox, 1964, British-U.S.
WHAT A WAY TO GO!   20th Century-Fox, 1964
MISTER MOSES   United Artists, 1965, British
THE WAY WEST   United Artists, 1967
EL DORADO   Paramount, 1967
VILLA RIDES   Paramount, 1968
ANZIO   Columbia, 1968, Italian
5 CARD STUD   Paramount, 1968
SECRET CEREMONY   Universal, 1968, British-U.S.
YOUNG BILLY YOUNG   United Artists, 1969
THE GOOD GUYS AND THE BAD GUYS   Warner Bros., 1969
RYAN'S DAUGHTER   MGM, 1970, British
GOING HOME   MGM, 1971
THE WRATH OF GOD   MGM, 1972
THE FRIENDS OF EDDIE COYLE   Paramount, 1973
THE YAKUZA   Warner Bros., 1975
FAREWELL, MY LOVELY   Avco Embassy, 1975
MIDWAY   Universal, 1976
THE LAST TYCOON   Paramount, 1976
THE AMSTERDAM KILL   Columbia, 1978, U.S.-Hong Kong
MATILDA   American International, 1978
THE BIG SLEEP   United Artists, 1978, British
TIME AFTER TIME   Orion/Warner Bros., 1979
BREAKTHROUGH   *SERGEANT STEINER*   Maverick Pictures
   International, 1978, German
NIGHTKILL   Cine Artists, 1980
AGENCY   Taft International, 1981, Canadian
ONE SHOE MAKES IT MURDER (TF)   The Fellows-Keegan
   Company/Lorimar Productions, 1982
THAT CHAMPIONSHIP SEASON   Cannon, 1982
THE WINDS OF WAR (MS)   Paramount TV/Dan Curtis
   Productions, 1983
A KILLER IN THE FAMILY (TF)   Stan Marguilies Productions/
   Sunn Classic Pictures, 1983
THE AMBASSADOR   MGM/UA/Cannon, 1984
MARIA'S LOVERS   Cannon, 1984
THE HEARST AND DAVIES AFFAIR (TF)   ABC Circle Films, 1985
PROMISES TO KEEP (TF)   Sandra Harmon Productions/Green-
   Epstein Productions/Telepictures, 1985
THE HEARST AND DAVIES AFFAIR (TF)   ABC Circle Films, 1985
REUNION AT FAIRBOROUGH (CTF)   HBO Premiere Films/Alan
   Wagner Productions/Alan King Productions/Columbia TV, 1985
THOMPSON'S LAST RUN (TF)   Cypress Point Productions, 1986
MR. NORTH   Samuel Goldwyn Company, 1988
SCROOGED   Paramount, 1988
WAR AND REMEMBRANCE (MS)   Dan Curtis Productions/ABC
   Circle Films, 1988-89
CAPE FEAR   Universal, 1991
TOMBSTONE   Buena Vista, 1993

KIM MIYORI
Agent: Susan Smith & Associates - Beverly Hills, 213/852-4777

WHEN THE BOUGH BREAKS (TF)   Taft Entertainment TV/TDF
   Productions, 1986
LOVERBOY   TriStar, 1989
THE BIG PICTURE   Columbia, 1989

ISAAC MIZRAHI
FOR LOVE OR MONEY   Universal, 1993

ALAINA MOBLEY
A SIMPLE TWIST OF FATE   Buena Vista, 1994

TONY MOCKUS, SR.
BACKDRAFT   Universal, 1991

MATTHEW MODINE
b. March 22, 1959 - Loma Linda, California
Agent: William Morris Agency - Beverly Hills, 310/274-7451

BABY IT'S YOU   Paramount, 1983
PRIVATE SCHOOL   Universal, 1983
THE HOTEL NEW HAMPSHIRE   Orion, 1984
BIRDY   TriStar, 1984
VISION QUEST   Warner Bros., 1985
MRS. SOFFEL   MGM/UA, 1984
FULL METAL JACKET   Warner Bros., 1987, British
ORPHANS   Lorimar, 1987
MARRIED TO THE MOB   Orion, 1988
GROSS ANATOMY   Buena Vista, 1989
PACIFIC HEIGHTS   20th Century Fox, 1990
MEMPHIS BELLE   Warner Bros., 1990
WIND   TriStar, 1992, U.S.-Japanese
AND THE BAND PLAYED ON (CTF)   HBO Pictures/Spelling
   Entertainment, 1993
SHORT CUTS   Fine Line Features/New Line Cinema, 1993
THE BROWNING VERSION   Paramount, 1994, British
FLUKE   MGM/UA, 1994
JACOB (CTF)   Turner Network TV, 1994
BYE BYE LOVE   20th Century Fox, 1995
MARTIN EDEN   Odyssey Entertainment, 1995
CUTTHROAT ISLAND   MGM/UA, 1995

DONALD MOFFAT
b. December 26, 1930 - Plymouth, England

ELEANOR AND FRANKLIN: THE WHITE HOUSE YEARS (TF)
   Talent Associates, 1977
THE RIGHT STUFF   The Ladd Company/Warner Bros., 1983
ALAMO BAY   TriStar, 1985
THE BEST OF TIMES   Universal, 1986
THE UNBEARABLE LIGHTNESS OF BEING   Orion, 1988
FAR NORTH   Alive Films, 1988
MUSIC BOX   TriStar, 1989
CLEAR AND PRESENT DANGER   Paramount, 1994
TRAPPED IN PARADISE   20th Century Fox, 1994

D.W. MOFFETT
Agent: William Morris Agency - Beverly Hills, 310/274-7451

BLACK WIDOW   20th Century Fox, 1987
LISA   MGM/UA, 1990

JACKIE MOFOKENG
A GOOD MAN IN AFRICA   Gramercy Pictures, 1994

ZAKES MOKAE
A DRY WHITE SEASON   MGM/UA, 1989
DAD   Universal, 1989
GROSS ANATOMY   Buena Vista, 1989
A RAGE IN HARLEM   Miramax Films, 1991, U.S.-British

ALFRED MOLINA
PRICK UP YOUR EARS   Samuel Goldwyn Company, 1987, British
NOT WITHOUT MY DAUGHTER   MGM-Pathe, 1991

WHITE FANG 2: MYTH OF THE WHITE WOLF   Buena Vista, 1994
THE PEREZ FAMILY   Samuel Goldwyn Company, 1994
HIDEAWAY   TriStar, 1995
SPECIES   MGM/UA, 1995

ANGELA MOLINA
CAMORRA   *UN COMPLICATO INTRIGO DI DONNE,
VICOLI E DELITTI*   Cannon, 1986, Italian

RICHARD MOLL
b. January 13, 1943 - Pasadena, California
Agent: Abrams Artists & Associates - Los Angeles, 310/859-0625

HOUSE   New World, 1986
THINK BIG   MPCA, 1990

DAN MONAHAN
FROM THE HIP   DEG, 1987

STEVE MONARQUE
Agent: J. Michael Bloom & Associates - Los Angeles, 310/275-6800

UNDER THE BOARDWALK   New World, 1989

CORBETT MONICA
BROADWAY DANNY ROSE   Orion, 1984

LAWRENCE MONOSON
Agent: Harris & Goldberg - Los Angeles, 310/553-5200

THE LAST AMERICAN VIRGIN   Cannon, 1982
FRIDAY THE 13TH - THE FINAL CHAPTER   Paramount, 1984
MASK   Universal, 1985
GABY - A TRUE STORY   TriStar, 1987, U.S.-Mexican
DANGEROUS LOVE   Motion Picture Corporation of America, 1988

RICARDO MONTALBAN
b. November 25, 1920 - Mexico City, Mexico

EL VERDUGO DE SEVILLA   1942, Mexican
SANTA   1943, Mexican
LA FUGA   1943, Mexican
LA HORA DE LA VERDAD   1944, Mexican
FIESTA   1947
ON AN ISLAND WITH YOU   1948
THE KISSING BANDIT   1948
NEPTUNE'S DAUGHTER   MGM, 1949
BORDER INCIDENT   1949
BATTLEGROUND   1949
MYSTERY STREET   1950
RIGHT CROSS   1950
TWO WEEKS WITH LOVE   MGM, 1950
ACROSS THE WIDE MISSOURI   MGM, 1951
MARK OF THE RENEGADE   1951
MY MAN AND I   1952
SOMBRERO   1953
LATIN LOVERS   MGM, 1953
THE SARACEN BLADE   1954
A LIFE IN THE BALANCE   1955
THREE FOR JAMIE DAWN   1956
SAYONARA   Warner Bros., 1957
LET NO MAN WRITE MY EPITAPH   1960
ADVENTURES OF A YOUNG MAN   1962
LOVE IS A BALL   1963
CHEYENNE AUTUMN   1964
THE MONEY TRAP   1966
MADAME X   1966
THE SINGING NUN   MGM, 1966
SOL MADRID   1968
BLUE   1968
SWEET CHARITY   Universal, 1969
THE DESERTER   LA SPINA DORSALE DEL DIAVOLO
1971, Spanish
ESCAPE FROM THE PLANET OF THE APES
20th Century-Fox, 1971
CONQUEST OF THE PLANET OF THE APES   20th Century-Fox, 1972
DESPERATE MISSION (TF)   20th Century-Fox TV, 1971
THE TRAIN ROBBERS   Warner Bros., 1973

JOE PANTHER   Artists Creation & Associates, 1976
HOW THE WEST WAS WON (MS)   MGM TV, 1977
FANTASY ISLAND (TF)   Spelling-Goldberg Productions, 1977
STAR TREK II: THE WRATH OF KHAN   Paramount, 1982
CANNONBALL RUN II   Warner Bros., 1984
THE NAKED GUN: FROM THE FILES OF POLICE SQUAD!
Paramount, 1988

BELINDA J. MONTGOMERY
THE TODD KILLINGS   National General, 1971
WOMEN IN CHAINS (TF)   Paramount TV, 1972
LETTERS FROM THREE LOVERS (TF)   Spelling-Goldberg
Productions, 1973
THE OTHER SIDE OF THE MOUNTAIN   Universal, 1975
BREAKING POINT   20th Century-Fox, 1976, Canadian
BLACKOUT   1978, Canadian-French
THE OTHER SIDE OF THE MOUNTAIN PART 2   Universal, 1978

ELIZABETH MONTGOMERY
b. April 15, 1933 - Hollywood, California

THE COURT-MARTIAL OF BILLY MITCHELL   Warner Bros., 1955
WHO'S BEEN SLEEPING IN MY BED?   Paramount, 1963
JOHNNY COOL   United Artists, 1963
THE VICTIM (TF)   1972
A CASE OF RAPE (TF)   Universal TV, 1974
THE LEGEND OF LIZZIE BORDEN (TF)   Paramount TV, 1975
DARK VICTORY (TF)   Universal TV, 1976
A KILLING AFFAIR   *BEHIND THE BADGE* (TF)   Columbia TV, 1977
THE AWAKENING LAND (MS)   Beven-Kuhn-Sagal Productions/
Warner Bros. TV, 1978
JENNIFER: A WOMAN'S STORY (TF)   Marble Arch Productions, 1979
ACT OF VIOLENCE (TF)   Emmett G. Lavery, Jr. Productions/
Paramount TV, 1979
BELLE STARR (TF)   Entheos Unlimited Productions/Hanna-Barbera
Productions, 1980
WHEN THE CIRCUS CAME TO TOWN (TF)   Entheos Unlimited
Productions/Meteor Films, 1981
THE RULES OF MARRIAGE (TF)   Entheos Unlimited Productions/
Brownstone Productions/20th Century-Fox TV, 1982
SECOND SIGHT: A LOVE STORY (TF)   Entheos Unlimited
Productions/J.T.C. Enterprises, 1984
FACE TO FACE (TF)   Qintex Productions, 1990

LEE MONTGOMERY
BURNT OFFERINGS   United Artists, 1976
GIRLS JUST WANT TO HAVE FUN   New World, 1985
THE MIDNIGHT HOUR (TF)   ABC Circle Films, 1985

LYNNE MOODY
THE ATLANTA CHILD MURDERS (MS)   Mann-Rafshoon
Productions/Finnegan Associates, 1985
LAST LIGHT (CTF)   Showtime Networks, Inc./Stillwater Prods., 1993

RON MOODY
(Ronald Moodnick)
b. January 8, 1924 - London, England

MAKE MINE MINK   1959, British
FOLLOW A STAR   1959, British
FIVE GOLDEN HOURS   1960, British
A PAIR OF BRIEFS   1962, British
SUMMER HOLIDAY   1963, British
THE MOUSE ON THE MOON   1963, British
LADIES WHO DO   1963, British
MURDER MOST FOUL   1964, British
EVERY DAY'S A HOLIDAY   1964, British
SAN FERRY ANN   1965, British
THE SANDWICH MAN   1965, British
OLIVER!   ★   Columbia, 1968, British
DAVID COPPERFIELD   1970, U.S.-British
THE TWELVE CHAIRS   UMC, 1970
FLIGHT OF THE DOVES   197
LEGEND OF THE WEREWOLF   1974
DOGPOUND SHUFFLE   Paramount, 1975, Canadian
DOMINIQUE   1978
THE WORD (TF)   1979
THE SPACEMAN AND KING ARTHUR   1979
ARTHUR   Orion, 1981
DIAL M FOR MURDER (TF)   1981
WRONG IS RIGHT   Columbia, 1982

DEMI MOORE
(Demi Guynes)
b. November 11, 1963 - Roswell, New Mexico
Agent: CAA - Beverly Hills, 310/288-4545

CHOICES   1981, Canadian
YOUNG DOCTORS IN LOVE   20th Century-Fox, 1982
PARASITE   Embassy, 1982
BLAME IT ON RIO   20th Century Fox, 1984
NO SMALL AFFAIR   Columbia, 1984
ST. ELMO'S FIRE   Columbia, 1985
ONE CRAZY SUMMER   Warner Bros., 1986
ABOUT LAST NIGHT...   TriStar, 1986
WISDOM   20th Century Fox, 1986
THE SEVENTH SIGN   TriStar, 1988
WE'RE NO ANGELS   Paramount, 1989
GHOST   Paramount, 1990
NOTHING BUT TROUBLE   Warner Bros., 1991
MORTAL THOUGHTS   Columbia, 1991
THE BUTCHER'S WIFE   Paramount, 1991
A FEW GOOD MEN   Columbia, 1992
INDECENT PROPOSAL   Paramount, 1993
DISCLOSURE   Warner Bros., 1994
A SCARLET LETTER   Buena Vista, 1995
GASLIGHT ADDITION   New Line Cinema, 1995
THE HUNCHBACK OF NOTRE DAME (AF)   Buena Vista, 1996 (voice)

DUDLEY MOORE
b. April 19, 1935 - Dagenham, England
Agent: ICM - Beverly Hills, 310/550-4000
Contact: PRS - London, 011-44-1-580-5544

THE WRONG BOX   Columbia, 1966, British
BEDAZZLED   20th Century-Fox, 1967, British
30 IS A DANGEROUS AGE, CYNTHIA   Columbia, 1968, British
THE BED SITTING ROOM   United Artists, 1969, British
THOSE DARING YOUNG MEN IN THEIR JAUNTY JALOPIES
   MONTE CARLO OR BUST   Paramount, 1969,
   British-Italian-French
ALICE'S ADVENTURES IN WONDERLAND   1972
THE HOUND OF THE BASKERVILLES   Atlantic Releasing
   Corporation, 1977, British
FOUL PLAY   Paramount, 1978
10   Orion/Warner Bros., 1979
WHOLLY MOSES   Columbia, 1980
DEREK AND CLIVE GET THE HORN (PF)   Peter Cook
   Productions, 1981, British
ARTHUR ★   Orion, 1981
SIX WEEKS   Universal, 1982
LOVESICK   The Ladd Company/Warner Bros., 1983
ROMANTIC COMEDY   MGM/UA, 1983
MICKI & MAUDE   Columbia, 1984
BEST DEFENSE   Paramount, 1984
UNFAITHFULLY YOURS   20th Century Fox, 1984
SANTA CLAUS: THE MOVIE   TriStar, 1985, U.S.-British
LIKE FATHER LIKE SON   TriStar, 1987
ARTHUR 2 ON THE ROCKS   Warner Bros., 1988
THE ADVENTURES OF MILO AND OTIS   Columbia,
   1989, Japanese (voice)
CRAZY PEOPLE   Paramount, 1990
BLAME IT ON THE BELLBOY   Buena Vista, 1992, British
PARALLEL LIVES (CTF)   Showtime Entertainment, 1994

JULIANNE MOORE
Agent: CAA - Beverly Hills, 310/288-4545

MONEY, POWER, MURDER (TF)   Skids Productions/CBS
   Entertainment, 1989
LOVECRAFT (CTF)   HBO Pictures/Pacific Western
   Productions, 1991
THE HAND THAT ROCKS THE CRADLE   Buena Vista, 1992
THE GUN IN BETTY LOU'S HANDBAG   Buena Vista, 1992
BODY OF EVIDENCE   MGM/UA, 1993
BENNY & JOON   MGM/UA, 1993
THE FUGITIVE   Warner Bros., 1993
SHORT CUTS   Fine Line Features/New Line Cinema, 1993
ROOMMATES   Buena Vista, 1994
NINE MONTHS   20th Century Fox, 1995

KEVIN MOORE
PRIME SUSPECT   Columbia, 1991

MARY TYLER MOORE
b. December 29, 1937 - Brooklyn, New York
Agent: William Morris Agency - Beverly Hills, 310/274-7451

X-15   United Artists, 1961
THOROUGHLY MODERN MILLIE   Universal, 1967
DON'T JUST STAND THERE!   Universal, 1968
WHAT'S SO BAD ABOUT FEELING GOOD?   Universal, 1968
CHANGE OF HABIT   Universal, 1969
RUN A CROOKED MILE (TF)   Universal TV, 1969
FIRST, YOU CRY (TF)   MTM Enterprises, 1978
ORDINARY PEOPLE ★   Paramount, 1980
SIX WEEKS   Universal, 1982
HEARTSOUNDS (TF)   Embassy TV, 1984
FINNEGAN BEGIN AGAIN (CTF)   HBO Premiere Films/Zenith
   Productions/Jennie & Co. Film Productions, 1985, U.S.-British
JUST BETWEEN FRIENDS   Orion, 1986
LINCOLN (MS)   Chris-Rose Productions/Finnegan-Pinchuk
   Company, 1988
THANKSGIVING DAY (TF)   Zacharias-Buhai Productions/NBC
   Productions, 1990
SOLEN BABIES (CTF)   ABC Video Enterprises/Sander-Moses
   Productions, 1993

MATTHEW MOORE
THE FLY II   20th Century Fox, 1989

MELBA MOORE
b. October 29, 1945 - New York, New York

HAIR   United Artists, 1979
ALL DOGS GO TO HEAVEN (AF)   MGM/UA, 1989 (voice)
DEF BY TEMPTATION   Troma, 1990

ROB MOORE
NATIONAL LAMPOON'S SENIOR TRIP   New Line Cinema, 1995

ROGER MOORE
b. October 14, 1928 - London, England

THE FULLER BRUSH MAN   1948
AS YOUNG AS YOU FEEL   1951
THE LAST TIME I SAW PARIS   MGM, 1954
INTERRUPTED MELODY   MGM, 1955
THE KING'S THIEF   MGM, 1955
DIANE   MGM, 1956
THE MIRACLE   Warner Bros., 1959
THE SINS OF RACHEL CADE   Warner Bros., 1961
GOLD OF THE SEVEN SAINTS   Warner Bros., 1961
RAPE OF THE SABINES   *IL RATTO DELLE SABINE*   1962, Italian
CROSSPLOT   United Artists, 1969, British
THE MAN WHO HAUNTED HIMSELF   Levitt-Pickman, 1970, British
LIVE AND LET DIE   United Artists, 1973, British
GOLD   Allied Artists, 1974, British
THE MAN WITH THE GOLDEN GUN   United Artists, 1974, British
THAT LUCKY TOUCH   Allied Artists, 1975, British
SHOUT AT THE DEVIL   American International, 1976, British
STREET PEOPLE   1976, U.S.-Italian
SHERLOCK HOLMES IN NEW YORK (TF)   20th Century-Fox TV, 1976
THE SPY WHO LOVED ME   United Artists, 1977, British-U.S.
THE WILD GEESE   Allied Artists, 1979, British
MOONRAKER   United Artists, 1979, British-French
ESCAPE TO ATHENA   AFD, 1979, British
ffolkes   *NORTH SEA HIJACK*   Universal, 1980, British
THE SEA WOLVES   Paramount, 1981, British
SUNDAY LOVERS   MGM/United Artists, 1981,
   U.S.-British-Italian-French
THE CANNONBALL RUN   20th Century-Fox, 1981
FOR YOUR EYES ONLY   United Artists, 1981, British
OCTOPUSSY   MGM/UA, 1983, British
THE NAKED FACE   Cannon, 1985
A VIEW TO A KILL   MGM/UA, 1985, British
BED AND BREAKFAST   Hemdale, 1992
THE QUEST   Universal, 1995

SHEILA MOORE
BYE BYE BLUES   Circle Releasing Corporation, 1990, Canadian

STEPHEN MOORE
CLOCKWISE   Universal, 1986, British
PRIME SUSPECT   Columbia, 1991

BILL MOORES
NORTH   Columbia, 1994
WILD BILL   MGM/UA, 1995

ESAI MORALES
Agent: William Morris Agency - Beverly Hills, 310/274-7451

FORTY-DEUCE   Island Alive, 1982
BAD BOYS   Universal/AFD, 1983
RAINY DAY FRIENDS   Powerdance Films, 1985
ON WINGS OF EAGLES (MS)   Edgar J. Scherick Productions/Taft
   Entertainment TV, 1986
LA BAMBA   Columbia, 1987
BLOODHOUNDS OF BROADWAY   Columbia, 1989
ULTRAVIOLET   Concorde, 1992
IN THE ARMY NOW   Buena Vista, 1994
RAPA NUI   Warner Bros., 1994
MI FAMILIA   New Line Cinema, 1995

SANTOS MORALES
CANNERY ROW   MGM/United Artists, 1982
WISDOM   20th Century Fox, 1986

RICK MORANIS
b. April 18, 1953 - Toronto, Ontario
Agent: CAA - Beverly Hills, 310/288-4545

GHOSTBUSTERS   Columbia, 1984
STREETS OF FIRE   Universal, 1984
CLUB PARADISE   Warner Bros., 1986
LITTLE SHOP OF HORRORS   The Geffen Company/
   Warner Bros., 1986
SPACEBALLS   MGM/UA, 1987
GHOSTBUSTERS II   Columbia, 1989
HONEY, I SHRUNK THE KIDS   Buena Vista, 1989
PARENTHOOD   Universal, 1989
MY BLUE HEAVEN   Warner Bros., 1990
L.A. STORY   TriStar, 1991
HONEY, I BLEW UP THE KID   Buena Vista, 1992
SPLITTING HEIRS   Universal, 1993, British-U.S.
THE FLINTSTONES   Universal, 1994
LITTLE GIANTS   Warner Bros., 1994

JEANNE MOREAU
Agent: William Morris Agency - Beverly Hills, 310/274-7451

MAP OF THE HUMAN HEART   Miramax Films, 1993,
   British-French-New Zealand

RITA MORENO
(Rosita Dolores Alverio)
b. December 11, 1931 - Humacao, Puerto Rico

A MEDAL FOR BENNY   Paramount, 1945
SO YOUNG, SO BAD   1950
THE TOAST OF NEW ORLEANS   MGM, 1950
PAGAN LOVE SONG   MGM, 1950
SINGIN' IN THE RAIN   MGM, 1952
THE RING   United Artists, 1952
LATIN LOVERS   MGM, 1953
FORT VENGEANCE   Allied Artists, 1953
JIVARO   1954
THE YELLOW TOMAHAWK   United Artists, 1954
GARDEN OF EVIL   20th Century-Fox, 1954
UNTAMED   20th Century-Fox, 1955
SEVEN CITIES OF GOLD   1955
THE LIEUTENANT WORE SKIRTS   20th Century-Fox, 1956
THE KING AND I   20th Century-Fox, 1956

THE VAGABOND KING   Paramount, 1956
THE DEERSLAYER   20th Century-Fox, 1957
THIS REBEL BREED   Warner Bros., 1960
WEST SIDE STORY ✪✪   United Artists, 1961
SUMMER AND SMOKE   Paramount, 1961
CRY OF BATTLE   Allied Artists, 1963
THE NIGHT OF THE FOLLOWING DAY   Universal, 1969
POPI   United Artists, 1969
CARNAL KNOWLEDGE   Avco Embassy, 1971
THE RITZ   Warner Bros., 1976
THE BOSS' SON   Circle Associates, 1978
HAPPY BIRTHDAY, GEMINI   United Artists, 1980
THE FOUR SEASONS   Universal, 1981
EVITA PERON (TF)   Hartwest Productions/Zephyr Productions, 1981
I LIKE IT LIKE THAT   Columbia, 1994

JEFFREY DEAN MORGAN
ANGELS IN RED   Concorde, 1991

HARRY MORGAN
(Harry Bratsburg/Henry Morgan)
b. April 10, 1915 - Detroit, Michigan

TO THE SHORES OF TRIPOLI   20th Century-Fox, 1942
CRASH DIVE   20th Century-Fox, 1943
THE OX BOW INCIDENT   20th Century-Fox, 1943
HAPPY LAND   20th Century-Fox, 1943
WING AND A PRAYER   20th Century-Fox, 1944
A BELL FOR ADANO   20th Century-Fox, 1945
STATE FAIR   20th Century-Fox, 1945
DRAGONWYCK   20th Century-Fox, 1946
FROM THIS DAY FORWARD   RKO Radio, 1946
THE GANGSTER   1947
ALL MY SONS   Universal, 1948
THE BIG CLOCK   Paramount, 1948
YELLOW SKY   20th Century-Fox, 1948
MOONRISE   Republic, 1948
MADAME BOVARY   MGM, 1949
THE SAXON SHARM   1949
DARK CITY   Paramount, 1950
THE WELL   1951
THE BLUE VEIL   RKO Radio, 1951
BEND OF THE RIVER   Universal, 1952
MY SIX CONVICTS   Universal, 1952
HIGH NOON   United Artists, 1952
WHAT PRICE GLORY?   20th Century-Fox, 1952
THUNDER BAY   Universal, 1953
TORCH SONG   MGM, 1953
THE GLENN MILLER STORY   Universal, 1954
NOT AS A STRANGER   United Artists, 1955
THE TEAHOUSE OF THE AUGUST MOON   MGM, 1956
INHERIT THE WIND   United Artists, 1960
HOW THE WEST WAS WON   MGM/Cinerama, 1963
JOHN GOLDFARB, PLEASE COME HOME   20th Century-Fox, 1965
WHAT DID YOU DO IN THE WAR, DADDY?   United Artists, 1966
FRANKIE AND JOHNNY   1966
THE FLIM-FLAM MAN   20th Century-Fox, 1967
SUPPORT YOUR LOCAL SHERIFF   United Artists, 1969
VIVA MAX!   Commonwealth United, 1969
THE BAREFOOT EXECUTIVE   Buena Vista, 1971
SUPPORT YOUR LOCAL GUNFIGHTER   United Artists, 1971
SCANDALOUS JOHN   Buena Vista, 1971
SNOWBALL EXPRESS   Buena Vista, 1972
JEREMIAH JOHNSON   Warner Bros., 1972
CHARLEY AND THE ANGEL   Buena Vista, 1973
THE APPLE DUMPLING GANG   Buena Vista, 1975
THE SHOOTIST   Paramount, 1976
THE CAT FROM OUTER SPACE   Buena Vista, 1978
THE APPLE DUMPLING GANG RIDES AGAIN   Buena Vista, 1979
DRAGNET   Universal, 1987
THE INCIDENT (TF)   Qintex Entertainment, 1990
AGAINST HER WILL: AN INCIDENT IN BALTIMORE (TF)
   RHI Entertainment, 1992
INCIDENT IN A SMALL TOWN (TF)   RHI Entertainment, 1994

RHIAN MORGAN
AUGUST   Granada Films, 1995

R I C H A R D   M O R G A N
FAREWELL TO THE KING   Orion, 1989

M A J A   M O R G E N S T E R N
NOSTRADAMUS   Orion Classics, 1994, British

C A T H Y   M O R I A R T Y
Agent: ICM - Beverly Hills, 310/550-4000

RAGING BULL ✪   United Artists, 1980
NEIGHBORS   Columbia, 1981
WHITE OF THE EYE   Palisades Entertainment, 1987, British
KINDERGARTEN COP   Universal, 1990
SOAPDISH   Paramount, 1991
THE MAMBO KINGS   Warner Bros., 1992
THE GUN IN BETTY LOU'S HANDBAG   Buena Vista, 1992
MATINEE   Universal, 1993
ANOTHER STAKEOUT   Buena Vista, 1993
CORRINA, CORRINA   New Line Cinema, 1994
PONTIAC MOON   Paramount, 1994
CASPER   Universal, 1995
FORGET PARIS   Columbia, 1995

M I C H A E L   M O R I A R T Y
b. April 5, 1941 - Detroit, Michigan

MY OLD MAN'S PLACE   *GLORY BOY*   Cinerama Releasing
   Corporation, 1972
HICKEY AND BOGGS   United Artists, 1972
BANG THE DRUM SLOWLY   Paramount, 1973
THE LAST DETAIL   Columbia, 1973
REPORT TO THE COMMISSIONER   United Artists, 1975
HOLOCAUST (MS)   Titus Productions, 1978
WHO'LL STOP THE RAIN   *DOG SOLDIERS*   United Artists, 1978
TOO FAR TO GO (TF)   Sea Cliff Productions, 1979
Q   *THE WINGED SERPENT*   United Film Distribution, 1982
ODD BIRDS   1985
PALE RIDER   Warner Bros., 1985
THE STUFF   New World, 1985
TROLL   Empire Pictures, 1986
THE HANOI HILTON   Cannon, 1987

N O R I Y U K I   " P A T "   M O R I T A
(Pat Morita)
b. June 28, 1932 - Isleton, California

THOROUGHLY MODERN MILLIE   Universal, 1967
MIDWAY   Universal, 1976
WHEN TIME RAN OUT   Warner Bros., 1980
SLAPSTICK OF ANOTHER KIND   *SLAPSTICK*   Entertainment
   Releasing Corporation/International Film Marketing, 1983
THE KARATE KID ✪   Columbia, 1984
THE LAS VEGAS STRIP WARS (TF)   George Englund
   Productions, 1984
THE KARATE KID PART II   Columbia, 1986
BABES IN TOYLAND (TF)   Orion TV/Finnegan-Pinchuk
   Company, 1986
CAPTIVE HEARTS   MGM/UA, 1987, Canadian
COLLISION COURSE   DEG, 1988
THE KARATE KID PART III   Columbia, 1989
ICE RUNNER   Triumph Releasing Corporation, 1991
LENA'S HOLIDAY   Crown International, 1991
HONEYMOON IN VEGAS   Columbia, 1992
EVEN COWGIRLS GET THE BLUES   Fine Line Features/
   New Line Cinema, 1994
THE NEXT KARATE KID   Columbia, 1994

R O B E R T   M O R L E Y
b. May 25, 1908 - Semley , England

MARIE ANTOINETTE ✪   MGM, 1938
MAJOR BARBARA   1941, British
THE YOUNG MR. PITT   1942, British
SOMEWHERE IN FRANCE   *THE FOREMAN WENT TO FRANCE*
   1942, British
A YANK IN LONDON   *I LIVE IN GROSVENOR SQARE*
   1945, British

THE SMALL BACK ROOM   1949, British
OUTCAST OF THE ISLANDS   1951, British
THE AFRICAN QUEEN   1952, British-U.S.
CURTAIN UP   1952, British
MELBA   1953
GILBERT AND SULLIVAN   *THE STORY OF GILBERT
   AND SULLIVAN*   1953, British
THE FINAL TEST   1953, British
BEAT THE DEVIL   1954, British-Italian
BEAU BRUMMEL   1954, U.S.-British
QUENTIN DURWARD   *THE ADVENTURES OF QUENTIN
   DURWARD*   1955, British
AROUND THE WORLD IN 80 DAYS   1956
LAW AND DISORDER   1958, British
THE JOURNEY   1959
THE DOCTOR'S DILEMMA   1959, British
LIBEL   1959, British
THE BATTLE OF THE SEXES   1959, British
OSCAR WILDE   1960, British
THE STORY OF JOSEPH AND HIS BRETHREN   1960, Italian
THE YOUNG ONES   1961
THE ROAD TO HONG KONG   1962, U.S.-British
THE BOYS   Gala, 1962, British
NINE HOURS TO RAMA   1963, U.S.-British
MURDER AT THE GALLOP   1963, British
THE OLD DARK HOUSE   1963, U.S.-British
TAKE HER—SHE'S MINE   1963
TOPKAPI   1964
OF HUMAN BONDAGE   1964, British
AGENT 8 3/4   *HOT ENOUGH FOR JUNE*   1964, British
THOSE MAGNIFICENT MEN IN THEIR FLYING MACHINES
   1965, British
A STUDY IN TERROR   1965, British-West German
LIFE AT THE TOP   1965, British
GENGHIS KHAN   1965, U.S.-British-West German
THE LOVED ONE   1965
THE ALPHABET MURDERS   1966, British
HOTEL PARADISO   1966, U.S.-British
TENDER SCOUNDREL   *TENDRE VOYOU*   1966, French-Italian
WAY...WAY OUT   1966
WOMAN TIMES SEVEN   *SEPT FOIS FEMME*   1967,
   French-Italian-U.S.
THE TRYGON FACTOR   1967, British
HOT MILLIONS   1968, British
SINFUL DAVEY   1969, British
CROMWELL   1970, British
SONG OF NORWAY   1970
WHEN EIGHT BELLS TOLL   1971, British
THEATRE OF BLOOD   1973, British
THE BLUE BIRD   1976, U.S.-Soviet
WHO IS KILLING THE GREAT CHEFS OF EUROPE?
   Warner Bros., 1978
SCAVENGER HUNT   20th Century-Fox, 1979
THE HUMAN FACTOR   United Artists, 1979, British
OH, HEAVENLY DOG!   20th Century-Fox, 1980
THE GREAT MUPPET CAPER   Universal/AFD, 1981, British
HIGH ROAD TO CHINA   Warner Bros., 1983, U.S.-Yugoslavian

M I K E   M O R O F F
CAGE   New Century/Vista, 1989
ANGEL TOWN   Taurus Entertainment, 1990

H A V I L A N D   M O R R I S
GREMLINS 2 THE NEW BATCH   Warner Bros., 1990

H O W A R D   M O R R I S
b. September 4, 1925 - New York, New York

END OF THE LINE   Orion Classics, 1988
LIFE STINKS   MGM-Pathe, 1991

J A N E   M O R R I S
FRANKIE & JOHNNY   Paramount, 1991

K E N N Y   M O R R I S O N
THE NEVERENDING STORY II: THE NEXT CHAPTER
   Warner Bros., 1991

TOMMY MORRISON
ROCKY V   MGM/UA, 1990

ROB MORROW
b. September 21, 1962 - New Rochelle, New York
Agent: William Morris Agency - Beverly Hills, 310/274-7451

QUIZ SHOW   Buena Vista, 1994

DAVID MORSE
Agent: Yvette Bikoff Agency - West Hollywood, 213/655-6123

INSIDE MOVES   AFD, 1980
SIX AGAINST THE ROCK (TF)   Schaefer-Karpf-Epstein
  Productions/Gaylord Production Company, 1987
DESPERATE HOURS   MGM/UA, 1990
THE INDIAN RUNNER   MGM-Pathe, 1991
THE GOOD SON   20th Century Fox, 1993
THE CROSSING GUARD   Miramax Films, 1994

ROBERT MORSE
b. May 18, 1931 - Newton, Massachusetts

WILD PALMS (MS)   Ixtlan Corporation/Greengrass
  Productions, Inc., 1993

GLENN MORSHOWER
84 CHARLIE MOPIC   New Century/Vista, 1989

VIGGO MORTENSEN
BOILING POINT   Warner Bros., 1993
CRIMSON TIDE   Buena Vista, 1995

GARY MORTON
POSTCARDS FROM THE EDGE   Columbia, 1990

JOE MORTON
b. October 18, 1947 - New York, New York
Agent: Judy Schoen & Associates - Los Angeles, 213/962-1950

THE BROTHER FROM ANOTHER PLANET   Cinecom, 1984
CROSSROADS   Columbia, 1986
TERRORIST ON TRIAL: THE UNITED STATES VS.
  SALIM AJAMI (TF)   George Englund Productions/Robert
  Papazian Productions, 1988
HOWARD BEACH: MAKING THE CASE FOR MURDER (TF)
  Patchett-Kaufmann Entertainment, 1989
CITY OF HOPE   Samuel Goldwyn Company, 1991
OF MICE AND MEN   MGM-Pathe Communications, 1992
SPEED   20th Century Fox, 1994

DAVID MOSCOW
b. November 14, 1974 - Manhattan, New York
Agent: J. Michael Bloom & Associates - Los Angeles, 310/275-6800

BIG   20th Century Fox, 1988
I'LL BE HOME FOR CHRISTMAS (TF)   NBC Productions, 1988
NEWSIES   Buena Vista, 1992

BILL MOSELEY
PINK CADILLAC   Warner Bros., 1989
WHITE FANG   Buena Vista, 1991
HONEY, I BLEW UP THE KID   Buena Vista, 1992

RICK MOSES
PLEASURES (TF)   Catalina Production Group/Columbia TV, 1986

WILLIAM R. MOSES
b. September 17, 1959 - Los Angeles, California
Agent: Gersh Agency - Beverly Hills, 310/274-6611

MYSTIC PIZZA   Samuel Goldwyn Company, 1988
PERRY MASON: THE CASE OF THE LETHAL LESSON (TF)
  The Fred Silverman Company/Dean Hargrove Productions/
  Viacom, 1989

PERRY MASON: THE CASE OF THE MUSICAL MURDER (TF)
  The Fred Silverman Company/Dean Hargrove Productions/
  Viacom, 1989
PERRY MASON: THE CASE OF THE ALL-STAR ASSASSIN (TF)
  The Fred Silverman Company/Dean Hargrove Productions/
  Viacom, 1989
ROCK HUDSON (TF)   The Konigsberg-Sanitsky Company, 1990
PERRY MASON: THE CASE OF THE PARISIAN PARADOX (TF)
  The Fred Silverman Company/Dean Hargrove Productions/
  Viacom, 1990
PERRY MASON: THE CASE OF THE POISONED PEN (TF)
  The Fred Silverman Company/Dean Hargrove Productions/
  Viacom, 1990
PERRY MASON: THE CASE OF THE DESPERATE
  DECEPTION (TF)   The Fred Silverman Company/Dean
  Hargrove Productions/Viacom, 1990
TRIAL BY JURY   Warner Bros., 1994

SERGIO MOSETTI
BIG   20th Century Fox, 1988

ROGER E. MOSLEY
Agent: Craig Agency - Los Angeles, 213/655-0236

THE NEW CENTURIONS   Columbia, 1972
HIT MAN   MGM, 1972
TERMINAL ISLAND   Dimension, 1973
LEADBELLY   Paramount, 1976
THE GREATEST   Columbia, 1977
SEMI-TOUGH   United Artists, 1977
ROOTS: THE NEXT GENERATION (MS)   Wolper Productions, 1978
THE JERICHO MILE (TF)   ABC Circle Films, 1979
UNLAWFUL ENTRY   20th Century Fox, 1992

JOSH MOSTEL
Agent: William Morris Agency - Beverly Hills, 310/274-7451

JESUS CHRIST SUPERSTAR   Universal, 1973
STAR 80   The Ladd Company/Warner Bros., 1983
ALMOST YOU   TLC Films/20th Century Fox, 1984
COMPROMISING POSITIONS   Paramount, 1985
RADIO DAYS   Orion, 1987
MATEWAN   Cinecom, 1987
WALL STREET   20th Century Fox, 1987
ANIMAL BEHAVIOR   Millimeter Films, 1989
CITY SLICKERS   Columbia, 1991
THE CHASE   20th Century Fox, 1994
CITY SLICKERS II: THE LEGEND OF CURLY'S GOLD   Columbia, 1994

COLLIN MOTHUPI
CHEETAH   Buena Vista, 1989

BRADLEY MOTT
THE ACCIDENTAL TOURIST   Warner Bros., 1988

PEGGY MOUNT
THE PRINCESS AND THE GOBLIN (AF)   Hemdale, 1994 (voice)

MAUREEN MUELLER
ENID IS SLEEPING   Vestron, 1990

ARMIN MUELLER-STAHL
Agent: Paul Kohner, Inc. - Los Angeles, 310/550-1060

MUSIC BOX   TriStar, 1989
AVALON   TriStar, 1990
NIGHT ON EARTH   Fine Line Features/New Line Cinema, 1991,
  U.S.-Japanese-French-German-British
THE POWER OF ONE   Warner Bros., 1992
THE HOUSE OF THE SPIRITS   Miramax Films, 1993, U.S.-German
A PYROMANIAC'S LOVE STORY   Buena Vista, 1995

MUHAMMAD ALI
(See Muhammad ALI)

DIANA MULDAUR
b. August 19, 1938 - New York, New York
Agent: The Artists Group - Los Angeles, 310/552-1100

THE SWIMMER   Columbia, 1968
NUMBER ONE   United Artists, 1969
THE LAWYER   Paramount, 1970
ONE MORE TRAIN TO ROB   Universal, 1971
THE OTHER   20th Century-Fox, 1972
McQ   Warner Bros., 1974
THE CHOSEN SURVIVORS   Columbia, 1974
CHARLIE'S ANGELS (TF)   Spelling-Goldberg Productions, 1976
PINE CANYON IS BURNING (TF)   Universal TV, 1977
BLACK BEAUTY (TF)   Universal TV, 1978
TO KILL A COP (TF)   David Gerber Company/Columbia TV, 1978
MANEATERS ARE LOOSE (TF)   Mona Productions/Finnegan
   Associates, 1978
THE WORD (MS)   Charles Fries Prods./Stonehenge Productions, 1978

KATE MULGREW
b. April 29, 1955 - Dubuque, Iowa

THE WORD (MS)   Charles Fries Prods./Stonehenge Productions, 1978
A TIME FOR MIRACLES (TF)   ABC Circle Films, 1980
LOVESPELL   Clar Productions, 1981, British
THE MANIONS OF AMERICA (MS)   Roger Gimbel Productions/
   EMI TV/Argonaut Films Ltd., 1981
A STRANGER IS WATCHING   MGM/United Artists, 1982
REMO WILLIAMS: THE ADVENTURE BEGINS   Orion, 1985
ROSES ARE FOR THE RICH (TF)   Phoenix Entertainment
   Group, 1987
THROW MOMMA FROM THE TRAIN   Orion, 1987

MATT MULHERN
EXTREME PREJUDICE   TriStar, 1987
BILOXI BLUES   Universal, 1988

CHRIS MULKEY
GHOST IN THE MACHINE   20th Century Fox, 1993

MARTIN MULL
b. August 18, 1943 - Chicago, New York
Agent: William Morris Agency - Beverly Hills, 310/274-7451

FM   Universal, 1978
MY BODYGUARD   20th Century-Fox, 1980
SERIAL   Paramount, 1980
MR. MOM   20th Century-Fox, 1983
CLUE   Paramount, 1985
RENTED LIPS   Cineworld, 1988
THINK BIG   MPCA, 1990
FAR OUT MAN   New Line Cinema, 1990
MR. WRITE   Shapiro-Glickenhaus Entertainment, 1994

LARRY MULLEN, JR.
U2: RATTLE AND HUM (FD)   Paramount, 1988

ROLF MULLER
CYBORG   Cannon, 1989

RICHARD MULLIGAN
b. November 13, 1932 - New York, New York
Agent: ICM - Beverly Hills, 310/550-4000

THE GROUP   United Artists, 1966
THE UNDEFEATED   20th Century-Fox, 1969
LITTLE BIG MAN   National General, 1970
THE BIG BUS   Paramount, 1976
SCAVENGER HUNT   20th Century-Fox, 1979
S.O.B.   Paramount, 1981
TRAIL OF THE PINK PANTHER   MGM/UA, 1982
MICKI & MAUDE   Columbia, 1984
TEACHERS   MGM/UA, 1984
THE HEAVENLY KID   Orion, 1985
A FINE MESS   Columbia, 1986
BABES IN TOYLAND (TF)   Orion TV/Finnegan-Pinchuk Co., 1986
LINCOLN (MS)   Chris-Rose Productions/Finnegan-Pinchuk
   Company, 1988

TERRY DAVID MULLIGAN
McCABE AND MRS. MILLER   Warner Bros., 1971
CHRISTINA   International Amusements, 1974
THE HAUNTING PASSION (TF)   BSR Productions/ITC, 1983
JANE DOE (TF)   ITC, 1983
THE BOY WHO COULD FLY   20th Century Fox, 1986
FIREFIGHTER (TF)   Forest Hills Productions/Embassy TV, 1986
THE GIRL WHO SPELLED FREEDOM (TF)   Knopf-Simons
   Productions/ITV Productions/Walt Disney Productions, 1986
SWORN TO SILENCE (TF)   Daniel H. Blatt-Robert Singer
   Productions, 1987
A STRANGER WAITS (TF)   Bruce Lansbury Productions/Edgar
   Lansbury Productions/Lewisfilm Ltd./New Century TV Prods., 1987
LOVE, MARY (TF)   CBS Entertainment, 1985
THE ACCUSED   Paramount, 1988

DEBORAH MULLOWNEY
CELLAR DWELLAR   Empire Pictures, 1988

DERMOT MULRONEY
Agent: CAA - Beverly Hills, 310/288-4545

DADDY (TF)   Robert Greenwald Productions, 1987
YOUNG GUNS   20th Century Fox, 1988
STAYING TOGETHER   Hemdale, 1989
SURVIVAL QUEST   MGM/UA, 1990
LONGTIME COMPANION   Samuel Goldwyn Company, 1990
CAREER OPPORTUNITIES   Universal, 1991
BRIGHT ANGEL   Hemdale, 1991
WHERE THE DAY TAKES YOU   New Line Cinema, 1992
POINT OF NO RETURN   Warner Bros., 1993
FAMILY PICTURES (TF)   Alexander, Enright & Associates/Hearst
   Entertainment, 1993
THE THING CALLED LOVE   Paramount, 1993
SILENT TONGUE   Trimark Pictures, 1994, U.S.-French
BAD GIRLS   20th Century Fox, 1994
THERE GOES MY BABY   Orion, 1994
HOW TO MAKE AN AMERICAN QUILT   Universal, 1995

KIERNAN MULRONEY
Agent: Bresler, Kelly & Kipperman - Encino, 818/905-1155

CAREER OPPORTUNITES   Universal, 1991

MEG MUNDY
FATAL ATTRACTION   Paramount, 1987

BOBBY MURCER
THE SCOUT   20th Century Fox, 1994

ALEC MURPHY
BEAUTY AND THE BEAST (AF)   Buena Vista, 1991 (voice)

CHARLES Q. MURPHY
HARLEM NIGHTS   Paramount, 1989

CHARLIE MURPHY
VAMPIRE IN BROOKLYN   Paramount, 1995

EDDIE MURPHY
b. April 3, 1961 - Brooklyn, New York
Agent: CAA - Beverly Hills, 310/288-4545

48 HRS.   Paramount, 1982
TRADING PLACES   Paramount, 1983
BEVERLY HILLS COP   Paramount, 1984
BEST DEFENSE   Paramount, 1984
THE GOLDEN CHILD   Paramount, 1986
BEVERLY HILLS COP II   Paramount, 1987
EDDIE MURPHY RAW   Paramount, 1987
COMING TO AMERICA   Paramount, 1988
HARLEM NIGHTS   Paramount, 1989 (also directed)
ANOTHER 48 HRS.   Paramount, 1990
BOOMERANG   Paramount, 1992
THE DISTINGUISHED GENTLEMAN   Buena Vista, 1992

BEVERLY HILLS COP III   Paramount, 1994
THE NUTTY PROFESSOR   Universal, 1995
VAMPIRE IN BROOKLYN   Paramount, 1995

MICHAEL MURPHY
b. May 5, 1938 - Los Angeles, California
Agent: ICM - Beverly Hills, 310/550-4000

COUNTDOWN   Warner Bros., 1968
THE ARRANGEMENT   Warner Bros., 1969
BREWSTER McCLOUD   MGM, 1970
M*A*S*H   20th Century-Fox, 1970
WHAT'S UP, DOC?   Warner Bros., 1972
THE THIEF WHO CAME TO DINNER   Warner Bros., 1973
NASHVILLE   Paramount, 1975
THE FRONT   Columbia, 1976
AN UNMARRIED WOMAN   20th Century-Fox, 1978
MANHATTAN   United Artists, 1979
THE YEAR OF LIVING DANGEROUSLY   MGM/UA,
   1983, Australian
CLOAK AND DAGGER   Universal, 1984
SALVADOR   Hemdale, 1986
SHOCKER   Universal, 1989
BATMAN RETURNS   Warner Bros., 1992
CLEAN SLATE   MGM/UA, 1994

ROSEMARY MURPHY
THAT NIGHT   Universal, 1957
THE YOUNG DOCTORS   United Artists, 1961
TO KILL A MOCKINGBIRD   Universal, 1962
ANY WEDNESDAY   Warner Bros., 1966
BEN   Cinerama Releasing Corporation, 1972
YOU'LL LIKE MY MOTHER   Universal, 1972
WALKING TALL   Cinerama Releasing Corporation, 1973
40 CARATS   Columbia, 1973
ACE ELI AND RODGER OF THE SKIES   20th Century-Fox, 1973
JULIA   20th Century-Fox, 1977
ELEANOR AND FRANKLIN (TF)   Talent Associates, 1976
ELEANOR AND FRANKLIN: THE WHITE HOUSE YEARS (TF)
   Talent Associates, 1977
SEPTEMBER   Orion, 1987

BILL MURRAY
b. September 21, 1950 - Chicago, Illinois
Agent: CAA - Beverly Hills, 310/288-4545

MEATBALLS   Paramount, 1979, Canadian
MR. MIKE'S MONDO VIDEO   New Line Cinema, 1979
SHAME OF THE JUNGLE (AF)   1979 (voice)
WHERE THE BUFFALO ROAM   Universal, 1980
CADDYSHACK   Orion/Warner Bros., 1980
LOOSE SHOES   COMING ATTRACTIONS   1980
STRIPES   Columbia, 1981
TOOTSIE   Columbia, 1982
NOTHING LASTS FOREVER   MGM/UA Classics, 1984
GHOSTBUSTERS   Columbia, 1984
THE RAZOR'S EDGE   Columbia, 1984
LITTLE SHOP OF HORRORS   The Geffen Company/
   Warner Bros., 1986
SCROOGED   Paramount, 1988
GHOSTBUSTERS II   Columbia, 1989
QUICK CHANGE   Warner Bros., 1990 (also co-directed)
WHAT ABOUT BOB?   Buena Vista, 1991
GROUNDHOG DAY   Columbia, 1993
MAD DOG AND GLORY   Universal, 1993
ED WOOD   Buena Vista, 1994

BRIAN DOYLE-MURRAY
(See Brian DOYLE-Murray)

DON MURRAY
b. July 31, 1929 - Hollywood, California
Agent: David Shapira & Associates - Sherman Oaks, 818/906-0322

BUS STOP ✪   20th Century-Fox, 1956
THE BACHELOR PARTY   United Artists, 1957
A HATFUL OF RAIN   20th Century-Fox, 1957

FROM HELL TO TEXAS   20th Century-Fox, 1958
THESE THOUSAND HILLS   20th Century-Fox, 1959
SHAKE HANDS WITH THE DEVIL   United Artists, 1959, British
ONE FOOT IN HELL   20th Century-Fox, 1960
THE HOODLUM PRIEST   United Artists, 1961
ADVISE AND CONSENT   Columbia, 1962
TUNNEL 28   ESCAPE FROM EAST BERLIN   MGM,
   1962, U.S.-West German
ONE MAN'S WAY   1964
BABY, THE RAIN MUST FALL   Columbia, 1965
KID RODELO   1966, U.S.-Spanish
THE PLAINSMAN   Universal, 1966
SWEET LOVE, BITTER   IT WON'T RUB OFF, BABY
   Peppercorn-Wormser, 1967
THE VIKING QUEEN   American International, 1967, British
THE BORGIA STICK (TF)   Universal TV, 1967
TALE OF THE COCK   CHILDISH THINGS   Filmworld,
   1969 (filmed in 1966)
DAUGHTER OF THE MIND (TF)   20th Century-Fox TV, 1969
THE INTRUDERS (TF)   Universal TV, 1970
HAPPY BIRTHDAY, WANDA JUNE   Columbia, 1971
CONQUEST OF THE PLANET OF THE APES
   20th Century-Fox, 1972
COTTER   1973
A GIRL NAMED SOONER (TF)   Frederick Brogger Associates/
   20th Century-Fox TV, 1974
THE SEX SYMBOL (FD)   Screen Gems/Columbia, 1974
THE GIRL ON THE LATE, LATE SHOW (TF)   Screen Gems/
   Columbia TV, 1974
DEADLY HERO   Avco Embassy, 1976
RAINBOW (TF)   Ten-Four Productions, 1978
CRISIS IN MID-AIR (TF)   CBS Entertainment, 1979
ENDLESS LOVE   Universal, 1981
A TOUCH OF SCANDAL (TF)   Doris M. Keating Productions/
   Columbia TV, 1984
PEGGY SUE GOT MARRIED   TriStar, 1986
SCORPION   Crown International, 1986
RADIOACTIVE DREAMS   DEG, 1986
SOMETHING IN COMMON (TF)   New World TV/Freyda Rothstein
   Productions/Littke-Grossbart Productions, 1986
MADE IN HEAVEN   Lorimar, 1987
STILLWATCH (TF)   Zev Braun Pictures/Interscope Communications/
   Potomac Productions, 1987
MISTRESS (TF)   Jaffe-Lansing Productions/Republic Pictures, 1987
A BRAND NEW LIFE: THE HONEYMOON (TF)
   NBC Productions, 1989
GHOSTS CAN'T DO IT   Triumph Releasing Corporation, 1990

JOHN MURRAY
SCROOGED   Paramount, 1988

PETER MURRAY
THE PRINCESS AND THE GOBLIN (AF)   Hemdale, 1994 (voice)

TONY MUSANTE
b. June 30, 1936 - Bridgeport, Connecticut

ONCE A THIEF   MGM, 1965, U.S.-French
THE INCIDENT   20th Century-Fox, 1967
THE DETECTIVE   20th Century-Fox, 1968
THE MERCENARY   IL MERCENARIO   United Artists,
   1969, Italian-Spanish
ONE NIGHT AT DINNER   METTI UNA SERA A CENA   1969, Italian
THE BIRD WITH THE CRYSTAL PLUMAGE   L'UCCELLO DALLE
   PIUME DI CRISTALLO   UMC, 1970, Italian-West German
THE ANONYMOUS VENETIAN   ANONIMO VENEZIANO
   1971, Italian
THE LAST RUN   MGM, 1971
THE GRISSOM GANG   Cinerama Releasing Corporation, 1971
EUTANASIA DI UN AMORE   1978, Italian
REARVIEW MIRROR (TF)   Simon-Asher Entertainment/Sunn
   Classic Pictures, 1984
NUTCRACKER: MONEY, MADNESS AND MURDER (MS)
   Green Arrow Productions/Warner Bros. TV, 1987

ELLEN MUTH
DOLORES CLAIBORNE   Columbia, 1994

ORNELLA MUTI
CASANOVA (TF)   Konigsberg-Sanitsky Company/Reteitalia,
   1987, U.S.-Italian
CHRONICLE OF A DEATH FORETOLD   Island Pictures, 1988
OSCAR   Buena Vista, 1991
ONCE UPON A CRIME   MGM-Pathe, 1992, U.S.-Italian
ESPECIALLY ON SUNDAY   Miramax Films, 1993

LOU MYERS
COBB   Warner Bros., 1994

MIKE MYERS
b. 1962 - Toronto, Ontario
Agent: UTA - Beverly Hills, 310/273-6700

WAYNE'S WORLD   Paramount, 1992
SO I MARRIED AN AXE MURDERER   TriStar, 1993
WAYNE'S WORLD 2   Paramount, 1993

N

JIM NABORS
b. June 12, 1933 - Sylacauga, Alabama

THE BEST LITTLE WHOREHOUSE IN TEXAS   Universal, 1982
STROKER ACE   Universal, 1983
CANNONBALL RUN II   Warner Bros., 1984
RETURN TO MAYBERRY (TF)   Strathmore Productions/Viacom
   Productions, 1986

MICHAEL NADER
LADY MOBSTER (TF)   Danjul Films/von Zerneck Productions, 1988
THE GREAT ESCAPE II: THE UNTOLD STORY (MS)
   Michael Jaffe Films/Spectacor Films, 1988
NICK KNIGHT (TF)   Barry Weitz Films/Robirdle Pictures/
   New World TV, 1989
JACKIE COLLINS' LUCKY CHANCES (MS)   NBC Productions, 1991
FORCED EXPOSURE   Concorde, 1991

JIMMY NAIL
MORONS FROM OUTER SPACE   Universal, 1985, British
CRUSOE   Island Pictures, 1988, U.S.-British
DIAMOND'S EDGE   Kings Road Entertainment, 1990

KATHY NAJIMY
Agent: ICM - Beverly Hills, 310/550-4000

TOPSY AND BUNKER
OTHER PEOPLE'S MONEY   Warner Bros., 1991
THE HARD WAY   Universal, 1991
THE FISHER KING   TriStar, 1991
SOAPDISH   Paramount, 1991
THIS IS MY LIFE   20th Century Fox, 1992
SISTER ACT   Buena Vista, 1992
HOCUS POCUS   Buena Vista, 1993
SISTER ACT 2: BACK IN THE HABIT   Buena Vista, 1993
IT'S PAT   Buena Vista, 1994
JEFFREY   1995
CATS DON'T DANCE (AF)   Turner Pictures, 1996 (voice)

SCOTT NAKAGAWA
ALOHA SUMMER   *HANAUMA BAY*   Spectrafilm, 1988

DANIEL NALBACH
THE GIG   Castle Hill Productions, 1985

JOE NAMATH
NORWOOD   Paramount, 1970
C.C. AND COMPANY   Avco Embassy, 1970
AVALANCHE EXPRESS   20th Century-Fox, 1979
MARRIAGE IS ALIVE AND WELL (TF)   Lorimar Productions, 1980
CHATTANOOGA CHOO CHOO   April Fools, 1984

JACK NANCE
ERASERHEAD   Libra, 1978
DUNE   Universal, 1984
GHOULIES   Empire Pictures, 1985
BLUE VELVET   DEG, 1986
BARFLY   Cannon, 1987

CHARLES NAPIER
CITIZENS BAND   *HANDLE WITH CARE*   Paramount, 1977
LAST EMBRACE   United Artists, 1979
RAMBO: FIRST BLOOD PART II   TriStar, 1985
THE NIGHT STALKER   PSO, 1987
DEEP SPACE   Trans World Entertainment, 1987
INSTANT JUSTICE   *MARINE ISSUE*   Warner Bros., 1987, Gibraltar
KIDNAPPED   Virgin Vision, 1987
HIT LIST   New Line Cinema, 1989
CENTER OF THE WEB   AIP, 1992
McNELLY'S RANGERS   Warner Bros., 1995

CHRIS NASH
MISCHIEF   20th Century Fox, 1985
SILENT WITNESS (TF)   Robert Greenwald Productions, 1985
MODERN GIRLS   Atlantic Releasing Corporation, 1986
SATISFACTION   20th Century Fox, 1988

LARRY NASH
DYING YOUNG   20th Century Fox, 1991

DAVID NAUGHTON
MIDNIGHT MADNESS   Buena Vista, 1980
AN AMERICAN WEREWOLF IN LONDON   Universal, 1981
GETTING PHYSICAL (TF)   CBS Entertainment, 1984
HOT DOG...THE MOVIE   MGM/UA, 1984
NOT FOR PUBLICATION   Samuel Goldwyn Company,
   1984, U.S.-British
THE BOY IN BLUE   20th Century-Fox, 1986, Canadian
SEPARATE VACATIONS   RSL Entertainment, 1986, Canadian
KIDNAPPED   Virgin Vision, 1987
GODDESS OF LOVE (TF)   Phil Margo Enterprises/New World TV/
   Phoenix Entertainment Group, 1988

JAMES NAUGHTON
b. July 6, 1946 - Middletown, Connecticut
Agent: ICM - Beverly Hills, 310/550-4000

THE PAPER CHASE   20th Century-Fox, 1973
THE BUNKER (TF)   Time-Life Productions/SFP France/Antenne-2,
   1981, U.S.-French
A STRANGER IS WATCHING   MGM/United Artists, 1982
SIN OF INNOCENCE (TF)   Renee Valente Productions/Jeremac
   Productions/20th Century Fox TV, 1986
THE GLASS MENAGERIE   Cineplex Odeon, 1987
NECESSITY (TF)   Barry-Enright Productions/Alexander
   Productions, 1988

JOHN NAVIN
THE TOUGHEST MAN IN THE WORLD (TF)   Guber-Peters
   Productions/Centerpoint Productions, 1984

THEMBA NDABA
A GOOD MAN IN AFRICA   Gramercy Pictures, 1994

BILLIE NEAL
DOWN BY LAW   Island Pictures, 1986
MORTAL THOUGHTS   Columbia, 1991
THE GUN IN BETTY LOU'S HANDBAG   Buena Vista, 1992

DONALD NEAL
THE ACCIDENTAL TOURIST   Warner Bros., 1988

PATRICIA NEAL
b. January 20, 1926 - Packard, Kentucky

JOHN LOVES MARY   Warner Bros., 1949
THE FOUNTAINHEAD   Warner Bros., 1949
IT'S A GREAT FEELING   Warner Bros., 1949
THE HASTY HEART   Warner Bros., 1950, U.S.-British
BRIGHT LEAF   Warner Bros., 1950
THREE SECRETS   Warner Bros., 1950
THE BREAKING POINT   Warner Bros., 1950
OPERATION PACIFIC   1951
RATON PASS   Warner Bros., 1951
THE DAY THE EARTH STOOD STILL   20th Century-Fox, 1951
WEEKEND WITH FATHER   Universal, 1952
DIPLOMATIC COURIER   20th Century-Fox, 1952
SOMETHING FOR THE BIRDS   MGM, 1952
WASHINGTON STORY   MGM, 1952
LA TUA DONNA   1954, Italian
STRANGER FROM VENUS   1954, British
A FACE IN THE CROWD   Warner Bros., 1957
BREAKFAST AT TIFFANY'S   Paramount, 1961
HUD ★★   Paramount, 1963
PSYCHE 59   Royal Films International, 1964, British
IN HARM'S WAY   Paramount, 1965
THE SUBJECT WAS ROSES ★   MGM, 1968
THE NIGHT DIGGER   THE ROAD BUILDER   MGM, 1971, British
THE HOMECOMING (TF)   Lorimar Productions, 1971
BAXTER   National General, 1973, British
HAPPY MOTHER'S DAY—LOVE, GEORGE
   RUN, STRANGER, RUN   Cinema 5, 1973
THINGS IN THEIR SEASON (TF)   Tomorrow Entertainment, 1974
ERIC (TF)   Lorimar Productions, 1975
TAIL GUNNER JOE (TF)   Universal TV, 1977
THE BASTARD (TF)   Universal TV, 1978
NIDO DE VIUDAS   1978, Spanish
THE PASSAGE   United Artists, 1979, British
ALL QUIET ON THE WESTERN FRONT (TF)   Norman Rosemont
   Productions/Marble Arch Productions, 1979
GHOST STORY   Universal, 1981
GLITTER (TF)   Aaron Spelling Productions, 1984
LOVE LEADS THE WAY (TF)   Hawkins-Permut Productions, 1984
AN UNREMARKABLE LIFE   Continental Film Group, 1989
CAROLINE? (TF)   Barry & Enright Productions, 1990

LESLIE NEALE
HONEY, I BLEW UP THE KID   Buena Vista, 1992

KEVIN NEALON
b. November 18, 1953 - Bridgeport, Connecticut

ALL I WANT FOR CHRISTMAS   Paramount, 1991

HOLLY NEAR
DOGFIGHT   Warner Bros., 1991

TED NEELEY
JESUS CHRIST SUPERSTAR   Universal, 1973
HARD COUNTRY   Universal/AFD, 1981

LIAM NEESON
(William John Neeson)
b. June 7, 1952
Agent: CAA - Beverly Hills, 310/288-4545

EXCALIBUR   Orion/Warner Bros., 1981, British-Irish
KRULL   Columbia, 1983, U.S.-British
THE BOUNTY   Orion, 1984, British
LAMB   Limehouse/Flickers/Channel Four, 1985, British
THE MISSION   Warner Bros., 1986, British
DUET FOR ONE   Cannon, 1986
A PRAYER FOR THE DYING   Samuel Goldwyn Company,
   1987, British
SWORN TO SILENCE (TF)   Daniel H. Blatt/Robert Singer
   Productions, 1987

SUSPECT   TriStar, 1987
SATISFACTION   20th Century Fox, 1988
THE DEAD POOL   Warner Bros., 1988
THE GOOD MOTHER   Buena Vista, 1988
HIGH SPIRITS   TriStar, 1988, British
NEXT OF KIN   Warner Bros., 1989
DARKMAN   Universal, 1990
THE BIG MAN   Miramax Films, 1990, British
THE OTHER WOMAN   Columbia, 1991
UNDER SUSPICION   Columbia, 1991, British
SHINING THROUGH   20th Century Fox, 1992
RUBY CAIRO   20th Century Fox, 1992
HUSBANDS AND WIVES   TriStar, 1992
LEAP OF FAITH   Paramount, 1992
ETHAN FROME   Miramax Films, 1993
SCHINDLER'S LIST ★   Universal, 1993
NELL   20th Century Fox, 1994
ROB ROY   MGM/UA, 1995
BEFORE AND AFTER   Buena Vista, 1995

TAYLOR NEGRON
YOUNG DOCTORS IN LOVE   20th Century-Fox, 1982
BAD MEDICINE   20th Century Fox, 1985
RIVER'S EDGE   Hemdale, 1987
NOTHING BUT TROUBLE   Warner Bros., 1991
THE LAST BOY SCOUT   The Geffen Company/Warner Bros., 1991

DAVID NEIDORF
HOOSIERS   Orion, 1986
PLATOON   Orion, 1986

HILDEGARD NEIL
THE MAN WHO HAUNTED HIMSELF   Levitt-Pickman, 1970, British
ENGLAND MADE ME   Cine Globe, 1973, British
ANTONY AND CLEOPATRA   Rank, 1973, British-Spanish-Swedish
A TOUCH OF CLASS   Avco Embassy, 1973, British
THE LEGACY   Universal, 1979
THE MIRROR CRACK'D   AFD, 1980, British

SAM NEILL
b. 1948 - New Zealand
Agent: ICM - Beverly Hills, 310/550-4000

SLEEPING DOGS   Aardvark Films, 1977, New Zealand
ATTACK FORCE Z   John McCallum Productions/Central Motion
   Picture Corporation, 1980, Australian-Taiwanese
MY BRILLIANT CAREER   Analysis, 1980, Australian
THE FINAL CONFLICT   20th Century-Fox, 1981
FROM A FAR COUNTRY: POPE JOHN PAUL II (TF)   Trans World
   Film/ITC/RAI/Film Polski, 1981, British-Italian-Polish
ENIGMA   Embassy, 1982, British-French
IVANHOE (TF)   1982
THE BLOOD OF OTHERS   LE SANG DES AUTRES (CMS)   HBO
   Premiere Films/ICC/Filmax Productions, 1984, Canadian-French
PLENTY   20th Century Fox, 1985, British
KANE AND ABEL (MS)   Schrekinger Communications/
   Embassy TV, 1985
THE GOOD WIFE   THE UMBRELLA WOMAN   Atlantic Releasing
   Corporation, 1986, Australian
AMERIKA (MS)   ABC Circle Films, 1987
A CRY IN THE DARK   Warner Bros., 1988, Australian
LEAP OF FAITH (TF)   Hart, Thomas & Berlin Productions, 1988
DEAD CALM   Warner Bros., 1989, Australian
THE HUNT FOR RED OCTOBER   Paramount, 1990
FEVER (CTF)   HBO Pictures/Saban-Scherick Productions, 1991
UNTIL THE END OF THE WORLD   Warner Bros., 1991,
   West German-French
MEMOIRS OF AN INVISIBLE MAN   Warner Bros., 1992
FAMILY PICTURES (TF)   Alexander, Enright & Associates/Hearst
   Entertainment, 1993
JURASSIC PARK   Universal, 1993
THE PIANO   Miramax Films, 1993, New Zealand-French
SIRENS   Miramax Films, 1993, Australian-British-German
THE JUNGLE BOOK   Buena Vista, 1994
RESTORATION   Miramax Films, 1994
VICTORY   Miramax Films, 1995

KATE NELLIGAN
b. March 16, 1951 - London, Ontario

THE ROMANTIC ENGLISHWOMAN   New World, 1975, British
THE COUNT OF MONTE CRISTO (TF)   Norman Rosemont
   Productions/ITC, 1975, U.S.-British
DRACULA   Universal, 1979
EYE OF THE NEEDLE   United Artists, 1981, U.S.-British
WITHOUT A TRACE   20th Century Fox, 1983
ELENI   Warner Bros., 1985
KOJAK: THE PRICE OF JUSTICE (TF)   MCA/Universal TV, 1987
LOVE AND HATE: A MARRIAGE MADE IN HELL (MS)
   CBC, 1990, Canadian
FRANKIE & JOHNNY   Paramount, 1991
THE PRINCE OF TIDES ✪   Columbia, 1991
SHADOWS AND FOG   Orion, 1992
FATAL INSTINCT   MGM/UA, 1993
WOLF   Columbia, 1994
HOW TO MAKE AN AMERICAN QUILT   Universal, 1995

CRAIG T. NELSON
b. April 4, 1946 - Spokane, Washington
Agent: ICM - Beverly Hills, 310/550-4000

...AND JUSTICE FOR ALL   Columbia, 1979
DIARY OF A TEENAGE HITCHHIKER (TF)   The Shpetner
   Company, 1979
THE FORMULA   MGM/United Artists, 1980
STIR CRAZY   Columbia, 1980
WHERE THE BUFFALO ROAM   Universal, 1980
PRIVATE BENJAMIN   Warner Bros., 1980
THE CHICAGO STORY (TF)   Eric Bercovici Productions/
   MGM TV, 1981
POLTERGEIST   MGM/UA, 1982
MAN, WOMAN AND CHILD   Paramount, 1983
THE OSTERMAN WEEKEND   20th Century-Fox, 1983
ALL THE RIGHT MOVES   20th Century-Fox, 1983
SILKWOOD   20th Century-Fox, 1983
THE KILLING FIELDS   Warner Bros., 1984, British
CALL TO GLORY (TF)   Tisch-Avnet Productions/
   Paramount TV, 1984
CALL TO GLORY: JFK (TF)   Tisch-Avnet Productions/
   Paramount TV, 1985
ALEX: THE LIFE OF A CHILD (TF)   Mandy Productions, 1986
POLTERGEIST II: THE OTHER SIDE   MGM/UA, 1986
THE TED KENNEDY, JR. STORY (TF)   Entertainment
   Partners, 1986
ACTION JACKSON   Lorimar, 1988
TROOP BEVERLY HILLS   Columbia, 1989
TURNER & HOOCH   Buena Vista, 1989
ME AND HIM   Columbia, 1989
DRUG WARS: THE CAMARENA STORY (MS)   ZZY, Inc.
   Productions/World International Network, 1990
THE JOSEPHINE BAKER STORY (CTF)   HBO Pictures/RHI
   Entertainment/Anglia TV/John Kemeny Productions, 1991

DAVID NELSON
CRY-BABY   Universal, 1990

ED NELSON
b. December 21, 1928 - New Orleans, Louisiana

ATTACK OF THE CRAB MONSTERS   Allied Artists, 1957
SHINING STAR   *THAT'S THE WAY OF THE WORLD*
   United Artists, 1975
MIDWAY   Universal, 1976
ACAPULCO GOLD   R.C. Riddell, 1978
FOR THE LOVE OF BENJI   Mulberry Square, 1977
THE RETURN OF FRANK CANNON (TF)   QM Productions, 1980
PEYTON PLACE: THE NEXT GENERATION (TF)
   Michael Filerman Productions/20th Century Fox TV, 1985
POLICE ACADEMY 3: BACK IN TRAINING   Warner Bros., 1986

JOHN ALLEN NELSON
HUNK   Crown International, 1987
QUANTUM LEAP (TF)   Belisarius Productions/Universal TV, 1989
ANGEL OF DESIRE   Trimark, 1994

JUDD NELSON
b. November 28, 1959 - Portland, Maine

MAKING THE GRADE   MGM/UA-Cannon, 1984
THE BREAKFAST CLUB   Universal, 1985
FANDANGO   Warner Bros., 1985
ST. ELMO'S FIRE   Columbia, 1985
BLUE CITY   Paramount, 1986
THE TRANSFORMERS (AF)   DEG, 1986 (voice)
BILLIONAIRE BOYS CLUB (MS)   Donald March/Gross-Weston
   Productions/ITC Productions, 1987
FROM THE HIP   DEG, 1987
RELENTLESS   New Line Cinema, 1989
HIROSHIMA: OUT OF THE ASHES (TF)   Robert Greenwald
   Productions, 1990
FAR OUT MAN   New Line Cinema, 1990
NEW JACK CITY   Warner Bros., 1991

RUTH NELSON
THE HAUNTING PASSION (TF)   BSR Productions/ITC, 1983
AWAKENINGS   Columbia, 1990

SEAN NELSON
FRESH   Miramax Films, 1994

TRACY NELSON
b. October 25, 1963 - Santa Monica, California

GLITTER (TF)   Aaron Spelling Productions, 1984
PLEASURES (TF)   Catalina Production Group/Columbia TV, 1986
DOWN AND OUT IN BEVERLY HILLS   Buena Vista, 1986
KATE'S SECRET (TF)   Andrea Baynes Productions/
   Columbia TV, 1986
TONIGHT'S THE NIGHT (TF)   Indieprod Productions/Phoenix
   Entertainment Group, 1987
IF IT'S TUESDAY, IT STILL MUST BE BELGIUM (TF)
   Eisenstock & Mintz Productions, 1987
FATAL CONFESSION: A FATHER DOWLING MYSTERY (TF)
   The Fred Silverman Company/Strathmore Productions/
   Viacom, 1987
FATHER DOWLING MYSTERIES: THE MISSING BODY
   MYSTERY (TF)   The Fred Silverman Company/Dean
   Hargrove Productions, 1989

WILLIE NELSON
b. April 30, 1933 - Abbott, Texas

THE ELECTRIC HORSEMAN   Columbia, 1979
HONEYSUCKLE ROSE   Warner Bros., 1980
THIEF   United Artists, 1981
BARBAROSA   Universal/AFD, 1982, West German
COMING OUT OF THE ICE (TF)   The Konigsberg Company, 1982
SONGWRITER   TriStar, 1984
THE LAST DAYS OF FRANK AND JESSE JAMES (TF)
   Joseph Cates Productions, 1986
STAGECOACH (TF)   Raymond Katz Productions/Heritage
   Entertainment, 1986
RED-HEADED STRANGER   Alive Films, 1987
AMAZONS   Concorde, 1987, U.S.-Argentine
ONCE UPON A TEXAS TRAIN (TF)   Robert Papazian Productions/
   Brigade Productions/Rastar, 1988
WHERE THE HELL'S THAT GOLD?!!? (TF)   Willie Nelson Prods./
   Brigade Productions/Konigsberg-Sanitsky Company, 1988
PAIR OF ACES (TF)   Pedernales Films/Once Upon A Time
   Films, Ltd., 1990

CORIN NEMEC
(Corky Nemec)
Agent: ICM - Beverly Hills, 310/550-4000

TUCKER - THE MAN AND HIS DREAM   Paramount, 1988
I KNOW MY FIRST NAME IS STEVEN (MS)   Andrew Adelson
   Company/Lorimar TV, 1989
DROP ZONE   Paramount, 1994

FRANCO NERO
b. 1942 - Italy

WILD WILD PLANET *I CRIMINALI DELLA GELASSIA*
  MGM, 1966, Italian
THE TRAMPLERS Embassy, 1966, Italian
THE HIRED KILLER 1966
THE BRUTE AND THE BEAST 1966
THE BIBLE 20th Century-Fox, 1966, Italian
CAMELOT Warner Bros., 1967
THE DAY OF THE OWL 1968
A QUIET PLACE IN THE COUNTRY United Artists,
  1968, Italian-French
MAFIA *IL GIORNO DELLA CIVETTA* American International,
  1968, Italian
THE GIRL Mafilm Studio, 1968, Hungarian
DETECTIVE BELLI 1969
CONFESSIONS OF A POLICE CAPTAIN *CONFESSIONE DE
  UN COMMISSARIO* 1970, Italian
THE MERCENARY United Artists, 1970, Italian-Spanish
TRISTANA Maron Films Limited, 1970, Spanish-French-Italian
THE VIRGIN AND THE GYPSY Chevron, 1970, British
THE BATTLE OF NERETVA 1971,
  Yugoslavian-U.S.-West German-Italian
COMPANEROS *VAMOS A MATAR COMPAÑEROS* 1971,
  Spanish-Italian-West German
DROPOUT Medusa/Lion Film, 1972, Italian
POPE JOAN Columbia, 1972, British
IL MONACO 1972
LA VACANZA Lion Film, 1972, Italian
WHITE FANG 1972, Italian-Spanish-French
DELITTO MATTEOTI 1973
DEAF SMITH AND JOHNNY EARS *LOS AMIGOS*
  1973, Spanish-Italian
HIGH CRIME 1973, Italian
THE LAST FOUR DAYS *MUSSOLINI—ULTIMO ATTO* Group 1,
  1974, Italian
CORRUZIONE AL PALAZZO DI GIUSTIZIA 1974
CHALLENGE TO WHITE FANG 1975
LEGEND OF VALENTINO (TF) Spelling-Goldberg
  Productions, 1975
SCANDALO 1975, Italian
PERCHE SI UCCIDE UN MAGISTRATO 1975, Italian
MARCIA TRIONFALE 1976, Italian
DJANGO—IL GRANDE RITORNO 1977, Italian
AUTOSTOP 1977, Italian
FORCE 10 FROM NAVARONE American International, 1978, British
THE VISITOR 1979, Italian
THE MAN WITH BOGART'S FACE *SAM MARLOW, PRIVATE EYE*
  20th Century-Fox, 1980
THE SALAMANDER ITC, 1981, British-Italian-U.S.
ENTER THE NINJA Cannon, 1981
QUERELLE Triumph/Columbia, 1983, West German
THE LAST DAYS OF POMPEII (MS) David Gerber Company/
  Columbia TV/Centerpoint Films/RAI, 1984, U.S.-British-Italian
TEN DAYS THAT SHOOK THE WORLD 1984
GARIBALDI 1986
KAMIKAZE Gaumont, 1987, French
SIDNEY SHELDON'S WINDMILLS OF THE GODS *WINDMILLS OF
  THE GODS* (MS) Dove Productions/ITC Productions, 1988
DIE HARD 2 20th Century Fox, 1990

LOIS NETTLETON
A FACE IN THE CROWD Warner Bros., 1957
PERIOD OF ADJUSTMENT MGM, 1962
COME FLY WITH ME MGM, 1963
MAIL ORDER BRIDE MGM, 1964
VALLEY OF MYSTERY 1967
BAMBOO SAUCER *COLLISION COURSE* 1968
THE GOOD GUYS AND THE BAD GUYS Warner Bros., 1969
DIRTY DINGUS MAGEE MGM, 1970
PIGEONS *SIDELONG GLANCES OF A PIGEON KICKER*
  MGM, 1971
THE FORGOTTEN MAN (TF) Walter Grauman Productions, 1971
THE HONKERS 1972
ECHOES OF A SUMMER Cine Artists, 1976, U.S.-Canadian
FEAR ON TRIAL (TF) Alan Landsburg Productions, 1975
WASHINGTON: BEHIND CLOSED DOORS (MS)
  Paramount TV, 1977

CENTENNIAL (MS) Universal TV, 1978
TOURIST (TF) Castle Combe Productions/Paramount TV, 1980
SOGGY BOTTOM USA Cinemax Marketing & Distribution, 1981
DEADLY BLESSING United Artists, 1981
BUTTERFLY Analysis, 1981, U.S.-Canadian
THE BEST LITTLE WHOREHOUSE IN TEXAS Universal, 1982
BRASS (TF) Carnan Productions/Jaygee Productions/Orion TV, 1985
MANHUNT FOR CLAUDE DALLAS (TF) London Films, Inc., 1986

BEBE NEUWIRTH
b. December 31 - Princeton, New Jersey
Agent: ICM - Beverly Hills, 310/550-4000

WITHOUT HER CONSENT (TF) Raymond Katz Enterprises/
  Half Pint Productions/Carla Singer Productions, 1990
GREEN CARD Buena Vista, 1990
WILD PALMS (MS) Ixtlan Corporation/Greengrass
  Productions, Inc., 1993
MALICE Columbia, 1993

AARON NEVILLE
ZANDALEE Electric Pictures/ITC Entertainment Group, 1991

JOHN NEVILLE
OSCAR WILDE Films Around the World, 1960, British
BILLY BUDD Allied Artists, 1962, British
THE UNEARTHLY STRANGER American International, 1964, British
A STUDY IN TERROR Columbia, 1966, British
THE ADVENTURES OF GERARD United Artists, 1970,
  British-Italian-Swedish
THE ADVENTURES OF BARON MUNCHAUSEN Columbia, 1989
BABY'S DAY OUT 20th Century Fox, 1994
THE ROAD TO WELLVILLE Columbia, 1994

GEORGE NEWBERN
Agent: UTA - Beverly Hills, 310/273-6700

ADVENTURES IN BABYSITTING Buena Vista, 1987
PARAMEDICS Vestron, 1988
FATHER OF THE BRIDE Buena Vista, 1991

BOB NEWHART
b. September 5, 1931 - Oak Park, Illinois
Agent: William Morris Agency - Beverly Hills, 310/274-7451

HELL IS FOR HEROES Paramount, 1962
HOT MILLIONS MGM, 1968, British
ON A CLEAR DAY YOU CAN SEE FOREVER Paramount, 1970
CATCH-22 Paramount, 1970
COLD TURKEY United Artists, 1971
THURSDAY'S GAME (TF) ABC Circle Films, 1974
THE RESCUERS (AF) Buena Vista, 1977 (voice)
MARATHON (TF) Alan Landsburg Productions, 1980
FIRST FAMILY Warner Bros., 1980
LITTLE MISS MARKER Universal, 1980
THE RESCUERS DOWN UNDER (AF) Buena Vista, 1990 (voice)

DANIEL NEWMAN
ROBIN HOOD: PRINCE OF THIEVES Warner Bros., 1991

LARAINE NEWMAN
TUNNELVISION World Wide, 1976
AMERICAN HOT WAX Paramount, 1978
MR. MIKE'S MONDO VIDEO New Line Cinema, 1979
WHOLLY MOSES! Columbia, 1980
STARDUST MEMORIES United Artists, 1980 (uncredited)
THIS WIFE FOR HIRE (TF) The Belle Company/Guillaume-Margo
  Productions/Comworld Productions, 1985
PERFECT Columbia, 1985
INVADERS FROM MARS Cannon, 1986
PROBLEM CHILD 2 Universal, 1991
CONEHEADS Paramount, 1993
THE FLINTSTONES Universal, 1994

PAUL NEWMAN
b. January 26, 1925 - Cleveland, Ohio
Agent: CAA - Beverly Hills, 310/288-4545

THE SILVER CHALICE   Warner Bros., 1955
SOMEBODY UP THERE LIKES ME   MGM, 1956
THE RACK   MGM, 1956
THE HELEN MORGAN STORY   Warner Bros., 1957
UNTIL THEY SAIL   MGM, 1957
THE LONG HOT SUMMER   MGM, 1958
THE LEFT-HANDED GUN   Warner Bros., 1958
CAT ON A HOT TIN ROOF ★   MGM, 1958
RALLY ROUND THE FLAG, BOYS!   20th Century-Fox, 1958
THE YOUNG PHILADELPHIANS   Warner Bros., 1959
FROM THE TERRACE   20th Century-Fox, 1960
EXODUS   United Artists, 1960
THE HUSTLER ★   20th Century-Fox, 1961
PARIS BLUES   United Artists, 1961
SWEET BIRD OF YOUTH   MGM, 1962
HEMINGWAY'S ADVENTURES OF A YOUNG MAN
    20th Century-Fox, 1962
HUD ★   Paramount, 1963
A NEW KIND OF LOVE   Paramount, 1963
THE PRIZE   MGM, 1963
WHAT A WAY TO GO!   20th Century-Fox, 1964
THE OUTRAGE   MGM, 1964
LADY L   MGM, 1965, U.S.-Italian-French
HARPER   Warner Bros., 1966
TORN CURTAIN   Universal, 1966
HOMBRE   20th Century-Fox, 1967
COOL HAND LUKE ★   Warner Bros., 1967
THE SECRET WAR OF HARRY FRIGG   Universal, 1968
WINNING   Universal, 1969
BUTCH CASSIDY AND THE SUNDANCE KID   20th Century-Fox, 1969
KING: A FILMED RECORD...MONTGOMERY TO MEMPHIS (FD)
    Maron Films Limited, 1970
WUSA   Paramount, 1970
SOMETIMES A GREAT NOTION   *NEVER GIVE AN INCH*
    Universal, 1971 (also directed)
POCKET MONEY   National General, 1972
THE LIFE AND TIMES OF JUDGE ROY BEAN   National General, 1972
THE MACKINTOSH MAN   Warner Bros., 1973, U.S.-British
THE STING   Universal, 1973
THE TOWERING INFERNO   20th Century-Fox/Warner Bros., 1974
THE DROWNING POOL   Warner Bros., 1975
SILENT MOVIE   20th Century-Fox, 1976 (uncredited)
BUFFALO BILL AND THE INDIANS or SITTING BULL'S
    HISTORY LESSON   United Artists, 1976
SLAP SHOT   Universal, 1977
QUINTET   20th Century-Fox, 1979
WHEN TIME RAN OUT   Warner Bros., 1980
FORT APACHE, THE BRONX   20th Century-Fox, 1981
ABSENCE OF MALICE ★   Columbia, 1981
THE VERDICT ★   20th Century-Fox, 1982
HARRY AND SON   Orion, 1984 (also directed)
THE COLOR OF MONEY ★★   Buena Vista, 1986
FAT MAN AND LITTLE BOY   Paramount, 1989
BLAZE   Buena Vista, 1989
MR. AND MRS. BRIDGE   Miramax Films, 1990
THE HUDSUCKER PROXY   Warner Bros., 1994
NOBODY'S FOOL   Paramount, 1994

JULIE NEWMAR
(Julie Newmeyer)
b. August 16, 1935 - Los Angeles, California

SEVEN BRIDES FOR SEVEN BROTHERS   MGM, 1954
LI'L ABNER   Paramount, 1959
THE ROOKIE   20th Century-Fox, 1960
THE MARRIAGE-GO-ROUND   20th Century-Fox, 1960
FOR LOVE OR MONEY   Universal, 1963
MACKENNA'S GOLD   Columbia, 1969
THE MALTESE BIPPY   MGM, 1969
HYSTERICAL   Embassy, 1983
STREETWALKIN'   Concorde, 1985
DEEP SPACE   Trans World Entertainment, 1987
GHOSTS CAN'T DO IT   Triumph Releasing Corporation, 1990
TO WONG FOO, THANKS FOR EVERYTHING, JULIE NEWMAR
    Universal, 1995

THANDIE NEWTON
INTERVIEW WITH THE VAMPIRE   Warner Bros., 1994
JEFFERSON IN PARIS   Buena Vista, 1995
THE JOURNEY OF AUGUST KING   Miramax Films, 1995

WAYNE NEWTON
b. April 3, 1942 - Norfolk, Virginia

80 STEPS TO JONAH   Warner Bros., 1969
LICENCE TO KILL   MGM/UA, 1989, British
THE ADVENTURES OF FORD FAIRLANE   20th Century Fox, 1990

OLIVIA NEWTON-JOHN
b. September 26, 1947 - Cambridge, England

GREASE   Paramount, 1978
XANADU   Universal, 1980
TWO OF A KIND   20th Century-Fox, 1983

MBONGENI NGEMA
SARAFINA!   Miramax Films/Buena Vista, 1992,
    South African-British-French

HAING S. NGOR
Agent: The Marion Rosenberg Office - Los Angeles, 213/653-7383

THE KILLING FIELDS ○○   Warner Bros., 1984, British
IN LOVE AND WAR (TF)   Carol Schreder Productions/Tisch-Avnet
    Productions, 1987
THE IRON TRIANGLE   Scotti Bros., 1989
AMBITION   Miramax Films, 1991
MY LIFE   Columbia, 1993
HEAVEN AND EARTH   Warner Bros., 1993

DUSTIN NGUYEN
HEAVEN AND EARTH   Warner Bros., 1993
3 NINJAS KICK BACK   TriStar, 1994

HO NGUYEN
ALAMO BAY   TriStar, 1985

DENISE NICHOLAS
(Denise Nicholas-Hill)
b. July 12, 1944 - Detroit, Michigan
Agent: Paul Kohner, Inc. - Los Angeles, 310/550-1060

BLACULA   American International, 1972
A PIECE OF THE ACTION   Warner Bros., 1977
MARVIN AND TIGE   *LIKE FATHER AND SON*   20th Century-Fox
    International Classics, 1983
SUPERCARRIER (TF)   Fries Entertainment/Richard Hayward-Real
    Tinsel Productions, 1988
GHOST DAD   Universal, 1990

HAROLD NICHOLAS
b. March 27, 1924 - Philadelphia, Pennsylvania

THE FIVE HEARTBEATS   20th Century Fox, 1991

PAUL NICHOLAS
STARDUST   Columbia, 1975, British
TOMMY   Columbia, 1975, British
LISZTOMANIA   Warner Bros., 1975, British
SGT. PEPPER'S LONELY HEARTS CLUB BAND   Universal, 1978
THE WORLD IS FULL OF MARRIED MEN   New Realm,
    1979, British
THE JAZZ SINGER   AFD, 1980
NUTCRACKER   Rank, 1983, British
INVITATION TO A WEDDING   Chancery Lane Films, 1984, British

THOMAS IAN NICHOLAS
ROOKIE OF THE YEAR   20th Century Fox, 1993

BILLY NICHOLS
MISS FIRECRACKER   Corsair Pictures, 1989

JENNY NICHOLS
CRIMES AND MISDEMEANORS   Orion, 1989

KYRA NICHOLS
GEORGE BALANCHINE'S THE NUTCRACKER
   Warner Bros., 1993

NICHELLE NICHOLS
Agent: The Artists Group - Los Angeles, 310/552-1100

MISTER BUDDWING   MGM, 1966
STAR TREK - THE MOTION PICTURE   Paramount, 1979
STAR TREK II: THE WRATH OF KHAN   Paramount, 1982
STAR TREK III: THE SEARCH FOR SPOCK   Paramount, 1984
THE SUPERNATURALS   Republic Entertainment/Sandy Howard
   Productions, 1986
STAR TREK IV: THE VOYAGE HOME   Paramount, 1986
STAR TREK V: THE FINAL FRONTIER   Paramount, 1989
STAR TREK VI: THE UNDISCOVERED COUNTRY
   Paramount, 1991

STEPHEN NICHOLS
SOAPDISH   Paramount, 1991

JACK NICHOLSON
b. April 22, 1937 - Neptune, New Jersey
Agent: Bresler Kelly Kipperman Agency - Encino, 818/905-1155

THE CRY BABY KILLER   Allied Artists, 1958
TOO SOON TO LOVE   Universal, 1960
THE WILD RIDE   The Filmgroup, 1960
STUDS LONIGAN   United Artists, 1960
THE LITTLE SHOP OF HORRORS   Filmgroup, 1960
THE BROKEN LAND   20th Century-Fox, 1962
THE RAVEN   American International, 1963
THE TERROR   American International, 1963
ENSIGN PULVER   Warner Bros., 1964
BACK DOOR TO HELL   20th Century-Fox, 1964
THE SHOOTING   American International, 1966
RIDE IN THE WHIRLWIND   American International, 1966
FLIGHT TO FURY   Harold Goldman Associates, 1966, U.S.-Filipino
THE ST. VALENTINE'S DAY MASSACRE   20th Century-Fox, 1967
HELL'S ANGELS ON WHEELS   American International, 1967
PSYCH-OUT   American International, 1968
EASY RIDER ✪   Columbia, 1969
REBEL ROUSERS   Four Star Excelsior, 1970
ON A CLEAR DAY YOU CAN SEE FOREVER   Paramount, 1970
FIVE EASY PIECES ★   Columbia, 1970
CARNAL KNOWLEDGE   Avco Embassy, 1971
A SAFE PLACE   Columbia, 1971
THE KING OF MARVIN GARDENS   Columbia, 1972
THE LAST DETAIL ★   Columbia, 1973
CHINATOWN ★   Paramount, 1974
TOMMY   Columbia, 1975, British
THE PASSENGER   PROFESSIONE: REPORTER
   MGM/United Artists, 1975, Italian-French-Spanish-U.S.
THE FORTUNE   Columbia, 1975
ONE FLEW OVER THE CUCKOO'S NEST ★★   United Artists, 1975
THE MISSOURI BREAKS   United Artists, 1976
THE LAST TYCOON   Paramount, 1976
GOIN' SOUTH   Paramount, 1979 (also directed)
THE SHINING   Warner Bros., 1980, British
THE POSTMAN ALWAYS RINGS TWICE   Paramount, 1981
REDS ✪   Paramount, 1981
THE BORDER   Universal, 1982
TERMS OF ENDEARMENT ✪✪   Paramount, 1983
PRIZZI'S HONOR ★   20th Century Fox, 1985
HEARTBURN   Paramount, 1986
THE WITCHES OF EASTWICK   Warner Bros., 1987
IRONWEED ★   TriStar, 1987
BROADCAST NEWS   20th Century Fox, 1987 (uncredited)
BATMAN   Warner Bros., 1989
THE TWO JAKES   Paramount, 1990 (also directed)
MAN TROUBLE   20th Century Fox, 1992
A FEW GOOD MEN ✪   Columbia, 1992
HOFFA   20th Century Fox, 1992
WOLF   Columbia, 1994
THE CROSSING GUARD   Miramax Films, 1994

BRIGITTE NIELSEN
RED SONJA   MGM/UA, 1985
ROCKY IV   MGM/UA, 1985
COBRA   Warner Bros., 1986
BEVERLY HILLS COP II   Paramount, 1987
BYE BYE BABY   Prism Entertainment, 1989
MURDER BY MOONLIGHT (TF)   Tamara Asseyev Productions/
   London Weekend TV/Viacom, 1989, U.S.-British

LESLIE NIELSEN
b. February 11, 1926 - Regina, Canada
Agent: Bresler-Kelly Agency - Encino, 818/905-1155

RANSOM   MGM, 1956
FORBIDDEN PLANET   MGM, 1956
THE VAGABOND KING   Paramount, 1956
THE OPPOSITE SEX   MGM, 1956
HOT SUMMER NIGHT   MGM, 1956
TAMMY AND THE BACHELOR   Universal, 1957
THE SHEEPMAN   MGM, 1958
NIGHT TRAIN TO PARIS   1965, British
HARLOW   Paramount, 1965
DARK INTRUDER   Universal, 1965
BEAU GESTE   Universal, 1966
THE PLAINSMAN   Universal, 1966
THE RELUCTANT ASTRONAUT   1967
GUNFIGHT IN ABILENE   Universal, 1967
ROSIE!   Universal, 1967
COUNTERPOINT   Universal, 1968
DAYTON'S DEVILS   Commonwealth United, 1968
HOW TO COMMIT MARRIAGE   Cinerama Releasing
   Corporation, 1969
CHANGE OF MIND   1969
FOUR RODE OUT   1969
THE RESURRECTION OF ZACHARY WHEELER   1971
THE POSEIDON ADVENTURE   20th Century-Fox, 1972
CAN ELLEN BE SAVED? (TF)   ABC Circle Films, 1974
PROJECT: KILL   1976
DAY OF THE ANIMALS   1977
SIXTH AND MAIN   National Cinema, 1977
VIVA KNIEVEL!   Warner Bros., 1977
THE AMSTERDAM KILL   Columbia, 1978, U.S.-Hong Kong
LITTLE MO (TF)   Mark VII, Ltd./Worldvision, 1978
CITY ON FIRE!   Avco Embassy, 1979, Canadian
RIEL   CBC/Green River Productions, 1979, Canadian
BACKSTAIRS AT THE WHITE HOUSE (MS)   Ed Friendly
   Productions, 1979
INSTITUTE FOR REVENGE (TF)   Gold-Driskill Productions/
   Columbia TV, 1979
AIRPLANE!   Paramount, 1980
PROM NIGHT   Avco Embassy, 1980, Canadian
THE CREATURE WASN'T NICE   SPACESHIP
   Almi Cinema 5, 1981
CREEPSHOW   Warner Bros., 1982
WRONG IS RIGHT   Columbia, 1982
SOUL MAN   New World, 1986
THE PATRIOT   Crown International, 1986
HOME IS WHERE THE HART IS   Atlantic Releasing Corporation,
   1987, Canadian
NIGHTSTICK   Production Distribution Company, 1987, Canadian
NUTS   Universal, 1987
FATAL CONFESSION: A FATHER DOWLING MYSTERY (TF)
   The Fred Silverman Company/Strathmore Productions/
   Viacom, 1987
THE NAKED GUN: FROM THE FILES OF POLICE SQUAD!
   Paramount, 1988
REPOSSESSED   New Line Cinema, 1990
THE NAKED GUN 2 1/2: THE SMELL OF FEAR   Paramount, 1991
ALL I WANT FOR CHRISTMAS   Paramount, 1991
SURF NINJAS   New Line Cinema, 1993
NAKED GUN 33 1/3: THE FINAL INSULT   Paramount, 1994

JULIE NIHILL
REBEL   Vestron, 1985, Australian

LEONARD NIMOY

b. March 26, 1931 - Boston, Massachusetts

QUEEN FOR A DAY   United Artists, 1951
RHUBARB   Paramount, 1951
KID MONK BARONI   Realart, 1952
FRANCIS GOES TO WEST POINT   Universal, 1952
OLD OVERLAND TRAIL   Republic, 1953
THEM!   Warner Bros., 1954
SATAN'S SATELLITES   1958
THE BALCONY   Continental, 1963
DEATHWATCH   Beverly Pictures, 1966
VALLEY OF MYSTERY   1967
CATLOW   MGM, 1971, U.S.-Spanish
THE ALPHA CAPER (TF)   Universal TV, 1973
INVASION OF THE BODY SNATCHERS   United Artists, 1978
STAR TREK - THE MOTION PICTURE   Paramount, 1979
A WOMAN CALLED GOLDA (TF)   Harve Bennett Productions/
   Paramount TV, 1982
STAR TREK II: THE WRATH OF KHAN   Paramount, 1982
STAR TREK III: THE SEARCH FOR SPOCK   Paramount,
   1984 (also directed)
THE TRANSFORMERS (AF)   DEG, 1986 (voice)
STAR TREK IV: THE VOYAGE HOME   Paramount,
   1986 (also directed)
STAR TREK V: THE FINAL FRONTIER   Paramount, 1989
STAR TREK VI: THE UNDISCOVERED COUNTRY
   Paramount, 1991
THE PAGEMASTER   20th Century Fox, 1994 (voice)

MIGUEL NIÑO

ABOVE THE LAW   Warner Bros., 1988

JOE NIPOTE

CASPER   Universal, 1995

MICHAEL NIRENBERG

SEARCHING FOR BOBBY FISCHER   Paramount, 1993

MICHAEL NISSMAN

FAREWELL TO THE KING   Orion, 1989

NIXAU

THE GODS MUST BE CRAZY   TLC Films/20th Century Fox,
   1987, Botswana
THE GODS MUST BE CRAZY 2   WEG/Columbia,
   1989, U.S.-Botswana

JAMES NOBLE

b. March 5, 1922 - Dallas, Texas

10   Orion/Warner Bros., 1979
WHEN THE BOUGH BREAKS (TF)   Taft Entertainment TV/
   TDF Productions, 1986
A TIGER'S TALE   Atlantic Releasing Corporation, 1987
CHANCES ARE   TriStar, 1989

PHILIPPE NOIRET

ESPECIALLY ON SUNDAY   Miramax Films, 1993

NICK NOLTE

b. February 8, 1941 - Omaha, Nebraska
Agent: ICM - Beverly Hills, 310/550-4000

THE CALIFORNIA KID (TF)   Universal TV, 1974
DEATH SENTENCE (TF)   Spelling-Goldberg Productions, 1974
THE RUNAWAY BARGE (TF)   Lorimar Productions, 1975
RETURN TO MACON COUNTY   American International, 1975
RICH MAN, POOR MAN (MS)   Universal TV, 1976
THE DEEP   Columbia, 1977
WHO'LL STOP THE RAIN   DOG SOLDIERS   United Artists, 1978
NORTH DALLAS FORTY   Paramount, 1979
HEART BEAT   Orion/Warner Bros., 1980
CANNERY ROW   MGM/United Artists, 1982
48 HRS.   Paramount, 1982

UNDER FIRE   Orion, 1983
TEACHERS   MGM/UA, 1984
GRACE QUIGLEY   THE ULTIMATE SOLUTION OF
   GRACE QUIGLEY   Cannon, 1985
DOWN AND OUT IN BEVERLY HILLS   Buena Vista, 1986
EXTREME PREJUDICE   TriStar, 1987
WEEDS   DEG, 1987
THREE FUGITIVES   Buena Vista, 1989
NEW YORK STORIES   Buena Vista, 1989
FAREWELL TO THE KING   Orion, 1989
EVERYBODY WINS   Orion, 1990
Q&A   TriStar, 1990
ANOTHER 48 HRS.   Paramount, 1990
CAPE FEAR   Universal, 1991
THE PRINCE OF TIDES ★   Columbia, 1991
THE PLAYER   Fine Line Features/New Line Cinema, 1992
LORENZO'S OIL   Universal, 1992
I'LL DO ANYTHING   Columbia, 1994
BLUE CHIPS   Paramount, 1994
I LOVE TROUBLE   Buena Vista, 1994
JEFFERSON IN PARIS   Buena Vista, 1995

MIKE NOMAN

APRIL FOOL'S DAY   Paramount, 1986

JOHN FORD NOONAN

ADVENTURES IN BABYSITTING   Buena Vista, 1987

KERRY NOONAN

FRIDAY THE 13TH, PART VI: JASON LIVES   Paramount, 1986

TOM NOONAN

HEAVEN'S GATE   United Artists, 1980
WOLFEN   Orion/Warner Bros., 1981
MANHUNTER   DEG, 1986
ROBOCOP 2   Orion, 1990
LAST ACTION HERO   Columbia, 1993
WHAT HAPPENED WAS...   Samuel Goldwyn Company,
   1994 (also directed)

LISA NORMAN

WILD HEARTS CAN'T BE BROKEN   Buena Vista, 1991

CHUCK NORRIS

(Carlos Ray)
b. March 10, 1940 - Ryan, Oklahoma

THE WRECKING CREW   Columbia, 1968
BREAKER BREAKER   American International, 1978
GOOD GUYS WEAR BLACK   American Cinema, 1979
AN EYE FOR AN EYE   Avco Embassy, 1981
FORCED VENGEANCE   MGM/United Artists, 1982
SILENT RAGE   Columbia, 1982
LONE WOLF McQUADE   Orion, 1983
MISSING IN ACTION   Cannon, 1984
MISSING IN ACTION 2 - THE BEGINNING   Cannon, 1985
CODE OF SILENCE   Orion, 1985
INVASION, U.S.A.   Cannon, 1985
THE DELTA FORCE   Cannon, 1986
FIREWALKER   Cannon, 1986
HERO AND THE TERROR   Cannon, 1988
BRADDOCK: MISSING IN ACTION III   Cannon, 1988
DELTA FORCE 2 - OPERATION STRANGLEHOLD   MGM/UA, 1990
THE HITMAN   Cannon, 1991

ALAN NORTH

SERPICO   Paramount, 1973
...AND JUSTICE FOR ALL   Columbia, 1979
THEIF OF HEARTS   Paramount, 1984
BILLY GALVIN   Vestron, 1986
LEAN ON ME   Warner Bros., 1989
SEE NO EVIL, HEAR NO EVIL   TriStar, 1989
PENN AND TELLER GET KILLED   Warner Bros., 1989
GLORY   TriStar, 1990
CRAZY PEOPLE   Paramount, 1990
THE JERKY BOYS   Buena Vista, 1994

JIM NORTON
HIDDEN AGENDA   Hemdale, 1990
MEMOIRS OF AN INVISIBLE MAN   Warner Bros., 1992

JACK NOSEWORTHY
THE BRADY BUNCH MOVIE   Paramount, 1995

MICHAEL NOURI
FLASHDANCE   Paramount, 1983
GOBOTS: BATTLE OF THE ROCK LORDS (AF)   Clubhouse/
   Atlantic Releasing Corporation, 1986 (voice)
RAGE OF ANGELS: THE STORY CONTINUES (MS)
   NBC Productions, 1986
THE HIDDEN   New Line Cinema, 1987
QUIET VICTORY: THE CHARLIE WEDEMEYER STORY (TF)
   The Landsburg Company, 1988
DANIELLE STEEL'S 'CHANGES' *CHANGES* (TF)   The Cramer
   Company/NBC Productions, 1991

BLAINE NOVAK
THEY ALL LAUGHED   United Artists Classics, 1981
STRANGER'S KISS   Orion, 1984

KIM NOVAK
(Marilyn Pauline Novak)
b. February 13, 1933 - Chicago, Illinois
Agent: William Morris Agency - Beverly Hills, 310/274-7451

THE FRENCH LINE   RKO Radio, 1953
PUSHOVER   Columbia, 1954
PHFFFT   Columbia, 1954
FIVE AGAINST THE HOUSE   Columbia, 1955
SON OF SINBAD   1955
PICNIC   Columbia, 1956
THE MAN WITH THE GOLDEN ARM   United Artists, 1955
THE EDDY DUCHIN STORY   Columbia, 1956
JEANNE EAGLES   Columbia, 1957
PAL JOEY   Columbia, 1957
VERTIGO   Paramount, 1958
BELL, BOOK AND CANDLE   Columbia, 1958
MIDDLE OF THE NIGHT   Columbia, 1959
STRANGERS WHEN WE MEET   Columbia, 1960
PEPE   Columbia, 1960
BOYS' NIGHT OUT   MGM, 1962
TH'E NOTORIOUS LANDLADY   Columbia, 1962
OF HUMAN BONDAGE   MGM, 1964, British
KISS ME, STUPID   Lopert, 1964
THE AMOROUS ADVENTURES OF MOLL FLANDERS
   Paramount, 1965, British
THE LEGEND OF LYLAH CLARE   MGM, 1968
THE GREAT BANK ROBBERY   Warner Bros., 1969
TALES THAT WITNESS MADNESS   Paramount, 1973, British
THE THIRD GIRL FROM THE LEFT (TF)
   Playboy Productions, 1973
SATAN'S TRIANGLE (TF)   Danny Thomas Productions, 1975
THE WHITE BUFFALO   United Artists, 1977
JUST A GIGOLO   United Artists Classics, 1978, West German
THE MIRROR CRACK'D   AFD, 1980, British
MALIBU (TF)   Hamner Productions/Columbia TV, 1983
ALFRED HITCHCOCK PRESENTS (TF)   Universal TV, 1985
LIEBESTRAUM   MGM-Pathe, 1991

DON NOVELLO
TUCKER - THE MAN AND HIS DREAM   Paramount, 1988
NEW YORK STORIES   Buena Vista, 1989

THOKO NTSHINGA
A DRY WHITE SEASON   MGM/UA, 1989

WINSTON NTSHONA
A DRY WHITE SEASON   MGM/UA, 1989

DANNY NUCCI
BOOK OF LOVE   New Line Cinema, 1991
CRIMSON TIDE   Buena Vista, 1995

TED NUGENT
STATE PARK   Atlantic Releasing Corporation, 1988

BILL NUNN
Agent: William Morris Agency - Beverly Hills, 310/274-7451

DO THE RIGHT THING   Universal, 1989
MO' BETTER BLUES   Universal, 1990
NEW JACK CITY   Warner Bros., 1991
REGARDING HENRY   Paramount, 1991
CANDYMAN 2: FAREWELL TO THE FLESH
   Gramercy Pictures, 1995

FRANCE NUYEN
(France Nguyen Vannga)
b. July 31, 1939 - Marseille, France
Agent: The Gage Group - Los Angeles, 213/859-8777

SOUTH PACIFIC   Magna, 1958
IN LOVE AND WAR   20th Century-Fox, 1958
THE LAST TIME I SAW ARCHIE   United Artists, 1961
SATAN NEVER SLEEPS   20th Century-Fox, 1962, U.S.-British
DIAMOND HEAD   Columbia, 1962
A GIRL NAMED TAMIKO   Paramount, 1963
THE MAN IN THE MIDDLE   20th Century-Fox, 1964, U.S.-British
DIMENSION 5   Feature Film Corporation of America, 1966
ONE MORE TRAIN TO ROB   Universal, 1971
BATTLE FOR THE PLANET OF THE APES   20th Century-Fox, 1973
THE HORROR AT 37,000 FEET (TF)   CBS, Inc., 1973
CHINA CRY   The Penland Company, 1990
THE JOY LUCK CLUB   Buena Vista, 1993

WILL NYE
BASIC TRAINING   The Movie Store, 1985

AMY OBERER
ALL I WANT FOR CHRISTMAS   Paramount, 1991

AUSTIN O'BRIEN
Agent: ICM - Beverly Hills, 310/550-4000

STEPHEN KING'S THE LAWNMOWER MAN
   New Line Cinema, 1992
LAST ACTION HERO   Columbia, 1993
MY GIRL 2   Columbia, 1994
THE LAWNMOWER MAN 2   New Line Cinema, 1995

DEVON O'BRIEN
TERMS OF ENDEARMENT   Paramount, 1983
PROMISES TO KEEP (TF)   NBC/Warner Bros. TV, 1990

ELAN OBERON
FAREWELL TO THE KING   Orion, 1989

NIALL O'BRIEN
KING RALPH   Universal, 1991

TOM O'BRIEN
THE ACCUSED   Paramount, 1988

RIC OCASEK
MADE IN HEAVEN   Lorimar, 1987
HAIRSPRAY   New Line Cinema, 1988

ANDREA OCCHIPINTI
BOLERO   Cannon, 1984

DEIRDRE O'CONNELL
STRAIGHT TALK   Buena Vista, 1992

EDDIE O'CONNELL
ABSOLUTE BEGINNERS   Orion, 1986, British

JERRY O'CONNELL
STAND BY ME   Columbia, 1986
CALENDAR GIRL   Columbia, 1993

PATRICK O'CONNELL
THE ENDLESS SUMMER II (FD)   New Line Cinema, 1994

CARROLL O'CONNOR
b. August 2, 1925 - Bronx, New York

A FEVER IN THE BLOOD   Warner Bros., 1961
PARRISH   Warner Bros., 1961
BY LOVE POSSESSED   United Artists, 1961
BELLE SOMMERS   Columbia, 1962
LAD: A DOG   Warner Bros., 1962
LONELY ARE THE BRAVE   Universal, 1962
CLEOPATRA   20th Century-Fox, 1963
IN HARM'S WAY   Paramount, 1965
WHAT DID YOU DO IN THE WAR, DADDY?   United Artists, 1966
HAWAII   United Artists, 1966
NOT WITH MY WIFE YOU DON'T!   Warner Bros., 1966
WARNING SHOT   Paramount, 1967
POINT BLANK   MGM, 1967
WATERHOLE #3   Paramount, 1967
THE DEVIL'S BRIGADE   United Artists, 1968
FOR LOVE OF IVY   Cinerama Releasing Corporation, 1968
DEATH OF A GUNFIGHTER   Universal, 1969
MARLOWE   MGM, 1969
KELLY'S HEROES   MGM, 1970, U.S.-Yugoslavian
DOCTORS' WIVES   Columbia, 1971
LAW AND DISORDER   Columbia, 1974
BRASS (TF)   Carnan Productions/Jaygee Productions/Orion TV, 1985
IN THE HEAT OF THE NIGHT (TF)   The Fred Silverman Company/
   Jadda Productions/MGM-UA TV, 1988

DERRICK O'CONNOR
Agent: Susan Smith & Associates - Beverly Hills, 213/852-4777

LETHAL WEAPON 2   Warner Bros., 1989
DEALERS   Skouras Pictures, 1989

DONALD O'CONNOR
b. August 28, 1925 - Chicago, Illinois

TOYS   20th Century Fox, 1992

GLYNNIS O'CONNOR
JEREMY   United Artists, 1973
SOMEONE I TOUCHED (TF)   Charles Fries Productions, 1975
ODE TO BILLY JOE   Warner Bros., 1976
CALIFORNIA DREAMING   American International, 1979
THOSE LIPS, THOSE EYES   United Artists, 1980
NIGHT CROSSING   Buena Vista, 1982, British
JOHNNY DANGEROUSLY   20th Century Fox, 1984
WHY ME?   Lorimar Productions, 1984
LOVE LEADS THE WAY (TF)   Hawkins-Permut Productions, 1984
TOO GOOD TO BE TRUE (TF)   Newland-Raynor Productions, 1988

HAZEL O'CONNOR
BREAKING GLASS   Paramount, 1980, British

KEVIN J. O'CONNOR
Agent: Gersh Agency - Beverly Hills, 310/274-6611

PEGGY SUE GOT MARRIED   TriStar, 1986
STEEL MAGNOLIAS   TriStar, 1989

LOVE AT LARGE   Orion, 1990
F/X 2 - THE DEADLY ART OF ILLUSION   Orion, 1991
HERO   Columbia, 1992
NO ESCAPE   Savoy Pictures, 1994
COLOR OF NIGHT   Buena Vista, 1994

RAYMOND O'CONNOR
MR. NANNY   New Line Cinema, 1993

HUGH O'CONOR
Agent: William Morris Agency - Beverly Hills, 310/274-7451

MY LEFT FOOT   Miramax Films, 1989, Irish-British

DAVID O'DELL
E.T. THE EXTRA-TERRESTRIAL   Universal, 1982

CHRIS O'DONNELL
Agent: CAA - Beverly Hills, 310/288-4545

MEN DON'T LEAVE   Warner Bros., 1990
FRIED GREEN TOMATOES   Universal, 1991
SCHOOL TIES   Paramount, 1992
SCENT OF A WOMAN   Universal, 1992
THE THREE MUSKETEERS   Buena Vista, 1993
BLUE SKY   Orion, 1994
CIRCLE OF FRIENDS   Savoy Pictures, 1995
BATMAN FOREVER   Warner Bros., 1995

ROSIE O'DONNELL
Agent: ICM - Beverly Hills, 310/550-4000

A LEAGUE OF THEIR OWN   Columbia, 1992
SLEEPLESS IN SEATTLE   TriStar, 1993
ANOTHER STAKEOUT   Buena Vista, 1993
CAR 54, WHERE ARE YOU?   Orion, 1994
I'LL DO ANYTHING   Columbia, 1994
THE FLINTSTONES   Universal, 1994
EXIT TO EDEN   Savoy Pictures, 1994
GASLIGHT ADDITION   New Line Cinema, 1995

GAIL O'GRADY
NOBODY'S PERFECT   Moviestore Entertainment, 1990

JACK O'HALLORAN
FAREWELL, MY LOVELY   Avco Embassy, 1975
KING KONG   Paramount, 1976
MARCH OR DIE   Columbia, 1977, British
SUPERMAN   Warner Bros., 1978, U.S.-British
THE BALTIMORE BULLET   Avco Embassy, 1980
SUPERMAN II   Warner Bros., 1981, U.S.-British
DRAGNET   Universal, 1987
HERO AND THE TERROR   Cannon, 1988

NATSUKO OHAMA
SPEED   20th Century Fox, 1994

CATHERINE O'HARA
Agent: ICM - Beverly Hills, 310/550-4000

AFTER HOURS   The Geffen Company/Warner Bros., 1985
REALLY WEIRD TALES (CTF)   HBO/Atlantis Films,
   1987, U.S.-Canadian
BEETLEJUICE   The Geffen Company/Warner Bros., 1988
DICK TRACY   Buena Vista, 1990
BETSY'S WEDDING   Buena Vista, 1990
HOME ALONE   20th Century Fox, 1990
HOME ALONE 2: LOST IN NEW YORK   20th Century Fox, 1992
TIM BURTON'S THE NIGHTMARE BEFORE CHRISTMAS
   Buena Vista, 1993 (voice)
THE PAPER   Universal, 1994
WYATT EARP   Warner Bros., 1994
A SIMPLE TWIST OF FATE   Buena Vista, 1994
TALL TALE   Buena Vista, 1994

F
I
L
M

A
C
T
O
R
S

JENNY O'HARA
ANGIE   Buena Vista, 1994

MAUREEN O'HARA
(Maureen FitzSimons)
b. August 17, 1920 - Millwall, Ireland

KICKING THE MOON AROUND   *THE PLAYBOY/MILLIONAIRE
   MERRY-GO-ROUND*   1938, British
MY IRISH MOLLY   1939, British
JAMAICA INN   Paramount, 1939, British
THE HUNCHBACK OF NOTRE DAME   RKO Radio, 1939
A BILL OF DIVORCEMENT   *NEVER TO LOVE*   RKO Radio, 1940
DANCE, GIRL, DANCE   RKO Radio, 1940
THEY MET IN ARGENTINA   RKO Radio, 1941
HOW GREEN WAS MY VALLEY   20th Century-Fox, 1941
TO THE SHORES OF TRIPOLI   20th Century-Fox, 1942
TEN GENTLEMEN FROM WEST POINT   20th Century-Fox, 1942
THE BLACK SWAN   20th Century-Fox, 1942
THE IMMORTAL SERGEANT   20th Century-Fox, 1943
THIS LAND IS MINE   RKO Radio, 1943
THE FALLEN SPARROW   RKO Radio, 1943
BUFFALO BILL   20th Century-Fox, 1944
THE SPANISH MAIN   RKO Radio, 1945
SENTIMENTAL JOURNEY   20th Century-Fox, 1946
DO YOU LOVE ME?   20th Century-Fox, 1946
SINBAD THE SAILOR   RKO Radio, 1947
THE HOMESTRETCH   20th Century-Fox, 1947
MIRACLE ON 34TH STREET   20th Century-Fox, 1947
THE FOXES OF HARROW   20th Century-Fox, 1947
SITTING PRETTY   20th Century-Fox, 1948
THE FORBIDDEN STREET   *BRITANNIA MEWS*
   20th Century-Fox, 1949, British
A WOMAN'S SECRET   RKO Radio, 1949
FATHER WAS A FULLBACK   20th Century-Fox, 1949
BAGDAD   Universal, 1949
COMANCHE TERRITORY   Universal, 1950
TRIPOLI   Paramount, 1950
RIO GRANDE   Republic, 1950
FLAME OF ARABY   Universal, 1951
AT SWORD'S POINT   RKO Radio, 1952
KANGAROO   20th Century-Fox, 1952
THE QUIET MAN   Republic, 1952
AGAINST ALL FLAGS   Universal, 1952
THE REDHEAD FROM WYOMING   Universal, 1953
WAR ARROW   Universal, 1953
FIRE OVER AFRICA   *MALAGA*   Columbia, 1954, British-U.S.
THE LONG GRAY LINE   Columbia, 1955
THE MAGNIFICENT MATADOR   20th Century-Fox, 1955
LADY GODIVA   Universal, 1955
LISBON   Republic, 1956
EVERYTHING BUT THE TRUTH   Universal, 1956
THE WINGS OF EAGLES   MGM, 1957
OUR MAN IN HAVANA   Columbia, 1960, British
THE PARENT TRAP   Buena Vista, 1961
THE DEADLY COMPANION   *TRIGGER HAPPY*
   Pathe-America, 1961
MR. HOBBS TAKES A VACATION   20th Century-Fox, 1962
SPENCER'S MOUNTAIN   Warner Bros., 1963
McLINTOCK!   United Artists, 1963
THE BATTLE OF THE VILLA FIORITA   Warner Bros.,
   1965, U.S.-British
THE RARE BREED   Universal, 1966
HOW DO I LOVE THEE?   Cinerama Releasing Corporation, 1970
BIG JAKE   National General, 1971
THE RED PONY (TF)   Universal TV/Omnibus Productions, 1973
ONLY THE LONELY   20th Century Fox, 1991

PAIGE O'HARA
BEAUTY AND THE BEAST (AF)   Buena Vista, 1991 (voice)

BRAD O'HARE
LONGTIME COMPANION   Samuel Goldwyn Company, 1990

DAN O'HERLIHY
(Daniel O'Herlihy)
b. May 1, 1919 - Wexford, Ireland

HUNGRY HILL   Universal, 1947, British
ODD MAN OUT   General Film Distributors, 1947, British
KIDNAPPED   Monogram, 1948
MACBETH   Republic, 1948
THE DESERT FOX   20th Century-Fox, 1951
SOLDIERS THREE   MGM, 1951
THE BLUE VEIL   RKO Radio, 1951
THE HIGHWAYMAN   Allied Artists, 1951
ACTORS AND SIN   United Artists, 1952
ADVENTURES OF ROBINSON CRUSOE ★   United Artists,
   1952, Mexican
AT SWORD'S POINT   RKO Radio, 1952
INVASION, U.S.A.   Columbia, 1952
OPERATION SECRET   Warner Bros., 1952
THE BLACK SHIELD OF FALWORTH   Universal, 1954
BENGAL BRIGADE   Columbia, 1954
THE PURPLE MASK   Universal, 1955
THE VIRGIN QUEEN   20th Century-Fox, 1955
CITY AFTER MIDNIGHT   *THAT WOMAN OPPOSITE*   RKO Radio,
   1957, British
HOME BEFORE DARK   Warner Bros., 1958
IMITATION OF LIFE   Universal, 1959
THE NIGHT FIGHTERS   *A TERRIBLE BEAUTY*   United Artists,
   1960, British
ONE FOOT IN HELL   20th Century-Fox, 1960
KING OF THE ROARING 20'S—THE STORY OF ARNOLD
   ROTHSTEIN   1961
THE CABINET OF CALIGARI   1962
FAIL-SAFE   Columbia, 1964
THE BIG CUBE   1969
100 RIFLES   20th Century-Fox, 1969
WATERLOO   Paramount, 1971, Italian-Soviet
THE CAREY TREATMENT   MGM, 1972
QB VII (TF)   Screen Gems/Columbia TV/The Douglas Cramer
   Company, 1974
THE TAMARIND SEED   Avco Embassy, 1974, British
MacARTHUR   Universal, 1977
HALLOWEEN III: SEASON OF THE WITCH   Universal, 1982
THE LAST STARFIGHTER   Universal, 1984
THE WHOOPEE BOYS   Paramount, 1986
ROBOCOP   Orion, 1987
THE DEAD   Vestron, 1987
ROBOCOP 2   Orion, 1990

MICHAEL O'KEEFE
THE GREAT SANTINI   *THE ACE* ✪   Orion/Warner Bros., 1980
FINDERS KEEPERS   Warner Bros., 1984
THE SLUGGER'S WIFE   Columbia, 1985
THE WHOOPEE BOYS   Paramount, 1986
UNHOLY MATRIMONY (TF)   Edgar J. Scherick Associates/Taft
   Entertainment TV, 1988
IN THE BEST INTEREST OF THE CHILD (TF)   Papazian-Hirsch
   Entertainment, 1990

MILES O'KEEFFE
TARZAN THE APE MAN   MGM/United Artists, 1981
CAMPUS MAN   Paramount, 1987
WAXWORK   Vestron, 1988
DEAD ON   New Line Cinema, 1991

YUJI OKUMOTO
THE KARATE KID PART II   Columbia, 1986
ALOHA SUMMER   *HANAUMA BAY*   Spectrafilm, 1988
MENENDEZ: A KILLING IN BEVERLY HILLS (MS)   Zev Braun
   Pictures/TriStar Television, 1994

KEN OLANDT
APRIL FOOL'S DAY   Paramount, 1986

DANIEL OLBRYCHSKI
THE UNBEARABLE LIGHTNESS OF BEING   Orion, 1988

WILL OLDHAM
MATEWAN   Cinecom, 1987

GARY OLDMAN
b. March 21, 1958 - London, England

SID AND NANCY   Samuel Goldwyn Company, 1986, British
PRICK UP YOUR EARS   Samuel Goldwyn Company, 1987, British
TRACK 29   Island Pictures, 1988
CRIMINAL LAW   Hemdale, 1989
CHATTAHOOCHEE   Hemdale, 1990
STATE OF GRACE   Orion, 1990
ROSENCRANTZ & GUILDENSTERN ARE DEAD   Cinecom, 1991
JFK   Warner Bros., 1991
BRAM STOKER'S DRACULA *DRACULA*   Columbia, 1992
TRUE ROMANCE   Warner Bros., 1993
ROMEO IS BLEEDING   Gramercy Pictures, 1994, U.S.-British
THE PROFESSIONAL   Columbia, 1994
MURDER IN THE FIRST   Warner Bros., 1994
IMMORTAL BELOVED   Columbia, 1994
A SCARLET LETTER   Buena Vista, 1995

GABRIEL OLDS
CALENDAR GIRL   Columbia, 1993

CASS OLE
THE BLACK STALLION RETURNS   MGM/UA, 1983

JOHN O'LEARY
AIRPLANE!   Paramount, 1980

WILLIAM O'LEARY
HOT SHOTS!   20th Century Fox, 1991
CANDYMAN 2: FAREWELL TO THE FLESH   Gramercy Pictures, 1995

KEN OLIN
b. July 30, 1954 - Chicago, Illinois
Agent: UTA - Beverly Hills, 310/273-6700

TONIGHT'S THE NIGHT (TF)   Indieprod Productions/Phoenix
   Entertainment Group, 1987
I'LL TAKE MANHATTAN (MS)   Steve Krantz Productions, 1987
A STONING IN FULHAM COUNTY (TF)   The Landsburg
   Company, 1988
GOOD NIGHT, SWEET WIFE: A MURDER IN BOSTON (TF)
   Arnold Shapiro Productions/CBS Entertainment Productions, 1990
QUEENS LOGIC   New Line Cinema, 1991

LENA OLIN
b. 1955 - Sweden
Agent: ICM - Beverly Hills, 310/550-4000

AFTER THE REHEARSAL   Triumph/Columbia, 1983,
   Swedish-West German
THE UNBEARABLE LIGHTNESS OF BEING   Orion, 1988
ENEMIES, A LOVE STORY ✪   20th Century Fox, 1989
HAVANA   Universal, 1990
MR. JONES   TriStar, 1993
ROMEO IS BLEEDING   Gramercy Pictures, 1994, U.S.-British

BARRET OLIVER
COCOON   20th Century Fox, 1985
COCOON: THE RETURN   20th Century Fox, 1988

MICHAEL OLIVER
PROBLEM CHILD   Universal, 1990
PROBLEM CHILD 2   Universal, 1991

ROCHELLE OLIVER
AN UNREMARKABLE LIFE   Continental Film Group, 1989

ROBERT OLIVERI
HONEY, I SHRUNK THE KIDS   Buena Vista, 1989
EDWARD SCISSORHANDS   20th Century Fox, 1990
HONEY, I BLEW UP THE KID   Buena Vista, 1992

WALTER OLKEWICZ
THE CLIENT   Warner Bros., 1994

EDWARD JAMES OLMOS
b. February 24, 1947 - Los Angeles, California
Agent: The Artists Agency - Los Angeles, 310/277-7779

ALOHA, BOBBY AND ROSE   Columbia, 1975
ALAMBRISTA!   Bobwin/Films Haus, 1977
WOLFEN   Orion/Warner Bros., 1981
BLADE RUNNER   The Ladd Company/Warner Bros., 1982
THE BALLAD OF GREGORIO CORTEZ   Embassy, 1983
SAVING GRACE   Columbia, 1986
STAND AND DELIVER ★   Columbia, 1988
TRIUMPH OF THE SPIRIT   Triumph Releasing Corporation, 1989
TALENT FOR THE GAME   Paramount, 1991
AMERICAN ME   Universal, 1992 (also directed)
MENENDEZ: A KILLING IN BEVERLY HILLS (MS)   Zev Braun
   Pictures/TriStar Television, 1994
A MILLION TO JUAN   Samuel Goldwyn Company, 1994
MI FAMILIA   New Line Cinema, 1995

SUSAN OLSEN
THE BRADY GIRLS GET MARRIED (TF)   Sherwood Schwartz
   Productions, 1981
THE BRADYS (TF)   Brady Productions/Paramount TV, 1990
THE BRADY BUNCH MOVIE   Paramount, 1995

JAMES OLSON
THE SHARKFIGHTERS   1956
THE STRANGE ONE   Columbia, 1957
RACHEL, RACHEL   Warner Bros., 1968
MOON ZERO TWO   Warner Bros., 1970, British
THE ANDROMEDA STRAIN   Universal, 1971
WILD ROVERS   MGM, 1971
THE GROUNDSTAR CONSPIRACY   Universal, 1972, Canadian
RAGTIME   Paramount, 1981
AMITYVILLE II: THE POSSESSION   Orion, 1982
COMMANDO   20th Century-Fox, 1985

GRIFFIN O'NEAL
THE ESCAPE ARTIST   Orion/Warner Bros., 1982
APRIL FOOL'S DAY   Paramount, 1986

PATRICK O'NEAL†
b. September 26, 1927 - Ocala, Florida
d. September 9, 1994

THE MAD MAGICIAN   Columbia, 1954
THE BLACK SHIELD OF FALWORTH   Universal, 1954
FROM THE TERRACE   20th Century-Fox, 1960
A MATTER OF MORALS   United Artists, 1960, U.S.-Swedish
THE CARDINAL   Columbia, 1963
IN HARM'S WAY   Paramount, 1965
KING RAT   Columbia, 1965, British
A FINE MADNESS   Warner Bros., 1966
ALVAREZ KELLY   Columbia, 1966
CHAMBER OF HORRORS   Warner Bros., 1966
WHERE WERE YOU WHEN THE LIGHTS WENT OUT?   MGM, 1968
THE SECRET LIFE OF AN AMERICAN WIFE   20th Century-Fox, 1968
ASSIGNMENT TO KILL   1968
STILETTO   Avco Embassy, 1969
CASTLE KEEP   Columbia, 1969
THE KREMLIN LETTER   20th Century-Fox, 1970
EL CONDOR   National General, 1970
CORKY *LOOKIN' GOOD*   1972
THE WAY WE WERE   Columbia, 1973
SILENT NIGHT, BLOODY NIGHT   Cannon, 1974
THE STEPFORD WIVES   Columbia, 1975
CROSSFIRE (TF)   QM Productions, 1975

ARTHUR HAILEY'S THE MONEYCHANGERS
THE MONEYCHANGERS (MS)   Ross Hunter Productions/
   Paramount TV, 1976
THE DEADLIEST SEASON (TF)   Titus Productions, 1977
THE LAST HURRAH (TF)   O'Connor-Becker Productions/
   Columbia TV, 1977
TO KILL A COP (TF)   David Gerber Company/Columbia TV, 1978
LIKE MOM, LIKE ME (TF)   CBS Entertainment, 1978
ALICE   Orion, 1990
UNDER SIEGE   Warner Bros., 1992

RON O'NEAL
b. September 1, 1937 - Utica, New York

MOVE   20th Century-Fox, 1970
THE ORGANIZATION   United Artists, 1971
SUPERFLY   1972
SUPERFLY T.N.T.   Paramount, 1973 (also directed)
THE MASTER GUNFIGHTER   Taylor-Laughlin, 1975
BROTHERS   Warner Bros., 1977
WHEN A STRANGER CALLS   Columbia, 1979
A FORCE OF ONE   American Cinema, 1979
THE FINAL COUNTDOWN   United Artists, 1980
GUYANA TRAGEDY: THE STORY OF JIM JONES (TF)
   The Konigsberg Company, 1980
ST. HELENS   Davis-Panzer Productions, 1981

RYAN O'NEAL
(Patrick Ryan O'Neal)
b. April 20, 1941 - Los Angeles, California

THE BIG BOUNCE   Warner Bros., 1969
THE GAMES   20th Century-Fox, 1970, British
LOVE STORY ★   Paramount, 1970
LOVE HATE LOVE (TF)   1970
WILD ROVERS   MGM, 1971
WHAT'S UP, DOC?   Warner Bros., 1972
THE THIEF WHO CAME TO DINNER   Warner Bros., 1973
PAPER MOON   Paramount, 1973
BARRY LYNDON   Warner Bros., 1975, British
NICKELODEON   Columbia, 1976
A BRIDGE TOO FAR   United Artists, 1977, British
THE DRIVER   20th Century-Fox, 1978
OLIVER'S STORY   Paramount, 1979
THE MAIN EVENT   Warner Bros., 1979
GREEN ICE   Universal/AFD, 1981, British
SO FINE   Warner Bros., 1981
PARTNERS   Paramount, 1982
IRRECONCILABLE DIFFERENCES   Warner Bros., 1984
FEVER PITCH   MGM/UA, 1985
TOUGH GUYS DON'T DANCE   Cannon, 1987
CHANCES ARE   TriStar, 1989
SMALL SACRIFICES (MS)   Louis Rudolph Films/Motown
   Productions/Allarcom Ltd./Fries Entertainment, 1989,
   U.S.-Canadian
THE MAN UPSTAIRS (TF)   Burt Reynolds Productions, 1992
FAITHFUL   Savoy Pictures, 1995

SHAQUILLE O'NEAL
BLUE CHIPS   Paramount, 1994

TATUM O'NEAL
b. November 5, 1963 - Los Angeles, California

PAPER MOON OO   Paramount, 1973
NICKELODEON   Columbia, 1976
THE BAD NEWS BEARS   Paramount, 1976
INTERNATIONAL VELVET   MGM/United Artists, 1978, British
LITTLE DARLINGS   Paramount, 1980
CIRCLE OF TWO   World Northal, 1980, Canadian
LITTLE NOISES   Monument Pictures, 1992

AMY O'NEILL
HONEY, I SHRUNK THE KIDS   Buena Vista, 1989
HONEY, I BLEW UP THE KID   Buena Vista, 1992

DICK O'NEILL
THE SECRET LIFE OF KATHY McCORMICK (TF)   Tamara Asseyev
   Productions/New World TV, 1988
SHE'S OUT OF CONTROL   Columbia, 1989

ED O'NEILL
b. 1946 - Youngstown, Ohio
Agent: ICM - Beverly Hills, 310/550-4000

K-9   Universal, 1989
DISORGANIZED CRIME   Buena Vista, 1989
THE ADVENTURES OF FORD FAIRLANE   20th Century Fox, 1990
SIBLING RIVALRY   Columbia, 1990
DUTCH   20th Century Fox, 1991
WAYNE'S WORLD   Paramount, 1992
BLUE CHIPS   Paramount, 1994
LITTLE GIANTS   Warner Bros., 1994

JENNIFER O'NEILL
b. February 20, 1948 - Rio de Janeiro, Brazil

FOR LOVE OF IVY   Cinerama Releasing Corporation, 1968
FUTZ   Commonwealth United, 1969
RIO LOBO   National General, 1970
SUMMER OF '42   Warner Bros., 1971
SUCH GOOD FRIENDS   Paramount, 1971
GLASS HOUSES   Columbia, 1972
THE CAREY TREATMENT   MGM, 1972
THE REINCARNATION OF PETER PROUD
   American International, 1975
WHIFFS   20th Century-Fox, 1975
THE INTRUDER   1976, Italian
CARAVANS   Universal, 1978, U.S.-Iranian
A FORCE OF ONE   American Cinema, 1979
CLOUD DANCER   Blossom, 1980
STEEL   *LOOK DOWN AND DIE/MEN OF STEEL*
   World Northal, 1980
SCANNERS   Avco Embassy, 1981, Canadian
COVER UP (TF)   Glen A. Larson Productions/20th Century
   Fox TV, 1984
FULL EXPOSURE: THE SEX TAPES SCANDAL (TF)
   von Zerneck-Sertner Films, 1989

MAGGIE O'NEILL
PRIME SUSPECT   Columbia, 1991

MICHAEL O'NEILL
Agent: Susan Smith & Associates - Beverly Hills, 213/852-4777

THE GUN IN BETTY LOU'S HANDBAG   Buena Vista, 1992

PAUL ONSONGO
CHEETAH   Buena Vista, 1989

MICHAEL ONTKEAN
b. January 24, 1946 - Vancouver, British Columbia
Agent: William Morris Agency - Beverly Hills, 310/274-7451

PICKUP ON 101   1972
NECROMANCY *THE WITCHING*   American International, 1972
SLAP SHOT   Universal, 1977
VOICES   MGM/United Artists, 1979
WILLIE AND PHIL   20th Century-Fox, 1980
MAKING LOVE   20th Century-Fox, 1982
THE BLOOD OF OTHERS *LE SANG DES AUTRES* (CMS)   HBO
   Premiere Films/ICC/Filmax Productions, 1984, Canadian-French
JUST THE WAY YOU ARE   MGM/UA, 1984
THE ALLNIGHTER   Universal, 1987
MAID TO ORDER   New Century/Vista, 1987
CLARA'S HEART   Warner Bros., 1988
BYE BYE BLUES   Circle Releasing Corporation, 1990, Canadian
TWIN PEAKS (TF)   Lynch-Frost Productions/Propaganda Films/
   World Vision Enterprises, 1990
POSTCARDS FROM THE EDGE   Columbia, 1990

DON OPPER
CRITTERS   New Line Cinema, 1986
SLAM DANCE   Island Pictures, 1987

TERRY O'QUINN
(Terrance O'Quinn)
WOMEN OF VALOR (TF)   Inter Planetary Productions/Jeni
   Productions, 1986
THE STEPFATHER   New Century/Vista, 1987
BLACK WIDOW   20th Century Fox, 1987
YOUNG GUNS   20th Century Fox, 1988
BLIND FURY   TriStar, 1990
PRISONERS OF THE SUN   Skouras Pictures, 1991
THE ROCKETEER   Buena Vista, 1991
THE CUTTING EDGE   MGM-Pathe Communications, 1992
MACSHAYNE: WINNER TAKES ALL (TF)   NBC, 1994

GERALDINE O'RAWE
CIRCLE OF FRIENDS   Savoy Pictures, 1995

JERRY ORBACH
b. October 20, 1935 - New York, New York

THE GANG THAT COULDN'T SHOOT STRAIGHT   MGM, 1971
THE SENTINEL   Universal, 1977
UNDERGROUND ACES   Filmways, 1981
PRINCE OF THE CITY   Orion/Warner Bros., 1981
BREWSTER'S MILLIONS   Universal, 1985
F/X   Orion, 1986
THE IMAGEMAKER   Castle Hill Productions, 1986
DIRTY DANCING   Vestron, 1987
SOMEONE TO WATCH OVER ME   Columbia, 1987
LOVE AMONG THIEVES (TF)   Robert A. Papazian
   Productions, 1987
OUT ON A LIMB (MS)   Stan Margulies Company/
   ABC Circle Films, 1987
THE LAW AND HARRY McGRAW: DEAD MEN DON'T MAKE
   PHONE CALLS (TF)   Universal TV, 1987
UPWORLD   Vestron, 1989
PERRY MASON: THE CASE OF THE MUSICAL MURDER (TF)
   The Fred Silverman Company/Dean Hargrove Productions/
   Viacom, 1989
CRIMES AND MISDEMEANORS   Orion, 1989
LAST EXIT TO BROOKLYN   Cinecom, 1989, West German-U.S.
OUT FOR JUSTICE   Warner Bros., 1991
DELIRIOUS   MGM-Pathe, 1991
DELUSION   I.R.S. Releasing, 1991
BEAUTY AND THE BEAST (AF)   Buena Vista, 1991 (voice)
STRAIGHT TALK   Buena Vista, 1992
UNIVERSAL SOLDIER   TriStar, 1992

CYRIL O'REILLY
AIRPLANE!   Paramount, 1980
NAVY SEALS   Orion, 1990

JULIA ORMOND
NOSTRADAMUS   Orion Classics, 1994, British
FIRST KNIGHT   Columbia, 1995
SABRINA   Paramount, 1995

ED O'ROSS
Agent: The Blake Agency - Beverly Hills, 310/246-0241

THE COTTON CLUB   Orion, 1984
THE POPE OF GREENWICH VILLAGE   MGM/UA, 1984
THE HIDDEN   New Line Cinema, 1987
LETHAL WEAPON   Warner Bros., 1987
FULL METAL JACKET   Warner Bros., 1987, British
ACTION JACKSON   Lorimar, 1988
RED HEAT   TriStar, 1988
ANOTHER 48 HRS.   Paramount, 1990
DICK TRACY   Buena Vista, 1990
UNIVERSAL SOLDIER   TriStar, 1992

MARINA ORSINI
EDDIE AND THE CRUISERS II: EDDIE LIVES   Scotti Bros., 1989

MADOLYN SMITH OSBORNE
(See Madolyn SMITH Osborne)

MILO O'SHEA
b. June 2, 1925 - Dublin, Ireland

YOU CAN'T BEAT THE IRISH   TALK OF A MILLION   1951
CARRY ON CABBY   Anglo-Amalgamated/Warner-Pathé,
   1963, British
NEVER PUT IT IN WRITING   Allied Artists, 1964, British
ULYSSES   Continental, 1967
ROMEO AND JULIET   Paramount, 1968, Italian-British
BARBARELLA   Paramount, 1968, Italian-French
THE ADDING MACHINE   1969, U.S.-British
THE ANGEL LEVINE   United Artists, 1970
PADDY   Allied Artists, 1970, Irish
SACCO AND VANZETTI   UMC, 1971, French-Italian
LOOT   Cinevision, 1972, British
THEATRE OF BLOOD   United Artists, 1973, British
THE HEBREW LESSON   1973
DIGBY, THE BIGGEST DOG IN THE WORLD   Cinerama Releasing
   Corporation, 1974, British
IT'S NOT THE SIZE THAT COUNTS   PERCY'S PROGRESS
   Joseph Brenner Associates, 1974, British
ARABIAN ADVENTURE   AFD, 1979, British
THE PILOT   Summit Features, 1979
THE VERDICT   20th Century-Fox, 1982
THE PURPLE ROSE OF CAIRO   Orion, 1985
THE DREAM TEAM   Universal, 1989
ONLY THE LONELY   20th Century Fox, 1991
THE PLAYBOYS   Samuel Goldwyn Company, 1992, Irish-British

BIBI OSTERWALD
STILLWATCH (TF)   Zev Braun Pictures/Interscope Communications/
   Potomac Productions, 1987

MAUREEN O'SULLIVAN
b. May 17, 1911 - Boyle, County Roscommon, Ireland

SONG O' MY HEART   20th Century-Fox, 1930
SO THIS IS LONDON   1930
JUST IMAGINE   20th Century-Fox, 1930
THE PRINCESS AND THE PLUMBER   1930
A CONNECTICUT YANKEE   20th Century-Fox, 1931
SKYLINE   1931
THE BIG SHOT   1931
TARZAN THE APE MAN   MGM, 1932
THE SILVER LINING   United Artists, 1932
FAST COMPANIONS   Universal, 1932
SKYSCRAPER SOULS   1932
INFORMATION KID   Universal, 1932
STRANGE INTERLUDE   MGM, 1932
OKAY AMERICA   Universal, 1932
PAYMENT DEFERRED   1932
ROBBERS' ROOST   1933
THE COHENS AND KELLYS IN TROUBLE   RKO Radio, 1933
TUGBOAT ANNIE   MGM, 1933
STAGE MOTHER   MGM, 1933
TARZAN AND HIS MATE   MGM, 1934
THE THIN MAN   MGM, 1934
HIDE-OUT   MGM, 1934
THE BARRETTS OF WIMPOLE STREET   MGM, 1934
DAVID COPPERFIELD   MGM, 1935
WEST POINT OF THE AIR   1935
CARDINAL RICHELIEU   United Artists, 1935
THE FLAME WITHIN   MGM, 1935
WOMAN WANTED   MGM, 1935
ANNA KARENINA   MGM, 1935
THE BISHOP MISBEHAVES   MGM, 1935
THE VOICE OF BUGLE ANN   MGM, 1936
THE DEVIL DOLL   MGM, 1936
TARZAN ESCAPES   MGM, 1936
A DAY AT THE RACES   MGM, 1937

THE EMPEROR'S CANDLESTICKS   MGM, 1937
BETWEEN TWO WOMEN   MGM, 1937
MY DEAR MISS ALDRICH   MGM, 1937
A YANK AT OXFORD   MGM, 1938
HOLD THAT KISS   MGM, 1938
PORT OF SEVEN SEAS   MGM, 1938
THE CROWD ROARS   MGM, 1938
SPRING MADNESS   Paramount, 1938
LET US LIVE   Columbia, 1939
TARZAN FINDS A SON   MGM, 1939
SPORTING BLOOD   MGM, 1940
PRIDE AND PREJUDICE   MGM, 1940
MAISIE WAS A LADY   MGM, 1941
TARZAN'S SECRET TREASURE   MGM, 1941
TARZAN'S NEW YORK ADVENTURE   MGM, 1942
THE BIG CLOCK   Paramount, 1948
WHERE DANGER LIVES   RKO Radio, 1950
BONZO GOES TO COLLEGE   1952
ALL I DESIRE   Universal, 1953
MISSION OVER KOREA   1953
DUFFY OF SAN QUENTIN   Warner Bros., 1954
THE STEEL CAGE   United Artists, 1954
THE TALL T   Columbia, 1957
WILD HERITAGE   1958
NEVER TOO LATE   Warner Bros., 1965
THE PHYNX   Warner Bros., 1970
THE CROOKED HEARTS (TF)   Lorimar Productions, 1972
THE GREAT HOUDINIS (TF)   ABC Circle Films, 1976
HANNAH AND HER SISTERS   Orion, 1986
PEGGY SUE GOT MARRIED   TriStar, 1986

CARRÉ OTIS

WILD ORCHID   Triumph Releasing Corporation, 1990

ANNETTE O'TOOLE

b. April 1, 1953 - Houston, Texas
Agent: ICM - Beverly Hills, 310/550-4000

THE GIRL MOST LIKELY TO... (TF)   ABC Circle Films, 1973
SMILE   United Artists, 1975
THE ENTERTAINER (TF)   RSO Rilms, 1975
ONE ON ONE   Warner Bros., 1977
THE WAR BETWEEN THE TATES (TF)   Talent Associates, 1977
KING OF THE GYPSIES   Paramount, 1978
FOO'LIN' AROUND   Columbia, 1978
CAT PEOPLE   Universal, 1982
48 HOURS   Paramount, 1982
SUPERMAN III   Warner Bros., 1983, U.S.-British
COPACABANA (TF)   Dick Clark Productions/Stiletto, Ltd., 1985
CROSS MY HEART   Universal, 1987
THE KENNEDYS OF MASSACHUSETTS (MS)   Edgar J. Scherick
   Associates/Orion TV, 1990
LOVE AT LARGE   Orion, 1990
IT (TF)   Konigsberg-Sanitsky Productions/Green-Epstein
   Productions/Lorimar TV, 1990

PETER O'TOOLE

b. August 2, 1932 - Connemara, Ireland
Agent: William Morris Agency - Beverly Hills, 310/274-7451

THE SAVAGE INNOCENTS   Paramount, 1959,
   Italian-French-British
THE DAY THEY ROBBED THE BANK OF ENGLAND
   MGM, 1960, British
KIDNAPPED   Buena Vista, 1960, British
LAWRENCE OF ARABIA ★   Columbia, 1962, British
BECKET ★   Paramount, 1964, British
LORD JIM   Columbia, 1965, British
WHAT'S NEW PUSSYCAT?   United Artists, 1965, British
THE SANDPIPER   MGM, 1965, British (voice)
THE BIBLE   20th Century-Fox, 1966, Italian
HOW TO STEAL A MILLION   Columbia, 1966
NIGHT OF THE GENERALS   Columbia, 1967, British-French
CASINO ROYALE   Columbia, 1967, British
THE LION IN WINTER ★   Avco Embassy, 1968, British
GREAT CATHERINE   Warner Bros., 1968, British

GOODBYE, MR. CHIPS ★   MGM, 1969, British
BROTHERLY LOVE   *COUNTRY DANCE*   MGM, 1969, British
MURPHY'S WAR   Paramount, 1971, British
UNDER MILK WOOD   Altura, 1973, British
THE RULING CLASS ★   Avco Embassy, 1972
MAN OF LA MANCHA   United Artists, 1972, Italian-U.S.
ROSEBUD   United Artists, 1975
MAN FRIDAY   Avco Embassy, 1976, British
FOXTROT   *OTHER SIDE OF PARADISE*   New World, 1976
ROGUE MALE (TF)   BBC, 1976, British
CALIGULA   *CALIGOLA*   Analysis Film Releasing,
   1977, Italian-U.S.
POWER PLAY   Magnum International Pictures/Cowry Film
   Productions, 1978, Canadian-British
ZULU DAWN   American Cinema, 1979, British
MASADA (MS)   Arnon Milchan Productions/Universal TV, 1981
THE STUNT MAN ★   20th Century-Fox, 1980
MY FAVORITE YEAR ★   MGM/UA, 1982
SVENGALI (TF)   Robert Halmi Productions, 1983
SUPERGIRL   Warner Bros., 1984, British
KIM (TF)   London Films, 1984, British
CREATOR   Universal, 1985
CLUB PARADISE   Warner Bros., 1986
THE LAST EMPEROR   Columbia, 1987, British-Chinese
HIGH SPIRITS   TriStar, 1988, British
CROSSING TO FREEDOM (TF)   Procter & Gamble Productions/
   Stan Margulies Productions/Granada TV, 1990, U.S.-British
THE NUTCRACKER PRINCE (AF)   Warner Bros., 1990 (voice)
KING RALPH   Universal, 1991

BARRY OTTO

BLISS   New World, 1985, Australian

PARK OVERALL

Agent: UTA - Beverly Hills, 310/273-6700

UNDERCOVER BLUES   MGM/UA, 1993

RICK OVERTON

Agent: Progressive Artists Agency - Beverly Hills, 310/553-8561
Manager: Amy Howard Management - Los Angeles, 310/475-6020

EARTH GIRLS ARE EASY   Vestron, 1989
BLIND FURY   TriStar, 1990

TIMOTHY OWEN

TERMINAL BLISS   Cannon, 1992

GARY OWENS

HOW I GOT INTO COLLEGE   20th Century Fox, 1989
I'M GONNA GIT YOU SUCKA   MGM/UA, 1989

FRANK OZ

b. May 25, 1944 - Herford, England
Agent: CAA - Beverly Hills, 310/288-4545

THE MUPPET MOVIE   AFD, 1979, British (voice)
THE EMPIRE STRIKES BACK   20th Century-Fox, 1980 (voice)
THE BLUES BROTHERS   Universal, 1980
THE GREAT MUPPET CAPER   Universal/AFD,
   1981, British (voice)
THE DARK CRYSTAL   Universal/AFD, 1982,
   British (voice; also co-directed)
RETURN OF THE JEDI   20th Century-Fox, 1983 (voice)
THE MUPPETS TAKE MANHATTAN   TriStar,
   1984 (voice; also directed)

P

FEDERICO PACIFICI
FLUKE   MGM/UA, 1994

AL PACINO
(Alberto Pacino)
b. April 25, 1940 - New York, New York
Agent: CAA - Beverly Hills, 310/288-4545

ME, NATALIE   1969
THE PANIC IN NEEDLE PARK   20th Century-Fox, 1971
THE GODFATHER ✪   Paramount, 1972
SCARECROW   Warner Bros., 1973
SERPICO ★   Paramount, 1973
THE GODFATHER, PART II ★   Paramount, 1974
DOG DAY AFTERNOON ★   Warner Bros., 1975
BOBBY DEERFIELD   Columbia, 1977
...AND JUSTICE FOR ALL ★   Columbia, 1979
CRUISING   United Artists, 1980
AUTHOR! AUTHOR!   20th Century-Fox, 1982
SCARFACE   Universal, 1983
REVOLUTION   Warner Bros., 1985, British-Norwegian
SEA OF LOVE   Universal, 1989
DICK TRACY ✪   Buena Vista, 1990
THE GODFATHER, PART III   Paramount, 1990
FRANKIE & JOHNNY   Paramount, 1991
GLENGARRY GLEN ROSS ✪   New Line Cinema, 1992
SCENT OF A WOMAN ★★   Universal, 1992
CARLITO'S WAY   Universal, 1993
TWO BITS   Miramax Films, 1994
CITY HALL   Columbia, 1995
HEAT   Warner Bros., 1995

DAVID PACKER
YOU CAN'T HURRY LOVE   MCEG, 1988

JOANNA PACULA
GORKY PARK   Orion, 1983
DEATH BEFORE DISHONOR   New World, 1987
ESCAPE FROM SOBRIBOR (TF)   Rule-Starger Productions/
   Zenith Productions, 1987, U.S.-British
BREAKING POINT (CTF)   Avnet-Kerner Company, 1989
MARKED FOR DEATH   20th Century Fox, 1990

HARRISON PAGE
LIONHEART   Universal, 1991
CARNOSAUR   New Horizons Pictures, 1993

KEN PAGE
TORCH SONG TRILOGY   New Line Cinema, 1988

SUZEE PAI
BIG TROUBLE IN LITTLE CHINA   20th Century Fox, 1986

HEIDI PAINE
SKIN DEEP   20th Century Fox, 1989

HOLLY PALANCE
UNDER FIRE   Orion, 1983
THE BEST OF TIMES   Universal, 1986

JACK PALANCE
(Walter Jack Palahnuik)
b. February 18, 1919 - Lattimer, Pennsylvania
Agent: Susan Smith & Associates - Beverly Hills, 213/852-4777

PANIC IN THE STREETS   1950
HALLS OF MONTEZUMA   20th Century-Fox, 1950
SUDDEN FEAR ✪   RKO Radio, 1952
SHANE ✪   Paramount, 1953
SECOND CHANCE   1953
ARROWHEAD   1953
FLIGHT TO TANGIER   1953
MAN IN THE ATTIC   1953
SIGN OF THE PAGAN   1954
THE SILVER CHALICE   1955
KISS OF FIRE   1955
THE BIG KNIFE   1955
I DIED A THOUSAND TIMES   1955
ATTACK!   1956
THE LONELY MAN   1957
HOUSE OF NUMBERS   1957
BEYOND ALL LIMITS   *FLOR DE MAYO*   1957, Mexican
THE MAN INSIDE   1958, British
TEN SECONDS TO HELL   1959, British-U.S.
AUSTERLITZ   1960, French-Italian
THE MONGOLS   *I MONGOLI*   1961, Italian-French
BARABBAS   *BARABBA*   1961, Italian
SWORD OF THE CONQUEROR   *ALBOINO E ROSMUNDA*
   1961, Italian
IL GIUDIZIO UNIVERSALE   1961, Italian
WARRIORS 5   *LA GUERRA CONTINUA*   1962, Italian-French
CONTEMPT   *LE MEPRIS*   1963, French-Italian
ONCE A THIEF   *LES TUEURS DE SAN FRANCISCO*
   1965, French-U.S.
THE PROFESSIONALS   1966
TORTURE GARDEN   1967, British
KILL A DRAGON   1967
A PROFESSIONAL GUN   1958
THEY CAME TO ROB LAS VEGAS   *LAS VEGAS 500 MILLONES*
   1968, Spanish-Italian-French-West German
THE MERCENARY   *IL MERCENARIO*   1969, Italian-Spanish
THE DESPERADOS   1969
CHE!   1969
THE COMPANEROS   1970
THE McMASTERS   1970
MONTE WALSH   1970
THE HORSEMEN   1971
CHATO'S LAND   1972
OKLAHOMA CRUDE   Columbia, 1973
DRACULA (TF)   1973
CRAZE   1974, British
THE FOUR DEUCES   1975, Israeli-British
AFRICA EXPRESS   1975, Italian
THE HATFIELDS AND THE McCOYS (TF)   Charles Fries
   Productions, 1975
THE GREAT ADVENTURE   1976, British
PAURA IN CITTA   1976, Italian
THE DIAMOND MERCENARIES   1976
GOD'S GUN   1977
WELCOME TO BLOOD CITY   1977, British-Canadian
KENNELL   1977
MR. SCARFACE   1977, Italian
ONE MAN JURY   1978
SEVEN FROM HEAVEN   1979
THE SHAPE OF THINGS TO COME (TF)   1979
COCAINE COWBOYS   1979
THE LAST RIDE OF THE DALTON GANG (TF)   NBC Productions/
   Dan Curtis Productions, 1979
HAWK THE SLAYER   1980
WITHOUT WARNING   1980
LADYFINGERS   1980
ALONE IN THE DARK   New Line Cinema, 1982
BAGDAD CAFE   *OUT OF ROSENHEIM*   Island Pictures, 1987,
   West German-U.S.
YOUNG GUNS   20th Century Fox, 1988
BATMAN   Warner Bros., 1989
TANGO & CASH   Warner Bros., 1989
CITY SLICKERS ✪✪   Columbia, 1991
COPS & ROBBERSONS   TriStar, 1994
CITY SLICKERS II: THE LEGEND OF CURLY'S GOLD   Columbia, 1994
BUFFALO GIRLS (MS)   Lauren Film Productions, Inc./CBS, 1995

MICHAEL PALIN
b. May 5, 1943 - England

AND NOW FOR SOMETHING COMPLETELY DIFFERENT
  1972, British
MONTY PYTHON AND THE HOLY GRAIL   Cinema 5, 1974, British
JABBERWOCKY   Cinema 5, 1977, British
MONTY PYTHON'S LIFE OF BRIAN   Orion/Warner Bros.,
  1979, British
TIME BANDITS   Avco Embassy, 1981, British
MONTY PYTHON LIVE AT THE HOLLYWOOD BOWL   Columbia,
  1982, British
THE MISSIONARY   Columbia, 1982, British
THE SECRET POLICEMAN'S OTHER BALL (FD)   Miramax Films,
  1982, British
MONTY PYTHON'S THE MEANING OF LIFE   Universal,
  1983, British
A PRIVATE FUNCTION   Island Alive, 1984, British
BRAZIL   Universal, 1985, British
A FISH CALLED WANDA   MGM/UA, 1988, British

GERALDINE PALLHAS
DON JUAN DE MARCO AND THE CENTERFOLD
  New Line Cinema, 1995

BETSY PALMER
b. November 1, 1929 - East Chicago, Indiana

THE LONG GRAY LINE   Columbia, 1955
QUEEN BEE   Columbia, 1955
THE TIN STAR   Paramount, 1957
THE LAST ANGRY MAN   Columbia, 1959
IT HAPPENED TO JANE   *TWINKLE AND SHINE*   Columbia, 1959
FRIDAY THE 13TH   Paramount, 1980
FRIDAY THE 13TH PART II   Paramount, 1981
GODDESS OF LOVE (TF)   Phil Margo Enterprises/New World TV/
  Phoenix Entertainment Group, 1988

CHAZZ PALMINTERI
Agent: William Morris Agency - Beverly Hills, 310/274-7451

PETER GUNN (TF)   The Blake Edwards Company/
  New World TV, 1990
OSCAR   Buena Vista, 1991
A BRONX TALE   Savoy Pictures, 1993
BULLETS OVER BROADWAY   Miramax Films, 1994
THE PEREZ FAMILY   Samuel Goldwyn Company, 1994
FAITHFUL   Savoy Pictures, 1995

CONRAD PALMISANO
AIRPLANE!   Paramount, 1980

GWYNETH PALTROW
HIGHER LEARNING   Columbia, 1994
FLESH AND BONE   Paramount, 1993
MRS. PARKER AND THE VICIOUS CIRCLE   Fine Line Features/
  New Line Cinema, 1994
JEFFERSON IN PARIS   Buena Vista, 1995
MOONLIGHT AND VALENTINO   Gramercy Pictures, 1995

RICHARD PANEBIANCO
CHINA GIRL   Vestron, 1987

STUART PANKIN
Agent: Metropolitan Talent Agency - Los Angeles, 213/857-4500

THE DIRT BIKE KID   Concorde/Cinema Group, 1986
A DIFFERENT AFFAIR (TF)   Rogers-Samuels Productions, 1987
FATAL ATTRACTON   Paramount, 1987
SECOND SIGHT   Warner Bros., 1989
ARACHNOPHOBIA   Buena Vista, 1990
MANNEQUIN TWO ON THE MOVE   20th Century Fox, 1991

JOHN PANKOW
Agent: William Morris Agency - Beverly Hills, 310/274-7451

TO LIVE AND DIE IN L.A.   MGM/UA, 1985
MONKEY SHINES   Orion, 1988
TALK RADIO   Universal, 1988
MORTAL THOUGHTS   Columbia, 1991
YEAR OF THE GUN   Columbia, 1991

JOE PANTOLIANO
Agent: UTA - Beverly Hills, 310/273-6700

ROAD MOVIE   Grove Press, 1974
FOR PETE'S SAKE   Columbia, 1974
THE GODFATHER, PART II   Paramount, 1974
SKIP TRACER   Highlight Propductions Ltd., 1977, Canadian
MORE THAN FRIENDS (TF)   Reiner-Mishkin Productions/
  Columbia TV, 1978
FROM HERE TO ETERNITY (MS)   Bennett-Katleman Productions/
  Columbia TV, 1979
ALCATRAZ: THE WHOLE SHOCKING STORY (TF)
  Pierre Cossette Productions, 1980
THE IDOLMAKER   United Artists, 1980
MONSIGNOR   20th Century-Fox, 1982
THE FINAL TERROR   Comworld, 1983
EDDIE AND THE CRUISERS   Embassy, 1983
RISKY BUSINESS   The Geffen Company/Warner Bros., 1983
THE MEAN SEASON   Orion, 1985
ROBERT KENNEDY AND HIS TIMES (MS)   Chris-Rose Productions/
  Columbia TV, 1985
THE GOONIES   Warner Bros., 1985
RUNNING SCARED   MGM/UA, 1986
DESTINATION AMERICA (TF)   Stephen J. Cannell
  Productions, 1987
LA BAMBA   Columbia, 1987
EMPIRE OF THE SUN   Warner Bros., 1987
SCENES FROM THE GOLDMINE   Hemdale, 1988
THE IN CROWD   Orion, 1988
MIDNIGHT RUN   Universal, 1988
EL DIABLO (CTF)   HBO Pictures/Wizan-Black Films, 1990
THE LAST OF THE FINEST   Orion, 1990
SHORT TIME   20th Century Fox, 1990
ZANDALEE   Electric Pictures/ITC Entertainment Group, 1991
USED PEOPLE   20th Century Fox, 1992
THREE OF HEARTS   New Line Cinema, 1993
THE FUGITIVE   Warner Bros., 1993
CALENDAR GIRL   Columbia, 1993
BABY'S DAY OUT   20th Century Fox, 1994
BAD BOYS   Columbia, 1995

ANNA PAQUIN
Agent: William Morris Agency - Beverly Hills, 310/274-7451

THE PIANO OO   Miramax Films, 1993, New Zealand-French

MICHAEL PARÉ
EDDIE AND THE CRUISERS   Embassy, 1983
THE PHILADELPHIA EXPERIMENT   New World, 1984
STREETS OF FIRE   Universal, 1984
SPACE RAGE   Vestron, 1985
THE WOMEN'S CLUB   Weintraub-Cloverleaf/Scorsese
  Productions, 1987
INSTANT JUSTICE   *MARINE ISSUE*   Warner Bros.,
  1987, Gibraltar
WORLD GONE WILD   Lorimar, 1988
EDDIE AND THE CRUISERS II: EDDIE LIVES   Scotti Bros., 1989
THE CLOSER   Ion Pictures, 1990
THE KILLING STREETS   21st Century Distribution, 1991

RANDI PAREIRA
b. March 24, 1963 - Miami, Florida
Agent: Joseph Heldfond & Rix, Inc. - Hollywood, 213/466-9111

THE IN CROWD   Orion, 1988
MY BLUE HEAVEN   Warner Bros., 1990
HOOK   TriStar, 1991
THE BEVERLY HILLBILLIES   20th Century Fox, 1993

JUDY PARFITT
GETTING IT RIGHT   MCEG, 1989, U.S.-British
DOLORES CLAIBORNE   Columbia, 1994

ANNE PARILLAUD
INNOCENT BLOOD   Warner Bros., 1992
MAP OF THE HUMAN HEART   Miramax Films, 1993,
   British-French-New Zealand

ANDREW PARIS
VIVA MAX!   Commonwealth United, 1969
HOW TO BREAK UP A HAPPY DIVORCE (TF)   Charles Fries
   Productions, 1976
POLICE ACADEMY 2: THEIR FIRST ASSIGNMENT
   Warner Bros., 1985
POLICE ACADEMY 3: BACK IN TRAINING   Warner Bros., 1986

ANDREA PARKER
Agent: Susan Smith & Associates - Beverly Hills, 213/852-4777

XXX'S & OOO'S (TF)   Moving Target Productions/New World
   Entertainment, 1994

COREY PARKER
SCREAM FOR HELP   Lorimar Distribution International, 1984
BILOXI BLUES   Universal, 1988
AT MOTHER'S REQUEST (TF)   Vista Organization, Ltd., 1987
HOW I GOT INTO COLLEGE   20th Century Fox, 1989
I'M DANGEROUS TONIGHT (CTF)   BBK Productions, 1990

ELEANOR PARKER
b. June 26, 1922 - Cedarville, Ohio

THEY DIED WITH THEIR BOOTS ON   Warner Bros., 1941
BUSSES ROAR   Warner Bros., 1942
MISSION TO MOSCOW   Warner Bros., 1943
THE MYSTERIOUS DOCTOR   Warner Bros., 1943
BETWEEN TWO WORLDS   Warner Bros., 1944
CRIME BY NIGHT   Warner Bros., 1944
THE LAST RIDE   Warner Bros., 1944
THE VERY THOUGHT OF YOU   Warner Bros., 1944
HOLLYWOOD CANTEEN   Warner Bros., 1944
PRIDE OF THE MARINES   Warner Bros., 1945
OF HUMAN BONDAGE   Warner Bros., 1946
NEVER SAY GOODBYE   Warner Bros., 1946
ESCAPE ME NEVER   Warner Bros., 1947
ALWAYS TOGETHER   Warner Bros., 1947
THE VOICE OF THE TURTLE   Warner Bros., 1947
THE WOMAN IN WHITE   Warner Bros., 1948
IT'S A GREAT FEELING   Warner Bros., 1949
CHAIN LIGHTNING   Warner Bros., 1950
CAGED ★   Warner Bros., 1950
THREE SECRETS   Warner Bros., 1950
VALENTINO   Columbia, 1951
A MILLIONAIRE FOR CHRISTY   20th Century-Fox, 1951
DETECTIVE STORY ★   Paramount, 1951
SCARAMOUCHE   MGM, 1952
ABOVE AND BEYOND   MGM, 1952
ESCAPE FROM FORT BRAVO   MGM, 1953
THE NAKED JUNGLE   Paramount, 1954
VALLEY OF THE KINGS   1954
MANY RIVERS TO CROSS   1955
INTERRUPTED MELODY ★   MGM, 1955
THE MAN WITH THE GOLDEN ARM   United Artists, 1955
THE KING AND FOUR QUEENS   United Artists, 1956
LIZZIE   1957
THE SEVENTH SIN   MGM, 1957
A HOLE IN THE HEAD   United Artists, 1959
HOME FROM THE HILL   MGM, 1960
RETURN TO PEYTON PLACE   20th Century-Fox, 1961
MADISON AVENUE   20th Century-Fox, 1962
PANIC BUTTON   Gorton, 1964
THE SOUND OF MUSIC   20th Century-Fox, 1965
THE OSCAR   Embassy, 1966
AN AMERICAN DREAM   1966
WARNING SHOT   Paramount, 1967

THE TIGER AND THE PUSSYCAT   *IL TIGRE*   Embassy,
   1967, Italian-U.S.
HOW TO STEAL THE WORLD   MGM, 1968
EYE OF THE CAT   1969
MAYBE I'LL COME HOME IN THE SPRING (TF)   Metromedia
   Productions, 1970
VANISHED (TF)   Universal TV, 1971
HOME FOR THE HOLIDAYS (TF)   ABC Circle Films, 1972
THE GREAT AMERICAN BEAUTY CONTEST (TF)
   ABC Circle Films, 1973
SHE'S DRESSED TO KILL   *SOMEONE'S KILLING THE WORLD'S*
   GREATEST MODELS (TF)   Grant-Case-McGrath Enterprises/
   Barry Weitz Films, 1979
SUNBURN   Paramount, 1979, U.S.-British

JAMESON PARKER
b. November 18, 1947 - Baltimore, Maryland

THE BELL JAR   Avco Embassy, 1979
A SMALL CIRCLE OF FRIENDS   United Artists, 1980
WHITE DOG   Paramount, 1982
WHO IS JULIA? (TF)   CBS Entertainment, 1986
PRINCE OF DARKNESS   Universal, 1987

LENI PARKER
MRS. PARKER AND THE VICIOUS CIRCLE   Fine Line Features/
   New Line Cinema, 1994

MARY-LOUISE PARKER
Agent: William Morris Agency - Beverly Hills, 310/274-7451

TOO YOUNG THE HERO (TF)   Rick-Dawn Productions/Pierre
   Cossette Productions/The Landsburg Company, 1988
SIGNS OF LIFE   Avenue Pictures, 1989
LONGTIME COMPANION   Samuel Goldwyn Company, 1990
GRAND CANYON   20th Century Fox, 1991
FRIED GREEN TOMATOES   Universal, 1991
MR. WONDERFUL   Warner Bros., 1993
NAKED IN NEW YORK   Fine Line Features/New Line Cinema, 1994
A PLACE FOR ANNIE (TF)   1994
THE CLIENT   Warner Bros., 1994
BULLETS OVER BROADWAY   Miramax Films, 1994
BOYS ON THE SIDE   Warner Bros., 1995

NATHANIEL PARKER
WIDE SARGASSO SEA   Fine Line Features/New Line Cinema,
   1993, British

NORMAN PARKER
LEAP OF FAITH (TF)   Hart, Thomas & Berlin Productions, 1988

SARAH JESSICA PARKER
b. March 25, 1965 - Nelsonville, Ohio
Agent: CAA - Beverly Hills, 310/288-4545

RICH KIDS   United Artists, 1979
SOMEWHERE TOMORROW   Comworld, 1983
FOOTLOOSE   Paramount, 1984
FIRSTBORN   Paramount, 1984
GIRLS JUST WANT TO HAVE FUN   New World, 1985
GOING FOR THE GOLD: THE BILL JOHNSON STORY (TF)
   ITC Productions/Sullivan-Carter Interests/Goodman-Rosen
   Productions, 1985
FLIGHT OF THE NAVIGATOR   Buena Vista, 1986
A YEAR IN THE LIFE (MS)   Universal TV, 1986
DADAH IS DEATH (MS)   Steve Krantz Prods./Roadshow, Coote &
   Carroll Productions/Samuel Goldwyn TV, 1988, U.S.-Australian
THE RYAN WHITE STORY (TF)   The Landsburg Company, 1989
L.A. STORY   TriStar, 1991
HONEYMOON IN VEGAS   Columbia, 1992
HOCUS POCUS   Buena Vista, 1993
STRIKING DISTANCE   Columbia, 1993
ED WOOD   Buena Vista, 1994

SUNSHINE PARKER
CANNERY ROW   MGM/United Artists, 1982

TREY PARKER
NEWSIES Buena Vista, 1992

JILL PARKER-JONES
THE SUBSTITUTE WIFE (TF) Frederick S. Pierce Company, 1994

MICHAEL PARKS
DEATH WISH V: THE FACE OF DEATH Trimark Pictures, 1994

KARYN PARSONS
MAJOR PAYNE Universal, 1995

ESTELLE PARSONS
b. November 20, 1927 - Lynn, Massachusetts

LADYBUG, LADYBUG United Artists, 1963
BONNIE AND CLYDE ○○ Warner Bros., 1967
RACHEL, RACHEL ○ Warner Bros., 1968
DON'T DRINK THE WATER Avco Embassy, 1969
WATERMELON MAN Columbia, 1970
I WALK THE LINE Columbia, 1970
I NEVER SANG FOR MY FATHER Columbia, 1970
TWO PEOPLE Universal, 1973
FOR PETE'S SAKE Columbia, 1974
OPEN ADMISSIONS (TF) The Mount Company/Viacom
   Productions, 1988
DICK TRACY Buena Vista, 1990
BOYS ON THE SIDE Warner Bros., 1995

DOLLY PARTON
b. January 19, 1946 - Sevierville, Tennessee

NINE TO FIVE 20th Century-Fox, 1980
THE BEST LITTLE WHOREHOUSE IN TEXAS Universal, 1982
RHINESTONE 20th Century Fox, 1984
A SMOKY MOUNTAIN CHRISTMAS (TF)
   Sandollar Productions, 1986
STEEL MAGNOLIAS TriStar, 1989
WILD TEXAS WIND (TF) NBC Productions, 1991
STRAIGHT TALK Buena Vista, 1992
THE BEVERLY HILLBILLIES 20th Century Fox, 1993

ISABELLE PASCO
PROSPERO'S BOOKS Miramax Films, 1991

ADRIAN PASDAR
TOP GUN Paramount, 1986
NEAR DARK DEG, 1987
COOKIE Warner Bros., 1989
VITAL SIGNS 20th Century Fox, 1990
TORN APART Castle Hill Productions, 1990

VINCENT PASTORE
THE JERKY BOYS Buena Vista, 1994

ROBERT PASTORELLI
OUTRAGEOUS FORTUNE Buena Vista, 1987
DANCES WITH WOLVES Orion, 1990
STRIKING DISTANCE Columbia, 1993

MICHAEL PATAKI
ROCKY IV MGM/UA, 1985
AMERICAN ANTHEM Columbia, 1986
HALLOWEEN IV - THE RETURN OF MICHAEL MYERS
   Galaxy, 1988

GEMMA PATERNOSTER
BLACK BEAUTY Warner Bros., 1994, British-U.S.

BILL PATERSON
DEFENSE OF THE REALM Hemdale, 1985, British
THE ADVENTURES OF BARON MUNCHAUSEN Columbia, 1989
DIAMOND'S EDGE Kings Road Entertainment, 1990

MANDY PATINKIN
b. November 30, 1952 - Chicago, Illinois
Agent: UTA - Beverly Hills, 310/273-6700

THE BIG FIX Universal, 1978
LAST EMBRACE United Artists, 1979
DANIEL Paramount, 1983
YENTL MGM/UA, 1983
MAXIE Orion, 1985
ALIEN NATION 20th Century Fox, 1988
DICK TRACY Buena Vista, 1990
IMPROMPTU Hemdale, 1990, U.S.-French
THE DOCTOR Buena Vista, 1991
TRUE COLORS Paramount, 1991

ANGELA PATON
TRAPPED IN PARADISE 20th Century Fox, 1994

JASON PATRIC
Agent: UTA - Beverly Hills, 310/273-6700

THE LOST BOYS Warner Bros., 1987
THE BEAST Columbia, 1988
AFTER DARK, MY SWEET Avenue Pictures, 1990
DENIAL *LOON* Filmstar, 1991
RUSH MGM-Pathe, 1991
GERONIMO - AN AMERICAN LEGEND Columbia, 1993
THE JOURNEY OF AUGUST KING Miramax Films, 1995

ROBERT PATRICK
Agent: UTA - Beverly Hills, 310/273-6700

TERMINATOR 2: JUDGMENT DAY TriStar, 1991
FIRE IN THE SKY Paramount, 1993

CHUCK PATTERSON
THE FIVE HEARTBEATS 20th Century Fox, 1991

FRANK PATTERSON
THE DEAD Vestron, 1987

JAY PATTERSON
STREET SMART Cannon, 1987
McBAIN Shapiro-Glickenhaus Entertainment, 1991

LORNA PATTERSON
AIRPLANE! Paramount, 1980

NEVA PATTERSON
WOMEN OF VALOR (TF) Inter Planetary Productions/Jeni
   Productions, 1986

WILL PATTON
Agent: William Morris Agency - Beverly Hills, 310/274-7451

AFTER HOURS The Geffen Company/Warner Bros., 1985
BELIZAIRE THE CAJUN Skouras Pictures, 1986
NO WAY OUT Orion, 1987
EVERYBODY WINS Orion, 1990
A SHOCK TO THE SYSTEM Corsair Pictures, 1990
COLD HEAVEN Hemdale, 1992
ROMEO IS BLEEDING Gramercy Pictures, 1994, U.S.-British
THE CLIENT Warner Bros., 1994
THE PUPPET MASTERS Buena Vista, 1994

ADRIAN PAUL
THE FAVORITE Kings Road, 1989
LOVE POTION #9 20th Century Fox, 1992

ALEXANDRA PAUL
CHRISTINE Columbia, 1983
JUST THE WAY YOU ARE MGM/UA, 1984
AMERICAN FLYERS Warner Bros., 1985
8 MILLION WAYS TO DIE TriStar, 1986
DRAGNET Universal, 1987

DAVID PAUL
(The Barbarian Brothers)
THINK BIG   MPCA, 1990

DON MICHAEL PAUL
DANGEROUSLY CLOSE   Cannon, 1986
ALOHA SUMMER   *HANAUMA BAY*   Spectrafilm, 1988
HEART OF DIXIE   Orion, 1989
RICH GIRL   Studio Three, 1991

NANCY PAUL
V.I. WARSHAWSKI   Buena Vista, 1991

PETER PAUL
(The Barbarian Brothers)
THINK BIG   MPCA, 1990

RICHARD JOSEPH PAUL
Agent: William Morris Agency - Beverly Hills, 310/274-7451

UNDER THE BOARDWALK   New World, 1989

SCOTT PAULIN
THE ACCUSED   Paramount, 1988
TRICKS OF THE TRADE (TF)   Leonard Hill Films, 1988
TURNER & HOOCH   Buena Vista, 1989
PUMP UP THE VOLUME   New Line Cinema, 1990

ROB PAULSEN
LAND BEFORE TIME (AF)   Universal, 1995 (voice)

RIA PAVIA
DREAM A LITTLE DREAM   Vestron, 1989

LUCIANO PAVAROTTI
b. October 12, 1935 - Modena, Italy

YES, GIORGIO   MGM/UA, 1982

JAMES PAX
KINJITE (FORBIDDEN SUBJECTS)   Cannon, 1989

BILL PAXTON
Agent: William Morris Agency - Beverly Hills, 310/274-7451

IMPULSE   20th Century Fox, 1984
ALIENS   20th Century Fox, 1986
NEAR DARK   DEG, 1987
NEXT OF KIN   Warner Bros., 1989
THE LAST OF THE FINEST   Orion, 1990
NAVY SEALS   Orion, 1990
PREDATOR 2   20th Century Fox, 1990
ONE FALSE MOVE   I.R.S. Releasing, 1992
HURRICANE   I.R.S. Releasing, 1992
THE VAGRANT   MGM-Pathe, 1992
INDIAN SUMMER   Buena Vista, 1993
BOXING HELENA   Orion Classics, 1993
TOMBSTONE   Buena Vista, 1993
TRUE LIES   20th Century Fox, 1994
FRANK AND JESSE   Trimark Pictures, 1994
APOLLO 13   Universal, 1995

COLLIN WILCOX PAXTON
FLUKE   MGM/UA, 1994

DAVID PAYMER
Agent: Susan Smith & Associates - Beverly Hills, 213/852-4777

THE IN-LAWS   Columbia, 1979
AIRPLANE II: THE SEQUEL   Paramount, 1982
IRRECONCILABLE DIFFERENCES   Warner Bros., 1984
PERFECT   Columbia, 1985
LOVE, MARY (TF)   CBS Entertainment, 1985
PLEASURES (TF)   Catalina Production Group/Columbia TV, 1986

NO WAY OUT   Orion, 1987
CRAZY PEOPLE   Paramount, 1990
CITY SLICKERS   Columbia, 1991
MR. SATURDAY NIGHT ✪   Columbia, 1992
HEART AND SOULS   Universal, 1993
SEARCHING FOR BOBBY FISCHER   Paramount, 1993
CITY SLICKERS II: THE LEGEND OF CURLY'S GOLD
    Columbia, 1994
QUIZ SHOW   Buena Vista, 1994
CAGNEY & LACEY: THE RETURN (TF)   The Rosenzweig
    Company, 1994
CAGNEY & LACEY: TOGETHER AGAIN (TF)   The Rosenzweig
    Company, 1995
CITY HALL   Columbia, 1995
THE AMERICAN PRESIDENT   Columbia, 1995

ALLEN PAYNE
CB4   Universal, 1993
JASON'S LYRIC   1994

BRUCE PAYNE
SWITCH   Warner Bros., 1991
PASSENGER 57   Warner Bros., 1992

AMANDA PAYS
Agent: William Morris Agency - Beverly Hills, 310/274-7451

OFF LIMITS   20th Century Fox, 1988

DANIEL PEACOCK
ROBIN HOOD: PRINCE OF THIEVES   Warner Bros., 1991

GUY PEARCE
THE ADVENTURES OF PRISCILLA, QUEEN OF THE DESERT
    Gramercy Pictures, 1994, Australian

BARRY PEARL
GREASE   Paramount, 1978
AVENGING ANGEL   New World, 1985

MALACHAI PEARSON
CASPER   Universal, 1995

ANTHONY PECK
DIE HARD 3   20th Century Fox, 1995

BOB PECK
JURASSIC PARK   Universal, 1993

CECILIA PECK
TORN APART   Castle Hill Productions, 1990
AMBITION   Miramax Films, 1991
THE PORTRAIT (CTF)   Robert Greenwald Productions/Atticus
    Corporation/Turner Network TV, 1993

J. EDDIE PECK
DANGEROUSLY CLOSE   Cannon, 1986
LAMBADA   Warner Bros., 1990

GREGORY PECK
(Eldred Gregory Peck)
b. April 5, 1916 - La Jolla, California

DAYS OF GLORY   RKO Radio, 1944
THE KEYS OF THE KINGDOM ★   20th Century-Fox, 1945
THE VALLEY OF DECISION   MGM, 1945
SPELLBOUND   United Artists, 1945
THE YEARLING ★   MGM, 1946
DUEL IN THE SUN   Selznick Releasing, 1946
THE MACOMBER AFFAIR   United Artists, 1947
GENTLEMAN'S AGREEMENT ★   20th Century-Fox, 1947
THE PARADINE CASE   Selznick Releasing, 1948
YELLOW SKY   20th Century-Fox, 1948
THE GREAT SINNER   MGM, 1949

TWELVE O'CLOCK HIGH ★   20th Century-Fox, 1949
THE GUNFIGHTER   20th Century-Fox, 1950
ONLY THE VALIANT   Warner Bros., 1951
DAVID AND BATHSHEBA   20th Century-Fox, 1951
CAPTAIN HORATIO HORNBLOWER   Warner Bros., 1951
THE SNOWS OF KILIMANJARO   20th Century-Fox, 1952
THE WORLD IN HIS ARMS   Universal, 1952
ROMAN HOLIDAY   Paramount, 1953
NIGHT PEOPLE   20th Century-Fox, 1954
THE MILLION POUND NOTE   *MAN WITH A MILLION*
   United Artists, 1954, British
THE PURPLE PLAIN   United Artists, 1954, British
THE MAN IN THE GRAY FLANNEL SUIT   20th Century-Fox, 1956
MOBY DICK   Warner Bros., 1956, British
DESIGNING WOMAN   MGM, 1957
THE BRAVADOS   20th Century-Fox, 1958
THE BIG COUNTRY   United Artists, 1958
PORK CHOP HILL   United Artists, 1959
BELOVED INFIDEL   20th Century-Fox, 1959
ON THE BEACH   United Artists, 1959
THE GUNS OF NAVARONE   Columbia, 1961, U.S.-British
TO KILL A MOCKINGBIRD ★★   Universal, 1962
CAPE FEAR   Universal, 1962
HOW THE WEST WAS WON   MGM/Cinerama, 1962
CAPTAIN NEWMAN, M.D.   Universal, 1963
BEHOLD A PALE HORSE   Columbia, 1964
MIRAGE   Universal, 1965
ARABESQUE   Universal, 1966, British-U.S.
THE STALKING MOON   National General, 1969
MACKENNA'S GOLD   Columbia, 1969
THE CHAIRMAN   *THE MOST DANGEROUS MAN IN THE WORLD*
   20th Century-Fox, 1969, British
MAROONED   Columbia, 1969
I WALK THE LINE   Columbia, 1970
SHOOT OUT   Universal, 1971
BILLY TWO HATS   *THE LADY AND THE OUTLAW*   United Artists,
   1972, British
THE OMEN   20th Century-Fox, 1976
MacARTHUR   Universal, 1977
THE BOYS FROM BRAZIL   20th Century-Fox, 1978
THE SEA WOLVES   Paramount, 1982, British
THE BLUE AND THE GRAY (MS)   Larry White-Lou Reda
   Productions/Columbia TV, 1982
THE SCARLET AND THE BLACK (TF)   Bill McCutchen Productions/
   ITC/RAI, 1983, U.S.-Italian
AMAZING GRACE AND CHUCK   TriStar, 1987
OLD GRINGO   Columbia, 1989
OTHER PEOPLE'S MONEY   Warner Bros., 1991
CAPE FEAR   Universal, 1991
THE PORTRAIT (CTF)   Robert Greenwald Productions/Atticus
   Corporation/Turner Network TV, 1993

T O N Y   P E C K
SLIVER   Paramount, 1993

J O E   P E C O R A R O
HARLEM NIGHTS   Paramount, 1989

N I A   P E E P L E S
DEEPSTAR SIX   TriStar, 1989
XXX'S & OOO'S (TF)   Moving Target Productions/New World
   Entertainment, 1994

A S H L E Y   P E L D O N
DECEIVED   Buena Vista, 1991
THE SECRETARY   Republic Pictures, 1995
CATS DON'TS DANCE (AF)   Turner Pictures, 1996 (voice)

C O U R T N E Y   P E L D O N
OUT ON A LIMB   Universal, 1992

L I S A   P E L I K A N
A BUNNY'S TALE (TF)   Stan Margulies Company/
   ABC Circle Films, 1985
LIONHEART   Universal, 1991
RETURN TO THE BLUE LAGOON   Columbia, 1991

E L I Z A B E T H   P E Ñ A
Agent: Paradigm - Los Angeles, 310/277-4400

EL SUPER   Columbia, 1979
TIMES SQUARE   AFD, 1980
THEY ALL LAUGHED   United Artists Classics, 1982
FOUND MONEY (TF)   Cypress Point Productions/
   Warner Bros. TV, 1983
CROSSOVER DREAMS   Miramax Films, 1985
DOWN AND OUT IN BEVERLY HILLS   Buena Vista, 1986
LA BAMBA   Columbia, 1987
BLUE STEEL   MGM/UA, 1990
JACOB'S LADDER   TriStar, 1990
THE WATERDANCE   Samuel Goldwyn Company, 1992
WILLY II: THE ADVENTURE HOME   Warner Bros., 1995

A U S T I N   P E N D L E T O N
Agent: The Blake Agency - Beverly Hills, 310/246-0241

SKIDOO   Paramount, 1969
WHAT'S UP, DOC?   Warner Bros., 1972
EVERY LITTLE CROOK AND NANNY   MGM, 1972
THE THIEF WHO CAME TO DINNER   Warner Bros., 1973
THE FRONT PAGE   Universal, 1974
THE GREAT SMOKEY ROADBLOCK   *THE LAST OF THE
   COWBOYS*   Dimension, 1978
STARTING OVER   Paramount, 1979
THE MUPPET MOVIE   AFD, 1979, British
FIRST FAMILY   Warner Bros., 1980
MR. AND MRS. BRIDGE   Miramax Films, 1990
MR. NANNY   New Line Cinema, 1993

C H R I S   P E N N
(Christopher Penn)
Agent: UTA - Beverly Hills, 310/273-6700

ALL THE RIGHT MOVES   20th Century-Fox, 1983
FOOTLOOSE   Paramount, 1984
AT CLOSE RANGE   Orion, 1986
BEST OF THE BEST   Taurus Entertainment/SVS Films, 1989
MOBSTERS   Universal, 1991
LEATHER JACKETS   Triumph Releasing Corporation, 1991
RESERVOIR DOGS   Miramax Films, 1992
THE PICKLE   Columbia, 1993
TRUE ROMANCE   Warner Bros., 1993
SHORT CUTS   Fine Line Features/New Line Cinema, 1993
JOSH AND S.A.M.   Columbia, 1993
BEETHOVEN'S 2ND   Universal, 1993

M A T T H E W   P E N N
DREAM LOVER   MGM/UA, 1986

S E A N   P E N N
b. August 17, 1960 - Burbank, California
Agent: William Morris Agency - Beverly Hills, 310/274-7451

THE KILLING OF RANDY WEBSTER (TF)   Roger Gimbel
   Productions/EMI TV, 1991
TAPS   20th Century-Fox, 1981
FAST TIMES AT RIDGEMONT HIGH   Universal, 1982
BAD BOYS   Universal/AFD, 1983
CRACKERS   Universal, 1984
RACING WITH THE MOON   Paramount, 1984
THE FALCON AND THE SNOWMAN   Orion, 1985
AT CLOSE RANGE   Orion, 1986
SHANGHAI SURPRISE   MGM/UA, 1986, British-U.S.
DEAR AMERICA: LETTERS HOME FROM VIETNAM (FD)
   Taurus Entertainment, 1987 (voice)
COLORS   Orion, 1988
JUDGMENT IN BERLIN   New Line Cinema, 1988
CASUALTIES OF WAR   Columbia, 1989
WE'RE NO ANGELS   Paramount, 1989
STATE OF GRACE   Orion, 1990
THE LAST PARTY (FD)   Triton Pictures, 1993
CARLITO'S WAY   Universal, 1993

JOE PENNY
b. September 14, 1956 - London, England

S.O.B.   Paramount, 1981
BLOOD VOWS: THE STORY OF A MAFIA WIFE (TF)
   Louis Rudolph Films/Fries Entertainment, 1987
ROSES ARE FOR THE RICH (MS)   Phoenix Entertainment
   Group, 1987
A WHISPER KILLS (TF)   Sandy Hook Productions/Steve Tisch
   Company/Phoenix Entertainment Group, 1988
THE OPERATION (TF)   Moress, Nanas, Golden Entertainment/
   Viacom, 1990

ARMANDO PENSO
BIG   20th Century Fox, 1988

MARCO PERELA
THE SUBSTITUTE WIFE (TF)   Frederick S. Pierce Company, 1994

SUSAN PERETZ
DOG DAY AFTERNOON   Warner Bros., 1975
SING   TriStar, 1989

JOSÉ PEREZ
STICK   Universal, 1985

ROSIE PEREZ
Agent: CAA - Beverly Hills, 310/288-4545

DO THE RIGHT THING   Universal, 1989
WHITE MEN CAN'T JUMP   20th Century Fox, 1992
UNTAMED HEART   MGM/UA, 1993
FEARLESS ✪   Warner Bros., 1993
IT COULD HAPPEN TO YOU   TriStar, 1994

ELIZABETH PERKINS
b. 1961 - Vermont
Agent: CAA - Beverly Hills, 310/288-4545

ABOUT LAST NIGHT...   TriStar, 1986
FROM THE HIP   DEG, 1987
BIG   20th Century Fox, 1988
SWEET HEARTS DANCE   TriStar, 1988
ENID IS SLEEPING   Vestron, 1990
LOVE AT LARGE   Orion, 1990
AVALON   TriStar, 1990
HE SAID, SHE SAID   Paramount, 1991
THE DOCTOR   Buena Vista, 1991
INDIAN SUMMER   Buena Vista, 1993
THE FLINTSTONES   Universal, 1994
MIRACLE ON 34TH STREET   20th Century Fox, 1994
MOONLIGHT AND VALENTINO   Gramercy Pictures, 1995

MILLIE PERKINS
b. May 12, 1938 - Passaic, New Jersey

THE DIARY OF ANNE FRANK   20th Century-Fox, 1959
WILD IN THE COUNTRY   1961
ENSIGN PULVER   Warner Bros., 1964
WILD IN THE STREETS   American International, 1968
COCKFIGHTER   BORN TO KILL/WILD DRIFTER/GAMBLIN' MAN
   New World, 1974
LADY COCOA   Dimension, 1975
THE WITCH WHO CAME FROM THE SEA   Moonstone, 1976
TABLE FOR FIVE   Warner Bros., 1983
AT CLOSE RANGE   Orion, 1986
JAKE SPEED   New World, 1986
SLAM DANCE   Island Pictures, 1987

MAX PERLICH
DRUGSTORE COWBOY   Avenue Pictures, 1989
GENUINE RISK   I.R.S. Releasing, 1990
THE BUTCHER'S WIFE   Paramount, 1991
RUSH   MGM-Pathe, 1991

RHEA PERLMAN
b. March 31, 1948 - Brooklyn, New York
Agent: CAA - Beverly Hills, 310/288-4545

INTIMATE STRANGERS (TF)   Charles Fries Productions, 1977
THE RATINGS GAME (CTF)   Imagination-New Street Prods., 1984
RADIO FLYER   Columbia, 1992
COACH   TriStar, 1995

RON PERLMAN
b. April 13, 1950 - New York, New York

QUEST FOR FIRE   20th Century-Fox, 1982, French-Canadian
THE NAME OF THE ROSE   20th Century Fox, 1986,
   West German-Italian-French
POLICE ACADEMY: MISSION TO MOSCOW   Warner Bros., 1994
FLUKE   MGM/UA, 1994

PAUL PERRI
DELTA FORCE 2 - OPERATION STRANGLEHOLD   MGM/UA, 1990
MEMOIRS OF AN INVISIBLE MAN   Warner Bros., 1992

MIREILLE PERRIER
CHOCOLAT   Orion Classics, 1988, French

JACQUES PERRIN
CINEMA PARADISO   NUOVO CINEMA PARADISO   Miramax Films,
   1989, Italian

VALERIE PERRINE
b. September 3, 1943 - Galveston, Texas
Agent: Borinstein-Oreck-Bogart - Los Angeles, 213/658-7500

SLAUGHTERHOUSE FIVE   Universal, 1972
THE LAST AMERICAN HERO   HARD DRIVER   20th Century-Fox, 1973
LENNY ★   United Artists, 1974
W.C. FIELDS AND ME   Universal, 1976
MR. BILLION   20th Century-Fox, 1977
ZIEGFELD: THE MAN AND HIS WOMEN (TF)
   Frankovich Productions/Columbia TV, 1978
SUPERMAN   Warner Bros., 1978
THE MAGICIAN OF LUBLIN   Cannon, 1979, Israeli-West German
THE ELECTRIC HORSEMAN   Columbia, 1979
CAN'T STOP THE MUSIC   AFD, 1980
AGENCY   Taft International, 1981, Canadian
SUPERMAN II   Warner Bros., 1981, U.S.-British
THE BORDER   Universal, 1982
WHEN YOUR LOVER LEAVES (TF)   Major H Productions, 1983
WATER   Atlantic Releasing Corporation, 1984, British
BRIGHT ANGEL   Hemdale, 1991

FELTON PERRY
ROBOCOP   Orion, 1987
CHECKING OUT   Warner Bros., 1989
ROBOCOP 3   Orion, 1993

JEFF PERRY
HARD PROMISES   Columbia, 1991

LUKE PERRY
b. October 11 - Fredericktown, Ohio

TERMINAL BLISS   Cannon, 1992
BUFFY THE VAMPIRE SLAYER   20th Century Fox, 1992
8 SECONDS   New Line Cinema, 1994

JOHN BENNETT PERRY
FAREWELL TO THE KING   Orion, 1989

LISA JANE PERSKY
THE GREAT SANTINI   THE ACE   Orion/Warner Bros., 1980
THE COTTON CLUB   Orion, 1984
SHARING RICHARD (TF)   Houston Motion Picture Entertainment/
   CBS Entertainment, 1988
WHEN HARRY MET SALLY...   Columbia, 1989

NEHEMIAH PERSOFF
b. August 14, 1920 - Jerusalem, Israel

THE NAKED CITY   Universal, 1948
ON THE WATERFRONT   Columbia, 1954
THE HARDER THEY FALL   Columbia, 1956
THE WILD PARTY   1956
THE WRONG MAN   Warner Bros., 1956
MEN IN WAR   United Artists, 1957
THIS ANGRY AGE   *LA DIGA SUL PACIFICO*   Columbia,
   1958, Italian
THE BADLANDERS   MGM, 1958
NEVER STEAL ANYTHING SMALL   1959
GREEN MANSIONS   MGM, 1959
AL CAPONE   Allied Artists, 1959
SOME LIKE IT HOT   United Artists, 1959
THE COMANCHEROS   20th Century-Fox, 1961
THE HOOK   MGM, 1963
A GLOBAL AFFAIR   MGM, 1964
FATE IS THE HUNTER   20th Century-Fox, 1964
THE GREATEST STORY EVER TOLD   United Artists, 1965
THE POWER   MGM, 1968
THE MONEY JUNGLE   1968
PANIC IN THE CITY   1968
MAFIA   *IL GIORNO DELLA CIVETTA*   American International,
   1968, Italian
THE PEOPLE NEXT DOOR   Avco Embassy, 1970
RED SKY AT MORNING   Universal, 1970
MRS. POLLIFAX—SPY   United Artists, 1971
PSYCHIC KILLER   Avco Embassy, 1975
VOYAGE OF THE DAMNED   Avco Embassy, 1976, British
THE WORD (MS)   Charles Fries Productions/Stonehenge
   Productions, 1978
YENTL   MGM/UA, 1983
AN AMERICAN TAIL (AF)   Universal, 1986 (voice)
AN AMERICAN TAIL: FIEVEL GOES WEST (AF)
   Universal, 1991 (voice)

FERN PERSONS
HOOSIERS   Orion, 1986

FRANK PESCE
TOP GUN   Paramount, 1986
29TH STREET   20th Century Fox, 1991

JOE PESCI
Agent: CAA - Beverly Hills, 310/288-4545
b. February 9, 1943 - Newark, New Jersey

DEATH COLLECTOR   *FAMILY ENFORCER*   1975
RAGING BULL ✪   United Artists, 1980
I'M DANCING AS FAST AS I CAN   Paramount, 1982
DEAR MR. WONDERFUL   Joachim von Vietinghoff Produktion/
   Westdeutscher Rundfunk/Sender Freis Berlin,
   1982, West German
EASY MONEY   Orion, 1983
EUREKA   MGM/UA Classics, 1984, British (filmed in 1981)
ONCE UPON A TIME IN AMERICA   The Ladd Company/
   Warner Bros., 1984, U.S.-Italian-Canadian
TUTTI DENTRO   Scena Film, 1984, Italian
MAN ON FIRE   TriStar, 1987, French-Italian
LETHAL WEAPON 2   Warner Bros., 1989
BETSY'S WEDDING   Buena Vista, 1990
GOODFELLAS ✪✪   Warner Bros., 1990
HOME ALONE   20th Century Fox, 1990
BACKTRACK   *CATCHFIRE*   Vestron, 1991 (uncredited)
THE SUPER   20th Century Fox, 1991
JFK   Warner Bros., 1991
MY COUSIN VINNY   20th Century Fox, 1992
LETHAL WEAPON 3   Warner Bros., 1992
THE PUBLIC EYE   Universal, 1992
HOME ALONE 2: LOST IN NEW YORK   20th Century Fox, 1992
A BRONX TALE   Savoy Pictures, 1993
JIMMY HOLLYWOOD   Paramount, 1994
WITH HONORS   Warner Bros., 1994
CASINO   Universal, 1995

LISA PESCIA
BODY CHEMISTRY   Concorde, 1990

BERNADETTE PETERS
b. February 28, 1948
Agent: William Morris Agency - Beverly Hills, 310/274-7451

ACE ELI AND RODGER OF THE SKIES   20th Century-Fox, 1973
THE LONGEST YARD   Paramount, 1974
SILENT MOVIE   20th Century-Fox, 1976
THE JERK   Universal, 1979
HEARTBEEPS   Universal, 1981
PENNIES FROM HEAVEN   MGM/United Artists, 1981
ANNIE   Columbia, 1982
DAVID (TF)   Tough Boys, Inc./Donald March Productions/ITC
   Entertainment Group, 1988
PINK CADILLAC   Warner Bros., 1989
SLAVES OF NEW YORK   TriStar, 1989
FALL FROM GRACE (TF)   NBC Productions, 1990
ALICE   Orion, 1990
IMPROMPTU   Hemdale, 1990, U.S.-French

BROCK PETERS
b. July 2, 1927 - New York, New York
Agent: Paradigm - Los Angeles, 310/277-4400

CARMEN JONES   20th Century-Fox, 1954
PORGY AND BESS   Columbia, 1959
TO KILL A MOCKINGBIRD   Universal, 1962
THE L-SHAPED ROOM   Columbia, 1963, British
HEAVENS ABOVE   1963, British
THE PAWNBROKER   Landau/Allied Artists, 1965
MAJOR DUNDEE   Columbia, 1965
P.J.   Universal, 1968
THE McMASTERS   Chevron, 1970
WELCOME HOME, JOHNNY BRISTOL (TF)   Cinema Center, 1971
BLACK GIRL   Cinerama Releasing Corporation, 1972
FRAMED   Paramount, 1975
TWO MINUTE WARNING   Universal, 1976
STAR TREK IV: THE VOYAGE HOME   Paramount, 1986
STAR TREK VI: THE UNDISCOVERED COUNTRY
   Paramount, 1991

ELISEABETH PETERS
SHE-DEVIL   Orion, 1989

WILLIAM L. PETERSEN
Agent: ICM - Beverly Hills, 310/550-4000

TO LIVE AND DIE IN L.A.   MGM/UA, 1985
MANHUNTER   DEG, 1986
AMAZING GRACE AND CHUCK   TriStar, 1987
LONG GONE (CTF)   HBO Pictures/The Landsburg Company, 1987
COUSINS   Paramount, 1989
THE KENNEDYS OF MASSACHUSETTS (MS)   Edgar J. Scherick
   Associates/Orion TV, 1990
YOUNG GUNS II   20th Century Fox, 1990
HARD PROMISES   Columbia, 1992
PASSED AWAY   Buena Vista, 1992
KEEP THE CHANGE (CTF)   The Steve Tisch Company/High
   Horse Films, 1992
NO FEAR   Universal, 1995

AMANDA PETERSON
EXPLORERS   Paramount, 1985
LOVE AND BETRAYAL (TF)   Gross-Weston Productions/ITC
   Entertainment Group, 1989
LISTEN TO ME   Columbia, 1989

CASSANDRA PETERSON
(Elvira)
b. September 17, 1951 - Manhattan, Kansas

ECHO PARK   Atlantic Releasing Corporation, 1986, U.S.-Austrian
PEE WEE'S BIG ADVENTURE   Warner Bros., 1986
ELVIRA, MISTRESS OF THE DARK   New World, 1988

LENKA PETERSON
PANIC IN THE STREETS   20th Century-Fox, 1950
THE PHENIX CITY STORY   Allied Artists, 1955
SOMEONE I TOUCHED (TF)   Charles Fries Productions, 1975
RETURNING HOME (TF)   Lorimar Productions/Samuel Goldwyn
    Productions, 1975
LIFEGUARD   Paramount, 1976
SO FINE   Warner Bros., 1981
WHE ME? (TF)   Lorimar Productions, 1984
CODE OF VENGEANCE (TF)   Universal TV, 1985
PALS (TF)   Robert Halmi, Inc., 1987
DRAGNET   Universal, 1987

PETE PETTIGREW
TOP GUN   Paramount, 1986

LORI PETTY
Agent: Gersh Agency - Beverly Hills, 310/274-6611

CADILLAC MAN   Orion, 1990
POINT BREAK   20th Century Fox, 1991
A LEAGUE OF THEIR OWN   Columbia, 1992
FREE WILLY   Warner Bros., 1993
DEMOLITION MAN   Warner Bros., 1993
IN THE ARMY NOW   Buena Vista, 1994
TANK GIRL   MGM/UA, 1995

TOM PETTY
b. October 20, 1953 - Gainesville, Florida

MADE IN HEAVEN   Lorimar, 1987

DEDEE PFEIFFER
VAMP   New World, 1986
THE ALLNIGHTER   Universal, 1987
FRANKIE & JOHNNY   Paramount, 1991

MICHELLE PFEIFFER
b. April 29, 1958 - Orange County, California
Agent: ICM - Beverly Hills, 310/550-4000

FALLING IN LOVE AGAIN   *IN LOVE*   International Picture Show
    Company, 1980
THE HOLLYWOOD KNIGHTS   Columbia, 1980
CHARLIE CHAN AND THE CURSE OF THE DRAGON QUEEN
    American Cinema, 1981
GREASE 2   Paramount, 1982
SCARFACE   Universal, 1983
INTO THE NIGHT   Universal, 1985
LADYHAWKE   Warner Bros., 1985
SWEET LIBERTY   Universal, 1986
AMAZON WOMEN ON THE MOON   Universal, 1987
THE WITCHES OF EASTWICK   Warner Bros., 1987
MARRIED TO THE MOB   Orion, 1988
TEQUILA SUNRISE   Warner Bros., 1988
DANGEROUS LIAISONS ✪   Warner Bros., 1988
THE FABULOUS BAKER BOYS ★   20th Century Fox, 1989
THE RUSSIA HOUSE   MGM-Pathe, 1990
FRANKIE & JOHNNY   Paramount, 1991
BATMAN RETURNS   Warner Bros., 1992
LOVE FIELD ★   Orion, 1992
THE AGE OF INNOCENCE   Columbia, 1993
WOLF   Columbia, 1994
MY POSSE DON'T DO HOMEWORK   Buena Vista, 1994
PRIVACY   New Line Cinema, 1995
UP CLOSE AND PERSONAL   Buena Vista, 1995

MICHAEL GATES PHENICIE
THE RESCUE   Buena Vista, 1988

MEKHI PHIFER
CLOCKERS   Universal, 1995

JOHN PHILBIN
MARTIANS GO HOME   Taurus Entertainment, 1990

CHYNNA PHILLIPS
Agent: CAA - Beverly Hills, 310/288-4545

THE COMEBACK (TF)   CBS Entertainment, 1989

ETHAN PHILLIPS
LEAN ON ME   Warner Bros., 1989
BLOODHOUNDS OF BROADWAY   Columbia, 1989

JOSEPH C. PHILLIPS
STRICTLY BUSINESS   Warner Bros., 1991

JULIANNE PHILLIPS
Agent: Gersh Agency - Beverly Hills, 310/274-6611

SEVEN HOURS TO JUDGMENT   Trans World Entertainment, 1988
SKIN DEEP   20th Century Fox, 1989
FLETCH LIVES   Universal, 1989

LESLIE PHILLIPS
EMPIRE OF THE SUN   Warner Bros., 1987
KING RALPH   Universal, 1991
AUGUST   Granada Films, 1995

LOU DIAMOND PHILLIPS
b. February 17, 1962 - Arlington, Texas
Agent: Innovative Artists - Los Angeles, 310/553-5200

LA BAMBA   Columbia, 1987
STAND AND DELIVER   Columbia, 1988
YOUNG GUNS   20th Century Fox, 1988
DAKOTA   Miramax Films , 1988
DISORGANIZED CRIME   Buena Vista, 1989
RENEGADES   Universal, 1989
THE FIRST POWER   Orion, 1990
A SHOW OF FORCE   Paramount, 1990
YOUNG GUNS II   20th Century Fox, 1990
AMBITION   Miramax Films, 1991
THE DARK WIND   New Line Cinema, 1991
SIOUX CITY   I.R.S. Releasing, 1994 (also directed)

MICHAEL PHILLIPS
THE TENDER   Triumph Releasing Corporation, 1990

MICHELLE PHILLIPS
b. June 4, 1944 - Long Beach, California
Agent: Ambrosio-Mortimer - Beverly Hills, 310/274-4274

AMERICAN ANTHEM   Columbia, 1986
TRENCHCOAT IN PARADISE (TF)   Ogiens-Kane Company
    Productions/The Finnegan-Pinchuk Company, 1990

NICHOLAS PHILLIPS
SCROOGED   Paramount, 1988

SIAN PHILLIPS
BECKET   Paramount, 1964, British
YOUNG CASSIDY   MGM, 1965, British
LAUGHTER IN THE DARK   Lopert, 1969, British
GOODBYE, MR. CHIPS   MGM, 1969, British
MURPHY'S WAR   Paramount, 1971, British
UNDER MILK WOOD   Altura, 1973, British
TINKER, TAILOR, SOLDIER, SPY (TF)   BBC/Paramount TV,
    1979, British
NIJINKSY   Paramount, 1980, British
CLASH OF THE TITANS   MGM/United Artists, 1981, British
DUNE   Universal, 1984
THE DOCTOR AND THE DEVILS   20th Century-Fox, 1985, British
EWOKS: THE BATTLE FOR ENDOR (TF)   Lucasfilm Ltd., 1985
THE TWO MRS. GRENVILLES (MS)   Lorimar-Telepictures, 1987
VALMONT   Orion, 1989, French

WENDY PHILLIPS
DEATH BE NOT PROUD (TF)   Good Housekeeping Productions/
    Westfall Productions, 1975
MIDNIGHT RUN   Universal, 1988
THE WIZARD   Universal, 1989
MACSHAYNE: WINNER TAKES ALL (TF)   NBC, 1994

JOAQUIN PHOENIX
PARENTHOOD   Universal, 1989
UNTITLED VAN SANT/ZISKIN   Columbia, 1995

LEAF PHOENIX
Agent: Iris Burton Agency - Los Angeles, 310/652-0954

RUSSKIES   New Century/Vista, 1987
PARENTHOOD   Universal, 1989

RAIN PHOENIX
Agent: Iris Burton Agency - Los Angeles, 310/652-0954

EVEN COWGIRLS GET THE BLUES   Fine Line Features/
    New Line Cinema, 1994

ROBERT PICARDO
EXPLORERS   Paramount, 1985
BACK TO SCHOOL   Orion, 1986
LOVERBOY   TriStar, 1989
GREMLINS 2 THE NEW BATCH   Warner Bros., 1990
FATAL DECEPTION: MRS. LEE HARVEY OSWALD (TF)
    David L. Wolper Productions/Bernard Sofronski/Warner Bros.
    Television, 1993
WAGONS EAST   TriStar, 1994

CINDY PICKETT
b. April 18, 1947 - Norman, Oklahoma

FERRIS BUELLER'S DAY OFF   Paramount, 1986
AMERIKA (MS)   ABC Circle Films, 1987
HOT TO TROT   Warner Bros., 1988
I KNOW MY FIRST NAME IS STEVEN (MS)   Andrew Adelson
    Company/Lorimar TV, 1989
DEEPSTAR SIX   TriStar, 1989
CROOKED HEARTS   MGM-Pathe, 1991

REBECCA PIDGEON
OLEANNA   Samuel Goldwyn Company, 1995

BRADLEY MICHAEL PIERCE
BEAUTY AND THE BEAST (AF)   Buena Vista, 1991 (voice)

CHARLES PIERCE
TORCH SONG TRILOGY   New Line Cinema, 1988

ALEXANDRA PIGG
CHICAGO JOE AND THE SHOWGIRL   New Line Cinema, 1990

MITCH PILEGGI
SHOCKER   Universal, 1989

MARK PILLOW
SUPERMAN IV: THE QUEST FOR PEACE   Warner Bros., 1987

BRONSON PINCHOT
b. May 20, 1959 - New York, New York

RISKY BUSINESS   The Geffen Company/Warner Bros., 1983
THE FLAMINGO KID   20th Century Fox, 1984
BEVERLY HILLS COP   Paramount, 1984
HOT RESORT   Cannon, 1985
AFTER HOURS   The Geffen Company/Warner Bros., 1985
SECOND SIGHT   Warner Bros., 1989
BLAME IT ON THE BELLBOY   Buena Vista, 1992, British
TRUE ROMANCE   Warner Bros., 1993
BEVERLY HILLS COP III   Paramount, 1994

MIGUEL PIÑERO
ALMOST YOU   TLC Films/20th Century Fox, 1984

JADA PINKETT
JASON'S LYRIC   1994
A LOW DOWN DIRTY SHAME   Buena Vista, 1994

TANYA PINKINS
ABOVE THE RIM   New Line Cinema, 1994

MARIANGELA PINO
Agent: Susan Smith & Associates - Beverly Hills, 213/852-4777

RICHIE RICH   Warner Bros., 1994

DOMINIQUE PINON
DIVA   United Artists Classics, 1982, French

LEAH KING PINSENT
APRIL FOOL'S DAY   Paramount, 1986

HAROLD PINTER
TURTLE DIARY   Samuel Goldwyn Company, 1985, British

RODDY PIPER
BODY SLAM   DEG, 1987
THEY LIVE   Universal, 1988
BUY & CELL   Empire Pictures, 1989

JOE PISCOPO
b. June 17, 1951 - Passaic, New Jersey

KING KONG   Paramount, 1976
JOHNNY DANGEROUSLY   20th Century Fox, 1984
WISE GUYS   MGM/UA, 1986
DEAD HEAT   New World, 1988

MARIE-FRANCE PISIER
COUSIN, COUSINE   Libra, 1975, French
CHANEL SOLITAIRE   United Film Distribution, 1981, French-British

MARIA PITILLO
Agent: William Morris Agency - Beverly Hills, 310/274-7451

BYE BYE LOVE   20th Century Fox, 1995

ANNE PITONIAK
AGNES OF GOD   Columbia, 1985
HOUSEKEEPING   Columbia, 1987
THE WIZARD OF LONELINESS   Skouras Pictures, 1988
OLD GRINGO   Columbia, 1989

BRAD PITT
Agent: CAA - Beverly Hills, 310/288-4545

THELMA & LOUISE   MGM-Pathe, 1991
JOHNNY SUEDE   Miramax Films, 1991
COOL WORLD   Paramount, 1992
A RIVER RUNS THROUGH IT   Columbia, 1992
KALIFORNIA   Gramercy Pictures, 1993
TRUE ROMANCE   Warner Bros., 1993
THE FAVOR   Orion, 1994
INTERVIEW WITH THE VAMPIRE   Warner Bros., 1994
LEGENDS OF THE FALL   TriStar, 1994

JEREMY PIVEN
JUDGMENT NIGHT   Universal, 1993
PCU   20th Century Fox, 1994
DR. JEKYLL AND MS. HYDE   Savoy Pictures, 1995

MARY KAY PLACE
Agent: ICM - Beverly Hills, 310/550-4000

BOUND FOR GLORY   United Artists, 1976
NEW YORK, NEW YORK   United Artists, 1977
MORE AMERICAN GRAFFITI   Universal, 1979
STARTING OVER   Paramount, 1979
PRIVATE BENJAMIN   Warner Bros., 1980
MODERN PROBLEMS   20th Century-Fox, 1981
THE BIG CHILL   Columbia, 1983
TERMS OF ENDEARMENT   Paramount, 1983, (voice)
EXPLORERS   Paramount, 1985
SMOOTH TALK   Spectrafilm, 1985
A NEW LIFE   Paramount, 1988
BRIGHT ANGEL   Hemdale, 1991
CAPTAIN RON   Buena Vista, 1992

TONY PLANA
BUY & CELL   Empire Pictures, 1989
ROMERO   Four Seasons Entertainment, 1989
ONE GOOD COP   Buena Vista, 1991

OLIVER PLATT
Agent: William Morris Agency - Beverly Hills, 310/274-7451

MARRIED TO THE MOB   Orion, 1988
WORKING GIRL   20th Century Fox, 1988
FLATLINERS   Columbia, 1990
BEETHOVEN   Universal, 1992
DIGGSTOWN   MGM-Pathe Entertainment, 1992
INDECENT PROPOSAL   Paramount, 1993
BENNY & JOON   MGM/UA, 1993
THE THREE MUSKETEERS   Buena Vista, 1993
TALL TALE   Buena Vista, 1994

BEGONIA PLAZA
DELTA FORCE 2 - OPERATION STRANGLEHOLD   MGM/UA, 1990

PLAY
(Kid N' Play)
Agent: William Morris Agency - Beverly Hills, 310/274-7451

A CLASS ACT   Warner Bros., 1992

DONALD PLEASENCE
b. October 5, 1919 - Worksop, Nottinghamshire, England

THE BEACHCOMBER   1954, British
1984   1956, British
STOWAWAY GIRL   *MANUELA*   1957, British
A TALE OF TWO CITIES   1958, British
LOOK BACK IN ANGER   1959, British
THE BIG DAY   1960, British
MANIA   *FLESH AND THE FIENDS*   1960, British
THE RISK   *SUSPECT*   1960, British
CIRCUS OF HORRORS   1960, British
SONS AND LOVERS   1960, British
THE HANDS OF ORLAC   *LES MAINS D'ORLAC*
   1961, French-British
NO LOVE FOR JOHNNIE   1961, British
LISA   *THE INSPECTOR*   1962, British
DR. CRIPPEN   1963, British
THE GREAT ESCAPE   1963
THE GUEST   *THE CARETAKER*   1963, British
MANIAC   1964, British
THE GREATEST STORY EVER TOLD   1965
THE HALLELUJAH TRAIL   1965
CUL-DE-SAC   1966, British
FANTASTIC VOYAGE   20th Century-Fox, 1966
NIGHT OF THE GENERALS   Columbia, 1967, British-French
EYE OF THE DEVIL   1967, British
MATCHLESS   1967, Italian
YOU ONLY LIVE TWICE   United Artists, 1967, British
WILL PENNY   Paramount, 1968
MR. FREEDOM   1969, French
THE MADWOMAN OF CHAILLOT   1969, British

SOLDIER BLUE   1970
THX 1138   1971
KIDNAPPED   1971, British
OUTBACK   1971, British
THE JERUSALEM FILE   1972, British
INNOCENT BYSTANDERS   1972, British
THE PIED PIPER   1972, British
HENRY VIII AND HIS SIX WIVES   1973, British
WEDDING IN WHITE   1973, British
RAW MEAT   1973, British
TALES THAT WITNESS MURDER   1973, British
THE MUTATIONS   1974, British
THE BLACK WINDMILL   1974
FROM BEYOND THE GRAVE   1975, British
ESCAPE TO WITCH MOUNTAIN   1975
HEARTS OF THE WEST   1975
JOURNEY INTO FEAR   1975, British
TRIAL BY COMBAT   1976
THE COUNT OF MONTE CRISTO   1976, British
DEVIL WITHIN HER   *I DON'T WANT TO BE BORN*   1976, British
DIRTY KNIGHTS' WORK   1976, British
THE PASSOVER PLOT   1976, U.S.-Israeli
THE LAST TYCOON   1976
THE EAGLE HAS LANDED   1976, British
OH, GOD!   Warner Bros., 1977
TELEFON   1977
JESUS OF NAZARETH (MS)   1978
BLOOD RELATIVES   *LES LIENS DE SANG*
   1978, French-Canadian
TOMORROW NEVER COMES   1978, British-Canadian
L'ORDRE ET LA SÉCURITÉ DU MONDE   1978, French
SGT. PEPPER'S LONELY HEARTS CLUB BAND   Universal, 1978
METEOR   1978
POWER PLAY   1978, Canadian-British
HALLOWEEN   Compass International, 1978
L'HOMME EN COLERE   1979, French-Canadian
JAGUAR LIVES   1979
GOOD LUCK, MISS WYCKOFF   1979
DRACULA   1979
ALL QUIET ON THE WESTERN FRONT (TF)   1979
ESCAPE FROM NEW YORK   1981
HALLOWEEN II   Universal, 1981
ALONE IN THE DARK   New Line Cinema, 1982
THE DEVONSVILLE TERROR   1983
WHERE IS PARSIFAL?   1984
ARCH OF TRIUMPH (TF)   1984
A BREED APART   Orion, 1984
THE LAST DAYS OF POMPEII (MS)   1985
SCOOP (TF)   1987
PRINCE OF DARKNESS   Universal, 1987
HANNA'S WAR   Cannon, 1988
GROUND ZERO   Avenue Pictures, 1988
HALLOWEEN 4 - THE RETURN OF MICHAEL MYERS
   Galaxy, 1988
THE GREAT ESCAPE II: THE UNTOLD STORY (MS)   Michael Jaffe
   Films/Spectacor Films, 1988
RIVER OF DEATH   Cannon, 1989, British
HALLOWEEN 5 - THE REVENGE OF MICHAEL MYERS
   Galaxy, 1989
SHADOWS AND FOG   Orion, 1992

JOHN PLESHETTE
S.O.B.   Paramount, 1981

SUZANNE PLESHETTE
b. January 31, 1937 - New York, New York

THE GEISHA BOY   Paramount, 1958
ROME ADVENTURE   Warner Bros., 1962
FORTY POUNDS OF TROUBLE   Universal, 1963
THE BIRDS   Universal, 1963
WALL OF NOISE   Warner Bros., 1963
A DISTANT TRUMPET   Warner Bros., 1964
FATE IS THE HUNTER   20th Century-Fox, 1964
YOUNGBLOOD HAWKE   Warner Bros., 1964
A RAGE TO LIVE   United Artists, 1965
THE UGLY DACHSHUND   1966
NEVADA SMITH   Paramount, 1966

MISTER BUDDWING   MGM, 1966
THE ADVENTURES OF BULLWHIP GRIFFIN   Buena Vista, 1967
WINGS OF FIRE (TF)   Universal TV, 1967
BLACKBEARD'S GHOST   Buena Vista, 1968
THE POWER   MGM, 1968
ALONG CAME A SPIDER (TF)   20th Century-Fox TV, 1969
IF IT'S TUESDAY, THIS MUST BE BELGIUM   United Artists, 1969
TARGET: HARRY   *HOW TO MAKE IT*   ABC Pictures
   International, 1969
SUPPOSE THEY GAVE A WAR AND NOBODY CAME?
   Cinerama Releasing Corporation, 1970
SUPPORT YOUR LOCAL GUNFIGHTER   United Artists, 1971
IN BROAD DAYLIGHT (TF)   Aaron Spelling Productions, 1971
BEYOND THE BERMUDA TRIANGLE (TF)
   Playboy Productions, 1975
THE LEGEND OF VALENTINO (TF)   Spelling-Goldberg
   Productions, 1975
RETURN OF THE PINK PANTHER   United Artists, 1975, British
THE SHAGGY D.A.   Buena Vista, 1976
KATE BLISS AND THE TICKERTAPE KID (TF)   Aaron Spelling
   Productions, 1978
FLESH AND BLOOD (TF)   The Jozak Company/Cypress Point
   Productions/Paramount TV, 1979
HOT STUFF   Columbia, 1979
OH, GOD! BOOK II   Warner Bros., 1980
A STRANGER WAITS (TF)   Bruce Lansbury Productions/
   Edgar Lansbury Productions/Lewisfilm Ltd./New Century TV
   Productions, 1987
LEONA HELMSLEY: THE QUEEN OF MEAN (TF)
   Fries Entertainment/Goiman-Taylor Entertainment, 1990

MARTHA PLIMPTON

Agent: ICM - Beverly Hills, 310/550-4000

THE RIVER RAT   Paramount, 1984
THE GOONIES   Warner Bros., 1985
THE MOSQUITO COAST   Warner Bros., 1986
SHY PEOPLE   Cannon, 1987
STARS AND BARS   Columbia, 1988
RUNNING ON EMPTY   Warner Bros., 1988
ANOTHER WOMAN   Orion, 1988
PARENTHOOD   Universal, 1989
SILENCE LIKE GLASS   Moviestore Entertainment,
   1989, West German
STANLEY & IRIS   MGM/UA, 1990
DAYBREAK (CTF)   Foundation Entertainment Productions/HBO
   Showcase, 1993
JOSH AND S.A.M.   Columbia, 1993
THE BEANS OF EGYPT, MAINE   I.R.S. Releasing, 1994
MRS. PARKER AND THE VICIOUS CIRCLE   Fine Line Features/
   New Line Cinema, 1994

JOAN PLOWRIGHT

b. October 28, 1929 - Brigg, England

TIME WITHOUT PITY   Astor, 1956, British
THE ENTERTAINER   Continental, 1960, British
EQUUS   United Artists, 1977, British
THE DIARY OF ANNE FRANK (TF)   Katz-Gallin/Half-Pint
   Productions/20th Century-Fox TV, 1980
BRITANNIA HOSPITAL   United Artists Classics, 1982, British
BRIMSTONE AND TREACLE   United Artists Classics, 1982, British
WAGNER (MS)   London Trust Productions/Richard Wagner
   Productions/Ladbroke Productions/Hungarofilm, 1983,
   British-Hungarian-Austrian
DROWNING BY NUMBERS   Galaxy International, 1988, British
I LOVE YOU TO DEATH   TriStar, 1990
AVALON   TriStar, 1990
ENCHANTED APRIL ✪   Miramax Films, 1991, British
LAST ACTION HERO   Columbia, 1993
DENNIS THE MENACE   Warner Bros., 1993
A PLACE FOR ANNIE (TF)   1994
WIDOWS' PEAK   Fine Line Features/New Line Cinema, 1994
ON PROMISED LAND (CTF)   The Disney Channel, 1994
A PYROMANIAC'S LOVE STORY   Buena Vista, 1995
THE GRASS HARP   New Line Cinema, 1995

EVE PLUMB

DAWN: PORTRAIT OF A TEENAGE RUNAWAY (TF)
   Douglas S. Cramer Productions, 1976
ALEXANDER: THE OTHER SIDE OF DAWN (TF)   Douglas Cramer
   Productions, 1977
THE BRADY GIRLS GET MARRIED (TF)   Sherwood Schwartz
   Productions, 1981
A VERY BRADY CHRISTMAS (TF)   Sherwood Schwartz
   Productions/Paramount TV, 1988
I'M GONNA GIT YOU SUCKA   MGM/UA, 1989
THE BRADYS (TF)   Brady Productions/Paramount TV, 1990
THE BRADY BUNCH MOVIE   Paramount, 1995

AMANDA PLUMMER

b. March 23, 1957 - New York, New York
Agent: Gersh Agency - Beverly Hills, 310/274-6611

DANIEL   Paramount, 1983
MADE IN HEAVEN   Lorimar, 1987
THE FISHER KING   TriStar, 1991
SO I MARRIED AN AXE MURDERER   TriStar, 1993
LAST LIGHT (CTF)   Showtime Networks, Inc./Stillwater
   Productions, 1993
NEEDFUL THINGS   Columbia, 1993
NOSTRADAMUS   Orion Classics, 1994, British
PULP FICTION   Miramax Films, 1994
SEARCH AND DESTROY   October Films, 1995

CHRISTOPHER PLUMMER
(Arthur Christopher Orme Plummer)
b. December 13, 1927 - Toronto, Ontario, Canada
Agent: ICM - Beverly Hills, 310/550-4000

STAGE STRUCK   RKO Radio, 1958
WIND ACROSS THE EVERGLADES   Warner Bros., 1958
THE FALL OF THE ROMAN EMPIRE   Paramount, 1964
THE SOUND OF MUSIC   20th Century-Fox, 1965
INSIDE DAISY CLOVER   Warner Bros., 1965
TRIPLE CROSS   Warner Bros., 1967, French-British
NIGHT OF THE GENERALS   Columbia, 1967, British-French
OEDIPUS THE KING   Regional, 1967, British
THE HIGH COMMISSIONER   *NOBODY RUNS FOREVER*
   Cinerama Releasing Corporation, 1968, British
THE ROYAL HUNT OF THE SUN   National General, 1969, British
BATTLE OF BRITAIN   United Artists, 1969, British
LOCK UP YOUR DAUGHTERS   1969, British
WATERLOO   Paramount, 1971, Italian-Soviet
THE PYX   Cinerama Releasing Corporation, 1973, Canadian
THE MAN WHO WOULD BE KING   Allied Artists, 1975, British
THE RETURN OF THE PINK PANTHER   United Artists,
   1975, British
CONDUCT UNBECOMING   Allied Artists, 1975, British
THE SPIRAL STAIRCASE   1975, British
ARTHUR HAILEY'S THE MONEYCHANGERS
   THE MONEYCHANGERS (MS)   Ross Hunter Productions/
   Paramount TV, 1976
ACES HIGH   Cinema Shares International, 1977, British
THE DAY THAT SHOOK THE WORLD   *ASSASSINATION AT
   SARAJEVO*   1976, Yugoslavian-Czechoslovakian
THE ASSIGNMENT   1977, Swedish
THE DISAPPEARANCE   Levitt-Pickman, 1977, Canadian
JESUS OF NAZARETH (MS)   Sir Lew Grade Productions/ITC,
   1978, British-Italian
INTERNATIONAL VELVET   MGM/United Artists, 1978, British
THE SILENT PARTNER   EMC Film/Aurora, 1978, Canadian
MURDER BY DECREE   Avco Embassy, 1979, Canadian-British
HANOVER STREET   Columbia, 1979
RIEL   CBC/Green River Productions, 1979, Canadian
STARCRASH   New World, 1979, Italian
SOMEWHERE IN TIME   Universal, 1980
HIGHPOINT   1980, Canadian
EYEWITNESS   20th Century-Fox, 1981
THE AMATEUR   20th Century-Fox, 1981, Canadian
LITTLE GLORIA...HAPPY AT LAST (MS)   Edgar J. Scherick
   Associates/Metromedia Producers Corporation, 1982,
   U.S.-Canadian-British
DREAMSCAPE   20th Century Fox, 1984
ORDEAL BY INNOCENCE   Cannon, 1984, British

LILY IN LOVE   New Line Cinema, 1985, U.S.-Hungarian
THE VELVETEEN RABBIT (AF)   1985 (voice)
CROSSINGS (MS)   Aaron Spelling Productions, 1986
THE BOY IN BLUE   20th Century Fox, 1986, Canadian
AN AMERICAN TAIL (AF)   Universal, 1986 (voice)
DRAGNET   Universal, 1987
WHERE THE HEART IS   Buena Vista, 1990
STAR TREK VI: THE UNDISCOVERED COUNTRY
   Paramount, 1991
ROCK-A-DOODLE (AF)   Samuel Goldwyn Company,
   1992 (voice)
WOLF   Columbia, 1994
DOLORES CLAIBORNE   Columbia, 1994

GLENN PLUMMER
HEATWAVE (CTF)   The Avnet-Kerner Company/
   Propaganda Films, 1990
ONE CUP OF COFFEE   Miramax Films, 1991
SPEED   20th Century Fox, 1994
STRANGE DAYS   20th Century Fox, 1995

ROBERT PLUNKET
AFTER HOURS   The Geffen Company/Warner Bros., 1985

TONG PO
KICKBOXER   Cannon, 1989

MARIE-SOPHIE POCHAT
A MAN AND A WOMAN: 20 YEARS LATER   Warner Bros.,
   1986, French

EMILY POE
ROCKET GIBRALTAR   Columbia, 1988

PRISCILLA POINTER
Agent: William Morris Agency - Beverly Hills, 310/274-7451

CARRIE   United Artists, 1976
BLUE VELVET   DEG, 1986

SIDNEY POITIER
b. February 20, 1924 - Miami, Florida
Agent: CAA - Beverly Hills, 310/288-4545

NO WAY OUT   20th Century-Fox, 1950
CRY, THE BELOVED COUNTRY   United Artists, 1951, British
RED BALL EXPRESS   Universal, 1952
GO, MAN, GO!   1954
THE BLACKBOARD JUNGLE   MGM, 1955
GOODBYE, MY LADY   Warner Bros., 1956
EDGE OF THE CITY   MGM, 1957
SOMETHING OF VALUE   MGM, 1957
BAND OF ANGELS   Warner Bros., 1957
THE MARK OF THE HAWK   1957
THE DEFIANT ONES ★   United Artists, 1958
PORGY AND BESS   Columbia, 1959
VIRGIN ISLAND   1959, British
ALL THE YOUNG MEN   Columbia, 1960
A RAISIN IN THE SUN   Columbia, 1961
PARIS BLUES   United Artists, 1961
PRESSURE POINT   United Artists, 1962
LILIES OF THE FIELD ★★   United Artists, 1963
THE LONG SHIPS   Columbia, 1964, British-Yugoslavian
THE GREATEST STORY EVER TOLD   United Artists, 1965
THE BEDFORD INCIDENT   Columbia, 1965
A PATCH OF BLUE   MGM, 1965
THE SLENDER THREAD   Paramount, 1965
DUEL AT DIABLO   United Artists, 1966
IN THE HEAT OF THE NIGHT   United Artists, 1967
TO SIR WITH LOVE   Columbia, 1967, British
GUESS WHO'S COMING TO DINNER   Columbia, 1967
FOR LOVE OF IVY   Cinerama Releasing Corporation, 1968
THE LOST MAN   1969
KING: A FILMED RECORD...MONTGOMERY TO MEMPHIS (FD)
   Maron Films Limited, 1970

THEY CALL ME MISTER TIBBS!   United Artists, 1970
THE ORGANIZATION   United Artists, 1971
BROTHER JOHN   Columbia, 1972
BUCK AND THE PREACHER   Columbia, 1972 (also directed)
A WARM DECEMBER   National General, 1973 (also directed)
UPTOWN SATURDAY NIGHT   Warner Bros., 1974 (also directed)
LET'S DO IT AGAIN   Warner Bros., 1975 (also directed)
THE WILBY CONSPIRACY   United Artists, 1975, British
A PIECE OF THE ACTION   Warner Bros., 1977 (also directed)
SHOOT TO KILL   Buena Vista, 1988
LITTLE NIKITA   Columbia, 1988
SNEAKERS   Universal, 1992

ROMAN POLANSKI
b. August 18, 1933 - Paris, France

THE FEARLESS VAMPIRE KILLERS, OR PARDON ME, BUT YOUR
   TEETH ARE IN MY NECK DANCE OF THE VAMPIRES MGM,
   1967, British (also directed)
THE MAGIC CHRISTIAN   Commonwealth United, 1970, British
WHAT?   Avco Embassy, 1973,
   Italian-French-West German (also directed)
CHINATOWN   Paramount, 1974 (also directed)
THE TENANT   Paramount, 1976, French-U.S. (also directed)

ASHLEY POLDON
THE SECRETARY   Republic Pictures, 1994

JON POLITO
FIRE WITH FIRE   Paramount, 1986
MILLER'S CROSSING   20th Century Fox, 1990
BARTON FINK   20th Century Fox, 1991
BLANKMAN   Columbia, 1994
FLUKE   MGM/UA, 1994

VIC POLIZOS
HARLEM NIGHTS   Paramount, 1989
STEPHEN KING'S GRAVEYARD SHIFT   Paramount, 1990

SYDNEY POLLACK
b. July 1, 1934 - South Bend, Indiana
Agent: CAA - Beverly Hills, 310/288-4545

WAR HUNT   United Artists, 1962
TOOTSIE   Columbia, 1982
THE PLAYER   Fine Line Features/New Line Cinema, 1992
DEATH BECOMES HER   Universal, 1992
HUSBANDS AND WIVES   TriStar, 1992

KEVIN POLLAK
AVALON   TriStar, 1990
L.A. STORY   TriStar, 1991
ANOTHER YOU   TriStar, 1991
RICOCHET   Warner Bros., 1991
A FEW GOOD MEN   Columbia, 1992
INDIAN SUMMER   Buena Vista, 1993
THE OPPOSITE SEX (AND HOW TO LIVE WITH THEM)
   Miramax Films, 1993
GRUMPY OLD MEN   Warner Bros., 1993
CLEAN SLATE   MGM/UA, 1994
CASINO   Universal, 1995

TRACY POLLAN
Agent: Harris & Goldberg Agency - Los Angeles, 310/553-5200

BABY IT'S YOU   Paramount, 1983
PROMISED LAND   Vestron, 1988
RUN   Buena Vista, 1991

MICHAEL J. POLLARD
(Michael J. Pollack)
b. May 30, 1939 - Pacific, New Jersey
Agent: Yvette Bikoff Agency - West Hollywood, 213/655-6123

HEMINGWAY'S ADVENTURES OF A YOUNG MAN
    20th Century-Fox, 1962
THE STRIPPER   20th Century-Fox, 1963
SUMMER MAGIC   Buena Vista, 1963
THE RUSSIANS ARE COMING, THE RUSSIANS ARE COMING
    United Artists, 1966
THE WILD ANGELS   American International, 1966
CAPRICE   20th Century-Fox, 1967
ENTER LAUGHING   Columbia, 1967
BONNIE AND CLYDE ✪   Warner Bros., 1967
JIGSAW   Universal, 1968
HANNIBAL BROOKS   United Artists, 1969, British
LITTLE FAUSS AND BIG HALSY   Paramount, 1970
DIRTY LITTLE BILLY   Columbia, 1972
SUNDAY IN THE COUNTRY   American International, 1973
BETWEEN THE LINES   Midwest Film Productions, 1977
MELVIN AND HOWARD   Universal, 1980
ROXANNE   Columbia, 1987
AMERICAN GOTHIC   Vidmark, 1987, British
SCROOGED   Paramount, 1988
NEXT OF KIN   Warner Bros., 1989
TANGO & CASH   Warner Bros., 1989
RIDER IN THE DARK   Cannon, 1989
RIDERS OF THE STORM   *THE AMERICAN WAY*   Miramax Films,
    1986, British
CRY DEVIL   Premiere Pictures, 1989
ENID IS SLEEPING   Vestron, 1990
DICK TRACY   Buena Vista, 1990
THE ARROWTOOTH WALTZ   Warner Bros., 1992

SARAH POLLEY
THE ADVENTURES OF BARON MUNCHAUSEN   Columbia, 1989

TERI POLO
Agent: William Morris Agency - Beverly Hills, 310/274-7451

THE PHANTOM OF THE OPERA (MS)   Saban-Scherick
    Productions, 1990
MYSTERY DATE   Orion, 1991
BORN TO RIDE   Warner Bros., 1991

MAX POMERANC
Agent: William Morris Agency - Beverly Hills, 310/274-7451

SEARCHING FOR BOBBY FISCHER   Paramount, 1993
FLUKE   MGM/UA, 1994

IGGY POP
CRY-BABY   Universal, 1990

PAULINA PORIZKOVA
Agent: CAA - Beverly Hills, 310/288-4545

ANNA   Vestron, 1987
HER ALIBI   Warner Bros., 1989
THE ARROWTOOTH WALTZ   Warner Bros., 1994

LOUISE PORTAL
THE DECLINE OF THE AMERICAN EMPIRE   Cineplex Odeon,
    1986, Canadian

ALISAN PORTER
CURLY SUE   Warner Bros., 1991

BILL PORTER
AIRPLANE!   Paramount, 1980

NATALIE PORTMAN
THE PROFESSIONAL   Columbia, 1994

RICHARD PORTNOW
HEART AND SOULS   Universal, 1993
TRIAL BY JURY   Warner Bros., 1994
MAN 2 MAN   Buena Vista, 1995

PARKER POSEY
Agent: William Morris Agency - Beverly Hills, 310/274-7451

SLEEP WITH ME   MGM/UA, 1994

PETE POSTLETHWAITE
DISTANT VOICES, STILL LIVES   Alive Films, 1988, British
IN THE NAME OF THE FATHER ✪   Universal, 1993, Irish-British
DRAGONHEART   Universal, 1995

MARKIE POST
b. November 4, 1950 - Palo Alto, California

TRICKS OF THE TRADE (TF)   Leonard Hill Films, 1988

TOM POSTON
b. October 17, 1927 - Columbus, Ohio

CITY THAT NEVER SLEEPS   1953
ZOTZ!   Columbia, 1962
SOLDIER IN THE RAIN   Allied Artists, 1963
THE OLD DARK HOUSE   Columbia, 1963
COLD TURKEY   United Artists, 1971
THE HAPPY HOOKER   Cannon, 1975
RABBIT TEST   Avco Embassy, 1978
MAD MAGAZINE PRESENTS UP THE ACADEMY
    UP THE ACADEMY   Warner Bros., 1980

ERU POTAKA-DEWES
THE PIANO   Miramax Films, 1993, New Zealand-French
RAPA NUI   Warner Bros., 1994

MADELEINE POTTER
THE BOSTONIANS   Almi Pictures, 1984
SLAVES OF NEW YORK   TriStar, 1989
BLOODHOUNDS OF BROADWAY   Columbia, 1989

ANNIE POTTS
b. October 28 - Nashville, Tennessee
Agent: UTA - Beverly Hills, 310/273-6700

GHOSTBUSTERS   Columbia, 1984
PRETTY IN PINK   Paramount, 1986
WHO'S HARRY CRUMB?   TriStar, 1989
GHOSTBUSTERS II   Columbia, 1989
TEXASVILLE   Columbia, 1990

C.C.H. POUNDER
Agent: Susan Smith & Associates - Beverly Hills, 213/852-4777

PRIZZI'S HONOR   20th Century Fox, 1985
BAGDAD CAFE   *OUT OF ROSENHEIM*   Island Pictures,
    1987, West German-U.S.
MURDER IN MISSISSIPPI (TF)   Wolper Productions/Bernard
    Sofronski Productions/Warner Bros. TV, 1990
POSTCARDS FROM THE EDGE   Columbia, 1990
COMMON GROUND (TF)   Daniel H. Blatt Prods./Lorimar TV, 1990
SLIVER   Paramount, 1993

BRITTNEY POWELL
AIRBORNE   Warner Bros., 1993

TYRONE POWER, JR.
COCOON   20th Century Fox, 1985
COCOON: THE RETURN   20th Century Fox, 1988

ALEXANDRA POWERS
SONNY BOY   Triumph Releasing Corporation, 1990
LOVECRAFT (CTF)   HBO Pictures/Pacific Western
    Productions, 1991

STEFANIE POWERS
(Stephania Federkiewicz)
b. November 2, 1942 - Hollywood, California

TAMMY TELL ME TRUE   1961
EXPERIMENT IN TERROR   Warner Bros., 1962
THE INTERNS   Columbia, 1962
IF A MAN ANSWERS   Universal, 1962
PALM SPRINGS WEEKEND   Warner Bros., 1963
McLINTOCK!   United Artists, 1963
THE NEW INTERNS   Columbia, 1964
LOVE HAS MANY FACES   Columbia, 1965
DIE! DIE! MY DARLING!   *FANATIC*   Columbia, 1965, British
THE YOUNG SINNER   United Screen Arts, 1965
STAGECOACH   20th Century-Fox, 1966
WARNING SHOT   Paramount, 1967
THE BOATNIKS   1970
THE MAGNIFICENT SEVEN RIDE!   United Artists, 1972
CRESCENDO   Warner Bros., 1972, British
HERBIE RIDES AGAIN   Buena Vista, 1974
GONE WITH THE WEST   International Cinefilm, 1975
WASHINGTON: BEHIND CLOSED DOORS (MS)
    Paramount TV, 1977
ESCAPE TO ATHENA   AFD, 1979, British
HART TO HART (TF)   Spelling-Goldberg Productions, 1979
FAMILY SECRETS (TF)   Katz-Gallin/Half-Pint Productions/
    Karoger Productions, 1984
MISTRAL'S DAUGHTER (MS)   Steve Krantz Productions/
    R.T.L. Productions/Antenne-2, 1984, U.S.-French
DECEPTIONS (TF)   Louis Rudolph Productions/Consolidated
    Productions/Columbia TV, 1985, U.S.-British
AT MOTHER'S REQUEST (TF)   Vista Organization, Ltd., 1987
BERYL MARKHAM: A SHADOW ON THE SUN (MS)
    Tamara Asseyev Productions/New World TV, 1988
SHE WAS MARKED FOR MURDER (TF)   Jack Grossbart
    Productions, 1988
LOVE AND BETRAYAL (TF)   Gross-Weston Productions/ITC
    Entertainment Group, 1989
HART TO HART: HOME IS WHERE THE HART IS (TF)   NBC, 1994
HART TO HART: OLD FRIENDS NEVER DIE (TF)   NBC, 1994

BEATA POZNIAK
JFK   Warner Bros., 1991

PAULA PRENTISS
(Paula Ragusa)
b. March 4, 1939 - San Antonio, Texas

WHERE THE BOYS ARE   MGM, 1960
THE HONEYMOON MACHINE   MGM, 1961
BACHELOR IN PARADISE   MGM, 1961
THE HORIZONTAL LIEUTENANT   MGM, 1962
FOLLOW THE BOYS   MGM, 1963
MAN'S FAVORITE SPORT?   Universal, 1964
THE WORLD OF HENRY ORIENT   United Artists, 1964
LOOKING FOR LOVE   MGM, 1964
IN HARM'S WAY   Paramount, 1964
WHAT'S NEW PUSSYCAT?   United Artists, 1965, British
CATCH-22   Paramount, 1970
MOVE   20th Century-Fox, 1970
BORN TO WIN   United Artists, 1971
LAST OF THE RED HOT LOVERS   Paramount, 1972
THE PARALLAX VIEW   Paramount, 1974
CRAZY JOE   Columbia, 1974, Italian-U.S.
THE STEPFORD WIVES   Columbia, 1975
HAVING BABIES II (TF)   The Jozak Company, 1977
THE BLACK MARBLE   Avco Embassy, 1980
BUDDY BUDDY   MGM/United Artists, 1981
SATURDAY THE 14TH   New World, 1981

PRISCILLA PRESLEY
b. May 24, 1946 - New York, New York
Agent: William Morris Agency - Beverly Hills, 310/274-7451

LOVE IS FOREVER (TF)   Michael Landon-Hall Bartlett Films/
    NBC-TV/20th Century-Fox TV, 1983
THE NAKED GUN: FROM THE FILES OF POLICE SQUAD!
    Paramount, 1988

THE ADVENTURES OF FORD FAIRLANE   20th Century Fox, 1990
THE NAKED GUN 2 1/2: THE SMELL OF FEAR   Paramount, 1991
NAKED GUN 33 1/3: THE FINAL INSULT   Paramount, 1994

GORDON PRESS
BIG   20th Century Fox, 1988

LAWRENCE PRESSMAN
THE HANOI HILTON   Cannon, 1987

JASON PRESSON
EXPLORERS   Paramount, 1985
LADY IN WHITE   New Century/Vista, 1988

J.A. PRESTON
BODY HEAT   The Ladd Company/Warner Bros., 1981

KELLY PRESTON
MISCHIEF   20th Century Fox, 1985
SPACECAMP   20th Century Fox, 1986
52 PICK-UP   Cannon, 1986
A TIGER'S TALE   Atlantic Releasing Corporation, 1987
SPELLBINDER   MGM/UA, 1988
TWINS   Universal, 1988
THE EXPERTS   Paramount, 1989
RUN   Buena Vista, 1991
LOVE IS A GUN   Trimark Pictures, 1994

MARC PRICE
b. February 23, 1968

THE RESCUE   Buena Vista, 1988

JASON PRIESTLEY
b. August 28, 1969 - Vancouver, British Columbia
Agent: UTA - Beverly Hills, 310/273-6700

CALENDAR GIRL   Columbia, 1993
TOMBSTONE   Buena Vista, 1993
COLDBLOODED   MPCA, 1995

BARRY PRIMUS
PUZZLE OF A DOWNFALL CHILD   Universal, 1970
BOXCAR BERTHA   American International, 1972
THE GRAVY TRAIN   *THE DION BROTHERS*   Columbia, 1974
NEW YORK, NEW YORK   United Artists, 1977
AVALANCHE   New World, 1978
THE ROSE   20th Century-Fox, 1979
HEARTLAND   Levitt-Pickman, 1979
ABSENCE OF MALICE   Columbia, 1981
PAPER DOLLS (TF)   Leonard Goldberg Productions, 1982
STILLWATCH (TF)   Zev Braun Pictures/Interscope Communications/
    Potomac Productions, 1987
BIG BUSINESS   Buena Vista, 1988
GUILTY BY SUSPICION   Warner Bros., 1991

PRINCE
(Prince Rogers Nelson)
b. June 7, 1958 - Minneapolis, Minnesota
Agent: CAA - Beverly Hills, 310/288-4545

PURPLE RAIN   Warner Bros., 1984
UNDER THE CHERRY MOON   Warner Bros., 1986 (also directed)
SIGN 'O' THE TIMES   Cineplex Odeon, 1987 (also directed)
GRAFFITI BRIDGE   Warner Bros., 1990 (also directed)

FAITH PRINCE
MY FATHER, THE HERO   Buena Vista, 1994

WILLIAM PRINCE
b. January 26, 1913 - Nichols, New York

DESTINATION TOKYO   1944
THE VERY THOUGHT OF YOU   1944
OBJECTIVE BURMA   1945

F
I
L
M

A
C
T
O
R
S

PILLOW TO POST   1945
CINDERELLA JONES   1946
DEAD RECKONING   1947
CARNEGIE HALL   1947
LUST FOR GOLD   1949
CYRANO DE BERGERAC   1950
THE VAGABOND KING   1956
SECRET OF TREASURE MOUNTAIN   1956
MACABRE   1958
SACCO AND VANZETTI   *SACCO E VANZETTI*   1971, Italian
THE HEARTBREAK KID   1972
BLADE   1973
THE STEPFORD WIVES   1975
FAMILY PLOT   1976
NETWORK   MGM/United Artists, 1976
THE GAUNTLET   1977
THE PROMISE   Universal, 1979
BRONCO BILLY   1980
LOVE AND MONEY   1982
MOVERS AND SHAKERS   1984
SPIES LIKE US   Warner Bros., 1985
SPONTANEOUS COMBUSTION   Taurus Entertainment, 1990

VICTORIA PRINCIPAL
b. January 3, 1950 - Japan
Agent: CAA - Beverly Hills, 310/288-4545

THE LIFE AND TIMES OF JUDGE ROY BEAN   National General, 1973
THE NAKED APE   Playboy Productions, 1973
EARTHQUAKE   Universal, 1974
I WILL, I WILL...FOR NOW   20th Century-Fox, 1976
VIGILANTE FORCE   United Artists, 1976
THE NIGHT THEY TOOK MISS BEAUTIFUL (TF)   Don Kirshner
    Productions, 1977
FANTASY ISLAND (TF)   Spelling-Goldberg Productions, 1977
MISTRESS (TF)   Jaffe-Lansing Productions/Republic Pictures, 1987
NAKED LIE (TF)   Shadowplay Films/Phoenix Entertainment
    Group, 1989
BLIND WITNESS (TF)   King Phoenix Entertainment Group, 1989
SPARKS: THE PRICE OF PASSION (TF)   Shadowplay Films/
    Victoria Principal Productions/King Phoenix Entertainment, 1990

ANDREW PRINE
THE MIRACLE WORKER   1962
COMPANY OF COWARDS   1964
THE DEVIL'S BRIGADE   1968
BANDOLERO   1968
A TIME FOR GIVING   1969
ONE LITTLE INDIAN   1973
GRIZZLY   1976
AMITYVILLE II: THE POSSESSION   Orion, 1982
ELIMINATORS   Empire Pictures, 1986

SANDRA PRINSLOO
THE GODS MUST BE CRAZY   TLC Films/20th Century-Fox,
    1979, Botswana

TED PRIOR
CENTER OF THE WEB   AIP, 1992

JÜRGEN PROCHNOW
LOVE IS FOREVER (TF)   Michael Landon-Hall Bartlett Films/
    NBC-TV/20th Century-Fox TV, 1983
DUNE   Universal, 1984
THE SEVENTH SIGN   TriStar, 1988
A DRY WHITE SEASON   MGM/UA, 1989
THE FOURTH WAR   Cannon, 1990
BODY OF EVIDENCE   MGM/UA, 1993
JUDGE DREDD   Buena Vista, 1995

ROBERT PROSKY
b. December 13, 1930 - Philadelphia, Pennsylvania
Agent: Gersh Agency - Beverly Hills, 310/274-6611

THIEF   United Artists, 1981
THE NATURAL   TriStar, 1984
OUTRAGEOUS FORTUNE   Buena Vista, 1987
BROADCAST NEWS   20th Century Fox, 1987

THINGS CHANGE   Columbia, 1988
GREMLINS 2 THE NEW BATCH   Warner Bros., 1990
LAST ACTION HERO   Columbia, 1993
MRS. DOUBTFIRE   20th Century Fox, 1993
MIRACLE ON 34TH STREET   20th Century Fox, 1994

PAUL PROVENZA
SURVIVAL QUEST   MGM/UA, 1990

DAVID PROWSE
STAR WARS   20th Century-Fox, 1977
THE EMPIRE STRIKES BACK   20th Century-Fox, 1980
RETURN OF THE JEDI   20th Century-Fox, 1983

HEYDON PROWSE
THE SECRET GARDEN   Warner Bros., 1993, U.S.-British

JONATHAN PRYCE
b. June 1, 1947 - Wales

VOYAGE OF THE DAMNED   1976
BREAKING GLASS   1980
LOOPHOLE   1980
THE DAY CHRIST DIED (TF)   1980
PRAYING MANTIS (TF)   1982
THE PLOUGHMAN'S LUNCH   1983
SOMETHING WICKED THIS WAY COMES   1983
BRAZIL   Universal, 1985, British
THE DOCTOR AND THE DEVILS   1986
HAUNTED HONEYMOON   1986
JUMPIN' JACK FLASH   20th Century Fox, 1986
THE ADVENTURES OF BARON MUNCHAUSEN   Columbia, 1989
THE RACHEL PAPERS   MGM/UA, 1989, U.S.-British
GLENGARRY GLEN ROSS   New Line Cinema, 1992
THE AGE OF INNOCENCE   Columbia, 1993
CARRINGTON   Gramercy Pictures, 1995

NICHOLAS PRYOR
SMILE   United Artists, 1975
AIRPLANE!   Paramount, 1980

RICHARD PRYOR
b. December 1, 1940 - Peoria, Illinois

THE BUSY BODY   Paramount, 1967
THE GREEN BERETS   Warner Bros., 1968
WILD IN THE STREETS   American International, 1968
THE PHYNX   Warner Bros., 1970
YOU'VE GOT TO WALK IT LIKE YOU TALK IT OR YOU'LL LOSE
    THAT BEAT   1971
DYNAMITE CHICKEN   EYR, 1972
LADY SINGS THE BLUES   Paramount, 1972
WATTSTAX (FD)   Columbia, 1973
THE MACK   Cinerama Releasing Corporation, 1973
THE HIT!   Paramount, 1973
SOME CALL IT LOVING   Cine Globe, 1973
UPTOWN SATURDAY NIGHT   Warner Bros., 1974
ADIOS AMIGO   Atlas, 1976
THE BINGO LONG TRAVELING ALL-STARS AND MOTOR KINGS
    Universal, 1976
CAR WASH   Universal, 1976
SILVER STREAK   20th Century-Fox, 1976
GREASED LIGHTNING   Warner Bros., 1977
WHICH WAY IS UP?   Universal, 1977
BLUE COLLAR   Universal, 1978
THE WIZ   Universal, 1978
CALIFORNIA SUITE   Columbia, 1978
RICHARD PRYOR LIVE IN CONCERT (FD)
    Special Event Entertainment, 1979
RICHARD PRYOR IS BACK LIVE IN CONCERT (FD)
    Special Event Entertainment, 1979
THE MUPPET MOVIE   AFD, 1979, British
IN GOD WE TRU$T   Universal, 1980
STIR CRAZY   Columbia, 1980
WHOLLY MOSES   Columbia, 1980
BUSTIN' LOOSE   Universal, 1981
SOME KIND OF HERO   1982

RICHARD PRYOR LIVE ON THE SUNSET STRIP (FD)
   Columbia, 1982
THE TOY   Columbia, 1982
RICHARD PRYOR HERE AND NOW (FD)   Columbia,
   1983 (also directed)
SUPERMAN III   Warner Bros., 1983, U.S.-British
BREWSTER'S MILLIONS   Universal, 1985
JO JO DANCER, YOUR LIFE IS CALLING   Columbia,
   1986 (also directed)
CRITICAL CONDITION   Paramount, 1987
MOVING   Warner Bros., 1988
SEE NO EVIL, HEAR NO EVIL   TriStar, 1989
HARLEM NIGHTS   Paramount, 1989
ANOTHER YOU   TriStar, 1991

TITO PUENTE
RADIO DAYS   Orion, 1987
THE MAMBO KINGS   Warner Bros., 1992

PASQUALE PUGLIESE
BIG   20th Century Fox, 1988

BILL PULLMAN
Agent: UTA - Beverly Hills, 310/273-6700

RUTHLESS PEOPLE   Buena Vista, 1986
SPACEBALLS   MGM/UA, 1987
ROCKET GIBRALTAR   Columbia, 1988
THE ACCIDENTAL TOURIST   Warner Bros., 1988
COLD FEET   Avenue Pictures, 1989
SIBLING RIVALRY   Columbia, 1990
BRIGHT ANGEL   Hemdale, 1991
NEWSIES   Buena Vista, 1992
A LEAGUE OF THEIR OWN   Columbia, 1992
SINGLES   Warner Bros., 1992
SOMMERSBY   Warner Bros., 1993
SLEEPLESS IN SEATTLE   TriStar, 1993
MALICE   Columbia, 1993
MR. JONES   TriStar, 1993
THE FAVOR   Orion, 1994
WYATT EARP   Warner Bros., 1994
THE LAST SEDUCTION   1994
CASPER   Universal, 1995
WHILE YOU WERE SLEEPING   Buena Vista, 1995

LEE PURCELL
SECRET SINS OF THE FATHER (TF)   Dick Clark Productions, 1994

CAROLYN PURDY-GORDON
FROM BEYOND   Empire Pictures, 1986

AMRISH PURI
INDIANA JONES AND THE TEMPLE OF DOOM   Paramount, 1984

OM PURI
CITY OF JOY   TriStar, 1992

LINDA PURL
ELEANOR AND FRANKLIN (TF)   Talent Associates, 1976
W.C. FIELDS AND ME   1976
TESTIMONY OF TWO MEN (TF)   1977
THE FLAME IS LOVE (TF)   1979
WOMEN AT WEST POINT (TF)   1980
THE NIGHT THE CITY SCREAMED (TF)   1981
VISITING HOURS   1982
PLEASURES (TF)   Catalina Production Group/Columbia TV, 1986

JACK PURVIS
THE ADVENTURES OF BARON MUNCHAUSEN   Columbia, 1989

WAYNE PYGRAM
FAREWELL TO THE KING   Orion, 1989

DENVER PYLE
MAVERICK   Warner Bros., 1994

Q

DENNIS QUAID
b. April 9, 1954 - Houston, Texas
Agent: ICM - Beverly Hills, 310/550-4000

9/30/55   *SEPTEMBER 30, 1955*   Universal, 1977
I NEVER PROMISED YOU A ROSE GARDEN   New World, 1977
THE SENIORS   Cinema Shares International, 1978
ARE YOU IN THE HOUSE ALONE? (TF)   Charles Fries
   Productions, 1978
AMATEUR NIGHT AT THE DIXIE BAR AND GRILL (TF)
   Motown/Universal TV, 1979
BREAKING AWAY   20th Century-Fox, 1979
THE LONG RIDERS   United Artists, 1980
ALL NIGHT LONG   Universal, 1981
BILL (TF)   Alan Landsburg Productions, 1981
CAVEMAN   United Artists, 1981
THE NIGHT THE LIGHTS WENT OUT IN GEORGIA
   Avco Embassy, 1981
BILL: ON HIS OWN (TF)   Alan Landsburg Productions, 1983
JAWS 3-D   Universal, 1983
THE RIGHT STUFF   The Ladd Company/Warner Bros., 1983
TOUGH ENOUGH   20th Century-Fox, 1983
DREAMSCAPE   20th Century Fox, 1984
ENEMY MINE   20th Century Fox, 1985
THE BIG EASY   Columbia, 1987
INNERSPACE   Warner Bros., 1987
SUSPECT   TriStar, 1987
D.O.A.   Buena Vista, 1988
EVERYBODY'S ALL-AMERICAN   Warner Bros., 1988
GREAT BALLS OF FIRE   Orion, 1989
POSTCARDS FROM THE EDGE   Columbia, 1990
COME SEE THE PARADISE   20th Century Fox, 1990
WILDER NAPALM   TriStar, 1993
UNDERCOVER BLUES   MGM/UA, 1993
FLESH AND BONE   Paramount, 1993
WYATT EARP   Warner Bros., 1994
DRAGONHEART   Universal, 1995
GRACE UNDER PRESSURE   Warner Bros., 1995

RANDY QUAID
b. October 1, 1950 - Houston, Texas

THE LAST PICTURE SHOW   Columbia, 1971
WHAT'S UP, DOC?   Warner Bros., 1972
THE LAST DETAIL ⊙   Columbia, 1973
LOLLY MADONNA XXX   *THE LOLLY-MADONNA WAR*   MGM, 1973
PAPER MOON   Paramount, 1973
THE APPRENTICESHIP OF DUDDY KRAVITZ   Paramount,
   1974, Canadian
BREAKOUT   Columbia, 1975
THE MISSOURI BREAKS   United Artists, 1976
BOUND FOR GLORY   United Artists, 1976
THE CHOIRBOYS   Universal, 1977
MIDNIGHT EXPRESS   Columbia, 1978, British
FOXES   United Artists, 1980
THE LONG RIDERS   United Artists, 1980
GUYANA TRAGEDY: THE STORY OF JIM JONES (TF)
   The Konigsberg Company, 1980
HEARTBEEPS   Universal, 1981
OF MICE AND MEN (TF)   Of Mice and Men Productions, 1981
NATIONAL LAMPOON'S VACATION   Warner Bros., 1983
THE WILD LIFE   Universal, 1984
FOOL FOR LOVE   Cannon, 1985
THE SLUGGER'S WIFE   *NEIL SIMON'S THE SLUGGER'S WIFE*
   Columbia, 1985
THE WRAITH   New Century/Vista, 1986
LBJ: THE EARLY YEARS (TF)   Louis Rudolph Films/Fries
   Entertainment, 1987
NO MAN'S LAND   Orion, 1987

MOVING   Warner Bros., 1988
CADDYSHACK II   Warner Bros., 1988
EVIL IN CLEAR RIVER (TF)   The Steve Tisch Company/Lionel
   Chetwynd Productions/Phoenix Entertainment Group, 1988
PARENTS   Vestron, 1989
OUT COLD   TriStar, 1989
BLOODHOUNDS OF BROADWAY   Columbia, 1989
NATIONAL LAMPOON'S CHRISTMAS VACATION
   Warner Bros., 1989
MARTIANS GO HOME   Taurus Entertainment, 1990
DAYS OF THUNDER   Paramount, 1990
QUICK CHANGE   Warner Bros., 1990
TEXASVILLE   Columbia, 1990
FREAKED   20th Century Fox, 1993
THE PAPER   Universal, 1994
MAJOR LEAGUE II   Warner Bros., 1994
NEXT DOOR (CTF)   Showtime, 1994
BYE BYE LOVE   20th Century Fox, 1995

KE HUY QUAN

INDIANA JONES AND THE TEMPLE OF DOOM   Paramount, 1984
THE GOONIES   Warner Bros., 1985

QUEEN LATIFAH

Agent: William Morris Agency - Beverly Hills, 310/274-7451

MY LIFE   Columbia, 1993

MAE QUESTEL

NEW YORK STORIES   Buena Vista, 1989

DIANA QUICK

NICHOLAS AND ALEXANDRA   Columbia, 1971, British
THE ODD JOB   Columbia, 1978, British
THE DUELLISTS   Paramount, 1978, British
THE BIG SLEEP   United Artists, 1978, British
BRIDESHEAD REVISITED (MS)   Granada TV/WNET-13/NDR
   Hamburg, 1982, British-U.S.-West German
THE PHANTOM OF THE OPERA (TF)   Robert Halmi, Inc., 1983
ORDEAL BY INNOCENCE   Cannon, 1984, British
NOSTRADAMUS   Orion Classics, 1994, British

TIM QUILL

HAMBURGER HILL   Paramount, 1987
LISTEN TO ME   Columbia, 1989
STAYING TOGETHER   Hemdale, 1989

DENIS QUILLEY

ANNE OF THE THOUSAND DAYS   Universal, 1969, British
THE BLACK WINDMILL   Universal, 1974, British
MURDER ON THE ORIENT EXPRESS   Paramount, 1974, British
MASADA (MS)   Arnon Milchan Productions/Universal TV, 1981
EVIL UNDER THE SUN   Universal/AFD, 1982, U.S.-British
PRIVATES ON PARADE   Orion Classics, 1983, British
KING DAVID   Paramount, 1985, U.S.-British
FOREIGN BODY   Orion, 1986, British
MEMED MY HAWK   Filmworld Distributors,
   1987, British-Yugoslavian
MISTER JOHNSON   Avenue Pictures, 1991

KATHLEEN QUINLAN

(Kathy Quinlan)
b. November 19, 1954
Agent: ICM - Beverly Hills, 310/550-4000

AMERICAN GRAFFITI   Universal, 1973
CAN ELLEN BE SAVED? (TF)   ABC Circle Films, 1974
WHERE HAVE ALL THE PEOPLE GONE? (TF)
   Metromedia Productions, 1974
THE ABDUCTION OF SAINT ANNE   *THEY'VE KIDNAPPED
   ANNE BENEDICT* (TF)   QM Productions, 1975
LIFEGUARD   Paramount, 1976
LITTLE LADIES OF THE NIGHT (TF)   Spelling-Goldberg
   Productions, 1977
AIRPORT '77   Universal, 1977
I NEVER PROMISED YOU A ROSE GARDEN   New World, 1977

THE PROMISE   Universal, 1979
THE RUNNER STUMBLES   20th Century-Fox, 1979
SHE'S IN THE ARMY NOW (TF)   ABC Circle Films, 1981
SUNDAY LOVERS   MGM/United Artists, 1981,
   U.S.-British-Italian-French
HANKY PANKY   Columbia, 1982
TWILIGHT ZONE—THE MOVIE   Warner Bros., 1983
INDEPENDENCE DAY   Warner Bros., 1983
THE LAST WINTER   Triumph/Columbia, 1983, Israeli
BLACKOUT (CTF)   HBO Premiere Films/Roger Gimbel Productions/
   Peregrine Entertainment Ltd./Lee Buck Industries/Alexander
   Smith & Parks, 1985, U.S.-Canadian
CHILDREN OF THE NIGHT (TF)   Robert Guenette Productions, 1985
WARNING SIGN   20th Century Fox, 1985
SUNSET   TriStar, 1988
CLARA'S HEART   Warner Bros., 1988
TRAPPED (CTF)   Cine Enterprises, 1989
THE OPERATION (TF)   Moress, Nanas, Golden Entertainment/
   Viacom, 1990
THE DOORS   TriStar, 1991
LAST LIGHT (CTF)   Showtime Networks, Inc./Stillwater
   Productions, 1993
TRIAL BY JURY   Warner Bros., 1994
APOLLO 13   Universal, 1995

AIDAN QUINN

b. March 8, 1959 - Chicago, Illinois
Agent: CAA - Beverly Hills, 310/288-4545

RECKLESS   MGM/UA, 1984
DESPERATELY SEEKING SUSAN   Orion, 1985
AN EARLY FROST (TF)   NBC Productions, 1985
THE MISSION   Warner Bros., 1986, British
STAKEOUT   Buena Vista, 1987
CRUSOE   Island Pictures, 1988, U.S.-British
PERFECT WITNESS (CTF)   HBO Pictures/Granger
   Productions, 1989
THE HANDMAID'S TALE   Cinecom, 1990
THE LEMON SISTERS   Miramax Films, 1990
AVALON   TriStar, 1990
AT PLAY IN THE FIELDS OF THE LORD   Universal, 1991
THE PLAYBOYS   Samuel Goldwyn Company, 1992, Irish-British
BENNY & JOON   MGM/UA, 1993
BLINK   New Line Cinema, 1994
MARY SHELLEY'S FRANKENSTEIN   TriStar, 1994
LEGENDS OF THE FALL   TriStar, 1994
THE STARS FELL ON HENRIETTA   Warner Bros., 1995

AILEEN QUINN

ANNIE   Columbia, 1982

ANTHONY QUINN

b. April 21, 1915 - Chihuahua, Mexico
Agent: William Morris Agency - Beverly Hills, 310/274-7451

PAROLE!   Universal, 1936
SWORN ENEMY   MGM, 1936
NIGHT WAITRESS   RKO Radio, 1936
THE PLAINSMAN   Paramount, 1936
SWING HIGH, SWING LOW   Paramount, 1937
WAIKIKI WEDDING   Paramount, 1937
THE LAST TRAIN FROM MADRID   Paramount, 1937
PARTNERS IN CRIME   Paramount, 1937
DAUGHTER OF SHANGHAI   Paramount, 1937
THE BUCCANEER   Paramount, 1938
DANGEROUS TO KNOW   Paramount, 1938
TIP-OFF GIRLS   Paramount, 1938
HUNTED MEN   Paramount, 1938
BULLDOG DRUMMOND IN AFRICA   Paramount, 1938
KING OF ALCATRAZ   Paramount, 1938
KING OF CHINATOWN   Paramount, 1939
UNION PACIFIC   Paramount, 1939
ISLAND OF LOST MEN   Paramount, 1939
TELEVISION SPY   Paramount, 1939
EMERGENCY SQUAD   Paramount, 1940
ROAD TO SINGAPORE   Paramount, 1940
PAROLE FIXER   Paramount, 1940
THE GHOST BREAKERS   Paramount, 1940

CITY FOR CONQUEST Warner Bros., 1940
TEXAS RANGERS RIDE AGAIN Paramount, 1940
BLOOD AND SAND 20th Century-Fox, 1941
KNOCKOUT 1941
THIEVES FALL OUT Warner Bros., 1941
BULLETS FOR O'HARA 1941
THEY DIED WITH THEIR BOOTS ON Warner Bros., 1941
THE PERFECT SNOB 1941
LARCENY, INC. Warner Bros., 1942
ROAD TO MOROCCO Paramount, 1942
THE BLACK SWAN 20th Century-Fox, 1942
THE OX-BOW INCIDENT 20th Century-Fox, 1943
GUADALCANAL DIARY 20th Century-Fox, 1943
BUFFALO BILL 20th Century-Fox, 1944
ROGER TOUHY—GANGSTER 20th Century-Fox, 1944
LADIES OF WASHINGTON 1944
IRISH EYES ARE SMILING 20th Century-Fox, 1944
CHINA SKY RKO Radio, 1945
WHERE DO WE GO FROM HERE? 20th Century-Fox, 1945
BACK TO BATAAN RKO Radio, 1945
CALIFORNIA Paramount, 1946
SINBAD THE SAILOR RKO Radio, 1947
THE IMPERFECT LADY Paramount, 1947
BLACK GOLD Allied Artists, 1947
TYCOON 1947
THE BRAVE BULLS Columbia, 1951
MASK OF THE AVENGER Columbia, 1951
VIVA ZAPATA! ○○ 20th Century-Fox, 1952
THE BRIGAND Columbia, 1952
THE WORLD IN HIS ARMS Universal, 1952
AGAINST ALL FLAGS Universal, 1952
CITY BENEATH THE SEA Universal, 1953
SEMINOLE Universal, 1953
RIDE VAQUERO MGM, 1953
EAST OF SUMATRA Universal, 1953
BLOWING WILD Warner Bros., 1953
FATAL DESIRE 1953, Italian
LA STRADA 1954, Italian
THE LONG WAIT 1954
ULYSSES 1955, Italian
THE MAGNIFICENT MATADOR 20th Century-Fox, 1955
THE NAKED STREET 1955
SEVEN CITIES OF GOLD 1955
ANGELS OF DARKNESS 1956, Italian
LUST FOR LIFE ○○ MGM, 1956
MAN FROM DEL RIO 1956
THE WILD PARTY 1956
THE HUNCHBACK OF NOTRE DAME NOTRE DAME DE PARIS
   RKO Radio, 1956, French
THE RIVER'S EDGE 20th Century-Fox, 1957
THE RIDE BACK 1957
WILD IS THE WIND ★ Paramount, 1957
HOT SPELL Paramount, 1958
ATTILA 1958, Italian-French
THE BLACK ORCHID Paramount, 1959
WARLOCK 20th Century-Fox, 1959
LAST TRAIN FROM GUN HILL Paramount, 1959
THE SAVAGE INNOCENTS Paramount, 1959,
   Italian-French-British-U.S.
HELLER IN PINK TIGHTS Paramount, 1960
PORTRAIT IN BLACK Universal, 1960
THE GUNS OF NAVARONNE Columbia, 1961, British-U.S.
BARABBAS Columbia, 1962, Italian
REQUIEM FOR A HEAVYWEIGHT Columbia, 1962
LAWRENCE OF ARABIA Columbia, 1962, British
BEHOLD A PALE HORSE Columbia, 1964
THE VISIT 20th Century-Fox, 1964,
   West German-French-Italian-U.S.
ZORBA THE GREEK ★ International Classics, 1964, Greek
A HIGH WIND IN JAMAICA 20th Century-Fox, 1965, British
MARCO THE MAGNIFICENT MGM, 1966,
   French-Italian-Egyptian-Afganistan-Yugoslavian
LOST COMMAND Columbia, 1966
THE 25TH HOUR MGM, 1967, French-Italian-Yugoslavian
THE HAPPENING Columbia, 1967
THE ROVER L'AVVENTURIERO Cinerama Releasing
   Corporation, 1967
GUNS FOR SAN SEBASTIAN LA BATAILLE DE SAN SEBASTIAN
   MGM, 1968, French-Italian-Mexican

THE SHOES OF THE FISHERMAN MGM, 1968
THE MAGUS 20th Century-Fox, 1968, British
THE SECRET OF SANTA VITTORIA United Artists, 1969
A DREAM OF KINGS National General, 1969
A WALK IN THE SPRING RAIN Columbia, 1970
R.P.M. Columbia, 1970
FLAP THE LAST WARRIOR Warner Bros., 1970
THE CITY (TF) Universal TV, 1971
ACROSS 110TH STREET United Artists, 1972
DEAF SMITH AND JOHNNY EARS LOS AMIGOS 1973
THE DON IS DEAD Universal, 1973
THE DESTRUCTORS THE MARSEILLES CONTRACT
   American International, 1974
THE INHERITANCE 1976, Italian
HIGH ROLLERS BLUFF 1976, Italian
TIGERS DON'T CRY 1976, South African
THE CON ARTISTS 1977, Italian
MOHAMMAD, MESSENGER OF GOD THE MESSAGE
   Tarik, 1977, British-Lebanese
JESUS OF NAZARETH (MS) Sir Lew Grade Productions/ITC,
   1978, British-Italian
THE GREEK TYCOON Universal, 1978
THE CHILDREN OF SANCHEZ Lone Star, 1978, U.S.-Mexican
CARAVANS Universal, 1978, U.S.-Iranian
THE PASSAGE United Artists, 1979, British
LION OF THE DESERT United Film Distribution,
   1981, Libyan-British
HIGH RISK American Cinema, 1981
THE SALAMANDER ITC, 1981, British-Italian-U.S.
MAN OF PASSION Golden Sun Productions, 1988, Spanish
RICHEST MAN IN THE WORLD: THE ARISTOTLE ONASSIS
   STORY (MS) The Konigsberg-Sanitsky Company, 1988
THE OLD MAN AND THE SEA (TF) Storke Enterprises/
   Green Pond Productions/Yorkshire TV, 1990
REVENGE Columbia, 1990
GHOSTS CAN'T DO IT Triumph Releasing Corporation, 1990
ONLY THE LONELY 20th Century Fox, 1991
JUNGLE FEVER Universal, 1991
MOBSTERS Universal, 1991
LAST ACTION HERO Columbia, 1993
THIS CAN'T BE LOVE (TF) Davis Entertainment/Pacific Motion
   Pictures/World International Network, 1994

DANIEL QUINN
SCANNER COP 2 Republic Pictures, 1994

DANIELE QUINN
BAND OF THE HAND TriStar, 1986

FRANCESCO QUINN
PLATOON Orion, 1986
THE OLD MAN AND THE SEA (TF) Storke Enterprises/
   Green Pond Productions/Yorkshire TV, 1990

GLENN QUINN
ALL SHOOK UP Universal, 1991

J.C. QUINN
AT CLOSE RANGE Orion, 1986
MAXIMUM OVERDRIVE DEG, 1986
BARFLY Cannon, 1987
THE ABYSS 20th Century Fox, 1989

MARTHA QUINN
b. May 11, 1959 - Albany, New York

EDDIE AND THE CRUISER II: EDDIE LIVES Scotti Bros., 1989
THE BRADYS (TF) Brady Productions/Paramount TV, 1990

PAT QUINN
ALICE'S RESTAURANT United Artists, 1969
ZACHARIAH Cinerama Releasing Corporation, 1971
AN UNMARRIED WOMAN 20th Century-Fox, 1978
CLEAN AND SOBER Warner Bros., 1988

VALENTINA QUINN
THE OLD MAN AND THE SEA (TF)   Storke Enterprises/
Green Pond Productions/Yorkshire TV, 1990

ADOLPHO "SHABBA-DOO" QUINONES
(Shabba-Doo)

BREAKIN'   MGM/UA/Cannon, 1984
BREAKIN' 2 ELECTRIC BOOGALOO   TriStar/Cannon, 1985
LAMBADA   Warner Bros., 1990

BEULAH QUO
CHINATOWN   Paramount, 1974
YES, GIORGIO   MGM/UA, 1982
AMERICAN GEISHA (TF)   Interscope Communications/
Stonehenge Productions, 1986

R

ELLIE RAAB
THE FABULOUS BAKER BOYS   20th Century Fox, 1989

FRANCISCO RABAL
CAMORRA   *UN COMPLICATO INTRIGO DI DONNE,
VICOLI E DELITTI*   Cannon, 1986, Italian

ALLESSANDRO RABELO
WHERE THE RIVER RUNS BLACK   MGM/UA, 1986

MARCELO RABELO
WHERE THE RIVER RUNS BLACK   MGM/UA, 1986

ALAN RACHINS
b. October 10, 1947 - Cambridge, Massachusetts

ALWAYS   Samuel Goldwyn Company, 1985

IVAN JORGE RADO
MAC AND ME   Orion, 1988

BOB RAFELSON
Agent: ICM - Beverly Hills, 310/550-4000

ALWAYS   Samuel Goldwyn Company, 1985

GARY RAFF
VASECTOMY, A DELICATE MATTER   Seymour Borde &
Associates, 1986

DEBORAH RAFFIN
b. March 13, 1953 - Los Angeles, California

40 CARATS   Columbia, 1973
THE DOVE   Paramount, 1974
JACQUELINE SUSANN'S ONCE IS NOT ENOUGH
ONCE IS NOT ENOUGH   Paramount, 1975
NIGHTMARE IN BADHAM COUNTY (TF)   ABC Circle Films, 1976
DEMON   *GOD TOLD ME TO*   New World, 1977
THE SENTINEL   Universal, 1977
RANSOM   *ASSAULT ON PARADISE/MANIAC*   New World, 1977
SKI LIFT TO DEATH (TF)   1978
HOW TO PICK UP GIRLS! (TF)   King-Hitzig Productions, 1978
WILLA (TF)   GJL Productions/Dove, Inc, 1979

TOUCHED BY LOVE   Columbia, 1980
THREESOME (TF)   CBS Entertainment, 1984
LACE II (MS)   Lorimar Productions, 1985
DEATH WISH 3   Cannon, 1985
JAMES CLAVELL'S NOBLE HOUSE   *NOBLE HOUSE* (MS)   Noble
House Productions, Ltd./De Laurentiis Entertainment Group, 1987
MORNING GLORY   Academy Entertainment, 1993

JOSEPH RAGNO
THE BABE   Universal, 1992

WILLIAM RAGSDALE
FRIGHT NIGHT   Columbia, 1985
FRIGHT NIGHT PART 2   New Century/Vista, 1989
MANNEQUIN TWO ON THE MOVE   20th Century Fox, 1991

STEVE RAILSBACK
THE STUNT MAN   20th Century-Fox, 1980
ARMED AND DANGEROUS   Columbia, 1986
DISTORTIONS   Cori Films, 1987

SHERYL LEE RALPH
THE MIGHTY QUINN   MGM/UA, 1989

HAROLD RAMIS
b. November 21, 1944 - Chicago, Illinois
Agent: CAA - Beverly Hills, 310/288-4545

STRIPES   Columbia, 1981
HEAVY METAL (AF)   Columbia, 1981, Canadian (voice)
GHOSTBUSTERS   Columbia, 1984
BABY BOOM   MGM/UA, 1987
STEALING HOME   Warner Bros., 1988
GHOSTBUSTERS II   Columbia, 1989
GROUNDHOG DAY   Columbia, 1993 (also directed)

CHARLOTTE RAMPLING
b. February 5, 1945 - Sturmer, England

THE KNACK...AND HOW TO GET IT   1965
ROTTEN TO THE CORE   1965
GEORGY GIRL   1966
THE LONG DUEL   1967
SEQUESTRO DI PERSONA   1968, Italian
THE DAMNED   *LA CADUTA DEGLI DEI*   1969,
Italian-West German
HOW TO MAKE IT   1969
THREE   1969, U.S.-French
'TIS PITY SHE'S A WHORE   *ADDIO FRATELLO CRUDELE*
1971, Italian
THE SKI BUM   1971
CORKY   *LOOKING GOOD*   1972
HENRY VIII AND HIS SIX WIVES   1973
ASYLUM   1973
THE NIGHT PORTER   *ZARDOZ, IL PORTIERE DI NOTTE*
Avco Embassy, 1974, Italian
CARAVAN TO VACCARES   1974, British-French
FAREWELL, MY LOVELY   Avco Embassy, 1975
YUPPI-DU   1975, Italian
OTHER SIDE OF PARADISE   *FOXTROT*   1976, Mexican-Swedish
SHERLOCK HOLMES IN NEW YORK (TF)   1976
FLESH OF THE ORCHID   1976
THE PURPLE TAXI   *UN TAXI MAUVE*   1977, French-Italian-Irish
ORCA   1977
STARDUST MEMORIES   United Artists, 1980
THE VERDICT   1982
THE VIVA LA VIE   1983
HE DIED WITH HIS EYES OPEN   1984
SADNESS AND BEAUTY   1985
MAX MY LOVE   1986
ANGEL HEART   TriStar, 1987
PARIS BY NIGHT   1988

ANNE ELIZABETH RAMSAY
A LEAGUE OF THEIR OWN   Columbia, 1992

BRUCE RAMSAY
Agent: UTA - Beverly Hills, 310/273-6700

ALIVE Buena Vista, 1993
KILLING ZOE October Films, 1994, U.S.-French
THE NEW AGE Warner Bros., 1994

LOGAN RAMSEY
THE SPORTING CLUB Avco Embassy, 1971
ANY WHICH WAY YOU CAN Warner Bros., 1980
SCROOGED Paramount, 1988
HOMER & EDDIE Skouras Pictures, 1990

MARION RAMSEY
POLICE ACADEMY The Ladd Company/Warner Bros., 1984
POLICE ACADEMY 2: THEIR FIRST ASSIGNMENT
  Warner Bros., 1985
POLICE ACADEMY 3: BACK IN TRAINING Warner Bros., 1986
POLICE ACADEMY 4: CITIZENS ON PATROL Warner Bros., 1987
POLICE ACADEMY 5: ASSIGNMENT MIAMI BEACH
  Warner Bros., 1988
POLICE ACADEMY 6: CITY UNDER SIEGE Warner Bros., 1989

ETHAN RANDALL
DUTCH 20th Century Fox, 1991
ALL I WANT FOR CHRISTMAS Paramount, 1991
A FAR OFF PLACE Buena Vista, 1993

LEXI RANDALL
THE WAR Universal, 1994

PETE RANDALL
THE ROOKIE Warner Bros., 1990

TONY RANDALL
(Leonard Rosenberg)
b. February 26, 1920 - Tulsa, Oklahoma
Agent: William Morris Agency - Beverly Hills, 310/274-7451

OH, MEN! OH, WOMEN! 20th Century-Fox, 1957
WILL SUCCESS SPOIL ROCK HUNTER? 20th Century-Fox, 1957
NO DOWN PAYMENT 20th Century-Fox, 1957
THE MATING GAME MGM, 1959
PILLOW TALK Universal, 1959
THE ADVENTURES OF HUCKLEBERRY FINN MGM, 1960
LET'S MAKE LOVE 20th Century-Fox, 1960
LOVER COME BACK Universal, 1961
BOYS' NIGHT OUT MGM, 1962
ISLAND OF LOVE Warner Bros., 1963
THE BRASS BOTTLE 1964
ROBIN AND THE SEVEN HOODS Warner Bros., 1964
THE SEVEN FACES OF DR. LAO MGM, 1964
SEND ME NO FLOWERS Universal, 1964
FLUFFY Universal, 1965
THE ALPHABET MURDERS *THE A.B.C. MURDERS* MGM, 1966, British
BANG! BANG! YOU'RE DEAD! *OUR MAN IN MARRAKESH*
  American International, 1966, British
HELLO DOWN THERE Paramount, 1969
EVERYTHING YOU ALWAYS WANTED TO KNOW ABOUT SEX*
  (*BUT WERE AFRAID TO ASK) United Artists, 1972
FOOLIN' AROUND Columbia, 1978
SCAVENGER HUNT 20th Century-Fox, 1979
SIDNEY SHORR: A GIRL'S BEST FRIEND (TF)
  Hajeno Productions/Warner Bros. TV, 1981
THE KING OF COMEDY 20th Century-Fox, 1983
AGATHA CHRISTIE'S 'THE MAN IN THE BROWN SUIT' (TF)
  Alan Shayne Productions/Warner Bros. TV, 1989
IT HAD TO BE YOU Limelight Studios, 1989
GREMLINS 2 THE NEW BATCH Warner Bros., 1990 (voice)
FATAL INSTINCT MGM/UA, 1993

MARY JO RANDLE
BAD BEHAVIOUR October Films, 1993, British

THERESA RANDLE
Agent: UTA - Beverly Hills, 310/273-6700

KING OF NEW YORK New Line Cinema, 1990
THE FIVE HEARTBEATS 20th Century Fox, 1991
JUNGLE FEVER Universal, 1991
MALCOLM X Warner Bros., 1992
SUGAR HILL 20th Century Fox, 1994
BEVERLY HILLS COPS III Paramount, 1994
BAD BOYS Columbia, 1995

JOHN RANDOLPH
b. June 1, 1915 - New York, New York

NAKED CITY Universal, 1948
SECONDS Paramount, 1966
PRETTY POISON 20th Century-Fox, 1968
THERE WAS A CROOKED MAN Warner Bros., 1970
LITTLE MURDERS 20th Century-Fox, 1971
SERPICO Paramount, 1973
KING KONG Paramount, 1976
WASHINGTON: BEHIND CLOSED DOORS (MS) Paramount TV, 1977
KILL ME IF YOU CAN (TF) Columbia TV, 1977
HEAVEN CAN WAIT Paramount, 1978
BLIND AMBITION (TF) Time-Life Productions, 1979
PRIZZI'S HONOR 20th Century Fox, 1985
THE WIZARD OF LONELINESS Skouras Pictures, 1988

MICHAEL RAPAPORT
Agent: Innovative Artists - Los Angeles, 310/553-5200

ZEBRAHEAD Triumph Releasing Corporation, 1992
POINT OF NO RETURN Warner Bros., 1993
POETIC JUSTICE Columbia, 1993
MONEY FOR NOTHING Buena Vista, 1993
TRUE ROMANCE Warner Bros., 1993
THE SCOUT 20th Century Fox, 1994
HIGHER LEARNING Columbia, 1994
KISS OF DEATH 20th Century Fox, 1995

LARRY RAPP
ONCE UPON A TIME IN AMERICA The Ladd Company/
  Warner Bros., 1984, U.S.-Italian-Canadian

ANTHONY RAPP
ADVENTURES IN BABYSITTING Buena Vista, 1987
SCHOOL TIES Paramount, 1992

STEPHEN RAPPAPORT
...AND GOD SPOKE Live Entertainment, 1994

DAVID RASCHE
COBRA Warner Bros., 1986
NATIVE SON Cinecom, 1986
MADE IN HEAVEN Lorimar, 1987
AN INNOCENT MAN Buena Vista, 1989
WICKED STEPMOTHER MGM, 1989
DELIRIOUS MGM-Pathe, 1991
BINGO! TriStar, 1991

THALMUS RASULALA
COOL BREEZE MGM, 1972
BLACULA American International, 1972
WILLIE DYNAMITE Universal, 1974
MR. RICCO MGM, 1975
BUCKTOWN American International, 1975
ADIOS AMIGO Atlas, 1976
FUN WITH DICK AND JANE Columbia, 1977
BULLETPROOF Cine Tel Films, 1987
ABOVE THE LAW Warner Bros., 1988

STACY LINN RAWSOWER
TANK GIRL MGM/UA, 1995

OLA RAY
FEAR CITY Chevy Chase Distribution, 1984

MARTHA RAYE†
(Margaret Teresa Yvonne O'Reed)
b. August 27, 1916 - Butte, Montana
d. October, 1994

RHYTHM ON THE RANGE   Paramount, 1936
THE BIG BROADCAST OF 1937   Paramount, 1936
COLLEGE HOLIDAY   Paramount, 1936
HIDEAWAY GIRL   Paramount, 1937
WAIKIKI WEDDING   Paramount, 1937
MOUNTAIN MUSIC   Paramount, 1937
ARTISTS AND MODELS   Paramount, 1937
DOUBLE OR NOTHING   Paramount, 1937
THE BIG BROADCAST OF 1938   Paramount, 1938
GIVE ME A SAILOR   Paramount, 1938
COLLEGE SWING   Paramount, 1938
TROPIC HOLIDAY   Paramount, 1938
NEVER SAY DIE   Paramount, 1939
$1,000 DOLLARS A TOUCHDOWN   Paramount, 1939
THE FARMER'S DAUGHTER   Paramount, 1940
THE BOYS FROM SYRACUSE   Universal, 1940
NAVY BLUES   Warner Bros., 1941
KEEP 'EM FLYING   Universal, 1941
HELLZAPOPPIN!   Universal, 1941
FOUR JILLS IN A JEEP   20th Century-Fox, 1944
PIN-UP GIRL   20th Century-Fox, 1944
MONSIEUR VERDOUX   United Artists, 1947
JUMBO *BILLY ROSE'S JUMBO*   MGM, 1962
THE PHYNX   Warner Bros., 1970
PUFNSTUF   1970 (voice)
THE CONCORDE—AIRPORT '79   Universal, 1979

DEVON RAYMOND
SINGLES   Warner Bros., 1992

PEGGY REA
IN COUNTRY   Warner Bros., 1989

STEPHEN REA
DANNY BOY *ANGEL*   Triumph/Columbia, 1982, Irish-British
THE COMPANY OF WOLVES   Cannon, 1984, British
LIFE IS SWEET   October Films, 1991, British
THE CRYING GAME ★   Miramax Films, 1992, Irish-British
BAD BEHAVIOUR   October Films, 1993, British
ANGIE   Buena Vista, 1994
PRINCESS CARABOO   TriStar, 1994
INTERVIEW WITH THE VAMPIRE   Warner Bros., 1994
PRET-A-PORTER   Miramax Films, 1994

JAMES READ
BLUE THUNDER   Columbia, 1983
LACE II (MS)   Lorimar Productions, 1985
ROBERT KENNEDY AND HIS TIMES (MS)   Chris-Rose
   Productions/Columbia TV, 1985
NORTH AND SOUTH (MS)   Wolper Productions/Warner
   Bros. TV, 1985
CELEBRATION FAMILY (TF)   Frank von Zerneck Films, 1987
POOR LITTLE RICH GIRL: THE BARBARA HUTTON STORY (MS)
   Lester Persky Productions/ITC Productions, 1987
EIGHT MEN OUT   Orion, 1988
BEACHES   Buena Vista, 1988

NANCY REAGAN
(See Nancy DAVIS)

RONALD REAGAN
b. February 6, 1911 - Tampico, Illinois

LOVE IS ON THE AIR   Warner Bros., 1937
HOLLYWOOD HOTEL   Warner Bros., 1937
SERGEANT MURPHY   Warner Bros., 1938
SWING YOUR LADY   Warner Bros., 1938
THE COWBOY FROM BROOKLYN   Warner Bros., 1938
BOY MEETS GIRL   Warner Bros., 1938
GIRLS ON PROBATION   Warner Bros., 1938
BROTHER RAT   Warner Bros., 1938

GOING PLACES   Warner Bros., 1938
ACCIDENTS WILL HAPPEN   Warner Bros., 1939
SECRET SERVICE OF THE AIR   Warner Bros., 1939
DARK VICTORY   Warner Bros., 1939
CODE OF THE SECRET SERVICE   Warner Bros., 1939
NAUGHTY BUT NICE   Warner Bros., 1939
HELL'S KITCHEN   Warner Bros., 1939
ANGELS WASH THEIR FACES   Warner Bros., 1939
SMASHING THE MONEY RING   Warner Bros., 1939
BROTHER RAT AND A BABY   Warner Bros., 1940
AN ANGEL FROM TEXAS   Warner Bros., 1940
MURDER IN THE AIR   Warner Bros., 1940
KNUTE ROCKNE, ALL AMERICAN   Warner Bros., 1940
TUGBOAT ANNIE SAILS AGAIN   Warner Bros., 1940
SANTA FE TRAIL   Warner Bros., 1940
THE BAD MAN   MGM, 1941
MILLION DOLLAR BABY   Warner Bros., 1941
NINE LIVES ARE NOT ENOUGH   Warner Bros., 1941
INTERNATIONAL SQUADRON   Warner Bros., 1941
KINGS ROW   Warner Bros., 1942
JUKE GIRL   Warner Bros., 1942
DESPERATE JOURNEY   Warner Bros., 1942
THIS IS THE ARMY   Warner Bros., 1943
STALLION ROAD   Warner Bros., 1947
THAT HAGEN GIRL   Warner Bros., 1947
THE VOICE OF THE TURTLE   *ONE FOR THE BOOK*
   Warner Bros., 1947
JOHN LOVES MARY   Warner Bros., 1949
NIGHT UNTO NIGHT   Warner Bros., 1949
THE GIRL FROM JONES BEACH   Warner Bros., 1949
IT'S A GREAT FEELING   Warner Bros., 1949 (uncredited)
THE HASTY HEART   Warner Bros., 1949, British
LOUISA   Universal, 1950
STORM WARNING   Warner Bros., 1951
BEDTIME FOR BONZO   Warner Bros., 1951
THE LAST OUTPOST   Warner Bros., 1951
HONG KONG   Warner Bros., 1951
THE WINNING TEAM   Warner Bros., 1952
SHE'S WORKING HER WAY THROUGH COLLEGE
   Warner Bros., 1952
TROPIC ZONE   1953
LAW AND ORDER   Universal, 1953
PRISONER OF WAR   MGM, 1954
CATTLE QUEEN OF MONTANA   RKO Radio, 1954
TENNESSEE'S PARTNER   RKO Radio, 1955
HELLCATS OF THE NAVY   Columbia, 1957
THE YOUNG DOCTORS   United Artists, 1961 (voice)
THE KILLERS   Universal, 1964

J.L. REATE
THE GOLDEN CHILD   Paramount, 1986

JAMES REBHORN
BLANK CHECK   Buena Vista, 1994
8 SECONDS   New Line Cinema, 1994

WINSTON RECKERT
AGNES OF GOD   Columbia, 1985

KEITH W. REDDIN
BIG   20th Century Fox, 1988

HELEN REDDY
b. October 25, 1941 - Melbourne, Australia

AIRPORT 1975   Universal, 1974
PETE'S DRAGON   Buena Vista, 1977

ROBERT REDFORD
(Charles Robert Redford)
b. August 18, 1937 - Santa Monica, California
Agent: CAA - Beverly Hills, 310/288-4545

WAR HUNT   United Artists, 1962
SITUATION HOPELESS—BUT NOT SERIOUS   Paramount, 1965
INSIDE DAISY CLOVER   Warner Bros., 1965

THE CHASE   Columbia, 1966
THIS PROPERTY IS CONDEMNED   Paramount, 1966
BAREFOOT IN THE PARK   Paramount, 1967
BUTCH CASSIDY AND THE SUNDANCE KID
   20th Century-Fox, 1969
DOWNHILL RACER   Paramount, 1969
TELL THEM WILLIE BOY IS HERE   Universal, 1969
LITTLE FAUSS AND BIG HALSY   Paramount, 1970
THE HOT ROCK   20th Century-Fox, 1972
THE CANDIDATE   Warner Bros., 1972
JEREMIAH JOHNSON   Warner Bros., 1972
THE WAY WE WERE   Columbia, 1973
THE STING ★   Universal, 1973
THE GREAT GATSBY   Paramount, 1974
THE GREAT WALDO PEPPER   Universal, 1975
THREE DAYS OF THE CONDOR   Paramount, 1975
ALL THE PRESIDENT'S MEN   Warner Bros., 1976
A BRIDGE TOO FAR   United Artists, 1977, British
THE ELECTRIC HORSEMAN   Columbia, 1979
BRUBAKER   20th Century-Fox, 1980
THE NATURAL   TriStar, 1984
OUT OF AFRICA   Universal, 1985
LEGAL EAGLES   Universal, 1986
YOSEMITE: THE FATE OF HEAVEN (FD)   1989 (narration)
HAVANA   Universal, 1990
INCIDENT AT OGLALA (FD)   Miramax Films, 1992 (narration)
SNEAKERS   Universal, 1992
A RIVER RUNS THROUGH IT   Columbia, 1992
   (narration; also directed)
INDECENT PROPOSAL   Paramount, 1993
UP CLOSE AND PERSONAL   Buena Vista, 1995

ROCKETS REDGLARE
AFTER HOURS   The Geffen Company/Warner Bros., 1985
DOWN BY LAW   Island Pictures, 1986
BIG   20th Century Fox, 1988
COOKIE   Warner Bros., 1989

CORIN REDGRAVE
FOUR WEDDINGS AND A FUNERAL   Gramercy Pictures,
   1994, British

JEMMA REDGRAVE
HOWARDS END   Sony Pictures Classics, 1992, British

LYNN REDGRAVE
b. March 8, 1943 - London, England

TOM JONES   Lopert, 1963, British
GIRL WITH GREEN EYES   United Artists, 1964, British
GEORGY GIRL ★   Columbia, 1966, British
THE DEADLY AFFAIR   Columbia, 1967, British
SMASHING TIME   Paramount, 1967, British
THE VIRGIN SOLDIERS   Columbia, 1969, British
BLOOD KIN   1969
THE LAST OF THE MOBILE HOTSHOTS   Warner Bros., 1970
KILLER FROM YUMA   1971
DON'T TURN THE OTHER CHEEK!   LOS GUERILLEROS
   1972, Spanish-Italian
VIVA LA MUERTE—TUA!   1972, Italian-West German
EVERY LITTLE CROOK AND NANNY   MGM, 1972
EVERYTHING YOU ALWAYS WANTED TO KNOW ABOUT SEX*
   (*BUT WERE AFRAID TO ASK)   United Artists, 1972
THE NATIONAL GENERAL   1973
THE HAPPY HOOKER   Cannon, 1975
THE BIG BUS   Paramount, 1976
SUNDAY LOVERS   MGM/UA, 1980, U.S.-British-Italian-French
GAUGUIN THE SAVAGE (TF)   Nephi Productions, 1980
REHEARSAL FOR MURDER (TF)   Levinson-Link Productions/
   Robert Papazian Productions, 1982
MORGAN STEWART'S COMING HOME   New Century/Vista, 1987
MIDNIGHT   SVS, 1989
GETTING IT RIGHT   MCEG, 1989, U.S.-British
WHAT EVER HAPPENED TO BABY JANE? (TF)   Steve White
   Productions, 1991

VANESSA REDGRAVE
b. January 30, 1937 - London, England

BEHIND THE MASK   Showcorporation, 1958, British
MORGAN!   MORGAN: A SUITABLE CASE FOR TREATMENT ★
   Cinema 5, 1966, British
A MAN FOR ALL SEASONS   Agamemnon Film/British Lion,
   1966, British
BLOW-UP   Premier, 1966, Italian-British
THE SAILOR FROM GIBRALTAR   Lopert, 1967, British
RED AND BLUE   1967, British
CAMELOT   Warner Bros., 1967
SMASHING TIME   Paramount, 1967, British
TONIGHT LET'S ALL MAKE LOVE IN LONDON (FD)   1968, British
THE CHARGE OF THE LIGHT BRIGADE   1968, British
ISADORA   THE LOVES OF ISADORA ★   Universal, 1968, British
THE SEA GULL   Warner Bros., 1968, U.S.-British
A QUIET PLACE IN THE COUNTRY   UN TRANQUILLO POSTO
   DI CAMGAPNA   United Artists, 1968, Italian-French
OH! WHAT A LOVELY WAR   Paramount, 1969
DROPOUT   Medusa/Lion Film, 1970, Italian
LA VACANZA   Lion Film, 1971, Italian
THE TROJAN WOMEN   Cinerama Releasing Corporation, 1972,
   U.S.-British-West German-Greek
THE DEVILS   Warner Bros., 1971, British-U.S.
MARY, QUEEN OF SCOTS ★   Universal, 1971
MURDER ON THE ORIENT EXPRESS   Paramount, 1974, British
OUT OF SEASON   Athenaeum, 1975
THE SEVEN-PER-CENT SOLUTION   Universal, 1976, British
JULIA ✪✪   20th Century-Fox, 1977
AGATHA   Warner Bros., 1979, British
YANKS   Universal, 1979, British
BEAR ISLAND   Taft International, 1980, British-Canadian
PLAYING FOR TIME (TF)   Syzygy Productions, 1980
WAGNER (MS)   London Trust Prods./Richard Wagner Productions/
   Ladbroke Productions/Hungarofilm, 1983, British-Hungarian-Austrian
MY BODY, MY CHILD (TF)   Titus Productions, 1982
THE BOSTONIANS ★   Almi Pictures, 1984
STEAMING   New World, 1985
WETHERBY   MGM/UA Classics, 1985, British
THREE SOVEREIGNS FOR SARAH (TF)   Night Owl
   Productions, 1985
PETER THE GREAT (MS)   PTG Productions/NBC Productions, 1986
SECOND SERVE (TF)   Linda Yellen Productions/
   Lorimar-Telepictures, 1986
PRICK UP YOUR EARS   Samuel Goldwyn Company, 1987, British
WHAT EVER HAPPENED TO BABY JANE? (TF)   Steve White
   Productions, 1991
HOWARDS END ✪   Sony Pictures Classics, 1992, British
THE HOUSE OF THE SPIRITS   Miramax Films, 1993, U.S.-German
MOTHER'S BOYS   Dimension/Miramax Films, 1994
JAMES AND THE GIANT PEACH   Buena Vista, 1995 (voice)

ALYSON REED
A CHORUS LINE   Columbia, 1985
SKIN DEEP   20th Century Fox, 1989

JERRY REED
b. March 20, 1937 - Atlanta, Georgia

W.W. AND THE DIXIE DANCEKINGS   20th Century-Fox, 1975
GATOR   United Artists, 1976
SMOKEY AND THE BANDIT   Universal, 1977
SMOKEY AND THE BANDIT II   Universal, 1980
SMOKEY AND THE BANDIT 3   Universal, 1983
THE SURVIVORS   Columbia, 1983
BAT 21   TriStar, 1988

OLIVER REED
b. February 13, 1938 - London, England

OLIVER!   Columbia, 1968, British
WOMEN IN LOVE   United Artists, 1970, British
Z.P.G.   Paramount, 1972, British
THE TRIPLE ECHO   Altura, 1973, British
THE THREE MUSKETEERS   20th Century-Fox, 1974, British
TOMMY   Columbia, 1975, British
THE FOUR MUSKETEERS   20th Century-Fox, 1975, British

F
I
L
M

A
C
T
O
R
S

TWO OF A KIND   20th Century-Fox, 1983
THE STING II   Universal, 1983
CASTAWAY   Cannon, 1986, British
THE ADVENTURES OF BARON MUNCHAUSEN   Columbia, 1989
THE RETURN OF THE MUSKETEERS   Universal, 1990
PRISONERS OF HONOR (CTF)   HBO Pictures/Dreyfuss-James
   Productions, 1991

PAMELA REED
Agent: ICM - Beverly Hills, 310/550-4000

YOUNG DOCTORS IN LOVE   20th Century-Fox, 1982
THE GOODBYE PEOPLE   Embassy, 1984
SCANDAL SHEET (TF)   Fair Dinkum Productions, 1985
THE CLAN OF THE CAVE BEAR   Warner Bros., 1986
THE BEST OF TIMES   Universal, 1986
CHATTAHOOCHEE   Hemdale, 1990
CADILLAC MAN   Orion, 1990
KINDERGARTEN COP   Universal, 1990
BOB ROBERTS   Paramount/Miramax Films, 1992
PASSED AWAY   Buena Vista, 1992
JUNIOR   Universal, 1994

STEVE REED
JFK   Warner Bros., 1991

ROGER REES
STAR 80   The Ladd Company/Warner Bros., 1983
MOUNTAINS OF THE MOON   TriStar, 1990
IF LOOKS COULD KILL   Warner Bros., 1991
STOP! OR MY MOM WILL SHOOT   Universal, 1992
ROBIN HOOD: MEN IN TIGHTS   20th Century Fox, 1993

DELLA REESE
b. July 6, 1931 - Detroit, Michigan
Agent: William Morris Agency - Beverly Hills, 310/274-7451

NIGHTMARE IN BADHAM COUNTY (TF)   ABC Circle Films, 1976
ROOTS: THE NEXT GENERATION (MS)
   Wolper Productions, 1979
HARLEM NIGHTS   Paramount, 1989

CHRISTOPHER REEVE
b. September 25, 1952 - New York, New York
Agent: William Morris Agency - Beverly Hills, 310/274-7451

GRAY LADY DOWN   Universal, 1978
SUPERMAN   Warner Bros., 1978
SOMEWHERE IN TIME   Universal, 1980
SUPERMAN II   Warner Bros., 1981, U.S.-British
DEATHTRAP   Warner Bros., 1982
MONSIGNOR   20th Century-Fox, 1982
SUPERMAN III   Warner Bros., 1983, U.S.-British
THE BOSTONIANS   Almi Pictures, 1984
THE AVIATOR   MGM/UA, 1985
ANNA KARENINA (TF)   Rastar Productions/Colgems
   Productions, 1985
SUPERMAN IV: THE QUEST FOR PEACE   Warner Bros., 1987
STREET SMART   Cannon, 1987
SWITCHING CHANNELS   Columbia, 1988
THE GREAT ESCAPE II: THE UNTOLD STORY (TF)   Michael Jaffe
   Films/Spectacor Films, 1988
THE ROSE AND THE JACKAL (CTF)   Steve White Productions/
   PWD Productions, 1990
NOISES OFF   Buena Vista, 1992
MORNING GLORY   Academy Entertainment, 1993
THE REMAINS OF THE DAY   Columbia, 1993, British
THE RHINEHART THEORY   Rysher Entertainment, 1994
SPEECHLESS   MGM/UA, 1994
VILLAGE OF THE DAMNED   Universal, 1995

DIANNE REEVES
GUILTY BY SUSPICION   Warner Bros., 1991

KEANU REEVES
b. September 2, 1964 - Beirut, Lebanon
Agent: CAA - Beverly Hills, 310/288-4545

UNDER THE INFLUENCE (TF)   CBS Entertainment, 1986
FLYING   Golden Harvest, 1986, Canadian
YOUNGBLOOD   MGM/UA, 1986
RIVER'S EDGE   Hemdale, 1987
THE NIGHT BEFORE   Kings Road Productions, 1988
THE PRINCE OF PENNSYLVANIA   New Line Cinema, 1988
PERMANENT RECORD   Paramount, 1988
DANGEROUS LIAISONS   Warner Bros., 1988
PARENTHOOD   Universal, 1989
BILL & TED'S EXCELLENT ADVENTURE   Orion, 1989
TUNE IN TOMORROW   Cinecom, 1990
I LOVE YOU TO DEATH   TriStar, 1990
BILL & TED'S BOGUS JOURNEY   Orion, 1991
MY OWN PRIVATE IDAHO   Fine Line Features/New Line Cinema, 1991
POINT BREAK   20th Century Fox, 1991
BRAM STOKER'S DRACULA   *DRACULA*   Columbia, 1992
MUCH ADO ABOUT NOTHING   Samuel Goldwyn Company,
   1993, British-U.S.
FREAKED   20th Century Fox, 1993 (uncredited)
EVEN COWGIRLS GET THE BLUES   Fine Line Features/
   New Line Cinema, 1994
LITTLE BUDDHA   Miramax Films, 1994, British-French
SPEED   20th Century Fox, 1994
JOHNNY MNEMONIC   TriStar, 1994
A WALK IN THE CLOUDS   20th Century Fox, 1995

PERREY REEVES
CHILD'S PLAY 3   Universal, 1991

SCOTT REEVES
FRIDAY THE 13TH PART VIII - JASON TAKES MANHATTAN
   Paramount, 1989

JOE REGALBUTO
b. August 24 - New York, New York

THAT SECRET SUNDAY (TF)   CBS Entertainment, 1986

FIONA REID
SWITCHING CHANNELS   Columbia, 1988
A NEW LIFE   Paramount, 1988

KATE REID
b. November 4, 1930 - London, England

THIS PROPERTY IS CONDEMNED   Paramount, 1966
THE ANDROMEDA STRAIN   Universal, 1971
A DELICATE BALANCE   American Film Theatre, 1973
DEATH AMONG FRIENDS (TF)   Douglas S. Cramer Productions/
   Warner Bros. TV, 1975
EQUUS   United Artists, 1977, British
ATLANTIC CITY   Paramount, 1981
FIRE WITH FIRE   Paramount, 1986
SWEET HEARTS DANCE   TriStar, 1988
BYE BYE BLUES   Circle Releasing Corporation, 1990, Canadian
DECEIVED   Buena Vista, 1991

TIM REID
b. December 19, 1944 - Norfolk, Virginia

DEAD-BANG   Warner Bros., 1989
THE FOURTH WAR   Cannon, 1990
IT (TF)   Konigsberg-Sanitsky Productions/Green-Epstein
   Productions/Lorimar TV, 1990

CHARLES NELSON REILLY
b. January 13, 1931 - New York, New York

CANNONBALL RUN II   Warner Bros., 1984
ALL DOGS GO TO HEAVEN (AF)   MGM/UA, 1989 (voice)
ROCK-A-DOODLE (AF)   Samuel Goldwyn Company, 1992 (voice)

JOHN C. REILLY
CASUALTIES OF WAR   Columbia, 1989
DAYS OF THUNDER   Paramount, 1990
WHAT'S EATING GILBERT GRAPE   Paramount, 1993
THE RIVER WILD   Universal, 1994
DOLORES CLAIBORNE   Columbia, 1994

LUKE REILLY
BYE BYE BLUES   Circle Releasing Corporation, 1990, Canadian

LUCY REINA
ROMERO   Four Season Entertainment, 1989

CARL REINER
b. March 20, 1922 - Bronx, New York

HAPPY ANNIVERSARY   United Artists, 1959
THE GAZEBO   MGM, 1960
GIDGET GOES HAWAIIAN   Columbia, 1961
THE THRILL OF IT ALL   Universal, 1963
IT'S A MAD MAD MAD MAD WORLD   United Artists, 1963
THE ART OF LOVE   Universal, 1965
ALICE OF WONDERLAND IN PARIS   Childhood Productions,
   1966 (voice)
DON'T WORRY, WE'LL THINK OF A TITLE   United Artists, 1966
THE RUSSIANS ARE COMING, THE RUSSIANS ARE COMING
   United Artists, 1966
A GUIDE FOR THE MARRIED MAN   20th Century-Fox, 1967
GENERATION   Avco Embassy, 1969
THE COMIC   Columbia, 1969 (also directed)
OH, GOD!   Warner Bros., 1977 (also directed)
THE END   United Artists, 1978
DEAD MEN DON'T WEAR PLAID   Universal, 1982
SUMMER SCHOOL   Paramount, 1987 (also directed)
BULLETS OVER BROADWAY   Miramax Films, 1994

ROB REINER
b. March 6, 1945 - Beverly Hills, California
Agent: CAA - Beverly Hills, 310/288-4545

THIS IS SPINAL TAP   Embassy, 1984 (also directed)
THROW MOMMA FROM THE TRAIN   Orion, 1987
POSTCARDS FROM THE EDGE   Columbia, 1990
SLEEPLESS IN SEATTLE   TriStar, 1993
BULLETS OVER BROADWAY   Miramax Films, 1994
LIFESAVERS   TriStar, 1994

TRACY REINER
BIG   20th Century Fox, 1988
FRANKIE & JOHNNY   Paramount, 1991
A LEAGUE OF THEIR OWN   Columbia, 1992

JUDGE REINHOLD
b. May 21, 1956 - Wilmington, Delaware
Agent: ICM - Beverly Hills, 310/550-4000

STRIPES   Columbia, 1981
FAST TIMES AT RIDGEMONT HIGH   Universal, 1982
PANDEMONIUM   MGM/UA, 1982
THE LORDS OF DISCIPLINE   Paramount, 1983
BEVERLY HILLS COP   Paramount, 1984
ROADHOUSE 66   Atlantic Releasing Corporation, 1984
GREMLINS   Warner Bros., 1984
RUTHLESS PEOPLE   Buena Vista, 1986
BEVERLY HILLS COP II   Paramount, 1987
PROMISED A MIRACLE (TF)   Dick Clark Productions/Republic
   Pictures/Roni Weisberg Productions, 1988
VICE VERSA   Columbia, 1988
ROSALIE GOES SHOPPING   Four Seasons Entertainment,
   1989, West German-U.S.
ENID IS SLEEPING   Vestron, 1990
DADDY'S DYIN'...WHO'S GOT THE WILL?   MGM/UA, 1990
ZANDALEE   Electric Pictures/ITC Entertainment Group, 1991
BANK ROBBER   I.R.S. Releasing, 1993
BEVERLY HILLS COP III   Paramount, 1994
THE SANTA CLAUSE   Buena Vista, 1994

ANN REINKING
b. November 10, 1950 - Seattle, Washington

MOVIE MOVIE   Warner Bros., 1978
ALL THAT JAZZ   20th Century-Fox, 1979
ANNIE   Columbia, 1982
MICKI & MAUDE   Columbia, 1984

PAUL REISER
Agent: UTA - Beverly Hills, 310/273-6700

DINER   MGM/United Artists, 1982
BEVERLY HILLS COP   Paramount, 1984
ALIENS   20th Century Fox, 1986
BEVERLY HILLS COP II   Paramount, 1987
CROSS MY HEART   Universal, 1987
CRAZY PEOPLE   Paramount, 1990
THE MARRYING MAN   Buena Vista, 1991
MR. WRITE   Shapiro-Glickenhaus Entertainment, 1994
BYE BYE LOVE   20th Century Fox, 1995

JAMES REMAR
THE COTTON CLUB   Orion, 1984
BAND OF THE HAND   TriStar, 1986
THE CLAN OF THE CAVE BEAR   Warner Bros., 1986
RENT-A-COP   Kings Road Productions, 1988
THE DREAM TEAM   Universal, 1989
DRUGSTORE COWBOY   Avenue Pictures, 1989
TALES FROM THE DARKSIDE: THE MOVIE   Paramount, 1990
WHITE FANG   Buena Vista, 1991
WEDLOCK (CTF)   HBO Pictures/Spectacor Films, 1991
BLINK   New Line Cinema, 1994
RENAISSANCE MAN   Buena Vista, 1994
MIRACLE ON 34TH STREET   20th Century Fox, 1994
BOYS ON THE SIDE   Warner Bros., 1995
WILD BILL   MGM/UA, 1995

BERT REMSEN
FUZZ   United Artists, 1972
CALIFORNIA SPLIT   Columbia, 1974
NASHVILLE   Paramount, 1975
THE STING II   Universal, 1983
WHO IS JULIA? (TF)   CBS Entertainment, 1986
MISS FIRECRACKER   Corsair Pictures, 1989
DICK TRACY   Buena Vista, 1990
ONLY THE LONELY   20th Century Fox, 1991
JACK THE BEAR   20th Century Fox, 1992

BRAD RENFRO
THE CLIENT   Warner Bros., 1994
THE CURE   Universal, 1995

DEBORAH RENNARD
LIONHEART   Universal, 1991

JEREMY RENNER
NATIONAL LAMPOON'S SENIOR TRIP   New Line Cinema, 1995

JEAN RENO
THE BIG BLUE   Columbia, 1988
THE PROFESSIONAL   Columbia, 1994
PARIS MATCH   20th Century Fox, 1995

KELLY RENO
THE BLACK STALLION   United Artists, 1979
THE BLACK STALLION RETURNS   MGM/UA, 1983
BRADY'S ESCAPE   THE LONG RUN   Satori, 1984, U.S.-Hungarian

SOPHIE RENOIR
BOYFRIENDS AND GIRLFRIENDS   1988, French
L'AMI DE MON AMIE   FRIEND OF A FRIEND/Orion Classics, 1988

MAGGIE RENZI
MATEWAN   Cinecom, 1987
EIGHT MEN OUT   Orion, 1988

FRANK RENZULLI
WILD HEARTS CAN'T BE BROKEN   Buena Vista, 1991

DEE DEE RESCHER
SKIN DEEP   20th Century Fox, 1989

MARY LOU RETTON
b. January 24, 1968

SCROOGED   Paramount, 1988
NAKED GUN 33 1/3: THE FINAL INSULT   Paramount, 1994

FAENZA REUBEN
RAPA NUI   Warner Bros., 1994

GLORIA REUBEN
TIMECOP   Universal, 1994

PAUL REUBENS
(Pee-Wee Herman)
b. August 27, 1952 - Peekskill, New York

CHEECH & CHONG'S NICE DREAMS   Columbia, 1981
PANDEMONIUM   MGM/UA, 1982
FLIGHT OF THE NAVIGATOR   Buena Vista,
    1986 (voice; uncredited)
PEE-WEE'S BIG ADVENTURE   Warner Bros., 1986
BACK TO THE BEACH   Paramount, 1987
BIG TOP PEE-WEE   Paramount, 1988
BATMAN RETURNS   Warner Bros., 1992
BUFFY THE VAMPIRE SLAYER   20th Century Fox, 1992
TIM BURTON'S THE NIGHTMARE BEFORE CHRISTMAS
    Buena Vista, 1993 (voice)

REYNALDO REY
COBB   Warner Bros., 1994

ERNIE REYES, JR.
SURF NINJAS   New Line Cinema, 1993

BURT REYNOLDS
b. February 11, 1936 - Waycross, Georgia
Agent: William Morris Agency - Beverly Hills, 310/274-7451

ANGEL BABY   Allied Artists, 1961
ARMORED COMMAND   Allied Artists, 1961
OPERATION C.I.A.   Allied Artists, 1965
NAVAJO JOE   United Artists, 1966, Italian-Spanish
FADE-IN   Paramount, 1968
SAM WHISKEY   United Artists, 1969
100 RIFLES   20th Century-Fox, 1969
SHARK! *MANEATER*   Heritage, 1969, U.S.-Mexican
IMPASSE   United Artists, 1969
SKULLDUGGERY   Universal, 1970
FUZZ   United Artists, 1972
DELIVERANCE   Warner Bros., 1972
EVERYTHING YOU ALWAYS WANTED TO KNOW ABOUT SEX*
    (*BUT WERE AFRAID TO ASK)   United Artists, 1972
SHAMUS   Columbia, 1973
THE MAN WHO LOVED CAT DANCING   MGM, 1973
WHITE LIGHTNING   United Artists, 1973
THE LONGEST YARD   Paramount, 1974
W.W. AND THE DIXIE DANCEKINGS   20th Century-Fox, 1975
AT LONG LAST LOVE   20th Century-Fox, 1975
LUCKY LADY   20th Century-Fox, 1975
HUSTLE   Paramount, 1975
SILENT MOVIE   20th Century-Fox, 1976 (uncredited)
GATOR   United Artists, 1976 (also directed)
NICKELODEON   Columbia, 1976
SMOKEY AND THE BANDIT   Universal, 1977
SEMI-TOUGH   United Artists, 1977
THE END   United Artists, 1978 (also directed)
HOOPER   Warner Bros., 1978
STARTING OVER   Paramount, 1979
SMOKEY AND THE BANDIT II   Universal, 1980

ROUGH CUT   Paramount, 1980
THE CANNONBALL RUN   20th Century-Fox, 1981
SHARKY'S MACHINE   Orion/Warner Bros., 1981 (also directed)
PATERNITY   Paramount, 1981
THE BEST LITTLE WHOREHOUSE IN TEXAS   Universal, 1982
BEST FRIENDS   Warner Bros., 1982
THE MAN WHO LOVED WOMEN   Columbia, 1983
STROKER ACE   Universal, 1983
SMOKEY AND THE BANDIT 3   Universal, 1983
CANNONBALL RUN II   Warner Bros., 1984
CITY HEAT   Warner Bros., 1984
STICK   Universal, 1985 (also directed)
HEAT   New Century/Vista, 1987
MALONE   Orion, 1987
RENT-A-COP   Kings Road Productions, 1988
SWITCHING CHANNELS   Columbia, 1988
PHYSICAL EVIDENCE   Columbia, 1989
BREAKING IN   Samuel Goldwyn Company, 1989
ALL DOGS GO TO HEAVEN (AF)   MGM/UA, 1989 (voice)
MODERN LOVE   Triumph Releasing Corporation, 1990
THE PLAYER   Fine Line Features/New Line Cinema, 1992
COP AND A HALF   Universal, 1993
THE MADDENING   Trimark Pictures, 1995

DEBBIE REYNOLDS
(Mary Frances Reynolds)
b. April 1, 1932 - El Paso, Texas

JUNE BRIDE   Warner Bros., 1948
THE DAUGHTER OF ROSIE O'GRADY   Warner Bros., 1950
THREE LITTLE WORDS   MGM, 1950
TWO WEEKS WITH LOVE   MGM, 1950
MR. IMPERIUM   MGM, 1951
SINGIN' IN THE RAIN   MGM, 1952
SKIRTS AHOY!   MGM, 1952
I LOVE MELVIN   MGM, 1953
THE AFFAIRS OF DOBIE GILLIS   MGM, 1953
GIVE A GIRL A BREAK   MGM, 1953
SUSAN SLEPT HERE   RKO Radio, 1954
ATHENA   MGM, 1954
HIT THE DECK   MGM, 1955
THE TENDER TRAP   MGM, 1955
THE CATERED AFFAIR   MGM, 1956
MEET ME IN LAS VEGAS   MGM, 1956
BUNDLE OF JOY   RKO Radio, 1956
TAMMY AND THE BACHELOR   Universal, 1957
THIS HAPPY FEELING   Universal, 1958
THE MATING GAME   MGM, 1959
SAY ONE FOR ME   20th Century-Fox, 1959
IT STARTED WITH A KISS   MGM, 1959
THE GAZEBO   MGM, 1959
THE RAT RACE   Paramount, 1960
PEPE   Columbia, 1960
THE PLEASURE OF HIS COMPANY   Paramount, 1961
THE SECOND TIME AROUND   20th Century-Fox, 1961
HOW THE WEST WAS WON   MGM/Cinerama, 1962
MY SIX LOVES   Paramount, 1963
MARY, MARY   Warner Bros., 1963
THE UNSINKABLE MOLLY BROWN ★   MGM, 1964
GOODBYE, CHARLIE   20th Century-Fox, 1964
THE SINGING NUN   MGM, 1966
DIVORCE AMERICAN STYLE   Columbia, 1967
HOW SWEET IT IS!   Buena Vista, 1968
WHAT'S THE MATTER WITH HELEN?   United Artists, 1971
CHARLOTTE'S WEB (AF)   Paramount, 1973 (voice)
THAT'S ENTERTAINMENT! (FD)   MGM/United Artists, 1974
SADIE AND SON (TF)   Norton Wright Productions/Kenny Rogers
    Organization/ITC Productions, 1987
PERRY MASON: THE CASE OF THE MUSICAL MURDER (TF)
    The Fred Silverman Company/Dean Hargrove Productions/
    Viacom, 1989
HEAVEN AND EARTH   Warner Bros., 1993
THAT'S ENTERTAINMENT! III (FD)   MGM/UA, 1994

PATRICK REYNOLDS
ELIMINATORS   Empire Pictures, 1986

VING RHAMES
Agent: William Morris Agency - Beverly Hills, 310/274-7451

PATTY HEARST   Atlantic Releasing Corporation, 1988
THE LONG WALK HOME   Miramax Films, 1990
FLIGHT OF THE INTRUDER   Paramount, 1991
DAVE   Warner Bros., 1993
THE SAINT OF FORT WASHINGTON   Warner Bros., 1993
PULP FICTION   Miramax Films, 1994

PHILLIP RHEE
BEST OF THE BEST   Taurus Entertainment/SVS Films, 1989

SIMON RHEE
BEST OF THE BEST   Taurus Entertainment, 1989

MICHAEL RHOADE
EDDIE AND THE CRUISERS: EDDIE LIVES   Scotti Bros., 1989

CYNTHIA RHODES
STAYING ALIVE   Paramount, 1983
RUNAWAY   TriStar, 1984
DIRTY DANCING   Vestron, 1987

HARI RHODES
SHARKY'S MACHINE   Orion/Warner Bros., 1981

PAUL RHYS
VINCENT & THEO   Hemdale, 1990, British-French
CHAPLIN   TriStar, 1992, U.S.-British

JOHN RHYS-DAVIES
SHOGUN (MS)   Paramount TV/NBC Entertainment,
   1980, U.S.-Japanese
SPHINX   Orion/Warner Bros., 1981
RAIDERS OF THE LOST ARK   Paramount, 1981
VICTOR/VICTORIA   MGM/United Artists, 1982
IVANHOE (TF)   1982
FIREWALKER   Cannon, 1986
THE LIVING DAYLIGHTS   MGM/UA, 1987, Brtish
PREDATOR   20th Century Fox, 1987
THE LITTLE MATCH GIRL (TF)   NBC Productions, 1987
WAXWORK   Vestron, 1988
INDIANA JONES AND THE LAST CRUSADE   Paramount, 1989
CATS DON'T DANCE (AF)   Turner Pictures, 1996 (voice)

CHRISTINA RICCI
b. February 12, 1980 - Santa Monica, California
Agent: ICM - Beverly Hills, 310/550-4000

MERMAIDS   Orion, 1990
THE HARD WAY   Universal, 1991
THE ADDAMS FAMILY   Paramount, 1991
THE CEMETERY CLUB   Buena Vista, 1993
ADDAMS FAMILY VALUES   Paramount, 1993
CASPER   Universal, 1995
GASLIGHT ADDITION   New Line Cinema, 1995
GOLD DIGGERS   Universal, 1995

MANDY RICE-DAVIES
ABSOLUTE BEGINNERS   Orion, 1986, British

ALAN RICH
GUILTY BY SUSPICION   Warner Bros., 1991

CHRISTOPHER RICH
FLIGHT OF THE INTRUDER   Paramount, 1991

EMILY RICHARD
EMPIRE OF THE SUN   Warner Bros., 1987

LITTLE RICHARD
(See LITTLE Richard)

PIERRE RICHARD
LES FUGITIFS   Gaumont, 1986, French

ARIANA RICHARDS
PRANCER   Orion, 1989
JURASSIC PARK   Universal, 1993

BEAH RICHARDS
THE MIRACLE WORKER   United Artists, 1962
GONE ARE THE DAYS! *PURLIE VICTORIOUS*   Trans-Lux, 1963
IN THE HEAT OF THE NIGHT   United Artists, 1967
GUESS WHO'S COMING TO DINNER ✪   Columbia, 1967
HURRY SUNDOWN   Paramount, 1967
THE GREAT WHITE HOPE   20th Century-Fox, 1970
MAHOGANY   Paramount, 1975
DRUGSTORE COWBOY   Avenue Pictures, 1989
HOMER & EDDIE   Skouras Pictures, 1990

EVAN RICHARDS
DOWN AND OUT IN BEVERLY HILLS   Buena Vista, 1986

MICHAEL RICHARDS
Agent: APA - Los Angeles, 310/273-0744

YOUNG DOCTORS IN LOVE   20th Century-Fox, 1982
UHF   Orion, 1989
AIRHEADS   20th Century Fox, 1994
UNSTRUNG HEROES   Buena Vista, 1995

LEE RICHARDSON
PRIZZI'S HONOR   20th Century-Fox, 1985
TRUE BELIEVERS   Orion, 1987
THE FLY II   20th Century Fox, 1989

IAN RICHARDSON
BURNING SECRET   Vestron, 1988, U.S.-British-West German
THE PLOT TO KILL HITLER (TF)   Wolper Productions/Bernard
   Sofronski Productions/Warner Bros. TV, 1990
ROSENCRANTZ & GUILDENSTERN ARE DEAD   Cinecom, 1991
M. BUTTERFLY   Warner Bros., 1993

JOELY RICHARDSON
KING RALPH   Universal, 1991
SHINING THROUGH   20th Century Fox, 1992
I'LL DO ANYTHING   Columbia, 1994
LOCH NESS   Gramercy Pictures, 1995

JULIET RICHARDSON
TRULY, MADLY, DEEPLY *CELLO*   Samuel Goldwyn Company,
   1991, British

LaTANYA RICHARDSON
LOSING ISAIAH   Paramount, 1995

LEE RICHARDSON
A STRANGER AMOUNG US   Buena Vista, 1992

MIRANDA RICHARDSON
Agent: Susan Smith & Associates - Beverly Hills, 213/852-4777

DANCE WITH A STRANGER   Samuel Goldwyn Company,
   1985, British
THE INNOCENT   TVS, Ltd./Tempest Films, 1985, British
UNDERWORLD   Empire Pictures, 1985, British
AFTER PILKINGTON (TF)   BBC, 1987, British
EMPIRE OF THE SUN   Warner Bros., 1987
ENCHANTED APRIL   Miramax Films, 1991, British
THE CRYING GAME   Miramax Films, 1992, Irish-British
DAMAGE ✪   New Line Cinema, 1992, French-British
INTERVIEW WITH THE VAMPIRE   Warner Bros., 1994

NATASHA RICHARDSON

Agent: ICM - Beverly Hills, 310/550-4000

GOTHIC   Vestron, 1986, British
PATTY HEARST   Atlantic Releasing Corporation, 1988
FAT MAN AND LITTLE BOY   Paramount, 1989
THE HANDMAID'S TALE   Cinecom, 1990
THE COMFORT OF STRANGERS   Skouras Pictures, 1990, British
THE FAVOR, THE WATCH, AND THE VERY BIG FISH
   Trimark Pictures, 1991, French-British
WIDOWS' PEAK   Fine Line Features/New Line Cinema, 1994
NELL   20th Century Fox, 1994

PATRICIA RICHARDSON

C.H.U.D.   New World, 1984
IN COUNTRY   Warner Bros., 1989

SALLI RICHARDSON

SIOUX CITY   I.R.S. Releasing, 1994
A LOW DOWN DIRTY SHAME   Buena Vista, 1994

SY RICHARDSON

KINJITE (FORBIDDEN SUBJECTS)   Cannon, 1989

WILLIAM RICHERT

THE CLIENT   Warner Bros., 1994

CARYN RICHMAN

A VERY BRADY CHRISTMAS (TF)   Sherwood Schwartz Produc-
   tions/Paramount TV, 1988

PETER MARK RICHMAN

FRIENDLY PERSUASION   Allied Artists, 1956
THE STRANGE ONE   END AS A MAN   Columbia, 1957
THE BLACK ORCHID   Paramount, 1959
GIRLS ON THE LOOSE   Universal, 1959
DARK INTRUDER   Universal, 1965
AGENT FOR H.A.R.M.   Universal, 1966
FOR SINGLES ONLY   Columbia, 1968
FRIDAY THE 13TH PART VIII - JASON TAKES MANHATTAN
   Paramount, 1989
THE NAKED GUN 2 1/2: THE SMELL OF FEAR   Paramount, 1991

DEBORAH RICHTER

SQUARE DANCE   Island Pictures, 1987
CYBORG   Cannon, 1989

JASON JAMES RICHTER

Agent: UTA - Beverly Hills, 310/273-6700

FREE WILLY   Warner Bros., 1993
COPS & ROBBERSONS   TriStar, 1994
THE NEVERENDING STORY III   1994, German-British
WILLY II: THE ADVENTURE HOME   Warner Bros., 1995

PATRICK RICHWOOD

PRETTY WOMAN   Buena Vista, 1990

DON RICKLES

b. May 8, 1926 - New York, New York

INNOCENT BLOOD   Warner Bros., 1992
CASINO   Universal, 1995

ALAN RICKMAN

Agent: UTA - Beverly Hills, 310/273-6700

DIE HARD   20th Century Fox, 1988
THE JANUARY MAN   MGM/UA, 1989
QUIGLEY DOWN UNDER   MGM/UA, 1990
CLOSET LAND   Universal, 1991
TRULY, MADLY, DEEPLY   CELLO   Samuel Goldwyn Company,
   1991, British
ROBIN HOOD: PRINCE OF THIEVES   Warner Bros., 1991
BOB ROBERTS   Paramount/Miramax Films, 1992

PETER RIEGERT

b. April 11, 1947 - New York, New York
Agent: UTA - Beverly Hills, 310/273-6700

NATIONAL LAMPOON'S ANIMAL HOUSE   Universal, 1978
LOCAL HERO   Warner Bros., 1983, British-Scottish
ELLIS ISLAND (MS)   Pantheon Pictures/Telepictures Productions,
   1984, U.S.-British
CROSSING DELANCEY   Warner Bros., 1988
A SHOCK TO THE SYSTEM   Corsair Pictures, 1990
THE OBJECT OF BEAUTY   Avenue Pictures, 1991
OSCAR   Buena Vista, 1991
PASSED AWAY   Buena Vista, 1992
GYPSY (TF)   RHI Entertainment, 1993
COLDBLOODED   MPCA, 1995
INFINITY   1995

RICHARD RIEHLE

PRELUDE TO A KISS   20th Century Fox, 1992
A DANGEROUS WOMAN   Gramercy Pictures, 1993

DIANA RIGG

b. July 20, 1938 - Doncaster, England

A MIDSUMMER NIGHT'S DREAM   Eagle, 1968, British
THE ASSASSINATION BUREAU   Paramount, 1968, British
ON HER MAJESTY'S SECRET SERVICE   United Artists,
   1969, British
JULIUS CAESAR   American International, 1970, British
THE HOSPITAL   United Artists, 1971
THEATRE OF BLOOD   United Artists, 1973, British
IN THIS HOUSE OF BREDE (TF)   Tomorrow Entertaiment, 1975
A LITTLE NIGHT MUSIC   New World, 1977, Austrian-U.S.
THE GREAT MUPPET CAPER   Universal/AFD, 1981, British
EVIL UNDER THE SUN   Universal/AFD, 1982, British
WITNESS FOR THE PROSECUTION (TF)   Norman Rosemont
   Productions/United Artists, 1982, U.S.-British
A GOOD MAN IN AFRICA   Gramercy Pictures, 1994

ROBIN RIKER

ALLIGATOR   Group 1, 1980

GARY RILEY

SUMMER SCHOOL   Paramount, 1987

LARRY RILEY

BADGE OF THE ASSASSIN (TF)   Blatt-Singer Productions/
   Columbia TV, 1985

MICHAEL RILEY

...AND GOD SPOKE   Live Entertainment, 1994

SHANE RIMMER

S*P*Y*S   20th Century-Fox, 1974, British-U.S.
THE PEOPLE THAT TIME FORGOT   American International,
   1977, British
SILVER BEARS   Columbia, 1978
ARABIAN ADVENTURE   AFD, 1979, British
HANOVER STREET   Columbia, 1979
CRUSOE   Island Pictures, 1988, U.S.-British
YEAR OF THE COMET   Columbia, 1992

MOLLY RINGWALD

b. February 17, 1968 - Rosewood, California
Agent: William Morris Agency - Beverly Hills, 310/274-7451

SIXTEEN CANDLES   Universal, 1984
THE BREAKFAST CLUB   Universal, 1985
PRETTY IN PINK   Paramount, 1986
KING LEAR   Cannon, 1987, U.S-Swiss
THE PICK-UP ARTIST   20th Century Fox, 1987
FOR KEEPS   TriStar, 1988
FRESH HORSES   WEG, 1988
STRIKE IT RICH   Millimeter Films, 1990
BETSY'S WEDDING   Buena Vista, 1990
STEPHEN KING'S THE STAND   THE STAND (MS)   ABC, 1994
MALICIOUS   Republic Pictures, 1995

GUILLERMO RIOS
OLD GRINGO Columbia, 1989

GENEVIEVE RIOUX
THE DECLINE OF THE AMERICAN EMPIRE Cineplex Odeon,
1986, Canadian

CARLOS RIQUELME
THE MILAGRO BEANFIELD WAR Universal, 1988

CHRIS RITCHIE
THE ADVENTURES OF MARK TWAIN (AF) Atlantic Releasing
Corporation, 1985 (voice)

JOHN RITTER
b. September 17, 1948 - Burbank, California

THE BAREFOOT EXECUTIVE Buena Vista, 1971
THE OTHER 20th Century-Fox, 1972
THE NIGHT THAT PANICKED AMERICA (TF) Paramount TV, 1975
NICKELODEON Columbia, 1976
AMERICATHON United Artists, 1979
HERO AT LARGE MGM/United Artists, 1980
WHOLLY MOSES Columbia, 1980
THEY ALL LAUGHED United Artists Classics, 1981
LETTING GO (TF) Adam Productions/ITC Productions, 1985
A SMOKY MOUNTAIN CHRISTMAS (TF)
Sandollar Productions, 1986
REAL MEN MGM/UA, 1987
TRICKS OF THE TRADE (TF) Leonard Hill Films, 1988
SKIN DEEP 20th Century Fox, 1989
MY BROTHER'S WIFE (TF) Robert Greenwald Productions/Adam
Productions, 1989
PROBLEM CHILD Universal, 1990
IT (TF) Konigsberg-Sanitsky Productions/Green-Epstein
Productions/Lorimar TV, 1990
PROBLEM CHILD 2 Universal, 1991
NOISES OFF Buena Vista, 1992
THE ONLY WAY OUT (TF) 1993
NORTH Columbia, 1994

MELISSA RIVERS
TEARS AND LAUGHTER: THE JOAN AND MELISSA
RIVERS STORY (TF) NBC, 1994

JOAN RIVERS
b. June 8, 1933 - New York, New York
Agent: William Morris Agency - Beverly Hills, 310/274-7451

THE SWIMMER Columbia, 1968
RABBIT TEST Avco Embassy, 1978 (also directed)
SPACEBALLS MGM/UA, 1987 (voice)
TEARS AND LAUGHTER: THE JOAN AND MELISSA
RIVERS STORY (TF) NBC, 1994

JASON ROBARDS
(Jason Robards, Jr.)
b. July 22, 1922 - Chicago, Illinois

THE JOURNEY MGM, 1959
BY LOVE POSSESSED United Artists, 1961
TENDER IS THE NIGHT 20th Century-Fox, 1962
LONG DAY'S JOURNEY INTO NIGHT Embassy, 1962
ACT ONE Warner Bros., 1963
A THOUSAND CLOWNS United Artists, 1965
A BIG HAND FOR THE LITTLE LADY Warner Bros., 1966
ANY WEDNESDAY Warner Bros., 1966
DIVORCE AMERICAN STYLE Columbia, 1967
HOUR OF THE GUN United Artists, 1967
THE ST. VALENTINE'S DAY MASSACRE 20th Century-Fox, 1967
THE NIGHT THEY RAIDED MINSKY'S United Artists, 1968
ISADORA *THE LOVES OF ISADORA* Universal, 1969, British
ONCE UPON A TIME IN THE WEST Paramount, 1969, Italian-U.S.
JULIUS CAESAR American International, 1970, British
THE BALLAD OF CABLE HOGUE Warner Bros., 1970
TORA! TORA! TORA! 20th Century-Fox, 1970, U.S.-Japanese

FOOLS Cinerama Releasing Corporation, 1970
JOHNNY GOT HIS GUN Cinemation, 1971
MURDERS IN THE RUE MORGUE American International, 1971, British
THE WAR BETWEEN MEN AND WOMEN National General, 1972
DEATH OF A STRANGER Delta Commerz, 1972, West German-Israeli
PAT GARRETT AND BILLY THE KID MGM, 1973
MR. SYCAMORE Film Ventures International, 1975
A BOY AND HIS DOG Pacific Film Enterprises, 1975
ALL THE PRESIDENT'S MEN ΦΦ Warner Bros., 1976
WASHINGTON: BEHIND CLOSED DOORS (MS) Paramount TV, 1977
JULIA ΦΦ 20th Century-Fox, 1977
COMES A HORSEMAN United Artists, 1978
HURRICANE Paramount, 1979
RAISE THE TITANIC AFD, 1980, British-U.S.
MELVIN AND HOWARD Φ Universal, 1980
CABOBLANCO Avco Embassy, 1981
THE LEGEND OF THE LONE RANGER Universal/AFD, 1981
MAX DUGAN RETURNS 20th Century-Fox, 1983
THE DAY AFTER (TF) ABC Circle Films, 1983
SOMETHING WICKED THIS WAY COMES Buena Vista, 1983
SAKHAROV (CTF) HBO Premiere Films/Titus Productions,
1984, U.S.-British
THE ATLANTA CHILD MURDERS (MS) Mann-Rafshoon
Productions/Finnegan Associates, 1985
JOHNNY BULL (TF) Titus Productions/Eugene O'Neill Memorial
Theatre Center, 1986
THE LAST FRONTIER (MS) McElroy & McElroy Productions,
1986, Australian
SQUARE DANCE Island Pictures, 1987
NORMAN ROCKWELL'S 'BREAKING HOME TIES'
BREAKING HOME TIES (TF) ABC, 1987
THE GOOD MOTHER Buena Vista, 1988
DREAM A LITTLE DREAM Vestron, 1989
PARENTHOOD Universal, 1989
QUICK CHANGE Warner Bros., 1990
THE PERFECT TRIBUTE (CTF) Dorothea Petrie Productions/
Proctor & Gamble Productions/World International Network, 1991
CHERNOBYL: THE FINAL WARNING (CTF) 1991
PURE LUCK Universal, 1991
BLACK RAINBOW Miramax Films, 1991, British
STORYVILLE 20th Century Fox, 1992
THE ADVENTURES OF HUCK FINN Buena Vista, 1993
PHILADELPHIA TriStar, 1993
THE PAPER Universal, 1994
LITTLE BIG LEAGUE Columbia, 1994

JASON ROBARDS, JR.
THE TRIAL Angelika Films, 1993

SAM ROBARDS
JACOBO TIMERMAN: PRISONER WITHOUT A NAME, CELL
WITHOUT A NUMBER (TF) Chrysalis-Yellin Productions, 1983
FANDANGO Warner Bros., 1985
CASUALTIES OF WAR Columbia, 1989
MRS. PARKER AND THE VICIOUS CIRCLE Fine Line Features/
New Line Cinema, 1994
PRET-A-PORTER Miramax Films, 1994

DAVID ROBB
THE DECEIVERS Cinecom, 1988

CAROL ROBBINS
'NIGHT, MOTHER Universal, 1986

MICHAEL ROBBINS
DIAMOND'S EDGE Kings Road Entertainment, 1990

TIM ROBBINS
b. October 16, 1958 - West Covina, California
Agent: ICM - Beverly Hills, 310/550-4000

THE SURE THING Embassy, 1985
HOWARD THE DUCK Universal, 1986
TOP GUN Paramount, 1986
FIVE CORNERS Cineplex Odeon, 1988
BULL DURHAM Orion, 1988
TAPEHEADS Avenue Pictures, 1988

MISS FIRECRACKER   Corsair Pictures, 1989
ERIK THE VIKING   Orion, 1989, British
CADILLAC MAN   Orion, 1990
JACOB'S LADDER   TriStar, 1990
THE PLAYER   Fine Line Features/New Line Cinema, 1992
BOB ROBERTS   Paramount/Miramax Films, 1992 (also directed)
SHORT CUTS   Fine Line Features/New Line Cinema, 1993
THE HUDSUCKER PROXY   Warner Bros., 1994
THE SHAWSHANK REDEMPTION   Columbia, 1994
I.Q.   Paramount, 1994
PRET-A-PORTER   Miramax Films, 1994

TOM ROBBINS
MADE IN HEAVEN   Lorimar, 1987

DORIS ROBERTS
b. November 4, 1929 - St. Louis, Missouri

REMINGTON STEELE: THE STEELE THAT WOULDN'T DIE (TF)
   MTM Productions, 1987
IF IT'S TUESDAY, IT STILL MUST BE BELGIUM (TF)
   Eisenstock & Mintz Productions, 1987
NATIONAL LAMPOON'S CHRISTMAS VACATION
   Warner Bros., 1989

DOUGLAS ROBERTS
FLIGHT OF THE INTRUDER   Paramount, 1991

ERIC ROBERTS
b. April 18, 1956 - Biloxi, Mississippi
Agent: UTA - Beverly Hills, 310/273-6700

KING OF THE GYPSIES   Paramount, 1978
RAGGEDY MAN   Universal, 1981
STAR 80   The Ladd Company/Warner Bros., 1983
THE POPE OF GREENWICH VILLAGE   MGM/UA, 1984
THE COCA COLA KID   Cinecom/Film Gallery, 1985, Australian
RUNAWAY TRAIN ✪   Cannon, 1985
NOBODY'S FOOL   Island Pictures, 1986
SLOW BURN (CTF)   Joel Schumacher Productions/
   Universal Pay TV, 1986
BLOOD RED   Hemdale, 1988
RUDE AWAKENING   Orion, 1989
BEST OF THE BEST   Taurus Entertainment/SVS Films, 1989
THE AMBULANCE   Triumph Releasing Corporation, 1991
FINAL ANALYSIS   Warner Bros., 1992
BY THE SWORD   The Movie Group, 1992
VOYAGE (CTF)   Davis Entertainment/Quinta Communications/
   USA Network, 1993
LOVE, CHEAT AND STEAL (CTF)   Showtime, 1993
BABYFEVER   Rainbow Releasing, 1994
LOVE IS A GUN   Trimark Pictures, 1994
THE SPECIALIST   Warner Bros., 1994
HEAVEN'S PRISONERS   Savoy Pictures, 1994
NATURE OF THE BEAST   New Line Cinema, 1995
McNELLY'S RANGERS   Warner Bros., 1995

FRANCESCA ROBERTS
HEART OF DIXIE   Orion, 1989

JULIA ROBERTS
b. October 25, 1967 - Smyrna, Georgia
Agent: ICM - Beverly Hills, 310/550-4000

BAJA OKLAHOMA (CTF)   HBO Pictures/Rastar Productions, 1988
BLOOD RED   Hemdale, 1988
SATISFACTION   20th Century Fox, 1988
MYSTIC PIZZA   Samuel Goldwyn Company, 1988
STEEL MAGNOLIAS ✪   TriStar, 1989
PRETTY WOMAN ★   Buena Vista, 1990
FLATLINERS   Columbia, 1990
SLEEPING WITH THE ENEMY   20th Century Fox, 1991
DYING YOUNG   20th Century Fox, 1991
HOOK   TriStar, 1991
THE PLAYER   Fine Line Features/New Line Cinema, 1992
THE PELICAN BRIEF   Warner Bros., 1993
I LOVE TROUBLE   Buena Vista, 1994

PRET-A-PORTER   Miramax Films, 1994
MARY REILLY   TriStar, 1995
GRACE UNDER PRESSURE   Warner Bros., 1995
THE WOMEN   New Line Cinema, 1995

TANYA ROBERTS
ZUMA BEACH (TF)   Edgar J. Scherick Associates/
   Warner Bros. TV, 1978
THE BEASTMASTER   MGM/UA, 1982
SHEENA   Columbia, 1984
A VIEW TO A KILL   MGM/UA, 1985, British
PURGATORY   New Star Entertainment, 1989
DEMON HUNTERS   Golden Harvest, 1989

TONY ROBERTS
b. October 22, 1939 - New York, New York
Agent: APA - Los Angeles, 310/273-0744

THE BEACH GIRLS AND THE MONSTER   U.S. Films, 1965
$1,000,000 DUCK   Buena Vista, 1971
STAR SPANGLED GIRL   Paramount, 1971
PLAY IT AGAIN, SAM   Paramount, 1972
SERPICO   Paramount, 1973
THE TAKING OF PELHAM 1-2-3   United Artists, 1974
LE SAUVAGE   1975, French
ANNIE HALL   United Artists, 1977
JUST TELL ME WHAT YOU WANT   Columbia, 1980
STARDUST MEMORIES   United Artists, 1980
A MIDSUMMER NIGHT'S SEX COMEDY   Orion/Warner Bros., 1982
AMITYVILLE 3-D   Orion, 1983
KEY EXCHANGE   TLC Films/20th Century Fox, 1985
HANNAH AND HER SISTERS   Orion, 1986
RADIO DAYS   Orion, 1987
POPCORN   Studio Three, 1991
SWITCH   Warner Bros., 1991
OUR SONS (TF)   Robert Greenwald Productions, 1991

CLIFF ROBERTSON
(Clifford Parker Robertson III)
b. September 9, 1925 - La Jolla, California
Agent: ICM - Beverly Hills, 310/550-4000

PICNIC   Columbia, 1955
AUTUMN LEAVES   Columbia, 1956
THE GIRL MOST LIKELY   Universal, 1957
THE NAKED AND THE DEAD   Warner Bros., 1958
GIDGET   Columbia, 1959
BATTLE OF THE CORAL SEA   Columbia, 1959
AS THE SEA RAGES   Columbia, 1960
ALL IN A NIGHT'S WORK   Paramount, 1961
UNDERWORLD, U.S.A.   Columbia, 1961
THE BIG SHOW   20th Century-Fox, 1961, U.S.-West German
THE INTERNS   Columbia, 1962
MY SIX LOVES   Paramount, 1963
PT-109   Warner Bros., 1963
SUNDAY IN NEW YORK   MGM, 1963
THE BEST MAN   United Artists, 1964
633 SQUADRON   United Artists, 1964, British
LOVE HAS MANY FACES   Columbia, 1965
MASQUERADE   United Artists, 1965, British
UP FROM THE BEACH   20th Century-Fox, 1965
THE HONEY POT   United Artists, 1967, British-U.S.-Italian
THE DEVIL'S BRIGADE   United Artists, 1968
CHARLY ★★   Cinerama Releasing Corporation, 1968
TOO LATE THE HERO   Cinerama Releasing Corporation, 1970
J.W. COOP   Columbia, 1972 (also directed)
THE GREAT NORTHFIELD, MINNESOTA RAID   Universal, 1972
ACE ELI AND RODGER OF THE SKIES   20th Century-Fox, 1973
MAN ON A SWING   Paramount, 1974
MY FATHER'S HOUSE (TF)   ABC Films, Inc., 1975
OUT OF SEASON   Athenaeum, 1975, British
THREE DAYS OF THE CONDOR   Paramount, 1975
SHOOT   Avco Embassy, 1976, Canadian
MIDWAY   Universal, 1976
OBSESSION   Columbia, 1976
WASHINGTON: BEHIND CLOSED DOORS (MS)
   Paramount TV, 1977
FRATERNITY ROW   Paramount, 1977 (voice)

THE PILOT   Summit Features, 1979 (also directed)
STAR 80   The Ladd Company/Warner Bros., 1983
BRAINSTORM   MGM/UA, 1983
WILD HEARTS CAN'T BE BROKEN   Buena Vista, 1991
WIND   TriStar, 1992, U.S.-Japanese
RENAISSANCE MAN   Buena Vista, 1994

GEORGE R. ROBERTSON
POLICE ACADEMY 4: CITIZENS ON PATROL   Warner Bros., 1987

KIMMY ROBERTSON
BEAUTY AND THE BEAST (AF)   Buena Vista, 1991 (voice)

ROBBIE ROBERTSON
Agent: CAA - Beverly Hills, 310/288-4545

CARNY   United Artists, 1980

TIM ROBERTSON
BLISS   New World, 1985, Australian

LAILA ROBINS
AN INNOCENT MAN   Buena Vista, 1989
WELCOME HOME ROXY CARMICHAEL   Paramount, 1990

OLIVER ROBINS
POLTERGEIST   MGM/UA, 1982
POLTERGEIST II: THE OTHER SIDE   MGM/UA, 1986

ANDREW ROBINSON
NOT MY KID (TF)   Beth Polson Productions/Finnegan
   Associates, 1985
COBRA   Warner Bros., 1986
SHOOT TO KILL   Buena Vista, 1988
LIBERACE (TF)   The Liberace Foundation/Dick Clark Productions/
   Republic Pictures, 1988
THE LADY FORGETS (TF)   Leonard Hill Films, 1989

CLAUDIA ROBINSON
WIDE SARGASSO SEA   Fine Line Features/New Line Cinema,
   1993, British

MADELEINE ROBINSON
CAMILLE CLAUDEL   Orion Classics, 1988, French

WAYNE ROBSON
BYE BYE BLUES   Circle Releasing Corporation, 1990, Canadian
THE RESCUERS DOWN UNDER (AF)   Buena Vista, 1990 (voice)

EUGENE ROCHE
b. September 22, 1928 - Boston, Massachusetts

THE LATE SHOW   Warner Bros., 1977
ETERNITY   Academy Entertainment, 1990

ALEX ROCCO
THE GODFATHER   Paramount, 1972
GOTCHA!   Universal, 1985
STICK   Universal, 1985
BADGE OF THE ASSASSIN (TF)   Blatt-Singer Productions/
   Columbia TV, 1985
LADY IN WHITE   New Century/Vista, 1988
DREAM A LITTLE DREAM   Vestron, 1989
WIRED   Taurus Entertainment, 1989
THE POPE MUST DIET   Miramax Films, 1991

SUZZY ROCHE
CROSSING DELANCEY   Warner Bros., 1988

LELA ROCHON
HARLEM NIGHTS   Paramount, 1989

CHRIS ROCK
Agent: William Morris Agency - Beverly Hills, 310/274-7451

NEW JACK CITY   Warner Bros., 1991
CB4   Universal, 1993
SO I MARRIED AN AXE MURDERER   TriStar, 1993

CHARLES ROCKET
DOWN TWISTED   Cannon, 1987
EARTH GIRLS ARE EASY   Vestron, 1989
HOW I GOT INTO COLLEGE   20th Century Fox, 1989
DANCES WITH WOLVES   Orion, 1990
DELIRIOUS   MGM-Pathe, 1991

ANTON RODGERS
DIRTY ROTTEN SCOUNDRELS   Orion, 1988
IMPROMPTU   Hemdale, 1990, U.S.-French

AGUSTIN RODRIGUEZ
FINAL ANALYSIS   Warner Bros., 1992

FREDDY RODRIQUEZ
A WALK IN THE CLOUDS   20th Century Fox, 1995

MARCO RODRIGUEZ
COBRA   Warner Bros., 1986
THE ROOKIE   Warner Bros., 1990

PAUL RODRIGUEZ
Agent: William Morris Agency - Beverly Hills, 310/274-7451

QUICKSILVER   Columbia, 1986
THE WHOOPEE BOYS   Paramount, 1986
BORN IN EAST L.A.   Universal, 1987
A MILLION TO JUAN   Samuel Goldwyn Company, 1994

DANIEL ROEBUCK
RIVER'S EDGE   Hemdale, 1987
DUDES   New Century/Vista, 1987
DISORGANIZED CRIME   Buena Vista, 1989
THE FUGITIVE   Warner Bros., 1993

GABRIELA ROEL
EL TRES DE COPAS   Casablanca Films/Conacine, 1987, Mexican
OLD GRINGO   Columbia, 1989

MAURICE ROEVES
HIDDEN AGENDA   Hemdale, 1990

KENNY ROGERS
b. August 21, 1938 - Houston, Texas

KENNY ROGERS AS THE GAMBLER (TF)   Kragen & Co., 1980
SIX PACK   20th Century-Fox, 1982
KENNY ROGERS AS THE GAMBLER—THE ADVENTURE
   CONTINUES (TF)   Lion Share Productions, 1983
WILD HORSES (TF)   Wild Horses Productions/Telepictures
   Productions, 1985
KENNY ROGERS AS THE GAMBLER III: THE LEGEND
   CONTINUES (TF)   Lion Share Productions, 1987
MACSHAYNE: WINNER TAKES ALL (TF)   NBC, 1994

MIMI ROGERS
b. January 27 - Coral Gables, Florida
Agent: CAA - Beverly Hills, 310/288-4545

STREET SMART   Cannon, 1987
SOMEONE TO WATCH OVER ME   Columbia, 1987
THE MIGHTY QUINN   MGM/UA, 1989
DESPERATE HOURS   MGM/UA, 1990
WEDLOCK (CTF)   HBO Pictures/Spectacor Films, 1991
THE RAPTURE   New Line Cinema, 1991
THE PLAYER   Fine Line Features/New Line Cinema, 1992

WHITE SANDS   Warner Bros., 1992
MONKEY TROUBLE   New Line Cinema, 1994
YELLOW DOG   20th Century Fox, 1994

TRISTAN ROGERS
THE RESCUERS DOWN UNDER (AF)   Buena Vista, 1990 (voice)

WAYNE ROGERS
ONCE IN PARIS...   Atlantic Releasing Corporation, 1978
THE TOP OF THE HILL (MS)   Fellows-Keegan Company/
   Paramount TV, 1980
HE'S FIRED, SHE'S HIRED (TF)   CBS, 1984
THE GIG   Castle Hill Productions, 1985
I DREAM OF JEANNIE: 15 YEARS LATER (TF)   Can't Sing Can't
   Dance Productions/Columbia TV, 1985
THE LADY FROM YESTERDAY (TF)   Barry Weitz Films/Comworld
   Productions, 1985
AMERICAN HARVEST (TF)   Roth-Stratton Productions/
   The Finnegan Company, 1987
DROP-OUT MOTHER (TF)   Fries Entertainment/Comco
   Productions, 1988
BLUEGRASS (MS)   The Landsburg Company, 1988

CLAYTON ROHNER
APRIL FOOL'S DAY   Paramount, 1986
MODERN GIRLS   Atlantic Releasing Corporation, 1986
BAT 21   TriStar, 1988
I, MADMAN   Trans World Entertainment, 1989
SNOW KILL (CTF)   Wilshire Court Productions, 1990

ESTHER ROLLE
b. November 8, 1933 - Pompano Beach, Florida
Agent: William Morris Agency - Beverly Hills, 310/274-7451

SUMMER OF MY GERMAN SOLDIER (TF)
   Highgate Productions, 1978
THE MIGHTY QUINN   MGM/UA, 1989
DRIVING MISS DAISY   Warner Bros., 1989
TO DANCE WITH THE WHITE DOG (TF)   Signboard Hill
   Productions, 1993

HENRY ROLLINS
Agent: William Morris Agency - Beverly Hills, 310/274-7451

THE CHASE   20th Century Fox, 1994
JOHNNY MNEMONIC   TriStar, 1994

HOWARD E. ROLLINS, JR.
b. October 17, 1950 - Baltimore, Maryland
Agent: William Morris Agency - Beverly Hills, 310/274-7451

RAGTIME ✪   Paramount, 1981
A SOLDIER'S STORY   Columbia, 1984
DEAR AMERICA: LETTERS HOME FROM VIETNAM (FD)
   Taurus Entertainment, 1987 (voice)

MARK ROLSTON
SURVIVAL QUEST   MGM/UA, 1990

ANNY ROMAND
DIVA   United Artists Classics, 1982, French

ANDY ROMANO
THE GUN IN BETTY LOU'S HANDBAG   Buena Vista, 1992
UNDER SIEGE   Warner Bros., 1992
DROP ZONE   Paramount, 1994

ROBERT ROMANUS
FAST TIMES AT RIDGEMONT HIGH   Universal, 1982
BAD MEDICINE   20th Century Fox, 1985

MAURICE RONET
THE DEADLY TRAP   *LA MAISON SOUS LES ARBRES*
   National General, 1971, French-Italian
LA BALANCE   Spectrafilm, 1982, French

LINDA RONSTADT
b. July 15, 1946 - Tucson, Arizona
Agent: William Morris Agency - Beverly Hills, 310/274-7451

FM   Universal, 1978
THE PIRATES OF PENZANCE   Universal, 1983

MICHAEL ROOKER
STREETS OF FIRE   Universal, 1984
HENRY   MPI Video, 1987
LIGHT OF DAY   TriStar, 1987
RENT-A-COP   Kings Road Productions, 1988
ABOVE THE LAW   Warner Bros., 1988
EIGHT MEN OUT   Orion, 1988
MISSISSIPPI BURNING   Orion, 1988
SEA OF LOVE   Universal, 1989
MUSIC BOX   TriStar, 1989
HENRY - PORTRAIT OF A SERIAL KILLER   Greycat Films, 1990
DAYS OF THUNDER   Paramount, 1990
JFK   Warner Bros., 1991
THE DARK HALF   Orion, 1993
CLIFFHANGER   TriStar, 1993
TOMBSTONE   Buena Vista, 1993

MICKEY ROONEY
(Joe Yule, Jr.)
b. September 23, 1920 - New York, New York

MANHATTAN MELODRAMA   MGM, 1934
AH! WILDERNESS   MGM, 1935
A MIDSUMMER NIGHT'S DREAM   Warner Bros., 1935
LITTLE LORD FAUNTLEROY   MGM, 1936
THE DEVIL IS A SISSY   MGM, 1936
CAPTAINS COURAGEOUS   MGM, 1937
A FAMILY AFFAIR   MGM, 1937
BOY'S TOWN   MGM, 1938
THE ADVENTURES OF HUCKLEBERRY FINN   MGM, 1939
BABES IN ARMS ★   MGM, 1939
YOUNG TOM EDISON   MGM, 1940
STRIKE UP THE BAND   MGM, 1940
GIRL CRAZY   MGM, 1943
THE HUMAN COMEDY ★   MGM, 1943
NATIONAL VELVET   MGM, 1945
THE BOLD AND THE BRAVE ✪   RKO Radio, 1956
BABY FACE NELSON   Allied Artists, 1957
EVERYTHING'S DUCKY   Columbia, 1961
BREAKFAST AT TIFFANY'S   Paramount, 1961
REQUIEM FOR A HEAVYWEIGHT   Columbia, 1962
THE EXTRAORDINARY SEAMAN   MGM, 1969
THE BLACK STALLION ✪   United Artists, 1979
BILL (TF)   Alan Landsburg Productions, 1981
THE FOX AND THE HOUND (AF)   Buena Vista, 1981 (voice)
BILL: ON HIS OWN (TF)   Alan Landsburg Productions, 1983
BLUEGRASS (MS)   The Landsburg Company, 1988
ERIK THE VIKING   Orion, 1989, British
MY HEROES HAVE ALWAYS BEEN COWBOYS   Samuel Goldwyn
   Company, 1991
THAT'S ENTERTAINMENT! III (FD)   MGM/UA, 1994

JENNIFER ROOSENDAHL
'NIGHT, MOTHER   Universal, 1986

ALEXANDRA ROOT
sex, lies, and videotape   Miramax Films, 1989

ROBBY ROSA
SALSA   Cannon, 1988

JAMIE ROSE
CHOPPER CHICKS IN ZOMBIETOWN   Troma, 1991

ROSEANNE
(Roseanne Barr/Roseanne Arnold)
b. November 3, 1952
Agent: William Morris Agency - Beverly Hills, 310/274-7451

SHE-DEVIL   Orion, 1989
LOOK WHO'S TALKING TOO   TriStar, 1990 (voice)
FREDDY'S DEAD: THE FINAL NIGHTMARE
   New Line Cinema, 1991
BACKFIELD IN MOTION (TF)   Think Entertainment/
   The Avnet-Kerner Company, 1991
EVEN COWGIRLS GET THE BLUES   Fine Line Features/
   New Line Cinema, 1994

RACHEL ROSENTHAL
THE NEW AGE   Warner Bros., 1994

SHEILA ROSENTHAL
NOT WITHOUT MY DAUGHTER   MGM-Pathe, 1991

ANNIE ROSS
Agent: William Morris Agency - Beverly Hills, 310/274-7451

SHORT CUTS   Fine Line Features/New Line Cinema, 1993

CHELCIE ROSS
ABOVE THE LAW   Warner Bros., 1988
THE LAST BOY SCOUT   The Geffen Company/Warner Bros., 1991
RICHIE RICH   Warner Bros., 1994

CLARINDA ROSS
FLUKE   MGM/UA, 1994

DIANA ROSS
b. March 26, 1944 - Detroit, Michigan
Agent: ICM - Beverly Hills, 310/550-4000

LADY SINGS THE BLUES ★   Paramount, 1972
MAHOGANY   Paramount, 1975
THE WIZ   Universal, 1978
OUT OF DARKNESS (TF)   ABC Theater, 1994

KATHARINE ROSS
b. January 29, 1942 - Los Angeles, California
Agent: Borinstein-Oreck-Bogart - Los Angeles, 213/658-7500

SHENANDOAH   Universal, 1965
THE SINGING NUN   MGM, 1966
MISTER BUDDWING   MGM, 1966
THE LONGEST HUNDRED MILES   *ESCAPE FROM BATAAN* (TF)
   Universal TV, 1967
GAMES   Universal, 1967
THE GRADUATE ✪   Avco Embassy, 1967
HELLFIGHTERS   Universal, 1969
BUTCH CASSIDY AND THE SUNDANCE KID
   20th Century-Fox, 1969
TELL THEM WILLIE BOY IS HERE   Universal, 1969
FOOLS   Cinerama Releasing Corporation, 1970
GET TO KNOW YOUR RABBIT   Warner Bros., 1972
THEY ONLY KILL THEIR MASTERS   MGM, 1973
LE HASARD ET LA VIOLENCE   1974, French
THE STEPFORD WIVES   Columbia, 1975
VOYAGE OF THE DAMNED   Avco Embassy, 1976, British
WANTED: THE SUNDANCE WOMAN   *MRS. SUNDANCE*
   RIDES AGAIN (TF)   20th Century-Fox TV, 1976
THE BETSY   Allied Artists, 1978
THE SWARM   Warner Bros., 1978
THE LEGACY   *THE LEGACY OF MAGGIE WALSH*
   Universal, 1979
MURDER BY NATURAL CAUSES (TF)   Richard Levinson-William
   Link Productions, 1979
THE FINAL COUNTDOWN   United Artists, 1980
MURDER IN TEXAS (TF)   Dick Clark Productions/
   Billy Hale Films, 1981

WRONG IS RIGHT   Columbia, 1982
THE SHADOW RIDERS (TF)   The Pegasus Group, Ltd./
   Columbia TV, 1982
TRAVIS McGEE (TF)   Hajeno Productions/Warner Bros. TV, 1983
HOUSTON: THE LEGEND OF TEXAS (TF)   Taft Entertainment TV/
   J.D. Feigelson Productions, 1986 (uncredited)

TED ROSS
THE WIZ   Universal, 1978
ARTHUR   Orion, 1981
AMITYVILLE II: THE POSSESSION   Orion, 1982

ISABELLA ROSSELLINI
b. June 18, 1952 - Rome, Italy
Agent: UTA - Beverly Hills, 310/273-6700

THE MEADOW   New Yorker, 1979, Italian-French
WHITE NIGHTS   Columbia, 1985
BLUE VELVET   DEG, 1986
SIESTA   Lorimar, 1987, British
TOUGH GUYS DON'T DANCE   Cannon, 1987
ZELLY AND ME   Columbia, 1988
COUSINS   Paramount, 1989
THE LAST ELEPHANT (CTF)   RHI Entertainment/Qintex
   Entertainment, 1990
WILD AT HEART   Samuel Goldwyn Company, 1990
DEATH BECOMES HER   Universal, 1992
FEARLESS   Warner Bros., 1993
THE INNOCENT   Miramax Films, 1994, U.S.-German
WYATT EARP   Warner Bros., 1994
IMMORTAL BELOVED   Columbia, 1994

LEO ROSSI
MR. BILLION   20th Century-Fox, 1976
HALLOWEEN II   Universal, 1981
HEART LIKE A WHEEL   20th Century-Fox, 1983
CIRCLE OF POWER   Televicine, 1983
KIDS DON'T TELL (TF)   Chris-Rose Productions/Viacom
   Productions, 1985
RUSSKIES   New Century/Vista, 1987
RIVER'S EDGE   Hemdale, 1987
BLACK WIDOW   20th Century Fox, 1987
CRACKED UP (TF)   Aaron Spelling Productions, 1987
THE ACCUSED   Paramount, 1988
RELENTLESS   New Line Cinema, 1989
HIT LIST   New Line Cinema, 1989
DEAD ON   New Line Cinema, 1991
SERIOUS MONEY   New Line Cinema, 1991

PAUL ROSSILLI
STAR TREK VI: THE UNDISCOVERED COUNTRY
   Paramount, 1991

RICK ROSSOVICH
THE LORDS OF DISCIPLINE   Paramount, 1983
STREETS OF FIRE   Universal, 1984
THE TERMINATOR   Orion, 1984
FAST FORWARD   Columbia, 1985
LET'S GET HARRY   TriStar, 1986
THE MORNING AFTER   20th Century Fox, 1986
TOP GUN   Paramount, 1986
ROXANNE   Columbia, 1987
SECRET INGREDIENT   Hemdale, 1988, U.S.-Yugoslavian
SPELLBINDER   MGM/UA, 1988
HEART RAGE   Winmill Entertainment, 1989
NAVY SEALS   Orion, 1990

TIM ROSSOVICH
CHEECH & CHONG'S NICE DREAMS   Columbia, 1981
AVENGING ANGEL   New World, 1985

JOANNA ROTH
ROSENCRANTZ & GUILDENSTERN ARE DEAD   Cinecom, 1991

TIM ROTH

b. May 14, 1961 - London, England
Agent: UTA - Beverly Hills, 310/273-6700

VINCENT & THEO   Hemdale, 1990, British-French
ROSENCRANTZ & GUILDENSTERN ARE DEAD   Cinecom, 1991
RESERVOIR DOGS   Miramax Films, 1992
MEANTIME   Channel Four/Mostpoint/Central Film, 1983
MADE IN BRITAIN (TF)   1985, British
BODIES, REST & MOTION   Mainline Films, 1993
LITTLE ODESSA   New Line Cinema, 1994
PULP FICTION   Miramax Films, 1994
ROB ROY   MGM/UA, 1995

JOHN ROTHMAN

BIG   20th Century Fox, 1988
COPYCAT   Warner Bros., 1995

CYNTHIA ROTHROCK

NO RETREAT, NO SURRENDER II   Shapiro-Glickenhaus
    Entertainment, 1989

RICHARD ROUNDTREE

b. September 7, 1942 - New Rochelle, New York

WHAT DO YOU SAY TO A NAKED LADY?   United Artists, 1970
SHAFT   MGM, 1971
SHAFT'S BIG SCORE!   MGM, 1972
EMBASSY   Hemdale, 1972, British
CHARLEY ONE-EYE   Paramount, 1973, British
SHAFT IN AFRICA   MGM, 1973
EARTHQUAKE   Universal, 1974
DIAMONDS   Avco Embassy, 1975, U.S.-Israeli-Swiss
MAN FRIDAY   Avco Embassy, 1976, British
GAME FOR VULTURES   New Line Cinema, 1979, British
ESCAPE TO ATHENS   AFD, 1979, British
INCHON!   MGM/UA, 1982, South Korean
Q THE WINGED SERPENT   United Film Distribution, 1982
ONE DOWN, TWO TO GO   Almi Films, 1982
THE BIG SCORE   Almi Distribution, 1983
CITY HEAT   Warner Bros., 1984
KILLPOINT   Crown International, 1984
OPPOSING FORCE HELLCAMP   Orion, 1986
CRY DEVIL   Premiere Pictures, 1989
CRACK HOUSE   Cannon, 1989

MICKEY ROURKE

b. 1953 - Miami, Florida

1941   Universal, 1979
CITY IN FEAR (TF)   Trans World International, 1980
FADE TO BLACK   American Cinema, 1980
ACT OF LOVE (TF)   Cypress Point Productions/
    Paramount TV, 1980
RAPE AND MARRIAGE: THE RIDEOUT CASE (TF)   Stonehenge
    Productions/Blue-Greene Productions/Lorimar Productions, 1980
HEAVEN'S GATE   United Artists, 1980
BODY HEAT   The Ladd Company/Warner Bros., 1981
DINER   MGM/United Artists, 1982
RUMBLE FISH   Universal, 1983
EUREKA   MGM/UA Classics, 1984, British (filmed in 1981)
THE POPE OF GREENWICH VILLAGE   MGM/UA, 1984
YEAR OF THE DRAGON   MGM/UA, 1985
9 1/2 WEEKS   MGM/UA, 1986
ANGEL HEART   TriStar, 1987
A PRAYER FOR THE DYING   Samuel Goldwyn Company,
    1987, British
BARFLY   Cannon, 1987
HOMEBOY   Redbury, Ltd./Elliott Kastner Productions, 1988
JOHNNY HANDSOME   TriStar, 1989
WILD ORCHID   Triumph Releasing Corporation, 1990
DESPERATE HOURS   MGM/UA, 1990
HARLEY DAVIDSON & THE MARLBORO MAN   MGM-Pathe, 1991
WHITE SANDS   Warner Bros., 1992

KELLY ROWAN

CANDYMAN 2: FAREWELL TO THE FLESH   Gramercy Pictures, 1995

GENA ROWLANDS

b. July 19, 1934 - Cambria, Wisconsin
Agent: ICM - Beverly Hills, 310/550-4000

THE HIGH COST OF LOVING   MGM, 1958
LONELY ARE THE BRAVE   Universal, 1962
THE SPIRAL ROAD   Universal, 1962
A CHILD IS WAITING   United Artists, 1963
TONY ROME   20th Century-Fox, 1967
FACES   Continental, 1968
MINNIE AND MOSKOWITZ   Universal, 1971
A WOMAN UNDER THE INFLUENCE ★   Faces International, 1974
TWO MINUTE WARNING   Universal, 1976
OPENING NIGHT   Faces International, 1978
THE BRINK'S JOB   Universal, 1978
GLORIA ★   Columbia, 1980
LOVE STREAMS   Cannon, 1984
LIGHT OF DAY   TriStar, 1987
ANOTHER WOMAN   Orion, 1988
MONTANA (CTF)   HBO Productions/Zoetrope Studios/Roger Gimbel
    Productions, 1990
ONCE AROUND   Universal, 1991
NIGHT ON EARTH   Fine Line Features/New Line Cinema, 1991,
    U.S.-Japanese-French-German-British
FACE OF A STRANGER (TF)   Linda Gottlieb Productions/Viacom
    Productions, 1991
PARALLEL LIVES (CTF)   Showtime Entertainment, 1994
THE NEON BIBLE   Miramax Films, 1995

PHIL RUBENSTEIN

ANOTHER YOU   TriStar, 1991

JAN RUBES

WITNESS   Paramount, 1985
DEAD OF WINTER   MGM/UA, 1987
BLOOD RELATIONS   Miramax Films, 1988
THE EXPERTS   Paramount, 1989
COURAGE MOUNTAIN   Triumph Releasing Corporation,
    1989, U.S.-French
D2: THE MIGHTY DUCKS   Buena Vista, 1994

JENNIFER RUBIN

A NIGHTMARE ON ELM STREET, PART 3: DREAM WARRIORS
    New Line Cinema, 1987
BLUEBERRY HILL   MGM/UA, 1988
PERMANENT RECORD   Paramount, 1988
BAD DREAMS   20th Century Fox, 1988
TOO MUCH SUN   New Line Cinema, 1991
THE DOORS   TriStar, 1991
DELUSION   I.R.S. Releasing, 1991
THE CRUSH   Warner Bros., 1993

SAUL RUBINEK

NOTHING PERSONAL   American International, 1980, Canadian
YOUNG DOCTORS IN LOVE   20th Century-Fox, 1982
SWEET LIBERTY   Universal, 1986
WALL STREET   20th Century Fox, 1987
THE BONFIRE OF THE VANITIES   Warner Bros., 1990
MAN TROUBLE   20th Century Fox, 1992
UNFORGIVEN   Warner Bros., 1992
TRUE ROMANCE   Warner Bros., 1993
AND THE BAND PLAYED ON (CTF)   HBO Pictures/Spelling
    Entertainment, 1993
DEATH WISH V: THE FACE OF DEATH   Trimark Pictures, 1994
GETTING EVEN WITH DAD   MGM/UA, 1994

JOHN RUBINSTEIN

b. December 8, 1946 - Los Angeles, California

LIBERACE (TF)   The Liberace Foundation/Dick Clark Productions/
    Republic Pictures, 1988

ZELDA RUBINSTEIN

POLTERGEIST   MGM/UA, 1982
POLTERGEIST II: THE OTHER SIDE   MGM/UA, 1986
ANGUISH   Spectrafilm, 1987, Spanish
POLTERGEIST III   MGM/UA, 1988

ALAN RUCK

FERRIS BUELLER'S DAY OFF   Paramount, 1986
THREE FOR THE ROAD   New Century/Vista, 1987
THREE FUGITIVES   Buena Vista, 1989
BLOODHOUNDS OF BROADWAY   Columbia, 1989
YOUNG GUNS II   20th Century Fox, 1990
SPEED   20th Century Fox, 1994

RITA RUDNER

PETER'S FRIENDS   Samuel Goldwyn Company, 1992, British

SARA RUE

ROCKET GIBRALTAR   Columbia, 1988

MERCEDES RUEHL

b. New York
Agent: UTA - Beverly Hills, 310/273-6700

THE WARRIORS   Paramount, 1979
FOUR FRIENDS   Filmways, 1981
HEARTBURN   Paramount, 1986
84 CHARING CROSS ROAD   Columbia, 1987, British
LEADER OF THE BAND   New Century/Vista, 1987
THE SECRET OF MY SUCCESS   Universal, 1987
RADIO DAYS   Orion, 1987
BIG   20th Century Fox, 1988
MARRIED TO THE MOB   Orion, 1988
SLAVES OF NEW YORK   1989
CRAZY PEOPLE   Paramount, 1990
ANOTHER YOU   TriStar, 1991
THE FISHER KING ○○   TriStar, 1991
LOST IN YONKERS   Columbia, 1993
LAST ACTION HERO   Columbia, 1993

ALLELON RUGGIERO

DEAD POETS SOCIETY   Buena Vista, 1989

VYTO RUGINIS

CLEAN SLATE   MGM/UA, 1994

RENE RUIZ

DIAMOND'S EDGE   Kings Road Entertainment, 1990

JANICE RULE

AMERICAN FLYERS   Warner Bros., 1985

JENNIFER RUNYON

A VERY BRADY CHRISTMAS (TF)   Sherwood Schwartz
   Productions/Paramount TV, 1988
QUANTUM LEAP (TF)   Belisarius Productions/Universal TV, 1989
CARNOSAUR   New Horizons Pictures, 1993

YING RUOCHENG

LITTLE BUDDHA   Miramax Films, 1994, British-French

DEBRA JO RUPP

BIG   20th Century Fox, 1988

AL RUSCIO

CAGE   New Century/Vista, 1989

DEBORAH RUSH

Agent: Gersh Agency - New York, 212/997-1818

COMPROMISING POSITIONS   Paramount, 1985
THE PURPLE ROSE OF CAIRO   Orion, 1985
FAMILY BUSINESS   TriStar, 1989

JARED RUSHTON

b. March 3, 1974 - Provo, Utah
Agent: Tyler Kjar Agency - Toluca Lake, 818/760-0321

LADY IN WHITE   New Century/Vista, 1988
OVERBOARD   MGM/UA, 1988
BIG   20th Century Fox, 1988
HONEY, I SHRUNK THE KIDS   Buena Vista, 1989
A CRY IN THE WILD   Concorde, 1990
PET SEMATARY II   Paramount, 1992

ROBERT RUSLER

VAMP   New World, 1986
TONIGHT'S THE NIGHT (TF)   Indieprod Productions/Phoenix
   Entertainment Group, 1987

TIM RUSS

FIRE WITH FIRE   Paramount, 1986

WILLIAM RUSS

Agent: Bresler Kelly Kipperman - Encino, 818/905-1155

WANTED DEAD OR ALIVE   New World, 1986
DEAD OF WINTER   MGM/UA, 1987
DISORGANIZED CRIME   Buena Vista, 1989
ONE CUP OF COFFEE   Miramax Films, 1991
TRACES OF RED   Samuel Goldwyn Company, 1992

BETSY RUSSELL

PRIVATE SCHOOL   Universal, 1983
AVENGING ANGEL   New World, 1985

HAROLD RUSSELL

b. 1914 - Sydney, Nova Scotia, Canada

THE BEST YEARS OF OUR LIVES ○○   RKO Radio, 1946
INSIDE MOVES   AFD, 1980

KERI RUSSELL

HONEY, I BLEW UP THE KID   Buena Vista, 1992

KIMBERLY RUSSELL

GHOST DAD   Universal, 1990

KURT RUSSELL

b. March 17, 1951 - Springfield, Massachusetts
Agent: CAA - Beverly Hills, 310/288-4545

IT HAPPENED AT THE WORLD'S FAIR   MGM, 1963
FOLLOW ME, BOYS!   Buena Vista, 1966
THE ONE AND ONLY GENUINE, ORIGINAL FAMILY BAND
   Buena Vista, 1968
THE HORSE IN THE GRAY FLANNEL SUIT   Buena Vista, 1968
THE COMPUTER WORE TENNIS SHOES   Buena Vista, 1970
THE BAREFOOT EXECUTIVE   Buena Vista, 1971
FOOLS' PARADE   Columbia, 1971
NOW YOU SEE HIM, NOW YOU DON'T   Buena Vista, 1972
CHARLEY AND THE ANGEL   Buena Vista, 1973
SUPERDAD   Buena Vista, 1974
THE STRONGEST MAN IN THE WORLD   Buena Vista, 1975
THE DEADLY TOWER (TF)   MGM TV, 1975
ELVIS (TF)   Dick Clark Productions, 1979
AMBER WAVES (TF)   Time-Life Productions, 1980
USED CARS   Columbia, 1980
ESCAPE FROM NEW YORK   Avco Embassy, 1981
THE FOX AND THE HOUND (AF)   Buena Vista, 1981 (voice)
THE THING   Universal, 1982
SILKWOOD   20th Century-Fox, 1983
SWING SHIFT   Warner Bros., 1984
THE MEAN SEASON   Orion, 1985
THE BEST OF TIMES   Universal, 1986
BIG TROUBLE IN LITTLE CHINA   20th Century Fox, 1986
OVERBOARD   MGM/UA, 1987
TEQUILA SUNRISE   Warner Bros., 1988
WINTER PEOPLE   Columbia, 1989

TANGO & CASH   Warner Bros., 1989
BACKDRAFT   Universal, 1991
UNLAWFUL ENTRY   20th Century Fox, 1992
CAPTAIN RON   Buena Vista, 1992
TOMBSTONE   Buena Vista, 1993
STARGATE   MGM/UA, 1994

LISA ANN RUSSELL
APEX   Republic Pictures, 1994

NIPSEY RUSSELL
b. October 13, 1925 - Atlanta, Georgia

THE WIZ   Universal, 1978
DREAM ONE   Columbia, 1984, British-French
WILDCATS   Warner Bros., 1986
CAR 54, WHERE ARE YOU?   Orion, 1994

THERESA RUSSELL
b. 1957 - San Diego, California
Agent: William Morris Agency - Beverly Hills, 310/274-7451

THE LAST TYCOON   Paramount, 1976
STRAIGHT TIME   Warner Bros., 1978
BAD TIMING/A SENSUAL OBSESSION   World Northal,
   1980, British
THE RAZOR'S EDGE   Columbia, 1984
EUREKA   MGM/UA Classics, 1984, British (filmed in 1981)
INSIGNIFICANCE   Island Alive, 1985, British
BLACK WIDOW   20th Century Fox, 1987
TRACK 29   Island Pictures, 1988
PHYSICAL EVIDENCE   Columbia, 1989
IMPULSE   Warner Bros., 1990
WHORE   Trimark Pictures International, 1991
COLD HEAVEN   Hemdale, 1992
FLIGHT OF THE DOVE   Concorde, 1995

JAMES RUSSO
FAST TIMES AT RIDGEMONT HIGH   Universal, 1982
EXPOSED   MGM/UA, 1983
EXTREMITIES   Atlantic Releasing Corporation, 1986
CHINA GIRL   Vestron, 1987
FREEWAY   New World, 1988
WE'RE NO ANGELS   Paramount, 1989
COLD HEAVEN   Hemdale, 1992
DANGEROUS GAME   MGM/UA, 1993
BAD GIRLS   20th Century Fox, 1994
THE SECRETARY   Republic Pictures, 1995

RAY RUSSO
b. January 22, 1957

CRIES UNHEARD: THE DONNA YAKLICH STORY (TF)
   Carla Singer Productions, 1994

RENE RUSSO
Agent: Progressive Artists - Beverly Hills, 310/553-8561

MAJOR LEAGUE   Paramount, 1989
MR. DESTINY   Buena Vista, 1990
ONE GOOD COP   Buena Vista, 1991
LETHAL WEAPON 3   Warner Bros., 1992
IN THE LINE OF FIRE   Columbia, 1993
OUTBREAK   Warner Bros., 1995

LEON RUSSOM
HOSTAGE (TF)   CBS Entertainment, 1988
STAR TREK VI: THE UNDISCOVERED COUNTRY
   Paramount, 1991

SUSAN RUTTAN
TAKE MY DAUGHTERS, PLEASE (TF)   NBC Productions, 1988
CHANCES ARE   TriStar, 1989

EILEEN RYAN
AT CLOSE RANGE   Orion, 1986

EVEANNA RYAN
WAR OF THE BUTTONS   Warner Bros., 1994

FRAN RYAN
CHANCES ARE   TriStar, 1989

JOHN P. RYAN
AVENGING FORCE   Cannon, 1986
RENT-A-COP   Kings Road Productions, 1988
CLASS OF 1999   Vestron, 1989
BEST OF THE BEST   Taurus Entertainment, 1989
DELTA FORCE 2 - OPERATION STRANGLEHOLD   MGM/UA, 1990
ETERNITY   Academy Entertainment, 1990
THE INNER CIRCLE   Columbia, 1991
BATMAN: MASK OF THE PHANTASM (AF)   Warner Bros.,
   1993 (voice)

MEG RYAN
b. November 19, 1961 - Fairfield, Connecticut
Agent: ICM - Beverly Hills, 310/550-4000

RICH AND FAMOUS   MGM/United Artists, 1981
AMITYVILLE 3-D   *AMITYVILLE: THE DEMON*   Orion, 1983
ARMED AND DANGEROUS   Columbia, 1986
TOP GUN   Paramount, 1986
INNERSPACE   Warner Bros., 1987
PROMISED LAND   Vestron, 1988
D.O.A.   Buena Vista, 1988
THE PRESIDIO   Paramount, 1988
WHEN HARRY MET SALLY...   Columbia, 1989
JOE VERSUS THE VOLCANO   Warner Bros., 1990
THE DOORS   TriStar, 1991
PRELUDE TO A KISS   20th Century Fox, 1992
SLEEPLESS IN SEATTLE   TriStar, 1993
FLESH AND BONE   Paramount, 1993
WHEN A MAN LOVES A WOMAN   Buena Vista, 1994
I.Q.   Paramount, 1994
RESTORATION   Miramax Films, 1994
PARIS MATCH   20th Century Fox, 1995
THE WOMEN   New Line Cinema, 1995

MITCHELL RYAN
LETHAL WEAPON   Warner Bros., 1987
WINTER PEOPLE   Columbia, 1989
THE RYAN WHITE STORY (TF)   The Landsburg Company, 1989
SPEECHLESS   MGM/UA, 1994

WILL RYAN
AN AMERICAN TAIL (AF)   Universal, 1986 (voice)
THE LITTLE MERMAID (AF)   Buena Vista, 1989 (voice)
HANS CHRISTIAN ANDERSEN'S THUMBELINA (AF)
   Warner Bros., 1994 (voice)

DEREK RYDALL
CRY DEVIL   Premiere Pictures, 1989
POPCORN   Studio Three, 1991

CHRIS RYDELL
(Christopher Rydell)
ON GOLDEN POND   Universal/AFD, 1981
GOTCHA!   Universal, 1985
HOW I GOT INTO COLLEGE   20th Century Fox, 1989
SIDE OUT   TriStar, 1990
FOR THE BOYS   20th Century Fox, 1991
BY THE SWORD   The Movie Group, 1992

MARK RYDELL
Agent: ICM - Beverly Hills, 310/550-4000

PUNCHLINE   Columbia, 1988

MICHAEL ALLEN RYDER
SURVIVAL QUEST   MGM/UA, 1990

WINONA RYDER
b. October 29, 1971 - Winona, Minnesota
Agent: CAA - Beverly Hills, 310/288-4545

LUCAS   20th Century Fox, 1986
SQUARE DANCE   Island Pictures, 1987
BEETLEJUICE   The Geffen Company/Warner Bros., 1988
1969   Atlantic Releasing Corporation, 1988
GREAT BALLS OF FIRE   Orion, 1989
HEATHERS   New World, 1989
WELCOME HOME, ROXY CARMICHAEL   Paramount, 1990
MERMAIDS   Orion, 1990
EDWARD SCISSORHANDS   20th Century Fox, 1990
NIGHT ON EARTH   Fine Line Features/New Line Cinema, 1991,
   U.S.-Japanese-French-German-British
BRAM STOKER'S DRACULA   *DRACULA*   Columbia, 1992
THE AGE OF INNOCENCE ✪   Columbia, 1993
THE HOUSE OF THE SPIRITS   Miramax Films, 1993, U.S.-German
REALITY BITES   Universal, 1994
LITTLE WOMEN   Columbia, 1994
BOYS   Buena Vista, 1995
HOW TO MAKE AN AMERICAN QUILT   Universal, 1995

PATRICK RYECART
LACE II (MS)   Lorimar Productions, 1985

ADAM RYEN
THE RESCUERS DOWN UNDER (AF)   Buena Vista, 1990 (voice)

MARK RYLANCE
ANGELS AND INSECTS   Samuel Goldwyn Company, 1995

ERNIE SABELLA
THE LION KING (AF)   Buena Vista, 1994 (voice)

NICK SADLER
MOBSTERS   Universal, 1991

WILLIAM SADLER
(Bill Sadler)
PROJECT X   20th Century Fox, 1987
HARD TO KILL   Warner Bros., 1990
DIE HARD 2   20th Century Fox, 1990
BILL & TED'S BOGUS JOURNEY   Orion, 1991
RUSH   MGM-Pathe, 1991
FREAKED   20th Century Fox, 1993
THE SHAWSHANK REDEMPTION   Columbia, 1994

JOE SAGAL
THE CHASE   20th Century Fox, 1994

JONATHAN SAGALLE
SCHINDLER'S LIST   Universal, 1993

MARIANNE SÄGEBRECHT
SUGARBABY   Kino International, 1985, West German
BAGDAD CAFE   *OUT OF ROSENHEIM*   Island Pictures, 1987,
   West German-U.S.
MOON OVER PARADOR   Universal, 1988, U.S.-Brazilian
THE WAR OF THE ROSES   20th Century Fox, 1989
ROSALIE GOES SHOPPING   Four Seasons Entertainment,
   1989, West German-U.S.

BOB SAGET
b. May 17, 1956 - Philadelphia, Pennsylvania

CRITICAL CONDITION   Paramount, 1987

MORT SAHL
(Morton Lyon Sahl)
b. May 11, 1926 - Montreal, Canada

IN LOVE AND WAR   20th Century-Fox, 1958
ALL THE YOUNG MEN   Columbia, 1960
JOHNNY COOL   United Artists, 1963
DOCTOR, YOU'VE GOT TO BE KIDDING   MGM, 1967
DON'T MAKE WAVES   MGM, 1967
NOTHING LASTS FOREVER   MGM/UA Classics, 1984

EVA MARIE SAINT
b. July 4, 1924 - Newark, New Jersey

ON THE WATERFRONT ✪✪   Columbia, 1954
THAT CERTAIN FEELING   Paramount, 1956
A HATFUL OF RAIN   20th Century-Fox, 1957
RAINTREE COUNTY   MGM, 1957
NORTH BY NORTHWEST   MGM, 1959
EXODUS   United Artists, 1960
ALL FALL DOWN   MGM, 1962
36 HOURS   MGM, 1964
THE SANDPIPER   MGM, 1965
THE RUSSIANS ARE COMING, THE RUSSIANS ARE COMING
   United Artists, 1966
GRAND PRIX   MGM, 1966
THE STALKING MOON   National General, 1969
LOVING   Columbia, 1970
CANCEL MY RESERVATION   Warner Bros., 1972
A CHRISTMAS TO REMEMBER (TF)   George Englund
   Productions, 1978
THE CURSE OF KING TUT'S TOMB (TF)   Stromberg-Kerby
   Productions/Columbia TV/HTV West, 1980
THE BEST LITTLE GIRL IN THE WORLD (TF)   Aaron Spelling
   Productions, 1981
MALIBU (TF)   Hamner Productions/Columbia TV, 1983
JANE DOE (TF)   ITC, 1983
LOVE LEADS THE WAY (TF)   Hawkins-Permut Productions, 1984
FATAL VISION (MS)   NBC Productions, 1984
THE LAST DAYS OF PATTON (TF)   Entertainment Partners, 1986
NOTHING IN COMMON   TriStar, 1986
NORMAN ROCKWELL'S 'BREAKING HOME TIES'
   BREAKING HOME TIES (TF)   ABC, 1987
I'LL BE HOME FOR CHRISTMAS (TF)   NBC Productions, 1988
PEOPLE LIKE US (TF)   ITC Productions, 1990

RAYMOND ST. JACQUES
(James Arthur Johnson)
b. 1930 - Hartford, Connecticut

BLACK LIKE ME   1964
THE PAWNBROKER   Landau/Allied Artists, 1965
MISTER MOSES   United Artists, 1965, British
MISTER BUDDWING   MGM, 1966
THE COMEDIANS   MGM, 1967
MADIGAN   Universal, 1968
THE GREEN BERETS   Warner Bros., 1968
IF HE HOLLERS, LET HIM GO!   1968
UP TIGHT   Paramount, 1968
CHANGE OF MIND   1969
COTTON COMES TO HARLEM   United Artists, 1970
COOL BREEZE   MGM, 1972
THE FINAL COMEDOWN   New World, 1972
COME BACK, CHARLESTON BLUE   Warner Bros., 1972
BOOK OF NUMBERS   Avco Embassy, 1973 (also directed)
LOST IN THE STARS   American Film Theatre, 1974
BLAST   1976
THE PRIVATE FILES OF J. EDGAR HOOVER
   American International, 1977
BORN AGAIN   Avco Embassy, 1978
KEY WEST CROSSING   1979
KILL CASTRO   1980

THE EVIL THAT MEN DO   TriStar, 1984
THE WILD PAIR   Transworld Entertainment, 1987
GLORY   TriStar, 1989 (uncredited)

SUSAN SAINT JAMES
(Susan Miller)
b. August 14, 1946 - Los Angeles, California
Agent: CAA - Beverly Hills, 310/288-4545

P.J.   Universal, 1968
WHERE ANGELS GO...TROUBLE FOLLOWS!   Columbia, 1968
WHAT'S SO BAD ABOUT FEELING GOOD   Universal, 1968
JIGSAW   Universal, 1968
MAGIC CARPET (TF)   Universal TV, 1971
OUTLAW BLUES   Warner Bros., 1977
DESPERATE WOMEN (TF)   Lorimar Productions, 1978
LOVE AT FIRST BITE   American International, 1979
S.O.S. TITANIC (TF)   Roger Gimbel Productions/EMI TV/Argonaut
   Films Ltd., 1979, U.S.-British
HOW TO BEAT THE HIGH COST OF LIVING
   American International, 1980
CARBON COPY   Avco Embassy, 1981
DON'T CRY, IT'S ONLY THUNDER   Sanrio, 1981, U.S.-Japanese

JILL ST. JOHN
(Jill Oppenheim)
b. August 19, 1940 - Los Angeles, California

THUNDER IN THE EAST   Paramount, 1953
SUMMER LOVE   1958
HOLIDAY FOR LOVERS   20th Century-Fox, 1959
THE LOST WORLD   20th Century-Fox, 1960
THE ROMAN SPRING OF MRS. STONE   Warner Bros., 1961
TENDER IS THE NIGHT   20th Century-Fox, 1962
COME BLOW YOUR HORN   Paramount, 1963
WHO'S MINDING THE STORE?   Paramount, 1963
WHO'S BEEN SLEEPING IN MY BED?   Paramount, 1963
HONEYMOON HOTEL   MGM, 1964
THE LIQUIDATOR   MGM, 1966, British
THE OSCAR   Embassy, 1966
TONY ROME   20th Century-Fox, 1967
EIGHT ON THE LAM   United Artists, 1967
BANNING   Universal, 1967
DIAMONDS ARE FOREVER   United Artists, 1971, British
SITTING TARGET   MGM, 1972, British
THE ACT   Artists Releasing Corporation/Film Ventures
   International, 1984

ROSS ST. PHILLIP
COBRA   Warner Bros., 1986

GENE SAKS
b. November 8, 1921 - New York, New York

A THOUSAND CLOWNS   United Artists, 1965
THE PRISONER OF SECOND AVENUE   Warner Bros., 1975
THE ONE AND ONLY   Paramount, 1978
LOVESICK   The Ladd Company/Warner Bros., 1983
THE GOODBYE PEOPLE   Embassy, 1984
I.Q.   Paramount, 1994

THERESA SALDANA
RAGING BULL   United Artists, 1980
SOPHIA LOREN: HER OWN STORY (TF)   Roger Gimbel
   Productions/EMI TV, 1980
VICTIMS FOR VICTIMS - THE THERESA SALDANA STORY (TF)
   Daniel L. Paulson-Loehr Spivey Productions/Orion TV, 1984
DOUBLE REVENGE   Smart Egg Releasing, 1988
ANGEL TOWN   Taurus Entertainment, 1990

MEREDITH SALENGER
APRIL MORNING (TF)   Robert Halmi, Inc./Samuel Goldwyn TV, 1988
DREAM A LITTLE DREAM   Vestron, 1989
VILLAGE OF THE DAMNED   Universal, 1995

SAM SALETTA
THE LITTLE RASCALS   Universal, 1994

DIANE SALINGER
THE MORNING AFTER   20th Century Fox, 1986

MATT SALINGER
MANHUNT FOR CLAUDE DALLAS (TF)   London Films, Inc., 1986
BABYFEVER   Rainbow Releasing, 1994

LEA SALONGA
ALADDIN (AF)   Buena Vista, 1992 (voice)

EMMA SAMMS
b. August 28, 1960 - London, England

AGATHA CHRISTIE'S "MURDER IN THREE ACTS" (TF)
   Warner Bros. TV, 1986
THE LADY AND THE HIGHWAYMAN (TF)   The Grade Company/
   Gainsborough Pictures, 1989, British
A CONNECTICUT YANKEE IN KING ARTHUR'S COURT (TF)
   Schaefer-Karpf Productions/Consolidated Productions, 1989
DELIRIOUS   MGM-Pathe, 1991

ROBERT SAMPSON
ROBOTJOX   Triumph Releasing Corporation, 1990

TIM SAMPSON
WAR PARTY   Hemdale, 1989

ALTANA SANCHEZ-GIJON
A WALK IN THE CLOUDS   20th Century Fox, 1995

PAUL SAND
THE HOT ROCK   20th Century-Fox, 1972
THE MAIN EVENT   Warner Bros., 1979
CAN'T STOP THE MUSIC   AFD, 1980
WHOLLY MOSES   Columbia, 1980

JAY O. SANDERS
THE PRINCE OF PENNSYLVANIA   New Line Cinema, 1988
V.I. WARSHAWSKI   Buena Vista, 1991
DEFENSELESS   New Line Cinema, 1991
JFK   Warner Bros., 1991

WILLIAM SANDERSON
b. January 10, 1948 - Memphis, Tennessee

BLADE RUNNER   The Ladd Company/Warner Bros., 1982
NIGHTMARES   Universal, 1983
CITY HEAT   Warner Bros., 1984
BLACK MOON RISING   New World, 1986
THE ROCKETEER   Buena Vista, 1991
THE CLIENT   Warner Bros., 1994

ADAM SANDLER
Agent: CAA - Beverly Hills, 310/288-4545

AIRHEADS   20th Century Fox, 1994
LIFESAVERS   TriStar, 1994
BILLY MADISON   Universal, 1995

DEBRA SANDLUND
TOUGH GUYS DON'T DANCE   Cannon, 1987

VAUGHN SANDMAN
BIG   20th Century Fox, 1988

MIGUEL SANDOVAL
CLEAR AND PRESENT DANGER   Paramount, 1994

JULIAN SANDS
Agent: ICM - Beverly Hills, 310/550-4000

OXFORD BLUES   MGM/UA, 1984, British
THE KILLING FIELDS   Warner Bros., 1984, British

THE DOCTOR AND THE DEVILS   20th Century Fox, 1985, British
A ROOM WITH A VIEW   Cinecom, 1986, British
GOTHIC   Vestron, 1986, British
SIESTA   Lorimar, 1987, British
VIBES   Columbia, 1988
TENNESSEE WALTZ   Condor Productions, 1989
ARACHNOPHOBIA   Buena Vista, 1990
IMPROMPTU   Hemdale, 1990, U.S.-French
WARLOCK   Trimark Pictures, 1991
NAKED LUNCH   20th Century Fox, 1992
BOXING HELENA   Orion Classics, 1993
WARLOCK: THE ARMAGEDDON   Trimark Pictures, 1993

LAURA SAN GIACOMO
sex, lies, and videotape   Miramax Films, 1989
VITAL SIGNS   20th Century Fox, 1990
PRETTY WOMAN   Buena Vista, 1990
QUIGLEY DOWN UNDER   MGM/UA, 1990
ONCE AROUND   Universal, 1991
THE OTHER WOMAN   Columbia, 1993
NINA TAKES A LOVER   1993
THE STAND (MS)   ABC, 1994
STUART SMALLEY   Paramount, 1995

RUBEN SANTIAGO-HUDSON
BLOWN AWAY   MGM, 1994

RENI SANTONI
ENTER LAUGHING   Columbia, 1967
ANZIO   THE BATTLE FOR ANZIO   Columbia, 1968,
   French-Italian-Spanish
DIRTY HARRY   Warner Bros., 1972
I NEVER PROMISED YOU A ROSE GARDEN   New World, 1977
THEY WENT THAT-A-WAY AND THAT-A-WAY   International Picture
   Show Company, 1978
DEAD MEN DON'T WEAR PLAID   Universal, 1982
BAD BOYS   Universal/AFD, 1983
COBRA   Warner Bros., 1986
THE PACKAGE   Orion, 1989

JOE SANTOS
SHAMUS   Columbia, 1973
ZANDY'S BRIDE   FOR BETTER, FOR WORSE   Warner Bros., 1974
FEAR CITY   Chevy Chase Distribution, 1984
MO' MONEY   Columbia, 1992
TRIAL BY JURY   Warner Bros., 1994

WILLIE SANTOS
THE SKATEBOARD KID II   Concorde, 1995

ADE SAPARA
CRUSOE   Island Pictures, 1988, U.S.-British

MIA SARA
LEGEND   Universal, 1986, British
FERRIS BUELLER'S DAY OFF   Paramount, 1986
APPRENTICE TO MURDER   New World, 1987, Canadian
QUEENIE (TF)   von Zerneck-Samuels Productions/Highgate
   Pictures, 1987
A STRANGER AMONG US   Buena Vista, 1992
BY THE SWORD   The Movie Group, 1992
TIMECOP   Universal, 1994

RICHARD SARAFIAN
DON JUAN DE MARCO AND THE CENTERFOLD
   New Line Cinema, 1995

CHRIS SARANDON
DOG DAY AFTERNOON ✪   Warner Bros., 1975
LIPSTICK   Paramount, 1976
THE SENTINEL   Universal, 1977
CUBA   United Artists, 1979
THE DAY CRIST DIED (TF)   Martin Manulis Productions/
   20th Century-Fox TV, 1980
A TALE OF TWO CITIES (TF)   Norman Rosemont Productions/
   Marble Arch Productions, 1980, U.S.-British

THE OSTERMAN WEEKEND   20th Century-Fox, 1983
PROTOCOL   Warner Bros., 1984
FRIGHT NIGHT   Columbia, 1985
THE PRINCESS BRIDE   20th Century Fox, 1987
CHILD'S PLAY   MGM/UA, 1988
SLAVES OF NEW YORK   TriStar, 1989

SUSAN SARANDON
(Susan Tomaling)
b. October 4, 1946 - New York, New York
Agent: ICM - Beverly Hills, 310/550-4000

JOE   Cannon, 1970
LADY LIBERTY   *MORTADELLA*   United Artists, 1971, Italian
F. SCOTT FITZGERALD AND "THE LAST OF THE BELLES" (TF)
   Titus Productions, 1974
LOVIN' MOLLY   Columbia, 1974
THE FRONT PAGE   Universal, 1974
THE ROCKY HORROR PICTURE SHOW   20th Century-Fox,
   1975, British
THE GREAT WALDO PEPPER   Universal, 1975
ONE SUMMER LOVE   *DRAGONFLY*   American International, 1976
CHECKERED FLAG OR CRASH   Universal, 1977
THE OTHER SIDE OF MIDNIGHT   20th Century-Fox, 1977
THE GREAT SMOKEY ROADBLOCK   *THE LAST OF
   THE COWBOYS*   Dimension, 1978
PRETTY BABY   Paramount, 1978
KING OF THE GYPSIES   Paramount, 1978
SOMETHING SHORT OF PARADISE   American International, 1979
LOVING COUPLES   20th Century-Fox, 1980
ATLANTIC CITY ★   Paramount, 1981
TEMPEST   Columbia, 1982
WHO AM I THIS TIME? (TF)   Rubicon Film Productions, 1982
THE HUNGER   MGM/UA, 1983, British
THE BUDDY SYSTEM   20th Century Fox, 1984
MUSSOLINI: THE DECLINE AND FALL OF IL DUCE (CMS)
   HBO Premiere Films/RAI/Antenne-2/Beta Film/TVE/RTSI, 1985,
   U.S.-Italian-French-West German
COMPROMISING POSITIONS   Paramount, 1985
WOMEN OF VALOR (TF)   Inter Planetary Prods./Jeni Prods., 1986
THE WITCHES OF EASTWICK   Warner Bros., 1987
BULL DURHAM   Orion, 1988
SWEET HEARTS DANCE   TriStar, 1988
THE JANUARY MAN   MGM/UA, 1989
A DRY WHITE SEASON   MGM/UA, 1989
ERIK THE VIKING   Orion, 1989, British
WHITE PALACE   Universal, 1990
THELMA & LOUISE ★   MGM-Pathe, 1991
THE PLAYER   Fine Line Features/New Line Cinema, 1992
BOB ROBERTS   Paramount/Miramax Films, 1992
LIGHT SLEEPER   Fine Line Features/New Line Cinema, 1992
LORENZO'S OIL ★   Universal, 1992
THE CLIENT   Warner Bros., 1994
SAFE PASSAGE   New Line Cinema, 1994
LITTLE WOMEN   Columbia, 1994

LEILANI SARELLE
BASIC INSTINCT   TriStar, 1992
SCAM   Viacom, 1993

DICK SARGENT
BERNARDINE   20th Century-Fox, 1957
OPERATION PETTICOAT   Universal, 1959
THAT TOUCH OF MINK   Universal, 1962
THE GHOST AND MR. CHICKEN   Universal, 1966
THE PRIVATE NAVY OF SERGEANT O'FARRELL   United Artists, 1968
RICH MAN, POOR MAN (MS)   Universal TV, 1976
HARDCORE   Columbia, 1979

MICHAEL SARRAZIN
b. May 22, 1940 - Quebec City, Canada

THE DOOMSDAY FLIGHT (TF)   Universal TV, 1966
GUNFIGHT IN ABILENE   Universal, 1967
THE FLIM-FLAM MAN   20th Century-Fox, 1967
JOURNEY TO SHILOH   Universal, 1968
THE SWEET RIDE   20th Century-Fox, 1968

THEY SHOOT HORSES, DON'T THEY?   Cinerama Releasing
    Corporation, 1969
EYE OF THE CAT   Universal, 1969
A MAN CALLED GANNON   Universal, 1969
IN SEARCH OF GREGORY   1970
THE PURSUIT OF HAPPINESS   Columbia, 1971
SOMETIMES A GREAT NOTION   *NEVER GIVE AN INCH*
    Universal, 1971
BELIEVE IN ME   MGM, 1971
THE GROUNDSTAR CONSPIRACY   Universal,
    1972, U.S.-Canadian
FRANKENSTEIN: THE TRUE STORY (TF)   Universal TV, 1973
HARRY IN YOUR POCKET   1973
FOR PETE'S SAKE   Columbia, 1974
THE REINCARNATION OF PETER PROUD
    American International, 1975
THE LIVES AND TIMES OF SCARAMOUCHE
    1976, Italian-Yugoslavian
THE GUMBALL RALLY   Warner Bros., 1976
A NIGHT FULL OF RAIN   Warner Bros., 1978, U.S.-Italian
CARAVANS   Universal, 1978, U.S.-Iranian
BEULAH LAND (MS)   David Gerber Company/Columbia TV, 1980
DOUBLE NEGATIVE   Best Film & Video, 1980, Canadian
THE SEDUCTION   Avco Embassy, 1982
FIGHTING BACK   Paramount, 1982
JOSHUA THEN AND NOW   20th Century-Fox, 1985, Canadian
KIDNAPPED   Virgin Vision, 1987
KEEPING TRACK   Shapiro Entertainment, 1987, Canadian
CAPTIVE HEARTS   MGM/UA, 1987, Canadian

GAILARD SARTAIN
HARD COUNTRY   Universal/AFD, 1981
BLAZE   Buena Vista, 1989
ERNEST GOES TO JAIL   Buena Vista, 1990
GUILTY BY SUSPICION   Warner Bros., 1991
FRIED GREEN TOMATOES   Universal, 1991
GETTING EVEN WITH DAD   MGM/UA, 1994
SPEECHLESS   MGM/UA, 1994

BEN SAVAGE
b. September 13, 1980 - Highland Park, Illinois

LITTLE MONSTERS   MGM/UA, 1989
STEPKIDS   New Line Cinema, 1991
WILD PALMS (MS)   Ixtlan Corporation/Greengrass
    Productions, Inc., 1993

FRED SAVAGE
b. July 9, 1976 - Highland Park, Illinois

THE BOY WHO COULD FLY   20th Century Fox, 1986
THE PRINCESS BRIDE   20th Century Fox, 1987
VICE VERSA   Columbia, 1988
LITTLE MONSTERS   MGM/UA, 1989
THE WIZARD   Universal, 1989

JOHN SAVAGE
BAD COMPANY   Paramount, 1972
ALL THE KIND STRANGERS (TF)   Cinemation TV, 1974
THE KILLING KIND   Media Trend, 1974
ERIC (TF)   Lorimar Productions, 1975
THE DEER HUNTER   Universal, 1978
HAIR   United Artists, 1979
THE ONION FIELD   Avco Embassy, 1979
INSIDE MOVES   AFD, 1980
CATTLE ANNIE AND LITTLE BRITCHES   Universal, 1981
THE AMATEUR   20th Century-Fox, 1981, Canadian
COMING OUT OF THE ICE (TF)   The Konigsberg Company, 1982
BRADY'S ESCAPE   *THE LONG RUN*   Satori,
    1984, U.S.-Hungarian
MARIA'S LOVERS   Cannon, 1984
SALVADOR   Hemdale, 1986
THE BEAT   Vestron, 1987
HOTEL COLONIAL   Hemdale, 1987, U.S.-Italian
DO THE RIGHT THING   Universal, 1989
THE GODFATHER, PART III   Paramount, 1990

KALA SAVAGE
b. October 16, 1978 - Highland Park, Illinois

LITTLE MONSTERS   MGM/UA, 1989

PIUS SAVAGE
WHITE FANG   Buena Vista, 1991
BLACK FEATHER   1995

DOUG SAVANT
TRICK OR TREAT   DEG, 1986
MASQUERADE   MGM/UA, 1988

CAMILLE SAVIOLA
BETSY'S WEDDING   Buena Vista, 1990
ALL I WANT FOR CHRISTMAS   Paramount, 1991

DEVON SAWA
LITTLE GIANTS   Warner Bros., 1994

JOHN SAXON
(Carmen Orrico)
b. August 5, 1935 - Brooklyn, New York

RUNNING WILD   1955
THE UNGUARDED MOMENT   1956
THE RESTLESS YEARS   1958
THE RELUCTANT DEBUTANTE   MGM, 1958
THIS HAPPY FEELING   Universal, 1958
SUMMER LOVE   1958
THE BIG FISHERMAN   Buena Vista, 1959
CRY TOUGH   United Artists, 1959
PORTRAIT IN BLACK   Universal, 1960
THE UNFORGIVEN   United Artists, 1960
THE PLUNDERERS   Allied Artists, 1960
POSSE FROM HELL   1961
MR. HOBBES TAKES A VACATION   20th Century-Fox, 1962
WAR HUNT   1962
THE EVIL EYE   American International, 1963, Italian
THE CARDINAL   Columbia, 1963
THE CAVERN   20th Century-Fox, 1965, Italian-German
THE RAVAGERS   Hemisphere, 1965, U.S.-Filipino
THE APPALOOSA   Universal, 1966
QUEEN OF BLOOD   *PLANET OF BLOOD*
    American International, 1966
THE NIGHT CALLER   *BLOOD BEAST FROM OUTER SPACE*
    1966, British
FOR SINGLES ONLY   Columbia, 1968
DEATH OF A GUNFIGHTER   Universal, 1969
COMPANY OF KILLERS   *THE PROTECTORS*   Universal, 1970
JOE KIDD   Universal, 1972
ENTER THE DRAGON   Warner Bros., 1973, U.S.-Hong Kong
CAN ELLEN BE SAVED? (TF)   ABC Circle Films, 1974
BLACK CHRISTMAS   *SILENT NIGHT, EVIL NIGHT*   Warner Bros.,
    1974, Canadian
FAMILY KILLER   1975, Italian
MITCHELL   Allied Artists, 1975
TOUGH TONY   *TONY SAITTA*   1975
THE SWISS CONSPIRACY   SJ International, 1975,
    U.S.-West German
NAPOLI VIOLENTA   1976, Italian
STRANGE SHADOWS IN AN EMPTY ROOM   *BLAZING MAGNUM*
    1977, Italian
MOONSHINE COUNTY EXPRESS   New World, 1977
E SPECIALISTE DEL 44   1977, Italian-Austrian
THE BEES   1978
SHALIMAR   *THE DEADLY THIEF*   Judson Productions/Laxmi
    Productions, 1978, Indian
FAST COMPANY   Topar, 1979, Canadian
THE ELECTRIC HORSEMAN   Columbia, 1979
BLOOD BEACH   Jerry Gross Organization, 1981
THE GLOVE   1981
HARDCASTLE AND McCORMICK (TF)   Stephen J. Cannell
    Productions, 1983
THE BIG SCORE   Almi Distribution, 1983
A NIGHTMARE ON ELM STREET   New Line Cinema, 1984

FEVER PITCH   MGM/UA, 1985
MY MOM'S A WEREWOLF   Crown International Pictures, 1989
BEVERLY HILLS COP III   Paramount, 1994

MITCH SAXTON
MISS FIRECRACKER   Corsair Pictures, 1989

JOHN SAYLES
b. September 28, 1950 - Schenectady, New York

RETURN OF THE SECAUCUS SEVEN   Libra/Specialty Films,
   1980 (also directed)
LIANNA   United Artists Classics, 1983 (also directed)
THE BROTHER FROM ANOTHER PLANET   Cinecom,
   1984 (also directed)
HARD CHOICES   Lorimar, 1986
SOMETHING WILD   Orion, 1986
MATEWAN   Cinecom, 1987 (also directed)
EIGHT MEN OUT   Orion, 1988 (also directed)
STRAIGHT TALK   Buena Vista, 1992

RAPHAEL SBARGE
Agent: Metropolitan Talent Agency - Los Angeles, 213/857-4500

PRISON FOR CHILDREN (TF)   Knopf-Simons Productions/
   Viacom Productions, 1987
CRACKED UP (TF)   Aaron Spelling Productions, 1987
BILLIONAIRE BOYS CLUB (MS)   Donald March/Gross-Weston
   Productions/ITC Productions, 1987
CARNOSAUR   New Horizons Pictures, 1993

GRETA SCACCHI
Agent: Susan Smith & Associates - Beverly Hills, 213/852-4777

HEAT AND DUST   Universal Classics, 1983, British
THE EBONY TOWER (TF)   Granada TV, 1984, British
CAMILLE (TF)   Rosemont Productions, 1984, U.S.-British
THE COCA COLA KID   Cinecom/Film Gallery, 1985, Australian
DEFENSE OF THE REALM   Hemdale, 1985, British
BURKE AND WILLS   Hemdale, 1985, Australian
GOOD MORNING, BABYLON   Vestron, 1987, Italian-French-U.S.
A MAN IN LOVE   Cinecom, 1987, French-Italian
WHITE MISCHIEF   Columbia, 1987, British
PRESUMED INNOCENT   Warner Bros., 1990
SHATTERED   MGM-Pathe, 1991
FIRES WITHIN   MGM-Pathe, 1991
THE PLAYER   Fine Line Features/New Line Cinema, 1992
THE BROWNING VERSION   Paramount, 1994, British
JEFFERSON IN PARIS   Buena Vista, 1995

PRUNELLA SCALES
THE BOYS FROM BRAZIL   20th Century-Fox, 1978
THE WICKED LADY   MGM/UA/Cannon, 1983, British
CONSUMING PASSIONS   Samuel Goldwyn Company,
   1988, British
HOWARDS END   Sony Pictures Classics, 1992, British
SECOND BEST   Warner Bros., 1994

JACK SCALIA
Agent: William Morris Agency - Beverly Hills, 310/274-7451

FEAR CITY   Chevy Chase Distribution, 1984
REMINGTON STEELE: THE STEELE THAT WOULDN'T DIE (TF)
   MTM Productions, 1987
I'LL TAKE MANHATTAN (MS)   Steve Krantz Productions, 1987
DEMON HUNTERS   Golden Harvest, 1989

GIAN-CARLO SCANDIUZZI
Personal Manager: Marc Rindner - Los Angeles, 213/461-6334

THE BONFIRE OF THE VANITIES   Warner Bros., 1990
ANOTHER YOU   1991
BUGSY   TriStar, 1991
INDECENCY   TriStar, 1991
THE PUBLIC EYE   Universal, 1992
KILLING ZOE   October Films, 1994, U.S.-French

KEVIN SCANNELL
SHOOT TO KILL   Buena Vista, 1988
MILK MONEY   Paramount, 1994

ALLAN SCARFE
IRON EAGLE II   TriStar, 1988, Canadian-Israeli

DIANA SCARWID
BATTERED (TF)   Henry Jaffe Enterprises, 1978
PRETTY BABY   Paramount, 1978
INSIDE MOVES ✪   Associated Film Distribution, 1980
GUYANA TRAGEDY: THE STORY OF JIM JONES (TF)
   The Konigsberg Company, 1980
MOMMIE DEAREST   Paramount, 1981
SILKWOOD   20th Century-Fox, 1983
STRANGE INVADERS   Orion, 1983, Canadian
A BUNNY'S TALE (TF)   Stan Margulies Company/
   ABC Circle Films, 1985
EXTREMITIES   Atlantic Releasing Corporation, 1986
THE LADIES CLUB   New Line Cinema, 1986
PSYCHO III   Universal, 1986
AFTER THE PROMISE (TF)   Tamara Asseyev Productions/
   New World TV, 1987
HEAT   New Century/Vista, 1987
BRENDA STARR   New World, 1989
THE NEON BIBLE   Miramax Films, 1995

WENDY SCHAAL
WHERE THE BOYS ARE '84   TriStar, 1984
CREATURE   *TITAN FIND*   Cardinal Releasing, 1985
THE 'BURBS   Universal, 1989

SAM SCHACHT
HEART OF MIDNIGHT   Virgin Vision, 1989

FELICE SCHACHTER
ZAPPED!   Embassy, 1982

ROY SCHEIDER
(Roy R. Sheider)
b. November 10, 1935 - Orange, New Jersey

THE CURSE OF THE LIVING CORPSE   1964
PAPER LION   United Artists, 1968
STILETTO   Avco Embassy, 1969
LOVING   Columbia, 1970
PUZZLE OF A DOWNFALL CHILD   Universal, 1970
KLUTE   Warner Bros., 1971
THE FRENCH CONNECTION ✪   20th Century-Fox, 1971
ASSIGNMENT: MUNICH (TF)   MGM TV, 1972
THE OUTSIDE MAN   *UN HOMME EST MORT*   United Artists,
   1973, French-Italian
THE FRENCH CONSPIRACY   *L'ATTENTAT*   1973,
   French-Italian-West German
THE SEVEN-UPS   20th Century-Fox, 1973
SHEILA LEVINE IS DEAD AND LIVING IN NEW YORK
   Paramount, 1975
JAWS   Universal, 1975
MARATHON MAN   Paramount, 1976
SORCERER   Paramount/Universal, 1977
JAWS 2   Universal, 1978
LAST EMBRACE   United Artists, 1979
ALL THAT JAZZ ★   20th Century-Fox, 1979
STILL OF THE NIGHT   MGM/UA, 1982
JACOBO TIMERMAN: PRISONER WITHOUT A NAME, CELL
   WITHOUT A NUMBER (TF)   Chrysalis-Yellin Productions, 1983
BLUE THUNDER   Columbia, 1983
TIGER TOWN (CTF)   Thompson Street Pictures, 1983
IN OUR HANDS   1984
2010   MGM/UA, 1984
MISHIMA: A LIFE IN FOUR CHAPTERS   Warner Bros., 1985,
   Japanese-U.S. (voice)
THE MEN'S CLUB   Atlantic Releasing Corporation, 1986
52 PICK-UP   Cannon, 1986
COHEN & TATE   Nelson Entertainment, 1989
LISTEN TO ME   Columbia, 1989

NIGHT GAME   Trans World Entertainment, 1989
SOMEBODY HAS TO SHOOT THE PICTURE (CTF)
   Alan Barnette Productions/Frank Pierson Films/MCA-TV
   Entertainment/Scholastic Productions, 1990
THE FOURTH WAR   Cannon, 1990
THE RUSSIA HOUSE   MGM-Pathe, 1990
NAKED LUNCH   20th Century Fox, 1991
ROMEO IS BLEEDING   Gramercy Pictures, 1994, U.S.-British

RAYNOR SCHEINE

FRIED GREEN TOMATOES   Universal, 1991

MARIA SCHELL

(Margarete Schell)
b. January 5, 1926 - Vienna, Austria

STEIBRUCH   1942, Swedish
DER ENGEL MIT DER POSAUNE   1948, Austrian-West German
ANGEL WITH THE TRUMPET   1949, British
DIE LETZTE NACHT   1949, West German
ES KOMMT EIN TAG   1950, West German
ANGELIKA   *DR. HOLL*   1951, West German
THE MAGIC BOX   Rank, 1951, British
SO LITTLE TIME   MacDonald, 1952, British
TAGEBUCH EINER VERLIEBTEN   1953, West German
DREAMING LIPS   *DER TRAUMENDE MUND*   1953, West German
THE HEART OF THE MATTER   1953, British
THE LAST BRIDGE   *DIE LETZTE BRUCKE*   1955,
   West German-Yugoslavian
NAPOLEON   1955, French
THE RATS   *DIE RATTEN*   1955, West German
GERVAISE   1956, French
LIEBE   1956, West German
THE SINS OF ROSE BERND   *ROSE BERND*   1957, West German
WHITE NIGHTS   *LE NOTTI BIANCHE*   1957, Italian-French
END OF DESIRE   *UNE VIE*   1958, French-Italian
THE BROTHERS KARAMAZOV   1958
AS THE SEA RAGES   *RAUBFISCHER IN HELLAS*   1959,
   West German-Yugoslavian
THE HANGING TREE   1959
CIMARRON   MGM, 1960
THE MARK   Continental, 1961, British
ONLY A WOMAN   *ICH BIN AUCH NUR EINE FRAU*   1962,
   West German
L'ASSASSIN CONNAIT LA MUSIQUE   1963, French
THE DEVIL BY THE TAIL   *LE DIABLE PAR LA QUEUE*
   1971, French-Italian
99 WOMEN   *99 MUJERES*   1969,
   Spanish-Italian-West German-British
NIGHT OF THE BLOOD MONSTER   1971,
   Spanish-West German-British
THE ODESSA FILE   Columbia, 1974, British-West German
FOLIES BOURGEOISES   1976, French
VOYAGE OF THE DAMNED   Avco Embassy, 1976, British
SO ODER SO IST DAS LEBEN   1976, West German
JUST A GIGOLO   United Artists Classics, 1978, West German
SUPERMAN   Warner Bros., 1978
PLAYERS   Paramount, 1979

MAXIMILIAN SCHELL

b. December 8, 1930 - Vienna, Austria

KINDER MÜTTER UND EIN GENERAL   1955, West German
DER 20. JULI   1956, West German
REIFENDE JUGEND   1956, West German
EIN HERZ KEHRT HEIM   1956, West German
THE YOUNG LIONS   20th Century-Fox, 1958
HAMLET (TF)   1950, West German
JUDGMENT AT NUREMBERG ★★   United Artists, 1961
FIVE FINGER EXERCISE   1962
THE RELUCTANT SAINT   1962, U.S.-Italian
THE CONDEMNED OF ALTONA   *I SEQUESTRATI DI ALTONA*
   1963, Italian-French
TOPKAPI   1964
RETURN FROM THE ASHES   1965, U.S.-British
THE DEADLY AFFAIR   1967, British

BEYOND THE MOUNTAINS   *THE DESPERATE ONES*
   1967, Spanish-U.S.
COUNTERPOINT   Universal, 1968
THE CASTLE   *DAS SCHLOSS*   1968, West German-Swedish
KRAKATOA EAST OF JAVA   1969
PAULINA 1880   1972, French
POPE JOAN   Columbia, 1972, British
THE ODESSA FILE   Columbia, 1974, British-West German
THE PEDESTRIAN   Cinerama Releasing Corporation, 1974,
   West German-Swedish-Israeli (also directed)
THE MAN IN THE GLASS BOOTH ★   American Film Theatre, 1975
ST. IVES   Warner Bros., 1976
THE DAY THAT SHOOK THE WORLD   *ASSASSINATION IN
   SARAJEVO*   1976, Yugoslavian-Czech
A BRIDGE TOO FAR   United Artists, 1977, British
CROSS OF IRON   1977, British-West German
JULIA ⊙   20th Century-Fox, 1977
AMO NON AMO   1978, Italian
AVALANCHE EXPRESS   20th Century-Fox, 1979
THE BLACK HOLE   Buena Vista, 1979
PLAYERS   Paramount, 1979
THE DIARY OF ANNE FRANK (TF)   Katz-Gallin/Half-Pint
   Productions/20th Century-Fox TV, 1981
THE CHOSEN   20th Century-Fox International Classics, 1981
MAN UNDER SUSPICION   1984
THE ASSISI UNDERGROUND   Cannon, 1985, Italian-British
PETER THE GREAT (MS)   PTG Productions/NBC
   Productions, 1986
THE FRESHMAN   TriStar, 1990

AUGUST SCHELLENBERG

FREE WILLY   Warner Bros., 1993
IRON WILL   Buena Vista, 1994
WILLY II: THE ADVENTURE HOME   Warner Bros., 1995

MARY KATE SCHELLHARDT

WILLY II: THE ADVENTURE HOME   Warner Bros., 1995

VINCENT SCHIAVELLI

COLD FEET   Avenue Pictures, 1989
GHOST   Paramount, 1990
WAITING FOR THE LIGHT   Triumph Releasing Corporation, 1990
FREEJACK   Warner Bros., 1992
BATMAN RETURNS   Warner Bros., 1992

EDWARD SCHICK

BIG   20th Century Fox, 1988

WILSON LAHTI SCHLAMME

MISS FIRECRACKER   Corsair Pictures, 1989

CHARLIE SCHLATTER

18 AGAIN   New World, 1988
BRIGHT LIGHTS, BIG CITY   MGM/UA, 1988
HEARTBREAK HOTEL   Buena Vista, 1988
POLICE ACADEMY: MISSION TO MOSCOW   Warner Bros., 1994

DAN SCHNEIDER

THE BIG PICTURE   Columbia, 1989
HAPPY TOGETHER   Borde Releasing Corporation, 1990

JOHN SCHNEIDER

b. April 8, 1954 - Mount Kisco, New York
Agent: William Morris Agency - Beverly Hills, 310/274-7451

EDDIE MACON'S RUN   Universal, 1983
STAGECOACH (TF)   Raymond Katz Productions/Heritage
   Entertainment, 1986
COCAINE WARS   Concorde, 1986, U.S.-Argentine
THE CURSE   Trans World Entertainment, 1987
CHRISTMAS COMES TO WILLOW CREEK (TF)   Blue Andre
   Productions/ITC Productions, 1987
OUTBACK BOUND (TF)   Andrew Gottlieb Productions/CBS
   Entertainment, 1988
MINISTRY OF VENGEANCE   MPCA, 1989

ROB SCHNEIDER
HOME ALONE 2: LOST IN NEW YORK   20th Century Fox, 1992
SURF NINJAS   New Line Cinema, 1993
DEMOLITION MAN   Warner Bros., 1993
THE BEVERLY HILLBILLIES   20th Century Fox, 1993
JUDGE DREDD   Buena Vista, 1995

MICHAEL SCHOEFFLING
SYLVESTER   Columbia, 1985
VISION QUEST   Warner Bros., 1985
BELIZAIRE THE CAJUN   Skouras Pictures, 1986
LET'S GET HARRY   TriStar, 1986
LONGTIME COMPANION   Samuel Goldwyn Company, 1990
MERMAIDS   Orion, 1990
WILD HEARTS CAN'T BE BROKEN   Buena Vista, 1991

JILL SCHOELEN
THE STEPFATHER   New Century/Vista, 1987
THE PHANTOM OF THE OPERA   Century Film Corporation, 1989
POPCORN   Studio Three, 1991
RICH GIRL   Studio Three, 1991

JASON SCHOMBING
TIMECOP   Universal, 1994

BITTY SCHRAM
A LEAGUE OF THEIR OWN   Columbia, 1992

AVERY SCHREIBER
b. April 9, 1935 - Chicago, Illinois

SWASHBUCKLER   Universal, 1976
GALAXINA   Crown International, 1980
LOOSE SHOES   *COMING ATTRACTIONS*   Atlantic Releasing
   Corporation, 1980
SILENT SCREAM   American Cinema, 1980
HUNK   Crown International, 1987

LIEV SCHREIBER
LIFESAVERS   TriStar, 1994

RICK SCHRODER
(Ricky Schroder)
b. April 3, 1970 - Staten Island, New York

THE CHAMP   MGM/United Artists, 1979
THE LAST FLIGHT OF NOAH'S ARK   Buena Vista, 1980
LITTLE LORD FAUNTLEROY (TF)   Norman Rosemont Productions,
   1980, U.S.-British
THE EARTHLING   1981, Australian
A REASON TO LIVE (TF)   Papazian Productions, 1985
A SON'S PROMISE (TF)   Marian Rees Associates, 1990
THERE GOES MY BABY   Orion, 1994

ERIK SCHRODY
JUDGMENT NIGHT   Universal, 1993

JOHN SCHUCK
M*A*S*H*   20th Century-Fox, 1970
HAMMERSMITH IS OUT   Cinerama Releasing Corporation, 1972
BLADE   Joseph Green Pictures, 1973
THIEVES LIKE US   United Artists, 1974
BUTCH AND SUNDANCE: THE EARLY DAYS
   20th Century-Fox, 1979
EARTHBOUND   Taft International, 1981
STAR TREK IV: THE VOYAGE HOME   Paramount, 1986
OUTRAGEOUS FORTUNE   Buena Vista, 1987
THE NEW ADVENTURES OF PIPPI LONGSTOCKING
   Columbia, 1988
DICK TRACY   Buena Vista, 1990
STAR TREK VI: THE UNDISCOVERED COUNTRY
   Paramount, 1991
HOLY MATRIMONY   Buena Vista, 1994

REBECCA SCHULL
MY LIFE   Columbia, 1993

DWIGHT SCHULTZ
ALONE IN THE DARK   New Line Cinema, 1982
THE A-TEAM (TF)   Stephen J. Cannell Productions, 1983
PERRY MASON: THE CASE OF THE SINISTER SPIRIT (TF)
   The Fred Silverman Company/Strathmore Productions/Viacom
   Productions, 1987
FAT MAN AND LITTLE BOY   Paramount, 1989
THE LONG WALK HOME   Miramax Films, 1990
THE TEMP   Paramount, 1993
MENENDEZ: A KILLING IN BEVERLY HILLS (MS)   Zev Braun
   Pictures/TriStar Television, 1994

JEFF SCHULZ
THE STEPFATHER   New Century/Vista, 1987

JERRY SCHUMACHER
Contact: 408/438-8717 or 408/625-5994

TURNER AND HOOCH   Buena Vista, 1989
THE ROOKIE   Warner Bros., 1990

IVYANN SCHWAN
PROBLEM CHILD 2   Universal, 1991

AARON SCHWARTZ
HEAVYWEIGHTS   Buena Vista, 1994

ARNOLD SCHWARZENEGGER
(Arnold Strong)
b. July 30, 1947 - Graz, Austria
Agent: ICM - Beverly Hills, 310/550-4000

HERCULES IN NEW YORK   *HERCULES GOES BANANAS/*
   HERCULES—THE MOVIE   Filmpartners, 1970
THE LONG GOODBYE   United Artists, 1973
STAY HUNGRY   United Artists, 1976
PUMPING IRON (FD)   Cinema 5, 1977
THE VILLAIN   Columbia, 1979
SCAVENGER HUNT   20th Century-Fox, 1979
THE JAYNE MANSFIELD STORY (TF)   Alan Landsburg
   Productions, 1980
CONAN THE BARBARIAN   Universal, 1982
CONAN THE DESTROYER   Universal, 1984
THE TERMINATOR   Orion, 1984
RED SONJA   MGM/UA, 1985
COMMANDO   20th Century Fox, 1985
RAW DEAL   DEG, 1986
PREDATOR   20th Century Fox, 1987
THE RUNNING MAN   TriStar, 1987
RED HEAT   TriStar, 1988
TWINS   Universal, 1988
TOTAL RECALL   TriStar, 1990
KINDERGARTEN COP   Universal, 1990
TERMINATOR 2: JUDGMENT DAY   TriStar, 1991
FEED (FD)   Original Cinema, 1992 (uncredited)
DAVE   Warner Bros., 1993
LAST ACTION HERO   Columbia, 1993
TRUE LIES   20th Century Fox, 1994
JUNIOR   Universal, 1994

ERIC SCHWEIG
THE LAST OF THE MOHICANS   20th Century Fox, 1992
INDIAN WARRIOR   Buena Vista, 1994
THE BROKEN CHAIN (CTF)   Turner Network Television, 1993
PONTIAC MOON   Paramount, 1994

HANNA SCHYGULLA
THE MARRIAGE OF MARIA BRAUN   New Yorker, 1978,
   West German
THE DELTA FORCE   Cannon, 1986
CASANOVA (TF)   Konigsberg-Sanitsky Company/Reteitalia,
   1987, U.S.-Italian
DEAD AGAIN   Paramount, 1991

ANNABELLA SCIORRA

Agent: CAA - Beverly Hills, 310/288-4545

TRUE LOVE   MGM/UA, 1989
INTERNAL AFFAIRS   Paramount, 1990
CADILLAC MAN   Orion, 1990
REVERSAL OF FORTUNE   Warner Bros., 1990
THE HARD WAY   Universal, 1991
JUNGLE FEVER   Universal, 1991
THE HAND THAT ROCKS THE CRADLE   Buena Vista, 1992
WHISPERS IN THE DARK   Paramount, 1992
THE NIGHT WE NEVER MET   Miramax Films, 1993
MR. WONDERFUL   Warner Bros., 1993
ROMEO IS BLEEDING   Gramercy Pictures, 1994, U.S.-British
THE CURE   Universal, 1995

PAUL SCOFIELD

b. January 21, 1922 - Hurstpierpoint, England

THAT LADY   20th Century-Fox, 1954, British
CARVE HER NAME WITH PRIDE   Lopert, 1958, British
THE TRAIN   United Artists, 1965 U.S.-French-Italian
A MAN FOR ALL SEASONS ★★   Columbia, 1966, British
TELL ME LIES   Continental, 1968, British
KING LEAR   Altura, 1971, British-Danish
BARTLEBY   Maron Films, Ltd., 1972, British
SCORPIO   United Artists, 1973
A DELICATE BALANCE   American Film Theatre Productions, 1973
ANNA KARENINA (TF)   Rastar Productions/Colgems
    Productions, 1985
THE ATTIC: THE HIDING OF ANNE FRANK (TF)
    Telecom Entertainment/Yorkshire TV, 1988, U.S.-British
WHEN THE WHALES CAME   20th Century Fox, 1989, British
HENRY V   Samuel Goldwyn Company, 1989, British
HAMLET   Warner Bros., 1990, British
QUIZ SHOW   Buena Vista, 1994

TRACY SCOGGINS

THE GUMSHOE KID   Argus Entertainment, 1989

PETER SCOLARI

b. New Rochelle, Illinois

FATAL CONFESSION: A FATHER DOWLING MYSTERY (TF)   The
    Fred Silverman Company/Strathmore Productions/Viacom, 1987
THE RYAN WHITE STORY (TF)   The Landsburg Company, 1989

MARTIN SCORSESE

b. November 17, 1942 - Flushing, New York
Agent: CAA - Beverly Hills, 310/288-4545

TAXI DRIVER   Columbia, 1976 (also directed)
AKIRA KUROSAWA'S DREAMS   *DREAMS*   Warner Bros.,
    1990, Japanese-U.S.
GUILTY BY SUSPICION   Warner Bros., 1991
THE AGE OF INNOCENCE   Columbia, 1993 (also directed)
QUIZ SHOW   Buena Vista, 1994

CAMPBELL SCOTT

b. July 19, 1961 - New York, New York
Agent: Paradigm - Los Angeles, 310/277-4400

FROM HOLLYWOOD TO DEADWOOD   Island Pictures, 1989
THE KENNEDYS OF MASSACHUSETTS (MS)   Edgar J. Scherick
    Associates/Orion TV, 1990
LONGTIME COMPANION   Samuel Goldwyn Company, 1990
THE SHELTERING SKY   Warner Bros., 1990, British
THE PERFECT TRIBUTE (CTF)   Dorothea Petrie Productions/
    Proctor & Gamble Productions/World International Network, 1991
DYING YOUNG   20th Century Fox, 1991
DEAD AGAIN   Paramount, 1991
SINGLES   Warner Bros., 1992
WHAT VENUS DID WITH MARS   Inside Out Productions, 1993
THE INNOCENT   Miramax Films, 1994, U.S.-German
MRS. PARKER AND THE VICIOUS CIRCLE   Fine Line Features/
    New Line Cinema, 1994
LET IT BE ME   Savoy Pictures, 1995
PASTA E FUSILLE   1995 (also co-directed)

DEBRALEE SCOTT

AMERICAN GRAFFITI   Universal, 1973
OUR TIME   Warner Bros., 1974
THE REINCARNATION OF PETER PROUD
    American International, 1975
POLICE ACADEMY   The Ladd Company/Warner Bros., 1984
POLICE ACADEMY 3: BACK IN TRAINING   Warner Bros., 1986

DONOVAN SCOTT

ZORRO, THE GAY BLADE   20th Century-Fox, 1981
THE BEST OF TIMES   Universal, 1986

GEORGE C. SCOTT

(George Campbell Scott)
b. October 18, 1927 - Wise, Virginia
Contact: Becker London and Kossow - New York, 212/541-7070

THE HANGING TREE   Warner Bros., 1959
ANATOMY OF A MURDER ✪   Columbia, 1959
THE HUSTLER ✪   20th Century-Fox, 1961
THE LIST OF ADRIAN MESSENGER   Universal, 1963
DR. STRANGELOVE OR: HOW I LEARNED TO STOP WORRYING
    AND LOVE THE BOMB   Columbia, 1964, British
THE YELLOW ROLLS-ROYCE   MGM, 1964, British
THE BIBLE...IN THE BEGINNING   20th Century-Fox, 1966, Italian
NOT WITH MY WIFE YOU DON'T!   Warner Bros., 1966
THE FLIM-FLAM MAN   20th Century-Fox, 1967
PETULIA   Warner Bros., 1968, U.S.-British
THIS SAVAGE LAND   Universal, 1968
PATTON ★★   20th Century-Fox, 1970
JANE EYRE (TF)   Omnibus Productions/Sagittarius Productions,
    1970, British-U.S.
THEY MIGHT BE GIANTS   Universal, 1971
THE LAST RUN   MGM, 1971
THE HOSPITAL ★   United Artists, 1971
THE NEW CENTURIONS   Columbia, 1972
RAGE   Warner Bros., 1972 (also directed)
OKLAHOMA CRUDE   Columbia, 1973
THE DAY OF THE DOLPHIN   Avco Embassy, 1973
BANK SHOT   United Artists, 1974
THE SAVAGE IS LOOSE   Campbell Devon, 1974 (also directed)
THE HINDENBURG   Universal, 1975
FEAR ON TRIAL (TF)   Alan Landsburg Productions, 1975
BEAUTY AND THE BEAST (TF)   Palms Films, Ltd., 1976, British
ISLANDS IN THE STREAM   Paramount, 1977
CROSSED SWORDS   *THE PRINCE AND THE PAUPER*
    Warner Bros., 1978, British
MOVIE MOVIE   Warner Bros., 1978
HARDCORE   Columbia, 1979
THE CHANGELING   AFD, 1980, Canadian
THE FORMULA   MGM/United Artists, 1980
TAPS   20th Century-Fox, 1981
OLIVER TWIST (TF)   Claridge Group Ltd./Grafton Films,
    1982, British
CHINA ROSE (TF)   Robert Halmi, Inc., 1983
FIRESTARTER   Universal, 1984
A CHRISTMAS CAROL (TF)   Entertainment Partners Ltd.,
    1984, U.S.-British
MUSSOLINI: THE UNTOLD STORY (MS)   Trian Productions, 1985
CHOICES (TF)   Robert Halmi, Inc., 1986
THE LAST DAYS OF PATTON (TF)   Entertainment Partners, 1986
THE MURDERS IN THE RUE MORGUE (TF)   Robert Halmi, Inc./
    International Film Productions, 1986
PALS (TF)   Robert Halmi, Inc., 1986
THE RYAN WHITE STORY (TF)   The Landsburg Company, 1989
DESCENDING ANGEL (CTF)   HBO Pictures, 1990
THE EXORCIST III   20th Century Fox, 1990
THE RESCUERS DOWN UNDER (AF)   Buena Vista, 1990 (voice)
FINDING THE WAY HOME (TF)   Peter K. Duchow Enterprises, 1991
MALICE   Columbia, 1993

JOAN SCOTT

GUILTY BY SUSPICION   Warner Bros., 1991

KIMBERLY SCOTT

THE ABYSS   20th Century Fox, 1989
THE CLIENT   Warner Bros., 1994

LARRY B. SCOTT

EXTREME PREJUDICE   TriStar, 1987

MARTHA SCOTT

b. September 22, 1914 - Jamesport, Missouri

OUR TOWN ★   United Artists, 1940
THE HOWARDS OF VIRGINIA   Columbia, 1940
CHEERS FOR MISS BISHOP   United Artists, 1941
THEY DARE NOT LOVE   Columbia, 1941
ONE FOOT IN HEAVEN   Warner Bros., 1941
HI DIDDLE DIDDLE *DIAMONDS AND CRIME*   RKO Radio, 1943
STAGE DOOR CANTEEN   United Artists, 1943
IN OLD OKLAHOMA *WAR OF THE WILDCATS*   Republic, 1943
SO WELL REMEMBERED   RKO Radio, 1947, British
STRANGE BARGAIN   RKO Radio, 1949
WHEN I GROW UP   United Artists, 1951
THE DESPERATE HOURS   Paramount, 1955
THE TEN COMMANDMENTS   Paramount, 1956
SAYONARA   Warner Bros., 1957
EIGHTEEN AND ANXIOUS   Republic, 1957
BEN-HUR   MGM, 1959
CHARLOTTE'S WEB (AF)   Paramount, 1973 (voice)
AIRPORT 1975   Universal, 1974
THE ABDUCTION OF SAINT ANNE *THEY'VE KIDNAPPED ANNE BENEDICT* (TF)   QM Productions, 1975
THE TURNING POINT   20th Century-Fox, 1977
THE WORD (MS)   Charles Fries Productions/Stonehenge Productions, 1978
CHARLESTON (TF)   Robert Stigwood Productions/RSO, Inc., 1979
BEULAH LAND (MS)   David Gerber Company/Columbia TV, 1980

TIM SCOTT

Agent: Susan Smith & Associates - Beverly Hills, 213/852-4777

SILENT TONGUE   Trimark Pictures, 1994, U.S.-French

STEVEN SEAGAL

b. April 10, 1951 - Lansing, Michigan
Agent: CAA - Beverly Hills, 310/288-4545

ABOVE THE LAW   Warner Bros., 1988
HARD TO KILL   Warner Bros., 1990
MARKED FOR DEATH   20th Century Fox, 1990
OUT FOR JUSTICE   Warner Bros., 1991
UNDER SIEGE   Warner Bros., 1992
ON DEADLY GROUND   Warner Bros., 1994 (also directed)
UNDER SIEGE 2   Warner Bros., 1995
FIRE DOWN BELOW   Columbia, 1995

JENNY SEAGROVE

THE GUARDIAN   Universal, 1990

DOUGLAS SEALE

THE RESCUERS DOWN UNDER (AF)   Buena Vista, 1990 (voice)
ALADDIN (AF)   Buena Vista, 1992 (voice)

DAVID SEAMAN JR.

THE NEW ADVENTURES OF PIPPI LONGSTOCKING   Columbia, 1988

NICK SEARCY

FRIED GREEN TOMATOES   Universal, 1991
NELL   20th Century Fox, 1994

KYLE SECOR

HEART OF DIXIE   Orion, 1989
DELUSION   I.R.S. Releasing, 1991
DROP ZONE   Paramount, 1994

JON SEDA

I LIKE IT LIKE THAT   Columbia, 1994

KYRA SEDGWICK

Agent: CAA - Beverly Hills, 310/288-4545

LEMON SKY   American Playhouse Theatrical Films, 1988
KANSAS   Trans World Entertainment, 1988
BORN ON THE FOURTH OF JULY   Universal, 1989
MR. AND MRS. BRIDGE   Miramax Films, 1990
WOMEN & MEN: IN LOVE THERE ARE NO RULES (CTF)   David Brown Productions/HBO Showcase, 1991
SINGLES   Warner Bros., 1992
FAMILY PICTURES (TF)   Alexander, Enright & Associates/Hearst Entertainment, 1993
HEART AND SOULS   Universal, 1993

GEORGE SEGAL

b. February 13, 1934 - New York, New York

THE YOUNG DOCTORS   United Artists, 1961
THE LONGEST DAY   20th Century-Fox, 1962
ACT ONE   Warner Bros., 1963
THE NEW INTERNS   Columbia, 1964
INVITATION TO A GUNFIGHTER   United Artists, 1964
SHIP OF FOOLS   Columbia, 1965
KING RAT   Columbia, 1965, British
WHO'S AFRAID OF VIRGINIA WOOLF? ✪   Warner Bros., 1966
LOST COMMAND   Columbia, 1966
THE QUILLER MEMORANDUM   Paramount, 1966, British
THE ST. VALENTINE'S DAY MASSACRE   20th Century-Fox, 1967
BYE BYE BRAVERMAN   Warner Bros., 1968
NO WAY TO TREAT A LADY   Paramount, 1968
THE GIRL WHO COULDN'T SAY NO *TENDERLY*   Italnoleggio, 1968, Italian
THE SOUTHERN STAR *L'ETOILE DU SUD*   Columbia, 1969, French-British
THE BRIDGE AT REMAGEN   United Artists, 1969
LOVING   Columbia, 1970
THE OWL AND THE PUSSYCAT   Columbia, 1970
WHERE'S POPPA?   United Artists, 1970
BORN TO WIN   United Artists, 1971
THE HOT ROCK   20th Century-Fox, 1972
A TOUCH OF CLASS   Avco Embassy, 1973
BLUME IN LOVE   Warner Bros., 1973
THE TERMINAL MAN   Warner Bros., 1974
CALIFORNIA SPLIT   Columbia, 1974
RUSSIAN ROULETTE   Avco Embassy, 1975, U.S.-Canadian
THE BLACK BIRD   Columbia, 1975
THE DUCHESS AND THE DIRTWATER FOX   20th Century-Fox, 1976
FUN WITH DICK AND JANE   Columbia, 1977
ROLLERCOASTER   Universal, 1977
WHO IS KILLING THE GREAT CHEFS OF EUROPE?   Warner Bros., 1978
LOST AND FOUND   Columbia, 1979
THE LAST MARRIED COUPLE IN AMERICA   Universal, 1980
CARBON COPY   Avco Embassy, 1981
TRACKDOWN: FINDING THE GOODBAR KILLER (TF)   Grosso-Jacobson Productions, 1983
THE COLD ROOM (CTF)   Jethro Films/Mark Forstater Productions, 1984, British
THE ZANY ADVENTURES OF ROBIN HOOD (TF)   Bobka Productions/Charles Fries Entertainment, 1984
NOT MY KID (TF)   Beth Polson Productions/Finnegan Associates, 1985
KILLING 'EM SOFTLY   Intermarket Pictures Corporation, 1985, Canadian
STICK   Universal, 1985
MANY HAPPY RETURNS (TF)   Alan M. Levin & Steven H. Stern Films, 1986, U.S.-Canadian
ALL'S FAIR   Moviestore Entertainment, 1989
LOOK WHO'S TALKING   TriStar, 1989
THE ENDLESS GAME (CTF)   TVS Films/Reteitalia/Pixit, 1990, British-Italian
FOR THE BOYS   20th Century Fox, 1991
ME MYSELF AND I   I.R.S. Releasing, 1992
LOOK WHO'S TALKING NOW   TriStar, 1993

PAMELA SEGALL
Agent: UTA - Beverly Hills, 310/273-6700

PLEASURES (TF)   Catalina Production Group/Columbia TV, 1986
GATE II   Triumph Releasing Corporation, 1992

EMMANUELLE SEIGNER
DETECTIVE   Spectrafilm, 1985, French
FRANTIC   Warner Bros., 1988
BITTER MOON   Fine Line Features/New Line Cinema,
    1993, French-British

TSUTOMU SEKINE
ERIK THE VIKING   Orion, 1989, British

DAVID SELBERG
MENENDEZ: A KILLING IN BEVERLY HILLS (MS)   Zev Braun
    Pictures/TriStar Television, 1994

DAVID SELBY
Agent: ICM - Beverly Hills, 310/550-4000

DYING YOUNG   20th Century Fox, 1991

MARIAN SELDES
THE GUN IN BETTY LOU'S HANDBAG   Buena Vista, 1992

TOM SELLECK
b. January 29, 1945 - Detroit, Michigan

THE MOVIE MURDERER (TF)   Universal TV, 1970
MYRA BRECKINRIDGE   20th Century-Fox, 1970
THE SEVEN MINUTES   20th Century-Fox, 1971
DAUGHTERS OF SATAN   United Artists, 1972
TERMINAL ISLAND   Dimension, 1973
A CASE OF RAPE (TF)   Universal TV, 1974
RETURNING HOME (TF)   Lorimar Productions/Samuel Goldwyn
    Productions, 1975
MOST WANTED (TF)   QM Productions, 1976
MIDWAY   Universal, 1976
THE WASHINGTON AFFAIR   1977
COMA   MGM/United Artists, 1978
THE SACKETTS (TF)   Douglas Netter Enterprises/M.B. Scott
    Productions/Shalako Enterprises, 1979
THE CONCRETE COWBOYS (TF)   Frankel Films, 1979
DIVORCE WARS: A LOVE STORY (TF)   Wrye-Konigsberg Films/
    Warner Bros. TV, 1982
THE SHADOW RIDERS (TF)   The Pegasus Group Ltd./
    Columbia TV, 1982
HIGH ROAD TO CHINA   Warner Bros., 1983, U.S.-Yugoslavian
LASSITER   Warner Bros., 1984
RUNAWAY   TriStar, 1984
THREE MEN AND A BABY   Buena Vista, 1987
HER ALIBI   Warner Bros., 1989
AN INNOCENT MAN   Buena Vista, 1989
THREE MEN AND A LITTLE LADY   Buena Vista, 1990
QUIGLEY DOWN UNDER   MGM/UA, 1990
FOLKS   20th Century Fox, 1992
MR. BASEBALL   Universal, 1992
CHRISTOPHER COLUMBUS: THE DISCOVERY   Warner Bros.,
    1992, British-Spanish

WILL SELTZER
THE WIZARD   Universal, 1989

JOE SENECA
CROSSROADS   Columbia, 1986
THE BLOB   TriStar, 1988
THE SAINT OF FORT WASHINGTON   Warner Bros., 1993

BRONWEN SENNISH
MISS FIRECRACKER   Corsair Pictures, 1989

YAHOO SERIOUS
(Greg Pead)
YOUNG EINSTEIN   Warner Bros., 1988, Australian

ASSUMPTA SERNA
WILD ORCHID   Triumph Releasing Corporation, 1990
NOSTRADAMUS   Orion Classics, 1994, British

PEPE SERNA
THE ROOKIE   Warner Bros., 1990

JOHN SESSIONS
PRINCESS CARABOO   TriStar, 1994

ROSHAN SETH
Agent: Susan Smith & Associates - Beverly Hills, 213/852-4777

GANDHI   Columbia, 1982, British-Indian
INDIANA JONES AND THE TEMPLE OF DOOM   Paramount, 1984
NOT WITHOUT MY DAUGHTER   MGM-Pathe, 1991

BRIAN SETZER
LA BAMBA   Columbia, 1987

JOAN SEVERANCE
SEE NO EVIL, HEAR NO EVIL   TriStar, 1989
NO HOLDS BARRED   New Line Cinema, 1989
BIRD ON A WIRE   Universal, 1990
ANGEL OF DESIRE   Trimark, 1994

RUFUS SEWELL
CARRINGTON   Gramercy Pictures, 1995

JANE SEYMOUR
b. February 15, 1951 - Middlesex, England
Agent: Metropolitan Talent Agency - Los Angeles, 213/857-4500

OH! WHAT A LOVELY WAR   Paramount, 1969, British
YOUNG WINSTON   Columbia, 1972, British
LIVE AND LET DIE   United Artists, 1973, British
FRANKENSTEIN: THE TRUE STORY (TF)   Universal TV, 1973
THE HANGED MAN (TF)   Fenady Associates/Bing Crosby
    Productions, 1974
SINBAD AND THE EYE OF THE TIGER   Columbia, 1977, British
CAPTAINS AND THE KINGS (MS)   Universal TV, 1976
LAS VEGAS UNDERCOVER (TF)   1977
SEVENTH AVENUE (MS)   Universal TV, 1977
KILLER ON BOARD (TF)   Lorimar Productions, 1977
THE FOUR FEATHERS (TF)   Norman Rosemont Productions/
    Trident Films, Ltd., 1977, U.S.-British
SOMEWHERE IN TIME   Universal, 1980
JOHN STEINBECK'S EAST OF EDEN *EAST OF EDEN* (MS)
    Mace Neufeld Productions, 1981
THE SCARLET PIMPERNEL (TF)   London Films, Ltd., 1982, British
JAMAICA INN (MS)   HTV/Metromedia Producers Corporation/United
    Media, Ltd./Jamaica Inn Productions, 1983, British-U.S.
THE SUN ALSO RISES (MS)   Furia-Oringer Productions/
    20th Century Fox TV, 1984
DARK MIRROR (TF)   Aaron Spelling Productions, 1984
OBSESSED WITH A MARRIED WOMAN (TF)   Sidaris-Camhe
    Productions/The Feldman-Meeker Company, 1985
CROSSINGS (MS)   Aaron Spelling Productions, 1986
THE WOMAN HE LOVED (TF)   The Larry Thompson Organization/
    HTV/New World TV, 1988, U.S.-British
JACK THE RIPPER (MS)   Euston Films/Thames TV/Hill-O'Connor
    Entertainment/Lorimar TV, 1988, British-U.S.
RICHEST MAN IN THE WORLD: THE ARISTOTLE ONASSIS
    STORY (MS)   The Konigsberg-Sanitsky Company, 1988
WAR AND REMEMBRANCE (MS)   Dan Curtis Productions/
    ABC Circle Films, 1988-89
KEYS TO FREEDOM   RPB Pictures/Queens Cross Productions, 1989

SHABBA-DOO
(See Adolpho "Shabba-Doo" QUINONES)

GLENN SHADIX
HEATHERS   New World, 1989
DEMOLITION MAN   Warner Bros., 1993

TUPAC SHAKUR
POETIC JUSTICE   Columbia, 1993
ABOVE THE RIM   New Line Cinema, 1994

TONY SHALHOUB
Agent: William Morris Agency - Beverly Hills, 310/274-7451

BARTON FINK   20th Century Fox, 1991
I.Q.   Paramount, 1994

DANIEL SHALIKAR
HONEY, I BLEW UP THE KID   Buena Vista, 1992

JOSHUA SHALIKAR
HONEY, I BLEW UP THE KID   Buena Vista, 1992

GARRY SHANDLING
b. November 29, 1949 - Tucson, Arizona

LOVE AFFAIR   Warner Bros., 1994
LIFESAVERS   TriStar, 1994

MICHAEL J. SHANNON
THE TED KENNEDY, JR. STORY (TF)   Entertainment
   Partners, 1986

JAMES ANTHONY SHANTA
THE ALLNIGHTER   Universal, 1987

OMAR SHARIF
(Michael Shalhoub)
b. April 10, 1932 - Alexandria, Egypt
Agent: William Morris Agency - Beverly Hills, 310/274-7451

THE STRUGGLE IN THE VALLEY   1953, Egyptian
DEVIL OF THE DESERT   1954, Egyptian
LAND OF PEACE   1955, Egyptian
GOHA   1957, Egyptian-French
SCANDAL AT ZAMALEK   1958, Egyptian
STRUGGLE ON THE NILE   1959, Egyptian
THE AGONY OF LOVE   1960, Egyptian
THE MAMELUKS   1963, Egyptian
LAWRENCE OF ARABIA ✪   Columbia, 1962, British
THE FALL OF THE ROMAN EMPIRE   Paramount, 1964
BEHOLD A PALE HORSE   Columbia, 1964
THE YELLOW ROLLS-ROYCE   MGM, 1965, British
GENGHIS KHAN   Columbia, 1965,
   U.S.-British-West German-Yugoslavian
MARCO THE MAGNIFICENT   MGM, 1965,
   French-Italian-Egyptian-Afghanistan
DOCTOR ZHIVAGO   MGM, 1965, British
THE POPPY IS ALSO A FLOWER   Cornet, 1966
NIGHT OF THE GENERALS   Columbia, 1967, British-French
MORE THAN A MIRACLE   MGM, 1967, Italian-French
FUNNY GIRL   Columbia, 1968
MAYERLING   MGM, 1968, British-French
MACKENNA'S GOLD   Columbia, 1969
CHE!   20th Century-Fox, 1969
THE APPOINTMENT   MGM, 1969
THE LAST VALLEY   Cinerama Releasing Corporation, 1971, British
THE HORSEMEN   Columbia, 1971
THE BURGLARS   *LE CASSE*   Columbia, 1972, French
THE RIGHT TO LOVE   *LE DROIT D'AIMER*   1972, French
THE MYSTERIOUS ISLAND OF CAPTAIN NEMO   Cinerama
   Releasing Corporation, 1973, French-Spanish
THE TAMARIND SEED   Avco Embassy, 1974
JUGGERNAUT   United Artists, 1974, British
FUNNY LADY   Columbia, 1975
CRIME AND PASSION   American International, 1976,
   U.S.-West German
ASHANTI   Columbia, 1979, Swiss-U.S.

SIDNEY SHELDON'S BLOODLINE   *BLOODLINE*   Paramount, 1979
THE BALTIMORE BULLET   Avco Embassy, 1980
OH, HEAVENLY DOG!   20th Century-Fox, 1980
GREEN ICE   Universal/AFD, 1981, British
INCHON!   MGM/UA, 1982, South Korean
TOP SECRET!   Paramount, 1984
ANASTASIA: THE MYSTERY OF ANNA (TF)   Telecom
   Entertainment/Consolidated Productions/Reteitalia,
   1986, U.S.-Italian
KEYS TO FREEDOM   RPB Pictures/Queens Cross
   Productions, 1989
MOUNTAINS OF THE MOON   TriStar, 1990
JOURNEY OF LOVE   *VIAGGIO D'AMORE*   Centaur Releasing,
   1990, Italian

MICHAEL SHARRETT
DEADLY FRIEND   Warner Bros., 1986

MELANIE SHATNER
OF UNKNOWN ORIGIN   Concorde, 1994

WILLIAM SHATNER
b. March 22, 1931 - Montreal, Quebec, Canada

THE BROTHERS KARAMAZOV   MGM, 1958
JUDGMENT AT NUREMBERG   United Artists, 1961
THE EXPLOSIVE GENERATION   United Artists, 1961
THE INTRUDER   *I HATE YOUR GUTS!/SHAME*
   Pathe American, 1961
THE OUTRAGE   MGM, 1964
HOUR OF VENGEANCE   1968, Italian
THE PEOPLE (TF)   Metromedia Productions/American
   Zoetrope, 1971
GO ASK ALICE (TF)   Metromedia Productions, 1972
HORROR AT 37,000 FEET (TF)   CBS, Inc., 1972
BIG BAD MAMA   New World, 1974
DEAD OF NIGHT   1974
THE DEVIL'S RAIN   Bryanston, 1975, U.S.-Mexican
IMPULSE   *WANT A RIDE, LITTLE GIRL?*   1975
A WHALE OF A TIME   1977
KINGDOM OF THE SPIDERS   Dimension, 1977
THE LAND OF NO RETURN   *SNOWMAN/CHALLENGE TO*
   SURVIVE   International Picture Show, 1978
THE THIRD WALKER   1978, Canadian
RIEL   CBC/Green River Productions, 1979, Canadian
STAR TREK - THE MOTION PICTURE   Paramount, 1979
THE KIDNAPPING OF THE PRESIDENT   Crown International,
   1980, U.S.-Canadian
STAR TREK II: THE WRATH OF KHAN   Paramount, 1982
VISITING HOURS   20th Century-Fox, 1982, Canadian
T.J. HOOKER (TF)   Spelling-Goldberg Productions, 1982
AIRPLANE II: THE SEQUEL   Paramount, 1982
SECRETS OF A MARRIED MAN (TF)   ITC Productions, 1984
STAR TREK III: THE SEARCH FOR SPOCK   Paramount, 1984
NORTH BEACH AND RAWHIDE (MS)   CBS Entertainment, 1985
STAR TREK IV: THE VOYAGE HOME   Paramount, 1986
BROKEN ANGEL (TF)   The Stan Margulies Company/
   MGM-UA TV, 1988
STAR TREK V: THE FINAL FRONTIER   Paramount,
   1989 (also directed)
STAR TREK VI: THE UNDISCOVERED COUNTRY
   Paramount, 1991
NATIONAL LAMPOON'S LOADED WEAPON 1
   New Line Cinema, 1993
STAR TREK GENERATIONS   Paramount, 1994

HELEN SHAVER
BEST DEFENSE   Paramount, 1984
DESERT HEARTS   Samuel Goldwyn Company, 1985
THE COLOR OF MONEY   Buena Vista, 1986
THE BELIEVERS   Orion, 1987
PAIR OF ACES (TF)   Pedernales Films/Once Upon A Time
   Films, Ltd., 1990
THAT NIGHT   Warner Bros., 1993
MORNING GLORY   Academy Entertainment, 1993
THE FORGET-ME-NOT MURDERS (TF)   CBS, 1994
KATIE   Warner Bros., 1995

FIONA SHAW

MY LEFT FOOT   Miramax Films, 1989, Irish-British
MOUNTAINS OF THE MOON   TriStar, 1990
THREE MEN AND A LITTLE LADY   Buena Vista, 1990
UNDERCOVER BLUES   MGM/UA, 1993

STAN SHAW

THE BINGO LONG TRAVELING ALL-STARS AND MOTOR KINGS
    Universal, 1976
ROCKY   United Artists, 1976
THE BOYS IN COMPANY C   Columbia, 1978
THE GREAT SANTINI   *THE ACE*   Orion/Warner Bros., 1980
SCARED STRAIGHT! ANOTHER STORY (TF)
    Golden West TV, 1980
RUNAWAY   TriStar, 1984
UNDER SIEGE (TF)   Ohlmeyer Communications Company/
    Telepictures Productions, 1986
THE MONSTER SQUAD   TriStar, 1987
BILLIONAIRE BOYS CLUB (MS)   Donald March/Gross-Weston
    Productions/ITC Productions, 1987
RED RIVER (TF)   Catalina Production Group/MGM-UA TV, 1988
HARLEM NIGHTS   Paramount, 1989
FRIED GREEN TOMATOES   Universal, 1991
HOUSEGUEST   Buena Vista, 1995

VINESSA SHAW

LADYBUGS   Paramount, 1992
HOCUS POCUS   Buena Vista, 1993

WALLACE SHAWN

Agent: William Morris Agency - Beverly Hills, 310/274-7451

STARTING OVER   Paramount, 1979
MANHATTAN   United Artists, 1979
MY DINNER WITH ANDRE   New Yorker, 1981
A LITTLE SEX   Universal, 1982
LOVESICK   The Ladd Company/Warner Bros., 1983
MICKI & MAUDE   Columbia, 1984
THE BEDROOM WINDOW   DEG, 1987
RADIO DAYS   Orion, 1987
THE MODERNS   Alive Films, 1988
SHE'S OUT OF CONTROL   Columbia, 1989
SCENES FROM THE CLASS STRUGGLE IN BEVERLY HILLS
    Cinecom, 1989
WE'RE NO ANGELS   Paramount, 1989
DICK AND MARGE SAVE THE WORLD   Warner Bros., 1992
MRS. PARKER AND THE VICIOUS CIRCLE   Fine Line Features/
    New Line Cinema, 1994

JOHN SHEA

Agent: William Morris Agency - Beverly Hills, 310/274-7451

HUSSY   Watchgrove Ltd., 1980, British
FAMILY REUNION (TF)   Creative Projects Inc./Columbia TV, 1981
MISSING   Universal, 1982
KENNEDY (MS)   Central Independent Television Productions/Alan
    Landsburg Productions, 1983, British-U.S.
WINDY CITY   Warner Bros., 1984
HONEYMOON   International Film Marketing, 1985,
    Canadian-French
HITLER'S S.S.: PORTRAIT IN EVIL (TF)   Colason Limited
    Productions/Edgar J. Scherick Associates, 1985, British-U.S.
THE IMPOSSIBLE SPY (CTF)   HBO Showcase/BBC/Quartet
    International/IMGC, 1987, British-Israeli
A NEW LIFE   Paramount, 1988
STEALING HOME   Warner Bros., 1988
BABY M (MS)   ABC Circle Films, 1988
DO YOU KNOW THE MUFFIN MAN? (TF)   The Avnet-Kerner
    Company, 1989
SMALL SACRIFICES (MS)   Louis Rudolph Films/Motown
    Productions/Allarcom Ltd./Fries Entertainment, 1989,
    U.S.-Canadian
FREEJACK   Warner Bros., 1992
HONEY, I BLEW UP THE KID   Buena Vista, 1992

RHONDA SHEAR

BASIC TRAINING   The Movie Store, 1985

HARRY SHEARER

THIS IS SPINAL TAP   Embassy, 1984
PURE LUCK   Universal, 1991
BLOOD AND CONCRETE   I.R.S. Releasing, 1991

ALLY SHEEDY

b. June 12, 1962 - New York, New York
Agent: William Morris Agency - Beverly Hills, 310/274-7451

THE BEST LITTLE GIRL IN THE WORLD (TF)   Aaron Spelling
    Productions, 1981
THE DAY THE LOVING STOPPED (TF)   Monash-Zeitman
    Productions, 1981
SPLENDOR IN THE GRASS (TF)   Katz-Gallin Productions/Half-Pint
    Productions/Warner Bros. TV, 1981
DEADLY LESSONS (TF)   1983
BAD BOYS   Universal/AFD, 1983
WARGAMES   MGM/UA, 1983
OXFORD BLUES   MGM/UA, 1984, British
THE BREAKFAST CLUB   Universal, 1985
ST. ELMO'S FIRE   Columbia, 1985
TWICE IN A LIFETIME   The Yorkin Company, 1985
BLUE CITY   Paramount, 1986
SHORT CIRCUIT   TriStar, 1986
WE ARE THE CHILDREN (TF)   Paulist Pictures/Dan Fauci-Ted
    Danson Productions/The Furia Organization, 1987
MAID TO ORDER   New Century/Vista, 1987
HEART OF DIXIE   Orion, 1989
BETSY'S WEDDING   Buena Vista, 1990
FEAR (CTF)   Richard Kobritz-Rockne S. O'Bannon Productions, 1990
ONLY THE LONELY   20th Century Fox, 1991
THE PICKLE   Columbia, 1993
MAN'S BEST FRIEND   New Line Cinema, 1993
PARALLEL LIVES (CTF)   Showtime Entertainment, 1994

BRIAN SHEEHAN

TOP GUN   Paramount, 1986

DOUG SHEEHAN

10   Orion/Warner Bros., 1979
STRANGER IN MY BED (TF)   Edgar J. Scherick Productions/Taft
    Entertainment TV, 1987
IN THE LINE OF DUTY: THE FBI MURDERS (TF)   Telecom
    Entertainment/World International Network, 1988

CHARLIE SHEEN

b. September 3, 1965 - New York, New York
Agent: William Morris Agency - Beverly Hills, 310/274-7451

THE EXECUTION OF PRIVATE SLOVIK (TF)   Universal TV, 1974
THE PREDATOR   1984 (unreleased)
RED DAWN   MGM/UA, 1984
THE BOYS NEXT DOOR   New World, 1985
FERRIS BUELLER'S DAY OFF   Paramount, 1986
WISDOM   20th Century Fox, 1986
LUCAS   20th Century Fox, 1986
THE WRAITH   New Century/Vista, 1986
PLATOON   Orion, 1986
THREE FOR THE ROAD   New Century/Vista, 1987
NO MAN'S LAND   Orion, 1987
WALL STREET   20th Century Fox, 1987
YOUNG GUNS   20th Century Fox, 1988
EIGHT MEN OUT   Orion, 1988
MAJOR LEAGUE   Paramount, 1989
COURAGE MOUNTAIN   Triumph Releasing Corporation,
    1989, U.S.-French
NAVY SEALS   Orion, 1990
MEN AT WORK   Triumph Releasing Corporation, 1990
THE ROOKIE   Warner Bros., 1990
BACKTRACK   *CATCHFIRE*   Vestron, 1991
CADENCE   New Line Cinema, 1991
HOT SHOTS!   20th Century Fox, 1991
HOT SHOTS! PART DEUX   20th Century Fox, 1993
THE THREE MUSKETEERS   Buena Vista, 1993
THE CHASE   20th Century Fox, 1994
MAJOR LEAGUE II   Warner Bros., 1994
TERMINAL VELOCITY   Buena Vista, 1994
MARTIN EDEN   1995

MARTIN SHEEN
(Ramon Estevez)
b. August 3, 1940 - Dayton, Ohio

THE INCIDENT   20th Century-Fox, 1967
THE SUBJECT WAS ROSES   MGM, 1968
CATCH-22   Paramount, 1970
GOODBYE, RAGGEDY ANN (TF)   Metromedia Producers
   Corporation, 1971
NO DRUMS, NO BUGLES   Cinerama Releasing Corporation, 1971
WELCOME HOME, JOHNNY BRISTOL (TF)   Cinema Center, 1971
WHEN THE LINE GOES THROUGH   1971 (unreleased)
THE FORESTS ARE NEARLY ALL GONE NOW   1972 (unreleased)
PICKUP ON 101   1972
PURSUIT (TF)   ABC Circle Films, 1972
RAGE   Warner Bros., 1972
THAT CERTAIN SUMMER (TF)   Universal TV, 1972
BADLANDS   Warner Bros., 1973
CATHOLICS (TF)   Sidney Glazier Productions, 1973, British
LETTERS FROM THREE LOVERS (TF)   Spelling-Goldberg
   Productions, 1973
MESSAGE TO MY DAUGHTER (TF)   Metromedia
   Productions, 1973
THE CALIFORNIA KID (TF)   Universal TV, 1974
THE EXECUTION OF PRIVATE SLOVIK (TF)   Universal TV, 1974
THE LEGEND OF EARL DURAND   1975
SWEET HOSTAGE (TF)   Brut Productions, 1975
THE CASSANDRA CROSSING   Avco Embassy, 1977,
   British-Italian-West German
THE LITTLE GIRL WHO LIVES DOWN THE LANE   American
   International, 1977, U.S.-Canadian-French
APOCALYPSE NOW   United Artists, 1979
EAGLE'S WING   International Picture Show, 1979, British
THE FINAL COUNTDOWN   United Artists, 1980
LOOPHOLE   MGM/United Artists, 1980, British
GANDHI   Columbia, 1982, British-Indian
THAT CHAMPIONSHIP SEASON   Cannon, 1982
ENIGMA   Embassy, 1982, British-French
MAN, WOMAN AND CHILD   Paramount, 1983
KENNEDY (MS)   Central Independent Television Productions/Alan
   Landsburg Productions, 1983, British-U.S.
THE DEAD ZONE   Paramount, 1983, Canadian
BROKEN RAINBOW (FD)   1985 (voice)
CONSENTING ADULT (TF)   Starger Company/David Lawrence and
   Ray Aghayan Productions, 1985
THE ATLANTA CHILD MURDERS (MS)   Mann-Rafshoon
   Productions/Finnegan Associates, 1985
OUT OF THE DARKNESS (TF)   Grosso-Jacobson Productions/
   Centerpoint Productions, 1985
SHATTERED SPIRITS (TF)   Sheen-Greenblatt Productions/Robert
   Greenwald Productions, 1986
NEWS AT ELEVEN (TF)   Turman-Foster Productions/Finnegan
   Associates, 1986
SAMARITAN: THE MITCH SNYDER STORY (TF)   Levine-Robbins
   Productions/Fries Entertainment, 1986
THE BELIEVERS   Orion, 1987
WALL STREET   20th Century Fox, 1987
DA   FilmDallas Pictures, 1988
PERSONAL CHOICE   Moviestore Entertainment, 1989
BEVERLY HILLS BRATS   Taurus Entertainment, 1989
CADENCE   New Line Cinema, 1991 (also directed)
ORIGINAL INTENT   Studio Three, 1991
GETTYSBURG   New Line Cinema, 1993
THE WAR AT HOME   Buena Vista, 1995
THE AMERICAN PRESIEDENT   Columbia, 1995

RUTH SHEEN
HIGH HOPES   Skouras Pictures, 1988, British

CRAIG SHEFFER
Agent: UTA - Beverly Hills, 310/273-6700

FIRE WITH FIRE   Paramount, 1986
SOME KIND OF WONDERFUL   Paramount, 1987
BABYCAKES (TF)   Konigsberg-Sanitsky Productions, 1989
NIGHTBREED   20th Century Fox, 1990
FIRE ON THE AMAZON   Concorde, 1991
A RIVER RUNS THROUGH IT   Columbia, 1992

FIRE IN THE SKY   Paramount, 1993
THE PROGRAM   Buena Vista, 1993
SLEEP WITH ME   MGM/UA, 1994
WINGS OF COURAGE   TriStar, 1995

JACK SHELDON
FOR THE BOYS   20th Century Fox, 1991

STEPHEN SHELLEN
THE STEPFATHER   New Century/Vista, 1987
DR. JEKYLL AND MS. HYDE   Savoy Pictures, 1995

ADRIENNE SHELLY
SLEEP WITH ME   MGM/UA, 1994

DEBORAH SHELTON
BODY DOUBLE   Columbia, 1984
HUNK   Crown International, 1987
PERFECT VICTIMS   Vertigo Pictures, 1988
NEMESIS   Imperial Entertainment, 1993

SLOANE SHELTON
JACKNIFE   Cineplex Odeon, 1989

PAUL SHENAR
ZIEGFELD: THE MAN AND HIS WOMEN (TF)   Frankovic
   Productions/Columbia TV, 1978
DREAM LOVER   MGM/UA, 1986
RAW DEAL   DEG, 1986
THE BEDROOM WINDOW   DEG, 1987
THE BIG BLUE   Columbia, 1988

ELIZABETH SHEPHARD
CRIMINAL LAW   Hemdale, 1989

SAM SHEPARD
(Samuel Shepard Rogers)
b. November 5, 1943 - Fort Sheridan, Illinois

RENALDO AND CLARA   Circuit, 1978
DAYS OF HEAVEN   Paramount, 1978
RESURRECTION   Universal, 1980
RAGGEDY MAN   Universal, 1981
FRANCES   Universal/AFD, 1982
THE RIGHT STUFF ✪   The Ladd Company/Warner Bros., 1983
COUNTRY   Buena Vista, 1984
FOOL FOR LOVE   Cannon, 1985
CRIMES OF THE HEART   DEG, 1986
BABY BOOM   MGM/UA, 1987
STEEL MAGNOLIAS   TriStar, 1989
DEFENSELESS   New Line Cinema, 1991
BRIGHT ANGEL   Hemdale, 1991
THUNDERHEART   TriStar, 1992
THE PELICAN BRIEF   Warner Bros., 1993
SAFE PASSAGE   New Line Cinema, 1994

CYBILL SHEPHERD
b. February 18, 1950 - Memphis, Tennessee
Agent: UTA - Beverly Hills, 310/273-6700

THE LAST PICTURE SHOW   Columbia, 1971
THE HEARTBREAK KID   20th Century-Fox, 1972
DAISY MILLER   Paramount, 1974
AT LONG LAST LOVE   20th Century-Fox, 1975
TAXI DRIVER   Columbia, 1976
SPECIAL DELIVERY   American International, 1976
SILVER BEARS   Columbia, 1978
THE LADY VANISHES   Rank, 1979, British
THE RETURN   THE ALIEN'S RETURN   Greydon Clark
   Productions, 1980
SECRETS OF A MARRIED MAN (TF)   ITC Productions, 1984
MOONLIGHTING (TF)   Picturemaker Productions/
   ABC Circle Films, 1985
SEDUCED (TF)   Catalina Production Group/Comworld
   Productions, 1985

THE LONG HOT SUMMER (MS)   Leonard Hill Productions, 1985
CHANCES ARE   TriStar, 1989
TEXASVILLE   Columbia, 1990
ALICE   Orion, 1990
ONCE UPON A CRIME   MGM-Pathe, 1992, U.S.-Italian
MARRIED TO IT   Orion, 1993

JACK SHEPHERD
NO ESCAPE   Savoy Pictures, 1994

SUZANNE SHEPHERD
THE JERKY BOYS   Buena Vista, 1994

ANTONY SHER
YANKS   Universal, 1979, British
SUPERMAN II   Warner Bros., 1981, U.S.-British
SHADEY   Skouras Pictures, 1985, British
ERIK THE VIKING   Orion, 1989, British

JAMEY SHERIDAN
STANLEY & IRIS   MGM/UA, 1990
ALL I WANT FOR CHRISTMAS   Paramount, 1991
TALENT FOR THE GAME   Paramount, 1992
WHISPERS IN THE DARK   Paramount, 1992
MY BREAST (TF)   CBS, 1994

NICOLLETTE SHERIDAN
Agent: ICM - Beverly Hills, 310/550-4000

THE SURE THING   Embassy, 1985
DECEPTIONS (CTF)   Sugar Entertainment/Alpha Entertainment
   Productions, 1990
JACKIE COLLINS' LUCKY CHANCES (MS)   NBC Productions, 1991
NOISES OFF   Buena Vista, 1992

ANTHONY SHERWOOD
EDDIE AND THE CRUISERS II: EDDIE LIVES   Scotti Bros., 1989

BROOKE SHIELDS
b. May 31, 1965 - New York, New York

ALICE, SWEET ALICE   COMMUNION/HOLY TERROR
   Allied Artists, 1977
KING OF THE GYPSIES   Paramount, 1978
PRETTY BABY   Paramount, 1978
TILT   Warner Bros., 1979
JUST YOU AND ME, KID   Columbia, 1979
WANDA NEVADA   United Artists, 1979
AN ALMOST PERFECT AFFAIR   Paramount, 1979
THE BLUE LAGOON   Columbia, 1980
ENDLESS LOVE   Universal, 1981
SAHARA   MGM/UA/Cannon, 1984
WET GOLD (TF)   Telepictures Productions, 1984
THE MUPPETS TAKE MANHATTAN   TriStar, 1984
THE DIAMOND TRAP (TF)   Jay Bernstein Productions/
   Columbia TV, 1988
SPEED ZONE   Orion, 1989, U.S.-Canadian
BRENDA STARR   New World, 1992
FREAKED   20th Century Fox, 1993

JAMES SHIGETA
b. 1933 - Hawaii

THE CRIMSON KIMONO   Columbia, 1959
WALK LIKE A DRAGON   Paramount, 1960
BRIDGE TO THE SUN   MGM, 1961, U.S.-French
FLOWER DRUM SONG   Universal, 1961
CRY FOR HAPPY   Columbia, 1961
PARADISE, HAWAIIAN STYLE   1966
NOBODY'S PERFECT   Universal, 1968
LOST HORIZON   Columbia, 1973
THE YAKUZA   Warner Bros., 1975
MIDWAY   Universal, 1976
DIE HARD   20th Century Fox, 1988
CAGE   New Century/Vista, 1989
CHINA CRY   The Penland Company, 1990

SAB SHIMONO
3 NINJAS KICK BACK   TriStar, 1994

DAVID SHINER
SILENT TONGUE   Trimark Pictures, 1994, U.S.-French
MAN 2 MAN   Buena Vista, 1995

TOSHI SHIOYA
MR. BASEBALL   Universal, 1992

TALIA SHIRE
(Talia Coppola)
b. April 25, 1947 - Lake Success, New York

THE WILD RACERS   American International, 1968
THE DUNWICH HORROR   American International, 1970
GAS-S-S-S   *GAS-S-S-S...OR, IT MAY BECOME NECESSARY
   TO DESTROY THE WORLD IN ORDER TO SAVE IT*
   American International, 1970
THE OUTSIDE MAN   *UN HOMME EST MORT*   United Artists,
   1973, French-Italian
THE GODFATHER   Paramount, 1972
THE GODFATHER, PART II ⊙   Paramount, 1974
ROCKY ★   United Artists, 1976
KILL ME IF YOU CAN (TF)   Columbia TV, 1977
OLD BOYFRIENDS   Avco Embassy, 1979
WINDOWS   United Artists, 1979
ROCKY II   United Artists, 1979
PROPHECY   Paramount, 1979
ROCKY III   MGM/UA, 1982
ROCKY IV   MGM/UA, 1985
RAD   TriStar, 1986
BLOOD VOWS: THE STORY OF A MAFIA WIFE (TF)
   Louis Rudolph Films/Fries Entertainment, 1987
NEW YORK STORIES   Buena Vista, 1989
ROCKY V   MGM/UA, 1990
THE GODFATHER, PART III   Paramount, 1990
COLD HEAVEN   Hemdale, 1992
BED AND BREAKFAST   Hemdale, 1992
FOR RICHER, FOR POORER   *FATHER, SON AND THE
   MISTRESS* (CTF)   Citadel Entertainment Productions, 1992

KIMBER SHOOP
THE TED KENNEDY, JR. STORY (TF)   Entertainment
   Partners, 1986

PAMELA SUSAN SHOOP
HALLOWEEN II   Universal, 1981

DAN SHOR
BLACK MOON RISING   New World, 1986
BILL & TED'S EXCELLENT ADVENTURE   Orion, 1989

PAULY SHORE
Agent: CAA - Beverly Hills, 310/288-4545

ENCINO MAN   Buena Vista, 1992
SON-IN-LAW   Buena Vista, 1993
IN THE ARMY NOW   Buena Vista, 1994
JURY DUTY   Sony Pictures, 1995
TO PROTECT AND SERVE   20th Century Fox, 1995

MARTIN SHORT
b. March 26, 1950 - Hamilton, Ontario
Agent: William Morris Agency - Beverly Hills, 310/274-7451

LOST AND FOUND   Columbia, 1979
THE OUTSIDER   Paramount, 1979, U.S.-Irish
THREE AMIGOS   Orion, 1986
REALLY WEIRD TALES (CTF)   HBO/Atlantis Films, 1987,
   U.S.-Canadian
CROSS MY HEART   Universal, 1987
INNERSPACE   Warner Bros., 1987
THREE FUGITIVES   Buena Vista, 1989
THE BIG PICTURE   Columbia, 1989 (uncredited)

PURE LUCK   Universal, 1991
FATHER OF THE BRIDE   Buena Vista, 1991
CAPTAIN RON   Buena Vista, 1992
WE'RE BACK! A DINOSAUR'S STORY (AF)   Universal,
   1993 (voice)
CLIFFORD   Orion, 1994
FATHER OF THE BRIDE 2   Buena Vista, 1995
THE PEBBLE AND THE PENGUIN (AF)   MGM/UA, 1995 (voice)

ROBIN SHOU
MORTAL KOMBAT   New Line Cinema, 1995

MAX SHOWALTER
(Casey Adams)
b. June 2, 1917 - Caldwell, Kansas

ALWAYS LEAVE THEM LAUGHING   Warner Bros., 1949
WITH A SONG IN MY HEART   20th Century-Fox, 1952
WHAT PRICE GLORY?   20th Century-Fox, 1952
NIAGRA   20th Century-Fox, 1953
DESTINATION GOBI   20th Century-Fox, 1953
VICKI   20th Century-Fox, 1953
DANGEROUS CROSSING   20th Century-Fox, 1953
NIGHT PEOPLE   20th Century-Fox, 1954
DOWN THREE DARK STREETS   1954
NAKED ALIBI   20th Century-Fox, 1954
THE RETURN OF JACK SLADE   Allied Artists, 1955
THE INDESTRUCTIBLE MAN   1956
BUS STOP   20th Century-Fox, 1956
DRAGOON WELLS MASSACRE   1957
THE MONSTER THAT CHALLENGED NEW YORK   1957
THE NAKED AND THE DEAD   Warner Bros., 1958
VOICE IN THE MIRROR   1958
ELMER GANTRY   United Artists, 1960
RETURN TO PEYTON PLACE   20th Century-Fox, 1961
SUMMER AND SMOKE   Paramount, 1961
BON VOYAGE!   Buena Vista, 1962
THE MUSIC MAN   Warner Bros., 1962
MY SIX LOVES   1963
MOVE OVER, DARLING   20th Century-Fox, 1963
FATE IS THE HUNTER   20th Century-Fox, 1964
SEX AND THE SINGLE GIRL   Warner Bros., 1965
HOW TO MURDER YOUR WIFE   United Artists, 1965
LORD LOVE A DUCK   United Artists, 1966
THE MOONSHINE WAR   MGM, 1970
THE ANDERSON TAPES   Columbia, 1971
SGT. PEPPER'S LONELY HEARTS CLUB BAND   Universal, 1978
10   Orion/Warner Bros., 1979

JOHN SHRAPNEL
HOW TO GET AHEAD IN ADVERTISING   Warner Bros.,
   1989, British

MARIA SHRIVER
LAST ACTION HERO   Columbia, 1993

ELISABETH SHUE
THE KARATE KID   Columbia, 1984
ADVENTURES IN BABYSITTING   Buena Vista, 1987
COCKTAIL   Buena Vista, 1988
BACK TO THE FUTURE PART II   Universal, 1989
BACK TO THE FUTURE PART III   Universal, 1990
THE MARRYING MAN   Buena Vista, 1991
SOAPDISH   Paramount, 1991
HEART AND SOULS   Universal, 1993
LEAVING LAS VEGAS   1995

RICHARD B. SHULL
b. February 24, 1929 - Evanston, Illinois

THE BIG BUS   Paramount, 1976
UNFAITHFULLY YOURS   20th Century Fox, 1984

MICHAEL SIBERRY
Agent: Susan Smith & Associates - Beverly Hills, 213/852-4777

BIGGLES   Compact Yellowbill/Tambarle, 1986, British
IF LOOKS COULD KILL   Warner Bros., 1991

SYLVIA SIDNEY
(Sophia Kosow)
b. August 8, 1910 - Bronx, New York

BROADWAY NIGHTS   1927
THRU DIFFERENT EYES   1929
CITY STREETS   Paramount, 1931
CONFESSIONS OF A CO-ED   *HER DILEMMA*   Paramount, 1931
AN AMERICAN TRAGEDY   Paramount, 1931
STREET SCENE   United Artists, 1931
LADIES OF THE BIG HOUSE   Paramount, 1931
THE MIRACLE MAN   Paramount, 1932
MERRILY WE GO TO HELL   Paramount, 1932
MAKE ME A STAR   Paramount, 1932
MADAME BUTTERFLY   Paramount, 1932
PICK-UP   Paramount, 1933
JENNIE GERHARDT   Paramount, 1933
GOOD DAME   *GOOD GIRL*   Paramount, 1934
THIRTY-DAY PRINCESS   Paramount, 1934
BEHOLD MY WIFE   Paramount, 1935
ACCENT ON YOUTH   Paramount, 1935
MARY BURNS, FUGITIVE   Paramount, 1935
THE TRAIL OF THE LONESOME PINE   Paramount, 1936
FURY   MGM, 1936
A WOMAN ALONE   *SABOTAGE*   Gaumont, 1936, British
YOU ONLY LIVE ONCE   United Artists, 1937
DEAD END   United Artists, 1937
YOU AND ME   Paramount, 1938
ONE THIRD OF A NATION   Paramount, 1939
THE WAGONS ROLL AT NIGHT   Warner Bros., 1941
BLOOD ON THE SUN   United Artists, 1945
THE SEARCHING WIND   Paramount, 1946
MR. ACE   United Artists, 1946
LOVE FROM A STRANGER   Eagle Lion, 1947
LES MISÉRABLES   20th Century-Fox, 1952
VIOLENT SATURDAY   20th Century-Fox, 1955
BEHIND THE HIGH WALL   1956
DO NOT FOLD, SPINDLE OR MUTILATE (TF)   Lee Rich
   Productions, 1971
SUMMER WISHES, WINTER DREAMS ✪   Columbia, 1973
DEATH AT LOVE HOUSE (TF)   Spelling-Goldberg
   Productions, 1976
GOD TOLD ME TO   New World, 1977
RAID ON ENTEBBE (TF)   Edgar J. Scherick Productions/
   20th Century-Fox TV, 1977
I NEVER PROMISED YOU A ROSE GARDEN   New World, 1977
SIEGE (TF)   Titus Productions, 1978
DAMIEN: OMEN II   20th Century-Fox, 1978
THE SHADOW BOX (TF)   The Shadow Box Film Company, 1980
HAMMETT   Orion/Warner Bros., 1983
CORRUPT   *ORDER OF DEATH/COP KILLERS*   1983, Italian
FINNEGAN BEGIN AGAIN (CTF)   HBO Premiere Films/Zenith
   Productions/Jennie & Co. Film Productions, 1985, U.S.-British
AN EARLY FROST (TF)   NBC Productions, 1985
PALS (TF)   Robert Halmi, Inc., 1987
BEETLEJUICE   The Geffen Company/Warner Bros., 1988
USED PEOPLE   20th Century Fox, 1992

CHARLES SIEBERT
Agent: David Shapira & Associates - Sherman Oaks, 818/906-0322

ALL NIGHT LONG   Universal, 1981

CASEY SIEMASZKO
BACK TO THE FUTURE   Universal, 1985
STAND BY ME   Columbia, 1986
GARDENS OF STONE   TriStar, 1987
THREE O'CLOCK HIGH   Universal, 1987
BILOXI BLUES   Universal, 1988
YOUNG GUNS   20th Century Fox, 1988
BREAKING IN   Samuel Goldwyn Company, 1989

BACK TO THE FUTURE PART II   Universal, 1989
OF MICE AND MEN   MGM-Pathe Communications, 1992
MILK MONEY   Paramount, 1994

NINA SIEMASZKO
TUCKER - THE MAN AND HIS DREAM   Paramount, 1988
BED AND BREAKFAST   Hemdale, 1992
THE SAINT OF FORT WASHINGTON   Warner Bros., 1993

GREGORY SIERRA
THE WRATH OF GOD   MGM, 1972
PAPILLON   Allied Artists, 1973
THE TOWERING INFERNO   20th Century-Fox/Warner Bros., 1974
THE PRISONER OF ZENDA   Universal, 1979
SOMETHING IS OUT THERE (MS)   Columbia TV, 1988
WHERE THE HELL'S THAT GOLD?!!? (TF)   Willie Nelson
   Productions/Brigade Productions/Konigsberg-Sanitsky
   Company, 1988
HONEY, I BLEW UP THE KID   Buena Vista, 1992
A LOW DOWN DIRTY SHAME   Buena Vista, 1994

TOM SIGNORELLI
THIEF   United Artists, 1981

CYNTHIA SIKES
THE MAN WHO LOVED WOMEN   Columbia, 1983
THAT'S LIFE!   Columbia, 1986
ARTHUR 2 ON THE ROCKS   Warner Bros., 1988
LOVE HURTS   Vestron, 1989

JAMES B. SIKKING
b. March 5, 1934 - Los Angeles, California
Agent: Metropolitan Talent Agency - Los Angeles, 213/857-4500

THE NEW CENTURIONS   Columbia, 1972
ORDINARY PEOPLE   Paramount, 1980
STAR TREK III: THE SEARCH FOR SPOCK   Paramount, 1984
TOO GOOD TO BE TRUE (TF)   Newland-Raynor Productions, 1988
NARROW MARGIN   TriStar, 1990
THE PELICAN BRIEF   Warner Bros., 1993

HENRY SILVA
b. 1928 - Brooklyn, New York

VIVA ZAPATA!   20th Century-Fox, 1952
CROWDED PARADISE   1956
A HATFUL OF RAIN   20th Century-Fox, 1957
THE LAW AND JAKE WADE   MGM, 1958
THE BRAVADOS   20th Century-Fox, 1958
GREEN MANSIONS   MGM, 1959
CINDERFELLA   Paramount, 1960
SERGEANTS 3   United Artists, 1962
THE MANCHURIAN CANDIDATE   United Artists, 1962
A GATHERING OF EAGLES   Universal, 1963
JOHNNY COOL   United Artists, 1963
THE SECRET INVASION   United Artists, 1964
HAIL! MAFIA   JE VOUS SALVE MAFIA   1965, French-Italian
THE RETURN OF MR. MOTO   1965
THE HILLS RUN RED   UN FIUME DI DOLLARI   United Artists,
   1965, Italian
THE REWARD   20th Century-Fox, 1965
THE PLAINSMAN   Universal, 1966
MATCHLESS   United Artists, 1967, Italian
ASSASSINATION   1967, Italian
NEVER A DULL MOMENT   Buena Vista, 1968
FIVE SAVAGE MEN   1970
THE ANIMALS   1971
MAN AND BOY   Levitt-Pickman, 1972
THE ITALIAN CONNECTION   LA MALA ORDINA   1972
LES HOMINES   1973, French
THE KIDNAP OF MARY LOU   1974, Italian
L'UOMO DELLA STRADA FA GIUSTIZIA   1976, Italian
SHOOT   Avco Embassy, 1976, Canadian
CRY OF A PROSTITUTE   1976
EVIOLENTI   1976, Italian
LOVE AND BULLETS   AFD, 1979, British
BUCK ROGERS IN THE 25TH CENTURY   Universal, 1979

THIRST   1979, Australian
ALLIGATOR   Group 1, 1980
SHARKY'S MACHINE   Orion/Warner Bros., 1981
WRONG IS RIGHT   Columbia, 1982
ALLAN QUATERMAIN AND THE LOST CITY OF GOLD
   Cannon, 1987
BULLETPROOF   CineTel Films, 1987
ABOVE THE LAW   Warner Bros., 1988
DICK TRACY   Buena Vista, 1990

ELAINE MELANIE SILVER
THE FLINTSTONES   Universal, 1994

RON SILVER
b. July 2, 1946 - New York, New York
Agent: ICM - Beverly Hills, 310/550-4000

BEST FRIENDS   Warner Bros., 1982
LOVESICK   The Ladd Company/Warner Bros., 1983
THE GOODBYE PEOPLE   Embassy, 1984
KANE AND ABEL (MS)   Schrekinger Communications/
   Embassy TV, 1985
TRAPPED IN SILENCE (TF)   Reader's Digest Productions, 1986
BILLIONAIRE BOYS CLUB (MS)   Donald March/Gross-Weston
   Productions/ITC Productions, 1987
ENEMIES, A LOVE STORY   20th Century Fox, 1989
BLUE STEEL   MGM/UA, 1990
REVERSAL OF FORTUNE   Warner Bros., 1990
MR. SATURDAY NIGHT   Columbia, 1992
MARRIED TO IT   Orion, 1993
TIMECOP   Universal, 1994

JONATHAN SILVERMAN
CHALLENGE OF A LIFETIME (TF)   Moonlight Productions, 1985
BRIGHTON BEACH MEMOIRS   Universal, 1986
CADDYSHACK II   Warner Bros., 1988
STEALING HOME   Warner Bros., 1988
WEEKEND AT BERNIE'S   20th Century Fox, 1989
GETTING THERE (CTF)   HBO Pictures/Citadel Entertainment, 1991
FOR RICHER, FOR POORER   FATHER, SON AND THE
   MISTRESS (CTF)   Citadel Entertainment Productions, 1992
WEEKEND AT BERNIE'S II   TriStar, 1993
LITTLE BIG LEAGUE   Columbia, 1994
TWO GUYS TALKING ABOUT GIRLS   Trimark Pictures, 1995

ALICIA SILVERSTONE
THE CRUSH   Warner Bros., 1993
HIDEAWAY   TriStar, 1995

BEN SILVERSTONE
THE BROWNING VERSION   Paramount, 1994, British

VASEK SIMEK
DEAD AGAIN   Paramount, 1991

GENE SIMMONS
b. August 25, 1949

RUNAWAY   TriStar, 1984
WANTED DEAD OR ALIVE   New World, 1986

J.K. SIMMONS
THE REF   Buena Vista, 1994

JEAN SIMMONS
b. January 31, 1929 - London, England
Agent: Susan Smith & Associates - Beverly Hills, 213/852-4777

GIVE US THE MOON   General Film Distributors, 1944, British
MR. EMMANUEL   1944, British
KISS THE BRIDE GOODBYE   1944, British
MEET SEXTON BLAKE   1944, British
JOHNNY IN THE CLOUDS   THE WAY TO THE STARS
   United Artists, 1945, British
CAESAR AND CLEOPATRA   United Artists, 1945, British

GREAT EXPECTATIONS   Universal, 1946, British
HUNGRY HILL   Universal, 1946, British
BLACK NARCISSUS   Universal, 1947, British
THE INHERITANCE   *UNCLE SILAS*   1947, British
THE WOMAN IN THE HALL   1947, British
HAMLET ⚬   Universal, 1948, British
THE BLUE LAGOON   1949, British
ADAM AND EVELYN   *ADAM AND EVELYNE*   1949, British
SO LONG AT THE FAIR   AFD, 1950, British
CAGE OF GOLD   Ellis Film, 1950, British
TRIO   Paramount, 1950, British
THE CLOUDED YELLOW   General Film Distributors, 1950, British
ANDROCLES AND THE LION   RKO Radio, 1953
ANGEL FACE   RKO Radio, 1953
YOUNG BESS   MGM, 1953
AFFAIR WITH A STRANGER   1953
THE ROBE   20th Century-Fox, 1953
THE ACTRESS   MGM, 1953
SHE COULDN'T SAY NO   RKO Radio, 1954
THE EGYPTIAN   20th Century-Fox, 1954
A BULLET IS WAITING   Columbia, 1954
DESIREE   20th Century-Fox, 1954
FOOTSTEPS IN THE FOG   Columbia, 1955, British
GUYS AND DOLLS   MGM, 1955
HILDA CRANE   1956
THIS COULD BE THE NIGHT   MGM, 1957
UNTIL THEY SAIL   MGM, 1957
THE BIG COUNTRY   United Artists, 1958
HOME BEFORE DARK   Warner Bros., 1958
THIS EARTH IS MINE   20th Century-Fox, 1959
ELMER GANTRY   United Artists, 1960
SPARTACUS   Universal, 1960
THE GRASS IS GREENER   Universal, 1960, British
ALL THE WAY HOME   1963
LIFE AT THE TOP   Columbia, 1965, British
MISTER BUDDWING   MGM, 1966
DIVORCE AMERICAN STYLE   Columbia, 1967
ROUGH NIGHT IN JERICHO   Universal, 1967
THE HAPPY ENDING ★   United Artists, 1969
SAY HELLO TO YESTERDAY   Cinerama Releasing Corporation,
   1971, British
MR. SYCAMORE   Film Ventures International, 1975
THE DAIN CURSE (TF) · Martin Poll Productions, 1978
DOMINIQUE   Sword and Sworcery Productions, 1979
BEGGARMAN THIEF (TF)   Universal TV, 1979
GOLDEN GATE (TF)   Lin Bolen Productions/Warner Bros. TV, 1980
THE THORN BIRDS (MS)   David L. Wolper-Stan Margulies
   Productions/Edward Lewis Productions/Warner Bros. TV, 1982
MIDAS VALLEY (TF)   Edward S. Feldman Company/
   Warner Bros. TV, 1984

PETER SIMMONS
RENAISSANCE MAN   Buena Vista, 1994

PAUL SIMON
b. October 13, 1941 - Newark, New Jersey

ANNIE HALL   United Artists, 1977
ONE-TRICK PONY   Warner Bros., 1980
MOTHER GOOSE ROCK 'N' RHYME (CTF)
   Think Entertainment, 1990

DON SIMPSON
Agent: CAA - Beverly Hills, 310/288-4545

DAYS OF THUNDER   Paramount, 1990
THE BIG BANG (FD)   Triton Pictures, 1990

FREDDIE SIMPSON
A LEAGUE OF THEIR OWN   Columbia, 1992

O.J. SIMPSON
(Orenthal James Simpson)
b. July 9, 1947 - San Francisco, California
Agent: ICM - Beverly Hills, 310/550-4000

THE KLANSMAN   Paramount, 1974
THE TOWERING INFERNO   20th Century-Fox/Warner Bros., 1974
THE CASSANDRA CROSSING   Avco Embassy, 1977,
   British-Italian-West German
ROOTS (MS)   Wolper Productions, 1977
A KILLING AFFAIR   *BEHIND THE BADGE*   (TF)   Columbia TV, 1977
CAPRICORN ONE   20th Century-Fox, 1978
FIREPOWER   AFD, 1979, British
GOLDIE AND THE BOXER (TF)   Orenthal Productions/
   Columbia TV, 1979
GOLDIE AND THE BOXER GO TO HOLLYWOOD (TF)
   Orenthal Productions/Columbia TV, 1981
HAMBONE AND HILLIE   New World, 1984
THE NAKED GUN: FROM THE FILES OF POLICE SQUAD!
   Paramount, 1988
THE NAKED GUN 2 1/2: THE SMELL OF FEAR   Paramount, 1991
NAKED GUN 33 1/3: THE FINAL INSULT   Paramount, 1994

FRANK SINATRA
b. December 12, 1915 - Hoboken, New Jersey

LAS VEGAS NIGHTS   Paramount, 1941
SHIP AHOY   MGM, 1942
REVEILLE WITH BEVERLY   Columbia, 1943
HIGHER AND HIGHER   RKO, 1943
STEP LIVELY   RKO, 1944
ANCHORS AWEIGH   MGM, 1945
THE HOUSE I LIVE IN   RKO, 1945
TILL THE CLOUDS ROLL BY   MGM, 1946
IT HAPPENED IN BROOKLYN   MGM, 1947
THE MIRACLE OF THE BELLS   RKO, 1948
THE KISSING BANDIT   MGM, 1948
TAKE ME OUT TO THE BALL GAME   MGM, 1949
ON THE TOWN   MGM, 1949
DOUBLE DYNAMITE   RKO, 1951
MEET DANNY WILSON   Universal/International, 1952
FROM HERE TO ETERNITY ⚬⚬   Columbia, 1953
SUDDENLY   United Artists, 1954
YOUNG AT HEART   Warner Bros., 1955
NOT AS A STRANGER   United Artists, 1955
THE TENDER TRAP   MGM, 1955
GUYS AND DOLLS   MGM, 1955
THE MAN WITH THE GOLDEN ARM ★   United Artists, 1955
MEET ME IN LAS VEGAS   MGM, 1956
JOHNNY CONCHO   United Artists, 1956
HIGH SOCIETY   MGM, 1956
AROUND THE WORLD IN 80 DAYS   United Artists, 1956
THE PRIDE AND THE PASSION   United Artists, 1957
THE JOKER IS WILD   Paramount, 1957
PAL JOEY   Columbia, 1957
KINGS GO FORTH   United Artists, 1958
SOME CAME RUNNING   MGM, 1958
A HOLE IN THE HEAD   United Artists, 1959
NEVER SO FEW   MGM, 1959
CAN-CAN   20th Century-Fox, 1960
OCEAN'S ELEVEN   Warner Bros., 1960
PEPE   Columbia, 1960
THE DEVIL AT 4 O'CLOCK   Columbia, 1961
SERGEANTS 3   United Artists, 1962
THE ROAD TO HONG KONG   United Artists, 1962
THE MANCHURIAN CANDIDATE   United Artists, 1962
COME BLOW YOUR HORN   Paramount, 1963
THE LIST OF ADRIAN MESSENGER   Universal, 1963
4 FOR TEXAS   Warner Bros., 1964
ROBIN AND THE SEVEN HOODS   Warner Bros., 1964
NONE BUT THE BRAVE   Warner Bros., 1964,
   U.S.-Japanese (also directed)
VON RYAN'S EXPRESS   20th Century-Fox, 1965
MARRIAGE ON THE ROCKS   Warner Bros., 1965
CAST A GIANT SHADOW   United Artists, 1966
THE OSCAR   Embassy Pictures, 1966
ASSAULT ON A QUEEN   Paramount, 1966
THE NAKED RUNNER   Warner Bros., 1967, British
TONY ROME   20th Century-Fox, 1967

THE DETECTIVE   20th Century-Fox, 1968
LADY IN CEMENT   20th Century-Fox, 1968
DIRTY DINGUS MAGEE   MGM, 1970
THAT'S ENTERTAINMENT! (FD)   MGM/United Artists, 1974
CONTRACT ON CHERRY STREET (TF)   Columbia, 1977
THE FIRST DEADLY SIN   Filmways, 1980
CANNONBALL RUN II   Warner Bros., 1984

SINBAD
b. November 10 - Benton Harbor, Michigan
Agent: William Morris Agency - Beverly Hills, 310/274-7451

NECESSARY ROUGHNESS   Paramount, 1991
THE METEOR MAN   MGM/UA, 1993
HOUSEGUEST   Buena Vista, 1995

JOHN GORDON SINCLAIR
ERIK THE VIKING   Orion, 1989, British

MADGE SINCLAIR
b. April 28, 1938 - Kingston, Jamaica

CONVOY   United Artists, 1978
GUYANA TRAGEDY: THE STORY OF JIM JONES (TF)
   The Konigsberg Company, 1980
COMING TO AMERICA   Paramount, 1988

LORI SINGER
Agent: CAA - Beverly Hills, 310/288-4545

FOOTLOOSE   Paramount, 1984
SUMMER HEAT   Atlantic Releasing Corporation, 1987
WARLOCK   Trimark Pictures, 1991
SHORT CUTS   Fine Line Features/New Line Cinema, 1993

MARC SINGER
Agent: David Shapira & Associates - Sherman Oaks, 818/906-0322

THE BEASTMASTER   MGM/UA, 1982
BODY CHEMISTRY   Concorde, 1990
THE DAY THE WALL CAME DOWN   Concorde, 1991
BEASTMASTER II   MGM-Pathe, 1991

STEPHEN SINGER
DON JUAN DE MARCO AND THE CENTERFOLD
   New Line Cinema, 1995

GARY SINISE
Agent: CAA - Beverly Hills, 310/288-4545

MY NAME IS BILL W (TF)   Garner-Duchow Productions, 1989
A MIDNIGHT CLEAR   Interstar Releasing, 1992
OF MICE AND MEN   MGM-Pathe Communications,
   1992 (also directed)
JACK THE BEAR   20th Century Fox, 1992
STEPHEN KING'S THE STAND   THE STAND (MS)   ABC, 1994
FORREST GUMP   Paramount, 1994
THE QUICK AND THE DEAD   TriStar, 1995
APOLLO 13   Universal, 1995

JOE SIROLA
LOVE IS A GUN   Trimark Pictures, 1994

MARINA SIRTIS
STAR TREK GENERATIONS   Paramount, 1994

JEREMY SISTO
HIDEAWAY   TriStar, 1995

TOM SIZEMORE
Agent: CAA - Beverly Hills, 310/288-4545

LOCK UP   TriStar, 1989
FLIGHT OF THE INTRUDER   Paramount, 1991
GUILTY BY SUSPICION   Warner Bros., 1991

HARLEY DAVIDSON & THE MARLBORO MAN   MGM-Pathe, 1991
PASSENGER 57   Warner Bros., 1992
HEART AND SOULS   Universal, 1993
STRIKING DISTANCE   Columbia, 1993
WYATT EARP   Warner Bros., 1994
NATURAL BORN KILLERS   Warner Bros., 1994
DEVIL IN A BLUE DRESS   TriStar, 1994
STRANGE DAYS   20th Century Fox, 1995

JIMMIE F. SKAGGS
GHOST TOWN   Empire Pictures, 1988

LILIA SKALA
LILIES OF THE FIELD ✪   United Artists, 1963
DEADLY HERO   Avco Embassy, 1976
ELEANOR AND FRANKLIN (TF)   Talent Associates, 1976
ROSELAND   Cinema Shares International, 1977
HEARTLAND   Levitt-Pickman, 1979
THE END OF AUGUST   1982
FLASHDANCE   Paramount, 1983
TESTAMENT   Paramount, 1983
HOUSE OF GAMES   Orion, 1987

STELLAN SKARSGARD
THE UNBEARABLE LIGHTNESS OF BEING   Orion, 1988
WIND   TriStar, 1992, U.S.-Japanese

TOM SKERRITT
b. August 25, 1933 - Detroit, Michigan
Agent: William Morris Agency - Beverly Hills, 310/274-7451

WAR HUNT   1962
ONE MAN'S WAY   1964
THOSE CALLAWAYS   Buena Vista, 1965
M*A*S*H   20th Century-Fox, 1970
WILD ROVERS   MGM, 1971
FUZZ   United Artists, 1972
THIEVES LIKE US   United Artists, 1974
BIG BAD MAMA   New World, 1974
THE DEVIL'S RAIN   Bryanston, 1975, U.S.-Mexican
THE TURNING POINT   20th Century-Fox, 1977
UP IN SMOKE   Paramount, 1978
ALIEN   20th Century-Fox, 1979, U.S.-British
ICE CASTLES   Columbia, 1979
SAVAGE HARVEST   20th Century-Fox, 1981
A DANGEROUS SUMMER   THE BURNING MAN   Filmco, Ltd.,
   1981, Australian
SILENCE OF THE NORTH   Universal, 1981, Canadian
FIGHTING BACK   Paramount, 1982
THE DEAD ZONE   Paramount, 1983, Canadian
A TOUCH OF SCANDAL (TF)   Doris M. Keating Productions/
   Columbia TV, 1984
TOP GUN   Paramount, 1986
OPPOSING FORCE   HELL CAMP   Orion, 1986
SPACECAMP   20th Century Fox, 1986
WISDOM   20th Century Fox, 1986
MAID TO ORDER   New Century/Vista, 1987
THE BIG TOWN   Columbia, 1987
POLTERGEIST III   MGM/UA, 1988
BIG MAN ON CAMPUS   Vestron, 1989
THE HEIST (CTF)   HBO Pictures/Chris-Rose Productions/
   Paramount TV, 1989
RED KING, WHITE KNIGHT (CTF)   HBO Pictures/Zenith
   Productions/John Kemeny Productions/Citadel Entertainment,
   1989, U.S.-British-Canadian
STEEL MAGNOLIAS   TriStar, 1989
CHILD IN THE NIGHT (TF)   Mike Robe Productions, 1990
HONOR BOUND   MGM/UA, 1990, U.S.-French
THE ROOKIE   Warner Bros., 1990
POISON IVY   New Line Cinema, 1992
A RIVER RUNS THROUGH IT   Columbia, 1992

PAT SKIPPER
MEMOIRS OF AN INVISIBLE MAN   Warner Bros., 1992

JERZY SKOLIMOWSKI
WHITE NIGHTS   Columbia, 1985

I O N E   S K Y E
STRANDED   New Line Cinema, 1987
RIVER'S EDGE   Hemdale, 1987
A NIGHT IN THE LIFE OF JIMMY REARDON
   20th Century Fox, 1988
SAY ANYTHING   20th Century Fox, 1989
THE RACHEL PAPERS   MGM/UA, 1989, U.S.-British

D E B O R A H   D A W N   S L A B O D A
FATAL DECEPTION: MRS. LEE HARVEY OSWALD (TF)
   David L. Wolper Productions/Bernard Sofronski/Warner Bros.
   Television, 1993

D E M I A N   S L A D E
BACK TO THE BEACH   Paramount, 1987

M A X   E L L I O T T   S L A D E
3 NINJAS KICK BACK   TriStar, 1994

C H R I S T I A N   S L A T E R
Agent: CAA - Beverly Hills, 310/288-4545

LIVING PROOF: THE HANK WILLIAMS, JR. STORY (TF)
   Procter & Gamble Productions/Telecom Entertainment/
   Melpomene Productions, 1983
THE LEGEND OF BILLIE JEAN   TriStar, 1985
THE NAME OF THE ROSE   20th Century Fox, 1986,
   West German-Italian-French
PERSONAL CHOICE   Moviestore Entertainment, 1988
TUCKER - THE MAN AND HIS DREAM   Paramount, 1988
GLEAMING THE CUBE   20th Century Fox, 1989
HEATHERS   New World, 1989
THE WIZARD   Universal, 1989
TALES FROM THE DARKSIDE: THE MOVIE   Paramount, 1990
PUMP UP THE VOLUME   New Line Cinema, 1990
YOUNG GUNS II   20th Century Fox, 1990
ROBIN HOOD: PRINCE OF THIEVES   Warner Bros., 1991
MOBSTERS   Universal, 1991
STAR TREK VI: THE UNDISCOVERED COUNTRY
   Paramount, 1991
TWISTED   1992 (made in 1986)
KUFFS   Universal, 1992
FERNGULLY...THE LAST RAINFOREST (AF)
   20th Century Fox, 1992 (voice)
UNTAMED HEART   MGM/UA, 1993
TRUE ROMANCE   Warner Bros., 1993
JIMMY HOLLYWOOD   Paramount, 1994
INTERVIEW WITH THE VAMPIRE   Warner Bros., 1994
MURDER IN THE FIRST   Warner Bros., 1994

H E L E N   S L A T E R
b. December 14, 1963 - Massapequa, New York

SUPERGIRL   Warner Bros., 1984, British
THE LEGEND OF BILLIE JEAN   TriStar, 1985
RUTHLESS PEOPLE   Buena Vista, 1986
THE SECRET OF MY SUCCESS   Universal, 1987
STICKY FINGERS   Spectrafilm, 1988
HAPPY TOGETHER   Borde Releasing Corporation, 1990
CITY SLICKERS   Columbia, 1991
LASSIE   Paramount, 1994
PARALLEL LIVES (CTF)   Showtime Entertainment, 1994

R Y A N   S L A T E R
RISE AND WALK: THE DENNIS BYRD STORY (TF)   1994
LITTLE PANDA   Warner Bros., 1995

G E N A   S L E E T E
THE SUBSTITUTE WIFE (TF)   Frederick S. Pierce Company, 1994

J A M E S   S L O Y A N
THE DISAPPEARANCE OF AIMEE (TF)   Tomorrow
   Entertainment, 1976
HER SECRET LIFE (TF)   Phoenix Entertainment Group, 1987

J E A N   S M A R T
Agent: William Morris Agency - Beverly Hills, 310/274-7451

FLASHPOINT   TriStar, 1984
FIRE WITH FIRE   Paramount, 1986
MISTRESS   Tribeca Films, 1992
HOMEWARD BOUND: THE INCREDIBLE JOURNEY
   Buena Vista, 1993
THE YEARLING (TF)   RHI Entertainment, 1994
THE BRADY BUNCH MOVIE   Paramount, 1995

S T I A N   S M E S T A D
SHIPWRECKED   Buena Vista, 1991

Y A K O V   S M I R N O F F
b. January 24, 1951 - Odessa, Russia

MOSCOW ON THE HUDSON   Columbia, 1984
BREWSTER'S MILLIONS   Universal, 1985
HEARTBURN   Paramount, 1986

A L L I S O N   S M I T H
b. December 9, 1969 - New York, New York

JASON GOES TO HELL—THE FINAL FRIDAY
   New Line Cinema, 1993

A N N A   D E A V E R E   S M I T H
DAVE   Warner Bros. 1993
THE AMERICAN PRESIDENT   Columbia, 1995

A N N A   N I C O L E   S M I T H
NAKED GUN 33 1/3: THE FINAL INSULT   Paramount, 1994

B R A N D O N   S M I T H
FATAL DECEPTION: MRS. LEE HARVEY OSWALD (TF)
   David L. Wolper Productions/Bernard Sofronski/Warner Bros.
   Television, 1993

B R O O K E   S M I T H
A CHORUS LINE   Columbia, 1985
THE MODERNS   Alive Films, 1988
ARTHUR 2 ON THE ROCKS   Warner Bros., 1988
SEE YOU IN THE MORNING   Warner Bros., 1989
THE SILENCE OF THE LAMBS   Orion, 1991

B U B B A   S M I T H
(Charles Smith)
STROKER ACE   Universal, 1983
POLICE ACADEMY   The Ladd Company/Warner Bros., 1984
POLICE ACADEMY 2: THEIR FIRST ASSIGNMENT
   Warner Bros., 1985
BLACK MOON RISING   New World, 1986
POLICE ACADEMY 3: BACK IN TRAINING   Warner Bros., 1986
POLICE ACADEMY 4: CITIZENS ON PATROL   Warner Bros., 1987
POLICE ACADEMY 5: ASSIGNMENT MIAMI BEACH
   Warner Bros., 1988
POLICE ACADEMY 6: CITY UNDER SIEGE   Warner Bros., 1989

C H A R L E S   M A R T I N   S M I T H
(Charlie Martin Smith)
b. October 30, 1953 - Van Nuys, California

AMERICAN GRAFFITI   Universal, 1973
NEVER CRY WOLF   Buena Vista, 1983
STARMAN   Columbia, 1984
TRICK OR TREAT   DEG, 1986 (also directed)
THE UNTOUCHABLES   Paramount, 1987
THE EXPERTS   Paramount, 1989
THE HOT SPOT   Orion, 1990
AND THE BAND PLAYED ON (CTF)   HBO Pictures/Spelling
   Entertainment, 1993
SPEECHLESS   MGM/UA, 1994

COTTER SMITH

A BUNNY'S TALE (TF)   Stan Margulies Company/
   Warner Bros., 1985
THE RAPE OF RICHARD BECK (TF)   Robert Papazian
   Productions/Henerson-Hirsch Productions, 1985
K-9   Universal, 1989

EDDIE SMITH

HARLEM NIGHTS   Paramount, 1989

HAL SMITH

BEAUTY AND THE BEAST (AF)   Buena Vista, 1991 (voice)

JACLYN SMITH

b. October 26, 1947 - Houston, Texas
Agent: William Morris Agency - Beverly Hills, 310/274-7451

THE ADVENTURERS   Paramount, 1970
PROBE (TF)   Warner Bros. TV, 1972
BOOTLEGGERS   *BOOTLEGGERS' ANGEL*
   Howco International, 1974
SWITCH (TF)   Universal TV, 1975
CHARLIE'S ANGELS (TF)   Spelling-Goldberg Productions, 1976
ESCAPE FROM BOGAN COUNTY (TF)   Paramount TV, 1977
THE USERS (TF)   Aaron Spelling Productions, 1978
NIGHTKILL (TF)   Cine Artists, 1980
JACQUELINE BOUVIER KENNEDY (TF)   ABC Circle Films, 1981
SIDNEY SHELDON'S RAGE OF ANGELS   *RAGE OF ANGELS* (MS)
   Furia-Oringer Productions/NBC Productions, 1983
GEORGE WASHINGTON (MS)   David Gerber Company/
   MGM-UA TV, 1984
SENTIMENTAL JOURNEY (TF)   Lucille Ball Productions/
   Smith-Richmond Productions/20th Century Fox TV, 1984
THE NIGHT THEY SAVED CHRISTMAS (TF)
   Robert Halmi, Inc., 1984
DÉJÀ VU   Cannon, 1985, British
FLORENCE NIGHTINGALE (TF)   Cypress Point Productions, 1985
RAGE OF ANGELS: THE STORY CONTINUES (MS)
   NBC Productions, 1986
SIDNEY SHELDON'S WINDMILLS OF THE GODS   *WINDMILLS OF
   THE GODS* (MS)   Dove Productions/ITC Productions, 1988
THE BOURNE IDENTITY (MS)   Alan Shayne Productions/Warner
   Bros. TV, 1988
SETTLE THE SCORE (TF)   Steve Sohmer Inc. Productions/ITC
   Entertainment Group, 1989
DANIELLE STEEL'S KALEIDOSCOPE   *KALEIDOSCOPE* (TF)
   The Cramer Company/NBC Productions, 1990
LIES BEFORE KISSES (TF)   Grossbart-Barnett Productions/
   Spectator Films, 1991
THE RAPE OF DR. WILLIS (TF)   Interprod Productions, 1991
IN THE ARMS OF A KILLER (TF)   RLC Productions/Monarch
   Pictures Corporation, 1992
NIGHTMARE IN THE DAYLIGHT (TF)   Smith-Richmond Productions/
   Saban-Scherick Productions, 1992
LOVE CAN BE MURDER (TF)   Konigsberg-Sanitsky
   Productions, 1992
CRIES UNHEARD: THE DONNA YAKLICH STORY (TF)
   Carla Singer Productions, 1994

KURTWOOD SMITH

Agent: Progressive Artists Agency, Inc. - Beverly Hills, 310/553-8561

ROBOCOP   Orion, 1987
HEART OF DIXIE   Orion, 1989
DEAD POETS SOCIETY   Buena Vista, 1989
STAR TREK VI: THE UNDISCOVERED COUNTRY
   Paramount, 1991
THE CRUSH   Warner Bros., 1993
BOXING HELENA   Orion Classics, 1993
UNTITLED VAN SANT/ZISKIN   Columbia, 1995
LAST OF THE DOGMEN   Savoy Pictures, 1995

LANE SMITH

NATIVE SON   Cinecom, 1986
KILLER INSTINCT (TF)   Millar-Bromberg Productions/ITC
   Entertainment, 1988
NIGHT GAME   Trans World Entertainment, 1989

AIR AMERICA   TriStar, 1990
THE MIGHTY DUCKS   Buena Vista, 1992
SON-IN-LAW   Buena Vista, 1993
THE SCOUT   20th Century Fox, 1994
FLIGHT OF THE DOVE   Concorde, 1995

LOIS SMITH

FIVE EASY PIECES   Columbia, 1970
NEXT STOP, GREENWICH VILLAGE   20th Century-Fox, 1976
RESURRECTION   Universal, 1980
RECKLESS   MGM/UA, 1984
BLACK WIDOW   20th Century Fox, 1987
HOLY MATRIMONY   Buena Vista, 1994

LIZ SMITH

APARTMENT ZERO   Skouras Pictures, 1989

MADOLYN SMITH OSBORNE
(Madolyn Smith)

Agent: UTA - Beverly Hills, 310/273-6700

ALL OF ME   Universal, 1984
DEADLY INTENTIONS (MS)   Green-Epstein Productions, 1985
FUNNY FARM   Warner Bros., 1988
THE PLOT TO KILL HITLER (TF)   Wolper Productions/Bernard
   Sofronski Productions/Warner Bros. TV, 1990
THE SUPER   20th Century Fox, 1991

MAGGIE SMITH

b. December 28, 1934 - Ilford, England

NOWHERE TO GO   MGM, 1958, British
GO TO BLAZES   1962, British
THE V.I.P.'S   MGM, 1963
THE PUMPKIN EATER   Royal International, 1964, British
YOUNG CASSIDY   MGM, 1965, British-U.S.
OTHELLO ✪   Warner Bros., 1965, British
THE HONEY POT   United Artists, 1967, British-U.S.-Italian
HOT MILLIONS   MGM, 1968, British
THE PRIME OF MISS JEAN BRODIE ★★   20th Century-Fox,
   1969, British
OH! WHAT A LOVELY WAR   Paramount, 1969, British
TRAVELS WITH MY AUNT ★   MGM, 1972
LOVE AND PAIN AND THE WHOLE DAMN THING   Columbia,
   1972, British-U.S.
MURDER BY DEATH   Columbia, 1976
DEATH ON THE NILE   Paramount, 1978, British
CALIFORNIA SUITE ✪✪   Columbia, 1978
CLASH OF THE TITANS   MGM/United Artists, 1981, British
QUARTET   New World, 1981, British-French
THE MISSIONARY   Columbia, 1982, British
EVIL UNDER THE SUN   Universal/AFD, 1982, British
BETTER LATE THAN NEVER   Warner Bros., 1982, British
A PRIVATE FUNCTION   Island Alive, 1985, British
LILY IN LOVE   1985
A ROOM WITH A VIEW ✪   Cinecom, 1986, British
THE LONELY PASSION OF JUDITH HEARNE   Island Films,
   1987, British
ROMEO-JULIET   1990
HOOK   TriStar, 1991
SISTER ACT   Buena Vista, 1992
SUDDENLY LAST SUMMER (TF)   BBC/WNET-13, 1993, British-U.S.
THE SECRET GARDEN   Warner Bros., 1993, U.S.-British
SISTER ACT 2: BACK IN THE HABIT   Buena Vista, 1993

REX SMITH

THE PIRATES OF PENZANCE   Universal, 1983

SHAWNEE SMITH

Agent: CAA - Beverly Hills, 310/288-4545

SUMMER SCHOOL   Paramount, 1987
THE BLOB   TriStar, 1988
WHO'S HARRY CRUMB?   TriStar, 1989
A BRAND NEW LIFE: THE HONEYMOON (TF)
   NBC Productions, 1989

T. RYDER SMITH
BRAINSCAN   Triumph Releasing Corporation, 1994

WILL SMITH
b. September 25, 1969 - Philadelphia, Pennsylvania

WHERE THE DAY TAKES YOU   New Line Cinema, 1992
SIX DEGREES OF SEPARATION   MGM/UA, 1993
BAD BOYS   Columbia, 1995

WILLIAM SMITH
ANY WHICH WAY YOU CAN   Warner Bros., 1980

YEARDLEY SMITH
GINGERALE AFTERNOON   Skouras Pictures, 1989
CITY SLICKERS   Columbia, 1991

J. SMITH-CAMERON
THAT NIGHT   Warner Bros., 1993

BILL SMITROVICH
A LITTLE SEX   Universal, 1982
WITHOUT A TRACE   20th Century-Fox, 1983
MARIA'S LOVERS   Cannon, 1984
SPLASH   Buena Vista, 1984
SILVER BULLET   STEPHEN KING'S SILVER BULLET
   Paramount, 1985
MANHUNTER   DEG, 1986
A KILLING AFFAIR   1988
RENEGADES   Universal, 1989
HER ALIBI   Warner Bros., 1989
CRAZY PEOPLE   Paramount, 1990

JIMMY SMITS
b. July 9, 1955 - New York, New York
Agent: CAA - Beverly Hills, 310/288-4545

RUNNING SCARED   MGM/UA, 1986
THE BELIEVERS   Orion, 1987
DANGEROUS AFFECTION (TF)   Freyda Rothstein Productions/
   Litke-Grossbart Productions/New World TV, 1987
GLITZ (TF)   Lorimar-Telepictures/Robert Cooper Films, 1988
OLD GRINGO   Columbia, 1989
VITAL SIGNS   20th Century Fox, 1990
SWITCH   Warner Bros., 1991
FIRES WITHIN   MGM-Pathe, 1991
MI FAMILIA   New Line Cinema, 1995

TOM SMOTHERS
b. February 2, 1937 - New York, New York

GET TO KNOW YOUR RABBIT   Warner Bros., 1972
SILVER BEARS   Columbia, 1978
THE KIDS ARE ALRIGHT (FD)   New World, 1979, British
THERE GOES THE BRIDE   Vanguard, 1979, British
SERIAL   Paramount, 1980
PANDEMONIUM   MGM/UA, 1982

VICKY SMURFIT
THE RUN OF THE COUNTRY   Columbia, 1995

WESLEY SNIPES
b. July 31, 1962 - Orlando, Florida
Agent: CAA - Beverly Hills, 310/288-4545

WILDCATS   Warner Bros., 1986
STREETS OF GOLD   20th Century Fox, 1986
MAJOR LEAGUE   Paramount, 1989
VIETNAM WAR STORY: THE LAST DAYS (CTF)   HBO, 1989
KING OF NEW YORK   New Line Cinema, 1990
MO' BETTER BLUES   Universal, 1990
NEW JACK CITY   Warner Bros., 1991
JUNGLE FEVER   Universal, 1991
WHITE MEN CAN'T JUMP   20th Century Fox, 1992
THE WATERDANCE   Samuel Goldwyn Company, 1992

PASSENGER 57   Warner Bros., 1992
BOILING POINT   Warner Bros., 1993
RISING SUN   20th Century Fox, 1993
DEMOLITION MAN   Warner Bros., 1993
SUGAR HILL   20th Century Fox, 1994
DROP ZONE   Paramount, 1994
TO WONG FOO, THANKS FOR EVERYTHING, JULIE NEWMAR
   Universal, 1995
THE MONEY TRAIN   Columbia, 1995

CARRIE SNODGRESS
b. October 27, 1946 - Chicago, Illinois

THE 48-HOUR MILE (TF)   1968
SILENT NIGHT, LONELY NIGHT (TF)   Universal TV, 1969
DIARY OF A MAD HOUSEWIFE ★   Universal, 1970
RABBIT, RUN   Warner Bros., 1970
THE FURY   20th Century-Fox, 1978
HOMEWORK   Jensen-Farley Pictures, 1982
TRICK OR TREATS   Lone Star, 1982
A NIGHT IN HEAVEN   20th Century-Fox, 1983
A REASON TO LIVE (TF)   Papazian Productions, 1985
PALE RIDER   Warner Bros., 1985
MURPHY'S LAW   Cannon, 1986
8 SECONDS   New Line Cinema, 1994
BLUE SKY   Orion, 1994

ARLEN DEAN SNYDER
KANSAS   Trans World Entertainment, 1988

JIMMY "THE GREEK" SNYDER
THE CANNONBALL RUN   20th Century-Fox, 1981

BARRY SOBEL
Agent: David Shapira & Associates - Sherman Oaks, 818/906-0322

MARTIANS GO HOME   Taurus Entertainment, 1990

P.J. SOLES
Agent: The Lawrence Agency - Los Angeles, 213/851-7711

CARRIE   United Artists, 1976
HALLOWEEN   Compass International, 1978
OUR WINNING SEASON   American International, 1978
ZUMA BEACH (TF)   Edgar J. Scherick Associates/Warner Bros. TV, 1978
STRIPES   Columbia, 1981

TODD SOLONDZ
FEAR, ANXIETY AND DEPRESSION   Samuel Goldwyn Company,
   1990 (also directed)

SUZANNE SOMERS
b. October 16, 1946 - San Bruno, California

AMERICAN GRAFFITI   Universal, 1973
IT HAPPENED AT LAKEWOOD MANOR   PANIC AT LAKEWOOD
   MANOR/ANTS (TF)   Alan Landsburg Productions, 1977
ZUMA BEACH (TF)   Edgar J. Scherick Associates/Warner Bros. TV, 1978
NOTHING PERSONAL   American International, 1980, Canadian
RICH MEN, SINGLE WOMEN (TF)   Aaron Spelling Productions, 1990
SERIAL MOM   Savoy Pictures, 1994

PHYLLIS SOMERVILLE
Agent: Susan Smith & Associates - Beverly Hills, 213/852-4777

LEAP OF FAITH   Paramount, 1992

JOSEF SOMMER
THE STEPFORD WIVES   Columbia, 1975
TOO FAR TO GO (TF)   Sea Cliff Productions, 1978
HIDE IN PLAIN SIGHT   MGM/United Artists, 1980
STILL OF THE NIGHT   MGM/UA, 1982
SOPHIE'S CHOICE   Universal/AFD, 1982 (voice)
HANKY PANKY   Columbia, 1982
ICEMAN   Universal, 1984

F
I
L
M

A
C
T
O
R
S

WITNESS   Paramount, 1985
THE BETTY FORD STORY (TF)   David L. Wolper Productions/
   Warner Bros. TV, 1987
CHANCES ARE   TriStar, 1989
BLOODHOUNDS OF BROADWAY   Columbia, 1989
MONEY, POWER, MURDER (TF)   Skids Productions/CBS
   Entertainment, 1989
MALICE   Columbia, 1993

TED SOREL
FROM BEYOND   Empire Pictures, 1986

ARLEEN SORKIN
Agent: Metropolitan Talent Agency - Los Angeles, 213/857-4500

IT'S PAT   Buena Vista, 1994

MIRA SORVINO
PARALLEL LIVES (CTF)   Showtime Entertainment, 1994

PAUL SORVINO
b. 1939 - New York, New York

WHERE'S POPPA?   United Artists, 1970
THE PANIC IN NEEDLE PARK   20th Century-Fox, 1971
CRY UNCLE   Cambist, 1971
MADE FOR EACH OTHER   20th Century-Fox, 1971
A TOUCH OF CLASS   1973, British
THE DAY OF THE DOLPHIN   Avco Embassy, 1973
THE GAMBLER   Avco Embassy, 1974
I WILL, I WILL..FOR NOW   20th Century-Fox, 1976
OH, GOD!   Warner Bros., 1977
THE BRINK'S JOB   Universal, 1978
BLOODBROTHERS   Warner Bros., 1978
SLOW DANCING IN THE BIG CITY   United Artists, 1978
LOST AND FOUND   Columbia, 1979
CRUISING   United Artists, 1980
REDS   Paramount, 1981
WITH INTENT TO KILL (TF)   London Productions, 1984
TURK 1982   20th Century-Fox, 1985
A FINE MESS   Columbia, 1986
VASECTOMY, A DELICATE MATTER   Seymour Borde &
   Associates, 1986
DICK TRACY   Buena Vista, 1990
GOODFELLAS   Warner Bros., 1990
THE ROCKETEER   Buena Vista, 1991
PARALLEL LIVES (CTF)   Showtime Entertainment, 1994

ANN SOTHERN
(Harriette Lake)
b. January 22, 1909 - Valley City, North Dakota

THE SHOW OF SHOWS   Warner Bros., 1929
DOUGHBOYS   MGM, 1930
BROADWAY THRU A KEYHOLE   20th Century-Fox/
   United Artists, 1933
LET'S FALL IN LOVE   Columbia, 1934
THE HELL CAT   Columbia, 1934
BLIND DATE   Columbia, 1934
KID MILLIONS   United Artists, 1934
FOLIES BERGERE   United Artists, 1935
HOORAY FOR LOVE   RKO Radio, 1935
THE GIRL FRIEND   Columbia, 1935
GRAND EXIT   Columbia, 1935
YOU MAY BE NEXT   Columbia, 1936
DON'T GAMBLE WITH LOVE   Columbia, 1936
MY AMERICAN WIFE   Paramount, 1936
WALKING ON AIR   RKO Radio, 1936
THE SMARTEST GIRL IN TOWN   1936
DANGEROUS NUMBER   MGM, 1937
FIFTY ROADS TO TOWN   20th Century-Fox, 1937
THERE GOES MY GIRL   RKO Radio, 1937
SUPER SLEUTH   RKO Radio, 1937
DANGER—LOVE AT WORK   20th Century-Fox, 1937
THERE GOES THE GROOM   RKO Radio, 1937
SHE'S GOT EVERYTHING   RKO Radio, 1937
TRADE WINDS   United Artists, 1939

MAISIE   MGM, 1939
HOTEL FOR WOMEN   20th Century-Fox, 1939
FAST AND FURIOUS   MGM, 1939
JOE AND ETHEL TURP CALL ON THE PRESIDENT   MGM, 1939
GOLD RUSH MAISIE   MGM, 1940
CONGO MAISIE   MGM, 1940
BROTHER ORCHID   Warner Bros., 1940
DULCY   MGM, 1940
MAISIE WAS A LADY   MGM, 1941
LADY BE GOOD   MGM, 1941
MAISIE GETS HER MAN   MGM, 1942
PANAMA HATTIE   MGM, 1942
THREE HEARTS FOR JULIA   MGM, 1943
THOUSANDS CHEER   MGM, 1943
CRY HAVOC   MGM, 1944
MAISIE GOES TO RENO   MGM, 1947
UP GOES MAISIE   MGM, 1946
UNDERCOVER MAISIE   MGM, 1947
APRIL SHOWERS   Warner Bros., 1948
LORDS AND MUSIC   MGM, 1948
A LETTER TO THREE WIVES   20th Century-Fox, 1949
THE JUDGE STEPS OUT   RKO Radio, 1949
SHADOW ON THE WALL   MGM, 1949
NANCY GOES TO RIO   MGM, 1950
THE BLUE GARDENIA   Warner Bros., 1953
THE BEST MAN   United Artists, 1964
LADY IN A CAGE   United Artists, 1964
SYLVIA   Paramount, 1965
CHUBASCO   Warner Bros., 1968
THE GREAT MAN'S WHISKERS (TF)   Universal TV, 1971
THE KILLING KIND   Media Cinema, 1973
GOLDEN NEEDLES   American International, 1974
CRAZY MAMA   New World, 1975
CAPTAINS AND THE KINGS (MS)   Universal TV, 1976
THE MANITOU   Avco Embassy, 1978
THE WHALES OF AUGUST ○   Alive Films, 1987

TALISA SOTO
LICENCE TO KILL   MGM/UA, 1989, British
DON JUAN DE MARCO AND THE CENTERFOLD
   New Line Cinema, 1995
MORTAL KOMBAT   New Line Cinema, 1995

KATH SOUCIE
BEAUTY AND THE BEAST (AF)   Buena Vista, 1991 (voice)

DAVID SOUL
b. August 28, 1943 - Chicago, Illinois

JOHNNY GOT HIS GUN   Cinemation, 1971
MAGNUM FORCE   Warner Bros., 1973
DOGPOUND SHUFFLE   Paramount, 1974, Canadian
STARSKY AND HUTCH (TF)   Spelling-Goldberg Productions, 1975
LITTLE LADIES OF THE NIGHT (TF)   Spelling-Goldberg
   Productions, 1977
THE STICK UP   Trident-Barber, 1978, British
SALEM'S LOT (TF)   Warner Bros. TV, 1979
SWAN SONG (TF)   Renee Valente Productions/Topanga
   Services, Ltd/20th Century-Fox TV, 1980
RAGE (TF)   Diane Silver Productions/Charles Fries Productions, 1980
THE FIFTH MISSILE (TF)   Bercovici-St. Johns Productions/
   MGM-UA TV, 1986
THE HANOI HILTON   Cannon, 1987
HARRY'S HONG KONG (TF)   Aaron Spelling Productions, 1987
IN THE LINE OF DUTY: THE FBI MURDERS (TF)   Telecom
   Entertainment/World International Network, 1988
SO PROUDLY WE HAIL (TF)   Lionel Chetwynd Productions/CBS
   Entertainment, 1990

JULIA NICKSON SOUL
CHINA CRY   The Penland Company, 1990

RENEE SOUTENDIJK
EVE OF DESTRUCTION   Orion, 1991

J.D. SOUTHER
MY GIRL 2   Columbia, 1994

SISSY SPACEK
(Mary Elizabeth Spacek)
b. December 25, 1949 - Quitman, Texas
Agent: CAA - Beverly Hills, 310/288-4545

PRIME CUT   National General, 1972
THE GIRLS OF HUNTINGTON HOUSE (TF)
   Lorimar Productions, 1973
GINGER IN THE MORNING   National Film, 1973
BADLANDS   Warner Bros., 1973
THE MIGRANTS (TF)   CBS, Inc., 1974
KATHERINE (TF)   The Jozak Company, 1975
CARRIE ★   United Artists, 1976
WELCOME TO L.A.   United Artists/Lions Gate, 1977
3 WOMEN   20th Century-Fox, 1977
HEART BEAT   Orion/Warner Bros., 1980
COAL MINER'S DAUGHTER ★★   Universal, 1980
RAGGEDY MAN   Universal, 1981
MISSING ★   Universal, 1982
THE MAN WITH TWO BRAINS   Warner Bros., 1983 (voice)
THE RIVER ★   Universal, 1984
MARIE   MGM/UA, 1985
VIOLETS ARE BLUE   Columbia, 1986
'NIGHT, MOTHER   Universal, 1986
CRIMES OF THE HEART ★   DEG, 1986
THE LONG WALK HOME   Miramax Films, 1990
JFK   Warner Bros., 1991
HARD PROMISES   Columbia, 1992
A PRIVATE MATTER (CTF)   HBO Pictures/Longbow Productions/
   Mirage Enterprises, 1992
A PLACE FOR ANNIE (TF)   1994
TRADING MOM   Trimark Pictures, 1994
THE GRASS HARP   New Line Cinema, 1995

KEVIN SPACEY
b. 1960 - South Orange, New Jersey

ROCKET GIBRALTAR   Columbia, 1988
SEE NO EVIL, HEAR NO EVIL   TriStar, 1989
DAD   Universal, 1989
FALL FROM GRACE (TF)   NBC Productions, 1990
A SHOW OF FORCE   Paramount, 1990
HENRY & JUNE   Universal, 1990
GLENGARRY GLEN ROSS   New Line Cinema, 1992
CONSENTING ADULTS   Buena Vista, 1992
IRON WILL   Buena Vista, 1994
THE REF   Buena Vista, 1994
REEL LIFE   1994
USUAL SUSPECTS   1995
OUTBREAK   Warner Bros., 1995

DAVID SPADE
POLICE ACADEMY 4: CITIZENS ON PATROL   Warner Bros., 1987
PCU   20th Century Fox, 1994
BILLY THE THIRD   Paramount, 1995

JAMES SPADER
b. February 7, 1960 - Boston, Massachusetts
Agent: ICM - Beverly Hills, 310/550-4000

ENDLESS LOVE   Universal, 1981
A KILLER IN THE FAMILY (TF)   Stan Margulies Productions/
   Sunn Classic Pictures, 1983
COCAINE: ONE MAN'S SEDUCTION (TF)   Charles Fries
   Productions/David Goldsmith Productions, 1983
THE NEW KIDS   Columbia, 1985
STARCROSSED (TF)   Fries Entertainment, 1985
TUFF TURF   New World, 1985
PRETTY IN PINK   Paramount, 1986
MANNEQUIN   20th Century Fox, 1987
BABY BOOM   MGM/UA, 1987
LESS THAN ZERO   20th Century Fox, 1987
WALL STREET   20th Century Fox, 1987
JACK'S BACK   Cinema Group, 1988
sex, lies, and videotape   Miramax Films, 1989
THE RACHEL PAPERS   MGM/UA, 1989, U.S.-British
BAD INFLUENCE   Triumph Releasing Corporation, 1990
WHITE PALACE   Universal, 1990

TRUE COLORS   Paramount, 1991
BOB ROBERTS   Paramount/Miramax Films, 1992
STORYVILLE   20th Century Fox, 1992
THE MUSIC OF CHANCE   I.R.S. Releasing, 1993
DREAM LOVER   Gramercy Pictures, 1994
WOLF   Columbia, 1994
STARGATE   MGM/UA, 1994

TIMOTHY SPALL
CRUSOE   Island Pictures, 1988, U.S.-British
THE SHELTERING SKY   Warner Bros., 1990, British

JOE SPANO
b. July 7, 1946 - San Francisco, California

THE BROTHERHOOD OF JUSTICE (TF)   Guber-Peters Productions/
   Phoenix Entertainment Group, 1986
DEEP DARK SECRETS (TF)   Gross-Weston Productions/
   Fries Entertainment, 1987
DISASTER AT SILO 7 (TF)   Mark Carliner Productions, 1988
CAST THE FIRST STONE (TF)   Mench Productions/Columbia TV, 1989

VINCENT SPANO
THE DOUBLE McGUFFIN   Mulberry Square, 1979
OVER THE EDGE   Orion/Warner Bros., 1979
THE BLACK STALLION RETURNS   MGM/UA, 1983
BABY IT'S YOU   Paramount, 1983
RUMBLEFISH   Universal, 1983
MARIA'S LOVERS   Cannon, 1984
ALPHABET CITY   Atlantic Releasing Corporation, 1984
CREATOR   Universal, 1985
GOOD MORNING, BABYLON   Vestron, 1987
AND GOD CREATED WOMAN   Vestron, 1988
OSCAR   Buena Vista, 1991
CITY OF HOPE   Samuel Goldwyn Company, 1991
ALIVE   Buena Vista, 1993
INDIAN SUMMER   Buena Vista, 1993
THE TIE THAT BINDS   Buena Vista, 1995

DANA SPARKS
THAT'S LIFE!   Columbia, 1986

WALTER SPARROW
ROBIN HOOD: PRINCE OF THIEVES   Warner Bros., 1991

JEFF SPEAKMAN
SIDE ROADS   1988
THE PERFECT WEAPON   Paramount, 1991

ARIES SPEARS
OUT OF SYNC   BET Films, 1994

DAVID SPECK
THE CLIENT   Warner Bros., 1994

GEORGINA SPELVIN
POLICE ACADEMY   The Ladd Company/Warner Bros., 1984
POLICE ACADEMY 3: BACK IN TRAINING   Warner Bros., 1986

JOHN SPENCER
b. 1946 - New Jersey

BLACK RAIN   Paramount, 1989
FORGET PARIS   Columbia, 1995

WENDIE JO SPERBER
BACK TO THE FUTURE   Universal, 1985

DAVID SPIELBERG
THE EFFECT OF GAMMA RAYS ON MAN-IN-THE-MOON
   MARIGOLDS   20th Century-Fox, 1972
NEWMAN'S LAW   Universal, 1974
HUSTLE   Paramount, 1975
THE CHOIRBOYS   Universal, 1977

THE END   United Artists, 1978
STONE (TF)   Stephen J. Cannell Productions/Universal TV, 1979
SWORN TO SILENCE (TF)   Daniel H. Blatt/Robert Singer
   Productions, 1987
ALICE   Orion, 1990

JOE SPINELL
THE GODFATHER, PART II   Paramount, 1974
TAXI DRIVER   Columbia, 1976
NIGHTHAWKS   Universal, 1981

STEPHEN SPINELLA
Agent: William Morris Agency - Beverly Hills, 310/274-7451

AND THE BAND PLAYED ON (CTF)   HBO Pictures/Spelling
   Entertainment, 1993

BRENT SPINER
MISS FIRECRACKER   Corsair Pictures, 1989
STAR TREK GENERATIONS   Paramount, 1994

VICTOR SPINETTI
THE PRINCESS AND THE GOBLIN (AF)   Hemdale, 1994 (voice)

TONY SPIRIDAKIS
QUEENS LOGIC   New Line Cinema, 1991

GREG SPORLEDER
RENAISSANCE MAN   Buena Vista, 1994

G.D. SPRADLIN
THE GODFATHER, PART II   Paramount, 1974
ONE ON ONE   Warner Bros., 1977
ROBERT KENNEDY AND HIS TIMES (MS)   Chris-Rose
   Productions/Columbia TV, 1985
RESTING PLACE (TF)   Marian Rees Associates, 1986
HOUSTON: THE LEGEND OF TEXAS (TF)   Taft Entertainment TV/
   J.D. Feigelson Productions, 1986
NUTCRACKER: MONEY, MADNESS AND MURDER (MS)
   Green Arrow Productions/Warner Bros. TV, 1987
THE WAR OF THE ROSES   20th Century Fox, 1989
ED WOOD   Buena Vista, 1994

RICK SPRINGFIELD
b. August 23, 1949 - Sydney, Australia

HARD TO HOLD   Universal, 1984
NICK KNIGHT (TF)   Barry Weitz Films/Robirdle Pictures/
   New World TV, 1989
DEAD RECKONING (CTF)   Houston Lady Productions, 1990

PAMELA SPRINGSTEEN
FAST TIMES AT RIDGEMONT HIGH   Universal, 1982
THE GUMSHOE KID   Argus Entertainment, 1989

VITTORIO SQUILLANTI
CAMORRA   *UN COMPLICATO INTRIGO DI DONNE,
   VICOLI E DELITTI*   Cannon, 1986, Italian

ROBERT STACK
b. January 13, 1919 - Los Angeles, California
Agent: The Blake Agency - Beverly Hills, 310/246-0241

FIRST LOVE   Universal, 1939
THE MORTAL STORM   MGM, 1940
A LITTLE BIT OF HEAVEN   1940
NICE GIRL?   Universal, 1941
BADLANDS OF DAKOTA   Universal, 1941
TO BE OR NOT TO BE   United Artists, 1942
MEN OF TEXAS   Universal, 1942
EAGLE SQUADRON   Universal, 1942
A DATE WITH JUDY   MGM, 1948
FIGHTER SQUADRON   Warner Bros., 1948
MISS TATLOCK'S MILLIONS   1948
MR. MUSIC   1950

MY OUTLAW BROTHER   Eagle Lion, 1951
THE BULLFIGHTER AND THE LADY   Republic, 1951
BWANA DEVIL   United Artists, 1952
WAR PAINT   United Artists, 1953
CONQUEST OF COCHISE   Columbia, 1953
SABRE JET   1953
THE HIGH AND THE MIGHTY   Warner Bros., 1954
THE IRON GLOVE   Columbia, 1954
HOUSE OF BAMBOO   20th Century-Fox, 1955
GOOD MORNING, MISS DOVE   20th Century-Fox, 1955
GREAT DAY IN THE MORNING   RKO Radio, 1956
WRITTEN ON THE WIND ✪   Universal, 1957
THE TARNISHED ANGELS   Universal, 1958
THE GIFT OF LOVE   20th Century-Fox, 1958
JOHN PAUL JONES   Warner Bros., 1959
THE LAST VOYAGE   MGM, 1960
THE SCARFACE MOB   Desilu, 1962
THE GUEST   *THE CARETAKERS*   Janus, 1963, British
IS PARIS BURNING?   *PARIS BRULE-T-IL?*   Paramount,
   1966, French-U.S.
THE CORRUPT ONES   Warner Bros., 1966,
   Italian-West German-French
THE ACTION MAN   *LE SOLEIL DES VOYOUS*
   H.K. Film Distribution, 1967, French-Italian
STORY OF A WOMAN   1970, Italian-U.S.
THE STRANGE AND DEADLY OCCURRENCE (TF)
   Metromedia Productions, 1974
MURDER ON FLIGHT 502 (TF)   Spelling-Goldberg Productions, 1975
ADVENTURES OF THE QUEEN (TF)   20th Century-Fox TV, 1975
A SECOND WIND   *UN SECOND SOUFFLE*   1978, French
1941   Universal/Columbia, 1979
AIRPLANE!   Paramount, 1980
UNCOMMON VALOUR   Paramount, 1983
BIG TROUBLE   Columbia, 1986
THE TRANSFORMERS (AF)   DEG, 1986 (voice)
PERRY MASON: THE CASE OF THE SINISTER SPIRIT (TF)
   The Fred Silverman Company/Strathmore Productions/Viacom
   Productions, 1987
CADDYSHACK II   Warner Bros., 1988
JOE VERSUS THE VOLCANO   Warner Bros., 1990

MICHELLE STACY
AIRPLANE!   Paramount, 1980

KATHY STAFF
MARY REILLY   TriStar, 1995

NICK STAHL
Agent: UTA - Beverly Hills, 310/273-6700

THE MAN WITHOUT A FACE   Warner Bros., 1993
TALL TALE   Buena Vista, 1994

JAMES STALEY
AMERICAN DREAMER   Warner Bros., 1984

FRANK STALLONE
STAYING ALIVE   Paramount, 1983
BARFLY   Cannon, 1987
CROSSING THE MOB (TF)   Bateman Company Productions/
   Interscope Communications, 1988
HEART OF MIDNIGHT   Virgin Vision, 1989
HUDSON HAWK   TriStar, 1991

SAGE STALLONE
ROCKY V   MGM/UA, 1990

SYLVESTER STALLONE
(Michael Sylvester Stallone)
b. July 6, 1946 - New York, New York
Agent: CAA - Beverly Hills, 310/288-4545

A PARTY AT KITTY AND STUD'S   *THE ITALIAN STALLION*   1970
BANANAS   United Artists, 1971 (uncredited)
THE LORDS OF FLATBUSH   Columbia, 1974
THE PRISONER OF SECOND AVENUE   Warner Bros., 1975
CAPONE   20th Century-Fox, 1975

DEATH RACE 2000   New World, 1975
FAREWELL, MY LOVELY   Avco Embassy, 1975
NO PLACE TO HIDE   American Films Ltd., 1975
CANNONBALL   New World, 1976
ROCKY ★   United Artists, 1976
F.I.S.T.   United Artists, 1978
PARADISE ALLEY   Universal, 1978 (also directed)
ROCKY II   United Artists, 1979 (also directed)
NIGHTHAWKS   Universal, 1981
VICTORY   Paramount, 1981
FIRST BLOOD   Orion, 1982, Canadian
ROCKY III   MGM/UA, 1982 (also directed)
RHINESTONE   20th Century Fox, 1984
RAMBO: FIRST BLOOD PART II   TriStar, 1985
ROCKY IV   MGM/UA, 1985 (also directed)
COBRA   Warner Bros., 1986
OVER THE TOP   Cannon, 1987
RAMBO III   TriStar, 1988
LOCK UP   TriStar, 1989
TANGO & CASH   Warner Bros., 1989
ROCKY V   MGM/UA, 1990
OSCAR   Buena Vista, 1991
STOP! OR MY MOM WILL SHOOT   Universal, 1992
CLIFFHANGER   TriStar, 1993
DEMOLITION MAN   Warner Bros., 1993
THE SPECIALIST   Warner Bros., 1994
JUDGE DREDD   Buena Vista, 1995
FAIR GAME   Warner Bros., 1995

JOHN STAMOS

Agent: William Morris Agency - Beverly Hills, 310/274-7451

DAUGHTER OF THE STREETS (TF)   Adam Productions/
    20th Century Fox TV, 1990
BORN TO RIDE   Warner Bros., 1991

TERENCE STAMP

b. July 23, 1939 - Stepney, East London, England

BILLY BUDD ✪   Allied Artists, 1962
TERM OF TRIAL   Warner Bros., 1963, British
THE COLLECTOR   Columbia, 1965, U.S.-British
MODESTY BLAISE   20th Century-Fox, 1966, British
FAR FROM THE MADDING CROWD   MGM, 1967, British
POOR COW   National General, 1967, British
BLUE   Paramount, 1968, British
SPIRITS OF THE DEAD   HISTOIRES EXTRAORDINAIRES
    American International, 1968, French-Italian
TEOREMA   Continental, 1968, Italian
THE MIND OF MR. SOAMES   Columbia, 1970, British
HU-NAN   1975, French
DIVINA CREATURA   1976, Italian
AMO NON AMO   1979, Italian
SUPERMAN   Warner Bros., 1978
MEETINGS WITH REMARKABLE MEN   Libra, 1979, British
THE THIEF OF BAGHDAD (TF)   Palm Films, Ltd., 1979, British
SUPERMAN II   Warner Bros., 1981, U.S.-British
THE HIT   Island Alive, 1984, British
THE COMPANY OF WOLVES   Cannon, 1984, British
LINK   Thorn EMI/Cannon, 1986, U.S.-British
THE SICILIAN   20th Century Fox, 1987
WALL STREET   20th Century Fox, 1987
YOUNG GUNS   20th Century Fox, 1988
ALIEN NATION   20th Century Fox, 1988
GENUINE RISK   I.R.S., 1990
THE REAL McCOY   Universal, 1993
THE ADVENTURES OF PRISCILLA, QUEEN OF THE DESERT
    Gramercy Pictures, 1994, Australian

LIONEL STANDER

b. January 11, 1908 - New York, New York

THE SCOUNDREL   Paramount, 1935
PAGE MISS GLORY   Warner Bros., 1935
SOAK THE RICH   Paramount, 1936
THE MILKY WAY   Paramount, 1936
MR. DEEDS GOES TO TOWN   Columbia, 1936
MEET NERO WOLFE   Columbia, 1936

A STAR IS BORN   United Artists, 1937
THE LEAGUE OF FRIGHTENED MEN   Columbia, 1937
THE LAST GANGSTER   1937
PROFESSOR BEWARE   Paramount, 1938
THE CROWD ROARS   MGM, 1938
WHAT A LIFE   1939
THE BRIDE WORE CRUTCHES   1941
HANGMEN ALSO DIE   United Artists, 1943
GUADALCANAL DIARY   20th Century-Fox, 1943
THE KID FROM BROOKLYN   1946
SPECTER OF THE ROSE   Republic, 1946
MAD WEDNESDAY   THE SIN OF HAROLD DIDDLEBLOCK
    RKO Radio, 1947
CALL NORTHSIDE 777   CALLING NORTHSIDE 777
    20th Century-Fox, 1948
UNFAITHFULLY YOURS   20th Century-Fox, 1948
ST. BENNY THE DIP   United Artists, 1951
THE LOVED ONE   MGM, 1965
CUL-DE-SAC   Sigma III, 1966, British
PROMISE HER ANYTHING   Paramount, 1966
A DANDY IN ASPIC   Columbia, 1968, British
ONCE UPON A TIME IN THE WEST   Paramount, 1969, Italian-U.S.
THE CROSS-EYED SAINT   PER GRAZIA RICEVUTA   1971, Italian
THE GANG THAT COULDN'T SHOOT STRAIGHT   MGM, 1971
TREASURE ISLAND   National General, 1972,
    British-French-West German-Spanish
PULP   United Artists, 1972, British
THE SENSUOUS MAN   THE SENSUOUS SICILIAN   1973, Italian
THE BLACK BIRD   Columbia, 1975
AH SI?...E IO LO DICO A ZORRO   1975, Italian
THE CASSANDRA CROSSING   Avco Embassy, 1977,
    British-Italian-West German
NEW YORK, NEW YORK   United Artists, 1977
MATILDA   American International, 1978
HART TO HART (TF)   Spelling-Goldberg Productions, 1979
THE TRANSFORMERS (AF)   DEG, 1986 (voice)
WICKED STEPMOTHER   MGM, 1988
COOKIE   Warner Bros., 1989
HART TO HART: HOME IS WHERE THE HART IS (TF)   NBC, 1994
HART TO HART: OLD FRIENDS NEVER DIE (TF)   NBC, 1994

JIM STANDIFORD

VIOLETS ARE BLUE   Columbia, 1986

BROOKE STANLEY

THE SKATEBOARD KID II   Concorde, 1995

FLORENCE STANLEY

Agent: William Morris Agency - Beverly Hills, 310/274-7451

TRAPPED IN PARADISE   20th Century Fox, 1994

KIM STANLEY

(Patricia Kimberly Reid)
b. February 11, 1925 - Tularosa, New Mexico

THE GODDESS   Columbia, 1958
SEANCE ON A WET AFTERNOON ★   Artixo, 1964, British
THREE SISTERS   NTA, 1966
FRANCES ✪   Universal/AFD, 1982
THE RIGHT STUFF   The Ladd Company/Warner Bros., 1983

LAUREN STANLEY

MAC AND ME   Orion, 1988

CLAIRE STANSFIELD

DROP ZONE   Paramount, 1994

HARRY DEAN STANTON

b. July 14, 1926 - Kentucky

DRAGOON WELLS MASSACRE   1957
HOW THE WEST WAS WON   MGM/Cinerama, 1963
THE MAN FROM THE DINER'S CLUB   Columbia, 1963
COOL HAND LUKE   Warner Bros., 1967
CISCO PIKE   Columbia, 1972

DILLINGER   American International, 1973
COCKFIGHTER   *BORN TO KILL/WILD DRIFTER/GAMBLIN' MAN*
   New World, 1974
ZANDY'S BRIDE   *FOR BETTER, FOR WORSE*
   Warner Bros., 1974
THE GODFATHER, PART II   Paramount, 1974
FAREWELL, MY LOVELY   Avco Embassy, 1975
THE MISSOURI BREAKS   United Artists, 1976
ALIEN   20th Century-Fox, 1979, U.S.-British
THE ROSE   20th Century-Fox, 1979
WISE BLOOD   New Line Cinema, 1979
THE BLACK MARBLE   Avco Embassy, 1980
PRIVATE BENJAMIN   Warner Bros., 1980
ONE FROM THE HEART   Columbia, 1982
YOUNG DOCTORS IN LOVE   20th Century-Fox, 1982
CHRISTINE   Columbia, 1983
PARIS, TEXAS   TLC Films/20th Century Fox, 1984,
   West German-French
RED DAWN   MGM/UA, 1984
REPO MAN   Universal, 1984
FOOL FOR LOVE   Cannon, 1985
ONE MAGIC CHRISTMAS   Buena Vista, 1985, U.S.-Canadian
PRETTY IN PINK   Paramount, 1986
SLAM DANCE   Island Pictures, 1987
MR. NORTH   Samuel Goldwyn Company, 1988
THE LAST TEMPTATION OF CHRIST   Universal, 1988
DREAM A LITTLE DREAM   Vestron, 1989
THE FOURTH WAR   Cannon, 1990
WILD AT HEART   Samuel Goldwyn Company, 1990
MAN TROUBLE   20th Century Fox, 1992
TWIN PEAKS: FIRE WALK WITH ME   New Line Cinema,
   992, U.S.-French

JOHN STANTON

TAI-PAN   DEG, 1986
RENT-A-COP   Kings Road Productions, 1988

MAVIS STAPLES

GRAFFITI BRIDGE   Warner Bros., 1990

JEAN STAPLETON

(Jeanne Murray)
b. January 19, 1923 - New York, New York

DAMN YANKEES   Warner Bros., 1958
BELLS ARE RINGING   MGM, 1960
SOMETHING WILD   United Artists, 1961
UP THE DOWN STAIRCASE   Warner Bros., 1967
COLD TURKEY   United Artists, 1971
KLUTE   Warner Bros., 1971
AGATHA CHRISTIE'S "DEAD MAN'S FOLLY" (TF)
   Warner Bros. TV, 1986, U.S.-British
MOTHER GOOSE ROCK 'N' RHYME (CTF)
   Think Entertainment, 1990

MAUREEN STAPLETON

b. June 21, 1925 - Troy, New York
Agent: ICM - Beverly Hills, 310/550-4000

LONELYHEARTS ✪   United Artists, 1958
THE FUGITIVE KIND   United Artists, 1960
A VIEW FROM THE BRIDGE   *VU DU PONT*   Allied Artists,
   1962, French-Italian
BYE BYE BIRDIE   Columbia, 1963
TRILOGY   Allied Artists, 1969
AIRPORT ✪   Universal, 1970
PLAZA SUITE   Paramount, 1971
TELL ME WHERE IT HURTS (TF)   Tomorrow Entertainment, 1974
QUEEN OF THE STARDUST BALLROOM (TF)
   Tomorrow Entertainment, 1975
THE GATHERING (TF)   Hanna-Barbera Productions, 1977
INTERIORS ✪   United Artists, 1978
THE RUNNER STUMBLES   20th Century-Fox, 1979
LOST AND FOUND   Columbia, 1979
THE GATHERING, PART II (TF)   Hanna-Barbera Productions, 1979
THE FAN   Paramount, 1981
REDS ✪✪   Paramount, 1981

JOHNNY DANGEROUSLY   20th Century Fox, 1984
SENTIMENTAL JOURNEY (TF)   Lucille Ball Productions/
   Smith-Richmond Productions/20th Century Fox TV, 1984
PRIVATE SESSIONS (TF)   The Belle Company/Seltzer-Gimbel
   Productions/Raven's Claw Productions/Comworld
   Productions, 1985
COCOON   20th Century Fox, 1985
THE COSMIC EYE (AF)   1985 (voice)
THE MONEY PIT   Universal, 1986
HEARTBURN   Paramount, 1986
SWEET LORRAINE   Angelika Films, 1987
MADE IN HEAVEN   Lorimar, 1987
LIBERACE: BEHIND THE MUSIC (TF)   Canadian International
   Studios/Kushner-Locke Productions, 1988, U.S.-Canadian
COCOON: THE RETURN   20th Century Fox, 1988
PASSED AWAY   Buena Vista, 1992
TRADING MOM   Trimark Pictures, 1994

NICOLA STAPLETON

COURAGE MOUNTAIN   Triumph Releasing Corporation,
   1989, U.S.-French

ANTHONY STARKE

LICENCE TO KILL   MGM/UA, 1989, British

BEAU STARR

HALLOWEEN 5 - THE REVENGE OF MICHAEL MYERS
   Galaxy, 1989

BLAZE STARR

BLAZE   Buena Vista, 1989

MIKE STARR

MAD DOG AND GLORY   Universal, 1993
ED WOOD   Buena Vista, 1994
A PYROMANIAC'S LOVE STORY   Buena Vista, 1994

RINGO STARR

(Richard Starkey)
b. July 7, 1940 - Liverpool, England

WHAT'S HAPPENING: THE BEATLES IN THE USA (FD)   1964
A HARD DAY'S NIGHT   United Artists, 1964, British
HELP!   United Artists, 1965, British
YELLOW SUBMARINE (AF)   1968, British (voice)
CANDY   1968
LET IT BE (FD)   United Artists, 1970, British
THE MAGIC CHRISTIAN   Commonwealth United, 1970, British
THE KIDS ARE ALRIGHT (FD)   New World, 1979, British
WATER   Atlantic Releasing Corporation, 1984, British (uncredited)

ROBERT STARR

AIRPLANE!   Paramount, 1980

ALISON STEADMAN

CLOCKWISE   Universal, 1986, British
THE ADVENTURES OF BARON MUNCHAUSEN   Columbia, 1989
LIFE IS SWEET   Republic Pictures, 1991
BLAME IT ON THE BELLBOY   Buena Vista, 1992, British

RED STEAGALL

BENJI THE HUNTED   Buena Vista, 1987

TED STEEDMAN

BILL & TED'S EXCELLENT ADVENTURE   Orion, 1989

AMY STEEL

FIRST STEPS (TF)   CBS Entertainment, 1985
APRIL FOOL'S DAY   Paramount, 1986

GEORGE "THE ANIMAL" STEELE

ED WOOD   Buena Vista, 1994

JESSICA STEEN
SING   TriStar, 1989

MARY STEENBURGEN
b. 1953 - Little Rock, Arkansas
Agent: William Morris Agency - Beverly Hills, 310/274-7451

GOIN' SOUTH   Paramount, 1978
RABBIT TEST   Avco Embassy, 1978
TIME AFTER TIME   Orion/Warner Bros., 1979
MELVIN AND HOWARD ○○   Universal, 1980
RAGTIME   Paramount, 1981
A MIDSUMMER NIGHT'S SEX COMEDY   Orion/Warner Bros., 1982
CROSS CREEK   Universal/AFD, 1983
ROMANTIC COMEDY   MGM/UA, 1983
ONE MAGIC CHRISTMAS   Buena Vista, 1985, U.S.-Canadian
DEAD OF WINTER   MGM/UA, 1987
THE WHALES OF AUGUST   Alive Films, 1987
END OF THE LINE   Orion Classics, 1988
THE ATTIC: THE HIDING OF ANNE FRANK (TF)
   Telecom Entertainment/Yorkshire TV, 1988, U.S.-British
MISS FIRECRACKER   Corsair Pictures, 1989
PARENTHOOD   Universal, 1989
BACK TO THE FUTURE PART III   Universal, 1990
THE LONG WALK HOME   Miramax Films, 1990 (voice)
THE BUTCHER'S WIFE   Paramount, 1991
WHAT'S EATING GILBERT GRAPE   Paramount, 1993
PHILADELPHIA   TriStar, 1993
CLIFFORD   Orion, 1994
IT RUNS IN THE FAMILY   MGM/UA, 1994
PONTIAC MOON   Paramount, 1994

ROD STEIGER
(Rodney Stephen Steiger)
b. April 14, 1925 - Westhampton, New York

TERESA   MGM, 1951
ON THE WATERFRONT ○   Columbia, 1954
OKLAHOMA!   Magna, 1955
THE BIG KNIFE   United Artists, 1955
THE COURT-MARTIAL OF BILLY MITCHELL   Warner Bros., 1955
JUBAL   Columbia, 1956
THE HARDER THEY FALL   Columbia, 1956
BACK FROM ETERNITY   RKO Radio, 1956
RUN OF THE ARROW   1957
ACROSS THE BRIDGE   1957, British
THE UNHOLY WIFE   Universal, 1957
CRY TERROR   MGM, 1958
AL CAPONE   Allied Artists, 1959
SEVEN THIEVES   20th Century-Fox, 1960
THE MARK   Continental, 1961, British
ON FRIDAY AT ELEVEN   British Lion, 1961, West German-British
THE WORLD IN MY POCKET   MGM, 1962,
   West German-French-Italian
13 WEST STREET   Columbia, 1962
CONVICTS FOUR   1962
THE LONGEST DAY   20th Century-Fox, 1962
HANDS OVER THE CITY   *LE MANI SULLA CITTA*   1963, Italian
TIME OF INDIFFERENCE   *GLI INDIFFERENTI*   1964, Italian
A MAN CALLED JOHN   1964
AND THERE CAME A MAN   *E VENNE UN UOMO*   Brandon,
   1965, Italian-French
THE PAWNBROKER ★   Landau/Allied Artists, 1965
THE LOVED ONE   1965
DOCTOR ZHIVAGO   MGM, 1965, British
THE GIRL AND THE GENERAL   *LA RAGAZZA E IL GENERALE*
   MGM, 1967, Italian-French
IN THE HEAT OF THE NIGHT ★★   United Artists, 1967
NO WAY TO TREAT A LADY   Paramount, 1968
THE SERGEANT   Warner Bros., 1968
THREE INTO TWO WON'T GO   1969, British
THE ILLUSTRATED MAN   Warner Bros., 1969
WATERLOO   Paramount, 1970, Soviet-Italian
HAPPY BIRTHDAY WANDA JUNE   Columbia, 1971
DUCK YOU SUCKER!   *A FISTFUL OF DYNAMITE/GIU LA TESTA*
   United Artists, 1972, Italian-U.S.
RE: LUCKY LUCIANO   *A PROPOSITO LUCIANO*   1973, Italian
LOLLY MADONNA XXX   MGM, 1973

THE HEROES   *GLI EROI*   1973, Italian
THE LAST FOUR DAYS   *LAST DAYS OF MUSSOLINI*   Group 1,
   1974, Italian
DIRTY HANDS   *LES INNOCENTS AUX MAINS SALES*
   New Line Cinema, 1975, French
HENNESSY   American International, 1975, British
W.C. FIELDS AND ME   Universal, 1976
JESUS OF NAZARETH (MS)   Sir Lew Grade Productions/ITC,
   1977, British-Italian
JIMBUCK   1977
WOLF LAKE   *THE HONOR GUARD*   Filmcorp Distribution,
   1978, Canadian
F.I.S.T.   United Artists, 1978
LOVE AND BULLETS   AFD, 1978, British
BREAKTHROUGH   *SERGEANT STEINER*   Maverick Pictures
   International, 1979, West German
THE AMITYVILLE HORROR   American International, 1979
THE LUCKY STAR   Pickman Films, 1980, Canadian
KLONDIKE FEVER   1979
CATTLE ANNIE AND LITTLE BRITCHES   Universal, 1979
LION OF THE DESERT   United Film Distribution,
   1981, Libyan-British
THE CHOSEN   20th Century-Fox International Classics, 1982
THE MAGIC MOUNTAIN   1982
THE GLORY BOYS (TF)   Yorkshire TV/Alan Landsburg Productions,
   1984, British-U.S.
HOLLYWOOD WIVES (MS)   Aaron Spelling Productions, 1984
THE NAKED FACE   Cannon, 1984
THE KINDRED   FM Entertainment, 1986
CATCH THE HEAT   *FEEL THE HEAT*   Trans World
   Entertainment, 1987
AMERICAN GOTHIC   Vidmark, 1987, British
THE JANUARY MAN   MGM/UA, 1989
TENNESSEE WALTZ   Condor Productions, 1989
MEN OF RESPECT   Columbia, 1991
GUILTY AS CHARGED   I.R.S. Releasing, 1991
THE PLAYER   Fine Line Features/New Line Cinema, 1992
THE SPECIALIST   Warner Bros., 1994

MARGARET SOPHIE STEIN
ENEMIES, A LOVE STORY   20th Century Fox, 1989

SAUL STEIN
NEW JERSEY DRIVE   Gramercy Pictures, 1994

DAVID STEINBERG
b. August 9, 1942 - Winnipeg, Canada

THE END   United Artists, 1978

GEORGE STEINBRENNER
THE SCOUT   20th Century Fox, 1994

JAKE STEINFELD
TOUGH GUYS   Buena Vista, 1986
COMING TO AMERICA   Paramount, 1988

ROBERT STEINMILLER, JR.
BINGO!   TriStar, 1991
JACK THE BEAR   20th Century Fox, 1992
THE REF   Buena Vista, 1994

ROBERT STEPHENS
b. July 14, 1931 - Bristol, England

CIRCLE OF DECEPTION   1961
PIRATES OF TORTUGA   1961
A TASTE OF HONEY   Continental, 1961, British
LISA   *THE INSPECTOR*   20th Century-Fox, 1962, British-U.S.
THE SMALL WORLD OF SAMMY LEE   7 Arts, 1963, British
CLEOPATRA   20th Century-Fox, 1963, British-U.S.
MORGAN!   *MORGAN—A SUITABLE CASE FOR TREATMENT*
   Cinema 5, 1966, British
ROMEO AND JULIET   Paramount, 1968, British-Italian
THE PRIME OF MISS JEAN BRODIE   20th Century-Fox,
   1969, British

THE PRIVATE LIFE OF SHERLOCK HOLMES   United Artists,
   1970, British-U.S.
THE ASPHYX   1972
TRAVELS WITH MY AUNT   MGM, 1972, British-U.S.
LUTHER   American Film Theatre, 1973, British-U.S.
QB VII (TF)   Screen Gems/Columbia TV/The Douglas Cramer
   Company, 1973
HOLOCAUST (MS)   Titus Productions, 1978
THE SHOUT   Films Inc., 1978, British
FORTUNES OF WAR (TF)   BBC/WGBH-TV/Primetime TV,
   1987, British-U.S.
EMPIRE OF THE SUN   Warner Bros., 1987
WAR AND REMEMBRANCE (MS)   Dan Curtis Productions/
   ABC Circle Films, 1987
HIGH SEASON   Hemdale, 1987, British
TESTIMONY (TF)   European Classics, 1987, British
HENRY V   Samuel Goldwyn Company, 1989, British
SEARCHING FOR BOBBY FISCHER   Paramount, 1993

PAMELA STEPHENSON

HISTORY OF THE WORLD—PART 1   20th Century-Fox, 1981
SUPERMAN III   Warner Bros., 1983, U.S.-British
SCANDALOUS   Orion, 1984
FINDERS KEEPERS   Warner Bros., 1984

DANIEL STERN
Agent: CAA - Beverly Hills, 310/288-4545

BREAKING AWAY   20th Century-Fox, 1979
IT'S MY TURN   Columbia, 1980
STARDUST MEMORIES   United Artists, 1980
DINER   MGM/United Artists, 1982
BLUE THUNDER   Columbia, 1983
HANNAH AND HER SISTERS   Orion, 1986
WEEKEND WAR (TF)   Pompian-Atamian Productions/
   Columbia TV, 1988
THE MILAGRO BEANFIELD WAR   Universal, 1988
D.O.A.   Buena Vista, 1988
LITTLE MONSTERS   MGM/UA, 1989
COUPE DE VILLE   Universal, 1990
HOME ALONE   20th Century Fox, 1990
CITY SLICKERS   Columbia, 1991
HOME ALONE 2: LOST IN NEW YORK   20th Century Fox, 1992
ROOKIE OF THE YEAR   20th Century Fox, 1993 (also directed)
CITY SLICKERS II: THE LEGEND OF CURLY'S GOLD
   Columbia, 1994
TENDERFOOTS   20th Century Fox, 1995

FRANCES STERNHAGEN
Agent: William Morris Agency - Beverly Hills, 310/274-7451

STARTING OVER   Paramount, 1979
OUTLAND   The Ladd Company/Warner Bros., 1981
INDEPENDENCE DAY   Warner Bros., 1983
ROMANTIC COMEDY   MGM/UA, 1983
AT MOTHER'S REQUEST (TF)   Vista Organization, Ltd., 1987
BRIGHT LIGHTS, BIG CITY   MGM/UA, 1988
SEE YOU IN THE MORNING   Warner Bros., 1989
COMMUNION   MCEG, 1989
FOLLOW YOUR HEART (TF)   Force Ten Productions/
   Danson-Fauci Productions/NBC Productions, 1990
MISERY   Columbia, 1990
DOC HOLLYWOOD   Warner Bros., 1991
RAISING CAIN   Universal, 1992

ROBYN STEVAN

BYE BYE BLUES   Circle Releasing Corporation, 1990, Canadian
STEPPING OUT   Paramount, 1991

ANDREW STEVENS
b. June 10, 1955 - Memphis, Tennessee

LAS VEGAS LADY   Crown International, 1976
VIGILANTE FORCE   United Artists, 1976
THE BASTARD (TF)   Universal TV, 1978
THE BOYS IN COMPANY C   Columbia, 1978
THE FURY   20th Century-Fox, 1978

WOMEN AT WEST POINT (TF)   Green-Epstein Productions/
   Alan Sacks Productions, 1979
TOPPER (TF)   Cosmo Prods./Robert A. Papazian Productions, 1980
MIRACLE ON ICE (TF)   Moonlight Productions/Filmways, 1981
THE SEDUCTION   Avco Embassy, 1982
TEN TO MIDNIGHT   1983
HOLLYWOOD WIVES (MS)   Aaron Spelling Productions, 1985
ONCE AN EAGLE (TF)   Universal TV, 1986
THE TERROR WITHIN   Concorde, 1988
THE TERROR WITHIN II   Concorde, 1991 (also directed)
THE SKATEBOARD KID II   Concorde, 1995

CONNIE STEVENS
(Concetta Ann Ingolia)
b. August 8, 1938 - Brooklyn, New York

EIGHTEEN AND ANXIOUS   1957
YOUNG AND DANGEROUS   20th Century-Fox, 1957
ROCK-A-BYE BABY   Paramount, 1958
THE PARTY CRASHERS   Paramount, 1958
PARRISH   Warner Bros., 1961
SUSAN SLADE   Warner Bros., 1961
PALM SPRINGS WEEKEND   Warner Bros., 1963
TWO ON A GUILLOTINE   Warner Bros., 1965
NEVER TOO LATE   Warner Bros., 1965
WAY...WAY OUT   20th Century-Fox, 1966
MISTER JERICHO (TF)   ITC, 1970. British
THE GRISSOM GANG   Cinerama Releasing Corporation, 1971
PLAYMATES (TF)   ABC Circle Films, 1972
THE SEX SYMBOL (TF)   Screen Gems/Columbia, 1973
SCORCHY   American International, 1976
BACK TO THE BEACH   Paramount, 1987
BRING ME THE HEAD OF DOBIE GILLIS (TF)
   20th Century Fox TV, 1988

FISHER STEVENS
Agent: William Morris Agency - Beverly Hills, 310/274-7451

THE BROTHER FROM ANOTHER PLANET   Cinecom, 1984
MY SCIENCE PROJECT   Buena Vista, 1985
SHORT CIRCUIT   TriStar, 1986
SHORT CIRCUIT 2   TriStar, 1988
BLOODHOUNDS OF BROADWAY   Columbia, 1989
REVERSAL OF FORTUNE   Warner Bros., 1990
THE MARRYING MAN   Buena Vista, 1991
MYSTERY DATE   Orion, 1991
ONLY YOU   TriStar, 1994

MORGAN STEVENS
A YEAR IN THE LIFE (MS)   Universal TV, 1986
ROSES ARE FOR THE RICH (MS)   Phoenix Entertainment
   Group, 1987
DEEP DARK SECRETS (TF)   Gross-Weston Productions/Fries
   Entertainment, 1987

SCOTT NEWTON STEVENS
FLIGHT OF THE INTRUDER   Paramount, 1991

SHADOE STEVENS
TRAXX   DEG, 1988

STELLA STEVENS
(Estelle Egglestone)
b. October 1, 1936 - Hot Coffee, Mississippi

SAY ONE FOR ME   20th Century-Fox, 1959
LI'L ABNER   Paramount, 1959
MAN-TRAP   1961
TOO LATE BLUES   Paramount, 1962
THE COURTSHIP OF EDDIE'S FATHER   MGM, 1963
THE NUTTY PROFESSOR   Paramount, 1963
ADVANCE TO THE REAR   MGM, 1964
SYNANON   Columbia, 1965
THE SECRET OF MY SUCCESS   MGM, 1965, British
THE SILENCERS   Columbia, 1966
HOW TO SAVE A MARRIAGE...AND RUIN YOUR LIFE
   Columbia, 1968

WHERE ANGELS GO...TROUBLE FOLLOWS!   Columbia, 1968
SOL MADRID   MGM, 1968
THE MAD ROOM   Columbia, 1969
THE BALLAD OF CABLE HOGUE   Warner Bros., 1970
A TOWN CALLED BASTARD   *A TOWN CALLED HELL*
   Scotia International, 1971, British-Spanish
STAND UP AND BE COUNTED   Columbia, 1971
SLAUGHTER   American International, 1972
THE POSEIDON ADVENTURE   20th Century-Fox, 1972
ARNOLD   Cinerama Releasing Corporation, 1973
CLEOPATRA JONES AND THE CASINO OF GOLD
   Warner Bros., 1975
LAS VEGAS LADY   Crown International, 1976
KISS ME, KILL ME (TF)   Columbia TV, 1976
NICKELODEON   Columbia, 1976
THE NIGHT THEY TOOK MISS BEAUTIFUL (TF)   Don Kirshner
   Productions, 1977
CRUISE INTO TERROR (TF)   Aaron Spelling Productions, 1978
THE MANITOU   1978
MAN AGAINST THE MOB (TF)   Frank von Zerneck Films, 1988
THE TERROR WITHIN II   Concorde, 1991

WARREN STEVENS
GUARDIAN ANGEL   PM Entertainment, 1994

CYNTHIA STEVENSON
Agent: William Morris Agency - Beverly Hills, 310/274-7451

THE PLAYER   Fine Line Features/New Line Cinema, 1992

JULIET STEVENSON
Agent: William Morris Agency - Beverly Hills, 310/274-7451

TRULY, MADLY, DEEPLY   Samuel Goldwyn Company, 1991

PARKER STEVENSON
b. June 4, 1952 - Philadelphia, Pennsylvania

STROKER ACE   Universal, 1983
THAT SECRET SUNDAY (TF)   CBS Entertainment, 1986
PROBE (TF)   MCA Television, Ltd., 1988
THE COVER GIRL AND THE COP (TF)   Barry & Enright
   Productions, 1989
BAYWATCH: PANIC AT MALIBU PIER (TF)
   GTG Entertainment, 1989

CATHERINE MARY STEWART
NIGHTHAWKS   Universal, 1981
WITH INTENT TO KILL (TF)   London Productions, 1984
MISCHIEF   20th Century Fox, 1985
MURDER BY THE BOOK (TF)   Nelson Productions/Orion TV, 1987
DUDES   New Century/Vista, 1987
PASSION AND PARADISE (MS)   Picturebase International/Primedia
   Productions/Leonard Hill Films, 1989, U.S.-Canadian
WEEKEND AT BERNIE'S   20th Century Fox, 1989

DON STEWART
AMERICAN NINJA   Cannon, 1985

JAMES STEWART
b. May 20, 1908 - Indiana, Pennsylvania

THE MURDER MAN   MGM, 1935
NEXT TIME WE LOVE   MGM, 1936
ROSE MARIE   MGM, 1936
WIFE VS. SECRETARY   MGM, 1936
SMALL TOWN GIRL   MGM, 1936
SPEED   MGM, 1936
THE GORGEOUS HUSSY   MGM, 1936
BORN TO DANCE   MGM, 1936
AFTER THE THIN MAN   MGM, 1936
SEVENTH HEAVEN   20th Century-Fox, 1937
THE LAST GANGSTER   1937
NAVY BLUE AND GOLD   MGM, 1937
OF HUMAN HEARTS   MGM, 1938
VIVACIOUS LADY   RKO Radio, 1938

THE SHOPWORN ANGEL   MGM, 1938
YOU CAN'T TAKE IT WITH YOU   Columbia, 1938
MADE FOR EACH OTHER   United Artists, 1939
ICE FOLLIES OF 1939   1939
IT'S A WONDERFUL WORLD   MGM, 1939
MR. SMITH GOES TO WASHINGTON ★   Columbia, 1939
DESTRY RIDES AGAIN   Universal, 1939
THE SHOP AROUND THE CORNER   MGM, 1940
THE MORTAL STORM   MGM, 1940
NO TIME FOR COMEDY   Warner Bros., 1940
THE PHILADELPHIA STORY ★★   MGM, 1940
COME LIVE WITH ME   MGM, 1941
POT O' GOLD   United Artists, 1941
ZIEGFELD GIRL   MGM, 1941
IT'S A WONDERFUL LIFE ★   RKO Radio, 1946
MAGIC TOWN   RKO Radio, 1947
ON OUR MERRY WAY   *A MIRACLE CAN HAPPEN*
   United Artists, 1948
CALL NORTHSIDE 777   20th Century-Fox, 1948
ROPE   Warner Bros., 1948, U.S.-British
YOU GOTTA STAY HAPPY   Universal, 1948
THE STRATTON STORY   MGM, 1949
MALAYA   MGM, 1950
WINCHESTER 73   Universal, 1950
BROKEN ARROW   20th Century-Fox, 1950
THE JACKPOT   20th Century-Fox, 1950
HARVEY ★   Universal, 1950
NO HIGHWAY IN THE SKY   *NO HIGHWAY*   20th Century-Fox,
   1951, British
THE GREATEST SHOW ON EARTH   Paramount, 1952
BEND OF THE RIVER   Universal, 1952
CARBINE WILLIAMS   MGM, 1952
THE NAKED SPUR   MGM, 1953
THUNDER BAY   Universal, 1953
THE GLENN MILLER STORY   Universal, 1954
REAR WINDOW   Paramount, 1954
THE FAR COUNTRY   Universal, 1955
STRATEGIC AIR COMMAND   Paramount, 1955
THE MAN FROM LARAMIE   Columbia, 1955
THE MAN WHO KNEW TOO MUCH   Paramount, 1956
THE SPIRIT OF ST. LOUIS   Warner Bros., 1957
NIGHT PASSAGE   Universal, 1957
VERTIGO   Paramount, 1958
BELL, BOOK AND CANDLE   Columbia, 1958
ANATOMY OF A MURDER ★   Columbia, 1959
THE FBI STORY   Warner Bros., 1959
THE MOUNTAIN ROAD   Columbia, 1960
X-15   United Artists, 1961 (voice)
TWO RODE TOGETHER   Columbia, 1961
THE MAN WHO SHOT LIBERTY VALANCE   Paramount, 1962
MR. HOBBS TAKES A VACATION   20th Century-Fox, 1962
HOW THE WEST WAS WON   MGM/Cinerama, 1962
TAKE HER SHE'S MINE   20th Century-Fox, 1963
CHEYENNE AUTUMN   Warner Bros., 1964
DEAR BRIGITTE   20th Century-Fox, 1965
SHENANDOAH   Universal, 1965
THE FLIGHT OF THE PHOENIX   20th Century-Fox, 1966
THE RARE BREED   Universal, 1966
FIRECREEK   Warner Bros., 1968
BANDOLERO!   20th Century-Fox, 1968
THE CHEYENNE SOCIAL CLUB   National General, 1970
FOOLS' PARADE   Columbia, 1971
THAT'S ENTERTAINMENT (FD)   MGM/United Artists, 1974
THE SHOOTIST   Paramount, 1976
AIRPORT '77   Universal, 1977
THE BIG SLEEP   United Artists, 1978, British
THE MAGIC OF LASSIE   International Picture Show, 1978
RIGHT OF WAY (CTF)   HBO Premiere Films/Schaefer-Karpf
   Productions/Post-Newsweek Video, 1983
NORTH AND SOUTH, BOOK II (MS)   Wolper Productions/
   Robert A. Papazian Productions/Warner Bros. TV, 1986
AN AMERICAN TAIL: FIEVEL GOES WEST (AF)   Universal,
   1991 (voice)

JEAN-PIERRE STEWART
NAPOLEON AND JOSEPHINE: A LOVE STORY (MS)   David L.
   Wolper Productions/Warner Bros. TV, 1987

JON STEWART
LIFESAVERS TriStar, 1994

PATRICK STEWART
Agent: ICM - Beverly Hills, 310/550-4000

HEDDA Brut Productions, 1975, British
EXCALIBUR Orion/Warner Bros., 1981, British-Irish
DUNE Universal, 1984
LADY JANE Paramount, 1985, British
L.A. STORY TriStar, 1991
ROBIN HOOD: MEN IN TIGHTS 20th Century Fox, 1993
GUNMEN Dimension/Miramax Films, 1994
THE PAGEMASTER 20th Century Fox, 1994 (voice)
STAR TREK GENERATIONS Paramount, 1994
LET IT BE ME Savoy Pictures, 1995

PHYLLIS YVONNE STICKNEY
WHAT'S LOVE GOT TO DO WITH IT Buena Vista, 1993
THE INKWELL Buena Vista, 1994

DAVID OGDEN STIERS
b. October 31, 1942 - Peoria, Illinois
Agent: Susan Smith & Associates - Beverly Hills, 213/852-4777

DRIVE, HE SAID Columbia, 1972
CHARLIE'S ANGELS (TF) Spelling-Goldberg Productions, 1976
OH, GOD! Warner Bros., 1977
THE CHEAP DETECTIVE Columbia, 1978
MAGIC 20th Century-Fox, 1978
THE BAD SEED (TF) Hajeno Productions/Warner Bros. TV, 1985
BETTER OFF DEAD Warner Bros., 1985
PERRY MASON: THE CASE OF THE SHOOTING STAR (TF)
    Intermedia Productions/Strathmore Productions/Viacom
    Productions, 1986
PERRY MASON: THE CASE OF THE LOST LOVE (TF) The Fred
    Silverman Company/Strathmore Productions/Viacom, 1987
PERRY MASON: THE CASE OF THE SINISTER SPIRIT (TF)
    The Fred Silverman Company/Strathmore Productions/Viacom
    Productions, 1987
PERRY MASON: THE CASE OF THE AVENGING ACE (TF) The
    Fred Silverman Company/Strathmore Productions/Viacom, 1988
PERRY MASON: THE CASE OF THE LADY IN THE LAKE (TF)
    The Fred Silverman Company/Strathmore Productions/
    Viacom, 1988
ANOTHER WOMAN Orion, 1988
THE ACCIDENTAL TOURIST Warner Bros., 1988
FINAL NOTICE (CTF) Wilshire Court Productions/Sharm Hill
    Productions, 1989
THE KISSING PLACE (CTF) Cynthia Cherbak Productions/Wilshire
    Court Productions, 1990
HOW TO MURDER A MILLIONAIRE (TF) Robert Greenwald
    Productions, 1990
DOC HOLLYWOOD Warner Bros., 1991
BEAUTY AND THE BEAST (AF) Buena Vista, 1991 (voice)
IRON WILL Buena Vista, 1994
THE TOOL SHED Buena Vista, 1994
POCAHONTAS (AF) Buena Vista, 1995 (voice)

BEN STILLER
b. June 8, 1928 - New York, New York

EMPIRE OF THE SUN Warner Bros., 1987
FRESH HORSES WEG, 1988
NEXT OF KIN Warner Bros., 1989
REALITY BITES Universal, 1994 (also directed)
HEAVYWEIGHTS Buena Vista, 1994

JERRY STILLER
HAIRSPRAY New Line Cinema, 1988
WOMEN & MEN: IN LOVE THERE ARE NO RULES (CTF)
    David Brown Productions/HBO Showcase, 1991
THE PICKLE Columbia, 1993
HEAVYWEIGHTS Buena Vista, 1994

F. BENJAMIN STIMLER
BIG 20th Century Fox, 1988

SARA STIMSON
LITTLE MISS MARKER Universal, 1980

STING
(Gordon Sumner)
b. October 2, 1951 - Newcastle, England
Agent: UTA - Beverly Hills, 310/273-6700

QUADROPHENIA World Northal, 1979, British
RADIO ON British Film Institute/Road Movies, 1979,
    British-West German
BRIMSTONE AND TREACLE United Artists Classics, 1982, British
THE SECRET POLICEMAN'S OTHER BALL (FD) Miramax,
    1982, British
DUNE Universal, 1984
THE BRIDE Columbia, 1985, British
PLENTY 20th Century-Fox, 1985, British
BRING ON THE NIGHT (FD) Samuel Goldwyn Company, 1985
JULIA AND JULIA Cinecom, 1987, Italian
STORMY MONDAY Atlantic Releasing Corporation, 1988, British
THE ADVENTURES OF BARON MUNCHAUSEN Columbia, 1989

AMY STOCK-POYNTON
GUTS AND GLORY: THE RISE AND FALL OF OLLIE NORTH (MS)
    Mike Robe Productions/Papazian-Hirsch Entertainment, 1989
BILL & TED'S EXCELLENT ADVENTURE Orion, 1989
BILL & TED'S BOGUS JOURNEY Orion, 1991

DEAN STOCKWELL
b. March 5, 1936 - North Hollywood, California
Agent: UTA - Beverly Hills, 310/273-6700

THE VALLEY OF DECISION MGM, 1945
ANCHORS AWEIGH MGM, 1945
ABBOTT AND COSTELLO IN HOLLYWOOD 1945
THE GREEN YEARS MGM, 1946
HOME SWEET HOMICIDE 20th Century-Fox, 1946
THE MIGHTY MCGURK 1947
THE ARNELO AFFAIR MGM, 1947
SONG OF THE THIN MAN MGM, 1947
THE ROMANCE OF ROSY RIDGE 1947
GENTLEMAN'S AGREEMENT 20th Century-Fox, 1947
DEEP WATERS 20th Century-Fox, 1948
THE BOY WITH GREEN HAIR RKO Radio, 1948
DOWN TO THE SEA IN SHIPS 20th Century-Fox, 1949
THE SECRET GARDEN 1949
THE HAPPY YEARS MGM, 1950
KIM MGM, 1950
STARS IN MY CROWN MGM, 1950
CATTLE DRIVE Universal, 1951
GUN FOR A COWARD 1957
THE CARELESS YEARS United Artists, 1957
COMPULSION 20th Century-Fox, 1959
SONS AND LOVERS 20th Century-Fox, 1960, British
LONG DAY'S JOURNEY INTO NIGHT Embassy, 1962
RAPTURE International Classics, 1965, British-French
PSYCH-OUT American International, 1968
THE DUNWICH HORROR American International, 1970
THE FAILING OF RAYMOND (TF) Universal TV, 1971
THE LAST MOVIE Universal, 1971
THE LONERS Fanfare, 1972
WEREWOLF OF WASHINGTON Diplomat, 1973
WIN, PLACE OR STEAL 1975
TRACKS Castle Hill Productions, 1976
WON TON TON, THE DOG WHO SAVED HOLLYWOOD
    Paramount, 1976
A KILLING AFFAIR *BEHIND THE BADGE* (TF) Columbia TV, 1977
SHE CAME TO THE VALLEY RGV Pictures, 1979
WRONG IS RIGHT Columbia, 1982
HUMAN HIGHWAY 1982
ALSINO AND THE CONDOR 1982, Cuban-Nicaraguan
DUNE Universal, 1984
PARIS, TEXAS TLC Films/20th Century Fox, 1984,
    West German-French
THE LEGEND OF BILLIE JEAN TriStar, 1985
TO LIVE AND DIE IN L.A. MGM/UA, 1985
BLUE VELVET DEG, 1986
BEVERLY HILLS COP II Paramount, 1987

GARDENS OF STONE   TriStar, 1987
KENNY ROGERS AS THE GAMBLER III: THE LEGEND
   CONTINUES (TF)   Lion Share Productions, 1987
THE BLUE IGUANA   Paramount, 1988
TUCKER - THE MAN AND HIS DREAM   Paramount, 1988
MARRIED TO THE MOB ✪   Orion, 1988
LIMIT UP   MCEG, 1989
QUANTUM LEAP (TF)   Belisarius Productions/Universal TV, 1989
BACKTRACK   *CATCHFIRE*   Vestron, 1991
THE PLAYER   Fine Line Features/New Line Cinema, 1992

JOHN STOCKWELL

TOP GUN   Paramount, 1986
DANGEROUSLY CLOSE   Cannon, 1986
RADIOACTIVE DREAMS   DEG, 1986
BILLIONAIRE BOYS CLUB (MS)   Donald March/Gross-Weston
   Productions/ITC Productions, 1987
BORN TO RIDE   Warner Bros., 1991

MINK STOLE

POLYESTER   New Line Cinema, 1981
CRY-BABY   Universal, 1990
SERIAL MOM   Savoy Pictures, 1994

BRAD STOLL

LOST IN YONKERS   Columbia, 1993

ERIC STOLTZ

b. September 30, 1961 - Whittier, California
Agent: CAA - Beverly Hills, 310/288-4545

FAST TIMES AT RIDGEMONT HIGH   Universal, 1982
A KILLER IN THE FAMILY (TF)   Stan Margulies Productions/
   Sunn Classic Pictures, 1983
SURF II   Arista, 1984
RUNNING HOT   New Line Cinema, 1984
THE WILD LIFE   Universal, 1984
MASK   Universal, 1985
THE NEW KIDS   Columbia, 1985
CODE NAME: EMERALD   MGM/UA, 1985
SOME KIND OF WONDERFUL   Paramount, 1987
LIONHEART   Orion, 1987
SISTER, SISTER   New World, 1987
MANIFESTO   Cannon, 1988, U.S.-Yugoslavian
HAUNTED SUMMER   Cannon, 1988
THE FLY II   20th Century Fox, 1989
SAY ANYTHING   20th Century Fox, 1989
MEMPHIS BELLE   Warner Bros., 1990
THE WATERDANCE   Samuel Goldwyn Company, 1992
SINGLES   Warner Bros., 1992
BODIES, REST & MOTION   Fine Line Features/New Line Cinema, 1993
NAKED IN NEW YORK   Fine Line Features/New Line Cinema, 1994
KILLING ZOE   October Films, 1994, U.S.-French
SLEEP WITH ME   MGM/UA, 1994
PULP FICTION   Miramax Films, 1994
FLUKE   MGM/UA, 1994
GOD'S ARMY   1994
ROOMMATES   Buena Vista, 1994
LITTLE WOMEN   Columbia, 1994
ROB ROY   MGM/UA, 1995

DANTON STONE

EIGHT MEN OUT   Orion, 1988
MARIA'S LOVERS   Cannon, 1984
JOY OF SEX   Paramount, 1984
CHECKING OUT   Warner Bros., 1989
CRAZY PEOPLE   Paramount, 1990
ONCE AROUND   Universal, 1991

DEE WALLACE STONE
(Dee Wallace)
10   Orion/Warner Bros., 1979
E.T. THE EXTRA-TERRESTRIAL   Universal, 1982
CUJO   Warner Bros., 1983
HOSTAGE FLIGHT (TF)   Frank von Zerneck Films, 1985
SIN OF INNOCENCE (TF)   Renee Valente Productions/
   Jeremac Productions/20th Century Fox TV, 1986

CRITTERS   New Line Cinema, 1986
STRANGER ON MY LAND (TF)   Edgar J. Scherick Associates/
   Taft Entertainment TV, 1988
ADDICTED TO HIS LOVE (TF)   Green-Epstein Productions/
   Columbia TV, 1988
I'M DANGEROUS TONIGHT (CTF)   BBK Productions, 1990
POPCORN   Studio Three, 1991
RESCUE ME   Cannon, 1993
MOMENT OF TRUTH: CRADLE OF CONSPIRACY (TF)
   O'Hara/Horowitz Productions, 1994
THE SKATEBOARD KID II   Concorde, 1995

OLIVER STONE

b. November 15, 1946 - New York, New York
Agent: CAA - Beverly Hills, 310/288-4545

THE HAND   Orion/Warner Bros., 1981 (also directed)
PLATOON   Orion, 1986 (also directed)
WALL STREET   20th Century Fox, 1987 (also directed)
BORN ON THE FOURTH OF JULY   Universal, 1989 (also directed)
THE DOORS   (also directed)
DAVE   Warner Bros., 1993

PHILIP STONE

INDIANA JONES AND THE TEMPLE OF DOOM   Paramount, 1984

SEAN STONE

WALL STREET   20th Century Fox, 1987
BORN ON THE FOURTH OF JULY   Universal, 1989

SHARON STONE

b. March 10, 1958 - Meadville, Pennsylvania
Agent: ICM - Beverly Hills, 310/550-4000

STARDUST MEMORIES   United Artists, 1980
DEADLY BLESSING   United Artists, 1981
BOLERO   Double 13/Sharp Features, 1982, French
IRRECONCILABLE DIFFERENCES   Warner Bros., 1984
KING SOLOMON'S MINES   Cannon, 1985
ALLAN QUATERMAIN AND THE LOST CITY OF GOLD
   Cannon, 1987
POLICE ACADEMY 4: CITIZENS ON PATROL   Warner Bros., 1987
COLD STEEL   CineTel, 1987
ABOVE THE LAW   Warner Bros., 1988
ACTION JACKSON   Lorimar, 1988
WAR AND REMEMBRANCE (MS)   Dan Curtis Productions/
   ABC Circle Films, 1988-89
PERSONAL CHOICE   *BEYOND THE STARS*
   Moviestore Entertainment, 1989
BLOOD AND SAND   1989, Spanish
TOTAL RECALL   TriStar, 1990
HE SAID, SHE SAID   Paramount, 1991
SCISSORS   DDM Film Corporation, 1991
YEAR OF THE GUN   Triumph Releasing Corporation, 1991
BASIC INSTINCT   TriStar, 1992
DIARY OF A HITMAN   Continental Film Group, 1992
SLIVER   Paramount, 1993
LAST ACTION HERO   Columbia, 1993
INTERSECTION   Paramount, 1994
THE SPECIALIST   Warner Bros., 1994
THE QUICK AND THE DEAD   TriStar, 1995
CASINO   Universal, 1995

ADAM STORKE

MYSTIC PIZZA   Samuel Goldwyn Company, 1988

MADELEINE STOWE

Agent: UTA - Beverly Hills, 310/273-6700

THE DEERSLAYER (TF)   Sunn Classic Productions, 1978
BLOOD AND ORCHIDS (MS)   Lorimar Productions, 1986
STAKEOUT   Buena Vista, 1987
WORTH WINNING   20th Century Fox, 1989
REVENGE   Columbia, 1990
THE TWO JAKES   Paramount, 1990
CLOSET LAND   Universal, 1991
UNLAWFUL ENTRY   20th Century Fox, 1992

THE LAST OF THE MOHICANS   20th Century Fox, 1992
SHORT CUTS   Fine Line Features/New Line Cinema, 1993
BLINK   New Line Cinema, 1994
CHINA MOON   Orion, 1994
BAD GIRLS   20th Century Fox, 1994

MICHAEL STOYANOV
FREAKED   20th Century Fox, 1993

BEATRICE STRAIGHT
b. August 2, 1918 - Old Westbury, New York

NETWORK OO   MGM/United Artists, 1976
KILLER ON BOARD (TF)   Lorimar Productions, 1977
SIDNEY SHELDON'S BLOODLINE *BLOODLINE*   Paramount, 1979
THE PROMISE   Universal, 1979
ENDLESS LOVE   Universal, 1981
POLTERGEIST   MGM/UA, 1982
TWO OF A KIND   20th Century-Fox, 1983
ROBERT KENNEDY AND HIS TIMES (MS)   Chris-Rose
   Productions/Columbia TV, 1985
POWER   20th Century Fox, 1986

GEORGE STRAIT
b. May 1, 1952 - Pearsall, Texas

PURE COUNTRY   Warner Bros., 1992

SUSAN STRASBERG
b. May 22, 1938 - New York, New York

THE COBWEB   MGM, 1955
PICNIC   Columbia, 1956
STAGE STRUCK   RKO Radio, 1958
KAPO   Vides/Zebra Film/Cineriz, 1960, Italian-French-Yugoslavian
SCREAM OF FEAR   *TASTE OF FEAR*   Columbia, 1961, British
DISORDER   *IL DISORDINE*   1962, Italian-French
HEMINGWAY'S ADVENTURES OF A YOUNG MAN
   20th Century-Fox, 1962
McGUIRE GO HOME!   *THE HIGH BRIGHT SUN*   Continental,
   1965, British
THE TRIP   American International, 1967
PSYCH-OUT   American International, 1968
CHUBASCO   1968
THE NAME OF THE GAME IS KILL! (TF)   Universal TV, 1968
THE BROTHERHOOD   Paramount, 1968
SWEET HUNTERS   1969, French
LEGEND OF HILLBILLY JOHN   *WHO FEARS THE DEVIL*
   Jack H. Harris Enterprises, 1973
SAMMY SOMEBODY   1976
ROLLERCOASTER   Universal, 1977
THE MANITOU   1978
IN PRAISE OF OLDER WOMEN   Avco Embassy, 1978, Canadian
THE RETURNING   1983
THE DELTA FORCE   Cannon, 1986

MARCIA STRASSMAN
HONEY, I SHRUNK THE KIDS   Buena Vista, 1989
HONEY, I BLEW UP THE KID   Buena Vista, 1992
ANOTHER STAKEOUT   Buena Vista, 1993

DAVID STRATHAIRN
RETURN OF THE SECAUCUS SEVEN   Libra/Specialty Films, 1980
LOVESICK   The Ladd Company/Warner Bros., 1983
SILKWOOD   20th Century-Fox, 1983
THE BROTHER FROM ANOTHER PLANET   Cinecom, 1984
ICEMAN   Universal, 1984
ENORMOUS CHANGES AT THE LAST MINUTE
   TC Films International, 1985
AT CLOSE RANGE   Orion, 1986
MATEWAN   Cinecom, 1987
EIGHT MEN OUT   Orion, 1988
THE JAMES BRADY STORY (CTF)   HBO Pictures/Enigma TV, 1991
SHADOWS AND FOG   Orion, 1992
O PIONEERS! (TF)   Craig Anderson Productions/Lorimar TV/
   Prairie Films, 1992
A LEAGUE OF THEIR OWN   Columbia, 1992

SNEAKERS   Universal, 1992
PASSION FISH   Miramax Films, 1992
LOST IN YONKERS   Columbia, 1993
THE FIRM   Paramount, 1993
A DANGEROUS WOMAN   Gramercy Pictures, 1993
THE RIVER WILD   Universal, 1994
DOLORES CLAIBORNE   Columbia, 1994
LOSING ISAIAH   Paramount, 1995

TAY STRATHAIRN
EIGHT MEN OUT   Orion, 1988

PETER STRAUSS
b. February 20, 1947 - New York, New York

SOLDIER BLUE (TF)   Avco Embassy, 1971
THE LAST TYCOON   Paramount, 1976
RICH MAN, POOR MAN (MS)   Universal TV, 1976
YOUNG JOE, THE FORGOTTEN KENNEDY (TF)
   ABC Circle Films, 1977
THE JERICHO MILE (TF)   ABC Circle Films, 1979
MASADA (TF)   Arnon Milchan Productions/Universal TV, 1980
SPACEHUNTER: ADVENTURES IN THE FORBIDDEN ZONE
   Columbia, 1983, Canadian-U.S.
TENDER IS THE NIGHT (TF)   Showtime/BBC/Seven Network, 1985,
   U.S.-British-Australian
KANE AND ABEL (MS)   Schrekinger Communications/
   Embassy TV, 1985
PROUD MEN (TF)   von Zerneck-Samuels Productions, 1987
PETER GUNN (TF)   The Blake Edwards Company/
   New World TV, 1990
THE YEARLING (TF)   RHI Entertainment, 1994

MAMIE STREEP
THE HOUSE OF THE SPIRITS   Miramax Films, 1993, U.S.-German

MERYL STREEP
(Mary Louise Streep)
b. June 22, 1949 - Summit, New Jersey
Agent: CAA - Beverly Hills, 310/288-4545

THE DEADLIEST SEASON (TF)   Titus Productions, 1977
JULIA   20th Century-Fox, 1977
HOLOCAUST (MS)   Titus Productions, 1978
THE DEER HUNTER O   Universal, 1978
MANHATTAN   United Artists, 1979
THE SEDUCTION OF JOE TYNAN   Universal, 1979
KRAMER VS. KRAMER OO   Columbia, 1979
THE FRENCH LIEUTENANT'S WOMAN ★   United Artists, 1981, British
SOPHIE'S CHOICE ★★   Universal/AFD, 1982
STILL OF THE NIGHT   MGM/UA, 1982
SILKWOOD ★   20th Century-Fox, 1983
IN OUR HANDS (FD)   1984
FALLING IN LOVE   Paramount, 1984
PLENTY   20th Century Fox, 1985, British
OUT OF AFRICA ★   Universal, 1985
HEARTBURN   Paramount, 1986
IRONWEED ★   TriStar, 1987
A CRY IN THE DARK ★   Warner Bros., 1988, Australian
SHE-DEVIL   Orion, 1989
POSTCARDS FROM THE EDGE ★   Columbia, 1990
DEFENDING YOUR LIFE   The Geffen Company/Warner Bros., 1991
DEATH BECOMES HER   Universal, 1992
THE HOUSE OF THE SPIRITS   Miramax Films, 1993, U.S.-German
THE RIVER WILD   Universal, 1994
THE BRIDGES OF MADISON COUNTY   Warner Bros., 1995
BEFORE AND AFTER   Buena Vista, 1995

BARBRA STREISAND
b. April 24, 1942 - Brooklyn, New York
Agent: CAA - Beverly Hills, 310/288-4545

FUNNY GIRL ★★   Columbia, 1968
HELLO, DOLLY!   20th Century-Fox, 1969
ON A CLEAR DAY, YOU CAN SEE FOREVER   Paramount, 1970
THE OWL AND THE PUSSYCAT   Columbia, 1970
WHAT'S UP, DOC?   Warner Bros., 1972

UP THE SANDBOX   National General, 1972
THE WAY WE WERE ★   Columbia, 1973
FOR PETE'S SAKE   Columbia, 1974
FUNNY LADY   Columbia, 1975
A STAR IS BORN   Warner Bros., 1976
THE MAIN EVENT   Warner Bros., 1979
ALL NIGHT LONG   Universal, 1981
YENTL   MGM/UA, 1983 (also directed)
NUTS   Warner Bros., 1987
LISTEN UP: THE LIVES OF QUINCY JONES (FD)
   Warner Bros., 1990
THE PRINCE OF TIDES   Columbia, 1991 (also directed)

GAIL STRICKLAND
THE DROWNING POOL   Warner Bros., 1975
ONE ON ONE   Warner Bros., 1977
NORMA RAE   20th Century-Fox, 1979
THE MAN IN THE MOON   MGM-Pathe, 1991

ELAINE STRITCH
b. February 2, 1926 - Detroit, Michigan
Agent: The Blake Agency - Beverly Hills, 310/246-0241

THE SCARLET HOUR   Paramount, 1956
THREE VIOLENT PEOPLE   Paramount, 1957
A FAREWELL TO ARMS   20th Century-Fox, 1957
THE PERFECT FURLOUGH   Universal, 1959
WHO KILLED TEDDY BEAR?   Magna, 1965
PIGEONS   THE SIDELONG GLANCES OF A PIGEON KICKER
   MGM, 1970
THE SPIRAL STAIRCASE   1975
PROVIDENCE   Cinema 5, 1977, French-Swiss
STRANDED (TF)   Tim Flack Productions/Columbia TV, 1986
SEPTEMBER   Orion, 1987
COCOON: THE RETURN   20th Century Fox, 1988
CADILLAC MAN   Orion, 1990 (uncredited)

WOODY STRODE
(Woodrow Strode)
b. 1914 - Los Angeles, California

SUNDOWN   United Artists, 1941
THE LION HUNTERS   1951
THE CITY BENEATH THE SEA   Universal, 1953
THE GAMBLER FROM NATCHEZ   20th Century-Fox, 1954
THE TEN COMMANDMENTS   1956
TARZAN'S FIGHT FOR LIFE   MGM, 1958
PORK CHOP HILL   United Artists, 1959
THE LAST VOYAGE   MGM, 1960
SERGEANT RUTLEDGE   Warner Bros., 1960
SPARTACUS   Universal, 1960
THE SINS OF RACHEL CADE   Warner Bros., 1961
TWO RODE TOGETHER   Columbia, 1961
THE MAN WHO SHOT LIBERTY VALANCE   Paramount, 1962
TARZAN'S THREE CHALLENGES   MGM, 1963, British
GENGHIS KHAN   Columbia, 1965,
   U.S.-British-West German-Yugoslavian
SEVEN WOMEN   MGM, 1966
THE PROFESSIONALS   American International, 1966, British
BLACK JESUS   SEDUTO ALLA SUA DESTRA   1968, Italian
ONCE UPON A TIME IN THE WEST   C'ERA UNA VOLTA IL WEST
   Paramount, 1968, Italian-U.S.
SHALAKO   Cinerama Releasing Corporation, 1968, British
CHE!   20th Century-Fox, 1969
THE DESERTER   LA SPINA DORSALE DEL DIAVOLO
   Paramount, 1971, Italian-Yugoslavian
THE LAST REBEL   1971
BLACK RODEO (FD)   Cinerama Releasing Corporation, 1972
THE REVENGERS   National General, 1972, U.S.-Mexican
THE ITALIAN CONNECTION   LA MALA ORDINA   1972, Italian
THE GATLING GUN   1973
WINTER HAWK   Howco International, 1975
LOADED GUNS   1976
OIL   1977, Italian
KINGDOM OF THE SPIDERS   Dimension, 1977
RAVAGERS   Columbia, 1979
JAGUAR LIVES   American International, 1979

KEY WEST CROSSING   1979
THE BLACK STALLION RETURNS   MGM/UA, 1983
VIGILANTE   Artists Releasing Corporation/Film Ventures
   International, 1983
THE COTTON CLUB   Orion, 1984

ANDREW STRONG
THE COMMITMENTS   20th Century Fox, 1991

DON STROUD
b. 1937 - Hawaii

GAMES   Universal, 1967
MADIGAN   Universal, 1968
JOURNEY TO SHILOH   Universal, 1968
COOGAN'S BLUFF   Universal, 1968
WHAT'S SO BAD ABOUT FEELING GOOD?   Universal, 1968
EXPLOSION   1970, Canadian
BLOODY MAMA   American International, 1970
ANGEL UNCHAINED   American International, 1970
tick...tick...tick...   MGM, 1970
VON RICHTHOFEN AND BROWN   United Artists, 1971
JOE KIDD   Universal, 1972
SLAUGHTER'S BIG RIP-OFF   1973
SCALAWAG   Paramount, 1973, Yugoslavian-Italian-U.S.
LIVE A LITTLE, STEAL A LOT   MURPH THE SURF
   American International, 1975
THE KILLER INSIDE ME   Warner Bros., 1976
THE HOUSE BY THE LAKE   DEATH WEEKEND
   American International, 1976, Canadian
SUDDEN DEATH   Topar, 1977, U.S.-Filipino
THE CHOIRBOYS   Universal, 1977
SEARCH AND DESTROY   STRIKING BACK   Film Ventures
   International, 1978
THE BUDDY HOLLY STORY   Columbia, 1978
THE AMITYVILLE HORROR   American International, 1979
ARMED AND DANGEROUS   Columbia, 1986
OF UNKNOWN ORIGIN   Concorde, 1994

DUKE STROUD
TOP GUN   Paramount, 1986

CAREL STRUYCKEN
SGT. PEPPER'S LONELY HEARTS CLUB BAND   Universal, 1978
THE ADDAMS FAMILY   Paramount, 1991
ADDAMS FAMILY VALUES   Paramount, 1993

HANS STRYDOM
THE GODS MUST BE CRAZY II   Columbia, 1990

BARBARA STUART
AIRPLANE!   Paramount, 1980
BACHELOR PARTY   20th Century Fox, 1984

MARY STUART MASTERSON
(See Mary Stuart MASTERSON)

IMOGEN STUBBS
A SUMMER STORY   Atlantic Releasing Corporation, 1988, British
ERIK THE VIKING   Orion, 1989, British
TRUE COLORS   Paramount, 1991

WES STUDI
DANCES WITH WOLVES   Orion, 1990
THE LAST OF THE MOHICANS   20th Century Fox, 1992
GERONIMO - AN AMERICAN LEGEND   Columbia, 1993
STREET FIGHTER   Universal, 1994

MIGUELANGEL SUAREZ
STIR CRAZY   Columbia, 1980

DAVID SUCHET
WHEN THE WHALES CAME   20th Century Fox, 1989, British

MOLLIE SUGDEN
THE PRINCESS AND THE GOBLIN (AF)   Hemdale, 1994 (voice)

ANNIE SUITE
THE SUBSTITUTE WIFE (TF)   Frederick S. Pierce Company, 1994

BARBARA SUKOWA
M. BUTTERFLY   Warner Bros., 1993
JOHNNY MNEMONIC   TriStar, 1994

BILLY L. SULLIVAN
LITTLE BIG LEAGUE   Columbia, 1994

BRAD SULLIVAN
FUNNY FARM   Warner Bros., 1988
GUILTY BY SUSPICION   Warner Bros., 1991
THE JERKY BOYS   Buena Vista, 1994

R. PATRICK SULLIVAN
TOUGH GUYS DON'T DANCE   Cannon, 1987

SUSAN SULLIVAN
b. November 18, 1944 - New York, New York

RAGE OF ANGELS: THE STORY CONTINUES (MS)
   NBC Productions, 1986

BUNNY SUMMERS
FROM BEYOND   Empire Pictures, 1986

DONALD SUMPTER
ROSENCRANTZ & GUILDENSTERN ARE DEAD   Cinecom, 1991

ELIZABETH SUNG
CHINA CRY   The Penland Company, 1990

PAUL SUTERA
THE BRADY BUNCH MOVIE   Paramount, 1995

DONALD SUTHERLAND
b. July 17, 1935 - St. John, N.B., Canada
Agent: CAA - Beverly Hills, 310/288-4545

THE WORLD TEN TIMES OVER   1963, British
CASTLE OF THE LIVING DEAD   IL CASTELLO DEI MORTI VIVI
   1964, Italian
THE BEDFORD INCIDENT   Columbia, 1965, British-U.S.
DR. TERROR'S HOUSE OF HORRORS   Paramount,
   1965, British-U.S.
DIE! DIE! MY DARLING!   FANATIC   Columbia, 1965, British
PROMISE HER ANYTHING   Paramount, 1966, British
THE DIRTY DOZEN   MGM, 1967, U.S.-British
BILLION DOLLAR BRAIN   United Artists, 1967, British
SEBASTIAN   Paramount, 1968, British
INTERLUDE   Columbia, 1968, British
OEDIPUS THE KING   Regional, 1968, British
THE SPLIT   MGM, 1968
JOANNA   20th Century-Fox, 1968, British
M*A*S*H   20th Century-Fox, 1970
START THE REVOLUTION WITHOUT ME   Warner Bros.,
   1970, British
KELLY'S HEROES   MGM, 1970, U.S.-Yugoslavian
ALEX IN WONDERLAND   MGM, 1970
ACT OF THE HEART   Universal, 1970, Canadian
LITTLE MURDERS   20th Century-Fox, 1971
KLUTE   Warner Bros., 1971
JOHNNY GOT HIS GUN   1971
F.T.A. (FD)   American International, 1972
STEELYARD BLUES   Warner Bros., 1973
LADY ICE   National General, 1973
ALIEN THUNDER   1973
DON'T LOOK NOW   Paramount, 1973, British-French-Italian
S*P*Y*S   20th Century-Fox, 1974, British-U.S.
DAN CANDY'S LAW   ALIEN THUNDER   1975, Canadian

END OF THE GAME   DER RICHTER UND SEIN HENKER
   20th Century-Fox, 1975, West German-Italian
THE DAY OF THE LOCUST   Paramount, 1975
1900   Paramount, 1976, Italian
CASANOVA   IL CASANOVA DI FREDERICO FELLINI
   Universal, 1976, Italian
THE EAGLE HAS LANDED   Columbia, 1976, British
THE KENTUCKY FRIED MOVIE   United Film Distribution, 1977
THE DISAPPEARANCE   Levitt-Pickman, 1977, Canadian
BLOOD RELATIONS   1978
LES LIENS DE SANG   Filmcorp, 1978, French-Canadian
NATIONAL LAMPOON'S ANIMAL HOUSE   Universal, 1978
INVASION OF THE BODY SNATCHERS   United Artists, 1978
THE GREAT TRAIN ROBBERY   THE FIRST GREAT TRAIN
   ROBBERY   United Artists, 1978, British
MURDER BY DECREE   Avco Embassy, 1979, British-Canadian
VERY BIG WITHDRAWAL   1979, Canadian
BEAR ISLAND   Taft International, 1979, British-Canadian
NOTHING PERSONAL   American International, 1979, Canadian
A MAN, A WOMAN AND A BANK   Avco Embassy,
   1979, Canadian
NOTHING PERSONAL   American International, 1980, Canadian
ORDINARY PEOPLE   Paramount, 1980
EYE OF THE NEEDLE   United Artists, 1981, U.S.-British
THRESHOLD   20th Century-Fox International Classics,
   1981, Canadian
GAS   Paramount, 1981, Canadian
MAX DUGAN RETURNS   20th Century-Fox, 1983
THE WINTER OF OUR DISCONTENT (TF)
   Lorimar Productions, 1983
CRACKERS   Universal, 1984
ORDEAL BY INNOCENCE   Cannon, 1984, British
HEAVEN HELP US   TriStar, 1985
REVOLUTION   Warner Bros., 1986, British-Norwegian
THE WOLF AT THE DOOR   OVIRI   International Film Marketing,
   1986, Danish-French
LOST ANGELS   Vestron, 1989
LOCK UP   TriStar, 1989
A DRY WHITE SEASON   MGM/UA, 1989
EMINENT DOMAIN   Triumph Releasing Corporation, 1990,
   Canadian-French-Israeli
BACKDRAFT   Universal, 1991
JFK   Warner Bros., 1991
BUFFY THE VAMPIRE SLAYER   20th Century Fox, 1992
BENEFIT OF THE DOUBT   Miramax Films, 1993
SIX DEGREES OF SEPARATION   MGM/UA, 1993
DR. BETHUNE   1994
THE WORLD'S OLDEST LIVING CONFEDERATE WIDOW
   TELLS ALL (MS)   CBS, 1994
THE PUPPET MASTERS   Buena Vista, 1994
DISCLOSURE   Warner Bros., 1994

KIEFER SUTHERLAND
b. December 20, 1966 - London, England
Agent: CAA - Beverly Hills, 310/288-4545

MAX DUGAN RETURNS   20th Century-Fox, 1983
THE BAY BOY   Orion, 1984, Canadian-French
AT CLOSE RANGE   Orion, 1986
TRAPPED IN SILENCE (TF)   Reader's Digest Productions, 1986
STAND BY ME   Columbia, 1986
CRAZY MOON   HUGGERS   Miramax Films, 1986, Canadian
THE BROTHERHOOD OF JUSTICE (TF)   Guber-Peters Productions/
   Phoenix Entertainment Group, 1986
THE LOST BOYS   Warner Bros., 1987
THE KILLING TIME   New World, 1987
PROMISED LAND   Vestron, 1988
BRIGHT LIGHTS, BIG CITY   MGM/UA, 1988
YOUNG GUNS   20th Century Fox, 1988
1969   Atlantic Releasing Corporation, 1988
RENEGADES   Universal, 1989
CHICAGO JOE AND THE SHOWGIRL   New Line Cinema, 1990
FLASHBACK   Paramount, 1990
FLATLINERS   Columbia, 1990
YOUNG GUNS II   20th Century Fox, 1990
THE NUTCRACKER PRINCE (AF)   Warner Bros., 1990 (voice)
ARTICLE 99   Orion, 1992
TWIN PEAKS: FIRE WALK WITH ME   New Line Cinema,
   1992, U.S.-French

A FEW GOOD MEN   Columbia, 1992
THE VANISHING   20th Century Fox, 1993
LAST LIGHT (CTF)   Showtime Entertainment/Stillwater Productions,
   1993 (also directed)
THE THREE MUSKETEERS   Buena Vista, 1993
THE COWBOY WAY   Universal, 1994

KRISTINE SUTHERLAND
HONEY, I SHRUNK THE KIDS   Buena Vista, 1989

JAMES SUTORIUS
MY BREAST (TF)   CBS, 1994

JANET SUZMAN
Agent: William Morris Agency - Beverly Hills, 310/274-7451

A DAY IN THE DEATH OF JOE EGG   Columbia, 1970, British
NICHOLAS AND ALEXANDRA ★   Columbia, 1971
THE BLACK WINDMILL   Universal, 1974, British
VOYAGE OF THE DAMNED   Avco Embassy, 1976, British
THE HOUSE ON GARIBALDI STREET (TF)   1979
NIJINSKY   Paramount, 1980
THE PRIEST OF LOVE   Filmways, 1981, British
THE DRAUGHTSMAN'S CONTRACT   United Artists Classics,
   1982, British
AND THE SHIP SAILS ON   Triumph/Columbia, 1984, Italian-French
MOUNTBATTEN (TF)   1985
A DRY WHITE SEASON   MGM/UA, 1989
NUNS ON THE RUN   20th Century Fox, 1990

BO SVENSON
THE GREAT WALDO PEPPER   Universal, 1975
PART 2, WALKING TALL   American International, 1975
SPECIAL DELIVERY   American International, 1976
BREAKING POINT   20th Century-Fox, 1976, Canadian
FINAL CHAPTER—WALKING TALL   American International, 1977
INGLORIOUS BASTARDS   COUNTERFEIT COMMANDOS
   1978, Italian
NORTH DALLAS FORTY   Paramount, 1979
HEARTBREAK RIDGE   Warner Bros., 1986
THE DELTA FORCE   Cannon, 1986

BOB SWAIM
b. November 2, 1943 - Evanston, Illinois
Agent: ICM - Beverly Hills, 310/550-4000

SPIES LIKE US   Warner Bros., 1985

HILARY SWANK
THE NEXT KARATE KID   Columbia, 1994

BRENDA SWANSON
SCANNER COP 2   Republic Pictures, 1994

KRISTY SWANSON
DEADLY FRIEND   Warner Bros., 1986
DIVING IN   Skouras Pictures, 1990
MANNEQUIN TWO ON THE MOVE   20th Century Fox, 1991
HOT SHOTS!   20th Century Fox, 1991
HIGHWAY TO HELL   Hemdale, 1991
BUFFY THE VAMPIRE SLAYER   20th Century Fox, 1992
THE PROGRAM   Buena Vista, 1993
THE CHASE   20th Century Fox, 1994
HIGHER LEARNING   Columbia, 1994

PATRICK SWAYZE
b. August 18, 1954 - Houston, Texas
Agent: William Morris Agency - Beverly Hills, 310/274-7451

SKATETOWN, U.S.A.   Columbia, 1979
THE COMEBACK KID (TF)   ABC Circle Films, 1980
RETURN OF THE REBELS (TF)   Moonlight Productions/
   Filmways, 1981
THE RENEGADES (TF)   Lawrence Gordon Productions/
   Paramount TV, 1982

THE OUTSIDERS   Warner Bros., 1983
UNCOMMON VALOR   Paramount, 1983
OFF SIDES (TF)   Ten-Four Productions, 1984, filmed in 1980
GRAND VIEW, U.S.A.   Warner Bros., 1984
RED DAWN   MGM/UA, 1984
NORTH AND SOUTH (MS)   Wolper Productions/Warner Bros. TV, 1985
NORTH AND SOUTH, BOOK II (MS)   Wolper Productions/
   Robert A. Papazian Productions/Warner Bros. TV, 1986
YOUNGBLOOD   MGM/UA, 1986
DIRTY DANCING   Vestron, 1987
STEEL DAWN   Vestron, 1987
TIGER WARSAW   Sony Pictures, 1988
ROAD HOUSE   MGM/UA, 1989
NEXT OF KIN   Warner Bros., 1989
GHOST   Paramount, 1990
POINT BREAK   20th Century Fox, 1991
CITY OF JOY   TriStar, 1992
HOMEWARD BOUND: THE INCREDIBLE JOURNEY
   Buena Vista, 1993 (voice)
FATHER HOOD   Buena Vista, 1993
TALL TALE   Buena Vista, 1994
TO WONG FOO, THANKS FOR EVERYTHING, JULIE NEWMAR
   Universal, 1995
THREE WISHES   Savoy Pictures, 1995

D.B. SWEENEY
(Daniel Bernard Sweeney)
POWER   20th Century Fox, 1986
FIRE WITH FIRE   Paramount, 1986
GARDENS OF STONE   TriStar, 1987
NO MAN'S LAND   Orion, 1987
EIGHT MEN OUT   Orion, 1988
MEMPHIS BELLE   Warner Bros., 1990
THE CUTTING EDGE   MGM-Pathe Communications, 1992
FIRE IN THE SKY   Paramount, 1993
ROOMMATES   Buena Vista, 1994

JULIA SWEENEY
Agent: William Morris Agency - Beverly Hills, 310/274-7451

HONEY, I BLEW UP THE KID   Buena Vista, 1992
IT'S PAT   Buena Vista, 1994
PULP FICTION   Miramax Films, 1994

INGA SWENSON
ADVISE AND CONSENT   Columbia, 1962
THE MIRACLE WORKER   United Artists, 1962
EARTH II (TF)   MGM TV, 1971
THE BETSY   Allied Artists, 1978

RICHARD SWINGLER
E.T. THE EXTRA-TERRESTRIAL   Universal, 1982

KITTY SWINK
PATTY HEARST   Atlantic Releasing Corporation, 1988

TILDA SWINTON
CARAVAGGIO   British Film Institute, 1986, British
ORLANDO   Sony Pictures Classics, 1992,
   British-Russian-Italian-French-Dutch

LORETTA SWIT
b. November 4, 1937 - Passaic, New Jersey

STAND UP AND BE COUNTED   Columbia, 1972
SHIRTS/SKINS (TF)   MGM TV, 1973
FREEBIE AND THE BEAN   Warner Bros., 1974
THE LAST DAY (TF)   Paramount TV, 1975
RACE WITH THE DEVIL   20th Century-Fox, 1975
THE HOSTAGE HEART (TF)   Andrew J. Fenady Associates, 1977
THE LOVE TAPES (TF)   Christiana Productions/MGM TV, 1980
S.O.B.   Paramount, 1981
CAGNEY & LACEY (TF)   Mace Neufeld Productions/Filmways, 1981
THE KID FROM NOWHERE (TF)   Cates-Bridges Company, 1982
FIRST AFFAIR (TF)   CBS Entertainment, 1983
THE EXECUTION (TF)   Newland-Raynor Prods./Comworld Prods., 1985
BEER   Orion, 1985

TRACY BROOKS SWOPE
THE BIG PICTURE Columbia, 1989

JEREMY SYLVERS
CHILD'S PLAY 3 Universal, 1991

KEITH SZARABAJKA
MARIE MGM/UA, 1985
BILLY GALVIN Vestron, 1986
STAYING TOGETHER Hemdale, 1989
A PERFECT WORLD Warner Bros., 1993
ANDRE Paramount, 1994
SIRINGO Rysher Entertainment, 1994

T

RICHARD TACCHINO
b. February 17, 1964 - Ogdensburg, New York
Agent: Chateau-Billings, Inc.

29TH STREET 20th Century Fox, 1991
MIRACLE ALLEY Starlight Pictures, 1992

CARY-HIROYUKI TAGAWA
Agent: The Agency - Los Angeles, 310/551-3000
Attorney: Marc Rindner - Los Angeles, 213/461-6334

THE LAST EMPEROR Columbia, 1987, British-Chinese
THE LAST WARRIOR SVS, 1989
LICENCE TO KILL MGM/UA, 1989, British
SHOWDOWN IN LITTLE TOKYO Warner Bros., 1991
AMERICAN ME Universal, 1992
RISING SUN 20th Century Fox, 1993
MORTAL KOMBAT New Line Cinema, 1995

RITA TAGGART
TORCHLIGHT International Film Marketing, 1984, U.S.-Mexican
WEEDS DEG, 1987
COUPE DE VILLE Universal, 1990

MIO TAKAKI
THE BERLIN AFFAIR Cannon, 1985, Italian-West German

WILLIAM TAKAKU
ROBINSON CRUSOE Miramax Films, 1995

KEN TAKAKURA
THE YAKUZA *BROTHERHOOD OF THE YAKUZA*
    Warner Bros., 1975
BLACK RAIN Paramount, 1989
MR. BASEBALL Universal, 1992

AYA TAKANASHI
MR. BASEBALL Universal, 1992

GEORGE TAKEI
WALK, DON'T RUN Columbia, 1966
THE GREEN BERETS Warner Bros., 1968
STAR TREK - THE MOTION PICTURE Paramount, 1979
STAR TREK II: THE WRATH OF KHAN Paramount, 1982
STAR TREK III: THE SEARCH FOR SPOCK Paramount, 1984
STAR TREK IV: THE VOYAGE HOME Paramount, 1986
STAR TREK V: THE FINAL FRONTIER Paramount, 1989
PRISONERS OF THE SUN Skouras Pictures, 1991
STAR TREK VI: THE UNDISCOVERED COUNTRY
    Paramount, 1991

TAKESHI
JOHNNY MNEMONIC TriStar, 1994

NITA TALBOT
BUNDLE OF JOY RKO Radio, 1956
ONCE UPON A HORSE Universal, 1958
WHO'S GOT THE ACTION? Paramount, 1962
GIRL HAPPY MGM, 1965
THAT FUNNY FEELING Universal, 1965
A VERY SPECIAL FAVOR Universal, 1965
THE COOL ONES Warner Bros., 1967
BUCK AND THE PREACHER Columbia, 1972
THE DAY OF THE LOCUST Paramount, 1975
SERIAL Paramount, 1980
NIGHT SHIFT The Ladd Company/Warner Bros., 1982

PATRICIA TALLMAN
NIGHT OF THE LIVING DEAD Columbia, 1990

RUSS TAMBLYN
(Rusty Tamblyn)
b. December 30, 1934 - Los Angeles, California

THE BOY WITH GREEN HAIR RKO Radio, 1948
THE KID FROM CLEVELAND Republic, 1949
SAMSON AND DELILAH Paramount, 1949
CAPTAIN CAREY, USA Paramount, 1950
FATHER OF THE BRIDE MGM, 1950
AS YOUNG AS YOU FEEL 1951
FATHER'S LITTLE DIVIDEND MGM, 1951
RETREAT, HELL! Warner Bros., 1952
TAKE THE HIGH GROUND MGM, 1953
SEVEN BRIDES FOR SEVEN BROTHERS MGM, 1954
MANY RIVERS TO CROSS MGM, 1955
HIT THE DECK MGM, 1955
THE LAST HUNT MGM, 1955
THE FASTEST GUN ALIVE MGM, 1956
THE YOUNG GUNS Allied Artists, 1956
DON'T GO NEAR THE WATER MGM, 1957
PEYTON PLACE ✪ 20th Century-Fox, 1957
HIGH SCHOOL CONFIDENTIAL MGM, 1958
TOM THUMB MGM, 1958
CIMARRON MGM, 1960
WEST SIDE STORY United Artists, 1961
THE WONDERFUL WORLD OF THE BROTHERS GRIMM
    MGM/Cinerama, 1962
HOW THE WEST WAS WON MGM, 1962
FOLLOW THE BOYS MGM, 1963
THE HAUNTING MGM, 1963, British-U.S.
THE LONG SHIPS Columbia, 1964, British-Yugoslavian
THE WAR OF THE GARGANTUANS 1966, U.S.-Japanese
SON OF A GUNFIGHTER MGM, 1966
SATAN'S SADISTS Independent-International, 1970
THE LAST MOVIE Universal, 1971 (uncredited)
DRACULA VS. FRANKENSTEIN Independent-International, 1973
WIN, PLACE OR STEAL 1975
BLACK HEAT Independent-International, 1976
HUMAN HIGHWAY 1982
CABIN BOY Buena Vista, 1994

JEFFREY TAMBOR
DESERT HEARTS Samuel Goldwyn Company, 1985
LIFE STINKS MGM-Pathe, 1991
ARTICLE 99 Orion, 1992
CROSSING THE BRIDGE Buena Vista, 1992
RADIOLAND MURDERS Universal, 1994
HEAVYWEIGHTS Buena Vista, 1994

KARLA TAMBURRELLI
CITY SLICKERS Columbia, 1991

PHILIP TAN
CHINA CRY The Penland Company, 1990

JESSICA TANDY†
b. June 7, 1909 - London, England
d. September 11, 1994

THE INDISCRETIONS OF EVE   1932, British
MURDER IN THE FAMILY   1938, British
THE SEVENTH CROSS   MGM, 1944
THE VALLEY OF DECISION   MGM, 1945
THE GREEN YEARS   MGM, 1946
DRAGONWYCK   20th Century-Fox, 1946
FOREVER AMBER   20th Century-Fox, 1947
A WOMAN'S VENGEANCE   Universal, 1947
SEPTEMBER AFFAIR   Paramount, 1950
THE DESERT FOX   20th Century-Fox, 1951
THE LIGHT IN THE FOREST   Buena Vista, 1958
HEMINGWAY'S ADVENTURES OF A YOUNG MAN
    20th Century-Fox, 1962
THE BIRDS   Universal, 1963
BUTLEY   American Film Theatre, 1974, British
HONKY TONK FREEWAY   Universal/AFD, 1981
THE WORLD ACCORDING TO GARP   Warner Bros., 1982
STILL OF THE NIGHT   MGM/UA, 1982
BEST FRIENDS   Warner Bros., 1982
THE BOSTONIANS   Almi Pictures, 1984
COCOON   20th Century Fox, 1985
*batteries not included   Universal, 1987
FOXFIRE (TF)   Marian Rees Associates, 1987
THE HOUSE ON CARROLL STREET   Orion, 1988
COCOON: THE RETURN   20th Century Fox, 1988
DRIVING MISS DAISY ★★   Warner Bros., 1989
FRIED GREEN TOMATOES ✪   Universal, 1991
USED PEOPLE   20th Century Fox, 1992
TO DANCE WITH THE WHITE DOG (TF)   Signboard Hill
    Productions, 1993
CAMILLA   Miramax Films, 1994, British-Canadian
NOBODY'S FOOL   Paramount, 1994

QUENTIN TARANTINO
Agent: William Morris Agency - Beverly Hills, 310/274-7451

RESERVOIR DOGS   (also directed)
SLEEP WITH ME   MGM/UA, 1994 (uncredited)
DESTINY TURNS ON THE RADIO   Savoy Pictures, 1995

IGNACIO LOPEZ TARSO
UNDER THE VOLCANO   Universal, 1984

LAHMARD J. TATE
JASON'S LYRIC   1994

TUVIA TAVI
PARADISE   Avco Embassy, 1982, Canadian

CHRISTINE TAYLOR
THE BRADY BUNCH MOVIE   Paramount, 1995

DUB TAYLOR
Agent: Gerler-Stevens - Los Angeles, 213/850-7386

BONNIE AND CLYDE   Warner Bros., 1967
GATOR   United Artists, 1976
BACK TO THE FUTURE PART III   Universal, 1990
FALLING FROM GRACE   Columbia, 1992

EARL T. TAYLOR
sex, lies, and videotape   Miramax Films, 1989

HOLLAND TAYLOR
UNTITLED VAN SANT/ZISKIN   Columbia, 1995

ELIZABETH TAYLOR
b. February 27, 1932 - London, England
Agent: William Morris Agency - Beverly Hills, 310/274-7451

THERE'S ONE BORN EVERY MINUTE   Universal, 1942
LASSIE COME HOME   MGM, 1943
JANE EYRE   RKO Radio, 1944
THE WHITE CLIFFS OF DOVER   MGM, 1944
NATIONAL VELVET   MGM, 1944
COURAGE OF LASSIE   Paramount, 1946
CYNTHIA   MGM, 1947
LIFE WITH FATHER   Warner Bros., 1947
A DATE WITH JUDY   MGM, 1948
JULIA MISBEHAVES   MGM, 1948
LITTLE WOMEN   MGM, 1949
CONSPIRATOR   MGM, 1950, British
THE BIG HANGOVER   MGM, 1950
FATHER OF THE BRIDE   MGM, 1950
QUO VADIS   MGM, 1951 (uncredited)
FATHER'S LITTLE DIVIDEND   MGM, 1951
A PLACE IN THE SUN   Paramount, 1951
CALLAWAY WENT THATAWAY   MGM, 1951
LOVE IS BETTER THAN EVER   *THE LIGHT FANTASTIC*   MGM, 1952
IVANHOE   MGM, 1952, British-U.S.
THE GIRL WHO HAD EVERYTHING   MGM, 1953
RHAPSODY   MGM, 1954
ELEPHANT WALK   Paramount, 1954
BEAU BRUMMELL   MGM, 1954, British
THE LAST TIME I SAW PARIS   MGM, 1954
GIANT   Warner Bros., 1956
RAINTREE COUNTY ★   MGM, 1957
CAT ON A HOT TIN ROOF ★   MGM, 1958
SUDDENLY LAST SUMMER ★   Columbia, 1959
SCENT OF MYSTERY   Todd, 1960, British (uncredited)
BUTTERFIELD 8 ★★   MGM, 1960
CLEOPATRA   20th Century-Fox, 1963
THE V.I.P.s   MGM, 1963
THE SANDPIPER   MGM, 1965
WHO'S AFRAID OF VIRGINIA WOOLF? ★★   Warner Bros., 1966
THE TAMING OF THE SHREW   Columbia, 1967, Italian-British
DOCTOR FAUSTUS   1967, British-Italian
REFLECTIONS IN A GOLDEN EYE   Warner Bros., 1967
THE COMEDIANS   MGM, 1967, British
BOOM!   Universal, 1968, British-U.S.
SECRET CEREMONY   Universal, 1968, British-U.S.
THE ONLY GAME IN TOWN   20th Century-Fox, 1970
X Y & ZEE   *ZEE & CO.*   Columbia, 1972, British
HAMMERSMITH IS OUT   Cinerama Releasing Corporation, 1972
UNDER MILK WOOD   Altura, 1973, British
DIVORCE HIS/DIVORCE HERS (TF)   World Film Services, 1973
NIGHT WATCH   Avco Embassy, 1973, British
ASH WEDNESDAY   Paramount, 1973
THE DRIVER'S SEAT   *IDENTIKIT*   1973, Italian
THAT'S ENTERTAINMENT! (FD)   MGM/United Artists, 1974
VICTORY AT ENTEBBE (MS)   1976
THE BLUE BIRD   20th Century-Fox, 1976, U.S.-Soviet
A LITTLE NIGHT MUSIC   New World, 1977, Austrian-U.S.
WINTER KILLS   Avco Embassy, 1979
THE MIRROR CRACK'D   AFD, 1980, British
BETWEEN FRIENDS (CTF)   HBO Premiere Films/Marian Rees
    Associates/Robert Cooper Films III/List-Estrin Productions,
    1983, U.S.-Canadian
MALICE IN WONDERLAND   *THE RUMOR MILL* (TF)
    ITC Productions, 1985
THERE MUST BE A PONY (TF)   R.J. Productions/Columbia TV, 1986
POKER ALICE (TF)   New World TV, 1987
TENNESSEE WILLIAMS' SWEET BIRD OF YOUTH   *SWEET BIRD
    OF YOUTH* (TF)   Atlantic/Kushner-Locke Productions, 1989
THE FLINTSTONES   Universal, 1994

HOLLAND TAYLOR
ALICE   Orion, 1990

LILI TAYLOR
MYSTIC PIZZA   Samuel Goldwyn Company, 1988
SAY ANYTHING   20th Century Fox, 1989
FAMILY OF SPIES (MS)   King Phoenix Entertainment, 1990
DOGFIGHT   Warner Bros., 1991

BRIGHT ANGEL   Hemdale, 1991
HOUSEHOLD SAINTS   Fine Line Features/New Line Cinema, 1993
SHORT CUTS   Fine Line Features/New Line Cinema, 1993
RUDY   TriStar, 1993
MRS. PARKER AND THE VICIOUS CIRCLE   Fine Line Features/
   New Line Cinema, 1994
PRET-A-PORTER   Miramax Films, 1994

MESHACH TAYLOR
MANNEQUIN   20th Century Fox, 1987
MANNEQUIN TWO ON THE MOVE   20th Century Fox, 1991

NOAH TAYLOR
THE YEAR MY VOICE BROKE   Avenue Pictures, 1988, Australian

RENEE TAYLOR
Agent: The Blake Agency - Beverly Hills, 310/246-0241

LAST OF THE RED HOT LOVERS   Paramount, 1972
LOVESICK   The Ladd Company/Warner Bros., 1983
IT HAD TO BE YOU   Limelight Studios, 1989
ALL I WANT FOR CHRISTMAS   Paramount, 1991

RIP TAYLOR
DUCK TALES THE MOVIE: THE SECRET OF THE LOST LAMP (AF)
   Buena Vista, 1990 (voice)
INDECENT PROPOSAL   Paramount, 1993

RUSSI TAYLOR
DUCK TALES THE MOVIE: THE SECRET OF THE LOST LAMP (AF)
   Buena Vista, 1990 (voice)

JONATHAN TAYLOR-THOMAS
MAN 2 MAN   Buena Vista, 1995

LEIGH TAYLOR-YOUNG
b. January 25, 1944 - Washington, D.C.
Agent: Don Buchwald & Associates - Los Angeles, 310/278-3600

I LOVE YOU, ALICE B. TOKLAS   Warner Bros., 1968
THE BIG BOUNCE   Warner Bros., 1969
THE GAMES   20th Century-Fox, 1970, British
THE BUTTERCUP CHAIN   Warner Bros., 1970, British
THE ADVENTURERS   Paramount, 1970
THE HORSEMEN   Columbia, 1971
THE GANG THAT COUDN'T SHOOT STRAIGHT   MGM, 1971
SOYLENT GREEN   MGM, 1973
CAN'T STOP THE MUSIC   AFD, 1980
LOOKER   The Ladd Company/Warner Bros., 1981
NAPOLEON AND JOSEPHINE: A LOVE STORY (MS)
   David L. Wolper Productions/Warner Bros. TV, 1987
WHO GETS THE FRIENDS? (TF)   CBS Entertainment, 1988

MARSHALL TEAGUE
ROAD HOUSE   MGM/UA, 1989

TRAVIS TEDFORD
THE LITTLE RASCALS   Universal, 1994

MAUREEN TEEFY
FAME   MGM/United Artists, 1980
SUPERGIRL   Warner Bros., 1984, British

TOM TEELEY
BEATLEMANIA   American Cinema, 1981

VICTORIA TENNANT
b. September 30, 1950 - London, England
Agent: Metropolitan Talent Agency - Los Angeles, 213/857-4500

THE RAGMAN'S DAUGHTER   Penelope Films, 1972, British
SPHINX   Orion/Warner Bros., 1981
THE DOGS OF WAR   United Artists, 1981, U.S.-British
INSEMINOID   *HORROR PLANET*   1982, British

DEMPSEY (TF)   Charles Fries Productions, 1983
THE WINDS OF WAR (MS)   Paramount TV/Dan Curtis
   Productions, 1983
CHIEFS (MS)   Highgate Pictures, 1983
STRANGER'S KISS   Orion, 1984
ALL OF ME   Universal, 1984
THE HOLCROFT COVENANT   Universal, 1985, British
UNDER SIEGE (TF)   Ohlmeyer Communications Company/
   Telepictures Productions, 1986
BEST SELLER   Orion, 1987
WAR AND REMEMBRANCE (TF)   Dan Curtis Productions/
   ABC Circle Films, 1988-89
THE HANDMAID'S TALE   Cinecom, 1990
L.A. STORY   TriStar, 1991

JON TENNEY
TOMBSTONE   Buena Vista, 1993
BEVERLY HILLS COP III   Paramount, 1994
LASSIE   Paramount, 1994
WILLY II: THE ADVENTURE HOME   Warner Bros., 1995

STUDS TERKEL
EIGHT MEN OUT   Orion, 1988

JOHN TERLESKY
THE ALLNIGHTER   Universal, 1987
LONGARM (TF)   Universal TV, 1988
WHEN HE'S NOT A STRANGER (TF)   Ohlmeyer Communications, 1989
CRAZY PEOPLE   Paramount, 1990

LEE TERRI
AIRPLANE!   Paramount, 1980

NIGEL TERRY
CARAVAGGIO   British Film Institute, 1986, British

JOHN TERRY
Agent: William Morris Agency - Beverly Hills, 310/274-7451

IN COUNTRY   Warner Bros., 1989
OF MICE AND MEN   MGM-Pathe Communications, 1992
A DANGEROUS WOMAN   Gramercy Pictures, 1993

JOHANNA TER STEEGE
IMMORTAL BELOVED   Columbia, 1994

JOHN TESH
SOAPDISH   Paramount, 1991

LAUREN TEWES
EYES OF A STRANGER   Warner Bros., 1981

TAB THACKER
(Talmadge "Tab" Thacker)
CITY HEAT   Warner Bros., 1984
WILDCATS   Warner Bros., 1986
POLICE ACADEMY 4: CITIZENS ON PATROL   Warner Bros., 1987

ERIC THAL
A STRANGER AMONG US   Buena Vista, 1992
THE GUN IN BETTY LOU'S HANDBAG   Buena Vista, 1992
THE PUPPET MASTERS   Buena Vista, 1994

JORDAN THALER
BIG   20th Century Fox, 1988

BENJ THALL
HOMEWARD BOUND: THE INCREDIBLE JOURNEY
   Buena Vista, 1993

BYRON THAMES
JOHNNY DANGEROUSLY   20th Century Fox, 1984
84 CHARLIE MOPIC   New Century/Vista, 1989

JOHN THAW
CHAPLIN TriStar, 1992, U.S.-British

PHYLLIS THAXTER
(Phyllis St. Felix Thaxter)
b. November 20, 1921 - Portland, Maine

THIRTY SECONDS OVER TOKYO MGM, 1944
BEWITCHED MGM, 1945
WEEKEND AT THE WALDORF MGM, 1945
THE SEA OF GRASS MGM, 1946
LIVING IN A BIG WAY MGM, 1947
TENTH AVENUE ANGEL MGM, 1948
THE SIGN OF THE RAM Columbia, 1948
BLOOD ON THE MOON RKO Radio, 1948
ACT OF VIOLENCE MGM, 1949
THE BREAKING POINT Warner Bros., 1950
JIM THORPE—ALL AMERICAN Warner Bros., 1951
COME FILL THE CUP Warner Bros., 1951
SPRINGFIELD RIFLE Warner Bros., 1952
OPERATION SECRET Warner Bros., 1952
WOMEN'S PRISON Columbia, 1955
MAN AFRAID 1957
THE WORLD OF HENRY ORIENT United Artists, 1964
THE LONGEST NIGHT (TF) Universal TV, 1972
SUPERMAN Warner Bros., 1978

BRYNN THAYER
BIG SHOTS 20th Century Fox, 1987
GHOST OF A CHANCE (TF) Stuart-Phoenix Productions/
   Thunder Bird Road Productions/Lorimar-Telepictures, 1987
HERO AND THE TERROR Cannon, 1988
THE COMEBACK (TF) CBS Entertainment, 1989

DAVID THEWLIS
b. Blackpool, England
Agent: ICM - Beverly Hills, 310/550-4000

THE SINGING DETECTIVE (TF) BBC/ABC Australia,
   1986, British-Australian
LITTLE DORRIT, PART I: NOBODY'S FAULT Cannon,
   1988, British
LITTLE DORRIT, PART II: LITTLE DORRIT'S STORY Cannon,
   1988, British
RESURRECTED Film Four International/British Screen/St. Pancras,
   1989, British
FILIPINA DREAM GIRLS (TF) BBC, 1991, British
LIFE IS SWEET October Films, 1991, British
AFRAID OF THE DARK Fine Line Features/New Line Cinema,
   1992, British-French
DAMAGE New Line Cinema, 1992, French-British
PRIME SUSPECT 3 (TF) Granada TV, 1993, British
THE TRIAL Angelika Films, 1993, British
NAKED Fine Line Features/New Line Cinema, 1993, British
BLACK BEAUTY Warner Bros., 1994, British-U.S.
RESTORATION Miramax Films, 1994
DRAGONHEART Universal, 1995
TOTAL ECLIPSE New Line Cinema, 1995

JACK THIBEAU
ACTION JACKSON Lorimar, 1988

LYNNE THIGPEN
TOOTSIE Columbia, 1982
LEAN ON ME Warner Bros., 1989
THE PAPER Universal, 1994

BETTY THOMAS
TROOP BEVERLY HILLS Columbia, 1989

HEATHER THOMAS
b. September 8, 1957

ZAPPED! Embassy, 1982

HENRY THOMAS
b. September 8, 1971

RAGGEDY MAN Universal, 1981
E.T. THE EXTRA-TERRESTRIAL Universal, 1982
MISUNDERSTOOD MGM/UA, 1984
CLOAK & DAGGER Universal, 1984
THE QUEST Miramax, 1986, Australian
VALMONT Orion, 1989, French
FIRE IN THE SKY Paramount, 1993

JAY THOMAS
b. July 12 - Kermit, Texas

C.H.U.D. New World, 1984
THE GIG Castle Hill Productions, 1985
STRAIGHT TALK Buena Vista, 1992
MR. HOLLAND'S OPUS Buena Vista, 1995

JONATHAN TAYLOR THOMAS
THE LION KING (AF) Buena Vista, 1994 (voice)

KRISTIN SCOTT THOMAS
A HANDFUL OF DUST New Line Cinema, 1988
BITTER MOON Fine Line Features/New Line Cinema,
   1993, French-British
FOUR WEDDINGS AND A FUNERAL Gramercy Pictures,
   1994, British
ANGELS AND INSECTS Samuel Goldwyn Company, 1995

MARLO THOMAS
(Margaret Thomas)
b. November 21, 1937 - Detroit, Michigan
Agent: CAA - Beverly Hills, 310/288-4545

THE KNACK...AND HOW TO GET IT Lopert, 1965, British
JENNY Cinerama Releasing Corporation, 1970
THIEVES Paramount, 1977
CONSENTING ADULT (TF) Starger Company/David Lawrence and
   Ray Aghayan Productions, 1985
NOBODY'S CHILD (TF) Joseph Feury Productions/Gaylord
   Production Company, 1986
IN THE SPIRIT Castle Hill Productions, 1990

RICHARD THOMAS
b. June 13, 1951 - New York, New York

WINNING Universal, 1969
LAST SUMMER Allied Artists, 1969
RED SKY AT MORNING Universal, 1971
THE HOMECOMING (TF) Lorimar Productions, 1971
YOU'LL LIKE MY MOTHER Universal, 1972
THE SILENCE (TF) Palomar Pictures International, 1975
9/30/55 SEPTEMBER 30, 1955 Universal, 1977
BATTLE BEYOND THE STARS New World, 1980
HOBSON'S CHOICE (TF) CBS Entertainment, 1983
GO TOWARD THE LIGHT (TF) Corapeak Productions/
   The Polson Company, 1988
IT (TF) Konigsberg-Sanitsky Productions/Green-Epstein
   Productions/Lorimar TV, 1990

ROBIN THOMAS
ABOUT LAST NIGHT... TriStar, 1986
SUMMER SCHOOL Paramount, 1987
MEMORIES OF MURDER (CTF) Houston Lady Productions/
   Viacom, 1990

SHARON THOMAS
YOUNG GUNS 20th Century Fox, 1988

TIM THOMERSON
TAKE THIS JOB AND SHOVE IT Avco Embassy, 1981
UNCOMMON VALOR Paramount, 1983
VOLUNTEERS TriStar, 1985
RATBOY Warner Bros., 1986

NEAR DARK   DEG, 1987
WHO'S HARRY CRUMB?   TriStar, 1989

BRIAN THOMPSON
COBRA   Warner Bros., 1986
LIONHEART   Universal, 1991

EMMA THOMPSON
Agent: William Morris Agency - Beverly Hills, 310/274-7451

HENRY V   Samuel Goldwyn Company, 1989, British
THE TALL GUY   Miramax Films, 1990
IMPROMPTU   Hemdale, 1991, U.S.-French
DEAD AGAIN   Paramount, 1991
HOWARDS END ★★   Sony Pictures Classics, 1992, British
PETER'S FRIENDS   Samuel Goldwyn Company, 1992, British
MUCH ADO ABOUT NOTHING   Samuel Goldwyn Company,
   1993, British-U.S.
THE REMAINS OF THE DAY ★   Columbia, 1993, British
IN THE NAME OF THE FATHER ✪   Universal, 1993, Irish-British
MY FATHER, THE HERO   Buena Vista, 1994
JUNIOR   Universal, 1994
CARRINGTON   Gramercy Pictures, 1995

ERNEST THOMPSON
STAR 80   The Ladd Company/Warner Bros., 1983

FRED DALTON THOMPSON
(Fred Thompson)
MARIE   MGM/UA, 1985
FEDS   Warner Bros., 1988
THE HUNT FOR RED OCTOBER   Paramount, 1990
DIE HARD 2   20th Century Fox, 1990
DAYS OF THUNDER   Paramount, 1990
CURLY SUE   Warner Bros., 1991
CAPE FEAR   Universal, 1991
IN THE LINE OF FIRE   Columbia, 1993

JACK THOMPSON
b. August 31, 1940 - Sydney, Australia

OUTBACK *WAKE IN FRIGHT*   United Artists, 1971, Australian
LIBIDO   Producers & Directors Guild of Australia, 1973, Australian
PETERSEN   Hexagon Productions, 1974, Australian
SUNDAY TOO FAR AWAY   1975, Australian
CADDIE   Atlantic Releasing Corporation, 1976, Australian
MAD DOG *MAD DOG MORGAN*   Cinema Shares International,
   1976, Australian
THE CHANT OF JIMMIE BLACKSMITH   New Yorker,
   1978, Australian
BREAKER MORANT   New World/Quartet, 1980, Australian
THE EARTHLING   1981, Australian
MERRY CHRISTMAS, MR. LAWRENCE   Universal,
   1983, British-Japanese
BURKE AND WILLS   Hemdale, 1985, Australian
FLESH + BLOOD   Orion, 1985, U.S.-Dutch
GROUND ZERO   Avenue Pictures, 1988
TROUBLE IN PARADISE (TF)   Qintex Entertainment,
   1989, U.S.-Australian
WIND   TriStar, 1992, U.S.-Japanese
A FAR OFF PLACE   Buena Vista, 1993

KENAN THOMPSON
HEAVYWEIGHTS   Buena Vista, 1994

LEA THOMPSON
b. May 31, 1961 - Rochester, Minnesota

ALL THE RIGHT MOVES   20th Century-Fox, 1983
RED DAWN   MGM/UA, 1984
THE WILD LIFE   Universal, 1984
BACK TO THE FUTURE   Universal, 1985
SOME KIND OF WONDERFUL   Paramount, 1987
THE WIZARD OF LONELINESS   Skouras Pictures, 1988
CASUAL SEX?   Universal, 1988
BACK TO THE FUTURE PART II   Universal, 1989

MONTANA (CTF)   HBO Productions/Zoetrope Studios/Roger
   Gimbel Productions, 1990
BACK TO THE FUTURE PART III   Universal, 1990
ARTICLE 99   Orion, 1992
DENNIS THE MENACE   Warner Bros., 1993
THE BEVERLY HILLBILLIES   20th Century Fox, 1993
THE SUBSTITUTE WIFE (TF)   Frederick S. Pierce Company, 1994

SHELLEY THOMPSON
LABYRINTH   TriStar, 1986, British

SUSANNA THOMPSON
LITTLE GIANTS   Warner Bros., 1994

ANNA THOMSON
UNFORGIVEN   Warner Bros., 1992

SCOTT THOMSON
FAST TIMES AT RIDGEMONT HIGH   Universal, 1982
JOHNNY DANGEROUSLY   20th Century-Fox, 1984
POLICE ACADEMY   The Ladd Company/Warner Bros., 1984
GHOULIES   Empire Pictures, 1985
POLICE ACADEMY 3: BACK IN TRAINING   Warner Bros., 1986

COURTNEY THORNE-SMITH
LUCAS   20th Century Fox, 1986
SUMMER SCHOOL   Paramount, 1987
SIDE OUT   TriStar, 1990

BILLY BOB THORNTON
Agent: William Morris Agency - Beverly Hills, 310/274-7451

ONE FALSE MOVE   I.R.S. Releasing, 1992
INDECENT PROPOSAL   Paramount, 1993

DAVID THORNTON
MRS. PARKER AND THE VICIOUS CIRCLE   Fine Line Features/
   New Line Cinema, 1994

SIGRID THORNTON
THE GETTING OF WISDOM   Atlantic Releasing Corporation,
   1977, Australian
THE DAY AFTER HALLOWEEN *SNAPSHOT*   Group 1,
   1979, Australian
THE MAN FROM SNOWY RIVER   20th Century-Fox,
   1982, Australian
ALL THE RIVERS RUN (CMS)   Crawford Productions/Nine Network,
   1984, Australian
SLATE, WYN AND ME   1987, Australian
THE MAN FROM SNOWY RIVER 2   Snowy Two Productions,
   1988, Australian

DAVID THRELFALL
WHEN THE WHALES CAME   20th Century Fox, 1989, British

CHRISTIANA THRONE
MISS FIRECRACKER   Corsair Pictures, 1989

BILL THURMAN
ALAMO BAY   TriStar, 1985

UMA THURMAN
Agent: CAA - Beverly Hills, 310/288-4545

JOHNNY BE GOOD   Orion, 1988
DANGEROUS LIAISONS   Warner Bros., 1988
THE ADVENTURES OF BARON MUNCHAUSEN   Columbia, 1989
WHERE THE HEART IS   Buena Vista, 1990
HENRY & JUNE   Universal, 1990
FINAL ANALYSIS   Warner Bros., 1992
JENNIFER EIGHT   Paramount, 1992
MAD DOG AND GLORY   Universal, 1993
EVEN COWGIRLS GET THE BLUES   Fine Line Features/
   New Line Cinema, 1994
PULP FICTION   Miramax Films, 1994

RACHEL TICOTIN

FORT APACHE, THE BRONX   20th Century-Fox, 1981
ROCKABYE (TF)   Roger Gimbel Productions/Peregrine
    Entertainment/Bertinelli Productions, 1986
CRITICAL CONDITION   Paramount, 1987
TOTAL RECALL   TriStar, 1990
ONE GOOD COP   Buena Vista, 1991
F/X 2 - THE DEADLY ART OF ILLUSION   Orion, 1991
WHERE THE DAY TAKES YOU   New Line Cinema, 1992
FALLING DOWN   Warner Bros., 1993
DON JUAN DE MARCO AND THE CENTERFOLD
    New Line Cinema, 1995

JACOB TIERNEY

JOSH AND S.A.M.   Columbia, 1993
THE NEON BIBLE   Miramax Films, 1995

LAWRENCE TIERNEY

b. March 15, 1919 - Brooklyn, New York

THE GHOST SHIP   RKO Radio, 1943
YOUTH RUNS WILD   RKO Radio, 1944
DILLINGER   1945
BACK TO BATAAN   RKO Radio, 1945
BADMAN'S TERRITORY   1946
STEP BY STEP   1946
SAN QUENTIN   RKO Radio, 1946
THE DEVIL THUMBS A RIDE   1947
BORN TO KILL   RKO Radio, 1947
BODYGUARD   Columbia, 1948
SHAKEDOWN   Universal, 1950
KILL OR BE KILLED   1950
THE HOODLUM   1951
THE GREATEST SHOW ON EARTH   Paramount, 1952
THE STEEL CAGE   United Artists, 1954
FEMALE JUNGLE   *THE HANGOVER*   1956
A CHILD IS WAITING   United Artists, 1963
CUSTER OF THE WEST   Cinerama Releasing Corporation,
    1968, U.S.-Spanish
ABDUCTION   United Film Distribution, 1975
ANDY WARHOL'S BAD   New World, 1977
MIDNIGHT   *BACKWOODS MASSACRE*   1981
PRIZZI'S HONOR   20th Century Fox, 1985
SILVER BULLET   *STEPHEN KING'S SILVER BULLET*
    Paramount, 1985
MURPHY'S LAW   Cannon, 1986
TOUGH GUYS DON'T DANCE   Cannon, 1987
RESERVOIR DOGS   Miramax Films, 1992

TIFFANY

b. August 31, 1940 - Norwalk, California

JETSONS: THE MOVIE (AF)   Universal, 1990 (voice)

KEVIN TIGHE

MATEWAN   Cinecom, 1987
EIGHT MEN OUT   Orion, 1988
K-9   Universal, 1989
ANOTHER 48 HRS.   Paramount, 1990
BRIGHT ANGEL   Hemdale, 1991
NEWSIES   Buena Vista, 1992
A MAN IN UNIFORM   I.R.S. Releasing, 1994

MEL TILLIS

b. August 8, 1932 - Tampa, Florida

THE CANNONBALL RUN   20th Century-Fox, 1981

JENNIFER TILLY

MOVING VIOLATIONS   20th Century Fox, 1985
REMOTE CONTROL   Vista Organization, 1988
RENTED LIPS   Cineworld, 1988
HIGH SPIRITS   TriStar, 1988
FAR FROM HOME   Vestron, 1989
LET IT RIDE   Paramount, 1989
THE FABULOUS BAKER BOYS   20th Century Fox, 1989

THE GETAWAY   Universal, 1994
BULLETS OVER BROADWAY   Miramax Films, 1994

MEG TILLY

Agent: UTA - Beverly Hills, 310/273-6700

TEX   Buena Vista, 1982
ONE DARK NIGHT   Comworld, 1983
THE BIG CHILL   Columbia, 1983
PSYCHO II   Universal, 1983
IMPULSE   20th Century Fox, 1984
AGNES OF GOD ✪   Columbia, 1985
OFF BEAT   Buena Vista, 1986
MASQUERADE   MGM/UA, 1988
THE GIRL IN A SWING   Millimeter Films, 1988, British-U.S.
VALMONT   Orion, 1989, French
IN THE BEST INTEREST OF THE CHILD (TF)   Papazian-Hirsch
    Entertainment, 1990
THE TWO JAKES   Paramount, 1990
LEAVING NORMAL   Universal, 1992
BODY SNATCHERS   Warner Bros., 1994
SLEEP WITH ME   MGM/UA, 1994

CHARLENE TILTON

FREAKY FRIDAY   Buena Vista, 1977
CENTER OF THE WEB   AIP, 1992

CHARLES TINGWELL

MALCOLM   Vestron, 1986, Australian

JAIME TIRELLI

BIG   20th Century Fox, 1988

JAMES TOBACK

EXPOSED   MGM/UA, 1983 (also directed)
THE PICK-UP ARTIST   20th Century Fox, 1987 (also directed)
THE BIG BANG (FD)   Triton Pictures, 1990 (also directed)
ALICE   Orion, 1990
BUGSY   TriStar, 1991

HEATHER TOBIAS

HIGH HOPES   Skouras Pictures, 1988, British

OLIVER TOBIAS

THE STUD   Trans-American, 1978, British
ARABIAN ADVENTURE   AFD, 1979, British
A NIGHTINGALE SANG IN BERKELEY SQUARE   S. Benjamin Fisz
    Productions/Nightingale Productions, 1980, British
THE WICKED LADY   MGM/UA/Cannon, 1983, British
MATA HARI   Cannon, 1985

STEPHEN TOBOLOWSKY

Agent: William Morris Agency - Beverly Hills, 310/274-7451

NOBODY'S FOOL   Island Pictures, 1986
GREAT BALLS OF FIRE   Orion, 1989
IN COUNTRY   Warner Bros., 1989
BREAKING IN   Samuel Goldwyn Company, 1989
BIRD ON A WIRE   Universal, 1990
MEMOIRS OF AN INVISIBLE MAN   Warner Bros., 1992
SINGLE WHITE FEMALE   Columbia, 1992
WHERE THE DAY TAKES YOU   New Line Cinema, 1992
JOSH AND S.A.M.   Columbia, 1993
RADOLAND MURDERS   Universal, 1994
DR. JEKYLL AND MS. HYDE   Savoy Pictures, 1995

BRIAN TOCHI

REVENGE OF THE NERDS   20th Century Fox, 1984
STITCHES   International Film Marketing, 1985
POLICE ACADEMY 3: BACK IN TRAINING   Warner Bros., 1986
POLICE ACADEMY 4: CITIZENS ON PATROL   Warner Bros., 1987

**F
I
L
M

A
C
T
O
R
S**

BEVERLY TODD
BABY BOOM   MGM/UA, 1987
MOVING   Warner Bros., 1988
CLARA'S HEART   Warner Bros., 1988
LEAN ON ME   Warner Bros., 1989

RYAN TODD
SCROOGED   Paramount, 1988
THE DREAMER OF OZ (TF)   Bedrock Productions/Adam
   Productions/Spelling Entertainment, 1990
DANIELLE STEEL'S PALOMINO   *PALOMINO* (TF)
   The Cramer Company/NBC Productions, 1991
MRS. LAMBERT REMEMBERS LOVE (TF)
   RHI Entertainment, 1991
BACKDRAFT   Universal, 1991
THE GIANT OF THUNDER MOUNTAIN
SPACED INVADERS
LAST ACTION HERO   Columbia, 1993
PONTIAC MOON   Paramount, 1994

SAIRA TODD
BAD BEHAVIOUR   October Films, 1993, British

TONY TODD
PLATOON   Orion, 1986
THE LAST ELEPHANT (CTF)   RHI Entertainment/Qintex
   Entertainment, 1990
NIGHT OF THE LIVING DEAD   Columbia, 1990
CANDYMAN 2: FAREWELL TO THE FLESH
   Gramercy Films, 1995

UGO TOGNAZZI
LA CAGE AUX FOLLES 3: THE WEDDING   1985, Italian-French

MARILYN TOKUDA
FAREWELL TO THE KING   Orion, 1989
CAGE   New Century/Vista, 1989

BERLINDA TOLBERT
HARLEM NIGHTS   Paramount, 1989

JAMES TOLKAN
THEY MIGHT BE GIANTS   Universal, 1971
BACK TO THE FUTURE   Universal, 1985
OFF BEAT   Buena Vista, 1986
TOP GUN   Paramount, 1986
WEEKEND WAR (TF)   Pompian-Atamian Productions/
   Columbia TV, 1988
LEAP OF FAITH (TF)   Hart, Thomas & Berlin Productions, 1988
MINISTRY OF VENGEANCE   MPCA, 1989
BACK TO THE FUTURE PART II   Universal, 1989
SUNSET BEAT (TF)   Patrick Hasburgh Productions, 1990
BACK TO THE FUTURE PART III   Universal, 1990
DICK TRACY   Buena Vista, 1990

LAUREN TOM
THE JOY LUCK CLUB   Buena Vista, 1993
WHEN A MAN LOVES A WOMAN   Buena Vista, 1994

NICHOLLE TOM
BEETHOVEN   Universal, 1992

CONCETTA TOMEI
Agent: Susan Smith & Associates - Beverly Hills, 213/852-4777

DON'T TELL MOM THE BABYSITTER'S DEAD   Warner Bros., 1991

MARISA TOMEI
Agent: William Morris Agency - Beverly Hills, 310/274-7451

THE FLAMINGO KID   20th Century Fox, 1984
OSCAR   Buena Vista, 1991
ZANDALEE   Electric Pictures/ITC Entertainment Group, 1991

MY COUSIN VINNY ⊙⊙   20th Century Fox, 1992
CHAPLIN   TriStar, 1992, U.S.-British
EQUINOX   I.R.S. Releasing, 1993
UNTAMED HEART   MGM/UA, 1993
THE PAPER   Universal, 1994
ONLY YOU   TriStar, 1994
THE PEREZ FAMILY   Samuel Goldwyn Company, 1994

FRANCES TOMELTY
THE FIELD   Avenue Pictures, 1990, Irish-British

TAMLYN TOMITA
THE KARATE KID PART II   Columbia, 1986
HIROSHIMA: OUT OF THE ASHES (TF)   Robert Greenwald
   Productions, 1990
COME SEE THE PARADISE   20th Century Fox, 1990
THE JOY LUCK CLUB   Buena Vista, 1993

LILY TOMLIN
(Mary Jean Tomlin)
b. September 1, 1939 - Detroit, Michigan
Agent: William Morris Agency - Beverly Hills, 310/274-7451

NASHVILLE ⊙   Paramount, 1975
THE LATE SHOW   Warner Bros., 1976
MOMENT BY MOMENT   Universal, 1978
NINE TO FIVE   20th Century-Fox, 1980
THE INCREDIBLE SHRINKING WOMAN   Universal, 1981
ALL OF ME   Universal, 1984
BIG BUSINESS   Buena Vista, 1988
THE SEARCH FOR SIGNS OF INTELLIGENT LIFE IN THE
   UNIVERSE   Orion Classics, 1991
SHADOWS AND FOG   Orion, 1992
THE PLAYER   Fine Line Features/New Line Cinema, 1992
AND THE BAND PLAYED ON (CTF)   HBO Pictures/Spelling
   Entertainment, 1993
SHORT CUTS   Fine Line Features/New Line Cinema, 1993
THE BEVERLY HILLBILLIES   20th Century Fox, 1993
EVEN COWGIRLS GET THE BLUES   Fine Line Features/
   New Line Cinema, 1994
GETTING AWAY WITH MURDER   Savoy Pictures, 1995

JASON TOMLINS
84 CHARLIE MOPIC   New Century/Vista, 1989

DAVID TOMLINSON
b. May 7, 1917 - Henley-on-Thames, England

QUIET WEDDING   1940, British
PIMPERNEL SMITH   *MISTER V*   Anglo-American, 1941, British
THE WAY TO THE STARS   *JOHNNY IN THE CLOUDS*
   United Artists, 1945, British
JOURNEY TOGETHER   RKO Radio, 1945, British
SCHOOL FOR SECRETS   *SECRET FLIGHT*   General Film
   Distributors, 1946, British
FAME IS THE SPUR   Two Cities, 1946, British
MASTER OF BANKDAM   1947, British
EASY MONEY   1948, British
SLEEPING CAR TO TRIESTE   1948, British
MIRANDA   Eagle-Lion, 1948, British
BROKEN JOURNEY   Eagle-Lion, 1948, British
MY BROTHER'S KEEPER   1949, British
THE CHILTREN HUNDREDS   *THE AMAZING MR. BEECHAM*
   1949, British
MARRY ME   1949, British
LANDFALL   Associated British Picture Corporation, 1949, British
SO LONG AT THE FAIR   GFD, 1950, British
THE WOODEN HORSE   1950, British
HOTEL SAHARA   United Artists, 1951, British
THE MAGIC BOX   Rank, 1951, British
CASTLE IN THE AIR   1952, British
THREE MEN IN A BOAT   DCA, 1956, British
CARRY ON ADMIRAL   *THE SHIP WAS LOADED*   Renown,
   1957, British
UP THE CREEK   Dominant, 1958, British
FOLLOW THAT HORSE!   1960, British

TOM JONES   Lopert, 1963, British
MARY POPPINS   Buena Vista, 1964
THE TRUTH ABOUT SPRING   Universal, 1965, British-U.S.
WAR-GODS OF THE DEEP   *CITY UNDER THE SEA*
    1965, U.S.-British
THE LIQUIDATOR   MGM, 1966, British
THE LOVE BUG   Buena Vista, 1969
BEDKNOBS AND BROOMSTICKS   Buena Vista, 1971
BON BAISERS DE HONG KONG   1975, French
THE WATER BABIES   Pethurst International/Film Polski,
    1978, British-Polish
THE FIENDISH PLOT OF DR. FU MANCHU   Orion/Warner Bros.,
    1980, British

ANGEL TOMPKINS

THE NAKED CAGE   Cannon, 1986
MURPHY'S LAW   Cannon, 1986

TONE LOC

POSSE   Gramercy Pictures, 1993, U.S.-British
POETIC JUSTICE   Columbia, 1993
SURF NINJAS   New Line Cinema, 1993
ACE VENTURA: PET DETECTIVE   Warner Bros., 1994
BLANK CHECK   Buena Vista, 1994

JACQUELINE TONG

HOW TO GET AHEAD IN ADVERTISING   Warner Bros.,
    1989, British

TOPOL

(Haym Topol)
b. September 9, 1935 - Tel Aviv, Israel

SALLAH   Palisades International, 1964, Israeli
CAST A GIANT SHADOW   United Artists, 1966
EVERY BASTARD A KING   1968, Israeli
BEFORE WINTER COMES   Columbia, 1969, British
A TALENT FOR LOVING   1969, British
THE ROOSTER   1971, Israeli
FIDDLER ON THE ROOF ★   United Artists, 1971
THE PUBLIC EYE   *FOLLOW ME*   Universal, 1972, British
GALILEO   American Film Theatre, 1975, British-Canadian
THE HOUSE ON GARIBALDI STREET (TF)   1979
FLASH GORDON   Universal, 1980, British
FOR YOUR EYES ONLY   United Artists, 1981, British
THE WINDS OF WAR (MS)   Paramount TV/Dan Curtis
    Productions, 1983
QUEENIE (MS)   von Zerneck-Samuels Productions/Highgate
    Pictures, 1987
WAR AND REMEMBRANCE (MS)   Dan Curtis Productions/
    ABC Circle Films, 1988-89

RIP TORN

(Elmore Rual Torn)
b. February 6, 1931 - Temple, Texas
Agent: Gersh Agency - Beverly Hills, 310/274-6611

BABY DOLL   Warner Bros., 1956
A FACE IN THE CROWD   Warner Bros., 1957
TIME LIMIT   1957
PORK CHOP HILL   United Artists, 1959
KING OF KINGS   MGM, 1961
SWEET BIRD OF YOUTH   MGM, 1962
CRITIC'S CHOICE   Warner Bros., 1963
THE CINCINNATI KID   MGM, 1965
ONE SPY TOO MANY   MGM, 1966
YOU'RE A BIG BOY NOW   7 Arts, 1966
BEACH RED   United Artists, 1967
SOL MADRID   MGM, 1968
BEYOND TH ELAW   1968, Italian
COMING APART   Kaleidescope, 1969
TROPIC OF CANCER   Paramount, 1970
MAIDSTONE   Supreme Mix, 1971
THE PRESIDENT'S PLANE IS MISSING (TF)
    ABC Circle Films, 1971
SLAUGHTER   American International, 1972

PAYDAY   Cinerama Releasing Corporation, 1973
CRAZY JOE   Columbia, 1973, Italian-U.S.
THE MAN WHO FELL TO EARTH   Cinema 5, 1976, British
BIRCH INTERVAL   Gamma III, 1977
NASTY HABITS   Brut Productions, 1977, British
THE PRIVATE FILES OF J. EDGAR HOOVER
    American International, 1977
BETRAYAL   Roger Gimbel Productions/EMI TV, 1978
COMA   MGM/United Artists, 1978
BLIND AMBITION (TF)   Time-Life Productions, 1979
A SHINING SEASON (TF)   Green-Epstein Productions/T-M
    Productions/Columbia TV, 1979
THE SEDUCTION OF JOE TYNAN   Universal, 1979
HEARTLAND   Levitt-Pickman, 1979
FIRST FAMILY   Warner Bros., 1980
ONE-TRICK PONY   Warner Bros., 1980
SOPHIA LOREN: HER OWN STORY (TF)   Roger Gimbel
    Productions/EMI TV, 1980
A STRANGER IS WATCHING   MGM/United Artists, 1982
THE BEASTMASTER   MGM/UA, 1982
AIRPLANE II: THE SEQUEL   Paramount, 1982
JINXED!   MGM/UA, 1982
CROSS CREEK ○   Universal/AFD, 1983
CITY HEAT   Warner Bros., 1984
SONGWRITER   TriStar, 1984
FLASHPOINT   TriStar, 1984
BEER   Orion, 1985
SUMMER RENTAL   Paramount, 1985
THE ATLANTA CHILD MURDERS (MS)   Mann-Rafshoon
    Productions/Finnegan Associates, 1985
THE EXECUTION (TF)   Newland-Raynor Productions/Comworld
    Productions, 1985
DREAM WEST (MS)   Sunn Classic Pictures, 1986
MANHUNT FOR CLAUDE DALLAS (TF)   London Films, Inc., 1986
NADINE   TriStar, 1987
EXTREME PREJUDICE   TriStar, 1987
COLD FEET   Avenue Pictures, 1989
HIT LIST   New Line Cinema, 1989
DEFENDING YOUR LIFE   Warner Bros., 1991
HARD PROMISES   Columbia, 1991
THE BLUE AND THE GRAY (MS)   Larry White-Lou Reda
    Productions/Columbia TV, 1982
FLASHPOINT   TriStar, 1984
MISUNDERSTOOD   MGM/UA, 1984
LAGUNA HEAT (CTF)   HBO Pictures/Jay Weston Productions, 1987
DESTINATION: AMERICA (TF)   Stephen J. Cannell
    Productions, 1987
APRIL MORNING (TF)   Robert Halmi, Inc./Samuel
    Goldwyn TV, 1988
THE GRAND TOUR (TF)   HBO Pictures, 1989
DEFENDING YOUR LIFE   The Geffen Company/Warner Bros., 1991
HOW TO MAKE AN AMERICAN QUILT   Universal, 1995

PIP TORRENS

EMINENT DOMAIN   Triumph Releasing Corporation, 1990,
    Canadian-French-Israeli

VINNIE TORRENTE

MAC AND ME   Orion, 1988

LIZ TORRES

KATE'S SECRET (TF)   Andrea Baynes Productions/
    Columbia TV, 1986

JOE TORRY

Agent: CAA - Beverly Hills, 310/288-4545

POETIC JUSTICE   Columbia, 1993
TALES FROM THE HOOD   Savoy Pictures, 1995

FRANK TOTH

E.T. THE EXTRA-TERRESTRIAL   Universal, 1982

SHEILA TOUSEY

THUNDERHEART   TriStar, 1992
SILENT TONGUE   Trimark Pictures, 1994, U.S.-French

LORRAINE TOUSSAINT
Agent: William Morris Agency - Beverly Hills, 310/274-7451

BREAKING IN   Samuel Goldwyn Company, 1989
HUDSON HAWK   TriStar, 1991

CONSTANCE TOWERS
Agent: Stone Manners Talent Agency - Los Angeles, 213/654-7575

SYLVESTER   Columbia, 1985

BUD TOWNSEND
ALWAYS   Samuel Goldwyn Company, 1985

JILL TOWNSEND
THE AWAKENING   Orion/Warner Bros., 1980

PATRICE TOWNSEND
ALWAYS   Samuel Goldwyn Company, 1985

ROBERT TOWNSEND
b. February 6, 1957 - Chicago, Illinois

A SOLDIER'S STORY   Columbia, 1984
AMERICAN FLYERS   Warner Bros., 1985
HOLLYWOOD SHUFFLE   Samuel Goldwyn Company,
   1987 (also directed)
THE MIGHTY QUINN   MGM/UA, 1989
I'M GONNA GIT YOU SUCKA   MGM/UA, 1989 (uncredited)
THE FIVE HEARTBEATS   20th Century Fox, 1991 (also directed)
THE METEOR MAN   MGM/UA, 1993 (also directed)

MARY ELLEN TRAINOR
LITTLE GIANTS   Warner Bros., 1994

TRUYER V. TRAN
ALAMO BAY   TriStar, 1985

FRED TRAVALENA
BUY & CELL   Empire Pictures, 1989

DANIEL J. TRAVANTI
b. March 7, 1940 - Kenosha, Wisconsin

ST. IVES   Warner Bros., 1976
ADAM (TF)   Alan Landsburg Productions, 1983
MURROW (CTF)   HBO Premiere Films/Titus Productions/TVS Ltd.
   Productions, 1986, U.S.-British
ADAM: HIS SONG CONTINUES (TF)   Alan Landsburg Prods., 1986
MIDNIGHT CROSSING   Vestron, 1988
MILLENNIUM   20th Century Fox, 1989
HOWARD BEACH: MAKING THE CASE FOR MURDER (TF)
   Patchett-Kaufmann Entertainment, 1989
JUST CAUSE   Warner Bros., 1995

NANCY TRAVIS
Agent: UTA - Beverly Hills, 310/273-6700

THREE MEN AND A BABY   Buena Vista, 1987
I'LL BE HOME FOR CHRISTMAS (TF)   NBC Productions, 1988
INTERNAL AFFAIRS   Paramount, 1990
AIR AMERICA   TriStar, 1990
THREE MEN AND A LITTLE LADY   Buena Vista, 1990
PASSED AWAY   Buena Vista, 1992
CHAPLIN   TriStar, 1992, U.S.-British
THE VANISHING   20th Century Fox, 1993
SO I MARRIED AN AXE MURDERER   TriStar, 1993
GREEDY   Universal, 1994
FLUKE   MGM/UA, 1994
DESTINY TURNS ON THE RADIO   Savoy Pictures, 1995

RANDY TRAVIS
b. May 4, 1959 - Marshville, North Carolina

FRANK AND JESSE   Trimark Pictures, 1994

JOEY TRAVOLTA
OSCAR   Buena Vista, 1991

JOHN TRAVOLTA
b. February 18, 1954 - Englewood, New Jersey
Agent: William Morris Agency - Beverly Hills, 310/274-7451

THE DEVIL'S RAIN   Bryanston, 1975, U.S.-Mexican
CARRIE   United Artists, 1976
THE BOY IN THE PLASTIC BUBBLE (TF)   Spelling-Goldberg
   Productions, 1976
SATURDAY NIGHT FEVER ★   Paramount, 1977
GREASE   Paramount, 1978
MOMENT BY MOMENT   Universal, 1978
URBAN COWBOY   Paramount, 1980
BLOW OUT   Filmways, 1981
STAYING ALIVE   Paramount, 1983
TWO OF A KIND   20th Century-Fox, 1983
PERFECT   Columbia, 1985
THE DUMB WAITER (TF)   Secret Castle Productions, 1987
THE EXPERTS   Paramount, 1989
LOOK WHO'S TALKING   TriStar, 1989
CHAINS OF GOLD   New Line Cinema, 1990
LOOK WHO'S TALKING TOO   TriStar, 1990
EYES OF AN ANGEL   1991
SHOUT   Universal, 1991
BORIS AND NATASHA   MCEG, 1992, filmed in 1988 (uncredited)
LOOK WHO'S TALKING NOW   TriStar, 1993
PULP FICTION   Miramax Films, 1994
GET SHORTY   MGM/UA, 1995

SUSAN TRAYLOR
SLEEP WITH ME   MGM/UA, 1994

ROBERT TREBOR
52 PICK-UP   Cannon, 1986
MY DEMON LOVER   New Line Cinema, 1987

WILLIAM TREGOE
AIRPLANE!   Paramount, 1980

JUDD TRICHTER
BIG   20th Century Fox, 1988

SARAH TRIGGER
PCU   20th Century Fox, 1994
THINGS TO DO IN DENVER WHEN YOU'RE DEAD
   Miramax Films, 1995

ZOE TRILLING
NIGHT OF THE DEMONS 2   Republic Pictures, 1994

JEAN-LOUIS TRINTIGNANT
b. December 11, 1930 - Fiolenc, France

A MAN AND A WOMAN   Allied Artists, 1966, French
THE OUTSIDE MAN   UN HOMME EST MORT   United Artists,
   1973, French-Italian
THE FRENCH CONSPIRACY   L'ATTENTAT   1973,
   French-Italian-West German
UNDER FIRE   Orion, 1983
A MAN AND A WOMAN: 20 YEARS LATER   Warner Bros.,
   1986, French
BETTY   MK2, 1993, French

LOUIS TRIPP
GATE II   Triumph Releasing Corporation, 1992

JEANNE TRIPPLEHORN
Agent: CAA - Beverly Hills, 310/288-4545

BASIC INSTINCT   TriStar, 1992
THE NIGHT WE NEVER MET   Miramax Films, 1993
THE FIRM   Paramount, 1993
WATERWORLD   Universal, 1995

JAN TRISKA
WORLD WAR II: THEN THERE WERE GIANTS (TF)
World International Network, 1994

CHAM TROTTER
MISS FIRECRACKER   Corsair Pictures, 1989

JIM TRUE
SINGLES   Warner Bros., 1992

DONALD TRUMP
GHOSTS CAN'T DO IT   Triumph Releasing Corporation, 1990
HOME ALONE 2: LOST IN NEW YORK   20th Century Fox,
1992 (uncredited)

STEVE "PATALAY" TSIGNOFF
ANGELO, MY LOVE   Cinecom, 1983

IRENE TSU
CAPRICE   20th Century-Fox, 1967
THE GREEN BERETS   Warner Bros., 1968
PAPER TIGER   Joseph E. Levine Presents, 1976, British
DOWN AND OUT IN BEVERLY HILLS   Buena Vista, 1986

LE TUAN
GLEAMING THE CUBE   20th Century Fox, 1989

BARRY TUBB
Agent: Susan Smith & Associates - Beverly Hills, 213/852-4777

TOP GUN   Paramount, 1986
BILLIONAIRE BOYS CLUB (MS)   Donald March/Gross-Weston
Productions/ITC Productions, 1987
WITHOUT HER CONSENT (TF)   Raymond Katz Enterprises/
Half Pint Productions/Carla Singer Productions, 1990

MARIA TUCCI
UNTITLED VAN SANT/ZISKIN   Columbia, 1995

STANLEY TUCCI
b. 1960 - New York, New York
Agent: William Morris Agency - Beverly Hills, 310/274-7451

FEAR, ANXIETY AND DEPRESSION   Samuel Goldwyn
Company, 1990
MEN OF RESPECT   Columbia, 1991
IN THE SOUP   Triton Pictures, 1992,
U.S.-Japanese-German-French-Spanish-Italian
BEETHOVEN   Universal, 1992
PRELUDE TO A KISS   20th Century Fox, 1992
UNDERCOVER BLUES   MGM/UA, 1993
THE PELICAN BRIEF   Warner Bros., 1993
MRS. PARKER AND THE VICIOUS CIRCLE   Fine Line Features/
New Line Cinema, 1994
KISS OF DEATH   20th Century Fox, 1995
JURY DUTY   Sony Pictures, 1995
PASTA E FUSILLE   1995 (also co-directed)

MICHAEL TUCKER
b. February 6, 1944 - Baltimore, Maryland

EYES OF LAURA MARS   Columbia, 1978
DINER   MGM/United Artists, 1982
THE GOODBYE PEOPLE   Embassy, 1984
THE PURPLE ROSE OF CAIRO   Orion, 1985
RADIO DAYS   Orion, 1987
CHECKING OUT   Warner Bros., 1989
FOR LOVE OR MONEY   Universal, 1993
D2: THE MIGHTY DUCKS   Buena Vista, 1994

ROBIN TUNNEY
EMPIRE   Warner Bros., 1995

PAIGE TURCO
TEENAGE MUTANT NINJA TURTLES II: THE SECRET OF
THE OOZE   New Line Cinema, 1991

ANN TURKEL
PAPER LION   United Artists, 1968
99 AND 44/100 % DEAD   20th Century-Fox, 1974
MATT HELM (TF)   1975
THE CASSANDRA CROSSING   1977
GOLDEN RENDEZVOUS   1978
HUMANOIDS FROM THE DEEP   1980

GLYNN TURMAN
GREMLINS   Warner Bros., 1984

ANGELA TURNER
MISS FIRECRACKER   Corsair Pictures, 1989

FRANK TURNER
THE FLY II   20th Century Fox, 1989

JANINE TURNER
b. December 6, 1962 - Lincoln, Nebraska

CLIFFHANGER   TriStar, 1993

KATHLEEN TURNER
b. June 19, 1954 - Springfield, Missouri
Agent: ICM - Beverly Hills, 310/550-4000

BODY HEAT   The Ladd Company/Warner Bros., 1981
THE MAN WITH TWO BRAINS   Warner Bros., 1983
ROMANCING THE STONE   20th Century Fox, 1984
A BREED APART   Orion, 1984
CRIMES OF PASSION   New World, 1984
PRIZZI'S HONOR   20th Century Fox, 1985
THE JEWEL OF THE NILE   20th Century Fox, 1985
PEGGY SUE GOT MARRIED ★   TriStar, 1986
JULIA AND JULIA   Cinecom, 1987, Italian
DEAR AMERICA: LETTERS HOME FROM VIETNAM (FD)
Taurus Entertainment, 1987 (voice)
SWITCHING CHANNELS   Columbia, 1988
WHO FRAMED ROGER RABBIT   Buena Vista,
1988 (voice; uncredited)
THE ACCIDENTAL TOURIST   Warner Bros., 1988
TUMMY TROUBLE (AS)   Buena Vista, 1989 (voice; uncredited)
THE WAR OF THE ROSES   20th Century Fox, 1989
ROLLERCOASTER RABBIT (AS)   Buena Vista,
1990 (voice; uncredited)
V.I. WARSHAWSKI   Buena Vista, 1991
HOUSE OF CARDS   Miramax Films, 1993
UNDERCOVER BLUES   MGM/UA, 1993
NAKED IN NEW YORK   Fine Line Features/New Line Cinema, 1994
SERIAL MOM   Savoy Pictures, 1994
MOONLIGHT AND VALENTINO   Gramercy Pictures, 1995

LANA TURNER
(Julia Jean Mildred Frances Turner)
b. February 8, 1920 - Wallace, Idaho

A STAR IS BORN   United Artists, 1937
THEY WON'T FORGET   Warner Bros., 1937
THE GREAT GARRICK   Warner Bros., 1937
THE ADVENTURES OF MARCO POLO   United Artists, 1938
FOUR'S A CROWD   Warner Bros., 1938
LOVE FINDS ANDY HARDY   MGM, 1938
THE CHASER   MGM, 1938
RICH MAN, POOR GIRL   1938
DRAMATIC SCHOOL   1938
CALLING DR. KILDARE   1939
THESE GLAMOUR GIRLS   1939
DANCING CO-ED   1939
TWO GIRLS ON BROADWAY   1940
WE WHO ARE YOUNG   1940
CHOOSE YOUR PARTNER   1940
ZIEGFELD GIRL   MGM, 1941

353

DR. JEKYLL AND MR. HYDE   MGM, 1941
HONKY TONK   MGM, 1941
JOHNNY EAGER   MGM, 1942
SOMEWHERE I'LL FIND YOU   MGM, 1942
SLIGHTLY DANGEROUS   MGM, 1943
THE YOUNGEST PROFESSION   MGM, 1943
DU BARRY WAS A LADY   MGM, 1943
MARRIAGE IS A PRIVATE AFFAIR   MGM, 1944
KEEP YOUR POWDER DRY   MGM, 1945
WEEK-END AT THE WALDORF   MGM, 1945
THE POSTMAN ALWAYS RINGS TWICE   MGM, 1946
GREEN DOLPHIN STREET   MGM, 1947
CASS TIMBERLANE   MGM, 1947
HOMECOMING   MGM, 1948
THE THREE MUSKETEERS   MGM, 1948
A LIFE OF HER OWN   MGM, 1950
MR. IMPERIUM   MGM, 1951
THE MERRY WIDOW   MGM, 1952
THE BAD AND THE BEAUTIFUL   MGM, 1952
LATIN LOVERS   MGM, 1953
FLAME AND THE FLESH   MGM, 1954
BETRAYED   1954
THE PRODIGAL   MGM, 1955
THE SEA CHASE   Warner Bros., 1955
THE RAINS OF RANCHIPUR   20th Century-Fox, 1955
DIANE   MGM, 1956
PEYTON PLACE ★   20th Century-Fox, 1957
THE LADY TAKES A FLYER   Universal, 1958
ANOTHER TIME, ANOTHER PLACE   Universal, 1958
IMITATION OF LIFE   Universal, 1959
PORTRAIT IN BLACK   Universal, 1960
BY LOVE POSSESSED   United Artists, 1961
BACHELOR IN PARADISE   MGM, 1961
WHO'S GOT THE ACTION?   Paramount, 1962
LOVE HAS MANY FACES   Columbia, 1965
MADAME X   Universal, 1966
THE BIG CUBE   1969, U.S.-Mexican
THE TERROR OF SHEBA   *PERSECUTION*   Blueberry Hill,
   1974, British
BITTERSWEET LOVE   Avco Embassy, 1976

TINA TURNER
(Anna Mae Bullock)
b. November 26, 1938 - Nutbush, Tennessee
Agent: CAA - Beverly Hills, 310/288-4545

TOMMY   Columbia, 1975, British
MAD MAX BEYOND THUNDERDOME   Warner Bros.,
   1985, Australian
WHAT'S LOVE GOT TO DO WITH IT   Buena Vista, 1993
LAST ACTION HERO   Columbia, 1993

AIDA TURTURRO
ANGIE   Buena Vista, 1994

JOHN TURTURRO
b. February 28, 1957 - Brooklyn, New York
Agent: ICM - Beverly Hills, 310/550-4000

RAGING BULL   United Artists, 1980
THE FLAMINGO KID   20th Century Fox, 1984
DESPERATELY SEEKING SUSAN   Orion, 1985
TO LIVE AND DIE IN L.A.   MGM/UA, 1985
HANNAH AND HER SISTERS   Orion, 1986
GUNG HO   Paramount, 1986
OFF BEAT   Buena Vista, 1986
THE COLOR OF MONEY   Buena Vista, 1986
THE SICILIAN   20th Century Fox, 1987
FIVE CORNERS   Cineplex Odeon, 1988
DO THE RIGHT THING   Universal, 1989
MO' BETTER BLUES   Universal, 1990
STATE OF GRACE   Orion, 1990
MILLER'S CROSSING   20th Century Fox, 1990
BACKTRACK   *CATCHFIRE*   Vestron, 1991
MEN OF RESPECT   Columbia, 1991
JUNGLE FEVER   Universal, 1991
BARTON FINK   20th Century Fox, 1991
BRAIN DONORS   Paramount, 1992
MAC   Samuel Goldwyn Company, 1992 (also directed)

FEARLESS   Warner Bros., 1993
BEING HUMAN   Warner Bros., 1994
QUIZ SHOW   Buena Vista, 1994
SEARCH AND DESTROY   October Films, 1995
UNSTRUNG HEROES   Buena Vista, 1995
CLOCKERS   Universal, 1995

SHANNON TWEED
HOT DOG...THE MOVIE   MGM/UA, 1984
THE HIGH PRICE OF PASSION (TF)   Edgar J. Scherick
   Productions, 1986

TWIGGY
b. September 19, 1949 - London, England

THE BOY FRIEND   MGM, 1971, British
"W"   *I WANT HER DEAD*   Cinerama Releasing Corporation,
   1974, British
THERE GOES THE BRIDE   Vanguard, 1979, British
THE DOCTOR AND THE DEVILS   20th Century Fox, 1985, British
CLUB PARADISE   Warner Bros., 1986
MADAME SOUSATZKA   Cineplex Odeon, 1988, British
THE DIAMOND TRAP (TF)   Jay Bernstein Prods./Columbia TV, 1988

ANNE TWOMEY
DEADLY FRIEND   Warner Bros., 1986
LAST RITES   MGM/United Artists, 1988
THE SCOUT   20th Century Fox, 1994

TYLER TYHURST
WANTED DEAD OR ALIVE   New World, 1986

LIV TYLER
SILENT FALL   Warner Bros., 1994
EMPIRE   Warner Bros., 1995

SUSAN TYRRELL
SHOOTOUT   Universal, 1971
THE STEAGLE   Avco Embassy, 1971
FAT CITY O   Columbia, 1972
CATCH MY SOUL   *SANTA FE SATAN*   Cinerama Releasing
   Corporation, 1974
ZANDY'S BRIDE   *FOR BETTER, FOR WORSE*   Warner Bros., 1974
THE KILLER INSIDE ME   Warner Bros., 1976
ISLANDS IN THE STREAM   Paramount, 1977
ANOTHER MAN, ANOTHER CHANCE   United Artists,
   1977, U.S.-French
ANDY WARHOL'S BAD   New World, 1977
I NEVER PROMISED YOU A ROSE GARDEN   New World, 1977
9/30/55   *SEPTEMBER 30, 1955*   Universal, 1977
LADY OF THE HOUSE   Metromedia Productions, 1978
FORBIDDEN ZONE   1980
LOOSE SHOES   *COMING ATTRACTIONS*   1980
NIGHT WARNING   Comworld, 1981
FAST-WALKING   Pickman Films, 1982
LIAR'S MOON   Crown International, 1982
TALES OF ORDINARY MADNESS   Fred Baker Films,
   1983, Italian-French
ANGEL   New World, 1984
FLESH + BLOOD   Orion, 1985, U.S.-Dutch
AVENGING ANGEL   New World, 1985
THOMPSON'S LAST RUN (TF)   Cypress Point Productions, 1986
IF TOMORROW COMES (MS)   CBS Entertainment, 1986
BIG TOP PEE-WEE   Paramount, 1988
CRY-BABY   Universal, 1990

CICELY TYSON
b. December 19, 1933 - New York, New York

A MAN CALLED ADAM   Embassy, 1966
THE COMEDIANS   MGM, 1967, British
THE HEART IS A LONELY HUNTER   Warner Bros., 1968
SOUNDER ★   20th Century-Fox, 1972
THE AUTOBIOGRAPHY OF MISS JANE PITTMAN (TF)
   Tomorrow Entertainment, 1974
WILMA (TF)   Cappy Productions, 1977
ROOTS (MS)   Wolper Productions, 1977

A HERO AIN'T NOTHIN' BUT A SANDWICH New World, 1977
KING (MS) Abby Mann Productions/Filmways, 1978
THE CONCORDE—AIRPORT '79 Universal, 1979
BUSTIN' LOOSE Universal, 1981
PLAYING WITH FIRE (TF) Zephyr Productions, 1985
ACCEPTABLE RISKS (TF) ABC Circle Films, 1986
SAMARITAN: THE MITCH SNYDER STORY (TF) Levine-Robbins
    Productions/Fries Entertainment, 1986
INTIMATE ENCOUNTERS (TF) Larry Thompson Productions/
    Donna Mills Productions/Columbia TV, 1986
HEATWAVE (CTF) The Avnet-Kerner Company/
    Propaganda Films, 1990
FRIED GREEN TOMATOES Universal, 1991
JEFFERSON IN PARIS Buena Vista, 1995
THE GRASS HARP New Line Cinema, 1995

RICHARD TYSON
THREE O'CLOCK HIGH Universal, 1987
TWO MOON JUNCTION Lorimar, 1988
KINDERGARTEN COP Universal, 1990

U

HECHTER UBARRY
"CROCODILE" DUNDEE II Paramount, 1988, U.S.-Australian
McBAIN Shapiro-Glickenhouse Entertainment, 1991

HATSUO UDA
AIRPLANE! Paramount, 1980

FABIANA UDENIO
IN THE ARMY NOW Buena Vista, 1994

BOB UECKER
b. January 26, 1935 - Milwaukee, Wisconsin
Agent: William Morris Agency - Beverly Hills, 310/274-7451

MAJOR LEAGUE Paramount, 1989
MAJOR LEAGUE II Warner Bros., 1994

LESLIE UGGAMS
b. May 25, 1943 - New York, New York

SUGAR HILL 20th Century Fox, 1994

TRACEY ULLMAN
b. December 30, 1959 - Slough, England
Agent: CAA - Beverly Hills, 310/288-4545

PLENTY 20th Century Fox, 1985, British
I LOVE YOU TO DEATH TriStar, 1990
ROBIN HOOD: MEN IN TIGHTS 20th Century Fox, 1993
HOUSEHOLD SAINTS Fine Line Features/New Line Cinema, 1993
I'LL DO ANYTHING Columbia, 1994
BULLETS OVER BROADWAY Miramax Films, 1994
PRET-A-PORTER Miramax Films, 1994

LIV ULLMANN
b. December 16, 1939 - Tokyo, Japan
Agent: The Lantz Office - New York, 212/586-0200

FJOLS TIL FJELLS 1957, Norwegian
THE WAYWARD GIRL 1959, Norwegian
TONNY 1962, Norwegian
SHORT IS THE SUMMER KORT AR SOMMAREN/PAN
    1962, Norwegian-Swedish
DE KALTE HAM SKARVEN 1964, Norwegian

UNG FLUKT 1966, Norwegian
PERSONA United Artists, 1966, Swedish
HOUR OF THE WOLF United Artists, 1968, Swedish
SHAME United Artists, 1968, Swedish
ANN-MAGRITT 1969, Norwegian-Swedish
THE PASSION OF ANNA PASSION United Artists,
    1969, Swedish
COLD SWEAT DE LA PART DES COPAINS 1970, French-Italian
THE NIGHT VISITOR 1971, Swish-Danish-U.S.
THE EMIGRANTS UTVANDRARNA ★ Warner Bros.,
    1972, Swedish
POPE JOAN THE DEVIL'S IMPOSTER Columbia, 1972, British
CRIES AND WHISPERS New World, 1972, Swedish
SCENES FROM A MARRIAGE Cinema 5, 1973, Swedish
LOST HORIZON Columbia, 1972
40 CARATS Columbia, 1973
THE NEW LAND NYBYGGARNA Warner Bros., 1973, Swedish
ZANDY'S BRIDE FOR BETTER, FOR WORSE
    Warner Bros., 1974
THE ABDICATION Warner Bros., 1974, British
LÉONOR 1975, French
FACE TO FACE ★ Paramount, 1976, Swedish
COULEUR CHAIR 1977, Belgian-French
A BRIDGE TOO FAR United Artists, 1977, British
THE SERPENT'S EGG 1977, U.S.-West German
AUTUMN SONATA New World, 1978, West German
PLAYERS 1979
RICHARD'S THINGS (TF) 1980
THE WILD DUCK 1982
BAY BOY 1984
DANGEROUS MOVES 1984
INGRID 1985
LET'S HOPE IT'S A GIRL 1985
JACOBO TIMERMAN: PRISONER WITHOUT A NAME, CELL
    WITHOUT A NUMBER (TF) Chrysalis-Yellin Productions, 1983
GABY - A TRUE STORY TriStar, 1987, U.S.-Mexican

BLAIR UNDERWOOD
b. August 25 - Tacoma, Washington
Agent: CAA - Beverly Hills, 310/288-4545

KRUSH GROOVE Warner Bros., 1985
THE COVER GIRL AND THE COP (TF) Barry & Enright
    Productions, 1989
MURDER IN MISSISSIPPI (TF) Wolper Productions/Bernard
    Sofronski Productions/Warner Bros. TV, 1990
HEATWAVE (CTF) The Avnet-Kerner Company/
    Propaganda Films, 1990
JUST CAUSE Warner Bros., 1995

JAY UNDERWOOD
(Jay D. Underwood)
THE BOY WHO COULD FLY 20th Century Fox, 1986
DESERT BLOOM Columbia, 1986
THE GUMSHOE KID Argus Entertainment, 1989

DEBORAH UNGER
WHISPERS IN THE DARK Paramount, 1992

ROBERT URICH
b. December 19, 1946 - Toronto, Ohio
Agent: ICM - Beverly Hills, 310/550-4000

MAGNUM FORCE Warner Bros., 1973
VEGA$ (TF) Aaron Spelling Productions, 1978
KILLING AT HELL'S GATE (TF) CBS Entertainment, 1981
ENDANGERED SPECIES MGM/UA, 1982
PRINCESS DAISY (TF) NBC Productions/Steve Krantz
    Productions, 1983
THE ICE PIRATES MGM/UA, 1984
MISTRAL'S DAUGHTER (MS) Steve Krantz Productions/
    R.T.L. Productions/Antenne-2, 1984, U.S.-French
SCANDAL SHEET (TF) Fair Dinkum Productions, 1985
TURK 182 20th Century Fox, 1985
SPENSER: FOR HIRE (TF) John Wilder Productions/
    Warner Bros. TV, 1985
AMERIKA (MS) ABC Circle Films, 1987

APRIL MORNING (TF)   Robert Halmi, Inc./Samuel Goldwyn TV, 1988
THE COMEBACK (TF)   CBS Entertainment, 1989
SHE KNOWS TOO MUCH (TF)   The Fred Silverman Company/
   Dinnegan-Pinchuk Productions/MGM-UA TV, 1989
LONESOME DOVE (MS)   Motown Productions/Pangaea/Qintex
   Entertainment, Inc., 1989
NIGHT WALK (TF)   CBS Entertainment/Galatea Productions, 1989
MURDER BY NIGHT (CTF)   Finnegan-Pinchuk Productions, 1989
SPOONER (CTF)   Pipeline Productions, Inc., 1989
BLIND FAITH (MS)   NBC Productions, 1990

PETER USTINOV

b. April 16, 1921 - London, England

HULLO FAME   1940, British
MEIN KAMPF MY CRIMES   1940, British
ONE OF OUR AIRCRAFT IS MISSING   United Artists, 1942, British
LET THE PEOPLE SING   1942, British
THE GOOSE STEPS OUT   United Artists, 1942, British
THE WAY AHEAD   *THE IMMORTAL BATTALION*
   20th Century-Fox, 1944, British
PRIVATE ANGELO   Associated British Picture Corporation,
   1949, British (also co-directed)
ODETTE   British Lion, 1950, British
HOTEL SAHARA   United Artists, 1951, British
THE MAGIC BOX   Rank, 1951, British
QUO VADIS ✪   MGM, 1951
HOUSE OF PLEASURE   *LE PLAISIR*   1952, French (voice)
THE EGYPTIAN   20th Century-Fox, 1954
BEAU BRUMMEL   1954, British-U.S.
WE'RE NO ANGELS   Paramount, 1956
THE SINS OF LOLA MONTES   *LOLA MONTES*   Brandon, 1955,
   French-West German
I GIROVAGHI   1956, Italian
THE MAN WHO WAGGED HIS TAIL   *UN ANGEL PASO POR*
   BROOKLYN   1957, Spanish-Italian
LES ESPIONS   1957, French
SPARTACUS ✪✪   Universal, 1960
THE SUNDOWNERS   Warner Bros., 1960, U.S.-British-Australian
DIG THAT JULIET   *ROMANOFF AND JULIET*   Universal,
   1961 (also directed)
BILLY BUDD   Allied Artists, 1962, British (also directed)
WOMEN OF THE WORLD   *LA DONNA NEL MONDO* (FD)
   1963, Italian (voice)
TOPKAPI ✪✪   United Artists, 1964
JOHN GOLDFARB, PLEASE COME HOME   20th Century-Fox, 1965
LADY L   MGM, 1965, Italian-French-U.S. (also directed)
THE COMEDIANS   MGM, 1968, U.S.-French
BLACKBEARD'S GHOST   Buena Vista, 1968
HOT MILLIONS   MGM, 1968, British
VIVA MAX!   Commonwealth United, 1969
HAMMERSMITH IS OUT   Cinerama Releasing Corporation,
   1972 (also directed)
ROBIN HOOD (AF)   Buena Vista, 1973 (voice)
ONE OF OUR DINOSAURS IS MISSING   Buena Vista,
   1975, U.S.-British
LOGAN'S RUN   MGM/United Artists, 1976
TREASURE OF MATECUMBE   Buena Vista, 1976
THE PURPLE TAXI   *UN TAXI MAUVE*   French-Italian-Irish
THE MOUSE AND HIS CHILD (AF)   Sanrio, 1977 (voice)
THE LAST REMAKE OF BEAU GESTE   1977
JESUS OF NAZARETH (MS)   Sir Lew Grade Productions/ITC,
   1978, British-Italian
DOPPIO DELITTO   1978, Italian-French
DEATH ON THE NILE   Paramount, 1978, British
ASHANTI   Columbia, 1979, Swiss-U.S.
THE THIEF OF BAGHDAD (TF)   Palm Films Ltd., 1979, British
CHARLIE CHAN AND THE CURSE OF THE DRAGON QUEEN
   American Cinema, 1981
EVIL UNDER THE SUN   Universal/AFD, 1982, British
MEMED MY HAWK   Filmworld Distributors, 1983,
   British-Yugoslavian (also directed)
MURDER WITH MIRRORS (TF)   1985
THIRTEEN AT DINNER (TF)   1985
DEAD MAN'S FOLLY (TF)   1986
LORENZO'S OIL   Universal, 1992

WILLIAM UTAY
COBB   Warner Bros., 1994

V

BRENDA VACCARO

b. November 18, 1939 - Brooklyn, New York

WHERE IT'S AT   United Artists, 1969
MIDNIGHT COWBOY   United Artists, 1969
I LOVE MY WIFE   Universal, 1970
SUMMERTREE   Columbia, 1971
GOING HOME   MGM, 1971
WHAT'S A NICE GIRL LIKE YOU...? (TF)   Universal TV, 1971
HONOR THY FATHER   Metromedia Productions, 1973
SUNSHINE (TF)   Universal TV, 1973
JACQUELINE SUSANN'S ONCE IS NOT ENOUGH   *ONCE IS NOT*
   ENOUGH ✪   Paramount, 1975
THE HOUSE BY THE LAKE   *DEATH WEEKEND*
   American International, 1977, Canadian
AIRPORT '77   Universal, 1977
CAPRICORN ONE   20th Century-Fox, 1978
FAST CHARLIE, THE MOONBEAM RIDER   *FAST CHARLIE AND*
   THE MOONBEAM   Universal, 1979
DEAR DETECTIVE (TF)   CBS, 1979
THE PRIDE OF JESSE HALLMAN (TF)   The Konigsberg
   Company, 1981
THE FIRST DEADLY SIN   Filmways, 1980
ZORRO, THE GAY BLADE   20th Century-Fox, 1981
SUPERGIRL   Warner Bros., 1984, British
WATER   Atlantic Releasing Corporation, 1984, British
COOKIE   Warner Bros., 1989
HEART OF MIDNIGHT   Virgin Vision, 1989
STOLEN: ONE HUSBAND (TF)   King Phoenix Entertainment, 1990

TRACY VACCARO
THE MAN WHO LOVED WOMEN   Columbia, 1983

WARREN VACHE
THE GIG   Castle Hill Productions, 1985

SAMUEL VALADEZ
OLD GRINGO   Columbia, 1989

MARIA VALDEZ
BETRAYED   MGM/UA, 1988

NANCY VALEN
LOVERBOY   TriStar, 1989

SCOTT VALENTINE
MY DEMON LOVER   New Line Cinema, 1987
WITHOUT HER CONSENT (TF)   Raymond Katz Enterprises/Half
   Pint Productions/Carla Singer Productions, 1990

KAREN VALENTINE
GIDGET GROWS UP (TF)   Screen Gems/Columbia TV, 1969
THE DAUGHTERS OF JOSHUA CABE (TF)   Spelling-Goldberg
   Productions, 1972
COFFEE, TEA OR ME? (TF)   CBS, Inc., 1973
THE GIRL WHO CAME GIFT-WRAPPED (TF)   Spelling-Goldberg
   Productions, 1974
HAVING BABIES (TF)   The Jozak Company, 1976
MURDER AT THE WORLD SERIES (TF)   ABC Circle Films, 1977
GO WEST, YOUNG GIRL (TF)   Bennett-Katleman Productions/
   Columbia TV, 1978
THE NORTH AVENUE IRREGULARS   Buena Vista, 1978
MUGGABLE MARY: STREET COP (TF)   CBS Entertainment, 1982

CHILDREN IN THE CROSSFIRE (TF)   Schaefer-Karpf
   Productions/Prendergast-Brittcadia Productions/Gaylord
   Production Company, 1984
HE'S FIRED, SHE'S HIRED (TF)   CBS Entertainment, 1984
PERFECT PEOPLE (TF)   Robert Greenwald Productions, 1988

TONY VALENTINO
ANGEL TOWN   Taurus Entertainment, 1990

FRANKIE VALLI
b. May 3, 1937 - Newark, New Jersey

MODERN LOVE   Triumph Releasing Corporation, 1990
ETERNITY   Academy Entertainment, 1990

RAF VALLONE
(Raffaele Vallone)
b. February 17, 1917 - Tropea, Italy

TWO WOMEN   Embassy, 1960, Italian-French
EL CID   Allied Artists, 1961, U.S.-Italian
A VIEW FROM THE BRIDGE   *VU DU PONT*   Allied Artists,
   1962, French-Italian
PHAEDRA   Lopert, 1962, West German-U.S.
THE CARDINAL   Columbia, 1963
THE SECRET INVASION   United Artists, 1964
A GUNFIGHT   Paramount, 1971
THE GREEK TYCOON   Universal, 1978
AN ALMOST PERFECT AFFAIR   Paramount, 1979
THE GODFATHER, PART III   Paramount, 1990

JOAN VAN ARK
b. June 16, 1943 - New York, New York
Agent: William Morris Agency - Beverly Hills, 310/274-7451

RED FLAG: THE ULTIMATE GAME (TF)   Marble Arch
   Productions, 1981
SHAKEDOWN ON THE SUNSET STRIP (TF)   CBS Entertainment, 1988
MY FIRST LOVE (TF)   The Avnet-Kerner Company, 1988
ALWAYS REMEMBER I LOVE YOU (TF)   Stephen J. Cannell/
   Gross-Weston Productions, Inc., 1990

COURTNEY B. VANCE
HAMBURGER HILL   Paramount, 1987
THE HUNT FOR RED OCTOBER   Paramount, 1990
THE ADVENTURES OF HUCK FINN   Buena Vista, 1993
PANTHER   Gramercy Pictures, 1995

JEAN-CLAUDE VAN DAMME
Agent: ICM - Beverly Hills, 310/550-4000

BLOODSPORT   Cannon, 1987
BLACK EAGLE   Taurus Entertainment, 1988
CYBORG   Cannon, 1989
KICKBOXER   Cannon, 1989
DEATH WARRANT   MGM/UA, 1990
LIONHEART   Universal, 1991
DOUBLE IMPACT   Columbia, 1991
UNIVERSAL SOLDIER   TriStar, 1992
NOWHERE TO RUN   Columbia, 1993
HARD TARGET   Universal, 1993
TIMECOP   Universal, 1994
STREET FIGHTER   Universal, 1994
THE QUEST   Universal, 1995
SUDDEN DEATH   Universal, 1995

NADINE VAN DER VELDE
CRITTERS   New Line Cinema, 1986

MILDRED R. VANDEVER
BIG   20th Century Fox, 1988

TRISH VAN DEVERE
(Patricia Dressel)
b. March 9, 1945 - Englewood Cliffs, New Jersey

THE LANDLORD   United Artists, 1970
WHERE'S POPPA?   United Artists, 1970
THE LAST RUN   MGM, 1971
ONE IS A LONELY NUMBER   MGM, 1972
HARRY IN YOUR POCKET   1973
THE DAY OF THE DOLPHIN   Avco Embassy, 1973
THE SAVAGE IS LOOSE   Campbell Devon, 1974
BEAUTY AND THE BEAST (TF)   Palms Films, Ltd., 1976, British
MOVIE MOVIE   Warner Bros., 1978
THE HEARSE   Crown International, 1980
THE CHANGELING   AFD, 1980, Canadian
MESSENGER OF DEATH   Cannon, 1988

JOHN VAN DREELEN
EVITA PERON (TF)   Hartwest Productions/Zephyr
   Productions, 1981

LUTHER VANDROSS
b. April 20, 1951 - New York, New York

THE METEOR MAN   MGM/UA, 1993

DICK VAN DYKE
b. December 13, 1925 - West Plains, Missouri
Agent: William Morris Agency - Beverly Hills, 310/274-7451

BYE BYE BIRDIE   Columbia, 1963
WHAT A WAY TO GO!   20th Century-Fox, 1964
MARY POPPINS   Buena Vista, 1964
THE ART OF LOVE   Universal, 1965
LT. ROBIN CRUSOE USN   Buena Vista, 1966
DIVORCE AMERICAN STYLE   Columbia, 1967
FITZWILLY   United Artists, 1967
NEVER A DULL MOMENT   Buena Vista, 1968
CHITTY CHITTY BANG BANG   United Artists, 1968, British
SOME KIND OF A NUT   United Artists, 1969
THE COMIC   Columbia, 1969
COLD TURKEY   United Artists, 1971
THE MORNING AFTER (TF)   Wolper Productions, 1974
THE RUNNER STUMBLES   20th Century-Fox, 1979
DROP-OUT FATHER (TF)   CBS Entertainment, 1982
FOUND MONEY (TF)   Cypress Point Prods./Warner Bros. TV, 1983
STRONG MEDICINE (TF)   Telepictures Productions/TVS Ltd.
   Productions, 1986, U.S.-British
GHOST OF A CHANCE (TF)   Stuart-Phoenix Productions/
   Thunder Bird Road Productions/Lorimar-Telepictures, 1987
DICK TRACY   Buena Vista, 1990

BRANT VAN HOFFMANN
POLICE ACADEMY   The Ladd Company/Warner Bros., 1984
RUSTLER'S RHAPSODY   Paramount, 1985
CHAPTER TWO   Columbia, 1980
POLICE ACADEMY 3: BACK IN TRAINING   Warner Bros., 1986

VANITY
52 PICK-UP   Cannon, 1986
ACTION JACKSON   Lorimar, 1988
MEMORIES OF MURDER (CTF)   Houston Lady Company/Viacom
   Productions, 1990

PETER VAN NORDEN
THE ACCUSED   Paramount, 1988

RENATA VANNI
LADY IN WHITE   New Century/Vista, 1988

NINA VAN PALLANDT
b. July 15, 1932 - Copenhagen, Denmark

THE LONG GOODBYE   United Artists, 1973
A WEDDING   20th Century-Fox, 1978

QUINTET   20th Century-Fox, 1979
AMERICAN GIGOLO   Paramount, 1980
CLOUD DANCER   Blossom, 1980

DICK VAN PATTEN
b. December 9, 1928 - Kew Gardens, New York

REG'LAR FELLERS   Producers Releasing Corporation, 1941
CHARLY   Cinerama Releasing Corporation, 1968
ZACHARIAH   Cinerama Releasing Corporation, 1971
MAKING IT   20th Century-Fox, 1971
JOE KIDD   Universal, 1972
DIRTY LITTLE BILLY   Columbia, 1972
SNOWBALL EXPRESS   Buena Vista, 1972
PSYCHOMANIA   *VIOLENT MIDNIGHT*   1973
SOYLENT GREEN   MGM, 1973
WESTWORLD   MGM, 1973
SUPERDAD   Buena Vista, 1974
THE STRONGEST MAN IN THE WORLD   Buena Vista, 1975
TREASURE OF MATECUMBE   Buena Vista, 1976
GUS   Buena Vista, 1976
THE SHAGGY D.A.   Buena Vista, 1976
FREAKY FRIDAY   Buena Vista, 1977
HIGH ANXIETY   20th Century-Fox, 1977
THE MIDNIGHT HOUR (TF)   ABC Circle Films, 1985
EIGHT IS ENOUGH: A FAMILY REUNION (TF)   Lorimar TV, 1987
THE NEW ADVENTURES OF PIPPI LONGSTOCKING
    Columbia, 1988
AN EIGHT IS ENOUGH WEDDING (TF)   Lorimar TV, 1989

JOYCE VAN PATTEN
b. March 9, 1934 - New York, New York

REG'LAR FELLERS   Producers Releasing Corporation, 1941
FOURTEEN HOURS   20th Century-Fox, 1951
THE GODDESS   Columbia, 1958
I LOVE YOU, ALICE B. TOKLAS!   Warner Bros., 1968
THE TROUBLE WITH GIRLS   MGM, 1969
PUSSYCAT, PUSSYCAT, I LOVE YOU   United Artists, 1970, British
MAKING IT   20th Century-Fox, 1971
SOMETHING BIG   National General, 1971
THE BRAVOS (TF)   Universal TV, 1972
BONE   Jack H. Harris Enterprises, 1972
MAME   Warner Bros., 1974
THE MANCHU EAGLE MURDER CAPER MYSTERY
    United Artists, 1975
THE BAD NEWS BEARS   Paramount, 1976
MIKEY AND NICKY   Paramount, 1976
BILLY GALVIN   Vestron, 1986
UNDER THE INFLUENCE (TF)   CBS Entertainment, 1986
MONKEY SHINES   Orion, 1988

MARIO VAN PEEBLES
b. January 15, 1957 - Mexico
Agent: ICM - Beverly Hills, 310/550-4000

THE CHILD SAVER (TF)   Michael Filerman Productions/
    NBC Productions, 1988
NEW JACK CITY   Warner Bros., 1991 (also directed)
POSSE   Gramercy Pictures, 1993, U.S.-British (also directed)
GUNMEN   Dimension/Miramax Films, 1994
PANTHER   Gramercy Films, 1995 (also directed)

MELVIN VAN PEEBLES
(Melvin Peebles)
b. August 21, 1932 - Chicago, Illinois

POSSE   Gramercy Pictures, 1993, U.S.-British
TERMINAL VELOCITY   Buena Vista, 1994

DEBORAH VAN VALKENBURGH
A BUNNY'S TALE (TF)   Stan Margulies Company/
    Warner Bros., 1985
GOING FOR THE GOLD: THE BILL JOHNSON STORY (TF)
    ITC Productions/Sullivan-Carter Interests/
    Goodman-Rosen Productions, 1985

JIM VARNEY
DR. OTTO AND THE RIDDLE OF THE GLOOM BEAN   1985
ERNEST GOES TO CAMP   Buena Vista, 1987
ERNEST SAVES CHRISTMAS   Buena Vista, 1988
ERNEST GOES TO JAIL   Buena Vista, 1990
ERNEST SCARED STUPID   Buena Vista, 1991
WILDER NAPALM   TriStar, 1993
THE BEVERLY HILLBILLIES   20th Century Fox, 1993
ERNEST RIDES AGAIN   Emshell Producers Group, 1993

NED VAUGHN
Agent: Metropolitan Talent Agency - Los Angeles, 213/857-4500

THE RESCUE   Buena Vista, 1988

PETER VAUGHN
SAPPHIRE   1959
VILLAGE OF THE DAMNED   1960
THE PUNCH AND JUDY MAN   1963
FANATIC   1965
THE NAKED RUNNER   1967
HAMMERHEAD   1968
THE BOFORS GUN   1968
ALFRED THE GREAT   1969
EYE WITNESS   1970
STRAW DOGS   1971
THE PIED PIPER   1972
11 HARROWHOUSE   1974
ZULU DAWN   1979
FOX (TF)   1980
TIME BANDITS   1981
THE FRENCH LIEUTENANT'S WOMAN   United Artists,
    1981, British
JAMAICA INN (TF)   1983
THE RAZOR'S EDGE   Columbia, 1984
BRAZIL   Universal, 1985, British
HAUNTED HONEYMOON   Orion, 1986
MONTE CARLO (MS)   1986
WAR AND REMEMBRANCE (MS)   Dan Curtis Productions/ABC
    Circle Films, 1988-89
THE BOURNE IDENTITY   Alan Shayne Productions/Warner
    Bros. TV, 1988
PRISONERS OF HONOR (CTF)   HBO Pictures/Dreyfuss-James
    Productions, 1991
THE REMAINS OF THE DAY   Columbia, 1993, British

ROBERT VAUGHN
b. November 30, 1932 - New York, New York

NO TIME TO BE YOUNG   1957
TEENAGE CAVE MAN   1958
THE YOUNG PHILADELPHIANS ✪   Warner Bros., 1959
THE MAGNIFICENT SEVEN   1960
THE BIG SHOW   1961
THE CARETAKERS   1963
TO TRAP A SPY   1966
ONE SPY TOO MANY   1966
THE VENETIAN AFFAIR   1967
THE HELICOPTER SPIES   1968
BULLITT   Warner Bros., 1968
THE BRIDGE AT REMAGEN   1969
THE MIND OF MR. SOAMES   1970, British
JULIUS CAESAR   1970, British
THE STATUE   *LA STATUA*   1971, Italian-British
CLAY PIGEON   1971
THE TOWERING INFERNO   20th Century-Fox/Warner Bros., 1974
BABYSITTER   1975, Italian-French-West German
KISS ME, KILL ME (TF)   Columbia TV, 1976
WASHINGTON: BEHIND CLOSED DOORS (MS)
    Paramount TV, 1977
DEMON SEED   1977
STARSHIP INVASION   1977, Canadian
BRASS TARGET   MGM/United Artists, 1978
GOOD LUCK MISS WYCKOFF   1979
KEY WEST CROSSING   1979
BATTLE BEYOND THE STARS   1980
S.O.B.   Paramount, 1981
INSIDE THE THIRD REICH (TF)   1982

THE RETURN OF THE MAN FROM U.N.C.L.E. (TF)   1983
SUPERMAN III   Warner Bros., 1983, U.S.-British
PRIVATE SESSIONS (TF)   1985
INTERNATIONAL AIRPORT (TF)   1985
BLACK MOON RISING   New World, 1986
THE DELTA FORCE   Cannon, 1986
PRINCE OF BEL AIR (TF)   Leonard Hill Films, 1986
HOUR OF THE ASSASSIN   Concorde, 1987, U.S.-Peruvian
RIVER OF DEATH   Cannon, 1989, British
NOBODY'S PERFECT   Moviestore Entertainment, 1990

RON VAWTER
sex, lies, and videotape   Miramax Films, 1989

EDDIE VELEZ
ROOFTOPS   New Visions, 1989
ROMERO   Four Seasons Entertainment, 1989

LAUREN VELEZ
I LIKE IT LIKE THAT   Columbia, 1994

REGINALD VELJOHNSON
"CROCODILE" DUNDEE   Paramount, 1986
DIE HARD   20th Century Fox, 1988
TURNER & HOOCH   Buena Vista, 1989
DIE HARD 2   20th Century Fox, 1990

CHICK VENNERA
THE MILAGRO BEANFIELD WAR   Universal, 1988
LAST RITES   MGM/United Artists, 1988
McBAIN   Shapiro-Glickenhouse Entertainment, 1991
THE TERROR WITHIN II   Concorde, 1991

DIANE VENORA
WOLFEN   Orion/Warner Bros., 1981
THE COTTON CLUB   Orion, 1984
F/X   Orion, 1986
BIRD   Warner Bros., 1988

VINCENT VENTRESCA
MENENDEZ: A KILLING IN BEVERLY HILLS (MS)   Zev Braun
   Pictures/TriStar Television, 1994

VICTORIA VERA
MAN OF PASSION   Golden Sun Productions, 1988, Spanish

GWEN VERDON
b. January 13, 1925 - Culver City, California

ON THE RIVIERA   20th Century-Fox, 1951
DAVID AND BATHSHEBA   20th Century-Fox, 1951
MEET ME AFTER THE SHOW   1951
THE MERRY WIDOW   MGM, 1952
THE I DON'T CARE GIRL   20th Century-Fox, 1953
THE MISSISSIPPI GAMBLER   Universal, 1953
THE FARMER TAKES A WIFE   20th Century-Fox, 1953
DAMN YANKEES   Warner Bros., 1958
LEGS (TF)   The Catalina Production Group/Radio City Music Hall
   Productions/Comworld Productions, 1983
THE COTTON CLUB   Orion, 1984
COCOON   20th Century Fox, 1985
NADINE   TriStar, 1987
COCOON: THE RETURN   20th Century Fox, 1988
ALICE   Orion, 1990

BEN VEREEN
b. October 10, 1946 - Miami, Florida

SWEET CHARITY   Universal, 1969
FUNNY LADY   Columbia, 1975
ROOTS (MS)   Wolper Productions, 1977
ALL THAT JAZZ   20th Century-Fox, 1979
TENSPEED AND BROWNSHOE (TF)   Stephen J. Cannell
   Productions, 1980
BUY & CELL   Empire Pictures, 1989

JOHN VERNON
b. February 24, 1932 - Montreal, Canada

1984   1956, British (voice)
NOBODY WAVED GOODBYE   1964, Canadian
POINT BLANK   1967
JUSTINE   1969
TOPAZ   Universal, 1969
TELL THEM WILLIE BOY IS HERE   Universal, 1969
ONE MORE TRAIN TO ROB   1971
DIRTY HARRY   1971
FEAR IS THE KEY   1973
CHARLEY VARRICK   1973
THE BLACK WINDMILL   1974, British-U.S.
SWEET MOVIE   1975, Yugoslavian-French
BRANNIGAN   1975, British-U.S.
THE OUTLAW JOSEY WALES   Warner Bros., 1976
A SPECIAL DAY   1976, Italian-Canadian
GOLDEN RENDEZVOUS   1977
ANGELA   1978, Canadian
NATIONAL LAMPOON'S ANIMAL HOUSE   Universal, 1978
IT RAINED ALL NIGHT THE DAY I LEFT   1979,
   Canadian-Israeli-French
CRUNCH   1979
HERBIE GOES BANANAS   Buena Vista, 1980
AIRPLANE II: THE SEQUEL   Paramount, 1982
I'M GONNA GIT YOU SUCKA   MGM/UA, 1989

CHRISTINA VIDAL
LIFE WITH MIKEY   Buena Vista, 1993

GORE VIDAL
Agent: CAA - Beverly Hills, 310/288-4545

BOB ROBERTS   Paramount/Miramax Films, 1992
WITH HONORS   Warner Bros., 1994

THEA VIDALE
DR. JEKYLL AND MS. HYDE   Savoy Pictures, 1995

STEVE VIGNARI
MARRIED TO THE MOB   Orion, 1988

ABE VIGODA
b. February 24, 1921 - New York, New York

THE GODFATHER   Paramount, 1972
THE DON IS DEAD   Universal, 1973
NEWMAN'S LAW   Universal, 1974
THE GODFATHER, PART II   Paramount, 1974
HAVING BABIES (TF)   The Jozak Company, 1976
THE CHEAP DETECTIVE   Columbia, 1978
THE COMEDY COMPANY (TF)   Merrit Malloy-Jerry Adler
   Productions, 1978
VASECTOMY, A DELICATE MATTER   Seymour Borde &
   Associates, 1986
LOOK WHO'S TALKING   TriStar, 1989
PRANCER   Orion, 1989
JOE VERSUS THE VOLCANO   Warner Bros., 1990
SUGAR HILL   20th Century Fox, 1994
NORTH   Columbia, 1994
JURY DUTY   Sony Pictures, 1995

ROBERT VIHARO
EVITA PERON (TF)   Hartwest Productions/Zephyr Productions, 1981

JOEY VILLA
ETERNITY   Academy Entertainment, 1990

CHUNCHUNA VILLAFANE
THE OFFICIAL STORY   Historias Cinematograficas,
   1985, Argentine

TOM VILLARD
THE TROUBLE WITH DICK   FilmDallas, 1988
POPCORN   Studio Three, 1991

F
I
L
M

A
C
T
O
R
S

DANIEL VILLARREAL
SPEED   20th Century Fox, 1994

CHRISTOPHER VILLIERS
TOP SECRET!   Paramount, 1984

JAMES VILLIERS
UNDER THE VOLCANO   Universal, 1984

PRUITT TAYLOR VINCE
I KNOW MY FIRST NAME IS STEVEN (MS)   Andrew Adelson
   Company/Lorimar TV, 1989
JACOB'S LADDER   TriStar, 1990
CITY SLICKERS II: THE LEGEND OF CURLY'S GOLD
   Columbia, 1994

ALEX VINCENT
CHILD'S PLAY   MGM/UA, 1988
CHILD'S PLAY 2   Universal, 1990

FRANK VINCENT
RAGING BULL   United Artists, 1980
MORTAL THOUGHTS   Columbia, 1991
JUNGLE FEVER   Universal, 1991
CASINO   Universal, 1995

JAN-MICHAEL VINCENT
(Michael Vincent)
b. July 15, 1944 - Denver, Colorado

LOS BANDIDOS   1967, Mexican
JOURNEY TO SHILOH   Universal, 1968
THE UNDEFEATED   20th Century-Fox, 1969
TRIBES (TF)   20th Century-Fox, 1970
GOING HOME   MGM, 1971
THE MECHANIC   United Artists, 1972
THE WORLD'S GREATEST ATHLETE   Buena Vista, 1973
BUSTER AND BILLIE   Columbia, 1974
BITE THE BULLET   Columbia, 1975
WHITE LINE FEVER   Columbia, 1975
VIGILANTE FORCE   United Artists, 1976
BABY BLUE MARINE   Columbia, 1976
SHADOW OF THE HAWK   Columbia, 1976, Canadian
DAMNATION ALLEY   20th Century-Fox, 1977
BIG WEDNESDAY   Warner Bros., 1978
HOOPER   Warner Bros., 1978
DEFIANCE   American International, 1980
HARD COUNTRY   Universal/AFD, 1981
THE WINDS OF WAR (MS)   Paramount TV/Dan Curtis Prods., 1983
LAST PLANE OUT   New World, 1983
SIX AGAINST THE ROCK (TF)   Schaefer-Karpf-Epstein
   Productions/Gaylord Production Company, 1987
HIT LIST   New Line Cinema, 1989

LEE VING
STREETS OF FIRE   Universal, 1984
BLACK MOON RISING   New World, 1986
DUDES   New Century/Vista, 1987

JACKEY VINSON
THE WIZARD   Universal, 1989

NEIL VIPOND
PARADISE   Avco Embassy, 1982, Canadian

FLOYD VIVINO
GOOD MORNING, VIETNAM   Buena Vista, 1987
CRAZY PEOPLE   Paramount, 1990

LYNN VOGT
A NEW LIFE   Paramount, 1988

PETER VOGT
L.A. STORY   TriStar, 1991

JON VOIGHT
b. December 29, 1938 - Yonkers, New York
Agent: CAA - Beverly Hills, 310/288-4545

HOUR OF THE GUN   United Artists, 1967
FEARLESS FRANK   *FRANK'S GREATEST ADVENTURE*
   American International, 1967
OUT OF IT   United Artists, 1969
MIDNIGHT COWBOY ★   United Artists, 1969
CATCH-22   Paramount, 1970
THE REVOLUTIONARY   United Artists, 1970
DELIVERANCE   Warner Bros., 1972
THE ALL-AMERICAN BOY   Warner Bros., 1973
CONRACK   20th Century-Fox, 1974
THE ODESSA FILE   Columbia, 1974, British-West German
END OF THE GAME   20th Century-Fox, 1976, West German-Italian
COMING HOME ★★   United Artists, 1978
THE CHAMP   MGM/United Artists, 1979
LOOKIN' TO GET OUT   Paramount, 1982
TABLE FOR FIVE   Warner Bros., 1983
RUNAWAY TRAIN ★   Cannon, 1985
DESERT BLOOM   Columbia, 1986
ETERNITY   Academy Entertainment, 1990
CHERNOBYL: THE FINAL WARNING (CTF)   1991

LENNY VON DOHLEN
TENDER MERCIES   Universal/AFD, 1983
ELECTRIC DREAMS   MGM/UA, 1984, British
BILLY GALVIN   Vestron, 1986

WILHELM von HOMBURG
GHOSTBUSTERS II   Columbia, 1989

KURT VONNEGUT, JR.
BACK TO SCHOOL   Orion, 1986

ALEC VON SOMMER
BIG   20th Century Fox, 1988

MAX von SYDOW
b. April 10, 1929 - Lund, Sweden
Agent: UTA - Beverly Hills, 310/273-6700

THE VIRGIN SPRING   Janus, 1960, Swedish
HAWAII   United Artists, 1966
HOUR OF THE WOLF   United Artists, 1968, Swedish
THE EXORCIST   Warner Bros., 1973
THREE DAYS OF THE CONDOR   Paramount, 1975
VOYAGE OF THE DAMNED   Avco Embassy, 1976, British
MARCH OR DIE   Columbia, 1977, British
EXORCIST II: THE HERETIC   Warner Bros., 1977
BRASS TARGET   MGM/United Artists, 1978
FLASH GORDON   Universal, 1980, British
DUET FOR ONE   Cannon, 1986
HANNAH AND HER SISTERS   Orion, 1986
PELLE THE CONQUEROR ★   Miramax Films,
   1988, Danish-Swedish
HIROSHIMA: OUT OF THE ASHES (TF)   Robert Greenwald
   Productions, 1990
AWAKENINGS   Columbia, 1990
A KISS BEFORE DYING   Universal, 1991
UNTIL THE END OF THE WORLD   Warner Bros.,
   1991, West German-French
NEEDFUL THINGS   Columbia, 1993
JUDGE DREDD   Buena Vista, 1995

DANIELLE von ZERNECK
SHARON: PORTRAIT OF A MISTRESS (TF)   Moonlight
   Productions/Paramount TV, 1977
LOIS GIBBS AND THE LOVE CANAL (TF)   Moonlight Productions/
   Filmways, 1982
IN THE CUSTODY OF STRANGERS (TF)   Moonlight Productions/
   Filmways, 1982
SUMMER FANTASIES (TF)   Moonlight Productions II, 1984
MY SCIENCE PROJECT   Buena Vista, 1985
A FIGHTING CHOICE (TF)   Walt Disney Productions, 1986
LA BAMBA   Columbia, 1987
UNDER THE BOARDWALK   New World, 1989

YORGO VOYAGIS
FRANTIC   Warner Bros., 1988
COURAGE MOUNTAIN   Triumph Releasing Corporation,
1989, U.S.-French

ERIC VU-AN
THE SHELTERING SKY   Warner Bros., 1990, British

KA VUNDLA
CHEETAH   Buena Vista, 1989

WAIGWA WACHIRA
GORILLAS IN THE MIST   Warner Bros./Universal, 1988

STEVEN WADDINGTON
Agent: Susan Smith & Associates - Beverly Hills, 213/852-4777

CARRINGTON   Gramercy Pictures, 1995

JACK WAGNER
MOVING TARGET (TF)   Lewis B. Chesler Productions/Bateman
Company Productions/Finnegan-Pinchuk Company/
MGM-UA TV, 1988

LINDSAY WAGNER
b. June 22, 1949 - Los Angeles, California

THE PAPER CHASE   20th Century-Fox, 1973
TWO PEOPLE   Universal, 1973
THE ROCKFORD FILES (TF)   Universal TV, 1974
SECOND WIND   Health and Entertainment Corporation of America,
1976, Canadian
THE INCREDIBLE JOURNEY OF DR. MEG LAUREL (TF)
Columbia TV, 1979
THE TWO WORLDS OF JENNIE LOGAN (TF)   Joe Wizan
TV Productions/Charles Fries Productions, 1979
CALLIE AND SON (TF)   Rosilyn Heller Productions/Hemdale
Presentation/City Films/Motown Productions, 1981
HIGH RISK   American Cinema, 1981
NIGHTHAWKS   Universal, 1981
PRINCESS DAISY (MS)   NBC Productions/Steve Krantz
Productions, 1983
MARTIN'S DAY   MGM/UA, 1984, British
JESSIE (TF)   Lindsay Wagner Productions/MGM-UA TV, 1984
PASSIONS (TF)   Carson Production Group/Wizan TV
Enterprises, 1984
THE OTHER LOVER (TF)   Larry Thompson Productions/
Columbia TV, 1985
THIS CHILD IS MINE (TF)   Beth Polson Productions/Finnegan
Associates/Telepictures Productions, 1985
CHILD'S CRY (TF)   Shoot the Moon Enterprises/Phoenix
Entertainment Group, 1986
CONVICTED (TF)   Larry A. Thompson Productions, 1986
RETURN OF THE SIX MILLION DOLLAR MAN AND THE BIONIC
WOMAN (TF)   Michael Sloan Productions/Universal TV, 1987
STRANGER IN MY BED (TF)   Edgar J. Scherick Productions/Taft
Entertainment TV, 1987
EVIL IN CLEAR RIVER (TF)   The Steve Tisch Company/Lionel
Chetwynd Productions/Phoenix Entertainment Group, 1988
THE TAKING OF FLIGHT 847: THE ULI DERICKSON STORY (TF)
Columbia TV, 1988
NIGHTMARE AT BITTER CREEK (TF)   Swanton Films/
Guber-Peters Entertainment Company/Phoenix
Entertainment Group, 1988

BIONIC SHOWDOWN: THE SIX MILLION DOLLAR MAN AND
THE BIONIC WOMAN (TF)   Universal TV, 1989
FROM THE DEAD OF NIGHT (TF)   Shadowplay Films/Phoenix
Entertainment Group, 1989
SHATTERED DREAMS (TF)   Roger Gimbel Productions/Carolco
Television Productions, 1990
RICOCHET   Warner Bros., 1991
DANIELLE STEEL'S ONCE IN A LIFETIME   *ONCE IN A
LIFETIME* (TF)   The Cramer Company/NBC Productions, 1994

ROBERT WAGNER
b. February 10, 1930 - Detroit, Michigan
Agent: William Morris Agency - Beverly Hills, 310/274-7451

THE HAPPY YEARS   MGM, 1950
HALLS OF MONTEZUMA   20th Century-Fox, 1950
THE FROGMEN   20th Century-Fox, 1951
LET'S MAKE IT LEGAL   20th Century-Fox, 1951
WITH A SONG IN MY HEART   20th Century-Fox, 1952
WHAT PRICE GLORY   20th Century-Fox, 1952
STARS AND STRIPES FOREVER   20th Century-Fox, 1952
TITANIC   20th Century-Fox, 1953
BENEATH THE 12 MILE REEF   20th Century-Fox, 1953
PRINCE VALIANT   20th Century-Fox, 1954
BROKEN LANCE   20th Century-Fox, 1954
WHITE FEATHER   20th Century-Fox, 1955
A KISS BEFORE DYING   United Artists, 1956
BETWEEN HEAVEN AND HELL   20th Century-Fox, 1956
THE MOUNTAIN   Paramount, 1956
THE TRUE STORY OF JESSE JAMES   20th Century-Fox, 1957
STOPOVER TOKYO   20th Century-Fox, 1957
THE HUNTERS   20th Century-Fox, 1958
IN LOVE AND WAR   20th Century-Fox, 1958
SAY ONE FOR ME   20th Century-Fox, 1959
ALL THE FINE YOUNG CANNIBALS   MGM, 1960
SAIL A CROOKED SHIP   1962
THE LONGEST DAY   20th Century-Fox, 1962
THE WAR LOVER   Columbia, 1962, British
THE CONDEMNED OF ALTONA   20th Century-Fox,
1963, Italian-French
THE PINK PANTHER   United Artists, 1964
HARPER   Warner Bros., 1966
BANNING   Universal, 1967
THE BIGGEST BUNDLE OF THEM ALL   MGM, 1968, U.S.-Italian
DON'T JUST STAND THERE!   Universal, 1968
WINNING   Universal, 1969
CITY BENEATH THE SEA (TF)   20th Century-Fox TV/Motion
Pictures International, 1971
THE STREETS OF SAN FRANCISCO (TF)   QM Productions, 1972
THE AFFAIR (TF)   Spelling-Goldberg Productions, 1973
THE TOWERING INFERNO   20th Century-Fox/Warner Bros., 1974
THE ABDUCTION OF SAINT ANNE   *THEY'VE KIDNAPPED
ANNE BENEDICT* (TF)   QM Productions, 1975
SWITCH (TF)   Universal TV, 1975
MIDWAY   Universal, 1976
DEATH AT LOVE HOUSE (TF)   Spelling-Goldberg
Productions, 1976
THE CONCORDE—AIRPORT '79   Universal, 1979
HART TO HART (TF)   Spelling-Goldberg Productions, 1979
CURSE OF THE PINK PANTHER   MGM/UA, 1983
I AM THE CHEESE   Libra Cinema 5, 1983
LIME STREET (TF)   R.J. Productions/Bloodworth-Thomason-Mozark
Productions/Columbia TV, 1985
THERE MUST BE A PONY (TF)   R.J. Productions/
Columbia TV, 1986
LOVE AMONG THIEVES (TF)   Robert A. Papazian
Productions, 1987
SIDNEY SHELDON'S WINDMILLS OF THE GODS   *WINDMILLS OF
THE GODS* (MS)   Dove Productions/ITC Productions, 1988
INDISCREET (TF)   Karen Mack Productions/HTV/Republic Pictures,
1988, U.S.-British
THIS GUN FOR HIRE (CTF)   USA Cable, 1991
DEEP TROUBLE (CTF)   USA Cable, 1993
HART TO HART: HOME IS WHERE THE HART IS (TF)   NBC, 1994
HART TO HART: OLD FRIENDS NEVER DIE (TF)   NBC, 1994
PARALLEL LIVES (CTF)   Showtime Entertainment, 1994

KEN WAHL

b. February 14, 1956 - Chicago, Illinois

THE BUDDY HOLLY STORY   Columbia, 1978
EVERY WHICH WAY BUT LOOSE   Warner Bros., 1978
THE CHAMP   MGM/United Artists, 1979
THE WANDERERS   Orion/Warner Bros., 1979
FORT APACHE, THE BRONX   20th Century-Fox, 1981
RACE TO THE YANKEE ZEPHYR *TREASURE OF THE
   YANKEE ZEPHYR*   Artists Releasing Corporation/Film
   Ventures International, 1981, Australian-New Zealand
JINXED!   MGM/UA, 1982
THE SOLDIER   Embassy, 1982
PURPLE HEARTS   The Ladd Company/Warner Bros., 1984
WISEGUY (TF)   Stephen J. Cannell Productions, 1987
THE TAKING OF BEVERLY HILLS   Nelson Entertainment, 1991
THE FAVOR   Orion, 1994

MARK WAHLBERG
(Marky Mark)
THE SUBSTITUTE (CTF)   Showtime, 1993
RENAISSANCE MAN   Buena Vista, 1994
THE BASKETBALL DIARIES   1995
NO FEAR   Universal, 1995

ERIC TSANG CHI WAI
EAT A BOWL OF TEA   Columbia, 1989, U.S.-Hong Kong

LOUDON WAINWRIGHT III
JACKNIFE   Cineplex Odeon, 1989

RALPH WAITE

b. June 22, 1929 - White Plains, New York

THE BODYGUARD   Warner Bros., 1992
CLIFFHANGER   TriStar, 1993
THE WALTONS THANKSGIVING REUNION (TF)   CBS, 1993
SIOUX CITY   I.R.S. Releasing, 1994

THOMAS G. WAITES
THE CLAN OF THE CAVE BEAR   Warner Bros., 1986

T.J. WAITES
McBAIN   Shapiro-Glickenhouse Entertainment, 1991

TOM WAITS
THE COTTON CLUB   Orion, 1984
DOWN BY LAW   Island Pictures, 1986
BIG TIME   Island Films, 1988
COLD FEET   Avenue Pictures, 1989
QUEENS LOGIC   New Line Cinema, 1991
AT PLAY IN THE FIELDS OF THE LORD   Universal, 1991
BRAM STOKER'S DRACULA *DRACULA*   Columbia, 1992
SHORT CUTS   Fine Line Features/New Line Cinema, 1993

SHAWNA WALDRON
LITTLE GIANTS   Warner Bros., 1994

CHRISTOPHER WALKEN

b. March 31, 1943 - Queens, New York
Agent: William Morris Agency - Beverly Hills, 310/274-7451

THE ANDERSON TAPES   Columbia, 1971
THE HAPPINESS CAGE *THE MIND SNATCHERS*
   Cinerama Releasing Corporation, 1972
NEXT STOP, GREENWICH VILLAGE   20th Century-Fox, 1976
THE SENTINEL   Universal, 1977
ANNIE HALL   United Artists, 1977
ROSELAND   Cinema Shares International, 1977
THE DEER HUNTER OO   Universal, 1978
LAST EMBRACE   United Artists, 1979
HEAVEN'S GATE   United Artists, 1980
THE DOGS OF WAR   United Artists, 1981, U.S.-British
PENNIES FROM HEAVEN   MGM/United Artists, 1981
BRAINSTORM   MGM/UA, 1983

THE DEAD ZONE   Paramount, 1983, Canadian
A VIEW TO A KILL   MGM/UA, 1985, British
AT CLOSE RANGE   Orion, 1986
DEADLINE   Skouras Pictures, 1987, West German-Israeli
BILOXI BLUES   Universal, 1988
THE MILAGRO BEANFIELD WAR   Universal, 1988
COMMUNION   MCEG, 1989
KING OF NEW YORK   New Line Cinema, 1990
THE COMFORT OF STRANGERS   Skouras Pictures, 1990, British
SARAH, PLAIN AND TALL (TF)   Self Help Productions/Trillium
   Productions, 1991
McBAIN   Shapiro-Glickenhaus Entertainment, 1991
BATMAN RETURNS   Warner Bros., 1992
MISTRESS   Tribeca Films, 1992
SKYLARK (TF)   Self Help Productions/Trillium Productions, 1993
TRUE ROMANCE   Warner Bros., 1993
WAYNE'S WORLD 2   Paramount, 1993
PULP FICTION   Miramax Films, 1994
SEARCH AND DESTROY   October Films, 1995
THE WILDSIDE   August Entertainment, 1995

ALLY WALKER
UNIVERSAL SOLDIER   TriStar, 1992

ARNETIA WALKER
SCENES FROM THE CLASS STRUGGLE IN BEVERLY HILLS
   Cinecom, 1989

CHRISTOPHER WALKER
ECHO PARK   Atlantic Releasing Corporation, 1986, U.S.-Austrian

CLINT WALKER

b. May 30, 1927 - Hartford, Illinois

THE TEN COMMANDMENTS   Paramount, 1956
FORT DOBBS   Warner Bros., 1958
YELLOWSTONE KELLY   Warner Bros., 1959
GOLD OF THE SEVEN SAINTS   Warner Bros., 1961
SEND ME NO FLOWERS   Universal, 1964
NONE BUT THE BRAVE   Warner Bros., 1964, U.S.-Japanese
THE NIGHT OF THE GRIZZLY   Paramount, 1966
MAYA   MGM, 1966
THE DIRTY DOZEN   MGM, 1967
MORE DEAD THAN ALIVE   1969
SAM WHISKEY   United Artists, 1969
THE GREAT BANK ROBBERY   Warner Bros., 1969
THE PHYNX   Warner Bros., 1970
YUMA (TF)   Aaron Spelling Productions, 1971
THE BOUNTY MAN (TF)   ABC Circle Films, 1972
PANCHO VILLA   1972, Spanish
BAKER'S HAWK   Doty-Dayton, 1976
THE WHITE BUFFALO   United Artists, 1977
HYSTERICAL   Embassy, 1983
MAVERICK   Warner Bros., 1994

JIMMIE WALKER
AIRPLANE!   Paramount, 1980
THE CONCORDE—AIRPORT '79   Universal, 1979
WATER   Atlantic Releasing Corporation, 1984, British

KERRY WALKER
THE PIANO   Miramax Films, 1993, New Zealand-French

KIM WALKER
HEATHERS   New World, 1989

LIZA WALKER
TWISTED OBSESSION   Majectic Films International, 1990

POLLY WALKER
Agent: UTA - Beverly Hills, 310/273-6700

SLIVER   Paramount, 1993
THE TRIAL   Angelika Films, 1993
RESTORATION   Miramax Films, 1994

ROBERT WALKER, JR.
b. April 15, 1940 - New York, New York

THE HOOK   MGM, 1963
THE CEREMONY   1963
ENSIGN PULVER   Warner Bros., 1964
THE HAPPENING   Columbia, 1967
THE WAR WAGON   Universal, 1967
THE SAVAGE SEVEN   American International, 1968
KILLERS THREE   American International, 1968
EASY RIDER   Columbia, 1969
YOUNG BILLY YOUNG   United Artists, 1969
ROAD TO SALINA   LA ROUTE DE SALINA   1970, French-U.S.
MAN FROM O.R.G.Y.   1970
BEWARE! THE BLOB   SON OF BLOB   Jack H. Harris Enterprises, 1972
HEX   1973
GONE WITH THE WEST   International Cinefilm, 1975
THE PASSOVER PLOT   Atlas, 1977, U.S.-Israeli

SARI WALKER
'NIGHT, MOTHER   Universal, 1986

SYDNEY WALKER†
b. 1921 - Philadelphia
d. September 30, 1994

LOVE STORY   Paramount, 1970
PRELUDE TO A KISS   20th Century Fox, 1992
MRS. DOUBTFIRE   20th Century Fox, 1993
GETTING EVEN WITH DAD

ZENA WALKER
THE HELLIONS   Columbia, 1962, British
THE TRAITORS   1963, British
THE DRESSER   Columbia, 1983, British

BILL WALLACE
AVENGING FORCE   Cannon, 1986

DEE WALLACE
(See Dee Wallace STONE)

JACK WALLACE
ABOVE THE LAW   Warner Bros., 1988
THE BEAR   TriStar, 1988, French

ZAC WALLACE
RAPA NUI   Warner Bros., 1994

ELI WALLACH
b. December 7, 1915 - Brooklyn, New York

BABY DOLL   Warner Bros., 1956
THE LINEUP   Columbia, 1958
SEVEN THIEVES   20th Century-Fox, 1960
THE MAGNIFICENT SEVEN   United Artists, 1960
THE MISFITS   United Artists, 1961
HEMINGWAY'S ADVENTURES OF A YOUNG MAN
   ADVENTURES OF A YOUNG MAN   20th Century-Fox, 1962
HOW THE WEST WAS WON   MGM/Cinerama, 1963
THE VICTORS   Columbia, 1963
ACT ONE   Warner Bros., 1963
THE MOON-SPINNERS   Buena Vista, 1964, U.S.-British
KISSES FOR MY PRESIDENT   Warner Bros., 1964
LORD JIM   Columbia, 1965
GENGHIS KHAN   Columbia, 1965,
   U.S.-British-West German-Yugoslavian
HOW TO STEAL A MILLION   Columbia, 1966
THE GOOD, THE BAD AND THE UGLY   United Artists,
   1967, Italian
THE TIGER MAKES OUT   Columbia, 1967
ACE HIGH   IL QUATTRO DELL'AVE MARIA   1969, Italian
HOW TO SAVE A MARRIAGE AND RUIN YOUR LIFE
   Columbia, 1968
A LOVELY WAY TO DIE   Universal, 1968
THE BRAIN   LE CERVEAU   Paramount, 1969, French-Italian

MACKENNA'S GOLD   Columbia, 1969
ZIGZAG   MGM, 1970
THE ANGEL LEVINE   United Artists, 1970
THE PEOPLE NEXT DOOR   Avco Embassy, 1970
THE ADVENTURES OF GERARD   United Artists, 1970,
   British-Italian-Swedish
ROMANCE OF A HORSETHIEF   Allied Artists, 1971
DON'T TURN THE OTHER CHEEK   LOS GUERILLEROS
   1973, Spanish-Italian
A COLD NIGHT'S DEATH (TF)   ABC Circle Films, 1973
CINDERELLA LIBERTY   20th Century-Fox, 1973
CRAZY JOE   Columbia, 1974, Italian-U.S.
INDICT AND CONVICT (TF)   Universal TV, 1974
EYE OF THE CAT   OCCHIO DEL GATTO   1975, Italian
PAURA   1976, Italian
NASTY HABITS   Brut Productions, 1977, British
THE SENTINEL   Universal, 1977
THE DOMINO PRINCIPAL   Avco Embassy, 1977
SEVENTH AVENUE (MS)   Universal TV, 1977
THE DEEP   Columbia, 1977
GIRLFRIENDS   Warner Bros., 1978
HAROLD ROBBINS' THE PIRATE   THE PIRATE (TF)
   Howard W. Koch Productions/Warner Bros. TV, 1978
MOVIE MOVIE   Warner Bros., 1978
WINTER KILLS   Avco Embassy, 1979
CIRCLE OF IRON   Avco Embassy, 1979
FIREPOWER   AFD, 1979, British
THE HUNTER   Paramount, 1980
THE PRIDE OF JESSE HALLAM (TF)   The Konigsberg Company, 1981
THE SALAMANDER   ITC, 1981, U.S.-British-Italian
THE EXECUTIONER'S SONG (TF)   Film Communications, Inc., 1982
ANATOMY OF AN ILLNESS (TF)   Hamner Productions/CBS
   Entertainment, 1984
SAM'S SON   Invictus Entertainment Corporation, 1984
CHRISTOPHER COLUMBUS (MS)   RAI/Clesi Cinematografica/
   Antenne-2/Bavaria Atelier/Lorimar Productions, 1985,
   Italian-West German-U.S.-French
MURDER: BY REASON OF INSANITY (TF)   LS Entertainment, 1985
SOMETHING IN COMMON (TF)   New World TV/Freyda Rothstein
   Productions/Littke-Grossbart Productions, 1986
TOUGH GUYS   Buena Vista, 1986
THE TWO JAKES   Paramount, 1990
THE GODFATHER, PART III   Paramount, 1990
ARTICLE 99   Orion, 1992
MISTRESS   Tribeca Films, 1992

ANGELA WALSH
DISTANT VOICES, STILL LIVES   Alive Films, 1988, British

CHARLES HUNTER WALSH
LOVERBOY   TriStar, 1989

DYLAN WALSH
BETSY'S WEDDING   Buena Vista, 1990
NOBODY'S FOOL   Buena Vista, 1994
CONGO   Paramount, 1995

J.T. WALSH
POWER   20th Century Fox, 1986
HANNAH AND HER SISTERS   Orion, 1986
TIN MEN   Buena Vista, 1987
HOUSE OF GAMES   Orion, 1987
GOOD MORNING, VIETNAM   Buena Vista, 1987
TEQUILA SUNRISE   Warner Bros., 1988
WIRED   Taurus Entertainment, 1989
THE BIG PICTURE   Columbia, 1989
DAD   Universal, 1989
CRAZY PEOPLE   Paramount, 1990
NARROW MARGIN   TriStar, 1990
THE RUSSIA HOUSE   MGM-Pathe, 1990
IRON MAZE   Castle Hill Productions, 1991, U.S.-Japanese
DEFENSELESS   New Line Cinema, 1991
BACKDRAFT   Universal, 1991
TRUE IDENTITY   Buena Vista, 1991
A FEW GOOD MEN   Columbia, 1992
SNIPER   TriStar, 1993
NEEDFUL THINGS   Columbia, 1993
MORNING GLORY   Academy Entertainment, 1993

RED ROCK WEST   1993
BLUE CHIPS   Paramount, 1994
THE CLIENT   Warner Bros., 1994
SILENT FALL   Warner Bros., 1994
MIRACLE ON 34TH STREET   20th Century Fox, 1994
THE AMERICAN PRESIDENT   Columbia, 1995

M. EMMET WALSH

MIDNIGHT COWBOY   United Artists, 1969
LITTLE BIG MAN   National General, 1970
THEY MIGHT BE GIANTS   Universal, 1971
WHAT'S UP, DOC?   Warner Bros., 1972
SERPICO   Paramount, 1973
STRAIGHT TIME   Warner Bros., 1978
THE JERK   Universal, 1979
ORDINARY PEOPLE   Paramount, 1980
REDS   Paramount, 1981
CANNERY ROW   MGM/United Artists, 1982
BLADE RUNNER   The Ladd Company/Warner Bros., 1982
SILKWOOD   20th Century-Fox, 1983
BLOOD SIMPLE   Circle Releasing Corporation, 1984
FLETCH   Universal, 1985
BACK TO SCHOOL   Orion, 1986
CRITTERS   New Line Cinema, 1986
WILDCATS   Warner Bros., 1986
THE BEST OF TIMES   Universal, 1986
THE ABDUCTION OF KARI SWENSON (TF)
   NBC Productions, 1987
RAISING ARIZONA   20th Century Fox, 1987
THE MILAGRO BEANFIELD WAR   Universal, 1988
CLEAN AND SOBER   Warner Bros., 1988
WAR PARTY   Hemdale, 1989
THE MIGHTY QUINN   MGM/UA, 1989
CHATTAHOOCHEE   Hemdale, 1990
NARROW MARGIN   TriStar, 1990
WHITE SANDS   Warner Bros., 1992
WILDER NAPALM   TriStar, 1993
CAMP NOWHERE   Buena Vista, 1994
WILLY II: THE ADVENTURE HOME   Warner Bros., 1995

SYDNEY WALSH

TO DIE FOR   Arrowhead Entertainment, 1989
TRENCHCOAT IN PARADISE (TF)   Ogiens-Kane Company
   Productions/The Finnegan-Pinchuk Company, 1990

RAY WALSTON
b. November 22, 1918 - New Orleans, Louisiana

KISS THEM FOR ME   20th Century-Fox, 1957
SOUTH PACIFIC   Magna, 1958
DAMN YANKEES   Warner Bros., 1958
SAY ONE FOR ME   20th Century-Fox, 1959
TALL STORY   Warner Bros., 1960
THE APARTMENT   United Artists, 1960
TALL STORY   Warner Bros., 1960
PORTRAIT IN BLACK   Universal, 1960
CONVICTS FOUR   1962
WIVES AND LOVERS   Paramount, 1963
WHO'S MINDING THE STORE?   Paramount, 1963
KISS ME, STUPID   Lopert, 1964
CAPRICE   20th Century-Fox, 1967
PAINT YOUR WAGON   Paramount, 1969
THE STING   Universal, 1973
SILVER STREAK   20th Century-Fox, 1976
THE HAPPY HOOKER GOES TO WASHINGTON   Cannon, 1977
INSTITUTE FOR REVENGE (TF)   Gold-Driskill Productions/
   Columbia TV, 1979
POPEYE   Paramount, 1981
GALAXY OF TERROR   *MINDWARP: AN INFINITY OF TERROR/
   PLANET OF HORRORS*   New World, 1981
FAST TIMES AT RIDGEMONT HIGH   Universal, 1982
O'HARA'S WIFE   Davis-Panzer Productions, 1982
PRIVATE SCHOOL   Universal, 1983
JOHNNY DANGEROUSLY   20th Century Fox, 1984
FOR LOVE OR MONEY (TF)   Robert Papazian Productions/
   Henerson-Hirsch Productions, 1984
RAD   TriStar, 1986
O.C. AND STIGGS   MGM/UA, 1987

RED RIVER (TF)   Catalina Production Group/MGM-UA TV, 1988
BLOOD RELATIONS   Miramax Films, 1988, Canadian
PARAMEDICS   Vestron, 1988
MAN OF PASSION   Golden Sun Productions, 1988, Spanish
I KNOW MY FIRST NAME IS STEVEN (MS)   Andrew Adelson
   Company/Lorimar TV, 1989
POPCORN   Studio Three, 1991
OF MICE AND MEN   MGM-Pathe Communications, 1992

JESSICA WALTER
b. January 31, 1940 - Brooklyn, New York

LILITH   Columbia, 1964
THE GROUP   United Artists, 1966
GRAND PRIX   MGM, 1967
BYE BYE BRAVERMAN   Warner Bros., 1968
NUMBER ONE   United Artists, 1969
PLAY MISTY FOR ME   Universal, 1971
WOMEN IN CHAINS (TF)   Paramount TV, 1971
HOME FOR THE HOLIDAYS (TF)   ABC Circle Films, 1972
VICTORY AT ENTEBBE (TF)   1976
SECRETS OF THREE HUNGRY WIVES (TF)
   Penthouse Productions, 1978
SHE'S DRESSED TO KILL (TF)   Grant-Case-McGrath Enterprises/
   Barry Weitz Films, 1979
GOLDENGIRL   Avco Embassy, 1979
SPRING FEVER   Comworld, 1983, Canadian
THE EXECUTION (TF)   Newland-Raynor Productions/Comworld
   Productions, 1985
KILLER IN THE MIRROR (TF)   Litke-Grossbart Productions/
   Warner Bros. TV, 1986
AARON'S WAY (TF)   Blinn-Thorpe Productions/Lorimar
   Telepictures, 1988
GHOST IN THE MACHINE   20th Century Fox, 1993
PCU   20th Century Fox, 1994

TRACEY WALTER

CONAN THE DESTROYER   Universal, 1984
AT CLOSE RANGE   Orion, 1986
BATMAN   Warner Bros., 1989
DELUSION   I.R.S. Releasing, 1991

ANTHONY WALTERS

BLACK BEAUTY   Warner Bros., 1994, British-U.S.

JAMIE WALTERS
Agent: UTA - Beverly Hills, 310/273-6700

ALL SHOOK UP   Universal, 1991

JULIE WALTERS
Agent: CAA - Beverly Hills, 310/288-4545

EDUCATING RITA ★   Columbia, 1983, British
CAR TROUBLE   CineTel, 1985, British
PRICK UP YOUR EARS   Samuel Goldwyn Company, 1987, British
PERSONAL SERVICES   Vestron, 1987, British
BUSTER   Hemdale, 1988, British
MACK THE KNIFE   21st Century Distribution, 1989
STEPPING OUT   Paramount, 1991
THE WEDDING GIFT   Miramax Films, 1994

SUSAN WALTERS

XXX'S & OOO'S (TF)   Moving Target Productions/New World
   Entertainment, 1994

EMMA WALTON

THAT'S LIFE!   Columbia, 1986

LISA WALTZ

BRIGHTON BEACH MEMOIRS   Universal, 1986

COLIN WARD

MOTHER'S BOYS   Dimension/Miramax Films, 1994

FRED WARD
b. December 30, 1942 - San Diego, California

ESCAPE FROM ALCATRAZ   Paramount, 1979
TILT   Warner Bros., 1979
CARNY   United Artists, 1980
CARDIAC ARREST   1981
SOUTHERN COMFORT   20th Century-Fox, 1981
THE RIGHT STUFF   The Ladd Company/Warner Bros., 1983
SILKWOOD   20th Century-Fox, 1983
TIMERIDER   Jensen Farley Pictures, 1983
UNCOMMON VALOR   Paramount, 1983
SWING SHIFT   Warner Bros., 1984
SECRET ADMIRER   Orion, 1985
UFORIA   Universal, 1984
REMO WILLIAMS: THE ADVENTURE BEGINS...   Orion, 1985
BIG BUSINESS   Buena Vista, 1988
OFF LIMITS   20th Century Fox, 1988
THE PRINCE OF PENNSYLVANIA   New Line Cinema, 1988
TREMORS   Universal, 1990
MIAMI BLUES   Orion, 1990
HENRY & JUNE   Universal, 1990
BACKTRACK   *CATCHFIRE*   Vestron, 1991
THE DARK WIND   New Line Cinema, 1991
LOVECRAFT (CTF)   HBO Pictures/Pacific Western
   Productions, 1991
THUNDERHEART   TriStar, 1992
THE PLAYER   Fine Line Features/New Line Cinema, 1992
BOB ROBERTS   Paramount/Miramax Films, 1992
SHORT CUTS   Fine Line Features/New Line Cinema, 1993
NAKED GUN 33 1/3: THE FINAL INSULT   Paramount, 1994
TWO SMALL BODIES   Castle Hill Pictures, 1994

JONATHAN WARD
A FATHER'S HOMECOMING (TF)   NBC Productions, 1988
MAC AND ME   Orion, 1988

LYMAN WARD
FERRIS BUELLER'S DAY OFF   Paramount, 1986
GUILTY AS CHARGED   I.R.S. Releasing, 1991

MEGAN WARD
ENCINO MAN   Buena Vista, 1992
FREAKED   20th Century Fox, 1993
PCU   20th Century Fox, 1994

RACHEL WARD
Agent: William Morris Agency - Beverly Hills, 310/274-7451

THE FINAL TERROR   Comworld, 1981
NIGHT SCHOOL   *TERROR EYES*   Paramount, 1981
SHARKY'S MACHINE   Orion/Warner Bros., 1981
DEAD MEN DON'T WEAR PLAID   Universal, 1982
THE THORN BIRDS (MS)   David L. Wolper-Stan Margulies
   Productions/Edward Lewis Productions/Warner Bros. TV, 1983
AGAINST ALL ODDS   Columbia, 1984
THE GOOD WIFE   *THE UMBRELLA WOMAN*   Atlantic Releasing
   Corporation, 1986, Australian
HOTEL COLONIAL   Hemdale, 1987, U.S.-Italian
HOW TO GET AHEAD IN ADVERTISING   Warner Bros.,
   1989, British
AFTER DARK, MY SWEET   Avenue Pictures, 1990
CHRISTOPHER COLUMBUS: THE DISCOVERY   Warner Bros.,
   1992, British-Spanish
WIDE SARGASSO SEA   Fine Line Features/New Line Cinema,
   1993, British

SELA WARD
Agent: ICM - Beverly Hills, 310/550-4000

NOTHING IN COMMON
THE FUGITIVE   Warner Bros., 1993

SIMON WARD
b. October 19, 1941 - London, England

FRANKENSTEIN MUST BE DESTROYED!   Warner Bros.,
   1970, British
QUEST FOR LOVE   Rank, 1971, British
I START COUNTING   United Artists, 1969, British
YOUNG WINSTON   Columbia, 1972, British
HITLER: THE LAST TEN DAYS   1973
DRACULA (TF)   Universal TV/Dan Curtis Productions, 1973
THE THREE MUSKETEERS   20th Century-Fox, 1974, British
DEADLY STRANGERS   20th Century-Fox-Rank, 1974, British
ALL CREATURES GREAT AND SMALL   Talent Associates/EMI TV,
   1974, British
THE FOUR MUSKETEERS   20th Century-Fox, 1975, British
CHILDREN OF RAGE   LSF, 1975, U.S.-Israeli
ACES HIGH   Cinema Shares International, 1976, British
HOLOCAUST 2000   *THE CHOSEN*   1978, British-Italian
BATTLE FLAG   1977
DOMINIQUE   *DOMINIQUE IS DEAD*   Sword and Sworcery
   Productions, 1978, British
ZULU DAWN   American Cinema, 1979, British
LA SABINA   El Iman/Svensk Filminstitut, 1979, Spanish-Swedish
THE MONSTER CLUB   ITC, 1980, British
SUPERGIRL   Warner Bros., 1984, British
THE CORSICAN BROTHERS (TF)   Rosemont Productions,
   1985, British-U.S.

SOPHIE WARD
A SUMMER STORY   Atlantic Releasing Corporation, 1988, British

VINCENT WARD
Agent: CAA - Beverly Hills, 310/288-4545
Personal Manager: Howard Askenase - Los Angeles, 213/461-3227

THE SHOT   Bread & Water Productions, 1994
LEAVING LAS VEGAS   1995

JACK WARDEN
b. September 18, 1920 - Newark, New Jersey

YOU'RE IN THE NAVY NOW   *U.S.S. TEAKETTLE*
   20th Century-Fox, 1951
THE FROGMEN   20th Century-Fox, 1951
RED BALL EXPRESS   Universal, 1952
FROM HERE TO ETERNITY   Columbia, 1953
EDGE OF THE CITY   MGM, 1957
THE BACHELOR PARTY   United Artists, 1957
TWELVE ANGRY MEN   United Artists, 1957
DARBY'S RANGERS   Warner Bros., 1958
RUN SILENT, RUN DEEP   United Artists, 1958
THAT KIND OF WOMAN   Paramount, 1959
WAKE ME WHEN IT'S OVER   20th Century-Fox, 1960
ESCAPE FROM ZAHRAIN   Paramount, 1962
DONOVAN'S REEF   Paramount, 1963
THE THIN RED LINE   Allied Artists, 1964
MIRAGE   Universal, 1965
BLINDFOLD   1966
BYE BYE BRAVERMAN   Warner Bros., 1968
WELCOME TO THE CLUB   1971
SUMMERTREE   Columbia, 1971
WHO IS HARRY KELLERMAN AND WHY IS HE SAYING THOSE
   TERRIBLE THINGS ABOUT ME?   National General, 1971
BILLY TWO HATS   *THE LADY AND THE OUTLAW*   United Artists,
   1972, British
THE MAN WHO LOVED CAT DANCING   MGM, 1973
THE APPRENTICESHIP OF DUDDY KRAVITZ   Paramount,
   1974, Canadian
SHAMPOO ✪   Columbia, 1975
ALL THE PRESIDENT'S MEN   Warner Bros., 1976
VOYAGE OF THE DAMNED   Avco Embassy, 1976, British
THE WHITE BUFFALO   United Artists, 1977
HEAVEN CAN WAIT ✪   Paramount, 1978
DEATH ON THE NILE   Paramount, 1978, British
THE CHAMP   MGM/United Artists, 1979
DREAMER   20th Century-Fox, 1979
BEYOND THE POSEIDON ADVENTURE   Warner Bros., 1979
...AND JUSTICE FOR ALL   Columbia, 1979

BEING THERE   United Artists, 1979
USED CARS   Columbia, 1980
A PRIVATE BATTLE (TF)   Procter & Gamble Productions/
   Robert Halmi, Inc., 1980
SO FINE   Warner Bros., 1981
THE VERDICT   20th Century-Fox, 1982
HOBSON'S CHOICE (TF)   CBS Entertainment, 1983
CRACKERS   Universal, 1984
THE AVIATOR   MGM/UA, 1985
STILL CRAZY LIKE A FOX (TF)   Schenck-Cardea Productions/
   Columbia TV, 1987
SEPTEMBER   Orion, 1987
THE THREE KINGS (TF)   Aaron Spelling Productions, 1987
THE PRESIDIO   Paramount, 1988
EVERYBODY WINS   Orion, 1990
PROBLEM CHILD   Universal, 1990
PROBLEM CHILD 2   Universal, 1991
PASSED AWAY   Buena Vista, 1992
NIGHT AND THE CITY   20th Century Fox, 1992
BEYOND INNOCENCE   Buena Vista, 1993
BULLETS OVER BROADWAY   Miramax Films, 1994
WHILE YOU WERE SLEEPING   Buena Vista, 1995

HERTA WARE
COCOON   20th Century Fox, 1985
COCOON: THE RETURN   20th Century Fox, 1988

MARSHA WARFIELD
CADDYSHACK II   Warner Bros., 1988

JORDAN WARKOL
THE LITTLE RASCALS   Universal, 1994

DAVID WARNER
b. July 29, 1941 - Manchester, England

TOM JONES   Lopert, 1963, British
MORGAN!   *MORGAN—A SUITABLE CASE FOR TREATMENT*
   Cinema 5, 1966
THE DEADLY AFFAIR   Columbia, 1967, British
WORK IS A FOUR-LETTER WORD   Universal, 1968, British
A MIDSUMMER NIGHT'S DREAM   Eagle, 1968, British
THE BOFORS GUN   Universal, 1968, British
THE FIXER   MGM, 1968, British
THE SEA GULL   Warner Bros., 1968, British
MICHAEL KOHLHAAS   Columbia, 1969, West German
THE BALLAD OF CABLE HOGUE   Warner Bros., 1970
PERFECT FRIDAY   Chevron, 1970, British
THE ENGAGEMENT   1970
STRAW DOGS   Cinerama Releasing Corporation, 1971, British
A DOLL'S HOUSE   Paramount, 1973, Canadian-U.S.
LITTLE MALCOLM   Multicetera Investments, 1974, British
FROM BEYOND THE GRAVE   Howard Mahler Films, 1975, British
MR. QUILP   Avco Embassy, 1975, British
THE OMEN   20th Century-Fox, 1976
VICTORY AT ENTEBBE (MS)   1976
AGE OF INNOCENCE   Rank, 1977, British-Canadian
PROVIDENCE   Cinema 5, 1977, French-Swiss
CROSS OF IRON   Avco Embassy, 1977, British-West German
THE DISAPPEARANCE   Levitt-Pickman, 1977, Canadian
SILVER BEARS   Columbia, 1978
HOLOCAUST (MS)   Titus Productions, 1978
THE THIRTY-NINE STEPS   International Picture Show Company,
   1978, British
NIGHTWING   Columbia, 1979
THE CONCORDE—AIRPORT '79   Universal, 1979
S.O.S. TITANIC (TF)   Roger Gimbel Productions/EMI TV/Argonaut
   Films, Ltd., 1979, U.S.-British
TIME AFTER TIME   Orion/Warner Bros., 1979
THE ISLANDS   Universal, 1980
TIME BANDITS   Avco Embassy, 1981, British
THE FRENCH LIEUTENANT'S WOMAN   United Artists,
   1981, British
IRON   1982
THE MAN WITH TWO BRAINS   Warner Bros., 1983
THE COMPANY OF WOLVES   Cannon, 1984, British
A CHRISTMAS CAROL (TF)   Entertainment Partners, Ltd.,
   1984, U.S.-British

HANSEL AND GRETEL   Cannon, 1987, U.S.-Israeli
MR. NORTH   Samuel Goldwyn Company, 1988
WAXWORK   Vestron, 1988
HANNA'S WAR   Cannon, 1988
STAR TREK V: THE FINAL FRONTIER   Paramount, 1989
TEENAGE MUTANT NINJA TURTLES II: THE SECRET OF
   THE OOZE   New Line Cinema, 1991
LOVECRAFT (CTF)   HBO Pictures/Pacific Western
   Productions, 1991
STAR TREK VI: THE UNDISCOVERED COUNTRY
   Paramount, 1991
WILD PALMS (MS)   Ixtlan Corporation/Greengrass
   Productions, Inc., 1993

JEREMIAH WARNER
THE WIZARD OF LONELINESS   Skouras Pictures, 1988

JULIE WARNER
Agent: CAA - Beverly Hills, 310/288-4545

DOC HOLLYWOOD   Warner Bros., 1991
MR. SATURDAY NIGHT   Columbia, 1992
INDIAN SUMMER   Buena Vista, 1993
THE PUPPET MASTERS   Buena Vista, 1994

MALCOLM JAMAL WARNER
b. August 18, 1970 - Jersey City, New Jersey
Agent: William Morris Agency - Beverly Hills, 310/274-7451

THE FATHER CLEMENTS STORY (TF)   Zev Braun Productions/
   Interscope Communications, 1987
DROP ZONE   Paramount, 1994

JENNIFER WARREN
NIGHT MOVES   Warner Bros., 1975
SLAP SHOT   Universal, 1977
ANOTHER MAN, ANOTHER CHANCE   United Artists,
   1977, U.S.-French
FIRST, YOU CRY (TF)   MTM Enterprises, 1978
ICE CASTLES   Columbia, 1979
PAPER DOLLS (TF)   Mandy Productions/MGM-UA TV, 1984

LESLEY ANN WARREN
b. August 16, 1946 - New York, New York

THE HAPPIEST MILLIONAIRE   1967
THE ONE AND ONLY GENUINE, ORIGINAL FAMILY BAND
   Buena Vista, 1968
SEVEN IN DARKNESS (TF)   Paramount TV, 1969
ASSIGNMENT: MUNICH (TF)   MGM TV, 1972
THE DAUGHTERS OF JOSHUA CABE (TF)   Spelling-Goldberg
   Productions, 1972
PICKUP ON 101   1972
HAROLD ROBBINS' 79 PARK AVENUE   *79 PARK AVENUE* (MS)
   Universal TV, 1978
BEULAH LAND (MS)   David Gerber Company/Columbia TV, 1980
PORTRAIT OF A STRIPPER (TF)   Moonlight Productions/
   Filmways, 1979
VICTOR/VICTORIA ○   MGM/United Artists, 1982
A NIGHT IN HEAVEN   20th Century-Fox, 1983
CHOOSE ME   Island Alive/New Cinema, 1984
SONGWRITER   TriStar, 1984
EVERGREEN (MS)   Edgar J. Scherick Associates/Metromedia
   Producers Corporation, 1985
CLUE   Paramount, 1985
A FIGHT FOR JENNY (TF)   Robert Greenwald Productions, 1986
BURGLAR   Warner Bros., 1987
COP   Atlantic Releasing Corporation, 1988
WORTH WINNING   20th Century Fox, 1989
FAMILY OF SPIES (MS)   King Phoenix Entertainment, 1990
LIFE STINKS   MGM-Pathe, 1991
PURE COUNTRY   Warner Bros., 1992
COLOR OF NIGHT   Buena Vista, 1994
JOSEPH (CTF)   Turner Network TV, 1994

DIONNE WARWICK
b. December 12, 1941 - East Orange, New Jersey
Agent: William Morris Agency - Beverly Hills, 310/274-7451

RENT-A-COP   Kings Road Productions, 1988

DENZEL WASHINGTON
b. December 28, 1954
Agent: ICM - Beverly Hills, 310/550-4000

WILMA (TF)   Cappy Productions, 1977
CARBON COPY   Avco Embassy, 1981
LICENSE TO KILL (TF)   Marian Rees Associates/D. Petrie
    Productions, 1984
A SOLDIER'S STORY   Columbia, 1984
POWER   20th Century Fox, 1986
THE GEORGE McKENNA STORY (TF)   Alan Landsburg
    Productions, 1986
CRY FREEDOM ✪   Universal, 1987, British-U.S.
FOR QUEEN AND COUNTRY   Atlantic Releasing Corporation,
    1988, British
THE MIGHTY QUINN   MGM/UA, 1989
GLORY ✪✪   TriStar, 1989
MO' BETTER BLUES   Universal, 1990
HEART CONDITION   New Line Cinema, 1990
RICOCHET   Warner Bros., 1991
MISSISSIPPI MASALA   Samuel Goldwyn Company,
    1992, U.S.-British
MALCOLM X ★   Warner Bros., 1992
MUCH ADO ABOUT NOTHING   Samuel Goldwyn Company,
    1993, British-U.S.
THE PELICAN BRIEF   Warner Bros., 1993
PHILADELPHIA   TriStar, 1993
DEVIL IN A BLUE DRESS   TriStar, 1994
CRIMSON TIDE   Buena Vista, 1995

ISAIAH WASHINGTON
CLOCKERS   Universal, 1995

TED WASS
CURSE OF THE PINK PANTHER   MGM/UA, 1983
OH GOD! YOU DEVIL   Warner Bros., 1984
TRIPLECROSS (TF)   TAP Productions/ABC Circle Films, 1986
PANCHO BARNES (MS)   Blue Andre Productions/Orion TV, 1988
SPARKS: THE PRICE OF PASSION (TF)   Shadowplay Films/
    Victoria Principal Productions/King Phoenix Entertainment, 1990

ALLAN WASSERMAN
BIG   20th Century Fox, 1988

CRAIG WASSON
THE BOYS IN COMPANY C   Columbia, 1978
ROLLERCOASTER   Universal, 1977
GO TELL THE SPARTANS   Avco Embassy, 1978
THE OUTSIDER   Paramount, 1979, U.S.-Irish
SCHIZOID   Cannon, 1980
FOUR FRIENDS   Filmways, 1981
GHOST STORY   Universal, 1981
BODY DOUBLE   Columbia, 1984
THE MEN'S CLUB   Atlantic Releasing Corporation, 1986

GEDDE WATANABE
GUNG HO   Paramount, 1986
VAMP   New World, 1986

LAURA WATERBURY
MAC AND ME   Orion, 1988

HARRY WATERS, JR.
BACK TO THE FUTURE PART II   Universal, 1989

JOHN WATERS
HOMER & EDDIE   Skouras Pictures, 1990

JAMES WATERSTON
DEAD POETS SOCIETY   Buena Vista, 1989

SAM WATERSTON
b. November 15, 1940 - Cambridge, Massachusetts

FITZWILLY   United Artists, 1967
GENERATION   Avco Embassy, 1969
THREE   United Artists, 1969, British
THE PLASTIC DOME OF NORMA JEAN   1970
COVER ME BABE   20th Century-Fox, 1970
WHO KILLED MARY WAT'S 'ERNAME?   Cannon, 1971
SAVAGES   Angelika, 1972
A DELICATE BALANCE   American Film Theatre, 1973
THE GREAT GATSBY   Paramount, 1974
RANCHO DeLUXE   United Artists, 1975
JOURNEY INTO FEAR   Stirling Gold, 1975, Canadian
SWEET REVENGE   DANDY, THE ALL AMERICAN GIRL
    MGM/United Artists, 1976
COUP DE FOUDRE   1977, French
CAPRICORN ONE   20th Century-Fox, 1978
INTERIORS   United Artists, 1978
EAGLE'S WING   International Picture Show, 1979, British
SWEET WILLIAM   Kendon Films, 1980, British
HEAVEN'S GATE   United Artists, 1980
HOPSCOTCH   Avco Embassy, 1980
OPPENHEIMER (MS)   BBC-TV/WGBH-Boston, 1982, British-U.S.
Q.E.D. (TF)   1982, British
DEMPSEY (TF)   Charles Fries Productions, 1983
THE KILLING FIELDS ★   Warner Bros., 1984, British
FINNEGAN BEGIN AGAIN (CTF)   HBO Premiere Films/Zenith
    Productions/Jennie & Co. Film Productions, 1985, U.S.-British
LOVE LIVES ON (TF)   ABC Circle Films, 1985
THE FIFTH MISSILE (TF)   Bercovici-St. Johns Productions/
    MGM-UA TV, 1986
HANNAH AND HER SISTERS   Orion, 1986
JUST BETWEEN FRIENDS   Orion, 1986
THE ROOM UPSTAIRS (TF)   Marian Rees Associates/The
    Alexander Group, 1987
SEPTEMBER   Orion, 1987
TERRORIST ON TRIAL: THE UNITED STATES VS.
    SALIM AJAMI (TF)   George Englund Productions/Robert
    Papazian Productions, 1988
LINCOLN (MS)   Chris-Rose Productions/Finnegan-Pinchuk
    Company, 1988
WELCOME HOME   Columbia, 1989
THE NIGHTMARE YEARS (CMS)   Consolidated Productions, 1989
CRIMES AND MISDEMEANORS   Orion, 1989
LANTERN HILL (CTF)   Sullivan Films/The Disney Channel, 1990
THE MAN IN THE MOON   MGM-Pathe, 1991
SERIAL MOM   Savoy Pictures, 1994

JAMES A. WATSON, JR.
AIRPLANE II: THE SEQUEL   Paramount, 1982

VERNEE WATSON
ALL NIGHT LONG   Universal, 1981

NATHAN WATT
UNSTRUNG HEROES   Buena Vista, 1995

MARTY WATT
ALMOST YOU   TLC Films/20th Century Fox, 1984

NAOMI WATTS
TANK GIRL   MGM/UA, 1995

DAMON WAYANS
b. 1960 - New York, New York
Agent: CAA - Beverly Hills, 310/288-4545

BEVERLY HILLS COP   Paramount, 1984
HOLLYWOOD SHUFFLE   Samuel Goldwyn Company, 1987
ROXANNE   Columbia, 1987
COLORS   Orion, 1988
PUNCHLINE   Columbia, 1988

EARTH GIRLS ARE EASY   Vestron, 1989
I'M GONNA GIT YOU SUCKA   MGM/UA, 1989
LOOK WHO'S TALKING TOO   TriStar, 1990 (voice)
THE LAST BOY SCOUT   The Geffen Company/Warner Bros., 1991
MO' MONEY   Columbia, 1992
BLANKMAN   Columbia, 1994
MAJOR PAYNE   Universal, 1995

KEENEN IVORY WAYANS
b. June 8, 1958 - New York, New York
Agent: CAA - Beverly Hills, 310/288-4545

STAR 80   The Ladd Company/Warner Bros., 1983
I'M GONNA GIT YOU SUCKA   MGM/UA, 1989 (also directed)
A LOW DOWN DIRTY SHAME   Buena Vista, 1994 (also directed)

MARLON WAYANS
Agent: UTA - Beverly Hills, 310/273-6700

I'M GONNA GIT YOU SUCKA   MGM/UA, 1989
BATMAN RETURNS   Warner Bros., 1992
MO' MONEY   Columbia, 1992
ABOVE THE RIM   New Line Cinema, 1994

KRISTINA WAYBORN
OCTOPUSSY   MGM/UA, 1983, British

PATRICK WAYNE
b. July 15, 1939 - Los Angeles, California

THE LONG GRAY LINE   Columbia, 1955
MISTER ROBERTS   Warner Bros., 1955
THE SEARCHERS   Warner Bros., 1956
THE ALAMO   United Artists, 1960
THE COMANCHEROS   20th Century-Fox, 1961
DONOVAN'S REEF   Paramount, 1963
McLINTOCK!   United Artists, 1963
CHEYENNE AUTUMN   Warner Bros., 1964
SHENANDOAH   Universal, 1965
AN EYE FOR AN EYE   Creative Film Enterprises, 1966
THE GREEN BERETS   Warner Bros., 1968
THE DESERTER *LA SPINA DORSALE DEL DIAVOLO*
   Paramount, 1971, Italian-Yugoslavian
BIG JAKE   National General, 1971
THE GATLING GUN   1972
BEYOND ATLANTIS   Dimension, 1973, U.S.-Filipino
THE BEARS AND I   Buena Vista, 1974
MUSTANG COUNTRY   1976
SINBAD AND THE EYE OF THE TIGER   Columbia, 1977, British
THE PEOPLE THAT TIME FORGOT   American International,
   1977, British
HER ALIBI   Warner Bros., 1989

SHAWN WEATHERLY
POLICE ACADEMY 3: BACK IN TRAINING   Warner Bros., 1986

CARL WEATHERS
Agent: William Morris Agency - Beverly Hills, 310/274-7451

BUCKTOWN   American International, 1975
FRIDAY FOSTER   American International, 1975
ROCKY   United Artists, 1976
CLOSE ENCOUNTERS OF THE THIRD KIND   Columbia, 1977
SEMI-TOUGH   United Artists, 1977
FORCE 10 FROM NAVARONE   American International,
   1978, British
ROCKY II   United Artists, 1979
DEATH HUNT   20th Century-Fox, 1981
ROCKY III   MGM/UA, 1982
ROCKY IV   MGM/UA, 1985
PREDATOR   20th Century Fox, 1987
ACTION JACKSON   Lorimar, 1988
DANGEROUS PASSION (TF)   Stormy Weathers Productions/Davis
   Entertainment TV, 1990

DENNIS WEAVER
b. June 4, 1924 - Joplin, Missouri
Agent: David Shapira & Associates - Sherman Oaks, 818/906-0322

HORIZONS WEST   Universal, 1952
THE LAWLESS BREED   Universal, 1952
THE RAIDERS   Universal, 1952
THE MISSISSIPPI GAMBLER   Universal, 1953
WAR ARROW   Universal, 1954
DANGEROUS MISSION   1954
THE BRIDGES OF TOKO-RI   Paramount, 1954
SEVEN ANGRY MEN   1955
STORM FEAR   United Artists, 1955
TOUCH OF EVIL   Universal, 1958
THE GALLANT HOURS   United Artists, 1960
DUEL AT DIABLO   United Artists, 1966
WAY WAY OUT!   20th Century-Fox, 1966
GENTLE GIANT   Paramount, 1967
MISSION BATANGAS   1968
McCLOUD: WHO KILLED MISS U.S.A.? (TF)   Universal TV, 1970
A MAN CALLED SLEDGE   1970
THE GREAT MAN'S WHISKERS (TF)   Universal TV, 1971
WHAT'S THE MATTER WITH HELEN?   United Artists, 1971
DUEL (TF)   Universal TV, 1971
THE FORGOTTEN MAN (TF)   Walter Grauman Productions, 1971
ROLLING MAN (TF)   ABC Circle Films, 1972
CENTENNIAL (MS)   Universal TV, 1977
INTIMATE STRANGERS (TF)   Charles Fries Productions, 1977
THE ISLANDER (TF)   Universal TV, 1978
PEARL (MS)   Siliphant-Konigsberg Productions/Warner
   Bros. TV, 1978
ISHI: THE LAST OF HIS TRIBE (TF)   Edward & Mildred Lewis
   Productions, 1978
THE ORDEAL OF PATTY HEARST (TF)   Finnegan Associates/
   David Paradine TV, 1979
THE ORDEAL OF DR. MUDD (TF)   BSR Productions/Marble Arch
   Productions, 1980
GOING FOR THE GOLD: THE BILL JOHNSON STORY (TF)
   ITC Productions/Sullivan-Carter Interests/Goodman-Rosen
   Productions, 1985

FRITZ WEAVER
b. January 19, 1926 - Pittsburgh, Pennsylvania

FAIL SAFE   Columbia, 1964
THE GUNS OF AUGUST (FD)   1964 (voice)
TO TRAP A SPY   MGM, 1966
THE BORGIA STICK (TF)   Universal TV, 1967
THE MALTESE BIPPY   MGM, 1969
A WALK IN THE SPRING RAIN   Columbia, 1970
COMPANY OF KILLERS   Universal, 1970
THE DAY OF THE DOLPHIN   Avco Embassy, 1973
MARATHON MAN   Paramount, 1976
DEMOND SEED   MGM/United Artists, 1977
BLACK SUNDAY   Paramount, 1977
THE BIG FIX   Universal, 1978
HOLOCAUST (MS)   Titus Productions, 1978
THE MARTAIN CHRONICLES (TF)   Charles Fries Productions/
   Stonehenge Productions, 1980
JAWS OF SATAN   1981
CREEPSHOW   Warner Bros., 1982
THE HEARST AND DAVIES AFFAIR (TF)   ABC Circle Films, 1985
DREAM WEST (MS)   Sunn Classic Pictures, 1986
POWER   20th Century-Fox, 1986

JASON WEAVER
THE LION KING (AF)   Buena Vista, 1994 (voice)

ROBERT "WINGNUT" WEAVER
THE ENDLESS SUMMER II (FD)   New Line Cinema, 1994

ROSE WEAVER
THE ACCUSED   Paramount, 1988

SIGOURNEY WEAVER
(Susan Alexandra Weaver)
b. October 8, 1949 - New York, New York
Agent: ICM - Beverly Hills, 310/550-4000

ANNIE HALL   United Artists, 1977
MADMAN   1978, Israeli
ALIEN   20th Century-Fox, 1979, U.S.-British
EYEWITNESS   20th Century-Fox, 1981
THE YEAR OF LIVING DANGEROUSLY   MGM/UA,
    1983, Australian
DEAL OF THE CENTURY   Warner Bros., 1983
GHOSTBUSTERS   Columbia, 1984
ONE WOMAN OR TWO   Orion Classics, 1985, French
ALIENS ★   20th Century Fox, 1986
HALF MOON STREET   20th Century Fox, 1986, British
GORILLAS IN THE MIST ★   Warner Bros./Universal, 1988
WORKING GIRL ⊙   20th Century Fox, 1988
GHOSTBUSTERS II   Columbia, 1989
ALIEN 3   20th Century Fox, 1992, U.S.-British
1492: CONQUEST OF PARADISE   Paramount,
    1992, British-Spanish
DAVE   Warner Bros., 1993
DEATH AND THE MAIDEN   Fine Line Features/
    New Line Cinema, 1994
JEFFREY   1995
COPYCAT   Warner Bros., 1995

HUGO WEAVING
FRAUDS   Australian Film Finance Corporation, 1993, Australian
THE ADVENTURES OF PRISCILLA, QUEEN OF THE DESERT
    Gramercy Pictures, 1994, Australian

CHLOE WEBB
SID AND NANCY   Samuel Goldwyn Company, 1986, British
CHINA BEACH (TF)   Sacret, Inc. Productions/Warner Bros. TV, 1988
TWINS   Universal, 1988
HEART CONDITION   New Line Cinema, 1990
QUEENS LOGIC   New Line Cinema, 1991
A DANGEROUS WOMAN   Gramercy Pictures, 1993

DANIEL WEBB
ALIEN 3   20th Century Fox, 1992, U.S.-British

ROBERT WEBBER
b. October 14, 1924 - Santa Ana, California

HIGHWAY 301   Warner Bros., 1950
TWELVE ANGRY MEN   United Artists, 1957
THE STRIPPER   20th Century-Fox, 1963
THE SANDPIPER   MGM, 1965
THE THIRD DAY   Warner Bros., 1965
HYSTERIA   1965, British
THE SILENCERS   Columbia, 1966
THE HIRED KILLER   *TECNICA DI UN OMICIDIO*
    1966, Italian-French
HARPER   Warner Bros., 1966
DEAD HEAT ON A MERRY-GO-ROUND   Paramount, 1966
DON'T MAKE WAVES   MGM, 1967
THE DIRTY DOZEN   MGM, 1967
THE BIG BOUNCE   Warner Bros., 1969
THE GREAT WHITE HOPE   20th Century-Fox, 1970
$ *DOLLARS*   Columbia, 1971
BRING ME THE HEAD OF ALFREDO GARCIA   United Artists, 1974
MIDWAY   Universal, 1976
PASSI DI MORTE PERDUTI NEL BUIO   1976, Italian
MADAME CLAUDE   1977, French
L'IMPRECATEUR   1977, French
THE CHOIRBOYS   Universal, 1977
CASEY'S SHADOW   Columbia, 1978
REVENGE OF THE PINK PANTHER   United Artists, 1978, British
GARDENIA   1979, Italian
10   Orion/Warner Bros., 1979
PRIVATE BENJAMIN   Warner Bros., 1980
S.O.B.   Paramount, 1981
WRONG IS RIGHT   Columbia, 1982
WILD GEESE II   Universal, 1985, British

STEVEN WEBER
SINGLE WHITE FEMALE   Columbia, 1992
JEFFREY   1995

ANN WEDGEWORTH
BANG THE DRUM SLOWLY   Paramount, 1973
SCARECROW   Warner Bros., 1973
THE CATAMOUNT KILLINGS   1974
BIRCH INTERVAL   Gamma III, 1976
ONE SUMMER LOVE   *DRAGONFLY*   American International, 1976
RIGHT TO KILL? (TF)   Wrye-Konigsberg Productions/Taper Media
    Enterprises/Telepictures Productions, 1985
SWEET DREAMS   TriStar, 1985
A TIGER'S TALE   Atlantic Releasing Corporation, 1987
A STRANGER WAITS (TF)   Bruce Lansbury Productions/
    Edgar Lansbury Productions/Lewisfilm Ltd./New Century TV
    Productions, 1987
MADE IN HEAVEN   Lorimar, 1987
FAR NORTH   Alive Films, 1988
MISS FIRECRACKER   Corsair Pictures, 1989
STEEL MAGNOLIAS   TriStar, 1989
GREEN CARD   Buena Vista, 1990

JIMMIE RAY WEEKS
KING KONG LIVES   DEG, 1986
FRANTIC   Warner Bros., 1988
THE ABYSS   20th Century Fox, 1989

SCOTT WEINGER
ALADDIN (AF)   Buena Vista, 1992 (voice)
THE RETURN OF JAFAR (AV)   Buena Vista, 1994 (voice)

ROBIN WEISMAN
THREE MEN AND A LITTLE LADY   Buena Vista, 1990

MICHAEL T. WEISS
JEFFREY   1995

SHAUN WEISS
HEAVYWEIGHTS   Buena Vista, 1994

JEFFREY WEISSMAN
BACK TO THE FUTURE PART II   Universal, 1989
BACK TO THE FUTURE PART III   Universal, 1990

MITCH WEISSMAN
BEATLEMANIA   American Cinema, 1981

DWIGHT WEIST
THE NAME OF THE ROSE   20th Century Fox, 1986,
    West German-Italian-French (voice)

BRUCE WEITZ
b. May 27, 1943 - Norwalk, Connecticut

A REASON TO LIVE (TF)   Papazian Productions, 1985
IF IT'S TUESDAY, IT STILL MUST BE BELGIUM (TF)
    Eisenstock & Mintz Productions, 1987

BARBARA WELCH
MISS FIRECRACKER   Corsair Pictures, 1989

RAQUEL WELCH
(Raquel Tejada)
b. September 5, 1940 - Chicago, Illinois

A HOUSE IS NOT A HOME   Embassy, 1964
ROUSTABOUT   Paramount, 1964
A SWINGIN' SUMMER   1965
SHOOT LOUD...LOUDER...I DON'T UNDERSTAND   *SPARA
    FORTE...PIU FORTE...NON CAPISCO*   1966, Italian
FANTASTIC VOYAGE   20th Century-Fox, 1966
ONE MILLION YEARS B.C.   20th Century-Fox, 1966, British

THE QUEENS   1966, Italian-French
THE OLDEST PROFESSION   *LE PLUS VIEUX MÉTIER
   DU MONDE*   1967, French-Italian-West German
FATHOM   20th Century-Fox, 1967, British
BEDAZZLED   20th Century-Fox, 1967, British
THE BIGGEST BUNDLE OF THEM ALL   MGM, 1968, U.S.-Italian
BANDOLERO!   20th Century-Fox, 1968
LADY IN CEMENT   20th Century-Fox, 1968
FLAREUP   MGM, 1969
100 RIFLES   20th Century-Fox, 1969
THE MAGIC CHRISTIAN   Commonwealth United, 1970, British
MYRA BRECKINRIDGE   20th Century-Fox, 1970
HANNIE CAULDER   Paramount, 1972, British
THE BELOVED   1972, West German
BLUEBEARD   Cinerama Releasing Corporation,
   1972, Italian-French-West German
FUZZ   United Artists, 1972
KANSAS CITY BOMBER   MGM, 1972
THE LAST OF SHEILA   Warner Bros., 1973
THE THREE MUSKETEERS   20th Century-Fox, 1974, British
THE FOUR MUSKETEERS   20th Century-Fox, 1975, British
THE WILD PARTY   American International, 1975
MOTHER, JUGS & SPEED   20th Century-Fox, 1976
CROSSED SWORDS   *THE PRINCE AND THE PAUPER*
   Warner Bros., 1978, British
L'ANIMAL   1977, French
THE LEGEND OF WALKS FAR WOMAN (TF)   Roger Gimbel
   Productions/EMI TV/Raquel Welch Productions/Lee Levinson
   Productions, 1984
RIGHT TO DIE (TF)   Ohlmeyer Communications, 1987
SCANDAL IN A SMALL TOWN (TF)   Carliner-Rappoport
   Productions, 1988
TROUBLE IN PARADISE (TF)   Qintex Entertainment,
   1989, U.S.-Australian
NAKED GUN 33 1/3: THE FINAL INSULT   Paramount, 1994

TAHNEE WELCH
COCOON   20th Century Fox, 1985
COCOON: THE RETURN   20th Century Fox, 1988

TUESDAY WELD
(Susan Ker Weld)
b. August 27, 1943 - New York, New York

ROCK ROCK ROCK   1956
RALLY ROUND THE FLAG BOYS!   20th Century-Fox, 1958
THE FIVE PENNIES   Paramount, 1959
BECAUSE THEY'RE YOUNG   Columbia, 1960
SEX KITTENS GO TO COLLEGE   Allied Artists, 1960
HIGH TIME   20th Century-Fox, 1960
THE PRIVATE LIVES OF ADAM AND EVE   Universal, 1960
RETURN TO PEYTON PLACE   20th Century-Fox, 1961
WILD IN THE COUNTRY   1961
BACHELOR FLAT   20th Century-Fox, 1961
SOLDIER IN THE RAIN   Allied Artists, 1963
THE CINCINNATI KID   MGM, 1965
I'LL TAKE SWEDEN   1965
LORD LOVE A DUCK   United Artists, 1966
PRETTY POISON   20th Century Fox, 1968
I WALK THE LINE   Columbia, 1970
A SAFE PLACE   Columbia, 1971
PLAY IT AS IT LAYS   Universal, 1972
LOOKING FOR MR. GOODBAR ✪   Paramount, 1977
WHO'LL STOP THE RAIN   *DOG SOLDIERS*   United Artists, 1978
A QUESTION OF GUILT (TF)   Lorimar Productions, 1978
SERIAL   Paramount, 1980
THIEF   United Artists, 1981
AUTHOR! AUTHOR!   20th Century-Fox, 1982
ONCE UPON A TIME IN AMERICA   The Ladd Company/
   Warner Bros., 1984, U.S.-Italian-Canadian
SOMETHING IN COMMON (TF)   New World TV/Freyda Rothstein
   Productions/Littke-Grossbart Productions, 1986
HEARTBREAK HOTEL   Buena Vista, 1988
FALLING DOWN   Warner Bros., 1993

FRANK WELKER
THE RESCUERS DOWN UNDER (AF)   Buena Vista, 1990 (voice)
BEAUTY AND THE BEAST (AF)   Buena Vista, 1991 (voice)
ALADDIN (AF)   Buena Vista, 1992 (voice)
THE PAGEMASTER   20th Century Fox, 1994 (voice)

PETER WELLER
Agent: CAA - Beverly Hills, 310/288-4545

JUST TELL ME WHAT YOU WANT   Columbia, 1980
SHOOT THE MOON   MGM/United Artists, 1982
FIRSTBORN   Paramount, 1984
THE ADVENTURES OF BUCKAROO BANZAI: ACROSS THE
   8TH DIMENSION   20th Century Fox, 1984
ROBOCOP   Orion, 1987
SHAKEDOWN   Universal, 1988
A KILLING AFFAIR   Hemdale, 1988
ROBOCOP 2   Orion, 1990
NAKED LUNCH   20th Century Fox, 1991, Canadian-British
THE SUBSTITUTE WIFE (TF)   Frederick S. Pierce Company, 1994
THE NEW AGE   Warner Bros., 1994

CLAUDIA WELLS
BACK TO THE FUTURE   Universal, 1985

TICO WELLS
THE FIVE HEARTBEATS   20th Century Fox, 1991

GWEN WELLES
CALIFORNIA SPLIT   Columbia, 1974
NASHVILLE   Paramount, 1976
BETWEEN THE LINES   Midwest Film Productions, 1977
DESERT HEARTS   Samuel Goldwyn Company, 1985
NEW YEAR'S DAY   International Rainbow Pictures, 1988

KEN WELSH
DEATH WISH V: THE FACE OF DEATH   Trimark Pictures, 1994

KENNETH WELSH
"CROCODILE" DUNDEE II   Paramount, 1988, U.S.-Australian

MARGARET WELSH
MR. AND MRS. BRIDGE   Miramax Films, 1990

MING-NA WEN
THE JOY LUCK CLUB   Buena Vista, 1993
STREET FIGHTER   Universal, 1994

GEORGE WENDT
b. October 17, 1948 - Chicago, Illinois
Agent: UTA - Beverly Hills, 310/273-6700

MY BODYGUARD   20th Century-Fox, 1980
DREAMSCAPE   20th Century Fox, 1984
THIEF OF HEARTS   Paramount, 1984
FLETCH   Universal, 1985
GUNG HO   Paramount, 1986
HOUSE   New World, 1986
PLAIN CLOTHES   Paramount, 1988
NEVER SAY DIE   Everard Films, 1988, New Zealand
GUILTY BY SUSPICION   Warner Bros., 1991
FOREVER YOUNG   Warner Bros., 1992
MAN 2 MAN   Buena Vista, 1995

JANN WENNER
PERFECT   Columbia, 1985

ALEXANDRA WENTWORTH
Agent: UTA - Beverly Hills, 310/273-6700

TENDERFOOTS   20th Century Fox, 1995

KIP WENTZ
POLTERGEIST III MGM/UA, 1988

ADAM WEST
(William Anderson)
b. September 19, 1928 - Walla Walla, Washington

THE YOUNG PHILADELPHIANS Warner Bros., 1959
GERONIMO United Artists, 1962
TAMMY AND THE DOCTOR 1963
SOLDIER IN THE RAIN 1963
ROBINSON CRUSOE ON MARS Paramount, 1964
MARA OF THE WILDERNESS 1965
BATMAN 20th Century-Fox, 1966
THE GIRL WHO KNEW TOO MUCH 1969
THE MARRIAGE OF A YOUNG STOCKBROKER
   20th Century-Fox, 1971
HELL RIVER *PARTISANI* 1974, Yugoslavian-U.S.
THE SPECIALIST Crown International, 1975
HOOPER Warner Bros., 1978
THE LAST PRECINCT (TF) Stephen J. Cannell Productions, 1986
ZOMBIE NIGHTMARE 1987
DOIN' TIME ON PLANET EARTH Cannon, 1988
THE NEW AGE Warner Bros., 1994

MARTIN WEST
MAC AND ME Orion, 1988

SAMUEL WEST
HOWARDS END Sony Pictures Classics, 1992, British

TEGAN WEST
SLEEP WITH ME MGM/UA, 1994

TIMOTHY WEST
TWISTED NERVE National General, 1969, British
NICHOLAS AND ALEXANDRA Columbia, 1971, British
THE DAY OF THE JACKAL Universal, 1973, British-French
HEDDA Brut Productions, 1975, British
AGATHA Warner Bros., 1979, British
THE THIRTY-NINE STEPS International Picture Show Company,
   1978, British
CHURCHILL AND THE GENERALS (TF) BBC/Le Vien International,
   1979, British
ROUGH CUT Paramount, 1980
MURDER IS EASY (TF) David L. Wolper-Stan Margulies
   Productions/Warner Bros. TV, 1982
OLIVER TWIST (TF) Claridge Group, Ltd./Grafton Films,
   1982, British
TENDER IS THE NIGHT (CMS) Showtime/BBC/Seven Network,
   1985, U.S.-British-Australian

CELIA WESTON
A NEW LIFE Paramount, 1988
STARS AND BARS Columbia, 1988

JACK WESTON
(Jack Weinstein)
b. August 21, 1925 - Cleveland, Ohio

STAGE STRUCK 1958
PLEASE DON'T EAT THE DAISIES MGM, 1960
ALL IN A NIGHT'S WORK Paramount, 1961
THE HONEYMOON MACHINE MGM, 1961
IT'S ONLY MONEY Paramount, 1962
PALM SPRINGS WEEKEND Warner Bros., 1963
THE INCREDIBLE MR. LIMPET Universal, 1964
MIRAGE Universal, 1965
THE CINCINNATI KID MGM, 1965
WAIT UNTIL DARK Warner Bros., 1967
THE COUNTERFEIT KILLER 1968
THE THOMAS CROWN AFFAIR United Artists, 1968
THE APRIL FOOLS National General, 1969
CACTUS FLOWER Columbia, 1969
A NEW LEAF Paramount, 1971

FUZZ United Artists, 1972
MARCO Cinerama Releasing Corporation, 1973
GATOR United Artists, 1976
THE RITZ Warner Bros., 1976
CUBA United Artists, 1979
CAN'T STOP THE MUSIC AFD, 1980
THE FOUR SEASONS Universal, 1981
HIGH ROAD TO CHINA Warner Bros., 1983, U.S.-Yugoslavian
RAD TriStar, 1986
ISHTAR Columbia, 1987
SHORT CIRCUIT 2 TriStar, 1988

PATRICIA WETTIG
Agent: ICM - Beverly Hills, 310/550-4000

GUILTY BY SUSPICION Warner Bros., 1991
CITY SLICKERS Columbia, 1991
CITY SLICKERS II: THE LEGEND OF CURLY'S GOLD
   Columbia, 1994
PARALLEL LIVES (CTF) Showtime Entertainment, 1994

MARIUS WEYERS
THE GODS MUST BE CRAZY TLC Films/20th Century-Fox,
   1979, Botswana
DEEPSTAR SIX TriStar, 1989
FAREWELL TO THE KING Orion, 1989
HAPPY TOGETHER Borde Releasing Corporation, 1990
BOPHA! Paramount, 1993

FRANK WHALEY
Agent: William Morris Agency - Beverly Hills, 310/274-7451

LITTLE MONSTERS MGM/UA, 1989
FIELD OF DREAMS Universal, 1989
BORN ON THE FOURTH OF JULY Universal, 1989
THE FRESHMAN TriStar, 1990
THE DOORS TriStar, 1991
CAREER OPPORTUNITIES Universal, 1991
A MIDNIGHT CLEAR Interstar Releasing, 1992
HOFFA 20th Century Fox, 1992
SWING KIDS Buena Vista, 1993
FATAL DECEPTION: MRS. LEE HARVEY OSWALD (TF)
   David L. Wolper Productions/Bernard Sofronski/Warner Bros.
   Television, 1993
TO DANCE WITH THE WHITE DOG (TF) Signboard Hill
   Productions, 1993
PULP FICTION Miramax Films, 1994
I.Q. Paramount, 1994

JUSTIN WHALIN
CHILD'S PLAY 3 Universal, 1991

JOANNE WHALLEY-KILMER
(Joanne Whalley)
A CHRISTMAS CAROL (TF) Entertainment Partners, Ltd.,
   1984, U.S.-British
THE GOOD FATHER Skouras Pictures, 1986, British
TO KILL A PRIEST Columbia, 1988, U.S.-French
WILLOW MGM/UA, 1988
SCANDAL Miramax Films, 1989
KILL ME AGAIN MGM/UA, 1989
NAVY SEALS Orion, 1990
THE BIG MAN Miramax Films, 1990, British
SHATTERED MGM-Pathe, 1991
STORYVILLE 20th Century Fox, 1992
MOTHER'S BOYS Dimension/Miramax Films, 1994
A GOOD MAN IN AFRICA Gramercy Pictures, 1994
TRIAL BY JURY Warner Bros., 1994
SCARLETT (MS) 1994

LIEM WHATLEY
THE IRON TRIANGLE Scotti Bros., 1989

WIL WHEATON
STAND BY ME Columbia, 1986
TOY SOLDIERS TriStar, 1991

IRA WHEELER
SEPTEMBER   Orion, 1987

MARK WHEELER
BACKDRAFT   Universal, 1991

DANA WHEELER-NICHOLSON
FLETCH   Universal, 1985

JILL WHELAN
AIRPLANE!   Paramount, 1980

BARBARA WHINNERY
CRAWLSPACE   Empire Pictures, 1986

FOREST WHITAKER
b. July 15, 1961 - Longview, Texas
Agent: ICM - Beverly Hills, 310/550-4000

FAST TIMES AT RIDGEMONT HIGH   Universal, 1982
VISION QUEST   Warner Bros., 1985
THE COLOR OF MONEY   Buena Vista, 1986
PLATOON   Orion, 1986
STAKEOUT   Buena Vista, 1987
GOOD MORNING, VIETNAM   Buena Vista, 1987
BLOODSPORT   Cannon, 1988
BIRD   Warner Bros., 1988
JOHNNY HANDSOME   TriStar, 1989
DOWNTOWN   20th Century Fox, 1990
A RAGE IN HARLEM   Miramax Films, 1991, U.S.-British
ARTICLE 99   Orion, 1992
CONSENTING ADULTS   Buena Vista, 1992
THE CRYING GAME   Miramax Films, 1992, Irish-British
LAST LIGHT (CTF)   Showtime Entertainment/Stillwater
   Productions, 1993
BANK ROBBER   I.R.S. Releasing, 1993
BODY SNATCHERS   Warner Bros., 1994
BLOWN AWAY   MGM/UA, 1994
JASON'S LYRIC   1994
PRET-A-PORTER   Miramax Films, 1994
SMOKE   Miramax Films, 1995
SPECIES   MGM/UA, 1995

AL WHITE
AIRPLANE!   Paramount, 1980
AIRPLANE II: THE SEQUEL   Paramount, 1982

ANDREW WHITE
AMERICAN ANTHEM   Columbia, 1986

DE'VOREAUX WHITE
DIE HARD   20th Century Fox, 1988

RICHARD WHITE
BEAUTY AND THE BEAST (AF)   Buena Vista, 1991 (voice)

VANNA WHITE
b. February 18, 1957 - North Myrtle Beach, South Carolina

GODDESS OF LOVE (TF)   Phil Margo Enterprises/New World TV/
   Phoenix Entertainment Group, 1988
NAKED GUN 33 1/3: THE FINAL INSULT   Paramount, 1994

PAXTON WHITEHEAD
BACK TO SCHOOL   Orion, 1986

BILLIE WHITELAW
b. June 6, 1932 - Coventry, England

THE FAKE   1954
BOBBIKINS   20th Century-Fox, 1959, British
HELL IS A CITY   Columbia, 1960, British
I LOVE MONEY   MR. TOPAZE   1960
MAKE MINE MINK   1960

NO LOVE FOR JOHNNIE   Embassy, 1961, British
PAYROLL   1961
THE COMEDY MAN   Continental, 1963, British
CHARLIE BUBBLES   Regional, 1968, British
TWISTED NERVE   National General, 1968, British
THE ADDING MACHINE   1969
START THE REVOLUTION WITHOUT ME   Warner Bros.,
   1970, British
LEO THE LAST   United Artists, 1970, British
EAGLE IN A CAGE   National General, 1971, British-Yugoslavian
GUMSHOE   Columbia, 1972, British
FRENZY   Universal, 1972, British
NIGHT WATCH   Avco Embassy, 1973, British
THE OMEN   20th Century-Fox, 1976
THE WATER BABIES   Pethurst International/Film Polski,
   1979, British-Polish
AN UNSUITABLE JOB FOR A WOMAN   Boyd's Co., 1982, British
JAMAICA INN (TF)   HTV/Metromedia Producers Corporation/United
   Media Ltd./Jamaica Inn Productions, 1983, British-U.S.
CAMILLE (TF)   Rosemont Productions, 1984, U.S.-British
THE CHAIN   Rank, 1986, British
SHADEY   Skouras Pictures, 1986, British
MAURICE   Cinecom, 1987, British
THE KRAYS   Miramax Films, 1990

LYNN WHITFIELD
Agent: ICM - Beverly Hills, 310/550-4000

JOHNNIE MAE GIBSON: FBI (TF)   Fool's Cap Productions, 1986
THE JOSEPHINE BAKER STORY (CTF)   HBO Pictures/
   RHI Entertainment/Anglia TV/John Kemeny Productions, 1991
IN THE ARMY NOW   Buena Vista, 1994

MITCHELL WHITFIELD
MY COUSIN VINNY   20th Century Fox, 1992

BRAD WHITFORD
(Bradley Whitford)
ADVENTURES IN BABYSITTING   Buena Vista, 1987
MY LIFE   Columbia, 1993
A PERFECT WORLD   Warner Bros., 1993
PHILADELPHIA   TriStar, 1993
THE CLIENT   Warner Bros., 1994
BILLY MADISON   Universal, 1995

STUART WHITMAN
b. February 1, 1926 - San Francisco, California

WHEN WORLDS COLLIDE   Paramount, 1951
THE DAY THE EARTH STOOD STILL   20th Century-Fox, 1951
RHAPSODY   MGM, 1954
SEVEN MEN FROM NOW   Warner Bros., 1956
WAR DRUMS   1957
JOHNNY TROUBLE   1957
DARBY'S RANGERS   Warner Bros., 1958
TEN NORTH FREDERICK   1958
THE DECKS RAN RED   1958
CHINA DOLL   United Artists, 1958
THE SOUND AND THE FURY   20th Century-Fox, 1959
THESE THOUSAND HILLS   20th Century-Fox, 1959
HOUND-DOG MAN   20th Century-Fox, 1960
THE STORY OF RUTH   20th Century-Fox, 1960
MURDER, INC.   20th Century-Fox, 1960
THE MARK ★   Continental, 1961, British
FRANCIS OF ASSISI   20th Century-Fox, 1961
THE FIERCEST HEART   20th Century-Fox, 1961
THE COMANCHEROS   20th Century-Fox, 1961
CONVICTS FOUR   1962
THE LONGEST DAY   20th Century-Fox, 1962
REPRIEVE   1963
THE DAY AND THE HOUR   *LE JOUR ET L'HEURE*   MGM,
   1963, French-Italian
SHOCK TREATMENT   1964
RIO CONCHOS   20th Century-Fox, 1964
THOSE MAGNIFICENT MEN IN THEIR FLYING MACHINES
   20th Century-Fox, 1965, British
SANDS OF THE KALAHARI   Paramount, 1965, British
SIGNPOST TO MURDER   MGM, 1965

AN AMERICAN DREAM 1966
THE LAST ESCAPE United Artists, 1970
THE INVINCIBLE SIX Continental, 1970, U.S.-Iranian
THE ONLY WAY OUT IS DEAD 1970, Canadian
CAPTAIN APACHE Scotia International, 1971, U.S.-British-Spanish
CITY BENEATH THE SEA (TF) 20th Century-Fox TV/Motion
  Pictures International, 1971
NIGHT OF THE LEPUS MGM, 1972
TENDER FLESH WELCOME TO ARROW BEACH 1974
CALL HIM MR. SHATTER Avco Embassy, 1975, British-Hong Kong
MEAN JOHNNY BARROWS Atlas, 1976
LAS VEGAS LADY Crown International, 1976
TOUGH TONY TONY SAITTA 1976, Italian
STRANGE SHADOWS IN AN EMPTY ROOM 1977, Italian
RUBY Dimension, 1977
THE WHITE BUFFALO United Artists, 1977
EATEN ALIVE DEATH TRAP Virgo International, 1977
RUN FOR THE ROSES THE THOROUGHBREDS
  Kodiak Films, 1977
MANIAC New World, 1977
OIL 1977, Italian
LA MUJER DE LA TIERRA CALIENTE 1978, Spanish-Italian
DELTA FOX 1979
GUYANA—CRIME OF THE CENTURY 1979
KEY WEST CROSSING 1979
SWEET DIRTY TONY 1981
BUTTERFLY Analysis, 1982
STILLWATCH (TF) Zev Braun Pictures/Interscope
  Communications/Potomac Productions, 1987
TRIAL BY JURY Warner Bros., 1994

STEVE WHITMIRE
THE MUPPET CHRISTMAS CAROL Buena Vista, 1992 (voice)

JAMES WHITMORE
b. October 1, 1921 - White Plains, New York

THE UNDERCOVER MAN Columbia, 1949
BATTLEGROUND ⊙ MGM, 1949
THE ASPHALT JUNGLE MGM, 1950
PLEASE BELIEVE ME MGM, 1950
THE NEXT VOICE YOU HEAR MGM, 1950
MRS. O'MALLEY AND MR. MALONE MGM, 1950
ACROSS THE WIDE MISSOURI MGM, 1951
IT'S A BIG COUNTRY MGM, 1952
BECAUSE YOU'RE MINE MGM, 1952
ABOVE AND BEYOND MGM, 1952
KISS ME KATE MGM, 1953
THEM Warner Bros., 1954
BATTLE CRY Warner Bros., 1955
THE McCONNELL STORY Warner Bros., 1955
OKLAHOMA! Magna, 1955
CRIME IN THE STREETS Allied Artists, 1956
THE EDDY DUCHIN STORY Columbia, 1956
THE DEEP SIX Warner Bros., 1958
WHO WAS THAT LADY? Columbia, 1960
BLACK LIKE ME 1964
CHUKA Paramount, 1967
PLANET OF THE APES 20th Century-Fox, 1968
MADIGAN Universal, 1968
THE SPLIT MGM, 1968
GUNS OF THE MAGNIFICENT SEVEN United Artists, 1969
TORA! TORA! TORA! 20th Century-Fox, 1970, U.S.-Japanese
IF TOMORROW COMES (TF) Aaron Spelling Productions, 1971
CHATO'S LAND United Artists, 1972
THE HARRAD EXPERIMENT Cinerama Releasing
  Corporation, 1973
WHERE THE RED FERN GROWS 1974
GIVE 'EM HELL, HARRY! ★ Avco Embassy, 1975
THE SERPENT'S EGG Paramount, 1977, West German-U.S.
THE WORD (TF) Charles Fries Productions/Stonehenge
  Productions, 1978
BULLY Maturo Image, 1978
THE FIRST DEADLY SIN Filmways, 1980
THE ADVENTURES OF MARK TWAIN (AF) Atlantic Releasing
  Corporation, 1985 (voice)
FAVORITE SON (MS) NBC Productions, 1988
THE SHAWSHANK REDEMPTION Columbia, 1994

JAMES WHITMORE, JR.
HUNTER (TF) Stephen J. Cannell Productions, 1984
TRICKS OF THE TRADE (TF) Leonard Hill Films, 1988

GRACE LEE WHITNEY
SOME LIKE IT HOT United Artists, 1959
IRMA LA DOUCE United Artists, 1963
STAR TREK - THE MOTION PICTURE Paramount, 1979
STAR TREK VI: THE UNDISCOVERED COUNTRY
  Paramount, 1991

MARGARET WHITTON
Agent: William Morris Agency - Beverly Hills, 310/274-7451

LOVE CHILD The Ladd Company/Warner Bros., 1982
THE BEST OF TIMES Universal, 1986
THE SECRET OF MY SUCCESS Universal, 1987
IRONWEED TriStar, 1987
MAJOR LEAGUE Paramount, 1989
LITTLE MONSTERS MGM/UA, 1989
THE MAN WITHOUT A FACE Warner Bros., 1993
MAJOR LEAGUE II Warner Bros., 1994
MENENDEZ: A KILLING IN BEVERLY HILLS (MS) Zev Braun
  Pictures/TriStar Television, 1994

JOHNNY WHITWORTH
BYE BYE LOVE 20th Century Fox, 1995
EMPIRE Warner Bros., 1995

MARY WICKES
(Mary Isabelle Wickenhauser)
b. 1916 - St. Louis, Missouri

THE MAN WHO CAME TO DINNER Warner Bros., 1942
PRIVATE BUCKAROO Universal, 1942
NOW, VOYAGER Warner Bros., 1942
WHO DONE IT? 1942
HAPPY LAND 20th Century-Fox, 1943
HIGHER AND HIGHER RKO, 1943
JUNE BRIDE Warner Bros., 1948
ANNA LUCASTA Columbia, 1949
THE PETTY GIRL Columbia, 1950
ON MOONLIGHT BAY Warner Bros., 1951
I'LL SEE YOU IN MY DREAMS Warner Bros., 1951
YOUNG MAN WITH IDEAS MGM, 1952
THE ACTRESS MGM, 1953
WHITE CHRISTMAS Paramount, 1954
GOOD MORNING, MISS DOVE 20th Century-Fox, 1955
DON'T GO NEAR THE WATER MGM, 1957
IT HAPPENED TO JANE TWINKLE AND SHINE Columbia, 1959
CIMARRON MGM, 1960
THE MUSIC MAN Warner Bros., 1962
DEAR HEART Warner Bros., 1964
HOW TO MURDER YOUR WIFE United Artists, 1965
THE TROUBLE WITH ANGELS Columbia, 1966
WHERE ANGELS GO...TROUBLE FOLLOWS Columbia, 1968
NAPOLEON AND SAMANTHA Buena Vista, 1972
SNOWBALL EXPRESS Buena Vista, 1972
THE CHRISTMAS GIFT (TF) Rosemont Productions/Sunn Classic
  Pictures, 1986
FATAL CONFESSION: A FATHER DOWLING MYSTERY (TF)
  The Fred Silverman Company/Strathmore Productions/
  Viacom, 1987
POSTCARDS FROM THE EDGE Columbia, 1990
SISTER ACT Buena Vista, 1992
SISTER ACT 2: BACK IN THE HABIT Buena Vista, 1993
LITTLE WOMEN Columbia, 1994

RICHARD WIDMARK
b. December 26, 1914 - Sunrise, Minnesota

KISS OF DEATH ⊙ 20th Century-Fox, 1947
THE STREET WITH NO NAME 20th Century-Fox, 1948
ROAD HOUSE 20th Century-Fox, 1948
YELLOW SKY 20th Century-Fox, 1948
DOWN TO THE SEA IN SHIPS 20th Century-Fox, 1949

SLATTERY'S HURRICANE   20th Century-Fox, 1949
NIGHT ANDTHE CITY   20th Century-Fox, 1950, British
PANIC IN THE STREETS   20th Century-Fox, 1950
NO WAY OUT   20th Century-Fox, 1950
HALLS OF MONTEZUMA   20th Century-Fox, 1950
THE FROGMEN   20th Century-Fox, 1951
RED SKIES OF MONTANA   1952
SMOKE JUMPERS   1952
DON'T BOTHER TO KNOCK   20th Century-Fox, 1952
O. HENRY'S FULL HOUSE   20th Century-Fox, 1952
MY PAL GUS   20th Century-Fox, 1952
DESTINATION GOBI   20th Century-Fox, 1953
PICKUP ON SOUTH STREET   20th Century-Fox, 1953
TAKE THE HIGH GROUND   MGM, 1953
HELL AND HIGH WATER   20th Century-Fox, 1954
GARDEN OF EVIL   20th Century-Fox, 1954
BROKEN LANCE   20th Century-Fox, 1954
A PRIZE OF GOLD   Columbia, 1955, British
THE COBWEB   MGM, 1955
BACKLASH   MGM, 1956
RUN FOR THE SUN   United Artists, 1956, British
THE LAST WAGON   20th Century-Fox, 1956
SAINT JOAN   United Artists, 1957, British
TIME LIMIT   1957
THE LAW AND JAKE WADE   MGM, 1958
TUNNEL OF LOVE   1958
THE TRAP   Paramount, 1959
WARLOCK   20th Century-Fox, 1959
THE ALAMO   United Artists, 1960
THE SECRET WAYS   Universal, 1961
TWO RODE TOGETHER   Columbia, 1961
JUDGMENT AT NUREMBERG   United Artists, 1961
HOW THE WEST WAS WON   MGM/Cinerama, 1963
FLIGHT FROM ASHIYA   United Artists, 1964
THE LONG SHIPS   Columbia, 1964, British-Yugoslvian
CHEYENNE AUTUMN   Warner Bros., 1964
THE BEDFORD INCIDENT   Columbia, 1965
ALVAREZ KELLY   Columbia, 1966
THE WAY WEST   Umited Artists, 1967
MADIGAN   Universal, 1968
A TALENT FOR LOVING   1968
DEATH OF A GUNFIGHTER   Universal, 1969
THE MOONSHINE WAR   MGM, 1970
BROCK'S LAST CASE (TF)   Talent Associates/Universal TV, 1971
VANISHED (TF)   Universal TV, 1971
WHEN THE LEGENDS DIE   20th Century-Fox, 1972
MURDER ON THE ORIENT EXPRESS   Paramount, 1974, British
MIDAS RUN   Cinerama Releasing Corporation, 1975, West German
THE SELL OUT   1976, British
TO THE DEVIL A DAUGHTER   EMI, 1976, British-West German
TWILIGHT'S LAST GLEAMING   Allied Artists,
   1977, U.S.-West German
THE DOMINO PRINCIPLE   Avco Embassy, 1977
ROLLERCOASTER   Universal, 1977
THE PERFECT KILLER   1977, Spanish
MR. HORN (TF)   Lorimar Productions, 1978
COMA   MGM/United Artists, 1978
THE SWARM   Warner Bros., 1978
DINERO MALDITO   1978 (filmed in 1971)
BEAR ISLAND   Taft International, 1979, British-Canadian
ALL GOD'S CHILDREN (TF)   Blinn-Thorpe Productions/
   Viacom, 1980
A WHALE FOR THE KILLING (TF)   Play Productions/Beowulf
   Productions, 1981
THE FINAL OPTION   *WHO DARES WINS*   MGM/UA, 1982, British
HANKY PANKY   Columbia, 1982
NATIONAL LAMPOON'S MOVIE MADNESS   United Artists, 1982
AGAINST ALL ODDS   Columbia, 1984
BLACKOUT   Norsk Film, 1983, Norwegian
A GATHERING OF OLD MEN (TF)   Consolidated Productions/
   Jennie & Company/Zenith Productions, 1987
ONCE UPON A TEXAS TRAIN (TF)   Robert Papazian Productions/
   Brigade Productions/Rastar, 1988
COLD SASSY TREE (CTF)   Faye Dunaway Productions/Ohlmeyer
   Communications/Turner Network TV, 1989
TRUE COLORS   Paramount, 1991

ALEX WIESENDANGER
LITTLE BUDDHA   Miramax Films, 1994, British-French

DIANNE WIEST
b. March 28, 1948 - Kansas City, Missouri

IT'S MY TURN   Columbia, 1980
THE WALL (TF)   Cinetex International/Time-Life Productions,
   1982, U.S.-Polish
INDEPENDENCE DAY   Warner Bros., 1983
FOOTLOOSE   Paramount, 1984
FALLING IN LOVE   Paramount, 1984
THE PURPLE ROSE OF CAIRO   Orion, 1985
HANNAH AND HER SISTERS ☮☮   Orion, 1986
THE LOST BOYS   Warner Bros., 1987
RADIO DAYS   Orion, 1987
SEPTEMBER   Orion, 1987
BRIGHT LIGHTS, BIG CITY   MGM/UA, 1988
PARENTHOOD ☮   Universal, 1989
COOKIE   Warner Bros., 1989
EDWARD SCISSORHANDS   20th Century Fox, 1990
LITTLE MAN TATE   Orion, 1991
COPS & ROBBERSONS   TriStar, 1994
THE SCOUT   20th Century Fox, 1994
BULLETS OVER BROADWAY   Miramax Films, 1994

MICHAEL WIKES
LIBERACE: BEHIND THE MUSIC (TF)   Canadian International
   Studios/Kushner-Locke Productions, 1988, U.S.-Canadian

JAMES WILBY
A SUMMER STORY   Atlantic Releasing Corporation, 1988, British
A HANDFUL OF DUST   New Line Cinema, 1988
HOWARDS END   Sony Pictures Classics, 1992, British

LARRY WILCOX
Agent: David Shapira & Associates - Sherman Oaks, 818/906-0322

RICH MEN, SINGLE WOMEN (TF)   Aaron Spelling
   Productions, 1990

LISA WILCOX
A NIGHTMARE ON ELM STREET 5: THE DREAM CHILD
   New Line Cinema, 1989

SHANNON WILCOX
Agent: Susan Smith & Associates - Beverly Hills, 213/852-4777

FRANKIE & JOHNNY   Paramount, 1991

GENE WILDER
(Gerald Silberman)
b. June 11, 1935 - Milwaukee, Wisconsin
Agent: CAA - Beverly Hills, 310/288-4545

BONNIE AND CLYDE   Warner Bros., 1967
THE PRODUCERS ☮   Avco Embassy, 1968
START THE REVOLUTION WITHOUT ME   Warner Bros.,
   1970, British
QUACKSER FORTUNE HAS A COUSIN IN THE BRONX
   FUN LOVING   UMC, 1970, British
WILLY WONKA AND THE CHOCOLATE FACTORY   Paramount,
   1971, British
EVERYTHING YOU ALWAYS WANTED TO KNOW ABOUT SEX*
   (*BUT WERE AFRAID TO ASK)   United Artists, 1972
RHINOCEROS   American Film Theatre, 1974
BLAZING SADDLES   Warner Bros., 1974
YOUNG FRANKENSTEIN   20th Century-Fox, 1974
THE LITTLE PRINCE   Paramount, 1974, British
THE ADVENTURE OF SHERLOCK HOLMES' SMARTER BROTHER
   20th Century-Fox, 1975 (also directed)
SILVER STREAK   20th Century-Fox, 1976
THE WORLD'S GREATEST LOVER   20th Century-Fox,
   1977 (also directed)
THE FRISCO KID   Warner Bros., 1979

STIR CRAZY   Columbia, 1980
SUNDAY LOVERS   MGM/United Artists, 1981,
   U.S.-British-French-Italian (also co-directed)
HANKY PANKY   Columbia, 1982
THE WOMAN IN RED   Orion, 1984 (also directed)
HAUNTED HONEYMOON   Orion, 1986 (also directed)
SEE NO EVIL, HEAR NO EVIL   TriStar, 1989
FUNNY ABOUT LOVE   Paramount, 1990
ANOTHER YOU   TriStar, 1991

JAMES WILDER
Agent: UTA - Beverly Hills, 310/273-6700

CRACKED UP (TF)   Aaron Spelling Productions, 1987

JASON WILES
HIGHER LEARNING   Columbia, 1994

KATHLEEN WILHOITE
EVERYBODY WINS   Orion, 1990

DONNA WILKES
ANGEL   New World, 1984

JUNE WILKINSON
VASECTOMY, A DELICATE MATTER   Seymour Borde &
   Associates, 1986

BARBARA WILLIAMS
TELL ME THAT YOU LOVE ME   Canadian-Israeli
THIEF OF HEARTS   Paramount, 1984
JO JO DANCER, YOUR LIFE IS CALLING   Columbia, 1986
TIGER WARSAW   Sony Pictures, 1988
WATCHERS   Universal, 1988
PETER GUNN (TF)   The Blake Edwards Company/
   New World TV, 1990

BARRY WILLIAMS
THE BRADY GIRLS GET MARRIED (TF)   Sherwood Schwartz
   Productions, 1981
A VERY BRADY CHRISTMAS (TF)   Sherwood Schwartz
   Productions/Paramount TV, 1988
THE BRADYS (TF)   Brady Productions/Paramount TV, 1990

BILLY DEE WILLIAMS
b. April 6, 1937 - New York, New York
Agent: David Shapira & Associates - Sherman Oaks, 818/906-0322

THE LAST ANGRY MAN   Columbia, 1959
THE OUT-OF-TOWNERS   Paramount, 1970
LOST FLIGHT (TF)   1970
BRIAN'S SONG (TF)   Screen Gems/Columbia TV, 1971
THE GLASS HOUSE   *TRUMAN CAPOTE'S THE GLASS
   HOUSE* (TF)   Tomorrow Entertainment, 1972
LADY SINGS THE BLUES   Paramount, 1972
THE FINAL COMEDOWN   New World, 1972
HIT!   Paramount, 1973
THE TAKE   1974
MAHOGANY   Paramount, 1975
THE BINGO LONG TRAVELING ALL-STARS AND MOTOR KINGS
   Universal, 1976
SCOTT JOPLIN   Universal, 1977
CHRISTMAS LILIES OF THE FIELD (TF)   Rainbow Productions/
   Osmond Productions, 1979
THE EMPIRE STRIKES BACK   20th Century-Fox, 1980
THE HOSTAGE TOWER (TF)   Jerry Leider Productions, 1980
NIGHTHAWKS   Universal, 1981
MARVIN AND TIGE   *LIKE FATHER AND SON*   20th Century-Fox
   International Classics, 1983
RETURN OF THE JEDI   20th Century-Fox, 1983
FEAR CITY   Chevy Chase Distribution, 1984
NUMBER ONE WITH A BULLET   Cannon, 1987
BATMAN   Warner Bros., 1989
DANGEROUS PASSION (TF)   Stormy Weathers Productions/
   Davis Entertainment TV, 1990

CINDY WILLIAMS
b. August 22, 1947 - Van Nuys, California

GAS-S-S-S   *GAS-S-S-S...OR, IT MAY BECOME NECESSARY
   TO DESTROY THE WORLD IN ORDER TO SAVE IT*
   American International, 1970
DRIVE, HE SAID   Columbia, 1971
TRAVELS WITH MY AUNT   MGM, 1972, British
AMERICAN GRAFFITI   Universal, 1973
THE KILLING KIND   Media Trend, 1974
THE CONVERSATION   Paramount, 1974
MR. RICCO   MGM, 1975
THE FIRST NUDIE MUSICAL   Paramount, 1976
MORE AMERICAN GRAFFITI   Universal, 1979
SPACESHIP   *THE CREATURE WASN'T NICE*   Almi Cinema 5, 1981
UFORIA   Universal, 1984
TRICKS OF THE TRADE (TF)   Leonard Hill Films, 1988
RUDE AWAKENING   Orion, 1989
BINGO!   TriStar, 1991

CLARENCE WILLIAMS III
PURPLE RAIN   Warner Bros., 1984
52 PICK-UP   Cannon, 1986
TOUGH GUYS DON'T DANCE   Cannon, 1987
PERFECT VICTIMS   Vertigo Pictures, 1988
SUGAR HILL   20th Century Fox, 1994
TALES FROM THE HOOD   Savoy Pictures, 1995

CYNDA WILLIAMS
MO' BETTER BLUES   Universal, 1990
ONE FALSE MOVE   I.R.S. Releasing, 1992

DEAN WILLIAMS
DISTANT VOICES, STILL LIVES   Alive Films, 1988, British

DICK ANTHONY WILLIAMS
MO' BETTER BLUES   Universal, 1990

ED WILLIAMS
THE NAKED GUN: FROM THE FILES OF POLICE SQUAD!
   Paramount, 1988
THE NAKED GUN II 1/2: THE SMELL OF FEAR   Paramount, 1991

ESTHER WILLIAMS
b. August 8, 1923 - Los Angeles, California

THAT'S ENTERTAINMENT! III (FD)   MGM/UA, 1994

GREGORY ALAN WILLIAMS
ABOVE THE LAW   Warner Bros., 1988

JoBETH WILLIAMS
b. 1953 - Houston, Texas
Agent: William Morris Agency - Beverly Hills, 310/274-7451

KRAMER VS. KRAMER   Columbia, 1979
STIR CRAZY   Columbia, 1980
THE DOGS OF WAR   United Artists, 1981, U.S.-British
POLTERGEIST   MGM/UA, 1982
ENDANGERED SPECIES   MGM/UA, 1982
THE BIG CHILL   Columbia, 1983
ADAM (TF)   Alan Landsburg Productions, 1983
THE DAY AFTER (TF)   ABC Circle Films, 1983
AMERICAN DREAMER   Warner Bros., 1984
TEACHERS   MGM/UA, 1984
DESERT BLOOM   Columbia, 1986
POLTERGEIST II: THE OTHER SIDE   MGM/UA, 1986
ADAM: HIS SONG CONTINUES (TF)   Alan Landsburg
   Productions, 1986
MURDER ORDAINED (TF)   Zev Braun Productions/Interscope
   Communications, 1987
BABY M (MS)   ABC Circle Films, 1988
MEMORIES OF ME   MGM/UA, 1988
WELCOME HOME   Columbia, 1989
CHILD IN THE NIGHT (TF)   Mike Robe Productions, 1990
SWITCH   Warner Bros., 1991

DUTCH   20th Century Fox, 1991
STOP! OR MY MOM WILL SHOOT   Universal, 1992
ME, MYSELF AND I   I.R.S. Releasing, 1992
WYATT EARP   Warner Bros., 1994
PARALLEL LIVES (CTF)   Showtime Entertainment, 1994

JOHNNY WILLIAMS
THE SKATEBOARD KID II   Concorde, 1995

JOSEPH WILLIAMS
THE LION KING (AF)   Buena Vista, 1994 (voice)

JUSTIN WILLIAMS
FLIGHT OF THE INTRUDER   Paramount, 1991

KELLI WILLIAMS
THERE GOES MY BABY   Orion, 1994

KIMBERLY WILLIAMS
FATHER OF THE BRIDE   Buena Vista, 1991
INDIAN SUMMER   Buena Vista, 1993
COLDBLOODED   MPCA, 1995
FATHER OF THE BRIDE 2   Buena Vista, 1995

LAURA WILLIAMS
THE LION KING (AF)   Buena Vista, 1994 (voice)

MICHELLE WILLIAMS
LASSIE   Paramount, 1994

PAUL WILLIAMS
b. September 19, 1940 - Omaha, Nebraska

THE LOVED ONE   MGM, 1965
THE CHASE   Columbia, 1966
WATERMELON MAN   Columbia, 1970
BATTLE FOR THE PLANET OF THE APES   20th Century-Fox, 1973
PHANTOM OF THE PARADISE   20th Century Fox, 1974
SMOKEY AND THE BANDIT   Universal, 1977
THE CHEAP DETECTIVE   Columbia, 1978
THE MUPPET MOVIE   AFD, 1979, British
THE WILD, WILD WEST REVISITED (TF)   CBS Entertainment, 1979
SMOKEY AND THE BANDIT II   Universal, 1980
ROOSTER (TF)   Glen A. Larson Productions/Tugboat Productions/
   20th Century-Fox TV, 1982
SMOKEY AND THE BANDIT 3   Universal, 1983

R.J. WILLIAMS
AMERICAN ANTHEM   Columbia, 1986
MAN OF PASSION   Golden Sun Productions, 1988, Spanish

ROBIN WILLIAMS
b. July 21, 1952 - Chicago, Illinois
Agent: CAA - Beverly Hills, 310/288-4545

CAN I DO IT...TIL I NEED GLASSES?   1977
POPEYE   Paramount, 1980
THE WORLD ACCORDING TO GARP   Warner Bros., 1982
THE SURVIVORS   Columbia, 1983
MOSCOW ON THE HUDSON   Columbia, 1984
THE BEST OF TIMES   Universal, 1986
CLUB PARADISE   Warner Bros., 1986
SEIZE THE DAY (TF)   Learning in Focus, 1986
DEAR AMERICA: LETTERS HOME FROM VIETNAM (FD)
   Taurus Entertainment, 1987 (voice)
GOOD MORNING, VIETNAM ★   Buena Vista, 1987
THE ADVENTURES OF BARON MUNCHAUSEN   Columbia,
   1989, British (uncredited)
DEAD POETS SOCIETY ★   Buena Vista, 1989
CADILLAC MAN   Orion, 1990
AWAKENINGS   Columbia, 1990
DEAD AGAIN   Paramount, 1991
THE FISHER KING ★   TriStar, 1991
HOOK   TriStar, 1991
FERNGULLY...THE LAST RAINFOREST (AF)
   20th Century Fox, 1992 (voice)

ALADDIN (AF)   Buena Vista, 1992 (voice)
TOYS   20th Century Fox, 1992
MRS. DOUBTFIRE   20th Century Fox, 1993
BEING HUMAN   Warner Bros., 1994

SPICE WILLIAMS
STAR TREK V: THE FINAL FRONTIER   Paramount, 1989

STEVEN WILLIAMS
JASON GOES TO HELL—THE FINAL FRIDAY   New Line Cinema, 1993

TREAT WILLIAMS
b. December 1, 1951 - Rowayton, Connecticut
Agent: UTA - Beverly Hills, 310/273-6700

THE RITZ   Warner Bros., 1976
THE EAGLE HAS LANDED   Columbia, 1977, British
HAIR   United Artists, 1979
1941   Universal, 1979
WHY WOULD I LIE?   MGM/United Artists, 1980
THE PURSUIT OF D.B. COOPER   Universal, 1981
PRINCE OF THE CITY   Orion/Warner Bros., 1981
DEMPSEY (TF)   Charles Fries Productions, 1983
FLASHPOINT   TriStar, 1984
ONCE UPON A TIME IN AMERICA   The Ladd Company/
   Warner Bros., 1984, U.S.-Italian-Canadian
A STREETCAR NAMED DESIRE (TF)   Keith Barish Productions, 1984
SMOOTH TALK   Spectrafilm, 1985
THE MEN'S CLUB   Atlantic Releasing Corporation, 1986
DEAD HEAT   New World, 1988
HEART OF DIXIE   Orion, 1989
MAX AND HELEN (CTF)   Citadel Entertainment, 1990
DRUG WARS: THE CAMARENA STORY (MS)   ZZY, Inc.
   Productions/World International Network, 1990
PARALLEL LIVES (CTF)   Showtime Entertainment, 1994
THINGS TO DO IN DENVER WHEN YOU'RE DEAD
   Miramax Films, 1995

VANESSA WILLIAMS
NEW JACK CITY   Warner Bros., 1991

VANESSA WILLIAMS
b. March 18, 1963 - New York, New York
Agent: William Morris Agency - Beverly Hills, 310/274-7451

THE PICK-UP ARTIST   20th Century Fox, 1987
FULL EXPOSURE: THE SEX TAPES SCANDAL (TF)
   von Zerneck-Sertner Films, 1989
ANOTHER YOU   TriStar, 1991
HARLEY DAVIDSON & THE MARLBORO MAN   MGM-Pathe, 1991

FRED WILLIAMSON
b. March 5, 1938 - Gary, Indiana

M*A*S*H*   20th Century-Fox, 1970
TELL ME THAT YOU LOVE ME JUNIE MOON   Paramount, 1970
THE LEGEND OF NIGGER CHARLEY   1972
HAMMER   United Artists, 1972
BLACK CAESAR   American International, 1973
THE SOUL OF NIGGER CHARLEY   Paramount, 1973
THAT MAN BOLT   Universal, 1973
HELL UP IN HARLEM   American International, 1973
THREE TOUGH GUYS   1973, Italian
CRAZY JOE   Columbia, 1973, Italian-U.S.
BLACK EYE   Warner Bros., 1974
THREE THE HARD WAY   1974
BOSS NIGGER   Dimension, 1975
BUCKTOWN   American International, 1975
TAKE A HARD RIDE   20th Century-Fox, 1975
ADIOS AMIGO   Atlas, 1976 (also directed)
MEAN JOHNNY BARROWS   Atlas, 1976 (also directed)
DEATH JOURNEY   Atlas, 1976 (also directed)
NO WAY BACK   Atlas, 1976 (also directed)
JOSHUA   Lone Star, 1976
MR. MEAN   *DESTINAZIONE ROMA*   Lone Star/Po' Boy, 1977,
   Italian-U.S. (also directed)
DUE NELLE STELLE   1979, Italian

FIST OF FEAR, TOUCH OF DEATH   1980
VIGILANTE   Artists Releasing Corporation/Film Ventures
    International, 1983
THE BIG SCORE   Almi Distribution, 1983 (also directed)

MYKELTI WILLIAMSON
(Mykel T. Williamson)
b. St. Louis, Missouri

ENTER THE DRAGON   Warner Bros., 1973, U.S.-Hong Kong
SUNNYSIDE   American International, 1979
PENITENTIARY   Jerry Gross Organization, 1980
WILDCATS   Warner Bros., 1986
NUMBER ONE WITH A BULLET   Cannon, 1987
MIRACLE MILE   Hemdale, 1989
THE FIRST POWER   Orion, 1990
FREE WILLY   Warner Bros., 1993
FORREST GUMP   Paramount, 1994
HOW TO MAKE AN AMERICAN QUILT   Universal, 1995

NICOL WILLIAMSON
b. September 14, 1938 - Hamilton, Scotland

SIX-SIDED TRIANGLE   1964
INADMISSIBLE EVIDENCE   Paramount, 1968, British
THE BOFORS GUN   Universal, 1968, British
LAUGHTER IN THE DARK   Lopert, 1969, British-French
THE RECKONING   Columbia, 1969, British
HAMLET   Columbia, 1969, British
THE JERUSALEM FILE   MGM, 1972, Israeli-British
THE WILBY CONSPIRACY   United Artists, 1975, British
ROBIN AND MARIAN   Columbia, 1976, British
THE SEVEN-PER-CENT SOLUTION   Universal, 1976, British
THE GOODBYE GIRL   Warner Bros., 1977
THE WORD (TF)   Charles Fries Productions/Stonehenge
    Productions, 1978
THE CHEAP DETECTIVE   Columbia, 1978
THE HUMAN FACTOR   United Artists, 1979, British
VENOM   Paramount, 1981, British
EXCALIBUR   Orion/Warner Bros., 1981, British-Irish
I'M DANCING AS FAST AS I CAN   Paramount, 1982
SAKHAROV (TF)   HBO Premiere Films/Titus Productions,
    1985, U.S.-British
RETURN TO OZ   Buena Vista, 1985
BLACK WIDOW   20th Century Fox, 1987
THE EXORCIST III   20th Century Fox, 1990
THE ADVOCATE   Miramax Films, 1994

NOBLE WILLINGHAM
QUIET VICTORY: THE CHARLIE WEDEMEYER STORY (TF)
    The Landsburg Company, 1988
BLIND FURY   TriStar, 1990
CITY SLICKERS   Columbia, 1991
ONE CUP OF COFFEE   Miramax Films, 1991
THE LAST BOY SCOUT   The Geffen Company/Warner Bros., 1991
CITY SLICKERS II: THE LEGEND OF CURLY'S GOLD
    Columbia, 1994

BRUCE WILLIS
b. March 19, 1955 - Germany
Agent: William Morris Agency - Beverly Hills, 310/274-7451

THE FIRST DEADLY SIN   Filmways, 1980
THE VERDICT   20th Century-Fox, 1982
MOONLIGHTING (TF)   Picturemaker Productions/
    ABC Circle Films, 1985
BLIND DATE   TriStar, 1987
SUNSET   TriStar, 1988
DIE HARD   20th Century Fox, 1988
LOOK WHO'S TALKING   TriStar, 1989 (voice)
IN COUNTRY   Warner Bros., 1989
DIE HARD 2   20th Century Fox, 1990
LOOK WHO'S TALKING TOO   TriStar, 1990 (voice)
THE BONFIRE OF THE VANITIES   Warner Bros., 1990
MORTAL THOUGHTS   Columbia, 1991
HUDSON HAWK   TriStar, 1991
BILLY BATHGATE   Buena Vista, 1991
THE LAST BOY SCOUT   The Geffen Company/Warner Bros., 1991

THE PLAYER   Fine Line Features/New Line Cinema, 1992
DEATH BECOMES HER   Universal, 1992
NATIONAL LAMPOON'S LOADED WEAPON 1   New Line Cinema,
    1993 (uncredited)
STRIKING DISTANCE   Columbia, 1993
NORTH   Columbia, 1994
COLOR OF NIGHT   Buena Vista, 1994
PULP FICTION   Miramax Films, 1994
NOBODY'S FOOL   Paramount, 1994 (uncredited)
DIE HARD 3   20th Century Fox, 1995

SUSAN WILLIS
WHAT ABOUT BOB?   Buena Vista, 1991

BRIDGETTE WILSON
LAST ACTION HERO   Columbia, 1993
BILLY MADISON   Universal, 1995

ELIZABETH WILSON
b. April 4, 1925 - Grand Rapids, Michigan

THE GRADUATE   Avco Embassy, 1967
LITTLE MURDERS   20th Century-Fox, 1971
NINE TO FIVE   20th Century-Fox, 1980
THE BELIEVERS   Orion, 1987
THE ADDAMS FAMILY   Paramount, 1991

LAMBERT WILSON
JEFFERSON IN PARIS   Buena Vista, 1995

MARA WILSON
Agent: Gold/Marshak & Associates - Burbank, 818/953-7689

MRS. DOUBTFIRE   20th Century Fox, 1993
MIRACLE ON 34TH STREET   20th Century Fox, 1994
MATILDA   Universal, 1995

MARY LOUISE WILSON
ZELIG   Orion/Warner Bros., 1983

RENEE WILSON
FATAL DECEPTION: MRS. LEE HARVEY OSWALD (TF)
    David L. Wolper Productions/Bernard Sofronski/Warner Bros.
    Television, 1993

RICHARD WILSON
HOW TO GET AHEAD IN ADVERTISING   Warner Bros.,
    1989, British

RITA WILSON
VOLUNTEERS   TriStar, 1985
THE BONFIRE OF THE VANITIES   Warner Bros., 1990
SLEEPLESS IN SEATTLE   TriStar, 1993
LIFESAVERS   TriStar, 1994
GASLIGHT ADDITION   New Line Cinema, 1995

SCOTT WILSON
IN COLD BLOOD   Columbia, 1967
THE GRISSOM GANG   Cinerama Releasing Corporation, 1971
THE NEW CENTURIONS   Columbia, 1972
LOLLY MADONNA XXX   *THE LOLLY-MADONNA WAR*
    MGM, 1973
THE GREAT GATSBY   Paramount, 1974
THE PASSOVER PLOT   Atlas, 1977, U.S.-Israeli
THE NINTH CONFIGURATION   *TWINKLE, TWINKLE,
    "KILLER" KANE*   Warner Bros., 1980
THE RIGHT STUFF   The Ladd Company/Warner Bros., 1983
ON THE LINE   Miramax, 1984, Spanish
THE AVIATOR   MGM/UA, 1985
BLUE CITY   Paramount, 1986
MALONE   Orion, 1987
JOHNNY HANDSOME   TriStar, 1989
THE EXORCIST III   20th Century Fox, 1990
PURE LUCK   Universal, 1991
JUDGE DREDD   Buena Vista, 1995

STUART WILSON

WALLENBERG: A HERO'S STORY (MS)   Dick Berg-Stonehenge
    Productions/Paramount TV, 1985
LETHAL WEAPON 3   Warner Bros., 1992
THE AGE OF INNOCENCE   Columbia, 1993
NO ESCAPE   Savoy Pictures, 1994
EXIT TO EDEN   Savoy Pictures, 1994
DEATH AND THE MAIDEN   Fine Line Features/
    New Line Cinema, 1994

THOMAS F. WILSON

BACK TO THE FUTURE   Universal, 1985
APRIL FOOL'S DAY   Paramount, 1986
ACTION JACKSON   Lorimar, 1988
BACK TO THE FUTURE PART II   Universal, 1989
BACK TO THE FUTURE PART III   Universal, 1990

PENELOPE WILTON

CLOCKWISE   Universal, 1986, British
CRY FREEDOM   Universal, 1987, British-U.S.
BLAME IT ON THE BELLBOY   Buena Vista, 1992, British

BRIAN WIMMER

Agent: William Morris Agency - Beverly Hills, 310/274-7451

LATE FOR DINNER   Columbia, 1991
TANK GIRL   MGM/UA, 1995
THE MADDENING   Trimark Pictures, 1995

MICHAEL WINCOTT

TALK RADIO   Universal, 1988
BLOODHOUNDS OF BROADWAY   Columbia, 1989
ROBIN HOOD: PRINCE OF THIEVES   Warner Bros., 1991
THE CROW   Dimension/Miramax Films, 1994
STRANGE DAYS   20th Century Fox, 1995

WILLIAM WINDOM

b. September 28, 1923 - New York, New York

TO KILL A MOCKINGBIRD   Universal, 1962
FOR LOVE OR MONEY   Universal, 1963
ONE MAN'S WAY   1964
THE AMERICANIZATION OF EMILY   MGM, 1964
THE DETECTIVE   20th Century-Fox, 1968
BREWSTER McCLOUD   MGM, 1970
FOOLS' PARADE   Columbia, 1971
NOW YOU SEE HIM, NOW YOU DON'T   Buena Vista, 1972
THE ABDUCTION OF SAINT ANNE   THEY'VE KIDNAPPED
    ANNE BENEDICT (TF)   QM Productions, 1975
ECHOES OF A SUMMER   Cine Artists, 1976, U.S.-Canadian
MEAN DOG BLUES   American International, 1978
GRANDVIEW, U.S.A.   Warner Bros., 1984
SHE'S HAVING A BABY   Paramount, 1988
MIRACLE ON 34TH STREET   20th Century Fox, 1994

PAUL WINFIELD

b. May 22, 1941 - Los Angeles, California

THE LOST MAN   1969
R.P.M.   Columbia, 1970
BROTHER JOHN   Columbia, 1971
SOUNDER ★   20th Century-Fox, 1972
GORDON'S WAR   20th Century-Fox, 1973
CONRACK   20th Century-Fox, 1974
HUSTLE   Paramount, 1975
DAMNATION ALLEY   20th Century-Fox, 1977
TWILIGHT'S LAST GLEAMING   Allied Artists, 1977,
    U.S.-West German
THE GREATEST   Columbia, 1977
BACKSTAIRS AT THE WHITE HOUSE (MS)   Ed Friendly
    Productions, 1978
KING (MS)   Abby Mann Productions/Filmways, 1978
ANGEL CITY (TF)   Factor-Newland Productions, 1980
STAR TREK II: THE WRATH OF KHAN   Paramount, 1982
ON THE RUN   1982
MIKE'S MURDER   The Ladd Company/Warner Bros., 1984
GO TELL IT ON THE MOUNTAIN (TF)   Learning in Focus, 1984

THE TERMINATOR   Orion, 1984
BLUE CITY   Paramount, 1986
PRESUMED INNOCENT   Warner Bros., 1990
DENNIS THE MENACE   Warner Bros., 1993

OPRAH WINFREY

b. January 29, 1954 - Kosciusko, Mississippi
Agent: CAA - Beverly Hills, 310/288-4545

THE COLOR PURPLE ✪   Warner Bros., 1985
NATIVE SON   Cinecom, 1986
THROW MOMMA FROM THE TRAIN   Orion, 1987
THE WOMEN OF BREWSTER PLACE (MS)   Harpo Productions/
    Phoenix Entertainment Group, 1989
THERE ARE NO CHILDREN HERE (TF)   ABC, 1993

CHOY CHANG WING

FAREWELL TO THE KING   Orion, 1989

LESLIE WING

RETRIBUTION   Taurus Entertainment, 1988

DEBRA WINGER

b. May 16, 1955 - Cleveland, Ohio
Agent: CAA - Beverly Hills, 310/288-4545

SLUMBER PARTY '57   Cannon, 1977
SPECIAL OLYMPICS   A SPECIAL KIND OF LOVE (TF)
    Roger Gimbel Productions/EMI TV, 1978
THANK GOD IT'S FRIDAY   Columbia, 1978
FRENCH POSTCARDS   Paramount, 1979
URBAN COWBOY   Paramount, 1980
AN OFFICER AND A GENTLEMAN ★   Paramount, 1982
E.T. THE EXTRA-TERRESTRIAL   Universal, 1982 (voice; uncredited)
CANNERY ROW   MGM/United Artists, 1982
TERMS OF ENDEARMENT ★   Paramount, 1983
MIKE'S MURDER   The Ladd Company/Warner Bros.,
    1984 (filmed in 1982)
LEGAL EAGLES   Universal, 1986
BLACK WIDOW   20th Century Fox, 1987
MADE IN HEAVEN   Lorimar, 1987 (uncredited)
BETRAYED   MGM/UA, 1988
EVERYBODY WINS   Orion, 1990
THE SHELTERING SKY   Warner Bros., 1990, British
LEAP OF FAITH   Paramount, 1992
WILDER NAPALM   TriStar, 1993
A DANGEROUS WOMAN   Gramercy Pictures, 1993
SHADOWLANDS ★   Savoy Pictures, 1993, U.S.-British
FORGET PARIS   Columbia, 1995

HENRY WINKLER

b. October 30, 1945 - New York, New York
Agent: ICM - Beverly Hills, 310/550-4000

CRAZY JOE   Columbia, 1974, Italian-U.S.
THE LORDS OF FLATBUSH   Columbia, 1974
HEROES   Universal, 1977
THE ONE AND ONLY   Paramount, 1978
NIGHT SHIFT   The Ladd Company/Warner Bros., 1982
ABSOLUTE STRANGERS (TF)   Cates-Doty Productions/Fries
    Entertainment, 1991

MARE WINNINGHAM

Agent: William Morris Agency - Beverly Hills, 310/274-7451

ONE-TRICK PONY   Warner Bros., 1980
THRESHOLD   20th Century-Fox International Classics,
    1983, Canadian
ST. ELMO'S FIRE   Columbia, 1985
A WINNER NEVER QUITS (TF)   Blatt-Singer Prods./Columbia TV, 1986
WHO IS JULIA? (TF)   CBS Entertainment, 1986
MADE IN HEAVEN   Lorimar, 1987
GOD BLESS THE CHILD (TF)   Indieprod Company/Phoenix
    Entertainment Group, 1988
MIRACLE MILE   Hemdale, 1989
TURNER & HOOCH   Buena Vista, 1989
CROSSING TO FREEDOM (TF)   Procter & Gamble Productions/
    Stan Margulies Productions/Granada TV, 1990, U.S.-British

HARD PROMISES   Columbia, 1991
WYATT EARP   Warner Bros., 1994
THE WAR   Universal, 1994

MICHAEL WINSLOW
b. September 6, 1960

CHEECH AND CHONG'S NEXT MOVIE   Universal, 1980
UNDERGROUND ACES   Filmways, 1981
TAG   New World, 1982
POLICE ACADEMY   The Ladd Company/Warner Bros., 1984
ALPHABET CITY   Atlantic Releasing Corporation, 1984
GRANDVIEW, U.S.A.   Warner Bros., 1984
LOVELINES   TriStar, 1984
POLICE ACADEMY 2: THEIR FIRST ASSIGNMENT
    Warner Bros., 1985
POLICE ACADEMY 3: BACK IN TRAINING   Warner Bros., 1986
POLICE ACADEMY 4: CITIZENS ON PATROL   Warner Bros., 1987
POLICE ACADEMY 5: ASSIGNMENT MIAMI BEACH
    Warner Bros., 1988
BUY & CELL   Empire Pictures, 1989
POLICE ACADEMY 6: CITY UNDER SIEGE   Warner Bros., 1989
THINK BIG   MPCA, 1990
FAR OUT MAN   New Line Cinema, 1990
POLICE ACADEMY: MISSION TO MOSCOW   Warner Bros., 1994

HATTIE WINSTON
CLARA'S HEART   Warner Bros., 1988

ALEX WINTER
BILL & TED'S EXCELLENT ADVENTURE   Orion, 1989
ROSALIE GOES SHOPPING   Four Seasons Entertainment,
    1989, West German-U.S.
BILL & TED'S BOGUS JOURNEY   Orion, 1991
FREAKED   20th Century Fox, 1993 (also co-directed)

JONATHAN WINTERS
b. November 11, 1925 - Dayton, Ohio

IT'S A MAD MAD MAD MAD WORLD   United Artists, 1963
THE LOVED ONE   MGM, 1965
THE RUSSIANS ARE COMING, THE RUSSIANS ARE COMING
    United Artists, 1966
PENELOPE   MGM, 1966
OH DAD, POOR DAD, MAMA'S HUNG YOU IN THE CLOSET
    AND I'M FEELING SO SAD   Paramount, 1967
EIGHT ON THE LAM   United Artists, 1967
VIVA MAX!   Commonwealth United, 1969
THE FISH THAT SAVED PITTSBURGH   United Artists, 1979
MOON OVER PARADOR   Universal, 1988, U.S.-Brazilian

SHELLEY WINTERS
(Shirley Schrift)
b. August 18, 1922 - St. Louis, Missouri

WHAT A WOMAN!   Columbia, 1943
THE RACKET MAN   1944
NINE GIRLS   1944
TWO-MAN SUBMARINE   Columbia, 1944
KNICKERBOCKER HOLIDAY   1944
SHE'S A SOLDIER, TOO   Columbia, 1944
SAILOR'S HOLIDAY   1944
COVER GIRL   Columbia, 1944
TONIGHT AND EVERY NIGHT   1945
A THOUSAND AND ONE NIGHTS   Columbia, 1945
LIVING IN A BIG WAY   MGM, 1947
THE GANGSTER   1947
A DOUBLE LIFE   Universal, 1948
LARCENY   Universal, 1948
RED RIVER   United Artists, 1948
CRY OF THE CITY   20th Century-Fox, 1948
TAKE ONE FALSE STEP   Universal, 1949
THE GREAT GATSBY   Paramount, 1949
JOHNNY STOOL PIGEON   Universal, 1949
SOUTH SEA SINNER   Universal, 1950
WINCHESTER '73   Universal, 1950
EAST OF JAVA   1951

FRENCHIE   1951
HE RAN ALL THE WAY   United Artists, 1951
A PLACE IN THE SUN ★   Paramount, 1951
BEHAVE YOURSLEF   1951
THE RAGING TIDE   Universal, 1951
PHONE CALL FROM A STRANGER   20th Century-Fox, 1952
MEET DANNY WILSON   Universal, 1952
UNTAMED FRONTIER   Universal, 1952
MY MAN AND I   MGM, 1952
SASKATCHEWAN   Universal, 1954
EXECUTIVE SUITE   MGM, 1954
TENNESSEE CHAMP   1954
PLAYGIRL   Universal, 1954
CASH ON DELIVERY *TO DOROTHY A SON*   1954, British
MAMBO   Paramount, 1955, Italian-U.S.
I AM A CAMERA   1955, British
THE NIGHT OF THE HUNTER   United Artists, 1955
THE BIG KNIFE   United Artists, 1955
I DIED A THOUSAND TIMES   Warner Bros., 1955
THE TREASURE OF PANCHO VILLA   Universal, 1955
THE DIARY OF ANNE FRANK ○○   20th Century-Fox, 1959
ODDS AGAINST TOMORROW   United Artists, 1959
LET NO MAN WRITE MY EPITAPH   Columbia, 1960
THE YOUNG SAVAGES   United Artists, 1961
LOLITA   MGM, 1962, British
THE CHAPMAN REPORT   Warner Bros., 1962
THE BALCONY   Continental, 1963
WIVES AND LOVERS   Paramount, 1963
TIME OF INDIFFERENCE *GLI INDIFFERENTI*   1964, Italian-French
A HOUSE IS NOT A HOME   Embassy, 1964
THE GREATEST STORY EVER TOLD   United Artists, 1965
A PATCH OF BLUE ○○   MGM, 1965
ALFIE   Paramount, 1966, British
HARPER   Warner Bros., 1966
ENTER LAUGHING   Columbia, 1967
THE SCALPHUNTERS   United Artists, 1968
WILD IN THE STREETS   American International, 1968
BUONA SERA MRS. CAMPBELL   United Artists, 1969
THE MAD ROOM   Columbia, 1969
ARTHUR! ARTHUR!   1969
BLOODY MAMA   American International, 1970
HOW DO I LOVE THEE?   Cinerama Releasing Corporation, 1970
FLAP *THE LAST WARRIOR*   Warner Bros., 1970
WHAT'S THE MATTER WITH HELEN?   United Artists, 1971
WHO SLEW AUNTIE ROO?   American International, 1971, British
REVENGE! (TF)   Mark Carliner Productions, 1971
SOMETHING TO HIDE   1972, British
THE DEVIL'S DAUGHTER (TF)   Paramount TV, 1972
THE POSEIDON ADVENTURE ○   20th Century-Fox, 1972
BLUME IN LOVE   Warner Bros., 1973
CLEOPATRA JONES   Warner Bros., 1973
BIG ROSE (TF)   20th Century-Fox TV, 1974
POOR PRETTY EDDIE   1975
DIAMONDS   Avco Embassy, 1975, Israeli-U.S.-Swedish
THAT LUCKY TOUCH   Allied Artists, 1975, British-Italian-French
JOURNEY INTO FEAR   Stirling Gold, 1975, Canadian-British
NEXT STOP, GREENWICH VILLAGE   20th Century-Fox, 1976
THE TENANT *LE LOCATAIRE*   Paramount, 1976, French-U.S.
LA DAHLIA SCARLATTA   1976, Italian
MIMI BLUETTE   1976, Italian
UN BORGHESE PICCOLO PICCOLO   Cineriz, 1977, Italian
TENTACLES   1977, Italian
PETE'S DRAGON   Buena Vista, 1977
GRAN BOLLITO   Triangolo Film, 1977, Italian
THE THREE SISTERS   NTA, 1977
BLACK JOURNEY   1977
THE MAGICIAN OF LUBLIN   Cannon, 1979,
    Israeli-West German-U.S.
CITY ON FIRE   Avco Embassy, 1979, Canadian
KING OF THE GYPSIES   Paramount, 1979
REDNECK COUNTY RAPE   1979
THE VISITOR   1979
ELVIS (TF)   Dick Clark Productions, 1979
S.O.B.   Paramount, 1981
OVER THE BROOKLYN BRIDGE   MGM/UA/Cannon, 1983
DEJA VU   Cannon, 1984, British
THE DELTA FORCE   Cannon, 1986
AN UNREMARKABLE LIFE   Continental Film Group, 1989
STEPPING OUT   Paramount, 1991
THE PICKLE   Columbia, 1993
JURY DUTY   Sony Pictures, 1995

BILLY WIRTH
THE LOST BOYS   Warner Bros., 1987
WAR PARTY   Hemdale 1989
BODY SNATCHERS   Warner Bros., 1994
BOYS ON THE SIDE   Warner Bros., 1995
HARD EVIDENCE   1995

RAY WISE
ROBOCOP   Orion, 1987
THE TAKING OF FLIGHT 847: THE ULI DERICKSON STORY (TF)
   Columbia TV, 1988
RACE FOR GLORY   New Century/Vista, 1989
TWIN PEAKS: FIRE WALK WITH ME   New Line Cinema,
   1992, U.S.-French
BOB ROBERTS   Paramount/Miramax Films, 1992
THE CHASE   20th Century Fox, 1994

WILLIAM WISE
FAREWELL TO THE KING   Orion, 1989

JOSEPH WISEMAN
b. May 15, 1918 - Montreal, Canada

WITH THESE HANDS   1950
DETECTIVE STORY   Paramount, 1951
VIVA ZAPATA!   20th Century-Fox, 1952
LES MISÉRABLES   20th Century-Fox, 1952
THE SILVER CHALICE   Warner Bros., 1954
THE PRODIGAL   MGM, 1955
THE GARMENT JUNGLE   Columbia, 1957
THE UNFORGIVEN   United Artists, 1960
THE HAPPY THIEVES   United Artists, 1962
DR. NO   United Artists, 1962, British
BYE BYE BRAVERMAN   Warner Bros., 1968
THE NIGHT THEY RAIDED MINSKY'S   United Artists, 1968
THE COUNTERFEIT KILLER   1968
STILETTO   Avco Embassy, 1969
LAWMAN   United Artists, 1971
THE VALACHI PAPERS   VALACHI: I SEGRETI DI COSA NOSTRA
   Columbia, 1972, Italian-French
THE APPRENTICESHIP OF DUDDY KRAVITZ   Paramount,
   1974, Canadian
JOURNEY INTO FEAR   Stirling Gold, 1975, Canadian
THE BETSY   Allied Artists, 1978
BUCK ROGERS IN THE 25TH CENTURY   Universal, 1979
JAGUAR LIVES   American International, 1979
RAGE OF ANGELS (TF)   Furia-Oringer Productions/
   NBC Productions, 1983

MICHAEL WISEMAN
JUDGMENT NIGHT   Universal, 1993

JILL WISOFF
FEAR, ANXIETY AND DEPRESSION   Samuel Goldwyn
   Company, 1990

GUY WITCHER
JAMES AND THE GIANT PEACH   Buena Vista, 1995 (voice)

JOHN WITHERSPOON
Agent: William Morris Agency - Beverly Hills, 310/274-7451

RATBOY   Warner Bros., 1986
HOLLYWOOD SHUFFLE   Samuel Goldwyn Company, 1987

REESE WITHERSPOON
THE MAN IN THE MOON   MGM-Pathe, 1991
A FAR OFF PLACE   Buena Vista, 1993
S.F.W.   Gramercy Pictures, 1994
NO FEAR   Universal, 1995

ALICIA WITT
Agent: APA - Los Angeles, 310/273-0744

BODIES, REST & MOTION   Fine Line Features/
   New Line Cinema, 1993
MR. HOLLAND'S OPUS   Buena Vista, 1995

KAREN WITTER
HERO AND THE TERROR   Cannon, 1988

DAMIAN WOETZEL
GEORGE BALANCHINE'S THE NUTCRACKER
   Warner Bros., 1993

KELLY WOLF
STEPHEN KING'S GRAVEYARD SHIFT   Paramount, 1990

TRACI WOLFE
LETHAL WEAPON   Warner Bros., 1987
LETHAL WEAPON 2   Warner Bros., 1989

B.D. WONG
MYSTERY DATE   Orion, 1991
JURASSIC PARK   Universal, 1993
AND THE BAND PLAYED ON (CTF)   HBO Pictures/Spelling
   Entertainment, 1993

MEL WONG
THE RESCUE   Buena Vista, 1988

RUSSELL WONG
TAI-PAN   DEG, 1986
EAT A BOWL OF TEA   Columbia, 1989, U.S.-Hong Kong
CHINA CRY   The Penland Company, 1990

VICTOR WONG
BIG TROUBLE IN LITTLE CHINA   20th Century Fox, 1986
THE GOLDEN CHILD   Paramount, 1986
EAT A BOWL OF TEA   Columbia, 1989, U.S.-Hong Kong
FORBIDDEN NIGHTS (TF)   Tristine Rainer Productions/
   Warner Bros. TV, 1990
3 NINJAS KICK BACK   TriStar, 1994

ELIJAH WOOD
Agent: William Morris Agency - Beverly Hills, 310/274-7451

BACK TO THE FUTURE PART II   Universal, 1989
PARADISE   Buena Vista, 1991
RADIO FLYER   Columbia, 1992
FOREVER YOUNG   Warner Bros., 1992
THE ADVENTURES OF HUCK FINN   Buena Vista, 1993
THE GOOD SON   20th Century Fox, 1993
NORTH   Columbia, 1994
THE WAR   Universal, 1994
ZOO   New Line Cinema, 1995

JOHN WOOD
THE PURPLE ROSE OF CAIRO   Orion, 1985
SHADOWLANDS   Savoy Pictures, 1993, U.S.-British

TOM WOOD
THE FUGITIVE   Warner Bros., 1993

ALFRE WOODARD
b. November 2, 1953 - Tulsa, Oklahoma
Agent: ICM - Beverly Hills, 310/550-4000

REMEMBER MY NAME   Columbia/Lagoon Associates, 1978
HEALTH   20th Century-Fox, 1980
CROSS CREEK ✪   Universal/AFD, 1983
GO TELL IT ON THE MOUNTAIN (TF)   Learning in Focus, 1984
EXTREMITIES   Atlantic Releasing Corporation, 1986
THE CHILD SAVER (TF)   Michael Filerman Productions/NBC
   Productions, 1988

SCROOGED   Paramount, 1988
MISS FIRECRACKER   Corsair Pictures, 1989
GRAND CANYON   20th Century Fox, 1991
THE GUN IN BETTY LOU'S HANDBAG   Buena Vista, 1992
PASSION FISH   Miramax Films, 1992
RICH IN LOVE   MGM/UA, 1993
HEART AND SOULS   Universal, 1993
BOPHA!   Paramount, 1993
BLUE CHIPS   Paramount, 1994
CROOKLYN   Universal, 1994
HOW TO MAKE AN AMERICAN QUILT   Universal, 1995

BOKEEM WOODBINE
JASON'S LYRIC   1994

KAREN WOODLEY
THE SNAPPER   Miramax Films, 1993, British

JAMES WOODS
b. April 18, 1947 - Vernal, New Jersey
Agent: ICM - Beverly Hills, 310/550-4000

HICKEY AND BOGGS   United Artists, 1972
THE WAY WE WERE   Columbia, 1973
DISTANCE   1975
NIGHT MOVES   Warner Bros., 1975
ALEX AND THE GYPSY   20th Century-Fox, 1976
THE DISAPPEARANCE OF AIMEE (TF)
   Tomorrow Entertainment, 1976
THE CHOIRBOYS   Universal, 1977
HOLOCAUST (MS)   Titus Productions, 1978
THE ONION FIELD   Avco Embassy, 1979
THE BLACK MARBLE   Avco Embassy, 1980
EYEWITNESS   20th Century-Fox, 1981
FAST-WALKING   Pickman Films, 1982
SPLIT IMAGE   Orion, 1982
VIDEODROME   Universal, 1983, Canadian
AGAINST ALL ODDS   Columbia, 1984
ONCE UPON A TIME IN AMERICA   The Ladd Company/
   Warner Bros., 1984, U.S.-Italian-Canadian
STEPHEN KING'S CAT'S EYE   CAT'S EYE   MGM/UA, 1985
JOSHUA THEN AND NOW   20th Century Fox, 1985, Canadian
BADGE OF THE ASSASSIN (TF)   Blatt-Singer Productions/
   Columbia TV, 1985
SALVADOR ★   Hemdale, 1986
PROMISE (TF)   Garner-Duchow Productions/Warner Bros. TV, 1986
IN LOVE AND WAR (TF)   Carol Schreder Productions/
   Tisch-Avnet Productions, 1987
BEST SELLER   Orion, 1987
COP   Atlantic Releasing Corporation, 1988
THE BOOST   TriStar, 1988
TRUE BELIEVER   Columbia, 1989
MY NAME IS BILL W. (TF)   Garner-Duchow Productions, 1989
IMMEDIATE FAMILY   Columbia, 1989
THE HARD WAY   Universal, 1991
THE BOYS (TF)   William Link Productions/Papazian-Hirsch
   Productions, 1991
STRAIGHT TALK   Buena Vista, 1992
DIGGSTOWN   MGM-Pathe Entertainment, 1992
CHAPLIN   TriStar, 1992, U.S.-British
THE GETAWAY   Universal, 1994
NEXT DOOR (CTF)   Showtime, 1994
THE SPECIALIST   Warner Bros., 1994
CURSE OF THE STARVING CLASS   Trimark Pictures, 1994
STRANGER THINGS   Columbia, 1995
CASINO   Universal, 1995

KEVIN WOODS
THE LITTLE RASCALS   Universal, 1994

MICHAEL WOODS
LADY BEWARE   Scotti Brothers, 1987

CAROL WOODS-COLEMAN
STEPPING OUT   Paramount, 1991

JOHN WOODVINE
AN AMERICAN WEREWOLF IN LONDON   Universal, 1981

EDWARD WOODWARD
b. June 1, 1930 - Croyden, England

WHERE THERE'S A WILL   1954
BECKET   Paramount, 1964, British
THE FILE ON THE GOLDEN GOOSE   United Artists, 1969, British
SITTING TARGET   MGM, 1972, British
THE WICKER MAN   Warner Bros., 1973, British
YOUNG WINSTON   Columbia, 1973, British
CALLAN   Cinema International, 1974, British
STAND UP VIRGIN SOLDIERS   1977
BREAKER MORANT   New World/Quartet, 1980, Australian
WINSTON CHURCHILL: THE WILDERNESS YEARS (TF)
   Southern Pictures Productions, 1981, British
THE FINAL OPTION   WHO DARES WINS   MGM/UA, 1982, British
LOVE IS FOREVER (TF)   Michael Landon-Hall Bartlett Films/
   NBC-TV/20th Century-Fox TV, 1983
A CHRISTMAS CAROL (TF)   Entertainment Partners, Ltd.,
   1984, U.S.-British
KING DAVID   Paramount, 1985, U.S.-British
AGATHA CHRISTIE'S 'THE MAN IN THE BROWN SUIT' (TF)
   Alan Shayne Productions/Warner Bros. TV, 1989
MISTER JOHNSON   Avenue Pictures, 1991

JOANNE WOODWARD
b. February 27, 1930 - Thomasville, Georgia
Agent: ICM - Beverly Hills, 310/550-4000

COUNT THREE AND PRAY   Universal, 1955
A KISS BEFORE DYING   United Artists, 1956
THE THREE FACES OF EVE ★★   20th Century-Fox, 1957
NO DOWN PAYMENT   20th Century-Fox, 1957
THE LONG HOT SUMMER   MGM, 1958
RALLY ROUND THE FLAG, BOYS!   20th Century-Fox, 1958
THE SOUND AND THE FURY   20th Century-Fox, 1959
THE FUGITIVE KIND   United Artists, 1960
FROM THE TERRACE   20th Century-Fox, 1960
PARIS BLUES   United Artists, 1961
THE STRIPPER   20th Century-Fox, 1963
A NEW KIND OF LOVE   Paramount, 1963
SIGNPOST TO MURDER   MGM, 1965
A BIG HAND FOR THE LITTLE LADY   Warner Bros., 1966
A FINE MADNESS   Warner Bros., 1966
RACHEL, RACHEL ★   Warner Bros., 1968
WINNING   Universal, 1969
KING: A FILMED RECORD...MONTGOMERY TO MEMPHIS (FD)
   Maron Films Limited, 1970
WUSA   Paramount, 1970
THEY MIGHT BE GIANTS   Universal, 1971
THE EFFECT OF GAMMA RAYS ON MAN-IN-THE-MOON
   MARIGOLDS   20th Century-Fox, 1972
SUMMER WISHES, WINTER DREAMS ★   Columbia, 1973
THE DROWNING POOL   Warner Bros., 1975
SYBIL (TF)   Lorimar Productions, 1976
SEE HOW SHE RUNS (TF)   CLN Productions, 1978
THE END   United Artists, 1978
A CHRISTMAS TO REMEMBER (TF)   George Englund
   Productions, 1978
THE STREETS OF L.A. (TF)   George Englund Productions, 1979
THE SHADOW BOX (TF)   The Shadow Box Film Company, 1980
CRISIS AT CENTRAL HIGH (TF)   Time-Life Productions, 1981
HARRY AND SON   Orion, 1984
PASSIONS (TF)   Carson Production Group/Wizan TV
   Enterprises, 1984
DO YOU REMEMBER LOVE? (TF)   Dave Bell Productions, 1985
THE GLASS MENAGERIE   Cineplex Odeon, 1987
MR. AND MRS. BRIDGE ★   Miramax Films, 1990
BLIND SPOT (TF)   Signboard Hill Productions/
   RHI Entertainment, 1993
THE AGE OF INNOCENCE   Columbia, 1993 (voice)
PHILADELPHIA   TriStar, 1993
BREATHING LESSONS (TF)   Signboard Hill Productions, 1994

SUSAN WOOLDRIDGE
HOW TO GET AHEAD IN ADVERTISING   Warner Bros.,
   1989, British
CROSSING TO FREEDOM (TF)   Procter & Gamble Productions/
   Stan Margulies Productions/Granada TV, 1990, U.S.-British

SHEB WOOLEY
HOOSIERS   Orion, 1986

MICHAEL WOOLSON
Agent: Metropolitan Talent Agency - Los Angeles, 213/857-4500

MENENDEZ: A KILLING IN BEVERLY HILLS (MS)
   Zev Braun Pictures/TriStar Television, 1994

JAIMZ WOOLVETT
UNFORGIVEN   Warner Bros., 1992

TOM WOPAT
BURNING RAGE (TF)   Gilbert Cates Productions, 1984
CHRISTMAS COMES TO WILLOW CREEK (TF)   Blue Andre
   Productions/ITC Productions, 1987

JIMMY WORKMAN
b. October 4, 1980 - Fairfax, Virginia

THE ADDAMS FAMILY   Paramount, 1991
CHRISTMAS IN CONNECTICUT (CTF)   Guber-Peters
   Entertainment/Turner Network TV, 1992
ADDAMS FAMILY VALUES   Paramount, 1993

JO ANNE WORLEY
BEAUTY AND THE BEAST (AF)   Buena Vista, 1991 (voice)

MARY WORONOV
Agent: Stone Manners Talent Agency - Los Angeles, 213/654-7575

EATING RAOUL   20th Century Fox International Classics, 1982
A BUNNY'S TALE (TF)   Stan Margulies Company/
   ABC Circle Films, 1985
SCENES FROM THE CLASS STRUGGLE IN BEVERLY HILLS
   Cinecom, 1989
DICK TRACY   Buena Vista, 1990

IRENE WORTH
b. June 23, 1916 - Nebraska
Agent: ICM - Beverly Hills, 310/550-4000

ONE NIGHT WITH YOU   Universal, 1948, British
ANOTHER SHORE   Rank, 1948, British
SECRET PEOPLE   1951
ORDERS TO KILL   United Motion Picture Organization,
   1958, British
THE SCAPEGOAT   MGM, 1959, British
SEVEN SEAS TO CALAIS   *IL DOMINATORE DEI SETTE MARI*
   MGM, 1963, Italian
KING LEAR   Altura, 1969, British-Danish
NICHOLAS AND ALEXANDRA   Columbia, 1971, British
RICH KIDS   United Artistts, 1979
DEATHTRAP   Warner Bros., 1982
LOST IN YONKERS   Columbia, 1993

NICHOLAS WORTH
ACTION JACKSON   Lorimar, 1988

SUZANNE WOUK
WANTED DEAD OR ALIVE   New World, 1986

AMY WRIGHT
NOT A PRETTY PICTURE   Films Incorporated, 1976
GIRLFRIENDS   Warner Bros., 1978
THE DEER HUNTER   Universal, 1978
WISE BLOOD   New Line Cinema, 1979
BREAKING AWAY   20th Century-Fox, 1979

THE AMITYVILLE HORROR   American International, 1979
HEARTLAND   Levitt-Pickman, 1980
STARDUST MEMORIES   United Artists, 1980
INSIDE MOVES   AFD, 1980
OFF BEAT   Buena Vista, 1986
THE TELEPHONE   New World, 1988
CROSSING DELANCEY   Warner Bros., 1988
THE ACCIDENTAL TOURIST   Warner Bros., 1988
MISS FIRECRACKER   Corsair Pictures, 1989
DADDY'S DYIN'...WHO'S GOT THE WILL?   MGM/UA, 1990
LOVE HURTS   Vestron, 1990
TO DANCE WITH THE WHITE DOG (TF)   Signboard Hill
   Productions, 1993

BEN WRIGHT
THE SOUND OF MUSIC   20th Century-Fox, 1965
THE LITTLE MERMAID (AF)   Buena Vista, 1989 (voice)

JENNY WRIGHT
NEAR DARK   DEG, 1987
I, MADMAN   Trans World Entertainment, 1989
A SHOCK TO THE SYSTEM   Corsair Pictures, 1990
QUEEN'S LOGIC   New Line Cinema, 1991
STEPHEN KING'S THE LAWNMOWER MAN
   New Line Cinema, 1992

MICHAEL WRIGHT
STREAMERS   United Artists Classics, 1983
THE FIVE HEARTBEATS   20th Century Fox, 1991
SUGAR HILL   20th Century Fox, 1994

N'BUSHE WRIGHT
FRESH   Miramax Films, 1994

ROBIN WRIGHT
b. Dallas, Texas
Agent: CAA - Beverly Hills, 310/288-4545

THE PRINCESS BRIDE   20th Century Fox, 1987
STATE OF GRACE   Orion, 1990
DENIAL   *LOON*   Filmstar, 1991
THE PLAYBOYS   Samuel Goldwyn Company, 1992, Irish-British
TOYS   20th Century Fox, 1992
FORREST GUMP   Paramount, 1994
THE CROSSING GUARD   Miramax Films, 1994

SAMUEL E. WRIGHT
THE LITTLE MERMAID (AF)   Buena Vista, 1989 (voice)

STEVEN WRIGHT
b. December 6, 1955 - New York, New York

MEN OF RESPECT   Columbia, 1991
NATURAL BORN KILLERS   Warner Bros., 1994
THE SWAN PRINCESS (AF)   New Line Cinema, 1995 (voice)

TERESA WRIGHT
(Muriel Teresa Wright)
b. October 27, 1918 - New York, New York

THE LITTLE FOXES ✪   RKO Radio, 1941
MRS. MINIVER ✪✪   MGM, 1942
THE PRIDE OF THE YANKEES ★   RKO Radio, 1942
SHADOW OF A DOUBT   Universal, 1943
CASANOVA BROWN   RKO Radio, 1944
THE BEST YEARS OF OUR LIVES   RKO Radio, 1946
PURSUED   Warner Bros., 1947
THE IMPERFECT LADY   Paramount, 1947
THE TROUBLE WITH WOMEN   Paramount, 1947
ENCHANTMENT   RKO Radio, 1948
THE CAPTURE   RKO Radio, 1950
THE MEN   *BATTLE STRIPE*   Columbia, 1950
SOMETHING TO LIVE FOR   Paramount, 1952
CALIFORNIA CONQUEST   Columbia, 1952
THE STEEL TRAP   20th Century-Fox, 1952
THE ACTRESS   MGM, 1953

COUNT THE HOURS   RKO Radio, 1953
TRACK OF THE CAT   Warner Bros., 1954
THE SEARCH FOR BRIDEY MURPHY   Paramount, 1956
ESCAPADE IN JAPAN   Universal, 1957
THE RESTLESS YEARS   Universal, 1958
HAIL, HERO!   National General, 1969
THE HAPPY ENDING   United Artists, 1969
CRAWLSPACE (TF)   Titus Productions, 1971
THE ELEVATOR (TF)   Universal TV, 1974
FLOOD! (TF)   Irwin Allen Productions/20th Century-Fox TV, 1976
ROSELAND   Cinema Shares International, 1977
SOMEWHERE IN TIME   Universal, 1980

WHITTNI WRIGHT
I'LL DO ANYTHING   Columbia, 1994

VIVIAN WU
THE JOY LUCK CLUB   Buena Vista, 1993
HEAVEN AND EARTH   Warner Bros., 1993

ROBERT WUHL
GOOD M ORNING, VIETNAM   Buena Vista, 1987
BULL DURHAM   Orion, 1988
BATMAN   Warner Bros., 1989
BLAZE   Buena Vista, 1989
MISTRESS   Tribeca Films, 1992
MISSING PIECES   Orion, 1992
COBB   Warner Bros., 1994

JANE WYATT
b. August 12, 1911 - Campgaw, New Jersey

ONE MORE RIVER   Universal, 1934
GREAT EXPECTATIONS   Universal, 1934
WE'RE ONLY HUMAN   RKO Radio, 1936
THE LUCKIEST GIRL IN THE WORLD   Universal, 1936
LOST HORIZON   Columbia, 1937
THE GIRL FROM GOD'S COUNTRY   Republic, 1940
KISSES FOR BREAKFAST   Warner Bros., 1941
WEEKEND FOR THREE   RKO Radio, 1941
ARMY SURGEON   RKO Radio, 1942
THE NAVY COMES THROUGH   RKO Radio, 1942
THE KANSAN   United Artists, 1943
BUCKSKIN FRONTIER   United Artists, 1943
NONE BUT THE LONELY HEART   RKO Radio, 1944
THE BACHELOR'S DAUGHTERS   United Artists, 1946
BOOMERANG   20th Century-Fox, 1947
GENTLEMAN'S AGREEMENT   20th Century-Fox, 1947
PITFALL   United Artists, 1948
NO MINOR VICES   MGM, 1948
BAD BOY   Allied Artists, 1949
CANADIAN PACIFIC   20th Century-Fox, 1949
TASK FORCE   Warner Bros., 1949
HOUSE BY THE RIVER   Republic, 1950
OUR VERY OWN   RKO Radio, 1950
MY BLUE HEAVEN   20th Century-Fox, 1950
THE MAN WHO CHEATED HIMSELF   20th Century-Fox, 1950
CRIMINAL LAWYER   Columbia, 1951
INTERLUDE   Universal, 1957
NEVER TOO LATE   Warner Bros., 1965
TOM SAWYER (TF)   1973
TREASURE OF MATECUMBE   Buena Vista, 1976
STAR TREK IV: THE VOYAGE HOME   Paramount, 1986
AMITYVILLE: THE EVIL ESCAPES (TF)   Steve White Productions/
   Spectacor Films,

NOAH WYLE
Agent: UTA - Beverly Hills, 310/273-6700

CROOKED HEARTS   MGM-Pathe, 1991

JANE WYMAN
(Sarah Jane Fulks)
b. January 4, 1914 - St. Joseph, Missouri

KING OF BURLESQUE   20th Century-Fox, 1935
GOLD DIGGERS OF 1937   Warner Bros., 1936
MY MAN GODFREY   Universal, 1936
STAGE STRUCK   First National, 1936
SMART BLONDE   Warner Bros., 1937
THE KING AND THE CHORUS GIRL   Warner Bros., 1937
READY, WILLING AND ABLE   Warner Bros., 1937
SLIM   Warner Bros., 1937
THE SINGING MARINE   Warner Bros., 1937
PUBLIC WEDDING   Warner Bros., 1937
MR. DODD TAKES THE AIR   Warner Bros., 1937
THE SPY RING   Warner Bros., 1938
HE COULDN'T SAY NO   Warner Bros., 1938
WIDE OPEN FACES   Columbia, 1938
FOOLS FOR SCANDAL   Warner Bros., 1938
THE CROWD ROARS   MGM, 1938
BROTHER RAT   Warner Bros., 1938
TAIL SPIN   20th Century-Fox, 1939
PRIVATE DETECTIVE   Warner Bros., 1939
THE KID FROM KOKOMO   Warner Bros., 1939
TORCHY PLAYS WITH DYNAMITE   Warner Bros., 1939
KID NIGHTINGALE   Warner Bros., 1939
BROTHER RAT AND A BABY   Warner Bros., 1940
AN ANGEL FROM TEXAS   Warner Bros., 1940
FLIGHT ANGELS   Warner Bros., 1940
MY LOVE CAME BACK   Warner Bros., 1940
TUGBOAT ANNIE SAILS AGAIN   Warner Bros., 1940
GAMBLING ON THE HIGH SEAS   Warner Bros., 1940
HONEYMOON FOR THREE   Warner Bros., 1941
BAD MEN OF MISSOURI   Warner Bros., 1941
YOU'RE IN THE ARMY NOW   Warner Bros., 1941
THE BODY DISAPPEARS   Warner Bros., 1941
LARCENY, INC.,   Warner Bros., 1942
MY FAVORITE SPY   RKO Radio, 1942
FOOTLIGHT SERENADE   20th Century-Fox, 1942
PRINCESS O'ROURKE   Warner Bros., 1943
MAKE YOUR OWN BED   Warner Bros., 1944
CRIME BY NIGHT   Warner Bros., 1944
THE DOUGHGIRLS   Warner Bros., 1944
HOLLYWOOD CANTEEN   Warner Bros., 1944
THE LOST WEEKEND   Paramount, 1945
ONE MORE TOMORROW   Warner Bros., 1946
NIGHT AND DAY   Warner Bros., 1946
THE YEARLING ★   MGM, 1946
CHEYENNE *THE WYOMING KID*   Warner Bros., 1947
MAGIC TOWN   RKO Radio, 1947
JOHNNY BELINDA ★★   Warner Bros., 1948
A KISS IN THE DARK   Warner Bros., 1949
IT'S A GREAT FEELING   Warner Bros., 1949
THE LADY TAKES A SAILOR   Warner Bros., 1949
STAGE FRIGHT   Warner Bros., 1950
THE GLASS MENAGERIE   Warner Bros., 1950
THREE GUYS NAMED MIKE   MGM, 1951
HERE COMES THE GROOM   Paramount, 1951
THE BLUE VEIL ★   RKO Radio, 1951
STARLIFT   Warner Bros., 1951
THE STORY OF WILL ROGERS   Warner Bros., 1952
JUST FOR YOU   Paramount, 1952
LET'S DO IT AGAIN   Columbia, 1953
SO BIG   Warner Bros., 1953
MAGNIFICENT OBSESSION ★   Universal, 1954
LUCY GALLANT   Paramount, 1955
ALL THAT HEAVEN ALLOWS   Universal, 1956
MIRACLE IN THE RAIN   Warner Bros., 1956
HOLIDAY FOR LOVERS   20th Century-Fox, 1959
POLLYANNA   Buena Vista, 1960
BON VOYAGE!   Buena Vista, 1962
HOW TO COMMIT MARRIAGE   Cinerama Releasing
   Corporation, 1969
THE FAILING OF RAYMOND (TF)   Universal TV, 1971
THE INCREDIBLE JOURNEY OF DR. MEG LAUREL (TF)
   Columbia TV, 1979

Wy

FILM
ACTORS
GUIDE

F
I
L
M

A
C
T
O
R
S

GEORGE WYNER
FLETCH LIVES   Universal, 1989
FOR RICHER, FOR POORER *FATHER, SON AND THE MISTRESS* (CTF)   Citadel Entertainment Productions, 1992

AMANDA WYSS
POWWOW HIGHWAY   Warner Bros., 1989, U.S.-British
TO DIE FOR   Arrowhead Entertainment, 1988

NELSON XAVIER
AT PLAY IN THE FIELDS OF THE LORD   Universal, 1991

"WEIRD AL" YANKOVIC
b. October 23, 1959

THE NAKED GUN: FROM THE FILES OF POLICE SQUAD!
   Paramount, 1988
UHF   Orion, 1989
NAKED GUN 33 1/3: THE FINAL INSULT   Paramount, 1994

AMY YASBECK
PROBLEM CHILD   Universal, 1990
PROBLEM CHILD 2   Universal, 1991
ROBIN HOOD: MEN IN TIGHTS   20th Century Fox, 1993

DOUG YASUDA
"CROCODILE" DUNDEE II   Paramount, 1988
SEE NO EVIL, HEAR NO EVIL   TriStar, 1989
CRAZY PEOPLE   Paramount, 1990

PATTI YASUTAKE
THE WASH   Skouras Pictures, 1988

CASSIE YATES
FM   Universal, 1978
CONVOY   United Artists, 1978
ST. HELENS   Davis-Panzer Productions, 1981
UNFAITHFULLY YOURS   20th Century Fox, 1984
DETECTIVE IN THE HOUSE (TF)   Lorimar-Telepictures, 1985

DWIGHT YOAKAM
Agent: CAA - Beverly Hills, 310/288-4545

WAR PARTY   TriStar, 1989

MALIK YOBA
COOL RUNNINGS   Buena Vista, 1993

ERICA YOHN
JACK THE BEAR   20th Century Fox, 1992

JOHN J. YORK
THUNDERBOAT ROW (TF)   Stephen J. Cannell Productions, 1989

KATHLEEN YORK
Agent: Metropolitan Talent Agency - Los Angeles, 213/857-4500

THOMPSON'S LAST RUN (TF)   Cypress Point Productions, 1986
CHECKING OUT   Warner Bros., 1989
COLD FEET   Avenue Pictures, 1989
SISTER ISLAND   1995

MICHAEL YORK
b. March 27, 1942 - Fulmer, England

THE TAMING OF THE SHREW   Columbia, 1967, Italian-British
ACCIDENT   Cinema 5, 1967, British
SMASHING TIME   Paramount, 1967, British
THE STRANGE AFFAIR   Paramount, 1968, British
ROMEO AND JULIET   Paramount, 1968, Italian-British
THE GURU   20th Century-Fox, 1969, British-Indian
JUSTINE   20th Century-Fox, 1969
ALFRED THE GREAT   MGM, 1969, British
SOMETHING FOR EVERYONE   National General, 1970, British
LA POUDRE D'ESCAMPETTE   Columbia, 1971, French-Italian
TOUCH AND GO *LA ROUTE AU SOLEIL*   Libra, 1971, French
ZEPPELIN   Warner Bros., 1971, British
CABARET   Allied Artists, 1972
BROTHER SUN, SISTER MOON   Paramount, 1973, Italian-British
LOST HORIZON   Columbia, 1973
ENGLAND MADE ME   Cineglobe, 1973, British
THE THREE MUSKETEERS   20th Century-Fox, 1974, British
MURDER ON THE ORIENT EXPRESS   Paramount, 1974, British
THE FOUR MUSKETEERS   20th Century-Fox, 1975, British
GREAT EXPECTATIONS   Transcontinental Film Productions,
   1974, British
CONDUCT UNBECOMING   Allied Artists, 1975, British
LOGAN'S RUN   MGM/United Artists, 1976
SEVEN NIGHTS IN JAPAN   EMI, 1976, British-French
THE LAST REMAKE OF BEAU GESTE   Universal, 1977
THE ISLAND OF DR. MOREAU   American International, 1977
JESUS OF NAZARETH (MS)   Sir Lew Grade Productions/ITC,
   1978, British-Italian
FEDORA   United Artists, 1978, West German-French
THE RIDDLE OF THE SANDS   Satori, 1979, British
A MAN CALLED INTREPID   1979, British-Canadian
THE WHITE LIONS   Alan Landsburg Productions, 1979
FINAL ASSIGNMENT   Almi Cinema 5, 1980, Canadian
PHANTOM OF THE OPERA (TF)   Robert Halmi, Inc., 1983
THE MASTER OF BALLANTRAE (TF)   Larry White-Hugh Benson
   Productions/HTV/Columbia TV, 1984, U.S.-British
SUCCESS IS THE BEST REVENGE   Triumph/Columbia,
   1984, British
SPACE (MS)   Stonehenge Productions/Paramount TV, 1985
DAWN   Odessa Films, 1986, French
SWORD OF GIDEON (CTF)   Alliance Entertainment/Les Films
   Ariane/HBO Premiere Films/CTV/Telefilm Canada/Rogers
   Cablesystems/Radio-Canada, 1986, British-Canadian
THE FAR COUNTRY (MS)   Crawford Productions, 1987, Australian
JUDITH KRANTZ'S TILL WE MEET AGAIN *TILL WE MEET
   AGAIN* (MS)   Steve Krantz Productions/Yorkshire TV,
   1989, U.S.-British
THE LADY AND THE HIGHWAYMAN (TF)   The Grade Company/
   Gainsborough Pictures, 1989, British
THE RETURN OF THE MUSKETEERS   Universal, 1989
WIDE SARGASSO SEA   Fine Line Features/New Line Cinema,
   1993, British

SUSANNAH YORK
(Susannah Yolande Fletcher)
b. January 9, 1941 - London, England
Agent: Susan Smith & Associates - Beverly Hills, 213/852-4777

TUNES OF GLORY   Lopert, 1960, British
THERE WAS A CROOKED MAN   United Artists, 1960, British
LOSS OF INNOCENCE *THE GREENGAGE SUMMER*
   Columbia, 1961, British
FREUD   Universal, 1962

384

TOM JONES   Lopert, 1963, British
THE SEVENTH DAWN   United Artists, 1964, U.S.-British
SCENE NUN, TAKE ONE   1964, British
SCRUGGS   1964, British
SANDS OF THE KALAHARI   Paramount, 1965, British
KALEIDOSCOPE   Warner Bros., 1966, British
A GAME CALLED SCRUGGS   1966, British
A MAN FOR ALL SEASONS   Columbia, 1966, British
SEBASTIAN   Paramount, 1968, British
DUFFY   Columbia, 1968, British
THE KILLING OF SISTER GEORGE   Cinerama Releasing
    Corporation, 1968
LOCK UP YOUR DAUGHTERS   1969, British
OH! WHAT A LOVELY WAR   Paramount, 1969, British
BATTLE OF BRITAIN   United Artists, 1969, British
THEY SHOOT HORSES, DON'T THEY? ✪   Cinerama Releasing
    Corporation, 1969
BROTHERLY LOVE   COUNTRY DANCE   MGM, 1969, British
JANE EYRE (TF)   Omnibus Productions/Sagittarius Productions,
    1970, British-U.S.
HAPPY BIRTHDAY, WANDA JUNE   Columbia, 1971
X Y & ZEE   ZEE & CO.   Columbia, 1972, British
IMAGES   Columbia, 1972, U.S.-British
GOLD   Allied Artists, 1974, British
THE MAIDS   American Film Theatre, 1975, British-Canadian
CONDUCT UNBECOMING   Allied Artists, 1975, British
THAT LUCKY TOUCH   Allied Artists, 1975, British
SKY RIDERS   20th Century-Fox, 1976
ELIZA FRASER   1976, Australian
SUPERMAN   Warner Bros., 1978, U.S.-British
THE SILENT PARTNER   EMC Film/Aurora, 1978, Canadian
THE SHOUT   Films, Inc., 1979, British
THE GOLDEN GATE MURDERS (TF)   Universal TV, 1979
THE RIDDLE OF THE SANDS   Satori, 1979, British
FALLING IN LOVE AGAIN   IN LOVE   International Picture Show
    Company, 1980
THE AWAKENING   Orion/Warner Bros., 1980
LOOPHOLE   MGM/United Artists, 1980, British
SUPERMAN II   Warner Bros., 1981, U.S.-British
YELLOWBEARD   Orion, 1983, British
A CHRISTMAS CAROL (TF)   Entertainment Partners, Ltd.,
    1984, U.S.-British
PRETTYKILL   Spectrafilm, 1987, Canadian
SUPERMAN IV: THE QUEST FOR PEACE   Warner Bros.,
    1987 (voice)
A SUMMER STORY   Atlantic Releasing Corporation, 1988, British

TINA YOTHERS

SHOOT THE MOON   MGM/United Artists, 1982
FAMILY TIES VACATION (TF)   Paramount TV/Ubu Productions/
    NBC Entertainment, 1985
CRASH COURSE (TF)   Fries Entertainment, 1988
THE LAKER GIRLS (TF)   Viacom Productions/The Finnegan-Pinchuk
    Company/Valente-Hamilton Productions, 1990

ALAN YOUNG

(Angus Young)
b. November 19, 1919 - North Shields, England

MARGIE   20th Century-Fox, 1946
CHICKEN EVERY SUNDAY   20th Century-Fox, 1948
MR. BELVEDERE GOES TO COLLEGE   20th Century-Fox, 1949
AARON SLICK FROM PUNKIN CRICK   1952
ANDROCLES AND THE LION   RKO Radio, 1953
GENTLEMEN MARRY BRUNETTES   1955
tom thumb   MGM, 1958
THE TIME MACHINE   MGM, 1960, British
BAKER'S HAWK   Doty-Dayton, 1976
THE CAT FROM OUTER SPACE   Buena Vista, 1978
DUCK TALES THE MOVIE: THE SECRET OF THE LOST LAMP (AF)
    Buena Vista, 1990 (voice)
BEVERLY HILLS COPS III   Paramount, 1994

BRUCE A. YOUNG

THREE ON A MATCH (TF)   Belisarius Productions/TriStar TV, 1987
BLINK   New Line Cinema, 1994

BURT YOUNG

b. April 30, 1940 - New York, New York

THE GAMBLER   Paramount, 1974
CHINATOWN   Paramount, 1974
THE KILLER ELITE   United Artists, 1975
ROCKY ✪   United Artists, 1976
THE CHOIRBOYS   Universal, 1977
TWILIGHT'S LAST GLEAMING   Allied Artists, 1977,
    U.S.-West German
CONVOY   United Artists, 1978
ROCKY II   United Artists, 1979
MURDER CAN HURT YOU (TF)   Aaron Spelling Productions, 1980
...ALL THE MARBLES   MGM/United Artists, 1981
BLOOD BEACH   Jerry Gross Organization, 1981
AMITYVILLE II: THE POSSESSION   Orion, 1982
LOOKIN' TO GET OUT   Paramount, 1982
ROCKY III   MGM/UA, 1982
ONCE UPON A TIME IN AMERICA   The Ladd Company/
    Warner Bros., 1984, U.S.-Italian-Canadian
A SUMMER TO REMEMBER (TF)   Interplanetary Productions, 1985
ROCKY IV   MGM/UA, 1985
BACK TO SCHOOL   Orion, 1986
BEVERLY HILLS BRATS   Taurus Entertainment, 1989
LAST EXIT TO BROOKLYN   Cinecom, 1989, West German-U.S.
BETSY'S WEDDING   Buena Vista, 1990
DIVING IN   Skouras Pictures, 1990
ROCKY V   MGM/UA, 1990
BRIGHT ANGEL   Hemdale, 1991

CEDRIC YOUNG

BACKDRAFT   Universal, 1991

CHRIS YOUNG

THE GREAT OUTDOORS   Universal, 1988
BOOK OF LOVE   New Line Cinema, 1991
PCU   20th Century Fox, 1994

KAREN YOUNG

ALMOST YOU   TLC Films/20th Century Fox, 1984
THE HIGH PRICE OF PASSION (TF)   Edgar J. Scherick
    Productions, 1986
TORCH SONG TRILOGY   New Line Cinema, 1988
CRIMINAL LAW   Hemdale, 1989
NIGHT GAME   Trans World Entertainment, 1989

KEONE YOUNG

NORTH   Columbia, 1994

NEIL YOUNG

b. November 12, 1945 - Toronto, Ontario

MADE IN HEAVEN   Lorimar, 1987
LOVE AT LARGE   Orion, 1990

NORMA YOUNG

WHEN DREAMS COME TRUE (TF)   I & C Productions, 1985

PAUL YOUNG

THE GIRL IN THE PICTURE   Samuel Goldwyn Company,
    1986, British

PAULA YOUNG

GOODFELLAS   Warner Bros., 1990

RICHARD YOUNG

AN INNOCENT MAN   Buena Vista, 1989

RUDY YOUNG

ALAMO BAY   TriStar, 1985

SEAN YOUNG
JANE AUSTEN IN MANHATTAN   Contemporary, 1980
STRIPES   Columbia, 1981
BLADE RUNNER   The Ladd Company/Warner Bros., 1982
YOUNG DOCTORS IN LOVE   20th Century-Fox, 1982
DUNE   Universal, 1984
BABY—SECRET OF THE LOST LEGEND   Buena Vista, 1985
BLOOD AND ORCHIDS (MS)   Lorimar Productions, 1986
NO WAY OUT   Orion, 1987
WALL STREET   20th Century Fox, 1987
THE BOOST   TriStar, 1988
COUSINS   Paramount, 1989
FIRE BIRDS   Buena Vista, 1990
A KISS BEFORE DYING   Universal, 1991
ONCE UPON A CRIME   MGM-Pathe, 1992, U.S.-Italian
LOVE CRIMES   Millimeter Films, 1992
FATAL INSTINCT   MGM/UA, 1993
ACE VENTURA: PET DETECTIVE   Warner Bros., 1994
WITNESS TO THE EXECUTION (TF)   NBC, 1994
EVEN COWGIRLS GET THE BLUES   Fine Line Features/
   New Line Cinema, 1994
BLUE ICE (CTF)   HBO, 1994
DR. JEKYLL AND MS. HYDE   Savoy Pictures, 1995

WILLIAM ALLEN YOUNG
OUTRAGE! (TF)   Irwin Allen Productions/Columbia TV, 1986
JOHNNIE MAE GIBSON: FBI (TF)   Fool's Cap Productions, 1986

JACK YOUNGBLOOD
C.A.T. SQUAD (TF)   NBC Productions, 1986
C.A.T. SQUAD: PYTHON WOLF (TF)   NBC Productions, 1988

BARRIE YOUNGFELLOW
THE LADY FROM YESTERDAY (TF)   Barry Weitz Films/
   Comworld Productions, 1985

HENNY YOUNGMAN
b. March 16, 1906 - Liverpool, England

GOODFELLAS   Warner Bros., 1990

CLINT B. YOUNGREEN
WHITE FANG   Buena Vista, 1991

GAIL YOUNGS
THE LAST DAYS OF FRANK AND JESSE JAMES (TF)
   Joseph Cates Productions, 1986
BELIZAIRE THE CAJUN   Skouras Pictures, 1986

JIM YOUNGS
FOOTLOOSE   Paramount, 1984

MARION YUE
THE WASH   Skouras Pictures, 1988

HARRIS YULIN
DOC   United Artists, 1971
THE MIDNIGHT MAN   1974
NIGHT MOVES   Warner Bros., 1975
ST. IVES   Warner Bros., 1976
THE LAST RIDE OF THE DALTON GANG (TF)   NBC Productions/
   Dan Curtis Productions, 1979
STEEL   LOOK DOWN AND DIE/MEN OF STEEL
   World Northal, 1980
SCARFACE   Universal, 1983
THE BELIEVERS   Orion, 1987
ANOTHER WOMAN   Orion, 1988
GHOSTBUSTERS II   Columbia, 1989
DAUGHTER OF THE STREETS (TF)   Adam Productions/
   20th Century Fox TV, 1990
CLEAR AND PRESENT DANGER   Paramount, 1994
STUART SMALLEY   Paramount, 1995

TARIQ YUNIS
THE DECEIVERS   Cinecom, 1988

Z

WILLIAM ZABKA
BACK TO SCHOOL   Orion, 1986
A TIGER'S TALE   Atlantic Releasing Corporation, 1987

GRACE ZABRISKIE
THE BURNING BED (TF)   Tisch-Avnet Productions, 1984
THE BIG EASY   Columbia, 1987
THE RYAN WHITE STORY (TF)   The Landsburg Company, 1989
DRUGSTORE COWBOY   Avenue Pictures, 1989
CHILD'S PLAY 2   Universal, 1990
WILD AT HEART   Samuel Goldwyn Company, 1990
AMBITION   Miramax Films, 1991
MY OWN PRIVATE IDAHO   Fine Line Features/
   New Line Cinema, 1991
COBB   Warner Bros., 1994
DROP ZONE   Paramount, 1994

PIA ZADORA
BUTTERFLY   Analysis, 1981, U.S.-Canadian
FAKE-OUT   Analysis, 1982
THE LONELY LADY   Universal, 1983
HAIRSPRAY   New Line Cinema, 1988
NAKED GUN 33 1/3: THE FINAL INSULT   Paramount, 1994

STEVE ZAHN
REALITY BITES   Universal, 1994

ROXANA ZAL
TESTAMENT   Paramount, 1983
SOMETHING ABOUT AMELIA (TF)   Leonard Goldberg
   Productions, 1984
RIVER'S EDGE   Hemdale, 1987
EVERYBODY'S BABY: THE RESCUE OF JESSICA McCLURE (TF)
   Dick Berg-Stonehenge Productions/The Campbell Soup Company/
   Interscope Productions, 1989
UNDER THE BOARDWALK   New World, 1989
DAUGHTER OF THE STREETS (TF)   Adam Productions/
   20th Century Fox TV, 1990

EDDIE ZAMMIT
LONG TIME GONE (TF)   Picturemaker Productions/
   ABC Circle Films, 1986

DEL ZAMORA
ROBOCOP   Orion, 1987

BILLY ZANE
Agent: CAA - Beverly Hills, 310/288-4545

BACK TO THE FUTURE   Universal, 1985
CRITTERS   New Line Cinema, 1986
DEAD CALM   Warner Bros., 1989, Australian
THE CASE OF THE HILLSIDE STRANGLER (TF)
   Kenwood Productions/Fries Entertainment, 1989
BACK TO THE FUTURE PART II   Universal, 1989
MEMPHIS BELLE   Warner Bros., 1990
BLOOD AND CONCRETE   I.R.S. Releasing, 1991
ORLANDO   Sony Pictures Classics, 1992,
   British-Russian-Italian-French-Dutch
SNIPER   TriStar, 1993
TOMBSTONE   Buena Vista, 1993
ONLY YOU   TriStar, 1994
DEMON KNIGHT   Universal, 1995
THE PHANTOM   Paramount, 1995

LISA ZANE
Agent: William Morris Agency - Beverly Hills, 310/274-7451

GROSS ANATOMY   Buena Vista, 1989
BAD INFLUENCE   Triumph Releasing Corporation, 1990
FREDDY'S DEAD: THE FINAL NIGHTMARE
   New Line Cinema, 1991

LORA ZANE
LIVE NUDE GIRLS   Republic Pictures, 1995

CARMEN ZAPATA
BOULEVARD NIGHTS   Warner Bros., 1979
BROKEN ANGEL (TF)   The Stan Margulies Company/
   MGM-UA TV, 1988

DWEEZIL ZAPPA
b. September 5, 1969

PRETTY IN PINK   Paramount, 1986

MOON ZAPPA
NIGHTMARES   Universal, 1983
THE BOYS NEXT DOOR   New World, 1985
PTERODACTYL WOMAN FROM BEVERLY HILLS
   Experimental Pictures, 1994

MICHAEL ZASLOW
YOU LIGHT UP MY LIFE   Columbia, 1977
SEVEN MINUTES IN HEAVEN   Warner Bros., 1986

RENEE ZELLWEGER
EMPIRE   Warner Bros., 1995

MICHAEL ZELNIKER
NAKED LUNCH   20th Century Fox, 1991

JACKLYN ZEMAN
Agent: Stone Manners Talent Agency - Los Angeles, 213/654-7575

NATIONAL LAMPOON'S CLASS REUNION
   20th Century-Fox, 1982
YOUNG DOCTORS IN LOVE   20th Century-Fox, 1982
JURY DUTY: THE COMEDY (TF)   Steve White Productions/
   Spectator Films, 1990

ANTHONY ZERBE
b. May 20, 1936 - Long Beach, California
Agent: Susan Smith & Associates - Beverly Hills, 213/852-4777

WILL PENNY   Paramount, 1968
THE LIBERATION OF L.B. JONES   Columbia, 1970
THE OMEGA MAN   Warner Bros., 1971
THE LIFE AND TIMES OF JUDGE ROY BEAN
   National General, 1972
THE LAUGHING POLICEMAN   20th Century-Fox, 1973
ROOSTER COGBURN   Universal, 1975
FAREWELL, MY LOVELY   Avco Embassy, 1975, British
THE TURNING POINT   20th Century-Fox, 1977
WHO'LL STOP THE RAIN   DOG SOLDIERS   United Artists, 1978
ATTICA (TF)   ABC Circle Films, 1980
THE FIRST DEADLY SIN   Filmways, 1980
THE DEAD ZONE   Paramount, 1983, Canadian
THE RETURN OF THE MAN FROM U.N.C.L.E. (TF)   Michael Sloan
   Productions/Viacom Productions, 1983
NORTH AND SOUTH (MS)   Wolper Productions/Warner
   Bros. TV, 1985
OPPOSING FORCE   HELL CAMP   Orion, 1986
ONE POLICE PLAZA (TF)   CBS Entertainment, 1986
INDEPENDENCE (TF)   Sunn Classic Pictures, 1987
PRIVATE INVESTIGATIONS   MGM/UA, 1987
RICHEST MAN IN THE WORLD: THE ARISTOTLE ONASSIS
   STORY (MS)   The Konigsberg-Sanitsky Company, 1988
SEE NO EVIL, HEAR NO EVIL   TriStar, 1989
LICENCE TO KILL   MGM/UA, 1989, British

CHIP ZIEN
GRACE QUIGLEY   THE ULTIMATE SOLUTION OF GRACE
   QUIGLEY   Cannon, 1985
HOWARD THE DUCK   Universal, 1986
MRS. PARKER AND THE VICIOUS CIRCLE   Fine Line Features/
   New Line Cinema, 1994

MADELINE ZIMA
THE HAND THAT ROCKS THE CRADLE   Buena Vista, 1992
MR. NANNY   New Line Cinema, 1993

EFREM ZIMBALIST, JR.
b. November 30, 1923 - New York, New York

HOUSE OF STRANGERS   20th Century-Fox, 1949
BAND OF ANGELS   Warner Bros., 1957
BOMBERS B-52   Warner Bros., 1957
THE DEEP SIX   Warner Bros., 1958
TOO MUCH, TOO SOON   1958
HOME BEFORE DARK   Warner Bros., 1958
THE CROWDED SKY   Warner Bros., 1960
A FEVER IN THE BLOOD   Warner Bros., 1961
BY LOVE POSSESSED   United Artists, 1961
THE CHAPMAN REPORT   Warner Bros., 1962
HARLOW (TF)   1965
THE REWARD   20th Century-Fox, 1965
WAIT UNTIL DARK   Warner Bros., 1967
AIRPORT 1975   Universal, 1974
WHO IS THE BLACK DAHLIA? (TF)   Douglas S. Cramer
   Productions, 1975
A FAMILY UPSIDE DOWN (TF)   Ross Hunter-Jacques Mapes Film/
   Paramount TV, 1978
TERROR OUT OF THE SKY   Alan Landsburg Productions, 1978
HOT SHOTS!   20th Century Fox, 1991
BATMAN: MASK OF THE PHANTASM (AF)   Warner Bros.,
   1993 (voice)

STEPHANIE ZIMBALIST
b. October 8, 1956
Agent: William Morris Agency - Beverly Hills, 310/274-7451

THE MAGIC OF LASSIE   International Picture Show, 1978
THE AWAKENING   Orion/Warner Bros., 1980
THE BABYSITTER (TF)   Moonlight Productions/Filmways, 1980
LOVE ON THE RUN (TF)   NBC Productions, 1985
A LETTER TO THREE WIVES (TF)   Michael Filerman Productions/
   20th Century Fox TV, 1985
REMINGTON STEELE: THE STEELE THAT WOULDN'T DIE (TF)
   MTM Productions, 1987
CELEBRATION FAMILY (TF)   Frank von Zerneck Films, 1987
AGATHA CHRISTIE'S 'THE MAN IN THE BROWN SUIT' (TF)
   Alan Shayne Productions/Warner Bros. TV, 1989
PERSONALS (CTF)   Sharmhill Productions/Wilshire Court
   Productions, 1990, Canadian-U.S.
CAROLINE? (TF)   Barry & Enright Productions, 1990
INCIDENT IN A SMALL TOWN (TF)   RHI Entertainment, 1994

JOEY ZIMMERMAN
MOTHER'S BOYS   Dimension/Miramax Films, 1994

HANNS ZISCHLER
THE BERLIN AFFAIR   Cannon, 1985, Italian-West German

DAN ZISKIE
ADVENTURES IN BABYSITTING   Buena Vista, 1987

ADRIAN ZMED
THE FINAL TERROR   Comworld, 1981
GREASE 2   Paramount, 1982
BACHELOR PARTY   20th Century Fox, 1984
VICTIMS FOR VICTIMS - THE THERESA SALDANA STORY (TF)
   Daniel L. Paulson-Loehr Spivey Productions/Orion TV, 1984

RICHARD ZOBEL
PARKER KANE (TF)   Parker Kane Productions/Silver Pictures TV/
    Orion TV, 1990

LOUIS ZORICH
DEATH OF A SALESMAN (TF)   Roxbury & Punch Productions, 1985
BLOODHOUNDS OF BROADWAY   Columbia, 1989

CHARLOTTE ZUCKER
AIRPLANE!   Paramount, 1980
THE NAKED GUN: FROM THE FILES OF POLICE SQUAD!
    Paramount, 1988

ALEX ZUCKERMAN
Agent: Triton Agency - Century City,

ME AND THE KID   Orion, 1993
BLANK CHECK   Buena Vista, 1994

JOSHUA ZUEHLKE
AMAZING GRACE AND CHUCK   TriStar, 1987

DAPHNE ZUNIGA
Agent: UTA - Beverly Hills, 310/273-6700

THE SURE THING   Embassy, 1985
STONE PILLOW (TF)   Schaefer-Karpf Productions/Gaylord
    Productions, 1985
MODERN GIRLS   Atlantic Releasing Corporation, 1986
SPACEBALLS   MGM/UA, 1987
LAST RITES   MGM/UA, 1988
THE FLY II   20th Century Fox, 1989
GROSS ANATOMY   Buena Vista, 1989
STAYING TOGETHER   Hemdale, 1989

MICHAEL ZWIENER
LITTLE GIANTS   Warner Bros., 1994

DARRELL ZWERLING
CHINATOWN   Paramount, 1974
DOC SAVAGE, THE MAN OF BRONZE   Warner Bros., 1975
GREASE   Paramount, 1978

★ ★ ★

INDEX BY FILM TITLE

INDEX OF FILM TITLES

NOTE: This is not a list of every film ever made or every cast member, only those listed in this directory.

† after an actor's name denotes deceased and only appear in the Index of Film Titles.

★★ = Academy Award Win for Best Performance by an Actor or Actress in a Leading Role
★ = Academy Award Nomination for Best Performance by an Actor or Actress in a Leading Role
◎◎ = Academy Award Win for Best Performance by an Actor or Actress in a Supporting Role
◎ = Academy Award Nomination for Best Performance by an Actor or Actress in a Supporting Role

$ .... GOLDIE HAWN	1941 .... DAN AYKROYD	40 CARATS .... GENE KELLY
$ .... ROBERT WEBBER	1941 .... JOHN BELUSHI†	40 CARATS .... LIV ULLMANN
$ .... WARREN BEATTY	1941 .... JOHN CANDY†	40 CARATS .... NANCY WALKER†
10 .... BO DEREK	1941 .... LORRAINE GARY	40 CARATS .... ROSEMARY MURPHY
10 .... BRIAN DENNEHY	1941 .... MICKEY ROURKE	40 GRADA SOTTO
10 .... DEE WALLACE STONE	1941 .... NANCY ALLEN	LE LENZUOLA .... URSULA ANDRESS
10 .... DON CALFA	1941 .... NED BEATTY	40 POUNDS OF TROUBLE .... STUBBY KAYE
10 .... DOUG SHEEHAN	1941 .... PENNY MARSHALL	48 HOURS .... ANNETTE O'TOOLE
10 .... DUDLEY MOORE	1941 .... PERRY LANG	48 HOURS .... FRANK McRAE
10 .... JAMES NOBLE	1941 .... ROBERT STACK	48 HRS. .... DENISE CROSBY
10 .... JULIA JENNINGS	1941 .... TREAT WILLIAMS	48 HRS. .... EDDIE MURPHY
10 .... JULIE ANDREWS	1969 .... BRUCE DERN	48 HRS. .... NICK NOLTE
10 .... MAX SHOWALTER	1969 .... JOANNA CASSIDY	48 HRS .... PETER JASON
10 .... ROBERT WEBBER	1969 .... KIEFER SUTHERLAND	48-HOUR MILE, THE (TF) .... CARRIE SNODGRESS
10 RILLINGTON PLACE .... JOHN HURT	1969 .... MARIETTE HARTLEY	49TH MAN, THE .... JOHN IRELAND
10 RILLINGTON PLACE .... PAT HEYWOOD	1969 .... ROBERT DOWNEY JR.	5 CARD STUD .... ROBERT MITCHUM
10 TO MIDNIGHT .... CHARLES BRONSON	1969 .... WINONA RYDER	500 POUND JERK, THE (TF) .... ALEXIS KARRAS
10 TO MIDNIGHT .... LISA EILBACHER	1984 .... DONALD PLEASENCE	500 POUND JERK, THE (TF) .... HOPE LANGE
10 TO MIDNIGHT .... WILFORD BRIMLEY	1984 .... JOHN HURT	52 PICK-UP .... ANN-MARGRET
100 RIFLES .... BURT REYNOLDS	1984 .... JOHN VERNON	52 PICK-UP .... CLARENCE WILLIAMS III
100 RIFLES .... DAN O'HERLIHY	200 MOTELS .... THEODORE BIKEL	52 PICK-UP .... DOUG McCLURE
100 RIFLES .... FERNANDO LAMAS†	20,000 LEAGES UNDER THE SEA .... KIRK DOUGLAS	52 PICK-UP .... JOHN GLOVER
100 RIFLES .... JIM BROWN	20,000 YEARS IN SING SING .... BETTE DAVIS†	52 PICK-UP .... KELLY PRESTON
100 RIFLES .... RAQUEL WELCH	2001: A SPACE ODYSSEY .... KEIR DULLEA	52 PICK-UP .... LONNY CHAPMAN
$1,000 DOLLARS A TOUCHDOWN .... MARTHA RAYE†	2010 .... HELEN MIRREN	52 PICK-UP .... ROBERT TREBOR
$1,000,000 DUCK, THE .... SANDY DUNCAN	2010 .... JAMES McEACHIN	52 PICK-UP .... ROY SCHEIDER
$1,000,000 DUCK, THE .... TONY ROBERTS	2010 .... JOHN LITHGOW	52 PICK-UP .... VANITY
$1,000,000 DUCK, THE .... DEAN JONES	2010 .... ROY SCHEIDER	55 DAYS AT PEKING .... AVA GARDNER†
$1,000,000 DUCK, THE ....JACK KRUSCHEN	23 PACES TO BAKER STREET .... VAN JOHNSON	55 DAYS AT PEKING .... CHARLTON HESTON
101 DALMATIONS (AF) .... J. PAT O'MALLEY†	23 PACES TO BAKER STREET .... VERA MILES	55 DAYS AT PEKING .... JOHN IRELAND
10TH VICTIM, THE .... URSULA ANDRESS	25TH HOUR, THE .... ANTHONY QUINN	633 SQUADRON .... CLIFF ROBERTSON
11 HARROWHOUSE .... CANDICE BERGEN	29TH STREET .... ADAM LaVORGNA	7 MORTS SUR
11 HARROWHOUSE .... CHARLES GRODIN	29TH STREET .... ANTHONY LaPAGLIA	ORDONNANCE .... GERARD DEPARDIEU
11 HARROWHOUSE .... JOHN GIELGUD	29TH STREET .... DANNY AIELLO	7 WOMEN .... ANNE BANCROFT
11 HARROWHOUSE .... PETER VAUGHN	29TH STREET .... GLORIA MANN	7 WOMEN .... EDDIE ALBERT
12 ANGRY MEN .... HENRY FONDA†	29TH STREET .... LAINIE KAZAN	79 PARK AVENUE (MS) .... LESLEY ANN WARREN
12 O'CLOCK HIGH ◎◎ .... DEAN JAGGER†	29TH STREET .... RICHARD TACCHINO	8 1/2 .... ANOUK AIMEE
13 MOST BEAUTIFUL WOMEN .... SALLY KIRKLAND	29TH STREET .... RICK AIELLO	8 1/2 .... MARCELLO MASTROIANNI
13 RUE MADELEINE .... E. G. MARSHALL	29TH STREET .... ROBERT FORSTER	8 MILLION WAYS TO DIE .... ALEXANDRA PAUL
13 RUE MADELEINE .... KARL MALDEN	3 NINJAS KICK BACK..................... DUSTIN NGUYEN	8 MILLION WAYS TO DIE .... ANDY GARCIA
13 RUE MADELEINE .... RED BUTTONS	3 NINJAS KICK BACK..................... EVAN BONIFANT	8 MILLION WAYS TO DIE .... JEFF BRIDGES
13 WEST STREET .... ROD STEIGER	3 NINJAS KICK BACK..............MAX ELLIOTT SLADE	8 MILLION WAYS TO DIE .... RANDY BROOKS
14 HOURS .... JOYCE VAN PATTEN	3 NINJAS KICK BACK..................... SAB SHIMONO	8 MILLION WAYS TO DIE .... ROSANNA ARQUETTE
1492: CONQUEST	3 NINJAS KICK BACK..................... SEAN FOX	8 SECONDS .... CARRIE SNODGRESS
OF PARADISE .... ARMAND ASSANTE	3 NINJAS KICK BACK..................... VICTOR WONG	8 SECONDS .... CYNTHIA GEARY
1492: CONQUEST	3 WOMEN .... SHELLEY DUVALL	8 SECONDS .... JAMES REBHORN
OF PARADISE .... GERARD DEPARDIEU	3 WOMEN .... SISSY SPACEK	8 SECONDS .... LUKE PERRY
1492: CONQUEST	30 IS A DANGEROUS	8 SECONDS .... RONNIE CLAIRE EDWARDS
OF PARADISE .... SIGOURNEY WEAVER	AGE, CYNTHIA .... DUDLEY MOORE	8 SECONDS .... STEPHEN BALDWIN
16 FATHOMS DEEP .... LLOYD BRIDGES	30 SECONDS OVER TOKYO .... ALAN NAPIER†	80 STEPS TO JONAH .... R.G. ARMSTRONG
1776 .... BLYTHE DANNER	30 WISHES .... MICHAEL J. FOX	80 STEPS TO JONAH .... WAYNE NEWTON
1776 .... HOWARD CAINE†	300 SPARTANS, THE .... DIANE BAKER	80,000 SUSPECTS .... CLAIRE BLOOM
1776 .... HOWARD DA SILVA†	300 YEAR WEEKEND, THE .... WILLIAM DEVANE	84 CHARING CROSS ROAD .... ANNE BANCROFT
1776 .... JOHN CULLUM	36 HOURS .... EVA MARIE SAINT	84 CHARING CROSS ROAD .... ANTHONY HOPKINS
1776 .... KEN HOWARD	36 HOURS .... JAMES GARNER	84 CHARING CROSS ROAD .... ELEANOR DAVID
1776 .... WILLIAM DANIELS	3:10 TO YUMA .... HENRY JONES	84 CHARING CROSS ROAD .... JEAN DEBAER
18 AGAIN .... ANITA MORRIS†	3:10 TO YUMA .... RICHARD JAECKEL	84 CHARING CROSS ROAD .... JUDI DENCH
18 AGAIN .... CHARLIE SCHLATTER	4 FOR TEXAS .... CHARLES BRONSON	84 CHARING CROSS ROAD .... MERCEDES RUEHL
18 AGAIN .... GEORGE BURNS	4 FOR TEXAS .... FRANK SINATRA	84 CHARLIE MOPIC .... BYRON THAMES
18 AGAIN .... RED BUTTONS	4 FOR TEXAS .... URSULA ANDRESS	84 CHARLIE MOPIC .... CHRISTOPHER BURGARD
1900 .... BURT LANCASTER†	4-D MAN .... PATTY DUKE	84 CHARLIE MOPIC .... GLENN MORSHOWER
1900 .... DONALD SUTHERLAND	40 CARATS .... BILLY GREEN BUSH	84 CHARLIE MOPIC .... JASON TOMLINS
1900 .... GERARD DEPARDIEU	40 CARATS .... DEBORAH RAFFIN	84 CHARLIE MOPIC .... JONATHAN EMERSON
1900 .... ROBERT DE NIRO	40 CARATS .... EDWARD ALBERT	84 CHARLIE MOPIC .... NICHOLAS CASCONE

† after an actor's name denotes deceased.

84 CHARLIE MOPIC ... RICHARD BROOKS
9 1/2 WEEKS ... CHRISTINE BARANSKI
9 1/2 WEEKS ... KIM BASINGER
9 1/2 WEEKS ... MICKEY ROURKE
9/30/55 ... DENNIS CHRISTOPHER
9/30/55 ... DENNIS QUAID
9/30/55 ... LISA BLOUNT
9/30/55 ... RICHARD THOMAS
9/30/55 ... SUSAN TYRRELL
9/30/55 ... TOM HULCE
92 IN THE SHADE ... BURGESS MEREDITH
92 IN THE SHADE ... ELIZABETH ASHLEY
92 IN THE SHADE ... MARGOT KIDDER
92 IN THE SHADE ... PETER FONDA
92 IN THE SHADE ... SYLVIA MILES
99 AND 44/100% DEAD ... ANN TURKEL
99 AND 44/100% DEAD ... BRADFORD DILLMAN
99 AND 44/100% DEAD ... CHUCK CONNORS†
99 AND 44/100% DEAD ... RICHARD HARRIS
99 MUJERES ... MARIA SCHELL
99 WOMEN ... MARIA SCHELL
99 WOMEN ... MERCEDES McCAMBRIDGE

A

A.B.C. MURDERS, THE ... TONY RANDALL
A BOUT DE SOUFFLE ... JEAN SEBERG†
A.D. (MS) ... AVA GARDNER†
A GIU LA TESTA ... ROD STEIGER
A LA FRANÇAISE ... CLAUDINE AUGER
A NOUS DEUX ... CATHERINE DENEUVE
A PROPOSITO LUCIANO ... ROD STEIGER
A-TEAM, THE (TF) ... DIRK BENEDICT
A-TEAM, THE (TF) ... DWIGHT SCHULTZ
A-TEAM, THE (TF) ... GEORGE PEPPARD†
A-TEAM, THE (TF) ... MR. T
AAMILY FOR JOE, A (TF) ... BARBARA BABCOCK
AARON LOVES ANGELA ... KEVIN HOOKS
AARON LOVES ANGELA ... MOSES GUNN
AARON SLICK FROM PUNKIN CRICK ... ALAN YOUNG
AARON SLICK FROM PUNKIN CRICK ... DINAH SHORE†
AARON'S WAY (TF) ... JESSICA WALTER
ABANDON SHIP! ... GORDAN JACKSON†
ABANDON SHIP! ... MAE ZETTERLING†
ABANDONED ... RAYMOND BURR†
ABATTRE ... CATHERINE DENEUVE
ABBOTT AND COSTELLO GO TO MARS ... BUD ABBOTT†
ABBOTT AND COSTELLO GO TO MARS ... LOU COSTELLO†
ABBOTT AND COSTELLO IN HOLLYWOOD ... BUD ABBOTT†
ABBOTT AND COSTELLO IN HOLLYWOOD ... DEAN STOCKWELL
ABBOTT AND COSTELLO IN HOLLYWOOD ... LOU COSTELLO†
ABBOTT AND COSTELLO IN THE FOREIGN LEGION ... BUD ABBOTT†
ABBOTT AND COSTELLO IN THE FOREIGN LEGION ... LOU COSTELLO†
ABBOTT AND COSTELLO MEET CAPTAIN KIDD ... BUD ABBOTT†
ABBOTT AND COSTELLO MEET CAPTAIN KIDD ... LOU COSTELLO†
ABBOTT AND COSTELLO MEET DR. JEKYLL AND MR. HYDE ... BUD ABBOTT†
ABBOTT AND COSTELLO MEET DR. JEKYLL AND MR. HYDE ... LOU COSTELLO†
ABBOTT AND COSTELLO MEET FRANKENSTEIN ... BUD ABBOTT†
ABBOTT AND COSTELLO MEET FRANKENSTEIN ... LOU COSTELLO†
ABBOTT AND COSTELLO MEET FRANKENSTEIN ... VINCENT PRICE†
ABBOTT AND COSTELLO MEET THE INVISIBLE MAN ... BUD ABBOTT†
ABBOTT AND COSTELLO MEET THE INVISIBLE MAN ... LOU COSTELLO†
ABBOTT AND COSTELLO MEET THE KEYSTONE COPS ... BUD ABBOTT†
ABBOTT AND COSTELLO MEET THE KEYSTONE COPS ... LOU COSTELLO†
ABBOTT AND COSTELLO MEET THE KILLER, BORIS KARLOFF ... BUD ABBOTT†
ABBOTT AND COSTELLO MEET THE KILLER, BORIS KARLOFF ... LOU COSTELLO†
ABBOTT AND COSTELLO MEET THE MUMMY ... BUD ABBOTT†
ABBOTT AND COSTELLO MEET THE MUMMY ... LOU COSTELLO†
ABBY ... WILLIAM MARSHALL
ABDICATION, THE ... LIV ULLMANN
ABDUCTION ... LAWRENCE TIERNEY
ABDUCTION OF KARI SWENSON, THE (TF) ... GEOFFREY BLAKE
ABDUCTION OF KARI SWENSON, THE (TF) ... JOE DON BAKER
ABDUCTION OF KARI SWENSON, THE (TF) ... M. EMMET WALSH
ABDUCTION OF SAINT ANNE, THE (TF) ... KATHLEEN QUINLAN
ABDUCTION OF SAINT ANNE, THE (TF) ... MARTHA SCOTT
ABDUCTION OF SAINT ANNE, THE (TF) ... ROBERT WAGNER
ABDUCTION OF SAINT ANNE, THE (TF) ... WILLIAM WINDOM
ABDUCTION OF SAINT ANNE, THE (TF) ... E. G. MARSHALL
ABE LINCOLN IN ILLINOIS ... ALAN BAXTER†
ABE LINCOLN IN ILLINOIS ... HOWARD DA SILVA†
ABE LINCOLN IN ILLINOIS ... MINOR WATSON†
ABE LINCOLN IN ILLINOIS ★ ... RAYMOND MASSEY†
ABIE'S IRISH ROSE ... ART BAKER†
ABILENE TOWN ... LLOYD BRIDGES
ABOMINABLE DR. PHIBES, THE ... VINCENT PRICE†
ABOMINABLE SNOWMAN ... FORREST TUCKER†
ABOMINABLE SNOWMAN ... RICHARD WATTIS†
ABOMINABLE SNOWMAN OF THE HIMALAYAS, THE ... FORREST TUCKER†
ABOMINABLE SNOWMAN OF THE HIMALAYAS, THE ... RICHARD WATTIS†
ABOUT FACE ... DICK WESSON†
ABOUT FACE ... GORDON MACRAE†
ABOUT FACE ... JOEL GREY
ABOUT LAST NIGHT ... DONNA GIBBONS†
ABOUT LAST NIGHT... ... DEMI MOORE
ABOUT LAST NIGHT... ... ELIZABETH PERKINS
ABOUT LAST NIGHT... ... GEORGE DICENZO
ABOUT LAST NIGHT... ... JAMES BELUSHI
ABOUT LAST NIGHT... ... JOE GRECO
ABOUT LAST NIGHT... ... MICHAEL ALLDREDGE
ABOUT LAST NIGHT... ... ROB LOWE
ABOUT LAST NIGHT... ... ROBIN THOMAS
ABOUT LAST NIGHT... ... TIM KAZURINSKY
ABOUT MRS. LESLIE ... ROBERT RYAN†
ABOVE AND BEYOND ... ELEANOR PARKER
ABOVE AND BEYOND ... JAMES WHITMORE
ABOVE AND BEYOND ... JIM BACKUS†
ABOVE SUSPICION ... CONRAD VEIDT†
ABOVE SUSPICION ... JOAN CRAWFORD†
ABOVE THE LAW ... CHELCIE ROSS
ABOVE THE LAW ... DANIEL FARALDO
ABOVE THE LAW ... DANNY GOLDRING
ABOVE THE LAW ... GENE BARGE
ABOVE THE LAW ... GREGORY ALAN WILLIAMS
ABOVE THE LAW ... HENRY GODINEZ
ABOVE THE LAW ... HENRY SILVA
ABOVE THE LAW ... INDIA COOPER
ABOVE THE LAW ... JACK WALLACE
ABOVE THE LAW ... JOE D. LAUCK
ABOVE THE LAW ... JOE GRECO
ABOVE THE LAW ... JOHN DRUMMOND
ABOVE THE LAW ... JOSEPH KOSALA
ABOVE THE LAW ... METTA DAVIS
ABOVE THE LAW ... MICHAEL ROOKER
ABOVE THE LAW ... MICHELLE HOARD
ABOVE THE LAW ... MIGUEL NINO
ABOVE THE LAW ... MIKE JAMES
ABOVE THE LAW ... NICHOLAS KUSENKO
ABOVE THE LAW ... PAM GRIER
ABOVE THE LAW ... RON DEAN
ABOVE THE LAW ... RONNIE BARRON
ABOVE THE LAW ... SHARON STONE
ABOVE THE LAW ... STEVEN SEAGAL
ABOVE THE LAW ... THALMUS RASULALA
ABOVE THE RIM ... BERNIE MAC
ABOVE THE RIM ... DUANE MARTIN
ABOVE THE RIM ... LEON
ABOVE THE RIM ... MARLON WAYANS
ABOVE THE RIM ... TANYA PINKINS
ABOVE THE RIM ... TUPAC SHAKUR
ABOVE US THE WAVES ... JOHN MILLS
ABSENCE OF MALICE ... BARRY PRIMUS
ABSENCE OF MALICE ... SALLY FIELD
ABSENCE OF MALICE ... WILFORD BRIMLEY
ABSENCE OF MALICE ★ ... PAUL NEWMAN
ABSENCE OF MALICE ✪ ... MELINDA DILLON
ABSENT-MINDED PROFESSOR, THE ... LEON AMES
ABSOLUTE BEGINNERS ... ANITA MORRIS†
ABSOLUTE BEGINNERS ... DAVID BOWIE
ABSOLUTE BEGINNERS ... EDDIE O'CONNELL
ABSOLUTE BEGINNERS ... EVE FERRET
ABSOLUTE BEGINNERS ... JAMES FOX
ABSOLUTE BEGINNERS ... LIONEL BLAIR
ABSOLUTE BEGINNERS ... MANDY RICE-DAVIES
ABSOLUTE BEGINNERS ... PATSY KENSIT
ABSOLUTE BEGINNERS ... RAY DAVIES
ABSOLUTE BEGINNERS ... SADE ADU
ABSOLUTE BEGINNERS ... STEVEN BERKOFF
ABSOLUTE STRANGERS (TF) ... AUDRA LINDLEY
ABSOLUTE STRANGERS (TF) ... HENRY WINKLER
ABSOLUTE STRANGERS (TF) ... KARL MALDEN
ABSOLUTE STRANGERS (TF) ... PATTY DUKE
ABSOLUTE STRANGERS (TF) ... RICHARD KILEY
ABSOLUTION ... RICHARD BURTON†
ABYSS, THE ... CHRIS ELLIOTT
ABYSS, THE ... ED HARRIS
ABYSS, THE ... J. C. QUINN
ABYSS, THE ... JIMMIE RAY WEEKS
ABYSS, THE ... JOHN BEDFORD LLOYD
ABYSS, THE ... KIMBERLY SCOTT
ABYSS, THE ... LEO BURMESTER
ABYSS, THE ... MARY ELIZABETH MASTRANTONIO
ABYSS, THE ... MICHAEL BIEHN
ABYSS, THE ... TODD GRAFF
ACAPULCO GOLD ... ED NELSON
ACAPULCO GOLD ... MARJOE GORTNER
ACCENT ON YOUTH ... SYLVIA SIDNEY
ACCEPTABLE RISKS (TF) ... BRIAN DENNEHY
ACCEPTABLE RISKS (TF) ... CHRISTINE EBERSOLE
ACCEPTABLE RISKS (TF) ... CICELY TYSON
ACCEPTABLE RISKS (TF) ... KENNETH McMILLAN†
ACCIDENT ... MICHAEL YORK
ACCIDENTAL TOURIST, THE ... AMANDA HOUCK
ACCIDENTAL TOURIST, THE ... AMY WRIGHT
ACCIDENTAL TOURIST, THE ... BILL PULLMAN
ACCIDENTAL TOURIST, THE ... BRADLEY MOTT
ACCIDENTAL TOURIST, THE ... CAROLINE HOUCK
ACCIDENTAL TOURIST, THE ... DAVID OGDEN STIERS
ACCIDENTAL TOURIST, THE ... DONALD NEAL
ACCIDENTAL TOURIST, THE ... ED BEGLEY JR.
ACCIDENTAL TOURIST, THE ... GREGORY GOUVER
ACCIDENTAL TOURIST, THE ... KATHLEEN TURNER
ACCIDENTAL TOURIST, THE ... PEGGY CONVERSE
ACCIDENTAL TOURIST, THE ... ROBERT GORMAN
ACCIDENTAL TOURIST, THE ... SETH GRANGER
ACCIDENTAL TOURIST, THE ... W.H. BROWN
ACCIDENTAL TOURIST, THE ... WILLIAM HURT
ACCIDENTAL TOURIST, THE ✪✪ ... GEENA DAVIS
ACCIDENTS WILL HAPPEN ... RONALD REAGAN
ACCUSED, THE ... BERNIE COULSON
ACCUSED, THE ... KELLY McGILLIS
ACCUSED, THE ... LEO ROSSI
ACCUSED, THE ... PETER VAN NORDEN
ACCUSED, THE ... ROSE WEAVER
ACCUSED, THE ... SCOTT PAULIN
ACCUSED, THE ... STEPHEN E. MILLER
ACCUSED, THE ... STEVE ANTIN
ACCUSED, THE ... TERRY DAVID MULLIGAN
ACCUSED, THE ... TOM McBEATH
ACCUSED, THE ... TOM O'BRIEN
ACCUSED, THE ... WOODY BROWN
ACCUSED, THE ★★ ... JODIE FOSTER

This is not a list of every film ever made or every cast member, only those listed in this directory.

ACE ELI AND RODGER
OF THE SKIES .... ALICE GHOSTLEY
ACE ELI AND RODGER
OF THE SKIES .... BERNADETTE PETERS
ACE ELI AND RODGER
OF THE SKIES .... CLIFF ROBERTSON
ACE ELI AND RODGER
OF THE SKIES .... ROSEMARY MURPHY
ACE ELI AND RODGER
OF THE SKIES .... ROYAL DANO
ACE HIGH .... ELI WALLACH
ACE HIGH .... KEVIN McCARTHY
ACE IN THE HOLE .... KIRK DOUGLAS
ACE OF ACES .... RALPH BELLAMY†
ACE OF SPADES .... GERALDINE FITZGERALD
ACE, THE .... BLYTHE DANNER
ACE, THE .... LISA JANE PERSKY
ACE, THE .... PAUL GLEASON
ACE, THE .... PAUL MANTEE
ACE, THE .... STAN SHAW
ACE, THE .... THERESA MERRITT
ACE, THE ★ .... ROBERT DUVALL
ACE, THE ❍ .... MICHAEL O'KEEFE
ACE UP MY SLEEVE, AN .... KAREN BLACK
ACE VENTURA:
PET DETECTIVE .... COURTENEY COX
ACE VENTURA: PET DETECTIVE .... DAN MARINO
ACE VENTURA: PET DETECTIVE .... JIM CARREY
ACE VENTURA: PET DETECTIVE .... SEAN YOUNG
ACE VENTURA: PET DETECTIVE .... TONE LOC
ACE VENTURA: PET DETECTIVE .... TROY EVANS
ACES HIGH .... CHRISTOPHER PLUMMER
ACES HIGH .... JOHN GIELGUD
ACES HIGH .... MALCOLM McDOWELL
ACES HIGH .... PETER FIRTH
ACES HIGH .... SIMON WARD
ACES: IRON
EAGLE III .... CHRISTOPHER CAZENOVE
ACES: IRON EAGLE III .... JUAN FERNANDEZ
ACES: IRON EAGLE III ..... LOUIS GOSSETT JR.
ACES: IRON EAGLE III .... PAUL FREEMAN
ACES: IRON EAGLE III .... PHILL LEWIS
ACES: IRON EAGLE III .... RACHEL McLISH
ACES: IRON EAGLE III .... SONNY CHIBA
ACROSS 110TH STREET .... ANTHONY QUINN
ACROSS 110TH
STREET .... ANTHONY (TONY) FRANCIOSA
ACROSS 110TH STREET .... YAPHET KOTTO
ACROSS THE BRIDGE .... ROD STEIGER
ACROSS THE MOON .... CHRISTINA APPLEGATE
ACROSS THE WIDE
MISSOURI .... JAMES WHITMORE
ACROSS THE WIDE
MISSOURI .... RICARDO MONTALBAN
ACROSS THE WIDE
MISSOURI .... RICHARD ANDERSON
ACROSS TO SINGAPORE .... JOAN CRAWFORD†
ACT OF AGGRESSION .... CATHERINE DENEUVE
ACT OF LOVE .... KIRK DOUGLAS
ACT OF LOVE (TF) .... MICKEY ROURKE
ACT OF THE HEART .... DONALD SUTHERLAND
ACT OF THE HEART .... GENEVIEVE BUJOLD
ACT OF THE HEART .... SHARON ACKER
ACT OF VENGEANCE (CTF) .... ELLEN BURSTYN
ACT OF VENGEANCE (CTF) .... WILFORD BRIMLEY
ACT OF VIOLENCE .... JANET LEIGH
ACT OF VIOLENCE .... PHYLLIS THAXTER
ACT OF
VIOLENCE (TF) .... ELIZABETH MONTGOMERY
ACT ONE .... ELI WALLACH
ACT ONE .... GEORGE HAMILTON
ACT ONE .... GEORGE SEGAL
ACT ONE .... JACK KLUGMAN
ACT ONE .... JASON ROBARDS
ACT, THE .... EDDIE ALBERT
ACT, THE .... JILL ST. JOHN
ACTE DU COEUR .... GENEVIEVE BUJOLD
ACTION JACKSON .... BILL DUKE
ACTION JACKSON .... CARL WEATHERS
ACTION JACKSON .... CRAIG T. NELSON
ACTION JACKSON .... ED O'ROSS
ACTION JACKSON .... JACK THIBEAU

ACTION JACKSON .... NICHOLAS WORTH
ACTION JACKSON .... PERRY LOPEZ
ACTION JACKSON .... ROBERT DAVI
ACTION JACKSON .... ROBERT DVI
ACTION JACKSON .... SHARON STONE
ACTION JACKSON .... SONNY LANDHAM
ACTION JACKSON .... THOMAS F. WILSON
ACTION JACKSON .... VANITY
ACTION MAN, THE .... ROBERT STACK
ACTION OF THE TIGER .... SEAN CONNERY
ACTION OF THE TIGER .... VAN JOHNSON
ACTORS AND SIN .... DAN O'HERLIHY
ACTORS AND SIN .... EDDIE ALBERT
ACTRESS, THE .... ANTHONY PERKINS†
ACTRESS, THE .... JEAN SIMMONS
ACTRESS, THE .... MARY WICKES
ACTRESS, THE .... TERESA WRIGHT
AD EST DI MARSA MATRUH .... SANDRA DEE
ADA .... DEAN MARTIN
ADA .... MARTIN BALSAM
ADAM (TF) .... DANIEL J. TRAVANTI
ADAM (TF) .... JoBETH WILLIAMS
ADAM (TF) .... MASON ADAMS
ADAM (TF) .... RICHARD MASUR
ADAM AND EVELYN .... JEAN SIMMONS
ADAM AND EVELYNE .... JEAN SIMMONS
ADAM AT SIX A.M. .... JOE DON BAKER
ADAM AT SIX A.M. .... MICHAEL DOUGLAS
ADAM HAD FOUR SONS .... INGRID BERGMAN†
ADAM HAD FOUR SONS .... JUNE LOCKHART
ADAM HAD FOUR SONS .... SUSAN HAYWARD†
ADAM: HIS SONG
CONTINUES (TF) .... DANIEL J. TRAVANTI
ADAM: HIS SONG
CONTINUES (TF) .... JoBETH WILLIAMS
ADAM: HIS SONG
CONTINUES (TF) .... RICHARD MASUR
ADAM'S RIB .... SPENCER TRACY†
ADAM'S RIB .... KATHERINE HEPBURN
ADAM'S WOMAN .... BEAU BRIDGES
ADDAMS FAMILY, THE .... ANJELICA HUSTON
ADDAMS FAMILY, THE .... CAREL STRUYCKEN
ADDAMS FAMILY, THE .... CHRISTINA RICCI
ADDAMS FAMILY, THE .... CHRISTOPHER HART
ADDAMS FAMILY, THE .... CHRISTOPHER LLOYD
ADDAMS FAMILY, THE .... DAN HEDAYA
ADDAMS FAMILY, THE .... DANA IVEY
ADDAMS FAMILY, THE .... ELIZABETH WILSON
ADDAMS FAMILY, THE .... JIMMY WORKMAN
ADDAMS FAMILY, THE .... JOHN FRANKLIN
ADDAMS FAMILY, THE .... JUDITH MALINA
ADDAMS FAMILY, THE .... PAUL BENEDICT
ADDAMS FAMILY, THE .... RAUL JULIA†
ADDAMS FAMILY VALUES .... ANJELICA HUSTON
ADDAMS FAMILY VALUES .... CAREL STRUYCKEN
ADDAMS FAMILY VALUES .... CAROL KANE
ADDAMS FAMILY VALUES .... CHRISTINA RICCI
ADDAMS FAMILY VALUES .... CHRISTOPHER HART
ADDAMS FAMILY VALUES .... CHRISTOPHER LLOYD
ADDAMS FAMILY VALUES .... DANA IVEY
ADDAMS FAMILY VALUES .... DAVID KRUMHOLTZ
ADDAMS FAMILY VALUES .... JIMMY WORKMAN
ADDAMS FAMILY VALUES .... JOAN CUSAK
ADDAMS FAMILY VALUES .... JOHN FRANKLIN
ADDAMS FAMILY VALUES .... RAUL JULIA†
ADDICTED TO HIS LOVE (TF) ...... BARRY BOSTWICK
ADDICTED TO HIS LOVE (TF) .... COLLEEN CAMP
ADDICTED TO
HIS LOVE (TF) .... DEE WALLACE STONE
ADDICTED TO HIS LOVE (TF) .... POLLY BERGEN
ADDING MACHINE, THE .... BILLIE WHITELAW
ADDING MACHINE, THE .... JULIAN GLOVER
ADDING MACHINE, THE .... MILO O'SHEA
ADDING MACHINE, THE .... PHYLLIS DILLER
ADDIO FRATELLO
CRUDELE .... CHARLOTTE RAMPLING
ADIEU L'AMI .... CHARLES BRONSON
ADIOS AMIGO .... FRED WILLIAMSON
ADIOS AMIGO .... RICHARD PRYOR
ADIOS AMIGO .... THALMUS RASULALA
ADOLESCENTS, THE .... GENEVIEVE BUJOLD

ADUA E LE
COMPAGNE .... MARCELLO MASTROIANNI
ADULTRESS, THE .... TYNE DALY
ADVANCE TO THE REAR .... STELLA STEVENS
ADVENTURE .... GREER GARSON
ADVENTURE FOR
TWO, AN .... CATHERINE DENEUVE
ADVENTURE ISLAND .... RORY CALHOUN
ADVENTURE OF SHERLOCK HOLMES'
SMARTER BROTHER, THE .... DOM DeLUISE
ADVENTURE OF SHERLOCK HOLMES'
SMARTER BROTHER, THE .... GENE WILDER
ADVENTURE OF SHERLOCK HOLMES'
SMARTER BROTHER, THE .... MADELINE KAHN
ADVENTURE OF SHERLOCK
HOLMES' SMARTER
BROTHER, THE .... THORLEY WALTERS†
ADVENTURERS, THE .... CANDICE BERGEN
ADVENTURERS, THE .... ERNEST BORGNINE
ADVENTURERS, THE .... JACLYN SMITH
ADVENTURERS, THE .... JOHN IRELAND
ADVENTURERS, THE .... LEIGH TAYLOR-YOUNG
ADVENTURERS, THE .... LOIS MAXWELL
ADVENTURERS, THE .... OLIVIA DE HAVILLAND
ADVENTURES IN BABYSITTING .... ALBERT COLLINS
ADVENTURES IN BABYSITTING ...... ALLAN AARONS
ADVENTURES IN BABYSITTING ...... ANTHONY RAPP
ADVENTURES IN BABYSITTING .... BRAD WHITFORD
ADVENTURES IN BABYSITTING ...... CALVIN LEVELS
ADVENTURES IN BABYSITTING .... DAN ZISKIE
ADVENTURES IN BABYSITTING ...... DAVID BLACKER
ADVENTURES IN BABYSITTING ... ELISABETH SHUE
ADVENTURES IN
BABYSITTING .... GEORGE NEWBERN
ADVENTURES IN BABYSITTING ... JOHN CHANDLER
ADVENTURES IN
BABYSITTING .... JOHN FORD NOONAN
ADVENTURES IN BABYSITTING ...... KEITH COOGAN
ADVENTURES IN
BABYSITTING .... LOLITA DAVIDOVICH
ADVENTURES IN BABYSITTING ...... MAIA BREWTON
ADVENTURES IN
BABYSITTING .... MARCIA BENNETT
ADVENTURES IN
BABYSITTING .... PENELOPE ANN MILLER
ADVENTURES IN BABYSITTING .... RON CANADA
ADVENTURES IN BABYSITTING ...... RUMMY BISHOP
ADVENTURES IN
BABYSITTING .... VINCENT D'ONOFRIO
ADVENTURES OF A
YOUNG MAN .... ELI WALLACH
ADVENTURES OF A
YOUNG MAN .... RICARDO MONTALBAN
ADVENTURES OF BARON
MUNCHAUSEN, THE .... ALISON STEADMAN
ADVENTURES OF BARON
MUNCHAUSEN, THE .... BILL PATERSON
ADVENTURES OF BARON
MUNCHAUSEN, THE .... CHARLES McKEOWN
ADVENTURES OF BARON
MUNCHAUSEN, THE .... ERIC IDLE
ADVENTURES OF BARON
MUNCHAUSEN, THE .... JACK PURVIS
ADVENTURES OF BARON
MUNCHAUSEN, THE .... JOHN NEVILLE
ADVENTURES OF BARON
MUNCHAUSEN, THE .... JONATHAN PRYCE
ADVENTURES OF BARON
MUNCHAUSEN, THE .... OLIVER REED
ADVENTURES OF BARON
MUNCHAUSEN, THE .... ROBIN WILLIAMS
ADVENTURES OF BARON
MUNCHAUSEN, THE .... SARAH POLLEY
ADVENTURES OF BARON
MUNCHAUSEN, THE .... STING
ADVENTURES OF BARON
MUNCHAUSEN, THE .... UMA THURMAN
ADVENTURES OF BARON
MUNCHAUSEN, THE .... WINSTON DENNIS
ADVENTURES OF BARRY
MCKENZIE, THE .... PETER COOK

ADVENTURES OF BUCKAROO
BANZAI: ACROSS THE
8TH DIMENSION, THE .... CHRISTOPHER LLOYD
ADVENTURES OF BUCKAROO
BANZAI: ACROSS THE
8TH DIMENSION, THE .... ELLEN BARKIN
ADVENTURES OF BUCKAROO
BANZAI: ACROSS THE
8TH DIMENSION, THE .... JAMIE LEE CURTIS
ADVENTURES OF BUCKAROO
BANZAI: ACROSS THE
8TH DIMENSION, THE .... JOHN LITHGOW
ADVENTURES OF BUCKAROO
BANZAI: ACROSS THE
8TH DIMENSION, THE .... PETER WELLER
ADVENTURES OF BUCKAROO
BONZAI: ACROSS THE
8TH DIMENSION, THE .... JEFF GOLDBLUM
ADVENTURES OF BULLWHIP
GRIFFIN, THE .... HARRY GUARDINO
ADVENTURES OF BULLWHIP
GRIFFIN, THE .... KARL MALDEN
ADVENTURES OF BULLWHIP
GRIFFIN, THE .... RODDY McDOWALL
ADVENTURES OF BULLWHIP
GRIFFIN, THE .... SUZANNE PLESHETTE
ADVENTURES OF
CAPTAIN FABIAN .... VINCENT PRICE†
ADVENTURES OF
DON JUAN, THE .... RAYMOND BURR†
ADVENTURES OF
FORD FAIRLANE, THE .... ANDREW DICE CLAY
ADVENTURES OF
FORD FAIRLANE, THE .... ED O'NEILL
ADVENTURES OF
FORD FAIRLANE, THE .... GILBERT GOTTFRIED
ADVENTURES OF
FORD FAIRLANE, THE .... LAUREN HOLLY
ADVENTURES OF
FORD FAIRLANE, THE .... MADDIE CORMAN
ADVENTURES OF
FORD FAIRLANE, THE .... MORRIS DAY
ADVENTURES OF
FORD FAIRLANE, THE .... PRISCILLA PRESLEY
ADVENTURES OF
FORD FAIRLANE, THE .... ROBERT ENGLUND
ADVENTURES OF
FORD FAIRLANE, THE .... TONE LOC
ADVENTURES OF
FORD FAIRLANE, THE .... WAYNE NEWTON
ADVENTURES OF GERARD, THE .... ELI WALLACH
ADVENTURES OF GERARD, THE ...... JOHN NEVILLE
ADVENTURES OF
HUCK FINN, THE .... COURTNEY B. VANCE
ADVENTURES OF
HUCK FINN, THE .... ELIJAH WOOD
ADVENTURES OF
HUCK FINN, THE .... JASON ROBARDS
ADVENTURES OF
HUCK FINN, THE .... ROBBIE COLTRANE
ADVENTURES OF HUCKLEBERRY
FINN, THE .... MICKEY ROONEY
ADVENTURES OF HUCKLEBERRY
FINN, THE .... ROYAL DANO
ADVENTURES OF HUCKLEBERRY
FINN, THE .... TONY RANDALL
ADVENTURES OF
MARCO POLO, THE .... LANA TURNER
ADVENTURES OF
MARK TWAIN, THE .... ALEXIS SMITH†
ADVENTURES OF
MARK TWAIN, THE (AF) .... CHRIS RITCHIE
ADVENTURES OF MARK
TWAIN, THE (AF) .... GARY KRUG
ADVENTURES OF MARK
TWAIN, THE (AF) .... JAMES WHITMORE
ADVENTURES OF MARK
TWAIN, THE (AF) .... MICHELE MARIANA
ADVENTURES OF MILO
AND OTIS, THE .... DUDLEY MOORE
ADVENTURES OF NICK
CARTER, THE (TF) .... ROBERT CONRAD

ADVENTURES OF PRISCILLA, QUEEN
OF THE DESERT, THE .... BILL HUNTER
ADVENTURES OF PRISCILLA, QUEEN
OF THE DESERT, THE .... GUY PEARCE
ADVENTURES OF PRISCILLA, QUEEN
OF THE DESERT, THE .... HUGO WEAVING
ADVENTURES OF PRISCILLA, QUEEN
OF THE DESERT, THE .... TERENCE STAMP
ADVENTURES OF QUENTIN
DURWARD, THE .... ROBERT MORLEY
ADVENTURES OF
ROBIN HOOD, THE .... OLIVIA DE HAVILLAND
ADVENTURES OF ROBINSON
CRUSOE ★ .... DAN O'HERLIHY
ADVENTURES OF SADIE, THE .... JOAN COLLINS
ADVENTURES OF
THE QUEEN (TF) .... DAVID HEDISON
ADVENTURES OF
THE QUEEN (TF) .... ROBERT STACK
ADVENTURESS, THE .... DEBORAH KERR
ADVISE AND CONSENT .... BURGESS MEREDITH
ADVISE AND CONSENT .... DON MURRAY
ADVISE AND CONSENT .... GEORGE GRIZZARD
ADVISE AND CONSENT .... INGA SWENSON
ADVOCATE, THE .... LYSETTE ANTHONY
AERIAL GUNNER .... ROBERT MITCHUM
AERODROME, THE (TF) .... PETER FIRTH
AFFAIR IN HAVANA .... RAYMOND BURR†
AFFAIR OF THE SKIN, AN .... KEVIN McCARTHY
AFFAIR OF THE SKIN, AN .... LEE GRANT
AFFAIR, THE (TF) .... BRUCE DAVISON
AFFAIR, THE (TF) .... ROBERT WAGNER
AFFAIR TO REMEMBER, AN .... CARY GRANT†
AFFAIR TO REMEMBER, AN .... DEBORAH KERR
AFFAIR WITH A STRANGER .... JEAN SIMMONS
AFFAIRS OF CELLINI ★ .... FRANK MORGAN†
AFFAIRS OF
DOBIE GILLIS, THE .... DEBBIE REYNOLDS
AFFAIRS OF
DOBIE GILLIS, THE .... KATHLEEN FREEMAN
AFFECTIONATELY YOURS .... RALPH BELLAMY†
AFRAID OF THE DARK .... DAVID THEWLIS
AFRAID OF THE DARK .... FANNY ARDANT
AFRAID OF THE DARK .... JAMES FOX
AFRAID OF THE DARK .... PAUL McGANN
AFRICA EXPRESS .... JACK PALANCE
AFRICA EXPRESS .... URSULA ANDRESS
AFRICA SOTTO I MARI .... SOPHIA LOREN
AFRICA—TEXAS STYLE! .... HAYLEY MILLS
AFRICAN QUEEN, THE .... ROBERT MORLEY
AFRICAN QUEEN, THE .... THEODORE BIKEL
AFRICAN QUEEN, THE ★ .... KATHERINE HEPBURN
AFRICAN QUEEN, THE ★★ .... HUMPHREY BOGART†
AFRICAN, THE .... CATHERINE DENEUVE
AFTER DARK, MY SWEET .... BRUCE DERN
AFTER DARK, MY SWEET ...... GEORGE DICKERSON
AFTER DARK, MY SWEET .... JASON PATRIC
AFTER DARK, MY SWEET .... RACHEL WARD
AFTER HOURS .... BRONSON PINCHOT
AFTER HOURS .... CATHERINE O'HARA
AFTER HOURS .... CHEECH MARIN
AFTER HOURS .... DICK MILLER
AFTER HOURS .... GRIFFIN DUNNE
AFTER HOURS .... JOHN HEARD
AFTER HOURS .... LINDA FIORENTINO
AFTER HOURS .... ROBERT PLUNKET
AFTER HOURS .... ROCKETS REDGLARE
AFTER HOURS .... ROSANNA ARQUETTE
AFTER HOURS .... TERI GARR
AFTER HOURS .... THOMAS CHONG
AFTER HOURS .... VERNA BLOOM
AFTER HOURS .... WILL PATTON
AFTER PILKINGTON (TF) .... MIRANDA RICHARDSON
AFTER THE FOX .... AKIM TAMIROFF†
AFTER THE FOX .... BRITT EKLAND
AFTER THE FOX .... MARTIN BALSAM
AFTER THE FOX .... PETER SELLERS†
AFTER THE PROMISE (TF) .... DIANA SCARWID
AFTER THE PROMISE (TF) .... MARK HARMON
AFTER THE REHEARSAL .... ERLAND JOSEPHSON
AFTER THE REHEARSAL .... LENA OLIN
AFTER THE THIN MAN .... JAMES STEWART

AFTERBURN (CTF) .... LAURA DERN
AGAINST ALL FLAGS .... ANTHONY QUINN
AGAINST ALL FLAGS .... JOHN ANDERSON
AGAINST ALL FLAGS .... MAUREEN O'HARA
AGAINST ALL ODDS .... ALEXIS KARRAS
AGAINST ALL ODDS .... BILL McKINNEY
AGAINST ALL ODDS .... DORIAN HAREWOOD
AGAINST ALL ODDS .... JAMES WOODS
AGAINST ALL ODDS .... JANE GREER
AGAINST ALL ODDS .... JEFF BRIDGES
AGAINST ALL ODDS .... RACHEL WARD
AGAINST ALL ODDS .... RICHARD WIDMARK
AGAINST ALL ODDS .... SWOOSIE KURTZ
AGAINST HER WILL: AN INCIDENT
IN BALTIMORE (TF) .... BRIAN KERWIN
AGAINST HER WILL: AN INCIDENT
IN BALTIMORE (TF) .... HARRY MORGAN
AGAINST HER WILL: AN INCIDENT
IN BALTIMORE (TF) .... SUSAN BLAKELY
AGAINST HER WILL: AN INCIDENT
IN BALTIMORE (TF) .... WALTER MATTHAU
AGAINST THE WIND .... GORDAN JACKSON†
AGATHA .... DUSTIN HOFFMAN
AGATHA .... TIMOTHY DALTON
AGATHA .... TIMOTHY WEST
AGATHA .... VANESSA REDGRAVE
AGATHA CHRISTIE'S "DEAD
MAN'S FOLLY" (TF) .... JEAN STAPLETON
AGATHA CHRISTIES'
ENDLESS NIGHT .... HAYLEY MILLS
AGATHA CHRISTIE'S 'A CARIBBEAN
MYSTERY' (TF) .... STEPHEN MACHT
AGATHA CHRISTIE'S 'A CARIBBEAN
MYSTERY' (TF) .... SWOOSIE KURTZ
AGATHA CHRISTIE'S "MURDER IN
THREE ACTS" (TF) .... EMMA SAMMS
AGATHA CHRISTIE'S "MURDER IN
THREE ACTS" (TF) .... TONY CURTIS
AGATHA CHRISTIE'S 'SPARKLING
CYANIDE' (TF) .... ANTHONY ANDREWS
AGATHA CHRISTIE'S 'THE
MAN IN THE
BROWN SUIT' (TF) .... EDWARD WOODWARD
AGATHA CHRISTIE'S 'THE MAN
IN THE BROWN SUIT' (TF) .... KEN HOWARD
AGATHA CHRISTIE'S 'THE
MAN IN THE
BROWN SUIT' (TF) .... RUE McCLANAHAN
AGATHA CHRISTIE'S 'THE
MAN IN THE
BROWN SUIT' (TF) .... STEPHANIE ZIMBALIST
AGATHA CHRISTIE'S 'THE MAN
IN THE BROWN SUIT' (TF) .... TONY RANDALL
AGATHA CHRISTIE'S "THIRTEEN
AT DINNER" (TF) .... FAYE DUNAWAY
AGE OF CONSENT .... HELEN MIRREN
AGE OF INNOCENCE .... DAVID WARNER
AGE OF INNOCENCE, THE .... ALEC McCOWEN
AGE OF INNOCENCE, THE ..... DANIEL DAY-LEWIS
AGE OF INNOCENCE, THE ..... JOANNE WOODWARD
AGE OF INNOCENCE, THE .... JONATHAN PRYCE
AGE OF INNOCENCE, THE .... MARTIN SCORSESE
AGE OF INNOCENCE, THE ...... MARY BETH HURT
AGE OF INNOCENCE, THE .... MICHELLE PFEIFFER
AGE OF INNOCENCE, THE ...... MIRIAM MARGOLYES
AGE OF INNOCENCE, THE .... RICHARD E. GRANT
AGE OF
INNOCENCE, THE .... ROBERT SEAN LEONARD
AGE OF INNOCENCE, THE .... STUART WILSON
AGE OF INNOCENCE, THE ● .... WINONA RYDER
AGENCY .... LEE MAJORS
AGENCY .... ROBERT MITCHUM
AGENCY .... VALERIE PERRINE
AGENT 8 3/4 .... ROBERT MORLEY
AGENT FOR H.A.R.M. .... PETER MARK RICHMAN
AGNES OF GOD .... ANNE PITONIAK
AGNES OF GOD .... GRATIEN GELINAS
AGNES OF GOD .... JANE FONDA
AGNES OF GOD .... WINSTON RECKERT
AGNES OF GOD ★ .... ANNE BANCROFT
AGNES OF GOD ● .... MEG TILLY

This is not a list of every film ever made or every cast member, only those listed in this directory.

AGONY AND THE
ECSTASY, THE .... ALEC McCOWEN
AGONY AND THE
ECSTASY, THE .... CHARLTON HESTON
AGONY OF LOVE, THE .... OMAR SHARIF
AGUIRRE, THE WRATH OF GOD ...... KLAUS KINSKI†
AH SI?...E IO LO DICO
A ZORRO .... LIONEL STANDER
AH WILDERNESS! .... CECILIA PARKER†
AH! WILDERNESS .... MICKEY ROONEY
AH! WILDERNESS .... WALLACE BEERY†
AIDA .... LOIS MAXWELL
AIDA .... SOPHIA LOREN
AIMEZ-VOUS BRAHMS? ...... ANTHONY PERKINS†
AIMEZ-VOUS BRAHMS? ...... DIAHANN CARROLL
AIN'T MISBEHAVIN' .... PIPER LAURIE
AIN'T MISBEHAVIN' .... RORY CALHOUN
AIR AMERICA .... ART LA FLEUR
AIR AMERICA .... BURT KWOUK
AIR AMERICA .... DAVID BOWE
AIR AMERICA ...... DAVID MARSHALL GRANT
AIR AMERICA .... KEN JENKINS
AIR AMERICA .... LANE SMITH
AIR AMERICA .... MARSHALL BELL
AIR AMERICA .... MEL GIBSON
AIR AMERICA .... NANCY TRAVIS
AIR AMERICA .... ROBERT DOWNEY JR.
AIR CADET .... ROCK HUDSON†
AIR HAWKS .... RALPH BELLAMY†
AIR MAIL .... RALPH BELLAMY†
AIR UP THERE, THE .... KEVIN BACON
AIRBORNE .... BRITTNEY POWELL
AIRBORNE .... SETH GREEN
AIRBORNE .... SHANE McDERMOTT
AIRHEADS .... ADAM SANDLER
AIRHEADS .... BRENDAN FRASER
AIRHEADS .... CHRIS FARLEY
AIRHEADS .... ERNIE HUDSON
AIRHEADS .... JOE MANTEGNA
AIRHEADS .... MARSHALL BELL
AIRHEADS .... MICHAEL RICHARDS
AIRHEADS .... STEVE BUSCEMI
AIRPLANE! .... AL WHITE
AIRPLANE! .... BARBARA BILLINGSLEY
AIRPLANE! .... BARBARA MALLORY
AIRPLANE! .... BARBARA STUART
AIRPLANE! .... BILL PORTER
AIRPLANE! .... CHARLOTTE ZUCKER
AIRPLANE! .... CONRAD PALMISANO
AIRPLANE! .... CRAIG BERENSON
AIRPLANE! .... CYRIL O'REILLY
AIRPLANE! .... DAVID HOLLANDER
AIRPLANE! .... DAVID LEISURE
AIRPLANE! .... ETHEL MERMAN†
AIRPLANE! .... FRANK ASHMORE
AIRPLANE! .... GREGORY ITZIN
AIRPLANE! .... HATSUO UDA
AIRPLANE! .... HOWARD HONIG
AIRPLANE! .... JAMES HONG
AIRPLANE! .... JESSE EMMETT
AIRPLANE! .... JILL WHELAN
AIRPLANE! .... JIM ABRAHAMS
AIRPLANE! .... JIMMIE WALKER
AIRPLANE! .... JOHN O'LEARY
AIRPLANE! .... JONATHAN BANKS
AIRPLANE! .... JOYCE BULIFANT
AIRPLANE! .... JULIE HAGERTY
AIRPLANE! .... KAREEM ABDUL-JABBAR
AIRPLANE! .... LEE BRYANT
AIRPLANE! .... LEE TERRI
AIRPLANE! .... LESLIE NIELSEN
AIRPLANE! .... LLOYD BRIDGES
AIRPLANE! .... LORNA PATTERSON
AIRPLANE! .... MAE E. CAMPBELL
AIRPLANE! .... MARCY GOLDMAN
AIRPLANE! .... MAUREEN McGOVERN
AIRPLANE! .... MAURICE HILL
AIRPLANE! .... MICHAEL LAURENCE
AIRPLANE! .... MICHELLE STACY
AIRPLANE! .... NICHOLAS PRYOR
AIRPLANE! .... PETER GRAVES
AIRPLANE! .... ROBERT HAYS

AIRPLANE! .... ROBERT STACK
AIRPLANE! .... ROBERT STARR
AIRPLANE! .... ROSSIE HARRIS
AIRPLANE! .... STEPHEN STUCKER†
AIRPLANE! .... WILLIAM TREGOE
AIRPLANE! .... ZACHARY LEWIS
AIRPLANE II: THE SEQUEL .... AL WHITE
AIRPLANE II: THE SEQUEL .... CHAD EVERETT
AIRPLANE II: THE SEQUEL ...... CHUCK CONNORS†
AIRPLANE II: THE SEQUEL ...... DAVID PAYMER
AIRPLANE II: THE SEQUEL ... JAMES A. WATSON JR.
AIRPLANE II: THE SEQUEL ...... JOHN DEHNER†
AIRPLANE II: THE SEQUEL ...... JOHN VERNON
AIRPLANE II: THE SEQUEL ...... JULIE HAGERTY
AIRPLANE II: THE SEQUEL ...... KENT McCORD
AIRPLANE II: THE SEQUEL ...... LLOYD BRIDGES
AIRPLANE II: THE SEQUEL ...... PETER GRAVES
AIRPLANE II: THE SEQUEL ...... RAYMOND BURR†
AIRPLANE II: THE SEQUEL .... RIP TORN
AIRPLANE II: THE SEQUEL ...... ROBERT HAYS
AIRPLANE II: THE SEQUEL ...... SONNY BONO
AIRPLANE II: THE SEQUEL ..... STEPHEN STUCKER†
AIRPLANE II: THE SEQUEL .... WILLIAM SHATNER
AIRPORT O .... MAUREEN STAPLETON
AIRPORT OO .... HELEN HAYES
AIRPORT .... BARBARA HALE
AIRPORT .... BURT LANCASTER†
AIRPORT .... DEAN MARTIN
AIRPORT .... GEORGE KENNEDY
AIRPORT .... JACQUELINE BISSET
AIRPORT .... JEAN SEBERG†
AIRPORT .... LLOYD NOLAN†
AIRPORT .... VAN HEFLIN†
AIRPORT 1975 .... CHARLTON HESTON
AIRPORT 1975 .... EFREM ZIMBALIST JR.
AIRPORT 1975 .... GEORGE KENNEDY
AIRPORT 1975 .... GLORIA SWANSON†
AIRPORT 1975 .... HELEN REDDY
AIRPORT 1975 .... KAREN BLACK
AIRPORT 1975 .... LINDA BLAIR
AIRPORT 1975 .... MARTHA SCOTT
AIRPORT 1975 .... SHARON GLESS
AIRPORT 1975 .... SID CAESAR
AIRPORT 1975 .... SUSAN CLARK
AIRPORT '77 .... BRENDA VACCARO
AIRPORT '77 .... CHRIS LEMMON
AIRPORT '77 .... DARREN McGAVIN
AIRPORT '77 .... GEORGE KENNEDY
AIRPORT '77 .... GIL GERARD
AIRPORT '77 .... JACK LEMMON
AIRPORT '77 .... JAMES STEWART
AIRPORT '77 .... KATHLEEN QUINLAN
AIRPORT '77 .... LEE GRANT
AIRPORT '77 .... OLIVIA DE HAVILLAND
AIRPORT '77 .... ROBERT HOOKS
AIRWOLF (TF) .... ERNEST BORGNINE
AKIRA KUROSAWA'S
DREAMS .... MARTIN SCORSESE
AL CAPONE .... LOUIS QUINN†
AL CAPONE .... MARTIN BALSAM
AL CAPONE .... NEHEMIAH PERSOFF
AL CAPONE .... ROD STEIGER
ALADDIN (AF) .... BRAD KANE
ALADDIN (AF) .... DOUGLAS SEALE
ALADDIN (AF) .... FRANK WELKER
ALADDIN (AF) .... GILBERT GOTTFRIED
ALADDIN (AF) .... JONATHAN FREEMAN
ALADDIN (AF) .... LEA SALONGA
ALADDIN (AF) .... LINDA LARKIN
ALADDIN (AF) .... ROBIN WILLIAMS
ALADDIN (AF) .... SCOTT WEINGER
ALAMBRISTA! .... EDWARD JAMES OLMOS
ALAMBRISTA! .... NED BEATTY
ALAMBRISTA! .... TRINIDAD SILVA JR.†
ALAMO: 13 DAYS TO
GLORY, THE (TF) .... ALEC BALDWIN
ALAMO: 13 DAYS TO
GLORY, THE (TF) .... BRIAN KEITH
ALAMO: 13 DAYS TO
GLORY, THE (TF) .... JAMES ARNESS
ALAMO: 13 DAYS TO
GLORY, THE (TF) .... RAUL JULIA†

ALAMO BAY .... AMY MADIGAN
ALAMO BAY .... BILL THURMAN
ALAMO BAY .... CYNTHIA CARLE
ALAMO BAY .... DONALD MOFFAT
ALAMO BAY .... ED HARRIS
ALAMO BAY .... HO NGUYEN
ALAMO BAY .... MARTINO LASALLE
ALAMO BAY .... RUDY YOUNG
ALAMO BAY .... TRUVER V. TRAN
ALAMO BAY ...... WILLIAM FRANKFATHER
ALAMO, THE .... FRANKIE AVALON
ALAMO, THE .... JOHN WAYNE†
ALAMO, THE .... LAURENCE HARVEY†
ALAMO, THE .... PATRICK WAYNE
ALAMO, THE .... RICHARD BOONE†
ALAMO, THE .... RICHARD WIDMARK
ALAMO, THE O .... CHILL WILLS†
ALAN AND NAOMI .... LUKAS HAAS
ALASKA .... MARGARET LINDSAY†
ALASKA SEAS .... BRIAN KEITH
ALASKA SEAS .... TIMOTHY CAREY
ALBOINO E ROSMUNDA .... JACK PALANCE
ALCATRAZ: THE WHOLE
SHOCKING STORY (TF) .... JOE PANTOLIANO
ALCATRAZ: THE WHOLE
SHOCKING STORY (TF) .... MICHAEL BECK
ALCATRAZ: THE WHOLE
SHOCKING STORY (TF) .... RICHARD LYNCH
ALEX AND THE GYPSY .... JAMES WOODS
ALEX IN WONDERLAND .... DONALD SUTHERLAND
ALEX IN WONDERLAND .... ELLEN BURSTYN
ALEX IN WONDERLAND .... MICHAEL LERNER
ALEX IN WONDERLAND .... PAUL MAZURSKY
ALEX & THE GYPSY .... GENEVIEVE BUJOLD
ALEX & THE GYPSY .... JACK LEMMON
ALEX: THE LIFE
OF A CHILD (TF) .... BONNIE BEDELIA
ALEX: THE LIFE
OF A CHILD (TF) .... CRAIG T. NELSON
ALEXANDER THE GREAT .... CLAIRE BLOOM
ALEXANDER: THE OTHER
SIDE OF DAWN (TF) .... EARL HOLLIMAN
ALEXANDER: THE OTHER
SIDE OF DAWN (TF) .... EVE PLUMB
ALEXANDER'S RAGTIME BAND .... DON AMECHE†
ALFIE ★ .... MICHAEL CAINE
ALFIE O .... VIVIEN MERCHANT†
ALFIE .... DENHOLM ELLIOTT†
ALFIE .... ELEANOR BRON
ALFIE .... SHELLEY WINTERS
ALFIE .... SHIRLEY ANNE FIELD
ALFIE DARLING .... JOAN COLLINS
ALFRED HITCHCOCK
PRESENTS (TF) .... KIM NOVAK
ALFRED HITCHCOCK
PRESENTS (TF) .... MELANIE GRIFFITH
ALFRED HITCHCOCK
PRESENTS (TF) .... NED BEATTY
ALFRED THE GREAT .... DAVID HEMMINGS
ALFRED THE GREAT .... JULIAN GLOVER
ALFRED THE GREAT .... MICHAEL YORK
ALFRED THE GREAT .... PETER VAUGHN
ALFREDO ALFREDO .... DUSTIN HOFFMAN
ALGIERS ★ .... CHARLES BOYER†
ALGIERS O .... GENE LOCKHART†
ALIAS BOSTON BLACKIE .... LLOYD BRIDGES
ALIAS JESSE JAMES .... BOB HOPE
ALIBI ★ .... CHESTER MORRIS†
ALIBI IKE .... OLIVIA DE HAVILLAND
ALICE .... ALEC BALDWIN
ALICE .... BERNADETTE PETERS
ALICE .... BLYTHE DANNER
ALICE .... BOB BALABAN
ALICE .... CAROLINE AARON
ALICE .... CYBILL SHEPHERD
ALICE .... DAVID SPIELBERG
ALICE .... GWEN VERDON
ALICE .... HOLLAND TAYLOR
ALICE .... JAMES TOBACK
ALICE .... JOE MANTEGNA
ALICE .... JUDITH IVEY
ALICE .... JUDY DAVIS

† after an actor's name denotes deceased.

INDEX OF FILM TITLES

ALICE ... JULIE KAVNER
ALICE ... KEYE LUKE†
ALICE ... MIA FARROW
ALICE ... PATRICK O'NEAL†
ALICE ... ROBIN BARTLETT
ALICE ... WILLIAM HURT
ALICE ADAMS ★ ... KATHERINE HEPBURN
ALICE ADAMS ... FRED MACMURRAY†
ALICE ADAMS ... FRED STONE†
ALICE ADAMS ... EVELYN VENABLE†
ALICE ADAMS ... FRANK ALBERTSON†
ALICE ADAMS ... HATTIE MCDANIEL
ALICE DOESN'T LIVE HERE ANYMORE ★★ ... ELLEN BURSTYN
ALICE DOESN'T LIVE HERE ANYMORE ○ ... DIANE LADD
ALICE DOESN'T LIVE HERE ANYMORE ... BILLY GREEN BUSH
ALICE DOESN'T LIVE HERE ANYMORE ... HARVEY KEITEL
ALICE DOESN'T LIVE HERE ANYMORE ... JODIE FOSTER
ALICE DOESN'T LIVE HERE ANYMORE ... KRIS KRISTOFFERSON
ALICE DOESN'T LIVE HERE ANYMORE ... LAURA DERN
ALICE IN WONDERLAND (AF) ... ED WYNN†
ALICE IN WONDERLAND (AF) ... STERLING HOLLOWAY†
ALICE IN WONDERLAND (MS) ... RED BUTTONS
ALICE IN WONDERLAND (MS) ... SCOTT BAIO
ALICE IN WONDERLAND (MS) ... SID CAESAR
ALICE OF WONDERLAND IN PARIS ... CARL REINER
ALICE OR THE LAST ESCAPADE ... SYLVIA KRISTEL
ALICE OU LA DERNIERE FUGUE ... SYLVIA KRISTEL
ALICE, SWEET ALICE ... BROOKE SHIELDS
ALICE'S RESTAURANT ... JAMES BRODERICK†
ALICE'S ADVENTURES IN WONDERLAND ... DUDLEY MOORE
ALICE'S ADVENTURES IN WONDERLAND ... MICHAEL CRAWFORD
ALICE'S RESTAURANT ... PAT QUINN
ALIEN ... HARRY DEAN STANTON
ALIEN ... IAN HOLM
ALIEN ... JOHN HURT
ALIEN ... SIGOURNEY WEAVER
ALIEN ... TOM SKERRITT
ALIEN ... VERONICA CARTWRIGHT
ALIEN ... YAPHET KOTTO
ALIEN 3 ... BRIAN GLOVER
ALIEN 3 ... CHARLES DANCE
ALIEN 3 ... CHARLES S. DUTTON
ALIEN 3 ... DANIEL WEBB
ALIEN 3 ... LANCE HENRIKSEN
ALIEN 3 ... PAUL McGANN
ALIEN 3 ... RALPH BROWN
ALIEN 3 ... SIGOURNEY WEAVER
ALIEN NATION ... JAMES CAAN
ALIEN NATION ... MANDY PATINKIN
ALIEN NATION ... TERENCE STAMP
ALIEN PREDATOR ... DENNIS CHRISTOPHER
ALIEN PREDATOR ... LYNN-HOLLY JOHNSON
ALIEN PREDATOR ... MARTIN HEWITT
ALIEN THUNDER ... DONALD SUTHERLAND
ALIEN THUNDER ... DONALD SUTHERLAND
ALIEN THUNDER ... KEVIN McCARTHY
ALIENS ... BILL PAXTON
ALIENS ... CARRIE HENN
ALIENS ... JENETTE GOLDSTEIN
ALIENS ... LANCE HENRIKSEN
ALIENS ... MICHAEL BIEHN
ALIENS ... PAUL REISER
ALIENS ... WILLIAM HOPE
ALIENS ★ ... SIGOURNEY WEAVER
ALIEN'S RETURN, THE ... CYBILL SHEPHERD
ALIEN'S RETURN, THE ... MARTIN LANDAU
ALIEN'S RETURN, THE ... RAYMOND BURR†
ALIVE ... BRUCE RAMSAY
ALIVE ... ETHAN HAWKE
ALIVE ... JOHN MALKOVICH
ALIVE ... JOSH HAMILTON
ALIVE ... VINCENT SPANO
ALIVE AND KICKING ... RICHARD HARRIS
ALL ABOUT EVE ... EDDIE FISHER
ALL ABOUT EVE ... MARILYN MONROE†
ALL ABOUT EVE ★ ... ANNE BAXTER†
ALL ABOUT EVE ★ ... BETTE DAVIS†
ALL ABOUT EVE ○ ... THELMA RITTER†
ALL ABOUT EVE ○○ ... GEORGE SANDERS†
ALL ABOUT EVE ○ ... CELESTE HOLM
ALL ABOUT EVE ... GARY MERRILL†
ALL ABOUT EVE ... HUGH MARLOWE†
ALL ABOUT EVE ... GREGORY RATOFF†
ALL-AMERICAN BOY, THE ... ANNE ARCHER
ALL-AMERICAN BOY, THE ... ART METRANO
ALL-AMERICAN BOY, THE ... JON VOIGHT
ALL-AMERICAN BOY, THE ... ROSALIND CASH
ALL-AMERICAN, THE ... TONY CURTIS
ALL AT SEA ... ALEC GUINNESS
ALL BY MYSELF (FD) ... EARTHA KITT
ALL CREATURES GREAT AND SMALL ... SIMON WARD
ALL CREATURES GREAT AND SMALL (TF) ... ANTHONY HOPKINS
ALL CREATURES GREAT AND SMALL (TF) ... PETER DAVISON
ALL DOGS GO TO HEAVEN (AF) ... BURT REYNOLDS
ALL DOGS GO TO HEAVEN (AF) ... CHARLES NELSON REILLY
ALL DOGS GO TO HEAVEN (AF) ... DOM DeLUISE
ALL DOGS GO TO HEAVEN (AF) ... JUDITH BARSI†
ALL DOGS GO TO HEAVEN (AF) ... LONI ANDERSON
ALL DOGS GO TO HEAVEN (AF) ... MELBA MOORE
ALL DOGS GO TO HEAVEN (AF) ... VIC TAYBACK†
ALL FALL DOWN ... ANGELA LANSBURY
ALL FALL DOWN ... EVA MARIE SAINT
ALL FALL DOWN ... KARL MALDEN
ALL FALL DOWN ... WARREN BEATTY
ALL GOD'S CHILDREN (TF) ... RICHARD WIDMARK
ALL HANDS ON DECK ... BARBARA EDEN
ALL HANDS ON DECK ... BUDDY HACKETT
ALL HANDS ON DECK ... PAT BOONE
ALL I DESIRE ... BARBARA STANWYCK†
ALL I DESIRE ... MAUREEN O'SULLIVAN
ALL I WANT FOR CHRISTMAS ... AMY OBERER
ALL I WANT FOR CHRISTMAS ... ANDREA MARTIN
ALL I WANT FOR CHRISTMAS ... CAMILLE SAVIOLA
ALL I WANT FOR CHRISTMAS ... ETHAN RANDALL
ALL I WANT FOR CHRISTMAS ... FELICITY LA FORTUNE
ALL I WANT FOR CHRISTMAS ... FRANK GIRARDEAU
ALL I WANT FOR CHRISTMAS ... HARLEY JANE KOZAK
ALL I WANT FOR CHRISTMAS ... JAMEY SHERIDAN
ALL I WANT FOR CHRISTMAS ... KEVIN NEALON
ALL I WANT FOR CHRISTMAS ... LAUREN BACALL
ALL I WANT FOR CHRISTMAS ... LESLIE NIELSEN
ALL I WANT FOR CHRISTMAS ... MICHAEL PATRICK CARTER
ALL I WANT FOR CHRISTMAS ... RENEE TAYLOR
ALL I WANT FOR CHRISTMAS ... THORA BIRCH
ALL IN A NIGHT'S WORK ... CLIFF ROBERTSON
ALL IN A NIGHT'S WORK ... DEAN MARTIN
ALL IN A NIGHT'S WORK ... JACK WESTON
ALL IN A NIGHT'S WORK ... SHIRLEY MacLAINE
ALL MINE TO GIVE ... ROYAL DANO
ALL MY SONS ... BURT LANCASTER†
ALL MY SONS ... HARRY MORGAN
ALL MY SONS ... HOWARD DUFF†
ALL MY SONS (TF) ... JOAN ALLEN
ALL NEAT IN BLACK STOCKINGS ... SUSAN GEORGE
ALL NIGHT LONG ... BARBRA STREISAND
ALL NIGHT LONG ... CHARLES SIEBERT
ALL NIGHT LONG ... DENNIS QUAID
ALL NIGHT LONG ... DIANE LADD
ALL NIGHT LONG ... GENE HACKMAN
ALL NIGHT LONG ... HAMILTON CAMP
ALL NIGHT LONG ... KEVIN DOBSON
ALL NIGHT LONG ... RALEIGH BOND
ALL NIGHT LONG ... RICHARD HARRIS
ALL NIGHT LONG ... TERRY KISER
ALL NIGHT LONG ... VERNEE WATSON
ALL NIGHT LONG ... WILLIAM DANIELS
ALL OF ME ... JASON BERNARD
ALL OF ME ... LILY TOMLIN
ALL OF ME ... MADOLYN SMITH OSBORNE
ALL OF ME ... PEGGY FEURY†
ALL OF ME ... RICHARD LIBERTINI
ALL OF ME ... STEVE MARTIN
ALL OF ME ... VICTORIA TENNANT
ALL QUIET ON THE WESTERN FRONT (TF) ... DONALD PLEASENCE
ALL QUIET ON THE WESTERN FRONT (TF) ... ERNEST BORGNINE
ALL QUIET ON THE WESTERN FRONT (TF) ... IAN HOLM
ALL QUIET ON THE WESTERN FRONT (TF) ... PATRICIA NEAL
ALL SHOOK UP ... GLENN QUINN
ALL SHOOK UP ... HEATHER GRAHAM
ALL SHOOK UP ... JAMIE WALTERS
ALL SHOOK UP ... MICHAEL BACALL
ALL SHOOK UP ... SCOTT COFFEY
ALL THAT HEAVEN ALLOWS ... JANE WYMAN
ALL THAT HEAVEN ALLOWS ... ROCK HUDSON†
ALL THAT JAZZ ... ANN REINKING
ALL THAT JAZZ ... BEN VEREEN
ALL THAT JAZZ ... CLIFF GORMAN
ALL THAT JAZZ ... JESSICA LANGE
ALL THAT JAZZ ... JOHN LITHGOW
ALL THAT JAZZ ★ ... ROY SCHEIDER
ALL THAT MONEY CAN BUY ... WALTER HUSTON†
ALL THAT MONEY CAN BUY ... JEFF COREY
ALL THE FINE YOUNG CANNIBALS ... GEORGE HAMILTON
ALL THE FINE YOUNG CANNIBALS ... ROBERT DAVIS†
ALL THE FINE YOUNG CANNIBALS ... ROBERT WAGNER
ALL THE KIND STRANGERS (TF) ... JOHN SAVAGE
ALL THE KIND STRANGERS (TF) ... SAMANTHA EGGAR
ALL THE KIND STRANGERS (TF) ... STACY KEACH
ALL THE KING'S MEN ○ ... JOHN IRELAND
ALL THE KING'S MEN ○○ ... MERCEDES McCAMBRIDGE
...ALL THE MARBLES ... BURT YOUNG
...ALL THE MARBLES ... PETER FALK
...ALL THE MARBLES ... RICHARD JAECKEL
ALL THE PRESIDENT'S MEN ... BASIL HOFFMAN
ALL THE PRESIDENT'S MEN ... DUSTIN HOFFMAN
ALL THE PRESIDENT'S MEN ... F. MURRAY ABRAHAM
ALL THE PRESIDENT'S MEN ... HAL HOLBROOK
ALL THE PRESIDENT'S MEN ... JACK WARDEN
ALL THE PRESIDENT'S MEN ... LINDSAY CROUSE
ALL THE PRESIDENT'S MEN ... MARTIN BALSAM
ALL THE PRESIDENT'S MEN ... MEREDITH BAXTER
ALL THE PRESIDENT'S MEN ... NED BEATTY
ALL THE PRESIDENT'S MEN ... POLLY HOLLIDAY
ALL THE PRESIDENT'S MEN ... ROBERT REDFORD
ALL THE PRESIDENT'S MEN ... STEPHEN COLLINS
ALL THE PRESIDENT'S MEN ○ ... JANE ALEXANDER
ALL THE PRESIDENT'S MEN ○○ ... JASON ROBARDS
ALL THE RIGHT MOVES ... CHRIS PENN
ALL THE RIGHT MOVES ... CRAIG T. NELSON
ALL THE RIGHT MOVES ... LEA THOMPSON
ALL THE RIGHT MOVES ... PAUL CARAFOTES
ALL THE RIGHT MOVES ... TOM CRUISE
ALL THE RIGHT NOISES ... LESLEY-ANNE DOWN
ALL THE RIVERS RUN (CMS) ... SIGRID THORNTON
ALL THE WAY ... EDDIE ALBERT
ALL THE WAY HOME ... DAVID HUDDLESTON
ALL THE WAY HOME ... JEAN SIMMONS
ALL THE WAY HOME ... PAT HINGLE
ALL THE YOUNG MEN ... MORT SAHL
ALL THE YOUNG MEN ... SIDNEY POITIER
ALL THESE WOMEN ... BIBI ANDERSSON
ALL THIS AND HEAVEN TOO ... BETTE DAVIS†
ALL THIS AND HEAVEN TOO ... JUNE LOCKHART
ALL THIS, AND HEAVEN TOO ○ ... BARBARA O'NEIL†

This is not a list of every film ever made or every cast member, only those listed in this directory.

ALL THROUGH
 THE NIGHT .... DAME JUDITH ANDERSON†
ALL TOGETHER NOW (TF) .... BILL MACY
ALL YOU NEED IS CASH .... ERIC IDLE
ALL'S FAIR .... GEORGE SEGAL
ALLAN QUATERMAIN AND THE LOST
 CITY OF GOLD .... HENRY SILVA
ALLAN QUATERMAIN AND THE LOST
 CITY OF GOLD .... JAMES EARL JONES
ALLAN QUATERMAIN AND THE LOST
 CITY OF GOLD .... RICHARD CHAMBERLAIN
ALLAN QUATERMAIN AND THE LOST
 CITY OF GOLD .... ROBERT DONNER
ALLAN QUATERMAIN AND THE LOST
 CITY OF GOLD .... SHARON STONE
ALLEZ FRANCE! .... MARK LESTER
ALLIGATOR .... DEAN JAGGER†
ALLIGATOR .... HENRY SILVA
ALLIGATOR .... PERRY LANG
ALLIGATOR .... ROBERT FORSTER
ALLIGATOR .... ROBIN RIKER
ALLNIGHTER, THE .... DEDEE PFEIFFER
ALLNIGHTER, THE .... JAMES ANTHONY SHANTA
ALLNIGHTER, THE .... JOAN CUSAK
ALLNIGHTER, THE .... JOHN TERLESKY
ALLNIGHTER, THE .... MICHAEL ONTKEAN
ALLNIGHTER, THE .... SUSANNA HOFFS
ALMOST AN ANGEL .... CHARLTON HESTON
ALMOST AN ANGEL .... ELIAS KOTEAS
ALMOST AN ANGEL .... LINDA KOZLOWSKI
ALMOST AN ANGEL .... PAUL HOGAN
ALMOST MARRIED .... RALPH BELLAMY†
ALMOST PARTNERS (TF) .... DORIS BELACK
ALMOST PERFECT AFFAIR, AN ... BROOKE SHIELDS
ALMOST PERFECT
 AFFAIR, AN .... FARRAH FAWCETT
ALMOST PERFECT
 AFFAIR, AN .... GEORGE PEPPARD†
ALMOST PERFECT
 AFFAIR, AN .... KEITH CARRADINE
ALMOST PERFECT AFFAIR, AN .... RAF VALLONE
ALMOST YOU .... BROOKE ADAMS
ALMOST YOU .... CHRISTINE ESTABROOK
ALMOST YOU .... DANA DELANY
ALMOST YOU .... GRIFFIN DUNNE
ALMOST YOU .... JOE LEON
ALMOST YOU .... JOE SILVER†
ALMOST YOU .... JOSH MOSTEL
ALMOST YOU .... KAREN YOUNG
ALMOST YOU .... LAURA DEAN
ALMOST YOU .... MARTY WATT
ALMOST YOU .... MIGUEL PINERO
ALMOST YOU .... SPALDING GRAY
ALOHA, BOBBY AND ROSE .... DIANNE HULL
ALOHA, BOBBY
 AND ROSE .... EDWARD JAMES OLMOS
ALOHA BOBBY AND ROSE .... PAUL LeMAT
ALOHA, BOBBY AND ROSE ..... ROBERT CARRADINE
ALOHA SUMMER .... ANDY BUMATAI
ALOHA SUMMER .... BLAINE KIA
ALOHA SUMMER .... CHRIS MAKEPEACE
ALOHA SUMMER .... DON MICHAEL PAUL
ALOHA SUMMER .... LORIE GRIFFIN
ALOHA SUMMER .... RIC MANCINI
ALOHA SUMMER .... SCOTT NAKAGAWA
ALOHA SUMMER .... SHO KOSUGI
ALOHA SUMMER .... TIA CARRERE
ALOHA SUMMER .... WARREN FABRO
ALOHA SUMMER .... YUJI OKUMOTO
ALOISE .... ISABELLE HUPPERT
ALOMA OF THE SOUTH SEAS ... DOROTHY LAMOUR
ALONE IN THE DARK .... DONALD PLEASENCE
ALONE IN THE DARK .... DWIGHT SCHULTZ
ALONE IN THE DARK .... JACK PALANCE
ALONE IN THE DARK .... MARTIN LANDAU
ALONE IN THE NEON
 JUNGLE (TF) .... DANNY AIELLO
ALONE IN THE NEON
 JUNGLE (TF) .... GEORG STANFORD BROWN
ALONG CAME
 A SPIDER (TF) .... SUZANNE PLESHETTE
ALONG THE GREAT DIVIDE .... KIRK DOUGLAS

ALPHA BETA .... ALBERT FINNEY
ALPHA CAPER, THE (TF) .... JAMES McEACHIN
ALPHA CAPER, THE (TF) .... LARRY HAGMAN
ALPHA CAPER, THE (TF) .... LEONARD NIMOY
ALPHABET CITY .... MICHAEL WINSLOW
ALPHABET CITY .... VINCENT SPANO
ALPHABET CITY .... ZOHRA LAMPERT
ALPHABET MURDERS, THE .... ROBERT MORLEY
ALPHABET MURDERS, THE .... TONY RANDALL
ALSINO AND THE CONDOR .... DEAN STOCKWELL
ALTA INFEDELTA .... JOHN PHILLIP LAW
ALTERED STATES .... BLAIR BROWN
ALTERED STATES .... BOB BALABAN
ALTERED STATES .... CHARLES HAID
ALTERED STATES .... DREW BARRYMORE
ALTERED STATES .... GEORGE GAYNES
ALTERED STATES .... WILLIAM HURT
ALVAREZ KELLY .... HARRY CAREY JR.
ALVAREZ KELLY .... HOWARD CAINE†
ALVAREZ KELLY .... PATRICK O'NEAL†
ALVAREZ KELLY .... RICHARD WIDMARK
ALVAREZ KELLY .... VICTORIA SHAW†
ALWAYS .... ALAN RACHINS
ALWAYS .... AMNON MESKIN
ALWAYS .... ANDRE GREGORY
ALWAYS .... AUDREY HEPBURN†
ALWAYS .... BOB RAFELSON
ALWAYS .... BRAD JOHNSON
ALWAYS .... BUD TOWNSEND
ALWAYS .... HENRY JAGLOM
ALWAYS .... HOLLY HUNTER
ALWAYS .... JOANNA FRANK
ALWAYS .... JOHN GOODMAN
ALWAYS .... JONATHAN KAUFER
ALWAYS .... KEITH DAVID
ALWAYS .... MARG HELGENBERGER
ALWAYS .... MELISSA LEO
ALWAYS .... MICHAEL EMIL
ALWAYS .... PATRICE TOWNSEND
ALWAYS .... RICHARD DREYFUSS
ALWAYS .... ROBERTS BLOSSOM
ALWAYS GOODBYE .... BARBARA STANWYCK†
ALWAYS LEAVE
 THEM LAUGHING .... MAX SHOWALTER
ALWAYS LEAVE
 THEM LAUGHING .... MILTON BERLE
ALWAYS REMEMBER
 I LOVE YOU (TF) .... DAVID BIRNEY
ALWAYS REMEMBER
 I LOVE YOU (TF) .... JOAN VAN ARK
ALWAYS REMEMBER
 I LOVE YOU (TF) .... PATTY DUKE
ALWAYS REMEMBER
 I LOVE YOU (TF) .... RICHARD MASUR
ALWAYS REMEMBER
 I LOVE YOU (TF) .... SAM WANAMAKER†
ALWAYS REMEMBER
 I LOVE YOU (TF) .... STEPHEN DORFF
ALWAYS TOGETHER .... ELEANOR PARKER
AMADEUS .... CHRISTINE EBERSOLE
AMADEUS .... ELIZABETH BERRIDGE
AMADEUS .... JEFFREY JONES
AMADEUS .... ROY DOTRICE
AMADEUS .... SIMON CALLOW
AMADEUS ★ .... TOM HULCE
AMADEUS ★★ .... F. MURRAY ABRAHAM
AMANTI .... MARCELLO MASTROIANNI
AMATEUR, THE .... ARTHUR HILL
AMATEUR, THE .... CHRISTOPHER PLUMMER
AMATEUR, THE .... JOHN SAVAGE
AMATEUR, THE .... MARTHE KELLER
AMATEUR NIGHT AT THE DIXIE
 BAR AND GRILL (TF) .... DENNIS QUAID
AMATEUR NIGHT AT THE DIXIE
 BAR AND GRILL (TF) .... DON JOHNSON
AMATEUR NIGHT AT THE DIXIE
 BAR AND GRILL (TF) .... HENRY GIBSON
AMATEUR NIGHT AT THE DIXIE
 BAR AND GRILL (TF) .... JAMIE FARR
AMAZING DOBERMANS, THE .... BARBARA EDEN
AMAZING DOBERMANS, THE .... BILLY BARTY

AMAZING
 DOBERMANS, THE .... JAMES FRANCISCUS†
AMAZING GRACE .... MOSES GUNN
AMAZING GRACE .... ROSALIND CASH
AMAZING GRACE AND CHUCK .... ALEX ENGLISH
AMAZING GRACE
 AND CHUCK .... FRANCES CONROY
AMAZING GRACE AND CHUCK .... GREGORY PECK
AMAZING GRACE
 AND CHUCK .... JAMIE LEE CURTIS
AMAZING GRACE
 AND CHUCK .... JOSHUA ZUEHLKE
AMAZING GRACE
 AND CHUCK .... WILLIAM L. PETERSEN
AMAZING HOWARD
 HUGHES, THE (TF) .... ED FLANDERS
AMAZING HOWARD
 HUGHES, THE (TF) .... ED HARRIS
AMAZING HOWARD
 HUGHES, THE (TF) .... TOMMY LEE JONES
AMAZING HOWARD
 HUGHES, THE (TF) .... TOYAH FELDSHUH
AMAZING MR.
 BEECHAM, THE .... DAVID TOMLINSON
AMAZON WOMEN ON
 THE MOON .... ARSSENIO HALL
AMAZON WOMEN ON
 THE MOON .... CARRIE FISHER
AMAZON WOMEN ON
 THE MOON .... HOWARD HESSEMAN
AMAZON WOMEN ON
 THE MOON .... MICHELLE PFEIFFER
AMAZON WOMEN ON
 THE MOON .... RALPH BELLAMY†
AMAZON WOMEN ON
 THE MOON .... ROSANNA ARQUETTE
AMAZON WOMEN ON THE MOON .... STEVE ALLEN
AMAZONS .... WILLIE NELSON
AMAZONS OF ROME .... LOUIS JOURDAN
AMBASSADOR, THE .... ELLEN BURSTYN
AMBASSADOR, THE .... ROBERT MITCHUM
AMBASSADOR'S
 DAUGHTER, THE .... JOHN FORSYTHE
AMBASSADOR'S
 DAUGHTER, THE .... OLIVIA DE HAVILLAND
AMBER WAVES (TF) .... KURT RUSSELL
AMBITION .... CECILIA PECK
AMBITION .... CLANCY BROWN
AMBITION .... GRACE ZABRISKIE
AMBITION .... HAING S. NGOR
AMBITION .... LOU DIAMOND PHILLIPS
AMBITION .... RICHARD BRADFORD
AMBULANCE, THE .... ERIC ROBERTS
AMBULANCE, THE .... JAMES EARL JONES
AMBULANCE, THE .... RED BUTTONS
AMBUSH .... LEON AMES
AMBUSH AT CIMARRON PASS .... CLINT EASTWOOD
AMBUSHERS, THE .... ALBERT SALMI†
AMBUSHERS, THE .... DEAN MARTIN
AMELIA EARHART (TF) .... STEPHEN MACHT
AMELIA EARHART (TF) .... SUSAN CLARK
AMELIA EARHART -
 THE FINAL FLIGHT (CTF) .... DIANE KEATON
AMELIA EARHART -
 THE FINAL FLIGHT (CTF) .... RUTGER HAUER
AMERICA AMERICA .... GREGORY ROZAKIS†
AMERICAN ANTHEM .... ANDREW WHITE
AMERICAN ANTHEM .... GOOGY GRESS
AMERICAN ANTHEM .... JANET JONES
AMERICAN ANTHEM .... JOHN APREA
AMERICAN ANTHEM .... MARIA ANZ
AMERICAN ANTHEM .... MICHAEL PATAKI
AMERICAN ANTHEM .... MICHELLE PHILLIPS
AMERICAN ANTHEM .... MITCH GAYLORD
AMERICAN ANTHEM .... PATRICE DONNELLY
AMERICAN ANTHEM .... R. J. WILLIAMS
AMERICAN ANTHEM .... STACY MALONEY
AMERICAN DREAM, AN .... ELEANOR PARKER
AMERICAN DREAM, AN .... J. D. CANNON
AMERICAN DREAM, AN .... JANET LEIGH
AMERICAN DREAM, AN .... PAUL MANTEE
AMERICAN DREAM, AN .... STUART WHITMAN

AMERICAN DREAM, THE (TF) .... STEPHEN MACHT
AMERICAN DREAMER .... GIANCARLO GIANNINI
AMERICAN DREAMER .... JAMES STALEY
AMERICAN DREAMER .... JoBETH WILLIAMS
AMERICAN DREAMER .... TOM CONTI
AMERICAN DREAMER, THE (FD) ... DENNIS HOPPER
AMERICAN FLYERS .... ALEXANDRA PAUL
AMERICAN FLYERS .... DAVID MARSHALL GRANT
AMERICAN FLYERS .... JANICE RULE
AMERICAN FLYERS .... JENNIFER GREY
AMERICAN FLYERS .... JOHN AMOS
AMERICAN FLYERS .... KEVIN COSTNER
AMERICAN FLYERS .... LUCA BERCOVICI
AMERICAN FLYERS .... RAE DAWN CHONG
AMERICAN FLYERS .... ROBERT TOWNSEND
AMERICAN FRIEND, THE .... BRUNO GANZ
AMERICAN FRIEND, THE .... DENNIS HOPPER
AMERICAN FRIENDS .... ALUN ARMSTRONG
AMERICAN GEISHA (TF) .... BEULAH QUO
AMERICAN GEISHA (TF) .... PAM DAWBER
AMERICAN GEISHA (TF) .... ROBERT ITO
AMERICAN GIGOLO .... BILL DUKE
AMERICAN GIGOLO .... FRANCES BERGEN
AMERICAN GIGOLO .... HECTOR ELIZONDO
AMERICAN GIGOLO .... LAUREN HUTTON
AMERICAN GIGOLO .... NINA VAN PALLANDT
AMERICAN GIGOLO .... RICHARD GERE
AMERICAN GOTHIC .... MICHAEL J. POLLARD
AMERICAN GOTHIC .... ROD STEIGER
AMERICAN GOTHIC .... YVONNE DE CARLO
AMERICAN GRAFFITI .... BO HOPKINS
AMERICAN GRAFFITI .... CHARLES MARTIN SMITH
AMERICAN GRAFFITI .... CINDY WILLIAMS
AMERICAN GRAFFITI .... DEBRALEE SCOTT
AMERICAN GRAFFITI .... HARRISON FORD
AMERICAN GRAFFITI .... KATHLEEN QUINLAN
AMERICAN GRAFFITI .... PAUL LeMAT
AMERICAN GRAFFITI .... RICHARD DREYFUSS
AMERICAN GRAFFITI .... RON HOWARD
AMERICAN GRAFFITI .... SUZANNE SOMERS
AMERICAN GRAFFITI ⊙ .... CANDY CLARK
AMERICAN HARVEST (TF) .... EARL HOLLIMAN
AMERICAN HARVEST (TF) .... JAY KERR
AMERICAN HARVEST (TF) .... JOHN ANDERSON
AMERICAN HARVEST (TF) .... WAYNE ROGERS
AMERICAN HEART .... EDWARD FURLONG
AMERICAN HEART .... JEFF BRIDGES
AMERICAN HEART .... LUCINDA JENNEY
AMERICAN HOT WAX .... JAY LENO
AMERICAN HOT WAX .... JEFF ALTMAN
AMERICAN HOT WAX .... JERRY LEE LEWIS
AMERICAN HOT WAX .... LARAINE NEWMAN
AMERICAN IN PARIS, AN .... GENE KELLY
AMERICAN IN PARIS, AN .... LESLIE CARON
AMERICAN IN PARIS, AN .... NINA FOCH
AMERICAN IN PARIS, AN .... OSCAR LEVANT†
AMERICAN IN ROME, AN .... URSULA ANDRESS
AMERICAN JUSTICE .... WILFORD BRIMLEY
AMERICAN ME .... CARY-HIROYUKI TAGAWA
AMERICAN ME .... EDWARD JAMES OLMOS
AMERICAN NINJA .... DON STEWART
AMERICAN NINJA .... GUICH KOOCK
AMERICAN NINJA .... JOHN FUJIOKA
AMERICAN NINJA .... JOHN LA MOTTA
AMERICAN NINJA .... JUDIE ARONSON
AMERICAN NINJA .... MICHAEL DUDIKOFF
AMERICAN NINJA .... STEVE JAMES
AMERICAN NINJA 3: BLOOD HUNT .... CALVIN JUNG
AMERICAN NINJA 3:
    BLOOD HUNT .... DAVID BRADLEY
AMERICAN NINJA 3:
    BLOOD HUNT .... MARJOE GORTNER
AMERICAN NINJA 3:
    BLOOD HUNT ....MICHELE CHAN
AMERICAN NINJA 3:
    BLOOD HUNT .... STEVE JAMES
AMERICAN NINJA 4:
    THE ANNIHILATION .... DAVID BRADLEY
AMERICAN NINJA 4:
    THE ANNIHILATION .... JAMES BOOTH
AMERICAN NINJA 4:
    THE ANNIHILATION .... MICHAEL DUDIKOFF
AMERICAN PRESIDENT, THE .... ANNETTE BENING

AMERICAN PRESIDENT, THE .... MICHAEL DOUGLAS
AMERICAN PRESIDENT, THE .... DAVID PAYMER
AMERICAN PRESIDENT, THE .... MARTIN SHEEN
AMERICAN PRESIDENT, THE .... MICHAEL J. FOX
AMERICAN PRESIDENT, THE .... MORGAN FREEMAN
AMERICAN PRESIDENT, THE .... J. T. WALSH
AMERICAN
    PRESIDENT, THE .... ANNA DEAVERE SMITH
AMERICAN ROULETTE .... ANDY GARCIA
AMERICAN STORY, AN (TF) .... BRAD JOHNSON
AMERICAN SUCCESS CO., THE .... JEFF BRIDGES
AMERICAN SUCCESS
    COMPANY, THE .... NED BEATTY
AMERICAN SUCCESS/SUCCESS .... NED BEATTY
AMERICAN TAIL, AN (AF) .... CATHIANNE BLORE
AMERICAN
    TAIL, AN (AF) .... CHRISTOPHER PLUMMER
AMERICAN TAIL, AN (AF) .... DOM DeLUISE
AMERICAN TAIL, AN (AF) .... JOHN FINNEGAN
AMERICAN TAIL, AN (AF) .... MADELINE KAHN
AMERICAN TAIL, AN (AF) .... NEHEMIAH PERSOFF
AMERICAN TAIL, AN (AF) .... PHILLIP GLASSER
AMERICAN TAIL, AN (AF) .... WILL RYAN
AMERICAN TAIL: FIEVEL
    GOES WEST, AN (AF) .... AMY IRVING
AMERICAN TAIL: FIEVEL
    GOES WEST, AN (AF) .... CATHY CAVADINI
AMERICAN TAIL: FIEVEL
    GOES WEST, AN (AF) .... DOM DeLUISE
AMERICAN TAIL: FIEVEL
    GOES WEST, AN (AF) .... JAMES STEWART
AMERICAN TAIL: FIEVEL
    GOES WEST, AN (AF) .... JOHN CLEESE
AMERICAN TAIL: FIEVEL
    GOES WEST, AN (AF) .... JON LOVITZ
AMERICAN TAIL: FIEVEL
    GOES WEST, AN (AF) .... NEHEMIAH PERSOFF
AMERICAN TAIL: FIEVEL
    GOES WEST, AN (AF) .... PHILLIP GLASSER
AMERICAN TRAGEDY, AN .... SYLVIA SIDNEY
AMERICAN WAY, THE .... DENNIS HOPPER
AMERICAN WAY, THE .... MICHAEL J. POLLARD
AMERICAN WEREWOLF IN
    LONDON, AN .... BRIAN GLOVER
AMERICAN WEREWOLF IN
    LONDON, AN .... DAVID NAUGHTON
AMERICAN WEREWOLF IN
    LONDON, AN .... GRIFFIN DUNNE
AMERICAN WEREWOLF IN
    LONDON, AN .... JENNY AGUTTER
AMERICAN WEREWOLF IN
    LONDON, AN .... JOHN WOODVINE
AMERICANA .... BARBARA HERSHEY
AMERICANA .... DAVID CARRADINE
AMERICANIZATION
    OF EMILY, THE .... JAMES COBURN
AMERICANIZATION
    OF EMILY, THE .... JAMES GARNER
AMERICANIZATION
    OF EMILY, THE .... JOYCE GRENFELL†
AMERICANIZATION
    OF EMILY, THE .... JULIE ANDREWS
AMERICANIZATION
    OF EMILY, THE .... KEENAN WYNN†
AMERICANIZATION
    OF EMILY, THE .... MELVYN DOUGLAS†
AMERICANIZATION
    OF EMILY, THE .... WILLIAM WINDOM
AMERICATHON .... HARVEY KORMAN
AMERICATHON .... JAY LENO
AMERICATHON .... JOHN RITTER
AMERIKA (MS) .... CHRISTINE LAHTI
AMERIKA (MS) .... CINDY PICKETT
AMERIKA (MS) .... DORIAN HAREWOOD
AMERIKA (MS) .... KRIS KRISTOFFERSON
AMERIKA (MS) .... LARA FLYNN BOYLE
AMERIKA (MS) .... MARIEL HEMINGWAY
AMERIKA (MS) .... ROBERT URICH
AMERIKA (MS) .... SAM NEILL
AMITYVILLE 1992: IT'S
    ABOUT TIME (MFV) .... STEPHEN MACHT
AMITYVILLE 3-D .... CANDY CLARK
AMITYVILLE 3-D .... MEG RYAN

AMITYVILLE 3-D .... TESS HARPER
AMITYVILLE 3-D .... TONY ROBERTS
AMITYVILLE HORROR, THE .... AMY WRIGHT
AMITYVILLE HORROR, THE .... DON STROUD
AMITYVILLE HORROR, THE .... JAMES BROLIN
AMITYVILLE HORROR, THE .... MARGOT KIDDER
AMITYVILLE HORROR, THE .... ROD STEIGER
AMITYVILLE II:
    THE POSSESSION .... ANDREW PRINE
AMITYVILLE II: THE POSSESSION .... BURT YOUNG
AMITYVILLE II: THE POSSESSION ..... DANNY AIELLO
AMITYVILLE II:
    THE POSSESSION .... DIANE FRANKLIN
AMITYVILLE II: THE POSSESSION ..... JACK MAGNER
AMITYVILLE II: THE POSSESSION ..... JAMES OLSON
AMITYVILLE II: THE POSSESSION ...... MOSES GUNN
AMITYVILLE II: THE POSSESSION ... RUTANYA ALDA
AMITYVILLE II: THE POSSESSION ... TED ROSS
AMITYVILLE: THE DEMON .... MEG RYAN
AMITYVILLE: THE DEMON .... TESS HARPER
AMITYVILLE: THE EVIL
    ESCAPES (TF) .... JANE WYATT
AMITYVILLE: THE EVIL
    ESCAPES (TF) .... PATTY DUKE
AMO NON AMO .... JACQUELINE BISSET
AMO NON AMO .... MAXIMILIAN SCHELL
AMO NON AMO .... TERENCE STAMP
AMORI E VELENI .... LOIS MAXWELL
AMOROUS ADVENTURES OF
    MOLL FLANDERS, THE .... ANGELA LANSBURY
AMOROUS ADVENTURES OF
    MOLL FLANDERS, THE .... KIM NOVAK
AMOROUS ADVENTURES OF
    MOLL FLANDERS, THE .... VITTORIO DE SICA†
AMOS (TF) .... KIRK DOUGLAS
AMSTERDAM KILL, THE .... BRADFORD DILLMAN
AMSTERDAM KILL, THE .... LESLIE NIELSEN
AMSTERDAM KILL, THE .... RICHARD EGAN†
AMSTERDAM KILL, THE .... ROBERT MITCHUM
AMY ....JENNY AGUTTER
AMY FISHER
    STORY, THE (TF) .... DREW BARRYMORE
ANASTASIA .... HELEN HAYES
ANASTASIA ★★ .... INGRID BERGMAN†
ANASTASIA: THE MYSTERY
    OF ANNA (MS) .... CLAIRE BLOOM
ANASTASIA: THE MYSTERY
    OF ANNA (MS) .... EDWARD FOX
ANASTASIA: THE MYSTERY
    OF ANNA (TF) .... AMY IRVING
ANASTASIA: THE MYSTERY
    OF ANNA (TF) .... OLIVIA DE HAVILLAND
ANASTASIA: THE MYSTERY
    OF ANNA (TF) .... OMAR SHARIF
ANASTASIA: THE MYSTERY
    OF ANNA (TF) .... REX HARRISON†
ANATOMY OF A MURDER .... BEN GAZZARA
ANATOMY OF A MURDER ★ .... JAMES STEWART
ANATOMY OF A
    MURDER ⊙ .... ARTHUR O'CONNELL†
ANATOMY OF A MURDER ⊙ ...... GEORGE C. SCOTT
ANATOMY OF AN ILLNESS (TF) .... ED ASNER
ANATOMY OF AN ILLNESS (TF) .... ELI WALLACH
ANATOMY OF
    LOVE, THE .... MARCELLO MASTROIANNI
ANATOMY OF LOVE, THE .... SOPHIA LOREN
ANCHORS AWEIGH .... DEAN STOCKWELL
ANCHORS AWEIGH .... FRANK SINATRA
ANCHORS AWEIGH ★ .... GENE KELLY
AND BABY
    MAKES SIX (TF) .... COLLEEN DEWHURST†
AND BABY MAKES SIX (TF) ..... TIMOTHY HUTTON
AND BABY MAKES THREE .... BARBARA HALE
AND GOD CREATED WOMAN ...... DONOVAN LEITCH
AND GOD CREATED WOMAN ...... FRANK LANGELLA
AND GOD CREATED
    WOMAN .... REBECCA DE MORNAY
AND GOD CREATED WOMAN .... VINCENT SPANO
...AND GOD SPOKE .... MICHAEL RILEY
...AND GOD SPOKE .... STEPHEN RAPPAPORT
AND I ALONE SURVIVED (TF) .... BLAIR BROWN
...AND JUSTICE FOR ALL .... ALAN NORTH
...AND JUSTICE FOR ALL .... CHRISTINE LAHTI

This is not a list of every film ever made or every cast member, only those listed in this directory.

...AND JUSTICE FOR ALL .... CRAIG T. NELSON
...AND JUSTICE FOR ALL .... JACK WARDEN
...AND JUSTICE FOR ALL .... JOHN FORSYTHE
...AND JUSTICE FOR ALL .... LEE STRASBERG†
...AND JUSTICE FOR ALL ★ .... AL PACINO
AND NOTHING BUT
    THE TRUTH .... GLENDA JACKSON
AND NOW FOR SOMETHING
    COMPLETELY DIFFERENT .... ERIC IDLE
AND NOW FOR SOMETHING COMPLETELY
    DIFFERENT .... GRAHAM CHAPMAN†
AND NOW FOR SOMETHING
    COMPLETELY DIFFERENT .... JOHN CLEESE
AND NOW FOR SOMETHING
    COMPLETELY DIFFERENT .... MICHAEL PALIN
AND NOW FOR SOMETHING
    COMPLETELY DIFFERENT .... TERRY GILLIAM
AND NOW FOR SOMETHING
    COMPLETELY DIFFERENT .... TERRY JONES
AND NOW MY LOVE .... MARTHE KELLER
AND ONCE UPON A TIME .... BO DEREK
AND SO THEY
    WERE MARRIED .... ROBERT MITCHUM
AND THE ANGELS SING .... DOROTHY LAMOUR
AND THE BAND PLAYED ON (CTF) .... ALAN ALDA
AND THE BAND
    PLAYED ON (CTF) .... ANJELICA HUSTON
AND THE BAND PLAYED ON (CTF) .... B. D. WONG
AND THE BAND
    PLAYED ON (CTF) .... CHARLES MARTIN SMITH
AND THE BAND
    PLAYED ON (CTF) .... CHRISTIAN CLEMENSON
AND THE BAND
    PLAYED ON (CTF) .... DAVID CLENNON
AND THE BAND PLAYED ON (CTF) ...... DAVID DUKES
AND THE BAND
    PLAYED ON (CTF) .... GLENNE HEADLY
AND THE BAND
    PLAYED ON (CTF) .... IAN MCKELLEN
AND THE BAND PLAYED ON (CTF) .... LILY TOMLIN
AND THE BAND
    PLAYED ON (CTF) .... MATTHEW MODINE
AND THE BAND PLAYED ON (CTF) ...... PHIL COLLINS
AND THE BAND
    PLAYED ON (CTF) .... RICHARD GERE
AND THE BAND
    PLAYED ON (CTF) .... RICHARD MASUR
AND THE BAND
    PLAYED ON (CTF) .... SAUL RUBINEK
AND THE BAND
    PLAYED ON (CTF) .... STEPHEN SPINELLA
AND THE BAND
    PLAYED ON (CTF) .... STEVE MARTIN
AND THE BAND
    PLAYED ON (CTF) .... SWOOSIE KURTZ
AND THE SHIP SAILS ON .... FREDDIE JONES
AND THE SHIP SAILS ON .... JANET SUZMAN
AND THEN THERE
    WERE NONE ...... DAME JUDITH ANDERSON†
AND THERE CAME A MAN .... ROD STEIGER
ANDERSON TAPES, THE .... ALAN KING
ANDERSON
    TAPES, THE .... CHRISTOPHER WALKEN
ANDERSON TAPES, THE .... DYAN CANNON
ANDERSON TAPES, THE .... MARTIN BALSAM
ANDERSON TAPES, THE .... MAX SHOWALTER
ANDERSON TAPES, THE .... SEAN CONNERY
ANDERSON TAPES, THE .... VAL AVERY
ANDRE .... CHELSEA FIELD
ANDRE .... JOSHUA JACKSON
ANDRE .... KEITH CARRADINE
ANDRE .... KEITH SZARABAJKA
ANDRE .... TINA MAJORINO
ANDROCLES AND THE LION .... ALAN YOUNG
ANDROCLES AND THE LION .... JEAN SIMMONS
ANDROMEDA STRAIN, THE .... ARTHUR HILL
ANDROMEDA STRAIN, THE .... JAMES OLSON
ANDROMEDA STRAIN, THE .... KATE REID
ANDY HARDY FILMS .... CECILIA PARKER†
ANDY HARDY'S DOUBLE LIFE .... ROBERT BLAKE
ANDY WARHOL'S BAD .... CARROLL BAKER
ANDY WARHOL'S BAD .... LAWRENCE TIERNEY
ANDY WARHOL'S BAD .... PERRY KING

ANDY WARHOL'S BAD .... SUSAN TYRRELL
ANDY WARHOL'S DRACULA ..... JOE DALLESANDRO
ANDY WARHOL'S
    FRANKENSTEIN .... JOE DALLESANDRO
ANGEL .... CLIFF GORMAN
ANGEL .... DICK SHAWN
ANGEL .... DONNA WILKES
ANGEL .... JOHN DIEHL
ANGEL .... RORY CALHOUN
ANGEL .... STEPHEN REA
ANGEL .... SUSAN TYRRELL
ANGEL ANGEL DOWN WE GO ...... JENNIFER JONES
ANGEL ANGEL DOWN WE GO ... RODDY McDOWALL
ANGEL BABY .... BURT REYNOLDS
ANGEL BABY .... GEORGE HAMILTON
ANGEL BABY .... HENRY JONES
ANGEL BABY .... JOAN BLONDELL†
ANGEL BABY .... MERCEDES McCAMBRIDGE
ANGEL BABY .... SALOME JENS
ANGEL CITY (TF) .... PAUL WINFIELD
ANGEL FACE .... JEAN SIMMONS
ANGEL FACE .... ROBERT MITCHUM
ANGEL FROM TEXAS, AN .... EDDIE ALBERT
ANGEL FROM TEXAS, AN .... JANE WYMAN
ANGEL FROM TEXAS, AN .... RONALD REAGAN
ANGEL HEART .... CHARLOTTE RAMPLING
ANGEL HEART .... LISA BONET
ANGEL HEART .... MICKEY ROURKE
ANGEL HEART .... ROBERT DE NIRO
ANGEL III .... MARK BLANKFIELD
ANGEL III .... MITZI KAPTURE
ANGEL IN GREEN (TF) .... BRUCE BOXLEITNER
ANGEL IN GREEN (TF) .... SUSAN DEY
ANGEL IN MY POCKET .... ANDY GRIFFITH
ANGEL LEVINE, THE .... ANNE JACKSON
ANGEL LEVINE, THE .... ELI WALLACH
ANGEL LEVINE, THE .... MILO O'SHEA
ANGEL OF CONTENTION, THE .... LILLIAN GISH†
ANGEL OF DESIRE .... ANTHONY DENISON
ANGEL OF DESIRE .... JOAN SEVERANCE
ANGEL OF DESIRE .... JOHN ALLEN NELSON
ANGEL ON MY SHOULDER (TF) .... RICHARD KILEY
ANGEL TOWN .... FRANK ARAGON
ANGEL TOWN .... MIKE MOROFF
ANGEL TOWN .... PETER KWONG
ANGEL TOWN .... THERESA SALDANA
ANGEL TOWN .... TONY VALNTINO
ANGEL UNCHAINED .... DON STROUD
ANGEL UNCHAINED .... TYNE DALY
ANGEL WITH THE TRUMPET .... MARIA SCHELL
ANGEL WORE RED, THE .... AVA GARDNER†
ANGELA .... JOHN VERNON
ANGELA .... SOPHIA LOREN
ANGELIKA .... MARIA SCHELL
ANGELO, MY LOVE .... ANGELO EVANS
ANGELO, MY LOVE ..... STEVE "PATALAY" TSIGNOFF
ANGELS AND INSECTS .... JEREMY KEMP
ANGELS AND INSECTS ..... KRISTIN SCOTT THOMAS
ANGELS AND INSECTS .... MARK RYLANCE
ANGELS AND INSECTS .... PATSY KENSIT
ANGELS HARD AS THEY COME .... SCOTT GLENN
ANGELS IN RED .... JEFFREY DEAN MORGAN
ANGELS IN RED .... LESLIE BEGA
ANGELS IN THE OUTFIELD .... BRENDA FRICKER
ANGELS IN THE
    OUTFIELD .... CHRISTOPHER LLOYD
ANGELS IN THE OUTFIELD .... DANNY GLOVER
ANGELS IN THE OUTFIELD .... JANET LEIGH
ANGELS IN THE OUTFIELD .... MILTON DAVIS JR.
ANGELS IN THE OUTFIELD .... TONY DANZA
ANGELS OF DARKNESS .... ANTHONY QUINN
ANGELS WASH THEIR FACES ...... RONALD REAGAN
ANGELS WITH DIRTY FACES ★ ..... JAMES CAGNEY†
ANGELS WITH DIRTY FACES .... PAT O'BRIEN†
ANGELS WITH
    DIRTY FACES .... HUMPHREY BOGART†
ANGELS WITH DIRTY FACES .... ANN SHERIDAN†
ANGELS WITH
    DIRTY FACES .... GEORGE BANCROFT†
ANGELS WITH DIRTY FACES .... BILLY HALOP†
ANGELS WITH DIRTY FACES .... LEO GORCEY†
ANGELS WITH DIRTY FACES .... HUNTZ HALL†
ANGELS WITH DIRTY FACES .... GABE DELL†

ANGELS WITH DIRTY FACES .... BOBBY JORDAN†
ANGELS WITH
    DIRTY FACES .... BERNARD PUNSLEY†
ANGIE .... AIDA TURTURRO
ANGIE .... GEENA DAVIS
ANGIE .... JAMES GANDOLFIINI
ANGIE .... JENNY O'HARA
ANGIE .... PHILIP BOSCO
ANGIE .... STEPHEN REA
ANGRY HILLS, THE .... ROBERT MITCHUM
ANGRY HILLS, THE .... THEODORE BIKEL
ANGRY RED PLANET, THE .... JACK KRUSCHEN
ANGUISH .... ZELDA RUBINSTEIN
ANIMA PERSA .... CATHERINE DENEUVE
ANIMAL BEHAVIOR .... ARMAND ASSANTE
ANIMAL BEHAVIOR .... HOLLY HUNTER
ANIMAL BEHAVIOR .... JOSH MOSTEL
ANIMAL BEHAVIOR .... KAREN ALLEN
ANIMAL BEHAVIOR .... RICHARD LIBERTINI
ANIMALS, THE .... HENRY SILVA
ANIMALYMPICS (AF) .... BILLY CRYSTAL
ANN JILLIAN STORY, THE (TF) .... ANN JILLIAN
ANN JILLIAN STORY, THE (TF) .... KATE LYNCH
ANN JILLIAN STORY, THE (TF) ...... TONY LoBIANCO
ANN JILLIAN STORY, THE (TF) ..... VIVECA LINDFORS
ANN-MARGRIT .... LIV ULLMANN
ANNA ★ .... SALLY KIRKLAND
ANNA .... PAULINA PORIZKOYA
ANNA AND THE KING
    OF SIAM I .... GALE SONDERGAARD†
ANNA CHRISTIE ★ .... GRETA GARBO†
ANNA KARENINA .... MAUREEN O'SULLIVAN
ANNA KARENINA .... MICHAEL GOUGH
ANNA KARENINA (TF) .... CHRISTOPHER REEVE
ANNA KARENINA (TF) .... JACQUELINE BISSET
ANNA KARENINA (TF) .... PAUL SCOFIELD
ANNA LUCASTA .... EARTHA KITT
ANNA LUCASTA .... JOHN IRELAND
ANNA LUCASTA .... MARY WICKES
ANNAPOLIS STORY, AN .... KEVIN McCARTHY
ANNE OF THE INDIES .... LOUIS JOURDAN
ANNE OF THE THOUSAND DAYS ..... DENIS QUILLEY
ANNE OF THE
    THOUSAND DAYS ★ .... GENEVIEVE BUJOLD
ANNE OF THE
    THOUSAND DAYS ★ .... RICHARD BURTON†
ANNIE .... AILEEN QUINN
ANNIE .... ALBERT FINNEY
ANNIE .... ANN REINKING
ANNIE .... BERNADETTE PETERS
ANNIE .... CAROL BURNETT
ANNIE .... EDWRAD HERRMANN
ANNIE .... GEOFFREY HOLDER
ANNIE .... TIM CURRY
ANNIE GET YOUR GUN .... HOWARD KEEL
ANNIE HALL .... BEVERLY D'ANGELO
ANNIE HALL .... CAROL KANE
ANNIE HALL .... CHRISTOPHER WALKEN
ANNIE HALL .... COLLEEN DEWHURST†
ANNIE HALL .... DICK CAVETT
ANNIE HALL .... JANET MARGOLIN
ANNIE HALL .... JEFF GOLDBLUM
ANNIE HALL .... JOHN GLOVER
ANNIE HALL .... PAUL SIMON
ANNIE HALL .... SHELLEY DUVALL
ANNIE HALL .... SHELLEY HACK
ANNIE HALL .... SIGOURNEY WEAVER
ANNIE HALL .... STANLEY DeSANTIS
ANNIE HALL .... TONY ROBERTS
ANNIE HALL ★ .... WOODY ALLEN
ANNIE HALL ★★ .... DIANE KEATON
ANNIE LAURIE .... LILLIAN GISH†
ANNIE OAKLEY .... BARBARA STANWYCK†
ANNIHILATOR, THE (TF) .... LISA BLOUNT
ANNIHILATOR, THE (TF) .... SUSAN BLAKELY
ANNIVERSARY, THE .... BETTE DAVIS†
ANNIVERSARY, THE .... JACK HEDLEY
ANONIMO VENEZIANO .... TONY MUSANTE
ANONYMOUS .... JULIE CHRISTIE
ANONYMOUS VENETIAN, THE .... TONY MUSANTE
ANOTHER 48 HRS. .... ANDREW DIVOFF
ANOTHER 48 HRS. .... BERNIE CASEY
ANOTHER 48 HRS. .... BRION JAMES

† after an actor's name denotes deceased.

INDEX OF FILM TITLES

ANOTHER 48 HRS. ...... DAVID ANTHONY MARSHALL
ANOTHER 48 HRS. ...... ED O'ROSS
ANOTHER 48 HRS. ...... EDDIE MURPHY
ANOTHER 48 HRS. ...... KEVIN TIGHE
ANOTHER 48 HRS. ...... NICK NOLTE
ANOTHER COUNTRY ...... COLIN FIRTH
ANOTHER COUNTRY ...... RUPERT EVERETT
ANOTHER LANGUAGE ...... HELEN HAYES
ANOTHER MAN, ANOTHER CHANCE ...... GENEVIEVE BUJOLD
ANOTHER MAN, ANOTHER CHANCE ... JAMES CAAN
ANOTHER MAN, ANOTHER CHANCE ...... JENNIFER WARREN
ANOTHER MAN, ANOTHER CHANCE ...... SUSAN TYRRELL
ANOTHER MAN'S POISON ...... BETTE DAVIS†
ANOTHER SHORE ...... IRENE WORTH
ANOTHER STAKEOUT ...... CATHY MORIARTY
ANOTHER STAKEOUT ...... DENNIS FARINA
ANOTHER STAKEOUT ...... EMILIO ESTEVEZ
ANOTHER STAKEOUT ...... MARCIA STRASSMAN
ANOTHER STAKEOUT ...... RICHARD DREYFUSS
ANOTHER STAKEOUT ...... ROSIE O'DONNELL
ANOTHER TIME, ANOTHER PLACE ...... LANA TURNER
ANOTHER TIME, ANOTHER PLACE ...... SEAN CONNERY
ANOTHER WOMAN ...... BETTY BUCKLEY
ANOTHER WOMAN ...... BLYTHE DANNER
ANOTHER WOMAN ...... DAVID OGDEN STIERS
ANOTHER WOMAN ...... GENA ROWLANDS
ANOTHER WOMAN ...... GENE HACKMAN
ANOTHER WOMAN ...... HARRIS YULIN
ANOTHER WOMAN ...... IAN HOLM
ANOTHER WOMAN ...... JOHN HOUSEMAN†
ANOTHER WOMAN ...... MARTHA PLIMPTON
ANOTHER WOMAN ...... MIA FARROW
ANOTHER WOMAN ...... PHILIP BOSCO
ANOTHER WOMAN ...... SANDY DENNIS†
ANOTHER YOU ...... BILLY BECK
ANOTHER YOU ...... GENE WILDER
ANOTHER YOU ...... GIAN-CARLO SCANDIUZZI
ANOTHER YOU ...... JERRY HOUSER
ANOTHER YOU ...... KEVIN POLLAK
ANOTHER YOU ...... MERCEDES RUEHL
ANOTHER YOU ...... PETER MICHAEL GOETZ
ANOTHER YOU ...... PHIL RUBENSTEIN
ANOTHER YOU ...... RICHARD PRYOR
ANOTHER YOU ...... STEPHEN LANG
ANOTHER YOU ...... VANESSA WILLIAMS
ANTEFATTO ...... CLAUDINE AUGER
ANTHONY ADVERSE ...... OLIVIA DE HAVILLAND
ANTHONY ADVERSE ✪✪ ...... GALE SONDERGAARD†
ANTOINE ET SEBASTIEN ...... KEITH CARRADINE
ANTONY AND CLEOPATRA ...... CHARLTON HESTON
ANTONY AND CLEOPATRA ...... FREDDIE JONES
ANTONY AND CLEOPATRA ...... HILDEGARD NEIL
ANTONY AND CLEOPATRA ...... JOHN CASTLE
ANY NUMBER CAN PLAY ...... ALEXIS SMITH†
ANY WEDNESDAY ...... DEAN JONES
ANY WEDNESDAY ...... JANE FONDA
ANY WEDNESDAY ...... JASON ROBARDS
ANY WEDNESDAY ...... ROSEMARY MURPHY
ANY WHICH WAY YOU CAN ...... ANN RAMSEY†
ANY WHICH WAY YOU CAN ...... BILL McKINNEY
ANY WHICH WAY YOU CAN ...... CLINT EASTWOOD
ANY WHICH WAY YOU CAN ...... GEOFFREY LEWIS
ANY WHICH WAY YOU CAN ...... HARRY GUARDINO
ANY WHICH WAY YOU CAN ...... LOGAN RAMSEY
ANY WHICH WAY YOU CAN ...... RUTH GORDON†
ANY WHICH WAY YOU CAN ...... SONDRA LOCKE
ANY WHICH WAY YOU CAN ...... WILLIAM SMITH
ANYONE CAN PLAY ...... CLAUDINE AUGER
ANYONE CAN PLAY ...... URSULA ANDRESS
ANYTHING CAN HAPPEN ...... JOSE FERRER†
ANYTHING FOR LOVE ...... CANDICE BERGEN
ANYTHING FOR LOVE ...... JOHN GIELGUD
ANYTHING TO SURVIVE (TF) ...... OCEAN HELLMAN
ANYTHING TO SURVIVE (TF) ...... ROBERT CONRAD
ANZIO ...... EARL HOLLIMAN
ANZIO ...... PETER FALK
ANZIO ...... RENI SANTONI
ANZIO ...... ROBERT MITCHUM
APACHE ...... BURT LANCASTER†
APACHE ...... CHARLES BRONSON
APACHE ...... JOHN DEHNER†
APACHE RIFLES ...... MICHAEL DANTE
APACHE TERRITORY ...... RORY CALHOUN
APACHE UPRISING ...... RORY CALHOUN
APACHE WAR SMOKE ...... ROBERT BLAKE
APACHE WOMAN ...... DICK MILLER
APACHE WOMAN ...... LLOYD BRIDGES
APARTMENT, THE ...... EDIE ADAMS
APARTMENT, THE ...... RAY WALSTON
APARTMENT, THE ★ ...... JACK LEMMON
APARTMENT, THE ★ ...... SHIRLEY MacLAINE
APARTMENT, THE ✪ ...... JACK KRUSCHEN
APARTMENT ZERO ...... COLIN FIRTH
APARTMENT ZERO ...... FABRIZIO BENTIVOGLIO
APARTMENT ZERO ...... HART BOCHNER
APARTMENT ZERO ...... LIZ SMITH
APEX ...... ADAM LAWSON
APEX ...... LISA ANN RUSSELL
APEX ...... MARCUS AURELIUS
APEX ...... MITCHELL COX
APEX ...... RICHARD KEATS
APOCALPYSE NOW ...... COLLEEN CAMP
APOCALPYSE NOW ...... SCOTT GLENN
APOCALYPSE NOW ...... DENNIS HOPPER
APOCALYPSE NOW ...... FREDERIC FORREST
APOCALYPSE NOW ...... HARRISON FORD
APOCALYPSE NOW ...... LAURENCE FISHBURNE
APOCALYPSE NOW ...... MARLON BRANDO
APOCALYPSE NOW ...... MARTIN SHEEN
APOCALYPSE NOW ...... SAM BOTTOMS
APOCALYPSE NOW ✪ ...... ROBERT DUVALL
APOLLO 13 ...... BILL PAXTON
APOLLO 13 ...... ED HARRIS
APOLLO 13 ...... GARY SINISE
APOLLO 13 ...... KATHLEEN QUINLAN
APOLLO 13 ...... KEVIN BACON
APOLLO 13 ...... TOM HANKS
APPALOOSA, THE ...... JOHN SAXON
APPALOOSA, THE ...... MARLON BRANDO
APPEARANCES (TF) ...... ERNEST BORGNINE
APPEARANCES (TF) ...... JAMES HANDY
APPLE DUMPLING GANG RIDES AGAIN, THE ...... DON KNOTTS
APPLE DUMPLING GANG RIDES AGAIN, THE ...... HARRY MORGAN
APPLE DUMPLING GANG RIDES AGAIN, THE ...... KENNETH MARS
APPLE DUMPLING GANG RIDES AGAIN, THE ...... RUTH BUZZI
APPLE DUMPLING GANG RIDES AGAIN, THE ...... TIM CONWAY
APPLE DUMPLING GANG RIDES AGAIN, THE ...... TIM MATHESON
APPLE DUMPLING GANG, THE ...... BILL BIXBY†
APPLE DUMPLING GANG, THE ...... DON KNOTTS
APPLE DUMPLING GANG, THE ...... HARRY MORGAN
APPLE DUMPLING GANG, THE ...... SUSAN CLARK
APPLE DUMPLING GANG, THE ...... TIM CONWAY
APPLE, THE ...... JOSS ACKLAND
APPOINTMENT, THE ...... ANOUK AIMEE
APPOINTMENT, THE ...... OMAR SHARIF
APPOINTMENT WITH DEATH ...... CARRIE FISHER
APPOINTMENT WITH DEATH ...... JOHN GIELGUD
APPOINTMENT WITH DEATH ...... LAUREN BACALL
APPOINTMENT WITH DEATH ...... PIPER LAURIE
APPOINTMENT WITH VENUS ...... DAVID NIVEN†
APPRENTICE TO MURDER ...... MIA SARA
APPRENTICE TO MURDER ...... RUTANYA ALDA
APPRENTICESHIP OF DUDDY KRAVITZ, THE ...... JACK WARDEN
APPRENTICESHIP OF DUDDY KRAVITZ, THE ...... JOSEPH WISEMAN
APPRENTICESHIP OF DUDDY KRAVITZ, THE ...... RANDY QUAID
APPRENTICESHIP OF DUDDY KRAVITZ, THE ...... RICHARD DREYFUSS
APPRENTICESHIP OF DUDDY KRAVTIZ, THE ...... DENHOLM ELLIOTT†
APRIL FOOLS, THE ...... CATHERINE DENEUVE
APRIL FOOLS, THE ...... HARVEY KORMAN
APRIL FOOLS, THE ...... JACK LEMMON
APRIL FOOLS, THE ...... JACK WESTON
APRIL FOOLS, THE ...... MELINDA DILLON
APRIL FOOLS, THE ...... SALLY KELLERMAN
APRIL FOOL'S DAY ...... AMY STEEL
APRIL FOOL'S DAY ...... CLAYTON ROHNER
APRIL FOOL'S DAY ...... DEBORAH FOREMAN
APRIL FOOL'S DAY ...... DEBORAH GOODRICH
APRIL FOOL'S DAY ...... GRIFFIN O'NEAL
APRIL FOOL'S DAY ...... JAY BAKER
APRIL FOOL'S DAY ...... KEN OLANDT
APRIL FOOL'S DAY ...... LEAH KING PINSENT
APRIL FOOL'S DAY ...... LLOYD BERRY
APRIL FOOL'S DAY ...... NIKE NOMAN
APRIL FOOL'S DAY ...... PAT BARLOW
APRIL FOOL'S DAY ...... THOMAS F. WILSON
APRIL FOOL'S DAY ...... TOM HEATON
APRIL IN PARIS ...... DORIS DAY
APRIL LOVE ...... PAT BOONE
APRIL LOVE ...... SHIRLEY JONES
APRIL MORNING (TF) ...... CHAD LOWE
APRIL MORNING (TF) ...... MEREDITH SALENGER
APRIL MORNING (TF) ...... RIP TORN
APRIL MORNING (TF) ...... ROBERT URICH
APRIL MORNING (TF) ...... SUSAN BLAKELY
APRIL MORNING (TF) ...... TOMMY LEE JONES
APRIL SHOWERS ...... ANN SOTHERN
AQUARIANS, THE (TF) ...... JOSE FERRER†
ARABESQUE ...... GREGORY PECK
ARABESQUE ...... SOPHIA LOREN
ARABIAN ADVENTURE ...... MILO O'SHEA
ARABIAN ADVENTURE ...... OLIVER TOBIAS
ARABIAN ADVENTURE ...... SHANE RIMMER
ARACHNOPHOBIA ...... HARLEY JANE KOZAK
ARACHNOPHOBIA ...... JAMES HANDY
ARACHNOPHOBIA ...... JEFF DANIELS
ARACHNOPHOBIA ...... JOHN GOODMAN
ARACHNOPHOBIA ...... JULIAN SANDS
ARACHNOPHOBIA ...... STUART PANKIN
ARCH OF TRIUMPH (TF) ...... ANTHONY HOPKINS
ARCH OF TRIUMPH (TF) ...... DONALD PLEASENCE
ARCH OF TRIUMPH (TF) ...... LESLEY-ANNE DOWN
ARCHIE: TO RIVERDALE AND BACK AGAIN (TF) ...... LAUREN HOLLY
ARE YOU IN THE HOUSE ALONE? (TF) ...... BLYTHE DANNER
ARE YOU IN THE HOUSE ALONE? (TF) ...... DENNIS QUAID
ARE YOU IN THE HOUSE ALONE? (TF) ...... KATHLEEN BELLER
ARENA, THE ...... CLAUDIA CHRISTIAN
ARENA, THE ...... HAMILTON CAMP
ARENA, THE ...... PAM GRIER
ARIA ...... BRIDGET FONDA
ARIA ...... BUCK HENRY
ARIA ...... JOHN HURT
ARISTOCATS, THE (AF) ...... EVA GABOR
ARISTOCATS, THE (AF) ...... STERLING HOLLOWAY†
ARIZONA BUSHWHACKERS ...... HOWARD KEEL
ARIZONA BUSHWHACKERS ...... JOHN IRELAND
ARIZONA BUSHWHACKERS ...... YVONNE DE CARLO
ARIZONA DREAMER ...... FAYE DUNAWAY
ARIZONA DREAMER ...... JERRY LEWIS
ARIZONA DREAMER ...... JOHNNY DEPP
ARIZONA MISSION ...... ANGIE DICKINSON
ARIZONA RAIDERS ...... MICHAEL DANTE
ARMED AND DANGEROUS ...... BRION JAMES
ARMED AND DANGEROUS ...... DON STROUD
ARMED AND DANGEROUS ...... EUGENE LEVY
ARMED AND DANGEROUS ...... JOHN CANDY†
ARMED AND DANGEROUS ...... JONATHAN BANKS
ARMED AND DANGEROUS ...... KENNETH McMILLAN†
ARMED AND DANGEROUS ...... LARRY HANKIN
ARMED AND DANGEROUS ...... MEG RYAN
ARMED AND DANGEROUS ...... ROBERT LOGGIA
ARMED AND DANGEROUS ...... STEVE RAILSBACK
ARMED RESPONSE ...... DAVID CARRADINE
ARMED RESPONSE ...... MAKO
ARMED RESPONSE ...... ROSS HAGEN
ARMORED COMMAND ...... BURT REYNOLDS
ARMORED COMMAND ...... EARL HOLLIMAN
ARMORED COMMAND ...... HOWARD KEEL
ARMORED COMMAND ...... TINA LOUISE

This is not a list of every film ever made or every cast member, only those listed in this directory.

ARMORED COMMAND .... WARNER ANDERSON†
ARMY OF DARKNESS .... BRUCE CAMPBELL
ARMY SURGEON .... JANE WYATT
ARNELO AFFAIR, THE .... DEAN STOCKWELL
ARNOLD .... RODDY McDOWALL
ARNOLD .... STELLA STEVENS
AROUND THE WORLD
  IN 80 DAYS .... ANDY DEVINE†
AROUND THE WORLD IN 80 DAYS ..... DAVID NIVEN†
AROUND THE WORLD
  IN 80 DAYS .... FRANK SINATRA
AROUND THE WORLD IN 80 DAYS .... JACK OAKIE†
AROUND THE WORLD
  IN 80 DAYS .... JOHN GIELGUD
AROUND THE WORLD IN 80 DAYS .... JOHN MILLS
AROUND THE WORLD
  IN 80 DAYS .... ROBERT MORLEY
AROUND THE WORLD
  IN 80 DAYS .... SHIRLEY MacLAINE
AROUND THE WORLD
  IN 80 DAYS (MS) .... ERIC IDLE
AROUND THE WORLD
  IN 80 DAYS (MS) .... JOHN HILLERMAN
AROUND THE WORLD
  IN 80 DAYS (MS) .... PIERCE BROSNAN
AROUND THE WORLD
  UNDER THE SEA .... DAVID McCALLUM
AROUND THE WORLD
  UNDER THE SEA .... LLOYD BRIDGES
AROUSERS, THE .... TAB HUNTER
ARRANGEMENT, THE .... DEBORAH KERR
ARRANGEMENT, THE .... FAYE DUNAWAY
ARRANGEMENT, THE .... HUME CRONYN
ARRANGEMENT, THE .... KIRK DOUGLAS
ARRANGEMENT, THE .... MICHAEL MURPHY
ARRANGEMENT, THE .... RICHARD BOONE†
ARRIVADERCI, BABY! .... JACQUELINE BISSET
ARRIVEDERCI, BABY! .... TONY CURTIS
ARRIVEDERCI, BABY! .... ZSA ZSA GABOR
ARROWHEAD .... BRIAN KEITH
ARROWHEAD .... CHARLTON HESTON
ARROWHEAD .... JACK PALANCE
ARROWHEAD .... KATHY JURADO
ARROWSMITH .... HELEN HAYES
ARROWTOOTH
  WALTZ, THE .... MICHAEL J. POLLARD
ARROWTOOTH
  WALTZ, THE .... PAULINA PORIZKOYA
ART OF CRIME, THE (TF) .... JILL CLAYBURGH
ART OF CRIME, THE (TF) .... RON LEIBMAN
ART OF LOVE, THE .... ANGIE DICKINSON
ART OF LOVE, THE .... CARL REINER
ART OF LOVE, THE .... DICK VAN DYKE
ART OF LOVE, THE .... JAMES GARNER
ARTHUR ○○ .... JOHN GIELGUD
ARTHUR ★ .... DUDLEY MOORE
ARTHUR .... GERALDINE FITZGERALD
ARTHUR .... JILL EIKENBERRY
ARTHUR .... LIZA MINELLI
ARTHUR .... LOU JACOBI
ARTHUR .... PAUL GLEASON
ARTHUR .... RON MOODY
ARTHUR .... STEPHEN ELLIOTT
ARTHUR .... TED ROSS
ARTHUR 2 ON THE ROCKS .... BROOKE SMITH
ARTHUR 2 ON THE ROCKS .... CYNTHIA SIKES
ARTHUR 2 ON THE ROCKS .... DANIEL GREENE
ARTHUR 2 ON THE ROCKS .... DUDLEY MOORE
ARTHUR 2 ON
  THE ROCKS .... GERALDINE FITZGERALD
ARTHUR 2 ON THE ROCKS .... JACK GILFORD†
ARTHUR 2 ON THE ROCKS .... JOHN GIELGUD
ARTHUR 2 ON THE ROCKS .... KATHY BATES
ARTHUR 2 ON THE ROCKS .... LIZA MINELLI
ARTHUR 2 ON THE ROCKS .... PAUL BENEDICT
ARTHUR 2 ON THE ROCKS .... RON CANADA
ARTHUR 2 ON THE ROCKS .... STEPHEN ELLIOTT
ARTHUR! ARTHUR! .... SHELLEY WINTERS
ARTHUR ARTHUR .... TAMMY GRIMES
ARTHUR HAILEY'S HOTEL (TF) .... JAMES BROLIN
ARTHUR HAILEY'S THE MONEY-
  CHANGERS (MS) .... CHRISTOPHER PLUMMER

ARTHUR HAILEY'S THE
  MONEYCHANGERS (MS) .... ROBERT LOGGIA
ARTHUR HAILEY'S THE
  MONEYCHANGERS (MS) .... HELEN HAYES
ARTHUR HAILEY'S THE
  MONEYCHANGERS (MS) .... JOAN COLLINS
ARTHUR HAILEY'S THE
  MONEYCHANGERS (MS) .... KIRK DOUGLAS
ARTHUR HAILEY'S THE
  MONEYCHANGERS (MS) .... PATRICK O'NEAL†
ARTHUR HAILEY'S THE
  MONEYCHANGERS (MS) .... RALPH BELLAMY†
ARTHUR HAILEY'S THE
  MONEYCHANGERS (MS) ...... TIMOTHY BOTTOMS
ARTHUR HAILEY'S WHEELS (MS) ...... BLAIR BROWN
ARTHUR HAILEY'S WHEELS (MS) .... JOHN BECK
ARTHUR HAILEY'S
  WHEELS (MS) .... LISA EILBACHER
ARTHUR HAILEY'S
  WHEELS (MS) .... RALPH BELLAMY†
ARTHUR THE KING (TF) .... CANDICE BERGEN
ARTHUR THE KING (TF) .... DYAN CANNON
ARTHUR THE KING (TF) .... MALCOLM McDOWELL
ARTICLE 99 .... ELI WALLACH
ARTICLE 99 .... FOREST WHITAKER
ARTICLE 99 .... JEFFREY TAMBOR
ARTICLE 99 .... JOHN C. McGINLEY
ARTICLE 99 .... JOHN MAHONEY
ARTICLE 99 .... KATHY BAKER
ARTICLE 99 .... KEITH DAVID
ARTICLE 99 .... KIEFER SUTHERLAND
ARTICLE 99 .... LEA THOMPSON
ARTICLE 99 .... MARK LOWENTHAL
ARTICLE 99 .... RAY LIOTTA
ARTICLE 99 .... TROY EVANS
ARTISTS AND MODELS .... DEAN MARTIN
ARTISTS AND MODELS .... EVA GABOR
ARTISTS AND MODELS .... JERRY LEWIS
ARTISTS AND MODELS .... MARTHA RAYE†
ARTISTS AND MODELS .... SHIRLEY MacLAINE
AS SUMMERS DIE (TF) .... JAMIE LEE CURTIS
AS THE SEA RAGES .... CLIFF ROBERTSON
AS THE SEA RAGES .... MARIA SCHELL
AS YOUNG AS YOU FEEL ...... MARILYN MONROE†
AS YOUNG AS YOU FEEL .... ROGER MOORE
AS YOUNG AS YOU FEEL .... RUSS TAMBLYN
ASH WEDNESDAY .... ELIZABETH TAYLOR
ASHANTI .... KABIR BEDI
ASHANTI .... MICHAEL CAINE
ASHANTI .... OMAR SHARIF
ASHANTI .... PETER USTINOV
ASK ANY GIRL .... SHIRLEY MacLAINE
ASPEN EXTREME .... FINOLA HUGHES
ASPEN (MS) .... BO HOPKINS
ASPEN (MS) .... PERRY KING
ASPEN (MS) .... SAM ELLIOTT
ASPHALT JUNGLE, THE .... JAMES WHITMORE
ASPHALT JUNGLE, THE ...... MARILYN MONROE†
ASPHALT JUNGLE, THE ○ .... SAM JAFFE†
ASPHYX, THE .... ROBERT STEPHENS
ASSAM GARDEN, THE .... ALEC McCOWEN
ASSAM GARDEN, THE .... DEBORAH KERR
ASSASSIN (TF) .... KAREN AUSTIN
ASSASSIN (TF) .... ROBERT CONRAD
ASSASSIN, THE .... MARCELLO MASTROIANNI
ASSASSINATION .... CHARLES BRONSON
ASSASSINATION .... HENRY SILVA
ASSASSINATION .... JAN GAN BOYD
ASSASSINATION† .... JILL IRELAND†
ASSASSINATION .... STEPHEN ELLIOTT
ASSASSINATION
  AT SARAJEVO .... CHRISTOPHER PLUMMER
ASSASSINATION BUREAU, THE .... DIANA RIGG
ASSASSINATION BUREAU, THE .... TELLY SAVALAS†
ASSASSINATION IN ROME .... CYD CHARISSE
ASSASSINATION
  IN SARAJEVO .... MAXIMILIAN SCHELL
ASSASSINIO/MADE IN ITALY .... CYD CHARISSE
ASSAULT AND
  MATRIMONY (TF) .... JILL EIKENBERRY
ASSAULT AND
  MATRIMONY (TF) .... JOHN HILLERMAN

ASSAULT ON
  A QUEEN .... ANTHONY (TONY) FRANCIOSA
ASSAULT ON A QUEEN .... FRANK SINATRA
ASSAULT ON
  PARADISE/MANIAC .... DEBORAH RAFFIN
ASSAULT ON
  PARADISE/MANIAC .... JOHN IRELAND
ASSAULT/TOWER
  OF TERROR .... LESLEY-ANNE DOWN
ASSIGNMENT K .... JEREMY KEMP
ASSIGNMENT:
  MUNICH (TF) .... LESLEY ANN WARREN
ASSIGNMENT: MUNICH (TF) .... ROY SCHEIDER
ASSIGNMENT, THE .... CHRISTOPHER PLUMMER
ASSIGNMENT TO KILL .... JOAN HACKETT†
ASSIGNMENT TO KILL .... JOHN GIELGUD
ASSIGNMENT TO KILL .... PATRICK O'NEAL†
ASSISI UNDERGROUND, THE .... BEN CROSS
ASSISI
  UNDERGROUND, THE .... MAXIMILIAN SCHELL
ASTRONAUT, THE (TF) .... JACKIE COOPER
ASTRONAUT, THE (TF) .... SUSAN CLARK
ASYLUM .... BRITT EKLAND
ASYLUM .... CHARLOTTE RAMPLING
ASYLUM .... GEOFFREY BAYLDON
AT CLOSE RANGE .... ALAN AUTRY
AT CLOSE RANGE .... CANDY CLARK
AT CLOSE RANGE .... CHRIS PENN
AT CLOSE RANGE .... CHRISTOPHER WALKEN
AT CLOSE RANGE .... CRISPIN GLOVER
AT CLOSE RANGE .... DAVID STRATHAIRN
AT CLOSE RANGE .... EILEEN RYAN
AT CLOSE RANGE .... J. C. QUINN
AT CLOSE RANGE .... JAKE DENGEL
AT CLOSE RANGE .... KIEFER SUTHERLAND
AT CLOSE RANGE .... MARY STUART MASTERSON
AT CLOSE RANGE .... MILLIE PERKINS
AT CLOSE RANGE .... R.D. CALL
AT CLOSE RANGE .... SEAN PENN
AT CLOSE RANGE .... STEPHEN GEOFFREYS
AT CLOSE RANGE .... TRACEY WALTER
AT LONG LAST LOVE .... BASIL HOFFMAN
AT LONG LAST LOVE .... BURT REYNOLDS
AT LONG LAST LOVE .... CYBILL SHEPHERD
AT LONG LAST LOVE .... EILEEN BRENNAN
AT LONG LAST LOVE .... JOHN HILLERMAN
AT LONG LAST LOVE .... MADELINE KAHN
AT MOTHER'S REQUEST (TF) .... COREY PARKER
AT MOTHER'S REQUEST (TF) .... DOUG McKEON
AT MOTHER'S REQUEST (TF) .... E. G. MARSHALL
AT MOTHER'S
  REQUEST (TF) .... FRANCES STERNHAGEN
AT MOTHER'S
  REQUEST (TF) .... STEFANIE POWERS
AT PLAY IN THE FIELDS
  OF THE LORD .... AIDAN QUINN
AT PLAY IN THE FIELDS
  OF THE LORD .... DARYL HANNAH
AT PLAY IN THE FIELDS
  OF THE LORD .... JOHN LITHGOW
AT PLAY IN THE FIELDS
  OF THE LORD .... KATHY BATES
AT PLAY IN THE FIELDS
  OF THE LORD .... NELSON XAVIER
AT PLAY IN THE FIELDS
  OF THE LORD .... STENIO GARCIA
AT PLAY IN THE FIELDS
  OF THE LORD .... TOM BERENGER
AT PLAY IN THE FIELDS
  OF THE LORD .... TOM WAITS
AT SWORD'S POINT .... DAN O'HERLIHY
AT SWORD'S POINT .... MAUREEN O'HARA
AT THE EARTH'S CORE .... DOUG McCLURE
AT WAR WITH THE ARMY .... DEAN MARTIN
AT WAR WITH THE ARMY .... JERRY LEWIS
ATAME .... ANTONIO BANDERAS
ATAME .... VICTORIA ABRIL
ATHENA .... DEBBIE REYNOLDS
ATHENA .... KATHLEEN FREEMAN
ATILLA .... SOPHIA LOREN
ATLANTA CHILD
  MURDERS, THE (MS) .... ANNE MARIE JOHNSON

† after an actor's name denotes deceased.

ATLANTA CHILD
  MURDERS, THE (MS) .... JAMES EARL JONES
ATLANTA CHILD
  MURDERS, THE (MS) .... JASON ROBARDS
ATLANTA CHILD
  MURDERS, THE (MS) .... LYNNE MOODY
ATLANTA CHILD
  MURDERS, THE (MS) .... MARTIN SHEEN
ATLANTA CHILD
  MURDERS, THE (MS) .... MORGAN FREEMAN
ATLANTA CHILD MURDERS, THE (MS) ...... RIP TORN
ATLANTIC CITY .... KATE REID
ATLANTIC CITY .... ROBERT GOULET
ATLANTIC CITY .... ROBERT JOY
ATLANTIC CITY ★ .... BURT LANCASTER†
ATLANTIC CITY ★ .... SUSAN SARANDON
ATLANTIC CONVOY .... LLOYD BRIDGES
ATTACK! .... EDDIE ALBERT
ATTACK! .... JACK PALANCE
ATTACK! .... RICHARD JAECKEL
ATTACK FORCE Z .... MEL GIBSON
ATTACK FORCE Z .... SAM NEILL
ATTACK OF THE 50-FOOT
  WOMAN (CTF) .... DANIEL BALDWIN
ATTACK OF THE 50-FOOT
  WOMAN (CTF) .... DARYL HANNAH
ATTACK OF THE 50-FOOT
  WOMAN (CTF) .... FRANCES FISHER
ATTACK OF THE CRAB MONSTERS ...... ED NELSON
ATTACK ON FEAR (TF) .... LINDA KELSEY
ATTACK ON TERROR: THE FBI VS.
  THE KU KLUX KLAN (TF) .... DABNEY COLEMAN
ATTACK ON TERROR: THE FBI VS.
  THE KU KLUX KLAN (TF) .... GEORGE GRIZZARD
ATTACK ON TERROR: THE FBI VS.
  THE KU KLUX KLAN (TF) .... NED BEATTY
ATTACK ON THE IRON COAST .... LLOYD BRIDGES
ATTIC: THE HIDING OF
  ANNE FRANK, THE (TF) ...... MARY STEENBURGEN
ATTIC: THE HIDING OF
  ANNE FRANK, THE (TF) .... PAUL SCOFIELD
ATTICA (TF) .... ANTHONY ZERBE
ATTILA .... ANTHONY QUINN
AU RENDEZ-VOUS DE
  LA MORT JOYEUSE .... GERARD DEPARDIEU
AUDREY ROSE .... ANTHONY HOPKINS
AUDREY ROSE .... JOHN BECK
AUDREY ROSE .... MARSHA MASON
AUDREY ROSE .... NORMAN LLOYD
AUNT MARY (TF) .... JULIA JENNINGS
AUNT MARY (TF) .... MARTIN BALSAM
AUNTIE MAME ★ .... ROSALAND RUSSELL†
AURORA (TF) .... SOPHIA LOREN
AUSTERLITZ .... JACK PALANCE
AUSTERLITZ .... LESLIE CARON
AUTHOR! AUTHOR! .... AL PACINO
AUTHOR! AUTHOR! .... ALAN KING
AUTHOR! AUTHOR! .... BOB DISHY
AUTHOR! AUTHOR! .... BOB ELLIOTT
AUTHOR! AUTHOR! .... DYAN CANNON
AUTHOR! AUTHOR! .... ERIC GURRY
AUTHOR! AUTHOR! .... JUDY GRAUBART
AUTHOR! AUTHOR! .... RAY GOULDING
AUTHOR! AUTHOR! .... TUESDAY WELD
AUTOBIOGRAPHY OF MISS
  JANE PITTMAN, THE (TF) ....CICELY TYSON
AUTOMATIC .... DAPHNE ASHBROOK
AUTOMATIC .... JOHN GLOVER
AUTOSTOP .... FRANCO NERO
AUTUMN LEAVES .... CLIFF ROBERTSON
AUTUMN LEAVES .... JOAN CRAWFORD†
AUTUMN LEAVES .... VERA MILES
AUTUMN SONATA .... ERLAND JOSEPHSON
AUTUMN SONATA .... LIV ULLMANN
AUTUMN SONATA ★ .... INGRID BERGMAN†
AVALANCHE .... BARRY PRIMUS
AVALANCHE .... MIA FARROW
AVALANCHE .... ROBERT FORSTER
AVALANCHE .... ROCK HUDSON†
AVALANCHE EXPRESS .... JOE NAMATH
AVALANCHE EXPRESS .... LINDA EVANS
AVALANCHE EXPRESS .... MAXIMILIAN SCHELL

AVALON .... AIDAN QUINN
AVALON .... ARMIN MUELLER-STAHL
AVALON .... ELIZABETH PERKINS
AVALON .... EVE GORDON
AVALON .... JOAN PLOWRIGHT
AVALON .... KEVIN POLLAK
AVALON .... LEO FUCHS
AVALON .... LOU JACOBI
AVANTI! .... JACK LEMMON
AVENGERS, THE .... DEBORAH KERR
AVENGING ANGEL .... BARRY PEARL
AVENGING ANGEL .... BETSY RUSSELL
AVENGING ANGEL .... OSSIE DAVIS
AVENGING ANGEL .... ROBERT F. LYONS
AVENGING ANGEL .... RORY CALHOUN
AVENGING ANGEL .... ROSS HAGEN
AVENGING ANGEL .... SUSAN TYRRELL
AVENGING ANGEL .... TIM ROSSOVICH
AVENGING ANGEL (CTF) .... TOM BERENGER
AVENGING FORCE .... BILL WALLACE
AVENGING FORCE .... JAMES BOOTH
AVENGING FORCE .... JOHN P. RYAN
AVENGING FORCE .... KARL JOHNSON
AVENGING FORCE .... MICHAEL DUDIKOFF
AVENGING FORCE .... STEVE JAMES
AVIATOR, THE .... CHRISTOPHER REEVE
AVIATOR, THE .... JACK WARDEN
AVIATOR, THE .... ROSANNA ARQUETTE
AVIATOR, THE .... SAM WANAMAKER†
AVIATOR, THE .... SCOTT WILSON
AVIATOR, THE .... TYNE DALY
AWAKENIGN
  LAND, THE (TF) .... ELIZABETH MONTGOMERY
AWAKENING .... JOAN CHEN
AWAKENING LAND, THE (TF) .... LOUISE LATHAM
AWAKENING LAND, THE (TF) .... STEVEN KEATS†
AWAKENING, THE .... CHARLTON HESTON
AWAKENING, THE .... JILL TOWNSEND
AWAKENING, THE .... STEPHANIE ZIMBALIST
AWAKENING, THE .... SUSANNAH YORK
AWAKENINGS .... ANNE MEARA
AWAKENINGS .... DEXTER GORDON†
AWAKENINGS .... JOHN HEARD
AWAKENINGS .... JULIE KAVNER
AWAKENINGS .... MAX von SYDOW
AWAKENINGS .... PENELOPE ANN MILLER
AWAKENINGS .... ROBIN WILLIAMS
AWAKENINGS .... RUTH NELSON
AWAKENINGS ★ .... ROBERT DE NIRO
AWFUL TRUTH, THE ○ .... RALPH BELLAMY†
AWFULLY BIG
  ADVENTURE, AN .... ALUN ARMSTRONG
AWFULLY BIG
  ADVENTURE, AN .... GEORGINA CATES
AWFULLY BIG ADVENTURE, AN .... HUGH GRANT
AWFULLY BIG ADVENTURE, AN .... PETER FIRTH

B

B.F.'S DAUGHTER .... BARBARA STANWYCK†
BABA YAGA .... CARROLL BAKER
BABA YAGA DEVIL WITCH .... CARROLL BAKER
BABE (TF) .... ALEXIS KARRAS
BABE (TF) .... SUSAN CLARK
BABE, THE .... BRUCE BOXLEITNER
BABE, THE .... JAMES CROMWELL
BABE, THE .... JOHN GOODMAN
BABE, THE .... JOSEPH RAGNO
BABE, THE .... KELLY McGILLIS
BABE, THE .... RALPH MARRERO
BABE, THE .... TRINI ALVARADO
BABES IN ARMS H .... MICKEY ROONEY
BABES IN TOYLAND .... ANNETTE FUNICELLO
BABES IN TOYLAND (TF) .... DREW BARRYMORE
BABES IN
  TOYLAND (TF) .... NORIYUKI "PAT" MORITA
BABES IN TOYLAND (TF) .... RICHARD MULLIGAN
BABS .... HELEN HAYES
BABY AND THE BATTLESHIP, THE .... JOHN MILLS
BABY BLUE MARINE .... JAN-MICHAEL VINCENT
BABY BLUE MARINE .... KATHERINE HELMOND
BABY BLUE MARINE .... RICHARD GERE

BABY BOOM .... BEVERLY TODD
BABY BOOM .... DIANE KEATON
BABY BOOM .... HAROLD RAMIS
BABY BOOM .... JAMES SPADER
BABY BOOM .... KRISTINA MARIE KENNEDY
BABY BOOM .... MARY GROSS
BABY BOOM .... MICHELLE LYNN KENNEDY
BABY BOOM .... PAT HINGLE
BABY BOOM .... ROBIN BARTLETT
BABY BOOM .... SAM SHEPARD
BABY BOOM .... SAM WANAMAKER†
BABY BOOM .... VICTORIA JACKSON
BABY COMES HOME (TF) .... COLLEEN DEWHURST†
BABY DOLL .... ELI WALLACH
BABY DOLL .... KARL MALDEN
BABY DOLL .... LONNY CHAPMAN
BABY DOLL .... RIP TORN
BABY DOLL ★ .... CARROLL BAKER
BABY DOLL ○ .... MILDRED DUNNOCK†
BABY FACE .... BARBARA STANWYCK†
BABY FACE NELSON .... MICKEY ROONEY
BABY GIRL SCOTT (TF) .... JOHN LITHGOW
BABY GIRL SCOTT (TF) .... LINDA KELSEY
BABY GIRL SCOTT (TF) .... MARY BETH HURT
BABY GIRL SCOTT (TF) .... MIMI KENNEDY
BABY IT'S YOU .... MATTHEW MODINE
BABY IT'S YOU .... ROBERT DOWNEY JR.
BABY IT'S YOU .... ROSANNA ARQUETTE
BABY IT'S YOU .... TRACY POLLAN
BABY IT'S YOU .... VINCENT SPANO
BABY M (MS) .... ANNE JACKSON
BABY M (MS) .... DABNEY COLEMAN
BABY M (MS) .... JoBETH WILLIAMS
BABY M (MS) .... JOHN SHEA
BABY MAKER, THE .... BARBARA HERSHEY
BABY MAKER, THE .... JEANNIE BERLIN
BABY MAKER, THE .... SCOTT GLENN
BABY—SECRET OF THE
  LOST LEGEND .... JULIAN FELLOWES
BABY—SECRET OF THE
  LOST LEGEND .... KYALO MATIVO
BABY—SECRET OF THE
  LOST LEGEND .... SEAN YOUNG
BABY—SECRET OF THE
  LOST LEGEND .... WILLIAM KATT
BABY SISTER (TF) .... PHOEBE CATES
BABY, THE RAIN MUST FALL .... DON MURRAY
BABY'S DAY OUT .... BRIAN HALEY
BABY'S DAY OUT .... JOE MANTEGNA
BABY'S DAY OUT .... JOE PANTOLIANO
BABY'S DAY OUT .... JOHN NEVILLE
BABY'S DAY OUT .... LARA FLYNN BOYLE
BABY'S DAY OUT .... MATTHEW GLAYE
BABYCAKES (TF) .... BETTY BUCKLEY
BABYCAKES (TF) .... CRAIG SHEFFER
BABYCAKES (TF) .... JOHN KARLEN
BABYCAKES (TF) .... PAUL BENEDICT
BABYCAKES (TF) .... RICKI LAKE
BABYFEVER .... DINAH LENNEY
BABYFEVER .... ERIC ROBERTS
BABYFEVER .... FRANCES FISHER
BABYFEVER .... MATT SALINGER
BABYFEVER .... VICTORIA FOYT
BABYSITTER .... ROBERT VAUGHN
BABYSITTER, THE (TF) .... QUINN CUMMINGS
BABYSITTER, THE (TF) .... STEPHANIE ZIMBALIST
BACHELOR FLAT .... CELESTE HOLM
BACHELOR FLAT .... TUESDAY WELD
BACHELOR IN PARADISE .... BOB HOPE
BACHELOR IN PARADISE .... LANA TURNER
BACHELOR IN PARADISE .... PAULA PRENTISS
BACHELOR MOTHER .... DAVID NIVEN†
BACHELOR PARTY .... ADRIAN ZMED
BACHELOR PARTY .... BARBARA STUART
BACHELOR PARTY .... GEORGE GRIZZARD
BACHELOR PARTY .... TAWNY KITAEN
BACHELOR PARTY .... TOM HANKS
BACHELOR PARTY, THE .... DON MURRAY
BACHELOR PARTY, THE .... E. G. MARSHALL
BACHELOR PARTY, THE .... JACK WARDEN
BACHELOR PARTY, THE .... NANCY MARCHAND
BACHELOR PARTY, THE ○ .... CAROLYN JONES†

This is not a list of every film ever made or every cast member, only those listed in this directory.

BACHELOR'S DAUGHTERS, THE .... JANE WYATT
BACK DOOR TO HELL .... JACK NICHOLSON
BACK FROM ETERNITY .... BARBARA EDEN
BACK FROM ETERNITY .... ROD STEIGER
BACK OF BEYOND .... PAUL MERCURIO
BACK ROADS .... DAVID KEITH
BACK ROADS .... SALLY FIELD
BACK ROADS .... TOMMY LEE JONES
BACK STREET .... JOHN GAVIN
BACK STREET .... VERA MILES
BACK TO BATAAN .... ANTHONY QUINN
BACK TO BATAAN .... LAWRENCE TIERNEY
BACK TO GOD'S COUNTRY .... ROCK HUDSON†
BACK TO SCHOOL .... ADRIENNE BARBEAU
BACK TO SCHOOL .... BURT YOUNG
BACK TO SCHOOL .... JASON HERVEY
BACK TO SCHOOL .... KEITH GORDON
BACK TO SCHOOL .... KURT VONNEGUT JR.
BACK TO SCHOOL .... M. EMMET WALSH
BACK TO SCHOOL .... NED BEATTY
BACK TO SCHOOL .... PAXTON WHITEHEAD
BACK TO SCHOOL .... ROBERT DOWNEY JR.
BACK TO SCHOOL .... ROBERT PICARDO
BACK TO SCHOOL .... RODNEY DANGERFIELD
BACK TO SCHOOL .... SALLY KELLERMAN
BACK TO SCHOOL .... SAM KINISON†
BACK TO SCHOOL .... SEVERN DARDEN
BACK TO SCHOOL .... TERRY FARRELL
BACK TO SCHOOL .... WILLIAM ZABKA
BACK TO THE BEACH .... ANNETTE FUNICELLO
BACK TO THE BEACH .... CONNIE STEVENS
BACK TO THE BEACH .... DEMIAN SLADE
BACK TO THE BEACH .... FRANKIE AVALON
BACK TO THE BEACH .... LORI LOUGHLIN
BACK TO THE BEACH .... PAUL REUBENS
BACK TO THE FUTURE .... BILLY ZANE
BACK TO THE FUTURE .... CASEY SIEMASZKO
BACK TO THE FUTURE .... CHRISTOPHER LLOYD
BACK TO THE FUTURE .... CLAUDIA WELLS
BACK TO THE FUTURE .... CRISPIN GLOVER
BACK TO THE FUTURE .... FRANCES LEE McCAIN
BACK TO THE FUTURE .... GEORGE DICENZO
BACK TO THE FUTURE .... HUEY LEWIS
BACK TO THE FUTURE .... JAMES TOLKAN
BACK TO THE FUTURE .... JASON HERVEY
BACK TO THE FUTURE .... JASON MARIN
BACK TO THE FUTURE .... JEFF COHEN
BACK TO THE FUTURE .... LEA THOMPSON
BACK TO THE FUTURE .... MARC McCLURE
BACK TO THE FUTURE .... MICHAEL J. FOX
BACK TO THE FUTURE .... THOMAS F. WILSON
BACK TO THE FUTURE .... WENDIE JO SPERBER
BACK TO THE FUTURE PART II .... BILLY ZANE
BACK TO THE FUTURE
PART II .... CASEY SIEMASZKO
BACK TO THE FUTURE
PART II .... CHARLES FLEISCHER
BACK TO THE FUTURE
PART II ....CHRISTOPHER LLOYD
BACK TO THE FUTURE PART II .... ELIJAH WOOD
BACK TO THE FUTURE PART II .... ELISABETH SHUE
BACK TO THE FUTURE
PART II .... HARRY WATERS JR.
BACK TO THE FUTURE PART II .... JAMES TOLKAN
BACK TO THE FUTURE
PART II .... JASON SCOTT LEE
BACK TO THE FUTURE
PART II .... JEFFREY WEISSMAN
BACK TO THE FUTURE PART II ...... JOE FLAHERTY
BACK TO THE FUTURE PART II ...... LEA THOMPSON
BACK TO THE FUTURE PART II .... MICHAEL J. FOX
BACK TO THE FUTURE
PART II .... THOMAS F. WILSON
BACK TO THE FUTURE
PART III .... CHRISTOPHER LLOYD
BACK TO THE FUTURE PART III .... DUB TAYLOR
BACK TO THE FUTURE PART III ... ELISABETH SHUE
BACK TO THE FUTURE
PART III .... HARRY CAREY JR.
BACK TO THE FUTURE PART III .... JAMES TOLKAN
BACK TO THE FUTURE
PART III .... JEFFREY WEISSMAN

BACK TO THE FUTURE PART III ..... LEA THOMPSON
BACK TO THE FUTURE
PART III .... MARY STEENBURGEN
BACK TO THE FUTURE PART III .... MATT CLARK
BACK TO THE FUTURE PART III ... MICHAEL J. FOX
BACK TO THE FUTURE
PART III .... RICHARD DYSART
BACK TO THE FUTURE
PART III .... THOMAS F. WILSON
BACKBEAT .... GARY BAKEWELL
BACKBEAT .... IAN HART
BACKBEAT .... JENNIFER EHLE
BACKBEAT .... SHERYL LEE
BACKBEAT .... STEPHEN DORFF
BACKDRAFT .... CEDRIC YOUNG
BACKDRAFT .... CLINT HOWARD
BACKDRAFT .... DONALD SUTHERLAND
BACKDRAFT .... J. T. WALSH
BACKDRAFT .... JACK McGEE
BACKDRAFT .... JASON GEDRICK
BACKDRAFT .... JENNIFER JASON LEIGH
BACKDRAFT .... KURT RUSSELL
BACKDRAFT .... MARK WHEELER
BACKDRAFT .... REBECCA DE MORNAY
BACKDRAFT .... ROBERT DE NIRO
BACKDRAFT .... RYAN TODD
BACKDRAFT .... SCOTT GLENN
BACKDRAFT .... TONY MOCKUS SR.
BACKDRAFT .... WILLIAM BALDWIN
BACKFIELD IN MOTION (TF) .... ROSEANNE
BACKFIELD IN MOTION (TF) .... TOM ARNOLD
BACKFIRE .... DEAN PAUL MARTIN†
BACKFIRE .... GORDON MacRAE†
BACKFIRE .... KAREN ALLEN
BACKFIRE .... KEITH CARRADINE
BACKLASH .... RICHARD WIDMARK
BACKSTAIRS AT THE
WHITE HOUSE (MS) .... CELESTE HOLM
BACKSTAIRS AT THE
WHITE HOUSE (MS) .... CLAIRE BLOOM
BACKSTAIRS AT THE
WHITE HOUSE (MS) .... CLORIS LEACHMAN
BACKSTAIRS AT THE
WHITE HOUSE (MS) .... ED FLANDERS
BACKSTAIRS AT THE
WHITE HOUSE (MS) .... EILEEN HECKART
BACKSTAIRS AT THE
WHITE HOUSE (MS) .... GEORGE KENNEDY
BACKSTAIRS AT THE
WHITE HOUSE (MS) .... JOHN ANDERSON
BACKSTAIRS AT THE
WHITE HOUSE (MS) .... JULIE HARRIS
BACKSTAIRS AT THE
WHITE HOUSE (MS) .... LEE GRANT
BACKSTAIRS AT THE
WHITE HOUSE (MS) .... LESLIE NIELSEN
BACKSTAIRS AT THE
WHITE HOUSE (MS) .... LOUIS GOSSETT JR.
BACKSTAIRS AT THE
WHITE HOUSE (MS) .... PAUL WINFIELD
BACKSTAIRS AT THE
WHITE HOUSE (MS) .... ROBERT HOOKS
BACKSTREET DREAMS .... NICK CASSAVETES
BACKTRACK .... CHARLIE SHEEN
BACKTRACK .... DEAN STOCKWELL
BACKTRACK .... DENNIS HOPPER
BACKTRACK .... DOUG McCLURE
BACKTRACK .... FRED WARD
BACKTRACK .... JODIE FOSTER
BACKTRACK .... JOE PESCI
BACKTRACK .... JOHN TURTURRO
BACKTRACK .... VINCENT PRICE†
BACKTRACK (TF) .... ROYAL DANO
BACKWOODS MASSACRE ...... LAWRENCE TIERNEY
BAD AND THE
BEAUTIFUL, THE .... KATHLEEN FREEMAN
BAD AND THE BEAUTIFUL, THE .... LANA TURNER
BAD AND THE BEAUTIFUL, THE .... STEVE FORREST
BAD AND THE
BEAUTIFUL, THE ★ .... KIRK DOUGLAS
BAD AND THE
BEAUTIFUL, THE ☾☾ .... GLORIA GRAHAME†

BAD BEHAVIOUR .... CLARE HIGGINS
BAD BEHAVIOUR .... MARY JO RANDLE
BAD BEHAVIOUR .... PHIL DANIELS
BAD BEHAVIOUR .... PHILIP JACKSON
BAD BEHAVIOUR .... SAIRA TODD
BAD BEHAVIOUR .... SINEAD CUSACK
BAD BEHAVIOUR .... STEPHEN REA
BAD BLOOD .... LINDA BLAIR
BAD BLOOD .... TROY DONAHUE
BAD BOY .... JANE WYATT
BAD BOYS .... ALLY SHEEDY
BAD BOYS .... ESAI MORALES
BAD BOYS .... JOE PANTOLIANO
BAD BOYS .... MARTIN LAWRENCE
BAD BOYS .... MARTIN LAWRENCE
BAD BOYS .... RENI SANTONI
BAD BOYS .... SEAN PENN
BAD BOYS .... TCHEKY KARYO
BAD BOYS .... TEA LEONI
BAD BOYS .... TEA LEONI
BAD BOYS .... THERESA RANDLE
BAD BOYS .... WILL SMITH
BAD COMPANY .... DAVID HUDDLESTON
BAD COMPANY .... JEFF BRIDGES
BAD COMPANY .... JOHN SAVAGE
BAD DAY AT BLACK ROCK .... DEAN JAGGER†
BAD DAY AT BLACK ROCK .... ERNEST BORGNINE
BAD DAY AT BLACK ROCK .... LEE MARVIN†
BAD DAY AT BLACK ROCK ★ ...... SPENCER TRACY†
BAD DREAMS .... JENNIFER RUBIN
BAD FOR EACH OTHER .... CHARLTON HESTON
BAD GEORGIA ROAD .... CAROL LYNLEY
BAD GIRL .... KENNETH HAIGH
BAD GIRLS .... ANDIE MacDOWELL
BAD GIRLS .... DERMOT MULRONEY
BAD GIRLS .... DREW BARRYMORE
BAD GIRLS .... JAMES RUSSO
BAD GIRLS .... MADELEINE STOWE
BAD GIRLS .... MARY STUART MASTERSON
BAD GIRLS .... ROBERT LOGGIA
BAD GUYS .... MIKE JOLLY
BAD GUYS .... RUTH BUZZI
BAD INFLUENCE .... CHRISTIAN CLEMENSON
BAD INFLUENCE .... JAMES SPADER
BAD INFLUENCE .... LISA ZANE
BAD INFLUENCE .... ROB LOWE
BAD LIEUTENANT, THE .... HARVEY KEITEL
BAD LORD BYRON, THE .... MAE ZETTERLING†
BAD MAN, THE .... RONALD REAGAN
BAD MANNERS .... KAREN BLACK
BAD MEDICINE .... ALAN ARKIN
BAD MEDICINE .... BILL MACY
BAD MEDICINE .... CURTIS ARMSTRONG
BAD MEDICINE .... JOE GRIFASI
BAD MEDICINE .... JULIE HAGERTY
BAD MEDICINE .... JULIE KAVNER
BAD MEDICINE .... ROBERT ROMANUS
BAD MEDICINE .... STEVE GUTTENBERG
BAD MEDICINE .... TAYLOR NEGRON
BAD MEN OF MISSOURI .... JANE WYMAN
BAD NEWS BEARS, THE .... JACKIE EARLE HALEY
BAD NEWS BEARS, THE .... JOYCE VAN PATTEN
BAD NEWS BEARS, THE .... TATUM O'NEAL
BAD NEWS BEARS, THE .... VIC MORROW†
BAD NEWS BEARS, THE .... WALTER MATTHAU
BAD NEWS BEARS GO
TO JAPAN, THE .... JACKIE EARLE HALEY
BAD NEWS BEARS GO
TO JAPAN, THE .... TONY CURTIS
BAD NEWS BEARS IN BREAKING
TRAINING, THE .... CLIFTON JAMES
BAD NEWS BEARS IN BREAKING
TRAINING, THE .... JACKIE EARLE HALEY
BAD NEWS BEARS IN BREAKING
TRAINING, THE .... WILLIAM DEVANE
BAD RONALD (TF) .... DABNEY COLEMAN
BAD RONALD (TF) .... SCOTT JACOBY
BAD SEED, THE .... HENRY JONES
BAD SEED, THE ☾ .... EILEEN HECKART
BAD SEED, THE (TF) .... BLAIR BROWN
BAD SEED, THE (TF) .... DAVID CARRADINE
BAD SEED, THE (TF) .... DAVID OGDEN STIERS

† after an actor's name denotes deceased.

BAD SEED, THE (TF) .... RICHARD KILEY
BAD SISTER .... BETTE DAVIS†
BAD TIMING: A SENSUAL
    OBSESSION .... DENHOLM ELLIOTT†
BAD TIMING/A SENSUAL
    OBSESSION .... ART GARFUNKEL
BAD TIMING/A SENSUAL
    OBSESSION .... HARVEY KEITEL
BAD TIMING/A SENSUAL
    OBSESSION .... THERESA RUSSELL
BADGE 373 .... ROBERT DUVALL
BADGE OF THE ASSASSIN (TF) .... ALEX ROCCO
BADGE OF THE ASSASSIN (TF) .... DAVID HARRIS
BADGE OF THE ASSASSIN (TF) ...... JAMES WOODS
BADGE OF THE ASSASSIN (TF) .... LARRY RILEY
BADGE OR THE CROSS, THE (TF) ...... DIANE BAKER
BADLANDERS, THE .... ERNEST BORGNINE
BADLANDERS, THE .... KATHY JURADO
BADLANDERS, THE .... NEHEMIAH PERSOFF
BADLANDS .... MARTIN SHEEN
BADLANDS .... SISSY SPACEK
BADLANDS OF DAKOTA .... ROBERT STACK
BADMAN'S TERRITORY .... LAWRENCE TIERNEY
BAGDAD .... MAUREEN O'HARA
BAGDAD .... VINCENT PRICE†
BAGDAD CAFE .... C. C. H. POUNDER
BAGDAD CAFE .... CHRISTINE KAUFMANN
BAGDAD CAFE .... JACK PALANCE
BAGDAD CAFE .... MARIANNE SAGEBRECHT
BAIT, THE (TF) .... DONNA MILLS
BAJA OKLAHOMA (CTF) .... CAROLE DAVIS
BAJA OKLAHOMA (CTF) .... JULIA ROBERTS
BAKER'S HAWK .... ALAN YOUNG
BAKER'S HAWK .... BURL IVES
BAKER'S HAWK .... CLINT WALKER
BAKER'S HAWK .... DIANE BAKER
BALCONY, THE .... JEFF COREY
BALCONY, THE .... LEE GRANT
BALCONY, THE .... LEONARD NIMOY
BALCONY, THE .... PETER FALK
BALCONY, THE .... RUBY DEE
BALCONY, THE .... SHELLEY WINTERS
BALL OF FIRE ★ .... BARBARA STANWYCK†
BALL OF FIRE .... GARY COOPER†
BALL OF FIRE .... DANA ANDREWS†
BALL OF FIRE .... OSCAR HOMOLKA†
BALL OF FIRE .... DAN DURYEA†
BALL OF FIRE .... S. Z. SAKALL†
BALL OF FIRE .... RICHARD HADYN†
BALL OF FIRE .... HENRY TRAVERS†
BALL OF FIRE .... TULLY MARSHALL†
BALL OF FIRE .... GENE KRUPA†
BALLAD OF ANDY
    CROCKER, THE (TF) .... LEE MAJORS
BALLAD OF CABLE
    HOGUE, THE .... DAVID WARNER
BALLAD OF CABLE
    HOGUE, THE .... JASON ROBARDS
BALLAD OF CABLE HOGUE, THE ...... L. Q. JONES
BALLAD OF CABLE
    HOGUE, THE .... R.G. ARMSTRONG
BALLAD OF CABLE
    HOGUE, THE .... STELLA STEVENS
BALLAD OF GREGORIO
    CORTEZ, THE .... BARRY CORBIN
BALLAD OF GREGORIO
    CORTEZ, THE .... BRUCE McGILL
BALLAD OF GREGORIO
    CORTEZ, THE .... EDWARD JAMES OLMOS
BALLAD OF GREGORIO
    CORTEZ, THE .... JAMES GAMMON
BALLAD OF GREGORIO
    CORTEZ, THE .... ROSANA DE SOTO
BALLAD OF JOSIE, THE .... DORIS DAY
BALLAD OF JOSIE, THE .... GEORGE KENNEDY
BALLAD OF JOSIE, THE .... PETER GRAVES
BALLAD OF LITTLE JO, THE .... DAVID CHUNG
BALLAD OF LITTLE JO, THE .... IAN MCKELLEN
BALLAD OF LITTLE JO, THE .... SUZY AMIS
BALTIMORE
    BULLET, THE .... BRUCE BOXLEITNER

BALTIMORE BULLET, THE .... JACK O'HALLORAN
BALTIMORE BULLET, THE .... JAMES COBURN
BALTIMORE BULLET, THE .... MICHAEL LERNER
BALTIMORE BULLET, THE .... OMAR SHARIF
BALTIMORE BULLET, THE .... RONEE BLAKLEY
BALTO (AF) .... BOB HOSKINS
BALTO (AF) .... BRENDAN FRASER
BALTO (AF) .... CHRISTINE CAVANAGH
BALTO (AF) .... JACK ANGEL
BALTO (AF) .... JENNIFER BLANC
BALTO (AF) .... JIM CARTER
BALTO (AF) .... JIM CUMMINGS
BALTO (AF) .... KEVIN ANDERSON
BALTO (AF) .... PHIL COLLINS
BALTO (AF) .... SANDRA DICKINSON
BAMBOO BLONDE, THE .... JANE GREER
BAMBOO PRISON, THE .... E. G. MARSHALL
BAMBOO SAUCER .... LOIS NETTLETON
BANACEK: DETOUR
    TO NOWHERE (TF) .... GEORGE PEPPARD†
BANANAS .... ALLEN GARFIELD
BANANAS .... CONRAD BAIN
BANANAS .... LOUISE LASSER
BANANAS .... SYLVESTER STALLONE
BANANAS .... WOODY ALLEN
BAND OF ANGELS .... EFREM ZIMBALIST JR.
BAND OF ANGELS .... SIDNEY POITIER
BAND OF ANGELS .... YVONNE DE CARLO
BAND OF THE HAND .... DANIELE QUINN
BAND OF THE HAND .... JAMES REMAR
BAND OF THE HAND ..... JOHN CAMERON MITCHELL
BAND OF THE HAND .... LAUREN HOLLY
BAND OF THE HAND .... STEPHEN LANG
BAND WAGON, THE .... AVA GARDNER†
BAND WAGON, THE .... CYD CHARISSE
BANDIDO .... ROBERT MITCHUM
BANDITS OF CORSICA, THE .... RAYMOND BURR†
BANDOLERO! .... ANDREW PRINE
BANDOLERO! .... DEAN MARTIN
BANDOLERO! .... GEORGE KENNEDY
BANDOLERO! .... HARRY CAREY JR.
BANDOLERO! .... JAMES STEWART
BANDOLERO! .... RAQUEL WELCH
BANDOLERO! .... SEAN McCLORY
BANG! BANG! YOU'RE DEAD! .... TONY RANDALL
BANG THE DRUM SLOWLY ...... ANN WEDGEWORTH
BANG THE DRUM SLOWLY ...... BARBARA BABCOCK
BANG THE DRUM SLOWLY .... DANNY AIELLO
BANG THE DRUM SLOWLY ...... MICHAEL MORIARTY
BANG THE DRUM SLOWLY .... ROBERT DE NIRO
BANG THE DRUM
    SLOWLY ○ .... VINCENT GARDENIA†
BANJO HACKETT:
    ROAMIN' FREE (TF) .... CHUCK CONNORS†
BANJO ON MY KNEE .... BARBARA STANWYCK†
BANK ROBBER .... FOREST WHITAKER
BANK ROBBER .... JUDGE REINHOLD
BANK ROBBER .... LISA BONET
BANK ROBBER .... MICHAEL JETER
BANK ROBBER .... OLIVIA D'ABO
BANK ROBBER .... PATRICK DEMPSEY
BANK SHOT .... CLIFTON JAMES
BANK SHOT .... GEORGE C. SCOTT
BANK SHOT .... JOANNA CASSIDY
BANNING .... GENE HACKMAN
BANNING .... JAMES FARENTINO
BANNING .... JILL ST. JOHN
BANNING .... ROBERT WAGNER
BANNING .... SUSAN CLARK
BANYON (TF) .... JOSE FERRER†
BAR 20 .... ROBERT MITCHUM
BARABBA .... JACK PALANCE
BARABBAS .... ANTHONY QUINN
BARABBAS .... ERNEST BORGNINE
BARABBAS .... JACK PALANCE
BARABBAS .... KATHY JURADO
BARBARELLA .... DAVID HEMMINGS
BARBARELLA .... JANE FONDA
BARBARELLA .... JOHN PHILLIP LAW
BARBARELLA .... MILO O'SHEA
BARBARIANS, THE .... RICHARD LYNCH

BARBAROSA .... GARY BUSEY
BARBAROSA .... WILLIE NELSON
BARBARY COAST .... DAVID NIVEN†
BARBARY COAST, THE (TF) .... BILL BIXBY†
BARBARY PIRATE .... JOHN DEHNER†
BARE ESSENCE (MS) .... DONNA MILLS
BAREFOOT CONTESSA, THE .... AVA GARDNER†
BAREFOOT
    CONTESSA, THE ○○ .... EDMOND O'BRIEN†
BAREFOOT EXECUTIVE, THE .... HARRY MORGAN
BAREFOOT EXECUTIVE, THE .... JOHN RITTER
BAREFOOT EXECUTIVE, THE .... KURT RUSSELL
BAREFOOT IN THE PARK .... HERB EDELMAN
BAREFOOT IN THE PARK .... JANE FONDA
BAREFOOT IN THE PARK .... ROBERT REDFORD
BARFLY .... ALICE KRIGE
BARFLY .... FAYE DUNAWAY
BARFLY .... FRANK STALLONE
BARFLY .... FRITZ FELD
BARFLY .... J. C. QUINN
BARFLY .... JACK NANCE
BARFLY .... MICKEY ROURKE
BARKER, THE ★ .... BETTY COMPSON†
BARNACLE BILL .... ALEC GUINNESS
BARNUM (TF) .... BURT LANCASTER†
BAROCCO .... GERARD DEPARDIEU
BAROCCO .... ISABELLE ADJANI
BARON AND THE KID, THE (TF) .... JOHNNY CASH
BARON OF ARIZONA, THE .... VINCENT PRICE†
BARQUERO .... MARIETTE HARTLEY
BARRETTS OF WIMPOLE
    STREET, THE .... JENNIFER JONES
BARRETTS OF WIMPOLE
    STREET, THE .... JOHN GIELGUD
BARRETTS OF WIMPOLE
    STREET, THE .... MAUREEN O'SULLIVAN
BARRETTS OF WIMPOLE
    STREET, THE ★ .... NORMA SHEARER†
BARRY LYNDON .... MARISA BERENSON
BARRY LYNDON .... RYAN O'NEAL
BARTLEBY .... JOHN McENERY
BARTLEBY .... PAUL SCOFIELD
BARTON FINK .... JOHN GOODMAN
BARTON FINK .... JOHN MAHONEY
BARTON FINK .... JOHN TURTURRO
BARTON FINK .... JON POLITO
BARTON FINK .... JUDY DAVIS
BARTON FINK .... TONY SHALHOUB
BARTON FINK ○ .... MICHAEL LERNER
BASIC INSTINCT .... DENIS ARNDT
BASIC INSTINCT .... GEORGE DZUNDZA
BASIC INSTINCT .... JEANNE TRIPPLEHORN
BASIC INSTINCT .... LEILANI SARELLE
BASIC INSTINCT .... MICHAEL DOUGLAS
BASIC INSTINCT .... SHARON STONE
BASIC TRAINING .... ANGELA AAMES
BASIC TRAINING .... ANN DUSENBERRY
BASIC TRAINING .... MARK LOWENTHAL
BASIC TRAINING .... RHONDA SHEAR
BASIC TRAINING .... WALTER GOTELL
BASIC TRAINING .... WILL NYE
BASKETBALL DIARIES, THE .... BRUNO KIRBY
BASKETBALL DIARIES, THE ...... ERNIE HUDSON
BASKETBALL DIARIES, THE .... JAMES MADDIO
BASKETBALL
    DIARIES, THE .... LEONARDO DICAPRIO
BASKETBALL DIARIES, THE ...... LORRAINE BRACCO
BASKETBALL DIARIES, THE .... MARK WAHLBERG
BASKETBALL DIARIES, THE ...... MICHAEL IMPERIOLI
BASKETBALL FIX, THE .... JOHN IRELAND
BASTARD, THE .... CLAUDINE AUGER
BASTARD, THE (TF) .... ANDREW STEVENS
BASTARD, THE (TF) .... PATRICIA NEAL
BASTARDS WITHOUT GLORY .... IAN BANNEN
BAT 21 .... CLAYTON ROHNER
BAT 21 .... DANNY GLOVER
BAT 21 .... DAVID MARSHALL GRANT
BAT 21 .... ERICH ANDERSON
BAT 21 .... GENE HACKMAN
BAT 21 .... JERRY REED
BAT 21 .... JOE DORSEY

BAT, THE .... VINCENT PRICE†
BATES MOTEL (TF) .... BUD CORT
BATES MOTEL (TF) .... JASON BATEMAN
BATES MOTEL (TF) .... MOSES GUNN
BATMAN .... ADAM WEST
BATMAN .... BILLY DEE WILLIAMS
BATMAN .... BURGESS MEREDITH
BATMAN .... JACK NICHOLSON
BATMAN .... JACK PALANCE
BATMAN .... JERRY HALL
BATMAN .... KIM BASINGER
BATMAN .... MICHAEL GOUGH
BATMAN .... MICHAEL KEATON
BATMAN .... PAT HINGLE
BATMAN .... ROBERT WUHL
BATMAN .... TRACEY WALTER
BATMAN FOREVER .... CHRIS O'DONNELL
BATMAN FOREVER .... JIM CARREY
BATMAN FOREVER .... NICOLE KIDMAN
BATMAN FOREVER .... TOMMY LEE JONES
BATMAN FOREVER .... VAL KILMER
BATMAN FOREVER .... MICHAEL GOUGH
BATMAN FOREVER .... PAT HINGLE
BATMAN: MASK OF
   THE PHANTASM (AF) .... DANA DELANY
BATMAN: MASK OF
   THE PHANTASM (AF) .... EFREM ZIMBALIST JR.
BATMAN: MASK OF
   THE PHANTASM (AF) .... HART BOCHNER
BATMAN: MASK OF
   THE PHANTASM (AF) .... JOHN P. RYAN
BATMAN: MASK OF
   THE PHANTASM (AF) .... KEVIN CONROY
BATMAN: MASK OF
   THE PHANTASM (AF) .... ROBERT COSTANZO
BATMAN RETURNS .... CHRISTOPHER WALKEN
BATMAN RETURNS .... DANNY DEVITO
BATMAN RETURNS .... DEBBIE LEE CARRINGTON
BATMAN RETURNS .... JAN HOOKS
BATMAN RETURNS .... MARLON WAYANS
BATMAN RETURNS .... MICHAEL GOUGH
BATMAN RETURNS .... MICHAEL KEATON
BATMAN RETURNS .... MICHAEL MURPHY
BATMAN RETURNS .... MICHELLE PFEIFFER
BATMAN RETURNS .... PAT HINGLE
BATMAN RETURNS .... PAUL REUBENS
BATMAN RETURNS .... VINCENT SCHIAVELLI
BATTERED (TF) .... DIANA SCARWID
BATTERED (TF) .... LeVAR BURTON
*BATTERIES NOT INCLUDED .... HUME CRONYN
*BATTERIES NOT INCLUDED .... JESSICA TANDY†
BATTLE AT ELDERBUSH
   GULCH, THE .... LILLIAN GISH†
BATTLE BEYOND
   THE STARS .... GEORGE PEPPARD†
BATTLE BEYOND THE STARS .... JEFF COREY
BATTLE BEYOND THE STARS .... RICHARD THOMAS
BATTLE BEYOND THE STARS ..... ROBERT VAUGHN
BATTLE CIRCUS .... JUNE ALLYSON
BATTLE CIRCUS .... STEVE FORREST
BATTLE CRY .... JAMES WHITMORE
BATTLE CRY .... TAB HUNTER
BATTLE FLAG .... SIMON WARD
BATTLE FLAME .... ROBERT BLAKE
BATTLE FOR ANZIO, THE .... RENI SANTONI
BATTLE FOR THE PLANET
   OF THE APES .... CLAUDE AKINS†
BATTLE FOR THE PLANET
   OF THE APES .... FRANCE NUYEN
BATTLE FOR THE PLANET
   OF THE APES .... PAUL WILLIAMS
BATTLE FOR THE PLANET
   OF THE APES .... RODDY McDOWALL
BATTLE FORCE .... SAMANTHA EGGAR
BATTLE HYMN .... ROCK HUDSON†
BATTLE OF ANZIO, THE .... EARL HOLLIMAN
BATTLE OF AUSTERLITZ, THE .... LESLIE CARON
BATTLE OF BRITAIN .... CHRISTOPHER PLUMMER
BATTLE OF BRITAIN .... CURT JURGENS†
BATTLE OF BRITAIN .... LAURENCE OLIVIER†
BATTLE OF BRITAIN .... MICHAEL CAINE
BATTLE OF BRITAIN .... SUSANNAH YORK
BATTLE OF BRITAIN .... TREVOR HOWARD†

BATTLE OF NERETVA, THE .... FRANCO NERO
BATTLE OF THE BULGE .... CHARLES BRONSON
BATTLE OF THE BULGE .... TELLY SAVALAS†
BATTLE OF THE CORAL SEA ..... CLIFF ROBERTSON
BATTLE OF THE
   RIVER PLATE, THE .... PATRICK MACNEE
BATTLE OF THE SEXES, THE .... LILLIAN GISH†
BATTLE OF THE SEXES, THE .... PATRICIA HAYES
BATTLE OF THE SEXES, THE ...... ROBERT MORLEY
BATTLE OF THE SEXES, THE ... SAM WANAMAKER†
BATTLE OF THE
   VILLA FIORITA, THE .... MAUREEN O'HARA
BATTLE SQUADRON .... VAN JOHNSON
BATTLE STATIONS .... CLAUDE AKINS†
BATTLE STRIPE .... MARLON BRANDO
BATTLE STRIPE .... TERESA WRIGHT
BATTLEGROUND .... JAMES ARNESS
BATTLEGROUND .... LEON AMES
BATTLEGROUND .... RICARDO MONTALBAN
BATTLEGROUND .... RICHARD JAECKEL
BATTLEGROUND .... VAN JOHNSON
BATTLEGROUND ○ .... JAMES WHITMORE
BATTLESTAR: GALACTICA .... DIRK BENEDICT
BATTLING BELLHOP, THE .... BETTE DAVIS†
BATTLING
   BELLHOP, THE .... EDWARD G. ROBINSON†
BAWDY ADVENTURES OF
   TOM JONES, THE .... JOAN COLLINS
BAXTER! .... BRITT EKLAND
BAXTER! .... PATRICIA NEAL
BAXTER! .... SCOTT JACOBY
BAXTER—VERA BAXTER .... GERARD DEPARDIEU
BAY BOY .... LIV ULLMANN
BAY BOY, THE .... KIEFER SUTHERLAND
BAY COVEN (TF) .... BARBARA BILLINGSLEY
BAY COVEN (TF) .... PAMELA SUE MARTIN
BAY COVEN (TF) .... TIM MATHESON
BAY COVEN (TF) .... WOODY HARRELSON
BAY OF ST. MICHEL, THE .... MAE ZETTERLING†
BAYWATCH: PANIC AT
   MALIBU PIER (TF) .... DAVID HASSELHOFF
BAYWATCH: PANIC AT
   MALIBU PIER (TF) .... PARKER STEVENSON
BEACH BLANKET BINGO .... ANNETTE FUNICELLO
BEACH BLANKET BINGO .... FRANKIE AVALON
BEACH BLANKET BINGO .... LINDA EVANS
BEACH BLANKET BINGO .... PAUL LYNDE†
BEACH GIRLS AND THE
   MONSTER, THE .... TONY ROBERTS
BEACH PARTY .... ANNETTE FUNICELLO
BEACH PARTY .... FRANKIE AVALON
BEACH PARTY .... VINCENT PRICE†
BEACH RED .... RIP TORN
BEACHCOMBER, THE .... DONALD PLEASENCE
BEACHES .... BARBARA HERSHEY
BEACHES .... BETTE MIDLER
BEACHES .... JAMES READ
BEACHES .... JOE GRIFASI
BEACHES .... JOHN HEARD
BEACHES .... LAINIE KAZAN
BEACHES .... NICKY BLAIR
BEACHES .... SPALDING GRAY
BEACHHEAD .... TONY CURTIS
BEAR, THE .... ANDRE LACOMBE
BEAR, THE .... GARY BUSEY
BEAR, THE .... JACK WALLACE
BEAR, THE .... TCHEKY KARYO
BEAR ISLAND .... DONALD SUTHERLAND
BEAR ISLAND .... LLOYD BRIDGES
BEAR ISLAND .... RICHARD WIDMARK
BEAR ISLAND .... VANESSA REDGRAVE
BEARS AND I, THE .... PATRICK WAYNE
BEAST, THE .... DON HARVEY
BEAST, THE .... GEORGE DZUNDZA
BEAST, THE .... JASON PATRIC
BEAST, THE .... STEPHEN BALDWIN
BEAST, THE .... STEVEN BAUER
BEAST OF BUDAPEST, THE .... ROBERT BLAKE
BEAST WITHIN, THE .... RONNY COX
BEASTMASTER, THE .... JOHN AMOS
BEASTMASTER, THE .... MARC SINGER
BEASTMASTER, THE .... RIP TORN
BEASTMASTER, THE .... TANYA ROBERTS

BEASTMASTER II .... MARC SINGER
BEASTMASTER II .... RICHARD BALIN
BEASTS ARE ON THE
   STREETS, THE (TF) .... CAROL LYNLEY
BEAT GIRL .... SHIRLEY ANNE FIELD
BEAT STREET .... DUANE JONES†
BEAT STREET .... GUY DAVIS
BEAT STREET .... JON CHARDIET
BEAT STREET .... RAE DAWN CHONG
BEAT, THE .... JOHN SAVAGE
BEAT THE DEVIL .... JENNIFER JONES
BEAT THE DEVIL .... ROBERT MORLEY
BEATLEMANIA .... DAVID LEON
BEATLEMANIA .... MITCH WEISSMAN
BEATLEMANIA .... RALPH CASTELLI
BEATLEMANIA .... TOM TEELEY
BEAU BRUMMEL .... PETER USTINOV
BEAU BRUMMEL .... ROBERT MORLEY
BEAU BRUMMEL .... ELIZABETH TAYLOR
BEAU GESTE .... DOUG McCLURE
BEAU GESTE .... GARY COOPER†
BEAU GESTE .... LESLIE NIELSEN
BEAU GESTE .... MICHAEL CONSTANTINE
BEAU GESTE .... RAY MILLAND†
BEAU GESTE .... ROBERT PRESTON†
BEAU GESTE .... TELLY SAVALAS†
BEAU GESTE ○ .... BRIAN DONLEVY†
BEAU JAMES .... ALEXIS SMITH†
BEAU JAMES .... BOB HOPE
BEAU JAMES .... DARREN McGAVIN
BEAU JAMES .... VERA MILES
BEAU PERE .... ARIEL BESSE
BEAU PERE .... PATRICK DEWAERE†
BEAUTY AND THE BEAST .... JOSETTE DAY†
BEAUTY AND THE BEAST (AF) .... ALEC MURPHY
BEAUTY AND THE BEAST (AF) ...... ALVIN EPSTEIN
BEAUTY AND THE
   BEAST (AF) .... ANGELA LANSBURY
BEAUTY AND THE
   BEAST (AF) .... BRADLEY MICHAEL PIERCE
BEAUTY AND THE BEAST (AF) ...... BRIAN CUMMINS
BEAUTY AND THE
   BEAST (AF) .... DAVID OGDEN STIERS
BEAUTY AND THE BEAST (AF) ...... FRANK WELKER
BEAUTY AND THE BEAST (AF) .... HAL SMITH
BEAUTY AND THE BEAST (AF) .... JERRY ORBACH
BEAUTY AND THE BEAST (AF) .... JESSE CORTI
BEAUTY AND THE BEAST (AF) .... JO ANNE WORLEY
BEAUTY AND THE BEAST (AF) .... KATH SOUCIE
BEAUTY AND THE
   BEAST (AF) .... KIMMY ROBERTSON
BEAUTY AND THE
   BEAST (AF) .... MARY KAY BERGMAN
BEAUTY AND THE BEAST (AF) ...... PAIGE O'HARA
BEAUTY AND THE BEAST (AF) ...... REX EVERHART
BEAUTY AND THE BEAST (AF) .... RICHARD WHITE
BEAUTY AND THE BEAST (AF) ...... ROBBY BENSON
BEAUTY AND THE BEAST (AF) .... TONY JAY
BEAUTY AND THE
   BEAST (TF) .... GEORGE C. SCOTT
BEAUTY AND THE
   BEAST (TF) .... TRISH VAN DEVERE
BECAUSE OF THE CATS .... SYLVIA KRISTEL
BECAUSE THEY'RE YOUNG .... DOUG McCLURE
BECAUSE THEY'RE YOUNG .... TUESDAY WELD
BECAUSE YOU'RE MINE .... JAMES WHITMORE
BECKET .... EDWARD WOODWARD
BECKET .... SIAN PHILLIPS
BECKET ★ .... PETER O'TOOLE
BECKET ★ .... RICHARD BURTON†
BECKET ○ .... JOHN GIELGUD
BECKY SHARP ★ .... MIRIAM HOPKINS†
BECOMING COLETTE ... KLAUS MARIA BRANDAUER
BED AND BREAKFAST .... COLLEEN DEWHURST†
BED AND BREAKFAST .... NINA SIEMASZKO
BED AND BREAKFAST .... ROGER MOORE
BED AND BREAKFAST .... TALIA SHIRE
BED SITTING ROOM, THE .... DUDLEY MOORE
BED-SITTING ROOM, THE .... PETER COOK
BEDAZZLED .... DUDLEY MOORE
BEDAZZLED .... ELEANOR BRON
BEDAZZLED .... PETER COOK

BEDAZZLED .... RAQUEL WELCH
BEDEVILLED .... STEVE FORREST
BEDFORD
    INCIDENT, THE .... DONALD SUTHERLAND
BEDFORD INCIDENT, THE .... MARTIN BALSAM
BEDFORD INCIDENT, THE .... RICHARD WIDMARK
BEDFORD INCIDENT, THE .... SIDNEY POITIER
BEDKNOBS AND
    BROOMSTICKS .... ANGELA LANSBURY
BEDKNOBS AND
    BROOMSTICKS .... DAVID TOMLINSON
BEDKNOBS AND
    BROOMSTICKS .... RODDY McDOWALL
BEDROOM EYES .... DAYLE HADDON
BEDROOM WINDOW, THE .... BRAD GREENQUIST
BEDROOM WINDOW, THE .... CARL LUMBLY
BEDROOM
    WINDOW, THE .... ELIZABETH McGOVERN
BEDROOM WINDOW, THE .... FRED COFFIN
BEDROOM WINDOW, THE .... ISABELLE HUPPERT
BEDROOM WINDOW, THE .... PAUL SHENAR
BEDROOM WINDOW, THE ...... STEVE GUTTENBERG
BEDROOM WINDOW, THE .... WALLACE SHAWN
BEDTIME FOR BONZO .... RONALD REAGAN
BEDTIME STORY .... DAVID NIVEN†
BEDTIME STORY .... MARLON BRANDO
BEDTIME STORY .... SHIRLEY JONES
BEER .... LORETTA SWIT
BEER .... RIP TORN
BEES, THE .... JOHN SAXON
BEETHOVEN .... BONNIE HUNT
BEETHOVEN .... CHARLES GRODIN
BEETHOVEN .... CHRISTOPHER CASTILE
BEETHOVEN .... DAVID CALE
BEETHOVEN .... DAVID DUCHOVNY
BEETHOVEN .... DEAN JONES
BEETHOVEN .... LAUREL CRONIN
BEETHOVEN .... NICHOLLE TOM
BEETHOVEN .... OLIVER PLATT
BEETHOVEN .... PATRICIA HEATON
BEETHOVEN .... SARAH ROSE KARR
BEETHOVEN .... STANLEY TUCCI
BEETHOVEN'S 2ND .... BONNIE HUNT
BEETHOVEN'S 2ND .... CHARLES GRODIN
BEETHOVEN'S 2ND .... CHRIS PENN
BEETHOVEN'S 2ND .... DEBI MAZAR
BEETLEJUICE .... ALEC BALDWIN
BEETLEJUICE .... CATHERINE O'HARA
BEETLEJUICE .... DICK CAVETT
BEETLEJUICE .... GEENA DAVIS
BEETLEJUICE .... JEFFREY JONES
BEETLEJUICE .... MICHAEL KEATON
BEETLEJUICE .... SYLVIA SIDNEY
BEETLEJUICE .... WINONA RYDER
BEFORE AND AFTER .... EDWARD FURLONG
BEFORE AND AFTER .... LIAM NEESON
BEFORE AND AFTER .... MERYL STREEP
BEFORE AND AFTER (TF) .... PATTY DUKE
BEFORE MIDNIGHT .... RALPH BELLAMY†
BEFORE SUNRISE .... ETHAN HAWKE
BEFORE SUNRISE .... JULIE DELPY
BEFORE WINTER COMES .... JOHN HURT
BEFORE WINTER COMES .... TOPOL
BEGGARMAN THIEF (TF) .... JEAN SIMMONS
BEGINNING OF THE END, THE .... PETER GRAVES
BEGINNING OR THE END, THE ...... HUME CRONYN
BEGINNING OR THE END, THE ...... HURD HATFIELD
BEGINNING OR THE END, THE ...... NORMAN LLOYD
BEGUILED, THE .... CLINT EASTWOOD
BEGUILED, THE .... GERALDINE PAGE†
BEHAVE YOURSELF .... SHELLEY WINTERS
BEHIND ENEMY LINES (TF) .... HAL HOLBROOK
BEHIND ENEMY LINES (TF) .... MARYAM D'ABO
BEHIND ENEMY LINES (TF) .... RAY SHARKEY†
BEHIND GREEN LIGHTS .... JOHN IRELAND
BEHIND THE BADGE (TF) .... DEAN STOCKWELL
BEHIND THE
    BADGE (TF) .... ELIZABETH MONTGOMERY
BEHIND THE BADGE (TF) .... O. J. SIMPSON
BEHIND THE HIGH WALL .... JOHN GAVIN
BEHIND THE HIGH WALL .... SYLVIA SIDNEY
BEHIND THE MASK .... VANESSA REDGRAVE
BEHOLD A PALE HORSE .... ANTHONY QUINN

BEHOLD A PALE HORSE .... GREGORY PECK
BEHOLD A PALE HORSE .... OMAR SHARIF
BEHOLD MY WIFE .... SYLVIA SIDNEY
BEING DIFFERENT (TD) .... BILLY BARTY
BEING HUMAN .... ANNA GALIENA
BEING HUMAN .... HECTOR ELIZONDO
BEING HUMAN .... JOHN TURTURRO
BEING HUMAN .... LINDSAY CROUSE
BEING HUMAN .... LORRAINE BRACCO
BEING HUMAN .... ROBIN WILLIAMS
BEING HUMAN .... VINCENT D'ONOFRIO
BEING, THE .... RUTH BUZZI
BEING THERE .... JACK WARDEN
BEING THERE .... SHIRLEY MacLAINE
BEING THERE .... WENDELL BURTON
BEING THERE ★ .... PETER SELLERS†
BEING THERE ○○ .... MELVYN DOUGLAS†
BELIEVE IN ME .... ALLEN GARFIELD
BELIEVE IN ME .... GERALDINE FITZGERALD
BELIEVE IN ME .... JACQUELINE BISSET
BELIEVE IN ME .... MICHAEL SARRAZIN
BELIEVERS, THE .... ELIZABETH WILSON
BELIEVERS, THE .... HARLEY CROSS
BELIEVERS, THE .... HARRIS YULIN
BELIEVERS, THE .... HELEN SHAVER
BELIEVERS, THE .... JIMMY SMITS
BELIEVERS, THE .... MALICK BOWENS
BELIEVERS, THE .... MARTIN SHEEN
BELIEVERS, THE .... RICHARD MASUR
BELIEVERS, THE .... ROBERT LOGGIA
BELIZAIRE THE CAJUN .... ARMAND ASSANTE
BELIZAIRE THE CAJUN .... GAIL YOUNGS
BELIZAIRE THE CAJUN ..... MICHAEL SCHOEFFLING
BELIZAIRE THE CAJUN .... NANCY BARRETT
BELIZAIRE THE CAJUN .... ROBERT DUVALL
BELIZAIRE THE CAJUN .... STEPHEN McHATTIE
BELIZAIRE THE CAJUN .... WILL PATTON
BELL, BOOK AND CANDLE .... JACK LEMMON
BELL, BOOK AND CANDLE .... JAMES STEWART
BELL, BOOK AND CANDLE .... KIM NOVAK
BELL FOR ADANO, A .... HARRY MORGAN
BELL JAR, THE .... ANNE JACKSON
BELL JAR, THE .... BARBARA BARRIE
BELL JAR, THE .... JAMESON PARKER
BELL JAR, THE .... JULIE HARRIS
BELL JAR, THE .... MARILYN HASSETT
BELL JAR, THE .... ROBERT KLEIN
BELLBOY, THE .... JERRY LEWIS
BELLBOY, THE .... MILTON BERLE
BELLE DU JOUR .... CATHERINE DENEUVE
BELLE OF THE YUKON .... DINAH SHORE†
BELLE SOMMERS .... CARROLL O'CONNOR
BELLE STARR (TF) .... ELIZABETH MONTGOMERY
BELLS ARE RINGING .... DEAN MARTIN
BELLS ARE RINGING .... JEAN STAPLETON
BELLS OF ST. MARY'S, THE ★ .... BING CROSBY†
BELLS OF ST.
    MARY'S, THE ★ .... INGRID BERGMAN†
BELLY OF AN ARCHITECT, THE .... BRIAN DENNEHY
BELOVED ENEMY .... DAVID NIVEN†
BELOVED INFIDEL .... DEBORAH KERR
BELOVED INFIDEL .... EDDIE ALBERT
BELOVED INFIDEL .... GREGORY PECK
BELOVED, THE .... RAQUEL WELCH
BELOW THE SEA .... RALPH BELLAMY†
BELSTONE FOX, THE .... JEREMY KEMP
BEN .... JOSEPH CAMPANELLA
BEN .... MEREDITH BAXTER
BEN .... ROSEMARY MURPHY
BEN-HUR .... JACK HAWKINS†
BEN-HUR .... MARTHA SCOTT
BEN-HUR .... STEPHEN BOYD†
BEN-HUR ★★ .... CHARLTON HESTON
BEN-HUR ○○ .... HUGH GRIFFITH†
BEND OF THE RIVER .... HARRY MORGAN
BEND OF THE RIVER .... JAMES STEWART
BEND OF THE RIVER .... ROCK HUDSON†
BEND OF THE RIVER .... ROYAL DANO
BENEATH THE 12 MILE REEF ...... ROBERT WAGNER
BENEATH THE PLANET
    OF THE APES .... CHARLTON HESTON
BENEATH THE PLANET
    OF THE APES .... JAMES FRANCISCUS†

BENEATH THE PLANET
    OF THE APES .... JEFF COREY
BENEATH THE TWELVE
    MILE REEF .... PETER GRAVES
BENEATH THE TWELVE
    MILE REEF .... HARRY CAREY JR.
BENEFIT OF THE DOUBT .... AMY IRVING
BENEFIT OF
    THE DOUBT .... CHRISTOPHER McDONALD
BENEFIT OF THE DOUBT ..... DONALD SUTHERLAND
BENEFIT OF THE DOUBT .... GRAHAM GREENE
BENGAL BRIGADE .... DAN O'HERLIHY
BENGAL BRIGADE .... ROCK HUDSON†
BENJAMIN .... CATHERINE DENEUVE
BENJI .... EDGAR BUCHANAN†
BENJI THE HUNTED .... RED STEAGALL
BENNY GOODMAN STORY, THE .... STEVE ALLEN
BENNY & JOON .... AIDAN QUINN
BENNY & JOON .... DAN HEDAYA
BENNY & JOON .... JOHNNY DEPP
BENNY & JOON .... JULIANNE MOORE
BENNY & JOON .... MARY STUART MASTERSON
BENNY & JOON .... OLIVER PLATT
BENNY'S PLACE (TF) .... LOUIS GOSSETT JR.
BEQUEST TO THE NATION, A .... GLENDA JACKSON
BERKELEY SQUARE ★ .... LESLIE HOWARD†
BERLIN AFFAIR, THE .... GUDRUN LANDGREBE
BERLIN AFFAIR, THE .... HANNS ZISCHLER
BERLIN AFFAIR, THE .... KEVIN McNALLY
BERLIN AFFAIR, THE .... MIO TAKAKI
BERLIN AFFAIR, THE .... PHILIPPE LEROY
BERLIN AFFAIR, THE .... WILLIAM BERGER
BERNARDINE .... DICK SARGENT
BERNARDINE .... PAT BOONE
BERSERK .... JOAN CRAWFORD†
BERSERK .... MICHAEL GOUGH
BERT RIGBY, YOU'RE A FOOL .... ANNE BANCROFT
BERT RIGBY, YOU'RE A FOOL .... BRUNO KIRBY
BERT RIGBY,
    YOU'RE A FOOL .... CATHRYN BRADLEY
BERT RIGBY, YOU'RE A FOOL ..... CORBIN BERNSEN
BERT RIGBY, YOU'RE A FOOL .... JACKIE GAYLE
BERT RIGBY,
    YOU'RE A FOOL .... ROBBIE COLTRANE
BERT RIGBY, YOU'RE A FOOL ...... ROBERT LINDSAY
BERYL MARKHAM: A SHADOW
    ON THE SUN (MS) .... FREDERIC FORREST
BERYL MARKHAM: A SHADOW
    ON THE SUN (MS) .... JAMES FOX
BERYL MARKHAM: A SHADOW
    ON THE SUN (MS) .... STEFANIE POWERS
BERYL MARKHAM: A SHADOW
    ON THE SUN (TF) .... CLAIRE BLOOM
BEST DEFENSE .... DUDLEY MOORE
BEST DEFENSE .... EDDIE MURPHY
BEST DEFENSE .... HELEN SHAVER
BEST DEFENSE .... KATE CAPSHAW
BEST FOOT FORWARD .... JUNE ALLYSON
BEST FOOT FORWARD .... LUCILLE BALL†
BEST FOOT FORWARD .... NANCY WALKER†
BEST FRIENDS .... AUDRA LINDLEY
BEST FRIENDS .... BARNARD HUGHES
BEST FRIENDS .... BURT REYNOLDS
BEST FRIENDS .... CAROL LOCATELL
BEST FRIENDS .... GOLDIE HAWN
BEST FRIENDS .... JESSICA TANDY†
BEST FRIENDS .... KEENAN WYNN†
BEST FRIENDS .... RICHARD LIBERTINI
BEST FRIENDS .... RON SILVER
BEST HOUSE IN
    LONDON, THE .... DAVID HEMMINGS
BEST HOUSE IN LONDON, THE .... JOHN CLEESE
BEST KEPT SECRETS (TF) ...... FREDERIC FORREST
BEST KEPT SECRETS (TF) .... PATTY DUKE
BEST LITTLE GIRL IN
    THE WORLD, THE (TF) .... ALLY SHEEDY
BEST LITTLE GIRL IN
    THE WORLD, THE (TF) .... EVA MARIE SAINT
BEST LITTLE WHOREHOUSE
    IN TEXAS, THE .... BARRY CORBIN
BEST LITTLE WHOREHOUSE
    IN TEXAS, THE .... BURT REYNOLDS

This is not a list of every film ever made or every cast member, only those listed in this directory.

BEST LITTLE WHOREHOUSE
IN TEXAS, THE .... DOLLY PARTON
BEST LITTLE WHOREHOUSE
IN TEXAS, THE .... DOM DeLUISE
BEST LITTLE WHOREHOUSE
IN TEXAS, THE .... JIM NABORS
BEST LITTLE WHOREHOUSE
IN TEXAS, THE .... LOIS NETTLETON
BEST LITTLE WHOREHOUSE
IN TEXAS, THE .... ROBERT MANDAN
BEST LITTLE WHOREHOUSE
IN TEXAS, THE .... STANLEY DeSANTIS
BEST LITTLE WHOREHOUSE
IN TEXAS, THE .... THERESA MERRITT
BEST LITTLE WHOREHOUSE
IN TEXAS, THE ○ .... CHARLES DURNING
BEST MAN, THE .... ANN SOTHERN
BEST MAN, THE .... CLIFF ROBERTSON
BEST MAN, THE .... EDIE ADAMS
BEST MAN, THE .... KEVIN McCARTHY
BEST MAN, THE ○ .... LEE TRACY†
BEST OF EVERYTHING, THE .... DIANE BAKER
BEST OF EVERYTHING, THE .... HOPE LANGE
BEST OF EVERYTHING, THE ..... JOAN CRAWFORD†
BEST OF EVERYTHING, THE .... LOUIS JOURDAN
BEST OF THE BEST .... CHRIS PENN
BEST OF THE BEST .... ERIC ROBERTS
BEST OF THE BEST .... JAMES EARL JONES
BEST OF THE BEST .... JOHN DYE
BEST OF THE BEST .... JOHN P. RYAN
BEST OF THE BEST .... LOUISE FLETCHER
BEST OF THE BEST .... PHILLIP RHEE
BEST OF THE BEST .... SALLY KIRKLAND
BEST OF THE BEST .... SIMON RHEE
BEST OF THE BEST .... TOM EVERETT
BEST OF TIMES, THE .... DONALD MOFFAT
BEST OF TIMES, THE .... DONAOVAN SCOTT
BEST OF TIMES, THE .... HOLLY PALANCE
BEST OF TIMES, THE .... KIRK CAMERON
BEST OF TIMES, THE .... KURT RUSSELL
BEST OF TIMES, THE .... M. EMMET WALSH
BEST OF TIMES, THE .... MARGARET WHITTON
BEST OF TIMES, THE .... PAMELA REED
BEST OF TIMES, THE .... R.G. ARMSTRONG
BEST OF TIMES, THE .... ROBIN WILLIAMS
BEST OF TIMES, THE .... ROBYN LIVELY
BEST REVENGE .... LEVON HELM
BEST SELLER .... BRIAN DENNEHY
BEST SELLER .... JAMES WOODS
BEST SELLER .... JENNY GAGO
BEST SELLER .... VICTORIA TENNANT
BEST THINGS IN LIFE
ARE FREE, THE .... ERNEST BORGNINE
BEST THINGS IN LIFE
ARE FREE, THE .... GORDON MACRAE†
BEST YEARS OF OUR
LIVES, THE .... TERESA WRIGHT
BEST YEARS OF OUR
LIVES, THE ★★ .... FREDRIC MARCH†
BEST YEARS OF OUR
LIVES, THE ○○ .... HAROLD RUSSELL
BETRAYAL .... BEN KINGSLEY
BETRAYAL .... JEREMY IRONS
BETRAYAL .... PATRICIA HODGE
BETRAYAL .... RIP TORN
BETRAYED .... ALBERT HALL
BETRAYED .... BETSY BLAIR
BETRAYED .... BRIAN BOSAK
BETRAYED .... DAVID CLENNON
BETRAYED .... DEBRA WINGER
BETRAYED .... JEFFREY DEMUNN
BETRAYED .... JOHN HEARD
BETRAYED .... JOHN MAHONEY
BETRAYED .... LANA TURNER
BETRAYED .... MARIA VALDEZ
BETRAYED .... RICHARD LIBERTINI
BETRAYED .... TED LEVINE
BETRAYED .... TOM BERENGER
BETRAYED BY
INNOCENCE (TF) .... BARRY BOSTWICK
BETRAYED BY INNOCENCE (TF) .... PHILIP BRUNS
BETSY, THE .... EDWRAD HERRMANN

BETSY, THE .... INGA SWENSON
BETSY, THE .... JANE ALEXANDER
BETSY, THE .... JOSEPH WISEMAN
BETSY, THE .... KATHERINE ROSS
BETSY, THE .... KATHLEEN BELLER
BETSY, THE .... LAURENCE OLIVIER†
BETSY, THE .... LESLEY-ANNE DOWN
BETSY, THE .... ROBERT DUVALL
BETSY, THE .... TOMMY LEE JONES
BETSY'S WEDDING .... JULIE BOYASSO†
BETSY'S WEDDING .... ALAN ALDA
BETSY'S WEDDING .... ALLY SHEEDY
BETSY'S WEDDING .... ANTHONY LaPAGLIA
BETSY'S WEDDING .... BIBI BESCH
BETSY'S WEDDING .... BURT YOUNG
BETSY'S WEDDING .... CAMILLE SAVIOLA
BETSY'S WEDDING .... CATHERINE O'HARA
BETSY'S WEDDING .... DYLAN WALSH
BETSY'S WEDDING .... JOE PESCI
BETSY'S WEDDING .... JOEY BISHOP
BETSY'S WEDDING .... MADELINE KAHN
BETSY'S WEDDING .... MOLLY RINGWALD
BETSY'S WEDDING .... NICOLAS COSTER
BETTER LATE THAN NEVER .... MAGGIE SMITH
BETTER LATE THAN NEVER (TF) .... TYNE DALY
BETTER OFF DEAD .... DAVID OGDEN STIERS
BETTER OFF DEAD .... JOHN CUSACK
BETTER OFF DEAD .... KIM DARBY
BETTY .... JEAN-LOUIS TRINTIGNANT
BETTY .... STEPHANE AUDRAN
BETTY BLUE .... BEATRICE DOLLE
BETTY BLUE .... CLEMENTINE CELARIE
BETTY BLUE .... CONSUELO DE HAVILLAND
BETTY BLUE .... GERARD DARMON
BETTY BLUE .... JAQUES MATHOU
BETTY BLUE .... JEAN-HUGUES ANGLADE
BETTY BLUE .... VINCENT LINDON
BETTY FORD STORY, THE (TF) ...... JOSEF SOMMER
BETWEEN FRIENDS (CTF) .... CAROL BURNETT
BETWEEN FRIENDS (CTF) .... ELIZABETH TAYLOR
BETWEEN HEAVEN AND HELL .... ROBERT WAGNER
BETWEEN THE LINES .... BRUNO KIRBY
BETWEEN THE LINES .... GWEN WELLES
BETWEEN THE LINES .... JEFF GOLDBLUM
BETWEEN THE LINES .... JILL EIKENBERRY
BETWEEN THE LINES .... JOHN HEARD
BETWEEN THE LINES .... LINDSAY CROUSE
BETWEEN THE LINES .... MARILU HENNER
BETWEEN THE LINES .... MICHAEL J. POLLARD
BETWEEN THE LINES .... STEPHEN COLLINS
BETWEEN TWO WOMEN ..... MAUREEN O'SULLIVAN
BETWEEN TWO WOMEN .... VAN JOHNSON
BETWEEN TWO
WOMEN (TF) .... COLLEEN DEWHURST†
BETWEEN TWO WOMEN (TF) .... FARRAH FAWCETT
BETWEEN TWO WORLDS .... ELEANOR PARKER
BEULAH LAND (MS) .... DON JOHNSON
BEULAH LAND (MS) .... LESLEY ANN WARREN
BEULAH LAND (MS) .... MARTHA SCOTT
BEULAH LAND (MS) .... MEREDITH BAXTER
BEULAH LAND (MS) .... MICHAEL SARRAZIN
BEVERLY HILLBILLIES, THE .... BUDDY EBSEN
BEVERLY HILLBILLIES, THE ...... CLORIS LEACHMAN
BEVERLY HILLBILLIES, THE ...... DABNEY COLEMAN
BEVERLY HILLBILLIES, THE .... DIEDRICH BADER
BEVERLY HILLBILLIES, THE .... DOLLY PARTON
BEVERLY HILLBILLIES, THE .... ERIKA ELENIAK
BEVERLY HILLBILLIES, THE .... JIM VARNEY
BEVERLY HILLBILLIES, THE .... LEA THOMPSON
BEVERLY HILLBILLIES, THE .... LILY TOMLIN
BEVERLY HILLBILLIES, THE .... RANDI PAREIRA
BEVERLY HILLBILLIES, THE .... ROB SCHNEIDER
BEVERLY HILLBILLIES, THE .... ROBERT EASTON
BEVERLY HILLBILLIES, THE .... ZSA ZSA GABOR
BEVERLY HILLS BRATS .... BURT YOUNG
BEVERLY HILLS BRATS .... MARTIN SHEEN
BEVERLY HILLS BRATS .... PETER BILLINGSLEY
BEVERLY HILLS COP .... BRONSON PINCHOT
BEVERLY HILLS COP .... DAMON WAYANS
BEVERLY HILLS COP .... EDDIE MURPHY
BEVERLY HILLS COP .... GILBERT R. HILL
BEVERLY HILLS COP .... JOHN ASHTON

BEVERLY HILLS COP .... JUDGE REINHOLD
BEVERLY HILLS COP .... LISA EILBACHER
BEVERLY HILLS COP .... PAUL REISER
BEVERLY HILLS COP .... RONNY COX
BEVERLY HILLS COP .... STEVEN BERKOFF
BEVERLY HILLS COP II .... BRIGITTE NIELSEN
BEVERLY HILLS COP II .... DEAN STOCKWELL
BEVERLY HILLS COP II .... EDDIE MURPHY
BEVERLY HILLS COP II .... JOHN ASHTON
BEVERLY HILLS COP II .... JUDGE REINHOLD
BEVERLY HILLS COP II .... PAUL REISER
BEVERLY HILLS COP II .... RONNY COX
BEVERLY HILLS COP III .... BRONSON PINCHOT
BEVERLY HILLS COP III .... EDDIE MURPHY
BEVERLY HILLS COP III .... JOHN SAXON
BEVERLY HILLS COP III .... JON TENNEY
BEVERLY HILLS COP III .... JUDGE REINHOLD
BEVERLY HILLS COP III .... TIMOTHY CARHART
BEVERLY HILLS COPS III .... ALAN YOUNG
BEVERLY HILLS COPS III .... HECTOR ELIZONDO
BEVERLY HILLS COPS III .... THERESA RANDLE
BEVERLY HILLS
COWGIRL BLUES (TF) .... DAVID HEMMINGS
BEVERLY HILLS
COWGIRL BLUES (TF) .... JAMES BROLIN
BEVERLY HILLS
COWGIRL BLUES (TF) .... LISA HARTMAN-BLACK
BEVERLY HILLS MADAM (TF) .... DONNA DIXON
BEVERLY HILLS MADAM (TF) .... FAYE DUNAWAY
BEVERLY HILLS MADAM (TF) .... LOUIS JOURDAN
BEVERLY HILLS
MADAM (TF) .... MELODY ANDERSON
BEVERLY HILLS MADAM (TF) .... ROBIN GIVENS
BEWARE MY BRETHREN .... TONY BECKLEY†
BEWARE OF CHILDREN .... FRANCESCA ANNIS
BEWARE! THE BLOB .... BURGESS MEREDITH
BEWARE! THE BLOB .... CAROL LYNLEY
BEWARE! THE BLOB .... LARRY HAGMAN
BEWARE! THE BLOB .... ROBERT WALKER JR.
BEWITCHED .... PHYLLIS THAXTER
BEYOND ALL LIMITS .... JACK PALANCE
BEYOND ATLANTIS .... PATRICK WAYNE
BEYOND ATLANTIS .... SID HAIG
BEYOND EVIL .... ERLAND JOSEPHSON
BEYOND EVIL .... MICHAEL DANTE
BEYOND GLORY .... CONRAD JANIS
BEYOND GLORY .... SEAN McCLORY
BEYOND INNOCENCE .... JACK WARDEN
BEYOND INNOCENCE .... STEPHEN LANG
BEYOND REASON .... TELLY SAVALAS†
BEYOND TH ELAW .... RIP TORN
BEYOND THE BERMUDA
TRIANGLE (TF) .... SUZANNE PLESHETTE
BEYOND THE
BLUE HORIZON .... DOROTHY LAMOUR
BEYOND THE DOOR .... TOM BERENGER
BEYOND THE FOREST .... BETTE DAVIS†
BEYOND THE LAST
FRONTIER .... ROBERT MITCHUM
BEYOND THE LIMIT .... BOB HOSKINS
BEYOND THE LIMIT .... ELPIDIA CARRILLO
BEYOND THE LIMIT .... MICHAEL CAINE
BEYOND THE LIMIT .... RICHARD GERE
BEYOND THE MOUNTAINS ...... MAXIMILIAN SCHELL
BEYOND THE POSEIDON
ADVENTURE .... JACK WARDEN
BEYOND THE POSEIDON
ADVENTURE .... KARL MALDEN
BEYOND THE POSEIDON
ADVENTURE .... MARK HARMON
BEYOND THE POSEIDON
ADVENTURE .... MICHAEL CAINE
BEYOND THE POSEIDON
ADVENTURE .... PETER BOYLE
BEYOND THE POSEIDON
ADVENTURE .... SALLY FIELD
BEYOND THE POSEIDON
ADVENTURE .... SHIRLEY JONES
BEYOND THE POSEIDON
ADVENTURE .... SHIRLEY KNIGHT
BEYOND THE POSEIDON
ADVENTURE .... TELLY SAVALAS†

INDEX OF FILM TITLES

BEYOND THE POSEIDON ADVENTURE ... VERONICA HAMEL
BEYOND THE STARS ... SHARON STONE
BEYOND THE VALLEY OF THE DOLLS ... PAM GRIER
BEYOND THERAPY ... GLENDA JACKSON
BEYOND THERAPY ... GORDAN JACKSON†
BEYOND THERAPY ... JEFF GOLDBLUM
BEYOND THERAPY ... JULIE HAGERTY
BEYOND THERAPY ... TOM CONTI
BEYOND THIS PLACE ... VAN JOHNSON
BEYOND THIS PLACE ... VERA MILES
BHOWANI JUNCTION ... AVA GARDNER†
BIANCO ROSSO E... ... SOPHIA LOREN
BIBLE...IN THE BEGINNING, THE ... GEORGE C. SCOTT
BIBLE, THE ... AVA GARDNER†
BIBLE, THE ... FRANCO NERO
BIBLE, THE ... JOHN HUSTON†
BIBLE, THE ... PETER O'TOOLE
BIBLE, THE ... RICHARD HARRIS
BIG ★ ... TOM HANKS
BIG ... ALEC VON SOMMER
BIG ... ALLAN WASSERMAN
BIG ... ARMANDO PENSO
BIG ... AUGUSTO MARIANI
BIG ... BERT GOLDSTEIN
BIG ... BRUCE JARCHOW
BIG ... CHRIS DOWDEN
BIG ... DANA KAMINSKI
BIG ... DAVID MOSCOW
BIG ... DEBRA JO RUPP
BIG ... DOLORES MESSINA
BIG ... EDWARD SCHICK
BIG ... ELIZABETH PERKINS
BIG ... ERIKA KATZ
BIG ... F. BENJAMIN STIMLER
BIG ... GARY KLAR
BIG ... GEORGE J. MANOS
BIG ... GORDON PRESS
BIG ... HARVEY MILLER
BIG ... JAIME TIRELLI
BIG ... JAMES ECKHOUSE
BIG ... JARED RUSHTON
BIG ... JOHN HEARD
BIG ... JOHN ROTHMAN
BIG ... JON LOVITZ
BIG ... JONATHAN ISAAC LANDAU
BIG ... JORDAN THALER
BIG ... JOSH CLARK
BIG ... JUDD TRICHTER
BIG ... KEITH W. REDDIN
BIG ... KEVIN MEANEY
BIG' ... KIMBERLEE M. DAVIS
BIG ... LELA IVEY
BIG ... LINDA GILLEN
BIG ... MARK BALLOU
BIG ... MERCEDES RUEHL
BIG ... MILDRED R. VANDEVER
BIG ... NANCY GILES
BIG ... OLIVER BLOCK
BIG ... PASQUALE PUGLIESE
BIG ... PAUL HERMAN
BIG ... PAUL J. Q. LEE
BIG ... PETER McROBBIE
BIG ... RICHARD DEVIA
BIG ... ROBERT LOGGIA
BIG ... ROCKETS REDGLARE
BIG ... SAMANTHA LARKIN
BIG ... SERGIO MOSETTI
BIG ... TEDDY HOLIAVKO
BIG ... TOM COVIELLO
BIG ... TRACY REINER
BIG ... VAUGHN SANDMAN
BIG ... VINNY CAPONE
BIG BAD MAMA ... ANGIE DICKINSON
BIG BAD MAMA ... DICK MILLER
BIG BAD MAMA ... ROYAL DANO
BIG BAD MAMA ... SALLY KIRKLAND
BIG BAD MAMA ... TOM SKERRITT
BIG BAD MAMA ... WILLIAM SHATNER
BIG BANG, THE (FD) ... DON SIMPSON
BIG BANG, THE (FD) ... JAMES TOBACK
BIG BIRD CAGE, THE ... PAM GRIER
BIG BLOCKADE, THE ... JOHN MILLS
BIG BLUE, THE ... GRIFFIN DUNNE
BIG BLUE, THE ... JEAN RENO
BIG BLUE, THE ... JEAN-MARC BARR
BIG BLUE, THE ... MARC DURET
BIG BLUE, THE ... PAUL SHENAR
BIG BLUE, THE ... ROSANNA ARQUETTE
BIG BLUE, THE ... SERGIO CASTELLITTO
BIG BOUNCE, THE ... JAMES DALY†
BIG BOUNCE, THE ... LEE GRANT
BIG BOUNCE, THE ... LEIGH TAYLOR-YOUNG
BIG BOUNCE, THE ... ROBERT WEBBER
BIG BOUNCE, THE ... RYAN O'NEAL
BIG BOUNCE, THE ... VAN HEFLIN†
BIG BRAWL, THE ... JOSE FERRER†
BIG BRAWL, THE ... MAKO
BIG BROADCAST OF 1936, THE ... GEORGE BURNS
BIG BROADCAST OF 1937, THE ... MARTHA RAYE†
BIG BROADCAST OF 1938, THE ... BOB HOPE
BIG BROADCAST OF 1938, THE ... DOROTHY LAMOUR
BIG BROADCAST OF 1938, THE ... MARTHA RAYE†
BIG BROADCAST, THE ... GEORGE BURNS
BIG BUS, THE ... BOB DISHY
BIG BUS, THE ... HAROLD GOULD
BIG BUS, THE ... HOWARD HESSEMAN
BIG BUS, THE ... JOHN BECK
BIG BUS, THE ... JOSE FERRER†
BIG BUS, THE ... JOSEPH BOLOGNA
BIG BUS, THE ... LARRY HAGMAN
BIG BUS, THE ... LYNN REDGRAVE
BIG BUS, THE ... NED BEATTY
BIG BUS, THE ... RENE AUBERJONOIS
BIG BUS, THE ... RICHARD B. SHULL
BIG BUS, THE ... RICHARD MULLIGAN
BIG BUS, THE ... RUTH GORDON†
BIG BUS, THE ... SALLY KELLERMAN
BIG BUS, THE ... STOCKARD CHANNING
BIG BUS, THE ... STUART MARGOLIN
BIG BUSINESS ... BARRY PRIMUS
BIG BUSINESS ... BETTE MIDLER
BIG BUSINESS ... EDWRAD HERRMANN
BIG BUSINESS ... FRED WARD
BIG BUSINESS ... LILY TOMLIN
BIG BUSINESS ... MICHAEL GROSS
BIG BUSINESS ... ROY BROCKSMITH
BIG CAPER, THE ... RORY CALHOUN
BIG CARNIVAL, THE ... KIRK DOUGLAS
BIG CHILL, THE ... DON GALLOWAY
BIG CHILL, THE ... JEFF GOLDBLUM
BIG CHILL, THE ... JoBETH WILLIAMS
BIG CHILL, THE ... KEVIN COSTNER
BIG CHILL, THE ... KEVIN KLINE
BIG CHILL, THE ... MARY KAY PLACE
BIG CHILL, THE ... MEG TILLY
BIG CHILL, THE ... TOM BERENGER
BIG CHILL, THE ... WILLIAM HURT
BIG CHILL, THE ○ ... GLENN CLOSE
BIG CIRCUS, THE ... RED BUTTONS
BIG CIRCUS, THE ... STEVE ALLEN
BIG CIRCUS, THE ... VINCENT PRICE†
BIG CITY, THE ... DANNY THOMAS†
BIG CLOCK, THE ... HARRY MORGAN
BIG CLOCK, THE ... MAUREEN O'SULLIVAN
BIG COMBO, THE ... EARL HOLLIMAN
BIG COUNTRY, THE ... CARROLL BAKER
BIG COUNTRY, THE ... CHARLTON HESTON
BIG COUNTRY, THE ... CHUCK CONNORS†
BIG COUNTRY, THE ... GREGORY PECK
BIG COUNTRY, THE ... JEAN SIMMONS
BIG COUNTRY, THE ∞ ... BURL IVES
BIG CUBE, THE ... DAN O'HERLIHY
BIG CUBE, THE ... LANA TURNER
BIG DAY, THE ... DONALD PLEASENCE
BIG DEAL ON MADONNA STREET, THE ... MARCELLO MASTROIANNI
BIG DOLL HOUSE, THE ... PAM GRIER
BIG EASY, THE ... DENNIS QUAID
BIG EASY, THE ... ELLEN BARKIN
BIG EASY, THE ... GRACE ZABRISKIE
BIG EASY, THE ... JOHN GOODMAN
BIG EASY, THE ... NED BEATTY
BIG FISHERMAN, THE ... HOWARD KEEL
BIG FISHERMAN, THE ... JOHN SAXON
BIG FIX, THE ... BONNIE BEDELIA
BIG FIX, THE ... F. MURRAY ABRAHAM
BIG FIX, THE ... FRITZ WEAVER
BIG FIX, THE ... JOHN LITHGOW
BIG FIX, THE ... MANDY PATINKIN
BIG FIX, THE ... RITA KARIN
BIG FIX, THE ... SUSAN ANSPACH
BIG GUY, THE ... JACKIE COOPER
BIG HAND FOR THE LITTLE LADY, A ... BURGESS MEREDITH
BIG HAND FOR THE LITTLE LADY, A ... HENRY FONDA†
BIG HAND FOR THE LITTLE LADY, A ... JASON ROBARDS
BIG HAND FOR THE LITTLE LADY, A ... JOANNE WOODWARD
BIG HAND FOR THE LITTLE LADY, A ... KEVIN McCARTHY
BIG HANGOVER, THE ... ELIZABETH TAYLOR
BIG HANGOVER, THE ... VAN JOHNSON
BIG HEAT, THE ... LEE MARVIN†
BIG HOUSE, THE ★ ... WALLACE BEERY†
BIG HOUSE, U.S.A. ... CHARLES BRONSON
BIG JAKE ... HARRY CAREY JR.
BIG JAKE ... MAUREEN O'HARA
BIG JAKE ... PATRICK WAYNE
BIG JIM McLAIN ... JAMES ARNESS
BIG KNIFE, THE ... JACK PALANCE
BIG KNIFE, THE ... ROD STEIGER
BIG KNIFE, THE ... SHELLEY WINTERS
BIG KNIFE, THE ... WESLEY ADDY
BIG LEAGUER, THE ... RICHARD JAECKEL
BIG MAN ON CAMPUS ... TOM SKERRITT
BIG MAN, THE ... BILLY CONNELLY
BIG MAN, THE ... IAN BANNEN
BIG MAN, THE ... JOANNE WHALLEY-KILMER
BIG MAN, THE ... LIAM NEESON
BIG MONEY, THE ... JILL IRELAND†
BIG MOUTH, THE ... JERRY LEWIS
BIG NOISE, THE ... ROBERT BLAKE
BIG PICTURE, THE ... DAN SCHNEIDER
BIG PICTURE, THE ... EMILY LONGSTRETH
BIG PICTURE, THE ... FRAN DRESCHER
BIG PICTURE, THE ... J. T. WALSH
BIG PICTURE, THE ... JASON GOULD
BIG PICTURE, THE ... JENNIFER JASON LEIGH
BIG PICTURE, THE ... KEVIN BACON
BIG PICTURE, THE ... KIM MIYORI
BIG PICTURE, THE ... MARTIN SHORT
BIG PICTURE, THE ... MICHAEL McKEAN
BIG PICTURE, THE ... TERI HATCHER
BIG PICTURE, THE ... TRACY BROOKS SWOPE
BIG POND, THE ★ ... MAURICE CHEVALIER†
BIG PUNCH, THE ... GORDON MACRAE†
BIG RED ONE, THE ... LEE MARVIN†
BIG RED ONE, THE ... MARK HAMILL
BIG RED ONE, THE ... PERRY LANG
BIG RED ONE, THE ... ROBERT CARRADINE
BIG ROSE (TF) ... SHELLEY WINTERS
BIG SCORE, THE ... ED LAUTER
BIG SCORE, THE ... FRED WILLIAMSON
BIG SCORE, THE ... JOHN SAXON
BIG SCORE, THE ... MICHAEL DANTE
BIG SCORE, THE ... RICHARD ROUNDTREE
BIG SHAKEDOWN, THE ... BETTE DAVIS†
BIG SHOT, THE ... HOWARD DA SILVA†
BIG SHOT, THE ... MAUREEN O'SULLIVAN
BIG SHOTS ... BRYNN THAYER
BIG SHOW, THE ... CLIFF ROBERTSON
BIG SHOW, THE ... ROBERT VAUGHN
BIG SKY, THE ... KIRK DOUGLAS
BIG SKY, THE ○ ... ARTHUR HUNNICUTT†
BIG SLEEP, THE ... CANDY CLARK
BIG SLEEP, THE ... DIANA QUICK
BIG SLEEP, THE ... HUMPHREY BOGART†
BIG SLEEP, THE ... JAMES STEWART
BIG SLEEP, THE ... JOAN COLLINS
BIG SLEEP, THE ... LAUREN BACALL

This is not a list of every film ever made or every cast member, only those listed in this directory.

BIG SLEEP, THE ... ROBERT MITCHUM
BIG SLEEP, THE ... SARAH MILES
BIG STEAL, THE ... JANE GREER
BIG STEAL, THE ... ROBERT MITCHUM
BIG STREET, THE ... LUCILLE BALL†
BIG TIME ... TOM WAITS
BIG TOP PEE-WEE ... KRIS KRISTOFFERSON
BIG TOP PEE-WEE ... PAUL REUBENS
BIG TOP PEE-WEE ... PENELOPE ANN MILLER
BIG TOP PEE-WEE ... SUSAN TYRRELL
BIG TOP PEE-WEE ... VALERIA GOLINO
BIG TOWN, THE ... BRUCE DERN
BIG TOWN, THE ... DAVID MARSHALL GRANT
BIG TOWN, THE ... DIANE LANE
BIG TOWN, THE ... LEE GRANT
BIG TOWN, THE ... LOLITA DAVIDOVICH
BIG TOWN, THE ... MATT DILLON
BIG TOWN, THE ... SUZY AMIS
BIG TOWN, THE ... TOM SKERRITT
BIG TOWN, THE ... TOMMY LEE JONES
BIG TREES, THE ... KIRK DOUGLAS
BIG TROUBLE ... ALAN ARKIN
BIG TROUBLE ... BEVERLY D'ANGELO
BIG TROUBLE ... CHARLES DURNING
BIG TROUBLE ... PAUL DOOLEY
BIG TROUBLE ... PETER FALK
BIG TROUBLE ... ROBERT STACK
BIG TROUBLE IN LITTLE CHINA ... DENNIS DUN
BIG TROUBLE IN LITTLE CHINA ... JAMES HONG
BIG TROUBLE IN LITTLE CHINA ... KATE BURTON
BIG TROUBLE IN LITTLE CHINA ... KIM CATTRALL
BIG TROUBLE IN LITTLE CHINA ... KURT RUSSELL
BIG TROUBLE IN LITTLE CHINA ... SUZEE PAI
BIG TROUBLE IN LITTLE CHINA ... VICTOR WONG
BIG WEDNESDAY ... BARBARA HALE
BIG WEDNESDAY ... GARY BUSEY
BIG WEDNESDAY ... JAN-MICHAEL VINCENT
BIG WEDNESDAY ... PATTI D'ARBANVILLE
BIG WEDNESDAY ... PERRY LANG
BIG WEDNESDAY ... WILLIAM KATT
BIGAMIST, THE ... MARCELLO MASTROIANNI
BIGFOOT, THE MYSTERIOUS MONSTER ... PETER GRAVES
BIGGER THAN LIFE ... WALTER MATTHAU
BIGGEST BUNDLE OF THEM ALL, THE ... RAQUEL WELCH
BIGGEST BUNDLE OF THEM ALL, THE ... ROBERT WAGNER
BIGGLES ... MICHAEL SIBERRY
BIKINI BEACH ... ANNETTE FUNICELLO
BIKINI BEACH ... FRANKIE AVALON
BIKINI BEACH ... TIMOTHY CAREY
BILITIS ... PATTI D'ARBANVILLE
BILL (TF) ... DENNIS QUAID
BILL (TF) ... MICKEY ROONEY
BILL OF DIVORCEMENT, A ... JOHN BARRYMORE†
BILL OF DIVORCEMENT, A ... KATHERINE HEPBURN
BILL OF DIVORCEMENT, A ... MAUREEN O'HARA
BILL: ON HIS OWN (TF) ... DENNIS QUAID
BILL: ON HIS OWN (TF) ... HELEN HUNT
BILL: ON HIS OWN (TF) ... MICKEY ROONEY
BILL & TED'S BOGUS JOURNEY ... ALEX WINTER
BILL & TED'S BOGUS JOURNEY ... AMY STOCK-POYNTON
BILL & TED'S BOGUS JOURNEY ... ANNETTE AZCUY
BILL & TED'S BOGUS JOURNEY ... DENNIS OTT†
BILL & TED'S BOGUS JOURNEY ... GEORGE CARLIN
BILL & TED'S BOGUS JOURNEY ... HAL LANDON JR.
BILL & TED'S BOGUS JOURNEY ... JOSS ACKLAND
BILL & TED'S BOGUS JOURNEY ... KEANU REEVES
BILL & TED'S BOGUS JOURNEY ... PAM GRIER
BILL & TED'S BOGUS JOURNEY ... WILLIAM SADLER
BILL & TED'S EXCELLENT ADVENTURE ... AL LEONG
BILL & TED'S EXCELLENT ADVENTURE ... ALEX WINTER
BILL & TED'S EXCELLENT ADVENTURE ... AMY STOCK-POYNTON
BILL & TED'S EXCELLENT ADVENTURE ... BERNIE CASEY
BILL & TED'S EXCELLENT ADVENTURE ... DAN SHOR
BILL & TED'S EXCELLENT ADVENTURE ... GEORGE CARLIN
BILL & TED'S EXCELLENT ADVENTURE ... KEANU REEVES
BILL & TED'S EXCELLENT ADVENTURE ... ROBERT V. BARRON
BILL & TED'S EXCELLENT ADVENTURE ... ROD LOOMIS
BILL & TED'S EXCELLENT ADVENTURE ... TED STEEDMAN
BILL & TED'S EXCELLENT ADVENTURE ... TONY CAMILIERI
BILLIE ... JANE GREER
BILLIE ... PATTY DUKE
BILLION DOLLAR BRAIN ... DONALD SUTHERLAND
BILLION DOLLAR BRAIN ... KARL MALDEN
BILLION DOLLAR BRAIN ... MICHAEL CAINE
BILLION DOLLAR BRAIN ... SUSAN GEORGE
BILLION DOLLAR HOBO, THE ... TIM CONWAY
BILLION DOLLAR THREAT, THE (TF) ... PATRICK MacNEE
BILLION DOLLAR THREAT, THE (TF) ... RALPH BELLAMY†
BILLION FOR BORIS, A ... TIM KAZURINSKY
BILLIONAIRE BOYS CLUB (MS) ... BARRY TUBB
BILLIONAIRE BOYS CLUB (MS) ... FREDERIC LEHNE
BILLIONAIRE BOYS CLUB (MS) ... JOHN STOCKWELL
BILLIONAIRE BOYS CLUB (MS) ... JUDD NELSON
BILLIONAIRE BOYS CLUB (MS) ... RAPHAEL SBARGE
BILLIONAIRE BOYS CLUB (MS) ... RON SILVER
BILLIONAIRE BOYS CLUB (MS) ... STAN SHAW
BILLY BATHGATE ... BRUCE WILLIS
BILLY BATHGATE ... DUSTIN HOFFMAN
BILLY BATHGATE ... LOREN DEAN
BILLY BATHGATE ... NICOLE KIDMAN
BILLY BUD ... MELVYN DOUGLAS†
BILLY BUDD ... DAVID McCALLUM
BILLY BUDD ... JOHN MEILLON
BILLY BUDD ... JOHN NEVILLE
BILLY BUDD ... PETER USTINOV
BILLY BUDD ✪ ... TERENCE STAMP
BILLY GALVIN ... ALAN NORTH
BILLY GALVIN ... BARTON HEYMAN
BILLY GALVIN ... JOYCE VAN PATTEN
BILLY GALVIN ... KARL MALDEN
BILLY GALVIN ... KEITH SZARABAJKA
BILLY GALVIN ... LENNY VON DOHLEN
BILLY GALVIN ... PAUL GUILFOYLE
BILLY GALVIN ... TONI KALEM
BILLY JACK GOES TO WASHINGTON ... LUCIE ARNAZ
BILLY LIAR ... JULIE CHRISTIE
BILLY LIAR ... TOM COURTENAY
BILLY MADISON ... ADAM SANDLER
BILLY MADISON ... BRAD WHITFORD
BILLY MADISON ... BRIDGETTE WILSON
BILLY MADISON ... LARRY HANKIN
BILLY MADISON ... MARK BELTZMAN
BILLY MADISON ... NORM McDONALD
BILLY: PORTRAIT OF A STREET KID (TF) ... LeVAR BURTON
BILLY ROSE'S JUMBO ... DORIS DAY
BILLY ROSE'S JUMBO ... MARTHA RAYE†
BILLY THE KID VS. DRACULA ... JOHN CARRADINE†
BILLY THE THIRD ... BO DEREK
BILLY THE THIRD ... BRIAN DENNEHY
BILLY THE THIRD ... CHRIS FARLEY
BILLY THE THIRD ... DAVID SPADE
BILLY THE THIRD ... ROB LOWE
BILLY TWO HATS ... DESI ARNAZ JR.
BILLY TWO HATS ... GREGORY PECK
BILLY TWO HATS ... JACK WARDEN
BILOXI BLUES ... CASEY SIEMASZKO
BILOXI BLUES ... CHRISTOPHER WALKEN
BILOXI BLUES ... COREY PARKER
BILOXI BLUES ... MATHHEW BRODERICK
BILOXI BLUES ... MATT MULHERN
BILOXI BLUES ... PENELOPE ANN MILLER
BINGO! ... CINDY WILLIAMS
BINGO! ... DAVID RASCHE
BINGO! ... ROBERT STEINMILLER JR.
BINGO LONG TRAVELING ALL-STARS AND MOTOR KINGS, THE ... BILLY DEE WILLIAMS
BINGO LONG TRAVELING ALL-STARS AND MOTOR KINGS, THE ... JAMES EARL JONES
BINGO LONG TRAVELING ALL-STARS AND MOTOR KINGS, THE ... RICHARD PRYOR
BINGO LONG TRAVELING ALL-STARS AND MOTOR KINGS, THE ... STAN SHAW
BIONIC SHOWDOWN: THE SIX MILLION DOLLAR MAN AND THE BIONIC WOMAN (TF) ... LEE MAJORS
BIONIC SHOWDOWN: THE SIX MILLION DOLLAR MAN AND THE BIONIC WOMAN (TF) ... LINDSAY WAGNER
BIONIC SHOWDOWN: THE SIX MILLION DOLLAR MAN AND THE BIONIC WOMAN (TF) ... RICHARD ANDERSON
BIONIC SHOWDOWN: THE SIX-MILLION DOLLAR MAN AND THE BIONIC WOMAN (TF) ... SANDRA BULLOCK
BIRCH INTERVAL ... ANN WEDGEWORTH
BIRCH INTERVAL ... EDDIE ALBERT
BIRCH INTERVAL ... RIP TORN
BIRD ... DIANE VENORA
BIRD ... FOREST WHITAKER
BIRD ... JAMES HANDY
BIRD OF PARADISE ... LOUIS JOURDAN
BIRD ON A WIRE ... BILL DUKE
BIRD ON A WIRE ... DAVID CARRADINE
BIRD ON A WIRE ... GOLDIE HAWN
BIRD ON A WIRE ... HARRY CAESAR
BIRD ON A WIRE ... JEFF COREY
BIRD ON A WIRE ... JOAN SEVERANCE
BIRD ON A WIRE ... MEL GIBSON
BIRD ON A WIRE ... STEPHEN TOBOLOWSKY
BIRD WITH THE CRYSTAL PLUMAGE, THE ... TONY MUSANTE
BIRDMAN OF ALCATRAZ ... KARL MALDEN
BIRDMAN OF ALCATRAZ ★ ... BURT LANCASTER†
BIRDMAN OF ALCATRAZ ✪ ... THELMA RITTER†
BIRDMAN OF ALCATRAZ ✪ ... TELLY SAVALAS†
BIRDS, THE ... JESSICA TANDY†
BIRDS, THE ... LONNY CHAPMAN
BIRDS, THE ... MORGAN BRITTANY
BIRDS, THE ... SUZANNE PLESHETTE
BIRDS, THE ... TIPPI HEDREN
BIRDS, THE ... VERONICA CARTWRIGHT
BIRDS II: LAND'S END, THE (CTF) ... BRAD JOHNSON
BIRDS II: LAND'S END, THE (CTF) ... CHELSEA FIELD
BIRDS II: LAND'S END, THE (CTF) ... MEGAN GALLACHER
BIRDS DO IT ... TAB HUNTER
BIRDY ... MATTHEW MODINE
BIRDY ... NICOLAS CAGE
BIRTH OF A NATION, THE ... LILLIAN GISH†
BIRTHDAY PRESENT, THE ... IAN BANNEN
BISCUIT EATER, THE ... EARL HOLLIMAN
BISHOP MISBEHAVES, THE ... MAUREEN O'SULLIVAN
BISHOP'S WIFE, THE ... DAVID NIVEN†
BITCH, THE ... JOAN COLLINS
BITCH, THE ... KENNETH HAIGH
BITE THE BULLET ... BEN JOHNSON
BITE THE BULLET ... CANDICE BERGEN
BITE THE BULLET ... DABNEY COLEMAN
BITE THE BULLET ... GENE HACKMAN
BITE THE BULLET ... IAN BANNEN
BITE THE BULLET ... JAMES COBURN
BITE THE BULLET ... JAN-MICHAEL VINCENT
BITE THE BULLET ... SALLY KIRKLAND
BITTER CREEK ... CLAUDE AKINS†
BITTER HARVEST (TF) ... ART CARNEY
BITTER MOON ... EMMANUELLE SEIGNER
BITTER MOON ... HUGH GRANT
BITTER MOON ... KRISTIN SCOTT THOMAS
BITTER MOON ... PETER COYOTE
BITTER TEA OF GENERAL YEN, THE ... BARBARA STANWYCK†
BITTERSWEET LOVE ... CELESTE HOLM
BITTERSWEET LOVE ... LANA TURNER

† after an actor's name denotes deceased.

BITTERSWEET LOVE .... MEREDITH BAXTER
BIX FIX, THE .... RICHARD DREYFUSS
BLACK AND WHITE .... DANA DELANY
BLACK BART .... YVONNE DE CARLO
BLACK BEAUTY .... ALUN ARMSTRONG
BLACK BEAUTY .... ANDREW KNOTT
BLACK BEAUTY .... ANTHONY WALTERS
BLACK BEAUTY .... DAVID THEWLIS
BLACK BEAUTY .... ELEANOR BRON
BLACK BEAUTY .... GEMMA PATERNOSTER
BLACK BEAUTY .... GEORGINA ARMSTRONG
BLACK BEAUTY .... JIM CARTER
BLACK BEAUTY .... JOHN McENERY
BLACK BEAUTY .... MARK LESTER
BLACK BEAUTY .... PETER COOK
BLACK BEAUTY .... PETER DAVISON
BLACK BEAUTY .... SEAN BEAN
BLACK BEAUTY (MS) .... EILEEN BRENNAN
BLACK BEAUTY (MS) .... WILLIAM DEVANE
BLACK BEAUTY (TF) .... DIANA MULDAUR
BLACK BELLY OF THE
  TARANTULA, THE .... CLAUDINE AUGER
BLACK BIRD, THE .... GEORGE SEGAL
BLACK BIRD, THE .... LIONEL STANDER
BLACK BOOK, THE .... NORMAN LLOYD
BLACK CAESAR .... FRED WILLIAMSON
BLACK CAESAR .... JULIUS HARRIS
BLACK CAESAR .... VAL AVERY
BLACK CHRISTMAS .... JOHN SAXON
BLACK CHRISTMAS .... MARGOT KIDDER
BLACK EAGLE .... JEAN-CLAUDE VAN DAMME
BLACK EYE .... FRED WILLIAMSON
BLACK EYE .... RICHARD ANDERSON
BLACK FEATHER .... PIUS SAVAGE
BLACK GIRL .... BROCK PETERS
BLACK GIRL .... RUBY DEE
BLACK GOLD .... ANTHONY QUINN
BLACK GOLD .... CLAUDE AKINS†
BLACK GUNN .... JIM BROWN
BLACK GUNN .... MARTIN LANDAU
BLACK HAND .... GENE KELLY
BLACK HEAT .... RUSS TAMBLYN
BLACK HOLE, THE .... ANTHONY PERKINS†
BLACK HOLE, THE .... ERNEST BORGNINE
BLACK HOLE, THE .... JOSEPH BOTTOMS
BLACK HOLE, THE .... MAXIMILIAN SCHELL
BLACK HOLE, THE .... ROBERT FORSTER
BLACK JACK .... GEORG STANFORD BROWN
BLACK JESUS .... WOODY STRODE
BLACK JOURNEY .... SHELLEY WINTERS
BLACK LIKE ME .... JAMES WHITMORE
BLACK LIKE ME .... RAYMOND ST. JACQUES
BLACK LIKE ME .... ROSCOE LEE BROWNE
BLACK MAGIC .... RAYMOND BURR†
BLACK MAMA, WHITE MAMA .... PAM GRIER
BLACK MARBLE, THE .... ANN RAMSEY†
BLACK MARBLE, THE .... HARRY DEAN STANTON
BLACK MARBLE, THE .... JAMES WOODS
BLACK MARBLE, THE .... PAULA PRENTISS
BLACK MARBLE, THE .... ROBERT FOXWORTH
BLACK MIDNIGHT .... RODDY McDOWALL
BLACK MOON RISING .... BUBBA SMITH
BLACK MOON RISING .... DAN SHOR
BLACK MOON RISING .... LEE VING
BLACK MOON RISING .... LINDA HAMILTON
BLACK MOON RISING .... NICK CASSAVETES
BLACK MOON RISING .... RICHARD JAECKEL
BLACK MOON RISING .... ROBERT VAUGHN
BLACK MOON RISING .... TOMMY LEE JONES
BLACK MOON RISING .... WILLIAM SANDERSON
BLACK NARCISSUS .... DEBORAH KERR
BLACK NARCISSUS .... JEAN SIMMONS
BLACK OAK CONSPIRACY .... ALBERT SALMI†
BLACK OAK CONSPIRACY .... SEYMOUR CASSEL
BLACK ORCHID, THE .... ANTHONY QUINN
BLACK ORCHID, THE .... PETER MARK RICHMAN
BLACK ORCHID, THE .... SOPHIA LOREN
BLACK RAIN .... ANDY GARCIA
BLACK RAIN .... JOHN SPENCER
BLACK RAIN .... KATE CAPSHAW
BLACK RAIN .... KEN TAKAKURA
BLACK RAIN .... MICHAEL DOUGLAS

BLACK RAIN .... SHIGERU KOYAMA
BLACK RAIN .... YUSAKU MATSUDA†
BLACK RAINBOW .... JASON ROBARDS
BLACK RAINBOW .... ROSANNA ARQUETTE
BLACK RAINBOW .... TOM HULCE
BLACK RODEO (FD) .... WOODY STRODE
BLACK ROSE, THE .... ROBERT BLAKE
BLACK SHEEP OF WHITEHALL, THE ..... JOHN MILLS
BLACK SHIELD OF
  FALWORTH, THE .... DAN O'HERLIHY
BLACK SHIELD OF FALWORTH, THE ... JANET LEIGH
BLACK SHIELD OF
  FALWORTH, THE .... PATRICK O'NEAL†
BLACK SHIELD OF
  FALWORTH, THE .... TONY CURTIS
BLACK SPURS .... RORY CALHOUN
BLACK STALLION, THE .... HOYT AXTON
BLACK STALLION, THE .... KELLY RENO
BLACK STALLION, THE .... TERI GARR
BLACK STALLION, THE ○ .... MICKEY ROONEY
BLACK STALLION
  RETURNS, THE .... ALLEN GARFIELD
BLACK STALLION RETURNS, THE .... CASS OLE
BLACK STALLION RETURNS, THE .... KELLY RENO
BLACK STALLION RETURNS, THE .... TERI GARR
BLACK STALLION
  RETURNS, THE .... VINCENT SPANO
BLACK STALLION
  RETURNS, THE .... WOODY STRODE
BLACK SUNDAY .... BRUCE DERN
BLACK SUNDAY .... FRITZ WEAVER
BLACK SUNDAY .... KRISTY McNICHOL
BLACK SUNDAY .... MARTHE KELLER
BLACK SUNDAY .... ROBERT SHAW†
BLACK SUNDAY .... STEVEN KEATS†
BLACK SUNDAY .... WILLIAM DANIELS
BLACK SWAN, THE .... ANTHONY QUINN
BLACK SWAN, THE .... MAUREEN O'HARA
BLACK TIGHTS .... CYD CHARISSE
BLACK TUESDAY .... PETER GRAVES
BLACK WHIP, THE .... ANGIE DICKINSON
BLACK WIDOW .... D.W. MOFFETT
BLACK WIDOW .... DEBRA WINGER
BLACK WIDOW .... DENNIS HOPPER
BLACK WIDOW .... LEO ROSSI
BLACK WIDOW .... LOIS SMITH
BLACK WIDOW .... NICOL WILLIAMSON
BLACK WIDOW .... SAMI FREY
BLACK WIDOW .... TERRY O'QUINN
BLACK WIDOW .... THERESA RUSSELL
BLACK WINDMILL, THE .... DENIS QUILLEY
BLACK WINDMILL, THE .... DONALD PLEASENCE
BLACK WINDMILL, THE .... JANET SUZMAN
BLACK WINDMILL, THE .... JOHN VERNON
BLACK WINDMILL, THE .... JOSS ACKLAND
BLACK WINDMILL, THE .... MICHAEL CAINE
BLACK ZOO .... MICHAEL GOUGH
BLACKBEARD'S GHOST .... DEAN JONES
BLACKBEARD'S GHOST .... PETER USTINOV
BLACKBEARD'S GHOST .... SUZANNE PLESHETTE
BLACKBOARD JUNGLE, THE .... PAUL MAZURSKY
BLACKBOARD JUNGLE, THE .... RICHARD KILEY
BLACKBOARD JUNGLE, THE .... SIDNEY POITIER
BLACKBOARD JUNGLE, THE .... VIC MORROW†
BLACKE'S MAGIC (TF) .... DAVID HUDDLESTON
BLACKE'S MAGIC (TF) .... MAUD ADAMS
BLACKMAILED .... MAE ZETTERLING†
BLACKOUT .... BELINDA J. MONTGOMERY
BLACKOUT .... JEAN-PIERRE AUMONT
BLACKOUT .... JESSE BORREGO
BLACKOUT .... JON SEDA
BLACKOUT .... JUNE ALLYSON
BLACKOUT .... RICHARD WIDMARK
BLACKOUT .... ROBERT CARRADINE
BLACKOUT (CTF) .... KATHLEEN QUINLAN
BLACKOUT (CTF) .... MICHAEL BECK
BLACULA .... DENISE NICHOLAS
BLACULA .... THALMUS RASULALA
BLACULA .... WILLIAM MARSHALL
BLADE .... JOHN SCHUCK
BLADE .... WILLIAM PRINCE
BLADE ON THE FEATHER (TF) .... TOM CONTI

BLADE RUNNER .... DARYL HANNAH
BLADE RUNNER .... EDWARD JAMES OLMOS
BLADE RUNNER .... HARRISON FORD
BLADE RUNNER .... JOANNA CASSIDY
BLADE RUNNER .... M. EMMET WALSH
BLADE RUNNER .... RUTGER HAUER
BLADE RUNNER .... SEAN YOUNG
BLADE RUNNER .... WILLIAM SANDERSON
BLAME IT ON RIO .... DEMI MOORE
BLAME IT ON RIO .... JOSEPH BOLOGNA
BLAME IT ON RIO .... MICHAEL CAINE
BLAME IT ON RIO .... MICHELLE JOHNSON
BLAME IT ON RIO .... VALERIE HARPER
BLAME IT ON THE BELLBOY ...... ALISON STEADMAN
BLAME IT ON
  THE BELLBOY .... ANDREAS KATSULAS
BLAME IT ON THE BELLBOY ..... BRONSON PINCHOT
BLAME IT ON THE BELLBOY ..... BRYON BROWN
BLAME IT ON THE BELLBOY .... DUDLEY MOORE
BLAME IT ON THE BELLBOY .... JIM CARTER
BLAME IT ON THE BELLBOY .... PATSY KENSIT
BLAME IT ON THE BELLBOY ..... PENELOPE WILTON
BLAME IT ON THE BELLBOY ... RICHARD GRIFFITHS
BLANCHE FURY .... MICHAEL GOUGH
BLANK CHECK .... ALEX ZUCKERMAN
BLANK CHECK .... BRIAN BONSALL
BLANK CHECK .... CHRIS DEMETRAL
BLANK CHECK .... DEBBIE ALLEN
BLANK CHECK .... JAMES REBHORN
BLANK CHECK .... JAYNE ATKINSON
BLANK CHECK .... KAREN DUFFY
BLANK CHECK .... MICHAEL FAUSTINO
BLANK CHECK .... MICHAEL LERNER
BLANK CHECK .... MIGUEL FERRER
BLANK CHECK .... RICK DUCOMMUN
BLANK CHECK .... TONE LOC
BLANKMAN .... DAMON WAYANS
BLANKMAN .... DAVID ALAN GRIER
BLANKMAN .... JASON ALEXANDER
BLANKMAN .... JON POLITO
BLANKMAN .... ROBIN GIVENS
BLAST .... RAYMOND ST. JACQUES
BLAST-OFF/JULES VERNE'S
  ROCKET TO THE MOON .... TROY DONAHUE
BLAZE .... BLAZE STARR
BLAZE .... GAILORD SARTAIN
BLAZE .... GARLAND BUNTING
BLAZE .... JEFFREY DEMUNN
BLAZE .... JERRY HARDIN
BLAZE .... LOLITA DAVIDOVICH
BLAZE .... PAUL NEWMAN
BLAZE .... RICHARD JENKINS
BLAZE .... ROBERT WUHL
BLAZE OF NOON .... HOWARD DA SILVA†
BLAZING MAGNUM .... JOHN SAXON
BLAZING MAGNUMS .... MARTIN LANDAU
BLAZING SADDLES .... ALEXIS KARRAS
BLAZING SADDLES .... CLEAVON LITTLE†
BLAZING SADDLES .... DAVID HUDDLESTON
BLAZING SADDLES .... DOM DeLUISE
BLAZING SADDLES .... GENE WILDER
BLAZING SADDLES .... HARVEY KORMAN
BLAZING SADDLES .... JOHN HILLERMAN
BLAZING SADDLES ○ .... MEL BROOKS
BLAZING SADDLES ○ .... MADELINE KAHN
BLEU-BLANC-ROUGE .... JULIETTE BINOCHE
BLIND ADVENTURE .... RALPH BELLAMY†
BLIND ALLEY .... RALPH BELLAMY†
BLIND AMBITION (TF) .... ANN RAMSEY†
BLIND AMBITION (TF) .... JOHN RANDOLPH
BLIND AMBITION (TF) .... RIP TORN
BLIND DATE .... ANN SOTHERN
BLIND DATE .... BRUCE WILLIS
BLIND DATE .... GEORGE COE
BLIND DATE .... JOHN LARROQUETTE
BLIND DATE .... JULIA JENNINGS
BLIND DATE .... KIM BASINGER
BLIND DATE .... KIRSTIE ALLEY
BLIND DATE .... WILLIAM DANIELS
BLIND FAITH (MS) .... DENNIS FARINA
BLIND FAITH (MS) .... JOANNA KERNS
BLIND FAITH (MS) .... ROBERT URICH

This is not a list of every film ever made or every cast member, only those listed in this directory.

BI-BI
FILM ACTORS GUIDE

INDEX OF FILM TITLES

BLIND FAITH (MS) .... WILLIAM FORSYTHE
BLIND FURY .... BRANDON CALL
BLIND FURY .... CHARLES COOPER
BLIND FURY .... LISA BLOUNT
BLIND FURY .... MEG FOSTER
BLIND FURY .... NICK CASSAVETES
BLIND FURY .... NOBLE WILLINGHAM
BLIND FURY .... RANDALL (TEX) COBB
BLIND FURY .... RICK OVERTON
BLIND FURY .... RUTGER HAUER
BLIND FURY .... TERRY O'QUINN
BLIND GODDESS, THE .... CLAIRE BLOOM
BLIND JUSTICE .... GERALDINE FITZGERALD
BLIND JUSTICE .... JOHN MILLS
BLIND JUSTICE (TF) .... ANNE HANEY
BLIND JUSTICE (TF) .... LISA EICHHORN
BLIND JUSTICE (TF) .... TIM MATHESON
BLIND SPOT .... MICHAEL CAINE
BLIND SPOT (TF) .... JOANNE WOODWARD
BLIND TERROR .... MIA FARROW
BLIND VENGEANCE (CTF) .... DON HOOD
BLIND VENGEANCE (CTF) .... GERALD McRANEY
BLIND VENGEANCE (CTF) .... MARG HELGENBERGER
BLIND WITNESS (TF) .... MATT CLARK
BLIND WITNESS (TF) .... PAUL LeMAT
BLIND WITNESS (TF) .... STEPHEN MACHT
BLIND WITNESS (TF) .... VICTORIA PRINCIPAL
BLINDFOLD .... JACK WARDEN
BLINK .... AIDAN QUINN
BLINK .... BRUCE A. YOUNG
BLINK .... JAMES REMAR
BLINK .... LAURIE METCALF
BLINK .... MADELEINE STOWE
BLINK .... PETER FRIEDMAN
BLISS .... BARRY OTTO
BLISS .... GIA CARIDES
BLISS .... HELEN JONES
BLISS .... LYNETTE CURRAN
BLISS .... MILES BUCHANAN
BLISS .... TIM ROBERTSON
BLISS OF MRS. BLOSSOM, THE .... FREDDIE JONES
BLISS OF MRS. BLOSSOM, THE .... SHIRLEY MacLAINE
BLOB, THE .... CANDY CLARK
BLOB, THE .... DONOVAN LEITCH
BLOB, THE .... JEFFREY DEMUNN
BLOB, THE .... JOE SENECA
BLOB, THE .... KEVIN DILLON
BLOB, THE .... SHAWNEE SMITH
BLONDE FEVER .... AVA GARDNER†
BLONDY .... BIBI ANDERSSON
BLOOD ALLEY .... LAUREN BACALL
BLOOD AND CONCRETE .... BILLY ZANE
BLOOD AND CONCRETE .... DARREN McGAVIN
BLOOD AND CONCRETE .... HARRY SHEARER
BLOOD AND CONCRETE .... JAMES LE GROS
BLOOD AND CONCRETE .... JENNIFER BEALS
BLOOD AND ORCHIDS (MS) .... JANE ALEXANDER
BLOOD AND ORCHIDS (MS) .... JOSE FERRER†
BLOOD AND ORCHIDS (MS) .... KRIS KRISTOFFERSON
BLOOD AND ORCHIDS (MS) .... MADELEINE STOWE
BLOOD AND ORCHIDS (MS) .... RICHARD DYSART
BLOOD AND ORCHIDS (MS) .... SEAN YOUNG
BLOOD AND ORCHIDS (MS) .... SUSAN BLAKELY
BLOOD AND ROSES .... MEL FERRER
BLOOD AND SAND .... ANTHONY QUINN
BLOOD AND SAND .... SHARON STONE
BLOOD BEACH .... BURT YOUNG
BLOOD BEACH .... JOHN SAXON
BLOOD BEAST FROM OUTER SPACE .... JOHN SAXON
BLOOD FEUD .... SOPHIA LOREN
BLOOD FEUD (MS) .... JOSE FERRER†
BLOOD FEUD (TF) .... DANNY AIELLO
BLOOD FEUD (TF) .... EDWARD ALBERT
BLOOD FEUD (TF) .... ERNEST BORGNINE
BLOOD FEUD (TF) .... MICHAEL LERNER
BLOOD FEUD (TF) .... ROBERT BLAKE
BLOOD FOR DRACULA .... JOE DALLESANDRO
BLOOD KIN .... LYNN REDGRAVE
BLOOD MONEY .... DAME JUDITH ANDERSON†
BLOOD OF HEROES, THE .... JOAN CHEN
BLOOD OF HEROES, THE .... RUTGER HAUER
BLOOD OF HEROES, THE .... VINCENT D'ONOFRIO
BLOOD OF OTHERS, THE (CMS) .... JEAN-PIERRE AUMONT
BLOOD OF OTHERS, THE (CMS) .... JODIE FOSTER
BLOOD OF OTHERS, THE (CMS) .... MICHAEL ONTKEAN
BLOOD OF OTHERS, THE (CMS) .... SAM NEILL
BLOOD ON THE MOON .... PHYLLIS THAXTER
BLOOD ON THE MOON .... ROBERT MITCHUM
BLOOD ON THE SUN .... SYLVIA SIDNEY
BLOOD RED .... DENNIS HOPPER
BLOOD RED .... ELIAS KOTEAS
BLOOD RED .... ERIC ROBERTS
BLOOD RED .... JULIA ROBERTS
BLOOD RELATIONS .... DONALD SUTHERLAND
BLOOD RELATIONS .... JAN RUBES
BLOOD RELATIONS .... KEVIN HICKS
BLOOD RELATIONS .... LYDIE DENIER
BLOOD RELATIONS .... RAY WALSTON
BLOOD RELATIVES .... DAVID HEMMINGS
BLOOD RELATIVES .... DONALD PLEASENCE
BLOOD SIMPLE .... DAN HEDAYA
BLOOD SIMPLE .... FRANCES McDORMAND
BLOOD SIMPLE .... JOHN GETZ
BLOOD SIMPLE .... M. EMMET WALSH
BLOOD TIES .... BRAD DAVIS†
BLOOD VOWS: THE STORY OF A MAFIA WIFE (TF) .... ANTHONY (TONY) FRANCIOSA
BLOOD VOWS: THE STORY OF A MAFIA WIFE (TF) .... EILEEN BRENNAN
BLOOD VOWS: THE STORY OF A MAFIA WIFE (TF) .... JOE PENNY
BLOOD VOWS: THE STORY OF A MAFIA WIFE (TF) .... MELISSA GILBERT
BLOOD VOWS: THE STORY OF A MAFIA WIFE (TF) .... TALIA SHIRE
BLOODBATH AT THE HOUSE OF DEATH .... VINCENT PRICE†
BLOODBROTHERS .... DANNY AIELLO
BLOODBROTHERS .... KENNETH McMILLAN†
BLOODBROTHERS .... MARILU HENNER
BLOODBROTHERS .... PAUL SORVINO
BLOODBROTHERS .... RICHARD GERE
BLOODBROTHERS .... TONY LoBIANCO
BLOODFIST VI .... STEVE GARVEY
BLOODHOUNDS OF BROADWAY .... ALAN RUCK
BLOODHOUNDS OF BROADWAY .... ANITA MORRIS†
BLOODHOUNDS OF BROADWAY .... BLACK-EYED SUSAN
BLOODHOUNDS OF BROADWAY .... CHARLES BRONSON
BLOODHOUNDS OF BROADWAY .... DINAH MANOFF
BLOODHOUNDS OF BROADWAY .... ESAI MORALES
BLOODHOUNDS OF BROADWAY .... ETHAN PHILLIPS
BLOODHOUNDS OF BROADWAY .... FISHER STEVENS
BLOODHOUNDS OF BROADWAY .... GOOGY GRESS
BLOODHOUNDS OF BROADWAY .... JENNIFER GREY
BLOODHOUNDS OF BROADWAY .... JOSEF SOMMER
BLOODHOUNDS OF BROADWAY .... JULIE HAGERTY
BLOODHOUNDS OF BROADWAY .... LOUIS ZORICH
BLOODHOUNDS OF BROADWAY .... MADELINE POTTER
BLOODHOUNDS OF BROADWAY .... MADONNA
BLOODHOUNDS OF BROADWAY .... MATT DILLON
BLOODHOUNDS OF BROADWAY .... MICHAEL WINCOTT
BLOODHOUNDS OF BROADWAY .... RANDY QUAID
BLOODHOUNDS OF BROADWAY .... RICHARD EDSON
BLOODHOUNDS OF BROADWAY .... RUTGER HAUER
BLOODHOUNDS OF BROADWAY .... STEPHEN McHATTIE
BLOODHOUNDS OF BROADWAY .... STEVE BUSCEMI
BLOODHOUNDS OF BROADWAY .... TIMOTHY CAREY
BLOODHOUNDS OF BROADWAY .... TONY LONGO
BLOODHOUNDS OF BROADWAY .... WILLIAM S. BURROUGHS
BLOODLINE .... AUDREY HEPBURN†
BLOODLINE .... BEATRICE STRAIGHT
BLOODLINE .... BEN GAZZARA
BLOODLINE .... OMAR SHARIF
BLOODSPORT .... FOREST WHITAKER
BLOODSPORT .... JEAN-CLAUDE VAN DAMME
BLOODY BROOD, THE .... PETER FALK
BLOODY BUSHIDO BLADE, THE .... JAMES EARL JONES
BLOODY MAMA .... BRUCE DERN
BLOODY MAMA .... DON STROUD
BLOODY MAMA .... PAT HINGLE
BLOODY MAMA .... ROBERT DE NIRO
BLOODY MAMA .... SHELLEY WINTERS
BLOODY MARY .... CARROLL BAKER
BLOOMFIELD .... RICHARD HARRIS
BLOSSOMS IN THE DUST ★ .... GREER GARSON
BLOW OUT .... DENNIS FRANZ
BLOW OUT .... JOHN LITHGOW
BLOW OUT .... JOHN TRAVOLTA
BLOW OUT .... NANCY ALLEN
BLOW OUT .... PETER BOYDEN
BLOW-UP .... DAVID HEMMINGS
BLOW-UP .... SARAH MILES
BLOW-UP .... VANESSA REDGRAVE
BLOWING WILD .... ANTHONY QUINN
BLOWING WILD .... BARBARA STANWYCK†
BLOWN AWAY .... CAITLIN CLARKE
BLOWN AWAY .... FOREST WHITAKER
BLOWN AWAY .... JEFF BRIDGES
BLOWN AWAY .... LLOYD BRIDGES
BLOWN AWAY .... LLOYD CATLETT
BLOWN AWAY .... RUBEN SANTIAGO-HUDSON
BLOWN AWAY .... SUZY AMIS
BLOWN AWAY .... TOMMY LEE JONES
BLUE .... JULIETTE BINOCHE
BLUE .... KARL MALDEN
BLUE .... RICARDO MONTALBAN
BLUE .... SALLY KIRKLAND
BLUE .... TERENCE STAMP
BLUE AND THE GRAY, THE (MS) .... GREGORY PECK
BLUE AND THE GRAY, THE (MS) .... LLOYD BRIDGES
BLUE AND THE GRAY, THE (MS) .... RIP TORN
BLUE ANGEL, THE .... GRETA GARBO
BLUE ANGEL, THE .... THEODORE BIKEL
BLUE BIRD, THE .... AVA GARDNER†
BLUE BIRD, THE .... ELIZABETH TAYLOR
BLUE BIRD, THE .... JANE FONDA
BLUE BIRD, THE .... PATSY KENSIT
BLUE BIRD, THE .... ROBERT MORLEY
BLUE BLOOD .... DEREK JACOBI
BLUE CHIPS .... ALFRE WOODARD
BLUE CHIPS .... BOBBY KNIGHT
BLUE CHIPS .... ED O'NEILL
BLUE CHIPS .... J. T. WALSH
BLUE CHIPS .... LARRY BIRD
BLUE CHIPS .... MARY McDONNELL
BLUE CHIPS .... NICK NOLTE
BLUE CHIPS .... SHAQUILLE O'NEAL
BLUE CITY .... ALLY SHEEDY
BLUE CITY .... ANITA MORRIS†
BLUE CITY .... DAVID CARUSO
BLUE CITY .... JUDD NELSON
BLUE CITY .... PAUL WINFIELD
BLUE CITY .... SCOTT WILSON
BLUE COLLAR .... CLIFF DE YOUNG
BLUE COLLAR .... ED BEGLEY JR.
BLUE COLLAR .... HARVEY KEITEL
BLUE COLLAR .... RICHARD PRYOR
BLUE COLLAR .... YAPHET KOTTO
BLUE DAHLIA, THE .... HOWARD DA SILVA†
BLUE DENIM .... CAROL LYNLEY
BLUE DESERT .... COURTENEY COX
BLUE GARDENIA, THE .... ANN SOTHERN
BLUE GARDENIA, THE .... RAYMOND BURR†
BLUE HAWAII .... ANGELA LANSBURY
BLUE HAWAII .... ELVIS PRESLEY†

† after an actor's name denotes deceased.

BLUE HEAVEN .... JAMES ECKHOUSE
BLUE ICE .... ALUN ARMSTRONG
BLUE ICE (CTF) .... MICHAEL CAINE
BLUE ICE (CTF) .... SEAN YOUNG
BLUE IGUANA, THE .... DEAN STOCKWELL
BLUE IGUANA, THE .... JESSICA HARPER
BLUE KNIGHT, THE (TF) .... EILEEN BRENNAN
BLUE KNIGHT, THE (TF) .... GEORGE KENNEDY
BLUE KNIGHT, THE (TF) .... JAMIE FARR
BLUE KNIGHT, THE (TF) .... SAM ELLIOTT
BLUE LAGOON, THE .... BROOKE SHIELDS
BLUE LAGOON, THE .... CHRISTOPHER ATKINS
BLUE LAGOON, THE .... JEAN SIMMONS
BLUE LAGOON, THE .... WILLIAM DANIELS
BLUE LIGHTNING, THE (TF) .... SAM ELLIOTT
BLUE MAX, THE .... GEORGE PEPPARD†
BLUE MAX, THE .... JEREMY KEMP
BLUE MAX, THE .... URSULA ANDRESS
BLUE MONKEY .... SUSAN ANSPACH
BLUE SKIES .... BING CROSBY†
BLUE SKIES .... FRED ASTAIRE†
BLUE SKIES .... JOAN CAULFIELD†
BLUE SKIES AGAIN .... ANDY GARCIA
BLUE SKIES AGAIN .... HARRY HAMLIN
BLUE SKY .... AMY LOCANE
BLUE SKY .... ANNA KLEMP
BLUE SKY .... CARRIE SNODGRESS
BLUE SKY .... CHRIS O'DONNELL
BLUE SKY .... JESSICA LANGE
BLUE SKY .... JESSICA LANGE
BLUE SKY .... POWERS BOOTHE
BLUE SKY .... TOMMY LEE JONES
BLUE SKY .... TOMMY LEE JONES
BLUE STEEL .... CLANCY BROWN
BLUE STEEL .... ELIZABETH PENA
BLUE STEEL .... JAMIE LEE CURTIS
BLUE STEEL .... LOUISE FLETCHER
BLUE STEEL .... PHILIP BOSCO
BLUE STEEL .... RON SILVER
BLUE THUNDER .... CANDY CLARK
BLUE THUNDER .... DANIEL STERN
BLUE THUNDER .... JAMES READ
BLUE THUNDER .... MALCOLM McDOWELL
BLUE THUNDER .... ROY SCHEIDER
BLUE THUNDER .... WARREN OATES†
BLUE VEIL, THE .... DAN O'HERLIHY
BLUE VEIL, THE .... HARRY MORGAN
BLUE VEIL, THE ★ .... JANE WYMAN
BLUE VEIL, THE ○ .... JOAN BLONDELL†
BLUE VELVET .... BRAD DOURIF
BLUE VELVET .... DEAN STOCKWELL
BLUE VELVET .... DENNIS HOPPER
BLUE VELVET .... GEORGE DICKERSON
BLUE VELVET .... HOPE LANGE
BLUE VELVET .... ISABELLA ROSSELLINI
BLUE VELVET .... JACK NANCE
BLUE VELVET .... KYLE MacLACHLAN
BLUE VELVET .... LAURA DERN
BLUE VELVET .... PRISCILLA POINTER
BLUE YONDER, THE (CTF) .... ART CARNEY
BLUEBEARD .... JOEY HEATHERTON
BLUEBEARD .... RAQUEL WELCH
BLUEBEARD'S EIGHTH WIFE ...... DAVID NIVEN†
BLUEBERRY HILL .... JENNIFER RUBIN
BLUEGRASS (MS) .... ANTHONY ANDREWS
BLUEGRASS (MS) .... BRIAN KERWIN
BLUEGRASS (MS) .... CHERYL LADD
BLUEGRASS (MS) .... DIANE LADD
BLUEGRASS (MS) .... MICKEY ROONEY
BLUEGRASS (MS) .... WAYNE ROGERS
BLUEPRINT FOR MURDER, A .... JACK KRUSCHEN
BLUES BROTHERS, THE .... ARETHA FRANKLIN
BLUES BROTHERS, THE .... CARRIE FISHER
BLUES BROTHERS, THE .... DAN AYKROYD
BLUES BROTHERS, THE .... FRANK OZ
BLUES BROTHERS, THE .... HENRY GIBSON
BLUES BROTHERS, THE .... JOHN BELUSHI†
BLUES BROTHERS, THE .... JOHN CANDY†
BLUES BROTHERS, THE .... KATHLEEN FREEMAN
BLUES BROTHERS, THE .... RAY CHARLES
BLUFF .... ANTHONY QUINN
BLUFFING IT (TF) .... JANET CARROLL

BLUME IN LOVE .... GEORGE SEGAL
BLUME IN LOVE .... KRIS KRISTOFFERSON
BLUME IN LOVE .... MARSHA MASON
BLUME IN LOVE .... PAUL MAZURSKY
BLUME IN LOVE .... SHELLEY WINTERS
BLUME IN LOVE .... SUSAN ANSPACH
BLUNT .... ANTHONY HOPKINS
BOARDWALK .... JANET LEIGH
BOARDWALK .... LEE STRASBERG†
BOATNIKS, THE .... DON AMECHE†
BOATNIKS, THE .... STEFANIE POWERS
BOB & CAROL & TED & ALICE .... NATALIE WOOD†
BOB & CAROL & TED & ALICE .... ROBERT CULP
BOB & CAROL & TED & ALICE ○ ..... DYAN CANNON
BOB & CAROL & TED & ALICE ○ ..... ELLIOTT GOULD
BOB ROBERTS .... ALAN RICKMAN
BOB ROBERTS .... FRED WARD
BOB ROBERTS .... GIANCARLO ESPOSITO
BOB ROBERTS .... GORE VIDAL
BOB ROBERTS .... HELEN HUNT
BOB ROBERTS .... JAMES SPADER
BOB ROBERTS .... JOHN CUSAK
BOB ROBERTS .... PAMELA REED
BOB ROBERTS .... PETER GALLAGHER
BOB ROBERTS .... RAY WISE
BOB ROBERTS .... SUSAN SARANDON
BOB ROBERTS .... TIM ROBBINS
BOBBIE JOE AND
THE OUTLAW .... MARJOE GORTNER
BOBBIKINS .... BILLIE WHITELAW
BOBBIKINS .... SHIRLEY JONES
BOBBY DEERFIELD .... AL PACINO
BOBBY DEERFIELD .... MARTHE KELLER
BOBO, THE .... BRITT EKLAND
BOCCACCIO 70 .... SOPHIA LOREN
BODIES .... SONJA G. ANDERSON
BODIES, REST & MOTION .... ALICIA WITT
BODIES, REST & MOTION .... BRIDGET FONDA
BODIES, REST & MOTION .... ERIC STOLTZ
BODIES, REST & MOTION .... PETER FONDA
BODIES, REST & MOTION .... PHOEBE CATES
BODIES, REST & MOTION .... TIM ROTH
BODY AND SOUL ★ .... JOHN GARFIELD†
BODY CHEMISTRY .... JOSEPH CAMPANELLA
BODY CHEMISTRY .... LISA PESCIA
BODY CHEMISTRY .... MARC SINGER
BODY CHEMISTRY .... MARY CROSBY
BODY DISAPPEARS, THE .... JANE WYMAN
BODY DOUBLE .... CRAIG WASSON
BODY DOUBLE .... DEBORAH SHELTON
BODY DOUBLE .... DENNIS FRANZ
BODY DOUBLE .... GREGG HENRY
BODY DOUBLE .... GUY BOYD
BODY DOUBLE .... MELANIE GRIFFITH
BODY HEAT .... J. A. PRESTON
BODY HEAT .... KATHLEEN TURNER
BODY HEAT .... MICKEY ROURKE
BODY HEAT .... RICHARD CRENNA
BODY HEAT .... TED DANSON
BODY HEAT .... WILLIAM HURT
BODY OF EVIDENCE .... ANNE ARCHER
BODY OF EVIDENCE .... JOE MANTEGNA
BODY OF EVIDENCE .... JORGEN PROCHNOW
BODY OF EVIDENCE .... JULIANNE MOORE
BODY OF EVIDENCE .... MADONNA
BODY OF EVIDENCE .... WILLEM DAFOE
BODY OF EVIDENCE (TF) .... BARRY BOSTWICK
BODY OF EVIDENCE (TF) .... CAROLINE KAVA
BODY OF EVIDENCE (TF) .... MARGOT KIDDER
BODY OF EVIDENCE (TF) .... TONY LoBIANCO
BODY PARTS .... JEFF FAHEY
BODY SLAM .... BILLY BARTY
BODY SLAM .... DIRK BENEDICT
BODY SLAM .... JOHN ASTIN
BODY SLAM .... RODDY PIPER
BODY SNATCHERS .... BILLY WIRTH
BODY SNATCHERS .... CHRISTINE ELISE
BODY SNATCHERS .... FOREST WHITAKER
BODY SNATCHERS .... GABRIELLE ANWAR
BODY SNATCHERS .... MEG TILLY
BODY SNATCHERS .... TERRY KINNEY
BODYGUARD .... LAWRENCE TIERNEY

BODYGUARD, THE .... BILL COBBS
BODYGUARD, THE .... GARY KEMP
BODYGUARD, THE .... KEVIN COSTNER
BODYGUARD, THE .... RALPH WAITE
BODYGUARD, THE .... WHITNEY HOUSTON
BOEING BOEING .... JERRY LEWIS
BOEING BOEING .... TONY CURTIS
BOFORS GUN, THE .... DAVID WARNER
BOFORS GUN, THE .... IAN HOLM
BOFORS GUN, THE .... NICOL WILLIAMSON
BOFORS GUN, THE .... PETER VAUGHN
BOGUS .... GERARD DEPARDIEU
BOGUS .... WHOOPI GOLDBERG
BOILING POINT .... DAN HEDAYA
BOILING POINT .... DENNIS HOPPER
BOILING POINT .... LOLITA DAVIDOVICH
BOILING POINT .... TONY LoBIANCO
BOILING POINT .... VIGGO MORTENSEN
BOILING POINT .... WESLEY SNIPES
BOLD AND THE BRAVE, THE ○ ..... MICKEY ROONEY
BOLERO .... ANDREA OCCHIPINTI
BOLERO .... BO DEREK
BOLERO .... GEORGE KENNEDY
BOLERO .... GERALDINE CHAPLIN
BOLERO .... JAMES CAAN
BOLERO .... OLIVIA D'ABO
BOLERO .... SHARON STONE
BOMBARDIER .... EDDIE ALBERT
BOMBERS B-52 .... EFREM ZIMBALIST JR.
BOMBERS B-52 .... KARL MALDEN
BON BAISERS DE
HONG KONG .... DAVID TOMLINSON
BON VOYAGE! .... JANE WYMAN
BON VOYAGE! .... MAX SHOWALTER
BONE .... JEANNIE BERLIN
BONE .... JOYCE VAN PATTEN
BONE .... YAPHET KOTTO
BONFIRE OF THE VANITIES, THE ...... BRUCE WILLIS
BONFIRE OF THE
VANITIES, THE .... DEBBIE LEE CARRINGTON
BONFIRE OF THE
VANITIES, THE .... F. MURRAY ABRAHAM
BONFIRE OF THE
VANITIES, THE .... GIAN-CARLO SCANDIUZZI
BONFIRE OF THE
VANITIES, THE .... JOHN HANCOCK
BONFIRE OF THE VANITIES, THE .... KEVIN DUNN
BONFIRE OF THE VANITIES, THE ...... KIM CATTRALL
BONFIRE OF THE
VANITIES, THE .... MELANIE GRIFFITH
BONFIRE OF THE
VANITIES, THE .... MORGAN FREEMAN
BONFIRE OF THE VANITIES, THE .... RITA WILSON
BONFIRE OF THE VANITIES, THE ...... SAUL RUBINEK
BONFIRE OF THE VANITIES, THE ...... TOM HANKS
BONJOUR TRISTESSE .... DEBORAH KERR
BONNIE AND CLYDE .... DUB TAYLOR
BONNIE AND CLYDE .... GENE WILDER
BONNIE AND CLYDE ★ .... FAYE DUNAWAY
BONNIE AND CLYDE ★ .... WARREN BEATTY
BONNIE AND CLYDE ○ .... GENE HACKMAN
BONNIE AND CLYDE ○ .... MICHAEL J. POLLARD
BONNIE AND CLYDE ○○ .... ESTELLE PARSONS
BONNIE PRINCE CHARLIE .... DAVID NIVEN†
BONZO GOES
TO COLLEGE .... KATHLEEN FREEMAN
BONZO GOES
TO COLLEGE .... MAUREEN O'SULLIVAN
BOOB, THE .... JOAN CRAWFORD†
BOOK OF LOVE .... BEAU BREMMAN
BOOK OF LOVE .... CHRIS YOUNG
BOOK OF LOVE .... DANNY NUCCI
BOOK OF LOVE .... JOSIE BISSETT
BOOK OF LOVE .... KEITH COOGAN
BOOK OF LOVE .... MICHAEL McKEAN
BOOK OF LOVE .... TRICIA LEIGH FISHER
BOOK OF NUMBERS .... RAYMOND ST. JACQUES
BOOM! .... ELIZABETH TAYLOR
BOOMERANG .... DAVID ALAN GRIER
BOOMERANG .... EDDIE MURPHY
BOOMERANG .... HALLE BERRY
BOOMERANG .... JANE WYATT

BOOMERANG .... KARL MALDEN
BOOMERANG .... ROBIN GIVENS
BOOST, THE .... JAMES WOODS
BOOST, THE .... SEAN YOUNG
BOOTLEGGERS .... JACLYN SMITH
BOOTLEGGERS' ANGEL .... JACLYN SMITH
BOPHA! .... ALFRE WOODARD
BOPHA! .... DANNY GLOVER
BOPHA! .... MALCOLM McDOWELL
BOPHA! .... MARIUS WEYERS
BORDER INCIDENT .... RICARDO MONTALBAN
BORDER PATROL .... ROBERT MITCHUM
BORDER RIVER .... YVONNE DE CARLO
BORDER, THE .... ELPIDIA CARRILLO
BORDER, THE .... HARVEY KEITEL
BORDER, THE .... JACK NICHOLSON
BORDER, THE .... VALERIE PERRINE
BORDERLINE .... ED HARRIS
BORDERLINE .... MICHAEL LERNER
BORDERLINE .... RAYMOND BURR†
BORDERLINE .... WILFORD BRIMLEY
BORDERTOWN .... BETTE DAVIS†
BORGIA STICK, THE (TF) ...... DON MURRAY
BORGIA STICK, THE (TF) ...... FRITZ WEAVER
BORIS AND NATASHA .... JOHN TRAVOLTA
BORIS AND NATASHA .... SALLY KELLERMAN
BORN AGAIN .... DEAN JONES
BORN AGAIN .... RAYMOND ST. JACQUES
BORN AMERICAN .... ALBERT SALMI†
BORN FOR GLORY .... JOHN MILLS
BORN FREE .... GEOFFREY KEEN
BORN IN EAST L.A. .... CHEECH MARIN
BORN IN EAST L.A. .... JASON SCOTT LEE
BORN IN EAST L.A. .... PAUL RODRIGUEZ
BORN INNOCENT (TF) .... LINDA BLAIR
BORN ON THE FOURTH
    OF JULY .... ABBIE HOFFMAN†
BORN ON THE FOURTH OF JULY ...... BRYAN LARKIN
BORN ON THE FOURTH
    OF JULY .... CAROLINE KAVA
BORN ON THE FOURTH OF JULY .... FRANK WHALEY
BORN ON THE FOURTH OF JULY ...... JERRY LEVINE
BORN ON THE FOURTH OF JULY .... JOHN GETZ
BORN ON THE FOURTH OF JULY .... JOSH EVANS
BORN ON THE FOURTH
    OF JULY .... KYRA SEDGWICK
BORN ON THE FOURTH OF JULY ..... OLIVER STONE
BORN ON THE FOURTH
    OF JULY .... RAYMOND J. BARRY
BORN ON THE FOURTH
    OF JULY .... ROBERT CAMILLETTI
BORN ON THE FOURTH
    OF JULY .... SEAN STONE
BORN ON THE FOURTH
    OF JULY .... STEPHEN BALDWIN
BORN ON THE FOURTH
    OF JULY .... TOM BERENGER
BORN ON THE FOURTH OF JULY ..... WILLEM DAFOE
BORN ON THE FOURTH OF JULY ★ ...... TOM CRUISE
BORN TO BE BAD .... MEL FERRER
BORN TO DANCE .... JAMES STEWART
BORN TO KILL .... ED BEGLEY JR.
BORN TO KILL .... LAWRENCE TIERNEY
BORN TO KILL/WILD DRIFTER/
    GAMBLIN' MAN .... HARRY DEAN STANTON
BORN TO KILL/WILD DRIFTER/
    GAMBLIN' MAN .... MILLIE PERKINS
BORN TO KILL/WILD DRIFTER/
    GAMBLIN' MAN .... TROY DONAHUE
BORN TO RIDE .... JOHN STAMOS
BORN TO RIDE.................... JOHN STOCKWELL
BORN TO RIDE .... TERI POLO
BORN TO WIN .... GEORGE SEGAL
BORN TO WIN .... HECTOR ELIZONDO
BORN TO WIN .... KAREN BLACK
BORN TO WIN .... PAULA PRENTISS
BORN TO WIN .... ROBERT DE NIRO
BORN YESTERDAY .... DON JOHNSON
BORN YESTERDAY .... JOHN GOODMAN
BORN YESTERDAY .... MELANIE GRIFFITH
BORN YESTERDAY ★★ .... JUDY HOLLIDAY†
BORROWERS, THE (TF) .... TAMMY GRIMES

BOSS NIGGER .... FRED WILLIAMSON
BOSS' SON, THE .... RITA MORENO
BOSTON STRANGLER, THE ...... GEORGE KENNEDY
BOSTON STRANGLER, THE ...... HURD HATFIELD
BOSTON STRANGLER, THE .... JAMES BROLIN
BOSTON STRANGLER, THE .... JEFF COREY
BOSTON STRANGLER, THE ...... SALLY KELLERMAN
BOSTON STRANGLER, THE ...... TONY CURTIS
BOSTON STRANGLER, THE ...... WILLIAM MARSHALL
BOSTONIANS, THE .... CHRISTOPHER REEVE
BOSTONIANS, THE .... JESSICA TANDY†
BOSTONIANS, THE .... LINDA HUNT
BOSTONIANS, THE .... MADELINE POTTER
BOSTONIANS, THE .... NANCY MARCHAND
BOSTONIANS, THE .... WESLEY ADDY
BOSTONIANS, THE ★ .... VANESSA REDGRAVE
BOULEVARD NIGHTS .... CARMEN ZAPATA
BOULEVARD NIGHTS .... DANNY DE LA PAZ
BOUND FOR GLORY .... DAVID CARRADINE
BOUND FOR GLORY .... MARY KAY PLACE
BOUND FOR GLORY .... MELINDA DILLON
BOUND FOR GLORY .... RANDY QUAID
BOUND FOR GLORY .... RONNY COX
BOUNTY HUNTER, THE .... ERNEST BORGNINE
BOUNTY MAN, THE (TF) .... CLINT WALKER
BOUNTY MAN, THE (TF) .... MARGOT KIDDER
BOUNTY, THE .... ANTHONY HOPKINS
BOUNTY, THE .... DANIEL DAY-LEWIS
BOUNTY, THE .... EDWARD FOX
BOUNTY, THE .... LAURENCE OLIVIER†
BOUNTY, THE .... LIAM NEESON
BOUNTY, THE .... MEL GIBSON
BOURNE IDENTITY, THE .... DENHOLM ELLIOTT†
BOURNE IDENTITY, THE .... PETER VAUGHN
BOURNE IDENTITY, THE (MS) ...... JACLYN SMITH
BOURNE
    IDENTITY, THE (MS) ...... RICHARD CHAMBERLAIN
BOWERY, THE .... JACKIE COOPER
BOXCAR BERTHA .... BARBARA HERSHEY
BOXCAR BERTHA .... BARRY PRIMUS
BOXCAR BERTHA .... DAVID CARRADINE
BOXER, THE .... ERNEST BORGNINE
BOXER, THE .... ROBERT BLAKE
BOXING HELENA .... ART GARFUNKEL
BOXING HELENA .... BETSY CLARK
BOXING HELENA .... BILL PAXTON
BOXING HELENA .... JULIAN SANDS
BOXING HELENA .... KURTWOOD SMITH
BOXING HELENA .... SHERILYN FENN
BOY AND HIS DOG, A .... DON JOHNSON
BOY AND HIS DOG, A .... JASON ROBARDS
BOY, DID I GET A
    WRONG NUMBER! ...... PHYLLIS DILLER
BOY, DID I GET THE
    WRONG NUMBER! .... BOB HOPE
BOY FRIEND, THE ...... GLENDA JACKSON
BOY FRIEND, THE .... TWIGGY
BOY IN BLUE, THE .... CHRISTOPHER PLUMMER
BOY IN BLUE, THE .... CYNTHIA DALE
BOY IN BLUE, THE .... DAVID NAUGHTON
BOY IN BLUE, THE .... MELODY ANDERSON
BOY IN BLUE, THE .... NICOLAS CAGE
BOY IN THE PLASTIC
    BUBBLE, THE (TF) ...... ANN RAMSEY†
BOY IN THE PLASTIC
    BUBBLE, THE (TF) ...... JOHN TRAVOLTA
BOY IN THE PLASTIC
    BUBBLE, THE (TF) ...... RALPH BELLAMY†
BOY MEETS GIRL ...... RALPH BELLAMY†
BOY MEETS GIRL ...... RONALD REAGAN
BOY NEXT DOOR, THE ...... LLOYD BRIDGES
BOY OF THE STREETS .... JACKIE COOPER
BOY ON A DOLPHIN .... SOPHIA LOREN
BOY WHO COULD FLY, THE .... BONNIE BEDELIA
BOY WHO COULD
    FLY, THE .... COLLEEN DEWHURST†
BOY WHO COULD FLY, THE .... FRED GWYNNE†
BOY WHO COULD FLY, THE .... FRED SAVAGE
BOY WHO COULD FLY, THE .... JAY UNDERWOOD
BOY WHO COULD FLY, THE .... LOUISE FLETCHER
BOY WHO COULD FLY, THE .... LUCY DEAKINS
BOY WHO COULD FLY, THE ...... MINDY COHN

BOY WHO COULD
    FLY, THE .... TERRY DAVID MULLIGAN
BOY WHO DRANK
    TOO MUCH, THE (TF) .... SCOTT BAIO
BOY WITH GREEN HAIR, THE .... BARBARA HALE
BOY WITH GREEN HAIR, THE ..... DEAN STOCKWELL
BOY WITH GREEN HAIR, THE .... RUSS TAMBLYN
BOYFRIENDS AND
    GIRLFRIENDS .... SOPHIE RENOIR
BOYS .... LUKAS HAAS
BOYS .... WINONA RYDER
BOYS FROM BRAZIL, THE .... ANNE MEARA
BOYS FROM BRAZIL, THE .... BRUNO GANZ
BOYS FROM BRAZIL, THE .... DENHOLM ELLIOTT†
BOYS FROM BRAZIL, THE .... GREGORY PECK
BOYS FROM BRAZIL, THE .... JAMES MASON†
BOYS FROM BRAZIL, THE .... JOHN DEHNER†
BOYS FROM BRAZIL, THE .... MICHAEL GOUGH
BOYS FROM BRAZIL, THE .... PRUNELLA SCALES
BOYS FROM BRAZIL, THE ...... STEVE GUTTENBERG
BOYS FROM BRAZIL, THE ...... WALTER GOTELL
BOYS FROM
    BRAZIL, THE ★ .... LAURENCE OLIVIER†
BOYS FROM SYRACUSE, THE .... MARTHA RAYE†
BOYS IN COMPANY C, THE .... ANDREW STEVENS
BOYS IN COMPANY C, THE .... CRAIG WASSON
BOYS IN COMPANY C, THE .... STAN SHAW
BOYS IN THE BAND, THE .... CLIFF GORMAN
BOYS IN THE BAND, THE .... LAURENCE LUCKINBILL
BOYS IN THE BAND, THE .... LEONARD FREY†
BOYS IN THE BAND, THE .... MAUD ADAMS
BOYS NEXT DOOR, THE .... CHARLIE SHEEN
BOYS NEXT
    DOOR, THE .... CHRISTOPHER McDONALD
BOYS NEXT DOOR, THE .... HANK GARRETT
BOYS NEXT DOOR, THE .... MAXWELL CAULFIELD
BOYS NEXT DOOR, THE .... MOON ZAPPA
BOYS NEXT DOOR, THE .... PATTI D'ARBANVILLE
BOYS' NIGHT OUT .... JAMES GARNER
BOYS' NIGHT OUT .... KIM NOVAK
BOYS' NIGHT OUT .... TONY RANDALL
BOYS' NIGHT OUT .... ZSA ZSA GABOR
BOYS ON THE SIDE .... AMY AQUINO
BOYS ON THE SIDE .... ANITA GILLETTE
BOYS ON THE SIDE .... BILLY WIRTH
BOYS ON THE SIDE .... DENNIS BOUTSIKARIS
BOYS ON THE SIDE .... DREW BARRYMORE
BOYS ON THE SIDE .... ESTELLE PARSONS
BOYS ON THE SIDE .... JAMES REMAR
BOYS ON THE SIDE .... MARY-LOUISE PARKER
BOYS ON THE SIDE .... MATTHEW McCONAUGHEY
BOYS ON THE SIDE .... WHOOPI GOLDBERG
BOYS, THE .... ROBERT MORLEY
BOYS, THE (TF) .... EVE GORDON
BOYS, THE (TF) .... JAMES WOODS
BOYS, THE (TF) .... JOANNA GLEASON
BOYS, THE (TF) .... JOHN LITHGOW
BOYS TOWN ★★ .... SPENCER TRACY†
BOYZ 'N THE HOOD .... ANGELA BASSETT
BOYZ 'N THE HOOD .... CUBA GOODING JR.
BOYZ 'N THE HOOD .... ICE CUBE
BOYZ 'N THE HOOD .... LAURENCE FISHBURNE
BOYZ 'N THE HOOD .... TYRA FERRELL
BOY'S TOWN .... MICKEY ROONEY
BRADDOCK: MISSING IN ACTION III .... AKI ALEONG
BRADDOCK: MISSING
    IN ACTION III .... CHUCK NORRIS
BRADY BUNCH MOVIE, THE .... ANN B. DAVIS
BRADY BUNCH MOVIE, THE ..... CHRISTINE TAYLOR
BRADY BUNCH
    MOVIE, THE .... CHRISTOPHER DANIEL BARNES
BRADY BUNCH
    MOVIE, THE .... CHRISTOPHER KNIGHT
BRADY BUNCH MOVIE, THE .... DAVID GRAF
BRADY BUNCH MOVIE, THE .... EVE PLUMB
BRADY BUNCH
    MOVIE, THE .... FLORENCE HENDERSON
BRADY BUNCH MOVIE, THE .... GARY COLE
BRADY BUNCH MOVIE, THE ...... HENRIETTE MANTEL
BRADY BUNCH MOVIE, THE ....JACK NOSEWORTHY
BRADY BUNCH MOVIE, THE .... JEAN SMART
BRADY BUNCH MOVIE, THE .... JENNIFER COX

BRADY BUNCH MOVIE, THE ... JESSE LEE
BRADY BUNCH MOVIE, THE ... MAUREEN McCORMICK
BRADY BUNCH MOVIE, THE ... MICHAEL McKEAN
BRADY BUNCH MOVIE, THE ... MIKE LOOKINLAND
BRADY BUNCH MOVIE, THE ... OLIVIA HACK
BRADY BUNCH MOVIE, THE ... PAUL SUTERA
BRADY BUNCH MOVIE, THE ... SHELLEY LONG
BRADY BUNCH MOVIE, THE ... SUSAN OLSEN
BRADY GIRLS GET MARRIED, THE (TF) ... ANN B. DAVIS
BRADY GIRLS GET MARRIED, THE (TF) ... BARRY WILLIAMS
BRADY GIRLS GET MARRIED, THE (TF) ... CHRISTOPHER KNIGHT
BRADY GIRLS GET MARRIED, THE (TF) ... EVE PLUMB
BRADY GIRLS GET MARRIED, THE (TF) ... FLORENCE HENDERSON
BRADY GIRLS GET MARRIED, THE (TF) ... JERRY HAUSER
BRADY GIRLS GET MARRIED, THE (TF) ... MAUREEN McCORMICK
BRADY GIRLS GET MARRIED, THE (TF) ... MIKE LOOKINLAND
BRADY GIRLS GET MARRIED, THE (TF) ... ROBERT REED†
BRADY GIRLS GET MARRIED, THE (TF) ... SUSAN OLSEN
BRADYS, THE (TF) ... ANN B. DAVIS
BRADYS, THE (TF) ... BARRY WILLIAMS
BRADYS, THE (TF) ... CHRISTOPHER KNIGHT
BRADYS, THE (TF) ... EVE PLUMB
BRADYS, THE (TF) ... FLORENCE HENDERSON
BRADYS, THE (TF) ... JERRY HAUSER
BRADYS, THE (TF) ... MARTHA QUINN
BRADYS, THE (TF) ... MIKE LOOKINLAND
BRADYS, THE (TF) ... ROBERT REED†
BRADYS, THE (TF) ... SUSAN OLSEN
BRADY'S ESCAPE ... JOHN SAVAGE
BRADY'S ESCAPE ... KELLY RENO
BRAIN DONORS ... JOHN TURTURRO
BRAIN, THE ... ELI WALLACH
BRAINSCAN ... AMY HARGREAVES
BRAINSCAN ... EDWARD FURLONG
BRAINSCAN ... FRANK LANGELLA
BRAINSCAN ... T. RYDER SMITH
BRAINSTORM ... CHRISTOPHER WALKEN
BRAINSTORM ... CLIFF ROBERTSON
BRAINSTORM ... LOUISE FLETCHER
BRAINSTORM ... NATALIE WOOD†
BRAINSTORM ... ROBYN LIVELY
BRAINWASHED ... CLAIRE BLOOM
BRAINWAVES ... TONY CURTIS
BRAM STOKER'S DRACULA ... ANTHONY HOPKINS
BRAM STOKER'S DRACULA ... BILL CAMPBELL
BRAM STOKER'S DRACULA ... CARY ELWES
BRAM STOKER'S DRACULA ... GARY OLDMAN
BRAM STOKER'S DRACULA ... KEANU REEVES
BRAM STOKER'S DRACULA ... RICHARD E. GRANT
BRAM STOKER'S DRACULA ... SADIE FROST
BRAM STOKER'S DRACULA ... TOM WAITS
BRAM STOKER'S DRACULA ... WINONA RYDER
BRAMBLE BUSH, THE ... ANGIE DICKINSON
BRAMBLE BUSH, THE ... HENRY JONES
BRAND NEW LIFE: THE HONEYMOON, A (TF) ... BARBARA EDEN
BRAND NEW LIFE: THE HONEYMOON, A (TF) ... DON MURRAY
BRAND NEW LIFE: THE HONEYMOON, A (TF) ... SHAWNEE SMITH
BRAND X ... SALLY KIRKLAND
BRANNIGAN ... JOHN VERNON
BRANNIGAN ... LESLEY-ANNE DOWN
BRANNIGAN ... MEL FERRER
BRASS (TF) ... CARROLL O'CONNOR
BRASS (TF) ... LARRY ATLAS
BRASS (TF) ... LOIS NETTLETON
BRASS BOTTLE, THE ... BARBARA EDEN
BRASS BOTTLE, THE ... BURL IVES
BRASS BOTTLE, THE ... TONY RANDALL
BRASS BOTTLE, THE ... VAN JOHNSON
BRASS LEGEND, THE ... RAYMOND BURR†
BRASS TARGET ... BRUCE DAVISON
BRASS TARGET ... GEORGE KENNEDY
BRASS TARGET ... JOHN CASSAVETES†
BRASS TARGET ... MAX von SYDOW
BRASS TARGET ... ROBERT VAUGHN
BRASS TARGET ... SOPHIA LOREN
BRAVADOS, THE ... ALBERT SALMI†
BRAVADOS, THE ... GREGORY PECK
BRAVADOS, THE ... HENRY SILVA
BRAVADOS, THE ... JOAN COLLINS
BRAVE BULLS, THE ... ANTHONY QUINN
BRAVE BULLS, THE ... MEL FERRER
BRAVE HEART ... CATHERINE McCORMACK
BRAVE HEART ... MEL GIBSON
BRAVE HEART ... SOPHIE MARCEAU
BRAVE LITTLE TOASTER (AF) ... JON LOVITZ
BRAVEHEART ... CATHERINE McCORMACK
BRAVEHEART ... MEL GIBSON
BRAVEHEART ... PATRICK McGOOHAN
BRAVEHEART ... SOPHIE MARCEAU
BRAVOS, THE (TF) ... GEORGE PEPPARD†
BRAVOS, THE (TF) ... JOYCE VAN PATTEN
BRAZIL ... BOB HOSKINS
BRAZIL ... IAN HOLM
BRAZIL ... JONATHAN PRYCE
BRAZIL ... KATHERINE HELMOND
BRAZIL ... KIM GREIST
BRAZIL ... MICHAEL PALIN
BRAZIL ... PETER VAUGHN
BRAZIL ... ROBERT DE NIRO
BREAK OF HEARTS ... KATHERINE HEPBURN
BREAKER BREAKER ... CHUCK NORRIS
BREAKER MORANT ... BRYON BROWN
BREAKER MORANT ... EDWARD WOODWARD
BREAKER MORANT ... JACK THOMPSON
BREAKFAST AT TIFFANY'S ... GEORGE PEPPARD†
BREAKFAST AT TIFFANY'S ... JOHN MCGIVER†
BREAKFAST AT TIFFANY'S ... MARTIN BALSAM
BREAKFAST AT TIFFANY'S ... MICKEY ROONEY
BREAKFAST AT TIFFANY'S ... PATRICIA NEAL
BREAKFAST AT TIFFANY'S ★ ... AUDREY HEPBURN†
BREAKFAST CLUB, THE ... ALLY SHEEDY
BREAKFAST CLUB, THE ... ANTHONY MICHAEL HALL
BREAKFAST CLUB, THE ... EMILIO ESTEVEZ
BREAKFAST CLUB, THE ... JUDD NELSON
BREAKFAST CLUB, THE ... MAUREEN McGOVERN
BREAKFAST CLUB, THE ... MOLLY RINGWALD
BREAKFAST CLUB, THE ... PAUL GLEASON
BREAKFAST FOR TWO ... BARBARA STANWYCK†
BREAKHEART PASS ... BEN JOHNSON
BREAKHEART PASS ... BILL McKINNEY
BREAKHEART PASS ... CHARLES BRONSON
BREAKHEART PASS ... CHARLES DURNING
BREAKHEART PASS ... JILL IRELAND†
BREAKHEART PASS ... RICHARD CRENNA
BREAKHEART PASS ... SALLY KIRKLAND
BREAKIN' ... ADOLPHO "SHABBA-DOO" QUINONES
BREAKIN' ... CHRISTOPHER McDONALD
BREAKIN' ... LUCINDA DICKEY
BREAKIN' ... MICHAEL CHAMBERS
BREAKIN' 2 ELECTRIC BOOGALOO ... ADOLPHO QUINONES
BREAKIN' 2 ELECTRIC BOOGALOO ... LUCINDA DICKEY
BREAKIN' 2 ELECTRIC BOOGALOO ... MICHAEL CHAMBERS
BREAKING AWAY ... AMY WRIGHT
BREAKING AWAY ... DANIEL STERN
BREAKING AWAY ... DENNIS CHRISTOPHER
BREAKING AWAY ... DENNIS QUAID
BREAKING AWAY ... HART BOCHNER
BREAKING AWAY ... JACKIE EARLE HALEY
BREAKING AWAY ... PAUL DOOLEY
BREAKING AWAY ... ROBYN DOUGLASS
BREAKING AWAY ✪ ... BARBARA BARRIE
BREAKING GLASS ... HAZEL O'CONNOR
BREAKING GLASS ... JONATHAN PRYCE
BREAKING GLASS ... PHIL DANIELS
BREAKING HOME TIES (TF) ... DOUG McKEON
BREAKING HOME TIES (TF) ... EVA MARIE SAINT
BREAKING HOME TIES (TF) ... JASON ROBARDS
BREAKING IN ... ALBERT SALMI†
BREAKING IN ... BURT REYNOLDS
BREAKING IN ... CASEY SIEMASZKO
BREAKING IN ... DAVID FRISHBERG
BREAKING IN ... HARRY CAREY JR.
BREAKING IN ... LORRAINE TOUSSAINT
BREAKING IN ... MAURY CHAVKIN
BREAKING IN ... SHEILA KELLEY
BREAKING IN ... STEPHEN TOBOLOWSKY
BREAKING OF BUMBO, THE ... JOANNA LUMLEY
BREAKING POINT ... BELINDA J. MONTGOMERY
BREAKING POINT ... BO SVENSON
BREAKING POINT ... ROBERT CULP
BREAKING POINT (CTF) ... CORBIN BERNSEN
BREAKING POINT (CTF) ... JOANNA PACULA
BREAKING POINT (CTF) ... JOHN GLOVER
BREAKING POINT, THE ... PATRICIA NEAL
BREAKING POINT, THE ... PHYLLIS THAXTER
BREAKING THE RULES ... JASON BATEMAN
BREAKING THROUGH THE SOUND BARRIER ... DENHOLM ELLIOTT†
BREAKING UP IS HARD TO DO (TF) ... BILLY CRYSTAL
BREAKING UP IS HARD TO DO (TF) ... GEORGE GAYNES
BREAKING UP IS HARD TO DO (TF) ... JEFF CONAWAY
BREAKING UP IS HARD TO DO (TF) ... ROBERT CONRAD
BREAKOUT ... CHARLES BRONSON
BREAKOUT ... JILL IRELAND†
BREAKOUT ... RANDY QUAID
BREAKOUT ... ROBERT DUVALL
BREAKOUT (TF) ... RED BUTTONS
BREAKTHROUGH ... ROBERT MITCHUM
BREAKTHROUGH ... ROD STEIGER
BREATH OF SCANDAL, A ... ANGELA LANSBURY
BREATH OF SCANDAL, A ... JOHN GAVIN
BREATH OF SCANDAL, A ... SOPHIA LOREN
BREATHING LESSONS (TF) ... JAMES GARNER
BREATHING LESSONS (TF) ... JOANNE WOODWARD
BREATHLESS ... ART METRANO
BREATHLESS ... JEAN SEBERG†
BREATHLESS ... RICHARD GERE
BREATHLESS ... VALERIE KAPRISKY
BREED APART, A ... DONALD PLEASENCE
BREED APART, A ... KATHLEEN TURNER
BREED APART, A ... POWERS BOOTHE
BREED APART, A ... RUTGER HAUER
BREEZY ... KAY LENZ
BRENDA STARR ... BROOKE SHIELDS
BRENDA STARR ... DIANA SCARWID
BRENDA STARR ... TIMOTHY DALTON
BREWSTER McCLOUD ... BUD CORT
BREWSTER McCLOUD ... MICHAEL MURPHY
BREWSTER McCLOUD ... RENE AUBERJONOIS
BREWSTER McCLOUD ... SALLY KELLERMAN
BREWSTER McCLOUD ... SHELLEY DUVALL
BREWSTER McCLOUD ... STACY KEACH
BREWSTER McCLOUD ... WILLIAM WINDOM
BREWSTER'S MILLIONS ... CONRAD JANIS
BREWSTER'S MILLIONS ... HUME CRONYN
BREWSTER'S MILLIONS ... JERRY ORBACH
BREWSTER'S MILLIONS ... JOHN CANDY†
BREWSTER'S MILLIONS ... LONETTE McKEE
BREWSTER'S MILLIONS ... PAT HINGLE
BREWSTER'S MILLIONS ... PETER JASON
BREWSTER'S MILLIONS ... RICHARD PRYOR
BREWSTER'S MILLIONS ... STEPHEN COLLINS
BREWSTER'S MILLIONS ... YAKOV SMIRNOFF
BRIAN'S SONG (TF) ... BILLY DEE WILLIAMS
BRIAN'S SONG (TF) ... JAMES CAAN
BRIBE, THE ... AVA GARDNER†
BRIBE, THE ... VINCENT PRICE†
BRIDAL PATH, THE ... GORDAN JACKSON†
BRIDE CAME C.O.D., THE ... BETTE DAVIS†
BRIDE GOES WILD, THE ... HUME CRONYN
BRIDE GOES WILD, THE ... JUNE ALLYSON
BRIDE GOES WILD, THE ... VAN JOHNSON
BRIDE IS MUCH TOO BEAUTIFUL, THE ... LOUIS JOURDAN

This is not a list of every film ever made or every cast member, only those listed in this directory.

BRIDE OF FRANKENSTEIN .... BORIS KARLOFF†
BRIDE OF
  FRANKENSTEIN, THE .... JOHN CARRADINE†
BRIDE OF THE GORILLA .... RAYMOND BURR†
BRIDE OF VENGEANCE .... RAYMOND BURR†
BRIDE, THE .... CLANCY BROWN
BRIDE, THE .... GERALDINE PAGE†
BRIDE, THE .... JENNIFER BEALS
BRIDE, THE .... STING
BRIDE TO BE .... SARAH MILES
BRIDE WALKS OUT, THE ..... BARBARA STANWYCK†
BRIDE WORE
  BOOTS, THE .... BARBARA STANWYCK†
BRIDE WORE CRUTCHES, THE .... LIONEL STANDER
BRIDE WORE RED, THE .... JOAN CRAWFORD†
BRIDESHEAD
  REVISITED (MS) .... ANTHONY ANDREWS
BRIDESHEAD REVISITED (MS) .... CLAIRE BLOOM
BRIDESHEAD REVISITED (MS) .... DIANA QUICK
BRIDESHEAD REVISITED (MS) .... JEREMY IRONS
BRIDESHEAD REVISITED (MS) .... JOHN GIELGUD
BRIDESMAIDS (TF) .... BROOKE ADAMS
BRIDESMAIDS (TF) .... HAMILTON CAMP
BRIDESMAIDS (TF) .... SHELLEY HACK
BRIDGE ACROSS TIME (TF) .... ADRIENNE BARBEAU
BRIDGE ACROSS TIME (TF) ..... DAVID HASSELHOFF
BRIDGE ACROSS TIME (TF) .... STEPHANIE KRAMER
BRIDGE AT REMAGEN, THE ..... BEN GAZZARA
BRIDGE AT REMAGEN, THE .... BO HOPKINS
BRIDGE AT REMAGEN, THE .... BRADFORD DILLMAN
BRIDGE AT REMAGEN, THE .... E. G. MARSHALL
BRIDGE AT REMAGEN, THE .... GEORGE SEGAL
BRIDGE AT REMAGEN, THE .... ROBERT VAUGHN
BRIDGE ON THE
  RIVER KWAI, THE ★★ .... ALEC GUINNESS
BRIDGE ON THE
  RIVER KWAI, THE ○○ .... SESSUE HAYAKAWA†
BRIDGE TO SILENCE (TF) .... MARLEE MATLIN
BRIDGE TO THE SUN .... CARROLL BAKER
BRIDGE TO THE SUN .... JAMES SHIGETA
BRIDGE TOO FAR, A .... ALUN ARMSTRONG
BRIDGE TOO FAR, A .... ANTHONY HOPKINS
BRIDGE TOO FAR, A .... ARTHUR HILL
BRIDGE TOO FAR, A .... EDWARD FOX
BRIDGE TOO FAR, A .... ELLIOTT GOULD
BRIDGE TOO FAR, A .... GENE HACKMAN
BRIDGE TOO FAR, A .... JAMES CAAN
BRIDGE TOO FAR, A .... JEREMY KEMP
BRIDGE TOO FAR, A .... LAURENCE OLIVIER†
BRIDGE TOO FAR, A .... LIV ULLMANN
BRIDGE TOO FAR, A .... MAXIMILIAN SCHELL
BRIDGE TOO FAR, A .... MICHAEL CAINE
BRIDGE TOO FAR, A .... ROBERT REDFORD
BRIDGE TOO FAR, A .... RYAN O'NEAL
BRIDGE TOO FAR, A .... SEAN CONNERY
BRIDGES AT TOKO-RI, THE .... COREY ALLEN
BRIDGES AT TOKO-RI, THE .... GRACE KELLY†
BRIDGES OF MADISON
  COUNTY, THE .... CLINT EASTWOOD
BRIDGES OF MADISON
  COUNTY, THE .... MERYL STREEP
BRIDGES OF MADISON
  COUNTY, THE .... ANNIE CORLEY
BRIDGES OF TOKO-RI, THE .... DENNIS WEAVER
BRIDGES OF TOKO-RI, THE .... EARL HOLLIMAN
BRIEF ENCOUNTER ★ .... CELIA JOHNSON†
BRIEF ENCOUNTER (TF) .... JACK HEDLEY
BRIEF ENCOUNTER (TF) .... ROSEMARY LEACH
BRIEF ENCOUNTER (TF) .... SOPHIA LOREN
BRIEF RAPTURE .... LOIS MAXWELL
BRIGADOON .... CYD CHARISSE
BRIGADOON .... GENE KELLY
BRIGADOON, THE .... VAN JOHNSON
BRIGAND, THE .... ANTHONY QUINN
BRIGHAM YOUNG .... DEAN JAGGER†
BRIGHAM YOUNG,
  FRONTIERSMAN .... VINCENT PRICE†
BRIGHT ANGEL .... BILL PULLMAN
BRIGHT ANGEL .... BURT YOUNG
BRIGHT ANGEL .... DERMOT MULRONEY
BRIGHT ANGEL .... KEVIN TIGHE
BRIGHT ANGEL .... LILI TAYLOR
BRIGHT ANGEL .... MARY KAY PLACE

BRIGHT ANGEL .... SAM SHEPARD
BRIGHT ANGEL .... VALERIE PERRINE
BRIGHT LEAF .... JEFF COREY
BRIGHT LEAF .... LAUREN BACALL
BRIGHT LEAF .... PATRICIA NEAL
BRIGHT LIGHTS, BIG CITY ..... CHARLIE SCHLATTER
BRIGHT LIGHTS, BIG CITY .... DIANNE WIEST
BRIGHT LIGHTS,
  BIG CITY .... FRANCES STERNHAGEN
BRIGHT LIGHTS, BIG CITY ..... KIEFER SUTHERLAND
BRIGHT LIGHTS, BIG CITY ..... MICHAEL J. FOX
BRIGHT LIGHTS, BIG CITY .... PHOEBE CATES
BRIGHT LIGHTS, BIG CITY .... SWOOSIE KURTZ
BRIGHT VICTORY .... ROCK HUDSON†
BRIGHTON BEACH MEMOIRS .... BLYTHE DANNER
BRIGHTON BEACH MEMOIRS .... BOB DISHY
BRIGHTON BEACH MEMOIRS ... BRIAN DRILLINGER
BRIGHTON BEACH MEMOIRS .... JAMES HANDY
BRIGHTON BEACH
  MEMOIRS .... JONATHAN SILVERMAN
BRIGHTON BEACH MEMOIRS .... JUDITH IVEY
BRIGHTON BEACH MEMOIRS .... LISA WALTZ
BRIGHTON BEACH MEMOIRS .... STACEY GLICK
BRILLIANT DISGUISE .... ANTHONY DENISON
BRILLIANT DISGUISE .... ROBIN GIVENS
BRIMSTONE AND TREACLE .... DENHOLM ELLIOTT†
BRIMSTONE AND TREACLE .... JOAN PLOWRIGHT
BRIMSTONE AND TREACLE .... STING
BRING ME THE HEAD OF
  ALFREDO GARCIA .... KRIS KRISTOFFERSON
BRING ME THE HEAD OF
  ALFREDO GARCIA .... ROBERT WEBBER
BRING ME THE HEAD OF
  DOBIE GILLIS (TF) .... CONNIE STEVENS
BRING ME THE HEAD OF
  DOBIE GILLIS (TF) .... DWAYNE HICKMAN
BRING ME THE HEAD OF
  DOBIE GILLIS (TF) .... MIKE JOLLY
BRING ON THE GIRLS .... YVONNE DE CARLO
BRING ON THE NIGHT (FD) .... STING
BRINGING UP BABY .... CARY GRANT†
BRINGING UP BABY .... KATHERINE HEPBURN
BRINK OF LIFE .... BIBI ANDERSSON
BRINKS JOB, THE .... ALLEN GARFIELD
BRINKS JOB, THE .... PETER BOYLE
BRINK'S JOB, THE .... GENA ROWLANDS
BRINK'S JOB, THE .... PAUL SORVINO
BRINK'S JOB, THE .... PETER FALK
BRITANNIA HOSPITAL .... ALAN BATES
BRITANNIA HOSPITAL .... BRIAN GLOVER
BRITANNIA HOSPITAL .... JOAN PLOWRIGHT
BRITANNIA HOSPITAL ...... MALCOLM McDOWELL
BRITANNIA HOSPITAL .... MARK HAMILL
BRITANNIA MEWS .... MAUREEN O'HARA
BRITANNIA OF BILLINGSGATE .... JOHN MILLS
BROADCAST NEWS ...... CHRISTIAN CLEMENSON
BROADCAST NEWS .... JACK NICHOLSON
BROADCAST NEWS .... JOAN CUSAK
BROADCAST NEWS .... JOHN CUSAK
BROADCAST NEWS .... LOIS CHILES
BROADCAST NEWS .... ROBERT PROSKY
BROADCAST NEWS ★ .... HOLLY HUNTER
BROADCAST NEWS ★ .... WILLIAM HURT
BROADCAST NEWS ○ .... ALBERT BROOKS
BROADWAY BOUND (TF) .... ANNE BANCROFT
BROADWAY DANNY ROSE .... CORBETT MONICA
BROADWAY DANNY ROSE .... JOE FRANKLIN
BROADWAY DANNY ROSE .... MIA FARROW
BROADWAY DANNY ROSE .... MILTON BERLE
BROADWAY DANNY ROSE ...... NICK APOLLO FORTE
BROADWAY DANNY ROSE .... SANDY BARON
BROADWAY DANNY ROSE .... WOODY ALLEN
BROADWAY MELODY, THE .... CHARLES KING†
BROADWAY MELODY, THE ★ .... BESSIE LOVE†
BROADWAY NIGHTS .... BARBARA STANWYCK†
BROADWAY NIGHTS .... SYLVIA SIDNEY
BROADWAY RHYTHM .... LENA HORNE
BROADWAY THRU A KEYHOLE .... ANN SOTHERN
BROADWAY TO HOLLYWOOD .... JACKIE COOPER
BROCK'S LAST CASE (TF) .... DAVID HUDDLESTON
BROCK'S LAST CASE (TF) .... RICHARD WIDMARK
BROKEN ANGEL (TF) .... CARMEN ZAPATA

BROKEN ANGEL (TF) .... JASON HORST
BROKEN ANGEL (TF) .... SUSAN BLAKELY
BROKEN ANGEL (TF) .... WILLIAM SHATNER
BROKEN ARROW .... JAMES STEWART
BROKEN ARROW ○ .... JEFF CHANDLER†
BROKEN BLOSSOMS .... LILLIAN GISH†
BROKEN CHAIN, THE (CTF) .... ERIC SCHWEIG
BROKEN JOURNEY .... DAVID TOMLINSON
BROKEN LANCE .... E. G. MARSHALL
BROKEN LANCE .... EARL HOLLIMAN
BROKEN LANCE .... RICHARD WIDMARK
BROKEN LANCE ○ .... ROBERT WAGNER
BROKEN LANCE ○ .... KATHY JURADO
BROKEN LAND, THE .... JACK NICHOLSON
BROKEN RAINBOW (FD) .... BURGESS MEREDITH
BROKEN RAINBOW (FD) .... MARTIN SHEEN
BROKEN VOWS (TF) .... TOMMY LEE JONES
BRONCO BILLY .... BILL McKINNEY
BRONCO BILLY .... CLINT EASTWOOD
BRONCO BILLY .... SAM BOTTOMS
BRONCO BILLY .... SCATMAN CROTHERS†
BRONCO BILLY .... SONDRA LOCKE
BRONCO BILLY .... WILLIAM PRINCE
BRONTE SISTERS, THE .... ISABELLE ADJANI
BRONX TALE, A .... CHAZZ PALMINTERI
BRONX TALE, A .... FRANCIS CAPRA
BRONX TALE, A .... JOE PESCI
BRONX TALE, A .... LILLO BRANCATO
BRONX TALE, A .... ROBERT DE NIRO
BRONX TALE, A .... TARAL HICKS
BROOD, THE .... SAMANTHA EGGAR
BROTHER FROM ANOTHER
  PLANET, THE .... DAVID STRATHAIRN
BROTHER FROM ANOTHER
  PLANET, THE .... FISHER STEVENS
BROTHER FROM ANOTHER
  PLANET, THE .... JOE MORTON
BROTHER FROM ANOTHER
  PLANET, THE .... JOHN SAYLES
BROTHER FROM ANOTHER
  PLANET, THE .... MICHAEL MANTELL
BROTHER JOHN .... BRADFORD DILLMAN
BROTHER JOHN .... PAUL WINFIELD
BROTHER JOHN .... SIDNEY POITIER
BROTHER ORCHID .... ANN SOTHERN
BROTHER ORCHID .... RALPH BELLAMY†
BROTHER RAT .... EDDIE ALBERT
BROTHER RAT .... JANE WYMAN
BROTHER RAT .... RONALD REAGAN
BROTHER RAT .... WILLIAM TRACY†
BROTHER RAT AND A BABY .... EDDIE ALBERT
BROTHER RAT AND A BABY .... JANE WYMAN
BROTHER RAT AND A BABY .... RONALD REAGAN
BROTHER SUN SISTER MOON .... ALEC GUINNESS
BROTHER SUN, SISTER MOON .... MICHAEL YORK
BROTHER SUN, SISTER MOON .... PETER FIRTH
BROTHERHOOD OF
  JUSTICE, THE (TF) .... JOE SPANO
BROTHERHOOD OF
  JUSTICE, THE (TF) .... KIEFER SUTHERLAND
BROTHERHOOD OF SATAN, THE .... L. Q. JONES
BROTHERHOOD OF
  THE BELL, THE (TF) .... DABNEY COLEMAN
BROTHERHOOD OF
  THE YAKUZA .... HERB EDELMAN
BROTHERHOOD OF
  THE YAKUZA .... KEN TAKAKURA
BROTHERHOOD, THE .... KIRK DOUGLAS
BROTHERHOOD, THE .... SUSAN STRASBERG
BROTHERHOOD, THE .... VAL AVERY
BROTHERLY LOVE .... BRIAN BLESSED
BROTHERLY LOVE .... PETER O'TOOLE
BROTHERLY LOVE .... SUSANNAH YORK
BROTHERLY LOVE (TF) .... GEORGE DZUNDZA
BROTHERLY LOVE (TF) .... JUDD HIRSCH
BROTHERS .... RON O'NEAL
BROTHERS IN LAW .... GEORGE ROSE†
BROTHERS KARAMAZOV, THE .... ALBERT SALMI†
BROTHERS KARAMAZOV, THE .... CLAIRE BLOOM
BROTHERS KARAMAZOV, THE .... MARIA SCHELL
BROTHERS
  KARAMAZOV, THE .... WILLIAM SHATNER

† after an actor's name denotes deceased.

BROTHERS KARAMAZOV, THE ✺ .... LEE J. COBB†
BROTHERS O'TOOLE, THE .... JOHN ASTIN
BROWNING VERSION, THE .... ALBERT FINNEY
BROWNING VERSION, THE .... BEN SILVERSTONE
BROWNING VERSION, THE .... GRETA SCACCHI
BROWNING VERSION, THE .... MATTHEW MODINE
BRUBAKER .... ALBERT SALMI†
BRUBAKER .... JANE ALEXANDER
BRUBAKER .... MATT CLARK
BRUBAKER .... ROBERT REDFORD
BRUBAKER .... WILFORD BRIMLEY
BRUBAKER .... YAPHET KOTTO
BRUSHFIRE! .... JOHN IRELAND
BRUTE AND THE BEAST, THE .... FRANCO NERO
BRUTE FORCE .... BURT LANCASTER†
BRUTE FORCE .... HOWARD DUFF†
BRUTE FORCE .... HUME CRONYN
BRUTE FORCE .... JEFF COREY
BRUTE FORCE .... YVONNE DE CARLO
BRUTE, THE .... JULIAN GLOVER
BUCCANEER, THE .... ANTHONY QUINN
BUCCANEER, THE .... CHARLTON HESTON
BUCCANEER, THE .... CLAIRE BLOOM
BUCCANEER, THE .... E. G. MARSHALL
BUCCANEER'S GIRL .... YVONNE DE CARLO
BUCK AND THE PREACHER .... NITA TALBOT
BUCK AND THE PREACHER .... RUBY DEE
BUCK AND THE PREACHER .... SIDNEY POITIER
BUCK ROGERS IN THE
     25TH CENTURY .... GIL GERARD
BUCK ROGERS IN THE
     25TH CENTURY .... HENRY SILVA
BUCK ROGERS IN THE
     25TH CENTURY .... JOSEPH WISEMAN
BUCKET OF BLOOD, A .... DICK MILLER
BUCKSKIN .... BARBARA HALE
BUCKSKIN .... JOAN CAULFIELD†
BUCKSKIN FRONTIER .... JANE WYATT
BUCKTOWN .... CARL WEATHERS
BUCKTOWN .... FRED WILLIAMSON
BUCKTOWN .... PAM GRIER
BUCKTOWN .... THALMUS RASULALA
BUD ABBOTT AND LOU COSTELLO
     IN HOLLYWOOD .... BUD ABBOTT†
BUD ABBOTTAND LOU COSTELLO
     IN HOLLYWOOD .... LOU COSTELLO†
BUD AND LOU (TF) .... BUDDY HACKETT
BUD AND LOU (TF) .... MICHELE LEE
BUDDY BUDDY .... JACK LEMMON
BUDDY BUDDY .... PAULA PRENTISS
BUDDY BUDDY .... WALTER MATTHAU
BUDDY HOLLY STORY, THE .... DON STROUD
BUDDY HOLLY STORY, THE .... KEN WAHL
BUDDY HOLLY STORY, THE ★ .... GARY BUSEY
BUDDY SYSTEM, THE .... NANCY ALLEN
BUDDY SYSTEM, THE .... RICHARD DREYFUSS
BUDDY SYSTEM, THE .... SUSAN SARANDON
BUFFALO BILL .... ANTHONY QUINN
BUFFALO BILL .... MAUREEN O'HARA
BUFFALO BILL AND THE INDIANS or
     SITTING BULL'S HISTORY
     LESSON .... BURT LANCASTER†
BUFFALO BILL AND THE INDIANS or
     SITTING BULL'S HISTORY
     LESSON .... GERALDINE CHAPLIN
BUFFALO BILL AND THE INDIANS or
     SITTING BULL'S HISTORY
     LESSON .... HARVEY KEITEL
BUFFALO BILL AND THE INDIANS or
     SITTING BULL'S HISTORY LESSON ..... JOEL GREY
BUFFALO BILL AND THE INDIANS or
     SITTING BULL'S HISTORY
     LESSON .... KEVIN McCARTHY
BUFFALO BILL AND THE INDIANS or
     SITTING BULL'S HISTORY
     LESSON .... PAUL NEWMAN
BUFFALO BILL AND THE INDIANS or
     SITTING BULL'S HISTORY
     LESSON .... SHELLEY DUVALL
BUFFALO GIRLS (MS) .... ANJELICA HUSTON
BUFFALO GIRLS (MS) .... GABRIEL BYRNE
BUFFALO GIRLS (MS) .... JACK PALANCE
BUFFALO GIRLS (MS) .... MELANIE GRIFFITH

BUFFALO GIRLS (MS) .... SAM ELLIOTT
BUFFET FROID .... GERARD DEPARDIEU
BUFFY THE VAMPIRE
     SLAYER .... DONALD SUTHERLAND
BUFFY THE VAMPIRE
     SLAYER .... KRISTY SWANSON
BUFFY THE VAMPIRE SLAYER .... LUKE PERRY
BUFFY THE VAMPIRE SLAYER .... PAUL REUBENS
BUFFY THE VAMPIRE SLAYER ...... RUTGER HAUER
BUG .... BRADFORD DILLMAN
BUG .... JOANNA MILES
BUGSY .... ANNETTE BENING
BUGSY .... BILLY GRAHAM
BUGSY .... ELLIOTT GOULD
BUGSY .... GIAN-CARLO SCANDIUZZI
BUGSY .... JAMES TOBACK
BUGSY .... JOE MANTEGNA
BUGSY ★ .... WARREN BEATTY
BUGSY ✺ .... BEN KINGSLEY
BUGSY ✺ .... HARVEY KEITEL
BUGSY MALONE .... JODIE FOSTER
BUGSY MALONE .... SCOTT BAIO
BULL DURHAM .... KEVIN COSTNER
BULL DURHAM .... ROBERT WUHL
BULL DURHAM .... SUSAN SARANDON
BULL DURHAM .... TIM ROBBINS
BULL DURHAM .... TREY WILSON†
BULLDOG BREED, THE .... MICHAEL CAINE
BULLDOG DRUMMOND ★ .... RONALD COLMAN†
BULLDOG DRUMMOND
     IN AFRICA .... ANTHONY QUINN
BULLET FOR A BADMAN .... DARREN McGAVIN
BULLET FOR SANDOVAL, A ...... ERNEST BORGNINE
BULLET IS WAITING, A .... JEAN SIMMONS
BULLET IS WAITING, A .... RORY CALHOUN
BULLETPROOF .... GARY BUSEY
BULLETPROOF .... HENRY SILVA
BULLETPROOF .... THALMUS RASULALA
BULLETPROOF HEART .... ANTHONY LaPAGLIA
BULLETS FOR O'HARA .... ANTHONY QUINN
BULLETS OVER BROADWAY .... ALAN ARKIN
BULLETS OVER BROADWAY .... CARL REINER
BULLETS OVER BROADWAY .... CHAZZ PALMINTERI
BULLETS OVER BROADWAY .... DEBI MAZAR
BULLETS OVER BROADWAY .... DIANNE WIEST
BULLETS OVER BROADWAY ... HARVEY FIERSTEIN
BULLETS OVER BROADWAY ... JACK WARDEN
BULLETS OVER BROADWAY ... JENNIFER TILLY
BULLETS OVER BROADWAY .... JOHN CUSAK
BULLETS OVER
     BROADWAY .... MARY-LOUISE PARKER
BULLETS OVER BROADWAY .... TRACEY ULLMAN
BULLFIGHTER AND
     THE LADY, THE .... KATHY JURADO
BULLFIGHTER AND
     THE LADY, THE .... ROBERT STACK
BULLIES .... BERNIE COULSON
BULLIES .... BILL CROFT
BULLIES .... DEHL BERTI
BULLIES .... JANET LAINE GREEN
BULLIES .... JONATHAN CROMBIE
BULLIES .... OLIVIA D'ABO
BULLIES .... STEPHEN B. HUNTER
BULLITT .... GEORG STANFORD BROWN
BULLITT .... JACQUELINE BISSET
BULLITT .... JOANNA CASSIDY
BULLITT .... NORMAN FELL
BULLITT .... ROBERT DUVALL
BULLITT .... ROBERT VAUGHN
BULLITT .... STEVE McQUEEN†
BULLSHOT! .... GEOFFREY BAYLDON
BULLY .... JAMES WHITMORE
BUNDLE OF JOY .... DEBBIE REYNOLDS
BUNDLE OF JOY .... EDDIE FISHER
BUNDLE OF JOY .... NITA TALBOT
BUNKER, THE (TF) .... ANTHONY HOPKINS
BUNKER, THE (TF) .... JAMES NAUGHTON
BUNKER, THE (TF) .... PIPER LAURIE
BUNKER, THE (TF) .... SUSAN BLAKELY
BUNNY LAKE IS MISSING .... CAROL LYNLEY
BUNNY O'HARE .... BETTE DAVIS†
BUNNY O'HARE .... ERNEST BORGNINE
BUNNY O'HARE .... JOHN ASTIN

BUNNY'S TALE, A (TF) .... COTTER SMITH
BUNNY'S
     TALE, A (TF) .... DEBORAH VAN VALKENBURGH
BUNNY'S TALE, A (TF) .... DELTA BURKE
BUNNY'S TALE, A (TF) .... DIANA SCARWID
BUNNY'S TALE, A (TF) .... JOANNA KERNS
BUNNY'S TALE, A (TF) .... KIRSTIE ALLEY
BUNNY'S TALE, A (TF) .... LISA PELIKAN
BUNNY'S TALE, A (TF) .... MARY WORONOY
BUONA SERA,
     MRS. CAMPBELL .... JANET MARGOLIN
BUONA SERA, MRS. CAMPBELL .... LEE GRANT
BUONA SERA,
     MRS. CAMPBELL .... SHELLEY WINTERS
BUONA SERA,
     MRS. CAMPBELL .... TELLY SAVALAS†
'BURBS, THE .... BROTHER THEODORE
'BURBS, THE .... BRUCE DERN
'BURBS, THE .... CARRIE FISHER
'BURBS, THE .... COREY FELDMAN
'BURBS, THE .... COURTNEY GAINS
'BURBS, THE .... DICK MILLER
'BURBS, THE .... HENRY GIBSON
'BURBS, THE .... RICK DUCOMMUN
'BURBS, THE .... TOM HANKS
'BURBS, THE .... WENDY SCHAAL
BUREAU OF MISSING PERSONS .... BETTE DAVIS†
BURGLAR .... ANNE DESALVO
BURGLAR .... BOB GOLDTHWAIT
BURGLAR .... G.W. BAILEY
BURGLAR .... JAMES HANDY
BURGLAR .... JOHN GOODMAN
BURGLAR .... LESLEY ANN WARREN
BURGLAR .... WHOOPI GOLDBERG
BURGLARS, THE .... DYAN CANNON
BURGLARS, THE .... OMAR SHARIF
BURGLAR'S DILEMMA, THE .... LILLIAN GISH†
BURIED ALIVE (CTF) .... HOYT AXTON
BURIED ALIVE (CTF) .... JENNIFER JASON LEIGH
BURIED ALIVE (CTF) .... TIM MATHESON
BURIED ALIVE (CTF) .... WILLIAM ATHERTON
BURKE AND WILLS .... GRETA SCACCHI
BURKE AND WILLS .... JACK THOMPSON
BURKE AND WILLS .... NIGEL HAYERS
BURN! .... MARLON BRANDO
BURNIN' LOVE .... DAVID GRAF
BURNING BED, THE (TF) .... FARRAH FAWCETT
BURNING BED, THE (TF) .... GRACE ZABRISKIE
BURNING BED, THE (TF) .... PAUL LeMAT
BURNING BED, THE (TF) .... RICHARD MASUR
BURNING BRIDGES (TF) .... DEREK DE LINT
BURNING BRIDGES (TF) .... LOIS CHILES
BURNING BRIDGES (TF) .... MEREDITH BAXTER
BURNING BRIDGES (TF) .... NICK MANCUSO
BURNING HILLS, THE .... CLAUDE AKINS†
BURNING HILLS, THE .... EARL HOLLIMAN
BURNING HILLS, THE .... TAB HUNTER
BURNING LOVE .... ANN RAMSEY†
BURNING MAN, THE .... TOM SKERRITT
BURNING RAGE (TF) .... BARBARA MANDRELL
BURNING RAGE (TF) .... CAROL KANE
BURNING RAGE (TF) .... EDDIE ALBERT
BURNING RAGE (TF) .... TOM WOPAT
BURNING SECRET .... DAVID EBERTS
BURNING SECRET .... FAYE DUNAWAY
BURNING SECRET .... IAN RICHARDSON
BURNING SECRET ..... KLAUS MARIA BRANDAUER
BURNING, THE .... HOLLY HUNTER
BURNT OFFERINGS .... BETTE DAVIS†
BURNT OFFERINGS .... BURGESS MEREDITH
BURNT OFFERINGS .... EILEEN HECKART
BURNT OFFERINGS .... KAREN BLACK
BURNT OFFERINGS .... LEE MONTGOMERY
BURY ME DEAD .... JUNE LOCKHART
BUS RILEY'S BACK IN TOWN .... ANN-MARGRET
BUS RILEY'S BACK IN TOWN ...... DAVID CARRADINE
BUS RILEY'S BACK IN TOWN ...... JANET MARGOLIN
BUS RILEY'S BACK IN TOWN ...... KIM DARBY
BUS STOP .... EILEEN HECKART
BUS STOP .... HOPE LANGE
BUS STOP .... MARILYN MONROE†
BUS STOP .... MAX SHOWALTER
BUS STOP ✺ .... DON MURRAY

This is not a list of every film ever made or every cast member, only those listed in this directory.

BUSHIDO BLADE, THE .... JAMES EARL JONES
BUSHIDO BLADE, THE .... MAKO
BUSHWHACKERS, THE .... JOHN IRELAND
BUSINESS AS USUAL .... GLENDA JACKSON
BUSINESS TRIP .... GERALDINE DANON
BUSSES ROAR .... ELEANOR PARKER
BUSTER .... JULIE WALTERS
BUSTER .... PHIL COLLINS
BUSTER AND BILLIE .... JAN-MICHAEL VINCENT
BUSTER AND BILLIE .... PAMELA SUE MARTIN
BUSTER KEATON
  STORY, THE .... RICHARD ANDERSON
BUSTIN' LOOSE .... CICELY TYSON
BUSTIN' LOOSE .... RICHARD PRYOR
BUSTING .... ALLEN GARFIELD
BUSTING .... ELLIOTT GOULD
BUSTING .... MICHAEL LERNER
BUSTING .... ROBERT BLAKE
BUSY BODY, THE .... ANNE BAXTER†
BUSY BODY, THE .... DOM DeLUISE
BUSY BODY, THE .... GEORGE JESSEL†
BUSY BODY, THE .... KAY MEDFORD†
BUSY BODY, THE .... RICHARD PRYOR
BUSY BODY, THE .... ROBERT RYAN†
BUSY BODY, THE .... SID CAESAR
BUT I DON'T WANT TO
  GET MARRIED (TF) .... SHIRLEY JONES
BUT NOT FOR ME .... CARROLL BAKER
BUTCH AND SUNDANCE:
  THE EARLY DAYS .... ARTHUR HILL
BUTCH AND SUNDANCE:
  THE EARLY DAYS .... BRIAN DENNEHY
BUTCH AND SUNDANCE:
  THE EARLY DAYS .... JEFF COREY
BUTCH AND SUNDANCE:
  THE EARLY DAYS .... JILL EIKENBERRY
BUTCH AND SUNDANCE:
  THE EARLY DAYS .... JOHN SCHUCK
BUTCH AND SUNDANCE:
  THE EARLY DAYS .... TOM BERENGER
BUTCH AND SUNDANCE:
  THE EARLY DAYS .... WILLIAM KATT
BUTCH CASSIDY AND THE
  SUNDANCE KID .... CLORIS LEACHMAN
BUTCH CASSIDY AND THE
  SUNDANCE KID .... HENRY JONES
BUTCH CASSIDY AND THE
  SUNDANCE KID .... JEFF COREY
BUTCH CASSIDY AND THE
  SUNDANCE KID .... KATHERINE ROSS
BUTCH CASSIDY AND THE
  SUNDANCE KID .... KENNETH MARS
BUTCH CASSIDY AND THE
  SUNDANCE KID .... PAUL NEWMAN
BUTCH CASSIDY AND THE
  SUNDANCE KID .... ROBERT REDFORD
BUTCH CASSIDY AND THE
  SUNDANCE KID .... STROTHER MARTIN†
BUTCH CASSIDY AND THE
  SUNDANCE KID .... TED CASSIDY†
BUTCHER'S WIFE, THE .... DEMI MOORE
BUTCHER'S WIFE, THE ...... FRANCES McDORMAND
BUTCHER'S WIFE, THE .... GEORGE DZUNDZA
BUTCHER'S WIFE, THE .... HELEN HANFT
BUTCHER'S WIFE, THE .... JEFF DANIELS
BUTCHER'S WIFE, THE .... MARGARET COLIN
BUTCHER'S WIFE, THE ..... MARY STEENBURGEN
BUTCHER'S WIFE, THE .... MAX PERLICH
BUTCHER'S WIFE, THE .... MIRIAM MARGOLYES
BUTLEY .... ALAN BATES
BUTLEY .... JESSICA TANDY†
BUTTERCUP CHAIN, THE .... LEIGH TAYLOR-YOUNG
BUTTERFIELD 8 .... DINA MERRILL
BUTTERFIELD 8 .... EDDIE FISHER
BUTTERFIELD 8 .... LAURENCE HARVEY†
BUTTERFIELD 8 .... MILDRED DUNNOCK†
BUTTERFIELD 8 ★★ .... ELIZABETH TAYLOR
BUTTERFLIES ARE FREE .... EDWARD ALBERT
BUTTERFLIES ARE FREE .... GOLDIE HAWN
BUTTERFLIES ARE FREE ○○ .... EILEEN HECKART
BUTTERFLY .... EDWARD ALBERT
BUTTERFLY .... JAMES FRANCISCUS†
BUTTERFLY .... LOIS NETTLETON

BUTTERFLY .... PIA ZADORA
BUTTERFLY .... STACY KEACH
BUTTERFLY .... STUART WHITMAN
BUY & CELL .... BEN VEREEN
BUY & CELL .... FRED TRAVELENA
BUY & CELL .... IMOGENE COCA
BUY & CELL .... LISE CUTTER
BUY & CELL .... MALCOLM McDOWELL
BUY & CELL .... MICHAEL GOODWIN
BUY & CELL .... MICHAEL WINSLOW
BUY & CELL .... RANDALL (TEX) COBB
BUY & CELL .... ROBERT CARRADINE
BUY & CELL .... RODDY PIPER
BUY & CELL .... TONY PLANA
BWANA DEVIL .... ROBERT STACK
BY DAWN'S EARLY LIGHT (CTF) ..... MARTIN LANDAU
BY DAWN'S
  EARLY LIGHT (CTF) .... POWERS BOOTHE
BY DAWN'S
  EARLY LIGHT (CTF) .... REBECCA DE MORNAY
BY LOVE POSSESSED .... CARROLL O'CONNOR
BY LOVE POSSESSED .... EFREM ZIMBALIST JR.
BY LOVE POSSESSED .... GEORGE HAMILTON
BY LOVE POSSESSED .... JASON ROBARDS
BY LOVE POSSESSED .... LANA TURNER
BY THE LIGHT OF THE
  SILVERY MOON .... DORIS DAY
BY THE LIGHT OF THE
  SILVERY MOON .... GORDON MACRAE†
BY THE SWORD .... CHRIS RYDELL
BY THE SWORD .... ERIC ROBERTS
BY THE SWORD .... F. MURRAY ABRAHAM
BY THE SWORD .... MIA SARA
BYE BYE BABY .... BRIGITTE NIELSEN
BYE BYE BABY .... CAROL ALT
BYE BYE BABY .... JASON CONNERY
BYE BYE BIRDIE .... ANN-MARGRET
BYE BYE BIRDIE .... DICK VAN DYKE
BYE BYE BIRDIE .... ED SULLIVAN†
BYE BYE BIRDIE .... JANET LEIGH
BYE BYE BIRDIE .... KIM DARBY
BYE BYE BIRDIE .... MAUREEN STAPLETON
BYE BYE BIRDIE .... PAUL LYNDE†
BYE BYE BLUES .... KATE REID
BYE BYE BLUES .... LUKE COOPER
BYE BYE BLUES .... LUKE REILLY
BYE BYE BLUES .... MICHAEL ONTKEAN
BYE BYE BLUES .... REBECCA JENKINS
BYE BYE BLUES .... ROBYN STEVEN
BYE BYE BLUES .... SHEILA MOORE
BYE BYE BLUES .... STUART MARGOLIN
BYE BYE BLUES .... WAYNE ROBSON
BYE BYE BRAVERMAN .... ALAN KING
BYE BYE BRAVERMAN .... GEORGE SEGAL
BYE BYE BRAVERMAN .... JACK WARDEN
BYE BYE BRAVERMAN .... JESSICA WALTER
BYE BYE BRAVERMAN .... JOSEPH WISEMAN
BYE BYE BRAVERMAN .... SORRELL BOOKE
BYE BYE BRAVERMAN .... ZOHRA LAMPERT
BYE BYE LOVE .... AMBER BENSON
BYE BYE LOVE .... AMY BRENNEMAN
BYE BYE LOVE .... ELIZA DUSHKU
BYE BYE LOVE .... JANEANE GAROFALO
BYE BYE LOVE .... JOHNNY WHITWORTH
BYE BYE LOVE .... LINDSAY CROUSE
BYE BYE LOVE .... MARIA PITILLO
BYE BYE LOVE .... MATTHEW MODINE
BYE BYE LOVE .... PAMELA DILLMAN
BYE BYE LOVE .... PAUL REISER
BYE BYE LOVE .... RANDY QUAID
BYE BYE MONKEY .... GERALDINE FITZGERALD
BYE BYE MONKEY .... GERARD DEPARDIEU

C

C.A.T. SQUAD:
  PYTHON WOLF (TF) .... JACK YOUNGBLOOD
C.A.T. SQUAD:
  PYTHON WOLF (TF) .... MIGUEL FERRER
C.A.T. SQUAD (TF) .... JACK YOUNGBLOOD
C.C. AND COMPANY .... ANN-MARGRET
C.C. AND COMPANY .... JOE NAMATH
C.C. AND COMPANY .... SID HAIG
C.H.O.M.P.S. .... RED BUTTONS
C.H.U.D. .... JOHN GOODMAN
C.H.U.D. .... KIM GREIST
C.H.U.D. .... JAY THOMAS
C.H.U.D. .... PATRICIA RICHARDSON
ÇA N'ARRIVE
  QU'AUX AUTRES .... CATHERINE DENEUVE
CABARET .... MARISA BERENSON
CABARET .... MICHAEL YORK
CABARET ★★ .... LIZA MINELLI
CABARET ○○ .... JOEL GREY
CABIN BOY .... RUSS TAMBLYN
CABIN BOY .... CHRIS ELLIOTT
CABIN BOY .... DAVID LETTERMAN
CABIN IN THE COTTON .... BETTE DAVIS†
CABIN IN THE SKY .... LENA HORNE
CABINET OF CALIGARI, THE, ... DAN O'HERLIHY
CABLE CAR MURDER (TF) .... CAROL LYNLEY
CABLE CAR MURDER (TF) .... ROBERT HOOKS
CABO BLANCO .... SIMON MacCORKINDALE
CABOBLANCO .... CHARLES BRONSON
CABOBLANCO .... JASON ROBARDS
CACTUS .... BANDUK MARIKA
CACTUS .... ISABELLE HUPPERT
CACTUS .... MONICA MAUGHAN
CACTUS .... NORMAN KAYE
CACTUS .... ROBERT MENZIES
CACTUS FLOWER .... INGRID BERGMAN†
CACTUS FLOWER .... JACK WESTON
CACTUS FLOWER .... WALTER MATTHAU
CACTUS FLOWER ○○ .... GOLDIE HAWN
CADDIE .... JACK THOMPSON
CADDY, THE .... DEAN MARTIN
CADDY, THE .... JERRY LEWIS
CADDYSHACK .... BILL MURRAY
CADDYSHACK .... CHEVY CHASE
CADDYSHACK .... RODNEY DANGERFIELD
CADDYSHACK .... TED KNIGHT†
CADDYSHACK II .... BRIAN McNAMARA
CADDYSHACK II .... CHEVY CHASE
CADDYSHACK II .... DAN AYKROYD
CADDYSHACK II .... DINA MERRILL
CADDYSHACK II .... DYAN CANNON
CADDYSHACK II .... JACKIE MASON
CADDYSHACK II .... JONATHAN SILVERMAN
CADDYSHACK II .... MARSHA WARFIELD
CADDYSHACK II .... PAUL BARTEL
CADDYSHACK II .... RANDY QUAID
CADDYSHACK II .... ROBERT STACK
CADENCE .... CHARLIE SHEEN
CADENCE .... LAURENCE FISHBURNE
CADENCE .... MARTIN SHEEN
CADENCE .... MICHAEL BEACH
CADENCE .... RAMON ESTEVEZ
CADILLAC MAN .... ANNABELLA SCIORRA
CADILLAC MAN .... ELAINE STRITCH
CADILLAC MAN .... FRAN DRESCHER
CADILLAC MAN .... LORI PETTY
CADILLAC MAN .... PAMELA REED
CADILLAC MAN .... ROBIN WILLIAMS
CADILLAC MAN .... TIM ROBBINS
CAESAR AND CLEOPATRA .... JEAN SIMMONS
CAFE MASCOT .... GERALDINE FITZGERALD
CAGE .... AL LEONG
CAGE .... AL RUSCIO
CAGE .... JAMES SHIGETA
CAGE .... LOU FERRIGNO
CAGE .... MARILYN TOKUDA
CAGE .... MICHAEL DANTE
CAGE .... MIKE MOROFF
CAGE .... REB BROWN
CAGE OF GOLD .... JEAN SIMMONS

CAGE WITHOUT A KEY (TF) .... SAM BOTTOMS
CAGE WITHOUT A KEY (TF) .... SUSAN DEY
CAGED ★ .... ELEANOR PARKER
CAGED O .... HOPE EMERSON†
CAGNEY & LACEY (TF) .... LORETTA SWIT
CAGNEY & LACEY (TF) .... TYNE DALY
CAGNEY & LACEY:
    THE RETURN (TF) ....DAVID PAYMER
CAGNEY & LACEY:
    THE RETURN (TF) .... JOHN KARLEN
CAGNEY & LACEY:
    THE RETURN (TF) .... SHARON GLESS
CAGNEY & LACEY:
    THE RETURN (TF) .... TYNE DALY
CAGNEY & LACEY:
    TOGETHER AGAIN (TF) .... DAVID PAYMER
CAGNEY & LACEY:
    TOGETHER AGAIN (TF) .... JOHN KARLEN
CAGNEY & LACEY:
    TOGETHER AGAIN (TF) .... SHARON GLESS
CAGNEY & LACEY:
    TOGETHER AGAIN (TF) .... TYNE DALY
CAHILL, U.S MARSHAL .... HARRY CAREY JR.
CAHILL, U.S. MARSHALL .... GEORGE KENNEDY
CAHILL, U.S. MARSHALL .... ROYAL DANO
CAINE MUTINY COURT
    MARTIAL, THE (TF) .... BRAD DAVIS†
CAINE MUTINY COURT
    MARTIAL, THE (TF) .... ERIC BOGOSIAN
CAINE MUTINY COURT
    MARTIAL, THE (TF) .... JEFF DANIELS
CAINE MUTINY COURT
    MARTIAL, THE (TF) .... PETER GALLAGHER
CAINE MUTINY, THE .... CLAUDE AKINS†
CAINE MUTINY, THE .... E. G. MARSHALL
CAINE MUTINY, THE .... JOSE FERRER†
CAINE MUTINY, THE .... VAN JOHNSON
CAINE MUTINY, THE ★ .... HUMPHREY BOGART†
CAINE MUTINY, THE O .... TOM TULLY†
CAL .... HELEN MIRREN
CALAMITY JANE .... DORIS DAY
CALAMITY JANE .... HOWARD KEEL
CALAMITY JANE AND
    SAM BASS .... LLOYD BRIDGES
CALAMITY JANE AND
    SAM BASS .... NORMAN LLOYD
CALAMITY JANE AND
    SAM BASS .... YVONNE DE CARLO
CALAMITY JANE (TF) .... FREDERIC FORREST
CALAMITY JANE (TF) .... JANE ALEXANDER
CALENDAR GIRL .... GABRIEL OLDS
CALENDAR GIRL .... JASON PRIESTLEY
CALENDAR GIRL .... JERRY O'CONNELL
CALENDAR GIRL .... JOE PANTOLIANO
CALIFORNIA .... ANTHONY QUINN
CALIFORNIA .... BARBARA STANWYCK†
CALIFORNIA .... RAY MILLAND†
CALIFORNIA CONQUEST .... TERESA WRIGHT
CALIFORNIA DREAMING ..... DENNIS CHRISTOPHER
CALIFORNIA DREAMING .... GLYNNIS O'CONNOR
CALIFORNIA DREAMING .... SEYMOUR CASSEL
CALIFORNIA GIRLS (TF) .... ROBBY BENSON
CALIFORNIA GIRLS (TF) .... TAWNY KITAEN
CALIFORNIA KID, THE (TF) .... MARTIN SHEEN
CALIFORNIA KID, THE (TF) .... NICK NOLTE
CALIFORNIA SPLIT .... BERT REMSEN
CALIFORNIA SPLIT .... ELLIOTT GOULD
CALIFORNIA SPLIT .... GEORGE SEGAL
CALIFORNIA SPLIT .... GWEN WELLES
CALIFORNIA SPLIT .... JEFF GOLDBLUM
CALIFORNIA SUITE .... ALAN ALDA
CALIFORNIA SUITE .... BILL COSBY
CALIFORNIA SUITE .... ELAINE MAY
CALIFORNIA SUITE .... GLORIA GIFFORD
CALIFORNIA SUITE .... HERB EDELMAN
CALIFORNIA SUITE .... JAMES COBURN
CALIFORNIA SUITE .... JANE FONDA
CALIFORNIA SUITE .... MICHAEL CAINE
CALIFORNIA SUITE .... RICHARD PRYOR
CALIFORNIA SUITE .... WALTER MATTHAU
CALIFORNIA SUITE OO .... MAGGIE SMITH
CALIGOLA .... JOHN GIELGUD
CALIGOLA .... PETER O'TOOLE

CALIGULA .... HELEN MIRREN
CALIGULA .... JOHN GIELGUD
CALIGULA .... MALCOLM McDOWELL
CALIGULA .... PETER O'TOOLE
CALL HER MOM (TF) .... CYD CHARISSE
CALL HIM MR. SHATTER .... STUART WHITMAN
CALL IT A DAY .... OLIVIA DE HAVILLAND
CALL ME .... PATRICIA CHARBONNEAU
CALL ME .... PATTI D'ARBANVILLE
CALL ME .... STEVE BUSCEMI
CALL ME BWANA .... BOB HOPE
CALL ME BWANA .... EDIE ADAMS
CALL ME MISTER .... DANNY THOMAS†
CALL NORTHSIDE 777 .... E. G. MARSHALL
CALL NORTHSIDE 777 .... JAMES STEWART
CALL NORTHSIDE 777 .... LIONEL STANDER
CALL OF THE WILD .... CHARLTON HESTON
CALL OF THE WILD, THE (TF) .... JOHN BECK
CALL TO DANGER, A (TF) .... CLU GULAGER
CALL TO DANGER (TF) .... PETER GRAVES
CALL TO GLORY (TF) .... CRAIG T. NELSON
CALL TO GLORY: JFK (TF) .... CRAIG T. NELSON
CALLAN .... EDWARD WOODWARD
CALLAN .... PETER EGAN
CALLAWAY WENT
    THATAWAY .... ELIZABETH TAYLOR
CALLAWAY WENT THATAWAY .... HOWARD KEEL
CALLE MAYOR .... LILA KEDROVA
CALLIE AND SON (TF) .... LINDSAY WAGNER
CALLING DR. GILLESPIE .... AVA GARDNER†
CALLING DR. KILDARE .... LANA TURNER
CALLING NORTHSIDE 777 .... LIONEL STANDER
CALYPSO HEAT WAVE .... JOEL GREY
CALYPSO JOE .... ANGIE DICKINSON
CAMELOT .... DAVID HEMMINGS
CAMELOT .... FRANCO NERO
CAMELOT .... RICHARD HARRIS
CAMELOT .... VANESSA REDGRAVE
CAMILA .... HECTOR ALTERIO
CAMILLA .... BRIDGET FONDA
CAMILLA .... JESSICA TANDY†
CAMILLE ★ .... GRETA GARBO†
CAMILLE (TF) .... BEN KINGSLEY
CAMILLE (TF) .... BILLIE WHITELAW
CAMILLE (TF) .... COLIN FIRTH
CAMILLE (TF) .... DENHOLM ELLIOTT†
CAMILLE (TF) .... GRETA SCACCHI
CAMILLE (TF) .... JOHN GIELGUD
CAMILLE CLAUDEL .... GERARD DEPARDIEU
CAMILLE CLAUDEL .... KATRINE BOORMAN
CAMILLE CLAUDEL .... LAURENT GREVILL
CAMILLE CLAUDEL .... MADELEINE ROBINSON
CAMILLE CLAUDEL ★ .... ISABELLE ADJANI
CAMORRA .... ANGELA MOLINA
CAMORRA .... DANIEL EZRALOW
CAMORRA .... FRANCISCO RABAL
CAMORRA .... HARVEY KEITEL
CAMORRA .... ISA DANIELI
CAMORRA .... PAOLO BONACELLI
CAMORRA .... VITTORIO SQUILLANTI
CAMPUS MAN .... MILES O'KEEFFE
CAMPUS MAN .... MORGAN FAIRCHILD
CAN ELLEN BE SAVED? (TF) .... JOHN SAXON
CAN ELLEN BE SAVED? (TF) .... KATHLEEN QUINLAN
CAN ELLEN BE SAVED? (TF) .... LESLIE NIELSEN
CAN ELLEN BE SAVED? (TF) ...... LOUISE FLETCHER
CAN ELLEN BE SAVED? (TF) .... RUTANYA ALDA
CAN HIERONYMOUS MERKIN EVER
    FORGET MERCY HUMPPE AND
    FIND TRUE HAPPINESS? ... JOAN COLLINS
CAN HIERONYMOUS MERKIN EVER
    FORGET MERCY HUMPPE AND
    FIND TRUE HAPPINESS? .... MILTON BERLE
CAN I DO IT...TIL I
    NEED GLASSES? .... ROBIN WILLIAMS
CAN SHE BAKE A CHERRY PIE? .... KAREN BLACK
CAN SHE BAKE A CHERRY PIE? .... MICHAEL EMIL
CAN YOU FEEL ME
    DANCING? (TF) .... JASON BATEMAN
CAN YOU FEEL ME
    DANCING? (TF) .... JUSTINE BATEMAN
CAN-CAN .... FRANK SINATRA
CAN-CAN .... LOUIS JOURDAN

CAN-CAN .... SHIRLEY MacLAINE
CANAAN'S WAY (CTF) .... ARMAND ASSANTE
CANADIAN BACON .... JOHN CANDY†
CANADIAN CONSPIRACY .... JOHN CANDY†
CANADIAN PACIFIC .... JANE WYATT
CANADIANS, THE .... JOHN DEHNER†
CANCEL MY RESERVATION .... ANNE ARCHER
CANCEL MY RESERVATION .... BOB HOPE
CANCEL MY RESERVATION .... EVA MARIE SAINT
CANCEL MY RESERVATION .... RALPH BELLAMY†
CANDIDATE, THE .... ALLEN GARFIELD
CANDIDATE, THE .... MICHAEL LERNER
CANDIDATE, THE .... PETER BOYLE
CANDIDATE, THE .... ROBERT REDFORD
CANDIDATE, THE .... TONY BECKLEY†
CANDIDATE FOR MURDER .... MICHAEL GOUGH
CANDLES AT NINE .... PATRICIA HAYES
CANDLESHOE .... HELEN HAYES
CANDLESHOE .... JODIE FOSTER
CANDY .... JAMES COBURN
CANDY .... JOHN ASTIN
CANDY .... MARLON BRANDO
CANDY .... RINGO STARR
CANDY .... WALTER MATTHAU
CANDY STRIPE NURSES .... SALLY KIRKLAND
CANDYMAN 2: FAREWELL
    TO THE FLESH .... BILL NUNN
CANDYMAN 2: FAREWELL
    TO THE FLESH .... FAY HAUSER
CANDYMAN 2: FAREWELL
    TO THE FLESH .... KELLY ROWAN
CANDYMAN 2: FAREWELL
    TO THE FLESH .... TIMOTHY CARHART
CANDYMAN 2: FAREWELL
    TO THE FLESH .... TONY TODD
CANDYMAN 2: FAREWELL
    TO THE FLESH .... VERONICA CARTWRIGHT
CANDYMAN 2: FAREWELL
    TO THE FLESH .... WILLIAM O'LEARY
CANNERY ROW .... AUDRA LINDLEY
CANNERY ROW .... DEBRA WINGER
CANNERY ROW .... FRANK McRAE
CANNERY ROW .... JAMES KEANE
CANNERY ROW .... JOHN HUSTON†
CANNERY ROW .... JOHN MALLOY
CANNERY ROW .... M. EMMET WALSH
CANNERY ROW .... NICK NOLTE
CANNERY ROW .... ROSANA DE SOTO
CANNERY ROW .... SANTOS MORALES
CANNERY ROW .... SUNSHINE PARKER
CANNERY ROW .... TOM MAHONEY
CANNIBALS, THE .... BRITT EKLAND
CANNON FOR CORDOBA .... GEORGE PEPPARD†
CANNONBALL .... BILL McKINNEY
CANNONBALL .... DAVID CARRADINE
CANNONBALL .... DICK MILLER
CANNONBALL .... JAMES KEACH
CANNONBALL .... PAUL BARTEL
CANNONBALL .... ROBERT CARRADINE
CANNONBALL .... SYLVESTER STALLONE
CANNONBALL .... VERONICA HAMEL
CANNONBALL RUN, THE .... BERT CONVY†
CANNONBALL RUN, THE .... BIANCA JAGGER
CANNONBALL RUN, THE .... BURT REYNOLDS
CANNONBALL RUN, THE .... DEAN MARTIN
CANNONBALL RUN, THE .... DOM DeLUISE
CANNONBALL RUN, THE .... FARRAH FAWCETT
CANNONBALL RUN, THE .... JACKIE CHAN
CANNONBALL RUN, THE .... JAMIE FARR
CANNONBALL
    RUN, THE .... JIMMY "THE GREEK" SNYDER
CANNONBALL RUN, THE .... JOHN FIELDLER
CANNONBALL RUN, THE .... MEL TILLIS
CANNONBALL RUN, THE .... PETER FONDA
CANNONBALL RUN, THE .... ROGER MOORE
CANNONBALL RUN, THE .... SAMMY DAVIS JR.†
CANNONBALL RUN, THE .... TERRY BRADSHAW
CANNONBALL RUN II .... BURT REYNOLDS
CANNONBALL RUN II .... CATHERINE BACH
CANNONBALL RUN II ...... CHARLES NELSON REILLY
CANNONBALL RUN II .... DEAN MARTIN
CANNONBALL RUN II .... DOM DeLUISE

This is not a list of every film ever made or every cast member, only those listed in this directory.

CANNONBALL RUN II	DOUG McCLURE
CANNONBALL RUN II	FRANK SINATRA
CANNONBALL RUN II	JAMIE FARR
CANNONBALL RUN II	JIM NABORS
CANNONBALL RUN II	MARILU HENNER
CANNONBALL RUN II	RICARDO MONTALBAN
CANNONBALL RUN II	SAMMY DAVIS JR.†
CANNONBALL RUN II	SHIRLEY MacLAINE
CANNONBALL RUN II	SID CAESAR
CANNONBALL RUN II	SUSAN ANTON
CANNONBALL RUN II	TELLY SAVALAS†
CANYON PASSAGE	LLOYD BRIDGES
CAN'T BUY ME LOVE	PATRICK DEMPSEY
CAN'T STOP THE MUSIC	BRUCE JENNER
CAN'T STOP THE MUSIC	JACK WESTON
CAN'T STOP THE MUSIC	LEIGH TAYLOR-YOUNG
CAN'T STOP THE MUSIC	PAUL SAND
CAN'T STOP THE MUSIC	STEVE GUTTENBERG
CAN'T STOP THE MUSIC	TAMMY GRIMES
CAN'T STOP THE MUSIC	VALERIE PERRINE
CAPE FEAR ★	ROBERT DE NIRO
CAPE FEAR ⊙	JULIETTE LEWIS
CAPE FEAR	FRED DALTON THOMPSON
CAPE FEAR	GREGORY PECK
CAPE FEAR	JACK KRUSCHEN
CAPE FEAR	JESSICA LANGE
CAPE FEAR	JOE DON BAKER
CAPE FEAR	MARTIN BALSAM
CAPE FEAR	NICK NOLTE
CAPE FEAR	ROBERT MITCHUM
CAPE FEAR (1962)	MARTIN BALSAM
CAPE FEAR (1962)	ROBERT MITCHUM
CAPE FEAR (1962)	TELLY SAVALAS†
CAPE FEAR (1962)	POLLY BERGEN
CAPE FEAR (1962)	GREGORY PECK
CAPETOWN AFFAIR	JACQUELINE BISSET
CAPITAL NEWS (TF)	CHRISTIAN CLEMENSON
CAPITAL NEWS (TF)	KURT FULLER
CAPITAL NEWS (TF)	LLOYD BRIDGES
CAPITAL NEWS (TF)	MARK BLUM
CAPONE	BEN GAZZARA
CAPONE	HARRY GUARDINO
CAPONE	ROYAL DANO
CAPONE	SUSAN BLAKELY
CAPONE	SYLVESTER STALLONE
CAPONE	TONY CURTIS
CAPRICE	DORIS DAY
CAPRICE	IRENE TSU
CAPRICE	JACK KRUSCHEN
CAPRICE	MICHAEL J. POLLARD
CAPRICE	RAY WALSTON
CAPRICE	RICHARD HARRIS
CAPRICORN ONE	BRENDA VACCARO
CAPRICORN ONE	DAVID HUDDLESTON
CAPRICORN ONE	ELLIOTT GOULD
CAPRICORN ONE	HAL HOLBROOK
CAPRICORN ONE	JAMES BROLIN
CAPRICORN ONE	KAREN BLACK
CAPRICORN ONE	O. J. SIMPSON
CAPRICORN ONE	SAM WATERSTON
CAPRICORN ONE	TELLY SAVALAS†
CAPTAIN APACHE	CARROLL BAKER
CAPTAIN APACHE	STUART WHITMAN
CAPTAIN AVENGER	KEVIN McCARTHY
CAPTAIN BLOOD	OLIVIA DE HAVILLAND
CAPTAIN CAREY, USA	RUSS TAMBLYN
CAPTAIN EDDIE	JOHN DEHNER†
CAPTAIN EO	ANJELICA HUSTON
CAPTAIN EO	MICHAEL JACKSON
CAPTAIN HORATIO HORNBLOWER	GREGORY PECK
CAPTAIN LIGHTFOOT	ROCK HUDSON†
CAPTAIN MACKLIN	LILLIAN GISH†
CAPTAIN NEMO AND THE UNDERWATER CITY	CHUCK CONNORS†
CAPTAIN NEWMAN, M.D.	ANGIE DICKINSON
CAPTAIN NEWMAN, M.D.	EDDIE ALBERT
CAPTAIN NEWMAN, M.D.	GREGORY PECK
CAPTAIN NEWMAN, M.D.	ROBERT DUVALL
CAPTAIN NEWMAN, M.D.	TONY CURTIS
CAPTAIN NEWMAN, M.D. ⊙	BOBBY DARIN†
CAPTAIN RON	KURT RUSSELL
CAPTAIN RON	MARTIN SHORT
CAPTAIN RON	MARY KAY PLACE
CAPTAINS AND THE KINGS (MS)	ANN SOTHERN
CAPTAINS AND THE KINGS (MS)	CELESTE HOLM
CAPTAINS AND THE KINGS (MS)	CHARLES DURNING
CAPTAINS AND THE KINGS (MS)	JANE SEYMOUR
CAPTAINS AND THE KINGS (MS)	PERRY KING
CAPTAINS AND THE KINGS (MS)	PATTY DUKE
CAPTAINS AND THE KINGS (MS)	RICHARD JORDAN†
CAPTAINS COURAGEOUS	MICKEY ROONEY
CAPTAINS COURAGEOUS ★★	SPENCER TRACY†
CAPTAINS COURAGEOUS (TF)	FRED GWYNNE†
CAPTAINS COURAGEOUS (TF)	KARL MALDEN
CAPTAIN'S PARADISE, THE	ALEC GUINNESS
CAPTAIN'S PARADISE, THE	YVONNE DE CARLO
CAPTIVE CITY, THE	JOHN FORSYTHE
CAPTIVE GIRL	JOHN DEHNER†
CAPTIVE HEART, THE	GORDAN JACKSON†
CAPTIVE HEARTS	MICHAEL SARRAZIN
CAPTIVE HEARTS	NORIYUKI "PAT" MORITA
CAPTURE, THE	TERESA WRIGHT
CAR, THE	JAMES BROLIN
CAR, THE	R.G. ARMSTRONG
CAR, THE	RONNY COX
CAR 54, WHERE ARE YOU?	AL LEWIS
CAR 54, WHERE ARE YOU?	DANIEL BALDWIN
CAR 54, WHERE ARE YOU?	DAVID JOHANSEN
CAR 54, WHERE ARE YOU?	FRAN DRESCHER
CAR 54, WHERE ARE YOU?	JOHN C. McGINLEY
CAR 54, WHERE ARE YOU?	NIPSEY RUSSELL
CAR 54, WHERE ARE YOU?	ROSIE O'DONNELL
CAR TROUBLE	JULIE WALTERS
CAR WASH	ANTONIO FARGAS
CAR WASH	FRANKLYN AJAYE
CAR WASH	MELANIE MAYRON
CAR WASH	RICHARD PRYOR
CARAVAGGIO	DEXTER FLETCHER
CARAVAGGIO	GARRY COOPER
CARAVAGGIO	MICHAEL GOUGH
CARAVAGGIO	NIGEL DAVENPORT
CARAVAGGIO	NIGEL TERRY
CARAVAGGIO	ROBBIE COLTRANE
CARAVAGGIO	SEAN BEAN
CARAVAGGIO	SPENCER LEIGH
CARAVAGGIO	TILDA SWINTON
CARAVAN TO VACCARES	CHARLOTTE RAMPLING
CARAVAN TO VACCARES	MICHAEL BRYANT
CARAVANS	ANTHONY QUINN
CARAVANS	JENNIFER O'NEILL
CARAVANS	JEREMY KEMP
CARAVANS	MICHAEL SARRAZIN
CARBINE WILLIAMS	JAMES ARNESS
CARBINE WILLIAMS	JAMES STEWART
CARBON COPY	DENZEL WASHINGTON
CARBON COPY	GEORGE SEGAL
CARBON COPY	SUSAN SAINT JAMES
CARD, THE	ALEC GUINNESS
CARDIAC ARREST	FRED WARD
CARDINAL, THE	BURGESS MEREDITH
CARDINAL, THE	CAROL LYNLEY
CARDINAL, THE	JOHN SAXON
CARDINAL, THE	OSSIE DAVIS
CARDINAL, THE	PATRICK O'NEAL†
CARDINAL, THE	RAF VALLONE
CARDINAL, THE ⊙	JOHN HUSTON†
CARDINAL RICHELIEU	MAUREEN O'SULLIVAN
CARE BEARS MOVIE II: A NEW GENERATION, THE (AF)	HADLEY KAY
CARE BEARS MOVIE II: A NEW GENERATION, THE (AF)	MAXINE MILLER
CARE BEARS MOVIE II: A NEW GENERATION, THE (AF)	PAM HYATT
CAREER	ANTHONY (TONY) FRANCIOSA
CAREER	DEAN MARTIN
CAREER	SHIRLEY MacLAINE
CAREER OPPORTUNITES	KIERNAN MULRONEY
CAREER OPPORTUNITES	WILLIAM FORSYTHE
CAREER OPPORTUNITIES	DERMOT MULRONEY
CAREER OPPORTUNITIES	FRANK WHALEY
CAREER OPPORTUNITIES	JENNIFER CONNELLY
CAREFREE	RALPH BELLAMY†
CARELESS YEARS, THE	DEAN STOCKWELL
CARETAKER, THE	ALAN BATES
CARETAKER, THE	DONALD PLEASENCE
CARETAKERS, THE	JOAN CRAWFORD†
CARETAKERS, THE	ROBERT STACK
CARETAKERS, THE	ROBERT VAUGHN
CAREY TREATMENT, THE	DAN O'HERLIHY
CAREY TREATMENT, THE	JAMES COBURN
CAREY TREATMENT, THE	JENNIFER O'NEILL
CAREY TREATMENT, THE	PAT HINGLE
CARGO TO CAPETOWN	JOHN IRELAND
CARIBBEAN MYSTERY, A (TF)	HELEN HAYES
CARLITO'S WAY	AL PACINO
CARLITO'S WAY	JOHN LEGUIZAMO
CARLITO'S WAY	PAUL MAZURSKY
CARLITO'S WAY	PENELOPE ANN MILLER
CARLITO'S WAY	SEAN PENN
CARLTON BROWNE OF THE FO	THORLEY WALTERS†
CARLTON BROWNE OF THE F.O.	IAN BANNEN
CARLY'S WEB (TF)	DAPHNE ASHBROOK
CARMEN	JULIA MIGENES
CARMEN JONES	BROCK PETERS
CARMEN JONES	DIAHANN CARROLL
CARMEN JONES ★	DOROTHY DANDRIDGE†
CARNABY M.D.	SHIRLEY ANNE FIELD
CARNAL KNOWLEDGE	ART GARFUNKEL
CARNAL KNOWLEDGE	CANDICE BERGEN
CARNAL KNOWLEDGE	CAROL KANE
CARNAL KNOWLEDGE	JACK NICHOLSON
CARNAL KNOWLEDGE	RITA MORENO
CARNAL KNOWLEDGE ⊙	ANN-MARGRET
CARNEGIE HALL	WILLIAM PRINCE
CARNEY	BILL McKINNEY
CARNIVAL IN COSTA RICA	CELESTE HOLM
CARNOSAUR	CLINT HOWARD
CARNOSAUR	DIANE LADD
CARNOSAUR	HARRISON PAGE
CARNOSAUR	JENNIFER RUNYON
CARNOSAUR	NED BELLAMY
CARNOSAUR	RAPHAEL SBARGE
CARNY	FRED WARD
CARNY	GARY BUSEY
CARNY	JODIE FOSTER
CARNY	KENNETH McMILLAN†
CARNY	MEG FOSTER
CARNY	ROBBIE ROBERTSON
CAROLINE? (TF)	GEORGE GRIZZARD
CAROLINE? (TF)	PATRICIA NEAL
CAROLINE? (TF)	STEPHANIE ZIMBALIST
CAROSELLO NAPOLITANO	SOPHIA LOREN
CAROUSEL	BARBARA RUICK†
CAROUSEL	GORDON MacRAE†
CAROUSEL	JOHN DEHNER†
CAROUSEL	ROBERT ROUNSEVILLE†
CAROUSEL	SHIRLEY JONES
CARPETBAGGERS, THE	CARROLL BAKER
CARPETBAGGERS, THE	ELIZABETH ASHLEY
CARPETBAGGERS, THE	GEORGE PEPPARD†
CARPETBAGGERS, THE	MARTIN BALSAM
CARRIE	AMY IRVING
CARRIE	BETTY BUCKLEY
CARRIE	EDDIE ALBERT
CARRIE	JENNIFER JONES
CARRIE	JOHN TRAVOLTA
CARRIE	NANCY ALLEN
CARRIE	P. J. SOLES
CARRIE	PRISCILLA POINTER
CARRIE	WILLIAM KATT
CARRIE ★	SISSY SPACEK
CARRIE ⊙	PIPER LAURIE
CARRINGTON	EMMA THOMPSON
CARRINGTON	JONATHAN PRYCE
CARRINGTON	RUFUS SEWELL
CARRINGTON	STEVEN WADDINGTON
CARRINGTON V.C.	DAVID NIVEN†
CARRY ON ADMIRAL	DAVID TOMLINSON
CARRY ON CABBY	MILO O'SHEA
CARRY ON NURSE	JILL IRELAND†
CARS THAT ATE PARIS, THE	JOHN MEILLON

† after an actor's name denotes deceased.

CARS THAT EAT PEOPLE, THE	JOHN MEILLON
CARTER'S ARMY (TF)	MOSES GUNN
CARTIER AFFAIR, THE (TF)	DAVID HASSELHOFF
CARTIER AFFAIR, THE (TF)	ED LAUTER
CARTIER AFFAIR, THE (TF)	JOAN COLLINS
CARTIER AFFAIR, THE (TF)	TELLY SAVALAS†
CARVE HER NAME WITH PRIDE	PAUL SCOFIELD
CASA RICORDI	MARCELLO MASTROIANNI
CASABLANCA	INGRID BERGMAN†
CASABLANCA ★	HUMPHREY BOGART†
CASABLANCA ✪	CLAUDE RAINS†
CASANOVA	DONALD SUTHERLAND
CASANOVA '70	MARCELLO MASTROIANNI
CASANOVA BROWN	TERESA WRIGHT
CASANOVA & CO.	BRITT EKLAND
CASANOVA & CO.	TONY CURTIS
CASANOVA E COMPAGNI	URSULA ANDRESS
CASANOVA (TF)	FAYE DUNAWAY
CASANOVA (TF)	HANNA SCHYGULLA
CASANOVA (TF)	ORNELLA MUTI
CASANOVA (TF)	RICHARD CHAMBERLAIN
CASANOVA (TF)	SYLVIA KRISTEL
CASANOVA'S BIG NIGHT	BOB HOPE
CASANOVA'S BIG NIGHT	RAYMOND BURR†
CASANOVA'S BIG NIGHT	VINCENT PRICE†
CASBAH	YVONNE DE CARLO
CASE AGAINST BROOKLYN, THE	DARREN McGAVIN
CASE CLOSED (TF)	CHARLES DURNING
CASE OF RAPE, A (TF)	ELIZABETH MONTGOMERY
CASE OF RAPE, A (TF)	TOM SELLECK
CASE OF THE HILLSIDE STRANGLER, THE (TF)	BILLY ZANE
CASE OF THE HILLSIDE STRANGLER, THE (TF)	DENNIS FARINA
CASE OF THE HILLSIDE STRANGLERS, THE (TF)	RICHARD CRENNA
CASEY'S SHADOW	ALEXIS SMITH†
CASEY'S SHADOW	ROBERT WEBBER
CASEY'S SHADOW	WALTER MATTHAU
CASH McCALL	HENRY JONES
CASH McCALL	JAMES GARNER
CASH McCALL	NINA FOCH
CASH ON DELIVERY	SHELLEY WINTERS
CASINO	JAMES WOODS
CASINO	JOE PESCI
CASINO	KEVIN POLLAK
CASINO	ROBERT DE NIRO
CASINO	SHARON STONE
CASINO	ALAN KING
CASINO	DON RICKLES
CASINO	FRANK VINCENT
CASINO	L. Q. JONES
CASINO ROYALE	CHARLES BOYER†
CASINO ROYALE	DAVID NIVEN†
CASINO ROYALE	DEBORAH KERR
CASINO ROYALE	GEOFFREY BAYLDON
CASINO ROYALE	GEORGE RAFT†
CASINO ROYALE	JACQUELINE BISSET
CASINO ROYALE	JOHN HUSTON†
CASINO ROYALE	ORSON WELLES†
CASINO ROYALE	PETER O'TOOLE
CASINO ROYALE	PETER SELLERS†
CASINO ROYALE	URSULA ANDRESS
CASINO ROYALE	WILLIAM HOLDEN†
CASINO ROYALE	WOODY ALLEN
CASPER	AMY BRENNEMAN
CASPER	BILL PULLMAN
CASPER	BRAD GARRETT
CASPER	CATHY MORIARTY
CASPER	CHRISTINA RICCI
CASPER	ERIC IDLE
CASPER	JOE ALASKEY
CASPER	JOE NIPOTE
CASPER	MALACHAI PEARSON
CASS TIMBERLANE	LANA TURNER
CASSANDRA CROSSING	JOHN PHILLIP LAW
CASSANDRA CROSSING, THE	ANN TURKEL
CASSANDRA CROSSING, THE	AVA GARDNER†
CASSANDRA CROSSING, THE	BURT LANCASTER†
CASSANDRA CROSSING, THE	LEE STRASBERG†
CASSANDRA CROSSING, THE	LIONEL STANDER
CASSANDRA CROSSING, THE	MARTIN SHEEN
CASSANDRA CROSSING, THE	O. J. SIMPSON
CASSANDRA CROSSING, THE	RICHARD HARRIS
CASSANDRA CROSSING, THE	SOPHIA LOREN
CAST A GIANT SHADOW	ANGIE DICKINSON
CAST A GIANT SHADOW	FRANK SINATRA
CAST A GIANT SHADOW	GORDAN JACKSON†
CAST A GIANT SHADOW	JEREMY KEMP
CAST A GIANT SHADOW	KIRK DOUGLAS
CAST A GIANT SHADOW	TOPOL
CAST A LONG SHADOW	JOHN DEHNER†
CAST THE FIRST STONE (TF)	JILL EIKENBERRY
CAST THE FIRST STONE (TF)	JOE SPANO
CASTAWAY	AMANDA DONOHOE
CASTAWAY	OLIVER REED
CASTAWAY COWBOY, THE	JAMES GARNER
CASTAWAY COWBOY, THE	ROBERT CULP
CASTAWAY COWBOY, THE	VERA MILES
CASTILIAN, THE	FRANKIE AVALON
CASTLE IN THE AIR	DAVID TOMLINSON
CASTLE KEEP	BRUCE DERN
CASTLE KEEP	BURT LANCASTER†
CASTLE KEEP	PATRICK O'NEAL†
CASTLE KEEP	PETER FALK
CASTLE KEEP	TONY BILL
CASTLE OF THE LIVING DEAD	DONALD SUTHERLAND
CASTLE ON THE HUDSON	BURGESS MEREDITH
CASTLE, THE	MAXIMILIAN SCHELL
CASUAL SEX?	ANDREW DICE CLAY
CASUAL SEX?	DALE MIDKIFF
CASUAL SEX?	LEA THOMPSON
CASUAL SEX?	MARY GROSS
CASUAL SEX?	VICTORIA JACKSON
CASUALTIES OF WAR	DON HARVEY
CASUALTIES OF WAR	ERIK KING
CASUALTIES OF WAR	JOHN C. REILLY
CASUALTIES OF WAR	JOHN LEGUIZAMO
CASUALTIES OF WAR	MICHAEL J. FOX
CASUALTIES OF WAR	SAM ROBARDS
CASUALTIES OF WAR	SEAN PENN
CASUALTIES OF WAR	THUY THU LE
CASUALTY OF WAR, A (CTF)	ALAN HOWARD
CASUALTY OF WAR, A (CTF)	BILL BAILEY
CASUALTY OF WAR, A (CTF)	SHELLEY HACK
CAT AND MOUSE	JEAN-PIERRE AUMONT
CAT AND THE CANARY, THE	BOB HOPE
CAT AND THE CANARY, THE	CAROL LYNLEY
CAT AND THE CANARY, THE	WENDY HILLER
CAT BALLOU	JANE FONDA
CAT BALLOU	STUBBY KAYE
CAT BALLOU ★★	LEE MARVIN†
CAT CREATURE, THE (TF)	DAVID HEDISON
CAT CREATURE, THE (TF)	MEREDITH BAXTER
CAT FROM OUTER SPACE, THE	ALAN YOUNG
CAT FROM OUTER SPACE, THE	HARRY MORGAN
CAT FROM OUTER SPACE, THE	RODDY McDOWALL
CAT FROM OUTER SPACE, THE	SANDY DUNCAN
CAT GANG, THE	FRANCESCA ANNIS
CAT O' NINE TAILS, THE	KARL MALDEN
CAT O'NINE TAILS, THE	JAMES FRANCISCUS†
CAT ON A HOT TIN ROOF	BURL IVES
CAT ON A HOT TIN ROOF	DAME JUDITH ANDERSON†
CAT ON A HOT TIN ROOF ★	ELIZABETH TAYLOR
CAT ON A HOT TIN ROOF ★	PAUL NEWMAN
CAT PEOPLE	ALAN NAPIER†
CAT PEOPLE	ANNETTE O'TOOLE
CAT PEOPLE	JOHN HEARD
CAT PEOPLE	MALCOLM McDOWELL
CAT PEOPLE	NASTASSJA KINSKI
CAT PEOPLE	RUBY DEE
CATAMOUNT KILLING, THE	POLLY HOLLIDAY
CATAMOUNT KILLINGS, THE	ANN WEDGEWORTH
CATCH ME A SPY	KIRK DOUGLAS
CATCH ME A SPY	TOM COURTENAY
CATCH MY SOUL	SEASON HUBLEY
CATCH MY SOUL	SUSAN TYRRELL
CATCH THE HEAT	ROD STEIGER
CATCH-22	ALAN ALDA
CATCH-22	ALAN ARKIN
CATCH-22	ANTHONY PERKINS†
CATCH-22	ART GARFUNKEL
CATCH-22	BOB NEWHART
CATCH-22	BUCK HENRY
CATCH-22	CHARLES GRODIN
CATCH-22	JON VOIGHT
CATCH-22	MARTIN BALSAM
CATCH-22	MARTIN SHEEN
CATCH-22	PAULA PRENTISS
CATCH-22	RICHARD BENJAMIN
CATCHFIRE	CHARLIE SHEEN
CATCHFIRE	DEAN STOCKWELL
CATCHFIRE	DENNIS HOPPER
CATCHFIRE	FRED WARD
CATCHFIRE	JODIE FOSTER
CATCHFIRE	JOE PESCI
CATCHFIRE	JOHN TURTURRO
CATERED AFFAIR, THE	BETTE DAVIS†
CATERED AFFAIR, THE	DEBBIE REYNOLDS
CATERED AFFAIR, THE	ERNEST BORGNINE
CATHERINE & CO.	JEAN-PIERRE AUMONT
CATHOLICS (TF)	MARTIN SHEEN
CATHY TIPPEL/ KATIE'S PASSION	RUTGER HAUER
CATLOW	JEFF COREY
CATLOW	LEONARD NIMOY
CATLOW	RICHARD CRENNA
CATS DON'T DANCE (AF)	ASHLEY PELDON
CATS DON'T DANCE (AF)	DON KNOTTS
CATS DON'T DANCE (AF)	DON KNOTTS
CATS DON'T DANCE (AF)	ED ASNER
CATS DON'T DANCE (AF)	HAL HOLBROOK
CATS DON'T DANCE (AF)	JOHN RHYS-DAVIES
CATS DON'T DANCE (AF)	KATHY NAJIMY
CATS DON'T DANCE (AF)	NATALIE COLE
CATS DON'T DANCE (AF)	SCOTT BAKULA
CATTLE ANNIE AND LITTLE BRITCHES	BURT LANCASTER†
CATTLE ANNIE AND LITTLE BRITCHES	JOHN SAVAGE
CATTLE ANNIE AND LITTLE BRITCHES	ROD STEIGER
CATTLE DRIVE	DEAN STOCKWELL
CATTLE KING	JOAN CAULFIELD†
CATTLE KING	ROBERT LOGGIA
CATTLE QUEEN OF MONTANA	BARBARA STANWYCK†
CATTLE QUEEN OF MONTANA	RONALD REAGAN
CATTLE STATION	VICTORIA SHAW†
CAT'S EYE	ALAN KING
CAT'S EYE	DREW BARRYMORE
CAT'S EYE	JAMES WOODS
CAT'S EYE	ROBERT HAYS
CAUGHT IN THE DRAFT	BOB HOPE
CAUGHT IN THE DRAFT	DOROTHY LAMOUR
CAVALCADE ★	DIANA WYNARD†
CAVEMAN	BARBARA BACH
CAVEMAN	DENNIS QUAID
CAVERN, THE	JOHN SAXON
CAXAMBU	JOHN IRELAND
CB4	ALLEN PAYNE
CB4	CHRIS ELLIOTT
CB4	CHRIS ROCK
CB4	PHIL HARTMAN
CEASE FIRE	LISA BLOUNT
CELEBRATION FAMILY (TF)	DIANE LADD
CELEBRATION FAMILY (TF)	ED BEGLEY JR.
CELEBRATION FAMILY (TF)	JAMES READ
CELEBRATION FAMILY (TF)	STEPHANIE ZIMBALIST
CELL 2455 DEATH ROW	VINCE EDWARDS
CELLAR DWELLAR	DEBORAH MULLOWNEY
CELLAR DWELLAR	JEFFREY COMBS
CELLAR DWELLAR	PAMELA BELLWOOD-WHEELER
CELLAR DWELLAR	VINCE EDWARDS
CELLAR DWELLAR	YVONNE DE CARLO
CELLO	ALAN RICKMAN
CELLO	JULIET RICHARDSON

420

This is not a list of every film ever made or every cast member, only those listed in this directory.

CEMENT
  GARDEN, THE .... CHARLOTTE GAINSBOURG
CEMETERY CLUB, THE .... CHRISTINA RICCI
CEMETERY CLUB, THE .... DANNY AIELLO
CEMETERY CLUB, THE .... DIANE LADD
CEMETERY CLUB, THE .... ELLEN BURSTYN
CEMETERY CLUB, THE .... LAINIE KAZAN
CEMETERY CLUB, THE .... OLYMPIA DUKAKIS
CENTENNIAL (MS) .... ALEXIS KARRAS
CENTENNIAL (MS) .... ANDY GRIFFITH
CENTENNIAL (MS) .... DENNIS WEAVER
CENTENNIAL (MS) .... GREGORY HARRISON
CENTENNIAL (MS) .... LOIS NETTLETON
CENTENNIAL (MS) .... MARK HARMON
CENTENNIAL (MS) .... RICHARD CHAMBERLAIN
CENTENNIAL (MS) .... ROBERT CONRAD
CENTENNIAL (MS) .... SHARON GLESS
CENTENNIAL (MS) .... STEPHEN McHATTIE
CENTER OF THE WEB .... BO HOPKINS
CENTER OF THE WEB .... CHARLENE TILTON
CENTER OF THE WEB .... CHARLES NAPIER
CENTER OF THE WEB .... ROBERT DAVI
CENTER OF THE WEB .... TED PRIOR
CENTER OF THE WEB .... TONY CURTIS
CEREMONY, THE .... JOHN IRELAND
CEREMONY, THE .... ROBERT WALKER JR.
CEREMONY, THE .... SARAH MILES
CERTAIN SACRIFICE, A .... MADONNA
CERTAIN SMILE, A .... BRADFORD DILLMAN
CERVANTES .... JOSE FERRER†
CERVANTES .... LOUIS JOURDAN
CESAR AND ROSALIE .... ISABELLE HUPPERT
CÉSAR ET ROSALIE .... ISABELLE HUPPERT
CHAD HANNA .... DOROTHY LAMOUR
CHADWICK FAMILY, THE (TF) ..... BARRY BOSTWICK
CHAIN LIGHTNING .... ELEANOR PARKER
CHAIN, THE .... BILLIE WHITELAW
CHAIN, THE .... NIGEL HAWTHORNE
CHAINED .... JOAN CRAWFORD†
CHAINED HEAT .... LINDA BLAIR
CHAINS OF GOLD .... JOHN TRAVOLTA
CHAIRMAN, THE .... ARTHUR HILL
CHAIRMAN, THE .... GREGORY PECK
CHALK GARDEN, THE .... DEBORAH KERR
CHALK GARDEN, THE .... HAYLEY MILLS
CHALK GARDEN, THE .... JOHN MILLS
CHALK GARDEN, THE ⊙ .... EDITH EVANS†
CHALLENGE OF A
  LIFETIME (TF) .... JONATHAN SILVERMAN
CHALLENGE OF A
  LIFETIME (TF) .... PENNY MARSHALL
CHALLENGE OF A
  LIFETIME (TF) .... RICHARD GILLILAND
CHALLENGE, THE .... SCOTT GLENN
CHALLENGE TO WHITE FANG .... FRANCO NERO
CHALLENGER (TF) .... BARRY BOSTWICK
CHALLENGER (TF) .... KAREN ALLEN
CHALLENGER (TF) .... PETER BOYLE
CHALLENGERS, THE (TF) .... SUSAN CLARK
CHAMBER OF HORRORS .... PATRICK O'NEAL†
CHAMBER OF HORRORS .... TONY CURTIS
CHAMP, THE .... ARTHUR HILL
CHAMP, THE .... FAYE DUNAWAY
CHAMP, THE .... JACK WARDEN
CHAMP, THE .... JACKIE COOPER
CHAMP, THE .... JOAN BLONDELL†
CHAMP, THE .... JON VOIGHT
CHAMP, THE .... KEN WAHL
CHAMP, THE .... RICK SCHRODER
CHAMP, THE .... STROTHER MARTIN†
CHAMP, THE ★★ .... WALLACE BEERY†
CHAMPAGNE FOR CAESAR .... CELESTE HOLM
CHAMPAGNE FOR CAESAR .... VINCENT PRICE†
CHAMPAGNE
  MURDERS, THE .... ANTHONY PERKINS†
CHAMPAGNE MURDERS, THE .... HENRY JONES
CHAMPION ★ .... KIRK DOUGLAS
CHAMPIONS .... JOHN HURT
CHAMPIONS .... KIRSTIE ALLEY
CHAMPIONS .... MICHAEL BYRNE
CHANCE MEETING
  BLIND DATE .... GORDAN JACKSON†

CHANCES ARE .... CHRISTOPHER McDONALD
CHANCES ARE .... CYBILL SHEPHERD
CHANCES ARE .... FRAN RYAN
CHANCES ARE .... JAMES NOBLE
CHANCES ARE .... JOSEF SOMMER
CHANCES ARE .... MARY STUART MASTERSON
CHANCES ARE .... ROBERT DOWNEY JR.
CHANCES ARE .... RYAN O'NEAL
CHANCES ARE .... SUSAN RUTTAN
CHANDLER .... LESLIE CARON
CHANDLERTOWN (CMS) .... POWERS BOOTHE
CHANEL SOLITAIRE .... KAREN BLACK
CHANEL SOLITAIRE .... LEILA FRECHET
CHANEL SOLITAIRE ...... MARIE-FRANCE PISIER
CHANEL SOLITAIRE .... RUTGER HAUER
CHANEL SOLITAIRE .... TIMOTHY DALTON
CHANGE IN THE WIND, A .... WILLIAM DEVANE
CHANGE OF HABIT .... ED ASNER
CHANGE OF HABIT .... ELVIS PRESLEY†
CHANGE OF HABIT .... MARY TYLER MOORE
CHANGE OF MIND .... LESLIE NIELSEN
CHANGE OF MIND .... RAYMOND ST. JACQUES
CHANGE OF SEASONS, A .... ANTHONY HOPKINS
CHANGE OF SEASONS, A .... BO DEREK
CHANGE OF SEASONS, A .... SHIRLEY MacLAINE
CHANGELING, THE .... GEORGE C. SCOTT
CHANGELING, THE .... TRISH VAN DEVERE
CHANGES (TF) .... CHERYL LADD
CHANGES (TF) .... MICHAEL NOURI
CHANT OF JIMMIE
  BLACKSMITH, THE .... BRYON BROWN
CHANT OF JIMMIE
  BLACKSMITH, THE .... JACK THOMPSON
CHAPLIN .... ANTHONY HOPKINS
CHAPLIN .... DAN AYKROYD
CHAPLIN .... DAVID DUCHOVNY
CHAPLIN .... DIANE LANE
CHAPLIN .... GERALDINE CHAPLIN
CHAPLIN .... JAMES WOODS
CHAPLIN .... JOHN THAW
CHAPLIN .... KEVIN DUNN
CHAPLIN .... KEVIN KLINE
CHAPLIN .... MARISA TOMEI
CHAPLIN .... MILLA JOVOICH
CHAPLIN .... MOIRA KELLY
CHAPLIN .... NANCY TRAVIS
CHAPLIN .... PAUL RHYS
CHAPLIN .... PENELOPE ANN MILLER
CHAPLIN ★ .... ROBERT DOWNEY JR.
CHAPMAN REPORT, THE .... CHAD EVERETT
CHAPMAN REPORT, THE .... CLAIRE BLOOM
CHAPMAN REPORT, THE .... CLORIS LEACHMAN
CHAPMAN REPORT, THE .... COREY ALLEN
CHAPMAN REPORT, THE ...... EFREM ZIMBALIST JR.
CHAPMAN REPORT, THE .... JANE FONDA
CHAPMAN REPORT, THE .... JOHN DEHNER†
CHAPMAN REPORT, THE .... SHELLEY WINTERS
CHAPTER TWO .... BRANT VAN HOFFMANN
CHAPTER TWO .... JAMES CAAN
CHAPTER TWO .... JOSEPH BOLOGNA
CHAPTER TWO .... VALERIE HARPER
CHAPTER TWO ★ .... MARSHA MASON
CHARADE .... AUDREY HEPBURN†
CHARADE .... CARY GRANT†
CHARADE .... GEORGE KENNEDY
CHARADE .... JAMES COBURN
CHARADE .... NED GLASS†
CHARADE .... WALTER MATTHAU
CHARGE AT FEATHER CREEK, THE ...... VERA MILES
CHARGE OF THE LIGHT
  BRIGADE, THE .... DAVID HEMMINGS
CHARGE OF THE LIGHT
  BRIGADE, THE .... DAVID NIVEN†
CHARGE OF THE LIGHT
  BRIGADE, THE .... JOHN GIELGUD
CHARGE OF THE LIGHT
  BRIGADE, THE .... OLIVIA DE HAVILLAND
CHARGE OF THE LIGHT
  BRIGADE, THE .... VANESSA REDGRAVE
CHARING CROSS ROAD .... JOHN MILLS
CHARIOTS OF FIRE .... ALICE KRIGE

CHARIOTS OF FIRE .... BEN CROSS
CHARIOTS OF FIRE .... BRAD DAVIS†
CHARIOTS OF FIRE .... CHERYL CAMPBELL
CHARIOTS OF FIRE .... DENNIS CHRISTOPHER
CHARIOTS OF FIRE .... IAN CHARLESON†
CHARIOTS OF FIRE .... JOHN GIELGUD
CHARIOTS OF FIRE .... LINDSAY ANDERSON
CHARIOTS OF FIRE .... NIGEL DAVENPORT
CHARIOTS OF FIRE .... NIGEL HAYERS
CHARIOTS OF FIRE .... PATRICK MAGEE†
CHARIOTS OF FIRE .... PETER EGAN
CHARIOTS OF FIRE ⊙ .... IAN HOLM
CHARLESTON (TF) .... MARTHA SCOTT
CHARLESTON (TF) .... RONALD LACEY
CHARLEY AND THE ANGEL .... CLORIS LEACHMAN
CHARLEY AND THE ANGEL .... HARRY MORGAN
CHARLEY AND THE ANGEL .... KURT RUSSELL
CHARLEY HANNAH (TF) ...... CHRISTIAN CONRAD
CHARLEY HANNAH (TF) .... ROBERT CONRAD
CHARLEY ONE-EYE .... RICHARD ROUNDTREE
CHARLEY VARRICK .... JOE DON BAKER
CHARLEY VARRICK .... JOHN VERNON
CHARLEY-ONE-EYE .... NIGEL DAVENPORT
CHARLIE BUBBLES .... ALBERT FINNEY
CHARLIE BUBBLES .... BILLIE WHITELAW
CHARLIE BUBBLES .... LIZA MINELLI
CHARLIE CHAN AND THE CURSE OF
  THE DRAGON QUEEN .... ANGIE DICKINSON
CHARLIE CHAN AND THE CURSE OF
  THE DRAGON QUEEN .... BRIAN KEITH
CHARLIE CHAN AND THE CURSE OF
  THE DRAGON QUEEN .... LEE GRANT
CHARLIE CHAN AND THE CURSE OF
  THE DRAGON QUEEN .... MICHELLE PFEIFFER
CHARLIE CHAN AND THE CURSE OF
  THE DRAGON QUEEN .... PETER USTINOV
CHARLIE CHAN ON BROADWAY .... LEON AMES
CHARLIE COBB: NICE NIGHT
  FOR A HANGING (TF) .... RALPH BELLAMY†
CHARLIE MUFFIN (TF) .... DAVID HEMMINGS
CHARLIE VARRICK .... WALTER MATTHAU
CHARLIE'S ANGELS (TF) .... DAVID DOYLE
CHARLIE'S ANGELS (TF) .... DAVID OGDEN STIERS
CHARLIE'S ANGELS (TF) .... DIANA MULDAUR
CHARLIE'S ANGELS (TF) .... FARRAH FAWCETT
CHARLIE'S ANGELS (TF) .... JACLYN SMITH
CHARLIE'S ANGELS (TF) .... JOHN FORSYTHE
CHARLIE'S ANGELS (TF) .... KATE JACKSON
CHARLIE'S ANGELS (TF) .... TOMMY LEE JONES
CHARLOTTE'S WEB (AF) .... PAUL LYNDE†
CHARLOTTE'S WEB (AF) .... DEBBIE REYNOLDS
CHARLOTTE'S WEB (AF) .... HENRY GIBSON
CHARLOTTE'S WEB (AF) .... MARTHA SCOTT
CHARLY .... CLAIRE BLOOM
CHARLY .... DICK VAN PATTEN
CHARLY ★★ .... CLIFF ROBERTSON
CHARRO! .... ELVIS PRESLEY†
CHASE (TF) .... TERRENCE KNOX
CHASE, THE .... ANGIE DICKINSON
CHASE, THE .... CHARLIE SHEEN
CHASE, THE .... CLAUDIA CHRISTIAN
CHASE, THE .... CLIFTON JAMES
CHASE, THE .... E. G. MARSHALL
CHASE, THE .... HENRY ROLLINS
CHASE, THE .... JANE FONDA
CHASE, THE .... JOE SAGAL
CHASE, THE .... JOSH MOSTEL
CHASE, THE .... KRISTY SWANSON
CHASE, THE .... MARLON BRANDO
CHASE, THE .... MICHAEL BALZARY
CHASE, THE .... PAUL WILLIAMS
CHASE, THE .... RAY WISE
CHASE, THE .... ROBERT DUVALL
CHASE, THE .... ROBERT REDFORD
CHASE, THE .... ROCKY CARROLL
CHASE FOR THE GOLDEN
  NEEDLES, THE .... BURGESS MEREDITH
CHASE FOR THE GOLDEN
  NEEDLES, THE .... ELIZABETH ASHLEY
CHASER, THE .... LANA TURNER
CHASERS .... ERIKA ELENIAK

INDEX OF FILM TITLES

CHASERS ... GRAND L. BUSH
CHASERS ... TOM BERENGER
CHASERS, THE ... ANOUK AIMEE
CHASING DREAMS ... KEVIN COSTNER
CHASTITY ... CHER
CHASTITY BELT, THE ... TONY CURTIS
CHATO'S LAND ... CHARLES BRONSON
CHATO'S LAND ... JACK PALANCE
CHATO'S LAND ... JAMES WHITMORE
CHATTAHOOCHEE ... DENNIS HOPPER
CHATTAHOOCHEE ... FRANCES McDORMAND
CHATTAHOOCHEE ... GARY OLDMAN
CHATTAHOOCHEE ... M. EMMET WALSH
CHATTAHOOCHEE ... NED BEATTY
CHATTAHOOCHEE ... PAMELA REED
CHATTANOOGA CHOO CHOO ... BARBARA EDEN
CHATTANOOGA CHOO CHOO ... GEORGE KENNEDY
CHATTANOOGA CHOO CHOO ... JOE NAMATH
CHATTANOOGA CHOO CHOO ... MELISSA ANDERSON
CHATTANOOGA CHOO CHOO ... CHRISTOPHER McDONALD
CHE! ... JACK PALANCE
CHE! ... OMAR SHARIF
CHE! ... ROBERT LOGGIA
CHE! ... WOODY STRODE
CHEAP DETECTIVE, THE ... ABE VIGODA
CHEAP DETECTIVE, THE ... ANN-MARGRET
CHEAP DETECTIVE, THE ... DAVID OGDEN STIERS
CHEAP DETECTIVE, THE ... DOM DeLUISE
CHEAP DETECTIVE, THE ... EILEEN BRENNAN
CHEAP DETECTIVE, THE ... LOUISE FLETCHER
CHEAP DETECTIVE, THE ... MADELINE KAHN
CHEAP DETECTIVE, THE ... MARSHA MASON
CHEAP DETECTIVE, THE ... NICOL WILLIAMSON
CHEAP DETECTIVE, THE ... PAUL WILLIAMS
CHEAP DETECTIVE, THE ... PETER FALK
CHEAP DETECTIVE, THE ... SID CAESAR
CHEAP DETECTIVE, THE ... STOCKARD CHANNING
CHEAPER TO KEEP HER ... ART METRANO
CHEAPER TO KEEP HER ... MAC DAVIS
CHEAPER TO KEEP HER ... TOYAH FELDSHUH
CHEATERS, THE ... DAYLE HADDON
CHECK IS IN THE MAIL, THE ... ANNE ARCHER
CHECKERED COAT, THE ... HURD HATFIELD
CHECKERED FLAG OR CRASH ... SUSAN SARANDON
CHECKING OUT ... ALLAN HAYEY
CHECKING OUT ... ANN MAGNUSON
CHECKING OUT ... DANTON STONE
CHECKING OUT ... FELTON PERRY
CHECKING OUT ... JEFF DANIELS
CHECKING OUT ... KATHLEEN YORK
CHECKING OUT ... MARK LOWENTHAL
CHECKING OUT ... MELANIE MAYRON
CHECKING OUT ... MICHAEL TUCKER
CHEECH AND CHONG'S NEXT MOVIE ... MICHAEL WINSLOW
CHEECH & CHONG'S NEXT MOVIE ... CHEECH MARIN
CHEECH & CHONG'S NEXT MOVIE ... THOMAS CHONG
CHEECH & CHONG'S NICE DREAMS ... CHEECH MARIN
CHEECH & CHONG'S NICE DREAMS ... PAUL REUBENS
CHEECH & CHONG'S NICE DREAMS ... STACY KEACH
CHEECH & CHONG'S NICE DREAMS ... THOMAS CHONG
CHEECH & CHONG'S NICE DREAMS ... TIM ROSSOVICH
CHEECH & CHONG: STILL SMOKIN' ... CHEECH MARIN
CHEECH & CHONG: STILL SMOKIN' ... THOMAS CHONG
CHEECH & CHONG'S THE CORSICAN BROTHERS ... CHEECH MARIN
CHEECH & CHONG'S THE CORSICAN BROTHERS ... THOMAS CHONG
CHEERS FOR MISS BISHOP ... MARTHA SCOTT

CHEETAH ... BREON GORMAN
CHEETAH ... COLLIN MOTHUPI
CHEETAH ... KA VUNDLA
CHEETAH ... KEITH COOGAN
CHEETAH ... KULDEEP BHAKOO
CHEETAH ... PAUL ONSONGO
CHEETAH ... TIMOTHY LANDFIELD
CHERNOBYL: THE FINAL WARNING (CTF) ... JASON ROBARDS
CHERNOBYL: THE FINAL WARNING (CTF) ... JON VOIGHT
CHERNOBYL: THE FINAL WARNING (CTF) ... SAMMI DAVIS
CHERRY 2000 ... DAVID ANDREWS
CHERRY 2000 ... MELANIE GRIFFITH
CHEYENNE ... JANE WYMAN
CHEYENNE AUTUMN ... CARROLL BAKER
CHEYENNE AUTUMN ... HARRY CAREY JR.
CHEYENNE AUTUMN ... JAMES STEWART
CHEYENNE AUTUMN ... KARL MALDEN
CHEYENNE AUTUMN ... PATRICK WAYNE
CHEYENNE AUTUMN ... RICARDO MONTALBAN
CHEYENNE AUTUMN ... RICHARD WIDMARK
CHEYENNE SOCIAL CLUB, THE ... JAMES STEWART
CHEYENNE SOCIAL CLUB, THE ... JOHN DEHNER†
CHEYENNE SOCIAL CLUB, THE ... SHIRLEY JONES
CHEYENNE SOCIAL CLUB, THE ... SUE ANE LANGDON
CHICAGO CONFIDENTIAL ... BRIAN KEITH
CHICAGO JOE AND THE SHOWGIRL ... ALEXANDRA PIGG
CHICAGO JOE AND THE SHOWGIRL ... EMILY LLOYD
CHICAGO JOE AND THE SHOWGIRL ... JOHN JUNKIN
CHICAGO JOE AND THE SHOWGIRL ... KEITH ALLEN
CHICAGO JOE AND THE SHOWGIRL ... KIEFER SUTHERLAND
CHICAGO JOE AND THE SHOWGIRL ... PATSY KENSIT
CHICAGO STORY, THE (TF) ... CRAIG T. NELSON
CHICAGO STORY, THE (TF) ... JOHN MAHONEY
CHICKEN CHRONICLES, THE ... ED LAUTER
CHICKEN CHRONICLES, THE ... STEVE GUTTENBERG
CHICKEN EVERY SUNDAY ... ALAN YOUNG
CHICKEN EVERY SUNDAY ... CELESTE HOLM
CHIEFS (MS) ... BRAD DAVIS†
CHIEFS (MS) ... CHARLTON HESTON
CHIEFS (MS) ... KEITH CARRADINE
CHIEFS (MS) ... TESS HARPER
CHIEFS (MS) ... VICTORIA TENNANT
CHILD BRIDE OF SHORT CREEK (TF) ... CHRISTOPHER ATKINS
CHILD IN THE NIGHT (TF) ... DARREN McGAVIN
CHILD IN THE NIGHT (TF) ... JoBETH WILLIAMS
CHILD IN THE NIGHT (TF) ... SEASON HUBLEY
CHILD IN THE NIGHT (TF) ... TOM SKERRITT
CHILD IS BORN, A ... GERALDINE FITZGERALD
CHILD IS WAITING, A ... BURT LANCASTER†
CHILD IS WAITING, A ... GENA ROWLANDS
CHILD IS WAITING, A ... LAWRENCE TIERNEY
CHILD IS WAITING, A ... STEVEN HILL
CHILD SAVER, THE (TF) ... ALFRE WOODARD
CHILD SAVER, THE (TF) ... MARIO VAN PEEBLES
CHILD SAVER, THE (TF) ... MARTIN BALSAM
CHILD STEALER, THE (TF) ... BEAU BRIDGES
CHILD STEALER, THE (TF) ... BLAIR BROWN
CHILD UNDER A LEAF ... DYAN CANNON
CHILDISH THINGS ... DON MURRAY
CHILDREN IN THE CROSSFIRE (TF) ... CHARLES HAID
CHILDREN IN THE CROSSFIRE (TF) ... KAREN VALENTINE
CHILDREN OF A LESSER GOD ... ALISON GOMPF
CHILDREN OF A LESSER GOD ... JOHN BASINGER
CHILDREN OF A LESSER GOD ... JOHN F. CLEARY
CHILDREN OF A LESSER GOD ... PHILIP BOSCO
CHILDREN OF A LESSER GOD ★ ... WILLIAM HURT
CHILDREN OF A LESSER GOD ★★ ... MARLEE MATLIN

CHILDREN OF A LESSER GOD ○ ... PIPER LAURIE
CHILDREN OF AN LAC, THE (TF) ... SHIRLEY JONES
CHILDREN OF RAGE ... SIMON WARD
CHILDREN OF SANCHEZ, THE ... ANTHONY QUINN
CHILDREN OF SANCHEZ, THE ... KATHY JURADO
CHILDREN OF THE CORN ... LINDA HAMILTON
CHILDREN OF THE CORN ... PETER HORTON
CHILDREN OF THE NIGHT (TF) ... KATHLEEN QUINLAN
CHILDREN OF THE NIGHT (TF) ... LAR PARK LINCOLN
CHILDREN OF THE NIGHT (TF) ... NICHOLAS CAMPBELL
CHILDREN OF TIMES SQUARE, THE (TF) ... JOANNA CASSIDY
CHILDREN PAY, THE ... LILLIAN GISH†
CHILDREN'S HOUR, THE ○ ... FAY BAINTER†
CHILDREN'S HOUR, THE ... AUDREY HEPBURN†
CHILDREN'S HOUR, THE ... JAMES GARNER
CHILDREN'S HOUR, THE ... SHIRLEY MacLAINE
CHILDREN'S HOUR, THE ... VERONICA CARTWRIGHT
CHILD'S CRY (TF) ... LINDSAY WAGNER
CHILD'S PLAY ... ALEX VINCENT
CHILD'S PLAY ... BEAU BRIDGES
CHILD'S PLAY ... BRAD DOURIF
CHILD'S PLAY ... CATHERINE HICKS
CHILD'S PLAY ... CHRIS SARANDON
CHILD'S PLAY ... DINAH MANOFF
CHILD'S PLAY ... MICHAEL PATRICK CARTER
CHILD'S PLAY 2 ... ALEX VINCENT
CHILD'S PLAY 2 ... BRAD DOURIF
CHILD'S PLAY 2 ... CHRISTINE ELISE
CHILD'S PLAY 2 ... GERRITT GRAHAM
CHILD'S PLAY 2 ... GRACE ZABRISKIE
CHILD'S PLAY 2 ... JENNY AGUTTER
CHILD'S PLAY 3 ... BRAD DOURIF
CHILD'S PLAY 3 ... DEAN JACOBSEN
CHILD'S PLAY 3 ... JEREMY SYLVERS
CHILD'S PLAY 3 ... JUSTIN WHALIN
CHILD'S PLAY 3 ... PERREY REEVES
CHILLY SCENES OF WINTER ... GRIFFIN DUNNE
CHILLY SCENES OF WINTER ... JOHN HEARD
CHILLY SCENES OF WINTER ... MARY BETH HURT
CHILTREN HUNDREDS, THE ... DAVID TOMLINSON
CHIMES AT MIDNIGHT ... JOHN GIELGUD
CHINA 9, LIBERTY 37 ... JENNY AGUTTER
CHINA BEACH (TF) ... CHLOE WEBB
CHINA BEACH (TF) ... CHRISTOPHER ALLPORT
CHINA BEACH (TF) ... DANA DELANY
CHINA BEACH (TF) ... MARG HELGENBERGER
CHINA CORSAIR ... ERNEST BORGNINE
CHINA CRY ... ELIZABETH SUNG
CHINA CRY ... FRANCE NUYEN
CHINA CRY ... JAMES SHIGETA
CHINA CRY ... JULIA NICKSON SOUL
CHINA CRY ... PHILIP TAN
CHINA CRY ... RUSSELL WONG
CHINA DOLL ... STUART WHITMAN
CHINA GATE ... ANGIE DICKINSON
CHINA GIRL ... DAVID CARUSO
CHINA GIRL ... JAMES RUSSO
CHINA GIRL ... RICHARD PANEBIANCO
CHINA GIRL ... SARI CHANG
CHINA LAKE MURDERS, THE (CTF) ... NANCY EVERHARD
CHINA MOON ... BENICIO DEL TORO
CHINA MOON ... CHARLES DANCE
CHINA MOON ... ED HARRIS
CHINA MOON ... MADELEINE STOWE
CHINA ROSE (TF) ... ALI MacGRAW
CHINA ROSE (TF) ... GEORGE C. SCOTT
CHINA SKY ... ANTHONY QUINN
CHINA SYNDROME, THE ... MICHAEL DOUGLAS
CHINA SYNDROME, THE ... PETER DONAT
CHINA SYNDROME, THE ... WILFORD BRIMLEY
CHINA SYNDROME, THE ★ ... JACK LEMMON
CHINA SYNDROME, THE ★ ... JANE FONDA
CHINATOWN ... BEULAH QUO
CHINATOWN ... BURT YOUNG
CHINATOWN ... DARRELL ZWERLING
CHINATOWN ... DIANE LADD

This is not a list of every film ever made or every cast member, only those listed in this directory.

CHINATOWN .... JAMES HONG
CHINATOWN .... JOHN HILLERMAN
CHINATOWN .... JOHN HUSTON†
CHINATOWN .... PERRY LOPEZ
CHINATOWN .... ROMAN POLANSKI
CHINATOWN ★ .... FAYE DUNAWAY
CHINATOWN ★ .... JACK NICHOLSON
CHINATOWN AT MIDNIGHT .... HURD HATFIELD
CHINO .... CHARLES BRONSON
CHIPS, THE WAR DOG (CTF) .... WILLIAM DEVANE
CHISUM .... BEN JOHNSON
CHISUM .... JOHN WAYNE†
CHISUM .... RICHARD JAECKEL
CHITTY CHITTY BANG BANG .... DICK VAN DYKE
CHOCOLAT .... CECILE DUCASSE
CHOCOLAT .... FRANCOIS CLUZET
CHOCOLAT .... GIULIA BOSCHI
CHOCOLAT .... ISAACH DE BANKOLE
CHOCOLAT .... JACQUES DENIS
CHOCOLAT .... JEAN CLAUDE ADELIN
CHOCOLAT .... MIREILLE PERRIER
CHOCOLATE WAR, THE .... JOHN GLOVER
CHOICE OF WEAPONS .... BARBARA HERSHEY
CHOICES .... DEMI MOORE
CHOICES (TF) .... GEORGE C. SCOTT
CHOICES (TF) .... JACQUELINE BISSET
CHOICES (TF) .... MELISSA GILBERT
CHOIRBOYS, THE .... BLAIR BROWN
CHOIRBOYS, THE .... BURT YOUNG
CHOIRBOYS, THE .... CHARLES DURNING
CHOIRBOYS, THE .... DAVID SPIELBERG
CHOIRBOYS, THE .... DON STROUD
CHOIRBOYS, THE .... JAMES WOODS
CHOIRBOYS, THE .... LOUIS GOSSETT JR.
CHOIRBOYS, THE .... PERRY KING
CHOIRBOYS, THE .... RANDY QUAID
CHOIRBOYS, THE .... ROBERT WEBBER
CHOIRBOYS, THE .... STEPHEN MACHT
CHOKE CANYON .... LANCE HENRIKSEN
CHOKE CANYON .... STEPHEN COLLINS
CHOOSE ME .... GENEVIEVE BUJOLD
CHOOSE ME .... KEITH CARRADINE
CHOOSE ME .... LESLEY ANN WARREN
CHOOSE ME .... RAE DAWN CHONG
CHOOSE YOUR PARTNER .... LANA TURNER
CHOPPER CHICKS IN
  ZOMBIETOWN .... CATHERINE CARLEN
CHOPPER CHICKS IN ZOMBIETOWN ... JAMIE ROSE
CHORUS LINE, A .... ALYSON REED
CHORUS LINE, A .... AUDREY LANDERS
CHORUS LINE, A .... BROOKE SMITH
CHORUS LINE, A .... GREGG BURGE
CHORUS LINE, A .... JANET JONES
CHORUS LINE, A .... MICHAEL DOUGLAS
CHORUS OF
  DISAPPROVAL, A .... ANTHONY HOPKINS
CHORUS OF DISAPPROVAL, A .... JEREMY IRONS
CHOSEN, THE .... KIRK DOUGLAS
CHOSEN, THE .... MAXIMILIAN SCHELL
CHOSEN, THE .... ROBBY BENSON
CHOSEN, THE .... ROD STEIGER
CHOSEN, THE .... SIMON WARD
CHOSEN SURVIVORS .... BARBARA BABCOCK
CHOSEN SURVIVORS .... BRADFORD DILLMAN
CHOSEN SURVIVORS .... JACKIE COOPER
CHOSEN SURVIVORS .... RICHARD JAECKEL
CHOSEN SURVIVORS, THE .... DIANA MULDAUR
CHRISTIAN LICORICE
  STORE, THE .... BEAU BRIDGES
CHRISTIAN LICORICE
  STORE, THE, THE .... MAUD ADAMS
CHRISTINA .... TERRY DAVID MULLIGAN
CHRISTINE .... ALEXANDRA PAUL
CHRISTINE .... HARRY DEAN STANTON
CHRISTINE .... KEITH GORDON
CHRISTINE .... ROMY SCHNEIDER†
CHRISTMAS CAROL, A .... JUNE LOCKHART
CHRISTMAS CAROL, A (TF) .... DAVID WARNER
CHRISTMAS
  CAROL, A (TF) .... EDWARD WOODWARD
CHRISTMAS CAROL, A (TF) .... GEORGE C. SCOTT

CHRISTMAS
  CAROL, A (TF) .... JOANNE WHALLEY-KILMER
CHRISTMAS CAROL, A (TF) .... LUCY GUTTERIDGE
CHRISTMAS CAROL, A (TF) .... NIGEL DAVENPORT
CHRISTMAS CAROL, A (TF) .... SUSANNAH YORK
CHRISTMAS COMES TO
  WILLOW CREEK (TF) .... ANTONY HOLLAND
CHRISTMAS COMES TO
  WILLOW CREEK (TF) .... HOYT AXTON
CHRISTMAS COMES TO
  WILLOW CREEK (TF) .... JOHN SCHNEIDER
CHRISTMAS COMES TO
  WILLOW CREEK (TF) .... KIM DELANEY
CHRISTMAS COMES TO
  WILLOW CREEK (TF) .... TOM WOPAT
CHRISTMAS EVE (TF) .... ARTHUR HILL
CHRISTMAS EVE (TF) .... RON LEIBMAN
CHRISTMAS EVE (TF) .... SEASON HUBLEY
CHRISTMAS GIFT, THE (TF) .... JANE KACZMAREK
CHRISTMAS GIFT, THE (TF) .... JOHN DENVER
CHRISTMAS GIFT, THE (TF) .... MARY WICKES
CHRISTMAS HOLIDAY .... GENE KELLY
CHRISTMAS IN
  CONNECTICUT .... BARBARA STANWYCK†
CHRISTMAS IN
  CONNECTICUT (CTF) .... DYAN CANNON
CHRISTMAS IN
  CONNECTICUT (CTF) .... JIMMY WORKMAN
CHRISTMAS IN
  CONNECTICUT (CTF) .... KRIS KRISTOFFERSON
CHRISTMAS LILIES OF
  THE FIELD (TF) .... BILLY DEE WILLIAMS
CHRISTMAS STAR, THE (TF) .... ED ASNER
CHRISTMAS STAR, THE (TF) .... FRED GWYNNE†
CHRISTMAS
  STAR, THE (TF) .... RENE AUBERJONOIS
CHRISTMAS TO
  REMEMBER, A (TF) .... EVA MARIE SAINT
CHRISTMAS TO
  REMEMBER, A (TF) .... JOANNE WOODWARD
CHRISTOPHER COLUMBUS (MS) .... ELI WALLACH
CHRISTOPHER
  COLUMBUS (MS) .... FAYE DUNAWAY
CHRISTOPHER
  COLUMBUS (MS) .... GABRIEL BYRNE
CHRISTOPHER COLUMBUS:
  THE DISCOVERY .... GEORGE CORRAFACE
CHRISTOPHER COLUMBUS:
  THE DISCOVERY .... MARLON BRANDO
CHRISTOPHER COLUMBUS:
  THE DISCOVERY .... RACHEL WARD
CHRISTOPHER COLUMBUS:
  THE DISCOVERY .... TOM SELLECK
CHRISTOPHER STRONG .... KATHERINE HEPBURN
CHRISTY (TF) .... TYNE DALY
CHRONICLE OF A DEATH
  FORETOLD .... ANTHONY DELON
CHRONICLE OF A DEATH
  FORETOLD .... ORNELLA MUTI
CHRONICLE OF A DEATH
  FORETOLD .... RUPERT EVERETT
CHU CHU AND THE PHILLY FLASH .... ALAN ARKIN
CHU CHU AND THE
  PHILLY FLASH .... CAROL BURNETT
CHU CHU AND THE
  PHILLY FLASH .... DANNY AIELLO
CHU CHU AND THE PHILLY FLASH .... RUTH BUZZI
CHUBASCO .... ANN SOTHERN
CHUBASCO .... SUSAN STRASBERG
CHUKA .... ERNEST BORGNINE
CHUKA .... JAMES WHITMORE
CHURCHILL AND THE
  GENERALS (TF) .... TIMOTHY WEST
CIAO! MANHATTAN .... EDIE SEDGWICK†
CIMARRON .... MARIA SCHELL
CIMARRON .... MARY WICKES
CIMARRON .... MERCEDES McCAMBRIDGE
CIMARRON .... ROYAL DANO
CIMARRON .... RUSS TAMBLYN
CIMARRON ★ .... RICHARD DIX†
CINCINATTI KID, THE .... JEFF COREY
CINCINNATI KID, THE .... ANN-MARGRET

CINCINNATI KID, THE .... JACK WESTON
CINCINNATI KID, THE .... KARL MALDEN
CINCINNATI KID, THE .... RIP TORN
CINCINNATI KID, THE .... TUESDAY WELD
CINDERELLA JONES .... WILLIAM PRINCE
CINDERELLA LIBERTY .... DABNEY COLEMAN
CINDERELLA LIBERTY .... ELI WALLACH
CINDERELLA LIBERTY .... JAMES CAAN
CINDERELLA LIBERTY .... SALLY KIRKLAND
CINDERELLA LIBERTY ★ .... MARSHA MASON
CINDERFELLA .... DAME JUDITH ANDERSON†
CINDERFELLA .... HENRY SILVA
CINDERFELLA .... JERRY LEWIS
CINEMA PARADISO .... ANTONELLA ATTILI
CINEMA PARADISO .... JACQUES PERRIN
CINEMA PARADISO .... PUPELLA MAGGIO
CINEMA PARADISO .... SALVATORE CASCIO
CINQUE ORE IN CONTANTI .... CYD CHARISSE
CIRCLE OF DECEIT .... BRUNO GANZ
CIRCLE OF DECEPTION .... BRADFORD DILLMAN
CIRCLE OF DECEPTION .... ROBERT STEPHENS
CIRCLE OF FRIENDS .... CHRIS O'DONNELL
CIRCLE OF FRIENDS .... GERALDINE O'RAWE
CIRCLE OF FRIENDS .... MINNIE DRIVER
CIRCLE OF FRIENDS .... SAFFRON BURROWS
CIRCLE OF IRON .... DAVID CARRADINE
CIRCLE OF IRON .... ELI WALLACH
CIRCLE OF IRON .... RODDY McDOWALL
CIRCLE OF LOVE .... JANE FONDA
CIRCLE OF POWER .... LEO ROSSI
CIRCLE OF TWO .... TATUM O'NEAL
CIRCLE OF VIOLENCE: A
  FAMILY DRAMA (TF) ...... GERALDINE FITZGERALD
CIRCLE OF VIOLENCE:
  A FAMILY DRAMA (TF) .... PETER BONERZ
CIRCLE, THE .... JOHN MILLS
CIRCUS OF HORRORS .... DONALD PLEASENCE
CIRCUS OF HORRORS .... KENNY BAKER
CIRCUS, THE ★ .... CHARLES CHAPLIN†
CISCO PIKE .... GENE HACKMAN
CISCO PIKE .... HARRY DEAN STANTON
CISCO PIKE .... KAREN BLACK
CISCO PIKE .... KRIS KRISTOFFERSON
CISCO PIKE .... ROSCOE LEE BROWNE
CISCO PIKE .... SEVERN DARDEN
CITADEL, THE ★ .... ROBERT DONAT†
CITIZEN KANE ★ .... ORSON WELLES†
CITIZENS BAND .... BRUCE McGILL
CITIZENS BAND .... CANDY CLARK
CITIZENS BAND .... CHARLES NAPIER
CITIZENS BAND .... PAUL LeMAT
CITTA VIOLENTA .... TELLY SAVALAS†
CITY ACROSS THE RIVER .... RICHARD JAECKEL
CITY ACROSS THE RIVER .... TONY CURTIS
CITY AFTER MIDNIGHT .... DAN O'HERLIHY
CITY BENEATH THE SEA .... ANTHONY QUINN
CITY BENEATH THE SEA (TF) ...... ROBERT WAGNER
CITY BENEATH THE SEA (TF) ...... STUART WHITMAN
CITY BENEATH THE SEA, THE .... WOODY STRODE
CITY FOR CONQUEST .... ANTHONY QUINN
CITY GIRL, THE .... COLLEEN CAMP
CITY HALL .... AL PACINO
CITY HALL .... BRIDGET FONDA
CITY HALL .... DANNY AIELLO
CITY HALL .... DAVID PAYMER
CITY HALL .... MARTIN LANDAU
CITY HALL .... JOHN CUSACK
CITY HEAT .... BURT REYNOLDS
CITY HEAT .... CLINT EASTWOOD
CITY HEAT .... IRENE CARA
CITY HEAT .... JANE ALEXANDER
CITY HEAT .... MADELINE KAHN
CITY HEAT .... RICHARD ROUNDTREE
CITY HEAT .... RIP TORN
CITY HEAT .... TAB THACKER
CITY HEAT .... TONY LoBIANCO
CITY HEAT .... WILLIAM SANDERSON
CITY IN FEAR (TF) .... MICKEY ROURKE
CITY IN FEAR (TF) .... WILLIAM DANIELS
CITY KILLER (TF) .... TERRENCE KNOX
CITY LIMITS .... ROBBY BENSON
CITY OF BAD MEN .... LLOYD BRIDGES
CITY OF FEAR .... VINCE EDWARDS

† after an actor's name denotes deceased.

CITY OF HOPE ... JOE MORTON
CITY OF HOPE ... TONY LoBIANCO
CITY OF HOPE ... VINCENT SPANO
CITY OF JO ... ART MALIK
CITY OF JOY ... OM PURI
CITY OF JOY ... PATRICK SWAYZE
CITY OF JOY ... PAULINE COLLINS
CITY OF JOY ... SHABANA AZMI
CITY ON FIRE ... AVA GARDNER†
CITY ON FIRE ... SHELLEY WINTERS
CITY ON FIRE ... SUSAN CLARK
CITY ON FIRE! ... JAMES FRANCISCUS†
CITY ON FIRE! ... LESLIE NIELSEN
CITY SLICKERS ... BILL HENDERSON
CITY SLICKERS ... BILLY CRYSTAL
CITY SLICKERS ... BRUNO KIRBY
CITY SLICKERS ... DANIEL STERN
CITY SLICKERS ... DAVID PAYMER
CITY SLICKERS ... DEAN HALLO
CITY SLICKERS ... HELEN SLATER
CITY SLICKERS ... JAYNE MEADOWS
CITY SLICKERS ... JOSH MOSTEL
CITY SLICKERS ... KARLA TANBURRELLI
CITY SLICKERS ... NOBLE WILLINGHAM
CITY SLICKERS ... PATRICIA WETTIG
CITY SLICKERS ... PHILL LEWIS
CITY SLICKERS ... WALKER BRAND
CITY SLICKERS ... YEARDLEY SMITH
CITY SLICKERS ∞ ... JACK PALANCE
CITY SLICKERS II: THE LEGEND OF CURLY'S GOLD ... BILL McKINNEY
CITY SLICKERS II: THE LEGEND OF CURLY'S GOLD ... BILLY CRYSTAL
CITY SLICKERS II: THE LEGEND OF CURLY'S GOLD ... BOB BALABAN
CITY SLICKERS II: THE LEGEND OF CURLY'S GOLD ... DANIEL STERN
CITY SLICKERS II: THE LEGEND OF CURLY'S GOLD ... DAVID PAYMER
CITY SLICKERS II: THE LEGEND OF CURLY'S GOLD ... JACK PALANCE
CITY SLICKERS II: THE LEGEND OF CURLY'S GOLD ... JON LOVITZ
CITY SLICKERS II: THE LEGEND OF CURLY'S GOLD ... JOSH MOSTEL
CITY SLICKERS II: THE LEGEND OF CURLY'S GOLD ... LINDSAY CRYSTAL
CITY SLICKERS II: THE LEGEND OF CURLY'S GOLD ... NOBLE WILLINGHAM
CITY SLICKERS II: THE LEGEND OF CURLY'S GOLD ... PATRICIA WETTIG
CITY SLICKERS II: THE LEGEND OF CURLY'S GOLD ... PRUITT TAYLOR VINCE
CITY STREETS ... SYLVIA SIDNEY
CITY THAT NEVER SLEEPS ... TOM POSTON
CITY, THE (TF) ... ANTHONY QUINN
CITY, THE (TF) ... DON JOHNSON
CITY, THE (TF) ... E. G. MARSHALL
CITY, THE (TF) ... MARK HAMILL
CITY UNDER THE SEA ... DAVID TOMLINSON
CITY UNDER THE SEA ... TAB HUNTER
CITY UNDER THE SEA ... VINCENT PRICE†
CLAMBAKE ... BILL BIXBY†
CLAMBAKE ... ELVIS PRESLEY†
CLAN OF THE CAVE BEAR, THE ... SALOME JENS
CLAN OF THE CAVE BEAR, THE ... CURTIS ARMSTRONG
CLAN OF THE CAVE BEAR, THE ... DARYL HANNAH
CLAN OF THE CAVE BEAR, THE ... JAMES REMAR
CLAN OF THE CAVE BEAR, THE ... JOHN DOOLITTLE
CLAN OF THE CAVE BEAR, THE ... PAMELA REED
CLAN OF THE CAVE BEAR, THE ... THOMAS G. WAITES
CLARA ET LES CHICS TYPES ... ISABELLE ADJANI
CLARA'S HEART ... BEVERLY TODD
CLARA'S HEART ... HATTIE WINSTON
CLARA'S HEART ... KATHLEEN QUINLAN
CLARA'S HEART ... MICHAEL ONTKEAN
CLARA'S HEART ... NEIL PATRICK HARRIS
CLARA'S HEART ... SPALDING GRAY
CLARA'S HEART ... WHOOPI GOLDBERG
CLARENCE (CTF) ... ROBERT CARRADINE
CLASH BY NIGHT ... BARBARA STANWYCK†
CLASH BY NIGHT ... MARILYN MONROE†
CLASH BY NIGHT ... ROBERT RYAN†
CLASH OF THE TITANS ... BURGESS MEREDITH
CLASH OF THE TITANS ... CLAIRE BLOOM
CLASH OF THE TITANS ... HARRY HAMLIN
CLASH OF THE TITANS ... MAGGIE SMITH
CLASH OF THE TITANS ... SIAN PHILLIPS
CLASH OF THE TITANS ... URSULA ANDRESS
CLASS ... ANDREW McCARTHY
CLASS ... JACQUELINE BISSET
CLASS ... JOHN CUSAK
CLASS ... LANCE KINSEY
CLASS ... ROB LOWE
CLASS ... STUART MARGOLIN
CLASS ACT, A ... KID
CLASS ACT, A ... PLAY
CLASS ACTION ... GENE HACKMAN
CLASS ACTION ... MARY ELIZABETH MASTRANTONIO
CLASS CRUISE (TF) ... MICHAEL DeLUISE
CLASS OF 1984 ... MICHAEL J. FOX
CLASS OF 1984 ... PERRY KING
CLASS OF 1984 ... RODDY McDOWALL
CLASS OF 1999 ... BRADLEY GREGG
CLASS OF 1999 ... JOHN P. RYAN
CLASS OF 1999 ... MALCOLM McDOWELL
CLASS OF 1999 ... PAM GRIER
CLASS OF 1999 ... STACY KEACH
CLASS OF 1999 ... TRACI LIN
CLASS OF '44 ... JOHN CANDY†
CLASS OF '44 ... SAM BOTTOMS
CLASS OF '44 ... WILLIAM ATHERTON
CLASS OF '63 (TF) ... JAMES BROLIN
CLASS OF '63 (TF) ... JOAN HACKETT†
CLASS OF MISS MACMICHAEL, THE ... GLENDA JACKSON
CLASS OF MISS MACMICHAEL, THE ... ROSALIND CASH
CLASSIFIED LOVE (TF) ... DINAH MANOFF
CLASSIFIED LOVE (TF) ... STEPHANIE FARACY
CLAUDELLE INGLISH ... CHAD EVERETT
CLAUDELLE INGLISH ... CLAUDE AKINS†
CLAUDINE ... JAMES EARL JONES
CLAUDINE ★ ... DIAHANN CARROLL
CLAY PIGEON ... BURGESS MEREDITH
CLAY PIGEON ... ROBERT VAUGHN
CLAY PIGEON ... TELLY SAVALAS†
CLAY PIGEON, THE ... BARBARA HALE
CLEAN AND SOBER ... BEN PIAZZA†
CLEAN AND SOBER ... BRIAN BENBEN
CLEAN AND SOBER ... CLAUDIA CHRISTIAN
CLEAN AND SOBER ... DAKIN MATTHEWS
CLEAN AND SOBER ... HENRY JUDD BAKER
CLEAN AND SOBER ... J. DAVID KRASSNER
CLEAN AND SOBER ... KATHY BAKER
CLEAN AND SOBER ... LUCA BERCOVICI
CLEAN AND SOBER ... M. EMMET WALSH
CLEAN AND SOBER ... MARY CATHERINE MARTIN
CLEAN AND SOBER ... MICHAEL KEATON
CLEAN AND SOBER ... MORGAN FREEMAN
CLEAN AND SOBER ... PAT QUINN
CLEAN AND SOBER ... TATE DONOVAN
CLEAN SLATE ... DANA CARVEY
CLEAN SLATE ... ISABELLE HUPPERT
CLEAN SLATE ... JAMES EARL JONES
CLEAN SLATE ... JAYNE BROOK
CLEAN SLATE ... KEVIN POLLAK
CLEAN SLATE ... MICHAEL GAMBON
CLEAN SLATE ... MICHAEL MURPHY
CLEAN SLATE ... MIKE JOLLY
CLEAN SLATE ... OLIVIA D'ABO
CLEAN SLATE ... VALERIA GOLINO
CLEAN SLATE ... VYTO RUGGIERO
CLEAR AND PRESENT DANGER ... ANNE ARCHER
CLEAR AND PRESENT DANGER ... DEAN JONES
CLEAR AND PRESENT DANGER ... DONALD MOFFAT
CLEAR AND PRESENT DANGER ... HARRIS YULIN
CLEAR AND PRESENT DANGER ... HARRISON FORD
CLEAR AND PRESENT DANGER ... HENRY CZERNY
CLEAR AND PRESENT DANGER ... HOPE LANGE
CLEAR AND PRESENT DANGER ... JAMES EARL JONES
CLEAR AND PRESENT DANGER ... JOAQUIM DE ALMEIDA
CLEAR AND PRESENT DANGER ... MIGUEL SANDOVAL
CLEAR AND PRESENT DANGER ... RAYMOND CRUZ
CLEAR AND PRESENT DANGER ... THORA BIRCH
CLEAR AND PRESENT DANGER ... TIM GRIMM
CLEAR AND PRESENT DANGER ... WILLEM DAFOE
CLEAR AND PRESENT DANGER, A (TF) ... E. G. MARSHALL
CLEAR AND PRESENT DANGER, A (TF) ... HAL HOLBROOK
CLEAR AND PRESENT DANGER, A (TF) ... SHARON ACKER
CLEAVER AND HAVEN (TF) ... ERNEST BORGNINE
CLEOPATRA ... CARROLL O'CONNOR
CLEOPATRA ... ELIZABETH TAYLOR
CLEOPATRA ... FRANCESCA ANNIS
CLEOPATRA ... HUME CRONYN
CLEOPATRA ... JEREMY KEMP
CLEOPATRA ... KENNETH HAIGH
CLEOPATRA ... MARTIN LANDAU
CLEOPATRA ... RICHARD BURTON†
CLEOPATRA ... ROBERT STEPHENS
CLEOPATRA ... RODDY McDOWALL
CLEOPATRA ★ ... REX HARRISON†
CLEOPATRA JONES ... ANTONIO FARGAS
CLEOPATRA JONES ... BILL McKINNEY
CLEOPATRA JONES ... SHELLEY WINTERS
CLEOPATRA JONES AND THE CASINO OF GOLD ... STELLA STEVENS
CLIENT, THE ... AMY HATHAWAY
CLIENT, THE ... ANTHONY EDWARDS
CLIENT, THE ... ANTHONY HEALD
CLIENT, THE ... ANTHONY LaPAGLIA
CLIENT, THE ... BRAD RENFRO
CLIENT, THE ... BRAD WHITFORD
CLIENT, THE ... DAVID SPECK
CLIENT, THE ... J. T. WALSH
CLIENT, THE ... JO HARVEY ALLEN
CLIENT, THE ... KIM COATES
CLIENT, THE ... KIMBERLY SCOTT
CLIENT, THE ... MARY-LOUISE PARKER
CLIENT, THE ... MICOLE MERCURIO
CLIENT, THE ... OSSIE DAVIS
CLIENT, THE ... RON DEAN
CLIENT, THE ... SUSAN SARANDON
CLIENT, THE ... TOMMY LEE JONES
CLIENT, THE ... WALTER OLKEWICZ
CLIENT, THE ... WILL PATTON
CLIENT, THE ... WILLIAM H. MACY
CLIENT, THE ... WILLIAM RICHERT
CLIENT, THE ... WILLIAM SANDERSON
CLIFFHANGER ... CAROLINE GOODALL
CLIFFHANGER ... JANINE TURNER
CLIFFHANGER ... JOHN LITHGOW
CLIFFHANGER ... LEON
CLIFFHANGER ... MICHAEL ROOKER
CLIFFHANGER ... RALPH WAITE
CLIFFHANGER ... REX LINN
CLIFFHANGER ... SYLVESTER STALLONE
CLIFFORD ... CHARLES GRODIN
CLIFFORD ... DABNEY COLEMAN
CLIFFORD ... MARTIN SHORT
CLIFFORD ... MARY STEENBURGEN
CLOAK AND DAGGER ... DABNEY COLEMAN
CLOAK AND DAGGER ... MICHAEL MURPHY
CLOAK & DAGGER ... HENRY THOMAS
CLOAK & DAGGER ... LOUIE ANDERSON
CLOAK & DAGGER ... WILLIAM FORSYTHE
CLOCK, THE ... JUDY GARLAND†
CLOCKERS ... DELROY LINDO
CLOCKERS ... HARVEY KEITEL
CLOCKERS ... ISAIAH WASHINGTON
CLOCKERS ... JOHN TURTURRO
CLOCKERS ... KEITH DAVID
CLOCKERS ... MEKHI PHIFER

This is not a list of every film ever made or every cast member, only those listed in this directory.

CLOCKWISE ..... ALISON STEADMAN
CLOCKWISE ..... JOHN CLEESE
CLOCKWISE ..... PENELOPE WILTON
CLOCKWISE ..... SHARON MAIDEN
CLOCKWISE ..... STEPHAN MOORE
CLOCKWORK ORANGE, A ..... MALCOLM McDOWELL
CLONE MASTER, THE (TF) ..... RALPH BELLAMY†
CLOSE ENCOUNTERS OF THE THIRD KIND ..... BASIL HOFFMAN
CLOSE ENCOUNTERS OF THE THIRD KIND ..... BOB BALABAN
CLOSE ENCOUNTERS OF THE THIRD KIND ..... CARL WEATHERS
CLOSE ENCOUNTERS OF THE THIRD KIND ..... FRANCOIS TRUFFAUT†
CLOSE ENCOUNTERS OF THE THIRD KIND ..... RICHARD DREYFUSS
CLOSE ENCOUNTERS OF THE THIRD KIND ..... TERI GARR
CLOSE ENCOUNTERS OF THE THIRD KIND ✪ ..... MELINDA DILLON
CLOSER, THE ..... DANNY AIELLO
CLOSER, THE ..... JUSTINE BATEMAN
CLOSER, THE ..... MICHAEL LERNER
CLOSER, THE ..... MICHAEL PARE
CLOSER, THE ..... RICK AIELLO
CLOSET LAND ..... ALAN RICKMAN
CLOSET LAND ..... MADELEINE STOWE
CLOUD DANCER ..... DAVID CARRADINE
CLOUD DANCER ..... HOYT AXTON
CLOUD DANCER ..... JENNIFER O'NEILL
CLOUD DANCER ..... JOSEPH BOTTOMS
CLOUD DANCER ..... NINA VAN PALLANDT
CLOUD DANCER ..... SALOME JENS
CLOUDED YELLOW, THE ..... JEAN SIMMONS
CLOWN MURDERS, THE ..... JOHN CANDY†
CLOWN, THE ..... JANE GREER
CLOWN, THE ..... STEVE FORREST
CLUB EXTINCTION ..... ALAN BATES
CLUB LIFE ..... TONY CURTIS
CLUB MED (TF) ..... LINDA HAMILTON
CLUB MED (TF) ..... PATRICK MacNEE
CLUB PARADISE ..... ANDREA MARTIN
CLUB PARADISE ..... BRIAN DOYLE-MURRAY
CLUB PARADISE ..... CAREY LOWELL
CLUB PARADISE ..... EUGENE LEVY
CLUB PARADISE ..... JIMMY CLIFF
CLUB PARADISE ..... JOANNA CASSIDY
CLUB PARADISE ..... JOE FLAHERTY
CLUB PARADISE ..... MARY GROSS
CLUB PARADISE ..... PETER O'TOOLE
CLUB PARADISE ..... RICK MORANIS
CLUB PARADISE ..... ROBIN DUKE
CLUB PARADISE ..... ROBIN WILLIAMS
CLUB PARADISE ..... SIMON JONES
CLUB PARADISE ..... STEVEN KAMPMANN
CLUB PARADISE ..... TWIGGY
CLUE ..... CHRISTOPHER LLOYD
CLUE ..... COLLEEN CAMP
CLUE ..... EILEEN BRENNAN
CLUE ..... LESLEY ANN WARREN
CLUE ..... MADELINE KAHN
CLUE ..... MARTIN MULL
CLUE ..... TIM CURRY
CLUE OF THE NEW PIN, THE ..... JOHN GIELGUD
CLUNY BROWN ..... JENNIFER JONES
COACH ..... MICHAEL BIEHN
COACH ..... RHEA PERLMAN
COAL MINER'S DAUGHTER ..... BEVERLY D'ANGELO
COAL MINER'S DAUGHTER ..... LEVON HELM
COAL MINER'S DAUGHTER ..... TOMMY LEE JONES
COAL MINER'S DAUGHTER ★★ ..... SISSY SPACEK
COAST GUARD ..... RALPH BELLAMY†
COAST TO COAST ..... DYAN CANNON
COAST TO COAST ..... MICHAEL LERNER
COAST TO COAST ..... ROBERT BLAKE
COBB ..... GRACE ZABRISKIE
COBB ..... J. KENNETH CAMPBELL
COBB ..... LOLITA DAVIDOVICH
COBB ..... LOU MYERS
COBB ..... REYNALDO REY
COBB ..... ROBERT WUHL
COBB ..... TOMMY LEE JONES
COBB ..... WILLIAM UTAY
COBRA ..... ANDREW ROBINSON
COBRA ..... ART LA FLEUR
COBRA ..... BRIAN THOMPSON
COBRA ..... BRIGITTE NIELSEN
COBRA ..... DAVID RASCHE
COBRA ..... JOHN HERZFELD
COBRA ..... LEE GARLINGTON
COBRA ..... MARCO RODRIGUEZ
COBRA ..... RENI SANTONI
COBRA ..... ROSS ST. PHILLIP
COBRA ..... SYLVESTER STALLONE
COBRA ..... VAL AVERY
COBWEB, THE ..... LAUREN BACALL
COBWEB, THE ..... LILLIAN GISH†
COBWEB, THE ..... RICHARD WIDMARK
COBWEB, THE ..... SUSAN STRASBERG
COCA COLA KID, THE ..... ERIC ROBERTS
COCA COLA KID, THE ..... GRETA SCACCHI
COCAINE COWBOYS ..... JACK PALANCE
COCAINE: ONE MAN'S SEDUCTION (TF) ..... JAMES SPADER
COCAINE WARS ..... JOHN SCHNEIDER
COCKEYED COWBOYS OF CALICO COUNTY, THE ..... STUBBY KAYE
COCKFIGHTER ..... ED BEGLEY JR.
COCKFIGHTER ..... HARRY DEAN STANTON
COCKFIGHTER ..... MILLIE PERKINS
COCKFIGHTER ..... TROY DONAHUE
COCKLESHELL HEROES, THE ..... JOSE FERRER†
COCKTAIL ..... BRYON BROWN
COCKTAIL ..... ELISABETH SHUE
COCKTAIL ..... TOM CRUISE
COCOON ..... BARRET OLIVER
COCOON ..... BRIAN DENNEHY
COCOON ..... CLINT HOWARD
COCOON ..... GWEN VERDON
COCOON ..... HERTA WARE
COCOON ..... HUME CRONYN
COCOON ..... JACK GILFORD†
COCOON ..... JESSICA TANDY†
COCOON ..... LINDA HARRISON
COCOON ..... MAUREEN STAPLETON
COCOON ..... STEVE GUTTENBERG
COCOON ..... TAHNEE WELCH
COCOON ..... TYRONE POWER JR.
COCOON ..... WILFORD BRIMLEY
COCOON ✪✪ ..... DON AMECHE†
COCOON: THE RETURN ..... BARRET OLIVER
COCOON: THE RETURN ..... BRIAN DENNEHY
COCOON: THE RETURN ..... COURTENEY COX
COCOON: THE RETURN ..... DON AMECHE†
COCOON: THE RETURN ..... ELAINE STRITCH
COCOON: THE RETURN ..... GWEN VERDON
COCOON: THE RETURN ..... HERTA WARE
COCOON: THE RETURN ..... HUME CRONYN
COCOON: THE RETURN ..... JACK GILFORD†
COCOON: THE RETURN ..... JESSICA TANDY†
COCOON: THE RETURN ..... MAUREEN STAPLETON
COCOON: THE RETURN ..... STEVE GUTTENBERG
COCOON: THE RETURN ..... TAHNEE WELCH
COCOON: THE RETURN ..... TYRONE POWER JR.
COCOON: THE RETURN ..... WILFORD BRIMLEY
CODE NAME: EMERALD ..... ED HARRIS
CODE NAME: EMERALD ..... ERIC STOLTZ
CODE OF HONOR/ BITTERSWEET REVENGE (TF) ..... ALEC BALDWIN
CODE OF SILENCE ..... CHUCK NORRIS
CODE OF SILENCE ..... JOHN MAHONEY
CODE OF THE SECRET SERVICE ..... RONALD REAGAN
CODE OF THE STREETS ..... LEON AMES
CODE OF THE WEST ..... RAYMOND BURR†
CODE OF VENGEANCE (TF) ..... LENKA PETERSON
CODENAME: FOXFIRE (TF) ..... HENRY JONES
CODENAME: FOXFIRE (TF) ..... JOANNA CASSIDY
CODENAME: KYRIL (TF) ..... JOHN McENERY
CODENAME: WILDGEESE ..... ERNEST BORGNINE
COFFEE, TEA OR ME? (TF) ..... JOHN DAVIDSON
COFFEE, TEA OR ME? (TF) ..... KAREN VALENTINE
COFFEE, TEA OR ME? (TF) ..... LOUISE LASSER
COFFY ..... PAM GRIER
COHEN & TATE ..... ADAM BALDWIN
COHEN & TATE ..... HARLEY CROSS
COHEN & TATE ..... ROY SCHEIDER
COHENS AND KELLYS IN TROUBLE, THE ..... MAUREEN O'SULLIVAN
COLD FEET ..... BILL PULLMAN
COLD FEET ..... GRIFFIN DUNNE
COLD FEET ..... JEFF BRIDGES
COLD FEET ..... KATHLEEN YORK
COLD FEET ..... KEITH CARRADINE
COLD FEET ..... RIP TORN
COLD FEET ..... SALLY KIRKLAND
COLD FEET ..... TOM WAITS
COLD FEET ..... VINCENT SCHIAVELLI
COLD HEAVEN ..... JAMES RUSSO
COLD HEAVEN ..... JULIE CARMEN
COLD HEAVEN ..... MARK HARMON
COLD HEAVEN ..... RICHARD BRADFORD
COLD HEAVEN ..... TALIA SHIRE
COLD HEAVEN ..... THERESA RUSSELL
COLD HEAVEN ..... WILL PATTON
COLD NIGHT'S DEATH, A (TF) ..... ELI WALLACH
COLD RIVER ..... RICHARD JAECKEL
COLD ROOM, THE (CTF) ..... GEORGE SEGAL
COLD SASSY TREE (CTF) ..... FAYE DUNAWAY
COLD SASSY TREE (CTF) ..... FRANCES FISHER
COLD SASSY TREE (CTF) ..... NEIL PATRICK HARRIS
COLD SASSY TREE (CTF) ..... RICHARD WIDMARK
COLD STEEL ..... ADAM ANT
COLD STEEL ..... BRAD DAVIS†
COLD STEEL ..... SHARON STONE
COLD SWEAT ..... CHARLES BRONSON
COLD SWEAT ..... LIV ULLMANN
COLD TURKEY ..... BOB NEWHART
COLD TURKEY ..... DICK VAN DYKE
COLD TURKEY ..... JEAN STAPLETON
COLD TURKEY ..... TOM POSTON
COLD TURKEY ..... VINCENT GARDENIA†
COLDBLOODED ..... JANEANE GAROFALO
COLDBLOODED ..... JASON PRIESTLEY
COLDBLOODED ..... JAY KOGEN
COLDBLOODED ..... KIMBERLY WILLIAMS
COLDBLOODED ..... PETER RIEGERT
COLDITZ STORY, THE ..... JOHN MILLS
COLDITZ STORY, THE ..... THEODORE BIKEL
COLLECTION, THE (TF) ..... ALAN BATES
COLLECTOR, THE ..... TERENCE STAMP
COLLECTOR, THE ★ ..... SAMANTHA EGGAR
COLLEGE CONFIDENTIAL ..... STEVE ALLEN
COLLEGE HOLIDAY ..... DOROTHY LAMOUR
COLLEGE HOLIDAY ..... GEORGE BURNS
COLLEGE HOLIDAY ..... MARTHA RAYE†
COLLEGE HUMOR ..... GEORGE BURNS
COLLEGE RHYTHM ..... DEAN JAGGER†
COLLEGE SWING ..... BOB HOPE
COLLEGE SWING ..... GEORGE BURNS
COLLEGE SWING ..... MARTHA RAYE†
COLLISION COURSE ..... LOIS NETTLETON
COLLISION COURSE ..... NORIYUKI "PAT" MORITA
COLONEL BLIMP ..... PATRICK MacNEE
COLONEL REDL ..... KLAUS MARIA BRANDAUER
COLOR OF EVENING, THE ..... KYLE CHANDLER
COLOR OF MONEY, THE ..... BILL COBBS
COLOR OF MONEY, THE ..... FOREST WHITAKER
COLOR OF MONEY, THE ..... HELEN SHAVER
COLOR OF MONEY, THE ..... JOHN TURTURRO
COLOR OF MONEY, THE ..... ROBERT AGINS
COLOR OF MONEY, THE ..... TOM CRUISE
COLOR OF MONEY, THE ★★ ..... PAUL NEWMAN
COLOR OF MONEY, THE ✪ ..... MARY ELIZABETH MASTRANTONIO
COLOR OF NIGHT ..... BRAD DOURIF
COLOR OF NIGHT ..... BRUCE WILLIS
COLOR OF NIGHT ..... JANE MARCH
COLOR OF NIGHT ..... KEVIN J. O'CONNOR
COLOR OF NIGHT ..... LANCE HENRIKSEN
COLOR OF NIGHT ..... LESLEY ANN WARREN
COLOR OF NIGHT ..... RUBEN BLADES
COLOR OF NIGHT ..... SCOTT BAKULA
COLOR PURPLE, THE ..... AKOSUA BUSIA

† after an actor's name denotes deceased.

COLOR PURPLE, THE .... DANA IVEY
COLOR PURPLE, THE .... LAURENCE FISHBURNE
COLOR PURPLE, THE .... RAE DAWN CHONG
COLOR PURPLE, THE ★ .... WHOOPI GOLDBERG
COLOR PURPLE, THE ○ .... MARGARET AVERY
COLOR PURPLE, THE ○ .... OPRAH WINFREY
COLORS .... DAMON WAYANS
COLORS .... GRAND L. BUSH
COLORS .... MARIA CONCHITA ALONSO
COLORS .... ROBERT DUVALL
COLORS .... SEAN PENN
COLORS .... TRINIDAD SILVA JR.†
COLOSSUS OF RHODES, THE .... RORY CALHOUN
COLOSSUS: THE FORBIN
    PROJECT .... GEORG STANFORD BROWN
COLOSSUS: THE FORBIN
    PROJECT .... SUSAN CLARK
COLPO SECCO .... JOHN PHILLIP LAW
COLT .45 .... LLOYD BRIDGES
COLT COMRADES .... ROBERT MITCHUM
COMA .... ED HARRIS
COMA .... ELIZABETH ASHLEY
COMA .... GENEVIEVE BUJOLD
COMA .... LOIS CHILES
COMA .... MICHAEL DOUGLAS
COMA .... RICHARD WIDMARK
COMA .... RIP TORN
COMA .... TOM SELLECK
COMANCHE STATION .... CLAUDE AKINS†
COMANCHE TERRITORY .... MAUREEN O'HARA
COMANCHEROS, THE .... HARRY CAREY JR.
COMANCHEROS, THE .... NEHEMIAH PERSOFF
COMANCHEROS, THE .... PATRICK WAYNE
COMANCHEROS, THE .... STUART WHITMAN
COMBAT HIGH (TF) .... DANA HILL
COMBAT HIGH (TF) .... JAMIE FARR
COMBAT HIGH (TF) .... KEITH GORDON
COMBAT HIGH (TF) .... SHERMAN HEMSLEY
COMBAT SQUAD .... JOHN IRELAND
COME AND GET IT ○○ .... WALTER BRENNAN†
COME BACK, CHARLESTON
    BLUE .... RAYMOND ST. JACQUES
COME BACK LITTLE SHEBA .... BURT LANCASTER†
COME BACK LITTLE SHEBA .... RICHARD JAECKEL
COME BACK TO THE 5 & DIME
    JIMMY DEAN, JIMMY DEAN .... CHER
COME BACK TO THE 5 & DIME
    JIMMY DEAN, JIMMY DEAN .... KAREN BLACK
COME BACK TO THE 5 & DIME
    JIMMY DEAN, JIMMY DEAN .... KATHY BATES
COME BACK TO THE 5 & DIME
    JIMMY DEAN, JIMMY DEAN .... MARTA HEFLIN
COME BACK TO THE 5 & DIME
    JIMMY DEAN, JIMMY DEAN .... SANDY DENNIS†
COME BACK TO THE 5 & DIME
    JIMMY DEAN, JIMMY DEAN .... SUDIE BOND
COME BLOW YOUR HORN .... FRANK SINATRA
COME BLOW YOUR HORN .... JILL ST. JOHN
COME BLOW YOUR HORN .... TONY BILL
COME FILL THE CUP .... PHYLLIS THAXTER
COME FILL THE CUP ○ .... GIG YOUNG†
COME FLY WITH ME .... KARL MALDEN
COME FLY WITH ME .... LOIS MAXWELL
COME FLY WITH ME .... LOIS NETTLETON
COME LIVE WITH ME .... JAMES STEWART
COME SEE THE PARADISE .... DENNIS QUAID
COME SEE THE PARADISE .... SHIZUKO HOSHI
COME SEE THE PARADISE .... STAN EGI
COME SEE THE PARADISE .... TAMLYN TOMITA
COME SEPTEMBER .... JOEL GREY
COME SEPTEMBER .... SANDRA DEE
COME SPY WITH ME ○ .... TROY DONAHUE
COME TO THE STABLE ○ .... ELSA LANCHESTER†
COME TO THE STABLE ○ .... CELESTE HOLM
COMEBACK, THE .... DAVID DOYLE
COMEBACK, THE (TF) .... BRYNN THAYER
COMEBACK, THE (TF) .... CHYNNA PHILLIPS
COMEBACK, THE (TF) .... MITCHELL ANDERSON
COMEBACK, THE (TF) .... ROBERT URICH
COMEBACK, THE (TF) .... RONNY COX
COMEBACK KID, THE (TF) .... PATRICK SWAYZE
COMEDIANS, THE .... ALEC GUINNESS

COMEDIANS, THE .... CICELY TYSON
COMEDIANS, THE .... ELIZABETH TAYLOR
COMEDIANS, THE .... GEORG STANFORD BROWN
COMEDIANS, THE .... JAMES EARL JONES
COMEDIANS, THE .... LILLIAN GISH†
COMEDIANS, THE .... PETER USTINOV
COMEDIANS, THE .... RAYMOND ST. JACQUES
COMEDIANS, THE .... ROSCOE LEE BROWNE
COMEDY COMPANY, THE (TF) .... ABE VIGODA
COMEDY MAN, THE .... BILLIE WHITELAW
COMEDY OF TERRORS, THE .... VINCENT PRICE†
COMES A HORSEMAN .... GEORGE GRIZZARD
COMES A HORSEMAN .... JAMES CAAN
COMES A HORSEMAN .... JAMES KEACH
COMES A HORSEMAN .... JANE FONDA
COMES A HORSEMAN .... JASON ROBARDS
COMES A HORSEMAN .... MARK HARMON
COMES A
    HORSEMAN ○ .... RICHARD FARNSWORTH
COMFORT OF
    STRANGERS, THE .... CHRISTOPHER WALKEN
COMFORT OF STRANGERS, THE ..... HELEN MIRREN
COMFORT OF
    STRANGERS, THE .... NATASHA RICHARDSON
COMFORT OF
    STRANGERS, THE .... RUPERT EVERETT
COMIC, THE .... CARL REINER
COMIC, THE .... DICK VAN DYKE
COMIC, THE .... MICHELE LEE
COMIC, THE .... STEVE ALLEN
COMING APART .... RIP TORN
COMING APART .... SALLY KIRKLAND
COMING ATTRACTIONS .... AVERY SCHREIBER
COMING ATTRACTIONS .... BILL MURRAY
COMING ATTRACTIONS .... BUDDY HACKETT
COMING ATTRACTIONS ...... HOWARD HESSEMAN
COMING ATTRACTIONS .... SUSAN TYRRELL
COMING HOME ★★ .... ROBERT CARRADINE
COMING HOME ★★ .... JANE FONDA
COMING HOME ★★ .... JON VOIGHT
COMING HOME ○ .... BRUCE DERN
COMING HOME ○ .... PENELOPE MILFORD
COMING OUT OF
    THE ICE (TF) .... FRANCESCA ANNIS
COMING OUT OF THE ICE (TF) .... JOHN SAVAGE
COMING OUT OF THE ICE (TF) .... WILLIE NELSON
COMING TO AMERICA .... ARSSENIO HALL
COMING TO AMERICA .... DON AMECHE†
COMING TO AMERICA .... EDDIE MURPHY
COMING TO AMERICA .... ERIQ LA SALLE
COMING TO AMERICA .... JAKE STEINFELD
COMING TO AMERICA .... JAMES EARL JONES
COMING TO AMERICA .... JOHN AMOS
COMING TO AMERICA .... LOUIE ANDERSON
COMING TO AMERICA .... MADGE SINCLAIR
COMING TO AMERICA .... PAUL BATES
COMING TO AMERICA .... RALPH BELLAMY†
COMING TO AMERICA .... SHARI HEADLEY
COMMAND DECISION .... VAN JOHNSON
COMMANDO .... ARNOLD SCHWARZENEGGER
COMMANDO .... JAMES OLSON
COMMANDO .... RAE DAWN CHONG
COMMANDO SQUAD .... ROSS HAGEN
COMMANDO SQUAD .... SID HAIG
COMMANDOS STRIKE
    AT DAWN, THE .... LILLIAN GISH†
COMMITMENTS, THE .... ANDREW STRONG
COMMITMENTS, THE .... ANGELINE BALL
COMMITMENTS, THE .... COLM MEANEY
COMMITMENTS, THE .... KEN McCLUSKEY
COMMITMENTS, THE .... MICHAEL AHERNE
COMMITMENTS, THE .... ROBERT ARKINS
COMMITMENTS, THE .... ROBERT ARKINS
COMMON GROUND (MS) .... JAMES FARENTINO
COMMON GROUND (MS) .... JANE CURTIN
COMMON GROUND (TF) .... C. C. H. POUNDER
COMMUNION .... ANDREAS KATSULAS
COMMUNION .... BASIL HOFFMAN
COMMUNION .... CHRISTOPHER WALKEN
COMMUNION .... FRANCES STERNHAGEN
COMMUNION .... JOEL CARLSON
COMMUNION .... LINDSAY CROUSE

COMMUNION .... TERRI HANAUER
COMMUNION/HOLY TERROR ...... BROOKE SHIELDS
COMMUNISTS ARE COMFORTABLE
    (AND THREE OTHER
    STORIES), THE .... SPALDING GRAY
COMMUNISTS ARE COMFORTABLE
    (AND THREE OTHER
    STORIES), THE .... WILLEM DAFOE
COMPANEROS .... FRANCO NERO
COMPANEROS, THE .... JACK PALANCE
COMPANIONS IN
    NIGHTMARE (TF) .... LOUIS GOSSETT JR.
COMPANY BUSINESS .... GENE HACKMAN
COMPANY BUSINESS .... MIKHAIL BARYSHNIKOV
COMPANY OF COWARDS .... ANDREW PRINE
COMPANY OF KILLERS .... FRITZ WEAVER
COMPANY OF KILLERS .... JOHN SAXON
COMPANY OF KILLERS .... VAN JOHNSON
COMPANY OF WOLVES, THE .... ANGELA LANSBURY
COMPANY OF WOLVES, THE .... DAVID WARNER
COMPANY OF WOLVES, THE .... STEPHEN REA
COMPANY OF WOLVES, THE .... TERENCE STAMP
COMPANY SHE KEEPS, THE .... JANE GREER
COMPANY SHE KEEPS, THE .... JEFF BRIDGES
COMPETITION, THE .... AMY IRVING
COMPETITION, THE .... BEN HAMMER
COMPETITION, THE .... RICHARD DREYFUSS†
COMPETITION, THE .... SAM WANAMAKER†
COMPROMISING POSITIONS .... ANNE DESALVO
COMPROMISING POSITIONS .... DEBORAH RUSH
COMPROMISING
    POSITIONS .... EDWARD HERRMANN
COMPROMISING POSITIONS .... JOAN ALLEN
COMPROMISING POSITIONS .... JOE MANTEGNA
COMPROMISING POSITIONS .... JOSH MOSTEL
COMPROMISING POSITIONS .... JUDITH IVEY
COMPROMISING POSITIONS ...... MARY BETH HURT
COMPROMISING POSITIONS .... RAUL JULIA†
COMPROMISING POSITIONS .... SUSAN SARANDON
COMPULSION .... BRADFORD DILLMAN
COMPULSION .... DEAN STOCKWELL
COMPULSION .... E. G. MARSHALL
COMPULSION .... RICHARD ANDERSON
COMPUTER WORE TENNIS
    SHOES, THE .... KURT RUSSELL
CON ARTISTS, THE .... ANTHONY QUINN
CONAN THE
    BARBARIAN .... ARNOLD SCHWARZENEGGER
CONAN THE BARBARIAN .... JAMES EARL JONES
CONAN THE BARBARIAN .... MAKO
CONAN THE
    DESTROYER .... ARNOLD SCHWARZENEGGER
CONAN THE DESTROYER .... GRACE JONES
CONAN THE DESTROYER .... JEFF COREY
CONAN THE DESTROYER .... MAKO
CONAN THE DESTROYER .... OLIVIA D'ABO
CONAN THE DESTROYER .... SARAH DOUGLAS
CONAN THE DESTROYER .... TRACEY WALTER
CONAN THE DESTROYER .... WILT CHAMBERLAIN
CONCORDE—
    AIRPORT '79, THE .... ANDREA MARCOVICCI
CONCORDE—
    AIRPORT '79, THE .... BIBI ANDERSSON
CONCORDE—AIRPORT '79, THE .... CHARO
CONCORDE—AIRPORT '79, THE .... CICELY TYSON
CONCORDE—AIRPORT '79, THE ...... DAVID WARNER
CONCORDE—AIRPORT '79, THE ...... ED BEGLEY JR.
CONCORDE—AIRPORT '79, THE .... EDDIE ALBERT
CONCORDE—
    AIRPORT '79, THE .... GEORGE KENNEDY
CONCORDE—AIRPORT '79, THE ...... JIMMIE WALKER
CONCORDE—
    AIRPORT '79, THE .... JOHN DAVIDSON
CONCORDE—AIRPORT '79, THE ..... MARTHA RAYE†
CONCORDE—
    AIRPORT '79, THE ...... MERCEDES McCAMBRIDGE
CONCORDE—
    AIRPORT '79, THE .... ROBERT WAGNER
CONCORDE—
    AIRPORT '79, THE .... SUSAN BLAKELY
CONCORDE—AIRPORT '79, THE .... SYLVIA KRISTEL
CONCRETE COWBOYS, THE (TF) ...... TOM SELLECK

426

CONCRETE JUNGLE, THE ....SAM WANAMAKER†	CONRACK ....JON VOIGHT	COOL HAND LUKE ....DENNIS HOPPER
CONDEMNED ★ .... RONALD COLMAN†	CONRACK .... PAUL WINFIELD	COOL HAND LUKE .... HARRY DEAN STANTON
CONDEMNED OF	CONSENTING ADULT (TF) .... MARLO THOMAS	COOL HAND LUKE .... J. D. CANNON
ALTONA, THE ....MAXIMILIAN SCHELL	CONSENTING ADULT (TF) .... MARTIN SHEEN	COOL HAND LUKE .... JOE DON BAKER
CONDEMNED OF	CONSENTING	COOL HAND LUKE ★ .... PAUL NEWMAN
ALTONA, THE ....ROBERT WAGNER	ADULTS .... BENJAMIN HENDRICKSOIN	COOL HAND LUKE ○○ .... GEORGE KENNEDY
CONDEMNED OF ALTONA, THE .... SOPHIA LOREN	CONSENTING ADULTS .... E. G. MARSHALL	COOL ONES, THE .... NITA TALBOT
CONDOMINIUM (TF) ....RALPH BELLAMY†	CONSENTING ADULTS .... FOREST WHITAKER	COOL ONES, THE .... RODDY McDOWALL
CONDORMAN .... JAMES HAMPTON	CONSENTING ADULTS .... KEVIN KLINE	COOL RUNNINGS .... DOUG E. DOUG
CONDUCT	CONSENTING ADULTS .... KEVIN SPACEY	COOL RUNNINGS .... JOHN CANDY†
UNBECOMING .... CHRISTOPHER PLUMMER	CONSENTING ADULTS .... KIMBERLY McCULLOUGH	COOL RUNNINGS .... LEON
CONDUCT UNBECOMING .... MICHAEL YORK	CONSENTING	COOL RUNNINGS .... MALIK YOBA
CONDUCT UNBECOMING .... STACY KEACH	ADULTS .... MARY ELIZABETH MASTRANTONIO	COOL RUNNINGS .... RAWLE D. LEWIS
CONDUCT UNBECOMING .... SUSANNAH YORK	CONSENTING ADULTS .... REBECCA MILLER	COOL WORLD .... BRAD PITT
CONEHEADS .... DAN AYKROYD	CONSPIRACY OF LOVE (TF) .... DREW BARRYMORE	COOL WORLD .... GABRIEL BYRNE
CONEHEADS .... JANE CURTIN	CONSPIRACY: TRIAL OF THE	COOL WORLD .... KIM BASINGER
CONEHEADS .... JASON ALEXANDER	CHICAGO 8 (CTF) .... ROBERT CARRADINE	COP .... CHARLES DURNING
CONEHEADS .... LARAINE NEWMAN	CONSPIRATOR .... ELIZABETH TAYLOR	COP .... CHARLES HAID
CONEHEADS .... MICHELLE BURKE	CONSTANT NYMPH, THE .... ALEXIS SMITH†	COP .... JAMES WOODS
CONEHEADS, THE .... CHRIS FARLEY	CONSUMING PASSIONS .... PRUNELLA SCALES	COP .... LESLEY ANN WARREN
CONFESSIONE DE UN	CONTEMPT .... JACK PALANCE	COP AND A HALF .... BURT REYNOLDS
COMMISSARIO .... FRANCO NERO	CONTINENTAL .... MARCELLO MASTROIANNI	COP AND A HALF .... NORMAN D. GOLDEN II
CONFESSIONE DI UN	CONTINENTAL DIVIDE .... ALLEN GARFIELD	COP AND A HALF .... RAY SHARKEY†
COMMISSARIO .... MARTIN BALSAM	CONTINENTAL DIVIDE .... BLAIR BROWN	COP AND A HALF .... RUBY DEE
CONFESSIONS OF A CO-ED .... SYLVIA SIDNEY	CONTINENTAL DIVIDE .... JOHN BELUSHI†	COP HATER .... ROBERT LOGGIA
CONFESSIONS OF A	CONTINENTAL DIVIDE .... TIM KAZURINSKY	COP HATER .... VINCENT GARDENIA†
FRUSTRATED HOUSEWIFE .... CARROLL BAKER	CONTRABAND SPAIN .... ANOUK AIMEE	COP ON THE BEAT (TF) .... EDIE ADAMS
CONFESSIONS OF A	CONTRACT ON CHERRY	COP ON THE BEAT (TF) .... LLOYD BRIDGES
MARRIED MAN (TF) .... MARY CROSBY	STREET (TF) .... STEVE INWOOD	COP-OUT .... GERALDINE CHAPLIN
CONFESSIONS OF A	CONTRACT ON CHERRY	COPACABANA (TF) .... ANNETTE O'TOOLE
MARRIED MAN (TF) .... ROBERT CONRAD	STREET (TF) .... FRANK SINATRA	COPACABANA (TF) .... BARRY MANILOW
CONFESSIONS OF A	CONTRACT, THE .... LESLIE CARON	COPACABANA (TF) .... ESTELLE GETTY
POLICE CAPTAIN .... FRANCO NERO	CONVERSATION PIECE .... BURT LANCASTER†	COPPER CANYON .... HARRY CAREY JR.
CONFESSIONS OF A	CONVERSATION, THE .... ALLEN GARFIELD	COPS AND ROBBERS .... CLIFF GORMAN
POLICE CAPTAIN .... MARTIN BALSAM	CONVERSATION, THE .... CINDY WILLIAMS	COPS AND ROBIN, THE (TF) .... CAROL LYNLEY
CONFESSIONS OF AN	CONVERSATION, THE .... FREDERIC FORREST	COPS & ROBBERSONS .... CHEVY CHASE
OPIUM EATER .... VINCENT PRICE†	CONVERSATION, THE .... GENE HACKMAN	COPS & ROBBERSONS .... DIANNE WIEST
CONFIDENCE GIRL .... JACK KRUSCHEN	CONVERSATION, THE .... HARRISON FORD	COPS & ROBBERSONS .... JACK PALANCE
CONFIDENTIAL AGENT .... LAUREN BACALL	CONVERSATION, THE .... ROBERT DUVALL	COPS & ROBBERSONS ...... JASON JAMES RICHTER
CONFIDENTIALLY CONNIE .... VAN JOHNSON	CONVERSATION, THE .... TIMOTHY CAREY	COPS & ROBBERSONS ...... ROBERT DAVI
CONFIDENTIALLY CONNIE .... JANET LEIGH	CONVICTED: A MOTHER'S	COPYCAT .... HOLLY HUNTER
CONFIRM OR DENY .... DON AMECHE†	STORY (TF) .... ANN JILLIAN	COPYCAT .... SIGOURNEY WEAVER
CONFIRM OR DENY .... RODDY McDOWALL	CONVICTED: A MOTHER'S	COPYCAT .... HARRY CONNICK JR.
CONFLICT .... ALEXIS SMITH†	STORY (TF) .... JENNY GAGO	COPYCAT .... JOHN ROTHMAN
CONGO .... DYLAN WALSH	CONVICTED (TF) ...... JOHN LARROQUETTE	COPYCAT .... WILLIAM MCNAMARA
CONGO .... ERNIE HUDSON	CONVICTED (TF) ...... LINDSAY WAGNER	COQUETTE ★★ .... MARY PICKFORD†
CONGO .... LAURA LINNEY	CONVICTS FOUR .... BEN GAZZARA	CORKY .... BEN JOHNSON
CONGO .... TIM CURRY	CONVICTS FOUR .... JACK KRUSCHEN	CORKY .... CHARLOTTE RAMPLING
CONGO .... GRANT HESLOV	CONVICTS FOUR .... RAY WALSTON	CORKY .... PATRICK O'NEAL†
CONGO MAISIE .... ANN SOTHERN	CONVICTS FOUR .... ROD STEIGER	CORKY .... ROBERT BLAKE
CONGRATULATIONS,	CONVICTS FOUR .... STUART WHITMAN	CORN IS GREEN, THE .... BETTE DAVIS†
IT'S A BOY! (TF) .... BILL BIXBY†	CONVICTS FOUR .... TIMOTHY CAREY	CORN IS GREEN, THE ○ .... JOHN DALL†
CONGRATULATIONS,	CONVICTS FOUR .... VINCENT PRICE†	CORN IS GREEN,
IT'S A BOY (TF) .... DIANE BAKER	CONVOY .... ALI MacGRAW	THE (TF) .... KATHERINE HEPBURN
CONNECTICUT	CONVOY .... BURT YOUNG	CORN IS GREEN, THE (TF) .... PATRICIA HAYES
YANKEE, A .... MAUREEN O'SULLIVAN	CONVOY .... CASSIE YATES	CORNBREAD, EARL
CONNECTICUT YANKEE IN KING	CONVOY .... ERNEST BORGNINE	AND ME .... LAURENCE FISHBURNE
ARTHUR'S COURT, A (TF) .... EMMA SAMMS	CONVOY .... FRANKLYN AJAYE	CORNBREAD EARL AND ME .... MOSES GUNN
CONNECTICUT YANKEE IN KING	CONVOY .... KRIS KRISTOFFERSON	CORNBREAD EARL AND ME .... ROSALIND CASH
ARTHUR'S COURT, A (TF) .... JEAN MARSH	CONVOY .... MADGE SINCLAIR	CORRIDOR OF MIRRORS .... LOIS MAXWELL
CONNECTICUT YANKEE IN KING	CONVOY .... SEYMOUR CASSEL	CORRINA, CORRINA .... CATHY MORIARTY
ARTHUR'S COURT, A (TF) .... MICHAEL GROSS	COOGAN'S BLUFF .... CLINT EASTWOOD	CORRINA, CORRINA .... DON AMECHE†
CONNECTICUT YANKEE IN KING	COOGAN'S BLUFF .... DON STROUD	CORRINA, CORRINA .... JENIFER LEWIS
ARTHUR'S COURT, A (TF) .... RENE AUBERJONOIS	COOGAN'S BLUFF .... SEYMOUR CASSEL	CORRINA, CORRINA .... JOAN CUSAK
CONNECTING ROOMS .... ALEXIS KANNER	COOGAN'S BLUFF .... SUSAN CLARK	CORRINA, CORRINA .... RAY LIOTTA
CONNECTING ROOMS .... BETTE DAVIS†	COOK, THE THIEF, HIS WIFE &	CORRINA, CORRINA .... TINA MAJORINO
CONNECTION, THE .... ROBERT BLAKE	HER LOVER, THE .... ALAN HOWARD	CORRINA, CORRINA .... WHOOPI GOLDBERG
CONNECTION, THE .... ROSCOE LEE BROWNE	COOK, THE THIEF, HIS WIFE &	CORRUPT .... HARVEY KEITEL
CONNECTION, THE (TF) .... CHARLES DURNING	HER LOVER, THE .... HELEN MIRREN	CORRUPT .... SYLVIA SIDNEY
CONQUERED CITY .... BEN GAZZARA	COOKIE .... ADRIAN PASDAR	CORRUPT ONES, THE .... ROBERT STACK
CONQUERED CITY .... MARTIN BALSAM	COOKIE .... BOB GUNTON	CORRUZIONE AL PALAZZO
CONQUEROR WORM, THE .... VINCENT PRICE†	COOKIE .... BRENDA VACCARO	DI GIUSTIZIA .... FRANCO NERO
CONQUEST ★ .... CHARLES BOYER†	COOKIE .... DIANNE WIEST	CORRUZIONE AL PALAZZO
CONQUEST OF COCHISE .... ROBERT STACK	COOKIE .... EMILY LLOYD	DI GIUSTIZIA .... MARTIN BALSAM
CONQUEST OF THE PLANET	COOKIE .... JERRY LEWIS	CORSICAN
OF THE APES .... DON MURRAY	COOKIE .... LIONEL STANDER	BROTHERS, THE (TF) .... GERALDINE CHAPLIN
CONQUEST OF THE PLANET	COOKIE .... MICHAEL V. GAZZO	CORSICAN BROTHERS, THE (TF) .... JEAN MARSH
OF THE APES .... GORDON JUMP	COOKIE .... PETER FALK	CORSICAN
CONQUEST OF THE PLANET	COOKIE .... RICKI LAKE	BROTHERS, THE (TF) .... NICHOLAS CLAY
OF THE APES .... RICARDO MONTALBAN	COOKIE .... ROCKETS REDGLARE	CORSICAN BROTHERS, THE (TF) .... SIMON WARD
CONQUEST OF THE PLANET	COOL BREEZE .... RAYMOND ST. JACQUES	CORVETTE K-225 .... ROBERT MITCHUM
OF THE APES .... RODDY McDOWALL	COOL BREEZE .... THALMUS RASULALA	CORVETTE SUMMER .... MARK HAMILL
CONRACK .... HUME CRONYN	COOL HAND LUKE .... CLIFTON JAMES	COSH BOY .... JOAN COLLINS

† after an actor's name denotes deceased.

COSI DOLCE...
COSI PERVERSA .... CARROLL BAKER
COSMIC EYE, THE (AF) .... MAUREEN STAPLETON
COTTAGE TO LET .... JOHN MILLS
COTTER .... CAROL LYNLEY
COTTER .... DON MURRAY
COTTON CLUB, THE .... ALLEN GARFIELD
COTTON CLUB, THE .... BOB HOSKINS
COTTON CLUB, THE .... DIANE LANE
COTTON CLUB, THE .... DIANE VENORA
COTTON CLUB, THE .... ED O'ROSS
COTTON CLUB, THE .... FRED GWYNNE†
COTTON CLUB, THE .... GREGORY HINES
COTTON CLUB, THE .... GWEN VERDON
COTTON CLUB, THE .... JAMES REMAR
COTTON CLUB, THE .... JENNIFER GREY
COTTON CLUB, THE .... PATTY DUKE
COTTON CLUB, THE .... JOE DALLESANDRO
COTTON CLUB, THE .... LAURENCE FISHBURNE
COTTON CLUB, THE .... LISA JANE PERSKY
COTTON CLUB, THE .... LONETTE McKEE
COTTON CLUB, THE .... MAURICE HINES
COTTON CLUB, THE .... NICK CORRI
COTTON CLUB, THE .... NICOLAS CAGE
COTTON CLUB, THE .... RICHARD GERE
COTTON CLUB, THE .... TOM WAITS
COTTON CLUB, THE .... WOODY STRODE
COTTON COMES TO HARLEM ..... CLEAVON LITTLE†
COTTON COMES TO HARLEM .... J. D. CANNON
COTTON COMES TO HARLEM ...... JOHN ANDERSON
COTTON COMES TO HARLEM .... LOU JACOBI
COTTON COMES
 TO HARLEM .... RAYMOND ST. JACQUES
COTTON COMES TO HARLEM .... REDD FOXX†
COUCH, THE .... SHIRLEY KNIGHT
COUCH TRIP, THE .... CHARLES GRODIN
COUCH TRIP, THE .... DAN AYKROYD
COUCH TRIP, THE .... WALTER MATTHAU
COULEUR CHAIR .... DENNIS HOPPER
COULEUR CHAIR .... LIV ULLMANN
COUNSELOR AT CRIME .... MARTIN BALSAM
COUNT DRACULA AND HIS
 VAMPIRE BRIDE .... FREDDIE JONES
COUNT DRACULA AND HIS
 VAMPIRE BRIDE .... JOANNA LUMLEY
COUNT OF MONTE
 CRISTO, THE .... DONALD PLEASENCE
COUNT OF MONTE CRISTO, THE .... LEON AMES
COUNT OF MONTE
 CRISTO, THE .... LOUIS JOURDAN
COUNT OF MONTE
 CRISTO, THE .... RICHARD CHAMBERLAIN
COUNT OF MONTE
 CRISTO, THE (TF) .... KATE NELLIGAN
COUNT OF MONTE
 CRISTO, THE (TF) .... LOUIS JOURDAN
COUNT OF MONTE
 CRISTO, THE (TF) .... TONY CURTIS
COUNT THE HOURS .... TERESA WRIGHT
COUNT THREE AND PRAY ..... JOANNE WOODWARD
COUNT THREE AND PRAY .... RAYMOND BURR†
COUNT YOUR BLESSINGS .... DEBORAH KERR
COUNTDOWN .... JAMES CAAN
COUNTDOWN .... MICHAEL MURPHY
COUNTDOWN .... ROBERT DUVALL
COUNTDOWN AT KUSINI .... OSSIE DAVIS
COUNTDOWN AT KUSINI .... RUBY DEE
COUNTERFEIT COMMANDOS .... BO SVENSON
COUNTERFEIT CONSTABLE, THE ..... MARK LESTER
COUNTERFEIT KILLER, THE ...... JACK WESTON
COUNTERFEIT KILLER, THE .... JOSEPH WISEMAN
COUNTERFEIT
 KILLER, THE .... MERCEDES McCAMBRIDGE
COUNTERFEIT KILLER, THE .... SHIRLEY KNIGHT
COUNTERFEIT LADY .... RALPH BELLAMY†
COUNTERFORCE .... ISAAC HAYES
COUNTERPOINT .... CHARLTON HESTON
COUNTERPOINT .... LESLIE NIELSEN
COUNTERPOINT .... MAXIMILIAN SCHELL
COUNTESS DRACULA .... LESLEY-ANNE DOWN
COUNTESS FROM
 HONG KONG, A .... MARLON BRANDO

COUNTESS FROM
 HONG KONG, A .... SOPHIA LOREN
COUNTESS FROM
 HONG KONG, A .... TIPPI HEDREN
COUNTESS FROM
 HONG KONG, THE .... GERALDINE CHAPLIN
COUNTRY ★ .... JESSICA LANGE
COUNTRY .... MATT CLARK
COUNTRY .... SAM SHEPARD
COUNTRY .... WILFORD BRIMLEY
COUNTRY DANCE .... BRIAN BLESSED
COUNTRY DANCE .... PETER O'TOOLE
COUNTRY DANCE .... SUSANNAH YORK
COUNTRY GIRL, THE ★ .... BING CROSBY†
COUNTRY GIRL, THE ★★ .... GRACE KELLY†
COUNTRY MUSIC HOLIDAY .... PATTY DUKE
COUP DE FOUDRE .... ISABELLE HUPPERT
COUP DE FOUDRE .... SAM WATERSTON
COUP DE TORCHON .... ISABELLE HUPPERT
COUPE DE VILLE .... ALAN ARKIN
COUPE DE VILLE .... ANNABETH GISH
COUPE DE VILLE .... ARYE GROSS
COUPE DE VILLE .... DANIEL STERN
COUPE DE VILLE .... JOSEPH BOLOGNA
COUPE DE VILLE .... PATRICK DEMPSEY
COUPE DE VILLE .... RITA TAGGART
COUPLE NEXT
 DOOR, THE (CTF) .... KATE CAPSHAW
COUPLE TAKES A WIFE, THE (TF) .... BILL BIXBY†
COURAGE .... LOIS CHILES
COURAGE (TF) .... DAN HEDAYA
COURAGE (TF) .... HECTOR ELIZONDO
COURAGE (TF) .... ROBIN BARTLETT
COURAGE (TF) .... SOPHIA LOREN
COURAGE MOUNTAIN .... CHARLIE SHEEN
COURAGE MOUNTAIN .... JAN RUBES
COURAGE MOUNTAIN .... JOANNA CLARKE
COURAGE MOUNTAIN .... JULIETTE CATON
COURAGE MOUNTAIN .... LAURA BETTI
COURAGE MOUNTAIN .... LESLIE CARON
COURAGE MOUNTAIN .... NICOLA STAPLETON
COURAGE MOUNTAIN .... YORGO VOYAGIS
COURAGE OF KAVIK THE
 WOLF DOG, THE .... JOHN IRELAND
COURAGE OF LASSIE .... ELIZABETH TAYLOR
COURAGEOUS MR. PENN .... DEBORAH KERR
COURT JESTER, THE .... ALAN NAPIER†
COURT JESTER, THE .... ANGELA LANSBURY
COURT MARTIAL OF BILLY
 MITCHELL, THE .... ELIZABETH MONTGOMERY
COURT-MARTIAL OF BILLY
 MITCHELL, THE .... DARREN McGAVIN
COURT-MARTIAL OF BILLY
 MITCHELL, THE .... PETER GRAVES
COURT-MARTIAL OF BILLY
 MITCHELL, THE .... RALPH BELLAMY†
COURT-MARTIAL OF BILLY
 MITCHELL, THE .... ROD STEIGER
COURTSHIP OF EDDIE'S
 FATHER, THE .... DINA MERRILL
COURTSHIP OF EDDIE'S
 FATHER, THE .... RON HOWARD
COURTSHIP OF EDDIE'S
 FATHER, THE .... SHIRLEY JONES
COURTSHIP OF EDDIE'S
 FATHER, THE .... STELLA STEVENS
COUSIN, COUSINE .... MARIE-FRANCE PISIER
COUSIN,
 COUSINE ★ .... MARIE-CHRISTINE BARRAULT
COUSINS .... GEORGE COE
COUSINS .... GINA DEANGELIS
COUSINS .... ISABELLA ROSSELLINI
COUSINS .... KEITH COOGAN
COUSINS .... LLOYD BRIDGES
COUSINS .... NORMA ALEANDRO
COUSINS .... SEAN YOUNG
COUSINS .... TED DANSON
COUSINS .... WILLIAM L. PETERSEN
COVENANT WITH DEATH, A .... EARL HOLLIMAN
COVENANT WITH DEATH, A .... GENE HACKMAN
COVENANT WITH DEATH, A .... KATHY JURADO
COVER GIRL .... GENE KELLY

COVER GIRL .... SHELLEY WINTERS
COVER GIRL AND
 THE COP, THE (TF) .... BLAIR UNDERWOOD
COVER GIRL AND
 THE COP, THE (TF) .... DAVID CARRADINE
COVER GIRL AND
 THE COP, THE (TF) .... DINAH MANOFF
COVER GIRL AND
 THE COP, THE (TF) .... JOHN KARLEN
COVER GIRL AND
 THE COP, THE (TF) .... PARKER STEVENSON
COVER GIRLS (TF) .... GEORGE LAZENBY
COVER ME BABE .... ROBERT FORSTER
COVER ME BABE .... SAM WATERSTON
COVER UP (TF) .... DOUG McCLURE
COVER UP (TF) .... JENNIFER O'NEILL
COVER UP (TF) .... RICHARD ANDERSON
COVERGIRL .... JEFF CONAWAY
COWARD OF THE COUNTY (TF) .... ANA ALICIA
COWBOY .... JACK LEMMON
COWBOY .... RICHARD JAECKEL
COWBOY AND THE
 BALLERINA, THE (TF) .... LEE MAJORS
COWBOY FROM
 BROOKLYN, THE .... RONALD REAGAN
COWBOY WAY, THE .... DYLAN McDERMOTT
COWBOY WAY, THE .... ERNIE HUDSON
COWBOY WAY, THE .... KIEFER SUTHERLAND
COWBOY WAY, THE .... KRISTIN BAER
COWBOY WAY, THE .... WOODY HARRELSON
COWBOYS, THE .... BRUCE DERN
COWBOYS, THE .... COLLEEN DEWHURST†
COWBOYS, THE .... JOHN WAYNE†
COWBOYS, THE .... LONNY CHAPMAN
COWBOYS, THE .... ROBERT CARRADINE
COWBOYS, THE .... ROSCOE LEE BROWNE
CRACK HOUSE .... ANTHONY GEARY
CRACK HOUSE .... JIM BROWN
CRACK HOUSE .... RICHARD ROUNDTREE
CRACK IN THE MIRROR .... BRADFORD DILLMAN
CRACK IN THE MIRROR .... SALLY KIRKLAND
CRACKDOWN .... CLIFF DE YOUNG
CRACKDOWN .... ROBERT BELTRAN
CRACKED UP (TF) .... ED ASNER
CRACKED UP (TF) .... JAMES WILDER
CRACKED UP (TF) .... KIM DELANEY
CRACKED UP (TF) .... LEO ROSSI
CRACKED UP (TF) .... RAPHAEL SBARGE
CRACKER FACTORY, THE (TF) .... PERRY KING
CRACKERS .... CHRISTINE BARANSKI
CRACKERS .... DONALD SUTHERLAND
CRACKERS .... JACK WARDEN
CRACKERS .... SEAN PENN
CRACKERS .... TRINIDAD SILVA JR.†
CRACKING UP .... DICK BUTKUS
CRACKING UP .... HERB EDELMAN
CRACKING UP .... JERRY LEWIS
CRASH! .... JOE DON BAKER
CRASH! .... JOSE FERRER†
CRASH COURSE (TF) .... HARVEY KORMAN
CRASH COURSE (TF) .... TINA YOTHERS
CRASH DIVE .... HARRY MORGAN
CRASH LANDING .... MAC DAVIS
CRASH McCALL .... E. G. MARSHALL
CRAWLSPACE .... BARBARA WHINNERY
CRAWLSPACE .... KLAUS KINSKI†
CRAWLSPACE .... SALLY BROWN
CRAWLSPACE .... TALIA BALSAM
CRAWLSPACE (TF) .... TERESA WRIGHT
CRAZE .... JACK PALANCE
CRAZY FROM THE
 HEART (CTF) .... RUBEN BLADES
CRAZY FROM THE
 HEART (CTF) .... CHRISTINE LAHTI
CRAZY IN LOVE (CTF) .... HOLLY HUNTER
CRAZY JOE .... ELI WALLACH
CRAZY JOE .... FRED WILLIAMSON
CRAZY JOE .... HENRY WINKLER
CRAZY JOE .... PAULA PRENTISS
CRAZY JOE .... PETER BOYLE
CRAZY JOE .... RIP TORN
CRAZY MAMA .... ANN SOTHERN

CRAZY MAMA .... CLORIS LEACHMAN
CRAZY MAMA .... SALLY KIRKLAND
CRAZY MOON .... KIEFER SUTHERLAND
CRAZY PEOPLE .... ALAN NORTH
CRAZY PEOPLE .... BEN HAMMER
CRAZY PEOPLE .... BILL SMITROVICH
CRAZY PEOPLE .... DANTON STONE
CRAZY PEOPLE .... DARYL HANNAH
CRAZY PEOPLE .... DAVID PAYMER
CRAZY PEOPLE .... DICK CUSAK
CRAZY PEOPLE .... DOUG YASUDA
CRAZY PEOPLE .... DUDLEY MOORE
CRAZY PEOPLE .... FLOYD VIVINO
CRAZY PEOPLE .... J. T. WALSH
CRAZY PEOPLE .... JOHN TERLESKY
CRAZY PEOPLE .... MERCEDES RUEHL
CRAZY PEOPLE .... PAUL BATES
CRAZY PEOPLE .... PAUL REISER
CRAZY QUILT .... BURGESS MEREDITH
CRAZY WORLD OF JULIUS VROODER, THE .... BARBARA HERSHEY
CRAZY WORLD OF JULIUS VROODER, THE .... TIMOTHY BOTTOMS
CREATOR .... JOHN DEHNER†
CREATOR .... MARIEL HEMINGWAY
CREATOR .... MIKE JOLLY
CREATOR .... PETER O'TOOLE
CREATOR .... VINCENT SPANO
CREATURE .... WENDY SCHAAL
CREATURE WASN'T NICE, THE .... CINDY WILLIAMS
CREATURE WASN'T NICE, THE .... LESLIE NIELSEN
CREATURES .... LESLEY-ANNE DOWN
CREEP SHOW .... ADRIENNE BARBEAU
CREEPER, THE .... HAL HOLBROOK
CREEPSHOW .... E. G. MARSHALL
CREEPSHOW .... ED HARRIS
CREEPSHOW .... FRITZ WEAVER
CREEPSHOW .... HAL HOLBROOK
CREEPSHOW .... LESLIE NIELSEN
CREEPSHOW .... TED DANSON
CREEPSHOW 2 .... DON HARVEY
CREEPSHOW 2 .... DOROTHY LAMOUR
CREEPSHOW 2 .... GEORGE KENNEDY
CREEPSHOW 2 .... LOIS CHILES
CRESCENDO .... JOSS ACKLAND
CRESCENDO .... STEFANIE POWERS
CREST OF THE WAVE .... GENE KELLY
CRIA! .... GERALDINE CHAPLIN
CRIA CUERVOS .... GERALDINE CHAPLIN
CRIES AND WHISPERS .... BIBI ANDERSSON
CRIES AND WHISPERS .... ERLAND JOSEPHSON
CRIES AND WHISPERS .... LIV ULLMANN
CRIES UNHEARD: THE DONNA YAKLICH STORY (TF) .... BRAD JOHNSON
CRIES UNHEARD: THE DONNA YAKLICH STORY (TF) .... CAROLYN McCORMICK
CRIES UNHEARD: THE DONNA YAKLICH STORY (TF) .... JACLYN SMITH
CRIES UNHEARD: THE DONNA YAKLICH STORY (TF) .... RAY RUSSO
CRIM EOF INNOCENCE (TF) .... ANDY GRIFFITH
CRIM EOF INNOCENCE (TF) .... DIANE LADD
CRIME AND PASSION .... JOSEPH BOTTOMS
CRIME AND PASSION .... KAREN BLACK
CRIME AND PASSION .... OMAR SHARIF
CRIME BOSS .... TELLY SAVALAS†
CRIME BY NIGHT .... ELEANOR PARKER
CRIME BY NIGHT .... JANE WYMAN
CRIME CLUB (TF) .... LLOYD BRIDGES
CRIME CLUB (TF) .... WILLIAM DEVANE
CRIME DOCTOR .... LEON AMES
CRIME DOCTOR'S DIARY, THE .... LOIS MAXWELL
CRIME IN THE STREETS .... JAMES WHITMORE
CRIME OF DR. HALLET, THE .... RALPH BELLAMY†
CRIME OF HELEN STANLEY, THE .... RALPH BELLAMY†
CRIME OF INNOCENCE (TF) .... STEVE INWOOD
CRIME OF PASSION .... BARBARA STANWYCK†
CRIME OF PASSION .... RAYMOND BURR†
CRIME OF PASSION .... ROYAL DANO
CRIME & PUNISHMENT, USA .... GEORGE HAMILTON
CRIME WAVE .... CHARLES BRONSON
CRIME WAVE .... RICHARD BENJAMIN
CRIME WAVE .... TIMOTHY CAREY
CRIME WITHOUT PASSION .... HELEN HAYES
CRIMES AND MISDEMEANORS .... ALAN ALDA
CRIMES AND MISDEMEANORS .... ANJELICA HUSTON
CRIMES AND MISDEMEANORS .... CAROLINE AARON
CRIMES AND MISDEMEANORS .... CLAIRE BLOOM
CRIMES AND MISDEMEANORS .... DARYL HANNAH
CRIMES AND MISDEMEANORS .... JENNY NICHOLS
CRIMES AND MISDEMEANORS .... JERRY ORBACH
CRIMES AND MISDEMEANORS .... JOANNA GLEASON
CRIMES AND MISDEMEANORS .... MIA FARROW
CRIMES AND MISDEMEANORS .... ROBIN BARTLETT
CRIMES AND MISDEMEANORS .... SAM WATERSTON
CRIMES AND MISDEMEANORS .... WOODY ALLEN
CRIMES AND MISDEMEANORS ✪ .... MARTIN LANDAU
CRIMES OF PASSION .... ANTHONY PERKINS†
CRIMES OF PASSION .... BRUCE DAVISON
CRIMES OF PASSION .... KATHLEEN TURNER
CRIMES OF THE HEART .... DAVID CARPENTER
CRIMES OF THE HEART .... DIANE KEATON
CRIMES OF THE HEART .... HURD HATFIELD
CRIMES OF THE HEART .... JESSICA LANGE
CRIMES OF THE HEART .... SAM SHEPARD
CRIMES OF THE HEART ★ .... SISSY SPACEK
CRIMES OF THE HEART ✪ .... TESS HARPER
CRIMINAL AFFAIR .... ANN-MARGRET
CRIMINAL JUSTICE (CTF) .... ANTHONY LaPAGLIA
CRIMINAL JUSTICE (CTF) .... JENNIFER GREY
CRIMINAL LAW .... ELIZABETH SHEPHARD
CRIMINAL LAW .... GARY OLDMAN
CRIMINAL LAW .... JOE DON BAKER
CRIMINAL LAW .... KAREN YOUNG
CRIMINAL LAW .... KEVIN BACON
CRIMINAL LAW .... TESS HARPER
CRIMINAL LAWYER .... JANE WYATT
CRIMINAL, THE .... SAM WANAMAKER†
CRIMSON BLADE, THE .... JACK HEDLEY
CRIMSON KIMONO, THE .... JAMES SHIGETA
CRIMSON KIMONO, THE .... VICTORIA SHAW†
CRIMSON PIRATE, THE .... BURT LANCASTER†
CRIMSON TIDE .... DANNY NUCCI
CRIMSON TIDE .... DENZEL WASHINGTON
CRIMSON TIDE .... GENE HACKMAN
CRIMSON TIDE .... GEORGE DZUNDZA
CRIMSON TIDE .... JAIME GOMEZ
CRIMSON TIDE .... JAMES GANDOLFINI
CRIMSON TIDE .... LILLO BRANCATO
CRIMSON TIDE .... MATT CRAVEN
CRIMSON TIDE .... MICHAEL MILHOAN
CRIMSON TIDE .... ROCKY CARROLL
CRIMSON TIDE .... VIGGO MORTENSEN
CRISIS .... JOSE FERRER†
CRISIS .... LEON AMES
CRISIS AT CENTRAL HIGH (TF) .... JOANNE WOODWARD
CRISIS IN MID AIR (TF) .... GEORGE PEPPARD†
CRISIS IN MID-AIR (TF) .... DON MURRAY
CRISS CROSS .... BURT LANCASTER†
CRISS CROSS .... RAYMOND BURR†
CRISS CROSS .... TONY CURTIS
CRISS CROSS .... YVONNE DE CARLO
CRISSCROSS .... ARLISS HOWARD
CRISSCROSS .... DAVID ARNOTT
CRISSCROSS .... GOLDIE HAWN
CRISSCROSS .... JAMES GAMMON
CRISSCROSS .... KEITH CARRADINE
CRITICAL CONDITION .... BOB DISHY
CRITICAL CONDITION .... BOB SAGET
CRITICAL CONDITION .... JOE DALLESANDRO
CRITICAL CONDITION .... JOE MANTEGNA
CRITICAL CONDITION .... RACHEL TICOTIN
CRITICAL CONDITION .... RANDALL (TEX) COBB
CRITICAL CONDITION .... RICHARD PRYOR
CRITICAL CONDITION .... RUBEN BLADES
CRITICAL CONDITION .... SYLVIA MILES
CRITICAL LIST, THE (TF) .... KEN HOWARD
CRITICAL LIST, THE (TF) .... LLOYD BRIDGES
CRITICAL LIST, THE (TF) .... LOUIS GOSSETT JR.
CRITICAL LIST, THE (TF) .... MELINDA DILLON
CRITIC'S CHOICE .... BOB HOPE
CRITIC'S CHOICE .... JOHN DEHNER†
CRITIC'S CHOICE .... RIP TORN
CRITTERS .... BILLY GREEN BUSH
CRITTERS .... BILLY ZANE
CRITTERS .... DEE WALLACE STONE
CRITTERS .... DON OPPER
CRITTERS .... M. EMMET WALSH
CRITTERS .... NADINE VAN DER VELDE
CRITTERS .... SCOTT GRIMES
CRITTERS .... TERRENCE MANN
"CROCODILE" DUNDEE .... DAVID GULPILIL
"CROCODILE" DUNDEE .... IRVING METZMAN
"CROCODILE" DUNDEE .... JOHN MEILLON
"CROCODILE" DUNDEE .... LINDA KOZLOWSKI
"CROCODILE" DUNDEE .... MARK BLUM
"CROCODILE" DUNDEE .... MICHAEL LOMBARD
"CROCODILE" DUNDEE .... PAUL HOGAN
"CROCODILE" DUNDEE .... REGINALD VELJOHNSON
"CROCODILE" DUNDEE II .... CHARLES S. DUTTON
"CROCODILE" DUNDEE II .... DOUG YASUDA
"CROCODILE" DUNDEE II .... ERNIE DINGO
"CROCODILE" DUNDEE II .... HECHTER UBARRY
"CROCODILE" DUNDEE II .... JACE ALEXANDER
"CROCODILE" DUNDEE II .... JOHN MEILLON
"CROCODILE" DUNDEE II .... JUAN FERNANDEZ
"CROCODILE" DUNDEE II .... KENNETH WELSH
"CROCODILE" DUNDEE II .... LINDA KOZLOWSKI
"CROCODILE" DUNDEE II .... PAUL HOGAN
CROMWELL .... ALEC GUINNESS
CROMWELL .... RICHARD HARRIS
CROMWELL .... ROBERT MORLEY
CROMWELL .... TIMOTHY DALTON
CRONACA FAMILIARE .... MARCELLO MASTROIANNI
CRONACHE DI POVERI AMANTI .... MARCELLO MASTROIANNI
CROOKED HEARTS .... CINDY PICKETT
CROOKED HEARTS .... JENNIFER JASON LEIGH
CROOKED HEARTS .... JULIETTE LEWIS
CROOKED HEARTS .... MARG HELGENBERGER
CROOKED HEARTS .... NOAH WYLE
CROOKED HEARTS .... PETER BERG
CROOKED HEARTS .... PETER COYOTE
CROOKED HEARTS .... VINCENT D'ONOFRIO
CROOKED HEARTS, THE (TF) .... MAUREEN O'SULLIVAN
CROOKLYN .... ALFRE WOODARD
CROOKLYN .... DELROY LINDO
CROOKLYN .... JOIE LEE
CROOKLYN .... SPIKE LEE
CROOKLYN .... ZELDA HARRIS
CROOKS .... JULIE CHRISTIE
CROOKS AND CORONETS .... TELLY SAVALAS†
CROSS AND THE SWITCHBLADE, THE .... PAT BOONE
CROSS COUNTRY .... MICHAEL IRONSIDE
CROSS CREEK .... DANA HILL
CROSS CREEK .... MALCOLM McDOWELL
CROSS CREEK .... MARY STEENBURGEN
CROSS CREEK ✪ .... ALFRE WOODARD
CROSS CREEK ✪ .... RIP TORN
CROSS CURRENT (TF) .... JOSE FERRER†
CROSS MY HEART .... ANNETTE O'TOOLE
CROSS MY HEART .... MARTIN SHORT
CROSS MY HEART .... PAUL REISER
CROSS OF FIRE (MS) .... JOHN HEARD
CROSS OF FIRE (MS) .... MEL HARRIS
CROSS OF FIRE (TF) .... LLOYD BRIDGES
CROSS OF IRON .... DAVID WARNER
CROSS OF IRON .... JAMES COBURN
CROSS OF IRON .... MAXIMILIAN SCHELL
CROSS OF LORRAINE, THE .... GENE KELLY
CROSS OF LORRAINE, THE .... HUME CRONYN
CROSS-EYED SAINT, THE .... LIONEL STANDER
CROSSCURRENT (TF) .... CAROL LYNLEY
CROSSCURRENT (TF) .... ROBERT HOOKS
CROSSED SWORDS .... CHARLTON HESTON
CROSSED SWORDS .... DAVID HEMMINGS

† after an actor's name denotes deceased.

CROSSED SWORDS .... ERNEST BORGNINE
CROSSED SWORDS .... GEORGE C. SCOTT
CROSSED SWORDS .... MARK LESTER
CROSSED SWORDS .... RAQUEL WELCH
CROSSFIRE .... ROBERT MITCHUM
CROSSFIRE ✪ .... GLORIA GRAHAME†
CROSSFIRE ✪ .... ROBERT RYAN†
CROSSFIRE (TF) .... PATRICK O'NEAL†
CROSSING DELANCEY .... AMY IRVING
CROSSING DELANCEY .... AMY WRIGHT
CROSSING DELANCEY .... GEORGE MARTIN
CROSSING DELANCEY .... JEROEN KRABBE
CROSSING DELANCEY .... PETER RIEGERT
CROSSING DELANCEY .... REIZL BOZYK†
CROSSING DELANCEY .... SUZZY ROCHE
CROSSING DELANCEY .... SYLVIA MILES
CROSSING GUARD, THE .... ANJELICA HUSTON
CROSSING GUARD, THE .... DAVID MORSE
CROSSING GUARD, THE .... JACK NICHOLSON
CROSSING GUARD, THE .... PRISCILLA BARNES
CROSSING GUARD, THE .... ROBIN WRIGHT
CROSSING THE BRIDGE .... JASON GEDRICK
CROSSING THE BRIDGE .... JEFFREY TAMBOR
CROSSING THE BRIDGE .... JOSH CHARLES
CROSSING THE BRIDGE .... STEPHEN BALDWIN
CROSSING, THE (MFV) .... RUSSELL CROWE
CROSSING THE MOB (TF) .... FRANK STALLONE
CROSSING THE MOB (TF) .... JASON BATEMAN
CROSSING THE MOB (TF) .... PATTI D'ARBANVILLE
CROSSING TO
  FREEDOM (TF) .... MARE WINNINGHAM
CROSSING TO
  FREEDOM (TF) .... MICHAEL KITCHEN
CROSSING TO FREEDOM (TF) .... PETER O'TOOLE
CROSSING TO
  FREEDOM (TF) .... SUSAN WOOLDRIDGE
CROSSINGS (MS) .... CHERYL LADD
CROSSINGS (MS) .... CHRISTOPHER PLUMMER
CROSSINGS (MS) .... JANE SEYMOUR
CROSSINGS (MS) .... LEE HORSLEY
CROSSOVER DREAMS .... ELIZABETH PENA
CROSSPLOT .... ALEXIS KANNER
CROSSPLOT .... ROGER MOORE
CROSSROADS .... HARRY CAREY JR.
CROSSROADS .... JAMI GERTZ
CROSSROADS .... JOE MORTON
CROSSROADS .... JOE SENECA
CROSSROADS .... RALPH MACCHIO
CROSSROADS .... ROBERT G. MIRANDA
CROSSROADS .... ROBERT JUDD
CROW, THE .... BAI LING
CROW, THE .... BRANDON LEE†
CROW, THE .... DAVID PATRICK KELLY
CROW, THE .... ERNIE HUDSON
CROW, THE .... MICHAEL WINCOTT
CROWD ROARS, THE .... JANE WYMAN
CROWD ROARS, THE .... LIONEL STANDER
CROWD ROARS, THE .... MAUREEN O'SULLIVAN
CROWDED PARADISE .... HENRY SILVA
CROWDED PARADISE .... HUME CRONYN
CROWDED SKY, THE .... EFREM ZIMBALIST JR.
CROWDED SKY, THE .... LOUIS QUINN†
CROWDED SKY, THE .... TROY DONAHUE
CROWHAVEN FARM (TF) .... HOPE LANGE
CRUEL SEA, THE .... DENHOLM ELLIOTT†
CRUISE INTO TERROR (TF) ..... DIRK BENEDICT
CRUISE INTO TERROR (TF) .... STELLA STEVENS
CRUISE MISSILE .... PETER GRAVES
CRUISING .... AL PACINO
CRUISING† .... KAREN ALLEN
CRUISING .... PAUL SORVINO
CRUNCH .... JOHN VERNON
CRUSH, THE .... ALICIA SILVERSTONE
CRUSH, THE .... CARY ELWES
CRUSH, THE .... JENNIFER RUBIN
CRUSH, THE .... KURTWOOD SMITH
CRUSH PROOF .... DENNIS HOPPER
CRUSING .... POWERS BOOTHE
CRUSOE .... ADE SAPARA
CRUSOE .... AIDAN QUINN
CRUSOE .... HEPBURN GRAHAM
CRUSOE .... JIMMY NAIL

CRUSOE .... MICHAEL HIGGINS
CRUSOE .... SHANE RIMMER
CRUSOE .... TIMOTHY SPALL
CRUSOE .... WARREN CLARKE
CRY BABY KILLER, THE .... JACK NICHOLSON
CRY BLOOD, APACHE .... ROBERT TESSIER†
CRY DEVIL .... ALLEN GARFIELD
CRY DEVIL .... DEREK RYAN
CRY DEVIL .... ELLIOTT GOULD
CRY DEVIL .... MICHAEL J. POLLARD
CRY DEVIL .... RICHARD ROUNDTREE
CRY FOR HAPPY .... JAMES SHIGETA
CRY FOR HELP, A .... LILLIAN GISH†
CRY FOR HELP, A (TF) .... JULIUS HARRIS
CRY FOR HELP, A (TF) .... ROBERT CULP
CRY FOR LOVE, A (TF) .... POWERS BOOTHE
CRY FOR LOVE, A (TF) .... SUSAN BLAKELY
CRY FREEDOM .... ALEC McCOWEN
CRY FREEDOM .... JULIAN GLOVER
CRY FREEDOM .... KEVIN KLINE
CRY FREEDOM .... PENELOPE WILTON
CRY FREEDOM ✪ .... DENZEL WASHINGTON
CRY HAVOC .... ANN SOTHERN
CRY HAVOC .... ROBERT MITCHUM
CRY IN THE DARK, A .... SAM NEILL
CRY IN THE DARK, A ★ .... MERYL STREEP
CRY IN THE NIGHT, A .... RAYMOND BURR†
CRY IN THE WILD, A .... JARED RUSHTON
CRY IN THE WILD, A .... NED BEATTY
CRY IN THE WILD, A .... PAMELA SUE MARTIN
CRY OF A PROSTITUTE .... HENRY SILVA
CRY OF BATTLE .... RITA MORENO
CRY OF THE BANSHEE .... VINCENT PRICE†
CRY OF THE CITY .... SHELLEY WINTERS
CRY OF THE PENGUINS .... HAYLEY MILLS
CRY OF THE PENGUINS .... JOHN HURT
CRY OF THE WEREWOLF .... NINA FOCH
CRY TERROR .... ANGIE DICKINSON
CRY TERROR .... JACK KLUGMAN
CRY TERROR .... JACK KRUSCHEN
CRY TERROR .... ROD STEIGER
CRY, THE BELOVED COUNTRY ...... SIDNEY POITIER
CRY TOUGH .... JOHN SAXON
CRY UNCLE! .... ALLEN GARFIELD
CRY UNCLE .... PAUL SORVINO
CRY WOLF .... BARBARA STANWYCK†
CRY-BABY .... AMY LOCANE
CRY-BABY .... DAVID NELSON
CRY-BABY .... IGGY POP
CRY-BABY .... JOE DALLESANDRO
CRY-BABY .... JOEY HEATHERTON
CRY-BABY .... JOHNNY DEPP
CRY-BABY .... MINK STOLE
CRY-BABY .... PATRICIA HEARST
CRY-BABY .... POLLY BERGEN
CRY-BABY .... RICKI LAKE
CRY-BABY .... STEPHEN MAILER
CRY-BABY .... SUSAN TYRRELL
CRY-BABY .... TRACI LORDS
CRY-BABY .... TROY DONAHUE
CRY-BABY .... WILLEM DAFOE
CRYING GAME, THE .... FOREST WHITAKER
CRYING GAME, THE .... MIRANDA RICHARDSON
CRYING GAME, THE ★ .... STEPHEN REA
CRYING GAME, THE ✪ .... JAYE DAVIDSON
CRYSTAL BALL, THE .... YVONNE DE CARLO
CRYSTAL MAN, THE .... JOHN PHILLIP LAW
CUBA .... BROOKE ADAMS
CUBA .... CHRIS SARANDON
CUBA .... DENHOLM ELLIOTT†
CUBA .... HECTOR ELIZONDO
CUBA .... JACK WESTON
CUBA .... MARTIN BALSAM
CUBA .... SEAN CONNERY
CUJO .... DEE WALLACE STONE
CUJO .... ED LAUTER
CUL-DE-SAC .... DONALD PLEASENCE
CUL-DE-SAC .... JACQUELINE BISSET
CUL-DE-SAC .... LIONEL STANDER
CULPEPPER CATTLE
  CO., THE .... BILLY GREEN BUSH

CULPEPPER CATTLE
  COMPANY, THE .... BO HOPKINS
CULPEPPER CATTLE
  COMPANY, THE .... ROYAL DANO
CULT OF THE DAMNED .... JENNIFER JONES
CULT OF THE DAMNED .... RODDY McDOWALL
CUORI SUL MARE .... SOPHIA LOREN
CURE, THE .... ANNABELLA SCIORRA
CURE, THE .... BRAD RENFRO
CURE, THE .... JOSEPH MAZZELLO
CURE, THE .... NICKY KATT
CURIOSITY KILLS (CTF) .... C. THOMAS HOWELL
CURIOSITY KILLS (CTF) .... COURTENEY COX
CURIOSITY KILLS (CTF) .... JEFF FAHEY
CURIOSITY KILLS (CTF) .... RAE DAWN CHONG
CURLY SUE .... ALISAN PORTER
CURLY SUE .... EDIE McCLURG
CURLY SUE .... FRED DALTON THOMPSON
CURLY SUE .... JAMES BELUSHI
CURLY SUE .... JOHN GETZ
CURLY SUE .... KELLY LYNCH
CURSE, THE .... CLAUDE AKINS†
CURSE, THE .... JOHN SCHNEIDER
CURSE, THE .... MALCOLM DANARE
CURSE OF KING TUT'S
  TOMB, THE (TF) .... EVA MARIE SAINT
CURSE OF KING TUT'S
  TOMB, THE (TF) .... RAYMOND BURR†
CURSE OF KING TUT'S
  TOMB, THE (TF) .... WENDY HILLER
CURSE OF THE BLACK
  WIDOW (TF) .... DONNA MILLS
CURSE OF THE BLACK
  WIDOW (TF) .... JUNE ALLYSON
CURSE OF THE FACELESS
  MAN, THE .... RICHARD ANDERSON
CURSE OF THE LIVING
  CORPSE, THE .... ROY SCHEIDER
CURSE OF THE PINK PANTHER .... BURT KWOUK
CURSE OF THE PINK PANTHER .... DAVID NIVEN†
CURSE OF THE PINK
  PANTHER .... HARVEY KORMAN
CURSE OF THE PINK
  PANTHER .... JOANNA LUMLEY
CURSE OF THE PINK
  PANTHER .... ROBERT LOGGIA
CURSE OF THE PINK
  PANTHER .... ROBERT WAGNER
CURSE OF THE PINK PANTHER .... TED WASS
CURSE OF THE
  STARVING CLASS .... KATHY BATES
CURTAIN CALL AT
  CACTUS CREEK .... VINCENT PRICE†
CURTAIN UP .... ROBERT MORLEY
CURTAINS .... SAMANTHA EGGAR
CUSTER OF THE WEST .... LAWRENCE TIERNEY
CUT AND RUN .... KAREN BLACK
CUT AND RUN .... LISA BLOUNT
CUT AND RUN .... WILLIE AAMES
CUTTER AND BONE .... JEFF BRIDGES
CUTTER AND BONE .... JOHN HEARD
CUTTER AND BONE .... LISA EICHHORN
CUTTER'S WAY .... JEFF BRIDGES
CUTTER'S WAY .... JOHN HEARD
CUTTER'S WAY .... LISA EICHHORN
CUTTHROAT ISLAND .... GEENA DAVIS
CUTTHROAT ISLAND .... MATTHEW MODINE
CUTTING EDGE, THE .... D. B. SWEENEY
CUTTING EDGE, THE .... MOIRA KELLY
CUTTING EDGE, THE .... ROY DOTRICE
CUTTING EDGE, THE .... TERRY O'QUINN
CYBER-TRACKER .... ABBY DALTON
CYBER-TRACKER .... JOHN APREA
CYBER-TRACKER .... STACIE FOSTER
CYBER-TRACKER .... STEVE BURTON
CYBORG .... ALEX DANIELS
CYBORG .... BLAISE LOONG
CYBORG .... DAYLE HADDON
CYBORG .... DEBORAH RICHTER
CYBORG .... JEAN-CLAUDE VAN DAMME
CYBORG .... ROLF MULLER

This is not a list of every film ever made or every cast member, only those listed in this directory.

CYBORG .... VINCENT KLYN
CYCLE SAVAGES .... BRUCE DERN
CYCLONE .... CARROLL BAKER
CYNTHIA .... ELIZABETH TAYLOR
CYRANO DE BERGERAC .... WILLIAM PRINCE
CYRANO DE BERGERAC ★ .... GERARD DEPARDIEU
CYRANO DE BERGERAC ★★ .... JOSE FERRER†
CYRANO ET D'ARTAGNAN .... JOSE FERRER†
CZARINA .... VINCENT PRICE†
C'ERA UNA VOLTA .... SOPHIA LOREN
C'ERA UNA VOLTA IL WEST .... WOODY STRODE

D

D.A.: CONSPIRACY
  TO KILL, THE (TF) .... ROBERT CONRAD
D.A.: MURDER ONE, THE (TF) .... DIANE BAKER
D.A.: MURDER ONE, THE (TF) ..... ROBERT CONRAD
D.A.R.Y.L. .... COLLEEN CAMP
D.A.R.Y.L. .... MARY BETH HURT
D.C. CAB .... GARY BUSEY
D.C. CAB .... IRENE CARA
D.C. CAB .... MR. T
D.C. CAB .... TIMOTHY CAREY
D.O.A. .... DANIEL STERN
D.O.A. .... DENNIS QUAID
D.O.A. .... MEG RYAN
D2: THE MIGHTY DUCKS .... BRANDON ADAMS
D2: THE MIGHTY DUCKS .... EMILIO ESTEVEZ
D2: THE MIGHTY DUCKS .... JAN RUBES
D2: THE MIGHTY DUCKS .... JOSHUA JACKSON
D2: THE MIGHTY DUCKS .... KATHRYN ERBE
D2: THE MIGHTY DUCKS .... MATT DOHERTY
D2: THE MIGHTY DUCKS .... MICHAEL TUCKER
DA .... BARNARD HUGHES
DA .... DOREEN HEPBURN
DA .... KARL HAYDEN
DA .... MARTIN SHEEN
DA .... WILLIAM HICKEY
DA UOMO A UOMO .... JOHN PHILLIP LAW
DAD .... CHRIS LEMMON
DAD .... ETHAN HAWKE
DAD .... J. T. WALSH
DAD .... JACK LEMMON
DAD .... JOHN APICELLA
DAD .... KATHY BAKER
DAD .... KEVIN SPACEY
DAD .... OLYMPIA DUKAKIS
DAD .... PETER MICHAEL GOETZ
DAD .... TED DANSON
DAD .... ZAKES MOKAE
DADAH IS DEATH (MS) .... JULIE CHRISTIE
DADAH IS DEATH (MS) .... KERRY ARMSTRONG
DADAH IS DEATH (MS) ...... SARAH JESSICA PARKER
DADAH IS DEATH (MS) .... VICTOR BANERJEE
DADDY LONG LEGS .... FRED ASTAIRE†
DADDY LONG LEGS .... LESLIE CARON
DADDY (TF) .... DANNY AIELLO
DADDY (TF) .... DERMOT MULRONEY
DADDY (TF) .... JOHN KARLEN
DADDY (TF) .... PATRICIA ARQUETTE
DADDY (TF) .... TESS HARPER
DADDY'S BOYS .... DARYL HANEY
DADDY'S DYIN'...WHO'S GOT
  THE WILL? .... AMY WRIGHT
DADDY'S DYIN'...WHO'S GOT
  THE WILL? .... BEAU BRIDGES
DADDY'S DYIN'...WHO'S GOT
  THE WILL? .... BEVERLY D'ANGELO
DADDY'S DYIN'...WHO'S GOT
  THE WILL? .... JUDGE REINHOLD
DADDY'S DYIN'...WHO'S GOT
  THE WILL? .... KEITH CARRADINE
DADDY'S DYIN'...WHO'S GOT
  THE WILL? .... MOLLY McCLURE
DADDY'S DYIN'...WHO'S GOT
  THE WILL? .... PATRIKA DARBO
DADDY'S DYIN'...WHO'S GOT
  THE WILL? .... TESS HARPER
DAIN CURSE, THE (MS) .... HECTOR ELIZONDO
DAIN CURSE, THE (TF) .... JAMES COBURN
DAIN CURSE, THE (TF) .... JASON MILLER

DAIN CURSE, THE (TF) .... JEAN SIMMONS
DAISY KENYON .... JOAN CRAWFORD†
DAISY MILLER .... CLORIS LEACHMAN
DAISY MILLER .... CYBILL SHEPHERD
DAISY MILLER .... EILEEN BRENNAN
DAKOTA .... LOU DIAMOND PHILLIPS
DAKOTA .... ROBERT BLAKE
DALLAS: THE EARLY YEARS (TF) ...... DALE MIDKIFF
DALLAS: THE EARLY
  YEARS (TF) .... DAVID MARSHALL GRANT
DALLAS: THE EARLY YEARS (TF) .... HOYT AXTON
DALLAS: THE EARLY
  YEARS (TF) .... LARRY HAGMAN
DALLAS: THE EARLY YEARS (TF) ..... MOLLY HAGAN
DAMAGE .... DAVID THEWLIS
DAMAGE .... IAN BANNEN
DAMAGE .... JEREMY IRONS
DAMAGE .... JULIETTE BINOCHE
DAMAGE .... LESLIE CARON
DAMAGE .... RUPERT GRAVES
DAMAGE ○ .... MIRANDA RICHARDSON
DAMIEN: OMEN II .... LEE GRANT
DAMIEN: OMEN II .... ROBERT FOXWORTH
DAMIEN: OMEN II .... SYLVIA SIDNEY
DAMN THE DEFIANT! .... ALEC GUINNESS
DAMN YANKEES .... GWEN VERDON
DAMN YANKEES .... JEAN STAPLETON
DAMN YANKEES .... RAY WALSTON
DAMN YANKEES .... TAB HUNTER
DAMNATION ALLEY .... GEORGE PEPPARD†
DAMNATION ALLEY .... JACKIE EARLE HALEY
DAMNATION ALLEY ..... JAN-MICHAEL VINCENT
DAMNATION ALLEY .... PAUL WINFIELD
DAMNED DON'T CRY, THE .... JOAN CRAWFORD†
DAMNED, THE .... CHARLOTTE RAMPLING
DAMNED, THE .... HELMUT BERGER
DAMNED, THE .... SHIRLEY ANNE FIELD
DAMNED, THE .... WALTER GOTELL
DAMSEL IN DISTRESS, A .... GEORGE BURNS
DAN CANDY'S LAW .... DONALD SUTHERLAND
DANCE, FOOLS, DANCE .... JOAN CRAWFORD†
DANCE, GIRL, DANCE .... MAUREEN O'HARA
DANCE, GIRL, DANCE .... RALPH BELLAMY†
DANCE LITTLE LADY .... MAE ZETTERLING†
DANCE OF THE VAMPIRES .... FIONA LEWIS
DANCE OF THE VAMPIRES .... ROMAN POLANSKI
DANCE WITH A STRANGER .... IAN HOLM
DANCE WITH A
  STRANGER .... MIRANDA RICHARDSON
DANCE WITH A STRANGER .... RUPERT EVERETT
DANCE WITH DEATH .... MARIA FORD
DANCE WITH DEATH .... MAXWELL CAULFIELD
DANCE WITH DEATH .... MIKE McDONALD
DANCE WITH DEATH .... RODGER HALL
DANCERS .... MIKHAIL BARYSHNIKOV
DANCES WITH WOLVES .... CHARLES ROCKET
DANCES WITH WOLVES .... MAURY CHAVKIN
DANCES WITH WOLVES .... ROBERT PASTORELLI
DANCES WITH WOLVES .... RODNEY A. GRANT
DANCES WITH WOLVES ★ .... WES STUDI
DANCES WITH WOLVES ★ .... KEVIN COSTNER
DANCES WITH WOLVES ○ .... GRAHAM GREENE
DANCES WITH WOLVES ○ .... MARY McDONNELL
DANCING CO-ED .... LANA TURNER
DANCING LADY .... JOAN CRAWFORD†
DANCING MASTERS, THE .... ROBERT MITCHUM
DANDELION DEAD (TF) .... MICHAEL KITCHEN
DANDY IN ASPIC, A .... LIONEL STANDER
DANDY IN ASPIC, A .... MIA FARROW
DANDY IN ASPIC, A .... PETER COOK
DANDY IN ASPIC, A .... TOM COURTENAY
DANDY, THE ALL
  AMERICAN GIRL .... SAM WATERSTON
DANDY, THE ALL
  AMERICAN GIRL .... STOCKARD CHANNING
DANGER DIABOLIK .... JOHN PHILLIP LAW
DANGER DOWN UNDER (TF) .... BRUCE HUGHES
DANGER DOWN UNDER (TF) .... LEE MAJORS
DANGER—LOVE AT WORK .... ANN SOTHERN
DANGER ROUTE .... CAROL LYNLEY
DANGER ROUTE .... GORDAN JACKSON†
DANGER ROUTE .... SAM WANAMAKER†

DANGEROUS ★★ .... BETTE DAVIS†
DANGEROUS AFFECTION (TF) .... JIMMY SMITS
DANGEROUS AGE, A .... BEN PIAZZA†
DANGEROUS COMPANY (TF) .... BEAU BRIDGES
DANGEROUS COMPANY (TF) .... RALPH MACCHIO
DANGEROUS CROSSING .... MAX SHOWALTER
DANGEROUS DAVIES - THE
  LAST DETECTIVE .... JOSS ACKLAND
DANGEROUS DAYS OF
  KIOWA JONES, THE .... DIANE BAKER
DANGEROUS DAYS OF
  KIOWA JONES, THE (TF) .... ROYAL DANO
DANGEROUS EXILE .... LOUIS JOURDAN
DANGEROUS FRIEND, A .... ED ASNER
DANGEROUS GAME .... HARVEY KEITEL
DANGEROUS GAME .... JAMES RUSSO
DANGEROUS GAME .... MADONNA
DANGEROUS GAME .... NANCY FERRARA
DANGEROUS INTRIGUE .... RALPH BELLAMY†
DANGEROUS LIAISONS .... JOHN MALKOVICH
DANGEROUS LIAISONS .... KEANU REEVES
DANGEROUS LIAISONS .... SWOOSIE KURTZ
DANGEROUS LIAISONS .... UMA THURMAN
DANGEROUS LIAISONS ★ .... GLENN CLOSE
DANGEROUS LIAISONS ○ .... MICHELLE PFEIFFER
DANGEROUS LIFE, A (CMS) .... GARY BUSEY
DANGEROUS LOVE .... ANTHONY GEARY
DANGEROUS LOVE .... BRENDA BAKKE
DANGEROUS LOVE .... ELLIOTT GOULD
DANGEROUS LOVE .... LAWRENCE MONOSON
DANGEROUS LOVE .... LISA FRIEDE
DANGEROUS LOVE .... PETER MARC
DANGEROUS LOVE .... TERI AUSTIN
DANGEROUS MISSION .... DENNIS WEAVER
DANGEROUS MISSION .... PIPER LAURIE
DANGEROUS MISSION .... VINCENT PRICE†
DANGEROUS MOVES .... LESLIE CARON
DANGEROUS MOVES .... LIV ULLMANN
DANGEROUS NUMBER .... ANN SOTHERN
DANGEROUS PASSION (TF) .... BILLY DEE WILLIAMS
DANGEROUS PASSION (TF) .... CARL WEATHERS
DANGEROUS PASSION (TF) .... LONETTE McKEE
DANGEROUS
  PURSUIT (CTF) .... GREGORY HARRISON
DANGEROUS SUMMER, A .... TOM SKERRITT
DANGEROUS TO KNOW .... ANTHONY QUINN
DANGEROUS WOMAN, A ... BARBARA HERSHEY
DANGEROUS WOMAN, A .... CHLOE WEBB
DANGEROUS WOMAN, A .... DAVID STRATHAIRN
DANGEROUS WOMAN, A .... DEBRA WINGER
DANGEROUS WOMAN, A .... GABRIEL BYRNE
DANGEROUS WOMAN, A .... JAN HOOKS
DANGEROUS WOMAN, A .... JOHN TERRY
DANGEROUS WOMAN, A .... LAURIE METCALF
DANGEROUS WOMAN, A .... PAUL DOOLEY
DANGEROUS WOMAN, A .... RICHARD RIEHLE
DANGEROUS WOMAN, A .... VIVEKA DAVIS
DANGEROUS YEARS .... MARILYN MONROE†
DANGEROUSLY CLOSE .... BRADFORD BANCROFT
DANGEROUSLY CLOSE .... CAREY LOWELL
DANGEROUSLY CLOSE .... DON MICHAEL PAUL
DANGEROUSLY CLOSE .... J. EDDIE PECK
DANGEROUSLY CLOSE .... JERRY DINOME
DANGEROUSLY CLOSE .... JOHN STOCKWELL
DANGEROUSLY CLOSE .... MADISON MASON
DANGEROUSLY CLOSE .... THOM MATHEWS
DANIEL .... AMANDA PLUMMER
DANIEL .... ED ASNER
DANIEL .... ELLEN BARKIN
DANIEL .... JULIE BOYASSO†
DANIEL .... LINDSAY CROUSE
DANIEL .... MANDY PATINKIN
DANIEL .... TIMOTHY HUTTON
DANIEL .... TOYAH FELDSHUH
DANIELLE STEEL'S
  'CHANGES' (TF) .... MICHAEL NOURI
DANIELLE STEEL'S
  'CHANGES' (TF) .... CHERYL LADD
DANIELLE STEEL'S
  KALEIDOSCOPE (TF) .... JACLYN SMITH
DANIELLE STEEL'S ONCE
  IN A LIFETIME (TF) .... BARRY BOSTWICK

DANIELLE STEEL'S ONCE
  IN A LIFETIME (TF) .... LINDSAY WAGNER
DANIELLE STEELE'S PALOMINO (TF) .... RYAN TODD
DANNY BOY .... STEPHEN REA
DANTON .... GERARD DEPARDIEU
DAPHNE AND THE PIRATE .... LILLIAN GISH†
DARBY O'GILL AND THE
  LITTLE PEOPLE .... SEAN CONNERY
DARBY'S RANGERS .... JACK WARDEN
DARBY'S RANGERS .... JAMES GARNER
DARBY'S RANGERS .... STUART WHITMAN
DARING DOBERMANS, THE .... JOAN CAULFIELD†
DARING GAME .... LLOYD BRIDGES
DARK, THE .... RICHARD JAECKEL
DARK, THE .... WILLIAM DEVANE
DARK ANGEL, THE ★ .... MERLE OBERON†
DARK AT THE TOP OF THE
  STAIRS, THE .... ANGELA LANSBURY
DARK AT THE TOP OF THE
  STAIRS, THE ⚬ .... SHIRLEY KNIGHT
DARK CITY .... CHARLTON HESTON
DARK CITY .... HARRY MORGAN
DARK CRYSTAL, THE .... FRANK OZ
DARK EYES ★ ...... MARCELLO MASTROIANNI
DARK HALF, THE .... AMY MADIGAN
DARK HALF, THE .... CHELSEA FIELD
DARK HALF, THE .... JULIE HARRIS
DARK HALF, THE .... KENT BROADHURST
DARK HALF, THE .... MICHAEL ROOKER
DARK HALF, THE .... ROBERT JOY
DARK HALF, THE .... RUTANYA ALDA
DARK HALF, THE .... TIMOTHY HUTTON
DARK HALF, THE .... TOM MARDIROSIAN
DARK HOLIDAY (TF) .... LEE REMICK†
DARK HOLIDAY (TF) .... NORMA ALEANDRO
DARK HORSE, THE .... BETTE DAVIS†
DARK INTRUDER .... LESLIE NIELSEN
DARK INTRUDER .... PETER MARK RICHMAN
DARK MANSIONS (TF) .... STEVE INWOOD
DARK MIRROR (TF) .... JANE SEYMOUR
DARK MIRROR, THE .... OLIVIA DE HAVILLAND
DARK OBSESSION .... AMANDA DONOHOE
DARK OF THE SUN .... JIM BROWN
DARK PASSAGE .... LAUREN BACALL
DARK PAST, THE .... LOIS MAXWELL
DARK PAST, THE .... NINA FOCH
DARK PLACES .... JOAN COLLINS
DARK PURPOSE .... SHIRLEY JONES
DARK SUN, THE .... JO CHAMP
DARK VICTORY .... GERALDINE FITZGERALD
DARK VICTORY .... RONALD REAGAN
DARK VICTORY ★ .... BETTE DAVIS†
DARK VICTORY (TF) .... ANTHONY HOPKINS
DARK VICTORY (TF) ...... ELIZABETH MONTGOMERY
DARK VICTORY (TF) .... MICHELE LEE
DARK WIND, THE .... FRED WARD
DARK WIND, THE .... GARY FARMER
DARK WIND, THE .... LOU DIAMOND PHILLIPS
DARKER THAN AMBER .... THEODORE BIKEL
DARKMAN .... COLIN FRIELS
DARKMAN .... FRANCES McDORMAND
DARKMAN .... JENNY AGUTTER
DARKMAN .... LARRY DRAKE
DARKMAN .... LIAM NEESON
DARLING .... LAURENCE HARVEY†
DARLING ★★ .... JULIE CHRISTIE
DARLING LILI .... JEREMY KEMP
DARLING LILI .... JULIE ANDREWS
DARLING LILI .... ROCK HUDSON†
DARWIN ADVENTURE, THE .... NICHOLAS CLAY
DAS HAUS DER TAUSEND
  FREUDEN .... VINCENT PRICE†
DAS NETZ .... MEL FERRER
DAS SCHLOSS .... MAXIMILIAN SCHELL
DATE WITH JUDY, A .... ELIZABETH TAYLOR
DATE WITH JUDY, A .... LEON AMES
DATE WITH JUDY, A .... ROBERT STACK
DATELINE DIAMONDS .... DAVID HEMMINGS
DAUGHTER OF ROSIE
  O'GRADY, THE .... GORDON MACRAE†
DAUGHTER OF ROSIE
  O'GRADY, THE .... DEBBIE REYNOLDS

DAUGHTER OF SHANGHAI .... ANTHONY QUINN
DAUGHTER OF THE MIND (TF) .... DON MURRAY
DAUGHTER OF THE STREETS (TF) .... HARRIS YULIN
DAUGHTER OF THE
  STREETS (TF) .... JANE ALEXANDER
DAUGHTER OF THE
  STREETS (TF) .... JOHN STAMOS
DAUGHTER OF THE STREETS (TF) ...... ROXANA ZAL
DAUGHTERS OF JOSHUA
  CABE, THE (TF) .... KAREN VALENTINE
DAUGHTERS OF JOSHUA
  CABE, THE (TF) .... LESLEY ANN WARREN
DAUGHTERS OF JOSHUA
  CABE, THE (TF) .... SANDRA DEE
DAUGHTERS OF SATAN .... TOM SELLECK
DAVE .... ANNA DEAVERE SMITH
DAVE .... ARNOLD SCHWARZENEGGER
DAVE .... BEN KINGSLEY
DAVE .... CHARLES GRODIN
DAVE .... FRANK LANGELLA
DAVE .... JAY LENO
DAVE .... KEVIN DUNN
DAVE .... KEVIN KLINE
DAVE .... OLIVER STONE
DAVE .... SIGOURNEY WEAVER
DAVE .... YING RHAMES
DAVID AND BATHSHEBA .... GREGORY PECK
DAVID AND BATHSHEBA .... GWEN VERDON
DAVID AND LISA .... CLIFTON JAMES
DAVID AND LISA .... HOWARD DA SILVA†
DAVID AND LISA .... JANET MARGOLIN
DAVID AND LISA .... KAREN LYNN GORNEY
DAVID COPPERFIELD .... MAUREEN O'SULLIVAN
DAVID COPPERFIELD .... RON MOODY
DAVID COPPERFIELD (TF) .... WENDY HILLER
DAVID (TF) .... BERNADETTE PETERS
DAVID (TF) .... CHRISTOPHER ALLPORT
DAVID (TF) .... DAN LAURIA
DAVID (TF) .... GEORGE GRIZZARD
DAVID (TF) .... JOHN GLOVER
DAVID (TF) .... MATTHEW LAWRENCE
DAVID'S MOTHER (TF) .... KIRSTIE ALLEY
DAWN .... MICHAEL YORK
DAWN AT SOCORRO .... PIPER LAURIE
DAWN AT SOCORRO .... RORY CALHOUN
DAWN PATROL, THE .... DAVID NIVEN†
DAWN: PORTRAIT OF A
  TEENAGE RUNAWAY (TF) .... EVE PLUMB
DAWNING, THE (TF) .... ANTHONY HOPKINS
DAY AFTER
  HALLOWEEN, THE .... SIGRID THORNTON
DAY AFTER, THE (TF) .... AMY MADIGAN
DAY AFTER, THE (TF) .... BIBI BESCH
DAY AFTER, THE (TF) .... JASON ROBARDS
DAY AFTER, THE (TF) .... JEFF EAST
DAY AFTER, THE (TF) .... JoBETH WILLIAMS
DAY AFTER, THE (TF) .... JOHN CULLUM
DAY AFTER, THE (TF) .... JOHN LITHGOW
DAY AFTER, THE (TF) .... LORI LETHIN
DAY AFTER, THE (TF) .... STEVE GUTTENBERG
DAY AND THE HOUR, THE .... STUART WHITMAN
DAY AT THE RACES, A .... MAUREEN O'SULLIVAN
DAY CHRIST DIED, THE (TF) .... HOPE LANGE
DAY CHRIST DIED, THE (TF) .... JONATHAN PRYCE
DAY CRIST DIED, THE (TF) .... CHRIS SARANDON
DAY FOR NIGHT .... FRANCOIS TRUFFAUT†
DAY FOR NIGHT .... JACQUELINE BISSET
DAY FOR NIGHT .... JEAN-PIERRE AUMONT
DAY FOR NIGHT .... NATHALIE BAYE
DAY IN COURT, A .... SOPHIA LOREN
DAY IN THE DEATH OF JOE EGG, A ..... ALAN BATES
DAY IN THE DEATH OF
  JOE EGG, A .... JANET SUZMAN
DAY OF THE ANIMALS .... LESLIE NIELSEN
DAY OF THE ANIMALS .... PAUL MANTEE
DAY OF THE ANIMALS .... RICHARD JAECKEL
DAY OF THE DOLPHIN, THE .... BUCK HENRY
DAY OF THE
  DOLPHIN, THE .... EDWRAD HERRMANN
DAY OF THE DOLPHIN, THE .... FRITZ WEAVER
DAY OF THE DOLPHIN, THE .... GEORGE C. SCOTT
DAY OF THE DOLPHIN, THE .... JOHN DEHNER†

DAY OF THE DOLPHIN, THE .... PAUL SORVINO
DAY OF THE DOLPHIN, THE ...... TRISH VAN DEVERE
DAY OF THE EVIL GUN .... JOHN ANDERSON
DAY OF THE EVIL GUN .... ROYAL DANO
DAY OF THE JACKAL, THE .... DEREK JACOBI
DAY OF THE JACKAL, THE .... TIMOTHY WEST
DAY OF THE LOCUST, THE .... BILLY BARTY
DAY OF THE LOCUST, THE .... BO HOPKINS
DAY OF THE
  LOCUST, THE .... DONALD SUTHERLAND
DAY OF THE LOCUST, THE .... JACKIE EARLE HALEY
DAY OF THE LOCUST, THE .... JOHN HILLERMAN
DAY OF THE LOCUST, THE .... KAREN BLACK
DAY OF THE LOCUST, THE .... MORGAN BRITTANY
DAY OF THE LOCUST, THE .... NITA TALBOT
DAY OF THE LOCUST, THE ...... WILLIAM ATHERTON
DAY OF THE
  LOCUST, THE ⚬ .... BURGESS MEREDITH
DAY OF THE NIGHTMARE .... JOHN IRELAND
DAY OF THE OUTLAW .... BURL IVES
DAY OF THE OUTLAW .... TINA LOUISE
DAY OF THE OWL, THE .... FRANCO NERO
DAY OF THE TRIFFIDS .... HOWARD KEEL
DAY ONE (TF) .... BARNARD HUGHES
DAY ONE (TF) .... BRIAN DENNEHY
DAY ONE (TF) .... HAL HOLBROOK
DAY ONE (TF) .... HUME CRONYN
DAY ONE (TF) .... RICHARD DYSART
DAY THAT SHOOK THE
  WORLD, THE .... CHRISTOPHER PLUMMER
DAY THAT SHOOK THE
  WORLD, THE .... MAXIMILIAN SCHELL
DAY THE EARTH CAUGHT
  FIRE, THE .... MICHAEL CAINE
DAY THE EARTH
  MOVED, THE (TF) .... JACKIE COOPER
DAY THE EARTH
  STOOD STILL, THE .... PATRICIA NEAL
DAY THE EARTH
  STOOD STILL, THE .... STUART WHITMAN
DAY THE FISH
  CAME OUT, THE .... CANDICE BERGEN
DAY THE FISH
  CAME OUT, THE .... SAM WANAMAKER†
DAY THE FISH
  CAME OUT, THE .... TOM COURTENAY
DAY THE LOVING
  STOPPED, THE (TF) .... ALLY SHEEDY
DAY THE SCREAMING
  STOPPED, THE .... DAVID DOYLE
DAY THE WALL CAME
  DOWN, THE .... MARC SINGER
DAY THE WALL CAME
  DOWN, THE .... MARY CROSBY
DAY THEY ROBBED THE BANK
  OF ENGLAND, THE .... PETER O'TOOLE
DAY WILL DAWN, THE .... DEBORAH KERR
DAYBREAK (CTF) .... CUBA GOODING JR.
DAYBREAK (CTF) .... MARTHA PLIMPTON
DAYBREAK (CTF) .... MOIRA KELLY
DAYDREAMER, THE .... BURL IVES
DAYDREAMER, THE .... HAYLEY MILLS
DAYS OF GLORY .... GREGORY PECK
DAYS OF HEAVEN .... BROOKE ADAMS
DAYS OF HEAVEN .... RICHARD GERE
DAYS OF HEAVEN .... SAM SHEPARD
DAYS OF HEAVEN .... STUART MARGOLIN
DAYS OF THUNDER .... CARY ELWES
DAYS OF THUNDER .... DON SIMPSON
DAYS OF THUNDER .... FRED DALTON THOMPSON
DAYS OF THUNDER .... JOHN C. REILLY
DAYS OF THUNDER .... MICHAEL ROOKER
DAYS OF THUNDER .... NICOLE KIDMAN
DAYS OF THUNDER .... RANDY QUAID
DAYS OF THUNDER .... ROBERT DUVALL
DAYS OF THUNDER .... TOM CRUISE
DAYS OF WINE AND ROSES .... JACK KLUGMAN
DAYS OF WINE AND ROSES ★ ...... JACK LEMMON
DAYS OF WINE AND ROSES ★ .... LEE REMICK†
DAYTON'S DEVILS .... GEORG STANFORD BROWN
DAYTON'S DEVILS .... LESLIE NIELSEN
DAYTON'S DEVILS .... RORY CALHOUN

This is not a list of every film ever made or every cast member, only those listed in this directory.

DAZZLED (TF) .... JAMES FARENTINO
DE KALTE HAM SKARVEN .... LIV ULLMANN
DE LA PART DES COPAINS .... CHARLES BRONSON
DE LA PART DES COPAINS .... LIV ULLMANN
DEAD, THE .... ANJELICA HUSTON
DEAD, THE .... CATHLEEN DELANY
DEAD, THE .... DAN O'HERLIHY
DEAD, THE .... DONAL DONNELLY
DEAD, THE .... DONAL McCANN
DEAD, THE .... FRANK PATTERSON
DEAD, THE .... HELENA CARROLL
DEAD, THE .... INGRID CRAIGIE
DEAD, THE .... MARIE KEAN
DEAD, THE .... RACHAEL DOWLING
DEAD, THE .... SEAN McCLORY
DEAD AGAIN .... ANDY GARCIA
DEAD AGAIN .... CAMPBELL SCOTT
DEAD AGAIN .... CHRISTINE EBERSOLE
DEAD AGAIN .... DEREK JACOBI
DEAD AGAIN .... EMMA THOMPSON
DEAD AGAIN .... GREGOR HESSE
DEAD AGAIN .... HANNA SCHYGULLA
DEAD AGAIN .... JO ANDERSON
DEAD AGAIN .... KENNETH BRANAGH
DEAD AGAIN .... MIRIAM MARGOLYES
DEAD AGAIN .... OBBA BABATUNDE
DEAD AGAIN .... RICHARD EASTON
DEAD AGAIN .... ROBIN WILLIAMS
DEAD AGAIN .... WAYNE KNIGHT
DEAD AGAIN .... YASEK SIMEK
DEAD AND BURIED .... JAMES FARENTINO
DEAD AND BURIED .... LISA BLOUNT
DEAD ARE ALIVE, THE .... SAMANTHA EGGAR
DEAD CALM .... BILLY ZANE
DEAD CALM .... NICOLE KIDMAN
DEAD CALM .... SAM NEILL
DEAD CERT .... JUDI DENCH
DEAD CERT .... JULIAN GLOVER
DEAD DON'T DIE, THE (TF) .... GEORGE HAMILTON
DEAD END .... SYLVIA SIDNEY
DEAD HEAT .... JOE PISCOPO
DEAD HEAT .... TREAT WILLIAMS
DEAD HEAT ON A MERRY-GO-ROUND .... HARRISON FORD
DEAD HEAT ON A MERRY-GO-ROUND .... JAMES COBURN
DEAD HEAT ON A MERRY-GO-ROUND .... ROBERT WEBBER
DEAD HEAT ON A MERRY-GO-ROUND .... SEVERN DARDEN
DEAD KIDS .... LOUISE FLETCHER
DEAD MAN ON THE RUN (TF) .... PETER GRAVES
DEAD MAN OUT (CTF) .... DANNY GLOVER
DEAD MAN OUT (CTF) .... RUBEN BLADES
DEAD MAN WALKING .... WINGS HAUSER
DEAD MAN'S FOLLY (TF) .... PETER USTINOV
DEAD MAN'S SHOES .... RODDY McDOWALL
DEAD MEN DON'T DIE .... ELLIOTT GOULD
DEAD MEN DON'T WEAR PLAID .... CARL REINER
DEAD MEN DON'T WEAR PLAID .... GEORGE GAYNES
DEAD MEN DON'T WEAR PLAID .... RACHEL WARD
DEAD MEN DON'T WEAR PLAID .... RENI SANTONI
DEAD MEN DON'T WEAR PLAID .... STEVE MARTIN
DEAD OF NIGHT .... WILLIAM SHATNER
DEAD OF WINTER .... JAN RUBES
DEAD OF WINTER .... MARY STEENBURGEN
DEAD OF WINTER .... RODDY McDOWALL
DEAD OF WINTER .... WILLIAM RUSS
DEAD ON .... LEO ROSSI
DEAD ON .... MEG FOSTER
DEAD ON .... MILES O'KEEFFE
DEAD ON .... RAY SHARKEY†
DEAD POETS SOCIETY .... ALLELON RUGGIERO
DEAD POETS SOCIETY .... DYLAN KUSSMAN
DEAD POETS SOCIETY .... ETHAN HAWKE
DEAD POETS SOCIETY .... GALE HANSEN
DEAD POETS SOCIETY .... JAMES WATERSTON
DEAD POETS SOCIETY .... JOSH CHARLES
DEAD POETS SOCIETY .... KURTWOOD SMITH
DEAD POETS SOCIETY .... NORMAN LLOYD
DEAD POETS SOCIETY .... ROBERT SEAN LEONARD
DEAD POETS SOCIETY ★ .... ROBIN WILLIAMS
DEAD POOL, THE .... CLINT EASTWOOD
DEAD POOL, THE .... EVAN KIM
DEAD POOL, THE .... JIM CARREY
DEAD POOL, THE .... LIAM NEESON
DEAD POOL, THE .... PATRICIA CLARKSON
DEAD RECKONING .... WILLIAM PRINCE
DEAD RECKONING (CTF) .... RICK SPRINGFIELD
DEAD RECKONING (CTF) .... SUSAN BLAKELY
DEAD RINGER .... BETTE DAVIS†
DEAD RINGER .... KARL MALDEN
DEAD RINGERS .... GENEVIEVE BUJOLD
DEAD RINGERS .... JEREMY IRONS
DEAD SLEEP .... LINDA BLAIR
DEAD SPACE .... JUDITH CHAPMAN
DEAD ZONE, THE .... ANTHONY ZERBE
DEAD ZONE, THE .... BROOKE ADAMS
DEAD ZONE, THE .... CHRISTOPHER WALKEN
DEAD ZONE, THE .... COLLEEN DEWHURST†
DEAD ZONE, THE .... MARTIN SHEEN
DEAD ZONE, THE .... TOM SKERRITT
DEAD-BANG .... BOB BALABAN
DEAD-BANG .... DON JOHNSON
DEAD-BANG .... EVANS EVANS
DEAD-BANG .... FRANK MILITARY
DEAD-BANG .... MICHAEL HIGGINS
DEAD-BANG .... PENELOPE ANN MILLER
DEAD-BANG .... TATE DONOVAN
DEAD-BANG .... TIM REID
DEAD-BANG .... WILLIAM FORSYTHE
DEADFALL .... MICHAEL BIEHN
DEADFALL .... MICHAEL CAINE
DEADFALL .... NICOLAS CAGE
DEADHEAD MILES .... ALAN ARKIN
DEADHEAD MILES .... CHARLES DURNING
DEADLIEST SEASON, THE (TF) .... JILL EIKENBERRY
DEADLIEST SEASON, THE (TF) .... MERYL STREEP
DEADLIEST SEASON, THE (TF) .... PATRICK O'NEAL†
DEADLINE .... CHRISTOPHER WALKEN
DEADLY AFFAIR, THE .... DAVID WARNER
DEADLY AFFAIR, THE .... KENNETH HAIGH
DEADLY AFFAIR, THE .... LYNN REDGRAVE
DEADLY AFFAIR, THE .... MAXIMILIAN SCHELL
DEADLY AFFAIR, THE .... MICHAEL BRYANT
DEADLY BLESSING .... ERNEST BORGNINE
DEADLY BLESSING .... JEFF EAST
DEADLY BLESSING .... LOIS NETTLETON
DEADLY BLESSING .... SHARON STONE
DEADLY BLESSING .... SUSAN BUCKNER
DEADLY BUSINESS, A (TF) .... ALAN ARKIN
DEADLY BUSINESS, A (TF) .... ARMAND ASSANTE
DEADLY CARE (TF) .... CHERYL LADD
DEADLY COMPANION, THE .... MAUREEN O'HARA
DEADLY COMPANIONS, THE .... BRIAN KEITH
DEADLY DECEPTION (TF) .... BONNIE BARTLETT
DEADLY DECEPTION (TF) .... LISA EILBACHER
DEADLY DREAM (TF) .... JANET LEIGH
DEADLY ENCOUNTER .... LEON AMES
DEADLY ENCOUNTER (TF) .... LARRY HAGMAN
DEADLY ENCOUNTER (TF) .... SUSAN ANSPACH
DEADLY FRIEND .... ANN RAMSEY†
DEADLY FRIEND .... ANNE TWOMEY
DEADLY FRIEND .... CHARLES FLEISCHER
DEADLY FRIEND .... KRISTY SWANSON
DEADLY FRIEND .... MATTHEW LABORTEAUX
DEADLY FRIEND .... MICHAEL SHARRETT
DEADLY FRIEND .... RICHARD MARCUS
DEADLY GAME (TF) .... ANDY GRIFFITH
DEADLY HARVEST (TF) .... PATTY DUKE
DEADLY HERO .... DON MURRAY
DEADLY HERO .... JAMES EARL JONES
DEADLY HERO .... LILIA SKALA
DEADLY HONEYMOON .... PAT HINGLE
DEADLY INTENTIONS (MS) .... CLIFF DE YOUNG
DEADLY INTENTIONS (MS) .... CLORIS LEACHMAN
DEADLY INTENTIONS (MS) .... MADOLYN SMITH OSBORNE
DEADLY INTENTIONS (MS) .... MICHAEL BIEHN
DEADLY INTENTIONS (MS) .... MORGANA KING
DEADLY LESSONS (TF) .... ALLY SHEEDY
DEADLY MESSAGES (TF) .... DENNIS FRANZ
DEADLY MESSAGES (TF) .... KATHLEEN BELLER
DEADLY MESSAGES (TF) .... MICHAEL BRANDON
DEADLY SILENCE, A (TF) .... CHARLES HAID
DEADLY SILENCE, A (TF) .... HEATHER FAIRFIELD
DEADLY SILENCE, A (TF) .... MIKE FARRELL
DEADLY STRANGERS .... HAYLEY MILLS
DEADLY STRANGERS .... SIMON WARD
DEADLY THIEF, THE .... JOHN SAXON
DEADLY THIEF, THE .... SYLVIA MILES
DEADLY TOWER, THE (TF) .... KURT RUSSELL
DEADLY TOWER, THE (TF) .... NED BEATTY
DEADLY TRACKERS, THE .... PEDRO ARMENDARIZ JR.
DEADLY TRACKERS, THE .... RICHARD HARRIS
DEADLY TRAP, THE .... FAYE DUNAWAY
DEADLY TRAP, THE .... FRANK LANGELLA
DEADLY TRAP, THE .... MAURICE RONET
DEADLY TREASURE OF THE PIRANHA .... KAREN BLACK
DEADLY TREASURE OF THE PIRANHA .... LEE MAJORS
DEADLY TREASURE OF THE PIRANHA .... MARGAUX HEMINGWAY
DEADLY TREASURE OF THE PIRANHA .... MARISA BERENSON
DEAF SMITH AND JOHNNY EARS .... ANTHONY QUINN
DEAF SMITH AND JOHNNY EARS .... FRANCO NERO
DEAL OF THE CENTURY .... CHEVY CHASE
DEAL OF THE CENTURY .... SIGOURNEY WEAVER
DEAL OF THE CENTURY .... VINCE EDWARDS
DEALERS .... DERRICK O'CONNOR
DEALERS .... PAUL McGANN
DEALERS .... REBECCA DE MORNAY
DEALING: OR THE BERKELEY-TO-BOSTON FORTY-BRICK LOST-BAG BLUES .... BARBARA HERSHEY
DEALING: OR THE BERKELEY-TO-BOSTON FORTY-BRICK LOST-BAG BLUES .... CHARLES DURNING
DEALING: OR THE BERKELEY-TO-BOSTON FORTY-BRICK LOST-BAG BLUES .... JOHN LITHGOW
DEAR AMERICA: LETTERS HOME FROM VIETNAM (FD) .... HARVEY KEITEL
DEAR AMERICA: LETTERS HOME FROM VIETNAM (FD) .... HOWARD E. ROLLINS JR.
DEAR AMERICA: LETTERS HOME FROM VIETNAM (FD) .... KATHLEEN TURNER
DEAR AMERICA: LETTERS HOME FROM VIETNAM (FD) .... MICHAEL J. FOX
DEAR AMERICA: LETTERS HOME FROM VIETNAM (FD) .... ROBERT DE NIRO
DEAR AMERICA: LETTERS HOME FROM VIETNAM (FD) .... ROBIN WILLIAMS
DEAR AMERICA: LETTERS HOME FROM VIETNAM (FD) .... SEAN PENN
DEAR AMERICA: LETTERS HOME FROM VIETNAM (FD) .... WILLEM DAFOE
DEAR BRIGITTE .... JACK KRUSCHEN
DEAR BRIGITTE .... JAMES STEWART
DEAR DETECTIVE (TF) .... BRENDA VACCARO
DEAR HEART .... ANGELA LANSBURY
DEAR HEART .... MARY WICKES
DEAR MR. PROHACK .... DENHOLM ELLIOTT†
DEAR MR. WONDERFUL .... JOE PESCI
DEAR RUTH .... JOAN CAULFIELD†
DEAR RUTH .... WILLIAM HOLDEN†
DEAR WIFE .... JOAN CAULFIELD†
DEATH AMONG FRIENDS (TF) .... KATE REID
DEATH AMONG FRIENDS (TF) .... MARTIN BALSAM
DEATH AND THE MAIDEN .... BEN KINGSLEY
DEATH AND THE MAIDEN .... SIGOURNEY WEAVER
DEATH AND THE MAIDEN .... STUART WILSON
DEATH AND THE MAIDEN (TF) .... BONNIE BEDELIA
DEATH AT LOVE HOUSE (TF) .... BILL MACY
DEATH AT LOVE HOUSE (TF) .... KATE JACKSON
DEATH AT LOVE HOUSE (TF) .... ROBERT WAGNER
DEATH AT LOVE HOUSE (TF) .... SYLVIA SIDNEY
DEATH BE NOT PROUD (TF) .... ARTHUR HILL
DEATH BE NOT PROUD (TF) .... JANE ALEXANDER
DEATH BE NOT PROUD (TF) .... RALPH CLANTON

† after an actor's name denotes deceased.

INDEX OF FILM TITLES

DEATH BE NOT PROUD (TF) .... ROBBY BENSON
DEATH BE NOT PROUD (TF) .... WENDY PHILLIPS
DEATH BECOMES HER .... BRUCE WILLIS
DEATH BECOMES HER .... GOLDIE HAWN
DEATH BECOMES HER .... ISABELLA ROSSELLINI
DEATH BECOMES HER .... MERYL STREEP
DEATH BECOMES HER .... SYDNEY POLLACK
DEATH BEFORE DISHONOR .... BRIAN KEITH
DEATH BEFORE DISHONOR .... JOANNA PACULA
DEATH CAR ON THE FREEWAY (TF) .... MORGAN BRITTANY
DEATH CAR ON THE FREEWAY (TF) .... PETER GRAVES
DEATH COLLECTOR .... JOE PESCI
DEATH CRUISE (TF) .... CELESTE HOLM
DEATH CRUISE (TF) .... KATE JACKSON
DEATH GAME .... SEYMOUR CASSEL
DEATH GAME .... SONDRA LOCKE
DEATH HUNT .... ANGIE DICKINSON
DEATH HUNT .... CARL WEATHERS
DEATH HUNT .... CHARLES BRONSON
DEATH HUNT .... LEE MARVIN†
DEATH IN CALIFORNIA, A (MS) .... ALEXIS SMITH†
DEATH IN CALIFORNIA, A (MS) .... CHERYL LADD
DEATH IN CALIFORNIA, A (MS) .... JOHN ASHTON
DEATH IN CALIFORNIA, A (MS) .... SAM ELLIOTT
DEATH IN CANAAN, A (TF) .... BRIAN DENNEHY
DEATH IN CANAAN, A (TF) .... CONCHATA FERRELL
DEATH IN SMALL DOSES .... CHUCK CONNORS†
DEATH IN VENICE .... MARISA BERENSON
DEATH JOURNEY .... FRED WILLIAMSON
DEATH MOON (TF) .... ROBERT FOXWORTH
DEATH OF A CENTERFOLD: THE DOROTHY STRATTEN STORY (TF) .... JAMIE LEE CURTIS
DEATH OF A GUNFIGHTER .... CARROLL O'CONNOR
DEATH OF A GUNFIGHTER .... HARRY CAREY JR.
DEATH OF A GUNFIGHTER .... JOHN SAXON
DEATH OF A GUNFIGHTER .... LENA HORNE
DEATH OF A GUNFIGHTER .... RICHARD WIDMARK
DEATH OF A SALESMAN ★ .... FREDRIC MARCH†
DEATH OF A SALESMAN ✪ .... MILDRED DUNNOCK†
DEATH OF A SALESMAN ✪ .... KEVIN McCARTHY
DEATH OF A SALESMAN (TF) .... CHARLES DURNING
DEATH OF A SALESMAN (TF) .... DUSTIN HOFFMAN
DEATH OF A SALESMAN (TF) .... JOHN MALKOVICH
DEATH OF A SALESMAN (TF) .... LOUIS ZORICH
DEATH OF A SALESMAN (TF) .... STEPHEN LANG
DEATH OF A SCOUNDREL .... YVONNE DE CARLO
DEATH OF A SCOUNDREL .... ZSA ZSA GABOR
DEATH OF A SOLDIER .... BELINDA DAVEY
DEATH OF A SOLDIER .... BILL HUNTER
DEATH OF A SOLDIER .... JAMES COBURN
DEATH OF A SOLDIER .... MAURIE FIELDS
DEATH OF A SOLDIER .... MAX FAIRCHILD
DEATH OF A SOLDIER .... REB BROWN
DEATH OF A STRANGER .... JASON ROBARDS
DEATH OF LOVE HOUSE (TF) .... DOROTHY LAMOUR
DEATH OF ME YET, THE (TF) .... MEG FOSTER
DEATH OF RICHIE, THE (TF) .... BEN GAZZARA
DEATH OF RICHIE, THE (TF) .... EILEEN BRENNAN
DEATH OF RICHIE, THE (TF) .... ROBBY BENSON
DEATH OF THE INCREDIBLE HULK, THE (TF) .... BILL BIXBY†
DEATH OF THE INCREDIBLE HULK, THE (TF) .... LOU FERRIGNO
DEATH ON THE NILE .... ANGELA LANSBURY
DEATH ON THE NILE .... BETTE DAVIS†
DEATH ON THE NILE .... GEORGE KENNEDY
DEATH ON THE NILE .... JACK WARDEN
DEATH ON THE NILE .... LOIS CHILES
DEATH ON THE NILE .... MAGGIE SMITH
DEATH ON THE NILE .... MIA FARROW
DEATH ON THE NILE .... PETER USTINOV
DEATH ON THE NILE .... SAM WANAMAKER†
DEATH ON THE NILE .... SIMON MacCORKINDALE
DEATH PLAY .... JAMES KEACH
DEATH RACE 2000 .... DAVID CARRADINE
DEATH RACE 2000 .... SYLVESTER STALLONE
DEATH RACE (TF) .... LLOYD BRIDGES
DEATH RIDES A HORSE .... JOHN PHILLIP LAW
DEATH SCREAM .... DIMITRA ARLYS
DEATH SCREAM .... ED ASNER
DEATH SCREAM .... KATE JACKSON
DEATH SCREAM .... LUCIE ARNAZ
DEATH SCREAM .... TINA LOUISE
DEATH SCREAM (TF) .... ART CARNEY
DEATH SCREAM (TF) .... CLORIS LEACHMAN
DEATH SCREAM (TF) .... DIAHANN CARROLL
DEATH SCREAM (TF) .... NANCY WALKER†
DEATH SCREAM (TF) .... RAUL JULIA†
DEATH SCREAM (TF) .... SALLY KIRKLAND
DEATH SENTENCE (TF) .... CLORIS LEACHMAN
DEATH SENTENCE (TF) .... LAURENCE LUCKINBILL
DEATH SENTENCE (TF) .... NICK NOLTE
DEATH SQUAD, THE (TF) .... CLAUDE AKINS†
DEATH SQUAD, THE (TF) .... ROBERT FORSTER
DEATH STALK (TF) .... CAROL LYNLEY
DEATH TRAP .... MEL FERRER
DEATH TRAP .... STUART WHITMAN
DEATH VALLEY .... PAUL LeMAT
DEATH VALLEY .... STEPHEN McHATTIE
DEATH VALLEY .... WILFORD BRIMLEY
DEATH WARRANT .... CYNTHIA GIBB
DEATH WARRANT .... GEORGE DICKERSON
DEATH WARRANT .... JEAN-CLAUDE VAN DAMME
DEATH WARRANT .... PATRICK KILPATRICK
DEATH WARRANT .... ROBERT GUILLAUME
DEATH WEEKEND .... BRENDA VACCARO
DEATH WEEKEND .... DON STROUD
DEATH WISH .... CHARLES BRONSON
DEATH WISH .... CHRISTOPHER GUEST
DEATH WISH .... HOPE LANGE
DEATH WISH .... JEFF GOLDBLUM
DEATH WISH .... OLYMPIA DUKAKIS
DEATH WISH .... STEPHEN ELLIOTT
DEATH WISH .... STEVEN KEATS†
DEATH WISH .... STUART MARGOLIN
DEATH WISH .... VINCENT GARDENIA†
DEATH WISH .... WILLIAM REDFIELD†
DEATH WISH II .... ANTHONY (TONY) FRANCIOSA
DEATH WISH II .... CHARLES BRONSON
DEATH WISH II .... J. D. CANNON
DEATH WISH II .... JILL IRELAND†
DEATH WISH II .... LAURENCE FISHBURNE
DEATH WISH II .... VINCENT GARDENIA†
DEATH WISH 3 .... CHARLES BRONSON
DEATH WISH 3 .... DEBORAH RAFFIN
DEATH WISH 3 .... ED LAUTER
DEATH WISH 3 .... MARTIN BALSAM
DEATH WISH 4: THE CRACKDOWN .... CHARLES BRONSON
DEATH WISH V: THE FACE OF DEATH .... CHARLES BRONSON
DEATH WISH V: THE FACE OF DEATH .... KEN WELSH
DEATH WISH V: THE FACE OF DEATH .... LESLEY-ANNE DOWN
DEATH WISH V: THE FACE OF DEATH .... MICHAEL PARKS
DEATH WISH V: THE FACE OF DEATH .... SAUL RUBINEK
DEATHMASK .... DANNY AIELLO
DEATHMASK .... LEE BRYANT
DEATHSTALKER IV .... BRET BAXTER CLARK
DEATHSTALKER IV .... MARIA FORD
DEATHSTALKER IV .... RICK HILL
DEATHTRAP .... CHRISTOPHER REEVE
DEATHTRAP .... DYAN CANNON
DEATHTRAP .... HENRY JONES
DEATHTRAP .... IRENE WORTH
DEATHTRAP .... JOE SILVER†
DEATHTRAP .... MICHAEL CAINE
DEATHWATCH .... HARVEY KEITEL
DEATHWATCH .... LEONARD NIMOY
DEATHWATCH .... PAUL MAZURSKY
DEBT OF HONOR .... GERALDINE FITZGERALD
DECAMERON NIGHTS .... JOAN COLLINS
DECAMERON NIGHTS .... LOUIS JOURDAN
DECEIVED .... ASHLEY PELDON
DECEIVED .... FRANCESCA BULLER
DECEIVED .... GOLDIE HAWN
DECEIVED .... JOHN HEARD
DECEIVED .... KATE REID
DECEIVED .... ROBIN BARTLETT
DECEIVED .... STANLEY ANDERSON
DECEIVED .... TOM IRWIN
DECEIVERS, THE .... DAVID ROBB
DECEIVERS, THE .... HELENA MICHELL
DECEIVERS, THE .... PIERCE BROSNAN
DECEIVERS, THE .... SAEED JAFFREY
DECEIVERS, THE .... SHASHI KAPOOR
DECEIVERS, THE .... TARIQ YUNIS
DECEPTION .... BETTE DAVIS†
DECEPTIONS (CTF) .... HARRY HAMLIN
DECEPTIONS (CTF) .... NICOLLETTE SHERIDAN
DECEPTIONS (CTF) .... ROBERT DAVI
DECEPTIONS (TF) .... BARRY BOSTWICK
DECEPTIONS (TF) .... STEFANIE POWERS
DECISION BEFORE DAWN .... KARL MALDEN
DECISION OF CHRISTOPHER BLAKE, THE .... ALEXIS SMITH†
DECISION OF CHRISTOPHER BLAKE, THE .... LOIS MAXWELL
DECKS RAN RED, THE .... JACK KRUSCHEN
DECKS RAN RED, THE .... STUART WHITMAN
DECLINE OF THE AMERICAN EMPIRE, THE .... DANIEL BRIERE
DECLINE OF THE AMERICAN EMPIRE, THE .... DOMINIQUE MICHEL
DECLINE OF THE AMERICAN EMPIRE, THE .... DOROTHEE BERRYMAN
DECLINE OF THE AMERICAN EMPIRE, THE .... GABRIEL ARCAND
DECLINE OF THE AMERICAN EMPIRE, THE .... GENEVIEVE RIOUX
DECLINE OF THE AMERICAN EMPIRE, THE .... LOUISE PORTAL
DECLINE OF THE AMERICAN EMPIRE, THE .... PIERRE CURZI
DECLINE OF THE AMERICAN EMPIRE, THE .... REMY GIRARD
DECLINE OF THE AMERICAN EMPIRE, THE .... YVES JACQUES
DECORATION DAY (TF) .... JAMES GARNER
DEEP, THE .... ELI WALLACH
DEEP, THE .... JACQUELINE BISSET
DEEP, THE .... LOUIS GOSSETT JR.
DEEP, THE .... NICK NOLTE
DEEP, THE .... ROBERT SHAW†
DEEP, THE .... ROBERT TESSIER†
DEEP BLUE SEA, THE .... ARTHUR HILL
DEEP COVER .... JEFF GOLDBLUM
DEEP DARK SECRETS (TF) .... JAMES BROLIN
DEEP DARK SECRETS (TF) .... JOE SPANO
DEEP DARK SECRETS (TF) .... MELODY ANDERSON
DEEP DARK SECRETS (TF) .... MORGAN STEVENS
DEEP DARK SECRETS (TF) .... PAMELA BELLWOOD-WHEELER
DEEP END .... BURT KWOUK
DEEP IN MY HEART .... CYD CHARISSE
DEEP IN MY HEART .... GENE KELLY
DEEP IN MY HEART .... HOWARD KEEL
DEEP IN MY HEART .... JOSE FERRER†
DEEP RED .... DAVID HEMMINGS
DEEP SIX, THE .... EFREM ZIMBALIST JR.
DEEP SIX, THE .... JAMES WHITMORE
DEEP SPACE .... CHARLES NAPIER
DEEP SPACE .... JULIE NEWMAR
DEEP TROUBLE (CTF) .... BEN CROSS
DEEP TROUBLE (CTF) .... ROBERT WAGNER
DEEP WATERS .... DEAN STOCKWELL
DEEPSTAR SIX .... CINDY PICKETT
DEEPSTAR SIX .... ELVA BASKIN
DEEPSTAR SIX .... GREG EVIGAN
DEEPSTAR SIX .... MARIUS WEYERS
DEEPSTAR SIX .... MATT McCOY
DEEPSTAR SIX .... MIGUEL FERRER
DEEPSTAR SIX .... NANCY EVERHARD
DEEPSTAR SIX .... NIA PEEPLES
DEEPSTAR SIX .... RON CARROLL
DEEPSTAR SIX .... TAUREAN BLACQUE
DEEPSTAR SIX .... THOMAS BRAY
DEER HUNTER, THE .... AMY WRIGHT
DEER HUNTER, THE .... GEORGE DZUNDZA

This is not a list of every film ever made or every cast member, only those listed in this directory.

DEER HUNTER, THE .... JOHN CAZALE†
DEER HUNTER, THE .... JOHN SAVAGE
DEER HUNTER, THE .... RUTANYA ALDA
DEER HUNTER, THE ★ .... ROBERT DE NIRO
DEER HUNTER, THE ○ .... MERYL STREEP
DEER HUNTER, THE ∞ ..... CHRISTOPHER WALKEN
DEERSLAYER, THE .... RITA MORENO
DEERSLAYER, THE .... YVONNE DE CARLO
DEERSLAYER, THE (TF) .... JOHN ANDERSON
DEERSLAYER, THE (TF) .... MADELINE STOWE
DEF BY TEMPTATION .... CYNTHIA BOND
DEF BY TEMPTATION .... JAMES BOND III
DEF BY TEMPTATION .... MELBA MOORE
DEFECTOR, THE .... RODDY McDOWALL
DEFENDING YOUR LIFE .... ALBERT BROOKS
DEFENDING YOUR LIFE .... BUCK HENRY
DEFENDING YOUR LIFE .... LEE GRANT
DEFENDING YOUR LIFE .... MERYL STREEP
DEFENDING YOUR LIFE .... RIP TORN
DEFENDING YOUR LIFE .... SHIRLEY MacLAINE
DEFENSE OF THE REALM .... BILL PATERSON
DEFENSE OF THE REALM .... DENHOLM ELLIOTT†
DEFENSE OF THE REALM .... FULTON MACKAY†
DEFENSE OF THE REALM .... GABRIEL BYRNE
DEFENSE OF THE REALM .... GRETA SCACCHI
DEFENSE OF THE REALM .... IAN BANNEN
DEFENSE OF THE REALM .... ROBBIE COLTRANE
DEFENSELESS .... BARBARA HERSHEY
DEFENSELESS .... J. T. WALSH
DEFENSELESS .... JAY O. SANDERS
DEFENSELESS .... MARK LOWENTHAL
DEFENSELESS .... MARY BETH HURT
DEFENSELESS .... SAM SHEPARD
DEFIANCE .... ART CARNEY
DEFIANCE .... DANNY AIELLO
DEFIANCE .... JAN-MICHAEL VINCENT
DEFIANT ONES, THE .... CLAUDE AKINS†
DEFIANT ONES, THE ★ .... SIDNEY POITIER
DEFIANT ONES, THE ★ .... TONY CURTIS
DEFIANT ONES, THE ○ .... THEODORE BIKEL
DÉJÀ VU .... JACLYN SMITH
DÉJÀ VU .... SHELLEY WINTERS
DELANCEY STREET (TF) .... LOUIS GOSSETT JR.
DELANCEY STREET: THE
   CRISIS WITHIN (TF) .... MARK HAMILL
DELIBERATE
   STRANGER, THE (MS) .... BEN MASTERS
DELIBERATE
   STRANGER, THE (MS) .... FRED COFFIN
DELIBERATE
   STRANGER, THE (MS) .... FREDERIC FORREST
DELIBERATE
   STRANGER, THE (MS) .... GEORGE GRIZZARD
DELIBERATE
   STRANGER, THE (MS) .... MARK HARMON
DELICATE BALANCE, A .... BETSY BLAIR
DELICATE BALANCE, A .... KATE REID
DELICATE BALANCE, A .... KATHERINE HEPBURN
DELICATE BALANCE, A .... PAUL SCOFIELD
DELICATE BALANCE, A .... SAM WATERSTON
DELICATE DELINQUENT, THE ..... DARREN McGAVIN
DELICATE DELINQUENT, THE .... JERRY LEWIS
DELIGHTFULLY DANGEROUS ..... RALPH BELLAMY†
DELIRIOUS .... CHARLES ROCKET
DELIRIOUS .... DAVID RASCHE
DELIRIOUS .... DYLAN BAKER
DELIRIOUS .... EMMA SAMMS
DELIRIOUS .... JERRY ORBACH
DELIRIOUS .... JOHN CANDY†
DELIRIOUS .... MARIEL HEMINGWAY
DELIRIOUS .... RAYMOND BURR†
DELITTO MATTEOTI .... FRANCO NERO
DELIVER US FROM EVIL (TF) .... DINA MERRILL
DELIVER US FROM EVIL (TF) .... PAT HINGLE
DELIVERANCE .... BILL McKINNEY
DELIVERANCE .... BURT REYNOLDS
DELIVERANCE .... CHARLEY BOORMAN
DELIVERANCE .... JON VOIGHT
DELIVERANCE .... NED BEATTY
DELIVERANCE .... RONNY COX
DELLA (TF) .... DIANE BAKER
DELPHI BUREAU, THE (TF) .... CELESTE HOLM

DELPHI BUREAU,
   THE (TF) .... LAURENCE LUCKINBILL
DELTA COUNTY, U.S.A. .... ROBERT HAYS
DELTA FACTOR, THE .... YVONNE DE CARLO
DELTA FORCE, THE .... ASSAF DAYAN
DELTA FORCE, THE .... BO SVENSON
DELTA FORCE, THE .... CHUCK NORRIS
DELTA FORCE, THE .... GEORGE KENNEDY
DELTA FORCE, THE .... HANNA SCHYGULLA
DELTA FORCE, THE .... JOEY BISHOP
DELTA FORCE, THE .... LAINIE KAZAN
DELTA FORCE, THE .... LEE MARVIN†
DELTA FORCE, THE .... MARTIN BALSAM
DELTA FORCE, THE .... ROBERT FORSTER
DELTA FORCE, THE .... ROBERT VAUGHN
DELTA FORCE, THE .... SHELLEY WINTERS
DELTA FORCE, THE .... SUSAN STRASBERG
DELTA FORCE 2 - OPERATION
   STRANGLEHOLD .... BEGONIA PLAZA
DELTA FORCE 2 - OPERATION
   STRANGLEHOLD .... BILLY DRAGO
DELTA FORCE 2 - OPERATION
   STRANGLEHOLD .... CHUCK NORRIS
DELTA FORCE 2 - OPERATION
   STRANGLEHOLD .... HECTOR MERCADO
DELTA FORCE 2 - OPERATION
   STRANGLEHOLD .... JOHN P. RYAN
DELTA FORCE 2 - OPERATION
   STRANGLEHOLD .... MATEO GOMEZ
DELTA FORCE 2 - OPERATION
   STRANGLEHOLD .... PAUL PERRI
DELTA FORCE 2 - OPERATION
   STRANGLEHOLD .... RICHARD JAECKEL
DELTA FOX .... RICHARD JAECKEL
DELTA FOX .... STUART WHITMAN
DELUSION .... JENNIFER RUBIN
DELUSION .... JERRY ORBACH
DELUSION .... KYLE SECOR
DELUSION .... ROBERT COSTANZO
DELUSION .... TRACEY WALTER
DEMENTIA 13 .... LUANA ANDERS
DEMETRIUS AND THE
   GLADIATORS .... ANNE BANCROFT
DEMETRIUS AND THE
   GLADIATORS .... ERNEST BORGNINE
DEMETRIUS AND THE
   GLADIATORS .... WILLIAM MARSHALL
DEMOLITION MAN .... ANDRE GREGORY
DEMOLITION MAN .... BENJAMIN BRATT
DEMOLITION MAN .... BOB GUNTON
DEMOLITION MAN .... DENIS LEARY
DEMOLITION MAN .... GLENN SHADIX
DEMOLITION MAN .... LORI PETTY
DEMOLITION MAN .... MELINDA DILLON
DEMOLITION MAN .... NIGEL HAWTHORNE
DEMOLITION MAN .... ROB SCHNEIDER
DEMOLITION MAN .... SANDRA BULLOCK
DEMOLITION MAN .... STEVE KAHAN
DEMOLITION MAN .... SYLVESTER STALLONE
DEMOLITION MAN .... WESLEY SNIPES
DEMON .... DEBORAH RAFFIN
DEMON .... SANDY DENNIS†
DEMON .... TONY LoBIANCO
DEMON HUNTERS .... JACK SCALIA
DEMON HUNTERS .... TANYA ROBERTS
DEMON KNIGHT .... BILLY ZANE
DEMON KNIGHT .... BRENDA BAKKE
DEMON KNIGHT .... THOMAS CHURCH
DEMON SEED .... JULIE CHRISTIE
DEMON SEED .... ROBERT VAUGHN
DEMOND SEED .... FRITZ WEAVER
DEMPSEY (TF) .... SAM WATERSTON
DEMPSEY (TF) .... TREAT WILLIAMS
DEMPSEY (TF) .... VICTORIA TENNANT
DENIAL .... JASON PATRIC
DENIAL .... ROBIN WRIGHT
DENNIS THE MENACE .... CHRISTOPHER LLOYD
DENNIS THE MENACE .... JOAN PLOWRIGHT
DENNIS THE MENACE .... LEA THOMPSON
DENNIS THE MENACE .... MASON GAMBLE
DENNIS THE MENACE .... PAUL WINFIELD
DENNIS THE MENACE .... WALTER MATTHAU

DEPARTMENT STORE ...... GERALDINE FITZGERALD
DER 20. JULI .... MAXIMILIAN SCHELL
DER AMERIKANISCHE FREUND .... DENNIS HOPPER
DER ENGEL MIT DER POSAUNE .... MARIA SCHELL
DER HIMMEL UBER BERLIN .... PETER FALK
DER RICHTER UND
   SEIN HENKER .... DONALD SUTHERLAND
DER TRAUMENDE MUND .... MARIA SCHELL
DEREK AND CLIVE GET
   THE HORN (PF) ....DUDLEY MOORE
DEREK AND CLIVE GET
   THE HORN (PF) .... PETER COOK
DES GENS SANS IMPORTANCE ...... LILA KEDROVA
DESCENDING ANGEL (CTF) ...... GEORGE C. SCOTT
DESERT BLOOM .... ALLEN GARFIELD
DESERT BLOOM .... ANNABETH GISH
DESERT BLOOM .... ELLEN BARKIN
DESERT BLOOM .... JAY UNDERWOOD
DESERT BLOOM .... JoBETH WILLIAMS
DESERT BLOOM .... JON VOIGHT
DESERT FOX .... SEAN McCLORY
DESERT FOX, THE .... DAN O'HERLIHY
DESERT FOX, THE .... JESSICA TANDY†
DESERT FURY .... BURT LANCASTER†
DESERT HAWK, THE .... ROCK HUDSON†
DESERT HAWK, THE .... YVONNE DE CARLO
DESERT HEARTS .... ANDRA AKERS
DESERT HEARTS .... AUDRA LINDLEY
DESERT HEARTS .... DEAN BUTLER
DESERT HEARTS .... GWEN WELLES
DESERT HEARTS .... HELEN SHAVER
DESERT HEARTS .... JEFFREY TAMBOR
DESERT HEARTS .... PATRICIA CHARBONNEAU
DESERT HELL .... BARBARA HALE
DESERT SHIELD .... EB LOTTIMER
DESERT SHIELD .... GALE HANSEN
DESERT SHIELD .... ROB LOWE
DESERT SHIELD .... TRACY GRIFFITH
DESERT SONG .... GORDON MACRAE†
DESERTER, THE .... ALBERT SALMI†
DESERTER, THE .... CHUCK CONNORS†
DESERTER, THE .... IAN BANNEN
DESERTER, THE .... PATRICK WAYNE
DESERTER, THE .... RICARDO MONTALBAN
DESERTER, THE .... RICHARD CRENNA
DESERTER, THE .... WOODY STRODE
DESIGNING WOMAN .... CHUCK CONNORS†
DESIGNING WOMAN .... GREGORY PECK
DESIGNING WOMAN .... LAUREN BACALL
DESIRE IN THE DUST .... RAYMOND BURR†
DESIRE ME .... GREER GARSON
DESIRE ME .... ROBERT MITCHUM
DESIRE UNDER THE ELMS ...... ANTHONY PERKINS†
DESIRE UNDER THE ELMS .... BURL IVES
DESIRE UNDER THE ELMS .... SOPHIA LOREN
DESIREE .... JEAN SIMMONS
DÉSIRÉE .... MARLON BRANDO
DESK SET .... DINA MERRILL
DESK SET .... KATHERINE HEPBURN
DESK SET .... SPENCER TRACY†
DESPERADO .... ANTONIO BANDERAS
DESPERADO .... CHEECH MARIN
DESPERADO .... RAUL JULIA†
DESPERADO .... STEVE BUSCEMI
DESPERADO: BADLANDS
   JUSTICE (TF) .... PATRICIA CHARBONNEAU
DESPERADO (TF) .... LISE CUTTER
DESPERADOES, THE .... VINCE EDWARDS
DESPERADOES, THE .... JACK PALANCE
DESPERATE .... RAYMOND BURR†
DESPERATE CHARACTERS .... CAROL KANE
DESPERATE CHARACTERS .... KENNETH MARS
DESPERATE CHARACTERS .... SHIRLEY MacLAINE
DESPERATE FOR LOVE (TF) .... TAMMY LAUREN
DESPERATE FOR
   LOVE (TF) .... VERONICA CARTWRIGHT
DESPERATE HOURS .... ANTHONY HOPKINS
DESPERATE HOURS .... DAVID MORSE
DESPERATE HOURS .... KELLY LYNCH
DESPERATE HOURS .... MICKEY ROURKE
DESPERATE HOURS .... MIMI ROGERS
DESPERATE HOURS, THE .... MARTHA SCOTT

DESPERATE JOURNEY .... RONALD REAGAN
DESPERATE
  MISSION (TF) .... RICARDO MONTALBAN
DESPERATE MOMENT .... MAE ZETTERLING†
DESPERATE MOMENT .... THEODORE BIKEL
DESPERATE ONES, THE ..... MAXIMILIAN SCHELL
DESPERATE SEARCH .... HOWARD KEEL
DESPERATE SEARCH .... JANE GREER
DESPERATE SIEGE .... JEFF COREY
DESPERATE WOMEN (TF) .... SUSAN SAINT JAMES
DESPERATELY SEEKING SUSAN .... AIDAN QUINN
DESPERATELY SEEKING SUSAN .... ANNA LEVINE
DESPERATELY SEEKING
  SUSAN .... JOHN TURTURRO
DESPERATELY SEEKING SUSAN .... MADONNA
DESPERATELY SEEKING SUSAN .... MARK BLUM
DESPERATELY SEEKING
  SUSAN .... RICHARD EDSON
DESPERATELY SEEKING SUSAN .... ROBERT JOY
DESPERATELY SEEKING
  SUSAN .... ROSANNA ARQUETTE
DESTINATION: AMERICA (TF) .... ALAN AUTRY
DESTINATION:
  AMERICA (TF) .... BRUCE GREENWOOD
DESTINATION: AMERICA (TF) .... JOE PANTOLIANO
DESTINATION: AMERICA (TF) .... RIP TORN
DESTINATION GOBI .... EARL HOLLIMAN
DESTINATION GOBI .... MAX SHOWALTER
DESTINATION GOBI .... RICHARD WIDMARK
DESTINATION MURDER .... HURD HATFIELD
DESTINATION TOKYO .... JOHN FORSYTHE
DESTINATION TOKYO .... WILLIAM PRINCE
DESTINATION UNKNOWN .... RALPH BELLAMY†
DESTINAZIONE ROMA .... FRED WILLIAMSON
DESTINY TURNS ON
  THE RADIO .... DYLAN McDERMOTT
DESTINY TURNS ON THE RADIO .... JAMES BELUSHI
DESTINY TURNS ON THE RADIO .... JAMES LeGROS
DESTINY TURNS ON THE RADIO ..... NANCY TRAVIS
DESTINY TURNS ON
  THE RADIO .... QUENTIN TARANTINO
DESTRUCTORS, THE .... ANTHONY QUINN
DESTRUCTORS, THE .... MICHAEL CAINE
DESTRY RIDES AGAIN .... JAMES STEWART
DETECTIVE .... EMMANUELLE SEIGNER
DETECTIVE BELLI .... FRANCO NERO
DETECTIVE IN THE HOUSE (TF) .... CASSIE YATES
DETECTIVE IN THE HOUSE (TF) .... JUDD HIRSCH
DETECTIVE STORY .... JOSEPH WISEMAN
DETECTIVE STORY .... KIRK DOUGLAS
DETECTIVE STORY ★ ...... ELEANOR PARKER
DETECTIVE STORY ✪ .... LEE GRANT
DETECTIVE, THE .... ALEC GUINNESS
DETECTIVE, THE .... FRANK SINATRA
DETECTIVE, THE .... JACK KLUGMAN
DETECTIVE, THE .... JACQUELINE BISSET
DETECTIVE, THE .... ROBERT DUVALL
DETECTIVE, THE .... TONY MUSANTE
DETECTIVE, THE .... WILLIAM WINDOM
DETENUOT IN ATTESA
  DI GIUDIZIO .... JEANNIE BERLIN
DEUX .... GERARD DEPARDIEU
DEUX HOMMES
  DANS LA VILLE .... GERARD DEPARDIEU
DEVIL AND DANIEL WEBSTER, THE ..... JEFF COREY
DEVIL AND DANIEL
  WEBSTER, THE ★ .... WALTER HUSTON†
DEVIL AND MAX DEVLIN, THE .... BILL COSBY
DEVIL AND MAX DEVLIN, THE .... ELLIOTT GOULD
DEVIL AND MAX DEVLIN, THE ...... SUSAN ANSPACH
DEVIL AND MISS
  JONES, THE ✪ .... CHARLES COBURN†
DEVIL AND THE TEN
  COMMANDMENTS, THE ...... MEL FERRER
DEVIL AT 4 O'CLOCK, THE .... FRANK SINATRA
DEVIL BY THE TAIL, THE .... MARIA SCHELL
DEVIL BY THE TAIL, THE .... MARTHE KELLER
DEVIL DOLL, THE .... MAUREEN O'SULLIVAN
DEVIL HAS SEVEN FACES, THE .... CARROLL BAKER
DEVIL IN A BLUE DRESS ...... DENZEL WASHINGTON
DEVIL IN A BLUE DRESS .... DON CHEADLE
DEVIL IN A BLUE DRESS .... JENNIFER BEALS

DEVIL IN A BLUE DRESS .... TOM SIZEMORE
DEVIL IN LOVE, THE .... CLAUDINE AUGER
DEVIL IS A SISSY, THE .... JACKIE COOPER
DEVIL IS A SISSY, THE .... MICKEY ROONEY
DEVIL IS A WOMAN, THE .... GLENDA JACKSON
DEVIL MAKES THREE, THE .... GENE KELLY
DEVIL OF THE DESERT .... OMAR SHARIF
DEVIL THUMBS
  A RIDE, THE .... LAWRENCE TIERNEY
DEVIL WITHIN HER .... DONALD PLEASENCE
DEVIL WITHIN HER, THE .... EILEEN ATKINS
DEVIL WITHIN HER, THE .... JOAN COLLINS
DEVIL'S DISCIPLE, THE .... GEORGE ROSE†
DEVIL'S HOLIDAY, THE ★ .... NANCY CARROLL†
DEVIL'S WIDOW, THE .... AVA GARDNER†
DEVILS, THE .... VANESSA REDGRAVE
DEVIL'S ADVOCATE, THE .... JASON MILLER
DEVIL'S ADVOCATE, THE .... LEIGH LAWSON
DEVIL'S BRIGADE, THE .... ANDREW PRINE
DEVIL'S BRIGADE, THE .... CARROLL O'CONNOR
DEVIL'S BRIGADE, THE .... CLAUDE AKINS†
DEVIL'S BRIGADE, THE .... CLIFF ROBERTSON
DEVIL'S BRIGADE, THE .... HARRY CAREY JR.
DEVIL'S BRIGADE, THE .... NORMAN ALDEN
DEVIL'S BRIGADE, THE .... RICHARD JAECKEL
DEVIL'S BRIGADE, THE .... VINCE EDWARDS
DEVIL'S
  DAUGHTER, THE (TF) .... ROBERT FOXWORTH
DEVIL'S
  DAUGHTER, THE (TF) .... SHELLEY WINTERS
DEVIL'S DISCIPLE, THE .... BURT LANCASTER†
DEVIL'S DISCIPLE, THE .... KIRK DOUGLAS
DEVIL'S EYE, THE .... BIBI ANDERSSON
DEVIL'S IMPOSTER, THE .... JEREMY KEMP
DEVIL'S IMPOSTER, THE .... LESLEY-ANNE DOWN
DEVIL'S IMPOSTER, THE .... LIV ULLMANN
DEVIL'S IMPOSTER, THE .... OLIVIA DE HAVILLAND
DEVIL'S RAIN, THE .... EDDIE ALBERT
DEVIL'S RAIN, THE .... ERNEST BORGNINE
DEVIL'S RAIN, THE .... JOHN TRAVOLTA
DEVIL'S RAIN, THE .... TOM SKERRITT
DEVIL'S RAIN, THE .... WILLIAM SHATNER
DEVIL'S TRIANGLE, THE (FD) .... VINCENT PRICE†
DEVIL'S WIDOW, THE .... JOANNA LUMLEY
DEVONSVILLE
  TERROR, THE .... DONALD PLEASENCE
DEVOTION .... OLIVIA DE HAVILLAND
DIABOLIK .... JOHN PHILLIP LAW
DIAL M FOR MURDER .... GRACE KELLY†
DIAL M FOR MURDER (TF) .... RON MOODY
DIAMOND HEAD .... CHARLTON HESTON
DIAMOND HEAD .... FRANCE NUYEN
DIAMOND HUNTERS .... DAVID McCALLUM
DIAMOND MERCENARIES, THE .... JACK PALANCE
DIAMOND MERCENARIES, THE .... PETER FONDA
DIAMOND MERCENARIES, THE ..... TELLY SAVALAS†
DIAMOND SKULLS .... AMANDA DONOHOE
DIAMOND TRAP, THE (TF) .... BROOKE SHIELDS
DIAMOND TRAP, THE (TF) ...... DARREN McGAVIN
DIAMOND TRAP, THE (TF) ...... ED MARINARO
DIAMOND TRAP, THE (TF) ..... HOWARD HESSEMAN
DIAMOND TRAP, THE (TF) .... TWIGGY
DIAMONDS .... BARBARA HERSHEY
DIAMONDS .... RICHARD ROUNDTREE
DIAMONDS .... SHELLEY WINTERS
DIAMONDS AND CRIME .... MARTHA SCOTT
DIAMONDS ARE FOREVER .... JILL ST. JOHN
DIAMONDS ARE FOREVER .... LOIS MAXWELL
DIAMONDS ARE FOREVER .... SEAN CONNERY
DIAMONDS ON WHEELS .... PETER FIRTH
DIAMOND'S EDGE .... BILL PATERSON
DIAMOND'S EDGE .... JIMMY NAIL
DIAMOND'S EDGE .... MICHAEL ROBBINS
DIAMOND'S EDGE .... NICKOLAS GRACE
DIAMOND'S EDGE .... PATRICIA HODGE
DIAMOND'S EDGE .... RENE RUIZ
DIAMOND'S EDGE .... SAEED JAFFREY
DIANE .... LANA TURNER
DIANE .... ROGER MOORE
DIANE .... SEAN McCLORY
DIANE OF THE FOLLIES .... LILLIAN GISH†

DIARY OF A
  CHAMBERMAID .... BURGESS MEREDITH
DIARY OF A CHAMBERMAID,
  THE .... DAME JUDITH ANDERSON†
DIARY OF A CHAMBERMAID,
  THE .... HURD HATFIELD
DIARY OF A HITMAN .... SHARON STONE
DIARY OF A MAD HOUSEWIFE .... FRANK LANGELLA
DIARY OF A MAD HOUSEWIFE .... PETER BOYLE
DIARY OF A MAD
  HOUSEWIFE .... RICHARD BENJAMIN
DIARY OF A MAD
  HOUSEWIFE ★ .... CARRIE SNODGRESS
DIARY OF A MADMAN .... VINCENT PRICE†
DIARY OF A PERFECT
  MURDER (TF) .... ANDY GRIFFITH
DIARY OF A PERFECT
  MURDER (TF) .... STEVE INWOOD
DIARY OF A TEENAGE
  HITCHHIKER (TF) .... CRAIG T. NELSON
DIARY OF A TEENAGE
  HITCHHIKER (TF) .... KATHERINE HELMOND
DIARY OF ANNE FRANK, THE .... DIANE BAKER
DIARY OF ANNE FRANK, THE .... LOU JACOBI
DIARY OF ANNE FRANK, THE .... MILLIE PERKINS
DIARY OF ANNE FRANK, THE ✪ .... ED WYNN†
DIARY OF ANNE
  FRANK, THE ✪✪ .... SHELLEY WINTERS
DIARY OF ANNE
  FRANK, THE (TF) .... JOAN PLOWRIGHT
DIARY OF ANNE
  FRANK, THE (TF) .... MAXIMILIAN SCHELL
DICE RULES (FD) .... ANDREW DICE CLAY
DICK AND MARGE SAVE
  THE WORLD .... DEBBIE LEE CARRINGTON
DICK AND MARGE SAVE THE WORLD .... ERIC IDLE
DICK AND MARGE SAVE
  THE WORLD .... JEFFREY JONES
DICK AND MARGE SAVE
  THE WORLD .... JON LOVITZ
DICK AND MARGE SAVE
  THE WORLD .... KATHY IRELAND
DICK AND MARGE SAVE
  THE WORLD .... TERI GARR
DICK AND MARGE SAVE
  THE WORLD .... WALLACE SHAWN
DICK TRACY ✪ .... AL PACINO
DICK TRACY .... ALLEN GARFIELD
DICK TRACY .... BERT REMSEN
DICK TRACY .... CATHERINE O'HARA
DICK TRACY .... CHARLES DURNING
DICK TRACY .... CHARLES FLEISCHER
DICK TRACY .... CHARLIE KORSMO
DICK TRACY .... DICK VAN DYKE
DICK TRACY .... DUSTIN HOFFMAN
DICK TRACY .... ED O'ROSS
DICK TRACY .... ESTELLE PARSONS
DICK TRACY .... FRANK CAMOANELLA
DICK TRACY .... GLENNE HEADLY
DICK TRACY .... HENRY JONES
DICK TRACY .... HENRY SILVA
DICK TRACY .... JAMES CAAN
DICK TRACY .... JAMES KEANE
DICK TRACY .... JAMES TOLKAN
DICK TRACY .... JOHN SCHUCK
DICK TRACY .... KATHY BATES
DICK TRACY .... MADONNA
DICK TRACY .... MANDY PATINKIN
DICK TRACY .... MARY WORONOV
DICK TRACY .... MICHAEL J. POLLARD
DICK TRACY .... PAUL SORVINO
DICK TRACY .... R.G. ARMSTRONG
DICK TRACY .... SEYMOUR CASSEL
DICK TRACY .... WARREN BEATTY
DICK TRACY .... WILLIAM FORSYTHE
DICK TRACY, DETECTIVE .... JANE GREER
DICK TRACY'S G-MEN .... JENNIFER JONES
DID YOU HEAR THE ONE ABOUT THE
  TRAVELING SALESLADY? .... PHYLLIS DILLER
DIE! DIE! MY DARLING! .... DONALD SUTHERLAND
DIE! DIE! MY DARLING! .... STEFANIE POWERS
DIE HARD .... ALAN RICKMAN

This is not a list of every film ever made or every cast member, only those listed in this directory.

DIE HARD	ALEXANDER GODUNOV
DIE HARD	BONNIE BEDELIA
DIE HARD	BRUCE WILLIS
DIE HARD	DE'VOREAUX WHITE
DIE HARD	GRAND L. BUSH
DIE HARD	HART BOCHNER
DIE HARD	JAMES SHIGETA
DIE HARD	PAUL GLEASON
DIE HARD	REGINALD VELJOHNSON
DIE HARD	RICK DUCOMMUN
DIE HARD	ROBERT DAVI
DIE HARD	SONJA G. ANDERSON
DIE HARD	WILLIAM ATHERTON
DIE HARD 2	BONNIE BEDELIA
DIE HARD 2	BRUCE WILLIS
DIE HARD 2	FRANCO NERO
DIE HARD 2	FRED DALTON THOMPSON
DIE HARD 2	JOHN AMOS
DIE HARD 2	REGINALD VELJOHNSON
DIE HARD 2	WILLIAM ATHERTON
DIE HARD 2	WILLIAM SADLER
DIE HARD 3	ANTHONY PECK
DIE HARD 3	BRUCE WILLIS
DIE HARD 3	COLLEEN CAMP
DIE HARD 3	GRAHAM GREENE
DIE HARD 3	JEREMY IRONS
DIE HARD 3	LARRY BRYGGMAN
DIE HARD 3	SAMUEL L. JACKSON
DIE LADY	CLAUDINE AUGER
DIE LAUGHING	BUD CORT
DIE LAUGHING	CHARLES DURNING
DIE LAUGHING	ROBBY BENSON
DIE LETZTE BRÜCKE	MARIA SCHELL
DIE LETZTE NACHT	MARIA SCHELL
DIE RATTEN	MARIA SCHELL
DIE SCREAMING MARIANNE	SUSAN GEORGE
DIFFERENT AFFAIR, A (TF)	ANNE ARCHER
DIFFERENT AFFAIR, A (TF)	STUART PANKIN
DIFFERENT STORY, A	MEG FOSTER
DIFFERENT STORY, A	PERRY KING
DIFFERENT STORY, A	PETER DONAT
DIG THAT JULIET	PETER USTINOV
DIGBY, THE BIGGEST DOG IN THE WORLD	MILO O'SHEA
DIGGSTOWN	BRUCE DERN
DIGGSTOWN	HEATHER GRAHAM
DIGGSTOWN	JAMES WOODS
DIGGSTOWN	LOUIS GOSSETT JR.
DIGGSTOWN	OLIVER PLATT
DIGITAL DREAMS	JAMES COBURN
DILLINGER	BEN JOHNSON
DILLINGER	CLORIS LEACHMAN
DILLINGER	HARRY DEAN STANTON
DILLINGER	LAWRENCE TIERNEY
DILLINGER	RICHARD DREYFUSS
DIMENSION 5	FRANCE NUYEN
DINER	DANIEL STERN
DINER	ELLEN BARKIN
DINER	KEVIN BACON
DINER	MICHAEL TUCKER
DINER	MICKEY ROURKE
DINER	PAUL REISER
DINER	STEVE GUTTENBERG
DINER	TIMOTHY DALY
DINERO MALDITO	RICHARD WIDMARK
DINKY	JACKIE COOPER
DINNER AT EIGHT (CTF)	CHARLES DURNING
DINNER AT EIGHT (CTF)	ELLEN GREENE
DINNER AT EIGHT (CTF)	HARRY HAMLIN
DINNER AT EIGHT (CTF)	LAUREN BACALL
DINNER AT EIGHT (CTF)	MARSHA MASON
DINNER AT THE RITZ	DAVID NIVEN†
DION BROTHERS, THE	BARRY PRIMUS
DION BROTHERS, THE	FREDERIC FORREST
DION BROTHERS, THE	MARGOT KIDDER
DION BROTHERS, THE	STACY KEACH
DIPLOMATIC COURIER	CHARLES BRONSON
DIPLOMATIC COURIER	KARL MALDEN
DIPLOMATIC COURIER	PATRICIA NEAL
DIRT BIKE KID, THE	STUART PANKIN
DIRTIEST GIRL I EVER MET, THE	STUBBY KAYE
DIRTY DANCING	CYNTHIA RHODES
DIRTY DANCING	JENNIFER GREY
DIRTY DANCING	JERRY ORBACH
DIRTY DANCING	KELLY BISHOP
DIRTY DANCING	PATRICK SWAYZE
DIRTY DINGUS MAGEE	ANNE JACKSON
DIRTY DINGUS MAGEE	FRANK SINATRA
DIRTY DINGUS MAGEE	GEORGE KENNEDY
DIRTY DINGUS MAGEE	HARRY CAREY JR.
DIRTY DINGUS MAGEE	HENRY JONES
DIRTY DINGUS MAGEE	JOHN DEHNER†
DIRTY DINGUS MAGEE	LOIS NETTLETON
DIRTY DOZEN, THE ○	JOHN CASSAVETES†
DIRTY DOZEN, THE	CHARLES BRONSON
DIRTY DOZEN, THE	CLINT WALKER
DIRTY DOZEN, THE	DICK MILLER
DIRTY DOZEN, THE	DONALD SUTHERLAND
DIRTY DOZEN, THE	ERNEST BORGNINE
DIRTY DOZEN, THE	GEORGE KENNEDY
DIRTY DOZEN, THE	JIM BROWN
DIRTY DOZEN, THE	LEE MARVIN†
DIRTY DOZEN, THE	RICHARD JAECKEL
DIRTY DOZEN, THE	ROBERT WEBBER
DIRTY DOZEN, THE	TELLY SAVALAS†
DIRTY DOZEN: THE DEADLY MISSION, THE (TF)	VINCE EDWARDS
DIRTY DOZEN: THE FATAL MISSION, THE (TF)	ERIK ESTRADA
DIRTY DOZEN: THE FATAL MISSION, THE (TF)	ERNEST BORGNINE
DIRTY DOZEN: THE FATAL MISSION, THE (TF)	ERNIE HUDSON
DIRTY DOZEN: THE FATAL MISSION, THE (TF)	TELLY SAVALAS†
DIRTY DOZEN: THE NEXT MISSION, THE (TF)	ERNEST BORGNINE
DIRTY DOZEN: THE NEXT MISSION, THE (TF)	TELLY SAVALAS†
DIRTY HANDS	ROD STEIGER
DIRTY HARRY	CLINT EASTWOOD
DIRTY HARRY	HARRY GUARDINO
DIRTY HARRY	JOHN VERNON
DIRTY HARRY	RENI SANTONI
DIRTY KNIGHTS' WORK	BARBARA HERSHEY
DIRTY KNIGHTS' WORK	DONALD PLEASENCE
DIRTY KNIGHT'S WORK	BRIAN GLOVER
DIRTY LITTLE BILLY	DICK VAN PATTEN
DIRTY LITTLE BILLY	GARY BUSEY
DIRTY LITTLE BILLY	MICHAEL J. POLLARD
DIRTY MARY, CRAZY LARRY	PETER FONDA
DIRTY MARY, CRAZY LARRY	RODDY McDOWALL
DIRTY MARY, CRAZY LARRY	SUSAN GEORGE
DIRTY MONEY	CATHERINE DENEUVE
DIRTY MONEY	RICHARD CRENNA
DIRTY ROTTEN SCOUNDRELS	ANTON RODGERS
DIRTY ROTTEN SCOUNDRELS	BARBARA HARRIS
DIRTY ROTTEN SCOUNDRELS	FRANCES CONROY
DIRTY ROTTEN SCOUNDRELS	GLENNE HEADLY
DIRTY ROTTEN SCOUNDRELS	MICHAEL CAINE
DIRTY ROTTEN SCOUNDRELS	STEVE MARTIN
DIRTY TRICKS	ARTHUR HILL
DIRTY TRICKS	ELLIOTT GOULD
DIRTY TRICKS	KATE JACKSON
DISAPPEARANCE OF AIMEE, THE (TF)	BETTE DAVIS†
DISAPPEARANCE OF AIMEE, THE (TF)	FAYE DUNAWAY
DISAPPEARANCE OF AIMEE, THE (TF)	JAMES SLOVAN
DISAPPEARANCE OF AIMEE, THE (TF)	JAMES WOODS
DISAPPEARANCE OF AIMEE, THE (TF)	SEVERN DARDEN
DISAPPEARANCE, THE	CHRISTOPHER PLUMMER
DISAPPEARANCE, THE	DAVID HEMMINGS
DISAPPEARANCE, THE	DAVID WARNER
DISAPPEARANCE, THE	DONALD SUTHERLAND
DISAPPEARANCE, THE	JOHN HURT
DISASTER AT SILO 7 (TF)	JOE SPANO
DISASTER AT SILO 7 (TF)	PATRICIA CHARBONNEAU
DISASTER AT SILO 7 (TF)	PERRY KING
DISCLOSURE	CAROLINE GOODALL
DISCLOSURE	DEMI MOORE
DISCLOSURE	DENNIS MILLER
DISCLOSURE	DONALD SUTHERLAND
DISCLOSURE	MICHAEL DOUGLAS
DISCLOSURE	ROMA MAFFIA
DISCREET CHARM OF THE BOURGEOISIE, THE	JEAN-PIERRE CASSEL
DISCREET CHARM OF THE BOURGEOISIE, THE	STEPHANE AUDRAN
DISORDER	LOUIS JOURDAN
DISORDER	SUSAN STRASBERG
DISORDERLIES	RALPH BELLAMY†
DISORDERLY CONDUCT	RALPH BELLAMY†
DISORDERLY ORDERLY, THE	JERRY LEWIS
DISORDERLY ORDERLY, THE	KATHLEEN FREEMAN
DISORGANIZED CRIME	CORBIN BERNSEN
DISORGANIZED CRIME	DANIEL ROEBUCK
DISORGANIZED CRIME	ED O'NEILL
DISORGANIZED CRIME	FRED GWYNNE†
DISORGANIZED CRIME	HOYT AXTON
DISORGANIZED CRIME	LOU DIAMOND PHILLIPS
DISORGANIZED CRIME	MARIA BUTLER KOUF
DISORGANIZED CRIME	RUBEN BLADES
DISORGANIZED CRIME	WILLIAM RUSS
DISPATCH FROM REUTERS, A	EDDIE ALBERT
DISPUTED PASSAGE	DOROTHY LAMOUR
DISRAELI ★★	GEORGE ARLISS†
DISTANCE	BIBI BESCH
DISTANCE	JAMES WOODS
DISTANCE	POLLY HOLLIDAY
DISTANT	LINDA BLAIR
DISTANT THUNDER	BLU MAKUMA
DISTANT THUNDER	JOHN LITHGOW
DISTANT THUNDER	RALPH MACCHIO
DISTANT TRUMPET, A	CLAUDE AKINS†
DISTANT TRUMPET, A	SUZANNE PLESHETTE
DISTANT TRUMPET, A	TROY DONAHUE
DISTANT VOICES, STILL LIVES	ANGELA WALSH
DISTANT VOICES, STILL LIVES	DEAN WILLIAMS
DISTANT VOICES, STILL LIVES	DEBI JONES
DISTANT VOICES, STILL LIVES	FREDA DOWIE
DISTANT VOICES, STILL LIVES	LORRAINE ASHBOURNE
DISTANT VOICES, STILL LIVES	PETE POSTLETHWAITE
DISTINGUISHED GENTLEMAN, THE	EDDIE MURPHY
DISTORTIONS	EDWARD ALBERT
DISTORTIONS	PIPER LAURIE
DISTORTIONS	RITA GAM
DISTORTIONS	STEVE RAILSBACK
DITES-LUI QUE JE L'AIME	GERARD DEPARDIEU
DIVA	ANNY ROMAND
DIVA	DOMINIQUE PINON
DIVA	FREDERIC ANDEI
DIVA	GERARD DARMON
DIVA	JAQUES FABBRI
DIVA	RICHARD BOHRINGER
DIVA	ROLAND BERTIN
DIVA	THUY AN LUU
DIVE BOMBER	ALEXIS SMITH†
DIVE BOMBER	RALPH BELLAMY†
DIVIDED HEART, THE	THEODORE BIKEL
DIVINA CREATURA	TERENCE STAMP
DIVINE MADNESS (FD)	BETTE MIDLER
DIVING IN	BURT YOUNG
DIVING IN	KRISTY SWANSON
DIVING IN	MATT ADLER
DIVING IN	MATT LATTANZI
DIVING IN	YOLANDA JILOT
DIVORCE AMERICAN STYLE	DEBBIE REYNOLDS
DIVORCE AMERICAN STYLE	DICK VAN DYKE
DIVORCE AMERICAN STYLE	EILEEN BRENNAN
DIVORCE AMERICAN STYLE	JASON ROBARDS
DIVORCE AMERICAN STYLE	JEAN SIMMONS
DIVORCE AMERICAN STYLE	LEE GRANT
DIVORCE AMERICAN STYLE	TIM MATHESON
DIVORCE AMERICAN STYLE	TOM BOSLEY
DIVORCE AMERICAN STYLE	VAN JOHNSON

† after an actor's name denotes deceased.

DIVORCE HIS/
DIVORCE HERS (TF) .... ELIZABETH TAYLOR
DIVORCE IN THE FAMILY .... JACKIE COOPER
DIVORCE ITALIAN STYLE ★ .... MARCELLO
MASTROIANNI
DIVORCE WARS:
A LOVE STORY (TF) .... TOM SELLECK
DIVORCÉE, THE ★★ .... NORMA SHEARER†
DIXIE .... DOROTHY LAMOUR
DJANGO—IL GRANDE RITORNO ...... FRANCO NERO
DO NOT DISTURB .... DORIS DAY
DO NOT FOLD, SPINDLE
OR MUTILATE (TF) .... HELEN HAYES
DO NOT FOLD, SPINDLE
OR MUTILATE (TF) .... SYLVIA SIDNEY
DO THE RIGHT THING .... BILL NUNN
DO THE RIGHT THING .... GIANCARLO ESPOSITO
DO THE RIGHT THING .... JOHN SAVAGE
DO THE RIGHT THING .... JOHN TURTURRO
DO THE RIGHT THING .... JOIE LEE
DO THE RIGHT THING .... OSSIE DAVIS
DO THE RIGHT THING .... PAUL BENJAMIN
DO THE RIGHT THING .... RICHARD EDSON
DO THE RIGHT THING .... RICK AIELLO
DO THE RIGHT THING .... ROSIE PEREZ
DO THE RIGHT THING .... RUBY DEE
DO THE RIGHT THING .... SPIKE LEE
DO THE RIGHT THING ◊ .... DANNY AIELLO
DO YOU KNOW THE
MUFFIN MAN? (TF) .... JOHN SHEA
DO YOU KNOW THE
MUFFIN MAN? (TF) .... PAM DAWBER
DO YOU KNOW THE
MUFFIN MAN? (TF) .... STEPHEN DORFF
DO YOU LOVE ME? .... MAUREEN O'HARA
DO YOU REMEMBER
LOVE? (TF) .... GERALDINE FITZGERALD
DO YOU REMEMBER
LOVE? (TF) .... JOANNE WOODWARD
DO YOU REMEMBER LOVE? (TF) .... RICHARD KILEY
DO YOU TAKE THIS
STRANGER? (TF) .... DIANE BAKER
DOC .... FAYE DUNAWAY
DOC .... HARRIS YULIN
DOC .... STACY KEACH
DOC HOLLYWOOD .... BARNARD HUGHES
DOC HOLLYWOOD .... BRIDGET FONDA
DOC HOLLYWOOD .... DAVID OGDEN STIERS
DOC HOLLYWOOD .... FRANCES STERNHAGEN
DOC HOLLYWOOD .... GEORGE HAMILTON
DOC HOLLYWOOD .... JULIE WARNER
DOC HOLLYWOOD .... MICHAEL J. FOX
DOC HOLLYWOOD .... ROBERTS BLOSSOM
DOC HOLLYWOOD .... WOODY HARRELSON
DOC SAVAGE, THE MAN
OF BRONZE .... DARRELL ZWERLING
DOCTEUR FRANÇOISE
GAILLAND .... ISABELLE HUPPERT
DOCTEUR POPAUL/
SCOUNDREL IN WHITE .... MIA FARROW
DOCTOR, THE .... ADAM ARKIN
DOCTOR, THE .... CHRISTINE LAHTI
DOCTOR, THE .... ELIZABETH PERKINS
DOCTOR, THE .... MANDY PATINKIN
DOCTOR, THE .... WILLIAM HURT
DOCTOR AND THE
DEVILS, THE .... JONATHAN PRYCE
DOCTOR AND THE DEVILS, THE .... JULIAN SANDS
DOCTOR AND THE DEVILS, THE .... SIAN PHILLIPS
DOCTOR AND THE
DEVILS, THE .... TIMOTHY DALTON
DOCTOR AND THE DEVILS, THE .... TWIGGY
DOCTOR AND THE GIRL, THE .... JANET LEIGH
DOCTOR AND THE GIRL, THE .... MAC DAVIS
DOCTOR CRIPPEN .... SAMANTHA EGGAR
DOCTOR DETROIT .... DAN AYKROYD
DOCTOR DETROIT .... DONNA DIXON
DOCTOR DETROIT .... FRAN DRESCHER
DOCTOR DETROIT .... HOWARD HESSEMAN
DOCTOR DOLITTLE .... REX HARRISON†
DOCTOR DOLITTLE .... SAMANTHA EGGAR
DOCTOR FAUSTUS .... ELIZABETH TAYLOR

DOCTOR IN CLOVER .... SHIRLEY ANNE FIELD
DOCTOR IN DISTRESS .... SAMANTHA EGGAR
DOCTOR, YOU'VE GOT
TO BE KIDDING .... BILL BIXBY†
DOCTOR, YOU'VE GOT
TO BE KIDDING! .... CELESTE HOLM
DOCTOR, YOU'VE GOT
TO BE KIDDING .... GEORGE HAMILTON
DOCTOR, YOU'VE GOT
TO BE KIDDING .... MORT SAHL
DOCTOR, YOU'VE GOT
TO BE KIDDING .... SANDRA DEE
DOCTOR ZHIVAGO .... ALEC GUINNESS
DOCTOR ZHIVAGO .... GERALDINE CHAPLIN
DOCTOR ZHIVAGO .... JULIE CHRISTIE
DOCTOR ZHIVAGO .... KLAUS KINSKI†
DOCTOR ZHIVAGO .... OMAR SHARIF
DOCTOR ZHIVAGO .... ROD STEIGER
DOCTOR ZHIVAGO ◊ .... TOM COURTENAY
DOCTORS' WIVES .... CARROLL O'CONNOR
DOCTORS' WIVES .... DYAN CANNON
DOCTORS' WIVES .... GENE HACKMAN
DOCTORS' WIVES .... GEORGE GAYNES
DOCTORS' WIVES .... RALPH BELLAMY†
DOCTORS' WIVES .... RICHARD ANDERSON
DOCTORS' WIVES .... RICHARD CRENNA
DOCTOR'S DILEMMA, THE .... LESLIE CARON
DOCTOR'S DILEMMA, THE .... ROBERT MORLEY
DOCTOR'S ORDERS .... JOHN MILLS
DODGE CITY .... OLIVIA DE HAVILLAND
DODSWORTH .... DAVID NIVEN†
DODSWORTH ★ .... WALTER HUSTON†
DODSWORTH ◊ .... MARIA OUSPENSKAYA†
DOG AND CAT (TF) .... KIM BASINGER
DOG DAY AFTERNOON .... CAROL KANE
DOG DAY AFTERNOON .... CHARLES DURNING
DOG DAY AFTERNOON .... SUSAN PERETZ
DOG DAY AFTERNOON ★ .... AL PACINO
DOG DAY AFTERNOON ◊ .... CHRIS SARANDON
DOG OF FLANDERS, A .... THEODORE BIKEL
DOG SOLDIERS .... ANTHONY ZERBE
DOG SOLDIERS .... MICHAEL MORIARTY
DOG SOLDIERS .... NICK NOLTE
DOG SOLDIERS .... RAY SHARKEY†
DOG SOLDIERS .... RICHARD MASUR
DOG SOLDIERS .... TUESDAY WELD
DOGFIGHT .... HOLLY NEAR
DOGFIGHT .... LILI TAYLOR
DOGFIGHT .... RIVER PHOENIX†
DOGPOUND SHUFFLE .... DAVID SOUL
DOGPOUND SHUFFLE .... RON MOODY
DOGS .... DAVID McCALLUM
DOGS OF WAR, THE .... CHRISTOPHER WALKEN
DOGS OF WAR, THE .... JoBETH WILLIAMS
DOGS OF WAR, THE .... TOM BERENGER
DOGS OF WAR, THE .... VICTORIA TENNANT
DOIN' TIME .... COLLEEN CAMP
DOIN' TIME .... JEFF ALTMAN
DOIN' TIME ON PLANET EARTH .... ADAM WEST
DOING LIFE (TF) .... MARA HOBEL
DOING LIFE (TF) .... TONY DANZA
DOING TIME ON MAPLE DRIVE (TF) ...... JIM CARREY
DOLLARS .... GOLDIE HAWN
DOLLARS .... ROBERT WEBBER
DOLLARS .... WARREN BEATTY
DOLLMAKER, THE (TF) .... JANE FONDA
DOLLMAKER, THE (TF) .... LEVON HELM
DOLL'S HOUSE, A .... ANTHONY HOPKINS
DOLL'S HOUSE, A .... CLAIRE BLOOM
DOLL'S HOUSE, A .... DAVID WARNER
DOLL'S HOUSE, A .... DENHOLM ELLIOTT†
DOLL'S HOUSE, A .... JANE FONDA
DOLORES CLAIBORNE .... BOB GUNTON
DOLORES CLAIBORNE .... CHRISTOPHER PLUMMER
DOLORES CLAIBORNE .... DAVID STRATHAIRN
DOLORES CLAIBORNE .... ELLEN MUTH
DOLORES CLAIBORNE .... ERIC BOGOSIAN
DOLORES CLAIBORNE ..... JENNIFER JASON LEIGH
DOLORES CLAIBORNE ..... JOHN BENJAMIN HICKEY
DOLORES CLAIBORNE .... JOHN C. REILLY
DOLORES CLAIBORNE .... JUDY PARFITT
DOLORES CLAIBORNE .... KATHY BATES

DOLORES CLAIBORNE .... ROY COOPER
DOMANI E TROPPO TARDI .... LOIS MAXWELL
DOMANI SAREMO RICCHI .... CARROLL BAKER
DOMINICK AND EUGENE .... JAMIE LEE CURTIS
DOMINICK AND EUGENE .... RAY LIOTTA
DOMINICK AND EUGENE .... TODD GRAFF
DOMINICK AND EUGENE .... TOM HULCE
DOMINIQUE .... JEAN SIMMONS
DOMINIQUE .... JENNY AGUTTER
DOMINIQUE .... RON MOODY
DOMINIQUE .... SIMON WARD
DOMINIQUE IS DEAD .... SIMON WARD
DOMINO PRINCIPLE, THE .... ELI WALLACH
DOMINO PRINCIPLE, THE .... CANDICE BERGEN
DOMINO PRINCIPLE, THE .... EDWARD ALBERT
DOMINO PRINCIPLE, THE .... GENE HACKMAN
DOMINO PRINCIPLE, THE .... RICHARD WIDMARK
DON IS DEAD, THE .... ABE VIGODA
DON IS DEAD, THE .... ANTHONY QUINN
DON IS DEAD, THE .... FREDERIC FORREST
DON IS DEAD, THE .... ROBERT FORSTER
DON JUAN DE MARCO AND
THE CENTERFOLD .... BOB DISHY
DON JUAN DE MARCO AND
THE CENTERFOLD .... CAITLIN BROWN
DON JUAN DE MARCO AND
THE CENTERFOLD .... FAYE DUNAWAY
DON JUAN DE MARCO AND
THE CENTERFOLD .... GERALDINE PALLHAS
DON JUAN DE MARCO AND
THE CENTERFOLD .... JOHNNY DEPP
DON JUAN DE MARCO AND
THE CENTERFOLD .... MARLON BRANDO
DON JUAN DE MARCO AND
THE CENTERFOLD .... RACHEL TICOTIN
DON JUAN DE MARCO AND
THE CENTERFOLD .... RICHARD SARAFIAN
DON JUAN DE MARCO AND
THE CENTERFOLD .... STEPHEN SINGER
DON JUAN DE MARCO AND
THE CENTERFOLD .... TALISA SOTO
DON QUIXOTE .... RUDOLF NUREYEV†
DON'T BOTHER TO KNOCK .... MARILYN MONROE†
DON'T DRINK THE WATER (TF) ..... JULIE KAVNER
DON'T DRINK THE WATER (TF) .... MICHAEL J. FOX
DON'T DRINK THE WATER (TF) .... WOODY ALLEN
DON'T WORRY, WE'LL
THINK OF A TITLE .... DANNY THOMAS†
DONA FLOR AND HER
TWO HUSBANDS .... SONIA BRAGA
DONDI .... LOUIS QUINN†
DONKEY SKIN .... CATHERINE DENEUVE
DONNER PASS: THE ROAD
TO SURVIVAL (TF) .... JOHN ANDERSON
DONNER PASS: THE ROAD
TO SURVIVAL (TF) .... ROYAL DANO
DONOVAN'S BRAIN .... MAC DAVIS
DONOVAN'S KID .... JACKIE COOPER
DONOVAN'S REEF .... DOROTHY LAMOUR
DONOVAN'S REEF .... JACK WARDEN
DONOVAN'S REEF .... PATRICK WAYNE
DON'T BE AFRAID OF THE DARK (TF) ..... KIM DARBY
DON'T BOTHER TO KNOCK .... ANNE BANCROFT
DON'T BOTHER TO KNOCK .... RICHARD WIDMARK
DON'T CRY, IT'S
ONLY THUNDER .... DENNIS CHRISTOPHER
DON'T CRY, IT'S
ONLY THUNDER .... SUSAN SAINT JAMES
DON'T DRINK THE WATER .... ESTELLE PARSONS
DON'T GAMBLE WITH LOVE .... ANN SOTHERN
DON'T GIVE UP THE SHIP .... CLAUDE AKINS†
DON'T GIVE UP THE SHIP .... DINA MERRILL
DON'T GIVE UP THE SHIP .... JERRY LEWIS
DON'T GO NEAR THE WATER .... EARL HOLLIMAN
DON'T GO NEAR THE WATER .... EVA GABOR
DON'T GO NEAR THE WATER .... MARY WICKES
DON'T GO NEAR THE WATER .... RUSS TAMBLYN
DON'T JUST LIE THERE,
SAY SOMETHING .... JOANNA LUMLEY
DON'T JUST STAND THERE! .... HARVEY KORMAN
DON'T JUST
STAND THERE! .... MARY TYLER MOORE

438

DON'T JUST STAND THERE! .... ROBERT WAGNER
DON'T LOOK BACK (FD) .... BOB DYLAN
DON'T LOOK BACK (TF) .... LOUIS GOSSETT JR.
DON'T LOOK NOW .... DONALD SUTHERLAND
DON'T LOOK NOW .... JULIE CHRISTIE
DON'T MAKE WAVES .... MORT SAHL
DON'T MAKE WAVES .... ROBERT WEBBER
DON'T MAKE WAVES .... TONY CURTIS
DON'T RAISE THE BRIDGE—
  LOWER THE RIVER .... JERRY LEWIS
DON'T TELL HER IT'S ME .... JAMI GERTZ
DON'T TELL HER IT'S ME .... KYLE MacLACHLAN
DON'T TELL HER IT'S ME .... SHELLEY LONG
DON'T TELL HER IT'S ME ...... STEVE GUTTENBERG
DON'T TELL MOM THE
  BABYSITTER'S DEAD ...... CHRISTINA APPLEGATE
DON'T TELL MOM THE
  BABYSITTER'S DEAD .... CONCETTA TOMEI
DON'T TELL MOM THE
  BABYSITTER'S DEAD .... EDA REISS MERIN
DON'T TELL MOM THE
  BABYSITTER'S DEAD .... JOANNA CASSIDY
DON'T TELL MOM THE
  BABYSITTER'S DEAD .... JOHN GETZ
DON'T TELL MOM THE
  BABYSITTER'S DEAD .... JOSH CHARLES
DON'T TELL MOM THE
  BABYSITTER'S DEAD .... KEITH COOGAN
DON'T TURN THE OTHER CHEEK! ...... ELI WALLACH
DON'T TURN THE
  OTHER CHEEK! .... LYNN REDGRAVE
DON'T WORRY, WE'LL THINK
  OF A TITLE .... CARL REINER
DON'T WORRY, WE'LL THINK
  OF A TITLE .... MILTON BERLE
DON'T WORRY, WE'LL THINK
  OF A TITLE .... STEVE ALLEN
DOOLINS OF OKLAHOMA, THE .... JOHN IRELAND
DOOMSDAY
  FLIGHT, THE (TF) .... MICHAEL SARRAZIN
DOOMSDAY GUN (CTF) .... FRANK LANGELLA
DOOMWATCH .... GEOFFREY KEEN
DOOMWATCH .... IAN BANNEN
DOOR-TO-DOOR MANIAC .... JOHNNY CASH
DOOR-TO-DOOR MANIAC .... RON HOWARD
DOORS, THE .... BILLY IDOL
DOORS, THE .... CRISPIN GLOVER
DOORS, THE .... DENNIS OTT†
DOORS, THE .... FRANK WHALEY
DOORS, THE .... JENNIFER RUBIN
DOORS, THE .... KATHLEEN QUINLAN
DOORS, THE .... KEVIN DILLON
DOORS, THE .... KYLE MacLACHLAN
DOORS, THE .... MEG RYAN
DOORS, THE .... MICHAEL MADSEN
DOORS, THE .... NICK CASSAVETES
DOORS, THE .... OLIVER STONE
DOORS, THE .... VAL KILMER
DOPPELGANGER: THE
  EVIL WITHIN (CTF) .... DREW BARRYMORE
DOPPIO DELITTO .... PETER USTINOV
DOUBLE CROSS: THE BARRY
  SEAL STORY (CTF) .... DENNIS HOPPER
DOUBLE CROSS: THE BARRY
  SEAL STORY (CTF) .... G.W. BAILEY
DOUBLE CROSSBONES .... ROCK HUDSON†
DOUBLE CROSSED CTF .... ROBERT CARRADINE
DOUBLE DYNAMITE .... FRANK SINATRA
DOUBLE IMPACT .... GEOFFREY LEWIS
DOUBLE IMPACT .... JEAN-CLAUDE VAN DAMME
DOUBLE INDEMNITY ★ .... BARBARA STANWYCK†
DOUBLE INDEMNITY (TF) .... RICHARD CRENNA
DOUBLE INDEMNITY (TF) .... SAMANTHA EGGAR
DOUBLE LIFE, A .... SHELLEY WINTERS
DOUBLE LIFE, A ★★ .... RONALD COLMAN†
DOUBLE MAN, THE .... BRITT EKLAND
DOUBLE McGUFFIN, THE .... ERNEST BORGNINE
DOUBLE McGUFFIN, THE .... GEORGE KENNEDY
DOUBLE McGUFFIN, THE .... VINCENT SPANO
DOUBLE NEGATIVE .... ANTHONY PERKINS†
DOUBLE NEGATIVE .... JOHN CANDY†
DOUBLE NEGATIVE .... MICHAEL SARRAZIN
DOUBLE NEGATIVE .... SUSAN CLARK

DOUBLE OR NOTHING .... MARTHA RAYE†
DOUBLE REVENGE .... JOE DALLESANDRO
DOUBLE REVENGE .... LEIGH McCLOSKEY
DOUBLE REVENGE .... NANCY EVERHARD
DOUBLE REVENGE .... THERESA SALDANA
DOUBLE STANDARD (TF) .... CHRISTIANNE HIRT
DOUBLE STANDARD (TF) .... MICHELLE GREENE
DOUBLE
  STANDARD (TF) .... PAMELA BELLWOOD-WHEELER
DOUBLE STANDARD (TF) .... ROBERT FOXWORTH
DOUBLE TROUBLE .... BARBARA EDEN
DOUBLE TROUBLE .... ELVIS PRESLEY†
DOUBLE YOUR PLEASURE (TF) .... DAN HEDAYA
DOUBLE YOUR
  PLEASURE (TF) .... RICHARD LAWSON
DOUBLETAKE (MS) .... BEVERLY D'ANGELO
DOUBLETAKE (MS) .... CLIFF GORMAN
DOUBLETAKE (MS) .... RICHARD CRENNA
DOUGHBOYS .... ANN SOTHERN
DOUGHBOYS IN IRELAND .... ROBERT MITCHUM
DOUGHGIRLS, THE .... ALEXIS SMITH†
DOUGHGIRLS, THE .... JANE WYMAN
DOVE, THE .... DABNEY COLEMAN
DOVE, THE .... DEBORAH RAFFIN
DOVE, THE .... GEORGE COE
DOVE, THE .... JOHN ANDERSON
DOVE, THE .... JOSEPH BOTTOMS
DOWN AMONG THE
  SHELTERING PALMS .... JANE GREER
DOWN AND OUT IN
  BEVERLY HILLS .... BETTE MIDLER
DOWN AND OUT IN
  BEVERLY HILLS .... ELIZABETH PENA
DOWN AND OUT IN
  BEVERLY HILLS .... EVAN RICHARDS
DOWN AND OUT IN BEVERLY HILLS .... IRENE TSU
DOWN AND OUT IN
  BEVERLY HILLS .... LITTLE RICHARD
DOWN AND OUT IN BEVERLY HILLS ..... NICK NOLTE
DOWN AND OUT IN
  BEVERLY HILLS .... PAUL MAZURSKY
DOWN AND OUT IN
  BEVERLY HILLS .... RICHARD DREYFUSS
DOWN AND OUT IN
  BEVERLY HILLS .... TRACY NELSON
DOWN AND OUT IN
  BEVERLY HILLS .... VALERIE CURTIN
DOWN ARGENTINE WAY .... DON AMECHE†
DOWN BY LAW .... BILLIE NEAL
DOWN BY LAW .... ELLEN BARKIN
DOWN BY LAW .... JOHN LURIE
DOWN BY LAW .... NICOLETTA BRASCHI
DOWN BY LAW .... ROBERTO BENIGNI
DOWN BY LAW .... ROCKETS REDGLARE
DOWN BY LAW .... TOM WAITS
DOWN BY LAW .... VERNEL BAGNERIS
DOWN MEMORY LANE .... STEVE ALLEN
DOWN THE ANCIENT STAIRS .... MARTHE KELLER
DOWN THREE DARK STREETS .... CLAUDE AKINS†
DOWN THREE DARK STREETS ... MAX SHOWALTER
DOWN TO THE SEA IN SHIPS ..... DEAN STOCKWELL
DOWN TO THE
  SEA IN SHIPS .... RICHARD WIDMARK
DOWN TWISTED .... CAREY LOWELL
DOWN TWISTED .... CHARLES ROCKET
DOWN TWISTED .... COURTENEY COX
DOWNHILL RACER .... DABNEY COLEMAN
DOWNHILL RACER .... GENE HACKMAN
DOWNHILL RACER .... ROBERT REDFORD
DOWNPAYMENT
  ON MURDER (TF) .... BEN GAZZARA
DOWNPAYMENT
  ON MURDER (TF) .... JONATHAN BANKS
DOWNTOWN .... ANTHONY EDWARDS
DOWNTOWN .... FOREST WHITAKER
DOWNTOWN .... RON CANADA
DR. BETHUNE .... DONALD SUTHERLAND
DR. BETHUNE .... HELEN MIRREN
DR. BLACK, MR. HYDE .... ROSALIND CASH
DR. COOK'S GARDEN (TF) .... BLYTHE DANNER
DR. CRIPPEN .... DONALD PLEASENCE
DR. DETROIT ....LANCE KINSEY

DR. FISCHER OF GENEVA (TF) .... ALAN BATES
DR. GILLESPIE'S NEW ASSISTANT ... VAN JOHNSON
DR. GOLDFOOT AND THE
  BIKINI MACHINE .... FRANKIE AVALON
DR. GOLDFOOT AND THE
  BIKINI MACHINE .... VINCENT PRICE†
DR. GOLDFOOT AND THE
  GIRL BOMBS .... VINCENT PRICE†
DR. HACKENSTEIN (unreleased) ... ANN RAMSEY†
DR. HOLL .... MARIA SCHELL
DR. JEKYLL AND MR. HYDE .... INGRID BERGMAN†
DR. JEKYLL AND MR. HYDE ... LANA TURNER
DR. JEKYLL AND MR. HYDE .... SPENCER TRACY†
DR. JEKYLL AND
  MR. HYDE ★★ .... FREDRIC MARCH†
DR. JEKYLL AND MS. HYDE .... JEREMY PIVEN
DR. JEKYLL AND MS. HYDE ... LYSETTE ANTHONY
DR. JEKYLL AND MS. HYDE .... POLLY BERGEN
DR. JEKYLL AND MS. HYDE .... SEAN YOUNG
DR. JEKYLL AND MS. HYDE .... SHEENA LARKIN
DR. JEKYLL AND MS. HYDE .... STEPHEN SHELLEN
DR. JEKYLL AND
  MS. HYDE .... STEPHEN TOBOLOWSKY
DR. JEKYLL AND MS. HYDE .... THEA VIDALE
DR. JEKYLL AND MS. HYDE .... TIMOTHY DALY
DR. JUSTICE .... JOHN PHILLIP LAW
DR. M .... ALAN BATES
DR. MAX (TF) .... KATHERINE HELMOND
DR. NO .... JOSEPH WISEMAN
DR. NO .... LOIS MAXWELL
DR. NO .... SEAN CONNERY
DR. NO .... URSULA ANDRESS
DR. OTTO AND THE RIDDLE OF
  THE GLOOM BEAN .... JIM VARNEY
DR. PHIBES RISES AGAIN .... FIONA LEWIS
DR. PHIBES RISES AGAIN .... VINCENT PRICE†
DR. SCORPION (TF) .... CHRISTINE LAHTI
DR. SCORPION (TF) .... NICK MANCUSO
DR. STRANGELOVE: OR HOW I
  LEARNED TO STOP WORRYING
  AND LOVE THE BOMB .... GEORGE C. SCOTT
DR. STRANGELOVE: OR HOW I
  LEARNED TO STOP WORRYING
  AND LOVE THE BOMB .... JAMES EARL JONES
DR. STRANGELOVE OR: HOW I
  LEARNED TO STOP WORRYING
  AND LOVE THE BOMB ★ .... PETER SELLERS†
DR. STRANGELOVE: OR HOW I
  LEARNED TO STOP WORRYING
  AND LOVE THE BOMB .... SLIM PICKENS†
DR. TERROR'S HOUSE
  OF HORRORS .... DONALD SUTHERLAND
DR. TERROR'S HOUSE
  OF HORRORS .... JEREMY KEMP
DR. TERROR'S HOUSE
  OF HORRORS .... MICHAEL GOUGH
DR. ZHIVAGO .... GEOFFREY KEEN
DRACULA (1931) .... BELA LUGOSI†
DRACULA (1979) .... DONALD PLEASENCE
DRACULA (1979) .... FRANK LANGELLA
DRACULA (1979) .... KATE NELLIGAN
DRACULA (1992) .... ANTHONY HOPKINS
DRACULA (1992) .... BILL CAMPBELL
DRACULA (1992) .... CARY ELWES
DRACULA (1992) .... GARY OLDMAN
DRACULA (1992) .... GEOFFREY BAYLDON
DRACULA (1992) .... KEANU REEVES
DRACULA (1992) .... MICHAEL GOUGH
DRACULA (1992) .... RICHARD E. GRANT
DRACULA (1992) .... SADIE FROST
DRACULA (1992) .... TOM WAITS
DRACULA (1992) .... WINONA RYDER
DRACULA (TF) .... FIONA LEWIS
DRACULA (TF) .... JACK PALANCE
DRACULA (TF) .... NIGEL DAVENPORT
DRACULA (TF) .... SIMON WARD
DRACULA, PRINCE
  OF DARKNESS .... THORLEY WALTERS†
DRACULA VS. FRANKENSTEIN .... RUSS TAMBLYN
DRACULA'S DOG .... JOSE FERRER†
DRAGNET .... ALEXANDRA PAUL
DRAGNET .... AVA FABIAN

DRAGNET .... BRUCE GRAY
DRAGNET .... CHRISTOPHER PLUMMER
DRAGNET .... DABNEY COLEMAN
DRAGNET† .... DAN AYKROYD
DRAGNET .... ELIZABETH ASHLEY
DRAGNET .... HARRY MORGAN
DRAGNET .... JACK O'HALLORAN
DRAGNET .... JULI DONALD
DRAGNET .... JULIA JENNINGS
DRAGNET .... KATHLEEN FREEMAN
DRAGNET .... KIMBERLY FOSTER
DRAGNET .... LENKA PETERSON
DRAGNET .... LISA ALIFF
DRAGNET .... TOM HANKS
DRAGON SEED .... HURD HATFIELD
DRAGON SEED .... KATHERINE HEPBURN
DRAGON: THE BRUCE
    LEE STORY .... JASON SCOTT LEE
DRAGON: THE BRUCE
    LEE STORY .... LAUREN HOLLY
DRAGON: THE BRUCE
    LEE STORY .... NANCY KWAN
DRAGONFLY .... ANN WEDGEWORTH
DRAGONFLY .... BEAU BRIDGES
DRAGONFLY .... SUSAN SARANDON
DRAGONHEART .... DAVID THEWLIS
DRAGONHEART .... DENNIS QUAID
DRAGONHEART .... DINA MEYER
DRAGONHEART .... JULIE CHRISTIE
DRAGONHEART .... PETE POSTLETHWAITE
DRAGONHEART .... SEAN CONNERY
DRAGONWYCK .... HARRY MORGAN
DRAGONWYCK .... JESSICA TANDY†
DRAGONWYCK .... VINCENT PRICE†
DRAGOON WELLS
    MASSACRE .... HARRY DEAN STANTON
DRAGOON WELLS MASSACRE ... MAX SHOWALTER
DRAMA DELLA
    GELOSIA .... MARCELLO MASTROIANNI
DRAMATIC SCHOOL .... LANA TURNER
DRAUGHTSMAN'S
    CONTRACT, THE .... JANET SUZMAN
DRAW! .... JAMES COBURN
DREAM A LITTLE DREAM .... ALEX ROCCO
DREAM A LITTLE DREAM .... COREY FELDMAN
DREAM A LITTLE DREAM .... COREY HAIM
DREAM A LITTLE DREAM ... HARRY DEAN STANTON
DREAM A LITTLE DREAM ...... JASON ROBARDS
DREAM A LITTLE DREAM .... JOSH EVANS
DREAM A LITTLE DREAM .... LALA
DREAM A LITTLE DREAM .... MATT ADLER
DREAM A LITTLE DREAM ...... MEREDITH SALENGER
DREAM A LITTLE DREAM .... PIPER LAURIE
DREAM A LITTLE DREAM .... RIA PAVIA
DREAM A LITTLE DREAM .... SUSAN BLAKELY
DREAM A LITTLE DREAM .... VICTORIA JACKSON
DREAM A LITTLE DREAM ...... WILLIAM McNAMARA
DREAM BREAKERS (TF) .... KYLE MacLACHLAN
DREAM BREAKERS (TF) .... ROBERT LOGGIA
DREAM DATE (TF) .... ANNE MARIE JOHNSON
DREAM DATE (TF) .... KADEEN HARDISON
DREAM LOVER .... BEN MASTERS
DREAM LOVER .... BESS ARMSTRONG
DREAM LOVER .... FREDERIC LEHNE
DREAM LOVER .... JAMES SPADER
DREAM LOVER .... JOHN McMARTIN
DREAM LOVER .... JOSEPH CULP
DREAM LOVER .... JUSTIN DEAS
DREAM LOVER .... KRISTY McNICHOL
DREAM LOVER .... LARRY MILLER
DREAM LOVER .... MADCHEN AMICK
DREAM LOVER .... MATTHEW PENN
DREAM LOVER .... PAUL SHENAR
DREAM MAKERS, THE (TF) .... DIANE BAKER
DREAM MAKERS, THE (TF) .... JAMES FRANCISCUS†
DREAM MAKERS, THE (TF) .... STEVEN KEATS†
DREAM MERCHANTS, THE (MS) ...... JOSE FERRER†
DREAM
    MERCHANTS, THE (MS) ...... VINCENT GARDENIA†
DREAM MERCHANTS, THE (TF) .... MARK HARMON
DREAM
    MERCHANTS, THE (TF) .... MORGAN FAIRCHILD

DREAM MERCHANTS, THE (TF) .... RED BUTTONS
DREAM OF KINGS, A .... ANTHONY QUINN
DREAM OF KINGS, A .... VAL AVERY
DREAM OF LOVE .... JOAN CRAWFORD†
DREAM OF PASSION, A .... ELLEN BURSTYN
DREAM ON .... ED HARRIS
DREAM ONE .... HARVEY KEITEL
DREAM ONE .... NIPSEY RUSSELL
DREAM TEAM, THE .... CHRISTOPHER LLOYD
DREAM TEAM, THE .... DENNIS BOUTSIKARIS
DREAM TEAM, THE .... JAMES REMAR
DREAM TEAM, THE .... LORRAINE BRACCO
DREAM TEAM, THE .... MICHAEL KEATON
DREAM TEAM, THE .... MILO O'SHEA
DREAM TEAM, THE .... PETER BOYLE
DREAM TEAM, THE .... PHILIP BOSCO
DREAM TEAM, THE .... STEPHEN FURST
DREAM WEST (MS) .... ALICE KRIGE
DREAM WEST (MS) .... BEN JOHNSON
DREAM WEST (MS) ...... F. MURRAY ABRAHAM
DREAM WEST (MS) .... FRITZ WEAVER
DREAM WEST (MS) .... JOHN ANDERSON
DREAM WEST (MS) .... MEL FERRER
DREAM WEST (MS) ...... RICHARD CHAMBERLAIN
DREAM WEST (MS) .... RIP TORN
DREAM WIFE .... DEBORAH KERR
DREAM WIFE .... STEVE FORREST
DREAMCHILD .... IAN HOLM
DREAMCHILD .... NIGEL HAWTHORNE
DREAMER .... JACK WARDEN
DREAMER .... SUSAN BLAKELY
DREAMER .... TIM MATHESON
DREAMER OF OZ, THE (TF) .... RYAN TODD
DREAMING LIPS .... MARIA SCHELL
DREAMS .... MARTIN SCORSESE
DREAMSCAPE .... CHRISTOPHER PLUMMER
DREAMSCAPE .... DENNIS QUAID
DREAMSCAPE .... EDDIE ALBERT
DREAMSCAPE .... GEORGE WENDT
DREAMSCAPE .... KATE CAPSHAW
DRESS GRAY (MS) .... ALEC BALDWIN
DRESS GRAY (MS) .... EDDIE ALBERT
DRESS GRAY (MS) .... HAL HOLBROOK
DRESS GRAY (MS) .... LLOYD BRIDGES
DRESS GRAY (MS) .... PATRICK CASSIDY
DRESS GRAY (MS) .... SUSAN HESS
DRESSED TO KILL .... ANGIE DICKINSON
DRESSED TO KILL .... BRANDON MAGGART
DRESSED TO KILL .... DAVID MARGULIES
DRESSED TO KILL .... DENNIS FRANZ
DRESSED TO KILL .... KEITH GORDON
DRESSED TO KILL .... MICHAEL CAINE
DRESSED TO KILL .... NANCY ALLEN
DRESSER, THE .... EILEEN ATKINS
DRESSER, THE .... MICHAEL GOUGH
DRESSER, THE .... ZENA WALKER
DRESSER, THE ★ .... ALBERT FINNEY
DRESSER, THE ★ .... TOM COURTENAY
DRIFTWOOD .... DEAN JAGGER†
DRIVE A CROOKED ROAD .... KEVIN McCARTHY
DRIVE HARD, DRIVE FAST (TF) .... JOAN COLLINS
DRIVE, HE SAID .... BRUCE DERN
DRIVE, HE SAID .... CINDY WILLIAMS
DRIVE, HE SAID .... DAVID OGDEN STIERS
DRIVE, HE SAID .... KAREN BLACK
DRIVER, THE .... BRUCE DERN
DRIVER, THE .... ISABELLE ADJANI
DRIVER, THE .... JAMES CAAN
DRIVER, THE .... PETER JASON
DRIVER, THE .... RONEE BLAKLEY
DRIVER, THE .... RYAN O'NEAL
DRIVER'S SEAT, THE .... ELIZABETH TAYLOR
DRIVER'S SEAT, THE .... IAN BANNEN
DRIVING MISS DAISY .... ESTHER ROLLE
DRIVING MISS DAISY .... PATTI LUPONE
DRIVING MISS DAISY ★ .... MORGAN FREEMAN
DRIVING MISS DAISY ★★ .... JESSICA TANDY†
DRIVING MISS DAISY ○ .... DAN AYKROYD
DROLE D'ENDROIT POUR
    UNE RENCONTRE .... GERARD DEPARDIEU
DROP DEAD, DARLING .... JACQUELINE BISSET
DROP DEAD, DARLING ....TONY CURTIS

DROP DEAD, DARLING .... ZSA ZSA GABOR
DROP DEAD FRED .... BRIDGET FONDA
DROP DEAD FRED .... CARRIE FISHER
DROP DEAD FRED .... MARSHA MASON
DROP DEAD FRED .... PHOEBE CATES
DROP DEAD FRED .... RIK MAYALL
DROP DEAD FRED .... TIM MATHESON
DROP ZONE .... ANDY ROMANO
DROP ZONE .... CLAIRE STANSFIELD
DROP ZONE .... CORIN NEMEC
DROP ZONE .... GARY BUSEY
DROP ZONE .... GRACE ZABRISKIE
DROP ZONE .... KYLE SECOR
DROP ZONE .... MALCOLM JAMAL WARNER
DROP ZONE .... MELANIE MAYRON
DROP ZONE .... MICHAEL JETER
DROP ZONE .... REX LINN
DROP ZONE .... ROBERT LaSARDO
DROP ZONE .... SAM HENNINGS
DROP ZONE .... WESLEY SNIPES
DROP ZONE .... YANCY BUTLER
DROP-OUT FATHER (TF) .... DICK VAN DYKE
DROP-OUT MOTHER (TF) .... CAROL KANE
DROP-OUT MOTHER (TF) .... VALERIE HARPER
DROP-OUT MOTHER (TF) .... WAYNE ROGERS
DROPOUT .... FRANCO NERO
DROPOUT .... VANESSA REDGRAVE
DROWNING BY NUMBERS .... JOAN PLOWRIGHT
DROWNING
    POOL, THE .... ANTHONY (TONY) FRANCIOSA
DROWNING POOL, THE .... GAIL STRICKLAND
DROWNING POOL, THE .... JOANNE WOODWARD
DROWNING POOL, THE .... MELANIE GRIFFITH
DROWNING POOL, THE .... MURRAY HAMILTON†
DROWNING POOL, THE .... PAUL NEWMAN
DROWNING POOL, THE .... RICHARD JAECKEL
DRUG WARS: THE CAMARENA
    STORY (MS) .... CRAIG T. NELSON
DRUG WARS: THE CAMARENA
    STORY (MS) .... STEVEN BAUER
DRUG WARS: THE CAMARENA
    STORY (MS) .... TREAT WILLIAMS
DRUGSTORE COWBOY .... BEAH RICHARDS
DRUGSTORE COWBOY .... ERIC HULL
DRUGSTORE COWBOY .... GRACE ZABRISKIE
DRUGSTORE COWBOY .... HEATHER GRAHAM
DRUGSTORE COWBOY .... JAMES LE GROS
DRUGSTORE COWBOY .... JAMES REMAR
DRUGSTORE COWBOY .... KELLY LYNCH
DRUGSTORE COWBOY .... MATT DILLON
DRUGSTORE COWBOY .... MAX PERLICH
DRUGSTORE COWBOY .... WILLIAM S. BURROUGHS
DRUM .... FIONA LEWIS
DRUM .... PAM GRIER
DRUM .... ROYAL DANO
DRUM .... YAPHET KOTTO
DRUM BEAT .... CHARLES BRONSON
DRUMS ALONG
    THE MOHAWK .... JOHN CARRADINE†
DRUMS ALONG
    THE MOHAWK ○ .... EDNA MAY OLIVER†
DRUMS OF AFRICA .... FRANKIE AVALON
DRUMS OF AFRICA .... MARIETTE HARTLEY
DRY WHITE SEASON, A .... DONALD SUTHERLAND
DRY WHITE SEASON, A .... JANET SUZMAN
DRY WHITE SEASON, A .... JORGEN PROCHNOW
DRY WHITE SEASON, A .... ROWAN ELMES
DRY WHITE SEASON, A .... SUSAN SARANDON
DRY WHITE SEASON, A .... SUSANNAH HARKER
DRY WHITE SEASON, A .... THOKO NTSHINGA
DRY WHITE SEASON, A .... WINSTON NTSHONA
DRY WHITE SEASON, A .... ZAKES MOKAE
DRY WHITE SEASON, A ○ .... MARLON BRANDO
DU BARRY WAS A LADY .... AVA GARDNER†
DU BARRY WAS A LADY .... GENE KELLY
DU BARRY WAS A LADY .... LANA TURNER
DUBIOUS PATRIOTS, THE .... CHARLES BRONSON
DUBIOUS PATRIOTS, THE .... TONY CURTIS
DUCHESS AND THE
    DIRTWATER FOX, THE .... CONRAD JANIS
DUCHESS AND THE
    DIRTWATER FOX, THE .... GEORGE SEGAL

This is not a list of every film ever made or every cast member, only those listed in this directory.

DUCHESS AND THE
DIRTWATER FOX, THE .... GOLDIE HAWN
DUCHESS AND THE DIRTWATER
FOX, THE .... RICHARD FARNSWORTH
DUCHESS OF IDAHO .... LENA HORNE
DUCHESS OF IDAHO .... VAN JOHNSON
DUCK TALES THE MOVIE:
THE SECRET OF THE
LOST LAMP (AF) .... ALAN YOUNG
DUCK TALES THE MOVIE:
THE SECRET OF THE
LOST LAMP (AF) .... CHRISTOPHER LLOYD
DUCK TALES THE MOVIE:
THE SECRET OF THE
LOST LAMP (AF) .... CHUCK McCANN
DUCK TALES THE MOVIE:
THE SECRET OF THE
LOST LAMP (AF) .... JOAN GERBER
DUCK TALES THE MOVIE:
THE SECRET OF THE
LOST LAMP (AF) .... JUNE FORAY
DUCK TALES THE MOVIE:
THE SECRET OF THE
LOST LAMP (AF) .... RICHARD LIBERTINI
DUCK TALES THE MOVIE:
THE SECRET OF THE
LOST LAMP (AF) .... RIP TAYLOR
DUCK TALES THE MOVIE:
THE SECRET OF THE
LOST LAMP (AF) .... RUSSI TAYLOR
DUCK TALES THE MOVIE:
THE SECRET OF THE
LOST LAMP (AF) .... TERENCE McGOVERN
DUCK YOU SUCKER! .... JAMES COBURN
DUCK YOU SUCKER! .... ROD STEIGER
DUDE GOES WEST, THE .... EDDIE ALBERT
DUDES .... CATHERINE MARY STEWART
DUDES .... DANIEL ROEBUCK
DUDES .... JON CRYER
DUDES .... LEE VING
DUE NELLE STELLE .... FRED WILLIAMSON
DUE NOTTI CON CLEOPATRA .... SOPHIA LOREN
DUEL (TF) .... DENNIS WEAVER
DUEL AT DIABLO .... BIBI ANDERSSON
DUEL AT DIABLO .... DENNIS WEAVER
DUEL AT DIABLO .... JAMES GARNER
DUEL AT DIABLO .... SIDNEY POITIER
DUEL IN THE SUN .... GREGORY PECK
DUEL IN THE SUN ★ .... JENNIFER JONES
DUEL IN THE SUN ❍ .... LILLIAN GISH†
DUELLISTS, THE .... ALBERT FINNEY
DUELLISTS, THE .... ALUN ARMSTRONG
DUELLISTS, THE .... DIANA QUICK
DUELLISTS, THE .... HARVEY KEITEL
DUELLISTS, THE .... JOHN McENERY
DUELLISTS, THE .... KEITH CARRADINE
DUELLISTS, THE .... TOM CONTI
DUET FOR ONE .... ALAN BATES
DUET FOR ONE .... CATHRYN HARRISON
DUET FOR ONE .... JULIE ANDREWS
DUET FOR ONE .... LIAM NEESON
DUET FOR ONE .... MACHA MERIL
DUET FOR ONE .... MARGARET COURTENAY
DUET FOR ONE .... MAX von SYDOW
DUET FOR ONE .... RACHEL LEVIN
DUET FOR ONE .... RUPERT EVERETT
DUFFY .... JAMES COBURN
DUFFY .... SUSANNAH YORK
DUFFY OF SAN QUENTIN ..... MAUREEN O'SULLIVAN
DUFFY'S TAVERN .... DOROTHY LAMOUR
DUFFY'S TAVERN .... JOAN CAULFIELD†
DUKE IS TOPS, THE .... LENA HORNE
DUKE STEPS OUT, THE .... JOAN CRAWFORD†
DULCY .... ANN SOTHERN
DUMB AND DUMBER .... JEFF DANIELS
DUMB AND DUMBER .... JIM CARREY
DUMB AND DUMBER .... LAUREN HOLLY
DUMB AND DUMBER .... SARAH JESSICA PARKER
DUMB AND DUMBER .... TERI GARR
DUMB WAITER, THE (TF) .... JOHN TRAVOLTA
DUMBO (AF) .... STERLING HOLLOWAY†
DUMMY (TF) .... LeVAR BURTON
DUNE .... BRAD DOURIF

DUNE .... DEAN STOCKWELL
DUNE .... EVERETT McGILL
DUNE .... FRANCESCA ANNIS
DUNE .... FREDDIE JONES
DUNE .... JACK NANCE
DUNE .... JORGEN PROCHNOW
DUNE .... JOSE FERRER†
DUNE .... KENNETH McMILLAN†
DUNE .... KYLE MacLACHLAN
DUNE .... LINDA HUNT
DUNE .... PATRICK STEWART
DUNE .... RICHARD JORDAN†
DUNE .... SEAN YOUNG
DUNE .... SIAN PHILLIPS
DUNE .... STING
DUNE .... VIRGINIA MADSEN
DUNERA BOYS, THE (TF) .... BOB HOSKINS
DUNKIRK .... JOHN MILLS
DUNWICH HORROR, THE .... DEAN STOCKWELL
DUNWICH HORROR, THE .... SANDRA DEE
DUNWICH HORROR, THE .... TALIA SHIRE
DUPONT LA JOIE .... ISABELLE HUPPERT
DURING THE ROUND-UP .... LILLIAN GISH†
DUTCH .... CHRISTOPHER McDONALD
DUTCH .... ED O'NEILL
DUTCH .... ETHAN RANDALL
DUTCH .... JoBETH WILLIAMS
DUTCH GIRLS (TF) .... COLIN FIRTH
DUTCHMAN .... SHIRLEY KNIGHT
DYING ROOM ONLY (TF) .... DABNEY COLEMAN
DYING ROOM ONLY (TF) .... NED BEATTY
DYING YOUNG .... A. J. JOHNSON
DYING YOUNG .... BEHROOZ AFRAKHAN
DYING YOUNG .... CAMPBELL SCOTT
DYING YOUNG .... COLLEEN DEWHURST†
DYING YOUNG .... DANIEL BEER
DYING YOUNG .... DAVID SELBY
DYING YOUNG .... DION ANDERSON
DYING YOUNG .... ELLEN BURSTYN
DYING YOUNG .... GEORGE MARTIN
DYING YOUNG .... JULIA ROBERTS
DYING YOUNG .... LARRY NASH
DYING YOUNG .... VINCENT D'ONOFRIO
DYNAMITE CHICKEN .... RICHARD PRYOR
DYNASTY (TF) .... BO HOPKINS
DYNASTY (TF) .... JOHN FORSYTHE
DYNASTY (TF) .... LINDA EVANS
DYNASTY (TF) .... PAMELA SUE MARTIN

E

E LOLLIPOP/LOLLIPOP .... JOSE FERRER†
E POI LO CHIAMORONO
IL MAGNIFICO .... HARRY CAREY JR.
E SPECIALISTE DEL 44 .... JOHN SAXON
E.T. THE EXTRA-TERRESTRIAL .... DAVID O'DELL
E.T. THE EXTRA-TERRESTRIAL .... DEBRA WINGER
E.T. THE EXTRA-
TERRESTRIAL .... DEE WALLACE STONE
E.T. THE EXTRA-
TERRESTRIAL .... DREW BARRYMORE
E.T. THE EXTRA-TERRESTRIAL .... ERIKA ELENIAK
E.T. THE EXTRA-TERRESTRIAL .... FRANK TOTH
E.T. THE EXTRA-TERRESTRIAL ...... HENRY THOMAS
E.T. THE EXTRA-TERRESTRIAL ...... K. C. MARTEL
E.T. THE EXTRA-
TERRESTRIAL .... MICHAEL DARRELL
E.T. THE EXTRA-TERRESTRIAL .... PETER COYOTE
E.T. THE EXTRA-
TERRESTRIAL .... RICHARD SWINGLER
E.T. THE EXTRA-
TERRESTRIAL .... ROBERT BARTON
E.T. THE EXTRA-TERRESTRIAL .... SEAN FRYE
E.T. THE EXTRA-TERRESTRIAL .... TOM HOWELL
E.T. THE EXTRA-
TERRESTRIAL .... ROBERT MacNAUGHTON
E VENNE UN UOMO .... ROD STEIGER
EAGLE HAS LANDED, THE ..... DONALD PLEASENCE
EAGLE HAS
LANDED, THE .... DONALD SUTHERLAND
EAGLE HAS LANDED, THE .... JEAN MARSH
EAGLE HAS LANDED, THE .... JEFF CONAWAY

EAGLE HAS LANDED, THE .... JENNY AGUTTER
EAGLE HAS LANDED, THE .... LARRY HAGMAN
EAGLE HAS LANDED, THE .... MICHAEL CAINE
EAGLE HAS LANDED, THE .... ROBERT DUVALL
EAGLE HAS LANDED, THE .... TREAT WILLIAMS
EAGLE IN A CAGE .... BILLIE WHITELAW
EAGLE IN A CAGE .... JOHN GIELGUD
EAGLE IN A CAGE .... KENNETH HAIGH
EAGLE IN A CAGE .... MOSES GUNN
EAGLE SQUADRON .... EDDIE ALBERT
EAGLE SQUADRON .... ROBERT STACK
EAGLE'S WING .... BRIAN KEITH
EAGLE'S WING .... HARVEY KEITEL
EAGLE'S WING .... JOHN CASTLE
EAGLE'S WING .... MARTIN SHEEN
EAGLE'S WING .... SAM WATERSTON
EAGLE'S WING .... STEPHANE AUDRAN
EARLY FROST, AN (TF) .... AIDAN QUINN
EARLY FROST, AN (TF) .... BEN GAZZARA
EARLY FROST, AN (TF) .... JOHN GLOVER
EARLY FROST, AN (TF) .... SYLVIA SIDNEY
EARTH II (TF) .... INGA SWENSON
EARTH II (TF) .... MARIETTE HARTLEY
EARTH GIRLS ARE EASY .... ANGELYNE
EARTH GIRLS ARE EASY .... CHARLES ROCKET
EARTH GIRLS ARE EASY .... DAMON WAYANS
EARTH GIRLS ARE EASY .... GEENA DAVIS
EARTH GIRLS ARE EASY .... JEFF GOLDBLUM
EARTH GIRLS ARE EASY .... JIM CARREY
EARTH GIRLS ARE EASY .... JULIE BROWN
EARTH GIRLS ARE EASY .... LARRY LINVILLE
EARTH GIRLS ARE EASY .... MICHAEL McKEAN
EARTH GIRLS ARE EASY .... RICK OVERTON
EARTHBOUND .... JOHN SCHUCK
EARTHBOUND (TF) .... BURL IVES
EARTHLING, THE .... JACK THOMPSON
EARTHLING, THE .... RICK SCHRODER
EARTHQUAKE .... AVA GARDNER†
EARTHQUAKE .... CHARLTON HESTON
EARTHQUAKE .... GENEVIEVE BUJOLD
EARTHQUAKE .... GEORGE KENNEDY
EARTHQUAKE .... LLOYD NOLAN†
EARTHQUAKE .... LORNE GREEN†
EARTHQUAKE .... MARJOE GORTNER
EARTHQUAKE .... PEDRO ARMENDARIZ JR.
EARTHQUAKE .... RICHARD ROUNDTREE
EARTHQUAKE .... VICTORIA PRINCIPAL
EARTHQUAKE .... WALTER MATTHAU
EAST OF EDEN .... BURL IVES
EAST OF EDEN .... JULIE HARRIS
EAST OF EDEN .... TIMOTHY CAREY
EAST OF EDEN ★ .... JAMES DEAN†
EAST OF EDEN (MS) .... BRUCE BOXLEITNER
EAST OF EDEN (MS) .... JANE SEYMOUR
EAST OF EDEN (MS) .... LLOYD BRIDGES
EAST OF EDEN (MS) .... RICHARD MASUR
EAST OF EDEN (MS) .... TIMOTHY BOTTOMS
EAST OF EDEN (MS) .... WENDELL BURTON
EAST OF ELEPHANT ROCK .... JEREMY KEMP
EAST OF ELEPHANT ROCK .... JOHN HURT
EAST OF JAVA .... SHELLEY WINTERS
EAST OF SUDAN .... JENNY AGUTTER
EAST OF SUMATRA .... ANTHONY QUINN
EAST SIDE, WEST SIDE .... AVA GARDNER†
EAST SIDE WEST SIDE .... BARBARA STANWYCK†
EAST SIDE, WEST SIDE .... CYD CHARISSE
EASTER SUNDAY .... RUTH BUZZI
EASY COME, EASY GO .... ELVIS PRESLEY†
EASY MONEY .... DAVID TOMLINSON
EASY MONEY .... GERALDINE FITZGERALD
EASY MONEY .... JENNIFER JASON LEIGH
EASY MONEY .... JOE PESCI
EASY MONEY .... RODNEY DANGERFIELD
EASY PREY (TF) .... KATE LYNCH
EASY RIDER .... DENNIS HOPPER
EASY RIDER .... KAREN BLACK
EASY RIDER .... LUANA ANDERS
EASY RIDER .... PETER FONDA
EASY RIDER .... ROBERT WALKER JR.
EASY RIDER ❍ .... JACK NICHOLSON
EASY STREET .... MILTON BERLE
EASY TO LOVE .... CARROLL BAKER

441

EASY TO LOVE ... CYD CHARISSE
EASY TO LOVE ... VAN JOHNSON
EASY TO WED ... VAN JOHNSON
EASY WHEELS ... EILEEN DAVIDSON
EASY WHEELS ... PAUL LeMAT
EAT A BOWL OF TEA ... CORA MIAO
EAT A BOWL OF TEA ... ERIC TSANG CHI WAI
EAT A BOWL OF TEA ... LAU SIU MING
EAT A BOWL OF TEA ... RUSSELL WONG
EAT A BOWL OF TEA ... VICTOR WONG
EAT MY DUST! ... CORBIN BERNSEN
EAT MY DUST! ... PAUL BARTEL
EAT MY DUST! ... RON HOWARD
EATEN ALIVE ... MEL FERRER
EATEN ALIVE ... STUART WHITMAN
EATING RAOUL ... ED BEGLEY JR.
EATING RAOUL ... MARY WORONOY
EATING RAOUL ... PAUL BARTEL
EATING RAOUL ... ROBERT BELTRAN
EAVESDROPPER, THE ... JANET MARGOLIN
EBONY TOWER, THE (TF) ... GRETA SCACCHI
ECHO PARK ... CASSANDRA PETERSON
ECHO PARK ... CHEECH MARIN
ECHO PARK ... CHRISTOPHER WALKER
ECHO PARK ... MICHAEL BOWEN
ECHO PARK ... SUSAN DEY
ECHO PARK ... TIMOTHY CAREY
ECHO PARK ... TOM HULCE
ECHOES IN THE DARKNESS (MS) ... GARY COLE
ECHOES IN THE DARKNESS (MS) ... PETER BOYLE
ECHOES IN THE DARKNESS (MS) ... PETER COYOTE
ECHOES IN THE DARKNESS (MS) ... ROBERT LOGGIA
ECHOES IN THE DARKNESS (MS) ... STOCKARD CHANNING
ECHOES OF A SUMMER ... GERALDINE FITZGERALD
ECHOES OF A SUMMER ... JODIE FOSTER
ECHOES OF A SUMMER ... LOIS NETTLETON
ECHOES OF A SUMMER ... RICHARD HARRIS
ECHOES OF A SUMMER ... WILLIAM WINDOM
ECOUTE VOIR... ... CATHERINE DENEUVE
ED AND HIS DEAD MOTHER ... JOHN GLOVER
ED AND HIS DEAD MOTHER ... NED BEATTY
ED AND HIS DEAD MOTHER ... STEVE BUSCEMI
ED WOOD ... JOHNNY DEPP
ED WOOD ... MARTIN LANDAU
ED WOOD ... PATRICIA ARQUETTE
ED WOOD ... SARAH JESSICA PARKER
ED WOOD ... STANLEY DeSANTIS
ED WOOD ... VINCENT D'ONOFRIO
EDDIE AND THE CRUISERS ... ELLEN BARKIN
EDDIE AND THE CRUISERS ... JOE PANTOLIANO
EDDIE AND THE CRUISERS ... MATTHEW LAURANCE
EDDIE AND THE CRUISERS ... MICHAEL PARE
EDDIE AND THE CRUISERS ... TOM BERENGER
EDDIE AND THE CRUISERS II: EDDIE LIVES ... MARTHA QUINN
EDDIE AND THE CRUISERS II: EDDIE LIVES ... BO DIDDLEY
EDDIE AND THE CRUISERS II: EDDIE LIVES ... LARRY KING
EDDIE AND THE CRUISERS II: EDDIE LIVES ... MICHAEL RHOADE
EDDIE AND THE CRUISERS II: EDDIE LIVES ... ANTHONY SHERWOOD
EDDIE AND THE CRUISERS II: EDDIE LIVES ... BERNIE COULSON
EDDIE AND THE CRUISERS II: EDDIE LIVES ... MARINA ORSINI
EDDIE AND THE CRUISERS II: EDDIE LIVES ... MICHAEL PARE
EDDIE MACON'S RUN ... JOHN SCHNEIDER
EDDIE MACON'S RUN ... KIRK DOUGLAS
EDDIE MURPHY RAW ... EDDIE MURPHY
EDDY DUCHIN STORY, THE ... JAMES WHITMORE
EDDY DUCHIN STORY, THE ... KIM NOVAK
EDDY DUCHIN STORY, THE ... VICTORIA SHAW†
EDGE OF DARKNESS ... DAME JUDITH ANDERSON†
EDGE OF ETERNITY ... VICTORIA SHAW†
EDGE OF THE CITY ... JACK WARDEN
EDGE OF THE CITY ... RUBY DEE
EDGE OF THE CITY ... SIDNEY POITIER
EDGE OF THE CITY ... VAL AVERY
EDUCATING RITA ★ ... JULIE WALTERS
EDUCATING RITA ★ ... MICHAEL CAINE
EDWARD MY SON ★ ... DEBORAH KERR
EDWARD SCISSORHANDS ... ALAN ARKIN
EDWARD SCISSORHANDS ... ANTHONY MICHAEL HALL
EDWARD SCISSORHANDS ... CAROLINE AARON
EDWARD SCISSORHANDS ... CONCHATA FERRELL
EDWARD SCISSORHANDS ... DIANNE WIEST
EDWARD SCISSORHANDS ... JOHN DAVIDSON
EDWARD SCISSORHANDS ... JOHNNY DEPP
EDWARD SCISSORHANDS ... KATHY BAKER
EDWARD SCISSORHANDS ... ROBERT OLIVERI
EDWARD SCISSORHANDS ... VINCENT PRICE†
EDWARD SCISSORHANDS ... WINONA RYDER
EFFECT OF GAMMA RAYS ON MAN-IN-THE-MOON MARIGOLDS, THE ... DAVID SPIELBERG
EFFECT OF GAMMA RAYS ON MAN-IN-THE-MOON MARIGOLDS, THE ... JOANNE WOODWARD
EFFICIENCY EXPERT, THE ... ANTHONY HOPKINS
EFFICIENCY EXPERT, THE ... BRUNO LAWRENCE
EGG AND I, THE ✪ ... MARJORIE MAIN†
EGYPTIAN, THE ... JEAN SIMMONS
EGYPTIAN, THE ... PETER USTINOV
EIGER SANCTION, THE ... CLINT EASTWOOD
EIGER SANCTION, THE ... GEORGE KENNEDY
EIGHT BELLS ... RALPH BELLAMY†
EIGHT IRON MEN ... RICHARD KILEY
EIGHT IS ENOUGH: A FAMILY REUNION (TF) ... DICK VAN PATTEN
EIGHT IS ENOUGH: A FAMILY REUNION (TF) ... WILLIE AAMES
EIGHT IS ENOUGH WEDDING, AN (TF) ... DICK VAN PATTEN
EIGHT IS ENOUGH WEDDING, AN (TF) ... WILLIE AAMES
EIGHT MEN OUT ... BILL IRWIN
EIGHT MEN OUT ... BRAD GARRETT
EIGHT MEN OUT ... CHARLIE SHEEN
EIGHT MEN OUT ... CHRISTOPHER LLOYD
EIGHT MEN OUT ... CLIFTON JAMES
EIGHT MEN OUT ... D. B. SWEENEY
EIGHT MEN OUT ... DANTON STONE
EIGHT MEN OUT ... DAVID STRATHAIRN
EIGHT MEN OUT ... DICK CUSAK
EIGHT MEN OUT ... DON HARVEY
EIGHT MEN OUT ... GORDON CLAPP
EIGHT MEN OUT ... JACE ALEXANDER
EIGHT MEN OUT ... JAMES READ
EIGHT MEN OUT ... JIM DESMOND
EIGHT MEN OUT ... JOHN ANDERSON
EIGHT MEN OUT ... JOHN CUSAK
EIGHT MEN OUT ... JOHN MAHONEY
EIGHT MEN OUT ... JOHN SAYLES
EIGHT MEN OUT ... KEVIN TIGHE
EIGHT MEN OUT ... MAGGIE RENZI
EIGHT MEN OUT ... MICHAEL LERNER
EIGHT MEN OUT ... MICHAEL MANTELL
EIGHT MEN OUT ... MICHAEL ROOKER
EIGHT MEN OUT ... PERRY LANG
EIGHT MEN OUT ... RICHARD EDSON
EIGHT MEN OUT ... STUDS TERKEL
EIGHT MEN OUT ... TAY STRATHAIRN
EIGHT ON THE LAM ... BOB HOPE
EIGHT ON THE LAM ... JILL ST. JOHN
EIGHT ON THE LAM ... JONATHAN WINTERS
EIGHT ON THE LAM ... PHYLLIS DILLER
EIGHTEEN AND ANXIOUS ... CONNIE STEVENS
EIGHTEEN AND ANXIOUS ... MARTHA SCOTT
EIN HERZ KEHRT HEIM ... MAXIMILIAN SCHELL
EL CHE GUEVARA ... JOHN IRELAND
EL CID ... CHARLTON HESTON
EL CID ... HURD HATFIELD
EL CID ... RAF VALLONE
EL CID ... SOPHIA LOREN
EL CLAN DE LOS IMMORALES ... JOSE FERRER†
EL CLAN DES LOS IMMORALES ... KEVIN McCARTHY
EL CONDOR ... JIM BROWN
EL CONDOR ... PATRICK O'NEAL†
EL DIABLO (CTF) ... ANTHONY EDWARDS
EL DIABLO (CTF) ... JOE PANTOLIANO
EL DIABLO (CTF) ... JOHN GLOVER
EL DIABLO (CTF) ... LOUIS GOSSETT JR.
EL DORADO ... ED ASNER
EL DORADO ... JAMES CAAN
EL DORADO ... R.G. ARMSTRONG
EL DORADO ... ROBERT MITCHUM
EL ELEGIDO ... KATHY JURADO
EL GRECO ... MEL FERRER
EL HOMBRE QUE SUPO AMAR ... TIMOTHY DALTON
EL RECURSO DEL METEDO ... KATHY JURADO
EL SEÑOR DE LA SALLE ... MEL FERRER
EL SUPER ... ELIZABETH PENA
EL TRES DE COPAS ... GABRIELA ROEL
EL VERDUGO DE SEVILLA ... RICARDO MONTALBAN
ELEANOR AND FRANKLIN (TF) ... DAVID HUFFMAN†
ELEANOR AND FRANKLIN (TF) ... ED FLANDERS
ELEANOR AND FRANKLIN (TF) ... EDWRAD HERRMANN
ELEANOR AND FRANKLIN (TF) ... JANE ALEXANDER
ELEANOR AND FRANKLIN (TF) ... LILIA SKALA
ELEANOR AND FRANKLIN (TF) ... LINDA KELSEY
ELEANOR AND FRANKLIN (TF) ... LINDA PURL
ELEANOR AND FRANKLIN (TF) ... LINDSAY CROUSE
ELEANOR AND FRANKLIN (TF) ... ROSEMARY MURPHY
ELEANOR AND FRANKLIN: THE WHITE HOUSE YEARS (TF) ... BLAIR BROWN
ELEANOR AND FRANKLIN: THE WHITE HOUSE YEARS (TF) ... DAVID HEALY
ELEANOR AND FRANKLIN: THE WHITE HOUSE YEARS (TF) ... DONALD MOFFAT
ELEANOR AND FRANKLIN: THE WHITE HOUSE YEARS (TF) ... EDWRAD HERRMANN
ELEANOR AND FRANKLIN: THE WHITE HOUSE YEARS (TF) ... JANE ALEXANDER
ELEANOR AND FRANKLIN: THE WHITE HOUSE YEARS (TF) ... LINDA KELSEY
ELEANOR AND FRANKLIN: THE WHITE HOUSE YEARS (TF) ... MARK HARMON
ELEANOR AND FRANKLIN: THE WHITE HOUSE YEARS (TF) ... ROSEMARY MURPHY
ELEANOR AND FRANKLIN: THE WHITE HOUSE YEARS (TF) ... WALTER McGINN†
ELECTRA GLIDE IN BLUE ... BILLY GREEN BUSH
ELECTRA GLIDE IN BLUE ... ROBERT BLAKE
ELECTRA GLIDE IN BLUE ... ROYAL DANO
ELECTRIC DREAMS ... BUD CORT
ELECTRIC DREAMS ... LENNY VON DOHLEN
ELECTRIC DREAMS ... VIRGINIA MADSEN
ELECTRIC HORSEMAN, THE ... BASIL HOFFMAN
ELECTRIC HORSEMAN, THE ... JANE FONDA
ELECTRIC HORSEMAN, THE ... JOHN SAXON
ELECTRIC HORSEMAN, THE ... ROBERT REDFORD
ELECTRIC HORSEMAN, THE ... VALERIE PERRINE
ELECTRIC HORSEMAN, THE ... WILFORD BRIMLEY
ELECTRIC HORSEMAN, THE ... WILLIE NELSON
ELENA ET LES HOMMES ... MEL FERRER
ELENI ... DIMITRA ARLYS
ELENI ... JOHN MALKOVICH
ELENI ... KATE NELLIGAN
ELENI ... LINDA HUNT
ELEPHANT MAN, THE ... ANNE BANCROFT
ELEPHANT MAN, THE ... ANTHONY HOPKINS
ELEPHANT MAN, THE ... FREDDIE JONES
ELEPHANT MAN, THE ... JOHN GIELGUD
ELEPHANT MAN, THE ... WENDY HILLER
ELEPHANT MAN, THE ★ ... JOHN HURT
ELEPHANT WALK ... ELIZABETH TAYLOR
ELEVATOR, THE (TF) ... CAROL LYNLEY
ELEVATOR, THE (TF) ... RODDY McDOWALL
ELEVATOR, THE (TF) ... TERESA WRIGHT
ELIMINATORS ... ANDREW PRINE
ELIMINATORS ... DENISE CROSBY
ELIMINATORS ... PATRICK REYNOLDS
ELIMINATORS ... ROY DOTRICE
ELISA, MY LOVE ... GERALDINE CHAPLIN
ELISA, VIDA MIA ... GERALDINE CHAPLIN
ELIZA FRASER ... SUSANNAH YORK
ELIZABETH THE QUEEN ... BETTE DAVIS†

This is not a list of every film ever made or every cast member, only those listed in this directory.

ELIZABETH THE QUEEN .... OLIVIA DE HAVILLAND
ELIZA'S HOROSCOPE .... LILA KEDROVA
ELLE COURT ELLE COURT
    LA BANLIEU .... MARTHE KELLER
ELLERY QUEEN AND THE
    MURDER RING .... LEON AMES
ELLERY QUEEN AND THE
    MURDER RING .... RALPH BELLAMY†
ELLERY QUEEN AND THE
    PERFECT CRIME .... RALPH BELLAMY†
ELLERY QUEEN—MASTER
    DETECTIVE .... RALPH BELLAMY†
ELLERY QUEEN'S PENTHOUSE
    MYSTERY .... RALPH BELLAMY†
ELLIE .... EDWARD ALBERT
ELLIS ISLAND (MS) .... ALICE KRIGE
ELLIS ISLAND (MS) .... CLAIRE BLOOM
ELLIS ISLAND (MS) .... KATE BURTON
ELLIS ISLAND (MS) .... PETER RIEGERT
ELMER GANTRY .... DEAN JAGGER†
ELMER GANTRY .... JEAN SIMMONS
ELMER GANTRY .... MAX SHOWALTER
ELMER GANTRY ★★ .... BURT LANCASTER†
ELMER GANTRY ○○ .... SHIRLEY JONES
ELUSIVE PIMPERNEL, THE .... DAVID NIVEN†
ELVIRA, MISTRESS OF
    THE DARK .... CASSANDRA PETERSON
ELVIRA, MISTRESS OF
    THE DARK .... DANIEL GREENE
ELVIRA, MISTRESS OF
    THE DARK .... JEFF CONAWAY
ELVIS AND ME (MS) .... DALE MIDKIFF
ELVIS AND ME (MS) .... HUGH GILLIN
ELVIS AND ME (MS) .... LINDA MILLER
ELVIS (TF) .... KURT RUSSELL
ELVIS (TF) .... SEASON HUBLEY
ELVIS (TF) .... SHELLEY WINTERS
ELVIS—THAT'S THE WAY IT IS ...... ELVIS PRESLEY†
EMBASSY .... CHUCK CONNORS†
EMBASSY .... RICHARD ROUNDTREE
EMBRYO .... BARBARA CARRERA
EMBRYO .... DIANE LADD
EMBRYO .... RODDY McDOWALL
EMERALD FOREST, THE .... CHARLEY BOORMAN
EMERALD FOREST, THE .... MEG FOSTER
EMERALD FOREST, THE .... POWERS BOOTHE
EMERGENCY SQUAD .... ANTHONY QUINN
EMERGENCY WEDDING .... BARBARA HALE
EMIGRANTS, THE .... LIV ULLMANN
EMINENT DOMAIN .... ANNE ARCHER
EMINENT DOMAIN .... ANTHONY BATE
EMINENT DOMAIN .... BERNARD HEPTON
EMINENT DOMAIN .... DENYS FOUQUERAY
EMINENT DOMAIN .... DONALD SUTHERLAND
EMINENT DOMAIN .... FRANCOISE MICHAUD
EMINENT DOMAIN .... JODHI MAY
EMINENT DOMAIN .... PIP TORRENS
EMINENT DOMAIN .... YVES BENEYTON
EMMA ★ .... MARIE DRESSLER†
EMMANUELLE .... SYLVIA KRISTEL
EMMANUELLE II .... SYLVIA KRISTEL
EMMANUELLE—JOYS OF
    A WOMAN .... SYLVIA KRISTEL
EMMENEZ-MOI AU RITZ .... CLAUDINE AUGER
EMPEROR OF THE NORTH .... ERNEST BORGNINE
EMPEROR OF THE NORTH .... KEITH CARRADINE
EMPEROR OF THE NORTH .... MATT CLARK
EMPEROR OF THE
    NORTH POLE .... ERNEST BORGNINE
EMPEROR OF THE
    NORTH POLE .... KEITH CARRADINE
EMPEROR OF THE NORTH POLE .... MATT CLARK
EMPEROR'S
    CANDLESTICKS, THE .... MAUREEN O'SULLIVAN
EMPEROR'S NEW CLOTHES, THE .... ART CARNEY
EMPEROR'S NEW CLOTHES, THE .... SID CAESAR
EMPIRE .... ANTHONY LaPAGLIA
EMPIRE .... JOHNNY WHITWORTH
EMPIRE .... LIV TYLER
EMPIRE .... RENEE ZELLWEGER
EMPIRE .... ROBIN TUNNEY
EMPIRE OF THE ANTS .... ALBERT SALMI†
EMPIRE OF THE ANTS .... JOAN COLLINS

EMPIRE OF THE SON .... BURT KWOUK
EMPIRE OF THE SON .... MASATO IBU
EMPIRE OF THE SON .... RUPERT FRAZER
EMPIRE OF THE SUN .... BEN STILLER
EMPIRE OF THE SUN .... CHRISTIAN BALE
EMPIRE OF THE SUN .... EMILY RICHARD
EMPIRE OF THE SUN .... JOE PANTOLIANO
EMPIRE OF THE SUN .... JOHN MALKOVICH
EMPIRE OF THE SUN .... LESLIE PHILLIPS
EMPIRE OF THE SUN .... MIRANDA RICHARDSON
EMPIRE OF THE SUN .... NIGEL HAYERS
EMPIRE OF THE SUN .... ROBERT STEPHENS
EMPIRE STATE .... MARTIN LANDAU
EMPIRE STRIKES BACK, THE .... ALEC GUINNESS
EMPIRE STRIKES BACK, THE .... ANTHONY DANIELS
EMPIRE STRIKES
    BACK, THE .... BILLY DEE WILLIAMS
EMPIRE STRIKES BACK, THE .... CARRIE FISHER
EMPIRE STRIKES BACK, THE .... DAVID PROWSE
EMPIRE STRIKES BACK, THE .... FRANK OZ
EMPIRE STRIKES BACK, THE .... HARRISON FORD
EMPIRE STRIKES
    BACK, THE .... JAMES EARL JONES
EMPIRE STRIKES BACK, THE .... KENNY BAKER
EMPIRE STRIKES BACK, THE .... MARK HAMILL
EMPIRE STRIKES BACK, THE .... PETER MAYHEW
EMPTY CANVAS, THE .... BETTE DAVIS†
ENCHANTED APRIL .... MICHAEL KITCHEN
ENCHANTED APRIL ...... MIRANDA RICHARDSON
ENCHANTED APRIL ○ .... JOAN PLOWRIGHT
ENCHANTMENT .... DAVID NIVEN†
ENCHANTMENT .... TERESA WRIGHT
ENCINO MAN .... BRENDAN FRASER
ENCINO MAN .... MARIETTE HARTLEY
ENCINO MAN .... MEGAN WARD
ENCINO MAN .... PAULY SHORE
ENCINO MAN .... RICHARD MASUR
ENCINO MAN .... SEAN ASTIN
END, THE .... BURT REYNOLDS
END, THE .... CARL REINER
END, THE .... DAVID SPIELBERG
END, THE .... DAVID STEINBERG
END, THE .... DOM DeLUISE
END, THE .... JOANNE WOODWARD
END, THE .... KRISTY McNICHOL
END, THE .... NORMAN FELL
END, THE .... PAT O'BRIEN†
END, THE .... ROBBY BENSON
END, THE .... SALLY FIELD
END AS A MAN .... BEN GAZZARA
END AS A MAN .... PAT HINGLE
END AS A MAN .... PETER MARK RICHMAN
END OF AUGUST, THE .... LILIA SKALA
END OF DESIRE .... MARIA SCHELL
END OF INNOCENCE, THE .... DYAN CANNON
END OF INNOCENCE, THE .... JOHN HEARD
END OF THE AFFAIR, THE .... DEBORAH KERR
END OF THE AFFAIR, THE .... JOHN MILLS
END OF THE AFFAIR, THE .... VAN JOHNSON
END OF THE GAME .... DONALD SUTHERLAND
END OF THE GAME .... JACQUELINE BISSET
END OF THE GAME .... JON VOIGHT
END OF THE LINE .... BARBARA BARRIE
END OF THE LINE .... BOB BALABAN
END OF THE LINE .... BRUCE McGILL
END OF THE LINE .... CLINT HOWARD
END OF THE LINE .... HOLLY HUNTER
END OF THE LINE .... HOWARD MORRIS
END OF THE LINE .... KEVIN BACON
END OF THE LINE .... LEVON HELM
END OF THE LINE .... MARY STEENBURGEN
END OF THE LINE .... WILFORD BRIMLEY
END OF THE ROAD .... JAMES EARL JONES
END OF THE ROAD .... STACY KEACH
END OF THE WORLD IN OUR
    USUAL BED IN A NIGHT
    FULL OF RAIN, THE .... CANDICE BERGEN
END OF THE WORLD IN OUR
    USUAL BED IN A NIGHT
    FULL OF RAIN, THE .... JILL EIKENBERRY
ENDANGERED SPECIES .... HARRY CAREY JR.
ENDANGERED SPECIES .... HOYT AXTON
ENDANGERED SPECIES .... JoBETH WILLIAMS

ENDANGERED SPECIES .... PAUL DOOLEY
ENDANGERED SPECIES .... ROBERT URICH
ENDLESS GAME, THE (CTF) .... ALBERT FINNEY
ENDLESS GAME, THE (CTF) .... GEORGE SEGAL
ENDLESS LOVE .... BEATRICE STRAIGHT
ENDLESS LOVE .... BROOKE SHIELDS
ENDLESS LOVE .... DON MURRAY
ENDLESS LOVE .... JAMES SPADER
ENDLESS LOVE .... MARTIN HEWITT
ENDLESS LOVE .... PENELOPE MILFORD
ENDLESS LOVE .... RICHARD KILEY
ENDLESS LOVE .... SHIRLEY KNIGHT
ENDLESS LOVE .... TOM CRUISE
ENDLESS NIGHT .... BRITT EKLAND
ENDLESS NIGHT .... HAYLEY MILLS
ENDLESS SUMMER II, THE (FD) .... BRUCE BROWN
ENDLESS SUMMER II,
    THE (FD) .... PATRICK O'CONNELL
ENDLESS SUMMER II,
    THE (FD) .... ROBERT "WINGBUT" WEAVER
ENEMIES, A LOVE STORY .... ALAN KING
ENEMIES, A LOVE STORY .... ELVA BASKIN
ENEMIES, A LOVE STORY .... JUDITH MALINA
ENEMIES, A LOVE
    STORY .... MARGARET SOPHIE STEIN
ENEMIES, A LOVE STORY .... PAUL MAZURSKY
ENEMIES, A LOVE STORY .... PHIL LEEDS
ENEMIES, A LOVE STORY .... RITA KARIN
ENEMIES, A LOVE STORY .... RON SILVER
ENEMIES, A LOVE STORY ○ .... ANJELICA HUSTON
ENEMIES, A LOVE STORY ○ .... LENA OLIN
ENEMY BELOW, THE .... DAVID HEDISON
ENEMY BELOW, THE .... DOUG McCLURE
ENEMY BELOW, THE .... ROBERT MITCHUM
ENEMY BELOW, THE .... THEODORE BIKEL
ENEMY GENERAL, THE .... VAN JOHNSON
ENEMY MINE .... DENNIS QUAID
ENEMY MINE .... LOUIS GOSSETT JR.
ENEMY OF THE PEOPLE, AN .... BIBI ANDERSSON
ENEMY OF THE PEOPLE, AN .... CHARLES DURNING
ENEMY, THE .... LILLIAN GISH†
ENFORCER, THE .... BRADFORD DILLMAN
ENFORCER, THE .... CLINT EASTWOOD
ENFORCER, THE .... HARRY GUARDINO
ENFORCER, THE .... TYNE DALY
ENGAGEMENT, THE .... DAVID WARNER
ENGLAND MADE ME .... HILDEGARD NEIL
ENGLAND MADE ME .... JOSS ACKLAND
ENGLAND MADE ME .... MICHAEL YORK
ENGLISHMAN ABROAD, AN (TF) .... ALAN BATES
ENGLISHMAN WHO WENT UP A
    HILL, BUT CAME DOWN A
    MOUNTAIN, THE .... FRASER CAINS
ENGLISHMAN WHO WENT UP A
    HILL, BUT CAME DOWN A
    MOUNTAIN, THE .... ROBERT BLYTHE
ENGLISHMAN WHO WENT UP A
    HILL, BUT CAME DOWN A
    MOUNTAIN, THE .... ROBERT ELSON
ENID IS SLEEPING .... ELIZABETH PERKINS
ENID IS SLEEPING .... JEFFREY JONES
ENID IS SLEEPING .... JUDGE REINHOLD
ENID IS SLEEPING .... MAUREEN MUELLER
ENID IS SLEEPING .... MICHAEL J. POLLARD
ENIGMA .... DEREK JACOBI
ENIGMA .... MARTIN SHEEN
ENIGMA .... SAM NEILL
ENOCH ARDEN .... LILLIAN GISH†
ENOLA GAY (TF) .... BILLY CRYSTAL
ENOLA GAY: THE MEN, THE MISSION,
    THE ATOMIC BOMB (TF) .... KIM DARBY
ENOLA GAY: THE MEN, THE MISSION,
    THE ATOMIC BOMB (TF) .... STEPHEN MACHT
ENORMOUS CHANGES AT
    THE LAST MINUTE .... DAVID STRATHAIRN
ENORMOUS CHANGES AT
    THE LAST MINUTE .... KEVIN BACON
ENOS ....JOHN DEHNER†
ENSIGN PULVER .... BURL IVES
ENSIGN PULVER .... JACK NICHOLSON
ENSIGN PULVER .... JAMES FARENTINO
ENSIGN PULVER .... LARRY HAGMAN
ENSIGN PULVER .... MILLIE PERKINS

† after an actor's name denotes deceased.

ENSIGN PULVER .... ROBERT WALKER JR.
ENSIGN PULVER .... WALTER MATTHAU
ENTER LAUGHING .... ELAINE MAY
ENTER LAUGHING .... JANET MARGOLIN
ENTER LAUGHING .... JOSE FERRER†
ENTER LAUGHING .... MICHAEL J. POLLARD
ENTER LAUGHING .... RENI SANTONI
ENTER LAUGHING .... SHELLEY WINTERS
ENTER THE DRAGON .... BRUCE LEE†
ENTER THE DRAGON .... JOHN SAXON
ENTER THE DRAGON ..... MYKELTI WILLIAMSON
ENTER THE NINJA .... FRANCO NERO
ENTER THE NINJA .... SUSAN GEORGE
ENTERTAINER, THE .... ALAN BATES
ENTERTAINER, THE .... ALBERT FINNEY
ENTERTAINER, THE .... JOAN PLOWRIGHT
ENTERTAINER, THE .... SHIRLEY ANNE FIELD
ENTERTAINER, THE ★ .... LAURENCE OLIVIER†
ENTERTAINER, THE (TF) .... ANNETTE O'TOOLE
ENTERTAINER, THE (TF) .... JACK LEMMON
ENTERTAINER, THE (TF) .... TYNE DALY
ENTITY, THE .... BARBARA HERSHEY
ENTRE NOUS .... ISABELLE HUPPERT
EQUAL JUSTICE (TF) .... LISE CUTTER
EQUINOX .... MARISA TOMEI
EQUUS .... EILEEN ATKINS
EQUUS .... JENNY AGUTTER
EQUUS .... JOAN PLOWRIGHT
EQUUS .... KATE REID
EQUUS ★ .... RICHARD BURTON†
EQUUS ○ .... PETER FIRTH
ERASERHEAD .... JACK NANCE
ERIC (TF) .... CLAUDE AKINS†
ERIC (TF) .... JOHN SAVAGE
ERIC (TF) .... MARK HAMILL
ERIC (TF) .... PATRICIA NEAL
ERIK THE VIKING .... ALEC GUINNESS
ERIK THE VIKING .... ANTHONY SHER
ERIK THE VIKING .... BOB HOSKINS
ERIK THE VIKING .... EARTHA KITT
ERIK THE VIKING .... FREDDIE JONES
ERIK THE VIKING .... IMOGEN STUBBS
ERIK THE VIKING .... JIM CARTER
ERIK THE VIKING .... JOHN CLEESE
ERIK THE VIKING .... JOHN GORDON SINCLAIR
ERIK THE VIKING .... MICKEY ROONEY
ERIK THE VIKING .... SEAN CONNERY
ERIK THE VIKING .... SUSAN SARANDON
ERIK THE VIKING .... TERRY JONES
ERIK THE VIKING .... TIM ROBBINS
ERIK THE VIKING .... TSUTOMU SEKINE
ERNEST GOES TO CAMP .... JIM VARNEY
ERNEST GOES TO JAIL .... GAILORD SARTAIN
ERNEST GOES TO JAIL .... JIM VARNEY
ERNEST GOES TO SCHOOL .... JIM VARNEY
ERNEST RIDES AGAIN .... DUKE ERNSBERGER
ERNEST RIDES AGAIN .... JIM VARNEY
ERNEST RIDES AGAIN .... LINDA KASH
ERNEST RIDES AGAIN .... RON K, JAMES
ERNEST RIDES AGAIN .... TOM BUTLER
ERNEST SAVES CHRISTMAS .... JIM VARNEY
ERNEST SCARED STUPID .... JIM VARNEY
EROTIQUE .... PRISCILLA BARNES
ERRAND BOY, THE .... JERRY LEWIS
ERRAND BOY, THE .... KATHLEEN FREEMAN
ES KOMMT EIN TAG .... MARIA SCHELL
ESCAPADE .... JOHN MILLS
ESCAPADE IN JAPAN .... CLINT EASTWOOD
ESCAPADE IN JAPAN .... TERESA WRIGHT
ESCAPE ARTIST, THE .... GRIFFIN O'NEAL
ESCAPE ARTIST, THE .... JOAN HACKETT†
ESCAPE ARTIST, THE .... RAUL JULIA†
ESCAPE FROM ALCATRAZ .... CLINT EASTWOOD
ESCAPE FROM ALCATRAZ .... FRED WARD
ESCAPE FROM BATAAN (TF) .... KATHERINE ROSS
ESCAPE FROM BOGAN
   COUNTY (TF) .... JACLYN SMITH
ESCAPE FROM EAST BERLIN .... DON MURRAY
ESCAPE FROM FORT BRAVO ..... ELEANOR PARKER
ESCAPE FROM FORT BRAVO .... JOHN FORSYTHE
ESCAPE FROM
   FORT BRAVO .... RICHARD ANDERSON
ESCAPE FROM NEW YORK ..... ADRIENNE BARBEAU

ESCAPE FROM NEW YORK .... DONALD PLEASENCE
ESCAPE FROM NEW YORK .... ERNEST BORGNINE
ESCAPE FROM NEW YORK .... KURT RUSSELL
ESCAPE FROM NEW YORK .... SEASON HUBLEY
ESCAPE FROM SOBRIBOR (TF) .... ALAN ARKIN
ESCAPE FROM
   SOBRIBOR (TF) .... HERTMUT BECKER
ESCAPE FROM SOBRIBOR (TF) ... JOANNA PACULA
ESCAPE FROM SOBRIBOR (TF) ..... RUTGER HAUER
ESCAPE FROM THE PLANET
   OF THE APES .... BRADFORD DILLMAN
ESCAPE FROM THE PLANET
   OF THE APES .... RICARDO MONTALBAN
ESCAPE FROM THE PLANET
   OF THE APES .... RODDY McDOWALL
ESCAPE FROM ZAHRAIN .... JACK WARDEN
ESCAPE IN THE FOG .... NINA FOCH
ESCAPE ME NEVER .... ELEANOR PARKER
ESCAPE ME NEVER ★ .... ELISABETH BEGNER†
ESCAPE TO ATHENA .... ELLIOTT GOULD
ESCAPE TO ATHENA .... ROGER MOORE
ESCAPE TO ATHENA .... STEFANIE POWERS
ESCAPE TO ATHENA .... TELLY SAVALAS†
ESCAPE TO ATHENS .... RICHARD ROUNDTREE
ESCAPE TO BURMA .... BARBARA STANWYCK†
ESCAPE TO THE SUN .... JOHN IRELAND
ESCAPE TO THE SUN .... LILA KEDROVA
ESCAPE TO WITCH
   MOUNTAIN .... DONALD PLEASENCE
ESCAPE TO WITCH MOUNTAIN .... EDDIE ALBERT
ESPECIALLY ON SUNDAY .... BRUNO GANZ
ESPECIALLY ON SUNDAY .... CHIARA CASELLI
ESPECIALLY ON
   SUNDAY .... JEAN-HUGUES ANGLADE
ESPECIALLY ON SUNDAY .... ORNELLA MUTI
ESPECIALLY ON SUNDAY .... PHILIPPE NOIRET
ESTHER AND THE KING .... JOAN COLLINS
ET MOURIR DE PLAISIR .... MEL FERRER
ETERNAL SEA, THE .... ALEXIS SMITH†
ETERNALLY YOURS .... DAVID NIVEN†
ETERNITY .... ARMAND ASSANTE
ETERNITY .... EILEEN DAVIDSON
ETERNITY .... EUGENE ROCHE
ETERNITY .... FRANKIE VALLI
ETERNITY .... JOEY VILLA
ETERNITY .... JOHN P. RYAN
ETERNITY .... JON VOIGHT
ETERNITY .... KAYE BALLARD
ETERNITY .... LAINIE KAZAN
ETERNITY .... STEVEN KEATS†
ETERNITY .... WILFORD BRIMLEY
ETHAN FROME .... LIAM NEESON
EUREKA .... ED LAUTER
EUREKA .... GENE HACKMAN
EUREKA .... JOE PESCI
EUREKA .... MICKEY ROURKE
EUREKA .... RUTGER HAUER
EUREKA .... THERESA RUSSELL
EUREKA STOCKADE .... GORDAN JACKSON†
EUROPA, EUROPA .... MARCO HOFSCHNEIDER
EUROPEANS, THE .... LEE REMICK†
EUROPEANS, THE .... LISA EICHHORN
EUROPEANS, THE .... WESLEY ADDY
EUTANASIA DI UN AMORE .... TONY MUSANTE
EVE OF DESTRUCTION .... GREGORY HINES
EVE OF DESTRUCTION .... KEVIN McCARTHY
EVE OF DESTRUCTION .... MIKE JOLLY
EVE OF DESTRUCTION .... RENEE SOUTENDIJK
EVE OF ST. MARK, THE .... VINCENT PRICE†
EVEL KNIEVEL .... GEORGE HAMILTON
EVEN COWGIRLS GET
   THE BLUES .... ANGIE DICKINSON
EVEN COWGIRLS GET THE BLUES ..... BUCK HENRY
EVEN COWGIRLS GET THE BLUES ..... CAROL KANE
EVEN COWGIRLS GET
   THE BLUES .... CRISPIN GLOVER
EVEN COWGIRLS GET
   THE BLUES .... ED BEGLEY JR.
EVEN COWGIRLS GET THE BLUES ...... JOHN HURT
EVEN COWGIRLS GET
   THE BLUES .... KEANU REEVES
EVEN COWGIRLS GET THE BLUES ...... LILY TOMLIN

EVEN COWGIRLS GET
   THE BLUES .... LORRAINE BRACCO
EVEN COWGIRLS GET
   THE BLUES .... NORIYUKI "PAT" MORITA
EVEN COWGIRLS GET
   THE BLUES .... RAIN PHOENIX
EVEN COWGIRLS GET THE BLUES .... ROSEANNE
EVEN COWGIRLS GET THE BLUES .... SEAN YOUNG
EVEN COWGIRLS GET
   THE BLUES .... UMA THURMAN
EVENING IN BYZANTIUM (TF) .... EDDIE ALBERT
EVENING IN BYZANTIUM (TF) ..... GEORGE LAZENBY
EVENING IN BYZANTIUM (TF) .... HARRY GUARDINO
EVENING IN BYZANTIUM (TF) .... SHIRLEY JONES
EVENING IN BYZANTIUM (TF) .... VINCE EDWARDS
EVENING STAR .... SHIRLEY MacLAINE
EVENSONG .... ALEC GUINNESS
EVER IN MY HEART .... BARBARA STANWYCK†
EVER IN MY HEART .... RALPH BELLAMY†
EVERGREEN (MS) .... ARMAND ASSANTE
EVERGREEN (MS) .... BETTY BUCKLEY
EVERGREEN (MS) .... BRIAN DENNEHY
EVERGREEN (MS) .... LESLEY ANN WARREN
EVERGREEN (MS) .... PATRICIA BARRY
EVERSMILE, NEW JERSEY .... DANIEL DAY-LEWIS
EVERY BASTARD A KING .... TOPOL
EVERY DAY'S A HOLIDAY .... RON MOODY
EVERY GIRL SHOULD
   HAVE ONE .... ZSA ZSA GABOR
EVERY LITTLE CROOK
   AND NANNY .... AUSTIN PENDLETON
EVERY LITTLE CROOK
   AND NANNY .... DOM DeLUISE
EVERY LITTLE CROOK AND NANNY ...... JOHN ASTIN
EVERY LITTLE CROOK
   AND NANNY .... LYNN REDGRAVE
EVERY MAN FOR HIMSELF .... ISABELLE HUPPERT
EVERY OTHER WEEKEND .... NATHALIE BAYE
EVERY TIME WE
   SAY GOODBYE .... CRISTINA MARSILLACH
EVERY TIME WE SAY GOODBYE .... TOM HANKS
EVERY WHICH WAY
   BUT LOOSE .... BEVERLY D'ANGELO
EVERY WHICH WAY BUT LOOSE ..... BILL McKINNEY
EVERY WHICH WAY
   BUT LOOSE .... CLINT EASTWOOD
EVERY WHICH WAY
   BUT LOOSE .... GEOFFREY LEWIS
EVERY WHICH WAY
   BUT LOOSE .... JAMES McEACHIN
EVERY WHICH WAY BUT LOOSE .... KEN WAHL
EVERY WHICH WAY
   BUT LOOSE ....RUTH GORDON†
EVERY WHICH WAY BUT LOOSE ... SONDRA LOCKE
EVERYBODY DOES IT .... CELESTE HOLM
EVERYBODY GO HOME! .... MARTIN BALSAM
EVERYBODY WINS .... DEBRA WINGER
EVERYBODY WINS .... JACK WARDEN
EVERYBODY WINS .... JUDITH IVEY
EVERYBODY WINS .... KATHLEEN WILHOITE
EVERYBODY WINS .... NICK NOLTE
EVERYBODY WINS .... WILL PATTON
EVERYBODY'S ALL-AMERICAN .... CARL LUMBLY
EVERYBODY'S ALL-AMERICAN .... DENNIS QUAID
EVERYBODY'S ALL-AMERICAN .... JESSICA LANGE
EVERYBODY'S ALL-AMERICAN ..... JOHN GOODMAN
EVERYBODY'S
   ALL-AMERICAN .... PATRICIA CLARKSON
EVERYBODY'S ALL-AMERICAN .. TIMOTHY HUTTON
EVERYBODY'S BABY: THE RESCUE
   OF JESSICA McCLURE (TF) .... BEAU BRIDGES
EVERYBODY'S BABY: THE RESCUE
   OF JESSICA McCLURE (TF) .... PAT HINGLE
EVERYBODY'S BABY: THE RESCUE
   OF JESSICA McCLURE (TF) .... PATTY DUKE
EVERYBODY'S BABY: THE RESCUE
   OF JESSICA McCLURE (TF) .... ROXANA ZAL
EVERYBODY'S FINE .... MARCELLO MASTROIANNI
EVERYTHING BUT THE TRUTH .... MAUREEN O'HARA
EVERYTHING YOU ALWAYS WANTED
   TO KNOW ABOUT SEX* (*BUT WERE
   AFRAID TO ASK) .... BURT REYNOLDS

This is not a list of every film ever made or every cast member, only those listed in this directory.

EVERYTHING YOU ALWAYS WANTED TO KNOW ABOUT SEX* (*BUT WERE AFRAID TO ASK) ... GENE WILDER
EVERYTHING YOU ALWAYS WANTED TO KNOW ABOUT SEX* (*BUT WERE AFRAID TO ASK) ... GEOFFREY HOLDER
EVERYTHING YOU ALWAYS WANTED TO KNOW ABOUT SEX* (*BUT WERE AFRAID TO ASK) ... JOHN CARRADINE†
EVERYTHING YOU ALWAYS WANTED TO KNOW ABOUT SEX* (BUT WERE AFRAID TO ASK) ... LOU JACOBI
EVERYTHING YOU ALWAYS WANTED TO KNOW ABOUT SEX* (*BUT WERE AFRAID TO ASK) ... LOUISE LASSER
EVERYTHING YOU ALWAYS WANTED TO KNOW ABOUT SEX* (*BUT WERE AFRAID TO ASK) ... LYNN REDGRAVE
EVERYTHING YOU ALWAYS WANTED TO KNOW ABOUT SEX* (*BUT WERE AFRAID TO ASK) ... MARCY GOLDMAN
EVERYTHING YOU ALWAYS WANTED TO KNOW ABOUT SEX* (BUT WERE AFRAID TO ASK) ... SIDNEY MILLER
EVERYTHING YOU ALWAYS WANTED TO KNOW ABOUT SEX* (*BUT WERE AFRAID TO ASK) ... TONY RANDALL
EVERYTHING YOU ALWAYS WANTED TO KNOW ABOUT SEX* (*BUT WERE AFRAID TO ASK) ... WOODY ALLEN
EVERYTHING'S DUCKY ... BUDDY HACKETT
EVERYTHING'S DUCKY ... JACKIE COOPER
EVERYTHING'S DUCKY ... MICKEY ROONEY
EVICTORS, THE ... JESSICA HARPER
EVIL, THE ... RICHARD CRENNA
EVIL EYE, THE ... JOHN SAXON
EVIL IN CLEAR RIVER (TF) ... LINDSAY WAGNER
EVIL IN CLEAR RIVER (TF) ... RANDY QUAID
EVIL IN THE DEEP ... CHERYL LADD
EVIL ROY SLADE (TF) ... EDIE ADAMS
EVIL ROY SLADE (TF) ... HENRY GIBSON
EVIL ROY SLADE (TF) ... JOHN ASTIN
EVIL ROY SLADE (TF) ... MILTON BERLE
EVIL THAT MEN DO, THE ... CHARLES BRONSON
EVIL THAT MEN DO, THE ... JOSE FERRER†
EVIL THAT MEN DO, THE ... RAYMOND ST. JACQUES
EVIL UNDER THE SUN ... DENIS QUILLEY
EVIL UNDER THE SUN ... DIANA RIGG
EVIL UNDER THE SUN ... MAGGIE SMITH
EVIL UNDER THE SUN ... NICHOLAS CLAY
EVIL UNDER THE SUN ... PETER USTINOV
EVIL UNDER THE SUN ... RODDY McDOWALL
EVIL UNDER THE SUN ... SYLVIA MILES
EVILSPEAK ... R.G. ARMSTRONG
EVIOLENTI ... HENRY SILVA
EVITA PERON (TF) ... FAYE DUNAWAY
EVITA PERON (TF) ... JAMES FARENTINO
EVITA PERON (TF) ... JEREMY KEMP
EVITA PERON (TF) ... JOHN VAN DREELEN
EVITA PERON (TF) ... JOSE FERRER†
EVITA PERON (TF) ... KATHY JURADO
EVITA PERON (TF) ... MICHAEL CONSTANTINE
EVITA PERON (TF) ... PEDRO ARMENDARIZ JR.
EVITA PERON (TF) ... RITA MORENO
EVITA PERON (TF) ... ROBERT VIHARO
EVITA PERON (TF) ... VIRGINIA GREGG
EWOK ADVENTURE, THE (TF) ... GUY BOYD
EWOK ADVENTURE, THE (TF) ... WARWICK DAVIS
EWOKS: THE BATTLE FOR ENDOR (TF) ... SIAN PHILLIPS
EWOKS: THE BATTLE FOR ENDOR (TF) ... WARWICK DAVIS
EWOKS: THE BATTLE FOR ENDOR (TF) ... WILFORD BRIMLEY
EX-LADY ... BETTE DAVIS†
EXCALIBUR ... GABRIEL BYRNE
EXCALIBUR ... HELEN MIRREN
EXCALIBUR ... LIAM NEESON
EXCALIBUR ... NICHOLAS CLAY
EXCALIBUR ... NICOL WILLIAMSON
EXCALIBUR ... PATRICK STEWART
EXECUTION OF PRIVATE SLOVIK, THE (TF) ... BEN HAMMER
EXECUTION OF PRIVATE SLOVIK, THE (TF) ... CHARLIE SHEEN
EXECUTION OF PRIVATE SLOVIK, THE (TF) ... GARY BUSEY
EXECUTION OF PRIVATE SLOVIK, THE (TF) ... MARTIN SHEEN
EXECUTION OF PRIVATE SLOVIK, THE (TF) ... NED BEATTY
EXECUTION, THE (TF) ... BARBARA BARRIE
EXECUTION, THE (TF) ... JESSICA WALTER
EXECUTION, THE (TF) ... LORETTA SWIT
EXECUTION, THE (TF) ... MICHAEL LERNER
EXECUTION, THE (TF) ... RIP TORN
EXECUTION, THE (TF) ... SANDY DENNIS†
EXECUTION, THE (TF) ... VALERIE HARPER
EXECUTIONER, THE ... GEORGE PEPPARD†
EXECUTIONER, THE ... JOAN COLLINS
EXECUTIONER'S SONG, THE (TF) ... CHRISTINE LAHTI
EXECUTIONER'S SONG, THE (TF) ... ELI WALLACH
EXECUTIONER'S SONG, THE (TF) ... ROSANNA ARQUETTE
EXECUTIONER'S SONG, THE (TF) ... STEVEN KEATS†
EXECUTIONER'S SONG, THE (TF) ... TOMMY LEE JONES
EXECUTIVE ACTION ... BURT LANCASTER†
EXECUTIVE ACTION ... ED LAUTER
EXECUTIVE ACTION ... JOHN ANDERSON
EXECUTIVE SUITE ... BARBARA STANWYCK†
EXECUTIVE SUITE ... DEAN JAGGER†
EXECUTIVE SUITE ... JUNE ALLYSON
EXECUTIVE SUITE ... SHELLEY WINTERS
EXECUTIVE SUITE ✪ ... NINA FOCH
EXIT TO EDEN ... DAN AYKROYD
EXIT TO EDEN ... DANA DELANY
EXIT TO EDEN ... HECTOR ELIZONDO
EXIT TO EDEN ... IMAN
EXIT TO EDEN ... PAUL MERCURIO
EXIT TO EDEN ... ROSIE O'DONNELL
EXIT TO EDEN ... STUART WILSON
EXODUS ... EVA MARIE SAINT
EXODUS ... HUGH GRIFFITH†
EXODUS ... LEE J. COBB†
EXODUS ... PAUL NEWMAN
EXODUS ... PETER LAWFORD†
EXODUS ... SIR FELIX AYLMER†
EXODUS ... SIR RALPH RICHARDSON†
EXODUS ✪ ... SAL MINEO†
EXORCIST, THE ... JACK MACGOWRAN†
EXORCIST, THE ... LEE J. COBB†
EXORCIST, THE ... MAX von SYDOW
EXORCIST, THE ... MERCEDES McCAMBRIDGE
EXORCIST, THE ★ ... ELLEN BURSTYN
EXORCIST, THE ✪ ... JASON MILLER
EXORCIST, THE ✪ ... LINDA BLAIR
EXORCIST II: THE HERETIC ... JAMES EARL JONES
EXORCIST II: THE HERETIC ... LINDA BLAIR
EXORCIST II: THE HERETIC ... LOUISE FLETCHER
EXORCIST II: THE HERETIC ... MAX von SYDOW
EXORCIST II: THE HERETIC ... NED BEATTY
EXORCIST II: THE HERETIC ... RICHARD BURTON†
EXORCIST III, THE ... BRAD DOURIF
EXORCIST III, THE ... ED FLANDERS
EXORCIST III, THE ... GEORGE C. SCOTT
EXORCIST III, THE ... JASON MILLER
EXORCIST III, THE ... NICOL WILLIAMSON
EXORCIST III, THE ... SCOTT WILSON
EXPERIMENT IN TERROR ... LEE REMICK†
EXPERIMENT IN TERROR ... NED GLASS†
EXPERIMENT IN TERROR ... STEFANIE POWERS
EXPERTS, THE ... ARYE GROSS
EXPERTS, THE ... BRIAN DOYLE-MURRAY
EXPERTS, THE ... CHARLES MARTIN SMITH
EXPERTS, THE ... DEBORAH FOREMAN
EXPERTS, THE ... JAMES KEACH
EXPERTS, THE ... JAN RUBES
EXPERTS, THE ... JOHN TRAVOLTA
EXPERTS, THE ... KELLY PRESTON
EXPERTS, THE ... RICK DUCOMMUN
EXPLORERS ... AMANDA PETERSON
EXPLORERS ... DICK MILLER
EXPLORERS ... ETHAN HAWKE
EXPLORERS ... JASON PRESSON
EXPLORERS ... MARY KAY PLACE
EXPLORERS ... RIVER PHOENIX†
EXPLORERS ... ROBERT PICARDO
EXPLOSION ... DON STROUD
EXPLOSIVE GENERATION, THE ... BEAU BRIDGES
EXPLOSIVE GENERATION, THE ... WILLIAM SHATNER
EXPOSED ... BIBI ANDERSSON
EXPOSED ... HARVEY KEITEL
EXPOSED ... JAMES RUSSO
EXPOSED ... JAMES TOBACK
EXPOSED ... NASTASSJA KINSKI
EXPOSED ... RUDOLF NUREYEV†
EXTERMINATOR, THE ... SAMANTHA EGGAR
EXTRAORDINARY SEAMAN, THE ... ALAN ALDA
EXTRAORDINARY SEAMAN, THE ... DAVID NIVEN†
EXTRAORDINARY SEAMAN, THE ... FAYE DUNAWAY
EXTRAORDINARY SEAMAN, THE ... JUANO HERNANDEZ†
EXTRAORDINARY SEAMAN, THE ... MICKEY ROONEY
EXTREME PREJUDICE ... CLANCY BROWN
EXTREME PREJUDICE ... LARRY B. SCOTT
EXTREME PREJUDICE ... MARIA CONCHITA ALONSO
EXTREME PREJUDICE ... MATT MULHERN
EXTREME PREJUDICE ... MICHAEL IRONSIDE
EXTREME PREJUDICE ... NICK NOLTE
EXTREME PREJUDICE ... POWERS BOOTHE
EXTREME PREJUDICE ... RIP TORN
EXTREME PREJUDICE ... WILLIAM FORSYTHE
EXTREMITIES ... ALFRE WOODARD
EXTREMITIES ... DIANA SCARWID
EXTREMITIES ... FARRAH FAWCETT
EXTREMITIES ... JAMES RUSSO
EYE FOR AN EYE, AN ... CHUCK NORRIS
EYE FOR AN EYE, AN ... NIGEL DAVENPORT
EYE FOR AN EYE, AN ... PATRICK WAYNE
EYE OF THE CAT ... ELEANOR PARKER
EYE OF THE CAT ... ELI WALLACH
EYE OF THE CAT ... MICHAEL SARRAZIN
EYE OF THE DEVIL ... DAVID HEMMINGS
EYE OF THE DEVIL ... DEBORAH KERR
EYE OF THE DEVIL ... DONALD PLEASENCE
EYE OF THE NEEDLE ... CHRISTOPHER CAZENOVE
EYE OF THE NEEDLE ... DONALD SUTHERLAND
EYE OF THE NEEDLE ... IAN BANNEN
EYE OF THE NEEDLE ... KATE NELLIGAN
EYE OF THE STRANGER ... DAVID HEAVENER
EYE OF THE STRANGER ... MARTIN LANDAU
EYE OF THE STRANGER ... SALLY KIRKLAND
EYE OF THE TIGER ... GARY BUSEY
EYE ON THE SPARROW (TF) ... CONCHATA FERRELL
EYE ON THE SPARROW (TF) ... KEITH CARRADINE
EYE WITNESS ... PETER VAUGHN
EYES OF A STRANGER ... GWEN LEIS
EYES OF A STRANGER ... JENNIFER JASON LEIGH
EYES OF A STRANGER ... JOHN DISANTI
EYES OF A STRANGER ... LAUREN TEWES
EYES OF A STRANGER ... PETER DUPRE
EYES OF AN ANGEL ... JOHN TRAVOLTA
EYES OF ANNIE JONES, THE ... FRANCESCA ANNIS
EYES OF LAURA MARS ... BRAD DOURIF
EYES OF LAURA MARS ... FAYE DUNAWAY
EYES OF LAURA MARS ... FRANK ADONIS
EYES OF LAURA MARS ... MICHAEL TUCKER
EYES OF LAURA MARS ... RAUL JULIA†
EYES OF LAURA MARS ... RENE AUBERJONOIS
EYES OF LAURA MARS ... TOMMY LEE JONES
EYES OF TERROR (TF) ... BARBARA EDEN
EYES OF TERROR (TF) ... MICHAEL DeGOOD
EYES OF TERROR (TF) ... MISSY CRIDER
EYEWITNESS ... CHRISTOPHER PLUMMER
EYEWITNESS ... JAMES WOODS
EYEWITNESS ... JEREMY KEMP
EYEWITNESS ... KENNETH McMILLAN†
EYEWITNESS ... MARK LESTER
EYEWITNESS ... SIGOURNEY WEAVER
EYEWITNESS ... SUSAN GEORGE
EYEWITNESS ... WILLIAM HURT

† after an actor's name denotes deceased.

F

F.I.S.T. .... MELINDA DILLON
F.I.S.T. .... PETER BOYLE
F.I.S.T. .... PETER DONAT
F.I.S.T. .... ROD STEIGER
F.I.S.T. .... SYLVESTER STALLONE
F.I.S.T. .... TONY LoBIANCO
F. SCOTT FITZGERALD AND "THE
  LAST OF THE BELLES" (TF) .... SUSAN SARANDON
F. SCOTT FITZGERALD IN
  HOLLYWOOD (TF) .... JASON MILLER
F.T.A. .... JANE FONDA
F.T.A. (FD) .... DONALD SUTHERLAND
F/X .... BRIAN DENNEHY
F/X .... BRYON BROWN
F/X .... CLIFF DE YOUNG
F/X .... DIANE VENORA
F/X .... JERRY ORBACH
F/X .... JOE GRIFASI
F/X .... MARTHA GEHMAN
F/X .... MASON ADAMS
F/X 2 - THE DEADLY ART
  OF ILLUSION .... BRIAN DENNEHY
F/X 2 - THE DEADLY ART
  OF ILLUSION .... BRYON BROWN
F/X 2 - THE DEADLY ART
  OF ILLUSION .... JOANNA GLEASON
F/X 2 - THE DEADLY ART
  OF ILLUSION .... KEVIN J. O'CONNOR
F/X 2 - THE DEADLY ART
  OF ILLUSION .... PHILIP BOSCO
F/X 2 - THE DEADLY ART
  OF ILLUSION .... RACHEL TICOTIN
FABULOUS BAKER BOYS, THE .... BEAU BRIDGES
FABULOUS BAKER BOYS, THE .... ELLIE RAAB
FABULOUS BAKER BOYS, THE .... JEFF BRIDGES
FABULOUS BAKER BOYS, THE .... JENNIFER TILLY
FABULOUS BAKER
  BOYS, THE ★ .... MICHELLE PFEIFFER
FACE IN THE CROWD, A .... ANDY GRIFFITH
FACE IN THE
  CROWD, A .... ANTHONY (TONY) FRANCIOSA
FACE IN THE CROWD, A .... LEE REMICK†
FACE IN THE CROWD, A .... LOIS NETTLETON
FACE IN THE CROWD, A .... PATRICIA NEAL
FACE IN THE CROWD, A .... RIP TORN
FACE IN THE CROWD, A ...... WALTER MATTHAU
FACE IN THE RAIN, A .... RORY CALHOUN
FACE OF A FUGITIVE .... JAMES COBURN
FACE OF A STRANGER .... JEREMY KEMP
FACE OF A STRANGER (TF) .... GENA ROWLANDS
FACE OF A STRANGER (TF) .... TYNE DALY
FACE OF FEAR, THE (TF) .... ELIZABETH ASHLEY
FACE OF FIRE .... ROYAL DANO
FACE OF THE ENEMY .... GEORGE DICENZO
FACE OF THE LADY .... JOHN CANDY†
FACE TO FACE .... ERLAND JOSEPHSON
FACE TO FACE ★ .... LIV ULLMANN
FACE TO FACE (TF) .... ELIZABETH MONTGOMERY
FACE TO FACE (TF) .... ROBERT FOXWORTH
FACES .... GENA ROWLANDS
FACES .... VAL AVERY
FACES ◊ .... SEYMOUR CASSEL
FACES IN THE DARK .... JOHN IRELAND
FACES IN THE DARK .... MAE ZETTERLING†
FACTS OF LIFE DOWN
  UNDER, THE (TF) .... CLORIS LEACHMAN
FACTS OF LIFE DOWN
  UNDER, THE (TF) .... MACKENZIE ASTIN
FACTS OF LIFE DOWN
  UNDER, THE (TF) .... MINDY COHN
FACTS OF LIFE, THE .... BOB HOPE
FACTS OF LIFE, THE .... LUCILLE BALL†
FADE TO BLACK .... DENNIS CHRISTOPHER
FADE TO BLACK .... MICKEY ROURKE
FADE-IN .... BARBARA LODEN†
FADE-IN .... BURT REYNOLDS
FAHRENHEIT 451 .... JULIE CHRISTIE
FAHRENHEIT 451 .... MARK LESTER
FAHRENHEIT 451 .... OSKAR WERNER†

FAIL SAFE .... DOM DELUISE
FAIL SAFE .... FRITZ WEAVER
FAIL SAFE .... LARRY HAGMAN
FAIL-SAFE .... DAN O'HERLIHY
FAIL-SAFE .... WALTER MATTHAU
FAILING OF
  RAYMOND, THE (TF) .... DEAN STOCKWELL
FAILING OF RAYMOND, THE (TF) .... JANE WYMAN
FAIR GAME .... SYLVESTER STALLONE
FAIR GAME .... WILLIAM BALDWIN
FAITHFUL .... CHAZZ PALMINTERI
FAITHFUL .... CHER
FAITHFUL .... PAUL MAZURSKY
FAITHFUL .... RYAN O'NEAL
FAKE, THE .... BILLIE WHITELAW
FAKE-OUT .... PIA ZADORA
FAKEOUT .... TELLY SAVALAS†
FALCON AND THE
  SNOWMAN, THE .... DORIAN HAREWOOD
FALCON AND THE SNOWMAN, THE ...... PAT HINGLE
FALCON AND THE SNOWMAN, THE ...... SEAN PENN
FALCON AND THE
  SNOWMAN, THE .... TIMOTHY HUTTON
FALCON IN HOLLYWOOD, THE .... BARBARA HALE
FALCON OUT WEST, THE .... BARBARA HALE
FALCON'S ALIBI, THE .... JANE GREER
FALL FROM GRACE (TF) .... BERNADETTE PETERS
FALL FROM GRACE (TF) .... KEVIN SPACEY
FALL FROM GRACE (TF) .... RICHARD HERD
FALL GUY, THE (TF) .... LEE MAJORS
FALL OF THE HOUSE
  OF USHER, THE (TF) .... DIMITRA ARLYS
FALL OF THE HOUSE
  OF USHER, THE (TF) .... ROBERT HAYS
FALL OF THE ROMAN
  EMPIRE, THE .... ALEC GUINNESS
FALL OF THE ROMAN
  EMPIRE, THE .... CHRISTOPHER PLUMMER
FALL OF THE ROMAN
  EMPIRE, THE .... JOHN IRELAND
FALL OF THE ROMAN EMPIRE, THE .... MEL FERRER
FALL OF THE ROMAN
  EMPIRE, THE .... OMAR SHARIF
FALL OF THE ROMAN
  EMPIRE, THE .... SOPHIA LOREN
FALLEN ANGEL (TF) .... DANA HILL
FALLEN ANGEL (TF) .... MELINDA DILLON
FALLEN ANGEL (TF) .... RICHARD MASUR
FALLEN ANGEL (TF) .... RONNY COX
FALLEN SPARROW, THE .... MAUREEN O'HARA
FALLING DOWN .... BARBARA HERSHEY
FALLING DOWN .... FREDERIC FORREST
FALLING DOWN .... MICHAEL DOUGLAS
FALLING DOWN .... RACHEL TICOTIN
FALLING DOWN .... ROBERT DUVALL
FALLING DOWN .... TUESDAY WELD
FALLING FROM GRACE .... CLAUDE AKINS†
FALLING FROM GRACE .... DUB TAYLOR
FALLING FROM GRACE .... JOHN MELLENCAMP
FALLING FROM GRACE .... KAY LENZ
FALLING FROM GRACE .... MARIEL HEMINGWAY
FALLING IN LOVE .... DAVID CLENNON
FALLING IN LOVE .... DIANNE WIEST
FALLING IN LOVE .... GEORGE MARTIN
FALLING IN LOVE .... HARVEY KEITEL
FALLING IN LOVE .... JANE KACZMAREK
FALLING IN LOVE .... MERYL STREEP
FALLING IN LOVE .... ROBERT DE NIRO
FALLING IN LOVE AGAIN .... ELLIOTT GOULD
FALLING IN LOVE AGAIN .... KAYE BALLARD
FALLING IN LOVE AGAIN .... MICHELLE PFEIFFER
FALLING IN LOVE AGAIN .... SUSANNAH YORK
FALSE COLORS .... ROBERT MITCHUM
FALSE IDENTITY .... GENEVIEVE BUJOLD
FALSE IDENTITY .... MIMI MAYNARD
FALSE IDENTITY .... STACY KEACH
FALSE IDENTITY .... TOBIN BELL
FALSE IDENTITY .... VERONICA CARTWRIGHT
FALSE WITNESS .... BRUNO GANZ
FALSE WITNESS (TF) .... GEORGE GRIZZARD
FALSTAFF .... JOHN GIELGUD
FALSTAFF .... TONY BECKLEY†
FAME .... ANNE MEARA

FAME .... BARRY MILLER
FAME .... IRENE CARA
FAME .... MAUREEN TEEFY
FAME .... PAUL McCRANE
FAME .... STEVE INWOOD
FAME IS THE SPUR .... DAVID TOMLINSON
FAMILY, THE .... CHARLES BRONSON
FAMILY, THE .... GEORGE KENNEDY
FAMILY, THE .... JO CHAMP
FAMILY, THE .... TELLY SAVALAS†
FAMILY AFFAIR, A .... MICKEY ROONEY
FAMILY BUSINESS .... BILL McCUTCHEON
FAMILY BUSINESS .... DEBORAH RUSH
FAMILY BUSINESS .... DUSTIN HOFFMAN
FAMILY BUSINESS .... JANET CARROLL
FAMILY BUSINESS .... MATTHEW BRODERICK
FAMILY BUSINESS .... ROSANA DE SOTO
FAMILY BUSINESS .... SEAN CONNERY
FAMILY BUSINESS .... VICTORIA JACKSON
FAMILY DIARY .... MARCELLO MASTROIANNI
FAMILY ENFORCER .... JOE PESCI
FAMILY FLIGHT (TF) .... JANET MARGOLIN
FAMILY FOR JOE, A (TF) .... MAIA BREWTON
FAMILY HONEYMOON .... WILLIAM DANIELS
FAMILY JEWELS, THE .... JERRY LEWIS
FAMILY KILLER .... JOHN SAXON
FAMILY NOBODY
  WANTED, THE (TF) .... SHIRLEY JONES
FAMILY OF SPIES (MS) .... GRAHAM BECKEL
FAMILY OF SPIES (MS) ..... LESLEY ANN WARREN
FAMILY OF SPIES (MS) .... LILI TAYLOR
FAMILY OF SPIES (MS) .... POWERS BOOTHE
FAMILY PICTURES (TF) .... ANJELICA HUSTON
FAMILY PICTURES (TF) .... DERMOT MULRONEY
FAMILY PICTURES (TF) .... KYRA SEDGWICK
FAMILY PICTURES (TF) .... SAM NEILL
FAMILY PLOT .... BARBARA HARRIS
FAMILY PLOT .... BRUCE DERN
FAMILY PLOT .... KAREN BLACK
FAMILY PLOT .... KATHERINE HELMOND
FAMILY PLOT .... WILLIAM DEVANE
FAMILY PLOT .... WILLIAM PRINCE
FAMILY PRAYERS .... ANNE ARCHER
FAMILY REUNION (TF) .... BETTE DAVIS†
FAMILY REUNION (TF) .... JOHN SHEA
FAMILY REUNION (TF) .... ROY DOTRICE
FAMILY RICO, THE (TF) .... BEN GAZZARA
FAMILY SECRETS (TF) .... STEFANIE POWERS
FAMILY SINS (TF) .... ANDREW BEDNARSKI
FAMILY SINS (TF) .... JAMES FARENTINO
FAMILY SINS (TF) .... JILL EIKENBERRY
FAMILY TIES VACATION (TF) ..... JUSTINE BATEMAN
FAMILY TIES VACATION (TF) ..... MEREDITH BAXTER
FAMILY TIES VACATION (TF) .... MICHAEL GROSS
FAMILY TIES VACATION (TF) .... MICHAEL J. FOX
FAMILY TIES VACATION (TF) .... TINA YOTHERS
FAMILY UPSIDE
  DOWN, A (TF) .... EFREM ZIMBALIST JR.
FAMILY UPSIDE DOWN, A (TF) .... HELEN HAYES
FAMILY UPSIDE DOWN, A (TF) .... PATTY DUKE
FAMILY WAY, THE .... HAYLEY MILLS
FAN, THE .... GRIFFIN DUNNE
FAN, THE .... HECTOR ELIZONDO
FAN, THE .... JAMES GARNER
FAN, THE .... LAUREN BACALL
FAN, THE .... MAUREEN STAPLETON
FAN, THE .... MICHAEL BIEHN
FANATIC .... DONALD SUTHERLAND
FANATIC .... PETER VAUGHN
FANATIC .... STEFANIE POWERS
FANCY PANTS .... BOB HOPE
FANDANGO .... BRIAN CESAK
FANDANGO .... CHUCK BUSH
FANDANGO .... JUDD NELSON
FANDANGO .... KEVIN COSTNER
FANDANGO .... MARVIN J. McINTYRE
FANDANGO .... SAM ROBARDS
FANDANGO .... SUZY AMIS
FANNY .... LESLIE CARON
FANNY ★ .... CHARLES BOYER†
FANTASIES .... BO DEREK
FANTASIST, THE .... CHRISTOPHER CAZENOVE
FANTASMI A ROMA .... MARCELLO MASTROIANNI

This is not a list of every film ever made or every cast member, only those listed in this directory.

FANTASTIC VOYAGE	DONALD PLEASENCE	
FANTASTIC VOYAGE	EDMOND O'BRIEN†	
FANTASTIC VOYAGE	JAMES BROLIN	
FANTASTIC VOYAGE	RAQUEL WELCH	
FANTASTIC VOYAGE	STEPHEN BOYD†	
FANTASTIC WORLD OF		
D.C. COLLINS, THE (TF)	GARY COLEMAN	
FANTASTICA	CLAUDINE AUGER	
FANTASY ISLAND (TF)	BILL BIXBY†	
FANTASY ISLAND (TF)	CAROL LYNLEY	
FANTASY ISLAND (TF)	RICARDO MONTALBAN	
FANTASY ISLAND (TF)	SANDRA DEE	
FANTASY ISLAND (TF)	VICTORIA PRINCIPAL	
FAN'S NOTES, A	BURGESS MEREDITH	
FAR AND AWAY	BARBARA BABCOCK	
FAR AND AWAY	NICOLE KIDMAN	
FAR AND AWAY	TOM CRUISE	
FAR COUNTRY, THE	JAMES STEWART	
FAR COUNTRY, THE	KATHLEEN FREEMAN	
FAR COUNTRY, THE	ROYAL DANO	
FAR COUNTRY, THE (MS)	MICHAEL YORK	
FAR EAST	BRYON BROWN	
FAR FROM HOME	DREW BARRYMORE	
FAR FROM HOME	JENNIFER TILLY	
FAR FROM HOME	MATT FREWER	
FAR FROM HOME	RICHARD MASUR	
FAR FROM THE MADDING CROWD	ALAN BATES	
FAR FROM THE		
MADDING CROWD	JULIE CHRISTIE	
FAR FROM THE		
MADDING CROWD	TERENCE STAMP	
FAR HORIZONS, THE	BARBARA HALE	
FAR HORIZONS, THE	CHARLTON HESTON	
FAR NORTH	ANN WEDGEWORTH	
FAR NORTH	CHARLES DURNING	
FAR NORTH	DONALD MOFFAT	
FAR NORTH	JESSICA LANGE	
FAR NORTH	PATRICIA ARQUETTE	
FAR NORTH	TESS HARPER	
FAR OFF PLACE, A	ETHAN RANDALL	
FAR OFF PLACE, A	JACK THOMPSON	
FAR OFF PLACE, A	REESE WITHERSPOON	
FAR OUT MAN	C. THOMAS HOWELL	
FAR OUT MAN	JUDD NELSON	
FAR OUT MAN	MARTIN MULL	
FAR OUT MAN	MICHAEL WINSLOW	
FAR OUT MAN	PAUL BARTEL	
FAR OUT MAN	RAE DAWN CHONG	
FAR OUT MAN	THOMAS CHONG	
FAR PAVILIONS, THE (CMS)	AMY IRVING	
FAR PAVILIONS, THE (CMS)	BEN CROSS	
FAR PAVILIONS, THE (CMS)	JOHN GIELGUD	
FAREWELL MY CONCUBINE	GONG LI	
FAREWELL, MY LOVELY	ANTHONY ZERBE	
FAREWELL, MY LOVELY	CHARLOTTE RAMPLING	
FAREWELL, MY LOVELY	HARRY DEAN STANTON	
FAREWELL, MY LOVELY	JACK O'HALLORAN	
FAREWELL, MY LOVELY	JOHN IRELAND	
FAREWELL, MY LOVELY	ROBERT MITCHUM	
FAREWELL, MY LOVELY	SYLVESTER STALLONE	
FAREWELL, MY LOVELY ⊙	SYLVIA MILES	
FAREWELL TO ARMS, A	ELAINE STRITCH	
FAREWELL TO ARMS, A	HELEN HAYES	
FAREWELL TO ARMS, A	JENNIFER JONES	
FAREWELL		
TO ARMS, A	MERCEDES McCAMBRIDGE	
FAREWELL TO ARMS, A ⊙	VITTORIO DE SICA†	
FAREWELL TO THE KING	AKI ALEONG	
FAREWELL TO THE KING	CHOY CHANG WING	
FAREWELL TO THE KING	ELAN OBERON	
FAREWELL TO THE KING	FRANK McRAE	
FAREWELL TO THE KING	GERRY LOPEZ	
FAREWELL TO THE KING	JAMES FOX	
FAREWELL TO THE KING	JOHN BENNETT PERRY	
FAREWELL TO THE KING	MARILYN TOKUDA	
FAREWELL TO THE KING	MARIUS WEYERS	
FAREWELL TO THE KING	MICHAEL NISSMAN	
FAREWELL TO THE KING	NICK NOLTE	
FAREWELL TO THE KING	NIGEL HAYERS	
FAREWELL TO THE KING	RICHARD MORGAN	
FAREWELL TO THE KING	WAYNE PYGRAM	
FAREWELL TO THE KING	WILLIAM WISE	
FARMER, THE	MICHAEL DANTE	
FARMER TAKES A WIFE, THE	GWEN VERDON	
FARMER'S DAUGHTER, THE	SPALDING GRAY	
FARMER'S		
DAUGHTER, THE ⊙	CHARLES BICKFORD†	
FARMER'S DAUGHTER, THE	JAMES ARNESS	
FARMER'S DAUGHTER, THE	MARTHA RAYE†	
FARRELL FOR THE PEOPLE (TF)	STEVE INWOOD	
FASHIONS OF 1934	BETTE DAVIS†	
FAST AND FURIOUS	ANN SOTHERN	
FAST AND THE FURIOUS, THE	JOHN IRELAND	
FAST BREAK	LAURENCE FISHBURNE	
FAST CHARLIE, THE		
MOONBEAM RIDER	BRENDA VACCARO	
FAST COMPANIONS	MAUREEN O'SULLIVAN	
FAST COMPANY	HOWARD KEEL	
FAST COMPANY	JOHN SAXON	
FAST COMPANY	NINA FOCH	
FAST FOOD	TRACI LORDS	
FAST FORWARD	RICK ROSSOVICH	
FAST GETAWAY	KEN LERNER	
FAST LADY, THE	JULIE CHRISTIE	
FAST TIMES AT		
RIDGEMONT HIGH	ANTHONY EDWARDS	
FAST TIMES AT		
RIDGEMONT HIGH	BRIAN BACKER	
FAST TIMES AT RIDGEMONT HIGH	ERIC STOLTZ	
FAST TIMES AT		
RIDGEMONT HIGH	FOREST WHITAKER	
FAST TIMES AT		
RIDGEMONT HIGH	JAMES RUSSO	
FAST TIMES AT		
RIDGEMONT HIGH	JENNIFER JASON LEIGH	
FAST TIMES AT		
RIDGEMONT HIGH	JUDGE REINHOLD	
FAST TIMES AT		
RIDGEMONT HIGH	MARTIN BREST	
FAST TIMES AT		
RIDGEMONT HIGH	PAMELA SPRINGSTEEN	
FAST TIMES AT		
RIDGEMONT HIGH	PHOEBE CATES	
FAST TIMES AT		
RIDGEMONT HIGH	RAY WALSTON	
FAST TIMES AT		
RIDGEMONT HIGH	ROBERT ROMANUS	
FAST TIMES AT		
RIDGEMONT HIGH	SCOTT THOMSON	
FAST TIMES AT RIDGEMONT HIGH	SEAN PENN	
FAST -WALKING	TIMOTHY CAREY	
FAST-WALKING	JAMES WOODS	
FAST-WALKING	ROBERT HOOKS	
FAST-WALKING	SUSAN TYRRELL	
FASTEST GUN ALIVE, THE	JOHN DEHNER†	
FASTEST GUN ALIVE, THE	RUSS TAMBLYN	
FAT CHANCE	MICHAEL CONSTANTINE	
FAT CITY	CANDY CLARK	
FAT CITY	JEFF BRIDGES	
FAT CITY	STACY KEACH	
FAT CITY ⊙	SUSAN TYRRELL	
FAT MAN AND LITTLE BOY	BONNIE BEDELIA	
FAT MAN AND LITTLE BOY	DWIGHT SCHULTZ	
FAT MAN AND LITTLE BOY	JOHN C. McGINLEY	
FAT MAN AND LITTLE BOY	JOHN CUSACK	
FAT MAN AND LITTLE BOY	LAURA DERN	
FAT MAN AND		
LITTLE BOY	NATASHA RICHARDSON	
FAT MAN AND LITTLE BOY	PAUL NEWMAN	
FAT MAN AND LITTLE BOY	RON FRAZIER	
FAT MAN, THE	ROCK HUDSON†	
FAT SPY, THE	PHYLLIS DILLER	
FATAL ATTRACTION (1987)	ELLEN FOLEY	
FATAL		
ATTRACTION (1987)	ELLEN HAMILTON LATZEN	
FATAL ATTRACTION (1987)	FRED GWYNNE†	
FATAL ATTRACTION (1980)	JOHN HUSTON†	
FATAL ATTRACTION (1980)	LAWRENCE DANE	
FATAL ATTRACTION (1987)	MEG MUNDY	
FATAL ATTRACTION (1987)	MICHAEL DOUGLAS	
FATAL ATTRACTION (1980)	SALLY KELLERMAN	
FATAL ATTRACTION (1980)	STEPHEN LACK	
FATAL ATTRACTION (1987) ★	GLENN CLOSE	
FATAL ATTRACTION (1987) ⊙	ANNE ARCHER	
FATAL ATTRACTON (1987)	STUART PANKIN	
FATAL BEAUTY	MIKE JOLLY	
FATAL BEAUTY	SAM ELLIOTT	
FATAL BEAUTY	WHOOPI GOLDBERG	
FATAL BOND	LINDA BLAIR	
FATAL CONFESSION: A FATHER		
DOWLING MYSTERY (TF)	LESLIE NIELSEN	
FATAL CONFESSION: A FATHER		
DOWLING MYSTERY (TF)	MARY WICKES	
FATAL CONFESSION: A FATHER		
DOWLING MYSTERY (TF)	PETER SCOLARI	
FATAL CONFESSION: A FATHER		
DOWLING MYSTERY (TF)	SUSAN BLAKELY	
FATAL CONFESSION: A FATHER		
DOWLING MYSTERY (TF)	TOM BOSLEY	
FATAL CONFESSION: A FATHER		
DOWLING MYSTERY (TF)	TRACY NELSON	
FATAL DECEPTION: MRS. LEE		
HARVEY OSWALD (TF)	BILL BOLENDER	
FATAL DECEPTION: MRS. LEE		
HARVEY OSWALD (TF)	BRANDON SMITH	
FATAL DECEPTION: MRS. LEE HARVEY		
OSWALD (TF)	DEBORAH DAWN SLABODA	
FATAL DECEPTION: MRS. LEE		
HARVEY OSWALD (TF)	FRANK WHALEY	
FATAL DECEPTION: MRS. LEE HARVEY		
OSWALD (TF)	HELENA BONHAM CARTER	
FATAL DECEPTION: MRS. LEE HARVEY		
OSWALD (TF)	INGEBORGA DAPKUNAITE	
FATAL DECEPTION: MRS. LEE		
HARVEY OSWALD (TF)	RENEE WILSON	
FATAL DECEPTION: MRS. LEE		
HARVEY OSWALD (TF)	ROBERT PICARDO	
FATAL DESIRE	ANTHONY QUINN	
FATAL GAMES	SALLY KIRKLAND	
FATAL INSTINCT	ARMAND ASSANTE	
FATAL INSTINCT	KATE NELLIGAN	
FATAL INSTINCT	SEAN YOUNG	
FATAL INSTINCT	SHERILYN FENN	
FATAL INSTINCT	TONY RANDALL	
FATAL JUDGMENT (TF)	PATTY DUKE	
FATAL VISION (MS)	ANDY GRIFFITH	
FATAL VISION (MS)	EVA MARIE SAINT	
FATAL VISION (MS)	GARY COLE	
FATAL VISION (MS)	KARL MALDEN	
FATE IS THE HUNTER	MAX SHOWALTER	
FATE IS THE HUNTER	NEHEMIAH PERSOFF	
FATE IS THE HUNTER	SUZANNE PLESHETTE	
FATHER BROWN	ALEC GUINNESS	
FATHER CLEMENTS		
STORY, THE (TF)	LOUIS GOSSETT JR.	
FATHER CLEMENTS		
STORY, THE (TF)	MALCOLM JAMAL WARNER	
FATHER DOWLING MYSTERIES: THE		
MISSING BODY MYSTERY (TF)	TOM BOSLEY	
FATHER DOWLING MYSTERIES: THE		
MISSING BODY MYSTERY (TF)	TRACY NELSON	
FATHER FIGURE (TF)	HAL LINDEN	
FATHER GOOSE	LESLIE CARON	
FATHER HOOD	HALLE BERRY	
FATHER HOOD	PATRICK SWAYZE	
FATHER OF HELL TOWN (TF)	JAMES GAMMON	
FATHER OF HELL TOWN (TF)	ROBERT BLAKE	
FATHER OF		
THE BRIDE (1950) ★	SPENCER TRACY†	
FATHER OF		
THE BRIDE (1950)	ELIZABETH TAYLOR	
FATHER OF THE BRIDE (1950)	RUSS TAMBLYN	
FATHER OF THE BRIDE	DIANE KEATON	
FATHER OF THE BRIDE	GEORGE NEWBERN	
FATHER OF THE BRIDE	KIERAN CULKIN	
FATHER OF THE BRIDE	KIMBERLY WILLIAMS	
FATHER OF THE BRIDE	MARTIN SHORT	
FATHER OF THE BRIDE	STEVE MARTIN	
FATHER OF THE BRIDE 2	DIANE KEATON	
FATHER OF THE BRIDE 2	KIMBERLY WILLIAMS	
FATHER OF THE BRIDE 2	MARTIN SHORT	
FATHER OF THE BRIDE 2	STEVE MARTIN	
FATHER, SON AND		
THE MISTRESS (CTF)	GEORGE WYNER	

† after an actor's name denotes deceased.

I
N
D
E
X

O
F

F
I
L
M

T
I
T
L
E
S

FATHER, SON AND
THE MISTRESS (CTF) .... JACK LEMMON
FATHER, SON AND
THE MISTRESS (CTF) .... JOANNA GLEASON
FATHER, SON AND
THE MISTRESS (CTF) .... JONATHAN SILVERMAN
FATHER, SON AND
THE MISTRESS (CTF) .... MADELINE KAHN
FATHER, SON AND
THE MISTRESS (CTF) .... TALIA SHIRE
FATHER WAS A FULLBACK .... MAUREEN O'HARA
FATHER WAS A FULLBACK .... NATALIE WOOD†
FATHER'S LITTLE DIVIDEND ..... SPENCER TRACY†
FATHERLAND (CTF) .... RUTGER HAUER
FATHER'S
HOMECOMING, A (TF) .... JONATHAN WARD
FATHER'S LITTLE DIVIDEND .... ELIZABETH TAYLOR
FATHER'S LITTLE DIVIDEND .... RUSS TAMBLYN
FATHER'S REVENGE, A (TF) .... BRIAN DENNEHY
FATHER'S REVENGE, A (TF) .... JOANNA CASSIDY
FATHOM .... ANTHONY (TONY) FRANCIOSA
FATHOM .... RAQUEL WELCH
FATSO .... ANNE BANCROFT
FATSO .... DOM DeLUISE
FATTI DI GENTE
PERBENE .... CATHERINE DENEUVE
FAUSTINE AND THE
BEAUTIFUL SUMMER .... ISABELLE ADJANI
FAUSTINE AND THE
BEAUTIFUL SUMMER .... ISABELLE HUPPERT
FAUSTINE ET LE BEL ETÉ .... ISABELLE HUPPERT
FAVOR, THE .... BILL PULLMAN
FAVOR, THE .... BRAD PITT
FAVOR, THE .... ELIZABETH McGOVERN
FAVOR, THE .... HARLEY JANE KOZAK
FAVOR, THE .... KEN WAHL
FAVOR, THE .... LARRY MILLER
FAVOR, THE WATCH, AND THE
VERY BIG FISH, THE .... BOB HOSKINS
FAVOR, THE WATCH, AND THE
VERY BIG FISH, THE .... JEFF GOLDBLUM
FAVOR, THE WATCH, AND THE
VERY BIG FISH, THE................... MICHEL BLANC
FAVOR, THE WATCH, AND THE
VERY BIG FISH, THE....... NATASHA RICHARDSON
FAVORITE, THE .... ADRIAN PAUL
FAVORITE, THE .... BARBARA CARRERA
FAVORITE SON (MS) .... HARRY HAMLIN
FAVORITE SON (MS) .... JAMES WHITMORE
FAVORITE SON (MS) .... JOHN MAHONEY
FAVORITE SON (MS) .... LANCE GUEST
FAVORITE SON (MS) .... LINDA KOZLOWSKI
FAVORITE SON (MS) .... ROBERT LOGGIA
FBI GIRL .... RAYMOND BURR†
FBI STORY, THE .... JAMES STEWART
FBI STORY, THE .... VERA MILES
FEAR .... DARREN McGAVIN
FEAR (CTF) .... ALLY SHEEDY
FEAR (CTF) .... LAUREN HUTTON
FEAR AND DESIRE .... PAUL MAZURSKY
FEAR, ANXIETY AND
DEPRESSION .... ALEXANDRA GERSTEN
FEAR, ANXIETY AND DEPRESSION ...... JILL WISOFF
FEAR, ANXIETY AND
DEPRESSION .... MAX CANTOR
FEAR, ANXIETY AND
DEPRESSION .... STANLEY TUCCI
FEAR, ANXIETY AND
DEPRESSION .... TODD SOLONDZ
FEAR, ANXIETY AND
DEPRESSION .... JANE HAMPER
FEAR CITY .... BILLY DEE WILLIAMS
FEAR CITY .... JACK SCALIA
FEAR CITY .... JOE SANTOS
FEAR CITY .... MELANIE GRIFFITH
FEAR CITY .... MICHAEL V. GAZZO
FEAR CITY .... OLA RAY
FEAR CITY .... RAE DAWN CHONG
FEAR CITY .... TOM BERENGER
FEAR IN THE NIGHT .... DEFOREST KELLEY
FEAR IN THE NIGHT .... JOAN COLLINS
FEAR IS THE KEY .... JOHN VERNON

FEAR ON TRIAL (TF) .... GEORGE C. SCOTT
FEAR ON TRIAL (TF) .... JUDD HIRSCH
FEAR ON TRIAL (TF) .... LOIS NETTLETON
FEAR ON TRIAL (TF) .... WILLIAM DEVANE
FEAR STALK (TF) .... JILL CLAYBURGH
FEAR STALK (TF) .... STEPHEN MACHT
FEAR STRIKES OUT .... ANTHONY PERKINS†
FEAR STRIKES OUT .... KARL MALDEN
FEARLESS .... ISABELLA ROSSELLINI
FEARLESS .... JEFF BRIDGES
FEARLESS .... JOHN TURTURRO
FEARLESS .... TOM HULCE
FEARLESS FAGAN .... JANET LEIGH
FEARLESS FRANK .... JON VOIGHT
FEARLESS ○ .... ROSIE PEREZ
FEARLESS VAMPIRE KILLERS,
OR PARDON ME, BUT YOUR
TEETH ARE IN MY NECK, THE .... FIONA LEWIS
FEARLESS VAMPIRE KILLERS,
OR PARDON ME, BUT YOUR TEETH
ARE IN MY NECK, THE .... ROMAN POLANSKI
FEATHER IN HER HAT, A .... DAVID NIVEN†
FEDORA .... JOSE FERRER†
FEDORA .... MARTHE KELLER
FEDORA .... MICHAEL YORK
FEDS .... FRED DALTON THOMPSON
FEDS .... KEN MARSHALL
FEDS .... MARY GROSS
FEDS .... REBECCA DE MORNAY
FEED (FD) .... ARNOLD SCHWARZENEGGER
FEEL THE HEAT .... ROD STEIGER
FÉLICIE NANTEUIL .... LOUIS JOURDAN
FEMALE ARTILLERY (TF) .... LINDA EVANS
FEMALE ARTILLERY (TF) .... NINA FOCH
FEMALE INSTINCT (TF) .... HELEN HAYES
FEMALE JUNGLE .... LAWRENCE TIERNEY
FEMALE ON THE BEACH .... JOAN CRAWFORD†
FEMALE, THE .... LILA KEDROVA
FEMININE TOUCH, THE .... DON AMECHE†
FEMINIST AND THE
FUZZ, THE (TF) .... BARBARA EDEN
FEMINIST AND THE
FUZZ, THE (TF) .... FARRAH FAWCETT
FEMINIST AND THE
FUZZ, THE (TF) .... PENNY MARSHALL
FER DE LANCE (TF) .... HOPE LANGE
FERNGULLY...THE LAST
RAINFOREST (AF) .... CHRISTIAN SLATER
FERNGULLY...THE LAST
RAINFOREST (AF) .... ROBIN WILLIAMS
FERNGULLY...THE LAST
RAINFOREST (AF) .... SAMANTHA MATHIS
FERRIS BUELLER'S DAY OFF .... ALAN RUCK
FERRIS BUELLER'S DAY OFF .... CHARLIE SHEEN
FERRIS BUELLER'S DAY OFF .... CINDY PICKETT
FERRIS BUELLER'S DAY OFF .... DEL CLOSE
FERRIS BUELLER'S DAY OFF .... EDIE McCLURG
FERRIS BUELLER'S DAY OFF .... JEFFREY JONES
FERRIS BUELLER'S DAY OFF .... JENNIFER GREY
FERRIS BUELLER'S DAY OFF .... LYMAN WARD
FERRIS BUELLER'S
DAY OFF .... MATTHEW BRODERICK
FERRIS BUELLER'S DAY OFF .... MIA SARA
FERRIS BUELLER'S DAY OFF .... RICHARD EDSON
FEVER (CTF) .... ARMAND ASSANTE
FEVER (CTF) .... SAM NEILL
FEVER IN THE BLOOD, A .... ANGIE DICKINSON
FEVER IN THE BLOOD, A .... CARROLL O'CONNOR
FEVER IN THE BLOOD, A .... DON AMECHE†
FEVER IN THE BLOOD, A .... EFREM ZIMBALIST JR.
FEVER PITCH .... CHAD EVERETT
FEVER PITCH .... JOHN SAXON
FEVER PITCH .... RYAN O'NEAL
FEW DAYS WITH ME, A .... DANIEL AUTEUIL
FEW DAYS WITH ME, A .... DANIELLE DARRIEUX
FEW DAYS WITH ME, A .... DOMINIQUE LAVANANT
FEW DAYS WITH ME, A ..... JEAN-PIERRE MARIELLE
FEW DAYS WITH ME, A .... SANDRINE BONNAIRE
FEW DAYS WITH ME, A .... TANYA LOPERT
FEW GOOD MEN, A .... CHRISTOPHER GUEST
FEW GOOD MEN, A .... DEMI MOORE
FEW GOOD MEN, A .... J. T. WALSH

FEW GOOD MEN, A .... JAMES MARSHALL
FEW GOOD MEN, A .... KEVIN BACON
FEW GOOD MEN, A .... KEVIN POLLAK
FEW GOOD MEN, A .... KIEFER SUTHERLAND
FEW GOOD MEN, A .... TOM CRUISE
FEW GOOD MEN, A ○ .... JACK NICHOLSON
ffolkes .... ANTHONY PERKINS†
ffolkes .... DAVID HEDISON
ffolkes .... ROGER MOORE
FIDDLER ON THE ROOF ★ .... TOPOL
FIDDLER ON THE ROOF ○ .... LEONARD FREY†
FIELD OF DREAMS .... AMY MADIGAN
FIELD OF DREAMS .... BURT LANCASTER†
FIELD OF DREAMS .... DWIER BROWN
FIELD OF DREAMS .... FRANK WHALEY
FIELD OF DREAMS .... GABY HOFFMAN
FIELD OF DREAMS .... JAMES EARL JONES
FIELD OF DREAMS .... KEVIN COSTNER
FIELD OF DREAMS .... RAY LIOTTA
FIELD OF DREAMS .... TIMOTHY BUSFIELD
FIELD, THE .... BRENDA FRICKER
FIELD, THE .... FRANCES TOMELTY
FIELD, THE .... JOHN HURT
FIELD, THE .... SEAN BEAN
FIELD, THE .... TOM BERENGER
FIELD, THE ★ .... RICHARD HARRIS
FIENDISH PLOT OF DR.
FU MANCHU, THE .... SID CAESAR
FIENDISH PLOT OF DR.
FU MANCHU, THE .... BURT KWOUK
FIENDISH PLOT OF DR.
FU MANCHU, THE .... DAVID TOMLINSON
FIENDISH PLOT OF DR.
FU MANCHU, THE .... HELEN MIRREN
FIERCEST HEART, THE .... GERALDINE FITZGERALD
FIERCEST HEART, THE .... STUART WHITMAN
FIESTA .... CYD CHARISSE
FIESTA .... RICARDO MONTALBAN
FIFTH FLOOR, THE .... BO HOPKINS
FIFTH FLOOR, THE .... DIANNE HULL
FIFTH FLOOR, THE .... MEL FERRER
FIFTH FLOOR, THE .... PATTI D'ARBANVILLE
FIFTH MISSILE, THE (TF) .... DAVID SOUL
FIFTH MISSILE, THE (TF) .... ROBERT CONRAD
FIFTH MISSILE, THE (TF) .... SAM WATERSTON
FIFTH MUSKETEER, THE .... BEAU BRIDGES
FIFTH MUSKETEER, THE .... JOSE FERRER†
FIFTH MUSKETEER, THE .... LLOYD BRIDGES
FIFTH MUSKETEER, THE .... OLIVIA DE HAVILLAND
FIFTH MUSKETEER, THE .... SYLVIA KRISTEL
FIFTH MUSKETEER, THE .... URSULA ANDRESS
FIFTY ROADS TO TOWN .... ANN SOTHERN
FIFTY ROADS TO TOWN ....DON AMECHE†
FIGHT FOR
JENNY, A (TF) .... LESLEY ANN WARREN
FIGHT FOR LIFE (TF) .... MORGAN FREEMAN
FIGHT FOR LIFE (TF) .... PATTY DUKE
FIGHTER SQUADRON .... ROBERT STACK
FIGHTER SQUADRON .... ROCK HUDSON†
FIGHTER, THE (TF) .... STEVE INWOOD
FIGHTING BACK .... MICHAEL SARRAZIN
FIGHTING BACK .... TOM SKERRITT
FIGHTING
CHOICE, A (TF) .... DANIELLE von ZERNECK
FIGHTING FATHER DUNNE .... RAYMOND BURR†
FIGHTING MAD .... PETER FONDA
FIGHTING MAD .... SCOTT GLENN
FIGHTING PRINCE
OF DONEGAL, THE .... GORDAN JACKSON†
FIGURES IN A
LANDSCAPE .... MALCOLM McDOWELL
FILE ON THE GOLDEN
GOOSE, THE .... EDWARD WOODWARD
FILIPINA DREAM GIRLS (TF) .... DAVID THEWLIS
FINAL ANALYSIS .... AGUSTIN RODRIGUEZ
FINAL ANALYSIS .... ERIC ROBERTS
FINAL ANALYSIS .... KEITH DAVID
FINAL ANALYSIS .... KIM BASINGER
FINAL ANALYSIS .... PAUL GUILFOYLE
FINAL ANALYSIS .... RICHARD GERE
FINAL ANALYSIS .... ROBERT HARPER
FINAL ANALYSIS .... UMA THURMAN

FINAL ASSIGNMENT	BURGESS MEREDITH
FINAL ASSIGNMENT	COLLEEN DEWHURST†
FINAL ASSIGNMENT	GENEVIEVE BUJOLD
FINAL ASSIGNMENT	MICHAEL YORK
FINAL CHAPTER—WALKING TALL	BO SVENSON
FINAL COMEDOWN, THE	BILLY DEE WILLIAMS
FINAL COMEDOWN, THE	RAYMOND ST. JACQUES
FINAL CONFLICT, THE	SAM NEILL
FINAL COUNTDOWN, THE	CHARLES DURNING
FINAL COUNTDOWN, THE	JAMES FARENTINO
FINAL COUNTDOWN, THE	KATHERINE ROSS
FINAL COUNTDOWN, THE	KIRK DOUGLAS
FINAL COUNTDOWN, THE	MARTIN SHEEN
FINAL COUNTDOWN, THE	RON O'NEAL
FINAL DAYS (TF)	ED FLANDERS
FINAL DAYS (TF)	RICHARD KILEY
FINAL HOUR, THE	RALPH BELLAMY†
FINAL JEOPARDY (TF)	JEFF COREY
FINAL NOTICE (CTF)	DAVID OGDEN STIERS
FINAL NOTICE (CTF)	GIL GERARD
FINAL NOTICE (CTF)	LOUISE FLETCHER
FINAL NOTICE (CTF)	MELODY ANDERSON
FINAL OPTION, THE	EDWARD WOODWARD
FINAL OPTION, THE	JUDY DAVIS
FINAL OPTION, THE	RICHARD WIDMARK
FINAL TERROR, THE	ADRIAN ZMED
FINAL TERROR, THE	DARYL HANNAH
FINAL TERROR, THE	DARYL HANNAH
FINAL TERROR, THE	JOE PANTOLIANO
FINAL TERROR, THE	RACHEL WARD
FINAL TEST, THE	ROBERT MORLEY
FIND THE LADY	JOHN CANDY†
FIND THE LADY	LAWRENCE DANE
FINDERS KEEPERS	BEVERLY D'ANGELO
FINDERS KEEPERS	ED LAUTER
FINDERS KEEPERS	LOUIS GOSSETT JR.
FINDERS KEEPERS	MICHAEL O'KEEFE
FINDERS KEEPERS	PAMELA STEPHENSON
FINDING THE WAY HOME (TF)	GEORGE C. SCOTT
FINE MADNESS, A	COLLEEN DEWHURST†
FINE MADNESS, A	JOANNE WOODWARD
FINE MADNESS, A	PATRICK O'NEAL†
FINE MADNESS, A	SEAN CONNERY
FINE MADNESS, A	SUE ANE LANGDON
FINE MADNESS, A	ZOHRA LAMPERT
FINE MESS, A	HOWIE MANDELL
FINE MESS, A	JENNIFER EDWARDS
FINE MESS, A	MARIA CONCHITA ALONSO
FINE MESS, A	PAUL SORVINO
FINE MESS, A	RICHARD MULLIGAN
FINE MESS, A	RICK DUCOMMUN
FINE MESS, A	STUART MARGOLIN
FINE MESS, A	TED DANSON
FINE ROMANCE, A	JULIE ANDREWS
FINGER MAN	TIMOTHY CAREY
FINGERS	DANNY AIELLO
FINGERS	HARVEY KEITEL
FINGERS	JIM BROWN
FINIAN'S RAINBOW	FRED ASTAIRE†
FINNEGAN BEGIN AGAIN (CTF)	MARY TYLER MOORE
FINNEGAN BEGIN AGAIN (CTF)	SAM WATERSTON
FINNEGAN BEGIN AGAIN (CTF)	SYLVIA SIDNEY
FIORILE	CLAUDIO BIGAGLI
FIRE!	ERNEST BORGNINE
FIRE AND RAIN (CTF)	ANGIE DICKINSON
FIRE AND RAIN (CTF)	CHARLES HAID
FIRE AND RAIN (CTF)	DEAN JONES
FIRE AND RAIN (CTF)	JOHN BECK
FIRE BIRDS	NICOLAS CAGE
FIRE BIRDS	SEAN YOUNG
FIRE BIRDS	TOMMY LEE JONES
FIRE DOWN BELOW (1957)	JACK LEMMON
FIRE DOWN BELOW (1957)	ROBERT MITCHUM
FIRE DOWN BELOW (1995)	STEVEN SEAGAL
FIRE IN THE SKY	CRAIG SHEFFER
FIRE IN THE SKY	D. B. SWEENEY
FIRE IN THE SKY	HENRY THOMAS
FIRE IN THE SKY	JAMES GARNER
FIRE IN THE SKY	PETER BERG
FIRE IN THE SKY	ROBERT PATRICK
FIRE IN THE SKY, A (TF)	DAVID DUKES
FIRE IN THE SKY, A (TF)	ELIZABETH ASHLEY
FIRE ON THE AMAZON	CRAIG SHEFFER
FIRE ON THE AMAZON	SANDRA BULLOCK
FIRE ONE	DON AMECHE†
FIRE OVER AFRICA	MAUREEN O'HARA
FIRE SALE	ALAN ARKIN
FIRE SALE	SID CAESAR
FIRE SALE	VINCENT GARDENIA†
FIRE! (TF)	ERIK ESTRADA
FIRE! TRAPPED ON THE 37TH FLOOR (TF)	LEE MAJORS
FIRE WITH FIRE	CRAIG SHEFFER
FIRE WITH FIRE	D. B. SWEENEY
FIRE WITH FIRE	JEAN SMART
FIRE WITH FIRE	JEFF COHEN
FIRE WITH FIRE	JON POLITO
FIRE WITH FIRE	KATE REID
FIRE WITH FIRE	TIM RUSS
FIRE WITH FIRE	VIRGINIA MADSEN
FIREBALL 500	ANNETTE FUNICELLO
FIREBALL 500	FRANKIE AVALON
FIREBALL FORWARD (TF)	BEN GAZZARA
FIREBALL FORWARD (TF)	EDDIE ALBERT
FIREBALL, THE	MARILYN MONROE†
FIRECHASERS, THE (TF)	CHAD EVERETT
FIRECREEK	JAMES STEWART
FIRECREEK	LOUISE LATHAM
FIREFIGHTER (TF)	GUY BOYD
FIREFIGHTER (TF)	TERRY DAVID MULLIGAN
FIREFOX	CLINT EASTWOOD
FIREFOX	DIMITRA ARLYS
FIREFOX	FREDDIE JONES
FIREFOX	NIGEL HAWTHORNE
FIREFOX	RONALD LACEY
FIREHOUSE	JOHN ANDERSON
FIREHOUSE (TF)	PAUL LeMAT
FIREPOWER	ANTHONY (TONY) FRANCIOSA
FIREPOWER	BILLY BARTY
FIREPOWER	ELI WALLACH
FIREPOWER	GEORGE GRIZZARD
FIREPOWER	JAMES COBURN
FIREPOWER	O. J. SIMPSON
FIREPOWER	SOPHIA LOREN
FIREPOWER	VINCENT GARDENIA†
FIRES WITHIN	GRETA SCACCHI
FIRES WITHIN	JIMMY SMITS
FIRESTARTER	ART CARNEY
FIRESTARTER	DREW BARRYMORE
FIRESTARTER	FREDDIE JONES
FIRESTARTER	GEORGE C. SCOTT
FIRESTARTER	LOUISE FLETCHER
FIRESTARTER	MOSES GUNN
FIRESTORM: 72 HOURS IN OAKLAND (TF)	LeVAR BURTON
FIRESTORM: 72 HOURS IN OAKLAND (TF)	JILL CLAYBURGH
FIRESTORM: 72 HOURS IN OAKLAND (TF)	MICHAEL GROSS
FIREWALKER	CHUCK NORRIS
FIREWALKER	JOHN RHYS-DAVIES
FIREWALKER	LOUIS GOSSETT JR.
FIRM, THE	BARBARA GARRICK
FIRM, THE	DAVID STRATHAIRN
FIRM, THE	ED HARRIS
FIRM, THE	GARY BUSEY
FIRM, THE	GENE HACKMAN
FIRM, THE	HAL HOLBROOK
FIRM, THE	JEANNE TRIPPLEHORN
FIRM, THE	JERRY HARDIN
FIRM, THE	KARINA LOMBARD
FIRM, THE	STEVEN HILL
FIRM, THE	TERRY KINNEY
FIRM, THE	TOM CRUISE
FIRM, THE	WILFORD BRIMLEY
FIRM, THE ○	HOLLY HUNTER
FIRST AFFAIR (TF)	LORETTA SWIT
FIRST AFFAIR (TF)	MELISSA ANDERSON
FIRST BLOOD	BILL McKINNEY
FIRST BLOOD	BRIAN DENNEHY
FIRST BLOOD	RICHARD CRENNA
FIRST BLOOD	SYLVESTER STALLONE
FIRST DEADLY SIN, THE	ANTHONY ZERBE
FIRST DEADLY SIN, THE	BRENDA VACCARO
FIRST DEADLY SIN, THE	BRUCE WILLIS
FIRST DEADLY SIN, THE	DAVID DUKES
FIRST DEADLY SIN, THE	FAYE DUNAWAY
FIRST DEADLY SIN, THE	FRANK SINATRA
FIRST DEADLY SIN, THE	GEORGE COE
FIRST DEADLY SIN, THE	JAMES WHITMORE
FIRST FAMILY	AUSTIN PENDLETON
FIRST FAMILY	BOB DISHY
FIRST FAMILY	BOB NEWHART
FIRST FAMILY	BUCK HENRY
FIRST FAMILY	GILDA RADNER†
FIRST FAMILY	HARVEY KORMAN
FIRST FAMILY	JULIUS HARRIS
FIRST FAMILY	MADELINE KAHN
FIRST FAMILY	RICHARD BENJAMIN
FIRST FAMILY	RIP TORN
FIRST GREAT TRAIN ROBBERY, THE	BRIAN GLOVER
FIRST GREAT TRAIN ROBBERY, THE	BROOKE ADAMS
FIRST GREAT TRAIN ROBBERY, THE	DONALD SUTHERLAND
FIRST GREAT TRAIN ROBBERY, THE	LESLEY-ANNE DOWN
FIRST KNIGHT	BEN CROSS
FIRST KNIGHT	JULIA ORMOND
FIRST KNIGHT	RICHARD GERE
FIRST KNIGHT	SEAN CONNERY
FIRST LEGION, THE	WESLEY ADDY
FIRST LOVE	ANOUK AIMEE
FIRST LOVE	BEVERLY D'ANGELO
FIRST LOVE	JOHN HEARD
FIRST LOVE	ROBERT LOGGIA
FIRST LOVE	ROBERT STACK
FIRST LOVE	SUSAN DEY
FIRST LOVE	SWOOSIE KURTZ
FIRST LOVE	WILLIAM KATT
FIRST MONDAY IN OCTOBER	JILL CLAYBURGH
FIRST MONDAY IN OCTOBER	RICHARD BALIN
FIRST MONDAY IN OCTOBER	WALTER MATTHAU
FIRST NUDIE MUSICAL, THE	CINDY WILLIAMS
FIRST OF THE FEW, THE	DAVID NIVEN†
FIRST OFFENSE	JOHN MILLS
FIRST POWER, THE	ELIZABETH ARLEN
FIRST POWER, THE	JEFF KOBER
FIRST POWER, THE	LOU DIAMOND PHILLIPS
FIRST POWER, THE	MYKELTI WILLIAMSON
FIRST POWER, THE	TRACY GRIFFITH
FIRST STEPS (TF)	AMY STEEL
FIRST STEPS (TF)	FRANCES LEE McCAIN
FIRST STEPS (TF)	JUDD HIRSCH
FIRST STEPS (TF)	KIM DARBY
FIRST TIME, THE	BARBARA HALE
FIRST TIME, THE	JACQUELINE BISSET
FIRST TIME, THE	SHARON ACKER
FIRST TO FIGHT	CHAD EVERETT
FIRST TO FIGHT	CLAUDE AKINS†
FIRST TO FIGHT	GENE HACKMAN
FIRST TRAVELING SALESLADY, THE	CLINT EASTWOOD
FIRST TRAVELLING SALESLADY, THE	JAMES ARNESS
FIRST YANK INTO TOKYO	BARBARA HALE
FIRST, YOU CRY (TF)	ANTHONY PERKINS†
FIRST, YOU CRY (TF)	JENNIFER WARREN
FIRST, YOU CRY (TF)	MARY TYLER MOORE
FIRSTBORN	CHRISTOPHER COLLET
FIRSTBORN	COREY HAIM
FIRSTBORN	PETER WELLER
FIRSTBORN	ROBERT DOWNEY JR.
FIRSTBORN	SARAH JESSICA PARKER
FIRSTBORN	TERI GARR
FISH CALLED WANDA, A	JAMIE LEE CURTIS
FISH CALLED WANDA, A	JOHN CLEESE
FISH CALLED WANDA, A	MICHAEL PALIN
FISH CALLED WANDA, A ○○	KEVIN KLINE
FISH THAT SAVED PITTSBURGH, THE	JONATHAN WINTERS
FISH THAT SAVED PITTSBURGH, THE	STOCKARD CHANNING

† after an actor's name denotes deceased.

FISHER KING, THE .... AMANDA PLUMMER
FISHER KING, THE .... JEFF BRIDGES
FISHER KING, THE .... KATHY NAJIMY
FISHER KING, THE .... MICHAEL JETER
FISHER KING, THE ★ .... ROBIN WILLIAMS
FISHER KING, THE ∞ .... MERCEDES RUEHL
FIST OF FEAR, TOUCH
  OF DEATH .... FRED WILLIAMSON
FISTFUL OF
  CHOPSTICKS, A .... MARGAUX HEMINGWAY
FISTFUL OF DOLLARS, A .... CLINT EASTWOOD
FISTFUL OF DYNAMITE, A .... ROD STEIGER
FITZCARRALDO .... KLAUS KINSKI†
FITZWILLY .... DICK VAN DYKE
FITZWILLY .... JOHN FIELDLER
FITZWILLY .... SAM WATERSTON
FIVE AGAINST THE HOUSE .... BRIAN KEITH
FIVE AGAINST THE HOUSE .... KIM NOVAK
FIVE BRANDED WOMEN .... HARRY GUARDINO
FIVE BRANDED WOMEN .... STEVE FORREST
FIVE BRANDED WOMEN .... VERA MILES
FIVE CARD STUD .... DEAN MARTIN
FIVE CARD STUD .... RODDY McDOWALL
FIVE CARD STUD .... YAPHET KOTTO
FIVE CORNERS .... ELIZABETH BERRIDGE
FIVE CORNERS .... GREGORY ROZAKIS†
FIVE CORNERS .... JODIE FOSTER
FIVE CORNERS .... JOHN TURTURRO
FIVE CORNERS .... MICHAEL MANTELL
FIVE CORNERS .... RODNEY HARVEY
FIVE CORNERS .... TIM ROBBINS
FIVE CORNERS .... TODD GRAFF
FIVE DAYS FROM HOME .... GEORGE PEPPARD†
FIVE DAYS ONE SUMMER .... SEAN CONNERY
FIVE DESPERATE WOMEN (TF) ..... JOAN HACKETT†
FIVE DESPERATE
  WOMEN (TF) .... ROBERT CONRAD
FIVE EASY PIECES .... FANNIE FLAGG
FIVE EASY PIECES .... LOIS SMITH
FIVE EASY PIECES .... SUSAN ANSPACH
FIVE EASY PIECES ★ .... JACK NICHOLSON
FIVE EASY PIECES ⊙ .... KAREN BLACK
FIVE FINGER EXERCISE .... MAXIMILIAN SCHELL
FIVE GATES TO HELL .... SHIRLEY KNIGHT
FIVE GOLDEN HOURS .... CYD CHARISSE
FIVE GOLDEN HOURS .... RON MOODY
FIVE HEARTBEATS, THE ..... ANNE MARIE JOHNSON
FIVE HEARTBEATS, THE .... CHUCK PATTERSON
FIVE HEARTBEATS, THE .... DIAHANN CARROLL
FIVE HEARTBEATS, THE .... HAROLD NICHOLAS
FIVE HEARTBEATS, THE .... HARRY J. LENNIX
FIVE HEARTBEATS, THE ...... HAWTHORNE JAMES
FIVE HEARTBEATS, THE .... LEON
FIVE HEARTBEATS, THE .... MICHAEL WRIGHT
FIVE HEARTBEATS, THE .... ROBERT TOWNSEND
FIVE HEARTBEATS, THE .... THERESA RANDLE
FIVE HEARTBEATS, THE .... TICO WELLS
FIVE MAN ARMY, THE .... PETER GRAVES
FIVE MILES TO MIDNIGHT .... ANTHONY PERKINS†
FIVE MILES TO MIDNIGHT .... SOPHIA LOREN
FIVE MINUTES TO LIVE .... JOHNNY CASH
FIVE MINUTES TO LIVE .... RON HOWARD
FIVE PENNIES, THE .... BOB HOPE
FIVE PENNIES, THE .... DANNY KAYE†
FIVE PENNIES, THE .... HARRY GUARDINO
FIVE PENNIES, THE .... LOUIS ARMSTRONG†
FIVE PENNIES, THE .... TUESDAY WELD
FIVE SAVAGE MEN .... HENRY SILVA
FIVE STAR FINAL .... EDWARD G. ROBINSON†
FIVE WEEKS IN A BALLOON .... BARBARA EDEN
FIVE WEEKS IN A BALLOON .... RED BUTTONS
FIXED BAYONETS .... JAMES DEAN†
FIXER, THE .... DAVID WARNER
FIXER, THE .... IAN HOLM
FIXER, THE ★ .... ALAN BATES
FJOLS TIL FJELLS .... LIV ULLMANN
FLAME .... TOM CONTI
FLAME AND THE
  ARROW, THE .... BURT LANCASTER†
FLAME AND THE ARROW, THE .... NORMAN LLOYD
FLAME AND THE FLESH .... LANA TURNER
FLAME IS LOVE, THE (TF) .... LINDA PURL

FLAME OF ARABY .... MAUREEN O'HARA
FLAME OF ARABY .... ROYAL DANO
FLAME OF THE ISLANDS .... JAMES ARNESS
FLAME OF THE ISLANDS .... YVONNE DE CARLO
FLAME OVER INDIA .... LAUREN BACALL
FLAME TREES OF
  THIKA, THE (TF) .... HAYLEY MILLS
FLAME WITHIN, THE .... MAUREEN O'SULLIVAN
FLAMING STAR .... BARBARA EDEN
FLAMING STAR .... ELVIS PRESLEY†
FLAMING STAR .... STEVE FORREST
FLAMINGO KID, THE .... BRONSON PINCHOT
FLAMINGO KID, THE .... CAROLE DAVIS
FLAMINGO KID, THE .... HECTOR ELIZONDO
FLAMINGO KID, THE .... JOHN TURTURRO
FLAMINGO KID, THE .... MARISA TOMEI
FLAMINGO KID, THE .... MATT DILLON
FLAMINGO KID, THE .... RICHARD CRENNA
FLAMINGO ROAD .... JOAN CRAWFORD†
FLAMINGO ROAD (TF) .... MARK HARMON
FLAMINGO ROAD (TF) .... MORGAN FAIRCHILD
FLANAGAN .... PHILIP BOSCO
FLAP .... ANTHONY QUINN
FLAP .... CLAUDE AKINS†
FLAP .... SHELLEY WINTERS
FLAP .... TONY BILL
FLAREUP .... RAQUEL WELCH
FLASH GORDON .... BRIAN BLESSED
FLASH GORDON .... MAX von SYDOW
FLASH GORDON .... TIMOTHY DALTON
FLASH GORDON .... TOPOL
FLASH OF GREEN, A .... BLAIR BROWN
FLASH OF GREEN, A .... ED HARRIS
FLASHBACK .... CAROL KANE
FLASHBACK .... CLIFF DE YOUNG
FLASHBACK .... DENNIS HOPPER
FLASHBACK .... KIEFER SUTHERLAND
FLASHBACK .... MICHAEL McKEAN
FLASHBACK .... PAUL DOOLEY
FLASHBACK .... RICHARD MASUR
FLASHDANCE .... BELINDA BAUER
FLASHDANCE .... JENNIFER BEALS
FLASHDANCE .... KYLE T. HEFFNER
FLASHDANCE .... LILIA SKALA
FLASHDANCE .... MICHAEL NOURI
FLASHPOINT .... JEAN SMART
FLASHPOINT .... KEVIN CONWAY
FLASHPOINT .... KRIS KRISTOFFERSON
FLASHPOINT .... MIGUEL FERRER
FLASHPOINT .... RIP TORN
FLASHPOINT .... RIP TORN
FLASHPOINT .... ROBERTS BLOSSOM
FLASHPOINT .... TESS HARPER
FLASHPOINT .... TREAT WILLIAMS
FLATBED ANNIE & SWEETIE PIE:
  LADY TRUCKERS (TF) .... KIM DARBY
FLATLINERS .... JULIA ROBERTS
FLATLINERS .... KEVIN BACON
FLATLINERS .... KIEFER SUTHERLAND
FLATLINERS .... OLIVER PLATT
FLATLINERS .... WILLIAM BALDWIN
FLEA IN HER EAR, A .... LOUIS JOURDAN
FLEET'S IN, THE .... DOROTHY LAMOUR
FLESH .... JOE DALLESANDRO
FLESH .... PATTI D'ARBANVILLE
FLESH AND BLOOD (TF) .... SUZANNE PLESHETTE
FLESH AND BLOOD (TF) .... TOM BERENGER
FLESH + BLOOD .... JACK THOMPSON
FLESH + BLOOD .... JENNIFER JASON LEIGH
FLESH + BLOOD .... PATRICK MacNEE
FLESH + BLOOD .... RUTGER HAUER
FLESH + BLOOD .... SUSAN TYRRELL
FLESH + BLOOD .... TOM BURLINSON
FLESH AND BONE .... DENNIS QUAID
FLESH AND BONE .... GWYNETH PALTROW
FLESH AND BONE .... JAMES CAAN
FLESH AND BONE .... MEG RYAN
FLESH AND BULLETS .... YVONNE DE CARLO
FLESH AND FANTASY .... BARBARA STANWYCK†
FLESH AND FLAME .... DEAN JONES
FLESH AND FURY .... HARRY GUARDINO
FLESH AND FURY .... TONY CURTIS

FLESH AND THE FIENDS .... DONALD PLEASENCE
FLESH FOR FRANKENSTEIN .... JOE DALLESANDRO
FLESH OF THE ORCHID ..... CHARLOTTE RAMPLING
FLETCH .... CHEVY CHASE
FLETCH .... DANA WHEELER-NICHOLSON
FLETCH .... GEENA DAVIS
FLETCH .... GEORGE WENDT
FLETCH .... JOE DON BAKER
FLETCH .... M. EMMET WALSH
FLETCH .... RICHARD LIBERTINI
FLETCH .... TIM MATHESON
FLETCH LIVES .... CHEVY CHASE
FLETCH LIVES .... CLEAVON LITTLE†
FLETCH LIVES .... GEOFFREY LEWIS
FLETCH LIVES .... GEORGE WYNER
FLETCH LIVES .... HAL HOLBROOK
FLETCH LIVES .... JULIANNE PHILLIPS
FLETCH LIVES .... LEE ERMEY
FLETCH LIVES .... PATRICIA KALEMBER
FLETCH LIVES .... PHIL HARTMAN
FLETCH LIVES .... RANDALL (TEX) COBB
FLETCH LIVES .... RICHARD BELZER
FLETCH LIVES .... RICHARD LIBERTINI
FLIC STORY .... CLAUDINE AUGER
FLIGHT 90: DISASTER ON
  THE POTOMAC (TF) .... STEPHEN MACHT
FLIGHT ANGELS .... JANE WYMAN
FLIGHT ANGELS .... RALPH BELLAMY†
FLIGHT FROM ASHIYA .... RICHARD WIDMARK
FLIGHT FROM ASHIYA .... SHIRLEY KNIGHT
FLIGHT FROM
  DESTINY .... GERALDINE FITZGERALD
FLIGHT OF THE DOVE .... LANE SMITH
FLIGHT OF THE DOVE .... SCOTT GLENN
FLIGHT OF THE DOVE .... THERESA RUSSELL
FLIGHT OF THE DOVES .... RON MOODY
FLIGHT OF THE INTRUDER .... BRAD JOHNSON
FLIGHT OF THE INTRUDER ...... CHRISTOPHER RICH
FLIGHT OF THE INTRUDER .... DANN FLOREK
FLIGHT OF THE INTRUDER .... DANNY GLOVER
FLIGHT OF THE INTRUDER ...... DOUGLAS ROBERTS
FLIGHT OF THE
  INTRUDER ....J. KENNETH CAMPBELL
FLIGHT OF THE INTRUDER .... JARED CHANDLER
FLIGHT OF THE INTRUDER .... JUSTIN WILLIAMS
FLIGHT OF THE INTRUDER .... MADISON MASON
FLIGHT OF THE INTRUDER .... MIKE JOLLY
FLIGHT OF THE
  INTRUDER .... ROSANNA ARQUETTE
FLIGHT OF THE
  INTRUDER .... SCOTT NEWTON STEVENS
FLIGHT OF THE INTRUDER .... TOM SIZEMORE
FLIGHT OF THE INTRUDER .... WILLEM DAFOE
FLIGHT OF THE INTRUDER .... YING RHAMES
FLIGHT OF THE NAVIGATOR .... CLIFF DE YOUNG
FLIGHT OF THE NAVIGATOR .... CLIFF DE YOUNG
FLIGHT OF THE
  NAVIGATOR .... HOWARD HESSEMAN
FLIGHT OF THE NAVIGATOR .... JOEY CRAMER
FLIGHT OF THE NAVIGATOR .... MATT ADLER
FLIGHT OF THE NAVIGATOR .... PAUL REUBENS
FLIGHT OF THE
  NAVIGATOR .... SARAH JESSICA PARKER
FLIGHT OF THE
  NAVIGATOR .... VERONICA CARTWRIGHT
FLIGHT OF THE
  PHOENIX, THE .... ERNEST BORGNINE
FLIGHT OF THE
  PHOENIX, THE .... GEORGE KENNEDY
FLIGHT OF THE PHOENIX, THE .... JAMES STEWART
FLIGHT OF THE PHOENIX, THE ⊙ .... IAN BANNEN
FLIGHT OF THE SPRUCE
  GOOSE, THE .... DENNIS CHRISTOPHER
FLIGHT TO FURY .... JACK NICHOLSON
FLIGHT TO HONG KONG .... RORY CALHOUN
FLIGHT TO TANGIER .... JACK PALANCE
FLIM FLAM MAN, THE .... ALICE GHOSTLEY
FLIM-FLAM MAN, THE .... ALBERT SALMI†
FLIM-FLAM MAN, THE .... GEORGE C. SCOTT
FLIM-FLAM MAN, THE .... HARRY MORGAN
FLIM-FLAM MAN, THE .... MICHAEL SARRAZIN
FLINTSTONES, THE .... ELAINE MELANIE SILVER

FLINTSTONES, THE	ELIZABETH PERKINS	
FLINTSTONES, THE	ELIZABETH TAYLOR	
FLINTSTONES, THE	HALLE BERRY	
FLINTSTONES, THE	JAY LENO	
FLINTSTONES, THE	JOHN GOODMAN	
FLINTSTONES, THE	KYLE MacLACHLAN	
FLINTSTONES, THE	LARAINE NEWMAN	
FLINTSTONES, THE	RICK DEES	
FLINTSTONES, THE	RICK MORANIS	
FLINTSTONES, THE	ROSIE O'DONNELL	
FLIPPER	CHUCK CONNORS†	
FLOOD! (TF)	BARBARA HERSHEY	
FLOOD! (TF)	CAROL LYNLEY	
FLOOD! (TF)	TERESA WRIGHT	
FLOODS OF FEAR	HOWARD KEEL	
FLOR DE MAYO	JACK PALANCE	
FLORENCE NIGHTINGALE (TF)	CLAIRE BLOOM	
FLORENCE NIGHTINGALE (TF)	JACLYN SMITH	
FLORENCE NIGHTINGALE (TF)	TIMOTHY DALTON	
FLORIDA STRAITS (CTF)	RAUL JULIA†	
FLOWER DRUM SONG	JAMES SHIGETA	
FLOWER WITH THE DEADLY		
STING, THE	CARROLL BAKER	
FLOWERS IN THE ATTIC	LOUISE FLETCHER	
FLUFFY	SHIRLEY JONES	
FLUFFY	TONY RANDALL	
FLUKE	BILL COBBS	
FLUKE	CLARINDA ROSS	
FLUKE	COLLIN WILCOX PAXTON	
FLUKE	ERIC STOLTZ	
FLUKE	FREDERICO PACIFICI	
FLUKE	JON POLITO	
FLUKE	MATTHEW MODINE	
FLUKE	MAX POMERANC	
FLUKE	NANCY TRAVIS	
FLUKE	RON PERLMAN	
FLY, THE (1958)	KATHLEEN FREEMAN	
FLY, THE (1958)	VINCENT PRICE†	
FLY, THE	DAVID CRONENBERG	
FLY, THE	DAVID HEDISON	
FLY, THE	GEENA DAVIS	
FLY, THE	JEFF GOLDBLUM	
FLY, THE	JOHN GETZ	
FLY, THE	JOY BOUSHEL	
FLY, THE	LES CARLSON	
FLY II, THE	ANN MARIE LEE	
FLY II, THE	DAPHNE ZUNIGA	
FLY II, THE	ERIC STOLTZ	
FLY II, THE	FRANK TURNER	
FLY II, THE	GARY CHALK	
FLY II, THE	HARLEY CROSS	
FLY II, THE	JOHN GETZ	
FLY II, THE	LEE RICHARDSON	
FLY II, THE	MATTHEW MOORE	
FLY II, THE	SAFFRON HENDERSON	
FLYING	KEANU REEVES	
FLYING DEVILS	RALPH BELLAMY†	
FLYING DOWN TO RIO	FRED ASTAIRE†	
FM	ALEXIS KARRAS	
FM	CASSIE YATES	
FM	CLEAVON LITTLE†	
FM	EILEEN BRENNAN	
FM	JAMES KEACH	
FM	LINDA RONSTADT	
FM	MARTIN MULL	
FM	MICHAEL BRANDON	
FM	NORMAN LLOYD	
FOG, THE	ADRIENNE BARBEAU	
FOG, THE	HAL HOLBROOK	
FOG, THE	JAMIE LEE CURTIS	
FOG, THE	JANET LEIGH	
FOG OVER FRISCO	BETTE DAVIS†	
FOLIES BERGERE	ANN SOTHERN	
FOLIES BOURGEOISES	ANN-MARGRET	
FOLIES BOURGEOISES	BRUCE DERN	
FOLIES BOURGEOISES	MARIA SCHELL	
FOLKS	DON AMECHE†	
FOLKS	TOM SELLECK	
FOLLOW A STAR	RON MOODY	
FOLLOW ME!	MIA FARROW	
FOLLOW ME	TOPOL	
FOLLOW ME, BOYS!	KURT RUSSELL	
FOLLOW ME, BOYS!	LILLIAN GISH†	
FOLLOW ME, BOYS!	VERA MILES	
FOLLOW THAT DREAM	ELVIS PRESLEY†	
FOLLOW THAT HORSE!	DAVID TOMLINSON	
FOLLOW THE BAND	ROBERT MITCHUM	
FOLLOW THE BOYS	DINAH SHORE†	
FOLLOW THE BOYS	PAULA PRENTISS	
FOLLOW THE BOYS	RUSS TAMBLYN	
FOLLOW THE FLEET	LUCILLE BALL†	
FOLLOW YOUR		
HEART (TF)	FRANCES STERNHAGEN	
FOLLOW YOUR HEART (TF)	PATRICK CASSIDY	
FOLLY OF ANNE, THE	LILLIAN GISH†	
FOOD OF THE GODS	MARJOE GORTNER	
FOOL, THE	ELEANOR BRON	
FOOL FOR LOVE	HARRY DEAN STANTON	
FOOL FOR LOVE	KIM BASINGER	
FOOL FOR LOVE	RANDY QUAID	
FOOL FOR LOVE	SAM SHEPARD	
FOOL KILLER, THE	ANTHONY PERKINS†	
FOOL KILLER, THE	EDWARD ALBERT	
FOOL KILLER, THE	SALOME JENS	
FOOLIN' AROUND	ANNETTE O'TOOLE	
FOOLIN' AROUND	CLORIS LEACHMAN	
FOOLIN' AROUND	EDDIE ALBERT	
FOOLIN' AROUND	GARY BUSEY	
FOOLIN' AROUND	TONY RANDALL	
FOOLS	JASON ROBARDS	
FOOLS	JOANNA CASSIDY	
FOOLS	KATHERINE ROSS	
FOOLS FOR SCANDAL	JANE WYMAN	
FOOLS FOR SCANDAL	RALPH BELLAMY†	
FOOLS OF FORTUNE	IAIN GLEN	
FOOLS OF FORTUNE	JULIE CHRISTIE	
FOOLS OF		
FORTUNE	MARY ELIZABETH MASTRANTONIO	
FOOLS' PARADE	DAVID HUDDLESTON	
FOOLS' PARADE	GEORGE KENNEDY	
FOOLS' PARADE	JAMES STEWART	
FOOLS' PARADE	KURT RUSSELL	
FOOLS' PARADE	WILLIAM WINDOM	
FOOTLIGHT SERENADE	JANE WYMAN	
FOOTLOOSE	CHRIS PENN	
FOOTLOOSE	DIANNE WIEST	
FOOTLOOSE	FRANCES LEE McCAIN	
FOOTLOOSE	JIM YOUNGS	
FOOTLOOSE	JOHN LITHGOW	
FOOTLOOSE	KEVIN BACON	
FOOTLOOSE	LORI SINGER	
FOOTLOOSE	SARAH JESSICA PARKER	
FOOTSTEPS IN THE DARK	RALPH BELLAMY†	
FOOTSTEPS IN THE FOG	JEAN SIMMONS	
FOOTSTEPS (TF)	CLU GULAGER	
FOOTSTEPS (TF)	NED BEATTY	
FOR A FEW DOLLARS MORE	CLINT EASTWOOD	
FOR BETTER, FOR WORSE	EILEEN HECKART	
FOR BETTER, FOR WORSE	GENE HACKMAN	
FOR BETTER,		
FOR WORSE	HARRY DEAN STANTON	
FOR BETTER, FOR WORSE	JOE SANTOS	
FOR BETTER, FOR WORSE	LIV ULLMANN	
FOR BETTER, FOR WORSE	SAM BOTTOMS	
FOR BETTER, FOR WORSE	SUSAN TYRRELL	
FOR KEEPS	CONCHATA FERRELL	
FOR KEEPS	HAILEY ELLEN AGNEW	
FOR KEEPS	KENNETH MARS	
FOR KEEPS	MIRIAM FLYNN	
FOR KEEPS	MOLLY RINGWALD	
FOR KEEPS	RANDALL BATINKOFF	
FOR KEEPS	SHARON BROWN	
FOR LADIES ONLY (TF)	GREGORY HARRISON	
FOR LADIES ONLY (TF)	LEE GRANT	
FOR LOVE OF IVY	BEAU BRIDGES	
FOR LOVE OF IVY	CARROLL O'CONNOR	
FOR LOVE OF IVY	JENNIFER O'NEILL	
FOR LOVE OF IVY	SIDNEY POITIER	
FOR LOVE OR MONEY	ANTHONY HIGGINS	
FOR LOVE OR MONEY	BOB BALABAN	
FOR LOVE OR MONEY	GABRIELLE ANWAR	
FOR LOVE OR MONEY	ISAAC MIZRAHI	
FOR LOVE OR MONEY	JULIE NEWMAR	
FOR LOVE OR MONEY	KIRK DOUGLAS	
FOR LOVE OR MONEY	MICHAEL J. FOX	
FOR LOVE OR MONEY	MICHAEL TUCKER	
FOR LOVE OR MONEY	UDO KIER	
FOR LOVE OR MONEY	WILLIAM WINDOM	
FOR LOVE OR MONEY (TF)	GIL GERARD	
FOR LOVE OR MONEY (TF)	JAMIE FARR	
FOR LOVE OR MONEY (TF)	RAY WALSTON	
FOR ME AND MY GAL	GENE KELLY	
FOR MEN ONLY	VERA MILES	
FOR PETE'S SAKE	ANN RAMSEY†	
FOR PETE'S SAKE	BILL McKINNEY	
FOR PETE'S SAKE	WILLIAM REDFIELD†	
FOR PETE'S SAKE	BARBRA STREISAND	
FOR PETE'S SAKE	ESTELLE PARSONS	
FOR PETE'S SAKE	JOE PANTOLIANO	
FOR PETE'S SAKE	MICHAEL SARRAZIN	
FOR QUEEN AND		
COUNTRY	DENZEL WASHINGTON	
FOR RICHER, FOR		
POORER (CTF)	GEORGE WYNER	
FOR RICHER, FOR POORER (CTF)	JACK LEMMON	
FOR RICHER, FOR		
POORER (CTF)	JOANNA GLEASON	
FOR RICHER, FOR		
POORER (CTF)	JONATHAN SILVERMAN	
FOR RICHER, FOR		
POORER (CTF)	MADELINE KAHN	
FOR RICHER, FOR POORER (CTF)	TALIA SHIRE	
FOR SINGLES ONLY	JOHN SAXON	
FOR SINGLES ONLY	MILTON BERLE	
FOR SINGLES ONLY	PETER MARK RICHMAN	
FOR THE BOYS	ARLISS HOWARD	
FOR THE BOYS	CHRIS RYDELL	
FOR THE BOYS	GEORGE SEGAL	
FOR THE BOYS	JACK SHELDON	
FOR THE BOYS	JAMES CAAN	
FOR THE BOYS	MELISSA MANCHESTER	
FOR THE BOYS	NORMAN FELL	
FOR THE BOYS ★	BETTE MIDLER	
FOR THE LOVE OF BENJI	ED NELSON	
FOR THE LOVE OF BENJI	PETER BOWLES	
FOR THE LOVE OF IT (TF)	TOM BOSLEY	
FOR THE TERM OF HIS		
NATURAL LIFE (TF)	ANTHONY PERKINS†	
FOR THOSE WHO		
THINK YOUNG	ELLEN BURSTYN	
FOR THOSE WHO THINK YOUNG	PAUL LYNDE†	
FOR THOSE WHO THINK YOUNG	TINA LOUISE	
FOR WHOM THE		
BELL TOLLS	YVONNE DE CARLO	
FOR WHOM THE		
BELL TOLLS ★	GARY COOPER†	
FOR WHOM THE		
BELL TOLLS ★	INGRID BERGMAN†	
FOR WHOM THE		
BELL TOLLS O	AKIM TAMIROFF†	
FOR WHOM THE		
BELL TOLLS OO	KATINA PAXINOU†	
FOR YOUR EYES ONLY	CAROLE BOUQUET	
FOR YOUR EYES ONLY	CHARLES DANCE	
FOR YOUR EYES ONLY	GEOFFREY KEEN	
FOR YOUR EYES ONLY	JACK HEDLEY	
FOR YOUR EYES ONLY	JULIAN GLOVER	
FOR YOUR EYES ONLY	LYNN-HOLLY JOHNSON	
FOR YOUR EYES ONLY	ROGER MOORE	
FOR YOUR EYES ONLY	TOPOL	
FOR YOUR EYES ONLY	WALTER GOTELL	
FORBIDDEN	BARBARA STANWYCK†	
FORBIDDEN	MEL FERRER	
FORBIDDEN	RALPH BELLAMY†	
FORBIDDEN	TONY CURTIS	
FORBIDDEN (CTF)	JACQUELINE BISSET	
FORBIDDEN DANCE, THE	JEFF JAMES	
FORBIDDEN DANCE, THE	LAURA HERRING	
FORBIDDEN DANCE, THE	RICHARD LYNCH	
FORBIDDEN DANCE, THE	SID HAIG	
FORBIDDEN NIGHTS (TF)	MELISSA GILBERT	
FORBIDDEN NIGHTS (TF)	VICTOR WONG	
FORBIDDEN PLANET	EARL HOLLIMAN	
FORBIDDEN PLANET	LESLIE NIELSEN	
FORBIDDEN PLANET	RICHARD ANDERSON	
FORBIDDEN STREET, THE	MAUREEN O'HARA	

Fl-Fo

FILM
ACTORS
GUIDE

INDEX OF FILM TITLES

451

† after an actor's name denotes deceased.

INDEX OF FILM TITLES

FORBIDDEN ZONE .... SUSAN TYRRELL
FORBIN PROJECT, THE .... GEORG STANFORD BROWN
FORBIN PROJECT, THE .... SUSAN CLARK
FORBUSH AND THE PENGUINS .... HAYLEY MILLS
FORCE 10 FROM NAVARONE .... BARBARA BACH
FORCE 10 FROM NAVARONE .... CARL WEATHERS
FORCE 10 FROM NAVARONE .... FRANCO NERO
FORCE 10 FROM NAVARONE .... HARRISON FORD
FORCE 10 FROM NAVARONE .... RICHARD KIEL
FORCE OF EVIL .... BEAU BRIDGES
FORCE OF ONE, A .... CLU GULAGER
FORCE OF ONE, A .... JENNIFER O'NEILL
FORCE OF ONE, A .... RON O'NEAL
FORCED EXPOSURE .... ART EVANS
FORCED EXPOSURE .... MICHAEL NADER
FORCED LANDING .... EVA GABOR
FORCED VENGEANCE .... CHUCK NORRIS
FOREIGN BODY .... AMANDA DONOHOE
FOREIGN BODY .... DENIS QUILLEY
FOREIGN BODY .... VICTOR BANERJEE
FOREIGN CORRESPONDENT ✪ .... ALBERT BASSERMAN†
FOREIGN INTRIGUE .... ROBERT MITCHUM
FOREIGN STUDENT .... MARCO HOFSCHNEIDER
FOREIGN STUDENT .... ROBIN GIVENS
FOREMAN WENT TO FRANCE, THE .... GORDAN JACKSON†
FOREMAN WENT TO FRANCE, THE .... ROBERT MORLEY
FOREPLAY .... ESTELLE PARSONS
FORESTS ARE NEARLY ALL GONE NOW, THE .... MARTIN SHEEN
FOREVER AMBER .... JESSICA TANDY†
FOREVER DARLING .... LUCILLE BALL†
FOREVER ENGLAND .... JOHN MILLS
FOREVER, LULU .... ALEC BALDWIN
FOREVER, LULU .... PAUL GLEASON
FOREVER YOUNG .... ELIJAH WOOD
FOREVER YOUNG .... GEORGE WENDT
FOREVER YOUNG .... ISABEL GLASSER
FOREVER YOUNG .... JAMIE LEE CURTIS
FOREVER YOUNG .... MEL GIBSON
FOREVER YOUNG, FOREVER FREE .... JOSE FERRER†
FORGET PARIS .... BILLY CRYSTAL
FORGET PARIS .... CATHY MORIARTY
FORGET PARIS .... DEBRA WINGER
FORGET PARIS .... JOE MANTEGNA
FORGET PARIS .... JOHN SPENCER
FORGET PARIS .... JULIE KAVNER
FORGET PARIS .... RICHARD MASUR
FORGET-ME-NOT MURDERS, THE (TF) .... HELEN SHAVER
FORGET-ME-NOT MURDERS, THE (TF) .... RICHARD CRENNA
FORGET-ME-NOT MURDERS, THE (TF) .... TYNE DALY
FORGOTTEN MAN, THE (TF) .... DENNIS WEAVER
FORGOTTEN MAN, THE (TF) .... LOIS NETTLETON
FORMULA, THE .... CRAIG T. NELSON
FORMULA, THE .... GEORGE C. SCOTT
FORMULA, THE .... JOHN GIELGUD
FORMULA, THE .... MARLON BRANDO
FORMULA, THE .... MARTHE KELLER
FORMULA, THE .... RICHARD LYNCH
FORREST GUMP .... GARY SINISE
FORREST GUMP .... HANNA R. HALL
FORREST GUMP .... MICHAEL CONNER HUMPHREYS
FORREST GUMP .... MIKE JOLLY
FORREST GUMP .... MYKELTI WILLIAMSON
FORREST GUMP .... ROBIN WRIGHT
FORREST GUMP .... SALLY FIELD
FORREST GUMP .... TOM HANKS
FORSAKING ALL OTHERS .... JOAN CRAWFORD†
FORSYTE SAGA, THE .... GREER GARSON
FORSYTE SAGA, THE .... JANET LEIGH
FORT ALGIERS .... RAYMOND BURR†
FORT ALGIERS .... YVONNE DE CARLO
FORT APACHE, THE BRONX .... DANNY AIELLO
FORT APACHE, THE BRONX .... ED ASNER
FORT APACHE, THE BRONX .... KATHLEEN BELLER
FORT APACHE, THE BRONX .... KEN WAHL
FORT APACHE, THE BRONX .... PAM GRIER
FORT APACHE, THE BRONX .... PAUL GLEASON
FORT APACHE, THE BRONX .... PAUL NEWMAN
FORT APACHE, THE BRONX .... RACHEL TICOTIN
FORT BOWIE .... BEN JOHNSON
FORT DEFIANCE .... BEN JOHNSON
FORT DEFIANCE .... PETER GRAVES
FORT DOBBS .... BRIAN KEITH
FORT DOBBS .... CLINT WALKER
FORT DOBBS .... MICHAEL DANTE
FORT SAGANNE .... CATHERINE DENEUVE
FORT SAGANNE .... GERARD DEPARDIEU
FORT UTAH .... JOHN IRELAND
FORT VENGEANCE .... RITA MORENO
FORTRESS .... CHRISTOPHER LAMBERT
FORTUNATE PILGRIM, THE (MS) .... HAL HOLBROOK
FORTUNATE PILGRIM, THE (MS) .... SOPHIA LOREN
FORTUNE AND MEN'S EYES .... WENDELL BURTON
FORTUNE COOKIE, THE .... JACK LEMMON
FORTUNE COOKIE, THE ✪✪ .... WALTER MATTHAU
FORTUNE, THE .... JACK NICHOLSON
FORTUNE, THE .... STOCKARD CHANNING
FORTUNE, THE .... WARREN BEATTY
FORTUNES OF WAR (TF) .... ROBERT STEPHENS
FORTY GUNS .... BARBARA STANWYCK†
FORTY LITTLE MOTHERS .... DAME JUDITH ANDERSON†
FORTY POUNDS OF TROUBLE .... SUZANNE PLESHETTE
FORTY POUNDS OF TROUBLE .... TONY CURTIS
FORTY-DEUCE .... ESAI MORALES
FORTY-DEUCE .... KEVIN BACON
FORTY-NINTH PARALLEL, THE .... LAURENCE OLIVIER†
FORTY-NINTH PARALLEL, THE .... LESLIE HOWARD†
FORTY-NINTH PARALLEL, THE .... RAYMOND MASSEY†
FOUL PLAY .... BILLY BARTY
FOUL PLAY .... BRIAN DENNEHY
FOUL PLAY .... BURGESS MEREDITH
FOUL PLAY .... CHEVY CHASE
FOUL PLAY .... DUDLEY MOORE
FOUL PLAY .... GOLDIE HAWN
FOUL PLAY .... RACHEL ROBERTS†
FOUND MONEY (TF) .... DICK VAN DYKE
FOUND MONEY (TF) .... ELIZABETH PENA
FOUNTAINHEAD, THE .... PATRICIA NEAL
FOUR BOYS AND A GUN .... JAMES FRANCISCUS†
FOUR DAUGHTERS ✪ .... JOHN GARFIELD†
FOUR DAYS IN DALLAS (TF) .... BRIAN DENNEHY
FOUR DAYS IN DALLAS (TF) .... GORDON JUMP
FOUR DAYS IN DALLAS (TF) .... MICHAEL LERNER
FOUR DEUCES, THE .... CAROL LYNLEY
FOUR DEUCES, THE .... JACK PALANCE
FOUR FEATHERS, THE (TF) .... BEAU BRIDGES
FOUR FEATHERS, THE (TF) .... JANE SEYMOUR
FOUR FOR TEXAS .... DEAN MARTIN
FOUR FOR TEXAS .... RICHARD JAECKEL
FOUR FOR TEXAS .... WESLEY ADDY
FOUR FRIENDS .... CRAIG WASSON
FOUR FRIENDS .... DAVID GRAF
FOUR FRIENDS .... MERCEDES RUEHL
FOUR GIRLS IN TOWN .... JOHN GAVIN
FOUR GIRLS IN TOWN .... ROCK HUDSON†
FOUR GUNS TO THE BORDER .... NINA FOCH
FOUR GUNS TO THE BORDER .... RORY CALHOUN
FOUR IN THE MORNING .... JUDI DENCH
FOUR JILLS IN A JEEP .... MARTHA RAYE†
FOUR MEN AND A PRAYER .... DAVID NIVEN†
FOUR MOTHERS .... EDDIE ALBERT
FOUR MUSKETEERS, THE .... CHARLTON HESTON
FOUR MUSKETEERS, THE .... FAYE DUNAWAY
FOUR MUSKETEERS, THE .... FRANK FINLAY†
FOUR MUSKETEERS, THE .... GERALDINE CHAPLIN
FOUR MUSKETEERS, THE .... JEAN-PIERRE CASSEL
FOUR MUSKETEERS, THE .... MICHAEL YORK
FOUR MUSKETEERS, THE .... OLIVER REED
FOUR MUSKETEERS, THE .... RAQUEL WELCH
FOUR MUSKETEERS, THE .... RICHARD CHAMBERLAIN
FOUR MUSKETEERS, THE .... SIMON WARD
FOUR RODE OUT .... LESLIE NIELSEN
FOUR SEASONS, THE .... ALAN ALDA
FOUR SEASONS, THE .... BEATRICE ALDA
FOUR SEASONS, THE .... BESS ARMSTRONG
FOUR SEASONS, THE .... CAROL BURNETT
FOUR SEASONS, THE .... ELIZABETH ALDA
FOUR SEASONS, THE .... JACK WESTON
FOUR SEASONS, THE .... LEN CARIOU
FOUR SEASONS, THE .... RITA MORENO
FOUR SEASONS, THE .... SANDY DENNIS†
FOUR SONS .... DON AMECHE†
FOUR WALLS .... JOAN CRAWFORD†
FOUR WEDDINGS AND A FUNERAL .... ANDIE MacDOWELL
FOUR WEDDINGS AND A FUNERAL .... CHARLOTTE COLEMAN
FOUR WEDDINGS AND A FUNERAL .... CORBIN REDGRAVE
FOUR WEDDINGS AND A FUNERAL .... DAVID BOWER
FOUR WEDDINGS AND A FUNERAL .... HUGH GRANT
FOUR WEDDINGS AND A FUNERAL .... JAMES FLEET
FOUR WEDDINGS AND A FUNERAL .... JOHN HANNAH
FOUR WEDDINGS AND A FUNERAL .... KRISTIN SCOTT THOMAS
FOUR WEDDINGS AND A FUNERAL .... ROWAN ATKINSON
FOUR WEDDINGS AND A FUNERAL .... SIMON CALLOW
FOUR WIVES .... EDDIE ALBERT
FOURTEEN HOURS .... GRACE KELLY†
FOURTEEN HOURS .... HOWARD DA SILVA†
FOURTEEN HOURS .... JEFF COREY
FOURTH PROTOCOL, THE .... JOANNA CASSIDY
FOURTH PROTOCOL, THE .... MICHAEL CAINE
FOURTH PROTOCOL, THE .... NED BEATTY
FOURTH PROTOCOL, THE .... PIERCE BROSNAN
FOURTH WAR, THE .... HARRY DEAN STANTON
FOURTH WAR, THE .... JORGEN PROCHNOW
FOURTH WAR, THE .... LARA HARRIS
FOURTH WAR, THE .... ROY SCHEIDER
FOURTH WAR, THE .... TIM REID
FOUR'S A CROWD .... LANA TURNER
FOUR'S A CROWD .... OLIVIA DE HAVILLAND
FOX (TF) .... PETER VAUGHN
FOX, THE .... SANDY DENNIS†
FOX AND THE HOUND, THE (AF) .... KURT RUSSELL
FOX AND THE HOUND, THE (AF) .... MICKEY ROONEY
FOX MOVIETONE FOLLIES .... JACKIE COOPER
FOXES .... JODIE FOSTER
FOXES .... LAURA DERN
FOXES .... RANDY QUAID
FOXES .... SALLY KELLERMAN
FOXES .... SCOTT BAIO
FOXES OF HARROW, THE .... MAUREEN O'HARA
FOXFIRE (TF) .... GARY GRUBBS
FOXFIRE (TF) .... HUME CRONYN
FOXFIRE (TF) .... JESSICA TANDY†
FOXFIRE (TF) .... JOHN DENVER
FOXHOLE IN CAIRO .... MICHAEL CAINE
FOXTROT .... CHARLOTTE RAMPLING
FOXTROT .... PETER O'TOOLE
FOXY BROWN .... PAM GRIER
FRAGMENT OF FEAR .... DAVID HEMMINGS
FRAMED .... BROCK PETERS
FRAMED .... JOE DON BAKER
FRANCES .... ANJELICA HUSTON
FRANCES .... KEVIN COSTNER
FRANCES .... SAM SHEPARD
FRANCES ★ .... JESSICA LANGE
FRANCES ✪ .... KIM STANLEY
FRANCIS .... TONY CURTIS
FRANCIS GARY POWERS: THE TRUE STORY OF THE U-2 SPY INCIDENT (TF) .... LEE MAJORS
FRANCIS GOES TO THE RACES .... PIPER LAURIE
FRANCIS GOES TO WEST POINT .... LEONARD NIMOY
FRANCIS IN THE NAVY .... CLINT EASTWOOD
FRANCIS OF ASSISI .... BRADFORD DILLMAN

FRANCIS OF ASSISI .... STUART WHITMAN
FRANK AND JESSE .... BILL PAXTON
FRANK AND JESSE .... RANDY TRAVIS
FRANK AND JESSE .... ROB LOWE
FRANK NITTI:
    THE ENFORCER (TF) .... ANTHONY LaPAGLIA
FRANK NITTI:
    THE ENFORCER (TF) .... TRINI ALVARADO
FRANKENSTEIN .... BORIS KARLOFF†
FRANKENSTEIN MUST
    BE DESTROYED! .... FREDDIE JONES
FRANKENSTEIN MUST
    BE DESTROYED! .... SIMON WARD
FRANKENSTEIN MUST
    BE DESTROYED .... THORLEY WALTERS†
FRANKENSTEIN (TF) .... ROBERT FOXWORTH
FRANKENSTEIN (TF) .... WILLIE AAMES
FRANKENSTEIN:
    TRUE STORY (TF) .... DAVID McCALLUM
FRANKENSTEIN: THE
    TRUE STORY (TF) .... JANE SEYMOUR
FRANKENSTEIN: THE
    TRUE STORY (TF) .... JOHN GIELGUD
FRANKENSTEIN: THE
    TRUE STORY (TF) .... MICHAEL SARRAZIN
FRANKENSTEIN UNBOUND .... BRIDGET FONDA
FRANKENSTEIN UNBOUND .... RAUL JULIA†
FRANKIE AND JOHNNY .... ELVIS PRESLEY†
FRANKIE AND JOHNNY .... HARRY MORGAN
FRANKIE AND JOHNNY .... PHIL LEEDS
FRANKIE & JOHNNY .... AL PACINO
FRANKIE & JOHNNY .... DEDEE PFEIFFER
FRANKIE & JOHNNY .... DIANE LANE
FRANKIE & JOHNNY .... HECTOR ELIZONDO
FRANKIE & JOHNNY .... JANE MORRIS
FRANKIE & JOHNNY .... K CALLAN
FRANKIE & JOHNNY .... KATE NELLIGAN
FRANKIE & JOHNNY .... LAURIE METCALF
FRANKIE & JOHNNY .... MICHELLE PFEIFFER
FRANKIE & JOHNNY .... NATHAN LANE
FRANKIE & JOHNNY .... SHANNON WILCOX
FRANKIE & JOHNNY .... TIM HOPPER
FRANKIE & JOHNNY .... TRACY REINER
FRANK'S GREATEST ADVENTURE .... JON VOIGHT
FRANTIC .... BETTY BUCKLEY
FRANTIC .... DAVID HUDDLESTON
FRANTIC .... EMMANUELLE SEIGNER
FRANTIC .... HARRISON FORD
FRANTIC .... JIMMIE RAY WEEKS
FRANTIC .... JOHN MAHONEY
FRANTIC .... YORGO VOYAGIS
FRATERNITY ROW .... CLIFF ROBERTSON
FRAUDS .... HUGO WEAVING
FRAUDS .... JOSEPHINE BYRNES
FRAUDS .... PHIL COLLINS
FRAULEIN .... MEL FERRER
FRAULEIN .... THEODORE BIKEL
FREAKED .... ALEX WINTER
FREAKED .... BOB GOLDTHWAIT
FREAKED .... BROOKE SHIELDS
FREAKED .... KEANU REEVES
FREAKED .... MEGAN WARD
FREAKED .... MICHAEL STOYANOV
FREAKED .... MR. T
FREAKED .... RANDY QUAID
FREAKED .... WILLIAM SADLER
FREAKY FRIDAY .... BARBARA HARRIS
FREAKY FRIDAY .... DICK VAN PATTEN
FREAKY FRIDAY .... JODIE FOSTER
FREAKY FRIDAY .... JOHN ASTIN
FREAKY FRIDAY .... KAYE BALLARD
FREAKY FRIDAY .... RUTH BUZZI
FREAKY FRIDAY .... CHARLENE TILTON
FREDDY'S DEAD: THE
    FINAL NIGHTMARE .... YAPHET KOTTO
FREDDY'S DEAD: THE
    FINAL NIGHTMARE .... ALICE COOPER
FREDDY'S DEAD: THE
    FINAL NIGHTMARE .... JOHNNY DEPP
FREDDY'S DEAD: THE
    FINAL NIGHTMARE .... LISA ZANE
FREDDY'S DEAD: THE
    FINAL NIGHTMARE .... ROBERT ENGLUND

FREDDY'S DEAD: THE
    FINAL NIGHTMARE .... ROSEANNE
FREDDY'S DEAD: THE
    FINAL NIGHTMARE .... TOM ARNOLD
FREE AND EASY .... DAME JUDITH ANDERSON†
FREE SOUL, A ★ .... NORMA SHEARER†
FREE SOUL, A ★★ .... LIONEL BARRYMORE†
FREE SPIRIT .... JEREMY KEMP
FREE THE ARMY .... JANE FONDA
FREE WILLY .... AUGUST SCHELLENBERG
FREE WILLY .... JASON JAMES RICHTER
FREE WILLY .... JAYNE ATKINSON
FREE WILLY .... LORI PETTY
FREE WILLY .... MICHAEL MADSEN
FREE WILLY .... MYKELTI WILLIAMSON
FREEBIE AND THE BEAN .... ALAN ARKIN
FREEBIE AND THE BEAN .... JACK KRUSCHEN
FREEBIE AND THE BEAN .... JAMES CAAN
FREEBIE AND THE BEAN .... LORETTA SWIT
FREEBIE AND THE BEAN .... VALERIE HARPER
FREEDOM FIGHTER (TF) .... DAVID McCALLUM
FREEDOM FIGHTER (TF) .... TONY DANZA
FREEDOM ROAD (TF) .... EDWRAD HERRMANN
FREEDOM ROAD (TF) .... KRIS KRISTOFFERSON
FREEDOM ROAD (TF) .... MUHAMMAD ALI
FREEJACK .... ANTHONY HOPKINS
FREEJACK .... DAVID JOHANSEN
FREEJACK .... EMILIO ESTEVEZ
FREEJACK .... JOHN SHEA
FREEJACK .... JONATHAN BANKS
FREEJACK .... MICK JAGGER
FREEJACK .... VINCENT SCHIAVELLI
FREEWAY .... BILLY DRAGO
FREEWAY .... DARLANNE FLEUGEL
FREEWAY .... JAMES RUSSO
FREEWAY .... RICHARD BELZER
FRENCH ATLANTIC
    AFFAIR, THE (TF) .... CHAD EVERETT
FRENCH ATLANTIC
    AFFAIR, THE (TF) .... JOSE FERRER†
FRENCH ATLANTIC
    AFFAIR, THE (TF) .... RICHARD JORDAN†
FRENCH ATLANTIC
    AFFAIR, THE (TF) .... TELLY SAVALAS†
FRENCH CAN CAN .... GENEVIEVE BUJOLD
FRENCH CONNECTION, THE .... TONY LoBIANCO
FRENCH
    CONNECTION, THE ★★ .... GENE HACKMAN
FRENCH CONNECTION, THE ⊙ .... ROY SCHEIDER
FRENCH CONNECTION II .... GENE HACKMAN
FRENCH
    CONSPIRACY, THE ..... JEAN-LOUIS TRINTIGNANT
FRENCH CONSPIRACY, THE .... ROY SCHEIDER
FRENCH LEAVE .... JACKIE COOPER
FRENCH LIEUTENANT'S
    WOMAN, THE .... ALUN ARMSTRONG
FRENCH LIEUTENANT'S
    WOMAN, THE .... DAVID WARNER
FRENCH LIEUTENANT'S
    WOMAN, THE .... JEREMY IRONS
FRENCH LIEUTENANT'S
    WOMAN, THE .... PETER VAUGHN
FRENCH LIEUTENANT'S
    WOMAN, THE ★ .... MERYL STREEP
FRENCH LINE, THE .... KIM NOVAK
FRENCH MISTRESS, A .... IAN BANNEN
FRENCH POSTCARDS ..... DAVID MARSHALL GRANT
FRENCH POSTCARDS .... DEBRA WINGER
FRENCH WOMAN, THE .... KLAUS KINSKI†
FRENCHIE .... SHELLEY WINTERS
FRENZY .... ALEC McCOWEN
FRENZY .... BILLIE WHITELAW
FRENZY .... MAE ZETTERLING†
FRESH .... GIANCARLO ESPOSITO
FRESH .... SAMUEL L. JACKSON
FRESH HORSES .... ANDREW McCARTHY
FRESH HORSES .... BEN STILLER
FRESH HORSES .... DOUG HUTCHISON
FRESH HORSES .... MOLLY RINGWALD
FRESH HORSES .... PATTI D'ARBANVILLE
FRESHMAN, THE .... BERT PARKS†
FRESHMAN, THE .... BRUNO KIRBY
FRESHMAN, THE .... FRANK WHALEY

FRESHMAN, THE .... MARLON BRANDO
FRESHMAN, THE .... MATTHEW BRODERICK
FRESHMAN, THE .... MAXIMILIAN SCHELL
FRESHMAN, THE .... PAUL BENEDICT
FRESHMAN, THE .... PENELOPE ANN MILLER
FRESNO (MS) .... CAROL BURNETT
FRESNO (MS) .... CHARLES GRODIN
FRESNO (MS) .... DABNEY COLEMAN
FRESNO (MS) .... GREGORY HARRISON
FRESNO (MS) .... LOUISE LATHAM
FRESNO (MS) .... MIKE JOLLY
FRESNO (MS) .... TERI GARR
FREUD .... DAVID McCALLUM
FREUD .... SUSANNAH YORK
FRIDAY FOSTER .... CARL WEATHERS
FRIDAY FOSTER .... EARTHA KITT
FRIDAY FOSTER .... PAM GRIER
FRIDAY FOSTER .... YAPHET KOTTO
FRIDAY THE 13TH .... BETSY PALMER
FRIDAY THE 13TH .... COREY FELDMAN
FRIDAY THE 13TH .... KEVIN BACON
FRIDAY THE 13TH PART II .... BETSY PALMER
FRIDAY THE 13TH PART 3 .... BRUCE MAHLER
FRIDAY THE 13TH, PART VI:
    JASON LIVES .... C. J. GRAHAM
FRIDAY THE 13TH, PART VI:
    JASON LIVES .... DAVID KAGEN
FRIDAY THE 13TH, PART VI:
    JASON LIVES .... JENNIFER COOKE
FRIDAY THE 13TH, PART VI:
    JASON LIVES .... KERRY NOONAN
FRIDAY THE 13TH, PART VI:
    JASON LIVES .... RENEE JONES
FRIDAY THE 13TH, PART VI:
    JASON LIVES .... THOM MATHEWS
FRIDAY THE 13TH, PART VI:
    JASON LIVES .... TOM FRIDLEY
FRIDAY THE 13TH PART VII - JASON
    TAKES MANHATTAN .... BARBARA BINGHAM
FRIDAY THE 13TH PART VII -
    THE NEW BLOOD .... LAR PARK LINCOLN
FRIDAY THE 13TH PART VIII - JASON
    TAKES MANHATTAN .... JENSEN DAGGETT
FRIDAY THE 13TH PART VIII - JASON
    TAKES MANHATTAN .... KANE HODDER
FRIDAY THE 13TH PART VIII - JASON
    TAKES MANHATTAN .... PETER MARK RICHMAN
FRIDAY THE 13TH PART VIII - JASON
    TAKES MANHATTAN .... SCOTT REEVES
FRIDAY THE 13TH PART VIII - JASON
    TAKES MANHATTAN .... SHARLENE MARTIN
FRIDAY THE 13TH PART VIII - JASON
    TAKES MANHATTAN .... V. C. DUPREE
FRIDAY THE 13TH - THE
    FINAL CHAPTER .... COREY FELDMAN
FRIDAY THE 13TH - THE
    FINAL CHAPTER .... ERICH ANDERSON
FRIDAY THE 13TH - THE
    FINAL CHAPTER .... KIMBERLY BECK
FRIDAY THE 13TH - THE
    FINAL CHAPTER .... LAWRENCE MONOSON
FRIED GREEN TOMATOES .... CHRIS O'DONNELL
FRIED GREEN TOMATOES .... CICELY TYSON
FRIED GREEN TOMATOES .... FANNIE FLAGG
FRIED GREEN TOMATOES .... GAILORD SARTAIN
FRIED GREEN TOMATOES .... GARY BASARABA
FRIED GREEN TOMATOES .... KATHY BATES
FRIED GREEN
    TOMATOES .... MARY STUART MASTERSON
FRIED GREEN
    TOMATOES .... MARY-LOUISE PARKER
FRIED GREEN TOMATOES .... NICK SEARCY
FRIED GREEN TOMATOES .... RAYNOR SCHEINE
FRIED GREEN TOMATOES .... STAN SHAW
FRIED GREEN TOMATOES ⊙ JACKSON .. JESSICA TANDY†
FRIEDA .... MAE ZETTERLING†
FRIEND OF A FRIEND .... ANNE-LAURE MEURY
FRIEND OF A FRIEND .... SOPHIE RENOIR
FRIENDLY FIRE (TF) .... CAROL BURNETT
FRIENDLY FIRE (TF) .... NED BEATTY
FRIENDLY FIRE (TF) .... TIMOTHY HUTTON
FRIENDLY PERSUASION .... GARY COOPER†

† after an actor's name denotes deceased.

I
N
D
E
X

O
F

F
I
L
M

T
I
T
L
E
S

FRIENDLY PERSUASION ..... PETER MARK RICHMAN
FRIENDLY PERSUASION ✪ ...... ANTHONY PERKINS†
FRIENDLY PERSUASION (TF) .... RICHARD KILEY
FRIENDS OF EDDIE COYLE, THE .... PETER BOYLE
FRIENDS OF
   EDDIE COYLE, THE .... RICHARD JORDAN†
FRIENDS OF
   EDDIE COYLE, THE .... ROBERT MITCHUM
FRIGHT .... IAN BANNEN
FRIGHT .... SUSAN GEORGE
FRIGHT NIGHT .... CHRIS SARANDON
FRIGHT NIGHT .... RODDY McDOWALL
FRIGHT NIGHT .... WILLIAM RAGSDALE
FRIGHT NIGHT PART 2 .... RODDY McDOWALL
FRIGHT NIGHT PART 2 .... WILLIAM RAGSDALE
FRIGHTENED BRIDE, THE .... MAE ZETTERLING†
FRIGHTENED CITY, THE .... SEAN CONNERY
FRISCO KID, THE .... GENE WILDER
FRISCO KID, THE .... HARRISON FORD
FROGMEN, THE .... JACK WARDEN
FROGMEN, THE .... RICHARD WIDMARK
FROGMEN, THE .... ROBERT WAGNER
FROGS .... SAM ELLIOTT
FROM A FAR
   COUNTRY .... CHRISTOPHER CAZENOVE
FROM A FAR COUNTRY:
   POPE JOHN PAUL II (TF) .... SAM NEILL
FROM BEYOND .... BARBARA CRAMPTON
FROM BEYOND .... BRUCE McGUIRE
FROM BEYOND .... BUNNY SUMMERS
FROM BEYOND .... CAROLYN PURDY-GORDON
FROM BEYOND .... JEFFREY COMBS
FROM BEYOND .... KEN FOREE
FROM BEYOND .... TED SOREL
FROM BEYOND THE GRAVE .... DAVID WARNER
FROM BEYOND
   THE GRAVE .... DONALD PLEASENCE
FROM BEYOND THE GRAVE .... IAN BANNEN
FROM BEYOND
   THE GRAVE .... LESLEY-ANNE DOWN
FROM HELL TO TEXAS .... DENNIS HOPPER
FROM HELL TO TEXAS .... DON MURRAY
FROM HELL TO TEXAS .... R.G. ARMSTRONG
FROM HELL TO VICTORY .... GEORGE HAMILTON
FROM HELL TO VICTORY .... GEORGE PEPPARD†
FROM HERE TO ETERNITY .... CLAUDE AKINS†
FROM HERE TO ETERNITY .... ERNEST BORGNINE
FROM HERE TO ETERNITY .... JACK WARDEN
FROM HERE TO ETERNITY ★ ... BURT LANCASTER†
FROM HERE TO ETERNITY ★ ...... DEBORAH KERR
FROM HERE TO
   ETERNITY ★ .... MONTGOMERY CLIFT†
FROM HERE TO ETERNITY ✪✪ .... DONNA REED†
FROM HERE TO ETERNITY ✪✪ ...... FRANK SINATRA
FROM HERE TO
   ETERNITY (MS) .... JOE PANTOLIANO
FROM HERE TO ETERNITY (MS) .... PETER BOYLE
FROM HERE TO ETERNITY (MS) .... SALOME JENS
FROM HERE TO
   ETERNITY (MS) .... WILLIAM DEVANE
FROM HERE TO ETERNITY (TF) ...... ANDY GRIFFITH
FROM HOLLYWOOD
   TO DEADWOOD .... CAMPBELL SCOTT
FROM NOON TILL THREE .... CHARLES BRONSON
FROM NOON TILL THREE .... JILL IRELAND†
FROM RUSSIA WITH LOVE .... LOIS MAXWELL
FROM RUSSIA WITH LOVE .... SEAN CONNERY
FROM THE DEAD
   OF NIGHT (TF) .... BRUCE BOXLEITNER
FROM THE DEAD
   OF NIGHT (TF) ....DIAHANN CARROLL
FROM THE DEAD
   OF NIGHT (TF) .... LINDSAY WAGNER
FROM THE DEAD OF NIGHT (TF) .... PETER JASON
FROM THE HIP .... DAN MONAHAN
FROM THE HIP .... DARREN McGAVIN
FROM THE HIP .... ELIZABETH PERKINS
FROM THE HIP .... JOHN HURT
FROM THE HIP .... JUDD NELSON
FROM THE HIP .... NANCY MARCHAND
FROM THE TERRACE .... BARBARA EDEN
FROM THE TERRACE .... GEORGE GRIZZARD

FROM THE TERRACE .... HOWARD CAINE†
FROM THE TERRACE .... JOANNE WOODWARD
FROM THE TERRACE .... LEON AMES
FROM THE TERRACE .... PATRICK O'NEAL†
FROM THE TERRACE .... PAUL NEWMAN
FROM THIS DAY FORWARD .... HARRY MORGAN
FRONT PAGE, THE .... ALLEN GARFIELD
FRONT PAGE, THE .... AUSTIN PENDLETON
FRONT PAGE, THE .... CAROL BURNETT
FRONT PAGE, THE .... CHARLES DURNING
FRONT PAGE, THE .... JACK LEMMON
FRONT PAGE, THE .... SUSAN SARANDON
FRONT PAGE, THE .... VINCENT GARDENIA†
FRONT PAGE, THE .... WALTER MATTHAU
FRONT PAGE, THE ★ .... ADOLPHE MENJOU†
FRONT PAGE WOMAN .... BETTE DAVIS†
FRONT, THE .... ANDREA MARCOVICCI
FRONT, THE .... DANNY AIELLO
FRONT, THE .... MICHAEL MURPHY
FRONT, THE .... POLLY HOLLIDAY
FRONT, THE .... WOODY ALLEN
FRONT, THE .... ZERO MOSTEL†
FRONTIER GAL .... YVONNE DE CARLO
FRONTIER MARSHALL .... JOHN CARRADINE†
FUGITIVE FAMILY (TF) .... MEL FERRER
FUGITIVE KIND, THE .... JOANNE WOODWARD
FUGITIVE KIND, THE .... MARLON BRANDO
FUGITIVE KIND, THE .... MAUREEN STAPLETON
FUGITIVE KIND, THE .... R.G. ARMSTRONG
FUGITIVE, THE .... ANDREAS KATSULAS
FUGITIVE, THE .... DANIEL ROEBUCK
FUGITIVE, THE .... HARRISON FORD
FUGITIVE, THE .... JEROEN KRABBE
FUGITIVE, THE .... JOE PANTOLIANO
FUGITIVE, THE .... JULIANNE MOORE
FUGITIVE, THE .... L. SCOTT CALDWELL
FUGITIVE, THE .... SELA WARD
FUGITIVE, THE .... TOM WOOD
FUGITIVE, THE ✪✪ .... TOMMY LEE JONES
FULFILLMENT OF MARY
   GRAY, THE (TF) .... CHERYL LADD
FULFILLMENT OF MARY
   GRAY, THE (TF) .... SHEILA KELLEY
FULL CIRCLE .... MIA FARROW
FULL CIRCLE .... TOM CONTI
FULL EXPOSURE: THE SEX
   TAPES SCANDAL (TF) .... JAMES AVERY
FULL EXPOSURE: THE SEX
   TAPES SCANDAL (TF) .... JENNIFER O'NEILL
FULL EXPOSURE: THE SEX
   TAPES SCANDAL (TF) .... LISA HARTMAN-BLACK
FULL EXPOSURE: THE SEX
   TAPES SCANDAL (TF) .... VANESSA WILLIAMS
FULL HOUSE .... KATHLEEN FREEMAN
FULL HOUSE .... MARILYN MONROE†
FULL METAL JACKET .... ADAM BALDWIN
FULL METAL JACKET .... DORIAN HAREWOOD
FULL METAL JACKET .... ED O'ROSS
FULL METAL JACKET .... LEE ERMEY
FULL METAL JACKET .... MATTHEW MODINE
FULL METAL JACKET .... VINCENT D'ONOFRIO
FULL MOON HIGH .... ALAN ARKIN
FULL MOON IN
   BLUE WATER .... BURGESS MEREDITH
FULL MOON IN BLUE WATER .... DAVID DOTY
FULL MOON IN BLUE WATER .... ELIAS KOTEAS
FULL MOON IN BLUE WATER .... ELIAS KOTEAS
FULL MOON IN BLUE WATER .... GENE HACKMAN
FULL MOON IN BLUE WATER .... KEVIN COONEY
FULL MOON IN BLUE WATER .... TERI GARR
FULLER BRUSH GIRL .... LUCILLE BALL†
FULLER BRUSH GIRL, THE .... EDDIE ALBERT
FULLER BRUSH MAN, THE .... ROGER MOORE
FULLY LOADED .... ANGELA GOETHALS
FULLY LOADED .... FRED COFFIN
FUN AND FANCY FREE .... DINAH SHORE
FUN IN ACAPULCO .... ELVIS PRESLEY†
FUN IN ACAPULCO .... URSULA ANDRESS
FUN LOVING .... GENE WILDER
FUN WITH DICK AND JANE .... GEORGE SEGAL
FUN WITH DICK AND JANE .... JANE FONDA
FUN WITH DICK AND JANE .... JOHN DEHNER†

FUN WITH DICK AND JANE ..... THALMUS RASULALA
FUNERAL IN BERLIN .... MARTHE KELLER
FUNERAL IN BERLIN .... MICHAEL CAINE
FUNHOUSE, THE .... ELIZABETH BERRIDGE
FUNNY ABOUT LOVE .... CHRISTINE LAHTI
FUNNY ABOUT LOVE .... GENE WILDER
FUNNY ABOUT
   LOVE .... MARY STUART MASTERSON
FUNNY FACE .... AUDREY HEPBURN†
FUNNY FACE .... FRED ASTAIRE†
FUNNY FARM .... BRAD SULLIVAN
FUNNY FARM .... CHEVY CHASE
FUNNY FARM .... JACK GILPIN
FUNNY FARM .... JOSEPH MAHUR
FUNNY FARM .... MACINTYRE DIXON
FUNNY FARM .... MADOLYN SMITH OSBORNE
FUNNY FARM, THE .... EILEEN BRENNAN
FUNNY GIRL .... OMAR SHARIF
FUNNY GIRL .... WALTER PIDGEON†
FUNNY GIRL ★★ .... BARBRA STREISAND
FUNNY GIRL ✪ .... KAY MEDFORD†
FUNNY LADY .... BARBRA STREISAND
FUNNY LADY .... BEN VEREEN
FUNNY LADY .... COLLEEN CAMP
FUNNY LADY .... JAMES CAAN
FUNNY LADY .... OMAR SHARIF
FUNNY LADY .... RODDY McDOWALL
FUNNY THING HAPPENED
   ON THE WAY TO THE
   FORUM, A .... MICHAEL CRAWFORD
FURIES, THE .... BARBARA STANWYCK†
FURIES, THE .... DAME JUDITH ANDERSON†
FURY .... SYLVIA SIDNEY
FURY, THE .... AMY IRVING
FURY, THE .... ANDREW STEVENS
FURY, THE .... CARRIE SNODGRESS
FURY, THE .... CHARLES DURNING
FURY, THE .... DARYL HANNAH
FURY, THE .... FIONA LEWIS
FURY, THE .... GORDON JUMP
FURY, THE .... KIRK DOUGLAS
FUTURE COP .... HELEN HUNT
FUTURE COP .... RICHARD HERD
FUTURE COP (TF) .... ERNEST BORGNINE
FUTUREKICK .... MEG FOSTER
FUTUREWORLD .... ARTHUR HILL
FUTUREWORLD .... BLYTHE DANNER
FUTUREWORLD .... PETER FONDA
FUTUREWORLD .... STUART MARGOLIN
FUTZ .... JENNIFER O'NEILL
FUTZ! .... SALLY KIRKLAND
FUZZ .... BERT REMSEN
FUZZ .... BURT REYNOLDS
FUZZ .... JACK WESTON
FUZZ .... JAMES McEACHIN
FUZZ .... RAQUEL WELCH
FUZZ .... STEVE IHNAT†
FUZZ .... TOM SKERRITT
FUZZ .... YUL BRYNNER†

G

G.I. BLUES .... ELVIS PRESLEY†
GABLE AND LOMBARD .... ALLEN GARFIELD
GABLE AND LOMBARD .... JAMES BROLIN
GABLE AND LOMBARD .... JILL CLAYBURGH
GABLE AND LOMBARD .... MELANIE MAYRON
GABLE AND LOMBARD .... MORGAN BRITTANY
GABLE AND LOMBARD .... RED BUTTONS
GABRIELA .... MARCELLO MASTROIANNI
GABRIELA .... SONIA BRAGA
GABY .... LESLIE CARON
GABY - A TRUE STORY .... LAWRENCE MONOSON
GABY - A TRUE STORY .... LIV ULLMANN
GABY - A TRUE STORY .... RACHEL LEVIN
GABY - A TRUE STORY .... ROBERT BELTRAN
GABY - A TRUE STORY .... ROBERT LOGGIA
GABY - A TRUE STORY ✪ .... NORMA ALEANDRO
GAILY GAILY .... BEAU BRIDGES
GAILY, GAILY .... BRIAN KEITH
GAILY, GAILY .... GEORGE KENNEDY
GAILY GAILY .... HUME CRONYN

This is not a list of every film ever made or every cast member, only those listed in this directory.

GAILY, GAILY .... MARGOT KIDDER
GAL WHO TOOK
  THE WEST, THE .... YVONNE DE CARLO
GALAXINA .... AVERY SCHREIBER
GALAXINA .... STEPHEN MACHT
GALAXY OF TERROR .... EDWARD ALBERT
GALAXY OF TERROR .... RAY WALSTON
GALILEO .... JOHN GIELGUD
GALILEO .... JOHN McENERY
GALILEO .... MICHAEL GOUGH
GALILEO .... TOM CONTI
GALILEO .... TOPOL
GALLANT HOURS, THE .... DENNIS WEAVER
GALLANT HOURS, THE .... RICHARD JAECKEL
GALLANT SONS .... JACKIE COOPER
GALLIPOLI .... MEL GIBSON
GAMBIT .... MICHAEL CAINE
GAMBIT .... SHIRLEY MacLAINE
GAMBLER, THE .... ANTONIO FARGAS
GAMBLER, THE .... BURT YOUNG
GAMBLER, THE .... JAMES CAAN
GAMBLER, THE .... LAUREN HUTTON
GAMBLER, THE .... PAUL SORVINO
GAMBLER FROM
  NATCHEZ, THE .... WOODY STRODE
GAMBLING LADY .... BARBARA STANWYCK†
GAMBLING ON THE HIGH SEAS .... JANE WYMAN
GAME, THE .... FREDERIC FORREST
GAME CALLED SCRUGGS, A ...... SUSANNAH YORK
GAME FOR VULTURES .... DENHOLM ELLIOTT†
GAME FOR VULTURES .... JOAN COLLINS
GAME FOR VULTURES .... RICHARD HARRIS
GAME FOR VULTURES .... RICHARD ROUNDTREE
GAME IS OVER, THE .... JANE FONDA
GAME OF DEATH .... COLLEEN CAMP
GAME OF DEATH .... DEAN JAGGER†
GAME OF DEATH .... KAREEM ABDUL-JABBAR
GAMES .... DON STROUD
GAMES .... JAMES CAAN
GAMES .... KATHERINE ROSS
GAMES, THE .... JEREMY KEMP
GAMES, THE .... LEIGH TAYLOR-YOUNG
GAMES, THE .... MICHAEL CRAWFORD
GAMES, THE .... RYAN O'NEAL
GAMES, THE .... SAM ELLIOTT
GAMES OF DESIRE .... CLAUDINE AUGER
GAMES THAT LOVERS PLAY .... JOANNA LUMLEY
GANDHI .... BERNARD HEPTON
GANDHI .... CANDICE BERGEN
GANDHI .... DANIEL DAY-LEWIS
GANDHI .... EDWARD FOX
GANDHI .... GERALDINE JAMES
GANDHI .... IAN BANNEN
GANDHI .... IAN CHARLESON†
GANDHI .... JOHN GIELGUD
GANDHI .... JOHN MILLS
GANDHI .... MARTIN SHEEN
GANDHI .... NIGEL HAWTHORNE
GANDHI .... ROSHAN SETH
GANDHI .... TREVOR HOWARD†
GANDHI ★★ .... BEN KINGSLEY
GANG THAT COULDN'T SHOOT
  STRAIGHT, THE .... LEIGH TAYLOR-YOUNG
GANG THAT COULDN'T SHOOT
  STRAIGHT, THE .... JERRY ORBACH
GANG THAT COULDN'T SHOOT
  STRAIGHT, THE .... LIONEL STANDER
GANG THAT COULDN'T SHOOT
  STRAIGHT, THE .... ROBERT DE NIRO
GANG WAR .... CHARLES BRONSON
GANGSTER STORY .... WALTER MATTHAU
GANGSTER, THE .... HARRY MORGAN
GANGSTER, THE .... JOHN IRELAND
GANGSTER, THE .... SHELLEY WINTERS
GANGSTER'S BOY .... JACKIE COOPER
GANJA AND HESS .... DUANE JONES†
GARBO TALKS .... ANNE BANCROFT
GARBO TALKS .... CARRIE FISHER
GARBO TALKS .... CATHERINE HICKS
GARDEN OF EDEN .... R.G. ARMSTRONG
GARDEN OF EVIL .... RICHARD WIDMARK
GARDEN OF EVIL .... RITA MORENO

GARDENIA .... ROBERT WEBBER
GARDENS OF STONE .... ANJELICA HUSTON
GARDENS OF STONE .... CASEY SIEMASZKO
GARDENS OF STONE .... D. B. SWEENEY
GARDENS OF STONE .... DEAN STOCKWELL
GARDENS OF STONE .... ELIAS KOTEAS
GARDENS OF STONE .... JAMES EARL JONES
GARDENS OF STONE .... LAURENCE FISHBURNE
GARDENS OF
  STONE .... MARY STUART MASTERSON
GARDENS OF STONE .... SAM BOTTOMS
GARIBALDI .... FRANCO NERO
GARMENT JUNGLE, THE .... JOSEPH WISEMAN
GARMENT JUNGLE, THE .... WESLEY ADDY
GAS .... DONALD SUTHERLAND
GAS .... SUSAN ANSPACH
GAS FOOD LODGING .... FAIRUZA BALK
GAS-S-S-S .... CINDY WILLIAMS
GAS-S-S-S .... TALIA SHIRE
GAS-S-S-S...OR, IT MAY BECOME
  NECESSARY TO DESTROY THE
  WORLD IN ORDER TO SAVE IT .... CINDY WILLIAMS
GAS-S-S-S...OR, IT MAY BECOME
  NECESSARY TO DESTROY THE
  WORLD IN ORDER TO SAVE IT .... TALIA SHIRE
GASLIGHT ★ .... CHARLES BOYER†
GASLIGHT ★★ .... INGRID BERGMAN†
GASLIGHT ○ .... ANGELA LANSBURY
GASLIGHT ADDITION .... CHRISTINA RICCI
GASLIGHT ADDITION .... DEMI MOORE
GASLIGHT ADDITION .... MELANIE GRIFFITH
GASLIGHT ADDITION .... RITA WILSON
GASLIGHT ADDITION .... ROSIE O'DONNELL
GASLIGHT ADDITION .... THORA BIRCH
GATE, THE .... STEPHEN DORFF
GATE II .... LOUIS TRIPP
GATE II .... PAMELA SEGALL
GATES TO PARADISE .... JENNY AGUTTER
GATEWAY .... DON AMECHE†
GATHERING, THE (TF) .... ED ASNER
GATHERING, THE (TF) .... MAUREEN STAPLETON
GATHERING,
  PART II, THE (TF) .... MAUREEN STAPLETON
GATHERING OF EAGLES, A .... HENRY SILVA
GATHERING OF EAGLES, A .... KEVIN McCARTHY
GATHERING OF
  EAGLES, A .... RICHARD ANDERSON
GATHERING OF
  OLD MEN, A (TF) .... HOLLY HUNTER
GATHERING OF
  OLD MEN, A (TF) .... LOUIS GOSSETT JR.
GATHERING OF
  OLD MEN, A (TF) .... RICHARD WIDMARK
GATLING GUN, THE .... PATRICK WAYNE
GATLING GUN, THE .... WOODY STRODE
GATOR .... ALICE GHOSTLEY
GATOR .... BURT REYNOLDS
GATOR .... DUB TAYLOR
GATOR .... JACK WESTON
GATOR .... JERRY REED
GATOR .... LAUREN HUTTON
GAUGUIN THE SAVAGE (TF) .... LYNN REDGRAVE
GAUNTLET, THE .... BILL McKINNEY
GAUNTLET, THE .... CLINT EASTWOOD
GAUNTLET, THE .... PAT HINGLE
GAUNTLET, THE .... SONDRA LOCKE
GAUNTLET, THE .... WILLIAM PRINCE
GAY ADVENTURE, THE .... BURGESS MEREDITH
GAY DIVORCEE, THE .... FRED ASTAIRE†
GAY PUR-EE (AF) .... RED BUTTONS
GAY SISTERS, THE .... BARBARA STANWYCK†
GAY SISTERS, THE .... GERALDINE FITZGERALD
GAZEBO, THE .... CARL REINER
GAZEBO, THE .... DEBBIE REYNOLDS
GAZEBO, THE .... MARTIN LANDAU
GEISHA BOY, THE .... JERRY LEWIS
GEISHA BOY, THE .... SUZANNE PLESHETTE
GENERAL DIED AT
  DAWN, THE ○ .... AKIM TAMIROFF†
GENERAL OF THE DEAD ARMY .... ANOUK AIMEE
GENERATION .... CARL REINER
GENERATION .... KIM DARBY

GENERATION .... SAM WATERSTON
GENESIS II (TF) .... MARIETTE HARTLEY
GENEVIEVE .... GEOFFREY KEEN
GENGHIS KHAN .... ELI WALLACH
GENGHIS KHAN .... OMAR SHARIF
GENGHIS KHAN .... ROBERT MORLEY
GENGHIS KHAN .... TELLY SAVALAS†
GENGHIS KHAN .... WOODY STRODE
GENTLE GIANT .... DENNIS WEAVER
GENTLE GIANT .... VERA MILES
GENTLE GUNMAN, THE .... JOHN MILLS
GENTLEMAN AT HEART, A .... MILTON BERLE
GENTLEMAN JIM .... ALEXIS SMITH†
GENTLEMAN'S AGREEMENT ...... DEAN STOCKWELL
GENTLEMAN'S AGREEMENT .... JANE WYATT
GENTLEMAN'S AGREEMENT ★ ...... GREGORY PECK
GENTLEMAN'S AGREEMENT ○○ .... CELESTE HOLM
GENTLEMEN MARRY BRUNETTES ..... ALAN YOUNG
GENTLEMEN PREFER
  BLONDES .... HARRY CAREY JR.
GENTLEMEN PREFER
  BLONDES .... MARILYN MONROE†
GENUINE RISK .... M. K. HARRIS
GENUINE RISK .... MAX PERLICH
GENUINE RISK .... MICHELLE JOHNSON
GENUINE RISK .... PETER BERG
GENUINE RISK .... TERENCE STAMP
GEORGE BALANCHINE'S
  THE NUTCRACKER .... BART ROBINSON COOK
GEORGE BALANCHINE'S
  THE NUTCRACKER .... DAMIAN WOETZEL
GEORGE BALANCHINE'S
  THE NUTCRACKER .... DARCI KISTLER
GEORGE BALANCHINE'S
  THE NUTCRACKER .... JESSICA LYNN COHEN
GEORGE BALANCHINE'S
  THE NUTCRACKER .... KEVIN KLINE
GEORGE BALANCHINE'S
  THE NUTCRACKER .... KYRA NICHOLS
GEORGE BALANCHINE'S
  THE NUTCRACKER .... MACAULAY CULKIN
GEORGE McKENNA
  STORY, THE (TF) .... AKOSUA BUSIA
GEORGE McKENNA
  STORY, THE (TF) .... DENZEL WASHINGTON
GEORGE McKENNA
  STORY, THE (TF) .... RICHARD MASUR
GEORGE WASHINGTON (MS) ..... BARRY BOSTWICK
GEORGE WASHINGTON (MS) .... JACLYN SMITH
GEORGE WASHINGTON (MS) .... JEREMY KEMP
GEORGE WASHINGTON II: THE
  FORGING OF A NATION (TF) ... BARRY BOSTWICK
GEORGE WASHINGTON II: THE
  FORGING OF A NATION (TF) .... JEFFREY JONES
GEORGE WASHINGTON II: THE
  FORGING OF A NATION (MS) .... PATTY DUKE
GEORGE WASHINGTON II: THE
  FORGING OF A NATION (MS) .... STEPHEN MACHT
GEORGE WHITE'S SCANDALS .... JANE GREER
GEORGY GIRL .... ALAN BATES
GEORGY GIRL .... CHARLOTTE RAMPLING
GEORGY GIRL ★ .... LYNN REDGRAVE
GEORGY GIRL ○ .... JAMES MASON†
GERMINAL .... GERARD DEPARDIEU
GERONIMO .... ADAM WEST
GERONIMO .... CHUCK CONNORS†
GERONIMO - AN AMERICAN
  LEGEND .... DAVID BARRY GRAY
GERONIMO - AN AMERICAN
  LEGEND .... GENE HACKMAN
GERONIMO - AN AMERICAN
  LEGEND .... JASON PATRIC
GERONIMO - AN AMERICAN
  LEGEND .... MATT DAMON
GERONIMO - AN AMERICAN
  LEGEND .... ROBERT DUVALL
GERONIMO - AN AMERICAN LEGEND .... WES STUDI
GERVAISE .... MARIA SCHELL
GET CARTER .... ALUN ARMSTRONG
GET CARTER .... BERNARD HEPTON
GET CARTER .... BRITT EKLAND
GET CARTER .... MICHAEL CAINE

INDEX OF FILM TITLES

† after an actor's name denotes deceased.

GET CRAZY .... ALLEN GARFIELD
GET CRAZY .... BILL HENDERSON
GET CRAZY .... FRANKLYN AJAYE
GET CRAZY .... MALCOLM McDOWELL
GET OUT YOUR HANDKERCHIEFS .... GERARD DEPARDIEU
GET SHORTY .... JOHN TRAVOLTA
GET SMART, AGAIN! (TF) .... DON ADAMS
GET SMART, AGAIN! (TF) .... HAROLD GOULD
GET SMART, AGAIN! (TF) .... KENNETH MARS
GET TO KNOW YOUR RABBIT .... ALLEN GARFIELD
GET TO KNOW YOUR RABBIT .... JOHN ASTIN
GET TO KNOW YOUR RABBIT .... KATHERINE ROSS
GET TO KNOW YOUR RABBIT .... TOM SMOTHERS
GET YOURSELF A COLLEGE GIRL .... CHAD EVERETT
GETAWAY, THE (1972) .... ALI MacGRAW
GETAWAY, THE .... ALEC BALDWIN
GETAWAY, THE .... BEN JOHNSON
GETAWAY, THE .... BO HOPKINS
GETAWAY, THE .... JAMES WOODS
GETAWAY, THE .... JENNIFER TILLY
GETAWAY, THE .... KIM BASINGER
GETAWAY, THE .... MICHAEL MADSEN
GETAWAY, THE .... RICHARD BRIGHT
GETAWAY, THE .... RICHARD FARNSWORTH
GETTING AWAY WITH MURDER .... BONNIE HUNT
GETTING AWAY WITH MURDER .... BRIAN KERWIN
GETTING AWAY WITH MURDER .... DAN AYKROYD
GETTING AWAY WITH MURDER .... JACK LEMMON
GETTING AWAY WITH MURDER .... LILY TOMLIN
GETTING EVEN .... EDWARD ALBERT
GETTING EVEN .... JOE DON BAKER
GETTING EVEN WITH DAD .... SYDNEY WALKER†
GETTING EVEN WITH DAD .... GAILORD SARTAIN
GETTING EVEN WITH DAD .... GLENNE HEADLY
GETTING EVEN WITH DAD .... HECTOR ELIZONDO
GETTING EVEN WITH DAD .... MACAULAY CULKIN
GETTING EVEN WITH DAD .... RON CANADA
GETTING EVEN WITH DAD .... SAUL RUBINEK
GETTING EVEN WITH DAD .... TED DANSON
GETTING IT RIGHT .... HELENA BONHAM CARTER
GETTING IT RIGHT .... JANE HORROCKS
GETTING IT RIGHT .... JESSE BIRDSALL
GETTING IT RIGHT .... JOHN GIELGUD
GETTING IT RIGHT .... JUDY PARFITT
GETTING IT RIGHT .... LYNN REDGRAVE
GETTING IT RIGHT .... PAT HEYWOOD
GETTING IT RIGHT .... PETER COOK
GETTING IT RIGHT .... RICHARD HUW
GETTING IT RIGHT .... SHIRLEY ANNE FIELD
GETTING MARRIED (TF) .... BESS ARMSTRONG
GETTING MARRIED (TF) .... KATHERINE HELMOND
GETTING MARRIED (TF) .... MARK HARMON
GETTING OF WISDOM, THE .... SIGRID THORNTON
GETTING PHYSICAL (TF) .... DAVID NAUGHTON
GETTING PHYSICAL (TF) .... JOHN APREA
GETTING STRAIGHT .... CANDICE BERGEN
GETTING STRAIGHT .... ELLIOTT GOULD
GETTING STRAIGHT .... HARRISON FORD
GETTING STRAIGHT .... JEANNIE BERLIN
GETTING STRAIGHT .... JEFF COREY
GETTING THERE (CTF) .... JONATHAN SILVERMAN
GETTYSBURG .... BRIAN MALLON
GETTYSBURG .... C. THOMAS HOWELL
GETTYSBURG .... JAMES LANCASTER
GETTYSBURG .... JEFF DANIELS
GETTYSBURG .... KEVIN CONWAY
GETTYSBURG .... MARTIN SHEEN
GETTYSBURG .... MAXWELL CAULFIELD
GETTYSBURG .... RICHARD JORDAN†
GETTYSBURG .... SAM ELLIOTT
GETTYSBURG .... STEPHEN LANG
GETTYSBURG .... TOM BERENGER
GHANDI .... MICHAEL BRYANT
GHOST .... ARMELIA McQUEEN
GHOST .... DEMI MOORE
GHOST .... GAIL BOGGS
GHOST .... PATRICK SWAYZE
GHOST .... PHIL LEEDS
GHOST .... RICK AVILES
GHOST .... TONY GOLDWYN
GHOST .... VINCENT SCHIAVELLI
GHOST ∞ .... WHOOPI GOLDBERG
GHOST AND MR. CHICKEN, THE .... DICK SARGENT
GHOST AND MR. CHICKEN, THE .... DON KNOTTS
GHOST BREAKERS, THE .... ANTHONY QUINN
GHOST BREAKERS, THE .... BOB HOPE
GHOST CAMERA, THE .... JOHN MILLS
GHOST DAD .... BILL COSBY
GHOST DAD .... DENISE NICHOLAS
GHOST DAD .... IAN BANNEN
GHOST DAD .... KIMBERLY RUSSELL
GHOST IN MONTE CARLO, A (CTF) .... SAMANTHA EGGAR
GHOST IN THE MACHINE .... CHRIS MULKEY
GHOST IN THE MACHINE .... JESSICA WALTER
GHOST IN THE MACHINE .... KAREN ALLEN
GHOST IN THE MACHINE .... TED MARCOUX
GHOST IN THE MACHINE .... WIL HORNEFF
GHOST OF A CHANCE (TF) .... BRYNN THAYER
GHOST OF A CHANCE (TF) .... DICK VAN DYKE
GHOST OF A CHANCE (TF) .... GEOFFREY HOLDER
GHOST OF A CHANCE (TF) .... REDD FOXX†
GHOST OF FRANKENSTEIN, THE .... RALPH BELLAMY†
GHOST SHIP, THE .... JOSS ACKLAND
GHOST SHIP, THE .... LAWRENCE TIERNEY
GHOST STORY .... ALICE KRIGE
GHOST STORY .... CRAIG WASSON
GHOST STORY .... LEIGH LAWSON
GHOST STORY .... PATRICIA NEAL
GHOST TOWN .... CATHERINE HICKLAND
GHOST TOWN .... FRANC LUZ
GHOST TOWN .... JIMMIE F. SKAGGS
GHOSTBUSTERS .... ANNIE POTTS
GHOSTBUSTERS .... BILL MURRAY
GHOSTBUSTERS .... DAN AYKROYD
GHOSTBUSTERS .... ERNIE HUDSON
GHOSTBUSTERS .... HAROLD RAMIS
GHOSTBUSTERS .... RICK MORANIS
GHOSTBUSTERS .... SIGOURNEY WEAVER
GHOSTBUSTERS .... WILLIAM ATHERTON
GHOSTBUSTERS II .... ANNIE POTTS
GHOSTBUSTERS II .... BILL MURRAY
GHOSTBUSTERS II .... DAN AYKROYD
GHOSTBUSTERS II .... DAVID MARGULIES
GHOSTBUSTERS II .... ERNIE HUDSON
GHOSTBUSTERS II .... HAROLD RAMIS
GHOSTBUSTERS II .... HARRIS YULIN
GHOSTBUSTERS II .... JANET MARGOLIN
GHOSTBUSTERS II .... KURT FULLER
GHOSTBUSTERS II .... PETER MacNICOL
GHOSTBUSTERS II .... RICK MORANIS
GHOSTBUSTERS II .... SIGOURNEY WEAVER
GHOSTBUSTERS II .... WILHELM von HOMBURG
GHOSTS CAN'T DO IT .... ANTHONY QUINN
GHOSTS CAN'T DO IT .... BO DEREK
GHOSTS CAN'T DO IT .... DON MURRAY
GHOSTS CAN'T DO IT .... DONALD TRUMP
GHOSTS CAN'T DO IT .... GEORGE GRIZZARD
GHOSTS CAN'T DO IT .... JULIE NEWMAR
GHOSTS CAN'T DO IT .... LEO DAMIAN
GHOSTS ITALIAN STYLE .... MARCELLO MASTROIANNI
GHOSTS ITALIAN STYLE .... SOPHIA LOREN
GHOSTS OF ROME .... MARCELLO MASTROIANNI
GHOSTS ON THE LOOSE .... AVA GARDNER†
GHOUL, THE .... JOHN HURT
GHOULIES .... JACK NANCE
GHOULIES .... SCOTT THOMSON
GIANT .... CARROLL BAKER
GIANT .... DENNIS HOPPER
GIANT .... EARL HOLLIMAN
GIANT .... ELIZABETH TAYLOR
GIANT ★ .... JAMES DEAN†
GIANT ★ .... ROCK HUDSON†
GIANT ⊙ .... MERCEDES McCAMBRIDGE
GIANT OF THUNDER MOUNTAIN, THE .... RICHARD KIEL
GIANT OF THUNDER MOUNTAIN, THE .... RYAN TODD
GIANT SPIDER INVASION, THE .... BARBARA HALE
GIDEON'S TRUMPET (TF) .... JOSE FERRER†
GIDGET .... CLIFF ROBERTSON
GIDGET .... DOUG McCLURE
GIDGET .... SANDRA DEE
GIDGET GETS MARRIED (TF) .... DON AMECHE†
GIDGET GOES HAWAIIAN .... CARL REINER
GIDGET GROWS UP (TF) .... KAREN VALENTINE
GIDGET GROWS UP (TF) .... NINA FOCH
GIFT, THE (TF) .... KEVIN BACON
GIFT OF LOVE: A CHRISTMAS STORY, THE (TF) .... ANGELA LANSBURY
GIFT OF LOVE: A CHRISTMAS STORY, THE (TF) .... LEE REMICK†
GIFT OF LOVE: A CHRISTMAS STORY, THE (TF) .... POLLY HOLLIDAY
GIFT OF LOVE, THE .... LAUREN BACALL
GIFT OF LOVE, THE .... ROBERT STACK
GIFTAS/MARRIED LIFE .... MAE ZETTERLING†
GIFTED ONE, THE (TF) .... G.W. BAILEY
GIFTED ONE, THE (TF) .... PETE KOWANKO
GIG, THE .... ANDREW DUNCAN
GIG, THE .... CLEAVON LITTLE†
GIG, THE .... DANIEL NALBACH
GIG, THE .... JAY THOMAS
GIG, THE .... JERRY MATZ
GIG, THE .... JOE SILVER†
GIG, THE .... WARREN VACHE
GIG, THE .... WAYNE ROGERS
GIGI .... EVA GABOR
GIGI .... HERMIONE GINGOLD†
GIGI .... LESLIE CARON
GIGI .... LOUIS JOURDAN
GIGI .... MAURICE CHEVALIER†
GIGOLETTE .... RALPH BELLAMY†
GILBERT AND SULLIVAN .... ROBERT MORLEY
GILDA LIVE (FD) .... GILDA RADNER†
GILDERSLEEVE'S BAD DAY .... BARBARA HALE
GIMME SHELTER (FD) .... MICK JAGGER
GINGER AND FRED .... FRANCO FABRIZI
GINGER AND FRED .... FREDERICK LEDEBUR
GINGER AND FRED .... MARCELLO MASTROIANNI
GINGER AND FRED .... MARTIN MARIA BLAU
GINGER AND FRED .... TOTO MIGNONE
GINGER IN THE MORNING .... SISSY SPACEK
GINGERALE AFTERNOON .... DANA ANDERSEN
GINGERALE AFTERNOON .... GENE BUTLER
GINGERALE AFTERNOON .... JOHN M. JACKSON
GINGERALE AFTERNOON .... YEARDLEY SMITH
GIORNI D'AMORE .... MARCELLO MASTROIANNI
GIRL, THE .... FRANCO NERO
GIRL AND THE GENERAL, THE .... ROD STEIGER
GIRL CALLED HATTER FOX, THE (TF) .... CONCHATA FERRELL
GIRL CAN'T HELP IT, THE .... HENRY JONES
GIRL CRAZY .... JUNE ALLYSON
GIRL CRAZY .... MICKEY ROONEY
GIRL FRIEND, THE .... ANN SOTHERN
GIRL FRO MPETROVKA, THE .... ANTHONY HOPKINS
GIRL FROM 10TH AVENUE, THE .... BETTE DAVIS†
GIRL FROM GOD'S COUNTRY, THE .... JANE WYATT
GIRL FROM JONES BEACH, THE .... RONALD REAGAN
GIRL FROM LORRAINE, THE .... NATHALIE BAYE
GIRL FROM MANHATTAN, THE .... DOROTHY LAMOUR
GIRL FROM PETROVKA, THE .... GOLDIE HAWN
GIRL FROM PETROVKA, THE .... HAL HOLBROOK
GIRL FROM THE RED CABARET .... MEL FERRER
GIRL HAPPY .... ELVIS PRESLEY†
GIRL HAPPY .... NITA TALBOT
GIRL HE LEFT BEHIND, THE .... ALAN KING
GIRL HE LEFT BEHIND, THE .... JAMES GARNER
GIRL HE LEFT BEHIND, THE .... TAB HUNTER
GIRL IN A SWING, THE .... MEG TILLY
GIRL IN BLACK STOCKINGS, THE .... ANNE BANCROFT
GIRL IN BLUE, THE .... MAUD ADAMS
GIRL IN DANGER .... RALPH BELLAMY†
GIRL IN THE EMPTY GRAVE, THE (TF) .... ANDY GRIFFITH
GIRL IN THE KREMLIN, THE .... ZSA ZSA GABOR
GIRL IN THE PAINTING, THE .... MAE ZETTERLING†
GIRL IN THE PICTURE, THE .... CAROLINE GUTHRIE
GIRL IN THE PICTURE, THE .... DAVID McKAY

This is not a list of every film ever made or every cast member, only those listed in this directory.

GIRL IN THE PICTURE, THE .... GREGOR FISHER
GIRL IN THE PICTURE, THE .... IRINA BROOK
GIRL IN THE
    PICTURE, THE .... JOHN GORDON-SINCLAIR
GIRL IN THE PICTURE, THE .... PAUL YOUNG
GIRL IN THE RED VELVET
    SWING, THE .... JOAN COLLINS
GIRL IN WHITE, THE .... JUNE ALLYSON
GIRL MOST LIKELY, THE .... CLIFF ROBERTSON
GIRL MOST LIKELY, THE .... KAYE BALLARD
GIRL MOST LIKELY
    TO..., THE (TF) .... ANNETTE O'TOOLE
GIRL MOST LIKELY
    TO..., THE (TF) .... STOCKARD CHANNING
GIRL NAMED
    SOONER, A (TF) .... CLORIS LEACHMAN
GIRL NAMED SOONER, A (TF) .... DON MURRAY
GIRL NAMED TAMIKO, A .... FRANCE NUYEN
GIRL ON THE LATE,
    LATE SHOW, THE (TF) .... DON MURRAY
GIRL ON THE LATE
    LATE SHOW, THE (TF) .... YVONNE DE CARLO
GIRL RUSH, THE .... EDDIE ALBERT
GIRL RUSH, THE .... ROBERT MITCHUM
GIRL TROUBLE .... DON AMECHE†
GIRL WHO CAME BETWEEN
    THEM, THE (TF) .... ANTHONY DENISON
GIRL WHO CAME BETWEEN
    THEM, THE (TF) .... CHERYL LADD
GIRL WHO CAME BETWEEN
    THEM, THE (TF) .... MELISSA CHAN
GIRL WHO CAME
    GIFT-WRAPPED, THE (TF) .... KAREN VALENTINE
GIRL WHO COULDN'T
    SAY NO, THE .... GEORGE SEGAL
GIRL WHO COULDN'T
    SAY NO, THE .... LILA KEDROVA
GIRL WHO HAD
    EVERYTHING, THE .... ELIZABETH TAYLOR
GIRL WHO KNEW TOO MUCH, THE .... ADAM WEST
GIRL WHO SPELLED
    FREEDOM, THE (TF) ...... TERRY DAVID MULLIGAN
GIRL WITH GREEN EYES .... LYNN REDGRAVE
GIRL WITH GREEN EYES, THE ..... JULIAN GLOVER
GIRL-GETTERS, THE .... DAVID HEMMINGS
GIRLFRIENDS .... AMY WRIGHT
GIRLFRIENDS .... ELI WALLACH
GIRLFRIENDS .... MELANIE MAYRON
GIRLS! GIRLS! GIRLS! .... ELVIS PRESLEY†
GIRLS JUST WANT TO
    HAVE FUN .... LEE MONTGOMERY
GIRLS JUST WANT TO
    HAVE FUN .... SARAH JESSICA PARKER
GIRLS OF HUNTINGTON
    HOUSE, THE (TF) ...... MERCEDES McCAMBRIDGE
GIRLS OF HUNTINGTON
    HOUSE, THE (TF) ...... PAMELA SUE MARTIN
GIRLS OF HUNTINGTON
    HOUSE, THE (TF) .... SHIRLEY JONES
GIRLS OF HUNTINGTON
    HOUSE, THE (TF) .... SISSY SPACEK
GIRLS ON PROBATION .... RONALD REAGAN
GIRLS ON THE LOOSE .... PETER MARK RICHMAN
GIRLS' SCHOOL .... RALPH BELLAMY†
GIRLY .... MICHAEL BRYANT
GIRO CITY .... GLENDA JACKSON
GIVE A GIRL A BREAK .... DEBBIE REYNOLDS
GIVE 'EM HELL, HARRY! ★ ..... JAMES WHITMORE
GIVE HER THE MOON .... MARTHE KELLER
GIVE ME A SAILOR .... BOB HOPE
GIVE ME A SAILOR .... MARTHA RAYE†
GIVE MY REGARDS TO
    BROAD STREET .... BRYON BROWN
GIVE MY REGARDS TO
    BROAD STREET .... BARBARA BACH
GIVE US THE MOON .... JEAN SIMMONS
GIVE US THIS DAY .... SAM WANAMAKER†
GLADIATOR .... BRIAN DENNEHY
GLADIATOR .... CARA BUONO
GLADIATOR .... CUBA GOODING JR.
GLADIATOR .... JAMES MARSHALL
GLADIATOR .... OSSIE DAVIS

GLADIATOR .... ROBERT LOGGIA
GLAMOUR BOY .... JACKIE COOPER
GLASS BOTTOM BOAT, THE .... DOM DeLUISE
GLASS BOTTOM BOAT, THE .... DORIS DAY
GLASS BOTTOM BOAT, THE .... PAUL LYNDE†
GLASS HOUSE, THE .... ALAN ALDA
GLASS HOUSE, THE .... DEAN JAGGER†
GLASS HOUSE, THE (TF) .... BILLY DEE WILLIAMS
GLASS HOUSE, THE (TF) .... CLU GULAGER
GLASS HOUSE, THE (TF) .... VIC MORROW†
GLASS HOUSES .... JENNIFER O'NEILL
GLASS MENAGERIE, THE .... JAMES NAUGHTON
GLASS MENAGERIE, THE .... JANE WYMAN
GLASS MENAGERIE, THE .... JOANNE WOODWARD
GLASS MENAGERIE, THE .... JOHN MALKOVICH
GLASS MENAGERIE, THE .... KAREN ALLEN
GLASS MENAGERIE, THE .... KIRK DOUGLAS
GLASS
    MENAGERIE, THE (TF) .... KATHERINE HEPBURN
GLASS SLIPPER, THE .... LESLIE CARON
GLASS WEB, THE .... JOHN FORSYTHE
GLEAMING THE CUBE .... CHARLES CYPHERS
GLEAMING THE CUBE .... CHRISTIAN SLATER
GLEAMING THE CUBE .... ED LAUTER
GLEAMING THE CUBE .... KIEU CHINH
GLEAMING THE CUBE .... LE TUAN
GLEAMING THE CUBE .... MICOLE MERCURIO
GLEAMING THE CUBE .... MIN LUONG
GLEAMING THE CUBE .... RICHARD HERD
GLEAMING THE CUBE .... STEVEN BAUER
GLENGARRY GLEN ROSS .... ALAN ARKIN
GLENGARRY GLEN ROSS .... ALEC BALDWIN
GLENGARRY GLEN ROSS .... ED HARRIS
GLENGARRY GLEN ROSS .... JACK LEMMON
GLENGARRY GLEN ROSS .... JONATHAN PRYCE
GLENGARRY GLEN ROSS .... KEVIN SPACEY
GLENGARRY GLEN ROSS ◊ .... AL PACINO
GLENN MILLER STORY, THE .... HARRY MORGAN
GLENN MILLER STORY, THE .... JAMES STEWART
GLENN MILLER STORY, THE .... JUNE ALLYSON
GLENORKY .... MARK HARMON
GLI AMANTI .... FAYE DUNAWAY
GLI EROI .... ROD STEIGER
GLI INDIFFERENTI .... ROD STEIGER
GLI INDIFFERENTI .... SHELLEY WINTERS
GLI INTOCCABILI .... BRITT EKLAND
GLI INTOCCABILI .... PETER FALK
GLITTER (TF) .... CHRISTOPHER MAYER
GLITTER (TF) .... DAVID BIRNEY
GLITTER (TF) .... MORGAN BRITTANY
GLITTER (TF) .... PATRICIA NEAL
GLITTER (TF) .... TRACY NELSON
GLITZ (TF) .... JIMMY SMITS
GLITZ (TF) .... JOHN DIEHL
GLOBAL AFFAIR, A .... BOB HOPE
GLOBAL AFFAIR, A .... NEHEMIAH PERSOFF
GLOBAL AFFAIR, A .... YVONNE DE CARLO
GLORIA .... BUCK HENRY
GLORIA ★ .... GENA ROWLANDS
GLORY .... ALAN NORTH
GLORY .... ANDRE BRAUGHER
GLORY .... BOB GUNTON
GLORY .... CARY ELWES
GLORY .... CLIFF DE YOUNG
GLORY .... DONOVAN LEITCH
GLORY .... JANE ALEXANDER
GLORY .... JIHMI KENNEDY
GLORY .... JOHN CULLUM
GLORY .... JOHN FINN
GLORY .... MATTHEW BRODERICK
GLORY .... MORGAN FREEMAN
GLORY ◊◊ .... RAYMOND ST. JACQUES
GLORY ◊◊ .... DENZEL WASHINGTON
GLORY ALLEY .... LESLIE CARON
GLORY BOY .... MICHAEL MORIARTY
GLORY BOY .... WILLIAM DEVANE
GLORY BOYS, THE (TF) .... ROD STEIGER
GLORY DAYS (TF) .... ROBERT CONRAD
GLORY GUYS, THE .... JAMES CAAN
GLORY STOMPERS, THE .... DENNIS HOPPER
GLOVE, THE .... JOHN SAXON
GO ASK ALICE (TF) .... WILLIAM SHATNER

GO FOR BROKE .... VAN JOHNSON
GO MAN GO! .... RUBY DEE
GO, MAN, GO! .... SIDNEY POITIER
GO NAKED IN
    THE WORLD .... ANTHONY (TONY) FRANCIOSA
GO NAKED IN THE WORLD ...... ERNEST BORGNINE
GO TELL IT ON THE
    MOUNTAIN (TF) .... ALFRE WOODARD
GO TELL IT ON THE
    MOUNTAIN (TF) .... PAUL WINFIELD
GO TELL THE SPARTANS .... BURT LANCASTER†
GO TELL THE SPARTANS .... CRAIG WASSON
GO TO BLAZES .... MAGGIE SMITH
GO TOWARD THE LIGHT (TF) ...... GARY BAYER
GO TOWARD THE LIGHT (TF) .... LINDA HAMILTON
GO TOWARD THE LIGHT (TF) ...... PIPER LAURIE
GO TOWARD THE LIGHT (TF) ..... RICHARD THOMAS
GO WEST, YOUNG GIRL (TF) ..... KAREN VALENTINE
GO-BETWEEN, THE .... ALAN BATES
GO-BETWEEN, THE .... JULIE CHRISTIE
GO-BETWEEN, THE .... MICHAEL GOUGH
GO-BETWEEN, THE ◊ .... MARGARET LEIGHTON†
GOBOTS: BATTLE OF THE
    ROCK LORDS (AF) .... MARGOT KIDDER
GOBOTS: BATTLE OF THE
    ROCK LORDS (AF) .... MICHAEL NOURI
GOBOTS: BATTLE OF THE
    ROCK LORDS (AF) .... RODDY McDOWALL
GOBOTS: BATTLE OF THE
    ROCK LORDS (AF) .... TELLY SAVALAS†
GOD BLESS THE CHILD (TF) ... DORIAN HAREWOOD
GOD BLESS THE CHILD (TF) ..... MARE WINNINGHAM
GOD TOLD ME TO .... DEBORAH RAFFIN
GOD TOLD ME TO .... SANDY DENNIS†
GOD TOLD ME TO .... SYLVIA SIDNEY
GOD TOLD ME TO .... TONY LoBIANCO
GOD'S LITTLE ACRE .... ALDO RAY†
GOD'S LITTLE ACRE .... MICHAEL LANDON†
GOD'S LITTLE ACRE .... ROBERT RYAN†
GODCHILD, THE (TF) .... KEITH CARRADINE
GODDESS OF LOVE (TF) .... BETSY PALMER
GODDESS OF LOVE (TF) .... DAVID LEISURE
GODDESS OF LOVE (TF) .... DAVID NAUGHTON
GODDESS OF LOVE (TF) .... LITTLE RICHARD
GODDESS OF LOVE (TF) .... VANNA WHITE
GODDESS, THE .... JOYCE VAN PATTEN
GODDESS, THE .... KIM STANLEY
GODDESS, THE .... LLOYD BRIDGES
GODDESS, THE .... PATTY DUKE
GODDESS, THE .... STEVEN HILL
GODFATHER, THE .... ABE VIGODA
GODFATHER, THE .... AL LETTIERI†
GODFATHER, THE .... ALEX ROCCO
GODFATHER, THE .... DIANE KEATON
GODFATHER, THE .... JOHN CAZALE†
GODFATHER, THE .... JOHN MARLEY†
GODFATHER, THE .... MORGANA KING
GODFATHER, THE .... RICHARD BRIGHT
GODFATHER, THE .... RICHARD CONTE†
GODFATHER, THE .... STERLING HAYDEN†
GODFATHER, THE .... TALIA SHIRE
GODFATHER, THE ★★ ..... MARLON BRANDO
GODFATHER, THE ◊ .... AL PACINO
GODFATHER, THE ◊ .... JAMES CAAN
GODFATHER, THE ◊ .... ROBERT DUVALL
GODFATHER, PART II, THE .... ABE VIGODA
GODFATHER, PART II, THE .... DANNY AIELLO
GODFATHER, PART II, THE .... DIANE KEATON
GODFATHER, PART II, THE .... G. D. SPRADLIN
GODFATHER,
    PART II, THE .... HARRY DEAN STANTON
GODFATHER, PART II, THE .... JAMES CAAN
GODFATHER, PART II, THE .... JOE PANTOLIANO
GODFATHER, PART II, THE .... JOE SPINELL
GODFATHER, PART II, THE .... JOHN CAZALE†
GODFATHER, PART II, THE .... KATHLEEN BELLER
GODFATHER, PART II, THE .... MORGANA KING
GODFATHER, PART II, THE .... PETER DONAT
GODFATHER, PART II, THE .... RICHARD BRIGHT
GODFATHER, PART II, THE .... ROBERT DUVALL
GODFATHER, PART II, THE .... TROY DONAHUE
GODFATHER, PART II, THE ★ .... AL PACINO

457

GODFATHER, PART II, THE ○ ...... LEE STRASBERG†
GODFATHER, PART II, THE ○ .... MICHAEL V. GAZZO
GODFATHER, PART II, THE ○ .... TALIA SHIRE
GODFATHER, PART II, THE ∞ .... ROBERT DE NIRO
GODFATHER, PART II, THE .... AL PACINO
GODFATHER, PART III, THE .... BRIDGET FONDA
GODFATHER, PART III, THE .... DIANE KEATON
GODFATHER, PART III, THE .... DONAL DONNELLY
GODFATHER, PART III, THE .... ELI WALLACH
GODFATHER, PART III, THE ..... FRANC D'AMBROSIO
GODFATHER, PART III, THE ..... GEORGE HAMILTON
GODFATHER, PART III, THE .... HELMUT BERGER
GODFATHER, PART III, THE .... JOE MANTEGNA
GODFATHER, PART III, THE .... JOHN SAVAGE
GODFATHER, PART III, THE .... RAF VALLONE
GODFATHER, PART III, THE .... SOFIA COPPOLA
GODFATHER, PART III, THE .... TALIA SHIRE
GODFATHER, PART III, THE ○ .... ANDY GARCIA
GODS MUST BE CRAZY, THE .... MARIUS WEYERS
GODS MUST BE CRAZY, THE .... NIXAU
GODS MUST BE CRAZY, THE ... SANDRA PRINSLOO
GODS MUST BE CRAZY II, THE ...... HANS STRYDOM
GODS MUST BE CRAZY II, THE .... LENA FARUGIA
GODS MUST BE CRAZY II, THE .... NIXAU
GODS OF SKID ROW, THE .... NICK CASSAVETES
GODZILLA 1985 .... RAYMOND BURR†
GODZILLA, KING OF
  THE MONSTERS .... RAYMOND BURR†
GOD'S GUN .... JACK PALANCE
GOD'S LITTLE ACRE .... BUDDY HACKETT
GOD'S LITTLE ACRE .... TINA LOUISE
GOD'S PAYROLL .... ANTHONY LaPAGLIA
GOD'S PAYROLL .... BRIAN BENBEN
GOHA .... OMAR SHARIF
GOIN' SOUTH .... ANN RAMSEY†
GOIN' SOUTH .... CHRISTOPHER LLOYD
GOIN' SOUTH .... DANNY DEVITO
GOIN' SOUTH .... JACK NICHOLSON
GOIN' SOUTH .... JOHN BELUSHI†
GOIN' SOUTH .... LUANA ANDERS
GOIN' SOUTH .... MARY STEENBURGEN
GOIN' SOUTH .... VERONICA CARTWRIGHT
GOING APE! .... ART METRANO
GOING APE! .... DANNY DEVITO
GOING APE! .... TONY DANZA
GOING BERSERK .... JOHN CANDY†
GOING BERSERK .... PAUL DOOLEY
GOING FOR THE GOLD: THE BILL
  JOHNSON STORY (TF) .... ANTHONY EDWARDS
GOING FOR THE GOLD:
  THE BILL JOHNSON
  STORY (TF) .... DEBORAH VAN VALKENBURGH
GOING FOR THE GOLD: THE BILL
  JOHNSON STORY (TF) .... DENNIS WEAVER
GOING FOR THE GOLD:
  THE BILL JOHNSON
  STORY (TF) .... SARAH JESSICA PARKER
GOING HOME .... BRENDA VACCARO
GOING HOME .... JAN-MICHAEL VINCENT
GOING HOME .... ROBERT MITCHUM
GOING HOME .... SALLY KIRKLAND
GOING IN STYLE .... ART CARNEY
GOING IN STYLE .... GEORGE BURNS
GOING IN STYLE .... LEE STRASBERG†
GOING MY WAY ★/∞ .... BARRY FITZGERALD†
GOING MY WAY ★★ .... BING CROSBY†
GOING PLACES .... GERARD DEPARDIEU
GOING PLACES .... ISABELLE HUPPERT
GOING PLACES .... RONALD REAGAN
GOING TO THE
  CHAPEL (TF) .... BARBARA BILLINGSLEY
GOING TO THE CHAPEL (TF) ..... CLORIS LEACHMAN
GOING TO THE CHAPEL (TF) .... EILEEN BRENNAN
GOING UP OF
  DAVID LEV, THE (TF) .... CLAIRE BLOOM
GOJIRA .... RAYMOND BURR†
GOLD .... BRADFORD DILLMAN
GOLD .... JOHN GIELGUD
GOLD .... ROGER MOORE
GOLD .... SUSANNAH YORK
GOLD .... TONY BECKLEY†
GOLD AND GLITTER .... LILLIAN GISH†

GOLD DIGGERS .... ANNA CHLUMSKY
GOLD DIGGERS .... ANNA CHLUMSKY
GOLD DIGGERS .... BRIAN KERWIN
GOLD DIGGERS .... CHRISTINA RICCI
GOLD DIGGERS .... POLLY DRAPER
GOLD DIGGERS OF 1937 .... JANE WYMAN
GOLD DIGGERS, THE .... JULIE CHRISTIE
GOLD IS WHERE
  YOU FIND IT .... OLIVIA DE HAVILLAND
GOLD OF NAPLES, THE .... SOPHIA LOREN
GOLD OF THE SEVEN SAINTS .... CLINT WALKER
GOLD OF THE SEVEN SAINTS .... ROGER MOORE
GOLD RUSH MAISIE .... ANN SOTHERN
GOLDEN ARROW, THE .... BETTE DAVIS†
GOLDEN ARROW, THE .... TAB HUNTER
GOLDEN BLADE, THE .... PIPER LAURIE
GOLDEN BLADE, THE .... ROCK HUDSON†
GOLDEN BOY .... BARBARA STANWYCK†
GOLDEN BOY .... WILLIAM HOLDEN†
GOLDEN CHILD, THE .... CHARLES DANCE
GOLDEN CHILD, THE .... CHARLOTTE LEWIS
GOLDEN CHILD, THE .... EDDIE MURPHY
GOLDEN CHILD, THE .... J. L. REATE
GOLDEN CHILD, THE .... JAMES HONG
GOLDEN CHILD, THE .... RANDALL (TEX) COBB
GOLDEN CHILD, THE .... VICTOR WONG
GOLDEN GATE .... BRUNO KIRBY
GOLDEN GATE .... JOAN CHEN
GOLDEN GATE .... MATT DILLON
GOLDEN GATE (TF) .... JEAN SIMMONS
GOLDEN GATE
  MURDERS, THE (TF) .... SUSANNAH YORK
GOLDEN GOOSE, THE .... CHARLES DURNING
GOLDEN HEAD, THE .... BUDDY HACKETT
GOLDEN
  HONEYMOON, THE (TF) .... STEPHEN ELLIOTT
GOLDEN NEEDLES .... ANN SOTHERN
GOLDEN NEEDLES .... BURGESS MEREDITH
GOLDEN NEEDLES .... ELIZABETH ASHLEY
GOLDEN NEEDLES .... JOE DON BAKER
GOLDEN RENDEZVOUS .... ANN TURKEL
GOLDEN RENDEZVOUS .... BURGESS MEREDITH
GOLDEN RENDEZVOUS .... GORDAN JACKSON†
GOLDEN RENDEZVOUS .... JOHN VERNON
GOLDEN RENDEZVOUS .... LEIGH LAWSON
GOLDEN RENDEZVOUS .... RICHARD HARRIS
GOLDEN SALAMANDER, THE .... ANOUK AIMEE
GOLDEN VOYAGE
  OF SINBAD, THE .... JOHN PHILLIP LAW
GOLDENEYE .... PIERCE BROSNAN
GOLDENGIRL .... HARRY GUARDINO
GOLDENGIRL .... JAMES COBURN
GOLDENGIRL .... JESSICA WALTER
GOLDENGIRL .... LESLIE CARON
GOLDENGIRL .... ROBERT CULP
GOLDENGIRL .... SUSAN ANTON
GOLDFINGER .... BURT KWOUK
GOLDFINGER .... HAROLD SAKATA†
GOLDFINGER .... HONOR BLACKMAN
GOLDFINGER .... LOIS MAXWELL
GOLDFINGER .... SEAN CONNERY
GOLDIE AND THE BOXER (TF) .... O. J. SIMPSON
GOLDIE AND THE BOXER GO
  TO HOLLYWOOD (TF) .... O. J. SIMPSON
GOLIATH AWAITS (MS) .... ROBERT FORSTER
GOLIATH AWAITS (TF) .... EDDIE ALBERT
GONE ARE THE DAYS! .... ALAN ALDA
GONE ARE THE DAYS! .... BEAH RICHARDS
GONE ARE THE DAYS! .... OSSIE DAVIS
GONE ARE THE DAYS! .... RUBY DEE
GONE ARE THE DAYS! .... SORRELL BOOKE
GONE ARE THE DAYS (CTF) .... SUSAN ANSPACH
GONE TO EARTH .... JENNIFER JONES
GONE WITH THE WEST .... JAMES CAAN
GONE WITH THE WEST .... ROBERT WALKER JR.
GONE WITH THE WEST .... STEFANIE POWERS
GONE WITH THE WIND .... LESLIE HOWARD†
GONE WITH THE WIND ★ .... CLARK GABLE†
GONE WITH THE WIND ★★ .... VIVIEN LEIGH†
GONE WITH THE WIND ∞ .... HATTIE MCDANIEL†
GONE WITH THE WIND ○ ...... OLIVIA DE HAVILLAND

GOOD COMPANIONS, THE .... JOHN GIELGUD
GOOD COMPANIONS, THE ..... SHIRLEY ANNE FIELD
GOOD DAME .... SYLVIA SIDNEY
GOOD DIE YOUNG, THE .... JOAN COLLINS
GOOD DIE YOUNG, THE .... JOHN IRELAND
GOOD FATHER, THE .... ANTHONY HOPKINS
GOOD FATHER, THE ..... JOANNE WHALLEY-KILMER
GOOD FATHER, THE .... MICHAEL BYRNE
GOOD FIGHT, THE (CTF) .... CHRISTINE LAHTI
GOOD GIRL .... SYLVIA SIDNEY
GOOD GUYS AND THE
  BAD GUYS, THE .... BUDDY HACKETT
GOOD GUYS AND THE
  BAD GUYS, THE .... DAVID CARRADINE
GOOD GUYS AND THE
  BAD GUYS, THE .... GEORGE KENNEDY
GOOD GUYS AND THE
  BAD GUYS, THE .... LOIS NETTLETON
GOOD GUYS AND THE
  BAD GUYS, THE .... MARTIN BALSAM
GOOD GUYS AND THE
  BAD GUYS, THE .... ROBERT MITCHUM
GOOD GUYS AND THE
  BAD GUYS, THE .... TINA LOUISE
GOOD GUYS WEAR BLACK .... ANNE ARCHER
GOOD GUYS WEAR BLACK .... CHUCK NORRIS
GOOD GUYS
  WEAR BLACK .... JAMES FRANCISCUS†
GOOD LUCK,
  MISS WYCKOFF .... DONALD PLEASENCE
GOOD LUCK, MISS WYCKOFF ...... ROBERT VAUGHN
GOOD MORNING, VIETNAM .... ROBERT WUHL
GOOD MAN IN AFRICA, A .... COLIN FRIELS
GOOD MAN IN AFRICA, A .... DIANA RIGG
GOOD MAN IN AFRICA, A .... JACKIE MOFOKENG
GOOD MAN IN
  AFRICA, A .... JOANNE WHALLEY-KILMER
GOOD MAN IN AFRICA, A .... JOHN LITHGOW
GOOD MAN IN AFRICA, A .... LOUIS GOSSETT JR.
GOOD MAN IN AFRICA, A .... MAYNARD EZIASHI
GOOD MAN IN AFRICA, A .... SARAH JANE FENTON
GOOD MAN IN AFRICA, A .... SEAN CONNERY
GOOD MAN IN AFRICA, A .... THEMBA NDABA
GOOD MORNING, BABYLON .... CHARLES DANCE
GOOD MORNING, BABYLON .... GRETA SCACCHI
GOOD MORNING, BABYLON .... VINCENT SPANO
GOOD MORNING MISS DOVE .... CHUCK CONNORS†
GOOD MORNING, MISS DOVE .... JENNIFER JONES
GOOD MORNING, MISS DOVE .... MARY WICKES
GOOD MORNING, MISS DOVE .... ROBERT STACK
GOOD MORNING, VIETNAM .... FLOYD VIVINO
GOOD MORNING, VIETNAM ..... FOREST WHITAKER
GOOD MORNING, VIETNAM .... J. T. WALSH
GOOD MORNING VIETNAM .... RICHARD EDSON
GOOD MORNING, VIETNAM ★ .... ROBIN WILLIAMS
GOOD MOTHER, THE .... DIANE KEATON
GOOD MOTHER, THE .... JASON ROBARDS
GOOD MOTHER, THE .... LIAM NEESON
GOOD MOTHER, THE .... RALPH BELLAMY†
GOOD NEIGHBOR SAM .... JACK LEMMON
GOOD NEWS .... JUNE ALLYSON
GOOD NIGHT, SWEET WIFE:
  A MURDER IN BOSTON (TF) .... KEN OLIN
GOOD OL' BOY .... ANN RAMSEY†
GOOD OLD BOYS, THE (CTF) .... TOMMY LEE JONES
GOOD SON, THE .... ASHLEY CROW
GOOD SON, THE .... DANIEL HUGH KELLY
GOOD SON, THE .... DAVID MORSE
GOOD SON, THE .... ELIJAH WOOD
GOOD SON, THE .... JACQUELINE BROOKES
GOOD SON, THE .... MACAULAY CULKIN
GOOD SON, THE .... QUINN CULKIN
GOOD SON, THE .... WENDY CREWSON
GOOD, THE BAD AND
  THE UGLY, THE .... CLINT EASTWOOD
GOOD, THE BAD AND
  THE UGLY, THE .... ELI WALLACH
GOOD TIMES .... CHER
GOOD TIMES .... SONNY BONO
GOOD TO GO .... ANJELICA HUSTON
GOOD TO GO .... ART GARFUNKEL
GOOD WIFE, THE .... BRYON BROWN

GOOD WIFE, THE .... RACHEL WARD
GOOD WIFE, THE .... SAM NEILL
GOODBYE AGAIN .... ANTHONY PERKINS†
GOODBYE AGAIN .... DIAHANN CARROLL
GOODBYE AND AMEN .... JOHN FORSYTHE
GOODBYE, CHARLIE .... DEBBIE REYNOLDS
GOODBYE, CHARLIE .... ELLEN BURSTYN
GOODBYE, CHARLIE .... JAMES BROLIN
GOODBYE, CHARLIE .... PAT BOONE
GOODBYE, CHARLIE .... TONY CURTIS
GOODBYE CHARLIE .... WALTER MATTHAU
GOODBYE, COLUMBUS .... ALI MacGRAW
GOODBYE, COLUMBUS .... JACK KLUGMAN
GOODBYE, COLUMBUS .... RICHARD BENJAMIN
GOODBYE EMMANUELLE .... SYLVIA KRISTEL
GOODBYE GEMINI .... ALEXIS KANNER
GOODBYE GEMINI .... FREDDIE JONES
GOODBYE GIRL, THE .... NICOL WILLIAMSON
GOODBYE GIRL, THE ★ .... MARSHA MASON
GOODBYE GIRL, THE ★★ .... RICHARD DREYFUSS
GOODBYE GIRL, THE ✪ .... QUINN CUMMINGS
GOODBYE, MR. CHIPS .... JACK HEDLEY
GOODBYE, MR. CHIPS .... JOHN MILLS
GOODBYE MR. CHIPS .... MICHAEL BRYANT
GOODBYE, MR. CHIPS .... PATRICIA HAYES
GOODBYE, MR. CHIPS .... SIAN PHILLIPS
GOODBYE, MR. CHIPS ★ .... GREER GARSON
GOODBYE, MR. CHIPS ★ .... PETER O'TOOLE
GOODBYE, MR. CHIPS ★★ .... ROBERT DONAT†
GOODBYE, MY FANCY .... JOAN CRAWFORD†
GOODBYE, MY LADY .... SIDNEY POITIER
GOODBYE, NEW YORK .... JULIE HAGERTY
GOODBYE PEOPLE, THE .... GENE SAKS
GOODBYE PEOPLE, THE .... JUDD HIRSCH
GOODBYE PEOPLE, THE .... MARTIN BALSAM
GOODBYE PEOPLE, THE .... MICHAEL TUCKER
GOODBYE PEOPLE, THE .... PAMELA REED
GOODBYE PEOPLE, THE .... RON SILVER
GOODBYE, RAGGEDY ANN (TF) .... ED FLANDERS
GOODBYE, RAGGEDY ANN (TF) .... MARTIN SHEEN
GOODBYE, RAGGEDY ANN (TF) .... MIA FARROW
GOODFELLAS .... ELAINE KAGAN
GOODFELLAS .... HENNY YOUNGMAN
GOODFELLAS .... PAUL SORVINO
GOODFELLAS .... PAULA YOUNG
GOODFELLAS .... RAY LIOTTA
GOODFELLAS .... ROBERT DE NIRO
GOODFELLAS ✪ .... LORRAINE BRACCO
GOODFELLAS ✪✪ .... JOE PESCI
GOODNIGHT, MIKE .... STACY KEACH
GOODNIGHT MY LOVE .... BARBARA BAIN
GOODNIGHT, SWEET WIFE (TF) .... JAMES HANDY
GOONIES, THE .... ANN RAMSEY†
GOONIES, THE .... COREY FELDMAN
GOONIES, THE .... JEFF COHEN
GOONIES, THE .... JOE PANTOLIANO
GOONIES, THE .... JOSH BROLIN
GOONIES, THE .... KE HUY QUAN
GOONIES, THE .... MARTHA PLIMPTON
GOONIES, THE .... ROBERT DAVI
GOONIES, THE .... SEAN ASTIN
GOOSE STEPS OUT, THE .... PETER USTINOV
GORDON IL PIRATO NERO .... VINCENT PRICE†
GORDON'S WAR .... PAUL WINFIELD
GORGEOUS HUSSY, THE .... JAMES STEWART
GORGEOUS HUSSY, THE .... JOAN CRAWFORD†
GORGEOUS HUSSY, THE ✪ .... BEULAH BONDI†
GORILLA AT LARGE .... ANNE BANCROFT
GORILLA AT LARGE .... RAYMOND BURR†
GORILLAS IN THE MIST .... BRYON BROWN
GORILLAS IN
THE MIST .... CONSTANTIN ALEXANDROV
GORILLAS IN THE MIST .... IAIN CUTHBERTSON
GORILLAS IN THE MIST .... JOHN OMIRAH MILUWI
GORILLAS IN THE MIST .... JULIE HARRIS
GORILLAS IN THE MIST .... WAIGWA WACHIRA
GORILLAS IN THE MIST ★ .... SIGOURNEY WEAVER
GORKY PARK .... BRIAN DENNEHY
GORKY PARK .... IAN BANNEN
GORKY PARK .... JOANNA PACULA
GORKY PARK .... LEE MARVIN†
GORKY PARK .... RICHARD GRIFFITHS
GORKY PARK .... WILLIAM HURT
GORP .... ROSANNA ARQUETTE
GOSPEL ACCORDING TO VIC .... DAVE ANDERSON
GOSPEL ACCORDING TO VIC .... TOM CONTI
GOSPEL ROAD, THE .... KRIS KRISTOFFERSON
GOTCHA! .... ALEX ROCCO
GOTCHA! .... ANTHONY EDWARDS
GOTCHA! .... CHRIS RYDELL
GOTCHA! .... LINDA FIORENTINO
GOTHIC .... GABRIEL BYRNE
GOTHIC .... JULIAN SANDS
GOTHIC .... NATASHA RICHARDSON
GOVERNMENT GIRL .... OLIVIA DE HAVILLAND
GRACE KELLY (TF) .... CHERYL LADD
GRACE KELLY (TF) .... DIANE LADD
GRACE KELLY (TF) .... LLOYD BRIDGES
GRACE QUIGLEY .... CHIP ZIEN
GRACE QUIGLEY .... JILL EIKENBERRY
GRACE QUIGLEY .... KATHERINE HEPBURN
GRACE QUIGLEY .... NICK NOLTE
GRACE UNDER PRESSURE .... DENNIS QUAID
GRACE UNDER PRESSURE .... JULIA ROBERTS
GRADUATE, THE .... ALICE GHOSTLEY
GRADUATE, THE .... BUCK HENRY
GRADUATE, THE .... ELIZABETH WILSON
GRADUATE, THE .... MARION LORNE†
GRADUATE, THE .... MIKE FARRELL
GRADUATE, THE .... MURRAY HAMILTON†
GRADUATE, THE .... NORMAN FELL
GRADUATE, THE .... RICHARD DREYFUSS
GRADUATE, THE .... WILLIAM DANIELS
GRADUATE, THE ★ .... ANNE BANCROFT
GRADUATE, THE ★ .... DUSTIN HOFFMAN
GRADUATE, THE ✪ .... KATHERINE ROSS
GRADUATION DAY .... RICHARD BALIN
GRAFFITI BRIDGE .... GEORGE CLINTON
GRAFFITI BRIDGE .... INGRID CHAVEZ
GRAFFITI BRIDGE .... JEROME BENTON
GRAFFITI BRIDGE .... JILL JONES
GRAFFITI BRIDGE .... MAVIS STAPLES
GRAFFITI BRIDGE .... MORRIS DAY
GRAFFITI BRIDGE .... PRINCE
GRAFFITI BRIDGE .... TEVIN CAMPBELL
GRAMBLING'S
WHITE TIGER (TF) .... LeVAR BURTON
GRAN BOLLITO .... SHELLEY WINTERS
GRAND CANYON .... ALFRE WOODARD
GRAND CANYON .... DANNY GLOVER
GRAND CANYON .... KEVIN KLINE
GRAND CANYON .... MARY McDONNELL
GRAND CANYON .... MARY-LOUISE PARKER
GRAND CANYON .... STEVE MARTIN
GRAND EXIT .... ANN SOTHERN
GRAND HOTEL .... GRETA GARBO†
GRAND HOTEL .... JOAN CRAWFORD†
GRAND HOTEL .... JOHN BARRYMORE†
GRAND HOTEL .... LIONEL BARRYMORE†
GRAND HOTEL .... WALLACE BEERY†
GRAND NATIONAL NIGHT .... GEORGE ROSE†
GRAND PRIX .... EVA MARIE SAINT
GRAND PRIX .... JAMES GARNER
GRAND PRIX .... JESSICA WALTER
GRAND SLAM .... JANET LEIGH
GRAND THEFT AUTO .... PAUL BARTEL
GRAND THEFT AUTO .... RON HOWARD
GRAND TOUR, THE (TF) .... RIP TORN
GRANDVIEW, U.S.A. .... PATRICK SWAYZE
GRANDVIEW, U.S.A. .... C. THOMAS HOWELL
GRANDVIEW, U.S.A. .... JAMIE LEE CURTIS
GRANDVIEW, U.S.A. .... JOHN CUSACK
GRANDVIEW, U.S.A. .... MICHAEL WINSLOW
GRANDVIEW, U.S.A. .... WILLIAM WINDOM
GRAPES OF WRATH, THE .... JOHN CARRADINE†
GRAPES OF WRATH, THE ★ .... HENRY FONDA†
GRAPES OF WRATH, THE ✪✪ .... JANE DARWELL†
GRASS HARP, THE .... CICELY TYSON
GRASS HARP, THE .... JACK LEMMON
GRASS HARP, THE .... JOAN PLOWRIGHT
GRASS HARP, THE .... SISSY SPACEK
GRASS HARP, THE .... WALTER MATTHAU
GRASS IS ALWAYS GREENER
OVER THE SEPTIC
TANK, THE (TF) .... CAROL BURNETT
GRASS IS ALWAYS GREENER
OVER THE SEPTIC
TANK, THE (TF) .... CHARLES GRODIN
GRASS IS GREENER, THE .... DEBORAH KERR
GRASS IS GREENER, THE .... JEAN SIMMONS
GRASS IS GREENER, THE .... ROBERT MITCHUM
GRASS IS SINGING, THE .... KAREN BLACK
GRASS WAS GREEN, THE .... PAT HINGLE
GRASSHOPPER, THE .... JACQUELINE BISSET
GRASSHOPPER, THE .... JIM BROWN
GRAVESIDE STORY, THE .... VINCENT PRICE†
GRAVY TRAIN, THE .... BARRY PRIMUS
GRAVY TRAIN, THE .... FREDERIC FORREST
GRAVY TRAIN, THE .... MARGOT KIDDER
GRAVY TRAIN, THE .... STACY KEACH
GRAY LADY DOWN .... CHARLTON HESTON
GRAY LADY DOWN .... CHRISTOPHER REEVE
GRAY LADY DOWN .... DAVID CARRADINE
GRAY LADY DOWN .... DORIAN HAREWOOD
GRAY LADY DOWN .... NED BEATTY
GRAY LADY DOWN .... STACY KEACH
GRAY LADY DOWN .... STEPHEN McHATTIE
GRAYEAGLE .... BEN JOHNSON
GREASE .... ALICE GHOSTLEY
GREASE .... BARRY PEARL
GREASE .... DARRELL ZWERLING
GREASE .... DIDI CONN
GREASE .... DINAH MANOFF
GREASE .... EDDIE DEEZEN
GREASE .... EVE ARDEN†
GREASE .... FANNIE FLAGG
GREASE .... FRANKIE AVALON
GREASE .... JEFF CONAWAY
GREASE .... JOAN BLONDELL†
GREASE .... JOHN TRAVOLTA
GREASE .... LORENZO LAMAS
GREASE .... OLIVIA NEWTON-JOHN
GREASE .... SID CAESAR
GREASE .... STOCKARD CHANNING
GREASE .... SUSAN BUCKNER
GREASE 2 .... ADRIAN ZMED
GREASE 2 .... CHRISTOPHER McDONALD
GREASE 2 .... DIDI CONN
GREASE 2 .... EVE ARDEN†
GREASE 2 .... MAXWELL CAULFIELD
GREASE 2 .... MICHELLE PFEIFFER
GREASE 2 .... SID CAESAR
GREASE 2 .... TAB HUNTER
GREASED LIGHTNING .... BEAU BRIDGES
GREASED LIGHTNING .... CLEAVON LITTLE†
GREASED LIGHTNING .... PAM GRIER
GREASED LIGHTNING .... RICHARD PRYOR
GREASED LIGHTNING .... VINCENT GARDENIA†
GREASER'S PALACE .... ROBERT DOWNEY JR.
GREAT ADVENTURE, THE .... JACK PALANCE
GREAT AMERICAN BEAUTY
CONTEST, THE (TF) .... ELEANOR PARKER
GREAT AMERICAN BEAUTY
CONTEST, THE (TF) .... FARRAH FAWCETT
GREAT AMERICAN
TRAGEDY, A (TF) .... GEORGE KENNEDY
GREAT BALLOON
ADVENTURE, THE .... KATHERINE HEPBURN
GREAT BALLS OF FIRE .... ALEC BALDWIN
GREAT BALLS OF FIRE .... DENNIS QUAID
GREAT BALLS OF FIRE .... JERRY LEE LEWIS
GREAT BALLS OF FIRE .... JOHN DOE
GREAT BALLS OF FIRE .... LISA BLOUNT
GREAT BALLS OF FIRE .... PETER COOK
GREAT BALLS OF FIRE .... STEPHEN TOBOLOWSKY
GREAT BALLS OF FIRE .... STEVE ALLEN
GREAT BALLS OF FIRE .... TREY WILSON†
GREAT BALLS OF FIRE .... WINONA RYDER
GREAT BANK HOAX, THE .... BURGESS MEREDITH
GREAT BANK HOAX, THE .... NED BEATTY
GREAT BANK ROBBERY, THE .... CLAUDE AKINS†
GREAT BANK ROBBERY, THE .... CLINT WALKER
GREAT BANK ROBBERY, THE .... KIM NOVAK
GREAT BATTLE, THE .... SAMANTHA EGGAR

† after an actor's name denotes deceased.

GREAT CATHERINE .... PETER O'TOOLE
GREAT DAY IN THE MORNING .... RAYMOND BURR†
GREAT DAY IN THE MORNING .... ROBERT STACK
GREAT DICTATOR, THE ★ .... CHARLES CHAPLIN†
GREAT DICTATOR, THE ⊙ .... JACK OAKIE†
GREAT ESCAPE, THE .... CHARLES BRONSON
GREAT ESCAPE, THE .... DAVID McCALLUM
GREAT ESCAPE, THE .... DONALD PLEASENCE
GREAT ESCAPE, THE .... GORDAN JACKSON†
GREAT ESCAPE, THE .... JAMES COBURN
GREAT ESCAPE, THE .... JAMES GARNER
GREAT ESCAPE, THE .... JILL IRELAND†
GREAT ESCAPE, THE .... STEVE MCQUEEN†
GREAT ESCAPE II: THE UNTOLD
    STORY, THE (MS) .... CHARLES HAID
GREAT ESCAPE II: THE UNTOLD
    STORY, THE (MS) .... CHRISTOPHER REEVE
GREAT ESCAPE II: THE UNTOLD
    STORY, THE (MS) .... DONALD PLEASENCE
GREAT ESCAPE II: THE UNTOLD
    STORY, THE (MS) .... JUDD HIRSCH
GREAT ESCAPE II: THE UNTOLD
    STORY, THE (MS) .... MICHAEL NADER
GREAT EXPECTATIONS .... ALEC GUINNESS
GREAT EXPECTATIONS .... JANE WYATT
GREAT EXPECTATIONS .... JEAN SIMMONS
GREAT EXPECTATIONS .... JOHN MILLS
GREAT EXPECTATIONS .... MICHAEL YORK
GREAT
    EXPECTATIONS (CMS) .... ANTHONY HOPKINS
GREAT EXPECTATIONS (TF) .... JOSS ACKLAND
GREAT EXPECTATIONS (TF) .... SARAH MILES
GREAT GARRICK, THE .... LANA TURNER
GREAT GARRICK, THE .... OLIVIA DE HAVILLAND
GREAT GATSBY, THE .... BRUCE DERN
GREAT GATSBY, THE .... EDWRAD HERRMANN
GREAT GATSBY, THE .... HOWARD DA SILVA†
GREAT GATSBY, THE .... KAREN BLACK
GREAT GATSBY, THE .... LOIS CHILES
GREAT GATSBY, THE .... MIA FARROW
GREAT GATSBY, THE .... PATSY KENSIT
GREAT GATSBY, THE .... ROBERT REDFORD
GREAT GATSBY, THE .... SAM WATERSTON
GREAT GATSBY, THE .... SCOTT WILSON
GREAT GATSBY, THE .... SHELLEY WINTERS
GREAT GATSBY, THE .... WILLIAM ATHERTON
GREAT
    HOUDINIS, THE (TF) .... MAUREEN O'SULLIVAN
GREAT HOUDINIS, THE (TF) .... NINA FOCH
GREAT IMPERSONATION, THE .... RALPH BELLAMY†
GREAT IMPOSTER, THE .... TONY CURTIS
GREAT IMPOSTOR, THE .... HARRY CAREY JR.
GREAT IMPOSTOR, THE .... KARL MALDEN
GREAT JOHN L., THE .... RORY CALHOUN
GREAT LIE, THE .... BETTE DAVIS†
GREAT LIE, THE ⊙⊙ .... MARY ASTOR†
GREAT LOVE, THE .... LILLIAN GISH†
GREAT LOVER, THE .... BOB HOPE
GREAT LOVER, THE .... JOSE FERRER†
GREAT MAN, THE .... JOSE FERRER†
GREAT MAN'S LADY, THE ... BARBARA STANWYCK†
GREAT MAN'S
    WHISKERS, THE (TF) .... ANN SOTHERN
GREAT MAN'S
    WHISKERS, THE (TF) .... DENNIS WEAVER
GREAT MOUSE
    DETECTIVE, THE (AF) .... CANDY CANDIDO
GREAT MOUSE
    DETECTIVE, THE (AF) .... EVE BRENNER
GREAT MR. NOBODY, THE .... EDDIE ALBERT
GREAT MUPPET CAPER, THE ..... CHARLES GRODIN
GREAT MUPPET
    CAPER, THE .... CHRISTINE NELSON†
GREAT MUPPET CAPER, THE .... DIANA RIGG
GREAT MUPPET CAPER, THE .... FRANK OZ
GREAT MUPPET CAPER, THE .... JIM HENSON†
GREAT MUPPET CAPER, THE .... ROBERT MORLEY
GREAT NORTHFIELD, MINNESOTA
    RAID, THE .... CLIFF ROBERTSON
GREAT NORTHFIELD, MINNESOTA
    RAID, THE .... R.G. ARMSTRONG
GREAT NORTHFIELD, MINNESOTA
    RAID, THE .... ROBERT DUVALL

GREAT NORTHFIELD,
    MINNESOTA RAID, THE .... ROYAL DANO
GREAT OUTDOORS, THE .... ANNETTE BENING
GREAT OUTDOORS, THE .... CHRIS YOUNG
GREAT OUTDOORS, THE .... DAN AYKROYD
GREAT OUTDOORS, THE .... JOHN CANDY†
GREAT OUTDOORS, THE .... STEPHANIE FARACY
GREAT RACE, THE .... JACK LEMMON
GREAT RACE, THE .... NATALIE WOOD†
GREAT RACE, THE .... PETER FALK
GREAT RACE, THE .... TONY CURTIS
GREAT SANTINI, THE .... BLYTHE DANNER
GREAT SANTINI, THE .... LISA JANE PERSKY
GREAT SANTINI, THE .... PAUL GLEASON
GREAT SANTINI, THE .... PAUL MANTEE
GREAT SANTINI, THE .... ROBERT DUVALL
GREAT SANTINI, THE .... STAN SHAW
GREAT SANTINI, THE .... THERESA MERRITT
GREAT SANTINI, THE ⊙ .... MICHAEL O'KEEFE
GREAT SCOUT AND CATHOUSE
    THURSDAY, THE .... ELIZABETH ASHLEY
GREAT SCOUT AND CATHOUSE
    THURSDAY, THE .... KAY LENZ
GREAT SCOUT AND CATHOUSE
    THURSDAY, THE .... ROBERT CULP
GREAT SCOUT AND CATHOUSE
    THURSDAY, THE .... SYLVIA MILES
GREAT SINNER, THE .... AVA GARDNER†
GREAT SINNER, THE .... GREGORY PECK
GREAT SIOUX
    MASSACRE, THE .... DARREN McGAVIN
GREAT SMOKEY
    ROADBLOCK, THE .... AUSTIN PENDLETON
GREAT SMOKEY
    ROADBLOCK, THE .... EILEEN BRENNAN
GREAT SMOKEY ROADBLOCK, THE .... JOHN BYNER
GREAT SMOKEY
    ROADBLOCK, THE .... SUSAN SARANDON
GREAT SPY MISSION, THE .... JEREMY KEMP
GREAT SPY MISSION, THE .... SOPHIA LOREN
GREAT SPY MISSION, THE .... TOM COURTENAY
GREAT TRAIN ROBBERY, THE .... BRIAN GLOVER
GREAT TRAIN
    ROBBERY, THE .... DONALD SUTHERLAND
GREAT TRAIN
    ROBBERY, THE .... LESLEY-ANNE DOWN
GREAT TRAIN ROBBERY, THE .... SEAN CONNERY
GREAT TRAIN
    ROBBERY, THE .... BROOKE ADAMS
GREAT WALDO PEPPER, THE .... BO SVENSON
GREAT WALDO
    PEPPER, THE .... EDWRAD HERRMANN
GREAT WALDO PEPPER, THE .... MARGOT KIDDER
GREAT WALDO
    PEPPER, THE .... ROBERT REDFORD
GREAT WALDO
    PEPPER, THE .... SUSAN SARANDON
GREAT WALLENDAS, THE (TF) .... BRITT EKLAND
GREAT WALLENDAS, THE (TF) .... LLOYD BRIDGES
GREAT WALTZ, THE ⊙ .... MILIZA KORJUS†
GREAT WHITE HOPE, THE .... ROBERT DAVIS†
GREAT WHITE HOPE, THE .... BEAH RICHARDS
GREAT WHITE HOPE, THE .... CHESTER MORRIS†
GREAT WHITE HOPE, THE .... HAL HOLBROOK†
GREAT WHITE HOPE, THE .... MOSES GUNN
GREAT WHITE HOPE, THE .... R.G. ARMSTRONG
GREAT WHITE HOPE, THE .... ROBERT WEBBER
GREAT WHITE HOPE, THE ★ .... JAMES EARL JONES
GREAT WHITE HOPE, THE ★ .... JANE ALEXANDER
GREAT ZIEGFELD, THE .... FANNY BRICE†
GREAT ZIEGFELD, THE .... FRANK MORGAN†
GREAT ZIEGFELD, THE .... WILLIAM POWELL†
GREATEST, THE .... BEN JOHNSON
GREATEST, THE .... DINA MERRILL
GREATEST, THE .... ERNEST BORGNINE
GREATEST, THE .... JAMES EARL JONES
GREATEST, THE .... JOHN MARLEY†
GREATEST, THE .... MUHAMMAD ALI
GREATEST, THE .... PAUL WINFIELD
GREATEST, THE .... ROBERT DUVALL
GREATEST, THE .... ROGER E. MOSLEY

GREATEST AMERICAN
    HERO, THE (TF) .... ROBERT CULP
GREATEST AMERICAN
    HERO, THE (TF) .... WILLIAM KATT
GREATEST GIFT, THE (TF) .... JULIE HARRIS
GREATEST MAN IN THE
    WORLD, THE (TF) .... BRAD DAVIS†
GREATEST QUESTION, THE .... LILLIAN GISH†
GREATEST SHOW ON EARTH, THE .... BOB HOPE
GREATEST SHOW ON
    EARTH, THE .... CHARLTON HESTON
GREATEST SHOW ON
    EARTH, THE .... DOROTHY LAMOUR
GREATEST SHOW ON
    EARTH, THE .... JAMES STEWART
GREATEST SHOW ON
    EARTH, THE .... KATHLEEN FREEMAN
GREATEST SHOW ON
    EARTH, THE .... LAWRENCE TIERNEY
GREATEST STORY
    EVER TOLD, THE .... ANGELA LANSBURY
GREATEST STORY
    EVER TOLD, THE .... CARROLL BAKER
GREATEST STORY
    EVER TOLD, THE .... CHARLTON HESTON
GREATEST STORY
    EVER TOLD, THE .... DAVID HEDISON
GREATEST STORY
    EVER TOLD, THE .... DAVID McCALLUM
GREATEST STORY
    EVER TOLD, THE .... DONALD PLEASENCE
GREATEST STORY
    EVER TOLD, THE .... JANET MARGOLIN
GREATEST STORY
    EVER TOLD, THE .... JOSE FERRER†
GREATEST STORY
    EVER TOLD, THE .... MARTIN LANDAU
GREATEST STORY
    EVER TOLD, THE .... NEHEMIAH PERSOFF
GREATEST STORY
    EVER TOLD, THE .... PAT BOONE
GREATEST STORY
    EVER TOLD, THE .... ROBERT BLAKE
GREATEST STORY
    EVER TOLD, THE .... ROBERT LOGGIA
GREATEST STORY
    EVER TOLD, THE .... RODDY McDOWALL
GREATEST STORY
    EVER TOLD, THE .... SHELLEY WINTERS
GREATEST STORY
    EVER TOLD, THE .... SIDNEY POITIER
GREATEST STORY
    EVER TOLD, THE .... TELLY SAVALAS†
GREATEST THING IN LIFE, THE .... LILLIAN GISH†
GREATEST THING THAT ALMOST
    HAPPENED, THE (TF) .... JAMES EARL JONES
GREEDY .... BOB BALABAN
GREEDY .... COLLEEN CAMP
GREEDY .... ED BEGLEY JR.
GREEDY .... JERE BURNS
GREEDY .... KIRK DOUGLAS
GREEDY .... MICHAEL J. FOX
GREEDY .... NANCY TRAVIS
GREEDY .... OLIVIA D'ABO
GREEDY .... PHIL HARTMAN
GREEDY .... SIOBHAN FALLON
GREEK TYCOON, THE .... ANTHONY QUINN
GREEK TYCOON, THE .... CHARLES DURNING
GREEK TYCOON, THE .... EDWARD ALBERT
GREEK TYCOON, THE .... JACQUELINE BISSET
GREEK TYCOON, THE .... JAMES FRANCISCUS†
GREEK TYCOON, THE .... RAF VALLONE
GREEN BERETS, THE .... GEORGE TAKEI
GREEN BERETS, THE .... IRENE TSU
GREEN BERETS, THE .... JOHN WAYNE†
GREEN BERETS, THE .... PATRICK WAYNE
GREEN BERETS, THE .... RAYMOND ST. JACQUES
GREEN BERETS, THE .... RICHARD PRYOR
GREEN CARD .... ANDIE MacDOWELL
GREEN CARD .... ANN WEDGEWORTH
GREEN CARD .... BEBE NEUWIRTH
GREEN CARD .... GERARD DEPARDIEU

GREEN COCKATOO, THE .... JOHN MILLS
GREEN DOLPHIN STREET .... LANA TURNER
GREEN FIRE .... GRACE KELLY†
GREEN GODDESS, THE ★ .... GEORGE ARLISS†
GREEN GRASS OF WYOMING .... BURL IVES
GREEN HELL .... VINCENT PRICE†
GREEN ICE .... ANNE ARCHER
GREEN ICE .... JOHN LARROQUETTE
GREEN ICE .... OMAR SHARIF
GREEN ICE .... RYAN O'NEAL
GREEN MANSIONS .... ANTHONY PERKINS†
GREEN MANSIONS .... AUDREY HEPBURN†
GREEN MANSIONS .... HENRY SILVA
GREEN MANSIONS .... NEHEMIAH PERSOFF
GREEN ROOM, THE .... NATHALIE BAYE
GREEN SLIME, THE .... RICHARD JAECKEL
GREEN YEARS, THE .... DEAN STOCKWELL
GREEN YEARS, THE .... HUME CRONYN
GREEN YEARS, THE .... JESSICA TANDY†
GREEN YEARS, THE .... NORMAN LLOYD
GREEN YEARS, THE ○ .... CHARLES COBURN†
GREEN-EYED DEVIL, THE .... LILLIAN GISH†
GREENGAGE SUMMER, THE .... SUSANNAH YORK
GREENWICH VILLAGE .... DON AMECHE†
GREETINGS .... ALLEN GARFIELD
GREETINGS .... ROBERT DE NIRO
GREMLINS .... COREY FELDMAN
GREMLINS .... DICK MILLER
GREMLINS .... EDWARD ANDREWS†
GREMLINS .... FRANCES LEE McCAIN
GREMLINS .... GLYNN TURMAN
GREMLINS .... HOYT AXTON
GREMLINS .... JONATHAN BANKS
GREMLINS .... JUDGE REINHOLD
GREMLINS .... KEYE LUKE†
GREMLINS .... PHOEBE CATES
GREMLINS .... POLLY HOLLIDAY
GREMLINS .... SCOTT BRADY†
GREMLINS .... ZACH GALLIGAN
GREMLINS 2 THE NEW BATCH .... DICK MILLER
GREMLINS 2 THE
   NEW BATCH .... HAVILAND MORRIS
GREMLINS 2 THE NEW BATCH .... JACKIE JOSEPH
GREMLINS 2 THE NEW BATCH .... JOHN GLOVER
GREMLINS 2 THE
   NEW BATCH .... KATHLEEN FREEMAN
GREMLINS 2 THE NEW BATCH .... KEYE LUKE†
GREMLINS 2 THE NEW BATCH .... PHOEBE CATES
GREMLINS 2 THE
   NEW BATCH .... ROBERT PICARDO
GREMLINS 2 THE NEW BATCH ..... ROBERT PROSKY
GREMLINS 2 THE NEW BATCH .... TONY RANDALL
GREMLINS 2 THE NEW BATCH ... ZACH GALLIGAN
GREY FOX, THE .... RICHARD FARNSWORTH
GREYSTOKE: THE LEGEND
   OF TARZAN, LORD
   OF THE APES .... ANDIE MacDOWELL
GREYSTOKE: THE LEGEND
   OF TARZAN, LORD
   OF THE APES .... CHRISTOPHER LAMBERT
GREYSTOKE: THE LEGEND
   OF TARZAN, LORD
   OF THE APES .... GLENN CLOSE
GREYSTOKE: THE LEGEND
   OF TARZAN, LORD OF THE APES .... IAN HOLM
GREYSTOKE: THE LEGEND
   OF TARZAN, LORD OF THE APES .... JAMES FOX
GREYSTOKE: THE LEGEND
   OF TARZAN, LORD
   OF THE APES .... RICHARD GRIFFITHS
GREYSTOKE: THE LEGEND
   OF TARZAN, LORD
   OF THE APES ○ .... SIR RALPH RICHARDSON†
GRIFFIN AND PHOENIX:
   A LOVE STORY (TF) .... JILL CLAYBURGH
GRIFFIN AND PHOENIX (TF) .... PETER FALK
GRIFTERS, THE .... JOHN CUSAK
GRIFTERS, THE .... PAT HINGLE
GRIFTERS, THE ★ .... ANJELICA HUSTON
GRIFTERS, THE ○ .... ANNETTE BENING
GRISSOM GANG, THE .... CONNIE STEVENS
GRISSOM GANG, THE .... DICK MILLER

GRISSOM GANG, THE .... KIM DARBY
GRISSOM GANG, THE .... SCOTT WILSON
GRISSOM GANG, THE .... TONY MUSANTE
GRISSOM GANG, THE .... WESLEY ADDY
GRIZZLY .... ANDREW PRINE
GRIZZLY .... RICHARD JAECKEL
GROSS ANATOMY .... ALICE CARTER
GROSS ANATOMY .... CHRISTINE LAHTI
GROSS ANATOMY .... DAPHNE ZUNIGA
GROSS ANATOMY .... JOHN SCOTT CLOUGH
GROSS ANATOMY .... LISA ZANE
GROSS ANATOMY .... MATTHEW MODINE
GROSS ANATOMY .... ROBERT DESIDERIO
GROSS ANATOMY .... TODD FIELD
GROSS ANATOMY .... ZAKES MOKAE
GROSSE POINT BLANK .... JOHN CUSAK
GROUND ZERO .... COLIN FRIELS
GROUND ZERO .... DONALD PLEASENCE
GROUND ZERO .... JACK THOMPSON
GROUNDHOG DAY .... ANDIE MacDOWELL
GROUNDHOG DAY .... BILL MURRAY
GROUNDHOG DAY .... CHRIS ELLIOTT
GROUNDHOG DAY .... HAROLD RAMIS
GROUNDS FOR MARRIAGE .... VAN JOHNSON
GROUNDSTAR
   CONSPIRACY, THE .... GEORGE PEPPARD†
GROUNDSTAR
   CONSPIRACY, THE .... JAMES OLSON
GROUNDSTAR
   CONSPIRACY, THE .... MICHAEL SARRAZIN
GROUP, THE .... CANDICE BERGEN
GROUP, THE .... GEORGE GAYNES
GROUP, THE .... HAL HOLBROOK
GROUP, THE .... JESSICA WALTER
GROUP, THE .... JOAN HACKETT†
GROUP, THE .... LARRY HAGMAN
GROUP, THE .... RICHARD MULLIGAN
GROUP, THE .... SHIRLEY KNIGHT
GROWING PAINS .... KAREN BLACK
GRUMPY OLD MEN .... ANN-MARGRET
GRUMPY OLD MEN .... BUCK HENRY
GRUMPY OLD MEN .... BURGESS MEREDITH
GRUMPY OLD MEN .... CHRISTOPHER McDONALD
GRUMPY OLD MEN .... DARYL HANNAH
GRUMPY OLD MEN .... JACK LEMMON
GRUMPY OLD MEN .... KEVIN POLLAK
GRUMPY OLD MEN .... OSSIE DAVIS
GRUMPY OLD MEN .... WALTER MATTHAU
GRUNT! THE WRESTLING
   MOVIE .... MARILYN DODDS FRANK
GRUNT! THE WRESTLING
   MOVIE .... ROBERT GLAUDINI
GRUNT! THE WRESTLING
   MOVIE .... STEVEN CEPELLO
GRUPPO DI FAMIGLIA
   IN UNO INTERO .... BURT LANCASTER†
GUADALCANAL DIARY .... ANTHONY QUINN
GUADALCANAL DIARY .... LIONEL STANDER
GUADALCANAL DIARY .... RICHARD JAECKEL
GUARDIAN, THE .... BRAD HALL
GUARDIAN, THE .... CAREY LOWELL
GUARDIAN, THE .... DWIER BROWN
GUARDIAN, THE .... JENNY SEAGROVE
GUARDIAN, THE (CTF) .... LOUIS GOSSETT JR.
GUARDIAN ANGEL .... ANNA DALVA
GUARDIAN ANGEL .... LYDIE DENIER
GUARDIAN ANGEL .... WARREN STEVENS
GUARDIAN OF THE
   WILDERNESS .... JACK KRUSCHEN
GUARDIAN OF THE
   WILDERNESS .... JOHN DEHNER†
GUARDIAN OF THE WILDERNESS ..... NORMAN FELL
GUARDING TESS .... NICOLAS CAGE
GUARDING TESS .... SHIRLEY MacLAINE
GUARDSMAN, THE ★ .... LYNN FONTANNE†
GUESS WHO'S COMING
   TO DINNER ★ .... SPENCER TRACY†
GUESS WHO'S COMING
   TO DINNER ○ .... CECIL KELLAWAY†
GUESS WHO'S COMING
   TO DINNER .... SIDNEY POITIER

GUESS WHO'S COMING
   TO DINNER ★★ ....KATHERINE HEPBURN
GUESS WHO'S COMING
   TO DINNER ○ .... BEAH RICHARDS
GUEST IN THE HOUSE .... RALPH BELLAMY†
GUEST, THE .... ALAN BATES
GUEST, THE .... DONALD PLEASENCE
GUEST, THE .... ROBERT STACK
GUEST WIFE .... DON AMECHE†
GUIDE FOR THE MARRIED MAN, A ...... ART CARNEY
GUIDE FOR THE MARRIED MAN, A ..... CARL REINER
GUIDE FOR THE MARRIED MAN, A .... SID CAESAR
GUIDE FOR THE MARRIED
   MAN, A .... SUE ANE LANGDON
GUIDE FOR THE MARRIED
   MAN, A .... WALTER MATTHAU
GUILT OF JANET AMES, THE .... NINA FOCH
GUILT OF JANET AMES, THE .... SID CAESAR
GUILTY AS CHARGED .... HEATHER GRAHAM
GUILTY AS CHARGED .... ISAAC HAYES
GUILTY AS CHARGED .... LAUREN HUTTON
GUILTY AS CHARGED .... LYMAN WARD
GUILTY AS CHARGED .... ROD STEIGER
GUILTY AS SIN .... DON JOHNSON
GUILTY AS SIN .... REBECCA DE MORNAY
GUILTY BY SUSPICION .... ADAM BALDWIN
GUILTY BY SUSPICION .... ALAN RICH
GUILTY BY SUSPICION .... ANNETTE BENING
GUILTY BY SUSPICION .... BARRY PRIMUS
GUILTY BY SUSPICION .... BEN PIAZZA†
GUILTY BY SUSPICION .... BILL BAILEY
GUILTY BY SUSPICION .... BRAD SULLIVAN
GUILTY BY SUSPICION .... CHRIS COOPER
GUILTY BY SUSPICION .... DIANNE REEVES
GUILTY BY SUSPICION .... GAILORD SARTAIN
GUILTY BY SUSPICION .... GENE KIRKWOOD
GUILTY BY SUSPICION .... GEORGE WENDT
GUILTY BY SUSPICION .... ILEANNA DOUGLAS
GUILTY BY SUSPICION .... JOAN SCOTT
GUILTY BY SUSPICION .... LUKE EDWARDS
GUILTY BY SUSPICION .... MARTIN SCORSESE
GUILTY BY SUSPICION .... PATRICIA WETTIG
GUILTY BY SUSPICION .... ROBERT DE NIRO
GUILTY BY SUSPICION .... ROBIN GAMMEL
GUILTY BY SUSPICION .... ROXANN BIGGS
GUILTY BY SUSPICION .... SAM WANAMAKER†
GUILTY BY SUSPICION .... STUART MARGOLIN
GUILTY BY SUSPICION .... TOM SIZEMORE
GUILTY CONSCIENCE (TF) .... ANTHONY HOPKINS
GUILTY CONSCIENCE (TF) .... BLYTHE DANNER
GUILTY CONSCIENCE (TF) .... SWOOSIE KURTZ
GUILTY CONSCIENCE (TF) .... WILEY HARKER
GUILTY OF INNOCENCE: THE LENELL
   GETER STORY (TF) .... DABNEY COLEMAN
GUILTY OF INNOCENCE: THE LENELL
   GETER STORY (TF) .... DORIAN HAREWOOD
GUILTY OF INNOCENCE: THE LENELL
   GETER STORY (TF) .... GARY GRUBBS
GUILTY OR INNOCENT:
   THE SAM SHEPPARD
   MURDER CASE (TF) .... GEORGE PEPPARD†
GUILTY UNTIL PROVEN
   INNOCENT (TF) .... BRENDAN FRASER
GULAG (CTF) .... JOHN McENERY
GULLIVER'S TRAVELS .... RICHARD HARRIS
GUMBALL RALLY, THE .... GARY BUSEY
GUMBALL RALLY, THE .... MICHAEL SARRAZIN
GUMSHOE .... ALBERT FINNEY
GUMSHOE .... BILLIE WHITELAW
GUMSHOE KID, THE .... JAY UNDERWOOD
GUMSHOE KID, THE .... PAMELA SPRINGSTEEN
GUMSHOE KID, THE .... TRACY SCOGGINS
GUMSHOE KID, THE .... VINCE EDWARDS
GUN AND THE
   PULPIT, THE (TF) .... DAVID HUDDLESTON
GUN AND THE
   PULPIT, THE (TF) .... PAMELA SUE MARTIN
GUN BELT .... TAB HUNTER
GUN FOR A COWARD .... DEAN STOCKWELL
GUN FURY .... ROCK HUDSON†
GUN HAWK, THE .... RORY CALHOUN

† after an actor's name denotes deceased.

GUN IN BETTY LOU'S
HANDBAG, THE .... ALFRE WOODARD
GUN IN BETTY LOU'S
HANDBAG, THE .... ANDY ROMANO
GUN IN BETTY LOU'S
HANDBAG, THE .... BILLIE NEAL
GUN IN BETTY LOU'S
HANDBAG, THE .... CATHY MORIARTY
GUN IN BETTY LOU'S
HANDBAG, THE .... CORDELL JACKSON
GUN IN BETTY LOU'S
HANDBAG, THE .... FAYE GRANT
GUN IN BETTY LOU'S
HANDBAG, THE .... GALE MAYRON
GUN IN BETTY LOU'S
HANDBAG, THE .... JULIANNE MOORE
GUN IN BETTY LOU'S
HANDBAG, THE .... MARIAN SELDES
GUN IN BETTY LOU'S
HANDBAG, THE .... MEAT LOAF
GUN IN BETTY LOU'S
HANDBAG, THE .... MICHAEL O'NEILL
GUN IN BETTY LOU'S
HANDBAG, THE .... RAY McKINNON
GUN IN BETTY LOU'S
HANDBAG, THE .... REATHEL BEAN
GUN IN BETTY LOU'S
HANDBAG, THE .... WILLIAM FORSYTHE
GUN IN BETTY LOU'S
HANDBAG, THE .... XANDER BERKELEY
GUN IN BETTY LOU'S HANDBAG, THE .... ERIC THAL
GUN IN BETTY LOU'S
HANDBAG, THE .... PENELOPE ANN MILLER
GUN RUNNERS, THE .... EDDIE ALBERT
GUN THE MAN DOWN .... ANGIE DICKINSON
GUNCRAZY .... DREW BARRYMORE
GUNFIGHT, A .... JANE ALEXANDER
GUNFIGHT, A .... JOHNNY CASH
GUNFIGHT, A .... KAREN BLACK
GUNFIGHT, A .... KEITH CARRADINE
GUNFIGHT, A .... KIRK DOUGLAS
GUNFIGHT, A .... RAF VALLONE
GUNFIGHT AT THE
O.K. CORRAL .... BURT LANCASTER†
GUNFIGHT AT THE
O.K. CORRAL .... DENNIS HOPPER
GUNFIGHT AT THE
O.K. CORRAL .... EARL HOLLIMAN
GUNFIGHT AT THE O.K. CORRAL ..... JOHN IRELAND
GUNFIGHT AT THE O.K. CORRAL ..... KIRK DOUGLAS
GUNFIGHT IN ABILENE .... LESLIE NIELSEN
GUNFIGHT IN ABILENE .... MICHAEL SARRAZIN
GUNFIGHTER, THE .... GREGORY PECK
GUNFIGHTER, THE .... KARL MALDEN
GUNFIGHTER, THE .... RICHARD JAECKEL
GUNG HO .... CLINT HOWARD
GUNG HO .... GEDDE WATANABE
GUNG HO .... GEORGE WENDT
GUNG HO .... JIHMI KENNEDY
GUNG HO .... JOHN TURTURRO
GUNG HO .... MICHAEL KEATON
GUNG HO .... MICHELLE JOHNSON
GUNG HO! .... ROBERT MITCHUM
GUNMAN'S WALK .... TAB HUNTER
GUNMEN .... CHRISTOPHER LAMBERT
GUNMEN .... DENIS LEARY
GUNMEN .... KADEEN HARDISON
GUNMEN .... MARIO VAN PEEBLES
GUNMEN .... PATRICK STEWART
GUNMEN .... SALLY KIRKLAND
GUNN .... ED ASNER
GUNPOINT .... ROYAL DANO
GUNRUNNER, THE .... KEVIN COSTNER
GUNS AT BATASI .... MIA FARROW
GUNS FOR SAN SEBASTIAN .... ANTHONY QUINN
GUNS FOR SAN SEBASTIAN .... CHARLES BRONSON
GUNS OF AUGUST, THE (FD) .... FRITZ WEAVER
GUNS OF DARKNESS .... LESLIE CARON
GUNS OF NAVARONE, THE .... GREGORY PECK
GUNS OF NAVARONE, THE .... RICHARD HARRIS
GUNS OF NAVARONE, THE .... WALTER GOTELL
GUNS OF NAVARONE, THE .... ANTHONY QUINN

GUNS OF THE MAGNIFICENT
SEVEN .... GEORGE KENNEDY
GUNS OF THE MAGNIFICENT
SEVEN .... JAMES WHITMORE
GUNS OF THE MAGNIFICENT
SEVEN .... JOE DON BAKER
GUNS OF THE TIMBERLAND .... FRANKIE AVALON
GUNS, SIN AND BATHTUB GIN ... LOUISE FLETCHER
GUNS, SIN AND
BATHTUB GIN .... PAMELA SUE MARTIN
GUNSLINGER, THE .... JOHN IRELAND
GUNSMOKE: RETURN
TO DODGE (TF) .... EARL HOLLIMAN
GUNSMOKE: RETURN
TO DODGE (TF) .... JAMES ARNESS
GUNSMOKE: RETURN
TO DODGE (TF) .... STEVE FORREST
GUNSMOKE: THE
LAST APACHE (TF) .... GEOFFREY LEWIS
GUNSMOKE: THE
LAST APACHE (TF) .... JAMES ARNESS
GUNSMOKE: THE
LAST APACHE (TF) .... RICHARD KILEY
GURU, THE .... MICHAEL YORK
GUS .... DICK VAN PATTEN
GUS .... DON KNOTTS
GUS .... ED ASNER
GUS .... TIM CONWAY
GUS .... TOM BOSLEY
GUTS AND GLORY:
THE RISE AND FALL OF
OLLIE NORTH (MS) .... AMY STOCK-POYNTON
GUTS AND GLORY: THE RISE AND
FALL OF OLLIE NORTH (MS) ... BARNARD HUGHES
GUTS AND GLORY: THE RISE AND
FALL OF OLLIE NORTH (MS) .... DAVID KEITH
GUTS AND GLORY: THE RISE AND
FALL OF OLLIE NORTH (MS) .... PETER BOYLE
GUY NAMED JOE, A .... SPENCER TRACY†
GUY NAMED JOE, A .... VAN JOHNSON
GUYANA—CRIME OF
THE CENTURY .... STUART WHITMAN
GUYANA: CULT OF
THE DAMNED .... BRADFORD DILLMAN
GUYANA: CULT OF THE DAMNED .... JOHN IRELAND
GUYANA: CULT OF THE DAMNED .... MEL FERRER
GUYANA: CULT OF
THE DAMNED .... YVONNE DE CARLO
GUYANA TRAGEDY: THE STORY
OF JIM JONES (TF) .... BRAD DOURIF
GUYANA TRAGEDY: THE STORY
OF JIM JONES (TF) .... COLLEEN DEWHURST†
GUYANA TRAGEDY: THE STORY
OF JIM JONES (TF) .... DIANA SCARWID
GUYANA TRAGEDY: THE STORY
OF JIM JONES (TF) .... DIANE LADD
GUYANA TRAGEDY: THE STORY
OF JIM JONES (TF) .... DIMITRA ARLYS
GUYANA TRAGEDY: THE STORY
OF JIM JONES (TF) .... IRENE CARA
GUYANA TRAGEDY: THE STORY
OF JIM JONES (TF) .... JAMES EARL JONES
GUYANA TRAGEDY: THE STORY
OF JIM JONES (TF) .... LeVAR BURTON
GUYANA TRAGEDY: THE STORY
OF JIM JONES (TF) .... MADGE SINCLAIR
GUYANA TRAGEDY: THE STORY
OF JIM JONES (TF) .... MEG FOSTER
GUYANA TRAGEDY: THE STORY
OF JIM JONES (TF) .... NED BEATTY
GUYANA TRAGEDY: THE STORY
OF JIM JONES (TF) .... POWERS BOOTHE
GUYANA TRAGEDY: THE STORY
OF JIM JONES (TF) .... RANDY QUAID
GUYANA TRAGEDY: THE STORY
OF JIM JONES (TF) .... RON O'NEAL
GUYANA TRAGEDY: THE STORY
OF JIM JONES (TF) .... ROSALIND CASH
GUYANA TRAGEDY: THE STORY
OF JIM JONES (TF) .... VERONICA CARTWRIGHT
GUYS AND DOLLS .... FRANK SINATRA
GUYS AND DOLLS .... JEAN SIMMONS

GUYS AND DOLLS .... MARLON BRANDO
GUYS AND DOLLS .... STUBBY KAYE
GUYVER, THE .... MARK HAMILL
GYPSY .... HARVEY KORMAN
GYPSY .... KARL MALDEN
GYPSY .... LOUIS QUINN†
GYPSY .... MORGAN BRITTANY
GYPSY .... NATALIE WOOD†
GYPSY .... ROSALAND RUSSELL†
GYPSY (TF) .... BETTE MIDLER
GYPSY (TF) .... CHRISTINE EBERSOLE
GYPSY (TF) .... CYNTHIA GIBB
GYPSY (TF) .... ED ASNER
GYPSY (TF) .... JEFFREY BROADHURST
GYPSY (TF) .... MICHAEL JETER
GYPSY (TF) .... PETER RIEGERT
GYPSY GIRL .... GEOFFREY BAYLDON
GYPSY GIRL, THE .... HAYLEY MILLS
GYPSY MOTHS, THE .... BONNIE BEDELIA
GYPSY MOTHS, THE .... BURT LANCASTER†
GYPSY MOTHS, THE .... DEBORAH KERR
GYPSY MOTHS, THE .... GENE HACKMAN

H

H.M.S. DEFIANT .... ALEC GUINNESS
H.P. LOVECRAFT'S
RE-ANIMATOR .... JEFFREY COMBS
HAIL, HERO! .... MICHAEL DOUGLAS
HAIL, HERO! .... TERESA WRIGHT
HAI! MAFIA .... HENRY SILVA
HAI! MAFIA! .... JACK KLUGMAN
HAIR .... BEVERLY D'ANGELO
HAIR .... ELLEN FOLEY
HAIR .... JOHN SAVAGE
HAIR .... MELBA MOORE
HAIR .... TREAT WILLIAMS
HAIR SPRAY .... RUTH BROWN
HAIRSPRAY .... DEBORAH HARRY
HAIRSPRAY .... DIVINE†
HAIRSPRAY .... JERRY STILLER
HAIRSPRAY .... JOSH CHARLES
HAIRSPRAY .... PIA ZADORA
HAIRSPRAY .... RIC O'CASEK
HAIRSPRAY .... RICKI LAKE
HAIRSPRAY .... SONNY BONO
HALF A LIFETIME (CTF) .... NICK MANCUSO
HALF MOON STREET .... KEITH BUCKLEY
HALF MOON STREET .... MICHAEL CAINE
HALF MOON STREET .... SIGOURNEY WEAVER
HALLELUJAH TRAIL, THE .... BRIAN KEITH
HALLELUJAH TRAIL, THE .... BURT LANCASTER†
HALLELUJAH TRAIL, THE .... DONALD PLEASENCE
HALLELUJAH TRAIL, THE .... JOHN ANDERSON
HALLELUJAH TRAIL, THE .... MARTIN LANDAU
HALLELUJAH TRAIL, THE .... VAL AVERY
HALLOWEEN .... CHARLES CYPHERS
HALLOWEEN .... DONALD PLEASENCE
HALLOWEEN .... JAMIE LEE CURTIS
HALLOWEEN .... NANCY LOOMIS
HALLOWEEN .... P. J. SOLES
HALLOWEEN II .... CHARLES CYPHERS
HALLOWEEN II .... DONALD PLEASENCE
HALLOWEEN II .... JAMIE LEE CURTIS
HALLOWEEN II .... LANCE GUEST
HALLOWEEN II .... LEO ROSSI
HALLOWEEN II .... PAMELA SUSAN SHOOP
HALLOWEEN III: SEASON
OF THE WITCH .... DAN O'HERLIHY
HALLOWEEN IV - THE RETURN OF
MICHAEL MYERS .... DANIELLE HARRIS
HALLOWEEN IV - THE RETURN OF
MICHAEL MYERS .... ELLIE CORNELL
HALLOWEEN IV - THE RETURN OF
MICHAEL MYERS .... MICHAEL PATAKI
HALLOWEEN IV - THE RETURN OF
MICHAEL MYERS .... DONALD PLEASENCE
HALLOWEEN 5 - THE REVENGE OF
MICHAEL MYERS .... BEAU STARR
HALLOWEEN 5 - THE REVENGE OF
MICHAEL MYERS .... DONALD PLEASENCE

HALLOWEEN 5 - THE REVENGE OF
MICHAEL MYERS .... ELLIE CORNELL
HALLOWEEN 5 - THE REVENGE OF
MICHAEL MYERS .... TAMARA GLYNN
HALLOWEEN 5 - THE REVENGE OF
MICHAEL MYERS .... WENDY KAPLAN
HALLOWEEN 5 - THE REVENGE OF
MICHAEL MYERS HARRIS ....
HALLS OF ANGER .... JEFF BRIDGES
HALLS OF MONTEZUMA .... JACK PALANCE
HALLS OF MONTEZUMA .... JACK WEBB†
HALLS OF MONTEZUMA .... KARL MALDEN
HALLS OF MONTEZUMA .... REGINALD GARDINER†
HALLS OF MONTEZUMA .... RICHARD WIDMARK
HALLS OF MONTEZUMA .... ROBERT WAGNER
HAMBONE AND HILLIE .... LILLIAN GISH†
HAMBONE AND HILLIE .... O. J. SIMPSON
HAMBONE AND HILLIE .... TIMOTHY BOTTOMS
HAMBURGER HILL .... COURTNEY B. VANCE
HAMBURGER HILL .... DYLAN McDERMOTT
HAMBURGER HILL .... TIM QUILL
HAMBURGER...THE
MOTION PICTURE .... DICK BUTKUS
HAMLET .... ALAN BATES
HAMLET .... ANJELICA HUSTON
HAMLET .... ANTHONY HOPKINS
HAMLET .... GEORGE ROSE†
HAMLET .... GLENN CLOSE
HAMLET .... GORDAN JACKSON†
HAMLET .... HELENA BONHAM CARTER
HAMLET .... HUME CRONYN
HAMLET .... IAN HOLM
HAMLET .... JOHN McENERY
HAMLET .... MEL GIBSON
HAMLET .... NICOL WILLIAMSON
HAMLET .... PATRICK MacNEE
HAMLET .... PAUL SCOFIELD
HAMLET ★★ .... LAURENCE OLIVIER†
HAMLET ⊙ .... JEAN SIMMONS
HAMLET (TF) .... MAXIMILIAN SCHELL
HAMMER .... FRED WILLIAMSON
HAMMERHEAD .... PETER VAUGHN
HAMMERHEAD .... VINCE EDWARDS
HAMMERSMITH IS OUT .... BEAU BRIDGES
HAMMERSMITH IS OUT .... ELIZABETH TAYLOR
HAMMERSMITH IS OUT .... JOHN SCHUCK
HAMMERSMITH IS OUT .... LEON AMES
HAMMERSMITH IS OUT .... PETER USTINOV
HAMMETT .... FREDERIC FORREST
HAMMETT .... MARILU HENNER
HAMMETT .... PETER BOYLE
HAMMETT .... R.G. ARMSTRONG
HAMMETT .... ROYAL DANO
HAMMETT .... SYLVIA SIDNEY
HAMSTER OF HAPPINESS, THE .... BARBARA HARRIS
HAMSTER OF HAPPINESS, THE .... ROBERT BLAKE
HANAUMA BAY .... ANDY BUMATAI
HANAUMA BAY .... BLAINE KIA
HANAUMA BAY .... CHRIS MAKEPEACE
HANAUMA BAY .... DON MICHAEL PAUL
HANAUMA BAY .... LORIE GRIFFIN
HANAUMA BAY .... RIC MANCINI
HANAUMA BAY .... SCOTT NAKAGAWA
HANAUMA BAY .... SHO KOSUGI
HANAUMA BAY .... TIA CARRERE
HANAUMA BAY .... WARREN FABRO
HANAUMA BAY .... YUJI OKUMOTO
HAND THAT ROCKS THE
CRADLE, THE .... ANNABELLA SCIORRA
HAND THAT ROCKS THE
CRADLE, THE .... ERNIE HUDSON
HAND THAT ROCKS THE
CRADLE, THE .... JULIANNE MOORE
HAND THAT ROCKS THE
CRADLE, THE .... MADELINE ZIMA
HAND THAT ROCKS THE
CRADLE, THE .... MATT McCOY
HAND THAT ROCKS THE
CRADLE, THE .... REBECCA DE MORNAY
HAND, THE .... MICHAEL CAINE
HAND, THE .... OLIVER STONE
HAND, THE .... VIVECA LINDFORS
HANDFUL OF DUST, A .... ALEC GUINNESS

HANDFUL OF DUST, A .... ANJELICA HUSTON
HANDFUL OF DUST, A .... JAMES WILBY
HANDFUL OF DUST, A .... JUDI DENCH
HANDFUL OF DUST, A ...... KRISTIN SCOTT THOMAS
HANDFUL OF DUST, A .... RUPERT GRAVES
HANDLE WITH CARE .... BRUCE McGILL
HANDLE WITH CARE .... CANDY CLARK
HANDLE WITH CARE .... CHARLES NAPIER
HANDLE WITH CARE .... DEAN JONES
HANDLE WITH CARE .... PAUL LeMAT
HANDLE WITH CARE .... ROYAL DANO
HANDMAID'S TALE, THE .... AIDAN QUINN
HANDMAID'S TALE, THE ..... ELIZABETH McGOVERN
HANDMAID'S TALE, THE .... FAYE DUNAWAY
HANDMAID'S TALE, THE ..... NATASHA RICHARDSON
HANDMAID'S TALE, THE .... ROBERT DUVALL
HANDMAID'S TALE, THE .... VICTORIA TENNANT
HANDS ACROSS THE TABLE .... RALPH BELLAMY†
HANDS OF A
MURDERER (TF) .... ANTHONY ANDREWS
HANDS OF A MURDERER (TF) ...... JOHN HILLERMAN
HANDS OF A STRANGER (MS) .... ARLISS HOWARD
HANDS OF A
STRANGER (MS) .... ARMAND ASSANTE
HANDS OF A
STRANGER (MS) .... BEVERLY D'ANGELO
HANDS OF A STRANGER (MS) .... BLAIR BROWN
HANDS OF A STRANGER (MS) ..... MICHAEL LERNER
HANDS OF CORMAC
JOYCE, THE (TF) .... COLLEEN DEWHURST†
HANDS OF ORLAC, THE .... DONALD PLEASENCE
HANDS OF ORLAC, THE .... MEL FERRER
HANDS OVER THE CITY .... ROD STEIGER
HANG 'EM HIGH .... BRUCE DERN
HANG 'EM HIGH .... CLINT EASTWOOD
HANG 'EM HIGH .... DENNIS HOPPER
HANG 'EM HIGH .... PAT HINGLE
HANGAR 18 .... DARREN McGAVIN
HANGAR 18 .... JAMES HAMPTON
HANGED MAN, THE (TF) .... JANE SEYMOUR
HANGED MAN, THE (TF) .... SHARON ACKER
HANGED MAN, THE (TF) .... VERA MILES
HANGIN' WITH THE HOMEBOYS ...... MARIO JOYNER
HANGING BY A THREAD (TF) .... PATTY DUKE
HANGING TREE, THE .... BEN PIAZZA†
HANGING TREE, THE .... GEORGE C. SCOTT
HANGING TREE, THE .... KARL MALDEN
HANGING TREE, THE .... MARIA SCHELL
HANGMAN, THE .... TINA LOUISE
HANGMEN ALSO DIE .... LIONEL STANDER
HANGOVER, THE .... LAWRENCE TIERNEY
HANKY PANKY .... GENE WILDER
HANKY PANKY .... GILDA RADNER†
HANKY PANKY .... JOSEF SOMMER
HANKY PANKY .... KATHLEEN QUINLAN
HANKY PANKY .... RICHARD WIDMARK
HANNAH AND HER SISTERS .... BARBARA HERSHEY
HANNAH AND HER SISTERS .... CARRIE FISHER
HANNAH AND
HER SISTERS .... CHRISTIAN CLEMENSON
HANNAH AND HER SISTERS .... DANIEL STERN
HANNAH AND HER SISTERS .... J. T. WALSH
HANNAH AND HER SISTERS ...... JOANNA GLEASON
HANNAH AND HER SISTERS .... JOHN TURTURRO
HANNAH AND
HER SISTERS .... JULIA LOUIS-DREYFUSS
HANNAH AND HER SISTERS .... JULIE KAVNER
HANNAH AND HER SISTERS .... LEWIS BLACK
HANNAH AND HER SISTERS .... LLOYD NOLAN†
HANNAH AND
HER SISTERS .... MAUREEN O'SULLIVAN
HANNAH AND HER SISTERS .... MAX von SYDOW
HANNAH AND HER SISTERS .... MIA FARROW
HANNAH AND HER SISTERS .... SAM WATERSTON
HANNAH AND HER SISTERS .... TONY ROBERTS
HANNAH AND HER SISTERS .... WOODY ALLEN
HANNAH AND HER SISTERS ∞ .... DIANNE WIEST
HANNAH AND HER SISTERS ∞ ..... MICHAEL CAINE
HANNAH K. .... GABRIEL BYRNE
HANNAH K. .... JILL CLAYBURGH
HANNA'S WAR .... ANTHONY ANDREWS
HANNA'S WAR .... DAVID WARNER

HANNA'S WAR .... DONALD PLEASENCE
HANNA'S WAR .... ELLEN BURSTYN
HANNA'S WAR .... MARUSCHKA DETMERS
HANNIBAL BROOKS .... MICHAEL J. POLLARD
HANNIE CAULDER .... ERNEST BORGNINE
HANNIE CAULDER .... RAQUEL WELCH
HANNIE CAULDER .... ROBERT CULP
HANOI HILTON, THE .... DAVID SOUL
HANOI HILTON, THE .... GLORIA CARLIN
HANOI HILTON, THE .... JEFFREY JONES
HANOI HILTON, THE .... LAWRENCE PRESSMAN
HANOI HILTON, THE .... MICHAEL MORIARTY
HANOI HILTON, THE .... PAUL LeMAT
HANOVER STREET .... ALEC McCOWEN
HANOVER STREET .... CHRISTOPHER PLUMMER
HANOVER STREET .... HARRISON FORD
HANOVER STREET .... LESLEY-ANNE DOWN
HANOVER STREET .... RICHARD MASUR
HANOVER STREET .... SHANE RIMMER
HANS CHRISTIAN ANDERSEN'S
THUMBELINA (AF) .... BARBARA COOK
HANS CHRISTIAN ANDERSEN'S
THUMBELINA (AF) .... CAROL CHANNING
HANS CHRISTIAN ANDERSEN'S
THUMBELINA (AF) .... CHARO
HANS CHRISTIAN ANDERSEN'S
THUMBELINA (AF) .... GARY IMHOFF
HANS CHRISTIAN ANDERSEN'S
THUMBELINA (AF) .... GILBERT GOTTFRIED
HANS CHRISTIAN ANDERSEN'S
THUMBELINA (AF) .... GINO CONFROTI
HANS CHRISTIAN ANDERSEN'S
THUMBELINA (AF) .... JOHN HURT
HANS CHRISTIAN ANDERSEN'S
THUMBELINA (AF) .... JUNE FORAY
HANS CHRISTIAN ANDERSEN'S
THUMBELINA (AF) .... KENDALL CUNNINGHAM
HANS CHRISTIAN ANDERSEN'S
THUMBELINA (AF) .... KENNETH MARS
HANS CHRISTIAN ANDERSEN'S
THUMBELINA (AF) ..... TAWNY SUNSHINE GLOVER
HANS CHRISTIAN ANDERSEN'S
THUMBELINA (AF) .... WILL RYAN
HANS CHRISTIAN ANDERSEN'S
THUMBELINA (AF) .... JODIE BENSON
HANSEL AND GRETEL .... CLORIS LEACHMAN
HANSEL AND GRETEL .... DAVID WARNER
HANUSSEN .... KLAUS MARIA BRANDAUER
HAPPENING, THE .... ANTHONY QUINN
HAPPENING, THE .... FAYE DUNAWAY
HAPPENING, THE .... JACK KRUSCHEN
HAPPENING, THE .... MILTON BERLE
HAPPENING, THE .... ROBERT WALKER JR.
HAPPIEST MILLIONAIRE, THE .... GREER GARSON
HAPPIEST MILLIONAIRE, THE .... JOHN DAVIDSON
HAPPIEST
MILLIONAIRE, THE .... LESLEY ANN WARREN
HAPPILY EVER AFTER (AF) .... CAROL CHANNING
HAPPILY EVER AFTER (AF) .... DOM DeLUISE
HAPPILY EVER AFTER (AF) .... ED ASNER
HAPPILY EVER AFTER (AF) .... PHYLLIS DILLER
HAPPILY EVER AFTER (AF) .... ZSA ZSA GABOR
HAPPINESS CAGE, THE ..... CHRISTOPHER WALKEN
HAPPINESS CAGE, THE .... JOSS ACKLAND
HAPPINESS CAGE, THE .... RONNY COX
HAPPY ANNIVERSARY .... CARL REINER
HAPPY ANNIVERSARY .... PATTY DUKE
HAPPY BIRTHDAY,
GEMINI .... DAVID MARSHALL GRANT
HAPPY BIRTHDAY, GEMINI .... MADELINE KAHN
HAPPY BIRTHDAY, GEMINI .... RITA MORENO
HAPPY BIRTHDAY TO ME .... FRANCES HYLAND
HAPPY BIRTHDAY TO ME .... JACK BLUM
HAPPY BIRTHDAY TO ME .... LAWRENCE DANE
HAPPY BIRTHDAY TO ME .... LISA LANGLOIS
HAPPY BIRTHDAY TO ME .... MATT CRAVEN
HAPPY BIRTHDAY TO ME .... MELISSA ANDERSON
HAPPY BIRTHDAY TO ME .... SHARON ACKER
HAPPY BIRTHDAY TO ME .... TRACY BREGMAN
HAPPY BIRTHDAY, WANDA JUNE ...... DON MURRAY
HAPPY BIRTHDAY
WANDA JUNE .... GEORGE GRIZZARD

HAPPY BIRTHDAY WANDA JUNE .... ROD STEIGER
HAPPY BIRTHDAY
    WANDA JUNE .... SUSANNAH YORK
HAPPY ENDING, THE .... JOHN FORSYTHE
HAPPY ENDING, THE .... LLOYD BRIDGES
HAPPY ENDING, THE .... SHIRLEY JONES
HAPPY ENDING, THE .... TERESA WRIGHT
HAPPY ENDING, THE ★ .... TINA LOUISE
HAPPY ENDING, THE ★ .... JEAN SIMMONS
HAPPY EVER AFTER .... DAVID NIVEN†
HAPPY GO LOVELY .... DAVID NIVEN†
HAPPY GO LOVELY .... GORDAN JACKSON†
HAPPY HOOKER GOES TO
    WASHINGTON, THE .... BILLY BARTY
HAPPY HOOKER GOES TO
    WASHINGTON, THE .... GEORGE HAMILTON
HAPPY HOOKER GOES TO
    WASHINGTON, THE .... JOEY HEATHERTON
HAPPY HOOKER GOES TO
    WASHINGTON, THE .... RAY WALSTON
HAPPY HOOKER, THE .... JEAN-PIERRE AUMONT
HAPPY HOOKER, THE .... LYNN REDGRAVE
HAPPY HOOKER, THE .... TOM POSTON
HAPPY LAND .... DON AMECHE†
HAPPY LAND .... HARRY MORGAN
HAPPY LAND .... MARY WICKES
HAPPY LANDING .... DON AMECHE†
HAPPY MOTHER'S DAY...
    LOVE, GEORGE .... CLORIS LEACHMAN
HAPPY MOTHER'S DAY—
    LOVE, GEORGE .... PATRICIA NEAL
HAPPY MOTHER'S DAY—
    LOVE, GEORGE .... RON HOWARD
HAPPY NEW YEAR .... CHARLES DURNING
HAPPY NEW YEAR .... PETER FALK
HAPPY NEW YEAR .... TOM COURTENAY
HAPPY ROAD, THE .... GENE KELLY
HAPPY (TF) .... DOM DeLUISE
HAPPY THIEVES, THE .... JOSEPH WISEMAN
HAPPY TIME, THE .... LOUIS JOURDAN
HAPPY TOGETHER .... BARBARA BABCOCK
HAPPY TOGETHER .... DAN SCHNEIDER
HAPPY TOGETHER .... HELEN SLATER
HAPPY TOGETHER .... MARIUS WEYERS
HAPPY TOGETHER .... PATRICK DEMPSEY
HAPPY VALLEY, THE (TF) .... DENHOLM ELLIOTT†
HAPPY YEARS, THE .... DEAN STOCKWELL
HAPPY YEARS, THE .... ROBERT WAGNER
HARD CHOICES .... JOHN SAYLES
HARD CHOICES .... LIANE CURTIS
HARD CHOICES .... SPALDING GRAY
HARD CONTRACT .... BURGESS MEREDITH
HARD CONTRACT .... JAMES COBURN
HARD CONTRACT .... KAREN BLACK
HARD COUNTRY .... DARYL HANNAH
HARD COUNTRY .... GAILORD SARTAIN
HARD COUNTRY .... JAN-MICHAEL VINCENT
HARD COUNTRY .... KIM BASINGER
HARD COUNTRY .... TED NEELEY
HARD DAY'S NIGHT, A .... JOHN LENNON†
HARD DAY'S NIGHT, A .... GEORGE HARRISON
HARD DAY'S NIGHT, A .... KENNETH HAIGH
HARD DAY'S NIGHT, A .... PAUL McCARTNEY
HARD DAY'S NIGHT, A .... RINGO STARR
HARD DRIVER .... GARY BUSEY
HARD DRIVER ....GERALDINE FITZGERALD
HARD DRIVER .... JEFF BRIDGES
HARD DRIVER .... VALERIE PERRINE
HARD EVIDENCE .... BILLY WIRTH
HARD EVIDENCE .... LEWIS BERGEN
HARD EVIDENCE .... RONNY COX
HARD KNOX (TF) .... ROBERT CONRAD
HARD PROMISES .... BRIAN KERWIN
HARD PROMISES .... JEFF PERRY
HARD PROMISES .... MARE WINNINGHAM
HARD PROMISES .... RIP TORN
HARD PROMISES .... SHIRLEY KNIGHT
HARD PROMISES .... SISSY SPACEK
HARD PROMISES .... WILLIAM L. PETERSEN
HARD RAIN .... TODD GRAFF
HARD RIDE TO RANTAN .... RICHARD CRENNA
HARD TARGET .... JEAN-CLAUDE VAN DAMME

HARD TARGET .... LANCE HENRIKSEN
HARD TARGET .... WILFORD BRIMLEY
HARD TARGET .... YANCY BUTLER
HARD TIMES .... CHARLES BRONSON
HARD TIMES .... JAMES COBURN
HARD TIMES .... JILL IRELAND†
HARD TO GET .... OLIVIA DE HAVILLAND
HARD TO HOLD .... ALBERT SALMI†
HARD TO HOLD .... JANET EILBER
HARD TO HOLD .... RICK SPRINGFIELD
HARD TO KILL .... FRED COFFIN
HARD TO KILL .... KELLY LeBROCK
HARD TO KILL .... STEVEN SEAGAL
HARD TO KILL .... WILLIAM SADLER
HARD TRUTH, THE (CTF) .... LYSETTE ANTHONY
HARD WAY, THE .... ANNABELLA SCIORRA
HARD WAY, THE .... CHRISTINA RICCI
HARD WAY, THE .... JAMES WOODS
HARD WAY, THE .... KATHY NAJIMY
HARD WAY, THE .... MICHAEL J. FOX
HARD WAY, THE .... PENNY MARSHALL
HARD WAY, THE .... STEPHEN LANG
HARDCASE (TF) .... ALEXIS KARRAS
HARDCASTLE AND
    McCORMICK (TF) .... BRIAN KEITH
HARDCASTLE AND
    McCORMICK (TF) .... DANIEL HUGH KELLY
HARDCASTLE AND
    McCORMICK (TF) .... JOHN SAXON
HARDCORE .... DICK SARGENT
HARDCORE .... GEORGE C. SCOTT
HARDCORE .... PETER BOYLE
HARDCORE .... SEASON HUBLEY
HARDER THEY COME, THE .... JIMMY CLIFF
HARDER THEY FALL, THE .... NEHEMIAH PERSOFF
HARDER THEY FALL, THE .... ROD STEIGER
HARDER THEY FALL, THE .... VAL AVERY
HARDHAT AND LEGS (TF) .... RAY LIOTTA
HARDHAT & LEGS (TF) .... SHARON GLESS
HARDLY WORKING .... BILLY BARTY
HARDLY WORKING .... JERRY LEWIS
HARE .... ALLEN GARFIELD
HAREM .... BEN KINGSLEY
HAREM .... NASTASSJA KINSKI
HAREM (MS) .... SARAH MILES
HAREM (MS) .... YAPHET KOTTO
HAREM SCAREM .... ELVIS PRESLEY†
HAREM (TF) .... AVA GARDNER†
HARLEM NIGHTS .... ARSSENIO HALL
HARLEM NIGHTS .... BERLINDA TOLBERT
HARLEM NIGHTS .... CHARLES Q. MURPHY
HARLEM NIGHTS .... DANNY AIELLO
HARLEM NIGHTS .... DAVID MARCIANO
HARLEM NIGHTS .... DELLA REESE
HARLEM NIGHTS .... EDDIE MURPHY
HARLEM NIGHTS .... EDDIE SMITH
HARLEM NIGHTS .... JASMINE GUY
HARLEM NIGHTS .... JOE PECORARO
HARLEM NIGHTS .... LELA ROCHON
HARLEM NIGHTS .... MICHAEL GOLDFINGER
HARLEM NIGHTS .... MICHAEL LERNER
HARLEM NIGHTS .... REDD FOXX†
HARLEM NIGHTS .... RICHARD PRYOR
HARLEM NIGHTS .... RICK AIELLO
HARLEM NIGHTS .... STAN SHAW
HARLEM NIGHTS .... TOMMY FORD
HARLEM NIGHTS .... VIC POLIZOS
HARLEY DAVIDSON & THE
    MARLBORO MAN .... CHELSEA FIELD
HARLEY DAVIDSON & THE
    MARLBORO MAN .... DANIEL BALDWIN
HARLEY DAVIDSON & THE
    MARLBORO MAN .... DON JOHNSON
HARLEY DAVIDSON & THE
    MARLBORO MAN .... JULIUS HARRIS
HARLEY DAVIDSON & THE
    MARLBORO MAN .... MICKEY ROURKE
HARLEY DAVIDSON & THE
    MARLBORO MAN .... ROBERT GINTY
HARLEY DAVIDSON & THE
    MARLBORO MAN .... TOM SIZEMORE

HARLEY DAVIDSON & THE
    MARLBORO MAN .... VANESSA WILLIAMS
HARLOW .... ANGELA LANSBURY
HARLOW .... CAROL LYNLEY
HARLOW .... CARROLL BAKER
HARLOW .... JACK KRUSCHEN
HARLOW .... LESLIE NIELSEN
HARLOW .... MARTIN BALSAM
HARLOW .... MICHAEL DANTE
HARLOW .... RED BUTTONS
HARLOW (TF) .... EFREM ZIMBALIST JR.
HARLOW (TF) .... HURD HATFIELD
HAROLD AND MAUDE .... BUD CORT
HAROLD AND MAUDE .... RUTH GORDON†
HAROLD ROBBINS' 79
    PARK AVENUE (MS) .... LESLEY ANN WARREN
HAROLD ROBBINS' THE PIRATE .... ANNE ARCHER
HAROLD ROBBINS'
    THE PIRATE .... ARMAND ASSANTE
HAROLD ROBBINS' THE PIRATE ..... DIMITRA ARLYS
HAROLD ROBBINS'
    THE PIRATE (TF) .... ELI WALLACH
HARPER .... ARTHUR HILL
HARPER .... JANET LEIGH
HARPER .... JULIE HARRIS
HARPER .... LAUREN BACALL
HARPER .... PAUL NEWMAN
HARPER .... ROBERT WAGNER
HARPER .... ROBERT WEBBER
HARPER .... SHELLEY WINTERS
HARPER VALLEY P.T.A. .... BARBARA EDEN
HARPER VALLEY P.T.A. .... WOODY HARRELSON
HARPY (TF) .... ELIZABETH ASHLEY
HARRAD EXPERIMENT, THE .... BRUNO KIRBY
HARRAD EXPERIMENT, THE .... DON JOHNSON
HARRAD
    EXPERIMENT, THE .... GREGORY HARRISON
HARRAD EXPERIMENT, THE .... JAMES WHITMORE
HARRAD EXPERIMENT, THE .... MELANIE GRIFFITH
HARRAD EXPERIMENT, THE .... TIPPI HEDREN
HARRIET CRAIG .... JOAN CRAWFORD†
HARRY AND SON .... ELLEN BARKIN
HARRY AND SON .... JOANNE WOODWARD
HARRY AND SON .... OSSIE DAVIS
HARRY AND SON .... PAUL NEWMAN
HARRY AND SON .... ROBBY BENSON
HARRY AND SON .... WILFORD BRIMLEY
HARRY AND THE HENDERSONS .... DON AMECHE†
HARRY AND THE HENDERSONS ..... JOHN LITHGOW
HARRY AND THE
    HENDERSONS .... MELINDA DILLON
HARRY AND TONTO .... CHIEF DAN GEORGE†
HARRY AND TONTO .... CLIFF DE YOUNG
HARRY AND TONTO .... ELLEN BURSTYN
HARRY AND TONTO .... GERALDINE FITZGERALD
HARRY AND TONTO .... LARRY HAGMAN
HARRY AND TONTO .... MELANIE MAYRON
HARRY AND TONTO ★★ .... ART CARNEY
HARRY AND WALTER GO
    TO NEW YORK .... CAROL KANE
HARRY AND WALTER GO
    TO NEW YORK .... CHARLES DURNING
HARRY AND WALTER GO
    TO NEW YORK .... DENNIS DUGAN
HARRY AND WALTER GO
    TO NEW YORK .... DIANE KEATON
HARRY AND WALTER GO
    TO NEW YORK .... ELLIOTT GOULD
HARRY AND WALTER GO
    TO NEW YORK .... GEORGE GAYNES
HARRY AND WALTER GO
    TO NEW YORK .... JAMES CAAN
HARRY AND WALTER GO
    TO NEW YORK .... MICHAEL CAINE
HARRY AND WALTER GO
    TO NEW YORK .... VAL AVERY
HARRY IN YOUR POCKET .... JAMES COBURN
HARRY IN YOUR POCKET .... MICHAEL SARRAZIN
HARRY IN YOUR POCKET .... TRISH VAN DEVERE
HARRY TRACY, DESPERADO .... BRUCE DERN
HARRY'S HONG KONG (TF) .... DAVID SOUL
HARRY'S HONG KONG (TF) .... DAVID HEMMINGS

I
N
D
E
X

O
F

F
I
L
M

T
I
T
L
E
S

This is not a list of every film ever made or every cast member, only those listed in this directory.

HARRY'S HONG KONG (TF) .... JAN GAN BOYD
HARRY'S HONG KONG (TF) .... MEL HARRIS
HARRY'S WAR .... EDWRAD HERRMANN
HARRY'S WAR .... SALOME JENS
HART TO HART: HOME IS WHERE
   THE HART IS (TF) .... LIONEL STANDER
HART TO HART: HOME IS WHERE
   THE HART IS (TF) .... ROBERT WAGNER
HART TO HART: HOME IS WHERE
   THE HART IS (TF) .... STEFANIE POWERS
HART TO HART: OLD FRIENDS
   NEVER DIE (TF) .... LIONEL STANDER
HART TO HART: OLD FRIENDS
   NEVER DIE (TF) .... ROBERT WAGNER
HART TO HART: OLD FRIENDS
   NEVER DIE (TF) .... STEFANIE POWERS
HART TO HART (TF) .... LIONEL STANDER
HART TO HART (TF) .... ROBERT WAGNER
HART TO HART (TF) .... STEFANIE POWERS
HARVARD HERE I COME! .... YVONNE DE CARLO
HARVEY GIRLS, THE .... ANGELA LANSBURY
HARVEY GIRLS, THE .... CYD CHARISSE
HARVEY ★ .... JAMES STEWART
HARVEY ∞ .... JOSEPHINE HULL†
HARVEY MIDDLEMAN,
   FIREMAN .... CHARLES DURNING
HAS ANYBODY SEEN MY GAL? .... JAMES DEAN†
HAS ANYBODY SEEN MY GAL? .... PIPER LAURIE
HAS ANYBODY SEEN MY GAL? ...... ROCK HUDSON†
HASTY HEART, THE .... PATRICIA NEAL
HASTY HEART, THE .... RONALD REAGAN
HATARI! .... RED BUTTONS
HATFIELDS AND THE
   McCOYS, THE (TF) .... JACK PALANCE
HATFUL OF RAIN, A .... DON MURRAY
HATFUL OF RAIN, A .... EVA MARIE SAINT
HATFUL OF RAIN, A .... HENRY SILVA
HATFUL OF
   RAIN, A ★ .... ANTHONY (TONY) FRANCIOSA
HATTER'S CASTLE .... DEBORAH KERR
HAUNTED HONEYMOON .... DOM DeLUISE
HAUNTED HONEYMOON .... GENE WILDER
HAUNTED HONEYMOON .... GILDA RADNER†
HAUNTED HONEYMOON .... JIM CARTER
HAUNTED HONEYMOON .... JONATHAN PRYCE
HAUNTED HONEYMOON .... PETER VAUGHN
HAUNTED HOUSE OF
   HORROR, THE .... FRANKIE AVALON
HAUNTED PALACE, THE .... VINCENT PRICE†
HAUNTED SUMMER .... ERIC STOLTZ
HAUNTED SUMMER .... LAURA DERN
HAUNTING, THE .... CLAIRE BLOOM
HAUNTING, THE .... JULIE HARRIS
HAUNTING, THE .... LOIS MAXWELL
HAUNTING, THE .... RUSS TAMBLYN
HAUNTING FEAR .... KAREN BLACK
HAUNTING OF HAMILTON
   HIGH, THE .... MICHAEL IRONSIDE
HAUNTING OF JULIA, THE .... MIA FARROW
HAUNTING OF JULIA, THE .... TOM CONTI
HAUNTING PASSION, THE (TF) .... RUTH NELSON
HAUNTING
   PASSION, THE (TF) .... TERRY DAVID MULLIGAN
HAUNTS OF THE
   VERY RICH (TF) .... CLORIS LEACHMAN
HAUNTS OF THE VERY RICH (TF) .... DONNA MILLS
HAUNTS OF THE
   VERY RICH (TF) .... LLOYD BRIDGES
HAUNTS OF THE VERY RICH (TF) ...... MOSES GUNN
HAVANA .... ALAN ARKIN
HAVANA .... LENA OLIN
HAVANA .... RAUL JULIA†
HAVANA .... ROBERT REDFORD
HAVING BABIES (TF) .... ABE VIGODA
HAVING BABIES (TF) .... KAREN VALENTINE
HAVING BABIES II (TF) .... CAROL LYNLEY
HAVING BABIES II (TF) .... PAULA PRENTISS
HAWAII .... BETTE MIDLER
HAWAII .... CARROLL O'CONNOR
HAWAII .... GENE HACKMAN
HAWAII .... GEORGE ROSE†
HAWAII .... JOHN CULLUM

HAWAII .... JULIE ANDREWS
HAWAII .... MAX von SYDOW
HAWAII .... MICHAEL CONSTANTINE
HAWAII .... RICHARD HARRIS
HAWAII .... TORIN THATCHER†
HAWAIIAN HEAT (TF) .... MAKO
HAWAIIAN HEAT (TF) .... ROBERT GINTY
HAWAIIANS, THE .... ALEC McCOWEN
HAWAIIANS, THE .... CHARLTON HESTON
HAWAIIANS, THE .... GERALDINE CHAPLIN
HAWAIIANS, THE .... JOHN PHILLIP LAW
HAWAIIANS, THE .... MAKO
HAWK, THE .... HELEN MIRREN
HAWK THE SLAYER .... JACK PALANCE
HAWKINS ON MURDER (TF) .... BONNIE BEDELIA
HAWKS .... ANTHONY EDWARDS
HAWKS .... TIMOTHY DALTON
HAWMPS! .... JAMES HAMPTON
HAZARD OF HEARTS, A (TF) .... EDWARD FOX
HAZARD OF
   HEARTS, A (TF) .... HELENA BONHAM CARTER
HAZEL'S PEOPLE .... PAT HINGLE
HE AND SHE .... HAROLD GOULD
HE COULDN'T SAY NO .... JANE WYMAN
HE DIED WITH HIS
   EYES OPEN .... CHARLOTTE RAMPLING
HE KNOWS YOU'RE ALONE .... TOM HANKS
HE RAN ALL THE WAY .... NORMAN LLOYD
HE RAN ALL THE WAY ...... SHELLEY WINTERS
HE RIDES TALL .... R.G. ARMSTRONG
HE SAID, SHE SAID .... ANTHONY LaPAGLIA
HE SAID, SHE SAID ...... ELIZABETH PERKINS
HE SAID, SHE SAID .... KEVIN BACON
HE SAID, SHE SAID .... SHARON STONE
HE WHO RIDES A TIGER .... JUDI DENCH
HE'S FIRED,
   SHE'S HIRED (TF) .... KAREN VALENTINE
HEAD .... TIMOTHY CAREY
HEAD OF THE FAMILY, THE .... CLAUDINE AUGER
HEAD OF THE FAMILY, THE .... LESLIE CARON
HEAD OFFICE .... DANNY DeVITO
HEAD OFFICE .... EDDIE ALBERT
HEAD OFFICE .... MERRITT BUTRICK†
HEAD OFFICE .... RON FRAZIER
HEAD ON .... JOHN HUSTON†
HEAD ON .... LAWRENCE DANE
HEAD ON .... SALLY KELLERMAN
HEAD ON .... STEPHEN LACK
HEAD OVER HEELS .... GRIFFIN DUNNE
HEAD OVER HEELS .... JOHN HEARD
HEAD OVER HEELS .... MARY BETH HURT
HEADLINE SHOOTERS .... RALPH BELLAMY†
HEALER, THE .... RALPH BELLAMY†
HEALERS, THE (TF) .... JOHN FORSYTHE
HEALTH .... ALFRE WOODARD
HEALTH .... CAROL BURNETT
HEALTH .... DICK CAVETT
HEALTH .... DINAH SHORE†
HEALTH .... GLENDA JACKSON
HEALTH .... HENRY GIBSON
HEALTH .... JAMES GARNER
HEALTH .... LAUREN BACALL
HEALTH .... PAUL DOOLEY
HEAR MY SONG .... NED BEATTY
HEAR MY SONG .... SHIRLEY ANNE FIELD
HEAR MY SONG .... TARA FITZGERALD
HEAR NO EVIL (TF) .... GIL GERARD
HEARSE, THE .... CHRISTOPHER McDONALD
HEARSE, THE .... TRISH VAN DEVERE
HEARST AND DAVIES
   AFFAIR, THE (TF) .... DORIS BELACK
HEARST AND DAVIES
   AFFAIR, THE (TF) .... FRITZ WEAVER
HEARST AND DAVIES
   AFFAIR, THE (TF) .... ROBERT MITCHUM
HEARST AND DAVIES
   AFFAIR, THE (TF) .... ROBERT MITCHUM
HEARST AND DAVIES
   AFFAIR, THE (TF) .... VIRGINIA MADSEN
HEART .... BRAD DAVIS†
HEART .... STEVE BUSCEMI
HEART AND SOULS .... ALFRE WOODARD

HEART AND SOULS .... BILL CALVERT
HEART AND SOULS .... CHARLES GRODIN
HEART AND SOULS .... DAVID PAYMER
HEART AND SOULS .... ELISABETH SHUE
HEART AND SOULS .... ERIC LLOYD
HEART AND SOULS .... ERNIE HUDSON
HEART AND SOULS .... KYRA SEDGWICK
HEART AND SOULS .... LISA LUCAS
HEART AND SOULS .... RICHARD PORTNOW
HEART AND SOULS .... ROBERT DOWNEY JR.
HEART AND SOULS .... TOM SIZEMORE
HEART BEAT .... JOHN HEARD
HEART BEAT .... JOHN LARROQUETTE
HEART BEAT .... NICK NOLTE
HEART BEAT .... RAY SHARKEY†
HEART BEAT .... SISSY SPACEK
HEART BEAT .... STEVE ALLEN
HEART CONDITION .... BOB HOSKINS
HEART CONDITION .... CHLOE WEBB
HEART CONDITION .... DENZEL WASHINGTON
HEART CONDITION .... MARK LOWENTHAL
HEART IS A LONELY
   HUNTER, THE .... CICELY TYSON
HEART IS A LONELY
   HUNTER, THE .... STACY KEACH
HEART IS A LONELY
   HUNTER, THE ★ .... ALAN ARKIN
HEART IS A LONELY
   HUNTER, THE ○ .... SONDRA LOCKE
HEART LIKE A WHEEL .... ANTHONY EDWARDS
HEART LIKE A WHEEL .... BEAU BRIDGES
HEART LIKE A WHEEL .... BILL McKINNEY
HEART LIKE A WHEEL .... BONNIE BEDELIA
HEART LIKE A WHEEL .... DEAN PAUL MARTIN†
HEART LIKE A WHEEL .... DICK MILLER
HEART LIKE A WHEEL .... HOYT AXTON
HEART LIKE A WHEEL .... LEO ROSSI
HEART LIKE A WHEEL .... PAUL BARTEL
HEART LIKE A WHEEL .... TERRENCE KNOX
HEART OF A CHAMPION: THE RAY
   MANCINI STORY (TF) .... DOUG McKEON
HEART OF A CHAMPION: THE RAY
   MANCINI STORY (TF) .... ROBERT BLAKE
HEART OF A NATION, THE .... LOUIS JOURDAN
HEART OF DIXIE .... ALLY SHEEDY
HEART OF DIXIE .... BARBARA BABCOCK
HEART OF DIXIE .... DON MICHAEL PAUL
HEART OF DIXIE .... FRANCESCA ROBERTS
HEART OF DIXIE .... KURTWOOD SMITH
HEART OF DIXIE .... KYLE SECOR
HEART OF DIXIE .... PHOEBE CATES
HEART OF DIXIE .... RICHARD BRADFORD
HEART OF DIXIE .... TREAT WILLIAMS
HEART OF DIXIE .... VIRGINIA MADSEN
HEART OF MIDNIGHT .... BRENDA VACCARO
HEART OF MIDNIGHT .... DENISE DUMMONT
HEART OF MIDNIGHT .... FRANK STALLONE
HEART OF MIDNIGHT .... GALE MAYRON
HEART OF MIDNIGHT ...... JENNIFER JASON LEIGH
HEART OF MIDNIGHT .... PETER COYOTE
HEART OF MIDNIGHT .... SAM SCHACHT
HEART OF STEEL (TF) .... GARY COLE
HEART OF THE
   MATTER, THE .... DENHOLM ELLIOTT†
HEART OF THE MATTER, THE ...... MARIA SCHELL
HEART RAGE .... REBECCA DE MORNAY
HEART RAGE .... RICK ROSSOVICH
HEARTACHES .... MARGOT KIDDER
HEARTACHES .... ROBERT CARRADINE
HEARTBEEPS .... ANDY KAUFMAN†
HEARTBEEPS .... BERNADETTE PETERS
HEARTBEEPS .... DICK MILLER
HEARTBEEPS .... MELANIE MAYRON
HEARTBEEPS .... RANDY QUAID
HEARTBREAK HOTEL .... CHARLIE SCHLATTER
HEARTBREAK HOTEL .... DAVID KEITH
HEARTBREAK HOTEL .... TUESDAY WELD
HEARTBREAK KID, THE .... AUDRA LINDLEY
HEARTBREAK KID, THE .... CHARLES GRODIN
HEARTBREAK KID, THE .... CYBILL SHEPHERD
HEARTBREAK KID, THE .... WILLIAM PRINCE
HEARTBREAK KID, THE ○ .... EDDIE ALBERT

† after an actor's name denotes deceased.

INDEX OF FILM TITLES

HEARTBREAK KID, THE ✪ ... JEANNIE BERLIN
HEARTBREAK RIDGE ... BO SVENSON
HEARTBREAK RIDGE ... BOYD GAINES
HEARTBREAK RIDGE ... CLINT EASTWOOD
HEARTBREAK RIDGE ... EILEEN HECKART
HEARTBREAK RIDGE ... MARSHA MASON
HEARTBREAK RIDGE ... MOSES GUNN
HEARTBREAK RIDGE ... PETER JASON
HEARTBREAKERS ... NICK MANCUSO
HEARTBREAKERS ... PETER COYOTE
HEARTBURN ... GERALDINE CHAPLIN
HEARTBURN ... JACK NICHOLSON
HEARTBURN ... JEFF DANIELS
HEARTBURN ... JOANNA GLEASON
HEARTBURN ... MAUREEN STAPLETON
HEARTBURN ... MERCEDES RUEHL
HEARTBURN ... MERYL STREEP
HEARTBURN ... RICHARD MASUR
HEARTBURN ... STEVEN HILL
HEARTBURN ... STOCKARD CHANNING
HEARTBURN ... YAKOV SMIRNOFF
HEARTLAND ... AMY WRIGHT
HEARTLAND ... BARRY PRIMUS
HEARTLAND ... CONCHATA FERRELL
HEARTLAND ... LILIA SKALA
HEARTLAND ... RIP TORN
HEARTS AND MINDS ... KIRK DOUGLAS
HEARTS OF FIRE ... BOB DYLAN
HEARTS OF FIRE ... RUPERT EVERETT
HEARTS OF THE WEST ... ALAN ARKIN
HEARTS OF THE WEST ... ANDY GRIFFITH
HEARTS OF THE WEST ... BLYTHE DANNER
HEARTS OF THE WEST ... DONALD PLEASENCE
HEARTS OF THE WEST ... JEFF BRIDGES
HEARTS OF THE WEST ... MATT CLARK
HEARTS OF THE WORLD ... LILLIAN GISH†
HEARTSOUNDS (TF) ... JAMES GARNER
HEARTSOUNDS (TF) ... MARY TYLER MOORE
HEARTSOUNDS (TF) ... SAM WANAMAKER†
HEAT ... AL PACINO
HEAT ... ROBERT DE NIRO
HEAT ... BURT REYNOLDS
HEAT ... DIANA SCARWID
HEAT ... HOWARD HESSEMAN
HEAT ... JOE DALLESANDRO
HEAT ... SYLVIA MILES
HEAT AND DUST ... CHRISTOPHER CAZENOVE
HEAT AND DUST ... GRETA SCACCHI
HEAT AND DUST ... JULIAN GLOVER
HEAT AND DUST ... JULIE CHRISTIE
HEAT OF ANGER (TF) ... TYNE DALY
HEATHERS ... CHRISTIAN SLATER
HEATHERS ... GLENN SHADIX
HEATHERS ... KIM WALKER
HEATHERS ... LANCE FENTON
HEATHERS ... LISANNE FALK
HEATHERS ... PENELOPE MILFORD
HEATHERS ... PHILL LEWIS
HEATHERS ... RENEE ESTEVEZ
HEATHERS ... SHANNEN DOHERTY
HEATHERS ... WINONA RYDER
HEATWAVE ... BILL HUNTER
HEATWAVE ... JUDY DAVIS
HEATWAVE (CTF) ... ADAM ARKIN
HEATWAVE (CTF) ... BLAIR UNDERWOOD
HEATWAVE (CTF) ... CICELY TYSON
HEATWAVE (CTF) ... GLENN PLUMMER
HEATWAVE (CTF) ... JAMES EARL JONES
HEATWAVE (CTF) ... MARGARET AVERY
HEATWAVE (CTF) ... ROBERT HOOKS
HEATWAVE (CTF) ... SALLY KIRKLAND
HEAT'S ON, THE ... LLOYD BRIDGES
HEAVEN AND EARTH ... DEBBIE REYNOLDS
HEAVEN AND EARTH ... DUSTIN NGUYEN
HEAVEN AND EARTH ... HAING S. NGOR
HEAVEN AND EARTH ... HIEP THI LE
HEAVEN AND EARTH ... JOAN CHEN
HEAVEN AND EARTH ... TOMMY LEE JONES
HEAVEN AND EARTH ... VIVIAN WU
HEAVEN CAN WAIT (1943) ... GENE TIERNEY†
HEAVEN CAN WAIT (1943) ... DON AMECHE†
HEAVEN CAN WAIT ... BUCK HENRY
HEAVEN CAN WAIT ... CHARLES GRODIN
HEAVEN CAN WAIT ... DOLPH SWEET†
HEAVEN CAN WAIT ... FRANK CAMOANELLA
HEAVEN CAN WAIT ... GEORGE J. MANOS
HEAVEN CAN WAIT ... HAMILTON CAMP
HEAVEN CAN WAIT ... JAMES MASON†
HEAVEN CAN WAIT ... JOHN RANDOLPH
HEAVEN CAN WAIT ... JOSEPH MAHUR
HEAVEN CAN WAIT ... JULIE CHRISTIE
HEAVEN CAN WAIT ... R.G. ARMSTRONG
HEAVEN CAN WAIT ... STEPHANIE FARACY
HEAVEN CAN WAIT ... VINCENT GARDENIA†
HEAVEN CAN WAIT ★ ... WARREN BEATTY
HEAVEN CAN WAIT ✪ ... DYAN CANNON
HEAVEN CAN WAIT ✪ ... JACK WARDEN
HEAVEN HELP US ... DONALD SUTHERLAND
HEAVEN HELP US ... JOHN HEARD
HEAVEN HELP US ... KEVIN DILLON
HEAVEN HELP US ... MARY STUART MASTERSON
HEAVEN HELP US ... PATRICK DEMPSEY
HEAVEN HELP US ... PHILIP BOSCO
HEAVEN KNOWS MR. ALLISON ... ROBERT MITCHUM
HEAVEN KNOWS MR. ALLISON ★ ... DEBORAH KERR
HEAVEN WITH A GUN ... BARBARA BABCOCK
HEAVEN WITH A GUN ... BARBARA HERSHEY
HEAVEN WITH A GUN ... DAVID CARRADINE
HEAVEN WITH A GUN ... JOHN ANDERSON
HEAVEN'S GATE ... TOM NOONAN
HEAVEN'S PRISONERS ... ALEC BALDWIN
HEAVEN'S PRISONERS ... BADJA DJOLA
HEAVEN'S PRISONERS ... ERIC ROBERTS
HEAVEN'S PRISONERS ... KELLY LYNCH
HEAVEN'S PRISONERS ... MARY STUART MASTERSON
HEAVEN'S PRISONERS ... PATRICIA ARQUETTE
HEAVEN'S PRISONERS ... SAMANTHA LAGPACAN
HEAVEN'S PRISONERS ... TERI HATCHER
HEAVENLY KID, THE ... RICHARD MULLIGAN
HEAVENLY PURSUITS ... DAVE ANDERSON
HEAVENLY PURSUITS ... TOM CONTI
HEAVENS ABOVE ... BROCK PETERS
HEAVEN'S GATE ... BRAD DOURIF
HEAVEN'S GATE ... CHRISTOPHER WALKEN
HEAVEN'S GATE ... ELIZABETH McGOVERN
HEAVEN'S GATE ... ISABELLE HUPPERT
HEAVEN'S GATE ... JEFF BRIDGES
HEAVEN'S GATE ... JOHN HURT
HEAVEN'S GATE ... KRIS KRISTOFFERSON
HEAVEN'S GATE ... MICKEY ROURKE
HEAVEN'S GATE ... RICHARD MASUR
HEAVEN'S GATE ... ROBIN BARTLETT
HEAVEN'S GATE ... SAM WATERSTON
HEAVEN'S GATE ... WILLEM DAFOE
HEAVY METAL (AF) ... HAROLD RAMIS
HEAVY PETTING ... SPALDING GRAY
HEAVYWEIGHTS ... AARON SCHWARTZ
HEAVYWEIGHTS ... ANNE MEARA
HEAVYWEIGHTS ... BEN STILLER
HEAVYWEIGHTS ... JEFFREY TAMBOR
HEAVYWEIGHTS ... JERRY STILLER
HEAVYWEIGHTS ... KENAN THOMPSON
HEAVYWEIGHTS ... LEAH LAIL
HEAVYWEIGHTS ... PAUL FEIG
HEAVYWEIGHTS ... SHAUN WEISS
HEAVYWEIGHTS ... TOM HODGES
HEAVYWEIGHTS ... TOM McGOWAN
HEBREW LESSON, THE ... MILO O'SHEA
HEC RAMSEY (TF) ... SHARON ACKER
HEDDA ... PATRICK STEWART
HEDDA ... TIMOTHY WEST
HEDDA ★ ... GLENDA JACKSON
HEIRESS, THE ★★ ... OLIVIA DE HAVILLAND
HEIRESS, THE ✪ ... SIR RALPH RICHARDSON†
HEIST (CTF) ... PIERCE BROSNAN
HEIST (CTF) ... WENDY HUGHES
HEIST, THE (CTF) ... TOM SKERRITT
HEIST, THE (TF) ... ELIZABETH ASHLEY
HELEN HAYES: PORTRAIT OF AN AMERICAN ACTRESS (FD) ... HELEN HAYES
HELEN MORGAN STORY, THE ... ALAN KING
HELEN MORGAN STORY, THE ... PAUL NEWMAN
HELICOPTER SPIES, THE ... BRADFORD DILLMAN
HELICOPTER SPIES, THE ... ROBERT VAUGHN
HELL AND HIGH WATER ... RICHARD WIDMARK
HELL BOATS ... JAMES FRANCISCUS†
HELL CAMP ... ANTHONY ZERBE
HELL CAMP ... LISA EICHHORN
HELL CAMP ... TOM SKERRITT
HELL CAT, THE ... ANN SOTHERN
HELL DRIVERS ... DAVID McCALLUM
HELL DRIVERS ... GORDAN JACKSON†
HELL DRIVERS ... JILL IRELAND†
HELL DRIVERS ... SEAN CONNERY
HELL HOLE ... MARJOE GORTNER
HELL IN KOREA ... MICHAEL CAINE
HELL IS A CITY ... BILLIE WHITELAW
HELL IS FOR HEROES ... BOB NEWHART
HELL IS FOR HEROES ... HARRY GUARDINO
HELL IS FOR HEROES ... JAMES COBURN
HELL IS SOLD OUT ... MAE ZETTERLING†
HELL NIGHT ... LINDA BLAIR
HELL RIVER ... ADAM WEST
HELL UP IN HARLEM ... FRED WILLIAMSON
HELL UP IN HARLEM ... JULIUS HARRIS
HELL WITH HEROES, THE ... HARRY GUARDINO
HELL'S HOUSE ... BETTE DAVIS†
HELLCAMP ... RICHARD ROUNDTREE
HELLCATS OF THE NAVY ... MAC DAVIS
HELLCATS OF THE NAVY ... RONALD REAGAN
HELLDORADO ... RALPH BELLAMY†
HELLER IN PINK TIGHTS ... ANTHONY QUINN
HELLER IN PINK TIGHTS ... EILEEN HECKART
HELLER IN PINK TIGHTS ... SOPHIA LOREN
HELLER IN PINK TIGHTS ... STEVE FORREST
HELLFIGHTERS ... KATHERINE ROSS
HELLFIGHTERS ... VERA MILES
HELLGATE ... TIMOTHY CAREY
HELLIONS, THE ... ZENA WALKER
HELLO AGAIN ... GABRIEL BYRNE
HELLO AGAIN ... JUDITH IVEY
HELLO AGAIN ... SHELLEY LONG
HELLO, DOLLY! ... BARBRA STREISAND
HELLO, DOLLY! ... MICHAEL CRAWFORD
HELLO, DOLLY! ... WALTER MATTHAU
HELLO DOWN THERE ... JANET LEIGH
HELLO DOWN THERE ... RICHARD DREYFUSS
HELLO DOWN THERE ... RODDY McDOWALL
HELLO DOWN THERE ... TONY RANDALL
HELLO—GOODBYE ... MICHAEL CRAWFORD
HELLO MARY LOU: PROM NIGHT II ... MICHAEL IRONSIDE
HELLZAPOPPIN! ... MARTHA RAYE†
HELL'S ANGELS ON WHEELS ... JACK NICHOLSON
HELL'S HORIZON ... JOHN IRELAND
HELL'S KITCHEN ... RONALD REAGAN
HELP! ... ELEANOR BRON
HELP! ... GEORGE HARRISON
HELP! ... PAUL McCARTNEY
HELP! ... RINGO STARR
HELTER SKELTER (MS) ... HOWARD CAINE†
HEMINGWAY'S ADVENTURES OF A YOUNG MAN ... DIANE BAKER
HEMINGWAY'S ADVENTURES OF A YOUNG MAN ... ELI WALLACH
HEMINGWAY'S ADVENTURES OF A YOUNG MAN ... JESSICA TANDY†
HEMINGWAY'S ADVENTURES OF A YOUNG MAN ... MICHAEL J. POLLARD
HEMINGWAY'S ADVENTURES OF A YOUNG MAN ... PAUL NEWMAN
HEMINGWAY'S ADVENTURES OF A YOUNG MAN ... SUSAN STRASBERG
HENNESSY ... LEE REMICK†
HENNESSY ... PETER EGAN
HENNESSY ... ROD STEIGER
HENRY ... MICHAEL ROOKER
HENRY & JUNE ... FRED WARD
HENRY & JUNE ... KEVIN SPACEY
HENRY & JUNE ... MARIA DE MEDEIROS
HENRY & JUNE ... RICHARD E. GRANT
HENRY & JUNE ... UMA THURMAN
HENRY - PORTRAIT OF A SERIAL KILLER ... MICHAEL ROOKER
HENRY V (1989) ... ALEC McCOWEN
HENRY V (1989) ... BRIAN BLESSED

This is not a list of every film ever made or every cast member, only those listed in this directory.

HENRY V (1989) ... CHARLES KAY
HENRY V (1989) ... CHRISTIAN BALE
HENRY V (1989) ... DEREK JACOBI
HENRY V (1989) ... EMMA THOMPSON
HENRY V (1989) ... GERALDINE McEWAN
HENRY V (1989) ... IAN HOLM
HENRY V (1989) ... JUDI DENCH
HENRY V (1989) ... MICHAEL MALONEY
HENRY V (1989) ... PAUL SCOFIELD
HENRY V (1989) ... RICHARD BRIERS
HENRY V (1989) ... ROBBIE COLTRANE
HENRY V (1989) ... ROBERT STEPHENS
HENRY V (1989) ★ ... KENNETH BRANAGH
HENRY V (1945) ★ ... LAURENCE OLIVIER†
HENRY VIII AND HIS SIX WIVES ... BERNARD HEPTON
HENRY VIII AND HIS SIX WIVES ... BRIAN BLESSED
HENRY VIII AND HIS SIX WIVES ... CHARLOTTE RAMPLING
HENRY VIII AND HIS SIX WIVES ... DONALD PLEASENCE
HENRY VIII AND HIS SIX WIVES ... MICHAEL GOUGH
HER ALIBI ... BILL SMITROVICH
HER ALIBI ... HURD HATFIELD
HER ALIBI ... JAMES FARENTINO
HER ALIBI ... JOAN COPELAND
HER ALIBI ... PATRICK WAYNE
HER ALIBI ... PAULINA PORIZKOVA
HER ALIBI ... RONALD GUTTMAN
HER ALIBI ... TESS HARPER
HER ALIBI ... TOM SELLECK
HER ALIBI ... VICTOR ARGO
HER ALIBI ... WILLIAM DANIELS
HER DILEMMA ... SYLVIA SIDNEY
HER FINAL FURY: BETTY BRODERICK, THE LAST CHAPTER (TF) ... MARCY GOLDMAN
HER FINAL FURY: BETTY BRODERICK, THE LAST CHAPTER (TF) ... MEREDITH BAXTER
HER FIRST AFFAIR ... LOUIS JOURDAN
HER FIRST BEAU ... JACKIE COOPER
HER HIGHNESS AND THE BELLBOY ... JUNE ALLYSON
HER JUNGLE LOVE ... DOROTHY LAMOUR
HER LIFE AS A MAN (TF) ... JOAN COLLINS
HER LIFE AS A MAN (TF) ... ROBYN DOUGLASS
HER SECRET LIFE (TF) ... CLIFF DE YOUNG
HER SECRET LIFE (TF) ... JAMES SLOVAN
HER SECRET LIFE (TF) ... KATE CAPSHAW
HER TWELVE MEN ... GREER GARSON
HER TWELVE MEN ... JAMES ARNESS
HER WICKED WAYS (TF) ... BARBARA EDEN
HERBIE GOES BANANAS ... CLORIS LEACHMAN
HERBIE GOES BANANAS ... HARVEY KORMAN
HERBIE GOES BANANAS ... JOHN VERNON
HERBIE GOES BANANAS ... RICHARD JAECKEL
HERBIE GOES TO MONTE CARLO ... DEAN JONES
HERBIE GOES TO MONTE CARLO ... DON KNOTTS
HERBIE RIDES AGAIN ... HELEN HAYES
HERBIE RIDES AGAIN ... STEFANIE POWERS
HERCULES— THE MOVIE ... ARNOLD SCHWARZENEGGER
HERCULES IN NEW YORK ... ARNOLD SCHWARZENEGGER
HERE COME THE GIRLS ... BOB HOPE
HERE COME THE NELSONS ... ROCK HUDSON†
HERE COME THE WAVES ... YVONNE DE CARLO
HERE COMES COOKIE ... GEORGE BURNS
HERE COMES MR. JORDAN ... LLOYD BRIDGES
HERE COMES MR. JORDAN ★ ... ROBERT MONTGOMERY†
HERE COMES MR. JORDAN ✪ ... JAMES GLEASON†
HERE COMES THE GROOM ... ALEXIS SMITH†
HERE COMES THE GROOM ... DOROTHY LAMOUR
HERE COMES THE GROOM ... JANE WYMAN
HERE WE GO 'ROUND THE MULBERRY BUSH ... DENHOLM ELLIOTT†
HERO ... ANDY GARCIA
HERO ... CHEVY CHASE
HERO ... DUSTIN HOFFMAN
HERO ... GEENA DAVIS
HERO ... JOAN CUSAK
HERO ... KEVIN J. O'CONNOR
HERO, THE ... RICHARD HARRIS
HERO AIN'T NOTHIN' BUT A SANDWICH, A ... CICELY TYSON
HERO AND THE TERROR ... BILLY DRAGO
HERO AND THE TERROR ... BRYNN THAYER
HERO AND THE TERROR ... CHUCK NORRIS
HERO AND THE TERROR ... JACK O'HALLORAN
HERO AND THE TERROR ... KAREN WITTER
HERO AND THE TERROR ... STEVE JAMES
HERO AT LARGE ... ANNE ARCHER
HERO AT LARGE ... JOHN RITTER
HERO AT LARGE ... KEVIN BACON
HEROES ... HARRISON FORD
HEROES ... HENRY WINKLER
HEROES ... SALLY FIELD
HEROES ... VAL AVERY
HEROES OF TELEMARK, THE ... GEOFFREY KEEN
HEROES OF TELEMARK, THE ... KIRK DOUGLAS
HEROES OF TELEMARK, THE ... RICHARD HARRIS
HEROES OF TELEMARK, THE ... ROY DOTRICE
HEROES, THE ... ROD STEIGER
HEROSTRATUS ... HELEN MIRREN
HESTER STREET ★ ... CAROL KANE
HETS/TORMENT ... MAE ZETTERLING†
HEX ... GARY BUSEY
HEX ... KEITH CARRADINE
HEX ... ROBERT WALKER JR.
HEX ... SCOTT GLENN
HEXED ... ARYE GROSS
HEXED ... CLAUDIA CHRISTIAN
HEY! HEY! USA ... RODDY McDOWALL
HEY, I'M ALIVE! (TF) ... ED ASNER
HE'S FIRED, SHE'S HIRED (TF) ... ELIZABETH ASHLEY
HE'S FIRED, SHE'S HIRED (TF) ... WAYNE ROGERS
HE'S NOT YOUR SON (TF) ... ANN DUSENBERRY
HE'S NOT YOUR SON (TF) ... DONNA MILLS
HE'S NOT YOUR SON (TF) ... KEN HOWARD
HI DIDDLE DIDDLE ... MARTHA SCOTT
HI, MOM! ... ALLEN GARFIELD
HI, MOM! ... CHARLES DURNING
HI, MOM! ... ROBERT DE NIRO
HIAWATHA ... VINCE EDWARDS
HICKEY AND BOGGS ... BILL COSBY
HICKEY AND BOGGS ... JAMES WOODS
HICKEY AND BOGGS ... MICHAEL MORIARTY
HICKEY AND BOGGS ... ROBERT CULP
HICKEY AND BOGGS ... ROSALIND CASH
HICKEY AND BOGGS ... VINCENT GARDENIA†
HIDDEN AGENDA ... BRAD DOURIF
HIDDEN AGENDA ... BRIAN COX
HIDDEN AGENDA ... DES McALEER
HIDDEN AGENDA ... FRANCES McDORMAND
HIDDEN AGENDA ... JIM NORTON
HIDDEN AGENDA ... JOHN BENFIELD
HIDDEN AGENDA ... MAE ZETTERLING†
HIDDEN AGENDA ... MAURICE ROEYES
HIDDEN GUNS ... ANGIE DICKINSON
HIDDEN, THE ... CLAUDIA CHRISTIAN
HIDDEN, THE ... ED O'ROSS
HIDDEN, THE ... KYLE MacLACHLAN
HIDDEN, THE ... MICHAEL NOURI
HIDDEN, THE ... RICHARD BROOKS
HIDE IN PLAIN SIGHT ... DANNY AIELLO
HIDE IN PLAIN SIGHT ... JAMES CAAN
HIDE IN PLAIN SIGHT ... JILL EIKENBERRY
HIDE IN PLAIN SIGHT ... JOSEF SOMMER
HIDE IN PLAIN SIGHT ... KENNETH McMILLAN†
HIDE-OUT ... MAUREEN O'SULLIVAN
HIDEAWAY ... ALFRED MOLINA
HIDEAWAY ... ALICIA SILVERSTONE
HIDEAWAY ... CHRISTINE LAHTI
HIDEAWAY ... JEFF GOLDBLUM
HIDEAWAY ... JEREMY SISTO
HIDEAWAY GIRL ... MARTHA RAYE†
HIDEOUT ... HOWARD KEEL
HIDING OUT ... ANNABETH GISH
HIDING OUT ... JON CRYER
HIDING OUT ... KEITH COOGAN
HIDING OUT ... NED EISENBERG
HIDING PLACE, THE ... EILEEN HECKART
HIDING PLACE, THE ... JULIE HARRIS
HIGH AND THE MIGHTY, THE ... ROBERT STACK
HIGH ANXIETY ... CLORIS LEACHMAN
HIGH ANXIETY ... DICK VAN PATTEN
HIGH ANXIETY ... HARVEY KORMAN
HIGH ANXIETY ... MADELINE KAHN
HIGH ANXIETY ... MEL BROOKS
HIGH BARBAREE ... JUNE ALLYSON
HIGH BARBAREE ... VAN JOHNSON
HIGH BRIGHT SUN, THE ... DENHOLM ELLIOTT†
HIGH BRIGHT SUN, THE ... SUSAN STRASBERG
HIGH COMMISSIONER, THE ... CHRISTOPHER PLUMMER
HIGH COST OF LOVING, THE ... GENA ROWLANDS
HIGH COST OF LOVING, THE ... JOSE FERRER†
HIGH COUNTRY, THE ... TIMOTHY BOTTOMS
HIGH CRIME ... FRANCO NERO
HIGH FLIGHT ... KENNETH HAIGH
HIGH HEELS ... MIA FARROW
HIGH HEELS ... VICTORIA ABRIL
HIGH HOPES ... DAVID BAMBER
HIGH HOPES ... EDNA DORE
HIGH HOPES ... HEATHER TOBIAS
HIGH HOPES ... LESLEY MANVILLE
HIGH HOPES ... PHILIP DAVIS
HIGH HOPES ... PHILIP JACKSON
HIGH HOPES ... RUTH SHEEN
HIGH INFIDELITY ... CLAIRE BLOOM
HIGH INFIDELITY ... JOHN PHILLIP LAW
HIGH MOUNTAIN RANGERS (TF) ... CHRISTIAN CONRAD
HIGH MOUNTAIN RANGERS (TF) ... ROBERT CONRAD
HIGH NOON ... GRACE KELLY†
HIGH NOON ... HARRY MORGAN
HIGH NOON ... KATHY JURADO
HIGH NOON ... LLOYD BRIDGES
HIGH NOON ★★ ... GARY COOPER†
HIGH PLAINS DRIFTER ... CLINT EASTWOOD
HIGH PRICE OF PASSION, THE (TF) ... KAREN YOUNG
HIGH PRICE OF PASSION, THE (TF) ... SHANNON TWEED
HIGH RISK ... ANTHONY QUINN
HIGH RISK ... BRUCE DAVISON
HIGH RISK ... CLEAVON LITTLE†
HIGH RISK ... ERNEST BORGNINE
HIGH RISK ... JAMES BROLIN
HIGH RISK ... JAMES COBURN
HIGH RISK ... LINDSAY WAGNER
HIGH ROAD TO CHINA ... BESS ARMSTRONG
HIGH ROAD TO CHINA ... BRIAN BLESSED
HIGH ROAD TO CHINA ... JACK WESTON
HIGH ROAD TO CHINA ... ROBERT MORLEY
HIGH ROAD TO CHINA ... TOM SELLECK
HIGH ROAD TO CHINA ... WILFORD BRIMLEY
HIGH ROLLERS ... ANTHONY QUINN
HIGH SCHOOL CONFIDENTIAL ... RUSS TAMBLYN
HIGH SCHOOL GIRL ... CECILIA PARKER†
HIGH SEASON ... JACQUELINE BISSET
HIGH SEASON ... KENNETH BRANAGH
HIGH SEASON ... ROBERT STEPHENS
HIGH SOCIETY ... BING CROSBY†
HIGH SOCIETY ... CELESTE HOLM
HIGH SOCIETY ... FRANK SINATRA
HIGH SOCIETY ... GRACE KELLY†
HIGH SPIRITS ... DARYL HANNAH
HIGH SPIRITS ... JENNIFER TILLY
HIGH SPIRITS ... LIAM NEESON
HIGH SPIRITS ... PETER O'TOOLE
HIGH SPIRITS ... STEVE GUTTENBERG
HIGH TERRACE, THE ... LOIS MAXWELL
HIGH TIDE ... COLIN FRIELS
HIGH TIDE ... JUDY DAVIS
HIGH TIME ... TUESDAY WELD
HIGH VELOCITY ... BEN GAZZARA
HIGH VELOCITY ... BRITT EKLAND
HIGH WIDE AND HANDSOME ... DOROTHY LAMOUR
HIGH WIND IN JAMAICA, A ... ANTHONY QUINN
HIGH WIND IN JAMAICA, A ... JAMES COBURN
HIGH WIND IN JAMAICA, A ... LILA KEDROVA
HIGH WIND IN JAMAICA, A ... NIGEL DAVENPORT
HIGH WINDOW, THE ... CONRAD JANIS
HIGH-BALLIN' ... PETER FONDA
HIGHER AND HIGHER ... BARBARA HALE
HIGHER AND HIGHER ... FRANK SINATRA

† after an actor's name denotes deceased.

HIGHER AND HIGHER .... MARY WICKES
HIGHER GROUND (TF) .... JOHN DENVER
HIGHER GROUND (TF) .... MARTIN KOVE
HIGHER LEARNING .... GWYNETH PALTROW
HIGHER LEARNING .... ICE CUBE
HIGHER LEARNING .... JASON WILES
HIGHER LEARNING .... JENNIFER CONNELLY
HIGHER LEARNING .... KRISTY SWANSON
HIGHER LEARNING .... LAURENCE FISHBURNE
HIGHER LEARNING .... MICHAEL RAPAPORT
HIGHER LEARNING .... OMAR EPPS
HIGHER LEARNING .... REGINA KING
HIGHER LEARNING .... TYRA BANKS
HIGHLANDER .... BEATIE EDNEY
HIGHLANDER .... CHRISTOPHER LAMBERT
HIGHLANDER .... CLANCY BROWN
HIGHLANDER .... ROXANNE HART
HIGHLANDER .... SEAN CONNERY
HIGHLANDER .... SHEILA GISH
HIGHLANDER II -
    THE QUICKENING .... CHRISTOPHER LAMBERT
HIGHLANDER II -
    THE QUICKENING .... JOHN C. McGINLEY
HIGHLANDER II -
    THE QUICKENING .... MICHAEL IRONSIDE
HIGHLANDER II -
    THE QUICKENING .... SEAN CONNERY
HIGHLANDER II -
    THE QUICKENING .... VIRGINIA MADSEN
HIGHPOINT .... CHRISTOPHER PLUMMER
HIGHPOINT .... RICHARD HARRIS
HIGHWAY 301 .... ROBERT WEBBER
HIGHWAY TO HEAVEN (TF) .... HELEN HAYES
HIGHWAY TO HEAVEN (TF) .... MICHAEL LANDON†
HIGHWAY TO HELL .... CHAD LOWE
HIGHWAY TO HELL .... KRISTY SWANSON
HIGHWAY TO HELL .... PATRICK BERGIN
HIGHWAYMAN, THE .... DAN O'HERLIHY
HIJACKING OF THE ACHILLE
    LAURO, THE (TF) .... E. G. MARSHALL
HIJACKING OF THE ACHILLE
    LAURO, THE (TF) .... KARL MALDEN
HIJACKING OF THE ACHILLE
    LAURO, THE (TF) .... LEE GRANT
HIJACKING OF THE ACHILLE
    LAURO, THE (TF) .... VERA MILES
HILDA CRANE .... JEAN SIMMONS
HILL IN KOREA, A .... MICHAEL CAINE
HILL, THE .... IAN BANNEN
HILL, THE .... OSSIE DAVIS
HILL, THE .... SEAN CONNERY
HILLS OF HOME .... JANET LEIGH
HILLS RUN RED, THE .... HENRY SILVA
HINDENBURG, THE .... ANNE BANCROFT
HINDENBURG, THE .... BURGESS MEREDITH
HINDENBURG, THE .... CHARLES DURNING
HINDENBURG, THE .... GEORGE C. SCOTT
HINDENBURG, THE .... GIG YOUNG†
HINDENBURG, THE .... PETER DONAT
HINDENBURG, THE .... RENE AUBERJONOIS
HINDENBURG, THE .... RICHARD DYSART
HINDENBURG, THE .... WILLIAM ATHERTON
HIRED GUN, THE .... CHUCK CONNORS†
HIRED GUN, THE .... RORY CALHOUN
HIRED GUN, THE .... VINCE EDWARDS
HIRED HAND, THE .... PETER FONDA
HIRED HAND, THE .... SEVERN DARDEN
HIRED KILLER, THE .... FRANCO NERO
HIRED KILLER, THE .... ROBERT WEBBER
HIRELING, THE .... PETER EGAN
HIRELING, THE .... SARAH MILES
HIROSHIMA: OUT OF
    THE ASHES (TF) .... JUDD NELSON
HIROSHIMA: OUT OF THE ASHES (TF) .... MAKO
HIROSHIMA: OUT OF
    THE ASHES (TF) .... MAX von SYDOW
HIROSHIMA: OUT OF
    THE ASHES (TF) .... TAMLYN TOMITA
HIS BROTHER'S WIFE .... BARBARA STANWYCK†
HIS DOUBLE LIFE .... LILLIAN GISH†
HIS EXCELLENCY .... GEOFFREY KEEN
HIS GIRL FRIDAY .... CARY GRANT†
HIS GIRL FRIDAY .... RALPH BELLAMY†

HIS GIRL FRIDAY .... ROSALAND RUSSELL†
HIS KIND OF WOMAN .... RAYMOND BURR†
HIS KIND OF WOMAN .... ROBERT MITCHUM
HIS KIND OF WOMAN .... VINCENT PRICE†
HIS MAJESTY O'KEEFE .... BURT LANCASTER†
HIS MISTRESS (TF) .... ANNE MARIE JOHNSON
HISTOIRES EXTRAORDINAIRES .... PETER FONDA
HISTOIRES
    EXTRAORDINAIRES .... TERENCE STAMP
HISTOIRES EXTRAORDINAIRES .... VINCENT PRICE†
HISTOIRES EXTRAORDINAIRES .... JANE FONDA
HISTORY OF MR. POLLY, THE .... JOHN MILLS
HISTORY OF THE WORLD—
    PART 1 .... CLORIS LEACHMAN
HISTORY OF THE WORLD—
    PART 1 .... DOM DeLUISE
HISTORY OF THE WORLD—
    PART 1 .... GREGORY HINES
HISTORY OF THE WORLD—
    PART 1 .... HARVEY KORMAN
HISTORY OF THE WORLD—
    PART 1 .... JOHN GAVIN
HISTORY OF THE WORLD—
    PART 1 .... JOHN HILLERMAN
HISTORY OF THE WORLD—PART 1 ...... JOHN HURT
HISTORY OF THE WORLD—
    PART 1 .... MADELINE KAHN
HISTORY OF THE WORLD—
    PART 1 .... MARY-MARGARET HUMES
HISTORY OF THE WORLD—PART 1 ... MEL BROOKS
HISTORY OF THE WORLD—
    PART 1 .... ORSON WELLES†
HISTORY OF THE WORLD—
    PART 1 .... PAMELA STEPHENSON
HISTORY OF THE WORLD—
    PART 1 .... PAUL MAZURSKY
HISTORY OF THE WORLD—PART 1 ...... RON CAREY
HISTORY OF THE WORLD—
    PART 1 .... SHECKY GREENE
HISTORY OF THE WORLD—PART 1 ..... SID CAESAR
HIT! .... BILLY DEE WILLIAMS
HIT, THE .... BILL HUNTER
HIT, THE .... JOHN HURT
HIT, THE .... RICHARD PRYOR
HIT, THE .... TERENCE STAMP
HIT LIST .... CHARLES NAPIER
HIT LIST .... HARRIET HALL
HIT LIST .... JAN-MICHAEL VINCENT
HIT LIST .... JERE BURNS
HIT LIST .... KEN LERNER
HIT LIST .... LANCE HENRIKSEN
HIT LIST .... LEO ROSSI
HIT LIST .... RIP TORN
HIT MAN .... PAM GRIER
HIT MAN .... ROGER E. MOSLEY
HIT PARADE OF 1947 .... EDDIE ALBERT
HIT THE DECK .... ALAN KING
HIT THE DECK .... DEBBIE REYNOLDS
HIT THE DECK .... RICHARD ANDERSON
HIT THE DECK .... RUSS TAMBLYN
HITCHER, THE .... C. THOMAS HOWELL
HITCHER, THE .... JEFFREY DeMUNN
HITCHER, THE .... JENNIFER JASON LEIGH
HITCHER, THE .... JOHN M. JACKSON
HITCHER, THE .... RUTGER HAUER
HITCHHIKE! (TF) .... CLORIS LEACHMAN
HITLER: THE LAST TEN DAYS .... ALEC GUINNESS
HITLER: THE LAST TEN DAYS .... JOSS ACKLAND
HITLER: THE LAST TEN DAYS .... SIMON WARD
HITLER'S MADMAN .... AVA GARDNER†
HITLER'S GOLD/
    THE GOLDEN HEIST .... ROBERT CULP
HITLER'S S.S.: PORTRAIT
    IN EVIL (TF) .... JOHN SHEA
HITLER'S S.S.: PORTRAIT
    IN EVIL (TF) .... JOSE FERRER†
HITLER'S S.S.: PORTRAIT
    IN EVIL (TF) .... LUCY GUTTERIDGE
HITLER'S SON .... BUD CORT
HITMAN, THE .... CHUCK NORRIS
HOBO'S CHRISTMAS, A (TF) ...... BARNARD HUGHES
HOBO'S CHRISTMAS, A (TF) .... WILLIAM HICKEY
HOBSON'S CHOICE .... JOHN MILLS

HOBSON'S CHOICE (TF) .... JACK WARDEN
HOBSON'S CHOICE (TF) .... LILLIAN GISH†
HOBSON'S CHOICE (TF) .... RICHARD THOMAS
HOBSON'S CHOICE (TF) .... ROBERT ENGLUND
HOBSON'S CHOICE (TF) .... SHARON GLESS
HOCUS POCUS .... BETTE MIDLER
HOCUS POCUS .... GARRY MARSHALL
HOCUS POCUS .... KATHY NAJIMY
HOCUS POCUS .... OMRI KATZ
HOCUS POCUS .... PENNY MARSHALL
HOCUS POCUS .... SARAH JESSICA PARKER
HOCUS POCUS .... THORA BIRCH
HOCUS POCUS .... VINESSA SHAW
HOFFA .... ARMAND ASSANTE
HOFFA .... DANNY DEVITO
HOFFA .... FRANK WHALEY
HOFFA .... JACK NICHOLSON
HOLCROFT
    COVENANT, THE .... ANTHONY ANDREWS
HOLCROFT COVENANT, THE .... MICHAEL CAINE
HOLCROFT
    COVENANT, THE .... VICTORIA TENNANT
HOLD BACK THE DAWN ★ ..... OLIVIA DE HAVILLAND
HOLD BACK THE NIGHT .... CHUCK CONNORS†
HOLD BACK TOMORROW .... HARRY GUARDINO
HOLD THAT KISS .... MAUREEN O'SULLIVAN
HOLD THE DREAM (TF) .... CLAIRE BLOOM
HOLE IN THE HEAD, A .... ELEANOR PARKER
HOLE IN THE HEAD, A .... FRANK SINATRA
HOLES, THE .... GERARD DEPARDIEU
HOLIDAY .... KATHERINE HEPBURN
HOLIDAY ★ .... ANN HARDING†
HOLIDAY AFFAIR .... JANET LEIGH
HOLIDAY AFFAIR .... ROBERT MITCHUM
HOLIDAY FOR LOVERS .... CAROL LYNLEY
HOLIDAY FOR LOVERS .... JANE WYMAN
HOLIDAY FOR LOVERS .... JILL ST. JOHN
HOLIDAY IN MEXICO .... RODDY McDOWALL
HOLIDAY IN SPAIN .... DENHOLM ELLIOTT†
HOLIDAY INN .... BING CROSBY†
HOLIDAY INN .... FRED ASTAIRE†
HOLLOW IMAGE (TF) .... ROBERT HOOKS
HOLLY AND THE IVY, THE ..... DENHOLM ELLIOTT†
HOLLYWOOD CANTEEN ...... BARBARA STANWYCK†
HOLLYWOOD CANTEEN .... BETTE DAVIS†
HOLLYWOOD CANTEEN .... ELEANOR PARKER
HOLLYWOOD CANTEEN .... JANE WYMAN
HOLLYWOOD CANTEEN .... JOAN CRAWFORD†
HOLLYWOOD CAVALCADE .... DON AMECHE†
HOLLYWOOD HOTEL .... RONALD REAGAN
HOLLYWOOD
    KNIGHTS, THE .... MICHELLE PFEIFFER
HOLLYWOOD MAVERICKS (TD) ..... DENNIS HOPPER
HOLLYWOOD OR BUST .... DEAN MARTIN
HOLLYWOOD OR BUST .... JERRY LEWIS
HOLLYWOOD REVUE
    OF 1929, THE .... JOAN CRAWFORD†
HOLLYWOOD SHUFFLE .... ANNE MARIE JOHNSON
HOLLYWOOD SHUFFLE .... DAMON WAYANS
HOLLYWOOD SHUFFLE .... JOHN WITHERSPOON
HOLLYWOOD SHUFFLE .... ROBERT TOWNSEND
HOLLYWOOD VICE SQUAD .... CARRIE FISHER
HOLLYWOOD WIVES (MS) .... ANDREW STEVENS
HOLLYWOOD WIVES (MS) .... ANGIE DICKINSON
HOLLYWOOD WIVES (MS) .... ANTHONY HOPKINS
HOLLYWOOD WIVES (MS) .... CANDICE BERGEN
HOLLYWOOD WIVES (MS) .... JOANNA CASSIDY
HOLLYWOOD WIVES (MS) .... ROD STEIGER
HOLLYWOOD WIVES (MS) .... STEVE FORREST
HOLOCAUST 2000 .... KIRK DOUGLAS
HOLOCAUST 2000 .... SIMON WARD
HOLOCAUST (MS) .... BLANCHE BAKER
HOLOCAUST (MS) .... DAVID WARNER
HOLOCAUST (MS) .... FRITZ WEAVER
HOLOCAUST (MS) .... GEORGE ROSE†
HOLOCAUST (MS) .... IAN HOLM
HOLOCAUST (MS) .... JAMES WOODS
HOLOCAUST (MS) .... JOSEPH BOTTOMS
HOLOCAUST (MS) .... MERYL STREEP
HOLOCAUST (MS) .... MICHAEL BECK
HOLOCAUST (MS) .... MICHAEL MORIARTY
HOLOCAUST (MS) .... ROBERT STEPHENS
HOLOCAUST (MS) .... SAM WANAMAKER†

HOLY MATRIMONY .... JOHN SCHUCK
HOLY MATRIMONY .... LOIS SMITH
HOLY MATRIMONY .... PATRICIA ARQUETTE
HOLY MATRIMONY .... TATE DONOVAN
HOMBRE .... MARTIN BALSAM
HOMBRE .... PAUL NEWMAN
HOMBRE .... VAL AVERY
HOME ALONE .... BILLIE BIRD
HOME ALONE .... CATHERINE O'HARA
HOME ALONE .... DANIEL STERN
HOME ALONE .... JOE PESCI
HOME ALONE .... JOHN CANDY†
HOME ALONE .... JOHN HEARD
HOME ALONE .... KIERAN CULKIN
HOME ALONE .... LARRY HANKIN
HOME ALONE .... MACAULAY CULKIN
HOME ALONE .... ROBERTS BLOSSOM
HOME ALONE 2:
    LOST IN NEW YORK .... BRENDA FRICKER
HOME ALONE 2:
    LOST IN NEW YORK .... CATHERINE O'HARA
HOME ALONE 2:
    LOST IN NEW YORK .... DANIEL STERN
HOME ALONE 2:
    LOST IN NEW YORK .... DONALD TRUMP
HOME ALONE 2:
    LOST IN NEW YORK .... EDDIE BRACKEN
HOME ALONE 2:
    LOST IN NEW YORK .... JOE PESCI
HOME ALONE 2:
    LOST IN NEW YORK .... JOHN HEARD
HOME ALONE 2:
    LOST IN NEW YORK .... KIERAN CULKIN
HOME ALONE 2:
    LOST IN NEW YORK .... MACAULAY CULKIN
HOME ALONE 2:
    LOST IN NEW YORK .... ROB SCHNEIDER
HOME ALONE 2:
    LOST IN NEW YORK .... RON CANADA
HOME ALONE 2:
    LOST IN NEW YORK .... TIM CURRY
HOME BEFORE DARK .... DAN O'HERLIHY
HOME BEFORE DARK .... EFREM ZIMBALIST JR.
HOME BEFORE DARK .... JEAN SIMMONS
HOME FIRES BURNING (TF) .... BARNARD HUGHES
HOME FIRES
    BURNING (TF) .... NEIL PATRICK HARRIS
HOME FOR THE
    HOLIDAYS (TF) .... ELEANOR PARKER
HOME FOR THE
    HOLIDAYS (TF) .... JESSICA WALTER
HOME FOR THE HOLIDAYS (TF) .... JULIE HARRIS
HOME FOR THE HOLIDAYS (TF) .... SALLY FIELD
HOME FROM THE HILL .... ELEANOR PARKER
HOME FROM THE HILL .... GEORGE HAMILTON
HOME FROM THE HILL .... GEORGE PEPPARD†
HOME FROM THE HILL .... ROBERT MITCHUM
HOME IS WHERE THE HART IS ...... LESLIE NIELSEN
HOME MOVIES .... KIRK DOUGLAS
HOME MOVIES .... NANCY ALLEN
HOME MOVIES .... VINCENT GARDENIA†
HOME OF OUR OWN, A............. EDWARD FURLONG
HOME OF OUR OWN, A .... KATHY BATES
HOME OF OUR OWN, A (TF) .... JASON MILLER
HOME OF THE BRAVE .... JEFF COREY
HOME OF THE BRAVE .... LLOYD BRIDGES
HOME SWEET HOME .... LILLIAN GISH†
HOME SWEET HOMICIDE .... DEAN STOCKWELL
HOMEBOY .... MICKEY ROURKE
HOMECOMING .... LANA TURNER
HOMECOMING, THE .... IAN HOLM
HOMECOMING, THE (TF) .... PATRICIA NEAL
HOMECOMING, THE (TF) .... RICHARD THOMAS
HOMER & EDDIE .... ANN RAMSEY†
HOMER & EDDIE .... BEAH RICHARDS
HOMER & EDDIE .... JAMES BELUSHI
HOMER & EDDIE .... JOHN WATERS
HOMER & EDDIE .... KAREN BLACK
HOMER & EDDIE .... LOGAN RAMSEY
HOMER & EDDIE .... WHOOPI GOLDBERG
HOMESTRETCH, THE.................. MAUREEN O'HARA
HOMETOWN STORY .... MARILYN MONROE†
HOMETOWN, U.S.A. .... SALLY KIRKLAND

HOMEWARD BOUND: THE
    INCREDIBLE JOURNEY .... BENJ THALL
HOMEWARD BOUND: THE
    INCREDIBLE JOURNEY .... DON AMECHE†
HOMEWARD BOUND: THE
    INCREDIBLE JOURNEY .... JEAN SMART
HOMEWARD BOUND: THE
    INCREDIBLE JOURNEY .... KEVIN CHEVALIA
HOMEWARD BOUND: THE
    INCREDIBLE JOURNEY .... KIM GREIST
HOMEWARD BOUND: THE
    INCREDIBLE JOURNEY .... MICHAEL J. FOX
HOMEWARD BOUND: THE
    INCREDIBLE JOURNEY ...... PATRICK SWAYZE
HOMEWARD BOUND: THE
    INCREDIBLE JOURNEY .... ROBERT HAYS
HOMEWARD BOUND: THE
    INCREDIBLE JOURNEY .... SALLY FIELD
HOMEWARD BOUND: THE
    INCREDIBLE JOURNEY .... VERONICA LAUREN
HOMEWORK .... CARRIE SNODGRESS
HOMICIDE .... JOE MANTEGNA
HONDO .... JAMES ARNESS
HONDO ❍ .... GERALDINE PAGE†
HONEY, I BLEW UP THE KID .... ANY O'NEILL
HONEY, I BLEW UP THE KID .... BILL MOSELY
HONEY, I BLEW UP THE KID .... DANIEL SHALIKAR
HONEY, I BLEW UP THE KID .... GREGORY SIERRA
HONEY, I BLEW UP THE KID .... JOHN SHEA
HONEY, I BLEW UP THE KID .... JOSHUA SHALIKAR
HONEY, I BLEW UP THE KID .... JULIA SWEENEY
HONEY, I BLEW UP THE KID .... KERI RUSSELL
HONEY, I BLEW UP THE KID .... LESLIE NEALE
HONEY, I BLEW UP THE KID .... LLOYD BRIDGES
HONEY, I BLEW
    UP THE KID .... MARCIA STRASSMAN
HONEY, I BLEW UP THE KID .... RICK MORANIS
HONEY, I BLEW UP THE KID .... ROBERT OLIVERI
HONEY, I BLEW UP THE KID .... RON CANADA
HONEY, I SHRUNK THE KIDS .... ANY O'NEILL
HONEY, I SHRUNK THE KIDS .... JARED RUSHTON
HONEY, I SHRUNK
    THE KIDS .... KRISTINE SUTHERLAND
HONEY, I SHRUNK
    THE KIDS .... MARCIA STRASSMAN
HONEY, I SHRUNK THE KIDS .... MATT FREWER
HONEY, I SHRUNK THE KIDS .... RICK MORANIS
HONEY, I SHRUNK THE KIDS .... ROBERT OLIVERI
HONEY, I SHRUNK THE KIDS .... THOMAS BROWN
HONEY POT, THE .... CLIFF ROBERTSON
HONEY POT, THE .... EDIE ADAMS
HONEY POT, THE .... MAGGIE SMITH
HONEYCOMB .... GERALDINE CHAPLIN
HONEYMOON .... JOHN SHEA
HONEYMOON FOR THREE .... JANE WYMAN
HONEYMOON HOTEL..................JILL ST. JOHN
HONEYMOON HOTEL................... ROBERT GOULET
HONEYMOON IN VEGAS .... ANNE BANCROFT
HONEYMOON IN VEGAS .... JAMES CAAN
HONEYMOON IN VEGAS .... LAINIE KAZAN
HONEYMOON IN VEGAS .... NICOLAS CAGE
HONEYMOON IN VEGAS ... NORIYUKI "PAT" MORITA
HONEYMOON IN VEGAS .... PETER BOYLE
HONEYMOON
    IN VEGAS .... SARAH JESSICA PARKER
HONEYMOON IN VEGAS .... SEYMOUR CASSEL
HONEYMOON KILLERS, THE .... TONY LoBIANCO
HONEYMOON MACHINE, THE........... JACK WESTON
HONEYMOON MACHINE, THE....... PAULA PRENTISS
HONEYMOON WITH
    A STRANGER (TF) .... JANET LEIGH
HONEYSUCKLE ROSE .... AMY IRVING
HONEYSUCKLE ROSE .... DYAN CANNON
HONEYSUCKLE ROSE .... SLIM PICKENS†
HONEYSUCKLE ROSE .... WILLIE NELSON
HONG KONG .... RONALD REAGAN
HONKERS, THE .... ANNE ARCHER
HONKERS, THE .... JAMES COBURN
HONKERS, THE .... LOIS NETTLETON
HONKERS, THE .... RICHARD ANDERSON
HONKYTONK MAN .... MATT CLARK
HONKY TONK .... LANA TURNER
HONKY TONK FREEWAY .... BEAU BRIDGES

HONKY TONK FREEWAY .... BEVERLY D'ANGELO
HONKY TONK FREEWAY .... FRANCES LEE McCAIN
HONKY TONK FREEWAY .... HUME CRONYN
HONKY TONK FREEWAY .... JESSICA TANDY†
HONKY TONK FREEWAY .... TERI GARR
HONKY TONK FREEWAY .... WILLIAM DEVANE
HONKY TONK (TF) .... MARGOT KIDDER
HONKYTONK MAN .... CLINT EASTWOOD
HONKYTONK MAN .... KYLE EASTWOOD
HONOLULU .... GEORGE BURNS
HONOR BOUND .... TOM SKERRITT
HONOR GUARD, THE .... ROD STEIGER
HONOR THY FATHER .... BRENDA VACCARO
HONOR THY FATHER AND MOTHER:
    THE TRUE STORY OF THE
    MENENDEZ BROTHERS (TF) ...... JILL CLAYBURGH
HONOR THY FATHER AND MOTHER:
    THE TRUE STORY OF THE
    MENENDEZ MURDERS (TF) .... JAMES FARENTINO
HONORARY CONSUL, THE .... BOB HOSKINS
HONORARY CONSUL, THE .... ELPIDIA CARRILLO
HONORARY CONSUL, THE .... MICHAEL CAINE
HONORARY CONSUL, THE .... RICHARD GERE
HOODLUM EMPIRE .... RICHARD JAECKEL
HOODLUM PRIEST, THE .... DON MURRAY
HOODLUM SAINT, THE .... ANGELA LANSBURY
HOODLUM, THE .... LAWRENCE TIERNEY
HOODWINK .... JUDY DAVIS
HOOK .... BOB HOSKINS
HOOK .... CHARLIE KORSMO
HOOK .... DUSTIN HOFFMAN
HOOK .... GLENN CLOSE
HOOK .... JULIA ROBERTS
HOOK .... MAGGIE SMITH
HOOK .... PHIL COLLINS
HOOK .... RANDI PAREIRA
HOOK .... ROBIN WILLIAMS
HOOK, THE .... KIRK DOUGLAS
HOOK, THE .... NEHEMIAH PERSOFF
HOOK, THE .... ROBERT WALKER JR.
HOOK, LINE AND SINKER .... JERRY LEWIS
HOOPER .... ADAM WEST
HOOPER .... BRIAN KEITH
HOOPER .... BURT REYNOLDS
HOOPER .... JAN-MICHAEL VINCENT
HOOPER .... JOHN MARLEY†
HOOPER .... ROBERT KLEIN
HOOPER .... ROBERT TESSIER†
HOOPER .... SALLY FIELD
HOORAY FOR LOVE .... ANN SOTHERN
HOOSIERS .... BARBARA HERSHEY
HOOSIERS .... BRAD BOYLE
HOOSIERS .... BRAD LONG
HOOSIERS .... DAVID NEIDORF
HOOSIERS .... FERN PERSONS
HOOSIERS .... GENE HACKMAN
HOOSIERS .... SHEB WOOLEY
HOOSIERS .... STEVE HOLLAR
HOOSIERS ❍ .... DENNIS HOPPER
HOPE AND GLORY .... IAN BANNEN
HOPE AND GLORY .... SAMMI DAVIS
HOPE AND GLORY .... SARAH MILES
HOPE AND GLORY .... SEBASTIAN RICE EDWARDS
HOPPY SERVES A WRIT .... ROBERT MITCHUM
HOPSCOTCH .... GLENDA JACKSON
HOPSCOTCH .... NED BEATTY
HOPSCOTCH .... SAM WATERSTON
HOPSCOTCH .... WALTER MATTHAU
HORIZONS WEST .... DENNIS WEAVER
HORIZONS WEST .... JAMES ARNESS
HORIZONS WEST .... RAYMOND BURR†
HORIZONS WEST .... ROCK HUDSON†
HORIZONTAL
    LIEUTENANT, THE .... PAULA PRENTISS
HORN BLOWS AT
    MIDNIGHT, THE .... ALEXIS SMITH†
HORN BLOWS AT
    MIDNIGHT, THE .... ROBERT BLAKE
HORNET'S NEST .... ROCK HUDSON†
HORROR AT 37,000 FEET (TF) .... TAMMY GRIMES
HORROR AT 37,000 FEET (TF) .... WILLIAM SHATNER
HORROR AT 37,000 FEET (TF) .... FRANCE NUYEN
HORROR EXPRESS .... TELLY SAVALAS†

INDEX OF FILM TITLES

HORROR HOUSE .... FRANKIE AVALON
HORROR OF DRACULA .... GEOFFREY BAYLDON
HORROR OF DRACULA .... MICHAEL GOUGH
HORROR OF IT ALL, THE .... PAT BOONE
HORROR PLANET .... VICTORIA TENNANT
HORRORS OF THE BLACK MUSEUM .... MICHAEL GOUGH
HORRORS OF THE BLACK MUSEUM .... SHIRLEY ANNE FIELD
HORSE IN THE GRAY FLANNEL SUIT, THE .... DEAN JONES
HORSE IN THE GRAY FLANNEL SUIT, THE .... DIANE BAKER
HORSE IN THE GRAY FLANNEL SUIT, THE .... KURT RUSSELL
HORSE SOLDIERS, THE .... JOHN WAYNE†
HORSEMEN, THE .... JACK PALANCE
HORSEMEN, THE .... LEIGH TAYLOR-YOUNG
HORSEMEN, THE .... OMAR SHARIF
HORSE'S MOUTH, THE .... ALEC GUINNESS
HORSE'S MOUTH, THE .... MICHAEL GOUGH
HOSPITAL, THE .... BARNARD HUGHES
HOSPITAL, THE .... DIANA RIGG
HOSPITAL, THE .... NANCY MARCHAND
HOSPITAL, THE .... STOCKARD CHANNING
HOSPITAL, THE ★ .... GEORGE C. SCOTT
HOSTAGE .... KAREN BLACK
HOSTAGE (TF) .... ANNETTE BENING
HOSTAGE (TF) .... CAROL BURNETT
HOSTAGE (TF) .... CARRIE HAMILTON
HOSTAGE (TF) .... LEON RUSSOM
HOSTAGE FLIGHT (TF) .... BARBARA BOSSON
HOSTAGE FLIGHT (TF) .... DEE WALLACE STONE
HOSTAGE FLIGHT (TF) .... NED BEATTY
HOSTAGE HEART, THE (TF) .... LORETTA SWIT
HOSTAGE HEART, THE (TF) .... SHARON ACKER
HOSTAGE TOWER, THE (TF) .... BILLY DEE WILLIAMS
HOSTAGE TOWER, THE (TF) .... BRITT EKLAND
HOSTAGE TOWER, THE (TF) .... CELIA JOHNSON†
HOSTAGE TOWER, THE (TF) .... KEIR DULLEA
HOSTAGE TOWER, THE (TF) .... MAUD ADAMS
HOSTAGE TOWER, THE (TF) .... PETER FONDA
HOSTAGE TOWER, THE (TF) .... RACHEL ROBERTS†
HOSTILE GUNS .... TAB HUNTER
HOSTILE GUNS .... YVONNE DE CARLO
HOT AND COLD .... ANDREW McCARTHY
HOT CHOCOLATE .... BO DEREK
HOT DEATH, THE .... MERCEDES McCAMBRIDGE
HOT DOG...THE MOVIE .... DAVID NAUGHTON
HOT DOG...THE MOVIE .... SHANNON TWEED
HOT ENOUGH FOR JUNE .... ROBERT MORLEY
HOT LEAD AND COLD FEET .... DARREN McGAVIN
HOT LEAD AND COLD FEET .... DON KNOTTS
HOT MILLIONS .... BOB NEWHART
HOT MILLIONS .... KARL MALDEN
HOT MILLIONS .... MAGGIE SMITH
HOT MILLIONS .... PETER USTINOV
HOT MILLIONS .... ROBERT MORLEY
HOT MONEY GIRL .... WALTER GOTELL
HOT PAINT (TF) .... GREGORY HARRISON
HOT PAINT (TF) .... JOHN GLOVER
HOT PAINT (TF) .... JOHN LARROQUETTE
HOT PURSUIT .... JOHN CUSAK
HOT PURSUIT .... PAUL BATES
HOT PURSUIT .... ROBERT LOGGIA
HOT RESORT .... BRONSON PINCHOT
HOT ROCK, THE .... GEORGE SEGAL
HOT ROCK, THE .... MOSES GUNN
HOT ROCK, THE .... PAUL SAND
HOT ROCK, THE .... ROBERT REDFORD
HOT ROCK, THE .... RON LEIBMAN
HOT ROD GIRL .... CHUCK CONNORS†
HOT ROD HULLABALLO .... MARSHA MASON
HOT SHOTS! .... BILL IRWIN
HOT SHOTS! .... CARY ELWES
HOT SHOTS! .... CHARLIE SHEEN
HOT SHOTS! .... EFREM ZIMBALIST JR.
HOT SHOTS! .... JON CRYER
HOT SHOTS! .... KEVIN DUNN
HOT SHOTS! .... KRISTY SWANSON
HOT SHOTS! .... LLOYD BRIDGES
HOT SHOTS! .... VALERIA GOLINO
HOT SHOTS! .... WILLIAM O'LEARY
HOT SHOTS! PART DEUX .... CHARLIE SHEEN
HOT SHOTS! PART DEUX .... LLOYD BRIDGES
HOT SHOTS! PART DEUX .... VALERIA GOLINO
HOT SPELL .... ANTHONY QUINN
HOT SPELL .... EARL HOLLIMAN
HOT SPELL .... EILEEN HECKART
HOT SPELL .... SHIRLEY MacLAINE
HOT SPOT, THE .... CHARLES MARTIN SMITH
HOT SPOT, THE .... DON JOHNSON
HOT SPOT, THE .... JENNIFER CONNELLY
HOT SPOT, THE .... VIRGINIA MADSEN
HOT STUFF .... DOM DeLUISE
HOT STUFF .... OSSIE DAVIS
HOT STUFF .... SUZANNE PLESHETTE
HOT SUMMER NIGHT .... CLAUDE AKINS†
HOT SUMMER NIGHT .... LESLIE NIELSEN
HOT TO TROT .... BOB GOLDTHWAIT
HOT TO TROT .... CINDY PICKETT
HOT TO TROT .... DABNEY COLEMAN
HOT TO TROT .... JIM METZLER
HOT TO TROT .... JOHN CANDY†
HOT TO TROT .... VIRGINIA MADSEN
HOTEL .... KARL MALDEN
HOTEL .... KEVIN McCARTHY
HOTEL COLONIAL .... JOHN SAVAGE
HOTEL COLONIAL .... RACHEL WARD
HOTEL COLONIAL .... ROBERT DUVALL
HOTEL FOR WOMEN .... ANN SOTHERN
HOTEL NEW HAMPSHIRE, THE .... BEAU BRIDGES
HOTEL NEW HAMPSHIRE, THE .... JODIE FOSTER
HOTEL NEW HAMPSHIRE, THE .... MATTHEW MODINE
HOTEL NEW HAMPSHIRE, THE .... NASTASSJA KINSKI
HOTEL NEW HAMPSHIRE, THE .... ROB LOWE
HOTEL NEW HAMPSHIRE, THE .... WILFORD BRIMLEY
HOTEL PARADISO .... ALEC GUINNESS
HOTEL PARADISO .... ROBERT MORLEY
HOTEL SAHARA .... DAVID TOMLINSON
HOTEL SAHARA .... PETER USTINOV
HOTEL SAHARA .... YVONNE DE CARLO
HOTEL (TF) .... JAMES BROLIN
HOUDINI .... JANET LEIGH
HOUDINI .... TONY CURTIS
HOUND DOG MAN .... CLAUDE AKINS†
HOUND DOG MAN .... ROYAL DANO
HOUND OF THE BASKERVILLES, THE .... DENHOLM ELLIOTT†
HOUND OF THE BASKERVILLES, THE .... DUDLEY MOORE
HOUND OF THE BASKERVILLES, THE .... PETER COOK
HOUND-DOG MAN .... CAROL LYNLEY
HOUND-DOG MAN .... STUART WHITMAN
HOUR OF GLORY .... MICHAEL GOUGH
HOUR OF THE ASSASSIN .... ERIK ESTRADA
HOUR OF THE ASSASSIN .... ROBERT VAUGHN
HOUR OF THE GUN .... ALBERT SALMI†
HOUR OF THE GUN .... JAMES GARNER
HOUR OF THE GUN .... JASON ROBARDS
HOUR OF THE GUN .... JON VOIGHT
HOUR OF THE PIG, THE .... JIM CARTER
HOUR OF THE WOLF .... ERLAND JOSEPHSON
HOUR OF THE WOLF .... LIV ULLMANN
HOUR OF THE WOLF .... MAX von SYDOW
HOUR OF VENGEANCE .... WILLIAM SHATNER
HOUSE .... GEORGE WENDT
HOUSE .... KAY LENZ
HOUSE .... RICHARD MOLL
HOUSE .... SUSAN FRENCH
HOUSE .... WILLIAM KATT
HOUSE BOAT .... CARY GRANT†
HOUSE BOAT .... SOPHIA LOREN
HOUSE BUILT UPON SAND, THE .... LILLIAN GISH†
HOUSE BY THE LAKE, THE .... BRENDA VACCARO
HOUSE BY THE LAKE, THE .... DON STROUD
HOUSE BY THE RIVER .... JANE WYATT
HOUSE CALLS .... ART CARNEY
HOUSE CALLS .... GLENDA JACKSON
HOUSE CALLS .... GORDON JUMP
HOUSE CALLS .... RICHARD BENJAMIN
HOUSE CALLS .... WALTER MATTHAU
HOUSE I LIVE IN, THE .... FRANK SINATRA
HOUSE II : THE SECOND STORY .... LAR PARK LINCOLN
HOUSE IS NOT A HOME, A .... KAYE BALLARD
HOUSE IS NOT A HOME, A .... RAQUEL WELCH
HOUSE IS NOT A HOME, A .... SHELLEY WINTERS
HOUSE OF 1000 DOLLS .... VINCENT PRICE†
HOUSE OF BAMBOO .... DEFOREST KELLEY
HOUSE OF BAMBOO .... ROBERT STACK
HOUSE OF CARDS .... GEORGE PEPPARD†
HOUSE OF CARDS .... KATHLEEN TURNER
HOUSE OF CARDS .... TOMMY LEE JONES
HOUSE OF DARKNESS, THE .... LILLIAN GISH†
HOUSE OF EXORCISM .... TELLY SAVALAS†
HOUSE OF GAMES .... J. T. WALSH
HOUSE OF GAMES .... JOE MANTEGNA
HOUSE OF GAMES .... LILIA SKALA
HOUSE OF GAMES .... LINDSAY CROUSE
HOUSE OF LONG SHADOWS, THE .... VINCENT PRICE†
HOUSE OF LOVERS, THE .... ANOUK AIMEE
HOUSE OF NUMBERS .... JACK PALANCE
HOUSE OF PLEASURE .... PETER USTINOV
HOUSE OF RICORDI .... MARCELLO MASTROIANNI
HOUSE OF STRANGERS .... EFREM ZIMBALIST JR.
HOUSE OF THE DAMNED .... RICHARD KIEL
HOUSE OF THE LIVING DEAD .... SHIRLEY ANNE FIELD
HOUSE OF THE SEVEN CORPSES, THE .... JOHN IRELAND
HOUSE OF THE SEVEN GABLES, THE .... VINCENT PRICE†
HOUSE OF THE SPIRITS, THE .... ANTONIO BANDERAS
HOUSE OF THE SPIRITS, THE .... ARMIN MUELLER-STAHL
HOUSE OF THE SPIRITS, THE .... GLENN CLOSE
HOUSE OF THE SPIRITS, THE .... JEREMY IRONS
HOUSE OF THE SPIRITS, THE .... MAMIE STREEP
HOUSE OF THE SPIRITS, THE .... MARIA CONCHITA ALONSO
HOUSE OF THE SPIRITS, THE .... MERYL STREEP
HOUSE OF THE SPIRITS, THE .... VANESSA REDGRAVE
HOUSE OF THE SPIRITS, THE .... VINCENT GALLO
HOUSE OF THE SPIRITS, THE .... WINONA RYDER
HOUSE OF USHER, THE .... VINCENT PRICE†
HOUSE OF WAX .... CHARLES BRONSON
HOUSE OF WAX .... VINCENT PRICE†
HOUSE OF WOMEN .... SHIRLEY KNIGHT
HOUSE ON 92ND STREET, THE .... E. G. MARSHALL
HOUSE ON CARROLL STREET, THE .... JEFF DANIELS
HOUSE ON CARROLL STREET, THE .... JESSICA TANDY†
HOUSE ON CARROLL STREET, THE .... KELLY McGILLIS
HOUSE ON GARIBALDI STREET, THE (TF) .... JANET SUZMAN
HOUSE ON GARIBALDI STREET, THE (TF) .... MARTIN BALSAM
HOUSE ON GARIBALDI STREET, THE (TF) .... NICK MANCUSO
HOUSE ON GARIBALDI STREET, THE (TF) ..... TOPOL
HOUSE ON GREENAPPLE ROAD, THE (TF) .... JANET LEIGH
HOUSE ON GREENAPPLE ROAD, THE (TF) .... JULIE HARRIS
HOUSE ON HAUNTED HILL .... VINCENT PRICE†
HOUSE ON THE SEVEN GABLES, THE .... ALAN NAPIER†
HOUSE PARTY 3 .... GILBERT GOTTFRIED
HOUSE PARTY 3 .... MICHAEL COLVAR
HOUSE PARTY 3 .... TISHA CAMPBELL
HOUSE THAT DRIPPED BLOOD, THE .... DENHOLM ELLIOTT†
HOUSE THAT DRIPPED BLOOD, THE .... JOSS ACKLAND
HOUSE WHERE EVIL DWELLS, THE .... DOUG McCLURE
HOUSE WHERE EVIL DWELLS, THE .... EDWARD ALBERT

HOUSEBOAT	....	HARRY GUARDINO
HOUSEGUEST	....	CHAUNCEY LEOPARDI
HOUSEGUEST	....	JEFFREY JONES
HOUSEGUEST	....	KIM GREIST
HOUSEGUEST	....	MASON ADAMS
HOUSEGUEST	....	PAUL BEN-VICTOR
HOUSEGUEST	....	PHIL HARTMAN
HOUSEGUEST	....	RON GLASS
HOUSEGUEST	....	SINBAD
HOUSEGUEST	....	STAN SHAW
HOUSEGUEST	....	TONY LONGO
HOUSEHOLD SAINTS	....	JUDITH MALINA
HOUSEHOLD SAINTS	....	LILI TAYLOR
HOUSEHOLD SAINTS	....	TRACEY ULLMAN
HOUSEHOLD SAINTS	....	VINCENT D'ONOFRIO
HOUSEKEEPING	....	ANNE PITONIAK
HOUSEKEEPING	....	CHRISTINE LAHTI
HOUSESITTER	....	DANA DELANY
HOUSESITTER	....	GOLDIE HAWN
HOUSESITTER	....	STEVE MARTIN
HOUSEWIFE	....	BETTE DAVIS†
HOUSTON STORY, THE	....	BARBARA HALE
HOUSTON: THE LEGEND OF TEXAS (TF)	....	BO HOPKINS
HOUSTON: THE LEGEND OF TEXAS (TF)	....	CLAUDIA CHRISTIAN
HOUSTON: THE LEGEND OF TEXAS (TF)	....	G. D. SPRADLIN
HOUSTON: THE LEGEND OF TEXAS (TF)	....	KATHERINE ROSS
HOUSTON: THE LEGEND OF TEXAS (TF)	....	MICHAEL BECK
HOUSTON: THE LEGEND OF TEXAS (TF)	....	SAM ELLIOTT
HOUSTON, WE'VE GOT A PROBLEM (TF)	....	SANDRA DEE
HOW AWFUL ABOUT ALLAN (TF)	....	ANTHONY PERKINS†
HOW AWFUL ABOUT ALLAN (TF)	....	JOAN HACKETT†
HOW AWFUL ABOUT ALLAN (TF)	....	JULIE HARRIS
HOW COME NOBODY'S ON OUR SIDE?	....	PENNY MARSHALL
HOW DO I LOVE THEE?	....	MAUREEN O'HARA
HOW DO I LOVE THEE?	....	SHELLEY WINTERS
HOW GREEN WAS MY VALLEY	....	MAUREEN O'HARA
HOW GREEN WAS MY VALLEY	....	RODDY McDOWALL
HOW GREEN WAS MY VALLEY ○	....	SARA ALLGOOD†
HOW GREEN WAS MY VALLEY ○○	....	DONALD CRISP†
HOW I GOT INTO COLLEGE	....	ANTHONY EDWARDS
HOW I GOT INTO COLLEGE	....	BRIAN DOYLE-MURRAY
HOW I GOT INTO COLLEGE	....	CHARLES ROCKET
HOW I GOT INTO COLLEGE	....	CHRIS RYDELL
HOW I GOT INTO COLLEGE	....	COREY PARKER
HOW I GOT INTO COLLEGE	....	FINN CARTER
HOW I GOT INTO COLLEGE	....	GARY OWENS
HOW I GOT INTO COLLEGE	.....	LARA FLYNN BOYLE
HOW I GOT INTO COLLEGE	....	NORA DUNN
HOW I GOT INTO COLLEGE	....	PHIL HARTMAN
HOW I WON THE WAR	....	MICHAEL CRAWFORD
HOW MUCH ARE THOSE CHILDREN IN THE WINDOW?	....	BEVERLY D'ANGELO
HOW MUCH ARE THOSE CHILDREN IN THE WINDOW?	....	ED BEGLEY JR.
HOW MUCH ARE THOSE CHILDREN IN THE WINDOW?	....	NELL CARTER
HOW MUCH ARE THOSE CHILDREN IN THE WINDOW?	....	STEVE LANDESBERG
HOW SWEET IT IS!	....	DEBBIE REYNOLDS
HOW SWEET IT IS!	....	JAMES GARNER
HOW SWEET IT IS!	....	PAUL LYNDE†
HOW SWEET IT IS!	....	PENNY MARSHALL
HOW THE WEST WAS WON	....	CARROLL BAKER
HOW THE WEST WAS WON	....	CLAUDE AKINS†
HOW THE WEST WAS WON	......	DEBBIE REYNOLDS
HOW THE WEST WAS WON	....	ELI WALLACH
HOW THE WEST WAS WON	....	GEORGE PEPPARD†
HOW THE WEST WAS WON	....	GREGORY PECK
HOW THE WEST WAS WON	....	HARRY DEAN STANTON
HOW THE WEST WAS WON	....	HARRY MORGAN
HOW THE WEST WAS WON	....	JAMES STEWART
HOW THE WEST WAS WON	....	KARL MALDEN
HOW THE WEST WAS WON	......	RICHARD WIDMARK
HOW THE WEST WAS WON	......	RUSS TAMBLYN
HOW THE WEST WAS WON (MS)	....	BRUCE BOXLEITNER
HOW THE WEST WAS WON (MS)	....	RICARDO MONTALBAN
HOW TO BEAT THE HIGH COST OF LIVING	....	ART METRANO
HOW TO BEAT THE HIGH COST OF LIVING	....	DABNEY COLEMAN
HOW TO BEAT THE HIGH COST OF LIVING	....	EDDIE ALBERT
HOW TO BEAT THE HIGH COST OF LIVING	....	JANE CURTIN
HOW TO BEAT THE HIGH COST OF LIVING	....	JESSICA LANGE
HOW TO BEAT THE HIGH COST OF LIVING	....	RICHARD BENJAMIN
HOW TO BEAT THE HIGH COST OF LIVING	....	SUSAN SAINT JAMES
HOW TO BREAK UP A HAPPY DIVORCE (TF)	....	ANDREW PARIS
HOW TO BREAK UP A HAPPY DIVORCE (TF)	....	BARBARA EDEN
HOW TO COMMIT MARRIAGE	....	BOB HOPE
HOW TO COMMIT MARRIAGE	....	JANE WYMAN
HOW TO COMMIT MARRIAGE	....	LESLIE NIELSEN
HOW TO COMMIT MARRIAGE	....	TINA LOUISE
HOW TO FRAME A FIGG	....	DON KNOTTS
HOW TO GET AHEAD IN ADVERTISING	....	HUGH ARMSTRONG
HOW TO GET AHEAD IN ADVERTISING	....	JACQUELINE TONG
HOW TO GET AHEAD IN ADVERTISING	....	JOHN SHRAPNEL
HOW TO GET AHEAD IN ADVERTISING	....	MICK FORD
HOW TO GET AHEAD IN ADVERTISING	....	RACHEL WARD
HOW TO GET AHEAD IN ADVERTISING	....	RICHARD E. GRANT
HOW TO GET AHEAD IN ADVERTISING	....	RICHARD WILSON
HOW TO GET AHEAD IN ADVERTISING	....	SUSAN WOOLDRIDGE
HOW TO MAKE AN AMERICAN QUILT	....	ALFRE WOODARD
HOW TO MAKE AN AMERICAN QUILT	....	ANNE BANCROFT
HOW TO MAKE AN AMERICAN QUILT	....	DERMOT MULRONEY
HOW TO MAKE AN AMERICAN QUILT	....	ELLEN BURSTYN
HOW TO MAKE AN AMERICAN QUILT	....	KATE NELLIGAN
HOW TO MAKE AN AMERICAN QUILT	....	MYKELTI WILLIAMSON
HOW TO MAKE AN AMERICAN QUILT	....	RIP TORN
HOW TO MAKE AN AMERICAN QUILT	....	SAMANTHA MATHIS
HOW TO MAKE AN AMERICAN QUILT	....	WINONA RYDER
HOW TO MAKE IT	....	CHARLOTTE RAMPLING
HOW TO MAKE IT	....	SUZANNE PLESHETTE
HOW TO MARRY A MILLIONAIRE	....	BETTY GRABLE†
HOW TO MARRY A MILLIONAIRE	....	LAUREN BACALL
HOW TO MARRY A MILLIONAIRE	....	MARILYN MONROE†
HOW TO MARRY A MILLIONAIRE	....	RORY CALHOUN
HOW TO MURDER A MILLIONAIRE (TF)	....	DAVID OGDEN STIERS
HOW TO MURDER A MILLIONAIRE (TF)	....	MORGAN FAIRCHILD
HOW TO MURDER A RICH UNCLE	....	MICHAEL CAINE
HOW TO MURDER A RICH UNCLE	....	WENDY HILLER
HOW TO MURDER YOUR WIFE	....	JACK LEMMON
HOW TO MURDER YOUR WIFE	....	MARY WICKES
HOW TO MURDER YOUR WIFE	...	MAX SHOWALTER
HOW TO PICK UP GIRLS!	....	BESS ARMSTRONG
HOW TO PICK UP GIRLS! (TF)	....	DEBORAH RAFFIN
HOW TO PICK UP GIRLS! (TF)	...	DESI ARNAZ JR.
HOW TO SAVE A MARRIAGE AND RUIN YOUR LIFE	....	ANNE JACKSON
HOW TO SAVE A MARRIAGE AND RUIN YOUR LIFE	....	DEAN MARTIN
HOW TO SAVE A MARRIAGE AND RUIN YOUR LIFE	....	ELI WALLACH
HOW TO SAVE A MARRIAGE...AND RUIN YOUR LIFE	....	STELLA STEVENS
HOW TO STEAL A MILLION	.....	AUDREY HEPBURN†
HOW TO STEAL A MILLION	....	ELI WALLACH
HOW TO STEAL A MILLION	....	PETER O'TOOLE
HOW TO STEAL THE WORLD	......	ELEANOR PARKER
HOW TO STUFF A WILD BIKINI	....	ANNETTE FUNICELLO
HOW TO STUFF A WILD BIKINI	.....	FRANKIE AVALON
HOW TO SUCCEED IN BUSINESS WITHOUT REALLY TRYING	....	MICHELE LEE
HOWARD BEACH: MAKING THE CASE FOR MURDER (TF)	....	DAN LAURIA
HOWARD BEACH: MAKING THE CASE FOR MURDER (TF)	......	DANIEL J. TRAVANTI
HOWARD BEACH: MAKING THE CASE FOR MURDER (TF)	....	JOE MORTON
HOWARD BEACH: MAKING THE CASE FOR MURDER (TF)	....	WILLIAM DANIELS
HOWARD THE DUCK	....	CHIP ZIEN
HOWARD THE DUCK	....	DEBBIE LEE CARRINGTON
HOWARD THE DUCK	....	JEFFREY JONES
HOWARD THE DUCK	....	PAUL GUILFOYLE
HOWARD THE DUCK	....	RICHARD EDSON
HOWARD THE DUCK	....	TIM ROBBINS
HOWARDS END	....	ANTHONY HOPKINS
HOWARDS END	....	HELENA BONHAM CARTER
HOWARDS END	....	JAMES WILBY
HOWARDS END	....	JEMMA REDGRAVE
HOWARDS END	....	PRUNELLA SCALES
HOWARDS END	....	SAMUEL WEST
HOWARDS END ★★	....	EMMA THOMPSON
HOWARDS END ○	....	VANESSA REDGRAVE
HOWARDS OF VIRGINIA, THE	......	MARTHA SCOTT
HOWLING, THE	....	KEVIN McCARTHY
HOWLING, THE	....	PATRICK MacNEE
HOWLING IN THE WOODS, A (TF)	....	BARBARA EDEN
HOWLING IN THE WOODS, A (TF)	....	LARRY HAGMAN
HOWLING IN THE WOODS, A (TF)	....	TYNE DALY
HU-NAN	....	TERENCE STAMP
HUCKLEBERRY FINN	....	HARVEY KORMAN
HUCKLEBERRY FINN (TF)	....	FREDERIC FORREST
HUCKLEBERRY FINN (TF)	....	ROYAL DANO
HUCKSTERS, THE	....	AVA GARDNER†
HUCKSTERS, THE	....	DEBORAH KERR
HUD	....	BRANDON DE WILDE†
HUD	....	VAL AVERY
HUD ★	....	PAUL NEWMAN
HUD ★★	....	PATRICIA NEAL
HUD ○○	....	MELVYN DOUGLAS†
HUDSON HAWK	....	ANDIE MacDOWELL
HUDSON HAWK	....	ANDREW BRYNIARSKI
HUDSON HAWK	....	BRUCE WILLIS
HUDSON HAWK	....	DANNY AIELLO
HUDSON HAWK	....	DAVID CARUSO
HUDSON HAWK	....	DON HARVEY
HUDSON HAWK	....	DONALD BURTON
HUDSON HAWK	....	FRANK STALLONE
HUDSON HAWK	....	JAMES COBURN
HUDSON HAWK	....	LORRAINE TOUSSAINT
HUDSON HAWK	....	RICHARD E. GRANT
HUDSON HAWK	....	SANDRA BERNHARD
HUDSON'S BAY	....	VINCENT PRICE†
HUDSUCKER PROXY, THE	....	CHARLES DURNING

† after an actor's name denotes deceased.

HUDSUCKER
PROXY, THE .... JENNIFER JASON LEIGH
HUDSUCKER PROXY, THE .... PAUL NEWMAN
HUDSUCKER PROXY, THE .... TIM ROBBINS
HUEY LONG (CTF) .... JOHN GOODMAN
HUGGERS .... KIEFER SUTHERLAND
HUGO THE HIPPO (AF) .... BURL IVES
HUGO THE HIPPO (AF) .... PAUL LYNDE†
HULLABALOO OVER GEORGIA &
BONNIE'S PICTURES .... PEGGY ASHCROFT†
HULLO FAME .... PETER USTINOV
HUMAN COMEDY, THE .... ROBERT MITCHUM
HUMAN COMEDY, THE .... VAN JOHNSON
HUMAN COMEDY, THE ★ .... MICKEY ROONEY
HUMAN DUPLICATORS, THE .... RICHARD KIEL
HUMAN FACTOR, THE .... DEREK JACOBI
HUMAN FACTOR, THE .... GEORGE KENNEDY
HUMAN FACTOR, THE .... JOHN GIELGUD
HUMAN FACTOR, THE .... NICOL WILLIAMSON
HUMAN FACTOR, THE .... ROBERT MORLEY
HUMAN FEELINGS (TF) .... BILLY CRYSTAL
HUMAN HIGHWAY .... DEAN STOCKWELL
HUMAN HIGHWAY .... DENNIS HOPPER
HUMAN HIGHWAY .... RUSS TAMBLYN
HUMAN HIGHWAY .... SALLY KIRKLAND
HUMAN JUNGLE, THE .... CHUCK CONNORS†
HUMAN JUNGLE, THE .... CLAUDE AKINS†
HUMAN SHIELD, THE .... MICHAEL DUDIKOFF
HUMAN SHIELD, THE .... STEVE INWOOD
HUMAN SHIELD, THE .... TOMMY HINKLEY
HUMANOID .... RICHARD KIEL
HUMANOIDS FROM THE DEEP .... ANN TURKEL
HUMANOIDS FROM THE DEEP .... DOUG McCLURE
HUMORESQUE .... JOAN CRAWFORD†
HUMORESQUE .... MILTON BERLE
HUMORESQUE .... ROBERT BLAKE
HUNCHBACK, THE .... LILLIAN GISH†
HUNCHBACK OF NOTRE
DAME, THE .... ANTHONY QUINN
HUNCHBACK OF NOTRE
DAME, THE .... MAUREEN O'HARA
HUNCHBACK OF NOTRE
DAME, THE (AF) .... DEMI MOORE
HUNCHBACK OF NOTRE
DAME, THE (AF) .... KEVIN KLINE
HUNCHBACK OF NOTRE
DAME, THE (AF) .... TOM HULCE
HUNCHBACK OF NOTRE
DAME, THE (TF) ...... ANTHONY HOPKINS
HUNCHBACK OF NOTRE
DAME, THE (TF) .... DEREK JACOBI
HUNCHBACK OF NOTRE
DAME, THE (TF) ...... LESLEY-ANNE DOWN
HUNCHBACK OF NOTRE
DAME, THE (TF) .... NIGEL HAWTHORNE
HUNGER, THE .... CATHERINE DENEUVE
HUNGER, THE .... CLIFF DE YOUNG
HUNGER, THE .... DAVID BOWIE
HUNGER, THE .... SUSAN SARANDON
HUNGER, THE .... WILLEM DAFOE
HUNGRY HILL .... DAN O'HERLIHY
HUNGRY HILL .... JEAN SIMMONS
HUNK .... AVERY SCHREIBER
HUNK .... DEBORAH SHELTON
HUNK .... JOHN ALLEN NELSON
HUNK .... STEVE LEVITT
HUNT FOR RED OCTOBER, THE ...... ALEC BALDWIN
HUNT FOR RED
OCTOBER, THE .... COURTNEY B. VANCE
HUNT FOR RED
OCTOBER, THE .... FRED DALTON THOMPSON
HUNT FOR RED
OCTOBER, THE .... JAMES EARL JONES
HUNT FOR RED
OCTOBER, THE .... RICK DUCOMMUN
HUNT FOR RED OCTOBER, THE .... SAM NEILL
HUNT FOR RED OCTOBER, THE ...... SCOTT GLENN
HUNT FOR RED OCTOBER, THE ...... SEAN CONNERY
HUNT FOR RED OCTOBER, THE .... TIM CURRY
HUNTED, THE .... CHRISTOPHER LAMBERT
HUNTED, THE .... JOAN CHEN
HUNTED, THE .... JOHN LONE
HUNTED LADY, THE (TF) .... DONNA MILLS

HUNTED MEN .... ANTHONY QUINN
HUNTER (TF) .... BRIAN DENNEHY
HUNTER (TF) .... FRED DRYER
HUNTER (TF) .... JAMES WHITMORE JR.
HUNTER (TF) .... JOANNA KERNS
HUNTER (TF) .... STEPHANIE KRAMER
HUNTER, THE .... BEN JOHNSON
HUNTER, THE .... ELI WALLACH
HUNTER, THE .... LeVAR BURTON
HUNTERS, THE .... ROBERT MITCHUM
HUNTERS, THE .... ROBERT WAGNER
HUNTERS ARE
FOR KILLING (TF) .... MARTIN BALSAM
HUNTERS OF THE REEF (TF) .... STEPHEN MACHT
HUNTER'S BLOOD .... CLU GULAGER
HUNTER'S BLOOD .... SAM BOTTOMS
HUNTING PARTY, THE .... CANDICE BERGEN
HUNTING PARTY, THE .... GENE HACKMAN
HUNTING PARTY, THE .... L. Q. JONES
HURRICANE .... BILL PAXTON
HURRICANE .... JAMES KEACH
HURRICANE .... JASON ROBARDS
HURRICANE .... JIM METZLER
HURRICANE .... MIA FARROW
HURRICANE .... TIMOTHY BOTTOMS
HURRICANE (TF) .... MICHAEL LEARNED
HURRICANE, THE .... DOROTHY LAMOUR
HURRICANE, THE ✿ .... THOMAS MITCHELL†
HURRICANE SMITH .... JOHN IRELAND
HURRICANE SMITH .... YVONNE DE CARLO
HURRY SUNDOWN .... BEAH RICHARDS
HURRY SUNDOWN .... BURGESS MEREDITH
HURRY SUNDOWN .... DIAHANN CARROLL
HURRY SUNDOWN .... FAYE DUNAWAY
HURRY SUNDOWN .... GEORGE KENNEDY
HURRY SUNDOWN .... JANE FONDA
HURRY SUNDOWN .... JIM BACKUS†
HURRY SUNDOWN .... JOHN PHILLIP LAW
HURRY SUNDOWN .... MICHAEL CAINE
HURRY SUNDOWN .... REX INGRAM†
HURRY SUNDOWN .... ROBERT HOOKS
HURRY SUNDOWN .... ROBERT REED†
HUSBANDS .... BEN GAZZARA
HUSBANDS .... PETER FALK
HUSBANDS AND WIVES .... BLYTHE DANNER
HUSBANDS AND WIVES .... JULIETTE LEWIS
HUSBANDS AND WIVES .... LIAM NEESON
HUSBANDS AND WIVES .... LYSETTE ANTHONY
HUSBANDS AND WIVES .... MIA FARROW
HUSBANDS AND WIVES .... SYDNEY POLLACK
HUSBANDS AND WIVES .... WOODY ALLEN
HUSBANDS AND WIVES ✿ .... JUDY DAVIS
HUSH...HUSH,
SWEET CHARLOTTE .... BETTE DAVIS†
HUSH...HUSH,
SWEET CHARLOTTE .... BRUCE DERN
HUSH...HUSH,
SWEET CHARLOTTE .... GEORGE KENNEDY
HUSH...HUSH,
SWEET CHARLOTTE .... OLIVIA DE HAVILLAND
HUSH...HUSH,
SWEET CHARLOTTE .... WESLEY ADDY
HUSH...HUSH,
SWEET CHARLOTTE ✿ ...... AGNES MOOREHEAD†
HUSSY .... HELEN MIRREN
HUSSY .... JOHN SHEA
HUSTLE .... BEN JOHNSON
HUSTLE .... BURT REYNOLDS
HUSTLE .... CATHERINE BACH
HUSTLE .... CATHERINE DENEUVE
HUSTLE .... DAVID SPIELBERG
HUSTLE .... DICK MILLER
HUSTLE .... EDDIE ALBERT
HUSTLE .... EILEEN BRENNAN
HUSTLE .... ERNEST BORGNINE
HUSTLE .... PAUL WINFIELD
HUSTLER, THE .... MICHAEL CONSTANTINE
HUSTLER, THE .... VINCENT GARDENIA†
HUSTLER, THE ★ .... PAUL NEWMAN
HUSTLER, THE ★ .... PIPER LAURIE
HUSTLER, THE ✿ .... JACKIE GLEASON†
HUSTLER, THE ✿ .... GEORGE C. SCOTT
HUSTLING (TF) .... JILL CLAYBURGH

HYSTERIA .... ROBERT WEBBER
HYSTERICAL .... CLINT WALKER
HYSTERICAL .... JULIE NEWMAR
HYSTERICAL .... RICHARD KIEL

I

I ACCUSE! .... JOSE FERRER†
I AIM AT THE STARS .... VICTORIA SHAW†
I AM A CAMERA .... JULIE HARRIS
I AM A CAMERA .... SHELLEY WINTERS
I AM A FUGITIVE FROM A
CHAIN GANG H .... PAUL MUNI†
I AM THE CHEESE .... HOPE LANGE
I AM THE CHEESE .... ROBERT WAGNER
I BELIEVE IN YOU .... JOAN COLLINS
I CLAUDIUS (MS) .... BRIAN BLESSED
I COME IN PEACE .... MARK LOWENTHAL
I COMPAGNI .... MARCELLO MASTROIANNI
I CONFESS .... KARL MALDEN
I CONSIGLIORI .... MARTIN BALSAM
I COULD GO ON SINGING .... JACK KLUGMAN
I CRIMINALI DELLA GELASSIA .... FRANCO NERO
I DIED A THOUSAND TIMES ...... DENNIS HOPPER
I DIED A THOUSAND TIMES .... EARL HOLLIMAN
I DIED A THOUSAND TIMES .... JACK PALANCE
I DIED A THOUSAND TIMES ...... SHELLEY WINTERS
I DON'T CARE GIRL, THE .... GWEN VERDON
I DON'T WANT TO
BE BORN .... DONALD PLEASENCE
I DON'T WANT TO BE BORN .... JOAN COLLINS
I DOOD IT .... LENA HORNE
I DREAM OF JEANNIE:
15 YEARS LATER (TF) .... BARBARA EDEN
I DREAM OF JEANNIE:
15 YEARS LATER (TF) .... WAYNE ROGERS
I ESCAPED FROM DEVIL'S ISLAND .... JIM BROWN
I GIRASOLI .... MARCELLO MASTROIANNI
I GIRASOLI .... SOPHIA LOREN
I GIROVAGHI .... PETER USTINOV
I HATE YOUR GUTS!/SHAME .... WILLIAM SHATNER
I KILLED RASPUTIN ...... GERALDINE CHAPLIN
I KILLED RASPUTIN .... JOSS ACKLAND
I KNOW MY FIRST NAME
IS STEVEN (MS) .... ARLISS HOWARD
I KNOW MY FIRST NAME
IS STEVEN (MS) .... CINDY PICKETT
I KNOW MY FIRST NAME
IS STEVEN (MS) .... CORIN NEMEC
I KNOW MY FIRST NAME
IS STEVEN (MS) .... JOHN ASHTON
I KNOW MY FIRST NAME
IS STEVEN (MS) .... LUKE EDWARDS
I KNOW MY FIRST NAME
IS STEVEN (MS) .... PRUITT TAYLOR VINCE
I KNOW MY FIRST NAME
IS STEVEN (MS) .... RAY WALSTON
I KNOW MY FIRST NAME
IS STEVEN (TF) .... STEPHEN DORFF
I KNOW WHERE I'M GOING ...... WENDY HILLER
I LANCIERI NERI .... MEL FERRER
I LIKE IT LIKE THAT .... GRIFFIN DUNNE
I LIKE IT LIKE THAT .... JESSE BORREGO
I LIKE IT LIKE THAT .... JON SEDA
I LIKE IT LIKE THAT .... LAUREN VELEZ
I LIKE IT LIKE THAT .... RITA MORENO
I LIVE IN GROSVENOR SQARE ..... ROBERT MORLEY
I LIVE MY LIFE .... JOAN CRAWFORD†
I LOVE A MYSTERY .... NINA FOCH
I LOVE MELVIN .... DEBBIE REYNOLDS
I LOVE MELVIN .... HOWARD KEEL
I LOVE MONEY .... BILLIE WHITELAW
I LOVE MY WIFE .... BRENDA VACCARO
I LOVE MY WIFE .... DABNEY COLEMAN
I LOVE MY WIFE .... ELLIOTT GOULD
I LOVE TROUBLE .... JULIA ROBERTS
I LOVE TROUBLE .... MARSHA MASON
I LOVE TROUBLE .... NICK NOLTE
I LOVE TROUBLE .... NORA DUNN
I LOVE TROUBLE .... OLYMPIA DUKAKIS
I LOVE TROUBLE .... RAYMOND BURR†
I LOVE TROUBLE .... ROBERT LOGGIA

This is not a list of every film ever made or every cast member, only those listed in this directory.

INDEX OF FILM TITLES

I LOVE YOU ALICE B. TOKLAS! ..... JOYCE VAN PATTEN
I LOVE YOU ALICE B. TOKLAS ..... LEIGH TAYLOR-YOUNG
I LOVE YOU, GOODBYE (TF) ..... EARL HOLLIMAN
I LOVE YOU, GOODBYE (TF) ..... HOPE LANGE
I LOVE YOU, I LOVE YOU NOT ..... JACQUELINE BISSET
I LOVE YOU PERFECT (TF) ..... ANTHONY DENISON
I LOVE YOU PERFECT (TF) ..... SUSAN DEY
I LOVE YOU TO DEATH ..... JOAN PLOWRIGHT
I LOVE YOU TO DEATH ..... KEANU REEVES
I LOVE YOU TO DEATH ..... KEVIN KLINE
I LOVE YOU TO DEATH ..... PHOEBE CATES
I LOVE YOU TO DEATH ..... RIVER PHOENIX†
I LOVE YOU TO DEATH ..... TRACEY ULLMAN
I LOVE YOU TO DEATH ..... WILLIAM HURT
I, MADMAN ..... CLAYTON ROHNER
I, MADMAN ..... JENNY WRIGHT
I MARRIED A CENTERFOLD (TF) ..... DIANE LADD
I MARRIED A CENTERFOLD (TF) ..... TIMOTHY DALY
I MARRIED A WOMAN ..... ANGIE DICKINSON
I MISERABILI ..... MARCELLO MASTROIANNI
I MONGOLI ..... JACK PALANCE
I NEVER PROMISED YOU A ROSE GARDEN ..... BEN PIAZZA†
I NEVER PROMISED YOU A ROSE GARDEN ..... BIBI ANDERSSON
I NEVER PROMISED YOU A ROSE GARDEN ..... DENNIS QUAID
I NEVER PROMISED YOU A ROSE GARDEN ..... KATHLEEN QUINLAN
I NEVER PROMISED YOU A ROSE GARDEN ..... LORRAINE GARY
I NEVER PROMISED YOU A ROSE GARDEN ..... RENI SANTONI
I NEVER PROMISED YOU A ROSE GARDEN ..... SUSAN TYRRELL
I NEVER PROMISED YOU A ROSE GARDEN ..... SYLVIA SIDNEY
I NEVER SANG FOR MY FATHER ..... ESTELLE PARSONS
I NEVER SANG FOR MY FATHER ★ ..... MELVYN DOUGLAS†
I NEVER SANG FOR MY FATHER ✪ ..... GENE HACKMAN
I OUGHT TO BE IN PICTURES ..... ANN-MARGRET
I OUGHT TO BE IN PICTURES ..... DINAH MANOFF
I OUGHT TO BE IN PICTURES ..... WALTER MATTHAU
I PASSED FOR WHITE ..... JAMES FRANCISCUS†
I.Q. ..... FRANK WHALEY
I.Q. ..... GENE SAKS
I.Q. ..... JOSEPH MAHUR
I.Q. ..... LOU JACOBI
I.Q. ..... MEG RYAN
I.Q. ..... STEPHEN FRY
I.Q. ..... TIM ROBBINS
I.Q. ..... TONY SHALHOUB
I.Q. ..... WALTER MATTHAU
I REMEMBER MAMA ✪ ..... OSCAR HOMOLKA†
I SAW WHAT YOU DID ..... JOAN CRAWFORD†
I SAW WHAT YOU DID ..... JOHN IRELAND
I SAW WHAT YOU DID (TF) ..... DAVID CARRADINE
I SAW WHAT YOU DID (TF) ..... ROBERT CARRADINE
I SAW WHAT YOU DID (TF) ..... TAMMY LAUREN
I SEE A DARK STRANGER ..... DEBORAH KERR
I SEQUESTRATI DI ALTONA ..... MAXIMILIAN SCHELL
I SEQUESTRATI DI ALTONA ..... SOPHIA LOREN
I SHOT JESSE JAMES ..... JOHN IRELAND
I SOLITI IGNOTI ..... MARCELLO MASTROIANNI
I SPY RETURNS (TF) ..... BILL COSBY
I SPY RETURNS (TF) ..... ROBERT CULP
I START COUNTING ..... JENNY AGUTTER
I START COUNTING ..... SIMON WARD
I STILL DREAM OF JEANNIE (TF) ..... BARBARA EDEN
I, THE JURY ..... ALAN KING
I, THE JURY ..... ARMAND ASSANTE
I TRE VOLTI ..... RICHARD HARRIS
I WALK ALONE ..... BURT LANCASTER†
I WALK ALONE ..... KIRK DOUGLAS
I WALK THE LINE ..... CHARLES DURNING
I WALK THE LINE ..... ESTELLE PARSONS
I WALK THE LINE ..... GREGORY PECK
I WALK THE LINE ..... TUESDAY WELD
I WANNA HOLD YOUR HAND ..... NANCY ALLEN
I WANT HER DEAD ..... TWIGGY
I WANT TO KEEP MY BABY (TF) ..... MARIEL HEMINGWAY
I WANT TO LIVE! ..... THEODORE BIKEL
I WANT TO LIVE! ★★ ..... SUSAN HAYWARD†
I WAS A MALE WAR BRIDE ..... ARTHUR HILL
I WAS A SHOPLIFTER ..... ROCK HUDSON†
I WAS A SHOPLIFTER ..... TONY CURTIS
I WAS A TEENAGE WEREWOLF ..... MICHAEL LANDON†
I WAS HAPPY HERE ..... JULIAN GLOVER
I WAS HAPPY HERE ..... SARAH MILES
I WAS MONTY'S DOUBLE ..... JOHN MILLS
I WILL FIGHT NO MORE FOREVER (TF) ..... SAM ELLIOTT
I WILL I WILL...FOR NOW ..... CANDY CLARK
I WILL I WILL...FOR NOW ..... DIANE KEATON
I WILL I WILL...FOR NOW ..... ELLIOTT GOULD
I WILL I WILL...FOR NOW ..... PAUL SORVINO
I WILL I WILL...FOR NOW ..... VICTORIA PRINCIPAL
I'LL CRY TOMORROW ★ ..... SUSAN HAYWARD†
I'LL DO ANYTHING ..... ALBERT BROOKS
I'LL DO ANYTHING ..... JOELY RICHARDSON
I'LL DO ANYTHING ..... JULIE KAVNER
I'LL DO ANYTHING ..... NICK NOLTE
I'LL DO ANYTHING ..... PATRICK CASSIDY
I'LL DO ANYTHING ..... ROSIE O'DONNELL
I'LL DO ANYTHING ..... TRACEY ULLMAN
I'LL DO ANYTHING ..... WHITTNI WRIGHT
I'LL DO ANYTHING ..... WOODY HARRELSON
I'LL SEE YOU IN MY DREAMS ..... DANNY THOMAS†
ICE CASTLES ..... COLLEEN DEWHURST†
ICE CASTLES ..... DAVID HUFFMAN†
ICE CASTLES ..... JENNIFER WARREN
ICE CASTLES ..... LYNN-HOLLY JOHNSON
ICE CASTLES ..... ROBBY BENSON
ICE CASTLES ..... TOM SKERRITT
ICE COLD IN ALEX ..... JOHN MILLS
ICE FOLLIES OF 1939 ..... JAMES STEWART
ICE FOLLIES OF 1939 ..... JOAN CRAWFORD†
ICE PALACE ..... SHIRLEY KNIGHT
ICE PIRATES, THE ..... ANJELICA HUSTON
ICE PIRATES, THE ..... MARY CROSBY
ICE PIRATES, THE ..... ROBERT URICH
ICE RUNNER ..... NORIYUKI "PAT" MORITA
ICE RUNNER ..... TIMOTHY BOTTOMS
ICE STATION ZEBRA ..... ERNEST BORGNINE
ICE STATION ZEBRA ..... JIM BROWN
ICE STATION ZEBRA ..... TONY BILL
ICEMAN ..... DANNY GLOVER
ICEMAN ..... DAVID STRATHAIRN
ICEMAN ..... JOHN LONE
ICEMAN ..... JOSEF SOMMER
ICEMAN ..... LINDSAY CROUSE
ICEMAN ..... TIMOTHY HUTTON
ICEMAN COMETH, THE ..... BRADFORD DILLMAN
ICEMAN COMETH, THE ..... CLIFTON JAMES
ICEMAN COMETH, THE ..... JEFF BRIDGES
ICEMAN COMETH, THE ..... MOSES GUNN
ICH BIN AUCH NUR EINE FRAU ..... MARIA SCHELL
IDAHO TRANSFER ..... KEITH CARRADINE
IDENTIKIT ..... ELIZABETH TAYLOR
IDIOT'S DELIGHT ..... BURGESS MEREDITH
IDOL, THE ..... JENNIFER JONES
IDOLMAKER, THE ..... JOE PANTOLIANO
IDOLMAKER, THE ..... PETER GALLAGHER
IDOLMAKER, THE ..... RAY SHARKEY†
IDOLMAKER, THE ..... TOYAH FELDSHUH
IERI OGGI DOMANI ..... MARCELLO MASTROIANNI
IERI OGGI E DOMANI ..... SOPHIA LOREN
IF.... ..... MALCOLM McDOWELL
IF A MAN ANSWERS ..... SANDRA DEE
IF A MAN ANSWERS ..... STEFANIE POWERS
IF EVER I SEE YOU AGAIN ..... SHELLEY HACK
IF HE HOLLERS LET HIM GO ..... KEVIN McCARTHY
IF HE HOLLERS, LET HIM GO! ..... RAYMOND ST. JACQUES
IF HE HOLLERS LET HIM GO ..... ROYAL DANO
IF I WERE KING ✪ ..... BASIL RATHBONE†
IF IT'S TUESDAY, IT STILL MUST BE BELGIUM (TF) ..... BRUCE WEITZ
IF IT'S TUESDAY, IT STILL MUST BE BELGIUM (TF) ..... CLAUDE AKINS†
IF IT'S TUESDAY, IT STILL MUST BE BELGIUM (TF) ..... COURTENEY COX
IF IT'S TUESDAY, IT STILL MUST BE BELGIUM (TF) ..... DAVID LEISURE
IF IT'S TUESDAY, IT STILL MUST BE BELGIUM (TF) ..... DORIS ROBERTS
IF IT'S TUESDAY, IT STILL MUST BE BELGIUM (TF) ..... PETER GRAVES
IF IT'S TUESDAY, IT STILL MUST BE BELGIUM (TF) ..... STEPHEN FURST
IF IT'S TUESDAY, IT STILL MUST BE BELGIUM (TF) ..... TRACY NELSON
IF IT'S TUESDAY, THIS MUST BE BELGIUM ..... BEN GAZZARA
IF IT'S TUESDAY, THIS MUST BE BELGIUM ..... MICHAEL CONSTANTINE
IF IT'S TUESDAY, THIS MUST BE BELGIUM ..... NORMAN FELL
IF IT'S TUESDAY, THIS MUST BE BELGIUM ..... SUZANNE PLESHETTE
IF LOOKS COULD KILL ..... CAROLE DAVIS
IF LOOKS COULD KILL ..... GABRIELLE ANWAR
IF LOOKS COULD KILL ..... GERALDINE JAMES
IF LOOKS COULD KILL ..... LINDA HUNT
IF LOOKS COULD KILL ..... MICHAEL SIBERRY
IF LOOKS COULD KILL ..... RICHARD GRIECO
IF LOOKS COULD KILL ..... ROBIN BARTLETT
IF LOOKS COULD KILL ..... ROGER REES
IF TOMORROW COMES (MS) ..... DAVID KEITH
IF TOMORROW COMES (MS) ..... RICHARD KILEY
IF TOMORROW COMES (MS) ..... SUSAN TYRRELL
IF TOMORROW COMES (MS) ..... TOM BERENGER
IF TOMORROW COMES (TF) ..... JAMES WHITMORE
IF TOMORROW COMES (TF) ..... PATTY DUKE
IF WINTER COMES ..... ANGELA LANSBURY
IF WINTER COMES ..... DEBORAH KERR
IF WINTER COMES ..... JANET LEIGH
IKE (MS) ..... DARREN McGAVIN
IKE (MS) ..... J. D. CANNON
IKE (MS) ..... LAURENCE LUCKINBILL
IKE: THE WAR YEARS (MS) ..... ROBERT DUVALL
IL BELL'ANTONIO ..... MARCELLO MASTROIANNI
IL BIGAMO ..... MARCELLO MASTROIANNI
IL CASANOVA DI FREDERICO FELLINI ..... DONALD SUTHERLAND
IL CASTELLO DEI MORTI VIVI ..... DONALD SUTHERLAND
IL COLTELLO DI GHIACCIO ..... CARROLL BAKER
IL COMMANDANTE ..... BRITT EKLAND
IL CORSARO NERO ..... MEL FERRER
IL COSOTTO ..... JODIE FOSTER
IL CUGINO AMERICANO (CTF) ..... BRAD DAVIS†
IL DISORDINE ..... LOUIS JOURDAN
IL DISORDINE ..... SUSAN STRASBERG
IL DOMINATORE DEI SETTE MARI ..... IRENE WORTH
IL GATTO A NOVE CODE ..... JAMES FRANCISCUS†
IL GATTOPARDO ..... BURT LANCASTER†
IL GIORNO DELLA CIVETTA ..... FRANCO NERO
IL GIORNO DELLA CIVETTA ..... NEHEMIAH PERSOFF
IL GIUDIZIO ITALIANI ..... ERNEST BORGNINE
IL GIUDIZIO UNIVERSALE ..... ANOUK AIMEE
IL GIUDIZIO UNIVERSALE ..... JACK PALANCE
IL GRANDE ROCKET ..... VINCENT GARDENIA†
IL LETTO IN PIAZZA ..... JOHN IRELAND
IL MAESTRO DI VIGEVANO ..... CLAIRE BLOOM
IL MERCENARIO ..... JACK PALANCE
IL MERCENARIO ..... TONY MUSANTE
IL MOMENTO PIU BELLO ..... MARCELLO MASTROIANNI
IL MONACO ..... FRANCO NERO
IL PADRE DI FAMIGLIA ..... CLAUDINE AUGER
IL PADRE DI FAMIGLIA ..... LESLIE CARON
IL PREZZO DEL POTERE ..... VAN JOHNSON
IL QUATTRO DELL'AVE MARIA ..... ELI WALLACH
IL RATTO DELLE SABINE ..... ROGER MOORE
IL RE DI POGGIOREALE ..... ERNEST BORGNINE
IL SEGNO DI VENERE ..... SOPHIA LOREN
IL SOGNO DI ZORRO ..... SOPHIA LOREN

IL SUCCESSO .... ANOUK AIMEE
IL TEMPO DEGLI ASSASSINI .... MARTIN BALSAM
IL TIGRE .... ANN-MARGRET
IL VIAGGIO .... SOPHIA LOREN
ILLEGAL .... NINA FOCH
ILLEGALLY YOURS .... COLLEEN CAMP
ILLEGALLY YOURS .... ROB LOWE
ILLICIT .... BARBARA STANWYCK†
ILLUSIONS .... ROBERT CARRADINE
ILLUSTRATED MAN, THE .... CLAIRE BLOOM
ILLUSTRATED MAN, THE .... ROD STEIGER
ILS SONT GRAND
    CES PETITS .... CATHERINE DENEUVE
IMAGE, THE (CTF) .... ALBERT FINNEY
IMAGE, THE (CTF) .... JOHN MAHONEY
IMAGE, THE (CTF) .... KATHY BAKER
IMAGE, THE (CTF) .... SWOOSIE KURTZ
IMAGEMAKER, THE .... JERRY ORBACH
IMAGEMAKER, THE .... JESSICA HARPER
IMAGES .... RENE AUBERJONOIS
IMAGES .... SUSANNAH YORK
IMAGINARY CRIMES .... FAIRUZA BALK
IMAGINARY CRIMES .... HARVEY KEITEL
IMAGINARY CRIMES .... KELLY LYNCH
IMAGINARY CRIMES ..... VINCENT D'ONOFRIO
IMITATION GENERAL .... DEAN JONES
IMITATION GENERAL .... RED BUTTONS
IMITATION OF LIFE .... DAN O'HERLIHY
IMITATION OF LIFE .... JOHN GAVIN
IMITATION OF LIFE .... LANA TURNER
IMITATION OF LIFE .... SANDRA DEE
IMITATION OF LIFE .... TROY DONAHUE
IMMEDIATE FAMILY .... GLENN CLOSE
IMMEDIATE FAMILY .... JAMES WOODS
IMMEDIATE FAMILY .... JANE GREER
IMMEDIATE FAMILY .... JESSICA JAMES
IMMEDIATE FAMILY .... KEVIN DILLON
IMMEDIATE FAMILY .... LINDA DARLOW
IMMEDIATE FAMILY ..... MARY STUART MASTERSON
IMMEDIATE FAMILY .... MIMI KENNEDY
IMMIGRANTS, THE (MS) .... SHARON GLESS
IMMIGRANTS, THE (MS) .... STEPHEN MACHT
IMMORTAL, THE (TF) .... RALPH BELLAMY†
IMMORTAL BATTALION, THE .... PETER USTINOV
IMMORTAL BELOVED .... ANTHONY HOPKINS
IMMORTAL BELOVED .... GARY OLDMAN
IMMORTAL BELOVED .... ISABELLA ROSSELINI
IMMORTAL BELOVED .... JEROEN KRABBE
IMMORTAL BELOVED .... JOHANNA TER STEEGE
IMMORTAL BELOVED .... MARCO HOFSCHNEIDER
IMMORTAL BELOVED .... VALERIA GOLINO
IMMORTAL SERGEANT, THE ...... MAUREEN O'HARA
IMPASSE .... BURT REYNOLDS
IMPASSE .... JEFF COREY
IMPERATIV (TF) .... LESLIE CARON
IMPERFECT LADY, THE .... ANTHONY QUINN
IMPERFECT LADY, THE .... TERESA WRIGHT
IMPOSSIBLE OBJECT .... ALAN BATES
IMPOSSIBLE SPY, THE (CTF) .... JOHN SHEA
IMPOSSIBLE YEARS, THE .... CHAD EVERETT
IMPOSTER, THE (TF) .... ANTHONY GEARY
IMPOSTOR, THE .... LLOYD BRIDGES
IMPROMPTU .... ANTON RODGERS
IMPROMPTU .... BERNADETTE PETERS
IMPROMPTU .... EMMA THOMPSON
IMPROMPTU .... GEORGE CORRAFACE
IMPROMPTU .... HUGH GRANT
IMPROMPTU .... JUDY DAVIS
IMPROMPTU .... JULIAN SANDS
IMPROMPTU .... MANDY PATINKIN
IMPROMPTU .... RALPH BROWN
IMPROPER CHANNELS .... ALAN ARKIN
IMPROPER CHANNELS .... MARIETTE HARTLEY
IMPULSE .... BILL PAXTON
IMPULSE .... GEORGE DZUNDZA
IMPULSE .... HUME CRONYN
IMPULSE .... JEFF FAHEY
IMPULSE .... JOHN KARLEN
IMPULSE .... MEG TILLY
IMPULSE .... THERESA RUSSELL
IMPULSE .... TIM MATHESON
IMPULSE .... WILLIAM SHATNER

IMPURE THOUGHTS .... BRAD DOURIF
IN A SHALLOW GRAVE .... PATRICK DEMPSEY
IN BROAD DAYLIGHT (TF) .... BRIAN DENNEHY
IN BROAD DAYLIGHT (TF) ..... SUZANNE PLESHETTE
IN CELEBRATION .... ALAN BATES
IN COLD BLOOD .... JEFF COREY
IN COLD BLOOD .... JOHN FORSYTHE
IN COLD BLOOD .... ROBERT BLAKE
IN COLD BLOOD .... SCOTT WILSON
IN COUNTRY .... BRUCE WILLIS
IN COUNTRY .... EMILY LLOYD
IN COUNTRY .... JIM BEAVER
IN COUNTRY .... JOAN ALLEN
IN COUNTRY .... JOHN TERRY
IN COUNTRY .... JUDITH IVEY
IN COUNTRY .... KEVIN ANDERSON
IN COUNTRY .... PATRICIA RICHARDSON
IN COUNTRY .... PEGGY REA
IN COUNTRY .... RICHARD HAMILTON
IN COUNTRY .... STEPHEN TOBOLOWSKY
IN CROWD, THE .... DONOVAN LEITCH
IN CROWD, THE .... JOE PANTOLIANO
IN CROWD, THE .... RANDI PAREIRA
IN DEFENSE
    OF KIDS (TF) .... GEORG STANFORD BROWN
IN ENEMY
    COUNTRY .... ANTHONY (TONY) FRANCIOSA
IN FONDO ALLA PISCINA .... CARROLL BAKER
IN GOD WE TRU$T .... LOUISE LASSER
IN GOD WE TRU$T .... MARTY FELDMAN†
IN GOD WE TRU$T .... PETER BOYLE
IN GOD WE TRU$T .... RICHARD PRYOR
IN GOD WE TRU$T .... SEVERN DARDEN
IN HARM'S WAY .... JOHN WAYNE†
IN HARM'S WAY .... BURGESS MEREDITH
IN HARM'S WAY .... CARROLL O'CONNOR
IN HARM'S WAY .... GEORGE KENNEDY
IN HARM'S WAY .... KIRK DOUGLAS
IN HARM'S WAY .... LARRY HAGMAN
IN HARM'S WAY .... PATRICIA NEAL
IN HARM'S WAY .... PATRICK O'NEAL†
IN HARM'S WAY .... PAULA PRENTISS
IN LIKE FLINT .... JAMES COBURN
IN LIKE FLYNN (TF) .... EDDIE ALBERT
IN LOVE .... ELLIOTT GOULD
IN LOVE .... KAYE BALLARD
IN LOVE .... MICHELLE PFEIFFER
IN LOVE .... SUSANNAH YORK
IN LOVE AND WAR .... BRADFORD DILLMAN
IN LOVE AND WAR .... FRANCE NUYEN
IN LOVE AND WAR .... HOPE LANGE
IN LOVE AND WAR .... MORT SAHL
IN LOVE AND WAR .... ROBERT WAGNER
IN LOVE AND WAR (TF) .... HAING S. NGOR
IN LOVE AND WAR (TF) .... JAMES WOODS
IN LOVE AND WAR (TF) .... JANE ALEXANDER
IN LOVE AND WAR (TF) .... STEVEN LEIGH
IN MEMORIAM .... GERALDINE CHAPLIN
IN OLD ARIZONA ★★ .... WARNER BAXTER†
IN OLD CHICAGO .... DON AMECHE†
IN OLD CHICAGO ∞∞ .... ALICE BRADY†
IN OLD OKLAHOMA .... MARTHA SCOTT
IN OLD SACRAMENTO .... ROBERT BLAKE
IN OUR HANDS .... ROY SCHEIDER
IN OUR HANDS (FD) .... MERYL STREEP
IN PRAISE OF OLDER WOMEN .... KAREN BLACK
IN PRAISE OF
    OLDER WOMEN .... SUSAN STRASBERG
IN PRAISE OF OLDER WOMEN .... TOM BERENGER
IN SEARCH OF AMERICA (TF) .... JEFF BRIDGES
IN SEARCH OF GREGORY .... JOHN HURT
IN SEARCH OF GREGORY .... JULIE CHRISTIE
IN SEARCH OF GREGORY .... MICHAEL SARRAZIN
IN SEARCH OF THE CASTAWAYS .... HAYLEY MILLS
IN SELF DEFENSE (TF) .... YAPHET KOTTO
IN TANDEM (TF) .... CLAUDE AKINS†
IN THE AISLES OF THE WILD .... LILLIAN GISH†
IN THE ARMS OF A KILLER (TF) .... JACLYN SMITH
IN THE ARMY NOW .... ANDY DICK
IN THE ARMY NOW .... ART LA FLEUR
IN THE ARMY NOW .... BRENDAN FRASER
IN THE ARMY NOW .... DAVID ALAN GRIER

IN THE ARMY NOW .... ESAI MORALES
IN THE ARMY NOW .... FABIANA UDENIO
IN THE ARMY NOW .... LORI PETTY
IN THE ARMY NOW .... LYNN WHITFIELD
IN THE ARMY NOW .... PAULY SHORE
IN THE BEST INTEREST
    OF THE CHILD (TF) .... ED BEGLEY JR.
IN THE BEST INTEREST
    OF THE CHILD (TF) .... MEG TILLY
IN THE BEST INTEREST
    OF THE CHILD (TF) .... MICHAEL O'KEEFE
IN THE COOL OF THE DAY .... ALEC McCOWEN
IN THE COOL OF THE DAY .... ANGELA LANSBURY
IN THE COOL OF THE DAY .... ARTHUR HILL
IN THE COOL OF THE DAY .... JANE FONDA
IN THE COOL OF THE DAY .... NIGEL DAVENPORT
IN THE CUSTODY OF
    STRANGERS (TF) .... DANIELLE von ZERNECK
IN THE DEVIL'S GARDEN .... LESLEY-ANNE DOWN
IN THE FRENCH STYLE .... CLAUDINE AUGER
IN THE FRENCH STYLE .... JACK HEDLEY
IN THE GLITTER PALACE (TF) .... SALOME JENS
IN THE GOOD OLD
    SUMMERTIME .... JUDY GARLAND†
IN THE GOOD OLD SUMMERTIME .... LIZA MINELLI
IN THE GOOD OLD SUMMERTIME ..... VAN JOHNSON
IN THE HEAT OF THE NIGHT .... BEAH RICHARDS
IN THE HEAT OF THE NIGHT .... LEE GRANT
IN THE HEAT OF THE NIGHT .... SIDNEY POITIER
IN THE HEAT OF THE NIGHT ★★ .... ROD STEIGER
IN THE HEAT OF
    THE NIGHT (TF) .... ANNE MARIE JOHNSON
IN THE HEAT OF
    THE NIGHT (TF) .... CARROLL O'CONNOR
IN THE HEAT OF
    THE NIGHT (TF) .... KEVIN McCARTHY
IN THE HEAT OF THE NIGHT (TF) .... DAVID HART
IN THE LINE OF DUTY:
    THE FBI MURDERS (TF) ...... BRUCE GREENWOOD
IN THE LINE OF DUTY:
    THE FBI MURDERS (TF) .... DAVID SOUL
IN THE LINE OF DUTY:
    THE FBI MURDERS (TF) .... DOUG SHEEHAN
IN THE LINE OF DUTY:
    THE FBI MURDERS (TF) .... MICHAEL GROSS
IN THE LINE OF FIRE .... CLINT EASTWOOD
IN THE LINE OF FIRE .... DYLAN McDERMOTT
IN THE LINE OF FIRE ..... FRED DALTON THOMPSON
IN THE LINE OF FIRE .... GARY COLE
IN THE LINE OF FIRE .... JAMES CURLEY
IN THE LINE OF FIRE .... JOHN HEARD
IN THE LINE OF FIRE .... JOHN MAHONEY
IN THE LINE OF FIRE .... RENE RUSSO
IN THE LINE OF FIRE ○ .... JOHN MALKOVICH
IN THE MOOD .... BEVERLY D'ANGELO
IN THE MOOD .... PATRICK DEMPSEY
IN THE MOUTH OF MADNESS .... JULIE CARMEN
IN THE NAME OF
    THE FATHER ★ .... DANIEL DAY-LEWIS
IN THE NAME OF
    THE FATHER ○ .... EMMA THOMPSON
IN THE NAME OF
    THE FATHER ○ .... PETE POSTLETHWAITE
IN THE NAVY .... BUD ABBOTT†
IN THE NAVY .... LOU COSTELLO†
IN THE SHADOW OF
    KILLMANJARO .... TIMOTHY BOTTOMS
IN THE SOUP .... SEYMOUR CASSEL
IN THE SOUP .... STANLEY TUCCI
IN THE SPIRIT .... ELAINE MAY
IN THE SPIRIT .... JEANNIE BERLIN
IN THE SPIRIT .... MARLO THOMAS
IN THE SPIRIT .... MELANIE GRIFFITH
IN THE SPIRIT .... OLYMPIA DUKAKIS
IN THE SPIRIT .... PETER FALK
IN THIS HOUSE OF BREDE (TF) .... DIANA RIGG
IN THIS OUR LIFE .... BETTE DAVIS†
IN THIS OUR LIFE .... OLIVIA DE HAVILLAND
IN WHICH WE SERVE .... JOHN MILLS
IN-LAWS, THE .... ALAN ARKIN
IN-LAWS, THE .... DAVID PAYMER
IN-LAWS, THE .... ED BEGLEY JR.

474

IN-LAWS, THE .... PETER FALK
IN-LAWS, THE .... ROSANA DE SOTO
INADMISSIBLE EVIDENCE .... EILEEN ATKINS
INADMISSIBLE EVIDENCE .... NICOL WILLIAMSON
INCHON! .... BEN GAZZARA
INCHON! .... JACQUELINE BISSET
INCHON! .... OMAR SHARIF
INCHON! .... RICHARD ROUNDTREE
INCIDENT, THE .... BEAU BRIDGES
INCIDENT, THE .... DONNA MILLS
INCIDENT, THE .... MARTIN SHEEN
INCIDENT, THE .... RUBY DEE
INCIDENT, THE .... TONY MUSANTE
INCIDENT, THE (TF) .... BARNARD HUGHES
INCIDENT, THE (TF) .... HARRY MORGAN
INCIDENT, THE (TF) .... PETER FIRTH
INCIDENT, THE (TF) .... ROBERT CARRADINE
INCIDENT, THE (TF) .... SUSAN BLAKELY
INCIDENT, THE (TF) .... WALTER MATTHAU
INCIDENT AT DARK RIVER (CTF) .... HELEN HUNT
INCIDENT AT DARK RIVER (CTF) ..... MIKE FARRELL
INCIDENT AT DARK RIVER (CTF) ..... TESS HARPER
INCIDENT AT OGLALA (FD) .... ROBERT REDFORD
INCIDENT AT PHANTOM HILL .... CLAUDE AKINS†
INCIDENT IN A
  SMALL TOWN (TF) .... HARRY MORGAN
INCIDENT IN A
  SMALL TOWN (TF) .... STEPHANIE ZIMBALIST
INCIDENT IN A
  SMALL TOWN (TF) .... WALTER MATTHAU
INCIDENT IN SAN
  FRANCISCO (TF) .... JULIUS HARRIS
INCONVENIENT
  WOMAN, AN (TF) .... CHELSEA FIELD
INCONVENIENT
  WOMAN, AN (TF) .... REBECCA DE MORNAY
INCREDIBLE HULK
  RETURNS, THE (TF) .... BILL BIXBY†
INCREDIBLE HULK
  RETURNS, THE (TF) .... LOU FERRIGNO
INCREDIBLE HULK, THE (TF) .... BILL BIXBY†
INCREDIBLE HULK, THE (TF) .... LOU FERRIGNO
INCREDIBLE JOURNEY OF DR.
  MEG LAUREL, THE (TF) .... JANE WYMAN
INCREDIBLE JOURNEY OF DR.
  MEG LAUREL, THE (TF) .... LINDSAY WAGNER
INCREDIBLE MR. LIMPET, THE .... DON KNOTTS
INCREDIBLE MR. LIMPET, THE .... JACK WESTON
INCREDIBLE SARAH, THE .... GLENDA JACKSON
INCREDIBLE SARAH, THE .... JOHN CASTLE
INCREDIBLE SHRINKING
  WOMAN, THE .... CHARLES GRODIN
INCREDIBLE SHRINKING
  WOMAN, THE .... HENRY GIBSON
INCREDIBLE SHRINKING
  WOMAN, THE .... LILY TOMLIN
INCREDIBLE SHRINKING
  WOMAN, THE .... NED BEATTY
INCREDIBLE SHRINKING
  WOMAN, THE .... SALLY KIRKLAND
INCREDIBLE TWO-HEADED
  TRANSPLANT, THE .... BRUCE DERN
INCUBUS, THE .... JOHN IRELAND
INDECENCY .... GIAN-CARLO SCANDIUZZI
INDECENT PROPOSAL .... BILLY BOB THORNTON
INDECENT PROPOSAL .... BILLY CONNOLLY
INDECENT PROPOSAL .... DEMI MOORE
INDECENT PROPOSAL .... HERBIE HANCOCK
INDECENT PROPOSAL .... JOEL BROOKS
INDECENT PROPOSAL .... OLIVER PLATT
INDECENT PROPOSAL .... PIERRE EPSTEIN
INDECENT PROPOSAL .... RIP TAYLOR
INDECENT PROPOSAL .... ROBERT REDFORD
INDECENT PROPOSAL .... SEYMOUR CASSEL
INDECENT PROPOSAL .... WOODY HARRELSON
INDEPENDENCE DAY .... DIANNE WIEST
INDEPENDENCE DAY .... FRANCES STERNHAGEN
INDEPENDENCE DAY .... KATHLEEN QUINLAN
INDEPENDENCE (TF) .... ANTHONY ZERBE
INDEPENDENCE (TF) .... ISABELLA HOFMANN
INDESTRUCTIBLE MAN, THE .... MAX SHOWALTER
INDIAN FIGHTER, THE .... KIRK DOUGLAS

INDIAN FIGHTER, THE .... WALTER MATTHAU
INDIAN RUNNER, THE .... CHARLES BRONSON
INDIAN RUNNER, THE .... DAVID MORSE
INDIAN RUNNER, THE .... DENNIS HOPPER
INDIAN RUNNER, THE .... PATRICIA ARQUETTE
INDIAN RUNNER, THE .... SANDY DENNIS†
INDIAN RUNNER, THE .... VALERIA GOLINO
INDIAN SUMMER .... ALAN ARKIN
INDIAN SUMMER .... BILL PAXTON
INDIAN SUMMER .... DIANE LANE
INDIAN SUMMER .... ELIZABETH PERKINS
INDIAN SUMMER .... JULIE WARNER
INDIAN SUMMER .... KEVIN POLLAK
INDIAN SUMMER .... KIMBERLY WILLIAMS
INDIAN SUMMER .... MATT CRAVEN
INDIAN SUMMER .... VINCENT SPANO
INDIAN WARRIOR .... ERIC SCHWEIG
INDIANA JONES AND THE
  LAST CRUSADE .... ALEX HYDE-WHITE
INDIANA JONES AND THE
  LAST CRUSADE .... ALISON DOODY
INDIANA JONES AND THE
  LAST CRUSADE .... DENHOLM ELLIOTT†
INDIANA JONES AND THE
  LAST CRUSADE .... HARRISON FORD
INDIANA JONES AND THE
  LAST CRUSADE .... JOHN RHYS-DAVIES
INDIANA JONES AND THE
  LAST CRUSADE .... JULIAN GLOVER
INDIANA JONES AND THE
  LAST CRUSADE .... MICHAEL BYRNE
INDIANA JONES AND THE
  LAST CRUSADE .... RIVER PHOENIX†
INDIANA JONES AND THE
  LAST CRUSADE .... SEAN CONNERY
INDIANA JONES AND THE
  TEMPLE OF DOOM .... AMRISH PURI
INDIANA JONES AND THE
  TEMPLE OF DOOM .... DAN AYKROYD
INDIANA JONES AND THE
  TEMPLE OF DOOM .... HARRISON FORD
INDIANA JONES AND THE
  TEMPLE OF DOOM .... KATE CAPSHAW
INDIANA JONES AND THE
  TEMPLE OF DOOM .... KE HUY QUAN
INDIANA JONES AND THE
  TEMPLE OF DOOM .... PHILIP STONE
INDIANA JONES AND THE
  TEMPLE OF DOOM .... ROSHAN SETH
INDIAN'S LOYALTY, AN .... LILLIAN GISH†
INDICT AND CONVICT (TF) .... BEN GAZZARA
INDICT AND CONVICT (TF) .... ED FLANDERS
INDICT AND CONVICT (TF) .... ELI WALLACH
INDICT AND CONVICT (TF) .... GEORGE GRIZZARD
INDISCREET (TF) .... LESLEY-ANNE DOWN
INDISCREET (TF) .... MAGGIE HENDERSON
INDISCREET (TF) .... ROBERT WAGNER
INDISCRETION OF AN
  AMERICAN WIFE .... JENNIFER JONES
INDISCRETIONS OF EVE, THE .... JESSICA TANDY†
INDOCHINE ★ .... CATHERINE DENEUVE
INFIDELITY (TF) .... KIRSTIE ALLEY
INFIDELITY (TF) .... LEE HORSLEY
INFIDELITY (TF) .... ROBERT ENGLUND
INFINITY .... CLIFF DE YOUNG
INFINITY .... JAMES LeGROS
INFINITY .... MATTHEW BRODERICK
INFINITY .... PATRICIA ARQUETTE
INFINITY .... PETER RIEGERT
INFINITY .... ZELJKO IVANEK
INFORMATION KID .... MAUREEN O'SULLIVAN
INFORMER, THE ★★ .... VICTOR McLAGLEN†
INGLORIOUS BASTARDS .... BO SVENSON
INGRID .... LIV ULLMANN
INHERIT THE WIND .... CLAUDE AKINS†
INHERIT THE WIND .... GENE KELLY
INHERIT THE WIND .... HARRY MORGAN
INHERIT THE WIND ★ .... SPENCER TRACY†
INHERIT THE WIND (TF) .... KIRK DOUGLAS
INHERIT THE
  WIND (TF) .... MEGAN POTTER FOLLOWS
INHERITANCE, THE .... ANTHONY QUINN

INHERITANCE, THE .... JEAN SIMMONS
INITIATION OF SARAH, THE (TF) .... ROBERT HAYS
INITIATION, THE .... RODNEY HARVEY
INKWELL, THE .... MORRIS CHESTNUT
INKWELL, THE .... PHYLLIS YVONNE STICKNEY
INKWELL, THE .... SUZANNE DOUGLAS
INKWELL, THE .... VANESSA BELL
INMATES: A LOVE STORY (TF) .... KATE JACKSON
INMATES: A LOVE STORY (TF) .... SHIRLEY JONES
INMATES: A LOVE STORY (TF) .... TONY CURTIS
INN OF THE DAMNED .... DAME JUDITH ANDERSON†
INN OF THE FRIGHTENED
  PEOPLE .... JOAN COLLINS
INNER CIRCLE, THE .... BESS MEYER
INNER CIRCLE, THE .... BOB HOSKINS
INNER CIRCLE, THE .... JOHN P. RYAN
INNER CIRCLE, THE .... LOLITA DAVIDOVICH
INNER CIRCLE, THE .... TOM HULCE
INNERSPACE .... DENNIS QUAID
INNERSPACE .... JENNY GAGO
INNERSPACE .... KEVIN HOOKS
INNERSPACE .... KEVIN McCARTHY
INNERSPACE .... MARTIN SHORT
INNERSPACE .... MEG RYAN
INNOCENT BLOOD .... ANNE PARILLAUD
INNOCENT BLOOD .... ANTHONY LaPAGLIA
INNOCENT BLOOD .... DON RICKLES
INNOCENT BLOOD .... ROBERT LOGGIA
INNOCENT BYSTANDERS ...... DONALD PLEASENCE
INNOCENT BYSTANDERS ...... GERALDINE CHAPLIN
INNOCENT MAGDALENE, AN .... LILLIAN GISH†
INNOCENT MAN, AN .... BADJA DJOLA
INNOCENT MAN, AN .... DAVID RASCHE
INNOCENT MAN, AN ...... F. MURRAY ABRAHAM
INNOCENT MAN, AN .... LAILA ROBINS
INNOCENT MAN, AN .... RICHARD YOUNG
INNOCENT MAN, AN .... TOM SELLECK
INNOCENT, THE .... ANTHONY HOPKINS
INNOCENT, THE .... CAMPBELL SCOTT
INNOCENT, THE .... ISABELLA ROSSELLINI
INNOCENT, THE .... MIRANDA RICHARDSON
INNOCENT VICTIM .... LAUREN BACALL
INNOCENTS IN PARIS .... CLAIRE BLOOM
INNOCENTS, THE .... DEBORAH KERR
INSEMINOID .... VICTORIA TENNANT
INSERTS .... BOB HOSKINS
INSERTS .... JESSICA HARPER
INSERTS .... RICHARD DREYFUSS
INSERTS .... VERONICA CARTWRIGHT
INSIDE DAISY CLOVER .... CHRISTOPHER PLUMMER
INSIDE DAISY CLOVER .... NATALIE WOOD†
INSIDE DAISY CLOVER .... ROBERT REDFORD
INSIDE DAISY CLOVER .... RODDY McDOWALL
INSIDE DAISY CLOVER ⊙ .... RUTH GORDON†
INSIDE MOVES .... AMY WRIGHT
INSIDE MOVES .... DAVID MORSE
INSIDE MOVES .... HAROLD RUSSELL
INSIDE MOVES .... JOHN SAVAGE
INSIDE MOVES ⊙ .... DIANA SCARWID
INSIDE OUT .... ELLIOTT GOULD
INSIDE OUT .... ROBERT CULP
INSIDE OUT .... TELLY SAVALAS†
INSIDE STRAIGHT .... MERCEDES McCAMBRIDGE
INSIDE THE THIRD REICH (MS) .... DEREK JACOBI
INSIDE THE THIRD REICH (MS) .... JOHN GIELGUD
INSIDE THE THIRD REICH (TF) ...... BLYTHE DANNER
INSIDE THE THIRD REICH (TF) ..... ROBERT VAUGHN
INSIDE THE THIRD REICH (TF) .... RUTGER HAUER
INSIGNIFICANCE .... MICHAEL EMIL
INSIGNIFICANCE .... THERESA RUSSELL
INSIGNIFICANCE .... TONY CURTIS
INSIGNIFIGANCE .... GARY BUSEY
INSPECTEUR LA BAVURE .... GERARD DEPARDIEU
INSPECTOR CLOUSEAU .... ALAN ARKIN
INSPECTOR, THE .... DONALD PLEASENCE
INSPECTOR, THE .... ROBERT STEPHENS
INSTANT JUSTICE .... CHARLES NAPIER
INSTANT JUSTICE .... MICHAEL PARE
INSTITUTE FOR
  REVENGE (TF) .... GEORGE HAMILTON
INSTITUTE FOR REVENGE (TF) .... LAUREN HUTTON
INSTITUTE FOR REVENGE (TF) ...... LESLIE NIELSEN

INSTITUTE FOR REVENGE (TF) .... RAY WALSTON
INSULT .... JOHN GIELGUD
INTERIORS .... DIANE KEATON
INTERIORS .... E. G. MARSHALL
INTERIORS .... MARY BETH HURT
INTERIORS .... RICHARD JORDAN†
INTERIORS .... SAM WATERSTON
INTERIORS ★ .... GERALDINE PAGE†
INTERIORS ○ .... MAUREEN STAPLETON
INTERLUDE .... DONALD SUTHERLAND
INTERLUDE .... JANE WYATT
INTERLUDE .... JOHN CLEESE
INTERLUDE .... JUNE ALLYSON
INTERMEZZO .... LESLIE HOWARD†
INTERNAL AFFAIRS .... ANDY GARCIA
INTERNAL AFFAIRS .... ANNABELLA SCIORRA
INTERNAL AFFAIRS .... LAURIE METCALF
INTERNAL AFFAIRS .... MICHAEL BEACH
INTERNAL AFFAIRS .... NANCY TRAVIS
INTERNAL AFFAIRS .... RICHARD BRADFORD
INTERNAL AFFAIRS .... RICHARD GERE
INTERNAL AFFAIRS .... WILLIAM BALDWIN
INTERNAL AFFAIRS (MS) .... CLIFF GORMAN
INTERNAL AFFAIRS (MS) .... KATE CAPSHAW
INTERNAL AFFAIRS (MS) .... RONALD HUNTER
INTERNATIONAL AIRPORT (TF) .... BILL BIXBY†
INTERNATIONAL AIRPORT (TF) .... GIL GERARD
INTERNATIONAL
    AIRPORT (TF) .... ROBERT VAUGHN
INTERNATIONAL HOUSE .... GEORGE BURNS
INTERNATIONAL SQUADRON .... RONALD REAGAN
INTERNATIONAL VELVET .... ANTHONY HOPKINS
INTERNATIONAL
    VELVET .... CHRISTOPHER PLUMMER
INTERNATIONAL VELVET .... TATUM O'NEAL
INTERNECINE PROJECT, THE .... JAMES COBURN
INTERNECINE PROJECT, THE .... LEE GRANT
INTERNS CAN'T
    TAKE MONEY .... BARBARA STANWYCK†
INTERNS, THE .... CLIFF ROBERTSON
INTERNS, THE .... STEFANIE POWERS
INTERNS, THE .... TELLY SAVALAS†
INTERRUPTED MELODY .... ROGER MOORE
INTERRUPTED MELODY ★ .... ELEANOR PARKER
INTERSECTION .... LOLITA DAVIDOVICH
INTERSECTION .... MARTIN LANDAU
INTERSECTION .... RICHARD GERE
INTERSECTION .... SHARON STONE
INTERVIEW WITH
    THE VAMPIRE .... ANTONIO BANDERAS
INTERVIEW WITH THE VAMPIRE .... BRAD PITT
INTERVIEW WITH
    THE VAMPIRE .... CHRISTIAN SLATER
INTERVIEW WITH THE VAMPIRE .... KIRSTEN DUNST
INTERVIEW WITH
    THE VAMPIRE .... MIRANDA RICHARDSON
INTERVIEW WITH THE VAMPIRE .... STEPHEN REA
INTERVIEW WITH
    THE VAMPIRE .... THANDIE NEWTON
INTERVIEW WITH THE VAMPIRE .... TOM CRUISE
INTIMATE ENCOUNTERS (TF) .... CICELY TYSON
INTIMATE ENCOUNTERS (TF) .... JAMES BROLIN
INTIMATE
    ENCOUNTERS (TF) .... VERONICA CARTWRIGHT
INTIMATE STRANGERS (TF) .... DENNIS WEAVER
INTIMATE STRANGERS (TF) .... LARRY HAGMAN
INTIMATE STRANGERS (TF) .... QUINN CUMMINGS
INTIMATE STRANGERS (TF) .... RHEA PERLMAN
INTIMATE STRANGERS (TF) .... STACY KEACH
INTIMATE STRANGERS (TF) .... TERI GARR
INTIMATE STRANGERS (TF) .... TYNE DALY
INTO THE NIGHT .... BRUCE McGILL
INTO THE NIGHT .... DAN AYKROYD
INTO THE NIGHT .... DAVID BOWIE
INTO THE NIGHT .... DON SIEGEL†
INTO THE NIGHT .... JEFF GOLDBLUM
INTO THE NIGHT .... KATHRYN HARROLD
INTO THE NIGHT .... MICHELLE PFEIFFER
INTO THE NIGHT .... PAUL MAZURSKY
INTO THE NIGHT .... VERA MILES
INTO THE WEST .... CIARAN FITZGERALD
INTO THE WEST .... ELLEN BARKIN

INTO THE WEST .... GABRIEL BYRNE
INTO THE WEST .... RUAIDHRI CONROY
INTO THIN AIR (TF) .... ELLEN BURSTYN
INTO THIN AIR (TF) .... TATE DONOVAN
INTOLERANCE .... LILLIAN GISH†
INTRIGUE (TF) .... ELEANOR BRON
INTRIGUE (TF) .... ROBERT LOGGIA
INTRIGUE (TF) .... SCOTT GLENN
INTRIGUE (TF) .... WILLIAM ATHERTON
INTRODUCTION TO
    THE ENEMY (FD) .... JANE FONDA
INTRUDER, THE .... JENNIFER O'NEILL
INTRUDER, THE .... WILLIAM SHATNER
INTRUDER WITHIN, THE (TF) .... CHAD EVERETT
INTRUDER WITHIN, THE (TF) ..... JOSEPH BOTTOMS
INTRUDERS, THE (TF) .... DON MURRAY
INTRUDERS, THE (TF) .... HARRISON FORD
INTRUSO .... VICTORIA ABRIL
INVADERS, THE .... LAURENCE OLIVIER†
INVADERS, THE .... LESLIE HOWARD†
INVADERS, THE .... RAYMOND MASSEY†
INVADERS FROM MARS .... BUD CORT
INVADERS FROM MARS .... HUNTER CARSON
INVADERS FROM MARS .... JAMES KAREN
INVADERS FROM MARS .... KAREN BLACK
INVADERS FROM MARS .... LARAINE NEWMAN
INVADERS FROM MARS .... LOUISE FLETCHER
INVADERS FROM MARS .... TIMOTHY BOTTOMS
INVASION OF JOHNSON
    COUNTY, THE (TF) .... BILL BIXBY†
INVASION OF THE
    BODY SNATCHERS .... BROOKE ADAMS
INVASION OF THE
    BODY SNATCHERS .... DON SIEGEL†
INVASION OF THE
    BODY SNATCHERS .... DONALD SUTHERLAND
INVASION OF THE
    BODY SNATCHERS .... JEFF GOLDBLUM
INVASION OF THE
    BODY SNATCHERS .... KEVIN McCARTHY
INVASION OF THE
    BODY SNATCHERS .... LEONARD NIMOY
INVASION OF THE
    BODY SNATCHERS .... ROBERT DUVALL
INVASION OF THE
    BODY SNATCHERS .... VERONICA CARTWRIGHT
INVASION, U.S.A. .... CHUCK NORRIS
INVASION, U.S.A. .... DAN O'HERLIHY
INVESTIGATION: INSIDE A TERRORIST
    BOMBING, THE (CTF) .... JOHN HURT
INVINCIBLE SIX, THE .... STUART WHITMAN
INVISIBLE MAN RETURNS, THE .... ALAN NAPIER†
INVISIBLE MAN RETURNS, THE ..... VINCENT PRICE†
INVISIBLE MAN, THE .... CLAUDE RAINS†
INVISIBLE MAN, THE (TF) .... JACKIE COOPER
INVITATION .... VAN JOHNSON
INVITATION TO A GUNFIGHTER .... GEORGE SEGAL
INVITATION TO A GUNFIGHTER ...... PAT HINGLE
INVITATION TO A WEDDING .... PAUL NICHOLAS
INVITATION TO THE DANCE .... CYD CHARISSE
INVITATION TO THE WEDDING ...... RONALD LACEY
INVITIATION TO THE DANCE .... GENE KELLY
INVITIATION TO THE WEDDING ...... JOHN GIELGUD
IPCRESS FILE, THE .... GORDAN JACKSON†
IPCRESS FILE, THE .... MICHAEL CAINE
IRIS AND THE LIEUTENANT .... MAE ZETTERLING†
IRISH EYES ARE SMILING .... ANTHONY QUINN
IRISH IN US, THE .... OLIVIA DE HAVILLAND
IRISH WHISKEY REBELLION .... WILLIAM DEVANE
IRMA LA DOUCE .... BILL BIXBY†
IRMA LA DOUCE .... GRACE LEE WHITNEY
IRMA LA DOUCE .... JACK LEMMON
IRMA LA DOUCE .... JAMES CAAN
IRMA LA DOUCE .... LOU JACOBI
IRMA LA DOUCE ★ .... SHIRLEY MacLAINE
IRON .... DAVID WARNER
IRON EAGLE .... JASON GEDRICK
IRON EAGLE .... JERRY LEVINE
IRON EAGLE .... LOUIS GOSSETT JR.
IRON EAGLE .... MICHAEL BOWEN
IRON EAGLE II .... ALLAN SCARFE
IRON EAGLE II .... LOUIS GOSSETT JR.

IRON EAGLE II .... MARK HUMPHREY
IRON EAGLE II .... MAURY CHAVKIN
IRON EAGLE II .... SARAH H. BRANDON
IRON EAGLE II .... STUART MARGOLIN
IRON FIST .... MICHAEL DELANO
IRON GLOVE, THE .... ROBERT STACK
IRON MAJOR, THE .... BARBARA HALE
IRON MAN .... ROCK HUDSON†
IRON MAZE .... BRIDGET FONDA
IRON MAZE .... J. T. WALSH
IRON MAZE .... JEFF FAHEY
IRON MAZE .... MARK LOWENTHAL
IRON PETTICOAT, THE .... BOB HOPE
IRON PETTICOAT, THE .... KATHERINE HEPBURN
IRON TRIANGLE, THE .... BEAU BRIDGES
IRON TRIANGLE, THE .... HAING S. NGOR
IRON TRIANGLE, THE .... JIM ISHIDA
IRON TRIANGLE, THE .... JOHNNY HALLYDAY
IRON TRIANGLE, THE .... LIEM WHATLEY
IRON WILL .... AUGUST SCHELLENBERG
IRON WILL .... BRIAN COX
IRON WILL .... DAVID OGDEN STIERS
IRON WILL .... GEORGE GERDES
IRON WILL .... KEVIN SPACEY
IRON WILL .... MACKENZIE ASTIN
IRONWEED .... BLACK-EYED SUSAN
IRONWEED .... CARROLL BAKER
IRONWEED .... MARGARET WHITTON
IRONWEED .... TED LEVINE
IRONWEED ★ .... JACK NICHOLSON
IRONWEED ★ .... MERYL STREEP
IRRECONCILABLE DIFFERENCES .... DAVID GRAF
IRRECONCILABLE
    DIFFERENCES .... DAVID PAYMER
IRRECONCILABLE
    DIFFERENCES .... DREW BARRYMORE
IRRECONCILABLE DIFFERENCES ..... JENNY GAGO
IRRECONCILABLE DIFFERENCES .... RYAN O'NEAL
IRRECONCILABLE
    DIFFERENCES .... SAM WANAMAKER†
IRRECONCILABLE
    DIFFERENCES .... SHARON STONE
IRRECONCILABLE
    DIFFERENCES .... SHELLEY LONG
IS PARIS BURNING? .... ANTHONY PERKINS†
IS PARIS BURNING? .... E. G. MARSHALL
IS PARIS BURNING? .... KIRK DOUGLAS
IS PARIS BURNING? .... LESLIE CARON
IS PARIS BURNING? .... ROBERT STACK
IS THERE SEX AFTER DEATH? ...... BUCK HENRY
IS THIS TRIP REALLY NECESSARY? ... CAROL KANE
ISABEL .... GENEVIEVE BUJOLD
ISADORA .... JASON ROBARDS
ISADORA ★ .... VANESSA REDGRAVE
ISHI: THE LAST OF
    HIS TRIBE (TF) .... DENNIS WEAVER
ISHTAR .... CAROL KANE
ISHTAR .... CHARLES GRODIN
ISHTAR .... DUSTIN HOFFMAN
ISHTAR .... ISABELLE ADJANI
ISHTAR .... JACK WESTON
ISHTAR .... TESS HARPER
ISHTAR .... WARREN BEATTY
ISLAND, THE .... BIBI ANDERSSON
ISLAND, THE .... MICHAEL CAINE
ISLAND AT THE TOP OF
    THE WORLD, THE .... MAKO
ISLAND IN THE SKY .... HARRY CAREY JR.
ISLAND IN THE SUN .... JOAN COLLINS
ISLAND OF DESIRE .... TAB HUNTER
ISLAND OF DR.
    MOREAU, THE .... BARBARA CARRERA
ISLAND OF DR.
    MOREAU, THE .... BURT LANCASTER†
ISLAND OF DR. MOREAU, THE .... MICHAEL YORK
ISLAND OF DR.
    MOREAU, THE .... NIGEL DAVENPORT
ISLAND OF LOST MEN .... ANTHONY QUINN
ISLAND OF LOVE .... MICHAEL CONSTANTINE
ISLAND OF LOVE .... TONY RANDALL
ISLAND OF LOVE .... WALTER MATTHAU

476

ISLAND OF THE BLUE DOLPHINS	GEORGE KENNEDY
ISLAND SONS (TF)	JOSEPH BOTTOMS
ISLAND SONS (TF)	SAM BOTTOMS
ISLAND SONS (TF)	TIMOTHY BOTTOMS
ISLANDER, THE (TF)	DENNIS WEAVER
ISLANDS IN THE STREAM	CLAIRE BLOOM
ISLANDS IN THE STREAM	DAVID HEMMINGS
ISLANDS IN THE STREAM	GEORGE C. SCOTT
ISLANDS IN THE STREAM	HART BOCHNER
ISLANDS IN THE STREAM	JULIUS HARRIS
ISLANDS IN THE STREAM	SUSAN TYRRELL
ISLANDS, THE	DAVID WARNER
ISN'T IT SHOCKING? (TF)	ALAN ALDA
ISN'T IT SHOCKING? (TF)	LOUISE LASSER
IT	CLARA BOW†
IT!	RODDY McDOWALL
IT (TF)	ANNETTE O'TOOLE
IT (TF)	DENNIS CHRISTOPHER
IT (TF)	JOHN RITTER
IT (TF)	RICHARD MASUR
IT (TF)	RICHARD THOMAS
IT (TF)	TIM CURRY
IT (TF)	TIM REID
IT CAME FROM HOLLYWOOD	JOHN CANDY†
IT CAME FROM HOLLYWOOD (FD)	CHEECH MARIN
IT CAME FROM HOLLYWOOD (FD)	DAN AYKROYD
IT CAME FROM HOLLYWOOD (FD)	GILDA RADNER†
IT CAME FROM HOLLYWOOD (FD)	THOMAS CHONG
IT CAME WITHOUT WARNING	MARTIN LANDAU
IT CONQUERED THE WORLD	PETER GRAVES
IT COULD HAPPEN TO YOU	ANN DOWD
IT COULD HAPPEN TO YOU	BRIDGET FONDA
IT COULD HAPPEN TO YOU	J. E. FREEMAN
IT COULD HAPPEN TO YOU	NICOLAS CAGE
IT COULD HAPPEN TO YOU	RED BUTTONS
IT COULD HAPPEN TO YOU	ROSIE PEREZ
IT COULD HAPPEN TO YOU	SEYMOUR CASSEL
IT COULDN'T HAPPEN TO A NICER GUY (TF)	MICHAEL LEARNED
IT GROWS ON TREES	RICHARD CRENNA
IT HAD TO BE YOU	DONNA DIXON
IT HAD TO BE YOU	EILEEN BRENNAN
IT HAD TO BE YOU	FRAN DRESCHER
IT HAD TO BE YOU	JOSEPH BOLOGNA
IT HAD TO BE YOU	RENEE TAYLOR
IT HAD TO BE YOU	TONY RANDALL
IT HAD TO BE YOU	WILLIAM HICKEY
IT HAPPENED AT LAKEWOOD MANOR	BRIAN DENNEHY
IT HAPPENED AT LAKEWOOD MANOR (TF)	ROBERT FOXWORTH
IT HAPPENED AT LAKEWOOD MANOR (TF)	SUZANNE SOMERS
IT HAPPENED AT THE WORLD'S FAIR	ELVIS PRESLEY†
IT HAPPENED AT THE WORLD'S FAIR	KURT RUSSELL
IT HAPPENED IN BROOKLYN	FRANK SINATRA
IT HAPPENED ONE NIGHT ★★	CLARK GABLE†
IT HAPPENED ONE NIGHT	CLAUDETTE COLBERT
IT HAPPENED TO JANE	BETSY PALMER
IT HAPPENED TO JANE	DORIS DAY
IT HAPPENED TO JANE	JACK LEMMON
IT HAPPENED TO JANE	MARY WICKES
IT HAPPENED TO JANE	STEVE FORREST
IT HAPPENS EVERY THURSDAY	JOHN FORSYTHE
IT IS RAINING ON SANTIAGO	BIBI ANDERSSON
IT LIVES AGAIN	FREDERIC FORREST
IT ONLY HAPPENS TO OTHERS	CATHERINE DENEUVE
IT RAINED ALL NIGHT THE DAY I LEFT	JOHN VERNON
IT RAINED ALL NIGHT THE DAY I LEFT	TONY CURTIS
IT RUNS IN THE FAMILY	CHARLES GRODIN
IT RUNS IN THE FAMILY	KIERAN CULKIN
IT RUNS IN THE FAMILY	MARY STEENBURGEN
IT SEEMED LIKE A GOOD IDEA AT THE TIME	JOHN CANDY†
IT SEEMED LIKE A GOOD IDEA AT THE TIME	YVONNE DE CARLO
IT SHOULD HAPPEN TO YOU	JACK LEMMON
IT STARTED IN NAPLES	CLARK GABLE†
IT STARTED IN NAPLES	SOPHIA LOREN
IT STARTED WITH A KISS	DEBBIE REYNOLDS
IT STARTED WITH A KISS	EVA GABOR
IT TAKES ALL KINDS	VERA MILES
IT TAKES TWO	LESLIE HOPE
IT WON'T RUB OFF, BABY	DON MURRAY
IT'S A GREAT FEELING	JOAN CRAWFORD†
IT'S A WONDERFUL LIFE	BEULAH BONDI†
IT'S A WONDERFUL LIFE	DONNA REED†
IT'S A WONDERFUL LIFE	FRANK FAYLEN†
IT'S A WONDERFUL LIFE	GLORIA GRAHAME†
IT'S A WONDERFUL LIFE	H. B. WARNER†
IT'S A WONDERFUL LIFE	HENRY TRAVERS†
IT'S A WONDERFUL LIFE	LIONEL BARRYMORE†
IT'S A WONDERFUL LIFE	SAMUEL S. HINDS†
IT'S A WONDERFUL LIFE	THOMAS MITCHELL†
IT'S A WONDERFUL LIFE	WARD BOND†
IT'S A WONDERFUL LIFE ★	JAMES STEWART
IT'S LOVE I'M AFTER	BETTE DAVIS†
IT'S A BIG COUNTRY	GENE KELLY
IT'S A BIG COUNTRY	JAMES WHITMORE
IT'S A BIG COUNTRY	JANET LEIGH
IT'S A BIG COUNTRY	LEON AMES
IT'S A BIG COUNTRY	MAC DAVIS
IT'S A BIG COUNTRY	VAN JOHNSON
IT'S A GREAT FEELING	DORIS DAY
IT'S A GREAT FEELING	ELEANOR PARKER
IT'S A GREAT FEELING	JANE WYMAN
IT'S A GREAT FEELING	PATRICIA NEAL
IT'S A GREAT FEELING	RONALD REAGAN
IT'S A MAD MAD MAD MAD WORLD	BUDDY HACKETT
IT'S A MAD MAD MAD MAD WORLD	CARL REINER
IT'S A MAD MAD MAD MAD WORLD	DON KNOTTS
IT'S A MAD MAD MAD MAD WORLD	EDIE ADAMS
IT'S A MAD MAD MAD MAD WORLD	JERRY LEWIS
IT'S A MAD MAD MAD MAD WORLD	JONATHAN WINTERS
IT'S A MAD MAD MAD MAD WORLD	MILTON BERLE
IT'S A MAD MAD MAD MAD WORLD	PETER FALK
IT'S A MAD MAD MAD MAD WORLD	SID CAESAR
IT'S A WONDERFUL WORLD	JAMES STEWART
IT'S ALIVE III: ISLAND OF THE ALIVE	KAREN BLACK
IT'S ALWAYS FAIR WEATHER	CYD CHARISSE
IT'S ALWAYS FAIR WEATHER	GENE KELLY
IT'S GOOD TO BE ALIVE (TF)	LOUIS GOSSETT JR.
IT'S GREAT TO BE YOUNG	JOHN MILLS
IT'S IN THE BAG	DON AMECHE†
IT'S LOVE I'M AFTER	OLIVIA DE HAVILLAND
IT'S MY TURN	CHARLES GRODIN
IT'S MY TURN	DANIEL STERN
IT'S MY TURN	DIANNE WIEST
IT'S MY TURN	JILL CLAYBURGH
IT'S MY TURN	MICHAEL DOUGLAS
IT'S MY TURN	STEVEN HILL
IT'S NEVER TOO LATE	SHIRLEY ANNE FIELD
IT'S NOT THE SIZE THAT COUNTS	ANTHONY ANDREWS
IT'S NOT THE SIZE THAT COUNTS	LEIGH LAWSON
IT'S NOT THE SIZE THAT COUNTS	MILO O'SHEA
IT'S NOT THE SIZE THAT COUNTS	VINCENT PRICE†
IT'S ONLY MONEY	JACK WESTON
IT'S ONLY MONEY	JERRY LEWIS
IT'S PAT	ARLEEN SORKIN
IT'S PAT	DAVID FOLEY
IT'S PAT	JULIA SWEENEY
IT'S PAT	KATHY NAJIMY
IT'S PAT	LARRY HANKIN
ITALIAN CONNECTION, THE	HENRY SILVA
ITALIAN CONNECTION, THE	WOODY STRODE
ITALIAN JOB, THE	MICHAEL CAINE
ITALIAN JOB, THE	TONY BECKLEY†
ITALIAN STALLION, THE	SYLVESTER STALLONE
ITALIANO BRAVA GENTE	PETER FALK
IVANHOE	ELIZABETH TAYLOR
IVANHOE (TF)	ANTHONY ANDREWS
IVANHOE (TF)	JOHN RHYS-DAVIES
IVANHOE (TF)	SAM NEILL
IZZY AND MOE (TF)	ART CARNEY
IZZY AND MOE (TF)	CYNTHIA HARRIS
I'D CLIMB THE HIGHEST MOUNTAIN	RORY CALHOUN
I'D RATHER BE RICH	ROBERT GOULET
I'D RATHER BE RICH	SANDRA DEE
I'LL BE HOME FOR CHRISTMAS (TF)	COURTENEY COX
I'LL BE HOME FOR CHRISTMAS (TF)	DAVID MOSCOW
I'LL BE HOME FOR CHRISTMAS (TF)	EVA MARIE SAINT
I'LL BE HOME FOR CHRISTMAS (TF)	HAL HOLBROOK
I'LL BE HOME FOR CHRISTMAS (TF)	NANCY TRAVIS
I'LL BE HOME FOR CHRISTMAS (TF)	PETER GALLAGHER
I'LL CRY TOMORROW	EDDIE ALBERT
I'LL CRY TOMORROW	PATTY DUKE
I'LL GET BY	STEVE ALLEN
I'LL SEE YOU IN MY DREAMS	DORIS DAY
I'LL SEE YOU IN MY DREAMS	MARY WICKES
I'LL TAKE MANHATTAN (MS)	BARRY BOSTWICK
I'LL TAKE MANHATTAN (MS)	FRANCESCA ANNIS
I'LL TAKE MANHATTAN (MS)	JACK SCALIA
I'LL TAKE MANHATTAN (MS)	JANE KACZMAREK
I'LL TAKE MANHATTAN (MS)	KEN OLIN
I'LL TAKE MANHATTAN (MS)	PAUL HECHT
I'LL TAKE MANHATTAN (MS)	PERRY KING
I'LL TAKE MANHATTAN (MS)	TIMOTHY DALY
I'LL TAKE MANHATTAN (MS)	VALERIE BERTINELLI
I'LL TAKE SWEDEN	BOB HOPE
I'LL TAKE SWEDEN	DINA MERRILL
I'LL TAKE SWEDEN	FRANKIE AVALON
I'LL TAKE SWEDEN	TUESDAY WELD
I'M DANCING AS FAST AS I CAN	JILL CLAYBURGH
I'M DANCING AS FAST AS I CAN	JOE PESCI
I'M DANCING AS FAST AS I CAN	JOHN LITHGOW
I'M DANCING AS FAST AS I CAN	NICOL WILLIAMSON
I'M DANCING AS FAST AS I CAN	RICHARD MASUR
I'M DANGEROUS TONIGHT (CTF)	ANTHONY PERKINS†
I'M DANGEROUS TONIGHT (CTF)	COREY PARKER
I'M DANGEROUS TONIGHT (CTF)	DAISY HALL
I'M DANGEROUS TONIGHT (CTF)	DEE WALLACE STONE
I'M DANGEROUS TONIGHT (CTF)	MADCHEN AMICK
I'M GONNA GIT YOU SUCKA	ANNE MARIE JOHNSON
I'M GONNA GIT YOU SUCKA	ANTONIO FARGAS
I'M GONNA GIT YOU SUCKA	BERNIE CASEY
I'M GONNA GIT YOU SUCKA	CLU GULAGER
I'M GONNA GIT YOU SUCKA	DAMON WAYANS
I'M GONNA GIT YOU SUCKA	DAWNN LEWIS
I'M GONNA GIT YOU SUCKA	EVE PLUMB
I'M GONNA GIT YOU SUCKA	GARY OWENS
I'M GONNA GIT YOU SUCKA	ISAAC HAYES
I'M GONNA GIT YOU SUCKA	JA'NET DUBOIS
I'M GONNA GIT YOU SUCKA	JIM BROWN
I'M GONNA GIT YOU SUCKA	JOHN VERNON
I'M GONNA GIT YOU SUCKA	KEENEN IVORY WAYANS
I'M GONNA GIT YOU SUCKA	MARLON WAYANS
I'M GONNA GIT YOU SUCKA	ROBERT TOWNSEND
I'M GONNA GIT YOU SUCKA	STEVE JAMES

Is-I'm

FILM
ACTORS
GUIDE

INDEX OF FILM TITLES

J.O.E. AND THE COLONEL (TF) ..... TERRENCE KNOX
J.W. COOP .... CLIFF ROBERTSON
J.W. COOP .... R.G. ARMSTRONG
JABBERWOCKY .... BRIAN GLOVER
JABBERWOCKY .... MICHAEL PALIN
JACK LONDON'S
    KLONDIKE FEVER .... ANGIE DICKINSON
JACK OF DIAMONDS .... CARROLL BAKER
JACK OF DIAMONDS .... GEORGE HAMILTON
JACK OF DIAMONDS .... ZSA ZSA GABOR
JACK THE BEAR .... ANDREA MARCOVICCI
JACK THE BEAR .... ART LA FLEUR
JACK THE BEAR .... BERT REMSEN
JACK THE BEAR .... DANNY DEVITO
JACK THE BEAR .... ERICA YOHN
JACK THE BEAR .... GARY SINISE
JACK THE BEAR .... JULIA LOUIS-DREYFUSS
JACK THE BEAR .... MIKO HUGHES
JACK THE BEAR .... ROBERT STEINMILLER JR.
JACK THE RIPPER .... GEORGE ROSE†
JACK THE RIPPER (MS) .... ARMAND ASSANTE
JACK THE RIPPER (MS) .... JANE SEYMOUR
JACK THE RIPPER (TF) .... MICHAEL CAINE
JACK THE RIPPER (TF) .... SUSAN GEORGE
JACKALS .... WILFORD BRIMLEY
JACKALS, THE .... VINCENT PRICE†
JACKIE COLLINS'
    LUCKY CHANCES (MS) .... ANNE MARIE JOHNSON
JACKIE COLLINS'
    LUCKY CHANCES (MS) .... MICHAEL NADER
JACKIE COLLINS'
    LUCKY CHANCES (MS) ... NICOLLETTE SHERIDAN
JACKIE ROBINSON STORY, THE .... RUBY DEE
JACKNIFE .... CHARLES S. DUTTON
JACKNIFE .... ED HARRIS
JACKNIFE .... KATHY BAKER
JACKNIFE .... LOUDON WAINWRIGHT III
JACKNIFE .... ROBERT DE NIRO
JACKNIFE .... SLOANE SHELTON
JACKPOT .... JAMES COBURN
JACKPOT .... NATALIE WOOD†
JACKPOT, THE .... BARBARA HALE
JACKPOT, THE .... JAMES STEWART
JACKSON COUNTY JAIL .... ROBERT CARRADINE
JACKSON COUNTY JAIL .... TOMMY LEE JONES
JACKSONS: AN AMERICAN
    DREAM, THE (TF) .... ANGELA BASSETT
JACK'S BACK .... JAMES SPADER
JACOB (CTF) .... MATTHEW MODINE
JACOBO TIMERMAN: PRISONER
    WITHOUT A NAME, CELL
    WITHOUT A NUMBER (TF) .... LIV ULLMANN
JACOBO TIMERMAN: PRISONER
    WITHOUT A NAME, CELL
    WITHOUT A NUMBER (TF) .... ROY SCHEIDER
JACOBO TIMERMAN: PRISONER
    WITHOUT A NAME, CELL
    WITHOUT A NUMBER (TF) .... SAM ROBARDS
JACOBO TIMERMAN: PRISONER
    WITHOUT A NAME, CELL
    WITHOUT A NUMBER (TF) .... ZACH GALLIGAN
JACOB'S LADDER .... DANNY AIELLO
JACOB'S LADDER .... ELIZABETH PENA
JACOB'S LADDER .... JASON ALEXANDER
JACOB'S LADDER .... MACAULAY CULKIN
JACOB'S LADDER .... MATT CRAVEN
JACOB'S LADDER .... PATRICIA KALEMBER
JACOB'S LADDER .... PRUITT TAYLOR VINCE
JACOB'S LADDER .... TIM ROBBINS
JACQUELINE BOUVIER
    KENNEDY (TF) .... JACLYN SMITH
JACQUELINE BOUVIER
    KENNEDY (TF) .... JAMES FRANCISCUS†
JACQUELINE SUSANN'S VALLEY
    OF THE DOLLS (MS) .... STEVE INWOOD
JACQUELINE SUSANN'S ONCE
    IS NOT ENOUGH .... ALEXIS SMITH†

JACQUELINE SUSANN'S ONCE
    IS NOT ENOUGH .... DEBORAH RAFFIN
JACQUELINE SUSANN'S ONCE
    IS NOT ENOUGH .... GEORGE HAMILTON
JACQUELINE SUSANN'S ONCE
    IS NOT ENOUGH .... KIRK DOUGLAS
JACQUELINE SUSANN'S ONCE
    IS NOT ENOUGH ❍ .... BRENDA VACCARO
JADE .... DAVID CARUSO
JAGGED EDGE .... BEN HAMMER
JAGGED EDGE .... GLENN CLOSE
JAGGED EDGE .... GUY BOYD
JAGGED EDGE .... JEFF BRIDGES
JAGGED EDGE .... JOHN DEHNER†
JAGGED EDGE .... PETER COYOTE
JAGGED EDGE ❍ .... ROBERT LOGGIA
JAGUAR LIVES .... DONALD PLEASENCE
JAGUAR LIVES .... JOSEPH WISEMAN
JAGUAR LIVES .... WOODY STRODE
JAILHOUSE ROCK .... DEAN JONES
JAILHOUSE ROCK .... ELVIS PRESLEY†
JAKE SPANNER,
    PRIVATE EYE (CTF) .... ERNEST BORGNINE
JAKE SPEED .... DENNIS CHRISTOPHER
JAKE SPEED .... JOHN HURT
JAKE SPEED .... LEON AMES
JAKE SPEED .... MILLIE PERKINS
JAKE SPEED .... WAYNE CRAWFORD
JAMAICA INN .... MAUREEN O'HARA
JAMAICA INN (MS) .... JANE SEYMOUR
JAMAICA INN (TF) .... BILLIE WHITELAW
JAMAICA INN (TF) .... JOHN McENERY
JAMAICA INN (TF) .... PETER VAUGHN
JAMBOREE .... FRANKIE AVALON
JAMES AND THE
    GIANT PEACH (AF) .... GUY WITCHER
JAMES AND THE
    GIANT PEACH (AF) .... MIRIAM MARGOLYES
JAMES AND THE
    GIANT PEACH (AF) .... VANESSA REDGRAVE
JAMES AT 15 (TF) .... KATE JACKSON
JAMES AT 15 (TF) .... MELISSA ANDERSON
JAMES BRADY
    STORY, THE (CTF) .... DAVID STRATHAIRN
JAMES BRADY STORY, THE (CTF) .... JOAN ALLEN
JAMES CLAVELL'S
    NOBLE HOUSE (MS) .... BEN MASTERS
JAMES CLAVELL'S
    NOBLE HOUSE (MS) .... DEBORAH RAFFIN
JAMES CLAVELL'S
    NOBLE HOUSE (MS) .... PIERCE BROSNAN
JAMES DEAN (TF) .... MEG FOSTER
JAMES DEAN (TF) .... ROBERT FOXWORTH
JAMES DEAN (TF) .... STEPHEN McHATTIE
JAMES MICHENER'S
    DYNASTY (TF) .... STACY KEACH
JANE AND THE LOST CITY .... MAUD ADAMS
JANE AUSTEN IN MANHATTAN .... SEAN YOUNG
JANE DOE (TF) .... EVA MARIE SAINT
JANE DOE (TF) .... TERRY DAVID MULLIGAN
JANE DOE (TF) .... WILLIAM DEVANE
JANE EYRE .... ELIZABETH TAYLOR
JANE EYRE (TF) .... GEORGE C. SCOTT
JANE EYRE (TF) .... IAN BANNEN
JANE EYRE (TF) .... SUSANNAH YORK
JANUARY MAN, THE .... ALAN RICKMAN
JANUARY MAN, THE .... DANNY AIELLO
JANUARY MAN, THE .... FAYE GRANT
JANUARY MAN, THE .... HARVEY KEITEL
JANUARY MAN, THE .... KEVIN KLINE
JANUARY MAN,
    THE .... MARY ELIZABETH MASTRANTONIO
JANUARY MAN, THE .... ROD STEIGER
JANUARY MAN, THE .... SUSAN SARANDON
JANUARY MAN, THE .... TANDY CRONYN
JASON GOES TO HELL—
    THE FINAL FRIDAY .... ALLISON SMITH
JASON GOES TO HELL—
    THE FINAL FRIDAY .... ERIN GRAY
JASON GOES TO HELL—
    THE FINAL FRIDAY .... JOHN D. LeMAY

JASON GOES TO HELL—
    THE FINAL FRIDAY .... KARI KEEGAN
JASON GOES TO HELL—
    THE FINAL FRIDAY .... STEVEN CULP
JASON GOES TO HELL—
    THE FINAL FRIDAY .... STEVEN WILLIAMS
JASON'S LYRIC .... ALLEN PAYNE
JASON'S LYRIC .... BOKEEM WOODBINE
JASON'S LYRIC .... EDDIE GRIFFIN
JASON'S LYRIC .... FOREST WHITAKER
JASON'S LYRIC .... JADA PINKETT
JASON'S LYRIC .... LAHMARD J. TATE
JASON'S LYRIC .... SUZZANNE DOUGLAS
JAWS .... LORRAINE GARY
JAWS .... MURRAY HAMILTON†
JAWS .... RICHARD DREYFUSS
JAWS .... ROBERT SHAW†
JAWS .... ROY SCHEIDER
JAWS 2 .... JOHN DUKAKIS
JAWS 2 .... LORRAINE GARY
JAWS 2 .... MURRAY HAMILTON†
JAWS 2 .... ROY SCHEIDER
JAWS 3-D .... BESS ARMSTRONG
JAWS 3-D .... DENNIS QUAID
JAWS 3-D .... LOUIS GOSSETT JR.
JAWS 3-D .... SIMON MacCORKINDALE
JAWS OF DEATH, THE .... RICHARD JAECKEL
JAWS OF SATAN .... FRITZ WEAVER
JAWS THE REVENGE .... JUDITH BARSI†
JAWS THE REVENGE .... LORRAINE GARY
JAWS THE REVENGE .... MICHAEL CAINE
JAYNE MANSFIELD
    STORY, THE (TF) .... ARNOLD SCHWARZENEGGER
JAYNE MANSFIELD
    STORY, THE (TF) .... LONI ANDERSON
JAZZ SINGER, THE .... CATLIN ADAMS
JAZZ SINGER, THE .... DANNY THOMAS†
JAZZ SINGER, THE .... FRANKLYN AJAYE
JAZZ SINGER, THE .... LAURENCE OLIVIER†
JAZZ SINGER, THE .... LUCIE ARNAZ
JAZZ SINGER, THE .... MIKE KELLIN†
JAZZ SINGER, THE .... NEIL DIAMOND
JAZZ SINGER, THE .... PAUL NICHOLAS
JAZZ SINGER, THE .... SULLY BOVAR
JE T'AIME MOI NON PLUS .... GERARD DEPARDIEU
JE VEUX RENTRER A
    LA MAISON .... GERARD DEPARDIEU
JE VOUS AIME .... GERARD DEPARDIEU
JE VOUS SALUE MAFFIA! .... JACK KLUGMAN
JE VOUS SALVE MAFIA .... HENRY SILVA
JEAN DE FLORETTE .... DANIEL AUTEUIL
JEAN DE FLORETTE .... GERARD DEPARDIEU
JEANNE EAGLES .... KIM NOVAK
JEFFERSON IN
    PARIS .... CHARLOTTE de TURCKHEIM
JEFFERSON IN PARIS .... CICELY TYSON
JEFFERSON IN PARIS .... DANIEL MESGUICH
JEFFERSON IN PARIS .... GRETA SCACCHI
JEFFERSON IN PARIS .... GWYNETH PALTROW
JEFFERSON IN PARIS .... LAMBERT WILSON
JEFFERSON IN PARIS .... MARISA BERENSON
JEFFERSON IN PARIS .... MICHAEL LONSDALE
JEFFERSON IN PARIS .... NICK NOLTE
JEFFERSON IN
    PARIS .... PHILIPPINE LEROY-BEAULIEU
JEFFERSON IN PARIS .... SIMON CALLOW
JEFFERSON IN PARIS .... THANDIE NEWTON
JEFFREY .... BRYAN BATT
JEFFREY .... KATHY NAJIMY
JEFFREY .... MICHAEL T. WEISS
JEFFREY .... OLYMPIA DUKAKIS
JEFFREY .... SIGOURNEY WEAVER
JEFFREY .... STEVEN WEBER
JEKYLL AND HYDE...
    TOGETHER AGAIN .... BESS ARMSTRONG
JEKYLL & HYDE (TF) .... CHERYL LADD
JEKYLL & HYDE (TF) .... JOSS ACKLAND
JEKYLL & HYDE (TF) .... MICHAEL CAINE
JENNIE GERHARDT .... SYLVIA SIDNEY
JENNIFER .... JEFF COREY
JENNIFER .... JOHN GAVIN

JENNIFER .... NINA FOCH
JENNIFER: A WOMAN'S
    STORY (TF) .... ELIZABETH MONTGOMERY
JENNIFER EIGHT .... ANDY GARCIA
JENNIFER EIGHT .... GRAHAM BECKEL
JENNIFER EIGHT .... JOHN MALKOVICH
JENNIFER EIGHT .... KATHY BAKER
JENNIFER EIGHT .... KEVIN CONWAY
JENNIFER EIGHT .... LANCE HENRIKSEN
JENNIFER EIGHT .... UMA THURMAN
JENNIFER ON MY MIND ...... BARRY BOSTWICK
JENNIFER ON MY MIND .... JEFF CONAWAY
JENNIFER ON MY MIND ..... ROBERT DE NIRO
JENNY .... ALAN ALDA
JENNY .... MARLO THOMAS
JENNY .... VINCENT GARDENIA†
JENNY'S WAR (TF) ... CHRISTOPHER CAZENOVE
JENNY'S WAR (TF) .... DYAN CANNON
JENNY'S WAR (TF) ...... NIGEL HAWTHORNE
JEOPARDY .... BARBARA STANWYCK†
JEREMIAH JOHNSON .... HARRY MORGAN
JEREMIAH JOHNSON .... ROBERT REDFORD
JEREMY .... GLYNNIS O'CONNOR
JEREMY .... ROBBY BENSON
JERICHO MILE, THE (TF) .... BILLY GREEN BUSH
JERICHO MILE, THE (TF) ...... PETER STRAUSS
JERICHO MILE, THE (TF) .... ROGER E. MOSLEY
JERK, THE .... BERNADETTE PETERS
JERK, THE .... CATLIN ADAMS
JERK, THE .... M. EMMET WALSH
JERK, THE .... STEVE MARTIN
JERKY BOYS, THE .... ALAN ARKIN
JERKY BOYS, THE .... ALAN NORTH
JERKY BOYS, THE .... BRAD SULLIVAN
JERKY BOYS, THE .... JAMES LORINZ
JERKY BOYS, THE .... JOHNNY B.
JERKY BOYS, THE .... KAMAL
JERKY BOYS, THE .... PAUL BARTEL
JERKY BOYS, THE ...... SUZANNE SHEPHERD
JERKY BOYS, THE .... VINCENT PASTORE
JERKY BOYS, THE .... WILLIAM HICKEY
JERUSALEM FILE, THE .... BRUCE DAVISON
JERUSALEM FILE, THE ..... DONALD PLEASENCE
JERUSALEM FILE, THE ...... NICOL WILLIAMSON
JESSE HAWKES (TF) ...... CHRISTIAN CONRAD
JESSE HAWKES (TF) ...... ROBERT CONRAD
JESSE JAMES .... HENRY FONDA†
JESSE JAMES .... RANDOLPH SCOTT†
JESSE OWENS
    STORY, THE (TF) .... DORIAN HAREWOOD
JESSE OWENS
    STORY, THE (TF) ...... GEORG STANFORD BROWN
JESSE OWENS STORY, THE (TF) .... TOM BOSLEY
JESSE (TF) .... RICHARD MARCUS
JESSICA .... ANGIE DICKINSON
JESSIE OWENS
    STORY, THE (TF) .... LeVAR BURTON
JESSIE (TF) .... CELESTE HOLM
JESSIE (TF) .... LINDSAY WAGNER
JESSIE (TF) .... RENEE JONES
JESSIE (TF) .... TONY LoBIANCO
JESUS CHRIST SUPERSTAR .... JOSH MOSTEL
JESUS CHRIST SUPERSTAR .... TED NEELEY
JESUS OF NAZARETH (MS) .... ANNE BANCROFT
JESUS OF NAZARETH (MS) .... ANTHONY QUINN
JESUS OF
    NAZARETH (MS) .... CHRISTOPHER PLUMMER
JESUS OF NAZARETH (MS) .... DONALD PLEASENCE
JESUS OF NAZARETH (MS) .... IAN HOLM
JESUS OF NAZARETH (MS) ...... JAMES EARL JONES
JESUS OF NAZARETH (MS) ...... JAMES FARENTINO
JESUS OF NAZARETH (MS) ...... MICHAEL YORK
JESUS OF NAZARETH (MS) ...... PETER USTINOV
JESUS OF NAZARETH (MS) .... ROD STEIGER
JESUS OF
    NAZARETH (MS) .... SIMON MacCORKINDALE
JESUS OF NAZARETH (MS) .... STACY KEACH
JESUS OF NAZARETH (MS) .... TONY LoBIANCO
JESUS OF NAZARETH (TF) .... ERNEST BORGNINE
JET PILOT .... JANET LEIGH
JET STORM .... GEORGE ROSE†

JET STORM .... MAE ZETTERLING†
JETSONS: THE MOVIE (AF) .... MEL BLANC†
JETSONS: THE MOVIE (AF) .... TIFFANY
JEU DE MASSACRE .... CLAUDINE AUGER
JEWEL IN THE
    CROWN, THE (MS) .... ROSEMARY LEACH
JEWEL IN THE
    CROWN, THE (TF) .... CHARLES DANCE
JEWEL OF THE NILE, THE .... DANNY DEVITO
JEWEL OF THE NILE, THE .... KATHLEEN TURNER
JEWEL OF THE NILE, THE .... MICHAEL DOUGLAS
JEZEBEL ★★ .... BETTE DAVIS†
JEZEBEL oo .... FAY BAINTER†
JFK o .... TOMMY LEE JONES
JFK .... BEATA POZNIAK
JFK .... BRIAN DOYLE-MURRAY
JFK .... DONALD SUTHERLAND
JFK .... ED ASNER
JFK .... GARY GRUBBS
JFK .... GARY OLDMAN
JFK .... JACK LEMMON
JFK .... JAY O. SANDERS
JFK .... JIM GARRISON
JFK .... JOE PESCI
JFK .... JOHN CANDY†
JFK .... KEVIN BACON
JFK .... KEVIN COSTNER
JFK .... LAURIE METCALF
JFK .... MICHAEL ROOKER
JFK .... NUMA BERTELL
JFK .... SALLY KIRKLAND
JFK .... SISSY SPACEK
JFK .... STEVE REED
JFK .... WALTER MATTHAU
JIGSAW† .... BRADFORD DILLMAN
JIGSAW .... HARRY GUARDINO
JIGSAW .... HOPE LANGE
JIGSAW .... MICHAEL J. POLLARD
JIGSAW .... PAT HINGLE
JIGSAW .... SUSAN SAINT JAMES
JIGSAW MAN, THE .... MICHAEL CAINE
JIGSAW MAN, THE .... SUSAN GEORGE
JIM THORPE—
    ALL AMERICAN .... BURT LANCASTER†
JIM THORPE—ALL AMERICAN .... PHYLLIS THAXTER
JIMBUCK .... ROD STEIGER
JIMMY HOLLYWOOD .... CHRISTIAN SLATER
JIMMY HOLLYWOOD .... HARRISON FORD
JIMMY HOLLYWOOD .... JASON BEGHE
JIMMY HOLLYWOOD .... JOE PESCI
JIMMY HOLLYWOOD .... JOHN COTHRAN JR.
JIMMY HOLLYWOOD .... VICTORIA ABRIL
JIMMY HOLLYWOOD .... VICTORIA BRILL
JIMMY THE GENT .... BETTE DAVIS†
JIMMY THE KID .... GARY COLEMAN
JIMMY THE KID .... PAUL LeMAT
JINXED! .... BETTE MIDLER
JINXED! .... KEN WAHL
JINXED! .... RIP TORN
JIVARO .... RITA MORENO
JO JO DANCER, YOUR
    LIFE IS CALLING .... ART EVANS
JO JO DANCER, YOUR
    LIFE IS CALLING ...... BARBARA WILLIAMS
JO JO DANCER, YOUR
    LIFE IS CALLING .... DEBBIE ALLEN
JO JO DANCER, YOUR
    LIFE IS CALLING .... DENNIS FARINA
JO JO DANCER, YOUR
    LIFE IS CALLING .... DIAHNNE ABBOTT
JO JO DANCER, YOUR
    LIFE IS CALLING .... E'LON COX
JO JO DANCER, YOUR
    LIFE IS CALLING ...... MICHAEL IRONSIDE
JO JO DANCER, YOUR
    LIFE IS CALLING .... RICHARD PRYOR
JO JO DANCER, YOUR
    LIFE IS CALLING .... TANYA BOYD
JO JO DANCER, YOUR LIFE
    IS CALLING .... VIRGINIA CAPERS
JO JO DANCER, YOUR LIFE
    IS CALLING .... WINGS HAUSER

JOAN OF ARC .... ALAN NAPIER†
JOAN OF ARC .... HURD HATFIELD
JOAN OF ARC .... JEFF COREY
JOAN OF ARC ★ .... JOHN IRELAND
JOAN OF ARC ★ .... INGRID BERGMAN†
JOAN OF ARC o .... JOSE FERRER†
JOANNA .... DONALD SUTHERLAND
JOANNA .... FIONA LEWIS
JOE .... K CALLAN
JOE .... PETER BOYLE
JOE .... SUSAN SARANDON
JOE AND ETHEL TURP CALL ON
    THE PRESIDENT .... ANN SOTHERN
JOE BUTTERFLY .... BURGESS MEREDITH
JOE DAKOTA .... CLAUDE AKINS†
JOE KIDD .... CLINT EASTWOOD
JOE KIDD .... DICK VAN PATTEN
JOE KIDD .... DON STROUD
JOE KIDD .... JOHN SAXON
JOE KIDD .... ROBERT DUVALL
JOE LOUIS STORY, THE .... OSSIE DAVIS
JOE PANTHER .... BRIAN KEITH
JOE PANTHER .... RICARDO MONTALBAN
JOE SMITH AMERICAN .... AVA GARDNER†
JOE VALACHI: I SEGRETI
    DI COSA NOSTRA .... CHARLES BRONSON
JOE VERSUS THE VOLCANO .... ABE VIGODA
JOE VERSUS THE VOLCANO ..... BARRY McGOVERN
JOE VERSUS THE VOLCANO .... DAN HEDAYA
JOE VERSUS THE VOLCANO .... LLOYD BRIDGES
JOE VERSUS THE VOLCANO .... MEG RYAN
JOE VERSUS THE VOLCANO .... OSSIE DAVIS
JOE VERSUS THE VOLCANO ..... ROBERT STACK
JOE VERSUS THE VOLCANO .... TOM HANKS
JOEY BOY .... THORLEY WALTERS†
JOHN AND MARY .... DUSTIN HOFFMAN
JOHN AND MARY .... MIA FARROW
JOHN AND MARY .... TYNE DALY
JOHN GOLDFARB, PLEASE
    COME HOME .... HARRY MORGAN
JOHN GOLDFARB, PLEASE
    COME HOME .... PETER USTINOV
JOHN GOLDFARB, PLEASE
    COME HOME .... RICHARD CRENNA
JOHN GOLDFARB, PLEASE
    COME HOME .... SHIRLEY MacLAINE
JOHN HUSTON AND
    THE DUBLINERS .... ANJELICA HUSTON
JOHN HUSTON: THE MAN,
    THE MOVIES, THE
    MAVERICK (CTD) .... ANJELICA HUSTON
JOHN LOVES MARY .... PATRICIA NEAL
JOHN LOVES MARY .... RONALD REAGAN
JOHN PAUL JONES .... BETTE DAVIS†
JOHN PAUL JONES .... ROBERT STACK
JOHN STEINBECK'S EAST
    OF EDEN (MS) .... BRUCE BOXLEITNER
JOHN STEINBECK'S EAST
    OF EDEN (MS) .... JANE SEYMOUR
JOHN STEINBECK'S EAST
    OF EDEN (MS) .... LLOYD BRIDGES
JOHN STEINBECK'S EAST
    OF EDEN (MS) .... RICHARD MASUR
JOHN STEINBECK'S EAST
    OF EDEN (MS) .... TIMOTHY BOTTOMS
JOHN STEINBECK'S EAST
    OF EDEN (MS) .... WENDELL BURTON
JOHNNIE MAE GIBSON:
    FBI (TF) .... LYNN WHITFIELD
JOHNNIE MAE GIBSON:
    FBI (TF) .... WILLIAM ALLEN YOUNG
JOHNNY ALLEGRO .... NINA FOCH
JOHNNY APOLLO .... DOROTHY LAMOUR
JOHNNY BE GOOD .... ANTHONY MICHAEL HALL
JOHNNY BE GOOD .... PAUL GLEASON
JOHNNY BE GOOD .... ROBERT DOWNEY JR.
JOHNNY BE GOOD .... UMA THURMAN
JOHNNY BELINDA .... ALAN NAPIER†
JOHNNY BELINDA ★★ .... JANE WYMAN
JOHNNY BELINDA o .... AGNES MOOREHEAD†
JOHNNY BELINDA o .... CHARLES BICKFORD†

JOHNNY BELINDA (TF) .... ROSANNA ARQUETTE
JOHNNY BULL (TF) .... COLLEEN DEWHURST†
JOHNNY BULL (TF) .... JASON ROBARDS
JOHNNY BULL (TF) .... KATHY BATES
JOHNNY BULL (TF) .... PETER MacNICOL
JOHNNY BULL (TF) .... SUZANNA HAMILTON
JOHNNY CONCHO .... CLAUDE AKINS†
JOHNNY CONCHO .... FRANK SINATRA
JOHNNY COOL .... ELIZABETH MONTGOMERY
JOHNNY COOL .... HENRY SILVA
JOHNNY COOL .... MORT SAHL
JOHNNY COOL .... RICHARD ANDERSON
JOHNNY COOL .... TELLY SAVALAS†
JOHNNY DANGEROUSLY .... BYRON THAMES
JOHNNY DANGEROUSLY .... DANNY DEVITO
JOHNNY DANGEROUSLY .... DICK BUTKUS
JOHNNY DANGEROUSLY .... DOM DeLUISE
JOHNNY DANGEROUSLY .... GLYNNIS O'CONNOR
JOHNNY DANGEROUSLY .... GRIFFIN DUNNE
JOHNNY DANGEROUSLY .... JOE PISCOPO
JOHNNY DANGEROUSLY .... MARILU HENNER
JOHNNY DANGEROUSLY .... MAUREEN STAPLETON
JOHNNY DANGEROUSLY .... MICHAEL KEATON
JOHNNY DANGEROUSLY .... PETER BOYLE
JOHNNY DANGEROUSLY .... RAY WALSTON
JOHNNY DANGEROUSLY .... RICHARD DIMITRI
JOHNNY DANGEROUSLY .... RON CAREY
JOHNNY DANGEROUSLY .... SCOTT THOMSON
JOHNNY DANGEROUSLY .... SUDIE BOND
JOHNNY DARK .... PIPER LAURIE
JOHNNY DARK .... TONY CURTIS
JOHNNY DOESN'T LIVE
    HERE ANY MORE .... ROBERT MITCHUM
JOHNNY EAGER .... LANA TURNER
JOHNNY EAGER ○○ .... VAN HEFLIN†
JOHNNY GOT HIS GUN .... DAVID SOUL
JOHNNY GOT HIS GUN .... DONALD SUTHERLAND
JOHNNY GOT HIS GUN .... JASON ROBARDS
JOHNNY GOT HIS GUN .... TIMOTHY BOTTOMS
JOHNNY GUITAR .... ERNEST BORGNINE
JOHNNY GUITAR .... JOAN CRAWFORD†
JOHNNY GUITAR .... MERCEDES McCAMBRIDGE
JOHNNY GUITAR .... ROYAL DANO
JOHNNY HANDSOME .... BLAKE CLARK
JOHNNY HANDSOME .... ELIZABETH McGOVERN
JOHNNY HANDSOME .... ELLEN BARKIN
JOHNNY HANDSOME .... FOREST WHITAKER
JOHNNY HANDSOME .... LANCE HENRIKSEN
JOHNNY HANDSOME .... MICKEY ROURKE
JOHNNY HANDSOME .... MORGAN FREEMAN
JOHNNY HANDSOME .... SCOTT WILSON
JOHNNY HANDSOME .... YVONNE BRYCELAND
JOHNNY IN THE CLOUDS .... DAVID TOMLINSON
JOHNNY IN THE CLOUDS .... JEAN SIMMONS
JOHNNY IN THE CLOUDS .... JOHN MILLS
JOHNNY MNEMONIC .... BARBARA SUKOWA
JOHNNY MNEMONIC .... DINA MEYER
JOHNNY MNEMONIC .... DOLPH LUNDGREN
JOHNNY MNEMONIC .... DON FRANCKS
JOHNNY MNEMONIC .... HENRY ROLLINS
JOHNNY MNEMONIC .... ICE-T
JOHNNY MNEMONIC .... KEANU REEVES
JOHNNY MNEMONIC .... TAKESHI
JOHNNY MNEMONIC .... UDO KIER
JOHNNY O'CLOCK .... NINA FOCH
JOHNNY RENO .... DEFOREST KELLEY
JOHNNY RYAN (TF) .... BRUCE ABBOTT
JOHNNY RYAN (TF) .... CLANCY BROWN
JOHNNY RYAN (TF) .... TERI AUSTIN
JOHNNY STOOL PIGEON .... SHELLEY WINTERS
JOHNNY STOOL PIGEON .... TONY CURTIS
JOHNNY TIGER .... CHAD EVERETT
JOHNNY TREMAIN .... ANNETTE FUNICELLO
JOHNNY TROUBLE .... STUART WHITMAN
JOHNNY, WE HARDLY
    KNEW YE (TF) .... BRIAN DENNEHY
JOHNNY, WE HARDLY
    KNEW YE (TF) .... TOM BERENGER
JOKE OF DESTINY LYING IN WAIT
    AROUND THE CORNER LIKE A
    STREET BANDIT, A .... VALERIA GOLINO
JOKER IS WILD, THE .... EDDIE ALBERT

JOKER IS WILD, THE .... FRANK SINATRA
JOKER, THE .... ANOUK AIMEE
JOKERS, THE .... MICHAEL CRAWFORD
JOLLY BAD FELLOW, A .... GEOFFREY BAYLDON
JOLSON SINGS AGAIN .... BARBARA HALE
JOLSON STORY, THE ★ .... LARRY PARKS†
JOLSON STORY, THE ○ .... WILLIAM DEMAREST†
JONATHAN LIVINGSTON
    SEAGULL .... HAL HOLBROOK
JONATHAN LIVINGSTON
    SEAGULL .... JAMES FRANCISCUS†
JORDAN CHANCE, THE (TF) .... RAYMOND BURR†
JORY .... ROBBY BENSON
JOSEPH ANDREWS .... ANN-MARGRET
JOSEPH ANDREWS .... JOHN GIELGUD
JOSEPH ANDREWS .... PEGGY ASHCROFT†
JOSEPH ANDREWS .... PETER FIRTH
JOSEPH (CTF) .... BEN KINGSLEY
JOSEPH (CTF) .... LESLEY ANN WARREN
JOSEPH (CTF) .... MARTIN LANDAU
JOSEPH (CTF) .... PAUL MERCURIO
JOSEPH WAMBAUGH'S ECHOES
    IN THE DARKNESS (MS) .... GARY COLE
JOSEPH WAMBAUGH'S ECHOES
    IN THE DARKNESS (MS) .... PETER BOYLE
JOSEPH WAMBAUGH'S ECHOES
    IN THE DARKNESS (MS) .... PETER COYOTE
JOSEPH WAMBAUGH'S ECHOES
    IN THE DARKNESS (MS) .... ROBERT LOGGIA
JOSEPH WAMBAUGH'S ECHOES
    IN THE DARKNESS (MS) ..... STOCKARD CHANNING
JOSEPHINE BAKER
    STORY, THE (CTF) .... CRAIG T. NELSON
JOSEPHINE BAKER
    STORY, THE (CTF) .... DAVID DUKES
JOSEPHINE BAKER
    STORY, THE (CTF) .... LOUIS GOSSETT JR.
JOSEPHINE BAKER
    STORY, THE (CTF) .... LYNN WHITFIELD
JOSEPHINE BAKER
    STORY, THE (CTF) .... RUBEN BLADES
JOSETTE .... DON AMECHE†
JOSH AND S.A.M. .... CHRIS PENN
JOSH AND S.A.M. .... JACOB TIERNEY
JOSH AND S.A.M. .... JOAN ALLEN
JOSH AND S.A.M. .... MARTHA PLIMPTON
JOSH AND S.A.M. .... NOAH FLEISS
JOSH AND S.A.M. .... RONALD GUTTMAN
JOSH AND S.A.M. .... STEPHEN TOBOLOWSKY
JOSHUA .... FRED WILLIAMSON
JOSHUA THEN AND NOW .... ALAN ARKIN
JOSHUA THEN AND NOW .... JAMES WOODS
JOSHUA THEN AND NOW .... MICHAEL SARRAZIN
JOSHUA THEN AND NOW .... PAUL HECHT
JOURNEY .... GENEVIEVE BUJOLD
JOURNEY BACK TO OZ (AF) .... DANNY THOMAS†
JOURNEY BACK TO OZ (AF) .... LIZA MINELLI
JOURNEY BACK TO OZ (AF) .... MILTON BERLE
JOURNEY BACK TO OZ (AF) .... PAUL LYNDE†
JOURNEY FROM
    DARKNESS (TF) .... DIRK BENEDICT
JOURNEY INTO FEAR .... DONALD PLEASENCE
JOURNEY INTO FEAR .... JOSEPH WISEMAN
JOURNEY INTO FEAR .... SAM WATERSTON
JOURNEY INTO FEAR .... SHELLEY WINTERS
JOURNEY INTO FEAR .... VINCENT PRICE†
JOURNEY OF AUGUST KING, THE .... JASON PATRIC
JOURNEY OF AUGUST KING, THE ..... LARRY DRAKE
JOURNEY OF AUGUST
    KING, THE .... THANDIE NEWTON
JOURNEY OF LOVE .... OMAR SHARIF
JOURNEY OF NATTY GANN, THE .... JOHN CUSAK
JOURNEY, THE .... ANNE JACKSON
JOURNEY, THE .... ANOUK AIMEE
JOURNEY, THE .... DEBORAH KERR
JOURNEY, THE .... E. G. MARSHALL
JOURNEY, THE .... JASON ROBARDS
JOURNEY, THE .... ROBERT MORLEY
JOURNEY, THE .... RON HOWARD
JOURNEY THROUGH
    ROSEBUD .... ROBERT FORSTER
JOURNEY TO SHILOH .... DON STROUD

JOURNEY TO SHILOH .... HARRISON FORD
JOURNEY TO SHILOH .... JAMES CAAN
JOURNEY TO SHILOH .... JAN-MICHAEL VINCENT
JOURNEY TO SHILOH .... MICHAEL SARRAZIN
JOURNEY TO THE CENTER
    OF THE EARTH .... ALAN NAPIER†
JOURNEY TO THE CENTER
    OF THE EARTH .... DIANE BAKER
JOURNEY TO THE CENTER
    OF THE EARTH .... PAT BOONE
JOURNEY TOGETHER .... DAVID TOMLINSON
JOVANKA E LE ALTRE .... HARRY GUARDINO
JOY HOUSE .... JANE FONDA
JOY IN THE MORNING ...... RICHARD CHAMBERLAIN
JOY LUCK CLUB, THE .... FRANCE NUYEN
JOY LUCK CLUB, THE .... KIEU CHINH
JOY LUCK CLUB, THE .... LAUREN TOM
JOY LUCK CLUB, THE .... LISA LU
JOY LUCK CLUB, THE .... MING-NA WEN
JOY LUCK CLUB, THE .... ROSALIND CHAO
JOY LUCK CLUB, THE .... TAMLYN TOMITA
JOY LUCK CLUB, THE .... TSAI CHIN
JOY LUCK CLUB, THE .... VIVIAN WU
JOY OF SEX .... CHRISTOPHER LLOYD
JOY OF SEX .... COLLEEN CAMP
JOY OF SEX .... DANTON STONE
JOY OF SEX .... ERNIE HUDSON
JOY OF SEX .... LISA LANGLOIS
JOYRIDE .... ANNE LOCKHART
JOYRIDE .... DESI ARNAZ JR.
JOYRIDE .... MELANIE GRIFFITH
JOYRIDE .... ROBERT CARRADINE
JOYSTICKS .... JOE DON BAKER
JUAREZ .... BETTE DAVIS†
JUAREZ ○ .... BRIAN AHERNE†
JUBAL .... CHARLES BRONSON
JUBAL .... ERNEST BORGNINE
JUBAL .... ROD STEIGER
JUDGE AND JAKE
    WYLER, THE (TF) .... DOUG McCLURE
JUDGE AND THE
    ASSASSIN, THE .... ISABELLE HUPPERT
JUDGE DREDD .... ARMAND ASSANTE
JUDGE DREDD .... BALTHAZAR GETTY
JUDGE DREDD .... DIANE LANE
JUDGE DREDD .... JOAN CHEN
JUDGE DREDD .... JOANNA MILES
JUDGE DREDD .... JURGEN PROCHNOW
JUDGE DREDD .... MAX VON SYDOW
JUDGE DREDD .... ROB SCHNEIDER
JUDGE DREDD .... SCOTT WILSON
JUDGE DREDD .... SYLVESTER STALLONE
JUDGE STEPS OUT, THE .... ANN SOTHERN
JUDGMENT AT NUREMBERG .... BURT LANCASTER†
JUDGMENT AT NUREMBERG .... HOWARD CAINE†
JUDGMENT AT
    NUREMBERG .... RICHARD WIDMARK
JUDGMENT AT NUREMBERG ..... WILLIAM SHATNER
JUDGMENT AT
    NUREMBERG ★ .... SPENCER TRACY†
JUDGMENT AT
    NUREMBERG ★★ .... MAXIMILIAN SCHELL
JUDGMENT AT NUREMBERG ○ ..... JUDY GARLAND†
JUDGMENT AT
    NUREMBERG ○ .... MONTGOMERY CLIFT†
JUDGMENT IN BERLIN .... SEAN PENN
JUDGMENT NIGHT .... CUBA GOODING JR.
JUDGMENT NIGHT .... DENIS LEARY
JUDGMENT NIGHT .... EMILIO ESTEVEZ
JUDGMENT NIGHT .... ERIK SCHRODY
JUDGMENT NIGHT .... JEREMY PIVEN
JUDGMENT NIGHT .... MICHAEL WISEMAN
JUDGMENT NIGHT .... PETER GREENE
JUDGMENT NIGHT .... STEPHEN DORFF
JUDITH .... SOPHIA LOREN
JUDITH KRANTZ'S TILL WE
    MEET AGAIN (MS) .... BARRY BOSTWICK
JUDITH KRANTZ'S TILL WE
    MEET AGAIN (MS) .... BRUCE BOXLEITNER
JUDITH KRANTZ'S TILL WE
    MEET AGAIN (MS) .... COURTENEY COX

This is not a list of every film ever made or every cast member, only those listed in this directory.

JUDITH KRANTZ'S TILL WE MEET AGAIN (MS) ... MICHAEL YORK
JUDITH OF BETHULIA ... LILLIAN GISH†
JUGGERNAUT ... ANTHONY HOPKINS
JUGGERNAUT ... CLIFTON JAMES
JUGGERNAUT ... DAVID HEMMINGS
JUGGERNAUT ... IAN HOLM
JUGGERNAUT ... JULIAN GLOVER
JUGGERNAUT ... OMAR SHARIF
JUGGERNAUT ... RICHARD HARRIS
JUGGERNAUT ... SHIRLEY KNIGHT
JUGGLER, THE ... KIRK DOUGLAS
JUICE ... OMAR EPPS
JUKE GIRL ... RONALD REAGAN
JULES VERNE'S ROCKET TO THE MOON ... BURL IVES
JULIA ... HAL HOLBROOK
JULIA ... JOHN GLOVER
JULIA ... MERYL STREEP
JULIA ... ROSEMARY MURPHY
JULIA ... SYLVIA KRISTEL
JULIA ★ ... JANE FONDA
JULIA ✪ ... MAXIMILIAN SCHELL
JULIA ✪✪ ... JASON ROBARDS
JULIA ✪✪ ... VANESSA REDGRAVE
JULIA AND JULIA ... GABRIEL BYRNE
JULIA AND JULIA ... KATHLEEN TURNER
JULIA AND JULIA ... STING
JULIA HAS TWO LOVERS ... DAPHNA KASTNER
JULIA HAS TWO LOVERS ... DAVID CHARLES
JULIA HAS TWO LOVERS ... DAVID DUCHOVNY
JULIA: INNOCENCE ONCE REMOVED ... SYLVIA KRISTEL
JULIA MISBEHAVES ... ELIZABETH TAYLOR
JULIA MISBEHAVES ... GREER GARSON
JULIE ... DORIS DAY
JULIE ... JACK KRUSCHEN
JULIE ... LOUIS JOURDAN
JULIUS CAESAR ... ALAN NAPIER†
JULIUS CAESAR ... CHARLTON HESTON
JULIUS CAESAR ... DEBORAH KERR
JULIUS CAESAR ... DIANA RIGG
JULIUS CAESAR ... GREER GARSON
JULIUS CAESAR ... JASON ROBARDS
JULIUS CAESAR ... JOHN GIELGUD
JULIUS CAESAR ... MICHAEL GOUGH
JULIUS CAESAR ... RICHARD CHAMBERLAIN
JULIUS CAESAR ... ROBERT VAUGHN
JULIUS CAESAR ★ ... MARLON BRANDO
JUMBO ... DEAN JAGGER†
JUMBO ... DORIS DAY
JUMBO ... MARTHA RAYE†
JUMPIN' JACK FLASH ... CAROL KANE
JUMPIN' JACK FLASH ... JAMES BELUSHI
JUMPIN' JACK FLASH ... JEROEN KRABBE
JUMPIN' JACK FLASH ... JON LOVITZ
JUMPIN' JACK FLASH ... JONATHAN PRYCE
JUMPIN' JACK FLASH ... PETER MICHAEL GOETZ
JUMPIN' JACK FLASH ... PHIL HARTMAN
JUMPIN' JACK FLASH ... ROSCOE LEE BROWNE
JUMPIN' JACK FLASH ... SARA BOTSFORD
JUMPIN' JACK FLASH ... STEPHEN COLLINS
JUMPIN' JACK FLASH ... WHOOPI GOLDBERG
JUMPING JACKS ... DEAN MARTIN
JUMPING JACKS ... JERRY LEWIS
JUNE BRIDE ... BETTE DAVIS†
JUNE BRIDE ... DEBBIE REYNOLDS
JUNE BRIDE ... MARY WICKES
JUNGLE BOOK, THE ... CARY ELWES
JUNGLE BOOK, THE ... JASON SCOTT LEE
JUNGLE BOOK, THE ... JOHN CLEESE
JUNGLE BOOK, THE ... LENA HEADEY
JUNGLE BOOK, THE ... SAM NEILL
JUNGLE BOOK, THE (AF) ... GEORGE SANDERS†
JUNGLE BOOK, THE (AF) ... PHIL HARRIS
JUNGLE BOOK, THE (AF) ... SEBASTIAN CABOT†
JUNGLE BOOK, THE (AF) ... STERLING HOLLOWAY†
JUNGLE FEVER ... ANNABELLA SCIORRA
JUNGLE FEVER ... ANTHONY QUINN
JUNGLE FEVER ... FRANK VINCENT
JUNGLE FEVER ... HALLE BERRY
JUNGLE FEVER ... JOHN TURTURRO
JUNGLE FEVER ... LONETTE McKEE
JUNGLE FEVER ... OSSIE DAVIS
JUNGLE FEVER ... RUBY DEE
JUNGLE FEVER ... SAMUEL L. JACKSON
JUNGLE FEVER ... SPIKE LEE
JUNGLE FEVER ... THERESA RANDLE
JUNGLE FEVER ... TYRA FERRELL
JUNGLE FEVER ... WESLEY SNIPES
JUNGLE FIGHTERS ... DAVID McCALLUM
JUNGLE FIGHTERS ... RICHARD HARRIS
JUNGLE HEAT ... JOHN AMOS
JUNGLE PATROL ... RICHARD JAECKEL
JUNGLE PRINCESS, THE ... DOROTHY LAMOUR
JUNGLE STREET ... DAVID McCALLUM
JUNGLE STREET GIRLS ... DAVID McCALLUM
JUNIOR ... ARNOLD SCHWARZENEGGER
JUNIOR ... DANNY DeVITO
JUNIOR ... EMMA THOMPSON
JUNIOR ... FRANK LANGELLA
JUNIOR ... PAMELA REED
JUNIOR BONNER ... BEN JOHNSON
JUNIOR BONNER ... BILL McKINNEY
JUNIOR BONNER ... JOE DON BAKER
JUPITER'S DARLING ... HOWARD KEEL
JURASSIC PARK ... ARIANA RICHARDS
JURASSIC PARK ... B. D. WONG
JURASSIC PARK ... BOB PECK
JURASSIC PARK ... JEFF GOLDBLUM
JURASSIC PARK ... JOSEPH MAZZELLO
JURASSIC PARK ... LAURA DERN
JURASSIC PARK ... MARTIN FERRERO
JURASSIC PARK ... RICHARD ATTENBOROUGH
JURASSIC PARK ... SAM NEILL
JURASSIC PARK ... SAMUEL L. JACKSON
JURASSIC PARK ... WAYNE KNIGHT
JURY DUTY ... BRIAN DOYLE MURRAY
JURY DUTY ... PAUL SHORE
JURY DUTY ... PAULY SHORE
JURY DUTY ... STANLEY TUCCI
JURY DUTY ... TIA CARRERE
JURY DUTY ... ABE VIGODA
JURY DUTY ... SHELLEY WINTERS
JURY DUTY: THE COMEDY (TF) ... BARBARA BOSSON
JURY DUTY: THE COMEDY (TF) ... JACKLYN ZEMAN
JURY OF ONE ... SOPHIA LOREN
JUST A GIGOLO ... DAVID BOWIE
JUST A GIGOLO ... DAVID HEMMINGS
JUST A GIGOLO ... KIM NOVAK
JUST A GIGOLO ... MARIA SCHELL
JUST A LITTLE INCONVENIENCE (TF) ... LEE MAJORS
JUST AN OLD SWEET SONG (TF) ... ROBERT HOOKS
JUST ANOTHER SECRET (CTF) ... ALAN HOWARD
JUST ANOTHER SECRET (CTF) ... BEAU BRIDGES
JUST BETWEEN FRIENDS ... CHRISTINE LAHTI
JUST BETWEEN FRIENDS ... JANE GREER
JUST BETWEEN FRIENDS ... MARY TYLER MOORE
JUST BETWEEN FRIENDS ... SALOME JENS
JUST BETWEEN FRIENDS ... SAM WATERSTON
JUST BETWEEN FRIENDS ... TED DANSON
JUST CAUSE ... BLAIR UNDERWOOD
JUST CAUSE ... DANIEL J. TRAVANTI
JUST CAUSE ... ED HARRIS
JUST CAUSE ... KATE CAPSHAW
JUST CAUSE ... LAURENCE FISHBURNE
JUST CAUSE ... SEAN CONNERY
JUST FOR YOU ... JANE WYMAN
JUST GOLD ... LILLIAN GISH†
JUST IMAGINE ... MAUREEN O'SULLIVAN
JUST ME AND YOU (TF) ... CHARLES GRODIN
JUST ME AND YOU (TF) ... JULIE BOYASSO†
JUST ME AND YOU (TF) ... LOUISE LASSER
JUST TELL ME WHAT YOU WANT ... ALAN KING
JUST TELL ME WHAT YOU WANT ... ALI MacGRAW
JUST TELL ME WHAT YOU WANT ... DINA MERRILL
JUST TELL ME WHAT YOU WANT ... PETER WELLER
JUST TELL ME WHAT YOU WANT ... TONY ROBERTS
JUST THE WAY YOU ARE ... ALEXANDRA PAUL
JUST THE WAY YOU ARE ... KRISTY McNICHOL
JUST THE WAY YOU ARE ... MICHAEL ONTKEAN
JUST THE WAY YOU ARE ... ROBERT CARRADINE
JUST THIS ONCE ... JANET LEIGH
JUST THIS ONCE ... RICHARD ANDERSON
JUST WILLIAM ... RODDY McDOWALL
JUST YOU AND ME, KID ... BROOKE SHIELDS
JUST YOU AND ME, KID ... BURL IVES
JUST YOU AND ME, KID ... GEORGE BURNS
JUST YOU AND ME, KID ... LEON AMES
JUST YOU AND ME, KID ... LORRAINE GARY
JUSTINE ... ANOUK AIMEE
JUSTINE ... CLIFF GORMAN
JUSTINE ... JOHN VERNON
JUSTINE ... MICHAEL YORK
JUSTINE ... ROBERT FORSTER
J'AI TUÉ RASPOUTINE ... GERALDINE CHAPLIN

K

K-9 ... COTTER SMITH
K-9 ... ED O'NEILL
K-9 ... JAMES BELUSHI
K-9 ... JAMES HANDY
K-9 ... KEVIN TIGHE
K-9 ... MEL HARRIS
KAFKA ... JEREMY IRONS
KALEIDOSCOPE ... SUSANNAH YORK
KALEIDOSCOPE ... WARREN BEATTY
KALEIDOSCOPE (TF) ... JACLYN SMITH
KALIFORNIA ... BRAD PITT
KALIFORNIA ... DAVID DUCHOVNY
KALIFORNIA ... JULIETTE LEWIS
KALIFORNIA ... MICHELLE FORBES
KAMIKAZE ... FRANCO NERO
KAMOURASKA ... GENEVIEVE BUJOLD
KAMOURASKA ... RICHARD JORDAN†
KANE AND ABEL (MS) ... JILL EIKENBERRY
KANE AND ABEL (MS) ... DAVID DUKES
KANE AND ABEL (MS) ... FRED GWYNNE†
KANE AND ABEL (MS) ... PETER STRAUSS
KANE AND ABEL (MS) ... RON SILVER
KANE AND ABEL (MS) ... SAM NEILL
KANE AND ABEL (MS) ... VERONICA HAMEL
KANGAROO ... JUDY DAVIS
KANGAROO ... MAUREEN O'HARA
KANSAN, THE ... JANE WYATT
KANSAS ... ANDREW McCARTHY
KANSAS ... ARLEN DEAN SNYDER
KANSAS ... KYRA SEDGWICK
KANSAS ... LESLIE HOPE
KANSAS ... MATT DILLON
KANSAS CITY BOMBER ... BILL McKINNEY
KANSAS CITY BOMBER ... KEVIN McCARTHY
KANSAS CITY BOMBER ... NORMAN ALDEN
KANSAS CITY BOMBER ... RAQUEL WELCH
KANSAS CITY BOMBER (TF) ... JODIE FOSTER
KANSAS RAIDERS ... TONY CURTIS
KAPO ... SUSAN STRASBERG
KARATE KID, THE ... ELISABETH SHUE
KARATE KID, THE ... MARTIN KOVE
KARATE KID, THE ... RALPH MACCHIO
KARATE KID, THE ✪ ... NORIYUKI "PAT" MORITA
KARATE KID PART II, THE ... DANNY KAMEKONA
KARATE KID PART II, THE ... MARTIN KOVE
KARATE KID PART II, THE ... NOBU McCARTHY
KARATE KID PART II, THE ... NORIYUKI "PAT" MORITA
KARATE KID PART II, THE ... RALPH MACCHIO
KARATE KID PART II, THE ... TAMLYN TOMITA
KARATE KID PART II, THE ... YUJI OKUMOTO
KARATE KID PART III, THE ... JONATHAN AVILDSEN
KARATE KID PART III, THE ... MARTIN KOVE
KARATE KID PART III, THE ... NORIYUKI "PAT" MORITA
KARATE KID PART III, THE ... RALPH MACCHIO
KARATE KID PART III, THE ... ROBYN LIVELY
KARATE KID PART III, THE ... SEAN KANAN
KARATE KID PART III, THE ... THOMAS IAN GRIFFITH
KAREN CARPENTER STORY, THE (TF) ... CYNTHIA GIBB

† after an actor's name denotes deceased.

KAREN CARPENTER
STORY, THE (TF) .... JAMES HONG
KAREN CARPENTER
STORY, THE (TF) .... LOUISE FLETCHER
KAREN CARPENTER
STORY, THE (TF) .... MITCHELL ANDERSON
KAREN CARPENTER
STORY, THE (TF) .... PETER MICHAEL GOETZ
KATE BLISS AND THE TICKERT
APE KID (TF) .... DAVID HUDDLESTON
KATE BLISS AND THE TICKERT
APE KID (TF) .... SUZANNE PLESHETTE
KATE McSHANE (TF) .... ANNE MEARA
KATE'S SECRET (TF) .... BEN MASTERS
KATE'S SECRET (TF) .... ED ASNER
KATE'S SECRET (TF) .... LIZ TORRES
KATE'S SECRET (TF) .... MEREDITH BAXTER
KATE'S
SECRET (TF) .... SHARI BELAFONTE-HARPER
KATE'S SECRET (TF) .... TRACY NELSON
KATHERINE (TF) .... ART CARNEY
KATHERINE (TF) .... SISSY SPACEK
KATIE .... HELEN SHAVER
KATIE .... JOHN C. McGINLEY
KATIE .... PETER BOYLE
KATIE .... WIL HORNEFF
KATIE: PORTRAIT OF
A CENTERFOLD (TF) .... KIM BASINGER
KAVIK THE WOLF DOG .... JOHN IRELAND
KAZAN .... LOIS MAXWELL
KEEGANS, THE (TF) .... JUDD HIRSCH
KEEP, THE .... GABRIEL BYRNE
KEEP 'EM FLYING .... MARTHA RAYE†
KEEP IT COOL .... CONRAD JANIS
KEEP THE CHANGE (CTF) ..... LOLITA DAVIDOVICH
KEEP THE CHANGE (CTF) ..... WILLIAM L. PETERSEN
KEEP YOUR POWDER DRY .... JUNE LOCKHART
KEEP YOUR POWDER DRY .... LANA TURNER
KEEPER OF THE CITY (CTF) .... ANTHONY LaPAGLIA
KEEPER OF THE FLAME .... KATHERINE HEPBURN
KEEPING TRACK .... MICHAEL SARRAZIN
KEETJE TIPPEL .... RUTGER HAUER
KELLY AND ME .... PIPER LAURIE
KELLY AND ME .... VAN JOHNSON
KELLY'S HEROES .... CARROLL O'CONNOR
KELLY'S HEROES .... CLINT EASTWOOD
KELLY'S HEROES .... DONALD SUTHERLAND
KELLY'S HEROES .... TELLY SAVALAS†
KENNEDY (MS) .... BLAIR BROWN
KENNEDY (MS) .... E. G. MARSHALL
KENNEDY (MS) .... GERALDINE FITZGERALD
KENNEDY (MS) .... JOHN SHEA
KENNEDY (MS) .... MARTIN SHEEN
KENNEDY (MS) .... VINCENT GARDENIA†
KENNEDYS OF MASSACHUSETTS,
THE (MS) .... ANNETTE O'TOOLE
KENNEDYS OF MASSACHUSETTS,
THE (MS) .... CAMPBELL SCOTT
KENNEDYS OF MASSACHUSETTS,
THE (MS) .... CHARLES DURNING
KENNEDYS OF MASSACHUSETTS,
THE (MS) .... WILLIAM L. PETERSEN
KENNELL .... JACK PALANCE
KENNER .... JIM BROWN
KENNY ROGERS AS THE
GAMBLER (TF) .... BRUCE BOXLEITNER
KENNY ROGERS AS THE
GAMBLER (TF) .... KENNY ROGERS
KENNY ROGERS AS THE
GAMBLER—THE ADVENTURE
CONTINUES (TF) .... BRUCE BOXLEITNER
KENNY ROGERS AS THE
GAMBLER—THE ADVENTURE
CONTINUES (TF) .... KENNY ROGERS
KENNY ROGERS AS THE
GAMBLER—THE ADVENTURE
CONTINUES (TF) .... LINDA EVANS
KENNY ROGERS AS THE
GAMBLER III: THE LEGEND
CONTINUES (TF) .... BRUCE BOXLEITNER

KENNY ROGERS AS THE
GAMBLER III: THE LEGEND
CONTINUES (TF) .... DEAN STOCKWELL
KENNY ROGERS AS THE
GAMBLER III: THE LEGEND
CONTINUES (TF) .... GEORGE KENNEDY
KENNY ROGERS AS THE
GAMBLER III: THE LEGEND
CONTINUES (TF) .... KENNY ROGERS
KENNY ROGERS AS THE
GAMBLER III: THE LEGEND
CONTINUES (TF) .... LINDA GRAY
KENNY ROGERS AS THE
GAMBLER III: THE LEGEND
CONTINUES (TF) .... MATT CLARK
KENT STATE (TF) .... DAVID MARSHALL GRANT
KENTUCKIAN, THE .... BURT LANCASTER†
KENTUCKIAN, THE .... WALTER MATTHAU
KENTUCKY ∞ .... WALTER BRENNAN†
KENTUCKY FRIED MOVIE .... JIM ABRAHAMS
KENTUCKY FRIED MOVIE, THE .... BILL BIXBY†
KENTUCKY FRIED
MOVIE, THE .... DONALD SUTHERLAND
KENTUCKY FRIED
MOVIE, THE .... MARCY GOLDMAN
KES .... BRIAN GLOVER
KETTLES ON OLD
MACDONALD'S FARM, THE .... CLAUDE AKINS†
KEY EXCHANGE .... BROOKE ADAMS
KEY EXCHANGE .... DANNY AIELLO
KEY EXCHANGE .... TONY ROBERTS
KEY LARGO .... LAUREN BACALL
KEY MAN .... ANGELA LANSBURY
KEY, THE .... MICHAEL CAINE
KEY, THE .... SOPHIA LOREN
KEY TO REBECCA, THE (MS) .... DAVID HEMMINGS
KEY TO THE CITY .... RAYMOND BURR†
KEY WEST CROSSING :........... ALBERT SALMI†
KEY WEST CROSSING .... RAYMOND ST. JACQUES
KEY WEST CROSSING .... ROBERT VAUGHN
KEY WEST CROSSING .... STUART WHITMAN
KEY WEST CROSSING .... WOODY STRODE
KEY WITNESS .... DENNIS HOPPER
KEYS OF THE
KINGDOM, THE .... RODDY McDOWALL
KEYS OF THE KINGDOM, THE ...... VINCENT PRICE†
KEYS OF THE
KINGDOM, THE ★ .... GREGORY PECK
KEYS TO FREEDOM .... DENHOLM ELLIOTT†
KEYS TO FREEDOM .... JANE SEYMOUR
KEYS TO FREEDOM .... OMAR SHARIF
KHARTOUM .... CHARLTON HESTON
KHYBER PATROL .... RAYMOND BURR†
KICKBOXER .... DENNIS ALEXIO
KICKBOXER .... DENNIS CHAN
KICKBOXER .... HASKELL V. ANDERSON
KICKBOXER .... JEAN-CLAUDE VAN DAMME
KICKBOXER .... ROCHELLE ASHANA
KICKBOXER .... TONG PO
KICKING THE MOON AROUND .... MAUREEN O'HARA
KICKS (TF) .... ANTHONY GEARY
KICKS (TF) .... IAN ABERCROMBIE
KICKS (TF) .... SHELLEY HACK
KID BLUE .... BEN JOHNSON
KID BLUE .... DENNIS HOPPER
KID BLUE .... PETER BOYLE
KID FOR TWO FARTHINGS, A .... LOU JACOBI
KID FROM BROOKLYN, THE .... LIONEL STANDER
KID FROM CLEVELAND, THE .... RUSS TAMBLYN
KID FROM KOKOMO, THE .... JANE WYMAN
KID FROM LEFT FIELD, THE .... ANNE BANCROFT
KID FROM LEFT FIELD, THE .... LLOYD BRIDGES
KID FROM LEFT FIELD, THE .... TAB HUNTER
KID FROM NOWHERE, THE (TF) .... BEAU BRIDGES
KID FROM NOWHERE, THE (TF) .... LORETTA SWIT
KID GALAHAD .... CHARLES BRONSON
KID GALAHAD .... EDWARD G. ROBINSON†
KID GALAHAD .... ELVIS PRESLEY†
KID GALAHAD .... MICHAEL DANTE
KID GALLAHAD .... BETTE DAVIS†
KID GLOVE KILLER .... AVA GARDNER†
KID MILLIONS .... ANN SOTHERN

KID MONK BARONI .... LEONARD NIMOY
KID NIGHTINGALE .... JANE WYMAN
KID RODELO .... DON MURRAY
KID RODELO .... JANET LEIGH
KID VENGEANCE .... JIM BROWN
KID VENGEANCE .... MATT CLARK
KID WITH THE 200 I.Q., THE (TF) .... DEAN BUTLER
KID WITH THE 200 I.Q., THE (TF) .... GARY COLEMAN
KID WITH THE BROKEN
HALO, THE (TF) .... GARY COLEMAN
KID WITH THE BROKEN
HALO, THE (TF) .... JUNE ALLYSON
KIDNAP OF MARY LOU, THE .... HENRY SILVA
KIDNAPPED .... CHARLES NAPIER
KIDNAPPED .... DAN O'HERLIHY
KIDNAPPED .... DAVID NAUGHTON
KIDNAPPED .... DONALD PLEASENCE
KIDNAPPED .... GORDAN JACKSON†
KIDNAPPED .... MICHAEL CAINE
KIDNAPPED .... MICHAEL SARRAZIN
KIDNAPPED .... PETER O'TOOLE
KIDNAPPED .... RODDY McDOWALL
KIDNAPPERS, THE .... BURGESS MEREDITH
KIDNAPPERS, THE .... THEODORE BIKEL
KIDNAPPING OF THE
PRESIDENT, THE .... AVA GARDNER†
KIDNAPPING OF THE
PRESIDENT, THE .... NICK MANCUSO
KIDNAPPING OF THE
PRESIDENT, THE .... WILLIAM SHATNER
KIDS ARE ALRIGHT, THE (FD) .... RINGO STARR
KIDS ARE ALRIGHT, THE (FD) .... STEVE MARTIN
KIDS ARE ALRIGHT, THE (FD) .... TOM SMOTHERS
KIDS DON'T TELL (TF) .... LEO ROSSI
KIDS LIKE THESE (TF) .... RICHARD CRENNA
KIDS LIKE THESE (TF) .... TYNE DALY
KIKA .... VICTORIA ABRIL
KILL A DRAGON .... JACK PALANCE
KILL CASTRO .... RAYMOND ST. JACQUES
KILL ME AGAIN .... JOANNE WHALLEY-KILMER
KILL ME AGAIN .... MICHAEL MADSEN
KILL ME AGAIN .... VAL KILMER
KILL ME IF YOU CAN (TF) .... ALAN ALDA
KILL ME IF YOU CAN (TF) .... BARNARD HUGHES
KILL ME IF YOU CAN (TF) .... BEN PIAZZA†
KILL ME IF YOU CAN (TF) .... JAMES KEACH
KILL ME IF YOU CAN (TF) .... JOHN HILLERMAN
KILL ME IF YOU CAN (TF) .... JOHN RANDOLPH
KILL ME IF YOU CAN (TF) .... TALIA SHIRE
KILL ME IF YOU CAN (TF) .... WALTER McGINN†
KILL ME TOMORROW .... LOIS MAXWELL
KILL OR BE KILLED .... LAWRENCE TIERNEY
KILLER BEES (TF) .... KATE JACKSON
KILLER BY NIGHT (TF) .... DIANE BAKER
KILLER BY
NIGHT (TF) .... MERCEDES McCAMBRIDGE
KILLER ELITE, THE .... ARTHUR HILL
KILLER ELITE, THE .... BO HOPKINS
KILLER ELITE, THE .... BURT YOUNG
KILLER ELITE, THE .... GIG YOUNG†
KILLER ELITE, THE .... JAMES CAAN
KILLER ELITE, THE .... MAKO
KILLER ELITE, THE .... ROBERT DUVALL
KILLER FISH .... KAREN BLACK
KILLER FISH .... LEE MAJORS
KILLER FISH .... MARGAUX HEMINGWAY
KILLER FISH .... MARISA BERENSON
KILLER FORCE .... MAUD ADAMS
KILLER FORCE .... PETER FONDA
KILLER FORCE .... TELLY SAVALAS†
KILLER FROM YUMA .... LYNN REDGRAVE
KILLER IN THE FAMILY, A (TF) .... ERIC STOLTZ
KILLER IN THE FAMILY, A (TF) .... JAMES SPADER
KILLER IN THE FAMILY, A (TF) .... ROBERT MITCHUM
KILLER IN THE MIRROR (TF) .... ANN JILLIAN
KILLER IN THE MIRROR (TF) .... JESSICA WALTER
KILLER IN THE MIRROR (TF) .... LEN CARIOU
KILLER INSIDE ME, THE .... DON STROUD
KILLER INSIDE ME, THE .... JOHN DEHNER†
KILLER INSIDE ME, THE .... ROYAL DANO
KILLER INSIDE ME, THE .... STACY KEACH
KILLER INSIDE ME, THE .... SUSAN TYRRELL

This is not a list of every film ever made or every cast member, only those listed in this directory.

Ki-Ki
FILM ACTORS GUIDE

KILLER INSTINCT (TF) ... LANE SMITH
KILLER INSTINCT (TF) ... MELISSA GILBERT
KILLER INSTINCT (TF) ... WOODY HARRELSON
KILLER IS ON THE PHONE, THE ... TELLY SAVALAS†
KILLER ON BOARD (TF) ... BEATRICE STRAIGHT
KILLER ON BOARD (TF) ... CLAUDE AKINS†
KILLER ON BOARD (TF) ... GEORGE HAMILTON
KILLER ON BOARD (TF) ... JANE SEYMOUR
KILLER ON BOARD (TF) ... PATTY DUKE
KILLER ON BOARD (TF) ... WILLIAM DANIELS
KILLER SHARK ... RODDY McDOWALL
KILLER TOMATOES GO TO FRANCE ... STEVE LUNDQUIST
KILLER WHO WOULDN'T DIE, THE (TF) ... CLU GULAGER
KILLER WHO WOULDN'T DIE, THE (TF) ... MARIETTE HARTLEY
KILLER WHO WOULDN'T DIE, THE (TF) ... ROBERT HOOKS
KILLER WHO WOULDN'T DIE, THE (TF) ... SAMANTHA EGGAR
KILLERS, THE ... ANGIE DICKINSON
KILLERS, THE ... AVA GARDNER†
KILLERS, THE ... BURT LANCASTER†
KILLERS, THE ... CLAUDE AKINS†
KILLERS, THE ... CLU GULAGER
KILLERS, THE ... JEFF COREY
KILLERS, THE ... RONALD REAGAN
KILLERS, THE ... SEYMOUR CASSEL
KILLERS THREE ... ROBERT WALKER JR.
KILLING, THE ... TIMOTHY CAREY
KILLING, THE ... VINCE EDWARDS
KILLING AFFAIR, A ... BILL SMITROVICH
KILLING AFFAIR, A ... ELIZABETH MONTGOMERY
KILLING AFFAIR, A ... JOHN GLOVER
KILLING AFFAIR, A ... KATHY BAKER
KILLING AFFAIR, A ... PETER WELLER
KILLING AFFAIR, A (TF) ... DEAN STOCKWELL
KILLING AFFAIR, A (TF) ... O. J. SIMPSON
KILLING AT HELL'S GATE (TF) ... ROBERT URICH
KILLING 'EM SOFTLY ... GEORGE SEGAL
KILLING FIELDS, THE ... CRAIG T. NELSON
KILLING FIELDS, THE ... JOHN MALKOVICH
KILLING FIELDS, THE ... JULIAN SANDS
KILLING FIELDS, THE ... SPALDING GRAY
KILLING FIELDS, THE ★ ... SAM WATERSTON
KILLING FIELDS, THE ∞ ... HAING S. NGOR
KILLING FLOOR, THE (TF) ... JOHN MAHONEY
KILLING GAME, THE ... CLAUDINE AUGER
KILLING HEAT ... KAREN BLACK
KILLING IN A SMALL TOWN (TF) ... BARBARA HERSHEY
KILLING IN A SMALL TOWN (TF) ... BRIAN DENNEHY
KILLING IN A SMALL TOWN (TF) ... LEE GARLINGTON
KILLING IN A SMALL TOWN (TF) ... RICHARD GILLILAND
KILLING KIND, THE ... ANN SOTHERN
KILLING KIND, THE ... CINDY WILLIAMS
KILLING KIND, THE ... JOHN SAVAGE
KILLING MACHINE ... MARGAUX HEMINGWAY
KILLING MACHINE ... WILLIE AAMES
KILLING OF A CHINESE BOOKIE, THE ... BEN GAZZARA
KILLING OF A CHINESE BOOKIE, THE ... SEYMOUR CASSEL
KILLING OF A CHINESE BOOKIE, THE ... TIMOTHY CAREY
KILLING OF RANDY WEBSTER, THE (TF) ... SEAN PENN
KILLING OF SISTER GEORGE, THE ... SUSANNAH YORK
KILLING STONE (TF) ... GIL GERARD
KILLING STONE (TF) ... J. D. CANNON
KILLING STREETS, THE ... LORENZO LAMAS
KILLING STREETS, THE ... MICHAEL PARE
KILLING TIME, THE ... BEAU BRIDGES
KILLING TIME, THE ... KIEFER SUTHERLAND
KILLING ZOE ... BRUCE RAMSAY
KILLING ZOE ... ERIC STOLTZ
KILLING ZOE ... GIAN-CARLO SCANDIUZZI
KILLJOY (TF) ... KIM BASINGER
KILLJOY (TF) ... STEPHEN MACHT
KILLPOINT ... RICHARD ROUNDTREE
KILROY WAS HERE ... JACKIE COOPER
KIM ... DEAN STOCKWELL
KIM (TF) ... BRYON BROWN
KIM (TF) ... PETER O'TOOLE
KIND HEARTS AND CORONETS ... ALEC GUINNESS
KIND LADY ... ANGELA LANSBURY
KIND OF LOVING, A ... ALAN BATES
KIND OF LOVING, A ... TONY BECKLEY†
KINDER MÜTTER UND EIN GENERAL ... MAXIMILIAN SCHELL
KINDERGARTEN ... KLAUS MARIA BRANDAUER
KINDERGARTEN ... SEREZHA GUSAK
KINDERGARTEN COP ... ARNOLD SCHWARZENEGGER
KINDERGARTEN COP ... CARROLL BAKER
KINDERGARTEN COP ... CATHY MORIARTY
KINDERGARTEN COP ... CHRISTIAN COUSINS
KINDERGARTEN COP ... JOSEPH COUSINS
KINDERGARTEN COP ... LINDA HUNT
KINDERGARTEN COP ... MIKO HUGHES
KINDERGARTEN COP ... PAMELA REED
KINDERGARTEN COP ... PENELOPE ANN MILLER
KINDERGARTEN COP ... RICHARD TYSON
KINDRED, THE ... ROD STEIGER
KING (MS) ... CICELY TYSON
KING (MS) ... CLIFF DE YOUNG
KING (MS) ... PAUL WINFIELD
KING: A FILMED RECORD...MONTGOMERY TO MEMPHIS (FD) ... BURT LANCASTER†
KING: A FILMED RECORD...MONTGOMERY TO MEMPHIS (FD) ... JAMES EARL JONES
KING: A FILMED RECORD...MONTGOMERY TO MEMPHIS (FD) ... JOANNE WOODWARD
KING: A FILMED RECORD...MONTGOMERY TO MEMPHIS (FD) ... PAUL NEWMAN
KING: A FILMED RECORD...MONTGOMERY TO MEMPHIS (FD) ... SIDNEY POITIER
KING AND COUNTRY ... TOM COURTENAY
KING AND FOUR QUEENS, THE ... ELEANOR PARKER
KING AND I, THE ... RITA MORENO
KING AND I, THE ★ ... DEBORAH KERR
KING AND I, THE ★★ ... YUL BRYNNER†
KING AND THE CHORUS GIRL, THE ... JANE WYMAN
KING CREOLE ... ELVIS PRESLEY†
KING CREOLE ... VAL AVERY
KING CREOLE ... WALTER MATTHAU
KING DAVID ... ALICE KRIGE
KING DAVID ... DENIS QUILLEY
KING DAVID ... EDWARD WOODWARD
KING DAVID ... RICHARD GERE
KING KONG ... CHARLES GRODIN
KING KONG ... CORBIN BERNSEN
KING KONG ... ED LAUTER
KING KONG ... JACK O'HALLORAN
KING KONG ... JEFF BRIDGES
KING KONG ... JESSICA LANGE
KING KONG ... JOE PISCOPO
KING KONG ... JOHN RANDOLPH
KING KONG ... JULIUS HARRIS
KING KONG ... RENE AUBERJONOIS
KING KONG LIVES ... JIMMIE RAY WEEKS
KING KONG LIVES ... JOHN ASHTON
KING KONG LIVES ... LINDA HAMILTON
KING KONG LIVES ... PETER MICHAEL GOETZ
KING LEAR ... BURGESS MEREDITH
KING LEAR ... IRENE WORTH
KING LEAR ... MOLLY RINGWALD
KING LEAR ... PAUL SCOFIELD
KING LEAR ... WOODY ALLEN
KING OF ALCATRAZ ... ANTHONY QUINN
KING OF BURLESQUE ... JANE WYMAN
KING OF CHINATOWN ... ANTHONY QUINN
KING OF COMEDY, THE ... JERRY LEWIS
KING OF COMEDY, THE ... LIZA MINELLI
KING OF COMEDY, THE ... ROBERT DE NIRO
KING OF COMEDY, THE ... SANDRA BERNHARD
KING OF COMEDY, THE ... TONY RANDALL
KING OF HEARTS ... ALAN BATES
KING OF HEARTS ... GENEVIEVE BUJOLD
KING OF KINGS ... HARRY GUARDINO
KING OF KINGS ... HURD HATFIELD
KING OF KINGS ... RIP TORN
KING OF KINGS ... ROYAL DANO
KING OF LOVE, THE (TF) ... NICK MANCUSO
KING OF MARVIN GARDENS, THE ... BRUCE DERN
KING OF MARVIN GARDENS, THE ... ELLEN BURSTYN
KING OF MARVIN GARDENS, THE ... JACK NICHOLSON
KING OF NEW YORK ... CHRISTOPHER WALKEN
KING OF NEW YORK ... DAVID CARUSO
KING OF NEW YORK ... GIANCARLO ESPOSITO
KING OF NEW YORK ... JANET JULIA
KING OF NEW YORK ... JOEY CHIN
KING OF NEW YORK ... LAURENCE FISHBURNE
KING OF NEW YORK ... PAUL CALDERON
KING OF NEW YORK ... STEVE BUSCEMI
KING OF NEW YORK ... THERESA RANDLE
KING OF NEW YORK ... VICTOR ARGO
KING OF NEW YORK ... WESLEY SNIPES
KING OF THE CITY ... TONY CURTIS
KING OF THE GYPSIES ... ANNETTE O'TOOLE
KING OF THE GYPSIES ... BROOKE SHIELDS
KING OF THE GYPSIES ... ERIC ROBERTS
KING OF THE GYPSIES ... JUDD HIRSCH
KING OF THE GYPSIES ... SHELLEY WINTERS
KING OF THE GYPSIES ... SUSAN SARANDON
KING OF THE HILL ... ELIZABETH McGOVERN
KING OF THE HILL ... JEROEN KRABBE
KING OF THE HILL ... JESSE BRADFORD
KING OF THE HILL ... KAREN ALLEN
KING OF THE HILL ... LISA EICHHORN
KING OF THE HILL ... SPALDING GRAY
KING OF THE MOUNTAIN ... DENNIS HOPPER
KING OF THE MOUNTAIN ... HARRY HAMLIN
KING OF THE MOUNTAIN ... JOSEPH BOTTOMS
KING OF THE ROARING 20'S—THE STORY OF ARNOLD ROTHSTEIN ... DAN O'HERLIHY
KING RALPH ... CAMILLE CODURI
KING RALPH ... JOELY RICHARDSON
KING RALPH ... JOHN GOODMAN
KING RALPH ... JOHN HURT
KING RALPH ... JULIAN GLOVER
KING RALPH ... LESLIE PHILLIPS
KING RALPH ... NIALL O'BRIEN
KING RALPH ... PETER O'TOOLE
KING RALPH ... RICHARD GRIFFITHS
KING RAT ... DENHOLM ELLIOTT†
KING RAT ... GEOFFREY BAYLDON
KING RAT ... GEORGE SEGAL
KING RAT ... PATRICK O'NEAL†
KING RAT ... TOM COURTENAY
KING SOLOMON'S MINES ... DEBORAH KERR
KING SOLOMON'S MINES ... RICHARD CHAMBERLAIN
KING SOLOMON'S MINES ... SHARON STONE
KING SOLOMON'S TREASURE ... BRITT EKLAND
KING SOLOMON'S TREASURE ... DAVID McCALLUM
KING SOLOMON'S TREASURE ... PATRICK MacNEE
KING'S THIEF, THE ... DAVID NIVEN†
KINGDOM OF THE SPIDERS ... WILLIAM SHATNER
KINGDOM OF THE SPIDERS ... WOODY STRODE
KINGFISH CAPER, THE ... DAVID McCALLUM
KINGFISH CAPER, THE ... HAYLEY MILLS
KINGS AND DESPERATE MEN ... ALEXIS KANNER
KINGS GO FORTH ... FRANK SINATRA
KINGS GO FORTH ... TONY CURTIS
KINGS OF THE SUN ... SHIRLEY ANNE FIELD
KINGS ROW ... DAME JUDITH ANDERSON†
KINGS ROW ... RONALD REAGAN
KING'S PIRATE, THE ... DOUG McCLURE
KING'S THIEF, THE ... ROGER MOORE
KINJITE (FORBIDDEN SUBJECTS) ... ALEX HYDE-WHITE
KINJITE (FORBIDDEN SUBJECTS) ... AMY HATHAWAY
KINJITE (FORBIDDEN SUBJECTS) ... BILL McKINNEY
KINJITE (FORBIDDEN SUBJECTS) ... CHARLES BRONSON
KINJITE (FORBIDDEN SUBJECTS) ... JAMES PAX

INDEX OF FILM TITLES

† after an actor's name denotes deceased.

KINJITE (FORBIDDEN SUBJECTS)	JUAN FERNANDEZ
KINJITE (FORBIDDEN SUBJECTS)	KUMIKO HAYAKAWA
KINJITE (FORBIDDEN SUBJECTS)	PEGGY LIPTON
KINJITE (FORBIDDEN SUBJECTS)	PERRY LOPEZ
KINJITE (FORBIDDEN SUBJECTS)	SY RICHARDSON
KISMET	HOWARD KEEL
KISMET	YVONNE DE CARLO
KISS BEFORE DYING, A	DIANE LADD
KISS BEFORE DYING, A	JOANNE WOODWARD
KISS BEFORE DYING, A	MATT DILLON
KISS BEFORE DYING, A	MAX von SYDOW
KISS BEFORE DYING, A	ROBERT WAGNER
KISS BEFORE DYING, A	SEAN YOUNG
KISS FOR CORLISS, A	DAVID NIVEN†
KISS IN THE DARK, A	DAVID NIVEN†
KISS IN THE DARK, A	JANE WYMAN
KISS ME A KILLER	GUY BOYD
KISS ME A KILLER	JULIE CARMEN
KISS ME DEADLY	CLORIS LEACHMAN
KISS ME DEADLY	WESLEY ADDY
KISS ME GOODBYE	JAMES CAAN
KISS ME GOODBYE	JEFF BRIDGES
KISS ME GOODBYE	PAUL DOOLEY
KISS ME GOODBYE	SALLY FIELD
KISS ME KATE	HOWARD KEEL
KISS ME KATE	JAMES WHITMORE
KISS ME, KILL ME (TF)	BRUCE BOXLEITNER
KISS ME, KILL ME (TF)	CLAUDE AKINS†
KISS ME, KILL ME (TF)	DABNEY COLEMAN
KISS ME, KILL ME (TF)	ROBERT VAUGHN
KISS ME, KILL ME (TF)	STELLA STEVENS
KISS ME, STUPID	DEAN MARTIN
KISS ME STUPID	HENRY GIBSON
KISS ME STUPID	JOHN FIELDLER
KISS ME, STUPID	KIM NOVAK
KISS ME, STUPID	RAY WALSTON
KISS OF DEATH	DAVID CARUSO
KISS OF DEATH	HELEN HUNT
KISS OF DEATH	KARL MALDEN
KISS OF DEATH	KATHRYN ERBE
KISS OF DEATH	MICHAEL RAPAPORT
KISS OF DEATH	NICOLAS CAGE
KISS OF DEATH	SAMUEL L. JACKSON
KISS OF DEATH	STANLEY TUCCI
KISS OF DEATH ○	RICHARD WIDMARK
KISS OF FIRE	JACK PALANCE
KISS OF THE SPIDER WOMAN	RAUL JULIA†
KISS OF THE SPIDER WOMAN	SONIA BRAGA
KISS OF THE SPIDER WOMAN ★★	WILLIAM HURT
KISS SHOT (TF)	DENNIS FRANZ
KISS SHOT (TF)	DORIAN HAREWOOD
KISS SHOT (TF)	WHOOPI GOLDBERG
KISS THE BLOOD OFF MY HANDS	BURT LANCASTER†
KISS THE BOYS GOODBYE	DON AMECHE†
KISS THE BRIDE GOODBYE	JEAN SIMMONS
KISS THEM FOR ME	RAY WALSTON
KISSES FOR BREAKFAST	JANE WYATT
KISSES FOR MY PRESIDENT	ELI WALLACH
KISSES FOR MY PRESIDENT	POLLY BERGEN
KISSIN' COUSINS	ELVIS PRESLEY†
KISSING BANDIT, THE	CYD CHARISSE
KISSING BANDIT, THE	FRANK SINATRA
KISSING BANDIT, THE	RICARDO MONTALBAN
KISSING PLACE, THE (CTF)	DAVID OGDEN STIERS
KISSING PLACE, THE (CTF)	MEREDITH BAXTER
KITTEN WITH A WHIP	ANN-MARGRET
KITTEN WITH A WHIP	JOHN FORSYTHE
KLANSMAN, THE	LINDA EVANS
KLANSMAN, THE	O. J. SIMPSON
KLONDIKE FEVER	ANGIE DICKINSON
KLONDIKE FEVER	ROD STEIGER
KLUTE	CHARLES CIOFFI
KLUTE	DONALD SUTHERLAND
KLUTE	JEAN STAPLETON
KLUTE	ROSALIND CASH
KLUTE	ROY SCHEIDER
KLUTE ★★	JANE FONDA

KNACK...AND HOW TO GET IT, THE	CHARLOTTE RAMPLING
KNACK...AND HOW TO GET IT, THE	JACQUELINE BISSET
KNACK...AND HOW TO GET IT, THE	MARLO THOMAS
KNACK...AND HOW TO GET IT, THE	MICHAEL CRAWFORD
KNICKERBOCKER HOLIDAY	SHELLEY WINTERS
KNIGHT MOVES	CHRISTOPHER LAMBERT
KNIGHT MOVES	DIANE LANE
KNIGHT RIDER (TF)	DAVID HASSELHOFF
KNIGHTRIDERS	ED HARRIS
KNIGHTS OF THE ROUND TABLE	AVA GARDNER†
KNIGHTS OF THE ROUND TABLE	MEL FERRER
KNOCK ON ANY DOOR	ROBERT DAVIS†
KNOCK ON WOOD	MAE ZETTERLING†
KNOCKOUT	ANTHONY QUINN
KNOTS LANDING (TVS)	AVA GARDNER†
KNUTE ROCKNE, ALL AMERICAN	RONALD REAGAN
KOJAK AND THE MARCUS-NELSON MURDERS (TF)	NED BEATTY
KOJAK: THE BELARUS FILE (TF)	TELLY SAVALAS†
KOJAK: THE PRICE OF JUSTICE (TF)	KATE NELLIGAN
KOJAK: THE PRICE OF JUSTICE (TF)	PAT HINGLE
KOJAK: THE PRICE OF JUSTICE (TF)	TELLY SAVALAS†
KONA COAST	VERA MILES
KONGA	MICHAEL GOUGH
KORT AR SOMMAREN/PAN	LIV ULLMANN
KOTCH ★	WALTER MATTHAU
KRAKATOA, EAST OF JAVA	BRIAN KEITH
KRAKATOA EAST OF JAVA	DIANE BAKER
KRAKATOA EAST OF JAVA	MAXIMILIAN SCHELL
KRAMER VS. KRAMER	GEORGE COE
KRAMER VS. KRAMER	HOWARD DUFF†
KRAMER VS. KRAMER	JoBETH WILLIAMS
KRAMER VS. KRAMER ★★	DUSTIN HOFFMAN
KRAMER VS. KRAMER ○	JANE ALEXANDER
KRAMER VS. KRAMER ○	JUSTIN HENRY
KRAMER VS. KRAMER ○○	MERYL STREEP
KRAYS, THE	BILLIE WHITELAW
KRAYS, THE	GARY KEMP
KREMLIN LETTER, THE	BIBI ANDERSSON
KREMLIN LETTER, THE	DEAN JAGGER†
KREMLIN LETTER, THE	LILA KEDROVA
KREMLIN LETTER, THE	PATRICK O'NEAL†
KRULL	ALUN ARMSTRONG
KRULL	FRANCESCA ANNIS
KRULL	FREDDIE JONES
KRULL	LIAM NEESON
KRULL	LYSETTE ANTHONY
KRUSH GROOVE	BLAIR UNDERWOOD
KUFFS	BRUCE BOXLEITNER
KUFFS	CHRISTIAN SLATER
KUFFS	MILLA JOVOICH
KUFFS	TONY GOLDWYN

L

L.A. LAW (TF)	CORBIN BERNSEN
L.A. LAW (TF)	HARRY HAMLIN
L.A. LAW (TF)	JILL EIKENBERRY
L.A. LAW (TF)	RICHARD DYSART
L.A. LAW (TF)	SUSAN DEY
L.A. STORY	CHEVY CHASE
L.A. STORY	KEVIN POLLAK
L.A. STORY	LARRY MILLER
L.A. STORY	MARILU HENNER
L.A. STORY	MARY KOHNERT
L.A. STORY	PATRICK STEWART
L.A. STORY	PETER VOGT
L.A. STORY	RICHARD E. GRANT
L.A. STORY	RICK MORANIS
L.A. STORY	SAM McMURRAY
L.A. STORY	SARAH JESSICA PARKER
L.A. STORY	SCOTT BAKULA

L.A. STORY	STEVE MARTIN
L.A. STORY	SUSAN FORRISTAL
L.A. STORY	VICTORIA TENNANT
L.A. STORY	WOODY HARRELSON
L'AFFAIRE CONCORDE	JAMES FRANCISCUS†
L-SHAPED ROOM, THE ★	LESLIE CARON
L-SHAPED ROOM, THE	BROCK PETERS
LA BALANCE	CHRISTOPHE MALAVOY
LA BALANCE	JEAN-PAUL CONNART
LA BALANCE	MAURICE RONET
LA BALANCE	NATHALIE BAYE
LA BALANCE	PHILIPPE LEOTARD
LA BALANCE	RICHARD BERRY
LA BAMBA	BRIAN SETZER
LA BAMBA	DANIELLE von ZERNECK
LA BAMBA	ELIZABETH PENA
LA BAMBA	ESAI MORALES
LA BAMBA	JOE PANTOLIANO
LA BAMBA	LOU DIAMOND PHILLIPS
LA BAMBA	MARSHALL CRENSHAW
LA BAMBA	RICK DEES
LA BAMBA	ROSANA DE SOTO
LA BANDA DE JAIDER	GERALDINE CHAPLIN
LA BANDA J.&S.—CRONACA CRIMINALE DEL WEST	TELLY SAVALAS†
LA BATAILLE DE SAN SEBASTIAN	ANTHONY QUINN
LA BATAILLE DE SAN SEBASTIAN	CHARLES BRONSON
LA BATTAGLIA D'INGHILTERRA	VAN JOHNSON
LA BELLA MUGNAIA	MARCELLO MASTROIANNI
LA BELLA MUGNAIA	SOPHIA LOREN
LA BELLE AVENTURE	LOUIS JOURDAN
LA BOHEME	LILLIAN GISH†
LA CADUTA DEGLI DEI	CHARLOTTE RAMPLING
LA CADUTA DEGLI DEI/ GOTTERDAMERUNG	HELMUT BERGER
LA CAGE AUX FOLLES 3: THE WEDDING	MICHEL GALABRU
LA CAGE AUX FOLLES 3: THE WEDDING	STEPHANE AUDRAN
LA CAGE AUX FOLLES 3: THE WEDDING	UGO TOGNAZZI
LA CAGNA	CATHERINE DENEUVE
LA CASA SIN FRONTERAS	GERALDINE CHAPLIN
LA CASTIGLIONE	YVONNE DE CARLO
LA CATENA DELL'ODIO	URSULA ANDRESS
LA CHAMADE	CATHERINE DENEUVE
LA CHASSE A L'HOMME	CATHERINE DENEUVE
LA CITTA PRIGIONIERA	BEN GAZZARA
LA CITTA PRIGIONIERA	MARTIN BALSAM
LA COULEUR DE TEMPS	ISABELLE HUPPERT
LA CURÉE	JANE FONDA
LA DAHLIA SCARLATTA	SHELLEY WINTERS
LA DÉCADE PRODIGIEUSE	ANTHONY PERKINS†
LA DECIMA VITTIMA	MARCELLO MASTROIANNI
LA DECIMA VITTIMA	URSULA ANDRESS
LA DENTELLIERE	ISABELLE HUPPERT
LA DERNIERE FEMME	GERARD DEPARDIEU
LA DIGA SUL PACIFICO	NEHEMIAH PERSOFF
LA DOLCE VITA	ANOUK AIMEE
LA DOLCE VITA	MARCELLO MASTROIANNI
LA DONNA DEL FIUME	SOPHIA LOREN
LA DONNA NEL MONDO (FD)	PETER USTINOV
LA FAMIGLIA	JO CHAMPA
LA FAVORITA	SOPHIA LOREN
LA FEMME ET LA PANTIN	LILA KEDROVA
LA FORTUNA DI ESSERE DONNA	MARCELLO MASTROIANNI
LA FORTUNA DI ESSERE DONNA	SOPHIA LOREN
LA FRECCIA D'ORO	TAB HUNTER
LA FUGA	ANOUK AIMEE
LA FUGA	RICARDO MONTALBAN
LA GRAN FIESTA	RAUL JULIA†
LA GRANDE BOURGEOISE	CATHERINE DENEUVE
LA GUERRA CONTINUA	JACK PALANCE
LA GUERRE EST FINIE	GENEVIEVE BUJOLD
LA HORA DE LA VERDAD	RICARDO MONTALBAN
LA LEGGENDA DEL SANTO BEVITORE	RUTGER HAUER
LA LOI/IL LEGGE	MARCELLO MASTROIANNI

This is not a list of every film ever made or every cast member, only those listed in this directory.

La-La
FILM ACTORS GUIDE

LA MADRIGUERA .... GERALDINE CHAPLIN
LA MAISON SOUS LA MER .... ANOUK AIMEE
LA MAISON SOUS LES ARBRES ..... FAYE DUNAWAY
LA MAISON SOUS LES ARBRES .... FRANK LANGELLA
LA MAISON SOUS LES ARBRES .... MAURICE RONET
LA MALA ORDINA .... HENRY SILVA
LA MALA ORDINA .... WOODY STRODE
LA MARGE .... SYLVIA KRISTEL
LA MARIÉE EST TROP BELLE .... LOUIS JOURDAN
LA MOGLIE VERGINE .... CARROLL BAKER
LA MUJER DE LA TIERRA CALIENTE .... STUART WHITMAN
LA NOTTE .... MARCELLO MASTROIANNI
LA NUIT AMERICAINE .... FRANCOIS TRUFFAUT†
LA NUIT AMERICAINE .... JACQUELINE BISSET
LA NUIT AMERICAINE .... JEAN-PIERRE AUMONT
LA NUIT AMERICAINE .... NATHALIE BAYE
LA NUIT DE VARENNES .... HARVEY KEITEL
LA NUIT TOUS LES CHATS SONT GRIS .... GERARD DEPARDIEU
LA PETITE FILLE EN VELOURS BLEU .... DENHOLM ELLIOTT†
LA POUDRE D'ESCAMPETTE .... MICHAEL YORK
LA PROMESSE .... JACQUELINE BISSET
LA PROVINCIALE .... NATHALIE BAYE
LA RAGAZZA E IL GENERALE .... ROD STEIGER
LA RAGAZZA IN PIGIAMA GIALLO .... MEL FERRER
LA RAISON DU PLUS FOU .... MARTHE KELLER
LA RONDE .... JANE FONDA
LA ROUTE AU SOLEIL .... MICHAEL YORK
LA ROUTE DE SALINA .... ROBERT WALKER JR.
LA SABINA .... SIMON WARD
LA SCOUMOUNE .... GERARD DEPARDIEU
LA SIRENE DE MISSISSIPPI .... CATHERINE DENEUVE
LA SPINA DORSALE DEL DIAVOLO .... IAN BANNEN
LA SPINA DORSALE DEL DIAVOLO .... PATRICK WAYNE
LA SPINA DORSALE DEL DIAVOLO .... RICARDO MONTALBAN
LA SPINA DORSALE DEL DIAVOLO .... WOODY STRODE
LA STATUA .... ROBERT VAUGHN
LA STRADA .... ANTHONY QUINN
LA TETE CONTRE LES MURS .... ANOUK AIMEE
LA TRATTA DELLA BIANCHE .... SOPHIA LOREN
LA TRUITE .... ISABELLE HUPPERT
LA TUA DONNA .... PATRICIA NEAL
LA VACANZA .... FRANCO NERO
LA VACANZA .... VANESSA REDGRAVE
LA VIE DE BOHEME .... LOUIS JOURDAN
LA VIE DE CHATEAU .... CATHERINE DENEUVE
LA VIE PRIVÉE .... MARCELLO MASTROIANNI
LA VIEILLE FILLE .... MARTHE KELLER
LABYRINTH .... CHRISTOPHER MALCOLM
LABYRINTH .... DAVID BOWIE
LABYRINTH .... JENNIFER CONNELLY
LABYRINTH .... NATALIE FINLAND
LABYRINTH .... SHELLEY THOMPSON
LABYRINTH .... TOBY FROUD
LACE (MS) .... ANGELA LANSBURY
LACE (MS) .... ANTHONY HIGGINS
LACE (MS) .... ARIELLE DOMBASLE
LACE (MS) .... BESS ARMSTRONG
LACE (MS) .... BROOKE ADAMS
LACE (MS) .... HONOR BLACKMAN
LACE (MS) .... LEIGH LAWSON
LACE (MS) .... PHOEBE CATES
LACE II (MS) .... ANTHONY HIGGINS
LACE II (MS) .... ARIELLE DOMBASLE
LACE II (MS) .... BROOKE ADAMS
LACE II (MS) .... CHRISTOPHER CAZENOVE
LACE II (MS) .... DEBORAH RAFFIN
LACE II (MS) .... FRANCOIS GUETARY
LACE II (MS) .... JAMES READ
LACE II (MS) .... MICHAEL GOUGH
LACE II (MS) .... PATRICK RYECART
LACE II (MS) .... PHOEBE CATES
LACEMAKER, THE .... ISABELLE HUPPERT
LACY AND THE MISSISSIPPI QUEEN (TF) .... JAMES KEACH
LAD, THE .... GERALDINE FITZGERALD
LAD: A DOG .... CARROLL O'CONNOR
LADIES AND GENTLEMEN, THE FABULOUS STAINS .... CHRISTINE LAHTI
LADIES AND GENTLEMEN, THE FABULOUS STAINS .... DIANE LANE
LADIES AND GENTLEMEN, THE FABULOUS STAINS .... LAURA DERN
LADIES CLUB, THE .... BRUCE DAVISON
LADIES CLUB, THE .... DIANA SCARWID
LADIES COURAGEOUS ..... GERALDINE FITZGERALD
LADIES' DAY .... EDDIE ALBERT
LADIES IN LOVE .... DON AMECHE†
LADIES' MAN, THE .... JERRY LEWIS
LADIES MAN, THE .... KATHLEEN FREEMAN
LADIES OF LEISURE .... BARBARA STANWYCK†
LADIES OF THE BIG HOUSE .... SYLVIA SIDNEY
LADIES OF THE CHORUS, THE .... MARILYN MONROE†
LADIES OF WASHINGTON .... ANTHONY QUINN
LADIES THEY TALK ABOUT .... BARBARA STANWYCK†
LADIES WHO DO .... RON MOODY
LADY AND THE HIGHWAYMAN, THE (TF) .... CHRISTOPHER CAZENOVE
LADY AND THE HIGHWAYMAN, THE (TF) .... CLAIRE BLOOM
LADY AND THE HIGHWAYMAN, THE (TF) .... EMMA SAMMS
LADY AND THE HIGHWAYMAN, THE (TF) .... MICHAEL YORK
LADY AND THE MOUSE, THE .... LILLIAN GISH†
LADY AND THE OUTLAW, THE .... DESI ARNAZ JR.
LADY AND THE OUTLAW, THE .... GREGORY PECK
LADY AND THE OUTLAW, THE .... JACK WARDEN
LADY BE GOOD .... ANN SOTHERN
LADY BEWARE .... DIANE LANE
LADY BEWARE .... MICHAEL WOODS
LADY BLUE (TF) .... DANNY AIELLO
LADY BLUE (TF) .... JIM BROWN
LADY BODYGUARD .... EDDIE ALBERT
LADY CAROLINE LAMB ..... RICHARD CHAMBERLAIN
LADY CAROLINE LAMB .... SARAH MILES
LADY CAROLINE LAMB .... TIMOTHY DALTON
LADY CHATTERLEY .... SEAN BEAN
LADY CHATTERLY'S LOVER .... NICHOLAS CLAY
LADY COCOA .... MILLIE PERKINS
LADY EVE, THE .... BARBARA STANWYCK†
LADY EVE, THE .... HENRY FONDA†
LADY FOR A DAY ★ .... MAY ROBSON†
LADY FORGETS, THE (TF) .... ANDREW ROBINSON
LADY FORGETS, THE (TF) .... DONNA MILLS
LADY FORGETS, THE (TF) .... GREG EVIGAN
LADY FORGETS, THE (TF) .... ROY DOTRICE
LADY FROM YESTERDAY, THE (TF) .... BARRIE YOUNGFELLOW
LADY FROM YESTERDAY, THE (TF) .... BONNIE BEDELIA
LADY FROM YESTERDAY, THE (TF) ...... PAT HINGLE
LADY FROM YESTERDAY, THE (TF) .... WAYNE ROGERS
LADY GAMBLES, THE .... BARBARA STANWYCK†
LADY GAMBLES, THE .... TONY CURTIS
LADY GODIVA .... CLINT EASTWOOD
LADY GODIVA .... MAUREEN O'HARA
LADY ICE .... DONALD SUTHERLAND
LADY ICE .... ROBERT DUVALL
LADY IN A CAGE .... ANN SOTHERN
LADY IN A CAGE .... JAMES CAAN
LADY IN A CAGE .... JEFF COREY
LADY IN A CAGE .... OLIVIA DE HAVILLAND
LADY IN A CAR WITH GLASSES AND A GUN, THE .... SAMANTHA EGGAR
LADY IN A CORNER (TF) .... BRIAN KEITH
LADY IN A CORNER (TF) ...... ROSCOE LEE BROWNE
LADY IN A JAM .... RALPH BELLAMY†
LADY IN CEMENT .... FRANK SINATRA
LADY IN CEMENT .... RAQUEL WELCH
LADY IN RED, THE .... LOUISE FLETCHER
LADY IN RED, THE .... PAMELA SUE MARTIN
LADY IN WHITE .... ALEX ROCCO
LADY IN WHITE .... ANGELO BERTOLINI
LADY IN WHITE .... JARED RUSHTON
LADY IN WHITE .... JASON PRESSON
LADY IN WHITE .... KATHERINE HELMOND
LADY IN WHITE .... LEN CARIOU
LADY IN WHITE .... LUKAS HAAS
LADY IN WHITE .... RENATA VANNI
LADY JANE .... CARY ELWES
LADY JANE .... HELENA BONHAM CARTER
LADY JANE .... JILL BENNETT
LADY JANE .... JOSS ACKLAND
LADY JANE .... PATRICK STEWART
LADY KILLER OF ROME, THE .... MARCELLO MASTROIANNI
LADY L .... PAUL NEWMAN
LADY L .... PETER USTINOV
LADY L .... SOPHIA LOREN
LADY LIBERTY .... BASIL HOFFMAN
LADY LIBERTY .... DANNY DEVITO
LADY LIBERTY .... DAVID DOYLE
LADY LIBERTY .... EDWRAD HERRMANN
LADY LIBERTY .... SOPHIA LOREN
LADY LIBERTY .... SUSAN SARANDON
LADY LIBERTY .... WILLIAM DEVANE
LADY LUCK .... BARBARA HALE
LADY MOBSTER (TF) .... MICHAEL NADER
LADY MOBSTER (TF) .... THOMAS BRAY
LADY OF BURLESQUE .... BARBARA STANWYCK†
LADY OF THE HOUSE .... SUSAN TYRRELL
LADY OF THE HOUSE (TF) .... ARMAND ASSANTE
LADY OF THE HOUSE (TF) .... DYAN CANNON
LADY ON A TRAIN .... RALPH BELLAMY†
LADY SAYS NO, THE .... DAVID NIVEN†
LADY SAYS NO, THE .... HENRY JONES
LADY SAYS NO, THE .... JOAN CAULFIELD†
LADY SCARFACE .... DAME JUDITH ANDERSON†
LADY SINGS THE BLUES .... BILLY DEE WILLIAMS
LADY SINGS THE BLUES .... RICHARD PRYOR
LADY SINGS THE BLUES ★ .... DIANA ROSS
LADY TAKES A FLYER, THE .... LANA TURNER
LADY TAKES A SAILOR, THE .... JANE WYMAN
LADY VANISHES, THE .... ANGELA LANSBURY
LADY VANISHES, THE .... ARTHUR LOWE†
LADY VANISHES, THE .... CYBILL SHEPHERD
LADY VANISHES, THE .... ELLIOTT GOULD
LADY WITH A LAMP, THE .... GORDAN JACKSON†
LADY WITH RED HAIR, THE .... ALEXIS SMITH†
LADY WITHOUT PASSPORT, A .... STEVEN HILL
LADYBUG, LADYBUG .... ESTELLE PARSONS
LADYBUG, LADYBUG .... NANCY MARCHAND
LADYBUG, LADYBUG .... WILLIAM DANIELS
LADYBUGS .... ILENE GRAF
LADYBUGS .... JACKEE
LADYBUGS .... JONATHAN BRANDIS
LADYBUGS .... RODNEY DANGERFIELD
LADYBUGS .... VINESSA SHAW
LADYFINGERS .... JACK PALANCE
LADYHAWKE .... MATHHEW BRODERICK
LADYHAWKE .... MICHELLE PFEIFFER
LADYHAWKE .... RUTGER HAUER
LADYKILLERS (TF) .... LESLEY-ANNE DOWN
LADYKILLERS (TF) .... MARILU HENNER
LADYKILLERS (TF) .... SUSAN BLAKELY
LADYKILLERS, THE .... ALEC GUINNESS
LADY'S CHATTERLEY'S LOVER ...... SYLVIA KRISTEL
LAFAYETTE ESCADRILLE .... CLINT EASTWOOD
LAFAYETTE ESCADRILLE .... TAB HUNTER
LAGUNA HEAT (CTF) .... HARRY HAMLIN
LAGUNA HEAT (CTF) .... RIP TORN
LAIR OF THE WHITE WORM, THE .... AMANDA DONOHOE
LAKER GIRLS, THE (TF) .... PAUL JOHANSSON
LAKER GIRLS, THE (TF) .... TINA YOTHERS
LAMB .... IAN BANNEN
LAMB .... LIAM NEESON
LAMBADA ...... ADOLPHO "SHABBA-DOO" QUINONES
LAMBADA .... BASIL HOFFMAN
LAMBADA .... DENNIS BURKLEY
LAMBADA .... J. EDDIE PECK
LAMBADA .... MELORA HARDIN
LANCASHIRE LAD .... WENDY HILLER
LAND BEFORE TIME (AF) .... CANDANCE HUTSON

INDEX OF FILM TITLES

† after an actor's name denotes deceased.

LAND BEFORE TIME (AF) .... HEATHER HOGAN
LAND BEFORE TIME (AF) ....JEFF BENNETT
LAND BEFORE TIME (AF) ....JOHN INGLE
LAND BEFORE TIME (AF) .... KENNETH MARS
LAND BEFORE TIME (AF) .... LINDA GARY
LAND BEFORE TIME (AF) .... ROB PAULSEN
LAND BEFORE TIME (AF) .... SCOTT McAFEE
LAND BEFORE TIME (AF) .... TRESS MacNELLIE
LAND OF NO RETURN, THE .... WILLIAM SHATNER
LAND OF PEACE .... OMAR SHARIF
LAND OF THE PHARAOHS .... JOAN COLLINS
LAND RAIDERS, THE .... TELLY SAVALAS†
LAND THAT TIME FORGOT, THE .... DOUG McCLURE
LANDFALL .... DAVID TOMLINSON
LANDLORD, THE .... BEAU BRIDGES
LANDLORD, THE .... LOUIS GOSSETT JR.
LANDLORD, THE .... SUSAN ANSPACH
LANDLORD, THE .... TRISH VAN DEVERE
LANDLORD, THE ○ .... LEE GRANT
LANIGAN'S RABBI (TF) .... ART CARNEY
LANIGAN'S RABBI (TF) .... JANET MARGOLIN
LANIGAN'S RABBI (TF) .... STUART MARGOLIN
LANTERN HILL (CTF) ...... COLLEEN DEWHURST†
LANTERN HILL (CTF) .... SAM WATERSTON
LARCENY .... JOAN CAULFIELD†
LARCENY .... SHELLEY WINTERS
LARCENY, INC. .... ANTHONY QUINN
LARCENY, INC. .... JANE WYMAN
LARRY (TF) .... FREDERIC FORREST
LAS VEGAS 500 MILLONES .... JACK PALANCE
LAS VEGAS LADY .... ANDREW STEVENS
LAS VEGAS LADY .... STELLA STEVENS
LAS VEGAS LADY .... STUART WHITMAN
LAS VEGAS NIGHTS .... FRANK SINATRA
LAS VEGAS STORY, THE .... VINCENT PRICE†
LAS VEGAS STRIP
   WARS, THE (TF) .... JAMES EARL JONES
LAS VEGAS STRIP
   WARS, THE (TF) .... NORIYUKI "PAT" MORITA
LAS VEGAS UNDERCOVER (TF) ...... JANE SEYMOUR
LASERBLAST .... RODDY McDOWALL
LASH, THE .... JOHN MILLS
LASSE-MAJA .... MAE ZETTERLING†
LASSIE .... BRITTANY BOYD
LASSIE .... FREDERIC FORREST
LASSIE .... HELEN SLATER
LASSIE .... JON TENNEY
LASSIE .... MICHELLE WILLIAMS
LASSIE .... RICHARD FARNSWORTH
LASSIE .... TOM GUIRY
LASSIE COME HOME .... ALAN NAPIER†
LASSIE COME HOME .... ELIZABETH TAYLOR
LASSIE COME HOME .... RODDY McDOWALL
LASSIE'S GREATEST
   ADVENTURE .... JUNE LOCKHART
LASSITER .... BOB HOSKINS
LASSITER .... ED LAUTER
LASSITER .... LAUREN HUTTON
LASSITER .... TOM SELLECK
LAST ACTION HERO .... ANTHONY QUINN
LAST ACTION
   HERO .... ARNOLD SCHWARZENEGGER
LAST ACTION HERO .... ART CARNEY
LAST ACTION HERO .... AUSTIN O'BRIEN
LAST ACTION HERO .... BRIDGETTE WILSON
LAST ACTION HERO .... CHARLES DANCE
LAST ACTION HERO .... CHEVY CHASE
LAST ACTION HERO ... F. MURRAY ABRAHAM
LAST ACTION HERO .... FRANK McRAE
LAST ACTION HERO .... JAMES BELUSHI
LAST ACTION HERO .... JOAN PLOWRIGHT
LAST ACTION HERO .... MARIA SHRIVER
LAST ACTION HERO .... MERCEDES RUEHL
LAST ACTION HERO .... ROBERT PROSKY
LAST ACTION HERO .... RYAN TODD
LAST ACTION HERO .... SHARON STONE
LAST ACTION HERO .... TINA TURNER
LAST ACTION HERO .... TOM NOONAN
LAST AMERICAN HERO, THE .... ED LAUTER
LAST AMERICAN HERO, THE .... GARY BUSEY
LAST AMERICAN
   HERO, THE .... GERALDINE FITZGERALD

LAST AMERICAN HERO, THE .... JEFF BRIDGES
LAST AMERICAN HERO, THE .... NED BEATTY
LAST AMERICAN HERO, THE .... VALERIE PERRINE
LAST AMERICAN VIRGIN, THE .... DIANE FRANKLIN
LAST AMERICAN
   VIRGIN, THE .... LAWRENCE MONOSON
LAST AMERICAN VIRGIN, THE .... STEVE ANTIN
LAST ANGRY MAN, THE .... BETSY PALMER
LAST ANGRY MAN, THE .... BILLY DEE WILLIAMS
LAST ANGRY MAN, THE ★ .... PAUL MUNI†
LAST BLITZKRIEG, THE .... VAN JOHNSON
LAST BOY SCOUT, THE .... BRUCE WILLIS
LAST BOY SCOUT, THE .... CHELCIE ROSS
LAST BOY SCOUT, THE .... CHELSEA FIELD
LAST BOY SCOUT, THE .... DAMON WAYANS
LAST BOY SCOUT, THE .... HALLE BERRY
LAST BOY SCOUT, THE .... NOBLE WILLINGHAM
LAST BOY SCOUT, THE .... TAYLOR NEGRON
LAST BRIDGE, THE .... MARIA SCHELL
LAST BUTTERFLY, THE .... TOM COURTENAY
LAST CASTLE, THE .... GERALDINE FITZGERALD
LAST CASTLE, THE .... JODIE FOSTER
LAST CASTLE, THE .... RICHARD HARRIS
LAST CHALLENGE, THE .... ANGIE DICKINSON
LAST CHALLENGE, THE .... CHAD EVERETT
LAST CHALLENGE, THE .... ROYAL DANO
LAST CHASE, THE .... BURGESS MEREDITH
LAST CHILD, THE (TF) .... BARBARA BABCOCK
LAST CHILD, THE (TF) .... JANET MARGOLIN
LAST COMMAND, THE .... ERNEST BORGNINE
LAST COMMAND, THE ★★ .... EMIL JANNINGS†
LAST CONVERTIBLE, THE (MS) .... EDWARD ALBERT
LAST CONVERTIBLE, THE (MS) .... KIM DARBY
LAST CONVERTIBLE, THE (MS) .... PERRY KING
LAST CONVERTIBLE, THE (TF) .... SAM ELLIOTT
LAST CONVERTIBLE, THE (TF) .... SHARON GLESS
LAST CROOKED MILE, THE .... JOHN DEHNER†
LAST CRY FOR HELP, A (TF) .... SHIRLEY JONES
LAST DAY, THE (TF) .... LORETTA SWIT
LAST DAY, THE (TF) .... ROBERT CONRAD
LAST DAYS OF FRANK AND JESSE
   JAMES, THE (TF) .... GAIL YOUNGS
LAST DAYS OF FRANK AND JESSE
   JAMES, THE (TF) .... JOHNNY CASH
LAST DAYS OF FRANK AND JESSE
   JAMES, THE (TF) .... KRIS KRISTOFFERSON
LAST DAYS OF FRANK AND JESSE
   JAMES, THE (TF) .... WILLIE NELSON
LAST DAYS OF MUSSOLINI .... ROD STEIGER
LAST DAYS OF PATTON, THE (TF) .... ED LAUTER
LAST DAYS OF
   PATTON, THE (TF) .... EVA MARIE SAINT
LAST DAYS OF
   PATTON, THE (TF) .... GEORGE C. SCOTT
LAST DAYS OF
   PATTON, THE (TF) .... MURRAY HAMILTON†
LAST DAYS OF
   PATTON, THE (TF) .... RICHARD DYSART
LAST DAYS OF
   POMPEII, THE (MS) .... DONALD PLEASENCE
LAST DAYS OF
   POMPEII, THE (MS) .... FRANCO NERO
LAST DAYS OF
   POMPEII, THE (MS) .... LESLEY-ANNE DOWN
LAST DAYS OF
   POMPEII, THE (MS) .... ERNEST BORGNINE
LAST DETAIL, THE .... CAROL KANE
LAST DETAIL, THE .... CLIFTON JAMES
LAST DETAIL, THE .... GILDA RADNER†
LAST DETAIL, THE .... MICHAEL MORIARTY
LAST DETAIL, THE .... NANCY ALLEN
LAST DETAIL, THE ★ .... JACK NICHOLSON
LAST DETAIL, THE ○ .... RANDY QUAID
LAST DINOSAUR, THE (TF) .... STEVEN KEATS†
LAST ELEPHANT,
   THE (CTF) ....ISABELLA ROSSELLINI
LAST ELEPHANT, THE (CTF) ..... JAMES EARL JONES
LAST ELEPHANT, THE (CTF) .... JOHN LITHGOW
LAST ELEPHANT, THE (CTF) .... OLEK KRUPPA
LAST ELEPHANT, THE (CTF) .... TONY TODD
LAST EMBRACE .... CHARLES NAPIER
LAST EMBRACE .... CHRISTOPHER WALKEN

LAST EMBRACE .... JANET MARGOLIN
LAST EMBRACE .... JOHN GLOVER
LAST EMBRACE .... MANDY PATINKIN
LAST EMBRACE .... ROY SCHEIDER
LAST EMPEROR, THE ...... CARY-HIROYUKI TAGAWA
LAST EMPEROR, THE .... DENNIS DUN
LAST EMPEROR, THE .... JOAN CHEN
LAST EMPEROR, THE .... JOHN LONE
LAST EMPEROR, THE .... PETER O'TOOLE
LAST ESCAPE, THE .... STUART WHITMAN
LAST EXIT TO BROOKLYN .... BURT YOUNG
LAST EXIT TO
   BROOKLYN .... JENNIFER JASON LEIGH
LAST EXIT TO BROOKLYN .... JERRY ORBACH
LAST EXIT TO BROOKLYN .... PETER DOBSON
LAST EXIT TO BROOKLYN .... RICK AIELLO
LAST EXIT TO BROOKLYN .... RICKI LAKE
LAST EXIT TO BROOKLYN .... STEPHEN LANG
LAST FLIGHT OF
   NOAH'S ARK, THE .... ELLIOTT GOULD
LAST FLIGHT OF
   NOAH'S ARK, THE .... GENEVIEVE BUJOLD
LAST FLIGHT OF
   NOAH'S ARK, THE .... RICK SCHRODER
LAST FLIGHT OF
   NOAH'S ARK, THE .... VINCENT GARDENIA†
LAST FLIGHT OUT (TF) .... ERIC BOGOSIAN
LAST FLIGHT OUT (TF) .... JAMES EARL JONES
LAST FOUR DAYS, THE .... FRANCO NERO
LAST FOUR DAYS, THE .... ROD STEIGER
LAST FRONTIER, THE .... ANNE BANCROFT
LAST FRONTIER, THE (MS) .... JASON ROBARDS
LAST FRONTIER, THE (TF) .... LINDA EVANS
LAST FRONTIER, THE (TF) .... TONY BONNER
LAST GANGSTER, THE .... JAMES STEWART
LAST GANGSTER, THE .... LIONEL STANDER
LAST GIRAFFE, THE (TF) .... GORDAN JACKSON†
LAST HARD MEN, THE .... BARBARA HERSHEY
LAST HARD MEN, THE .... CHARLTON HESTON
LAST HARD MEN, THE .... JAMES COBURN
LAST HOLIDAY .... ALEC GUINNESS
LAST HOURS BEFORE
   MORNING (TF) .... ED LAUTER
LAST HUNT, THE .... RUSS TAMBLYN
LAST HURRAH, THE (TF) .... MARIETTE HARTLEY
LAST HURRAH, THE (TF) .... PATRICK O'NEAL†
LAST INNOCENT MAN, THE (CTF) .... ED HARRIS
LAST LIGHT (CTF) .... AMANDA PLUMMER
LAST LIGHT (CTF) .... CLANCY BROWN
LAST LIGHT (CTF) .... FOREST WHITAKER
LAST LIGHT (CTF) .... KATHLEEN QUINLAN
LAST LIGHT (CTF) .... KIEFER SUTHERLAND
LAST LIGHT (CTF) .... LYNNE MOODY
LAST MAN ON EARTH, THE .... VINCENT PRICE†
LAST MARRIED COUPLE IN
   AMERICA, THE .... BOB DISHY
LAST MARRIED COUPLE IN
   AMERICA, THE .... DOM DeLUISE
LAST MARRIED COUPLE IN
   AMERICA, THE .... GEORGE SEGAL
LAST MARRIED COUPLE IN
   AMERICA, THE .... NATALIE WOOD†
LAST MARRIED COUPLE IN
   AMERICA, THE .... PRISCILLA BARNES
LAST MARRIED COUPLE IN
   AMERICA, THE .... RICHARD BENJAMIN
LAST MARRIED COUPLE IN
   AMERICA, THE .... VALERIE HARPER
LAST MÉTRO, THE .... CATHERINE DENEUVE
LAST METRO, THE .... GERARD DEPARDIEU
LAST MILE, THE .... MICHAEL CONSTANTINE
LAST MOVIE, THE .... DEAN STOCKWELL
LAST MOVIE, THE .... DENNIS HOPPER
LAST MOVIE, THE .... JOHN PHILLIP LAW
LAST MOVIE, THE .... KRIS KRISTOFFERSON
LAST MOVIE, THE .... PETER FONDA
LAST MOVIE, THE .... RUSS TAMBLYN
LAST MOVIE, THE .... SYLVIA MILES
LAST OF MRS.
   CHEYNEY, THE .... JOAN CRAWFORD†
LAST OF SHEILA, THE .... ANTHONY PERKINS†
LAST OF SHEILA, THE .... DYAN CANNON

LAST OF SHEILA, THE .... JAMES COBURN
LAST OF SHEILA, THE .... JOAN HACKETT†
LAST OF SHEILA, THE .... RAQUEL WELCH
LAST OF SHEILA, THE .... RICHARD BENJAMIN
LAST OF THE
 BELLES, THE (TF) .... RICHARD CHAMBERLAIN
LAST OF THE BUCCANEERS .... JOHN DEHNER†
LAST OF THE
 COWBOYS, THE .... AUSTIN PENDLETON
LAST OF THE COWBOYS, THE ..... EILEEN BRENNAN
LAST OF THE COWBOYS, THE .... JOHN BYNER
LAST OF THE
 COWBOYS, THE .... SUSAN SARANDON
LAST OF THE DOGMEN .... BARBARA HERSHEY
LAST OF THE DOGMEN .... KURTWOOD SMITH
LAST OF THE DOGMEN .... TOM BERENGER
LAST OF THE FINEST, THE .... BILL PAXTON
LAST OF THE FINEST, THE .... BRIAN DENNEHY
LAST OF THE
 FINEST, THE .... DEBORRA-LEE FURNESS
LAST OF THE FINEST, THE .... GUY BOYD
LAST OF THE FINEST, THE .... HENRY DARROW
LAST OF THE FINEST, THE .... JEFF FAHEY
LAST OF THE FINEST, THE .... JOE PANTOLIANO
LAST OF THE FINEST, THE .... RON CANADA
LAST OF THE MOBILE
 HOTSHOTS, THE .... JAMES COBURN
LAST OF THE MOBILE
 HOTSHOTS, THE .... LYNN REDGRAVE
LAST OF THE MOBILE
 HOTSHOTS, THE .... ROBERT HOOKS
LAST OF THE
 MOHICANS, THE .... DANIEL DAY-LEWIS
LAST OF THE MOHICANS, THE .... ERIC SCHWEIG
LAST OF THE MOHICANS, THE .... JODHI MAY
LAST OF THE
 MOHICANS, THE .... MADELEINE STOWE
LAST OF THE MOHICANS, THE .... WES STUDI
LAST OF THE RED HOT LOVERS .... ALAN ARKIN
LAST OF THE RED
 HOT LOVERS .... PAULA PRENTISS
LAST OF THE RED HOT LOVERS .... RENEE TAYLOR
LAST OF THE RED
 HOT LOVERS .... SALLY KELLERMAN
LAST OUTPOST, THE .... RONALD REAGAN
LAST PARTY, THE (FD) .... SEAN PENN
LAST PICTURE SHOW, THE .... CLU GULAGER
LAST PICTURE SHOW, THE .... CYBILL SHEPHERD
LAST PICTURE SHOW, THE .... EILEEN BRENNAN
LAST PICTURE SHOW, THE .... RANDY QUAID
LAST PICTURE SHOW, THE .... SAM BOTTOMS
LAST PICTURE SHOW, THE ...... TIMOTHY BOTTOMS
LAST PICTURE SHOW, THE ○ .... ELLEN BURSTYN
LAST PICTURE SHOW, THE ○ .... JEFF BRIDGES
LAST PICTURE SHOW, THE ○○ .... BEN JOHNSON
LAST PICTURE
 SHOW, THE ○○ .... CLORIS LEACHMAN
LAST PLANE OUT .... JAN-MICHAEL VINCENT
LAST PRECINCT, THE (TF) .... ADAM WEST
LAST REBEL, THE .... WOODY STRODE
LAST REMAKE OF
 BEAU GESTE, THE .... ANN-MARGRET
LAST REMAKE OF
 BEAU GESTE, THE .... BURT KWOUK
LAST REMAKE OF
 BEAU GESTE, THE .... HENRY GIBSON
LAST REMAKE OF
 BEAU GESTE, THE .... JAMES EARL JONES
LAST REMAKE OF
 BEAU GESTE, THE .... MARTY FELDMAN†
LAST REMAKE OF
 BEAU GESTE, THE .... MICHAEL YORK
LAST REMAKE OF
 BEAU GESTE, THE .... PETER USTINOV
LAST RESORT, THE .... CHARLES GRODIN
LAST RESORT, THE .... JON LOVITZ
LAST RIDE OF THE DALTON
 GANG, THE (TF) .... HARRIS YULIN
LAST RIDE OF THE DALTON
 GANG, THE (TF) .... JACK PALANCE
LAST RIDE, THE .... ELEANOR PARKER
LAST RITES .... ANNE TWOMEY

LAST RITES .... CHICK VENNERA
LAST RITES .... DAPHNE ZUNIGA
LAST RITES .... PAUL DOOLEY
LAST RITES .... TOM BERENGER
LAST RITES .... VASSILI LAMBRINOS
LAST ROUNDUP, THE .... ROBERT BLAKE
LAST RUN, THE .... COLLEEN DEWHURST†
LAST RUN, THE .... GEORGE C. SCOTT
LAST RUN, THE .... TONY MUSANTE
LAST RUN, THE .... TRISH VAN DEVERE
LAST SEDUCTION, THE .... BILL PULLMAN
LAST SEDUCTION, THE .... LINDA FIORENTINO
LAST STARFIGHTER, THE .... DAN O'HERLIHY
LAST SUMMER .... BARBARA HERSHEY
LAST SUMMER .... BRUCE DAVISON
LAST SUMMER .... RICHARD THOMAS
LAST SUNSET, THE .... CAROL LYNLEY
LAST SUNSET, THE .... KIRK DOUGLAS
LAST SURVIVORS, THE (TF) .... DIANE BAKER
LAST TANGO IN PARIS ★ .... MARLON BRANDO
LAST TEMPTATION OF
 CHRIST, THE .... BARBARA HERSHEY
LAST TEMPTATION OF
 CHRIST, THE .... DAVID BOWIE
LAST TEMPTATION OF
 CHRIST, THE .... HARRY DEAN STANTON
LAST TEMPTATION OF
 CHRIST, THE .... HARVEY KEITEL
LAST TEMPTATION OF
 CHRIST, THE .... WILLEM DAFOE
LAST TENANT, THE (TF) .... CHRISTINE LAHTI
LAST TIME I SAW ARCHIE, THE .... DON KNOTTS
LAST TIME I SAW ARCHIE, THE .... FRANCE NUYEN
LAST TIME I SAW
 ARCHIE, THE .... ROBERT MITCHUM
LAST TIME I SAW
 PARIS, THE .... ELIZABETH TAYLOR
LAST TIME I SAW PARIS, THE .... EVA GABOR
LAST TIME I SAW PARIS, THE .... ROGER MOORE
LAST TIME I SAW PARIS, THE .... VAN JOHNSON
LAST TO GO, THE (TF) .... TYNE DALY
LAST TRAIN FROM GUN HILL .... ANTHONY QUINN
LAST TRAIN FROM GUN HILL .... EARL HOLLIMAN
LAST TRAIN FROM GUN HILL .... KIRK DOUGLAS
LAST TRAIN FROM
 MADRID, THE .... ANTHONY QUINN
LAST TRAIN FROM
 MADRID, THE .... DOROTHY LAMOUR
LAST TYCOON, THE .... ANJELICA HUSTON
LAST TYCOON, THE .... DONALD PLEASENCE
LAST TYCOON, THE .... JACK NICHOLSON
LAST TYCOON, THE .... JEFF COREY
LAST TYCOON, THE .... JOHN CARRADINE†
LAST TYCOON, THE .... PEGGY FEURY†
LAST TYCOON, THE .... PETER STRAUSS
LAST TYCOON, THE .... ROBERT DE NIRO
LAST TYCOON, THE .... ROBERT MITCHUM
LAST TYCOON, THE .... SEYMOUR CASSEL
LAST TYCOON, THE .... THERESA RUSSELL
LAST TYCOON, THE .... TONY CURTIS
LAST UNICORN, THE (AF) .... JEFF BRIDGES
LAST VALLEY, THE .... MICHAEL CAINE
LAST VALLEY, THE .... NIGEL DAVENPORT
LAST VALLEY, THE .... OMAR SHARIF
LAST VOYAGE, THE .... JACK KRUSCHEN
LAST VOYAGE, THE .... ROBERT STACK
LAST VOYAGE, THE .... WOODY STRODE
LAST WAGON, THE .... RICHARD WIDMARK
LAST WAGON, THE .... TIMOTHY CAREY
LAST WARRIOR, THE .... ANTHONY QUINN
LAST WARRIOR, THE .... CARY-HIROYUKI TAGAWA
LAST WARRIOR, THE .... CLAUDE AKINS†
LAST WARRIOR, THE .... SHELLEY WINTERS
LAST WAVE, THE .... RICHARD CHAMBERLAIN
LAST WINTER, THE .... KATHLEEN QUINLAN
LAST WINTER, THE .... STEPHEN MACHT
LAST WOMAN, THE .... GERARD DEPARDIEU
LAST WORD, THE .... KAREN BLACK
LAST WORD, THE .... RICHARD HARRIS
LATE EDWINA
 BLAKE, THE .... GERALDINE FITZGERALD
LATE FOR DINNER .... BO BRUNDIN

LATE FOR DINNER .... BRIAN WIMMER
LATE FOR DINNER .... MARCIA GAY HARDEN
LATE FOR DINNER .... PETER BERG
LATE FOR DINNER .... PETER GALLAGHER
LATE LIZ, THE .... STEVE FORREST
LATE SHOW, THE .... ART CARNEY
LATE SHOW, THE .... BILL MACY
LATE SHOW, THE .... EUGENE ROCHE
LATE SHOW, THE .... HOWARD DUFF†
LATE SHOW, THE .... JOANNA CASSIDY
LATE SHOW, THE .... LILY TOMLIN
LATIN LOVERS .... LANA TURNER
LATIN LOVERS .... RICARDO MONTALBAN
LATIN LOVERS .... RITA MORENO
LATINO .... ROBERT BELTRAN
LAUGHING POLICEMAN, THE .... ANTHONY ZERBE
LAUGHING POLICEMAN, THE .... BRUCE DERN
LAUGHING
 POLICEMAN, THE .... FRANCES LEE McCAIN
LAUGHING POLICEMAN, THE .... JOANNA CASSIDY
LAUGHING POLICEMAN, THE .... VAL AVERY
LAUGHING POLICEMAN, THE ..... WALTER MATTHAU
LAUGHING SINNERS .... JOAN CRAWFORD†
LAUGHTER IN PARADISE .... AUDREY HEPBURN†
LAUGHTER IN THE DARK .... NICOL WILLIAMSON
LAUGHTER IN THE DARK .... SIAN PHILLIPS
LAUGHTERHOUSE .... IAN HOLM
LAURA .... DAME JUDITH ANDERSON†
LAURA .... VINCENT PRICE†
LAURA ○ .... CLIFTON WEBB†
LAURA LANSING
 SLEPT HERE (TF) .... JOEL HIGGINS
LAURA LANSING
 SLEPT HERE (TF) .... KAREN AUSTIN
LAURA LANSING
 SLEPT HERE (TF) .... KATHERINE HEPBURN
LAVENDER HILL MOB, THE ...... AUDREY HEPBURN†
LAVENDER HILL MOB, THE ★ ..... ALEC GUINNESS
LAW, THE (TF) .... GARY BUSEY
LAW, THE (TF) .... JOHN BECK
LAW, THE (TF) .... JUDD HIRSCH
LAW AND DISORDER .... CARROLL O'CONNOR
LAW AND DISORDER .... ERNEST BORGNINE
LAW AND DISORDER .... KAREN BLACK
LAW AND DISORDER .... ROBERT MORLEY
LAW AND HARRY McGRAW:
 DEAD MEN DON'T MAKE
 PHONE CALLS, THE (TF) .... JERRY ORBACH
LAW AND JAKE WADE, THE .... HENRY SILVA
LAW AND JAKE WADE, THE ...... RICHARD WIDMARK
LAW AND ORDER .... RONALD REAGAN
LAW AND THE LADY, THE .... GREER GARSON
LAW OF DESIRE .... ANTONIO BANDERAS
LAW OF THE LAND (TF) .... DON JOHNSON
LAW OF THE LAWLESS .... YVONNE DE CARLO
LAW OF THE RANGE, THE .... JOAN CRAWFORD†
LAWLESS BREED, THE .... DENNIS WEAVER
LAWLESS BREED, THE .... ROCK HUDSON†
LAWLESS STREET, A .... ANGELA LANSBURY
LAWLESS, THE .... TAB HUNTER
LAWMAN .... ALBERT SALMI†
LAWMAN .... BURT LANCASTER†
LAWMAN .... J. D. CANNON
LAWMAN .... JOHN BECK
LAWMAN .... JOSEPH WISEMAN
LAWMAN .... RICHARD JORDAN†
LAWMAN .... ROBERT DUVALL
LAWNMOWER MAN 2, THE .... AUSTIN O'BRIEN
LAWRENCE OF ARABIA .... ALEC GUINNESS
LAWRENCE OF ARABIA .... ANTHONY QUINN
LAWRENCE OF ARABIA .... CLAUDE RAINS†
LAWRENCE OF ARABIA .... JACK HAWKINS†
LAWRENCE OF ARABIA .... JACK HEDLEY
LAWRENCE OF ARABIA .... JOSE FERRER†
LAWRENCE OF ARABIA ★ .... PETER O'TOOLE
LAWRENCE OF ARABIA ○ .... OMAR SHARIF
LAWYER, THE .... DIANA MULDAUR
LAZARUS SYNDROME, THE (TF) ... E. G. MARSHALL
LAZARUS
 SYNDROME, THE (TF) .... LOUIS GOSSETT JR.
LAZARUS
 SYNDROME, THE (TF) .... RONALD HUNTER

† after an actor's name denotes deceased.

LBJ: THE EARLY
  YEARS (TF) .... MORGAN BRITTANY
LBJ: THE EARLY YEARS (TF) .... PAT HINGLE
LBJ: THE EARLY YEARS (TF) ...... R.G. ARMSTRONG
LBJ: THE EARLY YEARS (TF) .... RANDY QUAID
LE AVVENTURE DI
  GIACOMO CASANOVA .... URSULA ANDRESS
LE CAMION .... GERARD DEPARDIEU
LE CASSE .... DYAN CANNON
LE CASSE .... OMAR SHARIF
LE CAVALEUR .... LILA KEDROVA
LE CERVEAU .... ELI WALLACH
LE CHANT DU MONDE .... CATHERINE DENEUVE
LE CHAT ET LA SOURIS .... JEAN-PIERRE AUMONT
LE CHEVRE .... GERARD DEPARDIEU
LE CHOIX DES ARMES .... GERARD DEPARDIEU
LE COMTE DE MONTE CRISTO ..... LOUIS JOURDAN
LE CORSAIRE .... LOUIS JOURDAN
LE COUTEAU
  DANS LA PLAIE .... ANTHONY PERKINS†
LE COUTEAU DANS LA PLAIE .... SOPHIA LOREN
LE CRI DU CORMORAN LE
  SOIR AUDESSUS
  DES JONQUES .... GERARD DEPARDIEU
LE DEFROQUÉ .... LILA KEDROVA
LE DIABLE PAR LA QUEUE .... MARIA SCHELL
LE DIABLE PAR LA QUEUE .... MARTHE KELLER
LE DOLCI SIGNORE .... CLAUDINE AUGER
LE DOLCI SIGNORE .... URSULA ANDRESS
LE DROIT D'AIMER .... OMAR SHARIF
LE GLAIVE ET LA BALANCE ..... ANTHONY PERKINS†
LE GRAN DÉLIRE .... ISABELLE HUPPERT
LE GRAND
  EMBOUTEILLAGE .... GERARD DEPARDIEU
LE GRAND FRERE .... GERARD DEPARDIEU
LE GUEPIER .... MARTHE KELLER
LE HASARD ET LA VIOLENCE ...... KATHERINE ROSS
LE JEU AVE LE FEU .... SYLVIA KRISTEL
LE JOUR ET L'HEURE .... STUART WHITMAN
LE JUGE ET L'ASSASSIN .... ISABELLE HUPPERT
LE LOCATAIRE .... SHELLEY WINTERS
LE MAGNIFIQUE .... JACQUELINE BISSET
LE MANI SULLA CITTA .... ROD STEIGER
LE MEPRIS .... JACK PALANCE
LE NOTTI BIANCHE .... MARCELLO MASTROIANNI
LE NOTTI BIANCHE .... MARIA SCHELL
LE PETIT BOUGNAT .... ISABELLE ADJANI
LE PLAISIR .... PETER USTINOV
LE PLUS VIEUX MÉTIER
  DU MONDE .... RAQUEL WELCH
LE PROCES/DER PROZESS ..... ANTHONY PERKINS†
LE RAGAZZE DI PIAZZA
  DI SPAGNA .... MARCELLO MASTROIANNI
LE RAYON VEIT .... CARITA
LE RAYON VEIT .... VINCENT GAUTHIER
LE RIDEAU CRAMOISI .... ANOUK AIMEE
LE ROI DE COEUR .... ALAN BATES
LE ROI DE COEUR .... GENEVIEVE BUJOLD
LE SANG DES
  AUTRES (CMS) .... JEAN-PIERRE AUMONT
LE SANG DES AUTRES (CMS) .... JODIE FOSTER
LE SANG DES
  AUTRES (CMS) .... MICHAEL ONTKEAN
LE SANG DES AUTRES (CMS) .... SAM NEILL
LE SAUVAGE .... TONY ROBERTS
LE SAUVAGE/
  THE SAVAGE .... CATHERINE DENEUVE
LE SCANDALE .... HENRY JONES
LE SOLEIL DES VOYOUS .... ROBERT STACK
LE SUCRE .... GERARD DEPARDIEU
LE TARTUFFE .... GERARD DEPARDIEU
LE TESTAMENT D'ORPHÉE .... CLAUDINE AUGER
LE TUEUR .... GERARD DEPARDIEU
LE VEGINI DI ROMA .... LOUIS JOURDAN
LE VIAGER .... GERARD DEPARDIEU
LE VOLEUR .... GENEVIEVE BUJOLD
LEADBELLY .... ROGER E. MOSLEY
LEADER OF THE BAND .... MERCEDES RUEHL
LEAGUE OF FRIGHTENED
  MEN, THE .... LIONEL STANDER
LEAGUE OF THEIR OWN, A .... ANN CUSACK

LEAGUE OF THEIR
  OWN, A .... ANNE ELIZABETH RAMSAY
LEAGUE OF THEIR OWN, A .... BILL PULLMAN
LEAGUE OF THEIR OWN, A .... BITTY SCHRAM
LEAGUE OF THEIR OWN, A .... DAVID STRATHAIRN
LEAGUE OF THEIR OWN, A .... FREDDIE SIMPSON
LEAGUE OF THEIR OWN, A .... GARRY MARSHALL
LEAGUE OF THEIR OWN, A .... GEENA DAVIS
LEAGUE OF THEIR OWN, A .... JON LOVITZ
LEAGUE OF THEIR OWN, A .... LORI PETTY
LEAGUE OF THEIR OWN, A .... MADONNA
LEAGUE OF THEIR OWN, A .... MEGAN CAVANAGH
LEAGUE OF THEIR OWN, A .... ROSIE O'DONNELL
LEAGUE OF THEIR OWN, A .... TOM HANKS
LEAGUE OF THEIR OWN, A .... TRACY REINER
LEAN ON ME .... ALAN NORTH
LEAN ON ME .... BEVERLY TODD
LEAN ON ME .... ETHAN PHILLIPS
LEAN ON ME .... LYNNE THIGPEN
LEAN ON ME .... MICHAEL BEACH
LEAN ON ME .... MORGAN FREEMAN
LEAN ON ME .... ROBERT GUILLAUME
LEAN ON ME .... ROBIN BARTLETT
LEAP OF FAITH .... DEBRA WINGER
LEAP OF FAITH .... LIAM NEESON
LEAP OF FAITH .... LOLITA DAVIDOVICH
LEAP OF FAITH .... LUKAS HAAS
LEAP OF FAITH .... MEAT LOAF
LEAP OF FAITH .... PHYLLIS SOMERVILLE
LEAP OF FAITH .... STEVE MARTIN
LEAP OF FAITH (TF) .... ANNE ARCHER
LEAP OF FAITH (TF) .... JAMES TOLKAN
LEAP OF FAITH (TF) .... MICHAEL CONSTANTINE
LEAP OF FAITH (TF) .... NORMAN PARKER
LEAP OF FAITH (TF) .... SAM NEILL
LEASE OF LIFE .... DENHOLM ELLIOTT†
LEATHER BURNERS, THE .... ROBERT MITCHUM
LEATHER JACKETS .... BRIDGET FONDA
LEATHER JACKETS .... CARY ELWES
LEATHER JACKETS .... CHRIS PENN
LEATHER JACKETS .... JAMES LE GROS
LEAVE 'EM LAUGHING (TF) .... RED BUTTONS
LEAVE HER TO HEAVEN .... VINCENT PRICE†
LEAVE YESTERDAY
  BEHIND (TF) .... CARRIE FISHER
LEAVING LAS VEGAS .... ELISABETH SHUE
LEAVING LAS VEGAS .... NICOLAS CAGE
LEAVING LAS VEGAS .... VINCENT WARD
LEAVING NORMAL .... CHRISTINE LAHTI
LEAVING NORMAL .... MEG TILLY
LEFT HAND OF GOD, THE .... E. G. MARSHALL
LEFT-HANDED GUN, THE .... HURD HATFIELD
LEFT-HANDED GUN, THE .... JOHN DEHNER†
LEFT-HANDED GUN, THE .... PAUL NEWMAN
LEFT-HANDED MAN, THE .... LILLIAN GISH†
LEFT-HANDED
  WOMAN, THE .... GERARD DEPARDIEU
LEGACY OF MAGGIE
  WALSH, THE .... KATHERINE ROSS
LEGACY, THE .... HILDEGARD NEIL
LEGACY, THE .... KATHERINE ROSS
LEGACY, THE .... ROGER DALTRY
LEGACY, THE .... SAM ELLIOTT
LEGAL EAGLES .... BRIAN DENNEHY
LEGAL EAGLES .... DARYL HANNAH
LEGAL EAGLES .... DAVID CLENNON
LEGAL EAGLES .... DEBRA WINGER
LEGAL EAGLES .... ROBERT REDFORD
LEGAL EAGLES .... ROSCOE LEE BROWNE
LEGAL EAGLES .... STEVEN HILL
LEGEND .... BILLY BARTY
LEGEND .... DAVID BENNENT
LEGEND .... MIA SARA
LEGEND .... TIM CURRY
LEGEND .... TOM CRUISE
LEGEND IN LEOTARDS .... ALAN ARKIN
LEGEND OF
  BILLIE JEAN, THE .... CHRISTIAN SLATER
LEGEND OF BILLIE JEAN, THE ... DEAN STOCKWELL
LEGEND OF BILLIE JEAN, THE .... HELEN SLATER
LEGEND OF EARL
  DURAND, THE .... ALBERT SALMI†
LEGEND OF EARL DURAND, THE ..... MARTIN SHEEN

LEGEND OF HELL
  HOUSE, THE .... RODDY McDOWALL
LEGEND OF HILL BILLY JOHN ..... R.G. ARMSTRONG
LEGEND OF HILLBILLY
  JOHN .... SUSAN STRASBERG
LEGEND OF HILLBILLY
  JOHN, THE .... SEVERN DARDEN
LEGEND OF LIZZIE
  BORDEN, THE (TF) .... ED FLANDERS
LEGEND OF LIZZIE
  BORDEN, THE (TF) ...... ELIZABETH MONTGOMERY
LEGEND OF LIZZIE
  BORDEN, THE (TF) .... KATHERINE HELMOND
LEGEND OF LYLAH
  CLARE, THE .... ERNEST BORGNINE
LEGEND OF LYLAH
  CLARE, THE .... GEORGE KENNEDY
LEGEND OF LYLAH CLARE, THE .... KIM NOVAK
LEGEND OF NIGGER
  CHARLEY, THE .... FRED WILLIAMSON
LEGEND OF SLEEPY
  HOLLOW, THE .... MEG FOSTER
LEGEND OF THE
  HOLY DRINKER, THE .... RUTGER HAUER
LEGEND OF THE
  LONE RANGER, THE .... JASON ROBARDS
LEGEND OF THE
  LONE RANGER, THE .... MATT CLARK
LEGEND OF THE LOST .... SOPHIA LOREN
LEGEND OF THE WEREWOLF .... RON MOODY
LEGEND OF TOM
  DOOLEY, THE .... MICHAEL LANDON†
LEGEND OF VALENTINO (TF) .... FRANCO NERO
LEGEND OF VALENTINO, THE (TF) ..... JUDD HIRSCH
LEGEND OF
  VALENTINO, THE (TF) ....MILTON BERLE
LEGEND OF
  VALENTINO, THE (TF) .... SUZANNE PLESHETTE
LEGEND OF WALKS
  FAR WOMAN, THE (TF) .... NICK MANCUSO
LEGEND OF WALKS
  FAR WOMAN, THE (TF) .... RAQUEL WELCH
LEGENDS OF THE FALL .... AIDAN QUINN
LEGENDS OF THE FALL .... ANTHONY HOPKINS
LEGENDS OF THE FALL .... BRAD PITT
LEGENDS OF THE FALL .... KARINA LOMBARD
LEGGE DI GUERRA .... MEL FERRER
LEGS (TF) .... GWEN VERDON
LEMON DROP KID, THE .... BOB HOPE
LEMON SISTERS, THE .... AIDAN QUINN
LEMON SISTERS, THE .... CAROL KANE
LEMON SISTERS, THE .... DIANE KEATON
LEMON SISTERS, THE .... ELLIOTT GOULD
LEMON SISTERS, THE .... RUBEN BLADES
LEMON SKY .... KEVIN BACON
LEMON SKY .... KYRA SEDGWICK
LEMON SKY .... LINDSAY CROUSE
LENA: MY 100 CHILDREN (TF) .... LEONORE HARRIS
LENA: MY 100 CHILDREN (TF) .... LINDA LAVIN
LENA RIVERS .... MILTON BERLE
LENA'S HOLIDAY .... CHRIS LEMMON
LENA'S HOLIDAY .... NORIYUKI "PAT" MORITA
LENA'S HOLIDAY .... SUSAN ANTON
LENNY ★ .... DUSTIN HOFFMAN
LENNY ★ .... VALERIE PERRINE
LEO THE LAST .... BILLIE WHITELAW
LEO THE LAST .... MARCELLO MASTROIANNI
LEONA HELMSLEY: THE
  QUEEN OF MEAN (TF) .... LLOYD BRIDGES
LEONA HELMSLEY: THE
  QUEEN OF MEAN (TF) ...... SUZANNE PLESHETTE
LEONARD PART 6 .... BILL COSBY
LEONARD PART 6 .... JANE FONDA
LEONARD PART 6 .... TOM COURTENAY
LÉONOR .... LIV ULLMANN
LEOPARD, THE .... BURT LANCASTER†
LEOPARD IN THE SNOW .... JEREMY KEMP
LEPKE .... MILTON BERLE
LEPKE .... TONY CURTIS
LEPRECHAUN .... WARWICK DAVIS
LEPRECHAUN 2 .... WARWICK DAVIS
LES APPRENTIS SORCIERS .... DENNIS HOPPER

This is not a list of every film ever made or every cast member, only those listed in this directory.

LES CAPRICES DE MARIE	MARTHE KELLER
LES CHIENS	GERARD DEPARDIEU
LES COLLÉGIENNES	CATHERINE DENEUVE
LES COMPERES	GERARD DEPARDIEU
LES CRÉATURES	CATHERINE DENEUVE
LES DEMOISELLES DE ROCHEFORT	CATHERINE DENEUVE
LES DEMOISELLES DE ROCHEFORT	GENE KELLY
LES ESPIONS	PETER USTINOV
LES FÉLINS/THE LOVE CAGE	JANE FONDA
LES FUGITIFS	GERARD DEPARDIEU
LES FUGITIFS	PIERRE RICHARD
LES GASPARDS	GERARD DEPARDIEU
LES GIRLS	GENE KELLY
LES GIRLS	PATRICK MacNEE
LES GRANDS CHEMINS	ANOUK AIMEE
LES GUERRILLEROS	ERNEST BORGNINE
LES HOMINES	HENRY SILVA
LES INDIENS SONT ENCORE LOIN	ISABELLE HUPPERT
LES INNOCENTS AUX MAINS SALES	ROD STEIGER
LES LIENS DE SANG	DAVID HEMMINGS
LES LIENS DE SANG	DONALD PLEASENCE
LES LIENS DE SANG	DONALD SUTHERLAND
LES MAINS D'ORLAC	DONALD PLEASENCE
LES MAINS D'ORLAC	MEL FERRER
LES MAUVAISES RENCONTRES	ANOUK AIMEE
LES MISÉRABLES	JOSEPH WISEMAN
LES MISÉRABLES	SEAN McCLORY
LES MISÉRABLES	SYLVIA SIDNEY
LES MISÉRABLES (TF)	ANTHONY PERKINS†
LES MISÉRABLES (TF)	JOHN GIELGUD
LES MISÉRABLES (TF)	RICHARD JORDAN†
LES PARAPLUIES DE CHERBOURG	CATHERINE DENEUVE
LES PARISIENNES	CATHERINE DENEUVE
LES PETITS CHATS	CATHERINE DENEUVE
LES PORTES CLAQUENT	CATHERINE DENEUVE
LES QUATRE VÉRITÉS	LESLIE CARON
LES TRIBULATIONS D'UN CHINOIS EN CHINE	URSULA ANDRESS
LES TUEURS DE SAN FRANCISCO	JACK PALANCE
LES UNS ET LES AUTRES/ WITHIN MEMORY	GERALDINE CHAPLIN
LES UNS ET LES AUTRES/ WITHIN MEMORY	JAMES CAAN
LES VALSEUSES	GERARD DEPARDIEU
LES VALSEUSES	ISABELLE HUPPERT
LESS THAN ZERO	JAMES SPADER
LESS THAN ZERO	JAMI GERTZ
LESS THAN ZERO	ROBERT DOWNEY JR.
LET HIM HAVE IT	EILEEN ATKINS
LET HIM HAVE IT	MICHAEL GOUGH
LET IT BE (FD)	GEORGE HARRISON
LET IT BE (FD)	PAUL McCARTNEY
LET IT BE (FD)	RINGO STARR
LET IT BE ME	CAMPBELL SCOTT
LET IT BE ME	JAMIE GOODWIN
LET IT BE ME	JENNIFER BEALS
LET IT BE ME	LESLIE CARON
LET IT BE ME	PATRICK STEWART
LET IT BE ME	YANCY BUTLER
LET IT BE ME	ELLIOTT GOULD
LET IT BE ME	PERRY KING
LET IT RIDE	DAVID JOHANSEN
LET IT RIDE	JENNIFER TILLY
LET IT RIDE	RICHARD DREYFUSS
LET IT RIDE	TERI GARR
LET NO MAN WRITE MY EPITAPH	BURL IVES
LET NO MAN WRITE MY EPITAPH	RICARDO MONTALBAN
LET NO MAN WRITE MY EPITAPH	SHELLEY WINTERS
LET THE PEOPLE SING	PETER USTINOV
LET US LIVE	MAUREEN O'SULLIVAN
LET US LIVE	RALPH BELLAMY†
LETHAL WEAPON	DANNY GLOVER
LETHAL WEAPON	DARLENE LOVE
LETHAL WEAPON	ED O'ROSS
LETHAL WEAPON	GARY BUSEY
LETHAL WEAPON	MEL GIBSON
LETHAL WEAPON	MITCHELL RYAN
LETHAL WEAPON	TOM ATKINS
LETHAL WEAPON	TRACI WOLFE
LETHAL WEAPON 2	DANNY GLOVER
LETHAL WEAPON 2	DARLENE LOVE
LETHAL WEAPON 2	DERRICK O'CONNOR
LETHAL WEAPON 2	JOE PESCI
LETHAL WEAPON 2	JOSS ACKLAND
LETHAL WEAPON 2	MEL GIBSON
LETHAL WEAPON 2	PATSY KENSIT
LETHAL WEAPON 2	STEVE KAHAN
LETHAL WEAPON 2	TRACI WOLFE
LETHAL WEAPON 3	DANNY GLOVER
LETHAL WEAPON 3	DARLENE LOVE
LETHAL WEAPON 3	JOE PESCI
LETHAL WEAPON 3	MEL GIBSON
LETHAL WEAPON 3	RENE RUSSO
LETHAL WEAPON 3	STUART WILSON
LETTER, THE ★	BETTE DAVIS†
LETTER, THE ★	JEANNE EAGELS†
LETTER, THE ❍	JAMES STEPHENSON†
LETTER, THE (TF)	CHRISTOPHER CAZENOVE
LETTER FOR EVIE, A	HUME CRONYN
LETTER FROM AN UNKNOWN WOMAN	LOUIS JOURDAN
LETTER TO BREZHNEV	PETER FIRTH
LETTER TO THREE WIVES, A	ANN SOTHERN
LETTER TO THREE WIVES, A	CELESTE HOLM
LETTER TO THREE WIVES, A	KIRK DOUGLAS
LETTER TO THREE WIVES, A (TF)	BEN GAZZARA
LETTER TO THREE WIVES, A (TF)	CHARLES FRANK
LETTER TO THREE WIVES, A (TF)	LONI ANDERSON
LETTER TO THREE WIVES, A (TF)	MICHAEL GROSS
LETTER TO THREE WIVES, A (TF)	MICHELE LEE
LETTER TO THREE WIVES, A (TF)	STEPHANIE ZIMBALIST
LETTERS FROM THREE LOVERS (TF)	BELINDA J. MONTGOMERY
LETTERS FROM THREE LOVERS (TF)	MARTIN SHEEN
LETTI SELVAGGI	URSULA ANDRESS
LETTING GO (TF)	JOHN RITTER
LETTING GO (TF)	SHARON GLESS
LETTY LYNTON	JOAN CRAWFORD†
LET'S DO IT AGAIN	BILL COSBY
LET'S DO IT AGAIN	JANE WYMAN
LET'S DO IT AGAIN	JOHN AMOS
LET'S DO IT AGAIN	LEON AMES
LET'S DO IT AGAIN	OSSIE DAVIS
LET'S DO IT AGAIN	SIDNEY POITIER
LET'S DO IT AGAIN	VAL AVERY
LET'S FACE IT	BOB HOPE
LET'S FACE IT	YVONNE DE CARLO
LET'S FALL IN LOVE	ANN SOTHERN
LET'S GET HARRY	BEN JOHNSON
LET'S GET HARRY	CAROLE DAVIS
LET'S GET HARRY	GARY BUSEY
LET'S GET HARRY	JERE BURNS
LET'S GET HARRY	MARK HARMON
LET'S GET HARRY	MICHAEL SCHOEFFLING
LET'S GET HARRY	RICK ROSSOVICH
LET'S GET HARRY	ROBERT DUVALL
LET'S GET MARRIED	RALPH BELLAMY†
LET'S HOPE IT'S A GIRL	LIV ULLMANN
LET'S MAKE IT LEGAL	ROBERT WAGNER
LET'S MAKE IT LEGAL	MARILYN MONROE†
LET'S MAKE LOVE	MARILYN MONROE†
LET'S MAKE LOVE	YVES MONTAND†
LET'S MAKE LOVE	BING CROSBY†
LET'S MAKE LOVE	GENE KELLY
LET'S MAKE LOVE	MILTON BERLE
LET'S MAKE LOVE	TONY RANDALL
LET'S ROCK	CONRAD JANIS
LEVIATHAN	HECTOR ELIZONDO
LIANNA	JOHN SAYLES
LIAR'S MOON	HOYT AXTON
LIAR'S MOON	MATT DILLON
LIAR'S MOON	SUSAN TYRRELL
LIAR'S MOON	YVONNE DE CARLO
LIBEL	GEOFFREY BAYLDON
LIBEL	OLIVIA DE HAVILLAND
LIBEL	ROBERT MORLEY
LIBERACE: BEHIND THE MUSIC (TF)	MAUREEN STAPLETON
LIBERACE: BEHIND THE MUSIC (TF)	MICHAEL WIKES
LIBERACE: BEHIND THE MUSIC (TF)	PAUL HIPP
LIBERACE (TF)	ANDREW ROBINSON
LIBERACE (TF)	DEBORAH GOODRICH
LIBERACE (TF)	JOHN RUBINSTEIN
LIBERACE (TF)	RUE McCLANAHAN
LIBERATION OF L.B. JONES, THE	ANTHONY ZERBE
LIBERATION OF L.B. JONES, THE	BARBARA HERSHEY
LIBERATION OF L.B. JONES, THE	LEE MAJORS
LIBERATION OF L.B. JONES, THE	ROSCOE LEE BROWNE
LIBERATION OF L.B. JONES, THE	YAPHET KOTTO
LIBERATORS, THE (TF)	ROBERT CARRADINE
LIBERTY (TF)	CARRIE FISHER
LIBERTY (TF)	CLAIRE BLOOM
LIBERTY (TF)	FRANK LANGELLA
LIBERTY (TF)	GEORGE KENNEDY
LIBERTY (TF)	LeVAR BURTON
LIBIDO	JACK THOMPSON
LICENCE TO KILL	ANTHONY STARKE
LICENCE TO KILL	ANTHONY ZERBE
LICENCE TO KILL	BENICIO DEL TORO
LICENCE TO KILL	CAREY LOWELL
LICENCE TO KILL	CAROLINE BLISS
LICENCE TO KILL	CARY-HIROYUKI TAGAWA
LICENCE TO KILL	DAVID HEDISON
LICENCE TO KILL	DESMOND LLEWELYN
LICENCE TO KILL	EVERETT McGILL
LICENCE TO KILL	FRANK McRAE
LICENCE TO KILL	PEDRO ARMENDARIZ JR.
LICENCE TO KILL	PRISCILLA BARNES
LICENCE TO KILL	ROBERT BROWN
LICENCE TO KILL	ROBERT DAVI
LICENCE TO KILL	TALISA SOTO
LICENCE TO KILL	TIMOTHY DALTON
LICENCE TO KILL	WAYNE NEWTON
LICENSE TO DRIVE	CAROL KANE
LICENSE TO DRIVE	COREY FELDMAN
LICENSE TO DRIVE	COREY HAIM
LICENSE TO DRIVE	HEATHER GRAHAM
LICENSE TO DRIVE	RICHARD MASUR
LICENSE TO KILL (TF)	DENZEL WASHINGTON
LIEBE	MARIA SCHELL
LIEBESTRAUM	KEVIN ANDERSON
LIEBESTRAUM	KIM NOVAK
LIES BEFORE KISSES (TF)	JACLYN SMITH
LIEUTENANT SCHUSTER'S WIFE (TF)	LEE GRANT
LIEUTENANT WORE SKIRTS, THE	RITA MORENO
LIFE AND ASSASSINATION OF THE KINGFISH, THE (TF)	ED ASNER
LIFE AND DEATH OF COLONEL BLIMP, THE	DEBORAH KERR
LIFE AND DEATH OF COLONEL BLIMP, THE	PATRICK MacNEE
LIFE AND TIMES OF JUDGE ROY BEAN, THE	ANTHONY PERKINS†
LIFE AND TIMES OF JUDGE ROY BEAN, THE	ANTHONY ZERBE
LIFE AND TIMES OF JUDGE ROY BEAN, THE	AVA GARDNER†
LIFE AND TIMES OF JUDGE ROY BEAN, THE	BILL McKINNEY
LIFE AND TIMES OF JUDGE ROY BEAN, THE	JACQUELINE BISSET
LIFE AND TIMES OF JUDGE ROY BEAN, THE	NED BEATTY
LIFE AND TIMES OF JUDGE ROY BEAN, THE	PAUL NEWMAN
LIFE AND TIMES OF JUDGE ROY BEAN, THE	RODDY McDOWALL
LIFE AND TIMES OF JUDGE ROY BEAN, THE	STACY KEACH

Le-Li

FILM
ACTORS
GUIDE

INDEX OF FILM TITLES

489

INDEX OF FILM TITLES

LIFE AND TIMES OF JUDGE ROY BEAN, THE ... TAB HUNTER
LIFE AND TIMES OF JUDGE ROY BEAN, THE ... VICTORIA PRINCIPAL
LIFE AT STAKE, A ... ANGELA LANSBURY
LIFE AT THE TOP ... JEAN SIMMONS
LIFE AT THE TOP ... NIGEL DAVENPORT
LIFE AT THE TOP ... ROBERT MORLEY
LIFE BEGINS AT 17 ... LUANA ANDERS
LIFE FOR RUTH ... MICHAEL BRYANT
LIFE IN THE BALANCE, A ... ANNE BANCROFT
LIFE IN THE BALANCE, A ... RICARDO MONTALBAN
LIFE IS SWEET ... ALISON STEADMAN
LIFE IS SWEET ... DAVID THEWLIS
LIFE IS SWEET ... JANE HORROCKS
LIFE IS SWEET ... STEPHEN REA
LIFE OF EMILE ZOLA, THE ... GALE SONDERGAARD†
LIFE OF EMILE ZOLA, THE ★ ... PAUL MUNI†
LIFE OF EMILE ZOLA, THE ✪✪ ... JOSEPH SCHILDKRAUT†
LIFE OF HER OWN, A ... LANA TURNER
LIFE ON THE EDGE ... ANN RAMSEY†
LIFE STINKS ... HOWARD MORRIS
LIFE STINKS ... JEFFREY TAMBOR
LIFE STINKS ... LESLEY ANN WARREN
LIFE STINKS ... MEL BROOKS
LIFE WITH FATHER ... ELIZABETH TAYLOR
LIFE WITH FATHER ★ ... WILLIAM POWELL†
LIFE WITH HENRY ... JACKIE COOPER
LIFE WITH MIKEY ... CHRISTINA VIDAL
LIFE WITH MIKEY ... CYNDI LAUPER
LIFE WITH MIKEY ... MICHAEL J. FOX
LIFE WITH MIKEY ... NATHAN LANE
LIFE WITH THE LYONS ... ARTHUR HILL
LIFEBOAT ... HUME CRONYN
LIFEFORCE ... PETER FIRTH
LIFEGUARD ... ANNE ARCHER
LIFEGUARD ... KATHLEEN QUINLAN
LIFEGUARD ... LENKA PETERSON
LIFEGUARD ... SAM ELLIOTT
LIFESAVERS ... ADAM SANDLER
LIFESAVERS ... ANTHONY LaPAGLIA
LIFESAVERS ... GARRY SHANDLING
LIFESAVERS ... JON STEWART
LIFESAVERS ... JULIETTE LEWIS
LIFESAVERS ... LIEV SCHREIBER
LIFESAVERS ... MADELINE KAHN
LIFESAVERS ... RITA WILSON
LIFESAVERS ... ROB REINER
LIFESAVERS ... ROBERT KLEIN
LIFESAVERS ... STEVE MARTIN
LIGHT AT THE EDGE OF THE WORLD, THE ... KIRK DOUGLAS
LIGHT AT THE EDGE OF THE WORLD, THE ... SAMANTHA EGGAR
LIGHT FANTASTIC, THE ... ELIZABETH TAYLOR
LIGHT IN THE FOREST, THE ... CAROL LYNLEY
LIGHT IN THE FOREST, THE ... JESSICA TANDY†
LIGHT IN THE PIAZZA ... GEORGE HAMILTON
LIGHT IN THE PIAZZA, THE ... OLIVIA DE HAVILLAND
LIGHT OF DAY ... GENA ROWLANDS
LIGHT OF DAY ... JOAN JETT
LIGHT OF DAY ... MICHAEL J. FOX
LIGHT OF DAY ... MICHAEL McKEAN
LIGHT OF DAY ... MICHAEL ROOKER
LIGHT SLEEPER ... DANA DELANY
LIGHT SLEEPER ... SUSAN SARANDON
LIGHT SLEEPER ... WILLEM DAFOE
LIGHT YEARS (AF) ... GLENN CLOSE
LIGHTHORSEMEN, THE ... ANTHONY ANDREWS
LIGHTNING JACK ... BEVERLY D'ANGELO
LIGHTNING JACK ... CUBA GOODING JR.
LIGHTNING JACK ... PAUL HOGAN
LIGHTNING STRIKES TWICE ... MERCEDES McCAMBRIDGE
LIGHTNING, THE WHITE STALLION ... SUSAN GEORGE
LIGHTSHIP, THE ... ARLISS HOWARD
LIGHTSHIP, THE ... BADJA DJOLA
LIGHTSHIP, THE ... KLAUS MARIA BRANDAUER
LIGHTSHIP, THE ... ROBERT COSTANZO
LIGHTSHIP, THE ... ROBERT DUVALL
LIGHTSHIP, THE ... TOM BOWER
LIGHTSHIP, THE ... WILLIAM FORSYTHE
LIKE A CROW ON A JUNE BUG ... MERCEDES McCAMBRIDGE
LIKE FATHER AND SON ... BILLY DEE WILLIAMS
LIKE FATHER AND SON ... DENISE NICHOLAS
LIKE FATHER LIKE SON ... DUDLEY MOORE
LIKE FATHER, LIKE SON ... KIRK CAMERON
LIKE MOM, LIKE ME (TF) ... KRISTY McNICHOL
LIKE MOM, LIKE ME (TF) ... PATRICK O'NEAL†
LIKE NORMAL PEOPLE (TF) ... HOPE LANGE
LIKE NORMAL PEOPLE (TF) ... JAMES KEACH
LIKELY LADS, THE ... RONALD LACEY
LIKELY STORY, A ... BARBARA HALE
LILI ... MEL FERRER
LILI ... ZSA ZSA GABOR
LILI ★ ... LESLIE CARON
LILIES OF THE FIELD ★★ ... SIDNEY POITIER
LILIES OF THE FIELD ✪ ... LILIA SKALA
LILITH ... GENE HACKMAN
LILITH ... JESSICA WALTER
LILITH ... PETER FONDA
LILITH ... RENE AUBERJONOIS
LILITH ... WARREN BEATTY
LILLIAN RUSSELL ... DON AMECHE†
LILY (TF) ... SHELLEY DUVALL
LILY AND THE ROSE, THE ... LILLIAN GISH†
LILY IN LOVE ... CHRISTOPHER PLUMMER
LILY IN LOVE ... MAGGIE SMITH
LIMBO ... KATE JACKSON
LIMBO ... STUART MARGOLIN
LIME STREET (TF) ... ROBERT WAGNER
LIMELIGHT ... CLAIRE BLOOM
LIMELIGHT ... GERALDINE CHAPLIN
LIMELIGHT ... NORMAN LLOYD
LIMIT, THE ... YAPHET KOTTO
LIMIT UP ... BRAD HALL
LIMIT UP ... DEAN STOCKWELL
LIMIT UP ... NANCY ALLEN
LIMPING MAN, THE ... LLOYD BRIDGES
LINCOLN (MS) ... MARY TYLER MOORE
LINCOLN (MS) ... RICHARD MULLIGAN
LINCOLN (MS) ... SAM WATERSTON
LINCOLN CONSPIRACY, THE ... BRADFORD DILLMAN
LINCOLN CONSPIRACY, THE ... JOHN ANDERSON
LINCOLN CONSPIRACY, THE ... JOHN DEHNER†
LINDBERGH KIDNAPPING CASE, THE (TF) ... ANTHONY HOPKINS
LINDBERGH KIDNAPPING CASE, THE (TF) ... CLIFF DE YOUNG
LINDBERGH KIDNAPPING CASE, THE (TF) ... LAURENCE LUCKINBILL
LINDBERGH KIDNAPPING CASE, THE (TF) ... MARTIN BALSAM
LINEUP, THE ... ELI WALLACH
LINK ... JOE BELCHER
LINK ... RICHARD GARNETT
LINK ... TERENCE STAMP
LION HUNTERS, THE ... WOODY STRODE
LION IN WINTER, THE ... ANTHONY HOPKINS
LION IN WINTER, THE ... JOHN CASTLE
LION IN WINTER, THE ... TIMOTHY DALTON
LION IN WINTER, THE ★ ... PETER O'TOOLE
LION IN WINTER, THE ★★ ... KATHERINE HEPBURN
LION IS IN THE STREETS, A ... BARBARA HALE
LION KING, THE (AF) ... CHEECH MARIN
LION KING, THE (AF) ... ERNIE SABELLA
LION KING, THE (AF) ... JAMES EARL JONES
LION KING, THE (AF) ... JASON WEAVER
LION KING, THE (AF) ... JEREMY IRONS
LION KING, THE (AF) ... JIM CUMMINGS
LION KING, THE (AF) ... JONATHAN TAYLOR THOMAS
LION KING, THE (AF) ... JOSEPH WILLIAMS
LION KING, THE (AF) ... KRISTLE EDWARDS
LION KING, THE (AF) ... LAURA WILLIAMS
LION KING, THE (AF) ... MATHHEW BRODERICK
LION KING, THE (AF) ... NATHAN LANE
LION KING, THE (AF) ... ROBERT GUILLAUME
LION KING, THE (AF) ... ROWAN ATKINSON
LION KING, THE (AF) ... SALLY DWORSKY
LION KING, THE (AF) ... WHOOPI GOLDBERG
LION OF AFRICA, THE (CTF) ... BROOKE ADAMS
LION OF THE DESERT ... ANTHONY QUINN
LION OF THE DESERT ... JOHN GIELGUD
LION OF THE DESERT ... ROD STEIGER
LIONHEART ... BRIAN THOMPSON
LIONHEART ... DEBORAH RENNARD
LIONHEART ... ERIC STOLTZ
LIONHEART ... GABRIEL BYRNE
LIONHEART ... HARRISON PAGE
LIONHEART ... JEAN-CLAUDE VAN DAMME
LIONHEART ... LISA PELIKAN
LIPSTICK ... ANNE BANCROFT
LIPSTICK ... CHRIS SARANDON
LIPSTICK ... MARGAUX HEMINGWAY
LIPSTICK ... MARIEL HEMINGWAY
LIPSTICK ... PERRY KING
LIQUIDATOR, THE ... DAVID TOMLINSON
LIQUIDATOR, THE ... JILL ST. JOHN
LISA ... CHERYL LADD
LISA ... D.W. MOFFETT
LISA ... DONALD PLEASENCE
LISA ... ROBERT STEPHENS
LISA ... STACI KEANAN
LISA, BRIGHT AND DARK (TF) ... KAY LENZ
LISBON ... MAUREEN O'HARA
LIST OF ADRIAN MESSENGER, THE ... BURT LANCASTER†
LIST OF ADRIAN MESSENGER, THE ... FRANK SINATRA
LIST OF ADRIAN MESSENGER, THE ... GEORGE C. SCOTT
LIST OF ADRIAN MESSENGER, THE ... KIRK DOUGLAS
LIST OF ADRIAN MESSENGER, THE ... ROBERT MITCHUM
LIST OF ADRIAN MESSENGER, THE ... TONY CURTIS
LISTEN TO ME ... AMANDA PETERSON
LISTEN TO ME ... JAMI GERTZ
LISTEN TO ME ... KIRK CAMERON
LISTEN TO ME ... ROY SCHEIDER
LISTEN TO ME ... TIM QUILL
LISTEN TO YOUR HEART (TF) ... JOHN MAHONEY
LISTEN TO YOUR HEART (TF) ... KATE JACKSON
LISTEN UP: THE LIVES OF QUINCY JONES ... QUINCY JONES
LISTEN UP: THE LIVES OF QUINCY JONES (FD) ... BARBRA STREISAND
LISTZOMANIA ... ROGER DALTRY
LISZTOMANIA ... FIONA LEWIS
LISZTOMANIA ... PAUL NICHOLAS
LITTLE ADVENTURER ... MARK LESTER
LITTLE ARK, THE ... THEODORE BIKEL
LITTLE BIG HORN ... JOHN IRELAND
LITTLE BIG HORN ... LLOYD BRIDGES
LITTLE BIG LEAGUE ... ASHLEY CROW
LITTLE BIG LEAGUE ... BILLY L. SULLIVAN
LITTLE BIG LEAGUE ... DENNIS FARINA
LITTLE BIG LEAGUE ... JASON ROBARDS
LITTLE BIG LEAGUE ... JOHN ASHTON
LITTLE BIG LEAGUE ... JONATHAN SILVERMAN
LITTLE BIG LEAGUE ... KEVIN DUNN
LITTLE BIG LEAGUE ... LUKE EDWARDS
LITTLE BIG LEAGUE ... MILES FEULNER
LITTLE BIG LEAGUE ... TIMOTHY BUSFIELD
LITTLE BIG MAN ... DUSTIN HOFFMAN
LITTLE BIG MAN ... FAYE DUNAWAY
LITTLE BIG MAN ... JEFF COREY
LITTLE BIG MAN ... M. EMMET WALSH
LITTLE BIG MAN ... MARTIN BALSAM
LITTLE BIG MAN ... RICHARD MULLIGAN
LITTLE BIG MAN ✪ ... CHIEF DAN GEORGE†
LITTLE BIT OF HEAVEN, A ... ROBERT STACK
LITTLE BROTHER ... MILTON BERLE
LITTLE BUDDHA ... ALEX WIESENDANGER
LITTLE BUDDHA ... BRIDGET FONDA
LITTLE BUDDHA ... CHRIS ISAAK
LITTLE BUDDHA ... KEANU REEVES
LITTLE BUDDHA ... YING RUOCHENG
LITTLE DARLINGS ... ARMAND ASSANTE

This is not a list of every film ever made or every cast member, only those listed in this directory.

LITTLE DARLINGS .... KRISTY McNICHOL
LITTLE DARLINGS .... MATT DILLON
LITTLE DARLINGS .... TATUM O'NEAL
LITTLE DORRIT .... DEREK JACOBI
LITTLE DORRIT .... MIRIAM MARGOLYES
LITTLE DORRIT .... PATRICIA HAYES
LITTLE DORRIT ⊙ .... ALEC GUINNESS
LITTLE DORRIT, PART I:
    NOBODY'S FAULT .... DAVID THEWLIS
LITTLE DORRIT, PART I:
    NOBODY'S FAULT .... ELEANOR BRON
LITTLE DORRIT, PART I:
    NOBODY'S FAULT .... JOHN McENERY
LITTLE DORRIT, PART II: LITTLE
    DORRIT'S STORY .... DAVID THEWLIS
LITTLE DORRIT, PART II: LITTLE
    DORRIT'S STORY .... ELEANOR BRON
LITTLE DORRIT, PART II: LITTLE
    DORRIT'S STORY .... JOHN McENERY
LITTLE DRUMMER GIRL, THE .... DIANE KEATON
LITTLE DRUMMER GIRL, THE .... KLAUS KINSKI†
LITTLE DRUMMER
    GIRL, THE .... THORLEY WALTERS†
LITTLE FAUSS AND
    BIG HALSEY .... LAUREN HUTTON
LITTLE FAUSS AND
    BIG HALSY .... MICHAEL J. POLLARD
LITTLE FAUSS AND
    BIG HALSY .... ROBERT REDFORD
LITTLE FLOWER .... JOAN CHEN
LITTLE FOXES, THE ★ .... BETTE DAVIS†
LITTLE FOXES, THE ⊙ .... PATRICIA COLLINGE†
LITTLE FOXES, THE ⊙ .... TERESA WRIGHT
LITTLE GAME, A (TF) .... DIANE BAKER
LITTLE GIANTS .... DEVON SAWA
LITTLE GIANTS .... ED O'NEILL
LITTLE GIANTS .... EDDIE DERHAM
LITTLE GIANTS .... MARY ELLEN TRAINOR
LITTLE GIANTS .... MATTHEW McCURLEY
LITTLE GIANTS .... MICHAEL ZWIENER
LITTLE GIANTS .... RICK MORANIS
LITTLE GIANTS .... SHAWNA WALDRON
LITTLE GIANTS .... SUSANNA THOMPSON
LITTLE GIANTS .... TODD BOSLEY
LITTLE GIRL
    LOST (TF) .... CHRISTOPHER McDONALD
LITTLE GIRL LOST (TF) .... FREDERIC FORREST
LITTLE GIRL LOST (TF) .... PATRICIA KALEMBER
LITTLE GIRL LOST (TF) .... TESS HARPER
LITTLE GIRL WHO LIVES DOWN
    THE LANE, THE .... ALEXIS SMITH†
LITTLE GIRL WHO LIVES DOWN
    THE LANE, THE .... JODIE FOSTER
LITTLE GIRL WHO LIVES DOWN
    THE LANE, THE .... MARTIN SHEEN
LITTLE GIRL WHO LIVES DOWN
    THE LANE, THE .... SCOTT JACOBY
LITTLE GLORIA...HAPPY
    AT LAST (MS) .... ANGELA LANSBURY
LITTLE GLORIA...HAPPY
    AT LAST (MS) .... CHRISTOPHER PLUMMER
LITTLE GLORIA...HAPPY
    AT LAST (TF) .... MARTIN BALSAM
LITTLE HOUSE: BLESS ALL THE
    DEAR CHILDREN (TF) .... DEAN BUTLER
LITTLE HOUSE: BLESS ALL THE
    DEAR CHILDREN (TF) .... MELISSA GILBERT
LITTLE HOUSE: BLESS ALL THE
    DEAR CHILDREN (TF) .... MICHAEL LANDON†
LITTLE HOUSE: LOOK BACK
    TO YESTERDAY (TF) .... DEAN BUTLER
LITTLE HOUSE: LOOK BACK
    TO YESTERDAY (TF) .... MELISSA GILBERT
LITTLE HOUSE: LOOK BACK
    TO YESTERDAY (TF) .... MICHAEL LANDON†
LITTLE HOUSE ON
    THE PRAIRIE (TF) .... MELISSA ANDERSON
LITTLE HOUSE ON
    THE PRAIRIE (TF) .... MELISSA GILBERT
LITTLE HOUSE ON
    THE PRAIRIE (TF) .... MICHAEL LANDON†

LITTLE HOUSE: THE LAST
    FAREWELL (TF) .... DEAN BUTLER
LITTLE HOUSE: THE LAST
    FAREWELL (TF) .... MELISSA GILBERT
LITTLE HOUSE: THE LAST
    FAREWELL (TF) .... MICHAEL LANDON†
LITTLE HUT, THE .... AVA GARDNER†
LITTLE KIDNAPPERS, THE .... THEODORE BIKEL
LITTLE KIDNAPPERS,
    THE (CTF) .... BRUCE GREENWOOD
LITTLE KIDNAPPERS,
    THE (CTF) .... CHARLTON HESTON
LITTLE LADIES OF
    THE NIGHT (TF) .... DAVID SOUL
LITTLE LADIES OF
    THE NIGHT (TF) .... KATHLEEN QUINLAN
LITTLE LADIES OF
    THE NIGHT (TF) .... LOUIS GOSSETT JR.
LITTLE LAURA & BIG JOHN .... KAREN BLACK
LITTLE LORD FAUNTLEROY .... MICKEY ROONEY
LITTLE LORD
    FAUNTLEROY (TF) .... ALEC GUINNESS
LITTLE LORD
    FAUNTLEROY (TF) .... RICK SCHRODER
LITTLE MALCOLM .... DAVID WARNER
LITTLE MALCOLM AND HIS STRUGGLE
    AGAINST THE EUNUCHS .... JOHN HURT
LITTLE MAN TATE .... ADAM HANN-BYRD
LITTLE MAN TATE .... BOB BALABAN
LITTLE MAN TATE .... DIANNE WIEST
LITTLE MAN TATE .... HARRY CONNICK JR.
LITTLE MAN TATE .... JODIE FOSTER
LITTLE MATCH
    GIRL, THE (TF) .... JOHN RHYS-DAVIES
LITTLE MATCH
    GIRL, THE (TF) .... RUE McCLANAHAN
LITTLE MATCH GIRL, THE (TF) ..... WILLIAM DANIELS
LITTLE MERMAID, THE (AF) .... BEN WRIGHT
LITTLE MERMAID, THE (AF) .... BUDDY HACKETT
LITTLE MERMAID,
    THE (AF) .... CHRISTOPHER DANIEL BARNES
LITTLE MERMAID, THE (AF) .... EDIE McCLURG
LITTLE MERMAID, THE (AF) .... JASON MARIN
LITTLE MERMAID, THE (AF) .... JODIE BENSON
LITTLE MERMAID, THE (AF) .... KENNETH MARS
LITTLE MERMAID, THE (AF) .... PADDI EDWARDS
LITTLE MERMAID, THE (AF) .... PAT CARROLL
LITTLE MERMAID, THE (AF) ... RENE AUBERJONOIS
LITTLE MERMAID, THE (AF) ..... SAMUEL E. WRIGHT
LITTLE MERMAID, THE (AF) .... WILL RYAN
LITTLE MINISTER, THE .... KATHERINE HEPBURN
LITTLE MISS MARKER .... BOB NEWHART
LITTLE MISS MARKER .... BRIAN DENNEHY
LITTLE MISS MARKER .... JULIE ANDREWS
LITTLE MISS MARKER .... KENNETH McMILLAN†
LITTLE MISS MARKER .... LEE GRANT
LITTLE MISS MARKER .... SARA STIMSON
LITTLE MISS MARKER .... TONY CURTIS
LITTLE MISS MARKER .... WALTER MATTHAU
LITTLE MO (TF) .... CLAUDE AKINS†
LITTLE MO (TF) .... LESLIE NIELSEN
LITTLE MO (TF) .... MICHAEL LEARNED
LITTLE MONSTERS .... AMBER BARRETTO
LITTLE MONSTERS .... BEN SAVAGE
LITTLE MONSTERS .... DANIEL STERN
LITTLE MONSTERS .... FRANK WHALEY
LITTLE MONSTERS .... FRED SAVAGE
LITTLE MONSTERS .... HOWIE MANDELL
LITTLE MONSTERS .... KALA SAVAGE
LITTLE MONSTERS .... MARGARET WHITTON
LITTLE MONSTERS .... RICK DUCOMMUN
LITTLE MURDERS .... ALAN ARKIN
LITTLE MURDERS .... DONALD SUTHERLAND
LITTLE MURDERS .... ELIZABETH WILSON
LITTLE MURDERS .... ELLIOTT GOULD
LITTLE MURDERS .... JOHN RANDOLPH
LITTLE MURDERS .... LOU JACOBI
LITTLE MURDERS .... VINCENT GARDENIA†
LITTLE NELLIE KELLY .... CHARLES WINNINGER†
LITTLE NELLIE KELLY .... DOUGLAS MCPHAIL†
LITTLE NELLIE KELLY .... JUDY GARLAND†
LITTLE NIGHT MUSIC, A .... DIANA RIGG

LITTLE NIGHT MUSIC, A .... ELIZABETH TAYLOR
LITTLE NIGHT MUSIC, A .... HERMIONE GINGOLD†
LITTLE NIGHT MUSIC, A .... LEN CARIOU
LITTLE NIGHT MUSIC, A .... LESLEY-ANNE DOWN
LITTLE NIKITA .... CAROLINE KAVA
LITTLE NIKITA .... LORETTA DEVINE
LITTLE NIKITA .... LUCY DEAKINS
LITTLE NIKITA .... RICHARD BRADFORD
LITTLE NIKITA .... RICHARD JENKINS
LITTLE NIKITA .... RICHARD LYNCH
LITTLE NIKITA .... RIVER PHOENIX†
LITTLE NIKITA .... SIDNEY POITIER
LITTLE NOISES .... CRISPIN GLOVER
LITTLE NOISES .... TATE DONOVAN
LITTLE NOISES .... TATUM O'NEAL
LITTLE ODESSA .... EDWARD FURLONG
LITTLE ODESSA .... TIM ROTH
LITTLE PANDA .... RYAN SLATER
LITTLE PANDA .... STEPHEN LANG
LITTLE PANDA .... VI DING
LITTLE PRINCE, THE .... BOB FOSSE†
LITTLE PRINCE, THE .... GENE WILDER
LITTLE PRINCE, THE .... JOSS ACKLAND
LITTLE PRINCE, THE .... RICHARD KILEY
LITTLE PRINCESS, A .... ELEANOR BRON
LITTLE PRINCESS, A .... LIAM CUNNINGHAM
LITTLE PRINCESS, A .... LIESEL MATTHEWS
LITTLE RASCALS, THE .... BLAKE COLLINS
LITTLE RASCALS, THE .... BLAKE EWING
LITTLE
RASCALS, THE .... BRITTANY ASHTON HOLMES
LITTLE RASCALS, THE .... BUG HALL
LITTLE RASCALS, THE .... COURTLAND MEAD
LITTLE RASCALS, THE .... JORDAN WARKOL
LITTLE RASCALS, THE .... KEVIN WOODS
LITTLE RASCALS, THE .... MEL BROOKS
LITTLE RASCALS, THE .... ROSS BAGLEY
LITTLE RASCALS, THE .... SAM SALETTA
LITTLE RASCALS, THE .... TRAVIS TEDFORD
LITTLE RASCALS, THE .... ZACHARY MABRY
LITTLE ROMANCE .... THELONIOUS BERNARD
LITTLE ROMANCE, A .... ARTHUR HILL
LITTLE ROMANCE, A .... DAVID DUKES
LITTLE ROMANCE, A .... DIANE LANE
LITTLE ROMANCE, A .... LAURENCE OLIVIER†
LITTLE ROMANCE, A .... SALLY KELLERMAN
LITTLE SEX, A .... BILL SMITROVICH
LITTLE SEX, A .... EDWRAD HERRMANN
LITTLE SEX, A .... JOAN COPELAND
LITTLE SEX, A .... JOHN GLOVER
LITTLE SEX, A .... KATE CAPSHAW
LITTLE SEX, A .... MELINDA CULEA
LITTLE SEX, A .... SUSANNA DALTON
LITTLE SEX, A .... TIM MATHESON
LITTLE SEX, A .... WALLACE SHAWN
LITTLE SEX, A .... WENDIE MALICK
LITTLE SHEPHERD OF
    KINGDOM COME, THE .... GEORGE KENNEDY
LITTLE SHOP OF HORRORS .... BILL MURRAY
LITTLE SHOP OF
    HORRORS .... CHRISTOPHER GUEST
LITTLE SHOP OF HORRORS .... ELLEN GREENE
LITTLE SHOP OF HORRORS .... JAMES BELUSHI
LITTLE SHOP OF HORRORS .... JOHN CANDY†
LITTLE SHOP OF HORRORS .... RICK MORANIS
LITTLE SHOP OF HORRORS .... STEVE MARTIN
LITTLE SHOP OF
    HORRORS .... VINCENT GARDENIA†
LITTLE SHOP OF
    HORRORS, THE .... JACK NICHOLSON
LITTLE THIEF, THE .... CHARLOTTE GAINSBOURG
LITTLE THIEF, THE .... DIDIER BAZACE
LITTLE THIEF, THE .... SIMON DE LA BROSSE
LITTLE TREASURE .... BURT LANCASTER†
LITTLE TREASURE .... TED DANSON
LITTLE WHITE LIES (TF) .... ANN JILLIAN
LITTLE WOMEN (1933) .... KATHERINE HEPBURN
LITTLE WOMEN (1933) .... JOAN BENNETT†
LITTLE WOMEN (1933) .... PAUL LUKAS†
LITTLE WOMEN (1933) .... FRANCES DEE†
LITTLE WOMEN (1933) .... JEAN PARKER†
LITTLE WOMEN (1933) .... EDNA MAY OLIVER†

491

I N D E X   O F   F I L M   T I T L E S

LITTLE
 WOMEN (1933) .... DOUGLASS MONTGOMERY†
LITTLE WOMEN (1933) .... SPRING BYINGTON†
LITTLE WOMEN (1949) .... ELIZABETH TAYLOR
LITTLE WOMEN (1949) .... MARY ASTOR†
LITTLE WOMEN (1949) .... PETER LAWFORD†
LITTLE WOMEN (1949) .... MARGARET O'BRIEN†
LITTLE WOMEN (1949) .... JANET LEIGH
LITTLE WOMEN (1949) .... JUNE ALLYSON
LITTLE WOMEN .... CHRISTIAN BALE
LITTLE WOMEN .... CLAIRE DANES
LITTLE WOMEN .... ERIC STOLTZ
LITTLE WOMEN .... GABRIEL BYRNE
LITTLE WOMEN .... KIRSTEN DUNST
LITTLE WOMEN .... LEON AMES
LITTLE WOMEN .... MARY WICKES
LITTLE WOMEN .... SAMANTHA MATHIS
LITTLE WOMEN .... SUSAN SARANDON
LITTLE WOMEN .... TRINI ALVARADO
LITTLE WOMEN .... WINONA RYDER
LITTLE WOMEN (TF) .... GREER GARSON
LIVE A LITTLE, LOVE A LITTLE .... ELVIS PRESLEY†
LIVE A LITTLE, STEAL A LOT .... DON STROUD
LIVE AGAIN, DIE AGAIN (TF) .... DONNA MILLS
LIVE AND LET DIE .... BERNARD LEE†
LIVE AND LET DIE .... CLIFTON JAMES
LIVE AND LET DIE .... DAVID HEDISON
LIVE AND LET DIE .... GEOFFREY HOLDER
LIVE AND LET DIE .... JANE SEYMOUR
LIVE AND LET DIE .... LOIS MAXWELL
LIVE AND LET DIE .... ROGER MOORE
LIVE AND LET DIE .... YAPHET KOTTO
LIVE FOR LIFE .... CANDICE BERGEN
LIVE IT UP .... DAVID HEMMINGS
LIVE NOW, PAY LATER .... GEOFFREY KEEN
LIVE NUDE GIRLS .... DANA DELANY
LIVE NUDE GIRLS .... KIM CATTRALL
LIVE NUDE GIRLS .... LORA ZANE
LIVE NUDE GIRLS .... OLIVIA D'ABO
LIVELY SET, THE .... DOUG McCLURE
LIVES AND TIMES OF
 SCARAMOUCHE, THE .... MICHAEL SARRAZIN
LIVES OF JENNY
 DOLAN, THE (TF) .... DAVID HEDISON
LIVES OF JENNY
 DOLAND, THE (TF) .... SHIRLEY JONES
LIVIN' LARGE! .... BLANCHE BAKER
LIVIN' LARGE! .... JULIA CAMPBELL
LIVIN' LARGE! .... LISA C. ARRINDELL
LIVIN' LARGE .... TERENCE T. C. CARSON
LIVING APART TOGETHER .... SYLVIA KRISTEL
LIVING DAYLIGHTS, THE .... ART MALIK
LIVING DAYLIGHTS, THE .... GEOFFREY KEEN
LIVING DAYLIGHTS, THE .... JEROEN KRABBE
LIVING DAYLIGHTS, THE .... JOE DON BAKER
LIVING DAYLIGHTS, THE .... JOHN RHYS-DAVIES
LIVING DAYLIGHTS, THE .... MARYAM D'ABO
LIVING DAYLIGHTS, THE .... TIMOTHY DALTON
LIVING FREE .... GEOFFREY KEEN
LIVING FREE .... NIGEL DAVENPORT
LIVING IDOL, THE .... STEVE FORREST
LIVING IN A BIG WAY .... GENE KELLY
LIVING IN A BIG WAY .... PHYLLIS THAXTER
LIVING IN A BIG WAY .... SHELLEY WINTERS
LIVING IT UP .... DEAN MARTIN
LIVING IT UP .... JANET LEIGH
LIVING IT UP .... JERRY LEWIS
LIVING PROOF: THE HANK
 WILLIAMS, JR. STORY (TF) ..... CHRISTIAN SLATER
LIVING VENUS .... HARVEY KORMAN
LIZA .... CATHERINE DENEUVE
LIZZIE .... ELEANOR PARKER
LI'L ABNER .... JULIE NEWMAR
LI'L ABNER .... STELLA STEVENS
LI'L ABNER .... STUBBY KAYE
LO SBARCO DI ANZIO .... PETER FALK
LO STRANIERO .... MARCELLO MASTROIANNI
LOADED GUNS .... URSULA ANDRESS
LOADED GUNS .... WOODY STRODE
LOCAL HERO .... BURT LANCASTER†
LOCAL HERO .... DENIS LAWSON

LOCAL HERO .... PETER RIEGERT
LOCH NESS .... IAN HOLM
LOCH NESS .... JOELY RICHARDSON
LOCH NESS .... TED DANSON
LOCK UP .... DARLANNE FLEUGEL
LOCK UP .... DONALD SUTHERLAND
LOCK UP .... FRANK McRAE
LOCK UP .... JOHN AMOS
LOCK UP .... SONNY LANDHAM
LOCK UP .... SYLVESTER STALLONE
LOCK UP .... TOM SIZEMORE
LOCK UP YOUR
 DAUGHTERS .... CHRISTOPHER PLUMMER
LOCK UP YOUR DAUGHTERS .... IAN BANNEN
LOCK UP YOUR DAUGHTERS .... ROY DOTRICE
LOCK UP YOUR DAUGHTERS .... SUSANNAH YORK
LOCKED DOOR, THE .... BARBARA STANWYCK†
LOCKET, THE .... ROBERT MITCHUM
LOCUSTS (TF) .... KATHERINE HELMOND
LOG OF THE BLACK
 PEARL, THE (TF) .... RALPH BELLAMY†
LOGAN'S RUN .... FARRAH FAWCETT
LOGAN'S RUN .... JENNY AGUTTER
LOGAN'S RUN .... MICHAEL YORK
LOGAN'S RUN .... PETER USTINOV
LOGAN'S RUN .... RICHARD JORDAN†
LOGAN'S RUN .... ROSCOE LEE BROWNE
LOGAN'S RUN (TF) .... GREGORY HARRISON
LOIS GIBBS AND THE
 LOVE CANAL (TF) .... DANIELLE von ZERNECK
LOLA .... ANOUK AIMEE
LOLA .... CHARLES BRONSON
LOLA .... SUSAN GEORGE
LOLA MONTES .... PETER USTINOV
LOLITA .... LOIS MAXWELL
LOLITA .... SHELLEY WINTERS
LOLLY MADONNA XXX .... ED LAUTER
LOLLY MADONNA XXX .... GARY BUSEY
LOLLY MADONNA XXX .... JEFF BRIDGES
LOLLY MADONNA XXX .... RANDY QUAID
LOLLY MADONNA XXX .... ROD STEIGER
LOLLY MADONNA XXX .... SCOTT WILSON
LOLLY MADONNA XXX .... SEASON HUBLEY
LOLLY-MADONNA WAR, THE .... ED LAUTER
LOLLY-MADONNA WAR, THE .... GARY BUSEY
LOLLY-MADONNA WAR, THE .... JEFF BRIDGES
LOLLY-MADONNA WAR, THE .... RANDY QUAID
LOLLY-MADONNA WAR, THE .... SCOTT WILSON
LOLLY-MADONNA WAR, THE .... SEASON HUBLEY
LONDON AFFAIR, THE .... NIGEL DAVENPORT
LONDON AND DAVIS IN
 NEW YORK (TF) .... RODDY McDOWALL
LONDON AND DAVIS IN
 NEW YORK (TF) .... SEASON HUBLEY
LONDON CALLING .... DOUG E. DOUG
LONDON KILLS ME .... ALUN ARMSTRONG
LONE COWBOY .... JACKIE COOPER
LONE HAND .... BARBARA HALE
LONE HAND .... JAMES ARNESS
LONE RANGER AND THE LOST
 CITY OF GOLD, THE .... JAY SILVERHEELS†
LONE STAR .... AVA GARDNER†
LONE STAR TRAIL .... ROBERT MITCHUM
LONE WOLF McQUADE .... BARBARA CARRERA
LONE WOLF McQUADE .... CHUCK NORRIS
LONE WOLF McQUADE .... DAVID CARRADINE
LONE WOLF TAKES A
 CHANCE, THE .... LLOYD BRIDGES
LONELIEST
 RUNNER, THE (TF) .... MELISSA ANDERSON
LONELIEST
 RUNNER, THE (TF) .... MICHAEL LANDON†
LONELINESS OF THE LONG
 DISTANCE RUNNER, THE ...... ALEC McCOWEN
LONELINESS OF THE LONG
 DISTANCE RUNNER, THE .... TOM COURTENAY
LONELY ARE THE BRAVE .... BILL BIXBY†
LONELY ARE THE BRAVE ...... CARROLL O'CONNOR
LONELY ARE THE BRAVE ...... CHARLES BRONSON
LONELY ARE THE BRAVE .... GENA ROWLANDS
LONELY ARE THE BRAVE .... GEORGE KENNEDY

LONELY ARE THE BRAVE .... KIRK DOUGLAS
LONELY ARE THE BRAVE .... WALTER MATTHAU
LONELY GUY, THE .... ANDY GARCIA
LONELY GUY, THE .... CHARLES GRODIN
LONELY GUY, THE .... STEVE MARTIN
LONELY HEART BANDITS ...... KATHLEEN FREEMAN
LONELY HEARTS .... BEVERLY D'ANGELO
LONELY HEARTS .... JOANNA CASSIDY
LONELY HEARTS .... ROBERT GINTY
LONELY LADY, THE .... PIA ZADORA
LONELY LADY, THE .... RAY LIOTTA
LONELY MAN, THE .... ANTHONY PERKINS†
LONELY MAN, THE .... CLAUDE AKINS†
LONELY MAN, THE .... JACK PALANCE
LONELY PASSION OF
 JUDITH HEARNE, THE .... BOB HOSKINS
LONELY PASSION OF
 JUDITH HEARNE, THE .... MAGGIE SMITH
LONELY PASSION OF
 JUDITH HEARNE, THE .... WENDY HILLER
LONELYHEARTS o .... MAUREEN STAPLETON
LONERS, THE .... DEAN STOCKWELL
LONESOME DOVE (MS) .... ANJELICA HUSTON
LONESOME DOVE (MS) .... DANNY GLOVER
LONESOME DOVE (MS) .... DIANE LANE
LONESOME DOVE (MS) .... FREDERIC FORREST
LONESOME DOVE (MS) .... GLENNE HEADLY
LONESOME DOVE (MS) .... ROBERT DUVALL
LONESOME DOVE (MS) .... ROBERT URICH
LONESOME DOVE (MS) .... TOMMY LEE JONES
LONG AGO TOMORROW .... GEOFFREY BAYLDON
LONG AGO TOMORROW .... MALCOLM McDOWELL
LONG AND THE SHORT
 AND THE TALL, THE .... DAVID McCALLUM
LONG AND THE SHORT
 AND THE TALL, THE .... RICHARD HARRIS
LONG ARM, THE .... GEOFFREY KEEN
LONG ARM, THE .... IAN BANNEN
LONG, DARK NIGHT, THE ...... R.G. ARMSTRONG
LONG DAY'S DYING .... TONY BECKLEY†
LONG DAYS OF
 SUMMER, THE (TF) .... JOAN HACKETT†
LONG DAY'S DYING, THE .... DAVID HEMMINGS
LONG DAY'S JOURNEY
 INTO NIGHT .... DEAN STOCKWELL
LONG DAY'S JOURNEY
 INTO NIGHT .... JASON ROBARDS
LONG DAY'S JOURNEY
 INTO NIGHT ★ .... KATHERINE HEPBURN
LONG DAY'S JOURNEY
 INTO NIGHT (TF) .... JACK LEMMON
LONG DUEL, THE .... CHARLOTTE RAMPLING
LONG GONE (CTF) .... WILLIAM L. PETERSEN
LONG GOOD FRIDAY, THE .... BOB HOSKINS
LONG GOOD FRIDAY, THE .... HELEN MIRREN
LONG GOOD FRIDAY, THE .... MICHAEL BYRNE
LONG GOOD FRIDAY, THE .... PIERCE BROSNAN
LONG GOODBYE,
 THE .... ARNOLD SCHWARZENEGGER
LONG GOODBYE, THE .... ELLIOTT GOULD
LONG GOODBYE, THE .... NINA VAN PALLANDT
LONG GOODBYE, THE .... STERLING HAYDEN†
LONG GRAY LINE, THE .... BETSY PALMER
LONG GRAY LINE, THE .... HARRY CAREY JR.
LONG GRAY LINE, THE .... MAUREEN O'HARA
LONG GRAY LINE, THE .... PATRICK WAYNE
LONG GRAY LINE, THE .... PETER GRAVES
LONG HOT SUMMER, THE .... ANGELA LANSBURY
LONG HOT
 SUMMER, THE .... ANTHONY (TONY) FRANCIOSA
LONG HOT SUMMER, THE ..... JOANNE WOODWARD
LONG HOT SUMMER, THE .... LEE REMICK†
LONG HOT SUMMER, THE .... PAUL NEWMAN
LONG HOT SUMMER, THE ..... RICHARD ANDERSON
LONG HOT SUMMER, THE .... VAL AVERY
LONG HOT SUMMER,
 THE (MS) .... CYBILL SHEPHERD
LONG HOT SUMMER, THE (MS) .... DON JOHNSON
LONG HOT SUMMER, THE (TF) .... AVA GARDNER†
LONG HOT SUMMER, THE (TF) .... JUDITH IVEY
LONG JOURNEY HOME, THE (TF) ...... DAVID BIRNEY

This is not a list of every film ever made or every cast member, only those listed in this directory.

LONG JOURNEY
  HOME, THE (TF) .... MEREDITH BAXTER
LONG LIVE LIFE .... ANOUK AIMEE
LONG, LONG TRAILOR, THE .... DESI ARNAZ†
LONG, LONG TRAILOR, THE .... LUCILLE BALL†
LONG MEMORY, THE .... JOHN MILLS
LONG NIGHT, THE .... VINCENT PRICE†
LONG RIDE HOME, THE .... GEORGE HAMILTON
LONG RIDE HOME, THE .... HARRISON FORD
LONG RIDERS, THE .... DAVID CARRADINE
LONG RIDERS, THE .... DENNIS QUAID
LONG RIDERS, THE .... HARRY CAREY JR.
LONG RIDERS, THE .... JAMES KEACH
LONG RIDERS, THE .... KEITH CARRADINE
LONG RIDERS, THE .... PETER JASON
LONG RIDERS, THE .... RANDY QUAID
LONG RIDERS, THE .... ROBERT CARRADINE
LONG RIDERS, THE .... STACY KEACH
LONG RUN, THE .... JOHN SAVAGE
LONG RUN, THE .... KELLY RENO
LONG SHIPS, THE .... GORDAN JACKSON†
LONG SHIPS, THE .... RICHARD WIDMARK
LONG SHIPS, THE .... RUSS TAMBLYN
LONG SHIPS, THE .... SIDNEY POITIER
LONG SUMMER OF GEORGE
  ADAMS, THE (TF) .... DAVID GRAF
LONG SUMMER OF GEORGE
  ADAMS, THE (TF) .... JAMES GARNER
LONG SUMMER OF GEORGE
  ADAMS, THE (TF) .... JOAN HACKETT†
LONG TIME GONE (TF) .... EDDIE ZAMMIT
LONG WAIT, THE .... ANTHONY QUINN
LONG WALK HOME, THE .... DWIGHT SCHULTZ
LONG WALK HOME, THE .... DYLAN BAKER
LONG WALK HOME, THE .... MARY STEENBURGEN
LONG WALK HOME, THE .... SISSY SPACEK
LONG WALK HOME, THE .... WHOOPI GOLDBERG
LONG WALK HOME, THE .... YING RHAMES
LONGARM (TF) .... DAPHNE ASHBROOK
LONGARM (TF) .... JOHN TERLESKY
LONGARM (TF) .... RENE AUBERJONOIS
LONGEST DAY, THE .... EDDIE ALBERT
LONGEST DAY, THE .... GEORGE SEGAL
LONGEST DAY, THE .... HENRY FONDA†
LONGEST DAY, THE .... JOHN WAYNE†
LONGEST DAY, THE .... MEL FERRER
LONGEST DAY, THE .... PETER LAWFORD†
LONGEST DAY, THE .... RED BUTTONS
LONGEST DAY, THE .... RICHARD BURTON†
LONGEST DAY, THE .... ROBERT MITCHUM
LONGEST DAY, THE .... ROBERT WAGNER
LONGEST DAY, THE .... ROD STEIGER
LONGEST DAY, THE .... RODDY McDOWALL
LONGEST DAY, THE .... SEAN CONNERY
LONGEST DAY, THE .... STEVE FORREST
LONGEST DAY, THE .... STUART WHITMAN
LONGEST HUNDRED
  MILES, THE (TF) .... KATHERINE ROSS
LONGEST NIGHT, THE (TF) .... PHYLLIS THAXTER
LONGEST YARD, THE .... BERNADETTE PETERS
LONGEST YARD, THE .... BURT REYNOLDS
LONGEST YARD, THE .... ED LAUTER
LONGEST YARD, THE .... EDDIE ALBERT
LONGEST YARD, THE .... HARRY CAESAR
LONGEST YARD, THE .... JAMES HAMPTON
LONGEST YARD, THE .... MICHAEL CONRAD†
LONGEST YARD, THE .... MIKE HENRY
LONGEST YARD, THE .... RICHARD KIEL
LONGEST YARD, THE .... ROBERT TESSIER†
LONGSHOT, THE .... HARVEY KORMAN
LONGSHOT, THE .... TIM CONWAY
LONGTIME COMPANION .... BRAD O'HARE
LONGTIME COMPANION .... BRIAN COUSINS
LONGTIME COMPANION .... CAMPBELL SCOTT
LONGTIME COMPANION .... DERMOT MULRONEY
LONGTIME COMPANION .... JOHN DOSSETT
LONGTIME COMPANION .... MARK LAMOS
LONGTIME COMPANION ..... MARY-LOUISE PARKER
LONGTIME COMPANION ... MICHAEL SCHOEFFLING
LONGTIME COMPANION ... PATRICK CASSIDY
LONGTIME COMPANION ...... STEPHEN CAFFREY
LONGTIME COMPANION ◦ .... BRUCE DAVISON

LOOK BACK IN ANGER .... CLAIRE BLOOM
LOOK BACK IN ANGER .... DONALD PLEASENCE
LOOK BACK IN ANGER .... NIGEL DAVENPORT
LOOK DOWN AND DIE .... ALBERT SALMI†
LOOK DOWN AND DIE/
  MEN OF STEEL .... ART CARNEY
LOOK DOWN AND DIE/
  MEN OF STEEL .... GEORGE KENNEDY
LOOK DOWN AND DIE/
  MEN OF STEEL .... HARRIS YULIN
LOOK DOWN AND DIE/
  MEN OF STEEL .... JENNIFER O'NEILL
LOOK DOWN AND DIE/
  MEN OF STEEL .... LEE MAJORS
LOOK DOWN AND DIE/
  MEN OF STEEL .... RICHARD LYNCH
LOOK FOR THE
  SILVER LINING .... GORDON MACRAE†
LOOK WHAT'S HAPPENED TO
  ROSEMARY'S BABY (TF) .... STEPHEN McHATTIE
LOOK WHO'S TALKING .... ABE VIGODA
LOOK WHO'S TALKING .... BRUCE WILLIS
LOOK WHO'S TALKING .... GEORGE SEGAL
LOOK WHO'S TALKING .... JOHN TRAVOLTA
LOOK WHO'S TALKING .... KIRSTIE ALLEY
LOOK WHO'S TALKING .... OLYMPIA DUKAKIS
LOOK WHO'S TALKING NOW .... DANNY DEVITO
LOOK WHO'S TALKING NOW .... DIANE KEATON
LOOK WHO'S TALKING NOW .... GEORGE SEGAL
LOOK WHO'S TALKING NOW .... OLYMPIA DUKAKIS
LOOK WHO'S TALKING NOW .... JOHN TRAVOLTA
LOOK WHO'S TALKING NOW .... KIRSTIE ALLEY
LOOK WHO'S TALKING NOW ... LYSETTE ANTHONY
LOOK WHO'S TALKING TOO .... BRUCE WILLIS
LOOK WHO'S TALKING TOO .... DAMON WAYANS
LOOK WHO'S TALKING TOO .... ELIAS KOTEAS
LOOK WHO'S TALKING TOO .... JOHN TRAVOLTA
LOOK WHO'S TALKING TOO .... KIRSTIE ALLEY
LOOK WHO'S TALKING TOO .... OLYMPIA DUKAKIS
LOOK WHO'S TALKING TOO .... ROSEANNE
LOOKER .... ALBERT FINNEY
LOOKER .... DORIAN HAREWOOD
LOOKER .... JAMES COBURN
LOOKER .... LEIGH TAYLOR-YOUNG
LOOKER .... SUSAN DEY
LOOKIN' GOOD .... BEN JOHNSON
LOOKIN' GOOD .... PATRICK O'NEAL†
LOOKIN' TO GET OUT .... ANN-MARGRET
LOOKIN' TO GET OUT .... BURT YOUNG
LOOKIN' TO GET OUT .... JON VOIGHT
LOOKING FOR LOVE .... DANNY THOMAS†
LOOKING FOR LOVE .... GEORGE HAMILTON
LOOKING FOR LOVE .... PAULA PRENTISS
LOOKING FOR MR. GOODBAR .... DIANE KEATON
LOOKING FOR MR. GOODBAR .... JULIUS HARRIS
LOOKING FOR MR. GOODBAR .... LeVAR BURTON
LOOKING FOR MR. GOODBAR .... RICHARD GERE
LOOKING FOR MR. GOODBAR .... RICHARD KILEY
LOOKING FOR MR. GOODBAR .... TOM BERENGER
LOOKING FOR
  MR. GOODBAR .... WILLIAM ATHERTON
LOOKING FOR MR. GOODBAR ◦ ..... TUESDAY WELD
LOOKING GLASS WAR, THE .... ANTHONY HOPKINS
LOOKING GLASS WAR, THE .... SUSAN GEORGE
LOOKING GOOD .... CHARLOTTE RAMPLING
LOOKING GOOD .... ROBERT BLAKE
LOON .... JASON PATRIC
LOON .... ROBIN WRIGHT
LOOPHOLE .... ALBERT FINNEY
LOOPHOLE .... JONATHAN PRYCE
LOOPHOLE .... MARTIN SHEEN
LOOPHOLE .... SUSANNAH YORK
LOOSE CANNONS .... DAN AYKROYD
LOOSE CANNONS .... DOM DeLUISE
LOOSE CANNONS .... GENE HACKMAN
LOOSE CANNONS .... RONNY COX
LOOSE CHANGE (TF) .... STEPHEN MACHT
LOOSE SHOES .... AVERY SCHREIBER
LOOSE SHOES .... BILL MURRAY
LOOSE SHOES .... BUDDY HACKETT
LOOSE SHOES .... HOWARD HESSEMAN
LOOSE SHOES .... SUSAN TYRRELL

LOOT .... MILO O'SHEA
LOOTERS, THE .... ART EVANS
LOOTERS, THE .... ICE CUBE
LOOTERS, THE .... ICE-T
LORD CHUMLEY .... LILLIAN GISH†
LORD JIM .... ELI WALLACH
LORD JIM .... PETER O'TOOLE
LORD LOVE A DUCK .... HARVEY KORMAN
LORD LOVE A DUCK .... MAX SHOWALTER
LORD LOVE A DUCK .... RODDY McDOWALL
LORD LOVE A DUCK .... TUESDAY WELD
LORD OF THE FLIES .... MICHAEL GREENE
LORD OF THE RINGS, THE (AF) .... BILLY BARTY
LORDS AND MUSIC .... ANN SOTHERN
LORDS OF DISCIPLINE, THE .... BARBARA BABCOCK
LORDS OF DISCIPLINE, THE .... JUDGE REINHOLD
LORDS OF DISCIPLINE, THE .... RICK ROSSOVICH
LORDS OF FLATBUSH, THE .... HENRY WINKLER
LORDS OF FLATBUSH, THE .... PERRY KING
LORDS OF FLATBUSH, THE .... SUSAN BLAKELY
LORDS OF
  FLATBUSH, THE .... SYLVESTER STALLONE
LORENZO'S OIL .... NICK NOLTE
LORENZO'S OIL .... PETER USTINOV
LORENZO'S OIL ★ .... SUSAN SARANDON
LORNA DOONE .... BARBARA HALE
LORNA DOONE .... JOHN DEHNER†
LOS ALBANILES .... KATHY JURADO
LOS AMIGOS .... ANTHONY QUINN
LOS AMIGOS .... FRANCO NERO
LOS BANDIDOS .... JAN-MICHAEL VINCENT
LOS DESPERADOS .... ERNEST BORGNINE
LOS GUERILLEROS .... ELI WALLACH
LOS GUERILLEROS .... LYNN REDGRAVE
LOS OJOS VENDADOS .... GERALDINE CHAPLIN
LOSIN' IT .... JACKIE EARLE HALEY
LOSIN' IT .... TOM CRUISE
LOSING GROUND .... DUANE JONES†
LOSING ISAIAH .... CUBA GOODING JR.
LOSING ISAIAH .... DAISY EAGAN
LOSING ISAIAH .... DAVID STRATHAIRN
LOSING ISAIAH .... HALLE BERRY
LOSING ISAIAH .... JESSICA LANGE
LOSING ISAIAH .... JOIE LEE
LOSING ISAIAH .... LaTANYA RICHARDSON
LOSING ISAIAH .... MARK JOHN JEFFRIES
LOSING ISAIAH .... SAMUEL L. JACKSON
LOSS OF INNOCENCE .... SUSANNAH YORK
LOST AND FOUND .... GEORGE SEGAL
LOST AND FOUND .... GLENDA JACKSON
LOST AND FOUND .... JOHN CANDY†
LOST AND FOUND .... MARTIN SHORT
LOST AND FOUND .... MAUREEN STAPLETON
LOST AND FOUND .... PAUL SORVINO
LOST ANGEL .... AVA GARDNER†
LOST ANGELS .... ADAM HOROVITZ
LOST ANGELS .... AMY LOCANE
LOST ANGELS .... DONALD SUTHERLAND
LOST BOUNDARIES .... MEL FERRER
LOST BOYS, THE .... BARNARD HUGHES
LOST BOYS, THE .... BILLY WIRTH
LOST BOYS, THE .... COREY FELDMAN
LOST BOYS, THE .... COREY HAIM
LOST BOYS, THE .... DIANNE WIEST
LOST BOYS, THE .... EDWRAD HERRMANN
LOST BOYS, THE .... JAMI GERTZ
LOST BOYS, THE .... JASON PATRIC
LOST BOYS, THE .... KIEFER SUTHERLAND
LOST COMMAND .... ANTHONY QUINN
LOST COMMAND .... GEORGE SEGAL
LOST EMPIRE, THE .... ANGELA AAMES
LOST EMPIRES (TF) .... COLIN FIRTH
LOST FLIGHT (TF) .... BILLY DEE WILLIAMS
LOST FLIGHT (TF) .... LLOYD BRIDGES
LOST HONOR OF
  KATHRYN BECK, THE (TF) .... DICK CUSAK
LOST HORIZON .... GEORGE KENNEDY
LOST HORIZON .... JAMES SHIGETA
LOST HORIZON .... JANE WYATT
LOST HORIZON .... JOHN GIELGUD
LOST HORIZON .... LIV ULLMANN
LOST HORIZON .... MICHAEL YORK

LOST HORIZON ... SALLY KELLERMAN
LOST HORIZON ✪ ... H. B. WARNER†
LOST HOUSE, THE ... LILLIAN GISH†
LOST IN AMERICA ... ALBERT BROOKS
LOST IN AMERICA ... GARRY MARSHALL
LOST IN AMERICA ... JULIE HAGERTY
LOST IN SIBERIA ... ANTHONY ANDREWS
LOST IN THE STARS ... RAYMOND ST. JACQUES
LOST IN YONKERS ... BRAD STOLL
LOST IN YONKERS ... DAVID STRATHAIRN
LOST IN YONKERS ... IRENE WORTH
LOST IN YONKERS ... JACK LAUFER
LOST IN YONKERS ... MERCEDES RUEHL
LOST IN YONKERS ... MIKE DAMUS
LOST IN YONKERS ... RICHARD DREYFUSS
LOST IN YONKERS ... ROBERT G. MIRANDA
LOST LADY, A ... BARBARA STANWYCK†
LOST MAN, THE ... PAUL WINFIELD
LOST MAN, THE ... SIDNEY POITIER
LOST PEOPLE, THE ... MAE ZETTERLING†
LOST WEEKEND, THE ... HOWARD DA SILVA†
LOST WEEKEND, THE ... JANE WYMAN
LOST WEEKEND, THE ★★ ... RAY MILLAND†
LOST WORLD, THE ... DAVID HEDISON
LOST WORLD, THE ... JILL ST. JOHN
LOUIS ARMSTRONG— CHICAGO STYLE (TF) ... RED BUTTONS
LOUISA ... PIPER LAURIE
LOUISA ... RONALD REAGAN
LOUISIANA HAYRIDE ... LLOYD BRIDGES
LOUISIANA PURCHASE ... BOB HOPE
LOULOU ... GERARD DEPARDIEU
LOVE ... GRETA GARBO†
LOVE ... JOHN GILBERT†
LOVE A LA CARTE ... MARCELLO MASTROIANNI
LOVE A LITTLE, STEAL A LOT ... ROBERT CONRAD
LOVE AFFAIR (1932) ... HUMPHREY BOGART†
LOVE AFFAIR (1932) ... JACK KENNEDY†
LOVE AFFAIR (1932) ... DOROTHY MACKAILL†
LOVE AFFAIR (1932) ... BARBARA LEONARD†
LOVE AFFAIR (1932) ... ASTRID ALLWYN†
LOVE AFFAIR (1939) ✪ ... MARIA OUSPENSKAYA†
LOVE AFFAIR (1939) ... IRENE DUNNE†
LOVE AFFAIR (1939) ... CHARLES BOYER†
LOVE AFFAIR (1939) ... LEE BOWMAN†
LOVE AFFAIR (1939) ... ASTRID ALLWYN†
LOVE AFFAIR (1939) ... MAURICE MOSCOVICH†
LOVE AFFAIR ... ANNETTE BENING
LOVE AFFAIR ... GARRY SHANDLING
LOVE AFFAIR ... KATE CAPSHAW
LOVE AFFAIR ... KATHERINE HEPBURN
LOVE AFFAIR ... PIERCE BROSNAN
LOVE AFFAIR ... WARREN BEATTY
LOVE AFFAIR: THE ELEANOR AND LOU GEHRIG STORY, A (TF) ... BLYTHE DANNER
LOVE AFFAIR: THE ELEANOR AND LOU GEHRIG STORY, A (TF) ... EDWRAD HERRMANN
LOVE AMONG THE RUINS (TF) ... KATHERINE HEPBURN
LOVE AMONG THE RUINS (TF) ... LEIGH LAWSON
LOVE AMONG THIEVES (TF) ... AUDREY HEPBURN†
LOVE AMONG THIEVES (TF) ... JERRY ORBACH
LOVE AMONG THIEVES (TF) ... ROBERT WAGNER
LOVE AMONG THIEVES (TF) ... SAMANTHA EGGAR
LOVE AND BETRAYAL (TF) ... AMANDA PETERSON
LOVE AND BETRAYAL (TF) ... DAVID BIRNEY
LOVE AND BETRAYAL (TF) ... FRAN DRESCHER
LOVE AND BETRAYAL (TF) ... STEFANIE POWERS
LOVE AND BULLETS ... BRADFORD DILLMAN
LOVE AND BULLETS ... CHARLES BRONSON
LOVE AND BULLETS ... HENRY SILVA
LOVE AND BULLETS ... JILL IRELAND†
LOVE AND BULLETS ... ROD STEIGER
LOVE AND BULLETS ... VAL AVERY
LOVE AND DEATH ... DIANE KEATON
LOVE AND DEATH ... HAROLD GOULD
LOVE AND DEATH ... WOODY ALLEN
LOVE AND HATE: A MARRIAGE MADE IN HELL (MS) ... KATE NELLIGAN
LOVE AND LIES (TF) ... PETER GALLAGHER
LOVE AND MONEY ... ARMAND ASSANTE
LOVE AND MONEY ... KLAUS KINSKI†
LOVE AND MONEY ... RAY SHARKEY†
LOVE AND MONEY ... WILLIAM PRINCE
LOVE AND PAIN AND THE WHOLE DAMN THING ... MAGGIE SMITH
LOVE AND PAIN AND THE WHOLE DAMN THING ... TIMOTHY BOTTOMS
LOVE AND THE MIDNIGHT AUTO SUPPLY ... JOHN IRELAND
LOVE AND THE MIDNIGHT AUTO SUPPLY ... RORY CALHOUN
LOVE AND THE MIDNIGHT AUTO SUPPLY ... SCOTT JACOBY
LOVE AT FIRST BITE ... GEORGE HAMILTON
LOVE AT FIRST BITE ... RICHARD BENJAMIN
LOVE AT FIRST BITE ... SUSAN SAINT JAMES
LOVE AT FIRST SIGHT ... DAN AYKROYD
LOVE AT LARGE ... ANN MAGNUSON
LOVE AT LARGE ... ANNE ARCHER
LOVE AT LARGE ... ANNETTE O'TOOLE
LOVE AT LARGE ... ELIZABETH PERKINS
LOVE AT LARGE ... KATE CAPSHAW
LOVE AT LARGE ... KEVIN J. O'CONNOR
LOVE AT LARGE ... NEIL YOUNG
LOVE AT LARGE ... RUBY DEE
LOVE AT LARGE ... TED LEVINE
LOVE AT LARGE ... TOM BERENGER
LOVE AT STAKE ... DAVID GRAF
LOVE BAN, THE ... JOHN CLEESE
LOVE BOAT II (TF) ... CELESTE HOLM
LOVE BUG, THE ... BUDDY HACKETT
LOVE BUG, THE ... DAVID TOMLINSON
LOVE BUG, THE ... DEAN JONES
LOVE BUG, THE ... MICHELE LEE
LOVE CAN BE MURDER (TF) ... JACLYN SMITH
LOVE, CHEAT AND STEAL (CTF) ... ERIC ROBERTS
LOVE, CHEAT AND STEAL (CTF) ... JOHN LITHGOW
LOVE, CHEAT AND STEAL (CTF) ... MADCHEN AMICK
LOVE CHILD ... AMY MADIGAN
LOVE CHILD ... BEAU BRIDGES
LOVE CHILD ... MARGARET WHITTON
LOVE COMES QUIETLY ... BARBARA HERSHEY
LOVE CRIMES ... PATRICK BERGIN
LOVE CRIMES ... SEAN YOUNG
LOVE FIELD ... BRIAN KERWIN
LOVE FIELD ... DENNIS HAYSBERT
LOVE FIELD ... STEPHANIE
LOVE FIELD ★ ... MICHELLE PFEIFFER
LOVE FINDS ANDY HARDY ... LANA TURNER
LOVE FROM A STRANGER ... SYLVIA SIDNEY
LOVE GOD?, THE ... DON KNOTTS
LOVE HAPPY ... MARILYN MONROE†
LOVE HAPPY ... RAYMOND BURR†
LOVE HAS MANY FACES ... CLIFF ROBERTSON
LOVE HAS MANY FACES ... LANA TURNER
LOVE HAS MANY FACES ... STEFANIE POWERS
LOVE HATE LOVE (TF) ... RYAN O'NEAL
LOVE HURTS ... AMY WRIGHT
LOVE HURTS ... CLORIS LEACHMAN
LOVE HURTS ... CYNTHIA SIKES
LOVE HURTS ... JEFF DANIELS
LOVE HURTS ... JOHN MAHONEY
LOVE HURTS ... JUDITH IVEY
LOVE IN BLOOM ... GEORGE BURNS
LOVE IN THE AFTERNOON ... AUDREY HEPBURN†
LOVE IN THE AFTERNOON ... GARY COOPER†
LOVE IN THE AFTERNOON ... JOHN MCGIVER†
LOVE IN THE AFTERNOON ... MAURICE CHEVALIER†
LOVE IS A BALL ... HOPE LANGE
LOVE IS A BALL ... RICARDO MONTALBAN
LOVE IS A BALL ... TELLY SAVALAS†
LOVE IS A FUNNY THING ... FARRAH FAWCETT
LOVE IS A GUN ... ELIZA GARRETT
LOVE IS A GUN ... ERIC ROBERTS
LOVE IS A GUN ... JOE SIROLA
LOVE IS A GUN ... KELLY PRESTON
LOVE IS A MANY-SPLENDORED THING ★ ... JENNIFER JONES
LOVE IS BETTER THAN EVER ... ELIZABETH TAYLOR
LOVE IS FOREVER (TF) ... EDWARD WOODWARD
LOVE IS FOREVER (TF) ... JORGEN PROCHNOW
LOVE IS FOREVER (TF) ... MICHAEL LANDON†
LOVE IS FOREVER (TF) ... MOIRA CHEN
LOVE IS FOREVER (TF) ... PRISCILLA PRESLEY
LOVE IS NEVER SILENT (TF) ... BOB HUDDLESTON
LOVE IS NEVER SILENT (TF) ... CLORIS LEACHMAN
LOVE IS NEVER SILENT (TF) ... SID CAESAR
LOVE IS NEWS ... DON AMECHE†
LOVE IS ON THE AIR ... RONALD REAGAN
LOVE ISLAND ... EVA GABOR
LOVE LEADS THE WAY (TF) ... ARTHUR HILL
LOVE LEADS THE WAY (TF) ... ERNEST BORGNINE
LOVE LEADS THE WAY (TF) ... EVA MARIE SAINT
LOVE LEADS THE WAY (TF) ... GLYNNIS O'CONNOR
LOVE LEADS THE WAY (TF) ... PATRICIA NEAL
LOVE LEADS THE WAY (TF) ... RALPH BELLAMY†
LOVE LEADS THE WAY (TF) ... SUSAN DEY
LOVE LEADS THE WAY (TF) ... TIMOTHY BOTTOMS
LOVE LETTERS ... AMY MADIGAN
LOVE LETTERS ... BUD CORT
LOVE LETTERS ... JAMES KEACH
LOVE LETTERS ... JAMIE LEE CURTIS
LOVE LETTERS ... MATT CLARK
LOVE LETTERS ... SALLY KIRKLAND
LOVE LETTERS ★ ... JENNIFER JONES
LOVE LIVES ON (TF) ... CHRISTINE LAHTI
LOVE LIVES ON (TF) ... LOUISE LATHAM
LOVE LIVES ON (TF) ... MARY STUART MASTERSON
LOVE LIVES ON (TF) ... RICKY PAULL GOLDIN
LOVE LIVES ON (TF) ... SAM WATERSTON
LOVE LOTTERY, THE ... DAVID NIVEN†
LOVE LOTTERY, THE ... THEODORE BIKEL
LOVE MACHINE, THE ... DAVID HEMMINGS
LOVE MACHINE, THE ... DYAN CANNON
LOVE MACHINE, THE ... JACKIE COOPER
LOVE MACHINE, THE ... JOHN PHILLIP LAW
LOVE, MARY (TF) ... DAVID PAYMER
LOVE, MARY (TF) ... KRISTY McNICHOL
LOVE, MARY (TF) ... MATT CLARK
LOVE, MARY (TF) ... PIPER LAURIE
LOVE, MARY (TF) ... TERRY DAVID MULLIGAN
LOVE MATCH, THE ... PATRICIA HAYES
LOVE ME, LOVE MY DOG ... TONY BECKLEY†
LOVE ME OR LEAVE ME ... DORIS DAY
LOVE ME OR LEAVE ME ★ ... JAMES CAGNEY†
LOVE ME TENDER ... ELVIS PRESLEY†
LOVE NEST ... MARILYN MONROE†
LOVE ON THE DOLE ... DEBORAH KERR
LOVE ON THE GROUND ... GERALDINE CHAPLIN
LOVE ON THE RIVIERA ... MARCELLO MASTROIANNI
LOVE ON THE RUN ... JOAN CRAWFORD†
LOVE ON THE RUN (TF) ... ALEC BALDWIN
LOVE ON THE RUN (TF) ... ERNIE HUDSON
LOVE ON THE RUN (TF) ... STEPHANIE ZIMBALIST
LOVE OR MONEY ... TIMOTHY DALY
LOVE PARADE, THE ★ ... MAURICE CHEVALIER†
LOVE POTION #9 ... ADRIAN PAUL
LOVE POTION #9 ... ANNE BANCROFT
LOVE POTION #9 ... CHELSEA FIELD
LOVE POTION #9 ... DALE MIDKIFF
LOVE POTION #9 ... DYLAN BAKER
LOVE POTION #9 ... MARY MARA
LOVE POTION #9 ... SANDRA BULLOCK
LOVE POTION #9 ... TATE DONOVAN
LOVE STORY ... RAY MILLAND†
LOVE STORY ... TOMMY LEE JONES
LOVE STORY ... SYDNEY WALKER†
LOVE STORY ★ ... ALI MacGRAW
LOVE STORY ★ ... RYAN O'NEAL
LOVE STORY ✪ ... JOHN MARLEY†
LOVE STREAMS ... GENA ROWLANDS
LOVE TAPES, THE (TF) ... LORETTA SWIT
LOVE TAPES, THE (TF) ... MARTIN BALSAM
LOVE UNDER FIRE ... DON AMECHE†
LOVE WAR, THE (TF) ... ANGIE DICKINSON
LOVE WAR, THE (TF) ... LLOYD BRIDGES
LOVE WITH THE PROPER STRANGER ... EDIE ADAMS

This is not a list of every film ever made or every cast member, only those listed in this directory.

LOVE WITH THE
    PROPER STRANGER .... TOM BOSLEY
LOVE WITH THE
    PROPER STRANGER ★ .... NATALIE WOOD†
LOVECRAFT (CTF) .... ALEXANDRA POWERS
LOVECRAFT (CTF) .... CLANCY BROWN
LOVECRAFT (CTF) .... DAVID WARNER
LOVECRAFT (CTF) .... FRED WARD
LOVECRAFT (CTF) .... JULIANNE MOORE
LOVED ONE, THE .... HOWARD CAINE†
LOVED ONE, THE .... JAMES COBURN
LOVED ONE, THE .... JOHN GIELGUD
LOVED ONE, THE .... JONATHAN WINTERS
LOVED ONE, THE .... LIONEL STANDER
LOVED ONE, THE .... MILTON BERLE
LOVED ONE, THE .... PAUL WILLIAMS
LOVED ONE, THE .... ROBERT MORLEY
LOVED ONE, THE .... ROD STEIGER
LOVED ONE, THE .... RODDY McDOWALL
LOVED ONE, THE .... TAB HUNTER
LOVELESS, THE .... WILLEM DAFOE
LOVELINES .... MICHAEL WINSLOW
LOVELY TO LOOK AT .... HOWARD KEEL
LOVELY TO LOOK AT .... ZSA ZSA GABOR
LOVELY WAY TO DIE, A .... ALI MacGRAW
LOVELY WAY TO DIE, A .... DAVID HUDDLESTON
LOVELY WAY TO DIE, A .... ELI WALLACH
LOVELY WAY TO DIE, A .... KENNETH HAIGH
LOVELY WAY TO DIE, A .... KIRK DOUGLAS
LOVELY WAY TO DIE, A .... PHILIP BOSCO
LOVEMAKER, THE .... LILA KEDROVA
LOVER, THE .... JANE MARCH
LOVER, COME BACK .... DORIS DAY
LOVER COME BACK .... EDIE ADAMS
LOVER, COME BACK .... JACK KRUSCHEN
LOVER, COME BACK .... ROCK HUDSON†
LOVER COME BACK .... TONY RANDALL
LOVERBOY .... BARBARA CARRERA
LOVERBOY .... BERNIE COULSON
LOVERBOY .... CARRIE FISHER
LOVERBOY .... CHARLES HUNTER WALSH
LOVERBOY .... E. G. DAILY
LOVERBOY .... KATE JACKSON
LOVERBOY .... KIM MIYORI
LOVERBOY .... KIRSTIE ALLEY
LOVERBOY .... NANCY VALEN
LOVERBOY .... PATRICK DEMPSEY
LOVERBOY .... PETER KOCH
LOVERBOY .... RAY GIRARDIN
LOVERBOY .... ROBERT CAMILLETTI
LOVERBOY .... ROBERT GINTY
LOVERBOY .... ROBERT PICARDO
LOVERBOY .... VIC TAYBACK†
LOVERS AND LIARS .... CLAUDINE AUGER
LOVERS AND LIARS .... GOLDIE HAWN
LOVERS AND OTHER
    STRANGERS .... ANNE JACKSON
LOVERS AND OTHER STRANGERS .... ANNE MEARA
LOVERS AND OTHER
    STRANGERS .... BEATRICE ARTHUR
LOVERS AND OTHER STRANGERS .... BOB DISHY
LOVERS AND OTHER
    STRANGERS .... BONNIE BEDELIA
LOVERS AND OTHER
    STRANGERS .... CLORIS LEACHMAN
LOVERS AND OTHER
    STRANGERS .... DIANE KEATON
LOVERS AND OTHER STRANGERS ..... GIG YOUNG†
LOVERS AND OTHER
    STRANGERS .... HARRY GUARDINO
LOVERS AND OTHER
    STRANGERS .... MICHAEL BRANDON
LOVERS LIKE US .... CATHERINE DENEUVE
LOVERS OF VERONA, THE .... ANOUK AIMEE
LOVERS, THE .... VICTORIA ABRIL
LOVES AND TIMES OF
    SCARAMOUCHE, THE .... URSULA ANDRESS
LOVES OF ISADORA, THE .... JASON ROBARDS
LOVES OF
    ISADORA, THE ★ .... VANESSA REDGRAVE
LOVESICK .... ALAN KING
LOVESICK .... ALEC GUINNESS

LOVESICK .... DAVID STRATHAIRN
LOVESICK .... DUDLEY MOORE
LOVESICK .... ELIZABETH McGOVERN
LOVESICK .... GENE SAKS
LOVESICK .... JOHN HUSTON†
LOVESICK .... RENEE TAYLOR
LOVESICK .... RON SILVER
LOVESICK .... WALLACE SHAWN
LOVESPELL .... GERALDINE FITZGERALD
LOVESPELL .... KATE MULGREW
LOVESPELL .... NICHOLAS CLAY
LOVEY: A CIRCLE OF
    CHILDREN, PART II (TF) .... DANNY AIELLO
LOVE'S SAVAGE FURY (TF) .... PERRY KING
LOVE'S SAVAGE FURY (TF) .... RAYMOND BURR†
LOVIN' MOLLY .... ANTHONY PERKINS†
LOVIN' MOLLY .... BEAU BRIDGES
LOVIN' MOLLY .... BLYTHE DANNER
LOVIN' MOLLY .... SUSAN SARANDON
LOVING .... EVA MARIE SAINT
LOVING .... GEORGE SEGAL
LOVING .... ROY SCHEIDER
LOVING COUPLES .... JAMES COBURN
LOVING COUPLES .... SALLY KELLERMAN
LOVING COUPLES .... SHIRLEY MacLAINE
LOVING COUPLES .... STEPHEN COLLINS
LOVING COUPLES .... SUSAN SARANDON
LOVING YOU .... ELVIS PRESLEY†
LOW BLOW .... AKOSUA BUSIA
LOW DOWN DIRTY
    SHAME, A .... CHARLES S. DUTTON
LOW DOWN DIRTY SHAME, A ..... GREGORY SIERRA
LOW DOWN DIRTY
    SHAME, A .... KEENEN IVORY WAYANS
LOW DOWN DIRTY SHAME, A .... ANDREW DIVOFF
LOW DOWN DIRTY
    SHAME, A .... CHARLES S. DUTTON
LOW DOWN DIRTY SHAME, A ..... CORWIN HAWKINS
LOW DOWN DIRTY SHAME, A .... JADA PINKETT
LOW DOWN DIRTY
    SHAME, A .... KEENEN IVORY WAYANS
LOW DOWN DIRTY
    SHAME, A .... SALLI RICHARDSON
LT. DARING R.N. .... GERALDINE FITZGERALD
LT. ROBIN CRUSOE USN .... DICK VAN DYKE
LT. SCHUSTER'S WIFE (TF) .... EARTHA KITT
LUCAN (TF) .... NED BEATTY
LUCAN (TF) .... STOCKARD CHANNING
LUCAS .... CHARLIE SHEEN
LUCAS .... COREY HAIM
LUCAS .... COURTNEY THORNE-SMITH
LUCAS .... GUY BOYD
LUCAS .... KERRI GREEN
LUCAS .... WINONA RYDER
LUCK OF THE IRISH, THE ○ .... CECIL KELLAWAY†
LUCKIEST GIRL IN
    THE WORLD, THE .... JANE WYATT
LUCKIEST MAN IN
    THE WORLD, THE .... PHILIP BOSCO
LUCKY JIM .... SHARON ACKER
LUCKY JORDAN .... YVONNE DE CARLO
LUCKY LADY .... BURT REYNOLDS
LUCKY LADY .... GENE HACKMAN
LUCKY LADY .... GEOFFREY LEWIS
LUCKY LADY .... JOHN HILLERMAN
LUCKY LADY .... LIZA MINELLI
LUCKY LADY .... ROBBY BENSON
LUCKY LADY .... VAL AVERY
LUCKY LUCIANO .... VINCENT GARDENIA†
LUCKY ME .... ANGIE DICKINSON
LUCKY ME .... DORIS DAY
LUCKY STAR, THE .... LOU JACOBI
LUCKY STAR, THE .... LOUISE FLETCHER
LUCKY STAR, THE .... ROD STEIGER
LUCKY STIFF .... DONNA DIXON
LUCKY STIFF, THE .... DOROTHY LAMOUR
LUCKY TO BE
    A WOMAN .... MARCELLO MASTROIANNI
LUCKY TO BE A WOMAN .... SOPHIA LOREN
LUCY & DESI: BEFORE
    THE LAUGHTER (TF) .... FRANCES FISHER
LUCY GALLANT .... CHARLTON HESTON

LUCY GALLANT .... JANE WYMAN
LULLABY OF BROADWAY .... DORIS DAY
LULU BELLE .... DOROTHY LAMOUR
LUMIERE .... BRUNO GANZ
LUMIERE .... KEITH CARRADINE
LUNA .... FRED GWYNNE†
LUNA .... JILL CLAYBURGH
LUNA .... MATTHEW BARRY
LUNA .... VERONICA LAZAR
LUNCH HOUR .... SHIRLEY ANNE FIELD
LUST FOR GOLD .... WILLIAM PRINCE
LUST FOR LIFE ★ .... KIRK DOUGLAS
LUST FOR LIFE ○○ .... ANTHONY QUINN
LUST IN THE DUST .... TAB HUNTER
LUSTY MEN, THE .... ROBERT MITCHUM
LUTHER .... JOHN GIELGUD
LUTHER .... JUDI DENCH
LUTHER .... ROBERT STEPHENS
LUTHER .... STACY KEACH
LUV .... ELAINE MAY
LUV .... HARRISON FORD
LUV .... JACK LEMMON
LUV .... PETER FALK
LUV .... SEVERN DARDEN
LYDIA BAILEY .... WILLIAM MARSHALL
L'AFFAIRE DOMINICI .... GERARD DEPARDIEU
L'AGRESSION .... CATHERINE DENEUVE
L'AMI DE MON AMIE .... ANNE-LAURE MEURY
L'AMI DE MON AMIE .... SOPHIE RENOIR
L'AMOUR EN QUESTION .... BIBI ANDERSSON
L'AMPELOPEDE .... ISABELLE HUPPERT
L'ANIMAL .... RAQUEL WELCH
L'ANTI CRISTO .... MEL FERRER
L'APPAT .... CARROLL BAKER
L'ARCIDIAVOLO .... CLAUDINE AUGER
L'ARGENT DES AUTRES .... CATHERINE DENEUVE
L'ARLÉSIENNE .... LOUIS JOURDAN
L'ASSASSIN CONNAIT
    LA MUSIQUE .... MARIA SCHELL
L'ASSEDIO DI SIRACUSA .... TINA LOUISE
L'ATTENTAT .... JEAN-LOUIS TRINTIGNANT
L'ATTENTAT .... ROY SCHEIDER
L'AVVENTURIERO .... ANTHONY QUINN
L'ECHELLE BLANCHE .... JACQUELINE BISSET
L'ESPION .... RODDY McDOWALL
L'ETOILE DU SUD .... GEORGE SEGAL
L'ETOILE DU SUD .... URSULA ANDRESS
L'HAREM .... CARROLL BAKER
L'HOMME A FEMMES .... MEL FERRER
L'HOMME DE MARRAKECH .... CLAUDINE AUGER
L'HOMME DE MARRAKECH ...... GEORGE HAMILTON
L'HOMME EN COLERE ...... DONALD PLEASENCE
L'HOMME QUI AIMAIT
    LES FEMMES .... LESLIE CARON
L'IMPRECATEUR .... ROBERT WEBBER
L'INCHIESTA .... KEITH CARRADINE
L'INFERMIERA .... URSULA ANDRESS
L'INGORGO .... GERARD DEPARDIEU
L'INTRIGO .... SHIRLEY JONES
L'OCCHIO DEL RAGNO .... VAN JOHNSON
L'ORDRE ET LA SECURITE
    DU MONDE .... DENNIS HOPPER
L'ORDRE ET LA SECURITÉ
    DU MONDE .... DONALD PLEASENCE
L'ORO DI NAPOLI .... SOPHIA LOREN
L'UCCELLO DALLE PIUME
    DI CRISTALLO .... TONY MUSANTE
L'ULTIMA CHANCE .... URSULA ANDRESS
L'ULTIMO UOMO DELLA TERRA .... VINCENT PRICE†
L'UOMO DELLA STRADA
    FA GIUSTIZIA .... HENRY SILVA
L'UOMO SENZA PIETA .... MAUD ADAMS

† after an actor's name denotes deceased.

FILM
ACTORS
GUIDE

I
N
D
E
X

O
F

F
I
L
M

T
I
T
L
E
S

M .... HOWARD DA SILVA†
M .... NORMAN LLOYD
M .... RAYMOND BURR†
M.A.D.D.: MOTHERS AGAINST
    DRUNK DRIVERS (TF) .... MARIETTE HARTLEY
M*A*S*H .... BUD CORT
M*A*S*H .... DONALD SUTHERLAND
M*A*S*H .... ELLIOTT GOULD
M*A*S*H .... FRED WILLIAMSON
M*A*S*H .... JOHN SCHUCK
M*A*S*H .... MICHAEL MURPHY
M*A*S*H .... RENE AUBERJONOIS
M*A*S*H .... ROBERT DUVALL
M*A*S*H .... TOM SKERRITT
M*A*S*H ○ .... SALLY KELLERMAN
M. BUTTERFLY .... BARBARA SUKOWA
M. BUTTERFLY .... IAN RICHARDSON
M. BUTTERFLY .... JEREMY IRONS
M. BUTTERFLY .... JOHN LONE
MAC .... JOHN TURTURRO
MAC AND ME .... CHRISTINE EBERSOLE
MAC AND ME .... DANNY COOKSEY
MAC AND ME .... IVAN JORGE RADO
MAC AND ME .... JACK EISEMAN
MAC AND ME .... JADE CALEGORY
MAC AND ME .... JONATHAN WARD
MAC AND ME .... KATRINA CASPARY
MAC AND ME .... LAURA WATERBURY
MAC AND ME .... LAUREN STANLEY
MAC AND ME .... MARTIN WEST
MAC AND ME .... VINNIE TORRENTE
MACABRE .... WILLIAM PRINCE
MACAHANS, THE (TF) .... RICHARD KILEY
MACAO .... ROBERT MITCHUM
MACARONI .... JACK LEMMON
MacARTHUR .... DAN O'HERLIHY
MacARTHUR .... ED FLANDERS
MacARTHUR .... GREGORY PECK
MACBETH .... DAME JUDITH ANDERSON†
MACBETH .... DAN O'HERLIHY
MACBETH .... FRANCESCA ANNIS
MACBETH .... IAN BANNEN
MACBETH .... RODDY McDOWALL
MacGRUDER AND
    LOUD (TF) .... KATHRYN HARROLD
MACHINE GUN KELLY .... CHARLES BRONSON
MACHINE GUN McCAIN .... BRITT EKLAND
MACHINE GUN McCAIN .... PETER FALK
MACHO CALLAHAN .... BO HOPKINS
MACHO CALLAHAN .... DAVID CARRADINE
MACHO CALLAHAN .... DIANE LADD
MACHO CALLAHAN .... RICHARD ANDERSON
MACK, THE .... RICHARD PRYOR
MACK THE KNIFE .... ERIN DONOVAN
MACK THE KNIFE .... JULIA MIGENES
MACK THE KNIFE .... JULIE WALTERS
MACK THE KNIFE .... RAUL JULIA†
MACK THE KNIFE .... RICHARD HARRIS
MACK THE KNIFE .... ROGER DALTRY
MACKENNA'S GOLD .... BURGESS MEREDITH
MACKENNA'S GOLD .... ELI WALLACH
MACKENNA'S GOLD .... GREGORY PECK
MACKENNA'S GOLD .... JULIE NEWMAR
MACKENNA'S GOLD .... OMAR SHARIF
MACKENNA'S GOLD .... TELLY SAVALAS†
MACKINTOSH AND T.J. .... BILLY GREEN BUSH
MACKINTOSH AND T.J. .... JOAN HACKETT†
MACKINTOSH MAN, THE .... IAN BANNEN
MACKINTOSH MAN, THE .... PAUL NEWMAN
MACOMBER AFFAIR, THE .... GREGORY PECK
MACSHAYNE: WINNER
    TAKES ALL (TF) .... ANN JILLIAN
MACSHAYNE: WINNER
    TAKES ALL (TF) .... KENNY ROGERS
MACSHAYNE: WINNER
    TAKES ALL (TF) .... TERRY O'QUINN
MACSHAYNE: WINNER
    TAKES ALL (TF) .... WENDY PHILLIPS
MAD BOMBER, THE .... CHUCK CONNORS†

MAD BOMBER, THE .... VINCE EDWARDS
MAD BULL .... SUSAN ANSPACH
MAD BULL (TF) .... ALEXIS KARRAS
MAD BUTCHER, THE .... JOHN IRELAND
MAD DOG .... DENNIS HOPPER
MAD DOG .... JACK THOMPSON
MAD DOG AND GLORY .... BILL MURRAY
MAD DOG AND GLORY .... DAVID CARUSO
MAD DOG AND GLORY .... KATHY BAKER
MAD DOG AND GLORY .... MIKE STARR
MAD DOG AND GLORY .... ROBERT DE NIRO
MAD DOG AND GLORY .... UMA THURMAN
MAD DOG COLL .... GENE HACKMAN
MAD DOG COLL .... TELLY SAVALAS†
MAD DOG COLL .... VINCENT GARDENIA†
MAD DOG MORGAN .... DENNIS HOPPER
MAD DOG MORGAN .... JACK THOMPSON
MAD LITTLE ISLAND .... GORDAN JACKSON†
MAD LOVE .... DREW BARRYMORE
MAD LOVE .... JOAN ALLEN
MAD LOVE .... JUDE CICCOLELLA
MAD LOVE .... KEVIN DUNN
MAD LOVE .... T. J. LOWTHER
MAD MAGAZINE PRESENTS
    UP THE ACADEMY .... BARBARA BACH
MAD MAGAZINE PRESENTS
    UP THE ACADEMY .... RALPH MACCHIO
MAD MAGAZINE PRESENTS
    UP THE ACADEMY .... ROBERT DOWNEY JR.
MAD MAGAZINE PRESENTS
    UP THE ACADEMY .... RON LEIBMAN
MAD MAGAZINE PRESENTS
    UP THE ACADEMY .... TOM POSTON
MAD MAGAZINE PRESENTS
    UP THE ACADEMY .... WENDELL BROWN
MAD MAGICIAN, THE .... COREY ALLEN
MAD MAGICIAN, THE .... EVA GABOR
MAD MAGICIAN, THE .... PATRICK O'NEAL†
MAD MAGICIAN, THE .... VINCENT PRICE†
MAD MAX .... MEL GIBSON
MAD MAX 2 .... MEL GIBSON
MAD MAX BEYOND
    THUNDERDOME .... MEL GIBSON
MAD MAX BEYOND
    THUNDERDOME .... TINA TURNER
MAD MISS MANTON, THE .... BARBARA STANWYCK†
MAD MONSTER PARTY? (AF) .... PHYLLIS DILLER
MAD ROOM, THE .... SHELLEY WINTERS
MAD ROOM, THE .... STELLA STEVENS
MAD WEDNESDAY .... LIONEL STANDER
MADAM X ★ .... RUTH CHATTERTON†
MADAME .... SOPHIA LOREN
MADAME BOVARY .... HARRY MORGAN
MADAME BOVARY .... JENNIFER JONES
MADAME BOVARY .... LOUIS JOURDAN
MADAME BUTTERFLY .... SYLVIA SIDNEY
MADAME CLAUDE .... KLAUS KINSKI†
MADAME CLAUDE .... ROBERT WEBBER
MADAME CURIE .... VAN JOHNSON
MADAME CURIE ★ .... GREER GARSON
MADAME CURIE ★ .... WALTER PIDGEON†
MADAME SIN .... DENHOLM ELLIOTT†
MADAME SOUSATZKA .... GEOFFREY BAYLDON
MADAME SOUSATZKA .... LEIGH LAWSON
MADAME SOUSATZKA .... NAVIN CHOWDHRY
MADAME SOUSATZKA .... PEGGY ASHCROFT†
MADAME SOUSATZKA .... SHABANA AZMI
MADAME SOUSATZKA .... SHIRLEY MacLAINE
MADAME SOUSATZKA .... TWIGGY
MADAME X .... BURGESS MEREDITH
MADAME X .... JOHN FORSYTHE
MADAME X .... LANA TURNER
MADAME X .... RICARDO MONTALBAN
MADDENING, THE .... ANGIE DICKINSON
MADDENING, THE .... BRIAN WIMMER
MADDENING, THE .... BURT REYNOLDS
MADE FOR EACH OTHER .... JAMES STEWART
MADE FOR EACH OTHER .... PAUL SORVINO
MADE IN AMERICA .... TED DANSON
MADE IN AMERICA .... WHOOPI GOLDBERG
MADE IN BRITAIN (TF) .... TIM ROTH
MADE IN HEAVEN .... AMANDA PLUMMER

MADE IN HEAVEN .... ANN WEDGEWORTH
MADE IN HEAVEN .... DAVID RASCHE
MADE IN HEAVEN .... DEBRA WINGER
MADE IN HEAVEN .... DON MURRAY
MADE IN HEAVEN .... ELLEN BARKIN
MADE IN HEAVEN .... GARY LARSON
MADE IN HEAVEN .... KELLY McGILLIS
MADE IN HEAVEN .... MARE WINNINGHAM
MADE IN HEAVEN .... MARJ DUSAY
MADE IN HEAVEN .... MAUREEN STAPLETON
MADE IN HEAVEN .... NEIL YOUNG
MADE IN HEAVEN .... RAY GIDEON
MADE IN HEAVEN .... RIC O'CASEK
MADE IN HEAVEN .... TIMOTHY DALY
MADE IN HEAVEN .... TIMOTHY HUTTON
MADE IN HEAVEN .... TOM PETTY
MADE IN HEAVEN .... TOM ROBBINS
MADE IN PARIS .... ANN-MARGRET
MADE IN PARIS .... CHAD EVERETT
MADE IN PARIS .... EDIE ADAMS
MADE IN PARIS .... LOUIS JOURDAN
MADE IN PARIS .... RICHARD CRENNA
MADHOUSE .... ALISON LA PLACA
MADHOUSE .... BRADLEY GREGG
MADHOUSE .... DENNIS MILLER
MADHOUSE .... JESSICA LUNDY
MADHOUSE .... JOHN DIEHL
MADHOUSE .... JOHN LARROQUETTE
MADHOUSE .... KIRSTIE ALLEY
MADHOUSE .... ROBERT GINTY
MADHOUSE .... VINCENT PRICE†
MADHOUSE MANSION .... LEIGH LAWSON
MADIGAN .... DON STROUD
MADIGAN .... HARRY GUARDINO
MADIGAN .... JAMES WHITMORE
MADIGAN .... RAYMOND ST. JACQUES
MADIGAN .... RICHARD WIDMARK
MADIGAN .... SUSAN CLARK
MADIGAN'S MILLIONS .... DUSTIN HOFFMAN
MADISON AVENUE .... EDDIE ALBERT
MADISON AVENUE .... ELEANOR PARKER
MADMAN .... F. MURRAY ABRAHAM
MADMAN .... SIGOURNEY WEAVER
MADNESS OF
    GEORGE III, THE .... AMANDA DONOHOE
MADNESS OF GEORGE III, THE .... HELEN MIRREN
MADNESS OF GEORGE III, THE .... IAN HOLM
MADNESS OF
    GEORGE III, THE .... NIGEL HAWTHORNE
MADNESS OF
    GEORGE III, THE .... RUPERT EVERETT
MADNESS OF GEORGE III, THE .... RUPERT GRAVES
MADNESS OF LOVE, THE .... CARROLL BAKER
MADONNA OF THE STORM, THE .... LILLIAN GISH†
MADRON .... LESLIE CARON
MADWOMAN OF
    CHAILLOT, THE .... DONALD PLEASENCE
MADWOMAN OF CHAILLOT, THE .... JOHN GAVIN
MADWOMAN OF
    CHAILLOT, THE .... KATHERINE HEPBURN
MADWOMAN OF
    CHAILLOT, THE .... RICHARD CHAMBERLAIN
MAE WEST (TF) .... PIPER LAURIE
MAFIA .... FRANCO NERO
MAFIA .... NEHEMIAH PERSOFF
MAFIA PRINCESS (TF) .... TONY CURTIS
MAFU CAGE, THE .... CAROL KANE
MAFU CAGE, THE .... LEE GRANT
MAGEE AND THE LADY (TF) ...... SALLY KELLERMAN
MAGEE AND THE LADY (TF) .... TONY LoBIANCO
MAGIC .... ANN-MARGRET
MAGIC .... ANTHONY HOPKINS
MAGIC .... BURGESS MEREDITH
MAGIC .... DAVID OGDEN STIERS
MAGIC BOX, THE .... DAVID TOMLINSON
MAGIC BOX, THE .... MARIA SCHELL
MAGIC BOX, THE .... PETER USTINOV
MAGIC CARPET (TF) .... SUSAN SAINT JAMES
MAGIC CARPET, THE .... RAYMOND BURR†
MAGIC CHRISTIAN, THE .... LAURENCE HARVEY†
MAGIC CHRISTIAN, THE .... PETER SELLERS†
MAGIC CHRISTIAN, THE .... RAQUEL WELCH

This is not a list of every film ever made or every cast member, only those listed in this directory.

MAGIC CHRISTIAN, THE	RINGO STARR
MAGIC CHRISTIAN, THE	ROMAN POLANSKI
MAGIC CHRISTIAN, THE	YUL BRYNNER†
MAGIC FIRE	YVONNE DE CARLO
MAGIC MOUNTAIN, THE	ROD STEIGER
MAGIC OF LASSIE, THE	JAMES STEWART
MAGIC OF LASSIE, THE	STEPHANIE ZIMBALIST
MAGIC SWORD, THE	RICHARD KIEL
MAGIC TOWN	JAMES STEWART
MAGIC TOWN	JANE WYMAN
MAGICIAN, THE	BIBI ANDERSSON
MAGICIAN, THE	LOU JACOBI
MAGICIAN, THE (TF)	BILL BIXBY†
MAGICIAN, THE (TF)	ELIZABETH ASHLEY
MAGICIAN OF LUBLIN, THE	ALAN ARKIN
MAGICIAN OF LUBLIN, THE	LOUISE FLETCHER
MAGICIAN OF LUBLIN, THE	SHELLEY WINTERS
MAGICIAN OF LUBLIN, THE	VALERIE PERRINE
MAGNIFICENT AMBERSONS, THE ⊙	AGNES MOOREHEAD†
MAGNIFICENT DOLL	BURGESS MEREDITH
MAGNIFICENT DOLL	DAVID NIVEN†
MAGNIFICENT DOPE, THE	DON AMECHE†
MAGNIFICENT LIE, THE	RALPH BELLAMY†
MAGNIFICENT MAGNET OF SANTA MESA, THE (TF)	LONI ANDERSON
MAGNIFICENT MATADOR, THE	ANTHONY QUINN
MAGNIFICENT MATADOR, THE	MAUREEN O'HARA
MAGNIFICENT OBSESSION	ROCK HUDSON†
MAGNIFICENT OBSESSION ★	JANE WYMAN
MAGNIFICENT SEVEN RIDE, THE	PEDRO ARMENDARIZ JR.
MAGNIFICENT SEVEN RIDE!, THE	STEFANIE POWERS
MAGNIFICENT SEVEN, THE	CHARLES BRONSON
MAGNIFICENT SEVEN, THE	ELI WALLACH
MAGNIFICENT SEVEN, THE	JAMES COBURN
MAGNIFICENT SEVEN, THE	ROBERT VAUGHN
MAGNIFICENT SEVEN, THE	STEVE MCQUEEN†
MAGNIFICENT YANKEE, THE	RICHARD ANDERSON
MAGNIFICENT YANKEE, THE ★	LOUIS CALHERN†
MAGNUM FORCE	CLINT EASTWOOD
MAGNUM FORCE	DAVID SOUL
MAGNUM FORCE	HAL HOLBROOK
MAGNUM FORCE	ROBERT URICH
MAGNUM FORCE	TIM MATHESON
MAGUS, THE	ANTHONY QUINN
MAGUS, THE	CANDICE BERGEN
MAGUS, THE	MICHAEL CAINE
MAHOGANY	ANTHONY PERKINS†
MAHOGANY	BEAH RICHARDS
MAHOGANY	BILLY DEE WILLIAMS
MAHOGANY	DIANA ROSS
MAHOGANY	JEAN-PIERRE AUMONT
MAHOGANY	NINA FOCH
MAID IN AMERICA (TF)	SUSAN CLARK
MAID TO ORDER	ALLY SHEEDY
MAID TO ORDER	BEVERLY D'ANGELO
MAID TO ORDER	MERRY CLAYTON
MAID TO ORDER	MICHAEL ONTKEAN
MAID TO ORDER	TOM SKERRITT
MAIDS, THE	GLENDA JACKSON
MAIDS, THE	SUSANNAH YORK
MAIDSTONE	RIP TORN
MAIGRET (TF)	RICHARD HARRIS
MAIL ORDER BRIDE	LOIS NETTLETON
MAIN ATTRACTION, THE	MAE ZETTERLING
MAIN ATTRACTION, THE	PAT BOONE
MAIN EVENT, THE	BARBRA STREISAND
MAIN EVENT, THE	PAUL SAND
MAIN EVENT, THE	RYAN O'NEAL
MAIN STREET AFTER DARK	HUME CRONYN
MAIN STREET TO BROADWAY	HELEN HAYES
MAISIE	ANN SOTHERN
MAISIE GETS HER MAN	ANN SOTHERN
MAISIE GOES TO RENO	ANN SOTHERN
MAISIE GOES TO RENO	AVA GARDNER†
MAISIE WAS A LADY	ANN SOTHERN
MAISIE WAS A LADY	MAUREEN O'SULLIVAN
MAITRESSE	GERARD DEPARDIEU
MAJOR AND THE MINOR, THE	GRACE KELLY†
MAJOR BARBARA	DEBORAH KERR
MAJOR BARBARA	ROBERT MORLEY
MAJOR BARBARA	WENDY HILLER
MAJOR DUNDEE	BEN JOHNSON
MAJOR DUNDEE	BROCK PETERS
MAJOR DUNDEE	CHARLTON HESTON
MAJOR DUNDEE	JAMES COBURN
MAJOR DUNDEE	R.G. ARMSTRONG
MAJOR DUNDEE	RICHARD HARRIS
MAJOR LEAGUE	BOB UECKER
MAJOR LEAGUE	CHARLES CYPHERS
MAJOR LEAGUE	CHARLIE SHEEN
MAJOR LEAGUE	CORBIN BERNSEN
MAJOR LEAGUE	JAMES GAMMON
MAJOR LEAGUE	MARGARET WHITTON
MAJOR LEAGUE	RENE RUSSO
MAJOR LEAGUE	TOM BERENGER
MAJOR LEAGUE	WESLEY SNIPES
MAJOR LEAGUE II	ALISON DOODY
MAJOR LEAGUE II	BOB UECKER
MAJOR LEAGUE II	CHARLIE SHEEN
MAJOR LEAGUE II	CORBIN BERNSEN
MAJOR LEAGUE II	DAVID KEITH
MAJOR LEAGUE II	DENNIS HAYSBERT
MAJOR LEAGUE II	ERIC BRUSKOTTER
MAJOR LEAGUE II	JAMES GAMMON
MAJOR LEAGUE II	MARGARET WHITTON
MAJOR LEAGUE II	MICHELLE BURKE
MAJOR LEAGUE II	OMAR EPPS
MAJOR LEAGUE II	RANDY QUAID
MAJOR LEAGUE II	SKIP GRIPARIS
MAJOR LEAGUE II	TAKAAKI ISHIBASHI
MAJOR LEAGUE II	TOM BERENGER
MAJOR PAYNE	DAMON WAYANS
MAJOR PAYNE	KARYN PARSONS
MAJOR PAYNE	STEVEN MARTINI
MAJORITY OF ONE, A	ALEC GUINNESS
MAKE ME A STAR	SYLVIA SIDNEY
MAKE ME AN OFFER (TF)	SUSAN BLAKELY
MAKE MINE MINK	BILLIE WHITELAW
MAKE MINE MINK	JACK HEDLEY
MAKE MINE MINK	RON MOODY
MAKE MINE MUSIC	DINAH SHORE†
MAKE YOUR OWN BED	JANE WYMAN
MAKING IT	DICK VAN PATTEN
MAKING IT	JOHN FIELDLER
MAKING IT	JOYCE VAN PATTEN
MAKING IT	LOUISE LATHAM
MAKING LOVE	ARTHUR HILL
MAKING LOVE	HARRY HAMLIN
MAKING LOVE	KATE JACKSON
MAKING LOVE	MICHAEL ONTKEAN
MAKING LOVE	WENDY HILLER
MAKING MR. RIGHT	ANN MAGNUSON
MAKING MR. RIGHT	GLENNE HEADLY
MAKING MR. RIGHT	HART BOCHNER
MAKING MR. RIGHT	JOHN MALKOVICH
MAKING MR. RIGHT	LAURIE METCALF
MAKING MR. RIGHT	POLLY BERGEN
MAKING OF A MALE MODEL, THE (TF)	JOAN COLLINS
MAKING THE GRADE	ANDREW DICE CLAY
MAKING THE GRADE	JUDD NELSON
MAKO: THE JAWS OF DEATH	RICHARD JAECKEL
MALAGA	MAUREEN O'HARA
MALAYA	JAMES STEWART
MALCOLM	CHARLES TINGWELL
MALCOLM	CHRIS HAYWOOD
MALCOLM	COLIN FRIELS
MALCOLM X ★	DENZEL WASHINGTON
MALCOLM X	AL FREEMAN JR.
MALCOLM X	ALBERT HALL
MALCOLM X	ANGELA BASSETT
MALCOLM X	DELROY LINDO
MALCOLM X	SPIKE LEE
MALCOLM X	THERESA RANDLE
MALCOLM X	WILLIAM KUNSTLER
MALCOLM X (FD)	JAMES EARL JONES
MALCOLM X (FD)	OSSIE DAVIS
MALE ANIMAL, THE	OLIVIA DE HAVILLAND
MALE COMPANION	CATHERINE DENEUVE
MALE HUNT	CATHERINE DENEUVE
MALIBU (TF)	EVA MARIE SAINT
MALIBU (TF)	JAMES COBURN
MALIBU (TF)	KIM NOVAK
MALIBU (TF)	STEVE FORREST
MALIBU (TF)	TROY DONAHUE
MALIBU (TF)	WILLIAM ATHERTON
MALICE	ALEC BALDWIN
MALICE	ANNE BANCROFT
MALICE	BEBE NEUWIRTH
MALICE	BILL PULLMAN
MALICE	GEORGE C. SCOTT
MALICE	JOSEF SOMMER
MALICE	NICOLE KIDMAN
MALICE	PETER GALLAGHER
MALICE IN WONDERLAND	JANE ALEXANDER
MALICE IN WONDERLAND (TF)	ELIZABETH TAYLOR
MALICE IN WONDERLAND (TF)	RICHARD DYSART
MALICIOUS	MOLLY RINGWALD
MALICIOUS	PATRICK McGAW
MALLORY: CIRCUMSTANTIAL EVIDENCE (TF)	MARK HAMILL
MALLORY: CIRCUMSTANTIAL EVIDENCE (TF)	RAYMOND BURR†
MALONE	BURT REYNOLDS
MALONE	LAUREN HUTTON
MALONE	SCOTT WILSON
MALTA STORY, THE	ALEC GUINNESS
MALTESE BIPPY, THE	CAROL LYNLEY
MALTESE BIPPY, THE	FRITZ WEAVER
MALTESE BIPPY, THE	JULIE NEWMAR
MALTESE FALCON, THE	HUMPHREY BOGART†
MALTESE FALCON, THE ⊙	SIDNEY GREENSTREET†
MAMA DRACULA	LOUISE FLETCHER
MAMA, THERE'S A MAN IN YOUR BED	DANIEL AUTEUIL
MAMBO	SHELLEY WINTERS
MAMBO KINGS, THE	ANTONIO BANDERAS
MAMBO KINGS, THE	ARMAND ASSANTE
MAMBO KINGS, THE	CATHY MORIARTY
MAMBO KINGS, THE	CELIA CRUZ
MAMBO KINGS, THE	DESI ARNAZ JR.
MAMBO KINGS, THE	MARUSCHKA DETMERS
MAMBO KINGS, THE	TITO PUENTE
MAME	BEATRICE ARTHUR
MAME	BRUCE DAVISON
MAME	JOYCE VAN PATTEN
MAME	LUCILLE BALL†
MAME	ROBERT PRESTON†
MAMELUKS, THE	OMAR SHARIF
MAN, THE	BURGESS MEREDITH
MAN, THE	GEORG STANFORD BROWN
MAN, THE	JAMES EARL JONES
MAN, THE (TF)	MARTIN BALSAM
MAN 2 MAN	ART LA FLEUR
MAN 2 MAN	CHEVY CHASE
MAN 2 MAN	CHIEF LEONARD GEORGE
MAN 2 MAN	DAVID SHINER
MAN 2 MAN	FARRAH FAWCETT
MAN 2 MAN	GEORGE WENDT
MAN 2 MAN	JONATHAN TAYLOR-THOMAS
MAN 2 MAN	PETER APPEL
MAN 2 MAN	RICHARD PORTNOW
MAN, A WOMAN AND A BANK, A	BROOKE ADAMS
MAN, A WOMAN AND A BANK, A	DONALD SUTHERLAND
MAN, A WOMAN AND A BANK, A	PAUL MAZURSKY
MAN ABOUT TOWN	DOROTHY LAMOUR
MAN AFRAID	PHYLLIS THAXTER
MAN AFRAID	TROY DONAHUE
MAN AGAINST THE MOB (TF)	GEORGE PEPPARD†
MAN AGAINST THE MOB (TF)	KATHRYN HARROLD
MAN AGAINST THE MOB (TF)	STELLA STEVENS
MAN AGAINST THE MOB: THE CHINATOWN MURDERS (TF)	CHARLES HAID

---

† after an actor's name denotes deceased.

I
N
D
E
X

O
F

F
I
L
M

T
I
T
L
E
S

MAN AGAINST THE MOB:
THE CHINATOWN
MURDERS (TF) .... GEORGE PEPPARD†
MAN AGAINST THE MOB:
THE CHINATOWN
MURDERS (TF) .... URSULA ANDRESS
MAN ALONE, A .... RAYMOND BURR†
MAN AND
A WOMAN, A .... JEAN-LOUIS TRINTIGNANT
MAN AND A WOMAN ★ .... ANOUK AIMEE
MAN AND A WOMAN:
20 YEARS LATER, A .... ANOUK AIMEE
MAN AND A WOMAN:
20 YEARS LATER, A .... EVELYNE BOUIX
MAN AND A WOMAN:
20 YEARS LATER, A .... JEAN-LOUIS TRINTIGNANT
MAN AND A WOMAN:
20 YEARS LATER, A .... MARIE-SOPHIE POCHAT
MAN AND A WOMAN:
20 YEARS LATER, A .... RICHARD BERRY
MAN AND BOY .... BILL COSBY
MAN AND BOY .... HENRY SILVA
MAN AND BOY .... JOHN ANDERSON
MAN AND BOY .... YAPHET KOTTO
MAN AT THE TOP .... KENNETH HAIGH
MAN BETWEEN, THE .... CLAIRE BLOOM
MAN CALLED ADAM, A .... CICELY TYSON
MAN CALLED ADAM, A .... OSSIE DAVIS
MAN CALLED ADAM, A .... SAMMY DAVIS JR.†
MAN CALLED DAGGER, A .... RICHARD KIEL
MAN CALLED DAGGER, A .... STEVE ALLEN
MAN CALLED
GANNON, A .... ANTHONY (TONY) FRANCIOSA
MAN CALLED GANNON, A .... MICHAEL SARRAZIN
MAN CALLED
HORSE, A .... DAME JUDITH ANDERSON†
MAN CALLED HORSE, A .... RICHARD HARRIS
MAN CALLED INTREPID, A .... MICHAEL YORK
MAN CALLED JOHN, A .... ROD STEIGER
MAN CALLED NOON, THE .... RICHARD CRENNA
MAN CALLED SLEDGE, A .... CLAUDE AKINS†
MAN CALLED SLEDGE, A .... DENNIS WEAVER
MAN CALLED SLEDGE, A .... JAMES GARNER
MAN COULD GET
KILLED, A .... ANTHONY (TONY) FRANCIOSA
MAN COULD GET KILLED, A .... JAMES GARNER
MAN COULD GET KILLED, A .... SANDRA DEE
MAN FOR ALL SEASONS, A ★★ .... PAUL SCOFIELD
MAN FOR ALL SEASONS, A ○ .... ROBERT SHAW†
MAN FOR ALL SEASONS, A ○ .... WENDY HILLER
MAN FOR ALL SEASONS, A .... JOHN HURT
MAN FOR ALL SEASONS, A ...... NIGEL DAVENPORT
MAN FOR ALL SEASONS, A .... ORSON WELLES†
MAN FOR ALL SEASONS, A .... SUSANNAH YORK
MAN FOR ALL
SEASONS, A .... VANESSA REDGRAVE
MAN FOR ALL
SEASONS, A (CTF) .... CHARLTON HESTON
MAN FOR ALL
SEASONS, A (CTF) .... JOHN GIELGUD
MAN FRIDAY .... PETER O'TOOLE
MAN FRIDAY .... RICHARD ROUNDTREE
MAN FROM BUTTON
WILLOW, THE (AF) .... HOWARD KEEL
MAN FROM DEL RIO .... ANTHONY QUINN
MAN FROM DEL RIO .... KATHY JURADO
MAN FROM GALVESTON, THE .... JAMES COBURN
MAN FROM HONG KONG, THE ... GEORGE LAZENBY
MAN FROM LARAMIE, THE .... JAMES STEWART
MAN FROM O.R.G.Y. .... ROBERT WALKER JR.
MAN FROM SNOWY RIVER, THE ...... KIRK DOUGLAS
MAN FROM SNOWY
RIVER, THE .... SIGRID THORNTON
MAN FROM SNOWY
RIVER, THE .... TOM BURLINSON
MAN FROM SNOWY
RIVER 2, THE .... SIGRID THORNTON
MAN FROM THE
DINER'S CLUB, THE .... HOWARD CAINE†
MAN FROM THE
DINERS' CLUB, THE .... TELLY SAVALAS†

MAN FROM THE
DINER'S CLUB, THE .... GEORGE KENNEDY
MAN FROM THE
DINER'S CLUB, THE .... HARRY DEAN STANTON
MAN HUNT .... RODDY McDOWALL
MAN IN A COCKED HAT .... IAN BANNEN
MAN IN LOVE, A .... GRETA SCACCHI
MAN IN LOVE, A .... JAMIE LEE CURTIS
MAN IN THE ATTIC .... JACK PALANCE
MAN IN THE GLASS
BOOTH, THE ★ .... MAXIMILIAN SCHELL
MAN IN THE GRAY FLANNEL
SUIT, THE .... GREGORY PECK
MAN IN THE GRAY FLANNEL
SUIT, THE .... JENNIFER JONES
MAN IN THE IRON MASK, THE (TF) .... IAN HOLM
MAN IN THE IRON
MASK, THE (TF) .... JENNY AGUTTER
MAN IN THE IRON
MASK, THE (TF) .... LOUIS JOURDAN
MAN IN THE IRON
MASK, THE (TF) .... RICHARD CHAMBERLAIN
MAN IN THE MIDDLE .... ROBERT MITCHUM
MAN IN THE MIDDLE .... SAM WANAMAKER†
MAN IN THE MIDDLE .... SHIRLEY ANNE FIELD
MAN IN THE MIDDLE, THE .... FRANCE NUYEN
MAN IN THE MOON, THE .... GAIL STRICKLAND
MAN IN THE MOON, THE ...... REESE WITHERSPOON
MAN IN THE MOON, THE .... SAM WATERSTON
MAN IN THE MOON, THE .... TESS HARPER
MAN IN THE SANTA
CLAUS SUIT, THE .... JOHN BYNER
MAN IN THE SANTA
CLAUS SUIT, THE (TF) .... HAROLD GOULD
MAN IN THE SHADOW .... ROYAL DANO
MAN IN THE WHITE SUIT, THE ...... ALEC GUINNESS
MAN IN THE WHITE SUIT, THE ...... MICHAEL GOUGH
MAN IN THE WILDERNESS .... RICHARD HARRIS
MAN IN UNIFORM, A .... BRIGITTE BAKO
MAN IN UNIFORM, A .... DAVID HEMBLEN
MAN IN UNIFORM, A .... KEVIN TIGHE
MAN IN UNIFORM, A .... TOM McCAMUS
MAN INSIDE, THE .... JACK PALANCE
MAN OF A THOUSAND FACES .... JANE GREER
MAN OF LA MANCHA .... BRIAN BLESSED
MAN OF LA MANCHA .... JOHN CASTLE
MAN OF LA MANCHA .... PETER O'TOOLE
MAN OF LA MANCHA .... SOPHIA LOREN
MAN OF PASSION .... ANTHONY QUINN
MAN OF PASSION .... ELIZABETH ASHLEY
MAN OF PASSION .... JOSE MARIA CAFFAREL
MAN OF PASSION .... MAUD ADAMS
MAN OF PASSION .... R. J. WILLIAMS
MAN OF PASSION .... RAMON ESTEVEZ
MAN OF PASSION .... RAY WALSTON
MAN OF PASSION .... VICTORIA VERA
MAN OF THE WEST .... JOHN DEHNER†
MAN OF THE WEST .... ROYAL DANO
MAN ON A STRING .... COLLEEN DEWHURST†
MAN ON A STRING .... ERNEST BORGNINE
MAN ON A SWING .... CLIFF ROBERTSON
MAN ON A SWING .... JOEL GREY
MAN ON A TIGHTROPE .... JOHN DEHNER†
MAN ON FIRE .... DANNY AIELLO
MAN ON FIRE .... E. G. MARSHALL
MAN ON FIRE .... JOE PESCI
MAN ON THE EIFFEL
TOWER, THE .... BURGESS MEREDITH
MAN ON THE RUN .... BURGESS MEREDITH
MAN TROUBLE .... BEVERLY D'ANGELO
MAN TROUBLE .... DAVID CLENNON
MAN TROUBLE .... ELLEN BARKIN
MAN TROUBLE .... HARRY DEAN STANTON
MAN TROUBLE .... JACK NICHOLSON
MAN TROUBLE .... MICHAEL McKEAN
MAN TROUBLE .... PAUL MAZURSKY
MAN TROUBLE .... SAUL RUBINEK
MAN TROUBLE .... VERONICA CARTWRIGHT
MAN UNDER SUSPICION ...... MAXIMILIAN SCHELL
MAN UPSTAIRS, THE (TF) ..... KATHERINE HEPBURN
MAN UPSTAIRS, THE (TF) .... RYAN O'NEAL

MAN WHO CAME TO
DINNER, THE .... BETTE DAVIS†
MAN WHO CAME TO
DINNER, THE .... MARY WICKES
MAN WHO CHEATED HIMSELF, THE ... JANE WYATT
MAN WHO COULD TALK
TO KIDS, THE (TF) .... PETER BOYLE
MAN WHO FELL TO EARTH, THE .... BUCK HENRY
MAN WHO FELL TO EARTH, THE ...... CANDY CLARK
MAN WHO FELL TO EARTH, THE .... DAVID BOWIE
MAN WHO FELL TO EARTH, THE .... RIP TORN
MAN WHO FINALLY
DIED, THE .... MAE ZETTERLING†
MAN WHO HAUNTED
HIMSELF, THE .... HILDEGARD NEIL
MAN WHO HAUNTED
HIMSELF, THE .... ROGER MOORE
MAN WHO KNEW TOO MUCH, THE .... DORIS DAY
MAN WHO KNEW
TOO MUCH, THE .... JAMES STEWART
MAN WHO LIVED TWICE, THE ..... RALPH BELLAMY†
MAN WHO LOVED
CAT DANCING, THE .... BO HOPKINS
MAN WHO LOVED
CAT DANCING, THE .... BURT REYNOLDS
MAN WHO LOVED
CAT DANCING, THE .... GEORGE HAMILTON
MAN WHO LOVED
CAT DANCING, THE .... JACK WARDEN
MAN WHO LOVED
CAT DANCING, THE .... JAY SILVERHEELS†
MAN WHO LOVED
CAT DANCING, THE .... LEE J. COBB†
MAN WHO LOVED
CAT DANCING, THE .... ROBERT DONNER
MAN WHO LOVED
CAT DANCING, THE .... SARAH MILES
MAN WHO LOVED
REDHEADS, THE .... DENHOLM ELLIOTT†
MAN WHO LOVED WOMEN, THE ...... BARRY CORBIN
MAN WHO LOVED
WOMEN, THE .... BURT REYNOLDS
MAN WHO LOVED WOMEN, THE ...... CYNTHIA SIKES
MAN WHO LOVED
WOMEN, THE .... JENNIFER EDWARDS
MAN WHO LOVED WOMEN, THE .... JULIE ANDREWS
MAN WHO LOVED WOMEN, THE ...... KIM BASINGER
MAN WHO LOVED WOMEN, THE ...... LESLIE CARON
MAN WHO LOVED WOMEN, THE ... MARILU HENNER
MAN WHO LOVED
WOMEN, THE .... TRACY VACCARO
MAN WHO PLAYED GOD, THE .... BETTE DAVIS†
MAN WHO SHOT LIBERTY
VALANCE, THE .... JAMES STEWART
MAN WHO SHOT LIBERTY
VALANCE, THE .... VERA MILES
MAN WHO SHOT LIBERTY
VALANCE, THE .... WOODY STRODE
MAN WHO UNDERSTOOD
WOMEN, THE .... LESLIE CARON
MAN WHO WAGGED
HIS TAIL, THE .... PETER USTINOV
MAN WHO WANTED TO
LIVE FOREVER, THE .... BURL IVES
MAN WHO WANTED TO
LIVE FOREVER, THE .... SANDY DENNIS†
MAN WHO WASN'T THERE, THE ...... LISA LANGLOIS
MAN WHO WASN'T
THERE, THE .... STEVE GUTTENBERG
MAN WHO WATCHED
TRAINS GO BY, THE .... ANOUK AIMEE
MAN WHO WOULD
BE KING, THE .... CHRISTOPHER PLUMMER
MAN WHO WOULD
BE KING, THE .... MICHAEL CAINE
MAN WHO WOULD
BE KING, THE .... SEAN CONNERY
MAN WHO WOULDN'T DIE, THE .... JEFF COREY
MAN WHO WOULDN'T
TALK, THE .... ZSA ZSA GABOR
MAN WITH A CLOAK, THE ... BARBARA STANWYCK†
MAN WITH A CLOAK, THE .... LESLIE CARON

This is not a list of every film ever made or every cast member, only those listed in this directory.

MAN WITH A MILLION .... GREGORY PECK
MAN WITH BOGART'S FACE, THE .... FRANCO NERO
MAN WITH BOGART'S FACE, THE .... YVONNE DE CARLO
MAN WITH ONE RED SHOE, THE .... CARRIE FISHER
MAN WITH ONE RED SHOE, THE .... CHARLES DURNING
MAN WITH ONE RED SHOE, THE .... DABNEY COLEMAN
MAN WITH ONE RED SHOE, THE .... EDWRAD HERRMANN
MAN WITH ONE RED SHOE, THE .... JAMES BELUSHI
MAN WITH ONE RED SHOE, THE .... TOM HANKS
MAN WITH THE ALBATROSS, THE ..... TIPPI HEDREN
MAN WITH THE GOLDEN ARM, THE .... DARREN McGAVIN
MAN WITH THE GOLDEN ARM, THE .... ELEANOR PARKER
MAN WITH THE GOLDEN ARM, THE .... KIM NOVAK
MAN WITH THE GOLDEN ARM, THE ★ .... FRANK SINATRA
MAN WITH THE GOLDEN GUN, THE .... BERNARD LEE†
MAN WITH THE GOLDEN GUN, THE .... BRITT EKLAND
MAN WITH THE GOLDEN GUN, THE .... CLIFTON JAMES
MAN WITH THE GOLDEN GUN, THE .... DESMOND LLEWELYN
MAN WITH THE GOLDEN GUN, THE .... HERVE VILLECHAIZE†
MAN WITH THE GOLDEN GUN, THE .... LOIS MAXWELL
MAN WITH THE GOLDEN GUN, THE .... MAUD ADAMS
MAN WITH THE GOLDEN GUN, THE .... RICHARD LOO†
MAN WITH THE GOLDEN GUN, THE .... ROGER MOORE
MAN WITH THE GUN .... ANGIE DICKINSON
MAN WITH THE GUN .... ROBERT MITCHUM
MAN WITH TWO BRAINS, THE .... DAVID WARNER
MAN WITH TWO BRAINS, THE .... KATHLEEN TURNER
MAN WITH TWO BRAINS, THE .... SISSY SPACEK
MAN WITH TWO BRAINS, THE .... STEVE MARTIN
MAN WITHOUT A FACE, THE .... FAY MASTERSON
MAN WITHOUT A FACE, THE .... GABY HOFFMAN
MAN WITHOUT A FACE, THE .... GEOFFREY LEWIS
MAN WITHOUT A FACE, THE .... MARGARET WHITTON
MAN WITHOUT A FACE, THE .... MEL GIBSON
MAN WITHOUT A FACE, THE .... NICK STAHL
MAN WITHOUT A FACE, THE .... RICHARD MASUR
MAN WITHOUT A STAR .... KIRK DOUGLAS
MAN, WOMAN AND CHILD .... BLYTHE DANNER
MAN, WOMAN AND CHILD .... CRAIG T. NELSON
MAN, WOMAN AND CHILD .... DAVID HEMMINGS
MAN, WOMAN AND CHILD .... MARTIN SHEEN
MAN'S BEST FRIEND .... ALLY SHEEDY
MAN'S BEST FRIEND .... FREDERIC LEHNE
MAN'S BEST FRIEND .... LANCE HENRIKSEN
MAN'S BEST FRIEND .... ROBERT COSTANZO
MAN-TRAP .... STELLA STEVENS
MANCHU EAGLE MURDER CAPER MYSTERY, THE .... BARBARA HARRIS
MANCHU EAGLE MURDER CAPER MYSTERY, THE .... JOYCE VAN PATTEN
MANCHU EAGLE MURDER CAPER MYSTERY, THE .... VINCENT GARDENIA†
MANCHURIAN CANDIDATE, THE .... FRANK SINATRA
MANCHURIAN CANDIDATE, THE .... HENRY SILVA
MANCHURIAN CANDIDATE, THE .... JANET LEIGH
MANCHURIAN CANDIDATE, THE ✪ .... ANGELA LANSBURY
MANDINGO .... PERRY KING
MANDINGO .... SUSAN GEORGE
MANEATER .... BURT REYNOLDS
MANEATER (TF) .... BEN GAZZARA
MANEATERS ARE LOOSE! (TF) .... DABNEY COLEMAN
MANEATERS ARE LOOSE (TF) ...... DIANA MULDAUR
MANGO TREE, THE .... GERALDINE FITZGERALD
MANHANDLED .... DOROTHY LAMOUR
MANHATTAN .... ANNE BYRNE
MANHATTAN .... DIANE KEATON
MANHATTAN .... KAREN ALLEN
MANHATTAN .... MARK LINN-BAKER
MANHATTAN .... MERYL STREEP
MANHATTAN .... MICHAEL MURPHY
MANHATTAN .... WALLACE SHAWN
MANHATTAN .... WOODY ALLEN
MANHATTAN ✪ .... MARIEL HEMINGWAY
MANHATTAN MELODRAMA .... MICKEY ROONEY
MANHATTAN MURDER MYSTERY .... ALAN ALDA
MANHATTAN MURDER MYSTERY .... ANJELICA HUSTON
MANHATTAN MURDER MYSTERY ..... DIANE KEATON
MANHATTAN MURDER MYSTERY ..... WOODY ALLEN
MANHATTAN PROJECT, THE .... CHRISTOPHER COLLET
MANHATTAN PROJECT, THE .... JILL EIKENBERRY
MANHATTAN PROJECT, THE .... JOHN LITHGOW
MANHATTAN PROJECT, THE .... JOHN MAHONEY
MANHATTAN PROJECT, THE ...... RICHARD JENKINS
MANHATTAN PROJECT, THE .... SULLY BOVAR
MANHUNT FOR CLAUDE DALLAS (TF) .... CLAUDE AKINS†
MANHUNT FOR CLAUDE DALLAS (TF) .... LOIS NETTLETON
MANHUNT FOR CLAUDE DALLAS (TF) .... MATT SALINGER
MANHUNT FOR CLAUDE DALLAS (TF) .... PAT HINGLE
MANHUNT FOR CLAUDE DALLAS (TF) ...... RIP TORN
MANHUNT: SEARCH FOR THE NIGHT STALKER (TF) .... A MARTINEZ
MANHUNT: SEARCH FOR THE NIGHT STALKER (TF) .... LISA EILBACHER
MANHUNT: SEARCH FOR THE NIGHT STALKER (TF) .... RICHARD JORDAN†
MANHUNTER .... BILL SMITROVICH
MANHUNTER .... BRIAN COX
MANHUNTER .... CHRIS ELLIOT
MANHUNTER .... DENNIS FARINA
MANHUNTER .... JOAN ALLEN
MANHUNTER .... KIM GREIST
MANHUNTER .... STEPHEN LANG
MANHUNTER .... TOM NOONAN
MANHUNTER .... WILLIAM L. PETERSEN
MANHUNTER (TF) .... ROYAL DANO
MANHUNTER, THE (TF) .... SANDRA DEE
MANIA .... DONALD PLEASENCE
MANIAC .... DONALD PLEASENCE
MANIAC .... STUART WHITMAN
MANIFESTO .... ERIC STOLTZ
MANIFESTO .... GABRIELLE ANWAR
MANIONS OF AMERICA, THE (MS) .... KATE MULGREW
MANIONS OF AMERICA, THE (MS) .... PIERCE BROSNAN
MANIONS OF AMERICA, THE (MS) .... SIMON MacCORKINDALE
MANIONS OF AMERICA, THE (MS) .... STEVE FORREST
MANIPULATOR, THE .... LUANA ANDERS
MANITOU, THE .... ANN SOTHERN
MANITOU, THE .... BURGESS MEREDITH
MANITOU, THE .... STELLA STEVENS
MANITOU, THE .... SUSAN STRASBERG
MANITOU, THE .... TONY CURTIS
MANNEQUIN .... CAROLE DAVIS
MANNEQUIN .... JAMES SPADER
MANNEQUIN .... JOAN CRAWFORD†
MANNEQUIN .... KIM CATTRALL
MANNEQUIN .... MESHACH TAYLOR
MANNEQUIN TWO ON THE MOVE .... KRISTY SWANSON
MANNEQUIN TWO ON THE MOVE .... MESHACH TAYLOR
MANNEQUIN TWO ON THE MOVE .... STUART PANKIN
MANNEQUIN TWO ON THE MOVE .... TERRY KISER
MANNEQUIN TWO ON THE MOVE .... WILLIAM RAGSDALE
MANON 70 .... CATHERINE DENEUVE
MANON OF THE SPRING .... DANIEL AUTEUIL
MANUELA .... DONALD PLEASENCE
MANY HAPPY RETURNS .... GEORGE BURNS
MANY HAPPY RETURNS (TF) .... GEORGE SEGAL
MANY RIVERS TO CROSS .... ELEANOR PARKER
MANY RIVERS TO CROSS .... JAMES ARNESS
MANY RIVERS TO CROSS .... RUSS TAMBLYN
MAN'S ENEMY .... LILLIAN GISH†
MAN'S FAVORITE SPORT? .... NORMAN ALDEN
MAN'S FAVORITE SPORT? .... PAULA PRENTISS
MAP OF THE HUMAN HEART .... ANNE PARILLAUD
MAP OF THE HUMAN HEART ...... JASON SCOTT LEE
MAP OF THE HUMAN HEART .... JEANNE MOREAU
MAP OF THE HUMAN HEART .... JOHN CUSAK
MAP OF THE HUMAN HEART .... PATRICK BERGIN
MARA MARU .... RAYMOND BURR†
MARA OF THE WILDERNESS .... ADAM WEST
MARATHON MAN .... DUSTIN HOFFMAN
MARATHON MAN .... FRITZ WEAVER
MARATHON MAN .... MARTHE KELLER
MARATHON MAN .... RICHARD BRIGHT
MARATHON MAN .... ROY SCHEIDER
MARATHON MAN .... WILLIAM DEVANE
MARATHON MAN ✪ .... LAURENCE OLIVIER†
MARATHON (TF) .... BOB NEWHART
MARATHON (TF) .... HERB EDELMAN
MARATHON (TF) .... JULIA JENNINGS
MARCH OF THE SPRING .... ALLEN GARFIELD
MARCH OR DIE .... CATHERINE DENEUVE
MARCH OR DIE .... GENE HACKMAN
MARCH OR DIE .... IAN HOLM
MARCH OR DIE .... JACK O'HALLORAN
MARCH OR DIE .... LILA KEDROVA
MARCH OR DIE .... MAX von SYDOW
MARCIA TRIONFALE .... FRANCO NERO
MARCIANO (TF) .... RICHARD HERD
MARCIANO (TF) .... TONY LoBIANCO
MARCIANO (TF) .... VINCENT GARDENIA†
MARCO .... DESI ARNAZ JR.
MARCO .... JACK WESTON
MARCO POLO .... RORY CALHOUN
MARCO POLO (MS) .... ANNE BANCROFT
MARCO POLO (MS) .... BURT LANCASTER†
MARCO POLO (MS) .... JOHN GIELGUD
MARCO THE MAGNIFICENT .... ANTHONY QUINN
MARCO THE MAGNIFICENT .... OMAR SHARIF
MARCUS NELSON MURDERS, THE (TF) .... JOSE FERRER†
MARCUS NELSON MURDERS, THE (TF) .... MARJOE GORTNER
MARCUS NELSON MURDERS, THE (TF) .... TELLY SAVALAS†
MARCUS NELSON MURDERS, THE (TF) .... NED BEATTY
MARCUS WELBY, M.D. (TF) .... JAMES BROLIN
MARDI GRAS .... PAT BOONE
MARGARET BOURKE-WHITE (CTF) .... FARRAH FAWCETT
MARGIE .... ALAN YOUNG
MARGIE .... CONRAD JANIS
MARGIN FOR ERROR .... MILTON BERLE
MARIA'S LOVERS .... VINCENT SPANO
MARIA'S LOVERS .... BILL SMITROVICH
MARIA'S LOVERS .... BUD CORT
MARIA'S LOVERS .... DANTON STONE
MARIA'S LOVERS .... JOHN SAVAGE
MARIA'S LOVERS .... KEITH CARRADINE
MARIA'S LOVERS .... NASTASSJA KINSKI
MARIA'S LOVERS .... ROBERT MITCHUM
MARIE .... FRED DALTON THOMPSON
MARIE .... JEFF DANIELS
MARIE .... KEITH SZARABAJKA
MARIE .... SISSY SPACEK
MARIE ANTOINETTE ★ .... NORMA SHEARER†
MARIE ANTOINETTE ✪ .... ROBERT MORLEY
MARILYN (TF) .... ANN RAMSEY†
MARILYN: THE UNTOLD STORY (MS) .... HOWARD CAINE†
MARINE ISSUE .... CHARLES NAPIER

† after an actor's name denotes deceased.

MARINE ISSUE .... MICHAEL PARE
MARINES LET'S GO .... DAVID HEDISON
MARIO PUZO'S THE
    FORTUNATE PILGRIM .... SOPHIA LOREN
MARIO PUZO'S THE
    FORTUNATE PILGRIM (MS) .... HAL HOLBROOK
MARJORIE MORNINGSTAR .... GENE KELLY
MARJORIE MORNINGSTAR .... MARTIN BALSAM
MARJORIE MORNINGSTAR .... NATALIE WOOD†
MARK, THE .... MARIA SCHELL
MARK, THE .... ROD STEIGER
MARK, THE ★ .... STUART WHITMAN
MARK OF THE HAWK, THE .... EARTHA KITT
MARK OF THE HAWK, THE .... SIDNEY POITIER
MARK OF THE RENEGADE .... CYD CHARISSE
MARK OF THE
    RENEGADE .... RICARDO MONTALBAN
MARK OF ZORRO, THE .... MILTON BERLE
MARK OF ZORRO, THE (TF) .... ANNE ARCHER
MARK OF ZORRO, THE (TF) .... FRANK LANGELLA
MARK OF ZORRO, THE (TF) .... YVONNE DE CARLO
MARKED FOR DEATH .... JOANNA PACULA
MARKED FOR DEATH .... KEITH DAVID
MARKED FOR DEATH .... STEVEN SEAGAL
MARKED WOMAN .... BETTE DAVIS†
MARLOWE .... CARROLL O'CONNOR
MARLOWE .... JAMES GARNER
MARLOWE .... WILLIAM DANIELS
MARNIE .... ALAN NAPIER†
MARNIE .... BRUCE DERN
MARNIE .... DIANE BAKER
MARNIE .... LOUISE LATHAM
MARNIE .... MARIETTE HARTLEY
MARNIE .... MORGAN BRITTANY
MARNIE .... SEAN CONNERY
MARNIE .... TIPPI HEDREN
MAROC 7 .... CYD CHARISSE
MAROC 7 .... DENHOLM ELLIOTT†
MAROONED .... GENE HACKMAN
MAROONED .... GREGORY PECK
MAROONED .... JAMES FRANCISCUS†
MAROONED .... LEE GRANT
MAROONED .... MARIETTE HARTLEY
MAROONED .... RICHARD CRENNA
MARQUISE OF O..., THE .... BRUNO GANZ
MARRIAGE IS A PRIVATE AFFAIR ...... LANA TURNER
MARRIAGE IS ALIVE
    AND WELL (TF) .... JOE NAMATH
MARRIAGE IS ALIVE
    AND WELL (TF) .... SWOOSIE KURTZ
MARRIAGE ITALIAN
    STYLE .... MARCELLO MASTROIANNI
MARRIAGE ITALIAN STYLE ★ .... SOPHIA LOREN
MARRIAGE OF A YOUNG
    STOCKBROKER .... ELIZABETH ASHLEY
MARRIAGE OF A YOUNG
    STOCKBROKER, THE .... ADAM WEST
MARRIAGE OF A YOUNG
    STOCKBROKER, THE .... RICHARD BENJAMIN
MARRIAGE OF MARIA
    BRAUN, THE .... HANNA SCHYGULLA
MARRIAGE ON THE ROCKS .... DEAN MARTIN
MARRIAGE ON THE ROCKS .... DEBORAH KERR
MARRIAGE ON THE ROCKS .... FRANK SINATRA
MARRIAGE ON THE ROCKS ... KATHLEEN FREEMAN
MARRIAGE ON THE ROCKS .... TONY BILL
MARRIAGE: YEAR ONE (TF) .... SALLY FIELD
MARRIAGE-GO-ROUND, THE .... JULIE NEWMAR
MARRIED MAN, A (TF) .... ANTHONY HOPKINS
MARRIED TO IT .... BEAU BRIDGES
MARRIED TO IT .... CYBILL SHEPHERD
MARRIED TO IT .... MARY STUART MASTERSON
MARRIED TO IT .... ROBERT SEAN LEONARD
MARRIED TO IT .... RON SILVER
MARRIED TO IT .... STOCKARD CHANNING
MARRIED TO THE MOB .... AL LEWIS
MARRIED TO THE MOB .... ALEC BALDWIN
MARRIED TO THE MOB .... CHRIS ISAAK
MARRIED TO THE MOB .... ELLEN FOLEY
MARRIED TO THE MOB .... FRANK GIO
MARRIED TO THE MOB .... GARY KLAR
MARRIED TO THE MOB .... JOAN CUSAK

MARRIED TO THE MOB .... MATTHEW MODINE
MARRIED TO THE MOB .... MERCEDES RUEHL
MARRIED TO THE MOB .... MICHELLE PFEIFFER
MARRIED TO THE MOB .... O-LAN JONES
MARRIED TO THE MOB .... OLIVER PLATT
MARRIED TO THE MOB .... STEVE VIGNARI
MARRIED TO THE MOB ○ .... DEAN STOCKWELL
MARRY ME .... DAVID TOMLINSON
MARRYING KIND, THE .... CHARLES BRONSON
MARRYING MAN, THE .... ALEC BALDWIN
MARRYING MAN, THE .... ARMAND ASSANTE
MARRYING MAN, THE .... ELISABETH SHUE
MARRYING MAN, THE .... FISHER STEVENS
MARRYING MAN, THE .... KIM BASINGER
MARRYING MAN, THE .... PAUL REISER
MARRYING MAN, THE .... PETER DOBSON
MARRYING MAN, THE .... ROBERT LOGGIA
MARRYING MAN, THE .... STEPHEN HYTNER
MARSEILLES CONTRACT, THE ...... ANTHONY QUINN
MARSEILLES CONTRACT, THE .... MICHAEL CAINE
MARTAIN CHRONICLES, THE (TF) .... FRITZ WEAVER
MARTIAN CHRONICLES, THE ...... DARREN McGAVIN
MARTIANS GO HOME .... ANITA MORRIS†
MARTIANS GO HOME .... BARRY SOBEL
MARTIANS GO HOME .... JOHN PHILBIN
MARTIANS GO HOME .... MARGARET COLIN
MARTIANS GO HOME .... RANDY QUAID
MARTIANS GO HOME .... VIC DUNLOP
MARTIN EDEN .... CARY ELWES
MARTIN EDEN .... CHARLIE SHEEN
MARTIN EDEN .... MATTHEW MODINE
MARTIN'S DAY .... JAMES COBURN
MARTIN'S DAY .... JOHN IRELAND
MARTIN'S DAY .... JUSTIN HENRY
MARTIN'S DAY .... KAREN BLACK
MARTIN'S DAY .... LINDSAY WAGNER
MARTIN'S DAY .... RICHARD HARRIS
MARTY ★★ .... ERNEST BORGNINE
MARTY ○ .... BETSY BLAIR
MARVIN AND TIGE .... BILLY DEE WILLIAMS
MARVIN AND TIGE .... DENISE NICHOLAS
MARY BURNS, FUGITIVE .... SYLVIA SIDNEY
MARY JANE HARPER CRIED
    LAST NIGHT (TF) .... SUSAN DEY
MARY MAGDALENE .... YVONNE DE CARLO
MARY, MARY .... DEBBIE REYNOLDS
MARY OF SCOTLAND .... KATHERINE HEPBURN
MARY POPPINS .... ARTHUR TREACHER†
MARY POPPINS .... DAVID TOMLINSON
MARY POPPINS .... DICK VAN DYKE
MARY POPPINS .... ED WYNN†
MARY POPPINS .... ELSA LANCHESTER†
MARY POPPINS .... HERMIONE BADDELEY†
MARY POPPINS .... JANE DARWELL†
MARY POPPINS .... MATTHEW GARBER†
MARY POPPINS .... REGINALD OWEN†
MARY POPPINS ★★ .... JULIE ANDREWS
MARY QUEEN OF SCOTS .... GLENDA JACKSON
MARY QUEEN OF SCOTS .... IAN HOLM
MARY QUEEN OF SCOTS ...... NIGEL DAVENPORT
MARY, QUEEN OF SCOTS .... TIMOTHY DALTON
MARY, QUEEN
    OF SCOTS ★ .... VANESSA REDGRAVE
MARY REILLY .... GEORGE COLE
MARY REILLY .... GLENN CLOSE
MARY REILLY .... JOHN MALKOVICH
MARY REILLY .... JULIA ROBERTS
MARY REILLY .... KATHY STAFF
MARY SHELLEY'S FRANKENSTEIN .... AIDAN QUINN
MARY SHELLEY'S
FRANKENSTEIN .... HELENA BONHAM CARTER
MARY SHELLEY'S FRANKENSTEIN .... IAN HOLM
MARY SHELLEY'S FRANKENSTEIN .... JOHN CLEESE
MARY SHELLEY'S
FRANKENSTEIN .... KENNETH BRANAGH
MARY SHELLEY'S
FRANKENSTEIN .... RICHARD BRIERS
MARY SHELLEY'S
FRANKENSTEIN .... ROBERT DE NIRO
MARY SHELLEY'S FRANKENSTEIN .... TOM HULCE
MARY WHITE (TF) .... KATHLEEN BELLER
MASADA (MS) .... DENIS QUILLEY

MASADA (MS) .... PETER O'TOOLE
MASADA (TF) .... PETER STRAUSS
MASK .... BEN PIAZZA†
MASK .... CHER
MASK .... ERIC STOLTZ
MASK .... ESTELLE GETTY
MASK .... LAURA DERN
MASK .... LAWRENCE MONOSON
MASK .... NICK CASSAVETES
MASK .... SAM ELLIOTT
MASK, THE .... CAMERON DIAZ
MASK, THE .... JIM CARREY
MASK OF THE AVENGER ...... ANTHONY QUINN
MASKS OF DEATH, THE .... GORDAN JACKSON†
MASQUE OF THE RED
    DEATH, THE .... VINCENT PRICE†
MASQUERADE .... CLIFF ROBERTSON
MASQUERADE .... DOUG SAVANT
MASQUERADE .... JOHN GLOVER
MASQUERADE .... KIM CATTRALL
MASQUERADE .... MEG TILLY
MASQUERADE .... ROB LOWE
MASQUERADE IN MEXICO .... DOROTHY LAMOUR
MASQUERADE (TF) .... ERNEST BORGNINE
MASS APPEAL .... CHARLES DURNING
MASS APPEAL .... JACK LEMMON
MASSACRE AT
    CENTRAL HIGH .... ROBERT CARRADINE
MASSACRE AT FORT HOLMAN ...... JAMES COBURN
MASSACRE HILL .... GORDAN JACKSON†
MASSACRE RIVER .... RORY CALHOUN
MASTER
    GUNFIGHTER, THE .... BARBARA CARRERA
MASTER GUNFIGHTER, THE .... RON O'NEAL
MASTER OF
    BALLANTRAE, THE (TF) ... JOHN GIELGUD
MASTER OF
    BALLANTRAE, THE (TF) .... MICHAEL YORK
MASTER OF BANKDAM .... DAVID TOMLINSON
MASTER OF THE GAME (MS) .... DYAN CANNON
MASTER OF THE GAME (MS) .... JEAN MARSH
MASTER OF THE GAME (MS) .... LESLIE CARON
MASTER OF THE WORLD .... CHARLES BRONSON
MASTER OF THE WORLD .... VINCENT PRICE†
MASTER RACE, THE .... LLOYD BRIDGES
MASTERMIND .... BRADFORD DILLMAN
MASTERPIECE OF MURDER, A (TF) .... BOB HOPE
MASTERPIECE OF
    MURDER, A (TF) .... DON AMECHE†
MASTERPIECE OF
    MURDER, A (TF) .... YVONNE DE CARLO
MASTERS OF MENACE .... JOHN CANDY†
MASTERS OF THE UNIVERSE ...... COURTENEY COX
MASTERS OF THE UNIVERSE ... DOLPH LUNDGREN
MASTERS OF THE UNIVERSE ..... FRANK LANGELLA
MATA HARI .... CHRISTOPHER CAZENOVE
MATA HARI .... OLIVER TOBIAS
MATADOR .... ANTONIO BANDERAS
MATCHLESS .... DONALD PLEASENCE
MATCHLESS .... HENRY SILVA
MATCHMAKER, THE .... ANTHONY PERKINS†
MATCHMAKER, THE .... SHIRLEY MacLAINE
MATEWAN .... BOB GUNTON
MATEWAN .... CHRIS COOPER
MATEWAN .... DAVID STRATHAIRN
MATEWAN .... GORDON CLAPP
MATEWAN .... JACE ALEXANDER
MATEWAN .... JAMES EARL JONES
MATEWAN .... JOE GRIFASI
MATEWAN .... JOHN SAYLES
MATEWAN .... JOSH MOSTEL
MATEWAN .... KEVIN TIGHE
MATEWAN .... MAGGIE RENZI
MATEWAN .... MARY McDONNELL
MATEWAN .... MICHAEL MANTELL
MATEWAN .... WILL OLDHAM
MATILDA .... DANNY DEVITO
MATILDA .... ELLIOTT GOULD
MATILDA .... HARRY GUARDINO
MATILDA .... LIONEL STANDER
MATILDA .... MARA WILSON
MATILDA .... ROBERT MITCHUM

This is not a list of every film ever made or every cast member, only those listed in this directory.

MATINEE .... CATHY MORIARTY
MATINEE .... JOHN GOODMAN
MATINEE .... KELLIE MARTIN
MATINEE .... LISA JAKUB
MATINEE .... OMRO KATZ
MATINEE .... SIMON FENTON
MATING GAME, THE .... DEBBIE REYNOLDS
MATING GAME, THE .... TONY RANDALL
MATING SEASON, THE ❍ .... THELMA RITTER†
MATING SEASON, THE .... GENE TIERNEY†
MATING SEASON, THE .... JOHN LUND†
MATING SEASON, THE .... MIRIAM HOPKINS†
MATING SEASON, THE .... JAN STERLING†
MATING SEASON, THE .... LARRY KEATING†
MATING SEASON, THE .... JAMES LORIMER†
MATING SEASON, THE (TF) .... LUCIE ARNAZ
MATING SEASON, THE (TF) .... SWOOSIE KURTZ
MATING SEASON,
    THE (TF) .... LAURENCE LUCKINBILL
MATLOCK: THE HUNTING
    PARTY (TF) .... ANDY GRIFFITH
MATRIMONIO
    ALL'ITALIANA .... MARCELLO MASTROIANNI
MATT HELM (TF) .... ANN TURKEL
MATT HOUSTON (TF) .... LEE HORSLEY
MATTER OF DEGREES, A ...... JOHN F. KENNEDY JR.
MATTER OF HUMANITIES, A (TF) ...... JAMES BROLIN
MATTER OF INNOCENCE, A .... HAYLEY MILLS
MATTER OF LIFE AND DEATH, A .... DAVID NIVEN†
MATTER OF MORALS, A .... PATRICK O'NEAL†
MATTER OF TIME, A .... LIZA MINELLI
MAURICE .... BILLIE WHITELAW
MAURICE .... DENHOLM ELLIOTT†
MAURICE .... HELENA BONHAM CARTER
MAURICE .... HUGH GRANT
MAURICE .... SIMON CALLOW
MAVERICK .... CLINT BLACK
MAVERICK .... CLINT WALKER
MAVERICK .... DANNY GLOVER
MAVERICK .... DENVER PYLE
MAVERICK .... DOUG McCLURE
MAVERICK .... HENRY DARROW
MAVERICK .... JAMES COBURN
MAVERICK .... JAMES GARNER
MAVERICK .... JODIE FOSTER
MAVERICK .... MEL GIBSON
MAVERICK .... ROBERT FULLER
MAVERICK .... WILL HUTCHINS
MAVERICK QUEEN, THE ...... BARBARA STANWYCK†
MAX AND HELEN (CTF) .... ALICE KRIGE
MAX AND HELEN (CTF) .... MARTIN LANDAU
MAX AND HELEN (CTF) .... TREAT WILLIAMS
MAX DUGAN RETURNS .... DONALD SUTHERLAND
MAX DUGAN RETURNS .... JASON ROBARDS
MAX DUGAN RETURNS ...... KIEFER SUTHERLAND
MAX DUGAN RETURNS .... MARSHA MASON
MAX DUGAN RETURNS .... MATHHEW BRODERICK
MAX HAVELAAR .... RUTGER HAUER
MAX MY LOVE .... CHARLOTTE RAMPLING
MAXIE .... BARNARD HUGHES
MAXIE .... GLENN CLOSE
MAXIE .... GOOGY GRESS
MAXIE .... HARRY HAMLIN
MAXIE .... MANDY PATINKIN
MAXIE .... VALERIE CURTIN
MAXIMUM OVERDRIVE .... EMILIO ESTEVEZ
MAXIMUM OVERDRIVE .... J. C. QUINN
MAXIMUM OVERDRIVE .... PAT HINGLE
MAYA .... CLINT WALKER
MAYBE BABY (TF) .... DABNEY COLEMAN
MAYBE BABY (TF) .... DAVID DOYLE
MAYBE BABY (TF) .... JANE CURTIN
MAYBE I'LL COME HOME IN
    THE SPRING .... ELEANOR PARKER
MAYBE I'LL COME HOME IN
    THE SPRING (TF) .... JACKIE COOPER
MAYBE I'LL COME HOME IN
    THE SPRING (TF) .... SALLY FIELD
MAYERLING .... AVA GARDNER†
MAYERLING .... CATHERINE DENEUVE
MAYERLING .... OMAR SHARIF

MAYFLOWER MADAM (TF) .... CAITLIN CLARKE
MAYFLOWER MADAM (TF) .... CANDICE BERGEN
MAYFLOWER MADAM (TF) .... JIM ANTONIO
MAYFLOWER: THE PILGRIMS'
    ADVENTURE (TF) .... ANTHONY HOPKINS
MAYFLOWER: THE PILGRIMS'
    ADVENTURE (TF) .... MICHAEL BECK
MAZES AND MONSTERS (TF) .... TOM HANKS
McBAIN .... CHICK VENNERA
McBAIN .... CHRISTOPHER WALKEN
McBAIN .... HECHTER UBARRY
McBAIN .... JAY PATTERSON
McBAIN .... MARIA CONCHITA ALONSO
McBAIN .... MICHAEL IRONSIDE
McBAIN .... STEVE JAMES
McBAIN .... T. J. WAITES
McBAIN .... VICTOR ARGO
McCABE AND
    MRS. MILLER .... RENE AUBERJONOIS
McCABE AND MRS. MILLER .... SHELLEY DUVALL
McCABE AND
    MRS. MILLER .... TERRY DAVID MULLIGAN
McCABE AND MRS. MILLER .... WARREN BEATTY
McCABE AND MRS. MILLER .... WILLIAM DEVANE
McCABE & MRS. MILLER .... KEITH CARRADINE
McCABE & MRS. MILLER ★ .... JULIE CHRISTIE
McCLAIN'S LAW (TF) .... JAMES ARNESS
McCLOUD: WHO KILLED
    MISS U.S.A.? (TF) .... DENNIS WEAVER
McCONNELL STORY, THE .... JAMES WHITMORE
McCONNELL STORY, THE .... JUNE ALLYSON
McGUFFIN, THE .... CHARLES DANCE
McGUIRE GO HOME! .... DENHOLM ELLIOTT†
McGUIRE GO HOME! .... SUSAN STRASBERG
McHALE'S NAVY .... ERNEST BORGNINE
McHALE'S NAVY .... GEORGE KENNEDY
McHALE'S NAVY .... TIM CONWAY
McHALE'S NAVY JOINS THE
    AIR FORCE .... TIM CONWAY
McKENZIE BREAK, THE .... BRIAN KEITH
McLINTOCK! .... JACK KRUSCHEN
McLINTOCK! .... JOHN WAYNE†
McLINTOCK! .... MAUREEN O'HARA
McLINTOCK! .... PATRICK WAYNE
McLINTOCK! .... STEFANIE POWERS
McLINTOCK! .... YVONNE DE CARLO
McMASTERS, THE .... BROCK PETERS
McMASTERS, THE .... BURL IVES
McMASTERS, THE .... DAVID CARRADINE
McMASTERS, THE .... JACK PALANCE
McNAUGHTON'S
    DAUGHTER (TF) .... RALPH BELLAMY†
McQ .... CLU GULAGER
McQ .... COLLEEN DEWHURST†
McQ .... DIANA MULDAUR
McQ .... EDDIE ALBERT
McQ .... JOHN WAYNE†
McVICAR .... ADAM FAITH
McVICAR .... CHERYL CAMPBELL
McVICAR .... ROGER DALTRY
ME AND HIM .... CAREY LOWELL
ME AND HIM .... CRAIG T. NELSON
ME AND HIM .... ELLEN GREENE
ME AND HIM .... GRIFFIN DUNNE
ME AND HIM .... KELLY BISHOP
ME AND THE KID .... ALEX ZUCKERMAN
ME AND THE KID .... DANNY AIELLO
ME, MYSELF AND I .... GEORGE SEGAL
ME, MYSELF AND I .... JoBETH WILLIAMS
ME, NATALIE .... AL PACINO
ME, NATALIE .... BOB BALABAN
ME, NATALIE .... JAMES FARENTINO
ME, NATALIE .... MARTIN BALSAM
ME, NATALIE .... PATTY DUKE
ME, NATALIE .... SALOME JENS
MEADOW, THE .... ISABELLA ROSSELLINI
MEAL, THE .... DINA MERRILL
MEAL, THE .... LEON AMES
MEAN DOG BLUES .... GEORGE KENNEDY
MEAN DOG BLUES .... TINA LOUISE
MEAN DOG BLUES .... WILLIAM WINDOM

MEAN JOHNNY BARROWS .... ELLIOTT GOULD
MEAN JOHNNY BARROWS .... FRED WILLIAMSON
MEAN JOHNNY BARROWS .... RODDY McDOWALL
MEAN JOHNNY BARROWS .... STUART WHITMAN
MEAN SEASON, THE .... ANDY GARCIA
MEAN SEASON, THE .... JOE PANTOLIANO
MEAN SEASON, THE .... KURT RUSSELL
MEAN SEASON, THE .... MARIEL HEMINGWAY
MEAN SEASON, THE .... RICHARD JORDAN†
MEAN SEASON, THE .... RICHARD MASUR
MEAN STREETS .... DAVID CARRADINE
MEAN STREETS .... HARVEY KEITEL
MEAN STREETS .... ROBERT CARRADINE
MEAN STREETS .... ROBERT DE NIRO
MEANTIME .... TIM ROTH
MEATBALLS .... BILL MURRAY
MEATBALLS .... CHRIS MAKEPEACE
MEATBALLS III .... PATRICK DEMPSEY
MEATBALLS III .... SALLY KELLERMAN
MECHANIC, THE .... CHARLES BRONSON
MECHANIC, THE .... JAN-MICHAEL VINCENT
MEDAL FOR BENNY, A .... DOROTHY LAMOUR
MEDAL FOR BENNY, A .... RITA MORENO
MEDAL FOR BENNY, A ❍ .... J. CARROL NAISH†
MEDICAL STORY (TF) .... BEAU BRIDGES
MEDICAL STORY (TF) .... JOSE FERRER†
MEDICINE MAN .... LORRAINE BRACCO
MEDICINE MAN .... SEAN CONNERY
MEDIUM COOL .... PETER BOYLE
MEDIUM COOL .... ROBERT FORSTER
MEDIUM COOL .... VERNA BLOOM
MEDUSA TOUCH, THE .... DEREK JACOBI
MEDUSA TOUCH, THE .... GORDAN JACKSON†
MEDUSA
    TOUCH, THE .... MARIE-CHRISTINE BARRAULT
MEET DANNY WILSON .... FRANK SINATRA
MEET DANNY WILSON .... RAYMOND BURR†
MEET DANNY WILSON .... SHELLEY WINTERS
MEET JOHN DOE .... BARBARA STANWYCK†
MEET ME AFTER THE SHOW .... EDDIE ALBERT
MEET ME AFTER THE SHOW .... GWEN VERDON
MEET ME AFTER THE SHOW .... RORY CALHOUN
MEET ME IN LAS VEGAS .... CYD CHARISSE
MEET ME IN LAS VEGAS .... DEBBIE REYNOLDS
MEET ME IN LAS VEGAS .... FRANK SINATRA
MEET ME IN LAS VEGAS .... LENA HORNE
MEET ME IN ST. LOUIS .... JUDY GARLAND†
MEET ME IN ST. LOUIS .... JUNE LOCKHART
MEET ME IN ST. LOUIS .... LEON AMES
MEET MR. LUCIFER .... GORDAN JACKSON†
MEET NERO WOLFE .... LIONEL STANDER
MEET SEXTON BLAKE .... JEAN SIMMONS
MEET THE APPLEGATES .... DABNEY COLEMAN
MEET THE APPLEGATES .... ED BEGLEY JR.
MEET THE APPLEGATES ..... STOCKARD CHANNING
MEET THE PEOPLE .... JUNE ALLYSON
MEET THE WILDCAT .... RALPH BELLAMY†
MEETING VENUS .... ERLAND JOSEPHSON
MEETING VENUS .... GLENN CLOSE
MEETINGS WITH
    REMARKABLE MEN .... TERENCE STAMP
MEGAFORCE .... BARRY BOSTWICK
MEGAFORCE .... PERSIS KHAMBATTA
MEIN KAMPF MY CRIMES .... PETER USTINOV
MELBA .... ROBERT MORLEY
MELBA .... THEODORE BIKEL
MELODY .... MARK LESTER
MELTDOWN .... DOLPH LUNDGREN
MELVIN AND HOWARD .... DABNEY COLEMAN
MELVIN AND HOWARD .... MICHAEL J. POLLARD
MELVIN AND HOWARD .... PAUL LeMAT
MELVIN AND HOWARD ❍ .... JASON ROBARDS
MELVIN AND
    HOWARD ❍❍ .... MARY STEENBURGEN
MEMBER OF THE
    WEDDING, THE ★ .... JULIE HARRIS
MEMED MY HAWK .... DENIS QUILLEY
MEMED MY HAWK .... MICHAEL GOUGH
MEMED MY HAWK .... PETER USTINOV
MEMOIRS OF A SURVIVOR .... JULIE CHRISTIE
MEMOIRS OF AN INVISIBLE MAN ...... CHEVY CHASE

501

MEMOIRS OF AN INVISIBLE MAN .... DARYL HANNAH
MEMOIRS OF AN INVISIBLE MAN .... GREGORY PAUL MARTIN
MEMOIRS OF AN INVISIBLE MAN .... JIM NORTON
MEMOIRS OF AN INVISIBLE MAN .... MICHAEL McKEAN
MEMOIRS OF AN INVISIBLE MAN .... PAT SKIPPER
MEMOIRS OF AN INVISIBLE MAN .... PATRICIA HEATON
MEMOIRS OF AN INVISIBLE MAN .... PAUL PERRI
MEMOIRS OF AN INVISIBLE MAN .... RICHARD EPCAR
MEMOIRS OF AN INVISIBLE MAN .... SAM NEILL
MEMOIRS OF AN INVISIBLE MAN .... STEPHEN TOBOLOWSKY
MEMOIRS OF AN INVISIBLE MAN .... STEVEN BARR
MEMORIES OF ME .... ALAN KING
MEMORIES OF ME .... BILLY CRYSTAL
MEMORIES OF ME .... JoBETH WILLIAMS
MEMORIES OF ME .... SEAN CONNERY
MEMORIES OF MURDER (CTF) .... NANCY ALLEN
MEMORIES OF MURDER (CTF) .... ROBIN THOMAS
MEMORIES OF MURDER (CTF) .... VANITY
MEMORY OF EVA RYKER, THE (TF) .... MEL FERRER
MEMORY OF EVA RYKER, THE (TF) .... PETER GRAVES
MEMORY OF EVA RYKER, THE (TF) .... RALPH BELLAMY†
MEMPHIS BELLE .... BILLY ZANE
MEMPHIS BELLE .... COURTNEY GAINS
MEMPHIS BELLE .... D. B. SWEENEY
MEMPHIS BELLE .... ERIC STOLTZ
MEMPHIS BELLE .... HARRY CONNICK JR.
MEMPHIS BELLE .... JOHN LITHGOW
MEMPHIS BELLE .... MATTHEW MODINE
MEMPHIS BELLE .... NEIL GIUNTOLI
MEMPHIS BELLE .... REED EDWARD DIAMOND
MEMPHIS BELLE .... SEAN ASTIN
MEMPHIS BELLE .... TATE DONOVAN
MEN, THE .... MARLON BRANDO
MEN, THE .... TERESA WRIGHT
MEN AT WORK .... CHARLIE SHEEN
MEN AT WORK .... DARRELL LARSON
MEN AT WORK .... DEAN CAMERON
MEN AT WORK .... EMILIO ESTEVEZ
MEN AT WORK .... JOHN GETZ
MEN AT WORK .... KEITH DAVID
MEN AT WORK .... LESLIE HOPE
MEN DON'T LEAVE .... ARLISS HOWARD
MEN DON'T LEAVE .... CHARLIE KORSMO
MEN DON'T LEAVE .... CHRIS O'DONNELL
MEN DON'T LEAVE .... JESSICA LANGE
MEN DON'T LEAVE .... JIM HAYNIE
MEN DON'T LEAVE .... JOAN CUSAK
MEN DON'T LEAVE .... KATHY BATES
MEN IN WAR .... NEHEMIAH PERSOFF
MEN OF RESPECT .... DENNIS FARINA
MEN OF RESPECT .... JOHN TURTURRO
MEN OF RESPECT .... KATHERINE BOROWITZ
MEN OF RESPECT .... PETER BOYLE
MEN OF RESPECT .... ROD STEIGER
MEN OF RESPECT .... STANLEY TUCCI
MEN OF RESPECT .... STEVEN WRIGHT
MEN OF TEXAS .... JACKIE COOPER
MEN OF TEXAS .... RALPH BELLAMY†
MEN OF TEXAS .... ROBERT STACK
MEN OF THE FIGHTING LADY .... VAN JOHNSON
MENACE, THE .... BETTE DAVIS†
MENAGE .... BRUNO CREMER
MÉNAGE .... GERARD DEPARDIEU
MENAGE .... MICHEL BLANC
MENENDEZ: A KILLING IN BEVERLY HILLS (MS) .... BEVERLY D'ANGELO
MENENDEZ: A KILLING IN BEVERLY HILLS (MS) .... DAKIN MATHEWS
MENENDEZ: A KILLING IN BEVERLY HILLS (MS) .... DAMIAN CHAPA
MENENDEZ: A KILLING IN BEVERLY HILLS (MS) .... DAVID SELBERG

MENENDEZ: A KILLING IN BEVERLY HILLS (MS) .... DEBRAH FARENTINO
MENENDEZ: A KILLING IN BEVERLY HILLS (MS) .... DWIGHT SCHULTZ
MENENDEZ: A KILLING IN BEVERLY HILLS (MS) ..... EDWARD JAMES OLMOS
MENENDEZ: A KILLING IN BEVERLY HILLS (MS) .... H. RICHARD GREENE
MENENDEZ: A KILLING IN BEVERLY HILLS (MS) .... JACE ALEXANDER
MENENDEZ: A KILLING IN BEVERLY HILLS (MS) .... JO ANDERSON
MENENDEZ: A KILLING IN BEVERLY HILLS (MS) .... JOHN CAPODICE
MENENDEZ: A KILLING IN BEVERLY HILLS (MS) .... JOSHUA MALINA
MENENDEZ: A KILLING IN BEVERLY HILLS (MS) .... JULIO MECHOSO
MENENDEZ: A KILLING IN BEVERLY HILLS (MS) .... MARGARET WHITTON
MENENDEZ: A KILLING IN BEVERLY HILLS (MS) .... MICHAEL DURRELL
MENENDEZ: A KILLING IN BEVERLY HILLS (MS) .... MICHAEL WOOLSON
MENENDEZ: A KILLING IN BEVERLY HILLS (MS) .... MICHELLE JOHNSON
MENENDEZ: A KILLING IN BEVERLY HILLS (MS) .... ROBERT GOSSETT
MENENDEZ: A KILLING IN BEVERLY HILLS (MS) .... SHEILA McCARTHY
MENENDEZ: A KILLING IN BEVERLY HILLS (MS) .... TRAVIS FINE
MENENDEZ: A KILLING IN BEVERLY HILLS (MS) .... VINCENT VENTRESCA
MENENDEZ: A KILLING IN BEVERLY HILLS (MS) .... YUJI OKUMOTO
MEN'S CLUB, THE .... ANN DUSENBERRY
MEN'S CLUB, THE .... CRAIG WASSON
MEN'S CLUB, THE .... DAVID DUKES
MEN'S CLUB, THE .... FRANK LANGELLA
MEN'S CLUB, THE .... GINA GALLEGO
MEN'S CLUB, THE .... HARVEY KEITEL
MEN'S CLUB, THE .... JENNIFER JASON LEIGH
MEN'S CLUB, THE .... RACHEL LEVIN
MEN'S CLUB, THE .... RICHARD JORDAN†
MEN'S CLUB, THE .... ROY SCHEIDER
MEN'S CLUB, THE .... STOCKARD CHANNING
MEN'S CLUB, THE .... TREAT WILLIAMS
MEPHISTO .... KLAUS MARIA BRANDAUER
MEPHISTO WALTZ, THE .... ALAN ALDA
MEPHISTO WALTZ, THE .... BRADFORD DILLMAN
MEPHISTO WALTZ, THE .... JACQUELINE BISSET
MERCENARIES, THE .... JIM BROWN
MERCENARY, THE .... FRANCO NERO
MERCENARY, THE .... JACK PALANCE
MERCENARY, THE .... TONY MUSANTE
MERCY OR MURDER? (TF) .... EDDIE ALBERT
MERLIN & THE SWORD .... CANDICE BERGEN
MERMAIDS .... BOB HOSKINS
MERMAIDS .... CHER
MERMAIDS .... CHRISTINA RICCI
MERMAIDS .... MICHAEL SCHOEFFLING
MERMAIDS .... WINONA RYDER
MERRILL'S MARAUDERS .... CLAUDE AKINS†
MERRILY WE GO TO HELL .... SYLVIA SIDNEY
MERRILY WE LIVE ○ .... BILLIE BURKE†
MERRY CHRISTMAS MR. LAWRENCE .... DAVID BOWIE
MERRY CHRISTMAS, MR. LAWRENCE .... JACK THOMPSON
MERRY CHRISTMAS, MR. LAWRENCE .... TOM CONTI
MERRY WIDOW, THE .... GWEN VERDON
MERRY WIDOW, THE .... LANA TURNER
MESMERIZED .... JODIE FOSTER
MESMERIZED .... JOHN LITHGOW
MESSAGE, THE .... ANTHONY QUINN
MESSAGE TO GARCIA, A .... BARBARA STANWYCK†
MESSAGE TO MY DAUGHTER (TF) .... MARTIN SHEEN
MESSENGER OF DEATH .... CHARLES BRONSON
MESSENGER OF DEATH .... DANIEL BENZALI

MESSENGER OF DEATH .... JOHN IRELAND
MESSENGER OF DEATH ..... LAURENCE LUCKINBILL
MESSENGER OF DEATH ...... MARILYN HASSETT
MESSENGER OF DEATH .... TRISH VAN DEVERE
MESSIAH OF EVIL .... ROYAL DANO
METEOR .... BRIAN KEITH
METEOR .... DONALD PLEASENCE
METEOR .... KARL MALDEN
METEOR .... MARTIN LANDAU
METEOR .... NATALIE WOOD†
METEOR .... SEAN CONNERY
METEOR MAN, THE .... BILL COSBY
METEOR MAN, THE .... EDDIE GRIFFIN
METEOR MAN, THE .... JAMES EARL JONES
METEOR MAN, THE .... LUTHER VANDROSS
METEOR MAN, THE .... MARLA GIBBS
METEOR MAN, THE .... ROBERT GUILLAUME
METEOR MAN, THE .... ROBERT TOWNSEND
METEOR MAN, THE .... SINBAD
METTI UNA SERA A CENA .... TONY MUSANTE
MEXICALI ROSE .... BARBARA STANWYCK†
MI FAMILIA .... EDWARD JAMES OLMOS
MI FAMILIA .... ESAI MORALES
MI FAMILIA .... JIMMY SMITS
MIAMI BLUES .... ALEC BALDWIN
MIAMI BLUES .... FRED WARD
MIAMI BLUES .... JENNIFER JASON LEIGH
MIAMI BLUES .... NORA DUNN
MIAMI VICE (TF) .... DON JOHNSON
MICHAEL KOHLHAAS .... DAVID WARNER
MICKEY ONE .... HURD HATFIELD
MICKEY ONE .... JEFF COREY
MICKEY ONE .... WARREN BEATTY
MICKEY SPILLANE'S MIKE HAMMER: MURDER TAKES ALL (TF) .... LYNDA CARTER
MICKEY SPILLANE'S MIKE HAMMER: MURDER TAKES ALL (TF) .... STACY KEACH
MICKI & MAUDE .... AMY IRVING
MICKI & MAUDE .... ANN REINKING
MICKI & MAUDE .... DUDLEY MOORE
MICKI & MAUDE .... GEORGE GAYNES
MICKI & MAUDE .... RICHARD MULLIGAN
MICKI & MAUDE .... WALLACE SHAWN
MIDAS RUN .... RICHARD CRENNA
MIDAS RUN .... RICHARD WIDMARK
MIDAS RUN .... RODDY McDOWALL
MIDAS VALLEY (TF) .... JEAN SIMMONS
MIDDLE AGE CRAZY .... ANN-MARGRET
MIDDLE AGE CRAZY .... BRUCE DERN
MIDDLE OF THE NIGHT .... KIM NOVAK
MIDDLE OF THE NIGHT .... LEE GRANT
MIDDLE OF THE NIGHT .... MARTIN BALSAM
MIDNIGHT (1939) .... DON AMECHE†
MIDNIGHT (1939) .... CLAUDETTE COLBERT
MIDNIGHT (1939) .... JOHN BARRYMORE†
MIDNIGHT (1939) .... MARY ASTOR†
MIDNIGHT (1939) .... FRANCIS LEDERER†
MIDNIGHT (1939) .... HEDDA HOPPER†
MIDNIGHT (1939) .... MONTY WOOLLEY†
MIDNIGHT (1981) .... LAWRENCE TIERNEY
MIDNIGHT (1989) .... LYNN REDGRAVE
MIDNIGHT (1989) .... TONY CURTIS
MIDNIGHT AUTO SUPPLY .... JOHN IRELAND
MIDNIGHT AUTO SUPPLY .... RORY CALHOUN
MIDNIGHT AUTO SUPPLY .... SCOTT JACOBY
MIDNIGHT CLEAR, A .... ARYE GROSS
MIDNIGHT CLEAR, A .... ETHAN HAWKE
MIDNIGHT CLEAR, A .... FRANK WHALEY
MIDNIGHT CLEAR, A .... GARY SINISE
MIDNIGHT CLEAR, A .... JOHN C. McGINLEY
MIDNIGHT CLEAR, A .... KEVIN DILLON
MIDNIGHT CLEAR, A .... PETER BERG
MIDNIGHT COWBOY .... BARNARD HUGHES
MIDNIGHT COWBOY .... BOB BALABAN
MIDNIGHT COWBOY .... BRENDA VACCARO
MIDNIGHT COWBOY .... JOHN McGIVER†
MIDNIGHT COWBOY .... M. EMMET WALSH
MIDNIGHT COWBOY .... RUTH WHITE†
MIDNIGHT COWBOY ★ .... DUSTIN HOFFMAN
MIDNIGHT COWBOY ★ .... JON VOIGHT
MIDNIGHT COWBOY ○ .... SYLVIA MILES
MIDNIGHT CROSSING .... DANIEL J. TRAVANTI

This is not a list of every film ever made or every cast member, only those listed in this directory.

MIDNIGHT EXPRESS .... BO HOPKINS
MIDNIGHT EXPRESS .... BRAD DAVIS†
MIDNIGHT EXPRESS .... RANDY QUAID
MIDNIGHT EXPRESS ✪ .... JOHN HURT
MIDNIGHT HOUR, THE (TF) .... DICK VAN PATTEN
MIDNIGHT HOUR, THE (TF) .... KEVIN McCARTHY
MIDNIGHT HOUR, THE (TF) .... LEE MONTGOMERY
MIDNIGHT HOUR, THE (TF) .... LeVAR BURTON
MIDNIGHT
   HOUR, THE (TF) .... SHARI BELAFONTE-HARPER
MIDNIGHT LACE .... DORIS DAY
MIDNIGHT LACE .... JOHN GAVIN
MIDNIGHT LACE .... RODDY McDOWALL
MIDNIGHT LACE (TF) .... CELESTE HOLM
MIDNIGHT MADNESS .... DAVID NAUGHTON
MIDNIGHT MADNESS .... MICHAEL J. FOX
MIDNIGHT MADNESS .... STEPHEN FURST
MIDNIGHT MAN, THE .... BURT LANCASTER†
MIDNIGHT MAN, THE .... HARRIS YULIN
MIDNIGHT MAN, THE .... SUSAN CLARK
MIDNIGHT RUN .... CHARLES GRODIN
MIDNIGHT RUN .... DENNIS FARINA
MIDNIGHT RUN .... JOE PANTOLIANO
MIDNIGHT RUN .... JOHN ASHTON
MIDNIGHT RUN .... RICHARD FORONJY
MIDNIGHT RUN .... ROBERT DE NIRO
MIDNIGHT RUN .... ROBERT G. MIRANDA
MIDNIGHT RUN .... WENDY PHILLIPS
MIDNIGHT RUN .... YAPHET KOTTO
MIDNIGHT STORY, THE .... TONY CURTIS
MIDSHIPMAID, THE .... JOHN MILLS
MIDSUMMER NIGHT'S DREAM, A .... DAVID WARNER
MIDSUMMER NIGHT'S DREAM, A ..... DIANA RIGG
MIDSUMMER NIGHT'S DREAM, A ..... HELEN MIRREN
MIDSUMMER NIGHT'S DREAM, A .... IAN HOLM
MIDSUMMER NIGHT'S DREAM, A .... JUDI DENCH
MIDSUMMER NIGHT'S
   DREAM, A .... MICKEY ROONEY
MIDSUMMER NIGHT'S
   DREAM, A .... OLIVIA DE HAVILLAND
MIDSUMMER NIGHT'S
   SEX COMEDY, A .... JOSE FERRER†
MIDSUMMER NIGHT'S
   SEX COMEDY, A .... JULIE HAGERTY
MIDSUMMER NIGHT'S
   SEX COMEDY, A .... MARY STEENBURGEN
MIDSUMMER NIGHT'S
   SEX COMEDY, A .... MIA FARROW
MIDSUMMER NIGHT'S
   SEX COMEDY, A .... TONY ROBERTS
MIDSUMMER NIGHT'S
   SEX COMEDY, A .... WOODY ALLEN
MIDWAY .... CHARLTON HESTON
MIDWAY .... CHRISTOPHER GUEST†
MIDWAY .... CLIFF ROBERTSON
MIDWAY .... ED NELSON
MIDWAY .... EDWARD ALBERT
MIDWAY .... HAL HOLBROOK
MIDWAY .... HENRY FONDA†
MIDWAY .... JAMES COBURN
MIDWAY .... JAMES SHIGETA
MIDWAY .... KEVIN DOBSON
MIDWAY .... NORIYUKI "PAT" MORITA
MIDWAY .... ROBERT MITCHUM
MIDWAY .... ROBERT WAGNER
MIDWAY .... ROBERT WEBBER
MIDWAY .... TOM SELLECK
MIGHTY DUCKS, THE .... EMILIO ESTEVEZ
MIGHTY DUCKS, THE .... JOSHUA JACKSON
MIGHTY DUCKS, THE .... JOSS ACKLAND
MIGHTY DUCKS, THE .... LANE SMITH
MIGHTY JOE YOUNG .... BEN JOHNSON
MIGHTY McGURK, THE .... DEAN STOCKWELL
MIGHTY QUINN, THE .... ALEX COLON
MIGHTY QUINN, THE .... ART EVANS
MIGHTY QUINN, THE .... DENZEL WASHINGTON
MIGHTY QUINN, THE .... ESTHER ROLLE
MIGHTY QUINN, THE .... JAMES FOX
MIGHTY QUINN, THE .... M. EMMET WALSH
MIGHTY QUINN, THE .... MIMI ROGERS
MIGHTY QUINN, THE .... NORMAN BEATON
MIGHTY QUINN, THE .... ROBERT TOWNSEND

MIGHTY QUINN, THE .... SHERYL LEE RALPH
MIGRANTS, THE (TF) .... SISSY SPACEK
MIKEY AND NICKY .... JOYCE VAN PATTEN
MIKEY AND NICKY .... NED BEATTY
MIKE'S MURDER .... DEBRA WINGER
MIKE'S MURDER .... PAUL WINFIELD
MILAGRO BEANFIELD
   WAR, THE .... CARLOS RIQUELME
MILAGRO BEANFIELD
   WAR, THE .... CHICK VENNERA
MILAGRO BEANFIELD
   WAR, THE .... CHRISTOPHER WALKEN
MILAGRO BEANFIELD WAR, THE ...... DANIEL STERN
MILAGRO BEANFIELD
   WAR, THE .... FREDDY FENDER
MILAGRO BEANFIELD
   WAR, THE .... JAMES GAMMON
MILAGRO BEANFIELD WAR, THE ..... JERRY HARDIN
MILAGRO BEANFIELD WAR, THE .... JOHN HEARD
MILAGRO BEANFIELD WAR, THE ...... JULIE CARMEN
MILAGRO BEANFIELD
   WAR, THE .... M. EMMET WALSH
MILAGRO BEANFIELD
   WAR, THE .... MARIO ARRAMBIDE
MILAGRO BEANFIELD
   WAR, THE .... MELANIE GRIFFITH
MILAGRO BEANFIELD
   WAR, THE .... RICHARD BRADFORD
MILAGRO BEANFIELD
   WAR, THE .... ROBERT CARRICART
MILAGRO BEANFIELD
   WAR, THE .... RONALD G. JOSEPH
MILAGRO BEANFIELD WAR, THE .... RUBEN BLADES
MILAGRO BEANFIELD WAR, THE .... SONIA BRAGA
MILAGRO BEANFIELD WAR, THE ...... TOM CONNOR
MILAGRO BEANFIELD WAR, THE ..... TONY GENARO
MILAGRO BEANFIELD
   WAR, THE .... TRINIDAD SILVA JR.†
MILDRED PIERCE ★★ .... JOAN CRAWFORD†
MILDRED PIERCE ✪ .... EVE ARDEN†
MILES FROM HOME .... BRIAN DENNEHY
MILES FROM HOME .... JOHN MALKOVICH
MILES FROM HOME .... JUDITH IVEY
MILES FROM HOME .... KEVIN ANDERSON
MILES FROM HOME .... LAURIE METCALF
MILES FROM HOME .... PENELOPE ANN MILLER
MILES FROM HOME .... RICHARD GERE
MILES TO GO BEFORE
   I SLEEP (TF) .... MARTIN BALSAM
MILES TO GO... (TF) .... JILL CLAYBURGH
MILK MONEY .... ADAM LaVORGNA
MILK MONEY .... BRIAN CHRISTOPHER
MILK MONEY .... CASEY SIEMASZKO
MILK MONEY .... ED HARRIS
MILK MONEY .... KEVIN SCANNELL
MILK MONEY .... MALCOLM McDOWELL
MILK MONEY .... MELANIE GRIFFITH
MILK MONEY .... MICHAEL PATRICK CARTER
MILKMAN, THE .... PIPER LAURIE
MILKY WAY, THE .... LIONEL STANDER
MILL ON THE
   FLOSS, THE .... GERALDINE FITZGERALD
MILLENNIUM .... CHERYL LADD
MILLENNIUM .... DANIEL J. TRAVANTI
MILLENNIUM .... KRIS KRISTOFFERSON
MILLER'S BEAUTIFUL
   WIFE, THE .... MARCELLO MASTROIANNI
MILLER'S BEAUTIFUL WIFE, THE ..... SOPHIA LOREN
MILLER'S CROSSING .... ALBERT FINNEY
MILLER'S CROSSING .... GABRIEL BYRNE
MILLER'S CROSSING .... J. E. FREEMAN
MILLER'S CROSSING .... JOHN TURTURRO
MILLER'S CROSSING .... JON POLITO
MILLER'S CROSSING .... MARCIA GAY HARDEN
MILLION DOLLAR BABY .... RONALD REAGAN
MILLION DOLLAR MYSTERY .... TOM BOSLEY
MILLION EYES OF
   SU-MURU, THE .... FRANKIE AVALON
MILLION POUND NOTE, THE .... GREGORY PECK
MILLION TO JUAN, A .... EDWARD JAMES OLMOS

MILLION TO JUAN, A .... PAUL RODRIGUEZ
MILLIONAIRE FOR
   CHRISTY, A .... ELEANOR PARKER
MILLIONAIRE
   MERRY-GO-ROUND .... MAUREEN O'HARA
MILLIONAIRE, THE (TF) .... RALPH BELLAMY†
MILLIONAIRESS, THE .... SOPHIA LOREN
MILLIONS LIKE US .... GORDAN JACKSON†
MIMI BLUETTE .... SHELLEY WINTERS
MIN AND BILL ★★ .... MARIE DRESSLER†
MIND BENDERS, THE .... MICHAEL BRYANT
MIND OF MR. SOAMES, THE ...... NIGEL DAVENPORT
MIND OF MR. SOAMES, THE .... ROBERT VAUGHN
MIND OF MR. SOAMES, THE .... TERENCE STAMP
MIND SNATCHERS, THE ..... CHRISTOPHER WALKEN
MIND SNATCHERS, THE .... JOSS ACKLAND
MIND SNATCHERS, THE .... RONNY COX
MIND WARP .... BRUCE CAMPBELL
MINDWARP: AN INFINITY OF HORRORS/
   PLANET OF HORRORS .... EDWARD ALBERT
MINDWARP: AN INFINITY OF TERROR/
   PLANET OF HORRORS .... RAY WALSTON
MINE OWN EXECUTIONER ..... BURGESS MEREDITH
MINISTRY OF VENGEANCE .... APOLLONIA
MINISTRY OF VENGEANCE .... GEORGE KENNEDY
MINISTRY OF VENGEANCE .... JAMES TOLKAN
MINISTRY OF VENGEANCE .... JOHN SCHNEIDER
MINISTRY OF VENGEANCE .... NED BEATTY
MINISTRY OF VENGEANCE .... YAPHET KOTTO
MINIVER STORY, THE .... GREER GARSON
MINNIE AND MOSCOWITZ .... VAL AVERY
MINNIE AND MOSKOWITZ .... GENA ROWLANDS
MINNIE AND MOSKOWITZ .... SEYMOUR CASSEL
MINNIE AND MOSKOWITZ .... TIMOTHY CAREY
MIRACLE, THE .... BEVERLY D'ANGELO
MIRACLE, THE .... CARROLL BAKER
MIRACLE, THE .... NIALL BYRNE
MIRACLE, THE .... ROGER MOORE
MIRACLE ALLEY .... RICHARD TACCHINO
MIRACLE CAN HAPPEN, A .... BURGESS MEREDITH
MIRACLE CAN HAPPEN, A .... DOROTHY LAMOUR
MIRACLE CAN HAPPEN, A .... JAMES STEWART
MIRACLE IN THE RAIN .... ALAN KING
MIRACLE IN THE RAIN .... EILEEN HECKART
MIRACLE IN THE RAIN .... JANE WYMAN
MIRACLE IN THE RAIN .... VAN JOHNSON
MIRACLE MAN, THE .... SYLVIA SIDNEY
MIRACLE MILE .... ANTHONY EDWARDS
MIRACLE MILE .... MARE WINNINGHAM
MIRACLE MILE .... MYKELTI WILLIAMSON
MIRACLE OF KATHY
   MILLER, THE (TF) .... SHARON GLESS
MIRACLE OF THE BELLS, THE .... FRANK SINATRA
MIRACLE OF THE HEART: A BOYS
   TOWN STORY (TF) .... ART CARNEY
MIRACLE OF THE
   WHITE STALLIONS .... EDDIE ALBERT
MIRACLE OF THE
   WHITE STALLIONS .... JAMES FRANCISCUS†
MIRACLE ON 34TH
   STREET (1947) ✪✪ .... EDMUND GWENN†
MIRACLE ON 34TH
   STREET (1947) .... THELMA RITTER†
MIRACLE ON 34TH
   STREET (1947) .... WILLIAM FRAWLEY†
MIRACLE ON 34TH
   STREET (1947) .... MAUREEN O'HARA
MIRACLE ON 34TH
   STREET (1947) .... NATALIE WOOD†
MIRACLE ON 34TH
   STREET (1947) .... PORTER HALL†
MIRACLE ON 34TH
   STREET (1947) .... GENE LOCKHART†
MIRACLE ON 34TH
   STREET (1947) .... JACK ALBERTSON†
MIRACLE ON 34TH STREET ..... DYLAN McDERMOTT
MIRACLE ON 34TH STREET ..... ELIZABETH PERKINS
MIRACLE ON 34TH STREET .... J. T. WALSH
MIRACLE ON 34TH STREET .... JACK McGEE
MIRACLE ON 34TH STREET .... JAMES REMAR
MIRACLE ON 34TH STREET .... JOSS ACKLAND
MIRACLE ON 34TH STREET .... MARA WILSON

MIRACLE ON 34TH STREET ..... RICHARD ATTENBOROUGH
MIRACLE ON 34TH STREET ..... ROBERT PROSKY
MIRACLE ON 34TH STREET ..... SIMON JONES
MIRACLE ON 34TH STREET ..... WILLIAM WINDOM
MIRACLE ON 34TH STREET (TF) ..... DAVID DOYLE
MIRACLE ON 34TH STREET (TF) ..... JANE ALEXANDER
MIRACLE ON 34TH STREET (TF) ..... JIM BACKUS†
MIRACLE ON 34TH STREET (TF) ..... RODDY McDOWALL
MIRACLE ON 34TH STREET (TF) ..... SEBASTIAN CABOT†
MIRACLE ON 34TH STREET (TF) ..... TOM BOSLEY
MIRACLE ON ICE (TF) ..... ANDREW STEVENS
MIRACLE ON ICE (TF) ..... STEVE GUTTENBERG
MIRACLE WOMAN, THE ..... BARBARA STANWYCK†
MIRACLE WORKER, THE ..... ANDREW PRINE
MIRACLE WORKER, THE ..... BEAH RICHARDS
MIRACLE WORKER, THE ..... INGA SWENSON
MIRACLE WORKER, THE ★★ ..... ANNE BANCROFT
MIRACLE WORKER, THE ∞ ..... PATTY DUKE
MIRACLE WORKER, THE (TF) ..... MELISSA GILBERT
MIRACLE WORKER, THE (TF) ..... PATTY DUKE
MIRACLES ..... CHRISTOPHER LLOYD
MIRACLES ..... TERI GARR
MIRACLES ..... TOM CONTI
MIRACULOUS JOURNEY ..... RORY CALHOUN
MIRAGE ..... DIANE BAKER
MIRAGE ..... GEORGE KENNEDY
MIRAGE ..... GREGORY PECK
MIRAGE ..... JACK WARDEN
MIRAGE ..... JACK WESTON
MIRAGE ..... KEVIN McCARTHY
MIRAGE ..... WALTER MATTHAU
MIRANDA ..... DAVID TOMLINSON
MIRROR CRACK'D, THE ..... ROCK HUDSON†
MIRROR CRACK'D, THE ..... ANGELA LANSBURY
MIRROR CRACK'D, THE ..... ELIZABETH TAYLOR
MIRROR CRACK'D, THE ..... GERALDINE CHAPLIN
MIRROR CRACK'D, THE ..... HILDEGARD NEIL
MIRROR CRACK'D, THE ..... KIM NOVAK
MIRROR CRACK'D, THE ..... TONY CURTIS
MIRRORS (TF) ..... ANTONY HAMILTON
MIRRORS (TF) ..... TIMOTHY DALY
MISADVENTURES OF MERLIN JONES, THE ..... ANNETTE FUNICELLO
MISADVENTURES OF MERLIN JONES, THE ..... LEON AMES
MISCHIEF ..... CATHERINE MARY STEWART
MISCHIEF ..... CHRIS NASH
MISCHIEF ..... DOUG McKEON
MISCHIEF ..... KELLY PRESTON
MISERY ..... FRANCES STERNHAGEN
MISERY ..... JAMES CAAN
MISERY ..... LAUREN BACALL
MISERY ..... RICHARD FARNSWORTH
MISERY ★★ ..... KATHY BATES
MISFIT BRIGADE, THE ..... DAVID CARRADINE
MISFITS, THE ..... CLARK GABLE†
MISFITS, THE ..... ELI WALLACH
MISFITS, THE ..... KEVIN McCARTHY
MISFITS, THE ..... MARILYN MONROE†
MISFITS, THE ..... MONTGOMERY CLIFT†
MISHIMA: A LIFE IN FOUR CHAPTERS ..... ROY SCHEIDER
MISS ANNIE ROONEY ..... JUNE LOCKHART
MISS FIRECRACKER ..... ALFRE WOODARD
MISS FIRECRACKER ..... AMY WRIGHT
MISS FIRECRACKER ..... ANGELA TURNER
MISS FIRECRACKER ..... ANN WEDGEWORTH
MISS FIRECRACKER ..... AVRIL GENTLES
MISS FIRECRACKER ..... BARBARA WELCH
MISS FIRECRACKER ..... BERT REMSEN
MISS FIRECRACKER ..... BILLY NICHOLS
MISS FIRECRACKER ..... BRENT SPINER
MISS FIRECRACKER ..... BRONWEN SENNISH
MISS FIRECRACKER ..... CHAM TROTTER
MISS FIRECRACKER ..... CHRISTIANA THRONE
MISS FIRECRACKER ..... CHRISTINE LAHTI
MISS FIRECRACKER ..... GENE CALDWELL
MISS FIRECRACKER ..... GREG GERMANN
MISS FIRECRACKER ..... HOLLY HUNTER
MISS FIRECRACKER ..... JEWELL N. GUION
MISS FIRECRACKER ..... JODY LOVETT
MISS FIRECRACKER ..... JOHN BURGESS
MISS FIRECRACKER ..... KATHLEEN CHALFANT
MISS FIRECRACKER ..... LORI HAYES
MISS FIRECRACKER ..... MARY STEENBURGEN
MISS FIRECRACKER ..... MITCH SAXTON
MISS FIRECRACKER ..... ROBERT FIELDSTEEL
MISS FIRECRACKER ..... SCOTT GLENN
MISS FIRECRACKER ..... TIM ROBBINS
MISS FIRECRACKER ..... TREY WILSON†
MISS FIRECRACKER ..... VEANNE COX
MISS FIRECRACKER ..... WILSON LAHTI SCHLAMME
MISS JULIE ..... HELEN MIRREN
MISS MARY ..... JULIE CHRISTIE
MISS MARY ..... LUISINA BRANDO
MISS MARY ..... NACHA GUEVARA
MISS PILGRIM'S PROGRESS ..... ARTHUR HILL
MISS SADIE THOMPSON ..... CHARLES BRONSON
MISS SADIE THOMPSON ..... JOSE FERRER†
MISS SUSIE SLAGLE'S ..... JOAN CAULFIELD†
MISS SUSIE SLAGLE'S ..... LILLIAN GISH†
MISS SUSIE SLAGLE'S ..... LLOYD BRIDGES
MISS TATLOCK'S MILLIONS ..... ROBERT STACK
MISSING ★ ..... JACK LEMMON
MISSING ★ ..... SISSY SPACEK
MISSING ..... JOHN SHEA
MISSING ..... MELANIE MAYRON
MISSING ARE DEADLY, THE (TF) ..... JOSE FERRER†
MISSING CHILDREN: A MOTHER'S STORY (TF) ..... POLLY HOLLIDAY
MISSING IN ACTION ..... CHUCK NORRIS
MISSING IN ACTION ..... JAMES HONG
MISSING IN ACTION 2 - THE BEGINNING ..... CHUCK NORRIS
MISSING PIECES ..... ERIC IDLE
MISSING PIECES ..... JAMES HONG
MISSING PIECES ..... RICHARD BELZER
MISSING PIECES ..... ROBERT WUHL
MISSION, THE ..... AIDAN QUINN
MISSION, THE ..... DANIEL BERRIGAN
MISSION, THE ..... JEREMY IRONS
MISSION, THE ..... LIAM NEESON
MISSION, THE ..... ROBERT DE NIRO
MISSION BATANGAS ..... DENNIS WEAVER
MISSION: IMPOSSIBLE ..... TOM CRUISE
MISSION IMPOSSIBLE - THE GOLDEN SERPENT (TF) ..... PETER GRAVES
MISSION MARS ..... DARREN McGAVIN
MISSION OVER KOREA ..... MAUREEN O'SULLIVAN
MISSION TO MOSCOW ..... CYD CHARISSE
MISSION TO MOSCOW ..... ELEANOR PARKER
MISSIONARY, THE ..... DENHOLM ELLIOTT†
MISSIONARY, THE ..... MAGGIE SMITH
MISSIONARY, THE ..... MICHAEL PALIN
MISSISSIPPI BURNING ..... BRAD DOURIF
MISSISSIPPI BURNING ..... MICHAEL ROOKER
MISSISSIPPI BURNING ..... WILLEM DAFOE
MISSISSIPPI BURNING ★ ..... GENE HACKMAN
MISSISSIPPI BURNING O ..... FRANCES McDORMAND
MISSISSIPPI GAMBLER, THE ..... DENNIS WEAVER
MISSISSIPPI GAMBLER, THE ..... GWEN VERDON
MISSISSIPPI GAMBLER, THE ..... PIPER LAURIE
MISSISSIPPI MASALA ..... DENZEL WASHINGTON
MISSISSIPPI MERMAID ..... CATHERINE DENEUVE
MISSOURI BREAKS, THE ..... FREDERIC FORREST
MISSOURI BREAKS, THE ..... HARRY DEAN STANTON
MISSOURI BREAKS, THE ..... JACK NICHOLSON
MISSOURI BREAKS, THE ..... LUANA ANDERS
MISSOURI BREAKS, THE ..... MARLON BRANDO
MISSOURI BREAKS, THE ..... RANDY QUAID
MISTER 880 ..... BURT LANCASTER†
MISTER 880 O ..... EDMUND GWENN†
MISTER BUDDWING ..... ANGELA LANSBURY
MISTER BUDDWING ..... JAMES GARNER
MISTER BUDDWING ..... JEAN SIMMONS
MISTER BUDDWING ..... KATHERINE ROSS
MISTER BUDDWING ..... NICHELLE NICHOLS
MISTER BUDDWING ..... RAYMOND ST. JACQUES
MISTER BUDDWING ..... SUZANNE PLESHETTE
MISTER BUDDWING ..... WESLEY ADDY
MISTER CORY ..... TONY CURTIS
MISTER FROST ..... ALAN BATES
MISTER JERICHO (TF) ..... CONNIE STEVENS
MISTER JERICHO (TF) ..... PATRICK MacNEE
MISTER JOHNSON ..... BEATIE EDNEY
MISTER JOHNSON ..... DENIS QUILLEY
MISTER JOHNSON ..... EDWARD WOODWARD
MISTER JOHNSON ..... MAYNARD EZIASHI
MISTER JOHNSON ..... PIERCE BROSNAN
MISTER MOSES ..... CARROLL BAKER
MISTER MOSES ..... IAN BANNEN
MISTER MOSES ..... RAYMOND ST. JACQUES
MISTER MOSES ..... ROBERT MITCHUM
MISTER ROBERTS ..... HARRY CAREY JR.
MISTER ROBERTS ..... HENRY FONDA†
MISTER ROBERTS ..... JAMES CAGNEY†
MISTER ROBERTS ..... PATRICK WAYNE
MISTER ROBERTS ..... WILLIAM POWELL†
MISTER ROBERTS ∞ ..... JACK LEMMON
MISTER V ..... DAVID TOMLINSON
MISTRAL'S DAUGHTER (MS) ..... LEE REMICK†
MISTRAL'S DAUGHTER (MS) ..... JOANNA LUMLEY
MISTRAL'S DAUGHTER (MS) ..... ROBERT URICH
MISTRAL'S DAUGHTER (MS) ..... STACY KEACH
MISTRAL'S DAUGHTER (MS) ..... STEFANIE POWERS
MISTRAL'S DAUGHTER (MS) ..... TIMOTHY DALTON
MISTRESS ..... CHRISTOPHER WALKEN
MISTRESS ..... DANNY AIELLO
MISTRESS ..... ELI WALLACH
MISTRESS ..... ERNEST BORGNINE
MISTRESS ..... JEAN SMART
MISTRESS ..... LAURIE METCALF
MISTRESS ..... MARTIN LANDAU
MISTRESS ..... ROBERT DE NIRO
MISTRESS ..... ROBERT WUHL
MISTRESS (TF) ..... DON MURRAY
MISTRESS (TF) ..... VICTORIA PRINCIPAL
MISUNDERSTOOD ..... GENE HACKMAN
MISUNDERSTOOD ..... HENRY THOMAS
MISUNDERSTOOD ..... RIP TORN
MISUNDERSTOOD BOY, A ..... LILLIAN GISH†
MITCHELL ..... JOE DON BAKER
MITCHELL ..... JOHN SAXON
MITCHELL ..... LINDA EVANS
MITCHELL ..... MARTIN BALSAM
MIXED BLOOD ..... RODNEY HARVEY
MIXED COMPANY ..... BARBARA HARRIS
MIXED COMPANY ..... JOSEPH BOLOGNA
MIXED COMPANY ..... TOM BOSLEY
MO' BETTER BLUES ..... BILL NUNN
MO' BETTER BLUES ..... CYNDA WILLIAMS
MO' BETTER BLUES ..... DENZEL WASHINGTON
MO' BETTER BLUES ..... DICK ANTHONY WILLIAMS
MO' BETTER BLUES ..... GIANCARLO ESPOSITO
MO' BETTER BLUES ..... JOHN TURTURRO
MO' BETTER BLUES ..... JOIE LEE
MO' BETTER BLUES ..... SPIKE LEE
MO' BETTER BLUES ..... WESLEY SNIPES
MO' MONEY ..... DAMON WAYANS
MO' MONEY ..... HARRY J. LENNIX
MO' MONEY ..... JOE SANTOS
MO' MONEY ..... JOHN DIEHL
MO' MONEY ..... MARLON WAYANS
MO' MONEY ..... STACEY DASH
MOB, THE ..... CHARLES BRONSON
MOB, THE ..... ERNEST BORGNINE
MOB, THE ..... RICHARD KILEY
MOBILE TWO (TF) ..... JACKIE COOPER
MOBSTERS ..... ANTHONY QUINN
MOBSTERS ..... BILL BASTIANI
MOBSTERS ..... CHRIS PENN
MOBSTERS ..... CHRISTIAN SLATER
MOBSTERS ..... COSTAS MANDYLOR
MOBSTERS ..... F. MURRAY ABRAHAM
MOBSTERS ..... FRANK COLLISON
MOBSTERS ..... LARA FLYNN BOYLE
MOBSTERS ..... LESLIE BEGA
MOBSTERS ..... MICHAEL GAMBON
MOBSTERS ..... NICK SADLER
MOBSTERS ..... PATRICK DEMPSEY
MOBSTERS ..... RICHARD GRIECO
MOBY DICK ..... GREGORY PECK

This is not a list of every film ever made or every cast member, only those listed in this directory.

MOBY DICK .... ROYAL DANO
MODEL SHOP, THE .... ANOUK AIMEE
MODERN GIRLS .... CHRIS NASH
MODERN GIRLS .... CLAYTON ROHNER
MODERN GIRLS .... CYNTHIA GIBB
MODERN GIRLS .... DAPHNE ZUNIGA
MODERN GIRLS .... VIRGINIA MADSEN
MODERN LOVE .... BURT REYNOLDS
MODERN LOVE .... CLIFF BEMIS
MODERN LOVE .... FRANKIE VALLI
MODERN LOVE .... KARLA DEVITO
MODERN LOVE .... KAYE BALLARD
MODERN LOVE .... LOUISE LASSER
MODERN LOVE .... LYRIC BENSON
MODERN LOVE .... ROBBY BENSON
MODERN LOVE .... RUE McCLANAHAN
MODERN PROBLEMS .... BRIAN DOYLE-MURRAY
MODERN PROBLEMS .... CHEVY CHASE
MODERN PROBLEMS .... DABNEY COLEMAN
MODERN PROBLEMS .... MARY KAY PLACE
MODERN PROBLEMS .... PATTI D'ARBANVILLE
MODERN ROMANCE .... ALBERT BROOKS
MODERN ROMANCE .... GEORGE KENNEDY
MODERNS, THE .... BROOKE SMITH
MODERNS, THE .... GENEVIEVE BUJOLD
MODERNS, THE .... GERALDINE CHAPLIN
MODERNS, THE .... JOHN LONE
MODERNS, THE .... KEITH CARRADINE
MODERNS, THE .... LINDA FIORENTINO
MODERNS, THE .... WALLACE SHAWN
MODEST HERO, A .... LILLIAN GISH†
MODESTY BLAISE .... TERENCE STAMP
MODIGLIANI OF MONTPARNASSE .... LILA KEDROVA
MOGAMBO ★ .... AVA GARDNER†
MOGAMBO ◐ .... GRACE KELLY†
MOHAMMAD, MESSENGER
   OF GOD .... ANTHONY QUINN
MOI FLEUR BLEUE .... JODIE FOSTER
MOI FLEUR BLEUE .... LILA KEDROVA
MOKEY .... ROBERT BLAKE
MOLLY AND LAWLESS JOHN .... SAM ELLIOTT
MOLLY AND LAWLESS JOHN .... VERA MILES
MOLLY AND ME .... RODDY McDOWALL
MOLLY MAGUIRES, THE .... RICHARD HARRIS
MOLLY MAGUIRES, THE .... SAMANTHA EGGAR
MOLLY MAGUIRES, THE .... SEAN CONNERY
MOMENT BY MOMENT .... JOHN TRAVOLTA
MOMENT BY MOMENT .... LILY TOMLIN
MOMENT OF TRUTH: CRADLE
   OF CONSPIRACY (TF) .... CARMEN ARGENZIANO
MOMENT OF TRUTH: CRADLE
   OF CONSPIRACY (TF) .... DANICA McKELLAR
MOMENT OF TRUTH: CRADLE
   OF CONSPIRACY (TF) .... DEE WALLACE STONE
MOMENT OF TRUTH: CRADLE
   OF CONSPIRACY (TF) .... KURT DEUTSCH
MOMENT TO MOMENT .... ARTHUR HILL
MOMMIE DEAREST .... DIANA SCARWID
MOMMIE DEAREST .... FAYE DUNAWAY
MOMMIE DEAREST .... HARRY GOZ
MOMMIE DEAREST .... HOWARD DA SILVA†
MOMMIE DEAREST .... MARA HOBEL
MOMMIE DEAREST .... RUTANYA ALDA
MOMMIE DEAREST .... STEVE FORREST
MON ONCLE D'AMÉRIQUE ...... GERARD DEPARDIEU
MON PREMIER AMOUR .... ANOUK AIMEE
MONA LISA .... MICHAEL CAINE
MONA LISA .... ROBBIE COLTRANE
MONA LISA ★ .... BOB HOSKINS
MONEY FOR NOTHING .... DEBI MAZAR
MONEY FOR NOTHING .... JOHN CUSAK
MONEY FOR NOTHING .... MICHAEL MADSEN
MONEY FOR NOTHING .... MICHAEL RAPAPORT
MONEY FROM HOME .... DEAN MARTIN
MONEY FROM HOME .... JACK KRUSCHEN
MONEY FROM HOME .... JERRY LEWIS
MONEY JUNGLE, THE .... NEHEMIAH PERSOFF
MONEY ON THE SIDE (TF) .... JAMIE LEE CURTIS
MONEY PIT, THE .... ALEXANDER GODUNOV
MONEY PIT, THE .... MAUREEN STAPLETON
MONEY PIT, THE .... PHILIP BOSCO
MONEY PIT, THE .... SHELLEY LONG
MONEY PIT, THE .... TOM HANKS

MONEY, POWER, MURDER (TF) .... BLYTHE DANNER
MONEY, POWER, MURDER (TF) ..... JOSEF SOMMER
MONEY, POWER,
   MURDER (TF) .... JULIANNE MOORE
MONEY, POWER, MURDER (TF) .... KEVIN DOBSON
MONEY TO BURN (TF) .... E. G. MARSHALL
MONEY TO BURN (TF) .... MARTIN BALSAM
MONEY TRAIN, THE .... WESLEY SNIPES
MONEY TRAIN, THE .... WOODY HARRELSON
MONEY TRAP, THE............... RICARDO MONTALBAN
MONEYCHANGERS,
   THE (MS) .... CHRISTOPHER PLUMMER
MONEYCHANGERS, THE (MS) .... HELEN HAYES
MONEYCHANGERS, THE (MS) .... JOAN COLLINS
MONEYCHANGERS, THE (MS) .... KIRK DOUGLAS
MONEYCHANGERS, THE (MS) ..... PATRICK O'NEAL†
MONEYCHANGERS, THE (MS) .... RALPH BELLAMY†
MONEYCHANGERS, THE (MS) .... ROBERT LOGGIA
MONEYCHANGERS,
   THE (MS) .... TIMOTHY BOTTOMS
MONGOLS, THE .... JACK PALANCE
MONGO'S BACK IN TOWN (TF) .... JOE DON BAKER
MONITORS, THE .... ALAN ARKIN
MONK, THE (TF) .... JANET LEIGH
MONKEY BUSINESS .... CARY GRANT†
MONKEY BUSINESS .... HARRY CAREY JR.
MONKEY BUSINESS .... MARILYN MONROE†
MONKEY HUSTLE, THE .... ROSALIND CASH
MONKEY HUSTLE, THE .... YAPHET KOTTO
MONKEY SHINES .... JASON BEGHE
MONKEY SHINES .... JOHN PANKOW
MONKEY SHINES .... JOYCE VAN PATTEN
MONKEY SHINES .... KATE McNEIL
MONKEY TROUBLE .... CHRISTOPHER McDONALD
MONKEY TROUBLE .... HARVEY KEITEL
MONKEY TROUBLE .... MARCY GOLDMAN
MONKEY TROUBLE .... MIMI ROGERS
MONKEY TROUBLE .... ROBERT G. MIRANDA
MONKEY TROUBLE .... THORA BIRCH
MONKEYS, GO HOME! .... DEAN JONES
MONKEY'S UNCLE, THE .... ANNETTE FUNICELLO
MONKEY'S UNCLE, THE .... LEON AMES
MONSIEUR BEAUCAIRE .... BOB HOPE
MONSIEUR BEAUCAIRE .... JOAN CAULFIELD†
MONSIEUR VERDOUX .... MARTHA RAYE†
MONSIGNOR .... CHRISTOPHER REEVE
MONSIGNOR .... GENEVIEVE BUJOLD
MONSIGNOR .... JOE PANTOLIANO
MONSIGNOR QUIXOTE (TF) .... ALEC GUINNESS
MONSTER CLUB, THE .... BRITT EKLAND
MONSTER CLUB, THE .... SIMON WARD
MONSTER CLUB, THE .... VINCENT PRICE†
MONSTER IN A BOX (PF) .... SPALDING GRAY
MONSTER IN THE CLOSET .... CLAUDE AKINS†
MONSTER ON THE CAMPUS .... TROY DONAHUE
MONSTER SQUAD, THE .... STAN SHAW
MONSTER SQUAD, THE .... STEPHEN MACHT
MONSTER THAT CHALLENGED
   NEW YORK, THE .... MAX SHOWALTER
MONTANA .... ALEXIS SMITH†
MONTANA (CTF) .... GENA ROWLANDS
MONTANA (CTF) .... JUSTIN DEAS
MONTANA (CTF) .... LEA THOMPSON
MONTANA (CTF) .... RICHARD CRENNA
MONTANA MOON .... JOAN CRAWFORD†
MONTE CARLO BABY .... AUDREY HEPBURN†
MONTE CARLO (MS) .... GEORGE HAMILTON
MONTE CARLO (MS) .... JOAN COLLINS
MONTE CARLO (MS) .... LISA EILBACHER
MONTE CARLO (MS) .... MALCOLM McDOWELL
MONTE CARLO (MS) .... PETER VAUGHN
MONTE CARLO (MS) .... ROBERT CARRADINE
MONTE CARLO OR BUST .... DUDLEY MOORE
MONTE CARLO OR BUST .... PETER COOK
MONTE CARLO OR BUST .... TONY CURTIS
MONTE WALSH .... BO HOPKINS
MONTE WALSH .... JACK PALANCE
MONTE WALSH .... MATT CLARK
MONTENEGRO .... ERLAND JOSEPHSON
MONTENEGRO .... SUSAN ANSPACH
MONTENEGRO, OR PIGS
   AND PEARLS .... ERLAND JOSEPHSON

MONTENEGRO, OR PIGS
   AND PEARLS .... SUSAN ANSPACH
MONTH IN THE COUNTRY, A .... JIM CARTER
MONTH IN THE
   COUNTRY, A .... KENNETH BRANAGH
MONTPARNASSE 19 .... ANOUK AIMEE
MONTPARNASSE 19 .... LILA KEDROVA
MONTY PYTHON AND THE
   HOLY GRAIL .... ERIC IDLE
MONTY PYTHON AND THE
   HOLY GRAIL .... GRAHAM CHAPMAN†
MONTY PYTHON AND THE
   HOLY GRAIL .... JOHN CLEESE
MONTY PYTHON AND THE
   HOLY GRAIL .... MICHAEL PALIN
MONTY PYTHON AND THE
   HOLY GRAIL .... TERRY GILLIAM
MONTY PYTHON AND THE
   HOLY GRAIL .... TERRY JONES
MONTY PYTHON LIVE AT THE
   HOLLYWOOD BOWL .... ERIC IDLE
MONTY PYTHON LIVE AT THE
   HOLLYWOOD BOWL .... JOHN CLEESE
MONTY PYTHON LIVE AT THE
   HOLLYWOOD BOWL .... MICHAEL PALIN
MONTY PYTHON LIVE AT THE
   HOLLYWOOD BOWL .... TERRY GILLIAM
MONTY PYTHON LIVE AT THE
   HOLLYWOOD BOWL .... TERRY JONES
MONTY PYTHON'S LIFE
   OF BRIAN .... GRAHAM CHAPMAN†
MONTY PYTHON'S LIFE OF BRIAN .... ERIC IDLE
MONTY PYTHON'S LIFE OF BRIAN ..... JOHN CLEESE
MONTY PYTHON'S LIFE
   OF BRIAN .... MICHAEL PALIN
MONTY PYTHON'S LIFE
   OF BRIAN .... TERRY GILLIAM
MONTY PYTHON'S LIFE OF BRIAN ..... TERRY JONES
MONTY PYTHON'S THE
   MEANING OF LIFE .... GRAHAM CHAPMAN†
MONTY PYTHON'S THE
   MEANING OF LIFE .... ERIC IDLE
MONTY PYTHON'S THE
   MEANING OF LIFE .... JOHN CLEESE
MONTY PYTHON'S THE
   MEANING OF LIFE .... MICHAEL PALIN
MONTY PYTHON'S THE
   MEANING OF LIFE .... TERRY GILLIAM
MONTY PYTHON'S THE
   MEANING OF LIFE .... TERRY JONES
MOON IN SCORPIO .... BRITT EKLAND
MOON IN THE
   GUTTER, THE .... GERARD DEPARDIEU
MOON IN THE GUTTER, THE ..... NASTASSJA KINSKI
MOON IS BLUE, THE .... DAVID NIVEN†
MOON IS BLUE, THE ★ .... MAGGIE MCNAMARA†
MOON OF THE WOLF (TF) .... ROYAL DANO
MOON OVER BURMA .... DOROTHY LAMOUR
MOON OVER MIAMI .... DON AMECHE†
MOON OVER PARADOR .... CHARO
MOON OVER PARADOR .... ED ASNER
MOON OVER PARADOR .... JONATHAN WINTERS
MOON OVER
   PARADOR .... MARIANNE SAGEBRECHT
MOON OVER PARADOR .... PAUL MAZURSKY
MOON OVER PARADOR .... POLLY HOLLIDAY
MOON OVER PARADOR .... RAUL JULIA†
MOON OVER PARADOR .... RICHARD DREYFUSS
MOON OVER PARADOR ...... SAMMY DAVIS JR.†
MOON OVER PARADOR .... SONIA BRAGA
MOON PILOT .... BRIAN KEITH
MOON ZERO TWO .... JAMES OLSON
MOON-SPINNERS, THE .... ELI WALLACH
MOON-SPINNERS, THE .... HAYLEY MILLS
MOONFLEET .... SEAN McCLORY
MOONLIGHT AND
   VALENTINO .... ELIZABETH PERKINS
MOONLIGHT AND
   VALENTINO .... GWYNETH PALTROW
MOONLIGHT AND
   VALENTINO .... KATHLEEN TURNER
MOONLIGHT AND
   VALENTINO .... WHOOPI GOLDBERG

† after an actor's name denotes deceased.

MOONLIGHTER, THE .... BARBARA STANWYCK†
MOONLIGHTING .... JEREMY IRONS
MOONLIGHTING (TF) .... ALLYCE BEASLY
MOONLIGHTING (TF) .... BRUCE WILLIS
MOONLIGHTING (TF) .... CYBILL SHEPHERD
MOONRAKER .... GEOFFREY KEEN
MOONRAKER .... LOIS CHILES
MOONRAKER .... LOIS MAXWELL
MOONRAKER .... MICHAEL LONSDALE
MOONRAKER .... RICHARD KIEL
MOONRAKER .... ROGER MOORE
MOONRISE .... HARRY MORGAN
MOONRISE .... LLOYD BRIDGES
MOONSHINE COUNTY EXPRESS .... ALBERT SALMI†
MOONSHINE COUNTY EXPRESS .... JEFF COREY
MOONSHINE COUNTY EXPRESS .... JOHN SAXON
MOONSHINE WAR, THE .... ALAN ALDA
MOONSHINE WAR, THE .... HARRY CAREY JR.
MOONSHINE WAR, THE .... MAX SHOWALTER
MOONSHINE WAR, THE .... RICHARD WIDMARK
MOONSHINE WAR, THE .... TERI GARR
MOONSTRUCK .... ANITA GILLETTE
MOONSTRUCK .... DANNY AIELLO
MOONSTRUCK .... FEOFOR CHALIAPIN JR.
MOONSTRUCK .... JOHN MAHONEY
MOONSTRUCK .... JULIE BOYASSO†
MOONSTRUCK .... LOUIS GUSS
MOONSTRUCK .... NICOLAS CAGE
MOONSTRUCK .... ROBIN BARTLETT
MOONSTRUCK ★★ .... CHER
MOONSTRUCK ○ .... VINCENT GARDENIA†
MOONSTRUCK ○○ .... OLYMPIA DUKAKIS
MORE AMERICAN GRAFFITI .... BO HOPKINS
MORE AMERICAN GRAFFITI .... CANDY CLARK
MORE AMERICAN GRAFFITI .... CINDY WILLIAMS
MORE AMERICAN GRAFFITI .... MARY KAY PLACE
MORE AMERICAN GRAFFITI .... PAUL LeMAT
MORE AMERICAN GRAFFITI .... RON HOWARD
MORE AMERICAN
    GRAFFITI .... ROSANNA ARQUETTE
MORE DEAD THAN ALIVE .... CLINT WALKER
MORE DEAD THAN ALIVE .... VINCENT PRICE†
MORE THAN A MIRACLE .... OMAR SHARIF
MORE THAN A MIRACLE .... SOPHIA LOREN
MORE THAN FRIENDS (TF) .... JOE PANTOLIANO
MORE THE MERRIER, THE ★ .... JEAN ARTHUR†
MORE THE
    MERRIER, THE ○○ .... CHARLES COBURN†
MORGAN! ★ .... VANESSA REDGRAVE
MORGAN! .... DAVID WARNER
MORGAN! .... ROBERT STEPHENS
MORGAN—A SUITABLE CASE
    FOR TREATMENT .... DAVID WARNER
MORGAN—A SUITABLE CASE
    FOR TREATMENT .... ROBERT STEPHENS
MORGAN: A SUITABLE CASE
    FOR TREATMENT ★ .... VANESSA REDGRAVE
MORGAN STEWART'S
    COMING HOME .... LYNN REDGRAVE
MORGAN STEWART'S
    COMING HOME .... PAUL GLEASON
MORITURI .... JAMES BROLIN
MORITURI .... JANET MARGOLIN
MORITURI .... MARLON BRANDO
MORNING AFTER, THE .... DIANE SALINGER
MORNING AFTER, THE .... JEFF BRIDGES
MORNING AFTER, THE .... RAUL JULIA†
MORNING AFTER, THE .... RICHARD FORONJY
MORNING AFTER, THE .... RICK ROSSOVICH
MORNING AFTER, THE ★ .... JANE FONDA
MORNING AFTER, THE (TF) .... DICK VAN DYKE
MORNING DEPARTURE .... JOHN MILLS
MORNING GLORY .... CHRISTOPHER REEVE
MORNING GLORY .... DEBORAH RAFFIN
MORNING GLORY .... HELEN SHAVER
MORNING GLORY .... J. T. WALSH
MORNING GLORY .... LLOYD BOCHNER
MORNING GLORY .... NINA FOCH
MORNING GLORY ★★ .... KATHERINE HEPBURN
MORONS FROM OUTER SPACE .... JIMMY NAIL
MORT D'UN POURRI .... KLAUS KINSKI†
MORTADELLA .... BASIL HOFFMAN

MORTADELLA .... DANNY DEVITO
MORTADELLA .... DAVID DOYLE
MORTADELLA .... EDWRAD HERRMANN
MORTADELLA .... SOPHIA LOREN
MORTADELLA .... SUSAN SARANDON
MORTADELLA .... WILLIAM DEVANE
MORTAL KOMBAT .... CARY-HIROYUKI TAGAWA
MORTAL KOMBAT .... CHRISTOPHER LAMBERT
MORTAL KOMBAT .... KATHLEEN McCLELLAN
MORTAL KOMBAT .... LINDEN ASHBY
MORTAL KOMBAT .... ROBIN SHOU
MORTAL KOMBAT .... TALISA SOTO
MORTAL STORM, THE .... JAMES STEWART
MORTAL STORM, THE .... ROBERT STACK
MORTAL THOUGHTS .... BILLIE NEAL
MORTAL THOUGHTS .... BRUCE WILLIS
MORTAL THOUGHTS .... DEMI MOORE
MORTAL THOUGHTS .... FRANK VINCENT
MORTAL THOUGHTS .... GLENNE HEADLY
MORTAL THOUGHTS .... HARVEY KEITEL
MORTAL THOUGHTS .... JOHN PANKOW
MORTAL THOUGHTS .... PETER GALLAGHER
MORTUARY ACADEMY .... PERRY LANG
MOSCOW ON
    THE HUDSON .... CLEAVANT DERRICKS
MOSCOW ON THE HUDSON .... ELVA BASKIN
MOSCOW ON
    THE HUDSON ....MARIA CONCHITA ALONSO
MOSCOW ON THE HUDSON .... PAUL MAZURSKY
MOSCOW ON THE HUDSON .... ROBIN WILLIAMS
MOSCOW ON THE HUDSON .... SAVELY KRAMAROV
MOSCOW ON THE HUDSON .... YAKOV SMIRNOFF
MOSES (TF) .... BURT LANCASTER†
MOSQUITO COAST, THE .... ANDRE GREGORY
MOSQUITO COAST, THE .... HARRISON FORD
MOSQUITO COAST, THE .... HELEN MIRREN
MOSQUITO COAST, THE .... HILARY GORDON
MOSQUITO COAST, THE .... MARTHA PLIMPTON
MOSQUITO COAST, THE .... RIVER PHOENIX†
MOSQUITO SQUADRON .... DAVID McCALLUM
MOSS ROSE .... VINCENT PRICE†
MOST DANGEROUS MAN IN
    THE WORLD, THE .... GREGORY PECK
MOST WANTED (TF) .... TOM SELLECK
MOST WONDERFUL
    MOMENT, THE .... MARCELLO MASTROIANNI
MOTHER GOOSE
    ROCK 'N' RHYME (CTF) .... CYNDI LAUPER
MOTHER GOOSE
    ROCK 'N' RHYME (CTF) .... JEAN STAPLETON
MOTHER GOOSE
    ROCK 'N' RHYME (CTF) .... LITTLE RICHARD
MOTHER GOOSE
    ROCK 'N' RHYME (CTF) .... PAUL SIMON
MOTHER GOOSE
    ROCK 'N' RHYME (CTF) .... SHELLEY DUVALL
MOTHER GOOSE
    ROCK 'N' RHYME (CTF) .... TERI GARR
MOTHER IS A FRESHMAN .... VAN JOHNSON
MOTHER, JUGS & SPEED .... ALLEN GARFIELD
MOTHER, JUGS & SPEED .... BILL COSBY
MOTHER, JUGS & SPEED .... BRUCE DAVISON
MOTHER, JUGS & SPEED .... DICK BUTKUS
MOTHER, JUGS & SPEED .... HARVEY KEITEL
MOTHER, JUGS & SPEED .... L. Q. JONES
MOTHER, JUGS & SPEED .... LARRY HAGMAN
MOTHER, JUGS & SPEED .... RAQUEL WELCH
MOTHER LODE .... CHARLTON HESTON
MOTHER LODE .... JOHN MARLEY†
MOTHER LODE .... KIM BASINGER
MOTHER LODE .... NICK MANCUSO
MOTHERING HEART, THE .... LILLIAN GISH†
MOTHERS, DAUGHTERS
    AND LOVERS (TF) .... CLAUDE AKINS†
MOTHER'S BOYS .... COLIN WARD
MOTHER'S BOYS .... JAMIE LEE CURTIS
MOTHER'S BOYS .... JOANNE WHALLEY-KILMER
MOTHER'S BOYS .... JOEY ZIMMERMAN
MOTHER'S BOYS .... JOSS ACKLAND
MOTHER'S BOYS .... LUKE EDWARDS
MOTHER'S BOYS .... PETER GALLAGHER
MOTHER'S BOYS .... VANESSA REDGRAVE

MOTION AND EMOTION (TD) .... DENNIS HOPPER
MOTORAMA .... DREW BARRYMORE
MOULIN ROUGE .... ZSA ZSA GABOR
MOULIN ROUGE ★ .... JOSE FERRER†
MOUNTAIN MEN, THE .... BRIAN KEITH
MOUNTAIN MEN, THE .... CHARLTON HESTON
MOUNTAIN MEN, THE .... STEPHEN MACHT
MOUNTAIN MUSIC .... MARTHA RAYE†
MOUNTAIN ROAD, THE .... JAMES STEWART
MOUNTAIN, THE .... E. G. MARSHALL
MOUNTAIN, THE .... ROBERT WAGNER
MOUNTAINS OF THE MOON .... FIONA SHAW
MOUNTAINS OF THE MOON .... IAIN GLEN
MOUNTAINS OF THE MOON .... OMAR SHARIF
MOUNTAINS OF THE MOON .... PATRICK BERGIN
MOUNTAINS OF THE MOON .... ROGER REES
MOUNTBATTEN (TF) .... JANET SUZMAN
MOURNING BECOMES ELECTRA .... KIRK DOUGLAS
MOURNING BECOMES
    ELECTRA ★ .... MICHAEL REDGRAVE†
MOURNING BECOMES
    ELECTRA ★ .... ROSALAND RUSSELL†
MOUSE AND HIS
    CHILD, THE (AF) .... CLORIS LEACHMAN
MOUSE AND HIS
    CHILD, THE (AF) .... PETER USTINOV
MOUSE ON THE MOON, THE .... RON MOODY
MOUSEY CAT
    AND MOUSE (TF) .... SAM WANAMAKER†
MOUSEY (TF) .... KIRK DOUGLAS
MOVE .... ELLIOTT GOULD
MOVE .... JEANNIE BERLIN
MOVE .... PAULA PRENTISS
MOVE .... RON O'NEAL
MOVE OVER, DARLING .... CHUCK CONNORS†
MOVE OVER, DARLING .... DON KNOTTS
MOVE OVER, DARLING .... DORIS DAY
MOVE OVER, DARLING .... JAMES GARNER
MOVE OVER, DARLING .... MAX SHOWALTER
MOVERS AND SHAKERS .... WILLIAM PRINCE
MOVERS & SHAKERS .... BILL MACY
MOVERS & SHAKERS .... CHARLES GRODIN
MOVERS & SHAKERS .... GILDA RADNER†
MOVERS & SHAKERS .... LUANA ANDERS
MOVERS & SHAKERS .... MICHAEL LERNER
MOVERS & SHAKERS .... PENNY MARSHALL
MOVERS & SHAKERS .... STEVE MARTIN
MOVERS & SHAKERS .... TYNE DALY
MOVERS & SHAKERS .... VINCENT GARDENIA†
MOVERS & SHAKERS .... WALTER MATTHAU
MOVIE MAKER, THE .... DAVID HEDISON
MOVIE MOVIE .... ANN REINKING
MOVIE MOVIE .... ART CARNEY
MOVIE MOVIE .... BARBARA HARRIS
MOVIE MOVIE .... BARRY BOSTWICK
MOVIE MOVIE .... ELI WALLACH
MOVIE MOVIE .... GEORGE BURNS
MOVIE MOVIE .... GEORGE C. SCOTT
MOVIE MOVIE .... HARRY HAMLIN
MOVIE MOVIE .... RED BUTTONS
MOVIE MOVIE .... TRISH VAN DEVERE
MOVIE MURDERER, THE (TF) .... TOM SELLECK
MOVING .... BEVERLY TODD
MOVING .... DANA CARVEY
MOVING .... RANDY QUAID
MOVING .... RICHARD PRYOR
MOVING TARGET (TF) .... JACK WAGNER
MOVING TARGET (TF) .... JASON BATEMAN
MOVING TARGET (TF) .... JOHN GLOVER
MOVING TARGET (TF) .... RICHARD DYSART
MOVING VIOLATION .... EDDIE ALBERT
MOVING VIOLATION .... LONNY CHAPMAN
MOVING VIOLATION .... STEPHEN McHATTIE
MOVING VIOLATIONS .... JAMES KEACH
MOVING VIOLATIONS .... JENNIFER TILLY
MOVING VIOLATIONS .... SALLY KELLERMAN
MOVIOLA (MS) .... AUDRA LINDLEY
MOVIOLA (MS) .... BARRY BOSTWICK
MOVIOLA (MS) .... HAROLD GOULD
MOVIOLA (MS) .... TONY CURTIS
MOVIOLA (MS) .... SHARON GLESS
MR. ACE .... SYLVIA SIDNEY

This is not a list of every film ever made or every cast member, only those listed in this directory.

MR. AND MRS. BRIDGE .... AUSTIN PENDLETON
MR. AND MRS. BRIDGE .... BLYTHE DANNER
MR. AND MRS. BRIDGE .... GALE GARNETT
MR. AND MRS. BRIDGE .... JOHN BELL
MR. AND MRS. BRIDGE .... KYRA SEDGWICK
MR. AND MRS. BRIDGE .... MARGARET WELSH
MR. AND MRS. BRIDGE .... PAUL NEWMAN
MR. AND MRS. BRIDGE .... ROBERT SEAN LEONARD
MR. AND MRS. BRIDGE .... SIMON CALLOW
MR. AND MRS. BRIDGE ★ ...... JOANNE WOODWARD
MR. BASEBALL .... AVA TAKANASHI
MR. BASEBALL .... DENNIS HAYSBERT
MR. BASEBALL .... KEN TAKAKURA
MR. BASEBALL .... TOM SELLECK
MR. BASEBALL .... TOSHI SHIOYA
MR. BELVEDERE GOES
     TO COLLEGE .... ALAN YOUNG
MR. BELVEDERE GOES
     TO COLLEGE .... KATHLEEN FREEMAN
MR. BILLION .... LEO ROSSI
MR. BILLION .... R.G. ARMSTRONG
MR. BILLION .... VALERIE PERRINE
MR. CHRISTMAS DINNER .... DONNA DIXON
MR. DEEDS GOES
     TO TOWN .... DOUGLASS DUMBRILLE†
MR. DEEDS GOES TO TOWN .... JEAN ARTHUR†
MR. DEEDS GOES TO TOWN .... LIONEL STANDER
MR. DEEDS GOES
     TO TOWN .... RAYMOND WALBURN†
MR. DEEDS GOES TO TOWN ★ ...... GARY COOPER†
MR. DENNING DRIVES NORTH .... JOHN MILLS
MR. DENNING DRIVES
     NORTH .... SAM WANAMAKER†
MR. DESTINY .... BILL McCUTCHEON
MR. DESTINY .... COURTENEY COX
MR. DESTINY .... HART BOCHNER
MR. DESTINY .... JAMES BELUSHI
MR. DESTINY .... JON LOVITZ
MR. DESTINY .... LINDA HAMILTON
MR. DESTINY .... MICHAEL CAINE
MR. DESTINY .... RENE RUSSO
MR. DODD TAKES THE AIR .... JANE WYMAN
MR. EMMANUEL .... JEAN SIMMONS
MR. FORBUSH AND THE PENGUINS ..... JOHN HURT
MR. FORBUSH AND
     THE PENGUINS .... JOSS ACKLAND
MR. FREEDOM .... DONALD PLEASENCE
MR. HOBBS TAKES A VACATION .... JOHN SAXON
MR. HOBBS TAKES
     A VACATION .... JAMES STEWART
MR. HOBBS TAKES
     A VACATION .... MAUREEN O'HARA
MR. HOLLAND'S OPUS .... ALICIA WITT
MR. HOLLAND'S OPUS .... GLENNE HEADLY
MR. HOLLAND'S OPUS .... JAY THOMAS
MR. HOLLAND'S OPUS .... MIA KIRSHNER
MR. HOLLAND'S OPUS .... OLYMPIA DUKAKIS
MR. HOLLAND'S OPUS .... RICHARD DREYFUSS
MR. HOLLAND'S OPUS .... WILLIAM H. MACY
MR. HORN (TF) .... DAVID CARRADINE
MR. HORN (TF) .... KAREN BLACK
MR. HORN (TF) .... RICHARD WIDMARK
MR. IMPERIUM .... DEBBIE REYNOLDS
MR. IMPERIUM .... LANA TURNER
MR. JONES .... ANNE BANCROFT
MR. JONES .... BILL PULLMAN
MR. JONES .... DELROY LINDO
MR. JONES .... LENA OLIN
MR. JONES .... RICHARD GERE
MR. LUCKY .... CARY GRANT†
MR. MAJESTYK .... CHARLES BRONSON
MR. MEAN .... FRED WILLIAMSON
MR. MIKE'S MONDO VIDEO .... GILDA RADNER†
MR. MIKE'S MONDO VIDEO .... JOAN HACKETT†
MR. MIKE'S MONDO VIDEO .... BILL MURRAY
MR. MIKE'S MONDO VIDEO .... CARRIE FISHER
MR. MIKE'S MONDO VIDEO .... DAN AYKROYD
MR. MIKE'S MONDO VIDEO .... LARAINE NEWMAN
MR. MIKE'S MONDO VIDEO .... TERI GARR
MR. MOM .... CHRISTOPHER LLOYD
MR. MOM .... MARTIN MULL
MR. MOM .... MICHAEL KEATON

MR. MOM .... TERI GARR
MR. MUSIC .... ROBERT STACK
MR. NANNY .... AUSTIN PENDLETON
MR. NANNY .... DAVID JOHANSEN
MR. NANNY .... HULK HOGAN
MR. NANNY .... MADELINE ZIMA
MR. NANNY .... RAYMOND O'CONNOR
MR. NANNY .... ROBERT GORMAN
MR. NANNY .... SHERMAN HEMSLEY
MR. NORTH .... ANJELICA HUSTON
MR. NORTH .... ANTHONY EDWARDS
MR. NORTH .... DAVID WARNER
MR. NORTH .... HARRY DEAN STANTON
MR. NORTH .... LAUREN BACALL
MR. NORTH .... MARY STUART MASTERSON
MR. NORTH .... ROBERT MITCHUM
MR. NORTH .... TAMMY GRIMES
MR. NORTH .... VIRGINIA MADSEN
MR. PATMAN .... JAMES COBURN
MR. QUILP .... BRIAN GLOVER
MR. QUILP .... DAVID HEMMINGS
MR. QUILP .... DAVID WARNER
MR. RICCO .... CINDY WILLIAMS
MR. RICCO .... DEAN MARTIN
MR. RICCO .... THALMUS RASULALA
MR. SATURDAY NIGHT .... BILLY CRYSTAL
MR. SATURDAY NIGHT .... HELEN HUNT
MR. SATURDAY NIGHT .... JERRY LEWIS
MR. SATURDAY NIGHT .... JULIE WARNER
MR. SATURDAY NIGHT .... RON SILVER
MR. SATURDAY NIGHT ○ .... DAVID PAYMER
MR. SCARFACE .... JACK PALANCE
MR. SKEFFINGTON ★ .... BETTE DAVIS†
MR. SKEFFINGTON ○ .... CLAUDE RAINS†
MR. SMITH GOES TO
     WASHINGTON .... JEAN ARTHUR†
MR. SMITH GOES TO
     WASHINGTON ★ .... JAMES STEWART
MR. SMITH GOES TO
     WASHINGTON ○ .... CLAUDE RAINS†
MR. SMITH GOES TO
     WASHINGTON ○ .... HARRY CAREY†
MR. SUPERINVISIBLE .... DEAN JONES
MR. SYCAMORE .... JASON ROBARDS
MR. SYCAMORE .... JEAN SIMMONS
MR. SYCAMORE .... SANDY DENNIS†
MR. TOPAZE .... BILLIE WHITELAW
MR. UNIVERSE .... VINCE EDWARDS
MR. WONDERFUL .... ANNABELLA SCIORRA
MR. WONDERFUL .... MARY-LOUISE PARKER
MR. WONDERFUL .... MATT DILLON
MR. WONDERFUL .... WILLIAM HURT
MR. WRITE .... MARTIN MULL
MR. WRITE .... PAUL REISER
MRS. DELAFIELD WANTS
     TO MARRY (TF) .... DENHOLM ELLIOTT†
MRS. DELAFIELD WANTS
     TO MARRY (TF) .... HAROLD GOULD
MRS. DELAFIELD WANTS
     TO MARRY (TF) .... KATHERINE HEPBURN
MRS. DOUBTFIRE .... HARVEY FIERSTEIN
MRS. DOUBTFIRE .... LISA JAKUB
MRS. DOUBTFIRE .... MARA WILSON
MRS. DOUBTFIRE .... MATTHEW LAWRENCE
MRS. DOUBTFIRE .... PIERCE BROSNAN
MRS. DOUBTFIRE .... ROBERT PROSKY
MRS. DOUBTFIRE .... ROBIN WILLIAMS
MRS. DOUBTFIRE .... SALLY FIELD
MRS. DOUBTFIRE .... SYDNEY WALKER†
MRS. LAMBERT
     REMEMBERS LOVE (TF) .... RYAN TODD
MRS. MINIVER .... REGINALD OWEN†
MRS. MINIVER ★ .... WALTER PIDGEON†
MRS. MINIVER ★★ .... GREER GARSON
MRS. MINIVER ○ .... DAME MAY WHITTY†
MRS. MINIVER ○ .... HENRY TRAVERS†
MRS. MINIVER ○○ .... TERESA WRIGHT
MRS. O'MALLEY AND
     MR. MALONE .... JAMES WHITMORE
MRS. PARKER AND THE
     VICIOUS CIRCLE .... AMELIA CAMPBELL
MRS. PARKER AND THE
     VICIOUS CIRCLE .... ANDREW McCARTHY

MRS. PARKER AND THE
     VICIOUS CIRCLE .... CAMPBELL SCOTT
MRS. PARKER AND THE
     VICIOUS CIRCLE .... CHIP ZIEN
MRS. PARKER AND THE
     VICIOUS CIRCLE .... DAVID GOW
MRS. PARKER AND THE
     VICIOUS CIRCLE .... DAVID THORNTON
MRS. PARKER AND THE
     VICIOUS CIRCLE .... GARY BASARABA
MRS. PARKER AND THE
     VICIOUS CIRCLE .... GWYNETH PALTROW
MRS. PARKER AND THE
     VICIOUS CIRCLE .... HEATHER GRAHAM
MRS. PARKER AND THE
     VICIOUS CIRCLE .... J. M. HENRY
MRS. PARKER AND THE
     VICIOUS CIRCLE .... JAKE JOHANNSEN
MRS. PARKER AND THE
     VICIOUS CIRCLE .... JAMES LE GROS
MRS. PARKER AND THE
     VICIOUS CIRCLE .... JANE ADAMS
MRS. PARKER AND THE
     VICIOUS CIRCLE .... JENNIFER BEALS
MRS. PARKER AND THE
     VICIOUS CIRCLE .... JENNIFER JASON LEIGH
MRS. PARKER AND THE
     VICIOUS CIRCLE .... KEITH CARRADINE
MRS. PARKER AND THE
     VICIOUS CIRCLE .... LENI PARKER
MRS. PARKER AND THE
     VICIOUS CIRCLE .... LILI TAYLOR
MRS. PARKER AND THE
     VICIOUS CIRCLE .... MARTHA PLIMPTON
MRS. PARKER AND THE
     VICIOUS CIRCLE .... MATHHEW BRODERICK
MRS. PARKER AND THE
     VICIOUS CIRCLE .... MATT MALLOY
MRS. PARKER AND THE
     VICIOUS CIRCLE .... MINA BADIE
MRS. PARKER AND THE
     VICIOUS CIRCLE .... NICK CASSAVETES
MRS. PARKER AND THE
     VICIOUS CIRCLE .... PETER GALLAGHER
MRS. PARKER AND THE
     VICIOUS CIRCLE .... RANDY LOWELL
MRS. PARKER AND THE
     VICIOUS CIRCLE .... REBECCA MILLER
MRS. PARKER AND THE
     VICIOUS CIRCLE .... SAM ROBARDS
MRS. PARKER AND THE
     VICIOUS CIRCLE .... STANLEY TUCCI
MRS. PARKER AND THE
     VICIOUS CIRCLE .... STEPHEN BALDWIN
MRS. PARKER AND THE
     VICIOUS CIRCLE .... TOM McGOWAN
MRS. PARKER AND THE
     VICIOUS CIRCLE .... WALLACE SHAWN
MRS. PARKINGTON ★ .... GREER GARSON
MRS. PARKINGTON ○ .... AGNES MOOREHEAD†
MRS. POLLIFAX—SPY .... DARREN McGAVIN
MRS. POLLIFAX—SPY .... NEHEMIAH PERSOFF
MRS. SOFFEL .... DIANE KEATON
MRS. SOFFEL .... EDWRAD HERRMANN
MRS. SOFFEL .... MATTHEW MODINE
MRS. SOFFEL .... MEL GIBSON
MRS. SOFFEL .... TRINI ALVARADO
MRS. SUNDANCE
     RIDES AGAIN (TF) .... KATHERINE ROSS
MRS. SUNDANCE (TF) .... ROBERT FOXWORTH
MUCH ADO ABOUT
     NOTHING .... DENZEL WASHINGTON
MUCH ADO ABOUT NOTHING ..... EMMA THOMPSON
MUCH ADO ABOUT NOTHING .... KEANU REEVES
MUCH ADO ABOUT
     NOTHING .... KENNETH BRANAGH
MUCH ADO ABOUT NOTHING ...... MICHAEL KEATON
MUCH ADO ABOUT
     NOTHING .... ROBERT SEAN LEONARD
MUDLARK, THE .... ALEC GUINNESS
MUGGABLE MARY:
     STREET COP (TF) .... KAREN VALENTINE

† after an actor's name denotes deceased.

MUGGER, THE .... JAMES FRANCISCUS†
MULLIGAN'S STEW (TF) .... ALEXIS KARRAS
MUMMY, THE .... BORIS KARLOFF†
MUMSY, NANNY ,SONNY
    AND GIRLY .... MICHAEL BRYANT
MUNSTER, GO HOME .... AL LEWIS
MUNSTER, GO HOME .... FRED GWYNNE†
MUNSTER, GO HOME .... YVONNE DE CARLO
MUNSTERS'
    REVENGE, THE (TF) .... FRED GWYNNE†
MUNSTERS'
    REVENGE, THE (TF) .... YVONNE DE CARLO
MUPPET CHRISTMAS
    CAROL, THE .... MICHAEL CAINE
MUPPET CHRISTMAS
    CAROL, THE .... STEVE WHITMIRE
MUPPET MOVIE, THE .... AUSTIN PENDLETON
MUPPET MOVIE, THE .... BOB HOPE
MUPPET MOVIE, THE .... CAROL KANE
MUPPET MOVIE, THE .... CHARLES DURNING
MUPPET MOVIE, THE .... CLORIS LEACHMAN
MUPPET MOVIE, THE .... DOM DeLUISE
MUPPET MOVIE, THE .... EDGAR BERGEN
MUPPET MOVIE, THE .... ELLIOTT GOULD
MUPPET MOVIE, THE .... FRANK OZ
MUPPET MOVIE, THE .... JAMES COBURN
MUPPET MOVIE, THE .... JIM HENSON†
MUPPET MOVIE, THE .... MADELINE KAHN
MUPPET MOVIE, THE .... MEL BROOKS
MUPPET MOVIE, THE .... MILTON BERLE
MUPPET MOVIE, THE .... PAUL WILLIAMS
MUPPET MOVIE, THE .... RICHARD PRYOR
MUPPET MOVIE, THE .... STEVE MARTIN
MUPPET MOVIE, THE .... TELLY SAVALAS†
MUPPETS TAKE MANHATTAN, THE ..... ART CARNEY
MUPPETS TAKE
    MANHATTAN, THE .... BROOKE SHIELDS
MUPPETS TAKE
    MANHATTAN, THE .... DABNEY COLEMAN
MUPPETS TAKE
    MANHATTAN, THE .... ELLIOTT GOULD
MUPPETS TAKE MANHATTAN, THE .... FRANK OZ
MUPPETS TAKE MANHATTAN, THE ..... JULI DONALD
MUPPETS TAKE MANHATTAN, THE ..... LIZA MINELLI
MURDER AT THE GALLOP .... ROBERT MORLEY
MURDER AT THE
    WORLD SERIES (TF) .... JANET LEIGH
MURDER AT THE
    WORLD SERIES (TF) .... KAREN VALENTINE
MURDER BY CONTRACT .... VINCE EDWARDS
MURDER BY DEATH .... ALEC GUINNESS
MURDER BY DEATH .... DAVID NIVEN†
MURDER BY DEATH .... EILEEN BRENNAN
MURDER BY DEATH .... ELSA LANCHESTER†
MURDER BY DEATH .... JAMES COCO†
MURDER BY DEATH .... MAGGIE SMITH
MURDER BY DEATH .... NANCY WALKER†
MURDER BY DEATH .... PETER FALK
MURDER BY DEATH .... PETER SELLERS†
MURDER BY DEATH .... TRUMAN CAPOTE†
MURDER BY DECREE ...... CHRISTOPHER PLUMMER
MURDER BY DECREE .... DAVID HEMMINGS
MURDER BY DECREE .... DONALD SUTHERLAND
MURDER BY DECREE .... GENEVIEVE BUJOLD
MURDER BY DECREE .... JOHN GIELGUD
MURDER BY DECREE .... SUSAN CLARK
MURDER BY MOONLIGHT (TF) .... BRIAN COX
MURDER BY MOONLIGHT (TF) ... BRIGITTE NIELSEN
MURDER BY MOONLIGHT (TF) ... GERALD McRANEY
MURDER BY NATURAL
    CAUSES (TF) .... BARRY BOSTWICK
MURDER BY NATURAL
    CAUSES (TF) .... HAL HOLBROOK
MURDER BY NATURAL
    CAUSES (TF) .... KATHERINE ROSS
MURDER BY NIGHT (CTF) .... ROBERT URICH
MURDER BY PHONE .... RICHARD CHAMBERLAIN
MURDER: BY REASON
    OF INSANITY (TF) .... CANDICE BERGEN
MURDER: BY REASON
    OF INSANITY (TF) .... ELI WALLACH

MURDER: BY REASON
    OF INSANITY (TF) .... HECTOR ELIZONDO
MURDER BY
    THE BOOK (TF) .... CATHERINE MARY STEWART
MURDER BY THE BOOK (TF) .... CELESTE HOLM
MURDER BY THE BOOK (TF) .... FRED GWYNNE†
MURDER BY THE BOOK (TF) .... ROBERT HAYS
MURDER CAN BE DEADLY .... DAVID HEMMINGS
MURDER CAN HURT YOU (TF) .... BURT YOUNG
MURDER IN BLACK
    AND WHITE (TF) .... CLIFF GORMAN
MURDER IN BLACK
    AND WHITE (TF) .... DIAHANN CARROLL
MURDER IN BLACK
    AND WHITE (TF) .... FRED GWYNNE†
MURDER IN BLACK
    AND WHITE (TF) .... JOAN COPELAND
MURDER IN BLACK
    AND WHITE (TF) .... PHILIP BOSCO
MURDER IN BLACK
    AND WHITE (TF) .... RICHARD CRENNA
MURDER IN COWETA
    COUNTY (TF) .... JOHNNY CASH
MURDER IN
    MISSISSIPPI (TF) .... BLAIR UNDERWOOD
MURDER IN MISSISSIPPI (TF) ...... C. C. H. POUNDER
MURDER IN MISSISSIPPI (TF) .... JENNIFER GREY
MURDER IN MISSISSIPPI (TF) .... TOM HULCE
MURDER IN PARADISE (TF) .... MAGGIE HAN
MURDER IN PARADISE (TF) .... MAKO
MURDER IN PEYTON PLACE (TF) .... DAVID HEDISON
MURDER IN
    PEYTON PLACE (TF) .... JANET MARGOLIN
MURDER IN PEYTON PLACE (TF) .... ROYAL DANO
MURDER IN TEXAS (TF) .... DIMITRA ARLYS
MURDER IN TEXAS (TF) .... FARRAH FAWCETT
MURDER IN TEXAS (TF) .... KATHERINE ROSS
MURDER IN TEXAS (TF) .... SAM ELLIOTT
MURDER IN THE AIR .... RONALD REAGAN
MURDER IN THE BIG HOUSE .... VAN JOHNSON
MURDER IN THE FAMILY .... JESSICA TANDY†
MURDER IN THE FAMILY .... RODDY McDOWALL
MURDER IN THE FIRST .... CHRISTIAN SLATER
MURDER IN THE FIRST .... EMBETH DAVIDTZ
MURDER IN THE FIRST .... GARY OLDMAN
MURDER IN THE FIRST .... KEVIN BACON
MURDER IN THE HEARTLAND (TF) ... FAIRUZA BALK
MURDER, INC. .... JOSEPH CAMPANELLA
MURDER, INC. .... STUART WHITMAN
MURDER, INC. .... SYLVIA MILES
MURDER, INC. .... VINCENT GARDENIA†
MURDER, INC. ○ .... PETER FALK
MURDER IS EASY (TF) .... HELEN HAYES
MURDER IS EASY (TF) .... LEIGH LAWSON
MURDER IS EASY (TF) .... LESLEY-ANNE DOWN
MURDER IS EASY (TF) .... OLIVIA DE HAVILLAND
MURDER IS EASY (TF) .... TIMOTHY WEST
MURDER MAN, THE .... JAMES STEWART
MURDER MOST FOUL .... RON MOODY
MURDER OF MARY
    PHAGAN, THE (MS) .... JACK LEMMON
MURDER OF MARY
    PHAGAN, THE (MS) .... PETER GALLAGHER
MURDER OF MARY
    PHAGAN, THE (MS) .... RICHARD JORDAN†
MURDER ON FLIGHT 502 (TF) .... BROOKE ADAMS
MURDER ON FLIGHT 502 (TF) ..... FARRAH FAWCETT
MURDER ON FLIGHT 502 (TF) ...... RALPH BELLAMY†
MURDER ON FLIGHT 502 (TF) .... ROBERT STACK
MURDER ON FLIGHT 502 (TF) .... SONNY BONO
MURDER ON THE
    ORIENT EXPRESS .... ANTHONY PERKINS†
MURDER ON THE
    ORIENT EXPRESS .... COLIN BLAKELY†
MURDER ON THE
    ORIENT EXPRESS .... DENIS QUILLEY
MURDER ON THE
    ORIENT EXPRESS .... JACQUELINE BISSET
MURDER ON THE
    ORIENT EXPRESS .... JEAN-PIERRE CASSEL
MURDER ON THE
    ORIENT EXPRESS .... JOHN GIELGUD

MURDER ON THE
    ORIENT EXPRESS .... LAUREN BACALL
MURDER ON THE
    ORIENT EXPRESS .... MARTIN BALSAM
MURDER ON THE
    ORIENT EXPRESS .... MICHAEL YORK
MURDER ON THE
    ORIENT EXPRESS .... RACHEL ROBERTS†
MURDER ON THE
    ORIENT EXPRESS .... RICHARD WIDMARK
MURDER ON THE
    ORIENT EXPRESS .... SEAN CONNERY
MURDER ON THE
    ORIENT EXPRESS .... VANESSA REDGRAVE
MURDER ON THE
    ORIENT EXPRESS .... WENDY HILLER
MURDER ON THE
    ORIENT EXPRESS ★ .... ALBERT FINNEY
MURDER ON THE
    ORIENT EXPRESS ○○ .... INGRID BERGMAN†
MURDER ONCE REMOVED (TF) .... BARBARA BAIN
MURDER ONCE REMOVED (TF) .... JOHN FORSYTHE
MURDER ONCE REMOVED (TF) ...... RICHARD KILEY
MURDER ONE (TF) .... DIANE BAKER
MURDER ORDAINED (MS) .... TERRENCE KNOX
MURDER ORDAINED (TF) .... JoBETH WILLIAMS
MURDER ORDAINED (TF) .... KEITH CARRADINE
MURDER ORDAINED (TF) .... ROBERT HARPER
MURDER ORDAINED (TF) .... TERRY KINNEY
MURDER SHE SAID .... THORLEY WALTERS†
MURDER, SHE WROTE (TF) ...... ANGELA LANSBURY
MURDER, SHE WROTE (TF) .... ARTHUR HILL
MURDER, SHE WROTE (TF) .... BRIAN KEITH
MURDER, SHE WROTE (TF) .... NED BEATTY
MURDER THAT WOULDN'T
    DIE, THE (TF) .... SHARON ACKER
MURDER WITH MIRRORS (TF) .... HELEN HAYES
MURDER WITH MIRRORS (TF) .... PETER USTINOV
MURDERERS' ROW .... ANN-MARGRET
MURDERERS' ROW .... DEAN MARTIN
MURDERERS' ROW .... KARL MALDEN
MURDERS IN THE
    RUE MORGUE .... JASON ROBARDS
MURDERS IN THE RUE MORGUE .... LEON AMES
MURDERS IN THE RUE
    MORGUE, THE (TF) .... GEORGE C. SCOTT
MURDERS IN THE RUE
    MORGUE, THE (TF) .... REBECCA DE MORNAY
MURDERS IN THE RUE
    MORGUE, THE (TF) .... VAL KILMER
MURDOCK'S GANG (TF) .... JANET LEIGH
MURPH THE SURF .... DON STROUD
MURPHY'S LAW .... ANGEL TOMPKINS
MURPHY'S LAW .... BILL HENDERSON
MURPHY'S LAW .... CARRIE SNODGRESS
MURPHY'S LAW .... CHARLES BRONSON
MURPHY'S LAW .... LAWRENCE TIERNEY
MURPHY'S LAW .... ROBERT F. LYONS
MURPHY'S ROMANCE .... COREY HAIM
MURPHY'S ROMANCE .... SALLY FIELD
MURPHY'S ROMANCE ★ .... JAMES GARNER
MURPHY'S WAR .... JOHN HALLAM
MURPHY'S WAR .... PETER O'TOOLE
MURPHY'S WAR .... SIAN PHILLIPS
MURROW (CTF) .... DABNEY COLEMAN
MURROW (CTF) .... DANIEL J. TRAVANTI
MURROW (CTF) .... EDWRAD HERRMANN
MUSCLE BEACH PARTY .... ANNETTE FUNICELLO
MUSCLE BEACH PARTY .... BUDDY HACKETT
MUSCLE BEACH PARTY .... FRANKIE AVALON
MUSIC BOX .... ARMIN MUELLER-STAHL
MUSIC BOX .... DONALD MOFFAT
MUSIC BOX .... FREDERIC FORREST
MUSIC BOX .... LUKAS HAAS
MUSIC BOX .... MICHAEL ROOKER
MUSIC BOX ★ .... JESSICA LANGE
MUSIC FOR MILLIONS .... AVA GARDNER†
MUSIC FOR MILLIONS .... JUNE ALLYSON
MUSIC LOVERS, THE .... GLENDA JACKSON
MUSIC LOVERS, THE .... RICHARD CHAMBERLAIN
MUSIC MAN, THE .... BUDDY HACKETT
MUSIC MAN, THE .... MARY WICKES

This is not a list of every film ever made or every cast member, only those listed in this directory.

MUSIC MAN, THE .... MAX SHOWALTER
MUSIC MAN, THE .... ROBERT PRESTON†
MUSIC MAN, THE .... RON HOWARD
MUSIC MAN, THE .... SHIRLEY JONES
MUSIC OF CHANCE, THE .... CHARLES DURNING
MUSIC OF CHANCE, THE .... JAMES SPADER
MUSIC OF CHANCE, THE .... JOEL GREY
MUSKETEERS OF PIG ALLEY, THE .... LILLIAN GISH†
MUSSOLINI: THE DECLINE AND
  FALL OF IL DUCE (CMS) .... ANTHONY HOPKINS
MUSSOLINI: THE DECLINE AND
  FALL OF IL DUCE (CMS) .... BOB HOSKINS
MUSSOLINI: THE DECLINE AND
  FALL OF IL DUCE (CMS) .... SUSAN SARANDON
MUSSOLINI: THE UNTOLD
  STORY (MS) .... GABRIEL BYRNE
MUSSOLINI: THE UNTOLD
  STORY (MS) .... GEORGE C. SCOTT
MUSSOLINI: THE UNTOLD
  STORY (MS) .... LEE GRANT
MUSSOLINI: THE UNTOLD
  STORY (MS) .... MARY ELIZABETH MASTRANTONIO
MUSSOLINI: THE UNTOLD
  STORY (MS) .... MARY STUART MASTERSON
MUSSOLINI: THE UNTOLD
  STORY (MS) .... RAUL JULIA†
MUSSOLINI: THE UNTOLD
  STORY (MS) .... VIRGINIA MADSEN
MUSSOLINI—ULTIMO ATTO .... FRANCO NERO
MUSTANG COUNTRY .... PATRICK WAYNE
MUTATIONS, THE .... DONALD PLEASENCE
MUTINY .... ANGELA LANSBURY
MUTINY ON THE BOUNTY .... GORDAN JACKSON†
MUTINY ON THE BOUNTY .... MARLON BRANDO
MUTINY ON THE BOUNTY .... RICHARD HARRIS
MUTINY ON THE BOUNTY .... TREVOR HOWARD†
MUTINY ON THE
  BOUNTY ★ .... CHARLES LAUGHTON†
MUTINY ON THE BOUNTY ★ ...... CLARK GABLE†
MUTINY ON THE BOUNTY ★ .... FRANCHOT TONE†
MY AMERICAN WIFE .... ANN SOTHERN
MY BABY .... LILLIAN GISH†
MY BEAUTIFUL
  LAUNDRETTE .... DERRICK BRANCHE
MY BEAUTIFUL LAUNDRETTE .... SAEED JAFFREY
MY BEAUTIFUL
  LAUNDRETTE (TF) .... DANIEL DAY-LEWIS
MY BEAUTIFUL
  LAUNDRETTE (TF) .... SHIRLEY ANNE FIELD
MY BEST FRIEND'S GIRL .... ISABELLE HUPPERT
MY BLOOD RUNS COLD .... JOEY HEATHERTON
MY BLOOD RUNS COLD .... TROY DONAHUE
MY BLUE HEAVEN .... CAROL KANE
MY BLUE HEAVEN .... JANE WYATT
MY BLUE HEAVEN .... JOAN CUSAK
MY BLUE HEAVEN .... MELANIE MAYRON
MY BLUE HEAVEN .... RANDI PAREIRA
MY BLUE HEAVEN .... RICK MORANIS
MY BLUE HEAVEN .... ROBERT G. MIRANDA
MY BLUE HEAVEN .... STEVE MARTIN
MY BODY, MY CHILD (TF) .... VANESSA REDGRAVE
MY BODYGUARD .... CHRIS MAKEPEACE
MY BODYGUARD .... DICK CUSAK
MY BODYGUARD .... GEORGE WENDT
MY BODYGUARD .... JOAN CUSAK
MY BODYGUARD .... MARTIN MULL
MY BODYGUARD .... MATT DILLON
MY BODYGUARD .... TIM KAZURINSKY
MY BOYFRIEND'S BACK (TF) .... JILL EIKENBERRY
MY BOYFRIEND'S BACK (TF) .... SANDY DUNCAN
MY BOYFRIEND'S BACK (TF) .... STEPHEN MACHT
MY BREAST (TF) .... BARBARA BARRIE
MY BREAST (TF) .... JAMES SUTORIUS
MY BREAST (TF) .... JAMEY SHERIDAN
MY BREAST (TF) .... MEREDITH BAXTER
MY BREAST (TF) .... SARA BOTSFORD
MY BRILLIANT CAREER .... JUDY DAVIS
MY BRILLIANT CAREER .... SAM NEILL
MY BROTHER TOM (TF) .... GORDAN JACKSON†
MY BROTHER'S KEEPER .... DAVID TOMLINSON
MY BROTHER'S WIFE (TF) .... DAKIN MATTHEWS
MY BROTHER'S WIFE (TF) .... JOHN RITTER

MY BROTHER'S WIFE (TF) .... MEL HARRIS
MY BROTHER'S WIFE (TF) .... POLLY BERGEN
MY CHAUFFEUR .... DEBORAH FOREMAN
MY CHAUFFEUR .... HOWARD HESSEMAN
MY CHAUFFEUR .... PENN JILLETTE
MY COUSIN RACHEL .... OLIVIA DE HAVILLAND
MY COUSIN RACHEL ○ .... RICHARD BURTON†
MY COUSIN VINNY .... FRED GWYNNE†
MY COUSIN VINNY .... JOE PESCI
MY COUSIN VINNY .... MITCHELL WHITFIELD
MY COUSIN VINNY .... RALPH MACCHIO
MY COUSIN VINNY ○○ .... MARISA TOMEI
MY DARLING CLEMENTINE .... JOHN IRELAND
MY DEAR MISS ALDRICH ..... MAUREEN O'SULLIVAN
MY DEAR SECRETARY .... KIRK DOUGLAS
MY DEMON LOVER .... ALAN FUDGE
MY DEMON LOVER .... ARNOLD JOHNSON
MY DEMON LOVER .... CALVERT DEFOREST
MY DEMON LOVER .... GINA GALLEGO
MY DEMON LOVER .... MICHELLE LITTLE
MY DEMON LOVER .... ROBERT TREBOR
MY DEMON LOVER .... SCOTT VALENTINE
MY DINNER WITH ANDRE .... ANDRE GREGORY
MY DINNER WITH ANDRE .... WALLACE SHAWN
MY DREAM IS YOURS .... DORIS DAY
MY FAIR LADY .... ALAN NAPIER†
MY FAIR LADY .... AUDREY HEPBURN†
MY FAIR LADY .... HENRY DANIELL†
MY FAIR LADY .... ISOBEL ELSOM†
MY FAIR LADY .... THEODORE BIKEL
MY FAIR LADY .... WILFRID HYDE-WHITE†
MY FAIR LADY ★★ .... REX HARRISON†
MY FAIR LADY ○ .... DAME GLADYS COOPER†
MY FAIR LADY ○ .... STANLEY HOLLOWAY†
MY FATHER, MY SON (TF) .... KARL MALDEN
MY FATHER, MY SON (TF) .... KEITH CARRADINE
MY FATHER, MY SON (TF) .... MICHAEL HORTON
MY FATHER, THE HERO .... DALTON JAMES
MY FATHER, THE HERO .... EMMA THOMPSON
MY FATHER, THE HERO .... FAITH PRINCE
MY FATHER, THE HERO .... GERARD DEPARDIEU
MY FATHER, THE HERO .... KATHERINE HEIGL
MY FATHER, THE HERO .... LAUREN HUTTON
MY FATHER'S HOUSE (TF) .... CLIFF ROBERTSON
MY FATHER'S HOUSE (TF) .... EILEEN BRENNAN
MY FAVORITE BLONDE .... BOB HOPE
MY FAVORITE BRUNETTE .... BOB HOPE
MY FAVORITE BRUNETTE .... DOROTHY LAMOUR
MY FAVORITE SPY .... BOB HOPE
MY FAVORITE SPY .... JANE WYMAN
MY FAVORITE YEAR .... BASIL HOFFMAN
MY FAVORITE YEAR .... JESSICA HARPER
MY FAVORITE YEAR .... JOSEPH BOLOGNA
MY FAVORITE YEAR .... LAINIE KAZAN
MY FAVORITE YEAR .... LOU JACOBI
MY FAVORITE YEAR .... MARK LINN-BAKER
MY FAVORITE YEAR ★ .... PETER O'TOOLE
MY FIRST LOVE (TF) .... BARBARA BARRIE
MY FIRST LOVE (TF) .... BEATRICE ARTHUR
MY FIRST LOVE (TF) .... JOAN VAN ARK
MY FIRST LOVE (TF) .... RICHARD HERD
MY FIRST LOVE (TF) .... RICHARD KILEY
MY FOOLISH HEART ★ .... SUSAN HAYWARD†
MY FORBIDDEN PAST .... AVA GARDNER†
MY FORBIDDEN PAST .... ROBERT MITCHUM
MY FRIEND FLICKA .... JEFF COREY
MY FRIEND FLICKA .... RODDY McDOWALL
MY FRIEND IRMA .... DEAN MARTIN
MY FRIEND IRMA .... JERRY LEWIS
MY FRIEND IRMA GOES WEST .... DEAN MARTIN
MY FRIEND IRMA GOES WEST .... JERRY LEWIS
MY GEISHA .... SHIRLEY MacLAINE
MY GIRL .... ANNA CHLUMSKY
MY GIRL .... DAN AYKROYD
MY GIRL .... GRIFFIN DUNNE
MY GIRL .... JAMIE LEE CURTIS
MY GIRL .... MACAULAY CULKIN
MY GIRL .... RICHARD MASUR
MY GIRL 2 .... ANGELINE BALL
MY GIRL 2 .... ANNA CHLUMSKY
MY GIRL 2 .... AUSTIN O'BRIEN
MY GIRL 2 .... CHRISTINE EBERSOLE

MY GIRL 2 .... DAN AYKROYD
MY GIRL 2 .... J. D. SOUTHER
MY GIRL 2 .... JAMIE LEE CURTIS
MY GIRL 2 .... RICHARD MASUR
MY GIRL TISA .... SAM WANAMAKER†
MY HEROES HAVE ALWAYS
  BEEN COWBOYS .... BALTHAZAR GETTY
MY HEROES HAVE ALWAYS
  BEEN COWBOYS .... BEN JOHNSON
MY HEROES HAVE ALWAYS
  BEEN COWBOYS .... GARY BUSEY
MY HEROES HAVE ALWAYS
  BEEN COWBOYS .... KATE CAPSHAW
MY HEROES HAVE ALWAYS
  BEEN COWBOYS .... MICKEY ROONEY
MY HEROES HAVE ALWAYS
  BEEN COWBOYS .... SCOTT GLENN
MY HEROES HAVE ALWAYS
  BEEN COWBOYS .... TESS HARPER
MY IRISH MOLLY .... MAUREEN O'HARA
MY LEFT FOOT .... ADRIAN DUNBAR
MY LEFT FOOT .... FIONA SHAW
MY LEFT FOOT .... HUGH O'CONOR
MY LEFT FOOT .... RAY MCANALLY†
MY LEFT FOOT .... RUTH McCABE
MY LEFT FOOT ★★ .... DANIEL DAY-LEWIS
MY LEFT FOOT ○○ .... BRENDA FRICKER
MY LIFE .... BRAD WHITFORD
MY LIFE .... HAING S. NGOR
MY LIFE .... MICHAEL CONSTANTINE
MY LIFE .... MICHAEL KEATON
MY LIFE .... NICOLE KIDMAN
MY LIFE .... QUEEN LATIFAH
MY LIFE .... REBECCA SCHULL
MY LITTLE CHICKADEE .... MAE WEST†
MY LITTLE CHICKADEE .... W. C. FIELDS†
MY LITTLE GIRL .... MARY STUART MASTERSON
MY LITTLE PONY -
  THE MOVIE (AF) .... CLORIS LEACHMAN
MY LITTLE PONY -
  THE MOVIE (AF) .... DANNY DEVITO
MY LITTLE PONY -
  THE MOVIE (AF) .... MADELINE KAHN
MY LOVE CAME BACK .... EDDIE ALBERT
MY LOVE CAME BACK .... JANE WYMAN
MY LOVE CAME BACK .... OLIVIA DE HAVILLAND
MY LOVE LETTERS .... MATT CLARK
MY MAN AND I .... RICARDO MONTALBAN
MY MAN AND I .... SHELLEY WINTERS
MY MAN GODFREY .... EVA GABOR
MY MAN GODFREY .... JANE WYMAN
MY MAN GODFREY .... JUNE ALLYSON
MY MAN GODFREY ★ .... CAROLE LOMBARD†
MY MAN GODFREY ★ .... WILLIAM POWELL†
MY MAN GODFREY ○ .... ALICE BRADY†
MY MAN GODFREY ○ .... MISCHA AUER†
MY MOM'S A WEREWOLF .... JOHN SAXON
MY MOM'S A WEREWOLF .... SUSAN BLAKELY
MY NAME IS BILL W (TF) .... GARY SINISE
MY NAME IS BILL W. (TF) .... JAMES GARNER
MY NAME IS BILL W. (TF) .... JAMES WOODS
MY NAME IS JULIA ROSS .... NINA FOCH
MY NAME IS NOBODY .... R.G. ARMSTRONG
MY OLD MAN (TF) .... EILEEN BRENNAN
MY OLD MAN'S PLACE .... MICHAEL MORIARTY
MY OLD MAN'S PLACE .... PETER DONAT
MY OLD MAN'S PLACE .... WILLIAM DEVANE
MY OUTLAW BROTHER .... ROBERT STACK
MY OWN PRIVATE IDAHO .... GRACE ZABRISKIE
MY OWN PRIVATE IDAHO .... KEANU REEVES
MY OWN PRIVATE IDAHO .... RIVER PHOENIX†
MY PAL GUS .... RICHARD WIDMARK
MY POSSE DON'T DO
  HOMEWORK .... MICHELLE PFEIFFER
MY REPUTATION .... BARBARA STANWYCK†
MY SCIENCE PROJECT ..... DANIELLE von ZERNECK
MY SCIENCE PROJECT ..... DENNIS HOPPER
MY SCIENCE PROJECT .... FISHER STEVENS
MY SCIENCE PROJECT .... RICHARD MASUR
MY SIDE OF THE MOUNTAIN .... THEODORE BIKEL
MY SISTER EILEEN .... JACK LEMMON
MY SISTER EILEEN .... JANET LEIGH

† after an actor's name denotes deceased.

MY SISTER EILEEN ★ .... ROSALAND RUSSELL†
MY SISTER MY LOVE .... BIBI ANDERSSON
MY SISTER, MY LOVE/THE CAGE .... CAROL KANE
MY SISTER, MY LOVE/THE DAGE .... LEE GRANT
MY SIX CONVICTS .... CHARLES BRONSON
MY SIX CONVICTS .... HARRY MORGAN
MY SIX CONVICTS .... WESLEY ADDY
MY SIX LOVES .... ALICE GHOSTLEY
MY SIX LOVES .... CLIFF ROBERTSON
MY SIX LOVES .... DEBBIE REYNOLDS
MY SIX LOVES .... EILEEN HECKART
MY SIX LOVES .... MAX SHOWALTER
MY SON JOHN .... DEAN JAGGER†
MY SON JOHN .... HELEN HAYES
MY STEPMOTHER
    IS AN ALIEN .... ALYSON HANNIGAN
MY STEPMOTHER IS AN ALIEN .... DAN AYKROYD
MY STEPMOTHER IS AN ALIEN .... JON LOVITZ
MY STEPMOTHER IS AN ALIEN .... KIM BASINGER
MY SWEET CHARLIE (TF) .... PATTY DUKE
MY TUTOR .... KEVIN McCARTHY
MY TWO LOVES (TF) .... MARIETTE HARTLEY
MY WICKED, WICKED WAYS: THE
    LEGEND OF ERROL FLYNN (TF) .... HAL LINDEN
MYRA BRECKINRIDGE .... FARRAH FAWCETT
MYRA BRECKINRIDGE .... MAE WEST†
MYRA BRECKINRIDGE .... RAQUEL WELCH
MYRA BRECKINRIDGE .... TOM SELLECK
MYSTERIES .... SYLVIA KRISTEL
MYSTERIES OF THE
    DARK JUNGLE, THE (MS) .... GABRIELLE ANWAR
MYSTERIOUS DOCTOR, THE ...... ELEANOR PARKER
MYSTERIOUS ISLAND OF
    CAPTAIN NEMO, THE .... OMAR SHARIF
MYSTERIOUS MONSTERS, THE ...... PETER GRAVES
MYSTERIOUS MR. MOTO .... LEON AMES
MYSTERY DATE .... B. D. WONG
MYSTERY DATE .... BRIAN McNAMARA
MYSTERY DATE .... ETHAN HAWKE
MYSTERY DATE .... FISHER STEVENS
MYSTERY DATE .... TERI POLO
MYSTERY STREET .... RICARDO MONTALBAN
MYSTIC PIZZA .... ADAM STORKE
MYSTIC PIZZA .... ANNABETH GISH
MYSTIC PIZZA .... JULIA ROBERTS
MYSTIC PIZZA .... LILI TAYLOR
MYSTIC PIZZA .... VINCENT D'ONOFRIO
MYSTIC PIZZA .... WILLIAM R. MOSES
MYSTIC WARRIOR, THE (MS) ..... ROBERT BELTRAN

N

NADINE .... GLENNE HEADLY
NADINE .... GWEN VERDON
NADINE .... JEFF BRIDGES
NADINE .... KIM BASINGER
NADINE .... RIP TORN
NAILS (CTF) .... ANNE ARCHER
NAIROBI AFFAIR (TF) .... CHARLTON HESTON
NAIROBI AFFAIR (TF) .... MAUD ADAMS
NAKED .... DAVID THEWLIS
NAKED ALIBI .... CHUCK CONNORS†
NAKED ALIBI .... MAX SHOWALTER
NAKED AND THE DEAD, THE ..... CLIFF ROBERTSON
NAKED AND THE DEAD, THE ...... MAX SHOWALTER
NAKED AND THE DEAD, THE ..... RICHARD JAECKEL
NAKED APE, THE .... VICTORIA PRINCIPAL
NAKED CAGE, THE .... ANGEL TOMPKINS
NAKED CAGE, THE .... LUCINDA CROSBY
NAKED CITY .... HOWARD DUFF†
NAKED CITY .... JOHN RANDOLPH
NAKED CITY, THE .... KATHLEEN FREEMAN
NAKED CITY, THE .... NEHEMIAH PERSOFF
NAKED CIVIL SERVANT, THE (TF) ...... JOHN HURT
NAKED EDGE, THE .... DEBORAH KERR
NAKED FACE, THE .... ANNE ARCHER
NAKED FACE, THE .... ART CARNEY
NAKED FACE, THE .... DAVID HEDISON
NAKED FACE, THE .... ELLIOTT GOULD
NAKED FACE, THE .... ROD STEIGER
NAKED FACE, THE .... ROGER MOORE

NAKED GUN 2 1/2: THE SMELL
    OF FEAR, THE .... GEORGE KENNEDY
NAKED GUN 2 1/2: THE SMELL
    OF FEAR, THE .... LESLIE NIELSEN
NAKED GUN 2 1/2: THE SMELL
    OF FEAR, THE .... O. J. SIMPSON
NAKED GUN 2 1/2: THE SMELL
    OF FEAR, THE .... PETER MARK RICHMAN
NAKED GUN 2 1/2: THE SMELL
    OF FEAR, THE .... PRISCILLA PRESLEY
NAKED GUN 2 1/2: THE SMELL
    OF FEAR, THE .... ROBERT GOULET
NAKED GUN 2 1/2: THE SMELL
    OF FEAR, THE .... ZSA ZSA GABOR
NAKED GUN 2 1/2: THE SMELL
    OF FEAR, THE .... ED WILLIAMS
NAKED GUN 33 1/3:
    THE FINAL INSULT .... ANN B. DAVIS
NAKED GUN 33 1/3:
    THE FINAL INSULT .... ANNA NICOLE SMITH
NAKED GUN 33 1/3:
    THE FINAL INSULT .... FRED WARD
NAKED GUN 33 1/3:
    THE FINAL INSULT .... GEORGE KENNEDY
NAKED GUN 33 1/3:
    THE FINAL INSULT .... LESLIE NIELSEN
NAKED GUN 33 1/3:
    THE FINAL INSULT .... MARCY GOLDMAN
NAKED GUN 33 1/3:
    THE FINAL INSULT .... MARY LOU RETTON
NAKED GUN 33 1/3:
    THE FINAL INSULT .... O. J. SIMPSON
NAKED GUN 33 1/3:
    THE FINAL INSULT .... PIA ZADORA
NAKED GUN 33 1/3:
    THE FINAL INSULT .... PRISCILLA PRESLEY
NAKED GUN 33 1/3:
    THE FINAL INSULT .... RAQUEL WELCH
NAKED GUN 33 1/3:
    THE FINAL INSULT .... VANNA WHITE
NAKED GUN 33 1/3:
    THE FINAL INSULT .... "WEIRD AL" YANKOVIC
NAKED GUN: FROM THE FILES
    OF POLICE SQUAD!, THE .... CHARLOTTE ZUCKER
NAKED GUN: FROM THE FILES
    OF POLICE SQUAD!, THE .... ED WILLIAMS
NAKED GUN: FROM THE FILES
    OF POLICE SQUAD!, THE .... GEORGE KENNEDY
NAKED GUN: FROM THE FILES
    OF POLICE SQUAD!, THE .... JOHN HOUSEMAN†
NAKED GUN: FROM THE FILES
    OF POLICE SQUAD!, THE .... LESLIE NIELSEN
NAKED GUN: FROM THE FILES
    OF POLICE SQUAD!, THE .... NANCY MARCHAND
NAKED GUN: FROM THE FILES
    OF POLICE SQUAD!, THE .... O. J. SIMPSON
NAKED GUN: FROM THE FILES
    OF POLICE SQUAD!, THE ...... PRISCILLA PRESLEY
NAKED GUN: FROM THE FILES
    OF POLICE SQUAD!, THE .... REGGIE JACKSON
NAKED GUN: FROM THE FILES OF
    POLICE SQUAD!, THE .... RICARDO MONTALBAN
NAKED GUN: FROM THE FILES
    OF POLICE SQUAD!, THE ..... "WEIRD AL" YANKOVIC
NAKED IN NEW YORK .... ERIC STOLTZ
NAKED IN NEW YORK .... JILL CLAYBURGH
NAKED IN NEW YORK .... KATHLEEN TURNER
NAKED IN NEW YORK .... MARY-LOUISE PARKER
NAKED IN NEW YORK .... RALPH MACCHIO
NAKED IN NEW YORK .... TIMOTHY DALTON
NAKED IN NEW YORK .... TONY CURTIS
NAKED IN NEW YORK .... WHOOPI GOLDBERG
NAKED JUNGLE, THE .... CHARLTON HESTON
NAKED JUNGLE, THE .... ELEANOR PARKER
NAKED KISS, THE .... MICHAEL DANTE
NAKED LIE (TF) .... JAMES FARENTINO
NAKED LIE (TF) .... VICTORIA PRINCIPAL
NAKED LUNCH .... JUDY DAVIS
NAKED LUNCH .... JULIAN SANDS
NAKED LUNCH .... MICHAEL ZELNIKER
NAKED LUNCH .... MONIQUE MERCURE
NAKED LUNCH .... NICHOLAS CAMPBELL

NAKED LUNCH .... PETER WELLER
NAKED LUNCH .... ROY SCHEIDER
NAKED
    MAJA, THE .... ANTHONY (TONY) FRANCIOSA
NAKED MAJA, THE .... AVA GARDNER†
NAKED OBSESSION .... ROGER CRAIG
NAKED OBSESSION .... WILLIAM KATT
NAKED RUNNER, THE .... FRANK SINATRA
NAKED RUNNER, THE .... PETER VAUGHN
NAKED SPUR, THE .... JAMES STEWART
NAKED SPUR, THE .... JANET LEIGH
NAKED STREET, THE .... ANNE BANCROFT
NAKED STREET, THE .... ANTHONY QUINN
NAKED SUN, THE .... LEE MAJORS
NAKED TERROR (FD) .... VINCENT PRICE†
NAKIA (TF) .... ROBERT FORSTER
NAM ANGELS .... BRAD JOHNSON
NAME FOR EVIL, A .... SAMANTHA EGGAR
NAME OF THE GAME
    IS KILL!, THE (TF) .... SUSAN STRASBERG
NAME OF THE ROSE, THE .... CHRISTIAN SLATER
NAME OF THE ROSE, THE .... DWIGHT WEIST
NAME OF THE ROSE, THE .... ELVA BASKIN
NAME OF THE ROSE, THE ... F. MURRAY ABRAHAM
NAME OF THE
    ROSE, THE .... FEOFOR CHALIAPIN JR.
NAME OF THE ROSE, THE ... MICHAEL LONSDALE
NAME OF THE ROSE, THE .... RON PERLMAN
NAME OF THE ROSE, THE .... SEAN CONNERY
NAME OF THE ROSE, THE .... WILLIAM HICKEY
NAMELESS .... MICHAEL BIEHN
NAMELESS .... PATSY KENSIT
NAMELESS .... ROBERT CULP
NAMU, THE KILLER WHALE .... JOHN ANDERSON
NANCY ASTOR (TF) .... PIERCE BROSNAN
NANCY GOES TO RIO .... ANN SOTHERN
NANNY, THE .... BETTE DAVIS†
NAPOLÉON .... MARIA SCHELL
NAPOLEON AND JOSEPHINE:
    A LOVE STORY (MS) .... ANTHONY PERKINS†
NAPOLEON AND JOSEPHINE:
    A LOVE STORY (MS) .... ARMAND ASSANTE
NAPOLEON AND JOSEPHINE:
    A LOVE STORY (MS) .... JACQUELINE BISSET
NAPOLEON AND JOSEPHINE:
    A LOVE STORY (MS) .... JAN-PIERRE STEWART
NAPOLEON AND JOSEPHINE:
    A LOVE STORY (MS) .... LEIGH TAYLOR-YOUNG
NAPOLEON AND JOSEPHINE:
    A LOVE STORY (MS) .... PATRICK CASSIDY
NAPOLEON AND SAMANTHA .... JODIE FOSTER
NAPOLEON AND SAMANTHA .... MARY WICKES
NAPOLEON AND SAMANTHA .... MICHAEL DOUGLAS
NAPOLI VIOLENTA .... JOHN SAXON
NARROW CORNER, THE .... RALPH BELLAMY†
NARROW MARGIN .... ANNE ARCHER
NARROW MARGIN .... GENE HACKMAN
NARROW MARGIN .... J. T. WALSH
NARROW MARGIN .... JAMES B. SIKKING
NARROW MARGIN .... M. EMMET WALSH
NASHVILLE .... ALLEN GARFIELD
NASHVILLE .... BARBARA HARRIS
NASHVILLE .... BERT REMSEN
NASHVILLE .... ELLIOTT GOULD
NASHVILLE .... GERALDINE CHAPLIN
NASHVILLE .... GWEN WELLES
NASHVILLE .... HENRY GIBSON
NASHVILLE .... JEFF GOLDBLUM
NASHVILLE .... JULIE CHRISTIE
NASHVILLE .... KAREN BLACK
NASHVILLE .... KEENAN WYNN†
NASHVILLE .... KEITH CARRADINE
NASHVILLE .... MICHAEL MURPHY
NASHVILLE .... NED BEATTY
NASHVILLE .... ROBERT DOQUI
NASHVILLE .... SCOTT GLENN
NASHVILLE .... SHELLEY DUVALL
NASHVILLE .... SUSAN ANSPACH
NASHVILLE o .... LILY TOMLIN
NASHVILLE o .... RONEE BLAKLEY
NASTY BOYS (TF) .... BENJAMIN BRATT
NASTY HABITS .... ANNE JACKSON

This is not a list of every film ever made or every cast member, only those listed in this directory.

NASTY HABITS .... ANNE MEARA
NASTY HABITS .... ELI WALLACH
NASTY HABITS .... GLENDA JACKSON
NASTY HABITS .... RIP TORN
NASTY HABITS .... SANDY DENNIS†
NATALE IN CASA DI
   APPUNTAMENTO .... ERNEST BORGNINE
NATE AND HAYES .... TOMMY LEE JONES
NATHALIE GRANGER .... GERARD DEPARDIEU
NATIONAL GENERAL, THE .... LYNN REDGRAVE
NATIONAL HEALTH, THE .... BOB HOSKINS
NATIONAL LAMPOON GOES
   TO THE MOVIES .... ROBBY BENSON
NATIONAL LAMPOON'S
   ANIMAL HOUSE .... JOHN BELUSHI†
NATIONAL LAMPOON'S
   ANIMAL HOUSE .... STEPHEN FURST
NATIONAL LAMPOON'S
   CLASS REUNION .... ANN RAMSEY†
NATIONAL LAMPOON'S
   CLASS REUNION .... JACKLYN ZEMAN
NATIONAL LAMPOON'S
   CLASS REUNION .... STEPHEN FURST
NATIONAL LAMPOON'S
   LOADED WEAPON 1 .... BRUCE WILLIS
NATIONAL LAMPOON'S
   SENIOR TRIP .... ERIC EDWARDS
NATIONAL LAMPOON'S
   SENIOR TRIP .... JEREMY RENNER
NATIONAL LAMPOON'S
   SENIOR TRIP .... KEVIN McDONALD
NATIONAL LAMPOON'S
   SENIOR TRIP .... LARRY DANE
NATIONAL LAMPOON'S
   SENIOR TRIP .... MATT FREWER
NATIONAL LAMPOON'S
   SENIOR TRIP .... MICHAEL BLAKE
NATIONAL LAMPOON'S
   SENIOR TRIP .... ROB MOORE
NATIONAL LAMPOON'S
   SENIOR TRIP .... TARA CHARENDOFF
NATIONAL LAMPOON'S
   SENIOR TRIP .... TOMMY CHONG
NATIONAL LAMPOON'S
   SENIOR TRIP .... VALERIE MAHAFFEY
NATIONAL LAMPOON'S
   ANIMAL HOUSE .... BRUCE McGILL
NATIONAL LAMPOON'S
   ANIMAL HOUSE .... DONALD SUTHERLAND
NATIONAL LAMPOON'S
   ANIMAL HOUSE .... JOHN VERNON
NATIONAL LAMPOON'S
   ANIMAL HOUSE .... KAREN ALLEN
NATIONAL LAMPOON'S
   ANIMAL HOUSE .... KEVIN BACON
NATIONAL LAMPOON'S
   ANIMAL HOUSE .... PETER RIEGERT
NATIONAL LAMPOON'S
   ANIMAL HOUSE .... TIM MATHESON
NATIONAL LAMPOON'S
   ANIMAL HOUSE .... TOM HULCE
NATIONAL LAMPOON'S
   ANIMAL HOUSE .... VERNA BLOOM
NATIONAL LAMPOON'S
   CHRISTMAS VACATION .... BEVERLY D'ANGELO
NATIONAL LAMPOON'S
   CHRISTMAS VACATION .... CHEVY CHASE
NATIONAL LAMPOON'S
   CHRISTMAS VACATION .... DORIS ROBERTS
NATIONAL LAMPOON'S
   CHRISTMAS VACATION .... RANDY QUAID
NATIONAL LAMPOON'S
   CLASS REUNION .... MICHAEL LERNER
NATIONAL LAMPOON'S
   EUROPEAN VACATION .... BEVERLY D'ANGELO
NATIONAL LAMPOON'S
   EUROPEAN VACATION .... CHEVY CHASE
NATIONAL LAMPOON'S
   EUROPEAN VACATION .... DANA HILL
NATIONAL LAMPOON'S
   EUROPEAN VACATION .... ERIC IDLE

NATIONAL LAMPOON'S
   LOADED WEAPON 1 .... EMILIO ESTEVEZ
NATIONAL LAMPOON'S
   LOADED WEAPON 1 .... JON LOVITZ
NATIONAL LAMPOON'S
   LOADED WEAPON 1 .... KATHY IRELAND
NATIONAL LAMPOON'S
   LOADED WEAPON 1 .... SAMUEL L. JACKSON
NATIONAL LAMPOON'S
   LOADED WEAPON 1 .... TIM CURRY
NATIONAL LAMPOON'S
   LOADED WEAPON 1 .... WILLIAM SHATNER
NATIONAL LAMPOON'S
   MOVIE MADNESS .... RICHARD WIDMARK
NATIONAL LAMPOON'S
   MOVIE MADNESS .... ROBBY BENSON
NATIONAL LAMPOON'S
   VACATION .... ANTHONY MICHAEL HALL
NATIONAL LAMPOON'S
   VACATION .... BEVERLY D'ANGELO
NATIONAL LAMPOON'S
   VACATION .... CHEVY CHASE
NATIONAL LAMPOON'S
   VACATION .... CHRISTIE BRINKLEY
NATIONAL LAMPOON'S
   VACATION .... IMOGENE COCA
NATIONAL LAMPOON'S
   VACATION .... JAMES KEACH
NATIONAL LAMPOON'S
   VACATION .... JOHN CANDY†
NATIONAL LAMPOON'S VACATION .... RANDY QUAID
NATIONAL VELVET .... ANGELA LANSBURY
NATIONAL VELVET .... ELIZABETH TAYLOR
NATIONAL VELVET .... MICKEY ROONEY
NATIVE SON .... AKOSUA BUSIA
NATIVE SON .... ART EVANS
NATIVE SON .... CARROLL BAKER
NATIVE SON .... DAVID RASCHE
NATIVE SON .... ELIZABETH McGOVERN
NATIVE SON .... GERALDINE PAGE†
NATIVE SON .... JOHN KARLEN
NATIVE SON .... JOHN McMARTIN
NATIVE SON .... LANE SMITH
NATIVE SON .... MATT DILLON
NATIVE SON .... OPRAH WINFREY
NATIVE SON .... VICTOR LOVE
NATURAL, THE .... BARBARA HERSHEY
NATURAL, THE .... JOE DON BAKER
NATURAL, THE .... KIM BASINGER
NATURAL, THE .... MICHAEL MADSEN
NATURAL, THE .... RICHARD FARNSWORTH
NATURAL, THE .... ROBERT DUVALL
NATURAL, THE .... ROBERT PROSKY
NATURAL, THE .... ROBERT REDFORD
NATURAL, THE .... WILFORD BRIMLEY
NATURAL, THE ○ .... GLENN CLOSE
NATURAL BORN KILLERS .... JACK PALANCE
NATURAL BORN KILLERS .... JULIETTE LEWIS
NATURAL BORN KILLERS .... MARK HARMON
NATURAL BORN KILLERS .... ROBERT DOWNEY JR.
NATURAL BORN KILLERS .... TOMMY LEE JONES
NATURAL BORN KILLERS .... WOODY HARRELSON
NATURAL ENEMIES .... JOSE FERRER†
NATURE OF THE BEAST .... ERIC ROBERTS
NATURE OF THE BEAST .... LANCE HENRIKSEN
NAUGHTY BUT NICE .... RONALD REAGAN
NAVAJO JOE .... BURT REYNOLDS
NAVAJO JOE .... TANYA LOPERT
NAVY BLUE AND GOLD .... JAMES STEWART
NAVY BLUES .... MARTHA RAYE†
NAVY COMES THROUGH, THE .... JACKIE COOPER
NAVY COMES THROUGH, THE .... JANE WYATT
NAVY SEALS .... BILL PAXTON
NAVY SEALS .... CHARLIE SHEEN
NAVY SEALS .... CYRIL O'REILLY
NAVY SEALS .... JOANNE WHALLEY-KILMER
NAVY SEALS .... MICHAEL BIEHN
NAVY SEALS .... RICK ROSSOVICH
NAVY WIFE .... RALPH BELLAMY†
NAZI HUNTER: THE BEATE
   KLARSFELD STORY (TF) .... FARRAH FAWCETT

NAZI HUNTER: THE BEATE
   KLARSFELD STORY (TF) .... TOM CONTI
NAZI HUNTER: THE BEATE
   KLARSFELD STORY (TF) .... VINCENT GAUTHIER
NEAPOLITAN CAROUSEL .... SOPHIA LOREN
NEAR DARK .... ADRIAN PASDAR
NEAR DARK .... BILL PAXTON
NEAR DARK .... JENETTE GOLDSTEIN
NEAR DARK .... JENNY WRIGHT
NEAR DARK .... LANCE HENRIKSEN
NEAR DARK .... TIM THOMERSON
NECESSARY ROUGHNESS .... EVANDER HOLYFIELD
NECESSARY ROUGHNESS .... HARLEY JANE KOZAK
NECESSARY ROUGHNESS .... HECTOR ELIZONDO
NECESSARY ROUGHNESS .... JASON BATEMAN
NECESSARY ROUGHNESS .... KATHY IRELAND
NECESSARY ROUGHNESS .... ROBERT LOGGIA
NECESSARY ROUGHNESS .... SCOTT BAKULA
NECESSARY ROUGHNESS .... SINBAD
NECESSITY (TF) .... HARRIS LASKAWAY
NECESSITY (TF) .... JAMES NAUGHTON
NECESSITY (TF) .... JOHN HEARD
NECESSITY (TF) .... LONI ANDERSON
NECROMANCY .... MICHAEL ONTKEAN
NED BLESSING: THE STORY OF
   MY LIFE AND TIMES (TF) .... BRAD JOHNSON
NED KELLY .... MICK JAGGER
NEEDFUL THINGS .... AMANDA PLUMMER
NEEDFUL THINGS .... BONNIE BEDELIA
NEEDFUL THINGS .... ED HARRIS
NEEDFUL THINGS .... J. T. WALSH
NEEDFUL THINGS .... MAX von SYDOW
NEEDFUL THINGS .... VALRI BROMFIELD
NEFERTITE—REGINA DEL NILO .... VINCENT PRICE†
NEGATIVES .... GLENDA JACKSON
NEIGHBORS .... CATHY MORIARTY
NEIGHBORS .... DAN AYKROYD
NEIGHBORS .... JOHN BELUSHI†
NEIGHBORS .... TIM KAZURINSKY
NEIL SIMON'S BROADWAY
   BOUND (TF) .... ANNE BANCROFT
NEIL SIMON'S LOST
   IN YONKERS .... ROBERT G. MIRANDA
NEIL SIMON'S THE
   SLUGGER'S WIFE .... RANDY QUAID
NEIL SIMON'S THE
   SLUGGER'S WIFE .... REBECCA DE MORNAY
NELL .... JODIE FOSTER
NELL .... LIAM NEESON
NELL .... NATASHA RICHARDSON
NELL .... NICK SEARCY
NELSON AFFAIR, THE .... GLENDA JACKSON
NEMESIS .... DEBORAH SHELTON
NEMESIS .... OLIVIER GRUNER
NEON BIBLE, THE .... DENIS LEARY
NEON BIBLE, THE .... DIANA SCARWID
NEON BIBLE, THE .... GENA ROWLANDS
NEON BIBLE, THE .... JACOB TIERNEY
NEON CEILING, THE (TF) .... LEE GRANT
NEON EMPIRE (CMS) .... JULIE CARMEN
NEON EMPIRE (CMS) .... LINDA FIORENTINO
NEON EMPIRE (CMS) .... MARTIN LANDAU
NEPTUNE FACTOR, THE .... BEN GAZZARA
NEPTUNE FACTOR, THE .... ERNEST BORGNINE
NEPTUNE'S DAUGHTER .... RICARDO MONTALBAN
NERDS: THE NEXT
   GENERATION (TF) .... ROBERT CARRADINE
NEST, THE .... HECTOR ALTERIO
NEST, THE .... LISA LANGLOIS
NETWORK .... ROBERT DUVALL
NETWORK .... WESLEY ADDY
NETWORK .... WILLIAM PRINCE
NETWORK ★ .... WILLIAM HOLDEN†
NETWORK ★★ .... FAYE DUNAWAY
NETWORK ★★ .... PETER FINCH†
NETWORK ○ .... NED BEATTY
NETWORK ○○ .... BEATRICE STRAIGHT
NEVADA .... ROBERT MITCHUM
NEVADA SMITH .... BRIAN KEITH
NEVADA SMITH .... HOWARD DA SILVA†
NEVADA SMITH .... JANET MARGOLIN
NEVADA SMITH .... KARL MALDEN

† after an actor's name denotes deceased.

NEVADA SMITH .... MARTIN LANDAU
NEVADA SMITH .... PAT HINGLE
NEVADA SMITH .... SUZANNE PLESHETTE
NEVER A DULL MOMENT .... DICK VAN DYKE
NEVER A DULL MOMENT .... HENRY SILVA
NEVER CRY WOLF .... BRIAN DENNEHY
NEVER CRY WOLF .... CHARLES MARTIN SMITH
NEVER ENDING STORY, THE .... PATRICIA HAYES
NEVER GIVE AN INCH .... MICHAEL SARRAZIN
NEVER GIVE AN INCH .... PAUL NEWMAN
NEVER PUT IT IN WRITING .... MILO O'SHEA
NEVER PUT IT IN WRITING .... PAT BOONE
NEVER SAY DIE .... BILLY DRAGO
NEVER SAY DIE .... BOB HOPE
NEVER SAY DIE .... GEORGE WENDT
NEVER SAY DIE .... MARTHA RAYE†
NEVER SAY GOODBYE .... CLINT EASTWOOD
NEVER SAY GOODBYE .... ELEANOR PARKER
NEVER SAY GOODBYE .... ROCK HUDSON†
NEVER SAY NEVER AGAIN .... ALEC McCOWEN
NEVER SAY NEVER AGAIN ..... BARBARA CARRERA
NEVER SAY NEVER AGAIN .... KIM BASINGER
NEVER SAY
    NEVER AGAIN .... KLAUS MARIA BRANDAUER
NEVER SAY NEVER AGAIN .... SEAN CONNERY
NEVER SO FEW .... CHARLES BRONSON
NEVER SO FEW .... DEAN JONES
NEVER SO FEW .... FRANK SINATRA
NEVER STEAL
    ANYTHING SMALL .... NEHEMIAH PERSOFF
NEVER STEAL ANYTHING SMALL .... ROYAL DANO
NEVER STEAL
    ANYTHING SMALL .... SHIRLEY JONES
NEVER TO LOVE .... MAUREEN O'HARA
NEVER TOO LATE .... CONNIE STEVENS
NEVER TOO LATE .... HENRY JONES
NEVER TOO LATE .... JANE WYATT
NEVER TOO LATE .... MAUREEN O'SULLIVAN
NEVERENDING STORY II: THE
    NEXT CHAPTER, THE .... ALEXANDRA JOHNES
NEVERENDING STORY II: THE
    NEXT CHAPTER, THE .... CLARISSA BURT
NEVERENDING STORY II: THE
    NEXT CHAPTER, THE .... JONATHAN BRANDIS
NEVERENDING STORY II: THE
    NEXT CHAPTER, THE .... KENNY MORRISON
NEVERENDING
    STORY III, THE .... JASON JAMES RICHTER
NEW ADVENTURES OF PIPPI
    LONGSTOCKING, THE .... CHUB BAILEY
NEW ADVENTURES OF PIPPI
    LONGSTOCKING, THE .... CORY CROW
NEW ADVENTURES OF PIPPI
    LONGSTOCKING, THE .... DAVID SEAMAN JR.
NEW ADVENTURES OF PIPPI
    LONGSTOCKING, THE .... DENNIS DUGAN
NEW ADVENTURES OF PIPPI
    LONGSTOCKING, THE .... DIANNE HULL
NEW ADVENTURES OF PIPPI
    LONGSTOCKING, THE .... DICK VAN PATTEN
NEW ADVENTURES OF PIPPI
    LONGSTOCKING, THE .... EILEEN BRENNAN
NEW ADVENTURES OF PIPPI
    LONGSTOCKING, THE .... GEORGE DICENZO
NEW ADVENTURES OF PIPPI
    LONGSTOCKING, THE .... J. D. DICKINSON
NEW ADVENTURES OF PIPPI
    LONGSTOCKING, THE .... JOHN SCHUCK
NEW ADVENTURES OF PIPPI
    LONGSTOCKING, THE .... TAMI ERIN
NEW AGE, THE .... ADAM WEST
NEW AGE, THE .... BRUCE RAMSAY
NEW AGE, THE .... JOHN DIEHL
NEW AGE, THE .... JUDY DAVIS
NEW AGE, THE .... PATRICK BAUCHAU
NEW AGE, THE .... PETER WELLER
NEW AGE, THE .... RACHEL ROSENTHAL
NEW AGE, THE .... SAMUEL L. JACKSON
NEW CENTURIONS, THE .... ANN RAMSEY†
NEW CENTURIONS, THE .... CLIFTON JAMES
NEW CENTURIONS, THE .... ED LAUTER
NEW CENTURIONS, THE .... ERIK ESTRADA

NEW CENTURIONS, THE .... GEORGE C. SCOTT
NEW CENTURIONS, THE .... JAMES B. SIKKING
NEW CENTURIONS, THE .... JANE ALEXANDER
NEW CENTURIONS, THE .... ROGER E. MOSLEY
NEW CENTURIONS, THE .... ROSALIND CASH
NEW CENTURIONS, THE .... SCOTT WILSON
NEW CENTURIONS, THE .... STACY KEACH
NEW CENTURIONS, THE .... WILLIAM ATHERTON
NEW FACES .... ALICE GHOSTLEY
NEW FACES .... EARTHA KITT
NEW FACES .... PAUL LYNDE†
NEW FACES OF 1937 .... MILTON BERLE
NEW FRONTIER .... JENNIFER JONES
NEW INTERNS, THE .... BARBARA EDEN
NEW INTERNS, THE .... DEAN JONES
NEW INTERNS, THE .... GEORGE SEGAL
NEW INTERNS, THE .... STEFANIE POWERS
NEW INTERNS, THE .... TELLY SAVALAS†
NEW JACK CITY .... BILL NUNN
NEW JACK CITY .... CHRIS ROCK
NEW JACK CITY .... ICE-T
NEW JACK CITY .... JUDD NELSON
NEW JACK CITY .... MARIO VAN PEEBLES
NEW JACK CITY .... VANESSA WILLIAMS
NEW JACK CITY .... WESLEY SNIPES
NEW JERSEY DRIVE .... GABRIEL CASSEUS
NEW JERSEY DRIVE .... SAUL STEIN
NEW JERSEY DRIVE .... SHARON CORLEY
NEW KIDS, THE .... ERIC STOLTZ
NEW KIDS, THE .... JAMES SPADER
NEW KIND OF LOVE, A .... EVA GABOR
NEW KIND OF LOVE, A .... JOANNE WOODWARD
NEW KIND OF LOVE, A .... PAUL NEWMAN
NEW LAND, THE .... LIV ULLMANN
NEW LEAF, A .... ELAINE MAY
NEW LEAF, A .... GEORGE ROSE†
NEW LEAF, A .... JACK WESTON
NEW LEAF, A .... WALTER MATTHAU
NEW LIFE, A .... ALAN ALDA
NEW LIFE, A .... ANN-MARGRET
NEW LIFE, A .... BEATRICE ALDA
NEW LIFE, A .... BILL IRWIN
NEW LIFE, A .... CELIA WESTON
NEW LIFE, A .... FIONA REID
NEW LIFE, A .... HAL LINDEN
NEW LIFE, A .... JOHN KOZAKS
NEW LIFE, A .... JOHN SHEA
NEW LIFE, A .... LYNN VOGT
NEW LIFE, A .... MARY KAY PLACE
NEW LIFE, A .... PAUL HECHT
NEW LIFE, A .... VERONICA HAMEL
NEW MAVERICK, THE (TF) .... JAMES GARNER
NEW MEXICO .... RAYMOND BURR†
NEW ORIGINAL WONDER
    WOMAN, THE (TF) .... RED BUTTONS
NEW YEAR'S DAY .... HENRY JAGLOM
NEW YEAR'S DAY .... GWEN WELLES
NEW YORK CONFIDENTIAL .... ANNE BANCROFT
NEW YORK HAT, THE .... LILLIAN GISH†
NEW YORK, NEW YORK .... BARRY PRIMUS
NEW YORK, NEW YORK .... DIAHNNE ABBOTT
NEW YORK, NEW YORK .... LIONEL STANDER
NEW YORK, NEW YORK .... LIZA MINELLI
NEW YORK, NEW YORK .... MARY KAY PLACE
NEW YORK, NEW YORK .... ROBERT DE NIRO
NEW YORK NIGHTS .... WILLEM DAFOE
NEW YORK STORIES .... CAROLE BOUQUET
NEW YORK STORIES .... CHRIS ELLIOT
NEW YORK STORIES .... DEBORAH HARRY
NEW YORK STORIES .... DON NOVELLO
NEW YORK STORIES .... EDWARD I. KOCH
NEW YORK STORIES .... GIANCARLO GIANNINI
NEW YORK STORIES .... HEATHER McCOMB
NEW YORK STORIES .... JULIE KAVNER
NEW YORK STORIES .... MAE QUESTEL
NEW YORK STORIES .... MIA FARROW
NEW YORK STORIES .... NICK NOLTE
NEW YORK STORIES .... PETER GABRIEL
NEW YORK STORIES .... ROSANNA ARQUETTE
NEW YORK STORIES .... STEVE BUSCEMI
NEW YORK STORIES .... TALIA SHIRE
NEW YORK STORIES .... WOODY ALLEN

NEWMAN'S LAW .... ABE VIGODA
NEWMAN'S LAW .... DAVID SPIELBERG
NEWMAN'S LAW .... GEORGE PEPPARD†
NEWS AT ELEVEN (TF) .... BARBARA BABCOCK
NEWS AT ELEVEN (TF) .... MARTIN SHEEN
NEWSBOYS' HOME .... JACKIE COOPER
NEWSFRONT .... BILL HUNTER
NEWSFRONT .... BRYON BROWN
NEWSIES .... AARON LOHR
NEWSIES .... ANN-MARGRET
NEWSIES .... ARYIE LOWE JR.
NEWSIES .... BILL PULLMAN
NEWSIES .... CHARLES CIOFFI
NEWSIES .... CHRISTIAN BALE
NEWSIES .... DAVID MOSCOW
NEWSIES .... ELE KEATS
NEWSIES .... GABRIEL DAMON
NEWSIES .... KEVIN TIGHE
NEWSIES .... LUKE EDWARDS
NEWSIES .... MARK LOWENTHAL
NEWSIES .... MARTY BELAFSKY
NEWSIES .... MAX CASELLA
NEWSIES .... MICHAEL LERNER
NEWSIES .... ROBERT DUVALL
NEWSIES .... SHON GREENBLATT
NEWSIES .... TREY PARKER
NEXT DOOR (CTF) .... JAMES WOODS
NEXT DOOR (CTF) .... RANDY QUAID
NEXT KARATE KID, THE .... NORIYUKI "PAT" MORITA
NEXT MAN, THE .... SEAN CONNERY
NEXT OF KIN .... ADAM BALDWIN
NEXT OF KIN .... ANDREAS KATSULAS
NEXT OF KIN .... BEN STILLER
NEXT OF KIN .... BILL PAXTON
NEXT OF KIN .... HELEN HUNT
NEXT OF KIN .... LIAM NEESON
NEXT OF KIN .... MICHAEL J. POLLARD
NEXT OF KIN .... PATRICK SWAYZE
NEXT STOP, GREENWICH
    VILLAGE .... ANTONIO FARGAS
NEXT STOP, GREENWICH
    VILLAGE .... CHRISTOPHER WALKEN
NEXT STOP, GREENWICH
    VILLAGE .... ELLEN GREENE
NEXT STOP, GREENWICH
    VILLAGE .... JEFF GOLDBLUM
NEXT STOP, GREENWICH
    VILLAGE .... LOIS SMITH
NEXT STOP, GREENWICH
    VILLAGE .... LOU JACOBI
NEXT STOP, GREENWICH
    VILLAGE .... SHELLEY WINTERS
NEXT TIME WE LOVE .... JAMES STEWART
NEXT VOICE YOU HEAR, THE ..... JAMES WHITMORE
NIAGARA .... MARILYN MONROE†
NIAGRA .... MAX SHOWALTER
NICE GIRL? .... ROBERT STACK
NICE GIRLS DON'T EXPLODE ..... BARBARA HARRIS
NICE GUYS FINISH LAST (TF) .... NED BEATTY
NICE LITTLE BANK THAT SHOULD
    BE ROBBED, A .... DINA MERRILL
NICHOLAS AND ALEXANDRA .... DIANA QUICK
NICHOLAS AND ALEXANDRA .... IAN HOLM
NICHOLAS AND ALEXANDRA .... IRENE WORTH
NICHOLAS AND ALEXANDRA .... JOHN McENERY
NICHOLAS AND ALEXANDRA .... JULIAN GLOVER
NICHOLAS AND ALEXANDRA .... MICHAEL BRYANT
NICHOLAS AND ALEXANDRA .... ROY DOTRICE
NICHOLAS AND ALEXANDRA .... TIMOTHY WEST
NICHoLAS AND ALEXANDRA ★ ...... JANET SUZMAN
NICHOLAS NICKLEBY .... PATRICIA HAYES
NICK KNIGHT (TF) .... MICHAEL NADER
NICK KNIGHT (TF) .... RICK SPRINGFIELD
NICKEL RIDE, THE .... BO HOPKINS
NICKEL RIDE, THE .... JASON MILLER
NICKELODEON .... BRIAN KEITH
NICKELODEON .... BURT REYNOLDS
NICKELODEON .... GEORGE GAYNES
NICKELODEON .... HARRY CAREY JR.
NICKELODEON .... JOHN RITTER
NICKELODEON .... RYAN O'NEAL
NICKELODEON .... STELLA STEVENS

NICKELODEON .... TATUM O'NEAL
NIDO DE VIUDAS .... PATRICIA NEAL
NIGHT, THE .... MARCELLO MASTROIANNI
NIGHT AND DAY .... ALEXIS SMITH†
NIGHT AND DAY .... JANE WYMAN
NIGHT AND THE CITY .... ALAN KING
NIGHT AND THE CITY .... CLIFF GORMAN
NIGHT AND THE CITY .... JACK WARDEN
NIGHT AND THE CITY .... JESSICA LANGE
NIGHT AND THE CITY .... ROBERT DE NIRO
NIGHT AND THE CITY .... RICHARD WIDMARK
NIGHT ANGEL .... DEBRA FEUER
NIGHT ANGEL .... HELEN MARTIN
NIGHT ANGEL .... ISA ANDERSON
NIGHT ANGEL .... KAREN BLACK
NIGHT ANGEL .... LINDEN ASHBY
NIGHT BEFORE, THE .... KEANU REEVES
NIGHT CALLER, THE .... JOHN SAXON
NIGHT CHILD .... JOANNA CASSIDY
NIGHT CREATURE .... ROSS HAGEN
NIGHT CROSSING .... BEAU BRIDGES
NIGHT CROSSING .... GLYNNIS O'CONNOR
NIGHT CROSSING .... IAN BANNEN
NIGHT CROSSING .... JANE ALEXANDER
NIGHT CROSSING .... JOHN HURT
NIGHT DIGGER, THE .... NICHOLAS CLAY
NIGHT DIGGER, THE .... PATRICIA NEAL
NIGHT FIGHTERS, THE .... DAN O'HERLIHY
NIGHT FIGHTERS, THE .... RICHARD HARRIS
NIGHT FIGHTERS, THE .... ROBERT MITCHUM
NIGHT FLIGHT .... HELEN HAYES
NIGHT FULL OF RAIN, A .... CANDICE BERGEN
NIGHT FULL OF RAIN, A .... JILL EIKENBERRY
NIGHT FULL OF RAIN, A .... MICHAEL SARRAZIN
NIGHT GAME .... CARLIN GLYNN
NIGHT GAME .... KAREN YOUNG
NIGHT GAME .... LANE SMITH
NIGHT GAME .... PAUL GLEASON
NIGHT GAME .... RICHARD BRADFORD
NIGHT GAME .... ROY SCHEIDER
NIGHT GAMES (TF) .... ALBERT SALMI†
NIGHT HAIR CHILD .... BRITT EKLAND
NIGHT HAIR CHILD .... MARK LESTER
NIGHT HOLDS TERROR, THE .... VINCE EDWARDS
NIGHT IN HEAVEN, A .... ANDY GARCIA
NIGHT IN HEAVEN, A .... CARRIE SNODGRESS
NIGHT IN HEAVEN, A .... CHRISTOPHER ATKINS
NIGHT IN HEAVEN, A .... LESLEY ANN WARREN
NIGHT IN THE LIFE OF JIMMY
   REARDON, A .... ANN MAGNUSON
NIGHT IN THE LIFE OF JIMMY
   REARDON, A .... IONE SKYE
NIGHT IN THE LIFE OF JIMMY
   REARDON, A .... RIVER PHOENIX†
NIGHT INTO MORNING .... MAC DAVIS
NIGHT IS MY FUTURE .... MAE ZETTERLING†
'NIGHT, MOTHER .... ANNE BANCROFT
'NIGHT, MOTHER .... CAROL ROBBINS
'NIGHT, MOTHER .... CLAIRE MALIS
'NIGHT, MOTHER .... ED BERKE
'NIGHT, MOTHER .... JENNIFER ROOSENDAHL
'NIGHT, MOTHER .... MICHAEL KENWORTHY
'NIGHT, MOTHER .... SARI WALKER
'NIGHT, MOTHER .... SISSY SPACEK
NIGHT MOVES .... GENE HACKMAN
NIGHT MOVES .... HARRIS YULIN
NIGHT MOVES .... JAMES WOODS
NIGHT MOVES .... JENNIFER WARREN
NIGHT MOVES .... KENNETH MARS
NIGHT MOVES .... MELANIE GRIFFITH
NIGHT MOVES .... SUSAN CLARK
NIGHT MUST FALL .... ALBERT FINNEY
NIGHT MUST FALL ★ .... ROBERT MONTGOMERY†
NIGHT MUST FALL ❍ .... DAME MAY WHITTY†
NIGHT MY NUMBER
   CAME UP, THE .... DENHOLM ELLIOTT†
NIGHT MY NUMBER
   CAME UP, THE .... GEORGE ROSE†
NIGHT NURSE .... BARBARA STANWYCK†
NIGHT OF COURAGE (TF) .... BARNARD HUGHES
NIGHT OF COURAGE (TF) ...... DANIEL HUGH KELLY

NIGHT OF
   COURAGE (TF) .... GERALDINE FITZGERALD
NIGHT OF DARK SHADOWS .... KATE JACKSON
NIGHT OF TERROR (TF) .... DONNA MILLS
NIGHT OF TERROR (TF) .... MARTIN BALSAM
NIGHT OF THE BLOOD MONSTER .... MARIA SCHELL
NIGHT OF THE COMET .... ROBERT BELTRAN
NIGHT OF THE DEMONS 2 .... AMELIA KINKADE
NIGHT OF THE DEMONS 2 .... BOBBY JACOBY
NIGHT OF THE DEMONS 2 .... ZOE TRILLING
NIGHT OF THE FOLLOWING
   DAY, THE .... MARLON BRANDO
NIGHT OF THE FOLLOWING
   DAY, THE .... RITA MORENO
NIGHT OF THE
   GENERALS .... CHRISTOPHER PLUMMER
NIGHT OF THE GENERALS .... DONALD PLEASENCE
NIGHT OF THE GENERALS .... OMAR SHARIF
NIGHT OF THE GENERALS .... PETER O'TOOLE
NIGHT OF THE GENERALS .... TOM COURTENAY
NIGHT OF THE
   GENERALS, THE .... GORDAN JACKSON†
NIGHT OF THE GRIZZLY, THE......... CLINT WALKER
NIGHT OF THE HUNTER, THE .... COREY ALLEN
NIGHT OF THE HUNTER, THE .... LILLIAN GISH†
NIGHT OF THE HUNTER, THE .... PETER GRAVES
NIGHT OF THE HUNTER, THE ...... ROBERT MITCHUM
NIGHT OF THE HUNTER, THE .... SHELLEY WINTERS
NIGHT OF THE IGUANA .... AVA GARDNER†
NIGHT OF THE IGUANA .... RICHARD BURTON†
NIGHT OF THE IGUANA, THE .... DEBORAH KERR
NIGHT OF THE IGUANA, THE ❍ .... GRAYSON HALL†
NIGHT OF THE JUGGLER .... CLIFF GORMAN
NIGHT OF THE JUGGLER .... JAMES BROLIN
NIGHT OF THE JUGGLER .... STEVE INWOOD
NIGHT OF THE LEPUS .... JANET LEIGH
NIGHT OF THE LEPUS .... RORY CALHOUN
NIGHT OF THE LEPUS .... STUART WHITMAN
NIGHT OF THE LIVING DEAD .... DUANE JONES†
NIGHT OF THE LIVING DEAD ..... PATRICIA TALLMAN
NIGHT OF THE LIVING DEAD .... TONY TODD
NIGHT OF THE QUARTER MOON .... DEAN JONES
NIGHT OF THE RUNNING MAN .... JOHN GLOVER
NIGHT OF THE RUNNING MAN .... MARCY GOLDMAN
NIGHT OF THE RUNNING MAN .... SCOTT GLENN
NIGHT ON EARTH .... ARMIN MUELLER-STAHL
NIGHT ON EARTH .... GENA ROWLANDS
NIGHT ON EARTH .... WINONA RYDER
NIGHT PASSAGE .... JAMES STEWART
NIGHT PATROL .... BILLY BARTY
NIGHT PATROL .... LINDA BLAIR
NIGHT PEOPLE .... GREGORY PECK
NIGHT PEOPLE .... MAX SHOWALTER
NIGHT PORTER, THE .... CHARLOTTE RAMPLING
NIGHT RIDER, THE (TF) .... GEORGE GRIZZARD
NIGHT SCHOOL .... RACHEL WARD
NIGHT SHIFT .... HENRY WINKLER
NIGHT SHIFT .... KEVIN COSTNER
NIGHT SHIFT .... MICHAEL KEATON
NIGHT SHIFT .... NITA TALBOT
NIGHT SHIFT .... SHELLEY LONG
NIGHT SLAVES (TF) .... LEE GRANT
NIGHT STALKER, THE .... CHARLES NAPIER
NIGHT STALKER, THE (TF) .... CAROL LYNLEY
NIGHT STALKER, THE (TF) .... CLAUDE AKINS†
NIGHT STALKER, THE (TF) ...... DARREN McGAVIN
NIGHT STRANGLER, THE (TF) .... DARREN McGAVIN
NIGHT TERROR (TF) .... VALERIE HARPER
NIGHT THAT PANICKED
   AMERICA, THE (TF) .... CLIFF DE YOUNG
NIGHT THAT PANICKED
   AMERICA, THE (TF) .... EILEEN BRENNAN
NIGHT THAT PANICKED
   AMERICA, THE (TF) .... JOHN RITTER
NIGHT THAT PANICKED
   AMERICA, THE (TF) .... MEREDITH BAXTER
NIGHT THAT PANICKED
   AMERICA, THE (TF) .... TOM BOSLEY
NIGHT THAT PANICKED
   AMERICA, THE (TF) .... WALTER McGINN†
NIGHT THE BRIDGE FELL
   DOWN, THE (TF) .... DESI ARNAZ JR.

NIGHT THE CITY SCREAMED,
   THE (TF) .... GEORG STANFORD BROWN
NIGHT THE CITY
   SCREAMED, THE (TF) .... LINDA PURL
NIGHT THE CITY
   SCREAMED, THE (TF) .... RAYMOND BURR†
NIGHT THE LIGHTS WENT OUT
   IN GEORGIA, THE .... DENNIS QUAID
NIGHT THE LIGHTS WENT OUT
   IN GEORGIA, THE .... KRISTY McNICHOL
NIGHT THE LIGHTS WENT OUT
   IN GEORGIA, THE .... MARK HAMILL
NIGHT THEY RAIDED
   MINSKY'S, THE .... BRITT EKLAND
NIGHT THEY RAIDED
   MINSKY'S, THE .... DENHOLM ELLIOTT†
NIGHT THEY RAIDED
   MINSKY'S, THE .... ELLIOTT GOULD
NIGHT THEY RAIDED
   MINSKY'S, THE .... JASON ROBARDS
NIGHT THEY RAIDED
   MINSKY'S, THE .... JOSEPH WISEMAN
NIGHT THEY SAVED
   CHRISTMAS, THE (TF) .... ART CARNEY
NIGHT THEY SAVED
   CHRISTMAS, THE (TF) .... JACLYN SMITH
NIGHT THEY SAVED
   CHRISTMAS, THE (TF) .... JUNE LOCKHART
NIGHT THEY SAVED
   CHRISTMAS, THE (TF) .... MASON ADAMS
NIGHT THEY TOOK MISS
   BEAUTIFUL, THE (TF) .... CHUCK CONNORS†
NIGHT THEY TOOK MISS
   BEAUTIFUL, THE (TF) .... STELLA STEVENS
NIGHT THEY TOOK MISS
   BEAUTIFUL, THE (TF) .... VICTORIA PRINCIPAL
NIGHT TIDE .... DENNIS HOPPER
NIGHT TO REMEMBER, A .... DAVID McCALLUM
NIGHT TO REMEMBER, A .... GEORGE ROSE†
NIGHT TO REMEMBER, A .... SEAN CONNERY
NIGHT TRAIN TO PARIS .... LESLIE NIELSEN
NIGHT UNTO NIGHT .... RONALD REAGAN
NIGHT VISITOR, THE .... LIV ULLMANN
NIGHT WAITRESS .... ANTHONY QUINN
NIGHT WALK (TF) .... LESLEY-ANNE DOWN
NIGHT WALK (TF) .... ROBERT URICH
NIGHT WALKER, THE ..... BARBARA STANWYCK†
NIGHT WARNING .... SUSAN TYRRELL
NIGHT WATCH .... BILLIE WHITELAW
NIGHT WATCH .... ELIZABETH TAYLOR
NIGHT WE NEVER
   MET, THE .... ANNABELLA SCIORRA
NIGHT WE NEVER
   MET, THE .... JEANNE TRIPPLEHORN
NIGHT WE NEVER MET, THE ...... JUSTINE BATEMAN
NIGHT WE NEVER MET, THE .... KEVIN ANDERSON
NIGHT WE NEVER
   MET, THE .... MATTHEW BRODERICK
NIGHTBREED .... ANNE BOBBY
NIGHTBREED .... CHARLES HAID
NIGHTBREED .... CRAIG SHEFFER
NIGHTBREED .... DAVID CRONENBERG
NIGHTCOMERS, THE .... MARLON BRANDO
NIGHTFALL .... ALEXIS KANNER
NIGHTFALL .... ANDRA MILLIAN
NIGHTFALL .... ANNE BANCROFT
NIGHTFALL .... BRIAN KEITH
NIGHTFALL .... SARAH DOUGLAS
NIGHTFLYERS .... LISA BLOUNT
NIGHTFORCE .... LINDA BLAIR
NIGHTHAWKS .... BILLY DEE WILLIAMS
NIGHTHAWKS ...... CATHERINE MARY STEWART
NIGHTHAWKS .... JOE SPINELL
NIGHTHAWKS .... LINDSAY WAGNER
NIGHTHAWKS .... NIGEL DAVENPORT
NIGHTHAWKS .... PERSIS KHAMBATTA
NIGHTHAWKS .... RUTGER HAUER
NIGHTHAWKS .... SYLVESTER STALLONE
NIGHTINGALE SANG IN
   BERKELEY SQUARE, A .... OLIVER TOBIAS
NIGHTINGALES (TF) .... CHELSEA FIELD
NIGHTKILL .... ROBERT MITCHUM

NIGHTKILL (TF) .... JACLYN SMITH
NIGHTLIFE (CTF) .... BEN CROSS
NIGHTLIFE (CTF) .... MARYAM D'ABO
NIGHTMARE .... KEVIN McCARTHY
NIGHTMARE AT BITTER
   CREEK (TF) .... JOANNA CASSIDY
NIGHTMARE AT BITTER
   CREEK (TF) .... LINDSAY WAGNER
NIGHTMARE HONEYMOON .... PAT HINGLE
NIGHTMARE IN BADHAM
   COUNTY (TF) .... CHUCK CONNORS†
NIGHTMARE IN BADHAM
   COUNTY (TF) .... DEBORAH RAFFIN
NIGHTMARE IN BADHAM
   COUNTY (TF) .... DELLA REESE
NIGHTMARE IN BADHAM
   COUNTY (TF) .... RALPH BELLAMY†
NIGHTMARE IN THE
   DAYLIGHT (TF) .... JACLYN SMITH
NIGHTMARE IN THE SUN .... ROBERT DUVALL
NIGHTMARE IN THE SUN .... URSULA ANDRESS
NIGHTMARE ON ELM STREET, A .... JOHN SAXON
NIGHTMARE ON ELM STREET, A ..... JOHNNY DEPP
NIGHTMARE ON ELM STREET, A .... NICK CORRI
NIGHTMARE ON
   ELM STREET, A .... ROBERT ENGLUND
NIGHTMARE ON ELM STREET 2:
   FREDDY'S REVENGE, A .... CLU GULAGER
NIGHTMARE ON ELM STREET 2:
   FREDDY'S REVENGE, A .... HOPE LANGE
NIGHTMARE ON ELM STREET 2:
   FREDDY'S REVENGE, A .... MARSHALL BELL
NIGHTMARE ON ELM STREET 2:
   FREDDY'S REVENGE, A ...... ROBERT ENGLUND
NIGHTMARE ON ELM STREET 3:
   DREAM WARRIORS, A .... ROBERT ENGLUND
NIGHTMARE ON ELM STREET, PART 3:
   DREAM WARRIORS, A .... DICK CAVETT
NIGHTMARE ON ELM STREET, PART 3:
   DREAM WARRIORS, A .... JENNIFER RUBIN
NIGHTMARE ON ELM STREET,
   PART 3: DREAM
   WARRIORS, A .... LAURENCE FISHBURNE
NIGHTMARE ON ELM STREET 4:
   THE DREAM MASTER, A .... ROBERT ENGLUND
NIGHTMARE ON ELM STREET 5:
   THE DREAM CHILD, A .... LISA WILCOX
NIGHTMARE ON ELM STREET 5:
   THE DREAM CHILD, A .... ROBERT ENGLUND
NIGHTMARE (TF) .... CHUCK CONNORS†
NIGHTMARE (TF) .... PATTY DUKE
NIGHTMARE (TF) .... RICHARD CRENNA
NIGHTMARE YEARS,
   THE (CMS) .... MARTHE KELLER
NIGHTMARE YEARS,
   THE (CMS) .... SAM WATERSTON
NIGHTMARES .... EMILIO ESTEVEZ
NIGHTMARES .... LANCE HENRIKSEN
NIGHTMARES .... MOON ZAPPA
NIGHTMARES .... RICHARD MASUR
NIGHTMARES .... ROBIN GAMMEL
NIGHTMARES .... VERONICA CARTWRIGHT
NIGHTMARES .... WILLIAM SANDERSON
NIGHTS IN A HAREM .... VINCENT PRICE†
NIGHTSTICK .... LESLIE NIELSEN
NIGHTWING .... DAVID WARNER
NIGHTWING .... NICK MANCUSO
NIGHTWING .... STEPHEN MACHT
NIJINSKY .... SIAN PHILLIPS
NIJINSKY .... ALAN BADEL†
NIJINSKY .... ALAN BATES
NIJINSKY .... CARLA FRACCI
NIJINSKY .... COLIN BLAKELY†
NIJINSKY .... GEORGE DE LA PENA
NIJINSKY .... JANET SUZMAN
NIJINSKY .... JEREMY IRONS
NIJINSKY .... LESLIE BROWNE
NINA TAKES A LOVER .... LAURA SAN GIACOMO
NINE DAYS A QUEEN .... JOHN MILLS
NINE GIRLS .... NINA FOCH
NINE GIRLS .... SHELLEY WINTERS
NINE HOURS TO RAMA .... DIANE BAKER
NINE HOURS TO RAMA .... JOSE FERRER†

NINE HOURS TO RAMA .... ROBERT MORLEY
NINE LIVES ARE
   NOT ENOUGH .... RONALD REAGAN
NINE LIVES OF
   ELFEGO BACA, THE (TF) .... ROBERT LOGGIA
NINE MEN .... GORDAN JACKSON†
NINE MONTHS .... JEFF GOLDBLUM
NINE MONTHS .... HUGH GRANT
NINE MONTHS .... JOAN CUSACK
NINE MONTHS .... JULIANNE MOORE
NINE MONTHS .... TOM ARNOLD
NINE TO FIVE .... DABNEY COLEMAN
NINE TO FIVE .... DOLLY PARTON
NINE TO FIVE .... ELIZABETH WILSON
NINE TO FIVE .... HENRY JONES
NINE TO FIVE .... JANE FONDA
NINE TO FIVE ★ .... LILY TOMLIN
NINOTCHKA ★ .... GRETA GARBO†
NINTH CONFIGURATION, THE .... ED FLANDERS
NINTH CONFIGURATION, THE .... JASON MILLER
NINTH CONFIGURATION, THE .... MOSES GUNN
NINTH CONFIGURATION, THE ...... ROBERT LOGGIA
NINTH CONFIGURATION, THE .... SCOTT WILSON
NINTH CONFIGURATION, THE .... STACY KEACH
NO BLADE OF GRASS .... NIGEL DAVENPORT
NO DEPOSIT, NO RETURN .... DARREN McGAVIN
NO DEPOSIT, NO RETURN .... DON KNOTTS
NO DOWN PAYMENT .... JOANNE WOODWARD
NO DOWN PAYMENT .... PAT HINGLE
NO DOWN PAYMENT .... TONY RANDALL
NO DRUMS, NO BUGLES .... MARTIN SHEEN
NO ESCAPE .... ERNIE HUDSON
NO ESCAPE .... IAN McNEICE
NO ESCAPE .... JACK SHEPHERD
NO ESCAPE .... KEVIN DILLON
NO ESCAPE .... KEVIN J. O'CONNOR
NO ESCAPE .... LANCE HENRIKSEN
NO ESCAPE .... MICHAEL LERNER
NO ESCAPE .... RAY LIOTTA
NO ESCAPE .... STUART WILSON
NO FEAR .... MARK WAHLBERG
NO FEAR .... REESE WITHERSPOON
NO FEAR .... WILLIAM PETERSEN
NO FEAR .... ALYSSA MILANO
NO FEAR .... AMY BRENNEMAN
NO GREATER SIN .... LEON AMES
NO HIGHWAY .... JAMES STEWART
NO HIGHWAY IN THE SKY .... JAMES STEWART
NO HOLDS BARRED .... HULK HOGAN
NO HOLDS BARRED .... JOAN SEVERANCE
NO HOLDS BARRED .... KURT FULLER
NO HOLDS BARRED .... TINY LISTER
NO KIDDING .... FRANCESCA ANNIS
NO LEAVE, NO LOVE .... VAN JOHNSON
NO LOVE FOR JOHNNIE .... BILLIE WHITELAW
NO LOVE FOR JOHNNIE .... DONALD PLEASENCE
NO LOVE FOR JOHNNIE .... GEOFFREY KEEN
NO MAN OF HER OWN .... BARBARA STANWYCK†
NO MAN'S LAND .... CHARLIE SHEEN
NO MAN'S LAND .... D. B. SWEENEY
NO MAN'S LAND .... JENNY GAGO
NO MAN'S LAND .... RANDY QUAID
NO MERCY .... GARY BASARABA
NO MERCY .... GEORGE DZUNDZA
NO MERCY .... JEROEN KRABBE
NO MERCY .... KIM BASINGER
NO MERCY .... RICHARD GERE
NO MERCY .... TERRY KINNEY
NO MERCY .... WILLIAM ATHERTON
NO MINOR VICES .... BEAU BRIDGES
NO MINOR VICES .... JANE WYATT
NO MINOR VICES .... LOUIS JOURDAN
NO MINOR VICES .... NORMAN LLOYD
NO MORE LADIES .... JOAN CRAWFORD†
NO NUKES (FD) .... JANE FONDA
NO PLACE LIKE HOME (TF) .... CHRISTINE LAHTI
NO PLACE LIKE HOME (TF) .... JEFF DANIELS
NO PLACE TO HIDE .... SYLVESTER STALLONE
NO PLACE TO HIDE (TF) .... MARIETTE HARTLEY
NO PLACE TO LAND .... JOHN IRELAND
NO RESTING PLACE .... MICHAEL GOUGH
NO RETREAT,
   NO SURRENDER II .... CYNTHIA ROTHROCK

NO ROAD BACK .... SEAN CONNERY
NO ROOM FOR THE GROOM .... PIPER LAURIE
NO ROOM FOR THE GROOM .... TONY CURTIS
NO SMALL AFFAIR .... DEMI MOORE
NO TIME FOR BREAKFAST .... ISABELLE HUPPERT
NO TIME FOR COMEDY .... JAMES STEWART
NO TIME FOR SERGEANTS .... ANDY GRIFFITH
NO TIME FOR SERGEANTS .... DON KNOTTS
NO TIME TO BE YOUNG .... ROBERT VAUGHN
NO TIME TO KILL .... JOHN IRELAND
NO TREES IN THE STREET .... DAVID HEMMINGS
NO WAY BACK .... FRED WILLIAMSON
NO WAY BACK .... LILA KEDROVA
NO WAY OUT .... DAVID PAYMER
NO WAY OUT .... GENE HACKMAN
NO WAY OUT .... HOWARD DUFF†
NO WAY OUT .... KEVIN COSTNER
NO WAY OUT .... MATTHEW BARRY
NO WAY OUT .... OSSIE DAVIS
NO WAY OUT .... RICHARD WIDMARK
NO WAY OUT .... RUBY DEE
NO WAY OUT .... SEAN YOUNG
NO WAY OUT .... SIDNEY POITIER
NO WAY OUT .... WILL PATTON
NO WAY TO TREAT A LADY .... EILEEN HECKART
NO WAY TO TREAT A LADY .... GEORGE SEGAL
NO WAY TO TREAT A LADY .... ROD STEIGER
NOBLE HOUSE (MS) .... BEN MASTERS
NOBLE HOUSE (MS) .... DEBORAH RAFFIN
NOBLE HOUSE (MS) .... PIERCE BROSNAN
NOBODY LIVES
   FOREVER .... GERALDINE FITZGERALD
NOBODY RUNS
   FOREVER .... CHRISTOPHER PLUMMER
NOBODY WAVED GOODBYE .... JOHN VERNON
NOBODY'S CHILD (TF) .... CAROLINE KAVA
NOBODY'S CHILD (TF) .... KATHY BAKER
NOBODY'S CHILD (TF) .... MARLO THOMAS
NOBODY'S CHILD (TF) .... RAY BAKER
NOBODY'S CHILDREN (CTF) .... ANN-MARGRET
NOBODY'S FOOL .... BRUCE WILLIS
NOBODY'S FOOL .... JESSICA TANDY†
NOBODY'S FOOL .... MELANIE GRIFFITH
NOBODY'S FOOL .... PAUL NEWMAN
NOBODY'S FOOL .... CHARLIE BARNETT
NOBODY'S FOOL .... ERIC ROBERTS
NOBODY'S FOOL .... LEWIS ARQUETTE
NOBODY'S FOOL .... LOUISE FLETCHER
NOBODY'S FOOL .... ROSANNA ARQUETTE
NOBODY'S FOOL .... STEPHEN TOBOLOWSKY
NOBODY'S PERFECT .... CHAD LOWE
NOBODY'S PERFECT .... DOUG McCLURE
NOBODY'S PERFECT .... GAIL O'GRADY
NOBODY'S PERFECT .... JAMES SHIGETA
NOBODY'S PERFECT .... KIM FLOWERS
NOBODY'S PERFECT .... PATRICK BREEN
NOBODY'S PERFECT .... ROBERT VAUGHN
NOBODY'S PERFEKT .... ALEXIS KARRAS
NOBODY'S PERFEKT .... SUSAN CLARK
NOCTURNA .... YVONNE DE CARLO
NOISES OFF .... CAROL BURNETT
NOISES OFF .... CHRISTOPHER REEVE
NOISES OFF .... DENHOLM ELLIOTT†
NOISES OFF .... JOHN RITTER
NOISES OFF .... JULIE HAGERTY
NOISES OFF .... MARILU HENNER
NOISES OFF .... MARK LINN-BAKER
NOISES OFF .... MICHAEL CAINE
NOISES OFF .... NICOLLETTE SHERIDAN
NOMADS .... ADAM ANT
NOMADS .... LESLEY-ANNE DOWN
NOMADS .... PIERCE BROSNAN
NONE BUT THE BRAVE .... CLINT WALKER
NONE BUT THE BRAVE .... FRANK SINATRA
NONE BUT THE BRAVE .... TONY BILL
NONE BUT THE LONELY HEART .... JANE WYATT
NONE BUT THE
   LONELY HEART ★ .... CARY GRANT†
NONE BUT THE
   LONELY HEART ○○ .... ETHEL BARRYMORE†
NOOSE, THE ★ ...... RICHARD BARTHELMESS†
NORLISS TAPES, THE (TF) .... ANGIE DICKINSON

This is not a list of every film ever made or every cast member, only those listed in this directory.

NORLISS TAPES, THE (TF) .... HURD HATFIELD
NORMA RAE .... BEAU BRIDGES
NORMA RAE .... GAIL STRICKLAND
NORMA RAE .... LONNY CHAPMAN
NORMA RAE .... PAT HINGLE
NORMA RAE .... RON LEIBMAN
NORMA RAE ★★ .... SALLY FIELD
NORMAN...IS THAT YOU? .... REDD FOXX†
NORMAN LOVES ROSE .... CAROL KANE
NORMAN ROCKWELL'S 'BREAKING
    HOME TIES' (TF) .... DOUG McKEON
NORMAN ROCKWELL'S 'BREAKING
    HOME TIES' (TF) .... EVA MARIE SAINT
NORMAN ROCKWELL'S 'BREAKING
    HOME TIES' (TF) .... JASON ROBARDS
NOROIT .... GERALDINE CHAPLIN
NORSEMAN, THE .... LEE MAJORS
NORSEMEN, THE .... MEL FERRER
NORTH .... ABE VIGODA
NORTH .... ALAN ARKIN
NORTH .... ALANA AUSTIN
NORTH .... ALEXANDER GODUNOV
NORTH .... BRUCE WILLIS
NORTH .... DAN AYKROYD
NORTH .... ELIJAH WOOD
NORTH .... FAITH FORD
NORTH .... GRAHAM GREENE
NORTH .... JASON ALEXANDER
NORTH .... JOHN RITTER
NORTH .... JON LOVITZ
NORTH .... JULIA LOUIS-DREYFUSS
NORTH .... KATHY BATES
NORTH .... KELLY McGILLIS
NORTH .... KEONE YOUNG
NORTH .... MATTHEW McCURLEY
NORTH .... REBA McENTIRE
NORTH .... RICHARD BELZER
NORTH .... ROBERT COSTANZO
NORTH AND SOUTH (MS) .... ANTHONY ZERBE
NORTH AND SOUTH (MS) .... DAVID CARRADINE
NORTH AND SOUTH,
    SOUTH (MS) .... GEORG STANFORD BROWN
NORTH AND SOUTH (MS) .... JAMES READ
NORTH AND SOUTH (MS) .... KIRSTIE ALLEY
NORTH AND SOUTH (MS) .... LESLEY-ANNE DOWN
NORTH AND SOUTH (MS) .... PATRICK SWAYZE
NORTH AND SOUTH,
    BOOK II (MS) .... JAMES STEWART
NORTH AND SOUTH,
    BOOK II (MS) .... KIRSTIE ALLEY
NORTH AND SOUTH,
    BOOK II (MS) .... PATRICK SWAYZE
NORTH AVENUE
    IRREGULARS, THE .... BARBARA HARRIS
NORTH AVENUE
    IRREGULARS, THE .... CLORIS LEACHMAN
NORTH AVENUE
    IRREGULARS, THE .... EDWRAD HERRMANN
NORTH AVENUE
    IRREGULARS, THE .... JOAN HACKETT†
NORTH AVENUE
    IRREGULARS, THE .... KAREN VALENTINE
NORTH AVENUE
    IRREGULARS, THE .... MICHAEL CONSTANTINE
NORTH AVENUE
    IRREGULARS, THE .... SUSAN CLARK
NORTH BEACH AND
    RAWHIDE (MS) .... CONCHATA FERRELL
NORTH BEACH AND
    RAWHIDE (MS) .... TATE DONOVAN
NORTH BEACH AND
    RAWHIDE (MS) .... WILLIAM SHATNER
NORTH BY NORTHWEST .... CARY GRANT†
NORTH BY NORTHWEST .... EVA MARIE SAINT
NORTH BY NORTHWEST .... JAMES MASON†
NORTH BY NORTHWEST .... MARTIN LANDAU
NORTH DALLAS FORTY .... BO SVENSON
NORTH DALLAS FORTY .... CHARLES DURNING
NORTH DALLAS FORTY .... DABNEY COLEMAN
NORTH DALLAS FORTY .... DAYLE HADDON
NORTH DALLAS FORTY .... MAC DAVIS
NORTH DALLAS FORTY .... NICK NOLTE

NORTH DALLAS FORTY .... STEVE FORREST
NORTH SEA HIJACK .... ANTHONY PERKINS†
NORTH SEA HIJACK .... DAVID HEDISON
NORTH SEA HIJACK .... ROGER MOORE
NORTH SHORE .... MATT ADLER
NORTH TO ALASKA .... KATHLEEN FREEMAN
NORTH WEST FRONTIER .... LAUREN BACALL
NORWOOD .... CAROL LYNLEY
NORWOOD .... DOM DeLUISE
NORWOOD .... JOE NAMATH
NORWOOD .... KIM DARBY
NORWOOD .... PAT HINGLE
NOSFERATU THE VAMPYRE .... ISABELLE ADJANI
NOSFERATU THE VAMPYRE .... KLAUS KINSKI†
NOSFERATU THE VAMPYRE .... BRUNO GANZ
NOSTRADAMUS .... AMANDA PLUMMER
NOSTRADAMUS .... ANTHONY HIGGINS
NOSTRADAMUS .... ASSUMPTA SERNA
NOSTRADAMUS .... DIANA QUICK
NOSTRADAMUS .... F. MURRAY ABRAHAM
NOSTRADAMUS .... JULIA ORMOND
NOSTRADAMUS .... MAJA MORGENSTERN
NOSTRADAMUS .... MICHAEL GOUGH
NOSTRADAMUS .... RUTGER HAUER
NOSTRADAMUS .... TCHEKY KARYO
NOT A PENNY MORE, NOT A
    PENNY LESS (CMS) .... ED ASNER
NOT A PENNY MORE, NOT A
    PENNY LESS (CMS) .... ED BEGLEY JR.
NOT A PENNY MORE, NOT A
    PENNY LESS (CMS) .... MARYAM D'ABO
NOT A PRETTY PICTURE ....AMY WRIGHT
NOT AS A STRANGER .... FRANK SINATRA
NOT AS A STRANGER .... HARRY MORGAN
NOT AS A STRANGER .... OLIVIA DE HAVILLAND
NOT AS A STRANGER .... ROBERT MITCHUM
NOT FOR PUBLICATION .... DAVID NAUGHTON
NOT FOR PUBLICATION .... NANCY ALLEN
NOT FOR PUBLICATION .... PAUL BARTEL
NOT MY KID (TF) .... ANDREW ROBINSON
NOT MY KID (TF) .... GARY BAYER
NOT MY KID (TF) .... GEORGE SEGAL
NOT MY KID (TF) .... STOCKARD CHANNING
NOT MY KID (TF) ....VERONICA CARTWRIGHT
NOT OF THIS EARTH .... DICK MILLER
NOT OF THIS EARTH .... TRACI LORDS
NOT QUITE JERUSALEM .... SELINA CADRELL
NOT QUITE JERUSALEM .... TODD GRAFF
NOT QUITE PARADISE .... SELINA CADRELL
NOT QUITE PARADISE .... TODD GRAFF
NOT WITH MY WIFE YOU DON'T! .... BOB HOPE
NOT WITH MY WIFE
    YOU DON'T! .... CARROLL O'CONNOR
NOT WITH MY WIFE
    YOU DON'T! .... GEORGE C. SCOTT
NOT WITH MY WIFE YOU DON'T! .... TONY CURTIS
NOT WITHOUT MY DAUGHTER ..... ALFRED MOLINA
NOT WITHOUT MY DAUGHTER .... ROSHAN SETH
NOT WITHOUT MY DAUGHTER .... SALLY FIELD
NOT WITHOUT
    MY DAUGHTER .... SHEILA ROSENTHAL
NOTHING BUT A MAN .... MOSES GUNN
NOTHING BUT A MAN .... YAPHET KOTTO
NOTHING BUT THE BEST .... ALAN BATES
NOTHING BUT THE BEST .... DENHOLM ELLIOTT†
NOTHING BUT THE TRUTH .... BOB HOPE
NOTHING BUT TROUBLE .... CHEVY CHASE
NOTHING BUT TROUBLE .... DAN AYKROYD
NOTHING BUT TROUBLE .... DEMI MOORE
NOTHING BUT TROUBLE ....JOHN CANDY†
NOTHING BUT TROUBLE .... TAYLOR NEGRON
NOTHING BUT TROUBLE .... VALRI BROMFIELD
NOTHING IN COMMON .... SELA WARD
NOTHING IN COMMON .... BARRY CORBIN
NOTHING IN COMMON .... BESS ARMSTRONG
NOTHING IN COMMON .... CONRAD JANIS
NOTHING IN COMMON .... EVA MARIE SAINT
NOTHING IN COMMON .... HECTOR ELIZONDO
NOTHING IN COMMON .... JACKIE GLEASON†
NOTHING IN COMMON .... TOM HANKS
NOTHING LASTS FOREVER .... BILL MURRAY

NOTHING LASTS FOREVER .... DAN AYKROYD
NOTHING LASTS FOREVER .... EDDIE FISHER
NOTHING LASTS FOREVER .... IMOGENE COCA
NOTHING LASTS FOREVER .... JOHN CANDY†
NOTHING LASTS FOREVER .... MORT SAHL
NOTHING LASTS FOREVER .... ZACH GALLIGAN
NOTHING PERSONAL .... DABNEY COLEMAN
NOTHING PERSONAL .... DONALD SUTHERLAND
NOTHING PERSONAL .... LAWRENCE DANE
NOTHING PERSONAL .... ROSCOE LEE BROWNE
NOTHING PERSONAL .... SAUL RUBINEK
NOTHING PERSONAL .... SUZANNE SOMERS
NOTORIOUS .... CARY GRANT†
NOTORIOUS .... INGRID BERGMAN†
NOTORIOUS ✪ .... CLAUDE RAINS†
NOTORIOUS LANDLADY, THE .... JACK LEMMON
NOTORIOUS LANDLADY, THE .... KIM NOVAK
NOTRE DAME DE PARIS .... ANTHONY QUINN
NOVEMBER PLAN, THE .... MEREDITH BAXTER
NOW AND FOREVER .... CHERYL LADD
NOW, VOYAGER .... MARY WICKES
NOW, VOYAGER ★ .... BETTE DAVIS†
NOW, VOYAGER ✪ .... DAME GLADYS COOPER†
NOW YOU SEE HIM,
    NOW YOU DON'T .... ED BEGLEY JR.
NOW YOU SEE HIM,
    NOW YOU DON'T .... KURT RUSSELL
NOW YOU SEE HIM,
    NOW YOU DON'T .... WILLIAM WINDOM
NOW YOU SEE IT,
    NOW YOU DON'T (TF) .... STEVE ALLEN
NOWHERE TO GO .... MAGGIE SMITH
NOWHERE TO HIDE .... AMY MADIGAN
NOWHERE TO HIDE .... MICHAEL IRONSIDE
NOWHERE TO RUN .... JEAN-CLAUDE VAN DAMME
NOWHERE TO RUN .... KIERAN CULKIN
NOWHERE TO RUN .... ROSANNA ARQUETTE
NOWHERE TO RUN (TF) .... LINDA EVANS
NUDE BOMB, THE .... DON ADAMS
NUDE BOMB, THE .... NORMAN LLOYD
NUDE BOMB, THE .... SYLVIA KRISTEL
NUMBER ONE .... BRUCE DERN
NUMBER ONE .... CHARLTON HESTON
NUMBER ONE .... DIANA MULDAUR
NUMBER ONE .... JESSICA WALTER
NUMBER ONE WITH
    A BULLET .... BILLY DEE WILLIAMS
NUMBER ONE WITH
    A BULLET .... MYKELTI WILLIAMSON
NUMBER ONE WITH A BULLET .... PETER GRAVES
NUMBER ONE WITH
    A BULLET .... ROBERT CARRADINE
NUN'S STORY, THE .... COLLEEN DEWHURST†
NUNS ON THE RUN .... ERIC IDLE
NUNS ON THE RUN .... JANET SUZMAN
NUNS ON THE RUN .... ROBBIE COLTRANE
NUN'S STORY, THE .... DEAN JAGGER†
NUN'S STORY, THE .... EDITH EVANS†
NUN'S STORY, THE .... MILDRED DUNNOCK†
NUN'S STORY, THE .... PEGGY ASHCROFT†
NUN'S STORY, THE .... PETER FINCH†
NUN'S STORY, THE ★ .... AUDREY HEPBURN†
NUOVO CINEMA PARADISO .... ANTONELLA ATTILI
NUOVO CINEMA PARADISO .... JACQUES PERRIN
NUOVO CINEMA PARADISO .... PUPELLA MAGGIO
NUOVO CINEMA PARADISO ..... SALVATORE CASCIO
NUTCRACKER .... FINOLA HUGHES
NUTCRACKER .... JOAN COLLINS
NUTCRACKER .... PAUL NICHOLAS
NUTCRACKER: MONEY, MADNESS
    AND MURDER (MS) .... DAVID AYKROYD
NUTCRACKER: MONEY, MADNESS
    AND MURDER (MS) .... G. D. SPRADLIN
NUTCRACKER: MONEY, MADNESS
    AND MURDER (MS) .... JOHN GLOVER
NUTCRACKER: MONEY, MADNESS
    AND MURDER (MS) .... LINDA KELSEY
NUTCRACKER: MONEY, MADNESS
    AND MURDER (MS) .... TATE DONOVAN
NUTCRACKER: MONEY, MADNESS
    AND MURDER (MS) .... TONY MUSANTE

† after an actor's name denotes deceased.

NUTCRACKER PRINCE, THE (AF) ... KIEFER SUTHERLAND
NUTCRACKER PRINCE, THE (AF) ... MEGAN POTTER FOLLOWS
NUTCRACKER PRINCE, THE (AF) ... MIKE MacDONALD
NUTCRACKER PRINCE, THE (AF) ... PETER BORETSKI
NUTCRACKER PRINCE, THE (AF) ... PETER O'TOOLE
NUTCRACKER PRINCE, THE (AF) ... PHYLLIS DILLER
NUTCRACKER: THE MOTION PICTURE ... HUGH BIGNEY
NUTCRACKER: THE MOTION PICTURE ... JULIE HARRIS
NUTCRACKER: THE MOTION PICTURE ... PATRICIA BARKER
NUTCRACKER: THE MOTION PICTURE ... RUSSELL BURNETT
NUTS ... BARBRA STREISAND
NUTS ... KARL MALDEN
NUTS ... LESLIE NIELSEN
NUTS ... RICHARD DREYFUSS
NUTTY PROFESSOR, THE (1995) ... EDDIE MURPHY
NUTTY PROFESSOR, THE ... JERRY LEWIS
NUTTY PROFESSOR, THE ... KATHLEEN FREEMAN
NUTTY PROFESSOR, THE ... STELLA STEVENS
NYBYGGARNA ... LIV ULLMANN

O

O.C. AND STIGGS ... DENNIS HOPPER
O.C. AND STIGGS ... PAUL DOOLEY
O.C. AND STIGGS ... RAY WALSTON
O. HENRY'S FULL HOUSE ... RICHARD WIDMARK
O LUCKY MAN! ... HELEN MIRREN
O LUCKY MAN! ... MALCOLM McDOWELL
O LUCKY MAN! ... RACHEL ROBERTS†
O PIONEERS! (TF) ... DAVID STRATHAIRN
O PIONEERS! (TF) ... JESSICA LANGE
O.S.S. ... GERALDINE FITZGERALD
OBJECT OF BEAUTY, THE ... ANDIE MacDOWELL
OBJECT OF BEAUTY, THE ... JOHN MALKOVICH
OBJECT OF BEAUTY, THE ... JOSS ACKLAND
OBJECT OF BEAUTY, THE ... LOLITA DAVIDOVICH
OBJECT OF BEAUTY, THE ... PETER RIEGERT
OBJECT OF BEAUTY, THE ... RUDI DAVIES
OBJECTIVE BURMA ... WILLIAM PRINCE
OBLONG BOX, THE ... VINCENT PRICE†
OBSESSED, THE ... GERALDINE FITZGERALD
OBSESSED WITH A MARRIED WOMAN (TF) ... JANE SEYMOUR
OBSESSED WITH A MARRIED WOMAN (TF) ... RICHARD MASUR
OBSESSED WITH A MARRIED WOMAN (TF) ... TIM MATHESON
OBSESSION ... CLIFF ROBERTSON
OBSESSION ... GENEVIEVE BUJOLD
OBSESSION ... JOHN LITHGOW
OBSESSIVE LOVE (TF) ... SIMON MacCORKINDALE
OCCHIO DEL GATTO ... ELI WALLACH
OCEANS OF FIRE (TF) ... DAVID CARRADINE
OCEANS OF FIRE (TF) ... GREGORY HARRISON
OCEAN'S 11 ... SHIRLEY MacLAINE
OCEAN'S ELEVEN ... AKIM TAMIROFF†
OCEAN'S ELEVEN ... ANGIE DICKINSON
OCEAN'S ELEVEN ... DEAN MARTIN
OCEAN'S ELEVEN ... FRANK SINATRA
OCEAN'S ELEVEN ... JOEY BISHOP
OCEAN'S ELEVEN ... NORMAN FELL
OCEAN'S ELEVEN ... PETER LAWFORD†
OCEAN'S ELEVEN ... RICHARD CONTE†
OCEAN'S ELEVEN ... SAMMY DAVIS JR.†
OCTOBER MAN, THE ... JOHN MILLS
OCTOPUSSY ... DESMOND LLEWELYN
OCTOPUSSY ... KABIR BEDI
OCTOPUSSY ... KRISTINA WAYBORN
OCTOPUSSY ... LOIS MAXWELL
OCTOPUSSY ... LOUIS JOURDAN
OCTOPUSSY ... MAUD ADAMS
OCTOPUSSY ... ROGER MOORE
OCTOPUSSY ... STEVEN BERKOFF
OCTOPUSSY ... VIJAY ARMITRAJ
ODD BIRDS ... MICHAEL MORIARTY
ODD COUPLE, THE ... HERB EDELMAN
ODD COUPLE, THE ... JACK LEMMON
ODD COUPLE, THE ... JOHN FIELDLER
ODD COUPLE, THE ... WALTER MATTHAU
ODD JOB, THE ... DIANA QUICK
ODD MAN OUT ... DAN O'HERLIHY
ODDS AGAINST TOMORROW ... SHELLEY WINTERS
ODE TO BILLY JOE ... GLYNNIS O'CONNOR
ODE TO BILLY JOE ... ROBBY BENSON
ODESSA FILE, THE ... DEREK JACOBI
ODESSA FILE, THE ... JON VOIGHT
ODESSA FILE, THE ... MARIA SCHELL
ODESSA FILE, THE ... MAXIMILIAN SCHELL
ODETTE ... PETER USTINOV
OEDIPUS THE KING ... CHRISTOPHER PLUMMER
OEDIPUS THE KING ... DONALD SUTHERLAND
OF FLESH AND BLOOD ... ANOUK AIMEE
OF HUMAN BONDAGE ... ALEXIS SMITH†
OF HUMAN BONDAGE ... BETTE DAVIS†
OF HUMAN BONDAGE ... ELEANOR PARKER
OF HUMAN BONDAGE ... JACK HEDLEY
OF HUMAN BONDAGE ... KIM NOVAK
OF HUMAN BONDAGE ... LESLIE HOWARD†
OF HUMAN BONDAGE ... ROBERT MORLEY
OF HUMAN HEARTS ... JAMES STEWART
OF HUMAN HEARTS ✪ ... BEULAH BONDI†
OF LIFE AND LUST ... MAE ZETTERLING†
OF MICE AND MEN ... BURGESS MEREDITH
OF MICE AND MEN ... CASEY SIEMASZKO
OF MICE AND MEN ... GARY SINISE
OF MICE AND MEN ... JOE MORTON
OF MICE AND MEN ... JOHN MALKOVICH
OF MICE AND MEN ... JOHN TERRY
OF MICE AND MEN ... RAY WALSTON
OF MICE AND MEN ... SHERILYN FENN
OF MICE AND MEN (TF) ... RANDY QUAID
OF MICE AND MEN (TF) ... ROBERT BLAKE
OF UNKNOWN ORIGIN ... ALEX HYDE-WHITE
OF UNKNOWN ORIGIN ... DON STROUD
OF UNKNOWN ORIGIN ... LAWRENCE DANE
OF UNKNOWN ORIGIN ... MELANIE SHATNER
OF UNKNOWN ORIGIN ... RODDY McDOWALL
OF UNKNOWN ORIGIN ... RODGER HALLSTON
OFF AND RUNNING ... CYNDI LAUPER
OFF AND RUNNING ... DAVID KEITH
OFF BEAT ... AMY WRIGHT
OFF BEAT ... CLEAVANT DERRICKS
OFF BEAT ... FRED GWYNNE†
OFF BEAT ... HARVEY KEITEL
OFF BEAT ... JACQUES D'AMBOISE
OFF BEAT ... JAMES TOLKAN
OFF BEAT ... JOHN TURTURRO
OFF BEAT ... JULIE BOYASSO†
OFF BEAT ... MEG TILLY
OFF BEAT ... PENN JILLETTE
OFF BEAT ... VICTOR ARGO
OFF LIMITS ... AMANDA PAYS
OFF LIMITS ... BOB HOPE
OFF LIMITS ... FRED WARD
OFF LIMITS ... GREGORY HINES
OFF LIMITS ... SCOTT GLENN
OFF LIMITS ... WILLEM DAFOE
OFF SIDES (TF) ... PATRICK SWAYZE
OFF THE WALL ... ROSANNA ARQUETTE
OFFBEAT ... JOHN MEILLON
OFFBEAT ... MAE ZETTERLING†
OFFENCE, THE ... IAN BANNEN
OFFENCE, THE ... SEAN CONNERY
OFFICER AND A GENTLEMAN, AN ... DAVID KEITH
OFFICER AND A GENTLEMAN, AN ... LISA BLOUNT
OFFICER AND A GENTLEMAN, AN ... RICHARD GERE
OFFICER AND A GENTLEMAN, AN ... ROBERT LOGGIA
OFFICER AND A GENTLEMAN, AN ★ ... DEBRA WINGER
OFFICER AND A GENTLEMAN, AN ✪✪ ... LOUIS GOSSETT JR.
OFFICIAL STORY, THE ... ANALIA CASTRO
OFFICIAL STORY, THE ... CHUNCHUNA VILLAFANE
OFFICIAL STORY, THE ... HECTOR ALTERIO
OFFICIAL STORY, THE ... NORMA ALEANDRO
OFFICIAL STORY, THE ... PATRICIO CONTRERAS
OH! ALFIE ... JOAN COLLINS
OH DAD, POOR DAD, MAMA'S HUNG YOU IN THE CLOSET AND I'M FEELING SO SAD ... BARBARA HARRIS
OH DAD, POOR DAD, MAMA'S HUNG YOU IN THE CLOSET AND I'M FEELING SO SAD ... JONATHAN WINTERS
OH, GOD! ... BARNARD HUGHES
OH, GOD! ... CARL REINER
OH, GOD! ... DAVID OGDEN STIERS
OH, GOD! ... DINAH SHORE†
OH, GOD! ... DONALD PLEASENCE
OH, GOD! ... GEORGE BURNS
OH, GOD! ... JEFF COREY
OH, GOD! ... JOHN DENVER
OH, GOD! ... PAUL SORVINO
OH, GOD! ... RALPH BELLAMY†
OH, GOD! ... TERI GARR
OH, GOD! ... WILLIAM DANIELS
OH, GOD! BOOK II ... CONRAD JANIS
OH, GOD! BOOK II ... GEORGE BURNS
OH, GOD! BOOK II ... SUZANNE PLESHETTE
OH, GOD! YOU DEVIL ... BRANDY GOLD
OH, GOD! YOU DEVIL ... GEORGE BURNS
OH, GOD! YOU DEVIL ... TED WASS
OH, HEAVENLY DOG ... CHEVY CHASE
OH, HEAVENLY DOG! ... OMAR SHARIF
OH, HEAVENLY DOG! ... ROBERT MORLEY
OH, MEN! OH, WOMEN! ... TONY RANDALL
OH, ROSALINDA! ... MEL FERRER
OH! WHAT A LOVELY WAR ... IAN HOLM
OH! WHAT A LOVELY WAR ... JANE SEYMOUR
OH! WHAT A LOVELY WAR ... JEAN-PIERRE CASSEL
OH! WHAT A LOVELY WAR ... JOHN GIELGUD
OH! WHAT A LOVELY WAR ... MAGGIE SMITH
OH! WHAT A LOVELY WAR ... SUSANNAH YORK
OH! WHAT A LOVELY WAR ... VANESSA REDGRAVE
OHMS ... JOHN MILLS
OIL ... STUART WHITMAN
OIL ... WOODY STRODE
OIL AND WATER ... LILLIAN GISH†
OK CONNERY ... LOIS MAXWELL
OKAY AMERICA ... MAUREEN O'SULLIVAN
OKLAHOMA! ... CHARLOTTE GREENWOOD†
OKLAHOMA! ... EDDIE ALBERT
OKLAHOMA! ... GLORIA GRAHAME†
OKLAHOMA! ... GORDON MACRAE†
OKLAHOMA! ... JAMES WHITMORE
OKLAHOMA! ... JAY C. FLIPPEN†
OKLAHOMA! ... ROD STEIGER
OKLAHOMA! ... SHIRLEY JONES
OKLAHOMA CITY DOLLS, THE (TF) ... SUSAN BLAKELY
OKLAHOMA CRUDE ... FAYE DUNAWAY
OKLAHOMA CRUDE ... GEORGE C. SCOTT
OKLAHOMA CRUDE ... JACK PALANCE
OKLAHOMA CRUDE ... JOHN MILLS
OKLAHOMAN, THE ... BARBARA HALE
OLD ACQUAINTANCE ... BETTE DAVIS†
OLD BILL AND SON ... JOHN MILLS
OLD BOYFRIENDS ... BUCK HENRY
OLD BOYFRIENDS ... DAVID CARRADINE
OLD BOYFRIENDS ... JOHN BELUSHI†
OLD BOYFRIENDS ... KEITH CARRADINE
OLD BOYFRIENDS ... RICHARD JORDAN†
OLD BOYFRIENDS ... TALIA SHIRE
OLD CLOTHES ... JOAN CRAWFORD†
OLD CURIOSITY SHOP, THE ... BRIAN GLOVER
OLD CURIOSITY SHOP, THE ... DAVID HEMMINGS
OLD DARK HOUSE, THE ... ROBERT MORLEY
OLD DARK HOUSE, THE ... TOM POSTON
OLD ENOUGH ... DANNY AIELLO
OLD ENOUGH ... FRAN BRILL
OLD ENOUGH ... NEILL BARRY
OLD ENOUGH ... RAINBOW HARVEST
OLD ENOUGH ... ROXANNE HART
OLD ENOUGH ... SARAH BOYD
OLD ENOUGH ... SUSAN KINGSLEY

This is not a list of every film ever made or every cast member, only those listed in this directory.

OLD FRIENDS	HOLLY HUNTER
OLD FRIENDS	RALPH FIENNES
OLD GRINGO	ANNE PITONIAK
OLD GRINGO	GABRIELA ROEL
OLD GRINGO	GREGORY PECK
OLD GRINGO	GUILLERMO RIOS
OLD GRINGO	JANE FONDA
OLD GRINGO	JENNY GAGO
OLD GRINGO	JIM METZLER
OLD GRINGO	JIMMY SMITS
OLD GRINGO	PATRICIO CONTRERAS
OLD GRINGO	PEDRO ARMENDARIZ JR.
OLD GRINGO	SAMUEL VALADEZ
OLD GRINGO	SERGIO CALDERON
OLD MAID, THE	BETTE DAVIS†
OLD MAN AND THE SEA, THE ★	SPENCER TRACY†
OLD MAN AND THE SEA, THE (TF)	ANTHONY QUINN
OLD MAN AND THE SEA, THE (TF)	FRANCESCO QUINN
OLD MAN AND THE SEA, THE (TF)	GARY COLE
OLD MAN AND THE SEA, THE (TF)	VALENTINA QUINN
OLD MAN WHO CRIED WOLF, THE (TF)	DIANE BAKER
OLD MAN WHO CRIED WOLF, THE (TF)	MARTIN BALSAM
OLD OVERLAND TRAIL	LEONARD NIMOY
OLDEST PROFESSION, THE	RAQUEL WELCH
OLEANNA	DEBRA EISENSTADT
OLEANNA	REBECCA PIDGEON
OLEANNA	WILLIAM H. MACY
OLIVER! ★	RON MOODY
OLIVER!	HUGH GRIFFITH†
OLIVER!	MARK LESTER
OLIVER!	OLIVER REED
OLIVER & COMPANY (AF)	BETTE MIDLER
OLIVER & COMPANY (AF)	BILLY JOEL
OLIVER & COMPANY (AF)	CHEECH MARIN
OLIVER TWIST	ALEC GUINNESS
OLIVER TWIST (TF)	EILEEN ATKINS
OLIVER TWIST (TF)	GEORGE C. SCOTT
OLIVER TWIST (TF)	TIM CURRY
OLIVER TWIST (TF)	TIMOTHY WEST
OLIVER'S STORY	CANDICE BERGEN
OLIVER'S STORY	KENNETH McMILLAN†
OLIVER'S STORY	RYAN O'NEAL
OLLY OLLY OXEN FREE	KATHERINE HEPBURN
OMEGA MAN, THE	ANTHONY ZERBE
OMEGA MAN, THE	CHARLTON HESTON
OMEGA MAN, THE	ROSALIND CASH
OMEN, THE	BILLIE WHITELAW
OMEN, THE	DAVID WARNER
OMEN, THE	GREGORY PECK
OMEN, THE	LEE REMICK†
ON A CLEAR DAY, YOU CAN SEE FOREVER	BARBRA STREISAND
ON A CLEAR DAY YOU CAN SEE FOREVER	BOB NEWHART
ON A CLEAR DAY YOU CAN SEE FOREVER	JACK NICHOLSON
ON A CLEAR DAY YOU CAN SEE FOREVER	JEANNIE BERLIN
ON A CLEAR DAY YOU CAN SEE FOREVER	LEON AMES
ON AN ISLAND WITH YOU	CYD CHARISSE
ON AN ISLAND WITH YOU	RICARDO MONTALBAN
ON DEADLY GROUND	JOAN CHEN
ON DEADLY GROUND	JOHN C. McGINLEY
ON DEADLY GROUND	MICHAEL CAINE
ON DEADLY GROUND	STEVEN SEAGAL
ON FIRE (TF)	CARROLL BAKER
ON FIRE (TF)	GORDON JUMP
ON FIRE (TF)	JOHN FORSYTHE
ON FRIDAY AT ELEVEN	IAN BANNEN
ON FRIDAY AT ELEVEN	ROD STEIGER
ON GOLDEN POND	CHRIS RYDELL
ON GOLDEN POND	DABNEY COLEMAN
ON GOLDEN POND	DOUG McKEON
ON GOLDEN POND	WILLIAM LANTEAU
ON GOLDEN POND ★★	HENRY FONDA†
ON GOLDEN POND ★★	KATHERINE HEPBURN
ON GOLDEN POND O	JANE FONDA
ON HER MAJESTY'S SECRET SERVICE	BERNARD LEE†
ON HER MAJESTY'S SECRET SERVICE	DESMOND LLEWELYN
ON HER MAJESTY'S SECRET SERVICE	DIANA RIGG
ON HER MAJESTY'S SECRET SERVICE	GEORGE LAZENBY
ON HER MAJESTY'S SECRET SERVICE	JOANNA LUMLEY
ON HER MAJESTY'S SECRET SERVICE	LOIS MAXWELL
ON HER MAJESTY'S SECRET SERVICE	TELLY SAVALAS†
ON MOONLIGHT BAY	DORIS DAY
ON MOONLIGHT BAY	GORDON MACRAE†
ON MOONLIGHT BAY	LEON AMES
ON MOONLIGHT BAY	MARY WICKES
ON MY WAY TO THE CRUSADES I MET A GIRL WHO...	TONY CURTIS
ON OUR MERRY WAY	BURGESS MEREDITH
ON OUR MERRY WAY	DOROTHY LAMOUR
ON OUR MERRY WAY	JAMES STEWART
ON PROMISED LAND (CTF)	JOAN PLOWRIGHT
ON THE BEACH	ANTHONY PERKINS†
ON THE BEACH	AVA GARDNER†
ON THE BEACH	FRED ASTAIRE†
ON THE BEACH	GREGORY PECK
ON THE BEACH	JOHN MEILLON
ON THE EDGE	BILL BAILEY
ON THE EDGE	BRUCE DERN
ON THE EDGE	JIM HAYNIE
ON THE EDGE	PAM GRIER
ON THE FIDDLE	ALAN KING
ON THE FIDDLE	SEAN CONNERY
ON THE FIDDLE/ OPERATION WARHEAD	ALAN KING
ON THE LINE	SCOTT WILSON
ON THE RIGHT TRACK	GARY COLEMAN
ON THE RIGHT TRACK	NORMAN FELL
ON THE RIVIERA	GWEN VERDON
ON THE RUN	PAUL WINFIELD
ON THE SUNNY SIDE	RODDY McDOWALL
ON THE TOWN	FRANK SINATRA
ON THE TOWN	GENE KELLY
ON THE WATERFRONT	FRED GWYNNE†
ON THE WATERFRONT	MARTIN BALSAM
ON THE WATERFRONT	NEHEMIAH PERSOFF
ON THE WATERFRONT	PAT HINGLE
ON THE WATERFRONT ★★	MARLON BRANDO
ON THE WATERFRONT O	LEE J. COBB†
ON THE WATERFRONT O	KARL MALDEN
ON THE WATERFRONT O	ROD STEIGER
ON THE WATERFRONT OO	EVA MARIE SAINT
ON THE YARD	JOHN HEARD
ON VALENTINE'S DAY	CAROL GOODHEART
ON VALENTINE'S DAY	HALLIE FOOTE
ON VALENTINE'S DAY	HORTON FOOTE JR.
ON VALENTINE'S DAY	MATTHEW BRODERICK
ON VALENTINE'S DAY	MICHAEL HIGGINS
ON VALENTINE'S DAY	RICHARD JENKINS
ON VALENTINE'S DAY	STEVEN HILL
ON VALENTINE'S DAY	WILLIAM CONVERSE-ROBERTS
ON WINGS OF EAGLES (MS)	BURT LANCASTER†
ON WINGS OF EAGLES (MS)	ESAI MORALES
ON YOUR TOES	EDDIE ALBERT
ONCE A THIEF	ANN-MARGRET
ONCE A THIEF	JACK PALANCE
ONCE A THIEF	TONY MUSANTE
ONCE AN EAGLE (MS)	RALPH BELLAMY†
ONCE AN EAGLE (TF)	ANDREW STEVENS
ONCE AN EAGLE (TF)	SAM ELLIOTT
ONCE AROUND	DANNY AIELLO
ONCE AROUND	DANTON STONE
ONCE AROUND	GENA ROWLANDS
ONCE AROUND	GREG GERMANN
ONCE AROUND	GRIFFIN DUNNE
ONCE AROUND	HOLLY HUNTER
ONCE AROUND	LAURA SAN GIACOMO
ONCE AROUND	RICHARD DREYFUSS
ONCE AROUND	ROXANNE HART
ONCE AROUND	TIM GUINEE
ONCE BEFORE I DIE	URSULA ANDRESS
ONCE BITTEN	JIM CARREY
ONCE BITTEN	LAUREN HUTTON
ONCE IN A LIFETIME (TF)	BARRY BOSTWICK
ONCE IN A LIFETIME (TF)	LINDSAY WAGNER
ONCE IN PARIS...	WAYNE ROGERS
ONCE IS NOT ENOUGH	ALEXIS SMITH†
ONCE IS NOT ENOUGH	DEBORAH RAFFIN
ONCE IS NOT ENOUGH	GEORGE HAMILTON
ONCE IS NOT ENOUGH	KIRK DOUGLAS
ONCE IS NOT ENOUGH O	BRENDA VACCARO
ONCE MORE, WITH FEELING	SHIRLEY ANNE FIELD
ONCE TO EVERY WOMAN	RALPH BELLAMY†
ONCE UPON A CRIME	CYBILL SHEPHERD
ONCE UPON A CRIME	GEORGE HAMILTON
ONCE UPON A CRIME	GIANCARLO GIANNINI
ONCE UPON A CRIME	JAMES BELUSHI
ONCE UPON A CRIME	JOHN CANDY†
ONCE UPON A CRIME	ORNELLA MUTI
ONCE UPON A CRIME	RICHARD LEWIS
ONCE UPON A CRIME	SEAN YOUNG
ONCE UPON A FAMILY (TF)	BARRY BOSTWICK
ONCE UPON A HORSE	NITA TALBOT
ONCE UPON A TEXAS TRAIN (TF)	ANGIE DICKINSON
ONCE UPON A TEXAS TRAIN (TF)	CHUCK CONNORS†
ONCE UPON A TEXAS TRAIN (TF)	RICHARD WIDMARK
ONCE UPON A TEXAS TRAIN (TF)	SHAUN CASSIDY
ONCE UPON A TEXAS TRAIN (TF)	WILLIE NELSON
ONCE UPON A TIME IN AMERICA	BURT YOUNG
ONCE UPON A TIME IN AMERICA	DANNY AIELLO
ONCE UPON A TIME IN AMERICA	DARLANNE FLEUGEL
ONCE UPON A TIME IN AMERICA	ELIZABETH McGOVERN
ONCE UPON A TIME IN AMERICA	JAMES WOODS
ONCE UPON A TIME IN AMERICA	JENNIFER CONNELLY
ONCE UPON A TIME IN AMERICA	JOE PESCI
ONCE UPON A TIME IN AMERICA	LARRY RAPP
ONCE UPON A TIME IN AMERICA	ROBERT DE NIRO
ONCE UPON A TIME IN AMERICA	TREAT WILLIAMS
ONCE UPON A TIME IN AMERICA	TUESDAY WELD
ONCE UPON A TIME IN AMERICA	WILLIAM FORSYTHE
ONCE UPON A TIME IN THE WEST	CHARLES BRONSON
ONCE UPON A TIME IN THE WEST	JASON ROBARDS
ONCE UPON A TIME IN THE WEST	LIONEL STANDER
ONCE UPON A TIME IN THE WEST	WOODY STRODE
ONCE YOU KISS A STRANGER	CAROL LYNLEY
ONE AND ONLY GENUINE, ORIGINAL FAMILY BAND, THE	GOLDIE HAWN
ONE AND ONLY GENUINE, ORIGINAL FAMILY BAND, THE	JOHN DAVIDSON
ONE AND ONLY GENUINE, ORIGINAL FAMILY BAND, THE	KURT RUSSELL
ONE AND ONLY GENUINE, ORIGINAL FAMILY BAND, THE	LESLEY ANN WARREN
ONE AND ONLY ORIGINAL PHYLLIS DIXEY, THE (TF)	LESLEY-ANNE DOWN
ONE AND ONLY, THE	GENE SAKS
ONE AND ONLY, THE	HAROLD GOULD
ONE AND ONLY, THE	HENRY WINKLER
ONE AND ONLY, THE	HERVE VILLECHAIZE†
ONE AND ONLY, THE	KIM DARBY
ONE AND ONLY, THE	POLLY HOLLIDAY

517

ONE AND ONLY, THE .... WILLIAM DANIELS
ONE CRAZY SUMMER .... BILLIE BIRD
ONE CRAZY SUMMER .... BOB GOLDTHWAIT
ONE CRAZY SUMMER .... CURTIS ARMSTRONG
ONE CRAZY SUMMER .... DEMI MOORE
ONE CRAZY SUMMER .... JOE FLAHERTY
ONE CRAZY SUMMER .... JOHN CUSAK
ONE CRAZY SUMMER .... KIMBERLY FOSTER
ONE CRAZY SUMMER .... WILLIAM HICKEY
ONE CUP OF COFFEE .... GLENN PLUMMER
ONE CUP OF COFFEE .... NOBLE WILLINGHAM
ONE CUP OF COFFEE .... WILLIAM RUSS
ONE DARK NIGHT .... MEG TILLY
ONE DAY IN THE LIFE OF
    IVAN DENISOVITCH .... TOM COURTENAY
ONE DEADLY SUMMER .... SABELLE ADJANI
ONE DESIRE .... ROCK HUDSON†
ONE DOWN, TWO TO GO .... JIM BROWN
ONE DOWN, TWO TO GO ..... RICHARD ROUNDTREE
ONE FALSE MOVE .... BILL PAXTON
ONE FALSE MOVE .... BILLY BOB THORNTON
ONE FALSE MOVE .... CYNDA WILLIAMS
ONE FLEW OVER THE
    CUCKOO'S NEST .... SCATMAN CROTHERS†
ONE FLEW OVER THE
    CUCKOO'S NEST .... WILL SAMPSON†
ONE FLEW OVER THE
    CUCKOO'S NEST .... WILLIAM REDFIELD†
ONE FLEW OVER THE
    CUCKOO'S NEST .... CHRISTOPHER LLOYD
ONE FLEW OVER THE
    CUCKOO'S NEST .... DANNY DEVITO
ONE FLEW OVER THE
    CUCKOO'S NEST ★★ .... JACK NICHOLSON
ONE FLEW OVER THE
    CUCKOO'S NEST ★★ .... LOUISE FLETCHER
ONE FLEW OVER THE
    CUCKOO'S NEST ○ .... BRAD DOURIF
ONE FOOT IN HEAVEN .... MARTHA SCOTT
ONE FOOT IN HELL .... DAN O'HERLIHY
ONE FOOT IN HELL .... DON MURRAY
ONE FOR THE BOOK .... RONALD REAGAN
ONE FROM THE HEART .... ALLEN GARFIELD
ONE FROM THE HEART ...... FREDERIC FORREST
ONE FROM THE HEART ...... HARRY DEAN STANTON
ONE FROM THE HEART .... LUANA ANDERS
ONE FROM THE HEART .... NASTASSJA KINSKI
ONE FROM THE HEART .... RAUL JULIA†
ONE FROM THE HEART .... REBECCA DE MORNAY
ONE FROM THE HEART .... TERI GARR
ONE GOOD COP .... ANTHONY LaPAGLIA
ONE GOOD COP .... BENJAMIN BRATT
ONE GOOD COP .... KEVIN CONWAY
ONE GOOD COP .... MICHAEL KEATON
ONE GOOD COP .... RACHEL TICOTIN
ONE GOOD COP .... RENE RUSSO
ONE GOOD COP .... TONY PLANA
ONE IN A MILLION .... DON AMECHE†
ONE IN A MILLION: THE RON
    LeFLORE STORY (TF) .... LeVAR BURTON
ONE IS A LONELY NUMBER .... JANET LEIGH
ONE IS A LONELY NUMBER ...... TRISH VAN DEVERE
ONE IS GUILTY .... RALPH BELLAMY†
ONE LAST FLING .... ALEXIS SMITH†
ONE LITTLE INDIAN .... ANDREW PRINE
ONE LITTLE INDIAN .... JAMES GARNER
ONE LITTLE INDIAN .... JODIE FOSTER
ONE LITTLE INDIAN .... PAT HINGLE
ONE LITTLE INDIAN .... VERA MILES
ONE MAGIC CHRISTMAS .... ARTHUR HILL
ONE MAGIC CHRISTMAS .... ELIAS KOTEAS
ONE MAGIC CHRISTMAS .... HARRY DEAN STANTON
ONE MAGIC CHRISTMAS .... MARY STEENBURGEN
ONE MAN JURY .... JACK PALANCE
ONE MAN'S WAY .... DON MURRAY
ONE MAN'S WAY .... TOM SKERRITT
ONE MAN'S WAY .... WILLIAM WINDOM
ONE MILLION YEARS B.C. .... RAQUEL WELCH
ONE MINUTE TO ZERO .... ROBERT MITCHUM
ONE MORE MOUNTAIN (TF) .... MEREDITH BAXTER
ONE MORE RIVER .... JANE WYATT
ONE MORE SATURDAY NIGHT .... AL FRANKEN

ONE MORE TIME .... HARRY CAREY JR.
ONE MORE TOMORROW .... JANE WYMAN
ONE MORE TRAIN TO ROB .... DIANA MULDAUR
ONE MORE TRAIN TO ROB .... FRANCE NUYEN
ONE MORE TRAIN TO ROB ...... GEORGE PEPPARD†
ONE MORE TRAIN TO ROB .... JOHN VERNON
ONE NIGHT AT DINNER .... TONY MUSANTE
ONE NIGHT OF LOVE ★ .... GRACE MOORE†
ONE NIGHT WITH YOU .... IRENE WORTH
ONE OF MY WIVES
    IS MISSING .... ELIZABETH ASHLEY
ONE OF OUR AIRCRAFT
    IS MISSING .... PETER USTINOV
ONE OF OUR DINOSAURS
    IS MISSING .... HELEN HAYES
ONE OF OUR DINOSAURS
    IS MISSING .... JOSS ACKLAND
ONE OF OUR DINOSAURS
    IS MISSING .... PETER USTINOV
ONE OF OUR OWN (TF) .... GEORGE PEPPARD†
ONE OF THOSE THINGS .... ROY DOTRICE
ONE ON ONE .... ANNETTE O'TOOLE
ONE ON ONE .... G. D. SPRADLIN
ONE ON ONE .... GAIL STRICKLAND
ONE ON ONE .... LAMONT JOHNSON
ONE ON ONE .... MELANIE GRIFFITH
ONE ON ONE .... ROBBY BENSON
ONE ON TOP OF THE OTHER .... JOHN IRELAND
ONE PLUE TWO EQUALS FOUR .... JOE BURNS
ONE POLICE PLAZA (TF) .... ANTHONY ZERBE
ONE POLICE PLAZA (TF) .... GEORGE DZUNDZA
ONE POLICE PLAZA (TF) .... ROBERT CONRAD
ONE POTATO, TWO POTATO .... BARBARA BARRIE
ONE ROMANTIC NIGHT .... LILLIAN GISH†
ONE SHOE MAKES
    IT MURDER (TF) .... HOWARD HESSEMAN
ONE SHOE MAKES
    IT MURDER (TF) .... ROBERT MITCHUM
ONE SPY TOO MANY .... RIP TORN
ONE SPY TOO MANY .... ROBERT VAUGHN
ONE SUMMER LOVE .... ANN WEDGEWORTH
ONE SUMMER LOVE .... BEAU BRIDGES
ONE SUMMER LOVE .... SUSAN SARANDON
ONE TERRIFIC GUY (TF) .... GEOFFREY BLAKE
ONE TERRIFIC GUY (TF) .... MARIETTE HARTLEY
ONE THIRD OF A NATION .... SYLVIA SIDNEY
ONE TOUCH OF VENUS .... AVA GARDNER†
ONE TRICK PONY .... JOAN HACKETT†
ONE, TWO, THREE .... RED BUTTONS
ONE WAY STREET .... ROCK HUDSON†
ONE WILD OAT .... AUDREY HEPBURN†
ONE WOMAN OR TWO .... GERARD DEPARDIEU
ONE WOMAN OR TWO .... SIGOURNEY WEAVER
ONE-EYED JACKS .... BEN JOHNSON
ONE-EYED JACKS .... KARL MALDEN
ONE-EYED JACKS .... KATHY JURADO
ONE-EYED JACKS .... MARLON BRANDO
ONE-EYED JACKS .... SLIM PICKENS†
ONE-EYED JACKS .... TIMOTHY CAREY
ONE-TRICK PONY .... ALLEN GARFIELD
ONE-TRICK PONY .... BLAIR BROWN
ONE-TRICK PONY .... MARE WINNINGHAM
ONE-TRICK PONY .... PAUL SIMON
ONE-TRICK PONY .... RIP TORN
ONION FIELD, THE .... CHRISTOPHER LLOYD
ONION FIELD, THE .... DIANNE HULL
ONION FIELD, THE .... JAMES WOODS
ONION FIELD, THE .... JOHN SAVAGE
ONION FIELD, THE .... RONNY COX
ONION FIELD, THE .... TED DANSON
ONIONHEAD .... ANDY GRIFFITH
ONIONHEAD .... CLAUDE AKINS†
ONIONHEAD .... WALTER MATTHAU
ONKEL TOMS HÜTTE .... EARTHA KITT
ONLY A WOMAN .... MARIA SCHELL
ONLY GAME IN TOWN, THE ...... ELIZABETH TAYLOR
ONLY GAME IN TOWN, THE .... WARREN BEATTY
ONLY THE FRENCH CAN .... GENEVIEVE BUJOLD
ONLY THE LONELY .... ALLY SHEEDY
ONLY THE LONELY .... ANTHONY QUINN
ONLY THE LONELY .... BERT REMSEN
ONLY THE LONELY .... JAMES BELUSHI

ONLY THE LONELY .... JOHN CANDY†
ONLY THE LONELY .... KEVIN DUNN
ONLY THE LONELY .... MACAULAY CULKIN
ONLY THE LONELY .... MAUREEN O'HARA
ONLY THE LONELY .... MILO O'SHEA
ONLY THE VALIANT .... GREGORY PECK
ONLY THE VALIANT .... JEFF COREY
ONLY THING, THE .... JOAN CRAWFORD†
ONLY TWO CAN PLAY .... MAE ZETTERLING†
ONLY WAY HOME, THE .... BO HOPKINS
ONLY WAY OUT IS DEAD .... SANDY DENNIS†
ONLY WAY OUT IS DEAD, THE .... BURL IVES
ONLY WAY OUT
    IS DEAD, THE .... STUART WHITMAN
ONLY WAY OUT, THE (TF) .... JOHN RITTER
ONLY WHEN I LAUGH .... DAVID DUKES
ONLY WHEN I LAUGH .... KEVIN BACON
ONLY WHEN I LAUGH .... KRISTY McNICHOL
ONLY WHEN I LAUGH ★ .... MARSHA MASON
ONLY WHEN I LAUGH ○ .... JAMES COCO†
ONLY WHEN I LAUGH ○ .... JOAN HACKETT†
ONLY YOU .... BILLY ZANE
ONLY YOU .... BONNIE HUNT
ONLY YOU .... FISHER STEVENS
ONLY YOU .... JOAQUIM DE ALMEIDA
ONLY YOU .... MARISA TOMEI
ONLY YOU .... ROBERT DOWNEY JR.
OPEN ADMISSIONS (TF) .... DENNIS FARINA
OPEN ADMISSIONS (TF) .... ESTELLE PARSONS
OPEN ADMISSIONS (TF) .... JANE ALEXANDER
OPEN ADMISSIONS (TF) .... MICHAEL BEACH
OPEN ALL NIGHT .... GERALDINE FITZGERALD
OPEN SEASON .... JOHN PHILLIP LAW
OPEN SEASON .... PETER FONDA
OPEN SECRET .... JOHN IRELAND
OPENING NIGHT .... BEN GAZZARA
OPENING NIGHT .... GENA ROWLANDS
OPENING NIGHT .... ZOHRA LAMPERT
OPERATION, THE (TF) .... JASON BEGHE
OPERATION, THE (TF) .... JOE PENNY
OPERATION, THE (TF) .... KATHLEEN QUINLAN
OPERATION, THE (TF) .... LISA HARTMAN-BLACK
OPERATION BIKINI .... FRANKIE AVALON
OPERATION BIKINI .... MICHAEL DANTE
OPERATION BIKINI .... TAB HUNTER
OPERATION BOTTLENECK .... NORMAN ALDEN
OPERATION C.I.A. .... BURT REYNOLDS
OPERATION C.I.A. .... KIEU CHINH
OPERATION CROSSBOW .... GEORGE PEPPARD†
OPERATION CROSSBOW .... JEREMY KEMP
OPERATION CROSSBOW .... SOPHIA LOREN
OPERATION CROSSBOW .... TOM COURTENAY
OPERATION DAYBREAK .... ANTHONY ANDREWS
OPERATION DAYBREAK .... JOSS ACKLAND
OPERATION DISASTER .... JOHN MILLS
OPERATION DUMBO DROP .... DANNY GLOVER
OPERATION DUMBO DROP .... DENIS LEARY
OPERATION DUMBO DROP .... DOUG E. DOUG
OPERATION DUMBO DROP .... RAY LIOTTA
OPERATION KID BROTHER .... LOIS MAXWELL
OPERATION MAD BALL .... JACK LEMMON
OPERATION PACIFIC .... PATRICIA NEAL
OPERATION PETTICOAT .... DICK SARGENT
OPERATION PETTICOAT .... DINA MERRILL
OPERATION PETTICOAT .... TONY CURTIS
OPERATION PETTICOAT (TF) .... JACKIE COOPER
OPERATION PETTICOAT (TF) ..... JAMIE LEE CURTIS
OPERATION SECRET .... DAN O'HERLIHY
OPERATION SECRET .... KARL MALDEN
OPERATION SECRET .... PHYLLIS THAXTER
OPERATION SNAFU .... ALAN KING
OPERATION SNAFU .... PETER FALK
OPERATION SNAFU/
    OPERATION WARHEAD .... SEAN CONNERY
OPERATION THUNDERBOLT .... KLAUS KINSKI†
OPERAZIONE SAN GENNARO ..... CLAUDINE AUGER
OPERAZIONE SAN GENNARO ..... HARRY GUARDINO
OPPENHEIMER (MS) .... SAM WATERSTON
OPPORTUNITY KNOCKS .... DANA CARVEY
OPPORTUNITY KNOCKS .... JULIA CAMPBELL
OPPORTUNITY KNOCKS .... ROBERT LOGGIA
OPPORTUNITY KNOCKS .... TODD GRAFF

OPPOSING FORCE .... ANTHONY ZERBE
OPPOSING FORCE .... LISA EICHHORN
OPPOSING FORCE .... RICHARD ROUNDTREE
OPPOSING FORCE .... TOM SKERRITT
OPPOSITE SEX (AND HOW TO
  LIVE WITH THEM), THE .... ARYE GROSS
OPPOSITE SEX (AND HOW TO
  LIVE WITH THEM), THE .... COURTENEY COX
OPPOSITE SEX (AND HOW TO
  LIVE WITH THEM), THE .... KEVIN POLLAK
OPPOSITE SEX, THE .... JOAN COLLINS
OPPOSITE SEX, THE .... JUNE ALLYSON
OPPOSITE SEX, THE .... LESLIE NIELSEN
ORCA .... BO DEREK
ORCA .... CHARLOTTE RAMPLING
ORCA .... RICHARD HARRIS
ORCA .... ROBERT CARRADINE
ORDEAL BY INNOCENCE .... ANNETTE CROSBIE
ORDEAL BY
  INNOCENCE .... CHRISTOPHER PLUMMER
ORDEAL BY INNOCENCE .... DIANA QUICK
ORDEAL BY INNOCENCE ..... DONALD SUTHERLAND
ORDEAL BY INNOCENCE .... FAYE DUNAWAY
ORDEAL BY INNOCENCE .... SARAH MILES
ORDEAL OF BILL
  CARNEY, THE (TF) .... BETTY BUCKLEY
ORDEAL OF DR.
  MUDD, THE (TF) .... DENNIS WEAVER
ORDEAL OF PATTY
  HEARST, THE (TF) .... DENNIS WEAVER
ORDEAL OF PATTY
  HEARST, THE (TF) .... ROSANNA ARQUETTE
ORDER OF DEATH .... HARVEY KEITEL
ORDER OF DEATH/COP KILLERS ..... SYLVIA SIDNEY
ORDER TO KILL .... JOSE FERRER†
ORDER TO KILL .... KEVIN McCARTHY
ORDERS TO KILL .... EDDIE ALBERT
ORDERS TO KILL .... IRENE WORTH
ORDERS TO KILL .... LILLIAN GISH†
ORDINARY PEOPLE .... BASIL HOFFMAN
ORDINARY PEOPLE .... DINAH MANOFF
ORDINARY PEOPLE .... DONALD SUTHERLAND
ORDINARY PEOPLE ..... ELIZABETH McGOVERN
ORDINARY PEOPLE ..... JAMES B. SIKKING
ORDINARY PEOPLE ..... M. EMMET WALSH
ORDINARY PEOPLE ★ .... MARY TYLER MOORE
ORDINARY PEOPLE ✿ .... JUDD HIRSCH
ORDINARY PEOPLE ✿✿ .... TIMOTHY HUTTON
OREGON TRAIL, THE (TF) ..... DAVID HUDDLESTON
ORGANIZATION, THE .... ALLEN GARFIELD
ORGANIZATION, THE .... RON O'NEAL
ORGANIZATION, THE .... SIDNEY POITIER
ORGANIZER, THE .... MARCELLO MASTROIANNI
ORGASMO .... CARROLL BAKER
ORGY GIRLS '69 .... ALLEN GARFIELD
ORIGINAL INTENT .... CANDY CLARK
ORIGINAL INTENT .... KRIS KRISTOFFERSON
ORIGINAL INTENT .... MARTIN SHEEN
ORIGINAL SIN (TF) .... ANN JILLIAN
ORIGINAL SIN (TF) .... CHARLTON HESTON
ORIGINAL SIN (TF) .... ROBERT DESIDERIO
ORLANDO .... BILLY ZANE
ORLANDO .... QUENTIN CRISP
ORLANDO .... TILDA SWINTON
ORPHAN TRAIN (TF) .... GLENN CLOSE
ORPHAN TRAIN (TF) .... JILL EIKENBERRY
ORPHANS .... ALBERT FINNEY
ORPHANS .... KEVIN ANDERSON
ORPHANS .... MATTHEW MODINE
ORPHANS OF THE STORM .... LILLIAN GISH†
OSCAR .... ART LA FLEUR
OSCAR .... BRUCE DAVISON
OSCAR .... CHAZZ PALMINTERI
OSCAR .... DON AMECHE†
OSCAR .... EDDIE BRACKEN
OSCAR .... JOEY TRAVOLTA
OSCAR .... KEN HOWARD
OSCAR .... KIRK DOUGLAS
OSCAR .... LINDA GRAY
OSCAR .... MARISA TOMEI
OSCAR .... ORNELLA MUTI
OSCAR .... PETER RIEGERT

OSCAR .... SAM CHEW
OSCAR .... SYLVESTER STALLONE
OSCAR .... TIM CURRY
OSCAR .... VINCENT SPANO
OSCAR .... WILLIAM ATHERTON
OSCAR .... YVONNE DE CARLO
OSCAR, THE .... BOB HOPE
OSCAR, THE .... EDIE ADAMS
OSCAR, THE .... ELEANOR PARKER
OSCAR, THE .... ERNEST BORGNINE
OSCAR, THE .... FRANK SINATRA
OSCAR, THE .... JILL ST. JOHN
OSCAR, THE .... MILTON BERLE
OSCAR WILDE .... JOHN NEVILLE
OSCAR WILDE .... ROBERT MORLEY
OSTERMAN WEEKEND, THE ...... BURT LANCASTER†
OSTERMAN WEEKEND, THE ...... CHRIS SARANDON
OSTERMAN WEEKEND, THE .... CRAIG T. NELSON
OSTERMAN WEEKEND, THE ...... DENNIS HOPPER
OSTERMAN WEEKEND, THE .... JOHN HURT
OSTERMAN WEEKEND, THE ...... MEG FOSTER
OSTERMAN WEEKEND, THE .... RUTGER HAUER
OTELLO .... URBANO BARBERINI
OTHELLO ★ .... LAURENCE OLIVIER†
OTHELLO ✿ .... FRANK FINLAY†
OTHELLO ✿ .... MAGGIE SMITH
OTHER, THE .... DIANA MULDAUR
OTHER, THE .... JOHN RITTER
OTHER LOVE, THE .... BARBARA STANWYCK†
OTHER LOVE, THE (TF) .... DAVID NIVEN†
OTHER LOVER, THE (TF) .... LINDSAY WAGNER
OTHER MAN, THE (TF) .... JOAN HACKETT†
OTHER MAN, THE (TF) .... TAMMY GRIMES
OTHER PEOPLE'S MONEY .... DANNY DEVITO
OTHER PEOPLE'S MONEY .... DEAN JONES
OTHER PEOPLE'S MONEY .... GREGORY PECK
OTHER PEOPLE'S MONEY .... KATHY NAJIMY
OTHER PEOPLE'S
  MONEY .... PENELOPE ANN MILLER
OTHER PEOPLE'S MONEY .... PIPER LAURIE
OTHER SIDE OF BONNIE
  AND CLYDE, THE .... BURL IVES
OTHER SIDE OF HELL, THE (TF) .... ALAN ARKIN
OTHER SIDE OF MIDNIGHT, THE ...... CLU GULAGER
OTHER SIDE OF MIDNIGHT, THE .... DIMITRA ARLYS
OTHER SIDE OF MIDNIGHT, THE .... JOHN BECK
OTHER SIDE OF
  MIDNIGHT, THE .... SUSAN SARANDON
OTHER SIDE OF
  PARADISE .... CHARLOTTE RAMPLING
OTHER SIDE OF PARADISE .... PETER O'TOOLE
OTHER SIDE OF THE
  MOUNTAIN, THE .... BEAU BRIDGES
OTHER SIDE OF THE
  MOUNTAIN, THE .... BELINDA J. MONTGOMERY
OTHER SIDE OF THE
  MOUNTAIN, THE .... DABNEY COLEMAN
OTHER SIDE OF THE
  MOUNTAIN, THE .... MARILYN HASSETT
OTHER SIDE OF THE MOUNTAIN
  PART 2, THE .... BELINDA J. MONTGOMERY
OTHER SIDE OF THE MOUNTAIN
  PART 2, THE .... MARILYN HASSETT
OTHER SIDE OF THE MOUNTIAN
  PART 2, THE .... TIMOTHY BOTTOMS
OTHER WOMAN, THE .... LAURA SAN GIACOMO
OTHER WOMAN, THE .... LIAM NEESON
OTHER WOMAN, THE (TF) .... ANNE MEARA
OTHER WOMAN, THE (TF) .... HAL LINDEN
OTLEY .... FIONA LEWIS
OTLEY .... FREDDIE JONES
OTLEY .... GEOFFREY BAYLDON
OTLEY .... TOM COURTENAY
OTTO E MEZZO .... MARCELLO MASTROIANNI
OUR BLUSHING BRIDES .... JOAN CRAWFORD†
OUR DANCING DAUGHTERS ..... JOAN CRAWFORD†
OUR FAMILY BUSINESS (TF) ..... SAM WANAMAKER†
OUR FAMILY BUSINESS (TF) .... TED DANSON
OUR FAMILY BUSINESS (TF) .... VERA MILES
OUR FAMILY HONOR (TF) ...... KENNETH McMILLAN†
OUR FAMILY HONOR (TF) .... MICHAEL MADSEN
OUR GIRL FRIDAY .... JOAN COLLINS

OUR MAN FLINT .... JAMES BROLIN
OUR MAN FLINT .... JAMES COBURN
OUR MAN FLINT:
  DEAD ON TARGET (TF) .... SHARON ACKER
OUR MAN IN HAVANA .... ALEC GUINNESS
OUR MAN IN HAVANA .... BURL IVES
OUR MAN IN HAVANA .... MAUREEN O'HARA
OUR MAN IN HAVANA .... RACHEL ROBERTS†
OUR MAN IN MARRAKESH .... TONY RANDALL
OUR MISS BROOKS .... RICHARD CRENNA
OUR MISS FRED .... WALTER GOTELL
OUR MODERN MAIDENS .... JOAN CRAWFORD†
OUR MOTHER'S HOUSE .... MARK LESTER
OUR SONS (TF) .... ANN-MARGRET
OUR SONS (TF) .... HUGH GRANT
OUR SONS (TF) .... JULIE ANDREWS
OUR SONS (TF) .... TONY ROBERTS
OUR SONS (TF) .... ZELJKO IVANEK
OUR TIME .... DEBRALEE SCOTT
OUR TOWN ★ .... MARTHA SCOTT
OUR VERY OWN .... JANE WYATT
OUR WINNING SEASON .... P. J. SOLES
OUT COLD .... BRUCE McGILL
OUT COLD .... JOHN LITHGOW
OUT COLD .... LISA BLOUNT
OUT COLD .... RANDY QUAID
OUT COLD .... TERI GARR
OUT FOR JUSTICE .... JERRY ORBACH
OUT FOR JUSTICE .... JO CHAMP
OUT FOR JUSTICE .... STEVEN SEAGAL
OUT FOR JUSTICE .... WILLIAM FORSYTHE
OUT OF AFRICA .... IMAN
OUT OF AFRICA .... MALICK BOWENS
OUT OF AFRICA .... MICHAEL GOUGH
OUT OF AFRICA .... MICHAEL KITCHEN
OUT OF AFRICA .... ROBERT REDFORD
OUT OF AFRICA ★ .... MERYL STREEP
OUT OF AFRICA ✿ .... KLAUS MARIA BRANDAUER
OUT OF BOUNDS .... ANTHONY MICHAEL HALL
OUT OF BOUNDS .... RAYMOND J. BARRY
OUT OF CONTROL .... MARTIN HEWITT
OUT OF DARKNESS (TF) .... DIANA ROSS
OUT OF IT .... JON VOIGHT
OUT OF ROSENHEIM .... C. C. H. POUNDER
OUT OF ROSENHEIM .... JACK PALANCE
OUT OF ROSENHEIM .... MARIANNE SAGEBRECHT
OUT OF SEASON .... CLIFF ROBERTSON
OUT OF SEASON .... SUSAN GEORGE
OUT OF SEASON .... VANESSA REDGRAVE
OUT OF SYNC .... ARIES SPEARS
OUT OF SYNC .... HOWARD HESSEMAN
OUT OF SYNC .... ISAAC HAYES
OUT OF SYNC .... VICTORIA DILLARD
OUT OF SYNC .... YAPHET KOTTO
OUT OF THE BLUE .... DENNIS HOPPER
OUT OF THE BLUE .... RAYMOND BURR†
OUT OF THE DARK .... DIVINE†
OUT OF THE DARKNESS .... ROSS HAGEN
OUT OF THE
  DARKNESS (TF) .... HECTOR ELIZONDO
OUT OF THE DARKNESS (TF) .... MARTIN SHEEN
OUT OF THE DARKNESS (TF) .... MATT CLARK
OUT OF THE FOG .... EDDIE ALBERT
OUT OF THE PAST .... JANE GREER
OUT OF THE PAST .... KIRK DOUGLAS
OUT OF THE PAST .... ROBERT MITCHUM
OUT OF THE RAIN .... BRIDGET FONDA
OUT OF TIME (TF) .... ADAM ANT
OUT OF TIME (TF) .... BRUCE ABBOTT
OUT ON A LIMB .... COURTNEY PELDON
OUT ON A LIMB .... HEIDI KLING
OUT ON A LIMB .... JEFFREY JONES
OUT ON A LIMB .... MARIAN MERCER
OUT ON A LIMB .... MATTHEW BRODERICK
OUT ON A LIMB (MS) .... ANNE JACKSON
OUT ON A LIMB (MS) .... CHARLES DANCE
OUT ON A LIMB (MS) .... JENNY GAGO
OUT ON A LIMB (MS) .... JERRY ORBACH
OUT ON A LIMB (MS) .... JOHN HEARD
OUT ON A LIMB (MS) .... SHIRLEY MacLAINE
OUT ON THE EDGE (TF) .... RICHARD JENKINS
OUT-OF-TOWNERS, THE .... BILLY DEE WILLIAMS

† after an actor's name denotes deceased.

OUT-OF-TOWNERS, THE ... JACK LEMMON
OUT-OF-TOWNERS, THE ... SANDY DENNIS†
OUTBACK ... DONALD PLEASENCE
OUTBACK ... JACK THOMPSON
OUTBACK BOUND (TF) ... JOHN SCHNEIDER
OUTBACK BOUND (TF) ... NINA FOCH
OUTBACK BOUND (TF) ... ROBERT HARPER
OUTBREAK ... CUBA GOODING JR.
OUTBREAK ... DUSTIN HOFFMAN
OUTBREAK ... JOE DON BAKER
OUTBREAK ... KEVIN SPACEY
OUTBREAK ... MORGAN FREEMAN
OUTBREAK ... PATRICK DEMPSEY
OUTBREAK ... RENE RUSSO
OUTBREAK ... SUSAN LEE HOFFMAN
OUTCAST OF THE ISLANDS ... ROBERT MORLEY
OUTCAST OF THE ISLANDS ... WENDY HILLER
OUTFIT, THE ... BILL McKINNEY
OUTFIT, THE ... HENRY JONES
OUTFIT, THE ... JANE GREER
OUTFIT, THE ... JOANNA CASSIDY
OUTFIT, THE ... JOE DON BAKER
OUTFIT, THE ... KAREN BLACK
OUTFIT, THE ... RICHARD JAECKEL
OUTFIT, THE ... ROBERT DUVALL
OUTFIT, THE ... TIMOTHY CAREY
OUTLAND ... FRANCES STERNHAGEN
OUTLAND ... PETER BOYLE
OUTLAND ... SEAN CONNERY
OUTLAW BLUES ... MICHAEL LERNER
OUTLAW BLUES ... PETER FONDA
OUTLAW BLUES ... SUSAN SAINT JAMES
OUTLAW JOSEY WALES, THE ... BILL McKINNEY
OUTLAW JOSEY WALES, THE ... CLINT EASTWOOD
OUTLAW JOSEY WALES, THE ... JOHN VERNON
OUTLAW JOSEY WALES, THE ... ROYAL DANO
OUTLAW JOSEY WALES, THE ... SAM BOTTOMS
OUTLAW JOSEY WALES, THE ... SONDRA LOCKE
OUTLAW TERRITORY ... JOHN IRELAND
OUTRAGE! (TF) ... BEAU BRIDGES
OUTRAGE! (TF) ... MEL FERRER
OUTRAGE! (TF) ... WILLIAM ALLEN YOUNG
OUTRAGE, THE ... ALBERT SALMI†
OUTRAGE, THE ... CLAIRE BLOOM
OUTRAGE, THE ... HOWARD DA SILVA†
OUTRAGE, THE ... PAUL NEWMAN
OUTRAGE, THE ... WILLIAM SHATNER
OUTRAGEOUS FORTUNE ... ANTHONY HEALD
OUTRAGEOUS FORTUNE ... BETTE MIDLER
OUTRAGEOUS FORTUNE ... CHRISTOPHER McDONALD
OUTRAGEOUS FORTUNE ... GEORGE CARLIN
OUTRAGEOUS FORTUNE ... JOHN SCHUCK
OUTRAGEOUS FORTUNE ... PETER COYOTE
OUTRAGEOUS FORTUNE ... ROBERT PASTORELLI
OUTRAGEOUS FORTUNE ... ROBERT PROSKY
OUTRAGEOUS FORTUNE ... SHELLEY LONG
OUTSIDE MAN, THE ... ANGIE DICKINSON
OUTSIDE MAN, THE ... ANN-MARGRET
OUTSIDE MAN, THE ... JEAN-LOUIS TRINTIGNANT
OUTSIDE MAN, THE ... ROY SCHEIDER
OUTSIDE MAN, THE ... TALIA SHIRE
OUTSIDE WOMAN, THE (TF) ... SCOTT GLENN
OUTSIDE WOMAN, THE (TF) ... SHARON GLESS
OUTSIDER, THE ... CRAIG WASSON
OUTSIDER, THE ... GABRIEL BYRNE
OUTSIDER, THE ... JAMES FRANCISCUS†
OUTSIDER, THE ... MARTIN SHORT
OUTSIDER, THE ... RODDY McDOWALL
OUTSIDER, THE ... SUE ANE LANGDON
OUTSIDER, THE ... TONY CURTIS
OUTSIDERS, THE ... C. THOMAS HOWELL
OUTSIDERS, THE ... EMILIO ESTEVEZ
OUTSIDERS, THE ... MATT DILLON
OUTSIDERS, THE ... PATRICK SWAYZE
OUTSIDERS, THE ... RALPH MACCHIO
OUTSIDERS, THE ... TOM CRUISE
OVER MY DEAD BODY ... MILTON BERLE
OVER THE BROOKLYN BRIDGE ... MARGAUX HEMINGWAY
OVER THE BROOKLYN BRIDGE ... SHELLEY WINTERS
OVER THE BROOKLYN BRIDGE ... SID CAESAR
OVER THE EDGE ... MATT DILLON
OVER THE EDGE ... VINCENT SPANO
OVER THE TOP ... ROBERT LOGGIA
OVER THE TOP ... SUSAN BLAKELY
OVER THE TOP ... SYLVESTER STALLONE
OVER-EXPOSED ... RICHARD CRENNA
OVERBOARD ... EDWRAD HERRMANN
OVERBOARD ... GOLDIE HAWN
OVERBOARD ... JARED RUSHTON
OVERBOARD ... KATHERINE HELMOND
OVERBOARD ... KURT RUSSELL
OVERBOARD ... RAY COMBS
OVIRI ... DONALD SUTHERLAND
OWL AND THE PUSSYCAT, THE ... ALLEN GARFIELD
OWL AND THE PUSSYCAT, THE ... BARBRA STREISAND
OWL AND THE PUSSYCAT, THE ... BUCK HENRY
OWL AND THE PUSSYCAT, THE ... GEORGE SEGAL
OX BOW INCIDENT, THE ... HARRY MORGAN
OX-BOW INCIDENT, THE ... ANTHONY QUINN
OX-BOW INCIDENT, THE ... HENRY FONDA†
OXFORD BLUES ... ALLY SHEEDY
OXFORD BLUES ... CARY ELWES
OXFORD BLUES ... JULIAN SANDS
OXFORD BLUES ... ROB LOWE
O'HARA'S WIFE ... ED ASNER
O'HARA'S WIFE ... JODIE FOSTER
O'HARA'S WIFE ... RAY WALSTON
O'HARA'S WIFE ... TOM BOSLEY
O'SHAUGHNESSY'S BOY ... JACKIE COOPER

P

P.J. ... BROCK PETERS
P.J. ... GEORGE PEPPARD†
P.J. ... RAYMOND BURR†
P.J. ... SUSAN SAINT JAMES
P.O.W. THE ESCAPE ... CHARLES R. FLOYD
P.O.W. THE ESCAPE ... DAVID CARPENTER
P.O.W. THE ESCAPE ... PHIL BROCK
P.O.W. THE ESCAPE ... STEVE JAMES
PACIFIC BLACKOUT ... EVA GABOR
PACIFIC DESTINY ... DENHOLM ELLIOTT†
PACIFIC DESTINY ... GORDAN JACKSON†
PACIFIC HEIGHTS ... BEVERLY D'ANGELO
PACIFIC HEIGHTS ... CARL LUMBLY
PACIFIC HEIGHTS ... LAURIE METCALF
PACIFIC HEIGHTS ... MAKO
PACIFIC HEIGHTS ... MATTHEW MODINE
PACIFIC HEIGHTS ... MELANIE GRIFFITH
PACIFIC HEIGHTS ... MICHAEL KEATON
PACIFIC HEIGHTS ... TIPPI HEDREN
PACK, THE ... JOE DON BAKER
PACK, THE ... R.G. ARMSTRONG
PACK OF LIES (TF) ... ALAN BATES
PACK OF LIES (TF) ... DANIEL BENZALI
PACK OF LIES (TF) ... ELLEN BURSTYN
PACK OF LIES (TF) ... TERI GARR
PACKAGE, THE ... DENNIS FRANZ
PACKAGE, THE ... DICK CUSAK
PACKAGE, THE ... GENE HACKMAN
PACKAGE, THE ... JOANNA CASSIDY
PACKAGE, THE ... JOHN HEARD
PACKAGE, THE ... KEVIN CROWLEY
PACKAGE, THE ... PAM GRIER
PACKAGE, THE ... RENI SANTONI
PACKAGE, THE ... RON DEAN
PACKAGE, THE ... TOMMY LEE JONES
PACO ... ALLEN GARFIELD
PACO ... JOSE FERRER†
PAD AND HOW TO USE IT, THE ... JAMES FARENTINO
PADDY ... MILO O'SHEA
PADRI E FIGLI ... MARCELLO MASTROIANNI
PAGAN LOVE SONG ... HOWARD KEEL
PAGAN LOVE SONG ... RITA MORENO
PAGE MISS GLORY ... LIONEL STANDER
PAGEMASTER, THE ... CHARLES FLEISCHER
PAGEMASTER, THE ... CHRISOPHER LLOYD
PAGEMASTER, THE ... CHRISTOPHER LLOYD
PAGEMASTER, THE ... ED BEGLEY JR.
PAGEMASTER, THE ... FRANK WELKER
PAGEMASTER, THE ... LEONARD NIMOY
PAGEMASTER, THE ... MACAULAY CULKIN
PAGEMASTER, THE ... MEL HARRIS
PAGEMASTER, THE ... PATRICK STEWART
PAGEMASTER, THE ... PHIL HARTMAN
PAGEMASTER, THE ... WHOOPI GOLDBERG
PAID ... JOAN CRAWFORD†
PAINT YOUR WAGON ... ALAN BAXTER†
PAINT YOUR WAGON ... CLINT EASTWOOD
PAINT YOUR WAGON ... JEAN SEBERG†
PAINT YOUR WAGON ... LEE MARVIN†
PAINT YOUR WAGON ... RAY WALSTON
PAINTED SMILE, THE ... DAVID HEMMINGS
PAINTED VEIL, THE ... CECILIA PARKER†
PAIR OF ACES (TF) ... HELEN SHAVER
PAIR OF ACES (TF) ... JANE CAMERON
PAIR OF ACES (TF) ... KRIS KRISTOFFERSON
PAIR OF ACES (TF) ... WILLIE NELSON
PAIR OF BRIEFS, A ... RON MOODY
PAJAMA GAME, THE ... DORIS DAY
PAJAMA PARTY ... DOROTHY LAMOUR
PAJAMA PARTY ... FRANKIE AVALON
PAL JOEY ... FRANK SINATRA
PAL JOEY ... KIM NOVAK
PALE RIDER ... CARRIE SNODGRESS
PALE RIDER ... CLINT EASTWOOD
PALE RIDER ... MICHAEL MORIARTY
PALE RIDER ... RICHARD KIEL
PALEFACE, THE ... BOB HOPE
PALM SPRINGS ... DAVID NIVEN†
PALM SPRINGS WEEKEND ... CONNIE STEVENS
PALM SPRINGS WEEKEND ... JACK WESTON
PALM SPRINGS WEEKEND ... ROBERT CONRAD
PALM SPRINGS WEEKEND ... STEFANIE POWERS
PALM SPRINGS WEEKEND ... TROY DONAHUE
PALS (TF) ... DON AMECHE†
PALS (TF) ... GEORGE C. SCOTT
PALS (TF) ... LENKA PETERSON
PALS (TF) ... SYLVIA SIDNEY
PAN AMERICANA ... JANE GREER
PANACHE ... AMY IRVING
PANACHE (TF) ... RENE AUBERJONOIS
PANAMA HATTIE ... ANN SOTHERN
PANAMA HATTIE ... LENA HORNE
PANCHO BARNES (MS) ... CYNTHIA HARRIS
PANCHO BARNES (MS) ... TED WASS
PANCHO BARNES (MS) ... VALERIE BERTINELLI
PANCHO VILLA ... CHUCK CONNORS†
PANCHO VILLA ... CLINT WALKER
PANCHO VILLA ... TELLY SAVALAS†
PANDEMONIUM ... EILEEN BRENNAN
PANDEMONIUM ... JUDGE REINHOLD
PANDEMONIUM ... PAUL REUBENS
PANDEMONIUM ... TAB HUNTER
PANDEMONIUM ... TOM SMOTHERS
PANDORA AND THE FLYING DUTCHMAN ... AVA GARDNER†
PANE AMORE E... ... SOPHIA LOREN
PANIC AT LAKEWOOD MANOR/ANTS (TF) ... BRIAN DENNEHY
PANIC AT LAKEWOOD MANOR/ANTS (TF) ... SUZANNE SOMERS
PANIC BUTTON ... ELEANOR PARKER
PANIC IN NEEDLE PARK ... RICHARD BRIGHT
PANIC IN NEEDLE PARK, THE ... AL PACINO
PANIC IN NEEDLE PARK, THE ... PAUL SORVINO
PANIC IN NEEDLE PARK, THE ... RAUL JULIA†
PANIC IN THE CITY ... DENNIS HOPPER
PANIC IN THE CITY ... HOWARD DUFF†
PANIC IN THE CITY ... NEHEMIAH PERSOFF
PANIC IN THE PARLOR ... GORDAN JACKSON†
PANIC IN THE STREETS ... JACK PALANCE
PANIC IN THE STREETS ... LENKA PETERSON
PANIC IN THE STREETS ... RICHARD WIDMARK
PANIC IN YEAR ZERO! ... FRANKIE AVALON
PANIC ON THE 5.22 (TF) ... LAURENCE LUCKINBILL
PANTHER ... COURTNEY B. VANCE
PANTHER ... JOE DON BAKER
PANTHER ... KADEEN HARDISON

This is not a list of every film ever made or every cast member, only those listed in this directory.

PANTHER ... MARIO VAN PEEBLES
PAPA WAS A PREACHER ... IMOGENE COCA
PAPER, THE ... AMELIA CAMPBELL
PAPER, THE ... AUGUSTA DABNEY
PAPER, THE ... BRUCE ALTMAN
PAPER, THE ... CATHERINE O'HARA
PAPER, THE ... GLENN CLOSE
PAPER, THE ... JASON ALEXANDER
PAPER, THE ... JASON ROBARDS
PAPER, THE ... LYNNE THIGPEN
PAPER, THE ... MARISA TOMEI
PAPER, THE ... MICHAEL KEATON
PAPER, THE ... RANDY QUAID
PAPER, THE ... ROBERT DUVALL
PAPER, THE ... ROMA MAFFIA
PAPER, THE ... SIOBHAN FALLON
PAPER, THE ... SPALDING GRAY
PAPER CHASE, THE ... ALAN NAPIER†
PAPER CHASE, THE ... EDWRAD HERRMANN
PAPER CHASE, THE ... JAMES NAUGHTON
PAPER CHASE, THE ... LINDSAY WAGNER
PAPER CHASE, THE ... TIMOTHY BOTTOMS
PAPER CHASE, THE ○○ ... JOHN HOUSEMAN†
PAPER DOLLS (TF) ... BARRY PRIMUS
PAPER DOLLS (TF) ... DARYL HANNAH
PAPER DOLLS (TF) ... JENNIFER WARREN
PAPER DOLLS (TF) ... JOAN COLLINS
PAPER DOLLS (TF) ... LLOYD BRIDGES
PAPER DOLLS (TF) ... MORGAN FAIRCHILD
PAPER LION ... ALAN ALDA
PAPER LION ... ALEXIS KARRAS
PAPER LION ... ANN TURKEL
PAPER LION ... DAVID DOYLE
PAPER LION ... LAUREN HUTTON
PAPER LION ... ROY SCHEIDER
PAPER MASK ... AMANDA DONOHOE
PAPER MOON ... JOHN HILLERMAN
PAPER MOON ... KENNETH MARS
PAPER MOON ... RANDY QUAID
PAPER MOON ... RYAN O'NEAL
PAPER MOON ○ ... MADELINE KAHN
PAPER MOON ○○ ... TATUM O'NEAL
PAPER TIGER ... IRENE TSU
PAPER TIGER ... JEFF COREY
PAPER WEDDING, A ... GENEVIEVE BUJOLD
PAPERBACK HERO ... ELIZABETH ASHLEY
PAPILLON ... DUSTIN HOFFMAN
PAPILLON ... GREGORY SIERRA
PARACHUTE JUMPER ... BETTE DAVIS†
PARACHUTE JUMPER ... LEON AMES
PARADES ... DAVID DOYLE
PARADINE CASE, THE ... GREGORY PECK
PARADINE CASE, THE ... LOUIS JOURDAN
PARADINE CASE, THE ○ ... ETHEL BARRYMORE†
PARADISE ... AVIVA MARKS
PARADISE ... DON JOHNSON
PARADISE ... ELIJAH WOOD
PARADISE ... EVE GORDON
PARADISE ... LOUISE LATHAM
PARADISE ... MELANIE GRIFFITH
PARADISE ... NEIL VIPOND
PARADISE ... PHOEBE CATES
PARADISE ... RICHARD CURNOCK
PARADISE ... SHEILA McCARTHY
PARADISE ... THORA BIRCH
PARADISE ... TUVIA TAVI
PARADISE ... WILLIE AAMES
PARADISE ALLEY ... ANNE ARCHER
PARADISE ALLEY ... ARMAND ASSANTE
PARADISE ALLEY ... RAY SHARKEY†
PARADISE ALLEY ... SYLVESTER STALLONE
PARADISE HAWAIIAN STYLE ... ELVIS PRESLEY†
PARADISE, HAWAIIAN STYLE ... JAMES SHIGETA
PARALLAX VIEW, THE ... BILL McKINNEY
PARALLAX VIEW, THE ... HUME CRONYN
PARALLAX VIEW, THE ... KENNETH MARS
PARALLAX VIEW, THE ... PAULA PRENTISS
PARALLAX VIEW, THE ... WALTER MCGINN†
PARALLAX VIEW, THE ... WARREN BEATTY
PARALLAX VIEW, THE ... WILLIAM DANIELS
PARALLEL LIVES (CTF) ... ALLY SHEEDY
PARALLEL LIVES (CTF) ... BEN GAZZARA
PARALLEL LIVES (CTF) ... DAVID LANSBURY
PARALLEL LIVES (CTF) ... DUDLEY MOORE
PARALLEL LIVES (CTF) ... GENA ROWLANDS
PARALLEL LIVES (CTF) ... HELEN SLATER
PARALLEL LIVES (CTF) ... JACK KLUGMAN
PARALLEL LIVES (CTF) ... JAMES BELUSHI
PARALLEL LIVES (CTF) ... JAMES BROLIN
PARALLEL LIVES (CTF) ... JILL EIKENBERRY
PARALLEL LIVES (CTF) ... JoBETH WILLIAMS
PARALLEL LIVES (CTF) ... LeVAR BURTON
PARALLEL LIVES (CTF) ... LINDSAY CROUSE
PARALLEL LIVES (CTF) ... LIZA MINELLI
PARALLEL LIVES (CTF) ... MIRA SORVINO
PARALLEL LIVES (CTF) ... PATRICIA WETTIG
PARALLEL LIVES (CTF) ... PAUL SORVINO
PARALLEL LIVES (CTF) ... ROBERT WAGNER
PARALLEL LIVES (CTF) ... TREAT WILLIAMS
PARAMEDICS ... CHRISTOPHER McDONALD
PARAMEDICS ... GEORGE NEWBERN
PARAMEDICS ... LAWRENCE-HILTON JACOBS
PARAMEDICS ... RAY WALSTON
PARANOIA ... CARROLL BAKER
PARASITE ... DEMI MOORE
PARASITE ... ROBERT GLAUDINI
PARDNERS ... DEAN MARTIN
PARDNERS ... JERRY LEWIS
PARENT TRAP, THE ... BRIAN KEITH
PARENT TRAP, THE ... HAYLEY MILLS
PARENT TRAP, THE ... MAUREEN O'HARA
PARENT TRAP: HAWAIIAN HONEYMOON (TF) ... BARRY BOSTWICK
PARENT TRAP: HAWAIIAN HONEYMOON (TF) ... HAYLEY MILLS
PARENT TRAP II (CTF) ... HAYLEY MILLS
PARENT TRAP III (TF) ... BARRY BOSTWICK
PARENT TRAP III (TF) ... HAYLEY MILLS
PARENTHOOD ... DENNIS DUGAN
PARENTHOOD ... HARLEY JANE KOZAK
PARENTHOOD ... JASON ROBARDS
PARENTHOOD ... JOAQUIN PHOENIX
PARENTHOOD ... KEANU REEVES
PARENTHOOD ... LEAF PHOENIX
PARENTHOOD ... MARTHA PLIMPTON
PARENTHOOD ... MARY STEENBURGEN
PARENTHOOD ... RICK MORANIS
PARENTHOOD ... STEVE MARTIN
PARENTHOOD ... TOM HULCE
PARENTHOOD ○ ... DIANNE WIEST
PARENTS ... BRYAN MADORSKY
PARENTS ... JUNO MILLS-COCKELL
PARENTS ... MARY BETH HURT
PARENTS ... RANDY QUAID
PARENTS ... SANDY DENNIS†
PARIGI E SEMPRE PARIGI ... MARCELLO MASTROIANNI
PARIS ... JOAN CRAWFORD†
PARIS BLUES ... DIAHANN CARROLL
PARIS BLUES ... JOANNE WOODWARD
PARIS BLUES ... PAUL NEWMAN
PARIS BLUES ... SIDNEY POITIER
PARIS BRULE-T-IL? ... ANTHONY PERKINS†
PARIS BRULE-T-IL? ... KIRK DOUGLAS
PARIS BRULE-T-IL? ... LESLIE CARON
PARIS BRULE-T-IL? ... ROBERT STACK
PARIS BY NIGHT ... CHARLOTTE RAMPLING
PARIS DOES STRANGE THINGS ... MEL FERRER
PARIS EXPRESS, THE ... ANOUK AIMEE
PARIS HOLIDAY ... BOB HOPE
PARIS MATCH ... FRANCOIS CLUZET
PARIS MATCH ... JEAN RENO
PARIS MATCH ... KEVIN KLINE
PARIS MATCH ... MEG RYAN
PARIS MATCH ... TIMOTHY HUTTON
PARIS MODEL ... EVA GABOR
PARIS, TEXAS ... DEAN STOCKWELL
PARIS, TEXAS ... HARRY DEAN STANTON
PARIS, TEXAS ... NASTASSJA KINSKI
PARIS TROUT (CTF) ... BARBARA HERSHEY
PARIS TROUT (CTF) ... DENNIS HOPPER
PARIS TROUT (CTF) ... ED HARRIS
PARIS WHEN IT SIZZLES ... AUDREY HEPBURN†
PARIS WHEN IT SIZZLES ... MEL FERRER
PARIS WHEN IT SIZZLES ... TONY CURTIS
PARKER ... BRYON BROWN
PARKER KANE (TF) ... JEFF FAHEY
PARKER KANE (TF) ... RICHARD ZOBEL
PAROLE! ... ANTHONY QUINN
PAROLE FIXER ... ANTHONY QUINN
PAROLE GIRL ... RALPH BELLAMY†
PARRISH ... CARROLL O'CONNOR
PARRISH ... CONNIE STEVENS
PARRISH ... KARL MALDEN
PARRISH ... SYLVIA MILES
PARRISH ... TROY DONAHUE
PART 2, WALKING TALL ... BO SVENSON
PARTING GLANCES ... STEVE BUSCEMI
PARTISANI ... ADAM WEST
PARTNERS ... DENHOLM ELLIOTT†
PARTNERS ... JOHN HURT
PARTNERS ... KENNETH McMILLAN†
PARTNERS ... RYAN O'NEAL
PARTNERS IN CRIME ... ANTHONY QUINN
PARTNERS IN CRIME (TF) ... LEE GRANT
PARTY AT KITTY AND STUD'S, A ... SYLVESTER STALLONE
PARTY CRASHERS, THE ... CONNIE STEVENS
PARTY GIRL ... COREY ALLEN
PARTY GIRL ... CYD CHARISSE
PARTY GIRL ... JOHN IRELAND
PARTY'S OVER, THE ... EDDIE ALBERT
PAS SI MÉCHANT QUE ÇA ... GERARD DEPARDIEU
PASCALI'S ISLAND ... BEN KINGSLEY
PASCALI'S ISLAND ... CHARLES DANCE
PASCALI'S ISLAND ... HELEN MIRREN
PASS THE AMMO ... DENNIS BURKLEY
PASSAGE, THE ... ANTHONY QUINN
PASSAGE, THE ... KAY LENZ
PASSAGE, THE ... MALCOLM McDOWELL
PASSAGE, THE ... PATRICIA NEAL
PASSAGE TO INDIA, A ... ALEC GUINNESS
PASSAGE TO INDIA, A ... JAMES FOX
PASSAGE TO INDIA, A ... NIGEL HAYERS
PASSAGE TO INDIA, A ... VICTOR BANERJEE
PASSAGE TO INDIA, A ★ ... JUDY DAVIS
PASSAGE TO INDIA, A ○○ ... PEGGY ASHCROFT†
PASSED AWAY ... BLAIR BROWN
PASSED AWAY ... BOB HOSKINS
PASSED AWAY ... FRANCES McDORMAND
PASSED AWAY ... JACK WARDEN
PASSED AWAY ... MAUREEN STAPLETON
PASSED AWAY ... NANCY TRAVIS
PASSED AWAY ... PAMELA REED
PASSED AWAY ... PETER RIEGERT
PASSED AWAY ... TIM CURRY
PASSED AWAY ... WILLIAM L. PETERSEN
PASSENGER 57 ... BRUCE PAYNE
PASSENGER 57 ... TOM SIZEMORE
PASSENGER 57 ... WESLEY SNIPES
PASSENGER, THE ... JACK NICHOLSON
PASSI DI MORTE PERDUTI NEL BUIO ... ROBERT WEBBER
PASSION ... LIV ULLMANN
PASSION ... RAYMOND BURR†
PASSION ... YVONNE DE CARLO
PASSION, A ... ERLAND JOSEPHSON
PASSION AND PARADISE (MS) ... ARMAND ASSANTE
PASSION AND PARADISE (MS) ... CATHERINE MARY STEWART
PASSION AND PARADISE (MS) ... MARIETTE HARTLEY
PASSION FISH ... ALFRE WOODARD
PASSION FISH ... ANGELA BASSETT
PASSION FISH ... DAVID STRATHAIRN
PASSION FISH ... NORA DUNN
PASSION FISH ★ ... MARY McDONNELL
PASSION OF ANNA, THE ... BIBI ANDERSSON
PASSION OF ANNA, THE ... LIV ULLMANN
PASSIONATE THIEF, THE ... BEN GAZZARA
PASSIONS (TF) ... JOANNE WOODWARD
PASSIONS (TF) ... LINDSAY WAGNER
PASSIONS (TF) ... MASON ADAMS
PASSIONS (TF) ... RICHARD CRENNA
PASSOVER PLOT, THE ... DONALD PLEASENCE

† after an actor's name denotes deceased.

PASSOVER PLOT, THE .... ROBERT WALKER JR.
PASSOVER PLOT, THE .... SCOTT WILSON
PASSPORT TO SUEZ .... LLOYD BRIDGES
PASSPORT TO TREASON .... LOIS MAXWELL
PAST MIDNIGHT .... CLANCY BROWN
PAST MIDNIGHT .... RONNY COX
PAST MIDNIGHT (CTF) .... RUTGER HAUER
PAT AND MIKE .... CHARLES BRONSON
PAT AND MIKE .... CHUCK CONNORS†
PAT AND MIKE .... KATHERINE HEPBURN
PAT AND MIKE .... SPENCER TRACY†
PAT GARRETT AND
   BILLY THE KID .... JASON ROBARDS
PAT GARRETT AND BILLY THE KID .... JOHN BECK
PAT GARRETT AND
   BILLY THE KID .... KATHY JURADO
PAT GARRETT AND
   BILLY THE KID .... R.G. ARMSTRONG
PAT GARRETT & BILLY THE KID .... BOB DYLAN
PAT GARRETT & BILLY THE KID ..... JAMES COBURN
PAT GARRETT &
   BILLY THE KID .... KRIS KRISTOFFERSON
PAT GARRETT &
   BILLY THE KID .... RICHARD JAECKEL
PATCH OF BLUE, A .... SIDNEY POITIER
PATCH OF BLUE, A ★ .... ELIZABETH HARTMAN†
PATCH OF BLUE, A ∞ .... SHELLEY WINTERS
PATENT LEATHER
   KID, THE ★ .... RICHARD BARTHELMESS†
PATERNITY .... BEVERLY D'ANGELO
PATERNITY .... BURT REYNOLDS
PATERNITY .... ELIZABETH ASHLEY
PATERNITY .... LAUREN HUTTON
PATERNITY .... MIKE KELLIN†
PATERNITY .... NORMAN FELL
PATERNITY .... PAUL DOOLEY
PATHS OF GLORY .... KIRK DOUGLAS
PATHS OF GLORY .... RICHARD ANDERSON
PATHS OF GLORY .... TIMOTHY CAREY
PATHWAYS OF LIFE .... LILLIAN GISH†
PATRICIA NEAL
   STORY, THE (TF) .... GLENDA JACKSON
PATRIOT, THE .... GREGG HENRY
PATRIOT, THE .... JEFF CONAWAY
PATRIOT, THE .... LESLIE NIELSEN
PATRIOT, THE .... SIMONE GRIFFETH
PATRIOT, THE ★ .... LEWIS STONE†
PATRIOT GAMES .... ALUN ARMSTRONG
PATRIOT GAMES .... ANNE ARCHER
PATRIOT GAMES .... HARRISON FORD
PATRIOT GAMES .... JAMES EARL JONES
PATRIOT GAMES .... JAMES FOX
PATRIOT GAMES .... PATRICK BERGIN
PATRIOT GAMES .... RICHARD HARRIS
PATRIOT GAMES .... SEAN BEAN
PATRIOT GAMES .... THORA BIRCH
PATSY, THE .... JERRY LEWIS
PATTON .... KARL MALDEN
PATTON ★★ .... GEORGE C. SCOTT
PATTY HEARST .... DANA DELANY
PATTY HEARST .... FRANCES FISHER
PATTY HEARST .... JODI LONG
PATTY HEARST .... KITTY SWINK
PATTY HEARST .... NATASHA RICHARDSON
PATTY HEARST .... OLIVIA BARASH
PATTY HEARST .... WILLIAM FORSYTHE
PATTY HEARST .... YING RHAMES
PAULINA 1880 .... MAXIMILIAN SCHELL
PAULINE AT THE BEACH .... ARIELLE DOMBASLE
PAURA .... ELI WALLACH
PAURA IN CITTA .... JACK PALANCE
PAWNBROKER, THE .... BROCK PETERS
PAWNBROKER, THE .... GERALDINE FITZGERALD
PAWNBROKER, THE .... RAYMOND ST. JACQUES
PAWNBROKER, THE ★ .... ROD STEIGER
PAY DIRT .... HECTOR ELIZONDO
PAY OR DIE .... ERNEST BORGNINE
PAY OR DIE .... HOWARD CAINE†
PAY OR DIE .... ZOHRA LAMPERT
PAYDAY .... RIP TORN
PAYMENT DEFERRED .... MAUREEN O'SULLIVAN
PAYMENT ON DEMAND .... BETTE DAVIS†

PAYMENT ON DEMAND .... RICHARD ANDERSON
PAYROLL .... BILLIE WHITELAW
PCU .... CHRIS YOUNG
PCU .... DAVID SPADE
PCU .... JEREMY PIVEN
PCU .... JESSICA WALTER
PCU .... MEGAN WARD
PCU .... SARAH TRIGGER
PEARL (MS) .... ANGIE DICKINSON
PEARL (MS) .... AUDRA LINDLEY
PEARL (MS) .... BRIAN DENNEHY
PEARL (MS) .... DENNIS WEAVER
PEARL (TF) .... KATHERINE HELMOND
PEAU D'ANE .... CATHERINE DENEUVE
PEAU D'ESPION .... LOUIS JOURDAN
PEBBLE AND THE
   PENGUIN, THE (AF) .... ANNIE GOLDEN
PEBBLE AND THE
   PENGUIN, THE (AF) .... JAMES BELUSHI
PEBBLE AND THE
   PENGUIN, THE (AF) .... MARTIN SHORT
PEBBLE AND THE
   PENGUIN, THE (AF) .... TIM CURRY
PECCATO CHE SIA
   UNA CANAGLIA .... MARCELLO MASTROIANNI
PECCATO CHE SIA
   UNA CANAGLIA .... SOPHIA LOREN
PECK'S BAD BOY .... JACKIE COOPER
PEDESTRIAN, THE .... MAXIMILIAN SCHELL
PEDESTRIAN, THE .... PEGGY ASHCROFT†
PEE WEE'S BIG
   ADVENTURE .... CASSANDRA PETERSON
PEE-WEE'S BIG ADVENTURE .... JAMES BROLIN
PEE-WEE'S BIG ADVENTURE .... JAN HOOKS
PEE-WEE'S BIG
   ADVENTURE .... MORGAN FAIRCHILD
PEE-WEE'S BIG ADVENTURE .... PAUL REUBENS
PEEPER .... MICHAEL CAINE
PEEPER .... MICHAEL CONSTANTINE
PEEPER .... TIMOTHY CAREY
PEEPING TOM .... NIGEL DAVENPORT
PEEPING TOM .... SHIRLEY ANNE FIELD
PEGGY .... ROCK HUDSON†
PEGGY SUE GOT MARRIED .... BARBARA HARRIS
PEGGY SUE GOT MARRIED .... BARRY MILLER
PEGGY SUE GOT MARRIED .... CATHERINE HICKS
PEGGY SUE GOT MARRIED .... DON MURRAY
PEGGY SUE GOT MARRIED .... HARRY BASIL
PEGGY SUE GOT MARRIED .... HELEN HUNT
PEGGY SUE GOT MARRIED .... JIM CARREY
PEGGY SUE GOT MARRIED .... JOAN ALLEN
PEGGY SUE GOT MARRIED ...... JOHN CARRADINE†
PEGGY SUE GOT MARRIED ...... KEVIN J. O'CONNOR
PEGGY SUE GOT MARRIED .... LEON AMES
PEGGY SUE GOT MARRIED .... LUCINDA JENNEY
PEGGY SUE
   GOT MARRIED .... MAUREEN O'SULLIVAN
PEGGY SUE GOT MARRIED .... NICOLAS CAGE
PEGGY SUE GOT MARRIED .... RANDY BOURNE
PEGGY SUE GOT MARRIED .... SOFIA COPPOLA
PEGGY SUE
   GOT MARRIED ★ .... KATHLEEN TURNER
PELICAN BRIEF, THE .... DENZEL WASHINGTON
PELICAN BRIEF, THE .... HUME CRONYN
PELICAN BRIEF, THE .... JAMES B. SIKKING
PELICAN BRIEF, THE .... JOHN HEARD
PELICAN BRIEF, THE .... JOHN LITHGOW
PELICAN BRIEF, THE .... JULIA ROBERTS
PELICAN BRIEF, THE .... ROBERT CULP
PELICAN BRIEF, THE .... SAM SHEPARD
PELICAN BRIEF, THE .... STANLEY TUCCI
PELICAN BRIEF, THE .... TONY GOLDWYN
PELICAN BRIEF, THE .... WILLIAM ATHERTON
PELLE THE CONQUEROR ★ .... MAX von SYDOW
PENDULUM .... GEORGE PEPPARD†
PENDULUM .... RICHARD KILEY
PENELOPE .... IAN BANNEN
PENELOPE .... JONATHAN WINTERS
PENELOPE .... LILA KEDROVA
PENELOPE .... LOU JACOBI
PENELOPE .... NATALIE WOOD†
PENELOPE .... PETER FALK

PENITENT, THE .... RAUL JULIA†
PENITENTIARY .... MYKELTI WILLIAMSON
PENN AND TELLER GET KILLED .... ALAN NORTH
PENN OF PENNSYLVANIA .... DEBORAH KERR
PENNIES FROM HEAVEN .... BERNADETTE PETERS
PENNIES FROM
   HEAVEN .... CHRISTOPHER WALKEN
PENNIES FROM HEAVEN .... JESSICA HARPER
PENNIES FROM HEAVEN .... STEVE MARTIN
PENNIES FROM HEAVEN .... VERNEL BAGNERIS
PENNY GOLD .... JOSS ACKLAND
PENNY SERENADE ★ .... CARY GRANT†
PENTHOUSE, THE .... TONY BECKLEY†
PENTHOUSE, THE (TF) .... DAVID HEWLETT
PENTHOUSE, THE (TF) .... ROBERT GUILLAUME
PENTHOUSE, THE (TF) .... ROBIN GIVENS
PEOPLE ACROSS THE
   LAKE, THE (TF) .... BARRY CORBIN
PEOPLE ACROSS THE
   LAKE, THE (TF) .... DARYL ANDERSON
PEOPLE ACROSS THE
   LAKE, THE (TF) .... GERALD McRANEY
PEOPLE ACROSS THE
   LAKE, THE (TF) .... TAMMY LAUREN
PEOPLE ACROSS THE
   LAKE, THE (TF) .... VALERIE HARPER
PEOPLE AGAINST
   O'HARA, THE .... CHARLES BRONSON
PEOPLE AGAINST O'HARA, THE ..... JAMES ARNESS
PEOPLE AGAINST
   O'HARA, THE .... RICHARD ANDERSON
PEOPLE LIKE US (TF) .... BEN GAZZARA
PEOPLE LIKE US (TF) .... DENNIS FARINA
PEOPLE LIKE US (TF) .... EVA MARIE SAINT
PEOPLE NEXT DOOR, THE .... CLORIS LEACHMAN
PEOPLE NEXT DOOR, THE .... ELI WALLACH
PEOPLE NEXT DOOR, THE .... HAL HOLBROOK
PEOPLE NEXT DOOR, THE .... JULIE HARRIS
PEOPLE NEXT DOOR, THE ..... NEHEMIAH PERSOFF
PEOPLE NEXT DOOR, THE ...... STEPHEN McHATTIE
PEOPLE THAT TIME
   FORGOT, THE .... DOUG McCLURE
PEOPLE THAT TIME
   FORGOT, THE .... PATRICK WAYNE
PEOPLE THAT TIME
   FORGOT, THE .... SHANE RIMMER
PEOPLE THAT TIME
   FORGOT, THE .... THORLEY WALTERS†
PEOPLE, THE (TF) .... KIM DARBY
PEOPLE, THE (TF) .... WILLIAM SHATNER
PEOPLE VS. JEAN
   HARRIS, THE (TF) .... ELLEN BURSTYN
PEOPLE WILL TALK .... HUME CRONYN
PEPE .... DEBBIE REYNOLDS
PEPE .... FRANK SINATRA
PEPE .... GREER GARSON
PEPE .... JACK LEMMON
PEPE .... JANET LEIGH
PEPE .... KIM NOVAK
PEPE .... SHIRLEY JONES
PEPE .... TONY CURTIS
PEPE .... ZSA ZSA GABOR
PER GRAZIA RICEVUTA .... LIONEL STANDER
PER LE ANTICHE SCALE .... MARTHE KELLER
PERCHE?! .... LILA KEDROVA
PERCHE SI UCCIDE
   UN MAGISTRATO .... FRANCO NERO
PERCY .... BRITT EKLAND
PERCY .... DENHOLM ELLIOTT†
PERCY'S PROGRESS .... ANTHONY ANDREWS
PERCY'S PROGRESS .... LEIGH LAWSON
PERCY'S PROGRESS .... MILO O'SHEA
PERCY'S PROGRESS .... VINCENT PRICE†
PEREZ FAMILY, THE .... ALFRED MOLINA
PEREZ FAMILY, THE .... ANJELICA HUSTON
PEREZ FAMILY, THE .... CELIA CRUZ
PEREZ FAMILY, THE .... CHAZZ PALMINTERI
PEREZ FAMILY, THE .... MARISA TOMEI
PERFECT .... ANNE DESALVO
PERFECT .... DAVID PAYMER
PERFECT .... JAMIE LEE CURTIS
PERFECT .... JANN WENNER

PERFECT .... JOHN TRAVOLTA
PERFECT .... LARAINE NEWMAN
PERFECT .... MARILU HENNER
PERFECT .... STACY BAYNE
PERFECT .... STEFAN GIERASCH
PERFECT .... TRACY BAYNE
PERFECT ALIBI .... LYDIE DENIER
PERFECT ALIBI .... TERI GARR
PERFECT COUPLE, A .... DIMITRA ARLYS
PERFECT COUPLE, A .... HENRY GIBSON
PERFECT COUPLE, A .... PAUL DOOLEY
PERFECT FRIDAY .... DAVID WARNER
PERFECT FRIDAY .... URSULA ANDRESS
PERFECT FURLOUGH, THE .... ELAINE STRITCH
PERFECT FURLOUGH, THE .... JANET LEIGH
PERFECT FURLOUGH, THE .... TONY CURTIS
PERFECT FURLOUGH, THE .... TROY DONAHUE
PERFECT GENTLEMEN (TF) .... LAUREN BACALL
PERFECT GENTLEMEN (TF) .... SANDY DENNIS†
PERFECT KILLER, THE .... RICHARD WIDMARK
PERFECT MARRIAGE, THE .... DAVID NIVEN†
PERFECT MARRIAGE, THE .... EDDIE ALBERT
PERFECT MATCH, A (TF) ..... COLLEEN DEWHURST†
PERFECT PEOPLE (TF) .... DAVID LEISURE
PERFECT PEOPLE (TF) .... KAREN VALENTINE
PERFECT PEOPLE (TF) .... LAUREN HUTTON
PERFECT PEOPLE (TF) .... PERRY KING
PERFECT PEOPLE (TF) .... PRISCILLA BARNES
PERFECT PROFILE .... NANCY LIEBERMAN
PERFECT SNOB, THE .... ANTHONY QUINN
PERFECT STRANGERS .... DEBORAH KERR
PERFECT
  TRIBUTE, THE (CTF) .... CAMPBELL SCOTT
PERFECT TRIBUTE, THE (CTF) .... ED FLANDERS
PERFECT TRIBUTE, THE (CTF) ..... JASON ROBARDS
PERFECT TRIBUTE, THE (CTF) .... JOSE FERRER†
PERFECT
  TRIBUTE, THE (CTF) .... KATHERINE HELMOND
PERFECT TRIBUTE, THE (CTF) .... LUKAS HAAS
PERFECT VICTIMS .... CLARENCE WILLIAMS III
PERFECT VICTIMS .... DEBORAH SHELTON
PERFECT VICTIMS .... TOM DUGAN
PERFECT WEAPON, THE .... JAMES HONG
PERFECT WEAPON, THE .... JEFF SPEAKMAN
PERFECT WEAPON, THE .... JOHN DYE
PERFECT WEAPON, THE .... MAKO
PERFECT WITNESS (CTF) .... AIDAN QUINN
PERFECT WITNESS (CTF) .... BRIAN DENNEHY
PERFECT
  WITNESS (CTF) .... STOCKARD CHANNING
PERFECT WORLD, A .... BRAD WHITFORD
PERFECT WORLD, A .... CLINT EASTWOOD
PERFECT WORLD, A .... KEITH SZARABAJKA
PERFECT WORLD, A .... KEVIN COSTNER
PERFECT WORLD, A .... LAURA DERN
PERFECT WORLD, A .... LEO BURMESTER
PERFECT WORLD, A .... T. J. LOWTHER
PERFECTLY NORMAL .... ROBBIE COLTRANE
PERFORMANCE .... JAMES FOX
PERFORMANCE .... MICK JAGGER
PERILS OF PAULINE, THE .... MILTON BERLE
PERILS OF PAULINE, THE .... PAT BOONE
PERIOD OF
  ADJUSTMENT .... ANTHONY (TONY) FRANCIOSA
PERIOD OF ADJUSTMENT .... JANE FONDA
PERIOD OF ADJUSTMENT .... LOIS NETTLETON
PERMANENT RECORD .... JENNIFER RUBIN
PERMANENT RECORD .... KATHY BAKER
PERMANENT RECORD .... KEANU REEVES
PERMISSION TO KILL .... AVA GARDNER†
PERMISSION TO KILL .... FREDERIC FORREST
PERMISSION TO KILL .... TIMOTHY DALTON
PERRY MASON RETURNS (TF) .... BARBARA HALE
PERRY MASON RETURNS (TF) .... RAYMOND BURR†
PERRY MASON
  RETURNS (TF) .... RICHARD ANDERSON
PERRY MASON RETURNS (TF) .... WILLIAM KATT
PERRY MASON: THE CASE OF THE
  ALL-STAR ASSASSIN (TF) .... BARBARA HALE
PERRY MASON: THE CASE OF THE
  ALL-STAR ASSASSIN (TF) .... RAYMOND BURR†

PERRY MASON: THE CASE OF THE
  ALL-STAR ASSASSIN (TF) .... WILLIAM R. MOSES
PERRY MASON: THE CASE OF THE
  AVENGING ACE (TF) .... BARBARA HALE
PERRY MASON: THE CASE OF THE
  AVENGING ACE (TF) .... DAVID OGDEN STIERS
PERRY MASON: THE CASE OF
  THE AVENGING ACE (TF) .... PATTY DUKE
PERRY MASON: THE CASE OF
  THE AVENGING ACE (TF) .... RAYMOND BURR†
PERRY MASON: THE CASE OF
  THE AVENGING ACE (TF) .... WILLIAM KATT
PERRY MASON: THE CASE OF THE
  DESPERATE DECEPTION (TF) ..... BARBARA HALE
PERRY MASON: THE CASE OF THE
  DESPERATE DECEPTION (TF) .... IAN BANNEN
PERRY MASON: THE CASE
  OF THE DESPERATE
  DECEPTION (TF) .... RAYMOND BURR†
PERRY MASON: THE CASE
  OF THE DESPERATE
  DECEPTION (TF) .... WILLIAM R. MOSES
PERRY MASON: THE CASE OF THE
  LADY IN THE LAKE (TF) .... BARBARA HALE
PERRY MASON: THE CASE OF THE
  LADY IN THE LAKE (TF) .... DAVID HASSELHOFF
PERRY MASON: THE CASE OF THE
  LADY IN THE LAKE (TF) ...... DAVID OGDEN STIERS
PERRY MASON: THE CASE OF THE
  LADY IN THE LAKE (TF) .... JOHN BECK
PERRY MASON: THE CASE OF THE
  LADY IN THE LAKE (TF) .... RAYMOND BURR†
PERRY MASON: THE CASE OF THE
  LADY IN THE LAKE (TF) .... WILLIAM KATT
PERRY MASON: THE CASE OF THE
  LETHAL LESSON (TF) .... BARBARA HALE
PERRY MASON: THE CASE OF THE
  LETHAL LESSON (TF) .... RAYMOND BURR†
PERRY MASON: THE CASE OF THE
  LETHAL LESSON (TF) .... WILLIAM R. MOSES
PERRY MASON: THE CASE OF
  THE LOST LOVE (TF) .... BARBARA HALE
PERRY MASON: THE CASE OF
  THE LOST LOVE (TF) .... DAVID OGDEN STIERS
PERRY MASON: THE CASE OF
  THE LOST LOVE (TF) .... GORDON JUMP
PERRY MASON: THE CASE OF
  THE LOST LOVE (TF) .... RAYMOND BURR†
PERRY MASON: THE CASE OF
  THE LOST LOVE (TF) .... ROBERT MANDAN
PERRY MASON: THE CASE OF
  THE LOST LOVE (TF) .... WILLIAM KATT
PERRY MASON: THE CASE OF THE
  MURDERED MADAM (TF) .... ANN JILLIAN
PERRY MASON: THE CASE OF THE
  MURDERED MADAM (TF) .... BARBARA HALE
PERRY MASON: THE CASE OF THE
  MURDERED MADAM (TF) .... RAYMOND BURR†
PERRY MASON: THE CASE OF THE
  MURDERED MADAM (TF) .... WILLIAM KATT
PERRY MASON: THE CASE OF THE
  MUSICAL MURDER (TF) .... BARBARA HALE
PERRY MASON: THE CASE OF THE
  MUSICAL MURDER (TF) .... DEBBIE REYNOLDS
PERRY MASON: THE CASE OF THE
  MUSICAL MURDER (TF) .... JERRY ORBACH
PERRY MASON: THE CASE OF THE
  MUSICAL MURDER (TF) .... RAYMOND BURR†
PERRY MASON: THE CASE OF THE
  MUSICAL MURDER (TF) .... WILLIAM R. MOSES
PERRY MASON: THE CASE OF THE
  NOTORIOUS NUN (TF) .... ARTHUR HILL
PERRY MASON: THE CASE OF THE
  NOTORIOUS NUN (TF) .... BARBARA HALE
PERRY MASON: THE CASE OF THE
  NOTORIOUS NUN (TF) .... MICHELLE GREENE
PERRY MASON: THE CASE OF THE
  NOTORIOUS NUN (TF) .... RAYMOND BURR†
PERRY MASON: THE CASE OF THE
  NOTORIOUS NUN (TF) .... TIMOTHY BOTTOMS
PERRY MASON: THE CASE OF THE
  NOTORIOUS NUN (TF) .... TOM BOSLEY

PERRY MASON: THE CASE OF THE
  NOTORIOUS NUN (TF) .... WILLIAM KATT
PERRY MASON: THE CASE OF THE
  PARISIAN PARADOX (TF) .... BARBARA HALE
PERRY MASON: THE CASE OF THE
  PARISIAN PARADOX (TF) .... RAYMOND BURR†
PERRY MASON: THE CASE OF THE
  PARISIAN PARADOX (TF) .... WILLIAM R. MOSES
PERRY MASON: THE CASE OF THE
  POISONED PEN (TF) .... BARBARA HALE
PERRY MASON: THE CASE OF THE
  POISONED PEN (TF) .... RAYMOND BURR†
PERRY MASON: THE CASE OF THE
  POISONED PEN (TF) .... WILLIAM R. MOSES
PERRY MASON: THE CASE OF
  THE SCANDALOUS
  SCOUNDREL (TF) .... BARBARA HALE
PERRY MASON: THE CASE OF
  THE SCANDALOUS
  SCOUNDREL (TF) .... MORGAN BRITTANY
PERRY MASON: THE CASE OF
  THE SCANDALOUS
  SCOUNDREL (TF) .... RAYMOND BURR†
PERRY MASON: THE CASE OF
  THE SCANDALOUS
  SCOUNDREL (TF) .... ROBERT GUILLAUME
PERRY MASON: THE CASE OF
  THE SCANDALOUS
  SCOUNDREL (TF) .... WILLIAM KATT
PERRY MASON: THE CASE OF THE
  SHOOTING STAR (TF) .... BARBARA HALE
PERRY MASON: THE CASE OF THE
  SHOOTING STAR (TF) .... DAVID OGDEN STIERS
PERRY MASON: THE CASE OF THE
  SHOOTING STAR (TF) .... RAYMOND BURR†
PERRY MASON: THE CASE OF THE
  SHOOTING STAR (TF) .... WILLIAM KATT
PERRY MASON: THE CASE OF THE
  SILENCED SINGER (TF) .... RAYMOND BURR†
PERRY MASON: THE CASE OF THE
  SINISTER SPIRIT (TF) .... BARBARA HALE
PERRY MASON: THE CASE OF THE
  SINISTER SPIRIT (TF) .... DAVID OGDEN STIERS
PERRY MASON: THE CASE OF THE
  SINISTER SPIRIT (TF) .... DWIGHT SCHULTZ
PERRY MASON: THE CASE OF THE
  SINISTER SPIRIT (TF) .... RAYMOND BURR†
PERRY MASON: THE CASE OF THE
  SINISTER SPIRIT (TF) .... ROBERT STACK
PERRY MASON: THE CASE OF THE
  SINISTER SPIRIT (TF) .... WILLIAM KATT
PERSECUTION .... LANA TURNER
PERSECUTION AND ASSASSINATION
  OF JEAN-PAUL MARAT AS PERFORMED
  BY THE INMATES OF THE ASYLUM
  OF CHARENTON UNDER THE
  DIRECTION OF THE MARQUIS
  DE SADE, THE .... GLENDA JACKSON
PERSONA .... BIBI ANDERSSON
PERSONA .... LIV ULLMANN
PERSONAL BEST .... LUANA ANDERS
PERSONAL BEST .... MARIEL HEMINGWAY
PERSONAL BEST .... PATRICE DONNELLY
PERSONAL BEST .... SCOTT GLENN
PERSONAL CHOICE .... CHRISTIAN SLATER
PERSONAL CHOICE .... MARTIN SHEEN
PERSONAL CHOICE .... ROBERT FOXWORTH
PERSONAL CHOICE .... SHARON STONE
PERSONAL SERVICES .... ALEC McCOWEN
PERSONAL SERVICES .... JULIE WALTERS
PERSONALS (CTF) .... GINA GALLEGO
PERSONALS (CTF) .... STEPHANIE ZIMBALIST
PERSUADERS, THE .... TONY CURTIS
PET SEMATARY .... BLAZE BERDAHL
PET SEMATARY .... BRAD GREENQUIST
PET SEMATARY .... DALE MIDKIFF
PET SEMATARY .... DENISE CROSBY
PET SEMATARY .... FRED GWYNNE†
PET SEMATARY .... MICHAEL LOMBARD
PET SEMATARY .... MIKO HUGHES
PET SEMATARY .... STEPHEN KING
PET SEMATARY II .... ANTHONY EDWARDS

PET SEMATARY II .... CLANCY BROWN
PET SEMATARY II .... EDWARD FURLONG
PET SEMATARY II .... JARED RUSHTON
PETE KELLY'S BLUES .... JANET LEIGH
PETE N' TILLIE .... CAROL BURNETT
PETE 'N' TILLIE .... HENRY JONES
PETE N' TILLIE .... RENE AUBERJONOIS
PETE 'N' TILLIE .... WALTER MATTHAU
PETE 'N' TILLIE ○ .... GERALDINE PAGE†
PETER AND PAUL (TF) .... RAYMOND BURR†
PETER GUNN (TF) .... BARBARA WILLIAMS
PETER GUNN (TF) .... CHARLES CIOFFI
PETER GUNN (TF) .... CHAZZ PALMINTERI
PETER GUNN (TF) .... JENNIFER EDWARDS
PETER GUNN (TF) .... PETER STRAUSS
PETER LUNDY AND THE MEDICINE
    HAT STALLION (TF) .... JOHN ANDERSON
PETER THE GREAT (MS) .... MAXIMILIAN SCHELL
PETER THE GREAT (MS) .... VANESSA REDGRAVE
PETER THE GREAT (TF) .... JEREMY KEMP
PETERSEN .... JACK THOMPSON
PETER'S FRIENDS .... EMMA THOMPSON
PETER'S FRIENDS .... HUGH LAURIE
PETER'S FRIENDS .... KENNETH BRANAGH
PETER'S FRIENDS .... RITA RUDNER
PETER'S FRIENDS .... STEPHEN FRY
PETE'S DRAGON .... HELEN REDDY
PETE'S DRAGON .... RED BUTTONS
PETE'S DRAGON .... SHELLEY WINTERS
PETRIFIED FOREST, THE .... BETTE DAVIS†
PETTY GIRL, THE .... JOAN CAULFIELD†
PETTY GIRL, THE .... MARY WICKES
PETTY STORY, THE .... DARREN McGAVIN
PETULIA .... ARTHUR HILL
PETULIA .... GEORGE C. SCOTT
PETULIA .... JULIE CHRISTIE
PETULIA .... RENE AUBERJONOIS
PETULIA .... RICHARD CHAMBERLAIN
PETULIA .... SHIRLEY KNIGHT
PEYTON PLACE .... LEON AMES
PEYTON PLACE ★ .... LANA TURNER
PEYTON PLACE ○ .... HOPE LANGE
PEYTON PLACE ○ .... RUSS TAMBLYN
PEYTON PLACE: THE NEXT
    GENERATION (TF) .... ED NELSON
PHAEDRA .... ANTHONY PERKINS†
PHAEDRA .... RAF VALLONE
PHANTASM II .... JAMES LE GROS
PHANTASM II .... PAULA IRVINE
PHANTASM II .... REGGIE BANNISTER
PHANTOM, THE .... BILLY ZANE
PHANTOM, THE .... CAMERON DIAZ
PHANTOM CARAVAN .... DON AMECHE†
PHANTOM OF THE OPERA .... HUME CRONYN
PHANTOM OF THE OPERA (TF) .... MICHAEL YORK
PHANTOM OF THE OPERA, THE ..... JILL SCHOELEN
PHANTOM OF THE
    OPERA, THE .... MICHAEL GOUGH
PHANTOM OF THE
    OPERA, THE .... ROBERT ENGLUND
PHANTOM OF THE
    OPERA, THE (MS) .... BURT LANCASTER†
PHANTOM OF THE
    OPERA, THE (MS) .... CHARLES DANCE
PHANTOM OF THE
    OPERA, THE (MS) .... TERI POLO
PHANTOM OF THE
    OPERA, THE (TF) .... DIANA QUICK
PHANTOM OF THE PARADISE .... GERRITT GRAHAM
PHANTOM OF THE PARADISE ...... JESSICA HARPER
PHANTOM OF THE PARADISE ...... PAUL WILLIAMS
PHANTOM OF THE RUE MORGUE ..... KARL MALDEN
PHANTOM OF THE
    RUE MORGUE .... STEVE FORREST
PHANTOM PLANET, THE .... RICHARD KIEL
PHAR LAP .... TOM BURLINSON
PHASE IV .... NIGEL DAVENPORT
PHENIX CITY STORY, THE .... LENKA PETERSON
PHENIX CITY STORY, THE .... RICHARD KILEY
PHFFFT! .... JACK LEMMON
PHFFFT .... KIM NOVAK
PHILADELPHIA ★★ .... TOM HANKS
PHILADELPHIA .... ANTONIO BANDERAS

PHILADELPHIA .... BRAD WHITFORD
PHILADELPHIA .... DENZEL WASHINGTON
PHILADELPHIA .... JASON ROBARDS
PHILADELPHIA .... JOANNE WOODWARD
PHILADELPHIA .... MARY STEENBURGEN
PHILADELPHIA EXPERIMENT 2 ...... BRAD JOHNSON
PHILADELPHIA
    EXPERIMENT 2 .... GEOFFREY BLAKE
PHILADELPHIA
    EXPERIMENT 2 .... GERRITT GRAHAM
PHILADELPHIA EXPERIMENT 2 .... JAMES GREENE
PHILADELPHIA
    EXPERIMENT 2 .... JOHN CHRISTIAN GRAAS
PHILADELPHIA
    EXPERIMENT 2 .... MARJEAN HOLDEN
PHILADELPHIA
    EXPERIMENT, THE .... MICHAEL PARE
PHILADELPHIA EXPERIMENT, THE .... NANCY ALLEN
PHILADELPHIA STORY, THE .... CARY GRANT†
PHILADELPHIA
    STORY, THE ★ .... KATHERINE HEPBURN
PHILADELPHIA
    STORY, THE ★★ .... JAMES STEWART
PHILIP MARLOWE,
    PRIVATE EYE (CMS) .... POWERS BOOTHE
PHONE CALL FROM A STRANGER ..... BETTE DAVIS†
PHONE CALL FROM
    A STRANGER .... ROBERT DAVIS†
PHONE CALL FROM
    A STRANGER .... SHELLEY WINTERS
PHONE CALLS .... ANTHONY LaPAGLIA
PHONE CALLS .... BRIAN BENBEN
PHYNX, THE .... CLINT WALKER
PHYNX, THE .... DOROTHY LAMOUR
PHYNX, THE .... MARTHA RAYE†
PHYNX, THE .... MAUREEN O'SULLIVAN
PHYNX, THE .... RICHARD PRYOR
PHYSICAL EVIDENCE .... BURT REYNOLDS
PHYSICAL EVIDENCE .... KAY LENZ
PHYSICAL EVIDENCE .... NED BEATTY
PHYSICAL EVIDENCE .... THERESA RUSSELL
PIANO, THE .... GENEVIEVE LEMON
PIANO, THE .... HARVEY KEITEL
PIANO, THE .... KERRY WALKER
PIANO, THE .... SAM NEILL
PIANO, THE ★★ .... HOLLY HUNTER
PIANO, THE ○○ .... ANNA PAQUIN
PICASSO SUMMER, THE .... ALBERT FINNEY
PICASSO TRIGGER .... STEVE BOND
PICCADILLY THIRD STOP .... MAE ZETTERLING†
PICK-UP .... SYLVIA SIDNEY
PICK-UP ARTIST, THE .... BRIAN HAMILL
PICK-UP ARTIST, THE .... DANNY AIELLO
PICK-UP ARTIST, THE .... DENNIS HOPPER
PICK-UP ARTIST, THE .... HARVEY KEITEL
PICK-UP ARTIST, THE .... JAMES TOBACK
PICK-UP ARTIST, THE .... MILDRED DUNNOCK†
PICK-UP ARTIST, THE .... MOLLY RINGWALD
PICK-UP ARTIST, THE .... ROBERT DOWNEY JR.
PICK-UP ARTIST, THE .... VANESSA WILLIAMS
PICK-UP ARTIST, THE .... VICTORIA JACKSON
PICKING UP THE PIECES (TF) .... DAVID AYKROYD
PICKING UP THE PIECES (TF) .... MARGOT KIDDER
PICKLE, THE .... ALLY SHEEDY
PICKLE, THE .... BARRY MILLER
PICKLE, THE .... CHRIS PENN
PICKLE, THE .... CLOTILDE COURAU
PICKLE, THE .... DANNY AIELLO
PICKLE, THE .... DYAN CANNON
PICKLE, THE .... JERRY STILLER
PICKLE, THE .... PAUL MAZURSKY
PICKLE, THE .... SHELLEY WINTERS
PICKUP ON 101 .... LESLEY ANN WARREN
PICKUP ON 101 .... MARTIN SHEEN
PICKUP ON 101 .... MICHAEL ONTKEAN
PICKUP ON SOUTH STREET .... RICHARD KILEY
PICKUP ON SOUTH STREET ..... RICHARD WIDMARK
PICKUP ON SOUTH STREET ○ ..... THELMA RITTER†
PICKWICK PAPERS .... GEORGE ROSE†
PICNIC ○ .... ARTHUR O'CONNELL†
PICNIC .... CLIFF ROBERTSON
PICNIC .... KIM NOVAK
PICNIC .... SUSAN STRASBERG

PICNIC .... WILLIAM HOLDEN†
PICNIC AT HANGING ROCK ...... RACHEL ROBERTS†
PICTURA (FD) .... VINCENT PRICE†
PICTURE MOMMY DEAD .... DON AMECHE†
PICTURE MOMMY DEAD .... ZSA ZSA GABOR
PICTURE OF DORIAN
    GRAY, THE .... HURD HATFIELD
PICTURE OF DORIAN
    GRAY, THE ○ .... ANGELA LANSBURY
PICTURE SNATCHER .... RALPH BELLAMY†
PIECE OF THE ACTION, A .... BILL COSBY
PIECE OF THE ACTION, A .... DENISE NICHOLAS
PIECE OF THE ACTION, A .... JAMES EARL JONES
PIECE OF THE ACTION, A .... SIDNEY POITIER
PIECES OF DREAMS .... LAUREN HUTTON
PIECES OF DREAMS .... ROBERT FORSTER
PIED PIPER, THE .... DONALD PLEASENCE
PIED PIPER, THE .... JOHN HURT
PIED PIPER, THE .... PETER VAUGHN
PIED PIPER, THE .... RODDY McDOWALL
PIED PIPER, THE ★ .... MONTY WOOLLEY†
PIED PIPER MALONE .... BRIAN KEITH
PIED PIPER OF
    HAMELIN, THE (TF) .... VAN JOHNSON
PIGEON, THE (TF) .... PAT BOONE
PIGEON THAT TOOK
    ROME, THE .... CHARLTON HESTON
PIGEON THAT TOOK
    ROME, THE .... HARRY GUARDINO
PIGEONS .... ELAINE STRITCH
PIGEONS .... LOIS NETTLETON
PIGSKIN PARADE ○ .... STUART ERWIN†
PILLOW TALK .... ROCK HUDSON†
PILLOW TALK .... TONY RANDALL
PILLOW TALK ★ .... DORIS DAY
PILLOW TALK ○ .... THELMA RITTER†
PILLOW TO POST .... ROBERT BLAKE
PILLOW TO POST .... WILLIAM PRINCE
PILOT, THE .... CLIFF ROBERTSON
PILOT, THE .... GORDON MACRAE†
PILOT, THE .... MILO O'SHEA
PILOT NO. 5 .... AVA GARDNER†
PILOT NO. 5 .... GENE KELLY
PILOT NO. 5 .... VAN JOHNSON
PIMPERNEL SMITH .... DAVID TOMLINSON
PIN-UP GIRL .... MARTHA RAYE†
PINE CANYON IS BURNING (TF) .... DIANA MULDAUR
PINK CADILLAC .... BERNADETTE PETERS
PINK CADILLAC .... BILL MOSELY
PINK CADILLAC .... CATHERINE HICKLAND
PINK CADILLAC .... CLINT EASTWOOD
PINK CADILLAC .... GEOFFREY LEWIS
PINK CADILLAC .... JIM CARREY
PINK CHIQUITAS, THE .... EARTHA KITT
PINK FLAMINGOS .... DIVINE†
PINK FLOYD—THE WALL .... BOB HOSKINS
PINK JUNGLE, THE .... GEORGE KENNEDY
PINK JUNGLE, THE .... GEORGE ROSE†
PINK JUNGLE, THE .... JAMES GARNER
PINK JUNGLE, THE .... VAL AVERY
PINK MOTEL .... PHYLLIS DILLER
PINK PANTHER, THE .... BREANDA DE ANGELO†
PINK PANTHER, THE .... DAVID NIVEN†
PINK PANTHER, THE .... PETER SELLERS†
PINK PANTHER, THE .... ROBERT WAGNER
PINK PANTHER STRIKES
    AGAIN, THE .... BURT KWOUK
PINK PANTHER STRIKES
    AGAIN, THE .... COLIN BLAKELY†
PINK PANTHER STRIKES
    AGAIN, THE .... JULIE ANDREWS
PINK PANTHER STRIKES
    AGAIN, THE .... LEONARD ROSSITER†
PINK PANTHER STRIKES
    AGAIN, THE .... LESLEY-ANNE DOWN
PINK PANTHER STRIKES
    AGAIN, THE .... PETER SELLERS†
PINK STRINGS AND
    SEALING WAX .... GORDAN JACKSON†
PINK TELEPHONE, THE .... KIM DARBY
PINKY ○ .... ETHEL BARRYMORE†
PINKY ○ .... ETHEL WATERS†

This is not a list of every film ever made or every cast member, only those listed in this directory.

PIPE DREAMS .... SALLY KIRKLAND
PIRANHA .... BRADFORD DILLMAN
PIRANHA .... DICK MILLER
PIRANHA II: THE SPAWNING ..... LANCE HENRIKSEN
PIRATE, THE .... GENE KELLY
PIRATE, THE (TF) .... ANNE ARCHER
PIRATE, THE (TF) .... ARMAND ASSANTE
PIRATE, THE (TF) .... DIMITRA ARLYS
PIRATE, THE (TF) .... ELI WALLACH
PIRATE MOVIE, THE .... KRISTY McNICHOL
PIRATES .... CHARLOTTE LEWIS
PIRATES .... CRIS CAMPION
PIRATES .... WALTER MATTHAU
PIRATES OF
  PENZANCE, THE .... ANGELA LANSBURY
PIRATES OF PENZANCE, THE .... GEORGE ROSE†
PIRATES OF PENZANCE, THE .... KEVIN KLINE
PIRATES OF PENZANCE, THE ..... LINDA RONSTADT
PIRATES OF PENZANCE, THE .... REX SMITH
PIRATES OF PENZANCE, THE .... TONY AZITO
PIRATES OF TORTUGA .... ROBERT STEPHENS
PIRHANHA .... KEVIN McCARTHY
PIT AND THE PENDULUM, THE .... LUANA ANDERS
PIT AND THE PENDULUM, THE .... VINCENT PRICE†
PIT STOP .... ELLEN BURSTYN
PITFALL .... JANE WYATT
PITFALL .... RAYMOND BURR†
PIZZA TRIANGLE, THE .... MARCELLO MASTROIANNI
PLACE FOR ANNIE, A (TF) .... JOAN PLOWRIGHT
PLACE FOR
  ANNIE, A (TF) .... MARY-LOUISE PARKER
PLACE FOR ANNIE, A (TF) .... SISSY SPACEK
PLACE FOR LOVERS, A .... FAYE DUNAWAY
PLACE FOR
  LOVERS, A .... MARCELLO MASTROIANNI
PLACE IN THE SUN, A .... ELIZABETH TAYLOR
PLACE IN THE SUN, A .... KATHLEEN FREEMAN
PLACE IN THE SUN, A .... RAYMOND BURR†
PLACE IN THE SUN, A ★ .... MONTGOMERY CLIFT†
PLACE IN THE SUN, A ★ .... SHELLEY WINTERS
PLACE TO CALL HOME, A (TF) .... LINDA LAVIN
PLACE TO CALL
  HOME, A (TF) .... ROBERT MacNAUGHTON
PLACES IN THE HEART .... AMY MADIGAN
PLACES IN THE HEART .... ED HARRIS
PLACES IN THE HEART ★★ .... SALLY FIELD
PLACES IN THE HEART ○ .... JOHN MALKOVICH
PLACES IN THE HEART ○ .... LINDSAY CROUSE
PLAIN CLOTHES .... GEORGE WENDT
PLAIN CLOTHES .... LOREN DEAN
PLAIN CLOTHES .... SUZY AMIS
PLAINSMAN, THE .... ANTHONY QUINN
PLAINSMAN, THE .... BRADFORD DILLMAN
PLAINSMAN, THE .... DON MURRAY
PLAINSMAN, THE .... HENRY SILVA
PLAINSMAN, THE .... LESLIE NIELSEN
PLANES, TRAINS AND
  AUTOMOBILES .... EDIE McCLURG
PLANES, TRAINS AND
  AUTOMOBILES .... JOHN CANDY†
PLANES, TRAINS AND
  AUTOMOBILES .... KEVIN BACON
PLANES, TRAINS AND
  AUTOMOBILES .... STEVE MARTIN
PLANET EARTH (TF) .... JANET MARGOLIN
PLANET OF BLOOD .... JOHN SAXON
PLANET OF THE APES .... CHARLTON HESTON
PLANET OF THE APES .... JAMES WHITMORE
PLANET OF THE APES .... RODDY McDOWALL
PLASTIC DOME OF
  NORMA JEAN, THE .... SAM WATERSTON
PLATINUM HIGH SCHOOL .... RICHARD JAECKEL
PLATOON .... CHARLIE SHEEN
PLATOON .... DAVID NEIDORF
PLATOON .... FOREST WHITAKER
PLATOON .... FRANCESCO QUINN
PLATOON .... IVAN KANE
PLATOON .... JOHN C. McGINLEY
PLATOON .... JOHNNY DEPP
PLATOON .... KEITH DAVID
PLATOON .... KEVIN DILLON
PLATOON .... OLIVER STONE

PLATOON .... REGGIE JOHNSON
PLATOON .... RICHARD EDSON
PLATOON .... TONY TODD
PLATOON ○ .... TOM BERENGER
PLATOON ○ .... WILLEM DAFOE
PLAY DIRTY .... MICHAEL CAINE
PLAY DIRTY .... NIGEL DAVENPORT
PLAY IT AGAIN, SAM .... DIANE KEATON
PLAY IT AGAIN, SAM .... SUSAN ANSPACH
PLAY IT AGAIN, SAM .... TONY ROBERTS
PLAY IT AGAIN, SAM .... WOODY ALLEN
PLAY IT AS IT LAYS .... ANTHONY PERKINS†
PLAY IT AS IT LAYS .... RICHARD ANDERSON
PLAY IT AS IT LAYS .... TAMMY GRIMES
PLAY IT AS IT LAYS .... TUESDAY WELD
PLAY IT AS IT LAYS .... TYNE DALY
PLAY MISTY FOR ME .... CLINT EASTWOOD
PLAY MISTY FOR ME .... DONNA MILLS
PLAY MISTY FOR ME .... JAMES McEACHIN
PLAY MISTY FOR ME .... JESSICA WALTER
PLAY ROOM, THE .... CHRISTOPHER McDONALD
PLAYBOY, THE .... MAUREEN O'HARA
PLAYBOYS, THE .... AIDAN QUINN
PLAYBOYS, THE .... ALBERT FINNEY
PLAYBOYS, THE .... MILO O'SHEA
PLAYBOYS, THE .... ROBIN WRIGHT
PLAYER, THE .... ANDIE MacDOWELL
PLAYER, THE .... ANJELICA HUSTON
PLAYER, THE .... BRION JAMES
PLAYER, THE .... BRUCE WILLIS
PLAYER, THE .... BUCK HENRY
PLAYER, THE .... BURT REYNOLDS
PLAYER, THE .... CHER
PLAYER, THE .... CYNTHIA STEVENSON
PLAYER, THE .... DEAN STOCKWELL
PLAYER, THE .... DINA MERRILL
PLAYER, THE .... FRED WARD
PLAYER, THE .... GRETA SCACCHI
PLAYER, THE .... JACK LEMMON
PLAYER, THE .... JEFF GOLDBLUM
PLAYER, THE .... JOHN CUSACK
PLAYER, THE .... JULIA ROBERTS
PLAYER, THE .... KATHY IRELAND
PLAYER, THE .... LILY TOMLIN
PLAYER, THE .... LOUISE FLETCHER
PLAYER, THE .... LYLE LOVETT
PLAYER, THE .... MARLEE MATLIN
PLAYER, THE .... MIMI ROGERS
PLAYER, THE .... NICK NOLTE
PLAYER, THE .... PETER FALK
PLAYER, THE .... PETER GALLAGHER
PLAYER, THE .... RICHARD E. GRANT
PLAYER, THE .... ROD STEIGER
PLAYER, THE .... SCOTT GLENN
PLAYER, THE .... STEVE ALLEN
PLAYER, THE .... SUSAN SARANDON
PLAYER, THE .... SYDNEY POLLACK
PLAYER, THE .... TERI GARR
PLAYER, THE .... TIM ROBBINS
PLAYER, THE .... VINCENT D'ONOFRIO
PLAYER, THE .... WHOOPI GOLDBERG
PLAYERS .... ALI MacGRAW
PLAYERS .... DEAN PAUL MARTIN†
PLAYERS .... LIV ULLMANN
PLAYERS .... MARIA SCHELL
PLAYERS .... MAXIMILIAN SCHELL
PLAYERS .... STEVE GUTTENBERG
PLAYGIRL .... SHELLEY WINTERS
PLAYING FOR TIME (TF) .... JANE ALEXANDER
PLAYING FOR TIME (TF) .... MAUD ADAMS
PLAYING FOR TIME (TF) .... ROBIN BARTLETT
PLAYING FOR TIME (TF) .... VANESSA REDGRAVE
PLAYING WITH FIRE (TF) .... CICELY TYSON
PLAYING WITH FIRE (TF) .... GARY COLEMAN
PLAYING WITH FIRE (TF) .... YAPHET KOTTO
PLAYMATES (TF) .... ALAN ALDA
PLAYMATES (TF) .... CONNIE STEVENS
PLAYMATES (TF) .... DOUG McCLURE
PLAYMATES (TF) .... EILEEN BRENNAN
PLAYMATES (TF) .... SEVERN DARDEN
PLAZA SUITE .... BARBARA HARRIS
PLAZA SUITE .... LEE GRANT

PLAZA SUITE .... MAUREEN STAPLETON
PLAZA SUITE .... WALTER MATTHAU
PLAZA SUITE (TF) .... CAROL BURNETT
PLAZA SUITE (TF) .... DABNEY COLEMAN
PLAZA SUITE (TF) .... ERIN HAMILTON
PLAZA SUITE (TF) .... HAL HOLBROOK
PLAZA SUITE (TF) .... RICHARD CRENNA
PLEASE BELIEVE ME .... DEBORAH KERR
PLEASE BELIEVE ME .... JAMES WHITMORE
PLEASE DON'T EAT THE DAISIES .... DORIS DAY
PLEASE DON'T EAT THE DAISIES ..... JACK WESTON
PLEASE MURDER ME .... ANGELA LANSBURY
PLEASE MURDER ME .... RAYMOND BURR†
PLEASURE COVE (TF) .... JOAN HACKETT†
PLEASURE GARDEN, THE .... BIBI ANDERSSON
PLEASURE GIRLS, THE .... FRANCESCA ANNIS
PLEASURE GIRLS, THE .... KLAUS KINSKI†
PLEASURE OF HIS
  COMPANY, THE .... DEBBIE REYNOLDS
PLEASURE OF HIS COMPANY, THE ..... TAB HUNTER
PLEASURE OF THIS
  COMPANY, THE .... FRED ASTAIRE†
PLEASURE SEEKERS, THE .... ANN-MARGRET
PLEASURE
  SEEKERS, THE ...... ANTHONY (TONY) FRANCIOSA
PLEASURE SEEKERS, THE .... BRIAN KEITH
PLEASURE SEEKERS, THE .... CAROL LYNLEY
PLEASURE SEEKERS, THE .... DINA MERRILL
PLEASURES (TF) .... BARRY BOSTWICK
PLEASURES (TF) .... DAVID PAYMER
PLEASURES (TF) .... JOANNA CASSIDY
PLEASURES (TF) .... LINDA PURL
PLEASURES (TF) .... PAMELA SEGALL
PLEASURES (TF) .... RICK MOSES
PLEASURES (TF) .... TRACY NELSON
PLENTY .... BURT KWOUK
PLENTY .... CHARLES DANCE
PLENTY .... JOHN GIELGUD
PLENTY .... MERYL STREEP
PLENTY .... SAM NEILL
PLENTY .... STING
PLENTY .... TRACEY ULLMAN
PLOT TO KILL HITLER, THE (TF) .... BRAD DAVIS†
PLOT TO KILL
  HITLER, THE (TF) .... IAN RICHARDSON
PLOT TO KILL
  HITLER, THE (TF) ...... MADOLYN SMITH OSBORNE
PLOUGH AND THE
  STARS, THE .... BARBARA STANWYCK†
PLOUGHMAN'S LUNCH, THE ...... JONATHAN PRYCE
PLOUGHMAN'S LUNCH, THE .... TIM CURRY
PLUNDERERS, THE .... JOHN SAXON
PLYMOUTH ADVENTURE .... JOHN DEHNER†
PLYMOUTH ADVENTURE .... LLOYD BRIDGES
PLYMOUTH ADVENTURE .... VAN JOHNSON
POACHER'S DAUGHTER, THE .... JULIE HARRIS
POCAHONTAS (AF) .... CHRISTIAN BALE
POCAHONTAS (AF) .... DAVID OGDEN STIERS
POCAHONTAS (AF) .... IRENE BEDARD
POCAHONTAS (AF) .... JUDY KUHN
POCAHONTAS (AF) .... LINDA HUNT
POCAHONTAS (AF) .... MEL GIBSON
POCAHONTAS (AF) .... RUSSELL MEANS
POCKET MONEY .... HECTOR ELIZONDO
POCKET MONEY .... PAUL NEWMAN
POCKETFUL OF MIRACLES .... ANN-MARGRET
POCKETFUL OF MIRACLES .... BETTE DAVIS†
POCKETFUL OF MIRACLES .... HOPE LANGE
POCKETFUL OF MIRACLES ○ .... PETER FALK
POETIC JUSTICE .... JANET JACKSON
POETIC JUSTICE .... JOE TORRY
POETIC JUSTICE .... MICHAEL RAPAPORT
POETIC JUSTICE .... REGINA KING
POETIC JUSTICE .... TONE LOC
POETIC JUSTICE .... TUPAC SHAKUR
POETIC JUSTICE .... TYRA FERRELL
POINT BLANK .... ANGIE DICKINSON
POINT BLANK .... CARROLL O'CONNOR
POINT BLANK .... JOHN VERNON
POINT BLANK .... SHARON ACKER
POINT BREAK .... GARY BUSEY

† after an actor's name denotes deceased.

POINT BREAK .... GLORIA MANN
POINT BREAK .... KEANU REEVES
POINT BREAK .... LORI PETTY
POINT BREAK .... PATRICK SWAYZE
POINT OF NO RETURN .... ANNE BANCROFT
POINT OF NO RETURN .... BRIDGET FONDA
POINT OF NO RETURN .... DERMOT MULRONEY
POINT OF NO RETURN .... GABRIEL BYRNE
POINT OF NO RETURN .... HARVEY KEITEL
POINT OF NO RETURN .... MICHAEL RAPAPORT
POISON IVY .... CHERYL LADD
POISON IVY .... DREW BARRYMORE
POISON IVY .... SARA GILBERT
POISON IVY .... TOM SKERRITT
POISON IVY (TF) .... ADAM BALDWIN
POISON IVY (TF) .... MICHAEL J. FOX
POISON IVY (TF) .... ROBERT KLEIN
POISON PEN .... RODDY McDOWALL
POKER ALICE (TF) .... ELIZABETH TAYLOR
POKER ALICE (TF) .... GEORGE HAMILTON
POLICE .... GERARD DEPARDIEU
POLICE ACADEMY .... BRANT VAN HOFFMANN
POLICE ACADEMY .... BRUCE MAHLER
POLICE ACADEMY .... BUBBA SMITH
POLICE ACADEMY .... DAVID GRAF
POLICE ACADEMY .... DEBRALEE SCOTT
POLICE ACADEMY .... G.W. BAILEY
POLICE ACADEMY .... GEORGE GAYNES
POLICE ACADEMY .... GEORGINA SPELVIN
POLICE ACADEMY .... KIM CATTRALL
POLICE ACADEMY .... LESLIE EASTERBROOK
POLICE ACADEMY .... MARION RAMSEY
POLICE ACADEMY .... MICHAEL WINSLOW
POLICE ACADEMY .... SCOTT THOMSON
POLICE ACADEMY .... STEVE GUTTENBERG
POLICE AC ADEMY 2: THEIR
    FIRST ASSIGNMENT .... DAVID GRAF
POLICE ACADEMY 2: THEIR
    FIRST ASSIGNMENT .... ANDREW PARIS
POLICE ACADEMY 2: THEIR
    FIRST ASSIGNMENT .... ART METRANO
POLICE ACADEMY 2: THEIR
    FIRST ASSIGNMENT .... BOB GOLDTHWAIT
POLICE ACADEMY 2: THEIR
    FIRST ASSIGNMENT .... BRUCE MAHLER
POLICE ACADEMY 2: THEIR
    FIRST ASSIGNMENT .... BUBBA SMITH
POLICE ACADEMY 2: THEIR
    FIRST ASSIGNMENT .... COLLEEN CAMP
POLICE ACADEMY 2: THEIR
    FIRST ASSIGNMENT .... GEORGE GAYNES
POLICE ACADEMY 2: THEIR
    FIRST ASSIGNMENT .... HOWARD HESSEMAN
POLICE ACADEMY 2: THEIR
    FIRST ASSIGNMENT .... LANCE KINSEY
POLICE ACADEMY 2: THEIR
    FIRST ASSIGNMENT .... MARION RAMSEY
POLICE ACADEMY 2: THEIR
    FIRST ASSIGNMENT .... MICHAEL WINSLOW
POLICE ACADEMY 2: THEIR
    FIRST ASSIGNMENT .... STEVE GUTTENBERG
POLICE ACADEMY 2: THEIR
    FIRST ASSIGNMENT .... TIM KAZURINSKY
POLICE ACADEMY 3:
    BACK IN TRAINING .... ANDREW PARIS
POLICE ACADEMY 3:
    BACK IN TRAINING .... ART METRANO
POLICE ACADEMY 3:
    BACK IN TRAINING .... BOB GOLDTHWAIT
POLICE ACADEMY 3:
    BACK IN TRAINING .... BRANT VAN HOFFMANN
POLICE ACADEMY 3:
    BACK IN TRAINING .... BRIAN TOCHI
POLICE ACADEMY 3:
    BACK IN TRAINING .... BRUCE MAHLER
POLICE ACADEMY 3:
    BACK IN TRAINING .... BUBBA SMITH
POLICE ACADEMY 3:
    BACK IN TRAINING .... COLLEEN CAMP
POLICE ACADEMY 3:
    BACK IN TRAINING .... DAVID GRAF

POLICE ACADEMY 3:
    BACK IN TRAINING .... DAVID HUBAND
POLICE ACADEMY 3:
    BACK IN TRAINING .... DEBRALEE SCOTT
POLICE ACADEMY 3:
    BACK IN TRAINING .... ED NELSON
POLICE ACADEMY 3:
    BACK IN TRAINING .... GEORGE GAYNES
POLICE ACADEMY 3:
    BACK IN TRAINING .... GEORGINA SPELVIN
POLICE ACADEMY 3:
    BACK IN TRAINING .... LANCE KINSEY
POLICE ACADEMY 3:
    BACK IN TRAINING .... LESLIE EASTERBROOK
POLICE ACADEMY 3:
    BACK IN TRAINING .... MARION RAMSEY
POLICE ACADEMY 3:
    BACK IN TRAINING .... MICHAEL WINSLOW
POLICE ACADEMY 3:
    BACK IN TRAINING .... SCOTT THOMSON
POLICE ACADEMY 3:
    BACK IN TRAINING .... SHAWN WEATHERLY
POLICE ACADEMY 3:
    BACK IN TRAINING .... STEVE GUTTENBERG
POLICE ACADEMY 3:
    BACK IN TRAINING .... TIM KAZURINSKY
POLICE ACADEMY 4:
    CITIZENS ON PATROL .... BILLIE BIRD
POLICE ACADEMY 4:
    CITIZENS ON PATROL .... BOB GOLDTHWAIT
POLICE ACADEMY 4:
    CITIZENS ON PATROL .... BRIAN BACKER
POLICE ACADEMY 4:
    CITIZENS ON PATROL .... BRIAN TOCHI
POLICE ACADEMY 4:
    CITIZENS ON PATROL .... BUBBA SMITH
POLICE ACADEMY 4:
    CITIZENS ON PATROL .... COLLEEN CAMP
POLICE ACADEMY 4:
    CITIZENS ON PATROL .... DAVID GRAF
POLICE ACADEMY 4:
    CITIZENS ON PATROL .... DAVID SPADE
POLICE ACADEMY 4:
    CITIZENS ON PATROL .... DEREK McGRATH
POLICE ACADEMY 4:
    CITIZENS ON PATROL .... G.W. BAILEY
POLICE ACADEMY 4:
    CITIZENS ON PATROL .... GEORGE GAYNES
POLICE ACADEMY 4:
    CITIZENS ON PATROL ... GEORGE R. ROBERTSON
POLICE ACADEMY 4:
    CITIZENS ON PATROL .... LANCE KINSEY
POLICE ACADEMY 4:
    CITIZENS ON PATROL ...... LESLIE EASTERBROOK
POLICE ACADEMY 4:
    CITIZENS ON PATROL .... MARION RAMSEY
POLICE ACADEMY 4:
    CITIZENS ON PATROL .... MICHAEL WINSLOW
POLICE ACADEMY 4:
    CITIZENS ON PATROL .... SHARON STONE
POLICE ACADEMY 4:
    CITIZENS ON PATROL .... STEVE GUTTENBERG
POLICE ACADEMY 4:
    CITIZENS ON PATROL .... TAB THACKER
POLICE ACADEMY 4:
    CITIZENS ON PATROL .... TIM KAZURINSKY
POLICE ACADEMY 5: ASSIGNMENT
    MIAMI BEACH .... BUBBA SMITH
POLICE ACADEMY 5: ASSIGNMENT
    MIAMI BEACH .... DAVID GRAF
POLICE ACADEMY 5: ASSIGNMENT
    MIAMI BEACH .... G.W. BAILEY
POLICE ACADEMY 5: ASSIGNMENT
    MIAMI BEACH .... GEORGE GAYNES
POLICE ACADEMY 5: ASSIGNMENT
    MIAMI BEACH .... JANET JONES
POLICE ACADEMY 5: ASSIGNMENT
    MIAMI BEACH .... LANCE KINSEY
POLICE ACADEMY 5: ASSIGNMENT
    MIAMI BEACH .... LESLIE EASTERBROOK
POLICE ACADEMY 5: ASSIGNMENT
    MIAMI BEACH .... MARION RAMSEY

POLICE ACADEMY 5: ASSIGNMENT
    MIAMI BEACH .... MATT McCOY
POLICE ACADEMY 5: ASSIGNMENT
    MIAMI BEACH .... MICHAEL WINSLOW
POLICE ACADEMY 6:
    CITY UNDER SIEGE .... BRUCE MAHLER
POLICE ACADEMY 6:
    CITY UNDER SIEGE .... BUBBA SMITH
POLICE ACADEMY 6:
    CITY UNDER SIEGE .... DAVID GRAF
POLICE ACADEMY 6:
    CITY UNDER SIEGE .... G.W. BAILEY
POLICE ACADEMY 6:
    CITY UNDER SIEGE .... GEORGE GAYNES
POLICE ACADEMY 6:
    CITY UNDER SIEGE .... GERRITT GRAHAM
POLICE ACADEMY 6:
    CITY UNDER SIEGE .... KENNETH MARS
POLICE ACADEMY 6:
    CITY UNDER SIEGE .... LANCE KINSEY
POLICE ACADEMY 6:
    CITY UNDER SIEGE .... LESLIE EASTERBROOK
POLICE ACADEMY 6:
    CITY UNDER SIEGE .... MARION RAMSEY
POLICE ACADEMY 6:
    CITY UNDER SIEGE .... MATT McCOY
POLICE ACADEMY 6:
    CITY UNDER SIEGE .... MICHAEL WINSLOW
POLICE ACADEMY 6:
    CITY UNDER SIEGE .... DENNIS OTT†
POLICE ACADEMY:
    MISSION TO MOSCOW .... CHARLIE SCHLATTER
POLICE ACADEMY:
    MISSION TO MOSCOW .... CHRISTOPHER LEE
POLICE ACADEMY:
    MISSION TO MOSCOW .... CLAIRE FORIANI
POLICE ACADEMY:
    MISSION TO MOSCOW .... G.W. BAILEY
POLICE ACADEMY:
    MISSION TO MOSCOW .... GEORGE GAYNES
POLICE ACADEMY:
    MISSION TO MOSCOW .... GREGG BERGER
POLICE ACADEMY:
    MISSION TO MOSCOW ..... LESLIE EASTERBROOK
POLICE ACADEMY:
    MISSION TO MOSCOW .... MICHAEL WINSLOW
POLICE ACADEMY:
    MISSION TO MOSCOW .... RON PERLMAN
POLICE STORY: THE FREEWAY
    KILLINGS (TF) .... ANGIE DICKINSON
POLICE STORY: THE FREEWAY
    KILLINGS (TF) .... BEN GAZZARA
POLICE STORY: THE FREEWAY
    KILLINGS (TF) .... RICHARD CRENNA
POLITICAL PARTY, A .... JOHN MILLS
POLLYANNA .... HAYLEY MILLS
POLLYANNA .... JANE WYMAN
POLLYANNA .... KARL MALDEN
POLTERGEIST .... BEATRICE STRAIGHT
POLTERGEIST .... CRAIG T. NELSON
POLTERGEIST .... DOMINIQUE DUNNE†
POLTERGEIST .... HEATHER O'ROURKE†
POLTERGEIST .... JAMES KAREN
POLTERGEIST .... JoBETH WILLIAMS
POLTERGEIST .... OLIVER ROBINS
POLTERGEIST .... ZELDA RUBINSTEIN
POLTERGEIST II:
    THE OTHER SIDE .... CRAIG T. NELSON
POLTERGEIST II:
    THE OTHER SIDE .... GERALDINE FITZGERALD
POLTERGEIST II:
    THE OTHER SIDE .... HEATHER O'ROURKE†
POLTERGEIST II:
    THE OTHER SIDE .... JoBETH WILLIAMS
POLTERGEIST II:
    THE OTHER SIDE .... OLIVER ROBINS
POLTERGEIST II:
    THE OTHER SIDE .... WILL SAMPSON†
POLTERGEIST II:
    THE OTHER SIDE .... ZELDA RUBINSTEIN
POLTERGEIST III .... HEATHER O'ROURKE†
POLTERGEIST III .... KIP WENTZ
POLTERGEIST III .... LARA FLYNN BOYLE

This is not a list of every film ever made or every cast member, only those listed in this directory.

POLTERGEIST III .... NANCY ALLEN
POLTERGEIST III .... RICHARD FIRE
POLTERGEIST III .... TOM SKERRITT
POLTERGEIST III .... ZELDA RUBINSTEIN
POLYESTER .... DIVINE†
POLYESTER .... MINK STOLE
POLYESTER .... TAB HUNTER
POM-POM GIRLS, THE .... ROBERT CARRADINE
PONTIAC MOON .... CATHY MORIARTY
PONTIAC MOON .... ERIC SCHWEIG
PONTIAC MOON .... MARY STEENBURGEN
PONTIAC MOON .... RYAN TODD
PONTIAC MOON .... TED DANSON
PONY EXPRESS .... CHARLTON HESTON
PONY EXPRESS RIDER .... JOAN CAULFIELD†
POOR COW .... MALCOLM McDOWELL
POOR COW .... TERENCE STAMP
POOR LITTLE RICH GIRL: THE BARBARA
    HUTTON STORY (MS) .... BRUCE DAVISON
POOR LITTLE RICH GIRL: THE BARBARA
    HUTTON STORY (MS) .... BURL IVES
POOR LITTLE RICH GIRL: THE BARBARA
    HUTTON STORY (MS) .... DAVID AYKROYD
POOR LITTLE RICH GIRL: THE BARBARA
    HUTTON STORY (MS) .... FARRAH FAWCETT
POOR LITTLE RICH GIRL: THE BARBARA
    HUTTON STORY (MS) .... JAMES READ
POOR LITTLE RICH GIRL: THE BARBARA
    HUTTON STORY (MS) .... KEVIN McCARTHY
POOR PRETTY EDDIE .... SHELLEY WINTERS
POPCORN .... DEE WALLACE STONE
POPCORN .... DEREK RYAN
POPCORN .... ELLIOTT HURST
POPCORN .... JILL SCHOELEN
POPCORN .... KELLY JO MINTER
POPCORN .... MALCOLM DANARE
POPCORN .... RAY WALSTON
POPCORN .... TOM VILLARD
POPCORN .... TONY ROBERTS
POPE JOAN .... FRANCO NERO
POPE JOAN .... JEREMY KEMP
POPE JOAN .... LESLEY-ANNE DOWN
POPE JOAN .... LIV ULLMANN
POPE JOAN .... MAXIMILIAN SCHELL
POPE JOAN .... OLIVIA DE HAVILLAND
POPE MUST DIET, THE .... ALEX ROCCO
POPE MUST DIET, THE .... BALTHAZAR GETTY
POPE MUST DIET, THE .... BEVERLY D'ANGELO
POPE MUST DIET, THE .... PAUL BARTEL
POPE MUST DIET, THE .... ROBBIE COLTRANE
POPE OF GREENWICH
    VILLAGE, THE .... DARYL HANNAH
POPE OF GREENWICH VILLAGE, THE .... ED O'ROSS
POPE OF GREENWICH
    VILLAGE, THE .... ERIC ROBERTS
POPE OF GREENWICH
    VILLAGE, THE .... MICKEY ROURKE
POPE OF GREENWICH
    VILLAGE, THE .... PHILIP BOSCO
POPE OF GREENWICH
    VILLAGE, THE ⊙ .... GERALDINE PAGE†
POPEYE .... BILL IRWIN
POPEYE .... LINDA HUNT
POPEYE .... PAUL DOOLEY
POPEYE .... RAY WALSTON
POPEYE .... ROBIN WILLIAMS
POPEYE .... SHELLEY DUVALL
POPEYE DOYLE (TF) .... AUDREY LANDERS
POPEYE DOYLE (TF) .... CANDY CLARK
POPEYE DOYLE (TF) .... JAMES HANDY
POPI .... ALAN ARKIN
POPI .... RITA MORENO
POPPY IS ALSO A FLOWER, THE ... E. G. MARSHALL
POPPY IS ALSO A FLOWER, THE .... OMAR SHARIF
PORGY AND BESS .... BROCK PETERS
PORGY AND BESS .... CLAUDE AKINS†
PORGY AND BESS .... DIAHANN CARROLL
PORGY AND BESS .... SIDNEY POITIER
PORK CHOP HILL .... GEORGE PEPPARD†
PORK CHOP HILL .... GREGORY PECK
PORK CHOP HILL .... HARRY GUARDINO
PORK CHOP HILL .... MARTIN LANDAU
PORK CHOP HILL .... NORMAN FELL

PORK CHOP HILL .... RIP TORN
PORK CHOP HILL .... WOODY STRODE
PORKY'S .... SUSAN CLARK
PORT OF SEVEN SEAS .... MAUREEN O'SULLIVAN
PORTFOLIO .... CAROL ALT
PORTNOY'S COMPLAINT .... JEANNIE BERLIN
PORTNOY'S COMPLAINT .... JILL CLAYBURGH
PORTNOY'S COMPLAINT .... KAREN BLACK
PORTNOY'S COMPLAINT .... LEE GRANT
PORTNOY'S COMPLAINT .... RICHARD BENJAMIN
PORTRAIT FROM LIFE, A .... MAE ZETTERLING†
PORTRAIT IN BLACK .... ANTHONY QUINN
PORTRAIT IN BLACK .... JOHN SAXON
PORTRAIT IN BLACK .... LANA TURNER
PORTRAIT IN BLACK .... RAY WALSTON
PORTRAIT IN BLACK .... SANDRA DEE
PORTRAIT OF A LADY .... NICOLE KIDMAN
PORTRAIT OF A SHOWGIRL (TF) .... TONY CURTIS
PORTRAIT OF
    A STRIPPER (TF) .... EDWRAD HERRMANN
PORTRAIT OF
    A STRIPPER (TF) .... LESLEY ANN WARREN
PORTRAIT OF AN ESCORT (TF) .... CYD CHARISSE
PORTRAIT OF JENNIE .... JENNIFER JONES
PORTRAIT OF JENNIE .... LILLIAN GISH†
PORTRAIT OF THE ARTIST
    AS A YOUNG MAN, A .... JOHN GIELGUD
PORTRAIT, THE (CTF) .... CECILIA PECK
PORTRAIT, THE (CTF) .... DONNA MITCHELL
PORTRAIT, THE (CTF) .... GREGORY PECK
PORTRAIT, THE (CTF) .... LAUREN BACALL
PORTRAIT, THE (CTF) .... MITCHELL LAURANCE
PORTRAIT, THE (CTF) .... PAUL McCRANE
POSEIDON
    ADVENTURE, THE .... ARTHUR O'CONNELL†
POSEIDON ADVENTURE, THE .... CAROL LYNLEY
POSEIDON
    ADVENTURE, THE .... ERNEST BORGNINE
POSEIDON ADVENTURE, THE .... GENE HACKMAN
POSEIDON
    ADVENTURE, THE .... JACK ALBERTSON†
POSEIDON ADVENTURE, THE .... LESLIE NIELSEN
POSEIDON
    ADVENTURE, THE .... PAMELA SUE MARTIN
POSEIDON ADVENTURE, THE .... RED BUTTONS
POSEIDON
    ADVENTURE, THE .... RODDY McDOWALL
POSEIDON ADVENTURE, THE ...... STELLA STEVENS
POSEIDON
    ADVENTURE, THE ⊙ .... SHELLEY WINTERS
POSITIVELY TRUE ADVENTURES
    OF THE ALLEGED TEXAS
    CHEERLEADER-MURDERING
    MOM, THE (CTF) .... BEAU BRIDGES
POSITIVELY TRUE ADVENTURES
    OF THE ALLEGED TEXAS
    CHEERLEADER-MURDERING
    MOM, THE (CTF) .... HOLLY HUNTER
POSITIVELY TRUE ADVENTURES
    OF THE ALLEGED TEXAS
    CHEERLEADER-MURDERING
    MOM, THE (CTF) .... SWOOSIE KURTZ
POSSE .... BO HOPKINS
POSSE .... BRUCE DERN
POSSE .... KIRK DOUGLAS
POSSE .... MARIO VAN PEEBLES
POSSE .... MELVIN VAN PEEBLES
POSSE .... TONE LOC
POSSE FROM HELL .... JOHN SAXON
POSSE FROM HELL .... ROYAL DANO
POSSESSED ★ .... JOAN CRAWFORD†
POSSESSED, THE (TF) .... HARRISON FORD
POSSESSED, THE (TF) .... JOAN HACKETT†
POSSESSION .... ISABELLE ADJANI
POSSESSION OF JOEL
    DELANEY, THE .... PERRY KING
POSSESSION OF JOEL
    DELANEY, THE .... SHIRLEY MacLAINE
POSTCARDS FROM THE EDGE .... ANNETTE BENING
POSTCARDS FROM THE EDGE .... ANTHONY HEALD
POSTCARDS FROM THE EDGE ... C. C. H. POUNDER
POSTCARDS FROM THE EDGE .... CONRAD BAIN

POSTCARDS FROM THE EDGE .... DANA IVEY
POSTCARDS FROM THE EDGE .... DENNIS QUAID
POSTCARDS FROM THE EDGE .... GARY MORTON
POSTCARDS FROM THE EDGE ...... GENE HACKMAN
POSTCARDS FROM
    THE EDGE .... MARK LOWENTHAL
POSTCARDS FROM THE EDGE .... MARY WICKES
POSTCARDS FROM
    THE EDGE .... MICHAEL ONTKEAN
POSTCARDS FROM
    THE EDGE .... RICHARD DREYFUSS
POSTCARDS FROM THE EDGE .... ROB REINER
POSTCARDS FROM THE EDGE .... ROBIN BARTLETT
POSTCARDS FROM
    THE EDGE .... SHIRLEY MacLAINE
POSTCARDS FROM THE EDGE .... SIMON CALLOW
POSTCARDS FROM
    THE EDGE .... STANLEY DeSANTIS
POSTCARDS FROM
    THE EDGE ★ .... MERYL STREEP
POSTMAN ALWAYS
    RINGS TWICE, THE (1946) .... HUME CRONYN
POSTMAN ALWAYS
    RINGS TWICE, THE (1946) .... LANA TURNER
POSTMAN ALWAYS
    RINGS TWICE, THE (1946) .... LEON AMES
POSTMAN ALWAYS
    RINGS TWICE, THE (1981) .... ANJELICA HUSTON
POSTMAN ALWAYS
    RINGS TWICE, THE (1981) ...... JACK NICHOLSON
POSTMAN ALWAYS
    RINGS TWICE, THE (1981) .... JESSICA LANGE
POSTMAN ALWAYS
    RINGS TWICE, THE (1981) .... MICHAEL LERNER
POT BOUILLE .... ANOUK AIMEE
POT O' GOLD .... ART CARNEY
POT O' GOLD .... JAMES STEWART
POWDER RIVER .... RORY CALHOUN
POWER .... BEATRICE STRAIGHT
POWER .... D. B. SWEENEY
POWER .... DENZEL WASHINGTON
POWER .... E. G. MARSHALL
POWER .... FRITZ WEAVER
POWER .... GENE HACKMAN
POWER .... J. T. WALSH
POWER .... JULIE CHRISTIE
POWER .... KATE CAPSHAW
POWER .... RICHARD GERE
POWER (TF) .... JOE DON BAKER
POWER (TF) .... RALPH BELLAMY†
POWER, THE .... EARL HOLLIMAN
POWER, THE .... GEORGE HAMILTON
POWER, THE .... NEHEMIAH PERSOFF
POWER, THE .... SUZANNE PLESHETTE
POWER, THE .... YVONNE DE CARLO
POWER AND THE GLORY, THE (TF) ..... PATTY DUKE
POWER AND THE PRIZE, THE .... BURL IVES
POWER OF ONE, THE .... ARMIN MUELLER-STAHL
POWER OF ONE, THE .... JOHN GIELGUD
POWER OF ONE, THE .... MORGAN FREEMAN
POWER OF ONE, THE .... STEPHEN DORFF
POWER PLAY .... DAVID HEMMINGS
POWER PLAY .... DONALD PLEASENCE
POWER PLAY .... PETER O'TOOLE
POWER WITHIN, THE (TF) .... DAVID HEDISON
POWWOW HIGHWAY .... A MARTINEZ
POWWOW HIGHWAY .... AMANDA WYSS
POWWOW HIGHWAY .... GARY FARMER
PRACTICALLY YOURS .... YVONNE DE CARLO
PRANCER .... ABE VIGODA
PRANCER .... ARIANA RICHARDS
PRANCER .... CLORIS LEACHMAN
PRANCER .... MICHAEL CONSTANTINE
PRANCER .... REBECCA HARRELL
PRANCER .... RUTANYA ALDA
PRANCER .... SAM ELLIOTT
PRAY FOR THE .... WILDCATS (TF)
    ANGIE DICKINSON
PRAY FOR THE
    WILDCATS (TF) .... JANET MARGOLIN
PRAYER FOR THE DYING, A .... ALAN BATES
PRAYER FOR THE DYING, A .... ALISON DOODY

INDEX OF FILM TITLES

PRAYER FOR THE DYING, A .... BOB HOSKINS
PRAYER FOR THE DYING, A .... LIAM NEESON
PRAYER FOR THE DYING, A .... MICKEY ROURKE
PRAYING MANTIS (TF) .... JONATHAN PRYCE
PREDATOR .... ARNOLD SCHWARZENEGGER
PREDATOR .... CARL WEATHERS
PREDATOR .... JOHN RHYS-DAVIES
PREDATOR 2 .... BILL PAXTON
PREDATOR 2 .... DANNY GLOVER
PREDATOR 2 .... GARY BUSEY
PREDATOR 2 .... KENT McCORD
PREDATOR 2 .... KEVIN PETER HALL†
PREDATOR 2 .... MARIA CONCHITA ALONSO
PREDATOR 2 .... MORTON DOWNEY JR.
PREDATOR 2 .... RUBEN BLADES
PREDATOR, THE .... CHARLIE SHEEN
PRELUDE TO A KISS .... ALEC BALDWIN
PRELUDE TO A KISS .... KATHY BATES
PRELUDE TO A KISS .... MEG RYAN
PRELUDE TO A KISS .... NED BEATTY
PRELUDE TO A KISS .... PATTY DUKE
PRELUDE TO A KISS .... RICHARD RIEHLE
PRELUDE TO A KISS .... STANLEY TUCCI
PRELUDE TO A KISS .... SYDNEY WALKER†
PREMIER RENDEZ-VOUS .... LOUIS JOURDAN
PREMONITION, THE .... JEFF COREY
PRÉPAREZ VOS
   MOUCHOIRS .... GERARD DEPARDIEU
PREPPIE MURDER, THE (TF) .... DANNY AIELLO
PREPPIE MURDER, THE (TF) .... JAMES HANDY
PREPPIE MURDER, THE (TF) .... JOANNA KERNS
PREPPIE MURDER, THE (TF) .... LARA FLYNN BOYLE
PREPPIE MURDER, THE (TF) ...... WILLIAM BALDWIN
PREPPIE MURDER, THE (TF) ...... WILLIAM DEVANE
PRESCRIPTION: MURDER (TF) .... NINA FOCH
PRESCRIPTION MURDER (TF) .... PETER FALK
PRESIDENT'S ANALYST, THE .... JAMES COBURN
PRESIDENT'S ANALYST, THE ...... SEVERN DARDEN
PRESIDENT'S ANALYST, THE ...... WILLIAM DANIELS
PRESIDENT'S LADY, THE .... CHARLTON HESTON
PRESIDENT'S
   MISTRESS, THE (TF) .... BEAU BRIDGES
PRESIDENT'S PLANE IS
   MISSING, THE (TF) ..... MERCEDES McCAMBRIDGE
PRESIDENT'S PLANE
   IS MISSING, THE (TF) .... PETER GRAVES
PRESIDENT'S PLANE
   IS MISSING, THE (TF) .... RIP TORN
PRESIDIO, THE .... JACK WARDEN
PRESIDIO, THE .... MARK HARMON
PRESIDIO, THE .... MEG RYAN
PRESIDIO, THE .... SEAN CONNERY
PRESSURE POINT .... HOWARD CAINE†
PRESSURE POINT .... PETER FALK
PRESSURE POINT .... SIDNEY POITIER
PRESUMED INNOCENT .... BONNIE BEDELIA
PRESUMED INNOCENT .... BRIAN DENNEHY
PRESUMED INNOCENT .... GRETA SCACCHI
PRESUMED INNOCENT .... HARRISON FORD
PRESUMED INNOCENT .... PAUL WINFIELD
PRESUMED INNOCENT .... RAUL JULIA†
PRET-A-PORTER .... ANOUK AIMEE
PRET-A-PORTER .... DANNY AIELLO
PRET-A-PORTER .... FOREST WHITAKER
PRET-A-PORTER .... JULIA ROBERTS
PRET-A-PORTER .... KIM BASINGER
PRET-A-PORTER .... LAUREN BACALL
PRET-A-PORTER .... LILI TAYLOR
PRET-A-PORTER .... LINDA HUNT
PRET-A-PORTER .... LYLE LOVETT
PRET-A-PORTER .... MARCELLO MASTROIANNI
PRET-A-PORTER .... MICHEL BLANC
PRET-A-PORTER .... RICHARD E. GRANT
PRET-A-PORTER .... RUPERT EVERETT
PRET-A-PORTER .... SALLY KELLERMAN
PRET-A-PORTER .... SAM ROBARDS
PRET-A-PORTER .... SOPHIA LOREN
PRET-A-PORTER .... STEPHEN REA
PRET-A-PORTER .... TERI GARR
PRET-A-PORTER .... TIM ROBBINS
PRET-A-PORTER .... TRACEY ULLMAN
PRET-A-PORTER .... UTE LEMPER

PRETTY BABY .... ANTONIO FARGAS
PRETTY BABY .... BROOKE SHIELDS
PRETTY BABY .... DIANA SCARWID
PRETTY BABY .... KEITH CARRADINE
PRETTY BABY .... SUSAN SARANDON
PRETTY BOY FLOYD .... PETER FALK
PRETTY IN PINK .... ANDREW DICE CLAY
PRETTY IN PINK .... ANDREW McCARTHY
PRETTY IN PINK .... ANNIE POTTS
PRETTY IN PINK .... DWEEZIL ZAPPA
PRETTY IN PINK .... GINA GERSHON
PRETTY IN PINK .... HARRY DEAN STANTON
PRETTY IN PINK .... JAMES SPADER
PRETTY IN PINK .... JON CRYER
PRETTY IN PINK .... MARGARET COLIN
PRETTY IN PINK .... MOLLY RINGWALD
PRETTY LADIES .... JOAN CRAWFORD†
PRETTY MAIDS ALL IN A ROW ..... ANGIE DICKINSON
PRETTY MAIDS ALL
   IN A ROW .... RODDY McDOWALL
PRETTY MAIDS ALL IN A ROW .... TELLY SAVALAS†
PRETTY POISON .... ANTHONY PERKINS†
PRETTY POISON .... JOHN RANDOLPH
PRETTY POISON .... TUESDAY WELD
PRETTY POLLY .... HAYLEY MILLS
PRETTY WOMAN .... ALEX HYDE-WHITE
PRETTY WOMAN .... ELINOR DONAHUE
PRETTY WOMAN .... HECTOR ELIZONDO
PRETTY WOMAN .... JASON ALEXANDER
PRETTY WOMAN .... LARRY MILLER
PRETTY WOMAN .... LAURA SAN GIACOMO
PRETTY WOMAN .... PATRICK RICHWOOD
PRETTY WOMAN .... RALPH BELLAMY†
PRETTY WOMAN .... RICHARD GERE
PRETTY WOMAN ★ .... JULIA ROBERTS
PRETTYKILL .... SEASON HUBLEY
PRETTYKILL .... SUSANNAH YORK
PRETTYKILL .... YAPHET KOTTO
PRICE OF FREEDOM .... ANTHONY ANDREWS
PRICE OF FREEDOM .... JOSS ACKLAND
PRICE OF FREEDOM .... TIMOTHY BOTTOMS
PRICK UP YOUR EARS .... ALFRED MOLINA
PRICK UP YOUR EARS .... GARY OLDMAN
PRICK UP YOUR EARS .... JULIE WALTERS
PRICK UP YOUR EARS .... VANESSA REDGRAVE
PRIDE AND EXTREME
   PREJUDICE (CTF) .... ALAN HOWARD
PRIDE AND EXTREME
   PREJUDICE (CTF) .... BRIAN DENNEHY
PRIDE AND EXTREME
   PREJUDICE (CTF) .... LISA EICHHORN
PRIDE AND PREJUDICE .... GREER GARSON
PRIDE AND PREJUDICE .... MAUREEN O'SULLIVAN
PRIDE AND THE PASSION, THE ..... FRANK SINATRA
PRIDE AND THE PASSION, THE .... SOPHIA LOREN
PRIDE AND THE
   PASSION, THE .... THEODORE BIKEL
PRIDE OF JESSE
   HALLAM, THE (TF) .... ELI WALLACH
PRIDE OF JESSE
   HALLAM, THE (TF) .... JOHNNY CASH
PRIDE OF JESSE
   HALLMAN, THE (TF) .... BRENDA VACCARO
PRIDE OF ST. LOUIS, THE .... RICHARD CRENNA
PRIDE OF THE BLUE GRASS .... LLOYD BRIDGES
PRIDE OF THE BLUE GRASS .... VERA MILES
PRIDE OF THE MARINES .... ELEANOR PARKER
PRIDE OF THE
   YANKEES, THE ★ .... GARY COOPER†
PRIDE OF THE
   YANKEES, THE ★ .... TERESA WRIGHT
PRIEST OF LOVE .... JOHN GIELGUD
PRIEST OF LOVE .... SARAH MILES
PRIEST OF LOVE, THE .... JANET SUZMAN
PRIEST'S WIFE, THE .... SOPHIA LOREN
PRIME CUT .... GENE HACKMAN
PRIME CUT .... LEE MARVIN†
PRIME CUT .... SISSY SPACEK
PRIME MINISTER, THE .... JOHN GIELGUD
PRIME OF MISS
   JEAN BRODIE, THE .... GORDAN JACKSON†

PRIME OF MISS JEAN
   BRODIE, THE .... ROBERT STEPHENS
PRIME OF MISS JEAN
   BRODIE, THE ★★ .... MAGGIE SMITH
PRIME SUSPECT .... KENNETH CRANHAM
PRIME SUSPECT .... KEVIN MOORE
PRIME SUSPECT .... MAGGIE O'NEILL
PRIME SUSPECT .... STEPHAN MOORE
PRIME SUSPECT (TF) .... VERONICA CARTWRIGHT
PRIME SUSPECT 3 (TF) .... DAVID THEWLIS
PRIME TARGET (TF) .... ANGIE DICKINSON
PRIME TARGET (TF) .... CHARLES DURNING
PRIME TARGET (TF) .... JOSEPH BOLOGNA
PRIMROSE PATH ⊙ .... MARJORIE RAMBEAU†
PRINCE AND THE
   PAUPER, THE .... CHARLTON HESTON
PRINCE AND THE
   PAUPER, THE .... DAVID HEMMINGS
PRINCE AND THE
   PAUPER, THE .... ERNEST BORGNINE
PRINCE AND THE
   PAUPER, THE .... GEORGE C. SCOTT
PRINCE AND THE PAUPER, THE .... MARK LESTER
PRINCE AND THE PAUPER, THE .... RAQUEL WELCH
PRINCE AND THE
   SHOWGIRL, THE .... MARILYN MONROE†
PRINCE OF BEL AIR (TF) .... BART BRAVERMAN
PRINCE OF BEL AIR (TF) .... DEBORAH HARMON
PRINCE OF BEL AIR (TF) .... KIRSTIE ALLEY
PRINCE OF BEL AIR (TF) .... MARK HARMON
PRINCE OF BEL AIR (TF) .... MICHAEL HORTON
PRINCE OF BEL AIR (TF) ...... PATRICK LABORTEAUX
PRINCE OF BEL AIR (TF) .... ROBERT VAUGHN
PRINCE OF DARKNESS .... DENNIS DUN
PRINCE OF DARKNESS .... DONALD PLEASENCE
PRINCE OF DARKNESS .... JAMESON PARKER
PRINCE OF DARKNESS .... LISA BLOUNT
PRINCE OF DARKNESS .... PETER JASON
PRINCE OF PENNSYLVANIA, THE ..... AMY MADIGAN
PRINCE OF
   PENNSYLVANIA, THE .... BONNIE BEDELIA
PRINCE OF PENNSYLVANIA, THE .... FRED WARD
PRINCE OF
   PENNSYLVANIA, THE .... JAY O. SANDERS
PRINCE OF PENNSYLVANIA, THE .... JEFF HAYENGA
PRINCE OF PENNSYLVANIA, THE .... JOSEPH DELISI
PRINCE OF
   PENNSYLVANIA, THE .... KEANU REEVES
PRINCE OF THE CITY .... BOB BALABAN
PRINCE OF THE CITY .... JERRY ORBACH
PRINCE OF THE CITY .... STEVE INWOOD
PRINCE OF THE CITY .... TREAT WILLIAMS
PRINCE OF TIDES, THE .... BARBRA STREISAND
PRINCE OF TIDES, THE .... BLYTHE DANNER
PRINCE OF TIDES, THE .... GEORGE CARLIN
PRINCE OF TIDES, THE .... JASON GOULD
PRINCE OF TIDES, THE .... JEROEN KRABBE
PRINCE OF TIDES, THE ★ .... MELINDA DILLON
PRINCE OF TIDES, THE ★ .... NICK NOLTE
PRINCE OF TIDES, THE ⊙ .... KATE NELLIGAN
PRINCE VALIANT .... JANET LEIGH
PRINCE VALIANT .... ROBERT WAGNER
PRINCE WHO WAS A THIEF, THE ...... PIPER LAURIE
PRINCE WHO WAS A THIEF, THE .... TONY CURTIS
PRINCESS ACADEMY .... CAROLE DAVIS
PRINCESS ACADEMY .... LAR PARK LINCOLN
PRINCESS ACADEMY, THE .... EVA GABOR
PRINCESS AND THE
   GOBLIN, THE (AF) .... CLAIRE BLOOM
PRINCESS AND THE
   GOBLIN, THE (AF) ...... FRANK ROZELAAR GREEN
PRINCESS AND THE
   GOBLIN, THE (AF) .... JOSS ACKLAND
PRINCESS AND THE
   GOBLIN, THE (AF) .... MAXINE HOWE
PRINCESS AND THE
   GOBLIN, THE (AF) .... MOLLIE SUGDEN
PRINCESS AND THE
   GOBLIN, THE (AF) .... PEGGY MOUNT
PRINCESS AND THE
   GOBLIN, THE (AF) .... PETER MURRAY

This is not a list of every film ever made or every cast member, only those listed in this directory.

PRINCESS AND THE
GOBLIN, THE (AF) .... RIK MAYALL
PRINCESS AND THE
GOBLIN, THE (AF) .... ROBIN LYONS
PRINCESS AND THE
GOBLIN, THE (AF) .... ROY KINNEAR
PRINCESS AND THE
GOBLIN, THE (AF) .... SALLY ANN MARSH
PRINCESS AND THE
GOBLIN, THE (AF) .... STEVE LYONS
PRINCESS AND THE
GOBLIN, THE (AF) .... VICTOR SPINETTI
PRINCESS AND THE
GOBLIN, THE (AF) .... WILLIAM HOOTKINS
PRINCESS AND
THE PEA, THE .... BILLY BARTY
PRINCESS AND
THE PEA, THE .... HELENA BONHAM CARTER
PRINCESS AND THE PIRATE, THE .... BOB HOPE
PRINCESS AND THE
PLUMBER, THE .... MAUREEN O'SULLIVAN
PRINCESS BRIDE, THE .... BILLY CRYSTAL
PRINCESS BRIDE, THE .... CAROL KANE
PRINCESS BRIDE, THE .... CARY ELWES
PRINCESS BRIDE, THE .... CHRIS SARANDON
PRINCESS BRIDE, THE ...... CHRISTOPHER GUEST
PRINCESS BRIDE, THE .... FRED SAVAGE
PRINCESS BRIDE, THE .... PETER COOK
PRINCESS BRIDE, THE .... PETER FALK
PRINCESS BRIDE, THE .... ROBIN WRIGHT
PRINCESS CARABOO .... JIM BROADRENT
PRINCESS CARABOO .... JOHN LITHGOW
PRINCESS CARABOO .... JOHN SESSIONS
PRINCESS CARABOO .... KEVIN KLINE
PRINCESS CARABOO .... PHOEBE CATES
PRINCESS CARABOO .... STEPHEN REA
PRINCESS CARABOO .... WENDY HUGHES
PRINCESS DAISY (MS) .... HARRY CAREY JR.
PRINCESS DAISY (MS) .... LINDSAY WAGNER
PRINCESS DAISY (MS) .... STACY KEACH
PRINCESS DAISY (TF) .... ROBERT URICH
PRINCESS DAISY (TF) .... RUPERT EVERETT
PRINCESS O'ROURKE .... JANE WYMAN
PRINCESS O'ROURKE .... OLIVIA DE HAVILLAND
PRINCIPAL, THE .... JAMES BELUSHI
PRINCIPAL, THE .... KELLY JO MINTER
PRINCIPAL, THE .... LOUIS GOSSETT JR.
PRINCIPAL, THE .... RAE DAWN CHONG
PRISON FOR CHILDREN (TF) .... JOSH BROLIN
PRISON FOR CHILDREN (TF) ...... RAPHAEL SBARGE
PRISON SHIP .... NINA FOCH
PRISONER, THE .... ALEC GUINNESS
PRISONER OF SECOND
AVENUE, THE .... ANNE BANCROFT
PRISONER OF SECOND
AVENUE, THE .... GENE SAKS
PRISONER OF SECOND
AVENUE, THE .... JACK LEMMON
PRISONER OF SECOND
AVENUE, THE .... SYLVESTER STALLONE
PRISONER OF WAR .... RONALD REAGAN
PRISONER OF WAR .... STEVE FORREST
PRISONER OF ZENDA, THE .... DAVID NIVEN†
PRISONER OF ZENDA, THE .... DEBORAH KERR
PRISONER OF ZENDA, THE .... GREGORY SIERRA
PRISONER OF ZENDA, THE .... JANE GREER
PRISONER OF ZENDA, THE .... JEREMY KEMP
PRISONER OF ZENDA, THE .... STEPHANE AUDRAN
PRISONERS OF HONOR (CTF) .... BRIAN BLESSED
PRISONERS OF HONOR (CTF) .... JEREMY KEMP
PRISONERS OF HONOR (CTF) .... OLIVER REED
PRISONERS OF HONOR (CTF) .... PETER FIRTH
PRISONERS OF HONOR (CTF) .... PETER VAUGHN
PRISONERS OF
HONOR (CTF) .... RICHARD DREYFUSS
PRISONERS OF THE SUN .... BRYON BROWN
PRISONERS OF THE SUN .... GEORGE TAKEI
PRISONERS OF THE SUN .... TERRY O'QUINN
PRIVACY .... MICHELLE PFEIFFER
PRIVATE AFFAIRS OF
BEL AMI, THE .... ANGELA LANSBURY
PRIVATE ANGELO .... PETER USTINOV

PRIVATE BATTLE, A (TF) .... JACK WARDEN
PRIVATE BENJAMIN .... ALBERT BROOKS
PRIVATE BENJAMIN .... ARMAND ASSANTE
PRIVATE BENJAMIN .... BARBARA BARRIE
PRIVATE BENJAMIN .... CRAIG T. NELSON
PRIVATE BENJAMIN .... HARRY DEAN STANTON
PRIVATE BENJAMIN .... MARY KAY PLACE
PRIVATE BENJAMIN .... ROBERT WEBBER
PRIVATE BENJAMIN .... SALLY KIRKLAND
PRIVATE BENJAMIN ★ .... SAM WANAMAKER†
PRIVATE BENJAMIN ★ .... GOLDIE HAWN
PRIVATE BENJAMIN ○ .... EILEEN BRENNAN
PRIVATE BUCKAROO .... MARY WICKES
PRIVATE DETECTIVE .... JANE WYMAN
PRIVATE EYES, THE .... DON KNOTTS
PRIVATE EYES, THE .... TIM CONWAY
PRIVATE FILES OF J. EDGAR
HOOVER, THE .... CELESTE HOLM
PRIVATE FILES OF J. EDGAR
HOOVER, THE .... E. G. MARSHALL
PRIVATE FILES OF J. EDGAR
HOOVER, THE .... JOSE FERRER†
PRIVATE FILES OF J. EDGAR
HOOVER, THE .... RAYMOND ST. JACQUES
PRIVATE FILES OF J. EDGAR
HOOVER, THE .... RIP TORN
PRIVATE FUNCTION, A .... DENHOLM ELLIOTT†
PRIVATE FUNCTION, A .... JIM CARTER
PRIVATE FUNCTION, A .... MAGGIE SMITH
PRIVATE FUNCTION, A .... MICHAEL PALIN
PRIVATE FUNCTION, A .... RICHARD GRIFFITHS
PRIVATE INVESTIGATIONS .... ANTHONY ZERBE
PRIVATE INVESTIGATIONS .... PAUL LeMAT
PRIVATE INVESTIGATIONS (TF) ..... MARTIN BALSAM
PRIVATE LESSONS .... HOWARD HESSEMAN
PRIVATE LESSONS .... SYLVIA KRISTEL
PRIVATE LIFE OF
HENRY VIII, THE ★★ ...... CHARLES LAUGHTON†
PRIVATE LIFE OF SHERLOCK
HOLMES, THE .... ROBERT STEPHENS
PRIVATE LIVES OF ADAM
AND EVE, THE .... TUESDAY WELD
PRIVATE LIVES OF ELIZABETH
AND ESSEX, THE .... BETTE DAVIS†
PRIVATE LIVES OF ELIZABETH
AND ESSEX, THE .... OLIVIA DE HAVILLAND
PRIVATE LIVES OF ELIZABETH
AND ESSEX, THE .... VINCENT PRICE†
PRIVATE MATTER, A (CTF) .... SISSY SPACEK
PRIVATE NAVY OF SERGEANT
O'FARRELL, THE .... DICK SARGENT
PRIVATE NAVY OF SGT.
O'FARRELL, THE .... BOB HOPE
PRIVATE NAVY OF SGT.
O'FARRELL, THE .... PHYLLIS DILLER
PRIVATE POTTER .... TOM COURTENAY
PRIVATE PROPERTY .... COREY ALLEN
PRIVATE RESORT .... HECTOR ELIZONDO
PRIVATE RESORT .... JOHNNY DEPP
PRIVATE SCHOOL .... BETSY RUSSELL
PRIVATE SCHOOL .... MATTHEW MODINE
PRIVATE SCHOOL .... PHOEBE CATES
PRIVATE SCHOOL .... RAY WALSTON
PRIVATE SESSIONS (TF) ...... MAUREEN STAPLETON
PRIVATE SESSIONS (TF) .... MIKE FARRELL
PRIVATE SESSIONS (TF) .... ROBERT VAUGHN
PRIVATE SESSIONS (TF) .... TOM BOSLEY
PRIVATE WAR OF
MAJOR BENSON, THE .... CHARLTON HESTON
PRIVATE WAR OF
MAJOR PAYNE, THE .... DAMON WAYANS
PRIVATE'S PROGRESS .... THORLEY WALTERS†
PRIVATES ON PARADE .... DENIS QUILLEY
PRIVATES ON PARADE .... JOHN CLEESE
PRIVATE'S AFFAIR, A .... BARBARA EDEN
PRIVATE'S PROGRESS .... IAN BANNEN
PRIZE, THE .... DIANE BAKER
PRIZE, THE .... KEVIN McCARTHY
PRIZE, THE .... PAUL NEWMAN
PRIZE FIGHTER, THE .... TIM CONWAY
PRIZE OF GOLD, A .... MAE ZETTERLING†
PRIZE OF GOLD, A .... RICHARD WIDMARK

PRIZZI'S HONOR .... C. C. H. POUNDER
PRIZZI'S HONOR .... JOHN RANDOLPH
PRIZZI'S HONOR .... KATHLEEN TURNER
PRIZZI'S HONOR .... LAWRENCE TIERNEY
PRIZZI'S HONOR .... LEE RICHARDSON
PRIZZI'S HONOR .... ROBERT LOGGIA
PRIZZI'S HONOR ★ .... JACK NICHOLSON
PRIZZI'S HONOR ○ .... WILLIAM HICKEY
PRIZZI'S HONOR ○○ .... ANJELICA HUSTON
PRO & CON .... LEO DAMIAN
PROBE (TF) .... BURGESS MEREDITH
PROBE (TF) .... JACLYN SMITH
PROBE (TF) .... JOHN GIELGUD
PROBE (TF) .... PARKER STEVENSON
PROBLEM CHILD .... ANY YASBECK
PROBLEM CHILD .... JACK WARDEN
PROBLEM CHILD .... JOHN RITTER
PROBLEM CHILD .... MICHAEL OLIVER
PROBLEM CHILD 2 .... ANY YASBECK
PROBLEM CHILD 2 .... IVYANN SCHWAN
PROBLEM CHILD 2 .... JACK WARDEN
PROBLEM CHILD 2 .... JOHN RITTER
PROBLEM CHILD 2 .... LARAINE NEWMAN
PROBLEM CHILD 2 .... MICHAEL OLIVER
PRODIGAL, THE .... HOPE LANGE
PRODIGAL, THE .... JOHN DEHNER†
PRODIGAL, THE .... JOSEPH WISEMAN
PRODIGAL, THE .... LANA TURNER
PRODIGIOUS
HICKEY, THE (TF) .... STEPHEN BALDWIN
PRODUCERS, THE .... KENNETH MARS
PRODUCERS, THE ○ .... GENE WILDER
PROFESSIONAL, THE .... DANNY AIELLO
PROFESSIONAL, THE .... GARY OLDMAN
PROFESSIONAL, THE .... JEAN RENO
PROFESSIONAL, THE .... NATALIE PORTMAN
PROFESSIONAL GUN, A .... JACK PALANCE
PROFESSIONALS, THE .... BURT LANCASTER†
PROFESSIONALS, THE .... JACK PALANCE
PROFESSIONALS, THE .... RALPH BELLAMY†
PROFESSIONALS, THE .... WOODY STRODE
PROFESSIONE: REPORTER .... JACK NICHOLSON
PROFESSOR BEWARE .... LIONEL STANDER
PROFONDO ROSSO .... DAVID HEMMINGS
PROGRAM, THE .... CRAIG SHEFFER
PROGRAM, THE .... HALLE BERRY
PROGRAM, THE .... JAMES CAAN
PROGRAM, THE .... KRISTY SWANSON
PROGRAM, THE .... OMAR EPPS
PROIBITO .... MEL FERRER
PROJECT: KILL .... LESLIE NIELSEN
PROJECT X .... HELEN HUNT
PROJECT X .... HENRY JONES
PROJECT X .... MATTHEW BRODERICK
PROJECT X .... WILLIAM SADLER
PROJECTIONIST, THE .... RODNEY DANGERFIELD
PROM NIGHT .... JAMIE LEE CURTIS
PROM NIGHT .... LESLIE NIELSEN
PROMISE (TF) .... JAMES GARNER
PROMISE (TF) .... JAMES WOODS
PROMISE (TF) .... PETER MICHAEL GOETZ
PROMISE (TF) .... PIPER LAURIE
PROMISE, THE .... BEATRICE STRAIGHT
PROMISE, THE .... KATHLEEN QUINLAN
PROMISE, THE .... LAURENCE LUCKINBILL
PROMISE, THE .... STEPHEN COLLINS
PROMISE, THE .... WILLIAM PRINCE
PROMISE HER
ANYTHING .... DONALD SUTHERLAND
PROMISE HER ANYTHING .... LESLIE CARON
PROMISE HER ANYTHING .... LIONEL STANDER
PROMISE HER ANYTHING .... WARREN BEATTY
PROMISE HIM ANYTHING (TF) .... EDDIE ALBERT
PROMISE HIM
ANYTHING (TF) .... FREDERIC FORREST
PROMISE HIM ANYTHING (TF) .... STEVEN KEATS†
PROMISED A MIRACLE (TF) .... JUDGE REINHOLD
PROMISED A
MIRACLE (TF) .... ROSANNA ARQUETTE
PROMISED LAND .... JASON GEDRICK
PROMISED LAND .... KIEFER SUTHERLAND
PROMISED LAND .... MEG RYAN

529

† after an actor's name denotes deceased.

PROMISED LAND .... TRACY POLLAN
PROMISES IN THE DARK .... KATHLEEN BELLER
PROMISES IN THE DARK .... MARSHA MASON
PROMISES IN THE DARK .... NED BEATTY
PROMISES IN THE DARK .... SUSAN CLARK
PROMISES TO KEEP (TF) .... DEVON O'BRIEN
PROMISES TO KEEP (TF) .... ROBERT MITCHUM
PROMOTER, THE .... ALEC GUINNESS
PROOF .... RUSSELL CROWE
PROOF OF THE MAN .... GEORGE KENNEDY
PROPHECY .... ARMAND ASSANTE
PROPHECY .... ROBERT FOXWORTH
PROPHECY, THE .... TALIA SHIRE
PROPHET, THE .... ANN-MARGRET
PROSPERO'S BOOKS .... ERLAND JOSEPHSON
PROSPERO'S BOOKS .... ISABELLE PASCO
PROSPERO'S BOOKS .... JOHN GIELGUD
PROTECTOR, THE .... DANNY AIELLO
PROTECTORS, THE .... JOHN SAXON
PROTECTORS, THE .... VAN JOHNSON
PROTOCOL .... CHRIS SARANDON
PROTOCOL .... CLIFF DE YOUNG
PROTOCOL .... ED BEGLEY JR.
PROTOCOL .... GOLDIE HAWN
PROTOCOL .... KENNETH McMILLAN†
PROTOTYPE X29A .... MITCHELL COX
PROUD AND THE
    DAMNED, THE .... CHUCK CONNORS†
PROUD AND THE
    PROFANE, THE .... CLAUDE AKINS†
PROUD AND THE
    PROFANE, THE .... DEBORAH KERR
PROUD MEN (TF) .... ALAN AUTRY
PROUD MEN (TF) .... CHARLTON HESTON
PROUD MEN (TF) .... NAN MARTIN
PROUD MEN (TF) .... PETER STRAUSS
PROUD REBEL, THE .... OLIVIA DE HAVILLAND
PROVIDENCE .... DAVID WARNER
PROVIDENCE .... ELAINE STRITCH
PROVIDENCE .... ELLEN BURSTYN
PROVIDENCE .... JOHN GIELGUD
PRUDENCE AND THE PILL .... DEBORAH KERR
PSYCH-OUT .... BRUCE DERN
PSYCH-OUT .... DEAN STOCKWELL
PSYCH-OUT .... JACK NICHOLSON
PSYCH-OUT .... SUSAN STRASBERG
PSYCHE 59 .... IAN BANNEN
PSYCHE 59 .... PATRICIA NEAL
PSYCHE 59 .... SAMANTHA EGGAR
PSYCHIC KILLER .... NEHEMIAH PERSOFF
PSYCHO ◊ .... JANET LEIGH
PSYCHO .... ANTHONY PERKINS†
PSYCHO .... JOHN ANDERSON
PSYCHO .... JOHN GAVIN
PSYCHO .... JOHN McINTIRE†
PSYCHO .... MARTIN BALSAM
PSYCHO .... VERA MILES
PSYCHO II .... ANTHONY PERKINS†
PSYCHO II .... MEG TILLY
PSYCHO II .... ROBERT LOGGIA
PSYCHO II .... VERA MILES
PSYCHO III .... ANTHONY PERKINS†
PSYCHO III .... DIANA SCARWID
PSYCHO III .... HUGH GILLIN
PSYCHO III .... JEFF FAHEY
PSYCHO III .... LEE GARLINGTON
PSYCHO III .... ROBERT ALAN BROWNE
PSYCHO IV .... ANTHONY PERKINS†
PSYCHOMANIA .... DICK VAN PATTEN
PSYCHOMANIA .... JAMES FARENTINO
PSYCHOMANIA .... SYLVIA MILES
PT-109 .... CLIFF ROBERTSON
PT-109 .... ROBERT BLAKE
PT-109 .... ROBERT CULP
PTERODACTYL WOMAN FROM
    BEVERLY HILLS .... BEVERLY D'ANGELO
PTERODACTYL WOMAN FROM
    BEVERLY HILLS .... BRION JAMES
PTERODACTYL WOMAN FROM
    BEVERLY HILLS .... MOON ZAPPA
PTERODACTYL WOMAN FROM
    BEVERLY HILLS .... RUTA LEE

PTERODACTYL WOMAN FROM
    BEVERLY HILLS .... SHARON MARTIN
PUBLIC DEB No. 1 .... RALPH BELLAMY†
PUBLIC ENEMY NUMBER ONE .... ZSA ZSA GABOR
PUBLIC EYE, THE .... GIAN-CARLO SCANDIUZZI
PUBLIC EYE, THE .... JOE PESCI
PUBLIC EYE, THE .... BARBARA HERSHEY
PUBLIC EYE, THE (1972) .... MIA FARROW
PUBLIC EYE, THE (1972) .... TOPOL
PUBLIC WEDDING .... JANE WYMAN
PUFNSTUF .... MARTHA RAYE†
PULP .... LIONEL STANDER
PULP .... MICHAEL CAINE
PULP FICTION .... AMANDA PLUMMER
PULP FICTION .... BRUCE WILLIS
PULP FICTION .... CHRISTOPHER WALKEN
PULP FICTION .... ERIC STOLTZ
PULP FICTION .... FRANK WHALEY
PULP FICTION .... HARVEY KEITEL
PULP FICTION .... JOHN TRAVOLTA
PULP FICTION .... JULIA SWEENEY
PULP FICTION .... MARIA DE MEDEIROS
PULP FICTION .... ROSANNA ARQUETTE
PULP FICTION .... SAMUEL L. JACKSON
PULP FICTION .... TIM ROTH
PULP FICTION .... UMA THURMAN
PULP FICTION .... YING RHAMES
PUMP UP THE VOLUME .... CHRISTIAN SLATER
PUMP UP THE VOLUME .... ELLEN GREENE
PUMP UP THE VOLUME .... SAMANTHA MATHIS
PUMP UP THE VOLUME .... SCOTT PAULIN
PUMPING
    IRON (FD) .... ARNOLD SCHWARZENEGGER
PUMPKIN EATER, THE .... MAGGIE SMITH
PUMPKIN EATER, THE ★ .... ANNE BANCROFT
PUMPKINHEAD .... LANCE HENRIKSEN
PUNCH AND JUDY MAN, THE .... PETER VAUGHN
PUNCHLINE .... DAMON WAYANS
PUNCHLINE .... JOHN GOODMAN
PUNCHLINE .... KIM GREIST
PUNCHLINE .... MARK RYDELL
PUNCHLINE .... PAUL MAZURSKY
PUNCHLINE .... SALLY FIELD
PUNCHLINE .... TOM HANKS
PUNISHER, THE .... DOLPH LUNDGREN
PUNISHER, THE .... JEROEN KRABBE
PUNISHER, THE .... LOUIS GOSSETT JR.
PUPPET MASTERS, THE ...... DONALD SUTHERLAND
PUPPET MASTERS, THE .... ERIC THAL
PUPPET MASTERS, THE .... JULIE WARNER
PUPPET MASTERS, THE .... KEITH DAVID
PUPPET MASTERS, THE .... MARSHALL BELL
PUPPET MASTERS, THE .... RICHARD BELZER
PUPPET MASTERS, THE .... TODD BRYANT
PUPPET MASTERS, THE .... WILL PATTON
PURCHASE PRICE, THE ..... BARBARA STANWYCK†
PURE COUNTRY .... GEORGE STRAIT
PURE COUNTRY .... ISABEL GLASSER
PURE COUNTRY .... LESLEY ANN WARREN
PURE LUCK .... DANNY GLOVER
PURE LUCK .... HARRY SHEARER
PURE LUCK .... JASON ROBARDS
PURE LUCK .... MARTIN SHORT
PURE LUCK .... SAM WANAMAKER†
PURE LUCK .... SCOTT WILSON
PURE LUCK .... SHEILA KELLEY
PURGATORY .... TANYA ROBERTS
PURLIE VICTORIOUS .... ALAN ALDA
PURLIE VICTORIOUS .... BEAH RICHARDS
PURLIE VICTORIOUS .... OSSIE DAVIS
PURLIE VICTORIOUS .... RUBY DEE
PURLIE VICTORIOUS .... SORRELL BOOKE
PURPLE GANG, THE .... ROBERT BLAKE
PURPLE HEARTS .... CHERYL LADD
PURPLE HEARTS .... KEN WAHL
PURPLE MASK, THE .... ANGELA LANSBURY
PURPLE MASK, THE .... DAN O'HERLIHY
PURPLE MASK, THE .... TONY CURTIS
PURPLE PLAIN, THE .... GREGORY PECK
PURPLE RAIN .... APOLLONIA
PURPLE RAIN .... CLARENCE WILLIAMS III
PURPLE RAIN .... MORRIS DAY

PURPLE RAIN .... PRINCE
PURPLE ROSE OF CAIRO, THE .... DANNY AIELLO
PURPLE ROSE OF CAIRO, THE .... DEBORAH RUSH
PURPLE ROSE OF CAIRO, THE .... DIANNE WIEST
PURPLE ROSE
    OF CAIRO, THE .... EDWRAD HERRMANN
PURPLE ROSE OF CAIRO, THE .... JEFF DANIELS
PURPLE ROSE OF CAIRO, THE .... JOHN WOOD
PURPLE ROSE OF CAIRO, THE .... JULI DONALD
PURPLE ROSE OF CAIRO, THE .... KAREN AKERS
PURPLE ROSE OF CAIRO, THE .... MIA FARROW
PURPLE ROSE OF CAIRO, THE ... MICHAEL TUCKER
PURPLE ROSE OF CAIRO, THE .... MILO O'SHEA
PURPLE ROSE
    OF CAIRO, THE .... STEPHANIE FARROW
PURPLE ROSE OF CAIRO, THE .... VAN JOHNSON
PURPLE ROSE OF CAIRO, THE ...... ZOE CALDWELL
PURPLE TAXI, THE .... CHARLOTTE RAMPLING
PURPLE TAXI, THE .... EDWARD ALBERT
PURPLE TAXI, THE .... PETER USTINOV
PURSUED .... DAME JUDITH ANDERSON†
PURSUED .... HARRY CAREY JR.
PURSUED .... ROBERT MITCHUM
PURSUED .... TERESA WRIGHT
PURSUIT (TF) .... BEN GAZZARA
PURSUIT (TF) .... E. G. MARSHALL
PURSUIT (TF) .... MARTIN SHEEN
PURSUIT OF D.B. COOPER, THE .... ED FLANDERS
PURSUIT OF D.B. COOPER, THE ..... PAUL GLEASON
PURSUIT OF D.B.
    COOPER, THE .... ROBERT DUVALL
PURSUIT OF D.B.
    COOPER, THE .... TREAT WILLIAMS
PURSUIT OF HAPPINESS, THE .... ARTHUR HILL
PURSUIT OF
    HAPPINESS, THE .... BARBARA HERSHEY
PURSUIT OF
    HAPPINESS, THE .... CHARLES DURNING
PURSUIT OF HAPPINESS, THE .... E. G. MARSHALL
PURSUIT OF
    HAPPINESS, THE .... MICHAEL SARRAZIN
PURSUIT OF
    HAPPINESS, THE .... VINCENT GARDENIA†
PURSUIT OF HAPPINESS, THE ..... WILLIAM DEVANE
PURSUIT OF THE GRAF SPEE ...... PATRICK MacNEE
PUSHOVER .... E. G. MARSHALL
PUSHOVER .... KIM NOVAK
PUSSYCAT, PUSSYCAT,
    I LOVE YOU .... JOHN GAVIN
PUSSYCAT, PUSSYCAT,
    I LOVE YOU .... JOYCE VAN PATTEN
PUSSYCAT, PUSSYCAT,
    I LOVE YOU .... SEVERN DARDEN
PUTNEY SWOPE .... ALLEN GARFIELD
PUTNEY SWOPE .... ANTONIO FARGAS
PUTNEY SWOPE .... MEL BROOKS
PUZZLE OF A DOWNFALL CHILD ..... BARRY PRIMUS
PUZZLE OF A DOWNFALL CHILD ... FAYE DUNAWAY
PUZZLE OF A DOWNFALL CHILD ..... ROY SCHEIDER
PUZZLE OF A
    DOWNFALL CHILD .... VIVECA LINDFORS
PYGMALION ★ .... LESLIE HOWARD†
PYGMALION ★ .... WENDY HILLER
PYRATES .... KEVIN BACON
PYROMANIAC'S
    LOVE STORY, A .... ARMIN MUELLER-STAHL
PYROMANIAC'S LOVE STORY, A ... ERIKA ELENIAK
PYROMANIAC'S
    LOVE STORY, A .... JOAN PLOWRIGHT
PYROMANIAC'S
    LOVE STORY, A .... JOHN LEGUIZAMO
PYROMANIAC'S
    LOVE STORY, A .... JULIO MECHOSO
PYROMANIAC'S
    LOVE STORY, A .... MICHAEL LERNER
PYROMANIAC'S LOVE STORY, A .... MIKE STARR
PYROMANIAC'S LOVE STORY, A .... SADIE FROST
PYROMANIAC'S
    LOVE STORY, A .... WILLIAM BALDWIN
PYX, THE .... CHRISTOPHER PLUMMER
PYX, THE .... KAREN BLACK

530

Q

Q .... MICHAEL MORIARTY
Q .... RICHARD ROUNDTREE
Q.E.D. (TF) .... SAM WATERSTON
Q & A .... JENNY LUMET
Q&A .... ARMAND ASSANTE
Q&A .... CHARLES S. DUTTON
Q&A .... NICK NOLTE
Q&A .... TIMOTHY HUTTON
QB VII (MS) .... ANTHONY ANDREWS
QB VII (MS) .... ANTHONY HOPKINS
QB VII (MS) .... BEN GAZZARA
QB VII (MS) .... JOHN GIELGUD
QB VII (MS) .... LESLIE CARON
QB VII (TF) .... DAN O'HERLIHY
QB VII (TF) .... ROBERT STEPHENS
QUACKSER FORTUNE HAS A
  COUSIN IN THE BRONX .... GENE WILDER
QUACKSER FORTUNE HAS A
  COUSIN IN THE BRONX .... MARGOT KIDDER
QUADROPHENIA .... PHIL DANIELS
QUADROPHENIA .... STING
QUALITY STREET .... KATHERINE HEPBURN
QUANTEZ .... JOHN GAVIN
QUANTUM LEAP (TF) .... DEAN STOCKWELL
QUANTUM LEAP (TF) .... JENNIFER RUNYON
QUANTUM LEAP (TF) .... JOHN ALLEN NELSON
QUANTUM LEAP (TF) .... SCOTT BAKULA
QUARANTINED (TF) .... MARILYN HASSETT
QUARTERBACK PRINCESS (TF) .... HELEN HUNT
QUARTET .... ALAN BATES
QUARTET .... ISABELLE ADJANI
QUARTET .... MAE ZETTERLING†
QUARTET .... MAGGIE SMITH
QUEEN (MS) .... HALLE BERRY
QUEEN (MS) .... OSSIE DAVIS
QUEEN BEE .... BETSY PALMER
QUEEN BEE .... JOAN CRAWFORD†
QUEEN BEE .... JOHN IRELAND
QUEEN FOR A DAY .... DARREN McGAVIN
QUEEN FOR A DAY .... LEONARD NIMOY
QUEEN OF BLOOD .... DENNIS HOPPER
QUEEN OF BLOOD .... JOHN SAXON
QUEEN OF OUTER SPACE .... ZSA ZSA GABOR
QUEEN OF THE MOB .... RALPH BELLAMY†
QUEEN OF THE NILE .... VINCENT PRICE†
QUEEN OF THE STARDUST
  BALLROOM (TF) .... CHARLES DURNING
QUEEN OF THE STARDUST
  BALLROOM (TF) .... MAUREEN STAPLETON
QUEENIE (MS) .... CLAIRE BLOOM
QUEENIE (MS) .... LEIGH LAWSON
QUEENIE (MS) .... TOPOL
QUEENIE (TF) .... JOEL GREY
QUEENIE (TF) .... KIRK DOUGLAS
QUEENIE (TF) .... MARTIN BALSAM
QUEENIE (TF) .... MIA SARA
QUEENIE (TF) .... SARAH MILES
QUEENS, THE .... RAQUEL WELCH
QUEENS LOGIC .... CHLOE WEBB
QUEENS LOGIC .... JAMIE LEE CURTIS
QUEENS LOGIC .... JOE MANTEGNA
QUEENS LOGIC .... JOHN MALKOVICH
QUEENS LOGIC .... KEN OLIN
QUEENS LOGIC .... KEVIN BACON
QUEENS LOGIC .... LINDA FIORENTINO
QUEENS LOGIC .... TOM WAITS
QUEENS LOGIC .... TONY SPIRIDAKIS
QUEENS LOGIC .... JENNY WRIGHT
QUEIMADA! .... MARLON BRANDO
QUELQU'UN DERRIERE
  LA PORTE .... ANTHONY PERKINS†
QUENTIN DURWARD .... ROBERT MORLEY
QUERELLE .... BRAD DAVIS†
QUERELLE .... FRANCO NERO
QUEST, THE .... HENRY THOMAS
QUEST, THE .... JEAN-CLAUDE VAN DAMME
QUEST, THE .... ROGER MOORE
QUEST, THE (TF) .... BRIAN KEITH
QUEST FOR FIRE .... RAE DAWN CHONG

QUEST FOR FIRE .... RON PERLMAN
QUEST FOR LOVE .... DENHOLM ELLIOTT†
QUEST FOR LOVE .... JOAN COLLINS
QUEST FOR LOVE .... SIMON WARD
QUESTI FANTASMI .... MARCELLO MASTROIANNI
QUESTI FANTASMI .... SOPHIA LOREN
QUESTION OF GUILT, A (TF) .... RON LEIBMAN
QUESTION OF GUILT, A (TF) .... TUESDAY WELD
QUESTION OF HONOR, A (MS) .... STEVE INWOOD
QUESTION OF HONOR, A (TF) .... DANNY AIELLO
QUESTION OF LOVE, A (TF) .... BONNIE BEDELIA
QUESTION OF LOVE, A (TF) .... NED BEATTY
QUESTOR TAPES, THE (TF) .... ROBERT FOXWORTH
QUICK AND THE DEAD, THE .... GARY SINISE
QUICK AND THE DEAD, THE .... GENE HACKMAN
QUICK AND THE DEAD, THE .... KEITH DAVID
QUICK AND THE DEAD, THE .... KEVIN CONWAY
QUICK AND THE
  DEAD, THE .... LEONARDO DICAPRIO
QUICK AND THE DEAD, THE ... ROBERTS BLOSSOM
QUICK AND THE DEAD, THE .... RUSSELL CROWE
QUICK AND THE DEAD, THE .... SHARON STONE
QUICK AND THE DEAD, THE .... TOBIN BELL
QUICK AND THE DEAD, THE (CTF) .... SAM ELLIOTT
QUICK CHANGE .... BILL MURRAY
QUICK CHANGE .... GEENA DAVIS
QUICK CHANGE .... JASON ROBARDS
QUICK CHANGE .... PHILIP BOSCO
QUICK CHANGE .... RANDY QUAID
QUICK, LET'S GET MARRIED .... BARBARA EDEN
QUICKER THAN THE EYE .... BEN GAZZARA
QUICKER THAN THE EYE .... MARY CROSBY
QUICKSANDS, THE .... LILLIAN GISH†
QUICKSILVER .... JAMI GERTZ
QUICKSILVER .... KEVIN BACON
QUICKSILVER .... LAURENCE FISHBURNE
QUICKSILVER .... LOUIE ANDERSON
QUICKSILVER .... PAUL RODRIGUEZ
QUIET MAN, THE .... MAUREEN O'HARA
QUIET MAN, THE ◊ .... VICTOR McLAGLEN†
QUIET PLACE IN THE
  COUNTRY, A .... FRANCO NERO
QUIET PLACE IN THE
  COUNTRY, A .... VANESSA REDGRAVE
QUIET PLACE TO KILL, A .... CARROLL BAKER
QUIET VICTORY: THE CHARLIE
  WEDEMEYER STORY (TF) .... MICHAEL NOURI
QUIET VICTORY: THE CHARLIE
  WEDEMEYER STORY (TF) .... NOBLE WILLINGHAM
QUIET VICTORY: THE CHARLIE
  WEDEMEYER STORY (TF) .... PAM DAWBER
QUIET WEDDING .... DAVID TOMLINSON
QUIET WEDDING .... PEGGY ASHCROFT†
QUIGLEY DOWN UNDER .... ALAN RICKMAN
QUIGLEY DOWN UNDER .... CHRIS HAYWOOD
QUIGLEY DOWN UNDER .... LAURA SAN GIACOMO
QUIGLEY DOWN UNDER .... RON HADDRICK
QUIGLEY DOWN UNDER .... TOM SELLECK
QUIGLEY DOWN UNDER .... TONY BONNER
QUILLER MEMORANDUM, THE .... ALEC GUINNESS
QUILLER MEMORANDUM, THE .... GEORGE SEGAL
QUINCY, M.E. (TF) .... JACK KLUGMAN
QUINNS, THE (TF) .... BARRY BOSTWICK
QUINNS, THE (TF) .... BLAIR BROWN
QUINNS, THE (TF) .... GERALDINE FITZGERALD
QUINTET .... BIBI ANDERSSON
QUINTET .... NINA VAN PALLANDT
QUINTET .... PAUL NEWMAN
QUIZ SHOW .... BARRY LEVENSON
QUIZ SHOW .... CHRISTOPHER McDONALD
QUIZ SHOW .... HANK AZARIA
QUIZ SHOW .... JOHN TURTURRO
QUIZ SHOW .... MARTIN SCORSESE
QUIZ SHOW .... PAUL SCOFIELD
QUIZ SHOW .... RALPH FIENNES
QUIZ SHOW .... ROB MORROW
QUIZ SHOW .... TIMOTHY BUSFIELD
QUO VADIS? .... DEBORAH KERR
QUO VADIS .... ELIZABETH TAYLOR
QUO VADIS ◊ .... LEO GENN†
QUO VADIS ◊ .... PETER USTINOV
QUO VADIS (TF) .... FREDERIC FORREST

R

R.P.M. .... ANN-MARGRET
R.P.M. .... ANTHONY QUINN
R.P.M. .... PAUL WINFIELD
RABBIT, RUN .... ARTHUR HILL
RABBIT, RUN .... CARRIE SNODGRESS
RABBIT, RUN .... HENRY JONES
RABBIT, RUN .... JAMES CAAN
RABBIT TEST .... BILLY CRYSTAL
RABBIT TEST .... FANNIE FLAGG
RABBIT TEST .... IMOGENE COCA
RABBIT TEST .... JOAN RIVERS
RABBIT TEST .... MARY STEENBURGEN
RABBIT TEST .... PAUL LYNDE†
RABBIT TEST .... RODDY McDOWALL
RABBIT TEST .... TOM POSTON
RABBIT TRAP, THE .... ERNEST BORGNINE
RACCONTI D'ESTATE .... MARCELLO MASTROIANNI
RACE FOR GLORY .... ALEX McARTHUR
RACE FOR GLORY .... PAMELA LUDWIG
RACE FOR GLORY .... PETER BERG
RACE FOR GLORY .... RAY WISE
RACE FOR THE
  YANKEE ZEPHYR .... GEORGE PEPPARD†
RACE TO THE YANKEE ZEPHYR .... KEN WAHL
RACE WITH THE DEVIL .... LORETTA SWIT
RACE WITH THE DEVIL .... PETER FONDA
RACE WITH THE DEVIL .... R.G. ARMSTRONG
RACERS, THE .... KATHY JURADO
RACERS, THE .... KIRK DOUGLAS
RACHEL AND
  THE STRANGER .... ROBERT MITCHUM
RACHEL PAPERS, THE .... DEXTER FLETCHER
RACHEL PAPERS, THE .... IONE SKYE
RACHEL PAPERS, THE .... JAMES SPADER
RACHEL PAPERS, THE .... JONATHAN PRYCE
RACHEL RACHEL .... GERALDINE FITZGERALD
RACHEL, RACHEL ★ .... JAMES OLSON
RACHEL, RACHEL ★ .... JOANNE WOODWARD
RACHEL, RACHEL ◊ .... ESTELLE PARSONS
RACING WITH THE MOON .... CAROL KANE
RACING WITH THE MOON .... CRISPIN GLOVER
RACING WITH
  THE MOON .... ELIZABETH McGOVERN
RACING WITH THE MOON .... JOHN KARLEN
RACING WITH THE MOON .... NICOLAS CAGE
RACING WITH THE MOON .... RUTANYA ALDA
RACING WITH THE MOON .... SEAN PENN
RACING WITH THE MOON .... SUZANNE ADKINSON
RACK, THE .... CLORIS LEACHMAN
RACK, THE .... PAUL NEWMAN
RACKET, THE .... ROBERT MITCHUM
RACKET MAN, THE .... SHELLEY WINTERS
RAD .... BART CONNER
RAD .... BILL ALLEN
RAD .... JACK WESTON
RAD .... LORI LOUGHLIN
RAD .... RAY WALSTON
RAD .... TALIA SHIRE
RADIO CITY REVELS .... MILTON BERLE
RADIO DAYS .... DANNY AIELLO
RADIO DAYS .... DIANE KEATON
RADIO DAYS .... DIANNE WIEST
RADIO DAYS .... JEFF DANIELS
RADIO DAYS .... JOSH MOSTEL
RADIO DAYS .... JULIE KAVNER
RADIO DAYS .... KENNETH MARS
RADIO DAYS .... MERCEDES RUEHL
RADIO DAYS .... MIA FARROW
RADIO DAYS .... MICHAEL TUCKER
RADIO DAYS .... SETH GREEN
RADIO DAYS .... TITO PUENTE
RADIO DAYS .... TONY ROBERTS
RADIO DAYS .... WALLACE SHAWN
RADIO DAYS .... WOODY ALLEN
RADIO FLYER .... ADAM BALDWIN
RADIO FLYER .... ELIJAH WOOD
RADIO FLYER .... JOHN HEARD
RADIO FLYER .... JOSEPH MAZZELLO
RADIO FLYER .... LORRAINE BRACCO

† after an actor's name denotes deceased.

RADIO FLYER .... RHEA PERLMAN
RADIO FLYER .... TOM HANKS
RADIO ON .... STING
RADIOACTIVE DREAMS .... DON MURRAY
RADIOACTIVE DREAMS .... GEORGE KENNEDY
RADIOACTIVE DREAMS .... JOHN STOCKWELL
RADIOACTIVE DREAMS .... LISA BLOUNT
RADIOACTIVE DREAMS .... MICHAEL DUDIKOFF
RADIOACTIVE DREAMS .... MICHELLE LITTLE
RADIOLAND MURDERS .... CORBIN BERENSEN
RADIOLAND MURDERS .... BRIAN BENBEN
RADIOLAND MURDERS .... CHRISTOPHER LLOYD
RADIOLAND MURDERS .... JEFFREY TAMBOR
RADIOLAND
    MURDERS .... MARY STUART MASTERSON
RADIOLAND MURDERS .... MICHAEL LERNER
RADIOLAND MURDERS .... MICHAEL McKEAN
RADIOLAND MURDERS .... NED BEATTY
RADIOLAND
    MURDERS .... SCOTT MICHAEL CAMPBELL
RADIOLAND MURDERS ...... STEPHEN TOBOLOWSKY
RAFFERTY AND THE GOLD
    DUST TWINS .... ALAN ARKIN
RAFFERTY AND THE GOLD
    DUST TWINS .... SALLY KELLERMAN
RAFFLES .... DAVID NIVEN†
RAFFLES .... OLIVIA DE HAVILLAND
RAGE .... BARNARD HUGHES
RAGE .... GEORGE C. SCOTT
RAGE .... MARTIN SHEEN
RAGE (TF) .... DAVID SOUL
RAGE IN HARLEM, A .... BADJA DJOLA
RAGE IN HARLEM, A .... DANNY GLOVER
RAGE IN HARLEM, A .... FOREST WHITAKER
RAGE IN HARLEM, A .... GREGORY HINES
RAGE IN HARLEM, A .... ROBIN GIVENS
RAGE IN HARLEM, A .... TYLER COLLINS
RAGE IN HARLEM, A .... ZAKES MOKAE
RAGE OF ANGELS (MS) .... JACLYN SMITH
RAGE OF ANGELS (TF) .... JOSEPH WISEMAN
RAGE OF ANGELS: THE STORY
    CONTINUES (MS) .... ANGELA LANSBURY
RAGE OF ANGELS: THE STORY
    CONTINUES (MS) .... ARMAND ASSANTE
RAGE OF ANGELS: THE STORY
    CONTINUES (MS) .... BRAD DOURIF
RAGE OF ANGELS: THE STORY
    CONTINUES (MS) .... JACLYN SMITH
RAGE OF ANGELS: THE STORY
    CONTINUES (MS) .... KEN HOWARD
RAGE OF ANGELS: THE STORY
    CONTINUES (MS) .... MASON ADAMS
RAGE OF ANGELS: THE STORY
    CONTINUES (MS) .... MICHAEL NOURI
RAGE OF ANGELS: THE STORY
    CONTINUES (MS) .... SUSAN SULLIVAN
RAGE OF THE BUCCANEERS .... VINCENT PRICE†
RAGE TO LIVE, A .... BEN GAZZARA
RAGE TO LIVE, A .... BRADFORD DILLMAN
RAGE TO LIVE, A .... PETER GRAVES
RAGE TO LIVE, A .... SUZANNE PLESHETTE
RAGGEDY MAN .... ERIC ROBERTS
RAGGEDY MAN .... HENRY THOMAS
RAGGEDY MAN .... SAM SHEPARD
RAGGEDY MAN .... SISSY SPACEK
RAGGEDY RAWNEY, THE .... BOB HOSKINS
RAGING BULL .... FRANK ADONIS
RAGING BULL .... FRANK VINCENT
RAGING BULL .... JOHN TURTURRO
RAGING BULL .... NICHOLAS COLASANTO†
RAGING BULL .... THERESA SALDANA
RAGING BULL ★★ .... ROBERT DE NIRO
RAGING BULL ○ .... CATHY MORIARTY
RAGING BULL ○ .... JOE PESCI
RAGING MOON, THE .... GEOFFREY BAYLDON
RAGING MOON, THE .... MALCOLM McDOWELL
RAGING TIDE, THE .... SHELLEY WINTERS
RAGMAN'S DAUGHTER, THE .... VICTORIA TENNANT
RAGS TO RICHES (TF) .... JOSEPH BOLOGNA
RAGTIME .... BRAD DOURIF
RAGTIME .... JAMES OLSON
RAGTIME .... KENNETH McMILLAN†
RAGTIME .... MARY STEENBURGEN

RAGTIME .... MOSES GUNN
RAGTIME ○ .... ELIZABETH McGOVERN
RAGTIME ○ .... HOWARD E. ROLLINS JR.
RAID ON ENTEBBE (TF) .... CHARLES BRONSON
RAID ON ENTEBBE (TF) .... MARTIN BALSAM
RAID ON ENTEBBE (TF) ..... MICHAEL CONSTANTINE
RAID ON ENTEBBE (TF) .... STEPHEN MACHT
RAID ON ENTEBBE (TF) .... SYLVIA SIDNEY
RAID, THE .... ANNE BANCROFT
RAID, THE .... CLAUDE AKINS†
RAID, THE .... PETER GRAVES
RAIDERS OF THE
    LOST ARK .... DENHOLM ELLIOTT†
RAIDERS OF THE LOST ARK .... HARRISON FORD
RAIDERS OF THE LOST ARK .... JOHN RHYS-DAVIES
RAIDERS OF THE LOST ARK .... KAREN ALLEN
RAIDERS OF THE LOST ARK .... PAUL FREEMAN
RAIDERS OF THE LOST ARK .... RONALD LACEY
RAIDERS OF THE LOST ARK .... WOLF KAHLER
RAIDERS, THE .... BRIAN KEITH
RAIDERS, THE .... DENNIS WEAVER
RAIDERS, THE .... ROBERT CULP
RAILROADED .... JOHN IRELAND
RAILWAY CHILDREN, THE .... JENNY AGUTTER
RAIN .... JOAN CRAWFORD†
RAIN FOR A DUSTY SUMMER ... ERNEST BORGNINE
RAIN MAN .... BARRY LEVINSON
RAIN MAN .... TOM CRUISE
RAIN MAN .... VALERIA GOLINO
RAIN MAN ★★ .... DUSTIN HOFFMAN
RAIN PEOPLE, THE .... JAMES CAAN
RAIN PEOPLE, THE .... ROBERT DUVALL
RAIN PEOPLE, THE .... SHIRLEY KNIGHT
RAINBOW ISLAND .... DOROTHY LAMOUR
RAINBOW ISLAND .... YVONNE DE CARLO
RAINBOW (TF) .... DON MURRAY
RAINBOW (TF) .... MARTIN BALSAM
RAINBOW, THE .... AMANDA DONOHOE
RAINBOW, THE .... SAMMI DAVIS
RAINMAKER, THE .... BURT LANCASTER†
RAINMAKER, THE .... EARL HOLLIMAN
RAINMAKER, THE .... LLOYD BRIDGES
RAINMAKER, THE ★ .... KATHERINE HEPBURN
RAINS OF RANCHIPUR, THE .... JOAN CAULFIELD†
RAINS OF RANCHIPUR, THE .... LANA TURNER
RAINS OF RANCHIPUR, THE ..... RICHARD BURTON†
RAINTREE COUNTY .... EVA MARIE SAINT
RAINTREE COUNTY ★ .... ELIZABETH TAYLOR
RAINY DAY FRIENDS .... ESAI MORALES
RAISE THE TITANIC .... ALEC GUINNESS
RAISE THE TITANIC .... ANNE ARCHER
RAISE THE TITANIC .... J. D. CANNON
RAISE THE TITANIC .... JASON ROBARDS
RAISE THE TITANIC .... RICHARD JORDAN†
RAISIN IN THE SUN, A .... LOUIS GOSSETT JR.
RAISIN IN THE SUN, A .... RUBY DEE
RAISIN IN THE SUN, A .... SIDNEY POITIER
RAISING ARIZONA .... FRANCES McDORMAND
RAISING ARIZONA .... HOLLY HUNTER
RAISING ARIZONA .... JOHN GOODMAN
RAISING ARIZONA .... M. EMMET WALSH
RAISING ARIZONA .... NICOLAS CAGE
RAISING ARIZONA .... RANDALL (TEX) COBB
RAISING ARIZONA .... SAM McMURRAY
RAISING ARIZONA .... THOMAS JOSEPH (T.J.) KUHN
RAISING ARIZONA .... TREY WILSON†
RAISING ARIZONA .... WILLIAM FORSYTHE
RAISING CAIN .... FRANCES STERNHAGEN
RAISING CAIN .... JOHN LITHGOW
RAISING CAIN .... LOLITA DAVIDOVICH
RAISING CAIN .... STEVEN BAUER
RAISING THE WIND .... JILL IRELAND†
RALLY ROUND THE FLAG, BOYS! .... JOAN COLLINS
RALLY ROUND THE
    FLAG, BOYS! .... JOANNE WOODWARD
RALLY ROUND THE FLAG, BOYS! .. PAUL NEWMAN
RALLY ROUND THE
    FLAG, BOYS! .... TUESDAY WELD
RAMBLING ROSE .... JOHN HEARD
RAMBLING ROSE .... KEVIN CONWAY
RAMBLING ROSE .... LUKAS HAAS
RAMBLING ROSE .... ROBERT DUVALL

RAMBLING ROSE ★ .... LAURA DERN
RAMBLING ROSE ○ .... DIANE LADD
RAMBO: FIRST BLOOD PART II ..... CHARLES NAPIER
RAMBO: FIRST BLOOD
    PART II .... RICHARD CRENNA
RAMBO: FIRST BLOOD
    PART II .... SYLVESTER STALLONE
RAMBO III .... RICHARD CRENNA
RAMBO III .... SYLVESTER STALLONE
RAMONA .... DON AMECHE†
RAMPAGE .... ROBERT MITCHUM
RAMROD .... LLOYD BRIDGES
RANCHO DeLUXE .... ELIZABETH ASHLEY
RANCHO DeLUXE .... JEFF BRIDGES
RANCHO DeLUXE .... SAM WATERSTON
RANCHO NOTORIOUS .... MEL FERRER
RANDOM HARVEST .... GREER GARSON
RANDOM HARVEST ★ .... RONALD COLMAN†
RANDOM HARVEST ○ .... SUSAN PETERS†
RANSOM .... DEBORAH RAFFIN
RANSOM .... JOHN IRELAND
RANSOM .... LESLIE NIELSEN
RANSOM .... SEAN CONNERY
RANSOM FOR A DEAD MAN (TF) .... PETER FALK
RANSOM FOR ALICE! (TF) .... GIL GERARD
RAPE, THE .... BIBI ANDERSSON
RAPE AND MARRIAGE: THE
    RIDEOUT CASE (TF) .... CONCHATA FERRELL
RAPE AND MARRIAGE: THE
    RIDEOUT CASE (TF) .... MICKEY ROURKE
RAPE OF DR. WILLIS, THE (TF) .... JACLYN SMITH
RAPE OF DR. WILLIS, THE (TF) .... RICHARD BALIN
RAPE OF INNOCENCE .... ISABELLE HUPPERT
RAPE OF RICHARD
    BECK, THE (TF) .... COTTER SMITH
RAPE OF RICHARD
    BECK, THE (TF) .... FRANCES LEE McCAIN
RAPE OF RICHARD
    BECK, THE (TF) .... JOANNA KERNS
RAPE OF RICHARD
    BECK, THE (TF) .... MEREDITH BAXTER
RAPE OF RICHARD BECK, THE (TF) ...... PAT HINGLE
RAPE OF RICHARD
    BECK, THE (TF) .... RICHARD CRENNA
RAPE OF THE SABINES .... ROGER MOORE
RAPID FIRE .... BRANDON LEE†
RAPTURE .... DEAN STOCKWELL
RAPTURE, THE .... DAVID DUCHOVNY
RAPTURE, THE .... MIMI ROGERS
RAPTURE, THE .... PATRICK BAUCHAU
RARE BREED, A .... GEORGE KENNEDY
RARE BREED, THE .... BEN JOHNSON
RARE BREED, THE .... BRIAN KEITH
RARE BREED, THE .... HARRY CAREY JR.
RARE BREED, THE .... JAMES STEWART
RARE BREED, THE .... MAUREEN O'HARA
RASCAL .... STEVE FORREST
RASPUTIN AND THE
    EMPRESS .... LIONEL BARRYMORE†
RASPUTIN—THE MAD MONK .... JOSS ACKLAND
RAT RACE, THE .... DEBBIE REYNOLDS
RAT RACE, THE .... TONY CURTIS
RATBOY .... JOHN WITHERSPOON
RATBOY .... JON LOVITZ
RATBOY .... LOUIE ANDERSON
RATBOY .... SONDRA LOCKE
RATBOY .... TIM THOMERSON
RATINGS GAME, THE (CTF) .... DANNY DEVITO
RATINGS GAME, THE (CTF) .... RHEA PERLMAN
RATINGS GAME, THE (CTF) .... STEVE ALLEN
RATON PASS .... PATRICIA NEAL
RATS, THE .... MARIA SCHELL
RAUBFISCHER IN HELLAS .... MARIA SCHELL
RAVAGERS .... WOODY STRODE
RAVAGERS, THE .... JOHN SAXON
RAVEN, THE .... JACK NICHOLSON
RAVEN, THE .... VINCENT PRICE†
RAVISHING IDIOT, A .... ANTHONY PERKINS†
RAW COURAGE .... LOIS CHILES
RAW DEAL .... ARNOLD SCHWARZENEGGER
RAW DEAL .... BLANCHE BAKER
RAW DEAL .... ED LAUTER

RAW DEAL .... JOHN IRELAND
RAW DEAL .... KATHRYN HARROLD
RAW DEAL .... PAUL SHENAR
RAW DEAL .... RAYMOND BURR†
RAW DEAL .... ROBERT DAVI
RAW DEAL .... SAM WANAMAKER†
RAW DEAL .... STEVEN HILL
RAW EDGE .... RORY CALHOUN
RAW EDGE .... YVONNE DE CARLO
RAW MEAT .... DONALD PLEASENCE
RAWHIDE .... DEAN JAGGER†
RAWHIDE .... JEFF COREY
RAWHIDE YEARS, THE .... TONY CURTIS
RAZOR'S EDGE, THE ○ .... CLIFTON WEBB†
RAZOR'S EDGE, THE ○○ .... ANNE BAXTER†
RAZOR'S EDGE, THE .... BILL MURRAY
RAZOR'S EDGE, THE .... DENHOLM ELLIOTT†
RAZOR'S EDGE, THE .... JAMES KEACH
RAZOR'S EDGE, THE .... PETER VAUGHN
RAZOR'S EDGE, THE .... THERESA RUSSELL
RAZZIA .... LILA KEDROVA
RAZZIA SUR LA CHNOUFF .... LILA KEDROVA
RE: LUCKY LUCIANO .... ROD STEIGER
RE-ANIMATOR .... JEFFREY COMBS
REACH FOR GLORY .... ALEXIS KANNER
READY, WILLING AND ABLE .... JANE WYMAN
REAL AMERICAN HERO, A (TF) ..... BRIAN DENNEHY
REAL GENIUS .... GABE JARRET
REAL GENIUS .... MICHELLE MEYRINK
REAL GENIUS .... VAL KILMER
REAL GENIUS .... WILLIAM ATHERTON
REAL GLORY, THE .... DAVID NIVEN†
REAL LIFE .... ALBERT BROOKS
REAL LIFE .... CHARLES GRODIN
REAL LIFE .... FRANCES LEE McCAIN
REAL McCOY, THE .... KIM BASINGER
REAL McCOY, THE .... TERENCE STAMP
REAL McCOY, THE .... VAL KILMER
REAL McCOY, THE .... ZACH ENGLISH
REAL MEN .... JAMES BELUSHI
REAL MEN .... JOHN RITTER
REAL MEN .... LAWRENCE LOTT†
REALITY BITES .... ANDY DICK
REALITY BITES .... BEN STILLER
REALITY BITES .... ETHAN HAWKE
REALITY BITES .... JANEANE GAROFALO
REALITY BITES .... JOE DON BAKER
REALITY BITES .... JOHN MAHONEY
REALITY BITES .... STEVE ZAHN
REALITY BITES .... SWOOSIE KURTZ
REALITY BITES .... WINONA RYDER
REALLY WEIRD TALES (CTF) .... CATHERINE O'HARA
REALLY WEIRD TALES (CTF) .... JOHN CANDY†
REALLY WEIRD TALES (CTF) .... MARTIN SHORT
REALLY WEIRD TALES (CTF) .... OLIVIA D'ABO
REAR WINDOW .... GRACE KELLY†
REAR WINDOW .... JAMES STEWART
REAR WINDOW .... RAYMOND BURR†
REAR WINDOW .... THELMA RITTER†
REARVIEW MIRROR (TF) .... JIM ANTONIO
REARVIEW MIRROR (TF) .... LEE REMICK†
REARVIEW MIRROR (TF) .... MICHAEL BECK
REARVIEW MIRROR (TF) .... TONY MUSANTE
REASON TO LIVE, A REASON
   TO DIE, A .... JAMES COBURN
REASON TO LIVE, A REASON
   TO DIE, A .... TELLY SAVALAS†
REASON TO LIVE, A (TF) .... BRUCE WEITZ
REASON TO LIVE, A (TF) .... CARRIE SNODGRESS
REASON TO LIVE, A (TF) .... DIEDRE HALL
REASON TO LIVE, A (TF) .... PETER FONDA
REASON TO LIVE, A (TF) .... RICK SCHRODER
REASON TO LIVE, A (TF) .... TRACEY GOLD
REBECCA ★ .... LAURENCE OLIVIER†
REBECCA ○ .... DAME JUDITH ANDERSON†
REBECCA OF SUNNYBROOK
   FARM .... BILL ROBINSON†
REBECCA OF SUNNYBROOK FARM ... JACK HALEY†
REBECCA OF SUNNYBROOK
   FARM .... RALPH BELLAMY†
REBECCA OF SUNNYBROOK
   FARM .... RANDOLPH SCOTT†

REBEL .... BILL HUNTER
REBEL .... BRYON BROWN
REBEL .... DEBBIE BYRNE
REBEL .... JULIE NIHILL
REBEL .... KIM DEACON
REBEL .... MATT DILLON
REBEL ROUSERS .... DIANE LADD
REBEL ROUSERS .... JACK NICHOLSON
REBEL WITHOUT A CAUSE .... COREY ALLEN
REBEL WITHOUT A CAUSE .... DENNIS HOPPER
REBEL WITHOUT A CAUSE .... EDWARD PLATT†
REBEL WITHOUT A CAUSE .... JAMES DEAN†
REBEL WITHOUT A CAUSE .... JIM BACKUS†
REBEL WITHOUT A CAUSE .... NICK ADAMS†
REBEL WITHOUT A CAUSE .... ROCHELLE HUDSON†
REBEL WITHOUT A CAUSE .... WILLIAM HOPPER†
REBEL WITHOUT A CAUSE ○ .... NATALIE WOOD†
REBEL WITHOUT A CAUSE ○ .... SAL MINEO†
REBELLION OF KITTY BELLE, THE .... LILLIAN GISH†
REBELS (MS) .... DOUG McCLURE
REBELS, THE (TF) .... PETER GRAVES
REBORN .... DENNIS HOPPER
RECKLESS .... ADAM BALDWIN
RECKLESS .... AIDAN QUINN
RECKLESS .... CLIFF DE YOUNG
RECKLESS .... DAN HEDAYA
RECKLESS .... DARYL HANNAH
RECKLESS .... KENNETH McMILLAN†
RECKLESS .... LEON AMES
RECKLESS .... LOIS SMITH
RECKONING, THE .... NICOL WILLIAMSON
RED ALERT (TF) .... ADRIENNE BARBEAU
RED ALERT (TF) .... WILLIAM DEVANE
RED AND BLUE .... NIGEL DAVENPORT
RED AND BLUE .... VANESSA REDGRAVE
RED BADGE OF COURAGE, THE .... ROYAL DANO
RED BALL EXPRESS .... JACK WARDEN
RED BALL EXPRESS .... ROBERT DAVIS†
RED BALL EXPRESS .... SIDNEY POITIER
RED CANYON .... LLOYD BRIDGES
RED DANUBE, THE .... ANGELA LANSBURY
RED DANUBE, THE .... JANET LEIGH
RED DAWN .... BEN JOHNSON
RED DAWN .... C. THOMAS HOWELL
RED DAWN .... CHARLIE SHEEN
RED DAWN .... DAVID KEITH
RED DAWN .... HARRY DEAN STANTON
RED DAWN .... JENNIFER GREY
RED DAWN .... LEA THOMPSON
RED DAWN .... PATRICK SWAYZE
RED DAWN .... POWERS BOOTHE
RED DESERT .... RICHARD HARRIS
RED EARTH, WHITE
   EARTH (TF) .... GENEVIEVE BUJOLD
RED EARTH, WHITE
   EARTH (TF) .... RICHARD FARNSWORTH
RED EARTH, WHITE EARTH (TF) ...... TIMOTHY DALY
RED FLAG: THE
   ULTIMATE GAME (TF) .... BARRY BOSTWICK
RED FLAG: THE
   ULTIMATE GAME (TF) .... JOAN VAN ARK
RED FLAG: THE
   ULTIMATE GAME (TF) .... WILLIAM DEVANE
RED HEAT .... ARNOLD SCHWARZENEGGER
RED HEAT .... ED O'ROSS
RED HEAT .... JAMES BELUSHI
RED HEAT .... LAURENCE FISHBURNE
RED HEAT .... LINDA BLAIR
RED HEAT .... PETER BOYLE
RED HEAT .... RICHARD BRIGHT
RED, HOT AND BLUE .... JACK KRUSCHEN
RED HOUSE, THE .... DAME JUDITH ANDERSON†
RED HOUSE, THE .... RORY CALHOUN
RED KING, WHITE KNIGHT (CTF) .... HELEN MIRREN
RED KING, WHITE KNIGHT (CTF) ..... TOM SKERRITT
RED LIGHT .... RAYMOND BURR†
RED LINE 7000 .... JAMES CAAN
RED MOUNTAIN .... JEFF COREY
RED MOUNTAIN .... JOHN IRELAND
RED PLANET MARS .... PETER GRAVES
RED PONY, THE .... BEAU BRIDGES
RED PONY, THE .... ROBERT MITCHUM

RED PONY, THE (TF) .... MAUREEN O'HARA
RED RIVER .... HARRY CAREY JR.
RED RIVER .... JOHN IRELAND
RED RIVER .... SHELLEY WINTERS
RED RIVER (TF) .... BRUCE BOXLEITNER
RED RIVER (TF) .... GREGORY HARRISON
RED RIVER (TF) .... JAMES ARNESS
RED RIVER (TF) .... RAY WALSTON
RED RIVER (TF) .... STAN SHAW
RED ROCK WEST .... DENNIS HOPPER
RED ROCK WEST .... J. T. WALSH
RED ROCK WEST .... LARA FLYNN BOYLE
RED ROCK WEST .... NICOLAS CAGE
RED SALUTE .... BARBARA STANWYCK†
RED SCORPION .... DOLPH LUNDGREN
RED SKIES OF MONTANA .... CHARLES BRONSON
RED SKIES OF MONTANA .... RICHARD CRENNA
RED SKIES OF MONTANA .... RICHARD WIDMARK
RED SKY AT MORNING .... CLAIRE BLOOM
RED SKY AT MORNING .... DESI ARNAZ JR.
RED SKY AT MORNING .... HARRY GUARDINO
RED SKY AT MORNING .... NEHEMIAH PERSOFF
RED SKY AT MORNING .... RICHARD CRENNA
RED SKY AT MORNING .... RICHARD THOMAS
RED SONJA .... ARNOLD SCHWARZENEGGER
RED SONJA .... BRIGITTE NIELSEN
RED SONJA .... RONALD LACEY
RED SPIDER, THE (TF) .... JAMES FARENTINO
RED SUN SOLEIL ROUGE .... URSULA ANDRESS
RED SUNDOWN .... RORY CALHOUN
RED TENT, THE .... SEAN CONNERY
RED TOMAHAWK .... HOWARD KEEL
RED TOMAHAWK .... JOAN CAULFIELD†
RED-HEADED STRANGER .... WILLIE NELSON
RED-LIGHT STING, THE (TF) .... BEAU BRIDGES
RED-LIGHT STING, THE (TF) .... FARRAH FAWCETT
REDHEAD FROM
   WYOMING, THE .... MAUREEN O'HARA
REDNECK .... TELLY SAVALAS†
REDNECK COUNTY RAPE .... SHELLEY WINTERS
REDS .... EDWRAD HERRMANN
REDS .... GENE HACKMAN
REDS .... M. EMMET WALSH
REDS .... PAUL SORVINO
REDS .... R.G. ARMSTRONG
REDS .... WILLIAM DANIELS
REDS ★ .... DIANE KEATON
REDS ★ .... WARREN BEATTY
REDS ○ .... JACK NICHOLSON
REDS ○○ .... MAUREEN STAPLETON
REEL LIFE .... KEVIN SPACEY
REF, THE .... CHRISTINE BARANSKI
REF, THE .... DENIS LEARY
REF, THE .... GLYNIS JOHNS
REF, THE .... J. K. SIMMONS
REF, THE .... JUDY DAVIS
REF, THE .... KEVIN SPACEY
REF, THE .... RAYMOND J. BARRY
REF, THE .... RICHARD BRIGHT
REF, THE .... ROBERT STEINMILLER JR.
REFLECTING SKIN, THE .... JEREMY COOPER
REFLECTION OF FEAR, A .... SALLY KELLERMAN
REFLECTION OF FEAR, A .... SONDRA LOCKE
REFLECTIONS IN A GOLDEN EYE .... BRIAN KEITH
REFLECTIONS IN A
   GOLDEN EYE .... ELIZABETH TAYLOR
REFLECTIONS IN A GOLDEN EYE .... JULIE HARRIS
REFLECTIONS IN A
   GOLDEN EYE .... MARLON BRANDO
REFLECTIONS IN A
   GOLDEN EYE .... ROBERT FORSTER
REFLECTIONS OF
   MURDER (TF) .... JOAN HACKETT†
REFLECTIONS (TF) .... GABRIEL BYRNE
REFORM SCHOOL GIRL .... SALLY KELLERMAN
REFORMER AND THE
   REDHEAD, THE .... JUNE ALLYSON
REGARDING HENRY .... ANNETTE BENING
REGARDING HENRY .... BILL NUNN
REGARDING HENRY .... HARRISON FORD
REGARDING HENRY .... MIKKI ALLEN
REG'LAR FELLERS .... DICK VAN PATTEN

† after an actor's name denotes deceased.

REG'LAR FELLERS .... JOYCE VAN PATTEN
REHEARSAL FOR MURDER (TF) ... JEFF GOLDBLUM
REHEARSAL FOR
  MURDER (TF) .... LYNN REDGRAVE
REHEARSAL FOR
  MURDER (TF) .... WILLIAM DANIELS
REHEARSAL, THE .... STEVE INWOOD
REIFENDE JUGEND .... MAXIMILIAN SCHELL
REIGN OF TERROR .... NORMAN LLOYD
REINCARNATION OF
  PETER PROUD, THE .... DEBRALEE SCOTT
REINCARNATION OF
  PETER PROUD, THE .... JENNIFER O'NEILL
REINCARNATION OF
  PETER PROUD, THE .... MARGOT KIDDER
REINCARNATION OF
  PETER PROUD, THE .... MICHAEL SARRAZIN
REIVERS, THE .... BURGESS MEREDITH
REIVERS, THE .... CLIFTON JAMES
REIVERS, THE .... DIANE LADD
REIVERS, THE .... LONNY CHAPMAN
REIVERS, THE .... MICHAEL CONSTANTINE
REIVERS, THE ○ .... RUPERT CROSSE†
RELENTLESS .... JUDD NELSON
RELENTLESS .... LEO ROSSI
RELENTLESS .... MEG FOSTER
RELENTLESS .... ROBERT LOGGIA
RELUCTANT ASTRONAUT, THE .... DON KNOTTS
RELUCTANT ASTRONAUT, THE ..... LESLIE NIELSEN
RELUCTANT
  DEBUTANTE, THE .... ANGELA LANSBURY
RELUCTANT DEBUTANTE, THE .... JOHN SAXON
RELUCTANT DEBUTANTE, THE .... SANDRA DEE
RELUCTANT SAINT, THE .... MAXIMILIAN SCHELL
REMAINS OF THE
  DAY, THE .... CHRISTOPHER REEVE
REMAINS OF THE DAY, THE .... HUGH GRANT
REMAINS OF THE DAY, THE .... JAMES FOX
REMAINS OF THE DAY, THE ... MICHAEL LONSDALE
REMAINS OF THE DAY, THE .... PETER VAUGHN
REMAINS OF THE
  DAY, THE ★ .... ANTHONY HOPKINS
REMAINS OF THE
  DAY, THE ★ .... EMMA THOMPSON
REMAINS TO BE SEEN .... ANGELA LANSBURY
REMAINS TO BE SEEN .... JUNE ALLYSON
REMAINS TO BE SEEN .... VAN JOHNSON
REMEMBER? .... GREER GARSON
REMEMBER MY NAME .... ALFRE WOODARD
REMEMBER MY NAME .... ANTHONY PERKINS†
REMEMBER MY NAME .... JEFF GOLDBLUM
REMEMBER MY NAME .... MOSES GUNN
REMEMBER THE NIGHT ...... BARBARA STANWYCK†
REMEMBRANCE OF LOVE (TF) .... KIRK DOUGLAS
REMEMER MY NAME .... GERALDINE CHAPLIN
REMINGTON STEELE: THE STEELE THAT
  WOULDN'T DIE (TF) .... DORIS ROBERTS
REMINGTON STEELE: THE STEELE THAT
  WOULDN'T DIE (TF) .... JACK SCALIA
REMINGTON STEELE: THE STEELE THAT
  WOULDN'T DIE (TF) .... PIERCE BROSNAN
REMINGTON STEELE: THE STEELE THAT
  WOULDN'T DIE (TF) .... STEPHANIE ZIMBALIST
REMO WILLIAMS: THE
  ADVENTURE BEGINS... .... FRED WARD
REMO WILLIAMS: THE
  ADVENTURE BEGINS .... JOEL GREY
REMO WILLIAMS: THE
  ADVENTURE BEGINS .... KATE MULGREW
REMO WILLIAMS: THE
  ADVENTURE BEGINS .... WILFORD BRIMLEY
REMOTE CONTROL .... JENNIFER TILLY
RENAISSANCE MAN .... CLIFF ROBERTSON
RENAISSANCE MAN .... DANNY DEVITO
RENAISSANCE MAN .... ED BEGLEY JR.
RENAISSANCE MAN .... GREG SPORDLEDER
RENAISSANCE MAN .... GREGORY HINES
RENAISSANCE MAN .... JAMES REMAR
RENAISSANCE MAN .... JENIFER LEWIS
RENAISSANCE MAN .... KADEEN HARDISON
RENAISSANCE MAN .... LILLO BRANCATO

RENAISSANCE MAN .... MARK WAHLBERG
RENAISSANCE MAN .... PETER SIMMONS
RENAISSANCE MAN .... STACEY DASH
RENAISSANCE MAN .... TONY DANZA
RENALDO AND CLARA .... BOB DYLAN
RENALDO AND CLARA .... RONEE BLAKLEY
RENALDO AND CLARA .... SAM SHEPARD
RENDEZVOUS AT MIDNIGHT .... RALPH BELLAMY†
RENDEZVOUS WITH ANNIE .... EDDIE ALBERT
RENÉ LA CANNE .... GERARD DEPARDIEU
RENÉ LA CANNE .... SYLVIA KRISTEL
RENEGADES .... BILL SMITROVICH
RENEGADES .... JAMI GERTZ
RENEGADES .... KIEFER SUTHERLAND
RENEGADES .... LOU DIAMOND PHILLIPS
RENEGADES .... ROB KNEPPER
RENEGADES, THE (TF) .... PATRICK SWAYZE
RENT-A-COP .... BERNIE CASEY
RENT-A-COP .... BURT REYNOLDS
RENT-A-COP .... DIONNE WARWICK
RENT-A-COP .... JAMES REMAR
RENT-A-COP .... JOHN P. RYAN
RENT-A-COP .... JOHN STANTON
RENT-A-COP .... LIZA MINELLI
RENT-A-COP .... MICHAEL ROOKER
RENT-A-COP .... RICHARD MASUR
RENT-A-COP .... ROBBY BENSON
RENTED LIPS .... EILEEN BRENNAN
RENTED LIPS .... JENNIFER TILLY
RENTED LIPS .... MARTIN MULL
RENTED LIPS .... ROBERT DOWNEY JR.
REPO MAN .... EMILIO ESTEVEZ
REPO MAN .... HARRY DEAN STANTON
REPORT TO THE
  COMMISSIONER .... HECTOR ELIZONDO
REPORT TO THE
  COMMISSIONER .... MICHAEL MORIARTY
REPORT TO THE
  COMMISSIONER .... RICHARD GERE
REPORT TO THE
  COMMISSIONER .... SUSAN BLAKELY
REPORT TO THE
  COMMISSIONER .... WILLIAM DEVANE
REPORT TO THE
  COMMISSIONER .... YAPHET KOTTO
REPOSSESSED .... LESLIE NIELSEN
REPOSSESSED .... LINDA BLAIR
REPOSSESSED .... NED BEATTY
REPRIEVE .... JACK KRUSCHEN
REPRIEVE .... STUART WHITMAN
REPRIEVE .... TIMOTHY CAREY
REPULSION .... CATHERINE DENEUVE
REQUIEM FOR A
  HEAVYWEIGHT .... ANTHONY QUINN
REQUIEM FOR A
  HEAVYWEIGHT .... MICKEY ROONEY
REQUIEM FOR A HEAVYWEIGHT .... MUHAMMAD ALI
REQUIEM FOR A
  HEAVYWEIGHT .... RORY CALHOUN
REQUIEM FOR A HEAVYWEIGHT .... VAL AVERY
RESCUE, THE .... CHARLES HAID
RESCUE, THE .... CHRISTINA HARNOS
RESCUE, THE .... EDWARD ALBERT
RESCUE, THE .... IAN GIATTI
RESCUE, THE .... JAMES CROMWELL
RESCUE, THE .... KEVIN DILLON
RESCUE, THE .... MARC PRICE
RESCUE, THE .... MEL WONG
RESCUE, THE .... MICHAEL GATES PHENICIE
RESCUE, THE .... NED VAUGHN
RESCUE, THE .... TIMOTHY CARHART
RESCUE ME .... AMI DOLENZ
RESCUE ME .... DEE WALLACE STONE
RESCUE ME .... MICHAEL DUDIKOFF
RESCUE ME .... PETER DeLUISE
RESCUE ME .... STEPHEN DORFF
RESCUE ME .... WILLIAM LUCKING
RESCUERS DOWN UNDER, THE (AF) .... ADAM RYEN
RESCUERS DOWN
  UNDER, THE (AF) .... BOB NEWHART
RESCUERS DOWN
  UNDER, THE (AF) .... DOUGLAS SEALE

RESCUERS DOWN UNDER, THE (AF) .... EVA GABOR
RESCUERS DOWN
  UNDER, THE (AF) .... FRANK WELKER
RESCUERS DOWN
  UNDER, THE (AF) .... GEORGE C. SCOTT
RESCUERS DOWN
  UNDER, THE (AF) .... JOHN CANDY†
RESCUERS DOWN
  UNDER, THE (AF) ... TRISTAN ROGERS
RESCUERS DOWN
  UNDER, THE (AF) .... WAYNE ROBSON
RESCUERS, THE (AF) .... BOB NEWHART
RESCUERS, THE (AF) .... EVA GABOR
RESERVOIR DOGS .... CHRIS PENN
RESERVOIR DOGS .... HARVEY KEITEL
RESERVOIR DOGS .... LAWRENCE TIERNEY
RESERVOIR DOGS .... MICHAEL MADSEN
RESERVOIR DOGS .... QUENTIN TARANTINO
RESERVOIR DOGS .... STEVE BUSCEMI
RESERVOIR DOGS .... TIM ROTH
RESTING PLACE (TF) .... G. D. SPRADLIN
RESTING PLACE (TF) .... JOHN LITHGOW
RESTING PLACE (TF) .... MORGAN FREEMAN
RESTLESS BREED, THE .... ANNE BANCROFT
RESTLESS NATIVES .... NED BEATTY
RESTLESS YEARS, THE .... JOHN SAXON
RESTLESS YEARS, THE .... SANDRA DEE
RESTLESS YEARS, THE .... TERESA WRIGHT
RESTORATION .... DAVID THEWLIS
RESTORATION .... HUGH GRANT
RESTORATION .... MEG RYAN
RESTORATION .... POLLY WALKER
RESTORATION .... ROBERT DOWNEY JR.
RESTORATION .... SAM NEILL
RESTORATION .... SIR IAN McKELLAN
RESURRECTED .... DAVID THEWLIS
RESURRECTION .... LOIS SMITH
RESURRECTION .... RICHARD FARNSWORTH
RESURRECTION .... SAM SHEPARD
RESURRECTION ★ .... ELLEN BURSTYN
RESURRECTION OF ZACHARY
  WHEELER, THE .... ANGIE DICKINSON
RESURRECTION OF ZACHARY
  WHEELER, THE .... BRADFORD DILLMAN
RESURRECTION OF ZACHARY
  WHEELER, THE .... LESLIE NIELSEN
RETREAT, HELL! .... RUSS TAMBLYN
RETRIBUTION .... DENNIS LIPSCOMB
RETRIBUTION .... HOYT AXTON
RETRIBUTION .... LESLIE WING
RETURN .... FREDERIC FORREST
RETURN, THE .... CYBILL SHEPHERD
RETURN, THE .... MARTIN LANDAU
RETURN, THE .... RAYMOND BURR†
RETURN FROM THE ASHES .... MAXIMILIAN SCHELL
RETURN FROM THE ASHES ...... SAMANTHA EGGAR
RETURN FROM WITCH MOUNTAIN .... BETTE DAVIS†
RETURN OF A MAN
  CALLED HORSE, THE .... RICHARD HARRIS
RETURN OF BILLY JACK, THE ...... RODNEY HARVEY
RETURN OF CAPTAIN
  INVINCIBLE, THE .... ALAN ARKIN
RETURN OF
  DESPERADO, THE (TF) .... ROBERT FOXWORTH
RETURN OF FRANK
  CANNON, THE (TF) .... ED NELSON
RETURN OF FRANK
  JAMES, THE .... JACKIE COOPER
RETURN OF JACK SLADE, THE ... ANGIE DICKINSON
RETURN OF JACK SLADE, THE ... MAX SHOWALTER
RETURN OF
  JAFAR, THE (AV) .... DAN CASTELLANETA
RETURN OF
  JAFAR, THE (AV) .... GILBERT GOTTFRIED
RETURN OF
  JAFAR, THE (AV) .... JASON ALEXANDER
RETURN OF JAFAR, THE (AV) .... LINDA LARKIN
RETURN OF JAFAR, THE (AV) .... SCOTT WEINGER
RETURN OF JESSE JAMES, THE .... JOHN IRELAND
RETURN OF JOE
  FORRESTER, THE (TF) .... EDIE ADAMS

This is not a list of every film ever made or every cast member, only those listed in this directory.

RETURN OF JOE
 FORRESTER, THE (TF) .... LLOYD BRIDGES
RETURN OF MARTIN
 GUERRE, THE .... GERARD DEPARDIEU
RETURN OF MARTIN
 GUERRE, THE .... NATHALIE BAYE
RETURN OF MICKEY SPILLANE'S
 MIKE HAMMER, THE (TF) .... STACY KEACH
RETURN OF MICKEY SPILLANE'S
 MIKE HAMMER, THE (TF) .... STEPHEN MACHT
RETURN OF MR. MOTO, THE .... HENRY SILVA
RETURN OF RIN TIN TIN, THE .... ROBERT BLAKE
RETURN OF SAM
 McCLOUD, THE (TF) .... J. D. CANNON
RETURN OF SHERLOCK
 HOLMES, THE (TF) .... MARGARET COLIN
RETURN OF SHERLOCK
 HOLMES, THE (TF) .... WILLIAM HOOTKINS
RETURN OF THE BEVERLY
 HILLBILLIES (TF) .... IMOGENE COCA
RETURN OF THE FLY .... VINCENT PRICE†
RETURN OF THE
 FRONTIERSMAN .... GORDON MACRAE†
RETURN OF THE JEDI .... ALEC GUINNESS
RETURN OF THE JEDI .... ANTHONY DANIELS
RETURN OF THE JEDI .... BILLY DEE WILLIAMS
RETURN OF THE JEDI .... CARRIE FISHER
RETURN OF THE JEDI .... DAVID PROWSE
RETURN OF THE JEDI .... FRANK OZ
RETURN OF THE JEDI .... HARRISON FORD
RETURN OF THE JEDI .... JAMES EARL JONES
RETURN OF THE JEDI .... KENNY BAKER
RETURN OF THE JEDI .... MARK HAMILL
RETURN OF THE JEDI .... PETER MAYHEW
RETURN OF THE JEDI .... WARWICK DAVIS
RETURN OF THE LIVING
 DEAD, THE .... CLU GULAGER
RETURN OF THE LIVING
 DEAD PART II .... DANA ASHBROOK
RETURN OF THE LIVING
 DEAD PART II .... JAMES KAREN
RETURN OF THE LIVING
 DEAD PART II .... MARSHA DIETLEIN
RETURN OF THE LIVING
 DEAD PART II .... MICHAEL KENWORTHY
RETURN OF THE LIVING
 DEAD PART II .... PHILIP BRUNS
RETURN OF THE LIVING
 DEAD PART II .... THOM MATHEWS
RETURN OF THE MAN
 FROM U.N.C.L.E., THE (TF) .... ANTHONY ZERBE
RETURN OF THE MAN
 FROM U.N.C.L.E., THE (TF) .... DAVID McCALLUM
RETURN OF THE MAN
 FROM U.N.C.L.E., THE (TF) .... PATRICK MacNEE
RETURN OF THE MAN
 FROM U.N.C.L.E., THE (TF) .... ROBERT VAUGHN
RETURN OF THE
 MUSKETEERS, THE .... C. THOMAS HOWELL
RETURN OF THE
 MUSKETEERS, THE .... FRANK FINLAY†
RETURN OF THE
 MUSKETEERS, THE .... MICHAEL YORK
RETURN OF THE
 MUSKETEERS, THE .... OLIVER REED
RETURN OF THE
 MUSKETEERS, THE .... RICHARD CHAMBERLAIN
RETURN OF THE PINK
 PANTHER .... SUZANNE PLESHETTE
RETURN OF THE PINK
 PANTHER, THE .... BURT KWOUK
RETURN OF THE PINK
 PANTHER, THE .... CHRISTOPHER PLUMMER
RETURN OF THE PINK
 PANTHER, THE .... PETER ARNE†
RETURN OF THE PINK
 PANTHER, THE .... PETER SELLERS†
RETURN OF THE REBELS (TF) .... PATRICK SWAYZE
RETURN OF THE
 SECAUCUS SEVEN .... DAVID STRATHAIRN
RETURN OF THE
 SECAUCUS SEVEN .... GORDON CLAPP

RETURN OF THE
 SECAUCUS SEVEN .... JOHN SAYLES
RETURN OF THE SEVEN .... CLAUDE AKINS†
RETURN OF THE SIX MILLION
 DOLLAR MAN AND THE
 BIONIC WOMAN (TF) .... LEE MAJORS
RETURN OF THE SIX MILLION
 DOLLAR MAN AND THE
 BIONIC WOMAN (TF) .... LEE MAJORS II
RETURN OF THE SIX MILLION
 DOLLAR MAN AND THE
 BIONIC WOMAN (TF) .... LINDSAY WAGNER
RETURN OF THE SIX MILLION
 DOLLAR MAN AND THE
 BIONIC WOMAN (TF) .... RICHARD ANDERSON
RETURN OF THE SOLDIER .... GLENDA JACKSON
RETURN OF THE SOLDIER .... IAN HOLM
RETURN OF THE SOLDIER, THE .... ALAN BATES
RETURN OF THE SOLDIER, THE ...... ANN-MARGRET
RETURN OF THE SOLDIER, THE ..... JEREMY KEMP
RETURN OF THE SOLDIER, THE ..... JULIE CHRISTIE
RETURN OF THE VAMPIRE, THE .... NINA FOCH
RETURN TO GREEN ACRES (TF) ..... EDDIE ALBERT
RETURN TO GREEN ACRES (TF) .... EVA GABOR
RETURN TO HORROR HIGH .... VINCE EDWARDS
RETURN TO MACON COUNTY .... DON JOHNSON
RETURN TO MACON COUNTY .... NICK NOLTE
RETURN TO MAYBERRY (TF) .... ANDY GRIFFITH
RETURN TO MAYBERRY (TF) .... DON KNOTTS
RETURN TO MAYBERRY (TF) .... JIM NABORS
RETURN TO MAYBERRY (TF) .... RON HOWARD
RETURN TO OZ .... FAIRUZA BALK
RETURN TO OZ .... JEAN MARSH
RETURN TO OZ .... MATT CLARK
RETURN TO OZ .... NICOL WILLIAMSON
RETURN TO OZ .... PIPER LAURIE
RETURN TO PEYTON PLACE .... CAROL LYNLEY
RETURN TO PEYTON PLACE ...... ELEANOR PARKER
RETURN TO PEYTON PLACE ...... MAX SHOWALTER
RETURN TO PEYTON PLACE .... TUESDAY WELD
RETURN TO SNOWY RIVER .... BRYAN MARSHALL
RETURN TO SNOWY RIVER .... TOM BURLINSON
RETURN TO THE BLUE LAGOON ..... BRIAN KRAUSE
RETURN TO THE BLUE LAGOON .... LISA PELIKAN
RETURN TO THE BLUE LAGOON ..... MILLA JOVOVICH
RETURN TO TREASURE ISLAND .... TAB HUNTER
RETURNING, THE .... SUSAN STRASBERG
RETURNING HOME (TF) .... DABNEY COLEMAN
RETURNING HOME (TF) .... LENKA PETERSON
RETURNING HOME (TF) .... TOM SELLECK
REUBEN, REUBEN .... KELLY McGILLIS
REUBEN, REUBEN ★ .... TOM CONTI
REUNION AT
 FAIRBOROUGH (CTF) .... DEBORAH KERR
REUNION AT
 FAIRBOROUGH (CTF) .... RED BUTTONS
REUNION AT
 FAIRBOROUGH (CTF) .... ROBERT MITCHUM
REUNION IN FRANCE .... AVA GARDNER†
REUNION IN FRANCE .... JOAN CRAWFORD†
REVE DE SINGE .... GERARD DEPARDIEU
REVEALING EVIDENCE (TF) .... FINN CARTER
REVEALING EVIDENCE (TF) .... PERRY LANG
REVEILLE WITH BEVERLY .... FRANK SINATRA
REVENGE .... ANTHONY QUINN
REVENGE .... JAMES GAMMON
REVENGE .... KEVIN COSTNER
REVENGE .... MADELEINE STOWE
REVENGE .... SALLY KIRKLAND
REVENGE .... SOPHIA LOREN
REVENGE! (TF) .... SHELLEY WINTERS
REVENGE IN EL PASO .... KEVIN McCARTHY
REVENGE OF
 AL CAPONE, THE (TF) .... CHARLES HAID
REVENGE OF
 AL CAPONE, THE (TF) .... KEITH CARRADINE
REVENGE OF THE
 CREATURE .... CLINT EASTWOOD
REVENGE OF THE NERDS ...... ANTHONY EDWARDS
REVENGE OF THE NERDS .... BRIAN TOCHI
REVENGE OF THE NERDS ..... CURTIS ARMSTRONG
REVENGE OF THE NERDS .... JOHN GOODMAN

REVENGE OF THE NERDS ..... ROBERT CARRADINE
REVENGE OF THE NERDS .... TIMOTHY BUSFIELD
REVENGE OF THE NERDS II:
 NERDS IN PARADISE .... ANTHONY EDWARDS
REVENGE OF THE NERDS II:
 NERDS IN PARADISE .... CURTIS ARMSTRONG
REVENGE OF THE NERDS II:
 NERDS IN PARADISE .... ROBERT CARRADINE
REVENGE OF THE NERS II:
 NERDS IN PARADISE .... TIMOTHY BUSFIELD
REVENGE OF THE
 PINK PANTHER .... DYAN CANNON
REVENGE OF THE
 PINK PANTHER .... PETER SELLERS†
REVENGE OF THE
 PINK PANTHER .... ROBERT LOGGIA
REVENGE OF THE
 PINK PANTHER .... ROBERT WEBBER
REVENGE OF THE
 PINK PANTHER .... TONY BECKLEY†
REVENGERS, THE .... ERNEST BORGNINE
REVENGERS, THE .... WOODY STRODE
REVERSAL OF FORTUNE ...... ANNABELLA SCIORRA
REVERSAL OF FORTUNE ...... CHRISTINE BARANSKI
REVERSAL OF FORTUNE .... FISHER STEVENS
REVERSAL OF FORTUNE .... GLENN CLOSE
REVERSAL OF FORTUNE .... RON SILVER
REVERSAL OF FORTUNE ★★ .... JEREMY IRONS
REVOLT IN THE BIG HOUSE .... ROBERT BLAKE
REVOLT IN THE BIG HOUSE .... TIMOTHY CAREY
REVOLUTION ....AL PACINO
REVOLUTION .... DONALD SUTHERLAND
REVOLUTION .... NASTASSJA KINSKI
REVOLUTIONAR, THEY .... JON VOIGHT
REVOLUTIONARY, THE .... ROBERT DUVALL
REVOLUTIONARY, THE .... SEYMOUR CASSEL
REWARD, THE .... EFREM ZIMBALIST JR.
REWARD, THE .... HENRY SILVA
RHAPSODY .... ELIZABETH TAYLOR
RHAPSODY .... STUART WHITMAN
RHAPSODY IN AUGUST .... IGAWA HISASHI
RHAPSODY IN AUGUST .... RICHARD GERE
RHAPSODY IN BLUE .... ALEXIS SMITH†
RHINEHART
 THEORY, THE .... CHRISTOPHER REEVE
RHINEHART THEORY, THE .... JOE MANTEGNA
RHINEHART THEORY, THE .... KIM CATTRALL
RHINEHART THEORY, THE .... RON CANADA
RHINEMANN
 EXCHANGE, THE (MS) .... JEREMY KEMP
RHINESTONE .... DOLLY PARTON
RHINESTONE ....RICHARD FARNSWORTH
RHINESTONE .... RON LEIBMAN
RHINESTONE .... SYLVESTER STALLONE
RHINO! .... HARRY GUARDINO
RHINO! .... ROBERT CULP
RHINOCEROS .... GENE WILDER
RHINOCEROS .... KAREN BLACK
RHODES .... PEGGY ASHCROFT†
RHOES OF AFRICA .... PEGGY ASHCROFT†
RHUBARB .... LEONARD NIMOY
RHYTHM ON THE RANGE .... MARTHA RAYE†
RHYTHM PARADE .... YVONNE DE CARLO
RHYTHM ROMANCE .... BOB HOPE
RICH AND FAMOUS .... CANDICE BERGEN
RICH AND FAMOUS .... HART BOCHNER
RICH AND FAMOUS .... JACQUELINE BISSET
RICH AND FAMOUS .... MEG RYAN
RICH ARE ALWAYS
 WITH US, THE .... BETTE DAVIS†
RICH GIRL.............................. DON MICHAEL PAUL
RICH GIRL................................... JILL SCHOELEN
RICH GIRL..................................... PAUL GLEASON
RICH GIRL............................... RON KARABATSOS
RICH GIRL..................................... SEAN KANAN
RICH GIRL....................................... WILLIE DIXON
RICH IN LOVE .... ALBERT FINNEY
RICH IN LOVE .... ALFRE WOODARD
RICH IN LOVE .... ETHAN HAWKE
RICH IN LOVE .... JILL CLAYBURGH
RICH IN LOVE .... KATHRYN ERBE

† after an actor's name denotes deceased.

RICH IN LOVE .... KYLE MacLACHLAN
RICH IN LOVE .... PIPER LAURIE
RICH IN LOVE .... SUZY AMIS
RICH KIDS .... IRENE WORTH
RICH KIDS .... JILL EIKENBERRY
RICH KIDS .... JOHN LITHGOW
RICH KIDS .... PAUL DOOLEY
RICH KIDS .... SARAH JESSICA PARKER
RICH KIDS† .... TRINI ALVARADO
RICH MAN, POOR GIRL .... LANA TURNER
RICH MAN, POOR MAN (MS) ...... DICK SARGENT
RICH MAN, POOR MAN (MS) .... ED ASNER
RICH MAN, POOR MAN (MS) ...... GEORGE GAYNES
RICH MAN, POOR MAN (MS) .... JOHN GAVIN
RICH MAN, POOR MAN (MS) .... JULIUS HARRIS
RICH MAN, POOR MAN (MS) .... KAY LENZ
RICH MAN, POOR MAN (MS) .... KIM DARBY
RICH MAN, POOR MAN (MS) .... NICK NOLTE
RICH MAN, POOR MAN (MS) .... PETER STRAUSS
RICH MAN, POOR MAN (MS) .... SUSAN BLAKELY
RICH MAN, POOR MAN (MS) .... VAN JOHNSON
RICH MEN,
    SINGLE WOMEN (TF) .... DEBORAH ADAIR
RICH MEN,
    SINGLE WOMEN (TF) .... HEATHER LOCKLEAR
RICH MEN, SINGLE WOMEN (TF) ..... LARRY WILCOX
RICH MEN,
    SINGLE WOMEN (TF) .... SUZANNE SOMERS
RICHARD III .... CLAIRE BLOOM
RICHARD III .... JOHN GIELGUD
RICHARD III .... MICHAEL GOUGH
RICHARD III ★ .... LAURENCE OLIVIER†
RICHARD PRYOR HERE
    AND NOW (FD) .... RICHARD PRYOR
RICHARD PRYOR IS BACK
    LIVE IN CONCERT (FD) .... RICHARD PRYOR
RICHARD PRYOR LIVE
    IN CONCERT (FD) .... RICHARD PRYOR
RICHARD PRYOR LIVE ON
    THE SUNSET STRIP (FD) .... RICHARD PRYOR
RICHARD'S THINGS (TF) .... LIV ULLMANN
RICHEST MAN IN THE WORLD:
    THE ARISTOTLE ONASSIS
    STORY (MS) .... ANTHONY QUINN
RICHEST MAN IN THE WORLD:
    THE ARISTOTLE ONASSIS
    STORY (MS) .... ANTHONY ZERBE
RICHEST MAN IN THE WORLD:
    THE ARISTOTLE ONASSIS
    STORY (MS) .... JANE SEYMOUR
RICHEST MAN IN THE WORLD:
    THE ARISTOTLE ONASSIS
    STORY (MS) .... RAUL JULIA†
RICHEST MAN IN THE WORLD:
    THE ARISTOTLE ONASSIS
    STORY, THE (TF) .... DIMITRA ARLYS
RICHIE RICH .... CHELCIE ROSS
RICHIE RICH .... CHRISTINE EBERSOLE
RICHIE RICH .... EDWRAD HERRMANN
RICHIE RICH .... JOHN LARROQUETTE
RICHIE RICH .... JONATHAN HYDE
RICHIE RICH .... MACAULAY CULKIN
RICHIE RICH .... MARIANGELA PINO
RICHIE RICH .... MICHAEL McSHANE
RICOCHET .... DENZEL WASHINGTON
RICOCHET .... ICE-T
RICOCHET .... JOHN LITHGOW
RICOCHET .... JOSH EVANS
RICOCHET .... KEVIN POLLAK
RICOCHET .... LINDSAY WAGNER
RIDDLE OF THE SANDS, THE .... JENNY AGUTTER
RIDDLE OF THE SANDS, THE .... MICHAEL YORK
RIDDLE OF THE
    SANDS, THE .... SIMON MacCORKINDALE
RIDDLE OF THE SANDS, THE .... SUSANNAH YORK
RIDE A CROOKED TRAIL .... WALTER MATTHAU
RIDE BACK, THE .... ANTHONY QUINN
RIDE BEYOND VENGEANCE .... BILL BIXBY†
RIDE BEYOND VENGEANCE ...... CHUCK CONNORS†
RIDE BEYOND VENGEANCE .... CLAUDE AKINS†
RIDE BEYOND VENGEANCE .... JAMIE FARR
RIDE IN THE WHIRLWIND .... JACK NICHOLSON

RIDE LONESOME .... JAMES COBURN
RIDE OUT FOR REVENGE .... LLOYD BRIDGES
RIDE THE HIGH COUNTRY .... JOHN ANDERSON
RIDE THE HIGH COUNTRY .... MARIETTE HARTLEY
RIDE THE HIGH COUNTRY .... R.G. ARMSTRONG
RIDE THE HIGH IRON .... RAYMOND BURR†
RIDE THE HIGH WIND .... DARREN McGAVIN
RIDE THE PINK HORSE ❍ .... THOMAS GOMEZ†
RIDE THE WILD SURF .... BARBARA EDEN
RIDE THE WILD SURF .... TAB HUNTER
RIDE TO HANGMAN'S
    TREE, THE .... RICHARD ANDERSON
RIDE VAQUERO .... ANTHONY QUINN
RIDE VAQUERO! .... AVA GARDNER†
RIDE VAQUERO! .... HOWARD KEEL
RIDER IN THE DARK .... JENNIFER BEALS
RIDER IN THE DARK .... MICHAEL J. POLLARD
RIDER ON THE RAIN .... CHARLES BRONSON
RIDERS OF THE DEADLINE .... ROBERT MITCHUM
RIDERS OF THE STORM .... DENNIS HOPPER
RIDERS OF THE STORM .... MICHAEL J. POLLARD
RIDING HIGH .... DOROTHY LAMOUR
RIDING SHOTGUN .... CHARLES BRONSON
RIEL .... CHRISTOPHER PLUMMER
RIEL .... LESLIE NIELSEN
RIEL .... WILLIAM SHATNER
RIGHT CROSS .... JUNE ALLYSON
RIGHT CROSS .... MARILYN MONROE†
RIGHT CROSS .... RICARDO MONTALBAN
RIGHT HAND MAN, THE .... RUPERT EVERETT
RIGHT OF THE
    PEOPLE, THE (TF) .... JANE KACZMAREK
RIGHT OF WAY (CTF) .... JAMES STEWART
RIGHT STUFF, THE .... BARBARA HERSHEY
RIGHT STUFF, THE .... DENNIS QUAID
RIGHT STUFF, THE .... DONALD MOFFAT
RIGHT STUFF, THE .... ED HARRIS
RIGHT STUFF, THE .... FRED WARD
RIGHT STUFF, THE .... JEFF GOLDBLUM
RIGHT STUFF, THE .... JOHN DEHNER†
RIGHT STUFF, THE .... KATHY BAKER
RIGHT STUFF, THE .... KIM STANLEY
RIGHT STUFF, THE .... LEVON HELM
RIGHT STUFF, THE .... MARY JO DESCHANEL
RIGHT STUFF, THE .... ROYAL DANO
RIGHT STUFF, THE .... SCOTT GLENN
RIGHT STUFF, THE .... SCOTT WILSON
RIGHT STUFF, THE ❍ .... SAM SHEPARD
RIGHT TO DIE (TF) .... BONNIE BARTLETT
RIGHT TO DIE (TF) .... JOANNA MILES
RIGHT TO DIE (TF) .... MICHAEL GROSS
RIGHT TO DIE (TF) .... PETER MICHAEL GOETZ
RIGHT TO DIE (TF) .... RAQUEL WELCH
RIGHT TO KILL? (TF) .... ANN WEDGEWORTH
RIGHT TO KILL? (TF) .... CHRISTOPHER COLLET
RIGHT TO KILL? (TF) .... FREDERIC FORREST
RIGHT TO KILL? (TF) .... JUSTINE BATEMAN
RIGHT TO LOVE, THE .... OMAR SHARIF
RING, THE .... RITA MORENO
RING OF FEAR .... SEAN McCLORY
RING OF PASSION (TF) .... BRITT EKLAND
RING OF PASSION (TF) .... JULIUS HARRIS
RING OF PASSION (TF) .... STEPHEN MACHT
RING OF SPIES .... THORLEY WALTERS†
RINGER, THE .... MAE ZETTERLING†
RINGS AROUND THE WORLD (FD) ... DON AMECHE†
RIO BRAVO .... ANGIE DICKINSON
RIO BRAVO .... CLAUDE AKINS†
RIO BRAVO .... DEAN MARTIN
RIO BRAVO .... HARRY CAREY JR.
RIO BRAVO .... JOHN WAYNE†
RIO CONCHOS .... ANTHONY (TONY) FRANCIOSA
RIO CONCHOS .... JIM BROWN
RIO CONCHOS .... STUART WHITMAN
RIO GRANDE .... BEN JOHNSON
RIO GRANDE .... HARRY CAREY JR.
RIO GRANDE .... MAUREEN O'HARA
RIO LOBO .... DAVID HUDDLESTON
RIO LOBO .... JENNIFER O'NEILL
RIO LOBO .... JOHN WAYNE†
RIO LOBO .... MIKE HENRY
RIO LOBO .... PETER JASON

RIOT .... GENE HACKMAN
RIOT .... JIM BROWN
RIP-OFF, THE .... EDWARD ALBERT
RIP-OFF, THE .... KAREN BLACK
RIPPED OFF .... ERNEST BORGNINE
RIPPED OFF .... ROBERT BLAKE
RIPTIDE (TF) .... PERRY KING
RISATE DI GIOIA .... BEN GAZZARA
RISE .... DUANE JONES†
RISE AND FALL OF
    LEGS DIAMOND, THE .... DYAN CANNON
RISE AND RISE OF MICHAEL
    RIMMER, THE .... DENHOLM ELLIOTT†
RISE AND RISE OF MICHAEL
    RIMMER, THE .... JOHN CLEESE
RISE AND RISE OF MICHAEL
    RIMMER, THE .... PETER COOK
RISE AND SHINE .... MILTON BERLE
RISE AND WALK: THE DENNIS
    BYRD STORY (TF) .... RYAN SLATER
RISING SON (CTF) .... BRIAN DENNEHY
RISING SON (CTF) .... EMILY LONGSTRETH
RISING SON (CTF) .... MATT DAMON
RISING SON (CTF) .... PIPER LAURIE
RISING SUN .... CARY-HIROYUKI TAGAWA
RISING SUN .... HARVEY KEITEL
RISING SUN .... KEVIN ANDERSON
RISING SUN .... MAKO
RISING SUN .... SEAN CONNERY
RISING SUN .... TIA CARRERE
RISING SUN .... WESLEY SNIPES
RISK, THE .... DONALD PLEASENCE
RISK, THE .... IAN BANNEN
RISKY BUSINESS .... BRONSON PINCHOT
RISKY BUSINESS .... CURTIS ARMSTRONG
RISKY BUSINESS .... JOE PANTOLIANO
RISKY BUSINESS .... REBECCA DE MORNAY
RISKY BUSINESS .... RICHARD MASUR
RISKY BUSINESS .... TOM CRUISE
RITA HAYWORTH: THE LOVE
    GODDESS (TF) .... MICHAEL LERNER
RITES OF SUMMER .... KEVIN BACON
RITUALS .... HAL HOLBROOK
RITZ, THE .... F. MURRAY ABRAHAM
RITZ, THE .... JACK WESTON
RITZ, THE .... KAYE BALLARD
RITZ, THE .... RITA MORENO
RITZ, THE .... TREAT WILLIAMS
RIVALRY, THE (TF) .... CHARLES DURNING
RIVALS .... SCOTT JACOBY
RIVALS, THE .... JOAN HACKETT†
RIVE DROITE,
    RIVE GAUCHE .... GERARD DEPARDIEU
RIVER, THE .... MEL GIBSON
RIVER, THE .... SCOTT GLENN
RIVER, THE ★ .... SISSY SPACEK
RIVER LADY .... YVONNE DE CARLO
RIVER NIGER, THE .... JAMES EARL JONES
RIVER NIGER, THE .... LOUIS GOSSETT JR.
RIVER OF DEATH .... DONALD PLEASENCE
RIVER OF DEATH .... L. Q. JONES
RIVER OF DEATH .... MICHAEL DUDIKOFF
RIVER OF DEATH .... ROBERT VAUGHN
RIVER OF NO RETURN .... MARILYN MONROE†
RIVER OF NO RETURN .... ROBERT MITCHUM
RIVER OF NO RETURN .... RORY CALHOUN
RIVER RAT, THE .... BRIAN DENNEHY
RIVER RAT, THE .... MARTHA PLIMPTON
RIVER RAT, THE .... TOMMY LEE JONES
RIVER RUNS THROUGH IT, A .... BRAD PITT
RIVER RUNS THROUGH IT, A ..... BRENDA BLETHYN
RIVER RUNS THROUGH IT, A .... CRAIG SHEFFER
RIVER RUNS THROUGH IT, A .... EDIE McCLURG
RIVER RUNS THROUGH IT, A .... EMILY LLOYD
RIVER RUNS THROUGH IT, A ... ROBERT REDFORD
RIVER RUNS THROUGH IT, A .... TOM SKERRITT
RIVER WILD, THE .... DAVID STRATHAIRN
RIVER WILD, THE .... JOHN C. REILLY
RIVER WILD, THE .... JOSEPH MAZZELLO
RIVER WILD, THE .... KEVIN BACON
RIVER WILD, THE .... MERYL STREEP
RIVER WOLVES .... JOHN MILLS

RIVER'S EDGE	CRISPIN GLOVER
RIVER'S EDGE	DANIEL ROEBUCK
RIVER'S EDGE	DENNIS HOPPER
RIVER'S EDGE	IONE SKYE
RIVER'S EDGE	KEANU REEVES
RIVER'S EDGE	LEO ROSSI
RIVER'S EDGE	ROXANA ZAL
RIVER'S EDGE	TAYLOR NEGRON
RIVER'S EDGE, THE	ANTHONY QUINN
RIVER'S EDGE, THE	HARRY CAREY JR.
RIVIERA (TF)	BEN MASTERS
RIVKIN: BOUNTY HUNTER (TF)	RON LEIBMAN
ROAD BUILDER, THE	PATRICIA NEAL
ROAD GAMES	JAMIE LEE CURTIS
ROAD GAMES	STACY KEACH
ROAD HOUSE	BEN GAZZARA
ROAD HOUSE	CELESTE HOLM
ROAD HOUSE	KELLY LYNCH
ROAD HOUSE	MARSHALL TEAGUE
ROAD HOUSE	PATRICK SWAYZE
ROAD HOUSE	RICHARD WIDMARK
ROAD MOVIE	SAM ELLIOTT
ROAD MOVIE	JOE PANTOLIANO
ROAD RAIDERS, THE (TF)	BRUCE BOXLEITNER
ROAD TO BALI	BOB HOPE
ROAD TO BALI	DOROTHY LAMOUR
ROAD TO HONG KONG, THE	BOB HOPE
ROAD TO HONG KONG, THE	DOROTHY LAMOUR
ROAD TO HONG KONG, THE	FRANK SINATRA
ROAD TO HONG KONG, THE	JOAN COLLINS
ROAD TO HONG KONG, THE	ROBERT MORLEY
ROAD TO MOROCCO	ANTHONY QUINN
ROAD TO MOROCCO	BOB HOPE
ROAD TO MOROCCO	DOROTHY LAMOUR
ROAD TO MOROCCO	YVONNE DE CARLO
ROAD TO RIO	BOB HOPE
ROAD TO RIO	DOROTHY LAMOUR
ROAD TO SALINA	ROBERT WALKER JR.
ROAD TO SINGAPORE	ANTHONY QUINN
ROAD TO SINGAPORE	BOB HOPE
ROAD TO SINGAPORE	DOROTHY LAMOUR
ROAD TO UTOPIA	BING CROSBY†
ROAD TO UTOPIA	BOB HOPE
ROAD TO UTOPIA	DOROTHY LAMOUR
ROAD TO WELLVILLE, THE	ANTHONY HOPKINS
ROAD TO WELLVILLE, THE	BRIDGET FONDA
ROAD TO WELLVILLE, THE	DANA CARVEY
ROAD TO WELLVILLE, THE	JOHN CUSACK
ROAD TO WELLVILLE, THE	JOHN NEVILLE
ROAD TO WELLVILLE, THE	LARA FLYNN BOYLE
ROAD TO WELLVILLE, THE	MATHHEW BRODERICK
ROAD TO WELLVILLE, THE	ROY BROCKSMITH
ROAD TO ZANZIBAR	BOB HOPE
ROAD TO ZANZIBAR	DOROTHY LAMOUR
ROAD WARRIOR, THE	MEL GIBSON
ROADFLOWER	CHRISTOPHER LAMBERT
ROADHOUSE 66	JUDGE REINHOLD
ROADHOUSE 66	STEPHEN ELLIOTT
ROADHOUSE 66	WILLEM DAFOE
ROADIE	ART CARNEY
ROADSIDE PROPHETS	ADAM HOROVITZ
ROADSIDE PROPHETS	ARLO GUTHRIE
ROADSIDE PROPHETS	DAVID CARRADINE
ROADSIDE PROPHETS	JOHN CUSACK
ROADSIDE PROPHETS	JOHN DOE
ROADSIDE PROPHETS	TIMOTHY LEARY
ROAMING LADY	RALPH BELLAMY†
ROAR	MELANIE GRIFFITH
ROAR	TIPPI HEDREN
ROAR OF THE CROWD	HOWARD DUFF†
ROB ROY	BRIAN COX
ROB ROY	ERIC STOLTZ
ROB ROY	JESSICA LANGE
ROB ROY	JOHN HURT
ROB ROY	LIAM NEESON
ROB ROY	MICHAEL GOUGH
ROB ROY	TIM ROTH
ROBBERS' ROOST	MAUREEN O'SULLIVAN
ROBBERY UNDER ARMS	DAVID McCALLUM
ROBBERY UNDER ARMS	JILL IRELAND†
ROBE, THE	ANNE BANCROFT

ROBE, THE	DEAN JAGGER†
ROBE, THE	JEAN SIMMONS
ROBE, THE ★	RICHARD BURTON†
ROBERT KENNEDY AND HIS TIMES (MS)	BEATRICE STRAIGHT
ROBERT KENNEDY AND HIS TIMES (MS)	BRAD DAVIS†
ROBERT KENNEDY AND HIS TIMES (MS)	CLIFF DE YOUNG
ROBERT KENNEDY AND HIS TIMES (MS)	G. D. SPRADLIN
ROBERT KENNEDY AND HIS TIMES (MS)	JAMES READ
ROBERT KENNEDY AND HIS TIMES (MS)	JOE PANTOLIANO
ROBERT KENNEDY AND HIS TIMES (MS)	NED BEATTY
ROBERT KENNEDY AND HIS TIMES (MS)	VERONICA CARTWRIGHT
ROBERTA	LUCILLE BALL†
ROBIN AND MARIAN	AUDREY HEPBURN†
ROBIN AND MARIAN	DENHOLM ELLIOTT†
ROBIN AND MARIAN	IAN HOLM
ROBIN AND MARIAN	KENNETH HAIGH
ROBIN AND MARIAN	NICOL WILLIAMSON
ROBIN AND MARIAN	RICHARD HARRIS
ROBIN AND MARIAN	ROBERT SHAW†
ROBIN AND MARIAN	SEAN CONNERY
ROBIN AND THE SEVEN HOODS	ALLEN JENKINS†
ROBIN AND THE SEVEN HOODS	BING CROSBY†
ROBIN AND THE SEVEN HOODS	DEAN MARTIN
ROBIN AND THE SEVEN HOODS	EDWARD G. ROBINSON†
ROBIN AND THE SEVEN HOODS	FRANK SINATRA
ROBIN AND THE SEVEN HOODS	HANS CONRIED†
ROBIN AND THE SEVEN HOODS	JACK LARUE†
ROBIN AND THE SEVEN HOODS	PETER FALK
ROBIN AND THE SEVEN HOODS	SAMMY DAVIS JR.†
ROBIN AND THE SEVEN HOODS	SIG RUMAN†
ROBIN AND THE SEVEN HOODS	TONY RANDALL
ROBIN AND THE SEVEN HOODS	VICTOR BUONO†
ROBIN HOOD	DOUGLAS FAIRBANKS SR.†
ROBIN HOOD	WALLACE BEERY†
ROBIN HOOD (AF)	PETER USTINOV
ROBIN HOOD: MEN IN TIGHTS	ANY YASBECK
ROBIN HOOD: MEN IN TIGHTS	CARY ELWES
ROBIN HOOD: MEN IN TIGHTS	DAVE CHAPPELLE
ROBIN HOOD: MEN IN TIGHTS	DOM DeLUISE
ROBIN HOOD: MEN IN TIGHTS	ISAAC HAYES
ROBIN HOOD: MEN IN TIGHTS	MEL BROOKS
ROBIN HOOD: MEN IN TIGHTS	PATRICK STEWART
ROBIN HOOD: MEN IN TIGHTS	RICHARD LEWIS
ROBIN HOOD: MEN IN TIGHTS	ROGER REES
ROBIN HOOD: MEN IN TIGHTS	TRACEY ULLMAN
ROBIN HOOD: PRINCE OF THIEVES	ALAN RICKMAN
ROBIN HOOD: PRINCE OF THIEVES	BRIAN BLESSED
ROBIN HOOD: PRINCE OF THIEVES	CHRISTIAN SLATER
ROBIN HOOD: PRINCE OF THIEVES	DANIEL NEWMAN
ROBIN HOOD: PRINCE OF THIEVES	DANIEL PEACOCK
ROBIN HOOD: PRINCE OF THIEVES	GERALDINE McEWAN
ROBIN HOOD: PRINCE OF THIEVES	KEVIN COSTNER
ROBIN HOOD: PRINCE OF THIEVES	MARY ELIZABETH MASTRANTONIO
ROBIN HOOD: PRINCE OF THIEVES	MICHAEL WINCOTT
ROBIN HOOD: PRINCE OF THIEVES	MORGAN FREEMAN
ROBIN HOOD: PRINCE OF THIEVES	NICK BRIMBLE
ROBIN HOOD: PRINCE OF THIEVES	SEAN CONNERY
ROBIN HOOD: PRINCE OF THIEVES	SOO DROUET

ROBIN HOOD: PRINCE OF THIEVES	WALTER SPARROW
ROBINSON CRUSOE	PIERCE BROSNAN
ROBINSON CRUSOE	PIERCE BROSNAN
ROBINSON CRUSOE	WILLIAM TAKAKU
ROBINSON CRUSOE ON MARS	ADAM WEST
ROBINSON CRUSOE ON MARS	PAUL MANTEE
ROBOCOP	DAN O'HERLIHY
ROBOCOP	DEL ZAMORA
ROBOCOP	FELTON PERRY
ROBOCOP	KURTWOOD SMITH
ROBOCOP	MIGUEL FERRER
ROBOCOP	NANCY ALLEN
ROBOCOP	PAUL McCRANE
ROBOCOP	PETER WELLER
ROBOCOP	RAY WISE
ROBOCOP	ROBERT DOQUI
ROBOCOP	RONNY COX
ROBOCOP 2	BELINDA BAUER
ROBOCOP 2	DAN O'HERLIHY
ROBOCOP 2	GABRIEL DAMON
ROBOCOP 2	NANCY ALLEN
ROBOCOP 2	PETER WELLER
ROBOCOP 2	TOM NOONAN
ROBOCOP 3	BRUCE LOCKE
ROBOCOP 3	FELTON PERRY
ROBOCOP 3	JOHN CASTLE
ROBOCOP 3	NANCY ALLEN
ROBOCOP 3	ROBERT BURKE
ROBOCOP 3	ROBERT DOQUI
ROBOCOP 3	STANLEY ANDERSON
ROBOTJOX	ANNE MARIE JOHNSON
ROBOTJOX	DANNY KAMEKONA
ROBOTJOX	GARY GRAHAM
ROBOTJOX	HILARY MASON
ROBOTJOX	MICHAEL ALLDREDGE
ROBOTJOX	PAUL KOSLO
ROBOTJOX	ROBERT SAMPSON
ROCK HUDSON (TF)	DAPHNE ASHBROOK
ROCK HUDSON (TF)	THOMAS IAN GRIFFITH
ROCK HUDSON (TF)	WILLIAM R. MOSES
ROCK ROCK ROCK	TUESDAY WELD
ROCK-A-BYE BABY	CONNIE STEVENS
ROCK-A-BYE BABY	JERRY LEWIS
ROCK-A-DOODLE (AF)	CHARLES NELSON REILLY
ROCK-A-DOODLE (AF)	CHRISTOPHER PLUMMER
ROCK-A-DOODLE (AF)	EDDIE DEEZEN
ROCK-A-DOODLE (AF)	ELLEN GREENE
ROCK-A-DOODLE (AF)	GLEN CAMPBELL
ROCK-A-DOODLE (AF)	PHIL HARRIS
ROCK-A-DOODLE (AF)	SANDY DUNCAN
ROCKABYE (TF)	JASON ALEXANDER
ROCKABYE (TF)	RACHEL TICOTIN
ROCKABYE (TF)	VALERIE BERTINELLI
ROCKET GIBRALTAR	ANGELA GOETHALS
ROCKET GIBRALTAR	BILL PULLMAN
ROCKET GIBRALTAR	BURT LANCASTER†
ROCKET GIBRALTAR	DAN CORKILL
ROCKET GIBRALTAR	EMILY POE
ROCKET GIBRALTAR	FRANCES CONROY
ROCKET GIBRALTAR	JOHN BELL
ROCKET GIBRALTAR	JOHN GLOVER
ROCKET GIBRALTAR	KEVIN SPACEY
ROCKET GIBRALTAR	MACAULAY CULKIN
ROCKET GIBRALTAR	NICKY BRONSON
ROCKET GIBRALTAR	PATRICIA CLARKSON
ROCKET GIBRALTAR	SARA GOETHALS
ROCKET GIBRALTAR	SARA RUE
ROCKET GIBRALTAR	SINEAD CUSACK
ROCKET GIBRALTAR	SUZY AMIS
ROCKETEER, THE	ALAN ARKIN
ROCKETEER, THE	BILL CAMPBELL
ROCKETEER, THE	JAMES HANDY
ROCKETEER, THE	JENNIFER CONNELLY
ROCKETEER, THE	PAUL SORVINO
ROCKETEER, THE	ROBERT G. MIRANDA
ROCKETEER, THE	TERRY O'QUINN
ROCKETEER, THE	TIMOTHY DALTON
ROCKETEER, THE	WILLIAM SANDERSON
ROCKETS GALORE	GORDAN JACKSON†
ROCKETSHIP X-M	LLOYD BRIDGES
ROCKFORD FILES, THE (TF)	JAMES GARNER

ROCKFORD FILES, THE (TF) ... LINDSAY WAGNER
ROCKING HORSE WINNER, THE ... JOHN MILLS
ROCKY ... CARL WEATHERS
ROCKY ... RODDY McDOWALL
ROCKY ... STAN SHAW
ROCKY ... THAYER DAVID†
ROCKY ★ ... SYLVESTER STALLONE
ROCKY ★ ... TALIA SHIRE
ROCKY ○ ... BURGESS MEREDITH
ROCKY ○ ... BURT YOUNG
ROCKY II ... BURGESS MEREDITH
ROCKY II ... BURT YOUNG
ROCKY II ... CARL WEATHERS
ROCKY II ... SYLVESTER STALLONE
ROCKY II ... TALIA SHIRE
ROCKY III ... BURGESS MEREDITH
ROCKY III ... BURT YOUNG
ROCKY III ... CARL WEATHERS
ROCKY III ... MR. T
ROCKY III ... SYLVESTER STALLONE
ROCKY III ... TALIA SHIRE
ROCKY IV ... BRIGITTE NIELSEN
ROCKY IV ... BURT YOUNG
ROCKY IV ... CARL WEATHERS
ROCKY IV ... DOLPH LUNDGREN
ROCKY IV ... MICHAEL PATAKI
ROCKY IV ... SYLVESTER STALLONE
ROCKY IV ... TALIA SHIRE
ROCKY V ... BURGESS MEREDITH
ROCKY V ... BURT YOUNG
ROCKY V ... SAGE STALLONE
ROCKY V ... SYLVESTER STALLONE
ROCKY V ... TALIA SHIRE
ROCKY V ... TOMMY MORRISON
ROCKY HORROR PICTURE SHOW, THE ... BARRY BOSTWICK
ROCKY HORROR PICTURE SHOW, THE ... MEAT LOAF
ROCKY HORROR PICTURE SHOW, THE ... SUSAN SARANDON
ROCKY HORROR PICTURE SHOW, THE ... TIM CURRY
RODEO GIRL (TF) ... WILFORD BRIMLEY
ROE VS. WADE (TF) ... AMY MADIGAN
ROE VS. WADE (TF) ... HOLLY HUNTER
ROE VS. WADE (TF) ... KATHY BATES
ROGER CORMAN'S FRANKENSTEIN UNBOUND ... BRIDGET FONDA
ROGER CORMAN'S FRANKENSTEIN UNBOUND ... RAUL JULIA†
ROGER TOUHY—GANGSTER ... ANTHONY QUINN
ROGUE COP ... JANET LEIGH
ROGUE COP ... STEVE FORREST
ROGUE COP ... VINCE EDWARDS
ROGUE MALE (TF) ... PETER O'TOOLE
ROGUE RIVER ... PETER GRAVES
ROGUE RIVER ... RORY CALHOUN
ROGUE SONG, THE ★ ... LAWRENCE TIBBETT†
ROGUES' REGIMENT ... VINCENT PRICE†
ROLLER BOOGIE ... LINDA BLAIR
ROLLERBALL ... JAMES CAAN
ROLLERBALL ... MAUD ADAMS
ROLLERBALL ... MOSES GUNN
ROLLERCOASTER ... CRAIG WASSON
ROLLERCOASTER ... GEORGE SEGAL
ROLLERCOASTER ... HARRY GUARDINO
ROLLERCOASTER ... HENRY FONDA†
ROLLERCOASTER ... RICHARD WIDMARK
ROLLERCOASTER ... SUSAN STRASBERG
ROLLERCOASTER ... TIMOTHY BOTTOMS
ROLLERCOASTER RABBIT (AS) ... CHARLES FLEISCHER
ROLLERCOASTER RABBIT (AS) ... KATHLEEN TURNER
ROLLING MAN (TF) ... DENNIS WEAVER
ROLLING THUNDER ... TOMMY LEE JONES
ROLLING THUNDER ... WILLIAM DEVANE
ROLLING VENGEANCE ... LAWRENCE DANE
ROLLOVER ... HUME CRONYN
ROLLOVER ... JANE FONDA
ROLLOVER ... KRIS KRISTOFFERSON
ROLLOVER ... PAUL HECHT
ROMAN GREY (TF) ... JOSE FERRER†
ROMAN HOLIDAY ... GREGORY PECK
ROMAN HOLIDAY ★★ ... AUDREY HEPBURN†
ROMAN HOLIDAY ○ ... EDDIE ALBERT
ROMAN HOLIDAY (TF) ... ED BEGLEY JR.
ROMAN HOLIDAY (TF) ... PATRICK ALLEN
ROMAN HOLIDAY (TF) ... TOM CONTI
ROMAN SCANDALS ... LUCILLE BALL†
ROMAN SPRING OF MRS. STONE, THE ... JILL ST. JOHN
ROMAN SPRING OF MRS. STONE, THE ... VIVIEN LEIGH†
ROMAN SPRING OF MRS. STONE, THE ... WARREN BEATTY
ROMAN SPRING OF MRS. STONE, THE ○ ... LOTTE LENYA†
ROMANCE ★ ... GRETA GARBO†
ROMANCE IN THE JUGULAR VEIN ... VINCENT PRICE†
ROMANCE OF A HORSETHIEF ... ELI WALLACH
ROMANCE OF HAPPY VALLEY, A ... LILLIAN GISH†
ROMANCE OF ROSY RIDGE, THE ... DEAN STOCKWELL
ROMANCE OF ROSY RIDGE, THE ... JANET LEIGH
ROMANCE OF ROSY RIDGE, THE ... VAN JOHNSON
ROMANCE ON THE HIGH SEAS ... DORIS DAY
ROMANCE ON THE ORIENT EXPRESS (TF) ... CHERYL LADD
ROMANCE ON THE ORIENT EXPRESS (TF) ... JOHN GIELGUD
ROMANCE ON THE ORIENT EXPRESS (TF) ... RENEE ASHERSON
ROMANCING THE STONE ... DANNY DEVITO
ROMANCING THE STONE ... KATHLEEN TURNER
ROMANCING THE STONE ... MICHAEL DOUGLAS
ROMANOFF AND JULIET ... JOHN GAVIN
ROMANOFF AND JULIET ... PETER USTINOV
ROMANOFF AND JULIET ... SANDRA DEE
ROMANTIC AGE, THE ... MAE ZETTERLING†
ROMANTIC COMEDY ... DUDLEY MOORE
ROMANTIC COMEDY ... FRANCES STERNHAGEN
ROMANTIC COMEDY ... JANET EILBER
ROMANTIC COMEDY ... MARY STEENBURGEN
ROMANTIC COMEDY ... ROBYN DOUGLASS
ROMANTIC COMEDY ... RON LEIBMAN
ROMANTIC ENGLISHWOMAN, THE ... GLENDA JACKSON
ROMANTIC ENGLISHWOMAN, THE ... KATE NELLIGAN
ROMANTIC ENGLISHWOMAN, THE ... MICHAEL CAINE
ROMAULD ET JULIETTE ... DANIEL AUTEUIL
ROME ADVENTURE ... ANGIE DICKINSON
ROME ADVENTURE ... CHAD EVERETT
ROME ADVENTURE ... SUZANNE PLESHETTE
ROME ADVENTURE ... TROY DONAHUE
ROMEO AND JULIET ... JOHN GIELGUD
ROMEO AND JULIET ... JOHN McENERY
ROMEO AND JULIET ... MICHAEL YORK
ROMEO AND JULIET ... MILO O'SHEA
ROMEO AND JULIET ... PAT HEYWOOD
ROMEO AND JULIET ... ROBERT STEPHENS
ROMEO AND JULIET ★ ... NORMA SHEARER†
ROMEO AND JULIET ○ ... BASIL RATHBONE†
ROMEO IS BLEEDING ... ANNABELLA SCIORRA
ROMEO IS BLEEDING ... GARY OLDMAN
ROMEO IS BLEEDING ... JULIETTE LEWIS
ROMEO IS BLEEDING ... LENA OLIN
ROMEO IS BLEEDING ... ROY SCHEIDER
ROMEO IS BLEEDING ... WILL PATTON
ROMEO-JULIET ... MAGGIE SMITH
ROMERO ... ALEJANDRO BRACHO
ROMERO ... ANA ALICIA
ROMERO ... EDDIE VELEZ
ROMERO ... HAROLD GOULD
ROMERO ... LUCY REINA
ROMERO ... RAUL JULIA†
ROMERO ... RICHARD JORDAN†
ROMERO ... TONY PLANA
ROMOLA ... LILLIAN GISH†
ROMPER STOMPER ... RUSSELL CROWE
ROOFTOPS ... EDDIE VELEZ
ROOFTOPS ... JASON GEDRICK
ROOFTOPS ... TROY BEVER
ROOKIE, THE ... CHARLIE SHEEN
ROOKIE, THE ... CLINT EASTWOOD
ROOKIE, THE ... JERRY SCHUMACHER
ROOKIE, THE ... JULIE NEWMAR
ROOKIE, THE ... LARA FLYNN BOYLE
ROOKIE, THE ... MARCO RODRIGUEZ
ROOKIE, THE ... PEPE SERNA
ROOKIE, THE ... PETE RANDALL
ROOKIE, THE ... RAUL JULIA†
ROOKIE, THE ... SONIA BRAGA
ROOKIE, THE ... TOM SKERRITT
ROOKIE OF THE YEAR ... DAN HEDAYA
ROOKIE OF THE YEAR ... DANIEL STERN
ROOKIE OF THE YEAR ... EDDIE BRACKEN
ROOKIE OF THE YEAR ... GARY BUSEY
ROOKIE OF THE YEAR ... THOMAS IAN NICHOLAS
ROOM, THE (TF) ... LINDA HUNT
ROOM AT THE TOP ... JACK HEDLEY
ROOM AT THE TOP ★ ... LAURENCE HARVEY†
ROOM AT THE TOP ★★ ... SIMONE SIGNORET†
ROOM AT THE TOP ○ ... HERMIONE BADDELEY†
ROOM SERVICE ... LUCILLE BALL†
ROOM UPSTAIRS, THE (TF) ... LINDA HUNT
ROOM UPSTAIRS, THE (TF) ... SAM WATERSTON
ROOM UPSTAIRS, THE (TF) ... STOCKARD CHANNING
ROOM WITH A VIEW, A ... DANIEL DAY-LEWIS
ROOM WITH A VIEW, A ... HELENA BONHAM CARTER
ROOM WITH A VIEW, A ... JUDI DENCH
ROOM WITH A VIEW, A ... JULIAN SANDS
ROOM WITH A VIEW, A ... ROSEMARY LEACH
ROOM WITH A VIEW, A ... SIMON CALLOW
ROOM WITH A VIEW, A ○ ... DENHOLM ELLIOTT†
ROOM WITH A VIEW, A ○ ... MAGGIE SMITH
ROOMMATES ... ALLEN GARFIELD
ROOMMATES ... D. B. SWEENEY
ROOMMATES ... ELLEN BURSTYN
ROOMMATES ... ERIC STOLTZ
ROOMMATES ... JULIANNE MOORE
ROOMMATES ... PETER FALK
ROOSTER COGBURN ... ANTHONY ZERBE
ROOSTER COGBURN ... JOHN WAYNE†
ROOSTER COGBURN ... KATHERINE HEPBURN
ROOSTER COGBURN ... RICHARD JORDAN†
ROOSTER (TF) ... PAUL WILLIAMS
ROOSTER, THE ... TOPOL
ROOTS (MS) ... BEN VEREEN
ROOTS (MS) ... CHUCK CONNORS†
ROOTS (MS) ... CICELY TYSON
ROOTS (MS) ... ED ASNER
ROOTS (MS) ... GEORG STANFORD BROWN
ROOTS (MS) ... GEORGE HAMILTON
ROOTS (MS) ... LeVAR BURTON
ROOTS (MS) ... LLOYD BRIDGES
ROOTS (MS) ... LOUIS GOSSETT JR.
ROOTS (MS) ... O. J. SIMPSON
ROOTS (MS) ... OSSIE DAVIS
ROOTS (MS) ... SANDY DUNCAN
ROOTS OF HEAVEN, THE ... EDDIE ALBERT
ROOTS: THE GIFT (TF) ... LeVAR BURTON
ROOTS: THE GIFT (TF) ... LOUIS GOSSETT JR.
ROOTS: THE GIFT (TF) ... SHAUN CASSIDY
ROOTS: THE NEXT GENERATIONS (MS) ... ANDY GRIFFITH
ROOTS: THE NEXT GENERATION (MS) ... DELLA REESE
ROOTS: THE NEXT GENERATION (MS) ... ROGER E. MOSLEY
ROOTS: THE NEXT GENERATIONS (MS) ... GEORG STANFORD BROWN
ROOTS: THE NEXT GENERATIONS (MS) ... JAMES EARL JONES
ROOTS: THE NEXT GENERATIONS (MS) ... LeVAR BURTON
ROOTS: THE NEXT GENERATIONS (MS) ... MARLON BRANDO
ROOTS: THE NEXT GENERATIONS (MS) ... OLIVIA DE HAVILLAND
ROPE ... JAMES STEWART

This is not a list of every film ever made or every cast member, only those listed in this directory.

ROPE OF SAND	BURT LANCASTER†
ROSALIE GOES SHOPPING	ALEX WINTER
ROSALIE GOES SHOPPING	BRAD DAVIS†
ROSALIE GOES SHOPPING	JUDGE REINHOLD
ROSALIE GOES SHOPPING	MARIANNE SAGEBRECHT
ROSE, THE	ALAN BATES
ROSE, THE	BARRY PRIMUS
ROSE, THE	DAVID KEITH
ROSE, THE	HARRY DEAN STANTON
ROSE, THE ★	BETTE MIDLER
ROSE, THE ✪	FREDERIC FORREST
ROSE AND THE JACKAL, THE (CTF)	CHRISTOPHER REEVE
ROSE BERND	MARIA SCHELL
ROSE BOWL STORY, THE	VERA MILES
ROSE MARIE	DAVID NIVEN†
ROSE MARIE	HOWARD KEEL
ROSE MARIE	JAMES STEWART
ROSE TATTOO, THE	BURT LANCASTER†
ROSE TATTOO, THE ★★	ANNA MAGNANI†
ROSE-MARIE	JOAN CRAWFORD†
ROSEBUD	CLIFF GORMAN
ROSEBUD	ISABELLE HUPPERT
ROSEBUD	PETER O'TOOLE
ROSELAND	CHRISTOPHER WALKEN
ROSELAND	CONRAD JANIS
ROSELAND	GERALDINE CHAPLIN
ROSELAND	LILIA SKALA
ROSELAND	LOU JACOBI
ROSELAND	TERESA WRIGHT
ROSEMARY'S BABY ✪✪	RUTH GORDON†
ROSEMARY'S BABY	CHARLES GRODIN
ROSEMARY'S BABY	MIA FARROW
ROSEMARY'S BABY	RALPH BELLAMY†
ROSENCRANTZ & GUILDENSTERN ARE DEAD	DONALD SUMPTER
ROSENCRANTZ & GUILDENSTERN ARE DEAD	GARY OLDMAN
ROSENCRANTZ & GUILDENSTERN ARE DEAD	IAIN GLEN
ROSENCRANTZ & GUILDENSTERN ARE DEAD†	IAN RICHARDSON
ROSENCRANTZ & GUILDENSTERN ARE DEAD	JOANNA MILES
ROSENCRANTZ & GUILDENSTERN ARE DEAD	JOANNA ROTH
ROSENCRANTZ & GUILDENSTERN ARE DEAD	RICHARD DREYFUSS
ROSENCRANTZ & GUILDENSTERN ARE DEAD	TIM ROTH
ROSES ARE FOR THE RICH (MS)	BRUCE DERN
ROSES ARE FOR THE RICH (MS)	JOE PENNY
ROSES ARE FOR THE RICH (MS)	LISA HARTMAN-BLACK
ROSES ARE FOR THE RICH (MS)	MORGAN STEVENS
ROSES ARE FOR THE RICH (MS)	RICHARD MASUR
ROSES ARE FOR THE RICH (TF)	BETTY BUCKLEY
ROSES ARE FOR THE RICH (TF)	KATE MULGREW
ROSIE!	JAMES FARENTINO
ROSIE!	LESLIE NIELSEN
ROSIE!	SANDRA DEE
ROSY LA BOURRASQUE	GERARD DEPARDIEU
ROTTEN TO THE CORE	CHARLOTTE RAMPLING
ROTTEN TO THE CORE	IAN BANNEN
ROTTEN TO THE CORE	THORLEY WALTERS†
ROUGH CUT	AL MATTHEWS
ROUGH CUT	BURT REYNOLDS
ROUGH CUT	DAVID NIVEN†
ROUGH CUT	JOSS ACKLAND
ROUGH CUT	LESLEY-ANNE DOWN
ROUGH CUT	PATRICK MAGEE†
ROUGH CUT	TIMOTHY WEST
ROUGH MAGIC	BRIDGET FONDA
ROUGH MAGIC	JIM BROADBENT
ROUGH MAGIC	RUSSELL CROWE
ROUGH NIGHT IN JERICHO	DEAN MARTIN
ROUGH NIGHT IN JERICHO	GEORGE PEPPARD†
ROUGH NIGHT IN JERICHO	JEAN SIMMONS
ROUGH STUFF	HULK HOGAN
ROUGH STUFF	SHERMAN HEMSLEY
ROUGHNECKS (MS)	STEPHEN McHATTIE
ROUGHSHOD	JOHN IRELAND
'ROUND MIDNIGHT	FRANCOIS CLUZET
'ROUND MIDNIGHT	JOHN BERRY
ROUND MIDNIGHT ★	DEXTER GORDON†
ROUNDERS, THE	KATHLEEN FREEMAN
ROUNDERS, THE	SUE ANE LANGDON
ROUSTABOUT	BARBARA STANWYCK†
ROUSTABOUT	ELVIS PRESLEY†
ROUSTABOUT	RAQUEL WELCH
ROUSTERS, THE (TF)	CHAD EVERETT
ROVER DANGERFIELD (AF)	RODNEY DANGERFIELD
ROVER, THE	ANTHONY QUINN
ROXANNE	DAMON WAYANS
ROXANNE	DARYL HANNAH
ROXANNE	MICHAEL J. POLLARD
ROXANNE	RICK ROSSOVICH
ROXANNE	SHELLEY DUVALL
ROXANNE	STEVE MARTIN
ROXANNE: THE PRIZE PULITZER (TF)	PERRY KING
ROYAL CAVALCADE	JOHN MILLS
ROYAL FAMILY OF BROADWAY, THE ★	FREDRIC MARCH†
ROYAL FLASH	ALAN BATES
ROYAL FLASH	BOB HOSKINS
ROYAL FLASH	BRITT EKLAND
ROYAL FLASH	CHRISTOPHER CAZENOVE
ROYAL FLASH	JOSS ACKLAND
ROYAL FLASH	MALCOLM McDOWELL
ROYAL GAME, THE	CLAIRE BLOOM
ROYAL HUNT OF THE SUN, THE	CHRISTOPHER PLUMMER
ROYAL HUNT OF THE SUN, THE	NIGEL DAVENPORT
ROYAL ROMANCE OF CHARLES AND DIANA, THE (TF)	OLIVIA DE HAVILLAND
ROYAL SCANDAL, A	EVA GABOR
ROYAL SCANDAL, A	VINCENT PRICE†
ROYAL WAY, THE	RICHARD HARRIS
ROYAL WEDDING	FRED ASTAIRE†
ROYCE (CTF)	CHELSEA FIELD
ROYCE (CTF)	JAMES BELUSHI
ROYCE (CTF)	MIGUEL FERRER
ROYCE (CTF)	PETER BOYLE
RUBY	DANNY AIELLO
RUBY	PIPER LAURIE
RUBY	STUART WHITMAN
RUBY AND OSWALD	BRIAN DENNEHY
RUBY AND OSWALD (TF)	FREDERIC FORREST
RUBY AND OSWALD (TF)	GORDON JUMP
RUBY AND OSWALD (TF)	MICHAEL LERNER
RUBY CAIRO	LIAM NEESON
RUBY GENTRY	CHARLTON HESTON
RUBY GENTRY	JENNIFER JONES
RUBY GENTRY	KARL MALDEN
RUBY IN PARADISE	ASHLEY JUDD
RUCKUS	LINDA BLAIR
RUCKUS	RICHARD FARNSWORTH
RUDE AWAKENING	ANDREA MARTIN
RUDE AWAKENING	BUCK HENRY
RUDE AWAKENING	CHEECH MARIN
RUDE AWAKENING	CINDY WILLIAMS
RUDE AWAKENING	CLIFF DE YOUNG
RUDE AWAKENING	ERIC ROBERTS
RUDE AWAKENING	JULIE HAGERTY
RUDE AWAKENING	LAINIE KAZAN
RUDE AWAKENING	LOUISE LASSER
RUDE AWAKENING	ROBERT CARRADINE
RUDE JOURNÉE POUR LA REINE	GERARD DEPARDIEU
RUDY	CHARLES S. DUTTON
RUDY	LILI TAYLOR
RUDY	NED BEATTY
RUDY	SEAN ASTIN
RUE DE L'ESTRAPADE	LOUIS JOURDAN
RUE DU DÉPART	GERARD DEPARDIEU
RULE #3	MITCHELL COX
RULES OF MARRIAGE, THE (TF)	ELIZABETH MONTGOMERY
RULING CLASS, THE	MICHAEL BRYANT
RULING CLASS, THE ★	PETER O'TOOLE
RUMBLE FISH	DENNIS HOPPER
RUMBLE FISH	DIANE LANE
RUMBLE FISH	LAURENCE FISHBURNE
RUMBLE FISH	MATT DILLON
RUMBLE FISH	MICKEY ROURKE
RUMBLE FISH	NICOLAS CAGE
RUMBLE ON THE DOCKS	ROBERT BLAKE
RUMBLEFISH	VINCENT SPANO
RUMOR MILL, THE (TF)	ELIZABETH TAYLOR
RUMOR MILL, THE (TF)	JANE ALEXANDER
RUMOR OF WAR, A (TF)	BRAD DAVIS†
RUMOUR OF WAR, A (MS)	BRIAN DENNEHY
RUMPELSTILTSKIN	AMY IRVING
RUMPELSTILTSKIN	BILLY BARTY
RUN	KELLY PRESTON
RUN	PATRICK DEMPSEY
RUN	TRACY POLLAN
RUN A CROOKED MILE (TF)	LOUIS JOURDAN
RUN A CROOKED MILE (TF)	MARY TYLER MOORE
RUN FOR COVER	ERNEST BORGNINE
RUN FOR THE ROSES	STUART WHITMAN
RUN FOR THE ROSES	VERA MILES
RUN FOR THE SUN	JANE GREER
RUN FOR THE SUN	RICHARD WIDMARK
RUN FOR YOUR MONEY, A	ALEC GUINNESS
RUN HOME SLOW	MERCEDES McCAMBRIDGE
RUN OF THE ARROW	BRIAN KEITH
RUN OF THE ARROW	CHARLES BRONSON
RUN OF THE ARROW	ROD STEIGER
RUN OF THE COUNTRY, THE	ALBERT FINNEY
RUN OF THE COUNTRY, THE	ANTHONY BROPHY
RUN OF THE COUNTRY, THE	MATT KEESLAR
RUN OF THE COUNTRY, THE	VICKY SMURFIT
RUN, RUN, JOE!	KEITH CARRADINE
RUN SILENT, RUN DEEP	BURT LANCASTER†
RUN SILENT, RUN DEEP	JACK WARDEN
RUN SIMON, RUN (TF)	ROYAL DANO
RUN, STRANGER, RUN	CLORIS LEACHMAN
RUN, STRANGER, RUN	PATRICIA NEAL
RUN, STRANGER, RUN	RON HOWARD
RUN WILD, RUN FREE	GORDAN JACKSON†
RUN WILD, RUN FREE	MARK LESTER
RUNAWAY	CYNTHIA RHODES
RUNAWAY	G.W. BAILEY
RUNAWAY	GENE SIMMONS
RUNAWAY	JOEY CRAMER
RUNAWAY	KIRSTIE ALLEY
RUNAWAY	STAN SHAW
RUNAWAY	TOM SELLECK
RUNAWAY BARGE, THE (TF)	NICK NOLTE
RUNAWAY TRAIN	KENNETH McMILLAN†
RUNAWAY TRAIN	REBECCA DE MORNAY
RUNAWAY TRAIN ★	JON VOIGHT
RUNAWAY TRAIN ✪	ERIC ROBERTS
RUNNER STUMBLES, THE	BEAU BRIDGES
RUNNER STUMBLES, THE	DICK VAN DYKE
RUNNER STUMBLES, THE	KATHLEEN QUINLAN
RUNNER STUMBLES, THE	MAUREEN STAPLETON
RUNNER STUMBLES, THE	TAMMY GRIMES
RUNNING	MICHAEL DOUGLAS
RUNNING	SUSAN ANSPACH
RUNNING HOT	ERIC STOLTZ
RUNNING MAN, THE	ALAN BATES
RUNNING MAN, THE	ARNOLD SCHWARZENEGGER
RUNNING MAN, THE	JOHN MEILLON
RUNNING MAN, THE	MARIA CONCHITA ALONSO
RUNNING MAN, THE	RICHARD DAWSON
RUNNING MAN, THE	YAPHET KOTTO
RUNNING MATES (CTF)	DIANE KEATON
RUNNING MATES (CTF)	ED HARRIS
RUNNING ON EMPTY	CHRISTINE LAHTI
RUNNING ON EMPTY	JUDD HIRSCH
RUNNING ON EMPTY	MARTHA PLIMPTON
RUNNING ON EMPTY	STEVEN HILL
RUNNING ON EMPTY ✪	RIVER PHOENIX†
RUNNING OUT OF LUCK	DENNIS HOPPER
RUNNING OUT OF LUCK	JERRY HALL
RUNNING OUT OF LUCK	MICK JAGGER

I N D E X   O F   F I L M   T I T L E S

† after an actor's name denotes deceased.

RUNNING OUT OF LUCK .... RAE DAWN CHONG
RUNNING SCARED .... BILLY CRYSTAL
RUNNING SCARED .... DAN HEDAYA
RUNNING SCARED .... DARLANNE FLEUGEL
RUNNING SCARED .... GREGORY HINES
RUNNING SCARED .... JIMMY SMITS
RUNNING SCARED .... JOE PANTOLIANO
RUNNING SCARED .... JONATHAN GRIES
RUNNING SCARED .... STEVEN BAUER
RUNNING WILD .... DINA MERRILL
RUNNING WILD .... JOHN SAXON
RUNNING WILD .... LLOYD BRIDGES
RUNNING WILD .... PAT HINGLE
RUSH .... GREGG ALLMAN
RUSH .... JASON PATRIC
RUSH .... JENNIFER JASON LEIGH
RUSH .... MAX PERLICH
RUSH .... SAM ELLIOTT
RUSH .... TONY FRANK
RUSH .... WILLIAM SADLER
RUSSIA HOUSE, THE .... J. T. WALSH
RUSSIA HOUSE, THE .... JAMES FOX
RUSSIA HOUSE, THE .... JOHN MAHONEY
RUSSIA HOUSE, THE ... KLAUS MARIA BRANDAUER
RUSSIA HOUSE, THE .... MICHELLE PFEIFFER
RUSSIA HOUSE, THE .... ROY SCHEIDER
RUSSIA HOUSE, THE .... SEAN CONNERY
RUSSIAN ROULETTE .... DENHOLM ELLIOTT†
RUSSIAN ROULETTE .... GEORGE SEGAL
RUSSIAN ROULETTE .... GORDAN JACKSON†
RUSSIAN ROULETTE .... LOUISE FLETCHER
RUSSIAN ROULETTE .... PETER DONAT
RUSSIAN ROULETTE .... VAL AVERY
RUSSIANS ARE COMING, THE RUSSIANS
    ARE COMING, THE..................... BRIAN KEITH
RUSSIANS ARE COMING, THE RUSSIANS
    ARE COMING, THE.......................... CARL REINER
RUSSIANS ARE COMING, THE RUSSIANS
    ARE COMING, THE..................... EVA MARIE SAINT
RUSSIANS ARE COMING, THE RUSSIANS
    ARE COMING, THE.................... JOHN PHILLIP LAW
RUSSIANS ARE COMING, THE RUSSIANS
    ARE COMING, THE............... JONATHAN WINTERS
RUSSIANS ARE COMING, THE RUSSIANS
    ARE COMING, THE.............. MICHAEL J. POLLARD
RUSSIANS ARE COMING, THE RUSSIANS
    ARE COMING, THE..................... THEODORE BIKEL
RUSSIANS ARE COMING, THE
    RUSSIANS ARE COMING, THE ★ .... ALAN ARKIN
RUSSICUM (TF) .... DANNY AIELLO
RUSSKIES .... LEAF PHOENIX
RUSSKIES .... LEO ROSSI
RUSSKIES .... PETER BILLINGSLEY
RUSSKIES .... STEFAN DESALLE
RUSSKIES .... WHIP HUBLEY
RUSTLER'S RHAPSODY ..... BRANT VAN HOFFMANN
RUSTLER'S RHAPSODY .... G.W. BAILEY
RUSTLER'S RHAPSODY .... MARILU HENNER
RUSTLER'S RHAPSODY .... TOM BERENGER
RUTHLESS .... RAYMOND BURR†
RUTHLESS PEOPLE .... ANITA MORRIS†
RUTHLESS PEOPLE .... ART EVANS
RUTHLESS PEOPLE .... BETTE MIDLER
RUTHLESS PEOPLE .... BILL PULLMAN
RUTHLESS PEOPLE .... DANNY DEVITO
RUTHLESS PEOPLE .... HELEN SLATER
RUTHLESS PEOPLE .... JUDGE REINHOLD
RUTLES, THE (TF) .... ERIC IDLE
RYAN WHITE
    STORY, THE (TF) .... GEORGE C. SCOTT
RYAN WHITE
    STORY, THE (TF) .... GEORGE DZUNDZA
RYAN WHITE
    STORY, THE (TF) .... GRACE ZABRISKIE
RYAN WHITE STORY, THE (TF) .... JUDITH LIGHT
RYAN WHITE STORY, THE (TF) ...... LUKAS HAAS
RYAN WHITE STORY, THE (TF) .... MICHAEL BOWEN
RYAN WHITE STORY, THE (TF) ...... MITCHELL RYAN
RYAN WHITE STORY, THE (TF) ...... PETER SCOLARI
RYAN WHITE
    STORY, THE (TF) .... SARAH JESSICA PARKER

RYAN WHITE
    STORY, THE (TF) .... VALERIE LANDSBURG
RYAN'S DAUGHTER .... TREVOR HOWARD†
RYAN'S DAUGHTER .... ROBERT MITCHUM
RYAN'S DAUGHTER ★ .... SARAH MILES
RYAN'S DAUGHTER ○○ .... JOHN MILLS

S

S.F.W. .... REESE WITHERSPOON
S.F.W. .... STEPHEN DORFF
S.O.B. .... CORBIN BERNSEN
S.O.B. .... JENNIFER EDWARDS
S.O.B. .... JOE PENNY
S.O.B. .... JOHN PLESHETTE
S.O.B. .... JULIA JENNINGS
S.O.B. .... JULIE ANDREWS
S.O.B. .... LARRY HAGMAN
S.O.B. .... LORETTA SWIT
S.O.B. .... MARISA BERENSON
S.O.B. .... RICHARD MULLIGAN
S.O.B. .... ROBERT LOGGIA
S.O.B. .... ROBERT PRESTON†
S.O.B. .... ROBERT VAUGHN
S.O.B. .... ROBERT WEBBER
S.O.B. .... ROSANNA ARQUETTE
S.O.B. .... SHELLEY WINTERS
S.O.B. .... STUART MARGOLIN
S.O.B. .... WILLIAM HOLDEN†
S.O.S. TITANIC (TF) .... CLORIS LEACHMAN
S.O.S. TITANIC (TF) .... DAVID WARNER
S.O.S. TITANIC (TF) .... HELEN MIRREN
S.O.S. TITANIC (TF) .... IAN HOLM
S.O.S. TITANIC (TF) .... ROSEMARY LEACH
S.O.S. TITANIC (TF) .... SUSAN SAINT JAMES
S*P*Y*S .... DONALD SUTHERLAND
S*P*Y*S .... ELLIOTT GOULD
S*P*Y*S .... JOSS ACKLAND
S*P*Y*S .... SHANE RIMMER
S.W.A.L.K. .... MARK LESTER
SAADIA .... MEL FERRER
SABOTAGE .... SYLVIA SIDNEY
SABOTEUR .... NORMAN LLOYD
SABOTEUR, CODE NAME
    MORITURI, THE .... JAMES BROLIN
SABOTEUR, CODE NAME
    MORITURI, THE .... JANET MARGOLIN
SABOTEUR, CODE NAME
    MORITURI, THE .... MARLON BRANDO
SABRE JET .... ROBERT STACK
SABRINA (1954) .... FRANCIS X. BUSHMAN†
SABRINA (1954) .... HUMPHREY BOGART†
SABRINA (1954) .... JOHN WILLIAMS†
SABRINA (1954) .... WILLIAM HOLDEN†
SABRINA (1954) ★ .... AUDREY HEPBURN†
SABRINA (1995) .... HARRISON FORD
SABRINA (1995) .... JULIA ORMOND
SABRINA (1995) .... JULIA ORMOND
SACCO AND VANZETTI .... MILO O'SHEA
SACCO AND VANZETTI .... WILLIAM PRINCE
SACCO E VANZETTI .... WILLIAM PRINCE
SACKETS, THE (TF) .... SAM ELLIOTT
SACKETTS, THE (TF) ..... MERCEDES McCAMBRIDGE
SACKETTS, THE (TF) .... TOM SELLECK
SACRIFICE, THE .... ERLAND JOSEPHSON
SACRIFICE, THE .... GUDRUN GISLADOTTIR
SACRIFICE, THE .... SUSAN FLEETWOOD
SAD SACK, THE .... JERRY LEWIS
SADAT (MS) .... JEREMY KEMP
SADAT (TF) .... LOUIS GOSSETT JR.
SADDLE THE WIND .... ROYAL DANO
SADIE AND SON (TF) .... ALAR AEDMA
SADIE AND SON (TF) .... CYNTHIA DALE
SADIE AND SON (TF) .... DEBBIE REYNOLDS
SADIE AND SON (TF) .... PHIL AKIN
SADIE AND SON (TF) .... SAM WANAMAKER†
SADIE McKEE .... JOAN CRAWFORD†
SADIE THOMPSON ★ .... GLORIA SWANSON†
SADNESS AND BEAUTY ..... CHARLOTTE RAMPLING
SAFARI .... JANET LEIGH
SAFARI 3000 .... DAVID CARRADINE
SAFARI 3000 .... STOCKARD CHANNING

SAFE PASSAGE .... ROBERT SEAN LEONARD
SAFE PASSAGE .... SAM SHEPARD
SAFE PASSAGE .... SEAN ASTIN
SAFE PASSAGE .... SUSAN SARANDON
SAFE PLACE, A .... JACK NICHOLSON
SAFE PLACE, A .... TUESDAY WELD
SAFFO—VENERE DI LESBO .... TINA LOUISE
SAHARA .... BROOKE SHIELDS
SAHARA .... LLOYD BRIDGES
SAHARA ○ .... J. CARROL NAISH†
SAIGON - YEAR OF
    THE CAT (TF) .... CHARLES DANCE
SAIGON - YEAR OF
    THE CAT (TF) .... E. G. MARSHALL
SAIGON—YEAR OF
    THE CAT (TF) .... FREDERIC FORREST
SAIGON - YEAR OF THE CAT (TF) .... JUDI DENCH
SAIL A CROOKED SHIP .... ROBERT WAGNER
SAILOR BEWARE .... DEAN MARTIN
SAILOR BEWARE .... GORDAN JACKSON†
SAILOR BEWARE .... JAMES DEAN†
SAILOR BEWARE .... JERRY LEWIS
SAILOR BEWARE .... VINCE EDWARDS
SAILOR FROM GIBRALTAR, THE ...... IAN BANNEN
SAILOR FROM GIBRALTAR, THE .... JOHN HURT
SAILOR FROM
    GIBRALTAR, THE .... VANESSA REDGRAVE
SAILOR OF THE KING .... WENDY HILLER
SAILOR TAKES A WIFE, THE .... HUME CRONYN
SAILOR TAKES A WIFE, THE .... JUNE ALLYSON
SAILOR WHO FELL FROM GRACE
    WITH THE SEA, THE .... KRIS KRISTOFFERSON
SAILOR WHO FELL FROM GRACE
    WITH THE SEA, THE .... SARAH MILES
SAILOR'S HOLIDAY .... SHELLEY WINTERS
SAINT JACK .... BEN GAZZARA
SAINT JACK .... DENHOLM ELLIOTT†
SAINT JACK .... GEORGE LAZENBY
SAINT JACK .... JOSS ACKLAND
SAINT JOAN .... DAVID HEMMINGS
SAINT JOAN .... JOHN GIELGUD
SAINT JOAN .... KENNETH HAIGH
SAINT JOAN .... RICHARD WIDMARK
SAINT OF DEVIL'S ISLAND, THE .... EARTHA KITT
SAINT OF FORT
    WASHINGTON, THE .... DANNY GLOVER
SAINT OF FORT
    WASHINGTON, THE .... JOE SENECA
SAINT OF FORT
    WASHINGTON, THE .... MATT DILLON
SAINT OF FORT
    WASHINGTON, THE .... NINA SIEMASZKO
SAINT OF FORT
    WASHINGTON, THE .... RICK AVILES
SAINT OF FORT
    WASHINGTON, THE .... YING RHAMES
SAINTED SISTERS, THE .... JOAN CAULFIELD†
SAKHAROV (CTF) .... GLENDA JACKSON
SAKHAROV (CTF) .... JASON ROBARDS
SAKHAROV (CTF) .... MICHAEL BRYANT
SAKHAROV (TF) .... NICOL WILLIAMSON
SALAMANDER, THE .... ANTHONY QUINN
SALAMANDER, THE .... ELI WALLACH
SALAMANDER, THE .... FRANCO NERO
SALAMANDER, THE .... MARTIN BALSAM
SALEM'S LOT (TF) .... BARBARA BABCOCK
SALEM'S LOT (TF) .... DAVID SOUL
SALEM'S LOT (TF) .... ED FLANDERS
SALLAH .... TOPOL
SALLY, IRENE AND MARY .... JOAN CRAWFORD†
SALLY'S IRISH ROGUE .... JULIE HARRIS
SALOME .... DAME JUDITH ANDERSON†
SALOME .... JO CHAMP
SALOME—WHERE
    SHE DANCED .... YVONNE DE CARLO
SALON KITTY .... JOHN IRELAND
SALOON BAR .... RODDY McDOWALL
SALSA .... MAGALI GARCIA
SALSA .... ROBBY ROSA
SALSA .... RODNEY HARVEY
SALT TO THE DEVIL .... SAM WANAMAKER†
SALTY .... NINA FOCH
SALUTE FOR THREE .... YVONNE DE CARLO

SALUTE THE TOFF	ARTHUR HILL
SALVADOR	COLBY CHESTER
SALVADOR	CYNTHIA GIBB
SALVADOR	JAMES BELUSHI
SALVADOR	JOHN DOE
SALVADOR	JOHN SAVAGE
SALVADOR	MICHAEL MURPHY
SALVADOR ★	JAMES WOODS
SALZBURG	
CONNECTION, THE	KLAUS MARIA BRANDAUER
SAM MARLOW, PRIVATE EYE	FRANCO NERO
SAM MARLOW,	
PRIVATE EYE	YVONNE DE CARLO
SAM WHISKEY	ANGIE DICKINSON
SAM WHISKEY	BURT REYNOLDS
SAM WHISKEY	CLINT WALKER
SAM WHISKEY	OSSIE DAVIS
SAMARITAN: THE MITCH	
SNYDER STORY (TF)	CICELY TYSON
SAMARITAN: THE MITCH	
SNYDER STORY (TF)	MARTIN SHEEN
SAMARITAN: THE MITCH	
SNYDER STORY (TF)	ROXANNE HART
SAME TIME, NEXT YEAR	ALAN ALDA
SAME TIME, NEXT YEAR ★	ELLEN BURSTYN
SAMMY AND ROSIE GET LAID	CLAIRE BLOOM
SAMMY AND ROSIE GET LAID	FRANCES BARBER
SAMMY AND ROSIE GET LAID	ROLAND GIFT
SAMMY SOMEBODY	SUSAN STRASBERG
SAMSON AND DELILAH	ANGELA LANSBURY
SAMSON AND DELILAH	RUSS TAMBLYN
SAMSON AND DELILAH (TF)	STEPHEN MACHT
SAMURAI (TF)	MORGAN BRITTANY
SAM'S SON	ELI WALLACH
SAM'S SON (TF)	MICHAEL LANDON†
SAM'S SONG	ROBERT DE NIRO
SAN ANTONIO	ALEXIS SMITH†
SAN DEMETRIO, LONDON	GORDAN JACKSON†
SAN FERRY ANN	RON MOODY
SAN FRANCISCO ★	SPENCER TRACY†
SAN FRANCISCO DOCKS	BURGESS MEREDITH
SAN FRANCISCO INTERNATIONAL	
AIRPORT (TF)	CLU GULAGER
SAN FRANCISCO	
STORY, THE	YVONNE DE CARLO
SAN QUENTIN	LAWRENCE TIERNEY
SAN QUENTIN	RAYMOND BURR†
SANCTUARY	BRADFORD DILLMAN
SAND	RORY CALHOUN
SAND PEBBLES, THE	CANDICE BERGEN
SAND PEBBLES, THE	RICHARD CRENNA
SAND PEBBLES, THE ★	STEVE McQUEEN†
SAND PEBBLES, THE ✪	MAKO
SANDCASTLES (TF)	MARIETTE HARTLEY
SANDLOT, THE	TOM GUIRY
SANDPIPER, THE	CHARLES BRONSON
SANDPIPER, THE	ELIZABETH TAYLOR
SANDPIPER, THE	EVA MARIE SAINT
SANDPIPER, THE	PETER O'TOOLE
SANDPIPER, THE	ROBERT WEBBER
SANDS OF BEERSHEBA	DIANE BAKER
SANDS OF IWO JIMA	RICHARD JAECKEL
SANDS OF IWO JIMA ★	JOHN WAYNE†
SANDS OF THE KALAHARI	NIGEL DAVENPORT
SANDS OF THE KALAHARI	STUART WHITMAN
SANDS OF THE KALAHARI	SUSANNAH YORK
SANDS OF THE KALAHARI	THEODORE BIKEL
SANDWICH MAN, THE	RON MOODY
SANS TOIT NI LOI	ELAINE CORTADELLAS
SANS TOIT NI LOI	SANDRINE BONNAIRE
SANS TOIT NI LOI	STEPHANE FREISS
SANTA	RICARDO MONTALBAN
SANTA CLAUS: THE MOVIE	BURGESS MEREDITH
SANTA CLAUS: THE MOVIE	DAVID HUDDLESTON
SANTA CLAUS: THE MOVIE	DUDLEY MOORE
SANTA CLAUS: THE MOVIE	JOHN LITHGOW
SANTA CLAUSE, THE	DAVID KRUMHOLTZ
SANTA CLAUSE, THE	ERIC LLOYD
SANTA CLAUSE, THE	JUDGE REINHOLD
SANTA CLAUSE, THE	PETER BOYLE
SANTA CLAUSE, THE	TIM ALLEN
SANTA CLAUSE, THE	WENDY CREWSON

SANTA FE SATAN	SEASON HUBLEY
SANTA FE SATAN	SUSAN TYRRELL
SANTA FE TRAIL	OLIVIA DE HAVILLAND
SANTA FE TRAIL	RONALD REAGAN
SANTIAGO	ROYAL DANO
SAPPHIRE	PETER VAUGHN
SARABAND	MICHAEL GOUGH
SARABAND FOR	
DEAD LOVERS	MICHAEL GOUGH
SARACEN BLADE, THE	RICARDO MONTALBAN
SARAFINA!	JOHN KANI
SARAFINA!	LELETI KHUMALO
SARAFINA!	MBONGENI NGEMA
SARAFINA!	MIRIAM MAKEBA
SARAFINA!	WHOOPI GOLDBERG
SARAH AND SON ★	RUTH CHATTERTON†
SARAH, PLAIN	
AND TALL (TF)	CHRISTOPHER WALKEN
SARAH, PLAIN AND TALL (TF)	GLENN CLOSE
SARAH T - PORTRAIT OF A	
TEENAGE ALCOHOLIC (TF)	LINDA BLAIR
SARAH T - PORTRAIT OF A	
TEENAGE ALCOHOLIC (TF)	MARK HAMILL
SARATOGA TRUNK ✪	FLORA ROBSON†
SASKATCHEWAN	SHELLEY WINTERS
SATAN BUG, THE	ED ASNER
SATAN BUG, THE	JOHN ANDERSON
SATAN MET A LADY	BETTE DAVIS†
SATAN NEVER SLEEPS	FRANCE NUYEN
SATANIC RITES OF DRACULA	JOANNA LUMLEY
SATANIC RITES	
OF DRACULA, THE	FREDDIE JONES
SATAN'S CHEERLEADERS	JACK KRUSCHEN
SATAN'S CHEERLEADERS	JOHN IRELAND
SATAN'S CHEERLEADERS	YVONNE DE CARLO
SATAN'S SADISTS	RUSS TAMBLYN
SATAN'S SATELLITES	LEONARD NIMOY
SATAN'S SCHOOL	
FOR GIRLS (TF)	CHERYL LADD
SATAN'S SCHOOL	
FOR GIRLS (TF)	KATE JACKSON
SATAN'S TRIANGLE (TF)	KIM NOVAK
SATELLITE IN THE SKY	LOIS MAXWELL
SATISFACTION	CHRIS NASH
SATISFACTION	JULIA ROBERTS
SATISFACTION	JUSTINE BATEMAN
SATISFACTION	LIAM NEESON
SATISFACTION	TRINI ALVARADO
SATURDAY ISLAND	TAB HUNTER
SATURDAY NIGHT AND	
SUNDAY MORNING	ALBERT FINNEY
SATURDAY NIGHT AND	
SUNDAY MORNING	SHIRLEY ANNE FIELD
SATURDAY NIGHT FEVER	BARRY MILLER
SATURDAY NIGHT FEVER	FRAN DRESCHER
SATURDAY NIGHT FEVER	JULIE BOVASSO†
SATURDAY NIGHT FEVER	KAREN LYNN GORNEY
SATURDAY NIGHT FEVER	STANLEY DeSANTIS
SATURDAY NIGHT FEVER ★	JOHN TRAVOLTA
SATURDAY THE 14TH	PAULA PRENTISS
SATURDAY THE 14TH	RICHARD BENJAMIN
SATURDAY THE 14TH	SEVERN DARDEN
SATURN 3	FARRAH FAWCETT
SATURN 3	HARVEY KEITEL
SATURN 3	KIRK DOUGLAS
SAUVE QUI PEUT	ISABELLE HUPPERT
SAVAGE (TF)	MARTIN LANDAU
SAVAGE, THE	CHARLTON HESTON
SAVAGE DAWN	GEORGE KENNEDY
SAVAGE DAWN	KAREN BLACK
SAVAGE HARVEST	TOM SKERRITT
SAVAGE INNOCENTS, THE	ANTHONY QUINN
SAVAGE INNOCENTS, THE	PETER O'TOOLE
SAVAGE IS LOOSE, THE	GEORGE C. SCOTT
SAVAGE IS LOOSE, THE	TRISH VAN DEVERE
SAVAGE ISLAND	LINDA BLAIR
SAVAGE ISLANDS	TOMMY LEE JONES
SAVAGE MESSIAH	HELEN MIRREN
SAVAGE MESSIAH	MICHAEL GOUGH
SAVAGE SAM	BRIAN KEITH
SAVAGE SAM	ROYAL DANO
SAVAGE SEVEN, THE	PENNY MARSHALL

SAVAGE SEVEN, THE	ROBERT WALKER JR.
SAVAGE STREETS	LINDA BLAIR
SAVAGES	SALOME JENS
SAVAGES	SAM WATERSTON
SAVAGES	SUSAN BLAKELY
SAVAGES (TF)	SAM BOTTOMS
SAVANNAH SMILES	JOHN FIELDLER
SAVANNAH SMILES	PETER GRAVES
SAVE THE TIGER ★★	JACK LEMMON
SAVE THE TIGER ✪	JACK GILFORD†
SAVING GRACE	EDWARD JAMES OLMOS
SAVING GRACE	TOM CONTI
SAXON CHARM, THE	KATHLEEN FREEMAN
SAXON SHARM, THE	HARRY MORGAN
SAY ANYTHING	ERIC STOLTZ
SAY ANYTHING	IONE SKYE
SAY ANYTHING	JOAN CUSAK
SAY ANYTHING	JOHN CUSAK
SAY ANYTHING	JOHN MAHONEY
SAY ANYTHING	LOIS CHILES
SAY ANYTHING	LOREN DEAN
SAY HELLO TO YESTERDAY	JEAN SIMMONS
SAY ONE FOR ME	DEBBIE REYNOLDS
SAY ONE FOR ME	RAY WALSTON
SAY ONE FOR ME	ROBERT WAGNER
SAY ONE FOR ME	STELLA STEVENS
SAYONARA	JAMES GARNER
SAYONARA	MARTHA SCOTT
SAYONARA	RICARDO MONTALBAN
SAYONARA ★	MARLON BRANDO
SAYONARA ✪✪	RED BUTTONS
SCALAWAG	DANNY DEVITO
SCALAWAG	DON STROUD
SCALAWAG	KIRK DOUGLAS
SCALAWAG	LESLEY-ANNE DOWN
SCALAWAG	MARK LESTER
SCALPHUNTERS, THE	BURT LANCASTER†
SCALPHUNTERS, THE	DABNEY COLEMAN
SCALPHUNTERS, THE	OSSIE DAVIS
SCALPHUNTERS, THE	SHELLEY WINTERS
SCALPHUNTERS, THE	TELLY SAVALAS†
SCAM	LEILANI SARELLE
SCANDAL	BRIDGET FONDA
SCANDAL	BRITT EKLAND
SCANDAL	JOANNE WHALLEY-KILMER
SCANDAL	JOHN HURT
SCANDAL	ROLAND GIFT
SCANDAL AT SCOURIE	GREER GARSON
SCANDAL AT ZAMALEK	OMAR SHARIF
SCANDAL IN A SMALL TOWN (TF)	RAQUEL WELCH
SCANDAL IN SORRENTO	SOPHIA LOREN
SCANDAL SHEET (TF)	BURT LANCASTER†
SCANDAL SHEET (TF)	LAUREN HUTTON
SCANDAL SHEET (TF)	PAMELA REED
SCANDAL SHEET (TF)	ROBERT URICH
SCANDALO	FRANCO NERO
SCANDALOUS	JOHN GIELGUD
SCANDALOUS	PAMELA STEPHENSON
SCANDALOUS	ROBERT HAYS
SCANDALOUS JOHN	BRIAN KEITH
SCANDALOUS JOHN	HARRY MORGAN
SCANNER COP 2	BRENDA SWANSON
SCANNER COP 2	DANIEL QUINN
SCANNER COP 2	PATRICK KILPATRICK
SCANNER COP 2	ROBERT FORSTER
SCANNER COP 2	STEPHEN MENDEL
SCANNERS	JENNIFER O'NEILL
SCANNERS	LAWRENCE DANE
SCANNERS	MICHAEL IRONSIDE
SCAPEGOAT, THE	ALEC GUINNESS
SCAPEGOAT, THE	BETTE DAVIS†
SCAPEGOAT, THE	IRENE WORTH
SCARAMOUCHE	ELEANOR PARKER
SCARAMOUCHE	JANET LEIGH
SCARAMOUCHE	JOHN DEHNER†
SCARAMOUCHE	MEL FERRER
SCARAMOUCHE	NINA FOCH
SCARAMOUCHE	RICHARD ANDERSON
SCARAMOUCHE	URSULA ANDRESS
SCARECROW	AL PACINO
SCARECROW	ANN WEDGEWORTH
SCARECROW	EILEEN BRENNAN

SCARECROW .... GENE HACKMAN
SCARECROW .... RICHARD LYNCH
SCARED STIFF .... BOB HOPE
SCARED STIFF .... DEAN MARTIN
SCARED STIFF .... EARL HOLLIMAN
SCARED STIFF .... JERRY LEWIS
SCARED STRAIGHT!
    ANOTHER STORY (TF) .... STAN SHAW
SCARF, THE .... JOHN IRELAND
SCARF, THE .... MERCEDES McCAMBRIDGE
SCARFACE .... AL PACINO
SCARFACE .... ANGELA AAMES
SCARFACE .... F. MURRAY ABRAHAM
SCARFACE .... HARRIS YULIN
SCARFACE .... MARY ELIZABETH MASTRANTONIO
SCARFACE .... MICHELLE PFEIFFER
SCARFACE .... ROBERT LOGGIA
SCARFACE .... STEVEN BAUER
SCARFACE MOB, THE .... ROBERT STACK
SCARLET AND THE
    BLACK, THE (TF) .... GREGORY PECK
SCARLET AND THE
    BLACK, THE (TF) ..... JOHN GIELGUD
SCARLET ANGEL .... ROCK HUDSON†
SCARLET ANGEL .... YVONNE DE CARLO
SCARLET BLADE, THE .... JACK HEDLEY
SCARLET HOUR, THE .... E. G. MARSHALL
SCARLET HOUR, THE .... ELAINE STRITCH
SCARLET LETTER, A .... DEMI MOORE
SCARLET LETTER, A .... GARY OLDMAN
SCARLET LETTER, A .... ROBERT DUVALL
SCARLET LETTER, THE .... LILLIAN GISH†
SCARLET
    PIMPERNEL, THE (TF) .... ANTHONY ANDREWS
SCARLET PIMPERNEL, THE (TF) ..... JANE SEYMOUR
SCARLETT (MS) .... ANN-MARGRET
SCARLETT (MS) .... JOANNE WHALLEY-KILMER
SCARLETT (MS) .... STEPHEN COLLINS
SCARLETT (MS) .... TIMOTHY DALTON
SCARLETT O'HARA
    WARS, THE (MS) .... TONY CURTIS
SCATTERED DREAMS: THE KATHY
    MESSENGER STORY (TF) .... GERALD McRANEY
SCATTERED DREAMS: THE KATHY
    MESSENGER STORY (TF) .... TYNE DALY
SCAVENGER
    HUNT .... ARNOLD SCHWARZENEGGER
SCAVENGER HUNT .... CLEAVON LITTLE†
SCAVENGER HUNT .... CLORIS LEACHMAN
SCAVENGER HUNT .... DIRK BENEDICT
SCAVENGER HUNT .... RICHARD BENJAMIN
SCAVENGER HUNT .... RICHARD MASUR
SCAVENGER HUNT .... RICHARD MULLIGAN
SCAVENGER HUNT .... ROBERT MORLEY
SCAVENGER HUNT .... RODDY McDOWALL
SCAVENGER HUNT .... TONY RANDALL
SCAVENGER HUNT .... VINCENT PRICE†
SCAVENGER HUNT .... WILLIE AAMES
SCENE NUN, TAKE ONE .... SUSANNAH YORK
SCENE OF THE CRIME .... NORMAN LLOYD
SCENE OF THE CRIME .... VAN JOHNSON
SCENE OF THE CRIME (TF) .... GREG EVIGAN
SCENE OF THE
    CRIME, THE .... CATHERINE DENEUVE
SCENES FROM A MALL .... BETTE MIDLER
SCENES FROM A MALL .... BILL IRWIN
SCENES FROM A MALL .... PAUL MAZURSKY
SCENES FROM A MALL .... WOODY ALLEN
SCENES FROM A MARRIAGE .... BIBI ANDERSSON
SCENES FROM
    A MARRIAGE .... ERLAND JOSEPHSON
SCENES FROM A MARRIAGE .... LIV ULLMANN
SCENES FROM THE CLASS STRUGGLE
    IN BEVERLY HILLS .... ARNETIA WALKER
SCENES FROM THE CLASS STRUGGLE
    IN BEVERLY HILLS .... ED BEGLEY JR.
SCENES FROM THE CLASS STRUGGLE
    IN BEVERLY HILLS .... JACQUELINE BISSET
SCENES FROM THE CLASS STRUGGLE
    IN BEVERLY HILLS .... MARK LOWENTHAL
SCENES FROM THE CLASS STRUGGLE
    IN BEVERLY HILLS .... MARY WORONOV

SCENES FROM THE CLASS STRUGGLE
    IN BEVERLY HILLS .... PAUL BARTEL
SCENES FROM THE CLASS STRUGGLE
    IN BEVERLY HILLS .... PAUL MAZURSKY
SCENES FROM THE CLASS STRUGGLE
    IN BEVERLY HILLS .... RAY SHARKEY†
SCENES FROM THE CLASS STRUGGLE
    IN BEVERLY HILLS .... ROBERT BELTRAN
SCENES FROM THE CLASS STRUGGLE
    IN BEVERLY HILLS .... WALLACE SHAWN
SCENES FROM THE
    GOLDMINE .... JOE PANTOLIANO
SCENT OF A WOMAN .... CHRIS O'DONNELL
SCENT OF A WOMAN .... GABRIELLE ANWAR
SCENT OF A WOMAN ★★ .... AL PACINO
SCENT OF MYSTERY .... DENHOLM ELLIOTT†
SCENT OF MYSTERY .... ELIZABETH TAYLOR
SCHINDLER'S LIST .... BEN KINGSLEY
SCHINDLER'S LIST .... CAROLINE GOODALL
SCHINDLER'S LIST .... EMBETH DAVIDTZ
SCHINDLER'S LIST ⚬ .... JONATHAN SAGALLE
SCHINDLER'S LIST ○ .... RALPH FIENNES
SCHINDLER'S LIST ★ .... LIAM NEESON
SCHIZOID .... CRAIG WASSON
SCHIZOID .... RICHARD BALIN
SCHOOL DAZE .... A. J. JOHNSON
SCHOOL DAZE .... BRANFORD MARSALIS
SCHOOL DAZE .... GIANCARLO ESPOSITO
SCHOOL DAZE .... JOIE LEE
SCHOOL DAZE .... KASI LEMMONS
SCHOOL DAZE .... LAURENCE FISHBURNE
SCHOOL DAZE .... SPIKE LEE
SCHOOL FOR SECRETS .... DAVID TOMLINSON
SCHOOL TIES .... AMY LOCANE
SCHOOL TIES .... ANDREW LOWERY
SCHOOL TIES .... ANTHONY RAPP
SCHOOL TIES .... BEN AFFLECK
SCHOOL TIES .... BRENDAN FRASER
SCHOOL TIES .... CHRIS O'DONNELL
SCHOOL TIES .... COLE HAUSER
SCHOOL TIES .... MATT DAMON
SCHOOL TIES .... RANDALL BATINKOFF
SCIENTIFIC CARDPLAYER, THE .... BETTE DAVIS†
SCISSORS .... SHARON STONE
SCOOP (TF) .... DONALD PLEASENCE
SCORCHY .... CONNIE STEVENS
SCORNED AND
    SWINDLED (TF) .... KEITH CARRADINE
SCORPIO .... BURT LANCASTER†
SCORPIO .... PAUL SCOFIELD
SCORPION .... DON MURRAY
SCORPION .... JOHN ANDERSON
SCORPION .... KATHRYN DALEY
SCOTT JOPLIN .... ART CARNEY
SCOTT JOPLIN .... BILLY DEE WILLIAMS
SCOTT JOPLIN .... SEYMOUR CASSEL
SCOTT OF THE ANTARCTIC .... JOHN MILLS
SCOUNDREL, THE .... LIONEL STANDER
SCOUT, THE .... ALBERT BROOKS
SCOUT, THE .... ANNE TWOMEY
SCOUT, THE .... BOB COSTAS
SCOUT, THE .... BOBBY MERCER
SCOUT, THE .... BRENDAN FRASER
SCOUT, THE .... DIANNE WIEST
SCOUT, THE .... GEORGE STEINBRENNER
SCOUT, THE .... LANE SMITH
SCOUT, THE .... MICHAEL RAPAPORT
SCOUT, THE .... TONY BENNETT
SCOUTS TO THE RESCUE .... JACKIE COOPER
SCREAM AND SCREAM AGAIN ...... VINCENT PRICE†
SCREAM, BLACULA, SCREAM! .... PAM GRIER
SCREAM, BLACULA,
    SCREAM! .... WILLIAM MARSHALL
SCREAM FOR HELP .... COREY PARKER
SCREAM OF FEAR .... SUSAN STRASBERG
SCREAM OF THE WOLF (TF) .... PETER GRAVES
SCREAM PRETTY PEGGY (TF) ... TOYAH FELDSHUH
SCREAMING
    WOMAN, THE (TF) .... OLIVIA DE HAVILLAND
SCROOGE .... ALBERT FINNEY
SCROOGE .... ALEC GUINNESS
SCROOGE .... GEOFFREY BAYLDON

SCROOGE .... GORDAN JACKSON†
SCROOGED .... ALFRE WOODARD
SCROOGED .... ANN RAMSEY†
SCROOGED .... BILL MURRAY
SCROOGED .... BOB GOLDTHWAIT
SCROOGED .... BRIAN DOYLE-MURRAY
SCROOGED .... BUDDY HACKETT
SCROOGED .... CAROL KANE
SCROOGED .... DAVID JOHANSEN
SCROOGED .... JAMIE FARR
SCROOGED .... JOHN FORSYTHE
SCROOGED .... JOHN GLOVER
SCROOGED .... JOHN HOUSEMAN†
SCROOGED .... JOHN MURRAY
SCROOGED .... KAREN ALLEN
SCROOGED .... LEE MAJORS
SCROOGED .... LOGAN RAMSEY
SCROOGED .... MABEL KING
SCROOGED .... MARY LOU RETTON
SCROOGED .... MICHAEL J. POLLARD
SCROOGED .... NICHOLAS PHILLIPS
SCROOGED .... PAT McCORMICK
SCROOGED .... ROBERT GOULET
SCROOGED .... ROBERT MITCHUM
SCROOGED .... RYAN TODD
SCRUFFY .... RODDY McDOWALL
SCRUGGS .... SUSANNAH YORK
SCRUPLES (MS) .... NICK MANCUSO
SCRUPLES (TF) .... BARRY BOSTWICK
SCRUPLES II .... GEORGE GAYNES†
SEA CHASE, THE .... CLAUDE AKINS†
SEA CHASE, THE .... JAMES ARNESS
SEA CHASE, THE .... LANA TURNER
SEA CHASE, THE .... TAB HUNTER
SEA DEVILS .... ROCK HUDSON†
SEA GULL, THE .... DAVID WARNER
SEA GULL, THE .... DENHOLM ELLIOTT†
SEA GULL, THE .... VANESSA REDGRAVE
SEA OF GRASS .... KATHERINE HEPBURN
SEA OF GRASS, THE .... PHYLLIS THAXTER
SEA OF LOVE .... AL PACINO
SEA OF LOVE .... ELLEN BARKIN
SEA OF LOVE .... JOHN GOODMAN
SEA OF LOVE .... MICHAEL ROOKER
SEA OF LOVE .... PATRICIA BARRY
SEA SHALL NOT
    HAVE THEM, THE .... GEORGE ROSE†
SEA WALL, THE .... ANTHONY PERKINS†
SEA WIFE .... JOAN COLLINS
SEA WOLF, THE .... HOWARD DA SILVA†
SEA WOLVES, THE .... GREGORY PECK
SEA WOLVES, THE .... PATRICK MacNEE
SEA WOLVES, THE .... ROGER MOORE
SEAGULLS OVER SORRENTO .... GENE KELLY
SEANCE ON A
    WET AFTERNOON ★ .... KIM STANLEY
SEARCH, THE ★ .... MONTGOMERY CLIFT†
SEARCH AND DESTROY .... AMANDA PLUMMER
SEARCH AND DESTROY .... CHRISTOPHER WALKEN
SEARCH AND DESTROY .... DENNIS HOPPER
SEARCH AND DESTROY .... DON STROUD
SEARCH AND DESTROY .... ETHAN HAWKE
SEARCH AND DESTROY .... GRIFFIN DUNNE
SEARCH AND DESTROY .... ILEANNA DOUGLAS
SEARCH AND DESTROY .... JOHN TURTURRO
SEARCH AND DESTROY .... PERRY KING
SEARCH AND DESTROY .... ROSANNA ARQUETTE
SEARCH FOR BRIDEY
    MURPHY, THE .... RICHARD ANDERSON
SEARCH FOR BRIDEY
    MURPHY, THE .... TERESA WRIGHT
SEARCH FOR SIGNS OF INTELLIGENT
    LIFE IN THE UNIVERSE, THE .... LILY TOMLIN
SEARCH FOR THE GODS (TF) ..... RALPH BELLAMY†
SEARCH FOR
    THE GODS (TF) .... STEPHEN McHATTIE
SEARCH FOR THE MOTHER LODE: THE
    LAST GREAT TREASURE ...... CHARLTON HESTON
SEARCH FOR THE MOTHER LODE:
    THE LAST GREAT TREASURE...... JOHN MARLEY†
SEARCH FOR THE MOTHER LODE:
    THE LAST GREAT TREASURE .... KIM BASINGER

This is not a list of every film ever made or every cast member, only those listed in this directory.

SEARCH FOR THE MOTHER LODE:
    THE LAST GREAT TREASURE ...... NICK MANCUSO
SEARCHERS, THE .... HARRY CAREY JR.
SEARCHERS, THE .... JOHN WAYNE†
SEARCHERS, THE .... PATRICK WAYNE
SEARCHERS, THE .... VERA MILES
SEARCHING FOR
    BOBBY FISCHER .... BEN KINGSLEY
SEARCHING FOR
    BOBBY FISCHER .... DAVID PAYMER
SEARCHING FOR BOBBY FISCHER ...... JOAN ALLEN
SEARCHING FOR
    BOBBY FISCHER .... JOE MANTEGNA
SEARCHING FOR
    BOBBY FISCHER .... LAURENCE FISHBURNE
SEARCHING FOR
    BOBBY FISCHER .... MAX POMERANC
SEARCHING FOR
    BOBBY FISCHER .... MICHAEL NIRENBERG
SEARCHING FOR
    BOBBY FISCHER .... ROBERT STEPHENS
SEARCHING WIND, THE .... SYLVIA SIDNEY
SEASON OF DREAMS .... CHRISTINE LAHTI
SEASON OF DREAMS .... FREDERIC FORREST
SEASON OF PASSION .... ANGELA LANSBURY
SEASON OF PASSION .... ERNEST BORGNINE
SEBASTIAN .... DONALD SUTHERLAND
SEBASTIAN .... JOHN GIELGUD
SEBASTIAN .... NIGEL DAVENPORT
SEBASTIAN .... SUSANNAH YORK
SECOND BEST .... CHRISTOPHER CLEARY MILES
SECOND BEST .... JANE HORROCKS
SECOND BEST .... KEITH ALLEN
SECOND BEST .... PRUNELLA SCALES
SECOND BEST .... WILLIAM HURT
SECOND CHANCE .... ANOUK AIMEE
SECOND CHANCE .... CATHERINE DENEUVE
SECOND CHANCE .... JACK PALANCE
SECOND CHANCE .... ROBERT MITCHUM
SECOND CHANCE (TF) .... ELIZABETH ASHLEY
SECOND CHORUS .... BURGESS MEREDITH
SECOND HAND HEARTS .... BARBARA HARRIS
SECOND HAND HEARTS .... ROBERT BLAKE
SECOND HAND WIFE .... RALPH BELLAMY†
SECOND SERVE (TF) .... ALICE KRIGE
SECOND SERVE (TF) .... MARTIN BALSAM
SECOND SERVE (TF) .... VANESSA REDGRAVE
SECOND SIGHT .... BESS ARMSTRONG
SECOND SIGHT .... BRONSON PINCHOT
SECOND SIGHT .... JOHN LARROQUETTE
SECOND SIGHT .... STUART PANKIN
SECOND SIGHT (TF) ...... ELIZABETH MONTGOMERY
SECOND THOUGHTS .... KEN HOWARD
SECOND THOUGHTS .... LUCIE ARNAZ
SECOND TIME AROUND, THE .... ANDY GRIFFITH
SECOND TIME AROUND, THE .... DEBBIE REYNOLDS
SECOND TIME AROUND, THE .... STEVE FORREST
SECOND VICTORY, THE .... ANTHONY ANDREWS
SECOND WIND .... LINDSAY WAGNER
SECOND WIND, A .... ROBERT STACK
SECONDS .... JEFF COREY
SECONDS .... JOHN RANDOLPH
SECONDS .... RICHARD ANDERSON
SECONDS .... SALOME JENS
SECONDS .... WESLEY ADDY
SECRET, THE .... SAM WANAMAKER†
SECRET ADMIRER .... C. THOMAS HOWELL
SECRET ADMIRER .... COREY HAIM
SECRET ADMIRER .... FRED WARD
SECRET AGENT .... JOHN GIELGUD
SECRET BRIDE, THE .... BARBARA STANWYCK†
SECRET CEREMONY .... ELIZABETH TAYLOR
SECRET CEREMONY .... MIA FARROW
SECRET CEREMONY .... PEGGY ASHCROFT†
SECRET CEREMONY .... ROBERT MITCHUM
SECRET DIARY OF
    SIGMUND FREUD, THE .... CARROLL BAKER
SECRET FLIGHT .... DAVID TOMLINSON
SECRET FRIENDS .... ALAN BATES
SECRET GARDEN, THE .... ANDREW KNOTT
SECRET GARDEN, THE .... DEAN STOCKWELL
SECRET GARDEN, THE .... HEYDON PROWSE

SECRET GARDEN, THE .... KATE MABERLY
SECRET GARDEN, THE .... MAGGIE SMITH
SECRET GARDEN, THE (TF) .... DEREK JACOBI
SECRET HEART, THE .... JUNE ALLYSON
SECRET INGREDIENT .... RICK ROSSOVICH
SECRET INVASION, THE .... HENRY SILVA
SECRET INVASION, THE .... RAF VALLONE
SECRET LIFE OF AN
    AMERICAN WIFE, THE .... ANNE JACKSON
SECRET LIFE OF AN
    AMERICAN WIFE, THE .... PATRICK O'NEAL†
SECRET LIFE OF AN
    AMERICAN WIFE, THE .... WALTER MATTHAU
SECRET LIFE OF IAN
    FLEMING, THE (CTF) .... JASON CONNERY
SECRET LIFE OF IAN
    FLEMING, THE (CTF) .... JOSS ACKLAND
SECRET LIFE OF IAN
    FLEMING, THE (CTF) .... PATRICIA HODGE
SECRET LIFE OF KATHY
    McCORMICK, THE (TF) .... BARBARA EDEN
SECRET LIFE OF KATHY
    McCORMICK, THE (TF) .... DICK O'NEILL
SECRET NIGHT CALLER, THE (TF) .... HOPE LANGE
SECRET OF MY SUCCESS, THE ...... HELEN SLATER
SECRET OF MY
    SUCCESS, THE .... MARGARET WHITTON
SECRET OF MY
    SUCCESS, THE .... MERCEDES RUEHL
SECRET OF MY SUCCESS, THE ..... MICHAEL J. FOX
SECRET OF MY SUCCESS, THE ...... SHIRLEY JONES
SECRET OF MY
    SUCCESS, THE .... STELLA STEVENS
SECRET OF SANTA
    VITTORIA, THE .... ANTHONY QUINN
SECRET OF ST. IVES, THE .... JOHN DEHNER†
SECRET OF THE INCAS .... CHARLTON HESTON
SECRET OF THE
    PURPLE REEF, THE .... PETER FALK
SECRET OF THE
    PURPLE REEF, THE .... RICHARD CHAMBERLAIN
SECRET OF TREASURE
    MOUNTAIN .... WILLIAM PRINCE
SECRET OF TREASURE
    MOUNTAIN, THE .... RAYMOND BURR†
SECRET PEOPLE .... IRENE WORTH
SECRET PEOPLE, THE .... AUDREY HEPBURN†
SECRET PLACE, THE .... DAVID McCALLUM
SECRET PLACES .... CLAUDINE AUGER
SECRET PLACES .... JENNY AGUTTER
SECRET POLICEMAN'S
    OTHER BALL. THE (FD) .... ERIC CLAPTON
SECRET POLICEMAN'S
    OTHER BALL. THE (FD) .... JOHN CLEESE
SECRET POLICEMAN'S
    OTHER BALL. THE (FD) .... MICHAEL PALIN
SECRET POLICEMAN'S
    OTHER BALL. THE (FD) .... PETER COOK
SECRET POLICEMAN'S
    OTHER BALL. THE (FD) .... STING
SECRET SERVICE OF
    THE AIR .... RONALD REAGAN
SECRET SINS OF
    THE FATHER (TF) .... LEE PURCELL
SECRET SIX, THE .... RALPH BELLAMY†
SECRET WAR OF
    HARRY FRIGG, THE .... BUCK HENRY
SECRET WAR OF
    HARRY FRIGG, THE .... PAUL NEWMAN
SECRET WAR OF
    HARRY FRIGG, THE .... TOM BOSLEY
SECRET WAYS, THE .... RICHARD WIDMARK
SECRET WEAPON (CTF) .... GRIFFIN DUNNE
SECRET WEAPON (CTF) .... JEROEN KRABBE
SECRET WEAPON (CTF) .... KAREN ALLEN
SECRET WEAPONS (TF) .... GEENA DAVIS
SECRET WEAPONS (TF) .... LINDA HAMILTON
SECRET WEAPONS (TF) .... SALLY KELLERMAN
SECRET WEAPONS (TF) .... VIVECA LINDFORS
SECRET WORLD .... JACQUELINE BISSET
SECRETARY, THE .... ASHLEY PELDON
SECRETARY, THE .... ASHLEY POLDEN

SECRETARY, THE .... BARRY BOSTWICK
SECRETARY, THE .... JAMES RUSSO
SECRETARY, THE .... MEL HARRIS
SECRETARY, THE .... MIMI CRAVEN
SECRETARY, THE .... RAYMOND BAKER
SECRETARY, THE .... RICHARD HERD
SECRETARY, THE .... SHEILA KELLEY
SECRETARY, THE .... SONDRA CURRIE
SECRETS .... JACQUELINE BISSET
SECRETS .... SHIRLEY KNIGHT
SECRETS OF A
    MARRIED MAN (TF) .... CYBILL SHEPHERD
SECRETS OF A
    MARRIED MAN (TF) .... WILLIAM SHATNER
SECRETS OF THREE
    HUNGRY WIVES (TF) .... JESSICA WALTER
SECRETS (TF) .... SUSAN BLAKELY
SECURITY RISK .... JOHN IRELAND
SEDUCED (TF) .... CYBILL SHEPHERD
SEDUCED (TF) .... GEORGE HARRISON
SEDUCED (TF) .... GREGORY HARRISON
SEDUCED (TF) .... JOSE FERRER†
SEDUCED (TF) .... MEL FERRER
SEDUCERS, THE .... SEYMOUR CASSEL
SEDUCERS, THE .... SONDRA LOCKE
SEDUCTION OF JOE TYNAN, THE .... ALAN ALDA
SEDUCTION OF
    JOE TYNAN, THE .... BARBARA HARRIS
SEDUCTION OF
    JOE TYNAN, THE .... MELVYN DOUGLAS†
SEDUCTION OF
    JOE TYNAN, THE .... MERYL STREEP
SEDUCTION OF JOE TYNAN, THE .... RIP TORN
SEDUCTION OF
    MISS LEONA, THE (TF) .... CONCHATA FERRELL
SEDUCTION OF THE SOUTH .... ERNEST BORGNINE
SEDUCTION, THE .... ANDREW STEVENS
SEDUCTION, THE .... MICHAEL SARRAZIN
SEDUCTION, THE .... MORGAN FAIRCHILD
SEDUCTION, THE .... VINCE EDWARDS
SEDUTO ALLA SUA DESTRA .... WOODY STRODE
SEE HOW SHE RUNS (TF) ...... JOANNE WOODWARD
SEE HOW THEY RUN (TF) .... JOHN FORSYTHE
SEE NO EVIL .... MIA FARROW
SEE NO EVIL, HEAR NO EVIL .... ALAN NORTH
SEE NO EVIL, HEAR NO EVIL .... ANTHONY ZERBE
SEE NO EVIL, HEAR NO EVIL .... DOUG YASUDA
SEE NO EVIL, HEAR NO EVIL ...... GENE WILDER
SEE NO EVIL, HEAR NO EVIL ..... JOAN SEVERANCE
SEE NO EVIL, HEAR NO EVIL .... KEVIN SPACEY
SEE NO EVIL, HEAR NO EVIL ...... LOUIS GIAMBALVO
SEE NO EVIL, HEAR NO EVIL .... RICHARD PRYOR
SEE THE MAN RUN (TF) .... ANGIE DICKINSON
SEE THE MAN RUN (TF) .... EDDIE ALBERT
SEE THE MAN RUN (TF) .... ROBERT CULP
SEE YOU IN THE MORNING .... ALICE KRIGE
SEE YOU IN THE MORNING .... BROOKE SMITH
SEE YOU IN THE MORNING .... DAVID DUKES
SEE YOU IN THE MORNING ...... DREW BARRYMORE
SEE YOU IN THE MORNING .... FARRAH FAWCETT
SEE YOU IN THE
    MORNING .... FRANCES STERNHAGEN
SEE YOU IN THE MORNING .... GEORGE HEARN
SEE YOU IN THE MORNING .... HEATHER LILLY
SEE YOU IN THE MORNING .... JEFF BRIDGES
SEE YOU IN THE MORNING .... LINDA LAVIN
SEE YOU IN THE MORNING ...... LUKAS HAAS
SEE YOU IN THE MORNING ...... MACAULAY CULKIN
SEE YOU IN THE MORNING .... ROBIN BARTLETT
SEE YOU IN THE MORNING .... THEODORE BIKEL
SEED .... BETTE DAVIS†
SEEDING OF SARAH
    BURNS, THE (TF) .... MARTIN BALSAM
SEEMS LIKE OLD TIMES .... CHARLES GRODIN
SEEMS LIKE OLD TIMES .... CHEVY CHASE
SEEMS LIKE OLD TIMES .... GEORGE GRIZZARD
SEEMS LIKE OLD TIMES .... GOLDIE HAWN
SEEMS LIKE OLD TIMES .... HAROLD GOULD
SEEMS LIKE OLD TIMES .... ROBERT GUILLAUME
SEIZE THE DAY (TF) .... ROBIN WILLIAMS
SEIZURE .... TROY DONAHUE
SELL OUT, THE .... RICHARD WIDMARK

INDEX OF FILM TITLES

SELL OUT, THE ... SAM WANAMAKER†
SELLOUT, THE ... KARL MALDEN
SEMI-TOUGH ... BERT CONVY†
SEMI-TOUGH ... BRIAN DENNEHY
SEMI-TOUGH ... BURT REYNOLDS
SEMI-TOUGH ... CARL WEATHERS
SEMI-TOUGH ... JILL CLAYBURGH
SEMI-TOUGH ... KRIS KRISTOFFERSON
SEMI-TOUGH ... LOTTE LENYA†
SEMI-TOUGH ... NORMAN ALDEN
SEMI-TOUGH ... RICHARD MASUR
SEMI-TOUGH ... ROBERT PRESTON†
SEMI-TOUGH ... ROGER E. MOSLEY
SEMINOLE ... ANTHONY QUINN
SEMINOLE ... BARBARA HALE
SEMINOLE ... ROCK HUDSON†
SEND ME NO FLOWERS ... CHRISTINE NELSON†
SEND ME NO FLOWERS ... CLINT WALKER
SEND ME NO FLOWERS ... DORIS DAY
SEND ME NO FLOWERS ... PAUL LYNDE†
SEND ME NO FLOWERS ... TONY RANDALL
SENDER, THE ... KATHRYN HARROLD
SENDER, THE ... SHIRLEY KNIGHT
SENILITA ... ANTHONY (TONY) FRANCIOSA
SENIORS, THE ... DENNIS QUAID
SENSUAL MAN, THE ... LIONEL STANDER
SENSUALITA ... MARCELLO MASTROIANNI
SENSUOUS SICILIAN, THE ... LIONEL STANDER
SENTIMENTAL JOURNEY ... MAUREEN O'HARA
SENTIMENTAL JOURNEY (TF) ... DAVID DUKES
SENTIMENTAL JOURNEY (TF) ... JACLYN SMITH
SENTIMENTAL JOURNEY (TF) ... MAUREEN STAPLETON
SENTINEL, THE ... AVA GARDNER†
SENTINEL, THE ... BEVERLY D'ANGELO
SENTINEL, THE ... BURGESS MEREDITH
SENTINEL, THE ... CHRIS SARANDON
SENTINEL, THE ... CHRISTOPHER WALKEN
SENTINEL, THE ... DEBORAH RAFFIN
SENTINEL, THE ... ELI WALLACH
SENTINEL, THE ... JERRY ORBACH
SENTINEL, THE ... JOSE FERRER†
SENTINEL, THE ... MARTIN BALSAM
SENTINEL, THE ... SYLVIA MILES
SEPARATE LIVES ... JAMES BELUSHI
SEPARATE LIVES ... LINDA HAMILTON
SEPARATE TABLES ... BURT LANCASTER†
SEPARATE TABLES ★ ... DEBORAH KERR
SEPARATE TABLES ★★ ... DAVID NIVEN†
SEPARATE TABLES OO ... WENDY HILLER
SEPARATE VACATIONS ... DAVID NAUGHTON
SEPARATE WAYS ... KAREN BLACK
SEPARATE WAYS ... TONY LoBIANCO
SEPARATED BY MURDER (TF) ... SHARON GLESS
SEPT FOIS FEMME ... ROBERT MORLEY
SEPTEMBER ... DENHOLM ELLIOTT†
SEPTEMBER ... DIANNE WIEST
SEPTEMBER ... ELAINE STRITCH
SEPTEMBER ... IRA WHEELER
SEPTEMBER ... JACK WARDEN
SEPTEMBER ... JANE CECIL
SEPTEMBER ... MIA FARROW
SEPTEMBER ... ROSEMARY MURPHY
SEPTEMBER ... SAM WATERSTON
SEPTEMBER 30, 1955 ... DENNIS CHRISTOPHER
SEPTEMBER 30, 1955 ... DENNIS QUAID
SEPTEMBER 30, 1955 ... LISA BLOUNT
SEPTEMBER 30, 1955 ... RICHARD THOMAS
SEPTEMBER 30, 1955 ... SUSAN TYRRELL
SEPTEMBER 30, 1955 ... TOM HULCE
SEPTEMBER AFFAIR ... JESSICA TANDY†
SEQUESTRO DI PERSONA ... CHARLOTTE RAMPLING
SERAIL ... LESLIE CARON
SERENADE ... VINCE EDWARDS
SERENADE ... VINCENT PRICE†
SERGEANT DEADHEAD ... FRANKIE AVALON
SERGEANT MURPHY ... RONALD REAGAN
SERGEANT RUTLEDGE ... WOODY STRODE
SERGEANT RYKER ... BRADFORD DILLMAN
SERGEANT RYKER ... PETER GRAVES
SERGEANT RYKER ... VERA MILES
SERGEANT STEINER ... ROBERT MITCHUM
SERGEANT STEINER ... ROD STEIGER
SERGEANT, THE ... JOHN PHILLIP LAW
SERGEANT, THE ... ROD STEIGER
SERGEANT YORK ... JUNE LOCKHART
SERGEANT YORK ★★ ... GARY COOPER†
SERGEANT YORK O ... MARGARET WYCHERLY†
SERGEANT YORK O ... WALTER BRENNAN†
SERGEANTS 3 ... DEAN MARTIN
SERGEANTS 3 ... FRANK SINATRA
SERGEANTS 3 ... HENRY SILVA
SERIAL ... MARTIN MULL
SERIAL ... NITA TALBOT
SERIAL ... SALLY KELLERMAN
SERIAL ... TOM SMOTHERS
SERIAL ... TUESDAY WELD
SERIAL MOM ... KATHLEEN TURNER
SERIAL MOM ... MINK STOLE
SERIAL MOM ... PATRICIA HEARST
SERIAL MOM ... RICKI LAKE
SERIAL MOM ... SAM WATERSTON
SERIAL MOM ... SUZANNE SOMERS
SÉRIEUX COMME LE PLAISIR ... ISABELLE HUPPERT
SERIOUS MONEY ... DENNIS FARINA
SERIOUS MONEY ... LEO ROSSI
SERPENT OF THE NILE ... RAYMOND BURR†
SERPENT WARRIORS, THE ... EARTHA KITT
SERPENT'S EGG, THE ... DAVID CARRADINE
SERPENT'S EGG, THE ... JAMES WHITMORE
SERPENT'S EGG, THE ... LIV ULLMANN
SERPICO ... ALAN NORTH
SERPICO ... F. MURRAY ABRAHAM
SERPICO ... JOHN RANDOLPH
SERPICO ... M. EMMET WALSH
SERPICO ... TONY ROBERTS
SERPICO ★ ... AL PACINO
SERVANT, THE ... SARAH MILES
SERVICE DE LUXE ... VINCENT PRICE†
SESAME STREET PRESENTS: FOLLOW THAT BIRD ... JOHN CANDY†
SESSIONS (TF) ... DAVID MARSHALL GRANT
SESSIONS (TF) ... JILL EIKENBERRY
SESSIONS (TF) ... VERONICA HAMEL
SETTLE THE SCORE (TF) ... JACLYN SMITH
SETTLE THE SCORE (TF) ... JEFFREY DEMUNN
SETTLE THE SCORE (TF) ... RICHARD MASUR
SEVEN ANGRY MEN ... DENNIS WEAVER
SEVEN BEAUTIES ★ ... GIANCARLO GIANNINI
SEVEN BRIDES FOR SEVEN BROTHERS ... HOWARD KEEL
SEVEN BRIDES FOR SEVEN BROTHERS ... JULIE NEWMAR
SEVEN BRIDES FOR SEVEN BROTHERS ... RUSS TAMBLYN
SEVEN CITIES OF GOLD ... ANTHONY QUINN
SEVEN CITIES OF GOLD ... RITA MORENO
SEVEN DAYS IN MAY ... AVA GARDNER†
SEVEN DAYS IN MAY ... BURT LANCASTER†
SEVEN DAYS IN MAY ... KIRK DOUGLAS
SEVEN DAYS IN MAY ... MARTIN BALSAM
SEVEN DAYS IN MAY ... RICHARD ANDERSON
SEVEN DAYS IN MAY O ... EDMOND O'BRIEN†
SEVEN DAYS TO NOON ... JOSS ACKLAND
SEVEN DIFFERENT WAYS ... BARBARA EDEN
SEVEN FACES OF DR. LAO ... ROYAL DANO
SEVEN FACES OF DR. LAO, THE ... BARBARA EDEN
SEVEN FACES OF DR. LAO, THE ... TONY RANDALL
SEVEN FROM HEAVEN ... JACK PALANCE
SEVEN GRAVES FOR ROGAN ... EDWARD ALBERT
SEVEN HOURS TO JUDGMENT ... BEAU BRIDGES
SEVEN HOURS TO JUDGMENT ... JULIANNE PHILLIPS
SEVEN IN DARKNESS (TF) ... LESLEY ANN WARREN
SEVEN IN DARKNESS (TF) ... MILTON BERLE
SEVEN LITTLE FOYS, THE ... BOB HOPE
SEVEN MEN AT DAYBREAK ... TIMOTHY BOTTOMS
SEVEN MEN FROM NOW ... STUART WHITMAN
SEVEN MINUTES IN HEAVEN ... ALAN BOYCE
SEVEN MINUTES IN HEAVEN ... JENNIFER CONNELLY
SEVEN MINUTES IN HEAVEN ... MADDIE CORMAN
SEVEN MINUTES IN HEAVEN ... MICHAEL ZASLOW
SEVEN MINUTES IN HEAVEN ... SPALDING GRAY
SEVEN MINUTES, THE ... KATE JACKSON
SEVEN MINUTES, THE ... TOM SELLECK
SEVEN MINUTES, THE ... YVONNE DE CARLO
SEVEN MINUTES TO HEAVEN ... LAUREN HOLLY
SEVEN NIGHTS IN JAPAN ... MICHAEL YORK
SEVEN PER-CENT SOLUTION, THE ... SAMANTHA EGGAR
SEVEN PERCENT SOLUTION, THE ... ALAN ARKIN
SEVEN SEAS TO CALAIS ... IRENE WORTH
SEVEN THEIVES ... ROD STEIGER
SEVEN THIEVES ... ELI WALLACH
SEVEN THIEVES ... JOAN COLLINS
SEVEN THIEVES ... MICHAEL DANTE
SEVEN UPS, THE ... TONY LoBIANCO
SEVEN WAVES AWAY ... GORDAN JACKSON†
SEVEN WAVES AWAY ... MAE ZETTERLING†
SEVEN WOMEN ... WOODY STRODE
SEVEN-PER-CENT SOLUTION, THE ... JEREMY KEMP
SEVEN-PER-CENT SOLUTION, THE ... JOEL GREY
SEVEN-PER-CENT SOLUTION, THE ... NICOL WILLIAMSON
SEVEN-PER-CENT SOLUTION, THE ... ROBERT DUVALL
SEVEN-PER-CENT SOLUTION, THE ... VANESSA REDGRAVE
SEVEN-UPS, THE ... ROY SCHEIDER
SEVEN-YEAR ITCH, THE ... MARILYN MONROE†
SEVENTEEN ... JACKIE COOPER
SEVENTH AVENUE (MS) ... ELI WALLACH
SEVENTH AVENUE (MS) ... JANE SEYMOUR
SEVENTH AVENUE (TF) ... STEVEN KEATS†
SEVENTH CAVALRY ... BARBARA HALE
SEVENTH CROSS, THE ... JESSICA TANDY†
SEVENTH CROSS, THE O ... HUME CRONYN
SEVENTH DAWN, THE ... SUSANNAH YORK
SEVENTH HEAVEN ... JAMES STEWART
SEVENTH HEAVEN HH ... JANET GAYNOR†
SEVENTH SEAL, THE ... BIBI ANDERSSON
SEVENTH SIGN, THE ... DEMI MOORE
SEVENTH SIGN, THE ... HARRY BASIL
SEVENTH SIGN, THE ... JORGEN PROCHNOW
SEVENTH SIGN, THE ... MICHAEL BIEHN
SEVENTH SIGN, THE ... PETER FRIEDMAN
SEVENTH SIN, THE ... ELEANOR PARKER
SEVENTH VICTIM, THE ... BARBARA HALE
SEVERED HEAD, A ... CLAIRE BLOOM
SEVERED HEAD, A ... IAN HOLM
SEX AND THE COLLEGE GIRL ... CHARLES GRODIN
SEX AND THE MARRIED WOMAN (TF) ... FANNIE FLAGG
SEX AND THE SINGLE GIRL ... LAUREN BACALL
SEX AND THE SINGLE GIRL ... MAX SHOWALTER
SEX AND THE SINGLE GIRL ... MEL FERRER
SEX AND THE SINGLE GIRL ... NATALIE WOOD†
SEX AND THE SINGLE GIRL ... STUBBY KAYE
SEX AND THE SINGLE GIRL ... TONY CURTIS
SEX AND THE TEENAGER ... LLOYD BRIDGES
SEX, DRUGS, ROCK & ROLL ... ERIC BOGOSIAN
SEX KITTENS GO TO COLLEGE ... TUESDAY WELD
sex, lies, and videotape ... ALEXANDRA ROOT
sex, lies, and videotape ... ANDIE MacDOWELL
sex, lies, and videotape ... DAVID FOIL
sex, lies, and videotape ... EARL T. TAYLOR
sex, lies, and videotape ... JAMES SPADER
sex, lies, and videotape ... LAURA SAN GIACOMO
sex, lies, and videotape ... PETER GALLAGHER
sex, lies, and videotape ... RON VAWTER
sex, lies, and videotape ... STEVEN BRILL
SEX ON THE RUN ... TONY CURTIS
SEX SYMBOL, THE (FD) ... DON MURRAY
SEX SYMBOL, THE (TF) ... CONNIE STEVENS
SEX WITH A SMILE ... DAYLE HADDON
SEXTETTE ... DOM DeLUISE
SEXTETTE ... GEORGE HAMILTON
SEXTETTE ... MAE WEST†
SEXTETTE ... TIMOTHY DALTON
SEXTETTE ... TONY CURTIS
SGT. BILKO ... STEVE MARTIN
SGT. KABUKIMAN, NYPD ... SUSAN BYUN

This is not a list of every film ever made or every cast member, only those listed in this directory.

SGT. PEPPER'S LONELY
HEARTS CLUB BAND .... ALICE COOPER
SGT. PEPPER'S LONELY
HEARTS CLUB BAND .... BARRY GIBB
SGT. PEPPER'S LONELY
HEARTS CLUB BAND .... CAREL STRUYCKEN
SGT. PEPPER'S LONELY
HEARTS CLUB BAND .... DONALD PLEASENCE
SGT. PEPPER'S LONELY
HEARTS CLUB BAND .... GEORGE BURNS
SGT. PEPPER'S LONELY
HEARTS CLUB BAND .... KEITH CARRADINE
SGT. PEPPER'S LONELY
HEARTS CLUB BAND .... MAURICE GIBB
SGT. PEPPER'S LONELY
HEARTS CLUB BAND .... MAX SHOWALTER
SGT. PEPPER'S LONELY
HEARTS CLUB BAND .... PAUL NICHOLAS
SGT. PEPPER'S LONELY
HEARTS CLUB BAND .... ROBIN GIBB
SGT. PEPPER'S LONELY
HEARTS CLUB BAND .... STEVE MARTIN
SHADEY .... ANTHONY SHER
SHADEY .... BERNARD HEPTON
SHADEY .... BILLIE WHITELAW
SHADEY .... KATHERINE HELMOND
SHADEY .... PATRICK macNEE
SHADOW, THE .... ALEC BALDWIN
SHADOW, THE .... JOHN LONE
SHADOW, THE .... LARRY HANKIN
SHADOW, THE .... PENELOPE ANN MILLER
SHADOW, THE .... PETER BOYLE
SHADOW, THE .... TIM CURRY
SHADOW BOX, THE (TF) .... JOANNE WOODWARD
SHADOW BOX, THE (TF) .... SYLVIA SIDNEY
SHADOW CHASERS (TF) .... DENNIS DUGAN
SHADOW CHASERS (TF) .... NINA FOCH
SHADOW OF A DOUBT .... BING CROSBY†
SHADOW OF A DOUBT .... HUME CRONYN
SHADOW OF A DOUBT .... TERESA WRIGHT
SHADOW OF CHINA .... JOHN LONE
SHADOW OF CHINA .... SAMMI DAVIS
SHADOW OF THE HAWK ..... JAN-MICHAEL VINCENT
SHADOW ON THE LAND (TF) .... GENE HACKMAN
SHADOW ON THE LAND (TF) .... JACKIE COOPER
SHADOW ON THE WALL .... ANN SOTHERN
SHADOW ON THE WALL .... MAC DAVIS
SHADOW ON THE WINDOW .... COREY ALLEN
SHADOW OVER ELVERON (TF) .... DON AMECHE†
SHADOW PLAY .... CLORIS LEACHMAN
SHADOW RIDERS, THE (TF) .... JANE GREER
SHADOW RIDERS, THE (TF) .... KATHERINE ROSS
SHADOW RIDERS, THE (TF) .... SAM ELLIOTT
SHADOW RIDERS, THE (TF) .... TOM SELLECK
SHADOWLANDS .... ANTHONY HOPKINS
SHADOWLANDS .... EDWARD HARDWICKE
SHADOWLANDS .... JOHN WOOD
SHADOWLANDS .... JOSEPH MAZZELLO
SHADOWLANDS .... MICHAEL DENISON
SHADOWLANDS .... PETER FIRTH
SHADOWLANDS ★ .... DEBRA WINGER
SHADOWS AND FOG .... DAVID STRATHAIRN
SHADOWS AND FOG .... DONALD PLEASENCE
SHADOWS AND FOG .... FRED GWYNNE†
SHADOWS AND FOG .... JODIE FOSTER
SHADOWS AND FOG .... JOHN CUSACK
SHADOWS AND FOG .... JOHN MALKOVICH
SHADOWS AND FOG .... KATE NELLIGAN
SHADOWS AND FOG .... KATHY BATES
SHADOWS AND FOG .... KENNETH MARS
SHADOWS AND FOG .... LILY TOMLIN
SHADOWS AND FOG .... MADONNA
SHADOWS AND FOG .... MIA FARROW
SHADOWS AND FOG .... WOODY ALLEN
SHADOWS IN THE NIGHT .... NINA FOCH
SHADOWS RUN BLACK .... KEVIN COSTNER
SHAFT .... ANTONIO FARGAS
SHAFT .... MOSES GUNN
SHAFT .... RICHARD ROUNDTREE
SHAFT IN AFRICA .... RICHARD ROUNDTREE
SHAFT'S BIG SCORE .... JULIUS HARRIS
SHAFT'S BIG SCORE .... MOSES GUNN

SHAFT'S BIG SCORE! .... RICHARD ROUNDTREE
SHAG .... BRIDGET FONDA
SHAGGY D.A., THE .... DEAN JONES
SHAGGY D.A., THE .... DICK VAN PATTEN
SHAGGY D.A., THE .... JOHN FIELDLER
SHAGGY D.A., THE .... SUZANNE PLESHETTE
SHAGGY D.A., THE .... TIM CONWAY
SHAGGY DOG, THE .... ANNETTE FUNICELLO
SHAKE HANDS WITH THE DEVIL .... DON MURRAY
SHAKE HANDS WITH
THE DEVIL .... RICHARD HARRIS
SHAKEDOWN .... ANTONIO FARGAS
SHAKEDOWN .... BLANCHE BAKER
SHAKEDOWN .... LAWRENCE TIERNEY
SHAKEDOWN .... PATRICIA CHARBONNEAU
SHAKEDOWN .... PETER WELLER
SHAKEDOWN .... ROCK HUDSON†
SHAKEDOWN .... SAM ELLIOTT
SHAKEDOWN ON THE
SUNSET STRIP (TF) .... JOAN VAN ARK
SHAKEDOWN ON THE
SUNSET STRIP (TF) .... PERRY KING
SHAKEDOWN ON THE
SUNSET STRIP (TF) .... SEASON HUBLEY
SHAKES THE CLOWN .... BOB GOLDTHWAIT
SHAKES THE CLOWN .... JULIE BROWN
SHAKIEST GUN IN THE WEST, THE ..... DON KNOTTS
SHAKING THE TREE .... ARYE GROSS
SHAKING THE TREE .... COURTENEY COX
SHALAKO! .... SEAN CONNERY
SHALAKO .... WOODY STRODE
SHALIMAR .... JOHN SAXON
SHALIMAR .... SYLVIA MILES
SHALL WE DANCE .... FRED ASTAIRE†
SHAME .... DEBORRA-LEE FURNESS
SHAME .... LIV ULLMANN
SHAME .... SIMONE BUCHANAN
SHAME (CTF) .... FAIRUZA BALK
SHAME OF THE JUNGLE (AF) .... BILL MURRAY
SHAMPOO .... CARRIE FISHER
SHAMPOO .... GOLDIE HAWN
SHAMPOO .... JULIE CHRISTIE
SHAMPOO .... LUANA ANDERS
SHAMPOO .... SUSAN BLAKELY
SHAMPOO .... TONY BILL
SHAMPOO ○ .... WARREN BEATTY
SHAMPOO ○ .... JACK WARDEN
SHAMPOO ○○ .... LEE GRANT
SHAMUS .... BURT REYNOLDS
SHAMUS .... DYAN CANNON
SHAMUS .... JOE SANTOS
SHANE .... BEN JOHNSON
SHANE ○ .... BRANDON DE WILDE†
SHANE ○ .... JACK PALANCE
SHANGHAI SURPRISE .... GEORGE HARRISON
SHANGHAI SURPRISE .... MADONNA
SHANGHAI SURPRISE .... PAUL FREEMAN
SHANGHAI SURPRISE .... RICHARD GRIFFITHS
SHANGHAI SURPRISE .... SEAN PENN
SHANNON'S DEAL (TF) .... MIGUEL FERRER
SHAPE OF THINGS
TO COME, THE .... JOHN IRELAND
SHAPE OF THINGS
TO COME, THE (TF) .... CAROL LYNLEY
SHAPE OF THINGS
TO COME, THE (TF) .... JACK PALANCE
SHARING RICHARD (TF) .... ED MARINARO
SHARING RICHARD (TF) .... EILEEN DAVIDSON
SHARING RICHARD (TF) .... JANET CARROLL
SHARING RICHARD (TF) .... LISA JANE PERSKY
SHARK! .... BURT REYNOLDS
SHARKFIGHTERS, THE .... CLAUDE AKINS†
SHARKFIGHTERS, THE .... JAMES OLSON
SHARKS .... LEE MAJORS
SHARKS' TREASURE .... YAPHET KOTTO
SHARKY'S MACHINE .... BERNIE CASEY
SHARKY'S MACHINE .... BRIAN KEITH
SHARKY'S MACHINE .... BURT REYNOLDS
SHARKY'S MACHINE .... CHARLES DURNING
SHARKY'S MACHINE .... EARL HOLLIMAN
SHARKY'S MACHINE .... HARI RHODES
SHARKY'S MACHINE .... HENRY SILVA

SHARKY'S MACHINE .... JOHN FIELDLER
SHARKY'S MACHINE .... RACHEL WARD
SHARKY'S MACHINE .... RICHARD LIBERTINI
SHARON: PORTRAIT OF
A MISTRESS (TF) .... DANIELLE von ZERNECK
SHARON: PORTRAIT OF
A MISTRESS (TF) .... SALOME JENS
SHATTERED .... BOB HOSKINS
SHATTERED .... CORBIN BERNSEN
SHATTERED .... GRETA SCACCHI
SHATTERED .... JOANNE WHALLEY-KILMER
SHATTERED .... TOM BERENGER
SHATTERED DREAMS (TF) .... JAMES KAREN
SHATTERED DREAMS (TF) ..... LINDSAY WAGNER
SHATTERED INNOCENCE (TF) ...... MELINDA DILLON
SHATTERED SPIRITS (TF) .... LUKAS HAAS
SHATTERED SPIRITS (TF) .... MARTIN SHEEN
SHATTERED
SPIRITS (TF) .... MATTHEW LABORTEAUX
SHATTERED SPIRITS (TF) .... MELINDA DILLON
SHATTERED VOWS (TF) .... VALERIE BERTINELLI
SHAWSHANK REDEMPTION, THE ..... BOB GUNTON
SHAWSHANK
REDEMPTION, THE .... CLANCY BROWN
SHAWSHANK REDEMPTION, THE .... GIL BELLOWS
SHAWSHANK
REDEMPTION, THE .... JAMES WHITMORE
SHAWSHANK
REDEMPTION, THE .... MORGAN FREEMAN
SHAWSHANK REDEMPTION, THE .... TIM ROBBINS
SHAWSHANK
REDEMPTION, THE .... WILLIAM SADLER
SHE .... URSULA ANDRESS
SHE CAME TO THE VALLEY .... DEAN STOCKWELL
SHE CAME TO THE VALLEY .... RONEE BLAKLEY
SHE COULDN'T SAY NO .... JEAN SIMMONS
SHE COULDN'T SAY NO .... ROBERT MITCHUM
SHE CRIED MURDER (TF) .... TELLY SAVALAS†
SHE DANCES ALONE .... BUD CORT
SHE DEVILS .... YVONNE DE CARLO
SHE DONE HIM WRONG .... CARY GRANT†
SHE DONE HIM WRONG .... MAE WEST†
SHE KNOWS TOO MUCH (TF) .... ERIK ESTRADA
SHE KNOWS TOO MUCH (TF) .... MEREDITH BAXTER
SHE KNOWS TOO MUCH (TF) .... ROBERT URICH
SHE LIVES! (TF) .... DESI ARNAZ JR.
SHE LIVES! (TF) .... SEASON HUBLEY
SHE WAITS (TF) .... PATTY DUKE
SHE WAS MARKED
FOR MURDER (TF) .... LLOYD BRIDGES
SHE WAS MARKED
FOR MURDER (TF) .... POLLY BERGEN
SHE WAS MARKED
FOR MURDER (TF) .... STEFANIE POWERS
SHE WENT TO THE RACES .... AVA GARDNER†
SHE WORE A YELLOW RIBBON .... BEN JOHNSON
SHE WORE A
YELLOW RIBBON .... HARRY CAREY JR.
SHE'S BEEN AWAY .... PEGGY ASHCROFT†
SHE'S GOTTA HAVE IT .... JOIE LEE
SHE-DEVIL .... A MARTINEZ
SHE-DEVIL .... BRYAN LARKIN
SHE-DEVIL .... ED BEGLEY JR.
SHE-DEVIL .... ELIZABETH PETERS
SHE-DEVIL .... LINDA HUNT
SHE-DEVIL .... MERYL STREEP
SHE-DEVIL .... ROSEANNE
SHE-DEVIL .... SYLVIA MILES
SHE-WOLF OF LONDON, THE .... JUNE LOCKHART
SHEBA BABY .... PAM GRIER
SHEENA .... TANYA ROBERTS
SHEEPMAN, THE .... LESLIE NIELSEN
SHEEPMAN, THE .... SHIRLEY MacLAINE
SHEILA LEVINE IS DEAD AND
LIVING IN NEW YORK .... JEANNIE BERLIN
SHEILA LEVINE IS DEAD AND
LIVING IN NEW YORK .... ROY SCHEIDER
SHELL GAME (TF) .... JOHN DAVIDSON
SHELL SEEKERS, THE (TF) .... ANGELA LANSBURY
SHELL SEEKERS, THE (TF) .... SAM WANAMAKER†
SHELTERING SKY, THE .... CAMPBELL SCOTT
SHELTERING SKY, THE .... DEBRA WINGER

† after an actor's name denotes deceased.

SHELTERING SKY, THE .... ERIC VU-AN
SHELTERING SKY, THE .... JILL BENNETT
SHELTERING SKY, THE .... JOHN MALKOVICH
SHELTERING SKY, THE .... TIMOTHY SPALL
SHENANDOAH .... DOUG McCLURE
SHENANDOAH .... GEORGE KENNEDY
SHENANDOAH .... HARRY CAREY JR.
SHENANDOAH .... JAMES STEWART
SHENANDOAH .... KATHERINE ROSS
SHENANDOAH .... PATRICK WAYNE
SHENANIGANS/THE GREAT GEORGIA BANK HOAX .... BURGESS MEREDITH
SHENANIGANS/THE GREAT GEORGIA BANK HOAX .... NED BEATTY
SHERLOCK HOLMES IN NEW YORK (TF) .... CHARLOTTE RAMPLING
SHERLOCK HOLMES IN NEW YORK (TF) .... ROGER MOORE
SHE'LL BE SWEET (TF) .... SALLY KELLERMAN
SHE'LL BE SWEET (TF) .... TONY LoBIANCO
SHE'S A SOLDIER, TOO .... SHELLEY WINTERS
SHE'S BEEN AWAY .... GERALDINE JAMES
SHE'S DRESSED TO KILL (TF) .... ELEANOR PARKER
SHE'S DRESSED TO KILL (TF) .... JESSICA WALTER
SHE'S GOT EVERYTHING .... ANN SOTHERN
SHE'S GOTTA HAVE IT .... SPIKE LEE
SHE'S HAVING A BABY .... ALEC BALDWIN
SHE'S HAVING A BABY .... ELIZABETH McGOVERN
SHE'S HAVING A BABY .... KEVIN BACON
SHE'S HAVING A BABY .... PAUL GLEASON
SHE'S HAVING A BABY .... WILLIAM WINDOM
SHE'S IN THE ARMY NOW (TF) .... JAMIE LEE CURTIS
SHE'S IN THE ARMY NOW (TF) .... KATHLEEN QUINLAN
SHE'S IN THE ARMY NOW (TF) .... MELANIE GRIFFITH
SHE'S OUT OF CONTROL .... AMI DOLENZ
SHE'S OUT OF CONTROL .... CATHERINE HICKS
SHE'S OUT OF CONTROL .... DICK O'NEILL
SHE'S OUT OF CONTROL .... TONY DANZA
SHE'S OUT OF CONTROL .... WALLACE SHAWN
SHE'S WORKING HER WAY THROUGH COLLEGE .... RONALD REAGAN
SHIELD FOR MURDER .... CLAUDE AKINS†
SHIMMY LUGANO E TARANTELLE E VINO .... SOPHIA LOREN
SHINING, THE .... ANNE JACKSON
SHINING, THE .... JACK NICHOLSON
SHINING, THE .... SCATMAN CROTHERS†
SHINING, THE .... SHELLEY DUVALL
SHINING HOUR, THE .... JOAN CRAWFORD†
SHINING SEASON, A (TF) .... RIP TORN
SHINING SEASON, A (TF) .... TIMOTHY BOTTOMS
SHINING STAR .... BERT PARKS†
SHINING STAR .... ED NELSON
SHINING STAR .... HARVEY KEITEL
SHINING STAR .... MICHAEL DANTE
SHINING THROUGH .... JOELY RICHARDSON
SHINING THROUGH .... JOHN GIELGUD
SHINING THROUGH .... LIAM NEESON
SHINING THROUGH .... MELANIE GRIFFITH
SHINING THROUGH .... MICHAEL DOUGLAS
SHINING VICTORY .... GERALDINE FITZGERALD
SHIP AHOY .... FRANK SINATRA
SHIP COMES IN, A ★ .... LOUISE DRESSER†
SHIP OF FOOLS .... ELIZABETH ASHLEY
SHIP OF FOOLS .... GEORGE SEGAL
SHIP OF FOOLS .... JOSE FERRER†
SHIP OF FOOLS ★ .... OSKAR WERNER†
SHIP OF FOOLS ★ .... SIMONE SIGNORET†
SHIP OF FOOLS ✪ .... MICHAEL DUNN†
SHIP WAS LOADED, THE .... DAVID TOMLINSON
SHIPWRECKED .... GABRIEL BYRNE
SHIPWRECKED .... STIAN SMESTAD
SHIRALEE, THE (MS) .... BRYON BROWN
SHIRLEY VALENTINE .... TOM CONTI
SHIRLEY VALENTINE ★ .... PAULINE COLLINS
SHIRTS/SKINS (TF) .... LORETTA SWIT
SHOCK .... VINCENT PRICE†
SHOCK TO THE SYSTEM, A .... ELIZABETH McGOVERN
SHOCK TO THE SYSTEM, A .... JENNY WRIGHT
SHOCK TO THE SYSTEM, A .... MICHAEL CAINE
SHOCK TO THE SYSTEM, A .... PETER RIEGERT
SHOCK TO THE SYSTEM, A .... SWOOSIE KURTZ
SHOCK TO THE SYSTEM, A .... WILL PATTON
SHOCK TREATMENT .... CAROL LYNLEY
SHOCK TREATMENT .... CLIFF DE YOUNG
SHOCK TREATMENT .... JESSICA HARPER
SHOCK TREATMENT .... LAUREN BACALL
SHOCK TREATMENT .... OSSIE DAVIS
SHOCK TREATMENT .... RODDY McDOWALL
SHOCK TREATMENT .... STUART WHITMAN
SHOCK WAVES .... BROOKE ADAMS
SHOCKER .... CAMI COOPER
SHOCKER .... MICHAEL MURPHY
SHOCKER .... MITCH PILEGGI
SHOCKER .... PETER BERG
SHOES OF THE FISHERMAN, THE .... ANTHONY QUINN
SHOES OF THE FISHERMAN, THE .... JOHN GIELGUD
SHOGUN (MS) .... JOHN RHYS-DAVIES
SHOGUN (MS) .... RICHARD CHAMBERLAIN
SHOOT .... CLIFF ROBERTSON
SHOOT .... ERNEST BORGNINE
SHOOT .... HENRY SILVA
SHOOT LOUD...LOUDER... I DON'T UNDERSTAND .... RAQUEL WELCH
SHOOT OUT .... GREGORY PECK
SHOOT THE MOON .... ALBERT FINNEY
SHOOT THE MOON .... DANA HILL
SHOOT THE MOON .... DIANE KEATON
SHOOT THE MOON .... KAREN ALLEN
SHOOT THE MOON .... LEORA DANA†
SHOOT THE MOON .... PETER WELLER
SHOOT THE MOON .... TINA YOTHERS
SHOOT THE MOON .... TRACEY GOLD
SHOOT THE MOON .... VIVEKA DAVIS
SHOOT TO KILL .... ANDREW ROBINSON
SHOOT TO KILL .... BLU MAKUMA
SHOOT TO KILL .... CLANCY BROWN
SHOOT TO KILL .... FRED COFFIN
SHOOT TO KILL .... KEVIN SCANNELL
SHOOT TO KILL .... KIRSTIE ALLEY
SHOOT TO KILL .... RICHARD MASUR
SHOOT TO KILL .... SIDNEY POITIER
SHOOT TO KILL .... TOM BERENGER
SHOOT-OUT .... JEFF COREY
SHOOT-OUT AT MEDICINE BEND .... JAMES GARNER
SHOOTDOWN (TF) .... ANGELA LANSBURY
SHOOTDOWN (TF) .... GEORGE COE
SHOOTDOWN (TF) .... MOLLY HAGAN
SHOOTER (TF) .... CAROL HUSTON
SHOOTING PARTY, THE .... GORDAN JACKSON†
SHOOTING PARTY, THE .... JOHN GIELGUD
SHOOTING, THE .... JACK NICHOLSON
SHOOTIST, THE .... BILL McKINNEY
SHOOTIST, THE .... HARRY MORGAN
SHOOTIST, THE .... JAMES STEWART
SHOOTIST, THE .... JOHN WAYNE†
SHOOTIST, THE .... LAUREN BACALL
SHOOTIST, THE .... RICHARD BOONE†
SHOOTIST, THE .... RON HOWARD
SHOOTOUT .... SUSAN TYRRELL
SHOOTOUT AT MEDICINE BEND .... ANGIE DICKINSON
SHOP AROUND THE CORNER, THE .... JAMES STEWART
SHOP ON MAIN STREET, THE ★ .... IDA KAMINSKA†
SHOPWORN .... BARBARA STANWYCK†
SHOPWORN ANGEL, THE .... JAMES STEWART
SHORT CIRCUIT .... ALLY SHEEDY
SHORT CIRCUIT .... FISHER STEVENS
SHORT CIRCUIT .... G.W. BAILEY
SHORT CIRCUIT .... STEVE GUTTENBERG
SHORT CIRCUIT .... TIM BLANEY
SHORT CIRCUIT 2 .... CYNTHIA GIBB
SHORT CIRCUIT 2 .... FISHER STEVENS
SHORT CIRCUIT 2 .... JACK WESTON
SHORT CIRCUIT 2 .... MICHAEL McKEAN
SHORT CIRCUIT 2 .... TIM BLANEY
SHORT CUTS .... ANDIE MacDOWELL
SHORT CUTS .... ANNE ARCHER
SHORT CUTS .... ANNIE ROSS
SHORT CUTS .... BRUCE DAVISON
SHORT CUTS .... BUCK HENRY
SHORT CUTS .... CHRIS PENN
SHORT CUTS .... FRANCES McDORMAND
SHORT CUTS .... FRED WARD
SHORT CUTS .... HUEY LEWIS
SHORT CUTS .... JACK LEMMON
SHORT CUTS .... JENNIFER JASON LEIGH
SHORT CUTS .... JULIANNE MOORE
SHORT CUTS .... LILI TAYLOR
SHORT CUTS .... LILY TOMLIN
SHORT CUTS .... LORI SINGER
SHORT CUTS .... LYLE LOVETT
SHORT CUTS .... MADELEINE STOWE
SHORT CUTS .... MATTHEW MODINE
SHORT CUTS .... PETER GALLAGHER
SHORT CUTS .... ROBERT DOWNEY JR.
SHORT CUTS .... TIM ROBBINS
SHORT CUTS .... TOM WAITS
SHORT EYES .... BRUCE DAVISON
SHORT IS THE SUMMER .... BIBI ANDERSSON
SHORT IS THE SUMMER .... BRITT EKLAND
SHORT IS THE SUMMER .... LIV ULLMANN
SHORT TIME .... BARRY CORBIN
SHORT TIME .... DABNEY COLEMAN
SHORT TIME .... JOE PANTOLIANO
SHORT TIME .... MATT FREWER
SHORT TIME .... TERI GARR
SHORT WALK TO DAYLIGHT (TF) .... JAMES BROLIN
SHOT, THE .... VINCENT WARD
SHOT IN THE DARK, A .... PETER SELLERS†
SHOTGUN .... YVONNE DE CARLO
SHOUT .... JOHN TRAVOLTA
SHOUT, THE .... ALAN BATES
SHOUT, THE .... JOHN HURT
SHOUT, THE .... ROBERT STEPHENS
SHOUT, THE .... SUSANNAH YORK
SHOUT, THE .... TIM CURRY
SHOUT AT THE DEVIL .... IAN HOLM
SHOUT AT THE DEVIL .... ROGER MOORE
SHOW BOAT .... AVA GARDNER†
SHOW BOAT .... HOWARD KEEL
SHOW OF FORCE, A .... AMY IRVING
SHOW OF FORCE, A .... ANDY GARCIA
SHOW OF FORCE, A .... KEVIN SPACEY
SHOW OF FORCE, A .... LOU DIAMOND PHILLIPS
SHOW OF FORCE, A .... ROBERT DUVALL
SHOW OF SHOWS, THE .... ANN SOTHERN
SHOWDOWN .... DEAN MARTIN
SHOWDOWN .... SUSAN CLARK
SHOWDOWN AT BOOT HILL .... CHARLES BRONSON
SHOWDOWN IN LITTLE TOKYO .... BRANDON LEE†
SHOWDOWN IN LITTLE TOKYO .... CARY-HIROYUKI TAGAWA
SHOWDOWN IN LITTLE TOKYO .... DOLPH LUNDGREN
SHRIKE, THE .... JOSE FERRER†
SHRIKE, THE .... JUNE ALLYSON
SHRIMP ON THE BARBIE .... CAROLE DAVIS
SHRIMP ON THE BARBIE .... CHEECH MARIN
SHUT MY BIG MOUTH .... LLOYD BRIDGES
SHUTTERED ROOM, THE .... CAROL LYNLEY
SHY PEOPLE .... BARBARA HERSHEY
SHY PEOPLE .... JILL CLAYBURGH
SHY PEOPLE .... MARTHA PLIMPTON
SHY PEOPLE .... MERRITT BUTRICK†
SI C'ÉTAIT A REFAIRE .... ANOUK AIMEE
SI C'ÉTAIT A REFAIRE .... CATHERINE DENEUVE
SI JE SUIS COMME ÇA C'EST LA FAUTE A PAPA .... CATHERINE DENEUVE
SIBLING RIVALRY .... BILL PULLMAN
SIBLING RIVALRY .... CARRIE FISHER
SIBLING RIVALRY .... ED O'NEILL
SIBLING RIVALRY .... JAMI GERTZ
SIBLING RIVALRY .... KIRSTIE ALLEY
SIBLING RIVALRY .... SAM ELLIOTT
SIBLING RIVALRY .... SCOTT BAKULA
SICILIAN, THE .... CHRISTOPHER LAMBERT
SICILIAN, THE .... JOHN TURTURRO

This is not a list of every film ever made or every cast member, only those listed in this directory.

SICILIAN, THE .... JOSS ACKLAND
SICILIAN, THE .... TERENCE STAMP
SICILIAN CONNECTION, THE .... BEN GAZZARA
SID AND NANCY .... CHLOE WEBB
SID AND NANCY .... GARY OLDMAN
SID & NANCY .... DEBBY BISHOP
SID & NANCY .... PERRY BENSON
SIDE BY SIDE (TF) .... MILTON BERLE
SIDE BY SIDE (TF) .... MOREY AMSTERDAM
SIDE BY SIDE (TF) .... SID CAESAR
SIDE OUT .... C. THOMAS HOWELL
SIDE OUT .... CHRIS RYDELL
SIDE OUT .... COURTNEY THORNE-SMITH
SIDE OUT .... HARLEY JANE KOZAK
SIDE OUT .... PETER HORTON
SIDE ROADS .... JEFF SPEAKMAN
SIDE SHOW .... RED BUTTONS
SIDECAR RACERS .... PETER GRAVES
SIDEKICKS (TF) .... BLYTHE DANNER
SIDEKICKS (TF) .... JOHN BECK
SIDEKICKS (TF) .... LOUIS GOSSETT JR.
SIDELONG GLANCES OF A PIGEON KICKER .... LOIS NETTLETON
SIDELONG GLANCES OF A PIGEON KICKER, THE .... ELAINE STRITCH
SIDEWINDER ONE .... MARJOE GORTNER
SIDNEY SHELDON'S BLOODLINE .... AUDREY HEPBURN†
SIDNEY SHELDON'S BLOODLINE .... BEATRICE STRAIGHT
SIDNEY SHELDON'S BLOODLINE .... BEN GAZZARA
SIDNEY SHELDON'S BLOODLINE .... OMAR SHARIF
SIDNEY SHELDON'S RAGE OF ANGELS (MS) .... JACLYN SMITH
SIDNEY SHELDON'S WINDMILLS OF THE GODS (MS) .... CHRISTOPHER CAZENOVE
SIDNEY SHELDON'S WINDMILLS OF THE GODS (MS) .... DAVID AYKROYD
SIDNEY SHELDON'S WINDMILLS OF THE GODS (MS) .... FRANCO NERO
SIDNEY SHELDON'S WINDMILLS OF THE GODS (MS) .... JACLYN SMITH
SIDNEY SHELDON'S WINDMILLS OF THE GODS (MS) .... JEAN-PIERRE AUMONT
SIDNEY SHELDON'S WINDMILLS OF THE GODS (MS) .... ROBERT WAGNER
SIDNEY SHELDON'S WINDMILLS OF THE GODS (MS) .... RUBY DEE
SIDNEY SHORR: A GIRL'S BEST FRIEND (TF) .... TONY RANDALL
SIEGE (TF) .... SYLVIA SIDNEY
SIEGE AT RED RIVER, THE .... VAN JOHNSON
SIEGE OF SYRACUSE, THE .... TINA LOUISE
SIEGFIELD FOLLIES .... CYD CHARISSE
SIERRA .... BURL IVES
SIERRA .... TONY CURTIS
SIERRA BARON .... BRIAN KEITH
SIESTA .... ELLEN BARKIN
SIESTA .... GABRIEL BYRNE
SIESTA .... ISABELLA ROSSELLINI
SIESTA .... JODIE FOSTER
SIESTA .... JULIAN SANDS
SIGN 'O' THE TIMES .... PRINCE
SIGN OF FOUR, THE (TF) .... THORLEY WALTERS†
SIGN OF THE PAGAN .... JACK PALANCE
SIGN OF THE RAM, THE .... PHYLLIS THAXTER
SIGN OF VENUS, THE .... SOPHIA LOREN
SIGNPOST TO MURDER .... JOANNE WOODWARD
SIGNPOST TO MURDER .... STUART WHITMAN
SIGNS OF LIFE .... KATHY BATES
SIGNS OF LIFE .... MARY-LOUISE PARKER
SILAS MARNER (TF) .... JENNY AGUTTER
SILENCE LIKE GLASS .... MARTHA PLIMPTON
SILENCE OF THE HEART (TF) .... CHAD LOWE
SILENCE OF THE HEART (TF) .... DANA HILL
SILENCE OF THE HEART (TF) .... HOWARD HESSEMAN
SILENCE OF THE HEART (TF) .... MARIETTE HARTLEY
SILENCE OF THE LAMBS, THE .... ANTHONY HEALD
SILENCE OF THE LAMBS, THE .... BROOKE SMITH
SILENCE OF THE LAMBS, THE .... CHRIS ISAAK
SILENCE OF THE LAMBS, THE .... DIANE BAKER
SILENCE OF THE LAMBS, THE .... KASI LEMMONS
SILENCE OF THE LAMBS, THE .... SCOTT GLENN
SILENCE OF THE LAMBS, THE .... TED LEVINE
SILENCE OF THE LAMBS, THE ★★ .... ANTHONY HOPKINS
SILENCE OF THE LAMBS, THE ★★ ... JODIE FOSTER
SILENCE OF THE NORTH .... ELLEN BURSTYN
SILENCE OF THE NORTH .... TOM SKERRITT
SILENCE, THE (TF) .... RICHARD THOMAS
SILENCERS, THE .... CYD CHARISSE
SILENCERS, THE .... DEAN MARTIN
SILENCERS, THE .... KARL MALDEN
SILENCERS, THE .... ROBERT WEBBER
SILENCERS, THE .... STELLA STEVENS
SILENT ASSASSINS .... LINDA BLAIR
SILENT FALL .... BEN FAULKNER
SILENT FALL .... JOHN LITHGOW
SILENT FALL .... LINDA HAMILTON
SILENT FALL .... RICHARD DREYFUSS
SILENT FALL .... J. T. WALSH
SILENT FALL .... LIV TYLER
SILENT FLUTE, THE .... DAVID CARRADINE
SILENT GUN, THE (TF) .... JOHN BECK
SILENT GUN, THE (TF) .... LLOYD BRIDGES
SILENT LOVERS, THE (MS) .... BARRY BOSTWICK
SILENT MOVIE .... ANNE BANCROFT
SILENT MOVIE .... BERNADETTE PETERS
SILENT MOVIE .... BURT REYNOLDS
SILENT MOVIE .... DOM DeLUISE
SILENT MOVIE .... HAROLD GOULD
SILENT MOVIE .... JAMES CAAN
SILENT MOVIE .... LIZA MINELLI
SILENT MOVIE .... MARTY FELDMAN†
SILENT MOVIE .... MEL BROOKS
SILENT MOVIE .... PAUL NEWMAN
SILENT MOVIE .... RON CAREY
SILENT MOVIE .... SID CAESAR
SILENT NIGHT, BLOODY NIGHT .... PATRICK O'NEAL†
SILENT NIGHT, EVIL NIGHT .... JOHN SAXON
SILENT NIGHT, EVIL NIGHT/STRANGER IN THE HOUSE .... MARGOT KIDDER
SILENT NIGHT, LONELY NIGHT (TF) .... CARRIE SNODGRESS
SILENT NIGHT, LONELY NIGHT (TF) .... LLOYD BRIDGES
SILENT NIGHT, LONELY NIGHT (TF) .... SHIRLEY JONES
SILENT PARTNER, THE ... CHRISTOPHER PLUMMER
SILENT PARTNER, THE .... ELLIOTT GOULD
SILENT PARTNER, THE .... JOHN CANDY†
SILENT PARTNER, THE .... SUSANNAH YORK
SILENT RAGE .... CHUCK NORRIS
SILENT RAGE .... STEPHEN FURST
SILENT RAGE .... STEVEN KEATS†
SILENT RUNNING .... BRUCE DERN
SILENT SCREAM .... AVERY SCHREIBER
SILENT SCREAM .... YVONNE DE CARLO
SILENT TONGUE .... ALAN BATES
SILENT TONGUE .... BILL IRWIN
SILENT TONGUE .... DAVID SHINER
SILENT TONGUE .... DERMOT MULRONEY
SILENT TONGUE .... JERI ARREDONDO
SILENT TONGUE .... RICHARD HARRIS
SILENT TONGUE .... RIVER PHOENIX†
SILENT TONGUE .... SHEILA TOUSEY
SILENT TONGUE .... TANTOO CARDINAL
SILENT TONGUE .... TIM SCOTT
SILENT VICTORY: THE KITTY O'NEIL STORY (TF) .... COLLEEN DEWHURST†
SILENT VICTORY: THE KITTY O'NEIL STORY (TF) .... BRIAN DENNEHY
SILENT VICTORY: THE KITTY O'NEIL STORY (TF) .... EDWARD ALBERT
SILENT VICTORY: THE KITTY O'NEIL STORY (TF) .... STOCKARD CHANNING
SILENT WITNESS (TF) .... CHRIS NASH
SILENT WITNESS (TF) .... VALERIE BERTINELLI
SILENT WITNESS, THE .... GEORGE KENNEDY
SILK STOCKINGS .... CYD CHARISSE
SILK STOCKINGS .... FRED ASTAIRE†
SILKEN AFFAIR, THE .... SHIRLEY ANNE FIELD
SILKWOOD .... ANTHONY HEALD
SILKWOOD .... BRUCE McGILL
SILKWOOD .... CRAIG T. NELSON
SILKWOOD .... DAVID STRATHAIRN
SILKWOOD .... DIANA SCARWID
SILKWOOD .... FRED WARD
SILKWOOD .... KURT RUSSELL
SILKWOOD .... M. EMMET WALSH
SILKWOOD .... SUDIE BOND
SILKWOOD ★ .... MERYL STREEP
SILKWOOD ✪ .... CHER
SILVER BEARS .... CYBILL SHEPHERD
SILVER BEARS .... DAVID WARNER
SILVER BEARS .... JAY LENO
SILVER BEARS .... JOSS ACKLAND
SILVER BEARS .... LOUIS JOURDAN
SILVER BEARS .... MARTIN BALSAM
SILVER BEARS .... MICHAEL CAINE
SILVER BEARS .... SHANE RIMMER
SILVER BEARS .... STEPHANE AUDRAN
SILVER BEARS .... TOM SMOTHERS
SILVER BULLET .... BILL SMITROVICH
SILVER BULLET .... COREY HAIM
SILVER BULLET .... GARY BUSEY
SILVER BULLET .... LAWRENCE TIERNEY
SILVER CHALICE, THE .... E. G. MARSHALL
SILVER CHALICE, THE .... JACK PALANCE
SILVER CHALICE, THE .... JOSEPH WISEMAN
SILVER CHALICE, THE .... PAUL NEWMAN
SILVER CITY .... YVONNE DE CARLO
SILVER DREAM RACER .... BEAU BRIDGES
SILVER LINING, THE .... MAUREEN O'SULLIVAN
SILVER LODE, THE .... HARRY CAREY JR.
SILVER STREAK .... CLIFTON JAMES
SILVER STREAK .... GENE WILDER
SILVER STREAK .... JILL CLAYBURGH
SILVER STREAK .... NED BEATTY
SILVER STREAK .... RAY WALSTON
SILVER STREAK .... RICHARD KIEL
SILVER STREAK .... RICHARD PRYOR
SILVER STREAK .... SCATMAN CROTHERS†
SILVERADO .... BRIAN DENNEHY
SILVERADO .... DANNY GLOVER
SILVERADO .... JEFF GOLDBLUM
SILVERADO .... JOHN CLEESE
SILVERADO .... KEVIN COSTNER
SILVERADO .... KEVIN KLINE
SILVERADO .... LINDA HUNT
SILVERADO .... ROSANNA ARQUETTE
SILVERADO .... SCOTT GLENN
SIMON .... ALAN ARKIN
SIMON .... FRED GWYNNE†
SIMON .... MADELINE KAHN
SIMPLE TWIST OF FATE, A .... ALAINA MOBLEY
SIMPLE TWIST OF FATE, A .... CATHERINE O'HARA
SIMPLE TWIST OF FATE, A .... GABRIEL BYRNE
SIMPLE TWIST OF FATE, A .... LAURA LINNEY
SIMPLE TWIST OF FATE, A .... STEPHEN BALDWIN
SIMPLE TWIST OF FATE, A .... STEVE MARTIN
SIN OF HAROLD DIDDLEBLOCK, THE .... LIONEL STANDER
SIN OF INNOCENCE (TF) .... BILL BIXBY†
SIN OF INNOCENCE (TF) .... DEE WALLACE STONE
SIN OF INNOCENCE (TF) .... JAMES NAUGHTON
SIN OF INNOCENCE (TF) .... MEGAN POTTER FOLLOWS
SIN OF MADELON CLAUDET, THE ★★ .... HELEN HAYES
SINBAD AND THE EYE OF THE TIGER .... JANE SEYMOUR
SINBAD AND THE EYE OF THE TIGER .... PATRICK WAYNE
SINBAD AND THE EYE OF THE TIGER .... PETER MAYHEW
SINBAD THE SAILOR .... ANTHONY QUINN
SINBAD THE SAILOR .... JANE GREER
SINBAD THE SAILOR .... MAUREEN O'HARA
SINCE YOU WENT AWAY ✪ .... MONTY WOOLLEY†
SINCE YOU WENT AWAY ✪ .... JENNIFER JONES
SINCERELY, CHARLOTTE .... ISABELLE HUPPERT
SINCERELY CHARLOTTE .... NIELS ARESTRUP
SINFUL DAVEY .... ANJELICA HUSTON

† after an actor's name denotes deceased.

SINFUL DAVEY ... JOHN HURT
SINFUL DAVEY ... NIGEL DAVENPORT
SINFUL DAVEY ... ROBERT MORLEY
SING ... GEORGE DICENZO
SING ... JESSICA STEEN
SING ... LORRAINE BRACCO
SING ... LOUISE LASSER
SING ... PATTI LABELLE
SING ... PETER DOBSON
SING ... SUSAN PERETZ
SING AND SWING ... DAVID HEMMINGS
SINGAPORE ... AVA GARDNER†
SINGIN' IN THE RAIN ... CYD CHARISSE
SINGIN' IN THE RAIN ... DEBBIE REYNOLDS
SINGIN' IN THE RAIN ... GENE KELLY
SINGIN' IN THE RAIN ... KATHLEEN FREEMAN
SINGIN' IN THE RAIN ... RITA MORENO
SINGIN' IN THE RAIN ○ ... JEAN HAGEN†
SINGING DETECTIVE, THE (TF) ... DAVID THEWLIS
SINGING MARINE, THE ... JANE WYMAN
SINGING NUN, THE ... CHAD EVERETT
SINGING NUN, THE ... DEBBIE REYNOLDS
SINGING NUN, THE ... GREER GARSON
SINGING NUN, THE ... KATHERINE ROSS
SINGING NUN, THE ... RICARDO MONTALBAN
SINGLE BARS, SINGLE WOMEN (TF) ... CHRISTINE LAHTI
SINGLE BARS, SINGLE WOMEN (TF) ... KEITH GORDON
SINGLE BARS, SINGLE WOMEN (TF) ... SHELLEY HACK
SINGLE BARS, SINGLE WOMEN (TF) ... TONY DANZA
SINGLE PARENT ... SCOTT JACOBY
SINGLE STANDARD, THE ... LILLIAN GISH†
SINGLE WHITE FEMALE ... BRIDGET FONDA
SINGLE WHITE FEMALE ... JENNIFER JASON LEIGH
SINGLE WHITE FEMALE ... PETER FRIEDMAN
SINGLE WHITE FEMALE ... STEPHEN TOBOLOWSKY
SINGLE WHITE FEMALE ... STEVEN WEBER
SINGLE WOMEN, MARRIED MEN (TF) ... JULIE HARRIS
SINGLE WOMEN, MARRIED MEN (TF) ... LEE HORSLEY
SINGLE WOMEN, MARRIED MEN (TF) ... MICHELE LEE
SINGLEHANDED ... WENDY HILLER
SINGLES ... BILL PULLMAN
SINGLES ... BRIDGET FONDA
SINGLES ... CAMPBELL SCOTT
SINGLES ... DEVON RAYMOND
SINGLES ... ERIC STOLTZ
SINGLES ... JIM TRUE
SINGLES ... KYRA SEDGWICK
SINGLES ... MATT DILLON
SINGLES ... SHEILA KELLEY
SINS (MS) ... JOAN COLLINS
SINS (MS) ... TIMOTHY DALTON
SINS OF CASANOVA ... URSULA ANDRESS
SINS OF DORIAN GRAY, THE (TF) ... ANTHONY PERKINS†
SINS OF DORIAN GRAY, THE (TF) ... BELINDA BAUER
SINS OF DORIAN GRAY, THE (TF) ... JOSEPH BOTTOMS
SINS OF DORIAN GRAY, THE (TF) ... MICHAEL IRONSIDE
SINS OF LOLA MONTES, THE ... PETER USTINOV
SINS OF MAN ... DON AMECHE†
SINS OF RACHEL CADE, THE ... ANGIE DICKINSON
SINS OF RACHEL CADE, THE ... ROGER MOORE
SINS OF RACHEL CADE, THE ... WOODY STRODE
SINS OF ROSE BERND, THE ... MARIA SCHELL
SINS OF THE FATHER (TF) ... JAMES COBURN
SIOUX CITY ... LOU DIAMOND PHILLIPS
SIOUX CITY ... MELINDA DILLON
SIOUX CITY ... RALPH WAITE
SIOUX CITY ... SALLI RICHARDSON
SIR ARNE'S TREASURE ... BIBI ANDERSSON
SIRENS ... ELLE MACPHERSON
SIRENS ... HUGH GRANT
SIRENS ... KATE FISCHER
SIRENS ... PORTIA DE ROSSI
SIRENS ... SAM NEILL
SIRINGO ... BRAD JOHNSON
SIRINGO ... CHAD LOVE
SIRINGO ... CRYSTAL BERNARD
SIRINGO ... KEITH SZARABAJKA
SIRINGO ... STEPHEN MACHT
SISTER ACT ... HARVEY KEITEL
SISTER ACT ... KATHY NAJIMY
SISTER ACT ... MAGGIE SMITH
SISTER ACT ... MARY WICKES
SISTER ACT ... MIKE JOLLY
SISTER ACT ... ROBERT G. MIRANDA
SISTER ACT ... WENDY MAKKENA
SISTER ACT ... WHOOPI GOLDBERG
SISTER ACT 2: BACK IN THE HABIT ... BARNARD HUGHES
SISTER ACT 2: BACK IN THE HABIT ... JAMES COBURN
SISTER ACT 2: BACK IN THE HABIT ... KATHY NAJIMY
SISTER ACT 2: BACK IN THE HABIT ... LAURYN HILL
SISTER ACT 2: BACK IN THE HABIT ... MAGGIE SMITH
SISTER ACT 2: BACK IN THE HABIT ... MARY WICKES
SISTER ACT 2: BACK IN THE HABIT ... MICHAEL JETER
SISTER ACT 2: BACK IN THE HABIT ... WENDY MAKKENA
SISTER ACT 2: BACK IN THE HABIT ... WHOOPI GOLDBERG
SISTER ISLAND ... CARLENE CROCKETT
SISTER ISLAND ... ELLEN CRAWFORD
SISTER ISLAND ... ERIN BUCHANAN
SISTER ISLAND ... GUY BOYD
SISTER ISLAND ... KAREN BLACK
SISTER ISLAND ... KATHLEEN YORK
SISTER KENNEY ... DEAN JAGGER†
SISTER KENNY ★ ... ROSALAND RUSSELL†
SISTER, SISTER ... ERIC STOLTZ
SISTER, SISTER ... JENNIFER JASON LEIGH
SISTER, SISTER ... JUDITH IVEY
SISTERS ... BARNARD HUGHES
SISTERS ... CHARLES DURNING
SISTERS ... MARGOT KIDDER
SISTERS, THE ... BETTE DAVIS†
SISTERS, THE ... LILLIAN GISH†
SITTING DUCKS ... HENRY JAGLOM
SITTING PRETTY ... MAUREEN O'HARA
SITTING PRETTY ★ ... CLIFTON WEBB†
SITTING TARGET ... EDWARD WOODWARD
SITTING TARGET ... FREDDIE JONES
SITTING TARGET ... JILL ST. JOHN
SITUATION HOPELESS—BUT NOT SERIOUS ... ALEC GUINNESS
SITUATION HOPELESS—BUT NOT SERIOUS ... ROBERT REDFORD
SITUATION NORMAL ALL FOULED UP ... PETER FALK
SIX AGAINST THE ROCK (TF) ... CHARLES HAID
SIX AGAINST THE ROCK (TF) ... DAVID CARRADINE
SIX AGAINST THE ROCK (TF) ... DAVID MORSE
SIX AGAINST THE ROCK (TF) ... HOWARD HESSEMAN
SIX AGAINST THE ROCK (TF) ... JAN-MICHAEL VINCENT
SIX AGAINST THE ROCK (TF) ... RICHARD DYSART
SIX BRIDGES TO CROSS ... TONY CURTIS
SIX DEGREES OF SEPARATION ... BRUCE DAVISON
SIX DEGREES OF SEPARATION ... DONALD SUTHERLAND
SIX DEGREES OF SEPARATION ... IAN MCKELLEN
SIX DEGREES OF SEPARATION ... MARY BETH HURT
SIX DEGREES OF SEPARATION ... RICHARD MASUR
SIX DEGREES OF SEPARATION ... WILL SMITH
SIX DEGREES OF SEPARATION ★ ... STOCKARD CHANNING
SIX MILLION DOLLAR MAN, THE (TF) ... LEE MAJORS
SIX MILLION DOLLAR MAN, THE (TF) ... MARTIN BALSAM
SIX MILLION DOLLAR MAN, THE (TF) ... RICHARD ANDERSON
SIX OF A KIND ... GEORGE BURNS
SIX PACK ... KENNY ROGERS
SIX PACK ANNIE ... STUBBY KAYE
SIX WEEKS ... DUDLEY MOORE
SIX WEEKS ... KATHERINE HEALY
SIX WEEKS ... MARY TYLER MOORE
SIX-PACK ANNIE ... BRUCE BOXLEITNER
SIX-SIDED TRIANGLE ... NICOL WILLIAMSON
SIXTEEN ... MERCEDES McCAMBRIDGE
SIXTEEN CANDLES ... ANTHONY MICHAEL HALL
SIXTEEN CANDLES ... BILLIE BIRD
SIXTEEN CANDLES ... JOAN CUSAK
SIXTEEN CANDLES ... JOHN CUSAK
SIXTEEN CANDLES ... JUSTIN HENRY
SIXTEEN CANDLES ... MOLLY RINGWALD
SIXTEEN CANDLES ... PAUL DOOLEY
SIXTH AND MAIN ... LESLIE NIELSEN
SIXTH AND MAIN ... RODDY McDOWALL
SIZZLE BEACH, U.S.A. ... KEVIN COSTNER
SKAG (TF) ... PIPER LAURIE
SKATEBOARD ... ALLEN GARFIELD
SKATEBOARD KID II, THE ... ANDREA BARBER
SKATEBOARD KID II, THE ... ANDREW KEEGAN
SKATEBOARD KID II, THE ... ANDREW STEVENS
SKATEBOARD KID II, THE ... BROOKE STANLEY
SKATEBOARD KID II, THE ... BRUCE DAVISON
SKATEBOARD KID II, THE ... DEE WALLACE STONE
SKATEBOARD KID II, THE ... JOHNNY WILLIAMS
SKATEBOARD KID II, THE ... PABLO IRLANDO
SKATEBOARD KID II, THE ... TRENTON KNIGHT
SKATEBOARD KID II, THE ... TURHAN BAY
SKATEBOARD KID II, THE ... WILLIE SANTOS
SKATETOWN, U.S.A. ... BILLY BARTY
SKATETOWN, U.S.A. ... PATRICK SWAYZE
SKETCH ARTIST (CTF) ... DREW BARRYMORE
SKI BUM, THE ... CHARLOTTE RAMPLING
SKI BUM, THE ... DIMITRA ARLYS
SKI LIFT TO DEATH (TF) ... DEBORAH RAFFIN
SKI LIFT TO DEATH (TF) ... DON JOHNSON
SKI PARTY ... DICK MILLER
SKIDOO ... AUSTIN PENDLETON
SKIDOO ... BURGESS MEREDITH
SKIDOO ... FRANKIE AVALON
SKIDOO ... JOHN PHILLIP LAW
SKIDOO ... MICHAEL CONSTANTINE
SKIN DEEP ... ALYSON REED
SKIN DEEP ... BRYAN GENESSE
SKIN DEEP ... CHELSEA FIELD
SKIN DEEP ... DEE DEE RESCHER
SKIN DEEP ... DENISE CROSBY
SKIN DEEP ... DON GORDON
SKIN DEEP ... HEIDI PAINE
SKIN DEEP ... JOEL BROOKS
SKIN DEEP ... JOHN RITTER
SKIN DEEP ... JULIANNE PHILLIPS
SKIN DEEP ... MICHAEL KIDD
SKIN DEEP ... NINA FOCH
SKIN DEEP ... PETER DONAT
SKIN DEEP ... VINCENT GARDENIA†
SKIN GAME ... ED ASNER
SKIN GAME ... JAMES GARNER
SKIN GAME ... SUSAN CLARK
SKIN GAME, THE ... HENRY JONES
SKINHEADS ... BARBARA BAIN
SKINHEADS ... CHUCK CONNORS†
SKIP TRACER ... JOE PANTOLIANO
SKIPPY ★ ... JACKIE COOPER
SKIRTS AHOY! ... DEBBIE REYNOLDS
SKOKIE (TF) ... ROBIN BARTLETT
SKULL, THE ... MICHAEL GOUGH
SKULLDUGGERY ... BURT REYNOLDS
SKULLDUGGERY ... CHIPS RAFFERTY†
SKULLDUGGERY ... EDWARD FOX
SKULLDUGGERY ... RHYS WILLIAMS†
SKULLDUGGERY ... SUSAN CLARK
SKULLDUGGERY ... WILFRID HYDE-WHITE†

Sk-Sm
FILM ACTORS GUIDE
INDEX OF FILM TITLES

SKULLDUGGERY .... WILLIAM MARSHALL
SKY BANDITS .... RONALD LACEY
SKY IS FALLING, THE .... CARROLL BAKER
SKY IS FALLING, THE .... DENNIS HOPPER
SKY RIDERS .... JAMES COBURN
SKY RIDERS .... JOHN BECK
SKY RIDERS .... ROBERT CULP
SKY RIDERS .... SUSANNAH YORK
SKY WEST AND CROOKED .... GEOFFREY BAYLDON
SKY WEST AND CROOKED .... HAYLEY MILLS
SKY'S NO LIMIT, THE (TF) .... SHARON GLESS
SKY'S THE LIMIT, THE (TF) .... ANNE ARCHER
SKYJACKED .... CHARLTON HESTON
SKYJACKED .... CLAUDE AKINS†
SKYJACKED .... JAMES BROLIN
SKYJACKED .... MARIETTE HARTLEY
SKYJACKED .... MIKE HENRY
SKYJACKED .... SUSAN DEY
SKYLARK (TF) .... CHRISTOPHER WALKEN
SKYLARK (TF) .... GLENN CLOSE
SKYLINE .... MAUREEN O'SULLIVAN
SKYSCRAPER SOULS .... MAUREEN O'SULLIVAN
SLAGSKAMPEN .... DENNIS HOPPER
SLAM DANCE .... DON OPPER
SLAM DANCE .... HARRY DEAN STANTON
SLAM DANCE .... JOHN DOE
SLAM DANCE .... MILLIE PERKINS
SLAM DANCE .... TOM HULCE
SLAM DANCE .... VIRGINIA MADSEN
SLAMDANCE .... ADAM ANT
SLAMMER .... BRUCE DAVISON
SLAMS, THE .... JIM BROWN
SLANDER .... VAN JOHNSON
SLAP SHOT .... JENNIFER WARREN
SLAP SHOT .... LINDSAY CROUSE
SLAP SHOT .... MELINDA DILLON
SLAP SHOT .... MICHAEL ONTKEAN
SLAP SHOT .... PAUL DOOLEY
SLAP SHOT .... PAUL NEWMAN
SLAP, THE .... ISABELLE ADJANI
SLAPSTICK .... JERRY LEWIS
SLAPSTICK .... MADELINE KAHN
SLAPSTICK .... MERY GRIFFIN
SLAPSTICK .... NORIYUKI "PAT" MORITA
SLAPSTICK OF ANOTHER KIND .... JERRY LEWIS
SLAPSTICK OF ANOTHER KIND .... MADELINE KAHN
SLAPSTICK OF ANOTHER KIND .... MERY GRIFFIN
SLAPSTICK OF ANOTHER KIND .... NORIYUKI "PAT" MORITA
SLASHER, THE .... JOAN COLLINS
SLATE, WYN AND ME .... SIGRID THORNTON
SLATTERY'S HURRICANE .... RICHARD WIDMARK
SLAUGHTER .... JIM BROWN
SLAUGHTER .... RIP TORN
SLAUGHTER .... STELLA STEVENS
SLAUGHTER ON TENTH AVENUE .... WALTER MATTHAU
SLAUGHTERHOUSE FIVE .... JOHN DEHNER†
SLAUGHTERHOUSE FIVE .... PERRY KING
SLAUGHTERHOUSE FIVE .... RON LEIBMAN
SLAUGHTERHOUSE FIVE .... VALERIE PERRINE
SLAUGHTER'S BIG RIP-OFF .... DON STROUD
SLAUGHTER'S BIG RIP-OFF .... JIM BROWN
SLAVE GIRL .... YVONNE DE CARLO
SLAVE OF THE CANNIBAL GOD .... STACY KEACH
SLAVERS .... BRITT EKLAND
SLAVES .... DAVID HUDDLESTON
SLAVES .... JULIUS HARRIS
SLAVES .... OSSIE DAVIS
SLAVES OF NEW YORK .... ADAM COLEMAN HOWARD
SLAVES OF NEW YORK .... ANTHONY LaPAGLIA
SLAVES OF NEW YORK .... BERNADETTE PETERS
SLAVES OF NEW YORK .... CHRIS SARANDON
SLAVES OF NEW YORK .... MADELINE POTTER
SLAVES OF NEW YORK .... MARY BETH HURT
SLAVES OF NEW YORK .... MERCEDES RUEHL
SLAVES OF NEW YORK .... NICK CORRI
SLEEP MY LOVE .... DON AMECHE†
SLEEP MY LOVE .... RAYMOND BURR†
SLEEP WITH ME .... ADRIENNE SHELLY
SLEEP WITH ME .... AMARYLLIS BORREGO
SLEEP WITH ME .... CRAIG SHEFFER
SLEEP WITH ME .... DAVID KRIEGEL
SLEEP WITH ME .... DEAN CAMERON
SLEEP WITH ME .... ERIC STOLTZ
SLEEP WITH ME .... JOEY LAUREN ADAMS
SLEEP WITH ME .... JUNE LOCKHART
SLEEP WITH ME .... LEWIS ARQUETTE
SLEEP WITH ME .... MEG TILLY
SLEEP WITH ME .... PARKER POSEY
SLEEP WITH ME .... QUENTIN TARANTINO
SLEEP WITH ME .... SUSAN TRAYLOR
SLEEP WITH ME .... TEGAN WEST
SLEEP WITH ME .... THOMAS GIBSON
SLEEP WITH ME .... TODD FIELD
SLEEP WITH ME .... VANESSA ANGEL
SLEEPER .... DIANE KEATON
SLEEPER .... JOHN BECK
SLEEPER .... WOODY ALLEN
SLEEPING CAR TO TRIESTE .... DAVID TOMLINSON
SLEEPING DOGS .... SAM NEILL
SLEEPING TIGER, THE .... ALEXIS SMITH†
SLEEPING WITH THE ENEMY .... JULIA ROBERTS
SLEEPING WITH THE ENEMY .... KEVIN ANDERSON
SLEEPING WITH THE ENEMY .... PATRICK BERGIN
SLEEPLESS IN SEATTLE .... BILL PULLMAN
SLEEPLESS IN SEATTLE .... CAREY LOWELL
SLEEPLESS IN SEATTLE .... GABY HOFFMAN
SLEEPLESS IN SEATTLE .... MEG RYAN
SLEEPLESS IN SEATTLE .... RITA WILSON
SLEEPLESS IN SEATTLE .... ROB REINER
SLEEPLESS IN SEATTLE .... ROSIE O'DONNELL
SLEEPLESS IN SEATTLE .... ROSS MALINGER
SLEEPLESS IN SEATTLE .... TOM HANKS
SLEEPWALKERS .... MARK HAMILL
SLENDER THREAD, THE .... ANNE BANCROFT
SLENDER THREAD, THE .... DABNEY COLEMAN
SLENDER THREAD, THE .... ED ASNER
SLENDER THREAD, THE .... SIDNEY POITIER
SLENDER THREAD, THE .... STEVEN HILL
SLENDER THREAD, THE .... TELLY SAVALAS†
SLEUTH ★ .... LAURENCE OLIVIER†
SLEUTH ★ .... MICHAEL CAINE
SLIGHTLY DANGEROUS .... LANA TURNER
SLIGHTLY FRENCH .... DON AMECHE†
SLIGHTLY FRENCH .... DOROTHY LAMOUR
SLIGHTLY PREGNANT MAN, A .... CATHERINE DENEUVE
SLIM .... JANE WYMAN
SLIM CARTER .... BEN JOHNSON
SLIPPER AND THE ROSE: THE STORY OF CINDERELLA, THE .... RICHARD CHAMBERLAIN
SLIPSTREAM .... MARK HAMILL
SLITHER .... ALLEN GARFIELD
SLITHER .... JAMES CAAN
SLITHER .... LOUISE LASSER
SLITHER .... PETER BOYLE
SLITHER .... SALLY KELLERMAN
SLIVER .... AMANDA FOREMAN
SLIVER .... C. C. H. POUNDER
SLIVER .... COLLEEN CAMP
SLIVER .... KEENE CURTIS
SLIVER .... MARTIN LANDAU
SLIVER .... NINA FOCH
SLIVER .... POLLY WALKER
SLIVER .... SHARON STONE
SLIVER .... TOM BERENGER
SLIVER .... TONY PECK
SLIVER .... WILLIAM BALDWIN
SLOW BURN (CTF) .... BEVERLY D'ANGELO
SLOW BURN (CTF) .... ERIC ROBERTS
SLOW DANCING IN THE BIG CITY .... PAUL SORVINO
SLUGGER'S WIFE, THE .... MICHAEL O'KEEFE
SLUGGER'S WIFE, THE .... RANDY QUAID
SLUGGER'S WIFE, THE .... REBECCA DE MORNAY
SLUMBER PARTY '57 .... DEBRA WINGER
SMALL BACK ROOM, THE .... MICHAEL GOUGH
SMALL BACK ROOM, THE .... ROBERT MORLEY
SMALL CIRCLE OF FRIENDS, A .... BRAD DAVIS†
SMALL CIRCLE OF FRIENDS, A .... JAMESON PARKER
SMALL CIRCLE OF FRIENDS, A .... KAREN ALLEN
SMALL SACRIFICES (MS) .... FARRAH FAWCETT
SMALL SACRIFICES (MS) .... GORDON CLAPP
SMALL SACRIFICES (MS) .... JOHN SHEA
SMALL SACRIFICES (MS) .... RYAN O'NEAL
SMALL TOWN GIRL .... JAMES STEWART
SMALL TOWN IN TEXAS, A .... BO HOPKINS
SMALL TOWN IN TEXAS, A .... SUSAN GEORGE
SMALL TOWN IN TEXAS, A .... TIMOTHY BOTTOMS
SMALL VOICE, THE .... HOWARD KEEL
SMALL WORLD OF SAMMY LEE, THE .... ROBERT STEPHENS
SMART ALEC .... DAVID HEDISON
SMART BLONDE .... JANE WYMAN
SMARTEST GIRL IN TOWN, THE .... ANN SOTHERN
SMASH-UP .... EDDIE ALBERT
SMASH UP - THE STORY OF A WOMAN ★ .... SUSAN HAYWARD†
SMASH-UP ON INTERSTATE 5 (TF) .... DONNA MILLS
SMASH-UP ON INTERSTATE 5 (TF) .... ROBERT CONRAD
SMASH-UP ON INTERSTATE 5 (TF) .... TOMMY LEE JONES
SMASH-UP—THE STORY OF A WOMAN .... EDDIE ALBERT
SMASHING THE MONEY RING .... RONALD REAGAN
SMASHING THE SPY RING .... RALPH BELLAMY†
SMASHING TIME .... LYNN REDGRAVE
SMASHING TIME .... MICHAEL YORK
SMASHING TIME .... VANESSA REDGRAVE
SMILE .... ANNETTE O'TOOLE
SMILE .... BRUCE DERN
SMILE .... COLLEEN CAMP
SMILE .... GEOFFREY LEWIS
SMILE .... MELANIE GRIFFITH
SMILE .... MICHAEL KIDD
SMILE .... NICHOLAS PRYOR
SMILES OF A SUMMER NIGHT .... BIBI ANDERSSON
SMILEY'S PEOPLE (MS) .... ALEC GUINNESS
SMILEY'S PEOPLE (MS) .... BERNARD HEPTON
SMILING GHOST, THE .... ALEXIS SMITH†
SMOKE .... ASHLEY JUDD
SMOKE .... EARL HOLLIMAN
SMOKE .... FOREST WHITAKER
SMOKE .... HARVEY KEITEL
SMOKE .... KAY LENZ
SMOKE .... NED BEATTY
SMOKE .... STOCKARD CHANNING
SMOKE .... WILLIAM HURT
SMOKE JUMPERS .... RICHARD WIDMARK
SMOKE SIGNAL .... PIPER LAURIE
SMOKEY AND THE BANDIT .... BURT REYNOLDS
SMOKEY AND THE BANDIT .... JACKIE GLEASON†
SMOKEY AND THE BANDIT .... JERRY REED
SMOKEY AND THE BANDIT .... MIKE HENRY
SMOKEY AND THE BANDIT .... PAT McCORMICK
SMOKEY AND THE BANDIT .... PAUL WILLIAMS
SMOKEY AND THE BANDIT .... SALLY FIELD
SMOKEY AND THE BANDIT II .... BURT REYNOLDS
SMOKEY AND THE BANDIT II .... DAVID HUDDLESTON
SMOKEY AND THE BANDIT II .... DOM DeLUISE
SMOKEY AND THE BANDIT II .... JACKIE GLEASON†
SMOKEY AND THE BANDIT II .... JERRY REED
SMOKEY AND THE BANDIT II .... JOHN ANDERSON
SMOKEY AND THE BANDIT II .... MIKE HENRY
SMOKEY AND THE BANDIT II .... PAT McCORMICK
SMOKEY AND THE BANDIT II .... PAUL WILLIAMS
SMOKEY AND THE BANDIT II .... SALLY FIELD
SMOKEY AND THE BANDIT 3 .... BURT REYNOLDS
SMOKEY AND THE BANDIT 3 .... COLLEEN CAMP
SMOKEY AND THE BANDIT 3 .... JACKIE GLEASON†
SMOKEY AND THE BANDIT 3 .... JERRY REED
SMOKEY AND THE BANDIT 3 .... MIKE HENRY
SMOKEY AND THE BANDIT 3 .... PAT McCORMICK
SMOKEY AND THE BANDIT 3 .... PAUL WILLIAMS
SMOKY .... BURL IVES
SMOKY .... HOYT AXTON
SMOKY .... KATHY JURADO
SMOKY MOUNTAIN CHRISTMAS, A (TF) .... DOLLY PARTON
SMOKY MOUNTAIN CHRISTMAS, A (TF) .... JOHN RITTER

† after an actor's name denotes deceased.

INDEX OF FILM TITLES

SMOOTH TALK .... ELIZABETH BERRIDGE
SMOOTH TALK .... LAURA DERN
SMOOTH TALK .... LEVON HELM
SMOOTH TALK .... MARY KAY PLACE
SMOOTH TALK .... TREAT WILLIAMS
SMORGASBORD .... DICK BUTKUS
SMORGASBORD .... HERB EDELMAN
SMORGASBORD .... JERRY LEWIS
SMUGGLERS, THE (TF) .... CAROL LYNLEY
SNAFU .... CONRAD JANIS
SNAKE PIT, THE .... CELESTE HOLM
SNAKE PIT, THE ★ .... OLIVIA DE HAVILLAND
SNAPPER, THE .... COLM MEANEY
SNAPPER, THE .... KAREN WOODLEY
SNAPPER, THE .... PAT LAFFAN
SNAPPER, THE .... RUTH McCABE
SNAPPER, THE .... TINA KELLEGHER
SNAPSHOT .... SIGRID THORNTON
SNEAKERS .... BEN KINGSLEY
SNEAKERS .... DAN AYKROYD
SNEAKERS .... DAVID STRATHAIRN
SNEAKERS .... GEORGE HEARN
SNEAKERS .... JAMES EARL JONES
SNEAKERS .... MARY McDONNELL
SNEAKERS .... RIVER PHOENIX†
SNEAKERS .... ROBERT REDFORD
SNEAKERS .... SIDNEY POITIER
SNIPER .... BILLY ZANE
SNIPER .... J. T. WALSH
SNIPER .... TOM BERENGER
SNIPER, THE .... RICHARD KILEY
SNOOP SISTERS, THE (TF) .... HELEN HAYES
SNOW GOOSE, THE (TF) .... JENNY AGUTTER
SNOW GOOSE, THE (TF) .... RICHARD HARRIS
SNOW KILL (CTF) .... CLAYTON ROHNER
SNOW KILL (CTF) .... PATTI D'ARBANVILLE
SNOW KILL (CTF) .... TERRENCE KNOX
SNOW TREASURE .... JAMES FRANCISCUS†
SNOWBALL EXPRESS .... DEAN JONES
SNOWBALL EXPRESS .... DICK VAN PATTEN
SNOWBALL EXPRESS .... HARRY MORGAN
SNOWBALL EXPRESS .... MARY WICKES
SNOWMAN/CHALLENGE TO SURVIVE .... WILLIAM SHATNER
SNOWS OF KILIMANJARO, THE .... AVA GARDNER†
SNOWS OF KILIMANJARO, THE .... GREGORY PECK
SO BIG .... BARBARA STANWYCK†
SO BIG .... BETTE DAVIS†
SO BIG .... JANE WYMAN
SO BIG .... STEVE FORREST
SO CLOSE TO LIFE .... ERLAND JOSEPHSON
SO DEAR TO MY HEART .... BURL IVES
SO DEAR TO MY HEART .... HARRY CAREY JR.
SO EVIL MY LOVE .... GERALDINE FITZGERALD
SO FINE .... JACK WARDEN
SO FINE .... LENKA PETERSON
SO FINE .... RICHARD KIEL
SO FINE .... RYAN O'NEAL
SO GOES MY LOVE .... DON AMECHE†
SO I MARRIED AN AXE MURDERER .... ALAN ARKIN
SO I MARRIED AN AXE MURDERER .... AMANDA PLUMMER
SO I MARRIED AN AXE MURDERER .... ANTHONY LaPAGLIA
SO I MARRIED AN AXE MURDERER .... BRENDA FRICKER
SO I MARRIED AN AXE MURDERER .... CHARLES GRODIN
SO I MARRIED AN AXE MURDERER .... CHRIS ROCK
SO I MARRIED AN AXE MURDERER .... MIKE MYERS
SO I MARRIED AN AXE MURDERER .... NANCY TRAVIS
SO LITTLE TIME .... MARIA SCHELL
SO LONG AT THE FAIR .... DAVID TOMLINSON
SO LONG AT THE FAIR .... JEAN SIMMONS
SO ODER SO IST DAS LEBEN .... MARIA SCHELL
SO PROUDLY WE HAIL! .... YVONNE DE CARLO
SO PROUDLY WE HAIL (TF) .... DAVID SOUL
SO PROUDLY WE HAIL (TF) .... EDWRAD HERRMANN
SO PROUDLY WE HAIL (TF) .... GLORIA CARLIN
SO THIS IS LONDON .... MAUREEN O'SULLIVAN
SO THIS IS PARIS .... TONY CURTIS
SO WELL REMEMBERED .... JOHN MILLS
SO WELL REMEMBERED .... MARTHA SCOTT
SO YOUNG SO BAD .... ANNE JACKSON
SO YOUNG, SO BAD .... RITA MORENO
SOAK THE RICH .... LIONEL STANDER
SOAP BOX DERBY .... MICHAEL CRAWFORD
SOAPDISH .... CARRIE FISHER
SOAPDISH .... CATHY MORIARTY
SOAPDISH .... ELISABETH SHUE
SOAPDISH .... FINOLA HUGHES
SOAPDISH .... GARRY MARSHALL
SOAPDISH .... JOHN TESH
SOAPDISH .... KATHY NAJIMY
SOAPDISH .... KEVIN KLINE
SOAPDISH .... LEEZA GIBBONS
SOAPDISH .... PAUL JOHANSSON
SOAPDISH .... ROBERT CAMILLETTI
SOAPDISH .... ROBERT DOWNEY JR.
SOAPDISH .... SALLY FIELD
SOAPDISH .... STEPHEN NICHOLS
SOAPDISH .... TERI HATCHER
SOAPDISH .... WHOOPI GOLDBERG
SODOM AND GOMORRAH .... ANOUK AIMEE
SOFT BEDS AND HARD BATTLES .... LILA KEDROVA
SOGGY BOTTOM USA .... LOIS NETTLETON
SOL MADRID .... DAVID McCALLUM
SOL MADRID .... PAT HINGLE
SOL MADRID .... RICARDO MONTALBAN
SOL MADRID .... RIP TORN
SOL MADRID .... STELLA STEVENS
SOL MADRID .... TELLY SAVALAS†
SOLARBABIES .... CHARLES DURNING
SOLARBABIES .... JAMES LE GROS
SOLARBABIES .... JAMI GERTZ
SOLARBABIES .... LUKAS HAAS
SOLARBABIES .... RICHARD JORDAN†
SOLARBABIES .... SARAH DOUGLAS
SOLD FOR MARRIAGE .... LILLIAN GISH†
SOLDIER, THE .... KEN WAHL
SOLDIER BLUE .... CANDICE BERGEN
SOLDIER BLUE .... DONALD PLEASENCE
SOLDIER BLUE .... JOHN ANDERSON
SOLDIER BLUE (TF) .... PETER STRAUSS
SOLDIER IN THE RAIN .... ADAM WEST
SOLDIER IN THE RAIN .... JACKIE GLEASON†
SOLDIER IN THE RAIN .... STEVE McQUEEN†
SOLDIER IN THE RAIN .... TOM POSTON
SOLDIER IN THE RAIN .... TONY BILL
SOLDIER IN THE RAIN .... TUESDAY WELD
SOLDIER OF ORANGE .... RUTGER HAUER
SOLDIERS THREE .... DAN O'HERLIHY
SOLDIERS THREE .... DAVID NIVEN†
SOLDIER'S STORY, A .... DENZEL WASHINGTON
SOLDIER'S STORY, A .... HOWARD E. ROLLINS JR.
SOLDIER'S STORY, A .... PATTI LABELLE
SOLDIER'S STORY, A .... ROBERT TOWNSEND
SOLEIL ROUGE .... CHARLES BRONSON
SOLEN BABIES (CTF) .... MARY TYLER MOORE
SOLO FOR SPARROW .... MICHAEL CAINE
SOMBRERO .... CYD CHARISSE
SOMBRERO .... NINA FOCH
SOMBRERO .... RICARDO MONTALBAN
SOMBRERO .... YVONNE DE CARLO
SOME CALL IT LOVING .... RICHARD PRYOR
SOME CAME RUNNING .... DEAN MARTIN
SOME CAME RUNNING .... FRANK SINATRA
SOME CAME RUNNING ★ .... SHIRLEY MacLAINE
SOME GIRLS .... JENNIFER CONNELLY
SOME GIRLS DO .... JOANNA LUMLEY
SOME KIND OF A NUT .... DICK VAN DYKE
SOME KIND OF HERO .... MARGOT KIDDER
SOME KIND OF HERO .... RICHARD PRYOR
SOME KIND OF NUT .... ANGIE DICKINSON
SOME KIND OF WONDERFUL .... CRAIG SHEFFER
SOME KIND OF WONDERFUL .... ELIAS KOTEAS
SOME KIND OF WONDERFUL .... ERIC STOLTZ
SOME KIND OF WONDERFUL .... JOHN ASHTON
SOME KIND OF WONDERFUL .... LEA THOMPSON
SOME KIND OF WONDERFUL .... MARY STUART MASTERSON
SOME KIND OF WONDERFUL .... MOLLY HAGAN
SOME LIKE IT HOT .... BOB HOPE
SOME LIKE IT HOT .... GEORGE RAFT†
SOME LIKE IT HOT .... GRACE LEE WHITNEY
SOME LIKE IT HOT .... MARILYN MONROE†
SOME LIKE IT HOT .... NEHEMIAH PERSOFF
SOME LIKE IT HOT .... TONY CURTIS
SOME LIKE IT HOT ★ .... JACK LEMMON
SOME PEOPLE .... DAVID HEMMINGS
SOMEBODY HAS TO SHOOT THE PICTURE (CTF) .... ANDRE BRAUGHER
SOMEBODY HAS TO SHOOT THE PICTURE (CTF) .... ARLISS HOWARD
SOMEBODY HAS TO SHOOT THE PICTURE (CTF) .... BONNIE BEDELIA
SOMEBODY HAS TO SHOOT THE PICTURE (CTF) .... ROBERT CARRADINE
SOMEBODY HAS TO SHOOT THE PICTURE (CTF) .... ROY SCHEIDER
SOMEBODY KILLED HER HUSBAND .... FARRAH FAWCETT
SOMEBODY KILLED HER HUSBAND .... JEFF BRIDGES
SOMEBODY KILLED HER HUSBAND .... TAMMY GRIMES
SOMEBODY UP THERE LIKES ME .... EILEEN HECKART
SOMEBODY UP THERE LIKES ME .... PATTY DUKE
SOMEBODY UP THERE LIKES ME .... PAUL NEWMAN
SOMEBODY UP THERE LIKES ME .... ROBERT LOGGIA
SOMEONE BEHIND THE DOOR .... ANTHONY PERKINS†
SOMEONE BEHIND THE DOOR .... CHARLES BRONSON
SOMEONE I TOUCHED (TF) .... GLYNNIS O'CONNOR
SOMEONE I TOUCHED (TF) .... LENKA PETERSON
SOMEONE TO LOVE .... HENRY JAGLOM
SOMEONE TO LOVE .... MICHAEL EMIL
SOMEONE TO WATCH OVER ME .... JERRY ORBACH
SOMEONE TO WATCH OVER ME .... LORRAINE BRACCO
SOMEONE TO WATCH OVER ME .... MIMI ROGERS
SOMEONE TO WATCH OVER ME .... TOM BERENGER
SOMEONE'S WATCHING ME! (TF) .... ADRIENNE BARBEAU
SOMEONE'S WATCHING ME! (TF) .... LAUREN HUTTON
SOMETHING ABOUT AMELIA (TF) .... GLENN CLOSE
SOMETHING ABOUT AMELIA (TF) .... ROXANA ZAL
SOMETHING ABOUT AMELIA (TF) .... TED DANSON
SOMETHING BIG .... ALBERT SALMI†
SOMETHING BIG .... BEN JOHNSON
SOMETHING BIG .... BRIAN KEITH
SOMETHING BIG .... DEAN MARTIN
SOMETHING BIG .... HARRY CAREY JR.
SOMETHING BIG .... JOYCE VAN PATTEN
SOMETHING EVIL (TF) .... RALPH BELLAMY†
SOMETHING EVIL (TF) .... SANDY DENNIS†
SOMETHING FOR A LONELY MAN (TF) .... SUSAN CLARK
SOMETHING FOR EVERYONE .... ANGELA LANSBURY
SOMETHING FOR EVERYONE .... MICHAEL YORK
SOMETHING FOR JOEY (TF) .... KATHLEEN BELLER
SOMETHING FOR JOEY (TF) .... SCOTT BAIO
SOMETHING FOR JOEY (TF) .... STEVE GUTTENBERG
SOMETHING FOR THE BIRDS .... PATRICIA NEAL
SOMETHING FOR THE BOYS .... RORY CALHOUN
SOMETHING IN COMMON (TF) .... DON MURRAY
SOMETHING IN COMMON (TF) .... ELI WALLACH
SOMETHING IN COMMON (TF) .... ELLEN BURSTYN
SOMETHING IN COMMON (TF) .... PATRICK CASSIDY
SOMETHING IN COMMON (TF) .... TUESDAY WELD
SOMETHING IS OUT THERE .... PAUL MANTEE
SOMETHING IS OUT THERE .... RICHARD JAECKEL
SOMETHING IS OUT THERE (MS) .... GEORGE DZUNDZA
SOMETHING IS OUT THERE (MS) .... GREGORY SIERRA

This is not a list of every film ever made or every cast member, only those listed in this directory.

SOMETHING IS
   OUT THERE (MS) .... MARYAM D'ABO
SOMETHING IS OUT THERE (TF) .... KIM DELANEY
SOMETHING OF VALUE .... ROCK HUDSON†
SOMETHING OF VALUE .... SIDNEY POITIER
SOMETHING OF VALUE .... WENDY HILLER
SOMETHING OF VALUE .... WILLIAM MARSHALL
SOMETHING SHORT OF
   PARADISE .... SUSAN SARANDON
SOMETHING TO HIDE .... SHELLEY WINTERS
SOMETHING TO LIVE FOR .... TERESA WRIGHT
SOMETHING TO SHOUT ABOUT ...... CYD CHARISSE
SOMETHING TO SHOUT ABOUT .... DON AMECHE†
SOMETHING WICKED THIS
   WAY COMES .... DIANE LADD
SOMETHING WICKED THIS
   WAY COMES .... JASON ROBARDS
SOMETHING WICKED THIS
   WAY COMES .... JONATHAN PRYCE
SOMETHING WICKED THIS
   WAY COMES .... PAM GRIER
SOMETHING WICKED THIS
   WAY COMES .... ROYAL DANO
SOMETHING WILD .... ANNA LEVINE
SOMETHING WILD .... CARROLL BAKER
SOMETHING WILD .... DIANE LADD
SOMETHING WILD .... JACK GILPIN
SOMETHING WILD .... JEAN STAPLETON
SOMETHING WILD .... JEFF DANIELS
SOMETHING WILD .... JOHN CARPENTER
SOMETHING WILD .... JOHN SAYLES
SOMETHING WILD .... MARGARET COLIN
SOMETHING WILD .... MELANIE GRIFFITH
SOMETHING WILD .... RAY LIOTTA
SOMETIMES A GREAT
   NOTION .... MICHAEL SARRAZIN
SOMETIMES A GREAT NOTION .... PAUL NEWMAN
SOMETIMES A GREAT
   NOTION ❍ .... RICHARD JAECKEL
SOMEWHERE IN FRANCE .... GORDAN JACKSON†
SOMEWHERE IN FRANCE .... ROBERT MORLEY
SOMEWHERE IN TIME .... CHRISTOPHER PLUMMER
SOMEWHERE IN TIME ... CHRISTOPHER REEVE
SOMEWHERE IN TIME .... JANE SEYMOUR
SOMEWHERE IN TIME .... TERESA WRIGHT
SOMEWHERE IN TIME .... TIM KAZURINSKY
SOMEWHERE I'LL FIND YOU .... LANA TURNER
SOMEWHERE I'LL FIND YOU .... VAN JOHNSON
SOMEWHERE
   TOMORROW .... SARAH JESSICA PARKER
SOMMERSBY .... BILL PULLMAN
SOMMERSBY .... JAMES EARL JONES
SOMMERSBY .... JODIE FOSTER
SOMMERSBY .... RICHARD GERE
SON OF A GUNFIGHTER .... RUSS TAMBLYN
SON OF ALI BABA .... PIPER LAURIE
SON OF ALI BABA .... TONY CURTIS
SON OF BLOB .... BURGESS MEREDITH
SON OF BLOB .... CAROL LYNLEY
SON OF BLOB .... LARRY HAGMAN
SON OF BLOB .... ROBERT WALKER JR.
SON OF FLUBBER .... PAUL LYNDE†
SON OF FURY .... RODDY McDOWALL
SON OF LASSIE .... JUNE LOCKHART
SON OF LASSIE .... LEON AMES
SON OF PALEFACE .... BOB HOPE
SON OF ROBIN HOOD .... DAVID HEDISON
SON OF SINBAD .... KIM NOVAK
SON OF SINBAD .... VINCENT PRICE†
SON OF THE MORNING STAR (MS) .... GARY COLE
SON OF THE MORNING
   STAR (TF) .... RODNEY A. GRANT
SON-DAUGHTER, THE .... HELEN HAYES
SON-IN-LAW .... CARLA GUGINO
SON-IN-LAW .... LANE SMITH
SON-IN-LAW .... PAULY SHORE
SON-RISE: A MIRACLE
   OF LOVE (TF) .... JAMES FARENTINO
SONG O' MY HEART .... MAUREEN O'SULLIVAN
SONG OF BERNADETTE, THE .... ALAN NAPIER†
SONG OF BERNADETTE, THE .... VINCENT PRICE†

SONG OF
   BERNADETTE, THE ★★ .... JENNIFER JONES
SONG OF
   BERNADETTE, THE ❍ .... CHARLES BICKFORD†
SONG OF
   BERNADETTE, THE ❍ ..... DAME GLADYS COOPER†
SONG OF LOVE .... KATHERINE HEPBURN
SONG OF NORWAY .... FLORENCE HENDERSON
SONG OF NORWAY .... ROBERT MORLEY
SONG OF SCHEHEREZADE ...... YVONNE DE CARLO
SONG OF SURRENDER .... EVA GABOR
SONG OF THE THIN MAN .... DEAN STOCKWELL
SONG OF THE THIN MAN .... LEON AMES
SONG TO REMEMBER, A .... NINA FOCH
SONG WITHOUT END .... LOU JACOBI
SONGWRITER .... KRIS KRISTOFFERSON
SONGWRITER .... LESLEY ANN WARREN
SONGWRITER .... RIP TORN
SONGWRITER .... WILLIE NELSON
SONNY AND JED .... SUSAN GEORGE
SONNY AND JED .... TELLY SAVALAS†
SONNY BOY .... ALEXANDRA POWERS
SONNY BOY .... BRAD DOURIF
SONNY BOY .... CONRAD JANIS
SONNY BOY .... DAVID CARRADINE
SONNY BOY .... MICHAEL GRIFFIN
SONNY BOY .... SAVINA GERSAK
SONNY BOY .... STEVE CARLISLE
SONNY BOY .... SYDNEY LASSICK
SONS AND LOVERS .... DEAN STOCKWELL
SONS AND LOVERS .... DONALD PLEASENCE
SONS AND LOVERS .... WENDY HILLER
SONS AND LOVERS ★ .... TREVOR HOWARD†
SONS AND LOVERS ❍ .... MARY URE†
SONS OF KATIE ELDER, THE .... DEAN MARTIN
SONS OF KATIE ELDER, THE .... DENNIS HOPPER
SONS OF KATIE ELDER, THE .... EARL HOLLIMAN
SONS OF KATIE ELDER, THE .... GEORGE KENNEDY
SONS OF KATIE ELDER, THE .... JOHN WAYNE†
SON'S PROMISE, A (TF) .... DAVID ANDREWS
SON'S PROMISE, A (TF) .... RICK SCHRODER
SON'S PROMISE, A (TF) .... STEPHEN DORFF
SON'S PROMISE, A (TF) .... VERONICA CARTWRIGHT
SOOKY .... JACKIE COOPER
SOONER OR LATER (TF) .... JUDD HIRSCH
SOPHIA LOREN: HER
   OWN STORY (TF) .... JACK HEDLEY
SOPHIA LOREN: HER
   OWN STORY (TF) .... RIP TORN
SOPHIA LOREN: HER
   OWN STORY (TF) .... SOPHIA LOREN
SOPHIA LOREN: HER
   OWN STORY (TF) .... THERESA SALDANA
SOPHIE'S CHOICE .... JOSEF SOMMER
SOPHIE'S CHOICE .... KEVIN KLINE
SOPHIE'S CHOICE .... PETER MacNICOL
SOPHIE'S CHOICE ★★ .... MERYL STREEP
SOPHIE'S PLACE .... TELLY SAVALAS†
SORCERER .... ROY SCHEIDER
SORCERESS .... CATHERINE FROT
SORCERESS .... CHRISTINE BOISSON
SORCERESS .... FEODOR ATKINE
SORCERESS .... JEAN CARMET
SORCERESS .... RAOUL BILLEREY
SORCERESS .... TCHEKY KARYO
SORCERERS, THE .... SUSAN GEORGE
SORROWFUL JONES .... BOB HOPE
SORRY, WRONG NUMBER .... BURT LANCASTER†
SORRY, WRONG NUMBER (CTF) .... HAL HOLBROOK
SORRY, WRONG
   NUMBER (CTF) .... LONI ANDERSON
SORRY, WRONG
   NUMBER (CTF) .... PATRICK MacNEE
SORRY, WRONG
   NUMBER ★ .... BARBARA STANWYCK†
SOTTO CHOCK .... CLAUDINE AUGER
SOUL MAN .... ARYE GROSS
SOUL MAN .... C. THOMAS HOWELL
SOUL MAN .... JAMES EARL JONES
SOUL MAN .... JEFF ALTMAN
SOUL MAN .... JULIA LOUIS-DREYFUSS
SOUL MAN .... LESLIE NIELSEN

SOUL MAN .... MELORA HARDIN
SOUL MAN .... RAE DAWN CHONG
SOUL OF NIGGER
   CHARLEY, THE .... FRED WILLIAMSON
SOULS TRIUMPHANT .... LILLIAN GISH†
SOUND AND
   THE FURY, THE .... JOANNE WOODWARD
SOUND AND THE FURY, THE ...... STUART WHITMAN
SOUND BARRIER, THE .... DENHOLM ELLIOTT†
SOUND OF FURY, THE .... LLOYD BRIDGES
SOUND OF MUSIC, THE .... BEN WRIGHT
SOUND OF
   MUSIC, THE .... CHRISTOPHER PLUMMER
SOUND OF MUSIC, THE .... DORIS LLOYD†
SOUND OF MUSIC, THE .... ELEANOR PARKER
SOUND OF MUSIC, THE .... RICHARD HAYDN†
SOUND OF MUSIC, THE ★ .... JULIE ANDREWS
SOUND OF MUSIC, THE ❍ .... PEGGY WOOD†
SOUNDER .... KEVIN HOOKS
SOUNDER ★ .... CICELY TYSON
SOUNDER ★ .... PAUL WINFIELD
SOUTH OF RENO .... LISA BLOUNT
SOUTH OF ST. LOUIS .... ALEXIS SMITH†
SOUTH PACIFIC .... FRANCE NUYEN
SOUTH PACIFIC .... RAY WALSTON
SOUTH SEA SINNER .... SHELLEY WINTERS
SOUTH SEA WOMAN .... BURT LANCASTER†
SOUTH SEA WOMAN .... CHUCK CONNORS†
SOUTHERN COMFORT .... FRED WARD
SOUTHERN COMFORT .... KEITH CARRADINE
SOUTHERN COMFORT .... PETER COYOTE
SOUTHERN COMFORT .... POWERS BOOTHE
SOUTHERN STAR, THE .... GEORGE SEGAL
SOUTHERN STAR, THE .... URSULA ANDRESS
SOUTHERN YANKEE, A .... JOHN IRELAND
SOUTHERNER, THE .... NORMAN LLOYD
SOUTHWEST PASSAGE .... JOHN IRELAND
SOYLENT GREEN .... CHARLTON HESTON
SOYLENT GREEN .... CHUCK CONNORS†
SOYLENT GREEN .... DICK VAN PATTEN
SOYLENT GREEN .... LEIGH TAYLOR-YOUNG
SPACE (MS) .... BEAU BRIDGES
SPACE (MS) .... BLAIR BROWN
SPACE (MS) .... BRUCE DERN
SPACE (MS) .... DAVID DUKES
SPACE (MS) .... HARRY HAMLIN
SPACE (MS) .... JAMES GARNER
SPACE (MS) .... MARTIN BALSAM
SPACE (MS) .... MELINDA DILLON
SPACE (MS) .... MICHAEL YORK
SPACE (MS) .... RALPH BELLAMY†
SPACE (MS) .... SUSAN ANSPACH
SPACE RAGE .... MICHAEL PARE
SPACE RAGE .... RICHARD FARNSWORTH
SPACE RAIDERS .... VINCE EDWARDS
SPACEBALLS .... BILL PULLMAN
SPACEBALLS .... DAPHNE ZUNIGA
SPACEBALLS .... JOAN RIVERS
SPACEBALLS .... JOHN CANDY†
SPACEBALLS .... MEL BROOKS
SPACEBALLS .... RICK DUCOMMUN
SPACEBALLS .... RICK MORANIS
SPACECAMP .... KATE CAPSHAW
SPACECAMP .... KELLY PRESTON
SPACECAMP .... TATE DONOVAN
SPACECAMP .... TOM SKERRITT
SPACED INVADERS .... RYAN TODD
SPACEFLIGHT IC-1 .... MARK LESTER
SPACEHUNTER: ADVENTURES
   IN THE FORBIDDEN ZONE ...... MICHAEL IRONSIDE
SPACEHUNTER: ADVENTURES
   IN THE FORBIDDEN ZONE .... PETER STRAUSS
SPACEMAN AND KING
   ARTHUR, THE .... RON MOODY
SPACESHIP .... CINDY WILLIAMS
SPACESHIP .... LESLIE NIELSEN
SPALDING GRAY'S MONSTER
   IN A BOX (PF) .... SPALDING GRAY
SPANISH AFFAIR .... RICHARD KILEY
SPANISH MAIN, THE .... MAUREEN O'HARA
SPARA FORTE...PIU FORTE...
   NON CAPISCO .... RAQUEL WELCH

† after an actor's name denotes deceased.

SPARKLE .... DORIAN HAREWOOD
SPARKS: THE PRICE
OF PASSION (TF) .... TED WASS
SPARKS: THE PRICE
OF PASSION (TF) .... VICTORIA PRINCIPAL
SPARROWS .... MILTON BERLE
SPARTACUS .... CHARLES LAUGHTON†
SPARTACUS .... JEAN SIMMONS
SPARTACUS .... JOHN DALL†
SPARTACUS .... JOHN GAVIN
SPARTACUS .... JOHN IRELAND
SPARTACUS .... KIRK DOUGLAS
SPARTACUS .... LAURENCE OLIVIER†
SPARTACUS .... NINA FOCH
SPARTACUS .... TONY CURTIS
SPARTACUS ○○ .... WOODY STRODE
SPARTACUS ○○ .... PETER USTINOV
SPAWN OF THE NORTH .... DOROTHY LAMOUR
SPECIAL AGENT .... BETTE DAVIS†
SPECIAL DAY, A .... JOHN VERNON
SPECIAL DAY, A .... SOPHIA LOREN
SPECIAL DAY, A ★ .... MARCELLO MASTROIANNI
SPECIAL DELIVERY .... BO SVENSON
SPECIAL DELIVERY .... CYBILL SHEPHERD
SPECIAL DELIVERY .... MICHAEL C. GWYNNE
SPECIAL DELIVERY .... SORRELL BOOKE
SPECIAL DELIVERY .... TOM ATKINS
SPECIAL FRIENDSHIP, A (TF) .... AKOSUA BUSIA
SPECIAL FRIENDSHIP, A (TF) .... CYNTHIA HARRIS
SPECIAL FRIENDSHIP, A (TF) .... LeVAR BURTON
SPECIAL KIND
OF LOVE, A (TF) .... CHARLES DURNING
SPECIAL KIND OF LOVE, A (TF) .... DEBRA WINGER
SPECIAL OLYMPICS (TF) .... CHARLES DURNING
SPECIAL OLYMPICS (TF) .... DEBRA WINGER
SPECIAL PEOPLE: BASED ON
A TRUE STORY (TF) .... BROOKE ADAMS
SPECIALIST, THE .... ADAM WEST
SPECIALIST, THE .... ERIC ROBERTS
SPECIALIST, THE .... JAMES WOODS
SPECIALIST, THE .... JOHN ANDERSON
SPECIALIST, THE .... ROD STEIGER
SPECIALIST, THE .... SHARON STONE
SPECIALIST, THE .... SYLVESTER STALLONE
SPECIES .... ALFRED MOLINA
SPECIES .... BEN KINGSLEY
SPECIES .... FOREST WHITAKER
SPECIES .... MARG HELGENBERGER
SPECIES .... MICHAEL MADSEN
SPECIES .... NATASHA HENSTRIDGE
SPECTER OF
THE ROSE .... DAME JUDITH ANDERSON†
SPECTER OF THE ROSE .... LIONEL STANDER
SPECTRE (TF) .... GORDAN JACKSON†
SPECTRE (TF) .... JOHN HURT
SPEECHLESS .... BONNIE BEDELIA
SPEECHLESS .... CHARLES MARTIN SMITH
SPEECHLESS .... CHRISTOPHER REEVE
SPEECHLESS .... ERNIE HUDSON
SPEECHLESS .... GAILORD SARTAIN
SPEECHLESS .... GEENA DAVIS
SPEECHLESS .... MICHAEL KEATON
SPEECHLESS .... MITCHELL RYAN
SPEECHLESS .... RAY BAKER
SPEED .... ALAN RUCK
SPEED .... BETH GRANT
SPEED .... CARLOS CARRASCO
SPEED .... DANIEL VILLARREAL
SPEED .... DAVID KRIEGEL
SPEED .... DENNIS HOPPER
SPEED .... GLENN PLUMMER
SPEED .... HAWTHORNE JAMES
SPEED .... JAMES STEWART
SPEED .... JEFF DANIELS
SPEED .... JOE MORTON
SPEED .... KEANU REEVES
SPEED .... NATSUKO OHAMA
SPEED .... RICHARD LINEBACK
SPEED .... SANDRA BULLOCK
SPEED ZONE .... BROOKE SHIELDS
SPEED ZONE .... JOHN CANDY†
SPEEDTRAP .... JOE DON BAKER

SPEEDTRAP .... TIMOTHY CAREY
SPEEDTRAP .... TYNE DALY
SPEEDWAY .... BILL BIXBY†
SPEEDWAY .... ELVIS PRESLEY†
SPELL, THE (TF) .... LEE GRANT
SPELLBINDER .... ANTHONY CRIVELLO
SPELLBINDER .... KELLY PRESTON
SPELLBINDER .... RICK ROSSOVICH
SPELLBINDER .... TIMOTHY DALY
SPELLBOUND .... GREGORY PECK
SPELLBOUND .... NORMAN LLOYD
SPELLBOUND ○ .... MICHAEL CHEKHOV†
SPENCER'S MOUNTAIN .... MAUREEN O'HARA
SPENDOR IN THE GRASS .... ZOHRA LAMPERT
SPENSER: FOR HIRE (TF) .... ROBERT URICH
SPETTERS .... RUTGER HAUER
SPHINX .... FRANK LANGELLA
SPHINX .... JOHN GIELGUD
SPHINX .... JOHN RHYS-DAVIES
SPHINX .... LESLEY-ANNE DOWN
SPHINX .... VICTORIA TENNANT
SPIES, LIES AND
NAKED THIGHS (TF) .... ED BEGLEY JR.
SPIES LIKE US .... BERNIE CASEY
SPIES LIKE US .... BOB HOPE
SPIES LIKE US .... BOB SWAIM
SPIES LIKE US .... BRUCE DAVISON
SPIES LIKE US .... CHEVY CHASE
SPIES LIKE US .... DAN AYKROYD
SPIES LIKE US .... DONNA DIXON
SPIES LIKE US .... JOEL COEN
SPIES LIKE US .... MARTIN BREST
SPIES LIKE US .... MICHAEL APTED
SPIES LIKE US .... STEVE FORREST
SPIES LIKE US .... TERRY GILLIAM
SPIES LIKE US .... TOM HATTEN
SPIES LIKE US .... WILLIAM PRINCE
SPIKES GANG, THE .... RON HOWARD
SPINOUT .... ELVIS PRESLEY†
SPIRAL ROAD, THE .... BURL IVES
SPIRAL ROAD, THE .... GENA ROWLANDS
SPIRAL ROAD, THE .... GEOFFREY KEEN
SPIRAL
STAIRCASE, THE .... CHRISTOPHER PLUMMER
SPIRAL STAIRCASE, THE .... ELAINE STRITCH
SPIRAL STAIRCASE, THE .... JACQUELINE BISSET
SPIRAL
STAIRCASE, THE ○ .... ETHEL BARRYMORE†
SPIRIT, THE (TF) .... PHILIP BAKER HALL
SPIRIT IS WILLING, THE .... JOHN ASTIN
SPIRIT IS WILLING, THE .... SID CAESAR
SPIRIT IS WILLING, THE .... VERA MILES
SPIRIT OF CULVER .... JACKIE COOPER
SPIRIT OF ST. LOUIS, THE .... JAMES STEWART
SPIRITS .... CAROL LYNLEY
SPIRITS .... ERIK ESTRADA
SPIRITS OF THE DEAD .... JANE FONDA
SPIRITS OF THE DEAD .... PETER FONDA
SPIRITS OF THE DEAD .... TERENCE STAMP
SPIRITS OF THE DEAD .... VINCENT PRICE†
SPITFIRE .... KATHERINE HEPBURN
SPITFIRE .... RALPH BELLAMY†
SPLASH .... BILL SMITROVICH
SPLASH .... DARYL HANNAH
SPLASH .... JOHN CANDY†
SPLASH .... TOM HANKS
SPLENDOR .... DAVID NIVEN†
SPLENDOR IN THE GRASS .... PAT HINGLE
SPLENDOR IN THE GRASS .... PHYLLIS DILLER
SPLENDOR IN THE GRASS .... SANDY DENNIS†
SPLENDOR IN THE GRASS .... WARREN BEATTY
SPLENDOR IN THE GRASS ★ .... NATALIE WOOD†
SPLENDOR IN THE GRASS (TF) .... ALLY SHEEDY
SPLIT, THE .... DIAHANN CARROLL
SPLIT, THE .... DONALD SUTHERLAND
SPLIT, THE .... ERNEST BORGNINE
SPLIT, THE .... GENE HACKMAN
SPLIT, THE .... JACK KLUGMAN
SPLIT, THE .... JAMES WHITMORE
SPLIT, THE .... JIM BROWN
SPLIT, THE .... JULIE HARRIS
SPLIT DECISIONS .... GENE HACKMAN

SPLIT IMAGE .... BRIAN DENNEHY
SPLIT IMAGE .... ELIZABETH ASHLEY
SPLIT IMAGE .... JAMES WOODS
SPLIT IMAGE .... KAREN ALLEN
SPLIT IMAGE .... PETER FONDA
SPLIT SECOND .... ALEXIS SMITH†
SPLIT SECOND .... RUTGER HAUER
SPLITTING HEIRS .... BARBARA HERSHEY
SPLITTING HEIRS .... ERIC IDLE
SPLITTING HEIRS .... JOHN CLEESE
SPLITTING HEIRS .... RICK MORANIS
SPOILERS, THE .... RORY CALHOUN
SPONTANEOUS COMBUSTION .... BRAD DOURIF
SPONTANEOUS COMBUSTION .... MELINDA DILLON
SPONTANEOUS COMBUSTION ..... WILLIAM PRINCE
SPOONER (CTF) .... JANE KACZMAREK
SPOONER (CTF) .... ROBERT URICH
SPORTING BLOOD .... MAUREEN O'SULLIVAN
SPORTING CLUB, THE .... ANN RAMSEY†
SPORTING CLUB, THE .... LOGAN RAMSEY
SPOTSWOOD .... ANTHONY HOPKINS
SPOTSWOOD .... BRUNO LAWRENCE
SPRING AND PORT WINE .... SUSAN GEORGE
SPRING BREAK .... PERRY LANG
SPRING FEVER .... JESSICA WALTER
SPRING FEVER .... JOAN CRAWFORD†
SPRING FEVER .... SUSAN ANTON
SPRING MADNESS .... BURGESS MEREDITH
SPRING MADNESS .... MAUREEN O'SULLIVAN
SPRINGFIELD RIFLE .... PHYLLIS THAXTER
SPY (CTF) .... BRUCE GREENWOOD
SPY (CTF) .... CATHERINE HICKS
SPY IN THE GREEN HAT, THE .... JANET LEIGH
SPY RING, THE .... JANE WYMAN
SPY WHO CAME IN FROM
THE COLD, THE .... CLAIRE BLOOM
SPY WHO CAME IN FROM
THE COLD, THE .... SAM WANAMAKER†
SPY WHO CAME IN FROM
THE COLD, THE ★ .... RICHARD BURTON†
SPY WHO LOVED ME, THE .... BARBARA BACH
SPY WHO LOVED ME, THE .... CURT JURGENS†
SPY WHO LOVED ME, THE .... GEOFFREY KEEN
SPY WHO LOVED ME, THE .... LOIS MAXWELL
SPY WHO LOVED ME, THE .... RICHARD KIEL
SPY WHO LOVED ME, THE .... ROGER MOORE
SPY WHO LOVED ME, THE .... WALTER GOTELL
SPY WITH A COLD
NOSE, THE .... DENHOLM ELLIOTT†
SPY WITH MY FACE, THE .... DAVID McCALLUM
SQUADRA ANTIRUFFA .... DAVID HEMMINGS
SQUARE DANCE .... DEBORAH RICHTER
SQUARE DANCE .... ELBERT LEWIS
SQUARE DANCE .... GUICH KOOCK
SQUARE DANCE .... JANE ALEXANDER
SQUARE DANCE .... JASON ROBARDS
SQUARE DANCE .... ROB LOWE
SQUARE DANCE .... WINONA RYDER
SQUARE JUNGLE, THE .... ERNEST BORGNINE
SQUARE JUNGLE, THE .... TONY CURTIS
SQUEEZE, THE .... DAVID HEMMINGS
SQUEEZE, THE .... EDWARD ALBERT
SQUEEZE, THE .... KAREN BLACK
SQUEEZE, THE .... MICHAEL KEATON
SQUEEZE, THE .... STACY KEACH
ST. BENNY THE DIP .... LIONEL STANDER
ST. BENNY THE DIP .... NINA FOCH
ST. ELMO'S FIRE .... ALLY SHEEDY
ST. ELMO'S FIRE .... ANDIE MacDOWELL
ST. ELMO'S FIRE .... ANDREW McCARTHY
ST. ELMO'S FIRE .... DEMI MOORE
ST. ELMO'S FIRE .... EMILIO ESTEVEZ
ST. ELMO'S FIRE .... JUDD NELSON
ST. ELMO'S FIRE .... MARE WINNINGHAM
ST. ELMO'S FIRE .... MARTIN BALSAM
ST. ELMO'S FIRE .... ROB LOWE
ST. HELENS .... ALBERT SALMI†
ST. HELENS .... ART CARNEY
ST. HELENS .... BILL McKINNEY
ST. HELENS .... CASSIE YATES
ST. HELENS .... DAVID HUFFMAN†
ST. HELENS .... RON O'NEAL

ST. IVES .... CHARLES BRONSON
ST. IVES .... DANIEL J. TRAVANTI
ST. IVES .... HARRIS YULIN
ST. IVES .... HARRY GUARDINO
ST. IVES .... JACQUELINE BISSET
ST. IVES .... JOHN HOUSEMAN†
ST. IVES .... MAXIMILIAN SCHELL
ST. IVES .... MICHAEL LERNER
ST. LOUIS BLUES .... DOROTHY LAMOUR
ST. LOUIS BLUES .... EARTHA KITT
ST. LOUIS BLUES .... RUBY DEE
ST. VALENTINE'S DAY
    MASSACRE, THE .... BRUCE DERN
ST. VALENTINE'S DAY
    MASSACRE, THE .... GEORGE SEGAL
ST. VALENTINE'S DAY
    MASSACRE, THE .... JACK NICHOLSON
ST. VALENTINE'S DAY
    MASSACRE, THE .... JASON ROBARDS
ST. VALENTINE'S DAY
    MASSACRE, THE .... JOSEPH CAMPANELLA
STACKING .... CHRISTINE LAHTI
STACKING .... FREDERIC FORREST
STACY'S KNIGHTS .... KEVIN COSTNER
STAGE DOOR .... KATHERINE HEPBURN
STAGE DOOR .... LUCILLE BALL†
STAGE DOOR
    CANTEEN .... DAME JUDITH ANDERSON†
STAGE DOOR CANTEEN .... HELEN HAYES
STAGE DOOR CANTEEN ...... KATHERINE HEPBURN
STAGE DOOR CANTEEN ...... MARTHA SCOTT
STAGE DOOR CANTEEN .... RALPH BELLAMY†
STAGE DOOR ❍ .... ANDREA LEEDS†
STAGE FRIGHT .... JANE WYMAN
STAGE MOTHER .... MAUREEN O'SULLIVAN
STAGE STRUCK .... CHRISTOPHER PLUMMER
STAGE STRUCK .... JACK WESTON
STAGE STRUCK .... JANE WYMAN
STAGE STRUCK .... JOHN FIELDLER
STAGE STRUCK .... SUSAN STRASBERG
STAGECOACH .... ANN-MARGRET
STAGECOACH .... JOHN CARRADINE†
STAGECOACH .... RED BUTTONS
STAGECOACH ❍❍ .... STEFANIE POWERS
STAGECOACH ❍❍ .... THOMAS MITCHELL†
STAGECOACH (TF) ..... ANTHONY (TONY) FRANCIOSA
STAGECOACH (TF) .... ELIZABETH ASHLEY
STAGECOACH (TF) .... JOHN SCHNEIDER
STAGECOACH (TF) .... JOHNNY CASH
STAGECOACH (TF) .... KRIS KRISTOFFERSON
STAGECOACH (TF) .... MARY CROSBY
STAGECOACH (TF) .... WAYLON JENNINGS
STAGECOACH (TF) .... WILLIE NELSON
STAGECOACH TO
    DANCERS' ROCK .... MARTIN LANDAU
STAKEOUT .... AIDAN QUINN
STAKEOUT .... DAN LAURIA
STAKEOUT .... EMILIO ESTEVEZ
STAKEOUT .... FOREST WHITAKER
STAKEOUT .... MADELEINE STOWE
STAKEOUT .... RICHARD DREYFUSS
STALAG 17 .... PETER GRAVES
STALAG 17 ★ .... WILLIAM HOLDEN†
STALAG 17 ❍ .... ROBERT STRAUSS†
STALKING MOON, THE .... EVA MARIE SAINT
STALKING MOON, THE .... GREGORY PECK
STALKING MOON, THE .... ROBERT FORSTER
STALLION ROAD .... ALEXIS SMITH†
STALLION ROAD .... RONALD REAGAN
STAND, THE (MS) .... GARY SINISE
STAND, THE (MS) .... LAURA SAN GIACOMO
STAND, THE (MS) .... MOLLY RINGWALD
STAND, THE (MS) .... ROB LOWE
STAND ALONE .... CHARLES DURNING
STAND ALONE .... JAMES KEACH
STAND AND DELIVER .... ANDY GARCIA
STAND AND DELIVER .... LOU DIAMOND PHILLIPS
STAND AND DELIVER ★ .... EDWARD JAMES OLMOS
STAND BY ME .... CASEY SIEMASZKO
STAND BY ME .... COREY FELDMAN
STAND BY ME .... JERRY O'CONNELL
STAND BY ME .... JOHN CUSAK
STAND BY ME .... KIEFER SUTHERLAND

STAND BY ME .... RICHARD DREYFUSS
STAND BY ME .... RIVER PHOENIX†
STAND BY ME .... WIL WHEATON
STAND UP AND
    BE COUNTED .... HECTOR ELIZONDO
STAND UP AND
    BE COUNTED .... JACQUELINE BISSET
STAND UP AND
    BE COUNTED .... KATHLEEN FREEMAN
STAND UP AND BE COUNTED .... LORETTA SWIT
STAND UP AND
    BE COUNTED .... MEREDITH BAXTER
STAND UP AND BE COUNTED ..... STELLA STEVENS
STAND UP VIRGIN
    SOLDIERS .... EDWARD WOODWARD
STAND UP VIRGIN SOLDIERS .... NIGEL DAVENPORT
STANDING ROOM ONLY .... YVONNE DE CARLO
STANDING TALL (TF) .... CHUCK CONNORS†
STANDING TALL (TF) .... ROBERT FORSTER
STANLEY & IRIS .... FEOFOR CHALIAPIN JR.
STANLEY & IRIS .... HARLEY CROSS
STANLEY & IRIS .... JAMEY SHERIDAN
STANLEY & IRIS .... JANE FONDA
STANLEY & IRIS .... MARTHA PLIMPTON
STANLEY & IRIS .... ROBERT DE NIRO
STANLEY & IRIS .... SWOOSIE KURTZ
STAR! .... JENNY AGUTTER
STAR! .... JULIE ANDREWS
STAR! .... RICHARD CRENNA
STAR! .... ROBERT REED†
STAR, THE ★ .... BETTE DAVIS†
STAR 80 .... CARROLL BAKER
STAR 80 .... CLIFF ROBERTSON
STAR 80 .... DAVID CLENNON
STAR 80 .... ERIC ROBERTS
STAR 80 .... ERNEST THOMPSON
STAR 80 .... JORDAN CHRISTOPHER
STAR 80 .... JOSH MOSTEL
STAR 80 .... KEENEN IVORY WAYANS
STAR 80 .... MARIEL HEMINGWAY
STAR 80 .... ROGER REES
STAR 80 .... SIDNEY MILLER
STAR 80 .... STUART DAMON
STAR CHAMBER, THE .... HAL HOLBROOK
STAR CHAMBER, THE .... MICHAEL DOUGLAS
STAR CHAMBER, THE .... SHARON GLESS
STAR CHAMBER, THE .... YAPHET KOTTO
STAR FOR TWO, A .... LAUREN BACALL
STAR IN THE DUST .... CLINT EASTWOOD
STAR IS BORN, A (1937) ★ .... FREDRIC MARCH†
STAR IS BORN, A (1937) .... LIONEL STANDER
STAR IS BORN, A (1937) ★ .... JANET GAYNOR†
STAR IS BORN, A (1954) .... LANA TURNER
STAR IS BORN, A (1954) ★ .... JUDY GARLAND†
STAR IS BORN, A (1954) ★ .... JAMES MASON†
STAR IS BORN, A (1976) .... BARBRA STREISAND
STAR IS BORN, A (1976) .... GARY BUSEY
STAR IS BORN, A (1976) ...... KRIS KRISTOFFERSON
STAR IS BORN, A (1976) .... PAUL MAZURSKY
STAR IS BORN, A (1976) .... SALLY KIRKLAND
STAR MAKER, THE (TF) .... MELANIE GRIFFITH
STAR SPANGLED GIRL .... SANDY DUNCAN
STAR SPANGLED GIRL .... TONY ROBERTS
STAR SPANGLED RHYTHM .... BOB HOPE
STAR SPANGLED RHYTHM .... DOROTHY LAMOUR
STAR TREK: GENERATIONS .... BRENT SPINER
STAR TREK: GENERATIONS .... GATES McFADDEN
STAR TREK: GENERATIONS .... JAMES DOOHAN
STAR TREK: GENERATIONS ..... JONATHAN FRAKES
STAR TREK: GENERATIONS .... LeVAR BURTON
STAR TREK:
    GENERATIONS .... MALCOLM McDOWELL
STAR TREK: GENERATIONS .... MARINA SIRTIS
STAR TREK: GENERATIONS .... MICHAEL DORN
STAR TREK: GENERATIONS ..... PATRICK STEWART
STAR TREK: GENERATIONS .... WALTER KOENIG
STAR TREK: GENERATIONS ..... WHOOPI GOLDBERG
STAR TREK: GENERATIONS .... WILLIAM KOENIG
STAR TREK: GENERATIONS ...... WILLIAM SHATNER
STAR TREK II: THE WRATH
    OF KHAN .... BIBI BESCH
STAR TREK II: THE WRATH
    OF KHAN .... DEFOREST KELLEY

STAR TREK II: THE WRATH
    OF KHAN .... GEORGE TAKEI
STAR TREK II: THE WRATH
    OF KHAN .... JAMES DOOHAN
STAR TREK II: THE WRATH
    OF KHAN .... KIRSTIE ALLEY
STAR TREK II: THE WRATH
    OF KHAN .... LEONARD NIMOY
STAR TREK II: THE WRATH
    OF KHAN .... MERRITT BUTRICK†
STAR TREK II: THE WRATH
    OF KHAN .... NICHELLE NICHOLS
STAR TREK II: THE WRATH
    OF KHAN .... PAUL WINFIELD
STAR TREK II: THE WRATH
    OF KHAN .... RICARDO MONTALBAN
STAR TREK II: THE WRATH
    OF KHAN .... WILLIAM KOENIG
STAR TREK II: THE WRATH
    OF KHAN .... WILLIAM SHATNER
STAR TREK III: THE SEARCH
    FOR SPOCK .... CHRISTOPHER LLOYD
STAR TREK III: THE SEARCH
    FOR SPOCK .... DAME JUDITH ANDERSON†
STAR TREK III: THE SEARCH
    FOR SPOCK .... DEFOREST KELLEY
STAR TREK III: THE SEARCH
    FOR SPOCK .... DENNIS OTT†
STAR TREK III: THE SEARCH
    FOR SPOCK .... GEORGE TAKEI
STAR TREK III: THE SEARCH
    FOR SPOCK .... JAMES B. SIKKING
STAR TREK III: THE SEARCH
    FOR SPOCK .... JAMES DOOHAN
STAR TREK III: THE SEARCH
    FOR SPOCK .... JOHN LARROQUETTE
STAR TREK III: THE SEARCH
    FOR SPOCK .... LEONARD NIMOY
STAR TREK III: THE SEARCH
    FOR SPOCK .... MARK LENARD
STAR TREK III: THE SEARCH
    FOR SPOCK .... MERRITT BUTRICK†
STAR TREK III: THE SEARCH
    FOR SPOCK .... NICHELLE NICHOLS
STAR TREK III: THE SEARCH
    FOR SPOCK .... ROBERT HOOKS
STAR TREK III: THE SEARCH
    FOR SPOCK .... ROBIN CURTIS
STAR TREK III: THE SEARCH
    FOR SPOCK .... WILLIAM KOENIG
STAR TREK III: THE SEARCH
    FOR SPOCK .... WILLIAM SHATNER
STAR TREK IV:
    THE VOYAGE HOME .... BROCK PETERS
STAR TREK IV:
    THE VOYAGE HOME .... CATHERINE HICKS
STAR TREK IV:
    THE VOYAGE HOME .... DEFOREST KELLEY
STAR TREK IV:
    THE VOYAGE HOME .... GEORGE TAKEI
STAR TREK IV:
    THE VOYAGE HOME .... JAMES DOOHAN
STAR TREK IV:
    THE VOYAGE HOME .... JANE WYATT
STAR TREK IV:
    THE VOYAGE HOME .... JOHN SCHUCK
STAR TREK IV:
    THE VOYAGE HOME .... LEONARD NIMOY
STAR TREK IV:
    THE VOYAGE HOME .... MAJEL BARRETT
STAR TREK IV:
    THE VOYAGE HOME .... MARK LENARD
STAR TREK IV:
    THE VOYAGE HOME .... NICHELLE NICHOLS
STAR TREK IV:
    THE VOYAGE HOME .... ROBERT ELLENSTEIN
STAR TREK IV:
    THE VOYAGE HOME .... ROBIN CURTIS
STAR TREK IV:
    THE VOYAGE HOME .... WILLIAM KOENIG
STAR TREK IV:
    THE VOYAGE HOME .... WILLIAM SHATNER

† after an actor's name denotes deceased.

STAR TREK -
  THE MOTION PICTURE .... DEFOREST KELLEY
STAR TREK -
  THE MOTION PICTURE .... GEORGE TAKEI
STAR TREK -
  THE MOTION PICTURE .... GRACE LEE WHITNEY
STAR TREK -
  THE MOTION PICTURE .... JAMES DOOHAN
STAR TREK -
  THE MOTION PICTURE .... LEONARD NIMOY
STAR TREK -
  THE MOTION PICTURE .... MAJEL BARRETT
STAR TREK -
  THE MOTION PICTURE .... MARK LENARD
STAR TREK -
  THE MOTION PICTURE .... NICHELLE NICHOLS
STAR TREK -
  THE MOTION PICTURE .... PERSIS KHAMBATTA
STAR TREK -
  THE MOTION PICTURE .... STEPHEN COLLINS
STAR TREK -
  THE MOTION PICTURE .... WILLIAM KOENIG
STAR TREK -
  THE MOTION PICTURE ...... WILLIAM SHATNER
STAR TREK V: THE
  FINAL FRONTIER .... CHARLES COOPER
STAR TREK V: THE
  FINAL FRONTIER .... CYNTHIA GOUW
STAR TREK V: THE
  FINAL FRONTIER .... DAVID WARNER
STAR TREK V: THE
  FINAL FRONTIER .... DEFOREST KELLEY
STAR TREK V: THE
  FINAL FRONTIER .... GEORGE TAKEI
STAR TREK V: THE
  FINAL FRONTIER .... JAMES DOOHAN
STAR TREK V: THE
  FINAL FRONTIER .... LAURENCE LUCKINBILL
STAR TREK V: THE
  FINAL FRONTIER .... LEONARD NIMOY
STAR TREK V: THE
  FINAL FRONTIER .... NICHELLE NICHOLS
STAR TREK V: THE
  FINAL FRONTIER .... REX HOLMAN
STAR TREK V: THE
  FINAL FRONTIER .... SPICE WILLIAMS
STAR TREK V: THE
  FINAL FRONTIER .... TODD BRYANT
STAR TREK V: THE
  FINAL FRONTIER .... WILLIAM KOENIG
STAR TREK V: THE
  FINAL FRONTIER .... WILLIAM SHATNER
STAR TREK VI: THE UNDISCOVERED
  COUNTRY .... DENNIS OTT†
STAR TREK VI: THE UNDISCOVERED
  COUNTRY .... BROCK PETERS
STAR TREK VI: THE UNDISCOVERED
  COUNTRY .... CHRISTIAN SLATER
STAR TREK VI: THE UNDISCOVERED
  COUNTRY .... CHRISTOPHER PLUMMER
STAR TREK VI: THE UNDISCOVERED
  COUNTRY .... DAVID WARNER
STAR TREK VI: THE UNDISCOVERED
  COUNTRY .... DEFOREST KELLEY
STAR TREK VI: THE UNDISCOVERED
  COUNTRY .... GEORGE TAKEI
STAR TREK VI: THE UNDISCOVERED
  COUNTRY .... GRACE LEE WHITNEY
STAR TREK VI: THE UNDISCOVERED
  COUNTRY .... IMAN
STAR TREK VI: THE UNDISCOVERED
  COUNTRY .... JAMES DOOHAN
STAR TREK VI: THE UNDISCOVERED
  COUNTRY .... JOHN SCHUCK
STAR TREK VI: THE UNDISCOVERED
  COUNTRY .... KIM CATTRALL
STAR TREK VI: THE UNDISCOVERED
  COUNTRY .... KURTWOOD SMITH
STAR TREK VI: THE UNDISCOVERED
  COUNTRY .... LEON RUSSOM
STAR TREK VI: THE UNDISCOVERED
  COUNTRY .... LEONARD NIMOY

STAR TREK VI: THE UNDISCOVERED
  COUNTRY .... MARK LENARD
STAR TREK VI: THE UNDISCOVERED
  COUNTRY .... MICHAEL DORN
STAR TREK VI: THE UNDISCOVERED
  COUNTRY .... NICHELLE NICHOLS
STAR TREK VI: THE UNDISCOVERED
  COUNTRY .... PAUL ROSSILLI
STAR TREK VI: THE UNDISCOVERED
  COUNTRY .... ROSANA DE SOTO
STAR TREK VI: THE UNDISCOVERED
  COUNTRY .... WILLIAM KOENIG
STAR TREK VI: THE UNDISCOVERED
  COUNTRY .... WILLIAM SHATNER
STAR WARS .... ANTHONY DANIELS
STAR WARS .... CARRIE FISHER
STAR WARS .... DAVID PROWSE
STAR WARS .... HARRISON FORD
STAR WARS .... JAMES EARL JONES
STAR WARS .... KENNY BAKER
STAR WARS .... MARK HAMILL
STAR WARS ○ .... PETER MAYHEW
STAR WARS ○ .... ALEC GUINNESS
STARCRASH .... CHRISTOPHER PLUMMER
STARCRASH .... MARJOE GORTNER
STARCROSSED (TF) .... BELINDA BAUER
STARCROSSED (TF) .... JAMES SPADER
STARCROSSED (TF) .... PETE KOWANKO
STARDUST .... LARRY HAGMAN
STARDUST .... PAUL NICHOLAS
STARDUST MEMORIES .... AMY WRIGHT
STARDUST MEMORIES .... CHARLOTTE RAMPLING
STARDUST MEMORIES .... DANIEL STERN
STARDUST MEMORIES .... JESSICA HARPER
STARDUST MEMORIES .... LARAINE NEWMAN
STARDUST MEMORIES .... LOUISE LASSER
STARDUST
  MEMORIES .... MARIE-CHRISTINE BARRAULT
STARDUST MEMORIES .... SHARON STONE
STARDUST MEMORIES .... TONY ROBERTS
STARDUST MEMORIES .... WOODY ALLEN
STARFLIGHT ONE (TF) .... LAUREN HUTTON
STARFLIGHT ONE (TF) .... LEE MAJORS
STARFLIGHT ONE (TF) .... TESS HARPER
STARFLIGHT: THE PLANE
  THAT COULDN'T LAND .... LAUREN HUTTON
STARFLIGHT: THE PLANE
  THAT COULDN'T LAND (TF) .... LEE MAJORS
STARFLIGHT: THE PLANE
  THAT COULDN'T LAND (TF) .... TESS HARPER
STARGATE .... JAMES SPADER
STARGATE .... JAYE DAVIDSON
STARGATE .... KURT RUSSELL
STARGATE .... MILI AVITAL
STARK (TF) .... DENNIS HOPPER
STARK (TF) .... MARILU HENNER
STARK: MIRROR IMAGE (TF) .... DENNIS HOPPER
STARLIFT .... DORIS DAY
STARLIFT .... GORDON MACRAE†
STARLIFT .... JANE WYMAN
STARMAN .... CHARLES MARTIN SMITH
STARMAN .... JOHN ANDERSON
STARMAN .... KAREN ALLEN
STARMAN .... RICHARD JAECKEL
STARMAN ★ .... JEFF BRIDGES
STARS AND BARS .... CELIA WESTON
STARS AND BARS .... DANIEL DAY-LEWIS
STARS AND BARS .... MARTHA PLIMPTON
STARS AND BARS .... SPALDING GRAY
STARS AND STRIPES
  FOREVER .... ROBERT WAGNER
STARS FELL ON HENRIETTA, THE ...... AIDAN QUINN
STARS FELL ON
  HENRIETTA, THE .... BRIAN DENNEHY
STARS FELL ON
  HENRIETTA, THE .... FRANCES FISHER
STARS FELL ON
  HENRIETTA, THE .... ROBERT DUVALL
STARS IN MY CROWN .... DEAN STOCKWELL
STARSHIP INVASION .... ROBERT VAUGHN
STARSKY AND HUTCH (TF) .... DAVID SOUL
START THE REVOLUTION
  WITHOUT ME .... BILLIE WHITELAW

START THE REVOLUTION
  WITHOUT ME .... DONALD SUTHERLAND
START THE REVOLUTION
  WITHOUT ME .... GENE WILDER
START THE REVOLUTION
  WITHOUT ME .... HUGH GRIFFITH†
START THE REVOLUTION
  WITHOUT ME .... JACK MACGOWRAN†
START THE REVOLUTION
  WITHOUT ME .... ORSON WELLES†
STARTING OVER .... AUSTIN PENDLETON
STARTING OVER .... BURT REYNOLDS
STARTING OVER .... CHARLES DURNING
STARTING OVER .... FRANCES STERNHAGEN
STARTING OVER .... KEVIN BACON
STARTING OVER .... MARY KAY PLACE
STARTING OVER .... WALLACE SHAWN
STARTING OVER ★ .... JILL CLAYBURGH
STARTING OVER ○ .... CANDICE BERGEN
STATE FAIR .... ANN-MARGRET
STATE FAIR .... BOBBY DARIN†
STATE FAIR .... HARRY MORGAN
STATE FAIR .... PAT BOONE
STATE OF GRACE .... ED HARRIS
STATE OF GRACE .... GARY OLDMAN
STATE OF GRACE .... JOHN TURTURRO
STATE OF GRACE .... ROBIN WRIGHT
STATE OF GRACE .... SEAN PENN
STATE OF THE UNION .... ADOLPHE MENJOU†
STATE OF THE UNION .... ANGELA LANSBURY
STATE OF THE UNION .... KATHERINE HEPBURN
STATE OF THE UNION .... LEWIS STONE†
STATE OF THE UNION .... SPENCER TRACY†
STATE OF THE UNION .... VAN JOHNSON
STATE PARK .... TED NUGENT
STATION SIX—SAHARA .... CARROLL BAKER
STATION SIX—SAHARA .... DENHOLM ELLIOTT†
STATION SIX—SAHARA .... IAN BANNEN
STATION WEST .... BURL IVES
STATION WEST .... JANE GREER
STATION WEST .... RAYMOND BURR†
STATUE, THE .... ROBERT VAUGHN
STAVISKY .... GERARD DEPARDIEU
STAY AS YOU ARE .... NASTASSJA KINSKI
STAY AWAY, JOE .... BURGESS MEREDITH
STAY AWAY JOE .... ELVIS PRESLEY†
STAY AWAY JOE .... HENRY JONES
STAY AWAY JOE .... KATHY JURADO
STAY HUNGRY .... ARNOLD SCHWARZENEGGER
STAY HUNGRY .... ED BEGLEY JR.
STAY HUNGRY .... FANNIE FLAGG
STAY HUNGRY .... JEFF BRIDGES
STAY HUNGRY .... JOANNA CASSIDY
STAY HUNGRY .... R.G. ARMSTRONG
STAY HUNGRY .... SALLY FIELD
STAYING ALIVE .... CYNTHIA RHODES
STAYING ALIVE .... FINOLA HUGHES
STAYING ALIVE .... FRANK STALLONE
STAYING ALIVE .... JOHN TRAVOLTA
STAYING ALIVE .... JULIE BOYASSO†
STAYING ALIVE .... STEVE INWOOD
STAYING TOGETHER .... DAPHNE ZUNIGA
STAYING TOGETHER .... DERMOT MULRONEY
STAYING TOGETHER .... DINAH MANOFF
STAYING TOGETHER .... JIM HAYNIE
STAYING TOGETHER .... KEITH SZARABAJKA
STAYING TOGETHER .... LEVON HELM
STAYING TOGETHER .... MELINDA DILLON
STAYING TOGETHER .... SEAN ASTIN
STAYING TOGETHER .... SHEILA KELLEY
STAYING TOGETHER .... STOCKARD CHANNING
STAYING TOGETHER .... TIM QUILL
STAZIONE TERMINI .... JENNIFER JONES
STEAGLE, THE .... CLORIS LEACHMAN
STEAGLE, THE .... RICHARD BENJAMIN
STEAGLE, THE .... SUSAN TYRRELL
STEAL THE SKY (CTF) .... SAM GRAY
STEAL THE SKY (CTF) .... SASSON GABAI
STEALING HOME .... BLAIR BROWN
STEALING HOME .... CHRISTINE JONES
STEALING HOME .... HAROLD RAMIS
STEALING HOME .... HELEN HUNT

This is not a list of every film ever made or every cast member, only those listed in this directory.

STEALING HOME ... JODIE FOSTER
STEALING HOME ... JOHN SHEA
STEALING HOME ... JONATHAN SILVERMAN
STEALING HOME ... MARK HARMON
STEALING HOME ... RICHARD JENKINS
STEALING HOME ... THATCHER GOODWIN
STEALING HOME ... WILLIAM McNAMARA
STEAMING ... SARAH MILES
STEAMING ... VANESSA REDGRAVE
STEEL ... ALBERT SALMI†
STEEL ... ART CARNEY
STEEL ... GEORGE KENNEDY
STEEL ... HARRIS YULIN
STEEL ... JENNIFER O'NEILL
STEEL ... LEE MAJORS
STEEL ... RICHARD LYNCH
STEEL AGAINST THE SKY ... ALEXIS SMITH†
STEEL CAGE, THE ... JOHN IRELAND
STEEL CAGE, THE ... LAWRENCE TIERNEY
STEEL CAGE, THE ... MAUREEN O'SULLIVAN
STEEL COWBOY (TF) ... JAMES BROLIN
STEEL COWBOY (TF) ... MELANIE GRIFFITH
STEEL DAWN ... PATRICK SWAYZE
STEEL FIST, THE ... RODDY McDOWALL
STEEL JUNGLE, THE ... DENNIS HOPPER
STEEL MAGNOLIAS ... ANN WEDGEWORTH
STEEL MAGNOLIAS ... BILL McCUTCHEON
STEEL MAGNOLIAS ... DARYL HANNAH
STEEL MAGNOLIAS ... DOLLY PARTON
STEEL MAGNOLIAS ... DYLAN McDERMOTT
STEEL MAGNOLIAS ... KEVIN J. O'CONNOR
STEEL MAGNOLIAS ... OLYMPIA DUKAKIS
STEEL MAGNOLIAS ... SALLY FIELD
STEEL MAGNOLIAS ... SAM SHEPARD
STEEL MAGNOLIAS ... SHIRLEY MacLAINE
STEEL MAGNOLIAS ... TOM SKERRITT
STEEL MAGNOLIAS ✪ ... JULIA ROBERTS
STEEL TRAP, THE ... TERESA WRIGHT
STEELE JUSTICE ... MARTIN KOVE
STEELYARD BLUES ... DONALD SUTHERLAND
STEELYARD BLUES ... JANE FONDA
STEELYARD BLUES ... PETER BOYLE
STEIBRUCH ... MARIA SCHELL
STELLA ... BETTE MIDLER
STELLA ... EILEEN BRENNAN
STELLA ... JOHN GOODMAN
STELLA ... MARSHA MASON
STELLA ... STEPHEN COLLINS
STELLA ... TRINI ALVARADO
STELLA DALLAS ★ ... BARBARA STANWYCK†
STEP BY STEP ... LAWRENCE TIERNEY
STEP LIVELY ... FRANK SINATRA
STEP OUT OF LINE, A (TF) ... PETER FALK
STEPFATHER, THE ... CHARLES LANYER
STEPFATHER, THE ... JEFF SCHULZ
STEPFATHER, THE ... JILL SCHOELEN
STEPFATHER, THE ... SHELLEY HACK
STEPFATHER, THE ... STEPHEN SHELLEN
STEPFATHER, THE ... TERRY O'QUINN
STEPFORD CHILDREN, THE (TF) ... BARBARA EDEN
STEPFORD CHILDREN, THE (TF) ... RANDALL BATINKOFF
STEPFORD CHILDREN, THE (TF) ... RICHARD ANDERSON
STEPFORD CHILDREN, THE (TF) ... TAMMY LAUREN
STEPFORD WIVES, THE ... GEORGE COE
STEPFORD WIVES, THE ... JOSEF SOMMER
STEPFORD WIVES, THE ... KATHERINE ROSS
STEPFORD WIVES, THE ... MARY STUART MASTERSON
STEPFORD WIVES, THE ... PATRICK O'NEAL†
STEPFORD WIVES, THE ... PAULA PRENTISS
STEPFORD WIVES, THE ... TINA LOUISE
STEPFORD WIVES, THE ... WILLIAM PRINCE
STEPHEN KING'S SLEEPWALKERS ... ALICE KRIGE
STEPHEN KING'S SLEEPWALKERS ... BRIAN KRAUSE
STEPHEN KING'S SLEEPWALKERS ... MADCHEN AMICK
STEPHEN KING'S SLEEPWALKERS ... MARK HAMILL
STEPHEN KING'S THE STAND (MS) ... GARY SINISE
STEPHEN KING'S THE STAND (MS) ... MOLLY RINGWALD
STEPHEN KING'S CAT'S EYE ... ALAN KING
STEPHEN KING'S CAT'S EYE ... DREW BARRYMORE
STEPHEN KING'S CAT'S EYE ... JAMES WOODS
STEPHEN KING'S CAT'S EYE ... ROBERT HAYS
STEPHEN KING'S GRAVEYARD SHIFT ... ANDREW DIVOFF
STEPHEN KING'S GRAVEYARD SHIFT ... BRAD DOURIF
STEPHEN KING'S GRAVEYARD SHIFT ... DAVID ANDREWS
STEPHEN KING'S GRAVEYARD SHIFT ... KELLY WOLF
STEPHEN KING'S GRAVEYARD SHIFT ... STEPHEN MACHT
STEPHEN KING'S GRAVEYARD SHIFT ... VIC POLIZOS
STEPHEN KING'S PET SEMATARY ... BLAZE BERDAHL
STEPHEN KING'S PET SEMATARY ... BRAD GREENQUIST
STEPHEN KING'S PET SEMATARY ... DALE MIDKIFF
STEPHEN KING'S PET SEMATARY ... DENISE CROSBY
STEPHEN KING'S PET SEMATARY ... FRED GWYNNE†
STEPHEN KING'S PET SEMATARY ... MICHAEL LOMBARD
STEPHEN KING'S PET SEMATARY ... MIKO HUGHES
STEPHEN KING'S PET SEMATARY ... STEPHEN KING
STEPHEN KING'S SILVER BULLET ... BILL SMITROVICH
STEPHEN KING'S SILVER BULLET ... COREY HAIM
STEPHEN KING'S SILVER BULLET ... GARY BUSEY
STEPHEN KING'S SILVER BULLET ... LAWRENCE TIERNEY
STEPHEN KING'S THE LAWNMOWER MAN ... AUSTIN O'BRIEN
STEPHEN KING'S THE LAWNMOWER MAN ... GEOFFREY LEWIS
STEPHEN KING'S THE LAWNMOWER MAN ... JEFF FAHEY
STEPHEN KING'S THE LAWNMOWER MAN ... JENNY WRIGHT
STEPHEN KING'S THE LAWNMOWER MAN ... PIERCE BROSNAN
STEPKIDS ... BEN SAVAGE
STEPKIDS ... GRIFFIN DUNNE
STEPMOTHER, THE ... JOHN ANDERSON
STEPPING OUT ... ANDREA MARTIN
STEPPING OUT ... BILL IRWIN
STEPPING OUT ... CAROL WOODS-COLEMAN
STEPPING OUT ... ELLEN GREENE
STEPPING OUT ... JANE KRAKOWSKI
STEPPING OUT ... JULIE WALTERS
STEPPING OUT ... LIZA MINELLI
STEPPING OUT ... ROBYN STEVEN
STEPPING OUT ... SHEILA McCARTHY
STEPPING OUT ... SHELLEY WINTERS
STERILE CUCKOO, THE ... WENDELL BURTON
STERILE CUCKOO, THE ★ ... LIZA MINELLI
STEVIE ... ALEC McCOWEN
STEVIE ... GLENDA JACKSON
STICK ... ALEX ROCCO
STICK ... BURT REYNOLDS
STICK ... CANDICE BERGEN
STICK ... CHARLES DURNING
STICK ... GEORGE SEGAL
STICK ... JOSE PEREZ
STICK ... RICHARD LAWSON
STICK ... TRICIA LEIGH FISHER
STICK UP, THE ... DAVID SOUL
STICKFIGHTER ... KELY McCLUNG
STICKY FINGERS ... CAROL KANE
STICKY FINGERS ... CHRISTOPHER GUEST
STICKY FINGERS ... EILEEN BRENNAN
STICKY FINGERS ... HELEN SLATER
STICKY FINGERS ... MELANIE MAYRON
STILETTO ... BRITT EKLAND
STILETTO ... JOHN DEHNER†
STILETTO ... JOSEPH WISEMAN
STILETTO ... PATRICK O'NEAL†
STILETTO ... RAUL JULIA†
STILETTO ... ROY SCHEIDER
STILL CRAZY LIKE A FOX (TF) ... JACK WARDEN
STILL OF THE NIGHT ... JESSICA TANDY†
STILL OF THE NIGHT ... JOSEF SOMMER
STILL OF THE NIGHT ... MERYL STREEP
STILL OF THE NIGHT ... ROY SCHEIDER
STILL OF THE NIGHT ... SARA BOTSFORD
STILLWATCH (TF) ... ANGIE DICKINSON
STILLWATCH (TF) ... BARRY PRIMUS
STILLWATCH (TF) ... BIBI OSTERWALD
STILLWATCH (TF) ... DON MURRAY
STILLWATCH (TF) ... LYNDA CARTER
STILLWATCH (TF) ... STUART WHITMAN
STING, THE ... CHARLES DURNING
STING, THE ... DIMITRA ARLYS
STING, THE ... EILEEN BRENNAN
STING, THE ... HAROLD GOULD
STING, THE ... PAUL NEWMAN
STING, THE ... RAY WALSTON
STING, THE ... ROBERT SHAW†
STING, THE ... SALLY KIRKLAND
STING, THE ★ ... ROBERT REDFORD
STING II, THE ... BERT REMSEN
STING II, THE ... JACKIE GLEASON†
STING II, THE ... KARL MALDEN
STING II, THE ... MAC DAVIS
STING II, THE ... OLIVER REED
STING II, THE ... TERI GARR
STINGRAY (TF) ... NICK MANCUSO
STIR CRAZY ... BARRY CORBIN
STIR CRAZY ... CRAIG T. NELSON
STIR CRAZY ... GENE WILDER
STIR CRAZY ... GEORG STANFORD BROWN
STIR CRAZY ... JoBETH WILLIAMS
STIR CRAZY ... MIGUELANGEL SUAREZ
STIR CRAZY ... RICHARD PRYOR
STITCHES ... BRIAN TOCHI
STITCHES ... EDDIE ALBERT
STOLEN HOURS, THE ... DIANE BAKER
STOLEN LIFE, A ... BETTE DAVIS†
STOLEN: ONE HUSBAND (TF) ... BRENDA VACCARO
STOLEN: ONE HUSBAND (TF) ... ELLIOTT GOULD
STOLEN: ONE HUSBAND (TF) ... VALERIE HARPER
STONE (TF) ... DAVID SPIELBERG
STONE (TF) ... MARIETTE HARTLEY
STONE (TF) ... PAT HINGLE
STONE BOY, THE ... FREDERIC FORREST
STONE BOY, THE ... GLENN CLOSE
STONE BOY, THE ... ROBERT DUVALL
STONE BOY, THE ... WILFORD BRIMLEY
STONE COLD ... ARABELLA HOLZBOG
STONE COLD ... BRIAN BOSWORTH
STONE COLD ... SAM McMURRAY
STONE COLD ... WILLIAM FORSYTHE
STONE COLD DEAD ... RICHARD CRENNA
STONE KILLER, THE ... CHARLES BRONSON
STONE KILLER, THE ... MARTIN BALSAM
STONE KILLER, THE ... NORMAN FELL
STONE KILLER, THE ... STUART MARGOLIN
STONE PILLOW (TF) ... DAPHNE ZUNIGA
STONE PILLOW (TF) ... STEPHEN LANG
STONE PILLOW (TF) ... WILLIAM CONVERSE-ROBERTS
STONES FOR IBARRA (TF) ... ALFONSO ARAU
STONES FOR IBARRA (TF) ... GLENN CLOSE
STONES FOR IBARRA (TF) ... KEITH CARRADINE
STONESTREET (TF) ... JOAN HACKETT†
STONING IN FULHAM COUNTY, A (TF) ... GREGG HENRY
STONING IN FULHAM COUNTY, A (TF) ... JILL EIKENBERRY
STONING IN FULHAM COUNTY, A (TF) ... KEN OLIN
STOOGE, THE ... DEAN MARTIN
STOOGE, THE ... JERRY LEWIS
STOOGEMANIA ... SID CAESAR
STOP! OR MY MOM WILL SHOOT ... ESTELLE GETTY

† after an actor's name denotes deceased.

STOP! OR MY
MOM WILL SHOOT .... JoBETH WILLIAMS
STOP! OR MY MOM WILL SHOOT .... ROGER REES
STOP! OR MY
MOM WILL SHOOT .... SYLVESTER STALLONE
STOP TRAIN 349 .... JOSE FERRER†
STOPOVER TOKYO .... JOAN COLLINS
STOPOVER TOKYO .... ROBERT WAGNER
STORK BITES MAN .... JACKIE COOPER
STORM CENTER .... BETTE DAVIS†
STORM CENTER .... BRIAN KEITH
STORM FEAR .... DENNIS WEAVER
STORM FEAR .... LEE GRANT
STORM WARNING .... DORIS DAY
STORM WARNING .... RONALD REAGAN
STORMIN' HOME (TF) .... GIL GERARD
STORMIN' HOME (TF) .... JOANNA KERNS
STORMIN' HOME (TF) .... LISA BLOUNT
STORMY MONDAY .... MELANIE GRIFFITH
STORMY MONDAY .... SEAN BEAN
STORMY MONDAY .... STING
STORMY MONDAY .... TOMMY LEE JONES
STORMY WEATHER .... LENA HORNE
STORY OF A LOVE STORY .... ALAN BATES
STORY OF A MARRIAGE .... CAROL GOODHEART
STORY OF A MARRIAGE .... HALLIE FOOTE
STORY OF A MARRIAGE .... HORTON FOOTE JR.
STORY OF A MARRIAGE ..... MATTHEW BRODERICK
STORY OF A MARRIAGE .... MICHAEL HIGGINS
STORY OF A MARRIAGE .... RICHARD JENKINS
STORY OF A MARRIAGE .... STEVEN HILL
STORY OF A
MARRIAGE .... WILLIAM CONVERSE-ROBERTS
STORY OF A WOMAN .... JAMES FARENTINO
STORY OF A WOMAN .... ROBERT STACK
STORY OF ADELE H, THE .... ISABELLE ADJANI
STORY OF ALEXANDER
GRAHAM BELL, THE .... DON AMECHE†
STORY OF DR.
WASSELL, THE .... YVONNE DE CARLO
STORY OF ESTHER
COSTELLO, THE .... JOAN CRAWFORD†
STORY OF G.I. JOE, THE .... BURGESS MEREDITH
STORY OF G.I. JOE, THE ○ .... ROBERT MITCHUM
STORY OF GILBERT
AND SULLIVAN, THE .... ROBERT MORLEY
STORY OF JACOB AND
JOSEPH, THE (TF) .... ALAN BATES
STORY OF JACOB AND
JOSEPH, THE (TF) .... COLLEEN DEWHURST†
STORY OF JOSEPH AND
HIS BRETHREN, THE .... ROBERT MORLEY
STORY OF LOUIS
PASTEUR, THE ★★ .... PAUL MUNI†
STORY OF MANKIND, THE .... DENNIS HOPPER
STORY OF MANKIND, THE .... VINCENT PRICE†
STORY OF PRETTY BOY
FLOYD, THE (TF) .... STEVEN KEATS†
STORY OF RUTH, THE .... STUART WHITMAN
STORY OF THREE LOVES, THE ..... KIRK DOUGLAS
STORY OF THREE LOVES, THE .... LESLIE CARON
STORY OF THREE
LOVES, THE .... RICHARD ANDERSON
STORY OF THREE LOVES, THE ...... ZSA ZSA GABOR
STORY OF VERNON AND
IRENE CASTLE, THE .... FRED ASTAIRE†
STORY OF WILL ROGERS, THE .... JANE WYMAN
STORY ON PAGE
ONE, THE .... ANTHONY (TONY) FRANCIOSA
STORYVILLE .... JAMES SPADER
STORYVILLE .... JASON ROBARDS
STOWAWAY .... LEON AMES
STOWAWAY GIRL .... DONALD PLEASENCE
STOWAWAY TO THE MOON (TF) .... LLOYD BRIDGES
STRAIGHT FROM
THE SHOULDER .... RALPH BELLAMY†
STRAIGHT TALK .... CHARLES FLEISCHER
STRAIGHT TALK .... DEIDRE O'CONNELL
STRAIGHT TALK .... DOLLY PARTON
STRAIGHT TALK .... GRIFFIN DUNNE
STRAIGHT TALK .... JAMES WOODS
STRAIGHT TALK .... JAY THOMAS

STRAIGHT TALK .... JERRY ORBACH
STRAIGHT TALK .... JOHN SAYLES
STRAIGHT TALK .... MICHAEL MADSEN
STRAIGHT TALK .... PHILIP BOSCO
STRAIGHT TALK .... SPALDING GRAY
STRAIGHT TALK .... TERI HATCHER
STRAIGHT TIME .... DUSTIN HOFFMAN
STRAIGHT TIME .... GARY BUSEY
STRAIGHT TIME .... KATHY BATES
STRAIGHT TIME .... M. EMMET WALSH
STRAIGHT TIME .... THERESA RUSSELL
STRAIGHT TO HELL .... DENNIS HOPPER
STRAIGHT-JACKET .... JOAN CRAWFORD†
STRAIT-JACKET .... DIANE BAKER
STRAIT-JACKET .... GEORGE KENNEDY
STRANDED .... IONE SKYE
STRANDED (TF) .... ELAINE STRITCH
STRANDED (TF) .... JOEL BROOKS
STRANDED (TF) .... LONI ANDERSON
STRANDED (TF) .... PERRY KING
STRANGE AFFAIR OF
UNCLE HARRY, THE ...... GERALDINE FITZGERALD
STRANGE AFFAIR, THE .... JEREMY KEMP
STRANGE AFFAIR, THE .... MICHAEL YORK
STRANGE AFFAIR, THE .... NIGEL DAVENPORT
STRANGE AFFAIR, THE .... SUSAN GEORGE
STRANGE AND DEADLY
OCCURRENCE, THE (TF) .... ROBERT STACK
STRANGE BARGAIN .... MARTHA SCOTT
STRANGE BEHAVIOR .... LOUISE FLETCHER
STRANGE CARGO .... JOAN CRAWFORD†
STRANGE CONFESSION .... LLOYD BRIDGES
STRANGE DAYS .... ANGELA BASSETT
STRANGE DAYS .... BRIGITTE BAKO
STRANGE DAYS .... GLENN PLUMMER
STRANGE DAYS .... JULIETTE LEWIS
STRANGE DAYS .... MICHAEL WINCOTT
STRANGE DAYS .... RALPH FIENNES
STRANGE DAYS .... RICHARD EDSON
STRANGE DAYS .... TOM SIZEMORE
STRANGE DAYS .... VINCENT D'ONOFRIO
STRANGE DAYS .... WILLIAM FICHTNER
STRANGE INTERLUDE .... MAUREEN O'SULLIVAN
STRANGE INVADERS .... DIANA SCARWID
STRANGE INVADERS .... FIONA LEWIS
STRANGE INVADERS .... LOUISE FLETCHER
STRANGE INVADERS .... MICHAEL LERNER
STRANGE INVADERS .... NANCY ALLEN
STRANGE INVADERS .... PAUL LeMAT
STRANGE LADY IN TOWN .... GREER GARSON
STRANGE LOVE OF
MARTHA IVERS, THE .... BARBARA STANWYCK†
STRANGE LOVE OF MARTHA
IVERS, THE .... DAME JUDITH ANDERSON†
STRANGE LOVE OF
MARTHA IVERS, THE .... KIRK DOUGLAS
STRANGE ONE, THE .... BEN GAZZARA
STRANGE ONE, THE .... GEORGE PEPPARD†
STRANGE ONE, THE .... JAMES OLSON
STRANGE ONE, THE .... PAT HINGLE
STRANGE ONE, THE .... PETER MARK RICHMAN
STRANGE POSSESSION OF
MRS. OLIVER, THE (TF) .... GEORGE HAMILTON
STRANGE POSSESSION OF
MRS. OLIVER, THE (TF) .... KAREN BLACK
STRANGE SHADOWS IN
AN EMPTY ROOM .... JOHN SAXON
STRANGE SHADOWS IN
AN EMPTY ROOM .... MARTIN LANDAU
STRANGE SHADOWS IN
AN EMPTY ROOM .... STUART WHITMAN
STRANGE VENGEANCE
OF ROSALIE, THE .... BONNIE BEDELIA
STRANGE VENGEANCE
OF ROSALIE, THE .... KEN HOWARD
STRANGE VOICES (TF) .... NANCY McKEON
STRANGE VOICES (TF) .... STEPHEN MACHT
STRANGE VOICES (TF) .... TRICIA LEIGH FISHER
STRANGE VOICES (TF) .... VALERIE HARPER
STRANGE VOYAGE .... EDDIE ALBERT
STRANGER, THE .... MARCELLO MASTROIANNI
STRANGER, THE (TF) .... SHARON ACKER

STRANGER AMONG US, A .... ERIC THAL
STRANGER AMONG US, A .... MELANIE GRIFFITH
STRANGER AMONG US, A .... MIA SARA
STRANGER AMOUNG US, A .... LEE RICHARDSON
STRANGER FROM VENUS .... PATRICIA NEAL
STRANGER IN MY ARMS .... JUNE ALLYSON
STRANGER IN MY BED (TF) .... ARMAND ASSANTE
STRANGER IN MY BED (TF) .... DOUG SHEEHAN
STRANGER IN MY BED (TF) .... GABRIEL DAMON
STRANGER IN MY BED (TF) .... LINDSAY WAGNER
STRANGER IN THE HOUSE .... GERALDINE CHAPLIN
STRANGER IS WATCHING, A .... JAMES NAUGHTON
STRANGER IS WATCHING, A .... KATE MULGREW
STRANGER IS WATCHING, A .... RIP TORN
STRANGER LEFT
NO CARD, THE .... GEOFFREY BAYLDON
STRANGER ON HORSEBACK .... KEVIN McCARTHY
STRANGER ON MY LAND (TF) .... BEN JOHNSON
STRANGER ON
MY LAND (TF) .... DEE WALLACE STONE
STRANGER ON MY LAND (TF) .... PAT HINGLE
STRANGER ON
MY LAND (TF) .... TOMMY LEE JONES
STRANGER THAN PARADISE .... JOHN LURIE
STRANGER THAN PARADISE .... RICHARD EDSON
STRANGER THINGS .... BEATRICE ARTHUR
STRANGER THINGS .... JAMES WOODS
STRANGER THINGS .... JASON ALEXANDER
STRANGER THINGS .... JOE MANTEGNA
STRANGER THINGS .... LOLITA DAVIDOVICH
STRANGER THINGS .... ROBERT COSTANZO
STRANGER WAITS, A (TF) .... ANN WEDGEWORTH
STRANGER WAITS, A (TF) .... JUSTIN DEAS
STRANGER WAITS, A (TF) .... PAUL BENJAMIN
STRANGER WAITS, A (TF) .... SUZANNE PLESHETTE
STRANGER
WAITS, A (TF) .... TERRY DAVID MULLIGAN
STRANGER WHO LOOKS
LIKE ME, THE (TF) .... BEAU BRIDGES
STRANGER WHO LOOKS
LIKE ME, THE (TF) .... MEREDITH BAXTER
STRANGER WITHIN, THE (TF) .... BARBARA EDEN
STRANGER
WITHIN, THE (TF) .... GEORGE GRIZZARD
STRANGER WORE
A GUN, THE .... ERNEST BORGNINE
STRANGERS: THE STORY OF A
MOTHER AND A DAUGHTER (TF) ..... ROYAL DANO
STRANGERS WHEN WE MEET .... KIM NOVAK
STRANGERS WHEN WE MEET .... KIRK DOUGLAS
STRANGERS WHEN
WE MEET .... WALTER MATTHAU
STRANGER'S KISS .... BLAINE NOVAK
STRANGER'S KISS .... PETER COYOTE
STRANGER'S KISS .... VICTORIA TENNANT
STRAPLESS .... BLAIR BROWN
STRAPLESS .... BRIDGET FONDA
STRAPLESS .... BRUNO GANZ
STRATEGIC AIR COMMAND .... JAMES STEWART
STRATEGIC AIR COMMAND .... JUNE ALLYSON
STRATTON STORY, THE .... JAMES STEWART
STRATTON STORY, THE .... JUNE ALLYSON
STRAW DOGS .... DAVID WARNER
STRAW DOGS .... DUSTIN HOFFMAN
STRAW DOGS .... PETER VAUGHN
STRAW DOGS .... SUSAN GEORGE
STRAWBERRY
BLONDE, THE .... OLIVIA DE HAVILLAND
STRAWBERRY
STATEMENT, THE .... BRUCE DAVISON
STRAWBERRY
STATEMENT, THE .... JEANNIE BERLIN
STRAWBERRY STATEMENT, THE .... KIM DARBY
STREAMERS .... GEORGE DZUNDZA
STREAMERS .... GUY BOYD
STREAMERS .... MICHAEL WRIGHT
STREET ANGEL ★★ .... JANET GAYNOR†
STREET FIGHTER .... BYRON MANN
STREET FIGHTER .... DAMIAN CHAPA
STREET FIGHTER .... JEAN-CLAUDE VAN DAMME
STREET FIGHTER .... KYLIE MINOGUE

This is not a list of every film ever made or every cast member, only those listed in this directory.

STREET FIGHTER .... MING-NA WEN
STREET FIGHTER .... RAUL JULIA†
STREET FIGHTER .... WES STUDI
STREET GANG .... CAROL LYNLEY
STREET GANG .... ROBERT FORSTER
STREET KILLING (TF) .... HARRY GUARDINO
STREET OF CHANCE ...... BURGESS MEREDITH
STREET OF DREAMS (TF) .... BEN MASTERS
STREET OF DREAMS (TF) .... JOHN HILLERMAN
STREET OF DREAMS (TF) .... MORGAN FAIRCHILD
STREET PEOPLE .... ROGER MOORE
STREET PEOPLE .... STACY KEACH
STREET SCENE .... SYLVIA SIDNEY
STREET SMART .... ANDRE GREGORY
STREET SMART .... CHRISTOPHER REEVE
STREET SMART .... JAY PATTERSON
STREET SMART .... KATHY BAKER
STREET SMART .... MIMI ROGERS
STREET SMART O .... MORGAN FREEMAN
STREET WITH
  NO NAME, THE .... RICHARD WIDMARK
STREETCAR NAMED
  DESIRE, A ★ .... MARLON BRANDO
STREETCAR NAMED
  DESIRE, A ★★ .... VIVIEN LEIGH†
STREETCAR NAMED
  DESIRE, A OO .... KARL MALDEN
STREETCAR NAMED
  DESIRE, A (TF) .... ANN-MARGRET
STREETCAR NAMED
  DESIRE, A (TF) .... TREAT WILLIAMS
STREETFIGHTER .... KYLIE MINOGUE
STREETFIGHTER .... RAUL JULIA
STREETFIGHTER .... WES STUDI
STREETS OF FIRE .... AMY MADIGAN
STREETS OF FIRE .... DIANE LANE
STREETS OF FIRE .... ED BEGLEY JR.
STREETS OF FIRE .... LEE VING
STREETS OF FIRE .... MICHAEL PARE
STREETS OF FIRE .... MICHAEL ROOKER
STREETS OF FIRE .... PETER JASON
STREETS OF FIRE .... RICK MORANIS
STREETS OF FIRE .... RICK ROSSOVICH
STREETS OF FIRE .... WILLEM DAFOE
STREETS OF GOLD .... ELVA BASKIN
STREETS OF GOLD .... JOHN MAHONEY
STREETS OF GOLD .... KLAUS MARIA BRANDAUER
STREETS OF GOLD .... RAINBOW HARVEST
STREETS OF GOLD .... RICK AIELLO
STREETS OF GOLD .... WESLEY SNIPES
STREETS OF JUSTICE (TF) ...... JOHN HANCOCK
STREETS OF JUSTICE (TF) ...... LANCE HENRIKSEN
STREETS OF JUSTICE (TF) ..... ROBERT LOGGIA
STREETS OF
  L.A., THE (TF) .... JOANNE WOODWARD
STREETS OF NEW YORK ...... JACKIE COOPER
STREETS OF SAN
  FRANCISCO, THE (TF) ...... KARL MALDEN
STREETS OF SAN
  FRANCISCO, THE (TF) ...... MICHAEL DOUGLAS
STREETS OF SAN
  FRANCISCO, THE (TF) .... ROBERT WAGNER
STREETWALKIN' .... DALE MIDKIFF
STREETWALKIN' .... JULIE NEWMAR
STRICTLY BALLROOM .... PAUL MERCURIO
STRICTLY BUSINESS .... ANNE MARIE JOHNSON
STRICTLY BUSINESS .... DAVID MARSHALL GRANT
STRICTLY BUSINESS .... HALLE BERRY
STRICTLY BUSINESS .... JOSEPH C. PHILLIPS
STRICTLY BUSINESS .... KEVIN HOOKS
STRICTLY BUSINESS .... TOMMY DAVIDSON
STRICTLY DISHONORABLE .... JANET LEIGH
STRIKE FORCE (TF) .... CLIFF GORMAN
STRIKE FORCE (TF) .... RICHARD GERE
STRIKE IT RICH .... MOLLY RINGWALD
STRIKE IT RICH .... ROBERT LINDSAY
STRIKE UP THE BAND .... MICKEY ROONEY
STRIKING BACK .... DON STROUD
STRIKING BACK .... PERRY KING
STRIKING DISTANCE .... BRUCE WILLIS
STRIKING DISTANCE .... DENNIS FARINA
STRIKING DISTANCE .... JOHN MAHONEY

STRIKING DISTANCE .... ROBERT PASTORELLI
STRIKING DISTANCE .... SARAH JESSICA PARKER
STRIKING DISTANCE ...... TOM SIZEMORE
STRIPES .... BILL MURRAY
STRIPES .... HAROLD RAMIS
STRIPES .... JOHN CANDY†
STRIPES .... JOHN LARROQUETTE
STRIPES .... JUDGE REINHOLD
STRIPES .... P. J. SOLES
STRIPES .... SEAN YOUNG
STRIPES .... TIMOTHY BUSFIELD
STRIPES .... WARREN OATES†
STRIPPED TO KILL .... GREG EVIGAN
STRIPPED TO KILL .... KAY LENZ
STRIPPED TO KILL .... NORMAN FELL
STRIPPER, THE .... CAROL LYNLEY
STRIPPER, THE .... JOANNE WOODWARD
STRIPPER, THE .... MICHAEL J. POLLARD
STRIPPER, THE .... ROBERT WEBBER
STROKER ACE .... BUBBA SMITH
STROKER ACE .... BURT REYNOLDS
STROKER ACE .... FRANK O. HILL
STROKER ACE .... JIM NABORS
STROKER ACE .... JOHN BYNER
STROKER ACE .... LONI ANDERSON
STROKER ACE .... NED BEATTY
STROKER ACE .... PARKER STEVENSON
STRONG MEDICINE .... CAROL KANE
STRONG MEDICINE (TF) .... DICK VAN DYKE
STRONGEST MAN IN
  THE WORLD, THE ...... DICK VAN PATTEN
STRONGEST MAN IN
  THE WORLD, THE .... KURT RUSSELL
STRUGGLE IN THE VALLEY, THE ...... OMAR SHARIF
STRUGGLE ON THE NILE .... OMAR SHARIF
STUART SMALLEY .... AL FRANKEN
STUART SMALLEY .... HARRIS YULIN
STUART SMALLEY .... LAURA SAN GIACOMO
STUART SMALLEY .... LESLEY BOONE
STUART SMALLEY .... SHIRLEY KNIGHT
STUART SMALLEY .... VINCENT D'ONOFRIO
STUCK WITH EACH
  OTHER (TF) .... EILEEN HECKART
STUCK WITH EACH
  OTHER (TF) .... RICHARD CRENNA
STUCK WITH EACH
  OTHER (TF) .... ROSCOE LEE BROWNE
STUCK WITH EACH OTHER (TF) .... TYNE DALY
STUD, THE .... JOAN COLLINS
STUD, THE .... OLIVER TOBIAS
STUDENT PRINCE, THE .... RICHARD ANDERSON
STUDS LONIGAN .... JACK KRUSCHEN
STUDS LONIGAN .... JACK NICHOLSON
STUDS LONIGAN (MS) .... CHARLES DURNING
STUDS LONIGAN (MS) .... COLLEEN DEWHURST†
STUDS LONIGAN (MS) .... HARRY HAMLIN
STUDY IN TERROR, A .... JOHN NEVILLE
STUDY IN TERROR, A .... JUDI DENCH
STUDY IN TERROR, A .... ROBERT MORLEY
STUFF, THE .... DANNY AIELLO
STUFF, THE .... MICHAEL MORIARTY
STUFF, THE .... BROOKE ADAMS
STUNT MAN, THE .... ALLEN GARFIELD
STUNT MAN, THE .... BARBARA HERSHEY
STUNT MAN, THE .... STEVE RAILSBACK
STUNT MAN, THE ★ .... PETER O'TOOLE
STUNT SEVEN (TF) .... BILL MACY
STUNT SEVEN (TF) .... MORGAN BRITTANY
STUNTS .... FIONA LEWIS
STUNTS .... JOANNA CASSIDY
STUNTS .... RAY SHARKEY†
STUNTS .... ROBERT FORSTER
SUBJECT WAS ROSES, THE .... MARTIN SHEEN
SUBJECT WAS ROSES, THE ★ .... PATRICIA NEAL
SUBJECT WAS
  ROSES, THE OO .... JACK ALBERTSON†
SUBMARINE X-I .... JAMES CAAN
SUBSTITUTE, THE (CTF) .... AMANDA DONOHOE
SUBSTITUTE, THE (CTF) ...... MARK WAHLBERG
SUBSTITUTE WIFE, THE (TF) .... ANNIE SUITE
SUBSTITUTE WIFE, THE (TF) .... BABS GEORGE
SUBSTITUTE WIFE, THE (TF) ...... COLTON CONKLIN

SUBSTITUTE WIFE, THE (TF) .... CORY LLOYD
SUBSTITUTE WIFE, THE (TF) ...... FARRAH FAWCETT
SUBSTITUTE WIFE, THE (TF) .... GAIL CRONAUER
SUBSTITUTE WIFE, THE (TF) .... GENA SLEETE
SUBSTITUTE
  WIFE, THE (TF) .... JILL PARKER-JONES
SUBSTITUTE WIFE, THE (TF) ...... KARIS BRYANT
SUBSTITUTE WIFE, THE (TF) .... LEA THOMPSON
SUBSTITUTE WIFE, THE (TF) ...... MARCO PERELA
SUBSTITUTE WIFE, THE (TF) .... PETER WELLER
SUBSTITUTE WIFE, THE (TF) .... TONY FRANK
SUBSTITUTE WIFE, THE (TF) .... ZEKE MILLS
SUBTERFUGE .... JOAN COLLINS
SUBTERRANEANS, THE .... GEORGE PEPPARD†
SUBTERRANEANS, THE .... LESLIE CARON
SUBTERRANEANS, THE .... RODDY McDOWALL
SUBURBAN COMMANDO .... HULK HOGAN
SUBURBAN COMMANDO .... MARCY GOLDMAN
SUBURBAN COMMANDO .... SHELLEY DUVALL
SUBWAY .... CHRISTOPHER LAMBERT
SUBWAY .... ISABELLE ADJANI
SUBWAY IN THE SKY .... VAN JOHNSON
SUCCESS .... JEFF BRIDGES
SUCCESS IS THE BEST REVENGE .... ANOUK AIMEE
SUCCESS IS THE BEST REVENGE .... JOHN HURT
SUCCESS IS THE
  BEST REVENGE .... MICHAEL YORK
SUCH GOOD FRIENDS .... BURGESS MEREDITH
SUCH GOOD FRIENDS .... DYAN CANNON
SUCH GOOD FRIENDS .... JENNIFER O'NEILL
SUCH GOOD FRIENDS .... KEN HOWARD
SUCH GOOD FRIENDS .... LAURENCE LUCKINBILL
SUCH GOOD FRIENDS .... LOUISE LASSER
SUCH GOOD FRIENDS .... NINA FOCH
SUDDEN DEATH .... DON STROUD
SUDDEN DEATH .... JEAN-CLAUDE VAN DAMME
SUDDEN DEATH .... ROBERT CONRAD
SUDDEN FEAR ★ .... JOAN CRAWFORD†
SUDDEN FEAR O .... JACK PALANCE
SUDDEN IMPACT .... BRADFORD DILLMAN
SUDDEN IMPACT .... CLINT EASTWOOD
SUDDEN IMPACT .... PAT HINGLE
SUDDEN IMPACT .... SONDRA LOCKE
SUDDEN TERROR .... JEREMY KEMP
SUDDEN TERROR .... MARK LESTER
SUDDEN TERROR .... SUSAN GEORGE
SUDDENLY .... FRANK SINATRA
SUDDENLY LAST
  SUMMER .... MERCEDES McCAMBRIDGE
SUDDENLY LAST
  SUMMER ★ .... ELIZABETH TAYLOR
SUDDENLY, LAST
  SUMMER ★ .... KATHERINE HEPBURN
SUDDENLY LOVE (TF) .... EILEEN HECKART
SUDDENLY SINGLE .... HAL HOLBROOK
SUDDENLY SINGLE .... MARGOT KIDDER
SUDDENY LAST SUMMER (TF) .... MAGGIE SMITH
SUEZ .... LEON AMES
SUGAR HILL .... ABE VIGODA
SUGAR HILL .... CLARENCE WILLIAMS III
SUGAR HILL .... ERNIE HUDSON
SUGAR HILL .... LARRY JOSHUA
SUGAR HILL .... LESLIE UGGAMS
SUGAR HILL .... MICHAEL WRIGHT
SUGAR HILL .... THERESA RANDLE
SUGAR HILL .... WESLEY SNIPES
SUGARBABY .... MARIANNE SAGEBRECHT
SUGARLAND EXPRESS, THE .... BEN JOHNSON
SUGARLAND EXPRESS, THE .... GOLDIE HAWN
SUGARLAND EXPRESS, THE .... LOUISE LATHAM
SUGARLAND
  EXPRESS, THE ...... WILLIAM ATHERTON
SUMMER .... CARITA
SUMMER .... VINCENT GAUTHIER
SUMMER AND SMOKE .... EARL HOLLIMAN
SUMMER AND SMOKE .... MAX SHOWALTER
SUMMER AND SMOKE .... RITA MORENO
SUMMER AND SMOKE ★ .... GERALDINE PAGE†
SUMMER AND SMOKE O .... UNA MERKEL†
SUMMER CAMP NIGHTMARE .... CHUCK CONNORS†
SUMMER CITY .... MEL GIBSON

557

SUMMER DREAMS: THE STORY OF
  THE BEACH BOYS (TF) .... BRUCE GREENWOOD
SUMMER
  FANTASIES (TF) .... DANIELLE von ZERNECK
SUMMER HEAT .... ANTHONY EDWARDS
SUMMER HEAT .... KATHY BATES
SUMMER HEAT .... LORI SINGER
SUMMER HOLIDAY .... RON MOODY
SUMMER JOB .... PATRICK DEMPSEY
SUMMER JOB .... SALLY KELLERMAN
SUMMER LOVE .... JILL ST. JOHN
SUMMER LOVE .... JOHN SAXON
SUMMER LOVE .... TROY DONAHUE
SUMMER LOVERS .... DARYL HANNAH
SUMMER LOVERS .... PETER GALLAGHER
SUMMER MADNESS .... DARREN McGAVIN
SUMMER MADNESS ★ .... KATHERINE HEPBURN
SUMMER MAGIC .... BURL IVES
SUMMER MAGIC .... HAYLEY MILLS
SUMMER MAGIC .... MICHAEL J. POLLARD
SUMMER OF '42 .... JENNIFER O'NEILL
SUMMER OF MY GERMAN
  SOLDIER (TF) .... BARBARA BARRIE
SUMMER OF MY GERMAN
  SOLDIER (TF) .... BRUCE DAVISON
SUMMER OF MY GERMAN
  SOLDIER (TF) .... ESTHER ROLLE
SUMMER OF MY GERMAN
  SOLDIER (TF) .... KRISTY McNICHOL
SUMMER OF MY GERMAN
  SOLDIER (TF) .... MICHAEL CONSTANTINE
SUMMER OF THE
  17TH DOLL .... ANGELA LANSBURY
SUMMER OF THE 17TH DOLL .... JOHN MILLS
SUMMER OF THE
  SEVENTEENTH DOLL .... ERNEST BORGNINE
SUMMER PLACE, A .... SANDRA DEE
SUMMER PLACE, A .... TROY DONAHUE
SUMMER RENTAL .... JOHN CANDY†
SUMMER RENTAL .... RIP TORN
SUMMER SCHOOL .... CARL REINER
SUMMER SCHOOL .... COURTNEY THORNE-SMITH
SUMMER SCHOOL .... DEAN CAMERON
SUMMER SCHOOL .... GARY RILEY
SUMMER SCHOOL .... KIRSTIE ALLEY
SUMMER SCHOOL .... MARK HARMON
SUMMER SCHOOL .... PATRICK LABORTEAUX
SUMMER SCHOOL .... ROBIN THOMAS
SUMMER SCHOOL .... SHAWNEE SMITH
SUMMER STOCK .... GENE KELLY
SUMMER STORY, A .... IMOGEN STUBBS
SUMMER STORY, A .... JAMES WILBY
SUMMER STORY, A .... KEN COLLEY
SUMMER STORY, A .... SOPHIE WARD
SUMMER STORY, A .... SUSANNAH YORK
SUMMER TO
  REMEMBER, A (TF) .... BRIDGETTE ANDERSON
SUMMER TO REMEMBER, A (TF) .... BURT YOUNG
SUMMER TO
  REMEMBER, A (TF) .... JAMES FARENTINO
SUMMER TO
  REMEMBER, A (TF) .... LOUISE FLETCHER
SUMMER TO REMEMBER, A (TF) .... TESS HARPER
SUMMER WISHES,
  WINTER DREAMS .... MARTIN BALSAM
SUMMER WISHES,
  WINTER DREAMS ★ .... JOANNE WOODWARD
SUMMER WISHES,
  WINTER DREAMS ○ .... SYLVIA SIDNEY
SUMMER WITHOUT BOYS, A (TF) .... BARBARA BAIN
SUMMERTIME .... DARREN McGAVIN
SUMMERTIME .... KATHERINE HEPBURN
SUMMERTIME KILLER .... KARL MALDEN
SUMMERTREE .... BRENDA VACCARO
SUMMERTREE .... JACK WARDEN
SUMMERTREE .... MICHAEL DOUGLAS
SUN ALSO RISES, THE .... AVA GARDNER†
SUN ALSO RISES, THE .... EDDIE ALBERT
SUN ALSO RISES, THE .... MEL FERRER
SUN ALSO RISES, THE (MS) .... JANE SEYMOUR
SUN ALSO
  RISES, THE (MS) .... ROBERT CARRADINE

SUN ALSO RISES, THE (TF) .... HART BOCHNER
SUN VALLEY SERENADE .... MILTON BERLE
SUNBURN .... ART CARNEY
SUNBURN .... CHARLES GRODIN
SUNBURN .... ELEANOR PARKER
SUNBURN .... FARRAH FAWCETT
SUNBURN .... JACK KRUSCHEN
SUNBURN .... JOAN COLLINS
SUNBURN .... JOHN HILLERMAN
SUNBURST .... WILLIAM DANIELS
SUNBURST .... JAMES KEACH
SUNDAY, BLOODY SUNDAY ..... DANIEL DAY-LEWIS
SUNDAY, BLOODY SUNDAY .... PEGGY ASHCROFT†
SUNDAY, BLOODY
  SUNDAY ★ .... GLENDA JACKSON
SUNDAY, BLOODY SUNDAY ★ .... PETER FINCH†
SUNDAY IN NEW YORK .... CLIFF ROBERTSON
SUNDAY IN NEW YORK .... JANE FONDA
SUNDAY IN NEW YORK .... ROBERT CULP
SUNDAY IN THE COUNTRY .... ERNEST BORGNINE
SUNDAY IN THE COUNTRY .... MICHAEL J. POLLARD
SUNDAY LOVERS .... DENHOLM ELLIOTT†
SUNDAY LOVERS .... GENE WILDER
SUNDAY LOVERS .... KATHLEEN QUINLAN
SUNDAY LOVERS .... LYNN REDGRAVE
SUNDAY LOVERS .... ROGER MOORE
SUNDAY PUNCH .... AVA GARDNER†
SUNDAY TOO FAR AWAY .... JACK THOMPSON
SUNDAY WOMAN, THE .... JACQUELINE BISSET
SUNDOWN .... WOODY STRODE
SUNDOWNERS, THE .... DINA MERRILL
SUNDOWNERS, THE .... JOHN MEILLON
SUNDOWNERS, THE .... PETER USTINOV
SUNDOWNERS, THE .... ROBERT MITCHUM
SUNDOWNERS, THE ★ .... DEBORAH KERR
SUNFLOWER .... MARCELLO MASTROIANNI
SUNFLOWER .... SOPHIA LOREN
SUNNY SIDE UP .... JACKIE COOPER
SUNNYSIDE .... MYKELTI WILLIAMSON
SUNRISE ★★ .... JANET GAYNOR†
SUNRISE AT CAMPOBELLO .... HUME CRONYN
SUNRISE AT CAMPOBELLO ...... RALPH BELLAMY†
SUNRISE AT CAMPOBELLO ★ .... GREER GARSON
SUNSET .... BRUCE WILLIS
SUNSET .... JAMES GARNER
SUNSET .... JENNIFER EDWARDS
SUNSET .... JOE DALLESANDRO
SUNSET .... KATHLEEN QUINLAN
SUNSET .... MARIEL HEMINGWAY
SUNSET BEAT (TF) .... JAMES TOLKAN
SUNSET BEAT (TF) .... MICHAEL DeLUISE
SUNSET BOULEVARD ★ .... GLORIA SWANSON†
SUNSET BOULEVARD ★ .... WILLIAM HOLDEN†
SUNSET BOULEVARD ○ ..... ERICH VON STROHEIM†
SUNSET PASS .... JANE GREER
SUNSHINE BOYS, THE .... F. MURRAY ABRAHAM
SUNSHINE BOYS, THE .... HOWARD HESSEMAN
SUNSHINE BOYS, THE .... RICHARD BENJAMIN
SUNSHINE BOYS, THE ★ .... STEVE ALLEN
SUNSHINE BOYS, THE ○○ ...... WALTER MATTHAU
SUNSHINE BOYS, THE ○○ .... GEORGE BURNS
SUNSHINE CHRISTMAS (TF) .... EILEEN HECKART
SUNSHINE FOLLOWS RAIN .... MAE ZETTERLING†
SUNSHINE (TF) .... BRENDA VACCARO
SUNSHINE (TF) .... CLIFF DE YOUNG
SUNSHINE (TF) .... MEG FOSTER
SUPER, THE .... JOE PESCI
SUPER, THE .... MADOLYN SMITH OSBORNE
SUPER, THE .... RUBEN BLADES
SUPER, THE .... VINCENT GARDENIA†
SUPER COPS, THE .... PAT HINGLE
SUPER COPS, THE .... RON LEIBMAN
SUPER MARIO BROS. .... BOB HOSKINS
SUPER MARIO BROS. .... JOHN LEGUIZAMO
SUPER SLEUTH .... ANN SOTHERN
SUPERCARRIER (TF) .... ALEX HYDE-WHITE
SUPERCARRIER (TF) .... DENISE NICHOLAS
SUPERCARRIER (TF) .... PAUL GLEASON
SUPERCARRIER (TF) .... RICHARD JAECKEL
SUPERCARRIER (TF) .... ROBERT HOOKS
SUPERDAD .... DICK VAN PATTEN
SUPERDAD .... KURT RUSSELL

SUPERDOME (TF) .... DONNA MILLS
SUPERDOME (TF) .... KEN HOWARD
SUPERFLY .... JULIUS HARRIS
SUPERFLY .... RON O'NEAL
SUPERFLY T.N.T. .... RON O'NEAL
SUPERFLY T.N.T. .... ROSCOE LEE BROWNE
SUPERFUZZ .... ERNEST BORGNINE
SUPERGIRL .... BRENDA VACCARO
SUPERGIRL .... FAYE DUNAWAY
SUPERGIRL .... HART BOCHNER
SUPERGIRL .... HELEN SLATER
SUPERGIRL .... MARC McCLURE
SUPERGIRL .... MAUREEN TEEFY
SUPERGIRL .... MIA FARROW
SUPERGIRL .... PETER COOK
SUPERGIRL .... PETER O'TOOLE
SUPERGIRL .... SIMON WARD
SUPERGRASS, THE .... KEITH ALLEN
SUPERMAN .... CHRISTOPHER REEVE
SUPERMAN .... GENE HACKMAN
SUPERMAN .... JACK O'HALLORAN
SUPERMAN .... JACKIE COOPER
SUPERMAN .... MARGOT KIDDER
SUPERMAN .... MARIA SCHELL
SUPERMAN .... MARLON BRANDO
SUPERMAN .... NED BEATTY
SUPERMAN .... PHYLLIS THAXTER
SUPERMAN .... SUSANNAH YORK
SUPERMAN .... TERENCE STAMP
SUPERMAN .... TREVOR HOWARD†
SUPERMAN .... VALERIE PERRINE
SUPERMAN II .... ANTHONY SHER
SUPERMAN II .... CHRISTOPHER REEVE
SUPERMAN II .... CLIFTON JAMES
SUPERMAN II .... E. G. MARSHALL
SUPERMAN II .... GENE HACKMAN
SUPERMAN II .... JACK O'HALLORAN
SUPERMAN II .... JACKIE COOPER
SUPERMAN II .... MARC McCLURE
SUPERMAN II .... MARGOT KIDDER
SUPERMAN II .... NED BEATTY
SUPERMAN II .... SARAH DOUGLAS
SUPERMAN II .... SUSANNAH YORK
SUPERMAN II .... TERENCE STAMP
SUPERMAN II .... VALERIE PERRINE
SUPERMAN III .... ANNETTE O'TOOLE
SUPERMAN III .... CHRISTOPHER REEVE
SUPERMAN III .... JACKIE COOPER
SUPERMAN III .... MARC McCLURE
SUPERMAN III .... MARGOT KIDDER
SUPERMAN III .... PAMELA STEPHENSON
SUPERMAN III .... RICHARD PRYOR
SUPERMAN III .... ROBERT VAUGHN
SUPERMAN IV: THE QUEST
  FOR PEACE .... CHRISTOPHER REEVE
SUPERMAN IV: THE QUEST
  FOR PEACE .... GENE HACKMAN
SUPERMAN IV: THE QUEST
  FOR PEACE .... JACKIE COOPER
SUPERMAN IV: THE QUEST
  FOR PEACE .... MARGOT KIDDER
SUPERMAN IV: THE QUEST
  FOR PEACE .... MARIEL HEMINGWAY
SUPERMAN IV: THE QUEST
  FOR PEACE .... MARK PILLOW
SUPERMAN IV: THE QUEST
  FOR PEACE .... SAM WANAMAKER†
SUPERMAN IV: THE QUEST
  FOR PEACE .... SUSANNAH YORK
SUPERNATURALS, THE .... LeVAR BURTON
SUPERNATURALS, THE .... NICHELLE NICHOLS
SUPPORT YOUR LOCAL
  GUNFIGHTER .... CHUCK CONNORS†
SUPPORT YOUR LOCAL
  GUNFIGHTER .... HARRY MORGAN
SUPPORT YOUR LOCAL
  GUNFIGHTER .... HENRY JONES
SUPPORT YOUR LOCAL
  GUNFIGHTER .... JAMES GARNER
SUPPORT YOUR LOCAL
  GUNFIGHTER .... JOHN DEHNER†

This is not a list of every film ever made or every cast member, only those listed in this directory.

SUPPORT YOUR LOCAL GUNFIGHTER ... KATHLEEN FREEMAN
SUPPORT YOUR LOCAL GUNFIGHTER ... SUZANNE PLESHETTE
SUPPORT YOUR LOCAL SHERIFF ... BRUCE DERN
SUPPORT YOUR LOCAL SHERIFF ... HARRY MORGAN
SUPPORT YOUR LOCAL SHERIFF ... HENRY JONES
SUPPORT YOUR LOCAL SHERIFF ... JAMES GARNER
SUPPORT YOUR LOCAL SHERIFF ... JOAN HACKETT†
SUPPOSE THEY GAVE A WAR AND NOBODY CAME ... BRADFORD DILLMAN
SUPPOSE THEY GAVE A WAR AND NOBODY CAME? ... BRIAN KEITH
SUPPOSE THEY GAVE A WAR AND NOBODY CAME? ... DON AMECHE†
SUPPOSE THEY GAVE A WAR AND NOBODY CAME? ... ERNEST BORGNINE
SUPPOSE THEY GAVE A WAR AND NOBODY CAME? ... SUZANNE PLESHETTE
SUPPOSE THEY GAVE A WAR AND NOBODY CAME? ... TONY CURTIS
SUR UN ARBRE PERCHÉ ... GERALDINE CHAPLIN
SURE THING, THE ... ANTHONY EDWARDS
SURE THING, THE ... DAPHNE ZUNIGA
SURE THING, THE ... JOHN CUSAK
SURE THING, THE ... NICOLLETTE SHERIDAN
SURE THING, THE ... TIM ROBBINS
SURE THING, THE ... VIVECA LINDFORS
SURF II ... ERIC STOLTZ
SURF NINJAS ... ERNIE REYES JR.
SURF NINJAS ... JOHN KARLEN
SURF NINJAS ... LESLIE NIELSEN
SURF NINJAS ... NICHOLAS COWAN
SURF NINJAS ... ROB SCHNEIDER
SURF NINJAS ... TONE LOC
SURFACING ... JOSEPH BOTTOMS
SURRENDER ... MICHAEL CAINE
SURRENDER ... PETER BOYLE
SURRENDER ... RALPH BELLAMY†
SURRENDER ... SALLY FIELD
SURRENDER ... STEVE GUTTENBERG
SURROGATE, THE ... MICHAEL IRONSIDE
SURVIVAL OF DANA (TF) ... ROBERT CARRADINE
SURVIVAL QUEST ... BEN HAMMER
SURVIVAL QUEST ... CATHERINE KEENER
SURVIVAL QUEST ... DERMOT MULRONEY
SURVIVAL QUEST ... DOMINIC HOFFMAN
SURVIVAL QUEST ... LANCE HENRIKSEN
SURVIVAL QUEST ... MARK ROLSTON
SURVIVAL QUEST ... MICHAEL ALLEN RYDER
SURVIVAL QUEST ... PAUL PROVENZA
SURVIVAL QUEST ... STEVE ANTIN
SURVIVAL QUEST ... TRACI LIN
SURVIVING (TF) ... ELLEN BURSTYN
SURVIVING (TF) ... LEN CARIOU
SURVIVING (TF) ... MARSHA MASON
SURVIVING (TF) ... ZACH GALLIGAN
SURVIVING PICASSSO ... ANTHONY HOPKINS
SURVIVING THE GAME ... CHARLES S. DUTTON
SURVIVING THE GAME ... F. MURRAY ABRAHAM
SURVIVING THE GAME ... GARY BUSEY
SURVIVING THE GAME ... ICE-T
SURVIVING THE GAME ... JEFF COREY
SURVIVING THE GAME ... JOHN C. McGINLEY
SURVIVING THE GAME ... RUTGER HAUER
SURVIVING THE GAME ... WILLIAM McNAMARA
SURVIVOR, THE ... JENNY AGUTTER
SURVIVORS, THE ... JERRY REED
SURVIVORS, THE ... ROBIN WILLIAMS
SURVIVORS, THE ... WALTER MATTHAU
SUSAN AND GOD ... JOAN CRAWFORD†
SUSAN SLADE ... CONNIE STEVENS
SUSAN SLADE ... TROY DONAHUE
SUSAN SLEPT HERE ... DEBBIE REYNOLDS
SUSPECT ... CHER
SUSPECT ... DENNIS QUAID
SUSPECT ... DONALD PLEASENCE
SUSPECT ... IAN BANNEN
SUSPECT ... JOE MANTEGNA
SUSPECT ... JOHN MAHONEY
SUSPECT ... LIAM NEESON
SUSPECT ... PHILIP BOSCO
SUSPICION (TF) ... ANTHONY ANDREWS
SUSPIRIA ... JESSICA HARPER
SUSSURI NEL BUIO ... JOHN PHILLIP LAW
SVENGALI (TF) ... ELIZABETH ASHLEY
SVENGALI (TF) ... HOLLY HUNTER
SVENGALI (TF) ... JODIE FOSTER
SVENGALI (TF) ... PETER O'TOOLE
SWAMP THING ... ADRIENNE BARBEAU
SWAMP THING ... LOUIS JOURDAN
SWAN, THE ... ALEC GUINNESS
SWAN, THE ... GRACE KELLY†
SWAN, THE ... LOUIS JOURDAN
SWAN PRINCESS, THE (AF) ... JOHN CLEESE
SWAN PRINCESS, THE (AF) ... SANDY DUNCAN
SWAN PRINCESS, THE (AF) ... STEVEN WRIGHT
SWAN SONG (TF) ... DAVID SOUL
SWAN SONG (TF) ... JILL EIKENBERRY
SWANEE RIVER ... DON AMECHE†
SWANN IN LOVE ... JEREMY IRONS
SWARM, THE ... BEN JOHNSON
SWARM, THE ... BRADFORD DILLMAN
SWARM, THE ... HENRY FONDA†
SWARM, THE ... JOSE FERRER†
SWARM, THE ... KATHERINE ROSS
SWARM, THE ... LEE GRANT
SWARM, THE ... MICHAEL CAINE
SWARM, THE ... OLIVIA DE HAVILLAND
SWARM, THE ... PATTY DUKE
SWARM, THE ... RICHARD CHAMBERLAIN
SWARM, THE ... RICHARD WIDMARK
SWARM, THE ... SLIM PICKENS†
SWASHBUCKLER ... ANJELICA HUSTON
SWASHBUCKLER ... AVERY SCHREIBER
SWASHBUCKLER ... BEAU BRIDGES
SWASHBUCKLER ... GENEVIEVE BUJOLD
SWASHBUCKLER ... GEOFFREY HOLDER
SWASHBUCKLER ... JAMES EARL JONES
SWASHBUCKLER ... KABIR BEDI
SWASHBUCKLER ... PETER BOYLE
SWASHBUCKLER ... ROBERT SHAW†
SWEDISH MISTRESS, THE ... BIBI ANDERSSON
SWEENEY ... IAN BANNEN
SWEENEY 2 ... DENHOLM ELLIOTT†
SWEET BIRD OF YOUTH ... COREY ALLEN
SWEET BIRD OF YOUTH ... PAUL NEWMAN
SWEET BIRD OF YOUTH ... RIP TORN
SWEET BIRD OF YOUTH ★ ... GERALDINE PAGE†
SWEET BIRD OF YOUTH ✪✪ ... ED BEGLEY†
SWEET BIRD OF YOUTH ✪ ... SHIRLEY KNIGHT
SWEET BIRD OF YOUTH (TF) ... ELIZABETH TAYLOR
SWEET BIRD OF YOUTH (TF) ... MARK HARMON
SWEET BODY OF DEBORAH, THE ... CARROLL BAKER
SWEET CHARITY ... BEN VEREEN
SWEET CHARITY ... JOHN McMARTIN
SWEET CHARITY ... RICARDO MONTALBAN
SWEET CHARITY ... SHIRLEY MacLAINE
SWEET CHARITY ... STUBBY KAYE
SWEET COUNTRY ... JANE ALEXANDER
SWEET CREEK COUNTY WAR, THE ... ALBERT SALMI†
SWEET DIRTY TONY ... STUART WHITMAN
SWEET DREAMS ... ANN WEDGEWORTH
SWEET DREAMS ... DAVID CLENNON
SWEET DREAMS ... ED HARRIS
SWEET DREAMS ... JOHN GOODMAN
SWEET DREAMS ★ ... JESSICA LANGE
SWEET HEARTS DANCE ... DON JOHNSON
SWEET HEARTS DANCE ... ELIZABETH PERKINS
SWEET HEARTS DANCE ... JEFF DANIELS
SWEET HEARTS DANCE ... JUSTIN HENRY
SWEET HEARTS DANCE ... KATE REID
SWEET HEARTS DANCE ... SUSAN SARANDON
SWEET HOSTAGE (TF) ... LINDA BLAIR
SWEET HOSTAGE (TF) ... MARTIN SHEEN
SWEET HUNTERS ... SUSAN STRASBERG
SWEET KILL ... TAB HUNTER
SWEET LIBERTY ... ALAN ALDA
SWEET LIBERTY ... BOB HOSKINS
SWEET LIBERTY ... LILLIAN GISH†
SWEET LIBERTY ... LISE HILBOLDT
SWEET LIBERTY ... LOIS CHILES
SWEET LIBERTY ... MICHAEL CAINE
SWEET LIBERTY ... MICHELLE PFEIFFER
SWEET LIBERTY ... SAUL RUBINEK
SWEET LORRAINE ... GIANCARLO ESPOSITO
SWEET LORRAINE ... MAUREEN STAPLETON
SWEET LORRAINE ... TODD GRAFF
SWEET LORRAINE ... TRINI ALVARADO
SWEET LOVE, BITTER ... DON MURRAY
SWEET LOVE BITTER ... ROBERT HOOKS
SWEET MOVIE ... JOHN VERNON
SWEET NOVEMBER ... SANDY DENNIS†
SWEET NOVEMBER ... THEODORE BIKEL
SWEET REVENGE ... ALEC BALDWIN
SWEET REVENGE ... MARTIN LANDAU
SWEET REVENGE ... NANCY ALLEN
SWEET REVENGE ... SAM WATERSTON
SWEET REVENGE ... STOCKARD CHANNING
SWEET REVENGE (CTF) ... CARRIE FISHER
SWEET REVENGE (CTF) ... ROSANNA ARQUETTE
SWEET REVENGE (TF) ... KELLY McGILLIS
SWEET REVENGE (TF) ... KEVIN DOBSON
SWEET REVENGE (TF) ... WINGS HAUSER
SWEET RIDE, THE ... ANTHONY (TONY) FRANCIOSA
SWEET RIDE, THE ... JACQUELINE BISSET
SWEET RIDE, THE ... MICHAEL SARRAZIN
SWEET RIDE, THE ... SEYMOUR CASSEL
SWEET SAVIOR ... TROY DONAHUE
SWEET SMELL OF SUCCESS ... BURT LANCASTER†
SWEET SMELL OF SUCCESS ... TONY CURTIS
SWEET SWEETBACK'S BAADASSSSS SONG ... JOHN AMOS
SWEET TALKER ... BRYON BROWN
SWEET TALKER ... KAREN ALLEN
SWEET WILLIAM ... GERALDINE JAMES
SWEET WILLIAM ... JENNY AGUTTER
SWEET WILLIAM ... SAM WATERSTON
SWEETIE ... GENEVIEVE LEMON
SWEETIE ... KAREN COLSTON
SWEPT AWAY BY AN UNUSUAL DESTINY IN THE BLUE SEA OF AUGUST ... GIANCARLO GIANNINI
SWIM TEAM ... STEPHEN FURST
SWIMMER, THE ... BURT LANCASTER†
SWIMMER, THE ... DIANA MULDAUR
SWIMMER, THE ... JOAN RIVERS
SWIMMING TO CAMBODIA (PF) ... SPALDING GRAY
SWIMSUIT (TF) ... CYD CHARISSE
SWIMSUIT (TF) ... WILLIAM KATT
SWING FEVER ... AVA GARDNER†
SWING FEVER ... LENA HORNE
SWING HIGH, SWING LOW ... ANTHONY QUINN
SWING HIGH, SWING LOW ... DOROTHY LAMOUR
SWING KIDS ... BARBARA HERSHEY
SWING KIDS ... CHRISTIAN BALE
SWING KIDS ... FRANK WHALEY
SWING KIDS ... KENNETH BRANAGH
SWING KIDS ... ROBERT SEAN LEONARD
SWING SHIFT ... ED HARRIS
SWING SHIFT ... FRED WARD
SWING SHIFT ... GOLDIE HAWN
SWING SHIFT ... HOLLY HUNTER
SWING SHIFT ... KURT RUSSELL
SWING SHIFT ✪ ... CHRISTINE LAHTI
SWING TIME ... FRED ASTAIRE†
SWING YOUR LADY ... RONALD REAGAN
SWINGER, THE ... ANN-MARGRET
SWINGER, THE ... ANTHONY (TONY) FRANCIOSA
SWINGIN' ALONG ... BARBARA EDEN
SWINGIN' SUMMER, A ... RAQUEL WELCH
SWISS CONSPIRACY, THE ... JOHN IRELAND
SWISS CONSPIRACY, THE ... JOHN SAXON
SWISS FAMILY ROBINSON ... JOHN MILLS
SWITCH ... BRUCE PAYNE
SWITCH ... ELLEN BARKIN
SWITCH ... JIMMY SMITS
SWITCH ... JoBETH WILLIAMS
SWITCH ... LORRAINE BRACCO
SWITCH ... PERRY KING
SWITCH ... TONY ROBERTS
SWITCH (TF) ... CHARLES DURNING

† after an actor's name denotes deceased.

SWITCH (TF) .... JACLYN SMITH
SWITCH (TF) .... ROBERT WAGNER
SWITCH (TF) .... SHARON GLESS
SWITCHED AT BIRTH (MS) .... BONNIE BEDELIA
SWITCHED AT BIRTH (MS) .... BRIAN KERWIN
SWITCHED AT BIRTH (MS) .... ED ASNER
SWITCHING CHANNELS .... BURT REYNOLDS
SWITCHING CHANNELS .... CHRISTOPHER REEVE
SWITCHING CHANNELS .... FIONA REID
SWITCHING CHANNELS .... HENRY GIBSON
SWITCHING CHANNELS .... KATHLEEN TURNER
SWORD AND THE ROSE, THE .... MICHAEL GOUGH
SWORD AND THE SORCERER, THE .... JEFF COREY
SWORD AND THE SORCERER, THE .... RICHARD LYNCH
SWORD AND THE SORCERER, THE .... SIMON MacCORKINDALE
SWORD OF GIDEON (CTF) .... MICHAEL YORK
SWORD OF THE CONQUEROR .... JACK PALANCE
SWORD OF THE VALIANT .... LEIGH LAWSON
SWORD OF THE VALIANT .... LILA KEDROVA
SWORD OF THE VALIANT .... RONALD LACEY
SWORD OF THE VALIANT .... SEAN CONNERY
SWORN ENEMY .... ANTHONY QUINN
SWORN TO SILENCE (TF) .... CAROLINE McWILLIAMS
SWORN TO SILENCE (TF) .... DABNEY COLEMAN
SWORN TO SILENCE (TF) .... DAVID SPIELBERG
SWORN TO SILENCE (TF) .... LIAM NEESON
SWORN TO SILENCE (TF) .... PETER COYOTE
SWORN TO SILENCE (TF) .... TERRY DAVID MULLIGAN
SWORN TO VENGEANCE (TF) .... ROBERT CONRAD
SYBIL (TF) .... BRAD DAVIS†
SYBIL (TF) .... JOANNE WOODWARD
SYBIL (TF) .... SALLY FIELD
SYLVESTER .... ARLISS HOWARD
SYLVESTER .... CONSTANCE TOWERS
SYLVESTER .... MELISSA GILBERT
SYLVESTER .... MICHAEL SCHOEFFLING
SYLVESTER .... PETE KOWANKO
SYLVESTER .... RICHARD FARNSWORTH
SYLVIA .... ANN SOTHERN
SYLVIA .... CARROLL BAKER
SYLVIA .... EILEEN GLOVER
SYLVIA .... ELEANOR DAVID
SYLVIA .... JOSEPH GEORGE
SYLVIA SCARLETT .... KATHERINE HEPBURN
SYNANON .... CHUCK CONNORS†
SYNANON .... EARTHA KITT
SYNANON .... STELLA STEVENS
SYNCOPATION .... JACKIE COOPER
SYSKONBADD 1782 .... BIBI ANDERSSON
SYSTEM, THE .... DAVID HEMMINGS

T

T.J. HOOKER (TF) .... WILLIAM SHATNER
T.R. BASKIN .... CANDICE BERGEN
T.R. BASKIN .... JAMES CAAN
T.R. BASKIN .... PETER BOYLE
T. REX .... WHOOPI GOLDBERG
T-MEN .... JUNE LOCKHART
TABLE FOR FIVE .... JON VOIGHT
TABLE FOR FIVE .... KEVIN COSTNER
TABLE FOR FIVE .... MILLIE PERKINS
TABLE FOR FIVE .... RICHARD CRENNA
TABOOS OF THE WORLD (FD) .... VINCENT PRICE†
TAFFIN .... ALISON DOODY
TAFFIN .... PIERCE BROSNAN
TAFFIN .... RAY MCANALLY†
TAG .... MICHAEL WINSLOW
TAG: THE ASSASSINATION GAME .... ROBERT CARRADINE
TAGEBUCH EINER VERLIEBTEN .... MARIA SCHELL
TAGGART .... DAVID CARRADINE
TAI-PAN .... BILL LEADBETTER
TAI-PAN .... BRYON BROWN
TAI-PAN .... JOAN CHEN
TAI-PAN .... JOHN STANTON
TAI-PAN .... RUSSELL WONG
TAI-PAN .... TIM GUINEE
TAIL GUNNER JOE (TF) .... BURGESS MEREDITH
TAIL GUNNER JOE (TF) .... JOHN CARRADINE†
TAIL GUNNER JOE (TF) .... JOHN FORSYTHE
TAIL GUNNER JOE (TF) .... NED BEATTY
TAIL GUNNER JOE (TF) .... PATRICIA NEAL
TAIL GUNNER JOE (TF) .... PETER BOYLE
TAIL SPIN .... JANE WYMAN
TAILOR'S MAID, A .... MARCELLO MASTROIANNI
TAKE, THE .... ALBERT SALMI†
TAKE, THE .... BILLY DEE WILLIAMS
TAKE, THE .... EDDIE ALBERT
TAKE, THE .... FRANKIE AVALON
TAKE, THE (CTF) .... LISA HARTMAN-BLACK
TAKE, THE (CTF) .... RAY SHARKEY†
TAKE A GIANT STEP .... RUBY DEE
TAKE A GIRL LIKE YOU .... HAYLEY MILLS
TAKE A HARD RIDE .... FRED WILLIAMSON
TAKE A HARD RIDE .... HARRY CAREY JR.
TAKE A HARD RIDE .... JIM BROWN
TAKE DOWN .... EDWRAD HERRMANN
TAKE DOWN .... KEVIN HOOKS
TAKE DOWN .... STEPHEN FURST
TAKE HER, SHE'S MINE .... JAMES BROLIN
TAKE HER SHE'S MINE .... JAMES STEWART
TAKE HER—SHE'S MINE .... ROBERT MORLEY
TAKE HER, SHE'S MINE .... SANDRA DEE
TAKE ME OUT TO THE BALL GAME .... FRANK SINATRA
TAKE ME OUT TO THE BALL GAME .... GENE KELLY
TAKE MY DAUGHTERS, PLEASE (TF) .... DIEDRE HALL
TAKE MY DAUGHTERS, PLEASE (TF) .... KIM DELANEY
TAKE MY DAUGHTERS, PLEASE (TF) .... RUE McCLANAHAN
TAKE MY DAUGHTERS, PLEASE (TF) .... STEPHANIE KRAMER
TAKE MY DAUGHTERS, PLEASE (TF) .... SUSAN RUTTAN
TAKE ONE FALSE STEP .... SHELLEY WINTERS
TAKE THE HIGH GROUND .... KARL MALDEN
TAKE THE HIGH GROUND .... RICHARD WIDMARK
TAKE THE HIGH GROUND .... RUSS TAMBLYN
TAKE THE HIGH GROUND .... STEVE FORREST
TAKE THE MONEY AND RUN .... JANET MARGOLIN
TAKE THE MONEY AND RUN .... LOUISE LASSER
TAKE THE MONEY AND RUN .... WOODY ALLEN
TAKE THIS JOB AND SHOVE IT .... ART CARNEY
TAKE THIS JOB AND SHOVE IT .... BARBARA HERSHEY
TAKE THIS JOB AND SHOVE IT .... EDDIE ALBERT
TAKE THIS JOB AND SHOVE IT .... ROBERT HAYS
TAKE THIS JOB AND SHOVE IT .... ROYAL DANO
TAKE THIS JOB AND SHOVE IT .... TIM THOMERSON
TAKEN AWAY (TF) .... ANNA MARIA HORSFORD
TAKEN AWAY (TF) .... KEVIN DUNN
TAKEN AWAY (TF) .... VALERIE BERTINELLI
TAKING CARE OF BUSINESS .... ANNE DESALVO
TAKING CARE OF BUSINESS .... CHARLES GRODIN
TAKING CARE OF BUSINESS .... HECTOR ELIZONDO
TAKING CARE OF BUSINESS .... JAMES BELUSHI
TAKING CARE OF BUSINESS .... MAKO
TAKING CARE OF BUSINESS .... STANLEY DeSANTIS
TAKING CARE OF BUSINESS .... VERONICA HAMEL
TAKING OF BEVERLY HILLS, THE .... HARLEY JANE KOZAK
TAKING OF BEVERLY HILLS, THE .... KEN WAHL
TAKING OF BEVERLY HILLS, THE .... MATT FREWER
TAKING OF BEVERLY HILLS, THE .... ROBERT DAVI
TAKING OF FLIGHT 847: THE ULI DERICKSON STORY, THE (TF) .... ELI DANKER
TAKING OF FLIGHT 847: THE ULI DERICKSON STORY, THE (TF) .... LESLIE EASTERBROOK
TAKING OF FLIGHT 847: THE ULI DERICKSON STORY, THE (TF) .... LINDSAY WAGNER
TAKING OF FLIGHT 847: THE ULI DERICKSON STORY, THE (TF) .... RAY WISE
TAKING OF PELHAM 1-2-3, THE .... HECTOR ELIZONDO
TAKING OF PELHAM 1-2-3, THE .... KENNETH McMILLAN†
TAKING OF PELHAM 1-2-3, THE .... MARTIN BALSAM
TAKING OF PELHAM 1-2-3, THE .... TONY ROBERTS
TAKING OF PELHAM 1-2-3, THE .... WALTER MATTHAU
TAKING OFF .... ALLEN GARFIELD
TAKING OFF .... BUCK HENRY
TAKING OFF .... KATHY BATES
TALE OF THE COCK .... DON MURRAY
TALE OF TWO CITIES, A .... DONALD PLEASENCE
TALE OF TWO CITIES, A .... IAN BANNEN
TALE OF TWO CITIES, A (TF) .... ALICE KRIGE
TALE OF TWO CITIES, A (TF) .... CHRIS SARANDON
TALE OF TWO CITIES, A (TF) .... NIGEL HAWTHORNE
TALENT FOR LOVING, A .... RICHARD WIDMARK
TALENT FOR LOVING, A .... TOPOL
TALENT FOR THE GAME .... EDWARD JAMES OLMOS
TALENT FOR THE GAME .... JAMEY SHERIDAN
TALENT FOR THE GAME .... JEFF CORBETT
TALENT FOR THE GAME .... LORRAINE BRACCO
TALENT FOR THE GAME .... TERRY KINNEY
TALES FROM THE CRYPT .... JOAN COLLINS
TALES FROM THE DARKSIDE: THE MOVIE .... CHRISTIAN SLATER
TALES FROM THE DARKSIDE: THE MOVIE .... DAVID JOHANSEN
TALES FROM THE DARKSIDE: THE MOVIE .... DEBORAH HARRY
TALES FROM THE DARKSIDE: THE MOVIE .... JAMES REMAR
TALES FROM THE DARKSIDE: THE MOVIE .... RAE DAWN CHONG
TALES FROM THE DARKSIDE: THE MOVIE .... WILLIAM HICKEY
TALES FROM THE HOOD .... CLARENCE WILLIAMS III
TALES FROM THE HOOD .... CORBIN BERNSEN
TALES FROM THE HOOD .... DAVID ALAN GRIER
TALES FROM THE HOOD .... JOE TORRY
TALES FROM THE HOOD .... WINGS HAUSER
TALES OF ORDINARY MADNESS .... BEN GAZZARA
TALES OF ORDINARY MADNESS .... SUSAN TYRRELL
TALES OF PARIS .... CATHERINE DENEUVE
TALES OF TERROR .... VINCENT PRICE†
TALES THAT WITNESS MADNESS .... JOAN COLLINS
TALES THAT WITNESS MADNESS .... KIM NOVAK
TALES THAT WITNESS MURDER .... DONALD PLEASENCE
TALK OF A MILLION .... MILO O'SHEA
TALK OF THE TOWN, THE .... LLOYD BRIDGES
TALK RADIO .... ALEC BALDWIN
TALK RADIO .... ANNA LEVINE
TALK RADIO .... ELLEN GREENE
TALK RADIO .... ERIC BOGOSIAN
TALK RADIO .... JOHN C. McGINLEY
TALK RADIO .... JOHN PANKOW
TALK RADIO .... LESLIE HOPE
TALK RADIO .... MICHAEL WINCOTT
TALKIN' DIRTY AFTER DARK .... MARTIN LAWRENCE
TALKIN' DIRTY AFTER DARK .... TONE LOC
TALKING WALLS .... SALLY KIRKLAND
TALL, DARK AND HANDSOME .... MILTON BERLE
TALL GUY, THE .... EMMA THOMPSON
TALL GUY, THE .... GERALDINE JAMES
TALL GUY, THE .... JEFF GOLDBLUM
TALL GUY, THE .... ROWAN ATKINSON
TALL HEADLINES, THE .... MAE ZETTERLING†
TALL LIE, THE .... VERA MILES
TALL MAN RIDING .... JOHN DEHNER†
TALL STORY .... ANNE JACKSON
TALL STORY .... ANTHONY PERKINS†
TALL STORY .... JANE FONDA
TALL STORY .... RAY WALSTON
TALL T, THE .... MAUREEN O'SULLIVAN
TALL TALE .... CATHERINE O'HARA
TALL TALE .... NICK STAHL
TALL TALE .... OLIVER PLATT
TALL TALE .... PATRICK SWAYZE
TALL TALE .... ROGER AARON BROWN
TALL TALE .... SCOTT GLENN

This is not a list of every film ever made or every cast member, only those listed in this directory.

TALL TARGET, THE	RUBY DEE	
TALL TEXAN, THE	LLOYD BRIDGES	
TAM LIN	JOANNA LUMLEY	
TAMARIND SEED, THE	DAN O'HERLIHY	
TAMARIND SEED, THE	JULIE ANDREWS	
TAMARIND SEED, THE	OMAR SHARIF	
TAMARIND SEED, THE	OSCAR HOMOLKA†	
TAMING OF THE SHREW, THE	ELIZABETH TAYLOR	
TAMING OF THE SHREW, THE	MICHAEL YORK	
TAMMY AND THE BACHELOR	DEBBIE REYNOLDS	
TAMMY AND THE BACHELOR	LESLIE NIELSEN	
TAMMY AND THE DOCTOR	ADAM WEST	
TAMMY AND THE DOCTOR	PETER FONDA	
TAMMY AND THE DOCTOR	SANDRA DEE	
TAMMY TELL ME TRUE	JOHN GAVIN	
TAMMY TELL ME TRUE	SANDRA DEE	
TAMMY TELL ME TRUE	STEFANIE POWERS	
TANGO BAR	RAUL JULIA†	
TANGO & CASH	JACK PALANCE	
TANGO & CASH	KURT RUSSELL	
TANGO & CASH	MICHAEL J. POLLARD	
TANGO & CASH	SONJA G. ANDERSON	
TANGO & CASH	SYLVESTER STALLONE	
TANGO & CASH	TERI HATCHER	
TANK	C. THOMAS HOWELL	
TANK	GUY BOYD	
TANK	JAMES GARNER	
TANK GIRL	BRIAN WIMMER	
TANK GIRL	DON HARVEY	
TANK GIRL	ICE-T	
TANK GIRL	JEFF KOBER	
TANK GIRL	LORI PETTY	
TANK GIRL	MALCOLM McDOWELL	
TANK GIRL	NAOMI WATTS	
TANK GIRL	REG E. CATHEY	
TANK GIRL	SCOTT COFFEY	
TANK GIRL	STACY LINN RAWSOWER	
TAP	GREGORY HINES	
TAP	SAMMY DAVIS JR.†	
TAP	SAVION GLOVER	
TAP	SUZANNE DOUGLAS	
TAPEHEADS	JOHN CUSAK	
TAPEHEADS	TIM ROBBINS	
TAPS	GEORGE C. SCOTT	
TAPS	RONNY COX	
TAPS	SEAN PENN	
TAPS	TIMOTHY HUTTON	
TAPS	TOM CRUISE	
TARANTULA	CLINT EASTWOOD	
TARAS BULBA	SAM WANAMAKER†	
TARAS BULBA	TONY CURTIS	
TARGET	GENE HACKMAN	
TARGET	MATT DILLON	
TARGET EAGLE	GEORGE PEPPARD†	
TARGET EAGLE	MAUD ADAMS	
TARGET: HARRY	SUZANNE PLESHETTE	
TARGET OF SUSPICION (CTF)	LYSETTE ANTHONY	
TARGET RISK (TF)	MEREDITH BAXTER	
TARGET ZERO	CHARLES BRONSON	
TARGET ZERO	CHUCK CONNORS†	
TARGET ZERO	JOHN ANDERSON	
TARNISHED ANGELS, THE	ROBERT STACK	
TARNISHED ANGELS, THE	ROCK HUDSON†	
TARS AND SPARS	SID CAESAR	
TARZAN AND HIS MATE	MAUREEN O'SULLIVAN	
TARZAN AND JANE REGAINED...SORT OF	DENNIS HOPPER	
TARZAN AND THE GREAT RIVER	MIKE HENRY	
TARZAN AND THE JUNGLE BOY	MIKE HENRY	
TARZAN AND THE SHE-DEVIL	RAYMOND BURR†	
TARZAN AND THE SLAVE GIRL	HURD HATFIELD	
TARZAN AND THE VALLEY OF GOLD	MIKE HENRY	
TARZAN ESCAPES	MAUREEN O'SULLIVAN	
TARZAN FINDS A SON	MAUREEN O'SULLIVAN	
TARZAN IN MANHATTAN (TF)	TONY CURTIS	
TARZAN THE APE MAN	BO DEREK	
TARZAN, THE APE MAN	JOHN PHILLIP LAW	
TARZAN THE APE MAN	MAUREEN O'SULLIVAN	
TARZAN THE APE MAN	MILES O'KEEFFE	
TARZAN THE APE MAN	RICHARD HARRIS	
TARZAN'S FIGHT FOR LIFE	WOODY STRODE	
TARZAN'S GREATEST ADVENTURE	SEAN CONNERY	
TARZAN'S HIDDEN JUNGLE	VERA MILES	
TARZAN'S NEW YORK ADVENTURE	MAUREEN O'SULLIVAN	
TARZAN'S SECRET TREASURE	MAUREEN O'SULLIVAN	
TARZAN'S THREE CHALLENGES	WOODY STRODE	
TASK FORCE	JANE WYATT	
TASTE OF FEAR	SUSAN STRASBERG	
TASTE OF HONEY, A	ROBERT STEPHENS	
TASTE THE BLOOD OF DRACULA	GEOFFREY KEEN	
TATTOO	BRUCE DERN	
TATTOO	JOHN GETZ	
TATTOO	LEONARD FREY†	
TATTOO	MAUD ADAMS	
TATTOO	PETER IACHANGELO	
TATTOO	RIKKI BORGE	
TAXI	STUBBY KAYE	
TAXI DANCER, THE	JOAN CRAWFORD†	
TAXI DRIVER	ALBERT BROOKS	
TAXI DRIVER	CYBILL SHEPHERD	
TAXI DRIVER	HARVEY KEITEL	
TAXI DRIVER	JOE SPINELL	
TAXI DRIVER	MARTIN SCORSESE	
TAXI DRIVER	PETER BOYLE	
TAXI DRIVER ★	ROBERT DE NIRO	
TAXI DRIVER ✪	JODIE FOSTER	
TAZA SON OF COCHISE	ROCK HUDSON†	
TCHIN-TCHIN	JULIE ANDREWS	
TEA AND SYMPATHY	DEAN JONES	
TEA AND SYMPATHY	DEBORAH KERR	
TEA FOR TWO	DORIS DAY	
TEA FOR TWO	GORDON MACRAE†	
TEACHER'S PET ✪	GIG YOUNG†	
TEACHERS	ANTHONY HEALD	
TEACHERS	ART METRANO	
TEACHERS	JoBETH WILLIAMS	
TEACHERS	JULIA JENNINGS	
TEACHERS	LAURA DERN	
TEACHERS	LEE GRANT	
TEACHERS	MORGAN FREEMAN	
TEACHERS	NICK NOLTE	
TEACHERS	RICHARD MULLIGAN	
TEACHERS	RONALD HUNTER	
TEACHERS	ROYAL DANO	
TEACHERS	ZOHRA LAMPERT	
TEACHER'S PET	DORIS DAY	
TEAHOUSE OF THE AUGUST MOON	EDDIE ALBERT	
TEAHOUSE OF THE AUGUST MOON	MARLON BRANDO	
TEAHOUSE OF THE AUGUST MOON, THE	HARRY MORGAN	
TEAR THAT BURNED, THE	LILLIAN GISH†	
TEARS AND LAUGHTER: THE JOAN AND MELISSA RIVERS STORY (TF)	JOAN RIVERS	
TEARS AND LAUGHTER: THE JOAN AND MELISSA RIVERS STORY (TF)	MELISSA RIVERS	
TECNICA DI UN OMICIDIO	ROBERT WEBBER	
TED & VENUS	BUD CORT	
TED KENNEDY, JR. STORY, THE (TF)	CRAIG T. NELSON	
TED KENNEDY, JR. STORY, THE (TF)	DAVID HEALY	
TED KENNEDY, JR. STORY, THE (TF)	DENNIS CREAGHAN	
TED KENNEDY, JR. STORY, THE (TF)	KIMBER SHOOP	
TED KENNEDY, JR. STORY, THE (TF)	MICHAEL J. SHANNON	
TED KENNEDY, JR. STORY, THE (TF)	SUSAN BLAKELY	
TEEN WOLF	JAMES HAMPTON	
TEEN WOLF	MICHAEL J. FOX	
TEEN WOLF TOO	JAMES HAMPTON	
TEEN WOLF TOO	JASON BATEMAN	
TEEN WOLF TOO	KIM DARBY	
TEENAGE BAD GIRL/MY TEENAGE DAUGHTER	KENNETH HAIGH	
TEENAGE CAVE MAN	ROBERT VAUGHN	
TEENAGE MUTANT NINJA TURTLES	ELIAS KOTEAS	
TEENAGE MUTANT NINJA TURTLES	JUDITH HOAG	
TEENAGE MUTANT NINJA TURTLES II: THE SECRET OF THE OOZE	DAVID WARNER	
TEENAGE MUTANT NINJA TURTLES II: THE SECRET OF THE OOZE	PAIGE TURCO	
TELEFON	CHARLES BRONSON	
TELEFON	DONALD PLEASENCE	
TELEFON	TYNE DALY	
TELEPHONE, THE	AMY WRIGHT	
TELEPHONE, THE	ELLIOTT GOULD	
TELEPHONE, THE	JOHN HEARD	
TELEPHONE, THE	SEVERN DARDEN	
TELEPHONE, THE	WHOOPI GOLDBERG	
TELEPHONE BOOK, THE	JILL CLAYBURGH	
TELETHON (TF)	JANET LEIGH	
TELETHON (TF)	LLOYD BRIDGES	
TELETHON (TF)	RED BUTTONS	
TELEVISION SPY	ANTHONY QUINN	
TELL ME A RIDDLE	BROOKE ADAMS	
TELL ME A RIDDLE	LILA KEDROVA	
TELL ME LIES	GLENDA JACKSON	
TELL ME LIES	PAUL SCOFIELD	
TELL ME THAT YOU LOVE ME	BARBARA WILLIAMS	
TELL ME THAT YOU LOVE ME JUNIE MOON	FRED WILLIAMSON	
TELL ME THAT YOU LOVE ME, JUNIE MOON	KEN HOWARD	
TELL ME THAT YOU LOVE ME JUNIE MOON	LIZA MINELLI	
TELL ME THAT YOU LOVE ME, JUNIE MOON	NANCY MARCHAND	
TELL ME WHERE IT HURTS (TF)	MAUREEN STAPLETON	
TELL THEM WILLIE BOY IS HERE	JOHN VERNON	
TELL THEM WILLIE BOY IS HERE	KATHERINE ROSS	
TELL THEM WILLIE BOY IS HERE	ROBERT BLAKE	
TELL THEM WILLIE BOY IS HERE	ROBERT REDFORD	
TELL THEM WILLIE BOY IS HERE	SUSAN CLARK	
TEMP, THE	DWIGHT SCHULTZ	
TEMP, THE	FAYE DUNAWAY	
TEMP, THE	LARA FLYNN BOYLE	
TEMP, THE	TIMOTHY HUTTON	
TEMPEST	PAUL HECHT	
TEMPEST	PAUL MAZURSKY	
TEMPEST	SUSAN SARANDON	
TEMPEST, THE	MIA FARROW	
TEMPEST, THE	RAUL JULIA†	
TEMPI NOSTRI	MARCELLO MASTROIANNI	
TEMPI NOSTRI	SOPHIA LOREN	
TEMPTER, THE	GLENDA JACKSON	
TEMPTER, THE	MEL FERRER	
TEN CENTS A DANCE	BARBARA STANWYCK†	
TEN COMMANDMENTS, THE	ANNE BAXTER†	
TEN COMMANDMENTS, THE	CHARLTON HESTON	
TEN COMMANDMENTS, THE	CLINT WALKER	
TEN COMMANDMENTS, THE	DAME JUDITH ANDERSON†	
TEN COMMANDMENTS, THE	EDWARD G. ROBINSON†	
TEN COMMANDMENTS, THE	MARTHA SCOTT	
TEN COMMANDMENTS, THE	NINA FOCH	
TEN COMMANDMENTS, THE	SIR CEDRIC HARDWICKE†	
TEN COMMANDMENTS, THE	VINCENT PRICE†	
TEN COMMANDMENTS, THE	WOODY STRODE	
TEN COMMANDMENTS, THE	YUL BRYNNER†	
TEN COMMANDMENTS, THE	YVONNE DE CARLO	
TEN DAYS THAT SHOOK THE WORLD	FRANCO NERO	
TEN DAYS' WONDER	ANTHONY PERKINS†	
TEN FROM YOUR SHOW OF SHOWS	IMOGENE COCA	

† after an actor's name denotes deceased.

TEN FROM YOUR SHOW OF SHOWS ... SID CAESAR
TEN GENTLEMEN FROM
    WEST POINT .... MAUREEN O'HARA
TEN NORTH
    FREDERICK .... GERALDINE FITZGERALD
TEN NORTH FREDERICK .... STUART WHITMAN
TEN SECONDS TO HELL .... JACK PALANCE
TEN SECONDS TO HELL .... WESLEY ADDY
TEN TALL MEN .... BURT LANCASTER†
TEN TALL MEN .... JOHN DEHNER†
TEN THOUSAND BEDROOMS .... DEAN JONES
TEN THOUSAND BEDROOMS .... DEAN MARTIN
TEN TO MIDNIGHT .... ANDREW STEVENS
TEN TO MIDNIGHT .... TED LAUFER
TEN WHO DARED .... BRIAN KEITH
TENANT, THE .... ISABELLE ADJANI
TENANT, THE .... LILA KEDROVA
TENANT, THE .... MELVYN DOUGLAS†
TENANT, THE .... ROMAN POLANSKI
TENANT, THE .... SHELLEY WINTERS
TENDER, THE .... MICHAEL PHILLIPS
TENDER FLESH .... JOHN IRELAND
TENDER FLESH .... STUART WHITMAN
TENDER IS THE NIGHT .... JASON ROBARDS
TENDER IS THE NIGHT .... JENNIFER JONES
TENDER IS THE NIGHT .... JILL ST. JOHN
TENDER IS THE NIGHT (CMS) .... PIPER LAURIE
TENDER IS THE NIGHT (CMS) .... TIMOTHY WEST
TENDER IS THE NIGHT (TF) .... PETER STRAUSS
TENDER MERCIES .... BETTY BUCKLEY
TENDER MERCIES .... LENNY VON DOHLEN
TENDER MERCIES .... PAUL GLEASON
TENDER MERCIES .... TESS HARPER
TENDER MERCIES .... WILFORD BRIMLEY
TENDER MERCIES ★★ .... ROBERT DUVALL
TENDER SCOUNDREL .... ROBERT MORLEY
TENDER TRAP, THE .... CELESTE HOLM
TENDER TRAP, THE .... DEBBIE REYNOLDS
TENDER TRAP, THE .... FRANK SINATRA
TENDERFOOTS .... ALEXANDRA WENTWORTH
TENDERFOOTS .... DANIEL STERN
TENDERLY .... GEORGE SEGAL
TENDERLY .... LILA KEDROVA
TENDRE VOYOU .... ROBERT MORLEY
TENEBRAE .... ANTHONY (TONY) FRANCIOSA
TENNESSEE CHAMP .... CHARLES BRONSON
TENNESSEE CHAMP .... SHELLEY WINTERS
TENNESSEE WALTZ .... DENISE CROSBY
TENNESSEE WALTZ .... ED LAUTER
TENNESSEE WALTZ .... JULIAN SANDS
TENNESSEE WALTZ .... NED BEATTY
TENNESSEE WALTZ .... ROD STEIGER
TENNESSEE WALTZ .... STACEY DASH
TENNESSEE WILLIAMS' SWEET
    BIRD OF YOUTH (TF) .... ELIZABETH TAYLOR
TENNESSEE WILLIAMS' SWEET
    BIRD OF YOUTH (TF) .... MARK HARMON
TENNESSEE'S PARTNER .... ANGIE DICKINSON
TENNESSEE'S PARTNER .... RONALD REAGAN
TENSION .... CYD CHARISSE
TENSION AT TABLE ROCK .... ANGIE DICKINSON
TENSION AT TABLE ROCK .... ROYAL DANO
TENSPEED AND BROWNSHOE (TF) .... BEN VEREEN
TENSPEED AND
    BROWNSHOE (TF) .... JEFF GOLDBLUM
TENTACLES .... BO HOPKINS
TENTACLES† .... CLAUDE AKINS†
TENTACLES .... SHELLEY WINTERS
TENTH AVENUE ANGEL .... ANGELA LANSBURY
TENTH AVENUE ANGEL .... PHYLLIS THAXTER
TENTH LEVEL, THE (TF) .... STEPHEN MACHT
TENTH MAN, THE (TF) .... ANTHONY HOPKINS
TENTH MAN, THE (TF) .... DEREK JACOBI
TENTH VICTIM, THE .... MARCELLO MASTROIANNI
TENUE DE SOIREE .... BRUNO CREMER
TENUE DE SOIREE .... GERARD DEPARDIEU
TENUE DE SOIREE .... MICHEL BLANC
TEOREMA .... TERENCE STAMP
TEQUILA SUNRISE .... ANN MAGNUSON
TEQUILA SUNRISE .... J. T. WALSH
TEQUILA SUNRISE .... KURT RUSSELL
TEQUILA SUNRISE .... MEL GIBSON

TEQUILA SUNRISE .... MICHELLE PFEIFFER
TEQUILA SUNRISE .... RAUL JULIA†
TEQUILA SUNRISE .... LALA
TERESA .... ROD STEIGER
TERM OF TRIAL .... SARAH MILES
TERM OF TRIAL .... TERENCE STAMP
TERMINAL BLISS .... ALEXIS ARQUETTE
TERMINAL BLISS .... ESTEE CHANDLER
TERMINAL BLISS .... LUKE PERRY
TERMINAL BLISS .... MICAH GRANT
TERMINAL BLISS .... TIMOTHY OWEN
TERMINAL ISLAND .... ROGER E. MOSLEY
TERMINAL ISLAND .... TOM SELLECK
TERMINAL MAN, THE .... GEORGE SEGAL
TERMINAL MAN, THE .... JILL CLAYBURGH
TERMINAL MAN, THE .... JOAN HACKETT†
TERMINAL VELOCITY .... CHARLIE SHEEN
TERMINAL VELOCITY ..... CHRISTOPHER McDONALD
TERMINAL VELOCITY .... JAMES GANDOLFIINI
TERMINAL VELOCITY .... NASTASSJA KINSKI
TERMINAL VELOCITY .... MELVIN VAN PEEBLES
TERMINATOR, THE .... ARNOLD SCHWARZENEGGER
TERMINATOR, THE .... LINDA HAMILTON
TERMINATOR, THE .... MICHAEL BIEHN
TERMINATOR, THE .... PAUL WINFIELD
TERMINATOR, THE .... RICK ROSSOVICH
TERMINATOR 2:
    JUDGMENT DAY ..... ARNOLD SCHWARZENEGGER
TERMINATOR 2:
    JUDGMENT DAY .... EDWARD FURLONG
TERMINATOR 2:
    JUDGMENT DAY .... LINDA HAMILTON
TERMINATOR 2:
    JUDGMENT DAY .... ROBERT PATRICK
TERMS OF ENDEARMENT .... ALBERT BROOKS
TERMS OF ENDEARMENT .... DANNY DEVITO
TERMS OF ENDEARMENT .... DEVON O'BRIEN
TERMS OF ENDEARMENT .... JEFF DANIELS
TERMS OF ENDEARMENT .... LISA HART CARROLL
TERMS OF ENDEARMENT .... MARY KAY PLACE
TERMS OF ENDEARMENT .... TROY BISHOP
TERMS OF ENDEARMENT ★ .... DEBRA WINGER
TERMS OF
    ENDEARMENT ★★ .... SHIRLEY MacLAINE
TERMS OF ENDEARMENT ○ .... JOHN LITHGOW
TERMS OF ENDEARMENT ∞ ..... JACK NICHOLSON
TERRIBLE BEAUTY, A .... DAN O'HERLIHY
TERRIBLE BEAUTY, A .... RICHARD HARRIS
TERRIBLE BEAUTY, A .... ROBERT MITCHUM
TERROR, THE .... DICK MILLER
TERROR, THE .... JACK NICHOLSON
TERROR EYES .... RACHEL WARD
TERROR FROM UNDER THE
    HOUSE/REVENGE .... JOAN COLLINS
TERROR IN THE AISLES (FD) .... NANCY ALLEN
TERROR IN THE CITY .... LEE GRANT
TERROR IN THE CITY .... ROSCOE LEE BROWNE
TERROR OF SHEBA, THE .... LANA TURNER
TERROR ON
    HIGHWAY 91 (TF) .... GEORGE DZUNDZA
TERROR ON
    HIGHWAY 91 (TF) .... LARA FLYNN BOYLE
TERROR ON HIGHWAY 91 (TF) .... MATT CLARK
TERROR ON THE BEACH (TF) .... SUSAN DEY
TERROR OUT OF THE SKY ... EFREM ZIMBALIST JR.
TERROR OUT OF
    THE SKY (TF) .... TOYAH FELDSHUH
TERROR TRAIN .... BEN JOHNSON
TERROR TRAIN .... JAMIE LEE CURTIS
TERROR WITHIN, THE .... ANDREW STEVENS
TERROR WITHIN, THE .... GEORGE KENNEDY
TERROR WITHIN, THE .... STARR ANDREEFF
TERROR WITHIN II, THE .... ANDREW STEVENS
TERROR WITHIN II, THE .... CHICK VENNERA
TERROR WITHIN II, THE .... STELLA STEVENS
TERRORIST ON TRIAL:
    THE UNITED STATES VS.
    SALIM AJAMI (TF) .... FRANCES CONROY
TERRORIST ON TRIAL:
    THE UNITED STATES VS.
    SALIM AJAMI (TF) .... JOE MORTON

TERRORIST ON TRIAL:
    THE UNITED STATES VS.
    SALIM AJAMI (TF) .... ROBERT DAVI
TERRORIST ON TRIAL:
    THE UNITED STATES VS.
    SALIM AJAMI (TF) .... RON LEIBMAN
TERRORIST ON TRIAL:
    THE UNITED STATES VS.
    SALIM AJAMI (TF) .... SAM WATERSTON
TERRORISTS, THE .... SEAN CONNERY
TERRORVISION .... CHAD ALLEN
TERRORVISION .... DIANE FRANKLIN
TERRORVISION .... GERRITT GRAHAM
TERRORVISION .... JONATHAN GRIES
TERRORVISION .... RANDI BROOKS
TESS .... LEIGH LAWSON
TESS .... NASTASSJA KINSKI
TESS .... PETER FIRTH
TESS OF THE STORM COUNTRY .... DIANE BAKER
TESTAMENT .... KEVIN COSTNER
TESTAMENT .... LEON AMES
TESTAMENT .... LILIA SKALA
TESTAMENT .... LUKAS HAAS
TESTAMENT .... LURENE TUTTLE†
TESTAMENT .... MAKO
TESTAMENT .... PHILIP ANGLIM
TESTAMENT .... REBECCA DE MORNAY
TESTAMENT .... ROSS HARRIS
TESTAMENT .... ROXANA ZAL
TESTAMENT .... WILLIAM DEVANE
TESTAMENT ★ .... JANE ALEXANDER
TESTAMENT OF ORPHEUS .... CLAUDINE AUGER
TESTIMONY OF TWO MEN (TF) .... J. D. CANNON
TESTIMONY OF TWO MEN (TF) .... LINDA PURL
TESTIMONY OF TWO MEN (TF) ... RALPH BELLAMY†
TESTIMONY (TF) .... BEN KINGSLEY
TESTIMONY (TF) .... ROBERT STEPHENS
TEX .... BILL McKINNEY
TEX .... EMILIO ESTEVEZ
TEX .... FRANCES LEE McCAIN
TEX .... JIM METZLER
TEX .... MATT DILLON
TEX .... MEG TILLY
TEXAS ACROSS THE RIVER .... DEAN MARTIN
TEXAS ACROSS THE RIVER .... PETER GRAVES
TEXAS CARNIVAL .... HOWARD KEEL
TEXAS CHAINSAW
    MASSACRE 2, THE .... DENNIS HOPPER
TEXAS DETOUR .... R.G. ARMSTRONG
TEXAS LIGHTNING .... PETER JASON
TEXAS RANGERS RIDE AGAIN ...... ANTHONY QUINN
TEXASVILLE .... ANNIE POTTS
TEXASVILLE .... CLORIS LEACHMAN
TEXASVILLE .... CYBILL SHEPHERD
TEXASVILLE .... EILEEN BRENNAN
TEXASVILLE .... JEFF BRIDGES
TEXASVILLE .... RANDY QUAID
TEXASVILLE .... TIMOTHY BOTTOMS
TEXASVILLE .... WILLIAM McNAMARA
THADDEUS ROSE AND EDDIE (TF) .... BO HOPKINS
THADDEUS ROSE AND EDDIE (TF) ....DIANE LADD
THANK GOD IT'S FRIDAY .... DEBRA WINGER
THANK GOD IT'S FRIDAY .... JEFF GOLDBLUM
THANK YOU ALL VERY MUCH .... SANDY DENNIS†
THANK YOU JEEVES .... DAVID NIVEN†
THANK YOUR LUCKY STARS .... BETTE DAVIS†
THANK YOUR LUCKY STARS .... DINAH SHORE†
THANK YOUR
    LUCKY STARS .... OLIVIA DE HAVILLAND
THANKS FOR THE MEMORY .... BOB HOPE
THANKSGIVING DAY (TF) .... MARY TYLER MOORE
THANKSGIVING
    PROMISE, THE (TF) .... BEAU BRIDGES
THANKSGIVING
    PROMISE, THE (TF) .... JEFF BRIDGES
THANKSGIVING
    PROMISE, THE (TF) .... LLOYD BRIDGES
THAT CERTAIN AGE .... JACKIE COOPER
THAT CERTAIN FEELING .... BOB HOPE
THAT CERTAIN FEELING .... EVA MARIE SAINT
THAT CERTAIN SUMMER (TF) .... HAL HOLBROOK
THAT CERTAIN SUMMER (TF) .... HOPE LANGE

This is not a list of every film ever made or every cast member, only those listed in this directory.

THAT CERTAIN SUMMER (TF) .... MARTIN SHEEN
THAT CERTAIN WOMAN .... BETTE DAVIS†
THAT CHAMPIONSHIP SEASON .... BRUCE DERN
THAT CHAMPIONSHIP SEASON .... MARTIN SHEEN
THAT CHAMPIONSHIP
    SEASON .... ROBERT MITCHUM
THAT CHAMPIONSHIP SEASON .... STACY KEACH
THAT COLD DAY IN THE PARK .... LUANA ANDERS
THAT COLD DAY IN THE PARK .... SANDY DENNIS†
THAT DARN CAT .... DEAN JONES
THAT DARN CAT .... HAYLEY MILLS
THAT DARN CAT .... RODDY McDOWALL
THAT FORSYTE WOMAN .... GREER GARSON
THAT FORSYTE WOMAN .... JANET LEIGH
THAT FUNNY FEELING .... NITA TALBOT
THAT FUNNY FEELING .... SANDRA DEE
THAT HAGEN GIRL .... LOIS MAXWELL
THAT HAGEN GIRL .... RONALD REAGAN
THAT KIND OF WOMAN .... BEATRICE ARTHUR
THAT KIND OF WOMAN .... JACK WARDEN
THAT KIND OF WOMAN .... SOPHIA LOREN
THAT KIND OF WOMAN .... TAB HUNTER
THAT LADY .... OLIVIA DE HAVILLAND
THAT LADY .... PAUL SCOFIELD
THAT LUCKY TOUCH .... ROGER MOORE
THAT LUCKY TOUCH .... SHELLEY WINTERS
THAT LUCKY TOUCH .... SUSANNAH YORK
THAT MAN BOLT .... FRED WILLIAMSON
THAT MAN GEORGE! .... CLAUDINE AUGER
THAT MAN GEORGE! .... GEORGE HAMILTON
THAT NIGHT .... C. THOMAS HOWELL
THAT NIGHT .... ELIZA DUSHKU
THAT NIGHT .... HELEN SHAVER
THAT NIGHT .... J. SMITH-CAMERON
THAT NIGHT .... JOHN DOSSETT
THAT NIGHT .... JULIETTE LEWIS
THAT NIGHT .... ROSEMARY MURPHY
THAT NIGHT IN RIO .... DON AMECHE†
THAT SECRET SUNDAY (TF) .... DAPHNE ASHBROOK
THAT SECRET SUNDAY (TF) ..... GEORGE GRIZZARD
THAT SECRET SUNDAY (TF) ...... JAMES FARENTINO
THAT SECRET SUNDAY (TF) .... JOE REGALBUTO
THAT SECRET
    SUNDAY (TF) ...., PARKER STEVENSON
THAT TOUCH OF MINK .... CARY GRANT†
THAT TOUCH OF MINK .... DICK SARGENT
THAT TOUCH OF MINK .... DORIS DAY
THAT TOUCH OF MINK .... JOHN FIELDLER
THAT UNCERTAIN FEELING .... BURGESS MEREDITH
THAT WAS THEN, THIS IS NOW ..... EMILIO ESTEVEZ
THAT WAS THEN...
    THIS IS NOW .... MORGAN FREEMAN
THAT WOMAN OPPOSITE .... DAN O'HERLIHY
THAT TOUCH OF MINK .... JOHN ASTIN
THAT'LL BE THE DAY .... ROSEMARY LEACH
THAT'S ADEQUATE .... RICHARD BALIN
THAT'S DANCING! (FD) .... LIZA MINELLI
THAT'S
    ENTERTAINMENT! (FD) .... DEBBIE REYNOLDS
THAT'S
    ENTERTAINMENT! (FD) .... ELIZABETH TAYLOR
THAT'S ENTERTAINMENT! (FD) ...... FRANK SINATRA
THAT'S ENTERTAINMENT! (FD) .... GENE KELLY
THAT'S ENTERTAINMENT! (FD) ...... JAMES STEWART
THAT'S ENTERTAINMENT! (FD) .... LIZA MINELLI
THAT'S ENTERTAINMENT,
    PART 2 (FD) .... GENE KELLY
THAT'S ENTERTAINMENT! III (FD) .... ANN MILLER
THAT'S
    ENTERTAINMENT! III (FD) .... CYD CHARISSE
THAT'S
    ENTERTAINMENT! III (FD) .... DEBBIE REYNOLDS
THAT'S
    ENTERTAINMENT! III (FD) .... ESTHER WILLIAMS
THAT'S ENTERTAINMENT! III (FD) .... GENE KELLY
THAT'S ENTERTAINMENT! III (FD) ...... HOWARD KEEL
THAT'S ENTERTAINMENT! III (FD) .... JUNE ALLYSON
THAT'S ENTERTAINMENT! III (FD) .... LENA HORNE
THAT'S
    ENTERTAINMENT! III (FD) .... MICKEY ROONEY
THAT'S LIFE! .... CHRIS LEMMON
THAT'S LIFE! .... CYNTHIA SIKES

THAT'S LIFE! .... DANA SPARKS
THAT'S LIFE! .... EMMA WALTON
THAT'S LIFE! .... JACK LEMMON
THAT'S LIFE! .... JENNIFER EDWARDS
THAT'S LIFE! .... JULIE ANDREWS
THAT'S LIFE! .... MATT LATTANZI
THAT'S LIFE .... NICKY BLAIR
THAT'S LIFE! .... ROB KNEPPER
THAT'S LIFE! .... ROBERT LOGGIA
THAT'S LIFE! .... SALLY KELLERMAN
THAT'S MY BOY .... DEAN MARTIN
THAT'S MY BOY .... JERRY LEWIS
THAT'S MY MAN .... DON AMECHE†
THAT'S THE WAY OF THE WORLD .... BERT PARKS†
THAT'S THE WAY OF THE WORLD .... ED NELSON
THAT'S THE WAY OF
    THE WORLD .... HARVEY KEITEL
THAT'S THE WAY OF
    THE WORLD .... MICHAEL DANTE
THE GUN AND THE
    PULPIT, THE (TF) .... MARJOE GORTNER
THEATRE OF BLOOD .... DIANA RIGG
THEATRE OF BLOOD .... MILO O'SHEA
THEATRE OF BLOOD .... ROBERT MORLEY
THEATRE OF BLOOD .... VINCENT PRICE†
THIEF OF HEARTS .... ALAN NORTH
THEIR OWN DESIRE ★ .... NORMA SHEARER†
THELMA JORDAN .... BARBARA STANWYCK†
THELMA & LOUISE .... BRAD PITT
THELMA & LOUISE .... CHRISTOPHER McDONALD
THELMA & LOUISE .... HARVEY KEITEL
THELMA & LOUISE .... JASON BEGHE
THELMA & LOUISE .... LUCINDA JENNEY
THELMA & LOUISE .... MICHAEL MADSEN
THELMA & LOUISE ★ .... GEENA DAVIS
THELMA & LOUISE ★ .... SUSAN SARANDON
THEM! .... JAMES ARNESS
THEM .... JAMES WHITMORE
THEM! .... LEONARD NIMOY
THERE ARE NO
    CHILDREN HERE (TF) .... OPRAH WINFREY
THERE GOES MY BABY .... DERMOT MULRONEY
THERE GOES MY BABY .... KELLI WILLIAMS
THERE GOES MY BABY .... RICK SCHRODER
THERE GOES MY GIRL .... ANN SOTHERN
THERE GOES THE BRIDE .... MARTIN BALSAM
THERE GOES THE BRIDE .... TOM SMOTHERS
THERE GOES THE BRIDE .... TWIGGY
THERE GOES THE GROOM .... ANN SOTHERN
THERE GOES THE GROOM ..... BURGESS MEREDITH
THERE MUST
    BE A PONY (TF) .... ELIZABETH TAYLOR
THERE MUST BE A PONY (TF) ..... ROBERT WAGNER
THERE WAS A
    CROOKED MAN... .... BURGESS MEREDITH
THERE WAS A CROOKED MAN... ..... HUME CRONYN
THERE WAS A CROOKED MAN ... JOHN RANDOLPH
THERE WAS A CROOKED MAN .... KIRK DOUGLAS
THERE WAS A CROOKED MAN .... LEE GRANT
THERE WAS A CROOKED MAN .... SUSANNAH YORK
THERE'S A GIRL IN MY SOUP ...... PETER SELLERS†
THERE'S ALWAYS
    TOMORROW .... BARBARA STANWYCK†
THERE'S NO BUSINESS LIKE
    SHOW BUSINESS .... MARILYN MONROE†
THERE'S A GIRL IN MY SOUP .... GOLDIE HAWN
THERE'S ONE BORN
    EVERY MINUTE .... ELIZABETH TAYLOR
THESE ARE THE DAMNED ..... SHIRLEY ANNE FIELD
THESE GLAMOUR GIRLS .... LANA TURNER
THESE THOUSAND HILLS .... DON MURRAY
THESE THOUSAND HILLS .... ROYAL DANO
THESE THOUSAND HILLS .... STUART WHITMAN
THESE WILDER YEARS ...... BARBARA STANWYCK†
THEY ALL DIED LAUGHING .... GEOFFREY BAYLDON
THEY ALL KISSED
    THE BRIDE .... JOAN CRAWFORD†
THEY ALL LAUGHED .... AUDREY HEPBURN†
THEY ALL LAUGHED .... BEN GAZZARA
THEY ALL LAUGHED .... BLAINE NOVAK
THEY ALL LAUGHED .... COLLEEN CAMP
THEY ALL LAUGHED .... DOROTHY STRATTEN†

THEY ALL LAUGHED .... ELIZABETH PENA
THEY ALL LAUGHED .... JOHN RITTER
THEY CALL ME BRUCE? ..... MARGAUX HEMINGWAY
THEY CALL ME MISTER TIBBS! .... ED ASNER
THEY CALL ME MISTER TIBBS! .... JEFF COREY
THEY CALL ME MISTER TIBBS! ...... MARTIN LANDAU
THEY CALL ME MISTER TIBBS! ...... SIDNEY POITIER
THEY CAME FROM
    BEYOND SPACE .... MICHAEL GOUGH
THEY CAME TO CORDURA .... TAB HUNTER
THEY CAME TO ROB LAS VEGAS .... JACK PALANCE
THEY DARE NOT LOVE .... MARTHA SCOTT
THEY DIED WITH THEIR
    BOOTS ON .... ANTHONY QUINN
THEY DIED WITH THEIR
    BOOTS ON .... ELEANOR PARKER
THEY DIED WITH THEIR
    BOOTS ON .... OLIVIA DE HAVILLAND
THEY GOT ME COVERED .... BOB HOPE
THEY GOT ME COVERED .... DOROTHY LAMOUR
THEY KNEW WHAT
    THEY WANTED .... KARL MALDEN
THEY KNEW WHAT
    THEY WANTED ✪ .... WILLIAM GARGAN†
THEY LIVE .... MEG FOSTER
THEY LIVE .... RODDY PIPER
THEY LIVE BY NIGHT ...... HOWARD DA SILVA†
THEY MET IN ARGENTINA .... MAUREEN O'HARA
THEY MIGHT BE GIANTS .... AL LEWIS
THEY MIGHT BE GIANTS .... F. MURRAY ABRAHAM
THEY MIGHT BE GIANTS .... GEORGE C. SCOTT
THEY MIGHT BE GIANTS .... JACK GILFORD†
THEY MIGHT BE GIANTS .... JAMES TOLKAN
THEY MIGHT BE GIANTS .... JOANNE WOODWARD
THEY MIGHT BE GIANTS .... M. EMMET WALSH
THEY MIGHT BE GIANTS .... PAUL BENEDICT
THEY MIGHT BE GIANTS .... RUE McCLANAHAN
THEY MIGHT BE GIANTS .... SUDIE BOND
THEY MIGHT BE GIANTS .... THERESA MERRITT
THEY ONLY KILL
    THEIR MASTERS .... HAL HOLBROOK
THEY ONLY KILL
    THEIR MASTERS .... HARRY GUARDINO
THEY ONLY KILL
    THEIR MASTERS .... JAMES GARNER
THEY ONLY KILL
    THEIR MASTERS .... JUNE ALLYSON
THEY ONLY KILL
    THEIR MASTERS .... KATHERINE ROSS
THEY SHOOT HORSES,
    DON'T THEY? ✪✪ .... GIG YOUNG†
THEY SHOOT HORSES,
    DON'T THEY? .... ART METRANO
THEY SHOOT HORSES,
    DON'T THEY? .... BONNIE BEDELIA
THEY SHOOT HORSES,
    DON'T THEY? .... BRUCE DERN
THEY SHOOT HORSES,
    DON'T THEY? .... MARILYN HASSETT
THEY SHOOT HORSES,
    DON'T THEY? .... MICHAEL SARRAZIN
THEY SHOOT HORSES,
    DON'T THEY? .... PAUL MANTEE
THEY SHOOT HORSES,
    DON'T THEY? .... RED BUTTONS
THEY SHOOT HORSES,
    DON'T THEY? ★ .... JANE FONDA
THEY SHOOT HORSES,
    DON'T THEY? ✪ .... SUSANNAH YORK
THEY WENT THAT-A-WAY
    AND THAT-A-WAY .... RENI SANTONI
THEY WENT THAT-A-WAY
    AND THAT-A-WAY .... RICHARD KIEL
THEY WERE SISTERS .... THORLEY WALTERS†
THEY WERE SO YOUNG .... RAYMOND BURR†
THEY WHO DARE .... DENHOLM ELLIOTT†
THEY WON'T BELIEVE ME .... JANE GREER
THEY WON'T FORGET .... LANA TURNER
THEY'RE A WEIRD MOB .... JOHN MEILLON
THEY'VE KIDNAPPED
    ANNE BENEDICT (TF) .... KATHLEEN QUINLAN

† after an actor's name denotes deceased.

INDEX OF FILM TITLES

THEY'VE KIDNAPPED ANNE BENEDICT (TF) .... MARTHA SCOTT
THEY'VE KIDNAPPED ANNE BENEDICT (TF) .... ROBERT WAGNER
THEY'VE KIDNAPPED ANNE BENEDICT (TF) .... WILLIAM WINDOM
THIEF .... DENNIS FARINA
THIEF .... JAMES BELUSHI
THIEF .... JAMES CAAN
THIEF .... ROBERT PROSKY
THIEF .... TOM SIGNORELLI
THIEF .... TUESDAY WELD
THIEF .... WILLIE NELSON
THIEF (TF) .... ANGIE DICKINSON
THIEF (TF) .... HURD HATFIELD
THIEF (TF) .... RICHARD CRENNA
THIEF OF BAGHDAD, THE (TF) .... KABIR BEDI
THIEF OF BAGHDAD, THE (TF) .... PETER USTINOV
THIEF OF BAGHDAD, THE (TF) .... TERENCE STAMP
THIEF OF HEARTS .... BARBARA WILLIAMS
THIEF OF HEARTS .... GEORGE WENDT
THIEF OF HEARTS .... JOHN GETZ
THIEF OF HEARTS .... STEVEN BAUER
THIEF OF PARIS, THE .... GENEVIEVE BUJOLD
THIEF WHO CAME TO DINNER, THE .... AUSTIN PENDLETON
THIEF WHO CAME TO DINNER, THE .... JACQUELINE BISSET
THIEF WHO CAME TO DINNER, THE .... JILL CLAYBURGH
THIEF WHO CAME TO DINNER, THE .... MICHAEL MURPHY
THIEF WHO CAME TO DINNER, THE .... NED BEATTY
THIEF WHO CAME TO DINNER, THE .... RYAN O'NEAL
THIEVES .... CHARLES GRODIN
THIEVES .... HECTOR ELIZONDO
THIEVES .... MARLO THOMAS
THIEVES .... MERCEDES McCAMBRIDGE
THIEVES FALL OUT .... ANTHONY QUINN
THIEVES FALL OUT .... EDDIE ALBERT
THIEVES LIKE US .... JOHN SCHUCK
THIEVES LIKE US .... KEITH CARRADINE
THIEVES LIKE US .... LOUISE FLETCHER
THIEVES LIKE US .... SHELLEY DUVALL
THIEVES LIKE US .... TOM SKERRITT
THIN MAN, THE .... MAUREEN O'SULLIVAN
THIN MAN, THE ★ .... WILLIAM POWELL†
THIN MAN GOES HOME, THE .... LEON AMES
THIN RED LINE, THE .... JACK WARDEN
THING, THE .... JAMES ARNESS
THING, THE .... KURT RUSSELL
THING, THE .... RICHARD MASUR
THING, THE .... WILFORD BRIMLEY
THING CALLED LOVE, THE .... DERMOT MULRONEY
THING CALLED LOVE, THE .... RIVER PHOENIX†
THING CALLED LOVE, THE .... SAMANTHA MATHIS
THING CALLED LOVE, THE .... SANDRA BULLOCK
THINGS ARE TOUGH ALL OVER .... LANCE KINSEY
THINGS CHANGE .... DICK CUSAK
THINGS CHANGE .... DON AMECHE†
THINGS CHANGE .... JOE MANTEGNA
THINGS CHANGE .... ROBERT PROSKY
THINGS IN THEIR SEASON (TF) .... MEG FOSTER
THINGS IN THEIR SEASON (TF) .... PATRICIA NEAL
THINGS TO DO IN DENVER WHEN YOU'RE DEAD .... ANDY GARCIA
THINGS TO DO IN DENVER WHEN YOU'RE DEAD .... CHRISTOPHER LLOYD
THINGS TO DO IN DENVER WHEN YOU'RE DEAD .... GABRIELLE ANWAR
THINGS TO DO IN DENVER WHEN YOU'RE DEAD .... JAMES CAAN
THINGS TO DO IN DENVER WHEN YOU'RE DEAD .... JOSH CHARLES
THINGS TO DO IN DENVER WHEN YOU'RE DEAD .... SARA TRIGGER
THINGS TO DO IN DENVER WHEN YOU'RE DEAD .... SEYMOUR CASSEL
THINGS TO DO IN DENVER WHEN YOU'RE DEAD .... TREAT WILLIAMS
THINGS TO DO IN DENVER WHEN YOU'RE DEAD .... WILLIAM FORSYTHE
THINK BIG .... ARI MEYERS
THINK BIG .... CLAUDIA CHRISTIAN
THINK BIG .... DAVID CARRADINE
THINK BIG .... DAVID PAUL
THINK BIG .... MARTIN MULL
THINK BIG .... MICHAEL WINSLOW
THINK BIG .... PETER LUPUS
THINK BIG .... PETER PAUL
THINK BIG .... RICHARD KIEL
THINK BIG .... RICHARD MOLL
THINK BIG .... THOMAS GOTTSCHALK
THIRD DAY, THE .... ELIZABETH ASHLEY
THIRD DAY, THE .... GEORGE PEPPARD†
THIRD DAY, THE .... ROBERT WEBBER
THIRD DAY, THE .... SALLY KELLERMAN
THIRD DAY, THE .... VINCENT GARDENIA†
THIRD GIRL FROM THE LEFT, THE (TF) .... KIM NOVAK
THIRD GIRL FROM THE LEFT, THE (TF) .... TONY CURTIS
THIRD KEY, THE .... IAN BANNEN
THIRD MAN, THE .... ORSON WELLES†
THIRD MAN, THE .... JOSEPH COTTON†
THIRD MAN, THE .... TREVOR HOWARD†
THIRD MAN, THE .... VALLI†
THIRD MAN ON THE MOUNTAIN .... HELEN HAYES
THIRD SECRET, THE .... JUDI DENCH
THIRD SECRET, THE .... NIGEL DAVENPORT
THIRD SOLUTION, THE (TF) .... DANNY AIELLO
THIRD WALKER, THE .... COLLEEN DEWHURST†
THIRD WALKER, THE .... WILLIAM SHATNER
THIRST .... DAVID HEMMINGS
THIRST .... HENRY SILVA
THIRTEEN AT DINNER (TF) .... PETER USTINOV
THIRTEEN WOMEN .... LEON AMES
THIRTY .... JACK WEBB†
THIRTY SECONDS OVER TOKYO .... LEON AMES
THIRTY SECONDS OVER TOKYO .... PHYLLIS THAXTER
THIRTY SECONDS OVER TOKYO .... ROBERT MITCHUM
THIRTY SECONDS OVER TOKYO .... SPENCER TRACY†
THIRTY SECONDS OVER TOKYO .... VAN JOHNSON
THIRTY-DAY PRINCESS .... SYLVIA SIDNEY
THIRTY-NINE STEPS, THE .... DAVID WARNER
THIRTY-NINE STEPS, THE .... PEGGY ASHCROFT†
THIRTY-NINE STEPS, THE .... TIMOTHY WEST
THIS AMERICA THE MOVIE, NOT THE COUNTRY .... ROBERT DOWNEY JR.
THIS ANGRY AGE .... NEHEMIAH PERSOFF
THIS ANGRY AGE/ LA DIGA SUL PACIFICO .... ANTHONY PERKINS†
THIS BOY'S LIFE .... ELLEN BARKIN
THIS BOY'S LIFE .... LEONARDO DICAPRIO
THIS BOY'S LIFE .... ROBERT DE NIRO
THIS CAN'T BE LOVE (TF) .... ANTHONY QUINN
THIS CAN'T BE LOVE (TF) .... JAMI GERTZ
THIS CAN'T BE LOVE (TF) .... JASON BATEMAN
THIS CAN'T BE LOVE (TF) .... KATHERINE HEPBURN
THIS CAN'T BE LOVE (TF) .... MAXINE MILLER
THIS CAN'T BE LOVE (TF) .... MICHAEL FEINSTEIN
THIS CHILD IS MINE (TF) .... LINDSAY WAGNER
THIS COULD BE THE NIGHT .... ANTHONY (TONY) FRANCIOSA
THIS COULD BE THE NIGHT .... JEAN SIMMONS
THIS EARTH IS MINE .... JEAN SIMMONS
THIS ENGLAND .... RODDY McDOWALL
THIS GUN FOR HIRE .... YVONNE DE CARLO
THIS GUN FOR HIRE (CTF) .... FREDERIC LEHNE
THIS GUN FOR HIRE (CTF) .... JOHN HARKINS
THIS GUN FOR HIRE (CTF) .... NANCY EVERHARD
THIS GUN FOR HIRE (CTF) .... ROBERT WAGNER
THIS HAPPY BREED .... JOHN MILLS
THIS HAPPY FEELING .... ALEXIS SMITH†
THIS HAPPY FEELING .... DEBBIE REYNOLDS
THIS HAPPY FEELING .... JOHN SAXON
THIS HAPPY FEELING .... TROY DONAHUE
THIS IS MY AFFAIR .... BARBARA STANWYCK†
THIS IS MY LIFE .... CARRIE FISHER
THIS IS MY LIFE .... DAN AYKROYD
THIS IS MY LIFE .... GABY HOFFMAN
THIS IS MY LIFE .... JULIE KAVNER
THIS IS MY LIFE .... KATHY NAJIMY
THIS IS MY LIFE .... SAMANTHA MATHIS
THIS IS MY STREET .... JOHN HURT
THIS IS SPINAL TAP .... ANJELICA HUSTON
THIS IS SPINAL TAP .... BILLY CRYSTAL
THIS IS SPINAL TAP .... BRUNO KIRBY
THIS IS SPINAL TAP .... CHRISTOPHER GUEST
THIS IS SPINAL TAP .... ED BEGLEY JR.
THIS IS SPINAL TAP .... FRAN DRESCHER
THIS IS SPINAL TAP .... HARRY SHEARER
THIS IS SPINAL TAP .... JUNE CHADWICK
THIS IS SPINAL TAP .... MICHAEL McKEAN
THIS IS SPINAL TAP .... ROB REINER
THIS IS SPINAL TAP .... TONY HENDRA
THIS IS THE ARMY .... RONALD REAGAN
THIS IS THE WEST THAT WAS (TF) .... JANE ALEXANDER
THIS LAND IS MINE .... MAUREEN O'HARA
THIS MAN IS MINE .... RALPH BELLAMY†
THIS MAN STANDS ALONE (TF) .... LOUIS GOSSETT JR.
THIS MODERN AGE .... JOAN CRAWFORD†
THIS PROPERTY IS CONDEMNED .... CHARLES BRONSON
THIS PROPERTY IS CONDEMNED .... DABNEY COLEMAN
THIS PROPERTY IS CONDEMNED .... KATE REID
THIS PROPERTY IS CONDEMNED .... ROBERT BLAKE
THIS PROPERTY IS CONDEMNED .... ROBERT REDFORD
THIS REBEL BREED .... DYAN CANNON
THIS REBEL BREED .... RITA MORENO
THIS SAVAGE LAND .... GEORGE C. SCOTT
THIS SPORTING LIFE .... GLENDA JACKSON
THIS SPORTING LIFE ★ .... RACHEL ROBERTS†
THIS SPORTING LIFE ★ .... RICHARD HARRIS
THIS TIME FOR KEEPS .... AVA GARDNER†
THIS WIFE FOR HIRE (TF) .... LARAINE NEWMAN
THIS WIFE FOR HIRE (TF) .... PAM DAWBER
THIS WIFE FOR HIRE (TF) .... ROBERT KLEIN
THIS WOMAN IS DANGEROUS .... JOAN CRAWFORD†
THOMAS CROWN AFFAIR, THE .... FAYE DUNAWAY
THOMAS CROWN AFFAIR, THE .... JACK WESTON
THOMAS CROWN AFFAIR, THE .... STEVE MCQUEEN†
THOMAS CROWN AFFAIR, THE .... YAPHET KOTTO
THOMPSON'S LAST RUN (TF) .... SUSAN TYRRELL
THOMPSON'S LAST RUN (TF) .... KATHLEEN YORK
THOMPSON'S LAST RUN (TF) .... ROBERT MITCHUM
THOMPSON'S LAST RUN (TF) .... WILFORD BRIMLEY
THORN BIRDS, THE (MS) .... BRYON BROWN
THORN BIRDS, THE (MS) .... EARL HOLLIMAN
THORN BIRDS, THE (MS) .... JEAN SIMMONS
THORN BIRDS, THE (MS) .... KEN HOWARD
THORN BIRDS, THE (MS) .... PIPER LAURIE
THORN BIRDS, THE (MS) .... RACHEL WARD
THORN BIRDS, THE (MS) .... RICHARD CHAMBERLAIN
THOROUGHBRED .... VERA MILES
THOROUGHBREDS, THE .... STUART WHITMAN
THOROUGHLY MODERN MILLIE .... JAMES FOX
THOROUGHLY MODERN MILLIE .... JOHN GAVIN
THOROUGHLY MODERN MILLIE .... JULIE ANDREWS
THOROUGHLY MODERN MILLIE .... MARY TYLER MOORE
THOROUGHLY MODERN MILLIE .... NORIYUKI "PAT" MORITA
THOSE CALLAWAYS .... TOM SKERRITT
THOSE CALLOWAYS .... BRIAN KEITH
THOSE CALLOWAYS .... LINDA EVANS
THOSE CALLOWAYS .... VERA MILES
THOSE DARING YOUNG MEN IN THEIR JAUNTY JALOPIES .... DUDLEY MOORE
THOSE DARING YOUNG MEN IN THEIR JAUNTY JALOPIES .... PETER COOK
THOSE DARING YOUNG MEN IN THEIR JAUNTY JALOPIES .... TONY CURTIS
THOSE FANTASTIC FLYING FOOLS .... TROY DONAHUE

This is not a list of every film ever made or every cast member, only those listed in this directory.

THOSE FANTASTIC FLYING
    FOOLS/BLAST-OFF .... BURL IVES
THOSE LIPS, THOSE EYES .... FRANK LANGELLA
THOSE LIPS, THOSE EYES ...... GLYNNIS O'CONNOR
THOSE LIPS, THOSE EYES .... KEVIN McCARTHY
THOSE LIPS, THOSE EYES .... TOM HULCE
THOSE MAGNIFICENT MEN IN
    THEIR FLYING MACHINES .... GORDAN JACKSON†
THOSE MAGNIFICENT MEN IN
    THEIR FLYING MACHINES ..... JEAN-PIERRE CASSEL
THOSE MAGNIFICENT MEN IN
    THEIR FLYING MACHINES .... ROBERT MORLEY
THOSE MAGNIFICENT MEN IN
    THEIR FLYING MACHINES ...... SAM WANAMAKER†
THOSE MAGNIFICENT MEN IN
    THEIR FLYING MACHINES .... SARAH MILES
THOSE MAGNIFICENT MEN IN
    THEIR FLYING MACHINES .... STUART WHITMAN
THOSE SHE LEFT
    BEHIND (TF) .... COLLEEN DEWHURST†
THOSE SHE LEFT BEHIND (TF) .... GARY COLE
THOSE SHE LEFT BEHIND (TF) .... JOANNA KERNS
THOSE WERE THE DAYS .... JOHN MILLS
THOSE WERE THE
    HAPPY TIMES .... JENNY AGUTTER
THOSE WERE THE
    HAPPY TIMES .... JULIE ANDREWS
THOSE WERE THE
    HAPPY TIMES .... RICHARD CRENNA
THOSE WERE THE
    HAPPY TIMES .... ROBERT REED†
THOU SHALT NOT
    COMMIT ADULTERY (TF) .... LOUISE FLETCHER
THOU SHALT NOT KILL (TF) .... JAMES KEACH
THOUSAND AND
    ONE NIGHTS, A .... SHELLEY WINTERS
THOUSAND CLOWNS, A .... BARBARA HARRIS
THOUSAND CLOWNS, A .... GENE SAKS
THOUSAND CLOWNS, A .... JASON ROBARDS
THOUSAND CLOWNS, A .... WILLIAM DANIELS
THOUSAND CLOWNS, A ∞ .... MARTIN BALSAM
THOUSANDS CHEER .... ANN SOTHERN
THOUSANDS CHEER .... GENE KELLY
THOUSANDS CHEER .... JUNE ALLYSON
THOUSANDS CHEER .... LENA HORNE
THRASHIN' .... JOSH BROLIN
THRASHIN' .... PAMELA GILDAY
THREE .... CHARLOTTE RAMPLING
THREE .... SAM WATERSTON
THREE AMIGOS .... ALFONSO ARAU
THREE AMIGOS .... CHEVY CHASE
THREE AMIGOS .... JON LOVITZ
THREE AMIGOS .... MARTIN SHORT
THREE AMIGOS .... STEVE MARTIN
THREE BITES OF THE APPLE .... DAVID McCALLUM
THREE BITES OF THE APPLE .... HARVEY KORMAN
THREE BITES OF THE APPLE .... TAMMY GRIMES
THREE BLIND MICE .... DAVID NIVEN†
THREE BRAVE MEN .... ERNEST BORGNINE
THREE BRAVE MEN .... NINA FOCH
THREE CASES OF MURDER .... PATRICK MacNEE
THREE COINS IN
    THE FOUNTAIN .... LOUIS JOURDAN
THREE COMRADES ★ .... MARGARET SULLAVAN†
THREE DAYS OF THE CONDOR .... CARLIN GLYNN
THREE DAYS OF
    THE CONDOR .... CLIFF ROBERTSON
THREE DAYS OF THE CONDOR ..... FAYE DUNAWAY
THREE DAYS OF
    THE CONDOR .... JOHN HOUSEMAN†
THREE DAYS OF THE CONDOR ..... MAX von SYDOW
THREE DAYS OF
    THE CONDOR .... ROBERT REDFORD
THREE FABLES OF LOVE .... LESLIE CARON
THREE FACES OF EVE, THE .... VINCE EDWARDS
THREE FACES
    OF EVE, THE ★★ .... JOANNE WOODWARD
THREE FOR JAMIE DAWN .... RICARDO MONTALBAN
THREE FOR THE ROAD .... ALAN RUCK
THREE FOR THE ROAD .... CHARLIE SHEEN
THREE FOR THE SHOW .... JACK LEMMON
THREE FUGITIVES .... ALAN RUCK
THREE FUGITIVES .... JAMES EARL JONES

THREE FUGITIVES .... KENNETH McMILLAN†
THREE FUGITIVES .... MARTIN SHORT
THREE FUGITIVES .... NICK NOLTE
THREE FUGITIVES .... SARAH ROWLAND DOROFF
THREE GIRLS
    FROM ROME .... MARCELLO MASTROIANNI
THREE GODFATHERS .... BEN JOHNSON
THREE GODFATHERS .... HARRY CAREY JR.
THREE GUNS FOR TEXAS .... ALBERT SALMI†
THREE GUYS NAMED MIKE .... HOWARD KEEL
THREE GUYS NAMED MIKE .... JANE WYMAN
THREE GUYS NAMED MIKE .... VAN JOHNSON
THREE HEARTS FOR JULIA .... ANN SOTHERN
THREE HUSBANDS .... HOWARD DA SILVA†
THREE IN THE CELLAR .... LARRY HAGMAN
THREE INTO TWO
    WON'T GO .... PEGGY ASHCROFT†
THREE INTO TWO WON'T GO .... CLAIRE BLOOM
THREE INTO TWO WON'T GO .... ROD STEIGER
THREE KINGS, THE (TF) .... JACK WARDEN
THREE KINGS, THE (TF) .... JANE KACZMAREK
THREE LITTLE GIRLS IN BLUE .... CELESTE HOLM
THREE LITTLE WORDS .... DEBBIE REYNOLDS
THREE MEN AND A BABY .... CELESTE HOLM
THREE MEN AND A BABY .... LISA BLAIR
THREE MEN AND A BABY .... MARGARET COLIN
THREE MEN AND A BABY .... MICHELLE BLAIR
THREE MEN AND A BABY .... NANCY TRAVIS
THREE MEN AND A BABY .... PHILIP BOSCO
THREE MEN AND A BABY .... STEVE GUTTENBERG
THREE MEN AND A BABY .... TED DANSON
THREE MEN AND A BABY .... TOM SELLECK
THREE MEN AND A
    LITTLE LADY .... CHRISTOPHER CAZENOVE
THREE MEN AND A LITTLE LADY .... FIONA SHAW
THREE MEN AND A LITTLE LADY ..... NANCY TRAVIS
THREE MEN AND A
    LITTLE LADY .... ROBIN WEISMAN
THREE MEN AND A
    LITTLE LADY .... SHEILA HANCOCK
THREE MEN AND A
    LITTLE LADY .... STEVE GUTTENBERG
THREE MEN AND A LITTLE LADY .... TED DANSON
THREE MEN AND A LITTLE LADY .... TOM SELLECK
THREE MEN IN A BOAT .... DAVID TOMLINSON
THREE MEN IN A BOAT .... JILL IRELAND†
THREE MEN IN A BOAT .... LAURENCE HARVEY†
THREE MEN IN A BOAT .... MARTITA HUNT†
THREE MEN IN WHITE .... AVA GARDNER†
THREE MEN IN WHITE .... VAN JOHNSON
THREE MUSKETEERS, THE (1939) .... DON AMECHE†
THREE MUSKETEERS,
    THE (1948) .... ANGELA LANSBURY
THREE MUSKETEERS, THE (1948) ..... LANA TURNER
THREE MUSKETEERS,
    THE (1948) .... JUNE ALLYSON
THREE MUSKETEERS, THE (1948) .... GENE KELLY
THREE MUSKETEERS,
    THE (1948) .... VINCENT PRICE†
THREE MUSKETEERS,
    THE (1974) .... RICHARD CHAMBERLAIN
THREE MUSKETEERS, THE (1974) ...... SIMON WARD
THREE MUSKETEERS,
    THE (1974) .... CHARLTON HESTON
THREE MUSKETEERS,
    THE (1974) .... FAYE DUNAWAY
THREE MUSKETEERS,
    THE (1974) .... FRANK FINLAY†
THREE MUSKETEERS,
    THE (1974) .... GERALDINE CHAPLIN
THREE MUSKETEERS,
    THE (1974) .... JEAN-PIERRE CASSEL
THREE MUSKETEERS,
    THE (1974) .... OLIVER REED
THREE MUSKETEERS,
    THE (1974) .... RAQUEL WELCH
THREE MUSKETEERS,
    THE (1974) .... MICHAEL YORK
THREE MUSKETEERS,
    THE (1974) .... JOSS ACKLAND
THREE MUSKETEERS, THE .... JULIE DELPY
THREE
    MUSKETEERS, THE .... KIEFER SUTHERLAND

THREE MUSKETEERS, THE .... OLIVER PLATT
THREE MUSKETEERS, THE .... CHARLIE SHEEN
THREE MUSKETEERS, THE .... CHRIS O'DONNELL
THREE MUSKETEERS, THE ...... GABRIELLE ANWAR
THREE
    MUSKETEERS, THE .... REBECCA DE MORNAY
THREE MUSKETEERS, THE .... TIM CURRY
THREE NIGHTS OF LOVE .... JOHN PHILLIP LAW
THREE O'CLOCK HIGH .... MIKE JOLLY
THREE OF HEARTS .... JOE PANTOLIANO
THREE OF HEARTS .... KELLY LYNCH
THREE OF HEARTS .... LARA FLYNN BOYLE
THREE OF HEARTS .... SHERILYN FENN
THREE OF HEARTS .... WILLIAM BALDWIN
THREE ON A COUCH .... JANET LEIGH
THREE ON A COUCH .... JERRY LEWIS
THREE ON A COUCH .... KATHLEEN FREEMAN
THREE ON A DATE (TF) .... LONI ANDERSON
THREE ON A MATCH .... BETTE DAVIS†
THREE ON A MATCH (TF) .... BRUCE A. YOUNG
THREE ON A MATCH (TF) .... DAVID HEMMINGS
THREE ON A MATCH (TF) .... PATRICK CASSIDY
THREE O'CLOCK HIGH .... CASEY SIEMASZKO
THREE O'CLOCK HIGH .... RICHARD TYSON
THREE RING CIRCUS .... ZSA ZSA GABOR
THREE SAILORS
    AND A GIRL .... GORDON MACRAE†
THREE SECRETS .... ELEANOR PARKER
THREE SECRETS .... PATRICIA NEAL
THREE SHADES OF LOVE .... DYAN CANNON
THREE SISTERS .... ALAN BATES
THREE SISTERS .... KIM STANLEY
THREE SISTERS, THE .... KEVIN McCARTHY
THREE SISTERS, THE .... SANDY DENNIS†
THREE SISTERS, THE .... SHELLEY WINTERS
THREE SOVEREIGNS
    FOR SARAH (TF) .... RONALD HUNTER
THREE SOVEREIGNS
    FOR SARAH (TF) .... VANESSA REDGRAVE
THREE STEPS NORTH .... LLOYD BRIDGES
THREE STRANGERS .... GERALDINE FITZGERALD
THREE STRIPES IN THE SUN .... CHUCK CONNORS†
THREE THE HARD WAY .... FRED WILLIAMSON
THREE THE HARD WAY .... JIM BROWN
THREE TOUGH GUYS .... FRED WILLIAMSON
THREE VIOLENT PEOPLE .... CHARLTON HESTON
THREE VIOLENT PEOPLE .... ELAINE STRITCH
THREE WISE FOOLS .... CYD CHARISSE
THREE WISHES .... JOEY MAZZELLO
THREE WISHES .... PATRICK SWAYZE
THREE
    WISHES .... MARY ELIZABETH MASTRANTONIO
THREE WISHES OF BILLY
    GRIER, THE (TF) .... BETTY BUCKLEY
THREE WISHES OF BILLY
    GRIER, THE (TF) .... HAL HOLBROOK
THREE WISHES OF BILLY
    GRIER, THE (TF) .... RALPH MACCHIO
THREE WISHES OF BILLY
    GRIER, THE (TF) .... SEASON HUBLEY
THREE WITNESSES .... GERALDINE FITZGERALD
THREE-RING CIRCUS .... DEAN MARTIN
THREE-RING CIRCUS .... JERRY LEWIS
THREESOME .... JOSH CHARLES
THREESOME .... LARA FLYNN BOYLE
THREESOME .... STEPHEN BALDWIN
THREESOME (TF) .... DANA DELANY
THREESOME (TF) .... DEBORAH RAFFIN
THREESOME (TF) .... JOEL HIGGINS
THREESOME (TF) .... STEPHEN COLLINS
THRESHOLD .... DONALD SUTHERLAND
THRESHOLD .... JEFF GOLDBLUM
THRESHOLD .... MARE WINNINGHAM
THRILL OF A LIFETIME .... DOROTHY LAMOUR
THRILL OF A ROMANCE .... VAN JOHNSON
THRILL OF IT ALL, THE .... CARL REINER
THRILL OF IT ALL, THE .... DORIS DAY
THRILL OF IT ALL, THE .... JAMES GARNER
THROW MOMMA FROM
    THE TRAIN .... BILLY CRYSTAL
THROW MOMMA FROM
    THE TRAIN .... BRANFORD MARSALIS

† after an actor's name denotes deceased.

THROW MOMMA FROM THE TRAIN ... DANNY DEVITO
THROW MOMMA FROM THE TRAIN ... KIM GREIST
THROW MOMMA FROM THE TRAIN ... KATE MULGREW
THROW MOMMA FROM THE TRAIN ... OPRAH WINFREY
THROW MOMMA FROM THE TRAIN ... ROB REINER
THROW MOMMA FROM THE TRAIN ✪ ... ANN RAMSEY†
THRU DIFFERENT EYES ... SYLVIA SIDNEY
THUNDER ALLEY ... CLANCY BROWN
THUNDER ALLEY ... LISA EILBACHER
THUNDER AND LIGHTNING ... DAVID CARRADINE
THUNDER AND LIGHTNING ... KATE JACKSON
THUNDER BAY ... HARRY MORGAN
THUNDER BAY ... JAMES STEWART
THUNDER IN THE EAST ... DEBORAH KERR
THUNDER IN THE EAST ... JILL ST. JOHN
THUNDER OF DRUMS, A ... CHARLES BRONSON
THUNDER OF DRUMS, A ... GEORGE HAMILTON
THUNDER OF DRUMS, A ... RICHARD CHAMBERLAIN
THUNDER OVER HAWAII ... DICK MILLER
THUNDER OVER THE PLAINS ... RICHARD BENJAMIN
THUNDER PASS ... RAYMOND BURR†
THUNDER ROAD ... ROBERT MITCHUM
THUNDER RUN ... JOHN IRELAND
THUNDERBALL ... CLAUDINE AUGER
THUNDERBALL ... LOIS MAXWELL
THUNDERBALL ... SEAN CONNERY
THUNDERBOAT ROW (TF) ... CHAD EVERETT
THUNDERBOAT ROW (TF) ... DENNIS BOUTSIKARIS
THUNDERBOAT ROW (TF) ... JOHN J. YORK
THUNDERBOLT ★ ... GEORGE BANCROFT†
THUNDERBOLT AND LIGHTFOOT ... BILL McKINNEY
THUNDERBOLT AND LIGHTFOOT ... CLINT EASTWOOD
THUNDERBOLT AND LIGHTFOOT ... GEORGE KENNEDY
THUNDERBOLT AND LIGHTFOOT ✪ ... JEFF BRIDGES
THUNDERBOT AND LIGHTFOOT ... GARY BUSEY
THUNDERHEAD— HEAD OF FLICKA ... RODDY McDOWALL
THUNDERHEART ... FRED WARD
THUNDERHEART ... GRAHAM GREENE
THUNDERHEART ... SAM SHEPARD
THUNDERHEART ... SHEILA TOUSEY
THUNDERHEART ... VAL KILMER
THUNDERING JETS ... ROBERT CONRAD
THURSDAY'S GAME (TF) ... BOB NEWHART
THURSDAY'S GAME (TF) ... ELLEN BURSTYN
THURSDAY'S GAME (TF) ... VALERIE HARPER
THX 1138 ... DONALD PLEASENCE
THX 1138 ... ROBERT DUVALL
tick...tick...tick ... CLIFTON JAMES
tick...tick...tick... ... DON STROUD
tick...tick...tick ... GEORGE KENNEDY
TICK TICK TICK ... JIM BROWN
TICKET TO HEAVEN ... MEG FOSTER
TICKET TO HEAVEN ... NICK MANCUSO
TICKET TO TOMAHAWK, A ... MARILYN MONROE†
TICKET TO TOMAHAWK, A ... RORY CALHOUN
TICKLE ME ... ELVIS PRESLEY†
TICKLISH AFFAIR, A ... RED BUTTONS
TICKLISH AFFAIR, A ... SHIRLEY JONES
TIE ME UP! TIE ME DOWN! ... ANTONIO BANDERAS
TIE ME UP! TIE ME DOWN! ... VICTORIA ABRIL
TIE THAT BINDS, THE ... DARYL HANNAH
TIE THAT BINDS, THE ... KEITH CARRADINE
TIE THAT BINDS, THE ... MOIRA KELLY
TIE THAT BINDS, THE ... VINCENT SPANO
TIGER AND THE PUSSYCAT, THE ... ANN-MARGRET
TIGER AND THE PUSSYCAT, THE ... ELEANOR PARKER
TIGER BAY ... HAYLEY MILLS
TIGER BAY ... JOHN MILLS
TIGER MAKES OUT, THE ... ANNE JACKSON
TIGER MAKES OUT, THE ... BOB DISHY
TIGER MAKES OUT, THE ... DUSTIN HOFFMAN
TIGER MAKES OUT, THE ... ELI WALLACH
TIGER TOWN (CTF) ... JUSTIN HENRY
TIGER TOWN (CTF) ... ROY SCHEIDER
TIGER WALKS, A ... BRIAN KEITH
TIGER WALKS, A ... VERA MILES
TIGER WARSAW ... BARBARA WILLIAMS
TIGER WARSAW ... PATRICK SWAYZE
TIGERS DON'T CRY ... ANTHONY QUINN
TIGERS DON'T CRY ... JOHN PHILLIP LAW
TIGER'S TALE, A ... ANN WEDGEWORTH
TIGER'S TALE, A ... ANN-MARGRET
TIGER'S TALE, A ... C. THOMAS HOWELL
TIGER'S TALE, A ... CHARLES DURNING
TIGER'S TALE, A ... JAMES NOBLE
TIGER'S TALE, A ... KELLY PRESTON
TIGER'S TALE, A ... WILLIAM ZABKA
TIGHT LITTLE ISLAND ... GORDAN JACKSON†
TIGHT SPOT ... BRIAN KEITH
TIGHTROPE ... CLINT EASTWOOD
TIGHTROPE ... GENEVIEVE BUJOLD
TIJUANA STORY, THE ... ROBERT BLAKE
TILL THE CLOUDS ROLL BY ... ANGELA LANSBURY
TILL THE CLOUDS ROLL BY ... CYD CHARISSE
TILL THE CLOUDS ROLL BY ... DINAH SHORE†
TILL THE CLOUDS ROLL BY ... FRANK SINATRA
TILL THE CLOUDS ROLL BY ... JUNE ALLYSON
TILL THE CLOUDS ROLL BY ... LENA HORNE
TILL THE CLOUDS ROLL BY ... VAN JOHNSON
TILL THE END OF TIME ... ROBERT MITCHUM
'TILL WE MEET AGAIN ... GERALDINE FITZGERALD
TILL WE MEET AGAIN (MS) ... BARRY BOSTWICK
TILL WE MEET AGAIN (MS) ... BRUCE BOXLEITNER
TILL WE MEET AGAIN (MS) ... COURTENEY COX
TILL WE MEET AGAIN (MS) ... MICHAEL YORK
TILLIE'S PUNCTURED ROMANCE ... MILTON BERLE
TILT ... BROOKE SHIELDS
TILT ... CHARLES DURNING
TILT ... FRED WARD
TIM ... MEL GIBSON
TIM ... PIPER LAURIE
TIM BURTON'S THE NIGHTMARE BEFORE CHRISTMAS (AF) ... CATHERINE O'HARA
TIM BURTON'S THE NIGHTMARE BEFORE CHRISTMAS (AF) ... DANNY ELFMAN
TIM BURTON'S THE NIGHTMARE BEFORE CHRISTMAS (AF) ... PAUL REUBENS
TIMBER TRAMP ... CLAUDE AKINS†
TIMBER TRAMP ... LEON AMES
TIMBER TRAMP ... TAB HUNTER
TIMBUKTU ... JOHN DEHNER†
TIMBUKTU ... YVONNE DE CARLO
TIME AFTER TIME ... COREY FELDMAN
TIME AFTER TIME ... DAVID WARNER
TIME AFTER TIME ... MALCOLM McDOWELL
TIME AFTER TIME ... MARY STEENBURGEN
TIME AFTER TIME ... PATTI D'ARBANVILLE
TIME AFTER TIME ... ROBERT MITCHUM
TIME AFTER TIME ... SHELLEY HACK
TIME BANDITS ... DAVID WARNER
TIME BANDITS ... IAN HOLM
TIME BANDITS ... JOHN CLEESE
TIME BANDITS ... KATHERINE HELMOND
TIME BANDITS ... MICHAEL PALIN
TIME BANDITS ... PETER VAUGHN
TIME BANDITS ... SEAN CONNERY
TIME BANDITS ... SHELLEY DUVALL
TIME FLYER (CTF) ... ART CARNEY
TIME FOR GIVING, A ... ANDREW PRINE
TIME FOR KILLING, A ... GEORGE HAMILTON
TIME FOR KILLING, A ... HARRISON FORD
TIME FOR KILLING, A ... TIMOTHY CAREY
TIME FOR LOVING, A ... BRITT EKLAND
TIME FOR MIRACLES, A (TF) ... KATE MULGREW
TIME GUARDIAN, THE ... CARRIE FISHER
TIME LIMIT ... JUNE LOCKHART
TIME LIMIT ... MARTIN BALSAM
TIME LIMIT ... RICHARD WIDMARK
TIME LIMIT ... RIP TORN
TIME LIMIT/SPEED LIMIT 65 ... YAPHET KOTTO
TIME LOCK ... SEAN CONNERY
TIME LOST AND TIME REMEMBERED ... JULIAN GLOVER
TIME LOST AND TIME REMEMBERED ... SARAH MILES
TIME MACHINE, THE ... ALAN YOUNG
TIME MACHINE, THE (TF) ... JOHN BECK
TIME OF DESTINY, A ... MELISSA LEO
TIME OF DESTINY, A ... STOCKARD CHANNING
TIME OF DESTINY, A ... TIMOTHY HUTTON
TIME OF DESTINY, A ... WILLIAM HURT
TIME OF INDIFFERENCE ... ROD STEIGER
TIME OF INDIFFERENCE ... SHELLEY WINTERS
TIME OUT OF MIND ... EDDIE ALBERT
TIME RUNNER ... MARK HAMILL
TIME TO DIE, A ... EDWARD ALBERT
TIME TO LIVE, A (TF) ... COREY HAIM
TIME TO LIVE, A (TF) ... JEFFREY DEMUNN
TIME TO LIVE, A (TF) ... LIZA MINELLI
TIME TO LIVE, A (TF) ... SWOOSIE KURTZ
TIME TO LOVE AND A TIME TO DIE, A ... JOHN GAVIN
TIME TO TRIUMPH, A (TF) ... JOSEPH BOLOGNA
TIME TO TRIUMPH, A (TF) ... PATTY DUKE
TIME WITHOUT PITY ... ALEC McCOWEN
TIME WITHOUT PITY ... JOAN PLOWRIGHT
TIME WITHOUT PITY ... LOIS MAXWELL
TIMEBOMB ... PATSY KENSIT
TIMECOP ... BRUCE McGILL
TIMECOP ... GLORIA REUBEN
TIMECOP ... JASON SCHOMBING
TIMECOP ... JEAN-CLAUDE VAN DAMME
TIMECOP ... MIA SARA
TIMECOP ... RON SILVER
TIMELY INTERCEPTION, A ... LILLIAN GISH†
TIMERIDER ... FRED WARD
TIMES SQUARE ... ELIZABETH PENA
TIMES SQUARE ... TIM CURRY
TIMES SQUARE ... TRINI ALVARADO
TIMESTALKERS (TF) ... JAMES AVERY
TIMESTALKERS (TF) ... KLAUS KINSKI†
TIMESTALKERS (TF) ... LAUREN HUTTON
TIMESTALKERS (TF) ... WILLIAM DEVANE
TIMETABLE ... JACK KLUGMAN
TIMETABLE ... WESLEY ADDY
TIN DRUM, THE ... DAVID BENNENT
TIN MEN ... BARBARA HERSHEY
TIN MEN ... BRUNO KIRBY
TIN MEN ... DANNY DEVITO
TIN MEN ... J. T. WALSH
TIN MEN ... JACKIE GAYLE
TIN MEN ... JOHN MAHONEY
TIN MEN ... RICHARD DREYFUSS
TIN MEN ... SEYMOUR CASSEL
TIN MEN ... STANLEY BROCK
TIN STAR, THE ... ANTHONY PERKINS†
TIN STAR, THE ... BETSY PALMER
TINGLER, THE ... VINCENT PRICE†
TINKER, TAILOR, SOLDIER, SPY (TF) ... ALEC GUINNESS
TINKER, TAILOR, SOLDIER, SPY (TF) ... BERNARD HEPTON
TINKER, TAILOR, SOLDIER, SPY (TF) ... SIAN PHILLIPS
TIP-OFF GIRLS ... ANTHONY QUINN
'TIS PITY SHE'S A WHORE ... CHARLOTTE RAMPLING
TITAN FIND ... WENDY SCHAAL
TITANIC ... BARBARA STANWYCK†
TITANIC ... ROBERT WAGNER
TITLE SHOT ... TONY CURTIS
TO ALL MY FRIENDS ON SHORE (TF) ... BILL COSBY
TO BE OR NOT TO BE ... ANNE BANCROFT
TO BE OR NOT TO BE ... CHRISTOPHER LLOYD
TO BE OR NOT TO BE ... GEORGE GAYNES
TO BE OR NOT TO BE ... JOSE FERRER†
TO BE OR NOT TO BE ... MEL BROOKS
TO BE OR NOT TO BE ... ROBERT STACK
TO BE OR NOT TO BE ... TIM MATHESON
TO BE OR NOT TO BE ✪ ... CHARLES DURNING
TO CATCH A KILLER (TF) ... BRIAN DENNEHY
TO CATCH A SPY ... TOM COURTENAY
TO CATCH A THIEF ... GRACE KELLY†
TO COMMIT A MURDER ... LOUIS JOURDAN
TO DANCE WITH THE WHITE DOG (TF) ... AMY WRIGHT

This is not a list of every film ever made or every cast member, only those listed in this directory.

TO DANCE WITH THE
    WHITE DOG (TF) .... CHRISTINE BARANSKI
TO DANCE WITH THE
    WHITE DOG (TF) .... ESTHER ROLLE
TO DANCE WITH THE
    WHITE DOG (TF) .... FRANK WHALEY
TO DANCE WITH THE
    WHITE DOG (TF) .... HARLEY CROSS
TO DANCE WITH THE
    WHITE DOG (TF) .... HUME CRONYN
TO DANCE WITH THE
    WHITE DOG (TF) .... JESSICA TANDY†
TO DANCE WITH THE
    WHITE DOG (TF) .... TERRY BEAVER
TO DIE FOR .... AMANDA WYSS
TO DIE FOR .... BRENDAN HUGHES
TO DIE FOR .... SCOTT JACOBY
TO DIE FOR .... STEVE BOND
TO DIE FOR .... SYDNEY WALSH
TO DOROTHY A SON .... SHELLEY WINTERS
TO EACH HIS OWN ★★ .... OLIVIA DE HAVILLAND
TO ELVIS, WITH LOVE .... JOHN AMOS
TO FIND A MAN .... LLOYD BRIDGES
TO FIND A MAN .... PAMELA SUE MARTIN
TO FIND A MAN .... TOM BOSLEY
TO FIND A MAN/SEX AND
    THE TEENAGER .... PAMELA SUE MARTIN
TO FIND A MAN/SEX AND
    THE TEENAGER .... TOM BOSLEY
TO HAVE AND HAVE NOT .... LAUREN BACALL
TO HELL WITH HEROES .... KEVIN McCARTHY
TO KILL A CLOWN .... ALAN ALDA
TO KILL A CLOWN .... BLYTHE DANNER
TO KILL A COP (TF) .... DIANA MULDAUR
TO KILL A COP (TF) .... EARTHA KITT
TO KILL A COP (TF) .... JOE DON BAKER
TO KILL A COP (TF) .... LOUIS GOSSETT JR.
TO KILL A COP (TF) .... PATRICK O'NEAL†
TO KILL A COP (TF) .... ROBERT HOOKS
TO KILL A MOCKINGBIRD .... ALICE GHOSTLEY
TO KILL A MOCKINGBIRD .... BROCK PETERS
TO KILL A MOCKINGBIRD .... PAUL FIX†
TO KILL A MOCKINGBIRD .... ROBERT DUVALL
TO KILL A MOCKINGBIRD .... ROSEMARY MURPHY
TO KILL A MOCKINGBIRD .... RUTH WHITE†
TO KILL A MOCKINGBIRD .... WILLIAM WINDOM
TO KILL A MOCKINGBIRD ★★ .... GREGORY PECK
TO KILL A PRIEST .... CHRISTOPHER LAMBERT
TO KILL A PRIEST .... ED HARRIS
TO KILL A PRIEST .... JOANNE WHALLEY-KILMER
TO LIVE AND DIE IN L.A. .... DEAN STOCKWELL
TO LIVE AND DIE IN L.A. .... JOHN PANKOW
TO LIVE AND DIE IN L.A. .... JOHN TURTURRO
TO LIVE AND DIE IN L.A. .... WILLEM DAFOE
TO LIVE AND DIE IN L.A. .... WILLIAM L. PETERSEN
TO PARIS WITH LOVE .... ALEC GUINNESS
TO PLEASE A LADY .... BARBARA STANWYCK†
TO PROTECT AND SERVE .... PAULY SHORE
TO RACE THE WIND (TF) .... STEVE GUTTENBERG
TO SIR WITH LOVE .... GEOFFREY BAYLDON
TO SIR WITH LOVE .... SIDNEY POITIER
TO SLEEP WITH ANGER .... CARL LUMBLY
TO SLEEP WITH ANGER .... DANNY GLOVER
TO SLEEP WITH ANGER .... ROBERT DAVIS†
TO THE DEVIL A DAUGHTER ... DENHOLM ELLIOTT†
TO THE DEVIL A DAUGHTER ... NASTASSJA KINSKI
TO THE DEVIL A DAUGHTER .... RICHARD WIDMARK
TO THE SHORES OF TRIPOLI .... HARRY MORGAN
TO THE SHORES OF TRIPOLI ..... MAUREEN O'HARA
TO TRAP A SPY .... FRITZ WEAVER
TO TRAP A SPY .... ROBERT VAUGHN
TO TRAP A SPY .... VICTORIA SHAW†
TO TRAP A SPY .... WILLIAM MARSHALL
TO WONG FOO, THANKS FOR EVERYTHING,
    JULIE NEWMAR .... BETH GRANT
TO WONG FOO, THANKS FOR EVERYTHING,
    JULIE NEWMAR .... BLYTHE DANNER
TO WONG FOO, THANKS FOR EVERYTHING,
    JULIE NEWMAR .... JASON LONDON
TO WONG FOO, THANKS FOR EVERYTHING,
    JULIE NEWMAR .... JOHN LEGUIZAMO
TO WONG FOO, THANKS FOR EVERYTHING,
    JULIE NEWMAR .... JULIE NEWMAR

TO WONG FOO, THANKS FOR EVERYTHING,
    JULIE NEWMAR .... MELINDA DILLON
TO WONG FOO, THANKS FOR EVERYTHING,
    JULIE NEWMAR .... PATRICK SWAYZE
TO WONG FOO, THANKS FOR EVERYTHING,
    JULIE NEWMAR .... STOCKARD CHANNING
TO WONG FOO, THANKS FOR EVERYTHING,
    JULIE NEWMAR .... WESLEY SNIPES
TOAST OF NEW ORLEANS, THE .... DAVID NIVEN†
TOAST OF NEW ORLEANS, THE .... RITA MORENO
TOBRUK .... GEORGE PEPPARD†
TODAY WE LIVE .... JOAN CRAWFORD†
TODD KILLINGS, THE .... BELINDA J. MONTGOMERY
TODD KILLINGS, THE .... ED ASNER
TOGETHER? .... JACQUELINE BISSET
TOKYO POP .... CARRIE HAMILTON
TOM, DICK AND HARRY .... BURGESS MEREDITH
TOM HORN .... BILLY GREEN BUSH
TOM HORN .... LINDA EVANS
TOM HORN .... RICHARD FARNSWORTH
TOM HORN .... STEVE McQUEEN†
TOM JONES .... DAVID TOMLINSON
TOM JONES .... DAVID WARNER
TOM JONES .... JOAN GREENWOOD†
TOM JONES .... JULIAN GLOVER
TOM JONES .... LYNN REDGRAVE
TOM JONES .... SUSANNAH YORK
TOM JONES ★ .... ALBERT FINNEY
TOM JONES ○ .... EDITH EVANS†
TOM JONES ○ .... HUGH GRIFFITH†
TOM SAWYER .... CELESTE HOLM
TOM SAWYER .... HENRY JONES
TOM SAWYER .... JODIE FOSTER
TOM SAWYER (TF) .... JANE WYATT
tom thumb .... ALAN YOUNG
TOM THUMB .... RUSS TAMBLYN
TOMAHAWK .... ROCK HUDSON†
TOMAHAWK .... YVONNE DE CARLO
TOMAHAWK TRAIL .... CHUCK CONNORS†
TOMB OF LIGEIA, THE .... VINCENT PRICE†
TOMBSTONE .... BILL PAXTON
TOMBSTONE .... BILLY ZANE
TOMBSTONE .... CHARLTON HESTON
TOMBSTONE .... DANA DELANY
TOMBSTONE .... JASON PRIESTLEY
TOMBSTONE .... JOHN CORBETT
TOMBSTONE .... JON TENNEY
TOMBSTONE .... KURT RUSSELL
TOMBSTONE .... MICHAEL BIEHN
TOMBSTONE .... MICHAEL ROOKER
TOMBSTONE .... PAULA MALCOMSON
TOMBSTONE .... POWERS BOOTHE
TOMBSTONE .... ROBERT MITCHUM
TOMBSTONE .... SAM ELLIOTT
TOMBSTONE .... VAL KILMER
TOMMY .... ERIC CLAPTON
TOMMY .... JACK NICHOLSON
TOMMY .... OLIVER REED
TOMMY .... PAUL NICHOLAS
TOMMY .... ROGER DALTRY
TOMMY .... TINA TURNER
TOMMY ★ .... ANN-MARGRET
TOMORROW .... ROBERT DUVALL
TOMORROW IS TOO LATE .... LOIS MAXWELL
TOMORROW
    NEVER COMES .... DONALD PLEASENCE
TOMORROW NEVER COMES .... JOHN IRELAND
TOMORROW NEVER COMES ...... RAYMOND BURR†
TOMORROW NEVER COMES .... SUSAN GEORGE
TONIGHT AND EVERY NIGHT .... SHELLEY WINTERS
TONIGHT LET'S ALL MAKE LOVE
    IN LONDON (FD) .... MICHAEL CAINE
TONIGHT LET'S ALL MAKE LOVE
    IN LONDON (FD) .... VANESSA REDGRAVE
TONIGHT WE SING .... ANNE BANCROFT
TONIGHT'S THE NIGHT .... YVONNE DE CARLO
TONIGHT'S THE NIGHT (TF) .... BELINDA BAUER
TONIGHT'S THE NIGHT (TF) .... ED MARINARO
TONIGHT'S THE NIGHT (TF) .... KEN OLIN
TONIGHT'S THE NIGHT (TF) .... ROBERT RUSLER
TONIGHT'S THE NIGHT (TF) .... TRACY NELSON
TONNY .... LIV ULLMANN
TONY ROME .... FRANK SINATRA

TONY ROME .... GENA ROWLANDS
TONY ROME .... JILL ST. JOHN
TONY SAITTA .... JOHN SAXON
TONY SAITTA .... MARTIN LANDAU
TONY SAITTA .... STUART WHITMAN
TOO BAD SHE'S BAD ...... MARCELLO MASTROIANNI
TOO BAD SHE'S BAD .... SOPHIA LOREN
TOO BEAUTIFUL FOR YOU .... GERARD DEPARDIEU
TOO FAR TO GO (TF) .... BLYTHE DANNER
TOO FAR TO GO (TF) .... GLENN CLOSE
TOO FAR TO GO (TF) .... JOSEF SOMMER
TOO FAR TO GO (TF) .... MICHAEL MORIARTY
TOO GOOD TO
    BE TRUE (TF) .... GLYNNIS O'CONNOR
TOO GOOD TO BE TRUE (TF) ...... JAMES B. SIKKING
TOO GOOD TO BE TRUE (TF) .... JULIE HARRIS
TOO GOOD TO BE TRUE (TF) .... LARRY DRAKE
TOO GOOD TO BE TRUE (TF) .... LONI ANDERSON
TOO GOOD TO BE TRUE (TF) .... PATRICK DUFFY
TOO LATE BLUES .... SEYMOUR CASSEL
TOO LATE BLUES .... STELLA STEVENS
TOO LATE BLUES .... VAL AVERY
TOO LATE BLUES .... VINCE EDWARDS
TOO LATE THE HERO .... CLIFF ROBERTSON
TOO LATE THE HERO .... DENHOLM ELLIOTT†
TOO LATE THE HERO .... IAN BANNEN
TOO LATE THE HERO .... MICHAEL CAINE
TOO MANY GIRLS .... VAN JOHNSON
TOO MANY THIEVES (TF) .... BRITT EKLAND
TOO MANY THIEVES (TF) .... PETER FALK
TOO MUCH SUN .... ANDREA MARTIN
TOO MUCH SUN .... ERIC IDLE
TOO MUCH SUN .... HOWARD DUFF†
TOO MUCH SUN .... JENNIFER RUBIN
TOO MUCH SUN .... JIM HAYNIE
TOO MUCH SUN .... LAURA ERNST
TOO MUCH SUN .... RALPH MACCHIO
TOO MUCH SUN .... ROBERT DOWNEY JR.
TOO MUCH, TOO SOON .... EFREM ZIMBALIST JR.
TOO SCARED TO SCREAM .... ANNE ARCHER
TOO SOON TO LOVE .... JACK NICHOLSON
TOO YOUNG
    THE HERO (TF) .... MARY-LOUISE PARKER
TOO YOUNG TO DIE? (TF) .... ALAN FUDGE
TOO YOUNG TO KISS .... JUNE ALLYSON
TOO YOUNG TO KISS .... VAN JOHNSON
TOOL SHED, THE .... DAVID OGDEN STIERS
TOOL SHED, THE .... ELLEN BARKIN
TOOL SHED, THE .... GIA CARIDES
TOOL SHED, THE .... LAURENCE FISHBURNE
TOOL SHED, THE .... MICHAEL BEACH
TOOTSIE .... BILL MURRAY
TOOTSIE .... CHARLES DURNING
TOOTSIE .... DABNEY COLEMAN
TOOTSIE .... DORIS BELACK
TOOTSIE .... ESTELLE GETTY
TOOTSIE .... GEENA DAVIS
TOOTSIE .... GEORGE GAYNES
TOOTSIE .... LYNNE THIGPEN
TOOTSIE .... SYDNEY POLLACK
TOOTSIE ★ .... DUSTIN HOFFMAN
TOOTSIE ○ .... TERI GARR
TOOTSIE ○○ .... JESSICA LANGE
TOP GUN .... ADRIAN PASDAR
TOP GUN .... ANTHONY EDWARDS
TOP GUN .... BARRY TUBB
TOP GUN .... BRIAN SHEEHAN
TOP GUN .... CLARENCE GILVARD JR.
TOP GUN .... DUKE STROUD
TOP GUN .... FRANK PESCE
TOP GUN .... JAMES TOLKAN
TOP GUN .... JOHN STOCKWELL
TOP GUN .... KELLY McGILLIS
TOP GUN .... LINDA RAE JURGENS
TOP GUN .... MEG RYAN
TOP GUN .... MICHAEL IRONSIDE
TOP GUN .... PETE PETTIGREW
TOP GUN .... RANDALL BRADY
TOP GUN .... RICK ROSSOVICH
TOP GUN .... RON CLARK
TOP GUN .... TIM ROBBINS
TOP GUN .... TOM CRUISE
TOP GUN .... TOM SKERRITT

† after an actor's name denotes deceased.

TOP GUN .... TROY HUNTER
TOP GUN .... VAL KILMER
TOP GUN .... WHIP HUBLEY
TOP HAT .... FRED ASTAIRE†
TOP MAN .... LILLIAN GISH†
TOP O' THE MORNING .... HUME CRONYN
TOP OF THE HILL, THE (MS) .... WAYNE ROGERS
TOP OF THE HILL, THE (TF) .... MEL FERRER
TOP SECRET! .... CHRISTOPHER VILLIERS
TOP SECRET! .... HARRY DITSON
TOP SECRET! .... JEREMY KEMP
TOP SECRET! .... JIM CARTER
TOP SECRET! .... LUCY GUTTERIDGE
TOP SECRET! .... MICHAEL GOUGH
TOP SECRET! .... OMAR SHARIF
TOP SECRET! .... VAL KILMER
TOP SECRET AFFAIR .... KIRK DOUGLAS
TOP SECRET (TF) .... BILL COSBY
TOPAZ .... JOHN FORSYTHE
TOPAZ .... JOHN VERNON
TOPAZ .... ROSCOE LEE BROWNE
TOPKAPI .... MAXIMILIAN SCHELL
TOPKAPI .... ROBERT MORLEY
TOPKAPI ○○ .... PETER USTINOV
TOPPER .... CARY GRANT†
TOPPER .... CONSTANCE BENNETT†
TOPPER ○ .... ROLAND YOUNG†
TOPPER (TF) .... ANDREW STEVENS
TOPPER (TF) .... KATE JACKSON
TOPSY AND BUNKER .... KATHY NAJIMY
TORA! TORA! TORA! .... E. G. MARSHALL
TORA! TORA! TORA! .... JAMES WHITMORE
TORA! TORA! TORA! .... JASON ROBARDS
TORA! TORA! TORA! .... LEON AMES
TORA! TORA! TORA! .... MARTIN BALSAM
TORA! TORA! TORA ! .... NORMAN ALDEN
TORA! TORA! TORA! .... RICHARD ANDERSON
TORA! TORA! TORA! .... WESLEY ADDY
TORCH SONG .... HARRY MORGAN
TORCH SONG .... JOAN CRAWFORD†
TORCH SONG ○ .... MARJORIE RAMBEAU†
TORCH SONG TRILOGY .... ANNE BANCROFT
TORCH SONG TRILOGY .... BRIAN KERWIN
TORCH SONG TRILOGY .... CHARLES PIERCE
TORCH SONG TRILOGY .... HARVEY FIERSTEIN
TORCH SONG TRILOGY .... KAREN YOUNG
TORCH SONG TRILOGY .... KEN PAGE
TORCH SONG TRILOGY .... LAWRENCE LOTT†
TORCH SONG TRILOGY .... MATTHEW BRODERICK
TORCHLIGHT .... PAMELA SUE MARTIN
TORCHLIGHT .... RICHARD BALIN
TORCHLIGHT .... RITA TAGGART
TORCHY PLAYS WITH DYNAMITE ...... JANE WYMAN
TORN APART .... ADRIAN PASDAR
TORN APART .... CECILIA PECK
TORN BETWEEN
   TWO LOVERS (TF) .... GEORGE PEPPARD†
TORN BETWEEN
   TWO LOVERS (TF) .... NICK MANCUSO
TORN CURTAIN .... JULIE ANDREWS
TORN CURTAIN .... LILA KEDROVA
TORN CURTAIN .... PAUL NEWMAN
TORPEDO RUN .... DEAN JONES
TORPEDO RUN .... ERNEST BORGNINE
TORRENTS OF SPRING .... NASTASSJA KINSKI
TORRENTS OF SPRING .... TIMOTHY HUTTON
TORRENTS OF SPRING .... VALERIA GOLINO
TORRENTS OF SPRING .... WILLIAM FORSYTHE
TORTILLA FLAT ○ .... FRANK MORGAN†
TORTURE GARDEN .... BURGESS MEREDITH
TORTURE GARDEN .... JACK PALANCE
TORTURE GARDEN .... MICHAEL BRYANT
TOTAL ECLIPSE .... DAVID THEWLIS
TOTAL RECALL .... ARNOLD SCHWARZENEGGER
TOTAL RECALL ..... DEBBIE LEE CARRINGTON
TOTAL RECALL .... MARSHALL BELL
TOTAL RECALL .... MEL JOHNSON JR.
TOTAL RECALL .... MICHAEL CHAMPION
TOTAL RECALL .... MICHAEL IRONSIDE
TOTAL RECALL .... RACHEL TICOTIN
TOTAL RECALL .... RONNY COX
TOTAL RECALL .... ROY BROCKSMITH
TOTAL RECALL .... SHARON STONE

TOUCH, THE .... BIBI ANDERSSON
TOUCH, THE .... ELLIOTT GOULD
TOUCH AND GO .... JERE BURNS
TOUCH AND GO .... MARIA CONCHITA ALONSO
TOUCH AND GO .... MICHAEL KEATON
TOUCH AND GO .... MICHAEL YORK
TOUCH OF CLASS, A .... GEORGE SEGAL
TOUCH OF CLASS, A .... HILDEGARD NEIL
TOUCH OF CLASS, A .... PAUL SORVINO
TOUCH OF CLASS, A ★★ .... GLENDA JACKSON
TOUCH OF EVIL .... CHARLTON HESTON
TOUCH OF EVIL .... DENNIS WEAVER
TOUCH OF EVIL .... JANET LEIGH
TOUCH OF EVIL .... MERCEDES McCAMBRIDGE
TOUCH OF EVIL .... ZSA ZSA GABOR
TOUCH OF LARCENY, A .... VERA MILES
TOUCH OF LOVE, A .... SANDY DENNIS†
TOUCH OF SCANDAL, A (TF) .... ANGIE DICKINSON
TOUCH OF SCANDAL, A (TF) .... DON MURRAY
TOUCH OF SCANDAL, A (TF) .... JASON MILLER
TOUCH OF SCANDAL, A (TF) .... ROBERT LOGGIA
TOUCH OF SCANDAL, A (TF) .... TOM SKERRITT
TOUCHED .... NED BEATTY
TOUCHED .... ROBERT HAYS
TOUCHED BY LOVE .... CLU GULAGER
TOUCHED BY LOVE .... DEBORAH RAFFIN
TOUCHED BY LOVE .... JOHN AMOS
TOUCHED BY LOVE .... MICHAEL LEARNED
TOUGH ENOUGH .... BRUCE McGILL
TOUGH ENOUGH .... DENNIS QUAID
TOUGH ENOUGH .... WILFORD BRIMLEY
TOUGH GUY .... ERNEST BORGNINE
TOUGH GUY .... JACKIE COOPER
TOUGH GUYS .... ALEXIS SMITH†
TOUGH GUYS .... BILLY BARTY
TOUGH GUYS .... BURT LANCASTER†
TOUGH GUYS .... CHARLES DURNING
TOUGH GUYS .... DANA CARVEY
TOUGH GUYS .... DARLANNE FLEUGEL
TOUGH GUYS .... ELI WALLACH
TOUGH GUYS .... JAKE STEINFELD
TOUGH GUYS .... KIRK DOUGLAS
TOUGH GUYS .... MONTY ASH
TOUGH GUYS
   DON'T DANCE .... CLARENCE WILLIAMS III
TOUGH GUYS DON'T DANCE ...... DEBRA SANDLUND
TOUGH GUYS DON'T DANCE .... FRANCES FISHER
TOUGH GUYS
   DON'T DANCE .... ISABELLA ROSSELLINI
TOUGH GUYS
   DON'T DANCE .... JOHN BEDFORD LLOYD
TOUGH GUYS
   DON'T DANCE .... LAWRENCE TIERNEY
TOUGH GUYS DON'T DANCE .... PENN JILLETTE
TOUGH GUYS
   DON'T DANCE .... R. PATRICK SULLIVAN
TOUGH GUYS DON'T DANCE .... RYAN O'NEAL
TOUGH GUYS DON'T DANCE .... WINGS HAUSER
TOUGH TONY .... JOHN SAXON
TOUGH TONY .... MARTIN LANDAU
TOUGH TONY .... STUART WHITMAN
TOUGHEST MAN IN THE
   WORLD, THE (TF) .... DENNIS DUGAN
TOUGHEST MAN IN THE
   WORLD, THE (TF) .... JOHN NAVIN
TOUGHEST MAN IN THE
   WORLD, THE (TF) .... MR. T
TOUGHLOVE (TF) .... BRUCE DERN
TOUGHLOVE (TF) .... PIPER LAURIE
TOURIST (TF) .... LOIS NETTLETON
TOURIST TRAP .... CHUCK CONNORS†
TOUS LES MATINS DU MONDE ...... ANNE BROCHET
TOUS LES MATINS
   DU MONDE .... GERARD DEPARDIEU
TOUT VA BIEN .... JANE FONDA
TOUTE UNE VIE .... MARTHE KELLER
TOWARD THE UNKNOWN .... JAMES GARNER
TOWER OF LONDON .... VINCENT PRICE†
TOWERING INFERNO, THE .... DABNEY COLEMAN
TOWERING INFERNO, THE .... FAYE DUNAWAY
TOWERING INFERNO, THE .... GREGORY SIERRA
TOWERING INFERNO, THE .... JENNIFER JONES

TOWERING
   INFERNO, THE .... MAUREEN McGOVERN
TOWERING INFERNO, THE .... MIKE LOOKINLAND
TOWERING INFERNO, THE .... O. J. SIMPSON
TOWERING INFERNO, THE .... PAUL NEWMAN
TOWERING
   INFERNO, THE .... RICHARD CHAMBERLAIN
TOWERING INFERNO, THE .... ROBERT VAUGHN
TOWERING INFERNO, THE .... ROBERT WAGNER
TOWERING INFERNO, THE .... STEVE McQUEEN†
TOWERING INFERNO, THE .... SUSAN BLAKELY
TOWERING INFERNO, THE .... WILLIAM HOLDEN†
TOWERING INFERNO, THE ○ .... FRED ASTAIRE†
TOWN BULLY, THE (TF) .... BRUCE BOXLEITNER
TOWN BULLY, THE (TF) .... DAVID GRAF
TOWN BULLY, THE (TF) .... ISABELLA HOFMANN
TOWN BULLY, THE (TF) .... PAT HINGLE
TOWN CALLED BASTARD, A .... MARTIN LANDAU
TOWN CALLED BASTARD, A .... STELLA STEVENS
TOWN CALLED BASTARD, A .... TELLY SAVALAS†
TOWN CALLED HELL, A .... MARTIN LANDAU
TOWN CALLED HELL, A .... STELLA STEVENS
TOWN CALLED HELL, A .... TELLY SAVALAS†
TOWN LIKE ALICE, A (MS) .... BRYON BROWN
TOWN LIKE ALICE, A (TF) .... GORDAN JACKSON†
TOWN ON TRIAL .... ALEC McCOWEN
TOWN ON TRIAL .... JOHN MILLS
TOWN TAMER .... RICHARD JAECKEL
TOWN THAT DREADED
   SUNDOWN, THE .... BEN JOHNSON
TOWN WITHOUT PITY .... E. G. MARSHALL
TOWN WITHOUT PITY .... KIRK DOUGLAS
TOWN WITHOUT PITY .... RICHARD JAECKEL
TOWN WITHOUT PITY .... ROBERT BLAKE
TOY, THE .... NED BEATTY
TOY, THE .... RICHARD PRYOR
TOY SOLDIERS .... ANDREW DIVOFF
TOY SOLDIERS .... DENHOLM ELLIOTT†
TOY SOLDIERS .... KEITH COOGAN
TOY SOLDIERS .... LOUIS GOSSETT JR.
TOY SOLDIERS .... SEAN ASTIN
TOY SOLDIERS .... WIL WHEATON
TOYS .... DONALD O'CONNOR
TOYS .... JOAN CUSAK
TOYS .... LL COOL J
TOYS .... MICHAEL GAMBON
TOYS .... ROBIN WILLIAMS
TOYS .... ROBIN WRIGHT
TOYS IN THE ATTIC .... DEAN MARTIN
TOYS IN THE ATTIC .... WENDY HILLER
TRACES OF RED .... JAMES BELUSHI
TRACES OF RED .... LORRAINE BRACCO
TRACES OF RED .... TONY GOLDWYN
TRACES OF RED .... WILLIAM RUSS
TRACK 29 .... CHRISTOPHER LLOYD
TRACK 29 .... COLLEEN CAMP
TRACK 29 .... GARY OLDMAN
TRACK 29 .... SANDRA BERNHARD
TRACK 29 .... SEYMOUR CASSEL
TRACK 29 .... THERESA RUSSELL
TRACK OF THE CAT .... ROBERT MITCHUM
TRACK OF THE CAT .... TAB HUNTER
TRACK OF THE CAT .... TERESA WRIGHT
TRACKDOWN .... ANNE ARCHER
TRACKDOWN .... ERIK ESTRADA
TRACKDOWN .... RAY SHARKEY†
TRACKDOWN: FINDING
   THE GOODBAR KILLER (TF) .... GEORGE SEGAL
TRACKERS, THE (TF) .... ERNEST BORGNINE
TRACKS .... DEAN STOCKWELL
TRACKS .... DENNIS HOPPER
TRACKS .... MICHAEL EMIL
TRADE WINDS .... ANN SOTHERN
TRADE WINDS .... RALPH BELLAMY†
TRADING HEARTS .... RAUL JULIA†
TRADING MOM .... AARON MICHAEL METCHIK
TRADING MOM .... ANNA CHLUMSKY
TRADING MOM .... ASHER METCHIK
TRADING MOM .... MAUREEN STAPLETON
TRADING MOM .... SISSY SPACEK
TRADING PLACES .... DAN AYKROYD
TRADING PLACES .... DENHOLM ELLIOTT†
TRADING PLACES .... DON AMECHE†

This is not a list of every film ever made or every cast member, only those listed in this directory.

TRADING PLACES .... EDDIE MURPHY
TRADING PLACES .... JAMES BELUSHI
TRADING PLACES .... JAMIE LEE CURTIS
TRADING PLACES .... PAUL GLEASON
TRADING PLACES .... PHILIP BOSCO
TRADING PLACES .... RALPH BELLAMY†
TRAGEDY OF A RIDICULOUS MAN .... ANOUK AIMEE
TRAIL OF THE LONESOME PINE, THE .... SYLVIA SIDNEY
TRAIL OF THE PINK PANTHER .... BURT KWOUK
TRAIL OF THE PINK PANTHER .... HARVEY KORMAN
TRAIL OF THE PINK PANTHER ...... JOANNA LUMLEY
TRAIL OF THE PINK PANTHER .... RICHARD MULLIGAN
TRAIL OF THE PINK PANTHER ...... ROBERT LOGGIA
TRAIN, THE .... BURT LANCASTER†
TRAIN, THE .... PAUL SCOFIELD
TRAIN ROBBERS, THE .... ANN-MARGRET
TRAIN ROBBERS, THE .... BEN JOHNSON
TRAIN ROBBERS, THE .... RICARDO MONTALBAN
TRAITORS, THE .... ZENA WALKER
TRAMP, TRAMP, TRAMP .... JOAN CRAWFORD†
TRAMPLERS, THE .... FRANCO NERO
TRANCERS .... HELEN HUNT
TRANCERS .... RICHARD HERD
TRANSFORMERS, THE (AF) .... ERIC IDLE
TRANSFORMERS, THE (AF) .... JUDD NELSON
TRANSFORMERS, THE (AF) .... LEONARD NIMOY
TRANSFORMERS, THE (AF) .... LIONEL STANDER
TRANSFORMERS, THE (AF) .... ORSON WELLES†
TRANSFORMERS, THE (AF) .... ROBERT STACK
TRANSMUTATIONS .... DENHOLM ELLIOTT†
TRANSYLVANIA 6-5000 .... ED BEGLEY JR.
TRANSYLVANIA 6-5000 .... JEFF GOLDBLUM
TRANSYLVANIA 6-5000 .... JOHN BYNER
TRAP, THE .... EARL HOLLIMAN
TRAP, THE .... RICHARD WIDMARK
TRAP, THE .... TINA LOUISE
TRAPEZE .... BURT LANCASTER†
TRAPEZE .... KATHY JURADO
TRAPEZE .... TONY CURTIS
TRAPPED .... LLOYD BRIDGES
TRAPPED (TF) .... EARL HOLLIMAN
TRAPPED (TF) .... JAMES BROLIN
TRAPPED (TF) .... ROBERT HOOKS
TRAPPED (TF) .... SUSAN CLARK
TRAPPED (CTF) .... BRUCE ABBOTT
TRAPPED (CTF) .... KATHLEEN QUINLAN
TRAPPED BENEATH THE SEA (TF) .... MARTIN BALSAM
TRAPPED IN PARADISE .... ANGELA PATON
TRAPPED IN PARADISE .... DANA CARVEY
TRAPPED IN PARADISE .... DONALD MOFFAT
TRAPPED IN PARADISE .... FLORENCE STANLEY
TRAPPED IN PARADISE .... JOHN ASHTON
TRAPPED IN PARADISE .... JON LOVITZ
TRAPPED IN PARADISE .... MADCHEN AMICK
TRAPPED IN PARADISE .... NICOLAS CAGE
TRAPPED IN PARADISE .... PAUL LAZAR
TRAPPED IN PARADISE .... RICHARD JENKINS
TRAPPED IN SILENCE (TF) .... JOHN MAHONEY
TRAPPED IN SILENCE (TF) ..... KIEFER SUTHERLAND
TRAPPED IN SILENCE (TF) .... MARSHA MASON
TRAPPED IN SILENCE (TF) .... RON SILVER
TRASH .... JOE DALLESANDRO
TRAVELING EXECUTIONER, THE .... BUD CORT
TRAVELING EXECUTIONER, THE .... STACY KEACH
TRAVELING EXECUTIONER, THE .... VAL AVERY
TRAVELING MAN (CTF) .... JOHN LITHGOW
TRAVELS WITH ANITA .... CLAUDINE AUGER
TRAVELS WITH ANITA .... GOLDIE HAWN
TRAVELS WITH MY AUNT .... ALEC McCOWEN
TRAVELS WITH MY AUNT .... CINDY WILLIAMS
TRAVELS WITH MY AUNT .... LOUIS GOSSETT JR.
TRAVELS WITH MY AUNT .... ROBERT STEPHENS
TRAVELS WITH MY AUNT ★ .... MAGGIE SMITH
TRAVIS LOGAN, D.A. (TF) .... GEORGE GRIZZARD
TRAVIS McGEE (TF) .... KATHERINE ROSS
TRAVIS McGEE (TF) .... SAM ELLIOTT
TRAXX .... SHADOE STEVENS
TRE NOTTI D'AMORE .... JOHN PHILLIP LAW
TREASURE ISLAND .... JACKIE COOPER
TREASURE ISLAND .... LIONEL STANDER
TREASURE ISLAND .... MARTIN LANDAU
TREASURE ISLAND (CTF) .... CHARLTON HESTON
TREASURE ISLAND (CTF) .... JULIAN GLOVER
TREASURE OF JAMAICA REEF, THE .... CHERYL LADD
TREASURE OF MATECUMBE .... DICK VAN PATTEN
TREASURE OF MATECUMBE .... JANE WYATT
TREASURE OF MATECUMBE .... JOAN HACKETT†
TREASURE OF MATECUMBE .... PETER USTINOV
TREASURE OF MATECUMBE .... ROBERT FOXWORTH
TREASURE OF PANCHO VILLA, THE .... RORY CALHOUN
TREASURE OF PANCHO VILLA, THE .... SHELLEY WINTERS
TREASURE OF SAN GENNARO ... CLAUDINE AUGER
TREASURE OF SAN GENNARO .... HARRY GUARDINO
TREASURE OF SAN TERESA, THE .... WALTER GOTELL
TREASURE OF SIERRA MADRE ∞ .... WALTER HUSTON†
TREASURE OF THE GOLDEN CONDOR .... ANNE BANCROFT
TREASURE OF THE GOLDEN CONDOR .... ROBERT BLAKE
TREASURE OF THE SIERRA MADRE, THE .... ROBERT BLAKE
TREASURE OF THE YANKEE ZEPHYR .... KEN WAHL
TREAT 'EM ROUGH .... EDDIE ALBERT
TREE, THE .... EILEEN HECKART
TREE GROWS IN BROOKLYN, A ∞ .... JAMES DUNN†
TREE GROWS IN BROOKLYN, A (TF) .... DIANE BAKER
TREE OF HANDS .... LAUREN BACALL
TREMORS .... FRED WARD
TREMORS .... KEVIN BACON
TREMORS .... MICHAEL GROSS
TRENCHCOAT .... HOWARD CAINE†
TRENCHCOAT .... MARGOT KIDDER
TRENCHCOAT .... ROBERT HAYS
TRENCHCOAT IN PARADISE (TF) .... BRUCE DERN
TRENCHCOAT IN PARADISE (TF) .... DIRK BENEDICT
TRENCHCOAT IN PARADISE (TF) .... MICHELLE PHILLIPS
TRENCHCOAT IN PARADISE (TF) ... SYDNEY WALSH
TRESPASSER, THE ★ .... GLORIA SWANSON†
TRIAL .... KATHY JURADO
TRIAL, THE .... ANTHONY HOPKINS
TRIAL, THE .... ANTHONY PERKINS†
TRIAL, THE .... DAVID THEWLIS
TRIAL, THE .... JASON ROBARDS JR.
TRIAL, THE .... KYLE MacLACHLAN
TRIAL, THE .... POLLY WALKER
TRIAL BY COMBAT .... DONALD PLEASENCE
TRIAL BY COMBAT/ CHOICE OF WEAPONS .... BRIAN GLOVER
TRIAL BY JURY .... ARMAND ASSANTE
TRIAL BY JURY .... ED LAUTER
TRIAL BY JURY .... GABRIEL BYRNE
TRIAL BY JURY .... JOANNE WHALLEY-KILMER
TRIAL BY JURY .... JOE SANTOS
TRIAL BY JURY .... KATHLEEN QUINLAN
TRIAL BY JURY .... MARGARET WHITTON
TRIAL BY JURY .... RICHARD PORTNOW
TRIAL BY JURY .... STUART WHITMAN
TRIAL BY JURY .... WILLIAM HURT
TRIAL BY JURY .... WILLIAM R. MOSES
TRIAL OF CHAPLAIN JENSEN, THE (TF) .... CHARLES DURNING
TRIAL OF LEE HARVEY OSWALD, THE (MS) .... BEN GAZZARA
TRIAL OF THE INCREDIBLE HULK, THE (TF) .... BILL BIXBY†
TRIAL OF THE INCREDIBLE HULK, THE (TF) .... LOU FERRIGNO
TRIAL OF THE INCREDIBLE HULK, THE (TF) .... NANCY EVERHARD
TRIANGLE FACTORY FIRE SCANDAL, THE (TF) .... JANET MARGOLIN
TRIANGLE FACTORY FIRE SCANDAL, THE (TF) .... TOYAH FELDSHUH
TRIBES (TF) .... DARREN McGAVIN
TRIBES (TF) .... JAN-MICHAEL VINCENT
TRIBUTE .... COLLEEN DEWHURST†
TRIBUTE .... LEE REMICK†
TRIBUTE .... ROBBY BENSON
TRIBUTE ★ .... JACK LEMMON
TRIBUTE TO A BAD MAN .... ROYAL DANO
TRICK OR TREAT .... CHARLES MARTIN SMITH
TRICK OR TREAT .... DOUG SAVANT
TRICK OR TREAT .... TONY FIELDS
TRICK OR TREATS .... CARRIE SNODGRESS
TRICK OR TREATS .... PETER JASON
TRICKS OF THE TRADE (TF) .... CINDY WILLIAMS
TRICKS OF THE TRADE (TF) .... JAMES WHITMORE JR.
TRICKS OF THE TRADE (TF) .... JOHN RITTER
TRICKS OF THE TRADE (TF) .... MARKIE POST
TRICKS OF THE TRADE (TF) .... SCOTT PAULIN
TRIGGER HAPPY .... BRIAN KEITH
TRIGGER HAPPY .... MAUREEN O'HARA
TRILOGY .... MAUREEN STAPLETON
TRILOGY (TF) .... MARTIN BALSAM
TRILOGY OF TERROR (TF) .... KAREN BLACK
TRIO .... JEAN SIMMONS
TRIP, THE .... BRUCE DERN
TRIP, THE .... DENNIS HOPPER
TRIP, THE .... LUANA ANDERS
TRIP, THE .... PETER FONDA
TRIP, THE .... SUSAN STRASBERG
TRIP TO BOUNTIFUL, THE .... CARLIN GLYNN
TRIP TO BOUNTIFUL, THE .... JOHN HEARD
TRIP TO BOUNTIFUL, THE .... KEVIN COONEY
TRIP TO BOUNTIFUL, THE .... REBECCA DE MORNAY
TRIP TO BOUNTIFUL, THE ...... RICHARD BRADFORD
TRIP TO BOUNTIFUL, THE ★★ .... GERALDINE PAGE†
TRIPLE CROSS .... CHRISTOPHER PLUMMER
TRIPLE CROSS .... CLAUDINE AUGER
TRIPLE ECHO, THE .... GLENDA JACKSON
TRIPLE ECHO, THE .... OLIVER REED
TRIPLECROSS (TF) .... TED WASS
TRIPOLI .... MAUREEN O'HARA
TRISTAN AND ISOLDE ...... GERALDINE FITZGERALD
TRISTAN AND ISOLDE .... NICHOLAS CLAY
TRISTANA .... CATHERINE DENEUVE
TRISTANA .... FRANCO NERO
TRIUMPH OF A MAN CALLED HORSE .... RICHARD HARRIS
TRIUMPH OF A MAN CALLED HORSE .... MICHAEL BECK
TRIUMPH OF THE SPIRIT .... EDWARD JAMES OLMOS
TRIUMPH OF THE SPIRIT .... ROBERT LOGGIA
TRIUMPH OF THE SPIRIT .... WENDY GAZELLE
TRIUMPH OF THE SPIRIT .... WILLEM DAFOE
TROG .... JOAN CRAWFORD†
TROG .... MICHAEL GOUGH
TROJAN WOMEN, THE .... BRIAN BLESSED
TROJAN WOMEN, THE .... GENEVIEVE BUJOLD
TROJAN WOMEN, THE .... KATHERINE HEPBURN
TROJAN WOMEN, THE .... VANESSA REDGRAVE
TROLL .... ANNE LOCKHART
TROLL .... BRAD HALL
TROLL .... JENNY BECK
TROLL .... JULIA LOUIS-DREYFUSS
TROLL .... JUNE LOCKHART
TROLL .... MICHAEL MORIARTY
TROLL .... NOAH HATHAWAY
TROLL .... PHIL FONDACARO
TROLL .... SHELLEY HACK
TROLL .... SONNY BONO
TRON .... BARNARD HUGHES
TRON .... BRUCE BOXLEITNER
TRON .... JEFF BRIDGES
TROOP BEVERLY HILLS .... BETTY THOMAS
TROOP BEVERLY HILLS .... CRAIG T. NELSON
TROOP BEVERLY HILLS .... MARY GROSS
TROOP BEVERLY HILLS .... SHELLEY LONG
TROOPER HOOK .... BARBARA STANWYCK†
TROOPER HOOK .... EARL HOLLIMAN

† after an actor's name denotes deceased.

TROOPER HOOK .... ROYAL DANO
TROPIC HOLIDAY .... DOROTHY LAMOUR
TROPIC HOLIDAY .... MARTHA RAYE†
TROPIC OF CANCER .... ELLEN BURSTYN
TROPIC OF CANCER .... RIP TORN
TROPIC ZONE .... RONALD REAGAN
TROUBLE ALONG THE WAY .... JAMES DEAN†
TROUBLE COMES
  TO TOWN (TF) .... LLOYD BRIDGES
TROUBLE IN MIND .... GENEVIEVE BUJOLD
TROUBLE IN MIND .... KEITH CARRADINE
TROUBLE IN MIND .... KRIS KRISTOFFERSON
TROUBLE IN PARADISE (TF) .... JACK THOMPSON
TROUBLE IN
  PARADISE (TF) .... NICHOLAS HAMMOND
TROUBLE IN PARADISE (TF) .... RAQUEL WELCH
TROUBLE MAN .... ROBERT HOOKS
TROUBLE WITH ANGELS, THE .... HAYLEY MILLS
TROUBLE WITH ANGELS, THE .... MARY WICKES
TROUBLE WITH DICK, THE .... SUSAN DEY
TROUBLE WITH DICK, THE .... TOM VILLARD
TROUBLE WITH GIRLS, THE .... ELVIS PRESLEY†
TROUBLE WITH GIRLS, THE ...... JOYCE VAN PATTEN
TROUBLE WITH GIRLS, THE .... VINCENT PRICE†
TROUBLE WITH HARRY, THE ..... EDMUND GWENN†
TROUBLE WITH HARRY, THE .... JOHN FORSYTHE
TROUBLE WITH
  HARRY, THE .... MILDRED DUNNOCK†
TROUBLE WITH HARRY, THE .... ROYAL DANO
TROUBLE WITH HARRY, THE .... SHIRLEY MacLAINE
TROUBLE WITH WOMEN, THE .... TERESA WRIGHT
TROUBLEMAKER, THE .... BUCK HENRY
TROUT, THE .... ISABELLE HUPPERT
TRUCK TURNER .... YAPHET KOTTO
TRUCKIN' .... ALBERT SALMI†
TRUE BELIEVER .... JAMES WOODS
TRUE BELIEVER .... ROBERT DOWNEY JR.
TRUE BELIEVERS .... LEE RICHARDSON
TRUE BLUE (TF) .... RICH HALL
TRUE COLORS .... IMOGEN STUBBS
TRUE COLORS .... JAMES SPADER
TRUE COLORS .... JOHN CUSAK
TRUE COLORS .... MANDY PATINKIN
TRUE COLORS .... PHILIP BOSCO
TRUE COLORS .... RICHARD WIDMARK
TRUE CONFESSIONS .... BURGESS MEREDITH
TRUE CONFESSIONS .... CHARLES DURNING
TRUE CONFESSIONS .... ED FLANDERS
TRUE CONFESSIONS .... KENNETH McMILLAN†
TRUE CONFESSIONS .... ROBERT DE NIRO
TRUE CONFESSIONS .... ROBERT DUVALL
TRUE GRIT .... DENNIS HOPPER
TRUE GRIT .... JEFF COREY
TRUE GRIT .... JOHN FIELDLER
TRUE GRIT .... KIM DARBY
TRUE GRIT .... ROBERT DUVALL
TRUE GRIT ★★ .... JOHN WAYNE†
TRUE HEART SUSIE .... LILLIAN GISH†
TRUE IDENTITY .... ANDREAS KATSULAS
TRUE IDENTITY .... ANNE MARIE JOHNSON
TRUE IDENTITY .... FRANK LANGELLA
TRUE IDENTITY .... J. T. WALSH
TRUE IDENTITY .... LENNY HENRY
TRUE IDENTITY .... MICHAEL McKEAN
TRUE IDENTITY .... RUTH BROWN
TRUE LIES .... ARMEN KSAJIKIAN
TRUE LIES .... ARNOLD SCHWARZENEGGER
TRUE LIES .... ART MALIK
TRUE LIES .... BILL PAXTON
TRUE LIES .... CHARLTON HESTON
TRUE LIES .... ELIZA DUSHKU
TRUE LIES .... JAMIE LEE CURTIS
TRUE LIES .... TIA CARRERE
TRUE LIES .... TOM ARNOLD
TRUE LOVE .... ANNABELLA SCIORRA
TRUE ROMANCE .... BRAD PITT
TRUE ROMANCE .... BRONSON PINCHOT
TRUE ROMANCE .... CHRIS PENN
TRUE ROMANCE .... CHRISTIAN SLATER
TRUE ROMANCE .... CHRISTOPHER WALKEN
TRUE ROMANCE .... DENNIS HOPPER
TRUE ROMANCE .... GARY OLDMAN
TRUE ROMANCE .... MICHAEL RAPAPORT

TRUE ROMANCE .... PATRICIA ARQUETTE
TRUE ROMANCE .... SAUL RUBINEK
TRUE ROMANCE .... VAL KILMER
TRUE STORIES .... DAVID BYRNE
TRUE STORIES .... JO HARVEY ALLEN
TRUE STORIES .... JOHN GOODMAN
TRUE STORIES .... SPALDING GRAY
TRUE STORIES .... SWOOSIE KURTZ
TRUE STORY OF
  JESSE JAMES, THE .... HOPE LANGE
TRUE STORY OF
  JESSE JAMES, THE .... ROBERT WAGNER
TRUE STORY OF
  LYNN STUART, THE .... JOHN ANDERSON
TRUE TO LIFE .... YVONNE DE CARLO
TRULY, MADLY, DEEPLY ..... ALAN RICKMAN
TRULY, MADLY, DEEPLY ..... JULIET RICHARDSON
TRULY, MADLY, DEEPLY .... JULIET STEVENSON
TRUMAN CAPOTE'S THE
  GLASS HOUSE (TF) .... DEAN JAGGER†
TRUMAN CAPOTE'S THE
  GLASS HOUSE (TF) .... VIC MORROW†
TRUMAN CAPOTE'S THE
  GLASS HOUSE .... ALAN ALDA
TRUMAN CAPOTE'S THE
  GLASS HOUSE (TF) .... BILLY DEE WILLIAMS
TRUMAN CAPOTE'S THE
  GLASS HOUSE (TF) .... CLU GULAGER
TRUTH ABOUT SPRING, THE ...... DAVID TOMLINSON
TRUTH ABOUT SPRING, THE .... HAYLEY MILLS
TRUTH ABOUT WOMEN, THE .... EVA GABOR
TRUTH ABOUT WOMEN, THE .... JULIE HARRIS
TRUTH ABOUT WOMEN, THE ..... MAE ZETTERLING†
TRUTH OR DARE (FD) .... KEVIN COSTNER
TRUTH OR DARE (FD) .... MADONNA
TRUTH OR DARE (FD) .... WARREN BEATTY
TRY AND GET ME .... LLOYD BRIDGES
TRYGON FACTOR, THE .... ROBERT MORLEY
TUCKER - THE MAN AND
  HIS DREAM .... CHRISTIAN SLATER
TUCKER - THE MAN AND
  HIS DREAM .... CORIN NEMEC
TUCKER - THE MAN AND
  HIS DREAM .... DEAN GOODMAN
TUCKER - THE MAN AND
  HIS DREAM .... DEAN STOCKWELL
TUCKER - THE MAN AND
  HIS DREAM .... DON NOVELLO
TUCKER - THE MAN AND
  HIS DREAM .... ELIAS KOTEAS
TUCKER - THE MAN AND
  HIS DREAM .... FREDERIC FORREST
TUCKER - THE MAN AND
  HIS DREAM .... JEFF BRIDGES
TUCKER - THE MAN AND
  HIS DREAM .... JOAN ALLEN
TUCKER - THE MAN AND
  HIS DREAM .... LLOYD BRIDGES
TUCKER - THE MAN AND HIS DREAM .... MAKO
TUCKER - THE MAN AND
  HIS DREAM .... MARSHALL BELL
TUCKER - THE MAN AND
  HIS DREAM .... NINA SIEMASZKO
TUCKER - THE MAN AND
  HIS DREAM .... PATTI AUSTIN
TUCKER - THE MAN AND
  HIS DREAM .... PETER DONAT
TUCKER - THE MAN AND
  HIS DREAM ○ .... MARTIN LANDAU
TUDOR ROSE .... JOHN MILLS
TUFF TURF .... JAMES SPADER
TUFF TURF .... MATT CLARK
TUFF TURF .... ROBERT DOWNEY JR.
TUGBOAT ANNIE .... MAUREEN O'SULLIVAN
TUGBOAT ANNIE SAILS AGAIN .... JANE WYMAN
TUGBOAT ANNIE SAILS AGAIN ..... RONALD REAGAN
TUMMY TROUBLE (AS) .... CHARLES FLEISCHER
TUMMY TROUBLE (AS) .... KATHLEEN TURNER
TUNA CLIPPER .... RODDY McDOWALL
TUNE IN TOMORROW .... BARBARA HERSHEY
TUNE IN TOMORROW .... BUCK HENRY
TUNE IN TOMORROW .... KEANU REEVES
TUNE IN TOMORROW .... PETER FALK

TUNE IN TOMORROW .... PETER GALLAGHER
TUNES OF GLORY .... ALEC GUINNESS
TUNES OF GLORY .... GORDAN JACKSON†
TUNES OF GLORY .... JOHN MILLS
TUNES OF GLORY .... SUSANNAH YORK
TUNNEL 28 .... DON MURRAY
TUNNEL OF LOVE .... RICHARD WIDMARK
TUNNEL OF LOVE, THE .... DORIS DAY
TUNNELVISION .... CHEVY CHASE
TUNNELVISION .... HOWARD HESSEMAN
TUNNELVISION .... JOHN CANDY†
TUNNELVISION .... LARAINE NEWMAN
TURK 182 .... DARREN McGAVIN
TURK 182 .... KIM CATTRALL
TURK 182 .... PETER BOYLE
TURK 182 .... ROBERT CULP
TURK 182 .... ROBERT URICH
TURK 182 .... TIMOTHY HUTTON
TURK 1982 .... PAUL SORVINO
TURN BACK THE CLOCK (TF) .... DAVID DUKES
TURN BACK THE CLOCK (TF) .... JERE BURNS
TURN OF THE TIDE .... GERALDINE FITZGERALD
TURN THE KEY SOFTLY .... JOAN COLLINS
TURNER AND HOOCH .... JERRY SCHUMACHER
TURNER & HOOCH .... CRAIG T. NELSON
TURNER & HOOCH .... MARE WINNINGHAM
TURNER & HOOCH .... REGINALD VELJOHNSON
TURNER & HOOCH .... SCOTT PAULIN
TURNER & HOOCH .... TOM HANKS
TURNING POINT, THE .... ALEXIS SMITH†
TURNING POINT, THE .... ANTHONY ZERBE
TURNING POINT, THE .... MARTHA SCOTT
TURNING POINT, THE .... TOM SKERRITT
TURNING POINT, THE ★ .... ANNE BANCROFT
TURNING POINT, THE ★ .... SHIRLEY MacLAINE
TURNING POINT, THE ○ .... LESLIE BROWNE
TURNING POINT, THE ○ ... MIKHAIL BARYSHNIKOV
TURTLE DIARY .... BEN KINGSLEY
TURTLE DIARY .... ELEANOR BRON
TURTLE DIARY .... GLENDA JACKSON
TURTLE DIARY .... HAROLD PINTER
TURTLE DIARY .... MICHAEL GAMBON
TURTLE DIARY .... NIGEL HAWTHORNE
TURTLE DIARY .... ROSEMARY LEACH
TUSITALA (MS) .... JOHN McENERY
TUTTI A CASA .... MARTIN BALSAM
TUTTI DENTRO .... JOE PESCI
TWELVE ANGRY MEN .... E. G. MARSHALL
TWELVE ANGRY MEN .... JACK KLUGMAN
TWELVE ANGRY MEN .... JACK WARDEN
TWELVE ANGRY MEN .... JOHN FIELDLER
TWELVE ANGRY MEN .... MARTIN BALSAM
TWELVE ANGRY MEN .... ROBERT WEBBER
TWELVE CHAIRS, THE .... DOM DeLUISE
TWELVE CHAIRS, THE .... FRANK LANGELLA
TWELVE CHAIRS, THE .... MEL BROOKS
TWELVE CHAIRS, THE .... RON MOODY
TWELVE HOURS TO KILL .... BARBARA EDEN
TWELVE MILES OUT .... JOAN CRAWFORD†
TWELVE O'CLOCK HIGH .... RICHARD ANDERSON
TWELVE O'CLOCK HIGH ★ .... GREGORY PECK
TWENTY-ONE .... PATSY KENSIT
TWICE A WOMAN .... ANTHONY PERKINS†
TWICE IN A LIFETIME .... ALLY SHEEDY
TWICE IN A LIFETIME .... ANN-MARGRET
TWICE IN A LIFETIME .... BRIAN DENNEHY
TWICE IN A LIFETIME .... ELLEN BURSTYN
TWICE IN A LIFETIME .... GENE HACKMAN
TWICE IN A LIFETIME ○ .... AMY MADIGAN
TWICE IN A LIFETIME (TF) .... ERNEST BORGNINE
TWICE ROUND THE DAFFODILS .... JILL IRELAND†
TWICE TOLD TALES .... VINCENT PRICE†
TWILIGHT .... LOUIS JOURDAN
TWILIGHT FOR THE GODS .... CYD CHARISSE
TWILIGHT OF HONOR .... CLAUDE RAINS†
TWILIGHT OF HONOR .... JOEY HEATHERTON
TWILIGHT OF HONOR .... LINDA EVANS
TWILIGHT OF HONOR .... RICHARD CHAMBERLAIN
TWILIGHT OF HONOR ○ .... NICK ADAMS†
TWILIGHT PEOPLE .... PAM GRIER
TWILIGHT TIME .... KARL MALDEN
TWILIGHT ZONE—THE MOVIE .... ALBERT BROOKS
TWILIGHT ZONE—THE MOVIE .... DAN AYKROYD

I
N
D
E
X

O
F

F
I
L
M

T
I
T
L
E
S

This is not a list of every film ever made or every cast member, only those listed in this directory.

TWILIGHT ZONE—THE MOVIE .... JOHN LITHGOW
TWILIGHT ZONE—
THE MOVIE .... KATHLEEN QUINLAN
TWILIGHT ZONE—THE MOVIE ...... KEVIN McCARTHY
TWILIGHT ZONE—THE MOVIE .... VIC MORROW†
TWILIGHT'S LAST
GLEAMING .... MELVYN DOUGLAS†
TWILIGHT'S LAST GLEAMING .... BURT LANCASTER†
TWILIGHT'S LAST GLEAMING .... BURT YOUNG
TWILIGHT'S LAST
GLEAMING .... CHARLES DURNING
TWILIGHT'S LAST GLEAMING .... PAUL WINFIELD
TWILIGHT'S LAST GLEAMING .... RICHARD JAECKEL
TWILIGHT'S LAST
GLEAMING .... RICHARD WIDMARK
TWILIGHT'S LAST
GLEAMING .... ROSCOE LEE BROWNE
TWILIGHT'S LAST GLEAMING .... VERA MILES
TWILIGHT'S LAST
GLEAMING .... WILLIAM MARSHALL
TWIN DETECTIVES (TF) .... LILLIAN GISH†
TWIN PEAKS (TF) .... JOAN CHEN
TWIN PEAKS (TF) .... KYLE MacLACHLAN
TWIN PEAKS (TF) .... MICHAEL ONTKEAN
TWIN PEAKS (TF) .... PIPER LAURIE
TWIN PEAKS: FIRE WALK WITH ME .... CHRIS ISAAK
TWIN PEAKS: FIRE
WALK WITH ME .... DANA ASHBROOK
TWIN PEAKS: FIRE WALK WITH ME ... DAVID BOWIE
TWIN PEAKS: FIRE
WALK WITH ME .... DAVID LYNCH
TWIN PEAKS: FIRE
WALK WITH ME .... HARRY DEAN STANTON
TWIN PEAKS: FIRE
WALK WITH ME .... JAMES MARSHALL
TWIN PEAKS: FIRE
WALK WITH ME .... KIEFER SUTHERLAND
TWIN PEAKS: FIRE
WALK WITH ME .... KYLE MacLACHLAN
TWIN PEAKS: FIRE
WALK WITH ME .... MADCHEN AMICK
TWIN PEAKS: FIRE WALK WITH ME ... MOIRA KELLY
TWIN PEAKS: FIRE
WALK WITH ME .... PEGGY LIPTON
TWIN PEAKS: FIRE WALK WITH ME .... RAY WISE
TWIN PEAKS: FIRE WALK WITH ME ... SHERYL LEE
TWINIKLE AND SHINE .... BETSY PALMER
TWINKEY .... SUSAN GEORGE
TWINKLE AND SHINE .... DORIS DAY
TWINKLE AND SHINE .... MARY WICKES
TWINKLE, TWINKLE,
"KILLER" KANE .... ED FLANDERS
TWINKLE, TWINKLE,
"KILLER" KANE .... JASON MILLER
TWINKLE, TWINKLE,
"KILLER" KANE .... MOSES GUNN
TWINKLE, TWINKLE,
"KILLER" KANE .... ROBERT LOGGIA
TWINKLE, TWINKLE,
"KILLER" KANE .... SCOTT WILSON
TWINKLE, TWINKLE,
"KILLER" KANE .... STACY KEACH
TWINKY .... CHARLES BRONSON
TWINS .... ARNOLD SCHWARZENEGGER
TWINS .... BONNIE BARTLETT
TWINS .... CHLOE WEBB
TWINS .... DANNY DeVITO
TWINS .... KELLY PRESTON
TWIST, THE .... ANN-MARGRET
TWIST OF FATE (MS) .... BRUCE GREENWOOD
TWIST OF FATE (MS) .... VERONICA HAMEL
TWIST OF FATE (TF) .... JOHN GLOVER
TWIST OF SAND, A .... JEREMY KEMP
TWIST OF SAND, A .... ROY DOTRICE
TWISTED .... CHRISTIAN SLATER
TWISTED NERVE .... BILLIE WHITELAW
TWISTED NERVE .... HAYLEY MILLS
TWISTED NERVE .... TIMOTHY WEST
TWISTED OBSESSION .... ARIELLE DOMBASLE
TWISTED OBSESSION .... DANIEL CECCALDI
TWISTED OBSESSION .... DEXTER FLETCHER
TWISTED OBSESSION .... JEFF GOLDBLUM
TWISTED OBSESSION .... LIZA WALKER

TWISTER .... DYLAN McDERMOTT
TWO ARE GUILTY .... ANTHONY PERKINS†
TWO BITS .... AL PACINO
TWO BRIGHT BOYS .... JACKIE COOPER
TWO DAUGHTERS OF EVE .... LILLIAN GISH†
TWO FATHERS'
JUSTICE (TF) .... GEORGE HAMILTON
TWO FATHERS' JUSTICE (TF) ...... ROBERT CONRAD
TWO FOR THE
MONEY (TF) .... MERCEDES McCAMBRIDGE
TWO FOR THE ROAD .... ALBERT FINNEY
TWO FOR THE ROAD .... AUDREY HEPBURN†
TWO FOR THE ROAD .... ELEANOR BRON
TWO FOR THE ROAD .... JACQUELINE BISSET
TWO FOR THE ROAD .... WILLIAM DANIELS
TWO FOR THE SEESAW .... ROBERT MITCHUM
TWO FOR THE SEESAW .... SHIRLEY MacLAINE
TWO GIRLS AND A SAILOR .... AVA GARDNER†
TWO GIRLS AND A SAILOR .... JUNE ALLYSON
TWO GIRLS AND A SAILOR .... LENA HORNE
TWO GIRLS AND A SAILOR .... VAN JOHNSON
TWO GIRLS ON BROADWAY .... LANA TURNER
TWO GUYS FROM MILWAUKEE ..... LAUREN BACALL
TWO GUYS TALKING
ABOUT GIRLS .... DAN CORTESE
TWO GUYS TALKING
ABOUT GIRLS .... JONATHAN SILVERMAN
TWO JAKES, THE .... DAVID KEITH
TWO JAKES, THE .... ELI WALLACH
TWO JAKES, THE .... FREDERIC FORREST
TWO JAKES, THE .... HARVEY KEITEL
TWO JAKES, THE .... JACK NICHOLSON
TWO JAKES, THE .... MADELEINE STOWE
TWO JAKES, THE .... MEG TILLY
TWO JAKES, THE .... RICHARD FARNSWORTH
TWO JAKES, THE .... RUBEN BLADES
TWO LATINS FROM
MANHATTAN .... LLOYD BRIDGES
TWO LEFT FEET .... MICHAEL CRAWFORD
TWO LITTLE BEARS, THE .... EDDIE ALBERT
TWO LIVING, ONE DEAD .... MICHAEL CRAWFORD
TWO LOVES .... SHIRLEY MacLAINE
TWO MINUTE WARNING .... BEAU BRIDGES
TWO MINUTE WARNING .... BROCK PETERS
TWO MINUTE WARNING .... GENA ROWLANDS
TWO MINUTE WARNING .... MARILYN HASSETT
TWO MOON JUNCTION .... BURL IVES
TWO MOON JUNCTION .... KRISTY McNICHOL
TWO MOON JUNCTION .... LOUISE FLETCHER
TWO MOON JUNCTION .... RICHARD TYSON
TWO MOON JUNCTION .... SHERILYN FENN
TWO MRS. CARROLLS, THE .... ALEXIS SMITH†
TWO MRS.
CARROLLS, THE .... BARBARA STANWYCK†
TWO MRS.
GRENVILLES, THE (MS) .... ANN-MARGRET
TWO MRS.
GRENVILLES, THE (MS) .... ELIZABETH ASHLEY
TWO MRS.
GRENVILLES, THE (MS) .... SAM WANAMAKER†
TWO MRS. GRENVILLES, THE (MS) ... SIAN PHILLIPS
TWO MRS.
GRENVILLES, THE (MS) .... STEPHEN COLLINS
TWO MULES FOR
SISTER SARA .... CLINT EASTWOOD
TWO MULES FOR
SISTER SARA .... SHIRLEY MacLAINE
TWO NIGHTS WITH CLEOPATRA ..... SOPHIA LOREN
TWO OF A KIND .... BEATRICE STRAIGHT
TWO OF A KIND .... CHARLES DURNING
TWO OF A KIND .... GENE HACKMAN
TWO OF A KIND .... JOHN TRAVOLTA
TWO OF A KIND .... OLIVER REED
TWO OF A KIND ,................... OLIVIA NEWTON-JOHN
TWO OF A KIND .... SCATMAN CROTHERS†
TWO OF A KIND (TF) .... GEORGE BURNS
TWO ON A BENCH (TF) .... PATTY DUKE
TWO ON A GUILLOTINE .... CONNIE STEVENS
TWO ON A GUILLOTINE .... DEAN JONES
TWO O'CLOCK COURAGE .... JANE GREER
TWO PEOPLE .... ESTELLE PARSONS
TWO PEOPLE .... LINDSAY WAGNER
TWO PEOPLE .... PETER FONDA

TWO RODE TOGETHER .... JAMES STEWART
TWO RODE TOGETHER .... RICHARD WIDMARK
TWO RODE TOGETHER .... SHIRLEY JONES
TWO RODE TOGETHER .... WOODY STRODE
TWO SISTERS FROM BOSTON .... JUNE ALLYSON
TWO SMALL BODIES .... FRED WARD
TWO SMALL BODIES .... SUZY AMIS
TWO SOLITUDES .... STACY KEACH
TWO TICKETS TO BROADWAY .... JANET LEIGH
TWO TICKETS TO BROADWAY .... VERA MILES
TWO WEEKS IN ANOTHER TOWN .... CYD CHARISSE
TWO WEEKS IN
ANOTHER TOWN .... GEORGE HAMILTON
TWO WEEKS IN ANOTHER TOWN .... KIRK DOUGLAS
TWO WEEKS WITH LOVE .... DEBBIE REYNOLDS
TWO WEEKS WITH LOVE ..... RICARDO MONTALBAN
TWO WOMEN .... RAF VALLONE
TWO WOMEN ★★ .... SOPHIA LOREN
TWO WORLDS OF
JENNIE LOGAN, THE (TF) .... LINDSAY WAGNER
TWO-HEADED SPY, THE .... MICHAEL CAINE
TWO-MAN SUBMARINE .... SHELLEY WINTERS
TWO-MINUTE WARNING .... CHARLTON HESTON
TWO-MINUTE WARNING .... CHRISTINE NELSON†
TWO-MINUTE WARNING .... JACK KLUGMAN
TWO-MINUTE WARNING .... MARTIN BALSAM
TWO-WAY STRETCH .... THORLEY WALTERS†
TWOGETHER .... BRENDA BAKKE
TWOGETHER .... NICK CASSAVETES
TWOGETHER .... VIRGINIA CASSAVETES
TYCOON .... ANTHONY QUINN
TYCOON .... DAME JUDITH ANDERSON†
TYPHOON .... DOROTHY LAMOUR

U

U.S.S. TEAKETTLE .... EDDIE ALBERT
U.S.S. TEAKETTLE .... JACK WARDEN
U.S.S. TEAKETTLE .... JANE GREER
U-TURN .... MAUD ADAMS
U2: RATTLE AND HUM (FD) .... ADAM CLAYTON
U2: RATTLE AND HUM (FD) .... BONO
U2: RATTLE AND HUM (FD) .... EDGE
U2: RATTLE AND HUM (FD) .... LARRY MULLEN JR.
UFORIA .... CINDY WILLIAMS
UFORIA .... FRED WARD
UGLY AMERICAN, THE .... ARTHUR HILL
UGLY AMERICAN, THE .... MARLON BRANDO
UGLY AMERICAN, THE .... PAT HINGLE
UGLY DACHSHUND, THE .... DEAN JONES
UGLY DACHSHUND, THE ...... SUZANNE PLESHETTE
UHF .... ANTHONY GEARY
UHF .... DAVID BOWE
UHF .... FRAN DRESCHER
UHF .... KEVIN McCARTHY
UHF .... MICHAEL RICHARDS
UHF .... STANLEY BROCK
UHF .... VICTORIA JACKSON
UHF .... "WEIRD AL" YANKOVIC
ULTIMATE BETRAYAL (TF) .... HENRY CZERNY
ULTIMATE BETRAYAL (TF) .... KATHRYN DOWLING
ULTIMATE SOLUTION OF
GRACE QUIGLEY, THE .... CHIP ZIEN
ULTIMATE SOLUTION OF
GRACE QUIGLEY, THE .... JILL EIKENBERRY
ULTIMATE SOLUTION OF
GRACE QUIGLEY, THE ...... KATHERINE HEPBURN
ULTIMATE SOLUTION OF
GRACE QUIGLEY, THE .... NICK NOLTE
ULTIMATE THRILL, THE .... BRITT EKLAND
ULTIMATE WARRIOR, THE .... STEPHEN McHATTIE
ULTRAVIOLET .... ESAI MORALES
ULTRAVIOLET .... PATRICIA HEALY
ULYSSES .... ANTHONY QUINN
ULYSSES .... KIRK DOUGLAS
ULYSSES .... MILO O'SHEA
ULZANA'S RAID .... BRUCE DAVISON
ULZANA'S RAID .... BURT LANCASTER†
ULZANA'S RAID .... DICK MILLER
ULZANA'S RAID .... RICHARD JAECKEL
UMBRELLA WOMAN, THE .... BRYON BROWN
UMBRELLA WOMAN, THE .... RACHEL WARD

† after an actor's name denotes deceased.

UMBRELLA WOMAN, THE .... SAM NEILL
UMBRELLAS OF
    CHERBOURG, THE .... CATHERINE DENEUVE
UN AMERICANO A ROMA .... URSULA ANDRESS
UN ANGEL PASO POR
    BROOKLYN .... PETER USTINOV
UN BORGHESE PICCOLO
    PICCOLO .... SHELLEY WINTERS
UN COMPLICATO INTRIGO DI DONNE,
    VICOLI E DELITTI .... ANGELA MOLINA
UN COMPLICATO INTRIGO DI DONNE,
    VICOLI E DELITTI .... DANIEL EZRALOW
UN COMPLICATO INTRIGO DI DONNE,
    VICOLI E DELITTI .... FRANCISCO RABAL
UN COMPLICATO INTRIGO DI DONNE,
    VICOLI E DELITTI ....HARVEY KEITEL
UN COMPLICATO INTRIGO DI DONNE,
    VICOLI E DELITTI .... ISA DANIELI
UN COMPLICATO INTRIGO DI DONNE,
    VICOLI E DELITTI .... PAOLO BONACELLI
UN COMPLICATO INTRIGO DI DONNE,
    VICOLI E DELITTI ....VITTORIO SQUILLANTI
UN DEUX TROIS QUATRE/LES
    COLLANTS NOIRS .... CYD CHARISSE
UN DOLLARO A TESTA .... TANYA LOPERT
UN FIUME DI DOLLARI .... HENRY SILVA
UN FLIC .... CATHERINE DENEUVE
UN FLIC .... RICHARD CRENNA
UN GIORNO IN PRETURA .... SOPHIA LOREN
UN HOMME EST MORT .... ANGIE DICKINSON
UN HOMME EST MORT .... ANN-MARGRET
UN HOMME
    EST MORT .... JEAN-LOUIS TRINTIGNANT
UN HOMME EST MORT .... ROY SCHEIDER
UN HOMME EST MORT .... TALIA SHIRE
UN HOMME QUI ME PLAIT .... FARRAH FAWCETT
UN LINCEUL N'A PAS
    DE POCHES .... SYLVIA KRISTEL
UN MONSIEUR DE
    COMPAGNIE .... CATHERINE DENEUVE
UN PAPILLON SUR L'EPAULE ...... CLAUDINE AUGER
UN PEU DE SOLEIL DANS
    L'EAU FROIDE .... GERARD DEPARDIEU
UN SECOND SOUFFLE .... ROBERT STACK
UN TAXI MAUVE .... CHARLOTTE RAMPLING
UN TAXI MAUVE .... EDWARD ALBERT
UN TAXI MAUVE .... PETER USTINOV
UN TRANQUILLO POSTO
    DI CAMGAPNA .... VANESSA REDGRAVE
UNA DOMENICA
    D'AGOSTO .... MARCELLO MASTROIANNI
UNA GIORNATA SPECIALE .... SOPHIA LOREN
UNA STRANA COPPIO
    DI GANGSTERS .... URSULA ANDRESS
UNBEARABLE LIGHTNESS
    OF BEING, THE .... DANIEL DAY-LEWIS
UNBEARABLE LIGHTNESS
    OF BEING, THE .... DANIEL OLBRYCHSKI
UNBEARABLE LIGHTNESS
    OF BEING, THE...................... DEREK DE LINT
UNBEARABLE LIGHTNESS
    OF BEING, THE...................... DONALD MOFFAT
UNBEARABLE LIGHTNESS
    OF BEING, THE .... ERLAND JOSEPHSON
UNBEARABLE LIGHTNESS
    OF BEING, THE...................... JULIETTE BINOCHE
UNBEARABLE LIGHTNESS
    OF BEING, THE...................... LENA OLIN
UNBEARABLE LIGHTNESS
    OF BEING, THE...................... PAVEL LANDOVSKY
UNBEARABLE LIGHTNESS
    OF BEING, THE.................. STELLAN SKARSGARD
UNBORN, THE .... BROOKE ADAMS
UNBORN, THE .... JAMES KAREN
UNBORN, THE .... JANE CAMERON
UNBORN, THE .... JEFF HAYENGA
UNBORN, THE .... K CALLAN
UNBORN, THE .... RICK DEAN
UNCANNY, THE .... SAMANTHA EGGAR
UNCHAINED .... BARBARA HALE
UNCLE BUCK .... AMY MADIGAN
UNCLE BUCK .... GABY HOFFMAN
UNCLE BUCK .... JEAN LOUISA KELLY

UNCLE BUCK .... JOHN CANDY†
UNCLE BUCK .... MACAULAY CULKIN
UNCLE HARRY .... GERALDINE FITZGERALD
UNCLE SILAS .... JEAN SIMMONS
UNCLE TOM'S CABIN .... EARTHA KITT
UNCOMMON LOVE, AN (TF) .... HOLLY HUNTER
UNCOMMON VALOR .... FRED WARD
UNCOMMON VALOR .... GENE HACKMAN
UNCOMMON VALOR .... PATRICK SWAYZE
UNCOMMON VALOR .... TIM THOMERSON
UNCOMMON VALOUR .... ROBERT STACK
UNCONQUERED .... HOWARD DA SILVA†
UNCONQUERED (TF) .... TESS HARPER
UNDEAD, THE .... DICK MILLER
UNDEFEATED, THE .... BEN JOHNSON
UNDEFEATED, THE .... HARRY CAREY JR.
UNDEFEATED, THE .... JAN-MICHAEL VINCENT
UNDEFEATED, THE .... RICHARD MULLIGAN
UNDEFEATED, THE .... ROYAL DANO
UNDER FIRE .... ED HARRIS
UNDER FIRE .... GENE HACKMAN
UNDER FIRE .... HOLLY PALANCE
UNDER FIRE .... JEAN-LOUIS TRINTIGNANT
UNDER FIRE .... JENNY GAGO
UNDER FIRE .... JOANNA CASSIDY
UNDER FIRE .... NICK NOLTE
UNDER FIRE .... RICHARD MASUR
UNDER MILK WOOD .... ELIZABETH TAYLOR
UNDER MILK WOOD .... PETER O'TOOLE
UNDER MILK WOOD .... SIAN PHILLIPS
UNDER SIEGE .... ANDY ROMANO
UNDER SIEGE .... COLM MEANEY
UNDER SIEGE .... ERIKA ELENIAK
UNDER SIEGE .... GARY BUSEY
UNDER SIEGE .... NICK MANCUSO
UNDER SIEGE .... PATRICK O'NEAL†
UNDER SIEGE .... STEVEN SEAGAL
UNDER SIEGE .... TOMMY LEE JONES
UNDER SIEGE .... TROY EVANS
UNDER SIEGE 2 .... KATHERINE HEIGL
UNDER SIEGE 2 .... MORRIS CHESTNUT
UNDER SIEGE 2 .... STEVEN SEAGAL
UNDER SIEGE (TF) .... HAL HOLBROOK
UNDER SIEGE (TF) .... MASON ADAMS
UNDER SIEGE (TF) .... STAN SHAW
UNDER SIEGE (TF) .... VICTORIA TENNANT
UNDER SUSPICION .... LIAM NEESON
UNDER THE
    BOARDWALK .... DANIELLE von ZERNECK
UNDER THE BOARDWALK .... KEITH COOGAN
UNDER THE
    BOARDWALK .... RICHARD JOSEPH PAUL
UNDER THE BOARDWALK .... ROXANA ZAL
UNDER THE BOARDWALK .... STEVE MONARQUE
UNDER THE CHERRY MOON ..... FRANCESCA ANNIS
UNDER THE CHERRY MOON .... JEROME BENTON
UNDER THE CHERRY MOON .... PRINCE
UNDER THE CHERRY MOON ...... STEVEN BERKOFF
UNDER THE GUN .... ROYAL DANO
UNDER THE INFLUENCE (TF) .... ANDY GRIFFITH
UNDER THE INFLUENCE (TF) .... DANA ANDERSEN
UNDER THE
    INFLUENCE (TF) .... JOYCE VAN PATTEN
UNDER THE INFLUENCE (TF) .... KEANU REEVES
UNDER THE INFLUENCE (TF) .... SEASON HUBLEY
UNDER THE RAINBOW .... ADAM ARKIN
UNDER THE RAINBOW .... BILLY BARTY
UNDER THE RAINBOW .... CARRIE FISHER
UNDER THE RAINBOW .... CHEVY CHASE
UNDER THE RAINBOW .... JACK KRUSCHEN
UNDER THE RAINBOW .... MAKO
UNDER THE SUN
    OF SATAN .... GERARD DEPARDIEU
UNDER THE VOLCANO .... ANTHONY ANDREWS
UNDER THE VOLCANO .... IGNACIO LOPEZ TARSO
UNDER THE VOLCANO .... JACQUELINE BISSET
UNDER THE VOLCANO .... JAMES VILLIERS
UNDER THE VOLCANO ★ .... KATHY JURADO
UNDER THE VOLCANO ★ .... ALBERT FINNEY
UNDER THE YUM YUM TREE .... BILL BIXBY†
UNDER THE YUM YUM TREE .... CAROL LYNLEY
UNDER THE YUM YUM TREE .... DEAN JONES

UNDER THE YUM YUM TREE .... EDIE ADAMS
UNDER THE YUM YUM TREE .... IMOGENE COCA
UNDER THE YUM YUM TREE .... JACK LEMMON
UNDER THE YUM YUM TREE .... PAUL LYNDE†
UNDERCOVER BLUES .... DENNIS QUAID
UNDERCOVER BLUES .... FIONA SHAW
UNDERCOVER BLUES .... KATHLEEN TURNER
UNDERCOVER BLUES .... LARRY MILLER
UNDERCOVER BLUES .... PARK OVERALL
UNDERCOVER BLUES .... STANLEY TUCCI
UNDERCOVER BLUES .... TOM ARNOLD
UNDERCOVER GIRL........................ ALEXIS SMITH†
UNDERCOVER GIRL........................ ROYAL DANO
UNDERCOVER MAISIE .... ANN SOTHERN
UNDERCOVER MAN, THE .... JAMES WHITMORE
UNDERCOVER MAN, THE .... NINA FOCH
UNDERCOVERS HERO .... LILA KEDROVA
UNDERCURRENT .... KATHERINE HEPBURN
UNDERCURRENT .... ROBERT MITCHUM
UNDERGRADS, THE (CTF) .... ART CARNEY
UNDERGROUND ACES .... DIRK BENEDICT
UNDERGROUND ACES .... JERRY ORBACH
UNDERGROUND ACES .... MICHAEL WINSLOW
UNDERGROUND MAN, THE (TF) ...... CELESTE HOLM
UNDERGROUND MAN, THE (TF) ...... PETER GRAVES
UNDERSTANDING
    HEART, THE .... JOAN CRAWFORD†
UNDERTOW .... ROCK HUDSON†
UNDERWATER ODYSSEY/THE
    NEPTUNE DISASTER, AN .... BEN GAZZARA
UNDERWORLD .... MIRANDA RICHARDSON
UNDERWORLD, U.S.A. .... CLIFF ROBERTSON
UNE FEMME FIDELE .... SYLVIA KRISTEL
UNE PAGE D'AMOUR .... GERALDINE CHAPLIN
UNE RAVISSANTE IDIOTE .... ANTHONY PERKINS†
UNE VIE .... MARIA SCHELL
UNEARTHLY STRANGER, THE .... JOHN NEVILLE
UNFAITHFULLY YOURS .... ALBERT BROOKS
UNFAITHFULLY YOURS .... ARMAND ASSANTE
UNFAITHFULLY YOURS .... CASSIE YATES
UNFAITHFULLY YOURS .... DUDLEY MOORE
UNFAITHFULLY YOURS .... LIONEL STANDER
UNFAITHFULLY YOURS .... NASTASSJA KINSKI
UNFAITHFULLY YOURS .... RICHARD B. SHULL
UNFAITHFULLY YOURS .... RICHARD LIBERTINI
UNFINISHED DANCE, THE .... CYD CHARISSE
UNFINISHED DANCE, THE .... DANNY THOMAS†
UNFORGIVEN .... ANNA THOMSON
UNFORGIVEN .... ANTHONY JAMES
UNFORGIVEN .... FRANCES FISHER
UNFORGIVEN .... JAIMZ WOOLVETT
UNFORGIVEN .... MORGAN FREEMAN
UNFORGIVEN .... RICHARD HARRIS
UNFORGIVEN .... SAUL RUBINEK
UNFORGIVEN ★ .... CLINT EASTWOOD
UNFORGIVEN ○○ .... GENE HACKMAN
UNFORGIVEN, THE .... ALBERT SALMI†
UNFORGIVEN, THE .... AUDREY HEPBURN†
UNFORGIVEN, THE .... BURT LANCASTER†
UNFORGIVEN, THE .... DOUG McCLURE
UNFORGIVEN, THE .... JOHN SAXON
UNFORGIVEN, THE .... JOSEPH WISEMAN
UNFORGIVEN, THE .... LILLIAN GISH†
UNG FLUKT .... LIV ULLMANN
UNGUARDED MOMENT, THE .... JOHN SAXON
UNHOLY MATRIMONY (TF) .... CHARLES DURNING
UNHOLY MATRIMONY (TF) .... LISA BLOUNT
UNHOLY MATRIMONY (TF) .... MICHAEL O'KEEFE
UNHOLY MATRIMONY (TF) .... PATRICK DUFFY
UNHOLY WIFE, THE .... ROD STEIGER
UNION PACIFIC .... ANTHONY QUINN
UNION PACIFIC .... BARBARA STANWYCK†
UNIVERSAL SOLDIER .... ALLY WALKER
UNIVERSAL SOLDIER .... DOLPH LUNDGREN
UNIVERSAL SOLDIER .... ED O'ROSS
UNIVERSAL SOLDIER .... GEORGE LAZENBY
UNIVERSAL SOLDIER ... JEAN-CLAUDE VAN DAMME
UNIVERSAL SOLDIER .... JERRY ORBACH
UNKNOWN, THE .... JOAN CRAWFORD†
UNLAWFUL ENTRY .... KURT RUSSELL
UNLAWFUL ENTRY .... MADELEINE STOWE
UNLAWFUL ENTRY .... RAY LIOTTA

This is not a list of every film ever made or every cast member, only those listed in this directory.

UNLAWFUL ENTRY .... ROGER E. MOSLEY
UNMAN, WITTERING
AND ZINGO .... DAVID HEMMINGS
UNMARRIED WOMAN, AN .... ALAN BATES
UNMARRIED WOMAN, AN .... CLIFF GORMAN
UNMARRIED WOMAN, AN .... JILL EIKENBERRY
UNMARRIED WOMAN, AN .... KELLY BISHOP
UNMARRIED WOMAN, AN .... MICHAEL MURPHY
UNMARRIED WOMAN, AN .... PAT QUINN
UNMARRIED WOMAN, AN .... PAUL MAZURSKY
UNMARRIED WOMAN, AN ★ ... JILL CLAYBURGH
UNMASKED .... RAYMOND BURR†
UNNATURAL CAUSES (TF) .... PATTI LABELLE
UNREMARKABLE LIFE, AN ...... CHARLES S. DUTTON
UNREMARKABLE LIFE, AN .... JENNY CHRISINGER
UNREMARKABLE LIFE, AN .... LILY KNIGHT
UNREMARKABLE LIFE, AN .... MAKO
UNREMARKABLE LIFE, AN .... PATRICIA NEAL
UNREMARKABLE LIFE, AN .... ROCHELLE OLIVER
UNREMARKABLE LIFE, AN .... SHELLEY WINTERS
UNSANE .... ANTHONY (TONY) FRANCIOSA
UNSEEN ENEMY, AN .... LILLIAN GISH†
UNSEEN, THE .... BARBARA BACH
UNSEEN, THE .... NORMAN LLOYD
UNSEEN, THE .... STEPHEN FURST
UNSINKABLE MOLLY
BROWN, THE .... JACK KRUSCHEN
UNSINKABLE MOLLY
BROWN, THE ★ .... DEBBIE REYNOLDS
UNSPEAKABLE ACTS (TF) .... BRAD DAVIS†
UNSPEAKABLE ACTS (TF) .... JAMES HANDY
UNSPEAKABLE ACTS (TF) .... JILL CLAYBURGH
UNSPEAKABLE ACTS (TF) .... SEASON HUBLEY
UNSTOPPABLE MAN, THE .... LOIS MAXWELL
UNSTRUNG HEROES .... ANDIE MacDOWELL
UNSTRUNG HEROES .... JOHN TURTURRO
UNSTRUNG HEROES .... MAURY CHAVKIN
UNSTRUNG HEROES .... MICHAEL RICHARDS
UNSTRUNG HEROES .... NATHAN WATT
UNSUITABLE JOB FOR
A WOMAN, AN .... BILLIE WHITELAW
UNSUSPECTED, THE .... HURD HATFIELD
UNSUSPECTED, THE .... JOAN CAULFIELD†
UNTAMED .... JOAN CRAWFORD†
UNTAMED .... RITA MORENO
UNTAMED FRONTIER .... SHELLEY WINTERS
UNTAMED FURY .... E. G. MARSHALL
UNTAMED HEART .... CHRISTIAN SLATER
UNTAMED HEART .... MARISA TOMEI
UNTAMED HEART .... ROSIE PEREZ
UNTEL PERE ET FILS .... LOUIS JOURDAN
UNTIL SEPTEMBER .... KAREN ALLEN
UNTIL THE END OF
THE WORLD .... MAX von SYDOW
UNTIL THE END OF THE WORLD .... SAM NEILL
UUNTIL THE END OF
THE WORLD .... SOLVEIG DOMMARTIN
UNTIL THE END OF THE WORLD ...... WILLIAM HURT
UNTIL THEY SAIL .... JEAN SIMMONS
UNTIL THEY SAIL .... PAUL NEWMAN
UNTIL THEY SAIL .... PIPER LAURIE
UNTIL THEY SAIL .... SANDRA DEE
UNTITLED VAN SANT/ZISKIN .... ALISON FOLLAND
UNTITLED VAN SANT/ZISKIN .... CASEY AFFLECK
UNTITLED VAN SANT/ZISKIN ...... DAN HEDAYA
UNTITLED VAN SANT/ZISKIN ...... HOLLAND TAYLOR
UNTITLED VAN SANT/ZISKIN .... ILEANNA DOUGLAS
UNTITLED VAN SANT/ZISKIN ...... JOAQUIN PHOENIX
UNTITLED VAN SANT/ZISKIN ...... KURTWOOD SMITH
UNTITLED VAN SANT/ZISKIN ...... MARIA TUCCI
UNTITLED VAN SANT/ZISKIN ...... MATT DILLON
UNTITLED VAN SANT/ZISKIN ...... NICOLE KIDMAN
UNTITLED VAN SANT/ZISKIN ...... WAYNE KNIGHT
UNTOUCHABLES, THE .... ANDY GARCIA
UNTOUCHABLES, THE ...... CHARLES MARTIN SMITH
UNTOUCHABLES, THE .... CLIFTON JAMES
UNTOUCHABLES, THE .... DON HARVEY
UNTOUCHABLES, THE .... KEVIN COSTNER
UNTOUCHABLES, THE .... PATRICIA CLARKSON
UNTOUCHABLES, THE .... ROBERT DE NIRO
UNTOUCHABLES, THE .... ROBERT G. MIRANDA
UNTOUCHABLES, THE ∞ .... SEAN CONNERY

UNWELCOME GUEST, THE .... LILLIAN GISH†
UP CLOSE AND PERSONAL .... ROBERT REDFORD
UP CLOSE AND PERSONAL ..... MICHELLE PFEIFFER
UP FROM THE BEACH .... CLIFF ROBERTSON
UP FROM THE BEACH .... RED BUTTONS
UP GOES MAISIE .... ANN SOTHERN
UP IN ARMS .... DINAH SHORE†
UP IN CENTRAL PARK .... VINCENT PRICE†
UP IN SMOKE .... CHEECH MARIN
UP IN SMOKE .... EDIE ADAMS
UP IN SMOKE .... STACY KEACH
UP IN SMOKE .... STROTHER MARTIN†
UP IN SMOKE .... THOMAS CHONG
UP IN SMOKE .... TOM SKERRITT
UP IN THE CELLAR .... JOAN COLLINS
UP IN THE CELLAR .... LARRY HAGMAN
UP PERISCOPE .... JAMES GARNER
UP THE ACADEMY .... BARBARA BACH
UP THE ACADEMY .... RALPH MACCHIO
UP THE ACADEMY .... RON LEIBMAN
UP THE ACADEMY .... TOM POSTON
UP THE ACADEMY .... WENDELL BROWN
UP THE CREEK .... DAVID TOMLINSON
UP THE CREEK .... STEPHEN FURST
UP THE DOWN STAIRCASE .... EILEEN HECKART
UP THE DOWN STAIRCASE .... JEAN STAPLETON
UP THE DOWN STAIRCASE .... SANDY DENNIS†
UP THE FRONT .... ZSA ZSA GABOR
UP THE RIVER .... HUMPHREY BOGART†
UP THE RIVER .... SPENCER TRACY†
UP THE SANDBOX .... ANN RAMSEY†
UP THE SANDBOX .... BARBRA STREISAND
UP THE SANDBOX .... STOCKARD CHANNING
UP TIGHT .... RAYMOND ST. JACQUES
UP TIGHT .... ROSCOE LEE BROWNE
UP TO HIS EARS .... URSULA ANDRESS
UP YOUR ALLEY .... LINDA BLAIR
UPHILL ALL THE WAY .... BURL IVES
UPSTAIRS AND
DOWNSTAIRS .... SHIRLEY ANNE FIELD
UPTIGHT .... RUBY DEE
UPTOWN SATURDAY NIGHT .... BILL COSBY
UPTOWN SATURDAY NIGHT .... RICHARD PRYOR
UPTOWN SATURDAY NIGHT .... ROSALIND CASH
UPTOWN
SATURDAY NIGHT .... ROSCOE LEE BROWNE
UPTOWN SATURDAY NIGHT .... SIDNEY POITIER
UPWORLD .... ANTHONY MICHAEL HALL
UPWORLD .... CLAUDIA CHRISTIAN
UPWORLD .... JERRY ORBACH
URANUS .... GERARD DEPARDIEU
URANUS .... MICHEL BLANC
URBAN COWBOY .... DEBRA WINGER
URBAN COWBOY .... JAMES GAMMON
URBAN COWBOY .... JOHN TRAVOLTA
URBAN COWBOY .... SCOTT GLENN
USED CARS .... DICK MILLER
USED CARS .... GERRITT GRAHAM
USED CARS .... JACK WARDEN
USED CARS .... KURT RUSSELL
USED PEOPLE .... MARCIA GAY HARDEN
USED PEOPLE .... JESSICA TANDY†
USED PEOPLE .... JOE PANTOLIANO
USED PEOPLE .... KATHY BATES
USED PEOPLE .... MARCELLO MASTROIANNI
USED PEOPLE .... SHIRLEY MacLAINE
USED PEOPLE .... SYLVIA SIDNEY
USERS, THE (MS) .... JOHN FORSYTHE
USERS, THE (TF) .... GEORGE HAMILTON
USERS, THE (TF) .... JACLYN SMITH
USERS, THE (TF) .... RED BUTTONS
USERS, THE (TF) .... TONY CURTIS
USS TEAKETTLE .... CHARLES BRONSON
USUAL SUSPECTS .... GABRIEL BYRNE
USUAL SUSPECTS .... KEVIN SPACEY
USUAL SUSPECTS .... STEPHEN BALDWIN
UTILITIES .... BROOKE ADAMS
UTVANDRARNA ★ .... LIV ULLMANN

V

V.I.P.s, THE .... ELIZABETH TAYLOR
V.I.P.s, THE .... LOUIS JOURDAN
V.I.P.'S, THE .... MAGGIE SMITH
V.I.P.s, THE .... ORSON WELLES†
V.I.P.s, THE .... RICHARD BURTON†
V.I.P.'s, THE ∞ .... MARGARET RUTHERFORD†
V.I. WARSHAWSKI .... CHARLES DURNING
V.I. WARSHAWSKI .... CHARLES McCAUGHIN
V.I. WARSHAWSKI .... JAY O. SANDERS
V.I. WARSHAWSKI .... KATHLEEN TURNER
V.I. WARSHAWSKI .... NANCY PAUL
V.I. WARSHAWSKI .... STEPHEN MEADOWS
VACANCES
PORTUGAISES .... CATHERINE DENEUVE
VACATION FROM MARRIAGE .... DEBORAH KERR
VAGABOND .... ELAINE CORTADELLAS
VAGABOND .... SANDRINE BONNAIRE
VAGABOND .... STEPHANE FREISS
VAGABOND KING, THE .... LESLIE NIELSEN
VAGABOND KING, THE .... RITA MORENO
VAGABOND KING, THE .... VINCENT PRICE†
VAGABOND KING, THE .... WILLIAM PRINCE
VAGRANT, THE .... BILL PAXTON
VAGRANT, THE .... COLLEEN CAMP
VAGRANT, THE .... MARSHALL BELL
VAGRANT, THE .... MICHAEL IRONSIDE
VAGRANT, THE .... PATRIKA DARBO
VALACHI: I SEGRETI DI
COSA NOSTRA .... JOSEPH WISEMAN
VALACHI PAPERS, THE .... CHARLES BRONSON
VALACHI PAPERS, THE .... JILL IRELAND†
VALACHI PAPERS, THE .... JOSEPH WISEMAN
VALDEZ HORSES, THE .... CHARLES BRONSON
VALDEZ IS COMING .... BURT LANCASTER†
VALDEZ IS COMING .... HECTOR ELIZONDO
VALDEZ IS COMING .... RICHARD JORDAN†
VALDEZ IS COMING .... SUSAN CLARK
VALENTINO .... BILL McKINNEY
VALENTINO .... CAROL KANE
VALENTINO .... ELEANOR PARKER
VALENTINO .... LESLIE CARON
VALENTINO .... RUDOLF NUREYEV†
VALENTINO .... SEYMOUR CASSEL
VALENTINO RETURNS ...... VERONICA CARTWRIGHT
VALIANT, THE .... JOHN MEILLON
VALIANT, THE ★ .... PAUL MUNI†
VALIANT IS THE WORLD
FOR CARRIE ★ .... GLADYS GEORGE†
VALLEY GIRL .... DEBORAH FOREMAN
VALLEY GIRL .... FREDERIC FORREST
VALLEY GIRL .... NICOLAS CAGE
VALLEY GIRLS .... COLLEEN CAMP
VALLEY OF DECISION, THE .... DEAN STOCKWELL
VALLEY OF DECISION, THE .... GREGORY PECK
VALLEY OF DECISION, THE .... JESSICA TANDY†
VALLEY OF DECISION, THE ★ .... GREER GARSON
VALLEY OF GWANGI, THE ...... JAMES FRANCISCUS†
VALLEY OF MYSTERY .... HARRY GUARDINO
VALLEY OF MYSTERY .... LEONARD NIMOY
VALLEY OF MYSTERY .... LOIS NETTLETON
VALLEY OF MYSTERY .... PETER GRAVES
VALLEY OF THE DOLLS .... LEE GRANT
VALLEY OF THE DOLLS .... PATTY DUKE
VALLEY OF THE DOLLS .... RICHARD DREYFUSS
VALLEY OF THE DOLLS, THE .... SHARON TATE†
VALLEY OF THE KINGS .... ELEANOR PARKER
VALLEY OF THE SUN .... DEAN JAGGER†
VALMONT .... ANNETTE BENING
VALMONT .... COLIN FIRTH
VALMONT .... FABIA DRAKE
VALMONT .... FAIRUZA BALK
VALMONT .... HENRY THOMAS
VALMONT .... JEFFREY JONES
VALMONT .... MEG TILLY
VALMONT .... SIAN PHILLIPS
VAMOS A MATAR COMPAÑEROS .... FRANCO NERO
VAMP .... BILLY DRAGO
VAMP .... CHRIS MAKEPEACE
VAMP .... DEDEE PFEIFFER

Un-Va

FILM
ACTORS
GUIDE

INDEX OF FILM TITLES

573

VAMP .... GEDDE WATANABE
VAMP .... GRACE JONES
VAMP .... ROBERT RUSLER
VAMP .... SANDY BARON
VAMPIRE CIRCUS .... THORLEY WALTERS†
VAMPIRE IN BROOKLYN .... CHARLIE MURPHY
VAMPIRE IN BROOKLYN .... EDDIE MURPHY
VAMPIRE IN BROOKLYN .... VERNON LYNCH JR.
VAMPIRE (TF) .... RICHARD LYNCH
VAMPIRES .... DUANE JONES†
VAMPIRE'S KISS .... ELIZABETH ASHLEY
VAMPIRE'S KISS .... JENNIFER BEALS
VAMPIRE'S KISS .... KASI LEMMONS
VAMPIRE'S KISS .... MARIA CONCHITA ALONSO
VAMPIRE'S KISS .... NICOLAS CAGE
VAMPYRE, THE .... ISABELLE ADJANI
VAMPYRE, THE .... KLAUS KINSKI†
VAN, THE .... DANNY DEVITO
VANESSA, HER LOVE STORY .... HELEN HAYES
VANISHED (TF) .... E. G. MARSHALL
VANISHED (TF) .... ELEANOR PARKER
VANISHED (TF) .... LARRY HAGMAN
VANISHED (TF) .... RICHARD WIDMARK
VANISHING, THE .... GEORGE HEARN
VANISHING, THE .... JEFF BRIDGES
VANISHING, THE .... KIEFER SUTHERLAND
VANISHING, THE .... NANCY TRAVIS
VANISHING, THE .... SANDRA BULLOCK
VANISHING ACT (TF) .... ELLIOTT GOULD
VANISHING ACT (TF) .... FRED GWYNNE†
VANISHING ACT (TF) .... MARGOT KIDDER
VANISHING ACT (TF) .... MIKE FARRELL
VANISHING PAINT .... DEAN JAGGER†
VANISHING POINT .... CLEAVON LITTLE†
VANISHING POINT .... SEVERN DARDEN
VARIETY .... SPALDING GRAY
VARIETY GIRL .... BOB HOPE
VARIETY GIRL .... BURT LANCASTER†
VARIETY GIRL .... DOROTHY LAMOUR
VARIETY GIRL .... JOAN CAULFIELD†
VASECTOMY, A DELICATE MATTER ..... ABE VIGODA
VASECTOMY, A DELICATE
    MATTER .... CASSANDRA EDWARDS
VASECTOMY, A DELICATE MATTER .... GARY RAFF
VASECTOMY, A DELICATE
    MATTER .... JUNE WILKINSON
VASECTOMY, A DELICATE
    MATTER .... LORNE GREEN†
VASECTOMY, A DELICATE
    MATTER .... PAUL SORVINO
VASECTOMY, A DELICATE
    MATTER .... WILLIAM MARSHALL
VAULT OF HORROR, THE .... DENHOLM ELLIOTT†
VEGA$ (TF) .... RED BUTTONS
VEGA$ (TF) .... ROBERT URICH
VEGA$ (TF) .... TONY CURTIS
VELVET TOUCH, THE .... LEON AMES
VELVETEEN
    RABBIT, THE (AF) .... CHRISTOPHER PLUMMER
VENETIAN AFFAIR .... ED ASNER
VENETIAN AFFAIR, THE .... ROBERT VAUGHN
VENGEANCE IS MINE .... ERNEST BORGNINE
VENGEANCE: THE STORY
    OF TONY CIMO .... BRAD DAVIS†
VENGEANCE: THE STORY
    OF TONY CIMO (TF) .... BRAD DOURIF
VENGEANCE: THE STORY
    OF TONY CIMO (TF) .... ROXANNE HART
VENGEANCE VALLEY .... BURT LANCASTER†
VENGEANCE VALLEY .... JOHN IRELAND
VENOM .... NICOL WILLIAMSON
VENOM .... SARAH MILES
VENOM .... SUSAN GEORGE
VERA CRUZ .... BURT LANCASTER†
VERA CRUZ .... CHARLES BRONSON
VERA CRUZ .... ERNEST BORGNINE
VERANO SANGRIENTO .... JOHN IRELAND
VERDICT, THE .... BRUCE WILLIS
VERDICT, THE .... CHARLOTTE RAMPLING
VERDICT, THE .... JACK WARDEN
VERDICT, THE .... JAMES HANDY
VERDICT, THE .... LINDSAY CROUSE

VERDICT, THE .... MILO O'SHEA
VERDICT, THE .... SOPHIA LOREN
VERDICT, THE .... WESLEY ADDY
VERDICT, THE ★ .... PAUL NEWMAN
VERDICT, THE ✪ .... JAMES MASON†
VERFLUCHT
    DIES AMERIKA! .... GERALDINE CHAPLIN
VERNE MILLER .... SCOTT GLENN
VERTIGO .... HENRY JONES
VERTIGO .... JAMES STEWART
VERTIGO .... KIM NOVAK
VERY BIG WITHDRAWAL ...... DONALD SUTHERLAND
VERY BRADY CHRISTMAS, A (TF) ...... ANN B. DAVIS
VERY BRADY
    CHRISTMAS, A (TF) .... BARRY WILLIAMS
VERY BRADY
    CHRISTMAS, A (TF) .... CARYN RICHMAN
VERY BRADY
    CHRISTMAS, A (TF) ...... CHRISTOPHER KNIGHT
VERY BRADY CHRISTMAS, A (TF) .... EVE PLUMB
VERY BRADY
    CHRISTMAS, A (TF) .... FLORENCE HENDERSON
VERY BRADY
    CHRISTMAS, A (TF) .... JENNIFER RUNYON
VERY BRADY
    CHRISTMAS, A (TF) .... JERRY HAUSER
VERY BRADY
    CHRISTMAS, A (TF) .... MAUREEN McCORMICK
VERY BRADY
    CHRISTMAS, A (TF) .... MIKE LOOKINLAND
VERY BRADY
    CHRISTMAS, A (TF) .... ROBERT REED†
VERY LIKE A WHALE (TF) .... ALAN BATES
VERY PRIVATE
    AFFAIR, A .... MARCELLO MASTROIANNI
VERY SPECIAL FAVOR, A .... LESLIE CARON
VERY SPECIAL FAVOR, A .... NITA TALBOT
VERY THOUGHT
    OF YOU, THE .... ELEANOR PARKER
VERY THOUGHT OF YOU, THE .... WILLIAM PRINCE
VESTIGE OF HONOR (TF) ...... JASON SCOTT LEE
VIAGGIO D'AMORE .... OMAR SHARIF
VIBES .... AHARON IPALE
VIBES .... CYNDI LAUPER
VIBES .... GOOGY GRESS
VIBES .... JEFF GOLDBLUM
VIBES .... JULIAN SANDS
VIBES .... MICHAEL LERNER
VIBES .... PETER FALK
VIBES .... RODNEY KAGEYAMA
VIBES .... SUSAN BUGG
VICE AND VIRTUE .... CATHERINE DENEUVE
VICE ET LA VERTU .... CATHERINE DENEUVE
VICE VERSA .... FRED SAVAGE
VICE VERSA .... JUDGE REINHOLD
VICE VERSA .... SWOOSIE KURTZ
VICIOUS CIRCLE .... JOHN MILLS
VICKI .... MAX SHOWALTER
VICTIM, THE (TF) .... ELIZABETH MONTGOMERY
VICTIMS, THE (TF) .... KEN HOWARD
VICTIMS FOR VICTIMS - THE THERESA
    SALDANA STORY (TF) .... ADRIAN ZMED
VICTIMS FOR VICTIMS - THE THERESA
    SALDANA STORY (TF) .... THERESA SALDANA
VICTOR/VICTORIA .... ALEXIS KARRAS
VICTOR/VICTORIA .... JAMES GARNER
VICTOR/VICTORIA .... JOHN RHYS-DAVIES
VICTOR/VICTORIA .... PETER ARNE†
VICTOR/VICTORIA ★ .... JULIE ANDREWS
VICTOR/VICTORIA ✪ .... ROBERT PRESTON†
VICTOR/VICTORIA ✪ .... LESLEY ANN WARREN
VICTORS, THE .... ALBERT FINNEY
VICTORS, THE .... ELI WALLACH
VICTORS, THE .... GEORGE HAMILTON
VICTORS, THE .... GEORGE PEPPARD†
VICTORS, THE .... PETER FONDA
VICTORS, THE .... VINCE EDWARDS
VICTORY .... IRENE JACOB
VICTORY .... MICHAEL CAINE
VICTORY .... SAM NEILL
VICTORY .... SYLVESTER STALLONE
VICTORY .... WILLEM DAFOE

VICTORY .... WILLEM DAFOE
VICTORY AT ENTEBBE (TF) .... DAVID WARNER
VICTORY AT ENTEBBE (TF) ...... ELIZABETH TAYLOR
VICTORY AT ENTEBBE (TF) ...... ANTHONY HOPKINS
VICTORY AT ENTEBBE (TF) ...... BURT LANCASTER†
VICTORY AT ENTEBBE (TF) .... HELEN HAYES
VICTORY AT ENTEBBE (TF) .... JESSICA WALTER
VICTORY AT ENTEBBE (TF) .... JULIUS HARRIS
VICTORY AT ENTEBBE (TF) .... KIRK DOUGLAS
VICTORY AT ENTEBBE (TF) .... LINDA BLAIR
VICTORY AT ENTEBBE (TF) ... RICHARD DREYFUSS
VICTORY AT ENTEBBE (TF) .... THEODORE BIKEL
VIDEODROME .... DEBORAH HARRY
VIDEODROME .... JAMES WOODS
VIETNAM WAR STORY:
    THE LAST DAYS (CTF) .... WESLEY SNIPES
VIEW FROM THE
    BRIDGE, A .... MAUREEN STAPLETON
VIEW FROM THE BRIDGE, A .... RAF VALLONE
VIEW FROM THE
    BRIDGE, A .... VINCENT GARDENIA†
VIEW TO A KILL, A .... ALISON DOODY
VIEW TO A KILL, A .... CHRISTOPHER WALKEN
VIEW TO A KILL, A .... GEOFFREY KEEN
VIEW TO A KILL, A .... GRACE JONES
VIEW TO A KILL, A .... PATRICK MacNEE
VIEW TO A KILL, A .... ROGER MOORE
VIEW TO A KILL, A .... TANYA ROBERTS
VIGILANTE .... CAROL LYNLEY
VIGILANTE .... FRED WILLIAMSON
VIGILANTE .... ROBERT FORSTER
VIGILANTE .... WOODY STRODE
VIGILANTE FORCE .... ANDREW STEVENS
VIGILANTE FORCE ...... JAN-MICHAEL VINCENT
VIGILANTE FORCE ...... KRIS KRISTOFFERSON
VIGILANTE FORCE ...... VICTORIA PRINCIPAL
VIKING QUEEN, THE .... DON MURRAY
VIKINGS, THE .... ERNEST BORGNINE
VIKINGS, THE .... JANET LEIGH
VIKINGS, THE .... KIRK DOUGLAS
VIKINGS, THE .... TONY CURTIS
VILLA RIDES! .... CHARLES BRONSON
VILLA RIDES .... ROBERT MITCHUM
VILLAGE OF THE DAMNED .... MARK HAMILL
VILLAGE OF
    THE DAMNED .... CHRISTOPHER REEVE
VILLAGE OF THE DAMNED .... KIRSTIE ALLEY
VILLAGE OF THE DAMNED .... LINDA KOZLOWSKI
VILLAGE OF
    THE DAMNED .... MEREDITH SALENGER
VILLAGE OF THE DAMNED .... PETER VAUGHN
VILLAGE OF THE GIANTS .... BEAU BRIDGES
VILLAGE OF THE GIANTS .... RON HOWARD
VILLAIN .... FIONA LEWIS
VILLAIN .... JOSS ACKLAND
VILLAIN .... NIGEL DAVENPORT
VILLAIN, THE .... ANN-MARGRET
VILLAIN, THE .... ARNOLD SCHWARZENEGGER
VILLAIN, THE .... KIRK DOUGLAS
VILLAIN, THE .... PAUL LYNDE†
VILLAIN, THE .... RUTH BUZZI
VINCENT, FRANÇOIS, PAUL,
    AND THE OTHERS .... GERARD DEPARDIEU
VINCENT & THEO .... PAUL RHYS
VINCENT & THEO .... TIM ROTH
VINE BRIDGE, THE .... MAE ZETTERLING†
VINTAGE, THE .... MEL FERRER
VINTAGE, THE .... THEODORE BIKEL
VIOLANTA .... GERARD DEPARDIEU
VIOLENT CITY .... CHARLES BRONSON
VIOLENT CITY .... GEORGE KENNEDY
VIOLENT CITY .... JILL IRELAND†
VIOLENT MEN, THE .... BARBARA STANWYCK†
VIOLENT MEN, THE .... BRIAN KEITH
VIOLENT MEN, THE .... RICHARD JAECKEL
VIOLENT MIDNIGHT .... DICK VAN PATTEN
VIOLENT MIDNIGHT .... JAMES FARENTINO
VIOLENT MIDNIGHT .... SYLVIA MILES
VIOLENT ONES, THE .... DAVID CARRADINE
VIOLENT PLAYGROUND .... DAVID McCALLUM
VIOLENT SATURDAY .... ERNEST BORGNINE
VIOLENT SATURDAY .... SYLVIA SIDNEY
VIOLETS ARE BLUE .... AUGUSTA DABNEY

This is not a list of every film ever made or every cast member, only those listed in this directory.

VIOLETS ARE BLUE	BONNIE BEDELIA	
VIOLETS ARE BLUE	JIM STANDIFORD	
VIOLETS ARE BLUE	JOHN KELLOGG	
VIOLETS ARE BLUE	KEVIN KLINE	
VIOLETS ARE BLUE	SISSY SPACEK	
VIOLETTE	ISABELLE HUPPERT	
VIOLETTE ET FRANCOIS	ISABELLE ADJANI	
VIOLETTE NOZIERE	ISABELLE HUPPERT	
VIRGIN AND THE GYPSY, THE	FRANCO NERO	
VIRGIN ISLAND	RUBY DEE	
VIRGIN ISLAND	SIDNEY POITIER	
VIRGIN PRESIDENT, THE	PETER BOYLE	
VIRGIN QUEEN, THE	BETTE DAVIS†	
VIRGIN QUEEN, THE	DAN O'HERLIHY	
VIRGIN QUEEN, THE	JOAN COLLINS	
VIRGIN SOLDIERS, THE	DAVID BOWIE	
VIRGIN SOLDIERS, THE	LYNN REDGRAVE	
VIRGIN SOLDIERS, THE	NIGEL DAVENPORT	
VIRGIN SPRING, THE	MAX von SYDOW	
VISION QUEST	FOREST WHITAKER	
VISION QUEST	LINDA FIORENTINO	
VISION QUEST	MADONNA	
VISION QUEST	MATTHEW MODINE	
VISION QUEST	MICHAEL SCHOEFFLING	
VISIT, THE	ANTHONY QUINN	
VISIT TO A SMALL PLANET	EARL HOLLIMAN	
VISIT TO A SMALL PLANET	JERRY LEWIS	
VISITING HOURS	LEE GRANT	
VISITING HOURS	LINDA PURL	
VISITING HOURS	MICHAEL IRONSIDE	
VISITING HOURS	WILLIAM SHATNER	
VISITOR, THE	FRANCO NERO	
VISITOR, THE	SHELLEY WINTERS	
VITA DE CANE	MARCELLO MASTROIANNI	
VITAL SIGNS	ADRIAN PASDAR	
VITAL SIGNS	DIANE LANE	
VITAL SIGNS	JIMMY SMITS	
VITAL SIGNS	LAURA SAN GIACOMO	
VITAL SIGNS	NORMA ALEANDRO	
VITAL SIGNS	WILLIAM DEVANE	
VITAL SIGNS (TF)	BARBARA BARRIE	
VITAL SIGNS (TF)	ED ASNER	
VITAL SIGNS (TF)	GARY COLE	
VIVA KNIEVEL!	DABNEY COLEMAN	
VIVA KNIEVEL!	ALBERT SALMI†	
VIVA KNIEVEL!	GENE KELLY	
VIVA KNIEVEL!	LAUREN HUTTON	
VIVA KNIEVEL!	LESLIE NIELSEN	
VIVA KNIEVEL!	MARJOE GORTNER	
VIVA KNIEVEL!	RED BUTTONS	
VIVA LA MUERTE—TUA!	LYNN REDGRAVE	
VIVA LA VIE, THE	CHARLOTTE RAMPLING	
VIVA LAS VEGAS	ANN-MARGRET	
VIVA LAS VEGAS	ELVIS PRESLEY†	
VIVA LAS VEGAS	LENA HORNE	
VIVA MARIA!	GEORGE HAMILTON	
VIVA MAX!	ALICE GHOSTLEY	
VIVA MAX!	ANDREW PARIS	
VIVA MAX!	HARRY MORGAN	
VIVA MAX!	JOHN ASTIN	
VIVA MAX!	JONATHAN WINTERS	
VIVA MAX!	PETER USTINOV	
VIVA ZAPATA!	HENRY SILVA	
VIVA ZAPATA!	JOSEPH WISEMAN	
VIVA ZAPATA! ★	MARLON BRANDO	
VIVA ZAPATA! ○○	ANTHONY QUINN	
VIVACIOUS LADY	JAMES STEWART	
VIVRE POUR VIVRE	CANDICE BERGEN	
VOICE IN THE MIRROR, THE	MAX SHOWALTER	
VOICE IN THE MIRROR, THE	TROY DONAHUE	
VOICE IN THE MIRROR, THE	WALTER MATTHAU	
VOICE OF BUGLE		
ANN, THE	MAUREEN O'SULLIVAN	
VOICE OF THE TURTLE, THE	ELEANOR PARKER	
VOICE OF THE TURTLE, THE	RONALD REAGAN	
VOICES	AMY IRVING	
VOICES	DAVID HEMMINGS	
VOICES	MICHAEL ONTKEAN	
VOICES WITHIN: THE LIVES		
OF TRUDDI CASE (TF)	SHELLEY LONG	
VOLCANO	BRIAN KEITH	
VOLUNTEERS	JOHN CANDY†	

VOLUNTEERS	RITA WILSON	
VOLUNTEERS	TIM THOMERSON	
VOLUNTEERS	TOM HANKS	
VON RICHTHOFEN AND BROWN	DON STROUD	
VON RICHTHOFEN		
AND BROWN	HURD HATFIELD	
VON RICHTHOFEN		
AND BROWN	JOHN PHILLIP LAW	
VON RICHTHOFEN		
AND BROWN	STEPHEN McHATTIE	
VON RYAN'S EXPRESS	FRANK SINATRA	
VON RYAN'S EXPRESS	JAMES BROLIN	
VOYAGE (CTF)	ERIC ROBERTS	
VOYAGE (CTF)	RUTGER HAUER	
VOYAGE, THE	IAN BANNEN	
VOYAGE, THE	SOPHIA LOREN	
VOYAGE EN DOUCE	GERALDINE CHAPLIN	
VOYAGE OF THE DAMNED	BEN GAZZARA	
VOYAGE OF THE DAMNED	BERNARD HEPTON	
VOYAGE OF THE DAMNED	DENHOLM ELLIOTT†	
VOYAGE OF THE DAMNED	FAYE DUNAWAY	
VOYAGE OF THE DAMNED	JACK WARDEN	
VOYAGE OF THE DAMNED	JAMES MASON†	
VOYAGE OF THE DAMNED	JANET SUZMAN	
VOYAGE OF THE DAMNED	JONATHAN PRYCE	
VOYAGE OF THE DAMNED	JOSE FERRER†	
VOYAGE OF THE DAMNED	JULIE HARRIS	
VOYAGE OF THE DAMNED	KATHERINE ROSS	
VOYAGE OF THE DAMNED	LUTHER ADLER†	
VOYAGE OF THE		
DAMNED	MALCOLM McDOWELL	
VOYAGE OF THE DAMNED	MARIA SCHELL	
VOYAGE OF THE DAMNED	MAX von SYDOW	
VOYAGE OF THE		
DAMNED	MICHAEL CONSTANTINE	
VOYAGE OF THE DAMNED	NEHEMIAH PERSOFF	
VOYAGE OF THE DAMNED	ORSON WELLES†	
VOYAGE OF THE DAMNED	OSKAR WERNER†	
VOYAGE OF THE DAMNED	SAM WANAMAKER†	
VOYAGE OF THE DAMNED	WENDY HILLER	
VOYAGE OF THE DAMNED ○	LEE GRANT	
VOYAGE ROUND		
MY FATHER, A (TF)	ALAN BATES	
VOYAGE TO THE BOTTOM		
OF THE SEA	BARBARA EDEN	
VOYAGE TO THE BOTTOM		
OF THE SEA	FRANKIE AVALON	
VOYAGE TO THE BOTTOM		
OF THE SEA	PETER LORRE†	
VOYAGE TO THE BOTTOM		
OF THE SEA	WALTER PIDGEON†	
VOYEUR	JOHN MAHONEY	
VU DU PONT	MAUREEN STAPLETON	
VU DU PONT	RAF VALLONE	

W

"W"	TWIGGY	
W.B. BLUE AND THE BEAN	LINDA BLAIR	
W.C. FIELDS AND ME	BILLY BARTY	
W.C. FIELDS AND ME	LINDA PURL	
W.C. FIELDS AND ME	PAUL MANTEE	
W.C. FIELDS AND ME	ROD STEIGER	
W.C. FIELDS AND ME	VALERIE PERRINE	
W.W. AND THE DIXIE DANCEKINGS	ART CARNEY	
W.W. AND THE		
DIXIE DANCEKINGS	BURT REYNOLDS	
W.W. AND THE		
DIXIE DANCEKINGS	JAMES HAMPTON	
W.W. AND THE DIXIE DANCEKINGS	JERRY REED	
W.W. AND THE DIXIE DANCEKINGS	NED BEATTY	
W.W. AND THE		
DIXIE DANCEKINGS	POLLY HOLLIDAY	
WACKIEST SHIP IN		
THE ARMY, THE	JACK LEMMON	
WACKIEST SHIP IN		
THE ARMY, THE	RICHARD ANDERSON	
WACKO	ANDREW DICE CLAY	
WACO	HOWARD KEEL	
WACO & RHINEHART (TF)	CHARLES C. HILL	
WACO & RHINEHART (TF)	JUSTIN DEAS	
WACO & RHINEHART (TF)	WILLIAM HOOTKINS	

WACO & RINEHART (TF)	DANIEL FARALDO	
WAGNER (MS)	JOAN PLOWRIGHT	
WAGNER (MS)	JOHN GIELGUD	
WAGNER (MS)	VANESSA REDGRAVE	
WAGON MASTER	JAMES ARNESS	
WAGONMASTER	HARRY CAREY JR.	
WAGONMASTER, THE	BEN JOHNSON	
WAGONS EAST	JOHN CANDY†	
WAGONS EAST	RICHARD LEWIS	
WAGONS EAST	ROBERT PICARDO	
WAGONS EAST	THOMAS F. DUFFY	
WAGONS ROLL AT NIGHT, THE	EDDIE ALBERT	
WAGONS ROLL AT NIGHT, THE	SYLVIA SIDNEY	
WAIKIKI WEDDING	ANTHONY QUINN	
WAIKIKI WEDDING	MARTHA RAYE†	
WAIT UNTIL DARK	ALAN ARKIN	
WAIT UNTIL DARK	EFREM ZIMBALIST JR.	
WAIT UNTIL DARK	JACK WESTON	
WAIT UNTIL DARK	RICHARD CRENNA	
WAIT UNTIL DARK ★	AUDREY HEPBURN†	
WAITING FOR CAROLINE	SHARON ACKER	
WAITING FOR SALAZAR	JULIE CYPHER	
WAITING FOR SALAZAR	RUBEN BLADES	
WAITING FOR THE LIGHT	CLANCY BROWN	
WAITING FOR		
THE LIGHT	JOHN BEDFORD LLOYD	
WAITING FOR THE LIGHT	SHIRLEY MacLAINE	
WAITING FOR THE LIGHT	TERI GARR	
WAITING FOR THE LIGHT	VINCENT SCHIAVELLI	
WAITING FOR THE MOON	ANDREW McCARTHY	
WAITING FOR THE MOON	BERNADETTE LAFONT	
WAITING FOR THE MOON	BRUCE McGILL	
WAITING FOR THE MOON	JACQUES BOUDET	
WAITING FOR THE MOON	LINDA BASSETT	
WAITING FOR THE MOON	LINDA HUNT	
WAKE IN FRIGHT	JACK THOMPSON	
WAKE ISLAND ○	WILLIAM BENDIX†	
WAKE ME WHEN IT'S OVER	DON KNOTTS	
WAKE ME WHEN IT'S OVER	JACK WARDEN	
WALK A CROOKED MILE	RAYMOND BURR†	
WALK, DON'T RUN	GEORGE TAKEI	
WALK, DON'T RUN	SAMANTHA EGGAR	
WALK IN THE		
CLOUDS, A	ALTANA SANCHEZ-GIJON	
WALK IN THE CLOUDS, A	ANGELICA ARAGON	
WALK IN THE CLOUDS, A	DEBRA MESSING	
WALK IN THE		
CLOUDS, A	EVANGELINA ELIZONDO	
WALK IN THE CLOUDS, A	FREDDY RODRIQUEZ	
WALK IN THE CLOUDS, A	GIANCARLO GIANNINI	
WALK IN THE CLOUDS, A	KEANU REEVES	
WALK IN THE CLOUDS, A	KEANU REEVES	
WALK IN THE SHADOW	MICHAEL BRYANT	
WALK IN THE SPRING RAIN, A	ANTHONY QUINN	
WALK IN THE SPRING RAIN, A	FRITZ WEAVER	
WALK IN THE SUN, A	JOHN IRELAND	
WALK IN THE SUN, A	LLOYD BRIDGES	
WALK IN THE SUN, A	NORMAN LLOYD	
WALK LIKE A DRAGON	JAMES SHIGETA	
WALK LIKE A MAN	CLORIS LEACHMAN	
WALK LIKE A MAN	COLLEEN CAMP	
WALK LIKE A MAN	HOWIE MANDELL	
WALK ON THE WILD SIDE	BARBARA STANWYCK†	
WALK ON THE WILD SIDE	JANE FONDA	
WALK ON THE WILD SIDE	JOHN ANDERSON	
WALK ON THE WILD SIDE	LAURENCE HARVEY†	
WALK PROUD	ROBBY BENSON	
WALK PROUD	TRINIDAD SILVA JR.†	
WALK THE DARK STREET	CHUCK CONNORS†	
WALK THE PROUD LAND	ANNE BANCROFT	
WALK WITH LOVE		
AND DEATH, A	ANJELICA HUSTON	
WALK WITH LOVE		
AND DEATH, A	JOHN HUSTON†	
WALK WITH LOVE		
AND DEATH, A	MICHAEL GOUGH	
WALKABOUT	JENNY AGUTTER	
WALKER	ED HARRIS	
WALKER	PEDRO ARMENDARIZ JR.	
WALKER	RICHARD EDSON	
WALKING MY BABY		
BACK HOME	BUDDY HACKETT	

† after an actor's name denotes deceased.

WALKING MY BABY
  BACK HOME .... GEORGE CLEVELAND†
WALKING MY BABY BACK HOME .... JANET LEIGH
WALKING MY BABY
  BACK HOME .... SCATMAN CROTHERS†
WALKING ON AIR .... ANN SOTHERN
WALKING STICK, THE .... DAVID HEMMINGS
WALKING STICK, THE .... FRANCESCA ANNIS
WALKING STICK, THE .... SAMANTHA EGGAR
WALKING TALL .... JOE DON BAKER
WALKING TALL .... ROSEMARY MURPHY
WALKING TALL, PART 2 .... RICHARD JAECKEL
WALKING THROUGH THE FIRE (TF) ... J. D. CANNON
WALKING THROUGH
  THE FIRE (TF) .... RICHARD MASUR
WALKING THROUGH
  THE FIRE (TF) .... SWOOSIE KURTZ
WALL, THE (TF) .... DIANNE WIEST
WALL, THE (TF) .... GRIFFIN DUNNE
WALL, THE (TF) .... ROSANNA ARQUETTE
WALL, THE (TF) .... TOM CONTI
WALL OF NOISE .... SUZANNE PLESHETTE
WALL STREET .... ANNA LEVINE
WALL STREET .... CHARLIE SHEEN
WALL STREET .... DARYL HANNAH
WALL STREET .... FRANKLIN COVER
WALL STREET .... HAL HOLBROOK
WALL STREET .... JAMES KAREN
WALL STREET .... JAMES SPADER
WALL STREET .... JOHN C. McGINLEY
WALL STREET .... JOSH MOSTEL
WALL STREET .... MARTIN SHEEN
WALL STREET .... OLIVER STONE
WALL STREET .... SAUL RUBINEK
WALL STREET .... SEAN STONE
WALL STREET .... SEAN YOUNG
WALL STREET .... SYLVIA MILES
WALL STREET .... TERENCE STAMP
WALL STREET ★★ .... MICHAEL DOUGLAS
WALLENBERG: A HERO'S
  STORY (MS) .... ALICE KRIGE
WALLENBERG: A HERO'S
  STORY (MS) .... GUY DEGHY
WALLENBERG: A HERO'S
  STORY (MS) .... KEN COLLEY
WALLENBERG: A HERO'S
  STORY (MS) .... MELANIE MAYRON
WALLENBERG: A HERO'S
  STORY (MS) .... RICHARD CHAMBERLAIN
WALLENBERG: A HERO'S
  STORY (MS) .... STUART WILSON
WALLS OF JERICHO, THE .... KIRK DOUGLAS
WALTONS THANKSGIVING
  REUNION, THE (TF) .... RALPH WAITE
WALTZ ACROSS TEXAS .... ANNE ARCHER
WALTZ ACROSS TEXAS .... RICHARD FARNSWORTH
WALTZ OF THE
  TOREADORS .... MARGARET LEIGHTON†
WALTZ OF THE TOREADORS .... PETER SELLERS†
WANDA NEVADA .... BROOKE SHIELDS
WANDA NEVADA .... FIONA LEWIS
WANDA NEVADA .... PETER FONDA
WANDERERS, THE .... KAREN ALLEN
WANDERERS, THE .... KEN WAHL
WANDERERS, THE .... VAL AVERY
WANDERING JEW, THE .... PEGGY ASHCROFT†
WANT A RIDE, LITTLE GIRL? .... WILLIAM SHATNER
WANTED DEAD OR ALIVE .... DENNIS BURKLEY
WANTED DEAD OR ALIVE .... ELI DANKER
WANTED DEAD OR ALIVE .... GENE SIMMONS
WANTED DEAD OR ALIVE .... HUGH GILLIN
WANTED DEAD OR ALIVE .... JERRY HARDIN
WANTED DEAD OR ALIVE .... MEL HARRIS
WANTED DEAD OR ALIVE .... ROBERT GUILLAUME
WANTED DEAD OR ALIVE .... ROBERT HARPER
WANTED DEAD OR ALIVE .... RUTGER HAUER
WANTED DEAD OR ALIVE .... SUZANNE WOUK
WANTED DEAD OR ALIVE .... TYLER TYHURST
WANTED DEAD OR ALIVE .... WILLIAM RUSS
WANTED: THE SUNDANCE
  WOMAN (TF) .... KATHERINE ROSS

WANTED: THE SUNDANCE
  WOMAN (TF) .... STEVE FORREST
WAR, THE .... ELIJAH WOOD
WAR, THE .... KEVIN COSTNER
WAR, THE .... LEXI RANDALL
WAR, THE .... MARE WINNINGHAM
WAR AGAINST
  MRS. HADLEY, THE .... VAN JOHNSON
WAR AND PEACE .... AUDREY HEPBURN†
WAR AND PEACE .... JOHN MILLS
WAR AND PEACE .... MEL FERRER
WAR AND
  REMEMBRANCE (MS) .... BARRY BOSTWICK
WAR AND REMEMBRANCE (MS) .... BRIAN BLESSED
WAR AND REMEMBRANCE (MS) .... DAVID DUKES
WAR AND REMEMBRANCE (MS) ...... HART BOCHNER
WAR AND REMEMBRANCE (MS) .... JANE SEYMOUR
WAR AND REMEMBRANCE (MS) ...... JOHN GIELGUD
WAR AND REMEMBRANCE (MS) ..... PETER VAUGHN
WAR AND REMEMBRANCE (MS) ...... POLLY BERGEN
WAR AND
  REMEMBRANCE (MS) .... RALPH BELLAMY†
WAR AND
  REMEMBRANCE (MS) .... ROBERT MITCHUM
WAR AND
  REMEMBRANCE (MS) .... ROBERT STEPHENS
WAR AND REMEMBRANCE (MS) .... SAMI FREY
WAR AND REMEMBRANCE (MS) .... SHARON STONE
WAR AND REMEMBRANCE (MS) .... TOPOL
WAR AND
  REMEMBRANCE (TF) .... VICTORIA TENNANT
WAR ARROW .... DENNIS WEAVER
WAR ARROW .... MAUREEN O'HARA
WAR AT HOME, THE .... EMILIO ESTEVEZ
WAR AT HOME, THE .... MARTIN SHEEN
WAR BETWEEN MEN
  AND WOMEN, THE .... BARBARA HARRIS
WAR BETWEEN MEN
  AND WOMEN, THE .... JACK LEMMON
WAR BETWEEN MEN
  AND WOMEN, THE .... JASON ROBARDS
WAR BETWEEN MEN
  AND WOMEN, THE .... LISA EILBACHER
WAR BETWEEN MEN
  AND WOMEN, THE .... SEVERN DARDEN
WAR BETWEEN THE
  TATES, THE (TF) .... ANNETTE O'TOOLE
WAR BETWEEN THE
  TATES, THE (TF) .... ELIZABETH ASHLEY
WAR BETWEEN THE
  TATES, THE (TF) .... RICHARD CRENNA
WAR DRUMS .... BEN JOHNSON
WAR DRUMS .... STUART WHITMAN
WAR HUNT .... JOHN SAXON
WAR HUNT .... ROBERT REDFORD
WAR HUNT .... SYDNEY POLLACK
WAR HUNT .... TOM SKERRITT
WAR LORD, THE .... CHARLTON HESTON
WAR LORD, THE .... JAMES FARENTINO
WAR LOVER, THE .... MICHAEL CRAWFORD
WAR LOVER, THE .... ROBERT WAGNER
WAR LOVER, THE .... SHIRLEY ANNE FIELD
WAR OF CHILDREN, A (TF) ..... ANTHONY ANDREWS
WAR OF CHILDREN, A (TF) .... JENNY AGUTTER
WAR OF THE BUTTONS .... EVEANNA RYAN
WAR OF THE BUTTONS .... GREG FITZGERALD
WAR OF THE BUTTONS .... JOHN COFFEY
WAR OF THE BUTTONS .... LIAM CUNNINGHAM
WAR OF THE
  GARGANTUANS, THE .... RUSS TAMBLYN
WAR OF THE ROSES, THE .... DANNY DEVITO
WAR OF THE ROSES, THE ...... G. D. SPRADLIN
WAR OF THE ROSES, THE ...... HEATHER FAIRFIELD
WAR OF THE ROSES, THE ...... KATHLEEN TURNER
WAR OF THE
  ROSES, THE .... MARIANNE SAGEBRECHT
WAR OF THE ROSES, THE .... MICHAEL DOUGLAS
WAR OF THE ROSES, THE .... PETER DONAT
WAR OF THE ROSES, THE .... PETER HANSEN
WAR OF THE ROSES, THE .... ROY BROCKSMITH
WAR OF THE ROSES, THE .... SEAN ASTIN
WAR OF THE WILDCATS .... MARTHA SCOTT

WAR OF THE WORLDS, THE .... JACK KRUSCHEN
WAR PAINT .... ROBERT STACK
WAR PARTY .... BILLY WIRTH
WAR PARTY .... DWIGHT YOAKAM
WAR PARTY .... GUY BOYD
WAR PARTY .... KEVIN DILLON
WAR PARTY .... M. EMMET WALSH
WAR PARTY .... TIM SAMPSON
WAR WAGON, THE .... BRUCE DERN
WAR WAGON, THE .... HOWARD KEEL
WAR WAGON, THE .... KIRK DOUGLAS
WAR WAGON, THE .... ROBERT WALKER JR.
WAR-GODS OF THE DEEP ...... DAVID TOMLINSON
WAR-GODS OF THE DEEP .... TAB HUNTER
WAR-GODS OF THE DEEP .... VINCENT PRICE†
WARGAMES .... ALLY SHEEDY
WARGAMES .... BARRY CORBIN
WARGAMES .... DABNEY COLEMAN
WARGAMES .... MATTHEW BRODERICK
WARGAMES .... MICHAEL MADSEN
WARLOCK .... ANTHONY QUINN
WARLOCK .... DEFOREST KELLEY
WARLOCK .... JULIAN SANDS
WARLOCK .... LORI SINGER
WARLOCK .... RICHARD E. GRANT
WARLOCK: .... RICHARD WIDMARK
WARLOCK: THE ARMAGEDDON ...... JULIAN SANDS
WARLORDS OF ATLANTIS .... CYD CHARISSE
WARLORDS OF ATLANTIS .... DOUG McCLURE
WARM DECEMBER, A .... SIDNEY POITIER
WARM HEARTS, COLD FEET (TF) .... BARRY CORBIN
WARM HEARTS,
  COLD FEET (TF) .... ELIZABETH ASHLEY
WARM HEARTS,
  COLD FEET (TF) .... MARGARET COLIN
WARM HEARTS, COLD FEET (TF) ... TIM MATHESON
WARNING SHOT .... CARROLL O'CONNOR
WARNING SHOT .... ELEANOR PARKER
WARNING SHOT .... GEORGE GRIZZARD
WARNING SHOT .... JOAN COLLINS
WARNING SHOT .... LILLIAN GISH†
WARNING SHOT .... SAM WANAMAKER†
WARNING SHOT .... STEFANIE POWERS
WARNING SHOT .... STEVE ALLEN
WARNING SIGN .... KATHLEEN QUINLAN
WARNING SIGN .... YAPHET KOTTO
WARPATH .... HARRY CAREY JR.
WARRIOR EMPRESS, THE .... TINA LOUISE
WARRIORS .... MICHAEL BECK
WARRIORS 5 .... JACK PALANCE
WARRIORS, THE .... MERCEDES RUEHL
WASH, THE .... MAKO
WASH, THE .... MARION YUE
WASH, THE .... NOBU McCARTHY
WASH, THE .... PATTI YASUTAKE
WASH, THE .... SHIZUKO HOSHI
WASHINGTON AFFAIR, THE .... TOM SELLECK
WASHINGTON: BEHIND CLOSED
  DOORS (MS) .... ANDY GRIFFITH
WASHINGTON: BEHIND CLOSED
  DOORS (MS) .... CLIFF ROBERTSON
WASHINGTON: BEHIND CLOSED
  DOORS (MS) .... GEORGE GAYNES
WASHINGTON: BEHIND CLOSED
  DOORS (MS) .... HAROLD GOULD
WASHINGTON: BEHIND CLOSED
  DOORS (MS) .... JASON ROBARDS
WASHINGTON: BEHIND CLOSED
  DOORS (MS) .... JOHN RANDOLPH
WASHINGTON: BEHIND CLOSED
  DOORS (MS) .... LOIS NETTLETON
WASHINGTON: BEHIND CLOSED
  DOORS (MS) .... ROBERT VAUGHN
WASHINGTON: BEHIND CLOSED
  DOORS (MS) .... STEFANIE POWERS
WASHINGTON STORY .... PATRICIA NEAL
WASHINGTON STORY .... VAN JOHNSON
WATCH ON THE RHINE .... BETTE DAVIS†
WATCH ON THE RHINE ..... GERALDINE FITZGERALD
WATCH ON THE RHINE ★★ .... PAUL LUKAS†
WATCH ON THE RHINE O .... LUCILE WATSON†
WATCHED! .... STACY KEACH

This is not a list of every film ever made or every cast member, only those listed in this directory.

WATCHER IN THE WOODS, THE .... BETTE DAVIS†
WATCHER IN THE WOODS, THE .... CARROLL BAKER
WATCHER IN THE WOODS, THE .... DAVID McCALLUM
WATCHER IN THE WOODS, THE .... IAN BANNEN
WATCHER IN THE WOODS, THE .... LYNN-HOLLY JOHNSON
WATCHERS .... BARBARA WILLIAMS
WATCHERS .... BLU MAKUMA
WATCHERS .... COREY HAIM
WATCHERS .... LALA
WATCHERS .... MICHAEL IRONSIDE
WATER .... BILLY CONNELLY
WATER .... BRENDA VACCARO
WATER .... DENNIS DUGAN
WATER .... DICK SHAWN†
WATER .... ERIC CLAPTON
WATER .... FRED GWYNNE†
WATER .... GEORGE HARRISON
WATER .... JIMMIE WALKER
WATER .... LEONARD ROSSITER†
WATER .... MAUREEN LIPMAN
WATER .... MICHAEL CAINE
WATER .... RINGO STARR
WATER .... VALERIE PERRINE
WATER BABIES, THE .... BILLIE WHITELAW
WATER BABIES, THE .... DAVID TOMLINSON
WATERDANCE, THE .... ELIZABETH PENA
WATERDANCE, THE .... ERIC STOLTZ
WATERDANCE, THE .... HELEN HUNT
WATERDANCE, THE .... WESLEY SNIPES
WATERDANCE, THE .... WILLIAM FORSYTHE
WATERHOLE #3 .... BRUCE DERN
WATERHOLE #3 .... CARROLL O'CONNOR
WATERHOLE #3 .... CLAUDE AKINS†
WATERHOLE #3 .... JAMES COBURN
WATERHOLE #3 .... TIMOTHY CAREY
WATERLAND .... JEREMY IRONS
WATERLOO .... CHRISTOPHER PLUMMER
WATERLOO .... DAN O'HERLIHY
WATERLOO .... ROD STEIGER
WATERLOO BRIDGE .... BETTE DAVIS†
WATERLOO ROAD .... JOHN MILLS
WATERMELON MAN .... ESTELLE PARSONS
WATERMELON MAN .... HOWARD CAINE†
WATERMELON MAN .... PAUL WILLIAMS
WATERSHIP DOWN (AF) .... JOSS ACKLAND
WATERWORLD .... DENNIS HOPPER
WATERWORLD .... JEANNE TRIPPLEHORN
WATERWORLD .... KEVIN COSTNER
WATERWORLD .... LAURENCE FISHBURNE
WATERWORLD .... TINA MAJORINO
WATTSTAX (FD) .... RICHARD PRYOR
WAVELENGTH .... ROBERT CARRADINE
WAXWORK .... CHARLES McCAUGHIN
WAXWORK .... DANA ASHBROOK
WAXWORK .... DAVID WARNER
WAXWORK .... DEBORAH FOREMAN
WAXWORK .... J. KENNETH CAMPBELL
WAXWORK .... JOHN RHYS-DAVIES
WAXWORK .... MICHELLE JOHNSON
WAXWORK .... MILES O'KEEFFE
WAXWORK .... PATRICK MacNEE
WAXWORK .... ZACH GALLIGAN
WAY AHEAD, THE .... DAVID NIVEN†
WAY AHEAD, THE .... PETER USTINOV
WAY BACK HOME .... BETTE DAVIS†
WAY DOWN EAST .... LILLIAN GISH†
WAY OF A GAUCHO .... RORY CALHOUN
WAY OF ALL FLESH, THE ★★ .... EMIL JANNINGS†
WAY TO THE STARS, THE .... DAVID TOMLINSON
WAY TO THE STARS, THE .... JEAN SIMMONS
WAY TO THE STARS, THE .... JOHN MILLS
WAY...WAY OUT .... CONNIE STEVENS
WAY...WAY OUT .... DENNIS WEAVER
WAY...WAY OUT .... JERRY LEWIS
WAY...WAY OUT .... ROBERT MORLEY
WAY WE WERE, THE .... BRADFORD DILLMAN
WAY WE WERE, THE .... GEORGE GAYNES
WAY WE WERE, THE .... JAMES WOODS
WAY WE WERE, THE .... LOIS CHILES
WAY WE WERE, THE .... PATRICK O'NEAL†
WAY WE WERE, THE .... ROBERT REDFORD
WAY WE WERE, THE .... SALLY KIRKLAND
WAY WE WERE, THE .... SUSAN BLAKELY
WAY WE WERE, THE ★ .... BARBRA STREISAND
WAY WEST, THE .... HARRY CAREY JR.
WAY WEST, THE .... KIRK DOUGLAS
WAY WEST, THE .... RICHARD WIDMARK
WAY WEST, THE .... ROBERT MITCHUM
WAY WEST, THE .... SALLY FIELD
WAY WEST, THE .... STUBBY KAYE
WAYNE'S WORLD .... COLLEEN CAMP
WAYNE'S WORLD .... DONNA DIXON
WAYNE'S WORLD .... KURT FULLER
WAYNE'S WORLD .... LARA FLYNN BOYLE
WAYNE'S WORLD .... MICHAEL PATRICK CARTER
WAYNE'S WORLD .... ROB LOWE
WAYNE'S WORLD .... TIA CARRERE
WAYNE'S WORLD .... ALICE COOPER
WAYNE'S WORLD .... BRIAN DOYLE-MURRAY
WAYNE'S WORLD .... DANA CARVEY
WAYNE'S WORLD .... ED O'NEILL
WAYNE'S WORLD .... MIKE MYERS
WAYNE'S WORLD 2 .... KIM BASINGER
WAYNE'S WORLD 2 .... CHARLTON HESTON
WAYNE'S WORLD 2 .... CHRISTOPHER WALKEN
WAYNE'S WORLD 2 .... DANA CARVEY
WAYNE'S WORLD 2 .... HEATHER LOCKLEAR
WAYNE'S WORLD 2 .... MIKE MYERS
WAYNE'S WORLD 2 .... RALPH BROWN
WAYNE'S WORLD 2 .... TIA CARRERE
WAYWARD BUS, THE .... JOAN COLLINS
WAYWARD GIRL, THE .... BARBARA EDEN
WAYWARD GIRL, THE .... LIV ULLMANN
WE ARE THE CHILDREN (TF) .... ALLY SHEEDY
WE ARE THE CHILDREN (TF) .... JUDITH IVEY
WE ARE THE CHILDREN (TF) .... TED DANSON
WE DIVE AT DAWN .... JOHN MILLS
WE HAVE OUR MOMENTS .... DAVID NIVEN†
WE THINK THE WORLD OF YOU .... ALAN BATES
WE WERE DANCING .... AVA GARDNER†
WE WERE STRANGERS .... JENNIFER JONES
WE WHO ARE YOUNG .... LANA TURNER
WE'RE BACK! A DINOSAUR'S STORY (AF) .... JAY LENO
WE'RE BACK! A DINOSAUR'S STORY (AF) .... JOHN GOODMAN
WE'RE BACK! A DINOSAUR'S STORY (AF) .... JULIA CHILD
WE'RE BACK! A DINOSAUR'S STORY (AF) .... MARTIN SHORT
WE'RE NOT MARRIED! .... MARILYN MONROE†
WEAVERS OF LIFE, THE .... HELEN HAYES
WEB, THE .... VINCENT PRICE†
WEB OF EVIDENCE .... VAN JOHNSON
WEB OF EVIDENCE .... VERA MILES
WEBSTER BOY, THE .... GEOFFREY BAYLDON
WEDDING, A .... CAROL BURNETT
WEDDING, A .... DENNIS CHRISTOPHER
WEDDING, A .... DESI ARNAZ JR.
WEDDING, A .... DINA MERRILL
WEDDING, A .... GERALDINE CHAPLIN
WEDDING, A .... HOWARD DUFF†
WEDDING, A .... LAUREN HUTTON
WEDDING, A .... LILLIAN GISH†
WEDDING, A .... MIA FARROW
WEDDING, A .... NINA VAN PALLANDT
WEDDING, A .... PAUL DOOLEY
WEDDING GIFT, THE .... JULIE WALTERS
WEDDING IN WHITE .... CAROL KANE
WEDDING IN WHITE .... DONALD PLEASENCE
WEDDING NIGHT, THE .... RALPH BELLAMY†
WEDDING PARTY, THE .... JILL CLAYBURGH
WEDDING PARTY, THE .... ROBERT DE NIRO
WEDLOCK (CTF) .... JAMES REMAR
WEDLOCK (CTF) .... JOAN CHEN
WEDLOCK (CTF) .... MIMI ROGERS
WEDLOCK (CTF) .... RUTGER HAUER
WEEDS .... ANN RAMSEY†
WEEDS .... NICK NOLTE
WEEDS .... RITA TAGGART
WEEDS .... WILLIAM FORSYTHE
WEEKEND AT BERNIE'S .... ANDREW McCARTHY
WEEKEND AT BERNIE'S .... CATHERINE MARY STEWART
WEEKEND AT BERNIE'S .... JONATHAN SILVERMAN
WEEKEND AT BERNIE'S .... TERRY KISER
WEEKEND AT BERNIE'S II .... ANDREW McCARTHY
WEEKEND AT BERNIE'S II .... BARRY BOSTWICK
WEEKEND AT BERNIE'S II .... JONATHAN SILVERMAN
WEEKEND AT BERNIE'S II .... TERRY KISER
WEEKEND AT THE WALDORF .... PHYLLIS THAXTER
WEEKEND AT THE WALDORF .... VAN JOHNSON
WEEKEND AT THE WALDORF .... LANA TURNER
WEEKEND AT THE WALDORF .... LEON AMES
WEEKEND FOR THREE .... JANE WYATT
WEEKEND OF TERROR (TF) .... CAROL LYNLEY
WEEKEND OF TERROR (TF) .... LEE MAJORS
WEEKEND OF TERROR (TF) .... ROBERT CONRAD
WEEKEND WAR (TF) .... CHARLES HAID
WEEKEND WAR (TF) .... CHARLES KIMBROUGH
WEEKEND WAR (TF) .... DANIEL STERN
WEEKEND WAR (TF) .... JAMES TOLKAN
WEEKEND WAR (TF) .... STEPHEN COLLINS
WEEKEND WARRIORS .... LLOYD BRIDGES
WEEKEND WITH FATHER .... PATRICIA NEAL
WEG OHNE UMKEHR .... LILA KEDROVA
WEIRD SCIENCE .... ANTHONY MICHAEL HALL
WEIRD SCIENCE .... KELLY LeBROCK
WEIRD SCIENCE .... ROBERT DOWNEY JR.
WELCOME HOME .... BRIAN KEITH
WELCOME HOME .... JoBETH WILLIAMS
WELCOME HOME .... KRIS KRISTOFFERSON
WELCOME HOME .... SAM WATERSTON
WELCOME HOME, BOBBY (TF) .... JOHN KARLEN
WELCOME HOME, JOHNNY BRISTOL (TF) .... BROCK PETERS
WELCOME HOME, JOHNNY BRISTOL (TF) .... FORREST TUCKER†
WELCOME HOME, JOHNNY BRISTOL (TF) .... JANE ALEXANDER
WELCOME HOME, JOHNNY BRISTOL (TF) .... MARTIN LANDAU
WELCOME HOME, JOHNNY BRISTOL (TF) .... MARTIN SHEEN
WELCOME HOME, JOHNNY BRISTOL (TF) .... PAT O'BRIEN†
WELCOME HOME ROXY CARMICHAEL .... AVA FABIAN
WELCOME HOME ROXY CARMICHAEL .... DINAH MANOFF
WELCOME HOME ROXY CARMICHAEL .... JEFF DANIELS
WELCOME HOME ROXY CARMICHAEL .... LAILA ROBINS
WELCOME HOME, ROXY CARMICHAEL .... WINONA RYDER
WELCOME HOME SOLDIER BOYS .... JOE DON BAKER
WELCOME STRANGER .... JOAN CAULFIELD†
WELCOME TO 18 .... ERICH ANDERSON
WELCOME TO ARROW BEACH .... JOHN IRELAND
WELCOME TO ARROW BEACH .... STUART WHITMAN
WELCOME TO BLOOD CITY .... JACK PALANCE
WELCOME TO BLOOD CITY .... SAMANTHA EGGAR
WELCOME TO HARD TIMES .... JOHN ANDERSON
WELCOME TO HARD TIMES .... ROYAL DANO
WELCOME TO L.A. .... GERALDINE CHAPLIN
WELCOME TO L.A. .... HARVEY KEITEL
WELCOME TO L.A. .... JAMES KEACH
WELCOME TO L.A. .... KEITH CARRADINE
WELCOME TO L.A. .... LAUREN HUTTON
WELCOME TO L.A. .... SALLY KELLERMAN
WELCOME TO L.A. .... SISSY SPACEK
WELCOME TO L.A. .... VIVECA LINDFORS
WELCOME TO THE CLUB .... JACK WARDEN
WELL, THE .... HARRY MORGAN
WELL-GROOMED BRIDE, THE .... OLIVIA DE HAVILLAND
WEREWOLF OF WASHINGTON .... DEAN STOCKWELL

† after an actor's name denotes deceased.

WES CRAVEN'S
NEW NIGHTMARE .... HEATHER LANGENKAMP
WES CRAVEN'S NEW
NIGHTMARE .... MIKO HUGHES
WES CRAVEN'S NEW
NIGHTMARE .... ROBERT ENGLUND
WES CRAVEN'S NEW NIGHTMARE ..... WES CRAVEN
WEST OF BROADWAY .... RALPH BELLAMY†
WEST OF THE PECOS .... BARBARA HALE
WEST OF THE PECOS .... ROBERT MITCHUM
WEST POINT .... JOAN CRAWFORD†
WEST POINT OF THE AIR ..... MAUREEN O'SULLIVAN
WEST POINT STORY, THE .... DORIS DAY
WEST POINT STORY, THE .... GORDON MACRAE†
WEST SIDE STORY .... JOHN ASTIN
WEST SIDE STORY .... NATALIE WOOD†
WEST SIDE STORY .... RUSS TAMBLYN
WEST SIDE STORY ∞ .... RITA MORENO
WESTBOUND .... MICHAEL DANTE
WESTERN UNION .... DEAN JAGGER†
WESTERNER, THE ∞ .... WALTER BRENNAN†
WESTWORLD .... DICK VAN PATTEN
WESTWORLD .... JAMES BROLIN
WESTWORLD .... RICHARD BENJAMIN
WESTWORLD .... ROBERT DAVIS†
WESTWORLD .... VICTORIA SHAW†
WET GOLD (TF) .... BRIAN KERWIN
WET GOLD (TF) .... BROOKE SHIELDS
WETBACKS .... LLOYD BRIDGES
WETHERBY .... IAN HOLM
WETHERBY .... JUDI DENCH
WETHERBY .... VANESSA REDGRAVE
WE'RE NO ANGELS .... BRUNO KIRBY
WE'RE NO ANGELS .... DEMI MOORE
WE'RE NO ANGELS .... HOYT AXTON
WE'RE NO ANGELS .... JAMES RUSSO
WE'RE NO ANGELS .... PETER USTINOV
WE'RE NO ANGELS .... RAY MCANALLY†
WE'RE NO ANGELS .... ROBERT DE NIRO
WE'RE NO ANGELS .... SEAN PENN
WE'RE NO ANGELS .... WALLACE SHAWN
WE'RE NOT DRESSING .... GEORGE BURNS
WE'RE ONLY HUMAN .... JANE WYATT
WE'VE NEVER BEEN LICKED ..... ROBERT MITCHUM
WHALE FOR THE
KILLING, A (TF) ...... RICHARD WIDMARK
WHALE OF A TIME, A ...... WILLIAM SHATNER
WHALES OF AUGUST, THE .... BETTE DAVIS†
WHALES OF AUGUST, THE .... HARRY CAREY JR.
WHALES OF AUGUST, THE .... LILLIAN GISH†
WHALES OF AUGUST, THE ... MARY STEENBURGEN
WHALES OF AUGUST, THE ... VINCENT PRICE†
WHALES OF AUGUST, THE ○ .... ANN SOTHERN
WHAT? .... MARCELLO MASTROIANNI
WHAT? .... ROMAN POLANSKI
WHAT A LIFE .... JACKIE COOPER
WHAT A LIFE .... LIONEL STANDER
WHAT A WAY TO GO! .... DEAN MARTIN
WHAT A WAY TO GO! .... DICK VAN DYKE
WHAT A WAY TO GO! .... GENE KELLY
WHAT A WAY TO GO! .... PAUL NEWMAN
WHAT A WAY TO GO! .... ROBERT MITCHUM
WHAT A WAY TO GO! .... SHIRLEY MacLAINE
WHAT A WOMAN! .... SHELLEY WINTERS
WHAT ABOUT BOB? .... BILL MURRAY
WHAT ABOUT BOB? .... CHARLIE KORSMO
WHAT ABOUT BOB? .... JULIE HAGERTY
WHAT ABOUT BOB? .... KATHRYN ERBE
WHAT ABOUT BOB? .... RICHARD DREYFUSS
WHAT ABOUT BOB? .... SUSAN WILLIS
WHAT ABOUT BOB? .... TOM ALDRICH
WHAT ARE BEST FRIENDS FOR? (TF) .... LEE GRANT
WHAT CHANGED
CHARLEY FARTHING? .... DOUG McCLURE
WHAT CHANGED
CHARLEY FARTHING? .... HAYLEY MILLS
WHAT DID YOU DO IN
THE WAR, DADDY? .... CARROLL O'CONNOR
WHAT DID YOU DO IN
THE WAR, DADDY? .... HARRY MORGAN
WHAT DID YOU DO IN
THE WAR, DADDY? .... JAMES COBURN

WHAT DO YOU SAY TO
A NAKED LADY? .... RICHARD ROUNDTREE
WHAT EVER HAPPENED
TO BABY JANE? .... WESLEY ADDY
WHAT EVER HAPPENED
TO BABY JANE? ★ .... BETTE DAVIS†
WHAT EVER HAPPENED
TO BABY JANE? ○ .... VICTOR BUONO†
WHATEVER HAPPENED
TO BABY JANE? .... JOAN CRAWFORD†
WHAT EVER HAPPENED
TO BABY JANE? (TF) .... LYNN REDGRAVE
WHAT EVER HAPPENED
TO BABY JANE? (TF) .... VANESSA REDGRAVE
WHAT EVERY WOMAN KNOWS .... HELEN HAYES
WHAT HAPPENED TO THE MYSTERIOUS
MR. FOSTER? (TF) .... ERNEST BORGNINE
WHAT HAPPENED WAS... .... TOM NOONAN
WHAT HAVE I DONE TO
DESERVE THIS? .... CARMEN MAURA
WHAT HAVE I DONE TO
DESERVE THIS? .... CHUS LAMPREAVE
WHAT HAVE I DONE TO
DESERVE THIS? .... KITI MANYER
WHAT HAVE I DONE TO
DESERVE THIS? .... VERONICA FORQUE
WHAT PRICE GLORY? .... HARRY MORGAN
WHAT PRICE GLORY? .... MAX SHOWALTER
WHAT PRICE GLORY .... ROBERT WAGNER
WHAT PRICE VICTORY? (TF) ..... GEORGE KENNEDY
WHAT PRICE VICTORY? (TF) .... MAC DAVIS
WHAT PRICE VICTORY (TF) .... MIKE JOLLY
WHAT PRICE VICTORY? (TF) .... ROBERT CULP
WHAT PRICE VICTORY? (TF) .... SUSAN HESS
WHAT VENUS DID
WITH MARS .... CAMPBELL SCOTT
WHAT'S EATING
GILBERT GRAPE .... JOHN C. REILLY
WHAT'S EATING GILBERT GRAPE ..... JOHNNY DEPP
WHAT'S EATING
GILBERT GRAPE .... JULIETTE LEWIS
WHAT'S EATING
GILBERT GRAPE .... MARY STEENBURGEN
WHAT'S EATING
GILBERT GRAPE ○ .... LEONARDO DICAPRIO
WHAT'S NEW PUSSYCAT? .... PETER SELLERS†
WHAT'S NEW PUSSYCAT? .... ROMY SCHNEIDER†
WHAT'S A NICE GIRL
LIKE YOU...? (TF) .... BRENDA VACCARO
WHAT'S HAPPENING: THE
BEATLES IN THE USA (FD) ..... GEORGE HARRISON
WHAT'S HAPPENING: THE
BEATLES IN THE USA (FD) .... PAUL McCARTNEY
WHAT'S HAPPENING: THE
BEATLES IN THE USA (FD) .... RINGO STARR
WHAT'S LOVE GOT TO
DO WITH IT .... JENIFER LEWIS
WHAT'S LOVE GOT TO
DO WITH IT .... PHYLLIS YVONNE STICKNEY
WHAT'S LOVE GOT TO DO WITH IT .... TINA TURNER
WHAT'S LOVE GOT TO
DO WITH IT .... VANESSA BELL CALLOWAY
WHAT'S LOVE GOT TO
DO WITH IT ★ .... ANGELA BASSETT
WHAT'S LOVE GOT TO
DO WITH IT ★ .... LAURENCE FISHBURNE
WHAT'S NEW, PUSSYCAT? .... LOUISE LASSER
WHAT'S NEW PUSSYCAT? .... PAULA PRENTISS
WHAT'S NEW PUSSYCAT? .... PETER O'TOOLE
WHAT'S NEW PUSSYCAT? .... URSULA ANDRESS
WHAT'S NEW PUSSYCAT? .... WOODY ALLEN
WHAT'S SO BAD ABOUT
FEELING GOOD? .... CLEAVON LITTLE†
WHAT'S SO BAD ABOUT
FEELING GOOD? .... DOM DeLUISE
WHAT'S SO BAD ABOUT
FEELING GOOD? .... DON STROUD
WHAT'S SO BAD ABOUT
FEELING GOOD? .... GEORGE PEPPARD†
WHAT'S SO BAD ABOUT
FEELING GOOD? .... JOHN McMARTIN
WHAT'S SO BAD ABOUT
FEELING GOOD? .... MARY TYLER MOORE

WHAT'S SO BAD ABOUT
FEELING GOOD? .... MOSES GUNN
WHAT'S SO BAD ABOUT
FEELING GOOD .... SUSAN SAINT JAMES
WHAT'S SO BAD ABOUT
FEELING GOOD? .... THELMA RITTER†
WHAT'S THE MATTER
WITH HELEN? .... AGNES MOOREHEAD†
WHAT'S THE MATTER
WITH HELEN? .... DEBBIE REYNOLDS
WHAT'S THE MATTER
WITH HELEN? .... DENNIS WEAVER
WHAT'S THE MATTER
WITH HELEN? .... MICHAEL MACLIAMMOIR†
WHAT'S THE MATTER
WITH HELEN? .... SHELLEY WINTERS
WHAT'S THE MATTER
WITH HELEN? .... TIMOTHY CAREY
WHAT'S UP, DOC? .... AUSTIN PENDLETON
WHAT'S UP, DOC? .... BARBRA STREISAND
WHAT'S UP, DOC? .... JOHN BYNER
WHAT'S UP, DOC? .... KENNETH MARS
WHAT'S UP, DOC? .... M. EMMET WALSH
WHAT'S UP, DOC? .... MADELINE KAHN
WHAT'S UP, DOC? .... MICHAEL MURPHY
WHAT'S UP, DOC? .... RANDY QUAID
WHAT'S UP, DOC? .... RYAN O'NEAL
WHAT'S UP, DOC? .... SORRELL BOOKE
WHAT'S UP, TIGER LILY? .... LOUISE LASSER
WHAT'S UP, TIGER LILY? .... WOODY ALLEN
WHE ME? (TF) .... LENKA PETERSON
WHEELER AND MURDOCH (TF) .... DIANE BAKER
WHEELER DEALERS, THE .... JAMES GARNER
WHEELER DEALERS, THE .... JOHN ASTIN
WHEELS (MS) .... BLAIR BROWN
WHEELS (MS) .... JOHN BECK
WHEELS (MS) .... LISA EILBACHER
WHEELS OF TERROR .... DAVID CARRADINE
WHEELS OF TERROR (CTF) .... JOANNA CASSIDY
WHEN A FELLER NEEDS
A FRIEND .... JACKIE COOPER
WHEN A MAN LOVES A WOMAN .... ANDY GARCIA
WHEN A MAN LOVES A WOMAN ... ELLEN BURSTYN
WHEN A MAN LOVES A WOMAN ...... LAUREN TOM
WHEN A MAN LOVES A WOMAN .... MEG RYAN
WHEN A MAN LOVES A WOMAN ..... TINA MAJORINO
WHEN A STRANGER CALLS ...... CAROL KANE
WHEN A STRANGER CALLS ...... CHARLES DURNING
WHEN A STRANGER
CALLS .... COLLEEN DEWHURST†
WHEN A STRANGER CALLS ...... RACHEL ROBERTS†
WHEN A STRANGER CALLS .... RON O'NEAL
WHEN A STRANGER CALLS .... TONY BECKLEY†
WHEN A STRANGER
CALLS BACK (CTF) .... CAROL KANE
WHEN A STRANGER
CALLS BACK (CTF) .... CHARLES DURNING
WHEN DREAMS
COME TRUE (TF) .... JESSICA HARPER
WHEN DREAMS COME TRUE (TF) ...... LEE HORSLEY
WHEN DREAMS
COME TRUE (TF) .... NORMA YOUNG
WHEN EIGHT BELLS TOLL .... ANTHONY HOPKINS
WHEN EIGHT BELLS TOLL .... ROBERT MORLEY
WHEN HARRY MET SALLY... .... BILLY CRYSTAL
WHEN HARRY MET SALLY... .... BRUNO KIRBY
WHEN HARRY MET SALLY... .... CARRIE FISHER
WHEN HARRY MET SALLY... ...... LISA JANE PERSKY
WHEN HARRY MET SALLY... .... MEG RYAN
WHEN HARRY MET SALLY... .... STEVEN FORD
WHEN HELL BROKE LOOSE .... CHARLES BRONSON
WHEN HE'S NOT
A STRANGER (TF) .... ANNABETH GISH
WHEN HE'S NOT
A STRANGER (TF) .... JOHN TERLESKY
WHEN HE'S NOT
A STRANGER (TF) .... KEVIN DILLON
WHEN HE'S NOT
A STRANGER (TF) .... PAUL DOOLEY
WHEN I GROW UP .... MARTHA SCOTT
WHEN I LARF .... DAVID HEMMINGS
WHEN IN ROME .... VAN JOHNSON
WHEN LADIES MEET .... GREER GARSON

This is not a list of every film ever made or every cast member, only those listed in this directory.

WHEN LADIES MEET .... JOAN CRAWFORD†
WHEN MICHAEL CALLS (TF) .... BEN GAZZARA
WHEN MICHAEL CALLS (TF) ..... ELIZABETH ASHLEY
WHEN MICHAEL CALLS (TF) ..... MICHAEL DOUGLAS
WHEN MY BABY SMILES AT ME ★ .... DAN DAILEY†
WHEN STRANGERS MARRY .... ROBERT MITCHUM
WHEN THE BOUGH
   BREAKS (TF) .... DAVID HUDDLESTON
WHEN THE BOUGH BREAKS (TF) .... JAMES NOBLE
WHEN THE BOUGH BREAKS (TF) .... KIM MIYORI
WHEN THE BOUGH
   BREAKS (TF) .... RICHARD MASUR
WHEN THE BOUGH BREAKS (TF) .... TED DANSON
WHEN THE CIRCUS
   CAME TO TOWN .... EILEEN BRENNAN
WHEN THE CIRCUS CAME
   TO TOWN .... ELIZABETH MONTGOMERY
WHEN THE LEGENDS DIE ...... FREDERIC FORREST
WHEN THE LEGENDS DIE .... LUANA ANDERS
WHEN THE LEGENDS DIE .... RICHARD WIDMARK
WHEN THE LINE
   GOES THROUGH .... MARTIN SHEEN
WHEN THE TIME COMES (TF) .... BONNIE BEDELIA
WHEN THE TIME COMES (TF) .... BRAD DAVIS†
WHEN THE WHALES CAME .... BARBARA EWING
WHEN THE WHALES CAME .... DAVID SUCHET
WHEN THE WHALES CAME .... DAVID THRELFALL
WHEN THE WHALES CAME .... HELEN MIRREN
WHEN THE WHALES CAME .... JEREMY KEMP
WHEN THE WHALES CAME .... JOHN HALLAM
WHEN THE WHALES CAME .... PAUL SCOFIELD
WHEN TIME RAN OUT .... ALEXIS KARRAS
WHEN TIME RAN OUT .... BARBARA CARRERA
WHEN TIME RAN OUT .... BURGESS MEREDITH
WHEN TIME RAN OUT .... EDWARD ALBERT
WHEN TIME RAN OUT .... ERNEST BORGNINE
WHEN TIME RAN OUT .... JACQUELINE BISSET
WHEN TIME RAN OUT .... JAMES FRANCISCUS†
WHEN TIME RAN OUT ...... NORIYUKI "PAT" MORITA
WHEN TIME RAN OUT .... PAUL NEWMAN
WHEN TIME RAN OUT .... RED BUTTONS
WHEN TIME RAN OUT .... VERONICA HAMEL
WHEN TIME RAN OUT .... WILLIAM HOLDEN†
WHEN WE WERE YOUNG (TF) .... CYNTHIA GIBB
WHEN WE WERE YOUNG (TF) ... JACE ALEXANDER
WHEN WORLDS COLLIDE .... STUART WHITMAN
WHEN YOU COMIN' BACK,
   RED RYDER? .... AUDRA LINDLEY
WHEN YOU COMIN' BACK,
   RED RYDER? .... BILL McKINNEY
WHEN YOU COMIN' BACK,
   RED RYDER? .... CANDY CLARK
WHEN YOU COMIN' BACK,
   RED RYDER? .... HAL LINDEN
WHEN YOU COMIN' BACK,
   RED RYDER? .... LEE GRANT
WHEN YOU COMIN' BACK,
   RED RYDER? .... MARJOE GORTNER
WHEN YOU COMIN' BACK,
   RED RYDER? .... PAT HINGLE
WHEN YOU COMIN' BACK,
   RED RYDER? .... PETER FIRTH
WHEN YOU COMIN' BACK,
   RED RYDER? .... STEPHANIE FARACY
WHEN YOUR
   LOVER LEAVES (TF) ...... VALERIE PERRINE
WHERE ANGELS GO...
   TROUBLE FOLLOWS .... MARY WICKES
WHERE ANGELS GO...
   TROUBLE FOLLOWS! .... MILTON BERLE
WHERE ANGELS GO...
   TROUBLE FOLLOWS! .... STELLA STEVENS
WHERE ANGELS GO...
   TROUBLE FOLLOWS! .... SUSAN SAINT JAMES
WHERE ANGELS GO...
   TROUBLE FOLLOWS! .... VAN JOHNSON
WHERE ARE THE CHILDREN? .... JILL CLAYBURGH
WHERE ARE THE
   CHILDREN? (TF) .... FREDERIC FORREST
WHERE ARE YOUR CHILDREN? ..... JACKIE COOPER
WHERE DANGER LIVES .... MAUREEN O'SULLIVAN
WHERE DANGER LIVES .... ROBERT MITCHUM

WHERE DO WE
   GO FROM HERE? .... ANTHONY QUINN
WHERE DOES IT HURT? .... HAROLD GOULD
WHERE EAGLES DARE .... CLINT EASTWOOD
WHERE EAGLES DARE .... RICHARD BURTON†
WHERE HAVE ALL THE
   PEOPLE GONE? (TF) .... KATHLEEN QUINLAN
WHERE HAVE ALL THE
   PEOPLE GONE? (TF) .... PETER GRAVES
WHERE IS PARSIFAL? .... DONALD PLEASENCE
WHERE IT'S AT .... BRENDA VACCARO
WHERE LOVE HAS GONE .... BETTE DAVIS†
WHERE LOVE HAS GONE .... JANE GREER
WHERE LOVE HAS GONE .... JOEY HEATHERTON
WHERE PIGEONS GO TO DIE (TF) .... ART CARNEY
WHERE PIGEONS
   GO TO DIE (TF) .... CLIFF DE YOUNG
WHERE PIGEONS
   GO TO DIE (TF) .... MICHAEL LANDON†
WHERE SLEEPING DOGS LIE .... JOAN CHEN
WHERE THE BOYS ARE .... GEORGE HAMILTON
WHERE THE BOYS ARE .... PAULA PRENTISS
WHERE THE
   BOYS ARE '84 .... CHRISTOPHER McDONALD
WHERE THE
   BOYS ARE '84 .... LYNN-HOLLY JOHNSON
WHERE THE BOYS ARE '84 .... WENDY SCHAAL
WHERE THE BUFFALO ROAM .... BILL MURRAY
WHERE THE BUFFALO ROAM ...... BRUNO KIRBY
WHERE THE BUFFALO ROAM ...... CRAIG T. NELSON
WHERE THE BUFFALO ROAM .... MARK METCALF
WHERE THE BUFFALO ROAM .... PETER BOYLE
WHERE THE BUFFALO ROAM ...... R.G. ARMSTRONG
WHERE THE BUFFALO ROAM ...... RAFAEL CAMPOS
WHERE THE
   BUFFALO ROAM .... RENE AUBERJONOIS
WHERE THE DAY TAKES YOU .... ADAM BALDWIN
WHERE THE DAY TAKES YOU .... ALYSSA MILANO
WHERE THE DAY
   TAKES YOU .... BALTHAZAR GETTY
WHERE THE DAY
   TAKES YOU .... DERMOT MULRONEY
WHERE THE DAY TAKES YOU .... JAMES LE GROS
WHERE THE DAY
   TAKES YOU .... LARA FLYNN BOYLE
WHERE THE DAY TAKES YOU .... NANCY McKEON
WHERE THE DAY TAKES YOU .... PETER DOBSON
WHERE THE DAY TAKES YOU .... RACHEL TICOTIN
WHERE THE DAY TAKES YOU .... RICKI LAKE
WHERE THE DAY TAKES YOU .... SEAN ASTIN
WHERE THE DAY
   TAKES YOU .... STEPHEN TOBOLOWSKY
WHERE THE DAY TAKES YOU .... WILL SMITH
WHERE THE HEART IS .... CHRISTOPHER PLUMMER
WHERE THE HEART IS .... CRISPIN GLOVER
WHERE THE HEART IS .... DABNEY COLEMAN
WHERE THE HEART IS .... JOANNA CASSIDY
WHERE THE HEART IS .... SUZY AMIS
WHERE THE HEART IS .... UMA THURMAN
WHERE THE HELL'S
   THAT GOLD?!!? (TF) .... DELTA BURKE
WHERE THE HELL'S
   THAT GOLD?!! (TF) .... GERALD McRANEY
WHERE THE HELL'S
   THAT GOLD?!!? (TF) .... GREGORY SIERRA
WHERE THE HELL'S
   THAT GOLD?!!? (TF) .... WILLIE NELSON
WHERE THE HOT
   WIND BLOWS .... MARCELLO MASTROIANNI
WHERE THE RED
   FERN GROWS .... JAMES WHITMORE
WHERE THE RED
   FERN GROWS .... LONNY CHAPMAN
WHERE THE RIVER
   RUNS BLACK .... ALLESSANDRO RABELO
WHERE THE RIVER
   RUNS BLACK .... CASTULO GUERRA
WHERE THE RIVER
   RUNS BLACK .... CHARLES DURNING
WHERE THE RIVER
   RUNS BLACK .... CONCHATA FERRELL
WHERE THE RIVER RUNS BLACK ...... DANA DELANY

WHERE THE RIVER
   RUNS BLACK .... MARCELO RABELO
WHERE THE RIVER
   RUNS BLACK .... PETER HORTON
WHERE THE SIDEWALK ENDS .... KARL MALDEN
WHERE THE SPIES ARE .... NIGEL DAVENPORT
WHERE THERE'S A WILL ...... EDWARD WOODWARD
WHERE THERE'S LIFE .... BOB HOPE
WHERE WERE YOU WHEN THE
   LIGHTS WENT OUT? .... DORIS DAY
WHERE WERE YOU WHEN THE
   LIGHTS WENT OUT? .... PATRICK O'NEAL†
WHERE WERE YOU WHEN THE
   LIGHTS WENT OUT? .... STEVE ALLEN
WHERE'S JACK? .... FIONA LEWIS
WHERE'S POPPA? .... BARNARD HUGHES
WHERE'S POPPA? .... GEORGE SEGAL
WHERE'S POPPA? .... PAUL SORVINO
WHERE'S POPPA? .... RON LEIBMAN
WHERE'S POPPA? .... TRISH VAN DEVERE
WHERE'S POPPA? .... VINCENT GARDENIA†
WHICH WAY IS UP? .... RICHARD PRYOR
WHICH WAY TO THE FRONT? .... JERRY LEWIS
WHICH WAY TO THE FRONT? .... KAYE BALLARD
WHIFFS .... EDDIE ALBERT
WHIFFS .... ELLIOTT GOULD
WHIFFS .... JENNIFER O'NEILL
WHIFFS .... RICHARD MASUR
WHILE THE CITY SLEEPS .... VINCENT PRICE†
WHILE YOU WERE SLEEPING .... BILL PULLMAN
WHILE YOU WERE SLEEPING ... SANDRA BULLOCK
WHILE YOU WERE SLEEPING .... GLYNIS JOHNS
WHILE YOU WERE SLEEPING .... JACK WARDEN
WHILE YOU WERE SLEEPING .... MICOLE MERCURIO
WHILE YOU WERE SLEEPING .... PETER BOYLE
WHILE YOU WERE SLEEPING ..... PETER GALLAGHER
WHIP HAND, THE .... RAYMOND BURR†
WHIPLASH .... ALEXIS SMITH†
WHIRLPOOL .... JOSE FERRER†
WHISKY GALORE .... GORDAN JACKSON†
WHISPER KILLS, A (TF) ....JOE PENNY
WHISPER KILLS, A (TF) .... JUNE LOCKHART
WHISPER KILLS, A (TF) .... LONI ANDERSON
WHISPERERS, THE ★ .... EDITH EVANS†
WHISPERING GHOSTS .... MILTON BERLE
WHISPERS IN THE DARK .... ALAN ALDA
WHISPERS IN THE DARK ...... ANNABELLA SCIORRA
WHISPERS IN THE DARK ...... ANTHONY LaPAGLIA
WHISPERS IN THE DARK .... DEBORAH UNGER
WHISPERS IN THE DARK .... JAMEY SHERIDAN
WHISPERS IN THE DARK .... JILL CLAYBURGH
WHISPERS IN THE DARK .... JOHN LEGUIZAMO
WHISTLE AT EATON
   FALLS, THE .... ERNEST BORGNINE
WHISTLE AT EATON
   FALLS, THE .... LLOYD BRIDGES
WHISTLE BLOWER, THE .... GORDAN JACKSON†
WHISTLE BLOWER, THE .... JOHN GIELGUD
WHISTLE BLOWER, THE .... MICHAEL CAINE
WHISTLE BLOWER, THE .... NIGEL HAYERS
WHISTLE DOWN THE WIND .... ALAN BATES
WHISTLE DOWN THE WIND .... HAYLEY MILLS
WHISTLE STOP .... AVA GARDNER†
WHIT E ROCK (FD) .... JAMES COBURN
WHITE BANNERS .... JACKIE COOPER
WHITE BANNERS ★ .... FAY BAINTER†
WHITE BUFFALO, THE .... CHARLES BRONSON
WHITE BUFFALO, THE .... CLINT WALKER
WHITE BUFFALO, THE .... JACK WARDEN
WHITE BUFFALO, THE .... KIM NOVAK
WHITE BUFFALO, THE .... STUART WHITMAN
WHITE CHRISTMAS .... BING CROSBY†
WHITE CHRISTMAS .... DANNY KAYE†
WHITE CHRISTMAS .... DEAN JAGGER†
WHITE CHRISTMAS .... MARY WICKES
WHITE CLIFFS OF
   DOVER, THE .... ELIZABETH TAYLOR
WHITE CLIFFS OF DOVER, THE .... JUNE LOCKHART
WHITE CLIFFS OF
   DOVER, THE .... RODDY McDOWALL
WHITE CLIFFS OF DOVER, THE ...... VAN JOHNSON
WHITE DAWN, THE .... LOUIS GOSSETT JR.
WHITE DAWN, THE .... TIMOTHY BOTTOMS

WHITE DOG .... JAMESON PARKER
WHITE DOG .... KRISTY McNICHOL
WHITE FANG .... BILL MOSELY
WHITE FANG .... CLINT B. YOUNGREEN
WHITE FANG .... ETHAN HAWKE
WHITE FANG .... FRANCO NERO
WHITE FANG .... JAMES REMAR
WHITE FANG .... KLAUS MARIA BRANDAUER
WHITE FANG .... PIUS SAVAGE
WHITE FANG .... SEYMOUR CASSEL
WHITE FANG .... SUSAN HOGAN
WHITE FANG .... SUZANNE KENT
WHITE FANG 2: MYTH OF
   THE WHITE WOLF .... ALFRED MOLINA
WHITE FANG 2: MYTH OF
   THE WHITE WOLF .... CHARMAINE CRAIG
WHITE FANG 2: MYTH OF
   THE WHITE WOLF .... GEOFFREY LEWIS
WHITE FANG 2: MYTH OF
   THE WHITE WOLF .... MATTHEW COWLES
WHITE FANG 2: MYTH OF
   THE WHITE WOLF .... PAUL COEUR
WHITE FANG 2: MYTH OF
   THE WHITE WOLF .... SCOTT BAIRSTOW
WHITE FEATHER .... ROBERT WAGNER
WHITE HOT .... SALLY KIRKLAND
WHITE HUNTER,
   BLACK HEART .... ALUN ARMSTRONG
WHITE HUNTER,
   BLACK HEART .... CLINT EASTWOOD
WHITE HUNTER,
   BLACK HEART .... GEORGE DZUNDZA
WHITE HUNTER, BLACK HEART .... JEFF FAHEY
WHITE HUNTER,
   BLACK HEART .... MARISA BERENSON
WHITE LIGHTNING .... BO HOPKINS
WHITE LIGHTNING .... BURT REYNOLDS
WHITE LIGHTNING .... DIANE LADD
WHITE LIGHTNING .... LOUISE LATHAM
WHITE LIGHTNING .... MATT CLARK
WHITE LIGHTNING .... NED BEATTY
WHITE LIGHTNING .... R.G. ARMSTRONG
WHITE LINE FEVER .... JAN-MICHAEL VINCENT
WHITE LINE FEVER .... KAY LENZ
WHITE LINE FEVER .... R.G. ARMSTRONG
WHITE LIONS, THE .... MICHAEL YORK
WHITE MAMA (TF) .... ANN RAMSEY†
WHITE MAMA (TF) .... EILEEN HECKART
WHITE MEN CAN'T JUMP .... ROSIE PEREZ
WHITE MEN CAN'T JUMP .... TYRA FERRELL
WHITE MEN CAN'T JUMP .... WESLEY SNIPES
WHITE MEN CAN'T JUMP .... WOODY HARRELSON
WHITE MILE (CTF) .... FIONNULA FLANAGAN
WHITE MILE (CTF) .... PETER GALLAGHER
WHITE MILE (CTF) .... ROBERT LOGGIA
WHITE MISCHIEF .... CHARLES DANCE
WHITE MISCHIEF .... GRETA SCACCHI
WHITE MISCHIEF .... JOHN HURT
WHITE MISCHIEF .... JOSS ACKLAND
WHITE MISCHIEF .... SARAH MILES
WHITE NIGHTS .... GERALDINE PAGE†
WHITE NIGHTS .... GREGORY HINES
WHITE NIGHTS .... HELEN MIRREN
WHITE NIGHTS .... ISABELLA ROSSELLINI
WHITE NIGHTS .... JERZY SKOLIMOWSKI
WHITE NIGHTS .... MARCELLO MASTROIANNI
WHITE NIGHTS .... MARIA SCHELL
WHITE NIGHTS .... MIKHAIL BARYSHNIKOV
WHITE OF THE EYE .... ART EVANS
WHITE OF THE EYE .... CATHY MORIARTY
WHITE OF THE EYE .... DAVID KEITH
WHITE PALACE .... EILEEN BRENNAN
WHITE PALACE .... JAMES SPADER
WHITE PALACE .... KATHY BATES
WHITE PALACE .... SUSAN SARANDON
WHITE SANDS .... M. EMMET WALSH
WHITE
   SANDS .... MARY ELIZABETH MASTRANTONIO
WHITE SANDS .... MICKEY ROURKE
WHITE SANDS .... MIMI ROGERS
WHITE SANDS .... SAMUEL L. JACKSON
WHITE SANDS .... WILLEM DAFOE

WHITE SISTER .... SOPHIA LOREN
WHITE SISTER, THE .... HELEN HAYES
WHITE SISTER, THE .... LILLIAN GISH†
WHITE STAR .... DENNIS HOPPER
WHITE TOWER, THE .... LLOYD BRIDGES
WHITE VOICES .... ANOUK AIMEE
WHITE WATER SUMMER .... KEVIN BACON
WHITE WATER SUMMER .... MATT ADLER
WHITE WITCH DOCTOR .... ROBERT MITCHUM
WHITE WITCH DOCTOR .... TIMOTHY CAREY
WHO? .... ELLIOTT GOULD
WHO AM I THIS TIME? (TF) .... SUSAN SARANDON
WHO DARES WINS .... EDWARD WOODWARD
WHO DARES WINS .... JUDY DAVIS
WHO DARES WINS .... RICHARD WIDMARK
WHO DONE IT? .... MARY WICKES
WHO FEARS THE DEVIL .... R.G. ARMSTRONG
WHO FEARS THE DEVIL .... SEVERN DARDEN
WHO FEARS THE DEVIL .... SUSAN STRASBERG
WHO FRAMED ROGER RABBIT .... AMY IRVING
WHO FRAMED ROGER RABBIT .... BOB HOSKINS
WHO FRAMED
   ROGER RABBIT .... CHARLES FLEISCHER
WHO FRAMED
   ROGER RABBIT .... CHRISTOPHER LLOYD
WHO FRAMED ROGER RABBIT .... JOANNA CASSIDY
WHO FRAMED
   ROGER RABBIT .... KATHLEEN TURNER
WHO FRAMED ROGER RABBIT .... MEL BLANC†
WHO FRAMED ROGER RABBIT .... STUBBY KAYE
WHO GETS THE
   FRIENDS? (TF) .... JAMES FARENTINO
WHO GETS THE FRIENDS? (TF) .... JILL CLAYBURGH
WHO GETS THE
   FRIENDS? (TF) .... LEIGH TAYLOR-YOUNG
WHO GETS THE FRIENDS? (TF) .... LUCIE ARNAZ
WHO HAS SEEN THE WIND? .... JOSE FERRER†
WHO IS HARRY KELLERMAN, AND WHY
   IS HE SAYING THOSE TERRIBLE
   THINGS ABOUT ME? ○ .... BARBARA HARRIS
WHO IS HARRY KELLERMAN AND WHY
   IS HE SAYING THOSE TERRIBLE
   THINGS ABOUT ME? .... DUSTIN HOFFMAN
WHO IS HARRY KELLERMAN AND WHY
   IS HE SAYING THOSE TERRIBLE
   THINGS ABOUT ME? .... JACK WARDEN
WHO IS JULIA? (TF) .... BERT REMSEN
WHO IS JULIA? (TF) .... JAMESON PARKER
WHO IS JULIA? (TF) .... JONATHAN BANKS
WHO IS JULIA? (TF) .... MARE WINNINGHAM
WHO IS KILLING THE GREAT
   CHEFS OF EUROPE? .... GEORGE SEGAL
WHO IS KILLING THE GREAT
   CHEFS OF EUROPE? .... JACQUELINE BISSET
WHO IS KILLING THE GREAT
   CHEFS OF EUROPE? .... JEAN-PIERRE CASSEL
WHO IS KILLING THE GREAT
   CHEFS OF EUROPE? .... JOSS ACKLAND
WHO IS KILLING THE GREAT
   CHEFS OF EUROPE? .... ROBERT MORLEY
WHO IS KILLING THE
   STUNTMEN? .... JOANNA CASSIDY
WHO IS KILLING THE
   STUNTMEN? .... RAY SHARKEY†
WHO IS KILLING THE
   STUNTMENT? .... ROBERT FORSTER
WHO IS THE BLACK DAHLIA? (TF) ...... DONNA MILLS
WHO IS THE BLACK
   DAHLIA? (TF) .... EFREM ZIMBALIST JR.
WHO IS THE BLACK DAHLIA? (TF) ...... LUCIE ARNAZ
WHO IS THE BLACK
   DAHLIA? (TF) .... MERCEDES McCAMBRIDGE
WHO IS THE BLACK DAHLIA? (TF) .... TOM BOSLEY
WHO IS THE MAN? .... JOHN GIELGUD
WHO KILLED MARY
   WHAT'S 'ERNAME? .... SAM WATERSTON
WHO KILLED MARY
   WHAT'S'ER NAME? .... RED BUTTONS
WHO KILLED MARY
   WHAT'S'ER NAME? .... SYLVIA MILES
WHO KILLED TEDDY BEAR? .... ELAINE STRITCH
WHO MURDERED
   JOY MORGAN? (TF) .... KIM BASINGER

WHO SAYS I CAN'T RIDE
   A RAINBOW? .... JACK KLUGMAN
WHO SLEW AUNTIE ROO? .... MARK LESTER
WHO SLEW AUNTIE ROO? .... PAT HEYWOOD
WHO SLEW AUNTIE ROO? .... SHELLEY WINTERS
WHO WAS THAT LADY? .... DEAN MARTIN
WHO WAS THAT LADY? .... JAMES WHITMORE
WHO WAS THAT LADY? .... JANET LEIGH
WHO WAS THAT LADY? .... TONY CURTIS
WHO WILL LOVE
   MY CHILDREN? (TF) .... ANN-MARGRET
WHO WILL LOVE
   MY CHILDREN? (TF) .... FREDERIC FORREST
WHO'S AFRAID OF
   VIRGINIA WOOLF? ★ .... RICHARD BURTON†
WHO'S HARRY CRUMB? .... VALRI BROMFIELD
WHOLLY MOSES .... DOM DeLUISE
WHOLLY MOSES .... DUDLEY MOORE
WHOLLY MOSES .... JAMES COCO†
WHOLLY MOSES .... JOHN RITTER
WHOLLY MOSES .... LARAINE NEWMAN
WHOLLY MOSES .... MADELINE KAHN
WHOLLY MOSES .... PAUL SAND
WHOLLY MOSES .... RICHARD PRYOR
WHOOPEE BOYS, THE .... ANDY BUMATAI
WHOOPEE BOYS, THE .... DAN O'HERLIHY
WHOOPEE BOYS, THE .... DENHOLM ELLIOTT†
WHOOPEE BOYS, THE .... EDDIE DEEZEN
WHOOPEE BOYS, THE .... MICHAEL O'KEEFE
WHOOPEE BOYS, THE .... PAUL RODRIGUEZ
WHORE .... THERESA RUSSELL
WHOSE LIFE IS IT ANYWAY? .... BOB BALABAN
WHOSE LIFE IS IT ANYWAY? .... CHRISTINE LAHTI
WHOSE LIFE IS IT ANYWAY? .... JANET EILBER
WHOSE LIFE IS
   IT ANYWAY? .... RICHARD DREYFUSS
WHO'LL SAVE OUR
   CHILDREN? (TF) .... SHIRLEY JONES
WHO'LL STOP THE RAIN .... ANTHONY ZERBE
WHO'LL STOP THE RAIN ...... MICHAEL MORIARTY
WHO'LL STOP THE RAIN .... NICK NOLTE
WHO'LL STOP THE RAIN .... RAY SHARKEY†
WHO'LL STOP THE RAIN .... RICHARD MASUR
WHO'LL STOP THE RAIN .... TUESDAY WELD
WHO'S AFRAID OF
   VIRGINIA WOOLF? ★★ .... ELIZABETH TAYLOR
WHO'S AFRAID OF
   VIRGINIA WOOLF? ○ .... GEORGE SEGAL
WHO'S AFRAID OF
   VIRGINIA WOOLF? ○○ .... SANDY DENNIS†
WHO'S BEEN SLEEPING
   IN MY BED? .... CAROL BURNETT
WHO'S BEEN SLEEPING
   IN MY BED? .... DEAN MARTIN
WHO'S BEEN SLEEPING
   IN MY BED? .... ELIZABETH MONTGOMERY
WHO'S BEEN SLEEPING
   IN MY BED? .... JILL ST. JOHN
WHO'S BEEN SLEEPING
   IN MY BED? .... MARTIN BALSAM
WHO'S GOT THE ACTION? .... DEAN MARTIN
WHO'S GOT THE ACTION? .... EDDIE ALBERT
WHO'S GOT THE ACTION? .... LANA TURNER
WHO'S GOT THE ACTION? .... NITA TALBOT
WHO'S GOT THE ACTION? .... WALTER MATTHAU
WHO'S HARRY CRUMB? .... ANNIE POTTS
WHO'S HARRY CRUMB? .... BARRY CORBIN
WHO'S HARRY CRUMB? .... JAMES BELUSHI
WHO'S HARRY CRUMB? .... JEFFREY JONES
WHO'S HARRY CRUMB? .... JOHN CANDY†
WHO'S HARRY CRUMB? .... SHAWNEE SMITH
WHO'S HARRY CRUMB? .... TIM THOMERSON
WHO'S MINDING THE MINT? .... JAMIE FARR
WHO'S MINDING THE MINT? .... MILTON BERLE
WHO'S MINDING THE STORE? .... JERRY LEWIS
WHO'S MINDING THE STORE? .... JILL ST. JOHN
WHO'S MINDING THE STORE? .... RAY WALSTON
WHO'S THAT GIRL? .... GRIFFIN DUNNE
WHO'S THAT GIRL? .... MADONNA
WHO'S THAT KNOCKING
   AT MY DOOR? .... HARVEY KEITEL
WHY .... JEANNIE BERLIN

This is not a list of every film ever made or every cast member, only those listed in this directory.

WHY BOTHER TO KNOCK ... DAME JUDITH ANDERSON†
WHY ME? ... GLYNNIS O'CONNOR
WHY SHOOT THE TEACHER? ... BUD CORT
WHY SHOOT THE TEACHER? ... SAMANTHA EGGAR
WHY WOULD I LIE? ... SEVERN DARDEN
WHY WOULD I LIE? ... TREAT WILLIAMS
WICHITA ... LLOYD BRIDGES
WICHITA ... VERA MILES
WICKED LADY, THE ... ALAN BATES
WICKED LADY, THE ... DENHOLM ELLIOTT†
WICKED LADY, THE ... FAYE DUNAWAY
WICKED LADY, THE ... GLYNIS BARBER
WICKED LADY, THE ... JOHN GIELGUD
WICKED LADY, THE ... OLIVER TOBIAS
WICKED LADY, THE ... PRUNELLA SCALES
WICKED STEPMOTHER ... BARBARA CARRERA
WICKED STEPMOTHER ... BETTE DAVIS†
WICKED STEPMOTHER ... COLLEEN CAMP
WICKED STEPMOTHER ... DAVID RASCHE
WICKED STEPMOTHER ... LIONEL STANDER
WICKED STEPMOTHER ... TOM BOSLEY
WICKER MAN, THE ... BRITT EKLAND
WICKER MAN, THE ... EDWARD WOODWARD
WIDE OPEN FACES ... JANE WYMAN
WIDE SARGASSO SEA ... CLAUDIA ROBINSON
WIDE SARGASSO SEA ... KARINA LOMBARD
WIDE SARGASSO SEA ... MARTINE BESWICKE
WIDE SARGASSO SEA ... MICHAEL YORK
WIDE SARGASSO SEA ... NATHANIEL PARKER
WIDE SARGASSO SEA ... RACHEL WARD
WIDE SARGASSO SEA ... ROWENA KING
WIDOW (TF) ... MICHAEL LEARNED
WIDOWS' NEST ... LILA KEDROVA
WIDOWS' PEAK ... ADRIAN DUNBAR
WIDOWS' PEAK ... JIM BROADBENT
WIDOWS' PEAK ... JOAN PLOWRIGHT
WIDOWS' PEAK ... MIA FARROW
WIDOWS' PEAK ... NATASHA RICHARDSON
WIFE OF MONTE CRISTO, THE ... EVA GABOR
WIFE VS. SECRETARY ... JAMES STEWART
WILBY CONSPIRACY, THE ... MICHAEL CAINE
WILBY CONSPIRACY, THE ... NICOL WILLIAMSON
WILBY CONSPIRACY, THE ... SIDNEY POITIER
WILD AND THE WILLING, THE ... JOHN HURT
WILD AND THE WILLING, THE ... SAMANTHA EGGAR
WILD AND WONDERFUL ... TONY CURTIS
WILD ANGELS, THE ... BRUCE DERN
WILD ANGELS, THE ... DIANE LADD
WILD ANGELS, THE ... MICHAEL J. POLLARD
WILD ANGELS, THE ... PETER FONDA
WILD AT HEART ... CRISPIN GLOVER
WILD AT HEART ... GRACE ZABRISKIE
WILD AT HEART ... HARRY DEAN STANTON
WILD AT HEART ... ISABELLA ROSSELLINI
WILD AT HEART ... LAURA DERN
WILD AT HEART ... NICOLAS CAGE
WILD AT HEART ... SHERILYN FENN
WILD AT HEART ... WILLEM DAFOE
WILD AT HEART ✪ ... DIANE LADD
WILD BILL ... BRUCE DERN
WILD BILL ... CHRISTINA APPLEGATE
WILD BILL ... DAVID ARQUETTE
WILD BILL ... DIANE LANE
WILD BILL ... ELLEN BARKIN
WILD BILL ... JAMES GAMMON
WILD BILL ... JAMES REMAR
WILD BILL ... JEFF BRIDGES
WILD BILL ... JOHN HURT
WILD BILL ... KEITH CARRADINE
WILD BILL ... MARJOE GORTNER
WILD BILL ... ROBERT KNOTT
WILD BRIAN KENT ... RALPH BELLAMY†
WILD BUNCH, THE ... BEN JOHNSON
WILD BUNCH, THE ... BO HOPKINS
WILD BUNCH, THE ... ERNEST BORGNINE
WILD BUNCH, THE ... L. Q. JONES
WILD COUNTRY, THE ... RON HOWARD
WILD COUNTRY, THE ... STEVE FORREST
WILD COUNTRY, THE ... VERA MILES
WILD DUCK, THE ... JEREMY IRONS
WILD DUCK, THE ... LIV ULLMANN
WILD FOR KICKS ... SHIRLEY ANNE FIELD
WILD GEESE II ... BARBARA CARRERA
WILD GEESE II ... ROBERT WEBBER
WILD GEESE II ... SCOTT GLENN
WILD GEESE, THE ... JEFF COREY
WILD GEESE, THE ... RICHARD HARRIS
WILD GEESE, THE ... ROGER MOORE
WILD GIRL ... RALPH BELLAMY†
WILD HARVEST ... DOROTHY LAMOUR
WILD HARVEST ... KATHLEEN FREEMAN
WILD HEART, THE ... JENNIFER JONES
WILD HEARTS CAN'T BE BROKEN ... CLIFF ROBERTSON
WILD HEARTS CAN'T BE BROKEN ... DYLAN KUSSMAN
WILD HEARTS CAN'T BE BROKEN ... FRANK RENZULLI
WILD HEARTS CAN'T BE BROKEN ... GABRIELLE ANWAR
WILD HEARTS CAN'T BE BROKEN ... LISA NORMAN
WILD HEARTS CAN'T BE BROKEN ... MICHAEL SCHOEFFLING
WILD HERITAGE ... MAUREEN O'SULLIVAN
WILD HERITAGE ... TROY DONAHUE
WILD HORSE HANK ... LINDA BLAIR
WILD HORSES (TF) ... BEN JOHNSON
WILD HORSES (TF) ... DAVID ANDREWS
WILD HORSES (TF) ... KENNY ROGERS
WILD HORSES (TF) ... PAM DAWBER
WILD HORSES (TF) ... RICHARD MASUR
WILD IN THE COUNTRY ... ELVIS PRESLEY†
WILD IN THE COUNTRY ... HOPE LANGE
WILD IN THE COUNTRY ... JOHN IRELAND
WILD IN THE COUNTRY ... MILLIE PERKINS
WILD IN THE COUNTRY ... TUESDAY WELD
WILD IN THE SKY ... GEORG STANFORD BROWN
WILD IN THE STREETS ... HAL HOLBROOK
WILD IN THE STREETS ... MILLIE PERKINS
WILD IN THE STREETS ... RICHARD PRYOR
WILD IN THE STREETS ... SHELLEY WINTERS
WILD IS THE WIND ... ANTHONY (TONY) FRANCIOSA
WILD IS THE WIND ★ ... ANNA MAGNANI†
WILD IS THE WIND ★ ... ANTHONY QUINN
WILD LIFE, THE ... ERIC STOLTZ
WILD LIFE, THE ... HART BOCHNER
WILD LIFE, THE ... LEA THOMPSON
WILD LIFE, THE ... RANDY QUAID
WILD NORTH, THE ... CYD CHARISSE
WILD ON THE BEACH ... CHER
WILD ON THE BEACH ... SONNY BONO
WILD ONE, THE ... MARLON BRANDO
WILD ORCHID ... ASSUMPTA SERNA
WILD ORCHID ... CARRE OTIS
WILD ORCHID ... JACQUELINE BISSET
WILD ORCHID ... MICKEY ROURKE
WILD PAIR, THE ... BEAU BRIDGES
WILD PAIR, THE ... LLOYD BRIDGES
WILD PAIR, THE ... RAYMOND ST. JACQUES
WILD PALMS (MS) ... ANGIE DICKINSON
WILD PALMS (MS) ... BEBE NEUWIRTH
WILD PALMS (MS) ... BEN SAVAGE
WILD PALMS (MS) ... BOB GUNTON
WILD PALMS (MS) ... BRAD DOURIF
WILD PALMS (MS) ... CHARLES HALLAHAN
WILD PALMS (MS) ... DANA DELANY
WILD PALMS (MS) ... DAVID WARNER
WILD PALMS (MS) ... ERNIE HUDSON
WILD PALMS (MS) ... JAMES BELUSHI
WILD PALMS (MS) ... KIM CATTRALL
WILD PALMS (MS) ... NICK MANCUSO
WILD PALMS (MS) ... ROBERT LOGGIA
WILD PALMS (MS) ... ROBERT MORSE
WILD PARTY, THE ... ANTHONY QUINN
WILD PARTY, THE ... NEHEMIAH PERSOFF
WILD PARTY, THE ... PERRY KING
WILD PARTY, THE ... RAQUEL WELCH
WILD PARTY, THE ... ROYAL DANO
WILD RACERS, THE ... TALIA SHIRE
WILD RIDE, THE ... JACK NICHOLSON
WILD RIVER ... ALBERT SALMI†
WILD RIVER ... BRUCE DERN
WILD ROOTS OF LOVE ... CATHERINE DENEUVE
WILD ROVERS ... JAMES OLSON
WILD ROVERS ... JOE DON BAKER
WILD ROVERS ... KARL MALDEN
WILD ROVERS ... MOSES GUNN
WILD ROVERS ... RACHEL ROBERTS†
WILD ROVERS ... RYAN O'NEAL
WILD ROVERS ... TOM SKERRITT
WILD ROVERS ... WILLIAM HOLDEN†
WILD STRAWBERRIES ... BIBI ANDERSSON
WILD TEXAS WIND (TF) ... DOLLY PARTON
WILD THING ... ROBERT DAVI
WILD TIMES (TF) ... BRUCE BOXLEITNER
WILD TIMES (TF) ... DENNIS HOPPER
WILD TIMES (TF) ... SAM ELLIOTT
WILD WILD PLANET ... FRANCO NERO
WILD, WILD WEST REVISITED, THE (TF) ... PAUL WILLIAMS
WILD, WILD WEST REVISITED, THE (TF) ... ROBERT CONRAD
WILD WOMEN OF CHASTITY GULCH, THE (TF) ... JOAN COLLINS
WILD WOMEN OF CHASTITY GULCH, THE (TF) ... PAMELA BELLWOOD-WHEELER
WILD WOMEN OF CHASTITY GULCH, THE (TF) ... PRISCILLA BARNES
WILDCATS ... BRANDY GOLD
WILDCATS ... BRUCE McGILL
WILDCATS ... GOLDIE HAWN
WILDCATS ... JAMES KEACH
WILDCATS ... JAN HOOKS
WILDCATS ... M. EMMET WALSH
WILDCATS ... MYKELTI WILLIAMSON
WILDCATS ... NICK CORRI
WILDCATS ... NIPSEY RUSSELL
WILDCATS ... ROBYN LIVELY
WILDCATS ... SWOOSIE KURTZ
WILDCATS ... TAB THACKER
WILDCATS ... WESLEY SNIPES
WILDCATS ... WOODY HARRELSON
WILDCATS OF ST. TRINIAN'S, THE ... THORLEY WALTERS†
WILDER NAPALM ... ARLISS HOWARD
WILDER NAPALM ... DEBRA WINGER
WILDER NAPALM ... DENNIS QUAID
WILDER NAPALM ... JIM VARNEY
WILDER NAPALM ... M. EMMET WALSH
WILDROSE ... LISA EICHHORN
WILDSIDE, THE ... CHRISTOPHER WALKEN
WILDSIDE, THE ... JOAN CHEN
WILL: G. GORDON LIDDY (TF) ... ROBERT CONRAD
WILL JAMES' SAND ... RORY CALHOUN
WILL PENNY ... ANTHONY ZERBE
WILL PENNY ... BEN JOHNSON
WILL PENNY ... BRUCE DERN
WILL PENNY ... CHARLTON HESTON
WILL PENNY ... DONALD PLEASENCE
WILL PENNY ... JOAN HACKETT†
WILL PENNY ... LEE MAJORS
WILL PENNY ... MATT CLARK
WILL SUCCESS SPOIL ROCK HUNTER? ... HENRY JONES
WILL SUCCESS SPOIL ROCK HUNTER? ... TONY RANDALL
WILL THERE REALLY BE A MORNING? (TF) ... JOHN HEARD
WILL THERE REALLY BE A MORNING? (TF) ... LEE GRANT
WILL THERE REALLY BE A MORNING? (TF) ... ROYAL DANO
WILL THERE REALLY BE A MORNING? (TF) ... SUSAN BLAKELY
WILLA ... DIANE LADD
WILLA (TF) ... DEBORAH RAFFIN
WILLARD ... BRUCE DAVISON
WILLARD ... ERNEST BORGNINE
WILLARD ... MICHAEL DANTE
WILLARD ... SONDRA LOCKE
WILLIE AND PHIL ... LAURENCE FISHBURNE
WILLIE AND PHIL ... MARGOT KIDDER
WILLIE AND PHIL ... MICHAEL ONTKEAN
WILLIE AND PHIL ... RAY SHARKEY†

† after an actor's name denotes deceased.

WILLIE DYNAMITE .... THALMUS RASULALA
WILLOW .... BILLY BARTY
WILLOW .... JEAN MARSH
WILLOW .... JOANNE WHALLEY-KILMER
WILLOW .... VAL KILMER
WILLOW .... WARWICK DAVIS
WILLY II: THE ADVENTURE
    HOME .... AUGUST SCHELLENBERG
WILLY II: THE ADVENTURE
    HOME .... ELIZABETH PENA
WILLY II: THE ADVENTURE
    HOME .... FRANCIS CAPRA
WILLY II: THE ADVENTURE
    HOME .... JASON JAMES RICHTER
WILLY II: THE ADVENTURE
    HOME .... JAYNE ATKINSON
WILLY II: THE ADVENTURE HOME ...... JON TENNEY
WILLY II: THE ADVENTURE
    HOME .... M. EMMET WALSH
WILLY II: THE ADVENTURE
    HOME .... MARY KATE SCHELLHARDT
WILLY II: THE ADVENTURE
    HOME .... MICHAEL MADSEN
WILLY II: THE ADVENTURE HOME .... STEVE KAHAN
WILLY WONKA AND THE
    CHOCOLATE FACTORY .... GENE WILDER
WILLY WONKA AND THE
    CHOCOLATE FACTORY .... JACK ALBERTSON†
WILMA (TF) .... CICELY TYSON
WILMA (TF) .... DENZEL WASHINGTON
WILSON .... GERALDINE FITZGERALD
WILSON .... VINCENT PRICE†
WIN, PLACE OR STEAL .... DEAN STOCKWELL
WIN, PLACE OR STEAL .... RUSS TAMBLYN
WINCHESTER 73 .... JAMES STEWART
WINCHESTER 73 .... ROCK HUDSON†
WINCHESTER '73 .... SHELLEY WINTERS
WINCHESTER '73 .... TONY CURTIS
WIND .... CLIFF ROBERTSON
WIND .... JACK THOMPSON
WIND .... JENNIFER GREY
WIND .... MATTHEW MODINE
WIND .... REBECCA MILLER
WIND .... STELLAN SKARSGARD
WIND, THE .... LILLIAN GISH†
WIND ACROSS THE EVERGLADES .... BURL IVES
WIND ACROSS THE
    EVERGLADES .... CHRISTOPHER PLUMMER
WIND ACROSS THE EVERGLADES .... PETER FALK
WIND AND THE LION, THE .... BRIAN KEITH
WIND AND THE LION, THE .... CANDICE BERGEN
WIND AND THE LION, THE .... SEAN CONNERY
WIND OF CHANGE, THE .... DAVID HEMMINGS
WINDMILLS OF
    THE GODS (MS) .... CHRISTOPHER CAZENOVE
WINDMILLS OF THE GODS (MS) .... DAVID AYKROYD
WINDMILLS OF THE GODS (MS) .... FRANCO NERO
WINDMILLS OF THE GODS (MS) .... JACLYN SMITH
WINDMILLS OF
    THE GODS (MS) .... JEAN-PIERRE AUMONT
WINDMILLS OF
    THE GODS (MS) .... ROBERT WAGNER
WINDMILLS OF THE GODS (MS) .... RUBY DEE
WINDOW, THE .... BARBARA HALE
WINDOWS .... ELIZABETH ASHLEY
WINDOWS .... TALIA SHIRE
WINDS OF WAR, THE (MS) .... ALI MacGRAW
WINDS OF WAR, THE (MS) .... BEN HAMMER
WINDS OF WAR, THE (MS) .... DAVID DUKES
WINDS OF
    WAR, THE (MS) ...... JAN-MICHAEL VINCENT
WINDS OF WAR, THE (MS) .... JEREMY KEMP
WINDS OF WAR, THE (MS) .... LISA EILBACHER
WINDS OF WAR, THE (MS) .... PETER GRAVES
WINDS OF WAR, THE (MS) .... RALPH BELLAMY†
WINDS OF WAR, THE (MS) .... ROBERT MITCHUM
WINDS OF WAR, THE (MS) .... TOPOL
WINDS OF WAR, THE (MS) .... VICTORIA TENNANT
WINDY CITY .... JOHN SHEA
WINDY CITY .... KATE CAPSHAW
WING AND A PRAYER .... DON AMECHE†
WING AND A PRAYER .... HARRY MORGAN

WING AND A PRAYER .... RICHARD JAECKEL
WINGED SERPENT, THE .... MICHAEL MORIARTY
WINGED SERPENT, THE ...... RICHARD ROUNDTREE
WINGED VICTORY .... KARL MALDEN
WINGED VICTORY .... RED BUTTONS
WINGS OF COURAGE .... CRAIG SHEFFER
WINGS OF COURAGE .... ELIZABETH McGOVERN
WINGS OF COURAGE .... TOM HULCE
WINGS OF COURAGE .... VAL KILMER
WINGS OF DESIRE .... PETER FALK
WINGS OF EAGLES, THE .... MAUREEN O'HARA
WINGS OF FIRE (TF) .... RALPH BELLAMY†
WINGS OF FIRE (TF) .... SUZANNE PLESHETTE
WINGS OF THE NAVY .... OLIVIA DE HAVILLAND
WINNER NEVER QUITS, A (TF) .... DAVID HAID
WINNER NEVER QUITS, A (TF) .... G.W. BAILEY
WINNER NEVER QUITS, A (TF) ... KEITH CARRADINE
WINNER NEVER
    QUITS, A (TF) .... MARE WINNINGHAM
WINNER TAKE ALL (TF) .... LAURENCE LUCKINBILL
WINNER TAKE ALL (TF) .... SHIRLEY JONES
WINNERS OF
    THE WILDERNESS .... JOAN CRAWFORD†
WINNIE (TF) .... BARBARA BARRIE
WINNIE (TF) .... MEREDITH BAXTER
WINNIE THE POOH (AF) .... STERLING HOLLOWAY†
WINNING .... CLU GULAGER
WINNING .... JOANNE WOODWARD
WINNING .... PAUL NEWMAN
WINNING .... RICHARD THOMAS
WINNING .... ROBERT WAGNER
WINNING TEAM, THE .... DORIS DAY
WINNING TEAM, THE .... RONALD REAGAN
WINSTON CHURCHILL: THE WILDERNESS
    YEARS (TF) .... EDWARD WOODWARD
WINTER HAWK .... WOODY STRODE
WINTER KILL (TF) .... ANDY GRIFFITH
WINTER KILLS .... ANTHONY PERKINS†
WINTER KILLS .... ELI WALLACH
WINTER KILLS .... ELIZABETH TAYLOR
WINTER KILLS .... JEFF BRIDGES
WINTER MEETING .... BETTE DAVIS†
WINTER OF OUR
    DISCONTENT, THE (TF) .... DONALD SUTHERLAND
WINTER OF OUR
    DISCONTENT, THE (TF) .... E. G. MARSHALL
WINTER OF OUR
    DISCONTENT, THE (TF) .... MICHAEL V. GAZZO
WINTER OF OUR
    DISCONTENT, THE (TF) .... TERI GARR
WINTER OF OUR DREAMS .... BRYON BROWN
WINTER OF OUR DREAMS .... JUDY DAVIS
WINTER PEOPLE .... KELLY McGILLIS
WINTER PEOPLE .... KURT RUSSELL
WINTER PEOPLE .... LLOYD BRIDGES
WINTER PEOPLE .... MITCHELL RYAN
WINTERHAWK .... MICHAEL DANTE
WINTERSET .... BURGESS MEREDITH
WIRED .... ALEX ROCCO
WIRED .... GARY GROOMES
WIRED .... J. T. WALSH
WIRED .... JERE BURNS
WIRED .... LUCINDA JENNEY
WIRED .... MICHAEL CHIKLIS
WIRED .... PATTI D'ARBANVILLE
WIRED .... RAY SHARKEY†
WIRED TO KILL .... MERRITT BUTRICK†
WISDOM .... CHARLIE SHEEN
WISDOM .... DEMI MOORE
WISDOM .... EMILIO ESTEVEZ
WISDOM .... ERNIE BROWN
WISDOM .... SANTOS MORALES
WISDOM .... TOM SKERRITT
WISDOM .... VERONICA CARTWRIGHT
WISE BLOOD .... AMY WRIGHT
WISE BLOOD .... BRAD DOURIF
WISE BLOOD .... HARRY DEAN STANTON
WISE BLOOD .... NED BEATTY
WISE GUYS .... DANNY DEVITO
WISE GUYS .... HARVEY KEITEL
WISE GUYS .... JOE PISCOPO
WISE GUYS .... JULIE BOYASSO†

WISE GUYS .... LOU ALBANO
WISE GUYS .... PATTI LUPONE
WISEGUY (TF) .... KEN WAHL
WISEGUYS .... DAN HEDAYA
WISH YOU WERE HERE .... EMILY LLOYD
WISHBONE CUTTER .... SONDRA LOCKE
WITCH WHO CAME FROM
    THE SEA, THE .... MILLIE PERKINS
WITCHCRAFT .... JACK HEDLEY
WITCHERY .... LINDA BLAIR
WITCHES, THE .... ALEC McCOWEN
WITCHES, THE .... ANJELICA HUSTON
WITCHES, THE .... CLINT EASTWOOD
WITCHES, THE .... JIM CARTER
WITCHES, THE .... MAE ZETTERLING†
WITCHES' BREW .... RICHARD BENJAMIN
WITCHES OF EASTWICK, THE .... CHER
WITCHES OF EASTWICK, THE ..... JACK NICHOLSON
WITCHES OF
    EASTWICK, THE .... MICHELLE PFEIFFER
WITCHES OF
    EASTWICK, THE .... SUSAN SARANDON
WITCHES OF
    EASTWICK, THE .... VERONICA CARTWRIGHT
WITCHFINDER GENERAL .... VINCENT PRICE†
WITCHING, THE .... MICHAEL ONTKEAN
WITH A SONG IN MY HEART .... MAX SHOWALTER
WITH A SONG IN MY HEART .... ROBERT WAGNER
WITH A SONG IN MY HEART .... RORY CALHOUN
WITH A SONG IN
    MY HEART ★ .... SUSAN HAYWARD†
WITH A SONG IN MY HEART ○ ..... THELMA RITTER†
WITH HONORS .... BRENDAN FRASER
WITH HONORS .... GORE VIDAL
WITH HONORS .... JOE PESCI
WITH HONORS .... JOSH HAMILTON
WITH HONORS .... MOIRA KELLY
WITH HONORS .... PATRICK DEMPSEY
WITH INTENT
    TO KILL (TF) .... CATHERINE MARY STEWART
WITH INTENT TO KILL (TF) .... HOLLY HUNTER
WITH INTENT TO KILL (TF) .... KARL MALDEN
WITH INTENT TO KILL (TF) .... PAUL SORVINO
WITH INTENT TO KILL (TF) .... SHIRLEY KNIGHT
WITH SIX YOU GET EGG ROLL .... JAMIE FARR
WITH SIX YOU
    GET EGGROLL .... BARBARA HERSHEY
WITH SIX YOU GET EGGROLL .... BRIAN KEITH
WITH SIX YOU GET EGGROLL .... DORIS DAY
WITH THESE HANDS .... JOSEPH WISEMAN
WITHOUT A CLUE .... BEN KINGSLEY
WITHOUT A CLUE .... JEFFREY JONES
WITHOUT A CLUE .... LYSETTE ANTHONY
WITHOUT A CLUE .... MICHAEL CAINE
WITHOUT A CLUE .... PAUL FREEMAN
WITHOUT A TRACE .... BILL SMITROVICH
WITHOUT A TRACE .... DAVID DUKES
WITHOUT A TRACE .... JUDD HIRSCH
WITHOUT A TRACE .... KATE NELLIGAN
WITHOUT A TRACE .... STOCKARD CHANNING
WITHOUT HER CONSENT (TF) .... BARRY TUBB
WITHOUT HER CONSENT (TF) .... BEBE NEUWIRTH
WITHOUT HER CONSENT (TF) ..... MELISSA GILBERT
WITHOUT HER CONSENT (TF) .... SCOTT VALENTINE
WITHOUT LOVE .... KATHERINE HEPBURN
WITHOUT REGRET .... DAVID NIVEN†
WITHOUT RESERVATIONS .... RAYMOND BURR†
WITHOUT WARNING .... JACK PALANCE
WITHOUT WARNING .... MARTIN LANDAU
WITHOUT WARNING .... SUE ANE LANGDON
WITHOUT WARNING: THE JAMES
    BRADY STORY (CTF) .... BEAU BRIDGES
WITHOUT YOU I'M NOTHING .... STEVE ANTIN
WITHOUT YOU
    I'M NOTHING .... SANDRA BERNHARD
WITNESS ★ .... HARRISON FORD
WITNESS .... ALEXANDER GODUNOV
WITNESS .... DANNY GLOVER
WITNESS .... JAN RUBES
WITNESS .... JOSEF SOMMER
WITNESS .... KELLY McGILLIS
WITNESS .... LUKAS HAAS

This is not a list of every film ever made or every cast member, only those listed in this directory.

WITNESS .... PATTI LUPONE
WITNESS FOR THE
PROSECUTION ★ .... CHARLES LAUGHTON†
WITNESS FOR THE
PROSECUTION ๐ .... ELSA LANCHESTER†
WITNESS FOR THE
PROSECUTION (TF) .... BEAU BRIDGES
WITNESS FOR THE
PROSECUTION (TF) .... DEBORAH KERR
WITNESS FOR THE
PROSECUTION (TF) .... DIANA RIGG
WITNESS TO MURDER .... BARBARA STANWYCK†
WITNESS TO THE EXECUTION (TF) ...... LEN CARIOU
WITNESS TO THE EXECUTION (TF) .... SEAN YOUNG
WITNESS TO THE
EXECUTION (TF) .... TIMOTHY DALY
WIVES AND LOVERS .... JANET LEIGH
WIVES AND LOVERS .... RAY WALSTON
WIVES AND LOVERS .... SHELLEY WINTERS
WIVES AND LOVERS .... VAN JOHNSON
WIZ, THE .... DIANA ROSS
WIZ, THE .... LENA HORNE
WIZ, THE .... MABEL KING
WIZ, THE .... MICHAEL JACKSON
WIZ, THE .... NIPSEY RUSSELL
WIZ, THE .... RICHARD PRYOR
WIZ, THE .... TED ROSS
WIZ, THE .... THERESA MERRITT
WIZARD, THE .... BEAU BRIDGES
WIZARD, THE .... CHRISTIAN SLATER
WIZARD, THE .... FRANK McRAE
WIZARD, THE .... FRED SAVAGE
WIZARD, THE .... JACKEY VINSON
WIZARD, THE .... JENNY LEWIS
WIZARD, THE .... LUKE EDWARDS
WIZARD, THE .... SAM McMURRAY
WIZARD, THE .... WENDY PHILLIPS
WIZARD, THE .... WILL SELTZER
WIZARD OF BAGHDAD, THE .... DIANE BAKER
WIZARD OF LONELINESS, THE .... ANNE PITONIAK
WIZARD OF LONELINESS, THE .... DYLAN BAKER
WIZARD OF
LONELINESS, THE .... JEREMIAH WARNER
WIZARD OF LONELINESS, THE .... JOHN RANDOLPH
WIZARD OF LONELINESS, THE .... LANCE GUEST
WIZARD OF LONELINESS, THE ...... LEA THOMPSON
WIZARD OF LONELINESS, THE .... LUKAS HAAS
WIZARD OF
LONELINESS, THE .... STEVE HENDRICKSON
WIZARD OF OZ, THE .... BERT LAHR†
WIZARD OF OZ, THE .... BILLIE BURKE†
WIZARD OF OZ, THE .... CLARA BLANDICK†
WIZARD OF OZ, THE .... FRANK MORGAN†
WIZARD OF OZ, THE .... JACK HALEY†
WIZARD OF OZ, THE .... JUDY GARLAND†
WIZARD OF OZ, THE ..... MARGARET HAMILTON†
WIZARD OF OZ, THE .... RAY BOLGER†
WIZARDS (AF) .... MARK HAMILL
WOLF .... CHRISTOPHER PLUMMER
WOLF .... JACK NICHOLSON
WOLF .... JAMES SPADER
WOLF .... KATE NELLIGAN
WOLF .... MICHELLE PFEIFFER
WOLF .... RICHARD JENKINS
WOLF AT THE
DOOR, THE .... DONALD SUTHERLAND
WOLF LAKE .... ROD STEIGER
WOLF LARSEN .... PETER GRAVES
WOLF MAN, THE .... RALPH BELLAMY†
WOLFEN .... ALBERT FINNEY
WOLFEN .... DIANE VENORA
WOLFEN .... EDWARD JAMES OLMOS
WOLFEN .... GREGORY HINES
WOLFEN .... TOM NOONAN
WOLVES OF WILLOUGHBY
CHASE, THE .... GERALDINE JAMES
WOMAN ALONE, A .... SYLVIA SIDNEY
WOMAN CALLED GOLDA, A (TF) ..... ANNE JACKSON
WOMAN CALLED GOLDA, A (TF) .... JUDY DAVIS
WOMAN CALLED
GOLDA, A (TF) .... LEONARD NIMOY
WOMAN CALLED GOLDA, A (TF) .... NED BEATTY

WOMAN CALLED
GOLDA, A (TF) .... ROBERT LOGGIA
WOMAN CALLED MOSES, A (TF) .... ROBERT HOOKS
WOMAN FROM HELL, THE .... DEAN JAGGER†
WOMAN HE
LOVED, THE (TF) .... ANTHONY ANDREWS
WOMAN HE LOVED, THE (TF) .... JANE SEYMOUR
WOMAN HE LOVED, THE (TF) .... JULIE HARRIS
WOMAN HE
LOVED, THE (TF) .... LUCY GUTTERIDGE
WOMAN HE
LOVED, THE (TF) .... OLIVIA DE HAVILLAND
WOMAN HUNTER, THE (TF) .... BARBARA EDEN
WOMAN IN RED, THE .... BARBARA STANWYCK†
WOMAN IN RED, THE .... CHARLES GRODIN
WOMAN IN RED, THE .... GENE WILDER
WOMAN IN RED, THE .... GILDA RADNER†
WOMAN IN RED, THE .... JUDITH IVEY
WOMAN IN RED, THE .... KELLY LeBROCK
WOMAN IN ROOM 13, THE .... RALPH BELLAMY†
WOMAN IN THE DARK .... RALPH BELLAMY†
WOMAN IN THE HALL, THE .... JEAN SIMMONS
WOMAN IN THE ULTIMATE, A .... LILLIAN GISH†
WOMAN IN THE WINDOW .... ROBERT BLAKE
WOMAN IN WHITE, THE .... ALEXIS SMITH†
WOMAN IN WHITE, THE .... ELEANOR PARKER
WOMAN NEXT DOOR, THE ...... GERARD DEPARDIEU
WOMAN OF INDEPENDENT
MEANS, A (MS) .... SALLY FIELD
WOMAN OF STRAW .... SEAN CONNERY
WOMAN OF
SUBSTANCE, A (MS) .... DEBORAH KERR
WOMAN OF SUBSTANCE, A (MS) .... DIANE BAKER
WOMAN OF SUBSTANCE, A (MS) .... PETER EGAN
WOMAN OF
SUBSTANCE, A (TF) .... BARRY BOSTWICK
WOMAN OF THE RIVER .... SOPHIA LOREN
WOMAN OF THE YEAR .... SPENCER TRACY†
WOMAN OF THE YEAR ★ ...... KATHERINE HEPBURN
WOMAN REBELS, A .... KATHERINE HEPBURN
WOMAN SCORNED, A (TF) .... MEREDITH BAXTER
WOMAN TIMES SEVEN .... ALAN ARKIN
WOMAN TIMES SEVEN .... MICHAEL CAINE
WOMAN TIMES SEVEN .... ROBERT MORLEY
WOMAN TIMES SEVEN .... SHIRLEY MacLAINE
WOMAN UNDER THE INFLUENCE, A .... PETER FALK
WOMAN UNDER THE
INFLUENCE, A ★ .... GENA ROWLANDS
WOMAN WANTED .... MAUREEN O'SULLIVAN
WOMAN WHO CRIED
MURDER, THE (TF) .... ART CARNEY
WOMAN WHO CRIED
MURDER, THE (TF) .... CLORIS LEACHMAN
WOMAN WHO CRIED
MURDER, THE (TF) .... DIAHANN CARROLL
WOMAN WHO CRIED
MURDER, THE (TF) .... DIMITRA ARLYS
WOMAN WHO CRIED
MURDER, THE (TF) .... ED ASNER
WOMAN WHO CRIED
MURDER, THE (TF) .... KATE JACKSON
WOMAN WHO CRIED
MURDER, THE (TF) .... LUCIE ARNAZ
WOMAN WHO CRIED
MURDER, THE (TF) .... NANCY WALKER†
WOMAN WHO CRIED
MURDER, THE (TF) .... RAUL JULIA†
WOMAN WHO CRIED
MURDER, THE (TF) .... SALLY KIRKLAND
WOMAN WHO CRIED
MURDER, THE (TF) .... TINA LOUISE
WOMAN WITH RED
BOOTS, THE .... CATHERINE DENEUVE
WOMAN'S FACE, A .... JOAN CRAWFORD†
WOMAN'S WORLD .... JUNE ALLYSON
WOMAN'S ANGLE, THE .... LOIS MAXWELL
WOMAN'S SECRET, A .... MAUREEN O'HARA
WOMAN'S VENGEANCE, A .... JESSICA TANDY†
WOMAN'S WORLD .... LAUREN BACALL
WOMEN, THE .... JOAN CRAWFORD†
WOMEN, THE .... JULIA ROBERTS
WOMEN, THE .... MEG RYAN

WOMEN AT WEST POINT (TF) ... ANDREW STEVENS
WOMEN AT WEST POINT (TF) .... LINDA PURL
WOMEN IN
CHAINS (TF) .... BELINDA J. MONTGOMERY
WOMEN IN CHAINS (TF) .... JESSICA WALTER
WOMEN IN LIMBO .... KATE JACKSON
WOMEN IN LIMBO .... STUART MARGOLIN
WOMEN IN LOVE .... ALAN BATES
WOMEN IN LOVE ★★ .... GLENDA JACKSON
WOMEN IN LOVE .... ELEANOR BRON
WOMEN IN LOVE .... MICHAEL GOUGH
WOMEN IN LOVE ....OLIVER REED
WOMEN & MEN: IN LOVE THERE
ARE NO RULES (CTF) .... ANDIE MacDOWELL
WOMEN & MEN: IN LOVE THERE
ARE NO RULES (CTF) .... JERRY STILLER
WOMEN & MEN: IN LOVE THERE
ARE NO RULES (CTF) .... JULIETTE BINOCHE
WOMEN & MEN: IN LOVE THERE
ARE NO RULES (CTF) .... KYRA SEDGWICK
WOMEN & MEN: IN LOVE THERE
ARE NO RULES (CTF) .... MATT DILLON
WOMEN & MEN: IN LOVE THERE
ARE NO RULES (CTF) .... RAY LIOTTA
WOMEN & MEN: IN LOVE THERE
ARE NO RULES (CTF) .... SCOTT GLENN
WOMEN & MEN: STORIES
OF SEDUCTION (CTF) .... MELANIE GRIFFITH
WOMEN OF BREWSTER
PLACE, THE (MS) .... MOSES GUNN
WOMEN OF BREWSTER
PLACE, THE (MS) .... OPRAH WINFREY
WOMEN OF BREWSTER
PLACE, THE (MS) .... ROBIN GIVENS
WOMEN OF THE WORLD (FD) ... PETER USTINOV
WOMEN OF TWILIGHT .... LOIS MAXWELL
WOMEN OF VALOR (TF) .... KRISTY McNICHOL
WOMEN OF VALOR (TF) .... NEVA PATTERSON
WOMEN OF VALOR (TF) .... SUSAN SARANDON
WOMEN OF VALOR (TF) .... TERRY O'QUINN
WOMEN ON THE VERGE OF A
NERVOUS BREAKDOWN ..... ANTONIO BANDERAS
WOMEN'S CLUB, THE .... MAUD ADAMS
WOMEN'S CLUB, THE .... MICHAEL PARE
WOMEN'S PRISON .... PHYLLIS THAXTER
WOMEN'S ROOM, THE (TF) .... TOYAH FELDSHUH
WOMEN'S ROOM, THE (TF) .... TYNE DALY
WON TON TON, THE DOG THAT
SAVED HOLLYWOOD .... ERNEST BORGNINE
WON TON TON, THE DOG WHO
SAVED HOLLYWOOD .... ART CARNEY
WON TON TON, THE DOG WHO
SAVED HOLLYWOOD .... BRUCE DERN
WON TON TON, THE DOG WHO
SAVED HOLLYWOOD .... DEAN STOCKWELL
WON TON TON, THE DOG WHO
SAVED HOLLYWOOD .... DOROTHY LAMOUR
WON TON TON, THE DOG WHO
SAVED HOLLYWOOD .... MADELINE KAHN
WON TON TON, THE DOG WHO
SAVED HOLLYWOOD .... MILTON BERLE
WON TON TON, THE DOG WHO
SAVED HOLLYWOOD .... RON LEIBMAN
WON TON TON, THE DOG WHO
SAVED HOLLYWOOD .... YVONNE DE CARLO
WONDERFUL COUNTRY, THE .... ROBERT MITCHUM
WONDERFUL CROOK, THE ..... GERARD DEPARDIEU
WONDERFUL WORLD OF THE
BROTHERS GRIMM, THE .... BARBARA EDEN
WONDERFUL WORLD OF THE
BROTHERS GRIMM, THE .... BEULAH BONDI†
WONDERFUL WORLD OF THE
BROTHERS GRIMM, THE .... BUDDY HACKETT
WONDERFUL WORLD OF THE
BROTHERS GRIMM, THE .... CLAIRE BLOOM
WONDERFUL WORLD OF THE
BROTHERS GRIMM, THE .... JIM BACKUS†
WONDERFUL WORLD OF THE
BROTHERS GRIMM, THE ..... LAURENCE HARVEY†
WONDERFUL WORLD OF THE
BROTHERS GRIMM, THE .... MARTITA HUNT†

† after an actor's name denotes deceased.

WONDERFUL WORLD OF THE
  BROTHERS GRIMM, THE .... OSCAR HOMOLKA†
WONDERFUL WORLD OF THE
  BROTHERS GRIMM, THE .... RUSS TAMBLYN
WONDERFUL WORLD OF THE
  BROTHERS GRIMM, THE .... WALTER SLEZAK†
WOO WOO KID, THE .... BEVERLY D'ANGELO
WOO WOO KID, THE .... PATRICK DEMPSEY
WOODEN HORSE, THE .... DAVID TOMLINSON
WORD, THE (MS) .... DIANA MULDAUR
WORD, THE (MS) .... EDDIE ALBERT
WORD, THE (MS) .... EDWARD ALBERT
WORD, THE (MS) .... HURD HATFIELD
WORD, THE (MS) .... KATE MULGREW
WORD, THE (MS) .... MARTHA SCOTT
WORD, THE (MS) .... NEHEMIAH PERSOFF
WORD, THE (TF) .... JAMES WHITMORE
WORD, THE (TF) .... NICOL WILLIAMSON
WORD, THE (TF) .... RON MOODY
WORD OF HONOR (TF) .... KARL MALDEN
WORDS AND MUSIC .... CYD CHARISSE
WORDS AND MUSIC .... GENE KELLY
WORDS AND MUSIC .... JANET LEIGH
WORDS AND MUSIC .... JUNE ALLYSON
WORDS AND MUSIC .... LENA HORNE
WORK IS A
  FOUR-LETTER WORD .... DAVID WARNER
WORKING GIRL .... ALEC BALDWIN
WORKING GIRL .... HARRISON FORD
WORKING GIRL .... NORA DUNN
WORKING GIRL .... OLIVER PLATT
WORKING GIRL .... OLYMPIA DUKAKIS
WORKING GIRL .... PHILIP BOSCO
WORKING GIRL .... RICKI LAKE
WORKING GIRL .... ROBERT EASTON
WORKING GIRL ★ .... MELANIE GRIFFITH
WORKING GIRL ○ .... JOAN CUSAK
WORKING GIRL ○ .... SIGOURNEY WEAVER
WORKING MAN, THE .... BETTE DAVIS†
WORLD ACCORDING
  TO GARP, THE .... HUME CRONYN
WORLD ACCORDING
  TO GARP, THE .... JESSICA TANDY†
WORLD ACCORDING
  TO GARP, THE .... MARY BETH HURT
WORLD ACCORDING
  TO GARP, THE .... ROBIN WILLIAMS
WORLD ACCORDING
  TO GARP, THE .... SWOOSIE KURTZ
WORLD ACCORDING
  TO GARP, THE ○ .... GLENN CLOSE
WORLD ACCORDING
  TO GARP, THE ○ .... JOHN LITHGOW
WORLD APART, A .... BARBARA HERSHEY
WORLD APART, A .... JODHI MAY
WORLD GONE WILD .... ADAM ANT
WORLD GONE WILD .... BRUCE DERN
WORLD GONE WILD .... MICHAEL PARE
WORLD IN HIS ARMS, THE .... ANTHONY QUINN
WORLD IN HIS ARMS, THE .... GREGORY PECK
WORLD IN MY POCKET, THE .... ROD STEIGER
WORLD IS FULL OF MARRIED
  MEN, THE .... ANTHONY (TONY) FRANCIOSA
WORLD IS FULL OF
  MARRIED MEN, THE .... CARROLL BAKER
WORLD IS FULL OF
  MARRIED MEN, THE .... PAUL NICHOLAS
WORLD OF HENRY
  ORIENT, THE .... ANGELA LANSBURY
WORLD OF HENRY ORIENT, THE .... JOHN FIELDLER
WORLD OF HENRY
  ORIENT, THE .... PAULA PRENTISS
WORLD OF HENRY
  ORIENT, THE .... PETER SELLERS†
WORLD OF HENRY
  ORIENT, THE .... PHYLLIS THAXTER
WORLD OF HENRY ORIENT, THE .... TOM BOSLEY
WORLD TEN TIMES
  OVER, THE .... DONALD SUTHERLAND
WORLD, THE FLESH AND
  THE DEVIL, THE .... MEL FERRER

WORLD WAR II: THEN THERE
  WERE GIANTS (TF) .... BOB HOSKINS
WORLD WAR II: THEN THERE
  WERE GIANTS (TF) .... ED BEGLEY JR.
WORLD WAR II: THEN THERE
  WERE GIANTS (TF) .... JAN TRISKA
WORLD WAR II: THEN THERE
  WERE GIANTS (TF) .... JOHN LITHGOW
WORLD WAR II: THEN THERE
  WERE GIANTS (TF) .... MICHAEL CAINE
WORLD'S OLDEST LIVING
  CONFEDERATE WIDOW
  TELLS ALL, THE (MS) .... DIANE LANE
WORLD'S OLDEST LIVING
  CONFEDERATE WIDOW
  TELLS ALL, THE (MS) .... DONALD SUTHERLAND
WORLD'S GREATEST
  ATHLETE, THE .... JAN-MICHAEL VINCENT
WORLD'S GREATEST ATHLETE, THE .... JOHN AMOS
WORLD'S GREATEST
  ATHLETE, THE .... NANCY WALKER†
WORLD'S GREATEST
  ATHLETE, THE .... ROSCOE LEE BROWNE
WORLD'S GREATEST
  ATHLETE, THE .... TIM CONWAY
WORLD'S GREATEST LOVER, THE ...... CAROL KANE
WORLD'S GREATEST
  LOVER, THE .... DANNY DEVITO
WORLD'S GREATEST LOVER, THE ..... DOM DeLUISE
WORLD'S GREATEST LOVER, THE .... GENE WILDER
WORTH WINNING .... LESLEY ANN WARREN
WORTH WINNING .... MADELEINE STOWE
WORTH WINNING .... MARIA HOLYOE
WORTH WINNING .... MARK HARMON
WRAITH, THE .... CHARLIE SHEEN
WRAITH, THE .... NICK CASSAVETES
WRAITH, THE .... RANDY QUAID
WRATH OF GOD, THE .... FRANK LANGELLA
WRATH OF GOD, THE .... GREGORY SIERRA
WRATH OF GOD, THE .... ROBERT MITCHUM
WRECK OF THE MARY
  DEARE, THE .... CHARLTON HESTON
WRECK OF THE MARY
  DEARE, THE .... RICHARD HARRIS
WRECKING CREW, THE .... CHUCK NORRIS
WRECKING CREW, THE .... DEAN MARTIN
WRECKING CREW, THE .... TINA LOUISE
WRESTLING ERNEST
  HEMINGWAY .... PIPER LAURIE
WRESTLING ERNEST
  HEMINGWAY .... RICHARD HARRIS
WRESTLING ERNEST
  HEMINGWAY .... ROBERT DUVALL
WRESTLING ERNEST
  HEMINGWAY .... SANDRA BULLOCK
WRESTLING ERNEST
  HEMINGWAY .... SHIRLEY MacLAINE
WRITTEN ON THE WIND .... LAUREN BACALL
WRITTEN ON THE WIND .... ROCK HUDSON†
WRITTEN ON THE WIND .... ROBERT STACK
WRONG ARM OF THE LAW, THE .... MICHAEL CAINE
WRONG BOX, THE .... DUDLEY MOORE
WRONG BOX, THE .... MICHAEL CAINE
WRONG BOX, THE .... PETER COOK
WRONG BOX, THE .... THORLEY WALTERS†
WRONG GUYS, THE .... FRANKLYN AJAYE
WRONG IS RIGHT .... DEAN STOCKWELL
WRONG IS RIGHT .... HENRY SILVA
WRONG IS RIGHT .... KATHERINE ROSS
WRONG IS RIGHT .... LESLIE NIELSEN
WRONG IS RIGHT .... ROBERT CONRAD
WRONG IS RIGHT .... ROBERT WEBBER
WRONG IS RIGHT .... RON MOODY
WRONG IS RIGHT .... ROSALIND CASH
WRONG IS RIGHT .... SEAN CONNERY
WRONG MAN, THE .... NEHEMIAH PERSOFF
WRONG MAN, THE .... VERA MILES
WUSA .... ANTHONY PERKINS†
WUSA .... CLORIS LEACHMAN
WUSA .... DIANE LADD
WUSA .... JOANNE WOODWARD
WUSA .... MOSES GUNN

WUSA .... PAT HINGLE
WUSA .... PAUL NEWMAN
WUTHERING HEIGHTS .... DAVID NIVEN†
WUTHERING HEIGHTS .... JULIAN GLOVER
WUTHERING HEIGHTS .... TIMOTHY DALTON
WUTHERING HEIGHTS ★ .... LAURENCE OLIVIER†
WUTHERING
  HEIGHTS ○ .... GERALDINE FITZGERALD
WYATT EARP .... ADAM BALDWIN
WYATT EARP .... ANNABETH GISH
WYATT EARP .... BETTY BUCKLEY
WYATT EARP .... BILL PULLMAN
WYATT EARP .... CATHERINE O'HARA
WYATT EARP .... DAVID ANDREWS
WYATT EARP .... DENNIS QUAID
WYATT EARP .... GENE HACKMAN
WYATT EARP .... GREG AVELLONE
WYATT EARP .... IAN BOHEN
WYATT EARP .... ISABELLA ROSSELLINI
WYATT EARP .... JAMES CAVIEZEL
WYATT EARP .... JEFF FAHEY
WYATT EARP .... JOANNA GOING
WYATT EARP .... JoBETH WILLIAMS
WYATT EARP .... JOHN FURLONG
WYATT EARP .... KAREN GRASSLE
WYATT EARP .... KEVIN COSTNER
WYATT EARP .... KIRK FOX
WYATT EARP .... LINDEN ASHBY
WYATT EARP .... MARE WINNINGHAM
WYATT EARP .... MARK HARMON
WYATT EARP .... MICHAEL MADSEN
WYATT EARP .... TODD ALLEN
WYATT EARP .... TOM SIZEMORE
WYOMING KID, THE .... JANE WYMAN

X

X Y & ZEE .... ELIZABETH TAYLOR
X, Y & ZEE .... MICHAEL CAINE
X Y & ZEE .... SUSANNAH YORK
X-15 .... CHARLES BRONSON
X-15 .... JAMES STEWART
X-15 .... MARY TYLER MOORE
XANADU .... DIMITRA ARLYS
XANADU .... GENE KELLY
XANADU .... JULIA JENNINGS
XANADU .... MICHAEL BECK
XANADU .... OLIVIA NEWTON-JOHN
XXX'S & OOO'S (TF) .... ANDREA PARKER
XXX'S & OOO'S (TF) .... BRAD JOHNSON
XXX'S & OOO'S (TF) .... DAVID KEITH
XXX'S & OOO'S (TF) .... DEBRAH FARENTINO
XXX'S & OOO'S (TF) .... NIA PEEPLES
XXX'S & OOO'S (TF) .... PAUL GROSS
XXX'S & OOO'S (TF) .... SUSAN WALTERS

Y

YAKUZA, THE .... BRIAN KEITH
YAKUZA, THE .... HERB EDELMAN
YAKUZA, THE .... JAMES SHIGETA
YAKUZA, THE .... KEN TAKAKURA
YAKUZA, THE .... RICHARD JORDAN†
YAKUZA, THE .... ROBERT MITCHUM
YANK AT OXFORD, A .... MAUREEN O'SULLIVAN
YANK IN LONDON .... ROBERT MORLEY
YANKEE DOODLE DANDY ★★ .... JAMES CAGNEY†
YANKEE DOODLE DANDY ○ .... WALTER HUSTON†
YANKS .... ANTHONY SHER
YANKS .... LISA EICHHORN
YANKS .... RACHEL ROBERTS†
YANKS .... RICHARD GERE
YANKS .... VANESSA REDGRAVE
YANKS .... WILLIAM DEVANE
YEAR IN THE LIFE, A (MS) .... MORGAN STEVENS
YEAR IN THE LIFE, A (MS) .... RICHARD KILEY
YEAR IN THE
  LIFE, A (MS) .... SARAH JESSICA PARKER
YEAR MY VOICE
  BROKE, THE .... BEN MENDELSOHN

584

YEAR MY VOICE BROKE, THE .... LEONE CARMEN
YEAR MY VOICE BROKE, THE .... NOAH TAYLOR
YEAR OF LIVING
  DANGEROUSLY, THE .... MEL GIBSON
YEAR OF LIVING
  DANGEROUSLY, THE .... MICHAEL MURPHY
YEAR OF LIVING
  DANGEROUSLY, THE .... SIGOURNEY WEAVER
YEAR OF LIVING
  DANGEROUSLY, THE ○○ .... LINDA HUNT
YEAR OF THE COMET ...... PENELOPE ANN MILLER
YEAR OF THE COMET .... SHANE RIMMER
YEAR OF THE COMET .... TIMOTHY DALY
YEAR OF THE DRAGON .... DENNIS DUN
YEAR OF THE DRAGON .... JOHN LONE
YEAR OF THE DRAGON .... MICKEY ROURKE
YEAR OF THE GUN .... ANDREW McCARTHY
YEAR OF THE GUN .... JOHN PANKOW
YEAR OF THE GUN .... SHARON STONE
YEAR OF THE GUN .... VALERIA GOLINO
YEARLING, THE .... JUNE LOCKHART
YEARLING, THE ★ .... GREGORY PECK
YEARLING, THE ★ .... JANE WYMAN
YEARLING, THE (TF) .... JEAN SMART
YEARLING, THE (TF) .... PETER STRAUSS
YEARLING, THE (TF) .... WIL HORNEFF
YELLOW CANARY, THE .... BARBARA EDEN
YELLOW CANARY, THE .... JACK KLUGMAN
YELLOW CANARY, THE .... PAT BOONE
YELLOW CANARY, THE .... STEVE FORREST
YELLOW DOG .... BRUCE DAVISON
YELLOW DOG .... JESSE BRADFORD
YELLOW DOG .... MIMI ROGERS
YELLOW ROLLS-ROYCE, THE .... ART CARNEY
YELLOW ROLLS-ROYCE, THE ... GEORGE C. SCOTT
YELLOW ROLLS-ROYCE, THE .... OMAR SHARIF
YELLOW ROLLS-ROYCE, THE ... SHIRLEY MacLAINE
YELLOW SKY .... GREGORY PECK
YELLOW SKY .... HARRY MORGAN
YELLOW SKY .... RICHARD WIDMARK
YELLOW SUBMARINE (AF) ...... GEORGE HARRISON
YELLOW SUBMARINE (AF) .... PAUL McCARTNEY
YELLOW SUBMARINE (AF) .... RINGO STARR
YELLOW TOMAHAWK, THE .... RITA MORENO
YELLOWBEARD .... ERIC IDLE
YELLOWBEARD .... GRAHAM CHAPMAN†
YELLOWBEARD .... JOHN CLEESE
YELLOWBEARD .... MADELINE KAHN
YELLOWBEARD .... MARTY FELDMAN†
YELLOWBEARD .... PETER BOYLE
YELLOWBEARD .... PETER COOK
YELLOWBEARD .... SUSANNAH YORK
YELLOWSTONE KELLY .... CLAUDE AKINS†
YELLOWSTONE KELLY .... CLINT WALKER
YENTL .... BARBRA STREISAND
YENTL .... MANDY PATINKIN
YENTL .... NEHEMIAH PERSOFF
YENTL .... STEVEN HILL
YENTL ○ .... AMY IRVING
YES, GIORGIO .... BEULAH QUO
YES, GIORGIO .... EDDIE ALBERT
YES, GIORGIO .... KATHRYN HARROLD
YES, GIORGIO .... LUCIANO PAVAROTTI
YESTERDAY .... CLORIS LEACHMAN
YESTERDAY .... EDDIE ALBERT
YESTERDAY, TODAY
  AND TOMORROW .... MARCELLO MASTROIANNI
YESTERDAY, TODAY
  AND TOMORROW .... SOPHIA LOREN
YESTERDAY'S ENEMY .... GORDAN JACKSON†
YESTERDAY'S
  CHILD (TF) .... GERALDINE FITZGERALD
YESTERDAY'S CHILD (TF) .... SHIRLEY JONES
YIN AND YANG OF MR. GO, THE ...... JEFF BRIDGES
YOLANDA AND THE THIEF .... LEON AMES
YOSEMITE: THE FATE
  OF HEAVEN (FD) .... ROBERT REDFORD
YOU AND ME .... BARBARA HERSHEY
YOU AND ME .... DAVID CARRADINE
YOU AND ME .... KEITH CARRADINE
YOU AND ME .... SYLVIA SIDNEY
YOU BELONG TO ME .... BARBARA STANWYCK†

YOU BELONG TO ME .... DEAN JAGGER†
YOU CAN'T RUN AWAY FROM IT ...... JUNE ALLYSON
YOU CAN'T TAKE IT WITH YOU .... JEAN ARTHUR†
YOU CAN'T TAKE
  IT WITH YOU ○ .... SPRING BYINGTON†
YOU CAN'T BEAT THE IRISH .... MILO O'SHEA
YOU CAN'T GO
  HOME AGAIN (TF) .... HURD HATFIELD
YOU CAN'T GO HOME AGAIN (TF) .... LEE GRANT
YOU CAN'T GO
  HOME AGAIN (TF) .... TAMMY GRIMES
YOU CAN'T HAVE EVERYTHING .... DON AMECHE†
YOU CAN'T HURRY LOVE .... ANTHONY GEARY
YOU CAN'T HURRY LOVE .... BRIDGET FONDA
YOU CAN'T HURRY LOVE .... CHARLES GRODIN
YOU CAN'T HURRY LOVE .... DAVID LEISURE
YOU CAN'T HURRY LOVE .... DAVID PECKER
YOU CAN'T HURRY LOVE .... FRANK BONNER
YOU CAN'T HURRY LOVE .... KRISTY McNICHOL
YOU CAN'T HURRY LOVE .... SALLY KELLERMAN
YOU CAN'T RUN AWAY FROM IT ...... JACK LEMMON
YOU CAN'T TAKE IT WITH YOU .... JAMES STEWART
YOU CAN'T WIN 'EM ALL .... CHARLES BRONSON
YOU CAN'T WIN 'EM ALL .... TONY CURTIS
YOU FOR ME .... JANE GREER
YOU GOTTA STAY HAPPY .... EDDIE ALBERT
YOU GOTTA STAY HAPPY .... JAMES STEWART
YOU LIGHT UP MY LIFE .... DIDI CONN
YOU LIGHT UP MY LIFE .... MICHAEL ZASLOW
YOU MAY BE NEXT .... ANN SOTHERN
YOU MUST BE JOKING! .... DENHOLM ELLIOTT†
YOU ONLY LIVE ONCE .... SYLVIA SIDNEY
YOU ONLY LIVE TWICE .... BURT KWOUK
YOU ONLY LIVE TWICE .... DONALD PLEASENCE
YOU ONLY LIVE TWICE .... LOIS MAXWELL
YOU ONLY LIVE TWICE .... SEAN CONNERY
YOU SO CRAZY .... MARTIN LAWRENCE
YOU'RE A BIG BOY NOW ○ .... GERALDINE PAGE†
YOUNG AMERICA .... RALPH BELLAMY†
YOUNG AND DANGEROUS .... CONNIE STEVENS
YOUNG AND
  THE BRAVE, THE .... RICHARD JAECKEL
YOUNG AND WILLING .... JOHN HURT
YOUNG AND WILLING .... SAMANTHA EGGAR
YOUNG AS YOU FEEL .... CECILIA PARKER†
YOUNG AT HEART .... DORIS DAY
YOUNG AT HEART .... FRANK SINATRA
YOUNG AT HEART .... LONNY CHAPMAN
YOUNG BESS .... DEBORAH KERR
YOUNG BESS .... JEAN SIMMONS
YOUNG BILLY YOUNG .... ANGIE DICKINSON
YOUNG BILLY YOUNG .... DAVID CARRADINE
YOUNG BILLY YOUNG .... JOHN ANDERSON
YOUNG BILLY YOUNG .... ROBERT MITCHUM
YOUNG BILLY YOUNG .... ROBERT WALKER JR.
YOUNG CASSIDY .... JULIE CHRISTIE
YOUNG CASSIDY .... MAGGIE SMITH
YOUNG CASSIDY .... SIAN PHILLIPS
YOUNG COUNTRY, THE (TF) .... JOAN HACKETT†
YOUNG DILLINGER .... ROBERT CONRAD
YOUNG DOCTORS IN LOVE .... DABNEY COLEMAN
YOUNG DOCTORS IN LOVE .... DEMI MOORE
YOUNG DOCTORS IN LOVE .... ED BEGLEY JR.
YOUNG DOCTORS
  IN LOVE .... HARRY DEAN STANTON
YOUNG DOCTORS IN LOVE ...... HECTOR ELIZONDO
YOUNG DOCTORS IN LOVE ...... JACKLYN ZEMAN
YOUNG DOCTORS IN LOVE ...... MICHAEL McKEAN
YOUNG DOCTORS IN LOVE ..... MICHAEL RICHARDS
YOUNG DOCTORS IN LOVE ..... PAMELA REED
YOUNG DOCTORS IN LOVE ...... PATRICK MacNEE
YOUNG DOCTORS IN LOVE ...... SAUL RUBINEK
YOUNG DOCTORS IN LOVE .... SEAN YOUNG
YOUNG DOCTORS IN LOVE ...... TAYLOR NEGRON
YOUNG DOCTORS, THE .... ARTHUR HILL
YOUNG DOCTORS, THE .... BEN GAZZARA
YOUNG DOCTORS, THE .... EDDIE ALBERT
YOUNG DOCTORS, THE .... GEORGE SEGAL
YOUNG DOCTORS, THE .... RONALD REAGAN
YOUNG DOCTORS, THE .... ROSEMARY MURPHY
YOUNG EINSTEIN .... JOHN HOWARD
YOUNG EINSTEIN .... ODILE LE CLEZIO

YOUNG EINSTEIN .... YAHOO SERIOUS
YOUNG FRANKENSTEIN .... CLORIS LEACHMAN
YOUNG FRANKENSTEIN .... GENE HACKMAN
YOUNG FRANKENSTEIN .... GENE WILDER
YOUNG FRANKENSTEIN .... KENNETH MARS
YOUNG FRANKENSTEIN .... MADELINE KAHN
YOUNG FRANKENSTEIN .... MARTY FELDMAN†
YOUNG FRANKENSTEIN .... PETER BOYLE
YOUNG FRANKENSTEIN .... RICHARD HAYDN†
YOUNG FRANKENSTEIN .... TERI GARR
YOUNG FURY .... RORY CALHOUN
YOUNG GIRLS OF
  ROCHEFORT, THE .... CATHERINE DENEUVE
YOUNG GIRLS OF
  ROCHEFORT, THE .... GENE KELLY
YOUNG GUNS .... BRIAN KEITH
YOUNG GUNS .... CASEY SIEMASZKO
YOUNG GUNS .... CHARLIE SHEEN
YOUNG GUNS .... DERMOT MULRONEY
YOUNG GUNS .... EMILIO ESTEVEZ
YOUNG GUNS .... GEOFFREY BLAKE
YOUNG GUNS .... JACK PALANCE
YOUNG GUNS .... KIEFER SUTHERLAND
YOUNG GUNS .... LOU DIAMOND PHILLIPS
YOUNG GUNS .... SHARON THOMAS
YOUNG GUNS .... TERENCE STAMP
YOUNG GUNS .... TERRY O'QUINN
YOUNG GUNS II .... ALAN RUCK
YOUNG GUNS II .... BALTHAZAR GETTY
YOUNG GUNS II .... CHRISTIAN SLATER
YOUNG GUNS II .... EMILIO ESTEVEZ
YOUNG GUNS II .... KIEFER SUTHERLAND
YOUNG GUNS II .... LOU DIAMOND PHILLIPS
YOUNG GUNS II .... WILLIAM L. PETERSEN
YOUNG GUNS, THE .... RUSS TAMBLYN
YOUNG HARRY HOUDINI (TF) .... ROY DOTRICE
YOUNG IDEAS .... AVA GARDNER†
YOUNG JOE, THE FORGOTTEN
  KENNEDY (TF) .... PETER STRAUSS
YOUNG LAND, THE .... DENNIS HOPPER
YOUNG LIONS, THE .... DEAN MARTIN
YOUNG LIONS, THE .... HOPE LANGE
YOUNG LIONS, THE .... MARLON BRANDO
YOUNG LIONS, THE .... MAXIMILIAN SCHELL
YOUNG LOVE,
  FIRST LOVE (TF) .... TIMOTHY HUTTON
YOUNG LOVE,
  FIRST LOVE (TF) .... VALERIE BERTINELLI
YOUNG LOVERS, THE .... JOSEPH CAMPANELLA
YOUNG LOVERS, THE .... PETER FONDA
YOUNG MAN WITH A HORN .... DORIS DAY
YOUNG MAN WITH A HORN .... KIRK DOUGLAS
YOUNG MAN WITH A HORN .... LAUREN BACALL
YOUNG MAN WITH IDEAS .... MARY WICKES
YOUNG MAN WITH IDEAS .... NINA FOCH
YOUNG MR. LINCOLN .... HENRY FONDA†
YOUNG MR. PITT, THE .... JOHN MILLS
YOUNG MR. PITT, THE .... ROBERT MORLEY
YOUNG NURSES, THE .... SALLY KIRKLAND
YOUNG ONES, THE .... ROBERT MORLEY
YOUNG PHILADELPHIANS, THE .... ADAM WEST
YOUNG PHILADELPHIANS, THE .... ALEXIS SMITH†
YOUNG PHILADELPHIANS, THE .... BRIAN KEITH
YOUNG PHILADELPHIANS, THE .... PAUL NEWMAN
YOUNG
  PHILADELPHIANS, THE ○ .... ROBERT VAUGHN
YOUNG PIONEERS (TF) .... ROBERT HAYS
YOUNG PIONEERS'
  CHRISTMAS (TF) .... ROBERT HAYS
YOUNG RACERS, THE .... LUANA ANDERS
YOUNG REBEL, THE .... LOUIS JOURDAN
YOUNG RUNAWAYS, THE .... RICHARD DREYFUSS
YOUNG SAVAGES, THE .... BURT LANCASTER†
YOUNG SAVAGES, THE .... DINA MERRILL
YOUNG SAVAGES, THE .... SHELLEY WINTERS
YOUNG SAVAGES, THE .... TELLY SAVALAS†
YOUNG SINNER, THE .... STEFANIE POWERS
YOUNG TOM EDISON .... MICKEY ROONEY
YOUNG WARRIORS .... ERNEST BORGNINE
YOUNG WINSTON .... ANNE BANCROFT
YOUNG WINSTON .... ANTHONY HOPKINS
YOUNG WINSTON .... EDWARD WOODWARD

† after an actor's name denotes deceased.

I
N
D
E
X

O
F

F
I
L
M

T
I
T
L
E
S

YOUNG WINSTON .... IAN HOLM
YOUNG WINSTON .... JANE SEYMOUR
YOUNG WINSTON .... SIMON WARD
YOUNG WIVES' TALE .... AUDREY HEPBURN†
YOUNGBLOOD .... CYNTHIA GIBB
YOUNGBLOOD .... ED LAUTER
YOUNGBLOOD .... FIONNULA FLANAGAN
YOUNGBLOOD .... GEORGE FINN
YOUNGBLOOD .... KEANU REEVES
YOUNGBLOOD .... PATRICK SWAYZE
YOUNGBLOOD .... ROB LOWE
YOUNGBLOOD HAWKE .... EVA GABOR
YOUNGBLOOD HAWKE .... JAMES FRANCISCUS†
YOUNGBLOOD HAWKE .... JOHN DEHNER†
YOUNGBLOOD HAWKE .... MARTIN BALSAM
YOUNGBLOOD HAWKE .... SUZANNE PLESHETTE
YOUNGEST PROFESSION, THE ..... GREER GARSON
YOUNGEST PROFESSION, THE .... LANA TURNER
YOUR CHEATIN' HEART .... GEORGE HAMILTON
YOUR CHEATIN' HEART .... RED BUTTONS
YOUR HEAVEN, MY HELL .... JOHN PHILLIP LAW
YOUR MONEY OR
    YOUR WIFE (TF) .... ELIZABETH ASHLEY
YOUR MOTHER WEARS
    COMBAT BOOTS (TF) .... BARBARA EDEN
YOUR MOTHER WEARS
    COMBAT BOOTS (TF) .... CONCHATA FERRELL
YOUR MOTHER WEARS
    COMBAT BOOTS (TF) .... HECTOR ELIZONDO
YOUR THREE MINUTES ARE UP ...... BEAU BRIDGES
YOUR THREE
    MINUTES ARE UP .... JANET MARGOLIN
YOUR THREE MINUTES ARE UP .... RON LEIBMAN
YOUR TICKET IS NO
    LONGER VALID .... GEORGE PEPPARD†
YOUR TICKET IS NO
    LONGER VALID .... RICHARD HARRIS
YOURS, MINE AND OURS .... LUCILLE BALL†
YOURS, MINE AND OURS .... MORGAN BRITTANY
YOURS, MINE AND OURS .... TIM MATHESON
YOURS, MINE AND OURS .... TOM BOSLEY
YOURS MINE AND OURS .... VAN JOHNSON
YOUTH ON PARADE .... YVONNE DE CARLO
YOUTH RUNS WILD .... LAWRENCE TIERNEY
YOU'LL LIKE MY MOTHER .... PATTY DUKE
YOU'LL LIKE MY MOTHER .... RICHARD THOMAS
YOU'LL LIKE MY MOTHER .... ROSEMARY MURPHY
YOU'RE A BIG BOY NOW .... JULIE HARRIS
YOU'RE A BIG BOY NOW .... KAREN BLACK
YOU'RE A BIG BOY NOW .... RIP TORN
YOU'RE A BIG BOY NOW .... TONY BILL
YOU'RE IN THE ARMY NOW .... JANE WYMAN
YOU'RE IN THE ARMY NOW .... JOHN MILLS
YOU'RE IN THE NAVY NOW ..... CHARLES BRONSON
YOU'RE IN THE NAVY NOW .... EDDIE ALBERT
YOU'RE IN THE NAVY NOW .... JACK WARDEN
YOU'RE IN THE NAVY NOW .... JANE GREER
YOU'RE NEVER TOO YOUNG .... DEAN MARTIN
YOU'RE NEVER TOO YOUNG .... JERRY LEWIS
YOU'RE NEVER TOO YOUNG .... NINA FOCH
YOU'RE NEVER TOO YOUNG ...... RAYMOND BURR†
YOU'VE GOT TO WALK IT LIKE
    YOU TALK IT OR YOU'LL
    LOSE THAT BEAT .... RICHARD PRYOR
YOU'VE GOT TO WALK IT LIKE
    YOU TALK IT OR YOU'LL
    LOSE YOUR BEAT .... ALLEN GARFIELD
YOYO .... CLAUDINE AUGER
YUMA (TF) .... CLINT WALKER
YUPPI-DU .... CHARLOTTE RAMPLING
YURI NOSENKO, KGB (CTF) .... TOMMY LEE JONES

Z

Z.P.G. .... DON GORDON
Z.P.G. .... GERALDINE CHAPLIN
Z.P.G. .... OLIVER REED
ZABRISKIE POINT .... BEN HAMMER
ZABRISKIE POINT .... HARRISON FORD
ZACHARIAH .... DICK VAN PATTEN
ZACHARIAH .... DON JOHNSON
ZACHARIAH .... PAT QUINN
ZAMBA .... BEAU BRIDGES
ZANDALEE .... AARON NEVILLE
ZANDALEE .... ERIKA ANDERSON
ZANDALEE .... IAN ABERCROMBIE
ZANDALEE .... JOE PANTOLIANO
ZANDALEE .... JUDGE REINHOLD
ZANDALEE .... MARISA TOMEI
ZANDALEE .... NICOLAS CAGE
ZANDALEE .... VIVECA LINDFORS
ZANDALEE .... ZACH GALLIGAN
ZANDY'S BRIDE .... EILEEN HECKART
ZANDY'S BRIDE .... GENE HACKMAN
ZANDY'S BRIDE .... HARRY DEAN STANTON
ZANDY'S BRIDE .... JOE SANTOS
ZANDY'S BRIDE .... LIV ULLMANN
ZANDY'S BRIDE .... SAM BOTTOMS
ZANDY'S BRIDE .... SUSAN TYRRELL
ZANY ADVENTURES OF
    ROBIN HOOD, THE (TF) .... GEORGE SEGAL
ZAPPED! .... FELICE SCHACHTER
ZAPPED! .... GREG BRADFORD
ZAPPED! .... HEATHER THOMAS
ZAPPED! .... ROBERT MANDAN
ZAPPED! .... SCATMAN CROTHERS†
ZAPPED! .... SCOTT BAIO
ZAPPED! .... SUE ANE LANGDON
ZAPPED! .... WILLIE AAMES
ZARDOZ .... SEAN CONNERY
ZARDOZ, IL PORTIERE
    DI NOTTE .... CHARLOTTE RAMPLING
ZEBRAHEAD .... MICHAEL RAPAPORT
ZED AND TWO NOUGHTS, A .... JOSS ACKLAND
ZEE & CO. .... ELIZABETH TAYLOR
ZEE & CO. .... MICHAEL CAINE
ZEE & CO. .... SUSANNAH YORK
ZELIG .... GARRETT M. BROWN
ZELIG .... MARY LOUISE WILSON
ZELIG .... MIA FARROW
ZELIG .... SOL LOMITA
ZELIG .... STEPHANIE FARROW
ZELIG .... WILL HOLT
ZELIG .... WOODY ALLEN
ZELLY AND ME .... DAVID LYNCH
ZELLY AND ME .... ISABELLA ROSSELLINI
ZEPPELIN .... MICHAEL YORK
ZERO HOUR .... LINDA DARNELL†
ZERO HOUR .... STERLING HAYDEN†
ZERO TO SIXTY .... DARREN McGAVIN
ZERO TO SIXTY .... JOAN COLLINS
ZERO TO SIXTY .... SYLVIA MILES
ZIEGFELD FOLLIES .... GENE KELLY
ZIEGFELD FOLLIES .... HUME CRONYN
ZIEGFELD FOLLIES .... LENA HORNE
ZIEGFELD FOLLIES .... VAN JOHNSON
ZIEGFELD GIRL .... JACKIE COOPER
ZIEGFELD GIRL .... JAMES STEWART
ZIEGFELD GIRL .... LANA TURNER
ZIEGFELD: THE MAN AND
    HIS WOMEN (TF) .... PAUL SHENAR

ZIEGFELD: THE MAN AND
    HIS WOMEN (TF) .... SAMANTHA EGGAR
ZIEGFELD: THE MAN AND
    HIS WOMEN (TF) ....VALERIE PERRINE
ZIGGY STARDUST AND THE
    SPIDERS FROM MARS .... DAVID BOWIE
ZIGZAG .... ANNE JACKSON
ZIGZAG .... ELI WALLACH
ZIGZAG .... GEORGE KENNEDY
ZIGZAG .... STEVE IHNAT†
ZIGZAG .... WILLIAM MARSHALL
ZOMBIE NIGHTMARE .... ADAM WEST
ZOO .... ELIJAH WOOD
ZOO GANG, THE .... ERIC GURRY
ZOO GANG, THE .... JASON GEDRICK
ZOOT SUIT .... TYNE DALY
ZORBA THE GREEK .... ALAN BATES
ZORBA THE GREEK ★ .... ANTHONY QUINN
ZORBA THE GREEK ○○ .... LILA KEDROVA
ZORRO, THE GAY BLADE .... BRENDA VACCARO
ZORRO, THE GAY BLADE .... DONAOVAN SCOTT
ZORRO, THE GAY BLADE .... GEORGE HAMILTON
ZORRO, THE GAY BLADE .... JAMES BOOTH
ZORRO, THE GAY BLADE .... LAUREN HUTTON
ZORRO, THE GAY BLADE .... RON LEIBMAN
ZOTZI .... TOM POSTON
ZULU .... JACK HAWKINS†
ZULU .... JAMES BOOTH
ZULU .... MICHAEL CAINE
ZULU .... NIGEL GREEN†
ZULU .... ULLA JACOBSSON†
ZULU DAWN .... BOB HOSKINS
ZULU DAWN .... BURT LANCASTER†
ZULU DAWN .... CHRISTOPHER CAZENOVE
ZULU DAWN .... DENHOLM ELLIOTT†
ZULU DAWN .... NICHOLAS CLAY
ZULU DAWN .... NIGEL DAVENPORT
ZULU DAWN .... PETER O'TOOLE
ZULU DAWN .... PETER VAUGHN
ZULU DAWN .... RONALD LACEY
ZULU DAWN .... SIMON WARD
ZUMA BEACH (TF) .... KIMBERLY BECK
ZUMA BEACH (TF) .... MICHAEL BIEHN
ZUMA BEACH (TF) .... P. J. SOLES
ZUMA BEACH (TF) .... PERRY LANG
ZUMA BEACH (TF) .... ROSANNA ARQUETTE
ZUMA BEACH (TF) .... STEVEN KEATS†
ZUMA BEACH (TF) .... SUZANNE SOMERS
ZUMA BEACH (TF) .... TANYA ROBERTS
ZUMA BEACH (TF) .... TIMOTHY HUTTON

★★★

586

INDICES

ACADEMY AWARD NOMINEES AND WINNERS · INDEX BY ACTOR
INDEX OF ACTOR & AGENT · AGENTS & MANAGERS · ADVERTISERS

ACADEMY AWARD NOMINEES AND WINNERS
By Year
1927-1993

★★ = Academy Award Win for Best Performance by an Actor or Actress in a Leading Role

○○ = Academy Award Win for Best Performance by an Actor or Actress in a Supporting Role

1927-1928

Best Actor
Emil Jannings ★★ .... THE LAST COMMAND
Emil Jannings ★★ .... THE WAY OF ALL FLESH
Richard Barthelmess .... THE NOOSE
Richard Barthelmess .... THE PATENT LEATHER KID

Best Actress
Janet Gaynor ★★ .... SEVENTH HEAVEN
Janet Gaynor ★★ .... STREET ANGEL
Janet Gaynor ★★ .... SUNRISE
Louise Dresser .... A SHIP COMES IN
Gloria Swanson .... SADIE THOMPSON

1928-1929

Best Actor
Warner Baxter ★★ .... IN OLD ARIZONA
George Bancroft .... THUNDERBOLT
Chester Morris .... ALIBI
Paul Muni .... THE VALIANT
Lewis Stone .... THE PATRIOT

Best Actress
Mary Pickford ★★ .... COQUETTE
Ruth Chatterton .... MADAME X
Betty Compson .... THE BARKER
Jeanne Eagels .... THE LETTER
Corinne Griffith .... THE DIVINE LADY
Bessie Love .... BROADWAY MELODY

1929-1930

Best Actor
George Arliss ★★ .... DISRAELI
George Arliss .... THE GREEN GODDESS
Wallace Beery .... THE BIG HOUSE
Maurice Chevalier .... THE LOVE PARADE
Maurice Chevalier .... THE BIG POND
Ronald Colman .... BULLDOG DRUMMOND
Ronald Colman .... CONDEMNED
Lawrence Tibbett .... THE ROGUE SONG

Best Actress
Norma Shearer ★★ .... THE DIVORCÉE
Nancy Carroll .... THE DEVIL'S HOLIDAY
Ruth Chatterton .... SARAH AND SON
Greta Garbo .... ANNA CHRISTIE
Greta Garbo .... ROMANCE
Norma Shearer .... THEIR OWN DESIRE
Gloria Swanson .... THE TRESPASSER

1930-1931

Best Actor
Lionel Barrymore ★★ .... A FREE SOUL
Jackie Cooper .... SKIPPY
Richard Dix .... CIMARRON
Fredric March .... THE ROYAL FAMILY OF BROADWAY
Adolphe Menjou .... THE FRONT PAGE

Best Actress
Marie Dressler ★★ .... MIN AND BILL
Marlene Dietrich .... MOROCCO
Irene Dunne .... CIMARRON
Ann Harding .... HOLIDAY
Norma Shearer .... A FREE SOUL

1931-1932

Best Actor
Wallace Beery ★★ .... THE CHAMP
Fredric March ★★ .... DR. JEKYLL AND MR. HYDE
Alfred Lunt .... THE GUARDSMAN

Best Actress
Helen Hayes ★★ .... THE SIN OF MADELON CLAUDET
Marie Dressler .... EMMA
Lynn Fontanne .... THE GUARDSMAN

1932-1933

Best Actor
Charles Laughton ★★ ..... THE PRIVATE LIFE OF HENRY VIII
Leslie Howard .... BERKELEY SQUARE
Paul Muni .... I AM A FUGITIVE FROM A CHAIN GANG

Best Actress
Katharine Hepburn ★★ .... MORNING GLORY
May Robson .... LADY FOR A DAY
Diana Wynyard .... CAVALCADE

1934

Best Actor
Clark Gable ★★ ....IT HAPPENED ONE NIGHT
Frank Morgan .... AFFAIRS OF CELLINI
William Powell .... THE THIN MAN

Best Actress
Claudette Colbert ★★ .... IT HAPPENED ONE NIGHT
Grace Moore .... ONE NIGHT OF LOVE
Norma Shearer .... THE BARRETTS OF WIMPOLE STREET

1935

Best Actor

Victor McLaglen ★★ .... THE INFORMER
Clark Gable .... MUTINY ON THE BOUNTY
Charles Laughton .... MUTINY ON THE BOUNTY
Franchot Tone .... MUTINY ON THE BOUNTY

Best Actress

Bette Davis ★★ .... DANGEROUS
Elisabeth Bergner .... ESCAPE ME NEVER
Claudette Colbert .... PRIVATE WORLDS
Katharine Hepburn .... ALICE ADAMS
Miriam Hopkins .... BECKY SHARP
Merle Oberon .... THE DARK ANGEL

1936

Best Actor

Paul Muni ★★ .... THE STORY OF LOUIS PASTEUR
Gary Cooper .... MR. DEEDS GOES TO TOWN
Walter Huston .... DODSWORTH
William Powell .... MY MAN GODFREY
Spencer Tracy .... SAN FRANCISCO

Best Actress

Norma Shearer ★★ .... ROMEO AND JULIET
Irene Dunne .... THEODORA GOES WILD
Gladys George .... VALIANT IS THE WORD FOR CARRIE
Carole Lombard .... MY MAN GODFREY
Luise Rainer .... THE GREAT ZIEGFELD

Best Supporting Actor

Walter Brennan ○○ .... COME AND GET IT
Mischa Auer .... MY MAN GODFREY
Stuart Erwin .... PIGSKIN PARADE
Basil Rathbone .... ROMEO AND JULIET
Akim Tamiroff .... THE GENERAL DIED AT DAWN

Best Supporting Actress

Gale Sondergaard ○○ .... ANTHONY ADVERSE
Beulah Bondi .... THE GORGEOUS HUSSY
Alice Brady .... MY MAN GODFREY
Bonita Granville .... THESE THREE
Maria Ouspenskaya .... DODSWORTH

1937

Best Actor

Spencer Tracy ★★ .... CAPTAINS COURAGEOUS
Charles Boyer .... CONQUEST
Fredric March .... A STAR IS BORN
Robert Montgomery .... NIGHT MUST FALL
Paul Muni .... THE LIFE OF EMILE ZOLA

Best Actress

Luise Rainer ★★ .... THE GOOD EARTH
Irene Dunne .... THE AWFUL TRUTH
Greta Garbo .... CAMILLE
Janet Gaynor .... A STAR IS BORN
Barbara Stanwyck .... STELLA DALLAS

Best Supporting Actor

Joseph Schildkraut ○○ .... THE LIFE OF EMILE ZOLA
Ralph Bellamy .... THE AWFUL TRUTH
Thomas Mitchell .... THE HURRICANE
H. B. Warner .... LOST HORIZON
Roland Young .... TOPPER

Best Supporting Actress

Alice Brady ○○ .... IN OLD CHICAGO
Andrea Leeds .... STAGE DOOR
Anne Shirley .... STELLA DALLAS
Claire Trevor .... DEAD END
Dame May Whitty .... NIGHT MUST FALL

1938

Best Actor

Spencer Tracy ★★ .... BOYS TOWN
Charles Boyer .... ALGIERS
James Cagney .... ANGELS WITH DIRTY FACES
Robert Donat .... THE CITADEL
Leslie Howard .... PYGMALION

Best Actress

Bette Davis ★★ .... JEZEBEL
Fay Bainter .... WHITE BANNERS
Wendy Hiller .... PYGMALION
Norma Shearer .... MARIE ANTOINETTE
Margaret Sullavan .... THREE COMRADES

Best Supporting Actor

Walter Brennan ○○ .... KENTUCKY
John Garfield .... FOUR DAUGHTERS
Gene Lockhart .... ALGIERS
Robert Morley .... MARIE ANTOINETTE
Basil Rathbone .... IF I WERE KING

Best Supporting Actress

Fay Bainter ○○ .... JEZEBEL
Beulah Bondi .... OF HUMAN HEARTS
Billie Burke .... MERRILY WE LIVE
Spring Byington .... YOU CAN'T TAKE IT WITH YOU
Miliza Korjus .... THE GREAT WALTZ

1939

Best Actor

Robert Donat ★★ .... GOODBYE, MR. CHIPS
Clark Gable .... GONE WITH THE WIND
Laurence Olivier .... WUTHERING HEIGHTS
Mickey Rooney .... BABES IN ARMS
James Stewart .... MR. SMITH GOES TO WASHINGTON

Best Actress

Vivien Leigh ★★ .... GONE WITH THE WIND
Bette Davis .... DARK VICTORY
Irene Dunne .... LOVE AFFAIR
Greta Garbo .... NINOTCHKA
Greer Garson .... GOODBYE, MR. CHIPS

Best Supporting Actor

Thomas Mitchell ○○ .... STAGECOACH
Brian Aherne .... JUAREZ
Harry Carey .... MR. SMITH GOES TO WASHINGTON
Brian Donlevy .... BEAU GESTE
Claude Rains .... MR. SMITH GOES TO WASHINGTON

Best Supporting Actress

Hattie McDaniel ○○ .... GONE WITH THE WIND
Olivia De Havilland .... GONE WITH THE WIND
Geraldine Fitzgerald .... WUTHERING HEIGHTS
Edna May Oliver .... DRUMS ALONG THE MOHAWK
Maria Ouspenskaya .... LOVE AFFAIR

1940

Best Actor

James Stewart ★★ .... THE PHILADELPHIA STORY
Charles Chaplin ....THE GREAT DICTATOR
Henry Fonda .... THE GRAPES OF WRATH
Raymond Massey .... ABE LINCOLN IN ILLINOIS
Laurence Olivier .... REBECCA

Best Actress

Ginger Rogers ★★ ....KITTY FOYLE
Bette Davis .... THE LETTER
Joan Fontaine .... REBECCA
Katharine Hepburn .... THE PHILADELPHIA STORY
Martha Scott .... OUR TOWN

Best Supporting Actor

Walter Brennan ✪✪ .... THE WESTERNER
Albert Basserman .... FOREIGN CORRESPONDENT
William Gargan .... THEY KNEW WHAT THEY WANTED
Jack Oakie .... THE GREAT DICTATOR
James Stephenson ....THE LETTER

Best Supporting Actress

Jane Darwell ✪✪ .... THE GRAPES OF WRATH
Judith Anderson .... REBECCA
Ruth Hussey .... THE PHILADELPHIA STORY
Barbara O'Neil ....ALL THIS, AND HEAVEN TOO
Marjorie Rambeau ....PRIMROSE PATH

1941

Best Actor

Gary Cooper ★★ ....SERGEANT YORK
Cary Grant .... PENNY SERENADE
Walter Huston .... ALL THAT MONEY CAN BUY
            (AKA THE DEVIL AND DANIEL WEBSTER)
Robert Montgomery .... HERE COMES MR. JORDAN
Orson Welles .... CITIZEN KANE

Best Actress

Joan Fontaine ★★ .... SUSPICION
Bette Davis .... THE LITTLE FOXES
Greer Garson .... BLOSSOMS IN THE DUST
Olivia De Havilland ....HOLD BACK THE DAWN
Barbara Stanwyck.. BALL OF FIRE

Best Supporting Actor

Donald Crisp ✪✪ .... HOW GREEN WAS MY VALLEY
Walter Brennan .... SERGEANT YORK
Charles Coburn .... THE DEVIL AND MISS JONES
James Gleason .... HERE COMES MR. JORDAN
Sydney Greenstreet .... THE MALTESE FALCON

Best Supporting Actress

Mary Astor ✪✪ .... THE GREAT LIE
Sara Allgood .... HOW GREEN WAS MY VALLEY
Patricia Collinge .... THE LITTLE FOXES
Teresa Wright .... THE LITTLE FOXES
Margaret Wycherly ....SERGEANT YORK

1942

Best Actor

James Cagney ★★ .... YANKEE DOODLE DANDY
Ronald Colman ....RANDOM HARVEST
Gary Cooper .... THE PRIDE OF THE YANKEES
Walter Pidgeon ....MRS. MINIVER
Monty Woolley .... THE PIED PIPER

Best Actress

Greer Garson ★★ ....MRS. MINIVER
Bette Davis .... NOW, VOYAGER
Katharine Hepburn .... WOMAN OF THE YEAR
Rosalind Russell .... MY SISTER EILEEN
Teresa Wright .... THE PRIDE OF THE YANKEES

Best Supporting Actor

Van Heflin ✪✪ .... JOHNNY EAGER
William Bendix .... WAKE ISLAND
Walter Huston .... YANKEE DOODLE DANDY
Frank Morgan .... TORTILLA FLAT
Henry Travers .... MRS. MINIVER

Best Supporting Actress

Teresa Wright ✪✪ ....MRS. MINIVER
Gladys Cooper .... NOW, VOYAGER
Agnes Moorehead .... THE MAGNIFICENT AMBERSONS
Susan Peters .... RANDOM HARVEST
Dame May Whitty ....MRS. MINIVER

1943

Best Actor

Paul Lukas ★★ .... WATCH ON THE RHINE
Humphrey Bogart .... CASABLANCA
Gary Cooper .... FOR WHOM THE BELL TOLLS
Walter Pidgeon .... MADAME CURIE
Mickey Rooney .... THE HUMAN COMEDY

Best Actress

Jennifer Jones ★★ ....THE SONG OF BERNADETTE
Jean Arthur ....THE MORE THE MERRIER
Ingrid Bergman .... FOR WHOM THE BELL TOLLS
Joan Fontaine .... THE CONSTANT NYMPH
Greer Garson .... MADAME CURIE

Best Supporting Actor

Charles Coburn ✪✪ .... THE MORE THE MERRIER
Charles Bickford ....THE SONG OF BERNADETTE
J. Carrol Naish ....SAHARA
Claude Rains .... CASABLANCA
Akim Tamiroff .... FOR WHOM THE BELL TOLLS

Best Supporting Actress

Katina Paxinou ✪✪ .... FOR WHOM THE BELL TOLLS
Gladys Cooper ....THE SONG OF BERNADETTE
Paulette Goddard .... SO PROUDLY WE HAIL
Anne Revere .... THE SONG OF BERNADETTE
Lucile Watson .... WATCH ON THE RHINE

1944

Best Actor

Bing Crosby ★★ .... GOING MY WAY
Charles Boyer .... GASLIGHT
Barry Fitzgerald .... GOING MY WAY
Cary Grant .... NONE BUT THE LONELY HEART
Alexander Knox .... WILSON

Best Actress

Ingrid Bergman ★★ .... GASLIGHT
Claudette Colbert ....SINCE YOU WENT AWAY
Bette Davis .... MR. SKEFFINGTON
Greer Garson .... MRS. PARKINGTON
Barbara Stanwyck ....DOUBLE INDEMNITY

Best Supporting Actor

Barry Fitzgerald ✪✪ .... GOING MY WAY
Hume Cronyn .... THE SEVENTH CROSS
Claude Rains .... MR. SKEFFINGTON
Clifton Webb .... LAURA
Monty Woolley .... SINCE YOU WENT AWAY

Best Supporting Actress

Ethel Barrymore ✪✪ .... NONE BUT THE LONELY HEART
Jennifer Jones .... SINCE YOU WENT AWAY
Angela Lansbury .... GASLIGHT
Aline MacMahon .... DRAGON SEED
Agnes Moorehead .... MRS. PARKINGTON

1945

Best Actor

Ray Milland ★★ .... THE LOST WEEKEND
Bing Crosby .... THE BELLS OF ST. MARY'S
Gene Kelly .... ANCHORS AWEIGH
Gregory Peck .... THE KEYS OF THE KINGDOM
Cornel Wilde .... A SONG TO REMEMBER

Best Actress

Joan Crawford ★★ .... MILDRED PIERCE
Ingrid Bergman .... THE BELLS OF ST. MARY'S
Greer Garson .... THE VALLEY OF DECISION
Jennifer Jones .... LOVE LETTERS
Gene Tierney .... LEAVE HER TO HEAVEN

Best Supporting Actor

James Dunn ✪✪ .... A TREE GROWS IN BROOKLYN
Michael Chekhov .... SPELLBOUND
John Dall .... THE CORN IS GREEN
Robert Mitchum .... THE STORY OF G.I. JOE
J. Carrol Naish .... A MEDAL FOR BENNY

Best Supporting Actress

Anne Revere ✪✪ .... NATIONAL VELVET
Eve Arden .... MILDRED PIERCE
Ann Blyth .... MILDRED PIERCE
Angela Lansbury .... THE PICTURE OF DORIAN GRAY
Joan Lorring .... THE CORN IS GREEN

1946

Best Actor

Fredric March ★★ .... THE BEST YEARS OF OUR LIVES
Laurence Olivier .... HENRY V
Larry Parks .... THE JOLSON STORY
Gregory Peck .... THE YEARLING
James Stewart .... IT'S A WONDERFUL LIFE

Best Actress

Olivia De Havilland ★★ .... TO EACH HIS OWN
Celia Johnson .... BRIEF ENCOUNTER
Jennifer Jones .... DUEL IN THE SUN
Rosalind Russell .... SISTER KENNY
Jane Wyman .... THE YEARLING

Best Supporting Actor

Harold Russell ✪✪ .... THE BEST YEARS OF OUR LIVES
Charles Coburn .... THE GREEN YEARS
William Demarest .... THE JOLSON STORY
Claude Rains .... NOTORIOUS
Clifton Webb .... THE RAZOR'S EDGE

Best Supporting Actress

Anne Baxter ✪✪ .... THE RAZOR'S EDGE
Ethel Barrymore .... THE SPIRAL STAIRCASE
Lillian Gish .... DUEL IN THE SUN
Flora Robson .... SARATOGA TRUNK
Gale Sondergaard .... ANNA AND THE KING OF SIAM

1947

Best Actor

Ronald Colman ★★ .... A DOUBLE LIFE
John Garfield .... BODY AND SOUL
Gregory Peck .... GENTLEMAN'S AGREEMENT
William Powell .... LIFE WITH FATHER
Michael Redgrave .... MOURNING BECOMES ELECTRA

Best Actress

Loretta Young ★★ .... THE FARMER'S DAUGHTER
Joan Crawford .... POSSESSED
Susan Hayward ..... SMASH UP—THE STORY OF A WOMAN
Dorothy McGuire .... GENTLEMAN'S AGREEMENT
Rosalind Russell .... MOURNING BECOMES ELECTRA

Best Supporting Actor

Edmund Gwenn ✪✪ .... MIRACLE ON 34TH STREET
Charles Bickford .... THE FARMER'S DAUGHTER
Thomas Gomez .... RIDE THE PINK HORSE
Robert Ryan .... CROSSFIRE
Richard Widmark .... KISS OF DEATH

Best Supporting Actress

Celeste Holm ✪✪ .... GENTLEMAN'S AGREEMENT
Ethel Barrymore .... THE PARADINE CASE
Gloria Grahame .... CROSSFIRE
Marjorie Main .... THE EGG AND I
Anne Revere .... GENTLEMAN'S AGREEMENT

1948

Best Actor

Laurence Olivier ★★ .... HAMLET
Lew Ayres .... JOHNNY BELINDA
Montgomery Clift .... THE SEARCH
Dan Dailey .... WHEN MY BABY SMILES AT ME
Clifton Webb .... SITTING PRETTY

Best Actress

Jane Wyman ★★ .... JOHNNY BELINDA
Ingrid Bergman .... JOAN OF ARC
Olivia De Havilland .... THE SNAKE PIT
Irene Dunne .... I REMEMBER MAMA
Barbara Stanwyck .... SORRY, WRONG NUMBER

Best Supporting Actor

Walter Huston ✪✪ .... TREASURE OF SIERRA MADRE
Charles Bickford .... JOHNNY BELINDA
José Ferrer .... JOAN OF ARC
Oscar Homolka .... I REMEMBER MAMA
Cecil Kellaway .... THE LUCK OF THE IRISH

Best Supporting Actress

Claire Trevor ✪✪ .... KEY LARGO
Barbara Bel Geddes .... I REMEMBER MAMA
Ellen Corby .... I REMEMBER MAMA
Agnes Moorehead .... JOHNNY BELINDA
Jean Simmons .... HAMLET

1949

Best Actor
Broderick Crawford ★★ .... ALL THE KING'S MEN
Kirk Douglas .... CHAMPION
Gregory Peck .... 12 O'CLOCK HIGH
Richard Todd .... THE HASTY HEART
John Wayne .... SANDS OF IWO JIMA

Best Actress
Olivia De Havilland ★★ .... THE HEIRESS
Jeanne Crain .... PINKY
Susan Hayward .... MY FOOLISH HEART
Deborah Kerr .... EDWARD MY SON
Loretta Young .... COME TO THE STABLE

Best Supporting Actor
Dean Jagger ⊙⊙ .... 12 O'CLOCK HIGH
John Ireland .... ALL THE KING'S MEN
Arthur Kennedy .... CHAMPION
Ralph Richardson .... THE HEIRESS
James Whitmore .... BATTLEGROUND

Best Supprting Actress
Mercedes McCambridge ⊙⊙ .... ALL THE KING'S MEN
Ethel Barrymore .... PINKY
Celeste Holm .... COME TO THE STABLE
Elsa Lanchester .... COME TO THE STABLE
Ethel Waters .... PINKY

1950

Best Actor
José Ferrer ★★ .... CYRANO DE BERGERAC
Louis Calhern .... THE MAGNIFICENT YANKEE
William Holden .... SUNSET BOULEVARD
James Stewart .... HARVEY
Spencer Tracy .... FATHER OF THE BRIDE

Best Actress
Judy Holliday ★★ .... BORN YESTERDAY
Anne Baxter .... ALL ABOUT EVE
Bette Davis .... ALL ABOUT EVE
Eleanor Parker .... CAGED
Gloria Swanson .... SUNSET BOULEVARD

Best Supporting Actor
George Sanders ⊙⊙ .... ALL ABOUT EVE
Jeff Chandler .... BROKEN ARROW
Edmund Gwenn .... MISTER 880
Sam Jaffe .... THE ASPHALT JUNGLE
Erich Von Stroheim .... SUNSET BOULEVARD

Best Supporting Actress
Josephine Hull ⊙⊙ .... HARVEY
Hope Emerson .... CAGED
Celeste Holm .... ALL ABOUT EVE
Nancy Olson .... SUNSET BOULEVARD
Thelma Ritter .... ALL ABOUT EVE

1951

Best Actor
Humphrey Bogart ★★ .... THE AFRICAN QUEEN
Marlon Brando .... A STREETCAR NAMED DESIRE
Montgomery Clift .... A PLACE IN THE SUN
Arthur Kennedy .... BRIGHT VICTORY
Fredric March .... DEATH OF A SALESMAN

Best Actress
Vivien Leigh ★★ .... A STREETCAR NAMED DESIRE
Katharine Hepburn .... THE AFRICAN QUEEN
Eleanor Parker .... DETECTIVE STORY
Shelley Winters .... A PLACE IN THE SUN
Jane Wyman .... THE BLUE VEIL

Best Supporting Actor
Karl Malden ⊙⊙ .... A STREETCAR NAMED DESIRE
Leo Genn .... QUO VADIS
Kevin McCarthy .... DEATH OF A SALESMAN
Peter Ustinov .... QUO VADIS
Gig Young .... COME FILL THE CUP

Best Supporting Actress
Kim Hunter ⊙⊙ .... A STREETCAR NAMED DESIRE
Joan Blondell .... THE BLUE VEIL
Mildred Dunnock .... DEATH OF A SALESMAN
Lee Grant .... DETECTIVE STORY
Thelma Ritter .... THE MATING SEASON

1952

Best Actor
Gary Cooper ★★ .... HIGH NOON
Marlon Brando .... VIVA ZAPATA!
Kirk Douglas .... THE BAD AND THE BEAUTIFUL
José Ferrer .... MOULIN ROUGE
Alec Guinness .... THE LAVENDER HILL MOB

Best Actress
Shirley Booth ★★ .... COME BACK, LITTLE SHEBA
Joan Crawford ....SUDDEN FEAR
Bette Davis .... THE STAR
Julie Harris .... THE MEMBER OF THE WEDDING
Susan Hayward .... WITH A SONG IN MY HEART

Best Supporting Actor
Anthony Quinn ⊙⊙ .... VIVA ZAPATA!
Richard Burton .... MY COUSIN RACHEL
Arthur Hunnicutt .... THE BIG SKY
Victor McLaglen .... THE QUIET MAN
Jack Palance ....SUDDEN FEAR

Best Supporting Actress
Gloria Grahame ⊙⊙ .... THE BAD AND THE BEAUTIFUL
Jean Hagen .... SINGIN' IN THE RAIN
Colette Marchand .... MOULIN ROUGE
Terry Moore .... COME BACK, LITTLE SHEBA
Thelma Ritter .... WITH A SONG IN MY HEART

1953

Best Actor
William Holden ★★ .... STALAG 17
Marlon Brando .... JULIUS CAESAR
Richard Burton .... THE ROBE
Montgomery Clift .... FROM HERE TO ETERNITY
Burt Lancaster .... FROM HERE TO ETERNITY

Best Actress
Audrey Hepburn ★★ .... ROMAN HOLIDAY
Leslie Caron LILI
Ava Gardner .... MOGAMBO
Deborah Kerr .... FROM HERE TO ETERNITY
Maggie Mcnamara .... THE MOON IS BLUE

ACADEMY AWARDS

Best Supporting Actor
Frank Sinatra ○○ .... FROM HERE TO ETERNITY
Eddie Albert .... ROMAN HOLIDAY
Brandon De Wilde .... SHANE
Jack Palance .... SHANE
Robert Strauss .... STALAG 17

Best Supporting Actress
Donna Reed ○○ .... FROM HERE TO ETERNITY
Grace Kelly .... MOGAMBO
Geraldine Page .... HONDO
Marjorie Rambeau .... TORCH SONG
Thelma Ritter .... PICKUP ON SOUTH STREET

1954

Best Actor
Marlon Brando ★★ .... ON THE WATERFRONT
Humphrey Bogart .... THE CAINE MUTINY
Bing Crosby .... THE COUNTRY GIRL
James Mason .... A STAR IS BORN
Dan O'Herlihy ..... ADVENTURES OF ROBINSON CRUSOE

Best Actress
Grace Kelly ★★ .... THE COUNTRY GIRL
Dorothy Dandridge .... CARMEN JONES
Judy Garland .... A STAR IS BORN
Audrey Hepburn .... SABRINA
Jane Wyman .... MAGNIFICENT OBSESSION

Best Supporting Actor
Edmond O'Brien ○○ .... THE BAREFOOT CONTESSA
Lee J. Cobb .... ON THE WATERFRONT
Karl Malden .... ON THE WATERFRONT
Rod Steiger .... ON THE WATERFRONT
Tom Tully .... THE CAINE MUTINY

Best Supporting Actress
Eva Marie Saint ○○ .... ON THE WATERFRONT
Nina Foch .... EXECUTIVE SUITE
Katy Jurado .... BROKEN LANCE
Jan Sterling .... THE HIGH AND THE MIGHTY
Claire Trevor .... THE HIGH AND THE MIGHTY

1955

Best Actor
Ernest Borgnine ★★ .... MARTY
James Cagney .... LOVE ME OR LEAVE ME
James Dean .... EAST OF EDEN
Frank Sinatra .... THE MAN WITH THE GOLDEN ARM
Spencer Tracy .... BAD DAY AT BLACK ROCK

Best Actress
Anna Magnani ★★ .... THE ROSE TATTOO
Susan Hayward .... I'LL CRY TOMORROW
Katharine Hepburn .... SUMMERTIME
Jennifer Jones .... LOVE IS A MANY-SPLENDORED THING
Eleanor Parker .... INTERRUPTED MELODY

Best Supporting Actor
Jack Lemmon ○○ .... MISTER ROBERTS
Arthur Kennedy .... TRIAL
Joe Mantell .... MARTY
Sal Mineo .... REBEL WITHOUT A CAUSE
Arthur O'Connell .... PICNIC

Best Supporting Actress
Jo Van Fleet ○○ .... EAST OF EDEN
Betsy Blair .... MARTY
Peggy Lee .... PETE KELLY'S BLUES
Marisa Pavan .... THE ROSE TATTOO
Natalie Wood .... REBEL WITHOUT A CAUSE

1956

Best Actor
Yul Brynner ★★ .... THE KING AND I
James Dean .... GIANT
Kirk Douglas .... LUST FOR LIFE
Rock Hudson .... GIANT
Sir Laurence Olivier .... RICHARD III

Best Actress
Ingrid Bergman ★★ .... ANASTASIA
Carroll Baker .... BABY DOLL
Katharine Hepburn .... THE RAINMAKER
Nancy Kelly .... THE BAD SEED
Deborah Kerr .... THE KING AND I

Best Supporting Actor
Anthony Quinn ○○ .... LUST FOR LIFE
Don Murray .... BUS STOP
Anthony Perkins .... FRIENDLY PERSUASION
Mickey Rooney .... THE BOLD AND THE BRAVE
Robert Stack .... WRITTEN ON THE WIND

Best Supporting Actress
Dorothy Malone ○○ .... WRITTEN ON THE WIND
Mildred Dunnock .... BABY DOLL
Eileen Heckart .... THE BAD SEED
Mercedes McCambridge .... GIANT
Patty McCormack .... THE BAD SEED

1957

Best Actor
Alec Guinness ★★ .... THE BRIDGE ON THE RIVER KWAI
Marlon Brando .... SAYONARA
Anthony Franciosa .... A HATFUL OF RAIN
Charles Laughton ...... WITNESS FOR THE PROSECUTION
Anthony Quinn .... WILD IS THE WIND

Best Actress
Joanne Woodward ★★ .... THE THREE FACES OF EVE
Deborah Kerr .... HEAVEN KNOWS, MR. ALLISON
Anna Magnani .... WILD IS THE WIND
Elizabeth Taylor .... RAINTREE COUNTY
Lana Turner .... PEYTON PLACE

Best Supporting Actor
Red Buttons ○○ ....SAYONARA
Vittorio De Sica .... A FAREWELL TO ARMS
Sessue Hayakawa .... THE BRIDGE ON THE RIVER KWAI
Arthur Kennedy .... PEYTON PLACE
Russ Tamblyn .... PEYTON PLACE

Best Supporting Actress
Miyoshi Umeki ○○ ....SAYONARA
Carolyn Jones .... THE BACHELOR PARTY
Elsa Lanchester .... WITNESS FOR THE PROSECUTION
Hope Lange .... PEYTON PLACE
Diane Varsi .... PEYTON PLACE

1958

Best Actor
David Niven ★★ ....SEPARATE TABLES
Tony Curtis .... THE DEFIANT ONES
Paul Newman .... CAT ON A HOT TIN ROOF
Sidney Poitier............................. THE DEFIANT ONES
Spencer Tracy .... THE OLD MAN AND THE SEA

Best Actress
Susan Haywood ★★ .... I WANT TO LIVE!
Deborah Kerr .... SEPARATE TABLES
Shirley MaClaine .... SOME CAME RUNNING
Rosalind Russell ....AUNTIE MAME
Elizabeth Taylor .... CAT ON A HOT TIN ROOF

Best Supporting Actor
Burl Ives ◐◐ .... THE BIG COUNTRY
Theodore Bikel ....THE DEFIANT ONES
Lee J. Cobb .... THE BROTHERS KARAMAZOV
Arthur Kennedy .... SOME CAME RUNNING
Gig Young .... TEACHER'S PET

Best Supporting Actress
Wendy Hiller ◐◐ ....SEPARATE TABLES
Peggy Cass .... AUNTIE MAME
Martha Hyer .... SOME CAME RUNNING
Maureen Stapleton .... LONELYHEARTS
Cara Williams .... THE DEFIANT ONES

1959

Best Actor
Charlton Heston ★★ .... BEN-HUR
Laurence Harvey .... ROOM AT THE TOP
Jack Lemmon .... SOME LIKE IT HOT
Paul Muni .... THE LAST ANGRY MAN
James Stewart .... ANATOMY OF A MURDER

Best Actress
Simone Signoret ★★ .... ROOM AT THE TOP
Doris Day .... PILLOW TALK
Audrey Hepburn .... THE NUN'S STORY
Katharine Hepburn .... SUDDENLY, LAST SUMMER
Elizabeth Taylor .... SUDDENLY, LAST SUMMER

Best Supporting Actor
Hugh Griffith ◐◐ .... BEN-HUR
Arthur O'Connell ....ANATOMY OF A MURDER
George C. Scott .... ANATOMY OF A MURDER
Robert Vaughn .... THE YOUNG PHILADELPHIANS
Ed Wynn .... THE DIARY OF ANNE FRANK

Best Supporting Actress
Shelley Winters ◐◐ .... THE DIARY OF ANNE FRANK
Hermione Baddeley .... ROOM AT THE TOP
Susan Kohner .... IMITATION OF LIFE
Juanita Moore .... IMITATION OF LIFE
Thelma Ritter .... PILLOW TALK

1960

Best Actor
Burt Lancaster ★★ .... ELMER GANTRY
Trevor Howard .... SONS AND LOVERS
Jack Lemmon .... THE APARTMENT
Laurence Olivier.................... THE ENTERTAINER
Spencer Tracy .... INHERIT THE WIND

Best Actress
Elizabeth Taylor ★★ .... BUTTERFIELD 8
Greer Garson .... SUNRISE AT CAMPOBELLO
Deborah Kerr .... THE SUNDOWNERS
Shirley MaClaine .... THE APARTMENT
Melina Mercouri .... NEVER ON SUNDAY

Best Supporting Actor
Peter Ustinov ◐◐ ....SPARTACUS
Peter Falk .... MURDER, INC.
Jack Kruschen .... THE APARTMENT
Sal Mineo .... EXODUS
Chill Wills .... THE ALAMO

Best Supporting Actress
Shirley Jones ◐◐ .... ELMER GANTRY
Glynis Johns .... THE SUNDOWNERS
Shirley Knight ..... THE DARK AT THE TOP OF THE STAIRS
Janet Leigh .... PSYCHO
Mary Ure .... SONS AND LOVERS

1961

Best Actor
Maximilian Schell ★★ .... JUDGMENT AT NUREMBERG
Charles Boyer .... FANNY
Paul Newman .... THE HUSTLER
Spencer Tracy ....JUDGMENT AT NUREMBERG
Stuart Whitman .... THE MARK

Best Actress
Sophia Loren ★★ .... TWO WOMEN
Audrey Hepburn .... BREAKFAST AT TIFFANY'S
Piper Laurie .... THE HUSTLER
Geraldine Page .... SUMMER AND SMOKE
Natalie Wood .... SPLENDOR IN THE GRASS

Best Supporting Actor
George Chakiris ◐◐ .... WEST SIDE STORY
Montgomery Clift ....JUDGMENT AT NUREMBERG
Peter Falk ....POCKETFUL OF MIRACLES
Jackie Gleason ....THE HUSTLER
George C. Scott ....THE HUSTLER

Best Supporting Actress
Rita Moreno ◐◐..................... WEST SIDE STORY
Fay Bainter .... THE CHILDREN'S HOUR
Judy Garland .... JUDGMENT AT NUREMBERG
Lotte Lenya .... THE ROMAN SPRING OF MRS. STONE
Una Merkel .... SUMMER AND SMOKE

1962

Best Actor
Gregory Peck ★★ .... TO KILL A MOCKINGBIRD
Burt Lancaster ★★ .... BIRDMAN OF ALCATRAZ
Jack Lemmon .... DAYS OF WINE AND ROSES
Marcello Mastroianni.................. DIVORCE ITALIAN STYLE
Peter O'Toole .... LAWRENCE OF ARABIA

Best Actress
Anne Bancroft ★★ .... THE MIRACLE WORKER
Bette Davis ..... WHAT EVER HAPPENED TO BABY JANE?
Katharine Hepburn ..... LONG DAY'S JOURNEY INTO NIGHT
Geraldine Page .... SWEET BIRD OF YOUTH
Lee Remick .... DAYS OF WINE AND ROSES

A
C
A
D
E
M
Y

A
W
A
R
D
S

A
C
A
D
E
M
Y

A
W
A
R
D
S

Best Supporting Actor
Ed Begley ✪✪ .... SWEET BIRD OF YOUTH
Victor Buono ... WHAT EVER HAPPENED TO BABY JANE?
Telly Savalas .... BIRDMAN OF ALCATRAZ
Omar Sharif .... LAWRENCE OF ARABIA
Terence Stamp .... BILLY BUDD

Best Supporting Actress
Patty Duke ✪✪ .... THE MIRACLE WORKER
Mary Badham .... TO KILL A MOCKINGBIRD
Shirley Knight .... SWEET BIRD OF YOUTH
Angela Lansbury .... THE MANCHURIAN CANDIDATE
Thelma Ritter .... BIRDMAN OF ALCATRAZ

1963

Best Actor
Sidney Poitier ★★ .... LILIES OF THE FIELD
Albert Finney .... TOM JONES
Richard Harris .... THIS SPORTING LIFE
Rex Harrison .... CLEOPATRA
Paul Newman .... HUD

Best Actress
Patricia Neal ★★ .... HUD
Leslie Caron .... THE L-SHAPED ROOM
Shirley MacLaine .... IRMA LA DOUCE
Rachel Roberts .... THIS SPORTING LIFE
Natalie Wood .... LOVE WITH THE PROPER STRANGER

Best Supporting Actor
Melvyn Douglas ✪✪ .... HUD
Nick Adams .... TWILIGHT OF HONOR
Bobby Darin .... CAPTAIN NEWMAN, M.D.
Hugh Griffith .... TOM JONES
John Huston .... THE CARDINAL

Best Supporting Actress
Margaret Rutherford ✪✪ .... THE V.I.P.'s
Diane Cilento .... TOM JONES
Dame Edith Evans .... TOM JONES
Joyce Redman .... TOM JONES
Lilia Skala .... LILIES OF THE FIELD

1964

Best Actor
Rex Harrison ★★ .... MY FAIR LADY
Richard Burton .... BECKET
Peter O'Toole .... BECKET
Anthony Quinn .... ZORBA THE GREEK
Peter Sellers .... DR. STRANGELOVE OR: HOW I LEARNED
TO STOP WORRYING AND LOVE THE BOMB

Best Actress
Julie Andrews ★★ .... MARY POPPINS
Anne Bancroft .... THE PUMPKIN EATER
Sophia Loren .... MARRIAGE ITALIAN STYLE
Debbie Reynolds .... THE UNSINKABLE MOLLY BROWN
Kim Stanley .... SEANCE ON A WET AFTERNOON

Best Supporting Actor
Peter Ustinov ✪✪ .... TOPKAPI
John Gielgud .... BECKET
Stanley Holloway .... MY FAIR LADY
Edmond O'brien .... SEVEN DAYS IN MAY
Lee Tracy .... THE BEST MAN

Best Supporting Actress
Lila Kedrova ✪✪ .... ZORBA THE GREEK
Gladys Cooper .... MY FAIR LADY
Dame Edith Evans .... THE CHALK GARDEN
Grayson Hall .... THE NIGHT OF THE IGUANA
Agnes Moorehead ..... HUSH...HUSH, SWEET CHARLOTTE

1965

Best Actor
Lee Marvin ★★ .... CAT BALLOU
Richard Burton .... THE SPY WHO CAME IN
FROM THE COLD
Laurence Olivier .... OTHELLO
Rod Steiger .... THE PAWNBROKER
Oskar Werner .... SHIP OF FOOLS

Best Actress
Julie Christie ★★ .... DARLING
Julie Andrews .... THE SOUND OF MUSIC
Samantha Eggar .... THE COLLECTOR
Elizabeth Hartman .... A PATCH OF BLUE
Simone Signoret .... SHIP OF FOOLS

Best Supporting Actor
Martin Balsam ✪✪ .... A THOUSAND CLOWNS
Ian Bannen .... THE FLIGHT OF THE PHOENIX
Tom Courtenay .... DOCTOR ZHIVAGO
Michael Dunn .... SHIP OF FOOLS
Frank Finlay .... OTHELLO

Best Supporting Actress
Shelley Winters ✪✪ .... A PATCH OF BLUE
Ruth Gordon .... INSIDE DAISY CLOVER
Joyce Redman .... OTHELLO
Maggie Smith .... OTHELLO
Peggy Wood .... THE SOUND OF MUSIC

1966

Best Actor
Paul Scofield ★★ .... A MAN FOR ALL SEASONS
Alan Arkin .... THE RUSSIANS ARE COMING,
THE RUSSIANS ARE COMING
Richard Burton ...... WHO'S AFRAID OF VIRGINIA WOOLF?
Michael Caine .... ALFIE
Steve McQueen .... THE SAND PEBBLES

Best Actress
Elizabeth Taylor ★★ .... WHO'S AFRAID OF
VIRGINIA WOOLF?
Anouk Aimée .... A MAN AND A WOMAN
Ida Kaminska .... THE SHOP ON MAIN STREET
Lynn Redgrave .... GEORGY GIRL
Vanessa Redgrave .... MORGAN!

Best Supporting Actor
Walter Matthau ✪✪ .... THE FORTUNE COOKIE
Mako .... THE SAND PEBBLES
James Mason .... GEORGY GIRL
George Segal .... WHO'S AFRAID OF VIRGINIA WOOLF?
Robert Shaw .... A MAN FOR ALL SEASONS

Best Supporting Actress
Sandy Dennis ✪✪ ..... WHO'S AFRAID OF VIRGINIA WOOLF?
Wendy Hiller .... A MAN FOR ALL SEASONS
Jocelyn Lagarde .... HAWAII
Vivien Merchant .... ALFIE
Geraldine Page .... YOU'RE A BIG BOY NOW

1967

Best Actor
Rod Steiger ★★ .... IN THE HEAT OF THE NIGHt
Warren Beatty .... BONNIE AND CLYDE
Dustin Hoffman .... THE GRADUATE
Paul Newman .... COOL HAND LUKE
Spencer Tracy .... GUESS WHO'S COMING TO DINNER

Best Actress
Katharine Hepburn ★★ .... GUESS WHO'S COMING TO DINNER
Anne Bancroft .... THE GRADUATE
Faye Dunaway .... BONNIE AND CLYDE
Dame Edith Evans .... THE WHISPERERS
Audrey Hepburn .... WAIT UNTIL DARK

Best Supporting Actor
George Kennedy ○○ .... COOL HAND LUKE
John Cassavetes .... THE DIRTY DOZEN
Gene Hackman .... BONNIE AND CLYDE
Cecil Kellaway .... GUESS WHO'S COMING TO DINNER
Michael J. Pollard .... BONNIE AND CLYDE

Best Supporting Actress
Estelle Parsons ○○ .... BONNIE AND CLYDE
Carol Channing .... THOROUGHLY MODERN MILLIE
Mildred Natwick .... BAREFOOT IN THE PARK
Beah Richards .... GUESS WHO'S COMING TO DINNER
Katharine Ross .... THE GRADUATE

1968

Best Actor
Cliff Robertson ★★ .... CHARLY
Alan Arkin .... THE HEART IS A LONELY HUNTER
Alan Bates .... THE FIXER
Ron Moody .... OLIVER!
Peter O'Toole .... THE LION IN WINTER

Best Actress
Katharine Hepburn ★★ .... THE LION IN WINTER
Barbra Streisand ★★ .... FUNNY GIRL
Patricia Neal .... THE SUBJECT WAS ROSES
Vanessa Redgrave .... ISADORA
Joanne Woodward .... RACHEL, RACHEL

Best Supporting Actor
Jack Albertson ○○ .... THE SUBJECT WAS ROSES
Seymour Cassel .... FACES
Daniel Massey .... STAR!
Jack Wild .... OLIVER!
Gene Wilder .... THE PRODUCERS

Best Supporting Actress
Ruth Gordon ○○ .... ROSEMARY'S BABY
Lynn Carlin .... FACES
Sondra Locke .... THE HEART IS A LONELY HUNTER
Kay Medford .... FUNNY GIRL
Estelle Parsons .... RACHEL, RACHEL

1969

Best Actor
John Wayne ★★ .... TRUE GRIT
Richard Burton .... ANNE OF THE THOUSAND DAYS
Dustin Hoffman .... MIDNIGHT COWBOY
Peter O'Toole .... GOODBYE, MR. CHIPS
Jon Voight .... MIDNIGHT COWBOY

Best Actress
Maggie Smith ★★ ...... THE PRIME OF MISS JEAN BRODIE
Genevieve Bujold .... ANNE OF THE THOUSAND DAYS
Jane Fonda .... THEY SHOOT HORSES, DON'T THEY?
Liza Minnelli .... THE STERILE CUCKOO
Jean Simmons .... THE HAPPY ENDING

Best Supporting Actor
Gig Young ○○ ...... THEY SHOOT HORSES, DON'T THEY?
Rupert Crosse .... THE REIVERS
Elliott Gould .... BOB & CAROL & TED & ALICE
Jack Nicholson .... EASY RIDER
Anthony Quayle .... ANNE OF THE THOUSAND DAYS

Best Supporting Actress
Goldie Hawn ○○ .... CACTUS FLOWER
Catherine Burns .... LAST SUMMER
Dyan Cannon .... BOB & CAROL & TED & ALICE
Sylvia Miles .... MIDNIGHT COWBOY
Susannah York ..... THEY SHOOT HORSES, DON'T THEY?

1970

Best Actor
George C. Scott ★★ .... PATTON
Melvyn Douglas ....I NEVER SANG FOR MY FATHER
James Earl Jones .... THE GREAT WHITE HOPE
Jack Nicholson ....FIVE EASY PIECES
Ryan O'Neal .... LOVE STORY

Best Actress
Glenda Jackson ★★ .... WOMEN IN LOVE
Jane Alexander .... THE GREAT WHITE HOPE
Ali MacGraw .... LOVE STORY
Sarah Miles .... RYAN'S DAUGHTER
Carrie Snodgress .... DIARY OF A MAD HOUSEWIFE

Best Supporting Actor
John Mills ○○ .... RYAN'S DAUGHTER
Richard Castellano .... LOVERS AND OTHER STRANGERS
Chief Dan George .... LITTLE BIG MAN
Gene Hackman ....I NEVER SANG FOR MY FATHER
John Marley .... LOVE STORY

Best Supporting Actress
Helen Hayes ○○ ....AIRPORT
Karen Black .... FIVE EASY PIECES
Lee Grant .... THE LANDLORD
Sally Kellerman ....M*A*S*H
Maureen Stapleton ....AIRPORT

1971

Best Actor
Gene Hackman ★★ .... THE FRENCH CONNECTION
Peter Finch .... SUNDAY, BLOODY SUNDAY
Walter Matthau .... KOTCH
George C. Scott ....THE HOSPITAL
Topol .... FIDDLER ON THE ROOF

Best Actress
Jane Fonda ★★ .... KLUTE
Julie Christie .... MCCABE & MRS. MILLER
Glenda Jackson ....SUNDAY, BLOODY SUNDAY
Vanessa Redgrave .... MARY, QUEEN OF SCOTS
Janet Suzman .... NICHOLAS AND ALEXANDRA

Best Supporting Actor
Ben Johnson ✪✪ .... THE LAST PICTURE SHOW
Jeff Bridges .... THE LAST PICTURE SHOW
Leonard Frey .... FIDDLER ON THE ROOF
Richard Jaeckel .... SOMETIMES A GREAT NOTION
Roy Scheider .... THE FRENCH CONNECTION

Best Supporting Actress
Cloris Leachman ✪✪ .... THE LAST PICTURE SHOW
Ellen Burstyn .... THE LAST PICTURE SHOW
Barbara Harris ..... WHO IS HARRY KELLERMAN AND WHY
    IS HE SAYING THOSE TERRIBLE THINGS ABOUT ME?
Margaret Leighton .... THE GO-BETWEEN
Ann-Margret .... CARNAL KNOWLEDGE

1972

Best Actor
Marlon Brando ★★ .... THE GODFATHER
Michael Caine .... SLEUTH
Laurence Olivier .... SLEUTH
Peter O'Toole .... THE RULING CLASS
Paul Winfield .... SOUNDER

Best Actress
Liza Minnelli ★★ .... CABARET
Diana Ross .... LADY SINGS THE BLUES
Maggie Smith .... TRAVELS WITH MY AUNT
Cicely Tyson .... SOUNDER
Liv Ullmann .... THE EMIGRANTS

Best Supporting Actor
Joel Grey ✪✪ .... CABARET
Eddie Albert .... THE HEARTBREAK KID
James Caan .... THE GODFATHER
Robert Duvall .... THE GODFATHER
Al Pacino .... THE GODFATHER

Best Supporting Actress
Eileen Heckart ✪✪ .... BUTTERFLIES ARE FREE
Jeannie Berlin .... THE HEARTBREAK KID
Geraldine Page .... PETE 'N' TILLIE
Susan Tyrrell .... FAT CITY
Shelley Winters .... THE POSEIDON ADVENTURE

1973

Best Actor
Jack Lemmon ★★ .... SAVE THE TIGER
Marlon Brando .... LAST TANGO IN PARIS
Jack Nicholson .... THE LAST DETAIL
Al Pacino .... SERPICO
Robert Redford .... THE STING

Best Actress
Glenda Jackson ★★ ....A TOUCH OF CLASS
Ellen Burstyn .... THE EXORCIST
Marsha Mason .... CINDERELLA LIBERTY
Barbra Streisand ....THE WAY WE WERE
Joanne Woodward ..... SUMMER WISHES, WINTER DREAMS

Best Supporting Actor
John Houseman ✪✪ .... The Paper Chase
Vincent Gardenia .... BANG THE DRUM SLOWLY
Jack Gilford .... SAVE THE TIGER
Jason Miller .... THE EXORCIST
Randy Quaid .... THE LAST DETAIL

Best Supporting Actress
Tatum O'Neal ✪✪ .... PAPER MOON
Linda Blair .... THE EXORCIST
Candy Clark .... AMERICAN GRAFFITI
Madeline Kahn .... PAPER MOON
Sylvia Sidney .... SUMMER WISHES, WINTER DREAMS

1974

Best Actor
Art Carney ★★ .... HARRY AND TONTO
Albert Finney .... MURDER ON THE ORIENT EXPRESS
Dustin Hoffman .... LENNY
Jack Nicholson .... CHINATOWN
Al Pacino .... THE GODFATHER, PART II

Best Actress
Ellen Burstyn ★★ .... ALICE DOESN'T
    LIVE HERE ANYMORE
Diahann Carroll .... CLAUDINE
Faye Dunaway .... CHINATOWN
Valerie Perrine .... LENNY
Gena Rowlands .... A WOMAN UNDER THE INFLUENCE

Best Supporting Actor
Robert De Niro ✪✪ .... THE GODFATHER, PART II
Fred Astaire .... THE TOWERING INFERNO
Jeff Bridges .... THUNDERBOLT AND LIGHTFOOT
Michael V. Gazzo .... THE GODFATHER, PART II
Lee Strasberg .... THE GODFATHER, PART II

Best Supporting Actress
Ingrid Bergman ✪✪ ...... MURDER ON THE ORIENT EXPRESS
Valentina Cortese .... DAY FOR NIGHT
Madeline Kahn .... BLAZING SADDLES
Diane Ladd .... ALICE DOESN'T LIVE HERE ANYMORE
Talia Shire .... THE GODFATHER, PART II

1975

Best Actor
Jack Nicholson ★★ ....ONE FLEW OVER
    THE CUCKOO'S NEST
Walter Matthau .... THE SUNSHINE BOYS
Al Pacino .... DOG DAY AFTERNOON
Maximilian Schell .... THE MAN IN THE GLASS BOOTH
James Whitmore .... GIVE 'EM HELL, HARRY!

Best Actress
Louise Fletcher ★★ ....ONE FLEW OVER
    THE CUCKOO'S NEST
Isabelle Adjani .... THE STORY OF ADELE H
Ann-Margret .... TOMMY
Glenda Jackson .... HEDDA
Carol Kane .... HESTER STREET

Best Supporting Actor
George Burns ✪✪ .... THE SUNSHINE BOYS
Brad Dourif ....ONE FLEW OVER THE CUCKOO'S NEST
Burgess Meredith .... THE DAY OF THE LOCUST
Chris Sarandon .... DOG DAY AFTERNOON
Jack Warden .... SHAMPOO

Best Supporting Actress
Lee Grant ✪✪ .... SHAMPOO
Ronee Blakley .... NASHVILLE
Sylvia Miles .... FAREWELL, MY LOVELY
Lily Tomlin .... NASHVILLE
Brenda Vaccaro .... JACQUELINE SUSANN'S
    ONCE IS NOT ENOUGH

1976

Best Actor
Peter Finch ★★ .... NETWORK
Robert De Niro .... TAXI DRIVER
Giancarlo Giannini .... SEVEN BEAUTIES
William Holden .... NETWORK
Sylvester Stallone .... ROCKY

Best Actress
Faye Dunaway ★★ .... NETWORK
Marie-Christine Barrault .... COUSIN, COUSINE
Talia Shire .... ROCKY
Sissy Spacek .... CARRIE
Liv Ullmann .... FACE TO FACE

Best Supporting Actor
Jason Robards ✪✪ .... ALL THE PRESIDENT'S MEN
Ned Beatty .... NETWORK
Burgess Meredith .... ROCKY
Laurence Olivier .... MARATHAN MAN
Burt Young .... ROCKY

Best Supporting Actress
Beatrice Straight ✪✪ .... NETWORK
Jane Alexander .... ALL THE PRESIDENT'S MEN
Jodie Foster .... TAXI DRIVER
Lee Grant .... VOYAGE OF THE DAMNED
Piper Laurie .... CARRIE

1977

Best Actor
Richard Dreyfuss ★★ .... THE GOODBYE GIRL
Woody Allen .... ANNIE HALL
Richard Burton .... EQUUS
Marcello Mastroianni .... A SPECIAL DAY
John Travolta .... SATURDAY NIGHT FEVER

Best Actress
Diane Keaton ★★ .... ANNIE HALL
Anne Bancroft .... THE TURNING POINT
Jane Fonda .... JULIA
Shirley Maclaine .... THE TURNING POINT
Marsha Mason .... THE GOODBYE GIRL

Best Supporting Actor
Jason Robards ✪✪ .... JULIA
Mikhail Baryshnikov .... THE TURNING POINT
Peter Firth .... EQUUS
Alec Guinness .... STAR WARS
Maximilian Schell .... JULIA

Best Supporting Actress
Vanessa Redgrave ✪✪ .... JULIA
Leslie Browne .... THE TURNING POINT
Quinn Cummings .... THE GOODBYE GIRL
Melinda Dillon .... CLOSE ENCOUNTERS OF
THE THIRD KIND
Tuesday Weld .... LOOKING FOR MR. GOODBAR

1978

Best Actor
Jon Voight ★★ .... COMING HOME
Warren Beatty .... HEAVEN CAN WAIT
Gary Busey .... THE BUDDY HOLLY STORY
Robert De Niro .... THE DEER HUNTER
Laurence Olivier .... THE BOYS FROM BRAZIL

Best Actress
Jane Fonda ★★ .... COMING HOME
Ingrid Bergman .... AUTUMN SONATA
Ellen Burstyn .... SAME TIME, NEXT YEAR
Jill Clayburgh .... AN UNMARRIED WOMAN
Geraldine Page .... INTERIORS

Best Supporting Actor
Christopher Walken ✪✪ .... THE DEER HUNTER
Bruce Dern .... COMING HOME
Richard Farnsworth .... COMES A HORSEMAN
John Hurt .... MIDNIGHT EXPRESS
Jack Warden .... HEAVEN CAN WAIT

Best Supporting Actress
Maggie Smith ✪✪ .... CALIFORNIA SUITE
Dyan Cannon .... HEAVEN CAN WAIT
Penelope Milford .... COMING HOME
Maureen Stapleton .... INTERIORS
Meryl Streep .... THE DEER HUNTER

1979

Best Actor
Dustin Hoffman ★★ .... KRAMER VS. KRAMER
Jack Lemmon .... THE CHINA SYNDROME
Al Pacino .... AND JUSTICE FOR ALL
Roy Scheider .... ALL THAT JAZZ
Peter Sellers .... BEING THERE

Best Actress
Sally Field ★★ .... NORMA RAE
Jill Clayburgh .... STARTING OVER
Jane Fonda .... THE CHINA SYNDROME
Marsha Mason .... CHAPTER TWO
Bette Midler .... THE ROSE

Best Supporting Actor
Melvyn Douglas ✪✪ .... BEING THERE
Robert Duvall .... APOCALYPSE NOW
Frederic Forrest .... THE ROSE
Justin Henry .... KRAMER VS. KRAMER
Mickey Rooney .... THE BLACK STALLION

Best Supporting Actress
Meryl Streep ✪✪ .... KRAMER VS. KRAMER
Jane Alexander .... KRAMER VS. KRAMER
Barbara Barrie .... BREAKING AWAY
Candice Bergen .... STARTING OVER
Mariel Hemingway .... MANHATTAN

1980

Best Actor
Robert De Niro ★★ .... RAGING BULL
Robert Duvall .... THE GREAT SANTINI
John Hurt .... THE ELEPHANT MAN
Jack Lemmon .... TRIBUTE
Peter O'Toole .... THE STUNT MAN

Best Actress
Sissy Spacek ★★ .... COAL MINER'S DAUGHTER
Ellen Burstyn .... RESURRECTION
Goldie Hawn .... PRIVATE BENJAMIN
Mary Tyler Moore .... ORDINARY PEOPLE
Gena Rowlands .... GLORIA

A
C
A
D
E
M
Y

A
W
A
R
D
S

Best Supporting Actor
Timothy Hutton ✪✪ .... ORDINARY PEOPLE
Judd Hirsch .... ORDINARY PEOPLE
Michael O'Keefe .... THE GREAT SANTINI
Joe Pesci .... RAGING BULL
Jason Robards .... MELVIN AND HOWARD

Best Supporting Actress
Mary Steenburgen ✪✪ .... MELVIN AND HOWARD
Eileen Brennan .... PRIVATE BENJAMIN
Eva Le Gallienne .... RESURRECTION
Cathy Moriarty .... RAGING BULL
Diana Scarwid .... INSIDE MOVES

1981

Best Actor
Henry Fonda ★★ .... ON GOLDEN POND
Warren Beatty .... REDS
Burt Lancaster .... ATLANTIC CITY
Dudley Moore .... ARTHUR
Paul Newman .... ABSENCE OF MALICE

Best Actress
Katharine Hepburn ★★ .... ON GOLDEN POND
Diane Keaton .... REDS
Marsha Mason .... ONLY WHEN I LAUGH
Susan Sarandon .... ATLANTIC CITY
Meryl Streep .... THE FRENCH LIEUTENANT'S WOMAN

Best Supporting Actor
John Gielgud ✪✪ ....ARTHUR
James Coco .... ONLY WHEN I LAUGH
Ian Holm .... CHARIOTS OF FIRE
Jack Nicholson .... REDS
Howard E. Rollins, Jr. .... RAGTIME

Best Supporting Actress
Maureen Stapleton ✪✪ .... REDS
Melinda Dillon .... ABSENCE OF MALICE
Jane Fonda .... ON GOLDEN POND
Joan Hackett .... ONLY WHEN I LAUGH
Elizabeth McGovern .... RAGTIME

1982

Best Actor
Ben Kingsley ★★ ....GANDHI
Dustin Hoffman .... TOOTSIE
Jack Lemmon .... MISSING
Paul Newman .... THE VERDICT
Peter O'Toole .... MY FAVORITE YEAR

Best Actress
Meryl Streep ★★ .... SOPHIE'S CHOICE
Julie Andrews .... VICTOR/VICTORIA
Jessica Lange .... FRANCES
Sissy Spacek .... MISSING
Debra Winger .... AN OFFICER AND A GENTLEMAN

Best Supporting Actor
Louis Gossett, Jr. ✪✪ .... AN OFFICER AND A GENTLEMAN
Charles Durning .... THE BEST LITTLE
                          WHOREHOUSE IN TEXAS
John Lithgow .... THE WORLD ACCORDING TO GARP
James Mason .... THE VERDICT
Robert Preston .... VICTOR/VICTORIA

Best Supporting Actress
Jessica Lange ✪✪ .... TOOTSIE
Glenn Close .... THE WORLD ACCORDING TO GARP
Terri Garr .... TOOTSIE
Kim Stanley .... FRANCES
Lesley Ann Warren .... VICTOR/VICTORIA

1983

Best Actor
Robert Duvall ★★ .... TENDER MERCIES
Michael Caine .... EDUCATING RITA
Tom Conti .... REUBEN, REUBEN
Tom Courtenay .... THE DRESSER
Albert Finney .... THE DRESSER

Best Actress
Shirley MacLaine ★★ .... TERMS OF ENDEARMENT
Jane Alexander .... TESTAMENT
Meryl Streep .... SILKWOOD
Julie Walters .... EDUCATING RITA
Debra Winger .... TERMS OF ENDEARMENT

Best Supporting Actor
Jack Nicholson ✪✪ .... TERMS OF ENDEARMENT
Charles Durning .... TO BE OR NOT TO BE
John Lithgow .... TERMS OF ENDEARMENT
Sam Shepard .... THE RIGHT STUFF
Rip Torn .... CROSS CREEK

Best Supporting Actress
Linda Hunt ✪✪ ...... THE YEAR OF LIVING DANGEROUSLY
Cher .... SILKWOOD
Glenn Close .... THE BIG CHILL
Amy Irving .... YENTL
Alfre Woodard .... CROSS CREEK

1984

Best Actor
F. Murray Abraham ★★ .... AMADEUS
Jeff Bridges .... STARMAN
Albert Finney .... UNDER THE VOLCANO
Tom Hulce .... AMADEUS
Sam Waterston .... THE KILLING FIELDS

Best Actress
Sally Field ★★ .... PLACES IN THE HEART
Judy Davis .... A PASSAGE TO INDIA
Jessica Lange .... COUNTRY
Vanessa Redgrave .... THE BOSTONIANS
Sissy Spacek .... THE RIVER

Best Supporting Actor
Haing S. Ngor ✪✪ .... THE KILLING FIELDS
Adolph Caesar .... A SOLDIER'S STORY
John Malkovich .... PLACES IN THE HEART
Noriyuki "Pat" Morita .... THE KARATE KID
Ralph Richardson .... GREYSTOKE: THE LEGEND OF
                  .... TARZAN, LORD OF THE APES

Best Supporting Actress
Peggy Ashcroft ✪✪ .... A PASSAGE TO INDIA
Glenn Close .... THE NATURAL
Lindsay Crouse .... PLACES IN THE HEART
Christine Lahti .... SWING SHIFT
Geraldine Page .... THE POPE OF GREENWICH VILLAGE

1985

Best Actor
William Hurt ★★ .... KISS OF THE SPIDER WOMAN
Harrison Ford .... WITNESS
James Garner .... MURPHY'S ROMANCE
Jack Nicholson .... PRIZZI'S HONOR
Jon Voight .... RUNAWAY TRAIN

Best Actress
Geraldine Page ★★ .... THE TRIP TO BOUNTIFUL
Anne Bancroft .... AGNES OF GOD
Whoopi Goldberg .... THE COLOR PURPLE
Jessica Lange .... SWEET DREAMS
Meryl Streep .... OUT OF AFRICA

Best Supporting Actor
Don Ameche ○○ .... COCOON
Klaus Maria Brandauer .... OUT OF AFRICA
William Hickey .... PRIZZI'S HONOR
Robert Loggia .... JAGGED EDGE
Eric Roberts .... RUNAWAY TRAIN

Best Supporting Actress
Anjelica Huston ○○ .... PRIZZI'S HONOR
Margaret Avery .... THE COLOR PURPLE
Amy Madigan .... TWICE IN A LIFETIME
Meg Tilly .... AGNES OF GOD
Oprah Winfrey .... THE COLOR PURPLE

1986

Best Actor
Paul Newman ★★ .... THE COLOR OF MONEY
Dexter Gordon .... 'ROUND MIDNIGHT
Bob Hoskins .... MONA LISA
William Hurt .... CHILDREN OF A LESSER GOD
James Woods .... SALVADOR

Best Actress
Marlee Matlin ★★ .... CHILDREN OF A LESSER GOD
Jane Fonda .... THE MORNING AFTER
Sissy Spacek .... CRIMES OF THE HEART
Kathleen Turner .... PEGGY SUE GOT MARRIED
Sigourney Weaver .... ALIENS

Best Supporting Actor
Michael Caine ○○ .... HANNAH AND HER SISTERS
Tom Berenger .... PLATOON
Willem Dafoe .... PLATOON
Denholm Elliott .... A ROOM WITH A VIEW
Dennis Hopper .... HOOSIERS

Best Supporting Actress
Dianne Wiest ○○ .... HANNAH AND HER SISTERS
Tess Harper .... CRIMES OF THE HEART
Piper Laurie .... CHILDREN OF A LESSER GOD
Mary Elizabeth Mastrantonio .... THE COLOR OF MONEY
Maggie Smith .... A ROOM WITH A VIEW

1987

Best Actor
Michael Douglas ★★ .... WALL STREET
William Hurt .... BROADCAST NEWS
Robin Williams .... GOOD MORNING, VIETNAM
Marcello Mastroanni .... DARK EYES
Jack Nicholson .... IRONWEED

Best Actress
Cher ★★ .... MOONSTRUCK
Meryl Streep .... IRONWEED
Sally Kirkland .... ANNA
Glenn Close .... FATAL ATTRACTION
Holly Hunter .... BROADCAST NEWS

Best Supporting Actor
Sean Connery ○○ .... THE UNTOUCHABLES
Albert Brooks .... BROADCAST NEWS
Morgan Freeman .... STREET SMART
Vincent Gardenia .... MOONSTRUCK
Denzel Washington .... CRY FREEDOM

Best Supporting Actress
Olympia Dukakis ○○ .... MOONSTRUCK
Norma Aleandro .... GABY—A TRUE STORY
Anne Archer .... FATAL ATTRACTION
Anne Ramsey .... THROW MOMMA FROM THE TRAIN
Ann Sothern .... THE WHALES OF AUGUST

1988

Best Actor
Dustin Hoffman ★★ .... RAIN MAN
Gene Hackman .... MISSISSIPPI BURNING
Tom Hanks .... BIG
Edward James Olmos .... STAND AND DELIVER
Max Von Sydow .... PELLE THE CONQUEROR

Best Actress
Jodie Foster ★★ .... THE ACCUSED
Glenn Close .... DANGEROUS LIAISONS
Melanie Griffith .... WORKING GIRL
Meryl Streep .... A CRY IN THE DARK
Sigourney Weaver .... GORILLAS IN THE MIST

Best Supporting Actor
Kevin Kline ○○ .... A FISH CALLED WANDA
Martin Landau .... TUCKER—THE MAN AND HIS DREAM
River Phoenix .... RUNNING ON EMPTY
Dean Stockwell .... MARRIED TO THE MOB
Alec Guinness .... LITTLE DORRIT

Best Supporting Actress
Geena Davis ○○ .... THE ACCIDENTAL TOURIST
Joan Cusack .... WORKING GIRL
Frances McDormand ...... MISSISSIPPI BURNING
Michelle Pfeiffer .... DANGEROUS LIAISONS
Sigourney Weaver .... WORKING GIRL

1989

Best Actor
Daniel Day-Lewis ★★ .... MY LEFT FOOT
Kenneth Branagh .... HENRY V
Tom Cruise .... BORN ON THE FOURTH OF JULY
Morgan Freeman .... DRIVING MISS DAISY
Robin Williams .... DEAD POETS SOCIETY

Best Actress
Ijessica Tandy ★★ .... DRIVING MISS DAISY
Isabelle Adjani .... CAMILLE CLAUDEL
Pauline Collins .... SHIRLEY VALENTINE
Jessica Lange .... MUSIC BOX
Michelle Pfeiffer .... THE FABULOUS BAKER BOYS

Best Supporting Actor
Denzel Washington ✪✪ .... GLORY
Danny Aiello .... DO THE RIGHT THING
Dan Aykroyd .... DRIVING MISS DAISY
Marlon Brando .... A DRY WHITE SEASON
Martin Landau .... CRIMES AND MISDEMEANORS

Best Supporting Actress
Brenda Fricker ✪✪ .... MY LEFT FOOT
Anjelica Huston .... ENEMIES, A LOVE STORY
Lena Olin .... ENEMIES, A LOVE STORY
Julia Roberts .... STEEL MAGNOLIAS
Dianne Wiest .... PARENTHOOD

1990

Best Actor
Jeremy Irons ★★ .... REVERSAL OF FORTUNE
Kevin Costner .... DANCES WITH WOLVES
Robert De Niro .... AWAKENINGS
Gerard Dépardieu .... CYRANO DE BERGERAC
Richard Harris .... THE FIELD

Best Actress
Kathy Bates ★★ .... MISERY
Anjelica Huston .... THE GRIFTERS
Julia Roberts .... PRETTY WOMAN
Meryl Streep .... POSTCARDS FROM THE EDGE
Joanne Woodward .... MR. AND MRS. BRIDGE

Best Supporting Actor
Joe Pesci ✪✪ .... GOODFELLAS
Bruce Davison .... LONGTIME COMPANION
Andy Garcia .... THE GODFATHER, PART III
Graham Green .... DANCES WITH WOLVES
Al Pacino .... DICK TRACY

Best Supporting Actress
Whoopi Goldberg ✪✪ .... GHOST
Annette Bening .... THE GRIFTERS
Lorraine Bracco .... GOODFELLAS
Diane Ladd .... WILD AT HEART
Mary Mcdonnell .... DANCES WITH WOLVES

1991

Best Actor
Anthony Hopkins ★★ .... THE SILENCE OF THE LAMBS
Warren Beatty .... BUGSY
Robert De Niro .... CAPE FEAR
Nick Nolte .... THE PRINCE OF TIDES
Robin Williams .... THE FISHER KING

Best Actress
Jodie Foster ★★ .... THE SILENCE OF THE LAMBS
Geena Davis .... THELMA & LOUISE
Laura Dern .... RAMBLING ROSE
Bette Midler .... FOR THE BOYS
Susan Sarandon .... THELMA & LOUISE

Best Supporting Actor
Jack Palance ✪✪ .... CITY SLICKERS
Tommy Lee Jones .... JFK
Harvey Keitel .... BUGSY
Ben Kingsley .... BUGSY
Michael Lerner .... BARTON FINK

Best Supporting Actress
Mercedes Ruehl ✪✪ .... THE FISHER KING
Diane Ladd .... RAMBLING ROSE
Juliette Lewis .... CAPE FEAR
Kate Nelligan .... THE PRINCE OF TIDES
Jessica Tandy .... FRIED GREEN TOMATOES

1992

Best Actor
Al Pacino ★★ .... SCENT OF A WOMAN
Robert Downey, Jr. .... CHAPLIN
Clint Eastwood .... UNFORGIVEN
Stephen Rea .... THE CRYING GAME
Denzel Washington .... MALCOLM X

Best Actress
Emma Thompson ★★ .... HOWARD'S END
Catherine Deneuve .... INDOCHINE
Mary McDonnell .... PASSION FISH
Michelle Pfeiffer .... LOVE FIELD
Susan Sarandon .... LORENZO'S OIL

Best Supporting Actor
Gene Hackman ✪✪ .... UNFORGIVEN
Jaye Davidson .... THE CRYING GAME
Jack Nicholson .... A FEW GOOD MEN
Al Pacino .... GLENGARRY GLEN ROSS
David Paymer .... MR. SATURDAY NIGHT

Best Supporting Actress
Marisa Tomei ✪✪ .... MY COUSIN VINNY
Judy Davis .... HUSBANDS AND WIVES
Joan Plowright .... ENCHANTED APRIL
Vanessa Redgrave .... HOWARD'S END
Miranda Richardson .... DAMAGE

1993

Best Actor
Tom Hanks ★★ .... PHILADELPHIA
Daniel Day-Lewis .... IN THE NAME OF THE FATHER
Laurence Fishburne ....WHAT'S LOVE GOT TO DO WITH IT
Anthony Hopkins .... THE REMAINS OF THE DAY
Liam Neeson .... SCHINDLER'S LIST

Best Actress
Holly Hunter ★★ .... THE PIANO
Angela Bassett .... WHAT'S LOVE GOT TO DO WITH IT
Stockard Channing .... SIX DEGREES OF SEPARATION
Emma Thompson .... THE REMAINS OF THE DAY
Debra Winger .... SHADOWLANDS

Best Supporting Actor
Tommy Lee Jones ✪✪ .... THE FUGITIVE
Leonardo Di Caprio ...... WHAT'S EATING GILBERT GRAPE
Ralph Fiennes .... SCHINDLER'S LIST
John Malkovich .... IN THE LINE OF FIRE
Pete Postlethwaite .... IN THE NAME OF THE FATHER

Best Supporting Actress
Anna Paquin ✪✪ .... THE PIANO
Holly Hunter .... THE FIRM
Rosie Perez .... FEARLESS
Winona Ryder .... THE AGE OF INNOCENCE
Emma Thompson .... IN THE NAME OF THE FATHER

★★★★

ACADEMY AWARD NOMINEES AND WINNERS
By Actor
1927-1993

★★ = Academy Award Win for Best Performance by an Actor or Actress in a Leading Role

★ = Academy Award Nomination for Best Performance by an Actor or Actress in a Leading Role

◎◎ = Academy Award Win for Best Performance by an Actor or Actress in a Supporting Role

◎ = Academy Award Nomination for Best Performance by an Actor or Actress in a Supporting Role

A

F. MURRAY ABRAHAM
AMADEUS ★★ Orion, 1984

NICK ADAMS
TWILIGHT OF HONOR ◎ MGM, 1963

ISABELLE ADJANI
THE STORY OF ADELE H ★ New World, 1975, French
CAMILLE CLAUDEL ★ Orion Classics, 1988, French

BRIAN AHERNE
JUAREZ ◎ Warner Bros., 1939

DANNY AIELLO
DO THE RIGHT THING ◎ Universal, 1989

ANOUK AIMÉE
A MAN AND A WOMAN ★ Allied Artists, 1966, French

EDDIE ALBERT
ROMAN HOLIDAY ◎ Paramount, 1953
THE HEARTBREAK KID ◎ 20th Century-Fox, 1972

JACK ALBERTSON
THE SUBJECT WAS ROSES ◎◎ MGM, 1968

NORMA ALEANDRO
GABY - A TRUE STORY ◎ Tri-Star, 1987

JANE ALEXANDER
THE GREAT WHITE HOPE ★ 20th Century-Fox, 1970
ALL THE PRESIDENT'S MEN ◎ Warner Bros., 1976
KRAMER VS. KRAMER ◎ Columbia, 1979
TESTAMENT ★ Paramount, 1983

WOODY ALLEN
ANNIE HALL ★ United Artists, 1977

SARA ALLGOOD
HOW GREEN WAS MY VALLEY ◎ 20th Century-Fox, 1941

DON AMECHE
COCOON ◎◎ 20th Century Fox, 1985

JUDITH ANDERSON
REBECCA ◎ United Artists, 1940

JULIE ANDREWS
MARY POPPINS ★★ Buena Vista, 1964
THE SOUND OF MUSIC ★ 20th Century-Fox, 1965
VICTOR/VICTORIA ★ MGM/United Artists, 1982

ANN-MARGRET
CARNAL KNOWLEDGE ◎ Avco Embassy, 1971
TOMMY ★ Columbia, 1975, British

ANNE ARCHER
FATAL ATTRACTION ◎ Paramount, 1987

EVE ARDEN
MILDRED PIERCE ◎ Warner Bros., 1945

ALAN ARKIN
THE RUSSIANS ARE COMING, THE RUSSIANS ARE COMING ★
    United Artists, 1966
THE HEART IS A LONELY HUNTER ★ Warner Bros., 1968

GEORGE ARLISS
DISRAELI ★★ Warner Bros., 1929
THE GREEN GODDESS ★ Warner Bros., 1930

JEAN ARTHUR
THE MORE THE MERRIER ★ Columbia, 1943

PEGGY ASHCROFT
A PASSAGE TO INDIA ◎◎ Columbia, 1984, British

FRED ASTAIRE
THE TOWERING INFERNO ◎ 20th Century-Fox/Warner Bros., 1974

MARY ASTOR
THE GREAT LIE ◎◎ Warner Bros., 1941

MISCHA AUER
MY MAN GODFREY ◎ Universal, 1936

MARGARET AVERY
THE COLOR PURPLE ◎ Warner Bros., 1985

DAN AYKROYD
DRIVING MISS DAISY ◎ Warner Bros., 1989

LEW AYRES
JOHNNY BELINDA ★ Warner Bros., 1948

B

HERMIONE BADDELEY
ROOM AT THE TOP ◎ Continental, 1959, British

MARY BADHAM
TO KILL A MOCKINGBIRD ◎ Universal, 1962

FAY BAINTER
JEZEBEL ◎◎ Warner Bros., 1938
WHITE BANNERS ★ Warner Bros., 1938
THE CHILDREN'S HOUR ◎ United Artists, 1961

CARROLL BAKER
BABY DOLL ★ Warner Bros., 1956

MARTIN BALSAM
A THOUSAND CLOWNS ◎◎ United Artists, 1965

ANNE BANCROFT
THE MIRACLE WORKER ★★ United Artists, 1962
THE PUMPKIN EATER ★ Royal International, 1964, British
THE GRADUATE ★ Avco Embassy, 1967
THE TURNING POINT ★ 20th Century-Fox, 1977
AGNES OF GOD ★ Columbia, 1985

GEORGE BANCROFT
THUNDERBOLT ★ Paramount, 1929

IAN BANNEN
THE FLIGHT OF THE PHOENIX ◐ 20th Century-Fox, 1965

MARIE-CHRISTINE BARRAULT
COUSIN, COUSINE ★ Northal Films, 1976, French

BARBARA BARRIE
BREAKING AWAY ◐ 20th Century-Fox, 1979

ETHEL BARRYMORE
NONE BUT THE LONELY HEART ◐◐ RKO Radio, 1944
THE SPIRAL STAIRCASE ◐ RKO Radio, 1946
THE PARADINE CASE ◐ Selznick, 1947
PINKY ◐ 20th Century-Fox, 1949

LIONEL BARRYMORE
A FREE SOUL ★★ MGM, 1931

RICHARD BARTHELMESS
THE NOOSE ★ First National, 1927
THE PATENT LEATHER KID ★ First National, 1927

MIKHAIL BARYSHNIKOV
THE TURNING POINT ◐ 20th Century-Fox, 1977

ALBERT BASSERMAN
FOREIGN CORRESPONDENT ◐ United Artists, 1940

ANGELA BASSETT
WHAT'S LOVE GOT TO DO WITH IT ★ Buena Vista, 1993

ALAN BATES
THE FIXER ★ MGM, 1968, British

KATHY BATES
MISERY ★★ Columbia, 1990

ANNE BAXTER
THE RAZOR'S EDGE ◐◐ 20th Century-Fox, 1946
ALL ABOUT EVE ★ 20th Century-Fox, 1950

WARNER BAXTER
IN OLD ARIZONA ★★ Fox, 1929

NED BEATTY
NETWORK ◐ MGM/United Artists, 1976

WARREN BEATTY
BONNIE AND CLYDE ★ Warner Bros., 1967
HEAVEN CAN WAIT ★ Paramount, 1978
REDS ★ Paramount, 1981
BUGSY ★ TriStar, 1991

WALLACE BEERY
THE BIG HOUSE ★ MGM, 1930
THE CHAMP ★★ MGM, 1931

ED BEGLEY
SWEET BIRD OF YOUTH ◐◐ MGM, 1962

BARBARA BEL GEDDES
I REMEMBER MAMA ◐ RKO Radio, 1948

RALPH BELLAMY
THE AWFUL TRUTH ◐ Columbia, 1937

WILLIAM BENDIX
WAKE ISLAND ◐ Paramount, 1942

ANNETTE BENING
THE GRIFTERS ◐ Miramax Films, 1990

TOM BERENGER
PLATOON ◐ Orion, 1986

CANDICE BERGEN
STARTING OVER ◐ Paramount, 1979

INGRID BERGMAN
FOR WHOM THE BELL TOLLS ★ Paramount, 1943
GASLIGHT ★★ MGM, 1944
THE BELLS OF ST. MARY'S ★ RKO Radio, 1945
JOAN OF ARC ★ RKO Radio, 1948
ANASTASIA ★★ 20th Century-Fox, 1956
MURDER ON THE ORIENT EXPRESS ◐◐ Paramount, 1974
AUTUMN SONATA ★ New World, 1978, Swedish

ELISABETH BERGNER
ESCAPE ME NEVER ★ United Artists, 1935, British

JEANNIE BERLIN
THE HEARTBREAK KID ◐ 20th Century-Fox, 1972

CHARLES BICKFORD
THE SONG OF BERNADETTE ◐ 20th Century-Fox, 1943
THE FARMER'S DAUGHTER ◐ RKO Radio, 1947
JOHNNY BELINDA ◐ Warner Bros., 1948

THEODORE BIKEL
THE DEFIANT ONES ◐ United Artists, 1958

KAREN BLACK
FIVE EASY PIECES ◐ Columbia, 1970

BETSY BLAIR
MARTY ◐ United Artists, 1955

LINDA BLAIR
THE EXORCIST ◐ Warner Bros., 1973

RONEE BLAKLEY
NASHVILLE ◐ Paramount, 1975

JOAN BLONDELL
THE BLUE VEIL ◐ RKO Radio, 1951

ANN BLYTH
MILDRED PIERCE ◐ Warner Bros., 1945

HUMPHREY BOGART
CASABLANCA ★ Warner Bros., 1943
THE AFRICAN QUEEN ★★ United Artists, 1951
THE CAINE MUTINY ★ Columbia, 1954

BEULAH BONDI
THE GORGEOUS HUSSY ◐ MGM, 1936
OF HUMAN HEARTS ◐ MGM, 1938

SHIRLEY BOOTH
COME BACK, LITTLE SHEBA ★★ Paramount, 1952

ERNEST BORGNINE
MARTY ★★ United Artists, 1955

CHARLES BOYER
CONQUEST ★ MGM, 1937
ALGIERS ★ United Artists, 1938
GASLIGHT ★ MGM, 1944
FANNY ★ Warner Bros., 1961

LORRAINE BRACCO
GOODFELLAS ◐ Warner Bros., 1990

ALICE BRADY
MY MAN GODFREY ◐ Universal, 1936
IN OLD CHICAGO ◐◐ 20th Century-Fox, 1937

KENNETH BRANAGH
HENRY V ★ Samuel Goldwyn Company, 1989, British

KLAUS MARIA BRANDAUER
OUT OF AFRICA ◐ Universal, 1985

MARLON BRANDO
A STREETCAR NAMED DESIRE ★ Warner Bros., 1951
VIVA ZAPATA! ★ 20th Century-Fox, 1952
JULIUS CAESAR ★ MGM, 1953
ON THE WATERFRONT ★★ Columbia, 1954
SAYONARA ★ Warner Bros., 1957
THE GODFATHER ★★ Paramount, 1972
LAST TANGO IN PARIS ★ United Artists, 1973
A DRY WHITE SEASON ◐ MGM/UA, 1989

EILEEN BRENNAN
PRIVATE BENJAMIN ✪ Warner Bros., 1980

WALTER BRENNAN
COME AND GET IT ✪✪ United Artists, 1936
KENTUCKY ✪✪ 20th Century-Fox, 1938
THE WESTERNER ✪✪ United Artists, 1940
SERGEANT YORK ✪ Warner Bros., 1941

JEFF BRIDGES
THE LAST PICTURE SHOW ✪ Columbia, 1971
THUNDERBOLT AND LIGHTFOOT ✪ United Artists, 1974
STARMAN ★ Columbia, 1984

ALBERT BROOKS
BROADCAST NEWS ✪ 20th Century Fox, 1987

LESLIE BROWNE
THE TURNING POINT ✪ 20th Century-Fox, 1977

YUL BRYNNER
THE KING AND I ★★ 20th Century-Fox, 1956

GENEVIEVE BUJOLD
ANNE OF THE THOUSAND DAYS ★ Universal, 1969, British

VICTOR BUONO
WHAT EVER HAPPENED TO BABY JANE? ✪ Warner Bros., 1962

BILLIE BURKE
MERRILY WE LIVE ✪ MGM, 1938

CATHERINE BURNS
LAST SUMMER ✪ Allied Artists, 1969

GEORGE BURNS
THE SUNSHINE BOYS ✪✪ MGM/United Artists, 1975

ELLEN BURSTYN
THE LAST PICTURE SHOW ✪ Columbia, 1971
THE EXORCIST ★ Warner Bros., 1973
ALICE DOESN'T LIVE HERE ANYMORE ★★ Warner Bros., 1974
SAME TIME, NEXT YEAR ★ Universal, 1978
RESURRECTION ★ Universal, 1980

RICHARD BURTON
MY COUSIN RACHEL ✪ 20th Century-Fox, 1952
THE ROBE ★ 20th Century-Fox, 1953
BECKET ★ Paramount, 1964, British
THE SPY WHO CAME IN FROM THE COLD ★ Paramount, 1965, British
WHO'S AFRAID OF VIRGINIA WOOLF? ★ Warner Bros., 1966
ANNE OF THE THOUSAND DAYS ★ Universal, 1969, British
EQUUS ★ United Artists, 1977

GARY BUSEY
THE BUDDY HOLLY STORY ★ Columbia, 1978

RED BUTTONS
SAYONARA ✪✪ Warner Bros., 1957

SPRING BYINGTON
YOU CAN'T TAKE IT WITH YOU ✪ Columbia, 1938

C

JAMES CAAN
THE GODFATHER ✪ Paramount, 1972

ADOLPH CAESAR
A SOLDIER'S STORY ✪ Columbia, 1984

JAMES CAGNEY
ANGELS WITH DIRTY FACES ★ Warner Bros., 1938
YANKEE DOODLE DANDY ★★ Warner Bros., 1942
LOVE ME OR LEAVE ME ★ MGM, 1955

MICHAEL CAINE
ALFIE ★ Paramount, 1966, British
SLEUTH ★ 20th Century-Fox, 1972
EDUCATING RITA ★ Columbia, 1983, British
HANNAH AND HER SISTERS ✪✪ Orion, 1986

LOUIS CALHERN
THE MAGNIFICENT YANKEE ★ MGM, 1950

DYAN CANNON
BOB & CAROL & TED & ALICE ✪ Columbia, 1969
HEAVEN CAN WAIT ✪ Paramount, 1978

HARRY CAREY
MR. SMITH GOES TO WASHINGTON ✪ Columbia, 1939

LYNN CARLIN
FACES ✪ Continental, 1968

ART CARNEY
HARRY AND TONTO ★★ 20th Century-Fox, 1974

LESLIE CARON
LILI ★ MGM, 1953
THE L-SHAPED ROOM ★ Columbia, 1963, British

DIAHANN CARROLL
CLAUDINE ★ 20th Century-Fox, 1974

NANCY CARROLL
THE DEVIL'S HOLIDAY ★ Paramount, 1930

PEGGY CASS
AUNTIE MAME ✪ Warner Bros., 1958

JOHN CASSAVETES
THE DIRTY DOZEN ✪ MGM, 1967

SEYMOUR CASSEL
FACES ✪ Continental, 1968

RICHARD CASTELLANO
LOVERS AND OTHER STRANGERS ✪ Cinerama Releasing
    Corporation, 1970

GEORGE CHAKIRIS
WEST SIDE STORY ✪✪ United Artists, 1961

JEFF CHANDLER
BROKEN ARROW ✪ 20th Century-Fox, 1950

CAROL CHANNING
THOROUGHLY MODERN MILLIE ✪ Universal, 1967

STOCKARD CHANNING
SIX DEGREES OF SEPARATION ★ MGM/UA, 1993

CHARLES CHAPLIN
THE CIRCUS ★ United Artists, 1928
THE GREAT DICTATOR ★ United Artists, 1940

RUTH CHATTERTON
MADAM X ★ MGM, 1929
SARAH AND SON ★ Paramount, 1930

MICHAEL CHEKHOV
SPELLBOUND ✪ United Artists, 1945

CHER
SILKWOOD ✪ 20th Century-Fox, 1983
MOONSTRUCK ★★ MGM/UA, 1987

MAURICE CHEVALIER
THE LOVE PARADE ★ Paramount, 1929
THE BIG POND ★ Paramount, 1930

JULIE CHRISTIE
DARLING ★★ Embassy, 1965, British
McCABE & MRS. MILLER ★ Warner Bros., 1971

DIANE CILENTO
TOM JONES ✪ Lopert, 1963, British

CANDY CLARK
AMERICAN GRAFFITI ✪ Universal, 1973

JILL CLAYBURGH
AN UNMARRIED WOMAN ★ 20th Century-Fox, 1978
STARTING OVER ★ Paramount, 1979

MONTGOMERY CLIFT
THE SEARCH ★ MGM, 1948, Swiss
A PLACE IN THE SUN ★ Paramount, 1951
FROM HERE TO ETERNITY ★ Columbia, 1953
JUDGMENT AT NUREMBERG ⊙ United Artists, 1961

GLENN CLOSE
THE WORLD ACCORDING TO GARP ⊙ Warner Bros., 1982
THE BIG CHILL ⊙ Columbia, 1983
THE NATURAL ⊙ Tri-Star, 1984
FATAL ATTRACTION ★ Paramount, 1987
DANGEROUS LIAISONS ★ Warner Bros., 1988

LEE J. COBB
ON THE WATERFRONT ⊙ Columbia, 1954
THE BROTHERS KARAMAZOV ⊙ MGM, 1958

CHARLES COBURN
THE DEVIL AND MISS JONES ⊙ RKO Radio, 1941
THE MORE THE MERRIER ⊙⊙ Columbia, 1943
THE GREEN YEARS ⊙ MGM, 1946

JAMES COCO
ONLY WHEN I LAUGH ⊙ Columbia, 1981

CLAUDETTE COLBERT
IT HAPPENED ONE NIGHT ★★ Columbia, 1934
PRIVATE WORLDS ★ Paramount, 1935
SINCE YOU WENT AWAY ★ United Artists, 1944

PATRICIA COLLINGE
THE LITTLE FOXES ⊙ RKO Radio, 1941

PAULINE COLLINS
SHIRLEY VALENTINE ★ Paramount, 1989, British

RONALD COLMAN
BULLDOG DRUMMOND ★ United Artists, 1929
CONDEMNED ★ United Artists, 1929
RANDOM HARVEST ★ MGM, 1942
A DOUBLE LIFE ★★ Universal, 1947

BETTY COMPSON
THE BARKER ★ First National, 1928

SEAN CONNERY
THE UNTOUCHABLES ⊙⊙ Paramount, 1987

TOM CONTI
REUBEN, REUBEN ★ 20th Century-Fox International Classics, 1983

GARY COOPER
MR. DEEDS GOES TO TOWN ★ Columbia, 1936
SERGEANT YORK ★★ Warner Bros., 1941
THE PRIDE OF THE YANKEES ★ RKO Radio, 1942
FOR WHOM THE BELL TOLLS ★ Paramount, 1943
HIGH NOON ★★ United Artists, 1952

GLADYS COOPER
NOW, VOYAGER ⊙ Warner Bros., 1942
THE SONG OF BERNADETTE ⊙ 20th Century-Fox, 1943
MY FAIR LADY ⊙ Warner Bros., 1964

JACKIE COOPER
SKIPPY ★ Paramount, 1931

ELLEN CORBY
I REMEMBER MAMA ⊙ RKO Radio, 1948

VALENTINA CORTESE
DAY FOR NIGHT ⊙ Warner Bros., 1974, French

KEVIN COSTNER
DANCES WITH WOLVES ★ Orion, 1990

TOM COURTENAY
DOCTOR ZHIVAGO ⊙ MGM, 1965, British
THE DRESSER ★ Columbia, 1983, British

JEANNE CRAIN
PINKY ★ 20th Century-Fox, 1949

BRODERICK CRAWFORD
ALL THE KING'S MEN ★★ Columbia, 1949

JOAN CRAWFORD
MILDRED PIERCE ★★ Warner Bros., 1945
POSSESSED ★ Warner Bros., 1947
SUDDEN FEAR ★ RKO Radio, 1952

DONALD CRISP
HOW GREEN WAS MY VALLEY ⊙⊙ 20th Century-Fox, 1941

HUME CRONYN
THE SEVENTH CROSS ⊙ MGM, 1944

BING CROSBY
GOING MY WAY ★★ Paramount, 1944
THE BELLS OF ST. MARY'S ★ RKO Radio, 1945
THE COUNTRY GIRL ★ Paramount, 1954

RUPERT CROSSE
THE REIVERS ⊙ National General, 1969

LINDSAY CROUSE
PLACES IN THE HEART ⊙ Tri-Star, 1984

TOM CRUISE
BORN ON THE FOURTH OF JULY ★ Universal, 1989

QUINN CUMMINGS
THE GOODBYE GIRL ⊙ MGM/Warner Bros., 1977

TONY CURTIS
THE DEFIANT ONES ★ United Artists, 1958

JOAN CUSACK
WORKING GIRL ⊙ 20th Century Fox, 1988

D

WILLEM DAFOE
PLATOON ⊙ Orion, 1986

DAN DAILEY
WHEN MY BABY SMILES AT ME ★ 20th Century-Fox, 1948

JOHN DALL
THE CORN IS GREEN ⊙ Warner Bros., 1945

DOROTHY DANDRIDGE
CARMEN JONES ★ 20th Century-Fox, 1954

BOBBY DARIN
CAPTAIN NEWMAN, M.D. ⊙ Universal, 1963

JANE DARWELL
THE GRAPES OF WRATH ⊙⊙ 20th Century-Fox, 1940

JAYE DAVIDSON
THE CRYING GAME ⊙ Miramax Films, 1992, Irish-British

BETTE DAVIS
DANGEROUS ★★ Warner Bros., 1935
JEZEBEL ★★ Warner Bros., 1938
DARK VICTORY ★ Warner Bros., 1939
THE LETTER ★ Warner Bros., 1940
THE LITTLE FOXES ★ RKO Radio, 1941
NOW, VOYAGER ★ Warner Bros., 1942
MR. SKEFFINGTON ★ Warner Bros., 1944
ALL ABOUT EVE ★ 20th Century-Fox, 1950
THE STAR ★ 20th Century-Fox, 1952
WHAT EVER HAPPENED TO BABY JANE? ★ Warner Bros., 1962

GEENA DAVIS
THE ACCIDENTAL TOURIST ⊙⊙ Warner Bros., 1988
THELMA & LOUISE ★ MGM-Pathe, 1991

JUDY DAVIS
A PASSAGE TO INDIA ★ Columbia, 1984, British
HUSBANDS AND WIVES ⊙ TriStar, 1992

BRUCE DAVISON
LONGTIME COMPANION ⊙ Samuel Goldwyn Company, 1990

DORIS DAY
PILLOW TALK ★ Universal, 1959

DANIEL DAY-LEWIS
MY LEFT FOOT ★★ Miramax Films, 1989, Irish
IN THE NAME OF THE FATHER ★ Universal, 1993, Irish-British

JAMES DEAN
EAST OF EDEN ★ Warner Bros., 1955
GIANT ★ Warner Bros., 1956

OLIVIA de HAVILLAND
GONE WITH THE WIND ❍ MGM, 1939
HOLD BACK THE DAWN ★ Paramount, 1941
TO EACH HIS OWN ★★ Paramount, 1946
THE SNAKE PIT ★ 20th Century-Fox, 1948
THE HEIRESS ★★ Paramount, 1949

WILLIAM DEMAREST
THE JOLSON STORY ❍ Columbia, 1946

CATHERINE DENEUVE
INDOCHINE ★ Sony Pictures Classics, 1992, French

ROBERT DE NIRO
THE GODFATHER, PART II ❍❍ Paramount, 1974
TAXI DRIVER ★ Columbia, 1976
THE DEER HUNTER ★ Universal, 1978
RAGING BULL ★★ United Artists, 1980
AWAKENINGS ★ Columbia, 1990
CAPE FEAR ★ Universal, 1991

SANDY DENNIS
WHO'S AFRAID OF VIRGINIA WOOLF? ❍❍ Warner Bros., 1966

GERARD DÉPARDIEU
CYRANO DE BERGERAC ★ Orion Classics, 1990, French

BRUCE DERN
COMING HOME ❍ United Artists, 1978

LAURA DERN
RAMBLING ROSE ★ New Line Cinema, 1991

VITTORIO de SICA
A FAREWELL TO ARMS ❍ 20th Century-Fox, 1957

BRANDON de WILDE
SHANE ❍ Paramount, 1953

LEONARDO DI CAPRIO
WHAT'S EATING GILBERT GRAPE ❍ Paramount, 1993

MARLENE DIETRICH
MOROCCO ★ Paramount, 1930

MELINDA DILLON
CLOSE ENCOUNTERS OF THE THIRD KIND ❍ Columbia, 1977
ABSENCE OF MALICE ❍ Columbia, 1981

RICHARD DIX
CIMARRON ★ RKO Radio, 1931

ROBERT DONAT
THE CITADEL ★ MGM, 1938, British
GOODBYE, MR. CHIPS ★★ MGM, 1939, British

BRIAN DONLEVY
BEAU GESTE ❍ Paramount, 1939

KIRK DOUGLAS
CHAMPION ★ United Artists, 1949
THE BAD AND THE BEAUTIFUL ★ MGM, 1952
LUST FOR LIFE ★ MGM, 1956

MELVYN DOUGLAS
HUD ❍❍ Paramount, 1963
I NEVER SANG FOR MY FATHER ★ Columbia, 1970
BEING THERE ❍❍ United Artists, 1979

MICHAEL DOUGLAS
WALL STREET ★★ 20th Century Fox, 1987

BRAD DOURIF
ONE FLEW OVER THE CUCKOO'S NEST ❍ United Artists, 1975

ROBERT DOWNEY, JR.
CHAPLIN ★ Tri-Star, 1992, U.S.-British

LOUISE DRESSER
A SHIP COMES IN ★ Pathé-RKO Radio, 1927

MARIE DRESSLER
MIN AND BILL ★★ MGM, 1930
EMMA ★ MGM, 1931

RICHARD DREYFUSS
THE GOODBYE GIRL ★★ MGM/Warner Bros., 1977

OLYMPIA DUKAKIS
MOONSTRUCK ❍❍ MGM/UA, 1987

PATTY DUKE
THE MIRACLE WORKER ❍❍ United Artists, 1962

FAYE DUNAWAY
BONNIE AND CLYDE ★ Warner Bros., 1967
CHINATOWN ★ Paramount, 1974
NETWORK ★★ MGM/United Artists, 1976

JAMES DUNN
A TREE GROWS IN BROOKLYN ❍❍ 20th Century-Fox, 1945

MICHAEL DUNN
SHIP OF FOOLS ❍ Columbia, 1965

IRENE DUNNE
CIMARRON ★ RKO Radio, 1931
THEODORA GOES WILD ★ Columbia, 1936
THE AWFUL TRUTH ★ Columbia, 1937
LOVE AFFAIR ★ RKO Radio, 1939
I REMEMBER MAMA ★ RKO Radio, 1948

MILDRED DUNNOCK
DEATH OF A SALESMAN ❍ Columbia, 1951
BABY DOLL ❍ Warner Bros., 1956

CHARLES DURNING
THE BEST LITTLE WHOREHOUSE IN TEXAS ❍ Universal, 1982
TO BE OR NOT TO BE ❍ 20th Century-Fox, 1983

ROBERT DUVALL
THE GODFATHER ❍ Paramount, 1972
APOCALYPSE NOW ❍ United Artists, 1979
THE GREAT SANTINI ★ Orion/Warner Bros., 1980
TENDER MERCIES ★★ Universal/AFD, 1983

E

JEANNE EAGELS
THE LETTER ★ Paramount, 1929

CLINT EASTWOOD
UNFORGIVEN ★ Warner Bros., 1992

SAMANTHA EGGAR
THE COLLECTOR ★ Columbia, 1965, British

DENHOLM ELLIOTT
A ROOM WITH A VIEW ❍ Cinecom, 1986, British

HOPE EMERSON
CAGED ❍ Warner Bros., 1950

STUART ERWIN
PIGSKIN PARADE ❍ 20th Century-Fox, 1936

DAME EDITH EVANS
TOM JONES ❍ Lopert, 1963, British
THE CHALK GARDEN ❍ Universal, 1964, British
THE WHISPERERS ★ United Artists, 1967, British

ACADEMY AWARDS

607

F

PETER FALK
MURDER, INC. ✪ 20th Century-Fox, 1960
POCKETFUL OF MIRACLES ✪ United Artists, 1961

RICHARD FARNSWORTH
COMES A HORSEMAN ✪ United Artists, 1978

JOSÉ FERRER
JOAN OF ARC ✪ RKO Radio, 1948
CYRANO DE BERGERAC ★★ United Artists, 1950
MOULIN ROUGE ★ United Artists, 1952, British

SALLY FIELD
NORMA RAE ★★ 20th Century-Fox, 1979
PLACES IN THE HEART ★★ Tri-Star, 1984

RALPH FIENNES
SCHINDLER'S LIST ✪ Universal, 1993

PETER FINCH
SUNDAY, BLOODY SUNDAY ★ United Artists, 1971, British,
NETWORK ★★ MGM/United Artists, 1976

FRANK FINLAY
OTHELLO ✪ Warner Bros., 1965, British

ALBERT FINNEY
TOM JONES ★ Lopert, 1963, British
MURDER ON THE ORIENT EXPRESS ★ Paramount, 1974
THE DRESSER ★ Columbia, 1983, British
UNDER THE VOLCANO ★ Universal, 1984

PETER FIRTH
EQUUS ✪ United Artists, 1977

LAURENCE FISHBURNE
WHAT'S LOVE GOT TO DO WITH IT ★ Buena Vista, 1993

BARRY FITZGERALD
GOING MY WAY ★ Paramount, 1944
GOING MY WAY ✪✪ Paramount, 1944

GERALDINE FITZGERALD
WUTHERING HEIGHTS ✪ United Artists, 1939

LOUISE FLETCHER
ONE FLEW OVER THE CUCKOO'S NEST ★★ United Artists, 1975

NINA FOCH
EXECUTIVE SUITE ✪ MGM, 1954

HENRY FONDA
THE GRAPES OF WRATH ★ 20th Century-Fox, 1940
ON GOLDEN POND ★★ Universal/AFD, 1981

JANE FONDA
THEY SHOOT HORSES, DON'T THEY? ★ Cinerama Releasing
    Corporation, 1969
KLUTE ★★ Warner Bros., 1971
JULIA ★ 20th Century-Fox, 1977
COMING HOME ★★ United Artists, 1978
THE CHINA SYNDROME ★ Columbia, 1979
ON GOLDEN POND ✪ Universal/AFD, 1981
THE MORNING AFTER ★ 20th Century Fox, 1986

JOAN FONTAINE
REBECCA ★ United Artists, 1940
SUSPICION ★★ RKO Radio, 1941
THE CONSTANT NYMPH ★ Warner Bros., 1943

LYNN FONTANNE
THE GUARDSMAN ★ MGM, 1931

HARRISON FORD
WITNESS ★ Paramount, 1985

FREDERIC FORREST
THE ROSE ✪ 20th Century-Fox, 1979

JODIE FOSTER
TAXI DRIVER ✪ Columbia, 1976
THE ACCUSED ★★ Paramount, 1988
THE SILENCE OF THE LAMBS ★★ Orion, 1991

ANTHONY FRANCIOSA
A HATFUL OF RAIN ★ 20th Century-Fox, 1957

MORGAN FREEMAN
STREET SMART ✪ Cannon, 1987
DRIVING MISS DAISY ★ Warner Bros., 1989

LEONARD FREY
FIDDLER ON THE ROOF ✪ United Artists, 1971

BRENDA FRICKER
MY LEFT FOOT ✪✪ Miramax Films, 1989, Irish

G

CLARK GABLE
IT HAPPENED ONE NIGHT ★★ Columbia, 1934
MUTINY ON THE BOUNTY ★ MGM, 1935
GONE WITH THE WIND ★ MGM, 1939

GRETA GARBO
ANNA CHRISTIE ★ MGM, 1929
ROMANCE ★ MGM, 1930
CAMILLE ★ MGM, 1937
NINOTCHKA ★ MGM, 1939

ANDY GARCIA
THE GODFATHER, PART III ✪ Paramount, 1990

VINCENT GARDENIA
BANG THE DRUM SLOWLY ✪ Paramount, 1973
MOONSTRUCK ✪ MGM/UA, 1987

AVA GARDNER
MOGAMBO ★ MGM, 1953

JOHN GARFIELD
FOUR DAUGHTERS ✪ Warner Bros., 1938
BODY AND SOUL ★ United Artists, 1947

WILLIAM GARGAN
THEY KNEW WHAT THEY WANTED ✪ RKO Radio, 1940

JUDY GARLAND
A STAR IS BORN ★ Warner Bros., 1954
JUDGMENT AT NUREMBERG ✪ United Artists, 1961

JAMES GARNER
MURPHY'S ROMANCE ★ Columbia, 1985

TERRI GARR
TOOTSIE ✪ Columbia, 1982

GREER GARSON
GOODBYE, MR. CHIPS ★ MGM, 1939, British
BLOSSOMS IN THE DUST ★ MGM, 1941
MRS. MINIVER ★★ MGM, 1942
MADAME CURIE ★ MGM, 1943
MRS. PARKINGTON ★ MGM, 1944
THE VALLEY OF DECISION ★ MGM, 1945
SUNRISE AT CAMPOBELLO ★ Warner Bros., 1960

JANET GAYNOR
SEVENTH HEAVEN ★★ Fox, 1927
STREET ANGEL ★★ Fox, 1927
SUNRISE ★★ Fox, 1927
A STAR IS BORN ★ United Artists, 1937

MICHAEL V. GAZZO
THE GODFATHER, PART II ✪ Paramount, 1974

LEO GENN
QUO VADIS ✪ MGM, 1951

CHIEF DAN GEORGE
LITTLE BIG MAN ✪ National General, 1970

GLADYS GEORGE
VALIANT IS THE WORLD FOR CARRIE ★ Paramount, 1936

GIANCARLO GIANNINI
SEVEN BEAUTIES ★ Cinema 5, 1976, Italian

JOHN GIELGUD
BECKET ❍ Paramount, 1964, British
ARTHUR ❍❍ Orion, 1981

JACK GILFORD
SAVE THE TIGER ❍ Paramount, 1973

LILLIAN GISH
DUEL IN THE SUN ❍ Selznick International, 1946

JACKIE GLEASON
THE HUSTLER ❍ 20th Century-Fox, 1961

JAMES GLEASON
HERE COMES MR. JORDAN ❍ Columbia, 1941

PAULETTE GODDARD
SO PROUDLY WE HAIL ❍ Paramount, 1943

WHOOPI GOLDBERG
THE COLOR PURPLE ★ Warner Bros., 1985
GHOST ❍❍ Paramount, 1990

THOMAS GOMEZ
RIDE THE PINK HORSE ❍ Universal, 1947

DEXTER GORDON
'ROUND MIDNIGHT ★ Warner Bros., 1986

RUTH GORDON
INSIDE DAISY CLOVER ❍ Warner Bros., 1965
ROSEMARY'S BABY ❍❍ Paramount, 1968

LOUIS GOSSETT, JR.
AN OFFICER AND A GENTLEMAN ❍❍ Paramount, 1982

ELLIOTT GOULD
BOB & CAROL & TED & ALICE ❍ Columbia, 1969

GLORIA GRAHAME
CROSSFIRE ❍ RKO Radio, 1947
THE BAD AND THE BEAUTIFUL ❍❍ MGM, 1952

CARY GRANT
PENNY SERENADE ★ Columbia, 1941
NONE BUT THE LONELY HEART ★ RKO Radio, 1944

LEE GRANT
DETECTIVE STORY ❍ Paramount, 1951
THE LANDLORD ❍ United Artists, 1970
SHAMPOO ❍❍ Columbia, 1975
VOYAGE OF THE DAMNED ❍ Avco Embassy, 1976

BONITA GRANVILLE
THESE THREE ❍ United Artists, 1936

GRAHAM GREEN
DANCES WITH WOLVES ❍ Orion, 1990

SYDNEY GREENSTREET
THE MALTESE FALCON ❍ Warner Bros., 1941

JOEL GREY
CABARET ❍❍ Allied Artists, 1972

HUGH GRIFFITH
BEN-HUR ❍❍ MGM, 1959
TOM JONES ❍ Lopert, 1963, British

MELANIE GRIFFITH
WORKING GIRL ★ 20th Century Fox, 1988

ALEC GUINNESS
THE LAVENDER HILL MOB ★ Universal, 1951, British
THE BRIDGE ON THE RIVER KWAI ★★ Columbia, 1957, British
STAR WARS ❍ 20th Century-Fox, 1977
LITTLE DORRIT ❍ Cannon, 1987, British

EDMUND GWENN
MIRACLE ON 34TH STREET ❍❍ 20th Century-Fox, 1947
MISTER 880 ❍ 20th Century-Fox, 1950

H

JOAN HACKETT
ONLY WHEN I LAUGH ❍ Columbia, 1981

GENE HACKMAN
BONNIE AND CLYDE ❍ Warner Bros., 1967
I NEVER SANG FOR MY FATHER ❍ Columbia, 1970
THE FRENCH CONNECTION ★★ 20th Century-Fox, 1971
MISSISSIPPI BURNING ★ Orion, 1988
UNFORGIVEN ❍❍ Warner Bros., 1992

JEAN HAGEN
SINGIN' IN THE RAIN ❍ MGM, 1952

GRAYSON HALL
THE NIGHT OF THE IGUANA ❍ MGM, 1964

TOM HANKS
BIG ★ 20th Century Fox, 1988
PHILADELPHIA ★★ TriStar. 1993

ANN HARDING
HOLIDAY ★ RKO Pathé, 1931

TESS HARPER
CRIMES OF THE HEART ❍ DEG, 1986

BARBARA HARRIS
WHO IS HARRY KELLERMAN, AND WHY IS HE SAYING THOSE
TERRIBLE THINGS ABOUT ME? ❍ National General, 1971

JULIE HARRIS
THE MEMBER OF THE WEDDING ★ Columbia, 1952

RICHARD HARRIS
THIS SPORTING LIFE ★ Continental, 1962, British
THE FIELD ★ Avenue Pictures, 1990, British

REX HARRISON
CLEOPATRA ★ 20th Century-Fox, 1963
MY FAIR LADY ★★ Warner Bros., 1964

ELIZABETH HARTMAN
A PATCH OF BLUE ★ MGM, 1965

LAURENCE HARVEY
ROOM AT THE TOP ★ Continental, 1959, British

GOLDIE HAWN
CACTUS FLOWER ❍❍ Columbia, 1969
PRIVATE BENJAMIN ★ Warner Bros., 1980

SESSUE HAYAKAWA
THE BRIDGE ON THE RIVER KWAI ❍ Columbia, 1957, British

HELEN HAYES
THE SIN OF MADELON CLAUDET ★★ MGM, 1931
AIRPORT ❍❍ Universal, 1970

SUSAN HAYWARD
SMASH UP - THE STORY OF A WOMAN ★ Universal, 1947
MY FOOLISH HEART ★ RKO Radio, 1949
WITH A SONG IN MY HEART ★ 20th Century-Fox, 1952
I'LL CRY TOMORROW ★ MGM, 1955

SUSAN HAYWOOD
I WANT TO LIVE! ★★ United Artists, 1958

EILEEN HECKART
THE BAD SEED ❍ Warner Bros., 1956
BUTTERFLIES ARE FREE ❍❍ Columbia, 1972

VAN HEFLIN
JOHNNY EAGER ❍❍ MGM, 1942

MARIEL HEMINGWAY
MANHATTAN ❍ United Artists, 1979

JUSTIN HENRY
KRAMER VS. KRAMER ❍ Columbia, 1979

AUDREY HEPBURN
ROMAN HOLIDAY ★★ Paramount, 1953
SABRINA ★ Paramount, 1954
THE NUN'S STORY ★ Warner Bros., 1959
BREAKFAST AT TIFFANY'S ★ Paramount, 1961
WAIT UNTIL DARK ★ Warner Bros., 1967

KATHARINE HEPBURN
MORNING GLORY ★★ RKO Radio, 1933
ALICE ADAMS ★ RKO Radio, 1935
THE PHILADELPHIA STORY ★ MGM, 1940
WOMAN OF THE YEAR ★ MGM, 1942
THE AFRICAN QUEEN ★ United Artists, 1951
SUMMERTIME ★, United Artists, 1955, Anglo-American
THE RAINMAKER ★ Paramount, 1956
SUDDENLY, LAST SUMMER ★ Columbia, 1959
LONG DAY'S JOURNEY INTO NIGHT ★ Embassy, 1962
GUESS WHO'S COMING TO DINNER ★★ Columbia, 1967
THE LION IN WINTER ★★ Avco Embassy, 1968, British
ON GOLDEN POND ★★ Universal/AFD, 1981

CHARLTON HESTON
BEN-HUR ★★ MGM, 1959

WILLIAM HICKEY
PRIZZI'S HONOR ○ 20th Century Fox, 1985

WENDY HILLER
PYGMALION ★ MGM, 1938, British
SEPARATE TABLES ○○ United Artists, 1958
A MAN FOR ALL SEASONS ○ Columbia, 1966, British

JUDD HIRSCH
ORDINARY PEOPLE ○ Paramount, 1980

DUSTIN HOFFMAN
THE GRADUATE ★ Avco Embassy, 1967
MIDNIGHT COWBOY ★ United Artists, 1969
LENNY ★ United Artist, 1974
KRAMER VS. KRAMER ★★ Columbia, 1979
TOOTSIE ★ Columbia, 1982
RAIN MAN ★★ MGM/UA, 1988

WILLIAM HOLDEN
SUNSET BOULEVARD ★ Paramount, 1950
STALAG 17 ★ Paramount, 1953
NETWORK ★ MGM/United Artists, 1976

JUDY HOLLIDAY
BORN YESTERDAY ★★ Columbia, 1950

STANLEY HOLLOWAY
MY FAIR LADY ○ Warner Bros., 1964

CELESTE HOLM
GENTLEMAN'S AGREEMENT ○○ 20th Century-Fox, 1947
COME TO THE STABLE ○ 20th Century-Fox, 1949
ALL ABOUT EVE ○ 20th Century-Fox, 1950

IAN HOLM
CHARIOTS OF FIRE ○ The Ladd Company/Warner Bros., 1981, British

OSCAR HOMOLKA
I REMEMBER MAMA ○ RKO Radio, 1948

ANTHONY HOPKINS
THE SILENCE OF THE LAMBS ★★ Orion, 1991
THE REMAINS OF THE DAY ★ Columbia, 1993, British

MIRIAM HOPKINS
BECKY SHARP ★ RKO Radio, 1935

DENNIS HOPPER
HOOSIERS ○ Orion, 1986

BOB HOSKINS
MONA LISA ★ Island Pictures, 1986, British

JOHN HOUSEMAN
THE PAPER CHASE ○○ 20th Century-Fox, 1973

LESLIE HOWARD
BERKELEY SQUARE ★ Fox, 1933
PYGMALION ★ MGM, 1938, British

TREVOR HOWARD
SONS AND LOVERS ★ 20th Century-Fox, 1960

ROCK HUDSON
GIANT ★ Warner Bros., 1956

TOM HULCE
AMADEUS ★ Orion, 1984

JOSEPHINE HULL
HARVEY ○○ Universal, 1950

ARTHUR HUNNICUTT
THE BIG SKY ○ RKO Radio, 1952

LINDA HUNT
THE YEAR OF LIVING DANGEROUSLY ○○ MGM/UA, 1983, Australian

HOLLY HUNTER
BROADCAST NEWS ★ 20th Century Fox, 1987
THE PIANO ★★ Miramax Films, 1993, New Zealand-French
THE FIRM ○ Paramount, 1993

KIM HUNTER
A STREETCAR NAMED DESIRE ○○ Warner Bros., 1951

JOHN HURT
MIDNIGHT EXPRESS ○ Columbia, 1978
THE ELEPHANT MAN ★ Paramount, 1980

WILLIAM HURT
KISS OF THE SPIDER WOMAN ★★ Island Alive/FilmDallas, 1985, U.S.-Brazilian
CHILDREN OF A LESSER GOD ★ Paramount, 1986
BROADCAST NEWS ★ 20th Century Fox, 1987

RUTH HUSSEY
THE PHILADELPHIA STORY ○ MGM, 1940

ANJELICA HUSTON
PRIZZI'S HONOR ○○ 20th Century Fox, 1985
ENEMIES, A LOVE STORY ○ 20th Century-Fox, 1989
THE GRIFTERS ★ Miramax Films, 1990

JOHN HUSTON
THE CARDINAL ○ Columbia, 1963

WALTER HUSTON
DODSWORTH ★ United Artists, 1936
ALL THAT MONEY CAN BUY aka THE DEVIL AND DANIEL WEBSTER ★ RKO Radio, 1941
YANKEE DOODLE DANDY ○ Warner Bros., 1942
TREASURE OF SIERRA MADRE ○○ Warner Bros., 1948

TIMOTHY HUTTON
ORDINARY PEOPLE ○○ Paramount, 1980

MARTHA HYER
SOME CAME RUNNING ○ MGM, 1958

I

JOHN IRELAND
ALL THE KING'S MEN ○ Columbia, 1949

JEREMY IRONS
REVERSAL OF FORTUNE ★★ Warner Bros., 1990

AMY IRVING
YENTL ○ MGM/UA, 1983

BURL IVES
THE BIG COUNTRY ○○ United Artists, 1958

J

GLENDA JACKSON
WOMEN IN LOVE ★★ United Artists, 1970
SUNDAY, BLOODY SUNDAY ★ United Artists, 1971, British
A TOUCH OF CLASS ★ Avco Embassy, 1973
HEDDA ★ Brut Productions, 1975

RICHARD JAECKEL
SOMETIMES A GREAT NOTION ○ Universal, 1971

SAM JAFFE
THE ASPHALT JUNGLE ○ MGM, 1950

DEAN JAGGER
12 O'CLOCK HIGH ○○ 20th Century-Fox, 1949

EMIL JANNINGS
THE WAY OF ALL FLESH ★★ Paramount, 1927
THE LAST COMMAND ★★ Paramount, 1928

GLYNIS JOHNS
THE SUNDOWNERS ○ Warner Bros., 1960

BEN JOHNSON
THE LAST PICTURE SHOW ○○ Columbia, 1971

CELIA JOHNSON
BRIEF ENCOUNTER ★ Universal, 1946, British

CAROLYN JONES
THE BACHELOR PARTY ○ United Artists, 1957

JAMES EARL JONES
THE GREAT WHITE HOPE ★ 20th Century-Fox, 1970

JENNIFER JONES
THE SONG OF BERNADETTE ★★ 20th Century-Fox, 1943
SINCE YOU WENT AWAY ○ United Artists, 1944
LOVE LETTERS ★ Paramount, 1945
DUEL IN THE SUN ★ Selznick International, 1946, British
LOVE IS A MANY-SPLENDORED THING ★ 20th Century-Fox, 1955

TOMMY LEE JONES
JFK ○ Warner Bros., 1991
THE FUGITIVE ○○ Warner Bros., 1993

SHIRLEY JONES
ELMER GANTRY ○○ United Artists, 1960

KATY JURADO
BROKEN LANCE ○ 20th Century-Fox, 1954

K

MADELINE KAHN
PAPER MOON ○ Paramount, 1973
BLAZING SADDLES ○ Warner Bros., 1974

IDA KAMINSKA
THE SHOP ON MAIN STREET ★ Prominent Films, 1965,
    Czechoslovakian

CAROL KANE
HESTER STREET ★ Midwest Films, 1975

DIANE KEATON
ANNIE HALL ★★ United Artists, 1977
REDS ★ Paramount, 1981

LILA KEDROVA
ZORBA THE GREEK ○○ 20th Century-Fox/International Classics, 1964

HARVEY KEITEL
BUGSY ○ TriStar, 1991

CECIL KELLAWAY
THE LUCK OF THE IRISH ○ 20th Century-Fox, 1948
GUESS WHO'S COMING TO DINNER ○ Columbia, 1967

SALLY KELLERMAN
M*A*S*H ○ 20th Century-Fox, 1970

GENE KELLY
ANCHORS AWEIGH ★ MGM, 1945

GRACE KELLY
MOGAMBO ○ MGM, 1953
THE COUNTRY GIRL ★★ Paramount, 1954

NANCY KELLY
THE BAD SEED ★ Warner Bros., 1956

ARTHUR KENNEDY
CHAMPION ○ United Artists, 1949
BRIGHT VICTORY ★ Universal, 1951
TRIAL ○ MGM, 1955
PEYTON PLACE ○ 20th Century-Fox, 1957
SOME CAME RUNNING ○ MGM, 1958

GEORGE KENNEDY
COOL HAND LUKE ○○ Warner Bros., 1967

DEBORAH KERR
EDWARD MY SON ★ MGM, 1949
FROM HERE TO ETERNITY ★ Columbia, 1953
THE KING AND I ★ 20th Century-Fox, 1956
HEAVEN KNOWS, MR. ALLISON ★ 20th Century-Fox, 1957
SEPARATE TABLES ★ United Artists, 1958
THE SUNDOWNERS ★ Warner Bros., 1960

BEN KINGSLEY
GANDHI ★★ Columbia, 1982, British
BUGSY ○ TriStar, 1991

SALLY KIRKLAND
ANNA ★ Vestron, 1987

KEVIN KLINE
A FISH CALLED WANDA ○○ MGM/UA, 1988, British

SHIRLEY KNIGHT
THE DARK AT THE TOP OF THE STAIRS ○ Warner Bros., 1960
SWEET BIRD OF YOUTH ○ MGM, 1962

ALEXANDER KNOX
WILSON ★ 20th Century-Fox, 1944

SUSAN KOHNER
IMITATION OF LIFE ○ Universal, 1959

MILIZA KORJUS
THE GREAT WALTZ ○ MGM, 1938

JACK KRUSCHEN
THE APARTMENT ○ United Artists, 1960

L

DIANE LADD
ALICE DOESN'T LIVE HERE ANYMORE ○ Warner Bros., 1974
WILD AT HEART ○ Samuel Goldwyn Company, 1990
RAMBLING ROSE ○ New Line Cinema, 1991

JOCELYN LAGARDE
HAWAII ○ United Artists, 1966

CHRISTINE LAHTI
SWING SHIFT ○ Warner Bros., 1984

BURT LANCASTER
FROM HERE TO ETERNITY ★ Columbia, 1953
ELMER GANTRY ★★ United Artists, 1960
BIRDMAN OF ALCATRAZ ★ United Artists, 1962
ATLANTIC CITY ★ Paramount, 1981

ELSA LANCHESTER
COME TO THE STABLE ○ 20th Century-Fox, 1949
WITNESS FOR THE PROSECUTION ○ United Artists, 1957

MARTIN LANDAU
TUCKER - THE MAN AND HIS DREAM ○ Paramount, 1988
CRIMES AND MISDEMEANORS ○ Orion, 1989

HOPE LANGE
PEYTON PLACE ○ 20th Century-Fox, 1957

JESSICA LANGE
FRANCES ★ Universal/AFD, 1982
TOOTSIE ○○ Columbia, 1982
COUNTRY ★ Buena Vista, 1984
SWEET DREAMS ★ Tri-Star, 1985
MUSIC BOX ★ Tri-Star, 1989

ANGELA LANSBURY
GASLIGHT ○ MGM, 1944
THE PICTURE OF DORIAN GRAY ○ MGM, 1945
THE MANCHURIAN CANDIDATE ○ United Artists, 1962

CHARLES LAUGHTON
THE PRIVATE LIFE OF HENRY VIII ★★ United Artists, 1933, British
MUTINY ON THE BOUNTY ★ MGM, 1935
WITNESS FOR THE PROSECUTION ★ United Artists, 1957

PIPER LAURIE
THE HUSTLER ★ 20th Century-Fox, 1961
CARRIE ○ United Artists, 1976
CHILDREN OF A LESSER GOD ○ Paramount, 1986

EVA LE GALLIENNE
RESURRECTION ○ Universal, 1980

CLORIS LEACHMAN
THE LAST PICTURE SHOW ○○ Columbia, 1971

PEGGY LEE
PETE KELLY'S BLUES ○ Warner Bros., 1955

ANDREA LEEDS
STAGE DOOR ○ RKO Radio, 1937

JANET LEIGH
PSYCHO ○ Paramount, 1960

VIVIEN LEIGH
GONE WITH THE WIND ★★ MGM, 1939
A STREETCAR NAMED DESIRE ★★ Warner Bros., 1951

MARGARET LEIGHTON
THE GO-BETWEEN ○ Columbia, 1971

JACK LEMMON
MISTER ROBERTS ○○ Warner Bros., 1955
SOME LIKE IT HOT ★ United Artists, 1959
THE APARTMENT ★ United Artists, 1960
DAYS OF WINE AND ROSES ★ Warner Bros., 1962
SAVE THE TIGER ★★ Paramount, 1973
THE CHINA SYNDROME ★ Columbia, 1979
TRIBUTE ★ 20th Century-Fox, 1980
MISSING ★ Universal, 1982

LOTTE LENYA
THE ROMAN SPRING OF MRS. STONE ○ Warner Bros., 1961

MICHAEL LERNER
BARTON FINK ○ 20th Century Fox, 1991

JULIETTE LEWIS
CAPE FEAR ○ Universal, 1991

JOHN LITHGOW
THE WORLD ACCORDING TO GARP ○ Warner Bros., 1982
TERMS OF ENDEARMENT ○ Paramount, 1983

SONDRA LOCKE
THE HEART IS A LONELY HUNTER ○ Warner Bros., 1968

GENE LOCKHART
ALGIERS ○ United Artists, 1938

ROBERT LOGGIA
JAGGED EDGE ○ Columbia, 1985

CAROLE LOMBARD
MY MAN GODFREY ★ Universal, 1936

SOPHIA LOREN
TWO WOMEN ★★ Embassy, 1960, Italian
MARRIAGE ITALIAN STYLE ★ Embassy, 1964, Italian

JOAN LORRING
THE CORN IS GREEN ○ Warner Bros., 1945

BESSIE LOVE
THE BROADWAY MELODY ★ MGM, 1929

PAUL LUKAS
WATCH ON THE RHINE ★★ Warner Bros., 1943

ALFRED LUNT
THE GUARDSMAN ★ MGM, 1931

M

ALI MacGRAW
LOVE STORY ★ Paramount, 1970

SHIRLEY MacLAINE
SOME CAME RUNNING ★ MGM, 1958
THE APARTMENT ★ United Artists, 1960
IRMA LA DOUCE ★ United Artists, 1963
THE TURNING POINT ★ 20th Century-Fox, 1977
TERMS OF ENDEARMENT ★★ Paramount, 1983

ALINE MacMAHON
DRAGON SEED ○ MGM, 1944

AMY MADIGAN
TWICE IN A LIFETIME ○ The Yorkin Company, 1985

ANNA MAGNANI
THE ROSE TATTOO ★★ Paramount, 1955
WILD IS THE WIND ★ Paramount, 1957

MARJORIE MAIN
THE EGG AND I ○ Universal, 1947

MAKO
THE SAND PEBBLES ○ 20th Century-Fox, 1966

KARL MALDEN
A STREETCAR NAMED DESIRE ○○ Warner Bros., 1951
ON THE WATERFRONT ○ Columbia, 1954

JOHN MALKOVICH
PLACES IN THE HEART ○ Tri-Star, 1984
IN THE LINE OF FIRE ○ Columbia, 1993

DOROTHY MALONE
WRITTEN ON THE WIND ○○ Universal, 1956

JOE MANTELL
MARTY ○ United Artists, 1955

FREDRIC MARCH
THE ROYAL FAMILY OF BROADWAY ★ Paramount, 1930
DR. JEKYLL AND MR. HYDE ★★ Paramount, 1932
A STAR IS BORN ★ United Artists, 1937
THE BEST YEARS OF OUR LIVES ★★ RKO Radio, 1946
DEATH OF A SALESMAN ★ Columbia, 1951

COLETTE MARCHAND
MOULIN ROUGE ○ United Artists, 1952, British

JOHN MARLEY
LOVE STORY ○ Paramount, 1970

LEE MARVIN
CAT BALLOU ★★ Columbia, 1965

JAMES MASON
A STAR IS BORN ★ Warner Bros., 1954
GEORGY GIRL ○ Columbia, 1966, British
THE VERDICT ○ 20th Century-Fox, 1982

MARSHA MASON
CINDERELLA LIBERTY ★ 20th Century-Fox, 1973
THE GOODBYE GIRL ★ MGM/Warner Bros., 1977
CHAPTER TWO ★ Columbia, 1979
ONLY WHEN I LAUGH ★ Columbia, 1981

DANIEL MASSEY
STAR! ○ 20th Century-Fox, 1968

RAYMOND MASSEY
ABE LINCOLN IN ILLINOIS ★ RKO Radio, 1940

MARY ELIZABETH MASTRANTONIO
THE COLOR OF MONEY ✪ Buena Vista, 1986

MARCELLO MASTROIANNI
DIVORCE ITALIAN STYLE ★ Embassy, 1962, Italian
A SPECIAL DAY ★ Cinema 5, 1977, Italian
DARK EYES ★ Island Pictures, 1987, Italian

MARLEE MATLIN
CHILDREN OF A LESSER GOD ★★ Paramount, 1986

WALTER MATTHAU
THE FORTUNE COOKIE ✪✪ United Artists, 1966
KOTCH ★ Cinerama, 1971
THE SUNSHINE BOYS ★ MGM/United Artists, 1975

MERCEDES McCAMBRIDGE
ALL THE KING'S MEN ✪✪ Columbia, 1949
GIANT ✪ Warner Bros., 1956

KEVIN McCARTHY
DEATH OF A SALESMAN ✪ Columbia, 1951

PATTY McCORMACK
THE BAD SEED ✪ Warner Bros., 1956

HATTIE McDANIEL
GONE WITH THE WIND ✪✪ MGM, 1939

MARY McDONNELL
DANCES WITH WOLVES ✪ Orion, 1990
PASSION FISH ★ Miramax Films, 1992

FRANCES McDORMAND
MISSISSIPPI BURNING ✪ Orion, 1988

ELIZABETH McGOVERN
RAGTIME ✪ Paramount, 1981

DOROTHY McGUIRE
GENTLEMAN'S AGREEMENT ★ 20th Century-Fox, 1947

VICTOR McLAGLEN
THE INFORMER ★★ RKO Radio, 1935
THE QUIET MAN ✪ Republic, 1952

MAGGIE McNAMARA
THE MOON IS BLUE ★ United Artists, 1953

STEVE McQUEEN
THE SAND PEBBLES ★ 20th Century-Fox, 1966

KAY MEDFORD
FUNNY GIRL ✪ Columbia, 1968

ADOLPHE MENJOU
THE FRONT PAGE ★ United Artists, 1931

VIVIEN MERCHANT
ALFIE ✪ Paramount, 1966, British

MELINA MERCOURI
NEVER ON SUNDAY ★ Lopert, 1960, Greek

BURGESS MEREDITH
THE DAY OF THE LOCUST ✪ Paramount, 1975
ROCKY ✪ United Artists, 1976

UNA MERKEL
SUMMER AND SMOKE ✪ Paramount, 1961

BETTE MIDLER
THE ROSE ★ 20th Century-Fox, 1979
FOR THE BOYS ★ 20th Century Fox, 1991

SARAH MILES
RYAN'S DAUGHTER ★ MGM, 1970

SYLVIA MILES
MIDNIGHT COWBOY ✪ United Artists, 1969
FAREWELL, MY LOVELY ✪ Avco Embassy, 1975

PENELOPE MILFORD
COMING HOME ✪ United Artists, 1978

RAY MILLAND
THE LOST WEEKEND ★★ Paramount, 1945

JASON MILLER
THE EXORCIST ✪ Warner Bros., 1973

JOHN MILLS
RYAN'S DAUGHTER ✪✪ MGM, 1970

SAL MINEO
REBEL WITHOUT A CAUSE ✪ Warner Bros., 1955
EXODUS ✪ United Artists, 1960

LIZA MINNELLI
THE STERILE CUCKOO ★ Paramount, 1969
CABARET ★★ Allied Artists, 1972

THOMAS MITCHELL
THE HURRICANE ✪ United Artists, 1937
STAGECOACH ✪✪ United Artists, 1939

ROBERT MITCHUM
THE STORY OF G.I. JOE ✪ United Artists, 1945

ROBERT MONTGOMERY
NIGHT MUST FALL ★ MGM, 1937
HERE COMES MR. JORDAN ★ Columbia, 1941

RON MOODY
OLIVER! ★ Columbia, 1968, British

DUDLEY MOORE
ARTHUR ★ Orion, 1981

GRACE MOORE
ONE NIGHT OF LOVE ★ Columbia, 1934

JUANITA MOORE
IMITATION OF LIFE ✪ Universal, 1959

MARY TYLER MOORE
ORDINARY PEOPLE ★ Paramount, 1980

TERRY MOORE
COME BACK, LITTLE SHEBA ✪ Paramount, 1952

AGNES MOOREHEAD
THE MAGNIFICENT AMBERSONS ✪ RKO Radio, 1942
MRS. PARKINGTON ✪ MGM, 1944
JOHNNY BELINDA ✪ Warner Bros., 1948
HUSH...HUSH, SWEET CHARLOTTE ✪ 20th Century-Fox, 1964

RITA MORENO
WEST SIDE STORY ✪✪ United Artists, 1961

FRANK MORGAN
AFFAIRS OF CELLINI ★ United Artists, 1934
TORTILLA FLAT ✪ MGM, 1942

CATHY MORIARTY
RAGING BULL ✪ United Artists, 1980

NORIYUKI "PAT" MORITA
THE KARATE KID ✪ Columbia, 1984

ROBERT MORLEY
MARIE ANTOINETTE ✪ MGM, 1938

CHESTER MORRIS
ALIBI ★ United Artists, 1929

PAUL MUNI
THE VALIANT ★ Fox, 1929
I AM A FUGITIVE FROM A CHAIN GANG ★ Warner Bros., 1932
THE STORY OF LOUIS PASTEUR ★★ Warner Bros., 1936
THE LIFE OF EMILE ZOLA ★ Warner Bros., 1937
THE LAST ANGRY MAN ★ Columbia, 1959

DON MURRAY
BUS STOP ✪ 20th Century-Fox, 1956

N

J. CARROL NAISH
SAHARA ❍ Columbia, 1943
A MEDAL FOR BENNY ❍ Paramount, 1945

MILDRED NATWICK
BAREFOOT IN THE PARK ❍ Paramount, 1967

PATRICIA NEAL
HUD ★★ Paramount, 1963
THE SUBJECT WAS ROSES ★ MGM, 1968

LIAM NEESON
SCHINDLER'S LIST ★ Universal, 1993

KATE NELLIGAN
THE PRINCE OF TIDES ❍ Columbia, 1991

PAUL NEWMAN
CAT ON A HOT TIN ROOF ★ MGM, 1958
THE HUSTLER ★ 20th Century-Fox, 1961
HUD ★ Paramount, 1963
COOL HAND LUKE ★ Warner Bros., 1967
ABSENCE OF MALICE ★ Columbia, 1981
THE VERDICT ★ 20th Century-Fox, 1982
THE COLOR OF MONEY ★★ Buena Vista, 1986

HAING S. NGOR
THE KILLING FIELDS ❍❍ Warner Bros., 1984, British

JACK NICHOLSON
EASY RIDER ❍ Columbia, 1969
FIVE EASY PIECES ★ Columbia, 1970
THE LAST DETAIL ★ Columbia, 1973
CHINATOWN ★ Paramount, 1974
ONE FLEW OVER THE CUCKOO'S NEST ★★ United Artists, 1975
REDS ❍ Paramount, 1981
TERMS OF ENDEARMENT ❍❍ Paramount, 1983
PRIZZI'S HONOR ★ 20th Century Fox, 1985
IRONWEED ★ Tri-Star, 1987
A FEW GOOD MAN ❍ Columbia, 1992

DAVID NIVEN
SEPARATE TABLES ★★ United Artists, 1958

NICK NOLTE
THE PRINCE OF TIDES ★ Columbia, 1991

O

JACK OAKIE
THE GREAT DICTATOR ❍ United Artists, 1940

MERLE OBERON
THE DARK ANGEL ★ United Artists, 1935

EDMOND O'BRIEN
THE BAREFOOT CONTESSA ❍❍ United Artists, 1954, Italian
SEVEN DAYS IN MAY ❍ Paramount, 1964

ARTHUR O'CONNELL
PICNIC ❍ Columbia, 1955
ANATOMY OF A MURDER ❍ Columbia, 1959

DAN O'HERLIHY
ADVENTURES OF ROBINSON CRUSOE ★ United Artists, 1952, Mexican

MICHAEL O'KEEFE
THE GREAT SANTINI ❍ Orion/Warner Bros., 1980

LENA OLIN
ENEMIES, A LOVE STORY ❍ 20th Centruy-Fox, 1989

EDNA MAY OLIVER
DRUMS ALONG THE MOHAWK ❍ 20th Century-Fox, 1939

SIR LAURENCE OLIVIER
WUTHERING HEIGHTS ★ United Artists, 1939
REBECCA ★ United Artists, 1940
HENRY V ★ United Artists, 1946, British
HAMLET ★★ Universal, 1948, British
RICHARD III ★ Lopert, 1956, British
THE ENTERTAINER ★ Continental, 1960, British
OTHELLO ★ Warner Bros., 1965, British
SLEUTH ★ 20th Century-Fox, 1972
MARATHAN MAN ❍ Paramount, 1976
THE BOYS FROM BRAZIL ★ 20th Century-Fox, 1978

EDWARD JAMES OLMOS
STAND AND DELIVER ★ Columbia, 1988

NANCY OLSON
SUNSET BOULEVARD ❍ Paramount, 1950

RYAN O'NEAL
LOVE STORY ★ Paramount, 1970

TATUM O'NEAL
PAPER MOON ❍❍ Paramount, 1973

BARBARA O'NEIL
ALL THIS, AND HEAVEN TOO ❍ Warner Bros., 1940

PETER O'TOOLE
LAWRENCE OF ARABIA ★ Columbia, 1962, British
BECKET ★ Paramount, 1964, British
THE LION IN WINTER ★ Avco Embassy, 1968, British
GOODBYE, MR. CHIPS ★ MGM, 1969, British
THE RULING CLASS ★ Avco Embassy, 1972
THE STUNT MAN ★ 20th Century-Fox, 1980
MY FAVORITE YEAR ★ MGM/UA, 1982

MARIA OUSPENSKAYA
DODSWORTH ❍ United Artists, 1936
LOVE AFFAIR ❍ RKO Radio, 1939

P

AL PACINO
THE GODFATHER ❍ Paramount, 1972
SERPICO ★ Paramount, 1973
THE GODFATHER, PART II ★ Paramount, 1974
DOG DAY AFTERNOON ★ Warner Bros., 1975
...AND JUSTICE FOR ALL ★ Columbia, 1979
DICK TRACY ❍ Buena Vista, 1990
GLENGARRY GLEN ROSS ❍ New Line Cinema, 1992
SCENT OF A WOMAN ★★ Universal, 1992

GERALDINE PAGE
HONDO ❍ Warner Bros., 1953
SUMMER AND SMOKE ★ Paramount, 1961
SWEET BIRD OF YOUTH ★ MGM, 1962
YOU'RE A BIG BOY NOW ❍ Seven Arts, 1966
PETE 'N' TILLIE ❍ Universal, 1972
INTERIORS ★ United Artists, 1978
THE POPE OF GREENWICH VILLAGE ❍ MGM/UA, 1984
THE TRIP TO BOUNTIFUL ★★ Island Pictures/FilmDallas, 1985

JACK PALANCE
SUDDEN FEAR ❍ RKO Radio, 1952
SHANE ❍ Paramount, 1953
CITY SLICKERS ❍❍ Columbia, 1991

ANNA PAQUIN
THE PIANO ❍❍ Miramax Films, 1993, New Zealand-French

ELEANOR PARKER
CAGED ★ Warner Bros., 1950
DETECTIVE STORY ★ Paramount, 1951
INTERRUPTED MELODY ★ MGM, 1955

LARRY PARKS
THE JOLSON STORY ★ Columbia, 1946

ESTELLE PARSONS
BONNIE AND CLYDE ⊙⊙ Warner Bros., 1967
RACHEL, RACHEL ⊙ Warner Bros., 1968

MARISA PAVAN
THE ROSE TATTOO ⊙ Paramount, 1955

KATINA PAXINOU
FOR WHOM THE BELL TOLLS ⊙⊙ Paramount, 1943

DAVID PAYMER
MR. SATURDAY NIGHT ⊙ Columbia, 1992

GREGORY PECK
THE KEYS OF THE KINGDOM ★ 20th Century-Fox, 1945
THE YEARLING ★ MGM, 1946
GENTLEMAN'S AGREEMENT ★ 20th Century-Fox, 1947
12 O'CLOCK HIGH ★ 20th Century-Fox, 1949
TO KILL A MOCKINGBIRD ★★ Universal, 1962

ROSIE PEREZ
FEARLESS ⊙ Warner Bros., 1993

ANTHONY PERKINS
FRIENDLY PERSUASION ⊙ Allied Artists, 1956

VALERIE PERRINE
LENNY ★ United Artists, 1974

JOE PESCI
RAGING BULL ⊙ United Artists, 1980
GOODFELLAS ⊙⊙ Warner Bros., 1990

SUSAN PETERS
RANDOM HARVEST ⊙ MGM, 1942

MICHELLE PFEIFFER
DANGEROUS LIAISONS ⊙ Warner Bros., 1988
THE FABULOUS BAKER BOYS ★ 20th Century Fox, 1989
LOVE FIELD ★ Orion, 1992

RIVER PHOENIX
RUNNING ON EMPTY ⊙ Warner Bros., 1988

MARY PICKFORD
COQUETTE ★★ United Artists, 1929

WALTER PIDGEON
MRS. MINIVER ★ MGM, 1942
MADAME CURIE ★ MGM, 1943

JOAN PLOWRIGHT
ENCHANTED APRIL ⊙ Miramax Film, 1992, British

SIDNEY POITIER
THE DEFIANT ONES ★ United Artists, 1958
LILIES OF THE FIELD ★★ United Artists, 1963

MICHAEL J. POLLARD
BONNIE AND CLYDE ⊙ Warner Bros., 1967

PETE POSTLETHWAITE
IN THE NAME OF THE FATHER ⊙ Universal, 1993, Irish-British

WILLIAM POWELL
THE THIN MAN ★ MGM, 1934
MY MAN GODFREY ★ Universal, 1936
LIFE WITH FATHER ★ Warner Bros., 1947

ROBERT PRESTON
VICTOR/VICTORIA ⊙ MGM/United Artists, 1982

Q

RANDY QUAID
THE LAST DETAIL ⊙ Columbia, 1973

ANTHONY QUAYLE
ANNE OF THE THOUSAND DAYS ⊙ Universal, 1969, British

ANTHONY QUINN
VIVA ZAPATA! ⊙⊙ 20th Century-Fox, 1952
LUST FOR LIFE ⊙⊙ MGM, 1956
WILD IS THE WIND ★ Paramount, 1957
ZORBA THE GREEK ★ 20th Century Fox/International Classics, 1964

R

LUISE RAINER
THE GREAT ZIEGFELD ★★ MGM, 1936
THE GOOD EARTH ★★ MGM, 1937

CLAUDE RAINS
MR. SMITH GOES TO WASHINGTON ⊙ Columbia, 1939
CASABLANCA ⊙ Warner Bros., 1943
MR. SKEFFINGTON ⊙ Warner Bros., 1944
NOTORIOUS ⊙ RKO Radio, 1946

MARJORIE RAMBEAU
PRIMROSE PATH ⊙ RKO Radio, 1940
TORCH SONG ⊙ MGM, 1953

ANNE RAMSEY
THROW MOMMA FROM THE TRAIN ⊙ Orion, 1987

BASIL RATHBONE
ROMEO AND JULIET ⊙ MGM, 1936
IF I WERE KING ⊙ Paramount, 1938

STEPHEN REA
THE CRYING GAME ★ Miramax Films, 1992, Irish-British

ROBERT REDFORD
THE STING ★ Universal, 1973

LYNN REDGRAVE
GEORGY GIRL ★ Columbia, 1966, British

MICHAEL REDGRAVE
MOURNING BECOMES ELECTRA ★ RKO Radio, 1947

VANESSA REDGRAVE
MORGAN! ★ Cinema 5, 1966, British
ISADORA ★ Universal, 1968, British
MARY, QUEEN OF SCOTS ★ Universal, 1971
JULIA ⊙⊙ 20th Century-Fox, 1977
THE BOSTONIANS ★ Almi Pictures, 1984
HOWARD'S END ⊙ Sony Pictures Classics, 1992, British

JOYCE REDMAN
TOM JONES ⊙ Lopert, 1963, British
OTHELLO ⊙ Warner Bros., 1965, British

DONNA REED
FROM HERE TO ETERNITY ⊙⊙ Columbia, 1953

LEE REMICK
DAYS OF WINE AND ROSES ★ Warner Bros., 1962

ANNE REVERE
THE SONG OF BERNADETTE ⊙ 20th Century-Fox, 1943
NATIONAL VELVET ⊙⊙ MGM, 1945
GENTLEMAN'S AGREEMENT ⊙ 20th Century-Fox, 1947

DEBBIE REYNOLDS
THE UNSINKABLE MOLLY BROWN ★ MGM, 1964

BEAH RICHARDS
GUESS WHO'S COMING TO DINNER ⊙ Columbia, 1967

MIRANDA RICHARDSON
DAMAGE ⊙ New Line Cinema, 1992, French-British

RALPH RICHARDSON
THE HEIRESS ⊙ Paramount, 1949
GREYSTOKE: THE LEGEND OF TARZAN, LORD OF THE APES ⊙
     Warner Bros., 1984

THELMA RITTER
ALL ABOUT EVE ⊙ 20th Century-Fox, 1950
THE MATING SEASON ⊙ Paramount, 1951
WITH A SONG IN MY HEART ⊙ 20th Century-Fox, 1952
PICKUP ON SOUTH STREET ⊙ 20th Century-Fox, 1953
PILLOW TALK ⊙ Universal, 1959
BIRDMAN OF ALCATRAZ ⊙ United Artists, 1962

JASON ROBARDS
ALL THE PRESIDENT'S MEN ⊙⊙ Warner Bros., 1976
JULIA ⊙⊙ 20th Century-Fox, 1977
MELVIN AND HOWARD ⊙ Universal, 1980

A
C
A
D
E
M
Y

A
W
A
R
D
S

ERIC ROBERTS
RUNAWAY TRAIN ❍ Cannon, 1985

JULIA ROBERTS
STEEL MAGNOLIAS ❍ Tri-Star, 1989
PRETTY WOMAN ★ Buena Vista, 1990

RACHEL ROBERTS
THIS SPORTING LIFE ★ Continental, 1962, British

CLIFF ROBERTSON
CHARLY ★★ Cinerama Releasing Corporation, 1968

FLORA ROBSON
SARATOGA TRUNK ❍ Warner Bros., 1946

MAY ROBSON
LADY FOR A DAY ★ Columbia, 1933

GINGER ROGERS
KITTY FOYLE ★★ RKO Radio, 1940

HOWARD E. ROLLINS, JR.
RAGTIME ❍ Paramount, 1981

MICKEY ROONEY
BABES IN ARMS ★ MGM, 1939
THE HUMAN COMEDY ★ MGM, 1943
THE BOLD AND THE BRAVE ❍ RKO Radio, 1956
THE BLACK STALLION ❍ United Artists, 1979

DIANA ROSS
LADY SINGS THE BLUES ★ Paramount, 1972

KATHARINE ROSS
THE GRADUATE ❍ Avco Embassy, 1967

GENA ROWLANDS
A WOMAN UNDER THE INFLUENCE ★ Faces International, 1974
GLORIA ★ Columbia, 1980

MERCEDES RUEHL
THE FISHER KING ❍❍ TriStar, 1991

HAROLD RUSSELL
THE BEST YEARS OF OUR LIVES ❍❍ RKO Radio, 1946

ROSALIND RUSSELL
MY SISTER EILEEN ★ Columbia, 1942
SISTER KENNY ★ RKO Radio, 1946
MOURNING BECOMES ELECTRA ★ RKO Radio, 1947
AUNTIE MAME ★ Warner Bros., 1958

MARGARET RUTHERFORD
THE V.I.P.'S ❍❍ MGM, 1963

ROBERT RYAN
CROSSFIRE ❍ RKO Radio, 1947

WINONA RYDER
THE AGE OF INNOCENCE ❍ Columbia, 1993

S

EVA MARIE SAINT
ON THE WATERFRONT ❍❍ Columbia, 1954

GEORGE SANDERS
ALL ABOUT EVE ❍❍ 20th Century-Fox, 1950

CHRIS SARANDON
DOG DAY AFTERNOON ❍ Warner Bros., 1975

SUSAN SARANDON
ATLANTIC CITY ★ Paramount, 1981
THELMA & LOUISE ★ MGM-Pathe, 1991
LORENZO'S OIL ★ Universal, 1992

TELLY SAVALAS
BIRDMAN OF ALCATRAZ ❍ United Artists, 1962

DIANA SCARWID
INSIDE MOVES ❍ Associated Film Distribution, 1980

ROY SCHEIDER
THE FRENCH CONNECTION ❍ 20th Century-Fox, 1971
ALL THAT JAZZ ★ 20th Century-Fox, 1979

MAXIMILIAN SCHELL
JUDGMENT AT NUREMBERG ★★ United Artists, 1961
THE MAN IN THE GLASS BOOTH ★ American Film Theatre, 1975
JULIA ❍ 20th Century-Fox, 1977

JOSEPH SCHILDKRAUT
THE LIFE OF EMILE ZOLA ❍❍ Warner Bros., 1937

PAUL SCOFIELD
A MAN FOR ALL SEASONS ★★ Columbia, 1966, British

GEORGE C. SCOTT
ANATOMY OF A MURDER ❍ Columbia, 1959
THE HUSTLER ❍ 20th Century-Fox, 1961
PATTON ★★ 20th Century-Fox, 1970
THE HOSPITAL ★ United Artists, 1971

MARTHA SCOTT
OUR TOWN ★ United Artists, 1940

GEORGE SEGAL
WHO'S AFRAID OF VIRGINIA WOOLF? ❍ Warner Bros., 1966

PETER SELLERS
DR. STRANGELOVE OR: HOW I LEARNED TO STOP WORRYING
    AND LOVE THE BOMB ★ Columbia, 1964, British
BEING THERE ★ United Artists, 1979

OMAR SHARIF
LAWRENCE OF ARABIA ❍ Columbia, 1962, British

ROBERT SHAW
A MAN FOR ALL SEASONS ❍ Columbia, 1966, British

NORMA SHEARER
THEIR OWN DESIRE ★ MGM, 1929
THE DIVORCÉE ★★ MGM, 1930
A FREE SOUL ★ MGM, 1931
THE BARRETTS OF WIMPOLE STREET ★ MGM, 1934
ROMEO AND JULIET ★ MGM, 1936
MARIE ANTOINETTE ★ MGM, 1938

SAM SHEPARD
THE RIGHT STUFF ❍ The Ladd Company/Warner Bros., 1983

TALIA SHIRE
THE GODFATHER, PART II ❍ Paramount, 1974
ROCKY ★ United Artists, 1976

ANNE SHIRLEY
STELLA DALLAS ❍ United Artists, 1937

SYLVIA SIDNEY
SUMMER WISHES, WINTER DREAMS ❍ Columbia, 1973

SIMONE SIGNORET
ROOM AT THE TOP ★★ Continental, 1959, British
SHIP OF FOOLS ★ Columbia, 1965

JEAN SIMMONS
HAMLET ❍ Universal, 1948, British
THE HAPPY ENDING ★ United Artists, 1969

FRANK SINATRA
FROM HERE TO ETERNITY ❍❍ Columbia, 1953
THE MAN WITH THE GOLDEN ARM ★ United Artists, 1955

LILIA SKALA
LILIES OF THE FIELD ❍ United Artists, 1963

MAGGIE SMITH
OTHELLO ❍ Warner Bros., 1965, British
THE PRIME OF MISS JEAN BRODIE ★★ 20th Century-Fox, 1969,
    British
TRAVELS WITH MY AUNT ★ MGM, 1972
CALIFORNIA SUITE ❍❍ Columbia, 1978
A ROOM WITH A VIEW ❍ Cinecom, 1986, British

CARRIE SNODGRESS
DIARY OF A MAD HOUSEWIFE ★ Universal, 1970

GALE SONDERGAARD
ANTHONY ADVERSE ✪✪ Warner Bros., 1936
ANNA AND THE KING OF SIAM ✪ 20th Century-Fox, 1946

ANN SOTHERN
THE WHALES OF AUGUST ✪ Alive Films, 1987

SISSY SPACEK
CARRIE ★ United Artists, 1976
COAL MINER'S DAUGHTER ★★ Universal, 1980
MISSING ★ Universal, 1982
THE RIVER ★ Universal, 1984
CRIMES OF THE HEART ★ DEG, 1986

ROBERT STACK
WRITTEN ON THE WIND ✪ Universal, 1956

SYLVESTER STALLONE
ROCKY ★ United Artists, 1976

TERENCE STAMP
BILLY BUDD ✪ Allied Artists, 1962

KIM STANLEY
SEANCE ON A WET AFTERNOON ★ Artixo, 1964, British
FRANCES ✪ Universal/AFD, 1982

BARBARA STANWYCK
STELLA DALLAS ★ United Artists, 1937
BALL OF FIRE ★ RKO Radio, 1941
DOUBLE INDEMNITY ★ Paramount, 1944
SORRY, WRONG NUMBER ★ Paramount, 1948

MAUREEN STAPLETON
LONELYHEARTS ✪ United Artists, 1958
AIRPORT ✪ Universal, 1970
INTERIORS ✪ United Artists, 1978
REDS ✪✪ Paramount, 1981

MARY STEENBURGEN
MELVIN AND HOWARD ✪✪ Universal, 1980

ROD STEIGER
ON THE WATERFRONT ✪ Columbia, 1954
THE PAWNBROKER ★ Landau/Allied Artists, 1965
IN THE HEAT OF THE NIGHT ★★ United Artists, 1967

JAMES STEPHENSON
THE LETTER ✪ Warner Bros., 1940

JAN STERLING
THE HIGH AND THE MIGHTY ✪ Warner Bros., 1954

JAMES STEWART
MR. SMITH GOES TO WASHINGTON ★ Columbia, 1939
THE PHILADELPHIA STORY ★★ MGM, 1940
IT'S A WONDERFUL LIFE ★ RKO Radio, 1946
HARVEY ★ Universal, 1950
ANATOMY OF A MURDER ★ Columbia, 1959

DEAN STOCKWELL
MARRIED TO THE MOB ✪ Orion, 1988

LEWIS STONE
THE PATRIOT ★ Paramount, 1928

BEATRICE STRAIGHT
NETWORK ✪✪ MGM/United Artists, 1976

LEE STRASBERG
THE GODFATHER, PART II ✪ Paramount, 1974

ROBERT STRAUSS
STALAG 17 ✪ Paramount, 1953

MERYL STREEP
THE DEER HUNTER ✪ Universal, 1978
KRAMER VS. KRAMER ✪✪ Columbia, 1979
THE FRENCH LIEUTENANT'S WOMAN ★ United Artists, 1981, British
SOPHIE'S CHOICE ★★ Universal/AFD, 1982
SILKWOOD ★ 20th Century-Fox, 1983
OUT OF AFRICA ★ Universal, 1985
IRONWEED ★ Tri-Star, 1987
A CRY IN THE DARK ★ Warner Bros., 1988, Australian
POSTCARDS FROM THE EDGE ★ Columbia, 1990

BARBRA STREISAND
FUNNY GIRL ★★ Columbia, 1968
THE WAY WE WERE ★ Columbia, 1973

MARGARET SULLAVAN
THREE COMRADES ★ MGM, 1938

JANET SUZMAN
NICHOLAS AND ALEXANDRA ★ Columbia, 1971

GLORIA SWANSON
SADIE THOMPSON ★ United Artists, 1928
THE TRESPASSER ★ United Artists, 1929
SUNSET BOULEVARD ★ Paramount, 1950

T

RUSS TAMBLYN
PEYTON PLACE ✪ 20th Century-Fox, 1957

AKIM TAMIROFF
THE GENERAL DIED AT DAWN ✪ Paramount, 1936
FOR WHOM THE BELL TOLLS ✪ Paramount, 1943

JESSICA TANDY
DRIVING MISS DAISY ★★ Warner Bros., 1989
FRIED GREEN TOMATOES ✪ Universal, 1991

ELIZABETH TAYLOR
RAINTREE COUNTY ★ MGM, 1957
CAT ON A HOT TIN ROOF ★ MGM, 1958
SUDDENLY LAST SUMMER ★ Columbia, 1959
BUTTERFIELD 8 ★★ MGM, 1960
WHO'S AFRAID OF VIRGINIA WOOLF? ★★ Warner Bros., 1966

EMMA THOMPSON
HOWRD'S END ★★ Sony Pictures Classics, 1992, British
THE REMAINS OF THE DAY ★ Columbia, 1993, British
IN THE NAME OF THE FATHER ✪ Universal, 1993, Irish-British

LAWRENCE TIBBETT
THE ROGUE SONG ★ MGM, 1929

GENE TIERNEY
LEAVE HER TO HEAVEN ★ 20th Century-Fox, 1945

MEG TILLY
AGNES OF GOD ✪ Columbia, 1985

RICHARD TODD
THE HASTY HEART ★ Warner Bros., 1949

MARISA TOMEI
MY COUSIN VINNY ✪✪ 20th Century Fox. 1992

LILY TOMLIN
NASHVILLE ✪ Paramount, 1975

FRANCHOT TONE
MUTINY ON THE BOUNTY ★ MGM, 1935

TOPOL
FIDDLER ON THE ROOF ★ United Artists, 1971

RIP TORN
CROSS CREEK ✪ Universal/AFD, 1983

LEE TRACY
THE BEST MAN ✪ United Artists, 1964

SPENCER TRACY
SAN FRANCISCO ★ MGM, 1936
CAPTAINS COURAGEOUS ★★ MGM, 1937
BOYS TOWN ★★ MGM, 1938
FATHER OF THE BRIDE ★ MGM, 1950
BAD DAY AT BLACK ROCK ★ MGM, 1955
THE OLD MAN AND THE SEA ★ Warner Bros., 1958
INHERIT THE WIND ★ United Artists, 1960
JUDGMENT AT NUREMBERG ★ United Artists, 1961
GUESS WHO'S COMING TO DINNER ★ Columbia, 1967

HENRY TRAVERS
MRS. MINIVER ✪ MGM, 1942

JOHN TRAVOLTA
SATURDAY NIGHT FEVER ★ Paramount, 1977

CLAIRE TREVOR
DEAD END ○ United Artists, 1937
KEY LARGO ○○ Warner Bros., 1948
THE HIGH AND THE MIGHTY ○ Warner Bros., 1954

TOM TULLY
THE CAINE MUTINY ○ Columbia, 1954

KATHLEEN TURNER
PEGGY SUE GOT MARRIED ★ Tri-Star, 1986

LANA TURNER
PEYTON PLACE ★ 20th Century-Fox, 1957

SUSAN TYRRELL
FAT CITY ○ Columbia, 1972

CICELY TYSON
SOUNDER ★ 20th Century-Fox, 1972

U

LIV ULLMANN
THE EMIGRANTS ★ Warner Bros., 1972, Swedish
FACE TO FACE ★ Paramount, 1976, Swedish

MIYOSHI UMEKI
SAYONARA ○○ Warner Bros., 1957

MARY URE
SONS AND LOVERS ○ 20th Century-Fox, 1960

PETER USTINOV
QUO VADIS ○ MGM, 1951
SPARTACUS ○○ Universal, 1960
TOPKAPI ○○ United Artists, 1964

V

BRENDA VACCARO
JACQUELINE SUSANN'S ONCE IS NOT ENOUGH ○ Paramount, 1975

JO VAN FLEET
EAST OF EDEN ○○ Warner Bros., 1955

DIANE VARSI
PEYTON PLACE ○ 20th Century-Fox, 1957

ROBERT VAUGHN
THE YOUNG PHILADELPHIANS ○ Warner Bros., 1959

JON VOIGHT
MIDNIGHT COWBOY ★ United Artists, 1969
COMING HOME ★★ United Artists, 1978
RUNAWAY TRAIN ★ Cannon, 1985

ERICH von STROHEIM
SUNSET BOULEVARD ○ Paramount, 1950

MAX VON SYDOW
PELLE THE CONQUEROR ★ Miramax Films, 1988, Danish-Swedish

W

CHRISTOPHER WALKEN
THE DEER HUNTER ○○ Universal, 1978

JULIE WALTERS
EDUCATING RITA ★ Columbia, 1983, British

JACK WARDEN
SHAMPOO ○ Columbia, 1975
HEAVEN CAN WAIT ○ Paramount, 1978

J.B. WARNER
LOST HORIZON ○ Columbia, 1937

LESLEY ANN WARREN
VICTOR/VICTORIA ○ MGM/United Artists, 1982

DENZEL WASHINGTON
CRY FREEDOM ○ Universal, 1987, British
GLORY ○○ Tri-Star, 1989
MALCOLM X ★ Warner Bros., 1992

ETHEL WATERS
PINKY ○ 20th Century-Fox, 1949

SAM WATERSTON
THE KILLING FIELDS ★ Warner Bros., 1984, British

LUCILE WATSON
WATCH ON THE RHINE ○ Warner Bros., 1943

JOHN WAYNE
SANDS OF IWO JIMA ★ Republic, 1949
TRUE GRIT ★★ Paramount, 1969

SIGOURNEY WEAVER
ALIENS ★ 20th Century Fox, 1986
GORILLAS IN THE MIST ★ Warner Bros./Universal, 1988
WORKING GIRL ○ 20th Century Fox, 1988

CLIFTON WEBB
LAURA ○ 20th Century-Fox, 1944
THE RAZOR'S EDGE ○ 20th Century-Fox, 1946
SITTING PRETTY ★ 20th Century-Fox, 1948

TUESDAY WELD
LOOKING FOR MR. GOODBAR ○ Paramount, 1977

ORSON WELLES
CITIZEN KANE ★ RKO Radio, 1941

OSKAR WERNER
SHIP OF FOOLS ★ Columbia, 1965

STUART WHITMAN
THE MARK ★ Continental, 1961, British

JAMES WHITMORE
BATTLEGROUND ○ MGM, 1949
GIVE 'EM HELL, HARRY!, ★, Avco Embassy, 1975

DAME MAY WHITTY
NIGHT MUST FALL ○ MGM, 1937
MRS. MINIVER ○ MGM, 1942

RICHARD WIDMARK
KISS OF DEATH ○ 20th Century-Fox, 1947

DIANNE WIEST
HANNAH AND HER SISTERS ○○ Orion, 1986
PARENTHOOD ○ Universal, 1989

JACK WILD
OLIVER! ○ Columbia, 1968, British

CORNEL WILDE
A SONG TO REMEMBER ★ Columbia, 1945

GENE WILDER
THE PRODUCERS ○ Avco Embassy, 1968

CARA WILLIAMS
THE DEFIANT ONES ○ United Artists, 1958

ROBIN WILLIAMS
GOOD MORNING, VIETNAM ★ Buena Vista, 1987
DEAD POETS SOCIETY ★ Buena Vista, 1989
THE FISHER KING ★ TriStar, 1991

CHILL WILLS
THE ALAMO ○ United Artists, 1960

PAUL WINFIELD
SOUNDER ★ 20th Century-Fox, 1972

OPRAH WINFREY
THE COLOR PURPLE ○ Warner Bros., 1985

DEBRA WINGER
AN OFFICER AND A GENTLEMAN ★ Paramount, 1982
TERMS OF ENDEARMENT ★ Paramount, 1983
SHADOWLANDS ★ Savoy Pictures, 1993, U.S.-British

SHELLEY WINTERS
A PLACE IN THE SUN ★ Paramount, 1951
THE DIARY OF ANNE FRANK ✪✪ 20th Century-Fox, 1959
A PATCH OF BLUE ✪✪ MGM, 1965
THE POSEIDON ADVENTURE ✪ 20th Century-Fox, 1972

NATALIE WOOD
REBEL WITHOUT A CAUSE ✪ Warner Bros., 1955
SPLENDOR IN THE GRASS ★ Warner Bros., 1961
LOVE WITH THE PROPER STRANGER ★ Paramount, 1963

PEGGY WOOD
THE SOUND OF MUSIC ✪ 20th Century-Fox, 1965

ALFRE WOODARD
CROSS CREEK ✪ Universal/AFD, 1983

JAMES WOODS
SALVADOR ★ Hemdale, 1986

JOANNE WOODWARD
THE THREE FACES OF EVE ★★ 20th Century-Fox, 1957
RACHEL, RACHEL ★ Warner Bros., 1968
SUMMER WISHES, WINTER DREAMS ★ Columbia, 1973
MR. AND MRS. BRIDGE ★ Miramax Films, 1990

MONTY WOOLLEY
THE PIED PIPER ★ 20th Century-Fox, 1942
SINCE YOU WENT AWAY ✪ United Artists, 1944

TERESA WRIGHT
THE LITTLE FOXES ✪ RKO Radio, 1941
MRS. MINIVER ✪✪ MGM, 1942
THE PRIDE OF THE YANKEES ★ RKO Radio, 1942

MARGARET WYCHERLY
SERGEANT YORK ✪ Warner Bros., 1941

JANE WYMAN
THE YEARLING ★ MGM, 1946
JOHNNY BELINDA ★★ Warner Bros., 1948
THE BLUE VEIL ★ RKO Radio, 1951
MAGNIFICENT OBSESSION ★ Universal, 1954

ED WYNN
THE DIARY OF ANNE FRANK ✪ 20th Century-Fox, 1959

DIANA WYNYARD
CAVALCADE ★ Fox, 1933

Y

SUSANNAH YORK
THEY SHOOT HORSES, DON'T THEY? ✪ Cinerama Releasing
   Corporation, 1969

BURT YOUNG
ROCKY ✪ United Artists, 1976

GIG YOUNG
COME FILL THE CUP ✪ Warner Bros., 1951
TEACHER'S PET ✪ Paramount, 1958
THEY SHOOT HORSES, DON'T THEY? ✪✪ Cinerama Releasing
   Corporation, 1969

LORETTA YOUNG
THE FARMER'S DAUGHTER ★★ RKO Radio, 1947
COME TO THE STABLE ★ 20th Century-Fox, 1949

ROLAND YOUNG
TOPPER ✪ MGM, 1937

★★★

INDEX BY ACTOR
Male

Note: This is not a list of all male actors, only those
listed in the main listing section of this book.

A

Aames, Willie
Aarons, Allan
Abbott, Bruce
Abdul-Jabbar, Kareem
Abercrombie, Ian
Abraham, F. Murray
Abrahams, Jim
Ackland, Joss
Adams, Brandon
Adams, Don
Adams, Joey Lauren
Adams, Mason
Addy, Wesley
Adler, Matt
Adline, Jean Claude
Adonis, Frank
Aedma, Alar
Affleck, Ben
Affleck, Casey
Afrakhan, Behrooz
Agins, Robert
Aherne, Michael
Aiello, Danny
Aiello, Rick
Ajaye, Franklyn
Akin, Phil
Alaskey, Joe
Albano, Lou
Albert, Eddie
Albert, Edward
Alda, Alan
Alden, Norman
Aldrich, Tom
Aleong, Aki
Alexander, Jason
Alexandrov, Constantin
Alexio, Dennis
Ali, Muhammad
Alldredge, Michael
Allen, Bill
Allen, Chad

Allen, Corey
Allen, Keith
Allen, Patrick
Allen, Steve
Allen, Tim
Allen, Todd
Allen, Woody
Allman, Gregg
Allport, Christopher
Alterio, Hector
Altman, Bruce
Altman, Jeff
Alvarado, Trini
Ames, Leon
Amsterdam, Morey
Andersen, Dana
Anderson, Daryl
Anderson, Dave
Anderson, Dion
Anderson, Erich
Anderson, Harry
Anderson, Haskell V.
Anderson, John
Anderson, Kevin
Anderson, Louie
Anderson, Mitchell
Anderson, Richard
Anderson, Stanley
Andrei, Frederick
Andrews, Anthony
Andrews, David
Angel, Jack
Anglade, Jean-Hughes
Anglin, Philip
Ant, Adam
Antin, Steve
Antonio, Jim
Apicella, John
Appel, Peter
Aprea, John
Apted, Michael
Aragon, Frank
Arau, Alfonso

Arcard, Gabriel
Arestrup, Niels
Argo, Victor
Arkin, Adam
Arkin, Alan
Arkins, Robert
Armendariz, Pedro, Jr.
Armitraj, Vijay
Armstrong, Alun
Armstrong, Curtis
Armstrong, Hugh
Armstrong, R.G.
Arnaz, Desi, Jr.
Arndt, Denis
Arness, James
Arnold, Tom
Arnott, David
Arquette, David
Arquette, Lewis
Arrambide, Mario
Ash, Monty
Ashbrook, Dana
Ashby, Linden
Ashmore, Frank
Ashton, John
Asner, Ed
Assante, Armand
Astin, John
Astin, Mackenzie
Astin, Sean
Atherton, William
Atkine, Feodor
Atkins, Christopher
Atkins, Robert
Atkins, Tom
Atkinson, Rowan
Atlas, Larry
Attenborough, Richard
Auberjonois, René
Aumont, Jean-Pierre
Aurelius, Marcus
Auteuil, Daniel
Autry, Alan

Avalon, Frankie
Avellone, Greg
Avery, James
Avery, Val
Avildsen, Jonathan
Aviles, Rick
Axton, Hoyt
Aykroyd, Dan
Aykroyd, David
Azaria, Hank
Azito, Tony
Azmi, Shabana

B

Babatundé, Obba
Bacall, Michael
Backer, Brian
Bacon, Kevin
Bader, Diedrich
Bagley, Ross
Bagneris, Vernel
Bailey, Bill
Bailey, G. W.
Bailly, Chub
Bain, Conrad
Baio, Scott
Bairstow, Scott
Baker, Dylan
Baker, Henry Judd
Baker, Jay
Baker, Joe Don
Baker, Kenny
Baker, Ray
Baker, Raymond
Bakewell, Gary
Bakula, Scott
Balaban, Bob
Baldwin, Adam
Baldwin, Alec
Baldwin, Daniel
Baldwin, Stephen
Baldwin, William
Bale, Christian
Balin, Richard
Ballou, Mark
Balsam, Martin
Balzary, Michael
Bamber, David
Bancroft, Bradford
Banderas, Antonio
Banerjee, Victor
Banks, Jonathan
Bannen, Ian
Bannister, Reggie

Barberini, Urbano
Barge, Gene
Barlow, Pat
Barnes, Christopher Daniel
Barnett, Charlie
Baron, Sandy
Barr, Jean-Marc
Barr, Stephen
Barron, Robert V.
Barron, Ronnie
Barry, Matthew
Barry, Neill
Barry, Raymond J.
Bartel, Paul
Barton, Robert
Barty, Billy
Baryshnikov, Mikhail
Basaraba, Gary
Basil, Harry
Basinger, John
Baskin, Elya
Bastiani, Bill
Bate, Anthony
Bateman, Jason
Bates, Alan
Bates, Paul
Batinkoff, Randall
Batt, Bryan
Bauchau, Patrick
Bauer, Steven
Bay, Turhan
Bayer, Gary
Bayldon, Geoffrey
Beach, Michael
Bean, Sean
Beaton, Norman
Beatty, Ned
Beatty, Warren
Beaver, Jim
Beaver, Terry
Beck, Billy
Beck, John
Beck, Michael
Beckel, Graham
Becker, Hartmut
Bedi, Kabir
Bednarski, Andrew
Beer, Daniel
Beghe, Jason
Begley, Ed, Jr.
Belafsky, Marty
Belcher, Joe
Bell, John
Bell, Marshall
Bell, Tobin

Bellamy, Ned
Bellows, Gil
Beltran, Robert
Beltzman, Mark
Belushi, James
Belzer, Richards
Bemis, Cliff
Ben-Victor, Paul
Benben, Brian
Benedick, Paul
Benedict, Dirk
Beneyton, Yves
Benfield, John
Benigni, Roberto
Benjamin, Paul
Benjamin, Richard
Bennent, David
Bennett, Jeff
Bennett, Tony
Benson, Perry
Benson, Robby
Bentivoglio, Fabrizio
Benton, Jerome
Benzali, Daniel
Bercovici, Luca
Berenger, Tom
Berenson, Craig
Berg, Peter
Bergen, Lewis
Berger, Gregg
Berger, Helmut
Berger, William
Bergin, Patrick
Berke, Ed
Berkoff, Steven
Berle, Milton
Bernard, Jason
Bernard, Thelonious
Bernsen, Corbin
Berrigan, Daniel
Berry, John
Berry, Lloyd
Berry, Richard
Berti, Dehl
Bertin, Roland
Bertolini, Angelo
Beyer, Troy
Bezace, Didier
Bhakoo, Kuldeep
Biehl, Michael
Bigagli, Claudio
Bigney, Hugh
Bikel, Theodore
Bill, Tony
Billerey, Raoul

Billingsley, Peter
Bird, Larry
Birdsall, Jesse
Birney, David
Bishop, Joey
Bishop, Rummy
Bishop, Troy
Black, Clint
Black, Lewis
Blacker, David
Blacque, Taurean
Blades, Rubén
Blair, Lionel
Blair, Nicky
Blake, Geoffrey
Blake, Michael
Blake, Robert
Blanc, Michel
Blanche, Derrick
Blaney, Tim
Blankfield, Mark
Blau, Martin Maria
Blessed, Brain
Blethyn, Brenda
Block, Oliver
Blossom, Roberts
Blum, Jack
Blum, Mark
Blythe, Robert
Bochner, Hart
Bochner, Lloyd
Bohen, Ian
Bohringer, Richard
Bolender, Bill
Bologna, Joseph
Bonacelli, Paolo
Bond III, James
Bond, Raleigh
Bond, Steve
Bonerz, Peter
Bonifant, Evan
Bonner, Frank
Bonner, Tony
Bono
Bono, Sonny
Bonsall, Brian
Booke, Sorrell
Boone, Pat
Boorman, Charlie
Booth, James
Boothe, Powers
Boretski, Peter
Borgnine, Ernest
Borgosian, Eric
Borrego, Jesse

Bosco, Philip
Bosley, Todd
Bosley, Tom
Bostwick, Barry
Bosworth, Brian
Bottoms, Joseph
Bottoms, Sam
Bottoms, Timothy
Boudet, Jacques
Bourne, Randy
Boutsikaris, Dennis
Bowe, David
Bowen, Michael
Bower, David
Bower, Tom
Bowie, David
Bowles, Peter
Boxleitner, Bruce
Boyar, Sully
Boyce, Alan
Boyd, Guy
Boyden, Peter
Boyle, Brad
Boyle, Peter
Bozak, Brian
Bracho, Alejandro
Bracken, Eddie
Bradford, Greg
Bradford, Jesse
Bradford, Richard
Bradley, David
Bradshaw, Terry
Brady, Randall
Branagh, Kenneth
Brancato, Lillo
Brand, Walker
Brandauer, Klaus Maria
Brandis, Jonathan
Brando, Marlon
Brandon, Michael
Bratt, Benjamin
Braugher, Andre
Braverman, Bart
Bray, Thomas
Breen, Patrick
Bremann, Beau
Brest, Martin
Bridges, Beau
Bridges, Jeff
Bridges, Lloyd
Briere, Daniel
Briers, Richard
Bright, Richard
Brill, Steven
Brimble, Nick

Brimley, Wilford
Broadbent, Jim
Broadhurst, Jeffrey
Broadhurst, Kent
Brock, Phil
Brock, Stanley
Brocksmith, Roy
Broderick, Matthew
Brolin, James
Brolin, Josh
Bronson, Charles
Bronson, Nicky
Brooks, Albert
Brooks, Joel
Brooks, Mel
Brooks, Randy
Brooks, Richard
Brophy, Anthony
Brosnan, Pierce
Brother Theodore
Brown, Bruce
Brown, Bryan
Brown, Clancy
Brown, Dwier
Brown, Ernie
Brown, Garrett M.
Brown, Georg Stanford
Brown, Jim
Brown, Ralph
Brown, Reb
Brown, Robert
Brown, Roger Aaron
Brown, Thomas
Brown, W. H.
Brown, Wendell
Brown, Woody
Browne, Robert Alan
Browne, Roscoe Lee
Brundin, Bo
Bruns, Philip
Bruskotter, Eric
Bryant, Karis
Bryant, Michael
Bryant, Todd
Bryggman, Larry
Bryniarski, Andrew
Buchanan, Miles
Buckely, Keith
Bumatai, Andy
Bunting, Garland
Burgard, Christopher
Burge, Gregg
Burgess, John
Burke, Robert
Burkley, Dennis

Burlinson, Tom
Burmester, Leo
Burnett, Russell
Burns, George
Burns, Jere
Burns, Joe
Burroughs, William S.
Burton, Donald
Burton, Levar
Burton, Steve
Burton, Wendell
Buscemi, Steve
Busey, Gary
Busfield, Timothy
Bush, Billy Green
Bush, Chuck
Bush, Grand L.
Butkus, Dick
Butler, Dean
Butler, Gene
Butler, Tom
Buttons, Red
Byner, John
Byrne, David
Byrne, Gabriel
Byrne, Michael
Byrne, Niall

C

Caan, James
Caesar, Harry
Caesar, Sid
Caffarel, Jose Maria
Caffrey, Stephen
Cage, Nicolas
Caine, Michael
Cains, Fraser
Calderon, Paul
Calderon, Sergio
Caldwell, Gene
Cale, David
Calfa, Don
Calhoun, Rory
Call, Brandon
Call, R. D.
Callow, Simon
Calvert, Bill
Cameron, Dean
Cameron, Kirk
Camilieri, Tony
Camilletti, Robert
Camp, Hamilton
Campanella, Joseph
Campbell, Bill

Campbell, Bruce
Campbell, Glen
Campbell, J. Kenneth
Campbell, Nicholas
Campbell, Scott Michael
Campbell, Tevin
Campenella, Frank
Campion, Cris
Campos, Rafael
Canada, Ron
Cannon, J. D.
Cantor, Max
Capodice, John
Capone, Vinny
Capra, Francis
Carafotes, Paul
Cardinal, Tantoo
Carey, Harry, Jr.
Carey, Ron
Carey, Timothy
Carhart, Timothy
Cariou, Len
Carlin, George
Carlisle, Steve
Carlson, Joel
Carlson, Les
Carmen, Loene
Carmet, Jean
Carney, Art
Carpenter, David
Carpenter, John
Carradine, David
Carradine, Keith
Carradine, Robert
Carrasco, Carlos
Carrey, Jim
Carricart, Robert
Carroll, Rocky
Carroll, Ronn
Carson, Hunter
Carter, Jim
Carter, Michael Patrick
Caruso, David
Carvey, Dana
Cascio, Salvatore
Cascone, Nicholas
Casella, Max
Casey, Bernie
Cash, Johnny
Cassavetes, Nick
Cassel, Jean-Pierre
Cassel, Seymour
Casseus, Gabriel
Cassidy, Patrick
Cassidy, Shaun

Castellaneta, Dan
Castelli, Ralph
Castellitto, Sergio
Castile, Christopher
Castle, John
Cathey, Reg E.
Catlett, Lloyd
Caulfield, Maxwell
Cavett, Dick
Caviezel, James
Cazenove, Christopher
Ceccaldi, Daniel
Cepello, Steven
Cesak, Brian
Chaliapin, Feodor, Jr.
Chalk, Gary
Chamberlain, Richard
Chamberlain, Wilt
Chambers, Michael "Boogaloo
    Shrimp"
Champion
Chan, Dennis
Chan, Jackie
Chandler, Jared
Chandler, John
Chandler, Kyle
Chapa, Damian
Chapman, Lonny
Chappelle, Dave
Chardiet, Jon
Charles, David
Charles, Josh
Charles, Ray
Chase, Chevy
Chaykin, Maury
Cheadle, Don
Chester, Colby
Chestnut, Morris
Chevalia, Kevin
Chew, Sam
Chiba, Sonny
Chiklis, Michael
Chin, Joey
Chong, Thomas
Chowdhry, Navin
Christopher, Brian
Christopher, Dennis
Chung, David
Church, Thomas
Cioffi, Charles
Clanton, Ralph
Clapp, Gordon
Clapton, Eric
Clark, Blake
Clark, Bret Baxter

Clark, Josh
Clark, Matt
Clark, Ron
Clarke, Warren
Clay, Andrew Dice
Clay, Nicholas
Clayton, Adam
Cleary, John F.
Cleese, John
Clemenson, Christian
Clennon, David
Cliff, Jimmy
Clinton, George
Close, Del
Clough, John Scott
Cluzet, François
Coates, Kim
Cobb, Randall (Tex)
Cobbs, Bill
Coburn, James
Coe, George
Coen, Joel
Coeur, Paul
Coffey, John
Coffey, Scott
Coffin, Fred
Cohen, Jeff
Cole, Gary
Cole, George
Coleman, Dabney
Coleman, Gary
Collet, Christopher
Colley, Ken
Collins, Albert
Collins, Blake
Collins, Phil
Collins, Stephen
Collison, Frank
Colon, Alex
Coltrane, Robbie
Colyar, Michael
Combs, Jeffrey
Combs, Ray
Confroti, Gino
Conklin, Colton
Connart, Jean-Paul
Connelly, Billy
Connery, Sean
Connery, Thomas
Connick, Harry, Jr.
Connolly, Billy
Connor, Bart
Connor, Tom
Conrad, Christian
Conrad, Robert

Conroy, Kevin
Conroy, Ruaidhri
Constantine, Michael
Conti, Tom
Contreras, Patricio
Converse-Roberts, William
Conway, Jeff
Conway, Kevin
Conway, Time
Coogan, Keith
Cook, Bart Robinson
Cook, Peter
Cooksey, Danny
Cooney, Kevin
Cooper, Alice
Cooper, Charles
Cooper, Chris
Cooper, Garry
Cooper, Jackie
Cooper, Jeremy
Cooper, Luke
Cooper, Roy
Corbett, Jeff
Corbett, John
Corbin, Barry
Corey, Jeff
Corkill, Dan
Corraface, George
Corri, Nick
Cort, Bud
Cortese, Dan
Cosby, Bill
Costanzo, Robert
Costas, Bob
Coster, Nicolas
Costner, Kevin
Cothran, Jr., John
Coulson, Bernie
Courtenay, Tom
Cousins, Brian
Cousins, Christian
Cousins, Joseph
Cover, Franklin
Coviello, Tom
Cowan, Nicholas
Cowles, Matthew
Cox, Brian
Cox, E'Lon
Cox, Jennifer
Cox, Mitchell
Coyote, Peter
Craig, Roger
Cramer, Joey
Cranham, Kenneth
Craven, Matt

Craven, Wes
Crawford, Michael
Crawford, Wayne
Creaghan, Dennis
Cremeri, Bruno
Crenna, Richard
Crenshaw, Marshall
Crisp, Quentin
Crivello, Anthony
Croft, Bill
Crombie, Jonathan
Cromwell
Cronenberg, David
Cronkite, Walter
Cronyn, Hume
Cross, Ben
Crow, Cory
Crowe, Russell
Crowley, Kevin
Cruise, Tom
Cruz, Raymond
Cryer, Jon
Crystal, Billy
Culkin, Kieran
Culkin, Macaulay
Cullum, John
Culp, Joseph
Culp, Robert
Culp, Steven
Cummings, Jim
Cummins, Brian
Cunningham, Liam
Curley, James
Curnock, Richard
Curry, Tim
Curtis, Keene
Curtis, Tony
Curzi, Pierre
Cusack, Dick
Cusack, John
Cuthbertson, Iain
Cyphers, Charles
Czerny, Henry

D

Dafoe, Willem
Daggett, Jensen
Dallesandro, Joe
Dallesandro, Joe
Dalton, Timothy
Daltrey, Roger
Daly, Timothy
D'Amboise, Jacques
D'Ambrosio, Franc

Damian, Leo
Damon, Gabriel
Damon, Matt
Damon, Stuart
Damus, Mike
Danare, Malcolm
Dance, Charles
Dane, Lawrence
Dangerfield, Rodney
Daniels, Alex
Daniels, Anthony
Daniels, Jeff
Daniels, Phil
Daniels, William
Danker, Eli
Dano, Royal
Danson, Ted
Dante, Michael
Danza, Tony
Darden, Severn
Darmon, Gérard
Darrell, Michael
Darrow, Henry
Davenport, Nigel
Davi, Robert
David, Keith
Davidson, Jaye
Davidson, John
Davidson, Tommy
Davies, Ray
Davies, Rudi
Davis, Guy
Davis, Mac
Davis, Metta
Davis, Ossie
Davis, Philip
Davis, Warwick
Davison, Bruce
Davison, Peter
Dawson, Richard
Day, Morris
Day-Lewis, Daniel
Dayan, Assaf
Deacon, Kim
De Almeida, Joaquim
Dean, Loren
Dean, Rick
Dean, Ron
Deas, Justin
Dees, Rick
De Bankole, Isaach
Deezen, Eddie
Deforest, Calvert
Deghy, Guy
DeGood, Michael

Del Toro, Benecio
De La Brosse, Simon
Delano, Michael
De La Paz, Danny
De Lint, Derek
DeLisi, Joseph
Delon, Anthony
DeLuise, Dom
DeLuise, Michael
DeLuise, Peter
Dempsey, Patrick
DeMunn, Jeffrey
Dengel, Jake
DeNiro, Robert
Denis, Jacques
Denison, Anthony
Denison, Michael
Dennehy, Brian
Dennis, Winston
Denver, John
Depardieu, Gérard
Depp, Johnny
Derham, Eddie
Dern, Bruce
Derricks, Cleavant
Desalle, Stefan
DeSantis, Stanley
Desiderio, Robert
Desmond, Jim
Deutsch, Kurt
Devane, William
Devia, Richard
Devito, Danny
De Young, Cliff
Diamond, Cliff
Diamond, Reed Edward
DiCaprio, Leonardo
Dicenzo, George
Dick, Andy
Dickenson, J. D.
Dickerson, George
Diddley, Bo
Diehl, John
Dillman, Bradford
Dillon, Kevin
Dillon, Matt
Dimitri, Richard
Ding, Yi
Dingo, Ernie
Dinome, Jerry
Disanti, John
Dishy, Bob
Ditson, Harry
Divoff, Andrew
Dixon, Macintyre

Dixon, Willie
Djola, Badja
Dobson, Kevin
Dobson, Peter
Doe, John
Doherty, Matt
Donahue, Troy
Donat, Peter
D'Onofrio, Vincent
Donnelly, Donal
Donner, Robert
Donovan, Tate
Doohan, James
Dooley, Paul
Doolittle, John
Doqui, Robert
Dorff, Stephen
Dorn, Michael
Dorsey, Joe
Dossett, John
Dotrice, Roy
Doty, David
Doug, Doug E.
Douglas, Kirk
Douglas, Michael
Dourif, Brad
Dowden, Chris
Downey, Morton Jr.
Doyle, David
Doyle-Murray, Brian
Drago, Billy
Drake, Larry
Dreyfuss, Richard
Drillinger, Brian
Drummond, John
Dryer, Fred
Duchovny, David
Ducommun, Rick
Dudikoff, Michael
Duffy, Patrick
Duffy, Thomas F.
Dugan, Dennis
Dugan, Tom
Dukakis, John
Duke, Bill
Dukes, David
Dullea, Keir
Dun, Dennis
Dunbar, Adrian
Duncan, Andrew
Dunlop, Vic
Dunn, Kevin
Dunne, Griffin
Dupre, Peter
Dupree, V. C.

Duret, Marc
Durning, Charles
Durrell, Michael
Dutton, Charles
Duvall, Robert
Dvi, Robert
Dye, John
Dylan, Bob
Dysart, Richard
Dzunda, George

E

East, Jeff
Easton, Richard
Easton, Robert
Eastwood, Clint
Eastwood, Kyle
Eberts, David
Ebsen, Buddy
Eckhouse, James
Edelman, Herb
Edge
Edson, Richard
Edwards, Anthony
Edwards, Eric
Edwards, Luke
Edwards, Sebastian Rice
Edwards, Vince
Egan, Petar
Egi, Stan
Eiseman, Jack
Eisenberg, Ned
Elfman, Danny
Elizondo, Hector
Ellenstein, Robert
Elliot, Chris
Elliott, Bob
Elliott, Chris
Elliott, Sam
Elliott, Stephen
Elmes, Rowan
Elson, Robert
Elwes, Cary
Emerson, Jonathan
Emil, Michael
Emmett, Jesse
English, Alex
English, Zach
Englund, Robert
Epcar, Richard
Epps, Omar
Epstein, Alvin
Epstein, Pierre
Ermey, Lee

Ernsberger, Duke
Esposito, Giancarlo
Estevez, Emilio
Estevez, Ramon
Estrada, Erik
Evans, Angelo
Evans, Art
Evans, Josh
Evans, Troy
Everett, Chad
Everett, Rupert
Everett, Tom
Everhart, Rex
Evigan, Greg
Ewing, Blake
Eziashi, Maynard
Ezralow, Daniel

F

Fabri, Jaques
Fabrizi, Franco
Fabro, Warren
Fahey, Jeff
Fairchild, Max
Faith, Adam
Falk, Peter
Faraldo, Daniel
Farentino, James
Fargas, Antonio
Farina, Dennis
Farley, Chris
Farmer, Gary
Farnsworth, Richard
Farr, Jamie
Farrell, Mike
Faulkner, Ben
Faustino, Michael
Feig, Paul
Feinstein, Michael
Feld, Fritz
Feldman, Corey
Fell, Norman
Fellowes, Julian
Fender, Freddy
Fenton, Lance
Fenton, Simon
Fernandez, Juan
Ferrer, Mel
Ferrer, Miguel
Ferrero, Martin
Ferrigno, Lou
Feulner, Miles
Fichtner, William
Field, Todd

Fieldler, John
Fields, Maurie
Fields, Tony
Fieldsteel, Robert
Fiennes, Ralph
Fierstein, Harvey
Fine, Travis
Finn, George
Finn, John
Finnegan, John
Finney, Albert
Fire, Richard
Firth, Colin
Firth, Peter
Fishburne, Laurence
Fisher, Eddie
Fisher, Gregor
Fitzgerald, Ciaran
Fitzgerald, Greg
Flaherty, Joe
Flanders, Ed
Fleet, James
Fleischer, Charles
Fleiss, Noah
Fletcher, Dexter
Florek, Dann
Floyd, Charles R.
Foil, David
Foley, David
Fonda, Peter
Fondacaro, Phil
Foote, Horton
Ford, Harrison
Ford, Mick
Ford, Steven
Ford, Tommy
Foree, Ken
Foronjy, Richard
Forrest, Frederic
Forrest, Steve
Forster, Robert
Forsythe, John
Forsythe, William
Forte, Nick Apollo
Fouqueray, Denys
Fox, Edward
Fox, James
Fox, Kirk
Fox, Michael J.
Fox, Sean
Foxworth, Robert
Frakes, Jonathan
Franciosa, Anthony (Tony)
Francks, Don
Frank, Charles

Frank, Tony
Franken, Al
Frankfather, William
Franklin, Joe
Franklin, John
Franz, Dennis
Fraser, Brendan
Frazer, Rupert
Frazier, Ron
Freeman, J. E.
Freeman, Jonathan
Freeman, Jr., Al
Freeman, Morgan
Freeman, Paul
Freiss, Stephane
Frewer, Matt
Fridley, Tom
Friedman, Peter
Friels, Colin
Frishberg, David
Froud, Toby
Fry, Stephen
Frye, Sean
Fuchs, Leo
Fudge, Alan
Fujioka, John
Fuller, Kurt
Fuller, Robert
Furlong, Edward
Furlong, John
Furst, Stephen

G

Gabai, Sasson
Gabriel, Peter
Gains, Boyd
Galabru, Michel
Gallagher, Peter
Galligan, Zach
Gallo, Vincent
Galloway, Don
Gamble, Mason
Gambon, Michael
Gammel, Robin
Gammon, James
Gandolfini, James
Ganz, Bruno
Garcia, Andy
Garcia, Magali
Garcia, Stenio
Garfield, Allen
Garfunkel, Art
Garner, James
Garnett, Richard

Garrett, Brad
Garrett, Hank
Garrison, Jim
Garvey, Steve
Gauthier, Vincent
Gavin, John
Gayle, Jackie
Gaylord, Mitch
Gaynes, George
Gazzara, Ben
Gazzo, Michael V.
Geary, Anthony
Gedrick, Jason
Genaro, Tony
Genesse, Bryan
Geoffreys, Stephen
George, Chief Leonard
George, Joseph
Gerard, Gil
Gerdes, George
Gere, Richard
Germann, Greg
Getty, Balthazar
Getz, John
Giambalvo, Louis
Giannini, Giancarlo
Giatti, Ian
Gibb, Barry
Gibb, Maurice
Gibb, Robin
Gibson, Henry
Gibson, Mel
Gibson, Thomas
Gideon, Ray
Gielgud, Sir John
Giersach, Stefan
Gift, Roland
Gilliam, Terry
Gilliland, Richard
Gillin, Hugh
Gilpin, Jack
Ginty, Robert
Gio, Frank
Girard, Remy
Girardeau, Frank
Girardin, Ray
Giuntoli, Neil
Glass, Ron
Glasser, Phillip
Glaudini, Robert
Glave, Matthew
Gleason, Paul
Glen, Iain
Glenn, Scott
GLover, Savion

Glover, Brian
Glover, Crispin
Glover, Danny
Glover, John
Glover, Julian
Godinez, Henry
Godunov, Alexander
Goetz, Peter Michael
Goldblum, Jeff
Golden II, Norman D.
Goldfinger, Michael
Goldin, Ricky Paull
Goldring, Danny
Goldstein, Bert
Goldthwait, Bob
Goldwyn, Tony
Gomez, Jaime
Gomez, Mateo
Gooding, Cuba Jr.
Goodman, Dean
Goodman, John
Goodwin, Michael
Goodwin, Thatcher
Goorjian, Michael
Gordon, Don
Gordon, Keith
Gordon-Sinclair, John
Gorman, Cliff
Gorman, Robert
Gortner, Marjoe
Gossett, Louis Jr.
Gossett, Robert
Gotell, Walter
Gottfried, Gilbert
Gottschalk, Thomas
Gough, Michael
Gould, Elliott
Gould, Harold
Gould, Jason
Goulding, Ray
Goulet, Robert
Gouyer, Gregory
Gow, David
Goz, Harry
Graas, John Christian
Grace, Nickolas
Graf, David
Graff, Todd
Graham, Billy
Graham, C. J.
Graham, Gary
Graham, Gerritt
Graham, Hepburn
Granger, Seth
Grant, David Marshall

Grant, Hugh
Grant, Richard E.
Grant, Rodney
Graves, Peter
Graves, Rupert
Gray, Bruce
Gray, David Barry
Gray, Sam
Gray, Spalding
Greco, Joe
Green, Frank Rozelaar
Green, Seth
Greenblatt, Shon
Greene, Daniel
Greene, Graham
Greene, H. Richard
Greene, James
Greene, Michael
Greene, Peter
Greene, Shecky
Greenquist, Brad
Greenwood, Bruce
Gregg, Bradley
Gregory, Andre
Grevill, Laurent
Grey, Joel
Grieco, Richard
Grier, David Alan
Gries, Jonathan
Grifasi, Joe
Griffin, Eddie
Griffin, Merv
Griffin, Michael
Griffith, Andy
Griffith, Richards
Griffith, Thomas Ian
Griffiths, Richard
Grimes, Scott
Grimm, Tim
Griparis, Skip
Grizzard, George
Grodin, Charles
Groomes, Gary
Gross, Arye
Gross, Michael
Gross, Paul
Grubbs, Gary
Gruner, Olivier
Guardino, Harry
Guerra, Castulo
Guest, Christopher
Guest, Lance
Guetary, François
Guilfoyle, Paul
Guillaume, Robert

Guinee, Tim
Guiness, Alec
Guiry, Tom
Gulager, Clu
Gulpilil, David
Gunn, Moses
Gunton, Bob
Gunty, Morty
Gurry, Eric
Gusak, Serezha
Guss, Louis
Guthrie, Arlo
Guttenberg, Steve
Guttman, Ronald
Gwynne, Michael C.

H

Haas, Lukas
Hackett, Buddy
Hackman, Gene
Haddrick, Ron
Hagen, Ross
Hagman, Larry
Haid, Charles
Haid, David
Haig, Sid
Haigh, Kenneth
Haim, Corey
Haley, Brian
Haley, Jackie Earle
Hall, Albert
Hall, Anthony Michael
Hall, Arsenio
Hall, Brad
Hall, Bug
Hall, Philip Baker
Hall, Rich
Hall, Rodger
Hallahan, Charles
Hallam, John
Hallo, Dean
Hallston, Rodger
Hallyday, Johnny
Hamill, Brian
Hamill, Mark
Hamilton, Anthony
Hamilton, George
Hamilton, Josh
Hamilton, Richard
Hamlin, Harry
Hammer, Ben
Hammond, Nicholas
Hampton, James
Hancock, Herbie
Handy, James

Haney, Daryl
Hankin, Larry
Hanks, Tom
Hann-Byrd, Adam
Hannah, John
Hansen, Gale
Hansen, Peter
Hardin, Jerry
Hardison, Kadeem
Hardwicke, Edward
Harewood, Dorian
Harker, Wiley
Harkins, John
Harmon, Mark
Harper, Robert
Harrelson, Woody
Harris, David
Harris, Ed
Harris, Julius
Harris, M.K.
Harris, Neil Patrick
Harris, Phil
Harris, Richard
Harris, Ross
Harris, Rossie
Harrison, George
Harrison, Gregory
Hart, Christopher
Hart, David
Hart, Ian
Hart, Roxanne
Hartman, Phil
Harvey, Don
Harvey, Rodney
Hasselhoff, David
Hassett, Marilyn
Hatfield, Hurd
Hathaway, Noah
Hauer, Rutger
Hauser, Cole
Hauser, Jerry
Hauwer, Wings
Havers, Nigel
Havey, Allan
Hawke, Ethan
Hawkins, Corwin
Hawthorne, Nigel
Hayden, Karl
Hayenga, Jeff
Hayes, Isaac
Haynie, Him
Hays, Robert
Haysbert, Dennis
Heacock, John
Heald, Anthony

Healy, David
Heard, John
Hearn, George
Heaton, Tom
Heavener, David
Hecht, Paul
Hedaya, Dan
Hedison, David
Hedley, Jack
Heffner, Kyle T.
Hellman, Ocean
Helm, Levon
Hemblen, David
Hemmings, David
Hemsley, Sherman
Henare, George
Henderson, Bill
Henderson, Saffron
Hendra, Tony
Hendrickson, Benjamin
Hendrickson, Steve
Hennings, Sam
Henriksen, Lance
Henry, Buck
Henry, Gregg
Henry, J.M.
Henry, Justin
Henry, Lenny
Henry, Mike
Hepton, Bernard
Herd, Richard
Herman, Paul
Herman, Pee-Wee
    (See PAUL REUBENS)
Herrmann, Edward
Hervey, Jason
Herzfeld, John
Hesse, Gregor
Hesseman, Howard
Heston, Charlton
Hewitt, Martin
Hewlett, David
Heyman, Barton
Hickey, John Benjamin
Hickey, William
Hickman, Dwayne
Hicks, Kevin
Higgins, Joel
Higgins, Michael
Hill, Arthur
Hill, Charles, C.
Hill, Frank O.
Hill, Gilbert R.
Hill, Mauried
Hill, Rick

Hill, Steven
Hillerman, John
Hilton-Jacobs, Lawrence
Hines, Gregory
Hines, Maurice
Hinkley, Brent
Hinkley, Tommy
Hipp, Paul
Hirsch, Judd
Hisashi , Igawa
Hodder, Kane
Hodges, Tom
Hoffman, Basil
Hoffman, Dominic
Hoffman, Dustin
Hofschneider, Marco
Hogan, Hulk
Hogan, Paul
Holbrook, Hal
Holder, Geoffrey
Holland, Antony
Hollander, David
Hollar, Steve
Holliman, Earl
Holm, Ian
Holman, Rex
Holt, Will
Holyfield, Evander
Hong, James
Honig, Howard
Hood, Don
Hooks, Kevin
Hooks, Robert
Hootkins, William
Hope, Bob
Hope, William
Hopkins, Anthony
Hopkins, Bo
Hopper, Dennis
Hopper, Tim
Horneff, Wil
Horowitz, Adam
Horsley, Lee
Horst, Jason
Horton, Michael
Horton, Peter
Hoskins, Bob
Houser, Jerry
Howard, Adam Coleman
Howard, Alan
Howard, Arliss
Howard, Clint
Howard, John
Howard, Ken
Howard, Ron

Howell, C. Thomas
Howell, Tom
Huband, David
Hubley, Whip
Huddleston, Bob
Huddleston, David
Hudson, Ernie
Hughes, Barnard
Hughes, Brendan
Hughes, Bruce
Hughes, Miko
Hulce, Tom
Hull, Eric
Humphrey, Mark
Humphreys, Michael Conner
Hunter, Bill
Hunter, Ronald
Hunter, Stephen B.
Hunter, Tab
Hunter, Troy
Hurst, Elliott
Hurt William
Hurt, John
Hutchins, Will
Hutchison, Doug
Hutton, Timothy
Huw, Richard
Hyde, Jonathan
Hyde-White, Alex
Hytner, Stephen

I

Iachangelo, Peter
Ibu, Masato
Ice Cube
Ice T
Idle, Eric
Idol, Billy
Imhoff, Gary
Imperioli, Michael
Ingle, John
Ipale, Aharon
Ireland, John
Irlando, Pablo
Irons, Jeremy
Ironside, Michael
Irwin, Bill
Irwin, Tom
Isaak, Chris
Isha, Jim
Ishibashi, Takaaki
Ito, Robert
Itzin, Gregory
Ivanek, Zeljko
Ives, Burl

J

Jackson, John M.
Jackson, Joshua
Jackson, Michael
Jackson, Philip
Jackson, Reggie
Jackson, Samuel L.
Jacobi, Derek
Jacobi, Lou
Jacobsen, Dean
Jacoby, Bobby
Jacoby, Scott
Jacques, Yves
Jaeckel, Richard
Jaffrey, Saeed
Jagger, Mick
Jaglom, Henry
James, Anthony
James, Brion
James, Clifton
James, Dalton
James, Hawthorne
James, Jeff
James, Mike
James, Steve
Janis, Conrad
Jarchow, Bruce
Jarrett, Gabe
Jason, Peter
Jay, Tony
Jeffries, Mark John
Jenkins, Ken
Jenkins, Richard
Jenner, Bruce
Jennings, Waylon
Jeter, Michael
Jillette, Penn
Joel, Billy
Johannsen, Jake
Johansen, David
Johansson, Paul
Johnny B.
Johnson, Arnold
Johnson, Ben
Johnson, Brad
Johnson, Don
Johnson, Karl
Johnson, Lamont
Johnson, Mel, Jr.
Johnson, Reggie
Johnson, Van
Jolly, Mike
Jones, Dean
Jones, Freddie

Jones, Henry
Jones, James Earl
Jones, Jeggrte
Jones, O-Lan
Jones, Quincy
Jones, Simon
Jones, Terry
Jones, Tommy Lee
Jones,L. Q.
Joseph, Ronald G.
Josephson, Erland
Joshua, Larry
Jourdan, Louis
Joy, Robert
Joyner, Mario
Judd, Robert
Julia, Raoul
Jump, Gordon
Jung, Calvin
Junkin, John

K

Kagen, David
Kageyama, Rodney
Kahan, Steve
Kahler, Wolf
Kamal
Kamekona, Danny
Kampmann, Steven
Kanaly, Steve
Kanan, Sean
Kane, Brad
Kane, Ivan
Kani, John
Kapoor, Shashi
Karabtsos, Ron
Karen, James
Karlen, John
Karras, Alex
Karyo, Tcheky
Katsulas, Andreas
Katt, Nicky
Katt, William
Katz, Omri
Kaufer, Jonathan
Kay, Charles
Kay, Hadley
Kaye, Norman
Kaye, Stubby
Kazurinsky, Tim
Keach, James
Keach, Stacy
Keane, James
Keaton, Michael

Keats, Richard
Keegan, Andrew
Keel, Howard
Keen, Geoffrey
Keeslar, Mat
Keitel, Harvey
Keith, Brian
Keith, David
Kelley, Deforest
Kellogg, John
Kelly, Daniel Hugh
Kelly, David Patrick
Kelly, Gene
Kemp, Gary
Kemp, Jeremy
Kennedy, George
Kennedy, Jihmi
Kennedy, Jr., John F.
Kenworthy, Michael
Kerr, Jay
Kerwin, Brian
Kia, Blaine
Kid
Kidd, Michael
Kier, Udo
Kiley, Richard
Kilmer, Val
Kim, Evan
Kimbrough, Charles
King, Alan
King, Erik
King, Larry
King, Perry
King, Stephen
Kingsley, Ben
Kinnear, Roy
Kinney, Terry
Kinsey, Lance
Kirby, Bruno
Kirkpatrick, Patrick
Kirkwood, Gene
Kiser, Terry
Kitchen, Michael
Klar, Gary
Klein, Robert
Kline, Kevin
Klugman, Jack
Klyn, Vincent
Knepper, Rob
Knight, Bobby
Knight, Christopher
Knight, Trenton
Knight, Wayne
Knott, Andrew
Knott, Robert

Knotts, Don
Knox, Terence
Kober, Jeff
Koch, Edward I.
Koch, Peter
Koenig, Walter
Kogen, Jay
Koock, Guich
Korman, Harvey
Kosala, Joseph
Koslo, Paul
Kosmo, Charlie
Kosugi, Sho
Koteas, Elias
Kotto, Yaphet
Kove, Martin
Kowanko, Pete
Koyama, Shigeru
Kozak, John
Krabbe, Jeroen
Kramarov, Savely
Krassner, J. David
Krause, Brian
Kriegel, David
Kristofferson, Kris
Krug, Gary
Krumholtz, David
Kruppa, Olek
Kruschen, Jack
Ksajikian, Armen
Kuhn, Thomas Joseph (T.J.)
Kunstler, William
Kusenko, Nicholas
Kussman, Dylan
Kwong, Peter
Kwouk, Burt

L

Laborteaux, Matthew
Laborteaux, Patrick
Labrinos, Vassili
Lacey, Ronald
Lack, Stephen
Lacombe, Andre
Laffan, Pat
LaFleur, Art
Lamas, Lorenzo
Lambert, Christopher
Lamos, Mark
LaMotta, John
Lampreave, Chus
Lancaster, Burt
Lancaster, James
Landau, Jonathan Isaac

Landau, Martin
Landfield, Timothy
Landham, Sonny
Landon, Hal Jr.
Landovsky, Pavel
Lane, Nathan
Lang, Perry
Lang, Stephen
Langella, Frank
Lansbury, David
Lanteau, William
Lanyer, Charles
LaPaglia, Anthony
Larkin, Bryan
Larroquette, John
Larson, Darrell
Larson, Gary
Lasalle, Eriq
Lasalle, Martino
LaSardo, Robert
Laskaway, Harris
Lassick, Sydney
Lattanzi, Matt
Lauck, Joe D.
Laufer, Jack
Laufer, Ted
Laurance, Matthew
Laurance, Mitchell
Laurence, Michael
Lauria, Dan
Laurie, Hugh
Lauter, Ed
LaVorgna, Adam
Law, John Phillip
Lawrence, Bruno
Lawrence, Martin
Lawrence, Matthew
Lawson, Adam
Lawson, Denis
Lawson, Leigh
Lawson, Richard
Lazar, Paul
Lazenby, George
Le Gros, James
Leadbitter, Bill
Leary, Denis
Leary, Timory
LeClezio, Odile
Ledebur, Frederick
Lee, Christopher
Lee, Jason Scott
Lee, Jesse
Lee, Paul J. Q.
Lee, Spike
Leeds, Phil

Leguizamo, John
Lehne, Frederic
Leibman, Ron
Leigh, Spencer
Leigh, Steven
Leisure, David
Leitch, Donovan
LeMat, Paul
LeMay, John D.
Lemmon, Chris
Lemmon, Jack
Lenard, Mark
Lennix, Harry J.
Leno, Jay
Leon
Leon, David
Leon, Joe
Leonard, Robert Sean
Leong, Al
Leopardi, Chauncey
Leotard, Philippe
Lerner, Ken
Lerner, Michael
Leroy, Philippe
Lester, Mark
Letterman, David
Levels, Calvin
Levine, Jerry
Levine, Ted
Levinson, Barry
Levitt, Steve
Levy, Eugene
Lewis, Al
Lewis, Elbert
Lewis, Geoffrey
Lewis, Huey
Lewis, Jerry
Lewis, Jerry Lee
Lewis, Phill
Lewis, Rawle D.
Lewis, Richard
Lewis, Zachary
Libertini, Richard
Linden, Hal
Lindo, Delroy
Lindon, Vincent
Lindsay, Robert
Lineback, Richard
Linn, Rex
Linn-Baker, Mark
Linville, Larry
Liotta, Ray
Lipscomb, Dennis
Lister, Tiny
Lithgow, John

Little Richard
LL Cool J
Llewelyn, Desmond
Lloyd, Christopher
Lloyd, Cory
Lloyd, Eric
Lloyd, John Bedford
Lloyd, Norman
LoBianco, Tony
Loc, Tone
Locke, Bruce
Loggia, Robert
Lohr, Aaron
Lombard, Michael
Lomita, Sol
London, Jason
Lone, John
Long, Brad
Long, Jodi
Longo, Tony
Lonsdale, Michael
Lookinland, Mike
Loomis, Rod
Lopez, Gerry
Lopez, Perry
Lorinz, James
Lottimer, Eb
Love, Chad
Love, Victor
Lovett, Lyle
Lovitz, Jon
Lowe, Arvie, Jr.
Lowe, Chad
Lowe, Rob
Lowell, Randy
Lowery, Andrew
Lowther, T.J.
Luckinbill, Laurence
Lucking, William
Lumbly, Carl
Lundgren, Dolph
Lundquist, Steve
Luong, Min
Lupus, Peter
Lurie, John
Luz, Franc
Lynch, David
Lynch, Jr., Vernon
Lynch, Richard
Lyons, Robert F.
Lyons, Steve

M

Mabry, Zachary
Mac, Bernie
Macchio, Ralph
MacCorkindale, Simon
MacDonald, Mike
Macht, Stephen
MacLachlan, Kyle
MacNaughton, Robert
MacNee, Patrick
MacNicol, Peter
Macy, Bill
Macy, William H.
Madden, John
Maddio, James
Madorsky, Bryan
Madsen, Michael
Maggart, Brandon
Magner, Jack
Maher, Joseph
Mahler, Bruce
Mahoney, John
Mahoney, Tom
Mailer, Stephen
Majors, Lee
Makepeace, Chris
Mako
Makuma, Blu
Malavoy, Chrisophe
Malcolm, Christopher
Malden, Karl
Malik, Art
Malina, Joshua
Malinger, Ross
Malkovich, John
Mallon, Brian
Malloy, John
Malloy, Matt
Maloney, Michael
Mancini, Ric
Mancuso, Nick
Mandan, Robert
Mandell, Howie
Mandylor, Costas
Manilow, Barry
Mann, Byron
Mann, Terrence
Manos, George, J.
Mantee, Paul
Mantegna, Joe
Mantell, Michael
Manville, Lesley
Marc, Peter
Marciano, David

Marcoux, Ted
Marcus, Richard
Mardirosian, Tom
Margolin, Stuart
Margulies, David
Mariani, Augusto
Marielle, Jean-Pierre
Marika, Banduk
Marin, Cheech
Marin, Jason
Marinaro, Ed
Marino, Dan
Marky Mark
Marrero, Ralph
Mars, Kenneth
Marsalis, Branford
Marshall, Bryan
Marshall, David Anthony
Marshall, E. G.
Marshall, Garry
Marshall, James
Marshall, Ken
Marshall, William
Martel, K.C.
Martin, Dean
Martin, Duane
Martin, George
Martin, Gregory Paul
Martin, Steve
Martinez, A
Martini, Steven
Mason, Jackie
Mason, Madison
Masters, Ben
Mastroianni, Marcello
Masur, Richard
Matheson, Tim
Mathews, Dakin
Mathews, Thom
Mathou, Jaques
Mativo, Kyaloi
Matthau, Walter
Matthews, Al
Matthews, Dakin
Matz, Jerry
Mayall, Rik
Mayer, Christopher
Mayhew, Peter
Mayron, Gale
Mazello, Joseph
Mazursky, Paul
McAfee, Scott
McAleer, Des
McArthur, Alex
McBeath, Tom

McCallum, David
McCamus, Tom
McCann, Chuck
McCann, Donal
McCarthy, Andrew
McCarthy, Kevin
McCartney, Paul
McCaughin, Charles
McClory, Sean
McCloskey, Leigh
McClure, Doug
McClure, Marc
McCluskey, Ken
McConaughey, Matthew
McCord, Kent
McCormick, Pat
McCowen, AleC
McCoy, Matt
McCrane, Paul
McCurley, Matthew
McCutcheon, Bill
McDermott, Dylan
McDermott, Shane
McDonald, Christopher
McDonald, Kevin
McDonald, Mike
McDonald, Norm
McDowall, Roddy
McDowell, Malcolm
McEachin, James
McEnery, John
McGann, Paul
McGavin, Darren
McGaw, Patrick
McGee, Jack
McGill, Bruce
McGill, Everett
McGinley, John C.
McGoohan, Patrick
McGovern, Barry
McGovern, Terence
McGowan, Tom
McGrath, Derek
McGuire, Bruce
McHattie, Stephen
McIntyre, Marvin J.
McKay, David
McKean, Michael
McKellen, Ian
McKeon, Doug
McKeown, Charles
McKinney, Bill
McKinnon, Ray
McMartin, John
McMurray, Sam

McNally, Kevin
McNamara, Brian
McNamara, William
McNeice, Ian
McRae, Frank
McRaney, Gerald
McRobbie, Peter
McShane, Michael
Mead, Courtland
Meadows, Stephen
Meaney, Colm
Meaney, Kevin
Means, Russell
Meat Loaf
Mechoso, Julio
Meillon, John
Mellencamp, John
Mendel, Stephen
Mendelsohn, Ben
Menzies, Robert
Mercado, Hector
Mercurio, Paul
Meredith, Burgess
Meril, Macha
Mesguich, Daniel
Meskin, Amnon
Metcalf, Mark
Metchik, Aaron Michael
Metchik, Asher
Metrano, Art
Metzler, Jim
Metzman, Irving
Midkiff, Dale
Mignone, Toto
Miles, Christopher Cleary
Milhoan, Michael
Military, Frank
Miller, Barry
Miller, Dennis
Miller, Dick
Miller, Harvey
Miller, Jason
Miller, Larry
Miller, Sidney
Miller, Stephen E.
Mills, John
Mills, Zeke
Mills-Cockell, Juno
Miluwi, John Omirah
Ming, Lau Siu
Minter, Kelly Jo
Miranda, Robert G.
Mitchell, John Cameron
Mitchum, Robert
Mizrahi, Isaac

Mockus, Sr., Tony
Modine, Matthew
Moffat, Donald
Moffett, D. W.
Mokae, Zakes
Molina, Alfred
Moll, Richard
Monahan, Dan
Monarque, Steve
Monica, Corbett
Monoson, Lawrence
Montalban, Ricardo
Montgomery, Lee
Moody, Ron
Moore, Dudley
Moore, Kevin
Moore, Matthew
Moore, Rob
Moore, Roger
Moore, Stephen
Moores, Bill
Morales, Esai
Morales, Santos
Moranis, Rick
Morgan, Harry
Morgan, Jeffrey Dean
Morgan, Rhian
Morgan, Richard
Moriarty, Michael
Moriss, Howard
Morita, Noriyuki "Pat"
Morley, Robert
Moroff, Mike
Morrison, Tommy
Morrow, Rob
Morse, David
Morse, Robert
Morshower, Glenn
Mortensen, Viggo
Morton, Gary
Moscow, David
Moseley, Bill
Moses, Rick
Moses, William R.
Mosetti, Sergio
Mosley, Roger E.
Mostel, Josh
Mothupi, Collin
Mott, Bradley
Mr. T
Mueller-Stahl, Armin
Muhammad Ali
   (See Muhammad ALI)
Mulhern, Matt
Mulkey, Chris

Mull, Martin
Mullen, Larry Jr.
Muller, Rolf
Mulligan, Richard
Mulligan, Terry David
Mulroney, Dermot
Mulroney, Kiernan
Murcer, Bobby
Murphy, Alec
Murphy, Charles Q.
Murphy, Charlie
Murphy, Eddie
Murphy, Michael
Murray, Bill
Murray, Brian Doyle (See Brian
    DOYLE-Murray)
Murray, Don
Murray, John
Murray, Peter
Musante, Tony
Myers, Lou
Myers, Michael

N

Nabors, Jim
Nader, Michael
Nail, Jimmy
Nakagawa, Scott
Nalbach, Daniel
Namath, Joe
Nance, Jack
Napier, Charles
Nash, Chris
Nash, Larry
Naughton, David
Naughton, James
Navin, John
Ndaba, Themba
Neal, Donald
Nealon, Kevin
Neeley, Ted
Neeson, Liam
Negron, Taylor
Neidorf, David
Neill, Sam
Nelson, Craig T.
Nelson, David
Nelson, Ed
Nelson, John Allen
Nelson, Judd
Nelson, Sean
Nelson, Willie
Nemec, Corin
Nero, Franco

Neville, Aaron
Neville, John
Newbern, George
Newhart, Bob
Newman, Daniel
Newman, Paul
Newton, Wayne
Ngema, Mbongeni
Ngor, Haing S.
Nguyen, Dustin
Nguyen, Ho
Nicholas, Harold
Nicholas, Paul
Nicholas, Thomas Ian
Nichols, Billy
Nichols, Stephen
Nicholson, Jack
Nielsen, Leslie
Nimoy, Leonard
Niño, Miguel
Nipote, Joe
Nirenberg, Michael
Nissman, Michael
Nixau
Noble, James
Noiret, Philippe
Nolte, Nick
Noman, Mike
Noonan, John Ford
Noonan, Tom
Norris, Chuck
North, Alan
Norton, Jim
Noseworthy, Jack
Nouri, Michael
Novak, Blaine
Novello, Don
Ntshinga, Thoko
Ntshona, Winston
Nucci, Danny
Nugent, Ted
Nunn, Bill
Nye, Will

O

O'Brien, Austin
O'Brien, Niall
O'Brien, Tom
Ocasek, Ric
O'Connell, Eddie
O'Connell, Jerry
O'Connell, Patrick
O'Connor, Carroll
O'Connor, Derrick

O'Connor, Donald
O'Connor, Kevin J.
O'Connor, Raymond
O'Conor, Hugh
O'Dell, David
O'Donnell, Chris
O'Halloran, Jack
O'Hare, Brad
O'Herlihy, Dan
O'Keefe, Michael
O'Keeffe, Miles
Olbrychski, Daniel
Oldham, Will
Oldman, Gary
Olds, Gabriel
O'Leary, John
O'Leary, William
Olin, Ken
Oliver, Barret
Oliver, Michael
Oliveri, Robert
Olkewicz, Walter
Olmos, Edward James
Olson, James
O'Neal, Griffin
O'Neal, Ron
O'Neal, Ryan
O'Neal, Shaquille
O'Neill, Dick
O'Neill, Ed
O'Neill, Michael
Onsongo, Paul
Ontkean, Michael
Opper, Don
O'Quinn, Terry
Orbach, Jerry
O'Reilly, Cyril
Orlandt, Ken
O'Ross, Ed
O'Shea, Milo
O'Toole, Peter
Otto, Barry
Overton, Rick
Owen, Timothy
Owens, Gary
Oz, Frank

P

Pacifici, Federico
Pacino, Al
Packer, David
Page, Harrison
Page, Ken
Palance, Jack

Palin, Michael
Palminteri, Chazz
Palmisano, Conrad
Panebianco, Richard
Pankin, Stuart
Pankow, John
Pantoliano, Joe
Paré, Michael
Paris, Andrew
Parker, Corey
Parker, Jameson
Parker, Nathaniel
Parker, Norman
Parker, Trey
Parks, Michael
Parsons, Karyn
Pasdar, Adrian
Pastore, Vincent
Pastorelli, Robert
Pataki, Michael
Paterson, Bill
Patinkin, Mandy
Patric, Jason
Patrick, Robert
Patterson, Chuck
Patterson, Frank
Patterson, Jay
Patton, Will
Paul, Adrian
Paul, David
Paul, Don Michael
Paul, Peter
Paul, Richard Joseph
Paulin, Scott
Paulsen, Rob
Pavarotti, Luciano
Pax, James
Paxton, Bill
Paxton, Collin Wilcox
Paymer, David
Payne, Allen
Payne, Bruce
Peacock, Daniel
Pearce, Guy
Pearl, Barry
Pearson, Malachai
Peck, Anthony
Peck, Bob
Peck, Gregory
Peck, J. Eddie
Peck, Tony
Pecoraro, Joe
Pendleton, Austin
Penn, Chris
Penn, Matthew

Penn, Sean
Penny, Joe
Penso, Armando
Perela, Marco
Perez, José
Perlich, Max
Perlman, Ron
Perri, Paul
Perrin, Jacques
Perry, Felton
Perry, Jeff
Perry, John Bennett
Perry, Luke
Persoff, Nehemiah
Pesce, Frank
Pesci, Joe
Peters, Brock
Petersen, William L.
Pettigrew, Pete
Petty, Tom
Phenicie, Michael Gates
Phifer, Mekhi
Philbin, John
Phillips, Ethan
Phillips, Leslie
Phillips, Lou Diamond
Phillips, Michael
Phillips, Nicholas
Phoenix, Leaf
Picardo, Robert
Pierce, Bradley Michael
Pierce, Charles
Pileggi, Mitch
Pillow, Mark
Pinchot, Bronson
Piñero, Miguel
Pinter, Harold
Piper, Roddy
Piscopo, Joe
Pitt, Brad
Piven, Jeremy
Plana, Tony
Platt, Oliver
Play
Pleasance, Donald
Pleshette, John
Plummer, Christopher
Plummer, Glenn
Plunket, Robert
Po, Tong
Poitier, Sidney
Polanski, Roman
Polito, Jon
Polizos, Vic
Pollack, Kevin

Pollack, Sydney
Pollard, Michael J.
Pomeranc, Max
Pop, Iggy
Pop, Iggy
Porter, Bill
Portnow, Richard
Postlethwaite, Pete
Poston, Tom
Potaka-Dewes, Eru
Power, Tyrone Jr.
Press, Gordon
Pressman, Lawrence
Presson, Jason
Preston, J.A.
Price, Marc
Priestley, Jason
Primus, Barry
Prince
Prince, William
Prine, Andrew
Prior, Ted
Prochnow, Jürgen
Prosky, Robert
Provenza, Paul
Prowse, David
Prowse, Heydon
Pryce, Jonathan
Pryor, Nicholas
Pryor, Richard
Puente, Tito
Pugliese, Pasquale
Pullman, Bill
Puri, Amrish
Puri, Om
Purvis, Jack
Pygram, Wayne
Pyle, Denver

Q

Quaid, Dennis
Quaid, Randy
Quan, Ke Huy
Quill, Tim
Quilley, Denis
Quinn, Aidan
Quinn, Anthony
Quinn, Daniel
Quinn, Francesco
Quinn, Glenn
Quinn, J. C.
Quinones, Adolpho "Shabba-Doo"

R

Rabal, Francisco
Rabelo, Allessandro
Rachins, Alan
Rado, Ivan Jorge
Rafelson, Bob
Raffi, Gary
Ragno, Joseph
Ragsdale, William
Railsback, Steve
Ramis, Harold
Ramsey, Bruce
Ramsey, Logan
Randall, Ethan
Randall, Pete
Randall, Tony
Randolph, John
Rapaport, Michael
Rapp, Anthony
Rapp, Larry
Rappaport, Stephen
Rasche, David
Rasulala, Thalmus
Raymond, Devon
Rea, Stephen
Read, James
Reagan, Ronald
Reate, J. L.
Rebhorn, James
Reckert, Winston
Reddin, Keith W.
Redford, Robert
Redglare, Rockets
Redgrave, Corin
Reed, Jerry
Reed, Oliver
Reed, Steve
Rees, Roger
Reeve, Christopher
Reeves, Keanu
Reeves, Perrey
Reeves, Scott
Regalbuto, Joe
Reid, Tim
Reilly, Charles Nelson
Reilly, John C.
Reilly, Luke
Reiner, Carl
Reiner, Rob
Reinhold, Judge
Reiser, Paul
Remar, James
Remsen, Bert
Renfro, Brad

Renner, Jeremy
Reno, Jean
Reno, Kelly
Renzulli, Frank
Reubens, Paul
Rey, Reynaldo
Reyes, Jr., Ernie
Reynolds, Burt
Reynolds, Patrick
Rhames, Ving
Rhee, Phillip
Rhee, Simon
Rhoades, Hari
Rhoades, Michael
Rhys, Paul
Rhys-Davies John
Rich, Alan
Rich, Christopher
Richard, Little (see LITTLE Richard)
Richard, Pierre
Richards, Michael
Richards. Evan
Richardson, Ian
Richardson, Lee
Richardson, Sy
Richert, William
Richman, Peter Mark
Richter, Jason James
Richwood, Patrick
Rickles, Don
Rickman, Alan
Riegert, Peter
Riehle, Richard
Riley, Gary
Riley, Larry
Riley, Michael
Rimmer, Shane
Rios, Guillermo
Riquelme, Carlos
Ritchie, Chris
Ritter, John
Robards, Jason
Robards, Jr., Jason
Robards, Sam
Robb, David
Robbins, Michael
Robbins, Tim
Robbins, Tom
Roberts, Douglas
Roberts, Eric
Roberts, Tony
Robertson, Cliff
Robertson, George R.
Robertson, Robbie
Robertson, Tim

Robins, Oliver
Robinson, Andrew
Robson, Wayne
Rocco, Alex
Roche, Eugene
Rock, Chris
Rocket, Charles
Rodgers, Anton
Rodriguez, Agustin
Rodriguez, Marco
Rodriguez, Paul
Rodriquez, Freddy
Roebuck, Daniel
Roeves, Maurice
Rogers, Kenny
Rogers, Tristan
Rogers, Wayne
Rohner, Clayton
Rollins, Henry
Rollins, Howard E. Jr.
Rolston, Mark
Romano, Andy
Romanus, Robert
Ronet, Maurice
Rooker, Michael
Rooney, Mickey
Rosa, Bobby
Ross, Ted
Rossi, Leo
Rossilli, Paul
Rossovich, Rick
Rossovich, Tim
Roth, Tim
Rothman, John
Roundtree, Richard
Rourke, Mickey
Rubelo, Marcelo
Rubenstein, Phil
Rubes, Jan
Rubinek, Saul
Rubinstein, John
Ruck, Alan
Ruggiero, Allelon
Ruginis, Vyto
Ruiz, Rene
Ruocheng, Ying
Ruscio, Al
Rushton, Jared
Rusler, Robert
Russ, Tim
Russ, William
Russell, Harold
Russell, Kurt
Russell, Nipsey
Russo, James

Russo, Ray
Russom, Leon
Ryan, John P.
Ryan, Mitchell
Ryan, Will
Rydall, Derek
Rydell, Chris
Rydell, Mark
Ryder, Michael Allen
Ryecart, Patrick
Ryen, Adam
Rylance, Mark

S

Sabella, Ernie
Sadler, Nick
Sadler, William
Sagal, Joe
Sagalle, Jonathan
Saget, Bob
Sahl, Mort
Saks, Gene
Saletta, Sam
Salinger, Matt
Sampson, Robert
Sampson, Tim
Sand, Paul
Sanders, Jay O.
Sanderson, William
Sandler, Adam
Sandman, Vaughn
Sandoval, Miguel
Sands, Julian
Santiago-Hudson, Ruben
Santos, Joe
Santos, Willie
Sapara, Ade
Sarafian, Richard
Sarandon, Chris
Sargent, Dick
Sarrazin, Michael
Sartain, Gailard
Savage, Ben
Savage, Fred
Savage, John
Savage, Pius
Savant, Doug
Sawa, Devon
Saxon, John
Saxton, Mitch
Sayles, John
Sbarge, Raphael
Scalia, Jack
Scannell, Kevin

Scarfe, Allan
Schacht, Sam
Scheider, Roy
Schell, Maximilian
Schellenberg, August
Schiavelli, Vincent
Schick, Edward
Schlamme, Wilson Lahti
Schlatter, Charlie
Schneider, Dan
Schneider, John
Schneider, Rob
Schoeffling, Michael
Schombing, Jason
Schreiber, Avery
Schroder, Rick
Schrody, Erik
Schuck, John
Schultz, Dwight
Schulz, Jeff
Schwartz, Aaron
Schwarzenegger, Arnold
Schweig, Eric
Scofield, Paul
Scolari, Peter
Scorsese, Martin
Scott, Campbell
Scott, Donovan
Scott, George C.
Scott, Larry B.
Scott, Tim
Seagal, Steven
Seale, Douglas
Seaman, Jr., David
Searcy, Nick
Secor, Kyle
Seda, Jon
Segal, George
Sekine, Tsutomu
Selberg, David
Selby, David
Selleck, Tom
Seltzer, Will
Seneca, Joe
Serious, Yahoo
Serna, Pepe
Sessions, John
Seth, Roshan
Setzer, Brian
Sewell, Rufus
Shabba-Doo
Shadix, Glenn
Shakur, Tupac
Shalhoub, Tony
Shalikar, Daniel

Shalikar, Joshua
Shandling, Garry
Shannon, Michael J.
Shanta, James Anthony
Sharif, Omar
Sharrett, Michael
Shatner, William
Shaw, Stan
Shawn, Wallace
Shea, John
Shearer, Harry
Sheehan, Brian
Sheehan, Doug
Sheen, Charlie
Sheen, Martin
Sheffer, Craig
Sheldon, Jack
Shellen, Stephen
Shenar, Paul
Shepard, Sam
Shepherd, Jack
Sher, Antony
Sheridan, Jamey
Sherwood, Anthony
Shigeta, James
Shimono, Sab
Shiner, David
Shioya, Toshi
Shor, Dan
Shore, Pauly
Short, Martin
Showalter, Max
Shrapnel, John
Shull, Richard B.
Siberry, Michael
Siebert, Charles
Siemaszko, Casey
Sierra, Gregory
Signorelli, Tom
Sikking, James B.
Silva, Henry
Silver, Ron
Silverman, Jonathan
Silverstone, Ben
Simmons, Gene
Simmons, J.K.
Simmons, Peter
Simon, Paul
Simpson, Don
Simpson, O.J.
Sinatra, Frank
Sinbad
Sinclair, John Gordon
Singer, Marc
Singer, Stephen

Sinise, Gary
Sirola, Joe
Sisto, Jeremy
Sizemore, Tom
Skaggs, Jimmie F.
Skarsgard, Stellan
Skerritt, Tom
Skipper, Pat
Skolimowski, Jerzy
Slade, Demian
Slade, Max Elliott
Slater, Christian
Slater, Ryan
Sloyan, James
Smestad, Stian
Smirnoff, Yakov
Smith, Brandon
Smith, Bubba
Smith, Charles Martin
Smith, Cotter
Smith, Eddie
Smith, Hal
Smith, Kurtwood
Smith, Lane
Smith, Rex
Smith, T. Ryder
Smith, Will
Smith, William
Smith, Yeardley
Smitrovich, Bill
Smits, Jimmy
Smothers, Tom
Snipes, Wesley
Snyder, Arlen Dean
Snyder, Jimmy "The Greek"
Sobel, Barry
Solondz, Todd
Sommer, Josef
Sorel, Ted
Sorvino, Paul
Soul, David
Souther, J.D.
Spacey, Kevin
Spade, David
Spader, James
Spall, Timothy
Spano, Joe
Spano, Vincent
Sparrow, Walter
Speakman, Jeff
Spears, Aries
Speck, David
Spencer, John
Spielberg, David
Spinell, Joe

Spinella, Stephen
Spiner, Brent
Spinetti, Victor
Spiridakis, Tony
Sporleder, Greg
Spradlin, G.D.
Springfield, Rick
Squillanti, Vittorio
St. Jacques, Raymond
St. Phillip, Ross
Stack, Robert
Stahl, Nick
Staley, James
Stallone, Frank
Stallone, Sage
Stallone, Sylvester
Stamos, John
Stamp, Terence
Stander, Lionel
Standiford, Jim
Stanton, Harry Dean
Stanton, John
Starke, Anthony
Starr, Beau
Starr, Mike
Starr, Ringo
Starr, Robert
Steagall, Red
Steedman, Ted
Steele, George "The Animal"
Steiger, Rod
Stein, Saul
Steinberg, David
Steinbrenner, George
Steinfeld, Jake
Stephens, Robert
Stern, Daniel
Stevens, Andrew
Stevens, Fisher
Stevens, Morgan
Stevens, Scott Newton
Stevens, Shadoe
Stevens, Warren
Stevenson, Parker
Stewart, Don
Stewart, James
Stewart, Jean-Pierre
Stewart, Jon
Stewart, Patrick
Stiers, David Ogden
Stiller, Ben
Stiller, Jerry
Stimler, F. Benjamin
Sting
Stockwell, Dean

Stockwell, John
Stoll, Brad
Stoltz, Eric
Stone, Danton
Stone, Oliver
Stone, Philip
Stone, Sean
Storke, Adam
Stoyanov, Michael
Strait, George
Strathairn, David
Strathairn, Tay
Strauss, Peter
Strode, Woody
Strong, Andrew
Stroud, Don
Stroud, Duke
Struycken, Carel
Strydom, Hans
Studi, Wes
Suarez, Miguelangel
Suchet, David
Sullivan, Billy L.
Sullivan, Brad
Sullivan, R. Patrick
Sumpter, Donald
Sutera, Paul
Sutherland, Donald
Sutherland, Kiefer
Svenson, Bo
Swaim, Bob
Swayze, Patrick
Sweeney, D.B.
Swingler, Richard
Sylvers, Jeremy
Szarabajka, Keith

T

Tacchino, Richard
Tagawa, Cary-Hiroyuki
Takaki, Mio
Takaku, William
Takakura, Ken
Takei, George
Takeshi
Tamblyn, Russ
Tambor, Jeffrey
Tan, Philip
Tarantino, Quentin
Tarso, Ignacio Lopez
Taylor, Dub
Taylor, Earl T.
Taylor, Holland
Taylor, Meshach

Taylor, Noah
Taylor, Rip
Taylor-Thomas, Jonathan
Teague, Marshall
Tedford, Travis
Teeley, Tom
Tenney, Jon
Terkel, Studs
Terlesky, John
Terri, Lee
Terry, John
Terry, Nigel
Tesh, John
Thacker, Tab
Thal, Eric
Thaler, Jordan
Thall, Benj
Thames, Byron
Thaw, John
Thewlis, David
Thibeau, Jack
Thomas, Henry
Thomas, Jay
Thomas, Jonathan Taylor
Thomas, Richard
Thomerson, Tim
Thompson, Brian
Thompson, Ernest
Thompson, Fred Dalton
Thompson, Jack
Thompson, Kenan
Thomson, Scott
Thornton, Billy Bob
Thornton, David
Threlfall, David
Thurman, Bill
Tierney, Jacob
Tierney, Lawrence
Tighe, Kevin
Tillis, Mel
Tingwell, Charles
Toback, James
Tobias, Oliver
Tobolowsky, Stephen
Tochi, Brian
Todd, Ryan
Todd, Tony
Tognazzi, Ugo
Tolkan, James
Tomlins, Jason
Tomlinson, David
Tone Loc
Topol
Torn, Rip
Torrens, Pip

Torrente, Vinnie
Torry, Joe
Toth, Frank
Townsend, Bud
Townsend, Robert
Tran, Truyer V.
Travalena, Fred
Travanti, Daniel J.
Travis, Randy
Travolta, Joey
Travolta, John
Trebor, Robert
Tregoe, William
Trichter, Judd
Trintignant, Jean-Louis
Tripp, Louis
Trotter, Cham
True, Jim
Trump, Donald
Tsang Chi Wal, Eric
Tsignoff, Steve "Patalay"
Tuan, Le
Tubb, Barry
Tucci, Stanley
Tucker, Michael
Turner, Frank
Turturro, John
Tyhurst, Tyler
Tyson, Richard

U

Ubarry, Hechter
Uda, Hatsuo
Uecker, Bob
Underwood, Blair
Underwood, Jay
Urich, Robert
Ustinov, Peter
Utay, William

V

Vache, Warren
Valadez, Samuel
Valentine, Scott
Valentino, Tony
Valli, Frankie
Vallone, Raf
Van Damme, Jean-Claude
Van Dreelen, John
Van Dyke, Dick
Van Hoffmann, Brant
Van Norden, Peter
Van Patten, Dick
Van Peebles, Mario

Van Peebles, Melvin
Vance, Courtney B.
Vandross, Luther
Varney, Jim
Vaughn, Ned
Vaughn, Peter
Vaughn, Robert
Vawter, Ron
Velez, Eddie
Veljohnson, Reginald
Vennera, Chick
Ventresca, Vincent
Vereen, Ben
Vernon, John
Vidal, Gore
Vignari, Steve
Vigoda, Abe
Viharo, Robert
Villa, Joey
Villafane, Chunchuna
Villard, Tom
Villarreal, Daniel
Villiers, Christopher
Villiers, James
Vince, Pruitt Taylor
Vincent, Alex
Vincent, Frank
Vincent, Jan-Michael
Ving, Lee
Vinson, Jackey
Vipond, Neil
Vivino, Floyd
Vogt, Peter
Voight, Jon
Von Dohlen, Lenny
Von Sommer, Alec
von Homburg, Wilhelm
von Sydow, Max
Vonnegut, Jr., Kurt
Voyagis, Vorgo
Vu-An, Eric
Vundla, Ka

W

Wachira, Waigwa
Waddington, Steven
Wagner, Jack
Wagner, Robert
Wahl, Ken
Wahlberg, Mark
Wainwright III, Loudon
Waite, Ralph
Waites, T.J.
Waites, Thomas G.

Waits, Tom
Walken, Christopher
Walker, Christopher
Walker, Clint
Walker, Jimmie
Walker, Jr., Robert
Walker, Sydney
Wallace, Bill
Wallace, Jack
Wallace, Zac
Wallach, Eli
Walsh, Charles Hunter
Walsh, Dylan
Walsh, J.T.
Walsh, M. Emmet
Walsh, Sydney
Walston, Ray
Walter, Tracey
Walters, Anthony
Walters, Jamie
Ward, Colin
Ward, Fred
Ward, Jonathan
Ward, Lyman
Ward, Megan
Ward, Simon
Warden, Jack
Warkol, Jordan
Warner, David
Warner, Jeremiah
Warner, Malcolm Jamal
Washington, Denzel
Washington, Isaiah
Wass, Ted
Wasserman, Allan
Wasson, Craig
Watanabe, Gedde
Waters, John
Waters, Jr., Harry
Waterston, James
Waterston, Sam
Watson, Jr., James A.
Watt, Marty
Watt, Nathan
Wayans, Damon
Wayans, Keenen Ivory
Wayne, Patrick
Weathers, Carl
Weaver, Dennis
Weaver, Fritz
Weaver, Jason
Weaver, Robert "Wingnut"
Weaving, Hugo
Webb, Daniel
Webber, Robert

Weber, Steven
Weeks, Jimmie Ray
Weinger, Scott
Weiss, Michael T.
Weiss, Shaun
Weissman, Jeffrey
Weissman, Mitch
Weist, Dwight
Weitz, Bruce
Welker, Frank
Weller, Peter
Wells, Tico
Welsh, Ken
Welsh, Kenneth
Wendt, George
Wenner, Jann
Wentz, Kip
West, Adam
West, Martin
West, Samuel
West, Timothy
Weston, Jack
Weyers, Marius
Whaley, Frank
Whalin, Justin
Whatley, Liem
Wheaton, Wil
Wheeler, Mark
Whitaker, Forest
White, Al
White, Andrew
White, De'voreaux
White, Richard
Whitehead, Paxton
Whitfield, Mitchell
Whitford, Brad
Whitman, Stuart
Whitmire, Steve
Whitmore, James
Whitmore, Jr., James
Whitworth, Johnny
Widmark, Richard
Wiesendanger, Alex
Wikes, Michael
Wilby, James
Wilcox, Larry
Wilder, Gene
Wilder, James
Wiles, Jason
Williams III, Clarence
Williams, Barry
Williams, Billy Dee
Williams, Dean
Williams, Dick Anthony
Williams, Ed

Williams, Gregory Alan
Williams, Johnny
Williams, Joseph
Williams, Justin
Williams, Paul
Williams, R.J.
Williams, Robin
Williams, Spice
Williams, Steven
Williams, Treat
Williamson, Fred
Williamson, Mykelti
Williamson, Nicol
Willingham, Noble
Willis, Bruce
Wilson, Lambert
Wilson, Richard
Wilson, Scott
Wilson, Stuart
Wilson, Thomas F.
Wimmer, Brian
Wincott, Michael
Windom, William
Winfield, Paul
Wing, Choy Chang
Winkler, Henry
Winslow, Michael
Winter, Alex
Winters, Jonathan
Wirth, Billy
Wise, Ray
Wise, William
Wiseman, Joseph
Wiseman, Michael
Witcher, Guy
Witherspoon, John
Woetzel, Damian
Wong, B.D.
Wong, Mel
Wong, Russell
Wong, Victor
Wood, Elijah
Wood, John
Wood, Tom
Woodbine, Bokeem
Woods, James
Woods, Kevin
Woods, Michael
Woodvine, John
Woodward, Edward
Wooley, Sheb
Woolson, Michael
Woolvett, Jaimz
Wopat, Tom
Workman, Jimmy

Worth, Nicholas
Wright, Ben
Wright, Michael
Wright, Samuel E.
Wright, Steven
Wuhl, Robert
Wyle, Noah
Wyner, George

X

Xavier, Nelson

Y

Yankovic, "Weird Al"
Yasuda, Doug
Yoakam, Dwight
Yoba, Malik
York, John J.
York, Michael
Young, Alan
Young, Bruce A.
Young, Burt
Young, Cedric
Young, Chris
Young, Keone
Young, Neil
Young, Paul
Young, Richard
Young, Rudy
Young, William Allen
Youngblood, Jack
Youngman, Henny
Youngreen, Clint B.
Youngs, Jim
Yulin, Harris
Yunis, Tariq

Z

Zabka, William
Zahn, Steve
Zammit, Eddie
Zamora, Del
Zane, Billy
Zappa, Dweezil
Zaslow, Michael
Zelniker, Michael
Zerbe, Anthony
Zien, Chip
Zimbalist, Jr., Efrem
Zimmerman, Joey
Zischler, Hanns
Ziskie, Dan
Zmed, Adrian
Zobel, Richard
Zorich, Louis
Zuehlke, Joshua
Zwerling, Darrell
Zwiener, Michael

★ ★ ★

INDEX BY ACTOR
Female

Note: This is not a list of all female actors, only
those listed in the main listing section of this book.

A

Aames, Angela
Aaron, Caroline
Abbott, Diahnne
Abril, Victoria
Acker, Sharon
Adair, Deborah
Adams, Brooke
Adams, Catlin
Adams, Edie
Adams, Jane
Adams, Maud
Adjani, Isabelle
Adkinson, Suzanne
Adu, Sade
Agnew, Hailey Ellen
Agutter, Jenny
Aimée, Anouk
Akers, Andra
Akers, Karen
Alda, Beatrice
Alda, Elizabeth
Alda, Rutanya
Aleandro, Norma
Alexander, Jace
Alexander, Jane
Alicia, Ana
Aliff, Lisa
Allen, Debbie
Allen, Jo Harvey
Allen, Joan
Allen, Karen
Allen, Mikki
Allen, Nancy
Alley, Kirstie
Allyson, June
Alonso, Maria Conchita
Alt, Carol
Amick, Madchen
Amis, Suzy
Anders, Luana
Anderson, Bridgette

Anderson, Erika
Anderson, Isa
Anderson, Lindsay
Anderson, Loni
Anderson, Melissa
Anderson, Melody
Andersson, Bibi
Andeson, Jo
Andreeff, Starr
Andress, Ursula
Andrews, Julie
Angel, Vanessa
Angelyne
Ann-Margret
Annis, Francesca
Anspach, Susan
Anthony, Lysette
Anton, Susan
Anwar, Gabrielle
Anz, Maria
Apollonia
Applegate, Christina
Aquino, Amy
Aragon, Angelica
Archer, Anne
Ardant, Fanny
Argenziano, Carmen
Arlen, Elizabeth
Arlys, Dimitra
Armstrong, Bess
Armstrong, Georgina
Armstrong, Kerry
Arnaz, Lucie
Aronson, Judie
Arquette, Alexis
Arquette, Patricia
Arquette, Rosanna
Arredondo, Jeri
Arrindell, Lisa C.
Arthur, Beatrice
Ashana, Rochelle
Ashbourne, Lorraine
Ashbrook, Daphne

Asherson, Renee
Ashley, Elizabeth
Atkins, Eileen
Atkinson, Jayne
Attili, Atonella
Audran, Stéphane
Auger, Claudine
Austin, Alana
Austin, Karen
Austin, Patti
Austin, Teri
Avery, Margaret
Avital, Mili
Azcuy, Annette

B

Babcock, Barbara
Bacall, Lauren
Bach, Barbara
Bach, Catherine
Badie, Mina
Baer, Kristin
Bain, Barbara
Baker, Blanche
Baker, Carroll
Baker, Diane
Baker, Kathy
Bakke, Brenda
Bako, Bridgette
Balk, Fairuza
Ball, Angeline
Ballard, Kaye
Balsam, Talia
Bancroft, Anne
Banks, Tyra
Baranski, Christine
Barash, Olivia
Barbeau, Adrienne
Barber, Andrea
Barber, Frances
Barber, Glynnis
Barker, Patricia
Barkin, Ellen

Barnes, Priscilla
Barrault, Marie-Christine
Barrett, Majel
Barrett, Nancy
Barretto, Amber
Barrie, Barbara
Barry, Patricia
Barrymore, Drew
Bartlett, Bonnie
Bartlett, Robin
Basinger, Kim
Bassett, Angela
Bassett, Linda
Bateman, Justine
Bates, Kathy
Bauer, Belinda
Baxter, Meredith
Baye, Nathalie
Bayne, Stacy
Bayne, Tracy
Beals, Jennifer
Beasly, Allyce
Beck, Jenny
Beck, Kimberly
Bedard, Irene
Bedelia, Bonnie
Bega, Leslie
Belack, Doris
Belafonte-Harper, Shari
Bell, Vanessa
Beller, Kathleen
Bellwood-Wheeler, Pamela
Bening, Annette
Bennett, Jill
Bennett, Marcia
Benson, Amber
Benson, Jodi
Benson, Lyric
Berdahl, Blaze
Berenson, Marisa
Bergen, Candice
Bergen, Frances
Bergen, Polly
Bergman, Mary Kay
Berlin, Jeannie
Bernard, Crystal
Bernhard, Sandra
Berridge, Elizabeth
Berry, Halle
Berryman, Dorothée
Bertell, Numa
Bertinelli, Valerie
Besch, Bibi
Besse, Ariel
Beswicke, Martine

Betti, Laura
Biggs, Roxann
Billingsley, Barbara
Bingham, Barbara
Binoche, Juliette
Birch, Thora
Bird, Billie
Bishop, Debby
Bishop, Kelly
Bissett, Jacqueline
Bissett, Josie
Black, Karen
Black-Eyed Susan
Blackman, Honor
Blair, Betsy
Blair, Linda
Blair, Lisa
Blair, Michelle
Blakely, Susan
Blakley, Ronnie
Blanc, Jennifer
Bliss, Caroline
Bloom, Claire
Bloom, Verna
Blore, Cathianne
Blount, Lisa
Bobby, Anne
Boggs, Gail
Boisson, Christine
Bond, Cynthia
Bond, Sudie
Bonet, Lisa
Bonham Carter, Helena
Bonnaire, Sandrine
Boone, Lesley
Boorman, Katrine
Borge, Rikke
Borowitz, Katherine
Borrego, Amaryllis
Boschi, Giulia
Bosson, Barbara
Botsford, Sara
Bouix, Evelyne
Bouquet, Carole
Boushel, Joy
Bowens, Malick
Boyd, Brittany
Boyd, Jan Gan
Boyd, Sarah
Boyd, Tanya
Boyle, Lara Flynn
Bracco, Lorraine
Bradshaw, Cathryn
Braga, Sonia
Brando, Luisina

Brandon, Sharon H.
Braschi, Nicoletta
Bregman, Tracy
Brennan, Eileen
Brenneman, Amy
Brenner, Eve
Brewton, Maia
Brill, Fran
Brill, Victoria
Brinkley, Christie
Brittany, Morgan
Brochet, Anne
Bromfield, Valri
Bron, Eleanor
Brook, Irina
Brook, Jayne
Brookes, Jacqueline
Brooks, Randi
Brown, Blair
Brown, Caitlin
Brown, Julie
Brown, Ruth
Brown, Sally
Brown, Sharon
Browne, Leslie
Bryant, Lee
Bryceland, Yvonne
Buchanan, Erin
Buchanan, Simone
Buckley, Betty
Buckner, Susan
Bugg, Susan
Bujold, Genevieve
Bulifant, Joyce
Buller, Francesca
Bullock, Sandra
Buono, Cara
Burke, Delta
Burke, Michelle
Burnett, Carol
Burrows, Saffron
Burstyn, Ellen
Burt, Clarissa
Burton, Kate
Busia, Akosua
Butler, Yancy
Buzzi, Ruth
Byrne, Anne
Byrne, Debbie
Byrnes, Josephine
Byun, Susan

C

Cadrell, Selina
Caldwell, L. Scott
Caldwell, Zoe
Calegory, Jade
Callan, K
Calloway, Vanessa Bell
Cameron, Jane
Camp, Colleen
Campbell, Amelia
Campbell, Cheryl
Campbell, Julia
Campbell, Mae E.
Campbell, Tisha
Candido, Candy
Cannon, Dyan
Capers, Virginia
Capshaw, Kate
Cara, Irene
Carides, Gia
Carita
Carle, Cynthia
Carlin, Gloria
Carmen, Julie
Caron, Leslie
Carrera, Barbara
Carrere, Tia
Carrillo, Elpida
Carrington, Debbie Lee
Carroll, Diahann
Carroll, Helena
Carroll, Janet
Carroll, Lisa Hart
Carroll, Pat
Carter, Alice
Carter, Finn
Carter, Lynda
Carter, Nell
Cartwright, Veronica
Caselli, Chiara
Cash, Rosalind
Caspary, Katrina
Cassavetes, Virginia
Cassidy, Joanna
Castro, Analia
Cates, Georgina
Cates, Phoebe
Caton, Juliette
Cattrall, Kim
Cavadini, Cathy
Cavanagh, Christine
Cavanagh, Megan
Cecil, Jane
Célarie, Clementine

Chadwick, June
Chalfant, Kathleen
Champa, Jo
Chan, Melissa
Chan, Michele
Chandler, Estee
Chang, Sari
Channing, Carol
Channing, Stockard
Chao, Rosalind
Chaplin, Geraldine
Chapman, Judith
Charbonneau, Patricia
Charendoff, Tara
Charisse, Cyd
Charo
Chavez, Ingrid
Chen, Joan
Chen, Moira
Cher
Child, Julia
Chiles, Lois
Chin, Tsai
Chinh, Kieu
Chlumsky, Anna
Chong, Rae Dawn
Chrisinger, Jenny
Christiana, Claudia
Christie, Julie
Christopher, Jordan
Ciccolella, Jude
Clark, Betsy
Clark, Candy
Clark, Susan
Clarke, Caitlin
Clarke, Joanna
Clarkson, Patricia
Clayburgh, Jill
Clayton, Merry
Close, Glenn
Coca, Imogene
Coduri, Camille
Cohen, Jessica Lynn
Cohn, Mindy
Cole, Natalie
Coleman, Charlotte
Colin, Margaret
Collins, Joan
Collins, Pauline
Collins, Tyler
Colston, Karen
Conn, Didi
Connelly, Jennifer
Conroy, Frances
Converse, Peggy

Cook, Barbara
Cooke, Jennifer
Cooper, Cami
Cooper, India
Copeland, Joan
Coppola, Sofia
Corley, Sharon
Corman, Maddie
Cornell, Ellie
Cortadellas, Elaine
Courau, Clotilde
Courtenay, Margaret
Cox, Courteney
Cox, Yeanne
Craig, Charmaine
Craigie, Ingrid
Crampton, Barbara
Craven, Mimi
Crawford, Ellen
Crewson, Wendy
Crider, Missy
Crockett, Carlene
Cronauer, Gail
Cronin, Laurel
Cronyn, Tandy
Crosbie, Annette
Crosby, Denise
Crosby, Lucinda
Crosby, Mart
Cross, Harley
Crouse, Lindsay
Crow, Ashley
Cruz, Celia
Crystal, Lindsay
Culea, Melinda
Culkin, Quinn
Cummings, Quinn
Cunningham, Kendall
Curran, Lynnette
Currie, Sondra
Curtin, Jane
Curtin, Valerie
Curtis, Jamie Lee
Curtis, Liane
Curtis, Robin
Curtis, Sonia
Cusack, Ann
Cusack, Joan
Cusack, Sinead
Cutter, Lise
Cypher, Julie

D

Dabney, Augusta
D'Abo, Maryam
D'Abo, Olivia
Daily, E. G.
Daily, E. G.
Dale, Cynthia
Dale, Cynthia
Daley, Kathryn
Daley, Kathryn
Dalton, Abby
Dalton, Susanna
Dalva, Anna
Daly, Tyne
Dammartin, Solveig
Danes, Claire
D'Angelo, Beverly
Danieli, Isa
Danner, Blythe
Danon, Geraldine
Dapkunaite, Ingeborga
D'Arbanville, Patty
Darbo, Patrika
Darby, Kim
Darlow, Linda
Darrieux, Danielle
Dash, Stacey
Davey, Belinda
David, Eleanor
Davidovich, Lolita
Davidson, Eileeen
Davidtz, Embeth
Davis, Ann B.
Davis, Carole
Davis, Geena
Davis, Judy
Davis, Kimberlee M.
Davis, Nancy
Davis, Sammi
Davis, Viveka
Dawber, Pam
Day, Doris
Deakins, Lucy
Dean, Laura
Deangelis, Gina
Debaer, Jean
De Carlo, Yvonne
Dee, Ruby
Dee, Sandra
DeHavilland, Consuelo
De Havilland, Olivia
Delaney, Kim
Delany, Cathleen
Delany, Dana

De La Peña
Delpy, Julie
De Medeiros, Maria
DeMornay, Rebecca
Dench, Judi
Deneuve, Catherine
Denier, Lydie
Derek, Bo
Dern, Laura
DeSalvo, Anne
Deschanel, Mary Jo
De Soto, Rosana
Detmers, Maruschka
de Turckheim, Charlotte
Devine, Loretta
Devito, Karla
Dey, Susan
Diaz, Cameron
Dickey, Lucinda
Dickinson, Angie
Dickinson, Sandra
Dietlein, Marsha
Dillard, Victoria
Diller, Phyllis
Dillman, Pamela
Dillon, Melinda
Dixon, Donna
Doherty, Shannen
Dolenz, Ami
Dolle, Béatrice
Dombasle, Arielle
Dommartin, Solveig
Donahue, Elinor
Donald, Juli
Donnelly, Patrice
Donohoe, Amanda
Donovan, Erin
Doody, Alison
Dore, Edna
Doroff, Sara Rowland
Douglas, Ileanna
Douglas, Sarah
Dougias, Suzzanne
Douglass, Robyn
Dowd, Ann
Dowie, Freda
Dowling, Kathryn
Dowling, Rachel
Down, Lesley-Anne
Drake, Fabia
Draper, Polly
Drescher, Fran
Driver, Minnie
Drouet, Soo
Dubois, Ja'net

Ducasse, Cecile
Duffy, Karen
Dukakis, Olympia
Duke, Patty
Duke, Robin
Dummont, Denise
Dunaway, Faye
Duncan, Sandy
Dunn, Nora
Dunst, Kirsten
Dusay, Marj
Dusenberry, Ann
Dushku, Eliza
Duvall, Shelley
Dworsky, Sally

E

Eagan, Daisy
Easterbrook, Leslie
Ebersole, Christine
Eden, Barbara
Edney, Beatie
Edwards, Cassandra
Edwards, Jennifer
Edwards, Kristle
Edwards, Paddi
Edwards, Ronnie Claire
Eggar, Samantha
Ehle, Jennifer
Eichhorn, Lisa
Eikenberry, Jill
Eilbacher, Lisa
Eilber, Janet
Eisenstadt, Debra
Eklund, Britt
Eleniak, Erika
Elise, Christine
Elizondo, Evangelina
Erbe, Kathryn
Erin, Tami
Ernst, Laura
Estabrook, Christine
Estevez, Renee
Evans, Evans
Evans, Linda
Everhard, Nancy
Ewing, Barbara

F

Fabian, Ava
Fairchild, Morgan
Fairfield, Heather
Falk, Lisanne
Faracy, Stephanie

Farentino, Debrah
Farrell, Terry
Farrow, Mia
Farrow, Stephanie
Farugia, Lena
Fawcett, Farrah
Feldshuh, Tovah
Fenn, Sherilyn
Fenton, Sarah Jane
Ferrara, Nancy
Ferrell, Conchata
Ferrell, Tyra
Ferret, Eve
Feuer, Debra
Field, Chelsea
Field, Sally
Field, Shirley Anne
Finland, Natalie
Fiorentino, Linda
Fisher, Carrie
Fisher, Frances
Fisher, Tricia Leigh
Fitzgerald, Geraldine
Fitzgerald, Tara
Flagg, Fannie
Flanagan, Fionnula
Fleetwood, Susan
Fletcher, Louise
Flowers, Kim
Fluegel, Darlanne
Flynn, Miriam
Foch, Nina
Foley, Ellen
Folland, Alison
Follows, Megan Porter
Fonda, Bridget
Fonda, Jane
Foote, Hallie
Foray, June
Forbes, Michelle
Ford, Faith
Ford, Maria
Foreman, Amanda
Foreman, Deborah
Foriani, Claire
Forque, Veronica
Forristal, Susan
Foster, Jodie
Foster, Kimberly
Foster, Meg
Foster, Stacie
Foyt, Victoria
Fracci, Carla
Frank, Joanna
Frank, Marilyn Dodds

Franklin, Aretha
Franklin, Diane
Frechet, Leila
Freeman, Kathleen
French, Susan
Frey, Sami
Fricker, Brenda
Friede, Lisa
Frost, Sadie
Frot, Catherine
Funicello, Annette
Furness, Deborah-Lee

G

Gabor, Eva
Gabor, Zsa Zsa
Gago, Jenny
Gains, Courtney
Gainsburg, Charlotte
Galiena, Anna
Gallacher, Megan
Gallego, Gina
Gam, Rita
Garlington, Lee
Garnett, Gale
Garofalo, Janeane
Garr, Teri
Garrett, Eliza
Garrick, Barbara
Garson, Greer
Gary, Linda
Gary, Lorraine
Gazelle, Wendy
Geary, Cynthia
Gehman, Martha
Gelinas, Gratien
Gentles, Avril
George, Babs
George, Susan
Gerber, Joan
Gersak, Savina
Gershon, Gina
Gersten, Alexandra
Gertz, Jami
Getty, Estelle
Ghostley, Alice
Gibb, Cynthia
Gibbons, Leeza
Gibbs, Marla
Gifford, Gloria
Gilbert, Melissa
Gilbert, Sara
Gilday, Pamela
Giles, Nancy

Gillen, Linda
Gillette, Anita
Gish, Annabeth
Gish, Sheila
Gisladottir, Gudrun
Givens, Robin
Glasser, Isabel
Gleason, Joanna
Gless, Sharon
Glick, Stacey
Glover, Eileen
Glover, Tawny Sunshine
Glynn, Carlin
Glynn, Tamara
Goethals, Angela
Goethals, Sara
Going, Joanna
Gold, Brandy
Gold, Tracey
Goldberg, Whoopi
Golden, Annie
Goldman, Marcy
Goldstein, Jenette
Golino, Valeria
Gompf, Alison
Goodall, Caroline
Goodheart, Carol
Goodrich, Deborah
Goodwin, Jamie
Gordon, Eve
Gordon, Hilary
Gorman, Breon
Gorney, Karen Lynn
Gouw, Cynthia
Graff, Ilene
Graham, Heather
Grainger, Gawn
Grant, Beth
Grant, Faye
Grant, Lee
Grant, Micah
Grassle, Karen
Graubart, Judy
Gray, Erin
Gray, Linda
Green, Janet Laine
Green, Kerri
Greene, Ellen
Greene, Michelle
Greer, Jane
Gregg, Virginia
Greist, Kim
Gress, Googy
Grey, Jennifer
Grier, Pam

Griffeth, Simone
Griffin, Lorie
Griffith, Melanie
Griffith, Tracy
Grimes, Tammy
Gross, Mary
Guevara, Nacha
Gugino, Carla
Guion, Jewell N.
Guthrie, Caroline
Gutteridge, Lucy
Guy, Jasmine

H

Hack, Olivia
Hack, Shelley
Haddon, Dayle
Hagana, Molly
Hagerty, Julie
Hale, Barbara
Hall, Daisy
Hall, Diedre
Hall, Hanna R.
Hall, Harriet
Hall, Jerry
Hamel, Veronica
Hamilton, Carrie
Hamilton, Erin
Hamilton, Linda
Hamilton, Suzanna
Hamper, Jane
Han, Maggie
Hanauer, Terri
Hancock, Sheila
Haney, Anne
Hanft, Helen
Hannah, Daryl
Hannigan, Alyson
Harden, Marcia Gay
Hardin, Melora
Hargreaves, Amy
Harker, Susannah
Harmon, Deborah
Harnos, Christina
Harper, Tess
Harper, Valerie
Harrell, Rebecca
Harris, Barbara
Harris, Cynthia
Harris, Danielle
Harris, Julie
Harris, Lara
Harris, Leonore
Harris, Mel

Harris, Zelda
Harrision, Linda
Harrison, Cathryn
Harrold, Kathryn
Harry, Deborah
Hartley, Mariette
Hartman-Black, Lisa
Harvest, Rainbow
Hatcher, Teri
Hathaway, Amy
Hauser, Fay
Hawn, Goldie
Hayakawa, Kumiko
Hayes, Helen
Hayes, Lori
Hayes, Patricia
Headey, Lena
Headley, Glenne
Headley, Shari
Healy, Katherine
Healy, Patricia
Hearst, Patricia
Heatherton, Joey
Heaton, Patricia
Heckart, Eileen
Hedren, Tippi
Heflin, Marta
Heigl, Katherine
Helgenberger, Marg
Helmond, Katherine
Hemingway, Margaux
Hemingway, Mariel
Henderson, Florence
Henderson, Maggie
Henn, Carrie
Henner, Marilu
Henstridge, Natasha
Hepburn, Doreen
Hepburn, Katharine
Herring, Laura
Hershey, Barbara
Hess, Susan
Heywood, Pat
Hickland, Catherine
Hicks, Catherine
Hicks, Taral
Higgins, Clare
Hilboldt, Lise
Hill, Dana
Hill, Lauryn
Hiller, Wendy
Hirt, Christianne
Hoag, Judith
Hoard, Michelle
Hobel, Mara

Hodge, Patricia
Hoffman, Gaby
Hoffman, Isabella
Hoffman, Susan Lee
Hogan, Heather
Hogan, Susan
Holden, Marjean
Holiavko, Teddy
Holliday, Polly
Holly, Lauren
Holm, Celeste
Holmes, Brittany Ashton
Holt, Sandrine
Holvöe, Maria
Holzbog, Arabella
Hooks, Jan
Hope, Leslie
Horne, Lena
Horrocks, Jane
Horsford, Anna Maria
Hoshi, Shizuko
Houck, Amanda
Houck, Caroline
Houston, Whitney
Howe, Maxine
Hubley, Season
Hughes, Finola
Hughes, Wendy
Hull, Dianne
Humes, Mary-Margaret
Hunt, Bonnie
Hunt, Helen
Hunt, Linda
Hunter, Holly
Huppert, Isabelle
Hurt, Mary Beth
Huston, Angelica
Huston, Carol
Hutson, Candance
Hutton, Lauren
Hyatt, Pam
Hyland Frances

I

Iman
Ireland, Kathy
Irvine, Paula
Irving, Amy
Ivey, Dana
Ivey, Judith
Ivey, Lela

J

Jackée
Jackson, Anne
Jackson, Glenda
Jackson, Janet
Jackson, Kate
Jackson, Victoria
Jacob, Irene
Jagger, Bianca
Jakub, Lisa
James, Geraldine
James, Jessica
Jenkins, Rebecca
Jenney, Lucinda
Jennings, Julia
Jens, Salome
Jett, Joan
Jillian, Ann
Jilot, Yolanda
Johnes, Alesandra
Johns, Glynis
Johnson, A. J.
Johnson, Anne Marie
Johnson, Lynn-Holly
Johnson, Michelle
Jones, Christine
Jones, Debi
Jones, Grace
Jones, Helen
Jones, Janet
Jones, Jennifer
Jones, Jill
Jones, Renee
Jones, Shirley
Joseph, Jackie
Jovovich, Milla
Judd, Ashley
Julian, Janet
Jurado, Katy
Jurgens, Linda Rae

K

Kaczmarek, Jane
Kagan, Elaine
Kahn, Madeline
Kalem, Toni
Kalember, Patricia
Kaminski, Dana
Kane, Carol
Kaplan, Wendy
Kaprisky, Valerie
Kapture, Mitzi
Karin, Rita

Karr, Sarah Rose
Kash, Linda
Kastner, Daphna
Katz, Erika
Kaufmann, Christine
Kava, Caroline
Kavner, Julie
Kazan, Lainie
Kean, Marie
Keanan, Staci
Keaton, Diane
Keats, Ele
Keegan, Kari
Keener, Catherine
Kellegher, Tina
Keller, Marthe
Kellerman, Sally
Kelley, Sheila
Kelly, Jean Louisa
Kelly, Moira
Kelsey, Linda
Kennedy, Kristina Marie
Kennedy, Michelle Lynn
Kennedy, Mimi
Kensit, Patsy
Kent, Suzanne
Kerns, Joanna
Kerr, Deborah
Khambatta, Persis
Khumalo, Leleti
Kidder, Margot
Kidman, Nicole
King, Mabel
King, Morgana
King, Regina
King, Rowena
Kinglsey, Susan
Kinkade, Amelia
Kinski, Nastassja
Kirkland, Sally
Kirshner, Mia
Kistler, Darci
Kitaen, Tawny
Kitt, Eartha
Klemp, Anna
Kling, Heidi
Knight, Lily
Knight, Shirley
Kohnert, Mary
Kouf, Marie Butler
Kozak, Harley Jane
Kozlowski, Linda
Kramer, Stepfanie
Krawoski, Jane
Krige, Alice

Kristel, Sylvia
Kuhn, Judy
Kurtz, Swoosie
Kuzma, Nora (See Traci LORDS)
Kwan, Nancy

L

La Fortune, Felicity
Labelle, Patti
Ladd, Cheryl
Ladd, Diane
Lafont, Bernadette
Lagpacan, Samantha
Lahti, Christine
Lail, Leah
Lake, Ricki
Lala
Lamour, Dorothy
Lampert, Zohra
Landau, Juliet
Landers, Audrey
Landgrebe, Gudrun
Landsburg, Valeria
Lane, Diane
Langdon, Sue Ane
Lange, Hope
Lange, Jessica
Langenkamp, Heather
Langlois, Lisa
Lansbury, Angela
LaPlaca, Alison
Larkin, Linda
Larkin, Samantha
Larkin, Sheena
Lasser, Louise
Latham, Louise
Latzen, Ellen Hamilton
Lauper, Cyndi
Lauren, Tammy
Lauren, Veronica
Laurie, Piper
Lavanant, Dominique
Lavin, Linda
Lazar, Veronica
Le, Hiep Thi
Le, Thuy Thu
Leach, Rosemary
Leachman, Cloris
Learned, Michael
LeBrock, Kelly
Lee, Ann Marie
Lee, Joie
Lee, Michele
Lee, Ruta

Lee, Sheryl
Leigh, Janet
Leigh, Jennifer Jason
Lemmons, Kasi
Lemon, Genevieve
Lemper, Ute
Lenney, Dinah
Lenz, Kay
Leo, Melissa
Leoni, Tea
Leroy-Beaulieu, Philippine
Lethin, Lori
Levin, Rachel
Levine, Anna
Lewis, Charlotte
Lewis, Dawann
Lewis, Fiona
Lewis, Gwen
Lewis, Jenifer
Lewis, Jenny
Lewis, Juliette
Li, Gong
Lieberman, Nancy
Light, Judith
Lilly, Heather
Lin, Traci
Lincoln, Lar Park
Lindfors, Viveca
Lindley, Audra
Ling, Bai
Linney, Laura
Lipman, Maureen
Lipton, Peggy
Little, Michelle
Lively, Robyn
Lloyd, Emily
Locane, Amy
Locatell, Carol
Locke, Sondra
Lockhart, Anne
Lockhart, June
Locklear, Heather
Lombard, Karina
Long, Shelley
Longstreth, Emily
Loomis, Nancy
Loong, Blaise
Lopert, Tanya
Lords, Traci
Loren, Sophia
Loughlin, Lori
Louis-Dreyfuss, Julia
Louise, Tina
Love, Darlene
Lovett, Jody

Lowell, Carey
Lu, Lisa
Lucas, Lisa
Ludwig, Pamela
Lumet, Jenny
Lumley, Joanna
Lundy, Jessica
Lupone, Patti
Luu, Thuy An
Lynch, Kate
Lynch, Kelly
Lynley, Carol
Lyons, Robin

M

Maberly, Kate
MacDowell, Andie
MacGraw, Ali
MacLaine, Shirley
MacNellie, Tress
Macpherson, Elle
Madigan, Amy
Madonna
Madsen, Virginia
Maffia, Roma
Maggio, Pupella
Magnuson, Ann
Mahaffey, Valerie
Maiden, Sharon
Majorino, Tina
Makeba, Miriam
Makkena, Wendy
Malcomson, Paula
Malick, Wendie
Malina, Judith
Malis, Claire
Mallory, Barbara
Maloney, Stacy
Manchester, Melissa
Mandrell, Barbara
Mann, Gloria
Manoff, Dinah
Mantel, Henrietta
Manyer, Kiti
Mara, Mary
Marceau, Sophie
March, Jane
Marchand, Nancy
Marcovicci, Andrea
Margolin, Janet
Margolyes, Miriam
Margret, Ann (See ANN-Margret)
Mariana, Michele
Marie, Lisa
Marsh, Jean

Marsh, Sally Ann
Marshall, Penny
Martin, Andrea
Martin, Helen
Martin, Kellie
Martin, Mary Catherine
Martin, Nan
Martin, Pamela Sue
Martin, Sharlene
Martin, Sharon
Mason, Hilary
Mason, Marsha
Masterson, Fay
Masterson, Mary Stuart
Mastrantonio, Mary Elizabeth
Mathis, Samantha
Matlin, Marlee
Matthews, Liesel
Maughan, Monica
Maura, Carmen
Maxwell, Lois
May, Elaine
May, Jodhi
Maynard, Mimi
Mayron, Melanie
Mazar, Debi
McCabe, Ruth
McCain, Frances Lee
McCambridge, Mercedes
McCarthy, Nobu
McCarthy, Sheila
McClanahan, Rue
McClellan, Kathleen
McClung, Kely
McClure, Molly
McClurg, Edie
McComb, Heather
McCormack, Catherine
McCormick, Carolyn
McCormick, Maureen
McCullough, Kimberly
McDonnell, Mary
McDormand, Frances
McEntire, Reba
McEwan, Geraldine
McFadden, Gates
McFadden, Stephanie
McGillis, Kelly
McGovern, Elizabeth
McGovern, Maureen
McKee, Lonette
McKellar, Danica
McKeon, Nancy
McLish, Rachel
McNeil, Kate

McNichol, Kristy
McQueen, Armelia
McWilliams, Caroline
Meadows, Jayne
Meara, Anne
Mercer, Marian
Mercure, Monique
Mercurio, Micole
Merin, Eda Reiss
Merrill, Dina
Merritt, Theresa
Messina, Dolores
Messing, Debra
Metcalf, Laurie
Meury, Anne-Laure
Meyer, Bess
Meyer, Dina
Meyers, Ari
Meyrink, Michelle
Miao, Cora
Michaud, Françoise
Michel, Dominique
Michell, Helena
Midler, Bette
Migenes, Julia
Milano, Alyssa
Miles, Joanna
Miles, Sarah
Miles, Sylvia
Miles, Vera
Milford, Penelope
Millan, Andra
Miller, Ann
Miller, Linda
Miller, Maxine
Miller, Penelope Ann
Miller, Rebecca
Mills, Donna
Mills, Hayley
Minnelli, Liza
Minogue, Kylie
Mirren, Helen
Mitchell, Donna
Miyori, Kim
Mobley, Alaina
Mofokeng, Jackie
Molina, Angela
Montgomery, Belinda J.
Montgomery, Elizabeth
Moody, Lynne
Moore, Demi
Moore, Julianne
Moore, Mary Tyler
Moore, Melba
Moore, Sheila

Moreau, Jeanne
Moreno, Rita
Morgenstern, Maja
Moriarty, Cathy
Morris, Haviland
Morris, Jane
Mount, Peggy
Mueller, Maureen
Muldaur, Diana
Mulgrew, Kate
Mullowney, Deborah
Mundy, Meg
Murphy, Rosemary
Muth, Ellen
Muti, Ornella

N

Najimy, Kathy
Neal, Billie
Neal, Patricia
Neale, Leslie
Near, Holly
Neil, Hildegard
Nelligan, Kate
Nelson, Ruth
Nelson, Tracy
Nettleton, Lois
Neuwirth, Bebe
Newman, Laraine
Newmar, Julie
Newton, Thandie
Newton-John, Olivia
Nicholas, Denise
Nichols, Jenny
Nichols, Kyra
Nichols, Nichelle
Nielsen, Brigitte
Nihill, Julie
Noonan, Kerry
Norman, Lisa
Novak, Kim
Nuyen, France

O

Oberer, Amy
Oberon, Elan
O'Brien, Devon
Occipinti, Andrea
O'Connell, Deirdre
O'Connor, Glynnis
O'Connor, Hazel
O'Donnell, Rosie
O'Grady, Gail
Ohama, Natsuko

O'Hara, Catherine
O'Hara, Jenny
O'Hara, Maureen
O'Hara, Paige
Okumoto, Yuji
Ole, Cass
Olin, Lena
Oliver, Rochelle
Olsen, Susan
O'Neal, Tatum
O'Neill, Amy
O'Neill, Jennifer
O'Neill, Maggie
O'Rawe, Geraldine
Ormond, Julia
Orsini, Marina
Osborne, Madolyn Smith
  (see Madolyn SMITH)
Osterwald, Bibi
O'Sullivan, Maureen
Otis, Carré
O'Toole, Annette
Overall, Park

P

Pacula, Joanna
Pai, Suzee
Paine, Heidi
Palance, Holly
Pallhas, Geraldine
Palmer, Betsy
Paltrow, Gwyneth
Paquin, Anna
Pareira, Randi
Parfitt, Judy
Parillaud, Anne
Parker, Andrea
Parker, Eleanor
Parker, Leni
Parker, Mary-Louise
Parker, Sarah Jessica
Parker, Sunshine
Parker-Jones, Jill
Parsons, Estelle
Parton, Dolly
Pasco, Isabelle
Paternoster, Gemma
Paton, Angela
Patterson, Lorna
Patterson, Neva
Paul, Alexandra
Paul, Nancy
Pavia, Ria
Pays, Amanda

Peck, Cecilia
Peeples, Nia
Peldon, Ashley
Peldon, Courtney
Pelikan, Lisa
Peña, Elizabeth
Peretz, Susan
Perez, Rosie
Perkins, Elizabeth
Perkins, Millie
Perlman, Rhea
Perrier, Mireille
Perrine, Valerie
Persky, Lisa Jane
Persons, Fern
Pescia, Lisa
Peters, Bernadette
Peters, Eliseabeth
Peterson, Amanda
Peterson, Cassandra
Peterson, Lenka
Petty, Lori
Pfeiffer, Dedee
Pfeiffer, Michelle
Phillips, Chynna
Phillips, Julianne
Phillips, Michelle
Phillips, Sian
Phillips, Wendy
Phoenix, Rain
Pickett, Cindy
Pidgeon, Rebecca
Pigg, Alexandra
Pinkett, Jada
Pinkins, Tanya
Pino, Mariangela
Pinon, Dominique
Pisier, Marie-France
Pitillo, Maria
Pitoniak, Anne
Place, Mary Kay
Plaza, Begonia
Pleshette, Suzanne
Plimpton, Martha
Plowright, Joan
Plumb, Eve
Plummer, Amanda
Pochat, Marie-Sophie
Poe, Emily
Pointer, Priscilla
Poldon, Ashley
Pollan, Tracy
Polley, Sarah
Polo, Teri
Porizkova, Paulina

Portal, Louise
Porter, Alisan
Portman, Natalie
Posey, Parker
Post, Markie
Potter, Madeleine
Potts, Annie
Pounder, C. C. H.
Powell, Brittney
Powers, Alexandra
Powers, Stefanie
Pozniak, Beata
Prentiss, Paula
Present, Leah King
Presley, Priscilla
Preston, Kelly
Prince, Faith
Principal, Victoria
Prinsloo, Sandra
Purcell, Lee
Purdy-Gordon, Caroline
Purl, Linda

Q

Queen Latifah
Questel, Mae
Quick, Diana
Quinlan, Kathleen
Quinn, Aileen
Quinn, Daniele
Quinn, Martha
Quinn, Pat
Quinn, Valentina

R

Raab, Ellie
Raffin, Deborah
Ralph, Sheryl Lee
Rampling, Charlotte
Ramsay, Anne Elizabeth
Ramsey, Marion
Randall, Lexi
Randle, Mary Jo
Randle, Theresa
Rawsower, Stacy Linn
Ray, Ola
Raye, Martha
Rea, Peggy
Reagan, Nancy (see Nancy DAVIS)
Reddy, Helen
Redgrave, Jemma
Redgrave, Lynn
Redgrave, Vanessa
Reed, Alyson

Reed, Pamela
Reese, Della
Reeves, Dianne
Reid, Fiona
Reid, Kate
Reina, Lucy
Reiner, Tracy
Reinking, Ann
Rennard, Deborah
Renoir, Sophie
Renzi, Maggie
Rescher, Dee Dee
Retton, Mary Lou
Reuben, Faenza
Reuben, Gloria
Reynolds, Debbie
Rhodes, Cynthia
Ricci, Christina
Rice-Davies, Mandy
Richard, Emily
Richards, Ariana
Richards, Beah
Richardson, Joely
Richardson, LaTanya
Richardson, Miranda
Richardson, Natasha
Richardson, Patricia
Richardson, Salli
Richman, Caryn
Richter, Deborah
Rigg, Diana
Riker, Robin
Ringwald, Molly
Riouz, Genevieve
Rivers, Joan
Rivers, Melissa
Robbins, Carol
Roberts, Doris
Roberts, Francesca
Roberts, Julia
Roberts, Tanya
Robertson, Kimmy
Robins, Laila
Robinson, Claudia
Robinson, Madeleine
Roche, Suzzy
Rochon, Lela
Roel, Gabriella
Rogers, Mimi
Rolle, Esther
Romand, Anny
Ronstadt, Linda
Roosendahl, Jennifer
Root, Alexandra
Rose, Jamie

Roseanne
Rosenthal, Rachel
Rosenthal, Sheila
Ross, Annie
Ross, Chelcie
Ross, Clarinda
Ross, Diana
Ross, Katharine
Rossellini, Isabella
Roth, Joanna
Rothrock, Cynthia
Rowan, Kelly
Rowlands, Gena
Rubin, Jennifer
Rubinstein, Zelda
Rudner, Rita
Rue, Sara
Ruehl, Mercedes
Rule, Janice
Runyon, Jennifer
Rupp, Debra, Jo
Rush, Deborah
Russell, Betsy
Russell, Keri
Russell, Kimberly
Russell, Lisa Ann
Russell, Theresa
Russo, Rene
Ruttan, Susan
Ryan, Eileen
Ryan, Eveanna
Ryan, Fran
Ryan, Meg
Ryder, Winona

S

Sägebrecht, Marianne
Saint James, Susan
Saint, Eva Marie
Saldana, Theresa
Salenger, Meredith
Salinger, Diane
Salonga, Lea
Samms, Emma
San Giacomo, Laura San
Sanchez-Gijon, Altana
Sandlund, Debra
Santoni, Reni
Sara, Mia
Sarandon, Susan
Sarelle, Leilani
Savage, Kala
Saviola, Camille
Scacchi, Greta

Scales, Prunella
Scarwid, Diana
Schachter, Felice
Schellhardt, Mary Kate
Schoelen, Jill
Schram, Bitty
Schreiber, Liev
Schull, Rebecca
Schwan, Ivyann
Schygulla, Hanna
Sciorra, Annabella
Scoggins, Tracy
Scott, Debralee
Scott, Joan
Scott, Kimberly
Scott, Martha
Seagrove, Jenny
Sedgwick, Kyra
Segall, Pamela
Seigner, Emmanuelle
Seldes, Marian
Sennish, Bronwen
Serna, Assumpta
Severance, Joan
Seymour, Jane
Shatner, Melanie
Shaver, Helen
Shaw, Fiona
Shaw, Vinessa
Shear, Rhonda
Sheedy, Ally
Sheen, Ruth
Shelly, Adrienne
Shelton, Deborah
Shelton, Sloane
Shephard, Elizabeth
Shepherd, Cybill
Shepherd, Suzanne
Sheridan, Nicollette
Shields, Brooke
Shire, Talia
Shoop, Kimber
Shoop, Pamela Susan
Shou, Robin
Shriver, Maria
Shue, Elisabeth
Sidney, Sylvia
Siemaszko, Nina
Sikes, Cynthia
Silver, Elaine Melanie
Silverstone, Alicia
Simmons, Jean
Simpson, Freddie
Sinclair, Madge
Singer, Lori

Sirtis, Marina
Skala, Lilia
Skye, Ione
Slaboda, Deborah Dawn
Slater, Helen
Sleete, Gena
Smart, Jean
Smith Osborne, Madolyn
Smith, Allison
Smith, Anna Deavere
Smith, Anna Nicole
Smith, Brooke
Smith, Jaclyn
Smith, Liz
Smith, Lois
Smith, Maggie
Smith, Shawnee
Smith-Cameron, J.
Smurfit, Vicky
Snodgress, Carrie
Soles, P.J.
Somers, Suzanne
Somerville, Phyllis
Sorkin, Arleen
Sorvino, Mira
Sothern, Ann
Soto, Talisa
Soucie, Kath
Soul, Julia Nickson
Soutendijk, Renee
Spacek, Sissy
Sparks, Dana
Spelvin, Georgina
Sperber, Wendie Jo
Springsteen, Pamela
St. John, Jill
Stacy, Michelle
Staff, Kathy
Stanley, Brooke
Stanley, Florence
Stanley, Kim
Stanley, Lauren
Stansfield, Claire
Staples, Mavis
Stapleton, Jean
Stapleton, Maureen
Stapleton, Nicola
Starr, Blaze
Steadman, Alison
Steel, Amy
Steen, Jessica
Steenburgen, Mary
Stein, Margaret Sophie
Stephenson, Pamela
Sternhagen, Frances

Stevan, Robyn
Stevens, Connie
Stevens, Stella
Stevenson, Cynthia
Stevenson, Juliet
Stewart, Catherine Mary
Stickney, Phyllis Yvonne
Stimson, Sara
Stock-Poynton, Amy
Stole, Mink
Stone, Dee Wallace
Stone, Sharon
Stowe, Madeleine
Straight, Beatrice
Strasberg, Susan
Strassman, Marcia
Streep, Mamie
Streep, Meryl
Streisand, Barbra
Strickland, Gail
Stritch, Elaine
Stuart Masterson, Mary
    (See Mary Stuart MASTERSON)
Stuart, Barbara
Stubbs, Imogen
Sugden, Mollie
Suite, Annie
Sukowa, Barbara
Sullivan, Susan
Summers, Bunny
Sung, Elizabeth
Sutherland, Kristine
Sutorius, James
Suzman, Janet
Swank, Hilary
Swanson, Brenda
Swanson, Kristy
Sweeney, Julia
Swenson, Inga
Swink, Kitty
Swinton, Tilda
Swit, Loretta
Swope, Tracy Brooks

T

Taggart, Rita
Takanashi, Aya
Talbot, Nita
Tallman, Patricia
Tamburrelli, Karla
Tate, Lahmard J.
Tavi, Tuvia
Taylor, Christine
Taylor, Elizabeth

Taylor, Holland
Taylor, Lili
Taylor, Renee
Taylor-Young, Leigh
Teefy, Maureen
Tennant, Victoria
Ter Steege, Johanna
Tewes, Lauren
Thaxter, Phyllis
Thayer, Brynn
Thigpen, Lynne
Thomas, Betty
Thomas, Heather
Thomas, Marlo
Thomas, Robin
Thomas, Sharon
Thompson, Emma
Thompson, Lea
Thompson, Shelley
Thompson, Susanna
Thomson, Anna
Thorne-Smith, Courtney
Thornton, Sigrid
Throne, Christiana
Thurman, Uma
Ticotin, Rachel
Tiffany
Tilly, Jennifer
Tilly, Meg
Tilton, Charlene
Tirelli, Jaime
Tobias, Heather
Todd, Beverly
Todd, Saira
Tokuda, Marilyn
Tolbert, Berlinda
Tom, Lauren
Tom, Nicholle
Tomei, Concetta
Tomei, Marisa
Tomelty, Frances
Tomita, Tamlyn
Tomlin, Lily
Tompkins, Angel
Tong, Jacqueline
Torres, Liz
Tousey, Sheila
Toussaint, Lorraine
Towers, Constance
Townsend, Jill
Townsend, Patrice
Trainor, Mary Ellen
Travis, Nancy
Traylor, Susan
Trigger, Sarah

Trilling, Zoe
Tripplehorn, Jeanne
Tsu, Irene
Tucci, Maria
Tunney, Robin
Turco, Paige
Turkel, Ann
Turman, Glynn
Turner, Angela
Turner, Janine
Turner, Kathleen
Turner, Lana
Turner, Tina
Turturro, Aida
Tweed, Shannon
Twiggy
Twomey, Anne
Tyler, Liv
Tyrrell, Susan
Tyson, Cicely

U

Udenio, Fabiana
Uggams, Leslie
Ullman, Tracey
Ullmann, LIv
Unger, Deborah

V

Vaccaro, Brenda
Vaccaro, Tracy
Valdez, Maria
Valen, Nancy
Valentine, Karen
Van Ark, Joan
Van Der Velde, Nadine
Van Devere, Trish
Van Pallandt, Nina
Van Patten, Joyce
Van Valkenburgh, Deborah
Vandever, Mildred R.
Vanity
Vanni, Renata
Velez, Lauren
Venora, Diane
Vera, Victoria
Verdon, Gwen
Vidal, Christina
Vidale, Thea
Vogt, Lynn
von Zerneck, Danielle

W

Wagner, Lindsay
Waldron, Shawna
Walker, Ally
Walker, Arnetia
Walker, Kerry
Walker, Kim
Walker, Liza
Walker, Polly
Walker, Sari
Walker, Zena
Walsh, Angela
Walter, Jessica
Walters, Julie
Walters, Susan
Walton, Emma
Waltz, Lisa
Ward, Rachel
Ward, Sela
Ward, Sophie
Ware, Herta
Warfield, Marsha
Warner, Julie
Warren, Jennifer
Warren, Lesley Ann
Warwick, Dionne
Waterbury, Laura
Watson, Vernee
Watts, Naomi
Wayborn, Kristina
Weatherly, Shawn
Weaver, Rose
Weaver, Sigourney
Webb, Chloe
Wedgeworth, Ann
Weisman, Robin
Welch, Barbara
Welch, Raquel
Welch, Tahnee
Weld, Tuesday
Welles, Gwen
Wells, Claudia
Welsh, Margaret
Wen, Ming-Na
Wentworth, Alexandra
West, Tegan
Weston, Celia
Wettig, Patricia
Whalley-Kilmer, Joanne
Wheeler, Ira
Wheeler-Nicholson, Dana
Whelan, Jill
Whinnery, Barbara
White, Vanna

Whitelaw, Billie
Whitfield, Lynn
Whitney, Grace Lee
Whitton, Margaret
Wickes, Mary
Wiest, Dianne
Wilcox, Lisa
Wilcox, Shannon
Wilhoite, Kathleen
Wilkes, Donna
Wilkinson, June
Williams, Barbara
Williams, Cindy
Williams, Cynda
Williams, Esther
Williams, JoBeth
Williams, Kelli
Williams, Kimberly
Williams, Laura
Williams, Michelle
Williams, Vanessa
Willis, Susan
Wilson, Bridgette
Wilson, Elizabeth
Wilson, Mara
Wilson, Mary Louise
Wilson, Renee
Wilson, Rita
Wilton, Penelope
Winfery, Oprah
Wing, Leslie
Winger, Debra
Winningham, Mare
Winston, Hattie
Winters, Shelley
Wisoff, Jill
Witherspoon, Reese
Witt, Alicia
Witter, Karen
Wolf, Kelly
Wolfe, Traci
Woodard, Alfre
Woodley, Karen
Woods-Coleman, Carol
Woodward, Joanne
Wooldridge, Susan
Worley, Jo Anne
Woronov, Mary
Worth, Irene
Wouk, Suzanne
Wright, Amy
Wright, Jenny
Wright, N'Bushe
Wright, Robin
Wright, Teresa

Wright, Whittni
Wu, Vivian
Wyatt, Jane
Wyman, Jane
Wyss, Amanda

Y

Yasbeck, Amy
Yasutake, Patti
Yates, Cassie
Yohn, Erica
York, Kathleen
York, Susannah
Yothers, Tina
Young, Karen
Young, Norma
Young, Paula
Young, Sean
Youngfellow, Barrie
Youngs, Gail
Yue, Marion

Z

Zabriskie, Grace
Zadora, Pia
Zal, Roxana
Zane, Lisa
Zane, Lora
Zapata, Carmen
Zappa, Moon
Zellweger, Renee
Zeman, Jacklyn
Zima, Madeline
Zimbalist, Stephanie
Zucker, Charlotte
Zuniga, Daphne

★★★

INDEX OF ACTOR AND AGENT

Note: This is not a list of all actors and their agents, only those who have representation in the main listing section of this book.

A

CAROLINE AARON ....William Morris Agency
F. MURRAY ABRAHAM ....William Morris Agency
JIM ABRAHAMS ....UTA
SHARON ACKER ....The Characters Talent Agency, Ltd.
JOSS ACKLAND ....Susan Smith & Associates
BROOKE ADAMS ....Susan Smith & Associates
BEN AFFLECK .... Paradigm
BEHROOZ AFRAKHAN ....The Tyler Kjar Agency
JENNY AGUTTER .... Gersh Agency
DANNY AIELLO ....UTA
RICK AIELLO .... The Artists Agency
ALAN ALDA ....UTA
JACE ALEXANDER ....Writers & Artists Agency
JANE ALEXANDER ....William Morris Agency
JASON ALEXANDER ....William Morris Agency
WOODY ALLEN ....ICM
KIRSTIE ALLEY ....Metropolitan Talent Agency
CHRISTOPHER ALLPORT ....Susan Smith & Associates
JUNE ALLYSON ....Shapiro-Lichtman
JEFF ALTMAN ....David Shapira & Associates
TRINI ALVARADO ....J. Michael Bloom & Associates
SUZY AMIS ....ICM
JOHN AMOS .... The Artists Agency
LUANA ANDERS .... Media Artists Group
ERICH ANDERSON ....Paradigm
HARRY ANDERSON ....CAA
JOHN ANDERSON ....Paul Kohner, Inc.
KEVIN ANDERSON ....CAA
LONI ANDERSON ....CAA
MITCHELL ANDERSON .... Gersh Agency
STARR ANDREEFF .... Badgley/Connor
ANTHONY ANDREWS .... Gersh Agency
DAVID ANDREWS ....Paradigm
JULIE ANDREWS ....William Morris Agency
VANESSA ANGEL ....APA
JEAN-HUGUES ANGLADE ....William Morris Agency
PHILIP ANGLIM ....Writers & Artists Agency
ANN-MARGRET ....William Morris Agency
SUSAN ANSPACH .... Harris & Goldberg
ADAM ANT .... Harris & Goldberg
LYSETTE ANTHONY ....William Morris Agency

SUSAN ANTON ....The Irv Schechter Company
GABRIELLE ANWAR ....UTA
APOLLONIA ....Shapiro-Lichtman
JOHN APREA ....The Artists Group, Ltd.
MICHAEL APTED ....CAA
AMY AQUINO .... William Morris Agency
FRANK ARAGON ....Sutter/Walls Associates, Inc.
ANNE ARCHER ....ICM
ALAN ARKIN .... William Morris Agency
BESS ARMSTRONG ....William Morris Agency
CURTIS ARMSTRONG ....Paradigm
LUCIE ARNAZ .... William Morris Agency
TOM ARNOLD .... William Morris Agency
PATRICIA ARQUETTE .... UTA
ROSANNA ARQUETTE ....ICM
DANA ASHBROOK ....William Morris Agency
LINDEN ASHBY ....APA
ELIZABETH ASHLEY .... Gersh Agency
JOHN ASHTON ....Harris & Goldberg
ED ASNER .... Paradigm
ARMAND ASSANTE ....CAA
MACKENZIE ASTIN ....William Morris Agency
SEAN ASTIN .... William Morris Agency
WILLIAM ATHERTON .... Gersh Agency
TOM ATKINS .... Paradigm
JAYNE ATKINSON ....Susan Smith & Associates
ROWAN ATKINSON ....William Morris Agency
RICHARD ATTENBOROUGH ....CAA
FRANKIE AVALON ....ICM
RICK AVILES ....Writers & Artists Agency
HOYT AXTON ....Charles H. Stern Agency, Inc.
DAN AYKROYD ....CAA

B

OBBA BABATUNDÉ ....Stone Manners Talent Agency
BARBARA BABCOCK ....Paradigm
LAUREN BACALL ....William Morris Agency
BRIAN BACKER ....Abrams Artists & Associates
KEVIN BACON .... CAA
G.W. BAILEY ....Writers & Artists Agency
CONRAD BAIN .... Harris & Goldberg
SCOTT BAIO ....Shapiro-Lichtman

BLANCHE BAKER .... Abrams Artists & Associates
CARROLL BAKER .... Abrams Artists & Associates
DYLAN BAKER .... ICM
JAY BAKER .... Paradigm
JOE DON BAKER .... The Artists Agency
KATHY BAKER .... ICM
BRENDA BAKKE .... APA
SCOTT BAKULA .... UTA
ALEC BALDWIN .... CAA
DANIEL BALDWIN .... William Morris Agency
STEPHEN BALDWIN .... UTA
WILLIAM BALDWIN .... CAA
CHRISTIAN BALE .... William Morris Agency
FAIRUZA BALK .... William Morris Agency
MARK BALLOU .... Paul Kohner, Inc.
TALIA BALSAM .... Writers & Artists Agency
ANNE BANCROFT .... ICM
JONATHAN BANKS .... Paradigm
IAN BANNEN .... Harris & Goldberg
ELLEN BARKIN .... ICM
BARBARA BARRIE .... Gersh Agency
PATRICIA BARRY .... Paul Kohner Agency
DREW BARRYMORE .... UTA
PAUL BARTEL .... ICM
ROBIN BARTLETT .... Gersh Agency
MIKHAIL BARYSHNIKOV .... CAA
GARY BASARABA .... Paradigm
KIM BASINGER .... CAA
KATHY BATES .... Susan Smith & Associates
PAUL BATES .... Gersh Agency
RANDALL BATINKOFF .... Paradigm
BELINDA BAUER .... David Shapira & Associates
MEREDITH BAXTER .... William Morris Agency
MICHAEL BEACH .... Paradigm
JENNIFER BEALS .... UTA
SEAN BEAN .... ICM
WARREN BEATTY .... CAA
JIM BEAVER .... The Artists Agency
JOHN BECK .... Camden ITG
MICHAEL BECK .... David Shapira & Associates
DANIEL BEER .... Bauman, Hiller & Associates
ED BEGLEY, JR. .... APA
MARSHALL BELL .... UTA
KATHLEEN BELLER .... Paradigm
GIL BELLOWS .... William Morris Agency
PAMELA BELLWOOD-WHEELER .... Paul Kohner Agency
ROBERT BELTRAN .... Harris & Goldberg
CLIFF BEMIS .... Century Artists, Ltd.
BRIAN BENBEN .... UTA
DIRK BENEDICT .... Stone Manners Talent Agency
ANNETTE BENING .... Gersh Agency
RICHARD BENJAMIN .... Gersh Agency
ROBBY BENSON .... Gordon/Rosson Talent Agency
TOM BERENGER .... CAA
PETER BERG .... ICM
CANDICE BERGEN .... William Morris Agency
FRANCES BERGEN .... The Craig Agency
POLLY BERGEN .... William Morris Agency
PATRICK BERGIN .... William Morris Agency
STEVEN BERKOFF .... The Gage Group

MILTON BERLE .... Lenhoff/Robinson Agency
CRYSTAL BERNARD .... William Morris Agency
JASON BERNARD .... Paul Kohner, Inc.
CORBIN BERNSEN .... ICM
HALLE BERRY .... William Morris Agency
VALERIE BERTINELLI .... William Morris Agency
BIBI BESCH .... Barrett, Benson, McCartt & Weston
MICHAEL BIEHN .... ICM
ROXANN BIGGS .... Bauman, Hiller & Associates
THEODORE BIKEL .... The Artists Group, Ltd.
JULIETTE BINOCHE .... UTA
KELLY BISHOP .... Abrams Artists & Associates
JACQUELINE BISSET .... William Morris Agency
JOSIE BISSETT .... Paul Kohner Agency
CLINT BLACK .... CAA
TAUREAN BLACQUE .... Paradigm
RUBÉN BLADES .... UTA
LINDA BLAIR .... Schiowitz, Clay & Rose
GEOFFREY BLAKE .... Harris & Goldberg
MARK BLANKFIELD .... Gordon/Rosson Talent Agency
CLAIRE BLOOM .... Marion Rosenberg Office
ROBERTS BLOSSOM .... Gersh Agency
LISA BLOUNT .... William Morris Agency
MARK BLUM .... APA
HART BOCHNER .... Perry & Neidorf
ERIC BOGOSIAN .... William Morris Agency
JOSEPH BOLOGNA .... The Blake Agency
PETER BONERZ .... CAA
HELENA BONHAM CARTER .... UTA
FRANK BONNER .... Paradigm
JAMES BOOTH .... Hillard Elkins
ERNEST BORGNINE .... Selected Artists Agency
KATHERINE BOROWITZ .... Gersh Agency
PHILIP BOSCO .... Judy Schoen & Associates
TOM BOSLEY .... Shapiro-Lichtman
BRIAN BOSWORTH .... The Artists Agency
SAM BOTTOMS .... The Agency
TIMOTHY BOTTOMS .... Bresler, Kelly & Kipperman
MICHAEL BOWEN .... Harris & Goldberg
DAVID BOWIE .... ICM
BRUCE BOXLEITNER .... William Morris Agency
GUY BOYD .... Gersh Agency
LARA FLYNN BOYLE .... Judy Schoen & Associates
LORRAINE BRACCO .... CAA
ALEJANDRO BRACHO .... Writers & Artists Agency
EDDIE BRACKEN .... William Morris Agency
JESSE BRADFORD .... William Morris Agency
RICHARD BRADFORD .... Susan Smith & Associates
DAVID BRADLEY .... Fred Amsel & Associates
RANDALL BRADY .... Michel Keeler
SONIA BRAGA .... ICM
KENNETH BRANAGH .... Paradigm
LILLO BRANCATO .... William Morris Agency
KLAUS MARIA BRANDAUER .... ICM
MARLON BRANDO .... ICM
MICHAEL BRANDON .... The Artists Agency
THOMAS BRAY .... CAA
PATRICK BREEN .... Gersh Agency
EILEEN BRENNAN .... David Shapira & Associates
MARTIN BREST .... CAA

BEAU BRIDGES ....CAA
JEFF BRIDGES ....CAA
LLOYD BRIDGES ....William Morris Agency
STEVEN BRILL ....Writers & Artists Agency
JIM BROADBENT ....William Morris Agency
KENT BROADHURST ....Silver, Kass & Massetti Agency
ANNE BROCHET ....Susan Smith & Associates
MATTHEW BRODERICK .... CAA
JOSH BROLIN .... ICM
CHARLES BRONSON ....William Morris Agency
JACQUELINE BROOKES ....William Morris Agency
RANDY BROOKS ....Paul Kohner, Inc.
PIERCE BROSNAN ....CAA
BLAIR BROWN .... ICM
BRYAN BROWN ....CAA
CLANCY BROWN ....Paradigm
GARRETT M. BROWN .... Gersh Agency
JULIE BROWN .... William Morris Agency
RALPH BROWN .... Susan Smith & Associates
REB BROWN .... Fred Amsel & Associates
THOMAS BROWN ....Century Artists, Ltd.
WOODY BROWN .... Gordon/Rosson Talent Agency
ROSCOE LEE BROWNE .... Susan Smith & Associates
TODD BRYANT .... Ambrosio-Mortimer
GENEVIEVE BUJOLD .... The Blake Agency
FRANCESCA BULLER .... Susan Smith & Associates
SANDRA BULLOCK .... UTA
DENNIS BURKLEY .... The Artists Agency
TOM BURLINSON .... Harris & Goldberg Talent & Literary Agency
CAROL BURNETT .... ICM
JERE BURNS .... Harris & Goldberg Talent & Literary Agency
ELLEN BURSTYN ....CAA
LeVAR BURTON ....The Marion Rosenberg Office
WENDELL BURTON .... Don Gerler & Associates
STEVE BUSCEMI ....Ambrosio-Mortimer
GARY BUSEY .... ICM
TIMOTHY BUSFIELD ....William Morris Agency
RUTH BUZZI ....The Artists Group, Ltd.
GABRIEL BYRNE .... ICM
SUSAN BYUN .... The Rainford Agency

C

JAMES CAAN .... UTA
SID CAESAR ....The Artists Group, Ltd.
NICOLAS CAGE .... ICM
R.D. CALL .... The Agency
K CALLAN ....The Gage Group
BILL CALVERT .... Paradigm
KIRK CAMERON .... UTA
BRUCE CAMPBELL .... APA
JULIA CAMPBELL ....William Morris Agency
MAE E. CAMPBELL .... Artists First, Inc.
TEVIN CAMPBELL ....CAA
RON CANADA .... Stone Manners Talent Agency
DYAN CANNON .... APA
FRANCIS CAPRA ....William Morris Agency
KATE CAPSHAW .... ICM

PAUL CARAFOTES .... Badgley/Connor
TIMOTHY CARHART .... Bauman, Hiller & Associates
GIA CARIDES .... William Morris Agency
LEN CARIOU .... Paradigm
GEORGE CARLIN ....William Morris Agency
GLORIA CARLIN ....Marshak-Wyckoff & Associates
JULIE CARMEN .... Metropolitan Talent Agency
LESLIE CARON .... The Blake Agency
JOHN CARPENTER .... ICM
KEITH CARRADINE .... ICM
ROBERT CARRADINE .... Innovative Artists
TIA CARRERE .... ICM
JIM CARREY .... UTA
DEBBIE LEE CARRINGTON .... Coralie Jr. Agency
DIAHANN CARROLL .... APA
JANET CARROLL .... Harris & Goldberg
ROCKY CARROLL ....Paradigm
ALICE CARTER ....Bauman, Hiller & Associates
LYNDA CARTER ....William Morris Agency
NELL CARTER .... William Morris Agency
VERONICA CARTWRIGHT .... William Morris Agency
DAVID CARUSO .... UTA
NICHOLAS CASCONE .... Susan Smith & Associates
MAX CASELLA .... William Morris Agency
JOHNNY CASH .... APA
ROSALIND CASH .... John Sekura/A Talent Agency
KATRINA CASPARY .... Booh Schut Agency
SEYMOUR CASSEL .... William Morris Agency
JOHN CASTLE .... Paradigm
PHOEBE CATES .... UTA
KIM CATTRALL .... William Morris Agency
MAXWELL CAULFIELD .... Harris & Goldberg
CHRISTOPHER CAZENOVE .... Paul Kohner, Inc.
RICHARD CHAMBERLAIN ....CAA
JO CHAMPA .... Metropolitan Talent Agency
MICHELE CHAN .... Twentieth Century Artists
SARI CHANG .... Abrams Artists & Associates
STOCKARD CHANNING.. ICM
GERALDINE CHAPLIN ....William Morris Agency
LONNY CHAPMAN .... Contemporary Artists
PATRICIA CHARBONNEAU ....Harris & Goldberg
CYD CHARISSE .... Shapiro-Lichtman
RAY CHARLES .... William Morris Agency
CHEVY CHASE ....CAA
MAURY CHAYKIN .... Gersh Agency
JOAN CHEN .... William Morris Agency
CHER .... CAA
LOIS CHILES .... APA
KIEU CHINH .... The Light Company
ANNA CHLUMSKY ....William Morris Agency
RAE DAWN CHONG .... William Morris Agency
CLAUDIA CHRISTIAN .... Abrams Artists & Associates
JULIE CHRISTIE .... ICM
ERIC CLAPTON ....CAA
BLAKE CLARK .... APA
MATT CLARK .... Paul Kohner, Inc.
NICHOLAS CLAY .... Susan Smith & Associates
JILL CLAYBURGH ....William Morris Agency
CHRISTIAN CLEMENSON .... Susan Smith & Associates

GLENN CLOSE .... CAA
JOHN SCOTT CLOUGH .... APA
RANDALL (TEX) COBB .... The Blake Agency
GEORGE COE .... Gersh Agency
JOEL COEN .... UTA
SCOTT COFFEY .... Harris & Goldberg
FRED COFFIN .... Susan Smith & Associates
MINDY COHN .... The Light Company
GARY COLE .... ICM
NATALIE COLE .... William Morris Agency
DABNEY COLEMAN .... ICM
MARGARET COLIN .... ICM
PAULINE COLLINS .... Susan Smith & Associates
PHIL COLLINS .... Camden ITG
STEPHEN COLLINS .... William Morris Agency
ROBBIE COLTRANE .... William Morris Agency
JEFFREY COMBS .... Borinstein/Oreck/Bogart Agency
DIDI CONN .... The Agency
JENNIFER CONNELLY .... ICM
JASON CONNERY .... Paradigm
SEAN CONNERY .... CAA
ROBERT CONRAD .... David Shapira & Associates
KEVIN CONROY .... Paradigm
KEVIN CONWAY .... Badgley/Connor
KEVIN COONEY .... The Gage Group
CHRIS COOPER .... APA
JACKIE COOPER .... Contemporary Artists
ROY COOPER .... APA
JOHN CORBETT .... CAA
BARRY CORBIN .... Writers & Artists Agency
MADDIE CORMAN .... The Agency
ELLIE CORNELL .... The Gage Group, Inc.
GEORGE CORRAFACE .... William Morris Agency
NICK CORRI .... The Marion Rosenberg Office
BUD CORT .... Judy Schoen & Associates
DAN CORTESE .... William Morris Agency
BILL COSBY .... William Morris Agency
NICOLAS COSTER .... The Artists Group, Ltd.
KEVIN COSTNER .... CAA
CLOTILDE COURAU .... William Morris Agency
BRIAN COX .... The Marion Rosenberg Office
COURTENEY COX .... CAA
MITCHELL COX .... Marc Rindner
BARBARA CRAMPTON .... The Artists Agency
MATT CRAVEN .... ICM
RICHARD CRENNA .... CAA
JAMES CROMWELL .... Century Artists, Ltd.
DAVID CRONENBERG .... CAA
HUME CRONYN .... ICM
DENISE CROSBY .... Gersh Agency
BEN CROSS .... APA
HARLEY CROSS .... William Morris Agency
LINDSAY CROUSE .... Susan Smith & Associates
ASHLEY CROW .... William Morris Agency
RUSSELL CROWE .... ICM
TOM CRUISE .... CAA
BILLY CRYSTAL .... ICM
MACAULAY CULKIN .... ICM
JOHN CULLUM .... ICM
QUINN CUMMINGS .... Susan Smith & Associates

TIM CURRY .... UTA
VALERIE CURTIN .... CAA
JAMIE LEE CURTIS .... CAA
TONY CURTIS .... The Blake Agency
JOAN CUSACK .... ICM
JOHN CUSACK .... William Morris Agency
HENRY CZERNY .... William Morris Agency

D

OLIVIA D'ABO .... ICM
WILLEM DAFOE .... CAA
JENSEN DAGGETT .... The Agency
E.G. DAILY .... Flick East/West Talent, Inc.
JOE DALLESANDRO .... Flick East/West Talent, Inc.
TIMOTHY DALTON .... ICM
ROGER DALTREY .... APA
TIMOTHY DALY .... Gersh Agency
TYNE DALY .... The Blake Agency
FRANC D'AMBROSIO .... Gersh Agency
LEO DAMIAN .... CNA & Associates
MATT DAMON .... UTA
MALCOLM DANARE .... John Crosby
CHARLES DANCE .... William Morris Agency
LAWRENCE DANE .... The Artists Group, Ltd.
BEVERLY D'ANGELO .... William Morris Agency
ALEX DANIELS .... Herb Tannen & Associates
JEFF DANIELS .... ICM
WILLIAM DANIELS .... The Artists Agency
ELI DANKER .... The Actors Group Agency
TED DANSON .... CAA
TONY DANZA .... ICM
PATTI D'ARBANVILLE .... Harris & Goldberg
PATRIKA DARBO .... Booh Schut Agency
MICHAEL DARRELL .... Erika Wain Agency
STACEY DASH .... The Actors Group Agency
ROBERT DAVI .... APA
LOLITA DAVIDOVICH .... ICM
EILEEN DAVIDSON .... Metropolitan Talent Agency
TOMMY DAVIDSON .... William Morris Agency
EMBETH DAVIDTZ .... William Morris Agency
GEENA DAVIS .... CAA
OSSIE DAVIS .... The Artists Agency
VIVEKA DAVIS .... The Gordon/Rosson Company
BRUCE DAVISON .... William Morris Agency
PAM DAWBER .... ICM
DANIEL DAY-LEWIS .... William Morris Agency
RON DEAN .... The Geddes Agency
JUSTIN DEAS .... Paradigm
JEAN DEBAER .... Writers & Artists Agency
YVONNE DE CARLO .... Ruth Webb Enterprises, Inc.
RUBY DEE .... The Artists Agency
DANA DELANY .... ICM
DANNY DE LA PAZ .... The Agency
GEORGE DE LA PEÑA .... The Lantz Office
JULIE DELPY .... William Morris Agency
MARIA DE MEDEIROS .... William Morris Agency
REBECCA DE MORNAY .... ICM

PATRICK DEMPSEY ....CAA
LYDIE DENIER .... The Craig Agency
ROBERT DE NIRO ....CAA
ANTHONY DENISON ....Paradigm
BRIAN DENNEHY .... Susan Smith & Associates
JOHN DENVER .... William Morris Agency
GÉRARD DEPARDIEU ....CAA
JOHNNY DEPP .... ICM
BO DEREK .... ICM
BRUCE DERN .... CAA
LAURA DERN .... UTA
CLEAVANT DERRICKS .... Susan Smith & Associates
ANNE DESALVO .... Gersh Agency
MARY JO DESCHANEL .... Bauman Hiller & Associates
ROBERT DESIDERIO .... Gersh Agency
MARUSCHKA DETMERS .... William Morris Agency
WILLIAM DEVANE ....APA
DANNY DEVITO ....CAA
SUSAN DEY .... ICM
CAMERON DIAZ .... ICM
LEONARDO DICAPRIO ....CAA
GEORGE DICKERSON .... Badgley/Connor
ANGIE DICKINSON .... The Blake Agency
PHYLLIS DILLER .... Milton B. Suchin
BRADFORD DILLMAN .... The Artists Group, Ltd.
PAMELA DILLMAN ....Braverman, Gekis & Bloom
KEVIN DILLON .... ICM
MATT DILLON .... William Morris Agency
RICHARD DIMITRI ....Paradigm
JOHN DISANTI .... Stone Manners Talent Agency
KEVIN DOBSON .... Century Artists, Ltd.
JOHN DOE .... William Morris Agency
SHANNEN DOHERTY ....William Morris Agency
AMI DOLENZ .... Gersh Agency
ELINOR DONAHUE .... Fred Amsel & Associates, Inc.
PETER DONAT .... Gersh Agency
ROBERT DONNER .... J. Carter Gibson Agency
AMANDA DONOHOE ....William Morris Agency
ERIN DONOVAN .... Selected Artists Agency
TATE DONOVAN .... Gersh Agency
PAUL DOOLEY .... ICM
JOHN DOOLITTLE .... Badgley/Connor
ROBERT DOQUI .... The Gage Group
ROY DOTRICE ....The Lantz Office
DAVID DOTY .... The Gage Group
DOUG E. DOUG ....William Morris Agency
KIRK DOUGLAS ....CAA
MICHAEL DOUGLAS ....CAA
SARAH DOUGLAS .... Stone Manners Talent Agency
MORTON DOWNEY, JR. .... The Agency
ROBERT DOWNEY, JR. ....CAA
DAVID DOYLE .... The Gage Group
BRIAN DOYLE-MURRAY .... Abrams Artists & Associates
FRAN DRESCHER .... Gersh Agency
RICHARD DREYFUSS .... ICM
RICK DUCOMMUN ....William Morris Agency
MICHAEL DUDIKOFF .... The Craig Agency
PATRICK DUFFY ....Writers & Artists Agency
DENNIS DUGAN .... Gersh Agency
TOM DUGAN .... Atkins & Associates

OLYMPIA DUKAKIS ....William Morris Agency
PATTY DUKE ....William Morris Agency
DAVID DUKES .... ICM
DENISE DUMMONT .... Artists First, Inc.
FAYE DUNAWAY .... ICM
ADRIAN DUNBAR ....William Morris Agency
VIC DUNLOP .... CNA & Associates
KEVIN DUNN .... Paradigm
GRIFFIN DUNNE .... UTA
V.C. DUPREE .... Brooke, Dunn & Oliver
CHARLES DURNING ....Paradigm
MARJ DUSAY .... Fred Amsel & Associates
ANN DUSENBERRY .... J. Michael Bloom & Associates
CHARLES S. DUTTON ....CAA
ROBERT DUVALL ....William Morris Agency
SHELLEY DUVALL .... Gersh Agency
RICHARD DYSART .... Writers & Artists Agency

E

JEFF EAST .... The Artists Group, Ltd.
LESLIE EASTERBROOK .... The Marion Rosenberg Office
RICHARD EASTON .... Bauman, Hiller & Associates
CLINT EASTWOOD .... William Morris Agency
CHRISTINE EBERSOLE .... ICM
JAMES ECKHOUSE .... Writers & Artists Agency
BARBARA EDEN ....William Morris Agency
JENNIFER EDWARDS .... Gersh Agency
SAMANTHA EGGAR .... The Craig Agency
LISA EICHHORN .... Writers & Artists Agency
JILL EIKENBERRY ....William Morris Agency
LISA EILBACHER ....APA
JANET EILBER .... The Light Company
ERIKA ELENIAK .... Abrams Artists & Associates
HECTOR ELIZONDO ....William Morris Agency
CHRIS ELLIOTT ....William Morris Agency
SAM ELLIOTT .... William Morris Agency
STEPHEN ELLIOTT .... Harris & Goldberg
CARY ELWES .... UTA
OMAR EPPS .... Gersh Agency
KATHRYN ERBE ....William Morris Agency
LEE ERMEY .... Harris & Goldberg
GIANCARLO ESPOSITO .... Badgley/Connor
LINDA EVANS .... William Morris Agency
CHAD EVERETT .... Camden ITG
NANCY EVERHARD ....The Light Company
GREG EVIGAN .... The Blake Agency

F

MORGAN FAIRCHILD .... Camden ITG
LISANNE FALK................................. Gersh Agency
PETER FALK .... ICM
ANTONIO FARGAS .... Gersh Agency
DENNIS FARINA .... Getty's Agency
CHRIS FARLEY ....CAA

RICHARD FARNSWORTH .... Twentieth Century Artists
MIKE FARRELL .... Paradigm
TERRY FARRELL .... Flick East/West Talent, Inc.
MIA FARROW .... UTA
FARRAH FAWCETT .... William Morris Agency
COREY FELDMAN .... APA
TOVAH FELDSHUH .... William Morris Agency
SHERILYN FENN .... The Agency
MIGUEL FERRER .... William Morris Agency
MILES FEULNER .... Susan Smith & Associates
CHELSEA FIELD .... Gersh Agency
SALLY FIELD .... CAA
HARVEY FIERSTEIN .... Gersh Agency
TRAVIS FINE .... Susan Smith & Associates
JOHN FINN .... Susan Smith & Associates
ALBERT FINNEY .... ICM
LINDA FIORENTINO .... UTA
PETER FIRTH .... Susan Smith & Associates
LAURENCE FISHBURNE .... Paradigm
CARRIE FISHER .... CAA
FRANCES FISHER .... UTA
TRICIA LEIGH FISHER .... The Gordon/Rosson Company
TARA FITZGERALD .... William Morris Agency
FANNIE FLAGG .... CAA
CHARLES FLEISCHER .... APA
LOUISE FLETCHER .... Gersh Agency
DARLANNE FLEUGEL .... Harris & Goldberg
NINA FOCH .... William Morris Agency
DAVID FOLEY .... William Morris Agency
ELLEN FOLEY .... Gersh Agency
MEGAN PORTER FOLLOWS .... Susan Smith & Associates
BRIDGET FONDA .... UTA
JANE FONDA .... CAA
HALLIE FOOTE .... The Blake Agency
MICHELLE FORBES .... UTA
FAITH FORD .... UTA
HARRISON FORD .... McQueeney Management
FREDERIC FORREST .... Camden ITG
SUSAN FORRISTAL .... Flick East/West Talent, Inc.
ROBERT FORSTER .... APA
JOHN FORSYTHE .... Paradigm
WILLIAM FORSYTHE .... UTA
JODIE FOSTER .... ICM
KIMBERLY FOSTER .... APA
MICHAEL J. FOX .... CAA
ROBERT FOXWORTH .... APA
JONATHAN FRAKES .... Paradigm
ARETHA FRANKLIN .... William Morris Agency
DIANE FRANKLIN .... Special Artists Agency
DENNIS FRANZ .... Paradigm
BRENDAN FRASER .... William Morris Agency
RON FRAZIER .... Susan Smith & Associates
KATHLEEN FREEMAN .... Henderson/Hogan
MORGAN FREEMAN .... William Morris Agency
MATT FREWER .... Paradigm
BRENDA FRICKER .... Writers & Artists Agency
PETER FRIEDMAN .... Gersh Agency
STEPHEN FRY .... William Morris Agency

G

JENNY GAGO .... Paul Kohner, Inc.
CHARLOTTE GAINSBOURG .... William Morris Agency
PETER GALLAGHER .... ICM
GINA GALLEGO .... Belson & Klass Associates
MICHAEL GAMBON .... Paradigm
ROBIN GAMMEL .... The Blake Agency
JAMES GAMMON .... The Blake Agency
ANDY GARCIA .... Paradigm
LEE GARLINGTON .... Paul Kohner, Inc.
JAMES GARNER .... ICM
TERI GARR .... CAA
GEORGE GAYNES .... William Morris Agency
JASON GEDRICK .... UTA
MARTHA GEHMAN .... Flick East/West Talent, Inc.
RICHARD GERE .... ICM
SAVINA GERSAK .... Century Artists, Ltd.
JAMI GERTZ .... ICM
BALTHAZAR GETTY .... William Morris Agency
ESTELLE GETTY .... Jack Rose Agency
JOHN GETZ .... Gersh Agency
ALICE GHOSTLEY .... APA
LOUIS GIAMBALVO .... Gersh Agency
CYNTHIA GIBB .... William Morris Agency
LEEZA GIBBONS .... William Morris Agency
MEL GIBSON .... ICM
JOHN GIELGUD .... ICM
STEFAN GIERASCH .... Paradigm
MELISSA GILBERT .... William Morris Agency
SARA GILBERT .... William Morris Agency
NANCY GILES .... The Agency
LINDA GILLEN .... Gersh Agency
TERRY GILLIAM .... CAA
ANNABETH GISH .... ICM
MATTHEW GLAVE .... Susan Smith & Associates
SHARON GLESS .... William Morris Agency
DANNY GLOVER .... William Morris Agency
CARLIN GLYNN .... William Morris Agency
JOANNA GOING .... William Morris Agency
WHOOPI GOLDBERG .... CAA
RICKY PAULL GOLDIN .... Metropolitan Talent Agency
MARCY GOLDMAN .... Rickey Barr Agency
JENETTE GOLDSTEIN .... Harris & Goldberg
TONY GOLDWYN .... CAA
VALERIA GOLINO .... CAA
JOHN GOODMAN .... Gersh Agency
DEBORAH GOODRICH .... CNA & Associates
MICHAEL GOORJIAN .... APA
CLIFF GORMAN .... Paradigm
KAREN LYNN GORNEY .... Lucy Kroll Agency
LOUIS GOSSETT JR. .... CAA
GILBERT GOTTFRIED .... William Morris Agency
MICHAEL GOUGH .... Gersh Agency
ELLIOTT GOULD .... Shapira & Associates
GARY GRAHAM .... Metropolitan Talent Agency
GERRITT GRAHAM .... Gersh Agency
HEATHER GRAHAM .... CAA

DAVID MARSHALL GRANT ....ICM
LEE GRANT .... Camden ITG
RODNEY A. GRANT .... The Geddes Agency
RUPERT GRAVES ....William Morris Agency
ELLEN GREENE ....William Morris Agency
GRAHAM GREENE .... Susan Smith & Associates
BRUCE GREENWOOD .... APA
BRADLEY GREGG..Paradigm
ANDRE GREGORY ....William Morris Agency
JENNIFER GREY ....CAA
JOEL GREY .... William Morris Agency
RICHARD GRIECO ....CAA
DAVID ALAN GRIER ....William Morris Agency
PAM GRIER .... APA
JONATHAN GRIES .... Susan Smith & Associates
EDDIE GRIFFIN ....William Morris Agency
ANDY GRIFFITH ....William Morris Agency
MELANIE GRIFFITH ....ICM
RICHARD GRIFFITHS ....William Morris Agency
THOMAS IAN GRIFFITH ....CAA
SCOTT GRIMES .... Metropolitan Talent Agency
GEORGE GRIZZARD ....Paradigm
CHARLES GRODIN .... UTA
ARYE GROSS .... William Morris Agency
GARY GRUBBS ....Paradigm
HARRY GUARDINO .... The Artists Group
CASTULO GUERRA ....Paradigm
CHRISTOPHER GUEST ....CAA
CARLA GUGINO ....William Morris Agency
ROBERT GUILLAUME .... The Blake Agency
TIM GUINEE .... William Morris Agency
STEVE GUTTENBERG ....William Morris Agency
MICHAEL C. GWYNNE .... Susan Smith & Associates

MELORA HARDIN ....Writers & Artists Agency
JOHN HARKINS .... Susan Smith & Associates
MARK HARMON .... UTA
TESS HARPER .... William Morris Agency
VALERIE HARPER .... William Morris Agency
WOODY HARRELSON ....CAA
BARBARA HARRIS .... Bresler, Kelly & Kipperman
ED HARRIS .... CAA
JULIE HARRIS .... William Morris Agency
MEL HARRIS .... Gersh Agency
NEIL PATRICK HARRIS .... ICM
RICHARD HARRIS ....William Morris Agency
GREGORY HARRISON ....William Morris Agency
KATHRYN HARROLD ....William Morris Agency
DEBORAH HARRY ....William Morris Agency
PHIL HARTMAN ....William Morris Agency
LISA HARTMAN-BLACK .... David Shapira & Associates
DON HARVEY .... Abrams Artists & Associates
RODNEY HARVEY .... Flick East/West Talent, Inc.
TERI HATCHER ....William Morris Agency
RUTGER HAUER ....William Morris Agency
ALLAN HAVEY .... William Morris Agency
ETHAN HAWKE ....CAA
GOLDIE HAWN ....CAA
JEFF HAYENGA .... The Gage Group
DENNIS HAYSBERT ....Paradigm
SHARI HEADLEY .... Writers & Artists Agency
GLENNE HEADLY .... ICM
PAUL HECHT .... Susan Smith & Associates
EILEEN HECKART .... APA
DAVID HEDISON .... Fred Amsel & Associates
MARG HELGENBERGER .... Gersh Agency
KATHERINE HELMOND ....William Morris Agency
MARIEL HEMINGWAY .... ICM
FLORENCE HENDERSON .... APA
MARILU HENNER ....William Morris Agency
LANCE HENRIKSEN .... APA
BUCK HENRY .... William Morris Agency
GREGG HENRY .... Susan Smith & Associates
JUSTIN HENRY .... Susan Smith & Associates
LENNY HENRY .... William Morris Agency
RICHARD HERD .... Harris & Goldberg
EDWARD HERRMANN ....William Morris Agency
BARBARA HERSHEY ....CAA
HOWARD HESSEMAN .... APA
CHARLTON HESTON .... ICM
MARTIN HEWITT .... ICM
WILLIAM HICKEY .... Harris & Goldberg
CATHERINE HICKLAND .... Fred Amsel & Associates
CATHERINE HICKS .... Susan Smith & Associates
ANTHONY HIGGINS .... William Morris Agency
MICHAEL HIGGINS............................ The Artists Group, Ltd.
ARTHUR HILL .... CAA
DANA HILL .... The Artists Group, Ltd.
GREGORY HINES ....CAA
PAT HINGLE .... The Blake Agency
JUDITH HOAG .... Bauman, Hiller & Associates
PATRICIA HODGE .... Susan Smith & Associates
ISABELLA HOFMANN .... Susan Smith & Associates
DOMINIC HOFFMAN .... Silver, Kass & Massetti Agency, Ltd.

H

LUKAS HAAS .... CAA
GENE HACKMAN..CAA
CHARLES HAID ....William Morris Agency
COREY HAIM .... APA
BARBARA HALE ....David Shapira & Associates
ARSENIO HALL..CAA
DEAN HALLO .... Judy Schoen & Associates
VERONICA HAMEL................................William Morris Agency
MARK HAMILL .... APA
CARRIE HAMILTON .... The Blake Agency
GEORGE HAMILTON .... APA
JOSH HAMILTON ....William Morris Agency
LINDA HAMILTON .... ICM
JAMES HAMPTON .... The Artists Group, Ltd.
TERRI HANAUER ....Writers & Artists Agency
HERBIE HANCOCK ....CAA
JAMES HANDY .... APA
LARRY HANKIN .... Gold/Marshak & Associates
TOM HANKS.. CAA
DARYL HANNAH .... ICM
MARCIA GAY HARDEN ....William Morris Agency
JERRY HARDIN .... Susan Smith & Associates

DUSTIN HOFFMAN ....CAA
PAUL HOGAN .... CAA
POLLY HOLLIDAY ....The Blake Agency
POLLY HOLLIDAY ....The Lantz Office
LAUREN HOLLY ....UTA
CELESTE HOLM .... Mishkin Agency
IAN HOLM .... William Morris Agency
JAN HOOKS .... William Morris Agency
WILLIAM HOOTKINS .... Metropolitan Talent Agency
BOB HOPE .... ICM
LESLIE HOPE .... William Morris Agency
ANTHONY HOPKINS .... ICM
BO HOPKINS ....The Artists Group, Ltd.
DENNIS HOPPER ....CAA
WIL HORNEFF .... William Morris Agency
ADAM HOROVITZ .... Gersh Agency
LEE HORSLEY .... Harris & Goldberg
MICHAEL HORTON ....Paul Kohner, Inc.
PETER HORTON ....UTA
BOB HOSKINS ....CAA
WHITNEY HOUSTON .... William Morris Agency
RON HOWARD..CAA
C. THOMAS HOWELL .... William Morris Agency
ERNIE HUDSON .... Gersh Agency
FINOLA HUGHES .... Gersh Agency
TOM HULCE .... CAA
DIANNE HULL .... Contemporary Artists
HELEN HUNT ....CAA
LINDA HUNT .... William Morris Agency
HOLLY HUNTER .... ICM
ISABELLE HUPPERT ....UTA
JOHN HURT .... William Morris Agency
ANJELICA HUSTON .... ICM
DOUG HUTCHISON .... Gersh Agency
LAUREN HUTTON ....CAA
TIMOTHY HUTTON ....UTA
JONATHAN HYDE .... William Morris Agency

I

ICE CUBE .... William Morris Agency
ICE-T...UTA
ERIC IDLE .... William Morris Agency
MICHAEL IMPERIOLI .... William Morris Agency
JEREMY IRONS ....CAA
AMY IRVING .... William Morris Agency
BILL IRWIN .... ICM
CHRIS ISAAK ....UTA

J

JANET JACKSON ....CAA
JOSHUA JACKSON .... William Morris Agency
MICHAEL JACKSON ....CAA
VICTORIA JACKSON .... William Morris Agency
RICHARD JAECKEL .... David Shapira & Associates
RICHARD JENKINS .... William Morris Agency

SALOME JENS .... Badgley/Connor
PENN JILLETTE .... William Morris Agency
ANN JILLIAN .... William Morris Agency
GLYNIS JOHNS ....Susan Smith & Associates
ANNE MARIE JOHNSON .... Gordon/Rosson Talent Agency
BRAD JOHNSON ....CAA
DON JOHNSON .... ICM
MEL JOHNSON, JR. .... Gersh Agency
MIKE JOLLY .... Judy Schoen and Associates
DEAN JONES .... The Blake Agency
JAMES EARL JONES .... Bauman, Hiller & Associates
JEFFREY JONES .... J. Michael Bloom & Associates
QUINCY JONES .... William Morris Agency
RENEE JONES .... Harris & Goldberg
TOMMY LEE JONES .... ICM
RONALD G. JOSEPH .... Fred Amsel & Associates
ERLAND JOSEPHSON .... Susan Smith & Associates
ROBERT JOY .... William Morris Agency
ASHLEY JUDD .... William Morris Agency
RAUL JULIA .... William Morris Agency
CALVIN JUNG .... Fred Amsel & Associates

K

DAVID KAGEN .... Bauman, Hiller & Associates
STEVE KAHAN .... Paradigm
PATRICIA KALEMBER .... Gersh Agency
SEAN KANAN .... Harris & Goldberg
IVAN KANE .... Judy Schoen & Associates
MITZI KAPTURE .... David Shapira & Associates
JOHN KARLEN .... Gersh Agency
WILLIAM KATT .... APA
JAMES KEACH ....Metropolitan Talent Agency
STACY KEACH .... William Morris Agency
DIANE KEATON ....William Morris Agency
MICHAEL KEATON ....CAA
HOWARD KEEL .... Abrams Artists & Associates
HARVEY KEITEL.................................William Morris Agency
BRIAN KEITH .... The Blake Agency
DAVID KEITH .... William Morris Agency
SALLY KELLERMAN .... Gersh Agency
DEFOREST KELLEY .... The Blake Agency
SHEILA KELLEY ....UTA
LINDA KELSEY .... Harris & Goldberg
GEORGE KENNEDY .... Paradigm
BRIAN KERWIN .... William Morris Agency
KID .... William Morris Agency
MARGOT KIDDER .... Marion Rosenberg Office
NICOLE KIDMAN ....CAA
VAL KILMER .... CAA
CHARLES KIMBROUGH .... J. Michael Bloom & Associates
ALAN KING .... William Morris Agency
PERRY KING .... CAA
ROWENA KING .... William Morris Agency
STEPHEN KING ....CAA
BEN KINGSLEY .... ICM
TERRY KINNEY .... William Morris Agency
NASTASSJA KINSKI .... ICM

BRUNO KIRBY .... William Morris Agency
TERRY KISER .... Bauman, Hiller & Associates
ROBERT KLEIN .... APA
KEVIN KLINE .... CAA
SHIRLEY KNIGHT .... Gersh Agency
WAYNE KNIGHT .... Gersh Agency
JEFF KOBER .... Gersh Agency
MARY KOHNERT .... J. Michael Bloom & Associates
PAUL KOSLO .... The Artists Agency
YAPHET KOTTO .... The Artists Group, Ltd.
MARTIN KOVE .... Stone Manners Agency
HARLEY JANE KOZAK .... UTA
LINDA KOZLOWSKI .... William Morris Agency
JEROEN KRABBÉ .... The Marion Rosenberg Office
BRIAN KRAUSE .... William Morris Agency
KRIS KRISTOFFERSON .... ICM
DAVID KRUMHOLTZ .... Carson/Adler Agency
SWOOSIE KURTZ .... APA

L

RONALD LACEY .... The Marion Rosenberg Office
DIANE LADD .... The Marion Rosenberg Office
RICKI LAKE .... William Morris Agency
LORENZO LAMAS .... David Shapira & Associates
CHRISTOPHER LAMBERT .... UTA
DOROTHY LAMOUR .... Fred Amsel & Associates
BURT LANCASTER .... ICM
MARTIN LANDAU .... William Morris Agency
DIANE LANE .... William Morris Agency
NATHAN LANE .... William Morris Agency
STEPHEN LANG .... William Morris Agency
HOPE LANGE .... Century Artists, Ltd.
JESSICA LANGE .... CAA
FRANK LANGELLA .... Harris & Goldberg
LISA LANGLOIS .... Bauman, Hiller & Associates
ANGELA LANSBURY .... William Morris Agency
ALISON LA PLACA .... APA
JOHN LARROQUETTE .... CAA
LOUISE LATHAM .... Badgley/Connor
CYNDI LAUPER .... William Morris Agency
HUGH LAURIE .... William Morris Agency
PIPER LAURIE .... William Morris Agency
ED LAUTER .... Gersh Agency
RICHARD LAWSON .... ICM
CLORIS LEACHMAN .... Metropolitan Talent Agency
DENIS LEARY .... William Morris Agency
SHERYL LEE .... William Morris Agency
JAMES LE GROS .... William Morris Agency
JOHN LEGUIZAMO .... William Morris Agency
RON LEIBMAN .... Gersh Agency
JANET LEIGH .... Fred Amsel & Associates
JENNIFER JASON LEIGH .... ICM
DAVID LEISURE .... Harris & Goldberg
DONOVAN LEITCH .... William Morris Agency
CHRIS LEMMON .... Gordon/Rosson Talent Agency
JACK LEMMON .... CAA
HARRY J. LENNIX .... William Morris Agency

KAY LENZ .... The Gage Group
LEON .... UTA
ROBERT SEAN LEONARD .... William Morris Agency
KEN LERNER .... Fred Amsel & Associates
MICHAEL LERNER .... Gersh Agency
DAVID LETTERMAN .... CAA
ANNA LEVINE .... APA
BARRY LEVINSON .... CAA
STEVE LEVITT .... Badgley/Connor
EUGENE LEVY .... William Morris Agency
DAWNN LEWIS .... Badgley/Connor
GEOFFREY LEWIS .... William Morris Agency
JERRY LEWIS .... William Morris Agency
JULIETTE LEWIS .... William Morris Agency
PHILL LEWIS .... The Artists Agency
RICHARD LEWIS .... ICM
HAL LINDEN .... William Morris Agency
VIVECA LINDFORS .... Paul Kohner, Inc.
AUDRA LINDLEY .... Badgley/Connor
DELROY LINDO .... William Morris Agency
ROBERT LINDSAY .... William Morris Agency
LARRY LINVILLE .... Stone Manners Talent Agency
RAY LIOTTA .... CAA
DENNIS LIPSCOMB .... Harris & Goldberg
JOHN LITHGOW .... CAA
MICHELLE LITTLE .... The Agency
LITTLE RICHARD .... William Morris Agency
ROBYN LIVELY .... Abrams Artists & Associates
LL COOL J .... ICM
CHRISTOPHER LLOYD .... Gersh Agency
EMILY LLOYD .... William Morris Agency
TONY LoBIANCO .... David Shapira & Associates
SONDRA LOCKE .... Bauer Benedek Agency
JUNE LOCKHART .... APA
HEATHER LOCKLEAR .... William Morris Agency
ROBERT LOGGIA .... CAA
KARINA LOMBARD .... William Morris Agency
JASON LONDON .... William Morris Agency
JOHN LONE .... UTA
JODI LONG .... Flick East/West Talent, Inc.
SHELLEY LONG .... CAA
TONY LONGO .... Stone Manners Talent Agency
LORI LOUGHLIN .... William Morris Agency
JULIA LOUIS-DREYFUSS .... UTA
JON LOVITZ .... CAA
CHAD LOWE .... William Morris Agency
T.J. LOWTHER .... William Morris Agency
LISA LUCAS .... Susan Smith & Associates
CARL LUMBLY .... Writers & Artists Agency
DOLPH LUNDGREN .... William Morris Agency
JESSICA LUNDY .... William Morris Agency
PATTI LUPONE .... Gersh Agency
FRANC LUZ .... Judy Schoen & Associates
DAVID LYNCH .... CAA
KELLY LYNCH .... William Morris Agency

M

KATE MABERLY .... William Morris Agency
BERNIE MAC .... UTA
RALPH MACCHIO .... ICM
MIKE MacDONALD .... Spotlite Enterprises
ANDIE MacDOWELL .... ICM
KYLE MacLACHLAN .... UTA
SHIRLEY MacLAINE .... ICM
PATRICK MacNEE .... The Irv Schechter Company
BILL MACY .... Writers & Artists Agency
AMY MADIGAN .... William Morris Agency
MADONNA .... CAA
MICHAEL MADSEN .... CAA
JOSEPH MAHER .... Writers & Artists Agency
LEE MAJORS .... David Shapira & Associates
PAULA MALCOMSON .... Circle Talent Associates
KARL MALDEN .... CAA
WENDIE MALICK .... Camden ITG
NICK MANCUSO .... Gersh Agency
HOWIE MANDELL .... ICM
COSTAS MANDYLOR .... William Morris Agency
DINAH MANOFF .... Gersh Agency
PAUL MANTEE .... Flick
JOE MANTEGNA .... Peter Strain & Associates
PETER MARC .... Paul Kohner, Inc.
NANCY MARCHAND .... APA
DAVID MARCIANO .... Bauman, Hiller & Associates
STUART MARGOLIN .... ICM
MIRIAM MARGOLYES .... Susan Smith & Associates
CHEECH MARIN .... CAA
DAVID ANTHONY MARSHALL .... Geddes Agency
GARRY MARSHALL .... ICM
PENNY MARSHALL .... CAA
ANDREA MARTIN .... William Morris Agency
GEORGE MARTIN .... ICM
SHARON MARTIN .... Metropolitan Talent Agency
STEVE MARTIN .... ICM
A MARTINEZ .... William Morris Agency
MADISON MASON .... Craig Agency
MARSHA MASON .... ICM
BEN MASTERS .... J. Michael Bloom & Associates
FAY MASTERSON .... Susan Smith & Associates
MARY STUART MASTERSON .... William Morris Agency
MARY ELIZABETH MASTRANTONIO .... CAA
RICHARD MASUR .... Susan Smith & Associates
TIM MATHESON .... CAA
THOM MATHEWS .... Metropolitan Talent Agency
MARLEE MATLIN .... ICM
WALTER MATTHAU .... William Morris Agency
DAKIN MATTHEWS .... Henderson/Hogan Agency
CARMEN MAURA .... William Morris Agency
ELAINE MAY .... CAA
JODHI MAY .... William Morris Agency
PAUL MAZURSKY .... ICM
ALEX McARTHUR .... ICM
ANDREW McCARTHY .... ICM
RUE McCLANAHAN .... APA

MATTHEW McCONAUGHEY .... William Morris Agency
MATT McCOY .... Metropolitan Talent Agency
MATTHEW McCURLEY .... William Morris Agency
DYLAN McDERMOTT .... CAA
CHRISTOPHER McDONALD .... William Morris Agency
MARY McDONNELL .... William Morris Agency
FRANCES McDORMAND .... William Morris Agency
RODDY McDOWALL .... Harris & Goldberg Agency
REBA McENTIRE .... William Morris Agency
JACK McGEE .... Camden ITG
KELLY McGILLIS .... ICM
JOHN C. McGINLEY .... Harris & Goldberg
IAN McKELLEN .... APA
NANCY McKEON .... William Morris Agency
BILL McKINNEY .... The Barry Freed Company
GERALD McRANEY .... Karg-Weissenback & Associates
ANNE MEARA .... Innovative Artists
MEAT LOAF .... William Morris Agency
JOHN MELLENCAMP .... CAA
BEN MENDELSOHN .... Susan Smith & Associates
LAURIE METCALF .... ICM
DALE MIDKIFF .... Gersh Agency
BETTE MIDLER .... CAA
ALYSSA MILANO .... William Morris Agency
SARAH MILES .... Harris & Goldberg Agency
FRANK MILITARY .... William Morris Agency
DICK MILLER .... Contemporary Artists
PENELOPE ANN MILLER .... CAA
REBECCA MILLER .... William Morris Agency
HAYLEY MILLS .... Susan Smith & Associates
ROBERT G. MIRANDA .... Marc Rindner
JOHN CAMERON MITCHELL .... Geddes Agency
ROBERT MITCHUM .... ICM
KIM MIYORI .... Susan Smith & Associates
MATTHEW MODINE .... William Morris Agency
D.W. MOFFETT .... William Morris Agency
RICHARD MOLL .... Abrams Artists & Associates
STEVE MONARQUE .... J. Michael Bloom & Associates
LAWRENCE MONOSON .... Harris & Goldberg
DEMI MOORE .... CAA
DUDLEY MOORE .... ICM
JULIANNE MOORE .... CAA
MARY TYLER MOORE .... William Morris Agency
ESAI MORALES .... William Morris Agency
RICK MORANIS .... CAA
JEANNE MOREAU .... William Morris Agency
CATHY MORIARTY .... ICM
ROB MORROW .... William Morris Agency
DAVID MORSE .... Yvette Bikoff Agency
JOE MORTON .... Judy Schoen & Associates
DAVID MOSCOW .... J. Michael Bloom & Associates
WILLIAM R. MOSES .... Gersh Agency
ROGER E. MOSLEY .... Craig Agency
JOSH MOSTEL .... William Morris Agency
ARMIN MUELLER-STAHL .... Paul Kohner, Inc.
DIANA MULDAUR .... The Artists Group
MARTIN MULL .... William Morris Agency
RICHARD MULLIGAN .... ICM
DERMOT MULRONEY .... CAA
KIERNAN MULRONEY .... Bresler, Kelly & Kipperman

EDDIE MURPHY ....CAA
MICHAEL MURPHY .... ICM
BILL MURRAY ....CAA
DON MURRAY ....David Shapira & Associates
MIKE MYERS .... UTA

N

KATHY NAJIMY .... ICM
JAMES NAUGHTON .... ICM
LIAM NEESON .... CAA
SAM NEILL .... ICM
CRAIG T. NELSON .... ICM
CORIN NEMEC .... ICM
BEBE NEUWIRTH .... ICM
GEORGE NEWBERN .... UTA
BOB NEWHART ....William Morris Agency
PAUL NEWMAN ....CAA
HAING S. NGOR ....The Marion Rosenberg Office
DENISE NICHOLAS ....Paul Kohner, Inc.
NICHELLE NICHOLS .... The Artists Group
JACK NICHOLSON ....Bresler Kelly Kipperman Agency
LESLIE NIELSEN ....Bresler-Kelly Agency
NICK NOLTE .... ICM
KIM NOVAK .... William Morris Agency
BILL NUNN .... William Morris Agency
FRANCE NUYEN .... The Gage Group

O

AUSTIN O'BRIEN .... ICM
DERRICK O'CONNOR ....Susan Smith & Associates
KEVIN J. O'CONNOR .... Gersh Agency
HUGH O'CONOR ....William Morris Agency
CHRIS O'DONNELL .... CAA
ROSIE O'DONNELL .... ICM
CATHERINE O'HARA .... ICM
LENA OLIN .... ICM
EDWARD JAMES OLMOS .... The Artists Agency
ED O'NEILL .... ICM
MICHAEL O'NEILL .... Susan Smith & Associates
MICHAEL ONTKEAN ....William Morris Agency
ED O'ROSS .... The Blake Agency
ANNETTE O'TOOLE .... ICM
PETER O'TOOLE ....William Morris Agency
PARK OVERALL ....UTA
FRANK OZ .... CAA

P

AL PACINO .... CAA
JACK PALANCE ....Susan Smith & Associates
CHAZZ PALMINTERI ....William Morris Agency
STUART PANKIN ....Metropolitan Talent Agency
JOHN PANKOW ....William Morris Agency

JOE PANTOLIANO .... UTA
ANNA PAQUIN .... William Morris Agency
RANDI PAREIRA ....Joseph Heldfond & Rix, Inc.
ANDREA PARKER .... Susan Smith & Associates
MARY-LOUISE PARKER ....William Morris Agency
SARAH JESSICA PARKER .... CAA
MANDY PATINKIN .... UTA
JASON PATRIC .... UTA
ROBERT PATRICK .... UTA
WILL PATTON .... William Morris Agency
RICHARD JOSEPH PAUL ....William Morris Agency
BILL PAXTON .... William Morris Agency
DAVID PAYMER .... Susan Smith & Associates
AMANDA PAYS .... William Morris Agency
ELIZABETH PEÑA ....Paradigm
AUSTIN PENDLETON .... The Blake Agency
CHRIS PENN .... UTA
SEAN PENN .... CAA
ROSIE PEREZ .... CAA
ELIZABETH PERKINS .... CAA
RHEA PERLMAN ....CAA
VALERIE PERRINE ....Borinstein-Oreck-Bogart
JOE PESCI .... CAA
BERNADETTE PETERS ....William Morris Agency
BROCK PETERS ....Paradigm
WILLIAM L. PETERSEN .... ICM
LORI PETTY .... Gersh Agency
MICHELLE PFEIFFER .... ICM
CHYNNA PHILLIPS .... CAA
JULIANNE PHILLIPS .... Gersh Agency
LOU DIAMOND PHILLIPS .... Innovative Artists
MICHELLE PHILLIPS .... Ambrosio-Mortimer
LEAF PHOENIX .... Iris Burton Agency
RAIN PHOENIX .... Iris Burton Agency
MARIANGELA PINO .... Susan Smith & Associates
MARIA PITILLO .... William Morris Agency
BRAD PITT .... CAA
MARY KAY PLACE .... ICM
OLIVER PLATT .... William Morris Agency
PLAY .... William Morris Agency
MARTHA PLIMPTON .... ICM
AMANDA PLUMMER .... Gersh Agency
CHRISTOPHER PLUMMER ....ICM
PRISCILLA POINTER ....William Morris Agency
SIDNEY POITIER ....CAA
SYDNEY POLLACK ....CAA
TRACY POLLAN ....Harris & Goldberg Agency
MICHAEL J. POLLARD .... Yvette Bikoff Agency
TERI POLO .... William Morris Agency
MAX POMERANC ....William Morris Agency
PAULINA PORIZKOVA ....CAA
PARKER POSEY ....William Morris Agency
ANNIE POTTS .... UTA
C.C.H. POUNDER ....Susan Smith & Associates
PRISCILLA PRESLEY ....William Morris Agency
JASON PRIESTLEY .... UTA
PRINCE .... CAA
VICTORIA PRINCIPAL .... CAA
ROBERT PROSKY .... Gersh Agency
BILL PULLMAN .... UTA

Q

DENNIS QUAID .... ICM
QUEEN LATIFAH .... William Morris Agency
KATHLEEN QUINLAN .... ICM
AIDAN QUINN .... CAA
ANTHONY QUINN .... William Morris Agency

R

BOB RAFELSON .... ICM
HAROLD RAMIS .... CAA
BRUCE RAMSAY .... UTA
TONY RANDALL .... William Morris Agency
THERESA RANDLE .... UTA
MICHAEL R APAPORT .... Innovative Artists
ROBERT REDFORD .... CAA
PAMELA REED .... ICM
DELLA REESE .... William Morris Agency
CHRISTOPHER REEVE .... William Morris Agency
KEANU REEVES .... CAA
ROB REINER .... CAA
JUDGE REINHOLD .... ICM
PAUL REISER .... UTA
BURT REYNOLDS .... William Morris Agency
VING RHAMES .... William Morris Agency
CHRISTINA RICCI .... ICM
MICHAEL RICHARDS .... APA
MIRANDA RICHARDSON .... Susan Smith & Associates
NATASHA RICHARDSON .... ICM
JASON JAMES RICHTER .... UTA
ALAN RICKMAN .... UTA
PETER RIEGERT .... UTA
MOLLY RINGWALD .... William Morris Agency
JOAN RIVERS .... William Morris Agency
TIM ROBBINS .... ICM
ERIC ROBERTS .... UTA
JULIA ROBERTS .... ICM
TONY ROBERTS .... APA
CLIFF ROBERTSON .... ICM
ROBBIE ROBERTSON .... CAA
CHRIS ROCK .... William Morris Agency
PAUL RODRIGUEZ .... William Morris Agency
MIMI ROGERS .... CAA
ESTHER ROLLE .... William Morris Agency
HENRY ROLLINS .... William Morris Agency
HOWARD E. ROLLINS, JR. .... William Morris Agency
LINDA RONSTADT .... William Morris Agency
ROSEANNE .... William Morris Agency
ANNIE ROSS .... William Morris Agency
DIANA ROSS .... ICM
KATHARINE ROSS .... Borinstein-Oreck-Bogart
ISABELLA ROSSELLINI .... UTA
TIM ROTH .... UTA
GENA ROWLANDS .... ICM
MERCEDES RUEHL .... UTA

DEBORAH RUSH .... Gersh Agency
JARED RUSHTON .... Tyler Kjar Agency
WILLIAM RUSS .... Bresler Kelly Kipperman
KURT RUSSELL .... CAA
THERESA RUSSELL .... William Morris Agency
RENE RUSSO .... Progressive Artists
MEG RYAN .... ICM
MARK RYDELL .... ICM
WINONA RYDER .... CAA

S

SUSAN SAINT JAMES .... CAA
ADAM SANDLER .... CAA
JULIAN SANDS .... ICM
SUSAN SARANDON .... ICM
RAPHAEL SBARGE .... Metropolitan Talent Agency
GRETA SCACCHI .... Susan Smith & Associates
JACK SCALIA .... William Morris Agency
GIAN-CARLO SCANDIUZZI .... Marc Rindner
JOHN SCHNEIDER .... William Morris Agency
ARNOLD SCHWARZENEGGER .... ICM
ANNABELLA SCIORRA .... CAA
MARTIN SCORSESE .... CAA
CAMPBELL SCOTT .... Paradigm
GEORGE C. SCOTT .... Becker London and Kossow
TIM SCOTT .... Susan Smith & Associates
STEVEN SEAGAL .... CAA
KYRA SEDGWICK .... CAA
PAMELA SEGALL .... UTA
DAVID SELBY .... ICM
ROSHAN SETH .... Susan Smith & Associates
JANE SEYMOUR .... Metropolitan Talent Agency
TONY SHALHOUB .... William Morris Agency
OMAR SHARIF .... William Morris Agency
WALLACE SHAWN .... William Morris Agency
JOHN SHEA .... William Morris Agency
ALLY SHEEDY .... William Morris Agency
CHARLIE SHEEN .... ICM
CRAIG SHEFFER .... UTA
CYBILL SHEPHERD .... UTA
NICOLLETTE SHERIDAN .... ICM
PAULY SHORE .... CAA
MARTIN SHORT .... William Morris Agency
MICHAEL SIBERRY .... Susan Smith & Associates
CHARLES SIEBERT .... David Shapira & Associates
JAMES B. SIKKING .... Metropolitan Talent Agency
RON SILVER .... ICM
JEAN SIMMONS .... Susan Smith & Associates
DON SIMPSON .... CAA
O.J. SIMPSON .... ICM
SINBAD .... William Morris Agency
LORI SINGER .... CAA
MARC SINGER .... David Shapira & Associates
GARY SINISE .... CAA
TOM SIZEMORE .... CAA
TOM SKERRITT .... William Morris Agency
CHRISTIAN SLATER .... CAA

JEAN SMART .... William Morris Agency
JACLYN SMITH .... William Morris Agency
KURTWOOD SMITH .... Progressive Artists Agency, Inc.
MADOLYN SMITH OSBORNE .... UTA
SHAWNEE SMITH .... CAA
JIMMY SMITS .... CAA
WESLEY SNIPES ....CAA
BARRY SOBEL .... David Shapira & Associates
P.J. SOLES .... The Lawrence Agency
PHYLLIS SOMERVILLE .... Susan Smith & Associates
ARLEEN SORKIN .... Metropolitan Talent Agency
SISSY SPACEK .... CAA
JAMES SPADER .... ICM
STEPHEN SPINELLA .... William Morris Agency
ROBERT STACK .... The Blake Agency
NICK STAHL .... UTA
SYLVESTER STALLONE .... CAA
JOHN STAMOS .... William Morris Agency
FLORENCE STANLEY .... William Morris Agency
MAUREEN STAPLETON .... ICM
MARY STEENBURGEN .... William Morris Agency
DANIEL STERN ....CAA
FRANCES STERNHAGEN .... William Morris Agency
FISHER STEVENS .... William Morris Agency
CYNTHIA STEVENSON .... William Morris Agency
JULIET STEVENSON .... William Morris Agency
PATRICK STEWART .... ICM
DAVID OGDEN STIERS .... Susan Smith & Associates
STING .... UTA
DEAN STOCKWELL .... UTA
ERIC STOLTZ .... CAA
OLIVER STONE ....CAA
SHARON STONE .... ICM
MADELEINE STOWE .... UTA
MERYL STREEP ....CAA
BARBRA STREISAND ....CAA
ELAINE STRITCH .... The Blake Agency
DONALD SUTHERLAND ....CAA
KIEFER SUTHERLAND ....CAA
JANET SUZMAN .... William Morris Agency
BOB SWAIM .... ICM
PATRICK SWAYZE .... William Morris Agency
JULIA SWEENEY .... William Morris Agency

T

RICHARD TACCHINO .... Chateau-Billings, Inc.
CARY-HIROYUKI TAGAWA .... The Agency
QUENTIN TARANTINO .... William Morris Agency
DUB TAYLOR .... Gerler-Stevens
ELIZABETH TAYLOR .... William Morris Agency
RENEE TAYLOR...................................... The Blake Agency
LEIGH TAYLOR-YOUNG .... Don Buchwald & Associates
VICTORIA TENNANT .... Metropolitan Talent Agency
JOHN TERRY .... William Morris Agency
DAVID THEWLIS .... ICM
MARLO THOMAS ....CAA
EMMA THOMPSON .... William Morris Agency

BILLY BOB THORNTON .... William Morris Agency
UMA THURMAN ....CAA
MEG TILLY .... UTA
STEPHEN TOBOLOWSKY .... William Morris Agency
CONCETTA TOMEI .... Susan Smith & Associates
MARISA TOMEI .... William Morris Agency
LILY TOMLIN .... William Morris Agency
RIP TORN .... Gersh Agency
JOE TORRY .... CAA
LORRAINE TOUSSAINT .... William Morris Agency
CONSTANCE TOWERS .... Stone Manners Talent Agency
NANCY TRAVIS .... UTA
JOHN TRAVOLTA .... William Morris Agency
JEANNE TRIPPLEHORN .... CAA
BARRY TUBB .... Susan Smith & Associates
STANLEY TUCCI .... William Morris Agency
KATHLEEN TURNER .... ICM
TINA TURNER ....CAA
JOHN TURTURRO .... ICM

U

BOB UECKER .... William Morris Agency
TRACEY ULLMAN ....CAA
LIV ULLMANN .... The Lantz Office
BLAIR UNDERWOOD ....CAA
ROBERT URICH .... ICM

V

JOAN VAN ARK .... William Morris Agency
JEAN-CLAUDE VAN DAMME ....ICM
DICK VAN DYKE .... William Morris Agency
MARIO VAN PEEBLES .... ICM
NED VAUGHN .... Metropolitan Talent Agency
GORE VIDAL ....CAA
JON VOIGHT ....CAA
MAX von SYDOW .... UTA

W

STEVEN WADDINGTON .... Susan Smith & Associates
ROBERT WAGNER .... William Morris Agency
CHRISTOPHER WALKEN .... William Morris Agency
POLLY WALKER .... UTA
JAMIE WALTERS .... UTA
JULIE WALTERS ....CAA
RACHEL WARD .... William Morris Agency
SELA WARD .... ICM
VINCENT WARD .... Howard Askenase
JULIE WARNER ....CAA
MALCOLM JAMAL WARNER .... William Morris Agency
DIONNE WARWICK .... William Morris Agency
DENZEL WASHINGTON .... ICM

DAMON WAYANS .... CAA
KEENEN IVORY WAYANS .... CAA
MARLON WAYANS .... UTA
CARL WEATHERS .... William Morris Agency
DENNIS WEAVER .... David Shapira & Associates
SIGOURNEY WEAVER .... ICM
PETER WELLER .... CAA
GEORGE WENDT .... UTA
ALEXANDRA WENTWORTH .... UTA
PATRICIA WETTIG .... ICM
FRANK WHALEY .... William Morris Agency
FOREST WHITAKER .... ICM
LYNN WHITFIELD .... ICM
MARGARET WHITTON .... William Morris Agency
LARRY WILCOX .... David Shapira & Associates
SHANNON WILCOX .... Susan Smith & Associates
GENE WILDER .... CAA
JAMES WILDER .... UTA
BILLY DEE WILLIAMS .... David Shapira & Associates
JoBETH WILLIAMS .... William Morris Agency
ROBIN WILLIAMS .... CAA
TREAT WILLIAMS .... UTA
VANESSA WILLIAMS .... William Morris Agency
BRUCE WILLIS .... William Morris Agency
MARA WILSON .... Gold/Marshak & Associates
BRIAN WIMMER .... William Morris Agency
OPRAH WINFREY .... CAA
DEBRA WINGER .... CAA
HENRY WINKLER .... ICM
MARE WINNINGHAM .... William Morris Agency
JOHN WITHERSPOON .... William Morris Agency
ALICIA WITT .... APA
ELIJAH WOOD .... William Morris Agency
ALFRE WOODARD .... ICM
JAMES WOODS .... ICM
JOANNE WOODWARD .... ICM
MICHAEL WOOLSON .... Metropolitan Talent Agency
MARY WORONOV .... Stone Manners Talent Agency
IRENE WORTH .... ICM
ROBIN WRIGHT .... CAA
NOAH WYLE .... UTA

Y

DWIGHT YOAKAM .... CAA
KATHLEEN YORK .... Metropolitan Talent Agency
SUSANNAH YORK .... Susan Smith & Associates

Z

BILLY ZANE .... CAA
LISA ZANE .... William Morris Agency
JACKLYN ZEMAN .... Stone Manners Talent Agency
ANTHONY ZERBE .... Susan Smith & Associates
STEPHANIE ZIMBALIST .... William Morris Agency
ALEX ZUCKERMAN .... Triton Agency
DAPHNE ZUNIGA .... UTA

★ ★ ★

GUILDS

UNITED STATES

SCREEN ACTORS GUILD
5757 Wilshire Blvd.
Los Angeles, CA 90036
213/954-1600
213/549-6737

1515 Broadway
44th Floor
New York, NY 10036
212/944-1030

75 East Wacker Drive
14th Floor
Chicago, IL 60601
312/372-8081

AFTRA
6922 Hollywood Blvd.
8th Floor
Hollywood, CA 90028
213/461-8111

260 Madison Avenue
New York, NY 10016
212/532-0800

EQUITY
165 West 46th Street
New York, NY 10036
212/869-8530

6430 Sunset Blvd.
Suite 700
Hollywood, CA 90028
213/462-2334

DIRECTORS GUILD OF AMERICA
7920 Sunset Blvd.
Los Angeles, CA 90046
310/289-2000

110 West 57th Street
New York, NY 10019
212/581-0370

520 North Michigan Avenue
Suite 1026
Chicago, IL 60611
312/644-5050

CANADA

ACTRA
2239 Young Street
3rd Floor
Toronto, Ontario
Canada M4S 2B5
415/489-1311

UNION DES ARTISTES (UDA)
416/495-7670

FRANCE

ASSOCIATION DES COMEDIENS ET ARTISTES
40 Rue d'Enghien
75010 Paris, France
47 70 0902
42 02 4224

AGENTS AND MANAGERS

A

ABRAMS ARTISTS & ASSOCIATES
9200 Sunset Blvd.
Suite 625
Los Angeles, CA 90069
310/859-0625

420 Madison Ave.
Suite 1400
New York, NY 10017
212/935-8980

THE AGENCY
10351 Santa Monica Blvd.
Suite 211
Los Angeles, CA 90025
310/551-3000

AGENCY FOR THE PERFORMING ARTS, INC. (APA)
9000 Sunset Blvd.
Suite 1200
Los Angeles, CA 90069
310/273-0744
FAX 310/275-9401

888 Seventh Avenue
New York, NY 10106
212/582-1500
FAX 212/245-1647

ALL-STAR TALENT AGENCY
21416 Chase Street
Suite 2
Canoga Park, CA 91304
818/346-4313

THE ARTISTS AGENCY
10000 Santa Monica Blvd.
Suite 385
Los Angeles, CA 90067
310/277-7779
FAX 310/785-9338

THE ARTISTS GROUP, LTD.
1930 Century Park West
Suite 403
Los Angeles, CA 90067
310/552-1100
FAX 310/277-9513

ASSOCIATED TALENT AGENCY
9744 Wilshire Blvd.
Suite 312
Beverly Hills, CA 90212
310/271-4662

B

THE BENNETT AGENCY
150 S. Barrington Ave., Suite 1
Los Angeles, CA 90049
310/471-2251

J. MICHAEL BLOOM, LTD.
9255 Sunset Blvd.
Suite 710
Los Angeles, CA 90069
310/275-6800
FAX 310/275-6941

233 Park Avenue South
10th Floor
New York, NY 10003
212/529-6500

BRODER-KURLAND-WEBB-UFFNER AGENCY
9242 Beverly Blvd.
Suite 200
Beverly Hills, CA 90210
310/281-3400
FAX 310/276-3207

DON BUCHWALD & ASSOCIATES
9229 Sunset Blvd.
Suite 710
Los Angeles, CA 90069
310/278-3600

10 East 44th St.
New York, NY 10017
212/867-1200

C

CAMDEN-ITG
(In Association with Candace Lake Agency)
822 S. Robertson Blvd.
Suite 200
Los Angeles, CA 90035
310/289-2700
FAX 310/289-2718

729 Seventh Ave.
16th Floor
New York, NY 10019
212/221-7878

THE CHASIN AGENCY
8899 Beverly Blvd.
Beverly Hills, CA 90048
310/278-7505
FAX 310/275-6685

CREATIVE ARTISTS AGENCY (CAA)
9830 Wilshire Blvd.
Beverly Hills, CA 90212
310/288-4545
FAX 310/288-4800

D

DADE, SCHULTZ ASSOCIATES
11846 Ventura Blvd.
Suite 201
Studio City, CA 91604
818/760-3100

DOUROUX & CO.
445 S. Beverly Dr.
Suite 310
Beverly Hills, CA 90210
310/552-0900

F

FAVORED ARTISTS AGENCY
122 S. Robertson Blvd.
Suite 202
Los Angeles, CA 90048
310/247-1040
FAX 310/247-1048

G

THE GAGE GROUP, INC.
9255 Sunset Blvd.
Suite 515
Los Angeles, CA 90069
310/859-8777
FAX 310/859-8166

315 W. 57th St.
Suite 4H
New York, NY 10019
212/541-5258
FAX 212/956-7466

THE GERSH AGENCY
232 N. Cañon Dr.
Beverly Hills, CA 90210
310/274-6611
FAX 310/274-4035

138 West 42nd St.
Suite 2400
New York, NY 10036
212/997-1818

**A
G
E
N
T
S
&
M
A
N
A
G
E
R
S**

GOLD/MARSHAK & ASSOCIATES
3500 W. Olive Ave.
Burbank, CA 91505
818/972-4300
FAX 818/955-6411

I

ICM (INTERNATIONAL CREATIVE MANAGEMENT)
8942 Wilshire Blvd.
Beverly Hills, CA 90211
310/550-4000
FAX 310/550-4108

40 West 57th Street
New York, NY 10019
212/556-5600

76 Oxford House
London, England W1R 1RB
071/636-6565

INNOVATIVE ARTISTS
1999 Avenue of the Stars
Suite 2850
Los Angeles, CA 90067
310/553-5200
FAX 310/557-2211

130 West 57th Street, Suite 5B
New York, NY 10019-3316
212/315-4455
FAX 212/315-4688

K

THE KAPLAN-STAHLER AGENCY
8383 Wilshire Blvd.
Beverly Hills, CA 90211
213/653-4483

PATRICIA KARLAN AGENCY
3575 Cahuenga Blvd. West
Suite 210
Los Angeles, CA 90068
818/752-4800

PAUL KOHNER, INC.
9300 Wilshire Blvd.
Suite 555
Beverly Hills, CA 90212
310/550-1060
FAX 310/276-1083

KOPALOFF COMPANY
1930 Century Park West
Suite 403
Los Angeles, CA 90067
310/203-8430

L

THE CANDACE LAKE AGENCY
(In Association with Camden-ITG)
822 S. Robertson Blvd.
Suite 200
Los Angeles, CA 90035
310/289-0600
FAX 310/289-0619

M

MAJOR CLIENTS AGENCY
2121 Avenue of the Stars
Suite 2450
Los Angeles, CA 90067
310/284-6400
FAX 310/284-6499

MEDIA ARTISTS GROUP
8383 Wilshire Blvd.
Suite 954
Beverly Hills, CA 90211
213/658-7434
FAX 213/658-7871

METROPOLITAN TALENT AGENCY
4526 Wilshire Blvd.
Los Angeles, CA 90010
213/857-4500
FAX 213/857-4599

WILLIAM MORRIS AGENCY
151 El Camino Dr.
Beverly Hills, CA 90212
310/274-7451
FAX 310/859-4462

1325 Avenue of the Americas
New York, NY 10019
212/586-5100

2325 Crestmoore Road
Nashville, TN 37215
615/385-0310

31-32 Soho Square
London W12 5DG, England
01/434-2191

Via Giosue Carducci, 10
00187 Rome, Italy
48-6961

Lamonstrasse 9
Munich 80, West Germany
011/47/608-1234

P

PARADIGM
10100 Santa Monica Blvd.
25th Floor
Los Angeles, CA 90067
310/277-4400
FAX 310/277-7820

200 West 57th Street
Suite 900
New York, NY 10019
212/246-1030
FAX 212/246-1521

BARRY PERELMAN AGENCY
9200 Sunset Blvd.
Suite 531
Los Angeles, CA 90069
310/274-5999

PREFERRED ARTISTS
16633 Ventura Blvd.
Suite 1421
Encino, CA 91436
818/990-0305

JIM PREMINGER AGENCY
1650 Westwood Blvd.
Suite 201
Los Angeles, CA 90024
310/475-9491

S

SELECT ARTISTS
Suite 1B
New York, NY 10036
212/586-4300

DAVID SHAPIRA & ASSOCIATES
15301 Ventura Blvd.
Suite 345
Sherman Oaks, CA 91403
818/906-0322
FAX 818/783-2562

SUSAN SMITH & ASSOCIATES
121 N. San Vicente Blvd.
Beverly Hills, CA 90211
213/852-4777
FAX 213/658-7170

192 Lexington Ave.
New York, NY 10016
212/545-0500
FAX 212/545-7143

STONE MANNERS AGENCY
8091 Selma Ave.
Los Angeles, CA 90046
213/654-7575
FAX 213/654-7676

H.N. SWANSON, INC.
8523 Sunset Blvd.
Los Angeles, CA 90069
310/652-5385
FAX 310/652-3690

T

TWENTIETH CENTURY ARTISTS
14724 Ventura Blvd.
Suite 401
Sherman Oaks, CA 91403
818/788-5516
FAX 818/788-2070

U

UNITED TALENT AGENCY (UTA)
9560 Wilshire Blvd., 5th Floor
Beverly Hills, CA 90212
310/273-6700
FAX 310/247-1111

WRIGHT CONCEPT TALENT AGENCY
1811 W. Burbank Blvd.
Suite 201
Burbank, CA 91506
818/954-8943

WRITERS & ARTISTS AGENCY
924 Westwood Blvd.
Suite 900
Los Angeles, CA 90024
310/824-6300
FAX 310/824-6343

70 West 36th St.
Suite 501
New York, NY 10018
212/947-8765

CALLING ALL CREDITS!

The **Third Edition of FILM ACTORS GUIDE** is now in preparation. It will be published in the fall of 1995. We update our records continuously. If you qualify to be listed (please read HOW TO USE THIS BOOK for qualifications), then send us your listing information **ASAP.** All listings are free.
Photocopy the form on the next page.

Our editorial deadline is August 1, 1995
(Please do not wait until then.)

Send all listing information to:

FILMACTORS GUIDE
Third Edition
2337 Roscomare Road, Suite Nine
Los Angeles, CA 90077
310/471-8066 or 1/800-FILMBKS

If you are a director (*film or television*), a writer (*film or television*), film composer, cinematographer, production designer, costume designer, editor, film producer, agent, casting director, studio personnel, special effects person or stunt coordinator and want to find out about getting listed in our other directories, call **310/471-8066** or write to:

LONE EAGLE PUBLISHING COMPANY
2337 Roscomare Road, Suite Nine
Los Angeles, CA 90077-1851
310/471-8066 • 310/471-4969 (FAX) • 1/800-FILMBKS

• ALL LISTINGS ARE FREE •

Ask for *Lone Eagle* books at these fine bookstores.

The **THIRD EDITION** of

FILM ACTORS
GUIDE

☐ SAG
☐ EQUITY

ALL LISTINGS ARE FREE.

DON'T BE LEFT OUT!!! Include your *FREE* listing (read *How To Use This Book* for qualifications) by filling out and returning this form to us *IMMEDIATELY.* *(Photocopy as many times as necessary).*

PERSONAL INFORMATION

Name (as you prefer to be listed)

Company

Address

City/State/Zip

Area Code/Telephone

Birth Date & Place
☐ Home   ☐ Business
☐ Please list my home address and phone number in your directory.

REPRESENTATIVE'S INFORMATION
Agent ☐   Personal Manager ☐   Attorney ☐
Business Manager ☐   Other ☐
(List as many representatives as you would like. Continue listing on reverse, if necessary.)

Name (as you prefer to be listed)

Company

Address

City/State/Zip

Area Code/Telephone

CREDITS *(Attach a separate sheet, if necessary)*
List your credits as follows, noting title, type of work, distribution company, year of release, alternate titles in parentheses, Academy nominations/awards for your work, and country of origin.

STORMY MONDAY (Feature) Atlantic Releasing Corporation, 1988, British
LONESOME DOVE (Miniseries) Motown Productions/Pangaea/Qintex Entertainment, Inc. 1989
THE FUGITIVE (Feature) ✪✪ (Academy Award for Supporting Actor) Warner Bros., 1993
THE GOOD OLD BOYS (Cable Telefeature) Turner Network TV, 1995 (also directed)

_____

_____

_____

_____

_____

_____

MAIL form IMMEDIATELY to
FILM ACTORS GUIDE **Third Edition**
2337 Roscomare Road, Suite Nine
Los Angeles, CA 90077
310/471-8066 or 310/471-4969 (FAX)

Deadline:
August 1, 1995

Questions ???
Problems ???
Call 310/471-8066

INDEX OF ADVERTISERS

A special thanks to our advertisers whose support makes it possible to bring you the second edition of **FILM ACTORS Guide.**

The Drama Book Shop, Inc. 676

Lacy Street Production Center iv

Samuel French Theatre & Film Bookshops 676

ABOUT THE EDITOR

These days, Steve LuKanic is *always* in front of his computer. When he's not digging up film credits for actors and adding them to his "collection" he's busy pursuing a filmwriting career. He recently finished co-writing a feature script for a major Hollywood production company and has several other projects in various stages of development.

He spends his free time at the movies (jotting down credits in the dark) and avoiding paparazzi who routinely mistake him for Mel Gibson.

VINCENT WARD

SCOTT SHAW